# Koren Talmud Bavli

## BERAKHOT

# KOREN TALMUD BAVLI

## ברכות
## BERAKHOT

COMMENTARY BY

Rabbi Adin Even-Israel (Steinsaltz)

EDITOR-IN-CHIEF

Rabbi Dr Tzvi Hersh Weinreb

SENIOR CONTENT EDITOR

Rabbi Dr Shalom Z Berger

MANAGING EDITOR

Rabbi Joshua Schreier

•

SHEFA FOUNDATION
KOREN PUBLISHERS JERUSALEM

Supported by the Matanel Foundation

*Koren Talmud Bavli*
Volume 1: Tractate Berakhot
Daf Yomi Size

ISBN 978 965 301 608 8

First Hebrew/English Edition, 2012

Koren Publishers Jerusalem Ltd.
PO Box 4044, Jerusalem 91040, ISRAEL
PO Box 8531, New Milford, CT 06776, USA
www.korenpub.com

Shefa Foundation

*Shefa Foundation is the parent organization of institutions established by Rabbi Adin Even-Israel (Steinsaltz)*

PO Box 45187, Jerusalem 91450 ISRAEL
Telephone: +972 2 646 0900, Fax +972 2 624 9454
www.hashefa.co.il

*We dedicate this edition of Tractate Berakhot*

*with Berakhot – Blessings*

*for our sons*

*Jason, Ben, and David Pritzker*

## Translators

Amy Fay Kaplan Benoff
Betzalel Philip Edwards
Rabbi Elli Fischer
Gila Hoch
Stephen Lauber
Elie Leshem
Rabbi Eli Ozarowski
Gavriel Reiss
Yosef Rosen
Jay Shapiro
Rabbi Ami Silver
Eliana Kinderlehrer Silver
Avi Steinhart
Amiel Vick
Rabbi Abe Y. Weschler
Rabbi Yaakov Komisar
Rabbi Adin Krohn
Rabbi Jason Leib
Sally Mayer
Rabbi Jonathan Mishkin
Rabbi Jason Rappoport
Rabbi Noam Shapiro
Rabbi Michael Siev
Rabbi David Strauss

## Editors

Mali Brofsky
Rabbi David Jay Derovan
Rabbi Dov Karoll

## Proofreaders

Aliza Israel, *Proofreading Coordinator*
Bracha Hermon
Shira Finson
Ita Olesker
Nechama Unterman

## Language Consultants

Dr. Stephanie E. Binder, *Greek & Latin*
Yaakov Hoffman, *Arabic*
Dr. Shai Secunda, *Persian*

## Design & Typesetting

Raphaël Freeman, *Design & Typesetting*
Dena Landowne Bailey, *Typesetting*

## Images

Rabbi Eliahu Misgav, *Illustration*
Yehudit Cohen, *Image Acquisition*

## Digital Edition

Dena Landowne Bailey, *Concept*
Tani Bayer, *Graphic Design*
Rabbi Hanan Benayahu, *Concept*
Raphaël Freeman, *Team Leader*
Laura Messinger, *Commercial Liaison*
Eliyahu Skoczylas, *Senior Architect*

# Contents


Haskamot **viii**

Message from Rabbi Adin Even-Israel (Steinsaltz) **xii**

Introduction by the Editor-in-Chief **xiii**

Preface by the Managing Editor **xv**

Introduction by the Publisher **xvi**

Introduction to Berakhot **1**

Berakhot **5**

Index of Background **413**

Index of Language **416**

Index of Personalities **417**

Image Credits **417**

Hadran **418**


For the vocalized Vilna Shas layout, please open as a Hebrew book.

# Haskama
## Rabbi Moshe Feinstein

RABBI MOSES FEINSTEIN
455 F. D. R. DRIVE
New York, N. Y. 10002
OREGON 7-1222

משה פיינשטיין
ר"ם תפארת ירושלים
בנוא יארק

בע"ה

בזה ראיתי הפירוש החשוב של הרב הגאון מוהר"ר עדין שטיינזלץ שליט"א מעיה"ק ירושלים, על מסכתות ביצה ור"ה. באמת כבר ידוע לי פירושו של הרה"ג הנ"ל על מסכתות מתלמוד בבלי, וכבר כתבתי מכתב הסכמה עליהם. ובאתי בזה רק להדגיש מחדש איך שהחידושים של הרה"ג הנ"ל, שכולל פירוש חדש על הגמרא עצמו וגם פירוש שיש בו סיכום להלכה מהנידונים שבגמרא, נוסף לעוד כמה חלקים, הם באמת עבודה גדולה, שיכולים להיות לתועלת לא רק לאלו שכבר מורגלים בלמוד הגמרא, ורוצים להעמק יותר, אלא גם לאלו שמתחילים ללמוד, להדריכם בדרכי התורה איך להבין ולהעמיק בים התלמוד.

והריני מברך להרה"ג הנ"ל שיצליחהו השי"ת בספריו אלו ושיזכה לחבר עוד ספרים, להגדיל תורה ולהאדירה, לתפארת השם ותורתו.

ועל זה באתי על החתום לכבוד התורה ביום ז' לחודש אייר תשמ"ג.

משה פיינשטיין

משה פיינשטיין

...These new commentaries – which include a new interpretation of the Talmud, a halakhic summary of the debated issues, and various other sections – are a truly outstanding work; they can be of great benefit not only to those familiar with talmudic study who seek to deepen their understanding, but also to those who are just beginning to learn, guiding them through the pathways of the Torah and teaching them how to delve into the sea of the Talmud.

I would like to offer my blessing to this learned scholar. May the Holy One grant him success with these volumes and may he merit to write many more, to enhance the greatness of Torah, and bring glory to God and His word...

Rabbi Moshe Feinstein
New York, 7 Adar 5743

**ר׳ משה פיינשטיין שליט״א**

הנה ראיתי את מסכת אחת מהש״ס שנקד אותה וגם צייר צורות הצמחים וכדומה מדברים שלא ידוע לכמה אנשים הרה״ג ר׳ עדין שטייגזלץ מירושלים שליט״א וגם הוסיף שם בגליון פירושים וחידושים וניכר שהוא ת״ח וראויין לעיין בהם ת״ח ובני הישיבה וטוב גם לקנותם בבתי כנסיות ובבתי מדרשות שיש שיהיו להם לתועלת. — ועל זה באתי עה״ח ג׳ אדר ב׳ תש״ל.

נאם משה פיינשטיין
ר״מ תפארת ירושלים, ניו־יורק, ארה״ב

I have seen one tractate from the Talmud to which the great scholar Rabbi Adin Steinsaltz שליט״א has added *nikkud* (vowels) and illustrations to explain that which is unknown to many people; he has also added interpretations and innovations, and is evidently a *talmid hakham*. *Talmidei hakhamim* and yeshiva students ought to study these volumes, and synagogues and *batei midrash* would do well to purchase them, as they may find them useful.

Rabbi Moshe Feinstein
New York, Adar 5730

# Haskama

## Rabbi Menachem Mendel Schneerson

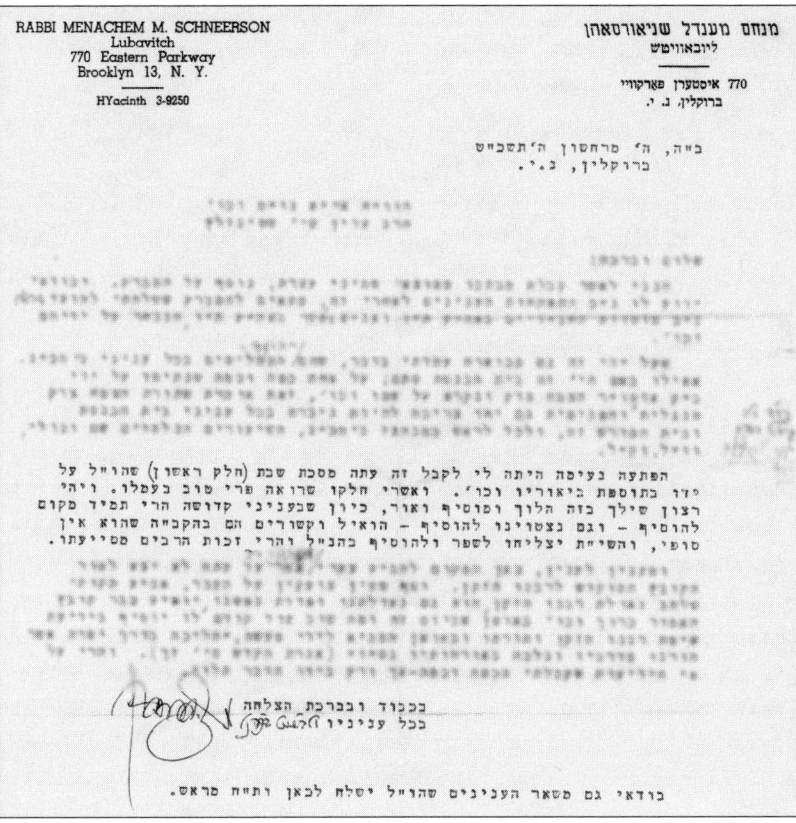

RABBI MENACHEM M. SCHNEERSON
Lubavitch
770 Eastern Parkway
Brooklyn 13, N. Y.

HYacinth 3-9250

מנחם מענדל שניאורסאהן
ליובאוויטש

770 איסטערן פארקוויי
ברוקלין, נ. י.

ב״ה, ה׳ מרחשון ה׳תשכ״ט
ברוקלין, נ.י.

הפתעה נעימה היתה לי לקבל זה עתה מסכת שבת (חלק ראשון) שהו״ל על ידו בתוספת ביאוריו וכו׳. ואשרי חלקו שרואה פרי טוב בעמלו. ויהי רצון שילך בזה הלוך ומוסיף ואור, כיון שבעניני קדושה הרי תמיד מקום להוסיף – וגם נצטוינו להוסיף – הואיל וקשורים הם בהקב״ה שהוא אין סופי, והשי״ת יצליחו לשפר ולהוסיף בהנ״ל והרי זכות הרבים מסייעתו.

בכבוד ובברכת הצלחה
בכל עניניו

בודאי גם משאר הענינים שהו״ל ישלח לכאן ותו״ח מראש.

…I have just had the pleasant surprise of receiving tractate *Shabbat* (part one), which has been published by [Rabbi Steinsaltz] along with his explanations, etc. Happy is the man who sees good fruits from his labors. May he continue in this path and increase light, for in the matters of holiness there is always room to add – and we have been commanded to add – for they are linked to the Holy One, Blessed be He, Who is infinite. And may the Holy One grant him success to improve and enhance this work, since the greater good strengthens his hand…

Rabbi Menachem Mendel Schneerson
The Lubavitcher Rebbe
Brooklyn, 5 Marḥeshvan, 5729

# Haskama

## Rabbi Moshe Zvi Neria

מכתבו של הרב משה צבי נריה

ב"ה

"ושמעו ביום ההוא החרשים דברי ספר"
(ישעי' כט' יח')

תרגום ספרי קדמונים לשפת דורות אחרונים – היא משימתם של חכמי דור ודור. ובישראל שמצוות "ושננתם לבניך" מקיפה את כל חלקי האומה, ודאי שהיתה זאת המשימה בכל עידן ועידן.

בכל דור כך, ובדורנו אשר רבים בו הקרובים שנתרחקו וחוזרים ומתקרבים – לא כל שכן. כי רבים היום האומרים "מי ישקנו מים מבאר" התלמוד, ומועטים הם הדולים ומשקים.

ראוי אפוא להערכה מיוחדת נסיונו המבורך של הצעיר המופלא, הרב עדין שטינזלץ, לפרש פרקי-תלמוד בהסברה מורחבת-תמציתית, אשר נוסף על הפרוש המלולי והעניני הוא מעלה גם את ההגיון של הדברים ומתרגמת אותם לשפת-המושגים של בן-דורנו.

דומה שכל הנגשים אל חומר למודי מתוך רצון להבינו – התלמיד החרוץ והמבוגר המשכיל – לא יתקלו בשום קושי בבואם ללמוד סוגיא תלמודית לפי פרוש זה. ולא עוד אלא שיש לקוות כי ההסברה הגיונית תעמידם מיד על טוב-הטעם של דף-הגמרא, והם ימשכו יותר ויותר אל הלמוד העיוני הזה אשר טובי המוחות בישראל לנו בעומקו, ואשר ממנו פינה, ממנו יתד לבנין חיינו.

נועם ד' על המפרש הנמרץ להמשיך במפעלו, וברוכים כל העוזרים להוצאתו לאור-עולם.

ביקר אורייתא

(חתימה)

The translation of the books of our past into the language of the present – this was the task of the sages of every generation. And in Israel, where the command to "teach them repeatedly to your children" applies to all parts of the nation, it was certainly the task of every era. This is true for every generation, and in our time – when many of those who have strayed far are once again drawing near – all the more so. For many today say, "Who will let us drink from the well" of Talmud, and few are those who offer up the waters to drink.

We must, therefore, particularly commend the blessed endeavor of Rabbi Adin Steinsaltz to explain the chapters of the Talmud in this extensive yet succinct commentary, which, in addition to its literal interpretation of the text, also explicates the latter's underlying logic and translates it into the language of our generation.

It appears that all those who seek to study Talmud – the diligent student and the learned adult – will have no difficulty understanding when using this commentary. Moreover, we may hope that the logical explanation will reveal to them the beauty of the talmudic page, and they will be drawn deeper and deeper into the intellectual pursuit which has engaged the best Jewish minds, and which serves as the cornerstone of our very lives…

Rabbi Moshe Zvi Neria

 THIS HASKAMA REFERS TO THE ORIGINAL HEBREW EDITION OF THE STEINSALTZ TALMUD, UPON WHICH THIS VOLUME IS BASED

ב"ה

**MORDECHAI ELIAHU**
FORMER CHIEF RABBI OF ISRAEL & RICHON LEZION

**מרדכי אליהו**
הראשון לציון והרב הראשי לישראל לשעבר

ז' בתשרי תשנ"ד
נד.5-137

מכתב ברכה

הגמרא בעירובין כ"א: אומרת: דרש רבא מאי דכתיב ויותר שהיה קהלת חכם, עוד לימד דעת את העם - ואזן וחקר תקן משלים הרבה". לימד דעת את העם - קבע כיצד לקרוא פסוק וסימנים בין תיבות המקרא וממשיכה הגמרא ואומרת: אמר עולא אמר ר' אליעזר בתחילה היתה תורה דומה לכפיפה שאין לה אזנים עד שבא שלמה ועשה לה אזנים". וכדברי רש"י שם: "וע"י כך אוחזין ישראל במצות שנתרחקו מן העבירה כדרך שנוח לאחוז בכלי שיש לו בית יד וכו' (ערובין כ"א, י').

דברים מעין אלו אפשר לאמר על האי גברא יקירא, על איש מורם מעם, משכמו ומעלה בתורה ובמידות. ויותר ממה שעשה בתורה שבע"פ עושה בתורה שבכתב - מלמד דעת את העם. ולא זו בלבד אלא גם עושה אזנים לתורה, היא תורת התלמוד שהוא חתום וסתום בפני רבים. ורק מעט מזער מבני עליה שהם מועטים ומי שלומד בישיבה יכל כיום ללמוד בש"ס ולהבין מה שלפניו, ואף שיש לנו פירוש רש"י, עדין לא הכל ממשמשין בו. עד שקם הרב הגדול מעוז ומגדול הרה"ג ר' **עדין שטיינזלץ** שליט"א ועשה אזנים לתורה, שאפשר לאחוז גמרא ביד וללמוד, ואפי' לפשוטי העם ועשה פרושים ושם אותם בצד הארון, פרושים נאים בשפה ברורה ונעימה דבר דבור על אופניו. ועם הסברים וציורים להבין ולהשכיל, כדי שמי שרוצה לקרבה אל מלאכת ה' ללמוד יכל לעשות זאת.

ועיני ראו ולא זר שבשיעורי תורה בגמרא הרבה באים עם גמרות בידם ואלה שבאים עם "פירוש הרב שטיינזלץ לתלמוד הבבלי" הם מוכנים ומבינים טוב יותר. כי כבר יש להם הקדמה מפרושיו ומבאוריו.
ואמינא לפועלו יישר ומן שמיא זכו ליה ללמד דעת את העם .

ויהי רצון שחפץ בידו יצלח, וכל אשר יפנה ישכיל ויצליח, ויזכה להגדיל תורה ולהאדירה, ויוסיף לנו עוד גמרות מבוארות כהנה וכהנה עד לסיומו , "וישראל עושה חיל".

ובזכות לימוד תורה ואני זאת בריתי וכו', ובא לציון גואל, בב"א.

מרדכי אליהו
ראשון לציון הרב הראשי לישראל לשעבר

# Haskama
## Rabbi Mordechai Eliyahu

The Talmud in *Eruvin* 21b states: "Rava continued to interpret verses homiletically. What is the meaning of the verse: 'And besides being wise, Kohelet also taught the people knowledge; and he weighed, and sought out, and set in order many proverbs'? (Ecclesiastes 12:9). He explains: He taught the people knowledge; he taught it with the accentuation marks in the Torah, and explained each matter by means of another matter similar to it. And he weighed [*izen*], and sought out, and set in order many proverbs; Ulla said that Rabbi Eliezer said: At first the Torah was like a basket without handles [*oznayim*] until Solomon came and made handles for it." And as Rashi there explains: "And thus were Israel able to grasp the mitzvot and distance themselves from transgressions – just as a vessel with handles is easily held, etc."

Such things may be said of this beloved and eminent man, a great sage of Torah and of virtue. And far more than he has done with the Oral Torah, he does with the Written Torah – teaching the people knowledge. And beyond that, he also affixes handles to the Torah, i.e., to the Talmud, which is obscure and difficult for many. Only the intellectual elite, which are a precious few, and those who study in yeshiva, can today learn the Talmud and understand what it says – and even though we have Rashi, still not everyone uses him. But now the great scholar Rabbi Adin Steinsaltz שליט"א has come and affixed handles to the Torah, allowing the Talmud to be held and studied, even by simple men. And he has composed a commentary alongside the text, a fine commentary in clear, comprehensible language, "a word fitly spoken" with explanations and illustrations, so that all those who seek to study the work of God can do so.

Rabbi Mordechai Eliyahu
Former Chief Rabbi of Israel, 7 Tishrei, 5754

# Message from Rabbi Adin Even-Israel (Steinsaltz)

The Talmud is the cornerstone of Jewish culture. True, our culture originated in the Bible and has branched out in directions besides the Talmud, yet the latter's influence on Jewish culture is fundamental. Perhaps because it was composed not by a single individual, but rather by hundreds and thousands of Sages in *batei midrash* in an ongoing, millennium-long process, the Talmud expresses not only the deepest themes and values of the Jewish people, but also of the Jewish spirit. As the basic study text for young and old, laymen and learned, the Talmud may be said to embody the historical trajectory of the Jewish soul. It is, therefore, best studied interactively, its subject matter coming together with the student's questions, perplexities, and innovations to form a single intricate weave. In the entire scope of Jewish culture, there is not one area that does not draw from or converse with the Talmud. The study of Talmud is thus the gate through which a Jew enters his life's path.

The *Koren Talmud Bavli* seeks to render the Talmud accessible to the millions of Jews whose mother tongue is English, allowing them to study it, approach it, and perhaps even become one with it.

This project has been carried out and assisted by several people, all of whom have worked tirelessly to turn this vision into an actual set of books to be studied. It is a joyful duty to thank the many partners in this enterprise for their various contributions. Thanks to Koren Publishers Jerusalem, both for the publication of this set and for the design of its very complex graphic layout. Thanks of a different sort are owed to the Shefa Foundation and its director, Rabbi Menachem Even-Israel, for their determination and persistence in setting this goal and reaching it. Many thanks to the translators, editors, and proofreaders for their hard and meticulous work. Thanks to the individuals and organizations that supported this project, chief among them the Matanel Foundation. And thanks in advance to all those who will invest their time, hearts, and minds in studying these volumes – to learn, to teach, and to practice.

Rabbi Adin Even-Israel (Steinsaltz)
Jerusalem 5772

# Introduction by the Editor-in-Chief

The vastly expanded audience of Talmud study in our generation is a phenomenon of historical proportions. The reasons for this phenomenon are many, and include the availability of a wide array of translations, commentaries, and study aids.

One outstanding example of such a work is the translation of the Talmud into modern Hebrew by Rabbi Adin Even-Israel (Steinsaltz). The product of a lifetime of intense intellectual labor, this translation stands out in its uniqueness.

Like all translations, it is also a commentary. Rabbi Steinsaltz excels in his ability to weave helpful explanations into the text without compromising its integrity. He has also supplemented the translation with informational notes, providing the readers with essential context for a full understanding of the subtleties of each talmudic passage: biographies of talmudic personalities, explanations of unfamiliar Aramaic terms and concepts, definitions of words and phrases drawn from languages such as Greek, Latin, Arabic, and Persian, intricate details about the lifestyle and botany of talmudic times, as well as summaries of the practical halahkic conclusions that were drawn from each passage.

In this masterful Hebrew translation, Rabbi Steinsaltz does not merely facilitate the task of the novice Talmud student. Rather, he provides the student with the skills to eventually study the text on his or her own, without resorting to the translation. In other words, he enables the transformation from novice to master.

The Steinsaltz Hebrew translation of the Talmud is to be found on the shelves of synagogues and school libraries all over the world. It has received the appreciation of beginners and the acclaim of scholars. The former are grateful for having gained the expertise necessary for more advanced study; the latter are impressed by the clarity and intellectual tour de force of Rabbi Steinsaltz.

But what can the interested student do if he or she does not comprehend the Hebrew, even in its modern form? Where is the English speaker who wishes to access this instructive material to turn?

The *Koren Talmud Bavli* that you hold in your hand is designed to be the answer to those questions.

This work is the joint effort of Rabbi Steinsaltz himself, his closest advisory staff, and Koren Publishers Jerusalem. It is my privilege to have been designated Editor-in-Chief of this important project, and to have worked in close collaboration with a team of translators and proofreaders, artists and graphic designers, scholars and editors.

Together we are presenting to the English-speaking world a translation that has all the merits of the original Hebrew work by Rabbi Steinsaltz, and provides assistance for the beginner of any age who seeks to obtain the necessary skills to become an adept talmudist.

This is the first volume of the project, tractate *Berakhot*. It includes the entire original text, in the traditional configuration and pagination of the famed Vilna edition of the

Talmud. This enables the student to follow the core text with the commentaries of Rashi, *Tosafot*, and the customary marginalia. It also provides a clear English translation in contemporary idiom, faithfully based upon the modern Hebrew edition.

At least equal to the linguistic virtues of this edition are the qualities of its graphic design. Rather than intimidate students by confronting them with a page-size block of text, we have divided the page into smaller thematic units. Thus, readers can focus their attention and absorb each discrete discussion before proceeding to the next unit. The design of each page allows for sufficient white space to ease the visual task of reading. The illustrations, one of the most innovative features of the Hebrew edition, have been substantially enhanced and reproduced in color.

The end result is a literary and artistic masterpiece. This has been achieved through the dedicated work of a large team of translators, headed by Rabbi Joshua Schreier, and through the unparalleled creative efforts of Raphaël Freeman and his gifted staff.

The group of individuals who surround Rabbi Steinsaltz and support his work deserve our thanks as well. I have come to appreciate their energy, initiative, and persistence. And I thank the indefatigable Rabbi Menachem Even-Israel, whom I cannot praise highly enough. The quality of his guidance and good counsel is surpassed only by his commitment to the dissemination and perpetuation of his father's precious teachings.

Finally, in humility, awe, and great respect, I acknowledge Rabbi Adin Even-Israel (Steinsaltz). I thank him for the inspirational opportunity he has granted me to work with one of the outstanding sages of our time.

Rabbi Tzvi Hersh Weinreb
Jerusalem 5772

# Preface by the Managing Editor

Towards the end of tractate *Berakhot* (63b), the well-known homiletic interpretation of Numbers 19:14 is cited: Matters of Torah are only retained by one who kills himself over it. In *Ein Ayah*, Rav Kook explains: While educators often try to make Torah study easier in the belief that doing so will lead students to accumulate more information and Torah knowledge, their approach is fundamentally flawed. The significance of Torah education is qualitative, not quantitative. It is not the sheer volume of knowledge amassed; it is the quality of the Torah wisdom that is attained. Simplistic, facile methods of study do not facilitate deep understanding. That can only be accomplished through hard work and serious effort.

The Hebrew Steinsaltz commentary has rendered the Talmud accessible to the multitudes and has allowed them to enter the world of talmudic discourse. The English *Koren Talmud Bavli* provides an even broader audience access to that world. This edition will help ensure that the hard work and serious effort to which Rav Kook alluded will indeed facilitate a profound understanding of the Gemara.

My involvement in the production of the *Koren Talmud Bavli* has been both a privilege and a pleasure. The Shefa Foundation, headed by Rabbi Menachem Even-Israel and devoted to the dissemination of the wide-ranging, monumental works of Rabbi Adin Even-Israel (Steinsaltz), constitutes the Steinsaltz side of this partnership; Koren Publishers Jerusalem, headed by Matthew Miller, with the day-to-day management in the able hands of Raphaël Freeman, constitutes the publishing side of this partnership. The outstanding quality of the *Koren Talmud Bavli* – in terms of both form and content – is a direct result of the inspiration of Shefa and the creativity and professionalism for which Koren is renowned, and which I have witnessed over the past two years.

I would like to express my appreciation for Rabbi Dr. Tzvi Hersh Weinreb, the Editor-in-Chief, whose insight and guidance have been invaluable. The contribution of my friend and colleague, Rabbi Dr. Shalom Z. Berger, the Senior Content Editor, cannot be overstated; his title does not begin to convey the excellent direction he has provided in all aspects of this project. The erudite and articulate men and women who serve as translators, editors and proofreaders have ensured that this project adheres to the highest standards.

There are several others whose contributions to this project cannot be overlooked. On the Steinsaltz side: Meir HaNegbi, Yacov Elbert, Rabbi Yaakov Komisar, Tsipora Ifrah and Oria Tubul; on the Koren side, my colleagues: Rabbi David Fuchs, Rabbi Hanan Benayahu, Efrat Gross, Rachel Hanstater Meghnagi and Eliyahu Misgav. Their assistance in all matters, large and small, is appreciated.

At the risk of being repetitious, I would like to thank Rabbi Dr. Berger for introducing me to the world of Steinsaltz. Finally, I would like to thank Rabbi Menachem Even-Israel, with whom it continues to be a pleasure to move forward in this great enterprise.

Rabbi Joshua Schreier
Jerusalem 5772

# Introduction by the Publisher

The Talmud has sustained and inspired Jews for thousands of years. Throughout Jewish history, an elite cadre of scholars has absorbed its learning and passed it on to succeeding generations. The Talmud has been the fundamental text of our people.

Beginning in the 1960s, Rabbi Adin Even-Israel (Steinsaltz) שליט״א created a revolution in the history of Talmud study. His translation of the Talmud, first into modern Hebrew and then into other languages, as well the practical learning aids he added to the text, have enabled millions of people around the world to access and master the complexity and context of the world of Talmud.

It is thus a privilege to present the *Koren Talmud Bavli*, an English translation of the talmudic text with the brilliant elucidation of Rabbi Steinsaltz. The depth and breadth of his knowledge are unique in our time. His rootedness in the tradition and his reach into the world beyond it are inspirational.

Working with Rabbi Steinsaltz on this remarkable project has been not only an honor, but a great pleasure. Never shy to express an opinion, with wisdom and humor, Rabbi Steinsaltz sparkles in conversation, demonstrating his knowledge (both sacred and worldly), sharing his wide-ranging interests, and, above all, radiating his passion. I am grateful for the unique opportunity to work closely with him, and I wish him many more years of writing and teaching.

Our intentions in publishing this new edition of the Talmud are threefold. First, we seek to fully clarify the talmudic page to the reader – textually, intellectually, and graphically. Second, we seek to utilize today's most sophisticated technologies, both in print and electronic formats, to provide the reader with a comprehensive set of study tools. And third, we seek to help readers advance in their process of Talmud study.

To achieve these goals, the *Koren Talmud Bavli* is unique in a number of ways:

- The classic *tzurat hadaf* of Vilna, used by scholars since the 1800s, has been reset for great clarity, and opens from the Hebrew "front" of the book. Full *nikkud* has been added to both the talmudic text and Rashi's commentary, allowing for a more fluent reading with the correct pronunciation; the commentaries of *Tosafot* have been punctuated. Upon the advice of many English-speaking teachers of Talmud, we have separated these core pages from the translation, thereby enabling the advanced student to approach the text without the distraction of the translation. This also reduces the number of volumes in the set. At bottom of each *daf,* there is a reference to the corresponding English pages. In addition, the Vilna edition was read against other manuscripts and older print editions, so that texts which had been removed by non-Jewish censors have been restored to their rightful place.
- The English translation, which starts on the English "front" of the book, reproduces the *menukad* Talmud text alongside the English translation (in bold) and commentary and explanation (in a lighter font). The Hebrew and Aramaic text is presented in logical paragraphs. This allows for a fluent reading of the text for the non-Hebrew or non-Aramaic reader. It also allows for the Hebrew reader to refer easily to the text alongside. Where the original text features dialogue or poetry, the English text is laid out in a manner appropriate to the genre. Each page refers to the relevant *daf.*

- Critical contextual tools surround the text and translation: personality notes, providing short biographies of the Sages; language notes, explaining foreign terms borrowed from Greek, Latin, Persian, or Arabic; and background notes, giving information essential to the understanding of the text, including history, geography, botany, archeology, zoology, astronomy, and aspects of daily life in the talmudic era.
- Halakhic summaries provide references to the authoritative legal decisions made over the centuries by the rabbis. They explain the reasons behind each halakhic decision as well as the ruling's close connection to the Talmud and its various interpreters.
- Photographs, drawings, and other illustrations have been added throughout the text – in full color in the Standard and Electronic editions, and in black and white in the Daf Yomi edition – to visually elucidate the text.

This is not an exhaustive list of features of this edition, it merely presents an overview for the English-speaking reader who may not be familiar with the "total approach" to Talmud pioneered by Rabbi Steinsaltz.

Several professionals have helped bring this vast collaborative project to fruition. My many colleagues are noted on the Acknowledgements page, and the leadership of this project has been exceptional.

RABBI MENACHEM EVEN-ISRAEL, DIRECTOR OF THE SHEFA FOUNDATION, was the driving force behind this enterprise. With enthusiasm and energy, he formed the happy alliance with Koren and established close relationships among all involved in the work.

RABBI DR. TZVI HERSH WEINREB שליט״א, EDITOR-IN-CHIEF, brought to this project his profound knowledge of Torah, intellectual literacy of Talmud, and erudition of Western literature. It is to him that the text owes its very high standard, both in form and content, and the logical manner in which the beauty of the Talmud is presented.

RABBI JOSHUA SCHREIER, MANAGING EDITOR, assembled an outstanding group of scholars, translators, editors, and proofreaders, whose standards and discipline enabled this project to proceed in a timely and highly professional manner.

RABBI MEIR HANEGBI, EDITOR OF THE HEBREW EDITION OF THE STEINSALTZ TALMUD, lent his invaluable assistance throughout the work process, supervising the reproduction of the Vilna pages.

RAPHAËL FREEMAN, EDITOR OF KOREN, created this Talmud's unique typographic design which, true to the Koren approach, is both elegant and user-friendly.

It has been an enriching experience for all of us at Koren Publishers Jerusalem to work with the Shefa Foundation and the Steinsaltz Center to develop and produce the *Koren Talmud Bavli*. We pray that this publication will be a source of great learning and, ultimately, greater *Avodat Hashem* for all Jews.

Matthew Miller, Publisher
Koren Publishers Jerusalem
Jerusalem 5772

# Introduction to **Berakhot**

Tractate *Berakhot* is the first tractate in the order of "Faith."[1] The primary focus of the tractate is the myriad ways in which a Jewish person expresses his faith throughout his life. The plethora of details with regard to the different blessings that one recites on various occasions over the course of his life, the prayer services and their customs, *Shema* with its associated blessings and *halakhot,* and numerous other laws connected with a person's the day-to-day existence are all comprehensively addressed in this tractate. In the background, the Gemara recounts in great detail the lives of Jews in Eretz Yisrael and Babylonia during the era of the Mishna and the Talmud. It describes their occupations, their prayers, their aspirations, and their dreams, from morning to evening, on weekdays and festivals, in felicitous times and calamitous times, citing numerous halakhic and aggadic sources to enlighten, guide, and explain.

With all of the different nuances and abundance of detail in the tractate, there is one central, unifying theme that recurs throughout all of the many *halakhot* and aspects touched upon within it, which transforms it into a cohesive unit: The principle that the abstract should be concretized and the sublime realized in a practical, detailed manner.

This theme is not unique to tractate *Berakhot*; to a certain degree, it appears in every tractate of the Talmud. In fact, it is one of the primary elements of the multifaceted world of *halakha*. Consequently, it is present in every Jewish literary work throughout history as an internal, essential characteristic.

In tractate *Berakhot,* this approach is more intensive and more conspicuous. This is because the theme of the tractate is faith: The total awareness in heart and mind that there is an everlasting connection between the Creator and man and that perpetual inspiration descends from the Creator to the world – inspiration which creates, generates, and sustains. Man reacts, thanking, requesting, praying, anticipating a response; waiting to be blessed, to be cured, for a miracle. This connection of faith, which in and of itself is exalted and sublime, achieves form and clarity when it is transformed into practical *halakha* through the *halakhot* of tractate *Berakhot*. Here, faith is manifest in the details of the *halakhot,* in the myriad blessings and in the formulation of prayer. However, alongside the de-emphasis of the abstract, faith as an integral part of real life is enhanced and established. This general consciousness evolves into *halakha,* guidance how to live one's life.

The choice in favor of practical manifestation of a concept, despite the rigidity of this form of expression, is multifaceted. The fundamental outlook of Judaism is that the essence of the Torah and the objective of creation are the actualization of the Torah as a living Torah. "It is not in the heavens";[2] rather, it was given to man and for man. The closer Torah is to man, the more concrete and practical it is, the closer it is to fulfilling its objective.

Therefore, the primary fulfillment and significance of most concepts in Judaism is when they are manifest in a concrete, practical manner. The manner and style in which they are actualized determine the significance of the concept. Therefore, throughout the generations, *halakha* has never stopped creating. As the structure and circumstances of life change, new forms and styles develop in order to actualize the general, abstract concepts in those specific circumstances.

Furthermore, faith, despite its broad scope, is not a palpable presence in one's daily life. True, faith as a *Weltanschauung* and as a general approach exists, in one form or another, in the hearts of all people, at different levels of consciousness and acceptance. However, the distance between that faith and real life is too significant. There is no comparison between accepting the fundamental tenets of faith in one's heart and fulfilling them in practice, especially at all of those minor, uninspiring opportunities that constitute a majority of one's life. If the abstract concepts of faith are not manifest in a practical manner in all of the details of a person's life, faith will lose its substance; consequently, all of life's details and actions will be rendered worthless and pointless. Indeed, the fundamental demand of religion is well characterized in the phrase: "If you devote your heart and your eyes to Me, I know that you are Mine."[3]

This issue of connecting abstract faith to real life is manifest in several verses in the Torah. Nowhere is that connection as conspicuous as in the section of *Shema* in Deuteronomy.[4] "Hear, Israel, the Lord is our God, the Lord is One" expresses the fundamental tenet of the Jewish faith; "And you shall love the Lord your God with all your heart, and with all your soul, and with all your might" expresses the essence of its accompanying feeling. However, together with those abstract ideas, this short section also includes instruction and guidance regarding how to translate them into the world of action: "And you shall teach them diligently unto your children"; "and you shall bind them for a sign upon your hand"; "and you shall write them upon the doorposts of your house." That is why this section constitutes the spiritual basis for the entire tractate of *Berakhot*. Not only do some of its chapters discuss the *halakhot* of *Shema*, but other chapters extrapolate from this approach, connecting pristine faith to its actualization by means of the meticulous fulfillment of mitzvot.

*Shema* consists of three sections[5] which, although they do not appear consecutively in the Torah, combine to form a single, meaningful unit. *Shema* is, first and foremost, a recitation of the fundamental tenets of Judaism. Reciting it each day provides the stabilizing foundation and the guidelines for Jewish life. It is conceivable that reciting *Shema* each morning and evening will not constitute a profound religious experience. However, it is accessible to all, and it provides the Jewish person with the ability to delve into the text and endow all of his thoughts and actions with the essence of *Shema*, thereby fulfilling the contents of those sections in the most profound sense.

Prayer is substantively different. From the outset, prayer constituted a portal through which one could address God whenever he desired, in times of distress and need as well as times of thanksgiving and gratitude. One's ability to recite his own personal prayer was never restricted. This is optional prayer, in which one pours out his heart before God in his own style and his own words. However, this was insufficient, and therefore, the greatest of the Sages throughout the generations established a set, defined, obligatory formula for prayer, to be recited at fixed times.

The establishment of set times for prayer and a set formula common to all has the capacity to crystallize that barely perceptible feeling which exists in the heart of even the simplest person. This is because, although religious feelings exist in the hearts of all people, these feelings are not easily expressed; not every individual is conscious of them, nor does he always understand them. Fixed prayer provides the desired expression, the coherent language for the person unable to appropriately articulate the feelings in his heart.

Furthermore, the very fact that prayer is, in its essence, communal, makes the person an integral member of the community at large. Each individual considers himself and is considered by those around him as belonging to a broad, all-encompassing world.

True, there is concern that the fixed nature of prayer, in terms of both the formula and the times that it may be recited, is liable to compromise the natural connection with God and one's ability to express himself in prayer, and could ultimately become a meaningless verbal framework. Therefore, unlike *Shema,* which one is obligated to recite regardless of the conditions and circumstances, the *halakha* is much more flexible regarding prayer in the sense that one principle supersedes all others: "Do not make your prayer fixed, rather make it a plea for mercy and an entreaty before God."[7]

*Shema* and prayer provide a general direction for integrating faith into daily life, with the eighteen blessings of the *Amida* prayer tying the fundamental tenets of faith that appear in *Shema* with all of the unique, specific problems that exist in the life of the Jewish people in general and in the life of each individual Jew in particular.

Blessings are an additional step in that direction. Tractate *Berakhot* discusses dozens of different types of blessings: Blessings in prayer, blessings of thanksgiving, blessings prior to the performance of mitzvot, blessings over food and delicacies, blessings as expressions of suffering and mourning, and blessings as expressions of joy and wonder. Despite the differences in details, formulas and meaning, there is a common intent to all of the blessings: They are a way of creating a bond of meaning between an action, incident, or object and God. Life is full of directionless, meaningless, purposeless phenomena; the blessing rescues them from that purposelessness, renders them significant, and connects them to their origins and their destiny.

The profusion of blessings is a result of the need for them; they draw a cloud of grace, sanctity, and meaning over the abundance of different phenomena in the world. Uniformity of formula and of custom can also lead to a general attitude of purposelessness toward the world around us, but the great number of blessings provide each object with a unique character, a significance all its own.

In addition to the halakhic portion of tractate *Berakhot,* there is also an aggadic portion. If, as mentioned above, the halakhic portion directed us from the abstract to the concrete, the direction provided by the aggadic section is from the concrete to the abstract. As a result, all actions, including the seemingly insignificant details among them, whether from the Torah or from human life, become paradigmatic and teeming with significance and meaning. Even matters that appear to be peripheral or of secondary importance are revealed in all their significance and centrality. Similarly, events that befell people in the distant past now become contemporary and extremely significant. In this way, personalities from the past are integrated in determining the character of the present. Even halakhic patterns – fixed, clearly defined templates – assume profundity and significance in the aggadic sections, in which they are tied to wide-ranging, sublime ideas, biblical verses, and the personalities of the great leaders throughout the generations.

The numerous aggadic sections in tractate *Berakhot,* as in all other tractates in the Talmud, are intermingled with the halakhic sections; they complement them and add additional perspective. There is no abrupt, disruptive transition between the practical world of *halakha,* which deals with matters that at first glance might seem inconsequential, and the *aggada,* which deals with the sublime mysteries of the world.

Heavenly worlds and our world, discussions that delve into the smallest details, and the enigmas of faith are all cited together, as all things that exist in this world, with all of their positive and negative aspects, are one.

Tractate *Berakhot*, which contains most of the *halakhot* of *Shema*, prayer, and blessing, is divided into nine chapters.

The first three chapters deal with *Shema*:

> Chapter One, in which the obligation to recite *Shema* is discussed, along with the times when it may be recited and the details of this obligation.
>
> Chapter Two, in which more specific problems related to the manner in which *Shema* may be recited are resolved, and regulations governing its recitation are discussed.
>
> Chapter Three, in which there is a discussion of special cases in which a person is exempt from reciting *Shema* and the *Amida* prayer.

The following two chapters deal with prayer:

> Chapter Four, in which, parallel to Chapter One, determination of the times of the various prayers is discussed.
>
> Chapter Five, in which the *halakhot* of prayer are elucidated in greater detail and depth, along with an explanation of the essence of prayer and regulations governing prayer.

The following three chapters deal with appropriate conduct at a meal as well as the blessings recited before and after eating:

> Chapter Six, in which the primary focus is on the blessings of enjoyment that one recites over food, drink, and other pleasures.
>
> Chapter Seven, which is devoted to Grace after Meals and the invitation [*zimmun*] to participate in joint recitation of Grace after Meals.
>
> Chapter Eight, in which, incidental to the discussion of blessings associated with a meal, a list of disputes between Beit Shammai and Beit Hillel with regard to appropriate conduct at a meal and the *halakhot* of blessings is cited.

The following chapter deals with blessings recited in response to various phenomena:

> Chapter Nine, in which the blessings recited in different circumstances are discussed – blessings which determine the attitude toward virtually every phenomenon, common and uncommon, that one encounters in the course of his life.

NOTES

1. This is the name given to the first of the six orders of the Mishna, the order of *Zera'im* (*Shabbat* 31a).
2. Deuteronomy 30:12.
3. Translation of tractate *Berakhot* in the Jerusalem Talmud 8:5.
4. Deuteronomy 6:4–9.
5. *Shema* – Deuteronomy 6:4–9; *VeHaya im Shamoa* – Deuteronomy 11:13–21; *VaYomer* – Numbers 15:37–41.
6. Rambam *Sefer Ahava, Hilkhot Tefilla* ch. 1.
7. *Avot* 2:12.

# Introduction to **Perek I**

*Hear, Israel, the Lord is our God, the Lord is One. And you shall love the Lord your God with all your heart, and with all your soul, and with all your might. And these words, which I command you this day, shall be upon your heart; and you shall teach them diligently unto your children, and shall talk of them when you sit in your house, and when you walk by the way, and when you lie down, and when you arise.*

(Deuteronomy 6:4–7)

The fundamental issue discussed in the first chapter of *Berakhot* is: What are the practical implications of the text of *Shema*? Particularly, how is one to understand the terms "When you lie down, and when you arise" as a precise, practical halakhic directive?

Based on a reading of the text of the Torah itself, one could understand the content of these verses as general encouragement to engage in the study of Torah at all times. However, in the oral tradition, the obligation to recite *Shema* is derived from these verses. Once this obligation is established, it is incumbent upon us to ascertain how it is to be fulfilled. The obligation of *Shema* involves reciting three sections from the Torah: (1) *Shema* (Deuteronomy 6:4–9); (2) *VeHaya im Shamoa* (Deuteronomy 11:13–21); and (3) *VaYomer* (Numbers 15:37–41). There is a twice-daily obligation to recite these sections, in the morning and the evening, as per the verse: "When you lie down, and when you arise." Through reciting these sections one expresses commitment to the fundamental tenets of the Torah and faith in God.

The first question is with regard to the meaning of: "When you lie down, and when you arise." Is the Torah merely establishing a time frame for reciting "these words," or is it also describing the manner and the circumstances in which those words should be recited?

Even if "when you lie down, and when you arise" merely establishes the time frame for reciting *Shema*, that time frame is not as clearly defined as it would have been had the Torah written "morning" and "evening." It remains to be determined whether "when you lie down" refers to the hour that people usually go to sleep or, perhaps, the entire duration of that sleep. Similarly, is "when you arise" referring to the entire period of the day during which people are awake, or is it perhaps referring to the specific hour when each individual awakens? In general, is there a direct correlation between "when you lie down and when you arise" and morning and evening?

These and many related questions are the primary focus of this chapter.

The beginning of tractate *Berakhot*, the first tractate in the first of the six orders of Mishna, opens with a discussion of the recitation of *Shema*,[N] as the recitation of *Shema* encompasses an acceptance of the yoke of Heaven and of the mitzvot, and as such, forms the basis for all subsequent teachings. The Mishna opens with the laws regarding the appropriate time to recite *Shema*:

מֵאֵימָתַי קוֹרִין אֶת ״שְׁמַע״ בְּעַרְבִין? – מִשָּׁעָה שֶׁהַכֹּהֲנִים נִכְנָסִים לֶאֱכוֹל בִּתְרוּמָתָן עַד סוֹף הָאַשְׁמוּרָה הָרִאשׁוֹנָה, דִּבְרֵי רַבִּי אֱלִיעֶזֶר.

**MISHNA** **From when,** that is, from what time, does **one recite** ***Shema*** **in the evening?**[H] **From the time when the priests enter to partake of their** ***teruma***.[NB] Until when does the time for the recitation of the evening *Shema* extend? **Until the end of the first watch.** The term used in the Torah (Deuteronomy 6:7) to indicate the time for the recitation of the evening *Shema* is *beshokhbekha*, when you lie down, which refers to the time in which individuals go to sleep. Therefore, the time for the recitation of *Shema* is the first portion of the night, when individuals typically prepare for sleep. **That is the statement of Rabbi Eliezer.**

וַחֲכָמִים אוֹמְרִים: עַד חֲצוֹת.

**The Rabbis say:** The time for the recitation of the evening *Shema* is **until midnight.**

רַבָּן גַּמְלִיאֵל אוֹמֵר: עַד שֶׁיַּעֲלֶה עַמּוּד הַשַּׁחַר.

**Rabban Gamliel**[P] **says:** One may recite *Shema* **until dawn,**[HB] indicating that *beshokhbekha* is to be understood as a reference to the entire time people sleep in their beds, the whole night.

מַעֲשֶׂה וּבָאוּ בָנָיו מִבֵּית הַמִּשְׁתֶּה, אָמְרוּ לוֹ: לֹא קָרִינוּ אֶת ״שְׁמַע״. אָמַר לָהֶם: אִם לֹא עָלָה עַמּוּד הַשַּׁחַר חַיָּיבִין אַתֶּם לִקְרוֹת. וְלֹא זוֹ בִּלְבַד אָמְרוּ, אֶלָּא כׇּל מַה שֶּׁאָמְרוּ חֲכָמִים עַד חֲצוֹת מִצְוָתָן עַד שֶׁיַּעֲלֶה עַמּוּד הַשַּׁחַר;

The mishna relates that Rabban Gamliel practiced in accordance with his ruling. There was an **incident** where Rabban Gamliel's **sons returned** very late **from a wedding hall. They said to him,** as they had been preoccupied with celebrating with the groom and bride: **We did not recite** ***Shema***. **He said to them: If the dawn has not** yet **arrived, you are obligated to recite** ***Shema***. Since Rabban Gamliel's opinion disagreed with that of the Rabbis, he explained to his sons that the Rabbis actually agree with him, **and** that it is **not only** with regard to the *halakha* of the recitation of *Shema*, **but rather, wherever the Sages say until midnight, the mitzva** may be performed **until dawn.**

### BACKGROUND

**Teruma – תְּרוּמָה:** Whenever the term *teruma* appears without qualification, it refers to *teruma gedola*. The Torah commands that "the first fruit of your oil, your wine, and your grain" be given to the priest (Numbers 18:12). The Sages extended the scope of this commandment to include all produce. This mitzva applies only in Eretz Yisrael. After the first fruits have been set aside, a certain portion of the produce must be set aside for the priests. The Torah does not specify the amount of *teruma* that must be set aside; one may even theoretically fulfill his obligation by separating a single kernel of grain from an entire crop. The Sages established a measure: one-fortieth for a generous gift, one-fiftieth for an average gift, and one-sixtieth for a miserly gift. One may not set aside the other tithes (*ma'asrot*) until he has set aside *teruma*. *Teruma* is considered sacred and may be eaten only by a priest and his household while they are in a state of ritual purity (Leviticus 22:9–15). To emphasize that state of ritual purity, the Sages obligated the priests to wash their hands before partaking of it. This is the source for the practice of washing one's hands prior to a meal. A ritually impure priest or a non-priest who eats *teruma* is subject to the penalty of death at the hand of Heaven. If *teruma* contracts ritual impurity, it may no longer be eaten and must be destroyed. Nevertheless, it remains the property of the priest and he may benefit from its destruction. Nowadays, *teruma* is not given to the priests because they have no definite proof of their priestly lineage. Nevertheless, the obligation to separate *teruma* still remains, although only a small portion of the produce is separated.

### NOTES

**Opening with the recitation of *Shema* – הַפְּתִיחָה בִּקְרִיאַת שְׁמַע:** Since this tractate discusses the laws of blessings and prayers, it opens with the laws of the recitation of *Shema*, a biblical commandment that applies every day and which constitutes the acceptance of the yoke of Heaven (*Tziyyun LeNefesh Ḥayya*).

**From the time when the priests enter to partake of their *teruma* – מִשָּׁעָה שֶׁהַכֹּהֲנִים נִכְנָסִים לֶאֱכוֹל בִּתְרוּמָתָן:** The priests would eat *teruma* in a state of purity. Failure to uphold this standard of purity with regard to *teruma* was punished by death at the hand of Heaven (Leviticus 22:3). Therefore, priests who became impure would immerse during the day and wait until the evening, or the emergence of the stars, when several stars are visible in the sky, before partaking of their *teruma* (Leviticus 22:6–7).

### PERSONALITIES

**Rabban Gamliel – רַבָּן גַּמְלִיאֵל:** *Nasi* of the Sanhedrin and one of the most important *tanna'im* in the period following the destruction of the Second Temple. Rabban Gamliel's father, Rabban Shimon ben Gamliel (the Elder), had also been *Nasi* of the Sanhedrin, as well as one of the leaders of the nation during the rebellion against Rome. Rabban Gamliel was taken to Yavne by Rabban Yoḥanan ben Zakkai after the destruction of the Temple, so that he became known as Rabban Gamliel of Yavne. After Rabban Yoḥanan ben Zakkai's death, Rabban Gamliel presided over the Sanhedrin.

Under Rabban Gamliel's leadership, Yavne became an important spiritual center. The greatest of the Sages gathered around him, including Rabbi Eliezer (Rabban Gamliel's brother-in-law), Rabbi Yehoshua, Rabbi Akiva, and Rabbi Elazar ben Azarya.

Rabban Gamliel sought to create a spiritual center for the Jews that would unite the entire people, a role filled by the Temple until its destruction. Therefore, he strove to enhance the prominence and central authority of the Sanhedrin and its *Nasi*. His strict and vigorous leadership eventually led his colleagues to remove him from his post for a brief period, replacing him with Rabbi Elazar ben Azarya. However, since everyone realized that his motives and actions were for the good of the people and were not based on personal ambition, they soon restored him to his position.

We do not possess many halakhic rulings explicitly in the name of Rabban Gamliel. However, in his time, and under his influence, some of the most important decisions in the history of Jewish spiritual life were made. These included the decision to follow Beit Hillel, the rejection of the halakhic system of Rabbi Eliezer, and the establishment of fixed formulas for prayers. In those halakhic decisions attributed to Rabban Gamliel, we find an uncompromising approach to the *halakha*; in reaching his conclusions, he was faithful to his principles. We know that two of his sons were Sages: Rabban Shimon ben Gamliel, who served as *Nasi* of the Sanhedrin after him, and Rabbi Ḥanina ben Gamliel.

### BACKGROUND

**Dawn – עַמּוּד הַשַּׁחַר:** The first light of the sun before sunrise. With regard to many *halakhot*, such as the eating of sacrifices at night, the recitation of *Shema* at night, and the permissibility of eating before a fast, dawn is considered the time when night ends. The definition of the precise time of dawn is uncertain. Nowadays, it is generally accepted that, in Eretz Yisrael, dawn is between approximately one-and-a-quarter and one-and-a-half hours before sunrise.

### HALAKHA

**From when does one recite *Shema* in the evening – מֵאֵימָתַי קוֹרִין אֶת שְׁמַע בְּעַרְבִין:** The beginning of the time for the recitation of the evening *Shema* is the emergence of the stars, defined as when three small stars are visible in the sky. Ideally, *Shema* should be recited as early as possible, as we hasten to perform mitzvot. This *halakha* is decided in accordance with our mishna, and although other tannaitic opinions are cited in the Gemara, the halakhic ruling in our mishna takes precedence over those cited in *baraitot*. Moreover, the Gemara itself follows the position articulated in our mishna. While it would be appropriate to consider the emergence of the stars to be when three medium stars are visible in the sky, due to concern lest *Shema* be recited too early, an added stringency was imposed to wait until three small stars are visible (*Magen Avraham*; Rambam *Sefer Ahava, Hilkhot Keriat Shema* 1:9; *Shulḥan Arukh, Oraḥ Ḥayyim* 235:1, 3).

**The Rabbis say until midnight. Rabban Gamliel says until dawn – וַחֲכָמִים אוֹמְרִים: עַד חֲצוֹת. רַבָּן גַּמְלִיאֵל אוֹמֵר: עַד שֶׁיַּעֲלֶה עַמּוּד הַשַּׁחַר:** One must recite the evening *Shema* before midnight. However, if one recited *Shema* after midnight, he fulfilled his obligation. According to Rabban Gamliel, even the Rabbis agree: When there are extenuating circumstances, one may recite *Shema* until dawn and one fulfills his obligation. That is the accepted halakhic ruling (*Kesef Mishne*; Rambam *Sefer Ahava, Hilkhot Keriat Shema* 1:9; *Shulḥan Arukh, Oraḥ Ḥayyim* 235:3).

הֶקְטֵר חֲלָבִים וְאֵבָרִים – מִצְוָתָן עַד שֶׁיַּעֲלֶה עַמּוּד הַשַּׁחַר, וְכָל הַנֶּאֱכָלִים לְיוֹם אֶחָד – מִצְוָתָן עַד שֶׁיַּעֲלֶה עַמּוּד הַשַּׁחַר, אִם כֵּן, לָמָּה אָמְרוּ חֲכָמִים עַד חֲצוֹת? – כְּדֵי לְהַרְחִיק אָדָם מִן הָעֲבֵירָה.

Rabban Gamliel cites several cases in support of his claim, such as **the burning of fats and limbs**[H] on the altar. Due to the quantity of offerings each day, the priests were often unable to complete the burning of all of the fats and limbs, so they continued to be burned into the night, as it is written: "This is the law of the burnt offering: The burnt offering shall remain upon the pyre on the altar all night until morning, while the fire on the altar burns it" (Leviticus 6:2). **And,** with regard to **all** sacrifices, such as the sin-offerings and the guilt-offerings **that are eaten for one day**[H] and night; although the Sages state that they may be eaten only until midnight, by Torah law they may be eaten **until dawn.** This is in accordance with the verse: "On the day on which it is offered must you eat. Do not leave it until the morning" (Leviticus 7:15). **If so, why did the Sages say** that they may be eaten only **until midnight?** This is **in order to distance a person from transgression,** as if one believes that he has until dawn to perform the mitzva, he might be negligent and postpone it until the opportunity to perform the mitzva has passed.

גמ׳ תַּנָּא הֵיכָא קָאֵי דְּקָתָנֵי "מֵאֵימָתַי"?

**GEMARA** The Mishna opens with the laws concerning the appropriate time to recite *Shema* with the question: From when does one recite *Shema* in the evening? With regard to this question, the Gemara asks: **On the basis of what** prior knowledge **does the *tanna***[B] of our mishna ask: **From when?** It would seem from his question that the obligation to recite *Shema* in the evening was already established, and that the *tanna* seeks only to clarify details that relate to it. But our mishna is the very first mishna in the Talmud.

וְתוּ, מַאי שְׁנָא דְּתָנֵי בְּעַרְבִית בְּרֵישָׁא? לִתְנֵי דְּשַׁחֲרִית בְּרֵישָׁא!

The Gemara asks: **And furthermore, what distinguishes the evening *Shema*,** that it was **taught first? Let** the *tanna* **teach** regarding the recitation of **the morning *Shema* first.** Since most mitzvot apply during the day, the *tanna* should discuss the morning *Shema* before discussing the evening *Shema*, just as the daily morning offering is discussed before the evening offering (*Tosefot HaRosh*).

תַּנָּא אַקְּרָא קָאֵי, דִּכְתִיב: "בְּשָׁכְבְּךָ וּבְקוּמֶךָ". וְהָכִי קָתָנֵי: זְמַן קְרִיאַת שְׁמַע דִּשְׁכִיבָה אֵימַת – מִשָּׁעָה שֶׁהַכֹּהֲנִים נִכְנָסִין לֶאֱכוֹל בִּתְרוּמָתָן.

The Gemara offers a single response to both questions: **The *tanna* bases himself on the verse as it is written:** "You will talk of them when you sit in your home, and when you walk along the way, **when you lie down, and when you arise**" (Deuteronomy 6:7). By teaching the laws of the evening *Shema* first, the *tanna* has established that the teachings of the Oral Torah correspond to that which is taught in the Written Torah. **And** based on the Written Torah, **the *tanna* teaches** the oral law: **When is the time for the recitation of *Shema* of lying down** as commanded in the Torah? **From when the priests enter to partake of their *teruma*.** Just as the Written Torah begins with the evening *Shema*, so too must the Oral Torah.

וְאִי בָּעֵית אֵימָא: יָלֵיף מִבְּרִיָּיתוֹ שֶׁל עוֹלָם, דִּכְתִיב: "וַיְהִי עֶרֶב וַיְהִי בֹקֶר יוֹם אֶחָד."

However, there is another possible explanation for why the mishna opens with the evening *Shema* rather than with the morning *Shema*. **If you wish,** you could **say** instead[B] that the *tanna* **derives** the precedence of the evening *Shema* **from the** order of the **creation of the world.**[N] **As it is written** in the story of creation: **"And there was evening, and there was morning, one day"** (Genesis 1:5). According to this verse, day begins with the evening and not the morning. For both of these reasons it was appropriate to open the discussion of the laws of the recitation of *Shema* with the evening *Shema*.

אִי הָכִי, סֵיפָא דְּקָתָנֵי "בַּשַּׁחַר מְבָרֵךְ שְׁתַּיִם לְפָנֶיהָ וְאַחַת לְאַחֲרֶיהָ, בָּעֶרֶב מְבָרֵךְ שְׁתַּיִם לְפָנֶיהָ וּשְׁתַּיִם לְאַחֲרֶיהָ" – לִתְנֵי דְּעַרְבִית בְּרֵישָׁא!

The Gemara asks: **If so,** why does the **latter clause**[B] of the mishna, which appears later in the chapter, **teach: In the morning one recites two** blessings **before** *Shema* **and one** blessing **afterward, and in the evening one recites two** blessings **before** *Shema* **and two afterward?**[H] Based upon the above reasoning, the mishna **should have taught** the blessing recited before and after the **evening** *Shema* **first.**

HALAKHA

**The burning of fats and limbs – הֶקְטֵר חֲלָבִים וְאֵבָרִים:** The fats and limbs of any sacrifice whose blood was sprinkled during the day may be burned throughout the night until dawn, in accordance with the opinion of Rabban Gamliel (Rambam *Sefer Avoda, Hilkhot Ma'aseh HaKorbanot* 4:2).

**All sacrifices that are eaten for one day – וְכָל הַנֶּאֱכָלִים לְיוֹם אֶחָד:** One must complete eating sacrifices that are eaten for one day and night, until midnight. Although by Torah law he is permitted to eat them until dawn, the Sages ruled stringently in order to prevent him from committing a transgression. That is the clear ruling in Chapter Five of tractate *Zevaḥim* (Rambam *Sefer Avoda, Hilkhot Ma'aseh Korbanot* 10:8).

**In the morning one recites two blessings before *Shema*… and in the evening… – בַּשַּׁחַר מְבָרֵךְ שְׁתַּיִם לְפָנֶיהָ...בָּעֶרֶב...:** When reciting *Shema*, one recites blessings beforehand and thereafter. During the day one recites two blessings beforehand: Who forms light and A great love/An everlasting love, and one thereafter: Who redeemed Israel; and at night one recites two blessings beforehand: Who brings on evenings and An everlasting love, and two thereafter: Who redeemed Israel and Help us lie down. One who recites *Shema* without reciting its blessings fulfills his obligation, but is required to recite the blessings without again reciting *Shema*. The *Shulḥan Arukh* writes in that case: It seems to me that it is preferable to recite *Shema* with its blessings (Rambam *Sefer Ahava, Hilkhot Keriat Shema* 1:5–6; *Shulḥan Arukh, Oraḥ Ḥayyim* 60:1–2, 236:1).

BACKGROUND

***Tanna* – תַּנָּא:** The *tanna'im* are Sages from the period of the Mishna. Some of them are cited in the Mishna itself, while others are cited only in other contemporaneous sources. The period of the *tanna'im* did not end all at once, and there was a transitional generation of Sages who lived during the era of the redaction of the Mishna. Later, in the amoraic period, the term *tanna* took on another meaning: one for whom tannaitic sources were his area of expertise but who was not himself one of the Sages.

**If you wish, you could say instead – אִי בָּעֵית אֵימָא:** This expression is used to introduce an additional answer to a question previously asked, or an additional explanation of a problem previously raised. When more than one solution is provided, it is generally an indication that each harbors some particular weakness (Rashba).

**Latter clause – סֵיפָא:** It means "the end"; the opposite of "the head," the first clause. These terms usually indicate the first and last sections of the mishna, although there are instances where the terms are relative: former and latter. Occasionally, this term does not refer to the last section of the mishna under discussion but rather to a mishna that appears later in the chapter. At times, the terms refer to two segments of a sentence or *halakha*. In certain cases, there is also a middle clause.

NOTES

**If you wish, you could say instead that he derives it from the creation of the world – וְאִי בָּעֵית אֵימָא: יָלֵיף מִבְּרִיָּיתוֹ שֶׁל עוֹלָם:** Although the first explanation seems adequate, this is not the case, as a dispute emerges (in the second chapter of this tractate) as to whether the verse "And you should speak of them…when you lie down and when you arise," applies specifically to the recitation of *Shema* or to Torah study in general. If one holds in accordance with the second opinion, one cannot rely on this verse as a proof. Therefore, another proof is cited here, explaining that, in any case, the evening precedes the morning (*Penei Yehoshua*).

תַּנָּא פָּתַח בְּעַרְבִית וַהֲדַר תָּנֵי בְּשַׁחֲרִית, עַד דְּקָאֵי בְּשַׁחֲרִית – פָּרֵישׁ מִילֵּי דְשַׁחֲרִית, וַהֲדַר פָּרֵישׁ מִילֵּי דְעַרְבִית.

The Gemara answers: Indeed, the ***tanna* began** by discussing the laws regarding the recitation of **the evening *Shema*, and then taught** the laws regarding the recitation of **the morning *Shema*. Once** he **was already dealing with the morning *Shema*, he explained the matters of the morning *Shema*, and then explained the matters of the evening *Shema*.**

אָמַר מָר: מִשָּׁעָה שֶׁהַכֹּהֲנִים נִכְנָסִים לֶאֱכוֹל בִּתְרוּמָתָן. מִכְּדִי, כֹּהֲנִים אֵימַת קָא אָכְלִי תְּרוּמָה – מִשְּׁעַת צֵאת הַכּוֹכָבִים, לִתְנֵי ״מִשְּׁעַת צֵאת הַכּוֹכָבִים״!

The Gemara proceeds to clarify the rest of the mishna. **The Master said**[B] in the mishna that the beginning of the period when one recites *Shema* in the evening is **when the priests enter to partake of their *teruma*.** However, this does not specify a definitive time. **When do the priests enter to partake of their *teruma*? From the time of the emergence of the stars.** If that is the case, then **let** the *tanna* **teach** that the time for the recitation of the evening *Shema* is **from the time of the emergence of the stars.**

מִלְּתָא אַגַּב אוֹרְחֵיהּ קָמַשְׁמַע לָן, כֹּהֲנִים אֵימַת קָא אָכְלִי בִּתְרוּמָה – מִשְּׁעַת צֵאת הַכּוֹכָבִים. וְהָא קָמַשְׁמַע לָן: דְּכַפָּרָה לָא מְעַכְּבָא. כִּדְתַנְיָא: ״וּבָא הַשֶּׁמֶשׁ וְטָהֵר״ – בִּיאַת שִׁמְשׁוֹ מְעַכַּבְתּוֹ מִלֶּאֱכוֹל בִּתְרוּמָה, וְאֵין כַּפָּרָתוֹ מְעַכַּבְתּוֹ מִלֶּאֱכוֹל בִּתְרוּמָה.

The Gemara responds: Indeed it would have been simpler to say that the time for the recitation of the evening *Shema* begins with the emergence of the stars, but the particular expression used by the *tanna* **teaches us** another **matter in passing: When do priests partake of their *teruma*? From the time of the emergence of the stars. And** the *tanna* **teaches us** a new *halakha* parenthetically: failure to bring an **atonement** offering **does not prevent** a priest from eating *teruma*.[N] In cases where an impure priest is required to immerse himself in a ritual bath and bring an atonement offering, even if he already immersed himself, he is not completely ritually pure until he brings the atonement offering. Nevertheless, he is still permitted to partake of *teruma*. Taught in passing in our mishna, this is articulated fully in a *baraita*, based on a close reading of the biblical passages. **As it was taught** in a *baraita*[B] with regard to the laws of ritual impurity, it is said: "One who touches it remains impure until evening. He should not eat of the consecrated items and he must wash his flesh with water. And the sun sets and it is purified. Afterwards, he may eat from the *teruma*, for it is his bread" (Leviticus 22:6–7). From the passage: **"And the sun sets and it is purified,"** that the absence of **the setting of his sun prevents him from partaking of *teruma*,**[H] **but** failure to bring **the atonement** offering **does not prevent him from partaking of *teruma*,** may be inferred.

וּמִמַּאי דְּהַאי ״וּבָא הַשֶּׁמֶשׁ״ בִּיאַת הַשֶּׁמֶשׁ, וְהַאי ״וְטָהֵר״ – טְהַר יוֹמָא,

The Gemara discusses the proof offered in the *baraita*: **From where** do we know **that the** phrase: **"And the sun sets"** refers to **the** complete **setting of the sun,** and therefore, **"and it is purified"** refers to the fact that **the day is pure,** i.e., and the sun sets and it is purified is one phrase meaning that the sun will set, the air will clear, and the stars will emerge (Rav Hai Gaon)?

### BACKGROUND

**The Master said** – **אָמַר מָר:** When the Gemara quotes a passage from a previously cited mishna or *baraita*, it introduces the passage with this honorific. This is usually followed by elucidation of several aspects of the topic under discussion.

**It was taught in a *baraita*** – **תַּנְיָא:** The literal meaning is "it was taught." This introduces a citation from a non-mishnaic tannaitic source. Usually, this term indicates a citation from a *baraita*. These sources are introduced with this term, "it was taught," as opposed to the term used to introduce a mishna, "we learned." The Mishna is something that we all learned, while the *baraita* was taught by a limited number of people and did not gain so extensive a readership.

### NOTES

**Failure to bring an atonement offering does not prevent him from eating *teruma*** – **וְאֵין כַּפָּרָתוֹ מְעַכַּבְתּוֹ מִלֶּאֱכוֹל בִּתְרוּמָה:** The preceding verses mention (among those prohibited to eat *teruma*) a *zav* and leper, who are required to bring a sacrifice in order to complete their purification process. These verses also offer an explanation for the leniency that allows a priest to eat *teruma* even though he is not completely purified: "For it is his bread." Since the *teruma* is the sustenance upon which his life depends, the Torah was not strict with him (*Seforno*).

### HALAKHA

**The absence of the setting of his sun prevents him from partaking of *teruma*** – **בִּיאַת שִׁמְשׁוֹ מְעַכַּבְתּוֹ מִלֶּאֱכוֹל בִּתְרוּמָה:** Priests who were ritually impure and immersed themselves during the day in order to purify themselves must wait until the emergence of three stars before partaking of their *teruma* (Rambam *Sefer Zera'im*, *Hilkhot Terumot* 7:2).

Perek **I**
Daf **2** Amud **b**

דִּילְמָא בִּיאַת אוֹרוֹ הוּא, וּמַאי ״וְטָהֵר״ – טְהַר גַּבְרָא!

**Perhaps** the expression: "And the sun sets and it is purified" refers to the very beginning of sunset, **the setting of** the sun's **light.** According to that explanation, **what does** the expression **and it is purified mean?** It means that **the person will become purified.** At the very beginning of sunset he will go and immerse himself and offer his sacrifice, and only then will he be able to eat of his *teruma* (*Tosafot*).

אָמַר רַבָּה בַּר רַב שֵׁילָא: אִם כֵּן לֵימָא קְרָא ״וְיִטְהַר״, מַאי ״וְטָהֵר״ – טְהַר יוֹמָא. כִּדְאָמְרִי אֱינָשֵׁי: ״אִיעֲרַב שִׁמְשָׁא וְאִדְּכִי יוֹמָא״.

**Rabba bar Rav Sheila said: If so,** that: And it is purified, means that the priest goes and purifies himself, then **let the verse say** unambiguously: **And he will become purified.** Since the Torah does not employ that language, the conclusion is: **What is** the meaning of the expression: **And it is purified?** It means **the day is pure,** no residue of day remains, **as people say**[B] colloquially: **The sun has set and the day is purified.**

### BACKGROUND

**People say** – **אָמְרִי אֱינָשֵׁי:** A term used to introduce a popular adage or saying. The Talmud incorporates many such sayings to explain the meaning of unusual terms, new ideas, or facts concerning everyday life.

בְּמַעְרְבָא הָא דְּרַבָּה בַּר רַב שֵׁילָא לָא שְׁמִיעַ לְהוּ, וּבְעוּ לַהּ מִיבַּעְיָא: הַאי "וּבָא הַשֶּׁמֶשׁ" – בִּיאַת שִׁמְשׁוֹ הוּא, וּמַאי "וְטָהֵר" – טְהַר יוֹמָא, אוֹ דִּילְמָא בִּיאַת אוֹרוֹ הוּא, וּמַאי "וְטָהֵר" – טְהַר גַּבְרָא?

**In the West,** Eretz Yisrael,[B] **they did not hear**[B] **this** explanation given **by Rabba bar Rav Sheila. They raised the dilemma: Does the expression: And the sun sets, refer to the** actual **setting of the sun, and does: And it is purified, mean the day clears away? Or perhaps it refers to the setting of its light** at sunset, in which case **what is** the meaning of: **And it is purified?** It refers to **the purification of the person.** In other words, in Eretz Yisrael, they attempted to clarify the *halakha* based on the biblical passage, but were unable to do so.

וַהֲדַר פַּשְׁטוּ לַהּ מִבָּרַיְיתָא, מִדְּקָתָנֵי בְּבָרַיְיתָא "סִימָן לַדָּבָר צֵאת הַכּוֹכָבִים" שְׁמַע מִינַּהּ: בִּיאַת שִׁמְשׁוֹ הוּא, וּמַאי 'וְטָהֵר' – טְהַר יוֹמָא.

**Ultimately they resolved**[B] this dilemma **from a** ***baraita*****.**[B] **It was taught in a baraita** that the time for the recitation of the evening *Shema* corresponds to the time when priests are permitted to eat of their *teruma*, **a sign for which is the emergence of the stars.** Therefore, **derive from here** that "and the sun sets" refers to **the complete sunset, and the expression "and it is purified"** means **the day clears away,** as the Sages in Babylonia concluded.

אָמַר מָר: "מִשָּׁעָה שֶׁהַכֹּהֲנִים נִכְנָסִין לֶאֱכוֹל בִּתְרוּמָתָן". וּרְמִינְהוּ: מֵאֵימָתַי קוֹרִין אֶת שְׁמַע בָּעֲרָבִין? מִשֶּׁהֶעָנִי נִכְנָס לֶאֱכוֹל פִּתּוֹ בְּמֶלַח, עַד שָׁעָה שֶׁעוֹמֵד לִיפָּטֵר מִתּוֹךְ סְעוּדָתוֹ.

In our mishna, **the Master said:** The beginning of the time for the recitation of the evening *Shema* is: **From the time when the priests enter to partake of their** ***teruma*****.** The Gemara **raises a contradiction**[B] to this opinion from a *baraita* that states that the time for the recitation of the evening *Shema* is: **From when a poor person enters to eat his bread with salt until he rises from his meal.**

סֵיפָא וַדַּאי פְּלִיגָא אַמַּתְנִיתִין; רֵישָׁא, מִי לֵימָא פְּלִיגֵי אַמַּתְנִיתִין?

The Gemara begins its analysis by clarifying whether there is an actual contradiction here, or whether different expressions are being employed to describe the same time. **The latter clause** of the *baraita*, which established that the time for the recitation of the evening *Shema* ends when a poor person rises from his meal, **certainly disagrees with our mishna.**[B] Since the poor person clearly does not continue eating until the end of the third watch, this *baraita* certainly contradicts our mishna. With regard to **the first clause** of the *baraita*, however, which establishes the beginning of the time for the recitation of the evening *Shema*, **shall we say that it disagrees with our mishna?**

לָא, עָנִי וְכֹהֵן חַד שִׁיעוּרָא הוּא.

The Gemara immediately rejects this idea: **No,** the time when **the poor person** eats **and** the time when **the priest** is purified and permitted to partake of his *teruma* **are one** and the same **time.**[N]

וּרְמִינְהוּ: מֵאֵימָתַי מַתְחִילִין לִקְרוֹת קְרִיאַת שְׁמַע בְּעַרְבִית? – מִשָּׁעָה שֶׁבְּנֵי אָדָם נִכְנָסִין לֶאֱכוֹל פִּתָּן בְּעַרְבֵי שַׁבָּתוֹת, דִּבְרֵי רַבִּי מֵאִיר. וַחֲכָמִים אוֹמְרִים: מִשָּׁעָה שֶׁהַכֹּהֲנִים זַכָּאִין לֶאֱכוֹל בִּתְרוּמָתָן, סִימָן לַדָּבָר: צֵאת הַכּוֹכָבִים. וְאַף עַל פִּי שֶׁאֵין רְאָיָה לַדָּבָר – זֵכֶר לַדָּבָר, שֶׁנֶּאֱמַר: "וַאֲנַחְנוּ עֹשִׂים בַּמְּלָאכָה וְחֶצְיָם מַחֲזִיקִים בָּרְמָחִים מֵעֲלוֹת הַשַּׁחַר עַד צֵאת הַכּוֹכָבִים", וְאוֹמֵר: "וְהָיוּ לָנוּ הַלַּיְלָה מִשְׁמָר וְהַיּוֹם מְלָאכָה".

The Gemara **raises a contradiction** from the *Tosefta*: **From when does one begin to recite** *Shema* **in the evening?**[N] **From the time when people enter to eat their bread on Shabbat eve.** This is **the statement of Rabbi Meir.** As they do in our mishna, **the Rabbis say: From the time when the priests are eligible to partake of their** ***teruma*****, a sign for which is the emergence of the stars. And although there is no** explicit **proof** that the emergence of the stars is when one may begin to recite the evening *Shema*, **there is an allusion** in the book of Nehemiah to the fact that the emergence of the stars is generally considered the beginning of the night. **As it is stated** with regard to the building of the walls of Jerusalem: **"And we perform the work, and half of them grasp their spears from dawn until the emergence of the stars"** (Nehemiah 4:15). **And it says: "That in the night they may be a guard to us, and may labor in the day"** (Nehemiah 4:17). From here we ascertain that the day ends with the emergence of the stars.

מַאי "וְאוֹמֵר"?

Even before analyzing these sources, the Gemara seeks to clarify a confusing element in the *Tosefta*. In their biblical proof, the Rabbis do not suffice with one verse, but rather they say: And it says… and they cite an additional verse. **What** is added by this use of: **And it says?** It seems superfluous, as the entire proof appears in the first verse.

וְכִי תֵּימָא: מִכִּי עָרְבָא שִׁמְשָׁא לֵילְיָא הוּא, וְאִינְהוּ דְּמַחְשְׁכִי וּמַקְדְּמִי, תָּא שְׁמַע: "וְהָיוּ לָנוּ הַלַּיְלָה מִשְׁמָר וְהַיּוֹם מְלָאכָה".

The Gemara answers that the first verse was not sufficient. **As, if you say that night begins when the sun sets, but** the workers **stayed late and arrived early;** i.e., due to the importance of their task they worked even into the night. In anticipation of this objection, the second verse was cited to teach: **Come and hear,** as it is stated: **"That in the night they may be a guard to us, and may labor in the day,"** the time between dawn and the emergence of the stars is explicitly referred to as "day," proving that night begins with the emergence of the stars.

## BACKGROUND

The West – מַעֲרָבָא: In the Babylonian Talmud, Eretz Yisrael is referred to as "the West," since it is southwest of Babylonia. In later periods, the customs in Israel were referred to as Western, as opposed to the Eastern customs of Babylonia.

They did not hear – לָא שְׁמִיעַ לְהוּ: This phrase often means exactly what it appears to mean, that they had not heard or were unaware of a particular *halakha*. Some, however, explain it here in the sense that it is employed elsewhere; they did not accept the particular opinion (*Adderet Eliyahu*).

They resolved this – פַּשְׁטוּ לַהּ: This phrase introduces the resolution of a problem that poses no difficulty to a particular Sage or opinion, but rather expresses difficulty in understanding a verse or a halakhic ruling.

*Baraita* – בָּרַיְיתָא: Literally, the word *baraita* means external or outside, and it is used to refer to tannaitic material, that was not included in the final compilation of the Mishna. When Rabbi Yehuda HaNasi redacted the collection of tannaitic material it was necessary to exclude much of it from the framework of the Mishna. This material, some of which comprises other collections, is known as *baraitot*, or "external *mishnayot*." These *baraitot* contain variant texts and other important material.

The Gemara raises a contradiction – וּרְמִינְהוּ: An expression used by the Gemara to introduce a contradiction between a biblical or tannaitic source about to be cited and the source of equal authority that had just been cited.

Our mishna – מַתְנִיתִין: The phrase may be used in general terms to refer to the Mishna of Rabbi Yehuda HaNasi, or more specifically, to the mishna that the Talmud is now discussing. It does not necessarily refer to the specific mishna at hand, and may refer to any mishna of the six orders.

## NOTES

The time of the poor person and the time of the priest are one and the same – עָנִי וְכֹהֵן חַד שִׁיעוּרָא הוּא: This explanation is based on a fundamental principle of talmudic thought: Do not intensify dispute. Whenever possible, what initially seem to be contradictory opinions are shown to actually be the same opinion expressed differently. Even when it is clear that a dispute does exist, an attempt is made to minimize the scope of the argument and find as many points of agreement between the opposing opinions as possible.

Establishing the time for the recitation of *Shema* – קְבִיעַת זְמַנֵּי קְרִיאַת שְׁמַע: These attempts to determine the time for *Shema* raise the question: Why did no one express the time to recite *Shema* in terms of hours? We will learn below that hours were, in fact, used to gauge time. The reason is not only because timepieces were rare in this era, but more importantly, because of the desire to correlate the times for the recitation of *Shema* as much as possible with the times when people actually went to sleep and arose, which varied in accordance with the changing lengths of the day and night. Fixed hours render this impossible.

קָא סָלְקָא דַּעְתָּךְ דְּעָנִי וּבְנֵי אָדָם חַד שִׁיעוּרָא הוּא, וְאִי אָמְרַתְּ עָנִי וְכֹהֵן חַד שִׁיעוּרָא הוּא – חֲכָמִים הַיְינוּ רַבִּי מֵאִיר!

In analyzing the three opinions regarding the beginning of the period for the recitation of the evening *Shema*, the Gemara begins with the supposition: **It might enter your mind** to say that the time when the **poor person** typically eats his meal and the time when ordinary **people** eat their Shabbat evening meal **are one** and the same **time,** since in both cases those eating would seek to begin their meals as early as possible, as, for different reasons, they are unable to kindle additional lights to illuminate their meal. And, **if you say** that the time of **the poor person's** meal **and** the time when **the priest** is purified and permitted to partake of his *teruma* **are one** and the same **time,** then the opinion of **the Rabbis is** identical to that of **Rabbi Meir.** What is their disagreement?

אֶלָּא שְׁמַע מִינַּהּ: עָנִי שִׁיעוּרָא לְחוּד וְכֹהֵן שִׁיעוּרָא לְחוּד! – לָא, עָנִי וְכֹהֵן חַד שִׁיעוּרָא הוּא, וְעָנִי וּבְנֵי אָדָם לָאו חַד שִׁיעוּרָא הוּא.

**Rather,** what we said previously must be rejected, and instead **learn from this** that there is **a separate time** for the **poor person and a separate time** for the **priest.** However, this conclusion is based on the assumption that the time of the poor person and the time of people are the same. That too can be rejected with the assertion that, **no,** the time of the **poor person and the priest are one** and the same **time,** and the time of **the poor person and people are not the same.** Accordingly, the opinion expressed by the *tanna* in our *baraita* is identical to that of the other *tanna'im,* and only Rabbi Meir disagrees with them.

וְעָנִי וְכֹהֵן חַד שִׁיעוּרָא הוּא? וּרְמִינְהוּ: מֵאֵימָתַי מַתְחִילִין לִקְרוֹת שְׁמַע בְּעַרְבִין? – מִשָּׁעָה שֶׁקָּדַשׁ הַיּוֹם בְּעַרְבֵי שַׁבָּתוֹת, דִּבְרֵי רַבִּי אֱלִיעֶזֶר. רַבִּי יְהוֹשֻׁעַ אוֹמֵר: מִשָּׁעָה שֶׁהַכֹּהֲנִים מְטוֹהָרִים לֶאֱכוֹל בִּתְרוּמָתָן. רַבִּי מֵאִיר אוֹמֵר: מִשָּׁעָה שֶׁהַכֹּהֲנִים טוֹבְלִין לֶאֱכוֹל בִּתְרוּמָתָן. אָמַר לוֹ רַבִּי יְהוּדָה: וַהֲלֹא כֹּהֲנִים מִבְּעוֹד יוֹם הֵם טוֹבְלִים! רַבִּי חֲנִינָא אוֹמֵר: מִשָּׁעָה שֶׁעָנִי נִכְנָס לֶאֱכוֹל פִּתּוֹ בְּמֶלַח. רַבִּי אַחַאי, וְאָמְרִי לַהּ רַבִּי אַחָא, אוֹמֵר: מִשָּׁעָה שֶׁרוֹב בְּנֵי אָדָם נִכְנָסִין לְהָסֵב.

**And is the time of the poor person and the priest the same?** The Gemara **raises a contradiction** to this approach from another *baraita,* in which other opinions regarding the time for the recitation of the evening *Shema* are cited: **From when does one begin to recite** the **evening** *Shema*?

**From the time when the day becomes sanctified on the eve of Shabbat, this is the statement of Rabbi Eliezer,** who established an earlier time for *Shema.*

**Rabbi Yehoshua,** like our mishna, **says: From the time when the priests are eligible to partake of their** *teruma.*

**Rabbi Meir says:** The time for the recitation of *Shema* begins before the priests were purified, **from when the priests immerse themselves in order to partake of their** *teruma.*

**Rabbi Yehuda said to** Rabbi Meir: How is it possible that the time for the recitation of the evening *Shema* corresponds to the time of the priests' immersion? **Do the priests not immerse themselves during the day,** so that with nightfall and the onset of a new day they will be purified? If so, how can that time be called night?

**Rabbi Ḥanina says** that the time for the recitation of the evening *Shema* begins **when the poor person enters to eat his bread with salt.**

But **Rabbi Aḥai, and some say Rabbi Aḥa, says: From the time when most people enter to recline** at their meal during the week.[N]

וְאִי אָמְרַתְּ עָנִי וְכֹהֵן חַד שִׁיעוּרָא הוּא – רַבִּי חֲנִינָא הַיְינוּ רַבִּי יְהוֹשֻׁעַ!

The preceding was the text of the *baraita.* Returning to our question, **if you say** that **the time of the poor person and the priest are one** and the same **time,** then the opinion of **Rabbi Ḥanina is** identical to that of **Rabbi Yehoshua.** However, the fact that they are cited together indicates that they are not, in fact, the same.

אֶלָּא לָאו שְׁמַע מִינַּהּ: שִׁיעוּרָא דְּעָנִי לְחוּד, וְשִׁיעוּרָא דְּכֹהֵן לְחוּד, שְׁמַע מִינַּהּ.

**Rather, must** one **not conclude from this the time for** the **poor person is separate and the time for** the **priest is separate?** Since no objection is raised, the Gemara concedes: Indeed, **conclude from this.**

הֵי מִינַּיְיהוּ מְאוּחָר? – מִסְתַּבְּרָא דְּעָנִי מְאוּחָר, דְּאִי אָמְרַתְּ דְּעָנִי מוּקְדָּם – רַבִּי חֲנִינָא הַיְינוּ רַבִּי אֱלִיעֶזֶר. אֶלָּא לָאו שְׁמַע מִינַּהּ דְּעָנִי מְאוּחָר, שְׁמַע מִינַּהּ.

Having established that the time of the poor person and that of the priest are different, the Gemara seeks to determine: **which one is later?** The Gemara suggests that **it is reasonable** to conclude that **the** time of the **poor person is later. As if you say** that **the poor person is earlier,** it would be impossible to establish a time earlier than that established by Rabbi Yehoshua, unless we hold that night begins with sunset, in which case the opinion of **Rabbi Ḥanina is** identical to that of **Rabbi Eliezer. Rather, must** one **not conclude from this that the poor person is later?** The Gemara notes: Indeed, **conclude from this.**

## NOTES

According to Rav Hai Gaon, the reasoning of the Sages of the *baraita* is as follows:

| The Sage | His Opinion | His Reasoning |
|---|---|---|
| Rabbi Eliezer | From the time when the day becomes sanctified on the eve of Shabbat | Night begins with sunset. The verse "and the sun sets" refers to the beginning of sunset. |
| Rabbi Yehoshua | From the time when the priests are eligible to eat their *teruma* | Night begins with the appearance of stars. The verse "and the sun sets" refers to the end of sunset. |
| Rabbi Meir | From when the priests immerse themselves in order to partake of their *teruma* | Agrees with Rabbi Yehoshua, but advances the time by a few minutes. |
| Rabbi Ḥanina | From when the poor person enters to eat his bread with salt | Rejects any connection between sunset and the recitation of *Shema.* The time of "lying down" is determined based solely on ordinary human activity. |
| Rabbi Aḥa | From the time when most people enter to recline | Agrees with Rabbi Ḥanina, but argues that the determination must be based on the general population rather than on the behavior of the poor. |

אָמַר מָר: אָמַר לֵיהּ רַבִּי יְהוּדָה, וַהֲלֹא כֹּהֲנִים מִבְּעוֹד יוֹם הֵם טוֹבְלִים.

We learned that **the Master said** in a *baraita* that the time for the recitation of the evening *Shema* according to Rabbi Meir begins with the time of the immersion of the priests. Regarding this, **Rabbi Yehuda said** to Rabbi Meir: **Do the priests not immerse themselves during the day?**

שַׁפִּיר קָאָמַר לֵיהּ רַבִּי יְהוּדָה לְרַבִּי מֵאִיר!

The Gemara notes: **What Rabbi Yehuda said to Rabbi Meir seems correct,** and how can Rabbi Meir respond? Rabbi Meir's response is connected to the fundamental dispute over when night begins. After sunset, a period begins which is neither day nor night. The *tanna'im* disagree over the precise duration of this period known as twilight [*bein hashemashot*]. Rabbi Yehuda holds that twilight extends a full hour after sunset. Rabbi Neḥemya agrees in principle, though he disagrees over the specifics. Rabbi Yosei maintains that twilight is very brief, and occurs immediately before the emergence of the stars, which marks the beginning of the night. Regarding Rabbi Meir's argument, Rabbi Yehuda asks that since the priests immerse themselves before twilight, they have a long wait until nightfall; clearly their immersion takes place while it is still day.

וְרַבִּי מֵאִיר, הָכִי קָאָמַר לֵיהּ: מִי סָבְרַתְּ דַּאֲנָא אַבֵּין הַשְּׁמָשׁוֹת דִּידָךְ קָא אָמִינָא? אֲנָא אַבֵּין הַשְּׁמָשׁוֹת דְּרַבִּי יוֹסֵי קָא אָמִינָא. דְּאָמַר רַבִּי יוֹסֵי: בֵּין הַשְּׁמָשׁוֹת כְּהֶרֶף עַיִן, זֶה נִכְנָס וְזֶה יוֹצֵא, וְאִי אֶפְשָׁר לַעֲמוֹד עָלָיו.

The Gemara answers that **Rabbi Meir said** to Rabbi Yehuda **as follows: Do you maintain that I am speaking of your** definition of **twilight? I am speaking of Rabbi Yosei's** definition of **twilight, as Rabbi Yosei said: Twilight is like the blink of an eye;** night **begins and** day **ends and** the time between them is so brief, **it is impossible to quantify.** According to this opinion, the priests immerse themselves just before the emergence of the stars, when it is already considered night.

Perek **I**
Daf **3** Amud **a**

קַשְׁיָא דְּרַבִּי מֵאִיר אַדְּרַבִּי מֵאִיר!

The previous *baraita* cited Rabbi Meir's opinion that the time for the recitation of *Shema* begins when the priests immerse before partaking of their *teruma*. In the *Tosefta*, it was taught that Rabbi Meir holds that one begins to recite *Shema* from when people enter to eat their meal on Shabbat eve. One opinion of **Rabbi Meir** seems to **contradict** another opinion of **Rabbi Meir.**

תְּרֵי תַּנָּאֵי אַלִּיבָּא דְּרַבִּי מֵאִיר.

The Gemara responds: **Two *tanna'im*,** students of Rabbi Meir, expressed different opinions **in accordance with Rabbi Meir's** opinion.

קַשְׁיָא דְּרַבִּי אֱלִיעֶזֶר אַדְּרַבִּי אֱלִיעֶזֶר!

So too, the opinion **of Rabbi Eliezer** cited in the mishna **contradicts** the opinion **of Rabbi Eliezer** cited in the *baraita*. In the mishna, Rabbi Eliezer holds that the time for the recitation of *Shema* begins with the emergence of the stars: From the time when the priests enter to partake of their *teruma*, while in the *baraita*, he states that the time for the recitation of *Shema* begins when the day becomes sanctified on the eve of Shabbat.

תְּרֵי תַּנָּאֵי אַלִּיבָּא דְּרַבִּי אֱלִיעֶזֶר. וְאִיבָּעֵית אֵימָא: רֵישָׁא לָאו רַבִּי אֱלִיעֶזֶר הִיא.

The Gemara responds: There are two possible resolutions to the apparent contradiction in Rabbi Eliezer's opinion. Either **two *tanna'im*** expressed different opinions **in accordance with Rabbi Eliezer's** opinion, **or if you wish, say** instead that **the first clause** of the mishna, according to which we begin to recite *Shema* when the priests enter to partake of their *teruma*, **is not** actually **Rabbi Eliezer's** opinion. Only the second half of the statement: Until the end of the first watch, was stated by Rabbi Eliezer.

"עַד סוֹף הָאַשְׁמוּרָה."

In the mishna, we learned that Rabbi Eliezer establishes that one may recite the evening *Shema* **until the end of the first watch.**[N] These watches are mentioned in the Bible as segments of the night, but it must established: Into precisely how many segments is the night divided, three or four? Moreover, why does Rabbi Eliezer employ such inexact parameters rather than a more precise definition of time (*Tosefot HaRosh*)?

מַאי קָסָבַר רַבִּי אֱלִיעֶזֶר? אִי קָסָבַר שָׁלֹשׁ מִשְׁמָרוֹת הָוֵי הַלַּיְלָה – לֵימָא "עַד אַרְבַּע שָׁעוֹת"! וְאִי קָסָבַר אַרְבַּע מִשְׁמָרוֹת הָוֵי הַלַּיְלָה – לֵימָא "עַד שָׁלֹשׁ שָׁעוֹת"!

**What does Rabbi Eliezer** actually **hold? If he holds that the night consists of three watches, let him say** explicitly that one recites the evening *Shema* **until the fourth hour. If he holds that the night consists of four watches, let him say** explicitly **until the third hour.**[N]

לְעוֹלָם קָסָבַר שָׁלֹשׁ מִשְׁמָרוֹת הָוֵי הַלַּיְלָה, וְהָא קָמַשְׁמַע לַן: דְּאִיכָּא מִשְׁמָרוֹת בָּרָקִיעַ וְאִיכָּא מִשְׁמָרוֹת בְּאַרְעָא. דְּתַנְיָא, רַבִּי אֱלִיעֶזֶר אוֹמֵר: שָׁלֹשׁ מִשְׁמָרוֹת הָוֵי הַלַּיְלָה, וְעַל כָּל מִשְׁמָר וּמִשְׁמָר יוֹשֵׁב הַקָּדוֹשׁ בָּרוּךְ הוּא וְשׁוֹאֵג כַּאֲרִי, שֶׁנֶּאֱמַר: "ה' מִמָּרוֹם יִשְׁאָג וּמִמְּעוֹן קָדְשׁוֹ יִתֵּן קוֹלוֹ שָׁאֹג יִשְׁאַג עַל נָוֵהוּ".

The Gemara responds: **Actually,** Rabbi Eliezer **holds that the night consists of three watches,** and he employs this particular language of watches **in order to teach us: There are watches in heaven and there are watches on earth;** just as our night is divided into watches, so too is the night in the upper worlds. **As it was taught** in a *baraita*: **Rabbi Eliezer says: The night consists of three watches, and over each and every watch, the Holy One, Blessed be He, sits and roars like a lion**[H] in pain over the destruction of the Temple. This imagery is derived from a reference in the Bible, **as it is stated: "The Lord roars [*yishag*] from on high, from His holy dwelling He makes His voice heard. He roars mightily [*shaog yishag*] over His dwelling place,** He cries out like those who tread grapes, against all the inhabitants of the earth" (Jeremiah 25:30). The three instances of the root *shin-alef-gimmel* in this verse correspond to the three watches of the night.

וְסִימָן לַדָּבָר: מִשְׁמָרָה רִאשׁוֹנָה – חֲמוֹר נוֹעֵר, שְׁנִיָּה – כְּלָבִים צוֹעֲקִים, שְׁלִישִׁית – תִּינוֹק יוֹנֵק מִשְּׁדֵי אִמּוֹ וְאִשָּׁה מְסַפֶּרֶת עִם בַּעְלָהּ.

**And signs of** the transition between each of **these** watches in the upper world can be sensed in this world: In **the first watch,**[N] **the donkey brays;** in **the second, dogs bark;** and in **the third** people begin to rise, **a baby nurses from its mother's breast and a wife converses with her husband.**

מַאי קָא חָשֵׁיב רַבִּי אֱלִיעֶזֶר? אִי תְּחִלַּת מִשְׁמָרוֹת קָא חָשֵׁיב – תְּחִלַּת מִשְׁמָרָה רִאשׁוֹנָה סִימָנָא לָמָּה לִי? אוּרְתָּא הוּא! אִי סוֹף מִשְׁמָרוֹת קָא חָשֵׁיב – סוֹף מִשְׁמָרָה אַחֲרוֹנָה לָמָּה לִי סִימָנָא? יְמָמָא הוּא!

With regard to these earthly manifestations of the three heavenly watches as established in the *baraita*, the Gemara asks: **What did Rabbi Eliezer enumerate? If** he **enumerated the beginning of the watch, why do I need a sign for the beginning of the first watch? It is** when **evening** begins; an additional sign is superfluous. **If he enumerated the end of the watches, why do I need a sign for the end of the last watch? It is** when **day** begins; an additional sign is similarly superfluous.

אֶלָּא: חָשֵׁיב סוֹף מִשְׁמָרָה רִאשׁוֹנָה וּתְחִלַּת מִשְׁמָרָה אַחֲרוֹנָה וְאֶמְצָעִית דְּאֶמְצָעִיתָא. וְאִיבָּעֵית אֵימָא: כּוּלְּהוּ סוֹף מִשְׁמָרוֹת קָא חָשֵׁיב, וְכִי תֵּימָא: אַחֲרוֹנָה לָא צְרִיךְ,

The Gemara answers: **Rather, he enumerated** the signs for **the end of the first watch and the beginning of the last watch,** both of which require a sign, as well as **the middle of the middle** watch. **And if you wish, say** instead: **He enumerated the ends of all** of the watches.[N] **And if you say** that a sign indicating the end of the **final** watch **is unnecessary** because it is day, nevertheless, that sign is useful.

**HALAKHA**

**Over each and every watch, the Holy One, Blessed be He, sits and roars like a lion – וְעַל כָּל מִשְׁמָר וּמִשְׁמָר יוֹשֵׁב הַקָּדוֹשׁ בָּרוּךְ הוּא וְשׁוֹאֵג כַּאֲרִי:** At those moments when the Holy One, Blessed be He, roars over the destruction of the Temple, it is appropriate for the God-fearing to rise and pray before God and mourn the exile. These are moments of divine compassion, as it is written: "Arise, sing at night, at the beginning of the watches" (Lamentations 2:19; see *Shulḥan Arukh, Oraḥ Ḥayyim* 1:2).

**NOTES**

**Until the end of the first watch – עַד סוֹף הָאַשְׁמוּרָה הָרִאשׁוֹנָה:** These watches were divisions of the night based on the changing of both the earthly military guard and the heavenly angelic guard, which recites songs of praise throughout the night (Rashi). This parallel between heaven and earth is in accordance with the principle: "Earthly kingdom is similar to divine kingdom," as discussed in this tractate (58a).

**The number of watches – מִנְיַן הַמִּשְׁמָרוֹת:** These watches, as their name indicates, parallel military watches that continue throughout the night. The disagreement between Rabbi Natan and Rabbi (3b) with regard to this issue is based upon the differences between standard procedure in the Greek army, which divided the night into three watches, and that in the Roman army, which divided the night into four watches (*vigiliae*). Given the existence of these two different systems, it was necessary to establish the traditional Jewish division of watches, based on an analysis of relevant verses in the Bible.

**And signs of these, the first watch – וְסִימָן לַדָּבָר: מִשְׁמָרָה רִאשׁוֹנָה:** This is not to say that the signs for the watches took place at a specific time. Rather, they continued, with interruptions, throughout the watch. Therefore, there is room to determine at what time these signs are most conspicuous.

**And if you wish, say instead: He enumerated the ends of all of the watches – וְאִיבָּעֵית אֵימָא: כּוּלְּהוּ:** This second explanation is given due to a difficulty with the first. Specifically, it is difficult to accept that the signs for the various watches are so incongruous; one sign indicates the beginning of one watch and a second indicates the end of another, while a third indicates the middle of yet another. On the other hand, there is a difficulty with the second explanation as well, as it is relevant only in special circumstances, i.e., for one sleeping in a dark house. Moreover, it contradicts Rabbi Eliezer's own opinion with regard to the time for reciting *Shema* in the morning (*Tosafot*). Due to the context in which it is discussed in the Gemara, as well as the reasons mentioned, some commentaries explain this as a metaphor for the stages of exile, which are comparable to the dark of night.

לְמַאי נַפְקָא מִינַּהּ – לְמִיקְרֵי קְרִיאַת שְׁמַע לְמַאן דְּגָנֵי בְּבַיִת אָפֵל וְלָא יָדַע זְמַן קְרִיאַת שְׁמַע אֵימַת, כֵּיוָן דְּאִשָּׁה מְסַפֶּרֶת עִם בַּעְלָהּ וְתִינוֹק יוֹנֵק מִשְּׁדֵי אִמּוֹ – לֵיקוּם וְלִיקְרֵי.

**What is the practical ramification** of this sign? It is relevant **to one who recites** *Shema* **while lying in a dark house,** who cannot see the dawn and **who does not know when the time for reciting** ***Shema*** arrives. That person is provided with a sign that **when a woman speaks with her husband and a baby nurses from its mother's breast,** the final watch of the night has ended and **he must rise and recite** *Shema.*

אָמַר רַב יִצְחָק בַּר שְׁמוּאֵל מִשְּׁמֵיהּ דְּרַב: שָׁלֹשׁ מִשְׁמָרוֹת הָוֵי הַלַּיְלָה, וְעַל כׇּל מִשְׁמָר וּמִשְׁמָר יוֹשֵׁב הַקָּדוֹשׁ בָּרוּךְ הוּא וְשׁוֹאֵג כַּאֲרִי, וְאוֹמֵר: ״אוֹי לִי שֶׁבַּעֲוֹנוֹתֵיהֶם הֶחֱרַבְתִּי אֶת בֵּיתִי וְשָׂרַפְתִּי אֶת הֵיכָלִי וְהִגְלִיתִים לְבֵין אוּמּוֹת הָעוֹלָם״.

**Rav Yitzḥak bar Shmuel said in the name of Rav: The night consists of three watches, and over each and every watch the Holy One, Blessed be He sits and roars like a lion,** because the Temple service was connected to the changing of these watches (*Tosefot HaRosh*), **and says: "Woe to Me, that due to their sins I destroyed My house, burned My Temple and exiled them among the nations of the world."**

תַּנְיָא, אָמַר רַבִּי יוֹסֵי: פַּעַם אַחַת הָיִיתִי מְהַלֵּךְ בַּדֶּרֶךְ, וְנִכְנַסְתִּי לְחוּרְבָּה אַחַת מֵחוּרְבוֹת יְרוּשָׁלַיִם לְהִתְפַּלֵּל. בָּא אֵלִיָּהוּ זָכוּר לַטּוֹב וְשָׁמַר לִי עַל הַפֶּתַח (וְהִמְתִּין לִי) עַד שֶׁסִּיַּימְתִּי תְּפִלָּתִי. לְאַחַר שֶׁסִּיַּימְתִּי תְּפִלָּתִי אָמַר לִי: ״שָׁלוֹם עָלֶיךָ, רַבִּי״! וְאָמַרְתִּי לוֹ: ״שָׁלוֹם עָלֶיךָ, רַבִּי וּמוֹרִי״! וְאָמַר לִי: בְּנִי, מִפְּנֵי מָה נִכְנַסְתָּ לְחוּרְבָּה זוֹ? אָמַרְתִּי לוֹ: לְהִתְפַּלֵּל. וְאָמַר לִי: הָיָה לְךָ לְהִתְפַּלֵּל בַּדֶּרֶךְ! וְאָמַרְתִּי לוֹ: מִתְיָרֵא הָיִיתִי שֶׁמָּא יַפְסִיקוּ בִּי עוֹבְרֵי דְרָכִים. וְאָמַר לִי: הָיָה לְךָ לְהִתְפַּלֵּל תְּפִלָּה קְצָרָה.

Incidental to the mention of the elevated significance of the night watches, the Gemara cites a related story: **It was taught** in a *baraita* that **Rabbi Yosei**[P] **said: I was once walking along the road when I entered** the ruins of an old, abandoned building **among the ruins of Jerusalem**[N] in order **to pray.** I noticed that **Elijah, of blessed memory, came and guarded the entrance for me and waited at the entrance until I finished my prayer. When I finished praying** and exited the ruin, Elijah **said to me,** deferentially as one would address a Rabbi: **Greetings to you, my Rabbi. I answered him: Greetings to you, my Rabbi, my teacher. And** Elijah **said to me: My son, why did you enter this ruin? I said to him:** In order **to pray. And** Elijah **said to me: You should have prayed on the road. And I said to him:** I was unable to pray along the road, because **I was afraid that I might be interrupted by travelers** and would be unable to focus. Elijah **said to me: You should have recited the abbreviated prayer** instituted for just such circumstances.

בְּאוֹתָהּ שָׁעָה לָמַדְתִּי מִמֶּנּוּ שְׁלֹשָׁה דְּבָרִים: לָמַדְתִּי שֶׁאֵין נִכְנָסִין לְחוּרְבָּה, וְלָמַדְתִּי שֶׁמִּתְפַּלְּלִין בַּדֶּרֶךְ, וְלָמַדְתִּי שֶׁהַמִּתְפַּלֵּל בַּדֶּרֶךְ – מִתְפַּלֵּל תְּפִלָּה קְצָרָה.

Rabbi Yosei concluded: **At that time,** from that brief exchange, **I learned from him, three things: I learned that one may not enter a ruin;**[H] **and I learned** that one need not enter a building to pray, but **he may pray along the road; and I learned that one who prays along the road recites an abbreviated prayer** so that he may maintain his focus.

וְאָמַר לִי: בְּנִי, מַה קּוֹל שָׁמַעְתָּ בְּחוּרְבָּה זוֹ? וְאָמַרְתִּי לוֹ: שָׁמַעְתִּי בַּת קוֹל שֶׁמְּנַהֶמֶת כַּיּוֹנָה וְאוֹמֶרֶת: ״אוֹי לַבָּנִים שֶׁבַּעֲוֹנוֹתֵיהֶם הֶחֱרַבְתִּי אֶת בֵּיתִי וְשָׂרַפְתִּי אֶת הֵיכָלִי וְהִגְלִיתִים לְבֵין הָאוּמּוֹת״. וְאָמַר לִי: חַיֶּיךָ וְחַיֵּי רֹאשְׁךָ, לֹא שָׁעָה זוֹ בִּלְבַד אוֹמֶרֶת כָּךְ, אֶלָּא בְּכׇל יוֹם וָיוֹם שָׁלֹשׁ פְּעָמִים אוֹמֶרֶת כָּךְ; וְלֹא זוֹ בִּלְבַד, אֶלָּא בְּשָׁעָה שֶׁיִּשְׂרָאֵל נִכְנָסִין לְבָתֵּי כְנֵסִיּוֹת וּלְבָתֵּי מִדְרָשׁוֹת וְעוֹנִין ״יְהֵא שְׁמֵיהּ הַגָּדוֹל מְבוֹרָךְ״, הַקָּדוֹשׁ בָּרוּךְ הוּא מְנַעְנֵעַ רֹאשׁוֹ וְאוֹמֵר: אַשְׁרֵי הַמֶּלֶךְ שֶׁמְּקַלְּסִין אוֹתוֹ בְּבֵיתוֹ כָּךְ, מַה לּוֹ לָאָב שֶׁהִגְלָה אֶת בָּנָיו, וְאוֹי לָהֶם לַבָּנִים שֶׁגָּלוּ מֵעַל שׁוּלְחַן אֲבִיהֶם.

And after this introduction, Elijah **said to me: What voice did you hear in that ruin?**

**I responded: I heard a Heavenly voice,** like an echo of that roar of the Holy One, Blessed be He (Maharsha), **cooing like a dove and saying: Woe to the children, due to whose sins I destroyed My house, burned My Temple, and exiled them among the nations.**

**And** Elijah **said to me:** By **your life and by your head, not only** did that voice **cry out in that moment, but it cries out three times each and every day. Moreover,** any time that God's greatness is evoked, such as **when Israel enters synagogues and study halls and answers** in the *kaddish* prayer, **May His great name be blessed, the Holy One, Blessed be He, shakes His head and says: Happy is the king who is thus praised in his house.** When the Temple stood, this praise was recited there, but now: **How** great is the pain of **the father who exiled his children, and woe to the children who were exiled from their father's table,** as their pain only adds to that of their father (Rabbi Shem Tov ibn Shaprut).

תָּנוּ רַבָּנַן, מִפְּנֵי שְׁלֹשָׁה דְּבָרִים אֵין נִכְנָסִין לְחוּרְבָּה: מִפְּנֵי חֲשָׁד, מִפְּנֵי הַמַּפּוֹלֶת וּמִפְּנֵי הַמַּזִּיקִין. ״מִפְּנֵי חֲשָׁד״ – וְתֵיפוֹק לֵיהּ מִשּׁוּם מַפּוֹלֶת!

**The Sages taught, for three reasons one may not enter a ruin: Because of suspicion**[N] of prostitution, **because** the ruin is liable **to collapse,** and **because of demons.** Three separate reasons seem extraneous, so the Gemara asks: Why was the reason **because of suspicion** necessary? **Let this** *halakha* **be derived because of collapse.**

## PERSONALITIES

**Rabbi Yosei – רַבִּי יוֹסֵי:** This is Rabbi Yosei ben Ḥalafta, one of the greatest of the *tanna'im*. He lived in the generation prior to the redaction of the Mishna, and the imprint of his teachings is evident throughout tannaitic literature.

His father, known as Abba Ḥalafta, was also considered one of the great Sages of his generation, and his family, according to one tradition, was descended from Yehonadav the son of Rekhav (see II Kings 10:15).

In addition to studying with his father, Rabbi Yosei was an outstanding student of Rabbi Akiva. Rabbi Yosei and his contemporaries, the other students of Rabbi Akiva, Rabbi Meir, Rabbi Yehuda, and Rabbi Shimon bar Yoḥai, formed the center of talmudic creativity of that entire generation. In his halakhic approach, as in his way of life, Rabbi Yosei was moderate; he refrained from taking extreme positions on halakhic issues. Because of his moderation and the logic of his teachings, the *halakha* is ruled in accordance with his opinion in every instance of disagreement with his colleagues. A well-known principle in the *halakha* is that "Rabbi Yosei's opinions are based on sound reasoning," and therefore the *halakha* is always in accordance with his opinion.

In addition to being a great master of *halakha*, Rabbi Yosei was also famous for his piety. The Talmud relates many stories about his modesty, his humility, and his sanctity. It is related that Elijah the prophet would reveal himself to him every day, and several conversations between him and Elijah are related in the Talmud. Rabbi Yosei was apparently the primary redactor of a series of *baraitot* on the history of the Jewish people known as *Seder Olam*. For many years he lived in Tzippori in the Galilee, and earned his living as a tanner.

Many of the prominent Sages of the following generation, including Rabbi Yehuda HaNasi, the redactor of the Mishna, were his students. But his main students were his five sons, all of whom were Sages in their generation. The most famous of them were Rabbi Eliezer the son of Rabbi Yosei, one of the great masters of *aggada*, and Rabbi Yishmael the son of Rabbi Yosei.

## NOTES

**I entered a ruin among the ruins of Jerusalem – וְנִכְנַסְתִּי לְחוּרְבָּה אַחַת מֵחוּרְבוֹת יְרוּשָׁלַיִם:** Beyond its simple meaning, there is a deeper message conveyed in this story. Rabbi Yosei was engrossed in thought and meditation, and as he entered a ruin among the ruins of Jerusalem, began to ruminate over the destruction of Jerusalem and Israel's resultant exile. He began to think of the Temple, praying that it would be rebuilt and that Jerusalem would be restored. In the midst of these prayers, Rabbi Yosei was interrupted by Elijah, who rebuked him and said that one should not become preoccupied with thoughts of destruction as that is a distraction from the task at hand. It is preferable to pray a brief, general prayer. In his vision, in the minor prophecy that Rabbi Yosei experienced in the ruin, he was told that the pain over the exile is not limited to Israel alone. Israel's pain in exile is God's pain as well, and one must hope that God will rebuild His sanctuary for His own sake as well as Israel's.

**Because of suspicion – מִפְּנֵי חֲשָׁד:** There are many *halakhot* based on the principle that one must avoid placing himself in a position that arouses suspicion. As it is said: "And you shall be clear before the Lord and before Israel" (see Numbers 32:22). In accordance with the talmudic principle that there is no guardian against licentiousness, no one is beyond suspicion.

## HALAKHA

**I learned that one may not enter a ruin – לָמַדְתִּי שֶׁאֵין נִכְנָסִין לְחוּרְבָּה:** One may not enter a ruin to pray, for the reasons outlined in the Gemara. For those same reasons, one may not enter a ruin for any other purpose either (Rambam *Sefer Ahava, Hilkhot Tefilla* 5:6, *Sefer Nezikin, Hilkhot Rotze'aḥ UShemirat HaNefesh* 12:6; *Shulḥan Arukh, Oraḥ Ḥayyim* 90:6).

בְּחֲדַתִּי.

The Gemara answers: This *halakha* applies even **in** the case of a **new**, sturdy ruin, where there is no danger of collapse. Therefore, the reason because of suspicion is cited in order to warn one not to enter a new ruin as well.

וְתִיפּוֹק לֵיהּ מִשּׁוּם מַזִּיקִין – בִּתְרֵי.

The Gemara continues to object: **And let this *halakha* be derived because of demons?** The Gemara answers: Demons are only a threat to individuals, so because of demons would not apply to a case **where two** people enter a ruin together.

אִי בִּתְרֵי – חֲשַׁד נַמִּי לֵיכָּא! – בִּתְרֵי וּפְרִיצֵי.

The Gemara objects: But **if there are two** people entering a ruin together, then **there is no suspicion either.** There is no prohibition against two men to be alone with a woman as, in that case, there is no suspicion of untoward behavior. Consequently, if two men enter a ruin together, there is no room for suspicion. The Gemara answers: If **two individuals** known to be **immoral** enter together, there is suspicion even though there are two of them.

״מִפְּנֵי הַמַּפּוֹלֶת״ – וְתִיפּוֹק לֵיהּ מִשּׁוּם חֲשַׁד וּמַזִּיקִין!

The Gemara considers why **because of collapse** is necessary. **Let the** prohibition **be derived from suspicion and demons.**

בִּתְרֵי וְכַשְׁרֵי.

The Gemara responds: There are times when this reason is necessary, e.g., when **two upstanding individuals** enter a ruin together. Although there is neither concern of suspicion nor of demons, there remains concern lest the ruin collapse.

״מִפְּנֵי הַמַּזִּיקִין״ – וְתִיפּוֹק לֵיהּ מִפְּנֵי חֲשַׁד וּמַפּוֹלֶת!

The Gemara considers the third reason, **because of demons.** Why is it necessary to include: Because of demons? **Let the** prohibition **be derived from suspicion and collapse.**

בְּחוּרְבָּה חֲדַתִּי, וּבִתְרֵי וְכַשְׁרֵי.

The Gemara responds: There are cases where this is the only concern, for example where it is a **new** ruin into which **two upstanding** individuals enter, so there is neither concern lest it collapse nor of suspicion.

אִי בִּתְרֵי – מַזִּיקִין נַמִּי לֵיכָּא!

The Gemara points out, however, that **if there are two people, there is also no** concern of **demons.** As such, the question remains: In what case can demons be the sole cause not to enter a ruin?

בִּמְקוֹמָן חָיְישִׁינַן. וְאִיבָּעֵית אֵימָא: לְעוֹלָם בְּחַד, וּבְחוּרְבָּה חֲדַתִּי דְּקָאֵי בְּדַבְרָא, דְּהָתָם מִשּׁוּם חֲשַׁד לֵיכָּא, דְּהָא אִשָּׁה בְּדַבְרָא לָא שְׁכִיחָא, וּמִשּׁוּם מַזִּיקִין אִיכָּא.

The Gemara responds: Generally speaking, two individuals need not be concerned about demons; but, if they are **in their place,** i.e., a place known to be haunted by demons (see Isaiah 13:21), **we are concerned** about demons even with two people. **And if you wish, say** instead: **Actually,** this refers **to** the case of **an individual** entering **a new ruin located in a field. There, there is no suspicion, as** finding **a woman in the field is uncommon;** and since it is a new ruin, there is no danger of collapse. **However, there is** still concern of **demons.**

תָּנוּ רַבָּנַן: אַרְבַּע מִשְׁמָרוֹת הָוֵי הַלַּיְלָה, דִּבְרֵי רַבִּי. רַבִּי נָתָן אוֹמֵר: שָׁלֹשׁ.

**The Sages taught** in a *Tosefta*: **The night is comprised of four watches;**[H] this is **the statement of Rabbi** Yehuda HaNasi. **Rabbi Natan**[P] **says:** The night is comprised of **three** watches.

מַאי טַעְמֵיהּ דְּרַבִּי נָתָן? – דִּכְתִיב: ״וַיָּבֹא גִדְעוֹן וּמֵאָה אִישׁ אֲשֶׁר אִתּוֹ בִּקְצֵה הַמַּחֲנֶה רֹאשׁ הָאַשְׁמֹרֶת הַתִּיכוֹנָה״, תָּנָא: אֵין ״תִּיכוֹנָה״ אֶלָּא שֶׁיֵּשׁ לְפָנֶיהָ וּלְאַחֲרֶיהָ.

The Gemara explains: **What is Rabbi Natan's reasoning? As it is written: "And Gideon, and the one hundred men who were with him, came to the edge of camp at the beginning of the middle watch"** (Judges 7:19). **It was taught** in the *Tosefta*: **Middle means nothing other than** that **there is one before it and one after it.** From the fact that the verse refers to a middle watch, the fact that the night is comprised of three watches may be inferred.

וְרַבִּי? מַאי ״תִּיכוֹנָה״ – אַחַת מִן הַתִּיכוֹנָה שֶׁבַּתִּיכוֹנוֹת.

**And** what does **Rabbi** Yehuda HaNasi say about this proof? He argues that it is inconclusive, as one could say: To **what** does **middle** refer? It refers to **one of the** two **middle** watches.

וְרַבִּי נָתָן? מִי כְּתִיב ״תִּיכוֹנָה שֶׁבַּתִּיכוֹנוֹת״? ״תִּיכוֹנָה״ כְּתִיב.

**And** how would **Rabbi Natan** respond? He would say: Despite Rabbi Yehuda HaNasi's objection, **is: One of the middle** watches, **written** in the verse? **The middle** watch **is written.** This indicates that the night is comprised of only three watches.

**HALAKHA**

**The night is comprised of four watches** – אַרְבַּע מִשְׁמָרוֹת הָוֵי הַלַּיְלָה, וכו׳: Though the Talmud does not arrive at a conclusion whether the night consists of three or four watches, the *halakha* is in accordance with the opinion of Rabbi Natan. Whenever the word "watch" is employed in this context, it refers to one-third of the night, as Rabbi Eliezer concurs; Rav employs language indicating that this is self-evident (see *Shulḥan Arukh, Oraḥ Ḥayyim* 1:2).

**PERSONALITIES**

**Rabbi Natan** – רַבִּי נָתָן: This is Rabbi Natan the Babylonian, who immigrated to Eretz Yisrael and was one of the greatest *tanna'im* during the generation prior to the redaction of the Mishna. Rabbi Natan was the son of the Exilarch in Babylonia. He was a member of a family descended from King David, the Jewish family with the noblest lineage. Because of his prominence as a Torah scholar and his noble lineage, he was named deputy to the *Nasi* of the Sanhedrin. He was famous for his profound knowledge of civil law. Similarly, he was known for his piety, and it is related that Elijah the Prophet would appear to him.

Rabbi Natan, together with Rabbi Meir, tried to alter the procedure for choosing the *Nasi* of the Sanhedrin. This effort failed, and as punishment it was decreed that Rabbi Natan's opinions would not be attributed to him by name in the Mishna, but that his teachings would be introduced anonymously with the phrase: Some say. But the decision was not always observed.

Rabbi Natan edited a number of collections of tannaitic pronouncements, and the tractate *Avot DeRabbi Natan* is named for him.

Many Sages of the following generation were his students, and prominent among them was Rabbi Yehuda HaNasi.

מַאי טַעְמֵיהּ דְּרַבִּי? – אָמַר רַבִּי זְרִיקָא אָמַר רַבִּי אַמִי אָמַר רַבִּי יְהוֹשֻׁעַ בֶּן לֵוִי, כָּתוּב אֶחָד אוֹמֵר: ״חֲצוֹת לַיְלָה אָקוּם לְהוֹדוֹת לָךְ עַל מִשְׁפְּטֵי צִדְקֶךָ״, וְכָתוּב אֶחָד אוֹמֵר: ״קִדְּמוּ עֵינַי אַשְׁמֻורוֹת״, הָא כֵּיצַד? – אַרְבַּע מִשְׁמָרוֹת הָוֵי הַלַּיְלָה.

What is Rabbi Yehuda HaNasi's **reasoning? Rabbi Zerika said** that **Rabbi Ami said** that **Rabbi Yehoshua ben Levi said: Rabbi** Yehuda HaNasi's opinion is based on a comparison of two verses. **One verse says: "At midnight I rise to give thanks for Your righteous laws"** (Psalms 119:62), **and the other verse says: "My eyes forestall the watches,** that I will speak of Your word" (Psalms 119:148). Taken together, these verses indicate that their author, King David, rose at midnight, two watches before dawn, in order to study Torah. **How is it** possible to reconcile these two verses? Only if **there are four watches in the night** does one who rises two watches before dawn rise at midnight.

וְרַבִּי נָתָן? סָבַר לַהּ כְּרַבִּי יְהוֹשֻׁעַ, דִּתְנַן: רַבִּי יְהוֹשֻׁעַ אוֹמֵר: עַד שָׁלֹשׁ שָׁעוֹת, שֶׁכֵּן דֶּרֶךְ מְלָכִים לַעֲמוֹד בְּשָׁלֹשׁ שָׁעוֹת: שִׁית דְּלֵילְיָא וְתַרְתֵּי דִּימָמָא, הָווּ לְהוּ שְׁתֵּי מִשְׁמָרוֹת.

**And** how does **Rabbi Natan** reconcile these two verses? He **holds in accordance with** the opinion of **Rabbi Yehoshua, for we learned** in a mishna that **Rabbi Yehoshua says:** One is permitted to recite the morning *Shema* during the time when people rise, **until the third hour** of the day, **as it is the custom of kings to rise during the third hour.** Since it is customary for kings to rise during the third hour of the day, if David rose at midnight, he would be awake for **six hours of the night and two hours of the day,** which amounts to **two watches.** Therefore King David could say that he "forestalls the watches," as he rose two watches before the rest of the kings in the world.

רַב אַשִׁי אָמַר: מִשְׁמָרָה וּפַלְגָא נַמִי ״מִשְׁמָרוֹת״ קָרוּ לְהוּ.

**Rav Ashi said** that the verses can be reconciled in accordance with Rabbi Natan's opinion in another way: **One and one-half watches are still called watches** in plural. Therefore King David could rise at midnight yet maintain that he "forestalls the watches."

וְאָמַר רַבִּי זְרִיקָא אָמַר רַבִּי אַמִי אָמַר רַבִּי יְהוֹשֻׁעַ בֶּן לֵוִי: אֵין אוֹמְרִין בִּפְנֵי הַמֵּת אֶלָּא דְּבָרָיו שֶׁל מֵת.

Following this discussion, another *halakha* that **Rabbi Zerika said** that **Rabbi Ami said** that **Rabbi Yehoshua ben Levi said** is cited: **Before the dead, one may speak only of matters relating to the dead,**[NH] as speaking of other matters appears to be contemptuous of the deceased, underscoring that he is unable to talk while those around him can. Therefore, one must remain fully engaged in matters relating to him.

אָמַר רַבִּי אַבָּא בַּר כָּהֲנָא: לָא אֲמָרַן אֶלָּא בְּדִבְרֵי תּוֹרָה, אֲבָל מִילֵּי דְעָלְמָא – לֵית לָן בָּהּ.

Two traditions exist with regard to the details of this *halakha* in the name of Rabbi Abba bar Kahana. According to one version, **Rabbi Abba bar Kahana said:** This *halakha* **was only said**[B] **with regard to matters of Torah.** Speaking of **other matters, however, is not** prohibited, since no contempt is expressed for the deceased by the fact that he is unable to speak of such topics.

וְאִיכָּא דְּאָמְרִי, אָמַר רַבִּי אַבָּא בַּר כָּהֲנָא: לָא אֲמָרַן אֶלָּא [אֲפִילּוּ] בְּדִבְרֵי תּוֹרָה, וְכָל שֶׁכֵּן מִילֵּי דְעָלְמָא.

**Others say** another version of this *halakha* in the name of Rabbi Abba bar Kahana: This *halakha* **was said even with regard to matters of Torah, and all the more so with regard to other matters.** If one must refrain from speaking of matters of Torah, regarding which one is commanded to speak, and limit himself to matters concerning the deceased, all the more so should he refrain from speaking of other matters, regarding which one is not commanded to speak.

וְדָוִד בְּפַלְגָא דְּלֵילְיָא הֲוָה קָאֵי? מֵאוּרְתָּא הֲוָה קָאֵי! דִּכְתִיב: ״קִדַּמְתִּי בַנֶּשֶׁף וָאֲשַׁוֵּעָה״, וּמִמַּאי דְּהַאי ״נֶשֶׁף״ אוּרְתָּא הוּא? דִּכְתִיב: ״בְּנֶשֶׁף בְּעֶרֶב יוֹם בְּאִישׁוֹן לַיְלָה וַאֲפֵלָה״!

Incidental to the Gemara's mention of King David, other sources are cited that describe his actions. Regarding that which was cited above, that he would rise in the middle of the night in order to serve his Creator, the Gemara asks: **Did David rise at midnight? He rose in the evening. As it is written: "I rose with the *neshef* and cried,** I hoped for Your word" (Psalms 119:147). **And how** do we know **that this *neshef* is the evening? As it is written: "In the *neshef*, in the evening of the day, in the blackness of night and the darkness"** (Proverbs 7:9). Apparently, King David did indeed rise when it was still evening.[N]

אָמַר רַב אוֹשַׁעְיָא אָמַר רַבִּי אַחָא, הָכִי קָאָמַר (דָּוִד): מֵעוֹלָם לֹא עָבַר עָלַי חֲצוֹת לַיְלָה בְּשֵׁינָה.

The Gemara suggests several ways to resolve this contradiction. **Rabbi Oshaya said** that **Rabbi Aḥa said: David said as follows: Midnight never passed me by in my sleep.** Sometimes I fulfilled the verse, "I rose with the *neshef* and cried," but I always, at least, fulfilled the verse, "At midnight I rise to give thanks for Your righteous laws."

### NOTES

**Before the dead, one may speak only of matters, etc.** – אֵין אוֹמְרִין בִּפְנֵי הַמֵּת וכו׳: There are many *halakhot* regarding respect for the deceased. Most of these fall under the rubric of "respect for living"; *halakhot* whose purpose is to respect the family of the deceased. The *halakhot* governing conduct in the presence of the dead were not established due to fear of the dead; rather, they are intended to protect those no longer capable of defending themselves. One who discusses Torah in the presence of the deceased flaunts, albeit unintentionally, his superiority over the deceased, which the Sages viewed as mocking the weak. This is based on the verse: "One who mocks the poor blasphemes his Maker" (Proverbs 17:5). One who disrespects the dead, disrespects God and the divine image that God imparts to every person.

**When did David arise from his sleep** – מָתַי קָם דָּוִד מִשְּׁנָתוֹ: The Jerusalem Talmud suggests an alternative resolution to the contradiction between the verses, based on Rabbi Natan's opinion: Two different cases are being discussed. When he dined at a royal meal that evening, David would rise at midnight; but when he did not, he would rise at the end of the first watch (Jerusalem Talmud, *Berakhot* 1:1).

### HALAKHA

**Before the dead, one may speak only of matters relating to the dead** – אֵין אוֹמְרִין בִּפְנֵי הַמֵּת אֶלָּא דְּבָרָיו שֶׁל מֵת: In the room in which the deceased lies, one may not discuss Torah matters even if he is more than four cubits from the body. One may speak only of matters relating to the burial and eulogy, or of other matters honoring the dead. Discussing other matters is prohibited within four cubits of the body, but permitted beyond that distance. One is permitted to discuss matters concerning the deceased within four cubits of his body (*Baḥ*). The halakhic ruling is in accordance with both opinions, though most decisors rule in accordance with the first. (Rambam *Sefer Shofetim*, *Hilkhot Evel* 13:9).

### BACKGROUND

**This *halakha* was only said** – לָא אֲמָרַן אֶלָּא: This phrase: This was only said with regard to case A but with regard to case B this *halakha* does not apply, is a standard formulation that restricts the application of a *halakha* that was presented as a general statement. The Gemara explains that it only applies to specific cases.

רַבִּי זֵירָא אָמַר: עַד חֲצוֹת לַיְלָה הָיָה מִתְנַמְנֵם כְּסוּס. מִכָּאן וְאֵילָךְ הָיָה מִתְגַּבֵּר כָּאֲרִי. רַב אַשִׁי אָמַר: עַד חֲצוֹת לַיְלָה הָיָה עוֹסֵק בְּדִבְרֵי תוֹרָה, מִכָּאן וְאֵילָךְ בְּשִׁירוֹת וְתִשְׁבָּחוֹת.

**Rabbi Zeira said: Until midnight,** David **would doze like a horse,** as a horse dozes, but never sleeps deeply. **From** midnight **on, he would gain the strength of a lion. Rav Ashi said: Until midnight, he would study Torah,** as it is written: "I rose with the *neshef* and cried, I hoped for Your word," **and from** midnight **on,** he would engage in **songs and praise,** as it is written: "At midnight I rise to give thanks."

וְ״נֶשֶׁף״ אוּרְתָּא הוּא? הָא ״נֶשֶׁף״ צַפְרָא הוּא! דִּכְתִיב: ״וַיַּכֵּם דָּוִד מֵהַנֶּשֶׁף וְעַד הָעֶרֶב לְמָחֳרָתָם״, מַאי לָאו מִצַּפְרָא וְעַד לֵילְיָא!

To this point, the discussion has been based on the assumption that *neshef* means evening. The Gemara asks: **Does *neshef*** really **mean evening? Doesn't *neshef* mean morning? As it is written: "And David slew them from the *neshef* until the evening of the next day"** (I Samuel 30:17). **Doesn't** this verse mean **from the morning until the night,** in which case *neshef* must mean morning?

לָא, מֵאוּרְתָּא וְעַד אוּרְתָּא.

The Gemara responds: **No,** this verse means that David slew them **from** one **evening until** the next **evening.**

אִי הָכִי, לִכְתּוֹב ״מֵהַנֶּשֶׁף וְעַד הַנֶּשֶׁף״ אוֹ ״מֵהָעֶרֶב וְעַד הָעֶרֶב״!

The Gemara rejects this response: **If so, let** the verse **be written: From the *neshef* until the *neshef*, or from the evening until the evening.** Why would the verse employ two different terms for a single concept?

אֶלָּא אָמַר רָבָא: תְּרֵי נִשְׁפֵי הָווּ, נְשַׁף לֵילְיָא וְאָתֵי יְמָמָא, נְשַׁף יְמָמָא וְאָתֵי לֵילְיָא.

**Rather, Rava said: There are two** times referred to as ***neshef,*** and the word can refer to either evening or morning. *Neshef* must be understood in accordance with its Aramaic root: **The night moves** past [*neshaf*] **and the day arrives, and the day moves** past [*neshaf*] **and the night arrives.**

וְדָוִד מִי הֲוָה יָדַע פַּלְגָּא דְלֵילְיָא אֵימַת? הַשְׁתָּא מֹשֶׁה רַבֵּינוּ לָא הֲוָה יָדַע, דִּכְתִיב: ״כַּחֲצוֹת הַלַּיְלָה אֲנִי יוֹצֵא בְּתוֹךְ מִצְרָיִם״,

When King David said: At midnight I rise, the assumption is that he rose precisely at midnight. The Gemara asks: **Did David know** exactly **when it was midnight?**[N] **Even Moses our teacher did not know** exactly when it was midnight. How do we know this about Moses? **As it is written** that he said to Pharaoh: "Thus said the Lord: **About midnight, I will go out into the midst of Egypt"** (Exodus 11:4). The word about indicates that it was only an approximation.

מַאי ״כַּחֲצוֹת״? אִילֵימָא דַּאֲמַר לֵיהּ קוּדְשָׁא בְּרִיךְ הוּא ״כַּחֲצוֹת״ – מִי אִיכָּא סְפֵיקָא קַמֵּי שְׁמַיָּא? אֶלָּא דַּאֲמַר לֵיהּ (לְמָחָר) ״בַּחֲצוֹת״ (כִּי הַשְׁתָּא), וַאֲתָא אִיהוּ וַאֲמַר: ״כַּחֲצוֹת״, אַלְמָא מְסַפְּקָא לֵיהּ – וְדָוִד הֲוָה יָדַע?

The Gemara clarifies: **What** is the meaning of the expression: **About midnight?** Did Moses say it or did God say it? **If we say** that **the Holy One, Blessed be He, Himself, said: About midnight,** to Moses, **is there doubt before** God in **heaven? Rather,** this must be understood as follows: **God told** Moses: **At midnight, but** from the fact that **when** Moses **came** to Pharaoh **he said: About midnight; apparently,** Moses **was uncertain** about the exact moment of midnight. Moses, the greatest of all the prophets, was uncertain, and **David knew?**

דָּוִד סִימָנָא הֲוָה לֵיהּ, דְּאָמַר רַב אַחָא בַּר בִּיזְנָא אָמַר רַבִּי שִׁמְעוֹן חֲסִידָא: כִּנּוֹר הָיָה תָּלוּי לְמַעְלָה מִמִּטָּתוֹ שֶׁל דָּוִד, וְכֵיוָן שֶׁהִגִּיעַ חֲצוֹת לַיְלָה בָּא רוּחַ צְפוֹנִית וְנוֹשֶׁבֶת בּוֹ וּמְנַגֵּן מֵאֵלָיו, מִיָּד הָיָה עוֹמֵד וְעוֹסֵק בַּתּוֹרָה עַד שֶׁעָלָה עַמּוּד הַשַּׁחַר. כֵּיוָן שֶׁעָלָה עַמּוּד הַשַּׁחַר נִכְנְסוּ חַכְמֵי יִשְׂרָאֵל אֶצְלוֹ, אָמְרוּ לוֹ: אֲדוֹנֵינוּ הַמֶּלֶךְ, עַמְּךָ יִשְׂרָאֵל צְרִיכִין פַּרְנָסָה. אָמַר לָהֶם: לְכוּ וְהִתְפַּרְנְסוּ זֶה מִזֶּה. אָמְרוּ לוֹ: אֵין הַקּוֹמֶץ מַשְׂבִּיעַ אֶת הָאֲרִי וְאֵין הַבּוֹר מִתְמַלֵּא מֵחוּלְיָתוֹ. אָמַר לָהֶם: לְכוּ וּפִשְׁטוּ יְדֵיכֶם בִּגְדוּד.

The Gemara offers several answers to this question:

**David had a sign** indicating when **it was midnight.** As **Rav Aḥa bar Bizna said** that **Rabbi Shimon Ḥasida said: A lyre**[B] **hung over David's bed, and once midnight arrived, the northern** midnight **wind would come and** cause **the lyre to play on its own.** David **would immediately rise** from his bed **and study Torah until the first rays of dawn.**

**Once dawn** arrived, **the Sages of Israel entered**[N] to advise **him** with regard to the various concerns of the nation and the economy. **They said to him: Our master, the king, your nation requires sustenance.**

**He said: Go and sustain one another,** provide each other with whatever is lacking.

The Sages of Israel **responded to him** with a parable: **A single handful** of food **does not satisfy a lion,**[N] **and a pit** will not **be filled** merely **from** the rain that falls directly into **its mouth,**[B] but other water must be piped in (*ge'onim*). So too, the nation cannot sustain itself using its own resources.

King David **told them: Go and take up arms with the troops** in battle in order to expand our borders and provide our people with the opportunity to earn a livelihood.

### NOTES

**Did David know when it was midnight – וְדָוִד מִי הֲוָה יָדַע פַּלְגָּא דְּלֵילְיָא אֵימַת:** Unlike noon, which is relatively easy to determine, the precise moment of midnight is difficult to ascertain. One would require precise clocks, and even then it would be difficult to be certain when it was midnight. On the other hand, one can rely on even the most primitive timepiece to approximate the time of midnight. Therefore, the Gemara questions how David knew the precise moment of midnight.

**The Sages of Israel entered – נִכְנְסוּ חַכְמֵי יִשְׂרָאֵל אֶצְלוֹ:** This story does not describe David's day-to-day affairs, but the events of a particular day in his life (Rabbi Yoshiyahu Pinto).

**The handful and the lion – הַקּוֹמֶץ וְהָאֲרִי:** The word we have translated as handful, *kometz,* can be explained in different ways. Some hold that it refers to a pit [*gometz*], rendering the passage: The pit, where the lion is located, cannot satisfy him, and the lion must leave in order to find food (Rav Hai Gaon). Others explain that it means "grasshopper" in Aramaic, rendering the passage: The grasshopper cannot satisfy the lion (*HaKotev; Shitta Mekubbetzet*).

### BACKGROUND

**Lyre – כִּנּוֹר:** This refers to a member of the lyre family. Strings are stretched across a special hollow box and when the instrument faces the proper direction, the strings produce music proportional to the force of the wind. If there is a fixed wind pattern, one could have the lyre play at a specific time and serve as a type of alarm clock (based on Rav Hai Gaon).

**The pit and its mouth – הַבּוֹר וְחוּלְיָתוֹ:** In places where pits are used to collect rainwater, the rain that falls directly into the pit is insufficient, because the stone structure surrounding the opening of the pit is small. Therefore, canals and pipelines are built to channel the water from a much larger area into the pit.

Stone structure surrounding the opening of a pit from the talmudic era

Ancient water canal that allows water to flow into a pit (from Tel Arad)

מִיָּד יוֹעֲצִים בַּאֲחִיתוֹפֶל וְנִמְלָכִין בְּסַנְהֶדְרִין, וְשׁוֹאֲלִין בְּאוּרִים וְתוּמִּים.

The Sages **immediately seek advice from Ahitophel** to determine whether or not it was appropriate to go to war at that time and how they should conduct themselves, **and they consult the Sanhedrin** in order to receive the requisite license to wage a war under those circumstances (*Tosefot HaRosh*). **And they ask the *Urim VeTummim*** whether or not they should go to war, and whether or not they would be successful.

אָמַר רַב יוֹסֵף: מַאי קְרָא? - דִּכְתִיב: "וְאַחֲרֵי אֲחִיתֹפֶל בְּנָיָהוּ בֶּן יְהוֹיָדָע וְאֶבְיָתָר וְשַׂר צָבָא לַמֶּלֶךְ יוֹאָב".

**Rav Yosef said:** Upon **what verse** is this *aggada* based? **As it is written: "And after Ahitophel was Yehoyada son of Benayahu and Evyatar, and the general of the king's army, Yoav"** (I Chronicles 27:34).

"אֲחִיתוֹפֶל" - זֶה יוֹעֵץ, וְכֵן הוּא אוֹמֵר: "וַעֲצַת אֲחִיתֹפֶל אֲשֶׁר יָעַץ בַּיָּמִים הָהֵם כַּאֲשֶׁר יִשְׁאַל אִישׁ בִּדְבַר הָאֱלֹהִים";

The individuals named in this verse correspond with the roles in the *aggada* as follows: **Ahitophel is the adviser** whose advice they sought first with regard to going to war, **and so it says: "Now the counsel of Ahitophel, which he counseled in those days, was as a man who inquires of the word of God;** so was the counsel of Ahitophel both with David and with Absalom" (II Samuel 16:23).

Perek **I**
Daf **4** Amud **a**

"בְּנָיָהוּ בֶּן יְהוֹיָדָע" - זֶה סַנְהֶדְרִין, "וְאֶבְיָתָר" - אֵלּוּ אוּרִים וְתוּמִּים,

**Benayahu ben Yehoyada** corresponds to **the Sanhedrin,** since he was the head of the Sanhedrin, and **Evyatar** corresponds to **the *Urim VeTummim*,** as Evyatar ben Ahimelekh the priest would oversee inquiries directed to the *Urim VeTummim* (see I Samuel 23:9).

וְכֵן הוּא אוֹמֵר: "וּבְנָיָהוּ בֶּן יְהוֹיָדָע עַל הַכְּרֵתִי וְעַל הַפְּלֵתִי"; וְלָמָּה נִקְרָא שְׁמָם "כְּרֵתִי וּפְלֵתִי"? "כְּרֵתִי" - שֶׁכּוֹרְתִים דִּבְרֵיהֶם, "פְּלֵתִי" - שֶׁמּוּפְלָאִים בְּדִבְרֵיהֶם; וְאַחַר כָּךְ "שַׂר צָבָא לַמֶּלֶךְ יוֹאָב".

**And so it says** regarding Benayahu ben Yehoyada's position as head of the Sanhedrin: **"And Benayahu ben Yehoyada was over the *Kereti* and over the *Peleti*"** (II Samuel 20:23).[N] **And why was** the Sanhedrin **called *Kereti UPeleti*?** It was called ***Kereti*** because **they were decisive [*koretim*] in their pronouncements.** It was called ***Peleti*** because **their pronouncements** and wisdom **were wondrous [*mufla'im*].** The head of the *Kereti UPeleti* was the head of the Sanhedrin. According to the order of the verse, upon being instructed by King David to go to war, the Sages first consulted with Ahitophel, then with the Sanhedrin, then they would ask the *Urim VeTummim*, **and** only **thereafter** was **the general of the king's army, Yoav,** given the command to ready the military for battle.

אָמַר רַב יִצְחָק בַּר אַדָּא, וְאָמְרִי לַהּ אָמַר רַב יִצְחָק בְּרֵיהּ דְּרַב אִידִי: מַאי קְרָא - "עוּרָה כְבוֹדִי עוּרָה הַנֵּבֶל וְכִנּוֹר אָעִירָה שָּׁחַר".

**Rav Yitzḥak bar Adda, and some say Rav Yitzḥak, son of Rav Idi, said:** From **what verse** is it derived[B] that David's lyre would wake him at midnight? **"Awake, my glory; awake, harp and lyre; I will wake the dawn"** (Psalms 57:9). This means that the playing lyre has already woken, and now I must engage in Torah study until dawn.

רַבִּי זֵירָא אָמַר: מֹשֶׁה לְעוֹלָם הֲוָה יָדַע, וְדָוִד נַמִּי הֲוָה יָדַע.

**Rabbi Zeira** offered a different solution to the question of whether Moses and David knew exactly when it was midnight and **said:** Moses **certainly knew** when it was midnight, **and David also knew.**

וְכֵיוָן דְּדָוִד הֲוָה יָדַע, כִּנּוֹר לָמָּה לֵיהּ? לְאִתְּעוֹרֵי מִשִּׁנְתֵיהּ.

The Gemara asks: **If David knew,** then **why did he need the lyre?** The Gemara answers: He needed the lyre **to wake him from his sleep.**

וְכֵיוָן דְּמֹשֶׁה הֲוָה יָדַע, לָמָּה לֵיהּ לְמֵימַר "כַּחֲצוֹת"? - מֹשֶׁה קָסָבַר: שֶׁמָּא יִטְעוּ אִצְטַגְנִינֵי פַרְעֹה וְיֹאמְרוּ מֹשֶׁה בַּדַּאי הוּא. דְּאָמַר מָר: לַמֵּד לְשׁוֹנְךָ לוֹמַר "אֵינִי יוֹדֵעַ", שֶׁמָּא תִּתְבַּדֶּה וְתֵאָחֵז.

Similarly with regard to Moses, **since** Moses **knew** the precise moment of midnight, **why did he say: About midnight,** instead of: At midnight? Moses did so because he **maintained: Lest Pharaoh's astrologers**[L] **err** and believe midnight to be earlier. Since no disaster would have occurred, **they would say: Moses is a liar.** Moses spoke in accordance with the principle **articulated by the Master: Accustom your tongue to say: I do not know, lest you become entangled in** a web of **deceit.**

**NOTES**

And Benayahu ben Yehoyada was over the *Kereti* and the *Peleti* – וּבְנָיָהוּ בֶּן יְהוֹיָדָע עַל הַכְּרֵתִי וְעַל הַפְּלֵתִי: The verse does not exist as quoted. In Chronicles it says: "And after Ahitophel was Yehoyada son of Benayahu." However, it seems likely that if Benayahu ben Yehoyada was the head of the Sanhedrin, as indicated in the verse in Samuel, his son Yehoyada ben Benayahu was also the head of the Sanhedrin. From the verse in Chronicles: "And after Ahitophel was Yehoyada son of Benayahu," the procedure is evident; they first consulted Ahitophel and then they consulted the Sanhedrin (*ge'onim*, *Tosafot*).

**BACKGROUND**

From what verse is it derived – מַאי קְרָא: Literally, this means: What is the verse? What is the biblical basis for this rabbinic statement? Most of the time the term is employed to connote a biblical allusion to something that seems to be of rabbinic origin.

**LANGUAGE**

Astrologers [*itztagninim*] – אִיצְטַגְנִינִים: The meaning of this word is clear from the context. Astrologers are star-gazers and magicians, possessors of secret wisdom. The source of the word is unclear. Some have suggested it is related to the Greek στεγανός, meaning hidden, concealed. Consequently, the meaning is allegorical, i.e., those who engage in hidden areas and similar fields. Other say that the source of the word is the Greek Θελγῖνες, meaning wizards.

רַב אַשִׁי אָמַר: בְּפַלְגָא אוּרְתָא דִּתְלֵיסַר נְגֵהִי אַרְבֵּסַר הֲוָה קָאֵי, וְהָכִי קָאָמַר מֹשֶׁה לְיִשְׂרָאֵל: אָמַר הַקָּדוֹשׁ בָּרוּךְ הוּא, לְמָחָר כַּחֲצוֹת הַלַּיְלָה כִּי הָאִידָּנָא, אֲנִי יוֹצֵא בְּתוֹךְ מִצְרַיִם.

**Rav Ashi said:** This question is unfounded, as Moses **was standing at midnight of the thirteenth, leading into the fourteenth,** when he pronounced his prophecy, **and Moses told Israel** that **the Holy One, Blessed be He, said** that **tomorrow,** at the exact time **like midnight tonight, I will go out into the midst of Egypt.** This indicates that the passage should not be understood to mean about midnight, an approximation; but rather, like midnight, as a comparison, likening midnight tomorrow to midnight tonight.

״לְדָוִד שָׁמְרָה נַפְשִׁי כִּי חָסִיד אָנִי״ – לֵוִי וְרַבִּי יִצְחָק: חַד אָמַר: כָּךְ אָמַר דָּוִד לִפְנֵי הַקָּדוֹשׁ בָּרוּךְ הוּא: רִבּוֹנוֹ שֶׁל עוֹלָם! לֹא חָסִיד אָנִי? שֶׁכָּל מַלְכֵי מִזְרָח וּמַעֲרָב יְשֵׁנִים עַד שָׁלֹשׁ שָׁעוֹת, וַאֲנִי ״חֲצוֹת לַיְלָה אָקוּם לְהוֹדוֹת לָךְ״.

The Gemara further explores King David's character. It is said: "A prayer **of David... Keep my soul, for I am pious**" (Psalms 86:1–2).[N] Levi and Rabbi Yitzḥak debated the meaning of this verse and how David's piety is manifest in the fact that he went beyond his fundamental obligations. **One said:** David's declaration of piety referred to his awakening during the night to pray, and **so said David before the Holy One, Blessed be He: Master of the Universe, am I not pious? As all of the kings of the East and the West sleep until the third hour** of the day, **but** although I am a king like them, **"At midnight I rise to give thanks"** (Psalms 119:62).

וְאִידָךְ: כָּךְ אָמַר דָּוִד לִפְנֵי הַקָּדוֹשׁ בָּרוּךְ הוּא: רִבּוֹנוֹ שֶׁל עוֹלָם, לֹא חָסִיד אָנִי? שֶׁכָּל מַלְכֵי מִזְרָח וּמַעֲרָב יוֹשְׁבִים אֲגוּדּוֹת אֲגוּדּוֹת בִּכְבוֹדָם, וַאֲנִי יָדַי מְלוּכְלָכוֹת בְּדָם וּבְשָׁפִיר וּבְשִׁלְיָא כְּדֵי לְטַהֵר אִשָּׁה לְבַעְלָהּ. וְלֹא עוֹד: אֶלָּא כׇּל מַה שֶּׁאֲנִי עוֹשֶׂה אֲנִי נִמְלָךְ בִּמְפִיבֹשֶׁת רַבִּי, וְאוֹמֵר לוֹ: ״מְפִיבֹשֶׁת רַבִּי! יָפֶה דַּנְתִּי? יָפֶה חִיַּיבְתִּי? יָפֶה זִכִּיתִי? יָפֶה טִהַרְתִּי? יָפֶה טִמֵּאתִי?״ וְלֹא בּוֹשְׁתִּי.

**And the other** Sage said: **David said the following before the Holy One, Blessed be He: Master of the Universe, am I not pious? For all of the kings of the East and the West sit in groups** befitting **their honored** status, but I sit as a judge who issues rulings for the people. Women come with questions of ritual impurity and **my hands become soiled with** their **blood** as I labor to determine whether or not it is blood of impurity and she has menstruating woman status, **and** with **a fetus that miscarried** at a stage of development before it was clear whether or not it is considered a birth, **and** with **placenta,** which women sometimes discharge unrelated to the birth of a child (see Leviticus 15:19–30 with regard to blood, and 12:1–8 with regard to miscarriage and placenta). King David went to all this trouble **in order to render a woman ritually pure** and consequently permitted **to her husband.** If, after examination, a Sage declares the woman ritually pure, she is permitted to be with her husband, which leads to increased love and affection, and ultimately to procreation (Rabbi Yoshiyahu Pinto). **And not only** do I engage in activity considered to be beneath the station of a king, **but I consult my teacher, Mefivoshet,** son of King Saul's son, Jonathan, with regard to **everything that I do. I say to him: Mefivoshet, my teacher, did I decide properly? Did I convict properly? Did I acquit properly? Did I rule** ritually **pure properly? Did I rule** ritually **impure properly? And I was not embarrassed.** Forgoing royal dignity should make me worthy to be called pious.

אָמַר רַבִּי יְהוֹשֻׁעַ בְּרֵיהּ דְּרַב אִידִי: מַאי קְרָא – ״וַאֲדַבְּרָה בְעֵדֹתֶיךָ נֶגֶד מְלָכִים וְלֹא אֵבוֹשׁ״.

**Rav Yehoshua, son of Rav Idi, said: What verse** alludes to this? **"And I speak Your testimonies before kings and I will not be ashamed"** (Psalms 119:46). This verse alludes both to David's commitment to Torah, in contrast to the kings of the East and the West, as well as to the fact that he was not ashamed to discuss matters of Torah with Mefivoshet, a descendant of kings. David was not afraid to have his mistakes corrected by Mefivoshet.

תָּנָא: לֹא ״מְפִיבֹשֶׁת״ שְׁמוֹ אֶלָּא ״אִישׁ בֹּשֶׁת״ שְׁמוֹ, וְלָמָּה נִקְרָא שְׁמוֹ ״מְפִיבֹשֶׁת״? – שֶׁהָיָה מְבַיֵּישׁ פְּנֵי דָוִד בַּהֲלָכָה. לְפִיכָךְ זָכָה דָּוִד וְיָצָא מִמֶּנּוּ כִּלְאָב.

**It was taught**[B] in a *Tosefta* from a tannaitic tradition: **His name was not Mefivoshet,**[N] **but rather Ish Boshet was his name. Why was** Ish Boshet **referred to as Mefivoshet? Because he would embarrass** [*mevayesh*] **David in matters of *halakha*.** According to this approach, Mefivoshet is an abbreviation of *boshet panim*, embarrassment. **Because** David was not embarrassed to admit his errors, **he merited that Kilav,**[N] who, according to tradition, was exceedingly wise, **would descend from him.**

וְאָמַר רַבִּי יוֹחָנָן: לֹא ״כִּלְאָב״ שְׁמוֹ אֶלָּא ״דָּנִיֵּאל״ שְׁמוֹ, וְלָמָּה נִקְרָא שְׁמוֹ ״כִּלְאָב״ – שֶׁהָיָה מַכְלִים פְּנֵי מְפִיבֹשֶׁת בַּהֲלָכָה,

**Rabbi Yoḥanan said: His name was not Kilav; rather, his name was Daniel,** as it appears in a different list of David's descendants. **Why was he called Kilav? Because he would embarrass** [*makhlim*] **Mefivoshet,** the teacher or authority figure [*av*] **in matters of *halakha*.**

## NOTES

**Of David…Keep my soul, for I am pious – לְדָוִד שָׁמְרָה נַפְשִׁי כִּי חָסִיד אָנִי:** This expression raises the question of how such unique piety was exhibited; upon what was David relying when he asked for special protection? The statements of the *amora'im* on this issue explore the inner soul of David as it is manifest in the book of Psalms: King David as a penitent. He sought to atone for his two most egregious sins, related to the episode with Bathsheba, quite literally getting his hands dirty in these areas of *halakha*. The reason he chose these specific areas was to counterbalance his wrongdoings. On the one hand, he facilitated procreation and increased the population, in atonement for his part in the death of Uriyya the Hittite. On the other hand, he facilitated intimacy between husbands and their wives as atonement for his conduct with Bathsheba. Therefore, he was able to assert: "Keep my soul, for I am pious" (*HaKotev*).

**His name was not Mefivoshet – לֹא מְפִיבֹשֶׁת שְׁמוֹ:** The medieval commentaries (*Tosafot* and others) question the version of the Gemara as it appears before us: "Mefivoshet was not his name, rather Ish Boshet was his name," as Mefivoshet and Ish Boshet were two different people and there is no indication of any confusion regarding their names. One solution is the suggestion of an alternative version of the text, "His name was not Mefivoshet, rather Meriv Ba'al was his name," referring to the son of Jonathan who actually had two different names (see I Chronicles 8:34; *Shitta Mekubbetzet*).

**Kilav – כִּלְאָב:** Several alternative explanations for his name were suggested. Kilav is related to the Hebrew *lekol av*, a father to all, which alludes to the fact he was a teacher who taught and issued rulings for all (Rabbi Yehonatan ben Korish). Others suggest that Kilav is similar to the Hebrew *ke'ilu av*, an allusion to his appearance, which was strikingly similar to that of his father, David (Rav Sa'adia Gaon).

## BACKGROUND

**It was taught – תָּנָא:** Literally, this word means: Taught, and is generally employed to introduce a quote from the *Tosefta*, although occasionally a *Tosefta* will be cited without this introduction. The *Tosefta* is a compendium of tannaitic statements that are second in importance only to the Mishna. The meaning of the word *tanna* falls somewhere between the term *tenan*, we learned, which introduces a mishna, and the weaker term *tanya*, it was taught, which introduces a *baraita*. The *Tosefta* cited does not necessarily appear in the compendium that constitutes the *Tosefta*, which is appended to each tractate, and may be part of collections no longer available to us.

## BACKGROUND

**Dots** – **נָקוּד**: These dots appear over certain words throughout the Torah, which, as a rule, is without punctuation or vocalization. Wherever they appear, these dots indicate that further investigation and exposition is necessary. Usually, they indicate a caveat regarding the simple understanding of the word or phrase, calling it into question or raising some uncertainty about it.

Dots over and under a word in Psalms 27:13

## NOTES

**Israel was worthy of having a miracle performed on its behalf in the time of Ezra…However, transgression caused the absence of a miracle** – **רְאוּיִם הָיוּ יִשְׂרָאֵל לֵיעָשׂוֹת לָהֶם נֵס בִּימֵי עֶזְרָא...אֶלָּא שֶׁגָּרַם הַחֵטְא**: In both the Rambam's *Mishne Torah, Hilkhot Yesodei HaTorah*, Chapter 10, and in his introduction to his commentary on the Mishna, he writes that promises made by God by means of a prophet will never be retracted and no sin can affect those promises. This appears to contradict the statement that transgression caused the rescission of Moses' promise to the Jewish people that entry into Eretz Yisrael during Ezra's time would be miraculous. One explanation for this discrepancy is that the Rambam wrote this in the context of explaining how to ascertain who is a true prophet. Positive prophecies made by a true prophet are always fulfilled lest questions be raised about the prophet's legitimacy. Since there is no question that Moses was a true prophet, even if one of his prophecies was not realized due to the people's transgression, no doubts would be raised with regard to his status as a prophet (*Anaf Yosef*).

וְעָלָיו אָמַר שְׁלֹמֹה בְּחָכְמָתוֹ: ״בְּנִי אִם חָכַם לִבֶּךָ יִשְׂמַח לִבִּי גַם אָנִי״, וְאוֹמֵר: ״חֲכַם בְּנִי וְשַׂמַּח לִבִּי וְאָשִׁיבָה חֹרְפִי דָבָר״.

In his book of **wisdom, Solomon said** about this wise son: **"My son, if your heart is wise, my heart will be glad, even mine"** (Proverbs 23:15), as David enjoyed witnessing his son Kilav develop into a Torah luminary to the extent that Kilav was able to respond to Mefivoshet. **And** Solomon **says** about Kilav: **"Be wise, my son, and make my heart glad, that I may respond to those who taunt me"** (Proverbs 27:11).

וְדָוִד מִי קָרֵי לְנַפְשֵׁיהּ ״חָסִיד״? וְהָכְתִיב: ״לוּלֵא הֶאֱמַנְתִּי לִרְאוֹת בְּטוּב ה׳ בְּאֶרֶץ חַיִּים״, וְתָנָא מִשְּׁמֵיהּ דְּרַבִּי יוֹסֵי: לָמָּה נָקוּד עַל ״לוּלֵא״? – אָמַר דָּוִד לִפְנֵי הַקָּדוֹשׁ בָּרוּךְ הוּא: רִבּוֹנוֹ שֶׁל עוֹלָם! מוּבְטָח אֲנִי בְּךָ שֶׁאַתָּה מְשַׁלֵּם שָׂכָר טוֹב לַצַּדִּיקִים לֶעָתִיד לָבוֹא, אֲבָל אֵינִי יוֹדֵעַ אִם יֵשׁ לִי חֵלֶק בֵּינֵיהֶם אִם לָאו!

With regard to David's statement, "Keep my soul, for I am pious," the Gemara asks: **Did David call himself pious? Isn't it written: "If I had not** [*luleh*] **believed to look upon the goodness of the Lord in the land of the living"** (Psalms 27:13). The dots that appear over the word *luleh* in the text indicate doubt and uncertainty of his piety, and whether he was deserving of a place in the land of the living (see *Avot De-Rabbi Natan* 34). **In the name of Rabbi Yosei, it was taught** in a *Tosefta*: **Why do dots**[B] appear **over the word** ***luleh***, as if there are some reservations? Because **David said before the Holy One, Blessed be He: Master of the Universe.** I have every **confidence in You that You grant an excellent reward to the righteous in the World-to-Come** since God's ultimate goodness is manifest in the land of eternal life, **but** I still harbor uncertainty with regard to myself, and **I do not know whether or not** I definitely **have a portion among them.** In any case, apparently David was uncertain whether or not he deserved to receive a portion of God's reward for the righteous; how, then, could he characterize himself as pious?

שֶׁמָּא יִגְרוֹם הַחֵטְא;

The Gemara responds: His concern does not prove anything, as King David knew that he was pious. He was simply concerned **lest a transgression** that he might commit in the future **will cause** him to lose his opportunity to look upon the goodness of the Lord in the land of the living.

כִּדְרַבִּי יַעֲקֹב בַּר אִידִי, דְּרַבִּי יַעֲקֹב בַּר אִידִי רָמֵי, כְּתִיב: ״וְהִנֵּה אָנֹכִי עִמָּךְ וּשְׁמַרְתִּיךָ בְּכֹל אֲשֶׁר תֵּלֵךְ״, וּכְתִיב: ״וַיִּירָא יַעֲקֹב מְאֹד״! – אָמַר: שֶׁמָּא יִגְרוֹם הַחֵטְא.

The Gemara cites a proof that there is room for one to fear lest he commit a transgression in the future **in accordance with** the opinion of **Rabbi Ya'akov bar Idi, as Rabbi Ya'akov bar Idi raised a contradiction** between two verses. **It is written** that God told Jacob in his vision of the ladder: **"Behold, I am with you and I guard you wherever you go"** (Genesis 28:15), yet when Jacob returned to Canaan and realized that Esau was coming to greet him, **it is written: "And Jacob became very afraid,** and he was pained" (Genesis 32:8). Why did Jacob not rely on God's promise? Jacob had concerns and **said** to himself: **Lest a transgression** that I might have committed after God made His promise to me **will cause** God to revoke His promise of protection.

כִּדְתַנְיָא: ״עַד יַעֲבֹר עַמְּךָ ה׳ עַד יַעֲבֹר עַם זוּ קָנִיתָ״;

Apparently, at times, transgression does cause God's promise to go unfulfilled, **as it was taught** explicitly in a *baraita* with regard to the ostensibly redundant language in a verse in the Song of the Sea: **"Until Your people will cross, Lord, until the people You have acquired will cross.** You bring them in and plant them in the mountain of Your inheritance, the place, Lord, which You made for Your dwelling" (Exodus 15:16–17).

״עַד יַעֲבֹר עַמְּךָ ה׳״ – זוֹ בִּיאָה רִאשׁוֹנָה, ״עַד יַעֲבֹר עַם זוּ קָנִיתָ״ – זוֹ בִּיאָה שְׁנִיָּה; מִכָּאן אָמְרוּ חֲכָמִים: רְאוּיִם הָיוּ יִשְׂרָאֵל לֵיעָשׂוֹת לָהֶם נֵס בִּימֵי עֶזְרָא כְּדֶרֶךְ שֶׁנַּעֲשָׂה לָהֶם בִּימֵי יְהוֹשֻׁעַ בִּן נוּן, אֶלָּא שֶׁגָּרַם הַחֵטְא.

The Gemara interprets homiletically that **until Your people will cross** refers to the **first entry** into Eretz Yisrael during the time of Joshua, while **until the people You have acquired pass over** refers to the **second entry** following the exile in Babylonia. **Based on** the juxtaposition of these two entries in this single verse, **the Sages said: Israel was worthy of having a miracle performed on its behalf in the time of Ezra** the scribe, just **as** one **was performed on their** behalf **in the time of Joshua bin Nun. However, transgression caused** the absence of a miracle.[N]

״וַחֲכָמִים אוֹמְרִים עַד חֲצוֹת״. חֲכָמִים כְּמַאן סְבִירָא לְהוּ? אִי כְּרַבִּי אֱלִיעֶזֶר סְבִירָא לְהוּ – לֵימְרוּ כְּרַבִּי אֱלִיעֶזֶר!

The Gemara returns to explain what we learned in the mishna: **And the Rabbis say:** The time for the recitation of the evening *Shema* is **until midnight.** The Gemara asks: **In accordance with whose** opinion **do they hold** in explaining the verse: "When you lie down"? **If** they explain this verse **in accordance with** the opinion of **Rabbi Eliezer,** who says that "when you lie down" is the time when people customarily go to sleep, then **let** the Rabbis also **say** that the time for the recitation of *Shema* extends, **in accordance with** the opinion of **Rabbi Eliezer,** until the end of the first watch.

וְאִי כְּרַבָּן גַּמְלִיאֵל סְבִירָא לְהוּ – לֵימְרוּ כְּרַבָּן גַּמְלִיאֵל!

**And if** they explain this verse **in accordance with** the opinion of **Rabban Gamliel** who says that "when you lie down" refers to the entire night, then **let** the Rabbis also **say** that one may recite the evening *Shema* until dawn, **in accordance with** the opinion of **Rabban Gamliel.**[N]

לְעוֹלָם כְּרַבָּן גַּמְלִיאֵל סְבִירָא לְהוּ, וְהָא דְּקָא אָמְרִי "עַד חֲצוֹת" – כְּדֵי לְהַרְחִיק אֶת הָאָדָם מִן הָעֲבֵירָה. כִּדְתַנְיָא: "חֲכָמִים עָשׂוּ סְיָיג לְדִבְרֵיהֶם, כְּדֵי שֶׁלֹּא יְהֵא אָדָם בָּא מִן הַשָּׂדֶה בָּעֶרֶב וְאוֹמֵר: "אֵלֵךְ לְבֵיתִי וְאוֹכַל קִימְעָא, וְאֶשְׁתֶּה קִימְעָא, וְאִישַׁן קִימְעָא, וְאַחַר כָּךְ אֶקְרָא קְרִיאַת שְׁמַע וְאֶתְפַּלֵּל", וְחוֹטַפְתּוֹ שֵׁינָה וְנִמְצָא יָשֵׁן כָּל הַלַּיְלָה; אֲבָל אָדָם בָּא מִן הַשָּׂדֶה בָּעֶרֶב, נִכְנָס לְבֵית הַכְּנֶסֶת, אִם רָגִיל לִקְרוֹת – קוֹרֵא, וְאִם רָגִיל לִשְׁנוֹת – שׁוֹנֶה, וְקוֹרֵא קְרִיאַת שְׁמַע וּמִתְפַּלֵּל, וְאוֹכֵל פִּתּוֹ וּמְבָרֵךְ;

The Gemara answers: **Actually,** the Rabbis **hold in accordance with** the opinion of **Rabban Gamliel,** and the fact **that they say until midnight is** in order **to distance a person from transgression. As it was taught** in a *baraita,* **the Rabbis created a "fence"**[N] **for their pronouncements** with regard to the recitation of *Shema* **in order to prevent** a situation where **a person comes home from the field in the evening,** tired from his day's work, and knowing that he is permitted to recite *Shema* until dawn **says** to himself: **I will go home, eat a little, drink a little, sleep a little and then I will recite** *Shema* **and recite** the evening prayer. In the meantime, **he is overcome by sleep and ends up sleeping all night.**[H] **However,** since one is concerned lest he fall asleep and fail to wake up before midnight in order to recite *Shema* at the appropriate time, **he will come from the field in the evening, enter the synagogue,** and until it is time to pray, he will immerse himself in Torah. **If he is accustomed to reading the Bible, he reads. If he is accustomed to learning** *mishnayot,* a more advanced level of study, **he learns. And** then **he recites** *Shema* **and prays** as he should. When he arrives home, **he eats his meal** with a contented heart **and recites a blessing.**

וְכָל הָעוֹבֵר עַל דִּבְרֵי חֲכָמִים חַיָּיב מִיתָה".

The *baraita* concludes with a warning: **Anyone who transgresses the pronouncements of the Sages is liable to** receive the **death** penalty.[N]

מַאי שְׁנָא בְּכָל דּוּכְתָּא דְּלָא קָתָנֵי "חַיָּיב מִיתָה", וּמַאי שְׁנָא הָכָא דְּקָתָנֵי "חַיָּיב מִיתָה"?

This is a startling conclusion. **What is different in all** other **places that it is not taught that one is liable** to receive **the death penalty and what is different here that it is taught that he is liable to** receive the **death penalty?** There is no unique stringency apparent in the rabbinic restriction on the recitation of *Shema.*

אִיבָּעֵית אֵימָא: מִשּׁוּם דְּאִיכָּא אוֹנֶס שֵׁינָה; וְאִיבָּעֵית אֵימָא: לְאַפּוּקֵי מִמַּאן דְּאָמַר תְּפִלַּת עַרְבִית רְשׁוּת, קָא מַשְׁמַע לַן דְּחוֹבָה.

The Gemara offers two answers, explaining that the conclusion of the *baraita* essentially stems not from the magnitude of the transgression, but rather from concern that the "fence" created around this particular mitzva may be neglected. **If you wish, say** that one returning from work is quite anxious to go to sleep, and due to the risk that he will be **overcome by sleep,** he must be particularly vigilant in the recitation of *Shema.* **And if you wish, say** instead that strong language is employed here in order **to exclude** the opinion of **he who says that** although the morning prayer and the afternoon prayer are mandatory, **the evening prayer is optional.** Therefore, **it teaches us** that the evening prayer **is mandatory,** and anyone who transgresses the pronouncement of the Sages in this regard is liable to receive the death penalty.

### HALAKHA

**In order to prevent a situation where a person comes home from the field in the evening – כְּדֵי שֶׁלֹּא יְהֵא אָדָם בָּא מִן הַשָּׂדֶה וכו׳:** A person may not eat or sleep (*Mishna Berura*) during the half-hour preceding the time for the recitation of the evening *Shema.* If one began to eat and that time arrived, he must interrupt his meal and recite *Shema* without its blessings before continuing his meal. After completing his meal, he recites *Shema* with its blessings and recites the evening prayer. This *halakha* is in accordance with the unchallenged *baraita* cited here (Rambam *Sefer Ahava, Hilkhot Tefilla* 6:7; *Shulḥan Arukh, Oraḥ Ḥayyim* 235:2).

### NOTES

**The opinions of the Rabbis and Rabban Gamliel – שִׁיטַת חֲכָמִים וְרַבָּן גַּמְלִיאֵל:** Although the Gemara's proposed solution seems to be the most straightforward based on the formulation of the mishna, there is another possible solution. One could assert that both the Rabbis and Rabbi Eliezer hold that the time when one goes to sleep lasts until midnight; and it was Rabbi Eliezer who issued a decree to prevent a situation where one would fail to recite *Shema* before midnight. Therefore, the discussion in the Gemara was necessary (*Derush VeHiddush*).

**Fence – סְיָיג:** This refers to a decree, generally a prohibition, issued by the Sages with regard to an action or an object which is essentially permitted. The decree is for the purpose of preventing people from sinning. Usually, decrees were enacted in connection with matters that were liable to ultimately lead to serious transgressions. However, occasionally the purpose of a decree was to establish consistent standards. For example, if people are permitted to perform one action, they may mistakenly believe that similar prohibited actions are permitted. Some decrees were also issued by the Sages because of an incident that occurred, in which the danger of transgression (either actual or potential) arose; they issued a decree prohibiting that action for all later generations.

**Anyone who transgresses the pronouncements of the Sages is liable to receive the death penalty – וְכָל הָעוֹבֵר עַל דִּבְרֵי חֲכָמִים חַיָּיב מִיתָה:** The special status accorded the Sages, and especially the "fences" that they erected around the Torah, could be rendered ineffectual if not practiced with the same stringency as the Torah itself. In several cases, the Gemara says: The Sages invested their pronouncements with more stringency than Torah laws. Since Torah laws were generally observed more vigilantly than rabbinic laws, it was necessary to insist upon fulfillment of the latter so that they would not be dismissed. Clearly, liable to receive the death penalty does not refer literally to a court-imposed death penalty, but rather comes to convey that one who transgresses rabbinic pronouncements is deserving of death because he committed a transgression before God.

אָמַר מָר: ״קוֹרֵא קְרִיאַת שְׁמַע וּמִתְפַּלֵּל״. מְסַיַּיע לֵיהּ לְרַבִּי יוֹחָנָן, דְּאָמַר רַבִּי יוֹחָנָן: אֵיזֶהוּ בֶּן הָעוֹלָם הַבָּא? – זֶה הַסּוֹמֵךְ גְּאוּלָּה לִתְפִלָּה שֶׁל עַרְבִית. רַבִּי יְהוֹשֻׁעַ בֶּן לֵוִי אוֹמֵר: תְּפִלּוֹת בְּאֶמְצַע תִּקְּנוּם.

In this *baraita*, **the Master said** that when one returns from work in the evening, he enters the synagogue, **recites *Shema*, and prays.** From this *baraita*, we see that at night, just as during the day, one first recites *Shema* and then prays. This **supports** the opinion of **Rabbi Yoḥanan, as Rabbi Yoḥanan said: Who** is assured **of** a place in **the World-to-Come? It is one who juxtaposes** the blessing of **redemption,** recited after *Shema*, **to the evening prayer.**[HN] **Rabbi Yehoshua ben Levi**[P] **says: The prayers were instituted** to be recited **between** the two recitations of *Shema*. According to Rabbi Yehoshua ben Levi, one recites the morning *Shema*, then recites all of the prayers and only after the recitation of the evening prayer does he recite the evening *Shema*.

בְּמַאי קָא מִיפַּלְגִי?

Although the practical difference between these two positions is clear, the Gemara seeks to determine: **With regard to what do they disagree?**[B] What is the basis of their argument?

אִי בָּעֵית אֵימָא קְרָא, אִי בָּעֵית אֵימָא סְבָרָא.

The Gemara answers: **If you wish, say** that they disagree over the interpretation of **a verse; if you wish, say** instead that they disagree on a point of **logic.**

אִי בָּעֵית אֵימָא סְבָרָא,

**If you say** that they disagree on a point of **logic,** then the argument relates to the redemption recited after *Shema*, whose focus is the exodus from Egypt, the first redemption. The question is whether that redemption began at night, which would render it appropriate to juxtapose redemption to the blessing of the evening prayers as well, in prayer for immediate redemption. Or, perhaps, the redemption from Egypt only began during the day.

דְּרַבִּי יוֹחָנָן סָבַר: גְּאוּלָּה מֵאוּרְתָּא נַמִי הָוֵי, אֶלָּא גְּאוּלָּה מְעַלַּיְיתָא לָא הָוְיָא אֶלָּא עַד צַפְרָא; וְרַבִּי יְהוֹשֻׁעַ בֶּן לֵוִי סָבַר: כֵּיוָן דְּלָא הָוְיָא אֶלָּא מִצַּפְרָא, לָא הָוְיָא גְּאוּלָּה מְעַלַּיְיתָא.

**Rabbi Yoḥanan holds: Redemption occurred in the evening as well;** however, **the full-fledged redemption was only in the morning.** Since the redemption began in the evening, it is appropriate to juxtapose the blessing of redemption to the daily evening prayer. **Rabbi Yehoshua ben Levi,** on the other hand, **holds: Since** full-fledged redemption **only occurred in the morning,** and the redemption of the previous evening **was not a full-fledged redemption,** there is no need to juxtapose the blessing of redemption to the evening prayer.

וְאִיבָּעֵית אֵימָא קְרָא – וּשְׁנֵיהֶם מִקְרָא אֶחָד דָּרְשׁוּ, דִּכְתִיב: ״בְּשָׁכְבְּךָ וּבְקוּמֶךָ״,

**And if you wish, say** instead that the dispute between Rabbi Yoḥanan and Rabbi Yehoshua ben Levi is not a difference over a point of logic, but over the interpretation of **a verse. Both derived their opinions from the same verse: "When you lie down, and when you rise."** Both interpreted that the juxtaposition in this verse of the recitation of *Shema* at night and the recitation of *Shema* in the morning draws a parallel between them.

רַבִּי יוֹחָנָן סָבַר: מַקִּישׁ שְׁכִיבָה לְקִימָה – מַה קִּימָה קְרִיאַת שְׁמַע וְאַחַר כָּךְ תְּפִלָּה, אַף שְׁכִיבָה נַמִי קְרִיאַת שְׁמַע וְאַחַר כָּךְ תְּפִלָּה; רַבִּי יְהוֹשֻׁעַ בֶּן לֵוִי סָבַר: מַקִּישׁ שְׁכִיבָה לְקִימָה – מַה קִּימָה קְרִיאַת שְׁמַע סָמוּךְ לְמִטָּתוֹ, אַף שְׁכִיבָה נַמִי קְרִיאַת שְׁמַע סָמוּךְ לְמִטָּתוֹ.

**Rabbi Yoḥanan holds:** The verse **juxtaposes lying down and rising. Just as when one rises, the recitation of *Shema* is followed by prayer,** as everyone agrees that in the morning one juxtaposes redemption to the morning prayer, **so too, when one lies down, the recitation of *Shema* is followed by prayer. And Rabbi Yehoshua ben Levi maintains:** The verse **juxtaposes lying down and rising** in a different sense. **Just as when one rises,** he recites *Shema* **adjacent to** rising from **his bed,** as the verse, when you rise, means when one awakens, **so too when one lies down, he recites *Shema* adjacent to** lying down in **his bed.** Therefore, the recitation of the evening *Shema* should be performed as close as possible to the moment when one actually lies down.

מְתִיב מָר בְּרֵיהּ דְּרָבִינָא: בָּעֶרֶב מְבָרֵךְ שְׁתַּיִם לְפָנֶיהָ וּשְׁתַּיִם לְאַחֲרֶיהָ; וְאִי אָמְרַתְּ בָּעֵי לִסְמוֹךְ, הָא לָא קָא סָמַךְ גְּאוּלָּה לִתְפִלָּה, דְּהָא בָּעֵי לְמֵימַר ״הַשְׁכִּיבֵנוּ״!

According to Rabbi Yoḥanan, it is a mitzva to recite *Shema* before the evening prayer. **Mar, son of Ravina, raises an objection** from a mishna: How can one do that? We learn in a later mishna: **In the evening, one recites two** blessings **prior to** the recitation of *Shema* **and two** blessings **afterward. And if you say** that **one must juxtapose** redemption to prayer, **doesn't he** does **fail to juxtapose redemption to prayer, as he must recite: Help us lie down** [*hashkivenu*], the blessing recited after the blessing of redemption, which constitutes an interruption between redemption and prayer?

**HALAKHA**

It is one who juxtaposes redemption to prayer – זֶה הַסּוֹמֵךְ גְּאוּלָּה לִתְפִלָּה: One must juxtapose redemption and prayer with no interruption between them, both in the morning prayer and in the evening prayer. However, those verses and blessings instituted by the Sages to be recited between redemption and prayer, such as: "Lord, open my lips," before prayer, or the blessing: May our eyes see, after redemption, are not considered interruptions. Rather, together with redemption they are considered one long blessing of redemption. While Rabbi Yoḥanan disagreed with Rabbi Yehoshua ben Levi, who is considered greater, the *halakha* was ruled in accordance with the opinion of Rabbi Yoḥanan, because the thrust of the discourse in the Gemara was conducted in accordance with his opinion. Although some halakhic decisors ruled otherwise, the accepted practice is in accordance with the opinion of Rabbi Yoḥanan (Rambam *Sefer Ahava, Hilkhot Tefilla* 7:17; *Shulḥan Arukh, Oraḥ Ḥayyim* 111:1, 236:2).

**NOTES**

Redemption and prayer – גְּאוּלָּה וּתְפִלָּה: The essence of the blessing of redemption is the recalling the redemption from Egypt, yet the Exodus is far more than an isolated incident. The Exodus was the birth of Judaism and its most basic image. Therefore, this is not only true regarding the Exodus as a whole, but also regarding each and every one of its details, which play a role in Judaism. Juxtaposing redemption and prayer is a continuation of the Exodus, with the Jewish people redeemed from their exile and travails and immediately turning to God in prayer. One who successfully connects, through his life and prayer, the blessing of redemption with his personal prayer to God, merits the World-to-Come; and is one whose life is conducted on a higher spiritual plane.

**PERSONALITIES**

Rabbi Yehoshua ben Levi – רַבִּי יְהוֹשֻׁעַ בֶּן לֵוִי: One of the greatest *amora'im* of the first generation in Eretz Yisrael, Rabbi Yehoshua ben Levi was, according to some opinions, the son of Levi ben Sisi, one of the outstanding students of Rabbi Yehuda HaNasi. Apparently, Rabbi Yehoshua ben Levi himself was one of Rabbi Yehuda HaNasi's younger students. Many halakhic disputes are recorded between him and Rabbi Yoḥanan, who was apparently his younger disciple-colleague. In general, the *halakha* is ruled in accordance with the opinion of Rabbi Yehoshua ben Levi, even against Rabbi Yoḥanan, who was the leading authority at that time.

Rabbi Yehoshua ben Levi was also a renowned teacher of *aggada*. Because of the great esteem in which he was held, aggadic statements in his name are cited at the end of the six orders of the Mishna.

A great deal is told of his piety and sanctity; he is regarded as one of the most righteous men who ever lived. Among other things, it is told that he would sit with the most dangerously infected lepers and study Torah. He was famous as a worker of miracles, to whom Elijah the Prophet appeared, and his prayers were always answered. According to tradition, the Angel of Death had no dominion over him, and he entered the Garden of Eden alive.

He taught many students. All of the Sages of the succeeding generation were his students to some degree, and cite Torah pronouncements in his name. His son, Rabbi Yosef, was also a Torah scholar, and married into the family of the *Nasi*.

**BACKGROUND**

With regard to what do they disagree – בְּמַאי קָא מִיפַּלְגִי: That is its literal meaning. This question is asked when the practical difference between the two opinions is clear, however, the underlying principle at the basis of the dispute is not. Clarifying this question is important not only in terms of understanding the dispute, but also in terms of extrapolating from the specific case regarding which they disagreed to cases regarding which they did not disagree explicitly and thereby arrive at additional halakhic conclusions. Compare this with: What is the practical difference between them?

אָמְרִי: כֵּיוָן דְּתַקִּינוּ רַבָּנַן "הַשְׁכִּיבֵנוּ", כִּגְאוּלָּה אֲרִיכְתָּא דָּמְיָא. דְּאִי לָא תֵּימָא הָכִי – שַׁחֲרִית הֵיכִי מָצֵי סָמֵיךְ? וְהָא אָמַר רַבִּי יוֹחָנָן, בַּתְּחִלָּה אוֹמֵר: "ה' שְׂפָתַי תִּפְתָּח", וּלְבַסּוֹף הוּא אוֹמֵר: "יִהְיוּ לְרָצוֹן אִמְרֵי פִי"!

**They say** in response: **Since the Sages instituted** the practice of reciting: **Help us lie down, it is considered one extended blessing of redemption,** and therefore does not constitute an interruption. **As if you fail to say** that the sections added by the Sages are considered no less significant than the original prayers, **then can one juxtapose redemption to prayer** even **in the morning? Didn't Rabbi Yoḥanan say: Before** every prayer **one recites** the verse: **"Lord, open my lips, that my mouth may declare Your glory"** (Psalms 51:17) as a prelude to prayer? **Afterward, one recites** the verse: **"May the words of my mouth and the meditations of my heart be acceptable before You"** (Psalms 19:15).[H] Doesn't the verse: Lord, open my lips, constitute an interruption between redemption and prayer?

אֶלָּא: הָתָם כֵּיוָן דְּתַקִּינוּ רַבָּנַן לְמֵימַר "ה' שְׂפָתַי תִּפְתָּח" – כִּתְפִלָּה אֲרִיכְתָּא דָּמְיָא, הָכָא נַמִי, כֵּיוָן דְּתַקִּינוּ רַבָּנַן לְמֵימַר "הַשְׁכִּיבֵנוּ" – כִּגְאוּלָּה אֲרִיכְתָּא דָּמְיָא.

**Rather, there, since the Sages instituted** that one must **recite: Lord, open my lips, it is considered as an extended prayer** and not as an interruption. **Here, too,** with regard to the evening prayer, **since the Sages instituted to recite** the blessing **Help us lie down, it is considered as one extended** blessing of **redemption.**

אָמַר רַבִּי אֶלְעָזָר אָמַר רַבִּי אָבִינָא: כָּל הָאוֹמֵר "תְּהִלָּה לְדָוִד" בְּכָל יוֹם שָׁלֹשׁ פְּעָמִים – מוּבְטָח לוֹ שֶׁהוּא בֶּן הָעוֹלָם הַבָּא.

Tangential to Rabbi Yoḥanan's statement that one who juxtaposes redemption and prayer is assured of a place in the World-to-Come, a similar statement is cited. **Rabbi Elazar said** that **Rabbi Avina said: Anyone who recites: "A Psalm of David"** (Psalms 145)[H] **three times every day is assured of** a place in **the World-to-Come.**

מַאי טַעְמָא?

This statement extolling the significance of this particular chapter of Psalms, usually referred to as *ashrei* because its recitation is preceded by recitation of the verse, "Happy [*ashrei*] are those who dwell in Your House, they praise You Selah" (Psalms 84:5), raises the question: **What is the reason** that such significance is ascribed to this particular chapter?[N]

אִילֵימָא מִשּׁוּם דְּאָתְיָא בְּאָלֶ"ף בֵּי"ת – נֵימָא "אַשְׁרֵי תְמִימֵי דָרֶךְ" דְּאָתְיָא בִּתְמָנְיָא אַפִּין!

**If you say that it is because it is arranged alphabetically,** then **let us say: "Happy are they who are upright in the way"** (Psalms 119) **where** the alphabetical arrangement **appears eight times.**

אֶלָּא מִשּׁוּם דְּאִית בֵּיהּ "פּוֹתֵחַ אֶת יָדֶךָ" – נֵימָא "הַלֵּל הַגָּדוֹל" דִּכְתִיב בֵּיהּ: "נֹתֵן לֶחֶם לְכָל בָּשָׂר"!

**Rather,** if you suggest that this particular chapter is recited **because it contains** praise for God's provision of sustenance to all of creation: **"You open Your hand** and satisfy every living thing with favor" (Psalms 145:16), then **let him recite the great *hallel*** (Psalms 136), **in which** numerous praises are **written,** including: **"Who provides food to all flesh,** Whose kindness endures forever" (Psalms 136:25).

אֶלָּא: מִשּׁוּם דְּאִית בֵּיהּ תַּרְתֵּי.

**Rather,** the reason why *tehilla leDavid* is accorded preference **is because it contains both** an alphabetic acrostic as well as mention of God's provision of sustenance to all creation.

אָמַר רַבִּי יוֹחָנָן: מִפְּנֵי מָה לֹא נֶאֱמַר נוּ"ן בְּ"אַשְׁרֵי"? מִפְּנֵי שֶׁיֵּשׁ בָּהּ מַפַּלְתָּן שֶׁל שׂוֹנְאֵי יִשְׂרָאֵל, דִּכְתִיב: "נָפְלָה לֹא תוֹסִיף קוּם בְּתוּלַת יִשְׂרָאֵל".

Additionally, with regard to this psalm, **Rabbi Yoḥanan said: Why is there no** verse beginning with the letter ***nun* in *ashrei*? Because it contains** an allusion to **the downfall of the enemies of Israel,**[B] a euphemism for Israel itself. **As it is written: "The virgin of Israel has fallen and she will rise no more;** abandoned in her land, none will raise her up" (Amos 5:2), which begins with the letter *nun*. Due to this verse, *ashrei* does not include a verse beginning with the letter *nun*.

בְּמַעְרְבָא מְתָרְצִי לָהּ הָכִי: "נָפְלָה וְלֹא תוֹסִיף לִנְפּוֹל עוֹד, קוּם בְּתוּלַת יִשְׂרָאֵל". אָמַר רַב נַחְמָן בַּר יִצְחָק: אֲפִילּוּ הָכִי חָזַר דָּוִד וּסְמָכָן בְּרוּחַ הַקֹּדֶשׁ, שֶׁנֶּאֱמַר: "סוֹמֵךְ ה' לְכָל הַנֹּפְלִים".

In order to ease the harsh meaning of this verse, **in the West,** in Eretz Yisrael, **they interpreted it** with a slight adjustment: **"She has fallen but she shall fall no more; rise, virgin of Israel." Rav Naḥman bar Yitzḥak** adds: **Even so, David went and** provided **support, through divine inspiration.** Although King David did not include a verse beginning with the letter *nun* alluding to Israel's downfall, he foresaw the verse that would be written by Amos through divine inspiration; and the very next verse, which begins with the letter *samekh*, reads: **"The Lord upholds the fallen** and raises up those who are bowed down" (Psalms 145:14). Therefore, through divine inspiration, David offered hope and encouragement; although the virgin of Israel may have fallen, the Lord upholds the fallen.

## HALAKHA

**Before, one recites: "Lord, open my lips, that my mouth may declare Your glory." Afterward, one recites: "May the words of my mouth and the meditations of my heart be acceptable before You" – בַּתְּחִלָּה אוֹמֵר: "ה' שְׂפָתַי תִּפְתָּח", וּלְבַסּוֹף הוּא אוֹמֵר: "יִהְיוּ לְרָצוֹן" וכו':** Every *Amida* prayer, on weekdays as well as on Shabbat and Festivals, begins with the verse: "Lord, open my lips, that my mouth may declare Your glory." Similarly, each of these prayers concludes with the verse: "May the words of my mouth and the meditations of my heart be acceptable before You," in accordance with the opinion of Rabbi Yoḥanan (Rambam *Sefer Ahava, Hilkhot Tefilla* 2:9; *Shulḥan Arukh, Oraḥ Ḥayyim* 111:1, 122:2).

**Anyone who recites: A Psalm of David – כָּל הָאוֹמֵר תְּהִלָּה לְדָוִד וכו':** Three times a day we recite *ashrei*, "A Psalm of David": Once in the context of the verses of praise preceding the *Amida* prayer, once following the *Amida* prayer, and once before the afternoon prayer. Some explained that this was instituted to parallel the times that *kedusha* is recited: Once in the repetition of the *Amida* prayer, once in the passage beginning, "And a Redeemer will come to Zion [*uva leTziyyon*]," and once during the afternoon prayer. This practice is based on the statement that Rabbi Elazar said that Rabbi Avina said (Rambam *Sefer Ahava, Hilkhot Tefilla* 7:12, 17–18; *Shulḥan Arukh, Oraḥ Ḥayyim* 51:7 and 131:1, 234:1 in the comment of the Rema).

## NOTES

**The significance of *ashrei* – מַעֲלַת אַשְׁרֵי:** Many have questioned the significance of reciting this specific psalm. Some explain that one who recites *ashrei* three times every day is likely to pray and be meticulous in the fulfillment of all other mitzvot. According to this interpretation, the recitation of this particular psalm itself has no particular significance; it is an indication of something much more significant (*HaKotev*). Others view this chapter as an expression of basic faith. Because of the acrostic nature of the psalm, each verse beginning with one of the letters of the aleph-bet, it represents the entire Torah which is comprised of those letters. But not only is this chapter an alphabetical acrostic, it also includes the verse which states that God opens His hand and sustains all living things, so that through recitation of this psalm, the essence of the Torah and its letters is tied to man's physical needs in the world. When one possesses this awareness, and reiterates it three times every day, one develops an approach which will lead him to the World-to-Come (*Penei Yehoshua, HaKotev*).

## BACKGROUND

**The enemies of Israel – שׂוֹנְאֵי יִשְׂרָאֵל:** The phrase: The downfall of the enemies of Israel, which uses enemies of Israel as a euphemism for Israel itself, is not unique to this instance. Any time Israel is cursed or the downfall of Israel is described, or where disrespect for God is shown, a euphemism is employed, i.e., enemies of Israel or enemies of the Holy One, Blessed be He. This is in order to refrain from having statements that desecrate the name of God or express contempt for Israel escape our lips. Although the true meaning of the phrase is evident, one should refrain from mentioning it explicitly.

אָמַר רַבִּי אֶלְעָזָר בַּר אָבִינָא: גָּדוֹל מַה שֶּׁנֶּאֱמַר בְּמִיכָאֵל יוֹתֵר מִמַּה שֶּׁנֶּאֱמַר בְּגַבְרִיאֵל, דְּאִילּוּ בְּמִיכָאֵל כְּתִיב: ״וַיָּעָף אֵלַי אֶחָד מִן הַשְּׂרָפִים״, וְאִילּוּ גַּבֵּי גַּבְרִיאֵל כְּתִיב: ״וְהָאִישׁ גַּבְרִיאֵל אֲשֶׁר רָאִיתִי בֶחָזוֹן בַּתְּחִלָּה מֻעָף בִּיעָף״ וגו׳.

After this discussion of the statement that Rabbi Elazar said that Rabbi Avina said, another statement of Rabbi Elazar is cited. **Rabbi Elazar bar Avina said: What was said about** the angel **Michael is greater than what was said about** the angel **Gabriel. As about Michael, it is written: "And one of the seraphim flew to me"** (Isaiah 6:6),[N] indicating that with a single flight, the seraph arrived and performed his mission, while **regarding Gabriel, it is written: "The man, Gabriel, whom I had seen at the beginning, in a vision, being caused to fly swiftly,** approached close to me about the time of the evening offering" (Daniel 9:21). The double language used in the phrase "to fly swiftly [*muaf biaf*]," indicates that he did not arrive at his destination in a single flight, but rather, that it took him two flights.

מַאי מַשְׁמַע דְּהַאי ״אֶחָד״ מִיכָאֵל הוּא?

To Rabbi Elazar bar Avina, it is clear that "one of the seraphim" refers to Michael, and the Gemara asks: **From where is it inferred that the one** mentioned in the verse **is Michael?**

אָמַר רַבִּי יוֹחָנָן: אָתְיָא ״אֶחָד״ ״אֶחָד״, כְּתִיב הָכָא: ״וַיָּעָף אֵלַי אֶחָד מִן הַשְּׂרָפִים״ וּכְתִיב הָתָם: ״וְהִנֵּה מִיכָאֵל אֶחָד (מִן) הַשָּׂרִים הָרִאשׁוֹנִים בָּא לְעָזְרֵנִי״.

**Rabbi Yoḥanan said: This is derived** through a verbal analogy between the words **one and one. Here, it is written: "And one of the seraphim flew to me"** (Isaiah 6:6), **and there, it is written: "And behold, Michael, one of the chief ministers of the king, came to my aid"** (Daniel 10:13). Since the verse from Daniel refers to Michael as "one," which aggadic midrash interprets as "the unique one," so, too, "one of the seraphs" described in Isaiah must also refer to the unique one, Michael.

תָּנָא: מִיכָאֵל – בְּאַחַת, גַּבְרִיאֵל – בִּשְׁתַּיִם, אֵלִיָּהוּ – בְּאַרְבַּע, וּמַלְאַךְ הַמָּוֶת – בִּשְׁמֹנֶה, וּבִשְׁעַת הַמַּגֵּפָה – בְּאַחַת.

This discussion in the Gemara concludes with a *Tosefta* that arrives at a hierarchy of angels based on the number of flights required by each to arrive at his destination. **It was taught** in a *Tosefta*: **Michael,** as stated above, **in one** flight; **Gabriel, in two** flights; **Elijah** the Prophet, **in four** flights; **and the Angel of Death, in eight** flights. **During a time of plague,** however, when the Angel of Death seems ubiquitous, he arrives everywhere **in one** flight.

אָמַר רַבִּי יְהוֹשֻׁעַ בֶּן לֵוִי: אַף עַל פִּי שֶׁקָּרָא אָדָם קְרִיאַת שְׁמַע בְּבֵית הַכְּנֶסֶת – מִצְוָה לִקְרוֹתוֹ עַל מִטָּתוֹ. אָמַר רַבִּי יוֹסֵי: מַאי קְרָא – ״רִגְזוּ וְאַל תֶּחֱטָאוּ אִמְרוּ בִלְבַבְכֶם עַל מִשְׁכַּבְכֶם וְדֹמּוּ סֶלָה״.

**Rabbi Yehoshua ben Levi said: Even though one recited *Shema* in the synagogue, it is a mitzva to recite it upon his bed**[H] in fulfillment of the verse: "When you lie down." **Rabbi Yosei said: What verse** alludes to the fact that one must recite *Shema* in the evening, upon his bed, as well? **"Tremble, and do not sin; say to your heart upon your bed and be still, Selah"** (Psalms 4:5). This is understood to mean: Recite *Shema*, about which it is written, "on your hearts," upon your bed, and afterward be still and sleep.

אָמַר רַב נַחְמָן:

With regard to Rabbi Yehoshua ben Levi's statement, **Rabbi Naḥman said:**

NOTES

**And one of the seraphim flew to me** – וַיָּעָף אֵלַי אֶחָד מִן הַשְּׂרָפִים: This midrash concerning the angels' flight contains an assessment of their virtues and their hierarchy as well as the attributes which they represent. The angel Michael is designated as the angel of Israel, "The Minister of Israel" (see Daniel 10:21). Gabriel is the angel through whom the prophets prophesy. Although he acts as defender of the Jewish people, he is essentially the Angel of Judgment and Minister of Fire, while Michael is the Minister of Loving-Kindness and Compassion. For this reason, Michael is capable of traveling anywhere in a single flight, while Gabriel must take two flights to reach his destination. This is the source for the *Tosefta* describing the hierarchy of the hosts of heaven. Michael and Gabriel are first because of the direct relationship between them and their missions. After them is Elijah, who is also considered by the Sages as one who represents Israel, as the Angel of the Covenant (see Malachi 3:1 and 3:23). Since Elijah is a human being who was elevated to the status of an angel, he is ranked below Gabriel. After Elijah is the "Angel of Death," or Satan, the evil inclination (*Bava Batra* 16a), who is the manifestation of evil in the world. He travels in eight flights, allowing a person time to repent before the Angel of Death carries out his mission (Rashba). However, during a plague, the Angel of Death arrives at his destination in a single bound and does not distinguish between the righteous and the wicked.

HALAKHA

**Even though one recited *Shema* in the synagogue, it is a mitzva to recite it upon his bed** – אַף עַל פִּי שֶׁקָּרָא אָדָם קְרִיאַת שְׁמַע בְּבֵית הַכְּנֶסֶת מִצְוָה לִקְרוֹתוֹ עַל מִטָּתוֹ: In addition to the *Shema* recited during the evening prayer in the synagogue, one must also recite *Shema* upon his bed. He need not actually recite it in bed, but it should be recited just before he actually goes to sleep. This recitation includes the first paragraph of *Shema*. According to some opinions, it includes all three paragraphs as well as several verses and prayers mentioning divine mercy, including: "In Your hand I entrust my soul" (Rambam *Sefer Ahava*, *Hilkhot Tefilla* 7:2; *Shulḥan Arukh*, *Oraḥ Ḥayyim* 239:1).

Perek **I**
Daf **5** Amud **a**

אִם תַּלְמִיד חָכָם הוּא – אֵין צָרִיךְ. אֲמַר אַבַּיֵי: אַף תַּלְמִיד חָכָם מִיבָּעֵי לֵיהּ לְמֵימַר חַד פְּסוּקָא דְּרַחֲמֵי, כְּגוֹן: ״בְּיָדְךָ אַפְקִיד רוּחִי פָּדִיתָה אוֹתִי ה׳ אֵל אֱמֶת״.

**If one is a Torah scholar, he need not** recite *Shema* on his bed since he is always engaged in the study of Torah and will likely fall asleep engrossed in matters of Torah. **Abaye said: Even a Torah scholar must recite at least one verse of prayer, such as: "Into Your hand I trust my spirit; You have redeemed me, Lord, God of truth"** (Psalms 31:6).

אָמַר רַבִּי לֵוִי בַּר חָמָא אָמַר רַבִּי שִׁמְעוֹן בֶּן לָקִישׁ: לְעוֹלָם יַרְגִּיז אָדָם יֵצֶר טוֹב עַל יֵצֶר הָרָע, שֶׁנֶּאֱמַר: ״רִגְזוּ וְאַל תֶּחֱטָאוּ״. אִם נִצְּחוֹ – מוּטָב, וְאִם לָאו – יַעֲסוֹק בַּתּוֹרָה, שֶׁנֶּאֱמַר: ״אִמְרוּ בִלְבַבְכֶם״; אִם נִצְּחוֹ – מוּטָב, וְאִם לָאו – יִקְרָא קְרִיאַת שְׁמַע, שֶׁנֶּאֱמַר: ״עַל מִשְׁכַּבְכֶם״; אִם נִצְּחוֹ – מוּטָב, וְאִם לָאו – יִזְכּוֹר לוֹ יוֹם הַמִּיתָה, שֶׁנֶּאֱמַר: ״וְדֹמּוּ סֶלָה״.

Incidental to the verse, "Tremble, and do not sin," the Gemara mentions that **Rabbi Levi bar Ḥama said** that **Rabbi Shimon ben Lakish**[P] **said: One should always incite his good inclination against his evil inclination,** i.e., that one must constantly struggle so that his evil inclination does not lead him to transgression.

If one succeeds and **subdues** his evil inclination, **excellent,** but **if** he does **not** succeed in subduing it, he should **study Torah,** as alluded to in **the verse: "Say to your heart."**

If he **subdues** his evil inclination, **excellent; if not, he should recite** ***Shema,*** which contains the acceptance of the yoke of God, and the concept of reward and punishment, **as it is stated** in the verse: **"Upon your bed,"** which alludes to *Shema*, where it says: "When you lie down."

If he **subdues** his evil inclination, **excellent; if not, he should remind himself of the day of death,** whose silence is alluded to in the continuation of **the verse: "And be still, Selah."**

וְאָמַר רַבִּי לֵוִי בַּר חָמָא אָמַר רַבִּי שִׁמְעוֹן בֶּן לָקִישׁ: מַאי דִּכְתִיב ״וְאֶתְּנָה לְךָ אֶת לֻחֹת הָאֶבֶן וְהַתּוֹרָה וְהַמִּצְוָה אֲשֶׁר כָּתַבְתִּי לְהוֹרֹתָם״, ״לֻחֹת״ – אֵלּוּ עֲשֶׂרֶת הַדִּבְּרוֹת, ״תּוֹרָה״ – זֶה מִקְרָא, ״וְהַמִּצְוָה״ – זוֹ מִשְׁנָה, ״אֲשֶׁר כָּתַבְתִּי״ – אֵלּוּ נְבִיאִים וּכְתוּבִים, ״לְהוֹרֹתָם״ – זֶה תַּלְמוּד; מְלַמֵּד שֶׁכּוּלָּם נִתְּנוּ לְמֹשֶׁה מִסִּינַי.

**And Rabbi Levi bar Ḥama said** that **Rabbi Shimon ben Lakish said:** God said to Moses, "Ascend to me on the mountain and be there, **and I will give you the stone tablets and the Torah and the mitzva that I have written that you may teach them"** (Exodus 24:12), meaning that God revealed to Moses not only the Written Torah, but all of Torah, as it would be transmitted through the generations.

**The "tablets" are the ten commandments** that were written on the tablets of the Covenant,

**the "Torah" is the five books of Moses.**

**The "mitzva" is the Mishna,** which includes explanations for the mitzvot and how they are to be performed.

**"That I have written" refers to the Prophets and Writings,** written with divine inspiration.

**"That you may teach them" refers to the Talmud,** which explains the Mishna.

These explanations are the foundation for the rulings of practical *halakha*. This verse **teaches** that **all** aspects of Torah **were given to** Moses **from Sinai.**

אָמַר רַבִּי יִצְחָק: כָּל הַקּוֹרֵא קְרִיאַת שְׁמַע עַל מִטָּתוֹ, כְּאִלּוּ אוֹחֵז חֶרֶב שֶׁל שְׁתֵּי פִיּוֹת בְּיָדוֹ, שֶׁנֶּאֱמַר: ״רוֹמְמוֹת אֵל בִּגְרוֹנָם וְחֶרֶב פִּיפִיּוֹת בְּיָדָם״. מַאי מַשְׁמַע? – אָמַר מָר זוּטְרָא וְאִיתֵּימָא רַב אַשִׁי: מֵרֵישָׁא דְּעִנְיָנָא, דִּכְתִיב: ״יַעְלְזוּ חֲסִידִים בְּכָבוֹד יְרַנְּנוּ עַל מִשְׁכְּבוֹתָם״, וּכְתִיב בָּתְרֵיהּ: ״רוֹמְמוֹת אֵל בִּגְרוֹנָם וְחֶרֶב פִּיפִיּוֹת בְּיָדָם״.

The Gemara continues its treatment of the recitation of *Shema* upon one's bed. **Rabbi Yitzḥak said: Anyone who recites** ***Shema*** **on his bed, it is as if he holds a double-edged sword,** guarding him from all evil, **as it is stated: "High praises of God in their mouths, and a double-edged sword in their hands"** (Psalms 149:6). The Gemara asks: **From where is it inferred** that this verse from Psalms refers to the recitation of *Shema*? **Mar Zutra, and some say Rav Ashi, said:** We derive it **from the preceding** verse, **as it is written: "Let the pious exult in glory; let them joyously sing upon their beds."** The praise of God from one's bed is the recitation of *Shema*. **And it is written thereafter: "High praises of God in their mouths, and a double-edged sword in their hands."**

וְאָמַר רַבִּי יִצְחָק: כָּל הַקּוֹרֵא קְרִיאַת שְׁמַע עַל מִטָּתוֹ – מַזִּיקִין בְּדֵילִין הֵימֶנּוּ, שֶׁנֶּאֱמַר: ״וּבְנֵי רֶשֶׁף יַגְבִּיהוּ עוּף״; וְאֵין ״עוּף״ אֶלָּא תּוֹרָה, שֶׁנֶּאֱמַר: ״הֲתָעִיף עֵינֶיךָ בּוֹ וְאֵינֶנּוּ״; וְאֵין ״רֶשֶׁף״ אֶלָּא מַזִּיקִין, שֶׁנֶּאֱמַר: ״מְזֵי רָעָב וּלְחֻמֵי רֶשֶׁף וְקֶטֶב מְרִירִי״.

**And Rabbi Yitzḥak said: Anyone who recites** ***Shema*** **upon his bed, demons stay away from him.** This is alluded to, **as it is stated:** "But man is born into trouble, **and the sparks [*reshef*] fly [*uf*] upward"** (Job 5:7). The verse is explained: The word **fly [*uf*]** means **nothing other than Torah,**[N] as Torah is difficult to grasp and easy to lose, like something that floats away, **as it is stated: "Will you set your eyes upon it? It is gone;** for riches certainly make themselves wings, like an eagle that flies into the heavens" (Proverbs 23:5). The word **"sparks"** means **nothing other than demons, as it is stated: "Wasting of hunger, and the devouring of the sparks [*reshef*] and bitter destruction [*ketev meriri*],** and the teeth of beasts I will send upon them, with the venom of crawling things of the dust" (Deuteronomy 32:24). Here we see *reshef* listed along with *ketev meriri*, both of which are understood by the Sages to be names of demons.

אָמַר רַבִּי שִׁמְעוֹן בֶּן לָקִישׁ: כָּל הָעוֹסֵק בַּתּוֹרָה – יִסּוּרִין בְּדֵילִין הֵימֶנּוּ, שֶׁנֶּאֱמַר: ״וּבְנֵי רֶשֶׁף יַגְבִּיהוּ עוּף״; וְאֵין ״עוּף״ אֶלָּא תּוֹרָה, שֶׁנֶּאֱמַר: ״הֲתָעִיף עֵינֶיךָ בּוֹ וְאֵינֶנּוּ״; וְאֵין ״רֶשֶׁף״ אֶלָּא יִסּוּרִין, שֶׁנֶּאֱמַר: ״מְזֵי רָעָב וּלְחֻמֵי רֶשֶׁף״.

Regarding this unclear verse, **Rabbi Shimon ben Lakish said: If one engages in Torah** study, **suffering stays away from him, as it is stated: "And the sparks fly upward."** And fly means **nothing other than Torah, and sparks** means **nothing other than suffering, as it is stated: "Wasting of hunger, and the devouring of the sparks,"** equating devouring sparks with wasting hunger, as both are types of suffering. From here, we derive that through Torah, fly, one is able to distance himself, upward, from suffering, sparks.

### PERSONALITIES

**Rabbi Shimon ben Lakish – רַבִּי שִׁמְעוֹן בֶּן לָקִישׁ:** Rabbi Shimon ben Lakish, typically referred to as Reish Lakish, was among the greatest *amora'im* in Eretz Yisrael. He was the friend and brother-in-law of Rabbi Yoḥanan.

Reish Lakish's life story is amazing. He studied Torah from a young age, but, perhaps due to dire financial straits, he sold himself to a Roman circus as a gladiator. There are many stories in the Talmud that attest to his great strength. Sometime later, in the wake of a meeting with Rabbi Yoḥanan, he resumed his Torah study, first as a student of Rabbi Yoḥanan, then as a friend and colleague. He married Rabbi Yoḥanan's sister.

Many halakhic disagreements between Reish Lakish and Rabbi Yoḥanan concerning central issues of *halakha* are recorded in the Talmud. His objective was not to disagree with Rabbi Yoḥanan but rather to help him hone his opinion through debate. Rabbi Yoḥanan related to him with great respect, often saying: My peer disagrees with me. He was well known for his strict piety, to the extent that one with whom Reish Lakish was seen conversing in public, was said to be able to borrow money without guarantors, as Reish Lakish only associated with people beyond reproach. When he died he was survived by his wife and son, who was a child prodigy. Nothing more is known about him.

### NOTES

**The word "fly" [*uf*] means nothing other than Torah – וְאֵין ״עוּף״ אֶלָּא תּוֹרָה:** The proof does not seem absolute, because the Gemara is seeking proof regarding *Shema* in particular and not regarding Torah study in general. This was explained through the dual implication of the word *uf* as well as an additional, secondary meaning of the verse: "Will you set [*hata'if*] your eyes upon it? It is gone." It is referring to portions of the Torah that one reads a short time before he goes to sleep, when he is about to shut his eyelids [*afapayim*]. Regarding that portion, it says: "Will you set your eyes upon it?" Others explain it based on an additional allusion from the word *uf*, which means double in Aramaic. In other words, that portion of the Torah that is recited twice daily, in the morning and evening.

אָמַר לֵיהּ רַבִּי יוֹחָנָן: הָא אֲפִילּוּ תִּינוֹקוֹת שֶׁל בֵּית רַבָּן יוֹדְעִין אוֹתוֹ, שֶׁנֶּאֱמַר: ״וַיֹּאמֶר אִם שָׁמוֹעַ תִּשְׁמַע לְקוֹל ה׳ אֱלֹהֶיךָ וְהַיָּשָׁר בְּעֵינָיו תַּעֲשֶׂה וְהַאֲזַנְתָּ לְמִצְוֹתָיו וְשָׁמַרְתָּ כׇּל חֻקָּיו כׇּל הַמַּחֲלָה אֲשֶׁר שַׂמְתִּי בְמִצְרַיִם לֹא אָשִׂים עָלֶיךָ כִּי אֲנִי ה׳ רֹפְאֶךָ״! אֶלָּא: כׇּל שֶׁאֶפְשָׁר לוֹ לַעֲסוֹק בַּתּוֹרָה וְאֵינוֹ עוֹסֵק – הַקָּדוֹשׁ בָּרוּךְ הוּא מֵבִיא עָלָיו יִסּוּרִין מְכוֹעָרִין וְעוֹכְרִין אוֹתוֹ, שֶׁנֶּאֱמַר: ״נֶאֱלַמְתִּי דוּמִיָּה הֶחֱשֵׁיתִי מִטּוֹב וּכְאֵבִי נֶעְכָּר״, וְאֵין ״טוֹב״ אֶלָּא תּוֹרָה, שֶׁנֶּאֱמַר: ״כִּי לֶקַח טוֹב נָתַתִּי לָכֶם תּוֹרָתִי אַל תַּעֲזֹבוּ״.

**Rabbi Yoḥanan said to him: Even schoolchildren,** who learn only the Written Torah, **know this** concept **as it is stated: "And He said you shall surely hear the voice of the Lord your God, and what is upright in His eyes you shall do and you shall listen to His mitzvot and guard His statutes; any disease that I have placed upon Egypt I will not place upon you for I am the Lord your healer"** (Exodus 15:26). **Rather,** one must interpret the verse: **Anyone who is able to engage in Torah** study **yet does not engage** in that study, not only does **the Holy One, Blessed be He,** fail to protect him, but He **brings upon him hideous afflictions,** that embarrass him **and trouble him, as it is stated: "I was mute with silence; I was silent from good, and my pain was strong"** (Psalms 39:3). The word **good** means **nothing other than Torah, as it is stated: "For I have given you a good portion, My Torah, do not abandon it"** (Proverbs 4:2). The verse should be understood: "I have been silent from the study of Torah, and my pain was strong."

אָמַר רַבִּי זֵירָא וְאִיתֵּימָא רַבִּי חֲנִינָא בַּר פַּפָּא: בֹּא וּרְאֵה שֶׁלֹּא כְּמִדַּת הַקָּדוֹשׁ בָּרוּךְ הוּא מִדַּת בָּשָׂר וָדָם, מִדַּת בָּשָׂר וָדָם – אָדָם מוֹכֵר חֵפֶץ לַחֲבֵירוֹ, מוֹכֵר – עָצֵב, וְלוֹקֵחַ – שָׂמֵחַ; אֲבָל הַקָּדוֹשׁ בָּרוּךְ הוּא אֵינוֹ כֵּן – נָתַן לָהֶם תּוֹרָה לְיִשְׂרָאֵל וְשָׂמַח, שֶׁנֶּאֱמַר: ״כִּי לֶקַח טוֹב נָתַתִּי לָכֶם תּוֹרָתִי אַל תַּעֲזֹבוּ״.

With regard to the verse: "For I have given you a good portion," **Rabbi Zeira, and some say Rabbi Ḥanina bar Pappa, said: Come and see how the characteristics of the Holy One, Blessed be He, are unlike the characteristics of flesh and blood. It is characteristic of flesh and blood that when one sells an object to another** person, **the seller grieves** the loss of his possession **and the buyer rejoices. With regard to the Holy One, Blessed be He,** however, **this is not so. He gave the Torah to Israel and rejoiced, as it is stated: "For I have given you a good portion, My Torah, do not abandon it."** A good portion is understood as a good purchase; although God sold Torah to Israel, He rejoices in the sale and praises the object before its new owner (Rabbi Yoshiyahu Pinto).

אָמַר רָבָא וְאִיתֵּימָא רַב חִסְדָּא: אִם רוֹאֶה אָדָם שֶׁיִּסּוּרִין בָּאִין עָלָיו – יְפַשְׁפֵּשׁ בְּמַעֲשָׂיו, שֶׁנֶּאֱמַר: ״נַחְפְּשָׂה דְרָכֵינוּ וְנַחְקֹרָה וְנָשׁוּבָה עַד ה׳״; פִּשְׁפֵּשׁ וְלֹא מָצָא – יִתְלֶה בְּבִטּוּל תּוֹרָה, שֶׁנֶּאֱמַר: ״אַשְׁרֵי הַגֶּבֶר אֲשֶׁר תְּיַסְּרֶנּוּ יָהּ וּמִתּוֹרָתְךָ תְלַמְּדֶנּוּ״.

Previously, the Gemara discussed suffering that results from one's transgressions. The Gemara shifts the focus and discusses suffering that does not result from one's transgressions and the suffering of the righteous. **Rava, and some say Rav Ḥisda, said: If a person sees that suffering has befallen him, he should examine his actions.**[N] Generally, suffering comes about as punishment for one's transgressions, **as it is stated: "We will search and examine our ways, and return to God"** (Lamentations 3:40). **If he examined** his ways and **found no** transgression[N] for which that suffering is appropriate, **he may attribute** his suffering **to dereliction** in the study **of Torah.** God punishes an individual for dereliction in the study of Torah in order to emphasize the gravity of the issue, **as it is stated: "Happy is the man whom You punish, Lord, and teach out of Your law"** (Psalms 94:12). This verse teaches us that his suffering will cause him to return to Your law.

וְאִם תָּלָה וְלֹא מָצָא – בְּיָדוּעַ שֶׁיִּסּוּרִין שֶׁל אַהֲבָה הֵם, שֶׁנֶּאֱמַר: ״כִּי אֶת אֲשֶׁר יֶאֱהַב ה׳ יוֹכִיחַ״.

**And if he did attribute** his suffering to dereliction in the study of Torah, **and did not find** this to be so, **he may be confident that these are afflictions of love,**[N] **as it is stated: "For whom the Lord loves, He rebukes,** as does a father the son in whom he delights" (Proverbs 3:12).

אָמַר רָבָא אָמַר רַב סְחוֹרָה אָמַר רַב הוּנָא: כׇּל שֶׁהַקָּדוֹשׁ בָּרוּךְ הוּא חָפֵץ בּוֹ – מְדַכְּאוֹ בְּיִסּוּרִין, שֶׁנֶּאֱמַר: ״וַה׳ חָפֵץ דַּכְּאוֹ הֶחֱלִי״;

So too, **Rava said** that **Rav Seḥora said** that **Rav Huna said: Anyone in whom the Holy One, Blessed be He, delights, He oppresses him with suffering, as it is stated: "Yet in whom the Lord delights, He oppresses him with disease;** to see if his soul would offer itself in guilt, that he might see his children, lengthen his days, and that the desire of the Lord might prosper by his hand" (Isaiah 53:10). This verse illustrates that in whomever God delights, he afflicts with illness.

יָכוֹל אֲפִילּוּ לֹא קִבְּלָם מֵאַהֲבָה – תַּלְמוּד לוֹמַר: ״אִם תָּשִׂים אָשָׁם נַפְשׁוֹ״, מָה אָשָׁם – לְדַעַת, אַף יִסּוּרִין – לְדַעַת.

I **might** have thought that God delights in him even **if he does not accept** his suffering **with love. Therefore the verse teaches: "If his soul would offer itself in guilt." Just as a guilt-offering is brought knowingly,** as it is one of the sacrifices offered willingly, without coercion, **so too his suffering** must be accepted **knowingly.**

וְאִם קִבְּלָם מַה שְּׂכָרוֹ – ״יִרְאֶה זֶרַע יַאֲרִיךְ יָמִים״; וְלֹא עוֹד אֶלָּא שֶׁתַּלְמוּדוֹ מִתְקַיֵּים בְּיָדוֹ, שֶׁנֶּאֱמַר: ״וְחֵפֶץ ה׳ בְּיָדוֹ יִצְלָח״.

**And if one accepts** that suffering with love, **what is his reward?** As the second part of the verse states: **"That he might see his children, lengthen his days." Moreover,** in addition to these earthly rewards, **his** Torah **study will endure** and his Torah study will be successful, **as it is stated: "The purpose of the Lord,"** the Torah, the revelation of God's will, **"might prosper by his hand."**

**NOTES**

**If a person sees that suffering has befallen him, he should examine his actions – רוֹאֶה אָדָם שֶׁיִּסּוּרִין בָּאִין עָלָיו יְפַשְׁפֵּשׁ בְּמַעֲשָׂיו:** The Gemara teaches that when one realizes that he is ill, he should not assume that it is happenstance and immediately turn to medical doctors. Rather, he should view it as an opportunity to examine his own actions and conduct. A doctor examines a patient to determine the cause of the illness so that he may prescribe effective medicine to counteract the illness and restore the patient to physical health. Similarly, an examination of the soul is required to determine the source of one's spiritual illness. The first step in curing the illness is abandoning the conduct that is deleterious to one's spiritual health (*Iyyun Ya'akov*).

**If he examined his ways and found no transgression – פִּשְׁפֵּשׁ וְלֹא מָצָא:** The question was raised: Is it feasible that one examined and found none? The verse states: "There is not a righteous man upon earth, that does good, and sins not" (Ecclesiastes 7:20) and immediately thereafter the Gemara suggests: Attribute it to dereliction in the study of Torah. Some commentaries answered that the suffering that one experiences is proportionate to the crime. Therefore, if he found that he did not violate a prohibition to warrant so severe a punishment or that the punishment does not fit the crime, then he should attribute it to dereliction in the study of Torah, as, no doubt, he did not study as much as he should have or did not expend the requisite effort (Rabbi Yoshiyahu Pinto, Maharsha).

**Afflictions of love – יִסּוּרִין שֶׁל אַהֲבָה:** Some explain this to mean that when one is young and healthy, it is easy to engage in the study of Torah and fulfillment of mitzvot. This is not the case when one is afflicted with suffering. Sometimes, God afflicts a person so that he will overcome those afflictions and engage in Torah study despite them. Through this process, one's ultimate reward is enhanced based on the principle that one's reward is proportional to his suffering (*Tziyyun LeNefesh Ḥayya*).

פְּלִיגִי בָּהּ רַבִּי יַעֲקֹב בַּר אִידִי וְרַבִּי אַחָא בַּר חֲנִינָא, חַד אָמַר: אֵלּוּ הֵם יִסּוּרִין שֶׁל אַהֲבָה – כֹּל שֶׁאֵין בָּהֶן בִּטּוּל תּוֹרָה, שֶׁנֶּאֱמַר: "אַשְׁרֵי הַגֶּבֶר אֲשֶׁר תְּיַסְּרֶנּוּ יָהּ וּמִתּוֹרָתְךָ תְלַמְּדֶנּוּ";

With regard to the acceptance of affliction with love and what exactly this entails, **Rabbi Ya'akov bar Idi and Rabbi Aḥa bar Ḥanina disagree. One of them said: Afflictions of love are any that do not cause dereliction** in the study **of Torah,** i.e., any which do not afflict his body to the extent that he is unable to study Torah, **as it is stated: "Happy is the man whom You afflict, Lord, and teach from Your Torah."** Afflictions of love are when You "teach from Your Torah."

וְחַד אָמַר: אֵלּוּ הֵן יִסּוּרִין שֶׁל אַהֲבָה – כֹּל שֶׁאֵין בָּהֶן בִּטּוּל תְּפִלָּה, שֶׁנֶּאֱמַר: "בָּרוּךְ אֱלֹהִים אֲשֶׁר לֹא הֵסִיר תְּפִלָּתִי וְחַסְדּוֹ מֵאִתִּי".

**And one said:**[B] **Afflictions of love are any that do not cause dereliction** in the recitation **of prayer, as it is stated: "Blessed is God Who did not turn away my prayer"** (Psalms 66:20). Despite his suffering, the afflicted is still capable of praying to God.

אָמַר לְהוּ רַבִּי אַבָּא בְּרֵיהּ דְּרַבִּי חִיָּיא בַּר אַבָּא, הָכִי אָמַר רַבִּי חִיָּיא בַּר אַבָּא אָמַר רַבִּי יוֹחָנָן: אֵלּוּ וָאֵלּוּ יִסּוּרִין שֶׁל אַהֲבָה הֵן, שֶׁנֶּאֱמַר: "כִּי אֶת אֲשֶׁר יֶאֱהַב ה' יוֹכִיחַ";

**Rabbi Abba, son of Rabbi Ḥiyya bar Abba, said:** My father, **Rabbi Ḥiyya bar Abba, said** that **Rabbi Yoḥanan said as follows: Both,** even afflictions that cause dereliction in the study of Torah and those that cause dereliction in the recitation of prayer, **are afflictions of love,** as with regard to one who suffers without transgression **it is stated: "For whom He loves, He rebukes,"** and inability to study Torah and to pray are among his afflictions.

אֶלָּא מָה תַּלְמוּד לוֹמַר "וּמִתּוֹרָתְךָ תְלַמְּדֶנּוּ"? – אַל תִּקְרֵי "תְלַמְּדֶנּוּ" אֶלָּא "תְלַמְּדֵנוּ"; דָּבָר זֶה מִתּוֹרָתְךָ תְּלַמְּדֵנוּ;

**What then,** is the meaning when **the verse states: "And teach him from Your Torah"? Do not read**[B] **and teach** to mean **and teach him,** rather, **and teach us. You teach us** the value of **this** affliction **from Your Torah.**

קַל וָחוֹמֶר מִשֵּׁן וָעַיִן: מָה שֵּׁן וָעַיִן שֶׁהֵן אֶחָד מֵאֵבָרָיו שֶׁל אָדָם – עֶבֶד יוֹצֵא בָּהֶן לְחֵירוּת, יִסּוּרִין שֶׁמְּמָרְקִין כׇּל גּוּפוֹ שֶׁל אָדָם – עַל אַחַת כַּמָּה וְכַמָּה.

This is taught through **an *a fortiori* inference**[B] **from** the law concerning **the tooth and eye** of a slave: **The tooth and eye are** each **a single limb of a person** and if his master damages either, **the slave thereby obtains his freedom; suffering that cleanses a person's entire body all the more so** that one attains freedom, atonement, from his sins.

וְהַיְינוּ דְּרַבִּי שִׁמְעוֹן בֶּן לָקִישׁ, דְּאָמַר רַבִּי שִׁמְעוֹן בֶּן לָקִישׁ: נֶאֱמַר "בְּרִית" בְּמֶלַח וְנֶאֱמַר "בְּרִית" בְּיִסּוּרִין; נֶאֱמַר "בְּרִית" בְּמֶלַח, דִּכְתִיב: "וְלֹא תַשְׁבִּית מֶלַח בְּרִית", וְנֶאֱמַר "בְּרִית" בְּיִסּוּרִין, דִּכְתִיב: "אֵלֶּה דִבְרֵי הַבְּרִית". מָה "בְּרִית" הָאָמוּר בְּמֶלַח – מֶלַח מְמַתֶּקֶת אֶת הַבָּשָׂר, אַף "בְּרִית" הָאָמוּר בְּיִסּוּרִין – יִסּוּרִין מְמָרְקִין כׇּל עֲוֹנוֹתָיו שֶׁל אָדָם.

**And that is** the statement of **Rabbi Shimon ben Lakish, as Rabbi Shimon ben Lakish said:** The word **covenant is used with regard to salt, and** the word **covenant is used with regard to afflictions.** The word **covenant is used with regard to salt, as it is written: "The salt of the covenant** with your God **should not be excluded** from your meal-offering; with all your sacrifices you must offer salt" (Leviticus 2:13). **And** the word **covenant is used with regard to afflictions, as it is written: "These are the words of the covenant"** (Deuteronomy 28:69). **Just as,** in **the covenant mentioned with regard to salt, the salt sweetens** the taste of **the meat** and renders it edible, **so too in the covenant mentioned with regard to suffering, the suffering cleanses a person's transgressions,** purifying him for a more sublime existence.

תַּנְיָא, רַבִּי שִׁמְעוֹן בֶּן יוֹחַאי אוֹמֵר: שָׁלֹשׁ מַתָּנוֹת טוֹבוֹת נָתַן הַקָּדוֹשׁ בָּרוּךְ הוּא לְיִשְׂרָאֵל, וְכוּלָּן לֹא נְתָנָן אֶלָּא עַל יְדֵי יִסּוּרִין. אֵלּוּ הֵן: תּוֹרָה וְאֶרֶץ יִשְׂרָאֵל וְהָעוֹלָם הַבָּא.

Additionally, **it was taught** in a *baraita* with regard to affliction: **Rabbi Shimon ben Yoḥai says: The Holy One, Blessed be He, gave Israel three precious gifts, all of which were given only by means of suffering,** which purified Israel so that they may merit to receive them. These gifts are: **Torah, Eretz Yisrael, and the World-to-Come.**

תּוֹרָה מִנַּיִן? שֶׁנֶּאֱמַר: "אַשְׁרֵי הַגֶּבֶר אֲשֶׁר תְּיַסְּרֶנּוּ יָהּ וּמִתּוֹרָתְךָ תְלַמְּדֶנּוּ".

**From where** is it derived that **Torah** is only acquired by means of suffering? **As it is said: "Happy is the man whom You afflict, Lord,"** after which it is said: **"And teach from Your Torah."**

אֶרֶץ יִשְׂרָאֵל – דִּכְתִיב: "כִּי כַּאֲשֶׁר יְיַסֵּר אִישׁ אֶת בְּנוֹ ה' אֱלֹהֶיךָ מְיַסְּרֶךָּ", וּכְתִיב בָּתְרֵיהּ: "כִּי ה' אֱלֹהֶיךָ מְבִיאֲךָ אֶל אֶרֶץ טוֹבָה".

**Eretz Yisrael, as it is written: "As a man rebukes his son, so the Lord your God rebukes you"** (Deuteronomy 8:5), **and it is written thereafter: "For the Lord your God will bring you to a good land."**

הָעוֹלָם הַבָּא – דִּכְתִיב: "כִּי נֵר מִצְוָה וְתוֹרָה אוֹר וְדֶרֶךְ חַיִּים תּוֹכְחוֹת מוּסָר".

**The World-to-Come, as it is written: "For the mitzva is a lamp, the Torah is light, and the reproofs of instruction are the way of life"** (Proverbs 6:23). One may arrive at the lamp of mitzva and the light of Torah that exists in the World-to-Come only by means of the reproofs of instruction in this world.

תָּנֵי תַּנָּא קַמֵּיהּ דְּרַבִּי יוֹחָנָן: כׇּל הָעוֹסֵק בַּתּוֹרָה וּבִגְמִילוּת חֲסָדִים

**A *tanna* taught** the following *baraita* **before Rabbi Yoḥanan:**[B] **If one engages in Torah and acts of charity**

## BACKGROUND

**One said…And one said** – **חַד אָמַר...וְחַד אָמַר**: This expression is used when a debate between two Sages is cited and it is not known which opinion was held by which of the Sages. Oftentimes the Gemara is not content with the ambiguity, and a lengthy debate ensues to determine who said what.

**Do not read** – **אַל תִּקְרֵי**: This method of homiletic interpretation does not imply that one should literally alter the way a particular verse is read; rather, it is a method employed to understanding a verse differently in order to shed new light on its meaning. Normally this approach changes the way a word is pronounced, without altering the letters of the word itself. This is possible because the text in the Torah scroll is not vocalized. Even though there is a tradition that teaches how each word should be read, perhaps the lack of vowels can be viewed as license to introduce homiletic interpretations by changing the pronunciation.

**An *a fortiori* inference** – **קַל וָחוֹמֶר**: One of the fundamental principles of rabbinic exegesis, an *a fortiori* inference appears in all of the standard lists of exegetical principles. In essence, it is a principle of logical argumentation where a comparison is drawn between two cases, one more lenient and the other more stringent. The *a fortiori* inference asserts that if the law is stringent in a case where the ruling is usually lenient, then all the more so will it be stringent in a more serious case; likewise, if the law is lenient in a case where the ruling is not usually lenient, then it will certainly be lenient in a less stringent case. *A fortiori* argumentation appears in the Bible, and the Sages compiled lists of verses in which *a fortiori* inferences appear. For example, "If you have run with the foot-soldiers, and they have wearied you, how can you contend with horses?" (Jeremiah 12:5).

**A *tanna* taught before Rabbi Yoḥanan** – **תָּנֵי תַּנָּא קַמֵּיהּ דְּרַבִּי יוֹחָנָן**: This expression describes a situation where a *baraita* was recited in the presence of the head of the Academy or study hall and the latter offered his comments on it. This *tanna* is not one of the Sages of the Mishna. Rather, this title refers to the later development in use of the term; a person with broad knowledge of tannaitic statements and *mishnayot*. Despite this knowledge, this person was not considered to be one of the Sages because he was unable to resolve difficult issues that arose in the texts that he recited. The *tanna* would recite the material in the presence of one of the Sages who would assess its accuracy and either confirm it or, if need be, correct it.

וְקוֹבֵר אֶת בָּנָיו – מוֹחֲלִין לוֹ עַל כָּל עֲוֹנוֹתָיו.

**and buries his sons, all his transgressions are forgiven.**

אֲמַר לֵיהּ רַבִּי יוֹחָנָן: בִּשְׁלָמָא תּוֹרָה וּגְמִילוּת חֲסָדִים – דִּכְתִיב: ״בְּחֶסֶד וֶאֱמֶת יְכֻפַּר עָוֺן״; ״חֶסֶד״ – זוֹ גְּמִילוּת חֲסָדִים, שֶׁנֶּאֱמַר: ״רוֹדֵף צְדָקָה וָחֶסֶד יִמְצָא חַיִּים צְדָקָה וְכָבוֹד״, ״אֱמֶת״ – זוֹ תּוֹרָה, שֶׁנֶּאֱמַר: ״אֱמֶת קְנֵה וְאַל תִּמְכֹּר״; אֶלָּא קוֹבֵר אֶת בָּנָיו – מִנַּיִן?

**Rabbi Yoḥanan**[P] **said to him:** What is your source for this? **Granted,** if one engages in **Torah and acts of charity,** his transgressions are forgiven, **as it is written: "With mercy and truth, iniquity is expiated"** (Proverbs 16:6); **mercy refers to acts of charity, as it is stated: "He who pursues charity and mercy finds life, charity and honor"** (Proverbs 21:21), mercy and charity are listed together. **And truth refers to Torah, as it is stated: "Buy truth and do not sell it;** also wisdom, guidance and understanding" (Proverbs 23:23). **However, from where is it derived** that the transgressions of **one who buries his sons** are also forgiven?

תְּנָא לֵיהּ הַהוּא סָבָא מִשּׁוּם רַבִּי שִׁמְעוֹן בֶּן יוֹחַאי: אָתְיָא ״עָוֺן״, ״עָוֺן״, כְּתִיב הָכָא: ״בְּחֶסֶד וֶאֱמֶת יְכֻפַּר עָוֺן״, וּכְתִיב הָתָם: ״וּמְשַׁלֵּם עֲוֺן אָבוֹת אֶל חֵיק בְּנֵיהֶם״.

An answer was provided to Rabbi Yoḥanan when **a certain elder taught him in the name of Rabbi Shimon bar Yoḥai:** This conclusion **is derived** from a verbal analogy between the words **iniquity** and **iniquity. Here, it is written: "With mercy and truth, iniquity is expiated," and there it is written: "He repays the iniquity of the fathers onto the bosom of their children"** (Jeremiah 32:18). Because he "repays the iniquity of the fathers onto the bosom of their children," the father's transgressions are forgiven.

אָמַר רַבִּי יוֹחָנָן: נְגָעִים וּבָנִים אֵינָן יִסּוּרִין שֶׁל אַהֲבָה.

**Rabbi Yoḥanan said: Leprosy**[B] **and** suffering due to **children are not afflictions of love.**

וּנְגָעִים לָא? וְהָתַנְיָא: כָּל מִי שֶׁיֵּשׁ בּוֹ אֶחָד מֵאַרְבָּעָה מַרְאוֹת נְגָעִים הַלָּלוּ – אֵינָן אֶלָּא מִזְבַּח כַּפָּרָה!

The Gemara asks: Is **leprosy not** an affliction of love? **Didn't we learn** in a *baraita*: **If one has any of the four signs of leprosy** (Leviticus 13) **they are nothing other than an altar of atonement?**

מִזְבַּח כַּפָּרָה הָווּ, יִסּוּרִין שֶׁל אַהֲבָה לָא הָווּ.

The Gemara answers: Although the signs of leprosy **are an altar of atonement** for one's transgressions, **they are not an affliction of love.**

וְאִי בָּעֵית אֵימָא: הָא – לָן וְהָא – לְהוּ.

**And if you wish, say** instead: **This** *baraita*, which says that leprosy is an affliction of love, **is for us** in Babylonia, because outside of Eretz Yisrael we are not as careful of the laws of ritual impurity, and one afflicted with leprosy may interact with others, mitigating his suffering. **And that** statement of Rabbi Yoḥanan, that leprosy is not an affliction of love, **is for them** in Eretz Yisrael, where they are exceedingly careful of the laws of ritual impurity and the suffering of a leper is great because he is banished from society (Rav Hai Gaon).

וְאִי בָּעֵית אֵימָא: הָא – בְּצִנְעָא, הָא – בְּפַרְהֶסְיָא.

**And if you wish, say** instead:[N] **This** *baraita*, which says that leprosy is an affliction of love, refers to **concealed** leprosy that only strikes the concealed areas of one's body. **But that** statement of Rabbi Yoḥanan refers to **visible** leprosy that causes those who see it to distance themselves from the leper.

**PERSONALITIES**

Rabbi Yoḥanan – רַבִּי יוֹחָנָן: This is Rabbi Yoḥanan bar Nappaḥa, one of the greatest *amora'im*, whose teachings are fundamental components of both the Babylonian and the Jerusalem Talmud. He resided in Tiberias and lived to an advanced age. Almost nothing is known of his family origins. He was orphaned at a young age and, although his family apparently owned considerable property, he spent virtually all of his resources in his devotion to the study of Torah, and he eventually became impoverished. In his youth, he had the privilege of studying under Rabbi Yehuda HaNasi, the redactor of the Mishna, but most of his Torah learning was accomplished under Rabbi Yehuda HaNasi's students: Ḥizkiya ben Ḥiyya, Rabbi Oshaya, Rabbi Ḥanina, and Rabbi Yannai, who lavished praise upon him. In time, he became the head of the yeshiva in Tiberias, at which point his fame and influence increased greatly. For a long time, Rabbi Yoḥanan was the leading rabbinic scholar in the entire Jewish world; not only in Eretz Yisrael, but in Babylonia, as well, where he was respected by the Babylonian Sages. Many of them ascended to Eretz Yisrael and became his outstanding students. He was a master of both *halakha* and *aggada*, his teachings in both disciplines are found throughout both of the Talmuds. In recognition of his intellectual and spiritual stature, the *halakha* is ruled in accordance with his opinion in almost every case, even when Rav or Shmuel, the preeminent *amora'im* of Babylonia, whom he treated deferentially, disagree with him. Only in disputes with his teachers in Eretz Yisrael, such as Rabbi Yannai and Rabbi Yehoshua ben Levi, is the *halakha* not ruled in accordance with his opinion.

Rabbi Yoḥanan was renowned for being handsome, and much was said in praise of his good looks. We know that his life was full of suffering. Ten of his sons died in his lifetime. There is a geonic tradition that one of his sons, Rabbi Mattana, a Babylonian *amora*, did not predecease him. The death of Rabbi Yoḥanan's disciple-colleague and brother-in-law, Reish Lakish, for which he considered himself responsible, hastened his own death.

Rabbi Yoḥanan had many students. In fact, all of the *amora'im* of Eretz Yisrael in succeeding generations were his students and benefited from his teachings, to the extent that he is considered the author of the Jerusalem Talmud. His greatest students were his brother-in-law Reish Lakish, Rabbi Elazar, Rabbi Ḥiyya bar Abba, Rabbi Abbahu, Rabbi Yosei bar Ḥanina, Rabbi Ami, and Rabbi Asi.

**BACKGROUND**

**Leprosy – נְגָעִים:** Traditionally rendered as "leprosy," the term employed by the Torah, *tzara'at*, is not necessarily identified medically with that illness. *Tzara'at* refers to symptoms that indicate severe ritual impurity. The laws governing these symptoms are detailed at length in Leviticus, chs. 13–15, and in the Mishna, tractate *Nega'im*. There can be leprosy of skin, of hair, of articles of clothing, and of houses. When a symptom appears, it is examined by a priest. Only a priest may determine whether to quarantine the affected person for a certain period or to declare immediately that the symptom is or is not leprosy. Leprosy is a primary source of ritual impurity. It is particularly severe in that it imparts ritual impurity to objects found in the same enclosure with it, as in the case of ritual impurity imparted by corpses. A person afflicted with leprosy is banished from the camp of Israel and must live alone until his affliction is cured. A garment affected by leprosy is burned, and a contaminated house is entirely destroyed, with its rubble thrown into a ritually impure place. A cured leper undergoes a ceremony outside the city and a special purification ceremony in the Temple. He must offer special sacrifices as part of his purification process.

**NOTES**

**If you wish, say…and if you wish, say – אִי בָּעֵית אֵימָא...וְאִי בָּעֵית אֵימָא:** Each of the three reasons offered in the Gemara to resolve the contradiction between the *baraita* describing leprosy as an altar of atonement and Rabbi Yoḥanan's statement that leprosy is not an affliction of love, has its own particular difficulty. That is why more than one explanation is offered. With regard to the first reason, it is difficult to accept that something described as an altar of atonement would not be considered an affliction of love, given that the altar represents an offering accepted by God (Rabbi Yoshiyahu Pinto). The second reason offered in the Gemara, that the *baraita* applies to those who live in Babylonia, outside Eretz Yisrael, while Rabbi Yoḥanan's statement applies only to those who live in Eretz Yisrael, is also difficult, as this distinction is not apparent in the statements themselves. This same problem exists with regard to the third reason, as the distinction between hidden and revealed leprosy is not apparent in the statements themselves.

וּבָנִים לָא? הֵיכִי דָּמֵי? אִילֵימָא דַּהֲווֹ לְהוּ וּמֵתוּ – וְהָא אָמַר רַבִּי יוֹחָנָן: דֵּין גַּרְמָא דַּעֲשִׂירָאָה בִּיר. אֶלָּא: הָא – דְּלָא הֲוֹו לֵיהּ כְּלָל, וְהָא – דַּהֲווֹ לֵיהּ וּמֵתוּ.

The Gemara continues to object: **And** suffering due to **children** is **not** an affliction of love? The Gemara clarifies: **What are the circumstances? If you say that he had** children **and they died, didn't Rabbi Yoḥanan** himself **say,** while consoling the victim of a catastrophe: **This is the bone of my tenth son?**[N] Rabbi Yoḥanan experienced the death of ten of his children, and he kept a small bone from his tenth child as a painful memorial. He would show that bone to others in order to console them, and since he showed it to them, the deaths of his children must certainly have been affliction of love. He consoled others by displaying that there is an element of intimacy with God that exists in that suffering (*Tosafot*). Why, then, would Rabbi Yoḥanan have said that suffering due to children is not afflictions of love? **Rather,** one must conclude that when Rabbi Yoḥanan said that those afflictions are not afflictions of love, he was speaking with regard to **one who has no** children, **and when one had** children **who died,** this could very well be considered afflictions of love.

רַבִּי חִיָּיא בַּר אַבָּא חֲלַשׁ, עָל לְגַבֵּיהּ רַבִּי יוֹחָנָן. אֲמַר לֵיהּ: חֲבִיבִין עָלֶיךָ יִסּוּרִין? אֲמַר לֵיהּ: לֹא הֵן וְלֹא שְׂכָרָן. אֲמַר לֵיהּ: הַב לִי יָדָךְ! יְהַב לֵיהּ יְדֵיהּ וְאוֹקְמֵיהּ.

The Gemara continues to address the issue of suffering and affliction: Rabbi Yoḥanan's student, **Rabbi Ḥiyya bar Abba, fell ill.** Rabbi Yoḥanan **entered to** visit **him, and said to him: Is your suffering dear to you?** Do you desire to be ill and afflicted? Rabbi Ḥiyya **said to him:** I welcome **neither** this suffering **nor its reward,** as one who welcomes this suffering with love is rewarded. Rabbi Yoḥanan **said to him: Give me your hand.** Rabbi Ḥiyya bar Abba **gave him his hand, and** Rabbi Yoḥanan **stood him up** and restored him to health.

רַבִּי יוֹחָנָן חֲלַשׁ, עָל לְגַבֵּיהּ רַבִּי חֲנִינָא. אֲמַר לֵיהּ: חֲבִיבִין עָלֶיךָ יִסּוּרִין? אֲמַר לֵיהּ: לֹא הֵן וְלֹא שְׂכָרָן. אֲמַר לֵיהּ: הַב לִי יָדָךְ! יְהַב לֵיהּ יְדֵיהּ וְאוֹקְמֵיהּ.

Similarly, **Rabbi Yoḥanan fell ill. Rabbi Ḥanina entered to** visit **him,** and **said to him: Is your suffering dear to you?** Rabbi Yoḥanan **said to him:** I welcome **neither** this suffering **nor its reward.** Rabbi Ḥanina **said to him: Give me your hand. He gave him his hand, and** Rabbi Ḥanina **stood him up** and restored him to health.

אַמַּאי? לוֹקִים רַבִּי יוֹחָנָן לְנַפְשֵׁיהּ!

The Gemara asks: **Why** did Rabbi Yoḥanan wait for Rabbi Ḥanina to restore him to health? If he was able to heal his student, **let Rabbi Yoḥanan stand himself up.**[N]

אָמְרִי: אֵין חָבוּשׁ מַתִּיר עַצְמוֹ מִבֵּית הָאֲסוּרִים.

The Gemara answers, **they say: A prisoner cannot** generally **free himself from prison,** but depends on others to release him from his shackles.

רַבִּי אֶלְעָזָר חֲלַשׁ, עָל לְגַבֵּיהּ רַבִּי יוֹחָנָן. חֲזָא דַּהֲוָה קָא גָּנֵי בְּבַיִת אָפֵל, גַּלְיֵיהּ לְדַרְעֵיהּ וּנְפַל נְהוֹרָא. חַזְיֵיהּ דַּהֲוָה קָא בָּכֵי רַבִּי אֶלְעָזָר. אֲמַר לֵיהּ: אַמַּאי קָא בָּכִית? אִי מִשּׁוּם תּוֹרָה דְּלָא אַפְּשְׁתְּ – שָׁנִינוּ: אֶחָד הַמַּרְבֶּה וְאֶחָד הַמַּמְעִיט וּבִלְבַד שֶׁיְּכַוֵּין לִבּוֹ לַשָּׁמַיִם! וְאִי מִשּׁוּם מְזוֹנֵי – לָא כָּל אָדָם זוֹכֶה לִשְׁתֵּי שֻׁלְחָנוֹת! וְאִי מִשּׁוּם בְּנֵי – דֵּין גַּרְמָא דַּעֲשִׂירָאָה בִּיר.

The Gemara relates that **Rabbi Elazar,** another of Rabbi Yoḥanan's students, **fell ill. Rabbi Yoḥanan entered** to visit him, and **saw that he was lying in a dark room.** Rabbi Yoḥanan **exposed his arm, and light** radiated from his flesh, **filling the house.** He **saw that** Rabbi Elazar **was crying,** and **said to him: Why are you crying?** Thinking that his crying was over the suffering that he endured throughout his life, Rabbi Yoḥanan attempted to comfort him: **If** you are weeping **because you did not study** as **much Torah** as you would have liked, **we learned: One who brings a substantial** sacrifice **and one who brings a meager** sacrifice have equal merit, **as long as he directs his heart toward Heaven. If** you are weeping **because** you lack **sustenance** and are unable to earn a livelihood, as Rabbi Elazar was, indeed, quite poor, **not every person merits** to eat off of **two tables,** one of wealth and one of Torah, so you need not bemoan the fact that you are not wealthy. **If** you are crying **over children** who have died, **this is the bone of my tenth son,** and suffering of that kind afflicts great people, and they are afflictions of love.

אֲמַר לֵיהּ: לְהַאי שׁוּפְרָא דְּבָלֵי בְּעַפְרָא קָא בָּכֵינָא. אֲמַר לֵיהּ: עַל דָּא וַדַּאי קָא בָּכֵית, וּבָכוּ תַּרְוַיְיהוּ.

Rabbi Elazar **said to** Rabbi Yoḥanan: **I am** not **crying** over my misfortune, but rather, **over this beauty** of yours **that will decompose in the earth,** as Rabbi Yoḥanan's beauty caused him to consider human mortality. **Rabbi Yoḥanan said to him: Over this, it is certainly** appropriate **to weep. Both cried** over the fleeting nature of beauty in the world and death that eventually overcomes all.

אַדְּהָכִי וְהָכִי, אֲמַר לֵיהּ: חֲבִיבִין עָלֶיךָ יִסּוּרִין? אֲמַר לֵיהּ: לֹא הֵן וְלֹא שְׂכָרָן. אֲמַר לֵיהּ: הַב לִי יָדָךְ, יְהַב לֵיהּ יְדֵיהּ וְאוֹקְמֵיהּ.

**Meanwhile,** Rabbi Yoḥanan **said to him: Is your suffering dear to you?** Rabbi Elazar **said to him:** I welcome **neither** this suffering **nor its reward.** Upon hearing this, Rabbi Yoḥanan **said to him: Give me your hand.** Rabbi Elazar **gave him his hand, and** Rabbi Yoḥanan **stood him up** and restored him to health.

**NOTES**

**This is the bone of my tenth son – דֵּין גַּרְמָא דַּעֲשִׂירָאָה בִּיר:** Many questions have been raised concerning Rabbi Yoḥanan's practice of carrying the bone of his son: How did he get the bone? Why would he carry with him an object that renders him ritually impure? Some say that this bone was in fact a tooth that his son lost while he was still alive and was therefore not impure. After his son passed away, Rabbi Yoḥanan kept it as a memorial (*Arukh*). Others say that it was not the bone of his son at all, but rather a bone from the meal eaten after his son's burial, which is called a *bir*, where the mourners are comforted. Therefore Rabbi Yoḥanan's statement means that this is a bone from the tenth such meal in which he partook after the passing of his children.

**Let Rabbi Yoḥanan stand himself up – לוֹקִים רַבִּי יוֹחָנָן לְנַפְשֵׁיהּ:** When Rabbi Ḥiyya bar Abba fell ill, the Gemara did not suggest that he heal himself. Rabbi Ḥiyya may have been unaware that suffering could be healed in this manner. Rabbi Yoḥanan, however, clearly knew that suffering could be cured this way. Therefore, the Gemara inquires why he could not heal himself (Maharsha).

## PERSONALITIES

**Rav Huna – רַב הוּנָא:** One of the great second generation Babylonian *amora'im*, Rav Huna was most closely associated with his teacher, Rav. Rav Huna was of aristocratic descent and descended from the House of the Exilarchs. Despite that lineage, he lived in abject poverty for many years. Later in life, he became wealthy and lived comfortably, and distributed his resources for the public good.

Rav Huna was the greatest of Rav's students, to the extent that Shmuel, Rav's colleague, used to treat him deferentially and direct questions to him. After Rav's death, Rav Huna became the head of the yeshiva of Sura and filled that position for about forty years. His prominence in Torah and his loftiness of character helped make the yeshiva of Sura the preeminent center of Torah for many centuries. Because of Rav Huna's extensive Torah knowledge, the *halakha* is almost invariably ruled in accordance with his opinion in disputes with all of his colleagues and contemporaries. The only exception was in civil law, where the rulings were in accordance with the opinion of Rav Naḥman.

Rav Huna had many students, some of whom studied exclusively with him; moreover, Rav's younger students remained to study with Rav Huna, his disciple, after his death. Rav Huna's son, Rabba bar Rav Huna, was one of the greatest Sages of the following generation.

## BACKGROUND

**Abba – אַבָּא:** An honorific used in reference to several tannaitic scholars, typically to those who are elderly and command respect. In some respects, this is similar to Mar, which was an honorific used in reference to certain Sages in Babylonia, although it was also used as a general, respectful form of address.

## HALAKHA

**That my prayer should be before my bed – עַל תְּפִלָּתִי שֶׁתְּהֵא...סָמוּךְ לְמִטָּתִי:** Most hold that Abba Binyamin's statement applies to the morning prayer as well. Once the time for prayer, dawn (Mishna Berura), has arrived, one may not eat or begin any work until he recites the morning prayer. Some, based on Rashi's opinion, prohibit even Torah study before prayer, but many are lenient, especially if it is communal Torah study (Rambam *Sefer Ahava, Hilkhot Tefilla,* 6:4; *Shulḥan Arukh, Oraḥ Ḥayyim* 89:3, 6).

**That my bed should be placed north to south – עַל מִטָּתִי שֶׁתְּהֵא נְתוּנָה בֵּין צָפוֹן לְדָרוֹם:** The Rambam holds that a person must make certain that he does not sleep east to west, even when sleeping alone in his bed; stringency is appropriate in this case. Therefore, one should place his bed north to south. The *Shulḥan Arukh*, however, rules that this applies only when a couple is in bed together. However, he concludes that it is appropriate to refrain from placing the bed east to west even when one is alone (Rambam *Sefer Avoda, Hilkhot Beit HaBeḥira,* 7:9; *Shulḥan Arukh, Oraḥ Ḥayyim* 3:6, 240:17).

**From where is it derived that one who prays should have nothing separating between him and the wall – מְנָיִן לַמִּתְפַּלֵּל שֶׁלֹּא יְהֵא דָּבָר חוֹצֵץ בֵּינוֹ לְבֵין הַקִּיר:** When a person prays there should be nothing between him and the wall, so as to avoid any potential distractions. An object that is secured in place and immobile, such as a closet or a bed which is not typically moved, is not considered a separation; similarly, neither a person nor an animal is considered a separation. The Rema holds that, although a person is indeed not considered a separation, an animal is (Rambam *Sefer Ahava, Hilkhot Tefilla,* 5:6; *Shulḥan Arukh, Oraḥ Ḥayyim* 90:21).

---

רַב הוּנָא תְּקִיפוּ לֵיהּ אַרְבַּע מְאָה דַּנֵּי דְּחַמְרָא. עָל לְגַבֵּיהּ רַב יְהוּדָה אֲחוּהּ דְּרַב סָלָּא חֲסִידָא וְרַבָּנַן, וְאָמְרִי לָהּ: רַב אַדָּא בַּר אַהֲבָה וְרַבָּנַן, וְאָמְרוּ לֵיהּ: לְעַיֵּין מָר בְּמִילֵּיהּ. אֲמַר לְהוּ: וּמִי חֲשִׁידְנָא בְּעֵינַיְיכוּ? אֲמַרוּ לֵיהּ: מִי חֲשִׁיד קוּדְשָׁא בְּרִיךְ הוּא דְּעָבֵיד דִּינָא בְּלָא דִּינָא?

אֲמַר לְהוּ: אִי אִיכָּא מַאן דִּשְׁמִיעַ עֲלַי מִלְּתָא – לֵימָא. אֲמַרוּ לֵיהּ: הָכִי שְׁמִיעַ לָן דְּלָא יָהֵיב מָר שִׁבְשָׁא לְאָרִיסֵיהּ.

אֲמַר לְהוּ: מִי קָא שָׁבֵיק לִי מִידֵּי מִינֵּיהּ? הָא קָא גָּנֵיב לֵיהּ כּוּלֵּיהּ!

אֲמַרוּ לֵיהּ: הַיְינוּ דְּאָמְרִי אִינָשֵׁי: בָּתַר גַּנָּבָא גְּנוֹב, וְטַעְמָא טְעֵים. אֲמַר לְהוּ: קַבֵּילְנָא עֲלַי דְּיָהֵיבְנָא לֵיהּ. אִיכָּא דְּאָמְרִי: הֲדַר חַלָּא וַהֲוָה חַמְרָא; וְאִיכָּא דְּאָמְרִי: אַיְיקַר חַלָּא וְאִיזְדַּבַּן בְּדָמֵי דְּחַמְרָא.

תָּנֵי, אַבָּא בִּנְיָמִין אוֹמֵר: עַל שְׁנֵי דְּבָרִים הָיִיתִי מִצְטַעֵר כָּל יָמַי – עַל תְּפִלָּתִי שֶׁתְּהֵא לִפְנֵי מִטָּתִי, וְעַל מִטָּתִי שֶׁתְּהֵא נְתוּנָה בֵּין צָפוֹן לְדָרוֹם. "עַל תְּפִלָּתִי שֶׁתְּהֵא לִפְנֵי מִטָּתִי" – מַאי "לִפְנֵי מִטָּתִי"? אִילֵּימָא לִפְנֵי מִטָּתִי מַמָּשׁ – וְהָאָמַר רַב יְהוּדָה אָמַר רַב וְאִיתֵימָא רַבִּי יְהוֹשֻׁעַ בֶּן לֵוִי: מְנַיִן לַמִּתְפַּלֵּל שֶׁלֹּא יְהֵא דָּבָר חוֹצֵץ בֵּינוֹ לְבֵין הַקִּיר? שֶׁנֶּאֱמַר: "וַיַּסֵּב חִזְקִיָּהוּ פָּנָיו אֶל הַקִּיר וַיִּתְפַּלֵּל". – לָא תֵּימָא "לִפְנֵי מִטָּתִי", אֶלָּא אֵימָא: "סָמוּךְ לְמִטָּתִי".

---

The Gemara relates another story regarding acknowledgement of the justice of divine punishment: **Four hundred barrels of Rav Huna's[P] wine fermented** and turned into vinegar, causing him great financial loss. **Rav Yehuda, the brother of Rav Sala the Pious, along with the Sages, and some say Rav Adda bar Ahava, along with the Sages, entered to visit him, and said: The Master should examine his actions,** as perhaps he committed a transgression for which he is being punished.

Rav Huna **said to them: Am I suspect in your eyes?** Have I committed a transgression on account of which you advise me to examine my behavior?

**They said to him: Is the Holy One, Blessed be He, suspect that He exacts punishment without justice?** Your loss was certainly just, and you must examine your conduct to find out why. The Sages were aware of a flaw in Rav Huna's conduct, to which they alluded (*Tosafot*).

Rav Huna **said to them: If someone has heard something** improper that I have done, **let him say so. They said to him: We have heard that the Master does not give** a share of his **grapevines to his tenant farmers.** A tenant farmer is entitled to a portion of the crop grown on his landlord's property, as well as a share of the vines planted during a given year.

Rav Huna **said to them: Does** this tenant farmer **leave me anything from** the produce that he grows on my property? **He steals it all.** Consequently, in denying him his share of the grapevines I am simply recouping that which was stolen from me by this tenant farmer.

**They said to him: That is the** meaning of the **folk saying: One who steals from a thief has a taste of theft.**[N] Despite the fact that the property was stolen to begin with, one nevertheless engages in theft. Although he did not violate a prohibition per se, it is still a form of theft, and one who is held to a higher standard than others will be punished for it.

**He said to them: I accept upon myself to give** my tenant farmer his portion in the future.

Thereupon, as a result of Rav Huna's repentance, God restored his loss. **Some say his vinegar turned back into wine, and some say that the price of vinegar rose and it was sold at the price of wine.**

The Gemara returns to the topic of prayer. **It was taught** in a *baraita* that the *tanna* **Abba**[B] **Binyamin** would say: **All of my life I have taken great pains with regard to two things: That my prayer should be before my bed**[H] **and that my bed should be placed north to south.**[NH] Abba Binyamin's statement requires explanation. With regard to his statement: **That my prayer should be before my bed,** the Gemara asks, **what does before my bed mean? If you say** that it **literally** means that he would stand **before his bed** and pray, it is difficult, as **Rav Yehuda said that Rav said, and some say that Rabbi Yehoshua ben Levi said: From where** is it derived **that one who prays should have nothing separating between him and the wall?**[H] **As it is stated: "And Hezekiah turned to face the wall and prayed"** (Isaiah 38:2), in order to facilitate his concentration during prayer. That being said, why would Abba Binyamin pray before his bed? Rather, **do not say** that **before my bed** refers to where he stood during prayer, but **rather, say** that he prayed **adjacent to** the time that he would retire to bed; he was careful to recite *Shema* and recite the evening prayer just before going to sleep (Rabbeinu Ḥananel).

---

## NOTES

**One who steals from a thief has a taste of theft – בָּתַר גַּנָּבָא גְּנוֹב וְטַעְמָא טְעֵים:** Some explain this expression to mean that although there is no inherent transgression in his action, one who steals from a thief has a theft-like experience, which is liable to become habitual (Rav Sa'adia Gaon).

**That my bed should be placed north to south – עַל מִטָּתִי שֶׁתְּהֵא נְתוּנָה בֵּין צָפוֹן לְדָרוֹם:** Some hold that this statement is an allusion to the positive aspect of placing the bed from north to south. North represents wealth; the golden shewbread table in the Temple was situated in the north of the Sanctuary because it is the symbol of plenty. South represents wisdom; the Temple candelabrum was situated in the south of the Sanctuary. One who places his bed north to south and prays to God, Who has dominion over all wealth and wisdom, will be rewarded with sons (*Talmidei Rabbeinu Yona*).

"וְעַל מִטָּתִי שֶׁתְּהֵא נְתוּנָה בֵּין צָפוֹן לְדָרוֹם"

Abba Binyamin's statement: **And my bed should be placed north to south** was in deference to the Divine Presence, which rests between east and west, the direction of the Temple; as the Holy of Holies was to the west, while the main entrance was to the east. Therefore, the Sages were careful not to perform actions inconsistent with that sanctity while facing east to west; and, therefore, Abba Binyamin was careful not to sleep in a bed that faced east to west.

דְּאָמַר רַבִּי חָמָא בְּרַבִּי חֲנִינָא אָמַר רַבִּי יִצְחָק: כָּל הַנּוֹתֵן מִטָּתוֹ בֵּין צָפוֹן לְדָרוֹם – הָוְיָין לֵיהּ בָּנִים זְכָרִים, שֶׁנֶּאֱמַר: "וּצְפוּנְךָ תְּמַלֵּא בִטְנָם יִשְׂבְּעוּ בָנִים".

In praise of that stringency, the Sages added that **Rabbi Ḥama said** that **Rabbi Ḥanina said** that **Rabbi Yitzḥak said: One who places his bed facing north to south will** be rewarded with **male children, as it is stated: "And whose belly You fill with Your treasure** [*utzfunekha*], **who have sons in plenty** and leave their abundance to their babies" (Psalms 17:14). This verse indicates that one who sets his bed facing north will be rewarded with sons in plenty, as north [*tzafon*] is etymologically similar to Your treasure [*tzfunekha*].

רַב נַחְמָן בַּר יִצְחָק אָמַר: אַף אֵין אִשְׁתּוֹ מַפֶּלֶת נְפָלִים; כְּתִיב הָכָא: "וּצְפוּנְךָ תְּמַלֵּא בִטְנָם", וּכְתִיב הָתָם: "וַיִּמְלְאוּ יָמֶיהָ לָלֶדֶת וְהִנֵּה תוֹמִים בְּבִטְנָהּ".

**Rav Naḥman bar Yitzḥak said: Moreover, his wife will not miscarry.** From where do we derive this? **It is written here: "And whose belly You fill** [*temaleh*] **with Your treasure," and it is written there,** concerning Rebecca's pregnancy: **"And her time to give birth was fulfilled** [*vayimle'u*] **and there were twins in her belly"** (Genesis 25:24), consequently: You fill with Your treasure refers to a pregnancy that proceeds without complication.

תַּנְיָא, אַבָּא בִנְיָמִין אוֹמֵר: שְׁנַיִם שֶׁנִּכְנְסוּ לְהִתְפַּלֵּל, וְקָדַם אֶחָד מֵהֶם לְהִתְפַּלֵּל וְלֹא הִמְתִּין אֶת חֲבֵרוֹ וְיָצָא – טוֹרְפִין לוֹ תְּפִלָּתוֹ בְּפָנָיו, שֶׁנֶּאֱמַר: טֹרֵף נַפְשׁוֹ בְּאַפּוֹ הַלְמַעַנְךָ תֵּעָזַב אָרֶץ.

Another of Abba Binyamin's statements with regard to the laws of prayer **was taught** in a *baraita*: **Abba Binyamin says: If two** people **enter** a synagogue outside of the city **in order to pray, and one began praying before** the other **and did not wait for the other** person to complete his prayer, **and left** him alone in the synagogue, **his prayer is thrown back in his face.**[NH] Because he left the other person alone and caused him to be distracted during his prayer, his own prayer is thrown back in his face, **as it is stated: "You who throw your soul in your face, for your sake will the earth be forsaken?** The Rock will be moved from its place" (Job 18:4). This verse indicates that one who left the other person alone effectively causes his soul, as prayer is the outpouring of the soul before God, to be thrown in his face. God says to that person: For your sake, do you think because you left, the earth will be forsaken, that God will leave the world and the prayer of the other person will go unheard?

וְלֹא עוֹד, אֶלָּא שֶׁגּוֹרֵם לַשְּׁכִינָה שֶׁתִּסְתַּלֵּק מִיִּשְׂרָאֵל, שֶׁנֶּאֱמַר: "וְיֶעְתַּק צוּר מִמְּקֹמוֹ"; וְאֵין "צוּר" אֶלָּא הַקָּדוֹשׁ בָּרוּךְ הוּא, שֶׁנֶּאֱמַר: "צוּר יְלָדְךָ תֶּשִׁי".

**Not only that, but it causes the Divine Presence to remove itself from Israel, as it is stated** in the continuation of the verse: **"The Rock will be moved from its place."** The rock, God, is forced to remove His presence. **And Rock means nothing other than the Holy One, Blessed be He, as it is stated: "Of the Rock that gave birth to you, you have been unmindful,** and you have forgotten God Who bore you" (Deuteronomy 32:18).

וְאִם הִמְתִּין לוֹ מַה שְּׂכָרוֹ?

**And if he waits for him** in the synagogue, what is his reward? Is his reward proportionate to the punishment received by one who failed to do so?

**NOTES**

**And did not wait for the other, his prayer is thrown back in his face** – **וְלֹא הִמְתִּין אֶת חֲבֵרוֹ וְיָצָא טוֹרְפִין לוֹ תְּפִלָּתוֹ בְּפָנָיו:** The *Amida* prayer is formulated in the plural in order to emphasize the communal aspect of our prayers. When one prays and thinks only of himself and his own needs, his prayer is rejected. The individual who does not wait for another displays a lack of concern for his welfare. Therefore, his prayers are rejected. He causes the Divine Presence, whose manifestation is dependent upon genuine fraternity among Jews, to remove itself from Israel (*Ein Ayah*).

**HALAKHA**

**If two people enter a synagogue in order to pray, and one began praying before the other and did not wait for the other** – **שְׁנַיִם שֶׁנִּכְנְסוּ לְהִתְפַּלֵּל, וְקָדַם אֶחָד מֵהֶם לְהִתְפַּלֵּל וְלֹא הִמְתִּין אֶת חֲבֵרוֹ:** When reciting the evening prayer in a synagogue outside the city, before leaving, one must wait for the other person present to finish his prayer. The same applies to a synagogue that is not outside the city. However, one need not wait for a person who begins after everyone else, or who began with everyone else but who extends his prayers with additional supplications. The Ri, one of the great tosafists, always waited for others to complete their prayers regardless of the circumstances. This was deemed a pious custom worthy of emulation whenever possible (Rambam *Sefer Ahava, Hilkhot Tefilla*, 9:11; *Shulḥan Arukh, Oraḥ Ḥayyim* 90:15).

### BACKGROUND

*Kalla* – כַּלָּה: The *kalla* is a uniquely Babylonian Jewish tradition, despite the fact that it appears to have its early roots in Eretz Yisrael. The *kalla* is essentially a gathering of all the Sages. It took place twice a year, in Adar and in Elul, and focused on a specific tractate, which the Sages would analyze and interpret. Thousands of people would attend the *yarḥei kalla*, which also served as an extraordinary occasion of paying homage to the Torah.

### LANGUAGE

Seal [*gushpanka*] – גּוּשְׁפַּנְקָא: The source of the word is from middle Persian or Parthian and it means seal, ring. The original word was apparently anguštpānak. The "t" was dropped from the word in Aramaic because words with three consecutive consonants are rare in Semitic languages.

### HALAKHA

**One's prayer is only heard in a synagogue** – **אֵין תְּפִלָּה שֶׁל אָדָם נִשְׁמַעַת אֶלָּא בְּבֵית הַכְּנֶסֶת**: One must strive to pray with the congregation in the synagogue. Even one who, due to circumstances beyond his control, is forced to pray alone, should do so in a synagogue, as one's prayers are always received in a synagogue. One who has a synagogue in his city but fails to pray there is called an evil neighbor (Rambam *Sefer Ahava*, *Hilkhot Tefilla*, 8:1; *Shulḥan Arukh*, *Oraḥ Ḥayyim* 90:9).

אָמַר רַבִּי יוֹסֵי בְּרַבִּי חֲנִינָא: זוֹכֶה לַבְּרָכוֹת הַלָּלוּ, שֶׁנֶּאֱמַר: ״לוּא הִקְשַׁבְתָּ לְמִצְוֹתָי וַיְהִי כַנָּהָר שְׁלוֹמֶךָ וְצִדְקָתְךָ כְּגַלֵּי הַיָּם. וַיְהִי כַחוֹל זַרְעֶךָ וְצֶאֱצָאֵי מֵעֶיךָ וגו׳״.

In terms of this reward, **Rabbi Yosei, son of Rabbi Ḥanina said:** One who waits in the synagogue for the other to finish his prayer **merits the following blessings, as it is stated: "If only you had listened to My mitzvot**[N] **then your peace would be as a river, and your righteousness as the waves of the sea. Your seed would be as the sand, and the offspring of your body** like the grains thereof; his name would be neither cut off nor destroyed from before Me" (Isaiah 48:18–19). The explanation of this passage is based on the etymological similarity between the word mitzva and the word *tzevet*, which means group. If he keeps the other person company and does not abandon him after his prayer, all of the blessings that appear later in the verse will be fulfilled in him (*Talmidei Rabbeinu Yona*).

תַּנְיָא, אַבָּא בִּנְיָמִין אוֹמֵר: אִלְמָלֵי נִתְּנָה רְשׁוּת לָעַיִן לִרְאוֹת, אֵין כָּל בְּרִיָּה יְכוֹלָה לַעֲמוֹד מִפְּנֵי הַמַּזִּיקִין.

In another *baraita* **it was taught** that **Abba Binyamin says: If the eye was given permission to see, no creature would be able to withstand the** abundance and ubiquity of the **demons** and continue to live unaffected by them.

אֲמַר אַבַּיֵי: אִינְהוּ נְפִישִׁי מִינַּן, וְקַיְימִי עֲלַן כִּי כִּסְלָא לְאוּגְיָא.

Similarly, **Abaye said: They are more numerous than we** are **and they stand over us like mounds of earth surrounding a pit.**

אֲמַר רַב הוּנָא: כָּל חַד וְחַד מִינַּן, אַלְפָּא מִשְּׂמָאלֵיהּ וְרִבְבָתָא מִימִינֵיהּ.

**Rav Huna said: Each and every one of us has a thousand** demons **to his left and ten thousand to his right.** God protects man from these demons, as it says in the verse: "A thousand may fall at your side, and ten thousand at your right hand; they will not approach you" (Psalms 91:7).

אֲמַר רָבָא: הַאי דּוּחֲקָא דְּהָוֵי בְּכַלָּה – מִנַּיְיהוּ הָוֵי; הָנֵי בִּרְכֵּי דְּשַׁלְהִי – מִנַּיְיהוּ; הָנֵי מָאנֵי דְּרַבָּנַן דְּבָלוּ – מֵחוּפְיָא דִּידְהוּ; הָנֵי כַּרְעֵי דְּמִנַּקְפָן – מִנַּיְיהוּ.

Summarizing the effects of the demons, **Rava said:**
**The crowding at the *kalla*,**[B] the gatherings for Torah study during Elul and Adar, **is from** the demons;
**those knees that are fatigued** even though one did not exert himself **is from** the demons;[N]
**those clothes of the Sages that wear out,** despite the fact that they do not engage in physical labor, **is from friction** with the demons;
**those feet that are in pain is from** the demons.

הַאי מַאן דְּבָעֵי לְמֵידַע לְהוּ – לֵיתֵי קִיטְמָא נְהִילָא וְנַהֲדַר אַפּוּרְיֵיהּ, וּבְצַפְרָא חָזֵי כִּי כַּרְעֵי דְּתַרְנְגוֹלָא. הַאי מַאן דְּבָעֵי לְמֶחֱזִינְהוּ – לֵיתֵי שִׁלְיְיתָא דְּשׁוּנָרְתָּא אוּכַּמְתָּא בַּת אוּכַּמְתָּא, בּוּכְרְתָא בַּת בּוּכְרְתָא, וְלִיקְלְיֵיהּ בְּנוּרָא, וְלִשְׁחֲקֵיהּ, וְלִימְלֵי עֵינֵיהּ מִנֵּיהּ, וְחָזֵי לְהוּ. וְלִשְׁדְּיֵיהּ בְּגוּבְתָּא דְּפַרְזְלָא וְלִחְתְּמֵיהּ בְּגוּשְׁפַּנְקָא דְּפַרְזְלָא, דִּילְמָא גָּנְבִי מִנֵּיהּ. וְלַחֲתוֹם פּוּמֵיהּ, כִּי הֵיכִי דְּלָא לִיתַּזַּק. רַב בֵּיבָי בַּר אַבַּיֵי עֲבַד הָכִי, חֲזָא וְאִתַּזַּק. בָּעוּ רַבָּנַן רַחֲמֵי עֲלֵיהּ וְאִתַּסִּי.

**One who seeks to know** that the demons exist **should place fine ashes around his bed, and in the morning** the demons' footprints **appear like chickens' footprints,** in the ash. **One who seeks to see them should take the afterbirth of a firstborn female black cat, born to a firstborn female black cat, burn it in the fire, grind it and place it in his eyes, and he will see them.** He must then **place** the ashes **in an iron tube sealed with an iron seal** [*gushpanka*][L] **lest the demons steal it from him, and then seal the opening** so **he will not be harmed. Rav Beivai bar Abaye performed this** procedure, **saw** the demons, **and was harmed. The Sages prayed for mercy** on his behalf **and he was healed.**

תַּנְיָא, אַבָּא בִּנְיָמִין אוֹמֵר: אֵין תְּפִלָּה שֶׁל אָדָם נִשְׁמַעַת אֶלָּא בְּבֵית הַכְּנֶסֶת, שֶׁנֶּאֱמַר: ״לִשְׁמֹעַ אֶל הָרִנָּה וְאֶל הַתְּפִלָּה״, בִּמְקוֹם רִנָּה – שָׁם תְּהֵא תְּפִלָּה.

**It was taught** in a *baraita* that **Abba Binyamin said: One's prayer is only** fully **heard in a synagogue,**[H] **as it is stated** with regard to King Solomon's prayer in the Temple: "Yet have You turned toward the prayer of Your servant and to his supplication, Lord my God, **to listen to the song and the prayer** which Your servant prays before You on this day" (1 Kings 8:28). The following verse concludes: "To hear the prayer Your servant directs toward this place" (1 Kings 8:29). We see that one's prayer is heard specifically in the Temple, of which the synagogue is a microcosm (Rav Yoshiyahu Pinto). It may be inferred that **in a place of song,** a synagogue where God's praises are sung, **there prayer should be.**

### NOTES

**If only you had listened to My mitzvot** – **לוּא הִקְשַׁבְתָּ לְמִצְוֹתָי**: The connection between this verse and waiting for another person to finish his prayer has been interpreted in different manners. Rashi explains the term listen in this context as waiting in anticipation. In other words, he is listening and waiting until he hears that the other person has completed his prayer and he thereby performs an act of kindness and is rewarded for that mitzva. Others explained that mitzvot in the plural refers to two mitzvot which he fulfills simultaneously. In addition to the mitzva of respect for God fulfilled by his waiting, there is the additional mitzva of performing an act of kindness for his counterpart.

**The crowding at the *kalla* is from them** – **הַאי דּוּחֲקָא דְּהָוֵי בְּכַלָּה מִנַּיְיהוּ הָוֵי**: Typically, some pronouncements of this kind are to be understood literally, while others are to be understood metaphorically. Some viewed this passage that ascribes the crowding at the *kalla* to demons as a critique of the overcrowding at these large gatherings. Many people stood and congregated far from where the Torah learning was concentrated with no intention to study. Rava mockingly said that it would be preferable if those people did not come and that it was the demons that pushed them there in order to cause overcrowding (*Otzar Balum*).

אָמַר רָבִין בַּר רַב אַדָּא אָמַר רַבִּי יִצְחָק: מִנַּיִן שֶׁהַקָּדוֹשׁ בָּרוּךְ הוּא מָצוּי בְּבֵית הַכְּנֶסֶת – שֶׁנֶּאֱמַר: "אֱלֹהִים נִצָּב בַּעֲדַת אֵל";

In explaining Abba Binyamin's statement, **Ravin bar Rav Adda said** that **Rabbi Yitzḥak said: From where** is it derived **that the Holy One, Blessed be He, is located in a synagogue? As it is stated: "God stands in the congregation of God;** in the midst of the judges He judges" (Psalms 82:1). The congregation of God is the place where people congregate to sing God's praises, and God is located among His congregation.

וּמִנַּיִן לַעֲשָׂרָה שֶׁמִּתְפַּלְּלִין שֶׁשְּׁכִינָה עִמָּהֶם – שֶׁנֶּאֱמַר: "אֱלֹהִים נִצָּב בַּעֲדַת אֵל";

**And from where** is it derived that **ten people who pray, the Divine Presence is with them? As it is stated: "God stands in the congregation of God,"** and the minimum number of people that constitute a congregation is a quorum of ten.

וּמִנַּיִן לִשְׁלֹשָׁה שֶׁיּוֹשְׁבִין בְּדִין שֶׁשְּׁכִינָה עִמָּהֶם – שֶׁנֶּאֱמַר: "בְּקֶרֶב אֱלֹהִים יִשְׁפֹּט";

**From where** is it derived **that three who sit in judgment, the Divine Presence is with them?** It is derived from this same verse, **as it is stated: "In the midst of the judges He judges,"** and the minimum number of judges that comprises a court is three.

וּמִנַּיִן לִשְׁנַיִם שֶׁיּוֹשְׁבִין וְעוֹסְקִין בַּתּוֹרָה שֶׁשְּׁכִינָה עִמָּהֶם – שֶׁנֶּאֱמַר: "אָז נִדְבְּרוּ יִרְאֵי ה' אִישׁ אֶל רֵעֵהוּ וַיַּקְשֵׁב ה'" וגו'.

**From where** is it derived **that two who sit and engage in Torah** study, **the Divine Presence is with them? As it is stated: "Then they that feared the Lord spoke one with the other, and the Lord listened,** and heard, and a book of remembrance was written before Him, for them that fear the Lord, and that think upon His name" (Malachi 3:16). The Divine Presence listens to any two God-fearing individuals who speak with each other.

מַאי "וּלְחֹשְׁבֵי שְׁמוֹ"? אָמַר רַב אַשִׁי: חָשַׁב אָדָם לַעֲשׂוֹת מִצְוָה וְנֶאֱנַס וְלֹא עֲשָׂאָהּ – מַעֲלֶה עָלָיו הַכָּתוּב כְּאִילּוּ עֲשָׂאָהּ.

With regard to this verse, the Gemara asks: **What** is the meaning of the phrase, **"And that think upon His name"? Rav Ashi said:** If **a person intended to perform a mitzva, but due to** circumstances **beyond** his **control, he did not perform it, the verse ascribes him** credit **as if he performed** the mitzva,[B] as he is among those that think upon His name.

וּמִנַּיִן שֶׁאֲפִילּוּ אֶחָד שֶׁיּוֹשֵׁב וְעוֹסֵק בַּתּוֹרָה שֶׁשְּׁכִינָה עִמּוֹ – שֶׁנֶּאֱמַר: "בְּכָל הַמָּקוֹם אֲשֶׁר אַזְכִּיר אֶת שְׁמִי אָבוֹא אֵלֶיךָ וּבֵרַכְתִּיךָ".

The Gemara returns to Ravin bar Rav Adda's statement: **And from where** is it derived **that when even one who sits and engages in Torah** study, **the Divine Presence is with him? As it is stated: "In every place where I cause My Name to be mentioned, I will come to you and bless you"** (Exodus 20:21); God blesses even a single person who mentions God's name, a reference to Torah study (*Iyyun Ya'akov*).

וְכִי מֵאַחַר דַּאֲפִילּוּ חַד – תְּרֵי מִבַּעְיָא? – תְּרֵי מִכַּתְבָן מִלַּיְיהוּ בְּסֵפֶר הַזִּכְרוֹנוֹת, חַד לָא מִכַּתְבָן מִלֵּיהּ בְּסֵפֶר הַזִּכְרוֹנוֹת.

The Gemara asks: **Since** the Divine Presence rests **even** upon **one** who engages in Torah study, **was it necessary** to say that the Divine Presence rests upon **two** who study Torah together? The Gemara answers: There is a difference between them. **Two** people, **their words** of Torah **are written in the book of remembrance,**[N] as it is stated: "And a book of remembrance was written"; however **a single** individual's **words** of Torah **are not written in a book of remembrance.**

וְכִי מֵאַחַר דַּאֲפִילּוּ תְּרֵי – תְּלָתָא מִבַּעְיָא? – מַהוּ דְּתֵימָא: דִּינָא שְׁלָמָא בְּעָלְמָא הוּא, וְלָא אָתְיָא שְׁכִינָה – קָמַשְׁמַע לָן דְּדִינָא נַמִי הַיְינוּ תּוֹרָה.

The Gemara continues: **Since** the Divine Presence rests **even** upon **two** who engage in Torah study, is it **necessary** to mention **three?** The Gemara answers: Here too, a special verse is necessary **lest you say that judgment is merely to** keep the **peace** among the citizenry, **and the Divine Presence does not come** and rest upon those who sit in judgment as they are not engaged in Torah study. Ravin bar Rav Adda **teaches us that** sitting in **judgment is also Torah.**

וְכִי מֵאַחַר דַּאֲפִילּוּ תְּלָתָא – עֲשָׂרָה מִבַּעְיָא? – עֲשָׂרָה – קָדְמָה שְׁכִינָה וְאָתְיָא, תְּלָתָא – עַד דְּיָתְבִי.

The Gemara asks: **Since** the Divine Presence rests **even** upon **three,** is it **necessary** to mention **ten?** The Gemara answers: **The Divine Presence arrives before a group of ten,** as the verse: "God stands in the congregation of God," indicates that when the ten individuals who comprise a congregation arrive, the Divine Presence is already there. For a group of **three** judges, however, the Divine Presence does not arrive **until they sit** and begin their deliberations, as in the midst of the judges He judges. God aids them in their judgment, but does not arrive before them.

אָמַר רַבִּי אָבִין בַּר רַב אַדָּא אָמַר רַבִּי יִצְחָק: מִנַּיִן שֶׁהַקָּדוֹשׁ בָּרוּךְ הוּא מַנִּיחַ תְּפִילִּין – שֶׁנֶּאֱמַר: "נִשְׁבַּע ה' בִּימִינוֹ וּבִזְרוֹעַ עֻזּוֹ";

The Gemara cites another aggadic statement: **Rabbi Avin bar Rav Adda said** that **Rabbi Yitzḥak said: From where** is it derived **that the Holy One, Blessed be He, wears phylacteries? As it is stated: "The Lord has sworn by His right hand, and by the arm of His strength"** (Isaiah 62:8). Since it is customary to swear upon holy objects, it is understood that His right hand and the arm of His strength are the holy objects upon which God swore.

**BACKGROUND**

**The verse ascribes him credit as if he performed the mitzva – מַעֲלֶה עָלָיו הַכָּתוּב כְּאִילּוּ עֲשָׂאָהּ:** This phrase: The verse, ascribes him credit, comes to indicate that, although a particular action is not that significant in and of itself, it is possible to derive its true value, or lack thereof, from the language of the verse. Although, in reality, one who thought to perform a mitzva and ultimately did not do so, did not fulfill the mitzva, nevertheless, the verse ascribes him credit as if he did.

**NOTES**

**Two, their words of Torah are written in the book of remembrance – תְּרֵי מִכַּתְבָן מִלַּיְיהוּ בְּסֵפֶר הַזִּכְרוֹנוֹת:** Despite the mishna: And all of your actions are written in the book (*Avot* 2:1), specifically two people engaged in Torah study are written in a book of remembrance because an individual who studies alone may fail to ascertain the true meaning of the Torah. Therefore, his words are not fit to be recorded in the book of remembrance before God. That is less likely when two people study, as presumably at least one of them will arrive at a true understanding, and thereby his counterpart, who was mistaken, will also have played a role in arriving at the correct conclusion. Therefore, his words will also be written before God under the rubric of Torah study (*Ḥatam Sofer*).

## NOTES

**The phylacteries of the Master of the world – תְּפִילִּין דְּמָרֵי עָלְמָא**: The mitzva to don phylacteries includes several profound ideas. This mitzva emphasizes the unique connection between God and the Jewish people. Tying God's word onto one's body symbolizes that bond, as the parchments have written on them biblical verses that express the deep spiritual significance of that relationship. Phylacteries are placed upon the arm and the head. While the verses on the arm are written on a single parchment and symbolize strength of action, the verses placed on the head represent thought and intellect; they are written on four separate parchments placed in four compartments, each with its own concept and message. On a parallel plane, God's phylacteries represent the connection between God's thoughts and actions with regard to the world, in general, and the Jewish people, in particular.

The discussion in the Gemara with regard to the specific verses and their placement in God's phylacteries is an attempt to draw an analogy between God's phylacteries, which represent God's aspirations with regard to His relationship with the Jewish people, and the phylacteries worn by the Jewish people, which represent our aspiration to forge a relationship with Him. Consequently, each of the verses underscores a different aspect of God's Providence and His direction of the Jewish people and of the world (Rashba, *HaKotev*, *Penei Yehoshua*).

Rav Hai Gaon takes a much simpler approach to this discussion, suggesting that the Gemara describes God wearing phylacteries in order to encourage every Jewish man to wear them as well.

## LANGUAGE

**Entity [*ḥativa*] – חֲטִיבָה**: In general, this term means something unique, exclusive. Rav Sa'adia Gaon explains that the root of the word is identical to the Arabic root خطب, meaning to speak, to say. However, its primary meaning is to seek a wife, to enter into a marriage. Therefore, the Gemara's affirmation that God is a single entity indicates that a marriage-like relationship was formed between God and the Jewish people, a concept that appears often in the Prophets.

## BACKGROUND

**Phylacteries compartments – בָּתֵּי הַתְּפִילִּין**: There are four compartments in the phylacteries of the head, which appear like thin slots. One of the four Torah portions, in which the mitzva of phylacteries is mentioned, is inserted into each of these slots. On the side of the phylacteries, the letter *shin* is carved into the leather, the first letter of one of God's names, *Shaddai*.

Phylacteries of the head

"בִּימִינוֹ" – זוֹ תּוֹרָה, שֶׁנֶּאֱמַר: "מִימִינוֹ אֵשׁ דָּת לָמוֹ", "וּבִזְרוֹעַ עֻזּוֹ" – אֵלּוּ תְּפִילִּין, שֶׁנֶּאֱמַר: "ה' עֹז לְעַמּוֹ יִתֵּן".

Specifically, **"His right hand" refers to the Torah, as it is stated** in describing the giving of the Torah: **"From His right hand, a fiery law for His people"** (Deuteronomy 33:2). **"The arm of His strength,"** His left hand, **refers to phylacteries, as it is stated: "The Lord gave strength to His nation"** (Psalms 29:11), in the form of the mitzva of phylacteries.

וּמְנַיִן שֶׁהַתְּפִילִּין עוֹז הֵם לְיִשְׂרָאֵל – דִּכְתִיב: "וְרָאוּ כָּל עַמֵּי הָאָרֶץ כִּי שֵׁם ה' נִקְרָא עָלֶיךָ וְיָרְאוּ מִמֶּךָּ", וְתַנְיָא, רַבִּי אֱלִיעֶזֶר הַגָּדוֹל אוֹמֵר: אֵלּוּ תְּפִילִּין שֶׁבָּרֹאשׁ.

The Gemara asks: **And from where** is it derived **that phylacteries provide strength for Israel? As it is written: "And all the nations of the land shall see that the name of the Lord is called upon you, and they will fear you"** (Deuteronomy 28:10). **It was taught** in a *baraita* that **Rabbi Eliezer the Great says: This is** a reference to **the phylacteries of the head,** upon which the name of God is written in fulfillment of the verse: "That the name of the Lord is called upon you."

אֲמַר לֵיהּ רַב נַחְמָן בַּר יִצְחָק לְרַב חִיָּיא בַּר אָבִין: הָנֵי תְּפִילִּין דְּמָרֵי עָלְמָא מַה כְּתִיב בְּהוּ? אֲמַר לֵיהּ: "וּמִי כְּעַמְּךָ יִשְׂרָאֵל גּוֹי אֶחָד בָּאָרֶץ".

**Rav Naḥman bar Yitzḥak said to Rav Ḥiyya bar Avin: What is written in the phylacteries of the Master of the world?**[N] **Rav Ḥiyya bar Avin replied:** It is written: **"Who is like Your people, Israel, one nation in the land?"** (I Chronicles 17:21). God's phylacteries serve to connect Him, in a sense, to the world, the essence of which is Israel.

וּמִי מִשְׁתַּבַּח קוּדְשָׁא בְּרִיךְ הוּא בְּשִׁבְחַיְיהוּ דְּיִשְׂרָאֵל? – אִין, דִּכְתִיב: "אֶת ה' הֶאֱמַרְתָּ הַיּוֹם" וּכְתִיב: "וַה' הֶאֱמִירְךָ הַיּוֹם" – אָמַר לָהֶם הַקָּדוֹשׁ בָּרוּךְ הוּא לְיִשְׂרָאֵל: אַתֶּם עֲשִׂיתוּנִי חֲטִיבָה אַחַת בָּעוֹלָם, וַאֲנִי אֶעֱשֶׂה אֶתְכֶם חֲטִיבָה אַחַת בָּעוֹלָם;

Rav Naḥman bar Yitzḥak continues: **Is the Holy One, Blessed be He, glorified through the glory of Israel?** Rav Ḥiyya bar Avin answered: **Yes,** as indicated by the juxtaposition of two verses; **as it is stated: "You have affirmed, this day,** that **the Lord** is your God, and that you will walk in His ways and keep His laws and commandments, and listen to His voice." **And the** subsequent **verse states: "And the Lord has affirmed, this day,** that **you** are His treasure, as He spoke to you, to keep His commandments" (Deuteronomy 26:17–18). From these two verses it is derived that **the Holy One, Blessed be He, said to Israel: You have made Me a single entity** [*ḥativa*][L] **in the world,** as you singled Me out as separate and unique. **And** because of this, **I will make you a single entity in the world,** and you will be a treasured nation, chosen by God.

אַתֶּם עֲשִׂיתוּנִי חֲטִיבָה אַחַת בָּעוֹלָם, שֶׁנֶּאֱמַר: "שְׁמַע יִשְׂרָאֵל ה' אֱלֹהֵינוּ ה' אֶחָד", וַאֲנִי אֶעֱשֶׂה אֶתְכֶם חֲטִיבָה אַחַת בָּעוֹלָם, שֶׁנֶּאֱמַר: "וּמִי כְּעַמְּךָ יִשְׂרָאֵל גּוֹי אֶחָד בָּאָרֶץ".

**You have made Me a single entity in the world, as it is stated** that Israel declares God's oneness by saying: **"Hear, Israel, the Lord is our God, the Lord is One"** (Deuteronomy 6:4). **And** because of this, **I will make you a single entity in the world,** unique and elevated with the utterance: **"Who is like Your people, Israel, one nation in the land?"** Consequently, the Holy One, Blessed be He, is glorified through the glory of Israel whose praises are written in God's phylacteries.

אֲמַר לֵיהּ רַב אַחָא בְּרֵיהּ דְּרָבָא לְרַב אַשִׁי: תֵּינַח בְּחַד בֵּיתָא, בִּשְׁאָר בָּתֵּי מַאי?

**Rav Aḥa, son of Rava said to Rav Ashi: It works out well** with regard to the contents of **one** of the four **compartments** of God's phylacteries of the head. However, all four compartments of Israel's phylacteries of the head contain portions of the Torah that praise God. **What** portions in praise of Israel are written in **the rest of the compartments** of God's phylacteries of the head?[B]

אֲמַר לֵיהּ: "כִּי מִי גוֹי גָּדוֹל", "וּמִי גּוֹי גָּדוֹל", "אַשְׁרֶיךָ יִשְׂרָאֵל", "אוֹ הֲנִסָּה אֱלֹהִים", "וּלְתִתְּךָ עֶלְיוֹן".

Rav Ashi **said to him:** In those three compartments it is written: **"For who is a great nation,** to whom God is close, like the Lord our God whenever we call upon Him?" (Deuteronomy 4:7); **"And who is a great nation,** who has righteous statutes and laws, like this entire Torah which I set before you today?" (Deuteronomy 4:8); **"Happy are you, Israel,** who is like you? A people saved by the Lord, the shield of your help, and that is the sword of your excellence. And your enemies shall dwindle away before you, and you shall tread upon their high places" (Deuteronomy 33:29); **"Or has God attempted** to go and take for Himself a nation from the midst of another nation, by trials, by signs and by wonders" (Deuteronomy 4:34); **"And to elevate you** above all nations that He has made, in praise, in name and in glory; that you may be a holy people to the Lord, your God, as He has spoken" (Deuteronomy 26:19).

אִי הָכִי נְפִישֵׁי לְהוּ טוּבֵי בָּתֵּי! אֶלָּא: "כִּי מִי גוֹי גָּדוֹל" "וּמִי גּוֹי גָּדוֹל" דְּדָמְיָין לַהֲדָדֵי – בְּחַד בֵּיתָא, "אַשְׁרֶיךָ יִשְׂרָאֵל" "וּמִי כְּעַמְּךָ יִשְׂרָאֵל" – בְּחַד בֵּיתָא, "אוֹ הֲנִסָּה אֱלֹהִים" – בְּחַד בֵּיתָא, "וּלְתִתְּךָ עֶלְיוֹן" – בְּחַד בֵּיתָא,

Rav Aḥa, son of Rava, raises an objection: **If** all of these verses are included in God's phylacteries of the head, **there are too many compartments** as more than four verses of praise were listed. **Rather,** the portions in God's phylacteries must be arranged as follows: The verses **"For who is a great nation" and "And who is a great nation"** are included **in one compartment,** as they are similar. **"Happy are you, Israel" is in one compartment. "Or has God attempted" is in one compartment and "And to elevate you" is in one compartment**

וְכוּלְּהוּ כְּתִיבִי בְּאֶדְרָעֵיהּ.

in the phylacteries of the head, where there are four separate compartments. **And all** of the verses **are written** together on one parchment **in** the phylacteries of the **arm**, which has only one compartment.

אָמַר רָבִין בַּר רַב אַדָּא אָמַר רַבִּי יִצְחָק: כָּל הָרָגִיל לָבֹא לְבֵית הַכְּנֶסֶת וְלֹא בָּא יוֹם אֶחָד – הַקָּדוֹשׁ בָּרוּךְ הוּא מְשָׁאִיל בּוֹ, שֶׁנֶּאֱמַר: ״מִי בָכֶם יְרֵא ה׳ שֹׁמֵעַ בְּקוֹל עַבְדּוֹ אֲשֶׁר הָלַךְ חֲשֵׁכִים וְאֵין נֹגַהּ לוֹ״;

Additionally, **Ravin bar Rav Adda said** that **Rabbi Yitzḥak said: One who is accustomed to come to the synagogue and did not come one day, the Holy One, Blessed be He, asks about him,** as it were, to determine what happened to him, **as it is stated: "Who among you fears the Lord? Who hears the voice of His servant? Though he walks in darkness and has no light,** let him trust in the name of the Lord, and rely upon his God" (Isaiah 50:10). In other words, God asks, who among you fears the Lord yet did not come to hear the voice of His servant the prayer leader, who engages in the service of God? He who went out before dawn and walks in darkness before prayer.

אִם לִדְבַר מִצְוָה הָלַךְ – נוֹגַהּ לוֹ, וְאִם לִדְבַר הָרְשׁוּת הָלַךְ – אֵין נוֹגַהּ לוֹ.

**If it is for a matter** involving **a mitzva that he went** and absented himself from prayer in the synagogue, then, despite the darkness, **there is light for him,** the aura of his mitzva will protect him. **But if it is for an optional matter,** some mundane purpose, **that he went** and absented himself from prayer in the synagogue, then, even once the day begins, **there is no light for him** (Maharsha).

״יִבְטַח בְּשֵׁם ה׳״, מַאי טַעְמָא? – מִשּׁוּם דַּהֲוָה לֵיהּ לִבְטוֹחַ בְּשֵׁם ה׳, וְלֹא בָּטַח.

The verse continues: **"Let him trust in the name of the Lord."** The Gemara asks: **What is the reason** that God is so exacting with this person? The Gemara answers: **Because he should have relied on the name of the Lord,** and trusted that he would not incur any loss if he postponed dealing with his mundane matters until after prayer in the synagogue, **and he did not rely** on God.

אָמַר רַבִּי יוֹחָנָן: בְּשָׁעָה שֶׁהַקָּדוֹשׁ בָּרוּךְ הוּא בָּא בְּבֵית הַכְּנֶסֶת וְלֹא מָצָא בָּהּ עֲשָׂרָה – מִיָּד הוּא כּוֹעֵס, שֶׁנֶּאֱמַר: ״מַדּוּעַ בָּאתִי וְאֵין אִישׁ קָרָאתִי וְאֵין עוֹנֶה״.

On this same topic, **Rabbi Yoḥanan said: When the Holy One, Blessed be He, enters a synagogue and does not find ten** people there, **He immediately becomes angry, as it is stated: "Why, when I came, was there no one? When I called, there was no one to answer…** Behold, with My rebuke I dry up the sea, I make the rivers a wilderness" (Isaiah 50:2).

אָמַר רַבִּי חֶלְבּוֹ אָמַר רַב הוּנָא: כָּל הַקּוֹבֵעַ מָקוֹם לִתְפִלָּתוֹ – אֱלֹהֵי אַבְרָהָם בְּעֶזְרוֹ.

Concerning another aspect of the constancy of prayer, **Rabbi Ḥelbo said that Rav Huna said: One who sets a fixed place for his prayer,**[H] **the God of Abraham assists him.** Since prayer parallels the Temple service, it is a sign of respect to set a fixed place for this sacred rite (Rabbi Yoshiyahu Pinto). The God of Abraham assists him because this pious custom evokes Abraham's conduct.

וּכְשֶׁמֵּת – אוֹמְרִים לוֹ: אִי עָנָיו, אִי חָסִיד, מִתַּלְמִידָיו שֶׁל אַבְרָהָם אָבִינוּ!

**When he dies,** those who eulogize one who set a fixed place for his prayer **say about him: "Where is the humble** one, **where is the pious** one, **of the disciples of our father Abraham?"** Presumably, one who sets a fixed place for prayer is a disciple of Abraham in every respect, including humility and piety (Rabbi Yoshiyahu Pinto).

וְאַבְרָהָם אָבִינוּ מְנָא לַן דְּקָבַע מָקוֹם? – דִּכְתִיב: ״וַיַּשְׁכֵּם אַבְרָהָם בַּבֹּקֶר אֶל הַמָּקוֹם אֲשֶׁר עָמַד שָׁם״, וְאֵין ״עֲמִידָה״ אֶלָּא תְּפִלָּה, שֶׁנֶּאֱמַר: ״וַיַּעֲמֹד פִּינְחָס וַיְפַלֵּל״.

The Gemara asks: **From where do we** derive **that Abraham our father set a fixed place** for his prayer? The Gemara answers: **As it is written: "And Abraham rose in the morning to the place where he had stood** before God" (Genesis 19:27), **and the** verb **"standing" means nothing other than prayer, as it is stated: "And Pinehas stood and prayed"** (Psalms 106:30).

אָמַר רַבִּי חֶלְבּוֹ אָמַר רַב הוּנָא: הַיּוֹצֵא מִבֵּית הַכְּנֶסֶת אַל יִפְסַע פְּסִיעָה גַּסָּה. אָמַר אַבָּיֵי: לָא אֲמַרַן אֶלָּא לְמִיפַּק, אֲבָל לְמֵיעַל – מִצְוָה לְמִרְהַט, שֶׁנֶּאֱמַר: ״נִרְדְּפָה לָדַעַת אֶת ה׳״.

**Rabbi Ḥelbo said** that **Rav Huna said: One who leaves the synagogue should not take large strides** because it creates the impression that he is eager to leave. **Abaye** explained Rav Huna's statement and **said:** This *halakha* **was only said** with regard **to leaving**[N] the synagogue, where large strides seem particularly disrespectful. **However,** with regard **to entering**[H] a synagogue, **it is a mitzva to run** and one is permitted to rush and take large strides (Rabbi Yoshiyahu Pinto). **As it is said:** "And let us know, **eagerly strive to know the Lord"** (Hosea 6:3). One who eagerly enters a synagogue displays his enthusiasm to follow the path of God.

**HALAKHA**

One who sets a fixed place for his prayer – כָּל הַקּוֹבֵעַ מָקוֹם לִתְפִלָּתוֹ וכו׳: One should establish a permanent place where he always prays. If he prays in a synagogue, it should always be the same synagogue. Even within the synagogue, he should establish a permanent place where he prays. If he prays alone in his house, e.g., if he lives in a village with no prayer quorum, he should establish a permanent place in his house for prayer (Rambam *Sefer Ahava, Hilkhot Tefilla*, 5:6; *Shulḥan Arukh, Oraḥ Ḥayyim* 90:19).

One who leaves the synagogue should not take large steps…However, with regard to entering – הַיּוֹצֵא מִבֵּית הַכְּנֶסֶת אַל יִפְסַע פְּסִיעָה גַּסָּה...אֲבָל לְמֵיעַל וכו׳: One should hurry on his way to the synagogue, especially when he nears the synagogue, where it is obvious that he is rushing to prayer. This is so even on Shabbat, when it is otherwise prohibited to take large steps. One should not rush when leaving the synagogue, unless it is obvious that he is leaving temporarily with the intention to return to his prayers, or if it is obvious that he is leaving the synagogue to proceed to the study hall (Rambam *Sefer Ahava, Hilkhot Tefilla*, 8:2; *Shulḥan Arukh, Oraḥ Ḥayyim* 90:12).

**NOTES**

This *halakha* was only said with regard to leaving – לָא אֲמַרַן אֶלָּא לְמִיפַּק: This statement of Abaye is problematic. It seems, on the one hand, that he is coming to explain Rav Huna's statement. On the other hand, he seems to be saying exactly the same thing. This anomaly was explained in different ways. Some said that Rav Huna's statement that one may not run when leaving the synagogue does not necessarily indicate that one is permitted to run when entering the synagogue. Conceivably, running into the synagogue could be interpreted that he is running into the synagogue in order to finish his prayers quickly, as they are a burden (*HaKotev*). Furthermore, while leaving the synagogue, the merit of his prayer protects him from any possible injury while running. Before he prays, he lacks that protection (*Iyyun Ya'akov*). Others suggested an alternative interpretation: It was only said with regard to leaving, means that this *halakha* only applies to one who leaves the synagogue and does not plan to return. However, with regard to entering, if he plans on returning to the synagogue, there is a mitzva to run (Rabbi Yoshiyahu Pinto). Or, one leaving the synagogue may not run as he left in order to go home, but "to enter" the study hall, it is a mitzva to run even when leaving a synagogue (Maharsha).

אָמַר רַבִּי זֵירָא: מֵרֵישׁ כִּי הֲוָה חָזֵינָא לְהוּ לְרַבָּנַן דְּקָא רָהֲטִי לְפִרְקָא בְּשַׁבְּתָא, אָמֵינָא: קָא מְחַלְּלִין רַבָּנַן שַׁבְּתָא. כֵּיוָן דִּשְׁמַעְנָא לְהָא דְּרַבִּי תַּנְחוּם אָמַר רַבִּי יְהוֹשֻׁעַ בֶּן לֵוִי: לְעוֹלָם יָרוּץ אָדָם לִדְבַר הֲלָכָה וַאֲפִילּוּ בְּשַׁבָּת, שֶׁנֶּאֱמַר: "אַחֲרֵי ה׳ יֵלְכוּ כְּאַרְיֵה יִשְׁאָג" וגו׳ – אֲנָא נַמִי רָהֵיטְנָא.

**Rabbi Zeira said: Initially, when I saw the Sages running to the** Rabbi's **lecture**[B] **on Shabbat, I said: These Sages are desecrating Shabbat.** One is prohibited from running on Shabbat in deference to the sanctity of the day. **Once I heard that which Rabbi Tanḥum said** that **Rabbi Yehoshua ben Levi** said: **One should always run for a matter of *halakha*, even on Shabbat,**[H] **as it is stated: "They shall walk after the Lord, who will roar like a lion"** (Hosea 11:10). In other words, one should rush as though he were chased by a lion (*Birkat Hashem*), **I too run.**

אָמַר רַבִּי זֵירָא: אַגְרָא דְּפִרְקָא – רְהָטָא.

**Rabbi Zeira said: The reward for** attending **the lecture is** for **running.**[N] Since most individuals attending the lecture did not fully understand the material taught, the primary reward for attendance was given for their intention to hear the Torah being taught, as evidenced by their rush to arrive.

אָמַר אַבָּיֵי: אַגְרָא דְּכַלָּה – דּוּחֲקָא.

Similarly, **Abaye said: The reward for** attending **the *kalla* is** for **the crowding.** Due to the large crowd, study was difficult, so the primary reward was given for their effort to hear and understand some part of the lecture.

אָמַר רָבָא: אַגְרָא דִּשְׁמַעְתָּא – סְבָרָא.

Similarly, **Rava said: The reward for** learning the halakhic **traditions** of the *amora'im* **is** for **the logical** analysis, as the primary reward for studying Talmud was not given for knowing the halakhic conclusions, but for the logical reasoning that led to those conclusions.

אָמַר רַב פָּפָּא: אַגְרָא דְּבֵי טַמְיָא – שְׁתִיקוּתָא.

**Rav Pappa said: The** primary **reward for** attending **a house of mourning** [***bei tammaya***][L] **is** for the **silence,** which is the optimal manner for those consoling the mourners to express their empathy.

אָמַר מָר זוּטְרָא: אַגְרָא דְּתַעֲנִיתָא – צְדָקְתָּא.

**Mar Zutra said: The** primary **reward for fasting is** for the **charity** given to the poor on the fast day (see Isaiah 58).

אָמַר רַב שֵׁשֶׁת: אַגְרָא דְּהֶסְפֵּדָא – דַּלּוּיֵי.

**Rav Sheshet said: The** primary **reward for** delivering **a eulogy is** for causing those in attendance to **raise their voices** and cry,[H] as that increases the grief over the deceased.

אָמַר רַב אַשִׁי: אַגְרָא דְּבֵי הִלּוּלֵי – מִילֵּי.

**Rav Ashi said: The** primary **reward for** participating in **a wedding is** for **the words,** i.e., the good wishes with which the guests regale the bride and groom.

אָמַר רַב הוּנָא: כָּל הַמִּתְפַּלֵּל אֲחוֹרֵי בֵית הַכְּנֶסֶת נִקְרָא "רָשָׁע", שֶׁנֶּאֱמַר: "סָבִיב רְשָׁעִים יִתְהַלָּכוּן".

Back to the topic of deference for a synagogue, the Gemara records that **Rav Huna said: One who prays behind the synagogue**[H] **is called wicked,** as while the entire congregation is facing one direction to pray, he faces the opposite direction creating the impression that he is treating the synagogue and its congregation with contempt. **As it is stated: "The wicked walk round about,** when vileness is exalted among the sons of men" (Psalms 12:9). In other words, only the wicked walk round about the synagogue in order to pray.

אָמַר אַבָּיֵי: לָא אֲמָרַן אֶלָּא דְּלָא מַהֲדַר אַפֵּיהּ לְבֵי כְנִישְׁתָּא, אֲבָל מַהֲדַר אַפֵּיהּ לְבֵי כְנִישְׁתָּא – לֵית לַן בַּהּ.

**Abaye said: This** *halakha* **was said only** in a case **where one does not turn his face toward the synagogue. But** where **he turns his face toward the synagogue** and prays **we have no** prohibition **in** that case.

הַהוּא גַּבְרָא דְּקָא מְצַלֵּי אֲחוֹרֵי בֵי כְנִישְׁתָּא, וְלָא מַהֲדַר אַפֵּיהּ לְבֵי כְנִישְׁתָּא. חֲלַף אֵלִיָּהוּ. חַזְיֵיהּ, אִידְּמִי לֵיהּ כְּטַיָּיעָא. אֲמַר לֵיהּ: כְּדוּ בַר קָיְימַתְּ קַמֵּי מָרָךְ? שְׁלַף סַפְסְרָא וְקַטְלֵיהּ.

To reinforce the gravity of this prohibition, the Gemara relates: **A certain individual prayed behind the synagogue and did not turn to face the synagogue.** Elijah the Prophet **passed by and appeared to him as an Arab** [***taya'a***].[NL] Elijah **said: "This is how** [***kadu bar***][L] **you stand before your Master?"** Elijah **drew a sword and killed him.**

## BACKGROUND

**Lecture – פִּרְקָא:** This was a lecture delivered by one of the Sages on matters of Torah to the general public. Specifically, the lecture delivered before each of the three Pilgrim Festivals addressed that Festival. The primary focus of these lectures was *halakha*. In attendance were the community at large, incapable of understanding the subject matter, and Torah scholars, who were already familiar with it. Therefore, the reward for attending the lecture is for running.

## NOTES

**The reward for attending the lecture is for running – אַגְרָא דְּפִרְקָא רְהָטָא וכו׳:** Some explain that this series of adages does not imply that the reward is exclusively for the crowding mentioned. Rather, the reward for attending the lecture includes a reward for running as well. The implication is that, although running and crowding seem tangential and not essential to the mitzva, one is, nevertheless, rewarded for that aspect as well, as it too is significant (*HaKotev*).

**Elijah passed by and appeared to him as an Arab – חֲלַף אֵלִיָּהוּ...אִידְּמִי לֵיהּ כְּטַיָּיעָא:** This text is difficult. Though the action described is reprehensible, it does not warrant the death penalty. Another version of the story reads: A certain Arab passed by and saw that he turned his face away from the synagogue, meaning that, it was not Elijah but an actual Arab who saw this individual act as contemptuous toward God. Even this non-Jew was offended by his actions. He took out his sword and killed the man in anger (Maharsha).

## LANGUAGE

**House of mourning [*bei tammaya*] – בֵּי טַמְיָא:** Many attempted to explain the source of this term. Some explained that the word *tammaya* means bones in Aramaic and therefore the term means house of the bones of the dead. Others interpreted homiletically through letter transformation that *tet-mem-aleph* becomes *aleph-bet-lamed* meaning mourner (*Arukh*). The *ge'onim* had a variant reading here: *Bei ta'ama*, the house of reason. This is because the house of mourning is a place where people attempt to console the mourners by seeking to rationalize the tragedy that befell them.

**Arab [*taya'a*] – טַיָּיעָא:** This term refers to an Arab, a member of the nomadic Arab tribes that were located, even in ancient times, along the Babylonian borders. The word derives from the name of one of those tribes, الطا, *al-Ta'i*, which apparently resided in those regions.

**This is how [*kadu bar*] – כְּדוּ בַר:** The *ge'onim* had a variant reading here in which these two words were condensed. This single word is comparable to the Arabic مستدبر, meaning to turn one's back on. After all, the one who said this was an Arab (Rav Sherira Gaon, *Arukh*).

## HALAKHA

**One should always run for a matter of *halakha*, even on Shabbat – לְעוֹלָם יָרוּץ אָדָם לִדְבַר הֲלָכָה וַאֲפִילּוּ בְּשַׁבָּת:** While one is otherwise prohibited to take large strides on Shabbat, he is, nevertheless, permitted to do so on his way to synagogue or the study hall (Rambam *Sefer Zemanim*, *Hilkhot Shabbat* 24:5; *Shulḥan Arukh*, *Oraḥ Ḥayyim* 301:1).

**The reward for a eulogy is causing people to raise their voices and cry – אַגְרָא דְּהֶסְפֵּדָא דַּלּוּיֵי:** Based on this statement, a eulogizer should speak in a loud, crying voice and speak the praises of the deceased so that those in attendance will be driven to tears (*Shulḥan Arukh*, *Yoreh De'a* 344:1).

**One who prays behind the synagogue – כָּל הַמִּתְפַּלֵּל אֲחוֹרֵי בֵית הַכְּנֶסֶת וכו׳:** One is prohibited from praying behind the synagogue. Behind the synagogue refers to the side where the entrance is located, facing the direction opposite the one faced by those praying in the synagogue. Others explain on the contrary: Behind the synagogue refers to behind the eastern wall in which there are no entrances at all, and he is praying with his back to the synagogue, even though he is facing in the same direction as those inside the synagogue. Everyone agrees that one who has his back to the synagogue and is facing in a direction other than the one faced by those in the synagogue is called wicked and it is to him that the Gemara referred when speaking of one who prayed behind the synagogue and did not turn his face toward the synagogue (Rambam *Sefer Ahava*, *Hilkhot Tefilla* 5:6; *Shulḥan Arukh*, *Oraḥ Ḥayyim* 90:7)

אָמַר לֵיהּ הַהוּא מֵרַבָּנַן לְרַב בֵּיבָי בַּר אַבָּיֵי, וְאָמְרִי לָהּ רַב בֵּיבָי לְרַב נַחְמָן בַּר יִצְחָק: מַאי ״כְּרֻם זֻלּוּת לִבְנֵי אָדָם״?

Rav Huna already explained the beginning of the verse, "The wicked walk round about." The Gemara explains the end of the verse: "When vileness is exalted among the sons of men." **One of the Sages said to Rav Beivai bar Abaye, and some say Rav Beivai said to Rav Naḥman bar Yitzḥak: What is** the meaning of: **"When vileness is exalted among the sons of men"?**

אָמַר לֵיהּ: אֵלּוּ דְּבָרִים שֶׁעוֹמְדִים בְּרוּמוֹ שֶׁל עוֹלָם וּבְנֵי אָדָם מְזַלְזְלִין בָּהֶן.

**He replied to: These are matters of utmost importance,** exalted, i.e., mitzvot or prayer, **which people** nonetheless **treat with contempt,** vileness among the sons of men.

רַבִּי יוֹחָנָן וְרַבִּי אֶלְעָזָר דְּאָמְרִי תַּרְוַיְיהוּ: כֵּיוָן שֶׁנִּצְטָרֵךְ אָדָם לַבְּרִיּוֹת – פָּנָיו מִשְׁתַּנּוֹת כִּכְרוּם, שֶׁנֶּאֱמַר: ״כְּרֻם זֻלּוּת לִבְנֵי אָדָם״.

**Rabbi Yoḥanan and** his student, **Rabbi Elazar, both said** an alternative explanation of this verse: **Once a person needs** the help of **others** and loses dignity in their eyes, vileness among the sons of men, **his face changes** and becomes **like a *kerum*, as it is stated: "When [*kerum*] vileness is exalted among the sons of men."**

מַאי ״כְּרוּם״? – כִּי אֲתָא רַב דִּימִי אָמַר: עוֹף אֶחָד יֵשׁ בִּכְרַכֵּי הַיָּם וּ״כְרוּם״ שְׁמוֹ, וְכֵיוָן שֶׁחַמָּה זוֹרַחַת – מִתְהַפֵּךְ לְכַמָּה גְּוָונִין.

**What is *kerum*** referred to by Rabbi Yoḥanan and Rabbi Elazar? **When Rav Dimi came**[B] to Babylonia from Eretz Yisrael **he said: There is a bird in the cities by the sea called *kerum***[B] **and when the sun rises,** the bird **changes several colors.** Similarly, one who becomes dependent upon others blushes in embarrassment.

רַבִּי אַמִּי וְרַבִּי אַסִּי דְּאָמְרִי תַּרְוַיְיהוּ: כְּאִלּוּ נִדּוֹן בִּשְׁנֵי דִּינִים, אֵשׁ וּמַיִם, שֶׁנֶּאֱמַר: ״הִרְכַּבְתָּ אֱנוֹשׁ לְרֹאשֵׁנוּ בָּאנוּ בָאֵשׁ וּבַמַּיִם״.

**Rabbi Ami and Rabbi Asi both said:** One who becomes dependent upon others, **it is as if he was punished with two punishments: Fire and water. As it is stated: "You have caused men to ride over our heads; we have gone through fire and water"** (Psalms 66:12).

וְאָמַר רַבִּי חֶלְבּוֹ אָמַר רַב הוּנָא: לְעוֹלָם יְהֵא אָדָם זָהִיר בִּתְפִלַּת הַמִּנְחָה, שֶׁהֲרֵי אֵלִיָּהוּ לֹא נַעֲנָה אֶלָּא בִּתְפִלַּת הַמִּנְחָה, שֶׁנֶּאֱמַר: ״וַיְהִי בַּעֲלוֹת הַמִּנְחָה וַיִּגַּשׁ אֵלִיָּהוּ הַנָּבִיא וַיֹּאמַר וגו׳. עֲנֵנִי ה׳ עֲנֵנִי״;

**And Rabbi Ḥelbo said** that **Rav Huna said: One must always be vigilant with regard to the afternoon prayer,**[NH] **as Elijah's** prayer **was only answered in the afternoon prayer, as it is stated: "And it was at the time of the afternoon offering that Elijah the Prophet came near, and he said:** Lord, God of Abraham, Isaac and Israel, let it be known on this day that You are God in Israel, and that I am Your servant, and that I have done all these things at Your word. **Answer me, Lord, answer me,** that this people will know that You, Lord, are God" (1 Kings 18:36–37). Because Elijah was answered in the afternoon prayer, it has particular significance.

״עֲנֵנִי״ – שֶׁתֵּרֵד אֵשׁ מִן הַשָּׁמַיִם, וַ״עֲנֵנִי״ – שֶׁלֹּא יֹאמְרוּ מַעֲשֵׂה כְשָׁפִים הֵם.

In passing, the Gemara explains why it was necessary for Elijah to repeat, "answer me, Lord, answer me": The first **answer me** was the request **that fire descend from the heavens, while** the second **answer me** was the request **that** Israel should accept complete faith in God and **not say that** the fire descending from the heavens **was an act of sorcery.**

רַבִּי יוֹחָנָן אָמַר: אַף בִּתְפִלַּת עַרְבִית, שֶׁנֶּאֱמַר: ״תִּכּוֹן תְּפִלָּתִי קְטֹרֶת לְפָנֶיךָ מַשְׂאַת כַּפַּי מִנְחַת עָרֶב״. רַב נַחְמָן בַּר יִצְחָק אָמַר: אַף תְּפִלַּת שַׁחֲרִית, שֶׁנֶּאֱמַר: ״ה׳ בֹּקֶר תִּשְׁמַע קוֹלִי בֹּקֶר אֶעֱרָךְ לְךָ וַאֲצַפֶּה״.

**Rabbi Yoḥanan** said: One must be vigilant **with regard to the evening prayer as well, as it is stated: "Let my prayer come forth as incense before You, the lifting of my hands as the evening offering"** (Psalms 141:2).

**Rav Naḥman bar Yitzḥak said:** One must be vigilant **with regard to the morning prayer as well, as it is stated: "Lord, in the morning You shall hear my voice; in the morning I will order my prayer unto You and will look forward"** (Psalms 5:4).

וְאָמַר רַבִּי חֶלְבּוֹ אָמַר רַב הוּנָא: כָּל הַנֶּהֱנֶה מִסְּעוּדַת חָתָן וְאֵינוֹ מְשַׂמְּחוֹ – עוֹבֵר בַּחֲמִשָּׁה קוֹלוֹת, שֶׁנֶּאֱמַר: ״קוֹל שָׂשׂוֹן וְקוֹל שִׂמְחָה קוֹל חָתָן וְקוֹל כַּלָּה קוֹל אוֹמְרִים הוֹדוּ אֶת ה׳ צְבָאוֹת״.

**And Rabbi Ḥelbo said** that **Rav Huna said: Anyone who benefits from the feast of a groom but does not cause him to rejoice violates the five voices** mentioned in this verse, **as it is stated: "The voice of joy and the voice of gladness, the voice of the groom and the voice of the bride, and the voice of those who say: Give thanks to the Lord of hosts,** for the Lord is good, for His mercy lasts forever, even of those who bring a thanks-offering to the house of the Lord. For I will restore the captivity of the land as it was in the beginning, says the Lord" (Jeremiah 33:11). These five voices in the context of a bride and groom correspond to the five voices mentioned in the context of the revelation at Sinai, as in Song of Songs, the day of the revelation at Sinai is alluded to by the phrase: His wedding day (Rabbi Yoshiyahu Pinto, Maharsha).

## BACKGROUND

**When Rav Dimi came – כִּי אֲתָא רַב דִּימִי:** Rav Dimi was one of the Sages who descended, or who would often travel from Eretz Yisrael to Babylonia, primarily to transmit the Torah of Eretz Yisrael to the Torah centers of the Diaspora, although occasionally, he traveled on business, as well. Consequently, many questions, particularly those concerning the Torah of Eretz Yisrael, remained unresolved, until the messenger from Zion would arrive and elucidate the *halakha*, the novel expression, or the unique circumstances pertaining to a particular statement that required clarification.

***Kerum* – כְּרוּם:** Some identify the *kerum* as the shining starling, *Lamprocolius splendidus*, which is indigenous to the area ranging from western, equatorial Africa to the Sudan. This starling, as well as another, *Spreo superbus*, indigenous to eastern Africa and banks of the Red Sea, have characteristics similar to the bird described by the Sages. The color of these birds' feathers is not the result of a pigment in the feathers themselves, but from the unique configuration of the feathers and the way the sun reflects off of them.

Starling

## NOTES

**One must always be vigilant with regard to the afternoon prayer – לְעוֹלָם יְהֵא אָדָם זָהִיר בִּתְפִלַּת הַמִּנְחָה:** There is room to issue a particular warning with regard to the afternoon prayer and to underscore its significance because there are many reasons liable to cause one to neglect to recite the afternoon prayer or to fail to recite it with the proper intent. Unlike the morning prayer, which one recites before he leaves for work, or the evening prayer, which he recites after returning home, often, one must interrupt his activities and recite the afternoon prayer. Therefore, he is warned more sternly with regard to that prayer. For that same reason, the afternoon prayer is highly significant, as one must disengage himself from all involvements in order to pray. Rabbi Yoḥanan, who underscored the significance of the evening prayer, did so because he believed that it too required reinforcement due to the fact that it is optional and, when one is tired, he is liable to take it lightly. Rav Naḥman bar Yitzḥak underscored the significance of the morning prayer as well because he was concerned that when one is hurrying to leave for work, he may neglect to recite the prayer and rely on the fact that he can recite the afternoon prayer twice (*Kli Yakar*, Rabbi Yoshiyahu Pinto).

## HALAKHA

**One must always be vigilant with regard to the afternoon prayer – לְעוֹלָם יְהֵא אָדָם זָהִיר בִּתְפִלַּת הַמִּנְחָה:** One must make an effort to recite the afternoon prayer at the appropriate time. The Sages cautioned with regard to the afternoon prayer in particular because its appointed time is in the middle of the day when one is engaged in his work or other business and he is liable, due to those distractions, to forget to pray. Nevertheless, if he prays properly, his reward is great (*Tur, Oraḥ Ḥayyim* 232).

PERSONALITIES

Rabbi Ḥelbo – רַבִּי חֶלְבּוֹ: Rabbi Ḥelbo, also known as Rav Ḥelbo, was a third generation Babylonian *amora* who ascended to Eretz Yisrael. He was the primary student of and learned most of his Torah from Rav Huna. Apparently, Rabbi Ḥelbo ascended to Eretz Yisrael towards the end of Rav Huna's life, and was already in Eretz Yisrael when Rav Huna's body was taken there for burial.

In Eretz Yisrael, Rabbi Ḥelbo had a colleague-disciple relationship with the more prominent students of Rabbi Yoḥanan and became one of the leaders and halakhic authorities of his generation. In the field of *aggada*, he was a disciple of Rabbi Shmuel bar Naḥmani and cites aggadic traditions in his name.

Rabbi Ḥelbo resided in Tiberias where he had ties with Rabbi Yehuda Nesia the second. The Talmud relates that he was not survived by children.

NOTES

The spoils of the poor is in your houses – גְּזֵלַת הֶעָנִי בְּבָתֵּיכֶם: Some tie the transgression of one who does not respond when another extended him a greeting to the verse: The spoils of the poor, in the following manner: Stealing from the poor [*ani*] is etymologically similar to stealing one's response [*ma'aneh*] by failing to reciprocate another's greeting (*Shitta Mekubbetzet, Kol Eliyahu*).

וְאִם מְשַׂמְּחוֹ מַה שְּׂכָרוֹ? – אָמַר רַבִּי יְהוֹשֻׁעַ בֶּן לֵוִי: זוֹכֶה לַתּוֹרָה שֶׁנִּתְּנָה בַּחֲמִשָּׁה קוֹלוֹת, שֶׁנֶּאֱמַר: ״וַיְהִי בַיּוֹם הַשְּׁלִישִׁי בִּהְיֹת הַבֹּקֶר וַיְהִי קֹלֹת וּבְרָקִים וְעָנָן כָּבֵד עַל הָהָר וְקֹל שׁוֹפָר״ וגו׳, ״וַיְהִי קוֹל הַשּׁוֹפָר״ וגו׳, ״וְהָאֱלֹהִים יַעֲנֶנּוּ בְקוֹל״.

What is his reward if he causes the groom to rejoice? He is privileged to acquire the Torah, which was given with five voices, as it is stated: "And it was on the third day, when it was morning, there were sounds [*kolot*], and lightning and a thick cloud upon the mountain, and the voice of the shofar" (Exodus 19:16). The plural *kolot* indicates at least two sounds, while "the voice of the shofar" is one more. The passage continues: "And when the voice of the shofar grew louder and louder, Moses spoke and God answered him by a voice" (Exodus 19:19). Along with the three previous voices, the second shofar and the voice with which God answered Moses amount to a total of five voices at the revelation at Sinai.

אִינִי? וְהָא כְּתִיב ״וְכָל הָעָם רוֹאִים אֶת הַקּוֹלֹת״!

The Gemara asks: **Is this so? Isn't it also written: "And the whole nation saw the voices** and the torches and the sound of the shofar" (Exodus 20:15)? Clearly more than five voices are mentioned with regard to the revelation at Sinai.

אוֹתָן קוֹלוֹת דְּקוֹדֶם מַתַּן תּוֹרָה הֲווּ.

The Gemara answers: **Those voices were** sounded **prior to the giving of the Torah,** so they are not included in this calculation of voices.

רַבִּי אַבָּהוּ אָמַר: כְּאִילּוּ הִקְרִיב תּוֹדָה, שֶׁנֶּאֱמַר: ״מְבִאִים תּוֹדָה בֵּית ה׳״. רַב נַחְמָן בַּר יִצְחָק אָמַר: כְּאִילּוּ בָּנָה אַחַת מֵחוּרְבוֹת יְרוּשָׁלַיִם, שֶׁנֶּאֱמַר: ״כִּי אָשִׁיב אֶת שְׁבוּת הָאָרֶץ כְּבָרִאשֹׁנָה אָמַר ה׳״.

**Rabbi Abbahu said:** The reward for causing a groom to rejoice **is** the same **as if one had offered a thanks-offering** in the Temple, for **as it is stated** later in the previously cited verse from Jeremiah: **"Those who bring a thanks-offering to the house of the Lord." And Rav Naḥman bar Yitzḥak said:** The reward for causing a groom to rejoice is the same **as if one rebuilt one of Jerusalem's ruins, as it is stated** later in the same verse: **"For I will restore the captivity of the land as it was in the beginning."**

וְאָמַר רַבִּי חֶלְבּוֹ אָמַר רַב הוּנָא: כׇּל אָדָם שֶׁיֵּשׁ בּוֹ יִרְאַת שָׁמַיִם – דְּבָרָיו נִשְׁמָעִין, שֶׁנֶּאֱמַר: ״סוֹף דָּבָר הַכֹּל נִשְׁמָע אֶת הָאֱלֹהִים יְרָא״ וגו׳.

**And Rabbi Ḥelbo said** that **Rav Huna said: Any person who has the fear of Heaven, his words are heeded, as it is stated: "The end of the matter, all having been heard: Fear God,** and keep His commandments; for this is all of man" (Ecclesiastes 12:13). The Gemara explains: "The end of the matter, all having been heard," refers to the words of one "who keeps His commandments; for this is all of man."

מַאי ״כִּי זֶה כׇּל הָאָדָם״? אָמַר רַבִּי אֶלְעָזָר, אָמַר הַקָּדוֹשׁ בָּרוּךְ הוּא: כׇּל הָעוֹלָם כּוּלּוֹ לֹא נִבְרָא אֶלָּא בִּשְׁבִיל זֶה.

With regard to the end of this verse, the Gemara asks: **What is** meant by, **"for this is all of man"? Rabbi Elazar said: The Holy One, Blessed be He, said** about him: **The entire world was created only for this** person. This is the ultimate person for which all of man was created.

רַבִּי אַבָּא בַּר כָּהֲנָא אָמַר: שָׁקוּל זֶה כְּנֶגֶד כׇּל הָעוֹלָם כּוּלּוֹ. רַבִּי שִׁמְעוֹן בֶּן עַזַּאי אוֹמֵר, וְאָמְרִי לַהּ רַבִּי שִׁמְעוֹן בֶּן זוֹמָא אוֹמֵר: כׇּל הָעוֹלָם כּוּלּוֹ לֹא נִבְרָא אֶלָּא לְצַוּוֹת לָזֶה.

**Rabbi Abba bar Kahana said:** The end of this verse teaches that **this is equivalent to the entire world,** all of man.
**Rabbi Shimon ben Azzai, and some say Rabbi Shimon ben Zoma, says:** Not only is he the equivalent of the entire world, but **the entire world was created** to serve **as companions for him,** so that he would have a society in which to live and with which to interact.

וְאָמַר רַבִּי חֶלְבּוֹ אָמַר רַב הוּנָא: כׇּל שֶׁיּוֹדֵעַ בַּחֲבֵרוֹ שֶׁהוּא רָגִיל לִיתֵּן לוֹ שָׁלוֹם – יַקְדִּים לוֹ שָׁלוֹם, שֶׁנֶּאֱמַר: ״בַּקֵּשׁ שָׁלוֹם וְרׇדְפֵהוּ״. וְאִם נָתַן לוֹ וְלֹא הֶחֱזִיר – נִקְרָא גַּזְלָן, שֶׁנֶּאֱמַר: ״וְאַתֶּם בִּעַרְתֶּם הַכֶּרֶם גְּזֵלַת הֶעָנִי בְּבָתֵּיכֶם״.

**And Rabbi Ḥelbo**[P] said that **Rav Huna said: One who is aware that another** person **is accustomed to greet him** is not only obligated to return his greeting, but **he** must **greet him first, as it is stated: "Seek peace and pursue it"** (Psalms 34:15). **If** the other person **extended** his **greeting to him and he did not respond, he is called a robber, as it is stated: "It is you who have eaten up the vineyard, the spoils of the poor is in your houses"** (Isaiah 3:14).[N] The only way to steal from a pauper who owns nothing is to rob him of his dignity by refusing to return his greeting.

אָמַר רַבִּי יוֹחָנָן מִשּׁוּם רַבִּי יוֹסֵי: מִנַּיִן שֶׁהַקָּדוֹשׁ בָּרוּךְ הוּא מִתְפַּלֵּל? – שֶׁנֶּאֱמַר: "וַהֲבִיאוֹתִים אֶל הַר קׇדְשִׁי וְשִׂמַּחְתִּים בְּבֵית תְּפִלָּתִי", "תְּפִלָּתָם" לֹא נֶאֱמַר אֶלָּא "תְּפִלָּתִי", מִכָּאן שֶׁהַקָּדוֹשׁ בָּרוּךְ הוּא מִתְפַּלֵּל.

Along the same lines, **Rabbi Yoḥanan said in the name of**[B] **Rabbi Yosei: From where** is it derived **that the Holy One, Blessed be He, prays? As it is stated: "I will bring them to My holy mountain, and make them joyful in the house of My prayer"** (Isaiah 56:7). The verse **does not say** the house of **their prayer, but rather, "**the house of **My prayer"; from here** we see **that the Holy One, Blessed be He, prays.**[N]

מַאי מְצַלֵּי?

The Gemara asks: **What does** God **pray?** To whom does God pray?

אָמַר רַב זוּטְרָא בַּר טוֹבִיָּה אָמַר רַב: "יְהִי רָצוֹן מִלְּפָנַי שֶׁיִּכְבְּשׁוּ רַחֲמַי אֶת כַּעֲסִי, וְיִגּוֹלּוּ רַחֲמַי עַל מִדּוֹתַי, וְאֶתְנַהֵג עִם בָּנַי בְּמִדַּת רַחֲמִים, וְאֶכָּנֵס לָהֶם לִפְנִים מִשּׁוּרַת הַדִּין".

**Rav Zutra bar Tovia said** that **Rav said:**
God says: **May it be My will that My mercy will overcome My anger** towards Israel for their transgressions,
**and may My mercy prevail over My** other **attributes** through which Israel is punished,
**and may I conduct** myself **toward My children,** Israel, **with the attribute of mercy,**
**and may I enter before them beyond the letter of the law.**

תַּנְיָא, אָמַר רַבִּי יִשְׁמָעֵאל בֶּן אֱלִישָׁע: פַּעַם אַחַת נִכְנַסְתִּי לְהַקְטִיר קְטוֹרֶת לִפְנַי וְלִפְנִים, וְרָאִיתִי אַכְתְּרִיאֵל יָהּ ה׳ צְבָאוֹת שֶׁהוּא יוֹשֵׁב עַל כִּסֵּא רָם וְנִשָּׂא, וְאָמַר לִי: "יִשְׁמָעֵאל בְּנִי, בָּרְכֵנִי"! – אָמַרְתִּי לוֹ: "יְהִי רָצוֹן מִלְּפָנֶיךָ שֶׁיִּכְבְּשׁוּ רַחֲמֶיךָ אֶת כַּעַסְךָ, וְיִגּוֹלּוּ רַחֲמֶיךָ עַל מִדּוֹתֶיךָ, וְתִתְנַהֵג עִם בָּנֶיךָ בְּמִדַּת הָרַחֲמִים, וְתִכָּנֵס לָהֶם לִפְנִים מִשּׁוּרַת הַדִּין", וְנִעְנַע לִי בְּרֹאשׁוֹ. וְקָמַשְׁמַע לַן שֶׁלֹּא תְּהֵא בִּרְכַּת הֶדְיוֹט קַלָּה בְּעֵינֶיךָ.

Similarly, **it was taught** in a *baraita* that **Rabbi Yishmael ben Elisha,** the High Priest, said: **Once,** on Yom Kippur, **I entered the innermost sanctum,** the Holy of Holies, **to offer incense, and** in a vision **I saw Akatriel Ya, the Lord of Hosts,** one of the names of God expressing His ultimate authority, **seated upon a high and exalted throne** (see Isaiah 6).
**And He said to me: Yishmael, My son, bless Me.**[N]
**I said to Him** the prayer that God prays: **"May it be Your will that Your mercy overcome Your anger,**
**and may Your mercy prevail over Your** other **attributes,**
**and may You act toward Your children with the attribute of mercy,**
**and may You enter before them beyond the letter of the law."**
The Holy One, Blessed be He, **nodded His head** and accepted the blessing. This event **teaches us that you should not take the blessing of an ordinary person lightly.** If God asked for and accepted a man's blessing, all the more so that a man must value the blessing of another man.

וְאָמַר רַבִּי יוֹחָנָן מִשּׁוּם רַבִּי יוֹסֵי: מִנַּיִן שֶׁאֵין מְרַצִּין לוֹ לְאָדָם בִּשְׁעַת כַּעֲסוֹ – דִּכְתִיב: "פָּנַי יֵלֵכוּ וַהֲנִחֹתִי לָךְ"; אָמַר לוֹ הַקָּדוֹשׁ בָּרוּךְ הוּא לְמֹשֶׁה: הַמְתֵּן לִי עַד שֶׁיַּעַבְרוּ פָּנִים שֶׁל זַעַם וְאָנִיחַ לָךְ.

**And Rabbi Yoḥanan said in the name of Rabbi Yosei: From where** is it derived **that one must not placate a person while** he is in the throes of **his anger,**[H] rather he should mollify him after he has calmed down? **As it is written,** when following the sin of the Golden Calf, Moses requested that the Divine Presence rest upon Israel as it had previously, God said to him: **"My face will go, and I will give you rest"** (Exodus 33:14). Rabbi Yoḥanan explained: **The Holy One, Blessed be He, said to** Moses: **Wait until My face of wrath will pass and I will grant your** request. One must wait for a person's anger to pass as well.

וּמִי אִיכָּא רִתְחָא קַמֵּיהּ דְּקוּדְשָׁא בְּרִיךְ הוּא?

The Gemara asks: **And is there anger before the Holy One, Blessed be He?** Can we speak of God using terms like anger?

אִין, דְּתַנְיָא: "וְאֵל זֹעֵם בְּכׇל יוֹם".

The Gemara answers: **Yes, as it was taught** in a *baraita,* God becomes angry, as it is stated: "God vindicates the righteous, **God is furious every day"** (Psalms 7:12).

וְכַמָּה זַעְמוֹ? – רֶגַע. וְכַמָּה רֶגַע? – אֶחָד מֵחֲמֵשֶׁת רִבּוֹא וּשְׁמוֹנַת אֲלָפִים וּשְׁמֹנֶה מֵאוֹת וּשְׁמוֹנִים וּשְׁמֹנָה בְּשָׁעָה, וְזוֹ הִיא "רֶגַע". וְאֵין כׇּל בְּרִיָּה יְכוֹלָה לְכַוֵּין אוֹתָהּ שָׁעָה, חוּץ מִבִּלְעָם הָרָשָׁע, דִּכְתִיב בֵּיהּ: "וְיֹדֵעַ דַּעַת עֶלְיוֹן".

**How much** time does **His anger** last? God's anger lasts **a moment.**[N] **And how long is a moment? One fifty-eight thousand, eight hundred and eighty-eighth of an hour, that is a moment.** The Gemara adds: **And no creature can** precisely **determine that moment** when God becomes angry, **except for Balaam the wicked, about whom it is written: "He who knows the knowledge of the Most High"** (Numbers 24:16).

**BACKGROUND**

In the name of – מִשּׁוּם: This phrase, in the name of Rabbi X, is employed to indicate that the one making the statement did not hear it directly from the person in whose name he is quoting it. In that case, the Gemara would say: Rabbi X said that Rabbi Y said. Rather, he heard it from others in the name of that Sage. Rabbi Yoḥanan, the *amora*, could not have heard firsthand a pronouncement made by Rabbi Yosei, the *tanna*. He only heard secondhand that that was what he said. In most cases where one Sage quotes a statement in the name of another, there is a generational gap between them. However, occasionally, a student quotes a statement in the name of his own Rabbi. The Gemara then explains that he was not present on the occasion when his Rabbi made that pronouncement and only heard it from other students.

**NOTES**

From here we see that the Holy One, Blessed be He, prays – מִכָּאן שֶׁהַקָּדוֹשׁ בָּרוּךְ הוּא מִתְפַּלֵּל: Much has been said with regard to these statements, and many homiletical and mystical interpretations were suggested in an effort to arrive at an understanding. Most commentaries hold that God's prayer is God's request of the individual and of mankind as a whole to turn to Him with all their heart. In other words, if people repent their sins and attempt to break the vicious cycle of "one transgression leads to another transgression," they will cause God's attribute of mercy to prevail over His attribute of justice, and even those deserving of punishment will be spared. That said, God's prayer, so to speak, is His wish/request of man: "And now, Israel, what does the Lord your God require of you, but to fear" (Deuteronomy 10:12).The fact that God's wish is characterized as a prayer means that God is showing His desire and His will, His prayer, that man will be better and worthy of His bountiful blessing (*Tziyyun LeNefesh Ḥayya*, Rashba).

Yishmael, My son, bless Me – יִשְׁמָעֵאל בְּנִי, בָּרְכֵנִי: This vision is also the object of many interpretations. While some say that Rabbi Yishmael, the High Priest, saw only the vision of an angel (Rav Hai Gaon), most commentaries maintain that this was a prophecy seen by the High Priest upon entering the Holy of Holies (Ḥayyim ben Yitzḥak and others). The revelation in this vision is not in God's desire for man's blessing, but in the essence of the blessing. The blessing which Rabbi Yishmael ben Elisha blesses God indicates the essence of all the blessings which we recite (Rav Shem Tov ibn Shaprut). The blessing does not offer praise or thanks to God, for God does not require our praise. Rather, it is a supplication that God will increase the bounty that He bestows upon the world. Blessing means adding to the good that already exists. God's will is to be blessed, meaning that God wills that people pray to Him and request that He continue to lead them with loving-kindness and mercy (Rashba).

Moment – רֶגַע: A moment does not denote a specific quantity of time. Rather, it is an expression usually denoting an extremely short, unquantifiable period of time. Therefore, the moment is explained in different places as being of various durations, without it being considered a contradiction. Consequently, a distinction must be drawn between this imprecise moment and the moment used in the precise mathematical sense, as it appears in the Talmud for astronomical calculations. The moment [*rega*] is 1/76 of a *ḥelek*, which is in turn 1/1,080 of an hour; a moment in that sense is 1/80,080 of an hour. A variant text of the Gemara establishes a *rega* at 0.044 seconds, which is close to the above calculation.

**HALAKHA**

One must not placate a person while he is in the throes of his anger – שֶׁאֵין מְרַצִּין לוֹ לְאָדָם בִּשְׁעַת כַּעֲסוֹ: Based on this Gemara, the Sages concluded that one should refrain from saying things, even positive things, when he is certain that they will not be accepted by his intended audience. This includes placating a person when he is angry. Rather, he should wait until his anger subsides somewhat (Rambam *Sefer HaMadda*, *Hilkhot De'ot* 5:7).

הַשְׁתָּא דַּעַת בְּהֶמְתּוֹ לָא הֲוָה יָדַע – דַּעַת עֶלְיוֹן הֲוָה יָדַע?

This should not be understood to mean that Balaam was a full-fledged prophet. Now, clearly, Balaam **did not know the mind of his animal; and he did know the mind of the Most High?** If he could not understand the rebuke of his donkey, he was certainly unable to understand the mind of the Most High.

אֶלָּא: מְלַמֵּד, שֶׁהָיָה יוֹדֵעַ לְכַוֵּין אוֹתָהּ שָׁעָה שֶׁהַקָּדוֹשׁ בָּרוּךְ הוּא כּוֹעֵס בָּהּ.

**Rather, this** verse from Numbers **teaches that** Balaam **was able** to precisely **determine the hour that the Holy One, Blessed be He, is angry.**[N] At that moment, Balaam would utter his curse and, through God's anger, it would be fulfilled.

וְהַיְינוּ דְּאָמַר לְהוּ נָבִיא לְיִשְׂרָאֵל: "עַמִּי זְכָר נָא מַה יָּעַץ בָּלָק מֶלֶךְ מוֹאָב" וגו׳. מַאי "לְמַעַן דַּעַת צִדְקוֹת ה׳"?

**And that is what the prophet said to Israel: "My nation, remember what Balak king of Moab advised,** and how Balaam, son of Beor, responded; from Shittim to Gilgal, so that you may know the righteous acts of the Lord" (Micah 6:5). **What is** meant by the statement: **"So that you may know the righteous acts of the Lord"?**

אָמַר רַבִּי אֶלְעָזָר, אָמַר לָהֶם הַקָּדוֹשׁ בָּרוּךְ הוּא לְיִשְׂרָאֵל: דְּעוּ כַּמָּה צְדָקוֹת עָשִׂיתִי עִמָּכֶם שֶׁלֹּא כָּעַסְתִּי בִּימֵי בִּלְעָם הָרָשָׁע, שֶׁאִלְמָלֵי כָּעַסְתִּי – לֹא נִשְׁתַּיֵּיר מִשּׂוֹנְאֵיהֶם שֶׁל יִשְׂרָאֵל שָׂרִיד וּפָלִיט;

**Rabbi Elazar said** that **the Holy One, Blessed be He, said to Israel: Know how many acts of kindness I performed on your behalf, that I did not become angry during the days of Balaam the wicked, for had I become angry, there would have been no remnant or survivor remaining among the enemies of Israel,** a euphemism for Israel itself. Instead, God restrained His anger and Balaam's curse went unfulfilled.

וְהַיְינוּ דְּקָאָמַר לֵיהּ בִּלְעָם לְבָלָק: "מָה אֶקֹּב לֹא קַבֹּה אֵל וּמָה אֶזְעֹם לֹא זָעַם ה׳", מְלַמֵּד, שֶׁכָּל אוֹתָן הַיָּמִים לֹא זָעַם.

**And that is what Balaam said to Balak: "How can I curse whom God has not cursed? And how can I condemn whom God has not condemned?"** (Numbers 23:8). This verse **teaches that all those days,** God **was not angry.**

וְכַמָּה זַעְמוֹ? – רֶגַע. וְכַמָּה "רֶגַע"? – אָמַר רַבִּי אָבִין וְאִיתֵּימָא רַבִּי אָבִינָא: רֶגַע כְּמֵימְרֵיהּ.

**And how long does His anger** last? God's anger lasts **a moment. And how long is a moment? Rabbi Avin, and some say Rabbi Avina, said:** A moment lasts as long as it takes **to say it** [*rega*].

וּמְנָא לַן דִּרְגַע רָתַח? – שֶׁנֶּאֱמַר: "כִּי רֶגַע בְּאַפּוֹ חַיִּים בִּרְצוֹנוֹ". וְאִי בָּעֵית אֵימָא, מֵהָכָא: "חֲבִי כִמְעַט רֶגַע עַד יַעֲבׇר זָעַם".

**From where do we** derive that God **is** only **angry for a moment? As it is stated: "His anger is but for a moment, His favor, for a lifetime"** (Psalms 30:6). **And if you wish, say** instead, **from here,** as it is stated: **"Hide yourself for a brief moment, until the anger passes"** (Isaiah 26:20), meaning that God's anger passes in a mere moment.

וְאֵימַת רָתַח? אָמַר אַבָּיֵי: בְּהָנָךְ תְּלָת שָׁעֵי קַמַּיְיתָא, כִּי חִיוְּרָא כַּרְבַּלְתָּא דְּתַרְנְגוֹלָא וְקָאֵי אַחַד כַּרְעָא.

The Gemara asks: **When is** the Holy One, Blessed be He, **angry? Abaye said:** God's anger is revealed through animals. **During the first three hours** of the day, **when the sun whitens the crest of the rooster**[B] **and it stands on one leg.** When it appears that its life has left him and he suddenly turns white, that is when God is angry.

כָּל שַׁעְתָּא וְשַׁעְתָּא נַמִי קָאֵי הָכִי!

The Gemara asks: The rooster **also stands that way every hour.** What kind of sign is this?

כָּל שַׁעְתָּא – אִית בֵּיהּ שׁוּרְיָיקֵי סוּמָּקֵי, בְּהַהִיא שַׁעְתָּא – לֵית בֵּיהּ שׁוּרְיָיקֵי סוּמָּקֵי.

The Gemara answers: The difference is that **every** other **hour** when the rooster stands in that way, **there are red streaks** in his crest. But **when** God is angry, **there are no red streaks** in his crest.

הַהוּא מִינָא דַּהֲוָה בְּשִׁבָבוּתֵיהּ דְּרַבִּי יְהוֹשֻׁעַ בֶּן לֵוִי, הֲוָה קָא מְצַעֵר לֵיהּ טוּבָא בִּקְרָאֵי. יוֹמָא חַד שְׁקַל תַּרְנְגוֹלָא וְאוֹקְמֵיהּ בֵּין כַּרְעֵיהּ דְּעַרְסָא וְעַיֵּין בֵּיהּ, סָבַר: כִּי מָטָא הַהִיא שַׁעְתָּא, אֲלַטְיֵיהּ. כִּי מָטָא הַהִיא שַׁעְתָּא נִיִּים. אָמַר: שְׁמַע מִינַּהּ לָאו אוֹרַח אַרְעָא לְמֶעְבַּד הָכִי, "וְרַחֲמָיו עַל כׇּל מַעֲשָׂיו" כְּתִיב,

The Gemara relates: **A certain heretic**[B] **who was in Rabbi Yehoshua ben Levi's neighborhood would upset him** by incessantly challenging the legitimacy of **verses. One day,** Rabbi Yehoshua ben Levi **took a rooster and placed it between the legs of the bed** upon which he sat **and looked at it. He thought: When the moment** of God's anger **arrives, I will curse him** and be rid of him. **When the moment** of God's anger **arrived,** Rabbi Yehoshua ben Levi **slept.** When he woke up, **he said** to himself: **Conclude from** the fact that I nodded off **that it is not proper conduct to do so,** to curse people, even if they are wicked. **"His mercy is over all His creations"** (Psalms 145:9) **is written** even with regard to sinners.

וּכְתִיב: "גַּם עֲנוֹשׁ לַצַּדִּיק לֹא טוֹב".

Moreover, it is inappropriate to cause the punishment of another, as **it is written: "Punishment, even for the righteous, is not good"** (Proverbs 17:26), even for a righteous person, it is improper to punish another.

### NOTES

**That the Holy One, Blessed be He, is angry – שֶׁהַקָּדוֹשׁ בָּרוּךְ הוּא כּוֹעֵס:** There are, of course, many verses in which the wrath of God is mentioned. However, the question was if there is a fixed period of anger each day, with no direct connection to specific transgressions (*Tziyyun LeNefesh Ḥayya*).

### BACKGROUND

**The crest of the rooster – כַּרְבַּלְתָּא דְּתַרְנְגוֹלָא:**

Rooster and its crest

**Heretic – מִינָא:** This heretic belonged to one of the many sects of heretics that were prevalent at that time. The heretics were primarily Christian and non-Christian Gnostics who had significant expertise in the Bible. They sought proof in the Bible for their belief in duality and in God's rejection of Israel. They also tried to undermine the significance of the Bible by raising internal contradictions.

In their war against Jews and Judaism, these heretics often resorted to incitement and slander before the Roman authorities. The problem became so acute that the Sages were forced to add a nineteenth blessing to the *Amida* prayer, the blessing of the heretics, praying for the demise of these heretics and slanderers.

תָּנָא מִשְּׁמֵיהּ דְּרַבִּי מֵאִיר: בְּשָׁעָה שֶׁהַחַמָּה זוֹרַחַת, וְכׇל מַלְכֵי מִזְרָח וּמַעֲרָב מַנִּיחִים כִּתְרֵיהֶם בְּרָאשֵׁיהֶם וּמִשְׁתַּחֲוִים לַחַמָּה, מִיָּד כּוֹעֵס הַקָּדוֹשׁ בָּרוּךְ הוּא.

Explaining the cause of God's anger, **it is taught in the name of Rabbi Meir: When the sun rises and the kings of the East and the West place their crowns on their heads and bow down to the sun, the Holy One, Blessed be He, immediately grows angry.** Since this occurs in the early hours every day, God becomes angry at His world at that moment every day.

וְאָמַר רַבִּי יוֹחָנָן מִשּׁוּם רַבִּי יוֹסֵי: טוֹבָה מַרְדּוּת אַחַת בְּלִבּוֹ שֶׁל אָדָם יוֹתֵר מִכַּמָּה מַלְקִיּוֹת, שֶׁנֶּאֱמַר: ״וְרִדְּפָה אֶת מְאַהֲבֶיהָ וגו׳ וְאָמְרָה אֵלְכָה וְאָשׁוּבָה אֶל אִישִׁי הָרִאשׁוֹן כִּי טוֹב לִי אָז מֵעַתָּה״; וְרֵישׁ לָקִישׁ אָמַר: יוֹתֵר מִמֵּאָה מַלְקִיּוֹת, שֶׁנֶּאֱמַר: ״תֵּחַת גְּעָרָה בְמֵבִין מֵהַכּוֹת כְּסִיל מֵאָה״.

**And Rabbi Yoḥanan said in the name of Rabbi Yosei: A single regret** or pang of guilt **in one's heart is preferable to many lashes**[N] administered by others that cause only physical pain, **as it is stated: "And she chases her lovers,** but she does not overtake them; she seeks them, but she will not find them; **and she will say 'I will go and return to my first husband; for it was better for me then than now'"** (Hosea 2:9). Remorse is more effective than any externally imposed punishment listed in the verses that follow (Hosea 2:11–19). **And Reish Lakish said** that in the Bible, it seems that such remorse is **preferable to one hundred lashes, as it is stated: "A rebuke enters deeper into a man of understanding than a hundred lashes to a fool"** (Proverbs 17:10).

וְאָמַר רַבִּי יוֹחָנָן מִשּׁוּם רַבִּי יוֹסֵי: שְׁלֹשָׁה דְּבָרִים בִּקֵּשׁ מֹשֶׁה מִלִּפְנֵי הַקָּדוֹשׁ בָּרוּךְ הוּא, וְנָתַן לוֹ. בִּקֵּשׁ שֶׁתִּשְׁרֶה שְׁכִינָה עַל יִשְׂרָאֵל, וְנָתַן לוֹ, שֶׁנֶּאֱמַר: ״הֲלוֹא בְּלֶכְתְּךָ עִמָּנוּ״.

**And Rabbi Yoḥanan said in the name of Rabbi Yosei** regarding Moses' request that the Divine Presence rest upon Israel as it once had: Moses **requested three things from the Holy One, Blessed be He,** at that time, **all of which were granted him. He requested that the Divine Presence rest upon Israel** and not leave, **and He granted** it **to him, as it is stated:** "For how can it be known that I have found grace in Your sight, I and Your people? **Is it not in that You go with us,** so that we are distinguished, I and Your people, from all the people that are on the face of the earth?" (Exodus 33:16). The request: Is it not in that You go with us, refers to the resting of the Divine Presence upon Israel.

בִּקֵּשׁ שֶׁלֹּא תִּשְׁרֶה שְׁכִינָה עַל אוּמּוֹת הָעוֹלָם, וְנָתַן לוֹ, שֶׁנֶּאֱמַר: ״וְנִפְלֵינוּ אֲנִי וְעַמְּךָ״.

Moses **requested that the Divine Presence not rest upon the nations of the world, and He granted** it **to him, as it is stated: "So that we are distinguished, I and Your people,** from all the people on the face of the earth" (Exodus 33:16).

בִּקֵּשׁ לְהוֹדִיעוֹ דְּרָכָיו שֶׁל הַקָּדוֹשׁ בָּרוּךְ הוּא, וְנָתַן לוֹ, שֶׁנֶּאֱמַר: ״הוֹדִיעֵנִי נָא אֶת דְּרָכֶיךָ״. אָמַר לְפָנָיו: רִבּוֹנוֹ שֶׁל עוֹלָם! מִפְּנֵי מָה יֵשׁ צַדִּיק וְטוֹב לוֹ, וְיֵשׁ צַדִּיק וְרַע לוֹ, יֵשׁ רָשָׁע וְטוֹב לוֹ, וְיֵשׁ רָשָׁע וְרַע לוֹ? אָמַר לוֹ: מֹשֶׁה, צַדִּיק וְטוֹב לוֹ – צַדִּיק בֶּן צַדִּיק, צַדִּיק וְרַע לוֹ – צַדִּיק בֶּן רָשָׁע, רָשָׁע וְטוֹב לוֹ – רָשָׁע בֶּן צַדִּיק, רָשָׁע וְרַע לוֹ – רָשָׁע בֶּן רָשָׁע.

Lastly, Moses **requested that the ways** in which **God** conducts the **world be revealed to him, and He granted it to him, as it is stated: "Show me Your ways** and I will know You" (Exodus 33:13).

Moses **said before** God: **Master of the Universe. Why is it that** the **righteous prosper, the righteous suffer,** the **wicked prosper,** the **wicked suffer?**

God **said to him: Moses, the righteous** person **who prospers is a righteous** person, **the son of a righteous** person, who is rewarded for the actions of his ancestors. **The righteous** person **who suffers is a righteous** person, **the son of a wicked** person, who is punished for the transgressions of his ancestors. **The wicked** person **who prospers is a wicked** person, **the son of a righteous** person, who is rewarded for the actions of his ancestors. **The wicked** person **who suffers is a wicked person, the son of a wicked person,** who is punished for the transgressions of his ancestors.

אָמַר מָר: צַדִּיק וְטוֹב לוֹ – צַדִּיק בֶּן צַדִּיק, צַדִּיק וְרַע לוֹ – צַדִּיק בֶּן רָשָׁע. אִינִי? וְהָא כְּתִיב: ״פֹּקֵד עֲוֹן אָבוֹת עַל בָּנִים״, וּכְתִיב: ״וּבָנִים לֹא יוּמְתוּ עַל אָבוֹת״, וּרְמִינַן קְרָאֵי אַהֲדָדֵי,

The Gemara expands upon these righteous and wicked individuals: **The Master said: The righteous** person **who prospers is a righteous** person, **the son of a righteous** person. **The righteous** person **who suffers is a righteous** person, **the son of a wicked** person. The Gemara asks: **Is it so** that one is always punished for his ancestors' transgressions? **Isn't it written: "He visits iniquity of the fathers upon the children,** and upon the children's children, unto the third and fourth generations" (Exodus 34:7). **And it is written** elsewhere: "Fathers shall not die for their children, **and children shall not be put to death for the fathers;** every man shall die for his own transgression" (Deuteronomy 24:16). **And** the Gemara **raises a contradiction between the two verses.**

וּמְשַׁנֵּינַן: לָא קַשְׁיָא, הָא – כְּשֶׁאוֹחֲזִין מַעֲשֵׂה אֲבוֹתֵיהֶם בִּידֵיהֶם, הָא – כְּשֶׁאֵין אוֹחֲזִין מַעֲשֵׂה אֲבוֹתֵיהֶם בִּידֵיהֶם!

The Gemara **resolves** the contradiction: **This is not difficult. This** verse from Exodus, which states that God punishes descendants for the transgressions of their ancestors, refers to a case **where they adopt the actions of their ancestors as their own. While this** verse from Deuteronomy, which states that descendants are not punished for the actions of their ancestors, refers to a case **where they do not adopt the actions of their ancestors as their own,** as it is stated: "I visit iniquity of the fathers upon the children, and upon the third and fourth generations of my enemies" (Exodus 20:5).

NOTES

**A single regret in one's heart is preferable to many lashes – טוֹבָה מַרְדּוּת אַחַת בְּלִבּוֹ שֶׁל אָדָם יוֹתֵר מִכַּמָּה מַלְקִיּוֹת:** With this statement, the Sages display a profound understanding of the essence of education. One does not learn a lesson by having it beaten into him; rather, he learns when he is approached in a sensitive manner. Genuine awe of God does not come through fear, but through profound love. This method of teaching, which is widely accepted in the contemporary world, has its roots in the prophetic statements of the Sages (*Ein Ayah*).

אֶלָּא, הָכִי קָאָמַר לֵיהּ: צַדִּיק וְטוֹב לוֹ – צַדִּיק גָּמוּר, צַדִּיק וְרַע לוֹ – צַדִּיק שֶׁאֵינוֹ גָּמוּר, רָשָׁע וְטוֹב לוֹ – רָשָׁע שֶׁאֵינוֹ גָּמוּר, רָשָׁע וְרַע לוֹ – רָשָׁע גָּמוּר.

A righteous person is clearly not punished for the transgressions of his ancestors. **Rather,** it must be that God **said to** Moses **as follows:**

**The righteous** person **who prospers is a completely righteous** person whose actions are entirely good and whose reward is entirely good both in this world and in the World-to-Come.

**The righteous** person **who suffers is** one who is **not a completely righteous** person. Because he does have some transgressions, he is punished in this world so that he will receive a complete reward in the World-to-Come.

**The wicked** person **who prospers is** one who is **not a completely wicked** person. God rewards him in this world for the good deeds that he performed, so that he will receive a complete punishment in the World-to-Come.

Finally, **the wicked** person **who suffers is a completely wicked** person. Since he performed absolutely no mitzvot and deserves no reward, he receives only punishment both in this world and in the World-to-Come (Maharsha).

וּפְלִיגָא דְּרַבִּי מֵאִיר, דְּאָמַר רַבִּי מֵאִיר: שְׁתַּיִם נָתְנוּ לוֹ וְאַחַת לֹא נָתְנוּ לוֹ, שֶׁנֶּאֱמַר: ״וְחַנֹּתִי אֶת אֲשֶׁר אָחֹן״ – אַף עַל פִּי שֶׁאֵינוֹ הָגוּן, ״וְרִחַמְתִּי אֶת אֲשֶׁר אֲרַחֵם״ – אַף עַל פִּי שֶׁאֵינוֹ הָגוּן.

Rabbi Yoḥanan's opinion, that God granted Moses all three of his requests, **disagrees with** that of **Rabbi Meir,** as **Rabbi Meir said: Two** of Moses' requests **were granted to him, and one was not granted to him.** God granted him that the Divine Presence would rest upon Israel and not leave, and that the Divine Presence would not rest upon the nations of the world, but God did not reveal to Moses the ways in which He conducts the world. **As it is said: "And I will be gracious to whom I will be gracious"** (Exodus 33:19); in His mercy, God bestows His grace upon every person, **even though he is not worthy.** Similarly, God says: **"And I will have mercy upon whom I will have mercy," even though he is not worthy.** According to Rabbi Meir, the way in which God conducts the world and bestows grace and mercy was not revealed even to Moses.

״וַיֹּאמֶר לֹא תוּכַל לִרְאוֹת אֶת פָּנָי״, תָּנָא מִשְּׁמֵיהּ דְּרַבִּי יְהוֹשֻׁעַ בֶּן קָרְחָה, כָּךְ אָמַר לוֹ הַקָּדוֹשׁ בָּרוּךְ הוּא לְמֹשֶׁה: כְּשֶׁרָצִיתִי – לֹא רָצִיתָ, עַכְשָׁיו שֶׁאַתָּה רוֹצֶה – אֵינִי רוֹצֶה.

The Gemara continues to cite the Sages' explanation of verses that require clarification on the same topic. With regard to God's statement to Moses, **"And He said: 'You cannot see My face,** for man shall not see Me and live'" (Exodus 33:20), **it was taught in the name of Rabbi Yehoshua ben Korḥa that the Holy One, Blessed be He, said to** Moses **as follows: When I wanted** to show you My glory at the burning bush, **you did not want** to see it, as it is stated: "And Moses concealed his face, fearing to gaze upon God" (Exodus 3:6). But **now that you want** to see My glory, as you said: "Show me Your glory," **I do not want**[N] to show it to you. Rabbi Yehoshua ben Korḥa interprets Moses' initial refusal to look upon God's glory negatively, as he rebuffed God's desire to be close to him.

וּפְלִיגָא דְּרַבִּי שְׁמוּאֵל בַּר נַחְמָנִי אָמַר רַבִּי יוֹנָתָן; דְּאָמַר רַבִּי שְׁמוּאֵל בַּר נַחְמָנִי אָמַר רַבִּי יוֹנָתָן, בִּשְׂכַר שָׁלֹשׁ זָכָה לְשָׁלֹשׁ:

This **disagrees with** that which **Rabbi Shmuel bar Naḥmani said** that Rabbi Yonatan said, as **Rabbi Shmuel bar Naḥmani said** that **Rabbi Yonatan said:** Specifically **as a reward for three** acts of humility in averting his glance at the burning bush, Moses **was privileged** to experience **three** great revelations:

בִּשְׂכַר ״וַיַּסְתֵּר מֹשֶׁה פָּנָיו״ – זָכָה לְקְלַסְתֵּר פָּנִים. בִּשְׂכַר ״כִּי יָרֵא״ – זָכָה לְ״וַיִּירְאוּ מִגֶּשֶׁת אֵלָיו״, בִּשְׂכַר ״מֵהַבִּיט״ – זָכָה לְ״וּתְמֻנַת ה׳ יַבִּיט״.

Because "Moses **concealed his face,** fearing to gaze upon God" (Exodus 3:6), **he was privileged to** have his **countenance** [*kelaster*][L] glow.

Because **he "feared," he was privileged that "they feared to approach him"** (Exodus 34:30).

Because he did not **"gaze," he was privileged to "behold the likeness of the Lord"** (Numbers 12:8).

״וַהֲסִרֹתִי אֶת כַּפִּי וְרָאִיתָ אֶת אֲחֹרָי״ – אָמַר רַב חָנָא בַּר בִּיזְנָא אָמַר רַבִּי שִׁמְעוֹן חֲסִידָא: מְלַמֵּד שֶׁהֶרְאָה הַקָּדוֹשׁ בָּרוּךְ הוּא לְמֹשֶׁה קֶשֶׁר שֶׁל תְּפִילִּין.

What did Moses see? It is said: **"And I will remove My hand, and you will see My back,** but My face you will not see" (Exodus 33:23). **Rav Ḥana bar Bizna said in the name of Rabbi Shimon Ḥasida,** the expression: "And you will see My back," should be understood as follows: **This teaches that the Holy One, Blessed be He,** Who, as mentioned above, wears phylacteries, **showed him the knot of the phylacteries**[B] of His head, which is worn on the back of the head.

NOTES

**When I wanted you did not want, now that you want, I do not want** – כְּשֶׁרָצִיתִי לֹא רָצִיתָ עַכְשָׁיו שֶׁאַתָּה רוֹצֶה אֵינִי רוֹצֶה: Although the continuation of the verse in Exodus cited by Rabbi Yehoshua ben Korḥa states: "For man shall not see Me and live," had Moses not concealed his face at the burning bush, he would have been permitted to witness God's glory. This statement should not be understood as an explanation of why Moses could not see God's glory. It is, rather, a promise to Moses that since he, master of all prophets, was not privileged to witness God's glory, no other man would be permitted to gaze upon God in the future. The burning bush took place at a moment just prior to the Exodus, at a time when Israel was on an elevated spiritual level and, as their leader, Moses would have merited a close encounter with God. Later, in the wake of their sins in the desert, that window of opportunity closed.

LANGUAGE

**Countenance** [*kelaster*]– קְלַסְתֵּר: The source of this word is unclear. Some maintain that it derives from the Latin caelatura, a graven image. Others claim that it derives from the Greek εἰκονάστηρ, meaning image or radiance of the countenance.

BACKGROUND

**Knot of the phylacteries** – קֶשֶׁר שֶׁל תְּפִילִּין: This is the knot tied on the phylacteries of the head in the back of the head in the form of an inverted *dalet*, another of the letters comprising God's name, *Shaddai*.

Knot of the phylacteries of the head

וְאָמַר רַבִּי יוֹחָנָן מִשּׁוּם רַבִּי יוֹסֵי: כָּל דִּבּוּר וְדִבּוּר שֶׁיָּצָא מִפִּי הַקָּדוֹשׁ בָּרוּךְ הוּא לְטוֹבָה, אֲפִילּוּ עַל תְּנַאי – לֹא חָזַר בּוֹ.

On this subject, **Rabbi Yoḥanan said in the name of Rabbi Yosei: Every statement** to a person or to a nation **that emerged from the mouth of the Holy One, Blessed be He,** with a promise **of good, even if it was conditional, He did not renege** on it. Ultimately, every promise made by God will be fulfilled.

מְנָא לָן? – מִמֹּשֶׁה רַבֵּינוּ שֶׁנֶּאֱמַר: "הֶרֶף מִמֶּנִּי וְאַשְׁמִידֵם וגו' וְאֶעֱשֶׂה אוֹתְךָ לְגוֹי עָצוּם". אַף עַל גַּב דִּבְעָא מֹשֶׁה רַחֲמֵי עֲלָהּ דְּמִלְּתָא וּבַטְלָהּ, אֲפִילּוּ הָכִי אוֹקְמָהּ בְּזַרְעֵיהּ, שֶׁנֶּאֱמַר: "בְּנֵי מֹשֶׁה גֵּרְשׁוֹם וֶאֱלִיעֶזֶר. וַיִּהְיוּ בְנֵי אֱלִיעֶזֶר רְחַבְיָה הָרֹאשׁ וגו' וּבְנֵי רְחַבְיָה רָבוּ לְמָעְלָה" וגו'.

**From where do we** derive that all of God's promises are fulfilled? We know this **from Moses our teacher,** as God promised and **said: "Leave Me alone; I will destroy them** and blot out their name from under heaven; **and I will make from you a nation mightier** and greater than they" (Deuteronomy 9:14). **Even though** Moses **prayed** to have the decree repealed, **and it was nullified, the promise was fulfilled** and Moses' **descendants** became a nation mightier and greater than the 600,000 Israelites in the desert. **As it is stated** with regard to the Levites: "**The sons of** Moses: **Gershom and Eliezer… and the sons of Eliezer were Reḥaviya the chief.** And Eliezer had no other sons; **and the sons of Reḥaviya were very many**" (I Chronicles 23:15–17).

וְתָנֵי רַב יוֹסֵף: "לְמָעְלָה" – מִשִּׁשִּׁים רִבּוֹא, אָתְיָא "רְבִיָּה" "רְבִיָּה", כְּתִיב הָכָא "רָבוּ לְמָעְלָה", וּכְתִיב הָתָם "וּבְנֵי יִשְׂרָאֵל פָּרוּ וַיִּשְׁרְצוּ וַיִּרְבּוּ".

**And Rav Yosef taught** in a *baraita*: **"Many"** means more **than 600,000.** This is learned through a verbal analogy between the words **many** and **many. It is written here** with regard to Reḥaviya's sons: **"Were very many." And it is written there** with regard to the Israelites in Egypt: **"And the children of Israel became numerous and multiplied and were very many,** and waxed exceeding mighty; and the land was filled with them" (Exodus 1:7). Just as when the children of Israel were in Egypt, very many meant that there were 600,000 of them, so too the descendants of Reḥaviya were 600,000.

Perek **I**
Daf **7** Amud **b**

אָמַר רַבִּי יוֹחָנָן מִשּׁוּם רַבִּי שִׁמְעוֹן בֶּן יוֹחַי: מִיּוֹם שֶׁבָּרָא הַקָּדוֹשׁ בָּרוּךְ הוּא אֶת הָעוֹלָם לֹא הָיָה אָדָם שֶׁקְּרָאוֹ לְהַקָּדוֹשׁ בָּרוּךְ הוּא "אָדוֹן", עַד שֶׁבָּא אַבְרָהָם וּקְרָאוֹ "אָדוֹן", שֶׁנֶּאֱמַר: "וַיֹּאמַר אֲדֹנָי אֱלֹהִים בַּמָּה אֵדַע כִּי אִירָשֶׁנָּה".

Until now, the Gemara has cited statements made by Rabbi Yoḥanan in the name of the *tanna*, Rabbi Yosei. Now, the Gemara begins to cite what **Rabbi Yoḥanan said in the name of Rabbi Shimon ben Yoḥai:**[P] **From the day that the Holy One, Blessed be He, created the world there was no person who called him "Lord" until Abraham came and called him Lord.**[N] **As it is stated: "And he said, 'My Lord, God, by what shall I know that I will inherit it?'"** (Genesis 15:8).

אָמַר רַב: אַף דָּנִיֵּאל לֹא נַעֲנָה אֶלָּא בִּשְׁבִיל אַבְרָהָם, שֶׁנֶּאֱמַר: "וְעַתָּה שְׁמַע אֱלֹהֵינוּ אֶל תְּפִלַּת עַבְדְּךָ וְאֶל תַּחֲנוּנָיו וְהָאֵר פָּנֶיךָ עַל מִקְדָּשְׁךָ הַשָּׁמֵם לְמַעַן אֲדֹנָי". "לְמַעַנְךָ" מִבָּעֵי לֵיהּ!

The Gemara cites another statement extolling that virtue of Abraham is mentioned, as **Rav said: Even Daniel's prayers were only answered on account of Abraham, as it is stated: "And now listen, God, to the prayer of Your servant and to his supplication; and cause Your face to shine upon Your desolate Temple, for the sake of the Lord"** (Daniel 9:17). The verse **should have said:** And cause Your face to shine upon Your desolate Temple, **for Your sake,** as Daniel was addressing the Lord.

אֶלָּא – לְמַעַן אַבְרָהָם שֶׁקְּרָאֲךָ "אָדוֹן".

**Rather,** this verse contains an allusion that the prayer should be accepted **for the sake of Abraham, who called You, Lord.** Daniel utilized that name of God in order to evoke Abraham's virtue and enhance his prayer.

**NOTES**

**There was no person who called him "Lord" until Abraham came – לֹא הָיָה אָדָם שֶׁקְּרָאוֹ לְהַקָּדוֹשׁ בָּרוּךְ הוּא "אָדוֹן" עַד שֶׁבָּא אַבְרָהָם וכו':** The virtue in calling Him Lord is not merely because of its novelty, but because of its essence. The name Lord expresses a new concept in the perception that God is the Lord of the world. He has the ability to implement His will in the world by using the laws of nature or by transcending them. This was the perception introduced by Abraham, who was the first to disseminate the concept of divine Providence in the world (*HaKotev; Tziyyun LeNefesh Ḥayya*).

**PERSONALITIES**

**Rabbi Shimon ben Yoḥai – רַבִּי שִׁמְעוֹן בֶּן יוֹחַי:** Rabbi Shimon ben Yoḥai is among the greatest *tanna'im* of the generation prior to the redaction of the Mishna. Rabbi Shimon was the preeminent student of Rabbi Akiva and he considered himself Rabbi Akiva's spiritual heir. Rabbi Akiva had a great deal of respect for his student, and said: It is enough for you that I and your Creator recognize your strength. Rabbi Shimon's greatness was manifest in his mastery of both *halakha* and *aggada*, and his statements can be found on all topics in every tractate of the Talmud. Although *halakha* is not always ruled in accordance with Rabbi Shimon ben Yoḥai's opinion, especially in disputes with Rabbi Yosei and Rabbi Yehuda, nevertheless, with regard to several core issues, the *halakha* is ruled in accordance with his opinion. He had his own, unique method of deriving *halakha* from the Torah. He factors in the rationale of the verse and infers halakhic conclusions from Bible based on the spirit and purpose of the law.

Rabbi Shimon traveled to Rome as an emissary of the people, but he harbored profound enmity toward the Romans. Because he made no attempt to conceal his feelings, he was sentenced to death and forced into hiding for many years.

He was an ascetic by nature who was very exacting, and was famous in his generation for his righteousness and his performance of miracles. There are many anecdotes related in the Talmud about miraculous acts that he performed.

The *Sifrei*, a collection of halakhic derivations on Numbers and Deuteronomy, was developed in his study hall. He is also the primary character in the fundamental book of kabbala, the *Zohar*. His greatest students were Rabbi Yehuda HaNasi, Rabbi Shimon ben Yehuda, and his son, Rabbi Elazar ben Rabbi Shimon, who was also among the most prominent *tanna'im*.

## NOTES

**No one thanked to the Holy One, Blessed be He, until Leah came** – **לֹא הָיָה אָדָם שֶׁהוֹדָה לְהַקָּדוֹשׁ בָּרוּךְ הוּא עַד שֶׁבָּאתָה לֵאָה וכו׳**: Thanksgiving in which one offers thanks for the good that has been bestowed upon him existed before Leah. Leah's innovation was offering thanks for what God had bestowed, and being satisfied with it (Rashba).

**See the difference between my son and the son of my father-in-law** – **רְאוּ מַה בֵּין בְּנִי לְבֶן חָמִי**: This midrash is aided by the similarity between the word son [*ben*] and the word between [*bein*]. It only uses the word *bein* once but it is understood as if it was written twice. This statement comes to praise Reuben. Although the impression one gets from Jacob's blessing is that Reuben was flawed, nevertheless, he had praiseworthy qualities as well.

**Who has made desolations** – **אֲשֶׁר שָׂם שַׁמּוֹת**: The emendation of this verse is also because it is difficult to accept it literally. It is difficult to accept: "Who has made desolations upon the earth" as praise for God. Therefore, an added layer of meaning is revealed: Do not read desolations [*shamot*]; rather, names [*shemot*]. The Holy One, Blessed be He, does not create and destroy things in the world, nor is He responsible for its ill fate. God only creates the external framework, i.e., the potential within which individuals are able to exercise their free will. Consequently, the name affects one's life indicates that God gives guidance and direction to a person's actions without obligating him to adopt a particular path, good or evil. The names given people enable them to realize their potential (*HaKotev*, Rashba).

**The war of Gog and Magog** – **מִלְחֶמֶת גּוֹג וּמָגוֹג**: According to tradition, the war of Gog and Magog is the suffering that will precede the advent of the Messiah. It is described most clearly in Ezekiel (38–39). However, with regard to this topic of the great war that will precede the redemption, the prophet said: "Of whom I spoke in old time by My servants the prophets of Israel, that prophesied in those days" (Ezekiel 38:17). In the words of the prophets, there are explicit and indirect references to this great war. One unique aspect of this war is that it will not merely be a war against Israel, but rather, against God Himself. Therefore, the war described in Psalms 2, where it is stated: "The kings of the earth stand up, and the rulers take counsel together, against the Lord, and against His Messiah," is identified as the war of Gog and Magog.

וְאָמַר רַבִּי יוֹחָנָן מִשּׁוּם רַבִּי שִׁמְעוֹן בֶּן יוֹחַי: מִנַּיִן שֶׁאֵין מְרַצִּין לוֹ לְאָדָם בִּשְׁעַת כַּעֲסוֹ? – שֶׁנֶּאֱמַר: ״פָּנַי יֵלֵכוּ וַהֲנִחֹתִי לָךְ״.

**And Rabbi Yoḥanan said in the name of Rabbi Shimon ben Yoḥai: From where** is it derived **that one must not placate a person while** the person in the throes of **his anger? As it is stated: "My face will go, and I will give you rest"** (Exodus 33:14).

וְאָמַר רַבִּי יוֹחָנָן מִשּׁוּם רַבִּי שִׁמְעוֹן בֶּן יוֹחַי: מִיּוֹם שֶׁבָּרָא הַקָּדוֹשׁ בָּרוּךְ הוּא אֶת עוֹלָמוֹ לֹא הָיָה אָדָם שֶׁהוֹדָה לְהַקָּדוֹשׁ בָּרוּךְ הוּא עַד שֶׁבָּאתָה לֵאָה וְהוֹדַתּוּ, שֶׁנֶּאֱמַר: ״הַפַּעַם אוֹדֶה אֶת ה׳״.

**And Rabbi Yoḥanan said in the name of Rabbi Shimon ben Yoḥai: From the day the Holy One, Blessed be He, created the world, no one thanked the Holy One, Blessed be He, until Leah came**[N] **and thanked Him, as it is stated:** "And she became pregnant and gave birth to a son, and she said, **'This time I will give thanks to God,'** and thus he was called Judah" (Genesis 29:35).

״רְאוּבֵן״ – אָמַר רַבִּי אֶלְעָזָר, אָמְרָה לֵאָה: רְאוּ מַה בֵּין בְּנִי לְבֶן חָמִי. דְּאִילּוּ בֶּן חָמִי, אַף עַל גַּב דְּמִדַּעְתֵּיהּ זַבְּנֵיהּ לִבְכֵירוּתֵיהּ, דִּכְתִיב: ״וַיִּמְכֹּר אֶת בְּכֹרָתוֹ לְיַעֲקֹב״, חֲזוּ מַה כְּתִיב בֵּיהּ: ״וַיִּשְׂטֹם עֵשָׂו אֶת יַעֲקֹב״,

Tangential to the mention of Leah's son, Judah, and the reason for his name, the Gemara explains the sources for other names, including **Reuben. Rabbi Elazar said:** Reuben's name should be considered a prophecy by Leah, as **Leah said: See** [*re'u*] **the difference between my son** [*beni*] **and the son of my father-in-law,**[N] Esau, son of Isaac. **Even though** Esau **knowingly sold his birthright** to his brother Jacob, **as it is written: "And he sold his birthright to Jacob"** (Genesis 25:33), nonetheless, **behold what is written** about **him: "And Esau hated Jacob"** (Genesis 27:41).

וּכְתִיב: ״וַיֹּאמֶר הֲכִי קָרָא שְׁמוֹ יַעֲקֹב וַיַּעְקְבֵנִי זֶה פַעֲמַיִם״ וגו׳.

Esau was not only angry over Isaac's blessing, but he was angry about another matter as well, **as it is written: "And he said, 'Is he not rightly named Jacob, for he has supplanted me twice?** He took my birthright, and behold, now he has taken my blessing'" (Genesis 27:36). Despite having sold his birthright, he refused to relinquish it.

וְאִילּוּ בְּנִי, אַף עַל גַּב דְּעַל כָּרְחֵיהּ שְׁקַלֵיהּ יוֹסֵף לִבְכֵירוּתֵיהּ מִנֵּיהּ, דִּכְתִיב: ״וּבְחַלְּלוֹ יְצוּעֵי אָבִיו נִתְּנָה בְּכֹרָתוֹ לִבְנֵי יוֹסֵף״, אֲפִילּוּ הָכִי לָא אִקַּנָּא בֵּיהּ, דִּכְתִיב: ״וַיִּשְׁמַע רְאוּבֵן וַיַּצִּלֵהוּ מִיָּדָם״.

**While my son,** Reuben, **even though Joseph took his birthright from him by force, as it is written:** "And the sons of Reuben the firstborn of Israel, for he was the firstborn; **but, since he defiled his father's bed, his birthright was given to the sons of Joseph,** son of Israel" (1 Chronicles 5:1). **Nevertheless, he was not jealous of him, as it is written** when Joseph's brothers sought to kill him: **"And Reuben heard and he saved him from their hands,** saying 'Let us not take his life'" (Genesis 37:21).

״רוּת״ – מַאי ״רוּת״? אָמַר רַבִּי יוֹחָנָן: שֶׁזָּכְתָה וְיָצָא מִמֶּנָּה דָּוִד שֶׁרִיוָּהוּ לְהַקָּדוֹשׁ בָּרוּךְ הוּא בְּשִׁירוֹת וְתִשְׁבָּחוֹת.

Continuing on the topic of names, the Gemara asks: **What is the** meaning of the name **Ruth? Rabbi Yoḥanan said: That she had the privilege that David, who inundated the Holy One, Blessed be He, with songs and praises, would descend from her.** The name Ruth [*Rut*] is etymologically similar in Hebrew to the word inundate [*riva*].

מְנָא לָן דִּשְׁמָא גָּרֵים? – אָמַר רַבִּי אֱלִיעֶזֶר דְּאָמַר קְרָא: ״לְכוּ חֲזוּ מִפְעֲלוֹת ה׳ אֲשֶׁר שָׂם שַׁמּוֹת בָּאָרֶץ״, אַל תִּקְרֵי ״שַׁמּוֹת״ אֶלָּא ״שֵׁמוֹת״.

Regarding the basic assumption that these homiletic interpretations of names are allusions to one's future, the Gemara asks: **From where do** we derive **that the name affects** one's life? **Rabbi Eliezer said** that **the verse says: "Go, see the works of the Lord, who has made desolations** [*shamot*][N] **upon the earth"** (Psalms 46:9). **Do not read** the word as ***shamot*, rather** as ***shemot*, names.** The names given to people are, therefore, "the works of the Lord upon the earth."

וְאָמַר רַבִּי יוֹחָנָן מִשּׁוּם רַבִּי שִׁמְעוֹן בֶּן יוֹחַי: קָשָׁה תַּרְבּוּת רָעָה בְּתוֹךְ בֵּיתוֹ שֶׁל אָדָם יוֹתֵר מִמִּלְחֶמֶת גּוֹג וּמָגוֹג, שֶׁנֶּאֱמַר: ״מִזְמוֹר לְדָוִד בְּבָרְחוֹ מִפְּנֵי אַבְשָׁלוֹם בְּנוֹ״, וּכְתִיב בַּתְרֵיהּ: ״ה׳ מָה רַבּוּ צָרָי רַבִּים קָמִים עָלָי״. וְאִילּוּ גַּבֵּי מִלְחֶמֶת גּוֹג וּמָגוֹג כְּתִיב: ״לָמָּה רָגְשׁוּ גוֹיִם וּלְאֻמִּים יֶהְגּוּ רִיק״, וְאִילּוּ ״מָה רַבּוּ צָרָי״ לָא כְּתִיב.

**And Rabbi Yoḥanan said** other aggadic statements **in the name of Rabbi Shimon ben Yoḥai:** The existence of **wayward** children **in a person's home is more troublesome than the war of Gog and Magog,**[N] the ultimate war, the climax of the travails of Messianic times. **As it is stated: "A Psalm of David, when he fled from his son, Absalom"** (Psalms 3:1). **And it is written thereafter: "Lord, how numerous are my enemies, many have risen against me"** (Psalms 3:2). **While** concerning the war of Gog and Magog, which is alluded to in the second chapter of Psalms, **it is written: "Why are the nations in an uproar? And why do the peoples speak for naught?** The kings of the earth stand up and the rulers take counsel together, against the Lord, and against His anointed… He that sits in heaven laughs, the Lord mocks them" (Psalms 2:1–4). **Yet** in this chapter describing the war of Gog and Magog **"how numerous are my enemies" is not written,** as it is not as difficult as raising a wayward son like Absalom.

"מִזְמוֹר לְדָוִד בְּבָרְחוֹ מִפְּנֵי אַבְשָׁלוֹם בְּנוֹ", "מִזְמוֹר לְדָוִד"? "קִינָה לְדָוִד" מִיבְּעֵי לֵיהּ!

Regarding the opening phrase of the psalm, which serves as its title, the Gemara wonders: It is said: **"A Psalm of David, when fleeing his son, Absalom." A Psalm of David? It should have** said: **A lament of David.**

אָמַר רַבִּי שִׁמְעוֹן בֶּן אֲבִישָׁלוֹם: מָשָׁל לְמָה הַדָּבָר דּוֹמֶה? – לְאָדָם שֶׁיָּצָא עָלָיו שְׁטַר חוֹב, קוֹדֶם שֶׁפְּרָעוֹ הָיָה עָצֵב, לְאַחַר שֶׁפְּרָעוֹ שָׂמַח

**Rabbi Shimon ben Avishalom said a parable: To what is this similar?** It is similar **to a person about whom a promissory note was issued** stating that he must repay a debt to the lender. **Before he repaid it,** he **was despondent,** worried how he will manage to repay the debt. **After he repaid it, he was glad.**

אַף כֵּן דָּוִד, כֵּיוָן שֶׁאָמַר לוֹ הַקָּדוֹשׁ בָּרוּךְ הוּא "הִנְנִי מֵקִים עָלֶיךָ רָעָה מִבֵּיתֶךָ" – הָיָה עָצֵב, אָמַר: שֶׁמָּא עֶבֶד אוֹ מַמְזֵר הוּא, דְּלָא חָיֵיס עֲלַי. כֵּיוָן דַּחֲזָא דְּאַבְשָׁלוֹם הוּא – שָׂמַח, מִשּׁוּם הָכִי אָמַר "מִזְמוֹר".

**So too** was the case with **David. When the Holy One, Blessed be He, told him,**[H] through Natan the prophet, after the incident with Bathsheba, **"Behold, I will raise up evil against you from your house"** (II Samuel 12:11), David **was despondent. He said: Perhaps** it will be **a slave or a** ***mamzer***[B] who will rise up in my house, a person of such lowly status, who **will have no pity on me. But once** David **saw that Absalom was the one** through whom the prophecy was to be fulfilled, **he rejoiced,** as he was certain that Absalom would show him mercy. **That is why** David **said a psalm,** not a lament, thanking God for punishing him in the least severe manner possible.

וְאָמַר רַבִּי יוֹחָנָן מִשּׁוּם רַבִּי שִׁמְעוֹן בֶּן יוֹחַי: מוּתָּר לְהִתְגָּרוֹת בָּרְשָׁעִים בָּעוֹלָם הַזֶּה, שֶׁנֶּאֱמַר: "עֹזְבֵי תוֹרָה יְהַלְלוּ רָשָׁע וְשֹׁמְרֵי תוֹרָה יִתְגָּרוּ בָם".

**And Rabbi Yoḥanan said in the name of Rabbi Shimon ben Yoḥai: One is permitted to provoke the wicked in this world.** Though the ways of the wicked prosper, one is still permitted to provoke them and need not fear (Maharsha), **as it is stated: "Those who abandon the Torah will praise wickedness, and the keepers of the Torah will fight them"** (Proverbs 28:4).

תַּנְיָא נַמִּי הָכִי, רַבִּי דּוֹסְתַּאי בְּרַבִּי מָתוּן אוֹמֵר: מוּתָּר לְהִתְגָּרוֹת בָּרְשָׁעִים בָּעוֹלָם הַזֶּה, שֶׁנֶּאֱמַר: "עֹזְבֵי תוֹרָה יְהַלְלוּ רָשָׁע" וגו׳. וְאִם לָחַשְׁךָ אָדָם לוֹמַר: וְהָא כְּתִיב "אַל תִּתְחַר בַּמְּרֵעִים אַל תְּקַנֵּא בְּעֹשֵׂי עַוְלָה"! אֱמוֹר לוֹ: מִי שֶׁלִּבּוֹ נוֹקְפוֹ אוֹמֵר כֵּן. אֶלָּא: "אַל תִּתְחַר בַּמְּרֵעִים" – לִהְיוֹת כַּמְּרֵעִים, "אַל תְּקַנֵּא בְּעֹשֵׂי עַוְלָה" – לִהְיוֹת כְּעוֹשֵׂי עַוְלָה,

**That** statement **was also taught** in a *baraita,* as **Rabbi Dostai, son of Rabbi Matun, says: One is permitted to provoke the wicked in this world, as it is stated: "Those who abandon the Torah will praise wickedness,** and the keepers of the Torah will fight them." **And if someone whispered to you, saying,** on the contrary, **isn't it** also **written: "Do not compete with evil-doers, and do not envy the unjust"** (Psalms 37:1), meaning that one should avoid provoking the wicked, **say to him:** Only **one whose heart strikes him** with pangs of conscience over sins that he committed **says this. Rather,** the true meaning of the verse is: **Do not compete with evil-doers, to be like the evil-doers, and do not envy the unjust to be like the unjust.**

וְאוֹמֵר: "אַל יְקַנֵּא לִבְּךָ בַּחַטָּאִים כִּי אִם בְּיִרְאַת ה׳ כָּל הַיּוֹם".

The Gemara cites proof from another verse. **And it says: "One shall not envy the unjust, but be in fear of the Lord all the day"** (Proverbs 23:17). In this context, to envy means to seek to emulate the unjust.

אִינִי?! וְהָאָמַר רַבִּי יִצְחָק: אִם רָאִיתָ רָשָׁע שֶׁהַשָּׁעָה מְשַׂחֶקֶת לוֹ – אַל תִּתְגָּרֶה בּוֹ, שֶׁנֶּאֱמַר: "יָחִילוּ דְרָכָיו בְּכָל עֵת". וְלֹא עוֹד אֶלָּא שֶׁזּוֹכֶה בַּדִּין, שֶׁנֶּאֱמַר: "מָרוֹם מִשְׁפָּטֶיךָ מִנֶּגְדּוֹ". וְלֹא עוֹד אֶלָּא שֶׁרוֹאֶה בְּצָרָיו, שֶׁנֶּאֱמַר: "כָּל צוֹרְרָיו יָפִיחַ בָּהֶם"!

From these verses in Psalms and Proverbs, it would seem that one is encouraged to provoke the wicked. The Gemara asks: **Is this so? Didn't Rabbi Yitzḥak say: If you see a wicked person upon whom the hour is smiling,**[N] **do not provoke him.** As long as he is enjoying good fortune, there is no point in confronting him. **As it is stated: "His ways prosper at all times;** Your judgments are far beyond him; as for his adversaries, he snorts at them" (Psalms 10:5). The verse teaches us that the ways of the wicked will always succeed. **And not only that, but he emerges victorious in judgment, as it is stated: "Your judgments are far beyond him,"** meaning that even when he is brought to justice, it does not affect him. **And not only that, but he witnesses his enemies'** downfall, **as it is stated: "As for all his adversaries, he snorts at them."**

לָא קַשְׁיָא: הָא – בְּמִילֵּי דִּידֵיהּ, הָא – בְּמִילֵּי דִּשְׁמַיָּא.

To resolve this contradiction with regard to whether or not one may provoke the wicked, the Gemara offers several explanations: **This is not difficult,** as it can be understood that **this,** which says that one may not provoke the wicked, is referring **to his** personal **matters, while that,** which says that it is a mitzva to confront them, is referring **to matters of Heaven.**

**HALAKHA**

**When the Holy One, Blessed be He, told him – כֵּיוָן שֶׁאָמַר לוֹ הַקָּדוֹשׁ בָּרוּךְ הוּא וכו׳:** The general principle that God does not renege on any promise of good, even if He made it contingent upon some condition that was not fulfilled, is extremely significant with regard to prophecy. The criterion through which the veracity of a prophecy can be determined is whether or not it came to pass. However, in a case where a prophet prophesied impending calamity, since it is known that God is "a gracious God, compassionate, long-suffering and abundant in mercy, repenting You of evil" (Jonah 4:2), it is possible for transgressors to repent and gain atonement. Therefore, a dire prophecy that is not fulfilled cannot serve as proof that it was a false prophecy (Rambam *Sefer HaMadda, Hilkhot Yesodei HaTorah* 10:4).

**BACKGROUND**

***Mamzer* – מַמְזֵר:** A *mamzer* is a child born from an incestuous or adulterous relationship, i.e., a child born from relations between a married woman and a man other than her husband, or between relatives who are forbidden to marry by Torah law, where the participants in such a relationship are subject to *karet*, excision. An exception to this rule is the offspring conceived with a menstruating woman with whom sexual relations are prohibited under penalty of *karet*. The offspring of an unmarried couple is not a *mamzer*. A *mamzer* inherits from his natural father and is halakhically considered his father's son in all respects. A *mamzer* may only marry a *mamzeret*, a female *mamzer*, or a convert to Judaism. Likewise, a *mamzeret* may only marry a *mamzer* or a convert. The offspring of that union is a *mamzer* as well.

**NOTES**

**A wicked person upon whom the hour is smiling – רָשָׁע שֶׁהַשָּׁעָה מְשַׂחֶקֶת לוֹ:** Several chapters in Psalms mention that there are times when a wicked person will be allowed to succeed in all his pursuits so that his ultimate downfall will be complete. At those times, his success is from God and even a righteous person who attempts to fight him will fail.

NOTES

**Service of Torah** – שִׁמּוּשָׁהּ שֶׁל תּוֹרָה: Some say that this phrase refers to more than service of Torah scholars. It primarily instructs that it is possible to learn a Torah study approach only through listening to Torah scholars discussing halakhic matters and arriving at halakhic conclusions. One who merely studies the pronouncements of the Sages is incapable of gaining a profound understanding of the rationales and the different aspects of the *halakhot* (*HaKotev* based on Rashi).

וְאִיבָּעֵית אֵימָא: הָא וְהָא בְּמִילֵּי דִשְׁמַיָּא, וְלָא קַשְׁיָא: הָא – בְּרָשָׁע שֶׁהַשָּׁעָה מְשַׂחֶקֶת לוֹ, הָא – בְּרָשָׁע שֶׁאֵין הַשָּׁעָה מְשַׂחֶקֶת לוֹ.

**And if you wish, say** instead **that this,** which says not to confront the wicked **and that,** which says to confront the wicked, are both referring **to matters of Heaven, and,** nevertheless, **it is not difficult. This,** which says that one may not provoke the wicked, is referring **to a wicked person upon whom the hour is smiling,** who is enjoying good fortune. **While that,** which says that it is a mitzva to confront them, is referring **to a wicked person upon whom the hour is not smiling.**

וְאִיבָּעֵית אֵימָא: הָא וְהָא בְּרָשָׁע שֶׁהַשָּׁעָה מְשַׂחֶקֶת לוֹ, וְלָא קַשְׁיָא, הָא – בְּצַדִּיק גָּמוּר, הָא – בְּצַדִּיק שֶׁאֵינוֹ גָּמוּר, דְּאָמַר רַב הוּנָא: מַאי דִּכְתִיב "לָמָּה תַבִּיט בּוֹגְדִים תַּחֲרִישׁ בְּבַלַּע רָשָׁע צַדִּיק מִמֶּנּוּ", וְכִי רָשָׁע בּוֹלֵעַ צַדִּיק? וְהָא כְּתִיב: "ה' לֹא יַעַזְבֶנּוּ בְיָדוֹ", וּכְתִיב: "לֹא יְאֻנֶּה לַצַּדִּיק כָּל אָוֶן"! – אֶלָּא: צַדִּיק מִמֶּנּוּ – בּוֹלֵעַ. צַדִּיק גָּמוּר – אֵינוֹ בּוֹלֵעַ.

**And if you wish, say** instead **that this,** which says not to confront **and that,** which says to confront, are both referring **to a wicked person upon whom the hour is smiling,** but the question of whether one is permitted to confront him depends on who is confronting him. **This,** which says that it is a mitzva to confront them, is referring **to a completely righteous person, while this,** which says that one may not confront the wicked, is referring **to one who is not completely righteous, as Rav Huna said: What is** the meaning of **that which is written: "Why do You look on those who deal treacherously and hold Your peace? When the wicked swallows the man more righteous than he?"** (Habakkuk 1:13). This verse is difficult to understand. **Do the wicked swallow the righteous? Isn't it written:** "The wicked looks to the righteous and seeks to kill him; **the Lord will not leave him in his hand,** nor allow him to be condemned when he is judged" (Psalms 37:32–33), **and it is written: "No mischief shall befall the righteous"** (Proverbs 12:21)? **Rather,** in light of these verses, the verse: "The wicked swallows the man more righteous than he" means: **The** man who is **more righteous than he,** but not completely righteous, **he swallows. The completely righteous he does not swallow.**

וְאִיבָּעֵית אֵימָא: שָׁעָה מְשַׂחֶקֶת לוֹ שָׁאנֵי.

**And if you wish, say:** In general, the wicked cannot swallow the righteous, but **when the hour is smiling upon him, it is different.** When the wicked are enjoying good fortune, even the righteous can be harmed (*Birkat Hashem*).

וְאָמַר רַבִּי יוֹחָנָן מִשּׁוּם רַבִּי שִׁמְעוֹן בֶּן יוֹחַי: כָּל הַקּוֹבֵעַ מָקוֹם לִתְפִלָּתוֹ – אוֹיְבָיו נוֹפְלִים תַּחְתָּיו, שֶׁנֶּאֱמַר: "וְשַׂמְתִּי מָקוֹם לְעַמִּי לְיִשְׂרָאֵל וּנְטַעְתִּיו וְשָׁכַן תַּחְתָּיו וְלֹא יִרְגַּז עוֹד וְלֹא יֹסִיפוּ בְנֵי עַוְלָה לְעַנּוֹתוֹ כַּאֲשֶׁר בָּרִאשׁוֹנָה".

**And Rabbi Yoḥanan said in the name of Rabbi Shimon ben Yoḥai:** Setting a fixed place for prayer is so important that **one who sets a fixed place for his prayer, his enemies fall beneath him, as it is said: "And I will appoint a place for My nation, Israel, and I will plant them, that they may dwell in their own place."** Through setting aside a place for prayer, they will merit to **"be disturbed no more; neither shall the children of wickedness afflict them anymore, as in the beginning"** (II Samuel 7:10).

רַב הוּנָא רָמֵי: כְּתִיב "לְעַנּוֹתוֹ" וּכְתִיב "לְכַלּוֹתוֹ"

This verse, cited by the Gemara, leads to an additional point. **Rav Huna raised a contradiction:** In the book of Samuel, in this verse **it is written: "To afflict them,"** while in the parallel verse in I Chronicles (17:9) **it is written: "To destroy them."**

בַּתְּחִילָּה "לְעַנּוֹתוֹ" וּלְבַסּוֹף "לְכַלּוֹתוֹ".

The Gemara resolves this contradiction: The enemies of Israel intend **first to afflict them, and, ultimately, to destroy them** entirely.

וְאָמַר רַבִּי יוֹחָנָן מִשּׁוּם רַבִּי שִׁמְעוֹן בֶּן יוֹחַי: גְּדוֹלָה שִׁמּוּשָׁהּ שֶׁל תּוֹרָה יוֹתֵר מִלִּמּוּדָהּ, שֶׁנֶּאֱמַר: "פֹּה אֱלִישָׁע בֶּן שָׁפָט אֲשֶׁר יָצַק מַיִם עַל יְדֵי אֵלִיָּהוּ", "לָמַד" לֹא נֶאֱמַר, אֶלָּא "יָצַק" – מְלַמֵּד שֶׁגְּדוֹלָה שִׁמּוּשָׁהּ יוֹתֵר מִלִּמּוּדָהּ.

**And Rabbi Yoḥanan said in the name of Rabbi Shimon ben Yoḥai: Service of Torah**[N] **is greater than its study,** i.e., serving a Torah scholar and spending time in his company is greater than learning Torah from him. Torah study is one component of a Torah life, but one who serves a Torah scholar learns about every aspect of life from his actions. This is derived from the verse that speaks in praise of Elisha, **as it is stated: "Here is Elisha son of Shafat, who poured water over Elijah's hands"** (II Kings 3:11). The verse **does not say** that **he learned** from Elijah, **rather** that **he poured** water, which **teaches** that **the service of Torah** represented by Elisha pouring water over Elijah's hands **is greater than its study.**

אֲמַר לֵיהּ רַבִּי יִצְחָק לְרַב נַחְמָן: מַאי טַעְמָא לָא אָתֵי מָר לְבֵי כְנִישְׁתָּא לְצַלּוֹיֵי? אֲמַר לֵיהּ: לָא יָכֵילְנָא. אֲמַר לֵיהּ: לִכַנְפֵי לְמָר עֲשָׂרָה וְלִיצַלֵּי. אֲמַר לֵיהּ: טְרִיחָא לִי מִלְּתָא. – וְלֵימָא לֵיהּ מָר לִשְׁלוּחָא דְצִבּוּרָא, בְּעִידָּנָא דִּמְצַלֵּי צִבּוּרָא לֵיתֵי וְלוֹדְעֵיהּ לְמָר.

As a prelude to another of the statements by Rabbi Yoḥanan in the name of Rabbi Shimon ben Yoḥai, the Gemara relates the following incident. **Rabbi Yitzḥak said to Rav Naḥman: Why did the Master not come to the synagogue**[H] **to pray?** Rav Naḥman **said to him: I was** weak and **unable** to come. Rabbi Yitzḥak **said to him: Let the Master gather ten** individuals, a prayer quorum, at your home **and pray.** Rav Naḥman **said to him: It is difficult for me** to impose upon the members of the community to come to my home to pray with me (*Sefer Mitzvot Gadol*). Rabbi Yitzḥak suggested another option: **The Master should tell the congregation** to send a **messenger when the congregation is praying to come and inform the Master** so you may pray at the same time.

אֲמַר לֵיהּ: מַאי כּוּלֵּי הַאי? אֲמַר לֵיהּ: דְּאָמַר רַבִּי יוֹחָנָן מִשּׁוּם רַבִּי שִׁמְעוֹן בֶּן יוֹחַי,

Rav Naḥman saw that Rabbi Yitzḥak was struggling to find a way for him to engage in communal prayer. **He asked: What is** the reason for **all this** fuss? Rabbi Yitzḥak **said to him: As Rabbi Yoḥanan said in the name of Rabbi Shimon ben Yoḥai:**

**HALAKHA**

Why did the Master not come to the synagogue – מַאי טַעְמָא לָא אָתֵי מָר לְבֵי כְנִישְׁתָּא וכו׳: One must strive to pray with the community in synagogue. If one cannot pray in a synagogue, he should at least try to pray at the time the community prays. Those who live in small cities, where there is no prayer quorum, must arrange for their prayer to coincide with the time when those in the nearest city are praying (Rambam, *Sefer Ahava, Hilkhot Tefilla* 8:1; *Shulḥan Arukh, Oraḥ Ḥayyim* 90:9).

Perek **I**
Daf **8** Amud **a**

מַאי דִּכְתִיב "וַאֲנִי תְפִלָּתִי לְךָ ה׳ עֵת רָצוֹן"? – אֵימָתַי עֵת רָצוֹן – בְּשָׁעָה שֶׁהַצִּבּוּר מִתְפַּלְּלִין.

**What is** the meaning of **that which is written: "But as for me, let my prayer be unto You, Lord, in a time of favor;** O God, in the abundance of Your mercy, answer me with the truth of Your salvation" (Psalms 69:14)? It appears that the individual is praying that his prayers will coincide with a special time of Divine favor. **When is a time of favor?** It is **at the time when the congregation is praying.**[N] It is beneficial to pray together with the congregation, for God does not fail to respond to the entreaties of the congregation.

רַבִּי יוֹסֵי בְּרַבִּי חֲנִינָא אָמַר, מֵהָכָא: "כֹּה אָמַר ה׳ בְּעֵת רָצוֹן עֲנִיתִיךָ".

**Rabbi Yosei, son of Rabbi Ḥanina, said that** the unique quality of communal prayer is derived **from here: "Thus said the Lord, in a time of acceptance I have answered you and on a day of salvation I have aided you"** (Isaiah 49:8).

רַבִּי אַחָא בְּרַבִּי חֲנִינָא אָמַר, מֵהָכָא: "הֵן אֵל כַּבִּיר וְלֹא יִמְאָס", וּכְתִיב: "פָּדָה בְשָׁלוֹם נַפְשִׁי מִקְּרָב לִי כִּי בְרַבִּים הָיוּ עִמָּדִי".

**Rabbi Aḥa, son of Rabbi Ḥanina, said** that it is derived **from here: "Behold, God is mighty, He despises no one"** (Job 36:5). He adopts an alternative reading of the verse: "Behold, God will not despise" the prayer of "the mighty," i.e., the community. **And it is written: "He has redeemed my soul in peace so that none came upon me; for there were many with me.** God shall hear and answer them…" (Psalms 55:19–20). This verse teaches that the prayer was answered because there were many with me when it was offered.

תַּנְיָא נַמִּי הָכִי, רַבִּי נָתָן אוֹמֵר: מִנַּיִן שֶׁאֵין הַקָּדוֹשׁ בָּרוּךְ הוּא מוֹאֵס בִּתְפִלָּתָן שֶׁל רַבִּים, שֶׁנֶּאֱמַר: "הֵן אֵל כַּבִּיר וְלֹא יִמְאָס", וּכְתִיב: "פָּדָה בְשָׁלוֹם נַפְשִׁי מִקְּרָב לִי" וגו׳. אָמַר הַקָּדוֹשׁ בָּרוּךְ הוּא: כָּל הָעוֹסֵק בַּתּוֹרָה וּבִגְמִילוּת חֲסָדִים וּמִתְפַּלֵּל עִם הַצִּבּוּר – מַעֲלֶה אֲנִי עָלָיו כְּאִילּוּ פְּדָאַנִי, לִי וּלְבָנַי, מִבֵּין אוּמּוֹת הָעוֹלָם.

That last proof **was also taught** in a *baraita*. **Rabbi Natan says: From where do we know that the Holy One, Blessed be He, does not despise the prayer of the masses? As it is stated: "Behold, God does not despise the mighty," and it is written: "He has redeemed my soul in peace so that none came upon me;** for there were many with me." Rabbi Natan interprets this not as David speaking about himself, but as God speaking to Israel. **The Holy One, Blessed be He, says: Anyone who engages in Torah** study, which is called peace in the verse: "All its ways are peace" (Proverbs 3:17); **and in acts of kindness, and prays with the congregation,**[N] **I ascribe to him** credit **as if he redeemed Me and My children from among the nations of the world.**

אָמַר רֵישׁ לָקִישׁ: כָּל מִי שֶׁיֵּשׁ לוֹ בֵּית הַכְּנֶסֶת בְּעִירוֹ וְאֵינוֹ נִכְנָס שָׁם לְהִתְפַּלֵּל – נִקְרָא "שָׁכֵן רָע", שֶׁנֶּאֱמַר: "כֹּה אָמַר ה׳ עַל כָּל שְׁכֵנַי הָרָעִים הַנֹּגְעִים בַּנַּחֲלָה אֲשֶׁר הִנְחַלְתִּי אֶת עַמִּי אֶת יִשְׂרָאֵל". וְלֹא עוֹד אֶלָּא שֶׁגּוֹרֵם גָּלוּת לוֹ וּלְבָנָיו, שֶׁנֶּאֱמַר: "הִנְנִי נֹתְשָׁם מֵעַל אַדְמָתָם וְאֶת בֵּית יְהוּדָה אֶתּוֹשׁ מִתּוֹכָם".

Continuing to extol communal prayer, **Reish Lakish said: One who has a synagogue** nearby **in his city but does not enter to pray there**[H] **is called an evil neighbor, as it is stated: "Thus said the Lord: As for all My evil neighbors who touch My inheritance which I have caused My people Israel to inherit,** behold, I will pluck them up from off their land, and will pluck the house of Judah up from among them" (Jeremiah 12:14). One who only touches, but does not enter the place of prayer, My inheritance, is considered an evil neighbor. **And furthermore,** he is punished in that **he causes himself and his children** to go into **exile, as it is stated: "Behold, I will pluck them up from off their land, and will pluck the house of Judah up from among them."**

**NOTES**

When is a time of favor? At the time when the congregation is praying – אֵימָתַי עֵת רָצוֹן בְּשָׁעָה שֶׁהַצִּבּוּר מִתְפַּלְּלִין: The Gemara's objective here is not to prove that communal prayer is greater and more readily accepted than individual prayer, as that is obvious from many other talmudic statements. Rabbi Shimon ben Yoḥai teaches that beyond participation in communal prayer, it is beneficial for an individual to join the congregation at the time when they are praying even if he does not actually participate in prayer with them. This idea is supported by the verses that are quoted. "But as for me, let my prayer be unto You, Lord," apparently refers to an individual praying in a time of favor, i.e., while the congregation is praying. Similarly, "He has redeemed my soul in peace so that none came upon me," refers to the acceptance of individual prayer, "for there were many with me" (Maharsha).

Anyone who engages in Torah study, and in acts of kindness, and prays with the congregation – כָּל הָעוֹסֵק בַּתּוֹרָה וּבִגְמִילוּת חֲסָדִים וּמִתְפַּלֵּל עִם הַצִּיבּוּר: These three elements are the foundation of the world, as it is taught in the mishna in tractate *Avot* (1:2): On three things the world stands: On the Torah, on the Temple service, and on acts of loving-kindness. Today, the Temple is no longer standing, and, consequently, there is no Temple service. Communal prayer stands in its stead, inasmuch as the daily prayers mirror the sacrificial service (Maharsha).

**HALAKHA**

One who has a synagogue in his city but does not enter to pray there – כָּל מִי שֶׁיֵּשׁ לוֹ בֵּית הַכְּנֶסֶת בְּעִירוֹ וְאֵינוֹ נִכְנָס שָׁם לְהִתְפַּלֵּל: One who has a synagogue in his city but does not go there to pray is called an "evil neighbor," and causes exile for himself and his offspring (Rambam *Sefer Ahava, Hilkhot Tefilla* 8:1; *Shulḥan Arukh, Oraḥ Ḥayyim* 90:11).

## HALAKHA

A person should always enter two doorways into the synagogue – לְעוֹלָם יִכָּנֵס אָדָם שְׁנֵי פְתָחִים בְּבֵית הַכְּנֶסֶת: One must enter a synagogue a distance equal to two doorways, and only then pray. In order to satisfy the demands of all of the various explanations of this *halakha*, one must make an effort to both enter more than eight handbreadths, which is equivalent to the minimum width of two doorways, into the synagogue and wait an interval equivalent to the time it would take to traverse eight handbreadths before beginning to pray. It is preferable that those who have a permanent seat adjacent to the door and, therefore, there is no suspicion that they intend to leave immediately, should see to it that the door remains closed so that they will not be distracted from their prayer by that which is transpiring outside (Rambam *Sefer Ahava, Hilkhot Tefilla* 8:2; *Shulḥan Arukh, Oraḥ Ḥayyim* 90:20).

## NOTES

A person should always enter two doorways into the synagogue – לְעוֹלָם יִכָּנֵס אָדָם שְׁנֵי פְתָחִים בְּבֵית הַכְּנֶסֶת: No consensus exists with regard to the explanation of this Gemara or the reasoning behind it. The *Tur*, based on the Jerusalem Talmud, holds that synagogues should be constructed in a manner that one must pass through two doors before arriving in the sanctuary. Based on this interpretation, it has become customary to build vestibules at the front of synagogues. From the Gemara, however, it would appear that one must take care to stand at a distance of two doorways, though there is a disagreement as to how this is to be interpreted. Some say that two doorways refers to a particular distance that one must enter so as to remove himself from the street, to avoid the appearance that he is preparing to leave, or to avoid being distracted from his prayers. Others maintain that one must wait a period of time sufficient to enter two doorways in order to compose himself for a moment before prayer.

אֲמַרוּ לֵיהּ לְרַבִּי יוֹחָנָן: אִיכָּא סָבֵי בְּבָבֶל. תְּמַהּ וְאָמַר: ״לְמַעַן יִרְבּוּ יְמֵיכֶם וִימֵי בְנֵיכֶם עַל הָאֲדָמָה״ כְּתִיב, אֲבָל בְּחוּצָה לָאָרֶץ – לָא! כֵּיוָן דְּאָמְרִי לֵיהּ: מַקְדְּמִי וּמַחְשְׁכִי לְבֵי כְנִישְׁתָּא, אֲמַר: הַיְינוּ דְּאַהֲנֵי לְהוּ.

The Gemara relates that when the Sages **told Rabbi Yoḥanan** that **there are elders in Babylonia, he was confounded and said: It is written: "So that your days will be lengthened and the days of your children upon the land** the Lord swore to your forefathers to give to them like the days of heaven on the earth" (Deuteronomy 11:21); lengthened in Eretz Yisrael **but not outside of the Land.** Why then, do the residents of Babylonia live long lives? **When they told him** that the people in Babylonia **go early** in the morning **and go late** in the evening **to the synagogue, he said: That is what was effective for them** in extending their lives.

דְּאָמַר רַבִּי יְהוֹשֻׁעַ בֶּן לֵוִי לִבְנֵיהּ: קְדִימוּ וְחֲשִׁיכוּ וְעַיְילוּ לְבֵי כְנִישְׁתָּא, כִּי הֵיכִי דְּתוֹרְכוּ חַיֵּי. אָמַר רַבִּי אַחָא בְּרַבִּי חֲנִינָא: מַאי קְרָא? – ״אַשְׁרֵי אָדָם שֹׁמֵעַ לִי לִשְׁקֹד עַל דַּלְתֹתַי יוֹם יוֹם לִשְׁמֹר מְזוּזֹת פְּתָחָי״, וּכְתִיב בָּתְרֵיהּ: ״כִּי מֹצְאִי מָצָא חַיִּים״.

**As Rabbi Yehoshua ben Levi said to his sons: Go early and go late and enter the synagogue, so that your lives will be extended.** And **Rabbi Aḥa, son of Rabbi Ḥanina, said:** Upon **what verse** is this based? As it is stated: **"Happy is the man who listens to Me, watching daily at My gates, guarding at My door posts"** (Proverbs 8:34). **And** the reward for doing so **is written thereafter: "For whoso finds Me finds life and obtains the favor of the Lord"** (Proverbs 8:35).

אָמַר רַב חִסְדָּא: לְעוֹלָם יִכָּנֵס אָדָם שְׁנֵי פְתָחִים בְּבֵית הַכְּנֶסֶת. שְׁנֵי פְתָחִים סָלְקָא דַעְתָּךְ?! – אֶלָּא, אֵימָא: שִׁיעוּר שְׁנֵי פְתָחִים, וְאַחַר כָּךְ יִתְפַּלֵּל.

Based on this verse, **Rav Ḥisda said: A person should always enter two doorways**[B] **into the synagogue.**[HN] This statement is unclear. Immediately, the Gemara asks: **Does it enter your mind** that Rav Ḥisda meant that one should enter **two doorways** literally? What if a synagogue only has a single doorway? Rather, emend his statement and **say** that Rav Ḥisda meant that **one should enter a distance of two doorways** into the synagogue **and then pray.** In entering a distance of two doorways, one fulfills the verse: Guarding at My door posts, in the plural.

״עַל זֹאת יִתְפַּלֵּל כָּל חָסִיד אֵלֶיךָ לְעֵת מְצֹא״, אָמַר רַבִּי חֲנִינָא: ״לְעֵת מְצֹא״ – זוֹ אִשָּׁה שֶׁנֶּאֱמַר: ״מָצָא אִשָּׁה מָצָא טוֹב״.

Having mentioned the verse, "For whoso finds Me finds life," the Gemara seeks to clarify its meaning. It is said, **"For this, let every pious man pray to You in the time of finding,** that the overflowing waters may not reach him" (Psalms 32:6). With regard to the phrase, the time of finding, **Rabbi Ḥanina said: The time of finding** refers to the time one must find **a wife,** that one should pray to find a suitable woman to marry. **As it is said: "He who finds [*matza*] a wife finds [*matza*] good** and obtains favor from the Lord" (Proverbs 18:22).

בְּמַעְרְבָא כִּי נָסֵיב אִינִשׁ אִתְּתָא, אָמְרִי לֵיהּ הָכִי: ״מָצָא״ אוֹ ״מוֹצֵא״? ״מָצָא״ – דִּכְתִיב: ״מָצָא אִשָּׁה מָצָא טוֹב וַיָּפֶק רָצוֹן מֵה׳״, ״מוֹצֵא״ דִּכְתִיב: ״וּמוֹצֶא אֲנִי מַר מִמָּוֶת אֶת הָאִשָּׁה״ וגו׳.

**In Eretz Yisrael,** the custom was that **when a man married a woman, they would ask him:** ***Matza*** **or** ***motzeh*****?** In other words, they would ask the groom whether the appropriate passage for his wife is the above verse from Proverbs that begins with the word ***matza*****, as it is written: "He who finds a wife finds good and obtains favor from the Lord"** or whether the more appropriate verse is the one beginning with the word ***motzeh*****, as it is written: "And I find [*motzeh*] the woman more bitter than death"** (Ecclesiastes 7:26).

רַבִּי נָתָן אוֹמֵר: ״לְעֵת מְצֹא״ – זוֹ תּוֹרָה, שֶׁנֶּאֱמַר: ״כִּי מֹצְאִי מָצָא חַיִּים״ וגו׳.

**Rabbi Natan says: The time of finding** refers to the time of finding **Torah, as it is stated** in a verse referring to Torah: **"He who finds Me finds life."** The Torah is the object most sought.

## BACKGROUND

Two doorways – שְׁנֵי פְתָחִים: As explained in the Jerusalem Talmud, synagogues were constructed with two entrances before the sanctuary.

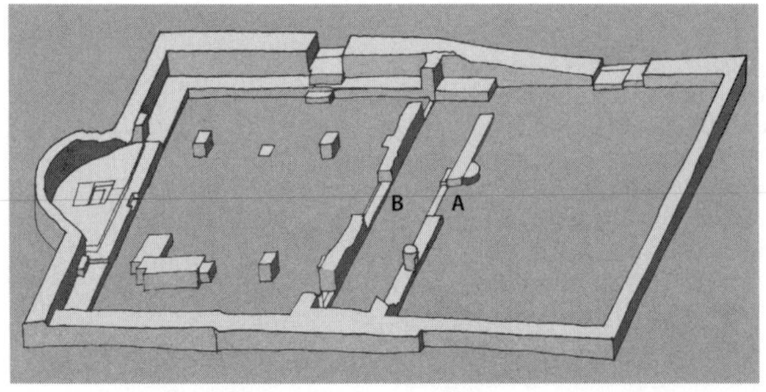


Structure of the synagogue in Beit Alfa

רַב נַחְמָן בַּר יִצְחָק אָמַר: ״לְעֵת מְצֹא״ – זוֹ מִיתָה, שֶׁנֶּאֱמַר: ״לַמָּוֶת תּוֹצָאוֹת״.

**Rav Naḥman bar Yitzḥak said: The time of finding** refers to **death.** One should pray that when death comes, he will leave the world peacefully, **as it is stated: "Issues [*totzaot*] of death"** (Psalms 68:21). Rav Naḥman bar Yitzḥak's statement is based on the etymological similarity between *totzaot* and *matza*, finding.

תַּנְיָא נַמִּי הָכִי: תְּשַׁע מֵאוֹת וּשְׁלֹשָׁה מִינֵי מִיתָה נִבְרְאוּ בָּעוֹלָם, שֶׁנֶּאֱמַר: ״לַמָּוֶת תּוֹצָאוֹת״ – ״תּוֹצָאוֹת״ בְּגִימַטְרִיָּא הָכִי הָווּ. קָשָׁה שֶׁבְּכוּלָּן – אַסְכָּרָא, נִיחָא שֶׁבְּכוּלָּן – נְשִׁיקָה. אַסְכָּרָא – דָּמְיָא כְּחִיזְרָא בְּגַבְבָא דְּעַמְרָא דִּלְאַחוֹרֵי נַשְׁרָא, וְאִיכָּא דְּאָמְרִי: כְּפִיטוּרֵי בְּפִי וֵשֶׁט. נְשִׁיקָה – דָּמְיָא כְּמִשְׁחַל בִּנִיתָא מֵחֲלָבָא.

**It was also taught** in a *baraita*: **Nine hundred and three types of death were created in the world, as it is stated: "Issues [*totzaot*] of death," and that,** 903, **is the numerical value [*gimatriya*][L] of *totzaot*.** The Gemara explains that **the most difficult of** all these types of death **is croup [*askara*],** while **the easiest is the kiss** of death. **Croup is like a thorn** entangled **in a wool fleece, which, when pulled out backwards,** tears the wool. **Some say that** croup **is like ropes**[B] **at the entrance to the esophagus,** which would be nearly impossible to insert and excruciating to remove. The **kiss** of death **is like drawing a hair from milk.** One should pray that he does not die a painful death.

רַבִּי יוֹחָנָן אָמַר: ״לְעֵת מְצֹא״ – זוֹ קְבוּרָה. אָמַר רַבִּי חֲנִינָא: מַאי קְרָא – ״הַשְּׂמֵחִים אֱלֵי גִיל יָשִׂישׂוּ כִּי יִמְצְאוּ קָבֶר״. אָמַר רַבָּה בַּר רַב שֵׁילָא, הַיְינוּ דְּאָמְרִי אֱינָשֵׁי: לִיבְעֵי אִינִישׁ רַחֲמֵי אֲפִילּוּ עַד זִיבּוּלָא בַּתְרַיְיתָא שְׁלָמָא.

**Rabbi Yoḥanan said: The time of finding** refers to a respectful **burial,** for which one should pray. Supporting Rabbi Yoḥanan's interpretation, **Rabbi Ḥanina said: What** is **the verse** that teaches that the time of finding refers to burial? **"Who rejoice in exultation and are glad when they can find a grave"** (Job 3:22), as there are situations in which one is relieved when his body finds a grave in which to rest. **Rabba bar Rav Sheila said, that is the** meaning of the **folk saying: A person should even pray for mercy until the final shovelful** of dirt **is thrown** upon his grave.

מָר זוּטְרָא אָמַר: ״לְעֵת מְצֹא״ – זֶה בֵּית הַכִּסֵּא. אָמְרִי בְּמַעְרְבָא: הָא דְּמָר זוּטְרָא עֲדִיפָא מִכּוּלְּהוּ.

**Mar Zutra said: The time of finding** refers to finding **a lavatory.** As most places did not have a sewage system, one was forced to relieve himself outside the city. Because of this unpleasantness, finding a suitable location was called by Mar Zutra, the time of finding. **In the West,** Eretz Yisrael, **they say: This** explanation **of Mar Zutra is preferable to all of them,** as the term *motza* is explicitly associated in the Bible (see II Kings 10:27) with the lavatory (Rabbi Abraham Moshe Horovitz).

אֲמַר לֵיהּ רָבָא לְרַפְרָם בַּר פָּפָּא: לֵימָא לַן מָר מֵהָנֵי מִילֵּי מְעַלְּיָיתָא דְּאָמְרַתְּ מִשְּׁמֵיהּ דְּרַב חִסְדָּא בְּמִילֵּי דְּבֵי כְנִישְׁתָּא.

Returning to the tractate's central topic, **Rava said to Rafram bar Pappa: Let the Master say to us some of those outstanding statements that you said in the name of Rav Ḥisda with regard to matters of the synagogue.**

אֲמַר לֵיהּ, הָכִי אָמַר רַב חִסְדָּא: מַאי דִּכְתִיב ״אֹהֵב ה׳ שַׁעֲרֵי צִיּוֹן מִכֹּל מִשְׁכְּנוֹת יַעֲקֹב״ – אוֹהֵב ה׳ שְׁעָרִים הַמְצוּיָּינִים בַּהֲלָכָה יוֹתֵר מִבָּתֵּי כְנֵסִיּוֹת וּמִבָּתֵּי מִדְרָשׁוֹת.

Rafram **said to him, Rav Ḥisda said as follows: What is** the meaning of the verse: **"The Lord loves the gates of Zion [*Tziyyon*] more than all the dwellings of Jacob"** (Psalms 87:2)? This means that **the Lord loves the gates distinguished [*metzuyanim*] through** the study of *halakha* as they are the gates of Zion, the outstanding gates, **more than the synagogues and study halls.** Although those places are the most outstanding of the dwellings of Jacob, they are not engaged in the study of *halakha*.

וְהַיְינוּ דְּאָמַר רַבִּי חִיָּיא בַּר אַמֵּי מִשְּׁמֵיהּ דְּעוּלָּא: מִיּוֹם שֶׁחָרַב בֵּית הַמִּקְדָּשׁ אֵין לוֹ לְהַקָּדוֹשׁ בָּרוּךְ הוּא בְּעוֹלָמוֹ אֶלָּא אַרְבַּע אַמּוֹת שֶׁל הֲלָכָה בִּלְבַד.

**And this** concept, that *halakha* is the most sublime pursuit, is expressed in that which **Rabbi Ḥiyya bar Ami said in the name of Ulla: Since the day the Temple,** where the Divine Presence rested in this world, **was destroyed, the Holy One, Blessed be He, has only** one place **in His world** where he reveals His presence exclusively; **only the four cubits** where the study **of *halakha***[N] is undertaken.

וְאָמַר אַבָּיֵי: מֵרֵישׁ הֲוָה גָּרֵיסְנָא בְּגוֹ בֵּיתָא וּמְצַלֵּינָא בְּבֵי כְנִישְׁתָּא, כֵּיוָן דִּשְׁמַעְנָא לְהָא דְּאָמַר רַבִּי חִיָּיא בַּר אַמֵּי מִשְּׁמֵיהּ דְּעוּלָּא: מִיּוֹם שֶׁחָרַב בֵּית הַמִּקְדָּשׁ אֵין לוֹ לְהַקָּדוֹשׁ בָּרוּךְ הוּא בְּעוֹלָמוֹ אֶלָּא אַרְבַּע אַמּוֹת שֶׁל הֲלָכָה בִּלְבַד – לָא הֲוָה מְצַלֵּינָא אֶלָּא הֵיכָא דְּגָרֵיסְנָא.

This statement has practical ramifications. **Abaye said: At first I studied in the house and prayed in the synagogue. Once I heard what Rabbi Ḥiyya bar Ami said in the name of Ulla: Since the day the Temple was destroyed, the Holy One, Blessed be He, has only** one place **in His world, only the four cubits of *halakha* alone,** from which I understood the significance of the four cubits of *halakha*, and **I pray only where I study.**[H]

### LANGUAGE

*Gimatriya* – גִּימַטְרִיָּא: The word derives from the Greek γεωμετρία, geometry, which means measurement or calculation in general, even though it was later designated for a specific type of calculation. In rabbinic literature, it also refers to mathematical calculations in general, although it was designated for tabulating the numerical value of the letters.

### BACKGROUND

Ropes – פִּיטוּרֵי: There are numerous explanations of this term. Some of the *ge'onim* explained that it refers to ropes placed through holes on a ship that pass through with great difficulty. That is the feeling experienced by one suffering from croup. Another geonic interpretation explains that it derives from the Aramaic for mushrooms. Croup feels like a person attempting to swallow a mushroom whole. It gets stuck in his esophagus and strangles him.

### NOTES

Four cubits of *halakha* – אַרְבַּע אַמּוֹת שֶׁל הֲלָכָה: This phrase refers to the place where *halakha* is located and revealed, where people engage in the study of *halakha*. Since *halakha* is a microcosm and revelation of the word of God, as it appears in the Torah, the *halakha* is a manifestation of God's will. Consequently, after the destruction of the Temple, which was the place where the will of God was revealed to man, the *halakha* remains as the conduit for the continued revelation of His will, God's spiritual-abstract Temple in the world. The conclusion drawn by Abaye from this concept was not the only practical conclusion. The Rif instituted the custom to sound the *shofar* on Rosh HaShana that occurred on Shabbat in his study hall, as if it was the Temple, based on the concept that the four cubits of *halakha* constitute the present-day Temple.

### HALAKHA

I pray only where I study – לָא הֲוָה מְצַלֵּינָא אֶלָּא הֵיכָא דְּגָרֵיסְנָא: A study hall dedicated to the study of the masses is more sanctified than a synagogue, and it is preferable to pray there if there is a prayer quorum. Some say that one for whom Torah is his profession is permitted to pray alone in a study hall instead of praying with the community (Rambam *Sefer Ahava*, *Hilkhot Tefilla* 8:3; *Shulḥan Arukh*, *Oraḥ Ḥayyim* 90:18).

רַבִּי אַמִי וְרַבִּי אַסִי אַף עַל גַּב דְּהָווּ לְהוּ תְּלֵיסַר בֵּי כְּנִישָׁתָא בִּטְבֶרְיָא לָא מְצַלּוּ אֶלָּא בֵּינֵי עַמּוּדֵי, הֵיכָא דַּהֲווּ גָּרְסִי.

Similarly, the Gemara relates that **Rabbi Ami and Rabbi Asi, despite** the fact **that they had thirteen synagogues in Tiberias, they would only pray between the pillars where they studied.**

וְאָמַר רַבִּי חִיָּיא בַּר אַמִי מִשְּׁמֵיהּ דְּעוּלָּא: גָּדוֹל הַנֶּהֱנֶה מִיגִיעוֹ יוֹתֵר מִירֵא שָׁמַיִם, דְּאִילּוּ גַּבֵּי יְרֵא שָׁמַיִם כְּתִיב: ״אַשְׁרֵי אִישׁ יָרֵא אֶת ה׳״, וְאִילּוּ גַּבֵּי נֶהֱנֶה מִיגִיעוֹ כְּתִיב: ״יְגִיעַ כַּפֶּיךָ כִּי תֹאכֵל אַשְׁרֶיךָ וְטוֹב לָךְ״, ״אַשְׁרֶיךָ״ – בָּעוֹלָם הַזֶּה, ״וְטוֹב לָךְ״ – לָעוֹלָם הַבָּא, וּלְגַבֵּי יְרֵא שָׁמַיִם ״וְטוֹב לָךְ״ לָא כְּתִיב בֵּיהּ.

**And Rabbi Ḥiyya bar Ami said in the name of Ulla: One who benefits from his hard labor is greater than a God-fearing** person,[N] i.e., one who is so enthralled by his fear of God that he sits idly by and does not work. **As with regard to a God-fearing** person, **it is written: "Happy is the man who fears the Lord,** who greatly desires His mitzvot" (Psalms 112:1), **while with regard to one who benefits from his hard work, it is written: "By the labor of your hands you will live; you are happy and it is good for you"** (Psalms 128:2). The Gemara explains this verse to mean that **you are happy in this world, and it is good for you in the World-to-Come. And regarding a God-fearing** person, happy is the man, is written about him but **and it is good for you, is not written about him.**

וְאָמַר רַבִּי חִיָּיא בַּר אַמִי מִשְּׁמֵיהּ דְּעוּלָּא: לְעוֹלָם יָדוּר אָדָם בִּמְקוֹם רַבּוֹ, שֶׁכָּל זְמַן שֶׁשִּׁמְעִי בֶּן גֵּרָא קַיָּים לֹא נָשָׂא שְׁלֹמֹה אֶת בַּת פַּרְעֹה.

**And Rabbi Ḥiyya bar Ami said in the name of Ulla: One should always live in the place where his teacher** lives; thereby he will avoid sin. **For as long as Shimi ben Gera,** who according to tradition was a great Torah scholar and teacher of Solomon (see *Gittin* 59a), **was alive, Solomon did not marry Pharaoh's daughter.** Immediately after the Bible relates the death of Shimi (1 Kings, end of ch. 2), Solomon's marriage to Pharaoh's daughter is recorded (beginning of ch. 3).

וְהָתַנְיָא: אַל יָדוּר!

The Gemara raises an objection: **Wasn't it taught** in a *baraita* that one **should not live** where his teacher lives?

לָא קַשְׁיָא: הָא – דְּכַיֵּיף לֵיהּ, הָא – דְּלָא כַּיֵּיף לֵיהּ.

The Gemara answers: **This is not difficult. This,** which says that one should live where his teacher lives, is referring to a case **where he is acquiescent to** his teacher and will heed his teaching and instruction. **While this** *baraita,* which says that one should not live where his teacher lives, is referring to a case **where he is not acquiescent to him** and that will lead them to quarrel.

אָמַר רַב הוּנָא בַּר יְהוּדָה אָמַר רַבִּי מְנַחֵם אָמַר רַבִּי אַמִי: מַאי דִּכְתִיב ״וְעוֹזְבֵי ה׳ יִכְלוּ״ – זֶה הַמַּנִּיחַ סֵפֶר תּוֹרָה, וְיוֹצֵא.

The Gemara again returns to the topic of the synagogue. **Rav Huna bar Yehuda said** that **Rabbi Menaḥem said** that **Rabbi Ami said: What is** the practical halakhic meaning of **that which is written: "They who forsake the Lord will perish"** (Isaiah 1:28)? **This** verse **refers to one who abandons the Torah** scroll when it was taken out to be read **and leaves**[H] the synagogue, as it appears that he is fleeing from God.

רַבִּי אַבָּהוּ נָפֵיק בֵּין גַּבְרָא לְגַבְרָא.

Practically speaking, the Gemara relates that **Rabbi Abbahu would go out between** one **person** who read the Torah **and the** next **person** who did so. Since the scroll was closed between readers, it was not considered to be a show of contempt.

בָּעֵי רַב פַּפָּא: בֵּין פְּסוּקָא לִפְסוּקָא מַהוּ?

**Rav Pappa raised a dilemma: What is** the ruling with regard to leaving **between** one **verse and** the next **verse?** Is one permitted to leave during a break in the Torah reading while the verse was translated into Aramaic?

תֵּיקוּ.

An answer to this question was not found, so the dilemma **stands** unresolved.

רַב שֵׁשֶׁת מַהֲדַר אַפֵּיהּ וְגָרֵיס, אָמַר: אֲנַן בְּדִידַן וְאִינְהוּ בְּדִידְהוּ.

The Gemara relates that **Rav Sheshet would turn his face**[N] away from the Torah while it was being read **and study.** Explaining this practice, **he said: We are** engaged **in ours,** the study of the Oral Torah **and they are** engaged **in theirs,** listening to the Written Torah. Since Rav Sheshet was engaged in Torah study, he is not considered one who forsakes the Lord.

אָמַר רַב הוּנָא בַּר יְהוּדָה אָמַר רַבִּי אַמִי: לְעוֹלָם יַשְׁלִים אָדָם פָּרָשִׁיּוֹתָיו עִם הַצִּבּוּר שְׁנַיִם מִקְרָא וְאֶחָד תַּרְגּוּם,

**Rav Huna bar Yehuda said** that **Rabbi Ami said: A person should always complete his** Torah **portions with the congregation.**[H] The congregation reads a particular Torah portion every Shabbat, and during the week prior to each Shabbat, one is required to read the **Bible** text of the weekly portion **twice** and the **translation once.**[N]

## NOTES

**One who benefits from his hard labor is greater than a God-fearing person** – גָּדוֹל הַנֶּהֱנֶה מִיגִיעוֹ יוֹתֵר מִירֵא שָׁמַיִם: This principle is emphasized here because otherwise one might assume that one who fears Heaven and devotes his life entirely to religious pursuits is preferable to one who works for a living and is unable to devote himself entirely to spiritual matters. On the contrary, the Gemara stresses that one who both benefits from his own labor and who has fear of Heaven is rewarded in this world because he is not reliant upon others, and is also rewarded in the World-to-Come. In this sense, he is more worthy than one who only fears Heaven (*HaKotev*, Rabbi Yoshiyahu Pinto).

**Rav Sheshet would turn his face** – רַב שֵׁשֶׁת מַהֲדַר אַפֵּיהּ: That Rav Sheshet would turn his face away and study while the community would read Torah is difficult to understand, and a number of explanations have been offered. The *ge'onim* hold that Rav Sheshet, specifically, was permitted to do so because he was blind. For others it was forbidden. Others maintain that Rav Sheshet's actions were permitted because he engaged in his own private Torah study quietly and did not prevent anyone from listening to the Torah reading. There was a prayer quorum without him, so his presence was not required. Yet others say that Rav Sheshet did this because Torah was his profession, and a person who spends all his days immersed in Torah becomes exempt from several mitzvot that can be fulfilled by others (*Tosafot*). Finally, some hold that Rav Sheshet did so before the congregation began the Torah reading (*Talmidei Rabbeinu Yona*) or between the verses (*Kehillat Ya'akov*).

**Read the Bible twice and translation once** – שְׁנַיִם מִקְרָא וְאֶחָד תַּרְגּוּם: The reason for the practice of reading the verses as well as their translation is clear, as the translation is itself a commentary on the text and it is appropriate for one reading the Torah to read an accompanying explanation so that he understands what he reads. However, the reason for reading each verse twice is not explained. Some say that this is based upon the way the Torah is read in the synagogue, where one person was called to read the Torah while another reads with him, after which the translator translates the verse. In that way, each verse is read twice and translated once (Ra'avan; see *Ma'adanei Yom Tov*).

## HALAKHA

**This refers to one who abandons the Torah and leaves** – זֶה הַמַּנִּיחַ סֵפֶר תּוֹרָה וְיוֹצֵא: One is forbidden to leave a synagogue while the Torah is open. Between portions, one may only leave when there are extenuating circumstances (*Magen Avraham*). In our generation, there is no public translation of the verses. Consequently, one is certainly prohibited from leaving between verses. Even in cases where there is a pause in the reading, the decisors of *halakha* are stringent in their ruling with regard to the uncertainty in the Gemara and one is prohibited from leaving (Rambam *Sefer Ahava, Hilkhot Tefilla* 12:9; *Shulḥan Arukh, Oraḥ Ḥayyim* 146:1).

**A person should always complete his portions with the congregation** – לְעוֹלָם יַשְׁלִים אָדָם פָּרָשִׁיּוֹתָיו עִם הַצִּבּוּר וכו׳: One should read each Torah portion twice and its translation once. Even those verses for which the translation is identical to the original Hebrew should be read in this manner. This reading along with the community should begin on the Sunday preceding the Shabbat when that particular Torah portion will be read. The beginning of that portion was already read at the Shabbat afternoon service the day before and ideally one should complete this reading before eating one's meal on Shabbat day. The reason for reading the portion in translation is to understand the verses according to their rabbinic interpretation. Therefore, one who reads Rashi's commentary on the Torah fulfills his obligation to read the translation. A God-fearing individual reads both the Aramaic translation and Rashi (Rambam *Sefer Ahava, Hilkhot Tefilla* 13:25; *Shulḥan Arukh, Oraḥ Ḥayyim* 285:1–4).

וַאֲפִילּוּ: "עֲטָרוֹת וְדִיבֹן", שֶׁכׇּל הַמַּשְׁלִים פָּרָשִׁיּוֹתָיו עִם הַצִּבּוּר מַאֲרִיכִין לוֹ יָמָיו וּשְׁנוֹתָיו.

This applies to every verse, **even** a verse like: **"Atarot and Divon**[N] and Yazer and Nimra and Ḥeshbon and Elaleh and Sevam and Nevo and Beon" (Numbers 32:3). While that verse is comprised entirely of names of places that are identical in Hebrew and Aramaic, one is nevertheless required to read the verse twice and its translation once, **as one who completes his** Torah **portions with the congregation** is rewarded that **his days and years are extended.**

רַב בֵּיבַי בַּר אַבָּיֵי סְבַר לְאַשְׁלוֹמִינְהוּ לְפָרָשִׁיָּיתָא דְּכוּלָּא שַׁתָּא בְּמַעֲלֵי יוֹמָא דְכִפּוּרֵי. תְּנָא לֵיהּ חִיָּיא בַּר רַב מִדִּפְתִּי: כְּתִיב "וְעִנִּיתֶם אֶת נַפְשֹׁתֵיכֶם בְּתִשְׁעָה לַחֹדֶשׁ בָּעֶרֶב",

**Rav Beivai bar Abaye thought to finish all the** Torah **portions of the entire year,**[N] which he had been unable to complete at their appointed time, **on the eve of Yom Kippur** when he would have time to do so. But **Ḥiyya bar Rav of Difti taught him: It is written** with regard to Yom Kippur: **"And you shall afflict your souls on the ninth day of the month in the evening,** from evening to evening you shall keep your Sabbath" (Leviticus 23:32).

וְכִי בְּתִשְׁעָה מִתְעַנִּין? וַהֲלֹא בַּעֲשָׂרָה מִתְעַנִּין! אֶלָּא לוֹמַר לָךְ: כׇּל הָאוֹכֵל וְשׁוֹתֶה בַּתְּשִׁיעִי – מַעֲלֶה עָלָיו הַכָּתוּב כְּאִילּוּ מִתְעַנֶּה תְּשִׁיעִי וַעֲשִׂירִי.

The Gemara wonders: **And does one fast on the ninth** of Tishrei? **Doesn't one fast on the tenth of Tishrei,** as the Torah says at the beginning of that portion: "However, on the tenth day of this seventh month is the Day of Atonement; there shall be a holy convocation for you, and you shall afflict your souls" (Leviticus 23:27)? **Rather,** this verse comes **to tell you: One who eats and drinks on the ninth** day of Tishrei in preparation for the fast the next day, **the verse ascribes him** credit **as if he fasted on** both **the ninth and the tenth** of Tishrei. Ḥiyya bar Rav of Difti cited this verse to Rav Beivai bar Abaye to teach him that Yom Kippur eve is dedicated to eating and drinking, not to completing the Torah portions one may have missed throughout the year.

סְבַר לְאַקְדּוֹמִינְהוּ, אֲמַר לֵיהּ הַהוּא סָבָא, תְּנֵינָא: וּבִלְבַד שֶׁלֹּא יַקְדִּים וְשֶׁלֹּא יְאַחֵר.

When Rav Beivai heard this, **he thought to** read the Torah portions **earlier,** before they were to be read by the community. **A certain** unnamed **elder**[B] **told him, we learned: As long as one does not** read the Torah portions **earlier or later** than the congregation. One must read them together with the congregation.

כִּדְאָמַר לְהוּ רַבִּי יְהוֹשֻׁעַ בֶּן לֵוִי לִבְנֵיהּ: אַשְׁלִימוּ פָּרָשִׁיּוֹתֵיכוֹ עִם הַצִּבּוּר שְׁנַיִם מִקְרָא וְאֶחָד תַּרְגּוּם,

**As Rabbi Yehoshua ben Levi told his sons: Complete your portions with the congregation, the Bible** text **twice and** the **translation once.**

וְהִזָּהֲרוּ בְּוָרִידִין כְּרַבִּי יְהוּדָה. דִּתְנַן: רַבִּי יְהוּדָה אוֹמֵר: עַד שֶׁיִּשְׁחוֹט אֶת הַוְּרִידִין.

He also advised them: **Be careful with the** jugular **veins, in accordance with** the opinion of **Rabbi Yehuda, as we learned** in a mishna with regard to the laws of ritual slaughter: **Rabbi Yehuda said:** Cutting the trachea and esophagus in the ritual slaughter of a bird does not render the bird kosher **until he slaughters the** jugular **veins**[B] as well. While this is not halakhically required, it is appropriate to do so to prevent significant amounts of blood from remaining in the bird.

וְהִזָּהֲרוּ בְּזָקֵן שֶׁשָּׁכַח תַּלְמוּדוֹ מֵחֲמַת אוֹנְסוֹ, דְּאָמְרִינַן: לוּחוֹת וְשִׁבְרֵי לוּחוֹת מוּנָּחוֹת בָּאָרוֹן.

Rabbi Yehoshua ben Levi further advised: **And be careful** to continue to respect **an elder who has forgotten his** Torah **knowledge due to** circumstances **beyond his control.** Even though he is no longer a Torah scholar, he must still be respected for the Torah that he once possessed. **As we say:** Both **the tablets** of the Covenant **and the broken tablets are placed in the Ark** of the Covenant in the Temple. Even though the first tablets were broken, their sanctity obligates one not to treat them with contempt. An elder who forgot the Torah knowledge he once possessed is likened to these broken tablets.

אֲמַר לְהוּ רָבָא לִבְנֵיהּ: כְּשֶׁאַתֶּם חוֹתְכִין בָּשָׂר – אַל תַּחְתְּכוּ עַל גַּב הַיָּד. אִיכָּא דְּאָמְרִי: מִשּׁוּם סַכָּנָה, וְאִיכָּא דְּאָמְרִי: מִשּׁוּם קִלְקוּל סְעוּדָה;

**Rava said to his sons** three bits of advice: **When you cut meat, do not cut it on your hand.** The Gemara offers two explanations for this. **Some say: Due to** the **danger** that one might accidentally cut his hand, **and some say: Due to** the fact that it could **ruin the meal,** as even if one only cut himself slightly, that small amount of blood could still spoil the meat and render it repulsive to eat.

**NOTES**

**Atarot and Divon – עֲטָרוֹת וְדִיבֹן:** The question was raised: Why were these particular places singled out? Some answered that it is because they have an Aramaic translation in the Jerusalem *Targum* that is different from the Hebrew (*Tosafot, Talmidei Rabbeinu Yona*), or because they were names of idolatry (*Adderet Eliyahu*).

**The Torah portions of the entire year – לְפָרָשִׁיָּיתָא דְּכוּלָּא שַׁתָּא:** The *ge'onim* had a variant reading: The Torah portions of the *kalla*, which refers to the great gatherings that took place during the months of Adar and Elul, when the community at large assembled to study Torah. Because Rav Beivai bar Abaye was busy tending to matters of the *kalla*, he did not have time to review the Torah portions during that month. At his first opportunity after the month of Elul, on the eve of Yom Kippur, he devoted himself to completing those portions that he missed.

**BACKGROUND**

**A certain elder – הַהוּא סָבָא:** This expression is used to note a certain unidentified elder. Generally, the Talmud records the names, even those of individuals who were not leading Torah scholars. And so, the question was raised as to the identity of this certain elder who is mentioned a number of times. Moreover, this certain elder usually comes to save a Sage from error or uncertainty (see below 43a), which led to the conjecture that this certain elder could be Elijah the prophet. *Tosafot*, however, reject this possibility because, in at least some of the stories, based on that assumption it would be impossible to understand the events that transpired.

**Rabbi Yehuda says until he slaughters the jugular veins – רַבִּי יְהוּדָה אוֹמֵר עַד שֶׁיִּשְׁחוֹט אֶת הַוְּרִידִין:** The term used by Rabbi Yehuda for veins is *veridim*, a word that does not appear in biblical Hebrew at all. It refers to the major blood vessels in the neck. The distinction that is made today between veins, which carry deoxygenated blood from the rest of the body to the heart, and arteries, which carry oxygenated blood from the heart to the rest of the body, is a modern concept. It was unknown in the time of the Gemara. According to the *Arukh HaShulḥan*, Rabbi Yehuda requires that the large veins in the neck just below skin level be cut, but most of the authorities, in the wake of the Rambam in his Commentary on the Mishna, understand that the reference is to the two arteries in the neck situated behind the esophagus and the trachea.

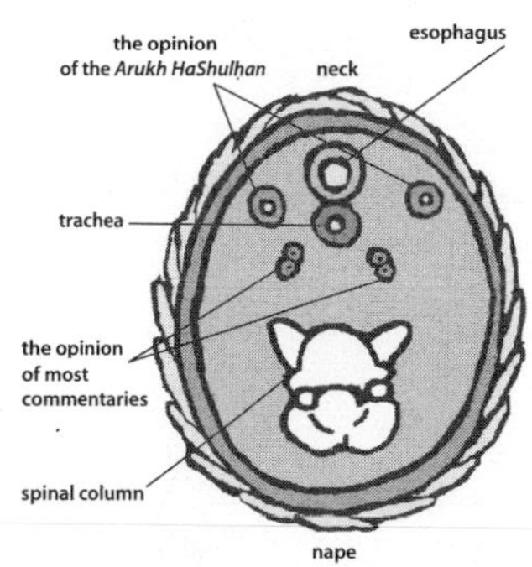

Schematic diagram of the neck

וְאַל תֵּשְׁבוּ עַל מִטַּת אֲרַמִּית; וְאַל תַּעַבְרוּ אֲחוֹרֵי בֵּית הַכְּנֶסֶת בְּשָׁעָה שֶׁהַצִּבּוּר מִתְפַּלְּלִין. ״וְאַל תֵּשְׁבוּ עַל מִטַּת אֲרַמִּית״ – אִיכָּא דְּאָמְרִי: לָא תִּגְנוּ בְּלָא קְרִיאַת שְׁמַע, וְאִיכָּא דְּאָמְרִי – דְּלָא תִּנְסְבוּ גִּיּוֹרְתָּא, וְאִיכָּא דְּאָמְרִי: אֲרַמִּית מַמָּשׁ,

And Rava also advised: **Do not sit on the bed of an Aramean woman, and do not pass by a synagogue when the community is praying.** The Gemara explains: **Some say: Do not sit on the bed of an Aramean woman** means **one should not go to sleep without reciting *Shema*,** as by doing so, it is tantamount to sleeping in the bed of a non-Jew, as his conduct is unbecoming a Jew. **Others say:** This means that **one should not marry a woman who converted,** and it is better to marry a woman who was born Jewish. **And some say:** It **literally** means that one should not sit on the bed of **an Aramean,** i.e., a non-Jewish **woman.**

וּמִשּׁוּם מַעֲשֶׂה דְּרַב פַּפָּא. דְּרַב פַּפָּא אֲזַל לְגַבֵּי אֲרַמִּית, הוֹצִיאָה לוֹ מִטָּה, אָמְרָה לוֹ: שֵׁב! אָמַר לָהּ: אֵינִי יוֹשֵׁב עַד שֶׁתַּגְבִּיהִי אֶת הַמִּטָּה. הִגְבִּיהָה אֶת הַמִּטָּה וּמָצְאוּ שָׁם תִּינוֹק מֵת. מִכָּאן אָמְרוּ חֲכָמִים: אָסוּר לֵישֵׁב עַל מִטַּת אֲרַמִּית.

This bit of advice was **due to an incident** involving **Rav Pappa.**[N] **Rav Pappa went to visit an Aramean woman. She took out a bed** and **she said to him: Sit. He said to her: I will not sit until you lift the** sheets covering the **bed.** She did so **and they found a dead baby there.** Had Rav Pappa sat upon the bed, he would have been blamed for killing the baby. **From** that incident, **the Sages said: One is prohibited from sitting on the bed of an Aramean woman.**

״וְאַל תַּעַבְרוּ אֲחוֹרֵי בֵּית הַכְּנֶסֶת בְּשָׁעָה שֶׁהַצִּבּוּר מִתְפַּלְּלִין״ – מְסַיֵּיעַ לֵיהּ לְרַבִּי יְהוֹשֻׁעַ בֶּן לֵוִי, דְּאָמַר רַבִּי יְהוֹשֻׁעַ בֶּן לֵוִי: אָסוּר לוֹ לְאָדָם שֶׁיַּעֲבוֹר אֲחוֹרֵי בֵּית הַכְּנֶסֶת בְּשָׁעָה שֶׁהַצִּבּוּר מִתְפַּלְּלִין.

And Rava's third bit of advice was, **do not pass behind a synagogue while the congregation is praying. This** statement **supports** the opinion of **Rabbi Yehoshua ben Levi,** as **Rabbi Yehoshua ben Levi said: One is prohibited from passing behind a synagogue while the congregation is praying**[H] because they will suspect that he does not want to pray, and it is a show of contempt for the synagogue.

אָמַר אַבַּיֵי: וְלָא אֲמַרַן אֶלָּא דְּלֵיכָּא פִּתְחָא אַחֲרִינָא, אֲבָל אִיכָּא פִּתְחָא אַחֲרִינָא – לֵית לָן בָּהּ. וְלָא אֲמַרַן אֶלָּא דְּלֵיכָּא בֵּי כְּנִישְׁתָּא אַחֲרִינָא, אֲבָל אִיכָּא בֵּי כְּנִישְׁתָּא אַחֲרִינָא – לֵית לָן בָּהּ. וְלָא אֲמַרַן אֶלָּא דְּלָא דָּרֵי טוּנָא וְלָא רָהֵיט, וְלָא מַנַּח תְּפִילִּין, אֲבָל אִיכָּא חַד מֵהָנָךְ – לֵית לָן בָּהּ.

**Abaye** introduced several caveats to Rabbi Yehoshua ben Levi's statement and **said:**

**We only said** this prohibition if **there is no other entrance** to the synagogue, **but** if **there is** another entrance, since it is possible that he will simply use the second entrance, they will not suspect him, and the prohibition **does not apply.**

**And we only said** this prohibition if **there is no other synagogue** in the city, **but** if **there is another synagogue,** the prohibition **does not apply.**

**And we only said** this prohibition when **he is not carrying a burden, and not running, and not wearing phylacteries. But** if **one of those** factors **applies,** the prohibition **does not apply.** If he is carrying a burden or running, clearly he is occupied with his work. If he is wearing phylacteries, it is evident that he is a God-fearing individual and they will not suspect him.

תַּנְיָא, אָמַר רַבִּי עֲקִיבָא: בִּשְׁלֹשָׁה דְּבָרִים אוֹהֵב אֲנִי אֶת הַמָּדִיִּים: כְּשֶׁחוֹתְכִין אֶת הַבָּשָׂר – אֵין חוֹתְכִין אֶלָּא עַל גַּבֵּי הַשּׁוּלְחָן, כְּשֶׁנּוֹשְׁקִין – אֵין נוֹשְׁקִין אֶלָּא עַל גַּב הַיָּד, וּכְשֶׁיּוֹעֲצִין – אֵין יוֹעֲצִין אֶלָּא בַּשָּׂדֶה.

The Gemara cites a statement from a *baraita*, along the lines of Rava's advice to refrain from cutting meat on one's hands: **Rabbi Akiva said: In three aspects** of their conduct, **I like the Medes,** and we should learn from their practices. **When they cut meat, they cut it only on the table** and not on their hands; **when they kiss,** either as a show of affection or honor, **they kiss only the back of the hand** and do not give the person being kissed an unpleasant feeling; and **when they hold counsel, they only hold counsel in the field** so others will not hear their secrets.

אָמַר רַב אַדָּא בַּר אַהֲבָה: מַאי קְרָאָה – ״וַיִּשְׁלַח יַעֲקֹב וַיִּקְרָא לְרָחֵל וּלְלֵאָה הַשָּׂדֶה אֶל צֹאנוֹ״.

**Rav Adda bar Ahava said:** From **what verse** is this derived? From the verse, **"And Jacob sent and he called Rachel and Leah to the field to his flock"** (Genesis 31:4); it was only there in the field that he held counsel with them.

תַּנְיָא, אָמַר רַבָּן גַּמְלִיאֵל: בִּשְׁלֹשָׁה דְּבָרִים אוֹהֵב אֲנִי אֶת הַפַּרְסִיִּים: הֵן צְנוּעִין בַּאֲכִילָתָן, וּצְנוּעִין בְּבֵית הַכִּסֵּא, וּצְנוּעִין בְּדָבָר אַחֵר.

**It was taught** in a *baraita*, **Rabban Gamliel said: In three aspects** of their conduct, **I like the Persians:** They are a modest people; **they are modest in their eating, they are modest in the lavatory, and they are modest in another matter,** i.e., sexual relations.

״אֲנִי צִוֵּיתִי לִמְקֻדָּשָׁי״. תָּנֵי רַב יוֹסֵף: אֵלּוּ הַפַּרְסִיִּים הַמְקוּדָּשִׁין וּמְזוּמָּנִין לְגֵיהִנָּם.

While they have been praised here regarding certain specific aspects of their conduct, the Gemara proceeds to offer another perspective on the Persians based on a verse describing the destruction of Babylonia at the hands of the Persian and Medean armies: **"I have commanded My consecrated ones;** I have also called My mighty ones for My anger, even My proudly exulting ones" (Isaiah 13:3). **Rav Yosef taught** a *baraita*: **These are the Persians who are consecrated and designated for Gehenna,** for they have been sent by God to carry out his mission of anger, and they will be sent to Gehenna.

## NOTES

**Due to an incident involving Rav Pappa – וּמִשּׁוּם מַעֲשֶׂה דְּרַב פַּפָּא:** According to a geonic tradition, this particular woman owed Rav Pappa money, and she thought that by accusing him she could force him to forgive her debt.

## HALAKHA

**One is prohibited from passing behind a synagogue while the congregation is praying – אָסוּר לוֹ לְאָדָם שֶׁיַּעֲבוֹר אֲחוֹרֵי בֵּית הַכְּנֶסֶת בְּשָׁעָה שֶׁהַצִּבּוּר מִתְפַּלְּלִין:** While the congregation is praying, one may not walk past the side of the synagogue where the entrance is situated. If he is carrying a load, donning phylacteries, if there is another synagogue in the area, if the synagogue has an additional entrance, or if he is riding an animal, it is permitted (Rambam *Sefer Ahava, Hilkhot Tefilla* 6:1; *Shulḥan Arukh, Oraḥ Ḥayyim* 90:8).

״רַבָּן גַּמְלִיאֵל אוֹמֵר״ וכו׳. אָמַר רַב יְהוּדָה אָמַר שְׁמוּאֵל: הֲלָכָה כְּרַבָּן גַּמְלִיאֵל.

The Gemara returns to explain the mishna, in which we learned that **Rabban Gamliel says:** One may recite *Shema* until dawn. **Rav Yehuda said** that **Shmuel said: The *halakha* is in accordance with** the opinion of **Rabban Gamliel.**

תַּנְיָא, רַבִּי שִׁמְעוֹן בֶּן יוֹחַי אוֹמֵר: פְּעָמִים שֶׁאָדָם קוֹרֵא קְרִיאַת שְׁמַע שְׁתֵּי פְעָמִים בַּלַּיְלָה, אַחַת קוֹדֶם שֶׁיַּעֲלֶה עַמּוּד הַשַּׁחַר, וְאַחַת לְאַחַר שֶׁיַּעֲלֶה עַמּוּד הַשַּׁחַר, וְיוֹצֵא בָּהֶן יְדֵי חוֹבָתוֹ, אַחַת שֶׁל יוֹם וְאַחַת שֶׁל לַיְלָה.

**It was taught** in a *baraita*: Based on Rabban Gamliel's ruling, **Rabbi Shimon ben Yoḥai said: At times, one recites *Shema* twice at night,**[H] once just **before dawn**[B] **and once just after dawn, and he thereby fulfills his obligation** to recite *Shema*, **one of the day and one of the night.** According to Rabban Gamliel, the *Shema* that he recited before dawn fulfills his evening obligation and the *Shema* that he recited after dawn fulfills his morning obligation.

הָא גוּפָא קַשְׁיָא! אָמְרַתְּ: ״פְּעָמִים שֶׁאָדָם קוֹרֵא קְרִיאַת שְׁמַע שְׁתֵּי פְעָמִים בַּלַּיְלָה״, אַלְמָא – לְאַחַר שֶׁיַּעֲלֶה עַמּוּד הַשַּׁחַר לֵילְיָא הוּא, וַהֲדַר תָּנֵי: ״יוֹצֵא בָּהֶן יְדֵי חוֹבָתוֹ אַחַת שֶׁל יוֹם וְאַחַת שֶׁל לַיְלָה״, אַלְמָא – יְמָמָא הוּא!

**This *Tosefta* is self-contradictory.**[B] Initially, **you said: At times one recites *Shema* twice at night. Apparently,** the time just **after dawn** is still **night. And then you taught: He thereby fulfills his obligation** to recite *Shema* **one of the day and one of the night. Apparently,** the time in question **is** considered **day,** as otherwise, he would not have fulfilled his obligation to recite *Shema* during the day. There is an internal contradiction with regard to the status of the time just after dawn. Is it considered day or night?

לָא, לְעוֹלָם לֵילְיָא הוּא, וְהָא דְּקָרֵי לֵיהּ ״יוֹם״ – דְּאִיכָּא אֱינָשֵׁי דְּקָיְימִי בְּהַהִיא שַׁעְתָּא.

The Gemara answers: **No,** there is no contradiction. **Actually,** the time just after dawn, when it is still dark, **is** considered **night and the fact that it is referred to** here as **day** is because **there are people who rise** from their sleep **at that time** and, if the need arises, it can be characterized as *bekumekha*, when you rise, despite the fact that it is still night.

אָמַר רַב אַחָא בַּר חֲנִינָא אָמַר רַבִּי יְהוֹשֻׁעַ בֶּן לֵוִי: הֲלָכָה כְּרַבִּי שִׁמְעוֹן בֶּן יוֹחַי.

**Rav Aḥa bar Ḥanina said** that **Rabbi Yehoshua ben Levi said: The** *halakha* **is in accordance with** the opinion of **Rabbi Shimon ben Yoḥai.**

אִיכָּא דְּמַתְנֵי לְהָא דְּרַב אַחָא בַּר חֲנִינָא אַהָא דְּתַנְיָא, רַבִּי שִׁמְעוֹן בֶּן יוֹחַי אוֹמֵר מִשּׁוּם רַבִּי עֲקִיבָא: פְּעָמִים שֶׁאָדָם קוֹרֵא קְרִיאַת שְׁמַע שְׁתֵּי פְעָמִים בַּיּוֹם, אַחַת קוֹדֶם הָנֵץ הַחַמָּה וְאַחַת לְאַחַר הָנֵץ הַחַמָּה, וְיוֹצֵא בָּהֶן יְדֵי חוֹבָתוֹ, אַחַת שֶׁל יוֹם וְאַחַת שֶׁל לַיְלָה.

**Some teach this** statement **of Rav Aḥa bar Ḥanina,** in which he ruled that the *halakha* is in accordance with the opinion of Rabbi Shimon ben Yoḥai, **with regard to this** *halakha*, which is stylistically similar to the previous *halakha*. **As it was taught** in a *baraita* that **Rabbi Shimon ben Yoḥai said in the name of Rabbi Akiva: At times, one recites *Shema* twice during the day,**[H] **once** just **before sunrise and once** just **after sunrise, and he thereby fulfills his** dual **obligation** to recite *Shema*: **One,** that he recites after sunrise, *Shema* **of the day, and one,** that he recites before sunrise, *Shema* **of the night.**

הָא גוּפָא קַשְׁיָא! אָמְרַתְּ: ״פְּעָמִים שֶׁאָדָם קוֹרֵא קְרִיאַת שְׁמַע שְׁתֵּי פְעָמִים בַּיּוֹם״, אַלְמָא – קוֹדֶם הָנֵץ הַחַמָּה יְמָמָא הוּא, וַהֲדַר תָּנֵי: ״יוֹצֵא בָּהֶן יְדֵי חוֹבָתוֹ אַחַת שֶׁל יוֹם וְאַחַת שֶׁל לַיְלָה״, אַלְמָא – לֵילְיָא הוּא!

**This *baraita* is self-contradictory.** Initially, **you said: "At times one recites *Shema* twice during the day." Apparently,** the time just **before sunrise is** considered **day. And then you taught: "He thereby fulfills his** dual **obligation** to recite *Shema*, **one of the day and one of the night." Apparently,** the time in question **is** considered **night,** as otherwise, he could not thereby fulfill his obligation to recite *Shema* during the night.

## HALAKHA

**At times, one recites *Shema* twice at night – פְּעָמִים שֶׁאָדָם קוֹרֵא קְרִיאַת שְׁמַע שְׁתֵּי פְעָמִים בַּלַּיְלָה וכו׳:** *Ab initio* one should recite *Shema* before midnight; however, he may recite it until dawn. If, due to circumstances beyond his control, he failed to recite *Shema* before dawn, he should recite it before sunrise. In any case, one who recites it then does not recite the blessing: Help us lie down. This ruling is in based on a combination of the various statements cited in the name of Rabbi Shimon ben Yoḥai. However, under no circumstances may one rely on the combination of those *halakhot* so as to recite both the evening and the daytime *Shema* during the same time period (Rambam *Sefer Ahava, Hilkhot Keriat Shema* 1:10; *Shulḥan Arukh, Oraḥ Ḥayyim* 58:5, 283:4).

**At times, one recites *Shema* twice during the day – פְּעָמִים שֶׁאָדָם קוֹרֵא קְרִיאַת שְׁמַע שְׁתֵּי פְעָמִים בַּיּוֹם וכו׳:** When, due to exigent circumstances, one is unable to delay recitation of *Shema* until sunrise, he may recite it after dawn. In any case, even where no exigent circumstances exist and he could have recited *Shema* later, if he recited *Shema* after dawn he fulfilled his obligation. This is in accordance with the opinion of Rabbi Shimon cited in our Gemara and the halakhic ruling in the second mishna (Rambam *Sefer Ahava, Hilkhot Keriat Shema* 1:12; *Shulḥan Arukh, Oraḥ Ḥayyim* 58:3–4, 235:4).

## BACKGROUND

**Dawn and sunrise – עַמּוּד הַשַּׁחַר וְהָנֵץ הַחַמָּה:** While the term *amud hashaḥar* is employed extensively in rabbinic literature, its meaning is not entirely clear. The first rays of dawn are not noticeable at one particular moment, although a similar phrase, *ayelet hashaḥar*, is defined as two rays of light shining from the east. The Sages debated the precise halakhic time of *alot hashaḥar*. The general consensus is that it is one hour and twelve minutes before sunrise, which is the amount of time required to walk eight thousand cubits. Between dawn and sunrise there is an intermediate period, called the illumination of the east [*he'ir hamizraḥ*] when the entire eastern horizon is illuminated prior to sunrise, which is at the moment that a portion of the sun itself is visible over the horizon. This is followed by the emergence of the sun [*yetziat hashemesh*] when the sun becomes visible in its entirety.

**This is self-contradictory – הָא גּוּפָא קַשְׁיָא:** This is one of the fundamental talmudic expressions, which indicates an internal contradiction within a previously cited mishna or *halakha*. Generally, challenges introduced by this phrase center on stylistic difficulties and incongruity of terms in the various sections of the source cited.

**BACKGROUND**

It was not said explicitly; rather, it was stated based on inference – לָאו בְּפֵירוּשׁ אִיתְּמַר אֶלָּא מִכְּלָלָא אִיתְּמַר: This comment, that a specific *halakha* was not stated explicitly but only inferred, is not uncommon in the Talmud. It is not merely an attempt to ascertain the precise manner in which the statement was transmitted. Rather, the Gemara is calling attention to the fact that one cannot rely on the formulation of a specific *halakha* as it appears, as the *halakha* was not stated in that form, but it was inferred from a statement made in a different context. In this case, the difference between the two versions is clear. At first, the *halakha* was presented as an absolute ruling, while the original version indicates that it is not standard practice, merely: Rabbi Shimon is worthy to rely upon in exigent circumstances.

לָא, לְעוֹלָם יְמָמָא הוּא, וְהַאי דְּקָרוּ לֵיהּ ״לֵילְיָא״ – דְּאִיכָּא אֱינָשֵׁי דְּגָנוּ בְּהַהִיא שַׁעְתָּא.

The Gemara answers: **No,** there is no contradiction. **Actually,** the time just before sunrise **is** considered **day and the fact that it is referred to** here as **night** is because **there are people who** are still **asleep at that time** and, if the need arises, it can be characterized as *beshokhbekha* [when you lie down] despite the fact that it is already day.

אָמַר רַבִּי אַחָא בְּרַבִּי חֲנִינָא אָמַר רַבִּי יְהוֹשֻׁעַ בֶּן לֵוִי: הֲלָכָה כְּרַבִּי שִׁמְעוֹן שֶׁאָמַר מִשּׁוּם רַבִּי עֲקִיבָא. אָמַר רַבִּי זֵירָא: וּבִלְבַד שֶׁלֹּא יֹאמַר ״הַשְׁכִּיבֵנוּ״.

**Rabbi Aḥa, son of Rabbi Ḥanina, said** that **Rabbi Yehoshua ben Levi said: The** ***halakha*** **is in accordance with** the opinion of **Rabbi Shimon who said it in the name of Rabbi Akiva. Rabbi Zeira said: As long as he will not recite: Help us lie down** [***hashkivenu***] as well, after reciting the evening *Shema* before sunrise, as the blessing: Help us lie down, is a prayer that we sleep in peace, which is inappropriate in the morning.

כִּי אֲתָא רַב יִצְחָק בַּר יוֹסֵף, אָמַר: הָא דְּרַבִּי אַחָא בְּרַבִּי חֲנִינָא אָמַר רַבִּי יְהוֹשֻׁעַ בֶּן לֵוִי, לָאו בְּפֵירוּשׁ אִיתְּמַר אֶלָּא מִכְּלָלָא אִיתְּמַר.

That is how the *halakha* was taught in the study hall. However, **when Rav Yitzḥak bar Yosef came** to Babylonia from Eretz Yisrael, where Rabbi Yehoshua ben Levi lived, **he said** that **this** ruling that **Rabbi Aḥa, son of Rabbi Ḥanina, said** that **Rabbi Yehoshua ben Levi** said, **was not said explicitly** by Rabbi Yehoshua ben Levi. **Rather, it was stated** that he held that the *halakha* is in accordance with the opinion of Rabbi Shimon who said it in the name of Rabbi Akiva **based on inference.**[B]

דְּהָהוּא זוּגָא דְּרַבָּנַן דְּאִשְׁתַּכּוּר בְּהִלּוּלָא דִּבְרֵיהּ דְּרַבִּי יְהוֹשֻׁעַ בֶּן לֵוִי, אֲתוֹ לְקַמֵּיהּ דְּרַבִּי יְהוֹשֻׁעַ בֶּן לֵוִי, אָמַר: כְּדַאי הוּא רַבִּי שִׁמְעוֹן לִסְמוֹךְ עָלָיו בִּשְׁעַת הַדְּחָק.

The incident was as follows: **This pair of Sages got drunk at the wedding of Rabbi Yehoshua ben Levi's son** and fell asleep before reciting the evening *Shema*. By the time they awoke, dawn had already passed. **They came before Rabbi Yehoshua ben Levi** and asked him if they could still recite the evening *Shema*. **He said** to them: **Rabbi Shimon is worthy to rely upon in exigent circumstances.** Rabbi Yehoshua ben Levi did not rule in accordance with the opinion of Rabbi Shimon, and, in a case where there are no exigent circumstances, one may not rely on this ruling.

״מַעֲשֶׂה שֶׁבָּאוּ בָּנָיו״ וכו׳.

The mishna relates that there was an **incident** where Rabban Gamliel's **sons returned** very late **from a wedding hall** and they asked their father if they were permitted to recite *Shema* after midnight.

וְעַד הָשְׁתָּא לָא שְׁמִיעַ לְהוּ הָא דְּרַבָּן גַּמְלִיאֵל?

The Gemara asks: **And until now, had they not heard this** ***halakha*** **of Rabban Gamliel?** Were they unaware that he held that one is permitted to recite the evening *Shema* after midnight?

הָכִי קָאָמְרִי לֵיהּ: רַבָּנַן פְּלִיגִי עִילָּוָךְ – וְיָחִיד וְרַבִּים הֲלָכָה כְּרַבִּים, אוֹ דִּלְמָא: רַבָּנַן כְּוָותָךְ סְבִירָא לְהוּ, וְהַאי דְּקָאָמְרִי ״עַד חֲצוֹת״ – כְּדֵי לְהַרְחִיק אָדָם מִן הָעֲבֵירָה? אָמַר לְהוּ: רַבָּנַן כְּוָותִי סְבִירָא לְהוּ, וְחַיָּיבִין אַתֶּם. וְהַאי דְּקָאָמְרִי ״עַד חֲצוֹת״ – כְּדֵי לְהַרְחִיק אָדָם מִן הָעֲבֵירָה.

The Gemara answers that Rabban Gamliel's sons did not ask him his opinion. Rather, **they said to him as follows: Do the Rabbis** fundamentally **disagree with you** concerning this *halakha*, holding that *Shema* may be recited only until midnight? If so, when there is a disagreement between **an individual** Sage **and many** Sages, **the** ***halakha*** **is in accordance with** the opinion of the **many,** in which case we must, in practice, follow the opinion of the Rabbis. **Or perhaps, do the Rabbis hold** in accordance with **your** opinion that the time of the evening *Shema* extends throughout the night, **and that which they say** that it may only be recited **until midnight** is **in order to distance a person from transgression?** If the latter is true, then, when there are extenuating circumstances, one may recite the evening *Shema* after midnight. Rabban Gamliel **replied to his sons: The Rabbis agree with me and you are** still **obligated** to recite *Shema*. The Rabbis **say** that *Shema* may only be recited **until midnight in order to distance a person from transgression,** but, after the fact, even the Rabbis permit recitation after midnight.

״וְלֹא זוֹ בִּלְבַד אָמְרוּ אֶלָּא״ וכו׳.

We learned in the mishna that Rabban Gamliel told his sons: **And** that is **not only** with regard to the *halakha* of the recitation of *Shema*, **but, rather,** wherever the Rabbis say until midnight, the mitzva may be performed until dawn.

וְרַבָּן גַּמְלִיאֵל מִי קָאָמַר ״עַד חֲצוֹת״ דְּקָתָנֵי ״וְלֹא זוֹ בִּלְבַד אָמְרוּ״?

The Gemara questions the formulation of the mishna: **Does Rabban Gamliel say until midnight, that he teaches: And not only did they say?** Rabban Gamliel does not restrict the time for the recitation of *Shema* until midnight, so why does he say, and not only do they say, implying that he agrees with that stringency?

הָכִי קָאָמַר לְהוּ רַבָּן גַּמְלִיאֵל לִבְנֵיהּ: אֲפִילּוּ לְרַבָּנַן דְּקָאָמְרִי ״עַד חֲצוֹת״ – מִצְוָתָהּ עַד שֶׁיַּעֲלֶה עַמּוּד הַשַּׁחַר, וְהַאי דְּקָא אָמְרִי ״עַד חֲצוֹת״ – כְּדֵי לְהַרְחִיק אָדָם מִן הָעֲבֵירָה.

The Gemara explains that **this is what Rabban Gamliel said to his sons: Even according to the Rabbis, who say** that the mitzva may be performed only **until midnight,** the biblical obligation to perform **the mitzva** continues **until dawn, and that which they say** that it may only be recited **until midnight** is **in order to distance a person from transgression.**

״הֶקְטֵר חֲלָבִים״ וכו׳.

In our mishna, Rabban Gamliel cites several cases where a mitzva that must be performed before midnight may actually be performed until dawn; among them, **the burning of fats and limbs** on the altar.

וְאִילּוּ אֲכִילַת פְּסָחִים לָא קָתָנֵי.

The Gemara notes: In our mishna, **the eating of the Paschal lamb was not taught** among those mitzvot that may be performed until dawn, indicating that the mitzva of eating the Paschal lamb does not extend until dawn.

וּרְמִינְהִי: קְרִיאַת שְׁמַע עַרְבִית, וְהַלֵּל בְּלֵילֵי פְּסָחִים, וַאֲכִילַת פֶּסַח – מִצְוָתָן עַד שֶׁיַּעֲלֶה עַמּוּד הַשַּׁחַר!

The Gemara **raises a contradiction** to this conclusion based on a *baraita*: **The mitzvot of the recitation of the evening** ***Shema,*** the recitation of ***hallel*** **on the nights of Passover** accompanying the sacrifice of the Paschal lamb, **as well as eating the Paschal lamb,** may all be performed **until dawn.**

אָמַר רַב יוֹסֵף לָא קַשְׁיָא, הָא – רַבִּי אֶלְעָזָר בֶּן עֲזַרְיָה, הָא – רַבִּי עֲקִיבָא. דְּתַנְיָא: ״וְאָכְלוּ אֶת הַבָּשָׂר בַּלַּיְלָה הַזֶּה״, רַבִּי אֶלְעָזָר בֶּן עֲזַרְיָה אוֹמֵר: נֶאֱמַר כָּאן ״בַּלַּיְלָה הַזֶּה״ וְנֶאֱמַר לְהַלָּן ״וְעָבַרְתִּי בְאֶרֶץ מִצְרַיִם בַּלַּיְלָה הַזֶּה״ – מָה לְהַלָּן עַד חֲצוֹת, אַף כָּאן עַד חֲצוֹת.

**Rav Yosef said: This is not difficult** as these two sources reflect two conflicting opinions. **This,** our mishna, **is in accordance with** the opinion of **Rabbi Elazar ben Azarya. While this,** the *baraita,* **is in accordance with** the opinion of **Rabbi Akiva.**[N] **As it was taught** in a *baraita* with regard to the verse discussing the mitzva to eat the Paschal lamb: **"And they shall eat of the meat on that night;** roasted over fire and *matzot* with bitter herbs shall they eat it" (Exodus 12:8); **Rabbi Elazar ben Azarya says: Here it is stated: "On that night,"** from which we cannot determine when night ends. The same expression is encountered later in the same chapter: **"And I will pass through the land of Egypt on that night** and I will strike every firstborn in the land of Egypt, from person to animal" (Exodus 12:12). We know when the firstborns were struck down based on the verse "Thus said the Lord: At about midnight, I will go out into the midst of Egypt and every firstborn in Egypt shall die" (Exodus 11:4–5). Therefore, **just as** in the verse **below,** the striking of the firstborns took place **until midnight,** as stated explicitly in the verse, **so too** in the verse **here,** the mitzva to eat the Paschal lamb continues **until midnight.**

אָמַר לֵיהּ רַבִּי עֲקִיבָא: וַהֲלֹא כְּבָר נֶאֱמַר ״בְּחִפָּזוֹן״ – עַד שְׁעַת חִפָּזוֹן! אִם כֵּן מָה תַּלְמוּד לוֹמַר ״בַּלַּיְלָה״

**Rabbi Akiva said to him: Was it not already said,** "Thus you shall eat it, with your loins girded, your shoes on your feet, your staffs in your hands and you will eat it **in haste** for it is the Paschal offering for the Lord" (Exodus 12:11)? Therefore the Paschal lamb may be eaten **until the time of haste.**[H] Since the time of haste is when Israel left Egypt, and it is said, "You will not leave, every man from his house, until the morning," then the Paschal lamb may be eaten until dawn. **If that is so, why does the verse state: On** that **night?**

יָכוֹל יְהֵא נֶאֱכָל כְּקָדָשִׁים בַּיּוֹם – תַּלְמוּד לוֹמַר: ״בַּלַּיְלָה״, בַּלַּיְלָה הוּא נֶאֱכָל, וְלֹא בַּיּוֹם.

The Gemara explains that the phrase on that night is necessary because without it I **might** have thought that the Paschal lamb **is eaten during the day, like** all other **sacrifices,** which must all be slaughtered and eaten during the day. Therefore, **the verse states: On** that **night,** to underscore that this particular sacrifice **is eaten at night and not during the day.**

### NOTES

**The dispute between Rabbi Akiva and Rabbi Elazar ben Azarya – מַחְלוֹקֶת רַבִּי עֲקִיבָא וְרַבִּי אֶלְעָזָר בֶּן עֲזַרְיָה:** The manner in which the Gemara clarifies the various stages of the dispute and the interpretation of the verses in accordance with both opinions is actually a means to prove the fundamental consensus between them. Ultimately, it becomes clear that the two *tanna'im* agree with regard to virtually all of the *halakhot* and the emphases in the verses. The difference between them is limited to the question whether the Torah's use of the word morning refers to the first or the second morning. The general approach of the Talmud is to minimize the scope of the dispute, reducing it to a dispute over logical reasoning. In that way, the opinion of each of the disputants is valid and each can remain committed to his opinion.

### HALAKHA

**And they shall eat of the meat on that night…until the time of haste – וְאָכְלוּ אֶת הַבָּשָׂר בַּלַּיְלָה הַזֶּה...עַד שְׁעַת חִפָּזוֹן:** The mitzva by Torah law to eat the Paschal lamb extends until dawn. However, in order to distance a person from transgression, the Sages instituted midnight as the deadline for eating the sacrifice. The Torah law is in accordance with the opinions of Rabbi Akiva, according to whom the *halakha* is established in disputes with his colleagues, and Rabbi Yehoshua, according to whom the *halakha* is established in disputes with Rabbi Eliezer. The ruling establishing the deadline at midnight is based on the opinion of the Rabbis in the mishna, who established a "fence" to distance a person from transgression (Rambam *Sefer Korbanot, Hilkhot Korban Pesaḥ* 8:15).

NOTES

**Sacrifices of lesser sanctity** – קָדָשִׁים קַלִּים: The sacrifices offered in the Temple are divided into two main categories: Sacrifices of the most sacred order and sacrifices of lesser sanctity. The sacrifices of the most sacred order include those offered on Yom Kippur, communal sin-offerings, burnt-offerings, and sin-offerings. The sacrifices of lesser sanctity include peace-offerings, animal tithes, the Paschal lamb, and the like. One of the primary differences between the two types of offerings is that sacrifices of the most sacred order are slaughtered only in the north of the Temple courtyard, while sacrifices of lesser sanctity may be slaughtered anywhere in the courtyard. However, the most fundamental difference between the two types of offerings is when the animal becomes sacred and when its sanctity is nullified through misuse. Sacrifices of the most sacred order are sacred and their sanctity can be nullified through misuse from the moment they are consecrated, while only certain parts of the sacrifices of lesser sanctity are considered sacred, and their sanctity takes effect only from the time they are slaughtered. Similarly, the sacrifices of the most sacred order may be consumed only one day and the following night, while most sacrifices of lesser sanctity may be consumed on the following day as well.

Essentially, the difference between these two opinions revolves around which word they deemed significant. Rabbi Elazar ben Azarya considered the word night as the key word, while Rabbi Akiva considered the word haste as the key word. The Gemara begins to analyze their statements.

בִּשְׁלָמָא לְרַבִּי אֶלְעָזָר בֶּן עֲזַרְיָה דְּאִית לֵיהּ גְּזֵירָה שָׁוָה – אִצְטְרִיךְ לְמִכְתַּב לֵיהּ "הַזֶּה", אֶלָּא לְרַבִּי עֲקִיבָא – הַאי "הַזֶּה" מַאי עָבֵיד לֵיהּ?

**Granted, according to Rabbi Elazar ben Azarya, who has** the tradition of **a verbal analogy** between the phrase, on that night, with regard to the eating of the Paschal lamb and the phrase, on that night, with regard to the striking of the firstborn in Egypt, **it was necessary** for the verse **to write "that"** in order to indicate that these times are parallel. **However, according to Rabbi Akiva,** who has no such tradition, **what does he do with "that"?** Why is it necessary to emphasize on that night?

לְמַעוֹטֵי לַיְלָה אַחֵר הוּא דְּאָתָא; סָלְקָא דַּעְתָּךְ אָמֵינָא: הוֹאִיל וּפֶסַח קָדָשִׁים קַלִּים, וּשְׁלָמִים קָדָשִׁים קַלִּים, מָה שְׁלָמִים נֶאֱכָלִין לִשְׁנֵי יָמִים וְלַיְלָה אֶחָד, אַף פֶּסַח נֶאֱכָל שְׁתֵּי לֵילוֹת בִּמְקוֹם שְׁנֵי יָמִים, וִיהֵא נֶאֱכָל לִשְׁנֵי לֵילוֹת וְיוֹם אֶחָד – קָמַשְׁמַע לַן: "בַּלַּיְלָה הַזֶּה" – בַּלַּיְלָה הַזֶּה הוּא נֶאֱכָל, וְאֵינוֹ נֶאֱכָל בַּלַּיְלָה אַחֵר.

The Gemara answers: On that night **comes to exclude another night,** as one might otherwise have concluded that the Paschal lamb may be eaten for two nights. **It would have entered your mind to say: Since the Paschal lamb** falls into the category of **sacrifices of lesser sanctity,**[N] **and peace-offerings are** also **sacrifices of lesser sanctity, just as peace-offerings may be eaten for two days and one night,** i.e., the day that they are sacrificed through the following day, as we learned in the Torah, **so too the Paschal lamb may be eaten for two nights instead of two days.** In other words, one might otherwise mistakenly conclude from its parallel to peace-offerings, that the Paschal lamb **is to be eaten for two nights and the day** between them. Therefore, the verse **teaches us** specifically **on that night,** i.e., **on that night it is eaten, and it is not eaten on another night.**

וְרַבִּי אֶלְעָזָר בֶּן עֲזַרְיָה?

The Gemara asks: If so, from where does **Rabbi Elazar ben Azarya** derive that the Paschal lamb cannot be eaten for two nights?

מִ"לֹּא תוֹתִירוּ עַד בֹּקֶר" נָפְקָא.

The Gemara answers: Rabbi Elazar ben Azarya **derives** this conclusion **from** the verse: **"It should not remain until the morning"** (Exodus 12:10). If one is prohibited from leaving over any part of the sacrifice until the morning, he is certainly prohibited from leaving it over until the following night. Therefore, it is unnecessary to cite an additional source to teach that the Paschal lamb may only be eaten on the first night.

וְרַבִּי עֲקִיבָא? אִי מֵהָתָם הֲוָה אָמֵינָא: מַאי "בֹּקֶר" – בֹּקֶר שֵׁנִי.

**And** why does **Rabbi Akiva** require "that" to derive that the Paschal lamb may not be eaten on the second night? According to Rabbi Akiva, **if** it was derived **from** the verse: "It should not remain until the morning," **I would have said: What** is the meaning of **morning?** It means the **second morning,** as the Torah does not specify until which morning the Paschal lamb may not be left; until the first morning or the second morning. Therefore, the Torah needed to write on that night and no other.

וְרַבִּי אֶלְעָזָר? אָמַר לָךְ: כָּל "בֹּקֶר" – בֹּקֶר רִאשׁוֹן הוּא.

**And** what would **Rabbi Elazar** ben Azarya respond? He **could have said to you:** If it is not otherwise noted, **every** unmodified mention of the word **morning** in the Bible **refers to the first,** i.e., the next, **morning.** If that were not the case, no biblical text could have any definite meaning.

וְהָנֵי תַּנָּאֵי כְּהָנֵי תַּנָּאֵי, דְּתַנְיָא: "שָׁם תִּזְבַּח אֶת הַפֶּסַח בָּעֶרֶב כְּבוֹא הַשֶּׁמֶשׁ מוֹעֵד צֵאתְךָ מִמִּצְרָיִם".

Concerning the tannaitic dispute between Rabbi Akiva and Rabbi Elazar ben Azarya regarding until when the Paschal lamb may be eaten, the Gemara remarks: The dispute between **these *tanna'im* is parallel to** the dispute between **those *tanna'im*,** who disagree over the same issue. **As it was taught** in a *baraita* with regard to the verse: **"There you will offer the Paschal lamb, in the evening when the sun sets at the time when you left the land of Egypt"** (Deuteronomy 16:6). Upon closer examination, it seems that this verse mentions three distinct times: In the evening, refers to the afternoon until sunset; when the sun sets, refers to the time of sunset itself; and the time when you left the land of Egypt refers to, as explained in Exodus, the early hours of the morning. Therefore it seems that these times parallel the different stages of the mitzva of the Paschal lamb, and it is regarding these details that the *tanna'im* disagree.

רַבִּי אֱלִיעֶזֶר אוֹמֵר: 'בָּעֶרֶב' אַתָּה זוֹבֵחַ, וּ'כְבוֹא הַשֶּׁמֶשׁ' אַתָּה אוֹכֵל, וּ'מוֹעֵד צֵאתְךָ מִמִּצְרָיִם' אַתָּה שׂוֹרֵף; רַבִּי יְהוֹשֻׁעַ אוֹמֵר: 'בָּעֶרֶב' אַתָּה זוֹבֵחַ, 'כְּבוֹא הַשֶּׁמֶשׁ' אַתָּה אוֹכֵל, וְעַד מָתַי אַתָּה אוֹכֵל וְהוֹלֵךְ – עַד 'מוֹעֵד צֵאתְךָ מִמִּצְרָיִם'.

**Rabbi Eliezer says: In the evening,** the afternoon, **you slaughter** the sacrifice, from **when the sun sets** until midnight **you eat it, and at the time when you left the land of Egypt you burn** what remains from the sacrifice, in accordance with the opinion of Rabbi Elazar ben Azarya.

**Rabbi Yehoshua says: In the evening,** the afternoon, **you slaughter** the sacrifice, from **when the sun sets, you eat it. And until when do you continue eating? Until the time when you left the land of Egypt,** meaning until morning, in accordance with the opinion of Rabbi Akiva.

אָמַר רַבִּי אַבָּא: הַכֹּל מוֹדִים, כְּשֶׁנִּגְאֲלוּ יִשְׂרָאֵל מִמִּצְרַיִם – לֹא נִגְאֲלוּ אֶלָּא בָּעֶרֶב, שֶׁנֶּאֱמַר: "הוֹצִיאֲךָ ה' אֱלֹהֶיךָ מִמִּצְרַיִם לָיְלָה", וּכְשֶׁיָּצְאוּ – לֹא יָצְאוּ אֶלָּא בַּיּוֹם, שֶׁנֶּאֱמַר: "מִמָּחֳרַת הַפֶּסַח יָצְאוּ בְנֵי יִשְׂרָאֵל בְּיָד רָמָה".

The Gemara cites an alternative explanation of the dispute between Rabbi Elazer ben Azarya and Rabbi Akiva. **Rabbi Abba said: Everyone agrees that when** the children of **Israel were redeemed from Egypt** were given permission to leave, **they were redeemed only in the evening, as it is stated:** "In the spring **the Lord, your God, took you out from Egypt at night"** (Deuteronomy 16:1). **And when they** actually **left, they left only during the day,**[N] **as it is stated:** "On the fifteenth of the first month, **on the day after the** offering of the **Paschal lamb, the children of Israel went out with a high hand** before the eyes of Egypt" (Numbers 33:3), indicating that they actually went out during the day.

עַל מָה נֶחְלְקוּ – עַל שְׁעַת חִפָּזוֹן. רַבִּי אֶלְעָזָר בֶּן עֲזַרְיָה סָבַר: מַאי "חִפָּזוֹן" – חִפָּזוֹן דְּמִצְרַיִם.

However, **with regard to what did they disagree?** They disagreed **with regard to the time of haste,** as it is written: "You will eat it in haste for it is the Paschal offering for the Lord" (Exodus 12:11). **Rabbi Elazar ben Azarya held: What is** the meaning of **haste?** It is **the haste of the Egyptians** at midnight, as they hurried to the houses of the people of Israel to send them away, in fear of the plague of the firstborn.

וְרַבִּי עֲקִיבָא סָבַר: מַאי "חִפָּזוֹן" – חִפָּזוֹן דְּיִשְׂרָאֵל.

**And Rabbi Akiva held: What is** the meaning of **haste?** It is **the haste of Israel** in the morning, as they rushed to leave Egypt.

תַּנְיָא נַמִי הָכִי: "הוֹצִיאֲךָ ה' אֱלֹהֶיךָ מִמִּצְרַיִם לָיְלָה" – וְכִי בַּלַּיְלָה יָצְאוּ? וַהֲלֹא לֹא יָצְאוּ אֶלָּא בַּיּוֹם, שֶׁנֶּאֱמַר: "מִמָּחֳרַת הַפֶּסַח יָצְאוּ בְנֵי יִשְׂרָאֵל בְּיָד רָמָה"! אֶלָּא: מְלַמֵּד שֶׁהִתְחִילָה לָהֶם גְּאוּלָּה מִבָּעֶרֶב.

Similar to Rabbi Abba's statement, **it was also taught** in a *baraita*, regarding the verse: **"The Lord, your God, took you out from Egypt at night,"** the question arises: **Did they leave at night? Didn't they leave during the day, as it is stated: "On the day after the offering of the Paschal lamb, the children of Israel went out with a high hand"? Rather, this teaches that the redemption began for them in the evening.**

"דַּבֶּר נָא בְּאָזְנֵי הָעָם" וגו' – אָמְרִי דְּבֵי רַבִּי יַנַּאי: אֵין "נָא" אֶלָּא לְשׁוֹן בַּקָּשָׁה, אָמַר לֵיהּ הַקָּדוֹשׁ בָּרוּךְ הוּא לְמֹשֶׁה: בְּבַקָּשָׁה מִמְּךָ, לֵךְ וֶאֱמוֹר לָהֶם לְיִשְׂרָאֵל: בְּבַקָּשָׁה מִכֶּם, שַׁאֲלוּ מִמִּצְרַיִם כְּלֵי כֶסֶף וּכְלֵי זָהָב, שֶׁלֹּא יֹאמַר

Since the last topic discussed in the Gemara revolved around the exodus from Egypt, the Gemara cites additional aggadic midrash on that subject. With regard to the verse: **"Speak, please [*na*] in the ears of the people,** and they should borrow, every man from his fellow and every woman from her fellow, silver and gold vessels" (Exodus 11:2), the word please [*na*] is unclear. The students of **the school of Rabbi Yannai said: Please [*na*] is nothing more than an expression of supplication.** Why would God employ an expression of supplication in approaching Israel? The Gemara explains that the **Holy One, Blessed be He, said to Moses: I beseech you,**[N] **go and tell Israel: I beseech you; borrow vessels of silver and vessels of gold from the Egyptians** in order to fulfill the promise I made to Abraham in the "Covenant between the Pieces," **so that**

NOTES

**When the children of Israel were redeemed from Egypt, they were redeemed only in the evening. And when they left, they left only during the day – כְּשֶׁנִּגְאֲלוּ יִשְׂרָאֵל מִמִּצְרַיִם לֹא נִגְאֲלוּ אֶלָּא בָּעֶרֶב...וּכְשֶׁיָּצְאוּ לֹא יָצְאוּ אֶלָּא בַּיּוֹם:** There are two separate elements to the transition from slavery to freedom. First, the slave acquires a personal sense of freedom and becomes master of his own fate. Second, he becomes free in the eyes of others, i.e., he is perceived by those surrounding him as a free man and has the potential to influence them. With regard to the children of Israel, the first element enabled them to receive the Torah and elevate themselves with the fulfillment of God's commandments. The second element provided Israel with the opportunity to become a "light unto the nations." Therefore, the redemption was divided into two stages. The first stage, in which they acquired private, personal freedom, took place at night; the second stage, which drew the attention of the world to the miracle of the Exodus, took place during the day (*Ein Ayah*).

NOTES

**I beseech you – בְּבַקָּשָׁה מִמְּךָ:** Many wondered why this request was necessary. The first explanation, based on what follows in the Gemara, is that Israel did not want to increase their burden or delay their redemption in order to attain the property. Others explain that, at first, Israel did not wish to engage in deceit in order to gain possession of the Egyptians' silver and gold. Therefore, it was necessary to request that they do so (Rabbi Yoshiyahu Pinto, *HaKotev*).

NOTES

**And they gave them what they requested – וַיַּשְׁאִלוּם:** The grammatical form of this word, which indicates that one caused another to act, leads one to surmise that there was coercion involved in this exchange of goods. From the verse it is unclear who forced whom: Did Israel force the Egyptians to give or did the Egyptians force Israel to take?

**And they emptied Egypt – וַיְנַצְּלוּ:** Here too, the word form leads to a unique interpretation. The Aramaic translation of the word is: And they emptied. The two homiletic interpretations of the word differ whether the Hebrew root of the word, *nun – tzaddi – lamed*, is etymologically more similar to the Hebrew word for trap or the Hebrew word for abyss.

**Like a trap in which there is no grain – כִּמְצוּדָה שֶׁאֵין בָּהּ דָּגָן:** According to this version of the text, this expression is understood as explained by Rashi: Grain is used to lure birds into the trap. This expression connotes a state of utter emptiness as in the verse: "Will a bird fall into a trap…if there is no lure for it?" (*Amos* 3:5). The variant reading of the text according to the *ge'onim* reads: "A threshing floor [*netzula*] without grain," which seems preferable because of both the simplicity of the metaphor and etymological similarity between the term in the verse, *vaynatzlu* and *netzula*.

**I was with you in this enslavement, and I will be with you in the enslavement of the kingdoms – אֲנִי הָיִיתִי עִמָּכֶם בְּשִׁעְבּוּד זֶה וַאֲנִי אֶהְיֶה עִמָּכֶם בְּשִׁעְבּוּד מַלְכֻיּוֹת:** In the verse in Exodus, God replies to Moses' question with regard to the manner in which he should represent Him to the children of Israel in two different manners. First, He said: "I will be that I will be," and, then, He merely stated: "I will be." The suggestion in the Gemara that God accepted Moses' argument is based on that difference. The Gemara explains this change by interjecting Moses' comment, i.e., that future tribulations should not be mentioned at this point. *Midrash Rabba* explains that God's original intent was to assure Moses that He would be with the children of Israel in future sufferings, as well. He never intended that Moses would share that message with the people. Moses misunderstood God's command and, therefore, God clarified His original intent (Maharsha).

אוֹתוֹ צַדִּיק: "וַעֲבָדוּם וְעִנּוּ אֹתָם" – קִיֵּים בָּהֶם, "וְאַחֲרֵי כֵן יֵצְאוּ בִּרְכֻשׁ גָּדוֹל" – לֹא קִיֵּים בָּהֶם.

**that righteous person,** Abraham, **will not say:** God **fulfilled** His pronouncement: **"And they will be enslaved and afflicted,"** but God **did not fulfill** His pronouncement: **"And afterward, they will leave with great possessions."** As God said to Abraham: "Surely you shall know that your descendants will be foreigners in a land that is not theirs, and they will be enslaved and afflicted for four hundred years. And also that nation who enslaves them will I judge. And afterward, they will leave with great possessions" (Genesis 15:13–14).

אָמְרוּ לוֹ: וּלְוַאי שֶׁנֵּצֵא בְּעַצְמֵנוּ. מָשָׁל לְאָדָם שֶׁהָיָה חָבוּשׁ בְּבֵית הָאֲסוּרִים, וְהָיוּ אוֹמְרִים לוֹ בְּנֵי אָדָם: מוֹצִיאִין אוֹתְךָ לְמָחָר מִבֵּית הָאֲסוּרִין וְנוֹתְנִין לְךָ מָמוֹן הַרְבֵּה, וְאוֹמֵר לָהֶם: בְּבַקָּשָׁה מִכֶּם, הוֹצִיאוּנִי הַיּוֹם, וְאֵינִי מְבַקֵּשׁ כְּלוּם.

The school of Rabbi Yannai continues: Israel **said to** Moses: **If only we could get out ourselves.** The Gemara offers **a parable to one who was incarcerated in prison, and people would say to him:** We promise, **we will release you tomorrow and give you much money. He says to them: I beseech you, release me today and I ask for nothing.** So too, Israel preferred leaving immediately empty handed rather than leaving later with great riches.

"וַיַּשְׁאִלוּם". אָמַר רַבִּי אַמֵּי: מְלַמֵּד, שֶׁהִשְׁאִילוּם בְּעַל כָּרְחָם. אִיכָּא דְּאָמְרִי: בְּעַל כָּרְחָם דְּמִצְרִים, וְאִיכָּא דְּאָמְרִי: בְּעַל כָּרְחָם דְּיִשְׂרָאֵל.

With regard to the spoils taken from Egypt described in the verse: "And the Lord gave the nation grace in the eyes of Egypt, **and they gave them what they requested**[N] and they emptied Egypt" (Exodus 12:36), **Rabbi Ami said: This teaches that** the Egyptians **gave them what they requested against their will.** There is a dispute with regard to the question: Against whose will? **Some say** it was given **against the will of the Egyptians, and some say** it was given **against the will of Israel.** The proponent of each position cites support for his opinion.

מַאן דְּאָמַר בְּעַל כָּרְחָם דְּמִצְרִים – דִּכְתִיב: "וּנְוַת בַּיִת תְּחַלֵּק שָׁלָל"; מַאן דְּאָמַר בְּעַל כָּרְחָם דְּיִשְׂרָאֵל – מִשּׁוּם מַשּׂוֹי.

**The one who said** that it was given **against the will of the Egyptians** cites the verse describing Israel's exit from Egypt, **as it is written: "And she who tarries at home divides the spoils"** (Psalms 68:13). That which the woman in the verse requested from her counterpart was actually spoils taken against the will of an enemy. **The one who said** that it was given **against the will of Israel,** claims that they did not want the vessels **because of the** burden of carrying a heavy **load** on a long journey.

"וַיְנַצְּלוּ אֶת מִצְרָיִם", אָמַר רַבִּי אַמֵּי: מְלַמֵּד שֶׁעֲשָׂאוּהָ כִּמְצוּדָה שֶׁאֵין בָּהּ דָּגָן. וְרֵישׁ לָקִישׁ אָמַר: עֲשָׂאוּהָ כִּמְצוּלָה שֶׁאֵין בָּהּ דָּגִים.

With regard to the continuation of the verse: **And they emptied Egypt,**[N] **Rabbi Ami said:** This indicates that **they made** Egypt **like a trap in which there is no grain**[N] that serves as bait to attract birds. **Reish Lakish said: They made** Egypt **like an abyss** in the sea **without fish.**

"אֶהְיֶה אֲשֶׁר אֶהְיֶה" – אָמַר לוֹ הַקָּדוֹשׁ בָּרוּךְ הוּא לְמֹשֶׁה, לֵךְ אֱמוֹר לָהֶם לְיִשְׂרָאֵל: אֲנִי הָיִיתִי עִמָּכֶם בְּשִׁעְבּוּד זֶה, וַאֲנִי אֶהְיֶה עִמָּכֶם בְּשִׁעְבּוּד מַלְכֻיּוֹת.

The Gemara proceeds to discuss the promise of redemption from Egypt that God made to Moses at the burning bush. When Moses asked God what to say when Israel asks him God's name, "and God said to Moses: **'I will be that I will be,'** and He said: 'Thus you will say unto the children of Israel: I will be has sent me to you'" (Exodus 3:14). **The Holy One, Blessed be He, told** Moses **to go and tell Israel: I was with you in this enslavement,** and in this redemption, **and I will be with you in the enslavement of the kingdoms**[N] in the future.

אָמַר לְפָנָיו: רִבּוֹנוֹ שֶׁל עוֹלָם! דַּיָּהּ לַצָּרָה בִּשְׁעָתָהּ. אָמַר לוֹ הַקָּדוֹשׁ בָּרוּךְ הוּא: לֵךְ אֱמוֹר לָהֶם "אֶהְיֶה שְׁלָחַנִי אֲלֵיכֶם".

Moses **said before Him: Master of the Universe, it is enough** for them to endure. Let **the** future **suffering** be endured **at its** appointed **time.** There is no need to mention their future enslavement. **The Holy One, Blessed be He,** agreed with Moses and **said to him: Go and tell** the children of Israel only that, **"I will be has sent me to you."**

"עֲנֵנִי ה' עֲנֵנִי". אָמַר רַבִּי אַבָּהוּ: לָמָּה אָמַר אֵלִיָּהוּ "עֲנֵנִי" שְׁתֵּי פְּעָמִים? – מְלַמֵּד שֶׁאָמַר אֵלִיָּהוּ לִפְנֵי הַקָּדוֹשׁ בָּרוּךְ הוּא: רִבּוֹנוֹ שֶׁל עוֹלָם! "עֲנֵנִי" – שֶׁתֵּרֵד אֵשׁ מִן הַשָּׁמַיִם וְתֹאכַל כָּל אֲשֶׁר עַל הַמִּזְבֵּחַ, וַ"עֲנֵנִי" – שֶׁתַּסִּיחַ דַּעְתָּם, כְּדֵי שֶׁלֹּא יֹאמְרוּ "מַעֲשֵׂה כְשָׁפִים הֵם", שֶׁנֶּאֱמַר: "וְאַתָּה הֲסִבֹּתָ אֶת לִבָּם אֲחֹרַנִּית".

Having explained the use of the double language of "I will be that I will be," the Gemara proceeds to explain the double language employed by Elijah on Mount Carmel: **"Answer me, Lord, answer me,"** that this people will know that You are the Lord, God, and You have turned their hearts backward" (1 Kings 18:37). **Rabbi Abbahu said: Why did** Elijah **say answer me twice?** This repetition **teaches that Elijah said before the Holy One, Blessed be He: Master of the Universe, answer me that fire will descend from heaven and consume everything that is on the altar, and answer me that You will divert their mind** from devising alternative explanations for what they witnessed so **that they will say that they were acts of sorcery. As it is stated** that Elijah said: **"And You have turned their hearts backward,"** God can restore them to the proper path as well.

מתני׳ מֵאֵימָתַי קוֹרִין אֶת ״שְׁמַע״ בְּשַׁחֲרִית? – מִשֶּׁיַּכִּיר בֵּין תְּכֵלֶת לְלָבָן. רַבִּי אֱלִיעֶזֶר אוֹמֵר: בֵּין תְּכֵלֶת לְכַרְתִּי. וְגוֹמְרָהּ עַד הָנֵץ הַחַמָּה. רַבִּי יְהוֹשֻׁעַ אוֹמֵר: עַד שָׁלֹשׁ שָׁעוֹת שֶׁכֵּן דֶּרֶךְ מְלָכִים לַעֲמוֹד בְּשָׁלֹשׁ שָׁעוֹת.

**MISHNA** **From when does one recite** ***Shema*** **in the morning?**[NH] **From** when a person **can distinguish between sky-blue** [*tekhelet*] **and white.**

**Rabbi Eliezer says:** From when one can distinguish **between sky-blue and leek-green.**[B]

And one must **finish** reciting *Shema* **until** the end of the period when you rise, i.e., **sunrise,** when the sun begins to shine.

**Rabbi Yehoshua says:** One may recite the morning *Shema* **until three hours** of the day, which this is still considered when you rise, **as that is the habit of kings to rise** from their sleep **at three hours** of the day.

הַקּוֹרֵא מִכָּאן וְאֵילָךְ – לֹא הִפְסִיד, כְּאָדָם הַקּוֹרֵא בַּתּוֹרָה.

While there is a set time frame for the recitation of *Shema,* **one who recites** *Shema* **from that time onward loses nothing.** Although he does not fulfill the mitzva of reciting of *Shema* at its appointed time, **he is** nevertheless considered **like one who reads the Torah,** and is rewarded accordingly.

גמ׳ מַאי ״בֵּין תְּכֵלֶת לְלָבָן״? אִילֵימָא בֵּין גִּבָּבָא דְעַמְרָא חִיוָּרָא לְגִבָּבָא דְעַמְרָא דְתִכְלְתָא – הָא בְּלֵילְיָא נַמִי מֵידַע יָדְעִי! אֶלָּא: בֵּין תְּכֵלֶת שֶׁבָּהּ לְלָבָן שֶׁבָּהּ.

**GEMARA** The mishna stated that the time for the recitation of the morning *Shema* begins when one can distinguish between sky-blue and white. The Gemara asks: To **what is between sky-blue**[B] **and white** referring? **If you say** that it means distinguishing between **a pile of white wool and a pile of sky-blue wool, wouldn't one know** the difference **at night, as well? Rather,** it must be a reference to ritual fringes made with sky-blue strings (see Numbers 15:38) along with white strings, and one must be able to distinguish **between the sky-blue** strings in the ritual fringes **and the white** strings **in** the ritual fringes.

With regard to the beginning of the time for the recitation of the morning *Shema,* a *baraita* cites additional opinions not cited in the mishna.

תַּנְיָא, רַבִּי מֵאִיר אוֹמֵר: מִשֶּׁיַּכִּיר בֵּין זְאֵב לְכֶלֶב. רַבִּי עֲקִיבָא אוֹמֵר: בֵּין חֲמוֹר לְעָרוֹד. וַאֲחֵרִים אוֹמְרִים: מִשֶּׁיִּרְאֶה אֶת חֲבֵרוֹ רָחוֹק אַרְבַּע אַמּוֹת וְיַכִּירֶנּוּ.

**It was taught** in a *baraita*:

**Rabbi Meir says** that the day begins when **one can distinguish between** two similar animals, e.g., **a wolf and a dog.**

**Rabbi Akiva** provides a different sign, and **says that the** day begins when there is sufficient light to distinguish **between a donkey and a wild donkey.**[B]

**And** ***Aḥerim*** **say: When one can see another** person, who is merely an acquaintance (Jerusalem Talmud) from **a distance of four cubits.**

אָמַר רַב הוּנָא: הֲלָכָה כַּאֲחֵרִים. אָמַר אַבָּיֵי: לִתְפִילִּין – כַּאֲחֵרִים, לִקְרִיאַת שְׁמַע – כְּוָתִיקִין. דְּאָמַר רַבִּי יוֹחָנָן: וָתִיקִין הָיוּ גּוֹמְרִין אוֹתָהּ עִם הָנֵץ הַחַמָּה.

**Rav Huna said: The** ***halakha*** **is in accordance with** ***Aḥerim.*** **Abaye said:** Regarding the time from which one may don **phylacteries,** a mitzva incumbent only by day, the *halakha* **is in accordance with** ***Aḥerim.*** But with regard to **the recitation of** ***Shema,*** one should conduct himself **in accordance with** the custom **of the** ***vatikin,***[H] pious individuals who were scrupulous in their performance of mitzvot. As **Rabbi Yoḥanan said: The** ***vatikin*** **would conclude** the recitation of *Shema* **with sunrise,** and one should act accordingly.

תַּנְיָא נַמִי הָכִי: וָתִיקִין הָיוּ גּוֹמְרִין אוֹתָהּ עִם הָנֵץ הַחַמָּה, כְּדֵי שֶׁיִּסְמוֹךְ גְּאוּלָּה לִתְפִלָּה וְנִמְצָא מִתְפַּלֵּל בַּיּוֹם.

**It was also taught** in a *baraita*: **The** ***vatikin*** **would conclude** the recitation of *Shema* **with sunrise in order to juxtapose** the blessing of **redemption,** which immediately follows the recitation of *Shema,* **with prayer, and pray during the day.**

אָמַר רַבִּי זֵירָא: מַאי קְרָאָה – ״יִירָאוּךָ עִם שָׁמֶשׁ וְלִפְנֵי יָרֵחַ דּוֹר דּוֹרִים״.

Regarding this custom of the *vatikin,* **Rabbi Zeira said: What verse** is the source for this tradition? **"They shall fear You with the sun, and before the moon for all generations"** (Psalms 72:5). This verse indicates that one should express one's awe of Heaven, they shall fear You, immediately before sunrise, with the sun.

### HALAKHA

**From when does one recite** ***Shema*** **in the morning** – **מֵאֵימָתַי קוֹרִין אֶת ״שְׁמַע״ בְּשַׁחֲרִית וכו׳**: The time for the recitation of the morning *Shema* is from when one can recognize an acquaintance from a distance of four cubits. This is in accordance with the opinion of *Aḥerim* and the ruling of Rav Huna, and based on the definition in the Jerusalem Talmud of the term *ḥavero* (Rambam *Sefer Ahava, Hilkhot Keriat Shema* 1:11, *Hilkhot Tefillin* 4:10; *Shulḥan Arukh Oraḥ Ḥayyim* 58:1).

**The recitation of the** ***Shema*** **in accordance with the** ***vatikin*** – **לִקְרִיאַת שְׁמַע כְּוָתִיקִין**: Optimally, the mitzva is to recite *Shema* adjacent to sunrise, in accordance with the custom of the *vatikin* (Rambam *Sefer Ahava, Hilkhot Keriat Shema* 1:11; *Shulḥan Arukh, Oraḥ Ḥayyim* 58:1).

### BACKGROUND

**Leek-green** – **כַּרְתִּי**: The leaves of this plant, see below p. 286 (44b), are a prototypical green, which served, even in other cultures, as an exemplar of color.

**Sky-blue** – **תְּכֵלֶת**: A special dye produced from a species of snail. In talmudic times, this dye was already quite rare, and the means of preparing it, including the species of snail used, were eventually forgotten. In recent generations, efforts have been made to identify the snail and to resume use of the dye. In the Torah, there is a positive commandment to use wool dyed this color for two purposes: For ritual fringes; one of the four threads of the fringes must be dyed with this special blue dye, and it is wound around the other threads. However, the mitzva to wear fringes is not contingent on one of the threads being dyed, and today virtually all ritual fringes are made without the dyed thread. In addition, in the priestly vestments, wool dyed this color is used in all or part of the sash, the entire cloak, the *ephod,* and the breastplate.

**Wild donkey** – **עָרוֹד**: The habitat of the wild donkey (*Assinus onager*) is in the desert, and today in the deserts of Asia. It is mentioned several times in the Bible as a symbol of freedom and wildness. The ability to distinguish between a wild and domesticated donkey can serve as an indicator for the amount of light at dusk and dawn.

Wild donkey

### NOTES

**From when does one recite** ***Shema*** **in the morning** – **מֵאֵימָתַי קוֹרִין אֶת ״שְׁמַע״ בְּשַׁחֲרִית וכו׳**: There is a basic explanation for the various determinations with regard to time for reciting *Shema.* In *Shema* it states: "When you walk along the way, when you lie down, and when you arise" (Deuteronomy 6:7). The time for reciting *Shema* is connected with the time people set out to travel. Since the two greatest dangers at night are wild animals and thieves, they are factors in determining the time of day when *Shema* is recited. People travel when they can distinguish between domesticated and wild animals, between a dog and a wolf, between a donkey and a wild donkey, or between an acquaintance and a stranger (*Penei Yehoshua*).

הֵעִיד רַבִּי יוֹסֵי בֶּן אֶלְיָקִים מִשּׁוּם קְהָלָא קַדִּישָׁא דְּבִירוּשָׁלַיִם: כׇּל הַסּוֹמֵךְ גְּאוּלָּה לִתְפִלָּה – אֵינוֹ נִזּוֹק כׇּל הַיּוֹם כּוּלּוֹ.

**Rabbi Yosei ben Elyakim testified in the name of the holy community**[B] **in Jerusalem,** a title accorded a particular group of Sages who lived there, that **one who juxtaposes redemption and prayer**[H] at sunrise **will incur no harm for the entire day.**

אָמַר רַבִּי זֵירָא: אִינִי? וְהָא אֲנָא סְמַכִי וְאִיתַּזַּקִי! אֲמַר לֵיהּ: בְּמַאי אִיתַּזַּקְתְּ – דְּאַמְטְיַית אָסָא לְבֵי מַלְכָּא; הָתָם נַמִי מִבָּעֵי לָךְ לְמֵיהַב אַגְרָא לְמֶחֱזֵי אַפֵּי מַלְכָּא, דְּאָמַר רַבִּי יוֹחָנָן: לְעוֹלָם יִשְׁתַּדֵּל אָדָם לָרוּץ לִקְרַאת מַלְכֵי יִשְׂרָאֵל, וְלֹא לִקְרַאת מַלְכֵי יִשְׂרָאֵל בִּלְבַד, אֶלָּא אֲפִילּוּ לִקְרַאת מַלְכֵי אוּמּוֹת הָעוֹלָם, שֶׁאִם יִזְכֶּה – יַבְחִין בֵּין מַלְכֵי יִשְׂרָאֵל לְמַלְכֵי אוּמּוֹת הָעוֹלָם.

**Rabbi Zeira said: Is that so? Didn't I juxtapose** redemption and prayer **and** nevertheless **I was harmed?** Rabbi Yosei ben Elyakim **asked** Rabbi Zeira: **How were you harmed? That you brought a myrtle branch to the king's palace?** The Gemara refers to Rabbi Zeira's responsibility as one of the respected members of the community to participate in a delegation that brought a crown of myrtle as a gift to the king, a dubious honor in which Rabbi Zeira had no interest. However, **there, too, you had to pay a price in order to see the face of the king, as Rabbi Yoḥanan said: One should always strive to run to greet the kings of Israel**[H] to witness them in their glory. **And not only** must one run **to greet the kings of Israel, but even to greet the kings of the nations of the world, so that if he will be privileged** to witness the redemption of Israel, **he will distinguish between the kings of Israel and the kings of the nations of the world,** to see how much greater the Jewish king will be and how his rule will be manifest. Therefore, it was a privilege for Rabbi Zeira that he was allowed to see the face of the king.

אֲמַר לֵיהּ רַבִּי אֶלְעָא לְעוּלָּא: כִּי עָיְילַתְּ לְהָתָם שְׁאֵיל בִּשְׁלָמָא דְּרַב בְּרוּנָא אָחִי בְּמַעֲמַד כׇּל הַחֲבוּרָה, דְּאָדָם גָּדוֹל הוּא וְשָׂמֵחַ בְּמִצְוֹת; זִימְנָא חֲדָא סְמַךְ גְּאוּלָּה לִתְפִלָּה וְלָא פְּסֵיק חוּכָא מִפּוּמֵּיהּ כּוּלֵּיהּ יוֹמָא.

**Rabbi El'a said to Ulla** before Ulla left for Babylonia: **When you go to** Babylonia, **ask after my brother, Rav Beruna, in the presence of the entire group, as he is a great man who rejoices in mitzvot,** and it is only fitting that he should be accorded respect. The Gemara provides proof that he was indeed a great man who rejoiced in mitzvot: **Once,** Rav Beruna **juxtaposed redemption and prayer** at sunrise, as per the custom of the *vatikin* (*Tosafot*), **and laughter** and joy **did not cease from his mouth for the entire day.**

הֵיכִי מָצֵי סָמֵיךְ? וְהָא אָמַר רַבִּי יוֹחָנָן: בַּתְּחִלָּה הוּא אוֹמֵר: ״ה׳ שְׂפָתַי תִּפְתָּח״, וּלְבַסּוֹף הוּא אוֹמֵר: ״יִהְיוּ לְרָצוֹן אִמְרֵי פִי״ וגו׳!

In practice, the Gemara asks: **How is one able to juxtapose redemption and prayer? Didn't Rabbi Yoḥanan say: At the beginning** of prayer, **one says: "Lord, open my lips,** that my mouth may declare Your glory" (Psalms 51:17), **and at the end** of prayer one says: **"May the words of my mouth** and the meditation of my heart **be acceptable**[N] before You, Lord, my Rock, and my Redeemer" (Psalms 19:15). If so, the first verse is an interruption between redemption and prayer.

אָמַר רַבִּי אֶלְעָזָר: תְּהֵא בִּתְפִלָּה שֶׁל עַרְבִית.

**Rabbi Elazar said: Let this** verse, "Lord, open my lips," be recited only **in the evening prayer** but not in the morning prayer.

וְהָא אָמַר רַבִּי יוֹחָנָן: אֵיזֶהוּ בֶּן הָעוֹלָם הַבָּא – זֶהוּ הַסּוֹמֵךְ גְּאוּלָּה שֶׁל עַרְבִית לִתְפִלָּה שֶׁל עַרְבִית!

The Gemara asks: **Didn't Rabbi Yoḥanan say: Who is worthy of** a place in **the World-to-Come? He who juxtaposes redemption of the evening prayer to the evening prayer.** Therefore, this verse from Psalms should not be recited before the evening prayer either.

אֶלָּא אָמַר רַבִּי אֶלְעָזָר: תְּהֵא בִּתְפִלַּת הַמִּנְחָה.

**Rather, Rabbi Elazar said: Let this** verse: "Lord, open my lips," be recited only before **the afternoon prayer.**

רַב אַשִׁי אָמַר: אֲפִילּוּ תֵּימָא אַכּוּלְּהוּ, וְכֵיוָן דִּקְבָעוּהָ רַבָּנַן בִּתְפִלָּה – כִּתְפִלָּה אֲרִיכְתָּא דָּמְיָא.

**Rav Ashi said** another explanation: **Even if you say** that Rabbi Yoḥanan holds that "Lord, open my lips" is recited before **all** prayers, including the morning and the evening prayers. **Since the Sages instituted** this verse, **it is considered as an extended prayer;** it is an inseparable part of the prayers, and if redemption is juxtaposed to this verse, it is no different than if redemption was juxtaposed to prayer directly.

דְּאִי לָא תֵּימָא הָכִי, עַרְבִית הֵיכִי מָצֵי סָמֵיךְ? וְהָא בָּעֵי לְמֵימַר ״הַשְׁכִּיבֵנוּ״! אֶלָּא, כֵּיוָן דְּתַקִּינוּ רַבָּנַן ״הַשְׁכִּיבֵנוּ״ – כִּגְאוּלָּה אֲרִיכְתָּא דָּמְיָא, הָכִי נַמִי, כֵּיוָן דִּקְבָעוּהָ רַבָּנַן בִּתְפִלָּה – כִּתְפִלָּה אֲרִיכְתָּא דָּמְיָא.

Rabbi Ashi supports his claim: **As if you do not say so, how does one juxtapose** redemption of the evening prayer to **the evening prayer? Mustn't one recite: Help us lie down** [*hashkivenu*] after redemption? **Rather, since the Sages instituted** the recitation of: **Help us lie down, it is considered as an extended blessing of redemption. So, too, since the Sages instituted** this verse **in prayer, it is considered as an extended prayer.**

מִכְּדֵי, הַאי ״יִהְיוּ לְרָצוֹן אִמְרֵי פִי״ – מַשְׁמַע לְבַסּוֹף, וּמַשְׁמַע מֵעִיקָּרָא, דְּבָעֵינָא לְמֵימַר. מַאי טַעְמָא תַּקְנוּהוּ רַבָּנַן לְאַחַר שְׁמוֹנֶה עֶשְׂרֵה בְּרָכוֹת? לֵימְרוּ מֵעִיקָּרָא!

With regard to the verse with which the prayer concludes, the Gemara deliberates: **Now, since this** verse: **"May the words of my mouth** and the meditation of my heart **be acceptable** before You," can **connote the end** of prayer, petitioning God that He accept the prayer that was just recited, **and** it can **connote the beginning** of the prayer **that he wants to recite:** May the words of my mouth which I am about to recite be acceptable before You. If so, the question arises: **Why did the Sages institute** that it is to be recited **after the eighteen blessings** that constitute the *Amida*? **Let it be recited at the beginning** of the prayer.

### BACKGROUND

**The holy community – קְהָלָא קַדִּישָׁא:** They were called by that appellation because they would divide their days into thirds: One third for prayer, one third for Torah study, and one third for labor. Others say that it is because they would engage in Torah during the winter and agriculture during the summer. As the Gemara explains, those who both benefit from the labor of their hands and are among the Torah luminaries of their generation are fit to be called "the holy community."

### HALAKHA

**One who juxtaposes redemption and prayer – כָּל הַסּוֹמֵךְ גְּאוּלָּה לִתְפִלָּה וכו׳:** One is required to juxtapose redemption and prayer and refrain from interrupting after completing the blessing: Who redeemed Israel, both morning and evening, even to respond amen. The only exception to this is the recitation of the verse: "Lord, open my lips," which was instituted by the Sages. Others hold that one is permitted to respond amen to the blessing: Who redeemed Israel, and that is the custom (*Tur*; Rambam *Sefer Ahava, Hilkhot Tefilla* 7:17; *Shulḥan Arukh, Oraḥ Ḥayyim* 66:8, 111:1 and in the Rema).

**One should always strive to run to greet the kings of Israel – לְעוֹלָם יִשְׁתַּדֵּל אָדָם לָרוּץ לִקְרַאת מַלְכֵי וכו׳:** Seeing the faces of kings, or of the prominent leaders of the kingdom (Jerusalem Talmud), even if they are not Jewish, is a mitzva. Furthermore, some rabbinic stringencies were suspended in order to facilitate going to greet kings, and a special blessing was instituted for just such an occasion (Rambam *Sefer Shofetim, Hilkhot Evel* 3:14; *Shulḥan Arukh, Oraḥ Ḥayyim* 224:9).

### NOTES

**The recitation of, "May the words of my mouth…be acceptable" – אֲמִירַת יִהְיוּ לְרָצוֹן:** Although the Gemara explains how this verse is appropriate both as a preface and as a conclusion to prayer, that does not entirely justify the question why it is not recited at the beginning. If the verse was recited at the beginning of the prayer, the question would be why is it not recited at the end. Therefore, the commentaries explained that there is a specific reason why it should open the prayer rather than close it. The verse reads, "May the words of my mouth and the meditations of my heart be acceptable before You, Lord, my Rock and my Redeemer." Were it recited before the prayer, it would be a form of juxtaposing redemption, my Redeemer, and prayer. Therefore, it was necessary to explain that, nevertheless, the fact that King David placed the verse at the end of the 18th Psalm (Rashba), is a more significant consideration in establishing where the verses will appear relative to the prayer (*Tosefot HaRosh*, *Tosefot Rabbeinu Yehuda HaḤasid*).

אָמַר רַבִּי יְהוּדָה בְּרֵיהּ דְּרַבִּי שִׁמְעוֹן בֶּן פָּזִי: הוֹאִיל וְלֹא אֲמָרוֹ דָּוִד אֶלָּא לְאַחַר שְׁמוֹנֶה עֶשְׂרֵה פָּרָשִׁיּוֹת, לְפִיכָךְ תִּקְּנוּ רַבָּנַן לְאַחַר שְׁמוֹנֶה עֶשְׂרֵה בְּרָכוֹת.

**Rabbi Yehuda, son of Rabbi Shimon ben Pazi, said:** This verse is recited after the eighteen blessings comprising the *Amida* **because David only said** this verse **after eighteen chapters** of Psalms (end of ch. 19). **Therefore, the Sages instituted** to recite it **after the eighteen blessings** of the *Amida*.

הָנֵי שְׁמוֹנֶה עֶשְׂרֵה? תְּשַׁע עֶשְׂרֵה הָוְיָין!

The Gemara asks: Are **these eighteen** psalms? **They are nineteen** chapters that precede that verse.[N]

"אַשְׁרֵי הָאִישׁ" וְ"לָמָּה רָגְשׁוּ גוֹיִם" חֲדָא פָּרָשָׁה הִיא.

The Gemara answers: **"Happy is the man,"** the first chapter of Psalms, **and "Why are the nations in an uproar,"** the second chapter, **constitute a single chapter,** so the nineteen chapters are actually eighteen.

דְּאָמַר רַבִּי יְהוּדָה בְּרֵיהּ דְּרַבִּי שִׁמְעוֹן בֶּן פָּזִי: מֵאָה וְשָׁלֹשׁ פָּרָשִׁיּוֹת אָמַר דָּוִד, וְלֹא אָמַר "הַלְלוּיָהּ" עַד שֶׁרָאָה בְּמַפַּלְתָּן שֶׁל רְשָׁעִים, שֶׁנֶּאֱמַר: "יִתַּמּוּ חַטָּאִים מִן הָאָרֶץ וּרְשָׁעִים עוֹד אֵינָם בָּרְכִי נַפְשִׁי אֶת ה' הַלְלוּיָהּ".

The Gemara cites proof that the first two chapters are in fact a single chapter. **As Rabbi Yehuda, son of Rabbi Shimon ben Pazi, said: David said one hundred and three chapters, and he did not say *Halleluya*** in any of them **until he saw the downfall of the wicked.** Only then could David could say *Halleluya* wholeheartedly. **As it is stated: "Let sinners cease from the earth, and let the wicked be no more. Bless the Lord, my soul, *Halleluya*"** (Psalms 104:35).

הָנֵי מֵאָה וְשָׁלֹשׁ? מֵאָה וְאַרְבַּע הָוְיָין! אֶלָּא שְׁמַע מִינַּהּ: "אַשְׁרֵי הָאִישׁ" וְ"לָמָּה רָגְשׁוּ גוֹיִם" חֲדָא פָּרָשָׁה הִיא.

Here too, the Gemara notes that the calculation appears inaccurate: Are **these one hundred and three** psalms? **They are one hundred and four. Rather, conclude from this** that **"Happy is the man"** and **"Why are the nations in uproar" constitute a single portion.**

דְּאָמַר רַבִּי שְׁמוּאֵל בַּר נַחְמָנִי אָמַר רַבִּי יוֹחָנָן:

Additional proof that these two chapters comprise a single portion is cited from what **Rabbi Shmuel bar Naḥmani said** that **Rabbi Yoḥanan said:**



כָּל פָּרָשָׁה שֶׁהָיְתָה חֲבִיבָה עַל דָּוִד, פָּתַח בָּהּ בְּ"אַשְׁרֵי" וְסִיֵּים בָּהּ בְּ"אַשְׁרֵי"; פָּתַח בְּ"אַשְׁרֵי" – דִּכְתִיב: "אַשְׁרֵי הָאִישׁ", וְסִיֵּים בְּ"אַשְׁרֵי" – דִּכְתִיב: "אַשְׁרֵי כָּל חוֹסֵי בוֹ".

**Every chapter that was dear to David, he began with "happy is"** and **concluded with "happy is."**[N] **He opened with "happy is," as it is written: "Happy is the man** who has not walked in the counsel of the wicked or stood in the way of sinners or sat in the dwelling place of the scornful" (Psalms 1:1). **And he concluded with "happy," as it is written** at the end of the chapter: "Pay homage in purity, lest He be angry, and you perish on the way when His anger is kindled suddenly. **Happy are those who take refuge in Him"** (Psalms 2:12). We see that these two chapters actually constitute a single chapter.

הָנְהוּ בִּרְיוֹנֵי דַּהֲווֹ בְּשִׁבָבוּתֵיהּ דְּרַבִּי מֵאִיר וַהֲווֹ קָא מְצַעֲרוּ לֵיהּ טוּבָא, הֲוָה קָא בָּעֵי רַבִּי מֵאִיר רַחֲמֵי עֲלַיְיהוּ כִּי הֵיכִי דְּלֵימוּתוּ. אָמְרָה לֵיהּ בְּרוּרְיָא דְּבֵיתְהוּ: מַאי דַּעְתָּךְ? – מִשּׁוּם דִּכְתִיב: "יִתַּמּוּ חַטָּאִים", מִי כְּתִיב "חוֹטְאִים"? "חַטָּאִים" כְּתִיב!

With regard to the statement of Rabbi Yehuda, son of Rabbi Shimon ben Pazi, that David did not say *Halleluya* until he saw the downfall of the wicked, the Gemara relates: **There were these hooligans in Rabbi Meir's neighborhood who caused him a great deal of anguish. Rabbi Meir prayed for** God to have **mercy on them, that they should die. Rabbi Meir's wife, Berurya,[P] said to him: What is your thinking?** On what basis do you pray for the death of these hooligans? Do you base yourself on the verse, **as it is written: "Let sins cease from the land"** (Psalms 104:35), which you interpret to mean that the world would be better if the wicked were destroyed? But **is it written, let sinners** cease?" Let **sins** cease, **is written.**[N] One should pray for an end to their transgressions, not for the demise of the transgressors themselves.

וְעוֹד, שְׁפִיל לְסֵיפֵיהּ דִּקְרָא: "וּרְשָׁעִים עוֹד אֵינָם", כֵּיוָן דְּ"יִתַּמּוּ חַטָּאִים" – "וּרְשָׁעִים עוֹד אֵינָם"? אֶלָּא, בְּעִי רַחֲמֵי עֲלַיְיהוּ דְּלִהְדְרוּ בִּתְשׁוּבָה – "וּרְשָׁעִים עוֹד אֵינָם".

**Moreover, go to the end of the verse,** where it says: **"And the wicked will be no more."** If, as you suggest, **transgressions shall cease** refers to the demise of the evildoers, how is it possible that **the wicked will be no more,** i.e., that they will no longer be evil? **Rather, pray for** God to have **mercy on them, that they should repent,** as if they repent, then the wicked will be no more, as they will have repented.

**NOTES**

**The number of Psalms** – מִסְפָּרָם שֶׁל מִזְמוֹרֵי הַתְּהִלִּים: While the book of Psalms as we know it, and apparently, as the Sages of the Talmud knew it, is divided into 150 Psalms, older traditions, cited in the midrash, divide it into 147. Chapters that now appear separately were once united. Since the first two chapters are similar in content, and since there is no introductory phrase in the second chapter, they can easily be integrated into a single chapter.

**NOTES**

**He began with "happy is" and concluded with "happy is"** – פָּתַח בָּהּ בְּ"אַשְׁרֵי" וְסִיֵּים בָּהּ בְּ"אַשְׁרֵי": It has been noted that the first two chapters of Psalms are the only instance where a psalm begins and ends with "happy is." Consequently, formulating a general principle: Every chapter that was dear to David, he began with "happy is" and concluded with "happy is," seems inappropriate, as it only applies to one case. However, some explained that this principle is not limited to psalms that begin and end with "happy is." Rather, it is a general principle with regard to any chapter of Psalms that opens and concludes with the same word, e.g., *Halleluya* (*Tosafot*).

**Is it written, let sinners cease? Let sins cease, is written** – מִי כְּתִיב חוֹטְאִים חַטָּאִים כְּתִיב: Berurya's interpretation of the term *ḥatta'im* is not literal. It is an interpretation based upon an allusion. The literal meaning of the word is, indeed, sinners. Some explain that the very fact that the verse opted to use the word *ḥatta'im*, which is open to various interpretations, as opposed to the unambiguous word *ḥotim*, opens the door to a more compassionate interpretation of the verse.

**PERSONALITIES**

**Berurya** – בְּרוּרְיָא: Berurya was the wife of the *tanna* Rabbi Meir. She was the daughter of the *tanna* Rabbi Ḥanina ben Teradyon, who was one of the ten martyrs. She was renowned not only for her character and personality, but also for her extensive Torah knowledge. Her aptitude for Torah study exemplified her exceptional genius. She disagreed with several Sages of her generation, and we find that the *halakha* in that dispute was ruled in accordance with her opinion.

As a result of decrees of persecution, nearly her entire family was martyred. Calamity continued to afflict her throughout her life when her two children died in a single day. The Gemara relates how she conducted herself with exceptional courage. From a story which is only alluded to in the Talmud, we know that her own death also came about in the wake of a series of painful events.

Aside from a few halakhic statements, we find several places in the Talmud where her modest and considerate characteristics are manifest even through sharp responses to various people.

## NOTES

**She opens her mouth with wisdom – פִּיהָ פָּתְחָה בְחָכְמָה:** According to the Gemara, Solomon said this verse about King David. The connection between this verse and King David can be explained as follows: Since this proverb, which praises the good woman, is interpreted in praise of the Torah and people who achieved excellence through its study, the verse: "She opens her mouth with wisdom," is speaking about the same theme. However, specifically vis-à-vis Solomon, the wisest of men, it is important to emphasize the essence of the wisdom mentioned in this verse. The wisdom lauded by Solomon in this proverb is unlike his own wisdom. Rather, it is the wisdom of the believer, of one who loves God. Therefore, "She opens her mouth with wisdom" refers to the great prophetic poet, King David of Israel.

**David…resided in five worlds and said a song of praise corresponding to each of them – דָּוִד...שֶׁדָּר בַּחֲמִשָּׁה עוֹלָמִים וְאָמַר שִׁירָה:** There is a tremendous difference between looking upon an experience in a superficial manner and reflecting upon it and contemplating it. An individual who merely sees the external will not come to understand the deeper, spiritual significance of a given experience or encounter. Natural events like pregnancy, birth, and nursing may seem to be mundane events experienced by humans and animals alike. However, one with a higher level of spiritual discernment will appreciate the vast difference between man and animal. King David's songs of praise, uttered at every stage of life, attest to the magnitude of his sensitivity to God's beneficence and to his appreciation of His role in the world (*Ein Ayah*).

בְּעָא רַחֲמֵי עִלָּוַיְהוּ וַהֲדַרוּ בִּתְשׁוּבָה.

Rabbi Meir saw that Berurya was correct **and he prayed for** God to have **mercy on them, and they repented.**

אֲמַר לָהּ הַהוּא מִינָא לִבְרוּרְיָא: כְּתִיב "רָנִּי עֲקָרָה לֹא יָלָדָה", מִשּׁוּם דְּלָא יָלְדָה – רָנִּי?!

The Gemara relates an additional example of Berurya's incisive insight: **A certain heretic said to Berurya: It is written: "Sing, barren woman who has not given birth,** open forth in song and cry, you did not travail, for more are the children of the desolate than the children of the married wife, said the Lord" (Isaiah 54:1). **Because she has not given birth,** she should **sing** and rejoice?

אָמְרָה לֵיהּ: שַׁטְיָא! שְׁפֵיל לְסֵיפֵיהּ דִּקְרָא, דִּכְתִיב: "כִּי רַבִּים בְּנֵי שׁוֹמֵמָה מִבְּנֵי בְעוּלָה אָמַר ה'".

Berurya responded to this heretic's mockery and **said: Fool! Go to the end of the verse, where it is written: "For the children of the desolate shall be more numerous than the children of the married wife, said the Lord."**

אֶלָּא מַאי "עֲקָרָה לֹא יָלָדָה" – רָנִּי כְּנֶסֶת יִשְׂרָאֵל שֶׁדּוֹמָה לְאִשָּׁה עֲקָרָה שֶׁלֹּא יָלְדָה בָּנִים לְגֵיהִנָּם כְּוָתַיְיכוּ.

**Rather, what** is the meaning of: **"Sing, barren woman who has not given birth"?** It means: **Sing congregation of Israel, which is like a barren woman who did not give birth to children who are** destined **for Gehenna like you.**

אֲמַר לֵיהּ הַהוּא מִינָא לְרַבִּי אַבָּהוּ, כְּתִיב: "מִזְמוֹר לְדָוִד בְּבָרְחוֹ מִפְּנֵי אַבְשָׁלוֹם בְּנוֹ", וּכְתִיב: "לְדָוִד מִכְתָּם בְּבָרְחוֹ מִפְּנֵי שָׁאוּל בַּמְּעָרָה", הֵי מַעֲשֶׂה הֲוָה בְּרֵישָׁא? מִכְּדֵי מַעֲשֵׂה שָׁאוּל הֲוָה בְּרֵישָׁא – לִכְתּוֹב בְּרֵישָׁא!

In explaining passages from Psalms, the Gemara relates another instance of a response to the question of a heretic: **A certain heretic said to Rabbi Abbahu, it is written: "A Psalm of David, when he fled from his son, Absalom"** (Psalms 3:1), **and** similarly **it is said:** "To the chief musician, *al tashḥet*, a *mikhtam* **of David when fleeing from Saul into the cave"** (Psalms 57:1). **Which event was first? Since the event with Saul was first,** it would have been appropriate **to write it first.**

אֲמַר לֵיהּ: אַתּוּן דְּלָא דָּרְשִׁיתוּן 'סְמוּכִין' – קַשְׁיָא לְכוּ, אֲנַן דְּדָרְשִׁינַן 'סְמוּכִים' – לָא קַשְׁיָא לַן,

Rabbi Abbahu **said to him:** For **you, who do** not employ the **homiletic** method **of juxtaposition** of verses, **it is difficult.** But for **us, who** employ the **homiletic** method **of juxtaposition** of verses, **it is not difficult,** as the Sages commonly homiletically infer laws and moral lessons from the juxtaposition of two verses.

דְּאָמַר רַבִּי יוֹחָנָן: 'סְמוּכִין' מִן הַתּוֹרָה מִנַּיִן – שֶׁנֶּאֱמַר: "סְמוּכִים לָעַד לְעוֹלָם עֲשׂוּיִם בֶּאֱמֶת וְיָשָׁר".

Regarding the juxtaposition of verses, **Rabbi Yoḥanan said: From where** in the Bible is it derived that one may draw homiletical inferences from the **juxtaposition** of verses? **As it is said:** "The works of His hands in truth and justice, all His commandments are sure. **Adjoined forever and ever, made in truth and uprightness"** (Psalms 111:7–8). Conclude from here that it is appropriate to draw inferences from the juxtaposition of God's commandments. Accordingly, David's fleeing from Absalom is situated where it is in order to juxtapose it to the next chapter, which mentions the war of Gog and Magog; the second chapter of Psalms opens: "Why are the nations in an uproar?"

לָמָּה נִסְמְכָה פָּרָשַׁת אַבְשָׁלוֹם לְפָרָשַׁת גּוֹג וּמָגוֹג – שֶׁאִם יֹאמַר לְךָ אָדָם: כְּלוּם יֵשׁ עֶבֶד שֶׁמּוֹרֵד בְּרַבּוֹ? אַף אַתָּה אֱמוֹר לוֹ: כְּלוּם יֵשׁ בֵּן שֶׁמּוֹרֵד בְּאָבִיו? אֶלָּא – הֲוָה, הָכָא נַמִּי – הֲוָה.

**Why was the chapter of Absalom juxtaposed with the chapter of Gog and Magog?** They are juxtaposed **so that if a person should say to you,** expressing doubt with regard to the prophecy of the war of Gog and Magog "against the Lord and against His anointed": **Is there a slave who rebels against his master?** Is there someone capable of rebelling against God? **You too say to him: Is there a son who rebels against his father** and severs the relationship with the one who brought him into the world and raised him? **Yet,** nevertheless, **there was** such a son, Absalom, and **so too there** can **be** a situation where people will seek to rebel against God.

אָמַר רַבִּי יוֹחָנָן מִשּׁוּם רַבִּי שִׁמְעוֹן בֶּן יוֹחַי, מַאי דִּכְתִיב: "פִּיהָ פָּתְחָה בְחָכְמָה וְתוֹרַת חֶסֶד עַל לְשׁוֹנָהּ", כְּנֶגֶד מִי אָמַר שְׁלֹמֹה מִקְרָא זֶה? – לֹא אֲמָרוֹ אֶלָּא כְּנֶגֶד דָּוִד אָבִיו, שֶׁדָּר בַּחֲמִשָּׁה עוֹלָמִים וְאָמַר שִׁירָה:

**Rabbi Yoḥanan said** explanations of other verses **in the name of Rabbi Shimon ben Yoḥai: What is** the meaning of **that which is written: "She opens her mouth with wisdom,[N] and the teaching of loving-kindness is on her tongue"** (Proverbs 31:26)? The Sages explain that this chapter discusses the wisdom of Torah and those who engage in its study, so **with reference to whom did Solomon say this verse? He said this** verse **about none other than his father, David,** who was the clearest example of one who opens his mouth in wisdom, and **who resided in five worlds** or stages of life **and** his soul **said a song** of praise corresponding to each of them.[N] Five times David said: "Bless the Lord, O my soul," each corresponding to a different stage of life.

דָּר בִּמְעֵי אִמּוֹ וְאָמַר שִׁירָה, שֶׁנֶּאֱמַר: "בָּרְכִי נַפְשִׁי אֶת ה׳ וְכָל קְרָבַי אֶת שֵׁם קׇדְשׁוֹ".

**He resided in his mother's womb,** his first world, **and said a song** of praise of the pregnancy, **as it is stated: "Of David. Bless the Lord, O my soul and all that is within me bless His holy name"** (Psalms 103:1), in which he thanks God for creating all that is within his mother, i.e., her womb.

יָצָא לַאֲוִיר הָעוֹלָם וְנִסְתַּכֵּל בְּכוֹכָבִים וּמַזָּלוֹת וְאָמַר שִׁירָה, שֶׁנֶּאֱמַר: "בָּרְכוּ ה׳ מַלְאָכָיו גִּבֹּרֵי כֹחַ עֹשֵׂי דְבָרוֹ לִשְׁמֹעַ בְּקוֹל דְּבָרוֹ בָּרְכוּ ה׳ כׇּל צְבָאָיו" וגו׳.

**He emerged into the atmosphere of the world,** his second world, **looked upon the stars and constellations and said a song** of praise of God for the entirety of creation, **as it is stated: "Bless the Lord, His angels, mighty in strength, that fulfill His word, listening to the voice of His word. Bless the Lord, all His hosts,** His servants, that do His will. Bless the Lord, all His works, in all places of His kingship, bless my soul, Lord" (Psalms 103:20–23). David saw the grandeur of all creation and recognized that they are mere servants, carrying out the will of their Creator (*Ma'ayan HaBerakhot*).

יָנַק מִשְּׁדֵי אִמּוֹ וְנִסְתַּכֵּל בְּדַדֶּיהָ וְאָמַר שִׁירָה, שֶׁנֶּאֱמַר: "בָּרְכִי נַפְשִׁי אֶת ה׳ וְאַל תִּשְׁכְּחִי כׇּל גְּמוּלָיו".

**He nursed from his mother's breast,** his third world, **and he looked upon her bosom and said a song** of praise, **as it is stated: "Bless the Lord, O my soul, and do not forget all His benefits** [*gemulav*]" (Psalms 103:2). The etymological association is between *gemulav* and *gemulei meḥalav*, which means weaned from milk (Isaiah 28:9).

מַאי "כׇּל גְּמוּלָיו"? אָמַר רַבִּי אַבָּהוּ: שֶׁעָשָׂה לָהּ דַּדִּים בִּמְקוֹם בִּינָה.

We still must understand, however, **what is** meant by **all His benefits?** What in particular is praiseworthy in what God provided, beyond merely providing for the infant? **Rabbi Abbahu said:** In contrast with most other animals, God **placed her breasts** near her heart, **the place** that is the source **of understanding.**

טַעְמָא מַאי? אָמַר רַב יְהוּדָה: כְּדֵי שֶׁלֹּא יִסְתַּכֵּל בִּמְקוֹם עֶרְוָה. רַב מַתָּנָא אָמַר: כְּדֵי שֶׁלֹּא יִינַק מִמְּקוֹם הַטִּנּוֹפֶת.

**What is the reason** that God did this? **Rav Yehuda said: So that** the nursing child **would not look upon the place of** his mother's **nakedness. Rav Mattana said: So that** the child **would not nurse from a place of uncleanliness.**

רָאָה בְּמַפַּלְתָּן שֶׁל רְשָׁעִים וְאָמַר שִׁירָה, שֶׁנֶּאֱמַר: "יִתַּמּוּ חַטָּאִים מִן הָאָרֶץ וּרְשָׁעִים עוֹד אֵינָם בָּרְכִי נַפְשִׁי אֶת ה׳ הַלְלוּיָהּ".

**He witnessed** in both vision and reality **the downfall of the wicked and he said a song** of praise, **as it is stated: "Let sinners cease from the earth, and let the wicked be no more. Bless the Lord, O my soul,** ***Halleluya*"** (Psalms 104:35).

נִסְתַּכֵּל בְּיוֹם הַמִּיתָה וְאָמַר שִׁירָה, שֶׁנֶּאֱמַר: "בָּרְכִי נַפְשִׁי אֶת ה׳, ה׳ אֱלֹהַי גָּדַלְתָּ מְּאֹד הוֹד וְהָדָר לָבָשְׁתָּ".

The fifth world was when David **looked upon the day of death and said a song** of praise, **as it is stated: "Bless the Lord, O my soul. Lord my God, You are very great; You are clothed in glory and majesty"** (Psalms 104:1); for even death is a time of transcendence for the righteous.

מַאי מַשְׁמַע דְּעַל יוֹם הַמִּיתָה נֶאֱמַר? אֲמַר רַבָּה בַּר רַב שֵׁילָא: מִסֵּיפָא דְּעִנְיָנָא, דִּכְתִיב: "תַּסְתִּיר פָּנֶיךָ יִבָּהֵלוּן תֹּסֵף רוּחָם יִגְוָעוּן" וגו׳.

The connection between this final praise and the day of death is unclear. The Gemara asks: **From where is it inferred** that **this** verse **was stated with regard to the day of death?** The Gemara answers: We can derive this **from** the verses at **the end of the matter,** where **it is written: "You hide Your face, they vanish; You gather Your breath, they perish** and return to the dust" (Psalms 104:29).

רַב שִׁימִי בַּר עוּקְבָא, וְאָמְרִי לָהּ מָר עוּקְבָא, הֲוָה שְׁכִיחַ קַמֵּיהּ דְּרַבִּי שִׁמְעוֹן בֶּן פָּזִי, וַהֲוָה מְסַדֵּר אַגַּדְתָּא קַמֵּיהּ דְּרַבִּי יְהוֹשֻׁעַ בֶּן לֵוִי. אֲמַר לֵיהּ: מַאי דִּכְתִיב "בָּרְכִי נַפְשִׁי אֶת ה׳ וְכׇל קְרָבַי אֶת שֵׁם קׇדְשׁוֹ"? אָמַר לֵיהּ: בֹּא וּרְאֵה שֶׁלֹּא כְּמִדַּת הַקָּדוֹשׁ בָּרוּךְ הוּא מִדַּת בָּשָׂר וָדָם. מִדַּת בָּשָׂר וָדָם – צָר צוּרָה עַל גַּבֵּי הַכּוֹתֶל, וְאֵינוֹ יָכוֹל לְהַטִּיל בָּהּ רוּחַ וּנְשָׁמָה, קְרָבַיִם וּבְנֵי מֵעַיִם. וְהַקָּדוֹשׁ בָּרוּךְ הוּא אֵינוֹ כֵּן, צָר צוּרָה בְּתוֹךְ צוּרָה, וּמַטִּיל בָּהּ רוּחַ וּנְשָׁמָה, קְרָבַיִם וּבְנֵי מֵעַיִם. וְהַיְינוּ דְּאָמְרָה חַנָּה: "אֵין קָדוֹשׁ כַּה׳ כִּי אֵין בִּלְתֶּךָ וְאֵין צוּר כֵּאלֹהֵינוּ".

Other interpretations of this verse exist. The Gemara relates how **Rav Shimi bar Ukva, and some say Mar Ukva, would regularly** study **before Rabbi Shimon ben Pazi,** who was well versed in *aggada* and **would arrange the** ***aggada*** **before Rabbi Yehoshua ben Levi.**

Once, Rabbi Shimon ben Pazi **said to him: What is** the meaning of **that which is written: "Bless the Lord, my soul, and all that is within me bless His Holy name"?**

Rav Shimi bar Ukva **said to** Rabbi Shimon ben Pazi: **Come and see that the attribute of the Holy One, Blessed be He, is not like the attribute of flesh and blood,** as this verse praises the formation of man in his mother's womb. **The attribute of flesh and blood is** such that he **shapes a form on the wall** for all to see, yet **he cannot instill it with a spirit and soul, bowels and intestines.** While **the Holy One, Blessed be He, is not so,** as God **shapes one form within another form,** a child in its mother's womb, **and instills it with spirit and soul, bowels and intestines. And this is** the explanation of **what Hannah said** with regard to the birth of Samuel: **"There is none holy like the Lord, for there is none like You, and there is no Rock like our God"** (I Samuel 2:2).

מַאי "אֵין צוּר כֵּאלֹהֵינוּ"? – אֵין צַיָּיר כֵּאלֹהֵינוּ.

**What is** the meaning of **there is no rock** [*tzur*] **like our God? There is no artist** [*tzayyar*][N] **like our God.**

**NOTES**

**There is no rock…there is no artist – אין צור...אין צייר:** The reason for the homiletic interpretation of the word *tzur* is that it is difficult to find a connection between its usual sense of strength, might, or stone, and Hannah's prayer. On the other hand, if it is interpreted to mean artist, the connection is clear: Hannah is thanking God for blessing her with a child.

## NOTES

**He said them about none other than the Holy One, Blessed be He, and corresponding to the soul – לֹא אֲמָרָן אֶלָּא כְּנֶגֶד הַקָּדוֹשׁ בָּרוּךְ הוּא וּכְנֶגֶד נְשָׁמָה:** According to *Nefesh HaHayyim*, while the Sages drew a parallel between God's connection to the world and the connection of the human soul to the body, it is impossible to suggest that they meant to say that they are comparable. This is eminently clear as verses throughout the Bible clearly indicate: "To whom then will you liken God? Or what likeness will you compare unto Him?" (Isaiah 40:18), God cannot be compared to any physical being. The point of the parallel is to provide us with the following understanding: One can only begin to comprehend anything about the human soul, a creation of God, in the context of the body. Similarly, it is only possible to gain any understanding of God in the context of His relationship with the world (*Etz Yosef*).

מַאי "כִּי אֵין בִּלְתֶּךָ"? – אָמַר רַבִּי יְהוּדָה בַּר מְנַסְיָא: אַל תִּקְרֵי "כִּי אֵין בִּלְתֶּךָ" אֶלָּא "אֵין לְבַלּוֹתְךָ", שֶׁלֹּא כְּמִדַּת הַקָּדוֹשׁ בָּרוּךְ הוּא מִדַּת בָּשָׂר וָדָם. מִדַּת בָּשָׂר וָדָם – מַעֲשֵׂה יָדָיו מְבַלִּין אוֹתוֹ, וְהַקָּדוֹשׁ בָּרוּךְ הוּא מְבַלֶּה מַעֲשָׂיו.

The Gemara continues to interpret the rest of that verse homiletically: **What is the meaning of "there is none like You"? Rabbi Yehuda ben Menasya said: Do not read** the verse to mean **"there is none like You** [*biltekha*]"; **rather, read** it to mean **"none can outlast You** [*levalotkha*]," **as the attribute of the Holy One, Blessed be He, is not like the attribute of flesh and blood: The attribute of flesh and blood is** such **that his creations outlast him,** but **the Holy One, Blessed be He, outlasts His actions.**

אֲמַר לֵיהּ: אֲנָא הָכִי קָא אָמִינָא לָךְ. הָנֵי חֲמִשָּׁה "בָּרְכִי נַפְשִׁי" כְּנֶגֶד מִי אֲמָרָן דָּוִד? – לֹא אֲמָרָן אֶלָּא כְּנֶגֶד הַקָּדוֹשׁ בָּרוּךְ הוּא וּכְנֶגֶד נְשָׁמָה:

This did not satisfy Rav Shimi bar Ukva, who **said to** Rabbi Shimon ben Pazi: **I** meant to **say to you as follows: Corresponding to whom did David say these five** instance of **"Bless** the Lord, **O my soul"?** He answered him: **He said them about none other than the Holy One, Blessed be He, and corresponding to the soul,**[N] as the verse refers to the relationship between man's soul and God. The five instances of "Bless the Lord, O my soul" correspond to the five parallels between the soul in man's body and God's power in His world.

מָה הַקָּדוֹשׁ בָּרוּךְ הוּא מָלֵא כָּל הָעוֹלָם – אַף נְשָׁמָה מְלֵאָה אֶת כָּל הַגּוּף; מָה הַקָּדוֹשׁ בָּרוּךְ הוּא רוֹאֶה וְאֵינוֹ נִרְאֶה – אַף נְשָׁמָה רוֹאָה וְאֵינָהּ נִרְאֵית; מָה הַקָּדוֹשׁ בָּרוּךְ הוּא זָן אֶת כָּל הָעוֹלָם כֻּלּוֹ – אַף נְשָׁמָה זָנָה אֶת כָּל הַגּוּף; מָה הַקָּדוֹשׁ בָּרוּךְ הוּא טָהוֹר – אַף נְשָׁמָה טְהוֹרָה; מָה הַקָּדוֹשׁ בָּרוּךְ הוּא יוֹשֵׁב בְּחַדְרֵי חֲדָרִים – אַף נְשָׁמָה יוֹשֶׁבֶת בְּחַדְרֵי חֲדָרִים; יָבֹא מִי שֶׁיֵּשׁ בּוֹ חֲמִשָּׁה דְּבָרִים הַלָּלוּ וִישַׁבֵּחַ לְמִי שֶׁיֵּשׁ בּוֹ חֲמִשָּׁה דְּבָרִים הַלָּלוּ.

**Just as the Holy One, Blessed be He, fills the entire world, so too the soul fills the entire body.**

**Just as the Holy One, Blessed be He, sees but is not seen, so too does the soul see, but is not seen.**

**Just as the Holy One, Blessed be He, sustains the entire world, so too the soul sustains the entire body.**

**Just as the Holy One, Blessed be He, is pure, so too is the soul pure.**

**Just as the Holy One, Blessed be He, resides in a chamber within a chamber,** in His inner sanctum, **so too the soul resides in a chamber within a chamber,** in the innermost recesses of the body.

Therefore, **that which has these five characteristics,** the soul, **should come and praise He Who has these five characteristics.**

אָמַר רַב הַמְנוּנָא, מַאי דִּכְתִיב: "מִי כְּהֶחָכָם וּמִי יוֹדֵעַ פֵּשֶׁר דָּבָר"? – מִי כְּהַקָּדוֹשׁ בָּרוּךְ הוּא שֶׁיּוֹדֵעַ לַעֲשׂוֹת פְּשָׁרָה בֵּין שְׁנֵי צַדִּיקִים, בֵּין חִזְקִיָּהוּ לִישַׁעְיָהוּ. חִזְקִיָּהוּ אֲמַר: לֵיתֵי יְשַׁעְיָהוּ גַּבַּאי, דְּהָכִי אַשְׁכַּחַן בְּאֵלִיָּהוּ דַּאֲזַל לְגַבֵּי אַחְאָב, שֶׁנֶּאֱמַר: "וַיֵּלֶךְ אֵלִיָּהוּ לְהֵרָאוֹת אֶל אַחְאָב". יְשַׁעְיָהוּ אֲמַר: לֵיתֵי חִזְקִיָּהוּ גַּבַּאי, דְּהָכִי אַשְׁכַּחַן בִּיהוֹרָם בֶּן אַחְאָב דַּאֲזַל לְגַבֵּי אֱלִישָׁע.

With regard to redemption and prayer, the Gemara tells the story of Hezekiah's illness, his prayer to God, and subsequent recuperation. **Rav Hamnuna said: What is** the meaning of **that which is written** praising the Holy One, Blessed be He: **"Who is like the wise man, and who knows the interpretation [*pesher*] of the matter"** (Ecclesiastes 8:1)? This verse means: **Who is like the Holy One, Blessed be He, Who knows how to effect compromise [*peshara*] between two righteous individuals, between Hezekiah,** the king of Judea, **and Isaiah** the prophet.[N] They disagreed over which of them should visit the other. **Hezekiah said: Let Isaiah come to me, as that is what we find with regard to Elijah** the prophet, **who went to Ahab,** the king of Israel, **as it is stated: "And Elijah went to appear to Ahab"** (I Kings 18:2). This proves that it is the prophet who must seek out the king. **And Isaiah said: Let Hezekiah come to me, as that is what we find with regard to Yehoram ben Ahab,** king of Israel, **who went to Elisha** the prophet, as it is stated: "So the king of Israel, Jehosaphat and the king of Edom went down to him" (II Kings 3:12).

מֶה עָשָׂה הַקָּדוֹשׁ בָּרוּךְ הוּא – הֵבִיא יִסּוּרִים עַל חִזְקִיָּהוּ, וְאָמַר לוֹ לִישַׁעְיָהוּ: לֵךְ וּבַקֵּר אֶת הַחוֹלֶה, שֶׁנֶּאֱמַר: "בַּיָּמִים הָהֵם חָלָה חִזְקִיָּהוּ לָמוּת וַיָּבֹא אֵלָיו יְשַׁעְיָהוּ בֶן אָמוֹץ הַנָּבִיא וַיֹּאמֶר אֵלָיו כֹּה אָמַר ה' צְבָאוֹת צַו לְבֵיתֶךָ כִּי מֵת אַתָּה וְלֹא תִחְיֶה" וגו'. מַאי "כִּי מֵת אַתָּה וְלֹא תִחְיֶה" – "מֵת אַתָּה" – בָּעוֹלָם הַזֶּה, "וְלֹא תִחְיֶה" – לָעוֹלָם הַבָּא.

**What did the Holy One, Blessed be He, do** to effect compromise between Hezekiah and Isaiah? **He brought the suffering** of illness **upon Hezekiah and told** Isaiah: **Go and visit the sick.** Isaiah did as God instructed, **as it is stated: "In those days Hezekiah became deathly ill, and Isaiah ben Amoz the prophet came and said to him: Thus says the Lord of Hosts: Set your house in order, for you will die and you will not live"** (Isaiah 38:1). This seems redundant; **what** is the meaning of **you will die and you will not live?** This repetition means: **You will die in this world, and you will not live,** you will have no share, **in the World-to-Come.**

## NOTES

**The dispute between Hezekiah and Isaiah – מַחְלוֹקֶת חִזְקִיָּהוּ וִישַׁעְיָהוּ:** This dispute should not be viewed as a petty argument between these two great individuals over honor, but rather as a dispute over a fundamental issue: On the one hand, a king must be greatly honored, and he may not waive that honor, as it is bestowed upon him by God; on the other hand, the prophet is a messenger of God, and as long as God has not commanded him to go to a certain place, it would be contemptuous of his divine dispatcher for him to do so and demean himself before another person. Therefore, there was mutual hesitation, which is why the meeting did not take place (*HaKotev*).

אֲמַר לֵיהּ: מַאי כּוּלֵּי הַאי? אֲמַר לֵיהּ: מִשּׁוּם דְּלָא עָסְקַתְּ בִּפְרִיָּה וּרְבִיָּה. אֲמַר לֵיהּ: מִשּׁוּם דַּחֲזַאי לִי בְּרוּחַ הַקֹּדֶשׁ דְּנָפְקִי מִינַּאי בְּנִין דְּלָא מַעֲלוּ.

Hezekiah **said to him: What is all of this?** For what transgression am I being punished?

Isaiah **said to him: Because you did not** marry and **engage in procreation.**[N]

Hezekiah apologized and **said:** I had no children **because I envisaged through divine inspiration that the children that emerge from me will not be virtuous.** Hezekiah meant that he had seen that his children were destined to be evil. In fact, his son Menashe sinned extensively, and he thought it preferable to have no children at all.

אֲמַר לֵיהּ: בַּהֲדֵי כַּבְשֵׁי דְּרַחֲמָנָא לָמָּה לָךְ? מַאי דְּמִפַּקְדַתְּ אִיבָּעֵי לָךְ לְמֶעְבַּד, וּמַה דְּנִיחָא קַמֵּיהּ קוּדְשָׁא בְּרִיךְ הוּא – לַעֲבִיד.

Isaiah **said to him: Why do you** involve **yourself with the secrets of the Holy One, Blessed be He? That which you have been commanded,** the mitzva of procreation, **you are required to perform, and that which is acceptable** in the eyes of **the Holy One, Blessed be He, let Him perform,** as He has so decided.

אֲמַר לֵיהּ: הַשְׁתָּא הַב לִי בְּרַתָּךְ, אֶפְשָׁר דְּגָרְמָא זְכוּתָא דִּידִי וְדִידָךְ וְנָפְקִי מִנַּאי בְּנִין דְּמַעֲלוּ. אֲמַר לֵיהּ: כְּבָר נִגְזְרָה עָלֶיךָ גְּזֵירָה. אֲמַר לֵיהּ: בֶּן אָמוֹץ, כַּלֵּה נְבוּאָתְךָ וָצֵא!

Hezekiah **said to** Isaiah: **Now give me your daughter**[N] as my wife; **perhaps my merit and your merit will cause virtuous children to emerge from me.**

Isaiah **said to him: The decree has already been decreed against you** and this judgment cannot be changed.

**Hezekiah said to him: Son of Amoz, cease your prophecy and leave.** As long as the prophet spoke as God's emissary, Hezekiah was obligated to listen to him. He was not, however, obligated to accept Isaiah's personal opinion that there was no possibility for mercy and healing.

כָּךְ מְקוּבְּלַנִי מִבֵּית אֲבִי אַבָּא: אֲפִילּוּ חֶרֶב חַדָּה מוּנַּחַת עַל צַוָּארוֹ שֶׁל אָדָם – אַל יִמְנַע עַצְמוֹ מִן הָרַחֲמִים.

Hezekiah continued: **I have received a tradition from the house of my father's father,**[N] from King David, the founding father of the dynasty of kings of Judea: **Even if a sharp sword rests upon a person's neck, he should not prevent himself from** praying for **mercy.** One may still hold out hope that his prayers will be answered, as was David himself when he saw the Angel of Destruction, but nonetheless prayed for mercy and his prayers were answered.

אִתְּמַר נַמִי, רַבִּי יוֹחָנָן וְרַבִּי אֱלִיעֶזֶר דְּאָמְרִי תַּרְוַיְיהוּ: אֲפִילּוּ חֶרֶב חַדָּה מוּנַּחַת עַל צַוָּארוֹ שֶׁל אָדָם – אַל יִמְנַע עַצְמוֹ מִן הָרַחֲמִים, שֶׁנֶּאֱמַר: "הֵן יִקְטְלֵנִי לוֹ אֲיַחֵל".

With regard to the fact that one should not despair of God's mercy, the Gemara cites that **it was also said** that **Rabbi Yoḥanan and Rabbi Eliezer both said: Even if a sharp sword is resting upon a person's neck, he should not prevent himself from** praying for **mercy, as it is stated** in the words of Job: **"Though He slay me, I will trust in Him"** (Job 13:15). Even though God is about to take his life, he still prays for God's mercy.

**NOTES**

**Because you did not engage in procreation – מִשּׁוּם דְּלָא עָסְקַתְּ בִּפְרִיָּה וּרְבִיָּה:** There is proof for these statements in the verses themselves. Since King Menashe was twelve years old when he assumed the throne (II Kings 21:1), and since Hezekiah lived for fifteen years after his recuperation (II Kings 20:7), it is evident that Menashe was born shortly after Hezekiah was healed (Maharsha). The severity of his punishment for having failed to procreate has been explained in various ways. Some consider dying without an heir as absolute death, while if one leaves heirs, they carry on his life's work to a large extent (Maharsha). Moreover, some viewed his failure to procreate as violation of a unique obligation in which a king is obligated to continue the Davidic line (*Iyyun Ya'akov*). In addition, they rely on the Gemara which states that if one does not engage in procreation, it is as if he spilled the blood of the children who would otherwise have been born, and he thereby loses his share in the World-to-Come (*Ahavat Eitan*).

**Give me your daughter – הַב לִי בְּרַתָּךְ:** The Bible does not mention the name of the father of Menashe's mother, but according to rabbinic tradition, Isaiah did actually give Hezekiah his daughter's hand in marriage. In fact, their merit did have an effect, and one of their descendants was the righteous King Josiah (*Iyyun Ya'akov*).

**Father's father – אֲבִי אַבָּא:** Some explain that the reference here is to King Jehosaphat who was a more immediate ancestor to Hezekiah than King David. When he was surrounded by the Arameans, he called out to God and was saved (I Kings 22; *Kol Eliyahu*).

Perek **I**
Daf **10** Amud **b**

אָמַר רַבִּי חָנָן: אֲפִילּוּ בַּעַל הַחֲלוֹמוֹת אוֹמֵר לוֹ לָאָדָם לְמָחָר הוּא מֵת – אַל יִמְנַע עַצְמוֹ מִן הָרַחֲמִים, שֶׁנֶּאֱמַר: "כִּי בְרֹב חֲלֹמוֹת וַהֲבָלִים וּדְבָרִים הַרְבֵּה כִּי אֶת הָאֱלֹהִים יְרָא".

Similarly, **Rabbi Ḥanan said: Even if the master of dreams,** in a true dream, an angel (*Ma'ayan HaBerakhot*) **tells a person that tomorrow he will die, he should not prevent himself from** praying for **mercy, as it is stated: "For in the multitude of dreams and vanities there are many words; but fear God"** (Ecclesiastes 5:6). Although the dream may seem real to him, that is not necessarily the case, and one must place his trust in God.

מִיָּד: "וַיַּסֵּב חִזְקִיָּהוּ פָּנָיו אֶל הַקִּיר וַיִּתְפַּלֵּל אֶל ה'".

Having heard Isaiah's harsh prophecy, **immediately "Hezekiah turned his face toward the wall and prayed to the Lord"** (Isaiah 38:2).

מַאי "קִיר"? אָמַר רַבִּי שִׁמְעוֹן בֶּן לָקִישׁ: מִקִּירוֹת לִבּוֹ, שֶׁנֶּאֱמַר: "מֵעַי מֵעַי אוֹחִילָה קִירוֹת לִבִּי" וגו'.

The Gemara asks: **What is** meant by the word **"wall [*kir*]"** in this context? Why did Hezekiah turn his face to a wall? **Rabbi Shimon ben Lakish said:** This symbolically alludes to the fact that Hezekiah prayed to God **from the chambers [*kirot*] of his heart,**[N] **as it is stated** elsewhere: **"My anguish, my anguish, I am in pain. The chambers of my heart.** My heart moans within me" (Jeremiah 4:19).

**NOTES**

**From the chambers [*kirot*] of his heart – מִקִּירוֹת לִבּוֹ:** Often prayer is viewed as an act that combines the spiritual and the intellectual. There is a cognitive awareness of the necessity to turn to God in our time of need. When there is a pressing need, calling for a higher level of prayer, there can be an authentic call emanating from a person's very heart, as the Psalmist declares: "My heart and my flesh sing for joy unto the living God" (Psalms 84:3; see *Ein Ayah*).

NOTES

**He suppressed the Book of Remedies** – **גָּנַז סֵפֶר רְפוּאוֹת**: According to Rashi, the reason for this is clear: As long as the Book of Cures was available, people would not turn to God in prayer but would use the medication prescribed in the Book of Remedies instead. Hezekiah's act was meant to renounce the physical benefits in the book because of the spiritual cost to the people who no longer turned to God in prayer. According to the Rambam, however, the book merely contained ineffectual charms. He maintains that it was because of the people's reliance upon these nonsensical beliefs that Hezekiah suppressed the book.

BACKGROUND

**The waters of the Gihon** – **מֵי גִּיחוֹן**: The stopping up of the waters of the Gihon, the Pool of Siloam, was connected to the excavation of the famous tunnel in the mountain, nearly half a kilometer in length, that was used to bring water from the spring into the city. This feat was an enormous undertaking, which required a massive investment of resources and effort. It is conceivable that the Sages of that generation doubted that the results justified the work invested in building the tunnel, and therefore opposed the stopping up of the waters of Gihon.

Hezekiah's tunnel

רַבִּי לֵוִי אָמַר: עַל עִסְקֵי הַקִּיר. אָמַר לְפָנָיו: רִבּוֹנוֹ שֶׁל עוֹלָם, וּמָה שׁוּנַמִּית שֶׁלֹּא עָשְׂתָה אֶלָּא קִיר אַחַת קְטַנָּה – הֶחֱיֵיתָ אֶת בְּנָהּ, אֲבִי אַבָּא שֶׁחִפָּה אֶת הַהֵיכָל כּוּלּוֹ בְּכֶסֶף וּבְזָהָב – עַל אַחַת כַּמָּה וְכַמָּה. ״זְכָר נָא אֵת אֲשֶׁר הִתְהַלַּכְתִּי לְפָנֶיךָ בֶּאֱמֶת וּבְלֵב שָׁלֵם וְהַטּוֹב בְּעֵינֶיךָ עָשִׂיתִי״

**Rabbi Levi said:** Hezekiah intended to evoke **matters** relating **to a wall,** and **he said before** God: **Master of the Universe, and if the woman from Shunem, who made only a single small wall** on the roof for the prophet Elisha, and **you revived her son, all the more so** should you bring life to the descendant of **my father's father,** King Solomon, **who covered the entire** Temple **Sanctuary with silver and gold.** In his prayer, Hezekiah said: "Please, Lord, **please remember that I walked before You in truth, and with a complete heart, and what was good in Your eyes I did.** And Hezekiah wept sore" (Isaiah 38:3).

מַאי ״וְהַטּוֹב בְּעֵינֶיךָ עָשִׂיתִי״? אָמַר רַב יְהוּדָה אָמַר רַב: שֶׁסָּמַךְ גְּאוּלָּה לִתְפִלָּה. רַבִּי לֵוִי אָמַר: שֶׁגָּנַז סֵפֶר רְפוּאוֹת.

The Gemara asks: To **what** specific action was he referring when he said: **"And what was good in your sight I did"?** Various opinions are offered: Mentioning Hezekiah's merits, **Rav Yehuda said in the name of Rav that he juxtaposed redemption and prayer** at sunrise instead of sleeping late, as was the custom of most kings (*Iyyun Ya'akov*). **Rabbi Levi said: He suppressed the Book of Remedies**[N] upon which everyone relied.

תָּנוּ רַבָּנַן: שִׁשָּׁה דְּבָרִים עָשָׂה חִזְקִיָּהוּ הַמֶּלֶךְ, עַל שְׁלֹשָׁה הוֹדוּ לוֹ, וְעַל שְׁלֹשָׁה לֹא הוֹדוּ לוֹ.

**The Sages taught: King Hezekiah performed six** innovative **actions. With regard to three** the Sages **agreed with him, and with regard to three they did not agree with him.**

עַל שְׁלֹשָׁה הוֹדוּ לוֹ: גָּנַז סֵפֶר רְפוּאוֹת – וְהוֹדוּ לוֹ, כִּתֵּת נְחַשׁ הַנְּחֹשֶׁת – וְהוֹדוּ לוֹ, גֵּירֵר עַצְמוֹת אָבִיו עַל מִטָּה שֶׁל חֲבָלִים – וְהוֹדוּ לוֹ.

**With regard to three** actions the Sages **agreed with him:**

**He suppressed the Book of Remedies, and they agreed with him.**

**He ground the copper snake** through which miracles were performed for Israel (Numbers 21:9), destroying it because it had been used in idol worship (II Kings 18:4), **and they agreed with him.**

**He dragged the bones of his** evil **father,** King Ahaz, **on a bed of ropes;** meaning he did not accord his father a funeral fit for a king (II Chronicles 28:27), **and they agreed with him.**

וְעַל שְׁלֹשָׁה לֹא הוֹדוּ לוֹ: סָתַם מֵי גִּיחוֹן – וְלֹא הוֹדוּ לוֹ, קִיצֵּץ דַּלְתוֹת הֵיכָל וְשִׁיגְּרָם לְמֶלֶךְ אַשּׁוּר – וְלֹא הוֹדוּ לוֹ, עִיבֵּר נִיסָן בְּנִיסָן – וְלֹא הוֹדוּ לוֹ.

Yet, **with regard to three** other innovations, the Sages of his generation **did not agree with him:**

**He stopped up the waters of the Gihon,**[B] the Pool of Siloam, diverting its water into the city by means of a tunnel (II Chronicles 32:30), **and they did not agree with him.**

**He cut off the doors of the Sanctuary and sent them to the king of Assyria** (II Kings 18:16), **and they did not agree with him.**

**He intercalated Nisan in Nisan,** creating a leap year by adding an extra month during the month of Nisan. That intercalation must be performed before the end of Adar (II Chronicles 30:2).

וּמִי לֵית לֵיהּ לְחִזְקִיָּהוּ: ״הַחֹדֶשׁ הַזֶּה לָכֶם רֹאשׁ חֳדָשִׁים״ – זֶה נִיסָן וְאֵין אַחֵר נִיסָן?!

With regard to his intercalation of Nisan, the Gemara asks: **Did Hezekiah not** accept the *halakha*: **"This month will be for you the first of the months;** it shall be the first for you of the months of the year" (Exodus 12:2)? By inference, **this** first month **is Nisan, and no other** month **is Nisan.** How could Hezekiah add an additional Nisan in violation of Torah law?

אֶלָּא, טָעָה בִּדְשְׁמוּאֵל; דְּאָמַר שְׁמוּאֵל: אֵין מְעַבְּרִין אֶת הַשָּׁנָה בְּיוֹם שְׁלֹשִׁים שֶׁל אֲדָר, הוֹאִיל וְרָאוּי לְקוֹבְעוֹ נִיסָן, סָבַר: ״הוֹאִיל וְרָאוּי״ לָא אָמְרִינַן.

The Gemara answers that the scenario was different. **Rather,** Hezekiah **erred with regard to** the halakhic opinion ascribed in later generations to **Shmuel,** as **Shmuel said: One may not intercalate the year on the thirtieth day of Adar, since it is fit to establish it** as the New Moon of **Nisan.** On the thirtieth day of each month, those who witnessed the new moon would come and testify before the court, which, based on their testimony, would declare that day the first day of the next month. Therefore, one may not declare a leap year on the thirtieth day of Adar, as it could potentially become the first of Nisan. Therefore, the Sages of Hezekiah's generation did not agree with his decision to intercalate the year on the thirtieth of Adar. Hezekiah **held** that **we do not say: Since** that day **is fit to establish it** as the New Moon is reason enough to refrain from intercalation of the year.

אָמַר רַבִּי יוֹחָנָן מִשּׁוּם רַבִּי יוֹסֵי בֶּן זִמְרָא: כׇּל הַתּוֹלֶה בִּזְכוּת עַצְמוֹ – תּוֹלִין לוֹ בִּזְכוּת אֲחֵרִים, וְכׇל הַתּוֹלֶה בִּזְכוּת אֲחֵרִים – תּוֹלִין לוֹ בִּזְכוּת עַצְמוֹ.

Stemming from the analysis of **Hezekiah's** prayer, **Rabbi Yoḥanan said in the name of Rabbi Yosei ben Zimra: Anyone who bases** his prayer or request **upon his own merit,** when God answers his prayer, **it is based upon the merit of others. And anyone who** modestly **bases** his prayer or request **upon the merit of others,** when God answers his prayer, **it is based upon his own merit.**

מֹשֶׁה תָּלָה בִּזְכוּת אֲחֵרִים, שֶׁנֶּאֱמַר: ״זְכֹר לְאַבְרָהָם לְיִצְחָק וּלְיִשְׂרָאֵל עֲבָדֶיךָ״ – תָּלוּ לוֹ בִּזְכוּת עַצְמוֹ, שֶׁנֶּאֱמַר: ״וַיֹּאמֶר לְהַשְׁמִידָם לוּלֵי מֹשֶׁה בְחִירוֹ עָמַד בַּפֶּרֶץ לְפָנָיו לְהָשִׁיב חֲמָתוֹ מֵהַשְׁחִית״;

The Gemara cites proof from Moses. When he prayed to God for forgiveness after the incident of the Golden Calf, **he based** his request **upon the merit of others, as it is stated: "Remember Abraham, Isaac and Israel your servants,** to whom You swore upon Yourself, and told them: I will increase your descendants like the stars of the heavens, and all of this land of which I have spoken, I will give to your descendants and they will inherit it forever" (Exodus 32:13). Yet when this story is related, God's forgiveness of Israel **is based upon Moses' own merit, as it is stated: "And He said He would destroy them, had Moses, His chosen, not stood before Him in the breach to turn back His destructive fury, lest He should destroy them"** (Psalms 106:23).

חִזְקִיָּהוּ תָּלָה בִּזְכוּת עַצְמוֹ, דִּכְתִיב: ״זְכׇר נָא אֵת אֲשֶׁר הִתְהַלַּכְתִּי לְפָנֶיךָ״ – תָּלוּ לוֹ בִּזְכוּת אֲחֵרִים, שֶׁנֶּאֱמַר: ״וְגַנּוֹתִי אֶל הָעִיר הַזֹּאת לְהוֹשִׁיעָהּ לְמַעֲנִי וּלְמַעַן דָּוִד עַבְדִּי״. וְהַיְינוּ דְּרַבִּי יְהוֹשֻׁעַ בֶּן לֵוִי. דְּאָמַר רַבִּי יְהוֹשֻׁעַ בֶּן לֵוִי, מַאי דִּכְתִיב: ״הִנֵּה לְשָׁלוֹם מַר לִי מָר״? – אֲפִילּוּ בְּשָׁעָה שֶׁשִּׁיגֵּר לוֹ הַקָּדוֹשׁ בָּרוּךְ הוּא שָׁלוֹם – מַר הוּא לוֹ.

**Hezekiah,** however, **based** his request **upon his own merit, as it is written: "Please, remember that I walked before You"** (Isaiah 38:3). When God answered his prayers, **it was based upon the merit of others** with no mention made of Hezekiah's own merit, **as it is stated: "And I will protect this city to save it, for My sake and for the sake of David, My servant"** (II Kings 19:34). **And that is what Rabbi Yehoshua ben Levi** said. **As Rabbi Yehoshua ben Levi said: What is** the meaning of **that which is written: "Behold, for my peace I had great bitterness;** but You have, in love to my soul, delivered it from the pit of corruption; for You have thrown all my sins behind Your back" (Isaiah 38:17)? This verse teaches that **even when the Holy One, Blessed be He, sent him peace** and told him that he would recover from his illness, **it was bitter for him,** because God did not take his merit into consideration.

״נַעֲשֶׂה נָּא עֲלִיַּת קִיר קְטַנָּה״.

Having mentioned the chamber on the roof built for Elisha by the woman from Shunem, the Gemara now describes the entire event. The woman from Shunem suggested to her husband: **"Let us make, I pray thee, a small chamber on the roof,** and let us place a bed, table, stool and candlestick for him there, and it will be, when he comes to us, that he will turn in there" (II Kings 4:10).

רַב וּשְׁמוּאֵל, חַד אָמַר: עֲלִיָּיה פְּרוּעָה הָיְתָה, וְקֵירוּהָ, וְחַד אָמַר: אַכְסַדְרָה גְּדוֹלָה הָיְתָה, וְחִלְּקוּהָ לִשְׁנַיִם.

**Rav and Shmuel** argued over the meaning of small chamber. **One** of them **said: They had an uncovered second story** on their roof, **over which they built a ceiling;** and **one** of them **said: There was an enclosed veranda** [***akhsadra***][L] **and they divided it in half.**

בִּשְׁלָמָא לְמַאן דְּאָמַר אַכְסַדְרָה – הַיְינוּ דִּכְתִיב ״קִיר״, אֶלָּא לְמַאן דְּאָמַר עֲלִיָּיה – מַאי ״קִיר״?

The Gemara comments: **Granted, according to the one who said that it was an enclosed veranda** which they divided in two, it makes sense **that** the term **wall** [***kir***] **was written. However, according to the one who said that they had an** open **second story, what is** the meaning of **wall?**

שֶׁקֵּירוּהָ.

The Gemara responds: The one who said that they had an uncovered second story interprets *kir* not as wall but as ceiling meaning that they **built a ceiling** [*kirui*] over it.

בִּשְׁלָמָא לְמַאן דְּאָמַר ״עֲלִיָּיה״ – הַיְינוּ דִּכְתִיב ״עֲלִיַּית״, אֶלָּא לְמַאן דְּאָמַר אַכְסַדְרָה – מַאי ״עֲלִיַּית״?

On the other hand, **granted, according to the one who said that they had an** uncovered **second story,** it makes sense **that** the term **second story** [***aliyat***] **was written. But according to the one who said** that it was **an enclosed veranda, what is** the meaning of the term **second story?**

מְעוּלָּה שֶׁבַּבָּתִּים.

The Gemara responds: The one who said that it was an enclosed veranda interprets *aliyat* not as second story, but **as the most outstanding** [***me'ula***] **of the rooms.**

LANGUAGE

**An enclosed veranda** [*akhsadra*] **– אַכְסַדְרָה:** This word comes from the Greek **ἐξέδρα**, or the Latin exedra, meaning an entrance room or sitting room.

Stone veranda

## NOTES

**One who seeks to enjoy…and one who does not seek to enjoy – הָרוֹצֶה לֵהָנוֹת...וְשֶׁאֵינוֹ רוֹצֶה לֵהָנוֹת וכו׳:** Many commented that these statements differ from those generally accepted throughout the Talmud, which are more in line with the verse: "He who hates gifts shall live" (Proverbs 15:27). The general view is that one should not benefit from the property of others, but from his own property alone. Therefore, they said that this talmudic statement should be understood as restrictive; even one who seeks to enjoy the property of others should do so only with the same conditions and in the same circumstances as Elisha. The gifts should be appropriate, both in terms of the intention of the benefactor and his respect for the one receiving the gift, as well as sensitivity to the needs of the recipient (Maharsha, *Iyyun Ya'akov*).

**A fly pass over his table – זְבוּב עוֹבֵר עַל שֻׁלְחָנוֹ:** It was said that, due to the sanctity of the Temple, a fly never passed near the sacrifices, so that no flying insect would defile them. Similarly, since the meal of a holy person is like the offering of a sacrifice, no fly would pass his table (Maharsha).

**To push her away – לְהָדְפָהּ:** Beyond the etymological similarity between *hodfa*, push her away, and *hod yofya*, the majesty of her beauty, there is also an allusion to this midrash in the verse itself: Elisha says to Geihazi: "Let her go" (II Kings 4:27). Apparently, he did not push her away, but instead grabbed her.

## HALAKHA

**A person should not stand in a high place and pray – אַל יַעֲמוֹד אָדָם בְּמָקוֹם גָּבוֹהַּ וְיִתְפַּלֵּל:** One is prohibited from praying while standing three handbreadths higher than the surrounding area. In addition, he may not stand on a bed or a chair, even if they are less than three handbreadths high (Rema). However one who is elderly or infirm, or a communal prayer leader seeking to be heard by the congregation, is permitted to do so if the elevated area is at least four cubits square or surrounded by partitions. The *Magen Avraham* writes that the practice today is for the communal prayer leader's position to be slightly lower than the rest of the synagogue, in keeping with the verse: "I called to You, Lord, from the depths" (Psalms 130:1; Rambam *Sefer Ahava, Hilkhot Tefilla* 5:7; *Shulḥan Arukh, Oraḥ Ḥayyim* 90:1–2 and the comments of the Rema).

## BACKGROUND

**Stool – שְׁרַפְרַף:**

Stool from the mishnaic period

"וְנָשִׂים לוֹ שָׁם מִטָּה וְשֻׁלְחָן וְכִסֵּא וּמְנוֹרָה".

Incidental to this discussion, the Gemara analyzes the statement made by the woman from Shunem to her husband with regard to the provisions that they would place in the room for Elisha: **"And let us place a bed, table, stool and candlestick for him there."**

אָמַר אַבָּיֵי, וְאִיתֵּימָא רַבִּי יִצְחָק: הָרוֹצֶה לֵהָנוֹת – יֵהָנֶה, כֶּאֱלִישָׁע, וְשֶׁאֵינוֹ רוֹצֶה לֵהָנוֹת – אַל יֵהָנֶה, כִּשְׁמוּאֵל הָרָמָתִי, שֶׁנֶּאֱמַר: "וּתְשֻׁבָתוֹ הָרָמָתָה כִּי שָׁם בֵּיתוֹ". וְאָמַר רַבִּי יוֹחָנָן: שֶׁכׇּל מָקוֹם שֶׁהָלַךְ שָׁם – בֵּיתוֹ עִמּוֹ.

**Abaye, and some say Rabbi Yitzḥak, said:** A great man **who seeks to enjoy** the contributions of those who seek to honor him **may enjoy** those gifts, **as Elisha** enjoyed gifts given him by the woman from Shunem, among others. **And one who does not seek to enjoy**[N] these gifts **should not enjoy them, as** was the practice of the prophet **Samuel from Rama,** who would not accept gifts from anyone at all. From where do we know that this was Samuel's custom? **As it is stated: "And he returned to Rama, for there was his house,** and there he judged Israel, and he built an altar to the Lord" (I Samuel 7:17). **And** similarly, **Rabbi Yoḥanan said: Every place where** Samuel **went, his house was with him,** so he would have everything that he needed and not be forced to benefit from public contributions. One may opt to conduct himself in accordance with either of these paths.

"וַתֹּאמֶר אֶל אִישָׁהּ הִנֵּה נָא יָדַעְתִּי כִּי אִישׁ אֱלֹהִים קָדוֹשׁ הוּא". אָמַר רַבִּי יוֹסֵי בְּרַבִּי חֲנִינָא: מִכָּאן, שֶׁהָאִשָּׁה מַכֶּרֶת בְּאוֹרְחִין יוֹתֵר מִן הָאִישׁ.

Regarding the woman from Shunem: **"And she said to her husband: Behold now, I perceive that he is a holy man of God** who passes by us continually" (II Kings 4:9). **Rabbi Yosei, son of Rabbi Ḥanina, said: From here,** where the woman from Shunem perceived the prophet's greatness before her husband did, derive **that a woman recognizes** the character of her **guests more than a man** does.

"קָדוֹשׁ הוּא", מְנָא יָדְעָה? רַב וּשְׁמוּאֵל, חַד אָמַר: שֶׁלֹּא רָאֲתָה זְבוּב עוֹבֵר עַל שֻׁלְחָנוֹ. וְחַד אָמַר: סָדִין שֶׁל פִּשְׁתָּן הִצִּיעָה עַל מִטָּתוֹ וְלֹא רָאֲתָה קֶרִי עָלָיו.

The Gemara notes that the woman from Shunem said that **"he is holy."** The Gemara asks: **From where did she know** that he was holy? **Rav and Shmuel** disagreed over this. **One** of them **said: She never saw a fly pass over his table;**[N] **and the other said: She spread a** white **linen sheet on his bed,** and despite that even the smallest stain is visible on white linen, and nocturnal seminal emissions are not uncommon, **she never saw** the residue of **a seminal emission on it.**

"קָדוֹשׁ הוּא" – אָמַר רַבִּי יוֹסֵי בְּרַבִּי חֲנִינָא: הוּא קָדוֹשׁ, וּמְשָׁרְתוֹ אֵינוֹ קָדוֹשׁ, שֶׁנֶּאֱמַר: "וַיִּגַּשׁ גֵּיחֲזִי לְהָדְפָהּ". אָמַר רַבִּי יוֹסֵי בְּרַבִּי חֲנִינָא: שֶׁאֲחָזָהּ בְּהוֹד יׇפְיָהּ.

With regard to the verse: **"He is holy," Rabbi Yosei, son of Rabbi Ḥanina, said:** The woman from Shunem intimated that: **He is holy,** but **his attendant,** Geihazi, **is not holy,** as she saw no indication of holiness in him (*Iyyun Ya'akov*). Here too, she correctly perceived the character of her guest, **as it is** later **stated: "And Geihazi approached her to push her away** [*lehodfa*]" (II Kings 4:27).[N] And **Rabbi Yosei, son of Rabbi Ḥanina, said: He grabbed her by the majesty of her beauty** [*hod yofya*], meaning that when he pushed her he grabbed her breasts in a licentious manner.

"עוֹבֵר עָלֵינוּ תָּמִיד" – אָמַר רַבִּי יוֹסֵי בְּרַבִּי חֲנִינָא מִשּׁוּם רַבִּי אֱלִיעֶזֶר בֶּן יַעֲקֹב: כׇּל הַמְאָרֵחַ תַּלְמִיד חָכָם בְּתוֹךְ בֵּיתוֹ וּמְהַנֵּהוּ מִנְּכָסָיו – מַעֲלֶה עָלָיו הַכָּתוּב כְּאִילּוּ מַקְרִיב תְּמִידִין.

With regard to the phrasing of the verse: "He is a holy man of God **who passes by us continually," Rabbi Yosei, son of Rabbi Ḥanina, said in the name of Rabbi Eliezer ben Ya'akov:** From this verse we derive that **one who hosts a Torah scholar in his home and lets him enjoy his possessions, the verse ascribes to him** credit **as if he is sacrificing the daily** [*tamid*] **offering,** as the verse states: "Passes by us continually [*tamid*]."

וְאָמַר רַבִּי יוֹסֵי בְּרַבִּי חֲנִינָא מִשּׁוּם רַבִּי אֱלִיעֶזֶר בֶּן יַעֲקֹב: אַל יַעֲמוֹד אָדָם בְּמָקוֹם גָּבוֹהַּ וְיִתְפַּלֵּל, אֶלָּא בְּמָקוֹם נָמוּךְ וְיִתְפַּלֵּל, שֶׁנֶּאֱמַר: "מִמַּעֲמַקִּים קְרָאתִיךָ ה׳".

With regard to the *halakhot* of prayer, **Rabbi Yosei, son of Rabbi Ḥanina, said in the name of Rabbi Eliezer ben Ya'akov: A person should not stand in a high place and pray;**[H] **rather,** he should stand **in a low place and pray, as it is stated: "I called to You, Lord, from the depths"** (Psalms 130:1).

תַּנְיָא נַמִי הָכִי: לֹא יַעֲמוֹד אָדָם לֹא עַל גַּבֵּי כִּסֵּא, וְלֹא עַל גַּבֵּי שְׁרַפְרַף, וְלֹא בְּמָקוֹם גָּבוֹהַּ וְיִתְפַּלֵּל, אֶלָּא בְּמָקוֹם נָמוּךְ וְיִתְפַּלֵּל, לְפִי שֶׁאֵין גַּבְהוּת לִפְנֵי הַמָּקוֹם, שֶׁנֶּאֱמַר: "מִמַּעֲמַקִּים קְרָאתִיךָ ה׳", וּכְתִיב: "תְּפִלָּה לְעָנִי כִי יַעֲטֹף".

**That was also taught** in a *baraita*: **One should neither stand upon a chair nor upon a stool,**[B] **nor in a high place and pray. Rather,** one should stand **in a low place and pray, for there is no haughtiness before God. As it is stated: "I called to You, Lord, from the depths"** and **it is written: "A prayer for the impoverished, when he is faint** and pours out his complaint before God" (Psalms 102:1). It is appropriate to feel impoverished when praying and make one's requests humbly.

וְאָמַר רַבִּי יוֹסֵי בְּרַבִּי חֲנִינָא מִשּׁוּם רַבִּי אֱלִיעֶזֶר בֶּן יַעֲקֹב: הַמִּתְפַּלֵּל צָרִיךְ שֶׁיְּכַוֵּין אֶת רַגְלָיו, שֶׁנֶּאֱמַר: "וְרַגְלֵיהֶם רֶגֶל יְשָׁרָה".

**And Rabbi Yosei, son of Rabbi Ḥanina, said in the name of Rabbi Eliezer ben Ya'akov: When praying, one should align his feet**[H] next to each other, as a single foot, in order to model oneself after the angels, with regard to whom **it is stated: "And their feet were a straight foot"** (Ezekiel 1:7).[N]

(אָמַר רַבִּי יִצְחָק אָמַר רַבִּי יוֹחָנָן) וְאָמַר רַבִּי יוֹסֵי בְּרַבִּי חֲנִינָא מִשּׁוּם רַבִּי אֱלִיעֶזֶר בֶּן יַעֲקֹב: מַאי דִּכְתִיב: "לֹא תֹאכְלוּ עַל הַדָּם" לֹא תֹּאכְלוּ קוֹדֶם שֶׁתִּתְפַּלְּלוּ עַל דִּמְכֶם.

**Rabbi Yitzḥak said** that **Rabbi Yoḥanan said and Rabbi Yosei, son of Rabbi Ḥanina, said in the name of Rabbi Eliezer ben Ya'akov: What is** the meaning **of that which is written: "You shall not eat with the blood"** (Leviticus 19:26)? **You may not eat before you pray for your blood.**[H] One may not eat before he prays.

אִיכָּא דְּאָמְרִי, אָמַר רַבִּי יִצְחָק אָמַר רַבִּי יוֹחָנָן אָמַר רַבִּי יוֹסֵי בְּרַבִּי חֲנִינָא מִשּׁוּם רַבִּי אֱלִיעֶזֶר בֶּן יַעֲקֹב: כׇּל הָאוֹכֵל וְשׁוֹתֶה וְאַחַר כָּךְ מִתְפַּלֵּל – עָלָיו הַכָּתוּב אוֹמֵר: "וְאֹתִי הִשְׁלַכְתָּ אַחֲרֵי גַוֶּךָ", אַל תִּקְרֵי "גַוֶּךָ" אֶלָּא "גֵאֶיךָ", אָמַר הַקָּדוֹשׁ בָּרוּךְ הוּא: לְאַחַר שֶׁנִּתְגָּאָה זֶה – קִיבֵּל עָלָיו מַלְכוּת שָׁמַיִם.

**Others say** that **Rabbi Yitzḥak said** that **Rabbi Yoḥanan said** that **Rabbi Yosei, son of Rabbi Ḥanina, said in the name of Rabbi Eliezer ben Ya'akov: One who eats and drinks and later prays, about him the verse states** the rebuke of the prophet in the name of God: **"And Me you have cast behind your back"** (1 Kings 14:9). One who sees to his own bodily needs by eating and drinking before prayer casts God aside, according his arrogance and ego priority over God (Maharsha). Indeed, **do not read your back [*gavekha*]; rather, your pride [*ge'ekha*]. The Holy One, Blessed be He, said: After this one has become arrogant** and engaged in satisfying his own needs, **he** only then **accepted upon himself the kingdom of Heaven.**

"רַבִּי יְהוֹשֻׁעַ אוֹמֵר, עַד שָׁלֹשׁ שָׁעוֹת". אָמַר רַב יְהוּדָה אָמַר שְׁמוּאֵל: הֲלָכָה כְּרַבִּי יְהוֹשֻׁעַ.

We learned in the mishna that **Rabbi Yehoshua says:** One may recite the morning *Shema* **until three hours** of the day. **Rav Yehuda said** that **Shmuel said: The *halakha* is in accordance with** the opinion of **Rabbi Yehoshua.**[H]

"הַקּוֹרֵא מִכָּאן וְאֵילָךְ – לֹא הִפְסִיד".

We also learned in the mishna that **one who recites *Shema* from that time onward loses nothing;**[N] although he does not fulfill the mitzva of reciting of *Shema* at its appointed time, **he is** nevertheless considered like one who reads the Torah, and is rewarded accordingly.

אָמַר רַב חִסְדָּא אָמַר מָר עוּקְבָא: וּבִלְבַד שֶׁלֹּא יֹאמַר "יוֹצֵר אוֹר".

With regard to this ruling, **Rav Ḥisda said** that **Mar Ukva said:** This only applies **provided one does not recite: Who forms light [*yotzer or*]**, or the rest of the blessings recited along with *Shema*, as they pertain only to the fulfillment of the mitzva of reciting of the morning *Shema*; after the third hour, they are inappropriate.

מֵיתִיבֵי: הַקּוֹרֵא מִכָּאן וְאֵילָךְ – לֹא הִפְסִיד, כְּאָדָם שֶׁהוּא קוֹרֵא בַּתּוֹרָה, אֲבָל מְבָרֵךְ הוּא שְׁתַּיִם לְפָנֶיהָ וְאַחַת לְאַחֲרֶיהָ – תְּיוּבְתָּא דְּרַב חִסְדָּא! תְּיוּבְתָּא.

The Gemara **raises an objection to** Rav Ḥisda's statement from a *baraita*: **One who recites *Shema* from that time onward loses nothing, and is considered like one who reads Torah, but he recites two blessings**[H] **beforehand and one** blessing **thereafter.** This directly contradicts Rav Ḥisda's statement, and the Gemara notes: Indeed, **the refutation** of the statement **of Rav Ḥisda is a** conclusive **refutation,**[B] and Rav Ḥisda's opinion is rejected in favor of that of the *baraita*.

אִיכָּא דְּאָמְרִי, אָמַר רַב חִסְדָּא אָמַר מָר עוּקְבָא: מַאי "לֹא הִפְסִיד" – שֶׁלֹּא הִפְסִיד בְּרָכוֹת. תַּנְיָא נַמִי הָכִי: הַקּוֹרֵא מִכָּאן וְאֵילָךְ – לֹא הִפְסִיד, כְּאָדָם שֶׁקּוֹרֵא בַּתּוֹרָה, אֲבָל מְבָרֵךְ הוּא שְׁתַּיִם לְפָנֶיהָ וְאַחַת לְאַחֲרֶיהָ.

**Some say that Rav Ḥisda said** that **Mar Ukva said** the opposite: **What is** the meaning of: **Loses nothing,** in the mishna? This means that one who recites *Shema* after the third hour **does not lose** the opportunity to recite **the blessings** and is permitted to recite them although the time for the recitation of *Shema* has passed. **That was also taught** in a *baraita*: **One who recites *Shema* after this time loses nothing, and is considered like one who reads the Torah, but he recites two blessings beforehand and one thereafter.**

אָמַר רַבִּי מָנִי: גָּדוֹל הַקּוֹרֵא קְרִיאַת שְׁמַע בְּעוֹנָתָהּ יוֹתֵר מֵהָעוֹסֵק בַּתּוֹרָה, מִדְּקָתָנֵי: "הַקּוֹרֵא מִכָּאן וְאֵילָךְ – לֹא הִפְסִיד, כְּאָדָם הַקּוֹרֵא בַּתּוֹרָה", מִכְּלָל דְּקוֹרֵא בְּעוֹנָתָהּ – עָדִיף.

With regard to our mishna, **Rabbi Mani said: Greater is one who recites *Shema* at its** appropriate **time**[N] **than one who engages in Torah** study. A proof is cited based on **what was taught** in the mishna: **One who recites *Shema* after this time loses nothing** and is considered **like one who reads the Torah.** This is proven **by inference,** since **one who recites *Shema* at its** appointed **time is greater** than one who does not, and one who does not is equal to one who reads the Torah, when one recites *Shema* at its appointed time he fulfills two mitzvot, that of Torah study and that of the recitation of *Shema*.

## NOTES

**A straight foot** – רֶגֶל יְשָׁרָה: The commentaries were not satisfied with the reason offered in the Gemara regarding why one should stand with his feet together while praying, and suggested additional reasons. There is an ancient tradition that it is an allusion to the binding of Isaac, whose feet were bound together on the altar. Standing this way also symbolizes submission and humility before God (Rashba, *Tur*).

**One who reads from that time onward loses nothing** – הַקּוֹרֵא מִכָּאן וְאֵילָךְ לֹא הִפְסִיד: Ostensibly, there is room to raise the question: Why would it enter my mind that reading *Shema* after its appointed time would be any worse than reading any other portion from the Torah? This statement seems superfluous. Some explain that, nevertheless, this statement was necessary. One might have thought that reading this portion, in which the prescribed time for reading it is explicitly mentioned, after its appointed time, would call his sin to mind and he would not even be rewarded for reading a portion from the Torah. Therefore, the Gemara states that he is rewarded (*Shitta Mekubbetzet*).

**Greater is one who recites *Shema* at its appropriate time** – גָּדוֹל הַקּוֹרֵא קְרִיאַת שְׁמַע בְּעוֹנָתָהּ: This statement appears to be self-evident, as it is obvious that one who recites *Shema* fulfills the mitzva of reciting *Shema* as well as the mitzva of Torah study. Therefore, this statement must be explained to mean that one who recites the *Shema* at its appropriate time is greater than one who recites other portions of the Torah, even if he studies them in depth (Rashba, *Me'iri*).

## HALAKHA

**When praying, one should align his feet** – הַמִּתְפַּלֵּל צָרִיךְ שֶׁיְּכַוֵּין אֶת רַגְלָיו: When reciting the *Amida* prayer, one must align his feet and bring them together as if they were one leg (Rambam *Sefer Ahava, Hilkhot Tefilla* 5:4; *Shulḥan Arukh, Oraḥ Ḥayyim* 95:1).

**You may not eat before you pray for your blood** – לֹא תֹאכְלוּ קוֹדֶם שֶׁתִּתְפַּלְּלוּ עַל דִּמְכֶם: One is prohibited from eating or drinking once the time for the morning prayer has arrived until he prays regardless of whether it is Shabbat or a weekday, unless there is a situation of duress or illness (Rambam *Sefer Ahava, Hilkhot Tefilla* 6:4; *Shulḥan Arukh, Oraḥ Ḥayyim* 89:3).

**Rabbi Yehoshua says until three hours of the day…the *halakha* is in accordance with Rabbi Yehoshua** – רַבִּי יְהוֹשֻׁעַ אוֹמֵר עַד שָׁלֹשׁ שָׁעוֹת...הֲלָכָה כְּרַבִּי יְהוֹשֻׁעַ: The time for reciting the morning *Shema* is until the end of the third hour, which is one quarter of the day, in accordance with the opinion of Rabbi Yehoshua. This is both because the *halakha* is generally ruled in accordance with the opinion of Rabbi Yehoshua in disputes with Rabbi Eliezer, and particularly because the Gemara explicitly states that the *halakha* is in accordance with his opinion (Rambam *Sefer Ahava, Hilkhot Keriat Shema* 1:11; *Shulḥan Arukh, Oraḥ Ḥayyim* 58:1).

**One who recites *Shema* from that time onward…but he recites two blessings…** – הַקּוֹרֵא מִכָּאן וְאֵילָךְ...אֲבָל מְבָרֵךְ הוּא שְׁתַּיִם וכו׳: If the time for reciting the morning *Shema*, the third hour of the day, has passed and he has not yet recited *Shema*, he may still do so with its blessings until the end of the fourth hour (*ge'onim*). However, his reward in that case does not equal the reward of one who recited *Shema* at its appointed time. If the fourth hour has passed, he may recite *Shema* all day; however, he does not recite it with its blessings, in accordance with the second version of Rav Ḥisda's statement and the *baraita* that supports his opinion (Rambam *Sefer Ahava, Hilkhot Keriat Shema* 1:13; *Shulḥan Arukh, Oraḥ Ḥayyim* 58:6).

## BACKGROUND

**This refutation of the statement of Rav X is a conclusive refutation** – תְּיוּבְתָּא דְּרַב...תְּיוּבְתָּא: This structure is one of the most fundamental talmudic expressions. When the statement of an *amora* is powerfully refuted by a tannaitic source, this term, which literally means return, in the sense that his statement is sent back to him, sums up the challenge. Occasionally responses are provided to these challenges, but in cases like the one in our Gemara, there is no resolution and his statement is rejected.

מַתְנִי׳ בֵּית שַׁמַּאי אוֹמְרִים: בָּעֶרֶב – כׇּל אָדָם יַטֶּה וְיִקְרָא, וּבַבֹּקֶר יַעֲמוֹד, שֶׁנֶּאֱמַר: ״וּבְשׇׁכְבְּךָ וּבְקוּמֶךָ״.

**MISHNA** Beit Shammai and Beit Hillel disputed the proper way to recite *Shema*. **Beit Shammai say: One should recite** *Shema* **in the manner indicated in the text of** *Shema* **itself. Therefore, in the evening every person must recline on his side and recite** *Shema*, in fulfillment of the verse: "When you lie down," **and in the morning he must stand and recite** *Shema*, in fulfillment of the verse: When you rise, **as it is stated: "When you lie down, and when you rise."**

וּבֵית הִלֵּל אוֹמְרִים: כׇּל אָדָם קוֹרֵא כְּדַרְכּוֹ, שֶׁנֶּאֱמַר: ״וּבְלֶכְתְּךָ בַדֶּרֶךְ״.

**And Beit Hillel say: Every person recites** *Shema* **as he is,**[H] and he may do so in whatever position is most comfortable for him, both day and night, **as it is stated: "And when you walk along the way,"** when one is neither standing nor reclining (*Me'iri*).

אִם כֵּן, לָמָּה נֶאֱמַר: ״וּבְשׇׁכְבְּךָ וּבְקוּמֶךָ״? – בְּשָׁעָה שֶׁבְּנֵי אָדָם שׁוֹכְבִים וּבְשָׁעָה שֶׁבְּנֵי אָדָם עוֹמְדִים.

**If so,** according to Beit Hillel, **why was it stated: "When you lie down, and when you rise"?** This is merely to denote time; **at the time when people lie down and the time when people rise.**

אָמַר רַבִּי טַרְפוֹן: אֲנִי הָיִיתִי בָּא בַּדֶּרֶךְ וְהִטֵּתִי לִקְרוֹת כְּדִבְרֵי בֵית שַׁמַּאי, וְסִכַּנְתִּי בְּעַצְמִי מִפְּנֵי הַלִּסְטִים.

With regard to this *halakha*, **Rabbi Tarfon said:** Once, **I was coming on the road** when I stopped and **reclined to recite** *Shema* **in accordance with the statement of Beit Shammai.** Although Rabbi Tarfon was a disciple of Beit Hillel, he thought that fulfilling the mitzva in accordance with the opinion of Beit Shammai would be a more meticulous fulfillment of the mitzva, acceptable to all opinions. Yet in so doing, **I endangered myself due to the highwaymen [*listim*]**[L] who accost travelers.

אָמְרוּ לוֹ: כְּדַי הָיִיתָ לָחוּב בְּעַצְמְךָ, שֶׁעָבַרְתָּ עַל דִּבְרֵי בֵית הִלֵּל.

The Sages **said to him: You deserved** to be in a position where you were **liable** to pay **with your life, as you transgressed the statement of Beit Hillel.** This statement will be explained in the Gemara.

**HALAKHA**

**Every person recites as he is – כׇּל אָדָם קוֹרֵא כְּדַרְכּוֹ:** One may recite *Shema* while walking, standing, reclining, or riding on an animal, but one may not do so while lying on his back. One who wishes to be stringent and who, when seated, stands in order to recite the *Shema* is called a transgressor, in accordance with the opinion of Beit Hillel (Rambam *Sefer Ahava*, *Hilkhot Keriat Shema* 2:2; *Shulḥan Arukh*, *Oraḥ Ḥayyim* 63:1–2).

**LANGUAGE**

**Highwaymen [*listim*] – לִסְטִים:** The source of the word is from the Greek ληστής, meaning thief or robber. The word originated in a misspelling.

In rabbinic literature, when used in the singular it generally refers to an unarmed thief. However, when used in the plural it refers to gangs of armed robbers, who primarily threaten travelers.

Perek **I**
Daf **11** Amud **a**

גְּמ׳ בִּשְׁלָמָא בֵּית הִלֵּל קָא מְפָרְשִׁי טַעֲמַיְיהוּ וְטַעְמָא דְּבֵית שַׁמַּאי, אֶלָּא בֵּית שַׁמַּאי – מַאי טַעְמָא לָא אָמְרִי כְּבֵית הִלֵּל?

**GEMARA** **The Gemara begins by clarifying the rationale for Beit Shammai's opinion. Granted, Beit Hillel explain the rationale for their opinion and the rationale for Beit Shammai's opinion. Beit Hillel explain both the verse that ostensibly supports Beit Shammai's opinion: When you lie down, at the time when people lie down, etc., and the verse that proves that their own explanation is more reasonable: "And when you walk along the way." However, what is the reason that Beit Shammai do not state their opinion in accordance with the opinion of Beit Hillel?**

אָמְרִי לָךְ בֵּית שַׁמַּאי: אִם כֵּן, נֵימָא קְרָא ׳בַּבֹּקֶר וּבָעֶרֶב׳, מַאי ׳בְּשׇׁכְבְּךָ וּבְקוּמֶךָ׳, בִּשְׁעַת שְׁכִיבָה – שְׁכִיבָה מַמָּשׁ, וּבִשְׁעַת קִימָה – קִימָה מַמָּשׁ.

The Gemara answers, **Beit Shammai** could **have said to you: If so** that the verse means only to denote the time for the recitation of *Shema*, as claimed by Beit Hillel, **then let the verse say: "In the morning and in the evening."** What is the meaning of the ambiguous formulation: **"When you lie down, and when you rise"?** It must mean that **at the time of lying down** one must recite *Shema* while **actually lying down, and at the time of arising** one must recite *Shema* while **actually risen.**

וּבֵית שַׁמַּאי, הַאי ׳וּבְלֶכְתְּךָ בַדֶּרֶךְ׳, מַאי עָבְדִי לְהוּ?

The Gemara continues, asking: **And what do Beit Shammai do with this** verse: **"And when you walk along the way,"** which Beit Hillel use to prove that every person recites *Shema* as he is?

הַהוּא מִבְּעֵי לְהוּ לְכִדְתַנְיָא: ׳בְּשִׁבְתְּךָ בְּבֵיתֶךָ׳ – פְּרָט לָעוֹסֵק בְּמִצְוָה, ׳וּבְלֶכְתְּךָ בַדֶּרֶךְ׳ – פְּרָט לֶחָתָן, מִכָּאן אָמְרוּ: הַכּוֹנֵס אֶת הַבְּתוּלָה – פָּטוּר, וְאֶת הָאַלְמָנָה – חַיָּיב.

The Gemara answers: Beit Shammai **need this** verse in order to derive other *halakhot*, **as it was taught** in a *baraita* which interpreted this verse that the obligation to recite *Shema* applies **when you sit in your home, to the exclusion of one who is engaged in** performance of **a mitzva,** who is exempt from the recitation of *Shema*; **and when you walk along the way, to the exclusion of a groom,** who is also exempt from the recitation of *Shema*. The *baraita* adds that **from here,** from this interpretation of the verses, **they said: One who marries a virgin**[H] **is exempt** from the recitation of *Shema* on his wedding night, **but one who marries a widow is obligated.**

**HALAKHA**

**One who marries a virgin – הַכּוֹנֵס אֶת הַבְּתוּלָה:** One who marries a virgin is exempt from reciting *Shema* for the first three days and four nights following his wedding (*Magen Avraham*) if he has not yet consummated the marriage. It was customary to exempt a groom from the recitation of *Shema* on his wedding night, but that is no longer the practice; see below (Rambam *Sefer Ahava*, *Hilkhot Keriat Shema* 4:1; *Shulḥan Arukh*, *Oraḥ Ḥayyim* 70:3).

מַאי מַשְׁמַע?

The Gemara clarifies the meaning of this *baraita*, and asks: **From where may it be inferred** that the verse, when you walk along the way, exempts a groom from the obligation to recite *Shema*?

אָמַר רַב פַּפָּא: כִּי דֶּרֶךְ, מַה דֶּרֶךְ רְשׁוּת, אַף כֹּל – רְשׁוּת.

**Rav Pappa said** that we learn: **Like the way; just as** the journey along a specific **way** described in the verse **is voluntary** and involves no mitzva, **so too all** of those who are obligated to recite *Shema* are engaged in **voluntary** activities. However, one engaged in the performance of a mitzva, like a groom, is exempt from the obligation to recite *Shema*.

מִי לָא עָסְקִינַן דְּקָא אָזֵיל לִדְבַר מִצְוָה, וַאֲפִילּוּ הָכִי אָמַר רַחֲמָנָא לִקְרֵי! – אִם כֵּן, לִכְתּוֹב רַחֲמָנָא ׳בְּשֶׁבֶת וּבְלֶכֶת׳, מַאי ׳בְּשִׁבְתְּךָ וּבְלֶכְתְּךָ׳? – בְּשֶׁבֶת דִּידָךְ וּבְלֶכֶת דִּידָךְ הוּא דְּמִחַיְּיבַתְּ, הָא דְּמִצְוָה – פְּטִירַתְּ.

The Gemara asks: **Are we not dealing with** a case where **one walks** along the way **to perform a mitzva?** The Torah did not designate the objective of his walk and, **nevertheless, the Torah said to recite** *Shema*, indicating that one is obligated even if he set out to perform a mitzva. Rather, the proof is from the formulation of the verse. **If so,** that the intention was to obligate in all cases, **let the Torah write: When sitting and when walking. What is** the meaning of: **When you sit and when you walk?** Certainly these additions come to emphasize **in your sitting down and in your walking,** meaning that when one does this for his own purposes and of his own volition, **he is obligated** to recite *Shema*, **but** when he does with the objective of performing **a mitzva, he is exempt** from reciting *Shema*, as in that case he is sitting or walking at God's behest.

אִי הָכִי, אֲפִילּוּ כּוֹנֵס אֶת הָאַלְמָנָה נָמֵי!

The conclusion is that anyone engaged in the performance of a mitzva is exempt from the recitation of *Shema*. **If so, even one who marries a widow should be** exempt, for he, too, is engaged in performance of a mitzva. That, however, contradicts the *baraita*.

הַאי טָרִיד וְהַאי לָא טָרִיד.

The Gemara responds that there is nevertheless a distinction between one marrying a virgin and one marrying a widow. **One** who marries a virgin **is preoccupied** by his concern lest he discover that his bride is not a virgin, while **one** who marries a widow **is not preoccupied.** The conclusion is that the groom is exempt from reciting *Shema* because he is preoccupied.

אִי מִשּׁוּם טִרְדָּא, אֲפִילּוּ טָבְעָה סְפִינָתוֹ בַּיָּם נָמֵי! וְכִי תֵּימָא הָכִי נָמֵי, אַלְמָה אָמַר רַבִּי אַבָּא בַּר זַבְדָּא אָמַר רַב: אָבֵל חַיָּיב בְּכׇל הַמִּצְוֹת הָאֲמוּרוֹת בַּתּוֹרָה, חוּץ מִן הַתְּפִילִּין, שֶׁהֲרֵי נֶאֱמַר בָּהֶם פְּאֵר, שֶׁנֶּאֱמַר: ״פְּאֵרְךָ חֲבוֹשׁ עָלֶיךָ״!

The Gemara asks: **If** the exemption is **due to preoccupation,** then **even one** who is preoccupied because **his ship sank at sea** should **also** be exempt. The Gemara reinforces its question: **And if you say** that **in this case as well,** when one's ship sank at sea, one is exempt, **why** then **did Rabbi Abba bar Zavda say** that **Rav said: A mourner is obligated in all the mitzvot mentioned in the Torah**[N] **except for** the mitzva to don **phylacteries,**[H] from which a mourner is exempt, **as** the term **splendor is stated** with regard to phylacteries, **as it is stated:** "Make no mourning for the dead, **bind your splendor upon yourself**" (Ezekiel 24:17). It is inappropriate for a mourner to wrap himself in phylacteries, with regard to which, the term splendor was employed (*Tosafot*). If a mourner, who is clearly pained and preoccupied, is obligated to recite *Shema*, then certainly all others who are preoccupied, even one whose ship sank at sea, whose loss was merely monetary (*Birkat Hashem*), should be obligated. Why, then, is a groom exempted because of his preoccupation and one who lost his property is not?

הָתָם – טָרִיד טִרְדָּא דְּמִצְוָה, הָכָא – טָרִיד טִרְדָּא דִּרְשׁוּת.

The Gemara answers: Nevertheless, there is a distinction between the cases. For **there,** in the case of a groom, **he is preoccupied with the preoccupation of a mitzva** that he must perform; **here,** in the case of a ship lost at sea, **he is preoccupied with the preoccupation of a voluntary** act that he chooses to perform.

וּבֵית שַׁמַּאי

Here, the Gemara returns to its initial question: **And** how do **Beit Shammai** explain the passage: "When you walk along the way" (Rashash)?

הַהוּא מִבְּעֵי לְהוּ: פְּרָט לִשְׁלוּחֵי מִצְוָה.

The Gemara answers: Beit Shammai **need this** passage in order to **exclude one who is on the path** to perform **a mitzva**[N] from the obligation to recite *Shema*.

וּבֵית הִלֵּל אָמְרִי: מִמֵּילָא שְׁמַע מִינַּהּ דַּאֲפִילּוּ בַּדֶּרֶךְ נָמֵי קָרֵי.

Beit Hillel also agree that one engaged in the performance of a mitzva is exempt from reciting *Shema*? If so, the *halakha* that they derived from: When you walk along the way lacks a source and is therefore unfounded. **And Beit Hillel say: Derive from this** *halakha* **itself** that one who is not an agent in the performance of a mitzva **recites** *Shema* **even along the way.**

**HALAKHA**

**A mourner is obligated in all the mitzvot…except for the mitzva of phylacteries – אָבֵל חַיָּיב בְּכׇל הַמִּצְוֹת...חוּץ מִן הַתְּפִילִּין:** One is prohibited from donning phylacteries on the day that he buries his deceased relative (Rambam *Sefer Ahava, Hilkhot Tefillin* 4:13, *Sefer Shofetim, Hilkhot Evel* 4:9; *Shulḥan Arukh, Oraḥ Ḥayyim* 38:5, *Yoreh De'a* 388:1).

**NOTES**

**One who marries a virgin…a mourner – הַכּוֹנֵס אֶת הַבְּתוּלָה...אָבֵל:** Ostensibly, one could ask why a mourner is not exempt from reciting *Shema*, as one cannot dismiss his preoccupation by characterizing it as preoccupation of a voluntary act; he is obligated to mourn the death of a family member. Nevertheless, there is a distinction between the preoccupation of a mourner and the preoccupation of the groom. The preoccupation of the mourner is his personal reaction, due to his personal pain over the death of his relative. However, not only is the preoccupation of the groom due to a mitzva, it is also preoccupation stemming from his preparation to perform that mitzva.

**Exclude one who is on the path to perform a mitzva – פְּרָט לִשְׁלוּחֵי מִצְוָה:** The authorities differed with regard to those on a path to perform a mitzva. Some say that they are exempt from the performance of another mitzva only if pursuing the second mitzva is likely to compromise fulfillment of that first mitzva, e.g., if searching for a *sukka* in which to sleep will take up valuable time that could have otherwise been devoted to pursuing the original mitzva. Others say that those on the path to perform a mitzva have the legal status of one engaged in the performance of a mitzva and are exempt from the performance of another mitzva, even if they could do so with no particular difficulty.

תָּנוּ רַבָּנַן, בֵּית הִלֵּל אוֹמְרִים: עוֹמְדִין וְקוֹרִין, יוֹשְׁבִין וְקוֹרִין, וּמַטִּין וְקוֹרִין, הוֹלְכִין בַּדֶּרֶךְ וְקוֹרִין, עוֹשִׂין בִּמְלַאכְתָּן וְקוֹרִין. וּמַעֲשֶׂה בְּרַבִּי יִשְׁמָעֵאל וְרַבִּי אֶלְעָזָר בֶּן עֲזַרְיָה שֶׁהָיוּ מְסוּבִּין בְּמָקוֹם אֶחָד, וְהָיָה רַבִּי יִשְׁמָעֵאל מוּטֶּה וְרַבִּי אֶלְעָזָר בֶּן עֲזַרְיָה זָקוּף. כֵּיוָן שֶׁהִגִּיעַ זְמַן קְרִיאַת שְׁמַע, הִטָּה רַבִּי אֶלְעָזָר וְזָקַף רַבִּי יִשְׁמָעֵאל. אָמַר לוֹ רַבִּי אֶלְעָזָר בֶּן עֲזַרְיָה לְרַבִּי יִשְׁמָעֵאל: יִשְׁמָעֵאל אָחִי, אֶמְשׁוֹל לְךָ מָשָׁל, לְמָה הַדָּבָר דּוֹמֶה? – מָשָׁל לְאֶחָד שֶׁאוֹמְרִים לוֹ זְקָנְךָ מְגוּדָּל, אָמַר לָהֶם: יִהְיֶה כְּנֶגֶד הַמַּשְׁחִיתִים. אַף כָּךְ אַתָּה, כָּל זְמַן שֶׁאֲנִי זָקוּף – אַתָּה מוּטֶּה, עַכְשָׁיו כְּשֶׁאֲנִי הִטֵּיתִי – אַתָּה זָקַפְתָּ!

**The Sages taught** in a *baraita* that **Beit Hillel say:** One may recite *Shema* in any situation: **Standing and reciting, sitting and reciting, reclining and reciting, walking and reciting** and even **working and reciting. And** in the *Tosefta* **an incident** is related where two *tanna'im*, **Rabbi Yishmael and Rabbi Elazar ben Azarya,** who were both disciples of Beit Hillel, **were reclining** at a meal **in one place** together with their students, **and Rabbi Yishmael was reclined** as was the customary dining position, **and Rabbi Elazar ben Azarya was upright. When the time to recite** the evening ***Shema*** **arrived, Rabbi Elazar reclined** to recite *Shema* in accordance with the opinion of Beit Shammai, **while Rabbi Yishmael** sat **upright** to recite *Shema*. **Rabbi Elazar ben Azarya** appeared to take offense, and **said to Rabbi Yishmael: Yishmael, my brother, I will tell you a parable to which this is similar. It is comparable to** a situation where **one to whom people say** as a compliment: **Your beard is full** and suits you. That man **says to them: May it be against those who** shave and **destroy** their beards, i.e., the only reason I grow my beard is to irritate those who cut their own (Rashba). **You are the same. As long as I am upright, you are reclined, and now when I reclined** lauding your conduct and emulating you, **you** sat **upright** as if to demonstrate that whatever I do, you do the opposite.

אָמַר לוֹ: אֲנִי עָשִׂיתִי כְּדִבְרֵי בֵּית הִלֵּל, וְאַתָּה עָשִׂיתָ כְּדִבְרֵי בֵּית שַׁמַּאי; וְלֹא עוֹד אֶלָּא שֶׁמָּא יִרְאוּ הַתַּלְמִידִים וְיִקְבְּעוּ הֲלָכָה לְדוֹרוֹת.

Rabbi Yishmael **said to him: I acted in accordance with** the opinion of **Beit Hillel,** according to whom one may recite *Shema* in any position, **while you acted in accordance with** the opinion of **Beit Shammai.** I am the one who acted in accordance with the *halakha*. **And furthermore,** I was concerned **lest the students see** your conduct **and establish the *halakha* for generations** accordingly. It was therefore necessary for me to demonstrate that there is no obligation to do so.

מַאי ״וְלֹא עוֹד״?

The Gemara asks: **What is** the meaning of: **And furthermore?** Why was it necessary for Rabbi Yishmael to add additional justification for his actions when the reason that he acted in accordance with the opinion of Beit Hillel was sufficient?

וְכִי תֵּימָא, בֵּית הִלֵּל נַמִּי אִית לְהוּ מַטִּין – הָנֵי מִילֵּי דְּמַטֶּה וַאֲתָא מֵעִיקָּרָא, אֲבָל הָכָא – כֵּיוָן דְּעַד הָשְׁתָּא הֲוֵית זָקוּף וְהָשְׁתָּא מוּטֶּה, אָמְרִי שְׁמַע מִינָּהּ כְּבֵית שַׁמַּאי סְבִירָא לְהוּ, שֶׁמָּא יִרְאוּ הַתַּלְמִידִים וְיִקְבְּעוּ הֲלָכָה לְדוֹרוֹת.

The Gemara answers: It was necessary for him to add this reason, as **if you say: Beit Hillel also hold** that one is permitted to recite *Shema* while **reclining** and Rabbi Yishmael could have remained reclining even in accordance with the opinion of Beit Hillel, but **this only applies when one had already been reclining originally,** in which case it is like any other position. **However, here, since until now he had been upright, and now he is reclined,** the students **will say: Conclude from this, that they hold in accordance with** the opinion of **Beit Shammai.** Due to the concern that **the students might see and establish the *halakha* for generations** in accordance with the opinion of Beit Shammai, it was necessary for Rabbi Yishmael to sit upright.

תָּנֵי רַב יְחֶזְקֵאל: עָשָׂה כְּדִבְרֵי בֵּית שַׁמַּאי – עָשָׂה, כְּדִבְרֵי בֵּית הִלֵּל – עָשָׂה.

**Rav Yeḥezkel**[P] **taught: One who acted in accordance with** the opinion of **Beit Shammai** has **acted** appropriately and is not in violation of the *halakha*. One who acted **in accordance with** the opinion of **Beit Hillel acted** appropriately as well. According to this opinion, Beit Hillel and Beit Shammai agree that one who acted in accordance with the opinion of the other fulfilled his obligation. Although the *halakha* was ruled in accordance with the opinion of Beit Hillel, Beit Hillel would agree that one who acted in accordance with the opinion of Beit Shammai fulfilled his obligation.

רַב יוֹסֵף אָמַר: עָשָׂה כְּדִבְרֵי בֵּית שַׁמַּאי – לֹא עָשָׂה וְלֹא כְלוּם, דִּתְנַן: מִי שֶׁהָיָה רֹאשׁוֹ וְרוּבּוֹ בַּסּוּכָּה וְשֻׁלְחָנוֹ בְּתוֹךְ הַבַּיִת – בֵּית שַׁמַּאי פּוֹסְלִין, וּבֵית הִלֵּל מַכְשִׁירִין.

However, **Rav Yosef said: One who acts in accordance with** the opinion of **Beit Shammai has done nothing** and must repeat *Shema* in accordance with the opinion of Beit Hillel, **as we learned** in the mishna with regard to the *halakhot* of a *sukka*: **One who had his head and most of his body in the *sukka*, and his table** upon which he was eating **inside the house, Beit Shammai invalidate** his action, as he is liable to be drawn after the table and end up eating outside the *sukka*. **And Beit Hillel validate** his action, since his head and most of his body remain inside the *sukka*.

**PERSONALITIES**

**Rav Yeḥezkel – רַב יְחֶזְקֵאל:** Rav Yeḥezkel was a first generation Babylonian *amora*. Much is not known about Rav Yeḥezkel aside from certain details that were preserved primarily on account of his famous sons. He was apparently one of the Babylonian Sages who learned all of his Torah in Babylonia, and was not influenced by the Torah of Eretz Yisrael. Therefore he was well-versed in traditions transmitted by the Sages of Babylonia who preceded him. While Rav Yeḥezkel was not renowned for his Torah knowledge, he was acclaimed for his performance of mitzvot, and due to his piety, even Shmuel, one of the greatest *amora'im* of his generation, respected him greatly.

Rav Yeḥezkel had two famous sons. One of them was Rav Yehuda ben Yeḥezkel, the Rav Yehuda frequently cited, a student of Shmuel, and one of the outstanding Sages of the Talmud. His other son, Rami, Rav Ami bar Yeḥezkel, was one of the sharpest Sages of his generation, who occasionally is cited disagreeing with his famous brother.

אָמְרוּ לָהֶם בֵּית הִלֵּל לְבֵית שַׁמַּאי: מַעֲשֶׂה שֶׁהָלְכוּ זִקְנֵי בֵית שַׁמַּאי וְזִקְנֵי בֵית הִלֵּל לְבַקֵּר אֶת רַבִּי יוֹחָנָן בֶּן הַחוֹרָנִית. מְצָאוּהוּ שֶׁהָיָה רֹאשׁוֹ וְרוּבּוֹ בַּסּוּכָּה וְשֻׁלְחָנוֹ בְּתוֹךְ הַבַּיִת, וְלֹא אָמְרוּ לוֹ כְּלוּם.

**Beit Hillel said to Beit Shammai** as a proof: **There was an incident where the elders of Beit Shammai and the elders of Beit Hillel went** on *Sukkot* **to visit Rabbi Yoḥanan ben HaḤoranit. They found him with his head and most of his** body **in the *sukka* and his table inside the house and they said nothing to him.** In other words, even Beit Shammai did not object.

אָמְרוּ לָהֶם: וּמִשָּׁם רְאָיָה? אַף הֵם אָמְרוּ לוֹ: אִם כֵּן הָיִיתָ נוֹהֵג, לֹא קִיַּימְתָּ מִצְוַת סוּכָּה מִיָּמֶיךָ.

Beit Shammai **said to them: And** is there **proof from there?** That is not what happened, rather **they said to him** explicitly: **If you have been** accustomed to **act in this manner, you have never in your life fulfilled the mitzva of *sukka*.** We see that Beit Shammai held that anyone who did not act in accordance with their opinion, did not fulfill his obligation at all. Similarly, since Beit Hillel's opinion was accepted as *halakha*, anyone who acts in accordance with the opinion of Beit Shammai fails to fulfill his obligation.

רַב נַחְמָן בַּר יִצְחָק אָמַר: עָשָׂה כְּדִבְרֵי בֵית שַׁמַּאי – חַיָּיב מִיתָה, דִּתְנַן אָמַר רַבִּי טַרְפוֹן: אֲנִי הָיִיתִי בָא בַּדֶּרֶךְ וְהִטֵּתִי לִקְרוֹת כְּדִבְרֵי בֵית שַׁמַּאי, וְסִכַּנְתִּי בְּעַצְמִי מִפְּנֵי הַלִּסְטִים. אָמְרוּ לוֹ: כְּדַאי הָיִיתָ לָחוּב בְּעַצְמְךָ, שֶׁעָבַרְתָּ עַל דִּבְרֵי בֵית הִלֵּל.

**Rav Naḥman bar Yitzḥak stated** an even more extreme opinion: **One who acted in accordance with** the opinion of **Beit Shammai** has acted so egregiously that he **is liable to** receive the **death** penalty,[N] **as we learned** in our mishna that **Rabbi Tarfon said** to his colleagues: Once, **I was coming on the road** when I stopped and **reclined to recite *Shema* in accordance with the statement of Beit Shammai.** Yet in so doing, **I endangered myself due to the highwaymen** who accost travelers. The Sages **said to him: You deserved** to be in a position where you were **liable** to pay **with your life, as you transgressed the statement of Beit Hillel.**

מתני׳ בַּשַּׁחַר מְבָרֵךְ שְׁתַּיִם לְפָנֶיהָ וְאַחַת לְאַחֲרֶיהָ, וּבָעֶרֶב מְבָרֵךְ שְׁתַּיִם לְפָנֶיהָ וּשְׁתַּיִם לְאַחֲרֶיהָ, אַחַת אֲרוּכָּה וְאַחַת קְצָרָה.

**MISHNA** From the laws of the recitation of *Shema* itself, the mishna proceeds to discuss the blessings recited in conjunction with *Shema*. Here, the order is established: **In** the **morning** when reciting *Shema*, **one recites two blessings beforehand,**[H] the first on the radiant lights and the second the blessing on the love of Torah, **and one thereafter,** which begins with: True and Firm [*emet veyatziv*]. **And in the evening one recites two blessings beforehand,** on the radiant lights and on the love of God, **and two thereafter,**[N] the blessing of redemption: True and Faithful [*emet ve'emuna*], and the blessing: Help us lie down. With regard to the blessing: True and Faithful, **whether** one recites it in its **long** formula **and whether** one recites it in its **short**[N] formula, he fulfills his obligation (*Tosafot*).

מָקוֹם שֶׁאָמְרוּ לְהַאֲרִיךְ – אֵינוֹ רַשַּׁאי לְקַצֵּר, לְקַצֵּר – אֵינוֹ רַשַּׁאי לְהַאֲרִיךְ, לַחְתּוֹם – אֵינוֹ רַשַּׁאי שֶׁלֹּא לַחְתּוֹם, שֶׁלֹּא לַחְתּוֹם – אֵינוֹ רַשַּׁאי לַחְתּוֹם.

However, the general principle is: **Where** the Sages **said** to recite a **long** blessing, **one may not shorten it,** and so too, wherever they said to recite **a short** blessing, **one may not lengthen it.**[H] Where the Sages said that a blessing **must conclude** with a second blessing at the end, **he may not fail to conclude** with that blessing. Similarly, if the Sages said that a blessing must **not conclude** with a second blessing, **one may not conclude** with a blessing.

גמ׳ מַאי מְבָרֵךְ?

**GEMARA** The Gemara begins by determining the formula of the two blessings preceding the morning *Shema*. The Gemara asks: **What blessing does one recite?**

אָמַר רַבִּי יַעֲקֹב אָמַר רַבִּי אוֹשַׁעְיָא:

**Rabbi Ya'akov said in the name of Rabbi Oshaya:** The blessing focuses on the verse:

### NOTES

**Liable to receive the death penalty – חַיָּיב מִיתָה:** Obviously, this is not to suggest that he would receive a court-imposed death penalty; rather, it is an expression that comes to underscore the severity of this matter. This stems from the fact that establishment of the *halakha* in accordance with the opinion of Beit Hillel is one of the central determinations in the development of *halakha*. Once this determination was made after a harsh, protracted dispute, anyone who does not accept it undermines the very foundation of halakhic decision-making.

**And two thereafter – וּשְׁתַּיִם לְאַחֲרֶיהָ:** The Jerusalem Talmud explains that an additional blessing was instituted at night in order to render it parallel to the day. Since in Eretz Yisrael the custom was not to recite the portion of the ritual fringes at night, because the mitzva does not apply at night, the Sages instituted an additional blessing to replace that portion.

**One long and one short – אַחַת אֲרוּכָּה וְאַחַת קְצָרָה:** The question of how to understand this simple phrase, one long and one short, is the subject of a vigorous and unresolved debate between the commentaries. According to Rashi, one long and one short refers to the two blessings recited after the evening *Shema*. However, Rabbeinu Tam shows that although this is the most expedient based on the language of the mishna, it is difficult to accept for other reasons. Therefore, he suggested alternative possibilities. One possibility is that the phrase refers to the blessing of *emet ve'emuna* and states a general principle: Whether a blessing is long or short, one may not alter its formula.

### HALAKHA

**In the morning when reciting *Shema* one recites two blessings beforehand – בַּשַּׁחַר מְבָרֵךְ שְׁתַּיִם לְפָנֶיהָ וכו׳:** Two blessing are recited before the morning *Shema* and one thereafter. Two blessings are recited before the evening *Shema* and two thereafter, in accordance with the ruling in our mishna (Rambam *Sefer Ahava, Hilkhot Keriat Shema* 1:5; *Shulḥan Arukh, Oraḥ Ḥayyim* 59:1, 60:1–2, 66:10, 236:1).

**Where the Sages said to recite a long blessing – מָקוֹם שֶׁאָמְרוּ לְהַאֲרִיךְ וכו׳:** One may not alter the formulas of blessings as formulated by the Sages. For example, one may neither lengthen the formula of a short blessing nor shorten the formula of a long blessing. On this basis, some prohibit adding liturgy in the middle of these blessings (*Tur, Oraḥ Ḥayyim* 68) although others permit it (Rema). Similarly, one may neither begin nor conclude a blessing with *barukh* if the Sages did not include it in the original formula of the blessing (Rambam *Sefer Ahava, Hilkhot Keriat Shema* 1:7; *Shulḥan Arukh, Oraḥ Ḥayyim* 68:1 and in the comments of the Rema).

"יוֹצֵר אוֹר וּבוֹרֵא חֹשֶׁךְ."

"**Who forms light and creates darkness,** Who makes peace and creates evil, I am the Lord Who does all these things" (Isaiah 45:7).

לֵימָא: יוֹצֵר אוֹר וּבוֹרֵא נוֹגַהּ!

With regard to this formula of the blessing, the Gemara asks: **Let him say** the following formula instead: **Who forms light and creates brightness,** so as not to mention darkness, which has negative connotations.

כְּדִכְתִיב קָאָמְרִינַן.

The Gemara answers: **We say** the blessing **as** the verse **is written** in the Bible and do not alter the formula that appears in the verse.

אֶלָּא מֵעַתָּה: "עֹשֶׂה שָׁלוֹם וּבוֹרֵא רָע," מִי קָא אָמְרִינַן כְּדִכְתִיב?! אֶלָּא, כְּתִיב "רָע" וְקָרֵינַן "הַכֹּל" לִישָּׁנָא מְעַלְּיָא, הָכָא נַמִי – לֵימָא "נוֹגַהּ" לִישָּׁנָא מְעַלְּיָא!

The Gemara strongly objects: **But if so,** what about the continuation of the verse: **"Who makes peace and creates evil"? Do we say** this blessing **as it is written** in the Bible? **Rather, it is written evil and we euphemistically recite** the blessing **all things** to avoid mention of evil. **Here, too, let us euphemistically say brightness** instead of darkness.

אֶלָּא אָמַר רָבָא: כְּדֵי לְהַזְכִּיר מִדַּת יוֹם בַּלַּיְלָה וּמִדַּת לַיְלָה בַּיּוֹם.

**Rather, Rava said:** The reason we recite: "Who creates darkness" is **in order to mention the attribute of day at night and the attribute of night during the day,** and thereby unify day and night as different parts of a single entity.

בִּשְׁלָמָא מִדַּת לַיְלָה בַּיּוֹם – כִּדְאָמְרִינַן: "יוֹצֵר אוֹר וּבוֹרֵא חֹשֶׁךְ," אֶלָּא מִדַּת יוֹם בַּלַּיְלָה הֵיכִי מַשְׁכַּחַתְּ לָהּ?

The Gemara continues and asks: **Granted, the attribute of night** is mentioned **during the day, as we say: Who forms light and creates darkness, but where do you find the attribute of day** mentioned **at night?** In the blessing over the radiant lights recited at night there is no mention of "Who forms light."

אָמַר אַבַּיֵי: "גּוֹלֵל אוֹר מִפְּנֵי חֹשֶׁךְ וְחֹשֶׁךְ מִפְּנֵי אוֹר."

**Abaye said:** Nevertheless, the attribute of day is mentioned at night in the words: **Rolling away light before the darkness and darkness before the light.**

וְאִידָךְ מַאי הִיא? – אָמַר רַב יְהוּדָה אָמַר שְׁמוּאֵל: "אַהֲבָה רַבָּה." וְכֵן אוֹרִי לֵיהּ רַבִּי אֶלְעָזָר לְרַבִּי פְּדָת בְּרֵיהּ: "אַהֲבָה רַבָּה."

The Gemara asks: **And what is** the formula of **the other** blessing recited before *Shema*? **Rav Yehuda said in the name of Shmuel: An abounding love [*ahava rabba*]. And Rabbi Elazar instructed his son, Rabbi Pedat, to** also say: **An abounding love.**

תַּנְיָא נַמִי הָכִי: אֵין אוֹמְרִים "אַהֲבַת עוֹלָם" אֶלָּא "אַהֲבָה רַבָּה." וְרַבָּנַן אָמְרִי: "אַהֲבַת עוֹלָם," וְכֵן הוּא אוֹמֵר "וְאַהֲבַת עוֹלָם אֲהַבְתִּיךְ עַל כֵּן מְשַׁכְתִּיךְ חָסֶד."

**That was also taught** in a *baraita*: **One does not recite: An eternal love [*ahavat olam*];**[N] **rather,** one recites: **An abounding love.**[H] **And the Rabbis say** that one recites: **An eternal love, and so it says: "And an eternal love I have loved you, therefore I have drawn you with kindness"** (Jeremiah 31:2).

אָמַר רַב יְהוּדָה אָמַר שְׁמוּאֵל: הִשְׁכִּים לִשְׁנוֹת, עַד שֶׁלֹּא קָרָא קְרִיאַת שְׁמַע צָרִיךְ לְבָרֵךְ, מִשֶּׁקָּרָא קְרִיאַת שְׁמַע אֵינוֹ צָרִיךְ לְבָרֵךְ, שֶׁכְּבָר נִפְטַר בְּאַהֲבָה רַבָּה.

The blessing: An abounding love, is about God's love for us and includes praise for His giving us the Torah. Therefore, **Rav Yehuda said** that **Shmuel said: One who arose to study, until he recites *Shema* he must recite** a special **blessing** over the Torah. **If he** already **recited *Shema* he need not recite** that **blessing,**[H] **as he has exempted** himself **by** reciting the blessing of: **An abounding love,** which includes the components of the blessing over the Torah.

אָמַר רַב הוּנָא: לְמִקְרָא – צָרִיךְ לְבָרֵךְ, וּלְמִדְרָשׁ – אֵינוֹ צָרִיךְ לְבָרֵךְ;

Having mentioned the blessing recited over Torah, the Gemara focuses on a dispute over what constitutes Torah in terms of requiring a blessing. **Rav Huna said: For** the study of **Bible, one must recite a blessing,** as it is the word of God, **and for** halakhic **midrash,** the derivation of *halakhot* from verses, **one need not recite a blessing.**

וְרַבִּי אֶלְעָזָר אָמַר: לְמִקְרָא וּלְמִדְרָשׁ – צָרִיךְ לְבָרֵךְ, לְמִשְׁנָה – אֵינוֹ צָרִיךְ לְבָרֵךְ;

**And Rabbi Elazar said: For Bible and midrash,** which includes *halakhot* derived from verses themselves, **one must recite a blessing; for Mishna,** which is only comprised of halakhic rulings issued by the Sages, **one need not recite a blessing.**

וְרַבִּי יוֹחָנָן אָמַר: אַף לְמִשְׁנָה נַמִי צָרִיךְ לְבָרֵךְ, [אֲבָל לְתַלְמוּד אֵינוֹ צָרִיךְ לְבָרֵךְ].

**And Rabbi Yoḥanan said: Even for Mishna,** which includes final, binding halakhic rulings, **one must recite a blessing as well, but for Talmud,** which comprises a study of the Mishna and the rationales for its rulings, **one need not recite a blessing.**

## HALAKHA

**One does not recite: An eternal love; rather: An abounding love – אֵין אוֹמְרִים "אַהֲבַת עוֹלָם," אֶלָּא "אַהֲבָה רַבָּה":** The formula for the beginning of the second blessing before *Shema* was not universally agreed upon in the time of the Talmud, as evidenced by this debate. Even in later eras, there was no consensus. Some *ge'onim* implemented a compromise between the two formulas and instituted: An abounding love, in the morning and: An everlasting love, at night. However, most *ge'onim* rejected this and held that one recites: An everlasting love, both in the morning and at night. Consequently, the custom among Sephardic Jews, based on the later *ge'onim*, the Rif and the Rambam, is to recite: An everlasting love, morning and night. The Vilna Gaon and Hasidic Jews adopted that custom as well. The non-Hasidic Ashkenazic custom, however, is to recite: An abounding love, in the morning and: An everlasting love, at night (Rambam *Sefer Ahava, Hilkhot Keriat Shema* 1:6; *Shulḥan Arukh, Oraḥ Ḥayyim* 60:1).

**If he recited *Shema* he need not recite that blessing – מִשֶּׁקָּרָא קְרִיאַת שְׁמַע אֵינוֹ צָרִיךְ לְבָרֵךְ:** One who has recited the blessing: An abounding love, need not recite the blessing on the Torah, as he has already fulfilled his obligation. However, because the Jerusalem Talmud restricts the cases where this *halakha* applies, the halakhic conclusion is that one must learn Torah immediately after reciting the blessing: An abounding love, in order for it to serve as a blessing on the Torah (Rambam *Sefer Ahava, Hilkhot Tefilla* 7:10; *Shulḥan Arukh, Oraḥ Ḥayyim* 47:7).

## NOTES

**An abounding love [*ahava rabba*]…An eternal love [*ahavat olam*] – אַהֲבָה רַבָּה...אַהֲבַת עוֹלָם:** We have inherited two kinds of love from our fathers, and both kinds can be considered a natural part of us in the sense that everyone can experience them with appropriate incentive and guidance. The first of these loves is abounding love, which is indeed vast and superior in every way. It is totally superior and, in contrast to earthly love, is not dependent on any external factor. It can only be achieved through an act of meditation and introspection. Love that sublime opens one up to a growing degree of awareness, of inner identity with divinity. It is a wholly internal experience, deeper, broader, and more sublime than any other.

On the one hand, one may justifiably wonder whether this sublime love is essential for one's immediate well-being. What is wrong with simply and naturally loving God with the second type of love, eternal love, like a son loves his father? Why can one not simply confess the soul's dependence on and yearning for God and leave the intellectual quest to fathom His greatness to those better qualified? After all, simple, natural love is within the capacity of all men, whereas the intellectual inquiry and meditative comprehension of the divine requires an elevated level of connection, attained by only a few.

On the other hand, if a son becomes conscious of his father's greatness and learns to appreciate his virtues and capabilities, that will enrich his love and provide it with breadth and vitality that may otherwise be lacking. The simple love then transcends its irrational, natural, and personal confines and becomes something that greatly enhances one's capacity to live in the world of God, Father to us all. It is as though one were to say: Even if God were not my own King and Father, I could not help loving Him in every way. The relationship gains an added dimension.

וְרָבָא אָמַר: אַף לְתַלְמוּד צָרִיךְ (לַחֲזוֹר וּלְבָרֵךְ) [לְבָרֵךְ];

And Rava said: Even for Talmud, which is the means to analyze the significance of the *halakhot*, and is the only form of Torah study that leads one to its true meaning, **one must recite a blessing.**[H]

דְּאָמַר רַב חִיָּיא בַּר אַשִׁי: זִימְנִין סַגִּיאִין הֲוָה קָאֵימְנָא קַמֵּיהּ דְּרַב לְתַנּוּיֵי פִּרְקִין בְּסִפְרָא דְּבֵי רַב, הֲוָה מַקְדִּים וְקָא מָשֵׁי יְדֵיהּ וּבָרֵיךְ, וּמַתְנֵי לַן פִּרְקִין.

This statement is supported by the practical *halakha* derived from observation of Rav's practice. His student, **Rav Ḥiyya bar Ashi, said: Many times I stood before Rav to study our chapter in the *Sifra*,** also known as *Torat Kohanim*, the halakhic midrash on Leviticus, **of the school of Rav,**[B] and I saw that Rav **would first wash his hands,** then **recite a blessing,** and only then **he would teach us our chapter.** This demonstrates that even before their study of *Torat Kohanim*, which, due to Rav's explanation of the reasons behind the *halakhot*, was the equivalent of studying Talmud, one must recite a blessing.

מַאי מְבָרֵךְ? אָמַר רַב יְהוּדָה אָמַר שְׁמוּאֵל: אֲשֶׁר קִדְּשָׁנוּ בְּמִצְוֹתָיו וְצִוָּנוּ לַעֲסוֹק בְּדִבְרֵי תוֹרָה.

The Gemara clarifies: **What** formula of **blessings does he recite?** There is a dispute over the formula of the blessings as well. **Rav Yehuda said** that **Shmuel said:** The formula of this blessing is like the standard formula for blessings recited over other mitzvot: Blessed are You, Lord our God, King of the universe, **Who sanctified us with his mitzvot and commanded us to engage in matters of Torah.**

וְרַבִּי יוֹחָנָן מְסַיֵּים בָּהּ הָכִי: הַעֲרֵב נָא ה׳ אֱלֹהֵינוּ אֶת דִּבְרֵי תוֹרָתְךָ בְּפִינוּ וּבְפִיפִיּוֹת עַמְּךָ בֵּית יִשְׂרָאֵל וְנִהְיֶה אֲנַחְנוּ וְצֶאֱצָאֵינוּ וְצֶאֱצָאֵי עַמְּךָ בֵּית יִשְׂרָאֵל כֻּלָּנוּ יוֹדְעֵי שְׁמֶךָ וְעוֹסְקֵי תוֹרָתֶךָ, בָּרוּךְ אַתָּה ה׳ הַמְלַמֵּד תּוֹרָה לְעַמּוֹ יִשְׂרָאֵל.

**And Rabbi Yoḥanan concludes** the blessing by adding **the following: Lord our God, make the words of Your Torah sweet in our mouths and in the mouths of Your people, the house of Israel, so that we and our descendants and the descendants of Your people, the house of Israel, may be those who know Your name and engage in Your Torah. Blessed are You, Lord, Who teaches Torah to His people Israel.**

וְרַב הַמְנוּנָא אָמַר: אֲשֶׁר בָּחַר בָּנוּ מִכָּל הָעַמִּים וְנָתַן לָנוּ אֶת תּוֹרָתוֹ. בָּרוּךְ אַתָּה ה׳ נוֹתֵן הַתּוֹרָה. אָמַר רַב הַמְנוּנָא: זוֹ הִיא מְעוּלָּה שֶׁבַּבְּרָכוֹת.

**And Rav Hamnuna said** an additional formula: **Who has chosen us from all the peoples and given us His Torah. Blessed are You, Lord, Giver of the Torah.** With regard to this formula, **Rav Hamnuna said: This** concise blessing **is the most outstanding of all the blessings** over the Torah, as it combines thanks to God for giving us the Torah as well as acclaim for the Torah and for Israel.

הִלְכָּךְ לֵימְרִינְהוּ לְכוּלְּהוּ.

Since several formulas for the blessing over Torah were suggested, each with its own distinct advantage, the Gemara concludes: **Therefore, let us recite them all** as blessings over the Torah.[H]

תְּנַן הָתָם, אָמַר לָהֶם הַמְמוּנֶּה: בָּרְכוּ בְּרָכָה אַחַת! וְהֵם בֵּרְכוּ, וְקָרְאוּ עֲשֶׂרֶת הַדִּבְּרוֹת, ״שְׁמַע,״ ״וְהָיָה אִם שָׁמוֹעַ,״ ״וַיֹּאמֶר,״ וּבֵרְכוּ אֶת הָעָם שָׁלֹשׁ בְּרָכוֹת: אֱמֶת וְיַצִּיב, וַעֲבוֹדָה, וּבִרְכַּת כֹּהֲנִים, וּבְשַׁבָּת מוֹסִיפִין בְּרָכָה אַחַת לַמִּשְׁמָר הַיּוֹצֵא.

The Gemara returns to dealing with the blessings that accompany *Shema*, and describes the practice in the Temple. **We learned there,** in a mishna in tractate *Tamid*: In the morning **the** deputy High Priest **appointed**[B] to oversee activity in the Temple, **said to** the priests who were members of the priestly watch [*mishmar*] on duty that week: **Recite a single blessing.** The members of the priestly watch **recited a blessing, and read the Ten Commandments,**[N] ***Shema, VeHaya im Shamoa* and *VaYomer*,** the standard recitation of *Shema*. Additionally, **they blessed the people** with **three blessings.** These blessings were: **True and Firm,** the blessing of redemption recited after *Shema*; ***Avoda***, service, the special blessing recited over God's acceptance of the sacrifices with favor, similar to the blessing of Temple Service recited in the *Amida* prayer; **and the priestly benediction,** recited in the form of a prayer without the outstretched hands that usually accompany that blessing (*Tosafot*). **And on Shabbat one blessing is added to** bless **the outgoing priestly watch,** as the watch serving in the Temple was replaced on Shabbat.

״מַאי בְּרָכָה אַחַת״? כִּי הָא דְּרַבִּי אַבָּא וְרַבִּי יוֹסֵי בַּר אַבָּא אִקְּלַעוּ לְהָהוּא אַתְרָא, בְּעוֹ מִינַּיְיהוּ: ״מַאי בְּרָכָה אַחַת״? לָא הֲוָה בִּידַיְיהוּ. וְאָתוּ שַׁיְילוּהוּ לְרַב מַתָּנָה, לָא הֲוָה בִּידֵיהּ. אָתוּ שַׁיְילוּהוּ לְרַב יְהוּדָה, אָמַר לְהוּ: הָכִי אָמַר שְׁמוּאֵל ״אַהֲבָה רַבָּה.״

Certain details in this mishna are not sufficiently clear. First, **what is the single blessing** that the deputy High Priest instructed the guards to recite? The Gemara relates: It is **like** the incident **where Rabbi Abba and Rabbi Yosei bar Abba happened to** visit **a certain** unnamed **place,** and the people there **asked them: What is the single blessing** mentioned in the mishna? They **did not have** an answer **readily available.** So **they came and asked Rav Mattana, and he** too **did not have** an answer **readily available. They came and asked Rav Yehuda,** and **he told them: Shmuel said as follows: An abounding love** is the single blessing recited by the priestly watch.

## HALAKHA

**For Bible…one needs to recite a blessing – לְמִקְרָא צָרִיךְ לְבָרֵךְ וכו׳:** One is obligated to recite the blessing on the Torah before engaging in the study of any form of Torah, i.e., Bible, Mishna, Gemara, or midrash. This is in accordance with the opinion of Rava, the last of the Sages to comment on this issue. His ruling is based on a practical application of the *halakha*, which overrules a *halakha* that was merely cited but not implemented (Rambam *Sefer Ahava, Hilkhot Tefilla* 7:10; *Shulḥan Arukh, Oraḥ Ḥayyim* 47:2 and in the comments of the Rema).

**What was the blessing?…Therefore, let us recite them all – מַאי מְבָרֵךְ…הִלְכָּךְ לֵימְרִינְהוּ לְכוּלְּהוּ:** Every morning one must recite the three blessings of the Torah, as per the ruling here (Rambam *Sefer Ahava, Hilkhot Tefilla* 7:10; *Shulḥan Arukh, Oraḥ Ḥayyim* 47:5).

## BACKGROUND

**The *Sifra* of the school of Rav – סִפְרָא דְּבֵי רַב:** The *Sifra*, book, of the school of Rav is a work of halakhic midrash on the book of Leviticus; it is also known as *Torat Kohanim*. This midrash consists primarily of tannaitic statements which derive various *halakhot* from verses.

The Talmud states that unattributed statements in the *Sifra* are in accordance with Rabbi Yehuda's opinion, although apparently the final redaction of the work was completed by Rav. Therefore, it is called the *Sifra* of the school of Rav. Rav also taught this halakhic midrash extensively, and its study became standard among the Sages to the extent that it became the most quoted work of halakhic midrash in the Talmud.

**The appointed one – הַמְמוּנֶּה:** Responsible for tasking the performance of the Temple service and for overseeing the other duties in the Temple, he was the most senior official in the Temple. As such, this individual was essentially the assistant to the High Priest, although from a halakhic perspective he had no privileged status and was no different from any other priest. He was appointed primarily to serve as a substitute for the High Priest; whenever the High Priest was unable to execute his duties due to illness or ritual impurity, this individual would replace him. As time went on, the responsibilities associated with the position grew; as the appointed one became responsible for tasking the performance of the Temple service, the status of this position grew to be one of the most influential in the Temple, second only to the High Priest.

## NOTES

**And they read the Ten Commandments – וְקָרְאוּ עֲשֶׂרֶת הַדִּבְּרוֹת:** The Jerusalem Talmud, in its explanation of this mishna, explains that there is a relationship between the Ten Commandments and the recitation of *Shema*, as allusions to all Ten Commandments can be found in the verses of *Shema*.

וְאָמַר רַבִּי זְרִיקָא אָמַר רַבִּי אַמִי אָמַר רַבִּי שִׁמְעוֹן בֶּן לָקִישׁ: "יוֹצֵר אוֹר." כִּי אֲתָא רַב יִצְחָק בַּר יוֹסֵף אֲמַר: הָא דְּרַבִּי זְרִיקָא לָאו בְּפֵירוּשׁ אִתְּמַר אֶלָּא מִכְּלָלָא אִתְּמַר, דְּאָמַר רַבִּי זְרִיקָא אָמַר רַבִּי אַמִי אָמַר רַבִּי שִׁמְעוֹן בֶּן לָקִישׁ: זֹאת אוֹמֶרֶת – בְּרָכוֹת אֵין מְעַכְּבוֹת זוֹ אֶת זוֹ.

**Rabbi Zerika said** that **Rabbi Ami said** that **Rabbi Shimon ben Lakish said** a different answer: This single blessing is: **Who creates light.** That was how Rabbi Shimon ben Lakish's statement was received in Babylonia, yet **when Rav Yitzḥak bar Yosef came** from Eretz Yisrael to Babylonia, **he said** that this *halakha* was not a direct quote of a statement by Rabbi Shimon ben Lakish. **That which Rabbi Zerika said was not stated explicitly** by Rabbi Shimon ben Lakish, but **rather it was inferred from** another statement. **As Rabbi Zerika said** that **Rabbi Ami said** that **Rabbi Shimon ben Lakish said:** From the expression: Recite a single blessing, in the mishna in tractate *Tamid*, **it follows** that failure to recite one of the **blessings** recited before *Shema* **does not prevent** one from reciting the **other.** This means that if only one of the blessings was recited, the obligation to recite that blessing was fulfilled, as the two blessings are not mutually dependent.

אִי אָמְרַתְּ בִּשְׁלָמָא "יוֹצֵר אוֹר" הֲווּ אָמְרִי – הַיְינוּ דִּבְרָכוֹת אֵין מְעַכְּבוֹת זוֹ אֶת זוֹ, דְּלָא קָא אָמְרִי "אַהֲבָה רַבָּה";

The conclusion was drawn from Rabbi Shimon ben Lakish's statement that he held that the single blessing recited was: Who creates light. The considerations that led the Sages to that conclusion were: **Granted, if you say that they would recite: Who creates light,** then the conclusion of Reish Lakish, that failure to recite one of the **blessings** recited before *Shema* **does not prevent one** from reciting the **other,** is understandable, as they recited: Who creates light, **and did not recite: An abounding love,** and they nonetheless fulfilled their obligation.

Perek **I**
Daf **12** Amud **a**

**BACKGROUND**

**The priestly watches** – מִשְׁמְרוֹת כְּהוּנָּה: Even before the Temple's construction was completed, there were already more priests than necessary to perform the sacred service. Therefore, King David and the prophet Samuel established priestly watches (see I Chronicles 24). Based on ancient criteria, the priests were grouped into twenty-four watches, each serving in the Temple for one week twice a year. Only during the Pilgrimage Festivals, when the entire nation ascended to Jerusalem, did all of the priests come to the Temple. During the Second Temple period, the watches were redivided; however, the basic divisions remained intact. Each watch was divided into six paternal families, each assigned to one day of the week, so that all of the members of the watch would serve. The changing of the watches took place each Shabbat, and they would then perform the ceremony and recite the blessing for the incoming priestly watch.

**If based on an inference, what of it** – אִי מִכְּלָלָא מַאי: This question appears quite often, following the statement: It was derived by inference. It is conceivable that although a statement is not stated explicitly, the conclusion derived from it is inevitable. At times, the second, inferred, version is clearer than the Sage's original statement. Then the Gemara asks: And if it is based on an inference, what of it? The Gemara generally answers that nevertheless, the conclusion is not inevitable.

**HALAKHA**

**The order of the blessings** – סֵדֶר בְּרָכוֹת: An error in the order of the blessings accompanying *Shema* does not prevent fulfillment of one's obligation to recite *Shema*. If he recited: An abounding love before reciting: Who creates light, he nevertheless fulfilled his obligation after the fact (*Mishna Berura*). This is based on the conclusion drawn from the statement of Rabbi Shimon ben Lakish (Rambam *Sefer Ahava, Hilkhot Keriat Shema* 1:8; *Shulḥan Arukh, Oraḥ Ḥayyim* 60:3).

אֶלָּא אִי אָמְרַתְּ "אַהֲבָה רַבָּה" הֲווּ אָמְרִי – מַאי "בְּרָכוֹת אֵין מְעַכְּבוֹת זוֹ אֶת זוֹ"? דִּלְמָא הַאי דְּלָא אָמְרִי "יוֹצֵר אוֹר" – מִשּׁוּם דְּלָא מְטָא זְמַן "יוֹצֵר אוֹר", וְכִי מְטָא זְמַן "יוֹצֵר אוֹר" – הֲווּ אָמְרִי!

**However, if you say that they** would omit: Who creates light, and **would recite: An abounding love,** on **what** basis would you conclude that failure to recite one of the **blessings** recited before *Shema* **does not prevent** one from reciting the **other?** In that case, one could offer another reason why only a single blessing is recited. **Perhaps** the fact **that they did not recite: Who creates light was because the time for the recitation of: Who creates light, had not yet arrived,** as the sun had yet to rise. The blessings of the priestly watch[B] are recited in the early morning hours, long before sunrise. **However,** afterward, **when the time** to recite: **Who creates light arrived, they would recite it.** From the conclusion drawn by Rabbi Shimon ben Lakish, that failure to recite one of the blessings recited before ***Shema*** does not prevent one from reciting the other, it is clear that the blessing recited by the members of the priestly watch was: Who creates light.

וְאִי מִכְּלָלָא מַאי?

As this deductive reasoning seems coherent and convincing, the Gemara asks: **And if** this *halakha* **is based on inference,** and not on an explicit statement, **what** of it?[B] There seems to be no other way to interpret Rabbi Shimon ben Lakish's statement.

דְּאִי מִכְּלָלָא, לְעוֹלָם "אַהֲבָה רַבָּה" הֲווּ אָמְרִי, וְכִי מְטָא זְמַן "יוֹצֵר אוֹר" – הֲווּ אָמְרִי לֵיהּ, וּמַאי "בְּרָכוֹת אֵין מְעַכְּבוֹת זוֹ אֶת זוֹ"? – סֵדֶר בְּרָכוֹת.

The Gemara answers: **If** this conclusion **were based on an inference,** one could say that **actually they recited: An abounding love, and when the time** to recite: **Who creates light arrived, they would recite it.** In that case, **what** is the meaning of: Failure to recite one of the **blessings** recited before *Shema* **does not prevent** one from reciting the **other?** Rabbi Shimon ben Lakish meant that failure to recite **the** correct **order of the blessings**[H] does not prevent one from fulfilling his obligation. Even if one recites: An abounding love before: Who creates light, he fulfills his obligation. Rabbi Shimon ben Lakish did not refer to a case where only one of the blessings was recited. Consequently, one cannot infer from his statement his opinion regarding the identity of the single blessing.

"וְקוֹרִין עֲשֶׂרֶת הַדִּבְּרוֹת שְׁמַע וְהָיָה אִם שָׁמוֹעַ וַיֹּאמֶר אֱמֶת וְיַצִּיב וַעֲבוֹדָה וּבִרְכַּת כֹּהֲנִים".

The Gemara related above that the priests in the Temple **read the Ten Commandments,** along with the sections of ***Shema, VeHaya im Shamoa, VaYomer,* True and Firm, *Avoda,* and the priestly benediction.**

אָמַר רַב יְהוּדָה אָמַר שְׁמוּאֵל: אַף בַּגְּבוּלִין בִּקְּשׁוּ לִקְרוֹת כֵּן, אֶלָּא שֶׁכְּבָר בִּטְּלוּם מִפְּנֵי תַּרְעוֹמֶת הַמִּינִין.

**Rav Yehuda said** that **Shmuel said: Even in the outlying areas,** outside the Temple, **they sought to recite** the Ten Commandments **in this manner** every day, as they are the basis of the Torah (Rambam), **but they had already abolished** recitation of the Ten Commandments **due to the grievance of the heretics,** who argued that the entire Torah, with the exception of the Ten Commandments, did not emanate from God (Jerusalem Talmud). If the Ten Commandments were recited daily, that would lend credence to their claim, so their recitation was expunged from the daily prayers.

תַּנְיָא נַמִּי הָכִי, רַבִּי נָתָן אוֹמֵר: בַּגְּבוּלִין בִּקְּשׁוּ לִקְרוֹת כֵּן, אֶלָּא שֶׁכְּבָר בִּטְּלוּם מִפְּנֵי תַּרְעוֹמֶת הַמִּינִין.

**That was also taught** in a *baraita* that **Rabbi Natan says: In the outlying areas, they sought to recite** the Ten Commandments **in this manner, but they had already abolished** their recitation **due to the grievance of the heretics.**

רַבָּה בַּר בַּר חָנָה סְבַר לְמִקְבְּעִינְהוּ בְּסוּרָא, אָמַר לֵיהּ רַב חִסְדָּא: כְּבָר בִּטְּלוּם מִפְּנֵי תַּרְעוֹמֶת הַמִּינִין.

The Gemara relates that several Sages sought to reinstitute recitation of the Ten Commandments, as **Rabba bar bar Ḥana thought to institute this in** the city of **Sura,**[B] but **Rav Ḥisda said to him: They already abolished them due to the grievance of the heretics.**

אַמֵימָר סְבַר לְמִקְבְּעִינְהוּ בִּנְהַרְדְּעָא, אָמַר לֵיהּ רַב אַשִׁי: כְּבָר בִּטְּלוּם מִפְּנֵי תַּרְעוֹמֶת הַמִּינִין.

So too, **Ameimar thought to institute this in** the city of **Neharde'a.**[B] **Rav Ashi,** the most prominent of the Sages in that generation, **said to him: They already abolished them due to the grievance of the heretics.**

"וּבְשַׁבָּת מוֹסִיפִין בְּרָכָה אַחַת לַמִּשְׁמָר הַיּוֹצֵא". מַאי בְּרָכָה אַחַת? אָמַר רַבִּי חֶלְבּוֹ: מִשְׁמָר הַיּוֹצֵא אוֹמֵר לַמִּשְׁמָר הַנִּכְנָס: מִי שֶׁשִּׁכֵּן אֶת שְׁמוֹ בַּבַּיִת הַזֶּה הוּא יַשְׁכִּין בֵּינֵיכֶם אַהֲבָה וְאַחֲוָה וְשָׁלוֹם וְרֵיעוּת.

We learned in a mishna in tractate *Tamid* that **on Shabbat a single blessing is added to** bless **the outgoing priestly watch.** The Gemara asks: **What is that single blessing? Rabbi Ḥelbo said:** As they finished their service, **the outgoing priestly watch would say to the incoming priestly watch: May He who caused His Name to dwell in this house cause love and brotherhood, peace and camaraderie to dwell among you.**[N]

"מָקוֹם שֶׁאָמְרוּ לְהַאֲרִיךְ". פְּשִׁיטָא, הֵיכָא דְּקָא נָקֵיט כָּסָא דְּחַמְרָא בִּידֵיהּ וְקָסָבַר דְּשִׁכְרָא הוּא וּפְתַח וּמְבָרֵךְ אַדַּעְתָּא דְּשִׁכְרָא וְסַיֵּים בְּדְחַמְרָא – יָצָא, דְּאִי נַמִּי אִם אָמַר "שֶׁהַכֹּל נִהְיָה בִּדְבָרוֹ" יָצָא, דְּהָא תְּנַן: "עַל כּוּלָּם אִם אָמַר "שֶׁהַכֹּל נִהְיָה בִּדְבָרוֹ" – יָצָא".

We learned in the mishna: **Where** the Sages **said** to recite **a long** blessing, one may not shorten it, and vice-versa. The Gemara proceeds to address a particular problem arising from conclusions drawn from this mishna. Before addressing the primary problem, however, a simpler, secondary issue is raised: **Obviously,**[B] **in a case where one took a cup of wine in his hand and thought it was beer, and began reciting the blessing thinking it was beer,** i.e., he intended to recite the appropriate blessing on beer: By Whose word all things came to be, **and** upon realizing that it was wine, **he concluded** the blessing **with that** which is recited over **wine:** Who creates the fruit of the vine, **he fulfilled** his obligation. In that case, **even had he recited: By Whose word all things came to be,** as he originally intended, **he** would have **fulfilled** his obligation, **as we learned** in a mishna: **If one** recited the general blessing: **By Whose word all things came to be, over all** food items, **he fulfilled** his obligation after the fact, even if *ab initio* another blessing was instituted to recite before eating that food. Therefore, if he reconsidered and concluded the blessing with the ending of the blessing over wine, he fulfilled his obligation.

אֶלָּא, הֵיכָא דְּקָא נָקֵיט כָּסָא דְּשִׁכְרָא בִּידֵיהּ וְקָסָבַר דְּחַמְרָא הוּא, פְּתַח וּבָרֵיךְ אַדַּעְתָּא דְּחַמְרָא, וְסַיֵּים בְּדְשִׁכְרָא, מַאי?

**However in a case where one took a cup of beer in his hand**[H] **and thought it was wine, and began reciting the blessing thinking it was wine,** meaning he intended to recite: Who creates the fruit of the vine, **and** upon realizing that it was beer **he concluded** the blessing **with that** which is recited over **beer:** By Whose word all things came to be, **what** is the *halakha*?

בָּתַר עִיקַּר בְּרָכָה אָזְלִינַן, אוֹ בָּתַר חֲתִימָה אָזְלִינַן?

Ostensibly, this blessing is comprised of two sections. The first section, during which he intended to recite: Who creates the fruit of the vine, cannot fulfill his obligation as it is an inappropriate blessing to recite over beer. However, in the second section he recited: By Whose word all things came to be, the appropriate blessing. The dilemma, then, is: **Do we follow the essence** of the blessing, the first section, **or do we follow the conclusion** of the blessing?

BACKGROUND

**Sura – סוּרָא:** A town in Southern Babylonia, Sura did not become an important Jewish community until the great *amora*, Rav, moved and established the yeshiva there (c. 220 CE). From then until the end of geonic period (c. 1000 CE), Sura was a major Torah center. The yeshiva in Sura, under the leadership of Rav and his closest disciples, was influenced by the halakhic traditions of Eretz Yisrael, and was renowned for its unique approach to Torah study. Among the great Sages and leaders in Sura were Rav, Rav Huna, Rav Ḥisda, Ravina, and Rav Ashi. The Babylonian Talmud was, for the most part, redacted in Sura. There was another city with the same name. In order to distinguish between them, the other city was called Sura on the Euphrates.

**Neharde'a – נְהַרְדְּעָא:** A city on the Euphrates near the Malka River, Neharde'a was one of the oldest Jewish communities in Babylonia. According to tradition, Jews lived in Neharde'a as early as First Temple times (sixth century BCE), beginning with the exile of King Jehoiachin of Judea. Neharde'a was one of the most important Jewish communities in Babylonia. It was a center of Torah study from an early period and its yeshiva was the oldest in Babylonia. Many of the greatest *tanna'im* visited Neharde'a, among them Rabbi Akiva, who intercalated the calendar there (*Yevamot* 122b). In Rav's time (the first half of the third century CE), Neharde'a's yeshiva was headed by Rav Sheila and then by Shmuel. Since the city was located near the border between the Roman and the Persian Empires, it frequently suffered from the wars between the two. Pappa ben Nazer Odonathus, king of Tadmor, destroyed it completely in 259 CE. Later, however, Jews resettled there, and many Torah scholars remained in Neharde'a even after its yeshiva moved to Meḥoza and Pumbedita.

**Obviously – פְּשִׁיטָא:** This style is employed at times as an introduction to raising a well formulated dilemma, as the parameters of the question must be established first. Therefore, the questioner, or the Gemara, explains what elements remain outside the parameters of the discussion, in order to isolate the central problem and focus upon it.

NOTES

**May He cause love and brotherhood, peace and camaraderie to dwell among you – הוּא יַשְׁכִּין בֵּינֵיכֶם אַהֲבָה וְאַחֲוָה וְשָׁלוֹם:** Some explain that the incoming priestly watch was blessed with this particular blessing because, at least for a brief period, the choice of the priest who would perform a particular service in the Temple was based on the result of competition between the priests. This competition sometimes led to calamitous results. Therefore, this blessing was recited in the hope that the incoming watch would be blessed with brotherhood and peace (Maharsha).

HALAKHA

**Where one took a cup of beer in his hand – הֵיכָא דְּקָא נָקֵיט כָּסָא דְּשִׁכְרָא בִּידֵיהּ וכו׳:** The case of one who mistakenly began to recite a blessing with the intention of reciting an incorrect blessing, as in the case of one who began to recite the blessing over wine on beer, is not resolved in the Gemara. Therefore, as per the rule in other cases of uncertainty with regard to blessing, the *halakha* and common practice is to be lenient, and therefore he is not required to recite another blessing. There are divergent opinions among the decisors of *halakha*, however, as the *ge'onim* had in their possession a variant reading of the Gemara, leading them to a different conclusion and a different ruling (Rambam *Sefer Ahava, Hilkhot Berakhot* 8:11; *Shulḥan Arukh, Oraḥ Ḥayyim* 209:1–2).

תָּא שְׁמַע: שַׁחֲרִית, פָּתַח בְּ״יוֹצֵר אוֹר״ וְסִיֵּים בְּ״מַעֲרִיב עֲרָבִים״ – לֹא יָצָא, פָּתַח בְּ״מַעֲרִיב עֲרָבִים״ וְסִיֵּים בְּ״יוֹצֵר אוֹר״ – יָצָא;

**Come and hear** a proof from what was taught in a *baraita* with regard to a similar case: If, in **the morning prayer**, one **began** the blessings prior to the recitation of *Shema* appropriately **with: Who creates light, and concluded with** the formula of the evening prayer: **Who brings on evenings, he did not fulfill** his obligation. However, if one did the opposite, and **commenced with: Who brings on evenings, and concluded with: Who creates light, he fulfilled** his obligation.

עַרְבִית, פָּתַח בְּ״מַעֲרִיב עֲרָבִים״ וְסִיֵּים בְּ״יוֹצֵר אוֹר״ – לֹא יָצָא, פָּתַח בְּ״יוֹצֵר אוֹר״ וְסִיֵּים בְּ״מַעֲרִיב עֲרָבִים״ – יָצָא;

Similarly, if, in **the evening prayer, one commenced** the recitation of *Shema* **with: Who brings on evenings and concluded with: Who creates light, he did not fulfill** his obligation. If **one commenced with: Who creates light and concluded with: Who brings on evenings, he fulfilled** his obligation.

כְּלָלוֹ שֶׁל דָּבָר: הַכֹּל הוֹלֵךְ אַחַר הַחִתּוּם.

The *baraita* summarizes that **the general principle is: Everything follows the conclusion** of the blessing. Based on this principle, the question with regard to a blessing recited over food and drink posed above can be resolved.

שָׁאנֵי הָתָם דְּקָאָמַר: ״בָּרוּךְ יוֹצֵר הַמְּאוֹרוֹת״.

This proof is rejected: **There,** in the case of the blessing recited over the radiant lights, **it is different, as one recites: Blessed**…Who **forms the radiant lights,** and similarly, in the evening one recites: Blessed…Who brings on evenings. Since these are long blessings that conclude with a second blessing summarizing their content, one could assert that everything follows the conclusion. However, in the case of short blessings, such as: By Whose word all things came to be, or: Who creates the fruit of the vine, ostensibly, if there is a problem with the first part of the blessing, the entire blessing is nullified.

הָנִיחָא לְרַב דְּאָמַר ״כָּל בְּרָכָה שֶׁאֵין בָּהּ הַזְכָּרַת הַשֵּׁם אֵינָהּ בְּרָכָה״ – שַׁפִּיר, אֶלָּא לְרַבִּי יוֹחָנָן דְּאָמַר: ״כָּל בְּרָכָה שֶׁאֵין בָּהּ מַלְכוּת אֵינָהּ בְּרָכָה״, מַאי אִיכָּא לְמֵימַר?

The distinction between the blessing recited over the radiant lights and the blessings recited over food and drink stems from the assumption that the conclusion: Blessed…Who fashions the radiant lights, is a complete, independent blessing. However, this is not necessarily so. **This works out well according to Rav, who said: Any blessing that does not include mention of God's name is not** considered **a blessing,** and since: Who creates light, includes God's name, it constitutes a complete, independent blessing. **However, according to Rabbi Yoḥanan, who said: Any blessing that does not include mention of** God's **sovereignty,** i.e., our God, King of the universe, **is not** considered **a blessing, what can be said** to distinguish between the conclusion of the blessings over food and drink and the blessing over the radiant lights? Since the conclusion: Who creates light, does not mention God's sovereignty, it does not constitute a complete, independent blessing.

אֶלָּא, כֵּיוָן דְּאָמַר רַבָּה בַּר עוּלָּא: וּכְדֵי לְהַזְכִּיר מִדַּת יוֹם בַּלַּיְלָה וּמִדַּת לַיְלָה בַּיּוֹם, כִּי קָאָמַר בְּרָכָה וּמַלְכוּת מֵעִיקָּרָא אַתַּרְוַיְיהוּ קָאָמַר.

The Gemara responds: **Rather,** Rabbi Yoḥanan also holds that the blessing over the radiant lights is a complete blessing. **Since Rabba bar Ulla said:** Who creates darkness, is mentioned during the day and: Rolling away the light before the darkness, is mentioned at night **in order to mention the attribute of day at night and the attribute of night in the day,** the beginning of the blessing in which God's sovereignty is mentioned day and night is appropriate to both day and night, and **when one recites the blessing** with God's name **and** mentions God's **sovereignty at the beginning of the blessing,** it refers **to both** day and night. Therefore, no proof can be cited from the blessing over the radiant lights to the blessings recited over food and drink.

תָּא שְׁמַע מִסֵּיפָא, ״כְּלָלוֹ שֶׁל דָּבָר: הַכֹּל הוֹלֵךְ אַחַר הַחִתּוּם״. ״כְּלָלוֹ שֶׁל דָּבָר״ לְאֵתוֹיֵי מַאי – לָאו לְאֵתוֹיֵי הָא דַּאֲמַרַן?

The Gemara attempts to cite an additional proof: **Come and hear** another solution based on what we learned **in the latter clause** of the *baraita* cited above: **The general principle is: Everything follows the conclusion** of the blessing. **What does** the phrase: The general principle is, come **to include** beyond the detailed example cited in the *baraita*? **Does it not come to include** the case **that we stated,** that both in the case of a long blessing and the case of a short blessing, the conclusion of the blessing is the determining factor?

לָא, לְאַתּוּיֵי נַהֲמָא וְתַמְרֵי. הֵיכִי דָּמֵי? אִילֵימָא דַּאֲכַל נַהֲמָא וְקָסָבַר דְּתַמְרֵי אֲכַל, וּפְתַח אַדַּעְתָּא דְּתַמְרֵי וְסַיֵּים בִּדְנַהֲמָא – הַיְינוּ בְּעָיָין!

The Gemara rejects this: **No,** the principle is cited **to include** a case of **bread and dates.** The Gemara clarifies: **What are the circumstances** of the dilemma with regard to the blessings on these food items? **If you say that** it is a case **where one ate bread and thought that he ate dates, and commenced** reciting the blessing **thinking it was dates;** then, upon realizing that it was bread, **he concluded** the blessing **with that** which is recited **over bread, isn't that our dilemma,** as this case is identical to the one involving wine and beer?

לָא צְרִיכָא: כְּגוֹן דַּאֲכַל תַּמְרֵי וְקָסָבַר נַהֲמָא אֲכַל, וּפְתַח בִּדְנַהֲמָא וְסַיֵּים בִּדְתַמְרֵי – [יָצָא], דַּאֲפִילּוּ סַיֵּים בִּדְנַהֲמָא נַמִי יָצָא;

The Gemara answers: **No; this** general principle **is** only **necessary** to teach a special **case, where one ate dates and thought that he ate bread, and commenced** reciting the blessing **thinking they were bread.** Upon realizing that they were dates, **he concluded** the blessing **with that** which is recited **over dates.** In that case **he fulfilled** his obligation, as **even had he concluded** the blessing **with that** which is recited **over bread, he** would have **fulfilled his obligation.**

מַאי טַעְמָא – דְּתַמְרֵי נַמִי מֵיזָן זָיְינִי.

**What is the reason** that had he concluded with the blessing recited over bread he would have fulfilled his obligation to recite a blessing over dates? This is **because dates also provide** a person **sustenance.** While *ab initio* one should not recite the blessing for bread over dates, after the fact, if one did so, he fulfilled his obligation. It is with regard to this particular situation that the *baraita* established the principle: Everything follows the conclusion of the blessing. Ultimately, the dilemma regarding a blessing with an inappropriate opening and an appropriate conclusion remains unresolved.

The Gemara proceeds to discuss the formula for the blessings recited along with *Shema*.

אָמַר רַבָּה בַּר חִינָּנָא סָבָא מִשְּׁמֵיהּ דְּרַב: כָּל שֶׁלֹּא אָמַר "אֱמֶת וְיַצִּיב" שַׁחֲרִית וֶ"אֱמֶת וֶאֱמוּנָה" עַרְבִית – לֹא יָצָא יְדֵי חוֹבָתוֹ, שֶׁנֶּאֱמַר: "לְהַגִּיד בַּבֹּקֶר חַסְדֶּךָ וֶאֱמוּנָתְךָ בַּלֵּילוֹת".

**Rabba bar Ḥinnana Sava said in the name of Rav: One who did not recite: True and Firm** [*emet veyatziv*] at the beginning of the blessing of redemption that follows *Shema* **in the morning prayer,**[N] **and: True and Trustworthy** [*emet ve'emuna*] **in the evening prayer,**[H] **he did not fulfill his obligation.** An allusion to the difference in formulation between morning and evening is, **as it is stated: "To declare Your kindness in the morning and Your faith in the nights"** (Psalms 92:3). In the morning, one must mention God's loving-kindness, while in the evening one is required to emphasize the aspect of faith.

וְאָמַר רַבָּה בַּר חִינָּנָא [סָבָא] מִשְּׁמֵיהּ דְּרַב: הַמִּתְפַּלֵּל, כְּשֶׁהוּא כּוֹרֵעַ – כּוֹרֵעַ בְּ"בָרוּךְ" וּכְשֶׁהוּא זוֹקֵף – זוֹקֵף בַּשֵּׁם.

**And Rabba bar Ḥinnana Sava said in the name of Rav: One who is praying, when he bows** in the appropriate places, **he bows when** he says: **Blessed, and when he** subsequently **stands upright,**[H] **he stands upright when he says** God's **name.**

אָמַר שְׁמוּאֵל: מַאי טַעְמָא דְּרַב – דִּכְתִיב: "ה' זוֹקֵף כְּפוּפִים".

**Shmuel,** who was Rav's colleague and significantly outlived him, **said: What is Rav's reason** for saying that one should stand upright at the mention of God's name? **As it is written: "The Lord, who raises the bowed"** (Psalms 146:8); one stands upright at the mention of God's name to recall that it is God who raises the bowed.

מֵתִיבֵי: "מִפְּנֵי שְׁמִי נִחַת הוּא"!

The Gemara **raises an objection** based on what we learned in praise of a priest: **"And he was afraid before My name"** (Malachi 2:5), indicating that one must be humbled and not upright before God's name.

מִי כְּתִיב "בִּשְׁמִי"? "מִפְּנֵי שְׁמִי" כְּתִיב.

The Gemara responds: **Is it written: At My name? Before My name, is written,** meaning that one is humbled and bows prior to the mention of God's name, when he says: Blessed.

אֲמַר לֵיהּ שְׁמוּאֵל לְחִיָּיא בַּר רַב: בַּר אוֹרְיָאן, תָּא וְאֵימָא לָךְ מִלְּתָא מְעַלַּיְיתָא דַּאֲמַר אֲבוּךְ! הָכִי אֲמַר אֲבוּךְ: כְּשֶׁהוּא כּוֹרֵעַ – כּוֹרֵעַ בְּבָרוּךְ, כְּשֶׁהוּא זוֹקֵף – זוֹקֵף בַּשֵּׁם.

The Gemara relates: **Shmuel said to Ḥiyya bar Rav: Son of Torah,**[B] **come and I will tell you a great saying that your father said. Your father said the following: When one bows, he bows when** he says: **Blessed, and when he stands upright, he stands upright when he says** God's **name.**

## NOTES

**"True and Firm" in the morning prayer – "אֱמֶת וְיַצִּיב" שַׁחֲרִית:** Times of trouble and exile are likened to night; while the period of redemption is likened to day. Consequently, the emphasis at night is on our faith in the future redemption. During the day, however, the emphasis is on the loving-kindness God has shown us in the past (*Me'iri*). Rashi explains that the emphasis in the morning is on God's love for us as demonstrated in the past, while at night the emphasis is on our faith in the present and future.

## HALAKHA

**One who did not recite: True and Firm, in the morning prayer and: True and Trustworthy, in the evening prayer – כָּל שֶׁלֹּא אָמַר "אֱמֶת וְיַצִּיב" שַׁחֲרִית וֶ"אֱמֶת וֶאֱמוּנָה" עַרְבִית:** One must recite: True and Firm, in the morning formula of the blessing, and: True and Trustworthy, at night. If one failed to do so, he did not fulfill his obligation to recite the blessing as instituted. In any case, he should recite the blessings after he prays and should repeat *Shema* (*Mishna Berura*; Rambam *Sefer Ahava, Hilkhot Keriat Shema* 1:7; *Shulḥan Arukh, Oraḥ Ḥayyim* 66:10).

**When one bows…and when one stands upright, etc. – כְּשֶׁהוּא כּוֹרֵעַ...וּכְשֶׁהוּא זוֹקֵף וכו':** When bowing during the *Amida* prayer, one bends his knees at the word: Blessed, and bows at the word: You, until the vertebrae of his spine pop. At the words: We give thanks, at the start of the blessing of thanksgiving, one bows his head and body together like a reed and remains in this position until the word: Lord, when he stands upright. This is in accordance with the undisputed opinion of Rav (Rambam *Sefer Ahava, Hilkhot Tefilla* 5:10, 12; *Shulḥan Arukh, Oraḥ Ḥayyim* 113:4, 7).

## BACKGROUND

**Son of Torah – בַּר אוֹרְיָאן:** Literally, son of our Torah. The phrase is used occasionally as a title for a Torah scholar.

Some claim, especially here, based on variant readings that support this approach, that it means son of the lion [*arya*]. In truth, those rare Sages who were addressed with this appellation were children of outstanding leaders of their generations, and it was appropriate to refer to them in that way.

רַב שֵׁשֶׁת כִּי כָּרַע – כָּרַע כְּחִיזְרָא, כִּי קָא זָקֵיף – זָקֵיף כְּחִיוְיָא.

With regard to bowing, the Gemara relates: **When Rav Sheshet bowed he bowed** all at once, **like a cane,**[BN] without delay. **When he stood upright he stood upright like a snake,**[BH] lifting himself slowly, demonstrating that the awe of God was upon him in the manner that he bowed and stood upright (*HaBoneh*).

וְאָמַר רַבָּה בַּר חִינָּנָא סָבָא מִשְּׁמֵיהּ דְּרַב: כׇּל הַשָּׁנָה כּוּלָּהּ אָדָם מִתְפַּלֵּל "הָאֵל הַקָּדוֹשׁ", "מֶלֶךְ אוֹהֵב צְדָקָה וּמִשְׁפָּט", חוּץ מֵעֲשָׂרָה יָמִים שֶׁבֵּין רֹאשׁ הַשָּׁנָה וְיוֹם הַכִּפּוּרִים שֶׁמִּתְפַּלֵּל "הַמֶּלֶךְ הַקָּדוֹשׁ" וְ"הַמֶּלֶךְ הַמִּשְׁפָּט".

**And,** with regard to the formulation of the blessings, **Rabba bar Ḥinnana Sava said in the name of Rav: Throughout the year a person prays** and concludes the third blessing of the *Amida* prayer with: **The holy God,** and concludes the blessing regarding the restoration of justice to Israel with: **King who loves righteousness and justice, with the exception of the ten days between Rosh HaShana and Yom Kippur,** the Ten Days of Atonement. These days are comprised of Rosh HaShana, Yom Kippur, and the seven days in between, when one emphasizes God's sovereignty, and so **when he prays** he concludes these blessings with: **The holy King and: The King of justice,** i.e., the King who reveals Himself through justice.

וְרַבִּי אֶלְעָזָר אָמַר: אֲפִילּוּ אָמַר 'הָאֵל הַקָּדוֹשׁ' – יָצָא, שֶׁנֶּאֱמַר: "וַיִּגְבַּהּ ה' צְבָאוֹת בַּמִּשְׁפָּט וְהָאֵל הַקָּדוֹשׁ נִקְדַּשׁ בִּצְדָקָה". אֵימָתַי "וַיִּגְבַּהּ ה' צְבָאוֹת בַּמִּשְׁפָּט" – אֵלּוּ עֲשָׂרָה יָמִים שֶׁמֵּרֹאשׁ הַשָּׁנָה וְעַד יוֹם הַכִּפּוּרִים, וְקָאָמַר 'הָאֵל הַקָּדוֹשׁ'.

In contrast, **Rabbi Elazar said** that one need not be exacting, and **even if he said: The holy God** during those ten days, he fulfilled his obligation, **as it is stated: "And the Lord of Hosts is exalted through justice, and the holy God is sanctified through righteousness"** (Isaiah 5:16). The Gemara explains: **When** is it appropriate to describe God with terms like: **And the Lord of Hosts is exalted through justice?** It is appropriate when God reveals Himself through justice, **during the ten days between Rosh HaShana and Yom Kippur,** yet the verse **says: The holy God.** This appellation sufficiently underscores God's transcendence, and there is no need to change the standard formula.

מַאי הֲוָה עֲלַהּ?

The Gemara asks: **What is** the conclusion that was reached **about this** *halakha*?

אָמַר רַב יוֹסֵף: 'הָאֵל הַקָּדוֹשׁ' וּ'מֶלֶךְ אוֹהֵב צְדָקָה וּמִשְׁפָּט'; רַבָּה אָמַר: 'הַמֶּלֶךְ הַקָּדוֹשׁ' וְ'הַמֶּלֶךְ הַמִּשְׁפָּט'. וְהִלְכְתָא כְּרַבָּה.

Here, too, opinions differ: **Rav Yosef said** in accordance with the opinion of Rabbi Elazar: There is no need to change the standard formula: **The holy God and: King Who loves righteousness and justice. Rabba said** in accordance with the opinion of Rav: **The holy King and: The King of justice.** The Gemara concludes: **The *halakha* is** in accordance **with** the opinion of **Rabba.**[H]

וְאָמַר רַבָּה בַּר חִינָּנָא סָבָא מִשְּׁמֵיהּ דְּרַב: כׇּל שֶׁאֶפְשָׁר לוֹ לְבַקֵּשׁ רַחֲמִים עַל חֲבֵירוֹ וְאֵינוֹ מְבַקֵּשׁ – נִקְרָא חוֹטֵא. שֶׁנֶּאֱמַר: "גַּם אָנֹכִי חָלִילָה לִּי מֵחֲטֹא לַה' מֵחֲדֹל לְהִתְפַּלֵּל בַּעַדְכֶם".

**And Rabba bar Ḥinnana Sava said in the name of Rav: Anyone who can ask for mercy on behalf of another, and does not ask is called a sinner, as it is stated** following Samuel's rebuke of the people: **"As for me, far be it from me that I should transgress against the Lord in ceasing to pray for you,** but I will teach you the good and the right way" (I Samuel 12:23). Had Samuel refrained from prayer, he would have committed a sin.

אָמַר רָבָא: אִם תַּלְמִיד חָכָם הוּא צָרִיךְ שֶׁיַּחֲלֶה עַצְמוֹ עָלָיו.

**Rava said: If** the one in need of mercy **is a Torah scholar,** it is insufficient to merely pray on his behalf. Rather, **one must make himself ill** worrying **about him.**

**BACKGROUND**

**Cane [*ḥizra*] – חִיזְרָא: This particular cane, *ḥizra*, called *ḥizran* in modern Hebrew, apparently refers to *Bambus*, a type of bamboo from the *Poaceae* family.**

The Talmud refers to a particular species, apparently *Bambusa arundinacea* (*B. Spinosa*), a thorny bush that grows to a height of 3–6 m. When the tree is young, its branches are flexible and pliant. Thorns emerge where the leaves and buds grow. Originally from southeastern Asia and India, by talmudic times this plant apparently reached Babylonia.

Bamboo stalks

**Snake – חִיוְיָא:** See the description on page 313 (49a) with regard to the manner in which a snake straightens.

**NOTES**

**He bowed like a cane – כָּרַע כְּחִיזְרָא:** The *ge'onim* explain that this refers to a type of thorn whose upper part is bent. The expression means that when one prostrates himself, he should do so in such a way that not only is his body bent, but his head too, expressing humility and self-abnegation.

**HALAKHA**

**When he bowed, he bowed like a cane; when he stood upright, he stood upright like a snake – כִּי כָּרַע כְּחִיזְרָא כִּי קָא זָקֵיף זָקֵיף כְּחִיוְיָא:** When one bows he should do so quickly and in a single movement, and bow his head as well. In so doing, he bows like both a cane according to Rashi's interpretation, and like a thorn whose top is bent, according to the interpretation of the *ge'onim*. When one stands upright he should do so slowly, first lifting his head. This *halakha* is derived from the undisputed practice of Rav Sheshet (Rambam *Sefer Ahava*, *Hilkhot Tefilla* 5:12; *Shulḥan Arukh*, *Oraḥ Ḥayyim* 113:6).

**The changes in the *Amida* prayer during the Ten Days of Atonement – הַשִּׁינּוּיִים בַּתְּפִלָּה בַּעֲשֶׂרֶת יְמֵי תְשׁוּבָה:** During the Ten Days of Atonement, the formula of some of the blessings of the *Amida* prayer is changed. The conclusion of the third blessing, the sanctification of God's name, is changed from: The holy God, which is customary throughout the year, to: The holy King. The conclusion of the eleventh blessing, the blessing of justice, is changed from: The King Who loves righteousness and justice, to: The King of justice. If one mistakenly said: The holy God or: The King Who loves righteousness and justice, or if one does not recall which he said, if the mistake was in the blessing of sanctification, one must repeat the *Amida* prayer, but if the mistake was in the blessing of justice, he need not repeat it. If one remembered his mistake immediately, within the time required to say: Greetings to you my master, my teacher, in Hebrew, and then recited it correctly, he fulfilled his obligation and may continue his prayer. If one mistakenly said: The holy God, and already began the fourth blessing of knowledge, even if the aforementioned period of time has not yet elapsed, he must return to the beginning of the *Amida* prayer (Rambam *Sefer Ahava*, *Hilkhot Tefilla* 2:18; *Shulḥan Arukh*, *Oraḥ Ḥayyim* 118:1 in the comment of the Rema).

מַאי טַעְמָא? אִילֵימָא מִשּׁוּם דִּכְתִיב "וְאֵין חֹלֶה מִכֶּם עָלַי וְאֵין גּוֹלֶה אֶת אׇזְנִי" – דִּילְמָא מֶלֶךְ שָׁאנֵי? – אֶלָּא, מֵהָכָא: "וַאֲנִי בַּחֲלוֹתָם לְבוּשִׁי וגו'".

The Gemara seeks to clarify the source of this *halakha*. **What is the reason** that one must make oneself ill over a Torah scholar in need of mercy? **If you say** that it is **because** of what Saul said to his men, **as it is written: "And there is none of you that is ill over me or tells unto me"** (I Samuel 22:8), meaning that because Saul was a Torah scholar, it would have been appropriate for people to make themselves ill worrying about him; this is not an absolute proof. **Perhaps a king is different,** and excessive worry is appropriate in that case. Rather, proof that one must make oneself ill over a Torah scholar in need for mercy is **from here:** When David speaks of his enemies, Doeg and Ahitophel, who were Torah scholars, he says: **"But for me, when they were sick, my clothing was sackcloth,** I afflicted my soul with fasting" (Psalms 35:13). One must be concerned to the extent that he dresses in sackcloth and fasts for the recovery of a Torah scholar.

וְאָמַר רַבָּה בַּר חִינָּנָא סָבָא מִשְּׁמֵיהּ דְּרַב: כׇּל הָעוֹשֶׂה דְּבַר עֲבֵירָה וּמִתְבַּיֵּישׁ בּוֹ – מוֹחֲלִין לוֹ עַל כׇּל עֲוֹנוֹתָיו, שֶׁנֶּאֱמַר: "לְמַעַן תִּזְכְּרִי וָבֹשְׁתְּ וְלֹא יִהְיֶה לָּךְ עוֹד פִּתְחוֹן פֶּה מִפְּנֵי כְּלִמָּתֵךְ בְּכַפְּרִי לָךְ לְכׇל אֲשֶׁר עָשִׂית נְאֻם ה' אֱלֹהִים".

**And Rabba bar Ḥinnana Sava said in the name of Rav: One who commits an act of transgression and is ashamed of it, all of his transgressions are forgiven.** Shame is a sign that one truly despises his transgressions and that shame has the power to atone for his actions (Rabbi Yoshiyahu Pinto), **as it is stated: "In order that you remember, and be embarrassed, and never open your mouth anymore, because of your shame, when I have forgiven you for all that you have done, said the Lord, God"** (Ezekiel 16:63).

דִּילְמָא צִבּוּר שָׁאנֵי? – אֶלָּא, מֵהָכָא: "וַיֹּאמֶר שְׁמוּאֵל אֶל שָׁאוּל לָמָּה הִרְגַּזְתַּנִי לְהַעֲלוֹת אֹתִי, וַיֹּאמֶר שָׁאוּל צַר לִי מְאֹד וּפְלִשְׁתִּים נִלְחָמִים בִּי וֵה' סָר מֵעָלַי וְלֹא עָנָנִי עוֹד גַּם בְּיַד הַנְּבִיאִים גַּם בַּחֲלֹמוֹת וָאֶקְרָאֶה לְךָ לְהוֹדִיעֵנִי מָה אֶעֱשֶׂה", וְאִילּוּ "אוּרִים וְתֻמִּים" לָא קָאָמַר

However this proof is rejected: **Perhaps a community is different,** as a community is forgiven more easily than an individual. **Rather,** proof that an individual ashamed of his actions is forgiven for his transgressions is cited **from here,** when King Saul consulted Samuel by means of a necromancer before his final the war with the Philistines: **"And Samuel said to Saul, why have you angered me to bring me up? And Saul said, I am very pained, and the Philistines are waging war against me, and God has removed Himself from me and answers me no more, neither by the hands of the prophets nor by dreams. And I call to you to tell me what to do"** (I Samuel 28:15). Saul says that he consulted prophets and dreams, but **he did not say** that he consulted **the *Urim VeTummim*.**

מִשּׁוּם דְּקַטְלֵיהּ לְנוֹב עִיר הַכֹּהֲנִים.

The reason for this is **because he killed** all the residents of **Nov, the city of priests,** and because of this transgression Saul was ashamed to consult the *Urim VeTummim*, which was accomplished by means of a priest.

וּמִנַּיִן דְּאַחִילוּ לֵיהּ מִן שְׁמַיָּא – שֶׁנֶּאֱמַר "וַיֹּאמֶר שְׁמוּאֵל אֶל שָׁאוּל [וּ]מָחָר אַתָּה וּבָנֶיךָ עִמִּי", וְאָמַר רַבִּי יוֹחָנָן: 'עִמִּי' – בִּמְחִיצָתִי.

The Gemara concludes: **And from where** is it derived **that Saul was pardoned by** God in **the heavens** for his transgressions? **As it is stated: "And Samuel said to Saul: Tomorrow you and your sons will be with me"** (I Samuel 28:19). **And Rabbi Yoḥanan said: With me** does not only mean that they will die, but also means, in a statement that contains an aspect of consolation, that they will be **in my company** among the righteous in heaven, as Saul was pardoned for his transgressions.

וְרַבָּנַן אָמְרִי, מֵהָכָא: "וְהוֹקַעֲנוּם לַה' בְּגִבְעַת שָׁאוּל בְּחִיר ה'", יָצְתָה בַּת קוֹל וְאָמְרָה: "בְּחִיר ה'".

**And the Rabbis say** that proof that Saul was pardoned is derived **from here,** from what the Gibeonites said to David: "Let seven men of his sons be given to us **and we will hang them up unto the Lord in the Giva of Saul, the chosen of the Lord"** (II Samuel 21:6). Certainly the Gibeonites, who were furious at Saul, would not refer to him as the chosen of the Lord. Therefore, this phrase must be understood as having been spoken by **a Heavenly Voice that emerged and said the chosen of the Lord,** because Saul had been pardoned for his transgressions and included among the completely righteous.

The Gemara returns to the primary focus of the chapter, the recitation of *Shema*.

אָמַר רַבִּי אַבָּהוּ בֶּן זוּטַרְתִּי אָמַר רַבִּי יְהוּדָה בַּר זְבִידָא: בִּקְּשׁוּ לִקְבּוֹעַ פָּרָשַׁת בָּלָק בִּקְרִיאַת שְׁמַע, וּמִפְּנֵי מָה לֹא קְבָעוּהָ – מִשּׁוּם טוֹרַח צִבּוּר.

**Rabbi Abbahu ben Zutarti said** that **Rabbi Yehuda bar Zevida said:** The Sages **sought to establish** the blessings of Balaam that appear in **the** Torah **portion of Balak,** as part of **the** twice-daily **recitation of *Shema*.**[N] **And why did they not establish it** there? **Because** extending *Shema* would place an **encumbrance on the congregation,** from which the Sages sought to refrain.

**NOTES**

**They sought to institute the portion of Balak (the blessings of Balaam) in the recitation of *Shema* – בִּקְּשׁוּ לִקְבּוֹעַ פָּרָשַׁת בָּלָק בִּקְרִיאַת שְׁמַע:** The mention of the verse: "He couched, He lay down like a lion," is linked to the recitation of *Shema* not only because it mentions lying down and arising, but also because it alludes to the reward for one who recites the *Shema* lying down and standing up (*Adderet Eliyahu*). Seemingly, this does not refer only to Balaam's prophecy but to the entire Torah portion, as that portion includes several references to Divine Providence and the Torah's heavenly origins. Indeed, because of the broad scope of the subjects included, the Sages were concerned lest the requirement to recite this portion would place an encumbrance upon the community (*Teshuvot Ḥatam Sofer*).

## BACKGROUND

They learned – גְּמִירִי: The term means, they learned, they were knowledgeable. However, it comes to define a fixed, established *halakha* which, even though it does not have a clear source, was nevertheless transmitted by means of a tradition of study throughout the generations.

Ritual fringes – צִיצִית: This refers to the positive biblical commandment to attach fringes to the four corners of a garment (Numbers 15:37–41). They are only attached to a garment with four corners, and the garment must be large enough to wrap around the person wearing it. Each fringe is comprised of four, generally wool, threads; the threads are folded in half, bringing their number to eight. The upper part of the fringe (*gedil*) is knotted in a prescribed manner, and the eight half-threads hang down from it. Their customs vary with regard to how precisely to knot the fringes. Originally ritual fringes included three white threads and one thread dyed blue (*petil tekhelet*). One is only obligated in the mitzva of ritual fringes if he is wearing a four-cornered garment. There is no obligation to wear such a garment. Nevertheless, it is customary to wear a large four-cornered garment [*tallit*] during the morning prayer and a smaller four-cornered garment [*tallit katan*] throughout the day. The mitzva of ritual fringes applies during daytime, but not at night. Consequently, its fulfillment is incumbent upon men, but not upon women.

## NOTES

The recitation of additional portions in the *Shema* – אֲמִירַת פָּרָשִׁיּוֹת נוֹסָפוֹת בִּקְרִיאַת שְׁמַע: Although the inclusion of the two paragraphs, *Shema* and *VeHaya im Shamoa* in the standard formula of *Shema* is obvious, as the recitation of *Shema* in the morning and the evening is mentioned therein, this is not the case with regard to the third paragraph. Apparently, there was a great deal of uncertainty with regard to the portion of ritual fringes, and many practices and customs developed over time with regard to its regular, complete recitation (see ch. 2). On the other hand, since in the Temple, the Ten Commandments were added to the standard formula, other additions were also considered (see *Me'iri*).

Because it includes five elements – מִפְּנֵי שֶׁיֵּשׁ בָּהּ חֲמִשָּׁה דְּבָרִים: Variant Gemara texts refer to six elements. However, others maintain that thoughts of heresy fall under the rubric of "thoughts of idolatry," there are only five (*Tosefot HaRosh*).

מַאי טַעְמָא? אִילֵימָא מִשּׁוּם דִּכְתִיב בָּהּ: "אֵל מוֹצִיאָם מִמִּצְרָיִם" – לֵימָא פָּרָשַׁת רִבִּית וּפָרָשַׁת מִשְׁקָלוֹת דִּכְתִיב בְּהֶן יְצִיאַת מִצְרַיִם!

The Gemara seeks: **Why** did the Sages seek to add the blessings of Balaam in the first place? **If you say** that they did so **because** the exodus from Egypt is mentioned, **as it is written therein: "God, who brought them forth out of Egypt,** is like the horns of the wild ram" (Numbers 23:22), certainly mention of the Exodus is not unique to this Torah portion. Many other portions mention the exodus as well. **Let us say the portion of usury** (Leviticus 25:35–38) or the **portion of weights** (Leviticus 19:35–37), **as the exodus from Egypt is written therein** as well. In addition, they are brief and would not constitute an encumbrance on the congregation.

אֶלָּא אָמַר רַבִּי יוֹסֵי בַּר אָבִין: מִשּׁוּם דִּכְתִיב בָּהּ הַאי קְרָא: "כָּרַע שָׁכַב כַּאֲרִי וּכְלָבִיא מִי יְקִימֶנּוּ".

**Rather, Rabbi Yosei bar Avin said:** The reason the Sages sought to establish the portion of Balak as part of the recitation of *Shema* is **because it is written therein: "He couched, He lay down like a lion and a lioness; who shall rouse Him?** Those who bless You are blessed and those who curse You are cursed" (Numbers 24:9). This is reminiscent of what is said in *Shema*: When you lie down, and when you rise.

וְלֵימָא הַאי פְּסוּקָא וְתוּ לָא!

On this, the Gemara asks: **And** if it is important to include this as part of *Shema* because of this single verse, then **let us say this verse and nothing more.**

גְּמִירִי: כׇּל פָּרָשָׁה דְּפַסְקַהּ מֹשֶׁה רַבֵּינוּ – פָּסְקִינַן, דְּלָא פַּסְקַהּ מֹשֶׁה רַבֵּינוּ – לָא פָּסְקִינַן.

The Gemara rejects this: It is impossible to do this, as **they learned**[B] through tradition that **any portion that Moses, our teacher, divided, we** too **divide** and read separately. However, a portion **that Moses, our teacher, did not divide, we do not divide** and read separately. And, as stated above, the Sages did not wish to institute the recitation of the entire portion of Balak to avoid placing an encumbrance on the congregation.

פָּרָשַׁת צִיצִית מִפְּנֵי מָה קְבָעוּהָ?

The Gemara continues: **Why was the portion of ritual fringes**[B] **established** as part of the recitation of *Shema* when its content is unrelated to that of the preceding portions?[N]

אָמַר רַבִּי יְהוּדָה בַּר חֲבִיבָא: מִפְּנֵי שֶׁיֵּשׁ בָּהּ חֲמִשָּׁה דְּבָרִים: מִצְוַת צִיצִית, יְצִיאַת מִצְרַיִם, עוֹל מִצְוֹת, וְדַעַת מִינִים, הִרְהוּר עֲבֵירָה, וְהִרְהוּר עֲבוֹדָה זָרָה.

**Rabbi Yehuda bar Ḥaviva said:** The portion of ritual fringes was added **because it includes five elements**[N] including the primary reason for its inclusion, the exodus from Egypt (*Melo HaRo'im*): **The mitzva of ritual fringes,** mention of **the exodus from Egypt,** the acceptance of **the yoke of mitzvot,** admonition against **the opinions of the heretics,** admonition against **thoughts of** the **transgressions** of licentiousness, **and** admonition against **thoughts of idolatry.**

בִּשְׁלָמָא הָנֵי תְּלָת – מְפָרְשָׁן; עוֹל מִצְוֹת – דִּכְתִיב: "וּרְאִיתֶם אֹתוֹ וּזְכַרְתֶּם אֶת כׇּל מִצְוֹת ה'", צִיצִית – דִּכְתִיב: "וְעָשׂוּ לָהֶם צִיצִית וגו'", יְצִיאַת מִצְרַיִם – דִּכְתִיב: "אֲשֶׁר הוֹצֵאתִי וגו'", אֶלָּא דַּעַת מִינִים, הִרְהוּר עֲבֵירָה, הִרְהוּר עֲבוֹדָה זָרָה מְנָלַן?

The Gemara clarifies: **Granted, these three are mentioned explicitly: The yoke of mitzvot** is mentioned in the portion of ritual fringes, **as it is written: "And you shall look upon them and remember all the mitzvot of the Lord** and you shall do them" (Numbers 15:39). **Ritual fringes** are mentioned explicitly, **as it is written: "And they will make for themselves ritual fringes"** (Numbers 15:38). **The exodus from Egypt** is also mentioned explicitly, **as it is written:** "I am the Lord, your God, **who took you out** from the Land of Egypt" (Numbers 15:41). **But where do we** derive the other elements mentioned above: Admonition against **the opinions of the heretics,** admonition against **thoughts of transgressions** of licentiousness, **and** admonition against **thoughts of idolatry?**

דְּתַנְיָא: "אַחֲרֵי לְבַבְכֶם" – זוֹ מִינוּת, וְכֵן הוּא אוֹמֵר "אָמַר נָבָל בְּלִבּוֹ אֵין אֱלֹהִים", "אַחֲרֵי עֵינֵיכֶם" – זֶה הִרְהוּר עֲבֵירָה, שֶׁנֶּאֱמַר: "וַיֹּאמֶר שִׁמְשׁוֹן אֶל אָבִיו אוֹתָהּ קַח לִי כִּי הִיא יָשְׁרָה בְעֵינָי", "אַתֶּם זוֹנִים" – זֶה הִרְהוּר עֲבוֹדָה זָרָה, וְכֵן הוּא אוֹמֵר: "וַיִּזְנוּ אַחֲרֵי הַבְּעָלִים".

In response, the Gemara cites a *baraita* where these elements were derived from allusions in the verse, "You shall stray neither after your hearts nor after your eyes, after which you would lust" (Numbers 15:39). **As it was taught: "After your hearts" refers to** following opinions **of heresy** that may arise in one's heart. The Gemara offers a proof, **as it is stated: "The fool said in his heart: 'There is no God';** they have been corrupt, they have acted abominably; there is none who does good" (Psalms 14:1). The phrase: **"After your eyes,"** in **this** verse refers to following **thoughts of transgressions** of licentiousness, that a person might see and desire, **as it is stated: "And Samson said to his father, 'That one take for me, for she is upright in my eyes'"** (Judges 14:3). The passage: **"You shall stray after"** refers to promiscuity, which in the parlance of the prophets is a metaphor for **idol worship, as it is stated:** "The children of Israel again **went astray after the Be'alim"** (Judges 8:33).

מתני׳ מַזְכִּירִין יְצִיאַת מִצְרַיִם בַּלֵּילוֹת. אָמַר רַבִּי אֶלְעָזָר בֶּן עֲזַרְיָה: הֲרֵי אֲנִי כְּבֶן שִׁבְעִים שָׁנָה, וְלֹא זָכִיתִי שֶׁתֵּאָמֵר יְצִיאַת מִצְרַיִם בַּלֵּילוֹת עַד שֶׁדְּרָשָׁהּ בֶּן זוֹמָא.

**MISHNA** It is a mitzva by Torah law to mention the exodus from Egypt at night, but some held that this mitzva was, like phylacteries or ritual fringes, fulfilled only during the day and not at night. For this reason it was decided: **The exodus from Egypt is mentioned at night,**[H] adjacent to the recitation of *Shema*. **Rabbi Elazar ben Azarya said: I am approximately seventy years old, and** although I have long held this opinion, **I was never privileged** to prevail (*Me'iri*) and prove that there is a biblical obligation to fulfill the accepted custom (Ra'avad) and have **the exodus from Egypt mentioned at night, until Ben Zoma**[P] **interpreted it homiletically** and proved it obligatory.

שֶׁנֶּאֱמַר: ״לְמַעַן תִּזְכֹּר אֶת יוֹם צֵאתְךָ מֵאֶרֶץ מִצְרַיִם כֹּל יְמֵי חַיֶּיךָ״. ״יְמֵי חַיֶּיךָ״ – הַיָּמִים, ״כֹּל יְמֵי חַיֶּיךָ״ – הַלֵּילוֹת;

Ben Zoma derived it **as it is stated: "That you may remember the day you went out of the land of Egypt all the days of your life"** (Deuteronomy 16:3). **The days of your life,** refers to daytime alone; however, the addition of the word all, as it is stated: **All the days of your life,** comes to add nights as well.

וַחֲכָמִים אוֹמְרִים: ״יְמֵי חַיֶּיךָ״ – הָעוֹלָם הַזֶּה, ״כֹּל״ – לְהָבִיא לִימוֹת הַמָּשִׁיחַ.

**And the Rabbis,** who posit that there is no biblical obligation to mention the exodus from Egypt at night, explain the word, all, differently and **say: The days of your life,** refers to the days in **this world, all** is added **to include the days of the Messiah.**

גמ׳ תַּנְיָא, אָמַר לָהֶם בֶּן זוֹמָא לַחֲכָמִים: וְכִי מַזְכִּירִין יְצִיאַת מִצְרַיִם לִימוֹת הַמָּשִׁיחַ? וַהֲלֹא כְּבָר נֶאֱמַר: ״הִנֵּה יָמִים בָּאִים נְאֻם ה׳ וְלֹא יֹאמְרוּ עוֹד חַי ה׳ אֲשֶׁר הֶעֱלָה אֶת בְּנֵי יִשְׂרָאֵל מֵאֶרֶץ מִצְרָיִם, כִּי אִם חַי ה׳ אֲשֶׁר הֶעֱלָה וַאֲשֶׁר הֵבִיא אֶת זֶרַע בֵּית יִשְׂרָאֵל מֵאֶרֶץ צָפוֹנָה וּמִכֹּל הָאֲרָצוֹת אֲשֶׁר הִדַּחְתִּים שָׁם״!

**GEMARA** The fundamental dispute between Ben Zoma and the Sages appears in the mishna, and the *baraita* cites its continuation. Disputing the position of the Sages that: All the days of your life, refers to both this world and the days of the Messiah, **it was taught** in a *baraita* that **Ben Zoma said to the Sages: And is the exodus from Egypt mentioned in the days of the Messiah? Was it not already said** that Jeremiah prophesied that in the days of the Messiah: **"Behold, days are coming, says the Lord, that they will no longer say: The Lord lives Who brought up the children of Israel out of the Land of Egypt. Rather: As the Lord lives, that brought up and led the seed of the house of Israel up out of the north country and from all the countries where I had driven them"** (Jeremiah 23:7–8).

אָמְרוּ לוֹ: לֹא שֶׁתֵּעָקֵר יְצִיאַת מִצְרַיִם מִמְּקוֹמָהּ, אֶלָּא שֶׁתְּהֵא שִׁעְבּוּד מַלְכֻיּוֹת עִיקָּר, וִיצִיאַת מִצְרַיִם טָפֵל לוֹ.

The Sages rejected this claim **and they said to him** that these verses do **not** mean **that** in the future **the exodus from Egypt will be uprooted from its place** and will be mentioned no more. **Rather,** redemption from **the subjugation of the kingdoms will be primary and the exodus from Egypt will be secondary.**

כַּיּוֹצֵא בּוֹ אַתָּה אוֹמֵר: ״לֹא יִקָּרֵא שִׁמְךָ עוֹד יַעֲקֹב כִּי אִם יִשְׂרָאֵל יִהְיֶה שְׁמֶךָ״.

**On a similar** note, **you say:** The meaning of the expressions: It will not say, and they will no longer mention, are not absolute, as in the verse: **"Your name shall no longer be called Jacob; rather, Israel will be your name"** (Genesis 35:10). There, too, the meaning is

### HALAKHA

**Mentioning the exodus from Egypt at night – הַזְכָּרַת יְצִיאַת מִצְרַיִם בַּלֵּילוֹת:** Although the mitzva of ritual fringes is not in effect at night, this passage is nevertheless recited at night because it mentions the exodus from Egypt, and there is a mitzva to recall the exodus from Egypt both during the day and at night. Therefore, one recites all three paragraphs of *Shema* on both occasions (Rambam *Sefer Ahava, Hilkhot Keriat Shema* 1:3).

### PERSONALITIES

**Ben Zoma – בֶּן זוֹמָא:** This is the *tanna*, Shimon ben Zoma.

Shimon ben Zoma was a contemporary of Rabbi Akiva, but he apparently died young and was never ordained. Therefore, he is generally referred to as Ben Zoma, rather than as Rabbi Shimon ben Zoma.

Ben Zoma was considered one of the greatest scholars of his generation, and the Gemara relates that he was fluent in seventy languages. He was especially gifted at homiletics, such that when he died the Sages said: When Ben Zoma died, the homiletic interpreters of the Bible were no more. Along with Rabbi Akiva, he is one of the four who entered the mystical orchard to engage in the esoterica of the Torah. According to the Gemara, of the four, only Rabbi Akiva emerged intact. Ben Zoma peeked and was harmed, indicating that he went insane. Apparently, he died soon thereafter. We know nothing of his family, his origins, or any other details of his life.

Perek **I**
Daf **13** Amud **a**

לֹא שֶׁיֵּעָקֵר יַעֲקֹב מִמְּקוֹמוֹ, אֶלָּא יִשְׂרָאֵל עִיקָּר וְיַעֲקֹב טָפֵל לוֹ; וְכֵן הוּא אוֹמֵר: ״אַל תִּזְכְּרוּ רִאשֹׁנוֹת וְקַדְמֹנִיּוֹת אַל תִּתְבֹּנָנוּ״, ״אַל תִּזְכְּרוּ רִאשֹׁנוֹת״ – זֶה שִׁעְבּוּד מַלְכֻיּוֹת, ״וְקַדְמֹנִיּוֹת אַל תִּתְבֹּנָנוּ״ – זוֹ יְצִיאַת מִצְרַיִם,

**not that** the name **Jacob will be** entirely **uprooted from its place, but that** the name **Israel** will be the **primary** name **to which** the name **Jacob** will be **secondary,** as the Torah continues to refer to him as Jacob after this event. **And it also says** that the ultimate redemption will overshadow the previous redemption in the verse: **"Do not remember the former events, and do not ponder things of old"** (Isaiah 43:18), and the Gemara explains: **"Do not remember the former events," that is the subjugation to the kingdoms, and "do not ponder things of old," that is the exodus from Egypt,** which occurred before the subjugation to the nations.

## NOTES

**Anyone who calls Abraham Abram transgresses a positive mitzva…a negative mitzva – כָּל הַקּוֹרֵא לְאַבְרָהָם ״אַבְרָם״ עוֹבֵר בַּעֲשֵׂה...עוֹבֵר בְּלָאו:** The Gemara did not reject either of these statements, that one who calls Abraham Abram transgresses a positive or a negative mitzva; however, neither is cited in most halakhic literature. Apparently, most authorities did not consider this a bona fide biblical prohibition that warranted inclusion in compendia of halakhic prohibitions (Maharsha). Others, however, deemed this a binding mitzva and cited it as *halakha* (*Magen Avraham*).

״הִנְנִי עֹשֶׂה חֲדָשָׁה עַתָּה תִצְמָח״ – תָּנֵי רַב יוֹסֵף: זוֹ מִלְחֶמֶת גּוֹג וּמָגוֹג.

With regard to the following verse: **"Behold, I will do new things, now it will spring forth"** (Isaiah 43:19), **Rav Yosef taught** a *baraita*: **This refers to the** future **war of Gog and Magog,** which will cause all earlier events to be forgotten.

מָשָׁל, לְמָה הַדָּבָר דּוֹמֶה – לְאָדָם שֶׁהָיָה מְהַלֵּךְ בַּדֶּרֶךְ וּפָגַע בּוֹ זְאֵב וְנִיצַּל מִמֶּנּוּ, וְהָיָה מְסַפֵּר וְהוֹלֵךְ מַעֲשֵׂה זְאֵב; פָּגַע בּוֹ אֲרִי וְנִיצַּל מִמֶּנּוּ, וְהָיָה מְסַפֵּר וְהוֹלֵךְ מַעֲשֵׂה אֲרִי; פָּגַע בּוֹ נָחָשׁ וְנִיצַּל מִמֶּנּוּ, שָׁכַח מַעֲשֵׂה שְׁנֵיהֶם וְהָיָה מְסַפֵּר וְהוֹלֵךְ מַעֲשֵׂה נָחָשׁ; אַף כָּךְ יִשְׂרָאֵל – צָרוֹת אַחֲרוֹנוֹת מְשַׁכְּחוֹת אֶת הָרִאשׁוֹנוֹת.

The Gemara cites **a parable: To what is this comparable? To a person who was walking along the way and a wolf accosted him and he survived it, and he continued to relate the story of the wolf. A lion accosted him and he survived it, and he continued to relate the story of the lion. A snake accosted him and he survived it, he forgot both** the lion and the wolf, **and he continued to relate the story of the snake.** Each encounter was more dangerous and each escape more miraculous than the last, so he would continue to relate the most recent story. **So too** with **Israel; more recent troubles cause the earlier** troubles **to be forgotten.**

״אַבְרָם הוּא אַבְרָהָם״,

Having mentioned the changing of Jacob's name, the Gemara addresses the changing of the names of Abraham and Sarah. What is the meaning of changing Abram's name to Abraham? As it is stated: **"Abram is Abraham"** (I Chronicles 1:27).

בַּתְּחִלָּה נַעֲשָׂה אָב לַאֲרָם, וּלְבַסּוֹף נַעֲשָׂה אָב לְכָל הָעוֹלָם כּוּלּוֹ.

The Gemara explains: **Initially he became a father,** a minister, and prominent person, only **to Aram,** so he was called Abram, father [*av*] of Aram, **and ultimately** with God's blessing **he became the father of the entire world,** so he was called Abraham, father of the masses [*av hamon*], as it is stated: "I have made you the father of a multitude of nations" (Genesis 17:5).

״שָׂרַי הִיא שָׂרָה״,

Similarly, what is the meaning of changing Sarai's name to Sarah? The same concept applies to Sarai as to Abram: **Sarai is Sarah."**

בַּתְּחִלָּה נַעֲשֵׂית שָׂרַי לְאוּמָּתָהּ, וּלְבַסּוֹף נַעֲשֵׂית שָׂרָה לְכָל הָעוֹלָם כּוּלּוֹ.

The Gemara explains: **Initially she was a princess** only **to her nation:** My princess [*Sarai*], **but ultimately she became Sarah,** a general term indicating that she was princess **for the entire world.**

תָּנֵי בַּר קַפָּרָא: כָּל הַקּוֹרֵא לְאַבְרָהָם ״אַבְרָם״ – עוֹבֵר בַּעֲשֵׂה, שֶׁנֶּאֱמַר: ״וְהָיָה שִׁמְךָ אַבְרָהָם״. רַבִּי אֱלִיעֶזֶר אוֹמֵר: עוֹבֵר בְּלָאו, שֶׁנֶּאֱמַר: ״וְלֹא יִקָּרֵא עוֹד [אֶת] שִׁמְךָ אַבְרָם״.

Also, with regard to Abraham's name, **bar Kappara taught: Anyone who calls Abraham Abram transgresses a positive mitzva, as it is stated: "And your name will be Abraham"** (Genesis 17:5). This is a positive mitzva to refer to him as Abraham. **Rabbi Eliezer says:** One who calls Abraham Abram **transgresses a negative mitzva,**[N] **as it is stated: "And your name shall no longer be called Abram,** and your name will be Abraham, for I have made you the father of a multitude of nations" (Genesis 17:5).

אֶלָּא מֵעַתָּה הַקּוֹרֵא לְשָׂרָה ״שָׂרַי״ הָכִי נַמֵי?

The Gemara asks: **But** if we consider these obligatory statements, then **from here** we must infer that **one who calls Sarah Sarai also** transgresses a positive or negative mitzva.

הָתָם, קוּדְשָׁא בְּרִיךְ הוּא אֲמַר לְאַבְרָהָם: ״שָׂרַי אִשְׁתְּךָ לֹא תִקְרָא אֶת שְׁמָהּ שָׂרָי כִּי שָׂרָה שְׁמָהּ״.

The Gemara answers: **There** in the case of Sarah, it is not a general mitzva rather **the Holy One, Blessed be He, said to Abraham** alone: "And God said to Abraham, **your wife Sarai, you shall not call her name Sarai; rather, Sarah is her name"** (Genesis 17:15). In contrast, this is stated regarding Abraham in general terms: "Your name shall no longer be called Abram."

אֶלָּא מֵעַתָּה, הַקּוֹרֵא לְיַעֲקֹב ״יַעֲקֹב״ הָכִי נַמֵי?

Again, the Gemara asks: **But if that is so, one who calls Jacob Jacob,** about whom it is written: "Your name shall no longer be Jacob, but Israel" (Genesis 32:29), **also** transgresses a mitzva.

שָׁאנֵי הָתָם, דַּהֲדַר אַהַדְרֵיהּ קְרָא, דִּכְתִיב ״וַיֹּאמֶר אֱלֹהִים לְיִשְׂרָאֵל בְּמַרְאוֹת הַלַּיְלָה וַיֹּאמֶר יַעֲקֹב יַעֲקֹב״.

The Gemara answers: **It is different there, as the verse reverts back** and God Himself refers to Jacob as Jacob, **as it is written** before his descent to Egypt **"And God said to Israel in the visions of the night, and said, Jacob, Jacob,** and he said, 'Here I am'" (Genesis 46:2).

מֵתִיב רַבִּי יוֹסֵי בַּר אָבִין וְאִיתֵּימָא רַבִּי יוֹסֵי בַּר זְבִידָא: ״אַתָּה הוּא ה׳ הָאֱלֹהִים אֲשֶׁר בָּחַרְתָּ בְּאַבְרָם״!

**Rabbi Yosei bar Avin, and some say Rabbi Yosei bar Zevida, raised an objection** to the statements of bar Kappara and Rabbi Eliezer based on what is said in the recounting of the history of the Jewish people: **"You are the Lord, God Who chose Abram** and took him out of Ur Kasdim and made his name Abraham" (Nehemiah 9:7). Here the Bible refers to him as Abram.

אֲמַר לֵיהּ: הָתָם נָבִיא הוּא דְּקָא מְסַדֵּר לְשִׁבְחֵיהּ דְּרַחֲמָנָא מַאי דַּהֲוָה מֵעִיקָּרָא.

The Gemara responds: **There, the prophet is recounting God's praises,** including **that which was** the situation **originally,** before his name was changed to Abraham. Indeed, the verse continues: "You took him out of Ur Kasdim and made his name Abraham, and found his heart faithful before You and made a covenant with him to give him the land of Canaan…to give to his descendants and You fulfilled Your words for You are righteous" (Nehemiah 9:7–8).

הדרן עלך מאימתי

# Summary of **Perek I**

Although not all of the problems related to *Shema* were resolved in the course of this chapter, the parameters of "when you lie down, and when you arise" were elucidated and the framework of the obligation of *Shema* was established.

In Beit Shammai's opinion, the phrase "when you lie down, and when you arise" includes instructions with regard to the specific manner in which *Shema* is to be recited. There were Sages, even those affiliated with Beit Hillel, e.g., Rabbi Tarfon and Rabbi Elazar ben Azarya, who ruled in accordance with this opinion. However, this opinion was not accepted as *halakha*. The accepted ruling was in accordance with the opinion of Beit Hillel, who hold that "when you lie down, and when you arise" merely establishes the time frame for reciting *Shema*.

There were many disputes with regard to the time defined by "when you lie down," in terms of both the beginning and the end of that period. The Gemara concluded that the beginning of this period is the time established as the beginning of the night in all *halakhot*, i.e., the emergence of the stars. The conclusion of this period in exigent circumstances is at the conclusion of the night, i.e., dawn. Due to the identity of the time of lying down with night, some of the blessings that accompany *Shema* were formulated to reflect the time that it may be recited: One of the two blessings recited prior to *Shema* is a blessing on the radiant lights: Who brings on evenings, and one of the two recited after *Shema* notes the preparation for sleep: Help us lie down.

The consensus with regard to *Shema* in the morning is that "when you arise" refers to the time when people arise from their beds, not the entire day. This period begins early in the morning, before sunrise, and ends early in the day, after one quarter of the day has passed, calculated either from dawn or from sunrise. Although the blessings accompanying *Shema* in the morning are fundamentally parallel to the blessings at night, with the exception of the blessing: Help us lie down, they are different in terms of their essence and emphasis.

Although the *halakhot* of prayer are not the topic of this chapter, the connection between *Shema* and the *Amida* prayer in the morning and evening is discussed. *Shema* is not always recited together with the *Amida* prayer, as in the case when it is recited in bed; nevertheless, the *halakha* is that *Shema* and the *Amida* prayer should be juxtaposed to every possible extent, as each complements the other.

*Shema* itself is analyzed in terms of the meaning of its component sections. The first two sections, *Shema* and *VeHaya im Shamoa*, include the mitzva of reciting *Shema* as well as the fundamental acceptance of the yoke of Heaven and the mitzvot. The third section, which deals with the mitzva of ritual fringes, mentions fulfillment of the mitzvot as well as the exodus from Egypt.

Although some opinions suggest reciting additional sections from the Torah, among them some that were recited during the Temple period, e.g., the Ten Commandments, these three sections alone were established as obligatory.

# Introduction to **Perek II**

*And these words, which I command you this day, shall be upon your heart; and you shall teach them diligently unto your children, and shall talk of them when you sit in your house, and when you walk along the way, and when you lie down, and when you arise.*

(Deuteronomy 6:6–7)

This chapter is a continuation of the previous one. In the previous chapter, the fundamental parameters of *Shema* were discussed and its framework was established; its component sections, the accompanying blessings and the time frame in which it is recited were discussed. In this chapter, a number of issues are raised with regard to the manner in which the mitzva of *Shema* is fulfilled, including how one should conduct himself when faced with situations and circumstances that do not enable him to fulfill the mitzva of *Shema* in an ideal manner. Although the various issues have no direct connection to one another, they all revolve around one central theme: What is the scope of the mitzva to recite *Shema*? In order to answer this question, one must answer an even more fundamental question: What is the basic requirement to recite *Shema*? Is there really a distinction between primary and secondary elements within *Shema*? If so, what are the practical ramifications of this distinction?

Although it is written: "You shall talk of them when you sit in your house, and when you walk along the way, and when you lie down, and when you arise," a question which is both theoretical and practical remains: What happens if the course of one's life does not allow one to recite *Shema* properly, in its entirety? What takes precedence? Hindrances of this kind are quite common and can be divided into three categories: those that originate with the person himself, due to physical or spiritual difficulties; those that are caused by other people or the circumstances in which one finds oneself; and those that occur in the course of daily life.

In order to answer these questions, it is necessary to clarify the fundamental question: Is *Shema*, as defined by *halakha*, a mitzva by Torah law? Or is it a mitzva by rabbinic law, in which case the verses cited by the Sages are merely biblical allusions to support their ordinance? Major differences in halakhic rulings are dependent upon the following basic question: To what extent can other factors, with varying degrees of significance, supersede *Shema*?

In addition, it is necessary to clarify the practical ramifications of the phrase: "Upon your heart." Does it add an obligation to pay special attention to the recited texts? Or perhaps, on the contrary, it creates a leniency by transforming the manner in which the mitzva is fulfilled from the realm of active speech to mere reflection? The phrase: "When you sit in your house, and when you walk by the way" also requires clarification. Does it mean that *Shema* should be treated as one of the various actions that one performs, in the sense that he must cease all of his usual activities, such as sitting, walking, and standing, in order to recite *Shema*? Or does it mean that the obligation to recite *Shema* is fulfilled in the context of a person's daily life, and it can be recited while one is engaged in mundane activities without interrupting or adjusting them?

The practical questions that arise in this chapter deal with a number of unusual cases: The sick, the weak, the deaf, the laborer at work, and the person walking in the street. However, the answers to these questions are drawn from a penetrating analysis of the chapter's central, fundamental question with regard to the essence of *Shema*, from which other more specific and, therefore, practical problems ensue.

מתני׳ הָיָה קוֹרֵא בַּתּוֹרָה וְהִגִּיעַ זְמַן הַמִּקְרָא, אִם כִּוֵּון לִבּוֹ – יָצָא.

**MISHNA** The first question discussed in the mishna is the question of intent. **One who was reading** the sections of **the Torah** which comprise *Shema*, **and the time for the recitation** of the morning or evening *Shema* **arrived,**[H] **if he focused his heart, he fulfilled** his obligation and need not repeat *Shema* in order to fulfill his obligation. This is true even if he failed to recite the requisite blessings (Rabbeinu Ḥananel).

בַּפְּרָקִים שׁוֹאֵל מִפְּנֵי הַכָּבוֹד וּמֵשִׁיב, וּבָאֶמְצַע – שׁוֹאֵל מִפְּנֵי הַיִּרְאָה וּמֵשִׁיב, דִּבְרֵי רַבִּי מֵאִיר.

*Ab initio*, one may not interrupt the recitation of *Shema*. The *tanna'im*, however, disagree over how strict one must be in this regard. They distinguish between interruptions between paragraphs and interruptions within each paragraph. **At the** breaks between **paragraphs, one may greet** an individual **due to the respect** that he is obligated to show him, **and one may respond** to another's greeting due to respect. **And in the middle** of each paragraph **one may greet** an individual **due to the fear**[N] that the individual may harm him if he fails do so (*Me'iri*) **and one may respond** to another's greeting due to fear. This is the **statement of Rabbi Meir.**

רַבִּי יְהוּדָה אוֹמֵר: בָּאֶמְצַע שׁוֹאֵל מִפְּנֵי הַיִּרְאָה וּמֵשִׁיב מִפְּנֵי הַכָּבוֹד, וּבַפְּרָקִים שׁוֹאֵל מִפְּנֵי הַכָּבוֹד וּמֵשִׁיב שָׁלוֹם לְכָל אָדָם.

**Rabbi Yehuda says:** There is a distinction between greeting someone and responding to his greeting. **In the middle** of each paragraph, one may **greet** another **due to fear and respond due to respect. In the** breaks between **paragraphs, one may greet** another **due to respect and respond with a greeting to any person**[H] who greets him, whether or not he is obligated to show him respect.

אֵלּוּ הֵן בֵּין הַפְּרָקִים: בֵּין בְּרָכָה רִאשׁוֹנָה לִשְׁנִיָּה, בֵּין שְׁנִיָּה לִשְׁמַע, בֵּין שְׁמַע לִוְהָיָה אִם שָׁמוֹעַ, בֵּין וְהָיָה אִם שָׁמוֹעַ לְוַיֹּאמֶר, בֵּין וַיֹּאמֶר לֶאֱמֶת וְיַצִּיב.

As for what constitutes a paragraph, **these are** the breaks **between the paragraphs:**[H] **Between the first blessing and the second, between the second and *Shema*, between *Shema* and** the second paragraph: **If you indeed heed** My commandments [***VeHaya im Shamoa***], **between *VeHaya im Shamoa* and** the third paragraph: **And the Lord spoke** [***VaYomer***] **and between *VaYomer* and True and Firm** [***emet veyatziv***], the blessing that follows *Shema*.

רַבִּי יְהוּדָה אוֹמֵר: בֵּין וַיֹּאמֶר לֶאֱמֶת וְיַצִּיב לֹא יַפְסִיק.

The Rabbis held that each blessing and each paragraph of *Shema* constitutes its own entity, and treat interruptions between them as between the paragraphs. **Rabbi Yehuda,** however, **says: Between *VaYomer* and *emet veyatziv***, which begins the blessing that follows *Shema*, **one may not interrupt** at all. According to Rabbi Yehuda, these must be recited consecutively.

אָמַר רַבִּי יְהוֹשֻׁעַ בֶּן קָרְחָה: לָמָּה קָדְמָה פָּרָשַׁת שְׁמַע לִוְהָיָה אִם שָׁמוֹעַ – כְּדֵי שֶׁיְּקַבֵּל עָלָיו עוֹל מַלְכוּת שָׁמַיִם תְּחִלָּה, וְאַחַר כָּךְ מְקַבֵּל עָלָיו עוֹל מִצְוֹת; וְהָיָה אִם שָׁמוֹעַ לְוַיֹּאמֶר – שֶׁוְּהָיָה אִם שָׁמוֹעַ נוֹהֵג בֵּין בַּיּוֹם וּבֵין בַּלַּיְלָה, וַיֹּאמֶר אֵינוֹ נוֹהֵג אֶלָּא בַּיּוֹם בִּלְבַד.

Since the paragraphs of *Shema* are not adjacent to one another in the Torah, and they are not recited in the order in which they appear, the mishna explains their placement. **Rabbi Yehoshua ben Korḥa said: Why,** in the mitzva of the recitation of *Shema*, **did the portion of *Shema* precede** that of ***VeHaya im Shamoa***? This is **so that one will first accept upon himself the yoke of the kingdom of Heaven,** the awareness of God and God's unity, **and only then accept upon himself the yoke of the mitzvot,** which appears in the paragraph of *VeHaya im Shamoa*. Why did ***VeHaya im Shamoa*** precede ***VaYomer***? Because the paragraph of ***VeHaya im Shamoa* is practiced both by day and by night,** while ***VaYomer***, which discusses the mitzva of ritual fringes, **is only practiced during the day.**

גמ׳ שְׁמַע מִינָּהּ: מִצְוֹת צְרִיכוֹת כַּוָּנָה!

**GEMARA** We learned in the mishna that one must focus his heart while reading the portion of *Shema* in the Torah in order to fulfill his obligation. From here, the Gemara seeks to conclude: **Learn from this** that **mitzvot require intent,**[HN] when one performs a mitzva, he must intend to fulfill his obligation. If he lacks that intention, he does not fulfill his obligation. With that statement, this Gemara hopes to resolve an issue that is raised several times throughout the Talmud.

### HALAKHA

**One who was reading the Torah and the time for the recitation of *Shema* arrived – הָיָה קוֹרֵא בַּתּוֹרָה וְהִגִּיעַ זְמַן וכו׳:** One who is reading the portion of the *Shema* in the Torah or if he was reviewing that portion in order to emend errors in the Torah scroll, if he focuses his heart while reciting the first verse, he fulfills his obligation (Rambam *Sefer Ahava, Hilkhot Keriat Shema* 2:1; *Shulḥan Arukh, Oraḥ Ḥayyim* 60:5).

**When may one interrupt the recitation of the Shema – מָתַי מַפְסִיק בִּקְרִיאַת שְׁמַע:** Between paragraphs, one may initiate greeting to a respected individual and one may reply to the greeting of any person, if that person is insistent that he respond (*Magen Avraham*). In the middle of a paragraph, one may interrupt only due to fear, such as the fear that one is required to show one's father, one's teacher, or an outstanding Torah scholar, or due to fear lest he will be harmed should he fail to greet that individual, as per the opinion of Rabbi Yehuda in his dispute with Rabbi Meir (Rambam *Sefer Ahava, Hilkhot Keriat Shema* 2:15–16; *Shulḥan Arukh, Oraḥ Ḥayyim* 66:1).

**Between the paragraphs – בֵּין הַפְּרָקִים:** Between the paragraphs refers to between the blessings or the portions of *Shema*. The *halakha* is in accordance with the opinion of Rabbi Yehuda, that one may not interrupt between *Shema* and *emet veyatziv*, the blessing that follows *Shema* (Rambam *Sefer Ahava, Hilkhot Keriat Shema* 2:17; *Shulḥan Arukh, Oraḥ Ḥayyim* 66:5).

**Mitzvot require intent – מִצְוֹת צְרִיכוֹת כַּוָּנָה:** The *halakha* is that mitzvot require intent, i.e., when performing a mitzva mandated by Torah law, one must have the intent to fulfill his obligation. Despite the fact that the Gemara did not arrive at a decisive conclusion, that appears to be the simple meaning of the mishna (Vilna Gaon). Mitzvot mandated by rabbinic law do not require intent (*Magen Avraham*; Rambam *Sefer Ahava, Hilkhot Keriat Shema* 2:1, *Sefer Zemanim, Hilkhot Shofar, Sukka VeLulav* 2:4; *Shulḥan Arukh, Oraḥ Ḥayyim* 60:4).

### NOTES

**Due to fear – מִפְּנֵי הַיִּרְאָה:** Rashi explains here that due to fear means fear for his life. This explanation is difficult because, if that is the case, there was no need for the mishna to say that he may interrupt *Shema*, as clearly, one need not sacrifice his life to recite *Shema*. Others explained in a totally different vein that due to fear refers to those whom the Torah requires him to respect to the point of fear, like his parents, about whom it is written: "You shall fear every man his mother, and his father" (Leviticus 19:3) or teacher. Others who command respect fall into the category of due to respect (*ge'onim*, Rashba).

**Mitzvot require intent – מִצְוֹת צְרִיכוֹת כַּוָּנָה:** This dispute, whether or not mitzvot require intent, appears several times throughout the Talmud. Some emphasize that the discussion is really whether or not one must have the intent to fulfill his obligation and not whether or not he is required to have intent for the essence of the mitzva (Maharam Ḥalu'a). Others say that he fulfills his obligation even if he acted unawares and had no intent to perform the action, as long as he did not have express intent not to fulfill his obligation (see *Me'iri*). Rav Hai Gaon wrote that, although the apparent conclusion in many of the discussions is that mitzvot do not require intent, it is proper to have intent. Certainly the ideal manner to perform a mitzva is with intent, the more the better. Many prayers have been composed to facilitate that objective.

מַאי אִם כִּוֵּון לִבּוֹ – לִקְרוֹת. לִקְרוֹת? וְהָא קָא קָרֵי!

The Gemara rejects this conclusion: **What is** the meaning of: **If one focused his heart?** It means that one had the intention **to read.** The Gemara attacks this explanation: How can you say that it means that one must have intention **to read? Isn't he already reading?** The case in the mishna refers to a person who is reading from the Torah. Therefore, focused his heart must refer to intention to perform a mitzva.

בְּקוֹרֵא לְהַגִּיהַּ.

The Gemara rejects this: Perhaps the mishna speaks of one who **is reading** the Torah not for the purpose of reciting the words, but **in order to emend**[N] mistakes in the text. Therefore, if he focused his heart and intended to read the words and not merely emend the text, he fulfills his obligation. He need not have the intention to fulfill his obligation.

תָּנוּ רַבָּנַן: קְרִיאַת שְׁמַע כִּכְתָבָהּ, דִּבְרֵי רַבִּי; וַחֲכָמִים אוֹמְרִים: בְּכָל לָשׁוֹן.

**The Sages taught** in a *baraita* that Rabbi Yehuda HaNasi and the Rabbis disagreed with regard to the language in which *Shema* must be recited. This dispute serves as an introduction to a broader analysis of the question of intent: ***Shema*** must be recited **as it is written,** in Hebrew, this is the **statement of Rabbi** Yehuda HaNasi. **And the Rabbis say:** *Shema* may be recited **in any language.**[NH]

מַאי טַעְמָא דְּרַבִּי? אָמַר קְרָא וְהָיוּ – בַּהֲוָיָיתָן יְהוּ.

The Gemara seeks to clarify: **What is the reason for Rabbi** Yehuda HaNasi's opinion? The Gemara answers: The source for his *halakha* lies in the emphasis on the word: **"And** these words, which I command you this day, **will be** upon your heart" (Deuteronomy 6:6). "Will be" means **as they are, so shall they be;** they should remain unchanged, in their original language.

וְרַבָּנַן מַאי טַעֲמַיְיהוּ? אָמַר קְרָא: שְׁמַע – בְּכָל לָשׁוֹן שֶׁאַתָּה שׁוֹמֵעַ.

The Gemara seeks to clarify further: **And what is the reason for the Rabbis'** opinion? The Gemara answers: The source upon which the Rabbis base their opinion is, **as it is stated: "Hear,** Israel" (Deuteronomy 6:4), which they understand to mean that *Shema* must be understood. Therefore, one may recite *Shema* **in any language that you** can **hear** and understand.

וּלְרַבִּי נַמִי, הָא כְּתִיב שְׁמַע! הַהוּא מִבְּעֵי לֵיהּ: הַשְׁמַע לְאָזְנֶיךָ מַה שֶּׁאַתָּה מוֹצִיא מִפִּיךָ.

The Gemara explains how Rabbi Yehuda HaNasi and the Rabbis each contend with the source cited by the other. **And according to Rabbi** Yehuda HaNasi, **isn't it also stated: "Hear,** Israel"? How does he explain this verse? The Gemara responds: **He requires this verse** in order to derive a different *halakha*: **Make your ears hear what your mouth utters,** i.e., one must recite *Shema* audibly so he hears it while reciting it.

וְרַבָּנַן? סָבְרִי לְהוּ כְּמַאן דְּאָמַר: לֹא הִשְׁמִיעַ לְאָזְנוֹ – יָצָא.

**And from** where do **the Rabbis** derive that one must recite *Shema* audibly? The Rabbis do not accept the literal interpretation of the word *Shema*; rather, **they hold in accordance with the one who said: One who recited** *Shema* in a manner **inaudible to his** own **ears, fulfilled** his obligation.

וּלְרַבָּנַן נַמִי הָא כְּתִיב וְהָיוּ! הַהוּא מִבְּעֵי לְהוּ שֶׁלֹּא יִקְרָא לְמַפְרֵעַ.

The Gemara asks: **And according to the Rabbis, isn't it also written: "And they will be"?** How do the Sages explain that emphasis in the verse? The Gemara answers: **They, too, require this** expression to derive **that one may not recite** *Shema* **out of order.** One may not begin reciting *Shema* from the end, but only in the order in which it is written.

וְרַבִּי, שֶׁלֹּא יִקְרָא לְמַפְרֵעַ מְנָא לֵיהּ? נָפְקָא לֵיהּ מִדְּבָרִים הַדְּבָרִים. וְרַבָּנַן? – דְּבָרִים הַדְּבָרִים לָא דָּרְשִׁי.

**And from where does Rabbi** Yehuda HaNasi derive the *halakha* **that one may not recite** *Shema* **out of order?** The Gemara answers: Rabbi Yehuda HaNasi **derives it** from an additional emphasis in the verse: "And the words [*hadevarim*], which I command you this day, will be upon your heart." The verse could have conveyed the same idea had it written: **Words [*devarim*]**, without the definite article. However, it says **the words [*hadevarim*]**, employing the definite article, emphasizing that it must be recited in the specific order in which it is written. **The Rabbis,** however, **do not derive** anything from the fact that **the words,** with the definite article, was written in place of **words,** without the definite article.

**NOTES**

**One who is reading in order to emend – בְּקוֹרֵא לְהַגִּיהַּ:** Some explained that in this context, one who is reading in order to correct the text is not reading the words with their appropriate vocalization. Rather, he is sounding out the words based solely on the letters. In this case, the Gemara says that if he begins reading the words with their vocalization he fulfills his obligation (*Tosafot*).

**The opinions of Rabbi and the Rabbis – שִׁיטַת רַבִּי וַחֲכָמִים:** The dispute between Rabbi Yehuda HaNasi and the Rabbis with regard to the language in which the Shema is recited reflects a broader argument over the meaning of reading. According to the opinion of Rabbi Yehuda HaNasi, the obligation to recite *Shema* is an obligation to recite a specific formula, similar to other obligations in which specific Hebrew phrases must be recited. He understands the term *Shema* as a practical directive to recite the passage in a manner audible to his own ears. The Rabbis understood that *Shema* means that one must understand what he says, and that the essence of reciting *Shema* is the acceptance of the yoke of the Kingdom of Heaven. Therefore, one may recite *Shema* in any language that he understands. On the other hand, since understanding is the crux of the mitzva, there is no obligation to hear the words as he recites them.

**HALAKHA**

***Shema* is recited as it is written…in any language – קְרִיאַת שְׁמַע כִּכְתָבָהּ...בְּכָל לָשׁוֹן:** If one does not understand Hebrew, he may recite *Shema* in any language, in accordance with the opinion of the Rabbis. This is not common practice, however, at least when praying with the congregation (Rambam *Sefer Ahava, Hilkhot Keriat Shema* 2:10; *Shulḥan Arukh, Oraḥ Ḥayyim* 62:2).

לְמֵימְרָא דְּסָבַר רַבִּי דְּכָל הַתּוֹרָה כּוּלָּהּ בְּכָל לָשׁוֹן נֶאֶמְרָה, דְּאִי סָלְקָא דַּעְתָּךְ בִּלְשׁוֹן הַקּוֹדֶשׁ נֶאֶמְרָה – וְהָיוּ דִּכְתַב רַחֲמָנָא לָמָּה לִי?

The Gemara seeks to link this debate to another: **Is that to say that Rabbi** Yehuda HaNasi **holds that the entire Torah,** i.e., any portion of the Torah which must be read publicly (*Tosafot*), or if one studies or reads the Torah in general (*Me'iri*), **may be recited in any language? As if it should enter your mind** to say **that** the entire Torah **may only be recited in the holy tongue** and not in any other, **then why do I need that which the Torah wrote: "And they will be"?** Prohibiting recitation of *Shema* in a language other than Hebrew is superfluous, if indeed one is prohibited from reciting any portion of the Torah in a language other than Hebrew. Since the Torah saw the need to specifically require *Shema* to be recited in Hebrew, it must be because the rest of the Torah may be recited in any language.

אִיצְטְרִיךְ, מִשּׁוּם דִּכְתִיב שְׁמַע.

The Gemara rejects this: This is not necessarily so, as the phrase: And they will be **is necessary** in this case **because *Shema*,** hear, **is** also **written.** Had it not been for the phrase: And they will be, I would have understood hear, to allow *Shema* to be recited in any language, in accordance with the opinion of the Rabbis. Therefore, and they will be, was necessary.

לְמֵימְרָא דְּסָבְרִי רַבָּנַן, דְּכָל הַתּוֹרָה כּוּלָּהּ בִּלְשׁוֹן הַקּוֹדֶשׁ נֶאֶמְרָה, דְּאִי סָלְקָא דַּעְתָּךְ בְּכָל לָשׁוֹן נֶאֶמְרָה – שְׁמַע דִּכְתַב רַחֲמָנָא לָמָּה לִי?

The Gemara attempts to clarify: **Is that to say that the Rabbis hold that the entire Torah may only be recited in the holy tongue** and not in any other? **As if it should enter your mind** to say **that** the Torah **may be recited in any language, then why do I require that which the Torah wrote: *Shema*,** hear? One is permitted to recite the entire Torah in any language, rendering a specific requirement regarding *Shema* superfluous.

אִיצְטְרִיךְ, מִשּׁוּם דִּכְתִיב וְהָיוּ.

The Gemara rejects this: *Shema* **is necessary** in any case, **because and they will be, is** also **written.** Had it not been for *Shema*, I would have understood this in accordance with the opinion of Rabbi Yehuda HaNasi, that one is prohibited from reciting *Shema* in any other language. Therefore, *Shema*, is necessary.

תָּנוּ רַבָּנַן: וְהָיוּ – שֶׁלֹּא יִקְרָא לְמַפְרֵעַ. הַדְּבָרִים עַל לְבָבֶךָ, יָכוֹל תְּהֵא כָּל הַפָּרָשָׁה צְרִיכָה כַּוָּונָה, תַּלְמוּד לוֹמַר: הָאֵלֶּה – עַד כָּאן צְרִיכָה כַּוָּונָה, מִכָּאן וְאֵילָךְ אֵין צְרִיכָה כַּוָּונָה, דִּבְרֵי רַבִּי אֱלִיעֶזֶר,

The interpretation of these verses is the source of a fundamental dispute concerning the obligation to recite *Shema* and the required intent during its recitation. **The Rabbis taught:** From: **And they will be,** it is derived that **one may not recite** *Shema* **out of order.** From: **These words…upon your heart,** it is derived that they must be recited with intent. I **might** have thought that **the entire paragraph requires intent? Therefore the verse teaches: These,** to indicate that **to this point, one must have intent,** but **from here on one need not have intent,** and even if he recites the rest of *Shema* without intent he fulfills his obligation. This is the **statement of Rabbi Eliezer.**

אָמַר לֵיהּ רַבִּי עֲקִיבָא: הֲרֵי הוּא אוֹמֵר

**Rabbi Akiva said to him: But** the verse **states:**

Perek **II**
Daf **13** Amud **b**

"אֲשֶׁר אָנֹכִי מְצַוְּךָ הַיּוֹם עַל לְבָבֶךָ" – מִכָּאן אַתָּה לָמֵד שֶׁכָּל הַפָּרָשָׁה כּוּלָּהּ צְרִיכָה כַּוָּונָה.

**"Which I command you this day, will be upon your heart."** Surely the word these, does not come to limit the mitzva of intent. On the contrary, **from here you derive that the entire portion requires intent.**[B]

אָמַר רַבָּה בַּר בַּר חָנָה אָמַר רַבִּי יוֹחָנָן: הֲלָכָה כְּרַבִּי עֲקִיבָא.

**Rabba bar bar Ḥana said that Rabbi Yoḥanan said: The *halakha* is in accordance with** the opinion of **Rabbi Akiva;** the entire portion requires intent.

**BACKGROUND**

Intent – כַּוָּונָה: This concept has two meanings with regard to mitzvot in general. The first meaning is awareness that the action being performed is a divine command. The second is appreciation of the spiritual significance of a commandment. This form of intent is strongly encouraged, though it is not an absolutely requirement for most mitzvot, with a few exceptions, notably reciting *Shema* and the *Amida* prayer.

## PERSONALITIES

**Rabbi Yoshiya – רַבִּי יֹאשִׁיָּה:** Rabbi Yoshiya was a member of the last generation of *tanna'im* and is, at times, considered to be a transitional figure between *tanna'im* and *amora'im*.

Rabbi Yoshiya and his counterpart, Rabbi Yonatan, are among the pairs in halakhic discourse, and arguments between them appear throughout the Talmud. Both Rabbi Yoshiya and Rabbi Yonatan were primary students of Rabbi Yishmael, and they were the main proponents of his approach to halakhic midrash.

There is room to conjecture that Rabbi Yoshiya fled to Babylonia and settled there. He may be the Rabbi Yoshiya of Hutzal who transformed that city into a significant Torah center, and to whom the verse: "But the righteous is an everlasting foundation" (Proverbs 10:25) was applied.

## BACKGROUND

**The placement of the phylacteries of the arm must be opposite the heart – שִׁימָה כְּנֶגֶד הַלֵּב:**

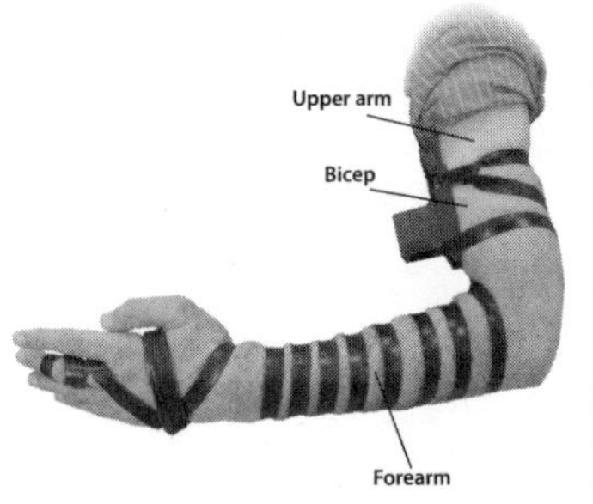


Placement of the phylacteries on the arm and hand

אִיכָּא דְּמַתְנֵי לָהּ אַהָא, דְּתַנְיָא: הַקּוֹרֵא אֶת שְׁמַע צָרִיךְ שֶׁיְּכַוֵּין אֶת לִבּוֹ; רַבִּי אַחָא מִשּׁוּם רַבִּי יְהוּדָה אוֹמֵר: כֵּיוָן שֶׁכִּוֵּון לִבּוֹ בְּפֶרֶק רִאשׁוֹן – שׁוּב אֵינוֹ צָרִיךְ. אָמַר רַבָּה בַּר בַּר חָנָה אָמַר רַבִּי יוֹחָנָן: הֲלָכָה כְּרַבִּי אַחָא שֶׁאָמַר מִשּׁוּם רַבִּי יְהוּדָה.

**Some teach this** *halakha* stated by Rabbi Yoḥanan **with regard to that which was taught** in a *Tosefta*, where there is a tannaitic dispute. The first *tanna* holds: **One who recites *Shema* must focus his heart** for the entire *Shema*. **Rabbi Aḥa says in the name of Rabbi Yehuda: Once he focused his heart for the first paragraph** alone, **he no longer requires** intent. With regard to this *Tosefta*, **Rabba bar bar Ḥana said** that **Rabbi Yoḥanan said: The *halakha* is in accordance with Rabbi Aḥa who said in the name of Rabbi Yehuda.** While this differs from the previous version in form, it arrives at the same conclusion.

תַּנְיָא אִידָךְ: "וְהָיוּ" – שֶׁלֹּא יִקְרָא לְמַפְרֵעַ. "עַל לְבָבֶךָ" – רַב זוּטְרָא אוֹמֵר: עַד כָּאן – מִצְוַת כַּוָּונָה, מִכָּאן וְאֵילָךְ – מִצְוַת קְרִיאָה; רַבִּי יֹאשִׁיָּה אוֹמֵר: עַד כָּאן – מִצְוַת קְרִיאָה, מִכָּאן וְאֵילָךְ – מִצְוַת כַּוָּונָה.

**It was taught** in **another** *baraita* on this subject, which cited different opinions. From: **And they will be,** recited in *Shema*, it is derived that **it may not be recited out of order.** From: **Upon your heart, Rav Zutra says: To this point,** there is **the mitzva of intent; from here on,** beginning with the second paragraph, there is only **the mitzva of recitation. Rabbi Yoshiya**[P] **says** that it means the opposite: **To this point,** there is **the mitzva of recitation; from here on** there is only **the mitzva of intent.**

מַאי שְׁנָא מִכָּאן וְאֵילָךְ מִצְוַת קְרִיאָה – דִּכְתִיב "לְדַבֵּר בָּם", הָכָא נַמִּי הָא כְּתִיב "וְדִבַּרְתָּ בָּם"!

At first the Gemara understands that Rav Zutra required recitation only in the second paragraph, while in the first paragraph only intent was required. Therefore, the Gemara asks: **What is different,** that **from here on,** beginning with the second paragraph, there is **the mitzva of recitation?** Is it because **it is written:** "And you shall teach them to your children, **to speak of them"** (Deuteronomy 11:19)? This is no proof, as **here too,** in the first paragraph **it is written: "And you shall speak of them."** The mitzva of recitation applies to the first paragraph as well.

הָכִי קָאָמַר: עַד כָּאן – מִצְוַת כַּוָּונָה וּקְרִיאָה, מִכָּאן וְאֵילָךְ – קְרִיאָה בְּלֹא כַּוָּונָה.

Rather, **he is saying as follows: To this point** there is **the mitzva of** both **intent and recitation,** but **from here on,** there is only the mitzva of **recitation without intent.**

וּמַאי שְׁנָא עַד כָּאן מִצְוַת כַּוָּונָה וּקְרִיאָה – דִּכְתִיב "עַל לְבָבֶךָ", "וְדִבַּרְתָּ בָּם", הָתָם נַמִּי הָא כְּתִיב "עַל לְבַבְכֶם", "לְדַבֵּר בָּם"!

Again the Gemara asks: According to Rav Zutra, **what is different,** that **to this point,** in the first paragraph, there is **the mitzva of** both **intent and recitation** because there are two requirements in the first paragraph, **as it is written: "Upon your heart… and you shall speak of them"? There, too,** in the second paragraph **it is also written: "And you shall place these words upon your heart… to speak of them,"** indicating that intent is also required in that paragraph.

הַהוּא מִבָּעֵי לֵיהּ לְכִדְרַבִּי יִצְחָק, דְּאָמַר: "וְשַׂמְתֶּם אֶת דְּבָרַי אֵלֶּה" – צְרִיכָה שֶׁתְּהֵא שִׂימָה כְּנֶגֶד הַלֵּב.

The Gemara responds: **That verse is necessary to derive** that which was taught by **Rabbi Yitzḥak, who said: "And you shall place these words"** refers literally to the paragraphs of *Shema* found in the phylacteries. The verse teaches **that the placement** of the phylacteries of the arm **must be opposite the heart.**[B]

אָמַר מָר, רַבִּי יֹאשִׁיָּה אוֹמֵר: עַד כָּאן – מִצְוַת קְרִיאָה, מִכָּאן וְאֵילָךְ – מִצְוַת כַּוָּונָה. מַאי שְׁנָא מִכָּאן וְאֵילָךְ מִצְוַת כַּוָּונָה – מִשּׁוּם דִּכְתִיב "עַל לְבַבְכֶם" – הָכָא נַמִּי הָא כְּתִיב "עַל לְבָבֶךָ"!

The Gemara now attempts to clarify the second opinion in the *baraita*. **The Master said, Rabbi Yoshiya says: To this point** at the end of the first paragraph, there is **the mitzva of recitation; from here on** there is **the mitzva of intent.** The Gemara asks: **What is different,** that **from here on,** beginning with the second paragraph, there is **the mitzva of intent?** Is it **because it is written** in the second paragraph: "And you shall place these words **upon your heart"? That is no proof, as **here too,** in the first paragraph **it is written: "Upon your heart."**

הָכִי קָאָמַר: עַד כָּאן – מִצְוַת קְרִיאָה וְכַוָּונָה, מִכָּאן וְאֵילָךְ – כַּוָּונָה בְּלֹא קְרִיאָה.

The Gemara responds that **he is saying as follows: To this point,** there is **the mitzva of** both **recitation and intent,** but **from here on,** there is only the mitzva of **recitation without intent.**

וּמַאי שְׁנָא עַד כָּאן מִצְוַת קְרִיאָה וְכַוָּונָה – דִּכְתִיב "עַל לְבָבֶךָ" "וְדִבַּרְתָּ בָּם" – הָתָם נַמִּי הָא כְּתִיב "עַל לְבַבְכֶם" "לְדַבֵּר בָּם"!

The Gemara continues: **And what is different,** that **to this point,** in the first paragraph, there is **the mitzva of recitation and intent** because there are two requirements, **as it is written: Upon your heart** as well as: **And you shall speak of them? There, too,** with regard to the second paragraph **isn't it written:** And you shall place these words **upon your heart**… and you shall teach them to your children, **to speak of them?**

הַהוּא בְּדִבְרֵי תוֹרָה כְּתִיב, וְהָכִי קָאָמַר רַחֲמָנָא: אַגְמִירוּ בְּנַיְיכוּ תּוֹרָה כִּי הֵיכִי דְּלִיגְרְסוּ בְּהוּ.

Rabbi Yoshiya responded: **That** verse refers to **Torah study** in general, not to the recitation of *Shema* in particular. **And the Torah says the following: Teach your children Torah, that they will be well-versed in them.**

תָּנוּ רַבָּנַן: שְׁמַע יִשְׂרָאֵל ה׳ אֱלֹהֵינוּ ה׳ אֶחָד – עַד כָּאן צְרִיכָה כַּוָּונַת הַלֵּב, דִּבְרֵי רַבִּי מֵאִיר. אָמַר רָבָא: הֲלָכָה כְּרַבִּי מֵאִיר.

**The Sages taught** in another *baraita* with regard to one who recites *Shema* and utters the verse, **"Hear, Israel, the Lord is our God, the Lord is One." Intent of the heart is** only **required to this point.**[H] This is **the statement of Rabbi Meir. Rava said:** In this matter, **the *halakha* is in accordance with** the opinion of **Rabbi Meir.**

תַּנְיָא, סוּמְכוֹס אוֹמֵר: כׇּל הַמַּאֲרִיךְ בְּאֶחָד – מַאֲרִיכִין לוֹ יָמָיו וּשְׁנוֹתָיו. אָמַר רַב אַחָא בַּר יַעֲקֹב: וּבְדָלֶ״ת. אָמַר רַב אַשִׁי: וּבִלְבַד שֶׁלֹּא יַחֲטוֹף בְּחֵי״ת.

**It was taught** in a *baraita*, **Sumakhos says: One who extends** his intonation **of the word One** [*eḥad*][H] while reciting *Shema*, is rewarded that **his days and years are extended. Rav Aḥa bar Ya'akov said:** This is only true if he extends **the letter *dalet*,** so the word *eḥad* is sounded in its entirety. **Rav Ashi said:** This is **only so long as one does not** pronounce the letter ***ḥet* hurriedly.**

רַבִּי יִרְמְיָה הֲוָה יָתֵיב קַמֵּיהּ דְּרַבִּי [חִיָּיא בַּר אַבָּא] חַזְיֵיהּ דַּהֲוָה מַאֲרִיךְ טוּבָא. אֲמַר לֵיהּ: כֵּיוָן דְּאַמְלֵיכְתֵּיהּ לְמַעְלָה וּלְמַטָּה וּלְאַרְבַּע רוּחוֹת הַשָּׁמַיִם, תּוּ לָא צְרִיכַתְּ.

The Gemara relates that **Rabbi Yirmeya was seated before Rabbi Ḥiyya bar Abba. He saw that he was greatly extending** his pronunciation of *eḥad*. **He said to him: Once you have crowned Him** in your thoughts **over** everything **above,** in Heaven, **below,** on earth, **and in the four corners of the heavens, you need not** extend any **further.**

אָמַר רַב נָתָן בַּר מָר עוּקְבָא אָמַר רַב יְהוּדָה: ״עַל לְבָבֶךָ״ בַּעֲמִידָה. ״עַל לְבָבֶךָ״ סָלְקָא דַּעְתָּךְ? אֶלָּא אֵימָא: עַד ״עַל לְבָבֶךָ״ – בַּעֲמִידָה, מִכָּאן וְאֵילָךְ – לָא. וְרַבִּי יוֹחָנָן אָמַר: כׇּל הַפָּרָשָׁה כּוּלָּהּ בַּעֲמִידָה.

**Rav Natan bar Mar Ukva said** that **Rav Yehuda said:** One must recite **upon your heart, while standing** in one place. The Gemara is perplexed: **Does it enter your mind** that **upon your heart** alone must be recited while standing in one place? What distinguishes that phrase from the rest of *Shema*? **Rather, say:** One must recite **until upon your heart** while **standing** in one place.[H] **From here on,** one need **not** stand in one place. **Rabbi Yoḥanan said:** One must recite **the entire** first **portion** while **standing** in one place.

וְאָזְדָא רַבִּי יוֹחָנָן לְטַעְמֵיהּ, דְּאָמַר רַבָּה בַּר בַּר חָנָה אָמַר רַבִּי יוֹחָנָן: הֲלָכָה כְּרַבִּי אַחָא שֶׁאָמַר מִשּׁוּם רַבִּי יְהוּדָה.

The Gemara notes: **Rabbi Yoḥanan** is consistent **and follows his reasoning** expressed elsewhere, as **Rabba bar bar Ḥana said** that **Rabbi Yoḥanan said: The *halakha* is in accordance with** the opinion **of Rabbi Aḥa who said in the name of Rabbi Yehuda;** one is required to recite the entire first paragraph of *Shema* with intent.

תָּנוּ רַבָּנַן: שְׁמַע יִשְׂרָאֵל ה׳ אֱלֹהֵינוּ ה׳ אֶחָד – זוֹ קְרִיאַת שְׁמַע שֶׁל רַבִּי יְהוּדָה הַנָּשִׂיא. אֲמַר לֵיהּ רַב לְרַבִּי חִיָּיא: לָא חֲזֵינָא לֵיהּ לְרַבִּי דִּמְקַבֵּל עֲלֵיהּ מַלְכוּת שָׁמַיִם. אֲמַר לֵיהּ: בַּר פַּחְתֵי! בְּשָׁעָה שֶׁמַּעֲבִיר יָדָיו עַל פָּנָיו מְקַבֵּל עָלָיו עוֹל מַלְכוּת שָׁמַיִם.

**The Sages taught** in a *baraita*: The single verse, **"Hear, Israel, the Lord is our God, the Lord is One"; this is Rabbi Yehuda HaNasi's recitation of *Shema*.** The Gemara relates: **Rav said to** his uncle, **Rabbi Ḥiyya: I did not see Rabbi** Yehuda HaNasi **accept the kingship of Heaven upon himself,** meaning that he did not see him recite *Shema*. Rabbi Ḥiyya **said to him: Son of noblemen [*bar paḥtei*],**[L] **when** Rabbi Yehuda HaNasi **passed his hands over his face**[HN] in the study hall in the middle of his lesson, **he accepted the yoke of the kingdom of Heaven upon himself,** as his *Shema* was comprised of a single verse.

חוֹזֵר וְגוֹמְרָהּ, אוֹ אֵינוֹ חוֹזֵר וְגוֹמְרָהּ? בַּר קַפָּרָא אוֹמֵר: אֵינוֹ חוֹזֵר וְגוֹמְרָהּ, רַבִּי שִׁמְעוֹן בְּרַבִּי אוֹמֵר: חוֹזֵר וְגוֹמְרָהּ. אֲמַר לֵיהּ בַּר קַפָּרָא לְרַבִּי שִׁמְעוֹן בְּרַבִּי: בִּשְׁלָמָא לְדִידִי דְּאָמֵינָא אֵינוֹ חוֹזֵר וְגוֹמְרָהּ – הַיְינוּ דִּמְהַדַּר רַבִּי אַשְׁמַעְתָּא דְּאִית בַּהּ יְצִיאַת מִצְרַיִם, אֶלָּא לְדִידָךְ דְּאָמְרַתְּ חוֹזֵר וְגוֹמְרָהּ, לָמָּה לֵיהּ לְאַהֲדוּרֵי?

Rabbi Yehuda HaNasi's students and members of his household disputed: **Does he complete** *Shema* **later or does he not complete it later? Bar Kappara says: He does not complete it later. Rabbi Shimon, son of Rabbi** Yehuda HaNasi, **says: He completes it later. Bar Kappara said to Rabbi Shimon, son of Rabbi** Yehuda HaNasi: **Granted, according to my** position, **that I say that** Rabbi Yehuda HaNasi **does not complete** *Shema* **later, that is why** when he taught, **Rabbi** Yehuda HaNasi would specifically **seek a topic that included the exodus from Egypt,** as by so doing he fulfills the mitzva to remember the Exodus; a mitzva that others fulfill in their recitation of the last paragraph of *Shema*. **But according to you, who says that he completes** his recitation of *Shema* **later, why,** when he teaches, **would** he specifically **seek** a topic that included the exodus from Egypt?

כְּדֵי לְהַזְכִּיר יְצִיאַת מִצְרַיִם בִּזְמַנָּהּ.

Rabbi Shimon responded: Rabbi Yehuda HaNasi did so **in order to mention the exodus from Egypt at its** appointed **time,** during the time of the recitation of *Shema*.

## HALAKHA

**Intent of the heart is required to this point – עַד כָּאן צְרִיכָה כַּוָּונַת הַלֵּב:** Lack of intent prevents one from fulfilling his obligation only in reciting the first verse of *Shema*. Therefore, if one recited *Shema* and did not have intent in the first verse, he did not fulfill his obligation. He must repeat it, and do so quietly (*Magen Avraham*). If he had intent only while reciting the first verse, he fulfilled his obligation (Rambam *Sefer Ahava, Hilkhot Keriat Shema* 2:1; *Shulḥan Arukh, Oraḥ Ḥayyim* 60:5, 63:4).

**One who extends his intonation of the word One – כׇּל הַמַּאֲרִיךְ בְּאֶחָד:** While reciting *Shema*, one must extend his intonation of the word "one" long enough to consider that God rules the entire world, in accordance with the opinions of Sumakhos and the *amora'im*. One should extend his *ḥet* slightly and his *dalet* considerably (*Magen Avraham*). Some say that one should not extend the *ḥet* at all, and that only the *dalet* should be extended. Nevertheless, he should not pronounce the *ḥet* hurriedly (Rambam *Sefer Ahava, Hilkhot Keriat Shema* 2:9; *Shulḥan Arukh, Oraḥ Ḥayyim* 61:6, 8).

**Until upon your heart while standing in one place – עַד עַל לְבָבְךָ בַּעֲמִידָה:** One who is walking and wishes to recite *Shema* must stand in one place for the first verse, in order to focus with the proper intent. This is in accordance with the opinion of Rabbi Natan who says that one must stand; however, it is in accordance with the opinion of Rabbi Meir as well, who holds that only the first verse requires intent (Rambam *Sefer Ahava, Hilkhot Keriat Shema* 2:3; *Shulḥan Arukh, Oraḥ Ḥayyim* 63:3).

**When he passed his hands over his face – בְּשָׁעָה שֶׁמַּעֲבִיר יָדָיו עַל פָּנָיו וכו׳:** It is customary to cover one's eyes with one's right hand (*Be'er Hetev*, based on kabbalistic sources) so that he will not be distracted. This is based on the practice of Rabbi Yehuda HaNasi who would cover his eyes when reciting *Shema* (*Shulḥan Arukh, Oraḥ Ḥayyim* 61:5).

## LANGUAGE

**Son of noblemen [*bar paḥtei*] – בַּר פַּחְתֵי:** This expression is normally interpreted as son of the great or son of ministers (Rabbi Shmuel ben Ḥafni), from the biblical word *peḥa* (see Malachi 1:8). Some suggest that Rav's father, who was Rabbi Ḥiyya's brother, actually held a high position in the Parthian government, and was addressed with this honorific.

Some of the *ge'onim* had a variant reading here: *Bar pa'atei*, as in *pa'atei Moav*, great men of Moab (Numbers 24:17; Rav Tzemaḥ Gaon), or because he was prominent in all areas of *halakha* (*Arukh*).

## NOTES

**When he passed his hands over his face – בְּשָׁעָה שֶׁמַּעֲבִיר יָדָיו עַל פָּנָיו וכו׳:** Various reasons for this passing of the hand were suggested. Some say that while accepting God's dominion over the entire world, one must direct his eyes in all directions. Therefore, Rabbi Yehuda HaNasi covered his eyes to conceal their movement (Rav Hai Gaon, *Arukh*). Others explained that passing his hands over his face was meant to keep all potential distractions from his sight in order to facilitate proper intent (Rosh).

אָמַר רַבִּי אִילָא בְּרֵיהּ דְּרַב שְׁמוּאֵל בַּר מָרְתָא מִשְּׁמֵיהּ דְּרַב: אָמַר ״שְׁמַע יִשְׂרָאֵל ה׳ אֱלֹהֵינוּ ה׳ אֶחָד״ וְנֶאֱנַס בְּשֵׁינָה – יָצָא. אֲמַר לֵיהּ רַב נַחְמָן לְדָרוּ עַבְדֵּיהּ: בִּפְסוּקָא קַמָּא – צַעֲרַן, טְפֵי – לָא תְּצַעֲרַן. אֲמַר לֵיהּ רַב יוֹסֵף לְרַב יוֹסֵף בְּרֵיהּ דְּרַבָּה: אֲבוּךְ הֵיכִי הֲוָה עָבֵיד? אֲמַר לֵיהּ: בִּפְסוּקָא קַמָּא הֲוָה קָא מְצַעֵר נַפְשֵׁיהּ, טְפֵי לָא הֲוָה מְצַעֵר נַפְשֵׁיהּ.

Based on this *halakha*, **Rabbi Ila, son of Rav Shmuel bar Marta, said in the name of Rav: One who recited** the verse, **"Hear, Israel, the Lord is our God, the Lord is One," and was** immediately **overcome by sleep, fulfilled** his obligation to recite *Shema*. Similarly, **Rav Naḥman said to his slave, Daru:** If you see that I have fallen asleep, **bother me** to recite **the first verse,**[NH] **do not bother me** to recite any **more** than that. Similarly, **Rav Yosef said to Rav Yosef, son of Rabba: What would your father do?** Rav Yosef, son of Rabba, **said to him: He would exert himself** not to fall asleep in order to recite **the first verse, he would not exert himself** to recite any **more** than that.

אָמַר רַב יוֹסֵף: פְּרַקְדָּן לֹא יִקְרָא קְרִיאַת שְׁמַע. מִקְרָא הוּא דְּלָא לִיקְרֵי, הָא מִיגְנָא – שַׁפִּיר דָּמֵי? וְהָא רַבִּי יְהוֹשֻׁעַ בֶּן לֵוִי לַיֵּיט אַמַּאן דְּגָנֵי אַפַּרְקִיד!

**Rav Yosef said: One who is lying** [*perakdan*][L] **on his back may not recite *Shema*,**[H] for lying that way is unbecoming. The Gemara asks: Is that to say that **one may not recite** *Shema* in this position, **but to sleep lying** in that position **is permissible? Didn't Rabbi Yehoshua ben Levi curse one who** sleeps **lying on his back?**

אָמְרִי: מִיגְנָא, כִּי מַצְלֵי – שַׁפִּיר דָּמֵי. מִקְרָא, אַף עַל גַּב דְּמַצְלֵי – נַמִי אָסוּר.

The Gemara answers: **If one** lies on his back **while leaning** slightly to the side, **it is permissible.** Nonetheless, **to recite** *Shema* in this position, **even though he is leaning, is prohibited.**

וְהָא רַבִּי יוֹחָנָן מַצְלֵי וְקָרֵי!

The Gemara asks: **Wouldn't Rabbi Yoḥanan** lie on his back, **lean** slightly **and recite** *Shema*?

שָׁאנֵי רַבִּי יוֹחָנָן דְּבַעַל בָּשָׂר הֲוָה.

The Gemara responds: The case of **Rabbi Yoḥanan is different,** because **he was corpulent** and it was difficult for him to read any other way.

בַּפְּרָקִים – שׁוֹאֵל וכו׳.

The mishna cited Rabbi Meir's statement: **At the** breaks between **paragraphs, one may greet** an individual due to the respect that he is obligated to show him, and may respond. And in the middle of each paragraph, one may greet an individual due to the fear that the individual may harm him if he fails do so, and may respond.

מֵשִׁיב מֵחֲמַת מַאי? אִילֵימָא מִפְּנֵי הַכָּבוֹד – הָשְׁתָּא מִשְׁאַל שָׁאֵיל, אַהֲדוּרֵי מִבַּעְיָא? אֶלָּא: שׁוֹאֵל מִפְּנֵי הַכָּבוֹד וּמֵשִׁיב שָׁלוֹם לְכָל אָדָם. אֵימָא סֵיפָא: וּבָאֶמְצַע – שׁוֹאֵל מִפְּנֵי הַיִּרְאָה וּמֵשִׁיב.

About this, the Gemara asks: He may **respond due to what** circumstance? **If you say** that one may respond **due to respect; now that** we learned that **one may greet** another due to respect, **is it necessary** to say that **one may respond** due to respect? **Rather,** it must be explained as follows: **One may greet due to respect and respond with a greeting to any person.** But if that is the case, **say the latter clause** of the mishna: **In the middle** of each paragraph **one may greet due to fear and return** another's greeting due to fear.

מֵשִׁיב מֵחֲמַת מַאי? אִילֵימָא מִפְּנֵי הַיִּרְאָה – הָשְׁתָּא מִשְׁאַל שָׁאֵיל, אַהֲדוּרֵי מִבַּעְיָא? אֶלָּא מִפְּנֵי הַכָּבוֹד: הַיְינוּ – דְּרַבִּי יְהוּדָה! דִּתְנַן, רַבִּי יְהוּדָה אוֹמֵר: בָּאֶמְצַע – שׁוֹאֵל מִפְּנֵי הַיִּרְאָה וּמֵשִׁיב מִפְּנֵי הַכָּבוֹד, וּבַפְּרָקִים – שׁוֹאֵל מִפְּנֵי הַכָּבוֹד וּמֵשִׁיב שָׁלוֹם לְכָל אָדָם!

Here too, it must be clarified: He may **respond due to what** circumstance? **If you say** that one may respond **due to fear; now that** we have learned that **one may greet** another due to fear, **is it necessary** to say that **one may respond** due to fear? **Rather,** it must mean that one may respond to another's greeting even **due to honor.** If so, **that is** identical to the opinion of **Rabbi Yehuda, as we learned** in the mishna: **In the middle** of each paragraph, **one may greet** another **due to fear and respond due to respect. At the** breaks between **paragraphs, one may greet** another **due to respect and respond with a greeting to any person.** If so, what is the dispute between them?

חַסּוּרֵי מִחַסְּרָא וְהָכִי קָתָנֵי: בַּפְּרָקִים – שׁוֹאֵל מִפְּנֵי הַכָּבוֹד וְאֵין צָרִיךְ לוֹמַר שֶׁהוּא מֵשִׁיב, וּבָאֶמְצַע – שׁוֹאֵל מִפְּנֵי הַיִּרְאָה וְאֵין צָרִיךְ לוֹמַר שֶׁהוּא מֵשִׁיב, דִּבְרֵי רַבִּי מֵאִיר; רַבִּי יְהוּדָה אוֹמֵר: בָּאֶמְצַע – שׁוֹאֵל מִפְּנֵי הַיִּרְאָה וּמֵשִׁיב מִפְּנֵי הַכָּבוֹד,

The Gemara says: The mishna **is incomplete;**[B] it is missing an important element, **and it teaches the following: At the** breaks between the **paragraphs, one may greet due to respect, and, needless to say,**[B] **he may respond** due to respect. **In the middle** of each paragraph **one may greet due to fear, and, needless to say, he may respond** due to fear. This is the **statement of Rabbi Meir. Rabbi Yehuda says: In the middle** of each paragraph **one may greet due to fear and respond due to respect.**

## NOTES

**Bother me to recite the first verse – בִּפְסוּקָא קַמָּא צַעֲרַן:** After the first verse, he could continue reciting *Shema* to the end while not fully awake, as the primary intent must be upon the first verse (*ge'onim*, *Talmidei Rabbeinu Yona*). Others explained that he wanted to be woken for the first verse and once he accepted the Kingdom of Heaven, he would not fall back asleep.

## HALAKHA

**Bother me to recite the first verse – בִּפְסוּקָא קַמָּא צַעֲרַן:** If one is sleeping, he must be roused from his sleep in order to recite the first verse of *Shema* fully awake. Thereafter, he may continue reciting *Shema* while nodding off (*Talmidei Rabbeinu Yona*; Rosh; Rambam *Sefer Ahava*, *Hilkhot Keriat Shema* 2:3; *Shulḥan Arukh*, *Oraḥ Ḥayyim*, 63:5).

**One who is lying on his back may not recite *Shema* – פְּרַקְדָּן לֹא יִקְרָא קְרִיאַת שְׁמַע:** One is prohibited from reciting *Shema* while lying on his back or stomach. If he leans to his side it is permitted. According to the *Shulḥan Arukh*, if it is not extremely burdensome, one should sit up. The Rema disagrees and is lenient (Rambam *Sefer Ahava*, *Hilkhot Keriat Shema* 2:2; *Shulḥan Arukh*, *Oraḥ Ḥayyim*, 63:1).

## LANGUAGE

**Lying [*perakdan*] – פְּרַקְדָּן:** This term can mean either lying on one's back, or on one's stomach. In addition to Rashi's explanation, some explained that this position is prohibited because it may lead to inappropriate sexual thoughts.

## BACKGROUND

**The mishna is incomplete – חַסּוּרֵי מִחַסְּרָא:** This method of explanation is often found in the Gemara; however, generally speaking, it does not suggest an actual emendation of the text of the mishna. The addition introduced by the Gemara is a necessary elaboration upon that which is written in the mishna, which is insufficiently clear in its current form. The addition provides the necessary clarification.

**And needless to say – וְאֵין צָרִיךְ לוֹמַר:** The addition of the words, and it goes without saying, resolves the difficulty raised in the Gemara by inference: Obviously, if one may initiate a greeting, one may respond. Why did the mishna write both? By inserting the phrase, and it goes without saying, it is clear that the mishna was also aware of the relationship between greeting and response and there is no difficulty.

וּבַפְּרָקִים – שׁוֹאֵל מִפְּנֵי הַכָּבוֹד וּמֵשִׁיב שָׁלוֹם לְכׇל אָדָם.

**And at the** breaks between the **paragraphs one may greet due to respect and respond with a greeting to any person.** And if that is the case, the mishna is no longer difficult.

תַּנְיָא נַמִי הָכִי: הַקּוֹרֵא אֶת שְׁמַע וּפָגַע בּוֹ רַבּוֹ אוֹ גָּדוֹל הֵימֶנּוּ, בַּפְּרָקִים – שׁוֹאֵל מִפְּנֵי הַכָּבוֹד וְאֵין צָרִיךְ לוֹמַר שֶׁהוּא מֵשִׁיב, וּבָאֶמְצַע – שׁוֹאֵל מִפְּנֵי הַיִּרְאָה וְאֵין צָרִיךְ לוֹמַר שֶׁהוּא מֵשִׁיב, דִּבְרֵי רַבִּי מֵאִיר; רַבִּי יְהוּדָה אוֹמֵר: בָּאֶמְצַע – שׁוֹאֵל מִפְּנֵי הַיִּרְאָה וּמֵשִׁיב מִפְּנֵי הַכָּבוֹד, וּבַפְּרָקִים – שׁוֹאֵל מִפְּנֵי הַכָּבוֹד וּמֵשִׁיב שָׁלוֹם לְכׇל אָדָם.

The Gemara remarks: **This** version of the dispute **was also taught** in a *baraita*: **One who is reciting *Shema* and happens upon his teacher or one who is greater than he, at the** breaks between the **paragraphs he may greet him due to respect and, needless to say, he may respond. And in the middle** of each paragraph, **he may greet** another **due to fear and, needless to say, he may respond.** This is the **statement of Rabbi Meir. Rabbi Yehuda says: In the middle** of each paragraph **one may greet due to fear and respond due to respect. And in the** breaks between the **paragraphs one may greet due to respect and respond with a greeting to any person.** The proposed additions to the mishna appear in the version of the dispute cited in the *baraita*.

בְּעָא מִינֵּיהּ אֲחַי תַּנָּא דְּבֵי רַבִּי חִיָּיא מֵרַבִּי חִיָּיא: בְּהַלֵּל וּבִמְגִילָּה מַהוּ שֶׁיַּפְסִיק? אָמְרִינַן קַל וָחוֹמֶר: קְרִיאַת שְׁמַע דְּאוֹרָיְיתָא פּוֹסֵק – הַלֵּל דְּרַבָּנַן מִבַּעְיָא, אוֹ דִּלְמָא פִּרְסוּמֵי נִיסָּא עֲדִיף?

**Aḥai, the *tanna*** who recited *mishnayot* **in the school of**[B] **Rabbi Ḥiyya, raised a dilemma before Rabbi Ḥiyya:**[N] **May one interrupt during** the recitation of ***hallel*** **and** the reading of **the Megilla,**[H] Esther, to greet someone? Do **we say that** it is an ***a fortiori*** **inference;** if in the middle of ***Shema*****, which is a biblical** obligation, **one may interrupt** in order to greet someone, **all the more so,** in the middle of ***hallel*****, which is a rabbinic** obligation, **one may interrupt? Or, perhaps, publicizing the miracle is more significant,** so one may not interrupt *hallel* or the Megilla at all.

אֲמַר לֵיהּ: פּוֹסֵק וְאֵין בְּכָךְ כְּלוּם. אָמַר רַבָּה: יָמִים שֶׁהַיָּחִיד גּוֹמֵר בָּהֶן אֶת הַהַלֵּל – בֵּין פֶּרֶק לְפֶרֶק פּוֹסֵק, בְּאֶמְצַע הַפֶּרֶק אֵינוֹ פּוֹסֵק; וְיָמִים שֶׁאֵין הַיָּחִיד גּוֹמֵר בָּהֶן אֶת הַהַלֵּל – אֲפִילּוּ בְּאֶמְצַע הַפֶּרֶק פּוֹסֵק.

Rabbi Ḥiyya **said to him: One interrupts and it is of no concern. Rabba said:** On **days when the individual completes** the entire ***hallel*****,**[N] i.e., the days on which there is a rabbinic obligation to recite *hallel*, an individual **may interrupt between one paragraph and another;** however, **one may not interrupt in the middle of the paragraph.** On **days where the individual does not complete** the entire ***hallel*****,** i.e., days on which the recitation of *hallel* is merely a custom, not a rabbinic obligation, **one may interrupt even in the middle of the paragraph.**[H]

אִינִי? וְהָא רַב בַּר שַׁבָּא אִיקְּלַע לְגַבֵּיהּ דְּרָבִינָא, וְיָמִים שֶׁאֵין הַיָּחִיד גּוֹמֵר אֶת הַהַלֵּל הֲוָה, וְלָא פְּסֵיק לֵיהּ!

The Gemara questions this: **It that so? Didn't Rav bar Shaba** once **happen** to come **before Ravina** on one of **the days when the individual does not complete** the entire ***hallel*****,** and Ravina **did not interrupt** his recitation of *hallel* to greet him?

שָׁאנֵי רַב בַּר שַׁבָּא דְּלָא חֲשִׁיב עֲלֵיהּ דְּרָבִינָא.

The Gemara responds: The case of Rav bar Shaba **is different, as Rav bar Shaba was not considered important** to **Ravina.** That is the reason that he did not interrupt his recitation of *hallel* to greet him.

בְּעִי מִינֵּיהּ אַשְׁיָאן תַּנָּא דְּבֵי רַבִּי אַמֵּי מֵרַבִּי אַמֵּי: הַשָּׁרוּי בְּתַעֲנִית מַהוּ שֶׁיִּטְעוֹם? אֲכִילָה וּשְׁתִיָּה קַבֵּיל עֲלֵיהּ – וְהָא לֵיכָּא, אוֹ דִּילְמָא הֲנָאָה קַבֵּיל עֲלֵיהּ – וְהָא אִיכָּא?

Having mentioned the dilemma raised by one of those who recite the *mishnayot* in the study hall, the Gemara cites that **Ashyan, the *tanna*** who recited *mishnayot* **in the school of Rabbi Ami, raised a dilemma before Rabbi Ami: May one who is fasting taste** the food that he is preparing to determine if it spiced properly? **Did he accept upon himself** to refrain from **eating and drinking, and that** is **not** eating and drinking; it is merely tasting? **Or, perhaps, he accepted upon himself** to refrain from deriving **pleasure** from food, **and that is** pleasure when he tastes.

**BACKGROUND**

**The *tanna* of the school – תַּנָּא דְּבֵי:** Even though writing the Oral Torah was permitted, most of it was not recorded. Some say that the Mishna itself was not written at the time of its redaction. Therefore, many rabbinic statements, such as the *Tosefta* and other *baraitot*, were preserved and transmitted orally. Each Sage was expected to commit the entire Mishna as well as a significant number of other tannaitic statements to memory; however, complete mastery of all of these sources was the province of the *tanna'im*, experts at memorization who memorized massive amounts of material and were capable of reciting it on demand. Often, the most prominent of these *tanna'im* were affiliated with the specific study hall of one of the Sages, where they served as living anthologies of this material.

**NOTES**

**Aḥai, the *tanna* who recited the *mishnayot*… raised a dilemma before Rabbi Ḥiyya – בְּעָא מִינֵּיהּ אֲחַי תַּנָּא...מֵרַבִּי חִיָּיא:** Despite the fact that these *tanna'im* were extremely well versed in the Mishna and *baraitot*, they often understood them on a superficial level, and rarely examined them critically. Therefore, these analytical dilemmas raised by these two *tanna'im* are cited in the Gemara. Others explain that these two dilemmas were cited together by the Gemara because in both cases, the one who raised the dilemma receives an answer more lenient than either of the options raised (*Tziyyun LeNefesh Ḥayya*).

**Days when the individual completes the entire *hallel* – יָמִים שֶׁהַיָּחִיד גּוֹמֵר בָּהֶן אֶת הַהַלֵּל:** The days on which *hallel* is recited are divided into two categories: Days when reciting *hallel* is a rabbinic ordinance: The first day of Passover (two days in the Diaspora), *Shavuot*, *Sukkot*, and Hanukka; and days when reciting *hallel* is merely a custom: The remaining days of Passover and the New Moon. On those days when reciting *hallel* is merely a custom, an abridged version of *hallel* is recited. With regard to those days, there are differing opinions among the authorities as to whether or not the congregation, as opposed to an individual, recites the entire *hallel*, and whether or not one recites a blessing over the abridged version of *hallel*.

**HALAKHA**

**And may one interrupt during the Megilla – וּבִמְגִילָּה מַהוּ שֶׁיַּפְסִיק:** One may not interrupt and engage in conversation during the reading the scroll of Esther. This ruling applies specifically to the listeners who are liable to miss hearing part of the reading if they do so. The reader, however, may interrupt his reading with the same restrictions as one reciting *Shema* (*Mishna Berura; Shulḥan Arukh, Oraḥ Ḥayyim* 692:2).

**Interruption in *hallel* – הַפְסָקָה בְּהַלֵּל:** On days when one recites the entire *hallel*, the same restrictions apply with regard to interruptions as one reciting *Shema*. On days when one does not recite the entire *hallel*, one may interrupt due to respect and respond with a greeting to any person, even in the middle of a paragraph (Rambam *Sefer Zemanim, Hilkhot Megilla VaḤanukka* 3:9; *Shulḥan Arukh, Oraḥ Ḥayyim* 422:4, 488:1, 644:1).

אָמַר לֵיהּ: טוֹעֵם וְאֵין בְּכָךְ כְּלוּם. תַּנְיָא נַמִי הָכִי: מַטְעֶמֶת אֵינָהּ טְעוּנָה בְּרָכָה, וְהַשָּׁרוּי בְּתַעֲנִית טוֹעֵם וְאֵין בְּכָךְ כְּלוּם.

Rabbi Ami **said to him: He tastes and it is of no concern. This was also taught** in a *baraita*: **Tasting** a cooked dish **does not require a blessing**[H] beforehand, **and one who is fasting** may **taste and it is of no concern.**[H]

עַד כַּמָּה?

The Gemara asks: **How much** may one who is fasting taste?

רַבִּי אַמִי וְרַבִּי אַסִי טָעֲמֵי עַד שִׁיעוּר רְבִיעְתָּא.

The Gemara responds: When **Rabbi Ami and Rabbi Asi** would fast, **they would taste up to a quarter** of a *log*.[B]

אָמַר רַב: כָּל הַנּוֹתֵן שָׁלוֹם לַחֲבֵירוֹ קוֹדֶם שֶׁיִּתְפַּלֵּל – כְּאִילּוּ עֲשָׂאוֹ בָּמָה, שֶׁנֶּאֱמַר: ״חִדְלוּ לָכֶם מִן הָאָדָם אֲשֶׁר נְשָׁמָה בְּאַפּוֹ כִּי בַמֶּה נֶחְשָׁב הוּא״, אַל תִּקְרֵי ״בַּמֶּה״ אֶלָּא ״בָּמָה״.

**Rav said: Anyone who greets another** person in the morning **before he prayed,**[NH] **it is as if he built an altar** for idol worship, **as it is stated: "Cease you from man, in whose nostrils there is breath, for how little is he to be accounted"** (Isaiah 2:22). When one's soul is breathed in through his nostrils in the morning (*ge'onim*) he should turn to no one other than God. **And do not read** it as it is written, ***bameh*, how; but rather,** read ***bama*, altar.**

וּשְׁמוּאֵל אָמַר: בַּמֶּה חֲשַׁבְתּוֹ לָזֶה וְלֹא לֶאֱלוֹהַּ.

**And Shmuel said:** The word *bameh* should not be taken in anything other than its literal connotation. The verse must therefore be understood: **How did you consider him** so significant, that you gave him priority **and not God?** Certainly you should have honored God first.

מְתִיב רַב שֵׁשֶׁת: ״בַּפְּרָקִים – שׁוֹאֵל מִפְּנֵי הַכָּבוֹד וּמֵשִׁיב״!

**Rav Sheshet raises an objection:** We learned in our mishna that **in the breaks** between the **paragraphs one may greet** an individual **due to respect, and respond** to another's greeting due to respect, despite the fact that the recitation of *Shema* precedes the *Amida* prayer.

תַּרְגְּמָהּ רַבִּי אַבָּא: בְּמַשְׁכִּים לְפִתְחוֹ.

**Rabbi Abba explained this:** The prohibition against greeting another in the morning refers specifically to **when one** sets out **early to** greet him at **his door.** If one simply happens to encounter another person, he is permitted to greet him.

אָמַר רַבִּי יוֹנָה אָמַר רַבִּי זֵירָא: כָּל הָעוֹשֶׂה חֲפָצָיו קוֹדֶם שֶׁיִּתְפַּלֵּל – כְּאִלּוּ בָּנָה בָּמָה. אָמְרוּ לוֹ: בָּמָה אֲמַרְתְּ? אָמַר לְהוּ: לָא, אָסוּר קָא אָמִינָא,

With regard to this same verse, **Rabbi Yona**[P] **said** that **Rabbi Zeira said: Anyone who tends to his own affairs before he prays, it is as though he built an altar. They said to** Rabbi Yona: **Did you say** that it was as if one built **an altar?** Rabbi Yona **responded to them: No; I said** simply that it is **prohibited.**

וְכִדְרַב אִידִי בַּר אָבִין. דְּאָמַר רַב אִידִי בַּר אָבִין אָמַר רַב יִצְחָק בַּר אָשְׁיָאן: אָסוּר לוֹ לָאָדָם לַעֲשׂוֹת חֲפָצָיו קוֹדֶם שֶׁיִּתְפַּלֵּל, שֶׁנֶּאֱמַר: ״צֶדֶק לְפָנָיו יְהַלֵּךְ וְיָשֵׂם לְדֶרֶךְ פְּעָמָיו״.

**And as Rav Idi bar Avin said** that **Rav Yitzḥak bar Ashyan said: A person is prohibited to attend to his own affairs before he prays,**[H] **as it is stated: "Righteousness shall go before Him, and shall make His footsteps on a path"** (Psalms 85:14). One should first pray and acknowledge the righteousness of his Creator, and only then should he set out on his way.

וְאָמַר רַב אִידִי בַּר אָבִין אָמַר רַב יִצְחָק בַּר אָשְׁיָאן: כָּל הַמִּתְפַּלֵּל וְאַחַר כָּךְ יוֹצֵא לַדֶּרֶךְ – הַקָּדוֹשׁ בָּרוּךְ הוּא עוֹשֶׂה לוֹ חֲפָצָיו, שֶׁנֶּאֱמַר: ״צֶדֶק לְפָנָיו יְהַלֵּךְ וְיָשֵׂם לְדֶרֶךְ פְּעָמָיו״.

And, **Rav Idi bar Avin said** that **Rav Yitzḥak bar Ashyan said: Anyone who** first **prays** and only **then sets out on his way, the Holy One, Blessed be He, tends to his affairs, as it is stated: "Righteousness shall go before Him, and shall make His footsteps on a path."** God will set righteousness before him and satisfy all his wishes, when he sets out on his way.

וְאָמַר רַבִּי יוֹנָה אָמַר רַבִּי זֵירָא: כָּל הַלָּן שִׁבְעַת יָמִים בְּלֹא חֲלוֹם נִקְרָא רַע, שֶׁנֶּאֱמַר: ״וְשָׂבֵעַ יָלִין בַּל יִפָּקֶד רָע״, אַל תִּקְרֵי שָׂבֵעַ אֶלָּא שֶׁבַע.

Having mentioned his name, the Gemara tangentially cites what **Rabbi Yona said** that **Rabbi Zeira said: One who goes seven nights without a dream, is called evil, as it is stated: "He who has it will abide satisfied [*save'a*], he will not be visited by evil"** (Proverbs 19:23). Rabbi Yona reinterprets the verse: **Do not read *save'a*, satisfied, but *sheva*, seven.** One who sleeps for seven nights without being visited by a dream, is called evil.

### BACKGROUND

**Quarter of a *log* – רְבִיעִית:** A unit of liquid volume, which serves as the standard unit of measurement in certain matters. For example, a quarter of a *log* is the minimum amount of wine over which *kiddush* may be recited; the amount of wine which a nazirite is flogged for drinking; and the minimum amount of certain foods for whose transfer from one domain to another one is liable on Shabbat. A quarter of a *log* of blood from a corpse imparts ritual impurity. In contemporary terms, the exact amount of a quarter of a *log* is subject to dispute among authorities with opinions ranging from 60 to 120 cubic centimeters.

### NOTES

**Anyone who greets another person before he prayed – הַנּוֹתֵן שָׁלוֹם לַחֲבֵירוֹ קוֹדֶם שֶׁיִּתְפַּלֵּל וכו׳:** Some explained that the prohibition is primarily due to the fact that when greeting a person, it is customary to politely bow. In so doing, it is as if one is bowing before another prior to bowing before God (*Halakhot Gedolot Asfamia; ge'onim*).

### PERSONALITIES

**Rabbi Yona – רַבִּי יוֹנָה:** One of the great *amora'im* of Eretz Yisrael, Rabbi Yona lived in the third generation of *amora'im* and was the primary student of Rabbi Zeira.

Rabbi Yona was among the prominent Sages of his generation in Eretz Yisrael, and was famous for his Torah erudition as well as his extreme righteousness. According to the Babylonian Talmud, he was one of "the mighty" of Eretz Yisrael. However, he was exceedingly humble and did not flaunt his greatness. Various stories illustrate his righteousness and describe miracles performed through the power of his prayer. His statements are rarely cited in the Babylonian Talmud; however, from the Jerusalem Talmud it is clear that he was one of the pillars of Torah in his generation, and many halakhic statements are cited in his name. Most Sages of the following generation in Eretz Yisrael were his students who transmitted his teachings. Rabbi Yona's son, Rabbi Mana, was one of the renowned Sages of the next generation.

### HALAKHA

**Tasting does not require a blessing – מַטְעֶמֶת אֵינָהּ טְעוּנָה בְּרָכָה:** If one takes a taste from a dish and spits it out, he need not recite a blessing at all, even if he tasted more than a quarter of a *log*. If he intends to swallow more than a quarter of a *log*, he must recite a blessing before tasting it. If he intends to swallow less than a quarter of a *log*, some say that he need not recite a blessing while others say that he does. The Rema rules that one need not recite a blessing because the *halakha* is lenient with regard to blessings in cases of uncertainty. The *Magen Avraham*, however, is strict (see *Ateret Zahav*; Rambam *Sefer Ahava, Hilkhot Berakhot* 1:2; *Shulḥan Arukh, Oraḥ Ḥayyim* 210:2 and Rema there).

**One who is fasting tastes and it is of no concern – וְהַשָּׁרוּי בְּתַעֲנִית טוֹעֵם וְאֵין בְּכָךְ כְּלוּם:** One who is fasting may taste up to a quarter of a *log*, as long as he spits it out. On Yom Kippur and the Ninth of Av, even that is prohibited. Others are strict and refrain from tasting on all communal fast days, and that is the common practice (*Tosafot*; Rambam *Sefer Zemanim, Hilkhot Ta'aniyot* 1:14; *Shulḥan Arukh, Oraḥ Ḥayyim* 567:1).

**Anyone who greets another person before he prayed – כָּל הַנּוֹתֵן שָׁלוֹם לַחֲבֵירוֹ קוֹדֶם שֶׁיִּתְפַּלֵּל:** One is prohibited from going to greet someone at his home before reciting the morning prayer. If he met him by chance, he may greet him, but not include "Shalom" in the greeting as it is one of God's names (Rambam *Sefer Ahava, Hilkhot Tefilla* 6:4; *Shulḥan Arukh, Oraḥ Ḥayyim* 89:2).

**A person is prohibited to attend to his own affairs before he prays – אָסוּר לוֹ לָאָדָם לַעֲשׂוֹת חֲפָצָיו קוֹדֶם שֶׁיִּתְפַּלֵּל:** Once the time for prayer has arrived, one may not attend to his own affairs or to travel before he prays. This law applies equally to all prayers (*Mishna Berura*; *Shulḥan Arukh, Oraḥ Ḥayyim* 89:3).

אֲמַר לֵיהּ רַב אַחָא בְּרֵיהּ דְּרַבִּי חִיָּיא בַּר אַבָּא, הָכִי אָמַר רַבִּי חִיָּיא אָמַר רַבִּי יוֹחָנָן: כׇּל הַמַּשְׂבִּיעַ עַצְמוֹ מִדִּבְרֵי תוֹרָה וְלָן – אֵין מְבַשְּׂרִין אוֹתוֹ בְּשׂוֹרוֹת רָעוֹת, שֶׁנֶּאֱמַר: וְשָׂבֵעַ יָלִין בַּל יִפָּקֶד רָע.

**Rav Aḥa, son of Rabbi Ḥiyya bar Abba, said to him: Rabbi Ḥiyya said** that **Rabbi Yoḥanan said as follows: Anyone who fills himself with matters of Torah and goes to sleep, they do not deliver evil tidings to him, as it is stated: "He who lies satisfied, will not be visited by evil."**

אֵלּוּ הֵן בֵּין הַפְּרָקִים וכו׳.

We learned in the mishna: **These are** the breaks **between the paragraphs** at which one is permitted to interrupt under certain circumstances. According to the first *tanna*, one may interrupt between the last paragraph of *Shema* and the blessing that follows it, but Rabbi Yehuda prohibits this.

אָמַר רַבִּי אַבָּהוּ אָמַר רַבִּי יוֹחָנָן: הֲלָכָה כְּרַבִּי יְהוּדָה דְּאָמַר, בֵּין ״אֱלֹהֵיכֶם״ לֶ״אֱמֶת וְיַצִּיב״ לֹא יַפְסִיק. אֲמַר רַבִּי אַבָּהוּ אָמַר רַבִּי יוֹחָנָן: מַאי טַעְמֵיהּ דְּרַבִּי יְהוּדָה – דִּכְתִיב:

**Rabbi Abbahu said** that **Rabbi Yoḥanan said: The *halakha* is in accordance with** the opinion of **Rabbi Yehuda who said that one may not interrupt between *eloheikhem* and *emet veyatziv*.**[H] Furthermore, **Rabbi Abbahu said** that **Rabbi Yoḥanan said: What is the reason for Rabbi Yehuda's** opinion? This phrase evokes the verse **as it is written:**

HALAKHA

**One may not interrupt between *eloheikhem* and *emet veyatziv* – בֵּין ״אֱלֹהֵיכֶם״ לֶ״אֱמֶת וְיַצִּיב״ לֹא יַפְסִיק:** One may not interrupt or pause between the end of the third paragraph of *Shema* and the beginning of the following blessing, *emet veyatziv*, in accordance with the opinion of Rabbi Yehuda (Rambam *Sefer Ahava, Hilkhot Keriat Shema* 2:17; *Shulḥan Arukh, Oraḥ Ḥayyim* 66:5).

Perek **II**
Daf **14** Amud **b**

״וַה׳ אֱלֹהִים אֱמֶת״.

**"And the Lord, God, is True"** (Jeremiah 10:10).

חוֹזֵר וְאוֹמֵר אֱמֶת, אוֹ אֵינוֹ חוֹזֵר וְאוֹמֵר אֱמֶת?

After the conclusion of the final paragraph of *Shema* along with the first word of the subsequent blessing, with the words: "The Lord, your God, is True [*Hashem Eloheikhem emet*]," the question is posed: **Does one repeat *emet*** when he begins the blessing of *emet veyatziv*, **or does he not repeat *emet*?**

אָמַר רַבִּי אַבָּהוּ אָמַר רַבִּי יוֹחָנָן: חוֹזֵר וְאוֹמֵר אֱמֶת. רַבָּה אָמַר: אֵינוֹ חוֹזֵר וְאוֹמֵר אֱמֶת. הַהוּא דְּנָחֵית קַמֵּיהּ דְּרַבָּה, שְׁמַעֵיהּ רַבָּה דַּאֲמַר אֱמֶת אֱמֶת תְּרֵי זִימְנֵי; אֲמַר רַבָּה: כׇּל אֱמֶת אֱמֶת תְּפַסֵּיהּ לְהַאי!

**Rabbi Abbahu said** that **Rabbi Yoḥanan said: He repeats *emet*. Rabba said: He does not repeat *emet*.**[H] The Gemara relates: **This person who descended** to lead the service **before Rabba, Rabba heard that he said *emet, emet*[N] twice. Rabba** mocked him and **said: Every *emet, emet* has caught this one;** he must be passionate about the pursuit of truth.

אֲמַר רַב יוֹסֵף: כַּמָּה מְעַלְיָא הָא שְׁמַעְתָּא, דְּכִי אֲתָא רַב שְׁמוּאֵל בַּר יְהוּדָה, אֲמַר, אָמְרִי בְּמַעֲרָבָא: עַרְבִית – ״דַּבֵּר אֶל בְּנֵי יִשְׂרָאֵל וְאָמַרְתָּ אֲלֵיהֶם אֲנִי ה׳ אֱלֹהֵיכֶם אֱמֶת״.

**Rav Yosef said: How excellent is this tradition** that I heard, **as when Rav Shmuel bar Yehuda came** from Eretz Yisrael to Babylonia he said: **In Eretz Yisrael, at the evening prayer** they do not recite the entire third portion of *Shema*, which deals with ritual fringes, as there is no obligation to wear ritual fringes at night. Rather, **they say**[N] a condensed version of that portion that includes an excerpt from the beginning and an excerpt from the end: **"Speak to the children of Israel and say to them… I am the Lord, your God, True"** (Numbers 15:38, 41).

אֲמַר לֵיהּ אַבַּיֵי: מַאי מַעַלְיוּתָא? וְהָא אָמַר רַב כָּהֲנָא אָמַר רַב: לֹא יַתְחִיל, וְאִם הִתְחִיל – גּוֹמֵר! וְכִי תֵּימָא וְאָמַרְתָּ אֲלֵיהֶם לָא הָוֵי הַתְחָלָה – וְהָאֲמַר רַב שְׁמוּאֵל בַּר יִצְחָק אָמַר רַב: דַּבֵּר אֶל בְּנֵי יִשְׂרָאֵל – לָא הָוֵי הַתְחָלָה, וְאָמַרְתָּ אֲלֵיהֶם – הָוֵי הַתְחָלָה!

**Abaye said to him: What is excellent** about this tradition? **Didn't Rav Kahana say** that **Rav said: One** should **not begin** to recite the portion of ritual fringes at night, **but if he does begin, he completes** it? **And if you say that:** Speak to the children of Israel **and say to them, is not considered the beginning** of the portion of ritual fringes, **didn't Rav Shmuel bar Yitzḥak say** that **Rav said: Speak to the children of Israel, is not** considered **a beginning** of the portion of ritual fringes, as many passages in the Torah begin this way; **and say to them,** is considered **a beginning.**

אֲמַר רַב פַּפָּא: קָסָבְרִי בְּמַעֲרָבָא, וְאָמַרְתָּ אֲלֵיהֶם – נַמִי לָא הָוְיָא הַתְחָלָה, עַד דְּאָמַר ״וְעָשׂוּ לָהֶם צִיצִת״.

**Rav Pappa said: In Eretz Yisrael, they hold** that **and say to them, is not** considered **a beginning, until he said: And make for them ritual fringes.**

אֲמַר אַבַּיֵי: הִלְכָּךְ, אֲנַן אַתְחוּלֵי מַתְחִלִינַן – דְּקָא מַתְחְלֵי בְּמַעֲרָבָא, וְכֵיוָן דְּאַתְחִלִינַן – מִגְמַר נַמִי גָּמְרִינַן, דְּהָא אָמַר רַב כָּהֲנָא אָמַר רַב: לֹא יַתְחִיל, וְאִם הִתְחִיל – גּוֹמֵר.

**Abaye said:** Therefore, **we begin** to recite the portion of ritual fringes, **since they begin** to recite it **in Eretz Yisrael. And once we begin** to recite it, **we complete it as well, as Rav Kahana said** that **Rav said:** One should **not begin** to recite the portion of ritual fringes at night, **but if he does begin, he completes** it.

HALAKHA

**He does not repeat *emet* – אֵינוֹ חוֹזֵר וְאוֹמֵר ״אֱמֶת״:** One who concluded the last paragraph of *Shema* with the word *emet* and stopped due to respect or fear, need not repeat *emet* when he begins to recite the blessing of *emet veyatziv*, in accordance with the statement and the practice of Rabba (*Shulḥan Arukh, Oraḥ Ḥayyim* 66:6).

NOTES

**Emet, emet – אֱמֶת, אֱמֶת:** One who repeats the word "true" following his recitation of the *Shema* does not thereby reinforce his declaration; rather, on the contrary, he undermines the unity of the "truth." It is similar to one who repeats *Shema* (*HaBoneh*).

**In Eretz Yisrael…they say – אָמְרִי בְּמַעֲרָבָא וכו׳:** That sequence of verses as recited in Eretz Yisrael creates various problems. Many commented on the halakhic problems inherent in truncating and dividing verses (Rashba). Some explained that although the passage recited is a fragment of the verse in Numbers, it does constitute an entire verse in Leviticus 18:2. That is why Rav Yosef was excited by this combination of verses; it was accomplished without dividing the verse (*Yad HaMelekh* and others).

חִיָּיא בַּר רַב אָמַר: אָמַר "אֲנִי ה' אֱלֹהֵיכֶם" – צָרִיךְ לוֹמַר "אֱמֶת", לֹא אָמַר "אֲנִי ה' אֱלֹהֵיכֶם" – אֵינוֹ צָרִיךְ לוֹמַר "אֱמֶת".

**Ḥiyya bar Rav**[P] **said: If** in the evening **one recited** the portion of ritual fringes concluding with: **I am the Lord, your God, he must recite: True** and Faithful [*emet ve'emuna*], and the entire blessing of redemption. However, **if he did not recite: I am the Lord, your God, he need not recite** ***emet*** *ve'emuna*.

וְהָא בָּעֵי לְאַדְכּוּרֵי יְצִיאַת מִצְרַיִם!

The Gemara asks: **Isn't he required to mention the exodus from Egypt** at night as well?

דְּאָמַר הָכִי: מוֹדִים אֲנַחְנוּ לָךְ ה' אֱלֹהֵינוּ שֶׁהוֹצֵאתָנוּ מֵאֶרֶץ מִצְרַיִם וּפְדִיתָנוּ מִבֵּית עֲבָדִים וְעָשִׂיתָ לָנוּ נִסִּים וּגְבוּרוֹת עַל הַיָּם וְשַׁרְנוּ לָךְ.

The Gemara responds: In place of reciting *emet ve'emuna* **he said the following** shorter passage: **We give thanks to You, Lord, our God, Who took us out from Egypt and redeemed us from the house of bondage, and performed miracles and mighty deeds on our behalf on the sea, and we sang unto You,** as this formula includes all of the content comprising *emet ve'emuna*.

אָמַר רַבִּי יְהוֹשֻׁעַ בֶּן קָרְחָה, לָמָּה קָדְמָה פָּרָשַׁת שְׁמַע וכו'.

We learned in the mishna: **Rabbi Yehoshua ben Korḥa**[P] **said: Why did the portion of** ***Shema*** **precede** that of *VeHaya im Shamoa*? So that one will first accept upon himself the yoke of the kingdom of Heaven and only then accept upon himself the yoke of the mitzvot.

תַּנְיָא, רַבִּי שִׁמְעוֹן בֶּן יוֹחַי אוֹמֵר: בְּדִין הוּא שֶׁיַּקְדִּים שְׁמַע לִוְהָיָה אִם שָׁמוֹעַ – שֶׁזֶּה לִלְמוֹד וְזֶה לְלַמֵּד; וְהָיָה אִם שָׁמוֹעַ לְוַיֹּאמֶר – שֶׁזֶּה לְלַמּוֹד וְזֶה לַעֲשׂוֹת.

**It was taught** in a *baraita* that **Rabbi Shimon ben Yoḥai** offers a different explanation for the order of the portions of *Shema*. He **says: By right,** ***Shema*** **should precede** ***VeHaya im Shamoa*** **because** the *Shema* includes the directive **to learn, while** *VeHaya im Shamoa* includes the directive **to teach.** Similarly, ***VeHaya im Shamoa*** should precede ***VaYomer,*** the final paragraph of *Shema*, because *VeHaya im Shamoa* includes the directive **to teach, while** the portion of ritual fringes includes the directive **to perform.**

אַטּוּ שְׁמַע, לִלְמוֹד אִית בֵּיהּ, לְלַמֵּד וְלַעֲשׂוֹת לֵית בֵּיהּ? וְהָא כְּתִיב: וְשִׁנַּנְתָּם, וּקְשַׁרְתָּם, וּכְתַבְתָּם! וְתוּ, וְהָיָה אִם שָׁמוֹעַ, לְלַמֵּד הוּא דְּאִית בֵּיהּ, וְלַעֲשׂוֹת לֵית בֵּיהּ? וְהָא כְּתִיב: וּקְשַׁרְתֶּם, וּכְתַבְתֶּם!

The Gemara asks: **Is that to say that** the portion of ***Shema*** **contains** the directive **to learn** but **it does not contain** the directive **to teach and perform? Isn't it written: "And you shall teach them** to your children" (Deuteronomy 6:7), a directive to teach, as well as: **"And you shall bind them** as a sign upon your arm" (Deuteronomy 6:8) and: **"And write them** on your door posts of your house" (Deuteronomy 6:9), directives to perform? **Furthermore, does** ***VeHaya im Shamoa*** **contain** the directive **to teach** but **it does not contain** the directive **to perform? Isn't it written: "And you shall bind them** as a sign upon your arm" (Deuteronomy 11:18), a directive to perform?

אֶלָּא הָכִי קָאָמַר: בְּדִין הוּא שֶׁתִּקְדַּם שְׁמַע לִוְהָיָה אִם שָׁמוֹעַ – שֶׁזֶּה לִלְמוֹד וּלְלַמֵּד וְלַעֲשׂוֹת, וְהָיָה אִם שָׁמוֹעַ לְוַיֹּאמֶר – שֶׁזֶּה יֵשׁ בָּהּ לְלַמֵּד וְלַעֲשׂוֹת, וַיֹּאמֶר – אֵין בָּהּ אֶלָּא לַעֲשׂוֹת בִּלְבַד.

**Rather,** Rabbi Shimon ben Yoḥai **said as follows: By right,** the portion of ***Shema*** **should precede** ***VeHaya im Shamoa*** **because** the portion of *Shema* includes the directives **to learn, to teach, and to perform,** while *VeHaya im Shamoa* includes the directives to teach and to perform. ***VeHaya im Shamoa*** **should precede** ***VaYomer*** **because** *VeHaya im Shamoa* includes the directives **to teach and to perform, while** *VaYomer* **only** includes the directive **to perform.**

וְתִיפּוֹק לֵיהּ מִדְּרַבִּי יְהוֹשֻׁעַ בֶּן קָרְחָה! חֲדָא וְעוֹד קָאָמַר; חֲדָא – כְּדֵי שֶׁיְּקַבֵּל עָלָיו עוֹל מַלְכוּת שָׁמַיִם תְּחִלָּה וְאַחַר כָּךְ יְקַבֵּל עָלָיו עוֹל מִצְוֹת, וְעוֹד – מִשּׁוּם דְּאִית בָּהּ הָנֵי מִילֵּי אַחֲרָנְיָיתָא.

The Gemara asks: **Let him derive this,** that the portion of *Shema* is recited first, **from** the statement of **Rabbi Yehoshua ben Korḥa.** The Gemara responds: **He stated one** reason **and another.** Rabbi Shimon ben Yoḥai does not disagree with Rabbi Yehoshua ben Korḥa; he simply suggested as additional explanation as follows: **One** reason the portion of *Shema* is recited first is **so that one will first accept the yoke of the kingdom of Heaven upon himself and afterward the yoke of the mitzvot; and** the second reason is **because** the portion of *Shema* **contains these other elements** as well.

**PERSONALITIES**

Ḥiyya bar Rav – חִיָּיא בַּר רַב: A Babylonian *amora*, the son of Rav. Although Rav had additional descendants, only Ḥiyya followed in his footsteps and became one of the prominent Sages of his generation.

We know that during Rav's life as well as after his death, Rav's students looked after Ḥiyya. Even Rav's close friend, Shmuel, treated Ḥiyya fondly, because of his relationship with his father.

Rav loved his son dearly, and even when he was a child, Rav took great pleasure in his son's wisdom. Since Ḥiyya suffered from ill health, Rav gave him various bits of medical advice.

Ḥiyya's son, Rav Shimi bar Ḥiyya, was among the great *amora'im* of the next generation.

Rabbi Yehoshua ben Korḥa – רַבִּי יְהוֹשֻׁעַ בֶּן קָרְחָה: One of the elder *tanna'im* in the generation of Rabban Shimon ben Gamliel II. Many commentaries (*Tosafot* and others) identify him as Rabbi Yehoshua the son of Rabbi Akiva, but others question this.

Little is known of Rabbi Yehoshua ben Korḥa's personality, and relatively few statements of *halakha* or *aggada* were cited in his name.

Rabbi Yehoshua ben Korḥa lived such a long life that he blessed Rabbi Yehuda HaNasi: May it be God's will that you reach half my days. Because he lived such a long life, he can be found in exchanges with Sages from several generations. By the end of his life, he was accepted and respected by all, the Sages of his generation sought his blessing and he would take the initiative to seek out others and offer them his guidance.

רַב מָשֵׁי יְדֵיהּ וּקְרָא קְרִיאַת שְׁמַע, וְאַנַּח תְּפִילִּין, וְצַלֵּי. וְהֵיכִי עָבֵיד הָכִי? וְהָתַנְיָא: הַחוֹפֵר כּוּךְ לְמֵת בְּקֶבֶר – פָּטוּר מִקְּרִיאַת שְׁמַע וּמִן הַתְּפִלָּה וּמִן הַתְּפִילִּין וּמִכָּל מִצְוֹת הָאֲמוּרוֹת בַּתּוֹרָה, הִגִּיעַ זְמַן קְרִיאַת שְׁמַע – עוֹלֶה וְנוֹטֵל יָדָיו וּמַנִּיחַ תְּפִילִּין וְקוֹרֵא קְרִיאַת שְׁמַע וּמִתְפַּלֵּל!

The Gemara relates: **Rav washed his hands, recited *Shema*,**[H] **donned phylacteries, and prayed** in that order. The Gemara asks: **How could he do that? Wasn't it taught** in a *baraita*: **One who digs a grave for the dead**[BH] in the wall of the family burial cave **is exempt from the recitation of *Shema*, from prayer, from phylacteries, and from all mitzvot mentioned in the Torah.**[N] When **the** appointed **time for the recitation of *Shema* arrives, he emerges** from the cave, **washes his hands, dons phylacteries, recites *Shema*, and prays.**

הָא גוּפָא קַשְׁיָא! רֵישָׁא אָמַר פָּטוּר, וְסֵיפָא חַיָּיב!

Before clarifying the problem, the Gemara comments: **This** *baraita* **itself is difficult;** it appears to be contradictory. **The first clause** of the *baraita* **stated** that one digging a grave **is exempt** from the recitation of *Shema*, **and the latter clause** stated that **he is obligated** to emerge and recite *Shema*

הָא לָא קַשְׁיָא: סֵיפָא – בִּתְרֵי, וְרֵישָׁא – בְּחַד.

The Gemara responds: **That is not difficult. The latter clause** of the *baraita* refers to a case **of two** individuals digging the grave together; one pauses to recite *Shema* while the other continues digging. **The first clause** of the *baraita* refers to a case **of one** individual digging alone, who may not stop.

מִכָּל מָקוֹם קַשְׁיָא לְרַב! – רַב כְּרַבִּי יְהוֹשֻׁעַ בֶּן קָרְחָה סְבִירָא לֵיהּ, דְּאָמַר: עוֹל מַלְכוּת שָׁמַיִם תְּחִלָּה וְאַחַר כָּךְ עוֹל מִצְוֹת.

**In any case, this** *baraita* **contradicts Rav** in terms of the order in which the mitzvot are performed. The Gemara responds: **Rav holds in accordance with** the opinion of **Rabbi Yehoshua ben Korḥa, who said** that the acceptance of **the yoke of the kingdom of Heaven** takes precedence and should **come first, followed by** the acceptance of **the yoke of the mitzvot.** Therefore, Rav first recited *Shema*, and only then donned phylacteries.

אֵימַר דְּאָמַר רַבִּי יְהוֹשֻׁעַ בֶּן קָרְחָה – לְהַקְדִּים קְרִיאָה לִקְרִיאָה, קְרִיאָה לַעֲשִׂיָּה מִי שָׁמְעַתְּ לֵיהּ?

The Gemara challenges: **Say that Rabbi Yehoshua ben Korḥa said** to **give precedence to recitation** of the portion concerning the acceptance of the yoke of the kingdom of Heaven over **recitation** of other portions. But **did you hear him** say the *halakha* gives precedence to **recitation over performance?**

וְתוּ, מִי סָבַר לֵיהּ כְּרַבִּי יְהוֹשֻׁעַ בֶּן קָרְחָה? וְהָאָמַר רַב חִיָּיא בַּר אַשִׁי: זִמְנִין סַגִּיאִין הֲוָה קָאֵימְנָא קַמֵּיהּ דְּרַב, וּמַקְדִּים וּמָשֵׁי יְדֵיהּ וּמְבָרֵךְ וּמַתְנֵי לָן פִּרְקִין, וּמַנַּח תְּפִילִּין וַהֲדַר קָרֵי קְרִיאַת שְׁמַע! וְכִי תֵּימָא בִּדְלָא מְטָא זְמַן קְרִיאַת שְׁמַע – אִם כֵּן, מַאי אַסְהֲדָתֵיהּ דְּרַב חִיָּיא בַּר אַשִׁי!

**And furthermore, does** Rav **really hold in accordance with** the opinion of **Rabbi Yehoshua ben Korḥa? But didn't Rav Ḥiyya bar Ashi say: Many times I stood before Rav, and he first washed his hands, recited a blessing, taught us our lesson, donned phylacteries, and then recited *Shema*. And if you say:** This was when **the time for the recitation of *Shema* had not** yet **arrived** and that is why he donned his phylacteries first, **then what is** the point of **the testimony of Rav Ḥiyya bar Ashi?**

לְאַפּוֹקֵי מִמַּאן דְּאָמַר לְמִשְׁנָה אֵין צָרִיךְ לְבָרֵךְ. קָמַשְׁמַע לָן דְּאַף לְמִשְׁנָה נַמִי צָרִיךְ לְבָרֵךְ.

The Gemara responds: Rav Ḥiyya bar Ashi's story comes **to exclude** the opinion of **the one who said that one need not recite the blessing** on Torah study **for** the study of **mishna. It teaches us that even for mishna, one must recite a blessing.**

מִכָּל מָקוֹם קַשְׁיָא לְרַב! – שְׁלוּחָא הוּא דְּעַוֵּית.

**In any case** this *baraita* **is difficult for Rav.** The Gemara responds: **The messenger was at fault** and brought Rav his phylacteries late, so Rav recited *Shema* at its appropriate time and later donned phylacteries.

אָמַר עוּלָּא: כָּל הַקּוֹרֵא קְרִיאַת שְׁמַע בְּלֹא תְּפִילִּין – כְּאִילּוּ מֵעִיד עֵדוּת שֶׁקֶר בְּעַצְמוֹ. אָמַר רַבִּי חִיָּיא בַּר אַבָּא אָמַר רַבִּי יוֹחָנָן: כְּאִילּוּ הִקְרִיב עוֹלָה בְּלֹא מִנְחָה וְזֶבַח בְּלֹא נְסָכִים.

With regard to the recitation of *Shema* without phylacteries, **Ulla said: Anyone who recites *Shema* without phylacteries,**[H] **it is as if he has borne false testimony against himself,**[N] as in *Shema*, he mentions his obligation to don phylacteries and in this case fails to don them himself (*Talmidei Rabbeinu Yona*). **Rabbi Ḥiyya bar Abba said that Rabbi Yoḥanan said:** One who recites *Shema* without phylacteries, **it is as if he has offered a burnt-offering without a meal-offering or a peace-offering without libations.** Despite the fact that he fulfilled his obligation, his offering is incomplete.

## HALAKHA

**He washed his hands and recited *Shema* – מָשֵׁי יְדֵיהּ וּקְרָא קְרִיאַת שְׁמַע:** If, due to circumstances beyond his control, one's phylacteries only became available after reciting *Shema*, he should don them immediately, even between the blessing of Redemption and the start of the *Amida* prayer. However, he should not recite the blessing over them until after he completes his prayer. Others hold that, even in that case, he recites a blessing over them immediately (*Peri Ḥadash*; *Shulḥan Arukh, Oraḥ Ḥayyim* 66:8).

**One who digs a grave for the dead – הַחוֹפֵר כּוּךְ לְמֵת:** One who is engaged in digging a grave for the deceased is exempt from reciting *Shema*. If there are two people digging the grave and it is impossible for them to dig together; while one is digging the other should recite *Shema*, and vice-versa. If it is possible for them to dig together they are both exempt (Rambam *Sefer Ahava, Hilkhot Keriat Shema* 4:3; *Shulḥan Arukh, Oraḥ Ḥayyim* 71:5–6).

**One who recites *Shema* without phylacteries – כָּל הַקּוֹרֵא קְרִיאַת שְׁמַע בְּלֹא תְּפִילִּין:** One must don phylacteries while reciting *Shema* (Rambam *Sefer Ahava, Hilkhot Tefillin UMezuza VeSefer Torah* 4:26; *Shulḥan Arukh, Oraḥ Ḥayyim* 25:4).

## BACKGROUND

**A grave for the dead – כּוּךְ לְמֵת:** The coffins, or sarcophagi, were placed in compartments chiseled in the cave walls. The grave would typically be hewn long in advance; however, on occasion they would only begin to dig when the individual died, in which case the work was urgent.

Talmudic era burial cave in Beit She'arim

## NOTES

**One who digs…is exempt from reciting *Shema*…and from all mitzvot mentioned in the Torah – הַחוֹפֵר...פָּטוּר מִקְּרִיאַת שְׁמַע...וּמִכָּל מִצְוֹת וכו׳:** There is an apparent redundancy in the *baraita* as it teaches that one is exempt from the recitation of *Shema* and from all mitzvot mentioned in the Torah. Given that the recitation of *Shema* is itself a mitzva mentioned in the Torah, its mention was unnecessary. Some explained that had the *baraita* merely stated: From all mitzvot mentioned in the Torah, one might have drawn the erroneous conclusion that it is referrinq only to those mitzvot with no set time, which may, therefore, be postponed; not to mitzvot like *Shema* whose time will pass (*Tosefot Rabbeinu Yehuda HaHasid*).

**Anyone who recites *Shema* without phylacteries, it is as if he has borne false testimony against himself – כָּל הַקּוֹרֵא קְרִיאַת שְׁמַע בְּלֹא תְּפִילִּין כְּאִילּוּ מֵעִיד עֵדוּת שֶׁקֶר:** The difference between the statements of Ulla and Rabbi Yoḥanan is that according to Ulla, apparently, reciting *Shema* without phylacteries is inherently flawed, as it is like false testimony. According to Rabbi Yoḥanan, that recitation is indeed lacking, but it may be remedied by donning phylacteries later, much like a libation or meal-offering, which is added after the sacrifice (*Alfasi Zuta*).

וְאָמַר רַבִּי יוֹחָנָן: הָרוֹצֶה שֶׁיְּקַבֵּל עָלָיו עוֹל מַלְכוּת שָׁמַיִם שְׁלֵמָה – יִפָּנֶה וְיִטּוֹל יָדָיו, וְיַנִּיחַ תְּפִילִּין וְיִקְרָא קְרִיאַת שְׁמַע וְיִתְפַּלֵּל, וְזוֹ הִיא מַלְכוּת שָׁמַיִם שְׁלֵמָה.

**And Rabbi Yoḥanan said: One who seeks to accept upon himself the complete yoke of the kingdom of Heaven, should relieve himself, wash his hands,**[H] **don phylacteries, recite *Shema*, and pray, and that is** acceptance of **the complete Kingdom of Heaven.**

אָמַר רַבִּי חִיָּיא בַּר אַבָּא אָמַר רַבִּי יוֹחָנָן: כָּל הַנִּפְנֶה וְנוֹטֵל יָדָיו וּמַנִּיחַ תְּפִילִּין וְקוֹרֵא קְרִיאַת שְׁמַע וּמִתְפַּלֵּל – מַעֲלֶה עָלָיו הַכָּתוּב כְּאִלּוּ בָּנָה מִזְבֵּחַ וְהִקְרִיב עָלָיו קָרְבָּן, דִּכְתִיב: ״אֶרְחַץ בְּנִקָּיוֹן כַּפָּי וַאֲסוֹבְבָה אֶת מִזְבַּחֲךָ ה׳״. אֲמַר לֵיהּ רָבָא: לָא סְבַר לָהּ מָר כְּאִילּוּ טָבַל? דִּכְתִיב: אֶרְחַץ [בְּנִקָּיוֹן] וְלָא כָּתַב, אַרְחִיץ [כַּפָּי].

On a similar note, **Rabbi Ḥiyya bar Abba said** that **Rabbi Yoḥanan said: Anyone who relieves himself, washes his hands, dons phylacteries, recites *Shema*, and prays, the verse ascribes** credit **to him as if he built an altar and offered a sacrifice upon it, as it is written: "I will wash in purity my hands, and I will encircle the altar of the Lord"** (Psalms 26:6). **Rava said to him: Do you not maintain, Master,** that one who does so, **it is as if he immersed** his entire body, **as it is written: "I will wash in purity," and it is not written: "I will wash my hands"?**

אֲמַר לֵיהּ רָבִינָא לְרָבָא: חֲזֵי מָר הַאי צוּרְבָא מֵרַבָּנַן דַּאֲתָא מִמַּעֲרְבָא וְאָמַר: מִי שֶׁאֵין לוֹ מַיִם לִרְחוֹץ יָדָיו – מְקַנֵּחַ יָדָיו בְּעָפָר וּבִצְרוֹר וּבְקֵסָמִית!

**Ravina said to Rava: My Master, look**[N] **at this Torah scholar** [*tzurva merabbanan*][L] **who came from** Eretz Yisrael **and said** something astonishing: **One who has no water with which to wash his hands,** it is sufficient that **he wipes his hands with earth,**[H] **a rock, or a sliver** of wood.

אֲמַר לֵיהּ: שַׁפִּיר קָאָמַר, מִי כְּתִיב, אֶרְחַץ בְּמַיִם? בְּנִקָּיוֹן כְּתִיב – כָּל מִידֵי דִּמְנַקֵּי. דְּהָא רַב חִסְדָּא לַיֵּיט אַמַּאן דִּמְהַדַּר אַמַּיָּא בְּעִידַּן צְלוֹתָא.

Rava **replied to** Ravina: **He spoke well, as, is it written: I will wash with water? In purity, is written** referring to anything that cleans, **as Rav Ḥisda** would **curse one who** went out of his way **to seek water at the time of prayer.**

וְהָנֵי מִילֵּי – לִקְרִיאַת שְׁמַע, אֲבָל לִתְפִלָּה – מְהַדַּר. וְעַד כַּמָּה? עַד פַּרְסָה. וְהָנֵי מִילֵּי – לְקַמֵּיהּ, אֲבָל לַאֲחוֹרֵיהּ – אֲפִילּוּ מִיל אֵינוֹ חוֹזֵר; [וּמִינָּהּ] – מִיל הוּא דְּאֵינוֹ חוֹזֵר, הָא פָּחוֹת מִמִּיל – חוֹזֵר.

With regard to seeking water, the Gemara comments: **This applies only to the recitation of *Shema*,** as the time for its recitation is limited, and if one goes seeking water he may run out of time. **However, for prayer,** which may be recited all day, **one** must go out of his way **to seek** water.[N] **And how** far must one go out of his way to seek water? **As far as a parasang** [*parsa*].[L] **And this,** one *parsa*, **applies only before him but behind him, he need not return even one *mil*.**[L] **From this** one may infer that **he need not return one *mil*, but one must return less than one *mil*.**[H]

מתני׳ הַקּוֹרֵא אֶת שְׁמַע וְלֹא הִשְׁמִיעַ לְאָזְנוֹ – יָצָא; רַבִּי יוֹסֵי אוֹמֵר: לֹא יָצָא.

**MISHNA** **One who recites *Shema* and did not** recite in a manner **audible to his own ear,**[H] either because he read inaudibly or because he is deaf, **fulfilled** his obligation. **Rabbi Yosei says: He did not fulfill** his obligation.

קָרָא וְלֹא דִּקְדֵּק בְּאוֹתִיּוֹתֶיהָ, רַבִּי יוֹסֵי אוֹמֵר: יָצָא, רַבִּי יְהוּדָה אוֹמֵר: לֹא יָצָא.

**One who recited** *Shema* and **was not** sufficiently **precise in** his enunciation of **its letters,**[H] **Rabbi Yosei says: He fulfilled** his obligation. **Rabbi Yehuda says: He did not fulfill** his obligation.

הַקּוֹרֵא לְמַפְרֵעַ – לֹא יָצָא, קָרָא וְטָעָה – יַחֲזוֹר לְמָקוֹם שֶׁטָּעָה.

**One who recited** *Shema* **out of order,**[H] meaning he did not read the verses sequentially, **he did not fulfill** his obligation. **One who recited and erred,**[H] **should return to the place** in *Shema* **that he erred.**

## NOTES

My master, look – חֲזֵי מָר: Ravina's intention was to draw Rava's attention to a seemingly unacceptable practice, until Rava provided a halakhic basis for it.

For prayer one goes out of his way to seek water – לִתְפִלָּה מְהַדַּר: Several reasons were suggested to explain why one need be more exacting with regard to washing his hands prior to prayer than he need be before *Shema*. One approach suggests that in prayer one addresses God directly, in the second person (*Sefer Mitzvot Gadol*). Others explained that this refers specifically to communal prayer in a synagogue (Rashi) but for individual prayer there is no difference between prayer and *Shema*. Yet others understand this *halakha* to the contrary: Since prayer is actually less significant than *Shema*, one may postpone praying to look for water, whereas reciting *Shema* may not be postponed as it has a set time (Rashi) and it is a mitzva by Torah law (Rashba).

## LANGUAGE

Torah scholar [*tzurva merabbanan*] – צוּרְבָא מֵרַבָּנַן: This appellation for a Torah scholar is commonly used throughout the Talmud; however, its source and precise meaning are unclear. Some say that it derives from the word *tzarav*, sear, as in something seared by the fire of Torah. Others say that the word *tzarav* derives from the Arabic word meaning hard and strong, in which case the phrase itself would refer to a Sage who is forceful and incisive (Rav Hai Gaon).

Parasang [*parsa*] – פַּרְסָה: The *parsa* is a Persian unit of distance. The word derives from the middle Persian frasang and the modern Persian farsang. From there, the word was adopted by other Semitic languages, such as the Syrian *parsha*, and the Greek παρασάγγης, *parasangès*. One *parsa* equals four *mil*.

*Mil* – מִיל: A unit of distance. Presumably, the word derives from the Roman *mille*, although their distance is almost certainly not identical. The Roman mile was 1,000 steps, about 1,490 m; however, the Sages established a *mil* as 2,000 cubits, which is certainly a shorter distance. Recent authorities disputed the length of this measurement. Rav Ḥayyim Na'e holds that one *mil* is about 960 m, while the Ḥazon Ish maintains that it is almost 1,200 m.

## HALAKHA

One should relieve himself and wash his hands – יִפָּנֶה וְיִטּוֹל יָדָיו: One must examine himself to determine whether or not he needs to relieve himself before prayer (*Shulḥan Arukh, Oraḥ Ḥayyim* 92:1).

If one has no water with which to wash his hands he wipes his hands with earth – מִי שֶׁאֵין לוֹ מַיִם לִרְחוֹץ יָדָיו מְקַנֵּחַ יָדָיו בְּעָפָר: If there is water available, one must wash his hands before prayer, even if they are not dirty. If there is no water available, he should wipe his hands with any substance that cleans (Rambam *Sefer Ahava, Hilkhot Keriat Shema* 3:1, *Hilkhot Tefilla* 4:2–3; *Shulḥan Arukh, Oraḥ Ḥayyim* 4:22, 92:4, 233:2).

Searching for water to wash before prayer – חִיפּוּשׂ מַיִם לִרְחוֹץ לִתְפִלָּה: One must seek water to wash his hands before prayer. If he is proceeding in the direction that he was originally headed, he must continue to look for water for up to a *parsa*; if he is retracing his steps, up to one *mil*. If he is concerned that while he is searching for water the time for prayer will pass, he need not search, but should instead wipe his hands on any substance that cleans (Rambam *Sefer Ahava, Hilkhot Keriat Shema* 3:1, *Hilkhot Tefilla* 4:2–3; *Shulḥan Arukh, Oraḥ Ḥayyim* 92:4).

One who recites *Shema* and did not recite it so it was audible to his own ear – הַקּוֹרֵא אֶת שְׁמַע וְלֹא הִשְׁמִיעַ לְאָזְנוֹ: One must recite *Shema* and its blessings in a manner that is audible to his own ear. If he did not recite it audibly, but mouthed the words, he fulfilled his obligation, in accordance with the opinion of Rabbi Yehuda (Rambam *Sefer Ahava, Hilkhot Keriat Shema* 2:8; *Shulḥan Arukh, Oraḥ Ḥayyim* 62:3).

One who recited *Shema* and was not precise in his enunciation of its letters – קָרָא וְלֹא דִּקְדֵּק בְּאוֹתִיּוֹתֶיהָ: It is a mitzva to enunciate each letter of *Shema* precisely; however, if he failed to do so, he fulfilled his obligation. This is in accordance with the opinion of Rabbi Yosei (Rambam *Sefer Ahava, Hilkhot Keriat Shema* 2:8; *Shulḥan Arukh, Oraḥ Ḥayyim* 62:1).

One who recited out of order – הַקּוֹרֵא לְמַפְרֵעַ: One who alters the sequence of the verses and recites *Shema* out of order has not fulfilled his obligation. Although *ab initio*, one may similarly not alter the sequence of the paragraphs, if he recited them out of order, after the fact, he fulfilled his obligation (Rambam *Sefer Ahava, Hilkhot Keriat Shema* 2:11; *Shulḥan Arukh, Oraḥ Ḥayyim* 64:1).

One who recited and erred – קָרָא וְטָעָה: One who erred in his recitation of *Shema* and knows where he erred; i.e., if he read the entire *Shema* but skipped a verse in the middle, he returns to the place that he erred and recites from there to the end. If he does not know where he erred, he returns to the beginning of the portion in which the error occurred (Rambam *Sefer Ahava, Hilkhot Keriat Shema* 2:13; *Shulḥan Arukh, Oraḥ Ḥayyim* 64:2).

גמ׳ מאי טַעְמָא דְּרַבִּי יוֹסֵי – מִשּׁוּם דִּכְתִיב: שְׁמַע – הַשְׁמַע לְאָזְנֶךָ מַה שֶּׁאַתָּה מוֹצִיא מִפִּיךָ. וְתַנָּא קַמָּא סָבַר: שְׁמַע – בְּכׇל לָשׁוֹן שֶׁאַתָּה שׁוֹמֵעַ.

GEMARA The discussion in our mishna dealt with the question of whether or not one who recites *Shema* without hearing it fulfilled his obligation. The Gemara clarifies the opinions cited in the mishna: **What is the reason for Rabbi Yosei's** opinion that one must recite *Shema* in a manner audible to his own ear? **Because it is written: *Shema*,** hear, and Rabbi Yosei holds that this is to be understood literally, meaning: **Make your ears hear what your mouth utters. The first *tanna*,** who holds that one fulfills his obligation even if he does not hear his recitation of *Shema*, **holds** that ***Shema*,** hear, comes to teach something else; one may recite *Shema* **in any language that one can hear** and understand, and there is no requirement to recite *Shema* specifically in Hebrew.

וְרַבִּי יוֹסֵי – תַּרְתֵּי שְׁמַע מִינַּהּ.

**And Rabbi Yosei** agrees with the principle derived by the first *tanna* from the word *Shema*; however Rabbi Yosei holds: **Derive two** *halakhot* **from** the word *Shema*; first, one may recite *Shema* in any language, and second, one must recite it in a manner audible to his own ears.

תְּנַן הָתָם: חֵרֵשׁ הַמְדַבֵּר וְאֵינוֹ שׁוֹמֵעַ – לֹא יִתְרוֹם, וְאִם תָּרַם – תְּרוּמָתוֹ תְּרוּמָה.

**We learned there** in a mishna regarding the laws of separating tithes: **A deaf person**[N] **who can speak but cannot hear may not separate *teruma***[H] ***ab initio*,** because he must recite a blessing over the separation of *teruma* and he is unable to hear the blessing. **But** after the fact, **if he did separate it, his *teruma*** is valid ***teruma*.**

מַאן תַּנָּא חֵרֵשׁ הַמְדַבֵּר וְאֵינוֹ שׁוֹמֵעַ, דִּיעֲבַד – אִין, לְכַתְּחִלָּה – לָא?

The Gemara asks: **Who is** this ***tanna*** who holds that if **a deaf person who can speak but cannot hear** separates *teruma*, **it is** considered *teruma* **after the fact,**[B] but *ab initio*[B] he may **not** do so?

אָמַר רַב חִסְדָּא: רַבִּי יוֹסֵי הִיא, דִּתְנַן: הַקּוֹרֵא אֶת שְׁמַע וְלֹא הִשְׁמִיעַ לְאׇזְנוֹ – יָצָא, דִּבְרֵי רַבִּי יְהוּדָה; רַבִּי יוֹסֵי אוֹמֵר: לֹא יָצָא.

**Rav Ḥisda said: It is Rabbi Yosei, as we learned** in our mishna: **One who recites *Shema* and did not** recite it so it was **audible to his own ear, he fulfilled** his obligation. **This is the statement of Rabbi Yehuda. Rabbi Yosei says: He did not fulfill** his obligation.

עַד כָּאן לֹא קָאָמַר רַבִּי יוֹסֵי לֹא יָצָא – אֶלָּא גַּבֵּי קְרִיאַת שְׁמַע דְּאוֹרָיְיתָא, אֲבָל תְּרוּמָה – מִשּׁוּם בְּרָכָה הוּא, וּבְרָכָה דְּרַבָּנַן, וְלָא בִּבְרָכָה תַּלְיָא מִילְּתָא.

Rav Ḥisda elaborates: **Rabbi Yosei only stated** that a deaf person **did not fulfill** his obligation even after the fact **with regard to the recitation of *Shema*,** which is a **biblical** obligation. **But** with regard to ***teruma*,** the concern is **due to the blessing recited over** its separation. **And the blessing is** by **rabbinic law,** and the separation of *teruma* itself **is not contingent upon the blessing.** The separation of *teruma* takes effect regardless of whether or not a blessing is recited, so in the case of a deaf person, he fulfilled his obligation after the fact.

וּמִמַּאי דְּרַבִּי יוֹסֵי הִיא? דִּילְמָא רַבִּי יְהוּדָה הִיא; וְאָמַר גַּבֵּי קְרִיאַת שְׁמַע נָמֵי: דִּיעֲבַד – אִין, לְכַתְּחִלָּה – לָא! תֵּדַע, דְּקָתָנֵי, הַקּוֹרֵא – דִּיעֲבַד אִין, לְכַתְּחִלָּה – לָא!

The Gemara challenges the assertion that this mishna is in accordance with the opinion of Rabbi Yosei: **And from where** do you infer that **this is** the opinion of **Rabbi Yosei? Perhaps it is** in accordance with the opinion of **Rabbi Yehuda, and he said that with regard to the recitation of *Shema* as well,** if one did not recite it in a manner audible to his own ears, **he has** fulfilled his obligation **after the fact,** but ***ab initio*** he may **not** do so. This opinion is identical to that of the *tanna* in the case of *teruma*. **Know** that this is true because **it was taught** in the mishna: **One who recites** *Shema* without it being audible to his own ear. The *tanna* formulated the dispute in a case which was **after the fact.** If one already recited *Shema* in this manner, **yes,** he fulfilled his obligation. The *tanna* did not formulate the case in the mishna using *ab initio* language, i.e., one may recite *Shema* in a manner inaudible to his own ears because, ***ab initio*,** he may **not** do so according to Rabbi Yehuda.

אָמְרִי: הַאי דְּקָתָנֵי, הַקּוֹרֵא – לְהוֹדִיעֲךָ כֹּחוֹ דְּרַבִּי יוֹסֵי דְּאָמַר: דִּיעֲבַד נָמֵי לָא, דְּאִי רַבִּי יְהוּדָה – אֲפִילּוּ לְכַתְּחִלָּה נָמֵי יָצָא.

The Gemara rejects this proof. In explanation, **they say:** The fact **that** the mishna **taught** the *halakha* utilizing the after the fact language: **One who recited,** does not prove that Rabbi Yehuda also holds that one may not *ab initio* recite *Shema* in a manner inaudible to his own ears. Rather, the mishna formulated the *halakha* in that manner **is to convey the far-reaching** nature of the opinion **of Rabbi Yosei, who said that** if one does so, even **after the fact, he did not fulfill** his obligation to recite *Shema*. **As, if it** sought to convey the opinion of **Rabbi Yehuda,** then **even *ab initio* he** may **fulfill** his obligation without hearing the recitation.

**NOTES**

**A deaf-mute – חֵרֵשׁ:** When the Sages employ the unmodified term, *ḥeresh*, the reference is to one who can neither hear nor speak. In the talmudic era, one with those disabilities did not, as a rule, have full mental capacity, and was consequently exempt from all of the mitzvot in the Torah. However, if he has full mental capacity, he is considered like anyone else and is obligated (see *Tosefot Rabbeinu Yehuda HaḤasid*).

**HALAKHA**

**A deaf person who can speak but cannot hear may not separate *teruma* – חֵרֵשׁ הַמְדַבֵּר וְאֵינוֹ שׁוֹמֵעַ לֹא יִתְרוֹם וכו׳:** A deaf person who is able to speak may not separate *teruma ab initio*; if he did so, it is considered valid *teruma* (Rambam *Sefer Zera'im*, *Hilkhot Terumot* 4:4).

**BACKGROUND**

**After the fact – (בְּ)דִיעֲבַד:** Literally, having been done. A situation where the legitimacy or validity of an action is considered after it was already performed.

***Ab initio* – לְכַתְּחִלָּה:** Literally, from the beginning. A situation where the legitimacy or validity of an action is being considered before one performs the action.

All are fit to read the Megilla – הַכֹּל כְּשֵׁרִים לִקְרוֹת
אֶת הַמְּגִילָּה וכו׳: All are fit to
read the Megilla except for
a deaf-mute, an imbecile,
and a minor (Rambam *Sefer
Zemanim, Hilkhot Megilla* 1:2;
*Shulḥan Arukh, Oraḥ Ḥayyim*
689:2).

בְּמַאי אוֹקִימְתָּא – כְּרַבִּי יוֹסֵי, וְאֶלָּא הָא דְּתַנְיָא: לֹא יְבָרֵךְ אָדָם בִּרְכַּת הַמָּזוֹן בְּלִבּוֹ, וְאִם בֵּירַךְ – יָצָא,

The Gemara challenges this conclusion: **How did you establish** the reasoning of the mishna dealing with the laws of *terumot*? **In accordance with** the opinion of **Rabbi Yosei,** who holds that one who does not hear his recitation does not fulfill his obligation even after the fact. **But** what about **that which was taught** in a *baraita*: **One may not recite the Grace after Meals,** which like *Shema* and unlike the blessing on separating *teruma* is a Torah commandment, **in his heart,** inaudibly, **and if he recited** the blessing in that manner, **he fulfilled** his obligation?

מַנִּי? לֹא רַבִּי יוֹסֵי וְלֹא רַבִּי יְהוּדָה; דְּאִי רַבִּי יְהוּדָה – הָא אָמַר: לְכַתְּחִלָּה נַמִי יָצָא, אִי רַבִּי יוֹסֵי – דִּיעֲבַד נַמִי לָא!

In accordance with **whose** opinion **is this** *baraita*? **It is** in accordance **neither** with the opinion of **Rabbi Yosei nor** with the opinion of **Rabbi Yehuda.** As if you say that it is in accordance **with** the opinion of **Rabbi Yehuda, didn't he say** according to the way the Gemara explained his position that even *ab initio* **he may fulfill** his obligation in that manner, **and he need not recite it audibly.** In that case, why should one refrain from reciting the blessing in his heart? And **if** you say that it is in accordance **with** the opinion of **Rabbi Yosei;** he holds that even **after the fact, he did not** fulfill his obligation.

אֶלָּא מַאי – רַבִּי יְהוּדָה, וְדִיעֲבַד – אִין, לְכַתְּחִלָּה – לָא?

**Rather, what** must we say? We must revert to the explanation that it is in accordance with the opinion of **Rabbi Yehuda** who holds that **after the fact, yes,** he fulfilled his obligation, but *ab initio*, **no,** one may not recite it in a manner inaudible to his own ears. Therefore the *baraita* concerning Grace after Meals is in accordance with the opinion of Rabbi Yehuda.

אֶלָּא הָא דְּתָנֵי רַבִּי יְהוּדָה בְּרֵיהּ דְּרַבִּי שִׁמְעוֹן בֶּן פַּזִּי: ״חֵרֵשׁ הַמְדַבֵּר וְאֵינוֹ שׁוֹמֵעַ תּוֹרֵם לְכַתְּחִלָּה״, מַנִּי?

The Gemara questions this: **But** what about **that** *baraita* **which was taught by Rabbi Yehuda, son of Rabbi Shimon ben Pazi: A deaf** person **who speaks but does not hear may,** *ab initio*, **separate** *teruma.* In accordance with **whose** opinion **is that** *baraita*?

לֹא רַבִּי יְהוּדָה וְלֹא רַבִּי יוֹסֵי; אִי רַבִּי יְהוּדָה – הָא אָמַר: דִּיעֲבַד – אִין, לְכַתְּחִלָּה – לֹא, אִי רַבִּי יוֹסֵי – הָא אָמַר: דִּיעֲבַד נַמִי לָא!

**According to** what we have said, **it is** in accordance **neither** with the opinion of **Rabbi Yehuda nor** with the opinion of **Rabbi Yosei.** As if you say that it is in accordance with the opinion of **Rabbi Yehuda, didn't he say** that **after the fact, yes,** he fulfilled his obligation, although it was inaudible in that manner, but *ab initio*, **no,** he may not fulfill his obligation in that manner? And **if** you say that it is in accordance with the opinion of **Rabbi Yosei, didn't he say** that if he does not hear himself, **even after the fact** he did **not** fulfill his obligation? If so, whose opinion is reflected in this *baraita*?

אֶלָּא, לְעוֹלָם רַבִּי יְהוּדָה, וַאֲפִילּוּ לְכַתְּחִלָּה נַמִי, וְלָא קַשְׁיָא: הָא דִּידֵיהּ, הָא דְּרַבֵּיהּ, דִּתְנַן, רַבִּי יְהוּדָה אוֹמֵר מִשּׁוּם רַבִּי אֶלְעָזָר בֶּן עֲזַרְיָה: הַקּוֹרֵא אֶת שְׁמַע – צָרִיךְ שֶׁיַּשְׁמִיעַ לְאָזְנוֹ, שֶׁנֶּאֱמַר: ״שְׁמַע יִשְׂרָאֵל ה׳ אֱלֹהֵינוּ ה׳ אֶחָד״; אָמַר לֵיהּ רַבִּי מֵאִיר: הֲרֵי הוּא אוֹמֵר ״אֲשֶׁר אָנֹכִי מְצַוְּךָ הַיּוֹם עַל לְבָבֶךָ״ – אַחַר כַּוָּנַת הַלֵּב הֵן הֵן הַדְּבָרִים.

**Rather, we must revert to the previous explanation but with a slight revision, and** say that **actually it is** in accordance with the opinion of **Rabbi Yehuda, and even** *ab initio*, a deaf person may **also** separate *teruma.* **And this is not difficult** and there is no contradiction between the mishna and the *baraita*, **as this is his own opinion and that is his teacher's** opinion. **As it was taught** in a *baraita*: **Rabbi Yehuda said in the name of Rabbi Elazar ben Azarya: One who recites** *Shema* **must make it audible to his ears, as it is stated:** "Hear, Israel, the Lord is our God, the Lord is One." This means that he must do so, but after the fact, if he failed to do so, he nevertheless fulfilled his obligation. The *baraita* continues: **Rabbi Meir said to him: It says:** "Which I command you this day, **upon your heart;"** which Rabbi Meir explains to mean that **the significance of the words follows the intention of the heart** and even *ab initio* one need not recite *Shema* audibly.

הַשְׁתָּא דְּאָתֵית לְהָכִי, אֲפִילּוּ תֵּימָא: רַבִּי יְהוּדָה כְּרַבֵּיהּ סְבִירָא לֵיהּ, וְלָא קַשְׁיָא לֵיהּ: הָא – רַבִּי מֵאִיר, הָא – רַבִּי יְהוּדָה.

The Gemara notes: **Now that you have arrived at this** point and the entire *baraita* has been cited, **even if you say** that **Rabbi Yehuda holds in accordance with** the opinion of **his teacher,** that only after the fact, does a deaf person fulfill his obligation, **it is,** nevertheless, **not difficult** and the different *baraitot* are not contradictory. As **this** *baraita* permitting a deaf person to separate *teruma ab initio* is in accordance with the opinion of **Rabbi Meir, while this** *baraita* that holds that he may not recite Grace after Meals *ab initio* but after the fact he fulfilled his obligation is in accordance with the opinion of **Rabbi Yehuda.**

תְּנַן הָתָם: הַכֹּל כְּשֵׁרִים לִקְרוֹת אֶת הַמְּגִילָּה חוּץ מֵחֵרֵשׁ שׁוֹטֶה וְקָטָן, וְרַבִּי יְהוּדָה מַכְשִׁיר בְּקָטָן.

The Gemara cites a similar discussion with regard to the reading of the Megilla: **We learned** in a mishna **there** in tractate *Megilla*: **All are fit to read the Megilla**[H] **except a deaf-mute, an imbecile, and a minor. And Rabbi Yehuda deems a minor fit.**

מַאן תְּנָא חֵרֵשׁ דִּיעֲבַד נַמִי לָא? אָמַר רַב מַתָּנָה: רַבִּי יוֹסֵי הִיא, דִּתְנַן: הַקּוֹרֵא אֶת שְׁמַע וְלֹא הִשְׁמִיעַ לְאָזְנוֹ – יָצָא, דִּבְרֵי רַבִּי יְהוּדָה; רַבִּי יוֹסֵי אוֹמֵר: לֹא יָצָא.

The Gemara clarifies: **Who is the** *tanna* who holds that even **after the fact,** the reading of **a deaf-mute is not** valid? **Rav Mattana said: It is Rabbi Yosei, as we learned** in our mishna: **One who recites** *Shema* **and did not** recite it so it was **audible to his own ear, fulfilled** his obligation. **Rabbi Yosei says: He did not fulfill** his obligation.

מִמַּאי דְּרַבִּי יוֹסֵי הִיא, וְדִיעֲבַד נַמִי לָא,

The Gemara asks: **From where** do you conclude that the mishna cited from tractate *Megilla* is in accordance with the opinion of **Rabbi Yosei, and** that **after the fact** his reading is **also not** valid?

דִּילְמָא רַבִּי יְהוּדָה הִיא וּלְכַתְּחִלָּה הוּא דְּלָא, הָא דִּיעֲבַד שַׁפִּיר דָּמֵי!

**Perhaps it is** in accordance with the opinion of **Rabbi Yehuda, and** although *ab initio* a deaf-mute may **not** read, **after the fact** his reading **is valid?**

לָא סָלְקָא דַּעְתָּךְ, דְּקָתָנֵי חֵרֵשׁ דּוּמְיָא דְּשׁוֹטֶה וְקָטָן; מָה שׁוֹטֶה וְקָטָן – דִּיעֲבַד נָמֵי לָא, אַף חֵרֵשׁ – דִּיעֲבַד נָמֵי לָא.

The Gemara responds: **This could not enter your mind, as it was taught:** A deaf-mute, an imbecile, and a minor, in one phrase in our mishna; to teach that **a deaf-mute** is **similar to an imbecile and a minor. Just as** in the case of **an imbecile and a minor, even after the fact,** their reading is **not** valid, **so too** the reading of **a deaf-mute, even after the fact,** is **not** valid.

וְדִילְמָא, הָא כִּדְאִיתָא וְהָא כִּדְאִיתָא?

The Gemara rejects this assertion based on their appearance in a common list: **And perhaps this** case is **as it is and that** case is **as it is;** although listed together, the circumstances of each case may be different, and no definite proof can be drawn from their juxtaposition.

וּמִי מָצֵית לְאוֹקְמַהּ כְּרַבִּי יְהוּדָה, וְהָא מִדְּקָתָנֵי סֵיפָא: רַבִּי יְהוּדָה מַכְשִׁיר בְּקָטָן – מִכְּלָל דְּרֵישָׁא לָאו רַבִּי יְהוּדָה הִיא!

The Gemara objects from a different perspective: **And can you** really **establish** that the first clause in the mishna is **in accordance with** the opinion of **Rabbi Yehuda? But from what was taught in the latter clause** of the mishna: **And Rabbi Yehuda deems a minor fit** to read the Megilla, this proves **by inference that the beginning** of the mishna **is not** in accordance with the opinion of **Rabbi Yehuda?**

וְדִילְמָא כּוּלַּהּ רַבִּי יְהוּדָה הִיא, וּתְרֵי גַּוְונֵי קָטָן, וְחַסּוּרֵי מִחַסְּרָא וְהָכִי קָתָנֵי: הַכֹּל כְּשֵׁרִין לִקְרוֹת אֶת הַמְּגִילָּה חוּץ מֵחֵרֵשׁ שׁוֹטֶה וְקָטָן, בַּמֶּה דְּבָרִים אֲמוּרִים – בְּקָטָן שֶׁלֹּא הִגִּיעַ לְחִינּוּךְ, אֲבָל קָטָן שֶׁהִגִּיעַ לְחִינּוּךְ – אֲפִילּוּ לְכַתְּחִלָּה כָּשֵׁר, דִּבְרֵי רַבִּי יְהוּדָה, שֶׁרַבִּי יְהוּדָה מַכְשִׁיר בְּקָטָן.

The Gemara rejects this challenge as well: **And perhaps the entire** mishna **is** in accordance with the opinion of **Rabbi Yehuda,**[N] and there are **two types of minors, and the mishna is incomplete and it teaches as follows: All are fit to read the Megilla except a deaf-mute, an imbecile, and a minor.**[N] **In what** case **is this said?** With regard to **a minor who has not** yet **reached** the age of **training** to fulfill the mitzvot. **However** in the case of **a minor**[N] **who has reached** the age of **training, even *ab initio* he is fit** to read the Megilla. This is the **statement of Rabbi Yehuda, as Rabbi Yehuda deems a minor fit,** and his statement here comes to elucidate and not to dispute.

בְּמַאי אוֹקֵימְתָּא – כְּרַבִּי יְהוּדָה, וְדִיעֲבַד – אִין, לְכַתְּחִלָּה – לָא, אֶלָּא הָא דְּתָנֵי רַבִּי יְהוּדָה בְּרֵיהּ דְּרַבִּי שִׁמְעוֹן בֶּן פָּזִי: חֵרֵשׁ הַמְדַבֵּר וְאֵינוֹ שׁוֹמֵעַ תּוֹרֵם לְכַתְּחִלָּה.

The Gemara asks: In accordance **with whose** opinion **did you establish** the mishna? **In accordance with** the opinion of **Rabbi Yehuda,** who holds that **after the fact, yes,** his reading is valid, but ***ab initio*, no,** he may not read? **However, that** *baraita* **which was taught by Rabbi Yehuda, son of Rabbi Shimon ben Pazi: A deaf** person **who speaks but does not hear may, *ab initio*, separate *teruma*.**

מַנִּי? לָא רַבִּי יְהוּדָה וְלָא רַבִּי יוֹסֵי; אִי רַבִּי יְהוּדָה, דִּיעֲבַד – אִין, לְכַתְּחִלָּה – לָא, אִי רַבִּי יוֹסֵי, דִּיעֲבַד נָמֵי לָא!

In accordance with **whose** opinion **is this** *baraita*? **Neither** the opinion of **Rabbi Yehuda nor** with the opinion of **Rabbi Yosei. As, if** you say that it is **Rabbi Yehuda's** opinion, didn't he say that **after the fact, yes,** he fulfilled his obligation, but ***ab initio*, no,** he may not fulfill his obligation in that manner? And **if** you say that it is **Rabbi Yosei's** opinion, didn't he say that **even after the fact he** did **not** fulfill his obligation?

אֶלָּא מַאי – רַבִּי יְהוּדָה, וַאֲפִילּוּ לְכַתְּחִלָּה נָמֵי? אֶלָּא הָא דְּתַנְיָא: לֹא יְבָרֵךְ אָדָם בִּרְכַּת הַמָּזוֹן בְּלִבּוֹ, וְאִם בֵּירַךְ – יָצָא, מַנִּי?

This Gemara rejects this objection: **But rather, what,** will you explain the *baraita* in accordance with the opinion of **Rabbi Yehuda, and a** deaf-mute is **also** fit to fulfill his obligation **even *ab initio*? However, that which was taught** in a *baraita*: **One may not recite the Grace after Meals in his heart,** inaudibly, **and if he recited** the blessing in that manner, **he fulfilled** his obligation, in accordance with **whose** opinion is that *baraita*?

לָא רַבִּי יְהוּדָה וְלָא רַבִּי יוֹסֵי; אִי רַבִּי יְהוּדָה – הָא אָמַר אֲפִילּוּ לְכַתְּחִלָּה נָמֵי, וְאִי רַבִּי יוֹסֵי – הָא אָמַר אֲפִילּוּ דִּיעֲבַד נָמֵי לָא!

It is in accordance **neither** with the opinion of **Rabbi Yehuda nor** with the opinion of **Rabbi Yosei.** As **if** you say that it is in accordance with the opinion of **Rabbi Yehuda, didn't he say** that even ***ab initio* he may fulfill** his obligation in that manner? And **if** you say that it is in accordance with the opinion of **Rabbi Yosei, didn't he say** that **even after the fact he** did **not** fulfill his obligation?

NOTES

**And perhaps the entire mishna is in accordance with the opinion of Rabbi Yehuda** – **וְדִילְמָא כּוּלַּהּ רַבִּי יְהוּדָה הִיא**: *Tosafot* commented on the unusual nature of this approach, which explains a mishna, which posed no difficulty, employing the method: The mishna is incomplete, etc. Some explained that the opinion of the Rabbis was difficult, as what reason would they have to deem the minor unfit in all circumstances? Therefore, the emendation was appropriate (*Tosefot Rabbi Shimshon of Saens; Tosefot Rabbeinu Yehuda HaḤasid*). Another suggestion is that the mishna itself is clearly lacking, as Rabbi Yehuda could not possibly have permitted a minor who did not yet reach the age of training to read the Megilla, so some emendation of the mishna was necessary (Rashbam in *Tosefot HaRosh*). Others explained that the emendation is not significant and is based on the notion that, instead of adopting the standard approach, i.e., that Rabbi Yehuda came to disagree with the previous statement, he came to comment on it. Based on that assumption, the emendation is logical.

**A deaf-mute, an imbecile, and a minor** – **חֵרֵשׁ שׁוֹטֶה וְקָטָן**: Members of these three categories are frequently grouped together because of their limited intellectual capacity and/or their inability to act responsibly. They are not obligated to perform mitzvot, nor are they held responsible for any damage they may cause. They also lack the legal capacity to act as agents. Though all three are often mentioned together, there are many differences between the laws governing each of them.

**A minor** – **קָטָן**: One who has not reached majority. A minor is not considered legally competent. He bears no criminal responsibility for his acts, and he is exempt from the obligation to perform mitzvot. Nevertheless several ordinances and customs were instituted to educate minors for adult life. Certain educational mitzvot are incumbent upon the child's father and mother, or upon the court as the child's guardian, in order to train the child to perform those mitzvot. One begins with mitzvot that a minor can become accustomed to performing properly. A minor boy may read from the Torah and he is entitled to read the additional portion from the Prophets. The Sages were divided as to whether one is obligated to prevent a minor from transgressing a prohibition from which he may derive enjoyment; for example, eating non-kosher food. Many of the mitzvot pertaining to a minor are actually the father's responsibility, e.g., circumcision and the redemption of the firstborn.

**HALAKHA**

**Hearing in all the mitzvot – שְׁמִיעָה בְּכָל הַמִּצְוֹת:** *Ab initio*, one who recites any blessing must recite it in a manner audible to his own ears. After the fact, if he failed to do so, he fulfilled his obligation. Some wrote that the majority of authorities agreed that if he failed to do so, he did not fulfill his obligation (*Be'er Heitev*, *Sefer Ḥaredim*). This is in accordance with the emended version of Rav Yosef's statement (Rambam *Sefer Ahava*, *Hilkhot Berakhot* 1:7; *Shulḥan Arukh*, *Oraḥ Ḥayyim* 185:2).

לְעוֹלָם רַבִּי יְהוּדָה הִיא, וַאֲפִילּוּ לְכַתְּחִלָּה נַמִי, וְלָא קַשְׁיָא: הָא דִּידֵיהּ, הָא דְּרַבֵּיהּ, דְּתַנְיָא, אָמַר רַבִּי יְהוּדָה מִשּׁוּם רַבִּי אֶלְעָזָר בֶּן עֲזַרְיָה: הַקּוֹרֵא אֶת שְׁמַע צָרִיךְ שֶׁיַּשְׁמִיעַ לְאׇזְנוֹ, שֶׁנֶּאֱמַר: שְׁמַע יִשְׂרָאֵל; אָמַר לוֹ רַבִּי מֵאִיר, הֲרֵי הוּא אוֹמֵר: אֲשֶׁר אָנֹכִי מְצַוְּךָ הַיּוֹם עַל לְבָבֶךָ – אַחַר כַּוָּונַת הַלֵּב הֵן הֵן הַדְּבָרִים.

The Gemara responds: **Actually,** we can explain that the *baraita*: A deaf person may, *ab initio*, separate *teruma*, **is** in accordance with the opinion of **Rabbi Yehuda,** according to whom a deaf-mute is **also** permitted to do so **even *ab initio*.** With regard to the opinion expressed that he is prohibited to recite *Shema* and Grace after Meals *ab initio*, **there is no difficulty, as this is his** own opinion **and that is his teacher's** opinion. **As it was taught** in a *baraita*: **Rabbi Yehuda said in the name of Rabbi Elazar ben Azarya: One who recites *Shema* must make it audible to his ears, as it is stated: "Hear, Israel,** the Lord is our God, the Lord is One." The *baraita* continues: **Rabbi Meir said to him: But it says: "Which I command you this day, upon your heart";** meaning that **the** significance of the **words follows the intention of the heart** and even *ab initio* one need not recite *Shema* audibly. The opinion that after the fact, a deaf person fulfilled his obligation to recite *Shema* is the opinion of Rabbi Elazar ben Azarya.

הָשְׁתָּא דְּאָתֵית לְהָכִי, אֲפִילּוּ תֵּימָא: רַבִּי יְהוּדָה כְּרַבֵּיהּ סְבִירָא לֵיהּ, וְלָא קַשְׁיָא, הָא – רַבִּי יְהוּדָה, הָא – רַבִּי מֵאִיר.

The Gemara notes: **Now that you have arrived at this** point and the entire *baraita* has been cited, **even** if **you say** that **Rabbi Yehuda holds in accordance with** the opinion of **his teacher, it is,** nevertheless, **not difficult.** As **this** *baraita* that holds that he may not recite Grace after Meals *ab initio* but after the fact he fulfilled his obligation is in accordance with the opinion of **Rabbi Yehuda,** while **this** *baraita* permitting a deaf person to separate *teruma ab initio* is in accordance with the opinion of **Rabbi Meir.**

אָמַר רַב חִסְדָּא אָמַר רַב שֵׁילָא: הֲלָכָה כְּרַבִּי יְהוּדָה שֶׁאָמַר מִשּׁוּם רַבִּי אֶלְעָזָר בֶּן עֲזַרְיָה, וַהֲלָכָה כְּרַבִּי יְהוּדָה.

**Rav Ḥisda said** that **Rav Sheila said: The *halakha* is in accordance with** the opinion of **Rabbi Yehuda who said in the name of Rabbi Elazar ben Azarya, and the *halakha* is in accordance with** the opinion of **Rabbi Yehuda** as cited in our mishna.

וּצְרִיכָא, דְּאִי אַשְׁמְעִינַן הֲלָכָה כְּרַבִּי יְהוּדָה – הֲוָה אָמֵינָא: אֲפִילּוּ לְכַתְּחִלָּה, קָמַשְׁמַע לַן: הֲלָכָה כְּרַבִּי יְהוּדָה שֶׁאָמַר מִשּׁוּם רַבִּי אֶלְעָזָר בֶּן עֲזַרְיָה.

The Gemara explains: **And** although that may seem redundant, both statements **are necessary, as had** Rav Ḥisda only **taught us** that **the *halakha* is in accordance with** the opinion of **Rabbi Yehuda, I would have said,** as was suggested in the Gemara above, that Rabbi Yehuda permits to do so **even *ab initio*.** Therefore, **he teaches us** that **the *halakha* is in accordance with** the opinion of **Rabbi Yehuda who said** it **in the name of** his teacher, **Rabbi Elazar ben Azarya;** *ab initio* one must recite *Shema* in a manner audible to his own ears.

וְאִי אַשְׁמְעִינַן הֲלָכָה כְּרַבִּי יְהוּדָה שֶׁאָמַר מִשּׁוּם רַבִּי אֶלְעָזָר בֶּן עֲזַרְיָה – הֲוָה אָמֵינָא: צָרִיךְ, וְאֵין לוֹ תַּקָּנָה, קָמַשְׁמַע לַן: הֲלָכָה כְּרַבִּי יְהוּדָה.

**And had** Rav Ḥisda only **taught us** that **the *halakha* is in accordance with Rabbi Yehuda in the name of Rabbi Elazar ben Azarya, I would have said** that the phrase: Must make it audible, means not only **must** he recite it that way *ab initio*, but **also** after the fact **he has no remedy** if he failed to do so. Therefore, **he teaches us** that **the *halakha* is in accordance with** the opinion of **Rabbi Yehuda;** *ab initio* one must recite *Shema* in a manner audible to his own ears, but if he failed to do so, after the fact his recitation is valid.

אָמַר רַב יוֹסֵף: מַחְלוֹקֶת בִּקְרִיאַת שְׁמַע, אֲבָל בִּשְׁאָר מִצְוֹת – דִּבְרֵי הַכֹּל לֹא יָצָא, דִּכְתִיב: הַסְכֵּת וּשְׁמַע יִשְׂרָאֵל.

**Rav Yosef said:** The **dispute** as to whether or not a deaf person fulfills his obligation **is** only **in** the case of **the recitation of *Shema*, but with regard to the rest of the mitzvot, everyone agrees that he does not fulfill** his obligation if he does not hear his recitation, **as it is written: "Pay attention, and hear, Israel"** (Deuteronomy 27:9); meaning that one is required to listen and hear.[H]

מֵיתִיבֵי: לֹא יְבָרֵךְ אָדָם בִּרְכַּת הַמָּזוֹן בְּלִבּוֹ, וְאִם בֵּירַךְ – יָצָא! אֶלָּא אִי אִתְּמַר, הָכִי אִתְּמַר: אָמַר רַב יוֹסֵף: מַחְלוֹקֶת בִּקְרִיאַת שְׁמַע, דִּכְתִיב: שְׁמַע יִשְׂרָאֵל, אֲבָל בִּשְׁאָר מִצְוֹת – דִּבְרֵי הַכֹּל יָצָא.

The Gemara **objects** based on what was taught in a *baraita*: **One may not recite the Grace after Meals in his heart,** inaudibly, **and if he recited** the blessing in that manner, **he fulfilled** his obligation. In this example of the rest of the mitzvot, the obligation to hear the recitation of the blessing is only *ab initio*. **Rather,** Rav Yosef's statement must be emended. **If this was said, it was said as follows; Rav Yosef said:** The **dispute** as to whether or not a deaf person fulfills his obligation **is** only **in** the case of **the recitation of *Shema*, as it is written: "Hear, Israel." But regarding the rest of the mitzvot, all agree that** a deaf-mute **fulfills** his obligation.

וְהָכְתִיב: הַסְכֵּת וּשְׁמַע יִשְׂרָאֵל!

The Gemara asks: **Isn't it written: "Pay attention, and hear, Israel"?**

הַהוּא בְּדִבְרֵי תוֹרָה כְּתִיב.

The Gemara responds: **That** verse **is written with regard to matters of Torah;** one must pay close attention to what is written in the Torah.

״קָרָא וְלֹא דִקְדֵּק בְּאוֹתִיּוֹתֶיהָ״.

We learned in the mishna: **One who recited** *Shema* and **was not** sufficiently **precise in** his enunciation of **its letters,** Rabbi Yosei says: He fulfilled his obligation. Rabbi Yehuda says: He did not fulfill his obligation. Similarly, there is a dispute whether or not one who recites *Shema* in a manner inaudible to his own ears fulfilled his obligation; the anonymous first *tanna* says: He fulfilled his obligation. Rabbi Yosei says: He did not fulfill his obligation.

אָמַר רַבִּי טָבִי אָמַר רַבִּי יֹאשִׁיָּה: הֲלָכָה כְּדִבְרֵי שְׁנֵיהֶם לְהָקֵל.

**Rabbi Tavi said** that **Rabbi Yoshiya said: The** ***halakha*** **is in accordance with the the statements in both** disputes that rule **leniently.**

וְאָמַר רַבִּי טָבִי אָמַר רַבִּי יֹאשִׁיָּה, מַאי דִּכְתִיב: ״שָׁלֹשׁ הֵנָּה לֹא תִשְׂבַּעְנָה שְׁאוֹל וְעֹצֶר רָחַם״, וְכִי מָה עִנְיַן שְׁאוֹל אֵצֶל רֶחֶם? אֶלָּא לוֹמַר לְךָ: מָה רֶחֶם מַכְנִיס וּמוֹצִיא – אַף שְׁאוֹל מַכְנִיס וּמוֹצִיא;

Incidental to citing one statement by this combination of Sages, the Gemara cites another statement in their name: **And Rabbi Tavi said** that **Rabbi Yoshiya said: What is** meant by that which is **written: "There are three that are never satisfied… the grave and the barren womb"** (Proverbs 30:15–16)? We have to ask: **What does a grave have to do with a womb?**[N] **Rather,** this juxtaposition comes **to tell you: Just as a womb takes in and gives forth, so too a grave takes in and gives forth** with the resurrection of the dead.

וַהֲלֹא דְּבָרִים קַל וָחוֹמֶר: וּמָה רֶחֶם שֶׁמַּכְנִיסִין בּוֹ בַּחֲשַׁאי – מוֹצִיאִין מִמֶּנּוּ בְּקוֹלֵי קוֹלוֹת, שְׁאוֹל שֶׁמַּכְנִיסִין בּוֹ בְּקוֹלֵי קוֹלוֹת – אֵינוֹ דִּין שֶׁמּוֹצִיאִין מִמֶּנּוּ בְּקוֹלֵי קוֹלוֹת! מִכָּאן תְּשׁוּבָה לָאוֹמְרִים אֵין תְּחִיַּית הַמֵּתִים מִן הַתּוֹרָה.

**And is this not an** ***a fortiori*** **inference: Just as** the fetus **is placed into the womb in private,** and the baby **is removed from it with loud cries** at childbirth; **the grave into which** the deceased **is placed with loud cries** of mourning at burial, **is it not right that** the body should **be removed with loud cries? From this** verse there is **a refutation to those who say that there is no Torah** source for the **resurrection of the dead.**

תָּנֵי רַבִּי אוֹשַׁעְיָא קַמֵּיהּ דְּרָבָא: וּכְתַבְתָּם – הַכֹּל בִּכְתָב, אֲפִילּוּ צַוָּאוֹת.

**Rabbi Oshaya taught** the following *baraita* **before Rava:** The verse, **"And you shall write them** [***ukhtavtam***] on the door posts of your house and your gates" (Deuteronomy 6:9), should be understood as though it were written: "And you shall write them completely [*ukhtav tam*]," i.e., in their entirety. **Everything must be in writing** in the *mezuza* or phylacteries, **even the commands** to write *mezuzot* and phylacteries.

אֲמַר לֵיהּ: דַּאֲמַר לָךְ מַנִּי – רַבִּי יְהוּדָה הִיא, דְּאָמַר גַּבֵּי סוֹטָה אָלוֹת כּוֹתֵב, צַוָּאוֹת אֵינוֹ כּוֹתֵב; וְהָתָם הוּא דִּכְתִיב: וְכָתַב אֶת הָאָלוֹת הָאֵלֶּה, אֲבָל הָכָא דִּכְתִיב וּכְתַבְתָּם – אֲפִילּוּ צַוָּאוֹת נַמִי.

Rava **said to him: Who said** this *baraita* **to you? It was Rabbi Yehuda,** who **said with regard to** the scroll of the ***sota*** that **one writes curses,** but **one does not write commands** and instructions how to administer the potion to the *sota*. According to Rabbi Yehuda, in the case of *mezuzot* and phylacteries the Torah taught that even the commands must be written in order to distinguish it from *sota*. **There,** in the case of the *sota*, **it is written: "And** the priest **shall write** [***vekhatav***] **these curses** in a scroll" (Numbers 5:23); only the curses are recorded in the scroll, and nothing more. **But here** in the case of *mezuza*, **where it is written: "And you shall write them** [***ukhtavtam***]," **even the commands** must **also** be written.

אַטּוּ טַעְמֵיהּ דְּרַבִּי יְהוּדָה מִשּׁוּם דִּכְתִיב וְכָתַב? טַעְמֵיהּ דְּרַבִּי יְהוּדָה מִשּׁוּם דִּכְתִיב אָלוֹת, אָלוֹת – אִין, צַוָּאוֹת – לָא!

The Gemara questions this: **Is that to say Rabbi Yehuda's reason** for writing only the curses in the *sota* scroll **is because** the verse in the portion of *sota* says: **"And** the priest **shall write** [***vekhatav***]," as opposed to: "And you shall write them [*ukhtavtam*]"? **Rabbi Yehuda's reason is because it is written** in the portion of the *sota*: These **curses,** meaning **curses, yes,** they must be recorded; **commands, no.** If that is Rabbi Yehuda's reasoning, there is no reason to derive the requirement to write the commands from the phrase: And you shall write them, in the case of the mitzva of *mezuza*. Derive it simply from the fact that the Torah did not distinguish between the various components of the portion.

אִצְטְרִיךְ, סָלְקָא דַּעְתָּךְ אָמִינָא: נֵילַף כְּתִיבָה כְּתִיבָה מֵהָתָם – מַה הָתָם – אָלוֹת – אִין, צַוָּאוֹת – לָא, אַף הָכָא נַמִי – צַוָּאוֹת לָא, כְּתַב רַחֲמָנָא, וּכְתַבְתָּם – אֲפִילּוּ צַוָּאוֹת.

The Gemara responds: "And you shall write them" **was necessary,** as otherwise **it might have entered your mind to say: Let us derive** it by means of a verbal analogy,[B] **writing** mentioned here **from writing** mentioned **there,** that **just as there curses, yes, commands, no; so too here, commands, no.** Therefore, **the Torah wrote: And you shall write them** in their entirety, **even the commands.**

## NOTES

**What does a grave have to do with a womb** – וְכִי מָה עִנְיַן שְׁאוֹל אֵצֶל רֶחֶם: The verse refers to three entities that are never satisfied: The grave, the womb, and the earth. It is only with regard to the earth that the verse specifies that it can never get enough water. With regard to the grave and the womb, the verse does not specify what it is of which they can never get enough. Therefore, the Gemara concludes: The verse remained silent with regard to these two juxtaposed entities to underscore a connection between them (Maharsha). Another explanation is that the four daughters mentioned in the verse represent the four primordial elements: The grave represents earth, the womb represents wind, the earth not satisfied with water represents water, and fire is, obviously, fire. The Gemara noted that rather than juxtapose the grave, representing earth, to earth not satisfied with water, the verse inserted the womb in between. This is because the earth and the womb have motherhood and birth in common, as man was created from the earth (Vilna Gaon on Proverbs 30:16).

## BACKGROUND

**Verbal analogy** – גְּזֵרָה שָׁוָה: A fundamental talmudic principle of biblical exegesis, appearing in all the standard lists of hermeneutical principles. If the same word or phrase appears in two places in the Torah, and a certain law is explicitly stated in one of these places, on the basis of verbal analogy, it is inferred that the same law applies in the other case as well.

Certain restrictions were placed on the use of this principle, to prevent unfounded conclusions from being drawn. Most significantly: One cannot infer a verbal analogy on his own, i.e., only a verbal analogy based on ancient tradition is valid.

תָּנֵי רַב עוֹבַדְיָה קַמֵּיהּ דְּרָבָא: וְלִמַּדְתֶּם – שֶׁיְּהֵא לִמּוּדְךָ תָּם, שֶׁיִּתֵּן רֶיוַח בֵּין הַדְּבֵקִים.

On a similar note: **Rav Ovadya taught** a *baraita* **before Rava:** That which was stated: **"And you shall teach them** [***velimadtem***] to your children" (Deuteronomy 11:19) teaches that **your teaching must be complete** [***tam***] **that one** should **leave space between adjacent** words,[H] where the last letter of the first and the first letter of the second are identical. One must distinguish between the words and enunciate each one clearly.

עָנֵי רָבָא בָּתְרֵיהּ: כְּגוֹן עַל לְבָבֶךָ, עַל לְבַבְכֶם, בְּכָל לְבָבְךָ, בְּכָל לְבַבְכֶם, עֵשֶׂב בְּשָׂדְךָ, וַאֲבַדְתֶּם מְהֵרָה, הַכָּנָף פְּתִיל, אֶתְכֶם מֵאֶרֶץ.

**Rava responded after him** by way of explanation: **For example,** one must enunciate ***al levavekha*** and not read them as one word. So too, ***al levavkhem, bekhol levavekha, bekhol levavkhem, esev besadkha, va'avadtem mehera, hakanaf petil,***[B] and ***etkhem me'eretz.*** Because the last letter of the first word and the first letter of the second are identical, the words are liable to be enunciated together and the correct meaning is liable to be obscured.

אָמַר רַבִּי חָמָא בְּרַבִּי חֲנִינָא: כָּל הַקּוֹרֵא קְרִיאַת שְׁמַע וּמְדַקְדֵּק בְּאוֹתִיּוֹתֶיהָ – מְצַנְּנִין לוֹ גֵּיהִנָּם, שֶׁנֶּאֱמַר: בְּפָרֵשׂ שַׁדַּי מְלָכִים בָּהּ תַּשְׁלֵג בְּצַלְמוֹן, אַל תִּקְרֵי בְּפָרֵשׂ אֶלָּא בְּפָרֵשׁ, אַל תִּקְרֵי בְּצַלְמוֹן אֶלָּא בְּצַלְמָוֶת.

On this same topic, **Rabbi Ḥama, son of Rabbi Ḥanina, said: Anyone who recites** ***Shema*** **and is punctilious in** enunciating **its letters, Gehenna is cooled for him, as it is stated: "When the Almighty scatters** [***befares***] **kings**[N] **over it, it will snow in Tzalmon"** (Psalms 68:15). **Do not read** ***befares,*** When He scatters, **but** ***befaresh,*** When he enunciates. When one enunciates the name of God with precision, God will fulfill the verse: It will snow in Tzalmon, on his behalf. **Do not read** ***beTzalmon,*** in Tzalmon, **but** ***betzalmavet,*** in the shadow of death, a reference to Gehenna. As reward for enunciating God's name precisely, God will cool Gehenna for him.

וְאָמַר רַבִּי חָמָא בְּרַבִּי חֲנִינָא: לָמָּה נִסְמְכוּ

**Rabbi Ḥama, son of Rabbi Ḥanina, also said: Why were**

**HALAKHA**

That one should leave space between adjacent words – שֶׁיִּתֵּן רֶיוַח בֵּין הַדְּבֵקִים: When reciting the Shema, one must be precise in his enunciation and create separation in cases where the last letter of the first word and the first letter of the second are identical (Rambam *Sefer Ahava, Hilkhot Keriat Shema* 2:8–9; *Shulḥan Arukh, Oraḥ Ḥayyim* 61:20).

**BACKGROUND**

*Hakanaf petil* – הַכָּנָף פְּתִיל: Failure to distinguish between the last syllable of one word and the first syllable of the next is easily understandable in words like *al levavekha*. However, it is a bit surprising with regard to *hakanaf petil*, as the *peh* at the end of the first word is soft and the one at the beginning of the second is hard. Apparently, at least in certain places, within Eretz Yisrael and without, there was no clear distinction between the pronunciation of hard and soft consonants, and certainly there were places where the soft consonants were read as though they had a *dagesh lene*, as is the practice in certain Jewish communities today. Or, perhaps, both were read as soft consonants, as appears to be the case in the Jerusalem Talmud, where both the soft and the hard *bet* are used interchangeably with the letter *vav*.

**NOTES**

"When the Almighty scatters kings" – "בְּפָרֵשׂ שַׁדַּי מְלָכִים": Even if, due to his transgressions, he is punished with the torment of Gehenna, his punishment will be eased because he was meticulous in the performance of mitzvot (Rav Hai Gaon). The homiletic interpretation of the verse is as follows: *Befaresh Shaddai*, when he enunciates the portion in which the Kingdom of God is mentioned; *melakhim ba*, the place where all the heathen kings are located; *tashleg beTzalmon*, Gehenna, will be cooled. The Gemara needed to emphasize that *beTzalmon* in this verse does not refer to mere darkness, as there is no significant connection between snow and darkness. Instead, *beTzalmavet*, in the Shadow of Death, is understood to refer to Gehenna, which is enveloped in absolute darkness (Rabbi Yoshiya Pinto).

Perek **II**
Daf **16** Amud **a**

אֹהָלִים לִנְחָלִים, דִּכְתִיב: כִּנְחָלִים נִטָּיוּ כְּגַנֹּת עֲלֵי נָהָר כַּאֲהָלִים נָטַע וגו׳, לוֹמַר לְךָ: מַה נְּחָלִים מַעֲלִין אֶת הָאָדָם מִטּוּמְאָה לְטָהֳרָה – אַף אֹהָלִים מַעֲלִין אֶת הָאָדָם מִכַּף חוֹבָה לְכַף זְכוּת.

**tents juxtaposed to streams, as it is written: "As streams stretched forth, as gardens by the riverside; as aloes** [***ahalim***] **planted** by the Lord, as cedars by the water" (Numbers 24:6)? The Gemara vocalizes the word *ohalim*, tents, rather than *ahalim*. They are juxtaposed in order **to tell you: Just as streams elevate a person from ritual impurity to purity** after he immerses himself in their water, **so too tents**[N] of Torah **elevate a person from the scale of guilt to the scale of merit.**

הַקּוֹרֵא לְמַפְרֵעַ לֹא יָצָא וכו׳.

We learned in our mishna: **One who recited** ***Shema*** **out of order did not fulfill** his obligation. One who recited and erred, should return to the place in *Shema* that he erred.

רַבִּי אַמִי וְרַבִּי אַסִי הָווּ קָא קָטְרִין לֵיהּ גְּנָנָא לְרַבִּי אֶלְעָזָר, אֲמַר לְהוּ: אַדְּהָכִי וְהָכִי אֵיזִיל וְאֶשְׁמַע מִלְּתָא דְּבֵי מִדְרְשָׁא, וְאֵיתֵי וְאֵימָא לְכוּ. אֲזַל אַשְׁכְּחֵיהּ לְתַנָּא דְּקָתָנֵי קַמֵּיהּ דְּרַבִּי יוֹחָנָן:

With regard to an error in the recitation of *Shema*, the Gemara recounts: **Rabbi Ami and Rabbi Asi were once tying a wedding canopy**[B] in preparation **for** the wedding of **Rabbi Elazar. He said to them: In the meantime,** until you finish, **I will go and hear something in the study hall, and I will come and say it to you. He went and found the** ***tanna*** who recited *mishnayot* in the study hall, **who was reciting** this *Tosefta* **before Rabbi Yoḥanan:**

**NOTES**

Just as streams…so too tents – מַה נְּחָלִים...אַף אֹהָלִים: Most commentaries explain that the word *ohalim* here is not the word that appears in the verse "As valleys stretched forth," etc., as there the word is *ahalim* and refers to a type of fragrant plant. Rather, the reference is to the adjacent verse: "How good are your tents [*ohalekha*], Jacob, your dwelling-places, Israel." In that context, *ohel* is generally understood as referring to the tents of Torah (*Tosafot*, Rashba, *Tosefot Rabbeinu Yehuda HaḤasid* and others).

**BACKGROUND**

Tying a wedding canopy – קָטְרִין גְּנָנָא: In talmudic times, a *huppa* was not merely a canopy spread over the couple, but a room in which the couple was secluded. Therefore, it was necessary to devote a considerable amount of time to its preparation. There is an ancient tradition that the custom in Judea was to plant a cedar at the birth of a son or an acacia tree at the birth of a daughter. When the children were to be married, branches would be taken from the trees in order to construct the *ḥuppa*. It is conceivable that they were doing the same for Rabbi Elazar.

קָרָא וְטָעָה וְאֵינוֹ יוֹדֵעַ לְהֵיכָן טָעָה, בְּאֶמְצַע הַפֶּרֶק – יַחֲזוֹר לָרֹאשׁ, בֵּין פֶּרֶק לְפֶרֶק – יַחֲזוֹר לְפֶרֶק רִאשׁוֹן, בֵּין כְּתִיבָה לִכְתִיבָה – יַחֲזוֹר לִכְתִיבָה רִאשׁוֹנָה.

**One who recited** ***Shema*** **and erred, and does not know where** exactly **he erred;**[H] if he was **in the middle of a paragraph** when he realized his error, **he must return to the beginning** of the paragraph; **if** he was **between one paragraph and another** when he realized his error but does not remember between which paragraphs, **he must return to the first** break between **paragraphs.** Similarly, **if one erred between writing and writing,** i.e., between the verse: "And you shall write them on the door posts of your house and on your gates" (Deuteronomy 6:9) in the first paragraph and the identical verse (Deuteronomy 11:20) in the second paragraph, **he must return to the first writing.**

אָמַר לֵיהּ רַבִּי יוֹחָנָן: לֹא שָׁנוּ אֶלָּא שֶׁלֹּא פָּתַח בְּ״לְמַעַן יִרְבּוּ יְמֵיכֶם״, אֲבָל פָּתַח בְּ״לְמַעַן יִרְבּוּ יְמֵיכֶם״ – סִרְכֵּיהּ נְקַט וְאָתֵי.

**Rabbi Yoḥanan said to him: They only taught** this *halakha* in a case **where one did not** yet **begin: "In order to lengthen your days"** (Deuteronomy 11:21) which follows that verse at the end of the second paragraph. **However, if he** already **began** to recite: **In order to lengthen your days,** he can assume that **he assumed his routine and continued** and completed the second paragraph.

אֲתָא וַאֲמַר לְהוּ. אֲמַרוּ לֵיהּ: אִלּוּ לֹא בָּאנוּ אֶלָּא לִשְׁמוֹעַ דָּבָר זֶה – דַּיֵּינוּ.

Rabbi Elazar **came and told** Rabbi Ami and Rabbi Asi what he heard. **They said to him: Had we come only to hear this, it would have been sufficient.**

מַתְנִי׳ הָאוּמָּנִין קוֹרִין בְּרֹאשׁ הָאִילָן וּבְרֹאשׁ הַנִּדְבָּךְ, מַה שֶּׁאֵינָן רַשָּׁאִין לַעֲשׂוֹת כֵּן בִּתְפִלָּה.

**MISHNA** The primary issue in this mishna is the requisite degree of concentration when reciting *Shema*. **Laborers** engaged in their work may **recite** ***Shema*** while standing **atop the tree**[H] **or atop the course of stones** in a wall under construction, **which they are not permitted to do for** the *Amida* **prayer,** which requires intent of the heart.

חָתָן פָּטוּר מִקְּרִיאַת שְׁמַע לַיְלָה הָרִאשׁוֹנָה, וְעַד מוֹצָאֵי שַׁבָּת אִם לֹא עָשָׂה מַעֲשֶׂה. וּמַעֲשֶׂה בְּרַבָּן גַּמְלִיאֵל שֶׁנָּשָׂא אִשָּׁה וְקָרָא לַיְלָה הָרִאשׁוֹנָה; אָמְרוּ לוֹ תַּלְמִידָיו: לִמַּדְתָּנוּ רַבֵּינוּ שֶׁחָתָן פָּטוּר מִקְּרִיאַת שְׁמַע! אָמַר לָהֶם: אֵינִי שׁוֹמֵעַ לָכֶם לְבַטֵּל הֵימֶנִּי מַלְכוּת שָׁמַיִם אֲפִילּוּ שָׁעָה אַחַת.

The mishna continues: **A groom is exempt from the recitation of** ***Shema***[H] **on the first night** of his marriage, which was generally Wednesday night, **until Saturday night,**[N] **if he has not taken action** and consummated the marriage, as he is preoccupied by concerns related to consummation of the marriage. The mishna relates that **there was an incident where Rabban Gamliel married a woman and recited** ***Shema*** even **the first night. His students said to him: Didn't our teacher teach us that a groom is exempt from the recitation of** ***Shema*****? He answered them:** Nevertheless, **I am not listening to you** to refrain from reciting *Shema*, and in so doing **preclude myself from** the acceptance of **the yoke of the Kingdom of Heaven, for even one moment.**

גמ׳ תָּנוּ רַבָּנַן: הָאוּמָּנִין קוֹרִין בְּרֹאשׁ הָאִילָן וּבְרֹאשׁ הַנִּדְבָּךְ, וּמִתְפַּלְּלִין בְּרֹאשׁ הַזַּיִת וּבְרֹאשׁ הַתְּאֵנָה, וּשְׁאָר כׇּל הָאִילָנוֹת – יוֹרְדִים לְמַטָּה וּמִתְפַּלְּלִין. וּבַעַל הַבַּיִת – בֵּין כָּךְ וּבֵין כָּךְ יוֹרֵד לְמַטָּה וּמִתְפַּלֵּל, לְפִי שֶׁאֵין דַּעְתּוֹ מְיוּשֶּׁבֶת עָלָיו.

**GEMARA** With regard to laborers, **the Sages taught** in a *Tosefta*: **Laborers,** while engaged in their labor, may **recite** ***Shema*** while standing **atop the tree or atop the course of stones** in a wall under construction. **And they** may **pray atop the olive tree or the fig tree,**[NH] as those trees have many branches close together, so one could stand on them and focus properly while praying. In the case of **all the rest of the trees,** however, **they must climb down and pray.** However, **the homeowner,** who is self-employed, **in all cases,** regardless of the type of tree, **must climb down**[N] **and pray, as he will be unable to focus appropriately.** Since, in contrast to the laborers, it is his prerogative to climb down and pray, the Sages did not permit him to pray atop the tree.

**NOTES**

**A groom is exempt from the recitation of the** ***Shema*** **until Saturday night – חָתָן פָּטוּר מִקְּרִיאַת שְׁמַע...וְעַד מוֹצָאֵי שַׁבָּת:** In the beginning of tractate *Ketubot*, the Gemara cites several reasons for the *halakha* in the mishna that a virgin bride's wedding was held on Wednesday. One, from a legal perspective, is that in the event that it was discovered she was not a virgin, he could go early the next morning and make his case before the court, which convened on Thursdays. Another reason for holding the wedding on Wednesday is because the blessing to "be fruitful and multiply" was given on the fifth day of creation, which began Wednesday night.

**Atop the olive tree or the fig tree – בְּרֹאשׁ הַזַּיִת וּבְרֹאשׁ הַתְּאֵנָה:** According to the Jerusalem Talmud, this is because these trees have numerous branches which makes it particularly difficult to climb up and down and tend to them. Furthermore, there is concern lest the branches will break due to the numerous climbs.

**The homeowner in all cases must climb down – בַּעַל הַבַּיִת בֵּין כָּךְ וּבֵין כָּךְ יוֹרֵד:** Some explain that this is because the homeowner is less accustomed to being up in a tree, and his fear will prevent him from praying with the proper intent (Rabbi Aharon HaLevi, Rosh, *Me'iri*).

**HALAKHA**

**If one recited** ***Shema*** **and erred, and does not know where he erred – קָרָא וְטָעָה וְאֵינוֹ יוֹדֵעַ לְהֵיכָן טָעָה:** One who erred in the recitation of *Shema* but does not know where he erred returns to the beginning of the paragraph. If he is uncertain which paragraph he was reciting, he returns to the beginning of the first paragraph. If he was reciting the verse: "And you shall write them," and is uncertain whether it is that verse in the first paragraph or the one in the second paragraph that he is reciting, he returns to the first. If he began reciting the verse: "In order to lengthen your days," he continues from there, as per the *baraita* and in accordance with the statement of Rabbi Yoḥanan (Rambam *Sefer Ahava, Hilkhot Keriat Shema* 2:13–14; *Shulḥan Arukh, Oraḥ Ḥayyim* 64:2–4).

**Laborers may recite atop the tree – הָאוּמָּנִין קוֹרִין בְּרֹאשׁ הָאִילָן:** One who was performing labor atop a tree or engaged in construction of a course of stones atop a wall may recite *Shema* there. No distinction is made between laborer and homeowner in this case, as no such distinction appears in the Gemara (*Tur*; Rambam *Sefer Ahava, Hilkhot Keriat Shema* 2:4; *Shulḥan Arukh, Oraḥ Ḥayyim* 63:8).

**A groom is exempt from the recitation of** ***Shema*** **– חָתָן פָּטוּר מִקְּרִיאַת שְׁמַע וכו׳:** Based on the ruling in the mishna, a groom is exempt from reciting *Shema* on his wedding night and three days thereafter as long as he did not consummate his marriage. Today, because, even under normal circumstances, one is incapable of achieving the appropriate level of intent when reciting *Shema*, even a groom is obligated to recite it (*Tosafot*; Rambam *Sefer Ahava, Hilkhot Keriat Shema* 4:1; *Shulḥan Arukh, Oraḥ Ḥayyim* 70:3).

**And they pray atop the olive tree or the fig tree – וּמִתְפַּלְּלִין בְּרֹאשׁ הַזַּיִת וּבְרֹאשׁ הַתְּאֵנָה:** Laborers engaged in labor for a homeowner at the top of a fig tree or an olive tree may pray there, but they may not pray atop other types of trees. A homeowner, however, must always climb down the tree, as per the *Tosefta* (Rambam *Sefer Ahava, Hilkhot Tefilla* 5:8; *Shulḥan Arukh, Oraḥ Ḥayyim* 90:3).

רָמֵי לֵיהּ רַב מָרִי בְּרָהּ דְּבַת שְׁמוּאֵל לְרָבָא, תְּנַן: הָאוּמָּנִין קוֹרִין בְּרֹאשׁ הָאִילָן וּבְרֹאשׁ הַנִּדְבָּךְ, אַלְמָא: לָא בָּעֵי כַּוָּונָה; וּרְמִינְהִי: הַקּוֹרֵא אֶת שְׁמַע צָרִיךְ שֶׁיְּכַוֵּין אֶת לִבּוֹ, שֶׁנֶּאֱמַר: שְׁמַע יִשְׂרָאֵל, וּלְהַלָּן הוּא אוֹמֵר: הַסְכֵּת וּשְׁמַע יִשְׂרָאֵל, מַה לְּהַלָּן בְּהַסְכָּמַת אַף כָּאן בְּהַסְכָּמַת!

**Rav Mari, son of the daughter of Shmuel,**[P] **raised a contradiction before Rava: We learned** in our mishna: **Laborers may recite** ***Shema*** **atop the tree or atop the course of stones** in a wall under construction. **We see that he does not require intent,** simple recitation is sufficient. **And he raised a contradiction** from the verbal analogy taught in a *baraita*: **One who recites** ***Shema*** **must focus his heart, as it is stated: "Hear [*Shema*], Israel." And below,** later in Deuteronomy, **it says: "Pay attention, and hear [*shema*], Israel"** (Deuteronomy 27:9). **Just as there** one must **pay attention, so too here** one must **pay attention.**

אִשְׁתֵּיק. אֲמַר לֵיהּ: מִידֵּי שְׁמִיעַ לָךְ בְּהָא? – אֲמַר לֵיהּ: הָכִי אָמַר רַב שֵׁשֶׁת: וְהוּא שֶׁבְּטֵלִין מִמְּלַאכְתָּן וְקוֹרִין.

Rava **was silent** as he had no response. But **he said to him: Have you heard anything on this** matter? **He replied: Rav Sheshet said as follows: And this** *halakha*, that laborers may recite *Shema* atop the tree only applies **when they are idle from their work and recite**[H] it so they can focus their hearts.

וְהָתַנְיָא, בֵּית הִלֵּל אוֹמְרִים: עוֹסְקִים בִּמְלַאכְתָּן וְקוֹרִין!

The Gemara challenges this: **But wasn't it taught** in a *baraita* that **Beit Hillel say:** Laborers **engage in their labor and recite** *Shema*?

לָא קַשְׁיָא: הָא בְּפֶרֶק רִאשׁוֹן, הָא בְּפֶרֶק שֵׁנִי.

The Gemara responds: **This is not difficult. This,** which says that laborers must be idle from their labor, is referring to a case when they are reciting **the first paragraph** of *Shema*, **while that,** which says that they may continue to work, is in a case when they are reciting **the second paragraph.**

תָּנוּ רַבָּנַן: הַפּוֹעֲלִים שֶׁהָיוּ עוֹשִׂין מְלָאכָה אֵצֶל בַּעַל הַבַּיִת – קוֹרִין קְרִיאַת שְׁמַע וּמְבָרְכִין לְפָנֶיהָ וּלְאַחֲרֶיהָ, וְאוֹכְלִין פִּתָּן וּמְבָרְכִין לְפָנֶיהָ וּלְאַחֲרֶיהָ, וּמִתְפַּלְּלִין תְּפִלָּה שֶׁל שְׁמוֹנֶה עֶשְׂרֵה אֲבָל אֵין יוֹרְדִין לִפְנֵי הַתֵּיבָה וְאֵין נוֹשְׂאִין כַּפֵּיהֶם.

**The Sages taught** in a *Tosefta*: **Laborers who were working for a homeowner** are obligated to **recite** ***Shema*** **and recite the blessings before it and after it; and** when they **eat their bread they** are obligated to **recite the blessing before and after it; and they** are obligated to **recite the** ***Amida*** **prayer. However, they do not descend before the ark** as communal prayer leaders **and** the priests among them **do not lift their hands** to recite the Priestly Blessing, so as not to be derelict in the duties they were hired to perform.

וְהָתַנְיָא: מֵעֵין שְׁמוֹנֶה עֶשְׂרֵה! – אָמַר רַב שֵׁשֶׁת, לָא קַשְׁיָא: הָא – רַבָּן גַּמְלִיאֵל, הָא רַבִּי יְהוֹשֻׁעַ.

The Gemara challenges this: **Didn't we learn** in a different *baraita* that laborers recite an abridged prayer consisting of **a microcosm of the** ***Amida*** **prayer** in place of the full *Amida* prayer? The Gemara responds: **This is not difficult. This** *baraita* obligating laborers to recite the full *Amida* prayer is in accordance with the opinion of **Rabban Gamliel,** as he holds that one must always recite the full eighteen blessings. **This** *baraita* which allows laborers to abridge their prayers is in accordance with the opinion of **Rabbi Yehoshua,** who permits one to abridge the *Amida* prayer.

אִי רַבִּי יְהוֹשֻׁעַ, מַאי אִירְיָא פּוֹעֲלִים, אֲפִילּוּ כָּל אָדָם נַמִי!

The Gemara objects: But **if** this *baraita* is in accordance with the opinion of **Rabbi Yehoshua, why** did the *baraita* **discuss** a case involving **laborers** in particular? Rabbi Yehoshua holds that **every person may also** recite an abridged version of the *Amida* prayer.

אֶלָּא, אִידִי וְאִידִי רַבָּן גַּמְלִיאֵל, וְלָא קַשְׁיָא: כָּאן – בְּעוֹשִׂין בִּשְׂכָרָן, כָּאן – בְּעוֹשִׂין בִּסְעוּדָתָן.

**Rather,** we must say that **this** *baraita* **and that** *baraita* are both in accordance with the opinion of **Rabban Gamliel, and this is not difficult: Here,** in the *baraita* where laborers pray the abridged version of the *Amida* prayer, refers to a case **where** laborers **work for their wage** beyond the meal provided by their employer; **while here,** in the *baraita* where laborers must pray the full *Amida* prayer, refers to a case **where** laborers **work** only **for their meal.**

וְהָתַנְיָא: הַפּוֹעֲלִים שֶׁהָיוּ עוֹשִׂים מְלָאכָה אֵצֶל בַּעַל – הַבַּיִת קוֹרִין קְרִיאַת שְׁמַע וּמִתְפַּלְּלִין, וְאוֹכְלִין פִּתָּן וְאֵין מְבָרְכִים לְפָנֶיהָ, אֲבָל מְבָרְכִין לְאַחֲרֶיהָ שְׁתַּיִם, כֵּיצַד – בְּרָכָה רִאשׁוֹנָה כְּתִקּוּנָהּ, שְׁנִיָּה – פּוֹתֵחַ בְּבִרְכַּת הָאָרֶץ וְכוֹלְלִין בּוֹנֵה יְרוּשָׁלַיִם בְּבִרְכַּת הָאָרֶץ;

**And** indeed **it was taught** in a *baraita*: **Laborers who were performing labor for the homeowner recite** ***Shema*** **and pray; and** when they **eat**[H] **their bread they do not recite a blessing beforehand** because the blessing recited before food is only an obligation by rabbinic law, **but they recite two** of the three blessings normally recited in **the blessing thereafter,** the Grace after Meals, which is an obligation by Torah law. **How so? The first blessing** is recited **in its standard** formula; **the second blessing, he begins** to recite **the blessing of the land and they include** the blessing: **Who builds Jerusalem within the blessing of the land,** at which point they conclude the Grace after Meals.

בַּמֶּה דְּבָרִים אֲמוּרִים – בְּעוֹשִׂין בִּשְׂכָרָן, אֲבָל עוֹשִׂין בִּסְעוּדָתָן אוֹ שֶׁהָיָה בַּעַל הַבַּיִת מֵיסֵב עִמָּהֶן – מְבָרְכִין כְּתִיקּוּנָהּ.

**In what** case **is this said?** This is said **with regard to** laborers **who work for their wage, but** if they **work for their meal or if the homeowner reclined** and ate the meal **with them, they recite the blessings in their standard** formula.

### PERSONALITIES

Rav Mari, son of the daughter of Shmuel – רַב מָרִי בְּרָהּ דְּבַת שְׁמוּאֵל: He is Rav Mari, the son of Rachel, a fourth-generation Babylonian *amora*, who was a contemporary of Rava. His unconventional appellation is explained by the history of Shmuel's family (see Rashi). The Gemara in *Ketubot* describes how the daughters of the *amora* Shmuel were taken into captivity. Two of them were brought to Eretz Yisrael, and one of them, Rachel, was married to a non-Jew, who later converted. From then he was called Issur the Convert and was close to the Torah luminaries in Babylonia.

Although he was born after his father converted, Rav Mari is generally mentioned without a patronymic because she was from a very prestigious family. There are several instances where Sages were called by the names of their famous mothers who were from prestigious families, even when their father's identity cast no aspersion on their lineage.

Rav Mari was apparently wealthy and engaged in commerce; however, he was also a significant Torah scholar, and was appointed to a lofty position on the court in Babylonia.

Rav Mari had three sons, all of whom were Torah scholars: Rav Aḥa Sava, Mar Zutra, and Rava bar Rav Mari.

### HALAKHA

When they are idle from their work and recite – וְהוּא שֶׁבְּטֵלִין מִמְּלַאכְתָּן וְקוֹרִין: Even laborers must stop working to recite the first paragraph of *Shema*, in accordance with the opinion of Rav Sheshet (Rambam *Sefer Ahava, Hilkhot Keriat Shema* 2:4; *Shulḥan Arukh, Oraḥ Ḥayyim* 63:7).

Laborers…recite the *Shema*, pray and eat – הַפּוֹעֲלִים...קוֹרִין קְרִיאַת שְׁמַע וּמִתְפַּלְּלִין וְאוֹכְלִין וכו׳: Laborers who are paid a salary recite an abridged *Amida* prayer and Grace after Meals. Today, all laborers recite the entire Grace after Meals, as they are hired on that basis (*Hagahot Maimoniyot*; Rambam *Sefer Ahava, Hilkhot Tefilla* 5:8, *Hilkhot Berakhot* 2:2; *Shulḥan Arukh, Oraḥ Ḥayyim* 191:1, 2).

חָתָן פָּטוּר מִקְּרִיאַת שְׁמַע. תָּנוּ רַבָּנַן: בְּשִׁבְתְּךָ בְּבֵיתֶךָ – פְּרָט לָעוֹסֵק בְּמִצְוָה, וּבְלֶכְתְּךָ בַדֶּרֶךְ – פְּרָט לְחָתָן, מִכָּאן אָמְרוּ: הַכּוֹנֵס אֶת הַבְּתוּלָה – פָּטוּר, וְאֶת הָאַלְמָנָה חַיָּיב.

We learned in the mishna that **a groom is exempt from the recitation of** ***Shema*** on the first night of his marriage. **The Sages taught** the source of this *halakha* in a *baraita* based on the verse: "When you sit in your home, and when you walk along the way." **When you sit in your home, to the exclusion of one who is engaged in** performance of a **mitzva,** who is exempt from the recitation of *Shema*; **and when you walk along the way, to the exclusion of a groom,** who is also exempt from the recitation of *Shema*. The *baraita* adds that **from here,** from this interpretation of the verses, **they said: One who marries a virgin is exempt** from the recitation of *Shema* on his wedding night, **but one who marries a widow is obligated.**

מַאי מַשְׁמַע? – אָמַר רַב פַּפָּא: כִּי דֶּרֶךְ, מָה דֶּרֶךְ – רְשׁוּת, אַף הָכָא נַמִי – רְשׁוּת.

The Gemara clarifies the meaning of this baraita, and asks: **From where is it inferred** that the verse: "When you walk along the way," enables us to derive that a groom is exempt from the obligation to recite Shema? **Rav Pappa said** that it is derived: **Like the way; just as** the journey along a specific **way** described in the verse **is voluntary** and involves no mitzva, **so too all** of those who are obligated to recite *Shema* are engaged in **voluntary activities.** However, one engaged in performance of a mitzva is exempt from the obligation to recite *Shema*.

מִי לָא עָסְקִינַן דְּקָאָזֵיל לִדְבַר מִצְוָה, וַאֲפִילּוּ הָכִי אָמַר רַחֲמָנָא לִיקְרֵי!

The Gemara asks: **Are we not dealing with** a case where one is walking along **on his way to** perform **a mitzva; nevertheless, the Torah said to recite** *Shema*, indicating that he is obligated even if he set out to perform a mitzva.

אִם כֵּן, לֵימָא קְרָא בְּלֶכֶת, מַאי בְּלֶכְתְּךָ – שְׁמַע מִינַּהּ: בְּלֶכֶת דִּידָךְ הוּא דְּמִחַיַּיבְתְּ, הָא דְּמִצְוָה – פְּטִירַתְּ.

The Gemara explains: **If so,** that the intention was to obligate in all cases, **let the Torah say: When walking** along the way. **What is** the meaning of: **When you walk** along the way? **Conclude from this: It is** in a case **of your walking,** meaning that when you do this for your own purposes and of your own volition, **you are obligated** to recite *Shema*, **but** when you go with the objective **of** performing a **mitzva, you are exempt.**

Perek **II**
Daf **16** Amud **b**

– אִי הָכִי מַאי אִירְיָא הַכּוֹנֵס אֶת הַבְּתוּלָה, אֲפִילּוּ כּוֹנֵס אֶת הָאַלְמָנָה נַמִי!

The Gemara questions this: **If so, why discuss** a case of **one who is marrying a virgin** in particular? **Even one who is marrying a widow** is performing a mitzva and should **also** be exempt.

הָכָא טָרִיד, וְהָכָא לָא טָרִיד.

The Gemara responds that nevertheless, there is a distinction between one marrying a virgin and one marrying a widow. **Here,** in the case of one who marries a virgin, the groom is **preoccupied** by his thoughts, **while here,** in the case of one who marries a widow, **he is not preoccupied.**

אִי מִשּׁוּם טִרְדָּא – אֲפִילּוּ טָבְעָה סְפִינָתוֹ בַּיָּם נַמִי! אַלְמָה אָמַר רַבִּי אַבָּא בַּר זַבְדָּא אָמַר רַב: אָבֵל חַיָּיב בְּכׇל מִצְוֹת הָאֲמוּרוֹת בַּתּוֹרָה, חוּץ מִן הַתְּפִילִּין, שֶׁהֲרֵי נֶאֱמַר בָּהֶן פְּאֵר, שֶׁנֶּאֱמַר: פְּאֵרְךָ חֲבוֹשׁ עָלֶיךָ וגו׳! –

The Gemara challenges: **If** a groom is exempt from the recitation of *Shema* simply **due to preoccupation,** then **even** one who is preoccupied because **his ship sank at sea should** be exempt. If so, **why then did Rabbi Abba bar Zavda say** that **Rav said: A mourner is obligated in all the mitzvot mentioned in the Torah except for** the mitzva to don **phylacteries, as** the term **splendor is stated** with regard to phylacteries, **as it is stated** that the prophet Ezekiel was prohibited to mourn and was told: **"Bind your splendor upon yourself"** (Ezekiel 24:17). If even a mourner, who is pained and preoccupied, is obligated to recite *Shema*, clearly preoccupation has no bearing upon one's obligation.

אָמְרִי: הָתָם טִרְדָּא דִּרְשׁוּת, הָכָא טִרְדָּא דְּמִצְוָה.

The Gemara responds: Nevertheless, there is a distinction between the cases. **There,** it is a case of **preoccupation with a voluntary** act, as there is no mitzva to be preoccupied with his mourning, but **here,** in the case of a groom, the cause of **the preoccupation is the mitzva** itself.

מתני׳ רָחַץ לַיְלָה הָרִאשׁוֹן שֶׁמֵּתָה אִשְׁתּוֹ, אָמְרוּ לוֹ תַּלְמִידָיו: לִמַּדְתָּנוּ רַבֵּינוּ שֶׁאָבֵל אָסוּר לִרְחוֹץ! אָמַר לָהֶם: אֵינִי כִּשְׁאָר בְּנֵי אָדָם, אִסְטְנִיס אֲנִי.

**MISHNA** The mishna relates another episode portraying unusual conduct by Rabban Gamliel. **He bathed on the first night after his wife died. His students said to him:** Have **you not taught us, our teacher, that a mourner is prohibited to bathe?**[H] He answered them: **I am not like other people, I am delicate** [***istenis***].[NL] For me, not bathing causes actual physical distress, and even a mourner need not suffer physical distress as part of his mourning.

**HALAKHA**

**A mourner is prohibited to bathe – שֶׁאָבֵל אָסוּר לִרְחוֹץ:** A mourner is prohibited to wash his entire body, as opposed to washing it incrementally, during the seven days of mourning, as we learned in the mishna. Today, the practice is to refrain from bathing for thirty days, and one should not deviate from this custom, as it is an ancient practice established by *vatikin* (Rema; Rambam *Sefer Shofetim, Hilkhot Evel* 5:3; *Shulḥan Arukh, Yoreh De'a* 381:1).

**NOTES**

**Delicate – אִסְטְנִיס:** The Sages said elsewhere that not every sensitive person is permitted to bathe when in mourning; only those who truly suffer. Some say only one who becomes physically ill from failure to bathe may do so when in mourning (*Peri Ḥadash*, see the Rosh).

**LANGUAGE**

**Delicate [*istenis*] – אִסְטְנִיס:** From the Greek ἀσθενής, *asthenès*, meaning weak or sickly.

וּכְשֶׁמֵּת טָבִי עַבְדּוֹ קִבֵּל עָלָיו תַּנְחוּמִין; אָמְרוּ לוֹ תַּלְמִידָיו: לִמַּדְתָּנוּ רַבֵּינוּ שֶׁאֵין מְקַבְּלִין תַּנְחוּמִין עַל הָעֲבָדִים! אָמַר לָהֶם: אֵין טָבִי עַבְדִּי כִּשְׁאָר כָּל הָעֲבָדִים, כָּשֵׁר הָיָה.

Another exceptional incident is related: **And when his slave, Tavi,**[P] **died,** Rabban Gamliel **accepted condolences for his** death[N] as one would for a close family member. **His students said to him: Have you** not **taught us, our teacher, that one does not accept condolences for** the death of **slaves?** Rabban Gamliel said to his students: **My slave, Tavi, is not like all the rest of the slaves, he was virtuous** and it is appropriate to accord him the same respect accorded to a family member.

חָתָן אִם רוֹצֶה לִקְרוֹת קְרִיאַת שְׁמַע לַיְלָה הָרִאשׁוֹן – קוֹרֵא. רַבָּן שִׁמְעוֹן בֶּן גַּמְלִיאֵל אוֹמֵר: לֹא כׇּל הָרוֹצֶה לִיטּוֹל אֶת הַשֵּׁם יִטּוֹל.

With regard to the recitation of *Shema* on one's wedding night, the Sages said that **if,** despite his exemption, **a groom wishes to recite *Shema* on the first night,**[H] he may do so. **Rabban Shimon ben Gamliel says: Not everyone who wishes to assume the reputation** of a God-fearing person **may assume** it, and consequently, not everyone who wishes to recite *Shema* on his wedding night may do so.

גמ׳ מַאי טַעְמָא דְּרַבָּן (שִׁמְעוֹן בֶּן) גַּמְלִיאֵל? קָסָבַר אֲנִינוּת לַיְלָה דְּרַבָּנַן, דִּכְתִיב: ״וְאַחֲרִיתָהּ כְּיוֹם מָר״, וּבְמָקוֹם אִיסְטְנִיס לָא גָּזְרוּ בֵּיהּ רַבָּנַן.

## GEMARA

With regard to Rabban Gamliel's bathing on the first night after the death of his wife, the Gemara asks: **What is the reason** that **Rabban Gamliel** did not practice the customs of mourning after his wife died? The Gemara answers: **He holds that** acute mourning [*aninut*] is in effect only on the day of the death itself, but **acute mourning at night is** only **by rabbinic law, as it is written:** "And I will turn your feasts into mourning, and all your songs into lamentations; I will bring sackcloth upon your loins and baldness upon every head; and I will make you like a mourner for an only child, **and the end will be like a bitter day"** (Amos 8:10). Therefore, by Torah law one's acute mourning is only during the day, like a bitter day, while the acute mourning at night that follows is only rabbinic. **And in the case of a delicate person, the Sages did not issue a decree** that one should afflict himself during the period of acute mourning.

וּכְשֶׁמֵּת טָבִי עַבְדּוֹ וכו׳.

We learned in our mishna that: **When his servant, Tavi, died,** Rabban Gamliel accepted condolences for him.

תָּנוּ רַבָּנַן: עֲבָדִים וּשְׁפָחוֹת אֵין עוֹמְדִין עֲלֵיהֶם בְּשׁוּרָה, וְאֵין אוֹמְרִים עֲלֵיהֶם בִּרְכַּת אֲבֵלִים וְתַנְחוּמֵי אֲבֵלִים.

**The Sages** taught in a *baraita*: For **slaves and maidservants** who die, **one does not stand in a row**[H] of comforters to console the mourners, **and one recites neither the blessing of the mourners nor the consolation of the mourners.**

מַעֲשֶׂה וּמֵתָה שִׁפְחָתוֹ שֶׁל רַבִּי אֱלִיעֶזֶר נִכְנְסוּ תַּלְמִידָיו לְנַחֲמוֹ. כֵּיוָן שֶׁרָאָה אוֹתָם עָלָה לַעֲלִיָּיה – וְעָלוּ אַחֲרָיו; נִכְנַס לָאַנְפִּילוֹן – נִכְנְסוּ אַחֲרָיו, נִכְנַס לִטְרַקְלִין – נִכְנְסוּ אַחֲרָיו; אָמַר לָהֶם: כִּמְדוּמֶּה אֲנִי שֶׁאַתֶּם נִכְוִים בְּפוֹשְׁרִים, עַכְשָׁיו אִי אַתֶּם נִכְוִים אֲפִילּוּ בְּחַמֵּי חַמִּין! לֹא כָּךְ שָׁנִיתִי לָכֶם: עֲבָדִים וּשְׁפָחוֹת אֵין עוֹמְדִים עֲלֵיהֶם בְּשׁוּרָה וְאֵין אוֹמְרִים עֲלֵיהֶם בִּרְכַּת אֲבֵלִים וְלֹא תַּנְחוּמֵי אֲבֵלִים? אֶלָּא מָה אוֹמְרִים עֲלֵיהֶם – כְּשֵׁם שֶׁאוֹמְרִים לוֹ לְאָדָם עַל שׁוֹרוֹ וְעַל חֲמוֹרוֹ שֶׁמֵּתוּ: הַמָּקוֹם יְמַלֵּא לָךְ חֶסְרוֹנְךָ, כָּךְ אוֹמְרִים לוֹ עַל עַבְדּוֹ וְעַל שִׁפְחָתוֹ: הַמָּקוֹם יְמַלֵּא לָךְ חֶסְרוֹנְךָ.

**An incident** is related that when **Rabbi Eliezer's maidservant died, his students entered to console him.**[N] **When he saw them** approaching **he went up to the second floor, and they went up after him. He entered the gatehouse** [*anpilon*],[L] **and they entered after him. He entered the banquet hall** [*teraklin*],[L] and **they entered after him.** Having seen them follow him everywhere, **he said to them: It seems to me that you would be burned by lukewarm water,** meaning that you could take a hint and when I went up to the second floor, you would understand that I did not wish to receive your consolations. **Now** I see that **you are not even burned by boiling hot water. Did I not teach you the following:** For **slaves and maidservants** who die, **one does not stand in a row** of comforters to console the mourners **and one neither recites the blessing of the mourners nor** does he recite **the consolation of the mourners,** as the relationship between master and slave is not like a familial relationship? **Rather, what does one say about them** when they die? **Just as we say to a person about his ox or donkey which died: May the Omnipresent replenish your loss, so too do we say for one's slave or maidservant** who died: **May the Omnipresent replenish your loss,** as the connection between a master and his slave is only financial in nature

### PERSONALITIES

Tavi – טָבִי: Tavi, the slave of Rabban Gamliel, is the most famous slave in the Talmud. Some go so far as to draw a parallel between Tavi, the slave of Rabban Gamliel, and Eliezer, the slave of Abraham.

Rabban Gamliel was very fond of Tavi and appreciated his character and Torah knowledge. The Gemara relates that when Rabban Gamliel thought he had discovered a way to free Tavi he was overjoyed. Ultimately, though, he did not free him, due to concern over the prohibition to free a slave. Despite this, Rabban Gamliel treated him as a member of his family and, therefore, he accepted condolences when Tavi died.

The Sages said about Tavi: There were many who were worthy to be ordained, like Tavi, the slave of Rabban Gamliel. Due to their lineage, they did not achieve that status.

### NOTES

**And when his slave, Tavi, died, he accepted condolences for him – וּכְשֶׁמֵּת טָבִי עַבְדּוֹ קִבֵּל עָלָיו תַּנְחוּמִין:** This does not contradict the principle that one does not accept condolences for slaves, as they commented in the Jerusalem Talmud: From here we see that a student is beloved like a son. A virtuous slave who was a student, like Tavi, is beloved like a son and therefore one may accept condolences for his death.

**His students entered to console him – נִכְנְסוּ תַּלְמִידָיו לְנַחֲמוֹ:** He knew that they were coming to console him and not to say, May the Omnipresent replenish your loss, because they entered in the manner of those coming to console a mourner (*Ḥefetz Hashem*).

### HALAKHA

**If a groom wishes to recite *Shema* the first night – חָתָן אִם הָיָה רוֹצֶה לִקְרוֹת קְרִיאַת שְׁמַע לַיְלָה הָרִאשׁוֹן:** A groom who wishes to recite *Shema* on his wedding night may not do so because it appears presumptuous, in accordance with the opinion of Rabban Shimon ben Gamliel. Today, however, all grooms recite it and, on the contrary, failure to recite it appears presumptuous. (Rambam *Sefer Ahava, Hilkhot Keriat Shema* 4:7; *Shulḥan Arukh, Oraḥ Ḥayyim* 70:3).

**For slaves and maidservants, one does not stand in a row – עֲבָדִים וּשְׁפָחוֹת אֵין עוֹמְדִין עֲלֵיהֶם בְּשׁוּרָה:** One neither stands in a row to console nor does one recite the consolation of mourners to the masters of slaves and maidservants who died. Instead, one says to him: "May the Omnipresent replenish your loss," as he would had his ox or donkey died (Rambam *Sefer Shofetim, Hilkhot Evel* 12:12; *Shulḥan Arukh, Yoreh De'a* 377:1).

### LANGUAGE

**Gatehouse [*anpilon*] – אַנְפִּילוֹן:** Apparently, from the Greek πυλών, meaning an anteroom or a small room built around a gate used as a corridor.

**Banquet hall [*teraklin*] – טְרַקְלִין:** From the Greek τρικλίνιον, this refers to a room with three divans; however, its meaning has been expanded to include any large room where guests are hosted.

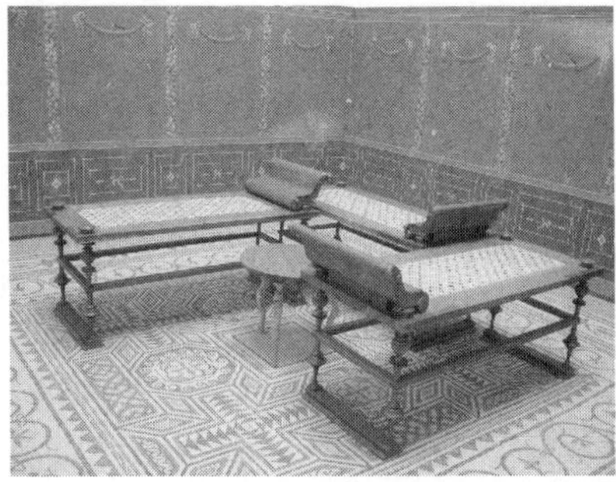

Roman banquet hall

תַּנְיָא אִידָךְ: עֲבָדִים וּשְׁפָחוֹת אֵין מַסְפִּידִין אוֹתָן; רַבִּי יוֹסֵי אוֹמֵר: אִם עֶבֶד כָּשֵׁר הוּא, אוֹמְרִים עָלָיו: הוֹי אִישׁ טוֹב וְנֶאֱמָן וְנֶהֱנֶה מִיגִיעוֹ! אָמְרוּ לוֹ: אִם כֵּן, מָה הִנַּחְתָּ לַכְּשֵׁרִים?

**It was taught in another** *baraita*: **One does not eulogize slaves and maidservants. Rabbi Yosei says: If he was a virtuous servant, one recites over him** a eulogy of sorts: **Alas, a good and loyal man who enjoyed** the fruits **of his hard labor. They said to him: If so, what** praise **have you left for virtuous** Jews? A Jewish person would be proud to be eulogized in that manner.

תָּנוּ רַבָּנַן: אֵין קוֹרִין אָבוֹת אֶלָּא לִשְׁלֹשָׁה, וְאֵין קוֹרִין אִמָּהוֹת אֶלָּא לְאַרְבַּע.

**The Sages taught** in a *baraita*: **One may only call three** people **patriarchs,**[N] Abraham, Isaac, and Jacob, but not Jacob's children. **And one may only call four** people **matriarchs,** Sarah, Rebecca, Rachel, and Leah.

אָבוֹת מַאי טַעְמָא? אִילֵימָא מִשּׁוּם דְּלָא יָדְעִינַן אִי מֵרְאוּבֵן קָא אָתֵינַן אִי מִשִּׁמְעוֹן קָא אָתֵינַן – אִי הָכִי, אִמָּהוֹת נַמִּי – לָא יָדְעִינַן אִי מֵרָחֵל קָא אָתֵינַן אִי מִלֵּאָה קָא אָתֵינַן! אֶלָּא: עַד הָכָא – חֲשִׁיבֵי, טְפֵי – לָא חֲשִׁיבֵי.

The Gemara asks: **What is the reason** for this exclusivity with regard to the **Patriarchs? If you say** that it is **because we do not know whether we descend from Reuben or from Simon,** so we cannot accurately say our father Reuben, for example, **if so,** with regard to the Matriarchs as well, **we do not know whether we descend from Rachel or from Leah,** and we should not call Rachel and Leah matriarchs either. **Instead,** the reason the sons of Jacob are not called patriarchs is not for that reason, but because **until** Jacob **they are significant** enough to be referred to as patriarchs, but **beyond** Jacob, **they are not significant** enough to be referred to as patriarchs.

תַּנְיָא אִידָךְ: עֲבָדִים וּשְׁפָחוֹת אֵין קוֹרִין אוֹתָם אַבָּא פְּלוֹנִי וְאִמָּא פְּלוֹנִית, וְשֶׁל רַבָּן גַּמְלִיאֵל הָיוּ קוֹרִים אוֹתָם אַבָּא פְּלוֹנִי וְאִמָּא פְּלוֹנִית.

This serves as an introduction; although older people are often referred to with the honorific: Father so-and-so, **it was taught in another** *baraita*: **One may not refer to slaves and maidservants as father** [*abba*] **so-and-so**[N] **or mother** [*imma*] **so-and-so. And they would call** the slaves and maidservants **of Rabban Gamliel "father so-and-so" and "mother so-and-so."**

מַעֲשֶׂה לִסְתּוֹר? – מִשּׁוּם דַּחֲשִׁיבֵי.

The Gemara asks: Is a **story** cited in order **to contradict**[B] the previously stated *halakha*? The Gemara answers: There is no contradiction; rather, **because** Rabban Gamliel's servants **were significant,** they were addressed with these honorifics.

אָמַר רַבִּי אֶלְעָזָר: מַאי דִּכְתִיב: ״כֵּן אֲבָרֶכְךָ בְחַיָּי בְּשִׁמְךָ אֶשָּׂא כַפָּי״ – ״כֵּן אֲבָרֶכְךָ בְחַיָּי״ – זוֹ קְרִיאַת שְׁמַע, ״בְּשִׁמְךָ אֶשָּׂא כַפָּי״ – זוֹ תְּפִלָּה. וְאִם עוֹשֶׂה כֵּן עָלָיו הַכָּתוּב אוֹמֵר: ״כְּמוֹ חֵלֶב וָדֶשֶׁן תִּשְׂבַּע נַפְשִׁי״, וְלֹא עוֹד אֶלָּא שֶׁנּוֹחֵל שְׁנֵי עוֹלָמִים, הָעוֹלָם הַזֶּה וְהָעוֹלָם הַבָּא, שֶׁנֶּאֱמַר: ״וְשִׂפְתֵי רְנָנוֹת יְהַלֶּל פִּי״.

The Gemara cites an aggadic statement concerning prayer and the recitation of *Shema*. **Rabbi Elazar said: What is** the meaning of **that which is written: "So I will bless You as I live, to Your name I will raise my hands"** (Psalms 63:5)? **So I will bless You as I live, refers to the recitation of** ***Shema*****,** and **to Your name I will raise my hands, refers to** the *Amida* **prayer,** which is characterized as lifting one's hands to God. **And if one does so,** recites *Shema* and prays, **the verse says about him: "As with fat and marrow, my soul will be satisfied"** (Psalms 63:6). **And not only** does he receive this reward, **but he inherits two worlds, this world and the World-to-Come, as it is stated: "With lips of joys [*renanot*], my mouth praises You"** (Psalms 63:6). The plural, joys, refers to two joys, that of this world and that of the World-to-Come.

רַבִּי אֶלְעָזָר בָּתַר דִּמְסַיֵּים צְלוֹתֵיהּ אָמַר הָכִי: יְהִי רָצוֹן מִלְּפָנֶיךָ ה׳ אֱלֹהֵינוּ שֶׁתַּשְׁכֵּן בְּפוּרֵינוּ אַהֲבָה וְאַחֲוָה וְשָׁלוֹם וְרֵיעוּת, וְתַרְבֶּה גְּבוּלֵנוּ בְּתַלְמִידִים, וְתַצְלִיחַ סוֹפֵנוּ אַחֲרִית וְתִקְוָה, וְתָשִׂים חֶלְקֵנוּ בְּגַן עֵדֶן, וְתַקְּנֵנוּ בְּחָבֵר טוֹב וְיֵצֶר טוֹב בְּעוֹלָמְךָ, וְנַשְׁכִּים וְנִמְצָא יִחוּל לְבָבֵנוּ לְיִרְאָה אֶת שְׁמֶךָ, וְתָבֹא לְפָנֶיךָ קוֹרַת נַפְשֵׁנוּ לְטוֹבָה.

The Gemara describes how **after Rabbi Elazar concluded his prayer, he said the following** additional prayer:
**May it be Your will, Lord our God,**
**to cause to dwell in our lot love and brotherhood, peace and friendship.**
**And may You make our borders rich in disciples**
**and cause us to ultimately succeed,** that we will have a good **end and hope.**
**And may You set our portion in the Garden of Eden,**
**and may You establish for us a good companion and a good inclination in Your world.**
**And may we rise early and find the aspiration of our hearts to fear Your name,**
**and may the satisfaction of our souls come before You,** i.e., may You hear our prayers that we may have spiritual contentment in this world **for the best.**

רַבִּי יוֹחָנָן בָּתַר דִּמְסַיֵּים צְלוֹתֵיהּ אָמַר הָכִי: יְהִי רָצוֹן מִלְּפָנֶיךָ ה׳ אֱלֹהֵינוּ שֶׁתָּצִיץ בְּבָשְׁתֵּנוּ וְתַבִּיט בְּרָעָתֵנוּ וְתִתְלַבֵּשׁ בְּרַחֲמֶיךָ וְתִתְכַּסֶּה בְּעֻזְּךָ וְתִתְעַטֵּף בַּחֲסִידוּתְךָ וְתִתְאַזֵּר בַּחֲנִינוּתְךָ וְתָבֹא לְפָנֶיךָ מִדַּת טוּבְךָ וְעַנְוְתָנוּתְךָ.

Similarly, the Gemara recounts that **after Rabbi Yoḥanan concluded his prayer, he said the following** additional prayer:
**May it be Your will, Lord our God,**
**that You look upon our shame and behold our plight,**
**that You clothe Yourself in Your mercy,**
**and cover Yourself with Your might,**
**that You wrap Yourself in Your loving-kindness,**
**and gird Yourself with Your grace,**
**and may Your attributes of goodness and humility come before You.**

NOTES

**One may only call three people patriarchs – אֵין קוֹרִין ״אָבוֹת״ אֶלָּא לִשְׁלֹשָׁה וכו׳:** Some explain that one who does not descend from these three patriarchs and four matriarchs is not eulogized, and that this is the connection between this passage and the laws of mourning for servants (Rav Sa'adia Gaon; see *Peri Ḥadash*).

**Father so-and-so – אַבָּא פְּלוֹנִי:** Some explain that one should not call a slave father so-and-so lest people conclude that the slave is actually his father, and his lineage will be called into question. Only Rabban Gamliel's slaves could be addressed in that manner, as they were distinguished and due to their renown, there would be no confusion (see *Shulḥan Arukh*, *Ḥoshen Mishpat* 279:5).

BACKGROUND

**A story to contradict – מַעֲשֶׂה לִסְתּוֹר:** This is a common question, raised when a mishna or *baraita* cites a story which contradicts the *halakha* cited immediately before. Generally, stories are cited to reinforce a stated *halakha* by demonstrating that it is not merely a *halakha* in theory but in practice as well. Therefore, when a story is incongruent with the previously cited *halakha*, it seems contradictory.

## PERSONALITIES

**Rav Safra – רַב סַפְרָא:** Rav Safra was a third-fourth generation Babylonian *amora*.

In the Talmud, Rav Safra is found engaging in halakhic discourse with the greatest of the third generation Sages, Rabba, Rav Yosef, and others. He was similarly active in the generation of their students, Abaye and Rava.

Apparently, Rav Safra was a merchant, who traveled on business to Eretz Yisrael where he engaged in halakhic discourse with various Sages, Rabbi Abba and Rabbi Abbahu among others. His primary focus was in the realm of *halakha* and dealt less in the disciplines of Bible and *aggada*. Rav Safra was renowned for his exemplary character, especially for distancing himself from all forms of dishonesty.

Since Rav Safra was an itinerant merchant, he never established his own yeshiva and did not spend much time in the study hall. Therefore, there were those among the Sages who held that he was unlike other Rabbis, that all are required to mourn their passing.

רַבִּי זֵירָא בָּתַר דִּמְסַיֵּים צְלוֹתֵיהּ אֲמַר הָכִי: יְהִי רָצוֹן מִלְּפָנֶיךָ ה׳ אֱלֹהֵינוּ שֶׁלֹּא נֶחֱטָא וְלֹא נֵבוֹשׁ וְלֹא נִכָּלֵם מֵאֲבוֹתֵינוּ.

Similarly, **after Rabbi Zeira concluded his prayers he said the following** additional prayer:
**May it be Your will, Lord our God,**
**that we not sin or shame ourselves,**
**and that we not disgrace ourselves before our forefathers,**
in the sense that our actions should not disgrace the actions of our forefathers.

רַבִּי חִיָּיא בָּתַר דִּמְצַלֵּי אֲמַר הָכִי: יְהִי רָצוֹן מִלְּפָנֶיךָ ה׳ אֱלֹהֵינוּ שֶׁתְּהֵא תּוֹרָתְךָ אוּמָּנוּתֵנוּ, וְאַל יִדְוֶה לִבֵּנוּ וְאַל יֶחְשְׁכוּ עֵינֵינוּ.

**After Rabbi Ḥiyya prayed he said the following:**
**May it be Your will, Lord our God,**
**that Your Torah should be our vocation,**
**and may our heart not become faint nor our eyes dim.**

רַב בָּתַר צְלוֹתֵיהּ אֲמַר הָכִי: יְהִי רָצוֹן מִלְּפָנֶיךָ ה׳ אֱלֹהֵינוּ שֶׁתִּתֵּן לָנוּ חַיִּים אֲרוּכִים, חַיִּים שֶׁל שָׁלוֹם, חַיִּים שֶׁל טוֹבָה, חַיִּים שֶׁל בְּרָכָה, חַיִּים שֶׁל פַּרְנָסָה, חַיִּים שֶׁל חִלּוּץ עֲצָמוֹת, חַיִּים שֶׁיֵּשׁ בָּהֶם יִרְאַת חֵטְא, חַיִּים שֶׁאֵין בָּהֶם בּוּשָׁה וּכְלִימָּה, חַיִּים שֶׁל עוֹשֶׁר וְכָבוֹד, חַיִּים שֶׁתְּהֵא בָנוּ אַהֲבַת תּוֹרָה וְיִרְאַת שָׁמַיִם, חַיִּים שֶׁתְּמַלֵּא לָנוּ אֶת כָּל מִשְׁאֲלוֹת לִבֵּנוּ לְטוֹבָה.

**After his prayer, Rav said the following:**
**May it be Your will, Lord our God,**
**that You grant us long life, a life of peace,**
**a life of goodness, a life of blessing,**
**a life of sustenance, a life of freedom of movement** from place to place, where we are not tied to one place,
**a life of dread of sin, a life without shame and disgrace,**
**a life of wealth and honor,**
**a life in which we have love of Torah and reverence for Heaven,**
**a life in which You fulfill all the desires of our heart for good.**

רַבִּי בָּתַר צְלוֹתֵיהּ אֲמַר הָכִי: יְהִי רָצוֹן מִלְּפָנֶיךָ ה׳ אֱלֹהֵינוּ וֵאלֹהֵי אֲבוֹתֵינוּ שֶׁתַּצִּילֵנוּ מֵעַזֵּי פָנִים וּמֵעַזּוּת פָּנִים, מֵאָדָם רָע וּמִפֶּגַע רָע, מִיֵּצֶר רָע, מֵחָבֵר רָע, מִשָּׁכֵן רָע, וּמִשָּׂטָן הַמַּשְׁחִית, וּמִדִּין קָשֶׁה וּמִבַּעַל דִּין קָשֶׁה, בֵּין שֶׁהוּא בֶן בְּרִית בֵּין שֶׁאֵינוֹ בֶן בְּרִית.

**After his prayer, Rabbi** Yehuda HaNasi **said the following:**
**May it be Your will, Lord our God, and God of our forefathers,**
**that You save us from the arrogant and from arrogance** in general,
**from a bad man, from a bad mishap,**
**from an evil instinct, from a bad companion,**
**from a bad neighbor, from the destructive Satan,**
**from a harsh trial and from a harsh opponent,**
**whether he is a member of the covenant,** a Jew,
**or whether he is not a member of the covenant.**

וְאַף עַל גַּב דְּקַיְימִי קָצוּצֵי עֲלֵיהּ דְּרַבִּי.

**And** the Gemara notes that Rabbi Yehuda HaNasi would recite this prayer every day **despite the fact that** royal **officers stood** watch **over Rabbi** Yehuda HaNasi for his protection; nevertheless, he prayed to avoid conflict or hindrance resulting from arrogance.

רַב סַפְרָא בָּתַר צְלוֹתֵיהּ אֲמַר הָכִי: יְהִי רָצוֹן מִלְּפָנֶיךָ ה׳ אֱלֹהֵינוּ שֶׁתָּשִׂים שָׁלוֹם

**After his prayer, Rav Safra**[P] **said the following:**
**May it be Your will, Lord our God, that You establish peace**

Perek **II**
Daf **17** Amud **a**

## NOTES

**In the heavenly entourage – בְּפָמַלְיָא שֶׁל מַעְלָה:** Since the reference is to Torah scholars who study polemically, there is room to emphasize the establishment of peace in the entire universe, in the heavens and on earth, as well as among those who study Torah.

**A lighted corner – בְּקֶרֶן אוֹרָה:** The word *keren*, corner, has a dual meaning in this context, as it also connotes exaltedness and loftiness (see I Samuel 2:10). Therefore, the term *keren ora*, a lighted corner, connotes ascending in a lighted path, while at the same time *keren* refers to a corner, in contrast to a darkened corner (see *Tziyyun LeNefesh Ḥayya*).

## LANGUAGE

**Entourage [*pamalia*] – פָּמַלְיָא:** This derives from the Latin familia, meaning extended family, the whole of the household including the servants; a company.

בְּפָמַלְיָא שֶׁל מַעְלָה וּבְפָמַלְיָא שֶׁל מַטָּה, וּבֵין הַתַּלְמִידִים הָעוֹסְקִים בְּתוֹרָתֶךָ, בֵּין עוֹסְקִין לִשְׁמָהּ בֵּין עוֹסְקִין שֶׁלֹּא לִשְׁמָהּ. וְכָל הָעוֹסְקִין שֶׁלֹּא לִשְׁמָהּ, יְהִי רָצוֹן שֶׁיְּהוּ עוֹסְקִין לִשְׁמָהּ.

**in the heavenly entourage** [*pamalia*][NL] of angels each of whom ministers to a specific nation (see Daniel 10), and whose infighting causes war on earth;
**and in the earthly entourage,** the Sages,
**and among the disciples engaged in** the study of **Your Torah,**
**whether they engage in its study for its own sake or not for its own sake.**
**And all those engaged** in Torah study **not for its own sake,**
**may it be** Your **will** that **they will come to engage** in its study **for its own sake.**

רַבִּי אֲלֶכְּסַנְדְּרִי בָּתַר צְלוֹתֵיהּ אֲמַר הָכִי: יְהִי רָצוֹן מִלְּפָנֶיךָ ה׳ אֱלֹהֵינוּ שֶׁתַּעֲמִידֵנוּ בְּקֶרֶן אוֹרָה וְאַל תַּעֲמִידֵנוּ בְּקֶרֶן חֲשֵׁכָה, וְאַל יִדְוֶה לִבֵּנוּ וְאַל יֶחְשְׁכוּ עֵינֵינוּ. אִיכָּא דְּאָמְרִי: הָא רַב הַמְנוּנָא מְצַלֵּי לַהּ, וְרַבִּי אֲלֶכְּסַנְדְּרִי בָּתַר דִּמְצַלֵּי אֲמַר הָכִי: רִבּוֹן הָעוֹלָמִים, גָּלוּי וְיָדוּעַ לְפָנֶיךָ שֶׁרְצוֹנֵנוּ לַעֲשׂוֹת רְצוֹנְךָ, וּמִי מְעַכֵּב? שְׂאוֹר שֶׁבָּעִיסָּה וְשִׁעְבּוּד מַלְכִיּוֹת; יְהִי רָצוֹן מִלְּפָנֶיךָ שֶׁתַּצִּילֵנוּ מִיָּדָם, וְנָשׁוּב לַעֲשׂוֹת חוּקֵּי רְצוֹנְךָ בְּלֵבָב שָׁלֵם.

**After his prayer, Rabbi Alexandri said the following:**
**May it be Your will, Lord our God,**
**that You station us in a lighted corner**[N] **and not in a darkened corner,**
**and do not let our hearts become faint nor our eyes dim.**
**Some say that this was the prayer that Rav Hamnuna would recite, and that after Rabbi Alexandri prayed, he would say the following:**
**Master of the Universe, it is revealed and known before You**
**that our will is to perform Your will, and what prevents us?**
On the one hand, **the yeast in the dough,** the evil inclination that is within every person;
**and the subjugation to the kingdoms** on the other.
**May it be Your will**
**that You will deliver us from their hands,** of both the evil inclination and the foreign kingdoms,
so that **we may return to perform the edicts of Your will with a perfect heart.**

רָבָא בָּתַר צְלוֹתֵיהּ אֲמַר הָכִי: אֱלֹהַי, עַד שֶׁלֹּא נוֹצַרְתִּי אֵינִי כְּדַאי וְעַכְשָׁיו שֶׁנּוֹצַרְתִּי כְּאִלּוּ לֹא נוֹצַרְתִּי, עָפָר אֲנִי בְּחַיַּי, קַל וָחוֹמֶר בְּמִיתָתִי, הֲרֵי אֲנִי לְפָנֶיךָ כִּכְלִי מָלֵא בוּשָׁה וּכְלִימָּה, יְהִי רָצוֹן מִלְּפָנֶיךָ ה׳ אֱלֹהַי שֶׁלֹּא אֶחֱטָא עוֹד, וּמַה שֶּׁחָטָאתִי לְפָנֶיךָ מָרֵק בְּרַחֲמֶיךָ הָרַבִּים אֲבָל לֹא עַל יְדֵי יִסּוּרִין וָחֳלָאִים רָעִים. וְהַיְינוּ וִידּוּי דְּרַב הַמְנוּנָא זוּטִי בְּיוֹמָא דְכִפּוּרֵי.

**After his prayer, Rava said the following:**
**My God, before I was created I was worthless,**
**and now that I have been created it is as if I had not been created,** I am no more significant.
**I am dust in life, all the more so in my death.**
**I am before You as a vessel filled with shame and humiliation.**
Therefore, **may it be Your will, Lord my God, that I will sin no more,**
**and that those** transgressions **that I have committed,**
**cleanse in Your abundant mercy;**
**but** may this cleansing **not be by means of suffering and serious illness,** but rather in a manner I will be able to easily endure.
**And this is the confession of Rav Hamnuna Zuti on Yom Kippur.**

מָר בְּרֵיהּ דְּרָבִינָא כִּי הֲוָה מְסַיֵּים צְלוֹתֵיהּ אֲמַר הָכִי: אֱלֹהַי, נְצוֹר לְשׁוֹנִי מֵרָע וְשִׂפְתוֹתַי מִדַּבֵּר מִרְמָה וְלִמְקַלְלַי נַפְשִׁי תִדּוֹם וְנַפְשִׁי כֶּעָפָר לַכֹּל תִּהְיֶה, פְּתַח לִבִּי בְּתוֹרָתֶךָ וּבְמִצְוֹתֶיךָ תִּרְדּוֹף נַפְשִׁי, וְתַצִּילֵנִי מִפֶּגַע רַע מִיֵּצֶר הָרָע וּמֵאִשָּׁה רָעָה וּמִכָּל רָעוֹת הַמִּתְרַגְּשׁוֹת לָבֹא בָּעוֹלָם, וְכָל הַחוֹשְׁבִים עָלַי רָעָה מְהֵרָה הָפֵר עֲצָתָם וְקַלְקֵל מַחְשְׁבוֹתָם, יִהְיוּ לְרָצוֹן אִמְרֵי פִי וְהֶגְיוֹן לִבִּי לְפָנֶיךָ ה׳ צוּרִי וְגוֹאֲלִי.

**When Mar, son of Ravina, would conclude his prayer, he said the following:**
**My God, guard**[H] **my tongue from evil and my lips from speaking deceit.**
**To those who curse me let my soul be silent**
**and may my soul be like dust to all.**
**Open my heart to Your Torah,**
**and may my soul pursue your mitzvot.**
**And save me from a bad mishap, from the evil inclination,**
**from a bad woman, and from all evils that suddenly come upon the world.**
**And all who plan evil against me,**
**swiftly thwart their counsel, and frustrate their plans.**
**May the words of my mouth and the meditation of my heart find favor before You,**
**Lord, my Rock and my Redeemer.**

רַב שֵׁשֶׁת כִּי הֲוָה יָתֵיב בְּתַעֲנִיתָא, בָּתַר דִּמְצַלֵּי אֲמַר הָכִי: רִבּוֹן הָעוֹלָמִים, גָּלוּי לְפָנֶיךָ, בִּזְמַן שֶׁבֵּית הַמִּקְדָּשׁ קַיָּים אָדָם חוֹטֵא וּמַקְרִיב קׇרְבָּן, וְאֵין מַקְרִיבִין מִמֶּנּוּ אֶלָּא חֶלְבּוֹ וְדָמוֹ וּמִתְכַּפֵּר לוֹ; וְעַכְשָׁיו יָשַׁבְתִּי בְּתַעֲנִית וְנִתְמַעֵט חֶלְבִּי וְדָמִי, יְהִי רָצוֹן מִלְּפָנֶיךָ שֶׁיְּהֵא חֶלְבִּי וְדָמִי שֶׁנִּתְמַעֵט כְּאִילּוּ הִקְרַבְתִּיו לְפָנֶיךָ עַל גַּבֵּי הַמִּזְבֵּחַ וְתִרְצֵנִי.

The Gemara recounts that **when Rav Sheshet would sit in** observance of **a fast, after he prayed he said as follows:**
**Master of the Universe, it is revealed before You**
that **when the Temple is standing, one sins and offers a sacrifice.**
**And** although **only its fat and blood were offered from** that sacrifice on the altar, his transgression **is atoned for him.**
**And now, I sat in** observance of **a fast and my fat and blood diminished.**
**May it be Your will that my fat and blood that diminished be** considered **as if I offered** a sacrifice **before You on the altar,**
**and may I find favor in Your eyes.**

Having cited statements that various Sages would recite after their prayers, the Gemara cites additional passages recited by the Sages on different occasions.

רַבִּי יוֹחָנָן כִּי הֲוָה מְסַיֵּים סִפְרָא דְּאִיּוֹב אֲמַר הָכִי: סוֹף אָדָם לָמוּת, וְסוֹף בְּהֵמָה לִשְׁחִיטָה, וְהַכֹּל לְמִיתָה הֵם עוֹמְדִים. אַשְׁרֵי מִי שֶׁגָּדַל בַּתּוֹרָה וַעֲמָלוֹ בַּתּוֹרָה וְעוֹשֶׂה נַחַת רוּחַ לְיוֹצְרוֹ, וְגָדַל בְּשֵׁם טוֹב וְנִפְטַר בְּשֵׁם טוֹב מִן הָעוֹלָם, וְעָלָיו אָמַר שְׁלֹמֹה טוֹב שֵׁם מִשֶּׁמֶן טוֹב וְיוֹם הַמָּוֶת מִיּוֹם הִוָּלְדוֹ.

**When Rabbi Yoḥanan would conclude** study of **the book of Job,**[N] **he said the following:**
**A person will ultimately die and an animal will ultimately be slaughtered, and all are destined for death.** Therefore, death itself is not a cause for great anguish.
Rather, **happy is he who grew up in Torah, whose labor is in Torah,**
**who gives pleasure to his Creator,**
**who grew up with a good name and who took leave of the world with a good name.**
Such a person lived his life fully, **and about him, Solomon said:**
**"A good name is better than fine oil, and the day of death than the day of one's birth"** (Ecclesiastes 7:1); one who was faultless in life reaches the day of his death on a higher level than he was at the outset.

מַרְגְּלָא בְּפוּמֵּיהּ דְּרַבִּי מֵאִיר: גְּמוֹר בְּכׇל לְבָבְךָ וּבְכׇל נַפְשְׁךָ לָדַעַת אֶת דְּרָכַי וְלִשְׁקוֹד עַל דַּלְתֵי תוֹרָתִי, נְצוֹר תּוֹרָתִי בְּלִבְּךָ וְנֶגֶד עֵינֶיךָ תִּהְיֶה יִרְאָתִי, שְׁמוֹר פִּיךָ מִכׇּל חֵטְא וְטַהֵר וְקַדֵּשׁ עַצְמְךָ מִכׇּל אַשְׁמָה וְעָוֹן, וַאֲנִי אֶהְיֶה עִמְּךָ בְּכׇל מָקוֹם.

**Rabbi Meir was wont to say**[B] the following idiom:
**Study with all your heart and with all your soul to know My ways**
**and to be diligent at the doors of My Torah.**
**Keep My Torah in your heart,**
**and fear of Me should be before your eyes.**
**Guard your mouth from all transgression,**
**and purify and sanctify yourself from all fault and iniquity.**
**And** if you do so, **I,** God, **will be with you everywhere.**

**HALAKHA**

**My God, guard – אֱלֹהַי, נְצוֹר:** In all prayer liturgies based on different customs and from different countries of origin, this prayer of Mar, the son of Ravina, with minor variations, appears at the conclusion of the *Amida* prayer (see *Tur*, *Oraḥ Ḥayyim* 122).

**NOTES**

**When he would conclude study of the book of Job – מְסַיֵּים סִפְרָא דְּאִיּוֹב:** The connection between this and the book of Job is that the book ends by noting the death of Job: "And Job died, being old and full of days" (Job 42:17). Even though his transgressions were cleansed and he was free of sin (*Iyyun Ya'akov*), he neither merited nor was he promised eternal corporeal life. The conclusion is that continued enjoyment of life in its physical form is not an objective, since all are destined for death. Rather, the objective is to be one who grew up with a good name (*HaKotev*).

**BACKGROUND**

**He was wont to say – מַרְגְּלָא בְּפוּמֵּיהּ:** These adages that were stated by these Sages on a regular basis, served as guidance for the ideal manner in which one should live his life. Even Rav's statement with regard to the World-to-Come underscores certain values, distinguishing between those that are temporal, with no impact on the World-to-Come, and those which are eternal, toward which one should aspire (*Iyyun Ya'akov*).

**HALAKHA**

The World-to-Come – הָעוֹלָם הַבָּא וכו׳: These statements about the World-to-Come serve as fundamental tenets of Jewish philosophy and are discussed primarily in Jewish philosophical literature. Nevertheless, disputes between the Sages over these issues appear in halakhic compositions as well (see Rambam *Sefer HaMadda*, *Hilkhot Teshuva* 8:2 and Ra'avad there).

**BACKGROUND**

Divine Presence – שְׁכִינָה: God's manifestation in the world.

**NOTES**

By what virtue do women merit – נָשִׁים בְּמַאי זָכְיָין: Once the Gemara stated that women receive a greater reward than men, the question arises: By what virtue is their reward so great, especially considering the fact that they are not obligated in the mitzva of Torah study? The answer is that women, too, play a role in fulfillment of this mitzva; they support and encourage their sons and husbands to study Torah. And the Sages said: One who causes others to perform a mitzva is greater than one who performs it himself, and his reward is commensurately greater (*Semikhat Ḥakhamim*; Rabbi Yoshiya Pinto).

מַרְגְּלָא בְּפוּמַּיְיהוּ דְּרַבָּנַן דְּיַבְנֶה: אֲנִי בְּרִיָּה וַחֲבֵרִי בְּרִיָּה, אֲנִי מְלַאכְתִּי בָּעִיר וְהוּא מְלַאכְתּוֹ בַּשָּׂדֶה, אֲנִי מַשְׁכִּים לִמְלַאכְתִּי וְהוּא מַשְׁכִּים לִמְלַאכְתּוֹ, כְּשֵׁם שֶׁהוּא אֵינוֹ מִתְגַּדֵּר בִּמְלַאכְתִּי כָּךְ אֲנִי אֵינִי מִתְגַּדֵּר בִּמְלַאכְתּוֹ, וְשֶׁמָּא תֹּאמַר: אֲנִי מַרְבֶּה וְהוּא מַמְעִיט – שָׁנִינוּ: אֶחָד הַמַּרְבֶּה וְאֶחָד הַמַּמְעִיט וּבִלְבַד שֶׁיְּכַוֵּין לִבּוֹ לַשָּׁמַיִם.

**The Sages in Yavne were wont to say:**
**I** who learn Torah **am** God's **creature and my counterpart** who engages in other labor **is** God's **creature.**
**My work is in the city and his work is in the field.**
**I rise early for my work and he rises early for his work.**
**And just as he does not presume to** perform **my work, so I do not presume to** perform **his work.**
**Lest you say: I** engage in Torah study **a lot, while he** only engages in Torah study **a little,** so I am better than he,
**it has** already **been taught:**
**One who brings a substantial** sacrifice **and one who brings a meager** sacrifice have equal merit,
**as long as he directs his heart towards Heaven** (Rav Hai Gaon, *Arukh*).

מַרְגְּלָא בְּפוּמֵּיהּ דְּאַבָּיֵי: לְעוֹלָם יְהֵא אָדָם עָרוּם בְּיִרְאָה, מַעֲנֶה רַךְ מֵשִׁיב חֵמָה וּמַרְבֶּה שָׁלוֹם עִם אֶחָיו וְעִם קְרוֹבָיו וְעִם כָּל אָדָם, וַאֲפִילּוּ עִם גּוֹי בַּשּׁוּק, כְּדֵי שֶׁיְּהֵא אָהוּב לְמַעְלָה וְנֶחְמָד לְמַטָּה, וִיהֵא מְקוּבָּל עַל הַבְּרִיּוֹת.

**Abaye was wont to say:**
**One must always be shrewd** and utilize every strategy **in** order to achieve **fear** of Heaven and performance of mitzvot.
One must fulfill the verse: **"A soft answer turns away wrath"** (Proverbs 15:1)
and take steps to **increase peace with one's brethren and with one's relatives,**
**and with all people, even with a non-Jew in the marketplace,** despite the fact that he is of no importance to him and does not know him at all (*Me'iri*),
**so that he will be loved above** in God's eyes,
**pleasant below** in the eyes of the people,
**and acceptable to all** of God's **creatures.**

אָמְרוּ עָלָיו עַל רַבָּן יוֹחָנָן בֶּן זַכַּאי שֶׁלֹּא הִקְדִּימוֹ אָדָם שָׁלוֹם מֵעוֹלָם וַאֲפִילּוּ גּוֹי בַּשּׁוּק.

Tangentially, the Gemara mentions that **they said about Rabban Yoḥanan ben Zakkai that no one ever preceded him in** issuing a **greeting, not even a non-Jew in the marketplace,** as Rabban Yoḥanan would always greet him first.

מַרְגְּלָא בְּפוּמֵּיהּ דְּרָבָא: תַּכְלִית חָכְמָה תְּשׁוּבָה וּמַעֲשִׂים טוֹבִים; שֶׁלֹּא יְהֵא אָדָם קוֹרֵא וְשׁוֹנֶה וּבוֹעֵט בְּאָבִיו וּבְאִמּוֹ וּבְרַבּוֹ וּבְמִי שֶׁהוּא גָּדוֹל מִמֶּנּוּ בְּחָכְמָה וּבְמִנְיָן, שֶׁנֶּאֱמַר: רֵאשִׁית חָכְמָה יִרְאַת ה׳ שֵׂכֶל טוֹב לְכָל עוֹשֵׂיהֶם. לְעוֹשִׂים לֹא נֶאֱמַר אֶלָּא לְעוֹשֵׂיהֶם – לְעוֹשִׂים לִשְׁמָהּ, וְלֹא לְעוֹשִׂים שֶׁלֹּא לִשְׁמָהּ. וְכָל הָעוֹשֶׂה שֶׁלֹּא לִשְׁמָהּ נוֹחַ לוֹ שֶׁלֹּא נִבְרָא.

**Rava was wont to say:**
**The objective of** Torah **wisdom** is to achieve **repentance and good deeds;**
**that one should not read** the Torah **and study** mishna and become arrogant
**and spurn his father and his mother and his teacher**
**and one who is greater than he in wisdom or in** the **number** of students who study before him,
**as it is stated: "The beginning of wisdom is fear of the Lord, a good understanding have all who fulfill them"** (Psalms 111:10).
**It is not stated** simply: **All who fulfill, but rather: All who fulfill them,** those who perform these actions as they ought to be performed, meaning **those who do** such deeds **for their own sake,** for the sake of the deeds themselves, **not those who do them not for their own sake.**
Rava continued: **One who does them not for their own sake,** it would have been **preferable for him had he not been created.**

מַרְגְּלָא בְּפוּמֵּיהּ דְּרַב: [לֹא כָּעוֹלָם הַזֶּה הָעוֹלָם הַבָּא], הָעוֹלָם הַבָּא אֵין בּוֹ לֹא אֲכִילָה וְלֹא שְׁתִיָּה וְלֹא פְּרִיָּה וּרְבִיָּה וְלֹא מַשָּׂא וּמַתָּן וְלֹא קִנְאָה וְלֹא שִׂנְאָה וְלֹא תַּחֲרוּת, אֶלָּא צַדִּיקִים יוֹשְׁבִין וְעַטְרוֹתֵיהֶם בְּרָאשֵׁיהֶם וְנֶהֱנִים מִזִּיו הַשְּׁכִינָה, שֶׁנֶּאֱמַר: וַיֶּחֱזוּ אֶת הָאֱלֹהִים וַיֹּאכְלוּ וַיִּשְׁתּוּ.

**Rav was wont to say:**
**The World-to-Come**[H] **is not like this world.**
**In the World-to-Come there is no eating, no drinking,**
**no procreation, no** business **negotiations,**
**no jealousy, no hatred, and no competition.**
**Rather, the righteous sit with their crowns upon their heads, enjoying the splendor of the Divine Presence,**[B] **as it is stated:**
**"And they beheld God, and they ate and drank"** (Exodus 24:11), meaning that beholding God's countenance is tantamount to eating and drinking.

גְּדוֹלָה הַבְטָחָה שֶׁהִבְטִיחָן הַקָּדוֹשׁ בָּרוּךְ הוּא לַנָּשִׁים יוֹתֵר מִן הָאֲנָשִׁים, שֶׁנֶּאֱמַר נָשִׁים שַׁאֲנַנּוֹת קֹמְנָה שְׁמַעְנָה קוֹלִי בָּנוֹת בֹּטְחוֹת הַאְזֵנָּה אִמְרָתִי.

The Gemara states: **Greater is the promise** for the future **made by the Holy One, Blessed be He, to women than to men, as it is stated: "Rise up, women at ease; hear My voice, confident daughters, listen to what I say"** (Isaiah 32:9). This promise of ease and confidence is not given to men.

אֲמַר לֵיהּ רַב לְרַבִּי חִיָּיא: נָשִׁים בְּמַאי זָכְיָין? בְּאַקְרוֹיֵי בְּנַיְיהוּ לְבֵי כְּנִישְׁתָּא, וּבְאַתְנוּיֵי גַּבְרַיְיהוּ בֵּי רַבָּנַן, וְנָטְרִין לְגַבְרַיְיהוּ עַד דְּאָתוּ מִבֵּי רַבָּנַן.

**Rav said to Rabbi Ḥiyya:** By **what** virtue **do women merit** to receive this reward?[N] Rabbi Ḥiyya answered: They merit this reward **for bringing their children to read** the Torah **in the synagogue, and for sending their husbands to study** mishna **in the study hall, and for waiting for their husbands until they return from the study hall.**

כִּי הֲווֹ מִפַּטְרִי רַבָּנַן מִבֵּי רַבִּי אַמֵי, וְאָמְרִי לָה מִבֵּי רַבִּי חֲנִינָא, אָמְרִי לֵיהּ הָכִי: עוֹלָמְךָ תִּרְאֶה בְּחַיֶּיךָ, וְאַחֲרִיתְךָ לְחַיֵּי הָעוֹלָם הַבָּא, וְתִקְוָתְךָ לְדוֹר דּוֹרִים. לִבְּךָ יֶהְגֶּה תְבוּנָה, פִּיךָ יְדַבֵּר חָכְמוֹת וּלְשׁוֹנְךָ יַרְחִישׁ רְנָנוֹת, עַפְעַפֶּיךָ יַיְשִׁירוּ נֶגְדֶּךָ, עֵינֶיךָ יָאִירוּ בִּמְאוֹר תּוֹרָה וּפָנֶיךָ יַזְהִירוּ כְּזוֹהַר הָרָקִיעַ, שְׂפָתוֹתֶיךָ יַבִּיעוּ דַעַת וְכִלְיוֹתֶיךָ תַּעֲלוֹזְנָה מֵישָׁרִים, וּפְעָמֶיךָ יָרוּצוּ לִשְׁמוֹעַ דִּבְרֵי עַתִּיק יוֹמִין.

When the Sages who had been studying there **took leave of the study hall of Rabbi Ami,** and some say it was **the study hall of Rabbi Ḥanina, they would say to him the following** blessing: **May you see your world,** may you benefit from all of the good in the world, **in your lifetime, and may your end be to life in the World-to-Come, and may your hope** be sustained **for many generations.** May **your heart meditate understanding, your mouth speak wisdom, and your tongue whisper with praise.** May **your eyelids look directly before you, your eyes shine in the light of Torah, and your face radiate like the brightness of the firmament.** May **your lips express knowledge, your kidneys rejoice in the upright, and your feet run to hear the words of the Ancient of Days,** God (see Daniel 7).

כִּי הֲווֹ מִפַּטְרִי רַבָּנַן מִבֵּי רַב חִסְדָּא וְאָמְרִי לָה מִבֵּי רַבִּי שְׁמוּאֵל בַּר נַחְמָנִי, אָמְרִי לֵיהּ הָכִי: אַלּוּפֵינוּ מְסֻבָּלִים וְגו'.

When the Sages **took leave of the study hall of Rav Ḥisda,** and **some say** it was **the study hall of Rabbi Shmuel bar Naḥmani, they would say to him the following,** in accordance with the verse: **"Our leaders are laden,** there is no breach and no going forth and no outcry in our open places" (Psalms 144:14).

אַלּוּפֵינוּ מְסֻבָּלִים. רַב וּשְׁמוּאֵל, וְאָמְרִי לָהּ רַבִּי יוֹחָנָן וְרַבִּי אֶלְעָזָר, חַד אָמַר: אַלּוּפֵינוּ בַּתּוֹרָה וּמְסֻבָּלִים בַּמִּצְוֹת. וְחַד אָמַר: אַלּוּפֵינוּ בַּתּוֹרָה וּבַמִּצְוֹת, וּמְסֻבָּלִים בְּיִסּוּרִים.

**Our leaders are laden. Rav and Shmuel, and some say Rabbi Yoḥanan and Rabbi Elazar,** disputed the proper understanding of this verse. **One said: Our leaders in Torah are laden with mitzvot. And one said: Our leaders in Torah and mitzvot are laden with suffering.**

## Perek II
## Daf 17 Amud b

"אֵין פֶּרֶץ" – שֶׁלֹּא תְהֵא סִיעָתֵנוּ כְּסִיעָתוֹ שֶׁל דָּוִד שֶׁיָּצָא מִמֶּנּוּ אֲחִיתוֹפֶל, "וְאֵין יוֹצֵאת" – שֶׁלֹּא תְהֵא סִיעָתֵנוּ כְּסִיעָתוֹ שֶׁל שָׁאוּל שֶׁיָּצָא מִמֶּנּוּ דּוֹאֵג הָאֲדוֹמִי, "וְאֵין צְוָחָה" – שֶׁלֹּא תְהֵא סִיעָתֵנוּ כְּסִיעָתוֹ שֶׁל אֱלִישָׁע שֶׁיָּצָא מִמֶּנּוּ גֵּחֲזִי, "בִּרְחוֹבוֹתֵינוּ" – שֶׁלֹּא יְהֵא לָנוּ בֵּן אוֹ תַלְמִיד שֶׁמַּקְדִּיחַ תַּבְשִׁילוֹ בָּרַבִּים, כְּגוֹן יֵשׁוּ הַנּוֹצְרִי.

**"There is no breach";**[N] that our faction of Sages **should not be like the faction of David, from which Ahitophel emerged,** who caused a breach in the kingdom of David. **"And no going forth"; that our faction should not be like the faction of Saul, from which Doeg the Edomite emerged,** who set forth on an evil path. **"And no outcry"; that our faction should not be like the faction of Elisha, from which Geihazi emerged. "In our open places"; that we should not have a child or student who overcooks his food in public,** i.e., who sins in public and causes others to sin, **as** in the well-known case of **Jesus the Nazarene.**[N]

"שִׁמְעוּ אֵלַי אַבִּירֵי לֵב הָרְחוֹקִים מִצְּדָקָה". רַב וּשְׁמוּאֵל, וְאָמְרִי לָהּ רַבִּי יוֹחָנָן וְרַבִּי אֶלְעָזָר, חַד אָמַר: כָּל הָעוֹלָם כּוּלּוֹ נִזּוֹנִין בִּצְדָקָה – וְהֵם נִזּוֹנִין בִּזְרוֹעַ; וְחַד אָמַר: כָּל הָעוֹלָם כּוּלּוֹ נִזּוֹנִין בִּזְכוּתָם, וְהֵם – אֲפִילוּ בִּזְכוּת עַצְמָן אֵין נִזּוֹנִין, כְּדָרַב יְהוּדָה אָמַר רַב,

Having cited a dispute with regard to the interpretation of a verse where we are uncertain whether the dispute is between Rav and Shmuel or Rabbi Yoḥanan and Rabbi Elazar, the Gemara cites another verse with regard to which there is a similar dispute. It is said: **"Hear Me, stubborn-hearted**[N] **who are far from charity"** (Isaiah 46:12). While both agree that the verse refers to the righteous, **Rav and Shmuel, and some say Rabbi Yoḥanan and Rabbi Elazar,** disagreed as to how to interpret the verse. **One said: The entire world is sustained** by God's **charity,** not because it deserves to exist, **while the righteous who are far from** God's **charity are sustained by force,** as due to their own good deeds they have the right to demand their sustenance. **And one said: The entire world is sustained by the merit of their** righteousness, **while they are not sustained** at all, **not even by their own merit,** in accordance **with** the statement that **Rav Yehuda** said that **Rav said.**

---

### NOTES

**There is no breach –** אֵין פֶּרֶץ: The *Arukh* explains that Doeg played a role in the destruction of the priestly city of Nov (see I Samuel 22) and Ahitofel gave advice to Absalom that was damaging to King David (see II Samuel 17).

**As in the well-known case of Jesus the Nazarene –** כְּגוֹן יֵשׁוּ הַנּוֹצְרִי: In standard versions of the Talmud, this story appears without the name Jesus the Nazarene, which was removed by censors due to sensitivity to the Christian society in which they lived.

Another example appears in tractate *Sota* (47a), where Rabbi Yehoshua ben Peraḥya is depicted as one who pushed aside Jesus the Nazarene with both hands. The Gemara relates that Yehoshua ben Peraḥya was returning to Jerusalem following his flight to Alexandria in Egypt, together with his student, Jesus the Nazarene. When they stopped in an inn and were treated well, Yehoshua ben Peraḥya mentioned to Jesus that the service was good. Jesus responded that the innkeeper was unattractive. This response led Yehoshua ben Peraḥya to ostracize Jesus. Yehoshua ben Peraḥya was unable to bring himself to revoke the ostracism until it was too late and Jesus turned away from traditional Judaism.

It should be noted, however, that the story of Yehoshua ben Peraḥya, who was driven from Jerusalem by the Hasmonean King Alexander Yannai, could not have taken place any later than 76 BCE. Consequently, the reference to Jesus the Nazarene cannot be connected with the individual surrounding whom the Christian faith was established. Many commentaries suggest that all talmudic references to Jesus refer to another person, or perhaps there was more than one person with that name who lived during the time of the Mishna.

**Stubborn-hearted –** אַבִּירֵי לֵב: The commentaries who understand the verse: "Stubborn-hearted, who are far from charity," as praise of the righteous rely on the subsequent verse, which promises rewards, which are certainly intended for the righteous (Rabbi Yoshiya Pinto).

HALAKHA

**Work on the Ninth of Av – מְלָאכָה בְּתִשְׁעָה בְּאָב:** In a place where the custom is to perform labor on the Ninth of Av, one may perform labor. In a place where the custom is not to perform labor on the Ninth of Av, one may not perform labor. And everywhere, Torah scholars are idle and do not perform labor. Anyone who seeks to emulate a Torah scholar in this regard is permitted to do so. The legal status of business dealings for profit is the same as that of labor, but business dealings should be curtailed from the start of the month of Av. In any case, even those accustomed to refrain from performing labor on the Ninth of Av do so only until noon. If by refraining from work he will suffer an irretrievable loss, he is permitted to perform that labor in a manner similar to that of the intermediate days of a Festival. One who performs labor on the Ninth of Av, even after noon, in a place where it is customary not to do so and even in a place where it is customary to perform labor (*Mishna Berura*), will see no blessing from the money he earns (Rambam *Sefer Zemanim, Hilkhot Ta'aniyot* 5:10; *Shulḥan Arukh, Oraḥ Ḥayyim* 554:22–24).

דְּאָמַר רַב יְהוּדָה אָמַר רַב: בְּכָל יוֹם וָיוֹם בַּת קוֹל יוֹצֵאת מֵהַר חוֹרֵב וְאוֹמֶרֶת: כָּל הָעוֹלָם כּוּלּוֹ נִזּוֹנִין בִּשְׁבִיל חֲנִינָא בְּנִי, וַחֲנִינָא בְּנִי – דַּי לוֹ בְּקַב חָרוּבִין מֵעֶרֶב שַׁבָּת לְעֶרֶב שַׁבָּת.

**As Rav Yehuda said** that **Rav said: Every day a Heavenly Voice emerges from Mount Horeb and says: The entire world is sustained by** the merit of **Ḥanina** ben Dosa, **my son, and for Ḥanina, my son, a** ***kav*** **of carobs is sufficient** to sustain him for an entire week, **from** one **Shabbat eve to** the next **Shabbat eve.**

וּפְלִיגָא דְּרַב יְהוּדָה, דַּאֲמַר רַב יְהוּדָה: מַאן ״אַבִּירֵי לֵב״ – גּוֹבָאֵי טִפְּשָׁאֵי. אֲמַר רַב יוֹסֵף: תֵּדַע, דְּהָא לָא אִיגַּיַּיר גִּיּוֹרָא מִינַּיְיהוּ.

**And** this exegesis **disagrees with** the opinion of **Rav Yehuda, as Rav Yehuda said, who are the stubborn-hearted?** They are the **foolish** heathens **of Gova'ei. Rav Yosef said: Know** that this is so, **as no convert has ever converted from their** ranks.

אֲמַר רַב אַשִׁי: בְּנֵי מָתָא מְחַסְיָא אַבִּירֵי לֵב נִינְהוּ, דְּקָא חָזוּ יְקָרָא דְּאוֹרַיְיתָא תְּרֵי זִמְנֵי בְּשַׁתָּא וְלָא קָמִגַּיַּיר גִּיּוֹרָא מִינַּיְיהוּ.

Similarly, **Rav Ashi said:** The heathen residents **of the city Mata Meḥasya are the stubborn-hearted, as they witness the glory of the Torah twice a year** at the *kalla* gatherings in Adar and Elul, when thousands of people congregate and study Torah *en masse*, **yet no convert has ever converted from their** ranks.

״חָתָן אִם רוֹצֶה לִקְרוֹת וכו׳״.

We learned in our mishna that **if a groom wishes to recite** ***Shema*** on the first night of his marriage, he may do so, and Rabban Shimon ben Gamliel prohibited doing so because of the appearance of presumptuousness.

לְמֵימְרָא, דְּרַבָּן שִׁמְעוֹן בֶּן גַּמְלִיאֵל חָיֵישׁ לְיוּהֲרָא וְרַבָּנַן לָא חָיְישֵׁי לְיוּהֲרָא – וְהָא אִיפְּכָא שָׁמְעִינַן לְהוּ! דִּתְנַן: מָקוֹם שֶׁנָּהֲגוּ לַעֲשׂוֹת מְלָאכָה בְּתִשְׁעָה בְּאָב – עוֹשִׂין, מָקוֹם שֶׁנָּהֲגוּ שֶׁלֹּא לַעֲשׂוֹת – אֵין עוֹשִׂין, וְכָל מָקוֹם תַּלְמִידֵי חֲכָמִים בְּטֵלִים; רַבָּן שִׁמְעוֹן בֶּן גַּמְלִיאֵל אוֹמֵר: לְעוֹלָם יַעֲשֶׂה כָּל אָדָם אֶת עַצְמוֹ כְּתַלְמִיד חָכָם.

The Gemara asks: **Is that to say that Rabban Shimon ben Gamliel is concerned about presumptuousness and the Rabbis are not concerned about presumptuousness? Didn't we learn** that **they** say **the opposite? As we learned** in a mishna: **A place where they were accustomed to perform labor on Ninth of Av,**[H] **one** may **perform** labor. **A place where they were accustomed not to perform** labor on Ninth of Av, **one** may **not perform** labor. **And everywhere, Torah scholars are idle** and do not perform labor. **Rabban Shimon ben Gamliel says:** With regard to performing labor on the Ninth of Av **one should always conduct himself as a Torah scholar.**

קַשְׁיָא דְּרַבָּנַן אַדְּרַבָּנַן, קַשְׁיָא דְּרַבָּן שִׁמְעוֹן בֶּן גַּמְלִיאֵל אַדְּרַבָּן שִׁמְעוֹן בֶּן גַּמְלִיאֵל!

If so, **there is a contradiction between** the statement of **the Rabbis** here **and** the statement of **the Rabbis** there. And, **there is a contradiction between** the statement of **Rabban Shimon ben Gamliel** here **and** the statement of **Rabban Shimon ben Gamliel** there.

אָמַר רַבִּי יוֹחָנָן: מוּחְלֶפֶת הַשִּׁיטָה. רַב שֵׁישָׁא בְּרֵיהּ דְּרַב אִידִי אָמַר: לְעוֹלָם לָא תַּחֲלִיף, דְּרַבָּנַן אַדְּרַבָּנַן לָא קַשְׁיָא: קְרִיאַת שְׁמַע כֵּיוָן דְּכוּלֵּי עָלְמָא קָא קָרוּ וְאִיהוּ נַמִי קָרֵי – לָא מֶיחֱזֵי כְּיוּהֲרָא, הָכָא, כֵּיוָן דְּכוּלֵּי עָלְמָא עָבְדִי מְלָאכָה וְאִיהוּ לָא קָא עָבֵיד – מֶיחֱזֵי כְּיוּהֲרָא;

**Rabbi Yoḥanan said: The attribution** of the opinions **is reversed** in one of the sources in the interest of avoiding contradiction. **Rav Sheisha, son of Rav Idi, said: Actually,** you need **not reverse** the opinions, as the contradiction between the statement of **the Rabbis** here **and** the statement of **the Rabbis** there **is not difficult.** In the case of **the recitation of** ***Shema*** on his wedding night, **since every one is reciting** *Shema* **and he is also reciting** ***Shema***, he is not conspicuous and **it does not appear as presumptuousness. Here,** in the case of the Ninth of Av, however, **since everyone is performing labor and he is not performing labor,** his idleness is conspicuous and **appears as presumptuousness.**

דְּרַבָּן שִׁמְעוֹן בֶּן גַּמְלִיאֵל אַדְּרַבָּן שִׁמְעוֹן בֶּן גַּמְלִיאֵל לָא קַשְׁיָא: הָתָם בְּכַוָּונָה תַּלְיָא מִילְּתָא, וַאֲנַן סָהֲדֵי דְּלָא מָצֵי לְכַוּוֹנֵי דַּעְתֵּיהּ. אֲבָל הָכָא, הָרוֹאֶה אוֹמֵר: מְלָאכָה הוּא דְּאֵין לוֹ, פּוּק חֲזֵי כַּמָּה בַּטְלָנֵי אִיכָּא בְּשׁוּקָא.

So too, the contradiction **between** the statement of **Rabban Shimon ben Gamliel** here **and** the statement of **Rabban Shimon ben Gamliel** there **is not difficult. There,** in the case of the recitation of *Shema* on his wedding night, **the matter is dependent upon his** capacity to **concentrate,** and **it is clear to all** that **he is unable to concentrate.** Reciting *Shema* under those circumstances is a display of presumptuousness. **But here,** in the case of the Ninth of Av, **one who sees** him idle **says: It is** because **he has no labor** to perform. **Go out and see how many idle people there are in the marketplace,** even on days when one is permitted to work. Consequently, his idleness is not conspicuous.

הדרן עלך היה קורא

# Summary of **Perek II**

Most of the discussion in this chapter did not focus upon the ideal manner in which to recite *Shema*. Rather, it dealt with questions with regard to what extent can the recitation of *Shema* be altered or even abandoned when circumstances do not allow its standard recitation.

Ideally, one should recite the entire *Shema* with all his heart; however, after the fact, if he only had the proper intention for the first verse alone and not for the rest of *Shema*, he fulfilled his obligation. The relative significance of the various component sections of *Shema* is manifest in the determination of where one may interrupt its recitation, due to honor that must be accorded or due to fear that one experiences, to greet another person or to respond to his greeting.

There is also room to distinguish between *ab initio* and after the fact with regard to the quality of the recitation. *Ab initio*, one must carefully pronounce each letter and avoid ambiguity or lack of clarity in reciting *Shema*. However, after the fact, even one who was not appropriately precise in reciting *Shema* fulfilled his obligation. Similarly, although one reciting *Shema* is required to recite it audibly, nevertheless, after the fact, one who did not recite it audibly fulfilled his obligation. The principle is that intent and understanding the meaning of the words are crucial; consequently, one may recite *Shema* in any language that he understands. For that same reason, even after the fact, one who recites *Shema* out of order has not fulfilled his obligation, as that subverts the fundamental intent.

Certain people, due to their unique situations, were permitted not to recite *Shema* or, at least, to read it with less devotion. Included among those people are hired laborers who, in order to assist them in the performance of their tasks, were permitted to recite *Shema* at their work site even though it is uncomfortable and their devotion is compromised. Beginning with the second section, they may even engage in their labor while reciting *Shema*. Work is not the only factor for which allowances are made in reciting *Shema*. Allowances are also made for one who is performing a mitzva or even preoccupied about performance of a mitzva. For that reason, a groom is exempt from the obligation to recite *Shema* on his wedding night. The Sages reluctantly permitted a groom who insists upon it to recite *Shema* on his wedding night.

Additional cases in which people are exempt from their obligation to recite *Shema* due to performance of a mitzva or preoccupation related to performance of a mitzva will be discussed in the next chapter.

# Introduction to **Perek III**

*When you go forth in camp against your enemies, then you shall keep yourself from every evil thing. If there be among you any man, that is not clean by reason of that which chance him by night, then shall he go abroad out of the camp, he shall not come within the camp. But it shall be, when evening comes on, he shall bathe himself in water; and when the sun is down, he may come within the camp. You shall have a place also without the camp, where you shall go forth abroad. And you shall have a paddle among thy weapons; and it shall be, when you sit down abroad, you shall dig with it, and shall turn back and cover that which comes from you. For the Lord your God walks in the midst of your camp, to deliver you, and to give up your enemies before you; therefore your camp shall be holy; that He see no unseemly thing in you, and turn away from you.*

(Deuteronomy 23:10–15)

This chapter is, in a sense, a continuation of the previous chapter. The previous chapter also dealt with problems that arise as a result of circumstances that hinder the recitation of *Shema*. However, those hindrances were primarily generated by external factors that prevent one from reciting *Shema* properly. In this chapter, hindrances of a different sort will be discussed; i.e., cases where one is in a place or a situation where it is inappropriate to engage in sacred activities.

One problem discussed in this chapter is how one should act as far as *Shema* and prayer are concerned in various conditions of mourning, both in terms of the mourner himself and in terms of those engaged in burial of the deceased.

Another problem related to the mitzvot of *Shema* and prayer is a by-product of their very essence; when a person accepts the fundamental tenets of his faith and stands before his Creator, he should do so while clean and ritually pure. However, there are circumstances which render a person ritually impure or constitute an unclean environment. Precise determinations are necessary to establish when those circumstances completely exempt one from the obligation to recite *Shema* and pray and when the obligation is merely postponed.

The verses in Deuteronomy, which warn a person to avoid ritual impurity and filth in an army camp, apply everywhere, at all times. A Jew is always obligated to acknowledge: "For the Lord your God walks in the midst of your camp," especially when engaged in sacred activities.

In *halakha*, this was consolidated into three categories: Ritual impurity, unseemly matters, and filth. Ritual impurity is not, in essence, tied to a concrete flaw; nevertheless, it is a spiritual flaw from which it is incumbent upon the person to purify himself before entering the camp. The Torah directive with regard to ritual impurity resulting from a seminal emission leads directly to the discussion of the ordinance instituted by Ezra. This ordinance established that one who is ritually impure due to a seminal emission, including a husband who engaged in conjugal relations with his wife, is forbidden to recite *Shema*, pray, or study Torah until he immerses himself and becomes ritually pure. Even though it never gained widespread acceptance, in many senses several appropriate modes of conduct with regard to caution and ritual purity while studying Torah and praying were established by virtue of that ordinance.

The concept of unseemly matters also has far-reaching applications. It includes any exposed limb in the human body that is usually covered. On the one hand, this was instituted to prevent arousing sexual desire while engaged in sacred activity. However, there is another aspect, as it says in the Torah: All nakedness involves contempt for God, and consequently, covering that nakedness is an acknowledgement of the sanctity of the matters in which one is involved.

What is true with regard to spiritual flaws also applies to actual filth. The Torah commandment to be vigilant about cleanliness within the camp was formulated as a general directive to avoid every evil thing. That includes avoiding all sights or smells that provoke disgust or unpleasantness, which should be avoided at all times, especially when reciting *Shema* and praying.

Defining and illuminating these elements, and determining their precise parameters, are the primary focus of this chapter.

Perek **III**
Daf **17** Amud **b**

מתני׳ מִי שֶׁמֵּתוֹ מוּטָּל לְפָנָיו – פָּטוּר מִקְּרִיאַת שְׁמַע, וּמִן הַתְּפִלָּה וּמִן הַתְּפִילִּין, וּמִכׇּל מִצְוֹת הָאֲמוּרוֹת בַּתּוֹרָה.

**MISHNA** **One whose deceased** relative **is laid out** unburied **before him is exempt from the recitation of** ***Shema***,[NH] **from** the *Amida* **prayer, and from** the mitzva to don **phylacteries, as well as all** positive **mitzvot mentioned in the Torah,** until the deceased has been buried.

נוֹשְׂאֵי הַמִּטָּה וְחִלּוּפֵיהֶן וְחִלּוּפֵי חִלּוּפֵיהֶן, אֶת שֶׁלִּפְנֵי הַמִּטָּה וְאֶת שֶׁלְּאַחַר הַמִּטָּה; אֶת שֶׁלִּפְנֵי הַמִּטָּה צוֹרֶךְ בָּהֶם – פְּטוּרִין, וְאֶת שֶׁלְּאַחַר הַמִּטָּה צוֹרֶךְ בָּהֶם – חַיָּיבִין, וְאֵלּוּ וְאֵלּוּ פְּטוּרִים מִן הַתְּפִלָּה.

With regard to **the pallbearers**[H] **and their replacements and the replacements of their replacements, those** located **before the bier** who have not yet carried the deceased **and those** located **after the bier. Those before the bier who are needed** to carry the bier **are exempt** from reciting *Shema*; **while those after the bier,** even if **they are** still **needed** to carry it, since they have already carried the deceased, they are **obligated** to recite *Shema*. However, both **these and those are exempt from** reciting the *Amida* **prayer,**[N] since they are preoccupied and are unable to focus and pray with the appropriate intent.

קָבְרוּ אֶת הַמֵּת וְחָזְרוּ, אִם יְכוֹלִין לְהַתְחִיל וְלִגְמוֹר עַד שֶׁלֹּא יַגִּיעוּ לַשּׁוּרָה – יַתְחִילוּ, וְאִם לָאו – לֹא יַתְחִילוּ.

After **they buried the deceased and returned, if they** have sufficient time to **begin** to recite *Shema* **and conclude before they arrive at the row,** formed by those who attended the burial, through which the bereaved family will pass in order to receive consolation, **they should begin. If** they do **not** have sufficient time to conclude reciting the entire *Shema*, then **they should not begin.**

הָעוֹמְדִים בַּשּׁוּרָה, הַפְּנִימִיִּים – פְּטוּרִים, וְהַחִיצוֹנִים – חַיָּיבִים. (נָשִׁים וַעֲבָדִים וּקְטַנִּים פְּטוּרִים מִקְּרִיאַת שְׁמַע וּמִן הַתְּפִילִּין וְחַיָּיבִין בִּתְפִלָּה וּבִמְזוּזָה וּבְבִרְכַּת הַמָּזוֹן.)

And **those standing in the row, those** in the **interior** row, directly before whom the mourners will pass and who will console them, **are exempt** from reciting *Shema*, while **those** in the **exterior** row, who stand there only to show their respect, **are obligated** to recite *Shema*. **Women, slaves and minors are exempt from the recitation of** ***Shema*** **and from phylacteries, but are obligated in prayer,** ***mezuza*** **and Grace after Meals.**

גמ׳ מוּטָּל לְפָנָיו – אִין, וְשֶׁאֵינוֹ מוּטָּל לְפָנָיו – לָא;

**GEMARA** We learned in the mishna that one whose deceased relative is laid out before him is exempt from the recitation of *Shema* and other positive mitzvot. The Gemara deduces: When the corpse is **laid out before him, yes,** he is exempt, but when the corpse is **not** physically **laid out before him, no,** he is not exempt from these mitzvot.

וּרְמִינְהִי: מִי שֶׁמֵּתוֹ מוּטָּל לְפָנָיו – אוֹכֵל בְּבַיִת אַחֵר, וְאִם אֵין לוֹ בַּיִת אַחֵר – אוֹכֵל בְּבֵית חֲבֵירוֹ, וְאִם אֵין לוֹ בֵּית חֲבֵירוֹ – עוֹשֶׂה מְחִיצָה וְאוֹכֵל, וְאִם אֵין לוֹ דָּבָר לַעֲשׂוֹת מְחִיצָה – מַחֲזִיר פָּנָיו וְאוֹכֵל, וְאֵינוֹ מֵיסֵב וְאוֹכֵל, וְאֵינוֹ אוֹכֵל בָּשָׂר וְאֵינוֹ שׁוֹתֶה יַיִן, וְאֵינוֹ מְבָרֵךְ וְאֵינוֹ מְזַמֵּן,

The Gemara **raises a contradiction** from a *baraita*: **One whose deceased** relative **is laid out before him eats in another room.**[H] **If he does not have another room, he eats in the house of a friend. If he does not have a friend's house** available, **he makes a partition** between him and the deceased **and eats. If he does not have material** with which **to make a partition, he averts his face** from the dead **and eats. And** in any case, **he does not recline while he eats,** as reclining is characteristic of a festive meal. **Furthermore, he neither eats meat nor drinks wine, and does not recite** a **blessing** before eating, **and does not** recite the formula to **invite** the participants in the meal to join together in the Grace after Meals [*zimmun*], i.e., he is exempt from the obligation of Grace after Meals.

Perek **III**
Daf **18** Amud **a**

וְאֵין מְבָרְכִין עָלָיו וְאֵין מְזַמְּנִין עָלָיו, וּפָטוּר מִקְּרִיאַת שְׁמַע וּמִן הַתְּפִלָּה וּמִן הַתְּפִילִּין וּמִכׇּל מִצְוֹת הָאֲמוּרוֹת בַּתּוֹרָה; וּבְשַׁבָּת – מֵיסֵב וְאוֹכֵל בָּשָׂר וְשׁוֹתֶה יַיִן, וּמְבָרֵךְ וּמְזַמֵּן, וּמְבָרְכִין עָלָיו וּמְזַמְּנִין עָלָיו, וְחַיָּיב בְּכׇל הַמִּצְוֹת הָאֲמוּרוֹת בַּתּוֹרָה; רַבָּן שִׁמְעוֹן בֶּן גַּמְלִיאֵל אוֹמֵר: מִתּוֹךְ שֶׁנִּתְחַיֵּיב בְּאֵלּוּ נִתְחַיֵּיב בְּכוּלָּן.

**And** there is no need for others **to recite a blessing** beforehand **on his behalf, nor do others invite him** to join in Grace after Meals, as he cannot be a member of the quorum of three required to recite the formula. **He is exempt from the recitation of** ***Shema***, **from** the *Amida* **prayer and from phylacteries, and from all mitzvot mentioned in the Torah. On Shabbat,** however, **he reclines** at the meal as per his custom, **and eats meat and drinks wine, and recites blessings and** recites the formula to **invite** the participants in the meal to join together in the Grace after Meals, **and others may recite blessings on his behalf and invite him** to join in Grace after Meals, **and he is obligated in all mitzvot mentioned in the Torah. Rabban Shimon ben Gamliel says: Just as he is obligated** on Shabbat **to** fulfill **these** mitzvot associated with Shabbat meals, **he is obligated to** fulfill **all** mitzvot.

**NOTES**

**One whose deceased relative is laid out unburied before him is exempt from the recitation of** ***Shema*** – **מִי שֶׁמֵּתוֹ מוּטָּל לְפָנָיו פָּטוּר מִקְּרִיאַת שְׁמַע**: In the Jerusalem Talmud, the verse: "That you may remember the day when you came forth out of the land of Egypt all the days of your life" (Deuteronomy 16:3) was cited in support of this *halakha*. Remember the Exodus on days that you are involved with the living and not on days when you are involved with the dead (Jerusalem Talmud, *Berakhot* 3:1).

**Both these and those are exempt from reciting the** ***Amida*** **prayer** – **אֵלּוּ וְאֵלּוּ פְּטוּרִים מִן הַתְּפִלָּה**: Although the bier no longer requires their services, nevertheless they are exempt from the obligation to pray because they are engaged in performance of a mitzva and the principle is: One who is engaged in a mitzva is exempt from a mitzva (*Magen Avraham*).

**HALAKHA**

**One whose deceased relative is laid out unburied before him is exempt from the recitation of** ***Shema*** – **מִי שֶׁמֵּתוֹ מוּטָּל לְפָנָיו פָּטוּר מִקְּרִיאַת שְׁמַע וכו׳**: A mourner is exempt from reciting *Shema* and prayer, and performing all other positive mitzvot, until the deceased he is mourning is buried (Rambam *Sefer Ahava, Hilkhot Keriat Shema* 4:3, *Sefer Shofetim, Hilkhot Evel* 4:6; *Shulḥan Arukh, Oraḥ Ḥayyim* 71:1).

**The pallbearers** – **נוֹשְׂאֵי הַמִּטָּה**: The pallbearers and their replacements, all of whom are needed to carry the bier, are exempt from reciting *Shema* and performing other positive mitzvot. If the replacements are not needed to carry the bier, they are obligated (Rambam *Sefer Ahava, Hilkhot Keriat Shema* 4:4; *Shulḥan Arukh, Oraḥ Ḥayyim* 72:1, *Yoreh De'a* 358:1). However, all of the pallbearers are exempt from prayer. (*Shulḥan Arukh, Oraḥ Ḥayyim* 106:1).

**One whose deceased relative is laid out before him eats in another room** – **מִי שֶׁמֵּתוֹ מוּטָּל לְפָנָיו אוֹכֵל בְּבַיִת אַחֵר וכו׳**: One whose deceased relative has not yet been buried, may not eat in the same house in which the body is located. In exigent circumstances, when there is no alternative, one may avert his face from the deceased and eat (Rambam *Sefer Shofetim, Hilkhot Evel* 4:6; *Shulḥan Arukh, Yoreh De'a* 341:1). On weekdays he is exempt from reciting blessings and does not join others in a *zimmun* (*Shulḥan Arukh, Oraḥ Ḥayyim* 199:5).

## HALAKHA

One who watches over the deceased – הַמְשַׁמֵּר אֶת הַמֵּת: One who is watching over the deceased, even if he is not a relative, is exempt from reciting it and exempt from all mitzvot in the Torah. However, if there were two people watching over the deceased in shifts, while one watches, the other recites *Shema* and vice-versa (Rambam *Sefer Ahava, Hilkhot Keriat Shema* 4:3; *Shulḥan Arukh, Oraḥ Ḥayyim* 71:3).

One may not walk in a cemetery with phylacteries on his head – לֹא יְהַלֵּךְ אָדָם בְּבֵית הַקְּבָרוֹת וּתְפִילִּין בְּרֹאשׁוֹ: It is prohibited to enter a cemetery or to come within four cubits of the deceased with exposed phylacteries, but if they are covered, it is permissible (Rambam *Sefer Ahava, Hilkhot Tefillin UMezuza VeSefer Torah* 4:23; *Shulḥan Arukh, Oraḥ Ḥayyim* 45:1, and see 71:7).

One may not walk in a cemetery with…a Torah scroll in his arm and read from it – לֹא יְהַלֵּךְ...וְסֵפֶר תּוֹרָה בִּזְרוֹעוֹ וְקוֹרֵא: It is prohibited to enter a cemetery with a Torah scroll, or to read the Torah in a cemetery, or to read it within four cubits of the deceased (Rambam *Sefer Shofetim, Hilkhot Evel* 14:13; *Shulḥan Arukh, Yoreh De'a* 282:4).

Prayer before the deceased – תְּפִלָּה בִּפְנֵי הַמֵּת: It is prohibited to recite *Shema* in a cemetery or within four cubits of the deceased. The same is true with regard to reciting all other sacred matters (*Mishna Berura*). One who recited *Shema* in the presence of the deceased is penalized by the Sages and they decreed that he did not fulfill his obligation (*Magen Avraham*). The *Ra'avad* ruled that he fulfilled his obligation. Since the Rambam ruled that he must repeat *Shema*, the ruling is that he repeats *Shema* but does not repeat its blessings (*Be'er Heitev*).

וְאָמַר רַבִּי יוֹחָנָן: מַאי בֵּינַיְיהוּ – תַּשְׁמִישׁ הַמִּטָּה אִיכָּא בֵּינַיְיהוּ,

**Rabbi Yoḥanan said: What is** the practical difference **between** the apparently identical statements of Rabban Shimon ben Gamliel and the first *tanna*? **The** practical difference **between them is** with regard to **conjugal relations.** The first *tanna* holds that although there is no mourning on Shabbat, since refraining from addressing his wife's conjugal rights would not be a public display of mourning, conjugal relations are prohibited. Rabban Shimon ben Gamliel holds that since there is no mourning on Shabbat, he must fulfill the mitzva of addressing his wife's conjugal rights.

קָתָנֵי מִיהַת ״פָּטוּר מִקְּרִיאַת שְׁמַע וּמִן הַתְּפִלָּה וּמִן הַתְּפִילִּין וּמִכׇּל מִצְוֹת הָאֲמוּרוֹת בַּתּוֹרָה״! אָמַר רַב פָּפָּא: תַּרְגְּמָא אַמַּחְזִיר פָּנָיו וְאוֹכֵל. רַב אָשֵׁי אָמַר: כֵּיוָן שֶׁמּוּטָּל עָלָיו לְקוֹבְרוֹ – כְּמוּטָּל לְפָנָיו דָּמֵי, שֶׁנֶּאֱמַר: ״וַיָּקׇם אַבְרָהָם מֵעַל פְּנֵי מֵתוֹ״, וְנֶאֱמַר: ״וְאֶקְבְּרָה מֵתִי מִלְּפָנָי״ – כׇּל זְמַן שֶׁמּוּטָּל עָלָיו לְקוֹבְרוֹ כְּמוּטָּל לְפָנָיו דָּמֵי.

**In any event,** the *baraita* **teaches** that **one is exempt from the recitation of *Shema*, from** the *Amida* **prayer and from phylacteries, and from all mitzvot mentioned in the Torah.** This is an apparent contradiction of our mishna which states that one is exempt only when the deceased is laid before him. To resolve this contradiction, **Rav Pappa said: Explain** the *baraita* as applicable only to the particular case when **one turns his face** away **and eats,** with the deceased laid out before him. In the other cases, when he is in a different room, he is obligated in all mitzvot. **Rav Ashi says:** The phrase: The deceased is laid out before him, is not to be taken literally, but rather, **since it is incumbent upon him to bury the deceased,** and he is not yet buried, it is **as if he is laid out before him, as it is stated: "And Abraham rose up from before his dead"** (Genesis 23:3), **and** when Abraham speaks with the Hittites, **it is stated: "So that I may bury my dead from before me"** (Genesis 23:4). **As long as it is incumbent upon him to bury him,** it is **like he is laid out before him.**

מֵתוֹ – אִין, אֲבָל מְשַׁמְּרוֹ – לָא,

From the mishna one can infer that when **his deceased** relative is laid out before him, **yes,** he is exempt from mitzvot. **But,** if it is not his relative and he is only **watching over** the deceased, **no,** he is not exempt.

וְהָתַנְיָא: הַמְשַׁמֵּר אֶת הַמֵּת אַף עַל פִּי שֶׁאֵינוֹ מֵתוֹ – פָּטוּר מִקְּרִיאַת שְׁמַע וּמִן הַתְּפִלָּה וּמִן הַתְּפִילִּין וּמִכׇּל מִצְוֹת הָאֲמוּרוֹת בַּתּוֹרָה. מְשַׁמְּרוֹ – אַף עַל פִּי שֶׁאֵינוֹ מֵתוֹ, מֵתוֹ – אַף עַל פִּי שֶׁאֵינוֹ מְשַׁמְּרוֹ.

The Gemara challenges: **Wasn't it taught** in a *baraita*: **One who watches over the deceased,**[H] **even if it is not his deceased** relative, **is exempt from the recitation of *Shema*, from prayer and from phylacteries, and from all mitzvot mentioned in the Torah?** The Gemara responds that these two sources should not be understood as contradictory, but as complementary. In both the cases, he is exempt; where **one watches over** the deceased, **but it is not his deceased** relative, as well as the case where **it is his deceased** relative, **but he is not watching over** the deceased.

מֵתוֹ וּמְשַׁמְּרוֹ אִין, אֲבָל מְהַלֵּךְ בְּבֵית הַקְּבָרוֹת – לָא, וְהָתַנְיָא: לֹא יְהַלֵּךְ אָדָם בְּבֵית הַקְּבָרוֹת וּתְפִילִּין בְּרֹאשׁוֹ וְסֵפֶר תּוֹרָה בִּזְרוֹעוֹ וְקוֹרֵא, וְאִם עוֹשֶׂה כֵּן עוֹבֵר מִשּׁוּם ״לוֹעֵג לָרָשׁ חֵרֵף עוֹשֵׂהוּ״!

The Gemara further challenges: We concluded that, in both cases, if it is **his deceased** relative or if he was **watching over** the unrelated deceased, **he is** exempt from mitzvot. **However, one walking in a cemetery is not** exempt. **Wasn't it taught** explicitly in a *baraita*: **One may not walk in a cemetery with phylacteries on his head**[H] **and a Torah scroll in his arm and read** from it?[H] **If one does so he commits** a transgression **due to** the verse: **"He who mocks the poor blasphemes his Creator"** (Proverbs 17:5). As the deceased is incapable of fulfilling mitzvot, fulfilling a mitzva in his presence is seen as mocking him.

הָתָם תּוֹךְ אַרְבַּע [אַמּוֹת] הוּא דְּאָסוּר, חוּץ לְאַרְבַּע אַמּוֹת חַיָּיב, דְּאָמַר מָר: מֵת תּוֹפֵס אַרְבַּע אַמּוֹת לִקְרִיאַת שְׁמַע, הָכָא – חוּץ לְאַרְבַּע אַמּוֹת נַמִי פָּטוּר.

The Gemara answers: **There,** when one walks in a cemetery, **within four cubits** of a grave, **that is prohibited.** However, **beyond four cubits** from a grave, **one is obligated** in prayer and phylacteries. **As the Master said: The deceased occupies four cubits** with regard to the exemption from the **recitation of *Shema*.** One who walks within four cubits of the deceased is exempt. **Here,** however, in the case where it is either his deceased relative or he is watching over an unrelated deceased, **beyond four cubits he is also exempt.**

גּוּפָא: הַמְשַׁמֵּר אֶת הַמֵּת אַף עַל פִּי שֶׁאֵינוֹ מֵתוֹ – פָּטוּר מִקְּרִיאַת שְׁמַע וּמִן הַתְּפִלָּה וּמִן הַתְּפִילִּין וּמִכׇּל מִצְוֹת הָאֲמוּרוֹת בַּתּוֹרָה. הָיוּ שְׁנַיִם – זֶה מְשַׁמֵּר וְזֶה קוֹרֵא, וְזֶה מְשַׁמֵּר וְזֶה קוֹרֵא. בֶּן עַזַּאי אוֹמֵר: הָיוּ בָּאִים בִּסְפִינָה – מַנִּיחוֹ בְּזָוִית זוֹ וּמִתְפַּלְּלִין שְׁנֵיהֶם בְּזָוִית אַחֶרֶת.

The Gemara discusses the **matter** of the *baraita* **itself.** It was taught in the *baraita*: **One who watches over the deceased, even though it is not his dead** relative, **is exempt from the recitation of *Shema*, from** the *Amida* **prayer**[H] **and from phylacteries, and from all mitzvot mentioned in the Torah.** The *baraita* continues: If **two** individuals **were** watching over the deceased, **this one watches and that** one **recites** *Shema*, and then **that** one **watches and this** one **recites** *Shema*. **Ben Azzai says:** If **they were traveling** with the deceased **on a boat,** they are permitted **to set** the deceased **down in this corner** of the boat **and both pray in another corner** of the boat.

מַאי בֵּינַיְיהוּ? אָמַר רָבִינָא: ״חוֹשְׁשִׁין לְעַכְבָּרִים״ אִיכָּא בֵּינַיְיהוּ. מָר סָבַר: חָיְישִׁינַן, וּמָר סָבַר: לָא חָיְישִׁינַן.

The Gemara asks: **What is** the practical difference **between these** two opinions? **Ravina said:** The practical difference **between them is** whether or not one need be **concerned about mice** even inside the boat. **The** first **Sage holds that we are concerned** about mice everywhere, and it is therefore inappropriate to leave the deceased unguarded, even on a boat, lest he be eaten by mice. The other **Sage,** ben Azzai, **maintains that we are not concerned about mice** on a boat.

תָּנוּ רַבָּנַן: הַמּוֹלִיךְ עֲצָמוֹת מִמָּקוֹם לְמָקוֹם – הֲרֵי זֶה לֹא יִתְּנֵם בְּדִסַּקְיָא וְיִתְּנֵם עַל גַּבֵּי חֲמוֹר וְיִרְכַּב עֲלֵיהֶם, מִפְּנֵי שֶׁנּוֹהֵג בָּהֶם מִנְהַג בִּזָּיוֹן. וְאִם הָיָה מִתְיָרֵא מִפְּנֵי גּוֹיִם וּמִפְּנֵי לִסְטִים – מוּתָּר, וּכְדֶרֶךְ שֶׁאָמְרוּ בַּעֲצָמוֹת כָּךְ אָמְרוּ בְּסֵפֶר תּוֹרָה.

The Gemara discusses other issues concerning the dignity of the deceased. **The Sages taught: One who transports bones from place to place**[HN] **may not place them in a saddlebag** [***disakaya***][L] **and place them on the donkey's back and ride on them,** as in doing so **he treats** the remains **disgracefully. However, if he is afraid of gentiles** or **highwaymen** and therefore must move quickly, **he is permitted** to do so. **And just as they said with regard to bones, so they said with regard to a Torah scroll.**[H]

אַהַיָּיא? אִילֵימָא אַרֵישָׁא – פְּשִׁיטָא, מִי גָּרַע סֵפֶר תּוֹרָה מֵעֲצָמוֹת! אֶלָּא אַסֵּיפָא.

With regard to this last statement, the Gemara asks: **To what** section of the *baraita* does the parallel to a Torah scroll refer? **If you say** that this refers to **the first clause** of the *baraita*, this is **obvious. Is a Torah scroll less** important **than bones** of the dead? Certainly one may not treat a Torah disgracefully. Rather, this statement must refer **to the latter clause** of the *baraita*, that in a dangerous situation, one is permitted to ride on a Torah scroll as well.

אָמַר רַחֲבָה אָמַר רַב יְהוּדָה: כׇּל הָרוֹאֶה הַמֵּת וְאֵינוֹ מְלַוֵּהוּ – עוֹבֵר מִשּׁוּם ״לֹעֵג לָרָשׁ חֵרֵף עֹשֵׂהוּ״. וְאִם הִלְוָהוּ מַה שְּׂכָרוֹ? אָמַר רַב אַסִי, עָלָיו הַכָּתוּב אוֹמֵר: ״מַלְוֵה ה׳ חוֹנֵן דָּל״, ״וּמְכַבְּדוֹ חֹנֵן אֶבְיוֹן״.

**Raḥava said** that **Rav Yehuda said: One who sees the deceased** taken to burial **and does not escort him**[H] **has committed a transgression due to** the verse: **"He who mocks the poor blasphemes his Creator." And if he does escort him, what is his reward? Rav Asi said: The verse says about him: "He who gives to the poor gives a loan to the Lord,** and the Lord will repay him" (Proverbs 19:17), and: "He who oppresses the poor blasphemes his Creator, **but he who is gracious to the poor honors Him"** (Proverbs 14:31).

רַבִּי חִיָּיא וְרַבִּי יוֹנָתָן הֲווּ שָׁקְלִי וְאָזְלִי בְּבֵית הַקְּבָרוֹת, הֲוָה קָשַׁדְיָא תְּכֶלְתָּא דְּרַבִּי יוֹנָתָן. אֲמַר לֵיהּ רַבִּי חִיָּיא: דַּלְיֵיהּ, כְּדֵי שֶׁלֹּא יֹאמְרוּ ״לְמָחָר בָּאִין אֶצְלֵנוּ וְעַכְשָׁיו מְחָרְפִין אוֹתָנוּ״.

The Gemara relates that **Rabbi Ḥiyya and Rabbi Yonatan were walking in a cemetery and the sky-blue string** of **Rabbi Yonatan's** ritual fringes **was cast** to the ground and dragging across the graves. **Rabbi Ḥiyya said** to him: **Lift it,** so the dead **will not say: Tomorrow,** when their day comes, they will **come to** be buried with **us, and now** they are **insulting us.**[H]

אֲמַר לֵיהּ: וּמִי יָדְעִי כּוּלֵּי הַאי? וְהָא כְּתִיב: ״וְהַמֵּתִים אֵינָם יוֹדְעִים מְאוּמָה״! אֲמַר לֵיהּ: אִם קָרִיתָ – לֹא שָׁנִיתָ, אִם שָׁנִיתָ – לֹא שִׁלַּשְׁתָּ, אִם שִׁלַּשְׁתָּ – לֹא פֵּירְשׁוּ לְךָ: ״כִּי הַחַיִּים יוֹדְעִים שֶׁיָּמֻתוּ״ – אֵלּוּ צַדִּיקִים שֶׁבְּמִיתָתָן נִקְרְאוּ חַיִּים, שֶׁנֶּאֱמַר: ״וּבְנָיָהוּ בֶן יְהוֹיָדָע בֶּן אִישׁ חַי רַב פְּעָלִים מִקַּבְצְאֵל הוּא הִכָּה אֵת שְׁנֵי אֲרִאֵל מוֹאָב וְהוּא יָרַד וְהִכָּה אֶת הָאֲרִי בְּתוֹךְ הַבּוֹר בְּיוֹם הַשָּׁלֶג״;

Rabbi Yonatan **said to him: Do** the dead **know so much? Isn't it stated: "And the dead know nothing"** (Ecclesiastes 9:5)? Rabbi Ḥiyya **said to him: If you read** the verse, **you did not** read it **a second time, and if you** read it a **second time, you did not** read it **a third time, and if you** read it **a third time, they did not explain it to you** properly. The meaning of the verse: "For the living know that they will die, and the dead know nothing and have no more reward, for their memory has been forgotten" (Ecclesiastes 9:5): **For the living know that they will die, these are the righteous, who even in their death are called living.** An allusion to this is **as it is stated: "And Benayahu, son of Yehoyada, son of a valiant man of Kabze'el, who had done mighty deeds, he smote the two altar-hearths of Moab; he went down also and slew a lion in the midst of a pit in time of snow"** (II Samuel 23:20).

A donkey carrying a saddlebag

### HALAKHA

**One who transports bones from place to place – הַמּוֹלִיךְ עֲצָמוֹת מִמָּקוֹם לְמָקוֹם:** One who transports the bones of the deceased should not ride upon them. However, as long as he does not sit on them, he is permitted to place them on the animal that he is riding (*Tosafot*). And if he was transporting them through a dangerous area, he may ride directly on them (Rambam *Sefer Shofetim, Hilkhot Evel* 14:14; *Shulḥan Arukh, Yoreh De'a* 403:10).

**One who transports a Torah scroll – הַמּוֹלִיךְ סֵפֶר תּוֹרָה:** One who travels from one place to another with a Torah scroll must not place it in a sack on the donkey's back and ride on it. Rather, he should hold it on his lap, opposite his heart. If he fears bandits, he may ride on it. Even in that case, halakhic authorities disagree whether or not it is permissible to sit directly on top of the Torah scroll. Some hold that it is preferable that the Torah scroll be stolen rather than have it treated with disrespect (*Baḥ*), while others disagree (*Shakh*). In dangerous circumstances, all necessary steps are permitted (*Shulḥan Arukh, Oraḥ Ḥayyim* 282:3).

**One who sees the deceased and does not escort him – כׇּל הָרוֹאֶה הַמֵּת וְאֵינוֹ מְלַוֵּהוּ:** One who sees a funeral procession is obligated to escort the deceased for a distance of at least four cubits, as less than that, it is not considered that he moved at all. If one fails to escort him, he violates the prohibition derived in the Gemara from the verse: "He who mocks the poor" (*Shulḥan Arukh, Yoreh De'a* 361:3).

**Ritual fringes in a cemetery – צִיצִית בְּבֵית הַקְּבָרוֹת:** In places where the custom is to attach ritual fringes to one's regular clothing, one may enter a cemetery with that garment, but he must make certain that the ritual fringes do not drag over the graves, in accordance with the opinion of Rabbi Ḥiyya. Nowadays, when the garment with the ritual fringes is designated exclusively for prayer, one is prohibited from wearing it in a cemetery even if the ritual fringes do not drag across the graves. If one wears the garment beneath his clothing, it is permitted to enter the cemetery (*Shulḥan Arukh, Yoreh De'a* 23:1).

### NOTES

**One who transports bones from place to place – הַמּוֹלִיךְ עֲצָמוֹת מִמָּקוֹם לְמָקוֹם:** During the mishnaic era, burial consisted of two stages. First, the body was buried in the ground. After the flesh decomposed, the bones were removed and placed in stone sarcophagi. That is why it was common for bones to be transported from one place to another.

### LANGUAGE

**Saddlebag [*disakaya*] – דִּסַּקְיָא:** The root of the word disakaya is the Greek δισάκκιον, *disakion*, which means a double bag, i.e., two bags tied together.

## NOTES

**Gnawing maggots are excruciating to the dead – קָשָׁה רִמָּה לְמֵת:** It is not that the body of the deceased feels the pain. Rather, his soul regrets the decomposition of his body, which served as its sanctuary (Sefer Ḥasidim, Rashba in his Responsa).

**There was an incident involving a pious man… and he went and slept in the cemetery – מַעֲשֶׂה בְּחָסִיד אֶחָד...וְהָלַךְ וְלָן בְּבֵית הַקְּבָרוֹת:** Nearly all of the commentaries interpret this incident and those that follow as dream-like visions of unique individuals. Some even explained that his sleeping in the cemetery itself was symbolic. In the wake of the quarrel with his wife, he was forced to descend from his lofty spiritual level to occupy himself with worldly matters and concerns for his livelihood (HaKotev).

**In a mat of reeds – בְּמַחֲצֶלֶת שֶׁל קָנִים:** Since the soul of the deceased maintains a connection with the body for as long as the body is intact (Shabbat 152b), and since the body of the girl buried in a mat of reeds was protected from decomposition for an extended period, her soul remained connected to her body (Tziyyun LeNefesh Ḥayya).

## LANGUAGE

**Curtain [pargod] – פַּרְגּוֹד:** The pargod, in one sense, refers to a type of screen. The word most likely comes from the Greek παραγαύδιον or the Latin paragauda, a garment with a purple border, which is derived from the Persian parigund.

## BACKGROUND

**A mat of reeds – מַחֲצֶלֶת שֶׁל קָנִים:** Mats are made from a variety of materials, the choicest being manufactured from the soft, inner portion of the reed, and the coarser, cheaper mats being manufactured from entire reeds tied together. Such mats were generally used as partitions or to cover roofs. There were also several different types of shrouds, and earlier generations were quite strict about burying the deceased in expensive fabrics, at times even beyond the means of the bereaved. Later, at the behest of Rabban Shimon ben Gamliel, they would also bury them in less expensive fabrics. Only the poorest of families, however, would be reduced to burying their deceased in cheap mats made from reeds, which is why the girl's mother was ashamed when this information was made public.

---

"בֶּן אִישׁ חַי", אַטּוּ כּוּלֵּי עָלְמָא בְּנֵי מֵתֵי נִינְהוּ? אֶלָּא, "בֶּן אִישׁ חַי" – שֶׁאֲפִילּוּ בְּמִיתָתוֹ קָרוּי חַי; "רַב פְּעָלִים מִקַּבְצְאֵל" – שֶׁרִיבָּה וְקִבֵּץ פּוֹעֲלִים לַתּוֹרָה; "וְהוּא הִכָּה אֶת שְׁנֵי אֲרִאֵל מוֹאָב" – שֶׁלֹּא הִנִּיחַ כְּמוֹתוֹ לֹא בְּמִקְדָּשׁ רִאשׁוֹן וְלֹא בְּמִקְדָּשׁ שֵׁנִי;

"וְהוּא יָרַד וְהִכָּה אֶת הָאֲרִי בְּתוֹךְ הַבּוֹר בְּיוֹם הַשָּׁלֶג" – אִיכָּא דְּאָמְרִי: דְּתַבַר גְּזִיזֵי דְּבַרְדָּא וְנָחֵת וּטְבַל, אִיכָּא דְּאָמְרִי דְּתָנֵי סִיפְרָא דְּבֵי רַב בְּיוֹמָא דְּסִיתְוָא.

"וְהַמֵּתִים אֵינָם יוֹדְעִים מְאוּמָה" – אֵלּוּ רְשָׁעִים שֶׁבְּחַיֵּיהֶן קְרוּיִין מֵתִים, שֶׁנֶּאֱמַר: "וְאַתָּה חָלָל רָשָׁע נְשִׂיא יִשְׂרָאֵל". וְאִי בָּעֵית אֵימָא, מֵהָכָא: "עַל פִּי שְׁנַיִם עֵדִים אוֹ (עַל פִּי) שְׁלֹשָׁה עֵדִים יוּמַת הַמֵּת". חַי הוּא! אֶלָּא: הַמֵּת מֵעִיקָּרָא.

בְּנֵי רַבִּי חִיָּיא נְפוּק לְקִרְיָיתָא אַיְיקַר לְהוּ תַּלְמוּדַיְיהוּ, הֲווּ קָא מְצַעֲרִי לְאַדְכּוּרֵיהּ. אֲמַר לֵיהּ חַד לְחַבְרֵיהּ: יָדַע אֲבוּן בְּהַאי צַעֲרָא? אֲמַר לֵיהּ אִידַךְ: מְנָא יָדַע וְהָא כְּתִיב: "יִכְבְּדוּ בָנָיו וְלֹא יֵדַע"!

אֲמַר לֵיהּ אִידַךְ: וְלָא יָדַע? וְהָא כְּתִיב: "אַךְ בְּשָׂרוֹ עָלָיו יִכְאָב וְנַפְשׁוֹ עָלָיו תֶּאֱבָל", וְאָמַר רַבִּי יִצְחָק: קָשָׁה רִמָּה לְמֵת כְּמַחַט בִּבְשַׂר הַחַי.

אָמְרִי: בְּצַעֲרָא דִּידְהוּ – יָדְעִי, בְּצַעֲרָא דַּאֲחֲרִינָא – לָא יָדְעִי.

וְלָא? וְהָתַנְיָא: מַעֲשֶׂה בְּחָסִיד אֶחָד שֶׁנָּתַן דִּינָר לְעָנִי בְּעֶרֶב רֹאשׁ הַשָּׁנָה בִּשְׁנֵי בַצּוֹרֶת, וְהִקְנִיטַתּוּ אִשְׁתּוֹ וְהָלַךְ וְלָן בְּבֵית הַקְּבָרוֹת. וְשָׁמַע שְׁתֵּי רוּחוֹת שֶׁמְּסַפְּרוֹת זוֹ לָזוֹ, אָמְרָה חֲדָא לַחֲבֶרְתָּהּ: חֲבֶרְתִּי, בּוֹאִי וְנָשׁוּט בָּעוֹלָם וְנִשְׁמַע מֵאֲחוֹרֵי הַפַּרְגּוֹד מַה פּוּרְעָנוּת בָּא לָעוֹלָם. אָמְרָה לָהּ חֲבֶרְתָּהּ: אֵינִי יְכוֹלָה שֶׁאֲנִי קְבוּרָה בְּמַחֲצֶלֶת שֶׁל קָנִים, אֶלָּא לְכִי אַתְּ וּמַה שֶּׁאַתְּ שׁוֹמַעַת אִמְרִי לִי. הָלְכָה הִיא וְשָׁטָה וּבָאָה. וְאָמְרָה לָהּ חֲבֶרְתָּהּ: חֲבֶרְתִּי, מַה שָּׁמַעַתְּ מֵאֲחוֹרֵי הַפַּרְגּוֹד? אָמְרָה לָהּ: שָׁמַעְתִּי, שֶׁכָּל הַזּוֹרֵעַ בִּרְבִיעָה רִאשׁוֹנָה בָּרָד מַלְקֶה אוֹתוֹ. הָלַךְ הוּא וְזָרַע בִּרְבִיעָה שְׁנִיָּה. שֶׁל כָּל הָעוֹלָם כּוּלּוֹ – לָקָה, שֶׁלּוֹ – לֹא לָקָה.

---

He was referred to in the verse as **son of a living man.** The Gemara wonders: **Is that to say,** the fact that the Bible referred to him with that appellation, **that all others are children of the dead? Rather,** the verse should be explained as follows: **The son of a living man** who lives forever, **who even in death is referred to as living. Man of Kabze'el who had done mighty deeds, as he accumulated and gathered many workers for** the sake of the **Torah. Who killed the two lion-hearted men** [**Ariel**] **of Moab,** as after his death **he left no one his equal, in either the First Temple or** the **Second Temple** periods, as the Temple is called *Ariel* (see Isaiah 29:1), and the two *Ariel* refers to the two Temples.

**The Sages disagreed over the interpretation of the rest of the verse: "And who descended and slew the lion in the pit on the snowy day." Some say** that this means **that he broke blocks of hail and descended and immersed himself** in the water to purify himself. **Others say that he learned** all of the *Sifra,* the halakhic midrash on the book of Leviticus **of the school of Rav, on a winter's day.**

In contrast to the righteous, who are referred to as living even after their death, the verse states explicitly: **"The dead know nothing." These are the wicked,** who even during their lives are called dead, as the prophet Ezekiel **said** in reference to a king of Israel who was alive: **"And you are a slain, wicked prince of Israel"** (Ezekiel 21:30). **And if you wish, say** instead that the proof is **from here: "At the mouth of two witnesses or three witnesses the dead shall be put to death"** (Deuteronomy 17:6). This is puzzling. As long as the accused has not been sentenced to death, he **is alive. Rather,** this person who is wicked is considered **dead from the outset.**

The Gemara relates a story on this topic: **The sons of Rabbi Ḥiyya went out to the villages** to oversee the laborers. **They forgot what they had learned** and were struggling to recall it. **One** of them said to the other: **Does our** deceased **father know of our anguish? The other said to him: From where would he know? Isn't it written: "His sons are honored yet he shall not know it,"** they come to sorrow and he shall not understand them" (Job 14:21)? The dead do not know.

**The other said** back **to him: And** do the dead truly **not know? Isn't it written: "Only in his flesh does he feel pain, in his soul does he mourn"** (Job 14:22)? Based on this verse **Rabbi Yitzḥak said: Gnawing maggots are as excruciating to the dead** as the stab of **a needle to the flesh of the living.** The dead must have the capacity to feel and know.

In order to reconcile this contradiction **they said: They know of their own pain but do not know of the pain of others.**

The Gemara challenges this: **And** is it so that the dead do **not know** of the pain of others? **Wasn't it taught** in a *baraita*: There was **an incident involving a pious man who gave a poor man a dinar on the eve of Rosh HaShana during drought years, and his wife mocked him** for giving so large a sum at so difficult a time? **And** in order to escape her incessant mockery, **he went and slept in the cemetery.** That night in his dream (Ritva, HaKotev, Maharsha), **he heard two spirits conversing with each other. One said to the other: My friend, let us roam the world and hear from behind the heavenly curtain** [**pargod**]**,** which separates the Divine Presence from the world, **what calamity will befall the world. The other spirit said to her: I cannot go with you, as I am buried in a mat of reeds,** but you go, and tell me what you hear. She went, and roamed, and came back. **The other spirit said: My friend, what did you hear from behind the heavenly curtain? She replied: I heard that anyone who sows during the first rainy season** of this year, **hail will fall and strike his** crops. Hearing this, the pious man **went and sowed** his seeds **during the second rainy season. Ultimately, the crops of the entire world were stricken** by hail **and his crops were not stricken.**

לַשָּׁנָה הָאַחֶרֶת הָלַךְ וְלָן בְּבֵית הַקְּבָרוֹת, וְשָׁמַע אוֹתָן שְׁתֵּי רוּחוֹת שֶׁמְּסַפְּרוֹת זוֹ עִם זוֹ. אָמְרָה חֲדָא לַחֲבֶרְתָּהּ: בּוֹאִי וְנָשׁוּט בָּעוֹלָם וְנִשְׁמַע מֵאֲחוֹרֵי הַפַּרְגּוֹד מַה פּוּרְעָנוּת בָּא לָעוֹלָם. אָמְרָה לָהּ: חֲבֶרְתִּי, לֹא כָּךְ אָמַרְתִּי לָךְ: אֵינִי יְכוֹלָה שֶׁאֲנִי קְבוּרָה בְּמַחֲצֶלֶת שֶׁל קָנִים? אֶלָּא לְכִי אַתְּ וּמַה שֶּׁאַתְּ שׁוֹמַעַת בּוֹאִי וְאִמְרִי לִי. הָלְכָה וְשָׁטָה וּבָאָה. וְאָמְרָה לָהּ חֲבֶרְתָּהּ: חֲבֶרְתִּי, מַה שָּׁמַעַתְּ מֵאֲחוֹרֵי הַפַּרְגּוֹד? אָמְרָה לָהּ: שָׁמַעְתִּי, שֶׁכָּל הַזּוֹרֵעַ בִּרְבִיעָה שְׁנִיָּה שִׁדָּפוֹן מַלְקֶה אוֹתוֹ. הָלַךְ וְזָרַע בִּרְבִיעָה רִאשׁוֹנָה. שֶׁל כָּל הָעוֹלָם כּוּלּוֹ – נִשְׁדַּף, וְשֶׁלּוֹ לֹא נִשְׁדַּף.

**The following year,** on the eve of Rosh HaShana, the same pious man **went and slept in the cemetery** at his own initiative, and again **he heard the two spirits conversing with each other. One said to the other: Let us roam the world and hear from behind the heavenly curtain what calamity will befall the world. She said to her: My friend, have I not** already **told you that I cannot, as I am buried in a mat of reeds? Rather, you go, and tell me what you hear. She went, and roamed, and returned. The other** spirit **said to her: My friend, what did you hear from behind the curtain? She said to her: I heard that those who sow during the second rainy season blight will strike his** crops. That pious man **went and sowed during the first rainy season.** Since everyone else sowed during the second rainy season, ultimately, the crops **of the entire world were blighted and his** crops **were not blighted.**

אָמְרָה לוֹ אִשְׁתּוֹ: מִפְּנֵי מָה אֶשְׁתָּקַד שֶׁל כָּל הָעוֹלָם כּוּלּוֹ לָקָה וְשֶׁלְּךָ לֹא לָקָה, וְעַכְשָׁיו שֶׁל כָּל הָעוֹלָם כּוּלּוֹ נִשְׁדַּף וְשֶׁלְּךָ לֹא נִשְׁדַּף? סָח לָהּ כָּל הַדְּבָרִים הַלָּלוּ. אָמְרוּ: לֹא הָיוּ יָמִים מוּעָטִים עַד שֶׁנָּפְלָה קְטָטָה בֵּין אִשְׁתּוֹ שֶׁל אוֹתוֹ חָסִיד וּבֵין אִמָּהּ שֶׁל אוֹתָהּ רִיבָה. אָמְרָה לָהּ: לְכִי וְאַרְאֵךְ בִּתֵּךְ שֶׁהִיא קְבוּרָה בְּמַחֲצֶלֶת שֶׁל קָנִים.

The pious man's **wife said to him: Why is it that last year,** the crops **of the entire world were stricken and yours were not stricken, and now** this year, the crops **of the entire world were blighted and yours were not blighted? He related to her the entire story. They said: It was not** even a few days later that **a quarrel fell between the pious man's wife and the mother of the young woman** who was buried there. The pious man's wife **said to her** scornfully: **Go and I will show you your daughter,** and you will see that **she is buried in a mat of reeds.**

לַשָּׁנָה הָאַחֶרֶת הָלַךְ וְלָן בְּבֵית הַקְּבָרוֹת וְשָׁמַע אוֹתָן רוּחוֹת שֶׁמְּסַפְּרוֹת זוֹ עִם זוֹ. אָמְרָה לָהּ: חֲבֶרְתִּי, בּוֹאִי וְנָשׁוּט בָּעוֹלָם וְנִשְׁמַע מֵאֲחוֹרֵי הַפַּרְגּוֹד מַה פּוּרְעָנוּת בָּא לָעוֹלָם. אָמְרָה לָהּ: חֲבֶרְתִּי, הַנִּיחִינִי, דְּבָרִים שֶׁבֵּינִי לְבֵינֵךְ כְּבָר נִשְׁמְעוּ בֵּין הַחַיִּים. אַלְמָא יָדְעִי!

**The following year,** he again **went and slept in the cemetery, and heard the same spirits conversing with each other. One said** to the other: **My friend, let us roam the world and hear from behind the heavenly curtain what calamity will befall the world. She said to her: My friend, leave me** alone, as **words that** we have privately exchanged **between us have already been heard among the living. Apparently,** the dead **know** what transpires in this world.

דִּילְמָא אִינִישׁ אַחֲרִינָא שָׁכֵיב וְאָזֵיל וַאֲמַר לְהוּ.

The Gemara responds: This is no proof; **perhaps another person,** who heard about the conversation of the spirits secondhand, **died** and he **went and told them** that they had been overheard.

תָּא שְׁמַע: דִּזְעֵירִי הֲוָה מַפְקִיד זוּזֵי גַּבֵּי אוּשְׁפִּיזִיכְתֵּיהּ, עַד דְּאָתֵי וְאָזֵיל לְבֵי רַב, שְׁכִיבָה. אֲזַל בַּתְרַהּ לַחֲצַר מָוֶת. אֲמַר לַהּ: זוּזֵי הֵיכָא? – אֲמַרָה לֵיהּ: זִיל שְׁקָלִינְהוּ מִתּוּתֵי בְּצִנּוֹרָא דְּדַשָּׁא בְּדוּךְ פְּלָן, וְאֵימָא לַהּ לְאִימָּא תְּשַׁדַּר לִי מַסְרְקַאי וְגוּבְתַּאי דְּכוּחְלָא בַּהֲדֵי פְּלָנִיתָא דְּאָתְיָא לִמְחָר. אַלְמָא יָדְעִי! –

With regard to the deceased's knowledge of what transpires, **come** and **hear** a proof, as it is told: **Ze'iri would deposit** his **dinars with his innkeeper. While he was going and coming to** and from **the school of Rav, she died,** and he did not know where she had put the money. **So he went after her to** her grave in **the cemetery**[N] **and said to her: Where are the dinars? She replied: Go and get them from beneath the hinge of the door in such and such a place, and tell my mother that she should send me my comb**[B] **and a tube of eyeshadow**[B] **with such and such a woman who will die and come here tomorrow. Apparently,** the dead **know** what transpires in this world.

דִּלְמָא דּוּמָה קָדֵים וּמַכְרִיז לְהוּ.

The Gemara rejects this proof: **Perhaps** the angel **Duma,** who oversees the dead, **comes beforehand and announces to them** that a particular individual will arrive the next day, but they themselves do not know.

תָּא שְׁמַע: דַּאֲבוּהּ דִּשְׁמוּאֵל הָווּ קָא מַפְקְדִי גַּבֵּיהּ זוּזֵי דְּיַתְמֵי, כִּי נָח נַפְשֵׁיהּ לָא הֲוָה שְׁמוּאֵל גַּבֵּיהּ. הָווּ קָא קָרוּ לֵיהּ בַּר אָכֵיל זוּזֵי דְּיַתְמֵי. אֲזַל אַבַּתְרֵיהּ לַחֲצַר מָוֶת. אֲמַר לְהוּ: בָּעֵינָא אַבָּא. אֲמַרוּ לֵיהּ: אַבָּא טוּבָא אִיכָּא הָכָא. אֲמַר לְהוּ: בָּעֵינָא אַבָּא בַּר אַבָּא. אֲמַרוּ לֵיהּ: אַבָּא בַּר אַבָּא נַמִי טוּבָא אִיכָּא הָכָא. אֲמַר לְהוּ: בָּעֵינָא אַבָּא בַּר אַבָּא אֲבוּהּ דִּשְׁמוּאֵל, הֵיכָא? – אֲמַרוּ לֵיהּ: סְלֵיק לִמְתִיבְתָּא דִּרְקִיעָא. אַדְּהָכִי חַזְיֵיהּ לְלֵוִי דְּיָתֵיב אַבָּרַאי. אֲמַר לֵיהּ: אַמַּאי יָתְבַתְּ אַבָּרַאי, מַאי טַעְמָא לָא סָלְקַתְּ? אֲמַר לֵיהּ, דְּאָמְרִי לִי: כָּל כִּי הָנָךְ שְׁנֵי דְּלָא סְלִיקַתְּ לִמְתִיבְתָּא דְּרַבִּי אָפֵס וְאַחֲלִישְׁתֵּיהּ לְדַעְתֵּיהּ – לָא מְעַיְּילִינַן לָךְ לִמְתִיבְתָּא דִּרְקִיעָא.

The Gemara cites another proof: **Come** and **hear,** as it is told: **They would deposit the money of orphans with Shmuel's father** for safekeeping. **When Shmuel's father died, Shmuel was not with him,** and did not learn from him the location of the money. Since he did not return it, Shmuel was called: **Son of** him who **consumes the money of orphans.** Shmuel **went after** his father **to the cemetery and said to** the dead: **I want Abba.** The dead **said to him: There are many Abbas here. He told them: I want Abba bar Abba. They said** to him: **There are also many** people named **Abba bar Abba here. He told them: I want Abba bar Abba, the father of Shmuel. Where** is he? **They replied: Ascend to the yeshiva on high. Meanwhile, he saw** his friend **Levi**[P] **sitting outside** the yeshiva, away from the rest of the deceased. **He asked him: Why do you sit outside? Why did you not ascend** to the yeshiva? **He replied: Because they tell me** that for **all those years that you didn't enter the yeshiva of Rabbi Afes,**[P] **and** thereby **upset him, we will not grant you entry to the yeshiva on high.**

NOTES

**To the cemetery [*hatzar mavet*] – לַחֲצַר מָוֶת:** Some interpreted *ḥatzar mavet* as referring to a cemetery (Rashi). Others explained this passage as a vision, as Shmuel was a priest and certainly did not go to a cemetery (*Ahavat Eitan*). Rather, *ḥatzar mavet* is a place where the dead who have yet to find rest in a more sublime world are in abeyance.

BACKGROUND

**Comb – מַסְרֵק:**

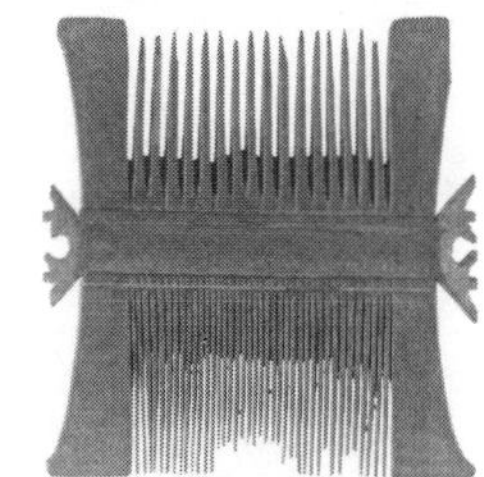

Comb from Eretz Yisrael in the mishnaic period

**Tube of eyeshadow – גּוּבְתָּא דְּכוּחְלָא:**

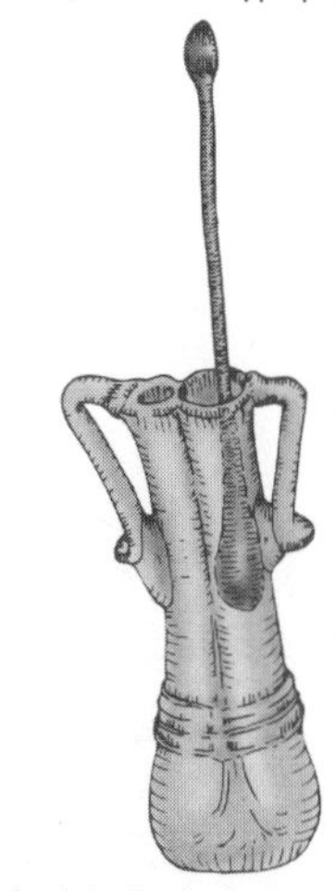

Tube of eyeshadow from the talmudic era

PERSONALITIES

**Levi and Rabbi Afes – לֵוִי וְרַבִּי אָפֵס:** The complicated chain of events that culminated in Levi not attending Rabbi Afes' yeshiva was set into motion by the will of Rabbi Yehuda HaNasi, in which he appointed Rabbi Ḥanina to succeed him at the helm of the yeshiva. Rabbi Ḥanina, however, foreswore the appointment in order to honor Rabbi Afes, who was Rabbi Ḥanina's senior in age, if not in wisdom. When Rabbi Afes was appointed to head the yeshiva, Rabbi Ḥanina could not attend as a student, so he sat outside the yeshiva. Rabbi Afes' friend Levi, who was his junior and who was not averse, in principle, to learning from him, joined Rabbi Ḥanina to keep him company. Rabbi Afes, however, was unaware of the reason for Levi's absence and was insulted. Shmuel and his father, who were close friends of Levi, likely knew that he had done so out of respect for Rabbi Ḥanina.

אַדְּהָכִי וְהָכִי אֲתָא אֲבוּהּ, חַזְיֵיהּ דַּהֲוָה קָא בָכֵי וְאָחֵיךְ. אֲמַר לֵיהּ: מַאי טַעְמָא קָא בָכֵית? אֲמַר לֵיהּ: דִּלְעֲגַל קָא אָתֵית. מַאי טַעְמָא אֲחֵיכַתְּ? – דַּחֲשִׁיבַת בְּהַאי עָלְמָא טוּבָא. אֲמַר לֵיהּ: אִי חֲשִׁיבְנָא – נְעַיְּילוּהּ לְלֵוִי, וְעַיְּילוּהוּ לְלֵוִי.

Meanwhile, Shmuel's **father came** and Shmuel **saw that he was crying and laughing.** Shmuel **said to** his father: **Why are you crying?** His father **replied:** Because **you will come here soon.** Shmuel continued and asked: **Why are you laughing?** His father replied: Because **you are extremely important in this world.** Shmuel **said to him: If I am important, then let them grant Levi entry** to the yeshiva. **And** so it was **that they granted Levi entry** to the yeshiva.

אֲמַר לֵיהּ: זוּזֵי דְּיַתְמֵי הֵיכָא? אֲמַר לֵיהּ: זִיל שְׁקָלִינְהוּ בְּאַמְתָא דְּרֵחְיָא, עִילָּאֵי וְתַתָּאֵי – דִּידַן, וּמִיצְעֵי – דְּיַתְמֵי. אֲמַר לֵיהּ: מַאי טַעְמָא עֲבַדְתְּ הָכִי? – אֲמַר לֵיהּ: אִי גָּנְבִי גַּנָּבֵי – מִגַּנְבוּ מִדִּידַן, אִי אָכְלָה אַרְעָא – אָכְלָה מִדִּידַן. אַלְמָא דְּיָדְעִי! – דִּילְמָא שָׁאנֵי שְׁמוּאֵל, כֵּיוָן דַּחֲשִׁיב – קָדְמִי וּמַכְרְזִי "פַּנּוּ מָקוֹם".

Shmuel **said to** his father: **Where is the orphans' money? He said to him: Go and** retrieve **it from the millhouse,** where you will find **the uppermost and the lowermost** money **is ours, and** the money **in the middle** belongs to **the orphans.** Shmuel **said to him: Why did you do that? He replied: If thieves stole, they would steal from our** money on top, which the thief would see first. **If the earth swallowed up** any of it, it would swallow **from our** money, on the bottom. **Apparently,** the dead, in this case Shmuel's father, **know** when others will die. Since Shmuel did not die the next day, clearly the angel Duma could not have informed them (*Tosafot*). The Gemara responds: **Perhaps Shmuel is different,** and **because he is so important they announce beforehand: Clear place** for his arrival.

וְאַף רַבִּי יוֹנָתָן הֲדַר בֵּיהּ, דְּאָמַר רַבִּי שְׁמוּאֵל בַּר נַחְמָנִי אָמַר רַבִּי יוֹנָתָן: מִנַּיִן לַמֵּתִים שֶׁמְּסַפְּרִים זֶה עִם זֶה? שֶׁנֶּאֱמַר: "וַיֹּאמֶר ה׳ אֵלָיו זֹאת הָאָרֶץ אֲשֶׁר נִשְׁבַּעְתִּי לְאַבְרָהָם לְיִצְחָק וּלְיַעֲקֹב לֵאמֹר", מַאי 'לֵאמֹר' – אָמַר הַקָּדוֹשׁ בָּרוּךְ הוּא לְמֹשֶׁה: לֵךְ אֱמוֹר לָהֶם לְאַבְרָהָם לְיִצְחָק וּלְיַעֲקֹב שְׁבוּעָה שֶׁנִּשְׁבַּעְתִּי לָכֶם כְּבָר קִיַּימְתִּיהָ לִבְנֵיכֶם.

In any case, with regard to the crux of the issue, **Rabbi Yonatan also reconsidered** his opinion, **as Rabbi Shmuel bar Naḥmani said** that **Rabbi Yonatan said: From where** is it derived **that the dead converse with each other? As it is stated: "And the Lord said to him, this is the land that I swore to Abraham, Isaac and Jacob, saying:** I will give it to your offspring" (Deuteronomy 34:4). **What is** the meaning of **"saying"?** It means that **God told Moses: Go and tell Abraham, Isaac, and Jacob,** that **the oath that I swore to you I have already fulfilled for your descendants.**

Perek **III**
Daf **19** Amud **a**

**LANGUAGE**

His skull [*arneka demoḥei*] – אַרְנְקָא דְמוֹחֵיהּ: *Arneka* is from the Greek ἀρνακίς meaning sheepskin. Ultimately, it included other items as well, especially, purses made from sheepskin.

**NOTES**

After the biers of Torah scholars – אַחַר מִטָּתָן: The standard explanation of this phrase is as a euphemism for "after their death," as the Sages said: The righteous, even after their death, are called alive (Maharsha). Variant readings have this explicitly as "after their death." Others explain: After the Torah scholars have strayed, which has an etymological similarity in Hebrew, from the path of righteousness evoking the verse: "Those who turn aside unto their crooked ways" (Psalms 125:5; see Rabbeinu Ḥananel).

וְאִי סָלְקָא דַּעְתָּךְ דְּלָא יָדְעִי – כִּי אָמַר לְהוּ מַאי הָוֵי? – אֶלָּא מַאי, דְּיָדְעִי? – לָמָּה לֵיהּ לְמֵימַר לְהוּ? – לְאַחֲזוּקֵי לֵיהּ טֵיבוּתָא לְמֹשֶׁה.

**And if it should enter your mind that** the dead **do not know, then what of it if he tells them?** The Gemara rejects this: **Rather what** will you say, **that** they **know?** Then **why does he** need **to tell them?** The Gemara replies: This is not difficult, as he is telling them so that **they will give credit to Moses.**

אָמַר רַבִּי יִצְחָק: כָּל הַמְסַפֵּר אַחֲרֵי הַמֵּת כְּאִלּוּ מְסַפֵּר אַחֲרֵי הָאֶבֶן. אִיכָּא דְּאָמְרִי: דְּלָא יָדְעִי; וְאִיכָּא דְּאָמְרִי: דְּיָדְעִי וְלָא אִיכְפַּת לְהוּ.

On this subject, **Rabbi Yitzḥak said: Anyone who speaks** negatively **after the deceased it is as if** he **speaks after the stone.** The Gemara offers two interpretations of this: **Some say** this is because the dead **do not know, and some say that they know,** but **they do not care** that they are spoken of in such a manner.

אִינִי? וְהָא אָמַר רַב פָּפָּא: חַד אִישְׁתָּעֵי מִילְּתָא בָּתְרֵיהּ דְּמָר שְׁמוּאֵל וּנְפַל קְנֵיא מִטַּלְּלָא וּבְזַעָא לְאַרְנְקָא דְמוֹחֵיהּ!

The Gemara asks: **Is that so? Didn't Rav Pappa say:** There was once **someone who spoke** disparagingly **after** the death of **Mar Shmuel and a reed fell from the ceiling, fracturing his skull?**[L] Obviously, the dead care when people speak ill of them.

שָׁאנֵי צוּרְבָא מֵרַבָּנַן, דְּקוּדְשָׁא בְּרִיךְ הוּא תָּבַע בִּיקָרֵיהּ.

The Gemara rejects this: This is no proof that the dead care. Rather, a **Torah scholar is different, as God** Himself **demands** that **his honor** be upheld.

אָמַר רַבִּי יְהוֹשֻׁעַ בֶּן לֵוִי: כָּל הַמְסַפֵּר אַחַר מִטָּתָן שֶׁל תַּלְמִידֵי חֲכָמִים נוֹפֵל בַּגֵּיהִנָּם, שֶׁנֶּאֱמַר: "וְהַמַּטִּים עֲקַלְקַלּוֹתָם יוֹלִיכֵם ה׳ אֶת פֹּעֲלֵי הָאָוֶן שָׁלוֹם עַל יִשְׂרָאֵל", אֲפִילּוּ בְּשָׁעָה שֶׁשָּׁלוֹם עַל יִשְׂרָאֵל "יוֹלִיכֵם ה׳ אֶת פֹּעֲלֵי הָאָוֶן".

Rabbi Yehoshua **ben Levi said** similarly: **One who speaks** disparagingly **after the biers of Torah scholars**[N] and maligns them after their death will **fall in Gehenna, as it is stated: "But those who turn aside unto their crooked ways, the Lord will lead them away with the workers of iniquity; peace be upon Israel"** (Psalms 125:5). **Even** if he speaks ill of them **when there is peace upon Israel,** after death, when they are no longer able to fight those denouncing them (*Tosafot*); nevertheless **the Lord will lead them away with the workers of iniquity,** to Gehenna.

תָּנָא דְּבֵי רַבִּי יִשְׁמָעֵאל: אִם רָאִיתָ תַּלְמִיד חָכָם שֶׁעָבַר עֲבֵירָה בַּלַּיְלָה – אַל תְּהַרְהֵר אַחֲרָיו בַּיּוֹם, שֶׁמָּא עָשָׂה תְשׁוּבָה. ״שֶׁמָּא״ סָלְקָא דַּעְתָּךְ? אֶלָּא: וַדַּאי עָשָׂה תְּשׁוּבָה. וְהָנֵי מִילֵּי – בִּדְבָרִים שֶׁבְּגוּפוֹ, אֲבָל בְּמָמוֹנָא – עַד דִּמְהַדַּר לְמָרֵיהּ.

On a similar note, **it was taught in the school of Rabbi Yishmael: If you saw a** Torah **scholar transgress a prohibition at night, do not think** badly **of him during the day; perhaps he has repented**[N] in the meantime. The Gemara challenges this: **Does it enter your mind** that only **perhaps** he has repented? Shouldn't he be given the benefit of the doubt? **Rather, he has certainly repented.** The Gemara notes: **The idea** that one must always give a Torah scholar the benefit of the doubt and assume that he has repented refers specifically to **matters** affecting **himself, but,** if one witnesses a Torah scholar committing a transgression **involving the property** of another, one is not required to give him the benefit of the doubt. Rather, he should not assume that he has repented **until** he sees him **return** the money to **its owner.**

וְאָמַר רַבִּי יְהוֹשֻׁעַ בֶּן לֵוִי: בְּעֶשְׂרִים וְאַרְבָּעָה מְקוֹמוֹת בֵּית דִּין מְנַדִּין עַל כְּבוֹד הָרַב, וְכוּלָּן שָׁנִינוּ בְּמִשְׁנָתֵנוּ. אֲמַר לֵיהּ רַבִּי אֶלְעָזָר: הֵיכָא? אֲמַר לֵיהּ: לְכִי תִּשְׁכַּח.

Since matters relating to the respect due Torah scholars were raised, the Gemara continues, citing **Rabbi Yehoshua ben Levi,** who **said: There are twenty-four places in which the court ostracizes**[N] **over** matters of **respect** due **the rabbi, and we learned them all in our Mishna. Rabbi Elazar said to him: Where** are those cases to be found? Rabbi Yehoshua ben Levi **said to him: When** you look, **you** will **find** them.

נְפַק דַּק וְאַשְׁכַּח תְּלָת: הַמְזַלְזֵל בִּנְטִילַת יָדַיִם, וְהַמְסַפֵּר אַחַר מִטָּתָן שֶׁל תַּלְמִידֵי חֲכָמִים, וְהַמֵּגִיס דַּעְתּוֹ כְּלַפֵּי מַעְלָה.

**He went out, analyzed, and found three** examples: **One who demeans** the ritual of **washing of the hands, one who speaks** disparagingly **after the bier**[H] **of Torah scholars, and one who is arrogant vis-à-vis Heaven.** The Gemara cites sources for each of these cases.

הַמְסַפֵּר אַחַר מִטָּתָן שֶׁל תַּלְמִידֵי חֲכָמִים מַאי הִיא? דִּתְנַן, הוּא הָיָה אוֹמֵר: אֵין מַשְׁקִין לֹא אֶת הַגִּיּוֹרֶת וְלֹא אֶת הַמְשׁוּחְרֶרֶת; וַחֲכָמִים אוֹמְרִים: מַשְׁקִין. וְאָמְרוּ לוֹ: מַעֲשֶׂה בְּכַרְכְּמִית, שִׁפְחָה מְשׁוּחְרֶרֶת בִּירוּשָׁלַיִם וְהִשְׁקוּהָ שְׁמַעְיָה וְאַבְטַלְיוֹן! – וְאָמַר לָהֶם: דּוּגְמָא הִשְׁקוּהָ; וְנִדּוּהוּ, וּמֵת בְּנִדּוּיוֹ, וְסָקְלוּ בֵּית דִּין אֶת אֲרוֹנוֹ.

**What is** the source for **one who speaks** disparagingly **after the biers of Torah scholars? As we learned** in the mishna: Akavya ben Mahalalel[P] **would say:** In the case of a woman whose husband suspects her of adultery, who was warned by her husband not to seclude herself with another man and she did not listen (see Numbers 5), the court **does not administer** the bitter water potion of a *sota* to **a convert or an emancipated** maidservant.[H] **And the Rabbis say:** The court **administers** the bitter water potion to them. **And** the Rabbis **said to him** as proof: **There is the story of Kharkemit, an emancipated maidservant in Jerusalem, and Shemaya and Avtalyon administered her** the bitter waters. Akavya ben Mahalalel **said to** the Sages: That is no proof. Shemaya and Avtalyon, who were also from families of converts, required the maidservant **to drink** the potion because she was **like them** [*dugma*].[NL] **And** since Akavya ben Mahalalel cast aspersion on the deceased Torah scholars, **he was ostracized and died** while **he** was still under the ban of **ostracism. And** in accordance with the *halakha* with regard to one who dies while under a ban of ostracism, the court **stoned his coffin.** Apparently, one who deprecates a deceased Torah scholar is sentenced to ostracism.

## NOTES

**Perhaps he has repented – שֶׁמָּא עָשָׂה תְּשׁוּבָה:** It is to be understood as follows: One who sees a Torah scholar sin should not think badly of him. One must assume that the scholar certainly, and not just might have, repented (Rav Yoshiya Pinto).

**Ostracism – נִדּוּי:** Ostracism is a lesser degree of excommunication. The primary *halakhot* that apply at this level of excommunication are that the individual must conduct himself as if he is in mourning and he is not included in a prayer quorum. This does not preclude the individual, however, from hiring laborers or hiring himself out as a laborer; in that sense, it is business as usual. The same is true in terms of studying and teaching Torah. On the other hand, one who does not take the necessary steps to have his ostracism lifted is then excommunicated. At that stage, all contacts with him are severed. The courts resorted to ostracism primarily in two cases: when an individual failed to pay his debts and there were no other measures at their disposal to compel him to pay, or as punishment for disparaging the Torah or Torah scholars.

**They required her to drink the potion because she was like them – דּוּגְמָא הִשְׁקוּהָ:** Some explain the phrase to mean that instead of the actual bitter waters, they had her drink colored water in order to scare her into confessing (Rabbeinu Ḥananel). According to Akavya they did so because, as descendants of converts themselves, they did not want it publicized that a convert does not drink the bitter waters. He was ostracized either for casting aspersion upon them (Rambam), or for suspecting that they acted improperly as substitution of colored water for the bitter waters was liable lead people to treat the actual bitter waters with disdain (Ra'avad).

## PERSONALITIES

**Akavya ben Mahalalel – עֲקַבְיָא בֶּן מַהֲלַלְאֵל:** One of the first *tanna'im* and a contemporary of Hillel the Elder (some 100 years before the destruction of the Temple), Akavya ben Mahalalel maintained stringent opinions that were at odds with most of the Sages of his generation. His eminence in Torah is evidenced by the fact that his fellow Sages told him that if he reneged upon three laws that they found unacceptable, he would be appointed head of the *beit din* of Israel. He famously replied: I would rather be called a fool for my entire life than be wicked for a single hour.

This firmness was based upon his piety and a profound fear of Heaven, as well as the conviction that he must pass on the *halakha* as he received it from his teachers. However, he told his son (who was also a Sage) to accept the opinion of the majority. Few of his halakhic and aggadic statements are recorded in the Mishna.

## LANGUAGE

**Like them [*dugma*] – דּוּגְמָא:** From the Greek δεῖγμα, *deigma*, meaning form or sample. Some, based on parallel sources, have a variant reading, *dukhma* or *dukma* from the Greek δοκιμή, *dokimè*, meaning test.

## HALAKHA

**Twenty-four places in which the court ostracizes over matters of respect due the rabbi…One who speaks disparagingly after the bier, etc. – בְּעֶשְׂרִים וְאַרְבָּעָה מְקוֹמוֹת בֵּית דִּין מְנַדִּין עַל כְּבוֹד הָרַב, וְהַמְסַפֵּר אַחַר מִטָּתָן וכו׳:** It is incumbent upon the court to ostracize one against whom there is testimony that he maligned a Torah scholar, even if he only did so verbally or not in his presence (Rema). His ostracism is not lifted until he appeases the scholar on whose account he was excommunicated. If he maligned a Torah scholar after his death, the court ostracizes him until he repents (Rambam *Sefer HaMadda, Hilkhot Talmud Torah* 6:14; *Shulḥan Arukh, Yoreh De'a* 243:7; 334:43).

**Administering the bitter waters to a convert or an emancipated maidservant – הַשְׁקָיַית הַגִּיּוֹרֶת וְהַשִּׁפְחָה הַמְשׁוּחְרֶרֶת בְּמֵי סוֹטָה:** A convert and an emancipated maidservant are administered the bitter water potion just like any other Jewish woman, in accordance with the opinion of the Rabbis, who constitute the majority in the dispute with the lone dissenting opinion (Rambam *Sefer Nashim, Hilkhot Sota* 2:6).

וְהַמְזַלְזֵל בִּנְטִילַת יָדַיִם מַאי הִיא? דִּתְנַן, אָמַר רַבִּי יְהוּדָה: חַס וְשָׁלוֹם שֶׁעֲקַבְיָא בֶּן מַהֲלַלְאֵל נִתְנַדָּה, שֶׁאֵין עֲזָרָה נִנְעֶלֶת עַל כׇּל אָדָם בְּיִשְׂרָאֵל בְּחׇכְמָה וּבְטׇהֳרָה וּבְיִרְאַת חֵטְא כַּעֲקַבְיָא בֶּן מַהֲלַלְאֵל, אֶלָּא אֶת מִי נִדּוּ – אֶת אֶלְעָזָר בֶּן חֲנוֹךְ שֶׁפִּקְפֵּק בִּנְטִילַת יָדַיִם; וּכְשֶׁמֵּת – שָׁלְחוּ בֵּית דִּין וְהִנִּיחוּ אֶבֶן גְּדוֹלָה עַל אֲרוֹנוֹ, לְלַמֶּדְךָ: שֶׁכׇּל הַמִּתְנַדֶּה וּמֵת בְּנִדּוּיוֹ – בֵּית דִּין סוֹקְלִין אֶת אֲרוֹנוֹ.

And **what is** the source for **one who demeans** the ritual of **washing of the hands?**[H] **We learned** later in the same mishna: **Rabbi Yehuda said:** That story related with regard to the ostracism of Akavya ben Mahalalel is completely untrue; **God forbid that Akavya ben Mahalalel was ostracized, as the Temple courtyard is not closed on any Jew,** meaning that even when all of Israel made the pilgrimage to Jerusalem, when each of the three groups that gathered to offer the Paschal lamb filled the courtyard, leading the Temple administration to close the courtyard, there was no one there as perfect **in wisdom, purity and fear of sin as Akavya ben Mahalalel. Rather, whom did they excommunicate? Elazar ben Ḥanokh,** because he **doubted** and demeaned the rabbinic ordinance of **washing of the hands. And when he died, the court sent** instructions **and they placed a large rock upon his coffin** in order **to teach you that one who is ostracized and dies in** a state of **ostracism, the court stones his coffin,**[H] as if symbolically stoning him. Apparently, one who makes light of the ritual of washing of the hands is sentenced to ostracism.

הַמֵּגִיס דַּעְתּוֹ כְּלַפֵּי מַעְלָה מַאי הִיא? דִּתְנַן, שָׁלַח לוֹ שִׁמְעוֹן בֶּן שָׁטָח לְחוֹנִי הַמְעַגֵּל: צָרִיךְ אַתָּה לְהִתְנַדּוֹת, וְאִלְמָלֵא חוֹנִי אַתָּה גּוֹזְרַנִי עָלֶיךָ נִדּוּי, אֲבָל מָה אֶעֱשֶׂה שֶׁאַתָּה מִתְחַטֵּא לִפְנֵי הַמָּקוֹם וְעוֹשֶׂה לְךָ רְצוֹנְךָ כְּבֵן שֶׁמִּתְחַטֵּא לִפְנֵי אָבִיו וְעוֹשֶׂה לוֹ רְצוֹנוֹ, וְעָלֶיךָ הַכָּתוּב אוֹמֵר ״יִשְׂמַח אָבִיךָ וְאִמֶּךָ וְתָגֵל יוֹלַדְתֶּךָ״.

**What is** the source for the third case, **one who is arrogant vis-à-vis Heaven?** The mishna relates that Ḥoni HaMe'aggel, the circle-drawer, drew a circle and stood inside it, and said that he would not leave the circle until it rained, and he went so far as to make demands in terms of the manner in which he wanted the rain to fall. After it rained, **Shimon ben Shataḥ,** the *Nasi* of the Sanhedrin, relayed to **Ḥoni HaMe'aggel:** Actually, **you should be ostracized** for what you said, **and if you were not Ḥoni, I would have decreed ostracism upon you, but what can I do? You nag God and He does your bidding, like a son who nags his father and** his father **does his bidding** without reprimand. After all, the rain fell as you requested. **About you, the verse states: "Your father and mother will be glad and she who bore you will rejoice"** (Proverbs 23:25). Apparently, one who is arrogant vis-à-vis Heaven would ordinarily merit excommunication.

וְתוּ לֵיכָּא? וְהָא אִיכָּא דְּתָנֵי רַב יוֹסֵף: תּוֹדוֹס אִישׁ רוֹמִי הִנְהִיג אֶת בְּנֵי רוֹמִי לְהַאֲכִילָן גְּדָיִים מְקוּלָּסִין בְּלֵילֵי פְסָחִים; שָׁלַח לֵיהּ שִׁמְעוֹן בֶּן שָׁטָח: אִלְמָלֵא תּוֹדוֹס אַתָּה גּוֹזְרַנִי עָלֶיךָ נִדּוּי, שֶׁאַתָּה מַאֲכִיל אֶת יִשְׂרָאֵל קָדָשִׁים בַּחוּץ!

The Gemara challenges this: **And are there no more** cases of excommunication or threats of excommunication? **Surely there are** additional cases like the one in the *baraita* **taught by Rav Yosef:** It is told that **Theodosius of Rome,**[P] leader of the Jewish community there, **instituted the custom for the Roman** Jews **to eat whole kids,** young goats roasted with their entrails over their heads, as was the custom when roasting the Paschal lamb, **on the eve of Passover,**[H] as they did in the Temple. **Shimon ben Shataḥ sent** a message **to him: If you were not Theodosius,** an important person, **I would have decreed ostracism upon you, as** it appears as if **you are feeding Israel consecrated food,** which may only be eaten in and around the Temple itself, **outside** the Temple.

בְּמִשְׁנָתֵנוּ קָאָמְרִינַן, וְהָא בָּרַיְיתָא הִיא.

The Gemara responds: This case should not be included, as Rabbi Yehoshua ben Levi said that there were twenty-four cases **in our Mishna,** and **this is** merely **a** ***baraita.***

וּבְמַתְנִיתִין לֵיכָּא? וְהָא אִיכָּא הָא דִּתְנַן: חֲתָכוֹ חוּלְיוֹת וְנָתַן חוֹל בֵּין חוּלְיָא לְחוּלְיָא, רַבִּי אֱלִיעֶזֶר מְטַהֵר, וַחֲכָמִים מְטַמְּאִים, וְזֶהוּ תַּנּוּרוֹ שֶׁל עַכְנַאי;

The Gemara asks: **And are there none in the Mishna? Isn't there that which we learned** in the mishna: **One** who **cut** an earthenware oven horizontally **into** ring-shaped **pieces and put sand between the pieces, Rabbi Eliezer deems** the oven **ritually pure,** i.e., it is no longer susceptible to ritual impurity. He holds that, although the fragments of the oven were pieced together, it is not considered an intact vessel but, rather, as a collection of fragments, and a broken earthenware vessel cannot become ritually impure. **And the Rabbis deem it ritually impure.** Since the oven continues to serve its original function, it is still considered a single entity and a whole vessel despite the sand put between the pieces. **And this is** called **the oven of** ***akhnai,*** **snake.**[HB]

מַאי עַכְנַאי? אָמַר רַב יְהוּדָה אָמַר שְׁמוּאֵל: מְלַמֵּד, שֶׁהִקִּיפוּהוּ הֲלָכוֹת כְּעַכְנַאי זֶה וְטִמְּאוּהוּ;

The Gemara asks: **What is** the meaning of oven of the **snake? Rav Yehuda said** that **Shmuel said:** It is called snake **to teach that** the Rabbis **surrounded** Rabbi Eliezer **with** ***halakhot*** and proofs **like a snake** surrounds its prey, **and declared** the oven and its contents **ritually impure.**

### HALAKHA

**One who demeans the ritual washing of the hands** – וְהַמְזַלְזֵל בִּנְטִילַת יָדַיִם: One must be vigilant with regard to the ritual washing of the hands, as the court is required to ostracize anyone who demeans that ritual, i.e., one who never in his life did so; Rashi, *Tosafot*. He will become impoverished and be uprooted from the world, in accordance with the mishna cited here (Rambam *Sefer Ahava, Hilkhot Berakhot* 6:19; *Shulḥan Arukh, Oraḥ Ḥayyim* 158:9).

**One who is ostracized and dies in a state of ostracism, the court stones his coffin** – שֶׁכׇּל הַמִּתְנַדֶּה וּמֵת בְּנִדּוּיוֹ בֵּית דִּין סוֹקְלִין אֶת אֲרוֹנוֹ: One who was ostracized due to contempt for Torah and mitzvot and died in that status, the court places a stone on his coffin, his relatives do not rend their clothing, he is not eulogized, and none of the rites instituted to honor the deceased are practiced. On the other hand, consoling the mourners, which is to honor the living, is permitted (*Shakh* based on the Ramban; Rambam *Sefer HaMadda, Hilkhot Talmud Torah* 7:4; *Shulḥan Arukh, Yoreh De'a* 334:3).

**Eating whole kids on the eve of Passover** – גְּדָיִים מְקוּלָּסִין בְּלֵילֵי פְּסָחִים: It is prohibited on Passover eve to eat a goat that was roasted whole, as it appears as if one is eating consecrated food outside of the Temple. Whether or not one is permitted to eat the meat if it was sliced and then roasted depends upon the local custom (Rambam *Sefer Zemanim, Hilkhot Ḥametz UMatza* 8:11; *Shulḥan Arukh, Oraḥ Ḥayyim* 476:1).

**The oven of** ***akhnai*** – תַּנּוּרוֹ שֶׁל עַכְנַאי: An oven that was cut into segments and sand was placed between the segments; if he subsequently plastered the surface of the oven, it has the legal status of a vessel and is susceptible to ritual impurity, as per the opinion of the Rabbis (Rambam *Sefer Tahara, Hilkhot Kelim* 16:3).

### PERSONALITIES

**Theodosius** – תּוֹדוֹס: Theodosius of Rome, who lived in the time of Shimon ben Shataḥ and King Alexander Yannai, was, apparently, the leader of the Jewish community in Rome. He was also charged with overseeing the transport of Jewish contributions to the Temple and the Sages. Theodosius was also a Sage, as evidenced by the inclusion in the Gemara of one of his aggadic statements with regard to the sanctification of God's name. Due to his renown and status as a leader, Shimon ben Shataḥ adopted a tone of respect when addressing him and did not excommunicate him.

### BACKGROUND

**The oven of** ***akhnai*** – תַּנּוּרוֹ שֶׁל עַכְנַאי: According to Rabbi Eliezer, if an oven was cut, according to the parallel lines in the illustration, it is considered a broken vessel incapable of contracting ritual impurity, even if it was later reassembled.

Likeness of the stove of *akhnai*

וְתַנְיָא: אוֹתוֹ הַיּוֹם הֵבִיאוּ כׇּל טְהָרוֹת שֶׁטִּיהֵר רַבִּי אֱלִיעֶזֶר וּשְׂרָפוּם לְפָנָיו, וּלְבַסּוֹף בֵּרְכוּהוּ!

**And it was taught** in a *baraita*: **On that day, they gathered all of the ritually pure** food items that had come into contact with the oven **that Rabbi Eliezer had declared ritually pure, and burned them before him,** and because he did not accept the decision of the majority, **in the end they "blessed,"** a euphemism for ostracized, **him.** This is another case that ended in ostracism.

אֲפִילּוּ הָכִי, נִדּוּי בְּמַתְנִיתִין לָא תְּנַן. אֶלָּא בְּעֶשְׂרִים וְאַרְבָּעָה מְקוֹמוֹת הֵיכָא מַשְׁכַּחַתְּ לְהוּ? – רַבִּי יְהוֹשֻׁעַ בֶּן לֵוִי מְדַמֶּה מִילְּתָא לְמִילְּתָא, וְרַבִּי אֶלְעָזָר לָא מְדַמֶּה מִילְּתָא לְמִילְּתָא.

The Gemara answers: **Even so, we did not learn** the ruling with regard to his **ostracism in the mishna.** The Gemara asks: Then **where do you find** the **twenty-four places** mentioned in Rabbi Yehoshua ben Levi's statement? The Gemara responds: **Rabbi Yehoshua ben Levi likens one matter to another** similar **matter.** Whenever he would encounter a case in a mishna where one of the Sages expressed himself inappropriately in reference to other Sages, he concluded that they should have been excommunicated. **Rabbi Elazar does not liken one matter to another** similar **matter,** and therefore located only three explicit cases of ostracism.

"נוֹשְׂאֵי הַמִּטָּה וְחִלּוּפֵיהֶן". תָּנוּ רַבָּנַן: אֵין מוֹצִיאִין אֶת הַמֵּת סָמוּךְ לִקְרִיאַת שְׁמַע, וְאִם הִתְחִילוּ אֵין מַפְסִיקִין. אִינִי? וְהָא רַב יוֹסֵף אַפְּקוּהוּ סָמוּךְ לִקְרִיאַת שְׁמַע! – אָדָם חָשׁוּב שָׁאנֵי.

We learned in the mishna that **the pallbearers and their replacements** are exempt from the recitation of *Shema*. On this subject, the Gemara cites that which the **Sages taught** in a *baraita*: **The deceased may not be taken out** to be buried **adjacent to** the time for **the recitation of *Shema*,**[H] but should be buried later. **And if they** already **started** to take him out, **they need not stop** in order to recite *Shema*. The Gemara challenges: **Is that so? Didn't they take Rav Yosef out** to be buried **adjacent to** the time for **the recitation of *Shema*?** The Gemara resolves this contradiction: The case of **an important person is different,** and they are more lenient in order to honor him at his burial.

"שֶׁלִּפְנֵי הַמִּטָּה וְשֶׁלְּאַחַר הַמִּטָּה". תָּנוּ רַבָּנַן: הָעוֹסְקִים בְּהֶסְפֵּד, בִּזְמַן שֶׁהַמֵּת מוּטָל לִפְנֵיהֶם – נִשְׁמָטִין אֶחָד אֶחָד וְקוֹרִין, אֵין הַמֵּת מוּטָל לִפְנֵיהֶם – הֵן יוֹשְׁבִין וְקוֹרִין וְהוּא יוֹשֵׁב וְדוֹמֵם, הֵם עוֹמְדִים וּמִתְפַּלְּלִין וְהוּא עוֹמֵד וּמַצְדִּיק עָלָיו אֶת הַדִּין, וְאוֹמֵר: רִבּוֹן הָעוֹלָמִים, הַרְבֵּה חָטָאתִי לְפָנֶיךָ וְלֹא נִפְרַעְתָּ מִמֶּנִּי אֶחָד מִנִּי אֶלֶף, יְהִי רָצוֹן מִלְּפָנֶיךָ ה׳ אֱלֹהֵינוּ שֶׁתִּגְדּוֹר פִּרְצוֹתֵינוּ וּפִרְצוֹת כׇּל עַמְּךָ בֵּית יִשְׂרָאֵל בְּרַחֲמִים.

In the mishna, we learned the *halakha* with regard to the pallbearers and their obligation to recite *Shema*, and a distinction was made between those **who are before the bier and** those **after the bier. Our Rabbis taught** in a *baraita*: **Those involved in eulogy**[H] **must slip away** from the eulogy **one by one while the deceased is laid out before them and recite** *Shema* elsewhere. And **if the deceased is not laid out before them,** the eulogizers must **sit and recite** *Shema* **while** the bereaved **sits silently. They stand and pray and he stands and justifies God's judgment, saying: Master of the Universe, I have sinned greatly against You, and You have not collected even one one-thousandth** of my debt. **May it be Your will, Lord our God, to mercifully repair the breaches in our** fence **and the breaches of Your nation, the House of Israel.**

אָמַר אַבָּיֵי לָא מִבְּעֵי לֵיהּ לְאִינִישׁ לְמֵימַר הָכִי דְּאָמַר רַבִּי שִׁמְעוֹן בֶּן לָקִישׁ וְכֵן תָּנָא מִשְּׁמֵיהּ דְּרַבִּי יוֹסֵי לְעוֹלָם אַל יִפְתַּח אָדָם פִּיו לַשָּׂטָן

**Abaye said: A person should not say that, as Rabbi Shimon ben Lakish said, and it was also taught in the name of Rabbi Yosei: One must never open his mouth to the Satan,**[HN] i.e., one must not leave room for or raise the possibility of disaster or evil. This formula, which states that the entire debt owed due to his transgressions has not been collected, raises the possibility that further payment will be exacted from him.

וְאָמַר רַב יוֹסֵף: מַאי קְרָאָה – שֶׁנֶּאֱמַר: "כִּמְעַט כִּסְדוֹם הָיִינוּ", מַאי אַהְדַר לְהוּ נָבִיא – "שִׁמְעוּ דְבַר ה׳ קְצִינֵי סְדוֹם".

**And Rav Yosef said: What is the verse** from which **it** is derived? **As it is stated: "We should have almost been as Sodom,** we should have been like unto Gomorrah" (Isaiah 1:9), after which **what did** the **prophet reply to them? "Hear the word of the Lord, rulers of Sodom;** give ear unto the law of our God, people of Gomorrah" (Isaiah 1:10).

"קָבְרוּ אֶת הַמֵּת וְחָזְרוּ וכו׳". אִם יְכוֹלִים לְהַתְחִיל וְלִגְמוֹר אֶת כּוּלָּהּ – אִין, אֲבָל פֶּרֶק אֶחָד אוֹ פָּסוּק אֶחָד – לָא. וּרְמִינְהוּ: קָבְרוּ אֶת הַמֵּת וְחָזְרוּ, אִם יְכוֹלִין לְהַתְחִיל וְלִגְמוֹר אֲפִילּוּ פֶּרֶק אֶחָד אוֹ פָּסוּק אֶחָד!

We learned in the mishna that, in a case when **they buried the deceased and returned,**[H] if they have sufficient time to begin to recite *Shema* and conclude before they arrive at the row formed by those who came to console the bereaved, they should begin. Here, the Gemara clarifies: This is the case only **if they can begin and complete** recitation of *Shema* **in its entirety. However,** if they can only complete **one chapter or one verse,** they should **not** stop to do so. The Gemara **raises a contradiction** from that which we learned in the *baraita*: After **they buried the deceased and returned, if they can begin** the recitation of *Shema* **and finish even a single chapter or verse,** they should begin.

הָכִי נָמֵי קָאָמַר: אִם יְכוֹלִין לְהַתְחִיל וְלִגְמוֹר אֲפִילּוּ פֶּרֶק אֶחָד אוֹ אֲפִילּוּ פָּסוּק אֶחָד עַד שֶׁלֹּא יַגִּיעוּ לַשּׁוּרָה – יַתְחִילוּ, וְאִם לָאו – לֹא יַתְחִילוּ.

The Gemara responds: **That is also what** the *tanna* of the mishna **said** and this is the conclusion drawn from his statement: **If one can begin and conclude even one chapter or one verse before they arrive at the row** of consolers, **they should begin. And if not, they should not begin.**

**HALAKHA**

**The deceased may not be taken out to be buried adjacent to the time for the recitation of *Shema* – אֵין מוֹצִיאִין אֶת הַמֵּת סָמוּךְ לִקְרִיאַת שְׁמַע:** The deceased may not be taken out for burial adjacent to the time when *Shema* must be recited, so that its recitation will not be abrogated. If the funeral procession already began, it is not interrupted to recite *Shema*. Nowadays, the custom is that even an important person is not taken out for burial adjacent to the time when *Shema* must be recited (*Taz*). There are those who are lenient with regard to the nighttime *Shema*. They begin the funeral procession adjacent to the time of its recital because one has the whole night to recite the *Shema* and in order to avoid delaying the burial until the next day. This opinion was cited by the Rema and adopted by the *Magen Avraham* (Rambam *Sefer Ahava, Hilkhot Keriat Shema* 4:4; *Shulḥan Arukh, Oraḥ Ḥayyim* 72:2 and *Yoreh De'a* 358:2).

**Those involved in eulogy with regard to reciting *Shema* – הָעוֹסְקִים בְּהֶסְפֵּד לְעִנְיַן קְרִיאַת שְׁמַע:** If the deceased was laid out before those engaged in eulogizing him, they slip out one at a time and recite *Shema* and pray. If the deceased is not before them, they recite *Shema* and pray where they are assembled, with the exception of the mourner who sits in silence (Rambam *Sefer Ahava, Hilkhot Keriat Shema* 4:5; *Shulḥan Arukh, Oraḥ Ḥayyim* 72:3).

**One must never open his mouth to the Satan – לְעוֹלָם אַל יִפְתַּח אָדָם פִּיו לַשָּׂטָן:** It is inappropriate for one to say that God has not punished him enough for his sins, as he thereby opens his mouth to Satan, as per the statements of Abaye and Reish Lakish (*Shulḥan Arukh, Yoreh De'a* 376:2, Rema).

**They buried the deceased and returned – קָבְרוּ אֶת הַמֵּת וְחָזְרוּ וכו׳:** If those who returned from the burial and are proceeding to form a row to console the mourners have enough time to recite even the first verse of *Shema*, they should begin and recite as much of *Shema* as they can (*Baḥ*). Some say that once they begin they should recite *Shema* in its entirety (*Beit Yosef*). If there is concern that the time for reciting *Shema* will pass, they should recite it (*Rema*) as per the *baraita* and the Gemara's conclusion (Rambam *Sefer Ahava, Hilkhot Keriat Shema* 4:6; *Shulḥan Arukh, Oraḥ Ḥayyim* 72:4).

**NOTES**

**One must never open his mouth to the Satan – לְעוֹלָם אַל יִפְתַּח אָדָם פִּיו לַשָּׂטָן:** The reason is that once a person justifies God's judgment, there is no more room for the attribute of mercy to be applied in his case. However, this restriction applies only to the future, but with regard to the past, it is an act of righteousness to declare that God punished him for his sins (*HaKotev*).

"הָעוֹמְדִים בַּשּׁוּרָה וכו׳". תָּנוּ רַבָּנַן: שׁוּרָה הָרוֹאָה פְּנִימָה – פְּטוּרָה, וְשֶׁאֵינָהּ רוֹאָה פְּנִימָה – חַיֶּיבֶת, רַבִּי יְהוּדָה אוֹמֵר: הַבָּאִים מֵחֲמַת הָאָבֵל – פְּטוּרִין, מֵחֲמַת עַצְמָן – חַיָּיבִין.

We learned in the mishna that **those standing in the row,**[H] those in the interior row, are exempt from reciting *Shema* and the others are obligated. **The Sages taught** this more expansively in the *Tosefta*: The consolers standing in **a row** from **which** one **sees inside** the area where the mourners are passing **are exempt, and** those standing in a row from which **one does not see inside are obligated. And Rabbi Yehuda** elaborates and **says:** The consolers standing in the row **who come on account of the bereaved**[N] **are exempt,** while those who come **on account of their own** curiosity **are obligated** to recite *Shema*.

אָמַר רַב יְהוּדָה אָמַר רַב: הַמּוֹצֵא כִּלְאַיִם בְּבִגְדוֹ פּוֹשְׁטָן אֲפִילּוּ בַּשּׁוּק, מַאי טַעְמָא – "אֵין חָכְמָה וְאֵין תְּבוּנָה וְאֵין עֵצָה לְנֶגֶד ה׳" – כָּל מָקוֹם שֶׁיֵּשׁ חִלּוּל הַשֵּׁם אֵין חוֹלְקִין כָּבוֹד לָרַב.

We learned that some who come to console the bereaved are exempt from *Shema* as a means of honoring the deceased. The Gemara expands the discussion to raise the general question: To what degree does preserving human dignity takes precedence over mitzvot enumerated in the Torah? **Rav Yehuda said** that **Rav said: One who discovers diverse kinds** [***kilayim***], i.e., a prohibited mixture of wool and linen, **in his garment,**[H] **must remove them even in the** public **marketplace.** He may not wait until he reaches home. **What is the reason** for this? As it is stated: **"There is neither wisdom, nor understanding, nor counsel against the Lord"** (Proverbs 21:30). From here, the general principle: **Anywhere that there is desecration of the Lord's name, one does not show respect to the teacher,** is derived.

מֵתִיבֵי: קָבְרוּ אֶת הַמֵּת וְחָזְרוּ, וְלִפְנֵיהֶם שְׁתֵּי דְרָכִים, אַחַת טְהוֹרָה וְאַחַת טְמֵאָה, בָּא בַּטְּהוֹרָה – בָּאִין עִמּוֹ בַּטְּהוֹרָה, בָּא בַּטְּמֵאָה – בָּאִין עִמּוֹ בַּטְּמֵאָה, מִשּׁוּם כְּבוֹדוֹ. אַמַּאי? לֵימָא: "אֵין חָכְמָה וְאֵין תְּבוּנָה לְנֶגֶד ה׳".

The Gemara cites several sources to challenge this principle. The Gemara **raised an objection** from a *baraita*: After **they buried the deceased and returned, and** on their way **there are two paths before them, one ritually pure and one ritually impure,** e.g., it passes through a cemetery, if the mourner **comes on the pure** path,[N] **they come with him on the pure** path; if **he comes on the impure** path, all of the funeral participants **accompany** him **on the impure** path in order to show **him respect. Why** would they do this? **Let us say** here too that, **"There is neither wisdom, nor understanding… against the Lord!"**

תַּרְגְּמַהּ רַבִּי אַבָּא בְּבֵית הַפְּרָס דְּרַבָּנַן.

**Rabbi Abba explained** that the *baraita* is referring to a path that passes **through an area where there is uncertainty with regard to the location of a grave or a corpse** [***beit haperas***].[BLH] For example, with regard to a field in which there is a grave that was plowed and no longer intact, the entire field is deemed impure due to concern that the plow scattered bones throughout the field. The field is impure only **by rabbinic law** but not according to Torah law. Since it is only prohibited by rabbinic law, one is permitted to walk through the field to show the mourner respect.

דְּאָמַר רַב יְהוּדָה אָמַר שְׁמוּאֵל: מְנַפֵּחַ אָדָם בֵּית הַפְּרָס וְהוֹלֵךְ; וְאָמַר רַב יְהוּדָה בַּר אַשִׁי מִשְּׁמֵיהּ דְּרַב: בֵּית הַפְּרָס שֶׁנִּדַּשׁ טָהוֹר.

The Gemara cites proof that the legal status of a *beit haperas* is unlike the legal status of impurity by Torah law: **Rav Yehuda said** that **Shmuel said: One** who passes through **a** ***beit haperas*** **may blow** on the dust before taking each step, so that if there is a bone beneath the dust, he will expose it, avoid it, **and walk.** One may not rely on that method of examination with regard to impurity by Torah law. **And Rav Yehuda bar Ashi said in the name of Rav: A** ***beit haperas*** **that has been trodden** underfoot,[H] creating a path, **is pure,** and one no longer need be concerned about bones. Clearly, the entire prohibition is a stringency decreed by the Sages.

### NOTES

**Those who come on account of the bereaved** – **הַבָּאִים מֵחֲמַת הָאָבֵל**: Rabbi Yehuda's statement can be interpreted in two ways. One possibility is that Rabbi Yehuda is more stringent with regard to those standing in the first row. If they did not come on account of the bereaved, they are obligated to recite *Shema*. Alternatively, it is possible that Rabbi Yehuda is more lenient with regard to those in the second row if they came on account of the bereaved (*Talmidei Rabbeinu Yona*). Some say that Rabbi Yehuda is merely explaining the statement of the previous *tanna*. He distinguishes between those in the first row who are there in deference to the bereaved and those standing in the other rows (*Alfasi Zuta*).

**He comes on the pure path** – **בָּא בַּטְּהוֹרָה**: The Ra'avad's version reads: If the community comes on the pure path, the priest comes with them on the pure path, etc. He prefers that version because it explains why the priest does not simply go off on his own, as the mourner would not notice the absence of one individual and, therefore, would not perceive it as an affront. Rather, it is in deference to the community, as it is inappropriate for one individual to separate himself from the community (*Shitta Mekubbetzet*).

### BACKGROUND

*Beit haperas* – **בֵּית הַפְּרָס**: This term is a general term referring to a place in which, by rabbinic law, ritual impurity imparted by a corpse is dispersed. Typically, it refers to a field in which a grave was plowed, causing the bones to be scattered throughout the field. A second field that falls into this category is one where it is known that there is a grave, but its exact location is unknown. The third field in this category is one where it was customary to place the bier while the deceased was eulogized. The concern is that limbs might have fallen in the field and remained there.

### LANGUAGE

*Beit haperas* – **בֵּית הַפְּרָס**: There are several interpretations of this term. Some hold that it stems from the Hebrew *perisa*, meaning spreading or expansion, i.e., a field in which the ritual impurity is spread throughout the entire field (Rambam's Commentary on the Mishna). Others suggest that it stems from the fact that a broken or sliced [*parus*] source of ritual impurity was found in the field (Rashi). Yet others maintain that the field is given that name because people's feet [*parsot*] do not tread there (*Tosafot*). Another school of thought holds that the name is foreign in origin. Some say that it is from the Latin forum or from the Greek πάρος, *paros*, meaning in front of (*Mosaf HaArukh*).

### HALAKHA

**Those standing in the row** – **הָעוֹמְדִים בַּשּׁוּרָה**: Those standing in the row of consolers; those in the interior row who are face-to-face with the mourners are exempt from reciting *Shema*, and those in the exterior rows who are not face-to-face with the mourners are obligated to recite it, in accordance with our mishna and the *Tosefta* here (Rambam *Sefer Ahava, Hilkhot Keriat Shema* 4:6; *Shulḥan Arukh, Oraḥ Ḥayyim* 72:5).

**One who discovers diverse kinds [*kilayim*] in his garment** – **הַמּוֹצֵא כִּלְאַיִם בְּבִגְדוֹ**: One who discovers a mixture of wool and linen, prohibited by Torah law, in the garment of another person, must remove the garment from him. He must do so even if they are in the marketplace, with no concern for the affront to his dignity, even if the individual in question was his teacher, as the dignity of a rabbi does not override the dignity of Heaven. If the mixture was only prohibited by rabbinic law, he may wait until the person wearing the garment returns home before removing it from him, as per the Gemara's conclusion that rabbinic decrees do not override human dignity. Furthermore, if the individual had worn the garment unwittingly, even if the mixture was prohibited by Torah law, human dignity takes precedence, and he should not remove the garment from him (*Tur* in the name of the Rosh; Rambam *Sefer Zera'im, Hilkhot Kilayim* 10:29; *Shulḥan Arukh, Yoreh De'a* 303:1).

**Consoling the mourners in a *beit haperas*** – **נִיחוּם אֲבֵלִים בְּבֵית הַפְּרָס**: A priest may enter a field in which a grave was plowed in order to console a mourner who is there (Rambam *Sefer Shofetim, Hilkhot Evel* 3:14; *Shulḥan Arukh, Yoreh De'a* 372:1).

**A *beit haperas* that has been trodden underfoot** – **בֵּית הַפְּרָס שֶׁנִּדַּשׁ**: One who passed through a field in which a grave was plowed, and a path had already been trodden, is ritually pure and eligible to offer the Paschal lamb. Similarly, if as he was passing through, he blew the dirt before him and did not encounter a bone capable of rendering him ritually impure, he is ritually pure and eligible to offer the Paschal lamb. The Sages did not apply their decree in a case involving *karet* (Rambam *Sefer Korbanot, Hilkhot Korban Pesaḥ* 6:8).

תָּא שְׁמַע, דְּאָמַר רַבִּי אֶלְעָזָר בַּר צָדוֹק: מְדַלְּגִין הָיִינוּ עַל גַּבֵּי אֲרוֹנוֹת שֶׁל מֵתִים לִקְרַאת מַלְכֵי יִשְׂרָאֵל, וְלֹא לִקְרַאת מַלְכֵי יִשְׂרָאֵל בִּלְבַד אָמְרוּ אֶלָּא אֲפִילּוּ לִקְרַאת מַלְכֵי אוּמּוֹת הָעוֹלָם, שֶׁאִם יִזְכֶּה – יַבְחִין בֵּין מַלְכֵי יִשְׂרָאֵל לְמַלְכֵי אוּמּוֹת הָעוֹלָם. אַמַּאי? לֵימָא: ״אֵין חׇכְמָה וְאֵין תְּבוּנָה וְאֵין עֵצָה לְנֶגֶד ה׳״!

The Gemara cites additional proof with regard to the extent to which human dignity overrides mitzvot in the Torah. **Come and hear, as Rabbi Elazar bar Tzadok** the priest **said:** I and my fellow priests **would jump over coffins**[B] **of the deceased**[H] in order to hurry **towards kings of Israel** to greet them. **And they did not say** this **only towards kings of Israel, but** they said this **even towards kings of the nations of the world, so that if one will be privileged** to witness the redemption of Israel, **he will distinguish between kings of Israel and kings of the nations of the world.** The priest violated the Torah prohibition to become ritually impure through contact with the dead, in order to show respect for a king. And **why** is this? **Let us say** here too: **"There is neither wisdom, nor understanding, nor counsel against the Lord."**

כִּדְרָבָא, דְּאָמַר רָבָא: דְּבַר תּוֹרָה, אֹהֶל, כׇּל שֶׁיֵּשׁ בּוֹ חֲלַל טֶפַח – חוֹצֵץ בִּפְנֵי הַטּוּמְאָה, וְשֶׁאֵין בּוֹ חֲלַל טֶפַח – אֵינוֹ חוֹצֵץ בִּפְנֵי הַטּוּמְאָה,

The Gemara responds to this challenge by saying that it must be understood **in accordance with** the opinion of **Rava, as Rava said: By Torah law, a tent** over a corpse, **as long as there is a handbreadth of space** between the corpse and the tent over it, **constitutes a barrier before** the spread of **impurity** and nothing above the tent can become ritually impure due to impurity imparted by the corpse. **And when there is not a handbreadth of space** between the corpse and the tent over it, the tent **does not constitute a barrier before** the spread of **impurity** and the "pressed" ritual impurity, can reach the heavens.

וְרוֹב אֲרוֹנוֹת יֵשׁ בָּהֶן חֲלַל טֶפַח, וְגָזְרוּ עַל שֶׁיֵּשׁ בָּהֶן מִשּׁוּם שֶׁאֵין בָּהֶן, וּמִשּׁוּם כְּבוֹד מְלָכִים לֹא גָּזְרוּ בְּהוּ רַבָּנַן.

**Most coffins have a handbreadth of space.** Consequently, their impurity does not spread above the coffin. However, the Sages **issued a decree regarding** coffins **in which there is** a handbreadth of space **because of** those coffins **in which there is not.** Nevertheless, **due to respect for kings,** the Sages **did not issue a decree** in a case involving **them** and the priests were permitted to jump over the coffins, as it is permitted by Torah law. Therefore, there is no proof from here regarding the question of whether or not human dignity overrides Torah law.

תָּא שְׁמַע: גָּדוֹל כְּבוֹד הַבְּרִיּוֹת שֶׁדּוֹחֶה [אֶת] לֹא תַעֲשֶׂה שֶׁבַּתּוֹרָה.

The Gemara cites an additional proof from a *baraita*: **Come and hear: Great is human dignity, as it overrides a prohibition in the Torah.**

וְאַמַּאי? לֵימָא: ״אֵין חׇכְמָה וְאֵין תְּבוּנָה וְאֵין עֵצָה לְנֶגֶד ה׳״! – תַּרְגְּמַהּ רַב בַּר שַׁבָּא קַמֵּיהּ דְּרַב כָּהֲנָא בְּלָאו דְּ״לֹא תָסוּר״. אַחִיכוּ עֲלֵיהּ: לָאו דְּ״לֹא תָסוּר״ דְּאוֹרָיְיתָא הִיא!

The Gemara asks: **Why? Let us** also **say** here: **"There is neither wisdom, nor understanding, nor counsel against the Lord." Rav bar Shaba interpreted this** prohibition, which is overridden by human dignity, **before Rav Kahana** as referring **to the prohibition of:** "According to the Torah taught to you and the ruling handed down to you, you shall do, **you shall not deviate** to the left or the right from that which they tell you" (Deuteronomy 17:11). The Yeshiva students **laughed at him,** as the **prohibition of "you shall not deviate" is by Torah law,** like all other Torah prohibitions. Why should human dignity override it any more than any other Torah prohibition?

אָמַר רַב כָּהֲנָא: גַּבְרָא רַבָּה אָמַר מִילְּתָא לָא תַּחִיכוּ עֲלֵיהּ, כׇּל מִילֵּי דְּרַבָּנַן אַסְמְכִינְהוּ עַל לָאו דְּ״לֹא תָסוּר״, וּמִשּׁוּם כְּבוֹדוֹ שָׁרוּ רַבָּנַן.

**Rav Kahana replied** to them: **A great man has spoken, do not laugh at him.** The Sages **based all rabbinic law on the prohibition of "you shall not deviate";**[N] **however, due to** concern for human **dignity, the Sages permitted** suspension of rabbinic law in cases where the two collide. All rabbinic decrees are predicated on the mitzva in the Torah to heed the judges in each generation and to never stray from their words. Therefore, when the Sages suspend a decree in the interest of preserving human dignity, human dignity is overriding a Torah prohibition. In any case, it only overrides rabbinic decrees.

תָּא שְׁמַע: ״וְהִתְעַלַּמְתָּ מֵהֶם״ – פְּעָמִים שֶׁאַתָּה מִתְעַלֵּם מֵהֶם וּפְעָמִים שֶׁאֵין אַתָּה מִתְעַלֵּם מֵהֶם;

The Gemara cites an additional proof from a *baraita*: **Come and hear:** With regard to the laws of returning a lost object, it is stated: "You shall not see the ox of your brother or his sheep go astray and ignore them; return them to your brother" (Deuteronomy 22:1). The *baraita* explains that the seemingly extraneous expression **and disregard them**[N] must be understood to give license that **at times you disregard** lost objects **and at times you do not disregard them.**

**BACKGROUND**

Coffins – אֲרוֹנוֹת: The ossuary is made of stone, as is its cover.

Stone ossuary from the end of the Second Temple era

**HALAKHA**

**We would jump over the coffins of the deceased – מְדַלְּגִין הָיִינוּ עַל אֲרוֹנוֹת:** A priest is permitted to run to greet the kings of Israel and disregard rabbinic decrees of impurity. Whether or not this allowance applies to gentile kings as well, see the Rambam and the *Magen Avraham* (Rambam *Sefer Shofetim, Hilkhot Evel* 3:14; *Shulḥan Arukh, Oraḥ Ḥayyim* 224:9, and see also the *Magen Avraham*).

**NOTES**

**The prohibition of: You shall not deviate – לָאו דְּלֹא תָסוּר:** Some explain that rabbinic decrees are overridden by concern for human dignity, despite the fact that the authority of rabbinic decrees and ordinances is itself based on a mitzva in the Torah. That mitzva only requires individuals to obey rulings of the Sanhedrin when there is a dispute between the Sages. However, the authority of rabbinic ordinances and decrees is alluded to by this prohibition and not based on it (*Alfei Menashe*).

**And disregard them – וְהִתְעַלַּמְתָּ מֵהֶם:** In the context in which it appears in the Torah, this phrase does not mean that one has license to ignore a lost object in certain circumstances. However, since the possibility of disregarding a lost object is mentioned, the inference is that this option exists in *halakha*, even though it is not the standard practice. The Sages interpreted it as an allusion to the established *halakha* that returning of a lost object is not incumbent upon every individual in every case.

HALAKHA

If he was a priest and the lost object was in the cemetery, or if he was an elder and it is beneath his dignity – אִם הָיָה כֹּהֵן וְהִיא בְּבֵית הַקְּבָרוֹת, אוֹ הָיָה זָקֵן וְאֵינָהּ לְפִי כְּבוֹדוֹ: A priest who sees a lost object in a cemetery is not obligated to tend to its return. An elder for whom it is undignified to handle an object of that kind even if it belonged to him, is similarly exempt. This *halakha* also applies to the mitzva to assist its owner to unload an animal that collapsed under its burden (Rambam *Sefer Nezikin, Hilkhot Gezela VeAveda* 11:18. See also *Shulḥan Arukh, Ḥoshen Mishpat* 272:2–3).

Or if he had more work to do – אוֹ שֶׁהָיְתָה מְלַאכְתּוֹ מְרוּבָּה: One who earns a high salary and is concerned that he will lose it if he interrupts his work to tend to a lost object, if he stipulated before the court that he will be reimbursed for any lost wages, he is obligated to return the lost object. If, however, there is no court before which he could make that stipulation, his wages take precedence, as per the Gemara here and in *Bava Metzia* 30a (*Shulḥan Arukh, Ḥoshen Mishpat* 265:1).

הָא כֵּיצַד? אִם הָיָה כֹּהֵן וְהִיא בְּבֵית הַקְּבָרוֹת, אוֹ הָיָה זָקֵן וְאֵינָהּ לְפִי כְּבוֹדוֹ, אוֹ שֶׁהָיְתָה מְלַאכְתּוֹ מְרוּבָּה מִשֶּׁל חֲבֵרוֹ, לְכָךְ נֶאֱמַר: ״וְהִתְעַלַּמְתָּ״. אַמַּאי? לֵימָא: ״אֵין חָכְמָה וְאֵין תְּבוּנָה וְאֵין עֵצָה לְנֶגֶד ה׳״!

**How so? If he was a priest and** the lost object **was in the cemetery, or if he was an elder and it is beneath his dignity**[H] to tend to a lost object of that kind, **or if he had more work to do**[H] **than another person** and he does not want to set it all aside when another person is available to tend to the lost object. **Therefore,** with regard to those cases **it is stated: And disregard them** to permit one to refrain from returning the object. **Why? Let us say** here, too: Although handling the lost object would be beneath his dignity, **"there is neither wisdom, nor understanding, nor counsel against the Lord."**

שָׁאנֵי הָתָם, דִּכְתִיב: ״וְהִתְעַלַּמְתָּ מֵהֶם״. וְלִיגְמַר מִינַּהּ! – אִיסּוּרָא מִמָּמוֹנָא לָא יָלְפִינַן.

The Gemara answers: **There it is different, as it is written: "And disregard them,"** indicating that under certain circumstances one is permitted to disregard a lost object. In that case, there is a biblical directive that creates an exception to the prohibition: "You may not disregard" (Deuteronomy 22:3). We found a case in which human dignity overrides a Torah prohibition. The Gemara suggests: **Let us derive** a general principle that human dignity takes precedence over all mitzvot in the Torah **from this** case. This possibility is rejected: **We do not derive** *halakhot* pertaining to **prohibitions** from **monetary** laws, and the case of the lost object merely entails a monetary loss, unlike other prohibitions.

תָּא שְׁמַע:

The Gemara cites an additional proof from a *baraita*. **Come** and **hear** what was said in the Torah with regard to the Nazirite: "He shall not become impure for his father or his mother or his brother or his sister in their death, for the crown of his God is on his head" (Numbers 6:7). Since it was already written with regard to the Nazirite: "He shall not come upon a dead body" (Numbers 6:6), why is it necessary to elaborate and specify his parents and siblings?

״וּלְאַחוֹתוֹ״ מַה תַּלְמוּד לוֹמַר? הֲרֵי שֶׁהָיָה הוֹלֵךְ לִשְׁחוֹט אֶת פִּסְחוֹ וְלָמוּל אֶת בְּנוֹ וְשָׁמַע שֶׁמֵּת לוֹ מֵת, יָכוֹל יַחֲזוֹר וְיִטַּמֵּא – אָמַרְתָּ לֹא יִטַּמָּא.

The Sages derived through halakhic midrash that each of these relationships come to teach a specific nuance of the law. They learned: To **what** purpose **did the verse state: And his sister?** To teach that one **who was going to slaughter his Paschal** lamb **and to circumcise his son,** both of which are positive mitzvot that if he fails to fulfill them, he is punished with *karet*, **and he heard that** a relative **of his died, I might have thought** that **he** should **return and become ritually impure** with the impurity imparted by a corpse. **You said: "He shall not become impure"**; the death of his relative will not override so significant a mitzva from the Torah.

יָכוֹל כְּשֵׁם שֶׁאֵינוֹ מִטַּמֵּא לָהֶם כָּךְ אֵינוֹ מִטַּמֵּא לְמֵת מִצְוָה, תַּלְמוּד לוֹמַר: ״וּלְאַחוֹתוֹ״ – לַאֲחוֹתוֹ הוּא דְּאֵינוֹ מִטַּמֵּא,

I **might** have thought: **Just as he does not become impure for** his relatives, **so he does not become impure for a corpse with no one to bury it** [*met mitzva*]. **The verse states: "And his sister"; he may not become impure for his sister,** as someone else can attend to her burial,

Perek **III**
Daf **20** Amud **a**

HALAKHA

But he does become impure for a *met mitzva* – אֲבָל מִטַּמֵּא הוּא לְמֵת מִצְוָה: One is required attend to the burial of a corpse with no one to bury it and become impure through contact with that corpse. This is true even for a High Priest, a Nazirite and one en route to offer the Paschal lamb or circumcise one's son, in accordance with the conclusion of the *baraita* cited in the Gemara (Rambam *Sefer Shofetim, Hilkhot Evel* 3:8; *Shulḥan Arukh, Yoreh De'a* 374:1).

אֲבָל מִטַּמֵּא הוּא לְמֵת מִצְוָה, אַמַּאי? לֵימָא: ״אֵין חָכְמָה וְאֵין תְּבוּנָה וְאֵין עֵצָה לְנֶגֶד ה׳״.

**but he does become impure for a** ***met mitzva***.[H] Here too, the question is asked: **Let us say** that the obligation to bury a *met mitzva*, which is predicated on the preservation of human dignity, should not override mitzvot explicitly written in the Torah, as it is stated: **"There is neither wisdom, nor understanding, nor counsel against the Lord."**

שָׁאנֵי הָתָם, דִּכְתִיב ״וּלְאַחוֹתוֹ״.

The Gemara answers: **There it is different, as it is** explicitly **written: "And his sister,"** from which we derive that although he may not become ritually impure to bury his sister, he must do so for a *met mitzva*.

וְלִיגְמַר מִינָּהּ! – שֵׁב וְאַל תַּעֲשֶׂה שָׁאנֵי.

The Gemara suggests: **Let us derive** a general principle that human dignity takes precedence over all mitzvot in the Torah **from this** case.[N] This possibility is rejected: This is a special case, because a case of **"sit and refrain from action"** [*shev ve'al ta'aseh*] **is different.**[N] Engaging in the burial of a *met mitzva* is not actually in contravention of a mitzva. Rather, by doing so he becomes ritually impure and is then rendered incapable of fulfilling that mitzva. We cannot derive a general principle from here that human dignity would also override a Torah prohibition in a case where that prohibition is directly contravened.

אֲמַר לֵיהּ רַב פַּפָּא לְאַבַּיֵי: מַאי שְׁנָא רִאשׁוֹנִים דְּאִתְרְחִישׁ לְהוּ נִיסָּא, וּמַאי שְׁנָא אֲנַן דְּלָא מִתְרְחִישׁ לָן נִיסָּא? אִי מִשּׁוּם תְּנוּיֵי – בִּשְׁנֵי דְּרַב יְהוּדָה כּוּלֵּי תְּנוּיֵי בִּנְזִיקִין הֲוָה, וַאֲנַן קָא מַתְנֵינַן שִׁיתָּא סִדְרֵי! וְכִי הֲוָה מָטֵי רַב יְהוּדָה בְּעוּקְצִין "הָאִשָּׁה שֶׁכּוֹבֶשֶׁת יָרָק בַּקְּדֵרָה" וְאָמְרִי לָהּ "זֵיתִים שֶׁכְּבָשָׁן בְּטַרְפֵיהֶן טְהוֹרִים" אֲמַר: "הֲוָיוֹת דְּרַב וּשְׁמוּאֵל קָא חָזֵינָא הָכָא", וַאֲנַן קָא מַתְנֵינַן בְּעוּקְצִין תְּלֵיסַר מְתִיבָתָא! וְאִילּוּ רַב יְהוּדָה, כִּי הֲוָה שָׁלֵיף חַד מְסָאנֵיהּ – אָתֵי מִטְרָא, וַאֲנַן קָא מְצַעֲרִינַן נַפְשִׁין וּמִצְוַח קָא צָוְחִינַן – וְלֵית דְּמַשְׁגַּח בָּן! –

The Gemara responds: In the context of the discussion whether or not human dignity overrides honoring God in the sense of fulfilling his mitzvot, **Rav Pappa said to Abaye: What is different about the earlier** generations, **for whom miracles occurred and what is different about us, for whom miracles do not occur? If it is because of** Torah **study; in the years of Rav Yehuda all of their learning was** confined to **the** order of ***Nezikin*****, while we learn** all **six orders!** Moreover, **when Rav Yehuda would reach in** tractate ***Okatzin*****,**[N] which discusses the extent to which the stems of various fruits and vegetables are considered an integral part of the produce in terms of becoming ritually impure, the *halakha* that **a woman who pickles a vegetable in a pot, and some say** when he would reach the *halakha* that **olives pickled with their leaves are pure,** because after pickling, it is no longer possible to lift the fruit by its leaves, they are no longer considered part of the fruit; he would find it difficult to understand. He **would say:** Those are **the disputes between Rav and Shmuel that we see here. And we,** in contrast, **learn thirteen versions of *Okatzin*. While,** with regard to miracles, after declaring a fast to pray for a drought to end, **when Rav Yehuda would remove one of his shoes**[N] **the rain would** immediately **fall, whereas we torment ourselves and cry out and no one notices us.**

אֲמַר לֵיהּ: קַמָּאֵי הָווּ קָא מָסְרִי נַפְשַׁיְיהוּ אַקְּדוּשַּׁת הַשֵּׁם, אֲנַן לָא מָסְרִינַן נַפְשִׁין אַקְּדוּשַּׁת הַשֵּׁם. כִּי הָא דְּרַב אַדָּא בַּר אַהֲבָה חַזְיֵיהּ לְהַהִיא כּוּתִית דַּהֲוַת לְבִישָׁא כַּרְבַּלְתָּא בְּשׁוּקָא, סְבַר דְּבַת יִשְׂרָאֵל הִיא, קָם קַרְעֵיהּ מִינַּהּ; אִגַּלַּאי מִילְּתָא דְּכוּתִית הִיא, שַׁיְּימוּהָ בְּאַרְבַּע מְאָה זוּזֵי. אֲמַר לָהּ: מָה שְׁמֵךְ? אֲמַרָה לֵיהּ: מָתוּן. אֲמַר לָהּ: מָתוּן מָתוּן אַרְבַּע מְאָה זוּזֵי שָׁוְיָא.

Abaye **said to** Rav Pappa: **The previous** generations were wholly **dedicated to the sanctification of God's name,** while **we are not** as **dedicated to the sanctification of God's name.** Typical of the earlier generations' commitment, the Gemara relates: **Like this** incident involving **Rav Adda bar Ahava who saw a non-Jewish woman who was wearing a garment made of a forbidden mixture of wool and linen** [*karbalta*][N] **in the marketplace.** Since he **thought** that **she was Jewish, he stood and ripped it from her. It was** then **divulged that she was a non-Jew** and he was taken to court due to the shame that he caused her, and **they assessed** the payment for the shame that he caused **her** at **four hundred *zuz*.** Ultimately, Rav Adda **said to her: What is your name? She replied: Matun.** In a play on words, **he said to her: Matun,** her name, plus ***matun*****,** the Aramaic word for two hundred, **is worth four hundred *zuz*.**

רַב גִּידֵּל הֲוָה רָגִיל דַּהֲוָה קָא אָזֵיל וְיָתֵיב אַשַּׁעֲרֵי דִּטְבִילָה, אֲמַר לְהוּ: הָכִי טְבִילוּ וְהָכִי טְבִילוּ. אָמְרִי לֵיהּ רַבָּנַן: לָא קָא מִסְתְּפֵי מָר מִיֵּצֶר הָרָע? אֲמַר לְהוּ: דַּמְיָין בְּאַפַּאי כִּי קָאקֵי חִיוָּרֵי.

It was also related about the earlier generations, that they would degrade themselves in the desire to glorify God. **Rav Giddel was accustomed to go and sit at the gates of the** women's **immersion** sites. **He said to them: Immerse yourselves in this way, and immerse yourselves in that way. The Sages said to him: Master,** do you **not fear the evil inclination? He said to them: In my eyes,** they **are comparable to white geese.**

רַבִּי יוֹחָנָן הֲוָה רָגִיל דַּהֲוָה קָא אָזֵיל וְיָתֵיב אַשַּׁעֲרֵי דִּטְבִילָה, אֲמַר: כִּי סָלְקָן בְּנוֹת יִשְׂרָאֵל וְאָתְיָין מִטְּבִילָה מִסְתַּכְּלָן בִּי, וְנֶהֱוֵי לְהוּ זַרְעָא דְּשַׁפִּירֵי כְּוָותִי. אָמְרִי לֵיהּ רַבָּנַן: לָא קָא מִסְתְּפֵי מָר מֵעֵינָא בִּישָׁא? אֲמַר לְהוּ: אֲנָא מִזַּרְעָא דְּיוֹסֵף קָא אָתֵינָא, דְּלָא שָׁלְטָא בֵּיהּ עֵינָא בִּישָׁא, דִּכְתִיב: "בֵּן פּוֹרָת יוֹסֵף בֵּן פּוֹרָת עֲלֵי עָיִן", וְאָמַר רַבִּי אַבָּהוּ: אַל תִּקְרֵי "עֲלֵי עָיִן" אֶלָּא "עוֹלֵי עַיִן".

Similarly, the Gemara relates that **Rabbi Yoḥanan was accustomed to go and sit at the gates of the** women's **immersion** sites. Rabbi Yoḥanan, who was known for his extraordinary good looks, explained this and **said: When the daughters of Israel emerge from their immersion, they will look at me, and will have children as beautiful as I. The Sages asked him: Master, do you not fear the evil eye? He said to them: I descend from the seed of Joseph over whom the evil eye has no dominion, as it is written: "Joseph is a bountiful vine, a bountiful vine on a spring** [*alei ayin*]**"** (Genesis 49:22). *"Ayin"* can mean both "spring" and "eye." **And Rabbi Abbahu said** a homiletic interpretation: **Do not read** it *alei ayin*, **rather *olei ayin*,** above the eye; they transcend the influence of the evil eye.

## NOTES

**Let us derive from this case – וְלִיגְמַר מִינָּהּ:** The logical flow of the discussion is as follows: The *halakha* concerning lost objects constitutes a challenge to the principle that preventing desecration of God's name overrides concerns of human dignity. This challenge is in two stages. First, the Gemara cites the *baraita* as an example that contradicts the principle. The Gemara rejects the challenge by pointing out unique circumstances extant in the case in the *baraita*. The second stage is more general: Since there is one clear case, whatever the reason, where human dignity overrides a mitzva in the Torah, it can serve as a paradigm from which a general principle can be extrapolated. Employing the hermeneutic principle of analogy, even though the paradigm was derived from a proof unique to that case, once established, it can serve as the basis for a general principle. Therefore the rejection of the second stage is not based on emphasizing the unique aspect of the specific case but rather in proving that this case falls into a special category and, consequently, general conclusions may not be drawn.

**"Sit and refrain from action" [*shev ve'al ta'aseh*] is different – שֵׁב וְאַל תַּעֲשֶׂה שָׁאנֵי:** *Tosafot* pointed out the difficulty with this explanation. It explains the situation where one is en route to bring his Paschal lamb and becomes ritually impure due to contact with a corpse, i.e., where the mitzva is not uprooted directly by his action, but rather as a consequence of his status. However, that is not the case in a situation where a priest, and certainly the High Priest or a nazirite, becomes ritually impure as a result of tending to the burial of a *met mitzva*. There he directly violates the prohibition with his action. *Tosafot* (in *Bava Metzia* and *Shevuot*) explain that demeaning the dead is far more severe than the standard concern for human dignity. Alternatively, one could distinguish and assert that the cases of a priest and a Nazirite are not paradigmatic, as the prohibition in each of those cases is less severe than a standard prohibition. Since a nazirite can approach a Sage for dissolution of his nazirite vow, it is a conditional, non-absolute and, therefore, less severe prohibition. The prohibition in the case of the priest is, by definition, limited to the priest and, therefore, relative to universal prohibitions, is less severe.

**In tractate *Okatzin* – בְּעוּקְצִין:** The *halakhot* of ritual purity and impurity include numerous definitions with regard to what is considered part of the fruit or vegetable and what is considered ancillary to and not actually part of the fruit, e.g., the leaves, stem, peel, etc. In the *mishnayot* in tractates *Okatzin* and *Teharot* that deal with this issue, much attention is paid to the distinctions between the various parts and why one is considered part of the fruit while the other is not. This constitutes one of the most intricate areas of halakhic discourse.

**Remove one of his shoes – שָׁלֵיף חַד מְסָאנֵיהּ:** It is prohibited to wear shoes on a public fast proclaimed due to drought. As soon as Rav Yehuda began his preparations for the fast, removing one of his shoes, the rain immediately began to fall.

**A garment made of a forbidden mixture of wool and linen [*karbalta*] – כַּרְבַּלְתָּא:** Some say that this is a red garment, which is considered immodest and that is why Rav Adda ripped it off her (*Arukh*). According to Rashi, who explained that it is an expensive garment, it is inappropriate to walk in public dressed in such finery without wearing an outer layer to cover it (Maharshal).

HALAKHA

**The obligation of women to recite *Shema* – נָשִׁים בְּחוֹבַת קְרִיאַת שְׁמַע:** Women are exempt from reciting *Shema* and the accompanying blessings (*Mishna Berura*). They are not even obligated to do so by rabbinic law (*Mishna Berura*). There are those who ruled that women are obligated to recite the first verse of *Shema*, because it includes acceptance of the yoke of Heaven (*Beit Yosef* and *Baḥ; Shulḥan Arukh, Oraḥ Ḥayyim* 70:1).

**The obligation of minors to recite the Shema – קְטַנִּים בִּקְרִיאַת שְׁמַע:** The commentaries disagree whether the minors mentioned in the mishna as exempt from reciting *Shema* are only those who have not yet reached the age of training to fulfill mitzvot (Rabbeinu Tam) or whether even those who reached that age are exempt (Rashi). One should adopt the custom that a child who reached the age of training to fulfill mitzvot recites *Shema*, in accordance with the opinion of Rabbeinu Tam (*Shulḥan Arukh, Oraḥ Ḥayyim* 70:2).

רַבִּי יוֹסֵי בְּרַבִּי חֲנִינָא אָמַר מֵהָכָא: "וְיִדְגּוּ לָרֹב בְּקֶרֶב הָאָרֶץ" מָה דָּגִים שֶׁבַּיָּם מַיִם מְכַסִּין עֲלֵיהֶם וְאֵין עַיִן הָרָע שׁוֹלֶטֶת בָּהֶם – אַף זַרְעוֹ שֶׁל יוֹסֵף אֵין עַיִן הָרָע שׁוֹלֶטֶת בָּהֶם.

**Rabbi Yosei, son of Rabbi Ḥanina,** cited a different proof, from Jacob's blessing of Joseph's sons, Ephraim and Menashe: "The angel who redeems me from all evil shall bless the young and in them may my name be recalled, and the name of my fathers, Abraham and Isaac, **and may they multiply [*veyidgu*] in the midst of the earth"** (Genesis 48:16). *Veyidgu* is related etymologically to the word fish [*dag*]. **Just as the fish in the sea, water covers them and the evil eye has no dominion over them, so too the seed of Joseph, the evil eye has no dominion over them.**

וְאִי בָּעֵית אֵימָא: עַיִן שֶׁלֹּא רָצְתָה לָזוּן מִמַּה שֶּׁאֵינוֹ שֶׁלּוֹ – אֵין עַיִן הָרָע שׁוֹלֶטֶת בּוֹ.

**And if you wish, say** instead: Joseph's **eye, which did not seek to feast on that which was not his,** Potiphar's wife, **the evil eye has no dominion over him.**

מתני׳ נָשִׁים וַעֲבָדִים וּקְטַנִּים פְּטוּרִין מִקְּרִיאַת שְׁמַע

**MISHNA** **Women,**[H] **slaves, and minors,**[H] who have parallel obligations in various mitzvot, **are exempt from the recitation of *Shema***



HALAKHA

**Those exempt from the mitzva of phylacteries – הַפְּטוּרִים מִתְּפִילִּין:** Women and slaves are exempt from phylacteries. If women want to assume a stringency and don phylacteries they should be rebuked (Rambam *Sefer Ahava, Hilkhot Tefillin UMezuza VeSefer Torah* 4:13; *Shulḥan Arukh, Oraḥ Ḥayyim* 38:3).

**Those obligated in prayer – הַחַיָּבִים בִּתְפִלָּה:** Everyone is obligated to pray, even women and slaves, in accordance with the *mishna*, and it is a mitzva to train minors to pray. Some rule that women fulfill their obligation by means of reciting an entreaty once daily. In the opinion of the Rambam, that is their obligation to pray by Torah law (*Magen Avraham*; Rambam *Sefer Ahava, Hilkhot Tefilla* 1:2; *Shulḥan Arukh, Oraḥ Ḥayyim* 106:1).

**Those obligated in the mitzva of *mezuza* – הַחַיָּבִים בִּמְזוּזָה:** Everyone, including women and slaves, is obligated to affix a *mezuza* to his doorways. Even minors are trained to affix a *mezuza* to their doorways (Rambam *Sefer Ahava, Hilkhot Tefillin Mezuza VeSefer Torah* 5:10; *Shulḥan Arukh, Yoreh De'a* 291:3).

**Those obligated in the mitzva of Grace after Meals – הַחַיָּבִים בְּבִרְכַּת הַמָּזוֹן:** Women are obligated to recite Grace after Meals in accordance with the *mishna*, and it is a mitzva to instruct minors to do so as well (Rambam *Sefer Ahava, Hilkhot Berakhot* 5:1; *Shulḥan Arukh, Oraḥ Ḥayyim* 186:1–2).

NOTES

**Women's obligation in prayer – נָשִׁים בְּחוֹבַת תְּפִלָּה:** This question is based on a more fundamental dilemma: Is prayer a mitzva by Torah or by rabbinic law? According to the opinion that it is rabbinic, the language of the Gemara: Like a time-bound positive mitzva is problematic. On the other hand, even those who hold that the basic mitzva of prayer is by Torah law, assert that the mitzva of turning to God is by Torah law, while the formula and the times for prayer are by rabbinic law. Therefore, it is possible for women to fulfill the mitzva of prayer by means of any request addressed to God.

וּמִן הַתְּפִילִּין, וְחַיָּיבִין בִּתְפִילָּה וּבִמְזוּזָה וּבְבִרְכַּת הַמָּזוֹן.

**and from phylacteries,**[H] **but** they **are obligated in** the mitzvot of **prayer,**[HN] ***mezuza*,**[H] **and Grace after Meals.**[H] The Gemara explains the rationale for these exemptions and obligations.

גמ׳ "קְרִיאַת שְׁמַע", פְּשִׁיטָא! מִצְוַת עֲשֵׂה שֶׁהַזְּמַן גְּרָמָא הוּא, וְכׇל מִצְוַת עֲשֵׂה שֶׁהַזְּמַן גְּרָמָא נָשִׁים פְּטוּרוֹת!

**GEMARA** With regard to the mishna's statement that women are exempt from **the recitation of *Shema*,** the Gemara asks: That is **obvious,** as *Shema* is a **time-bound, positive mitzva, and** the halakhic principle is: **Women are exempt from any time-bound, positive mitzva,** i.e., any mitzva whose performance is only in effect at a particular time. *Shema* falls into that category as its recitation is restricted to the morning and the evening. Why then did the mishna need to mention it specifically?

מַהוּ דְּתֵימָא: הוֹאִיל וְאִית בַּהּ מַלְכוּת שָׁמַיִם – קָמַשְׁמַע לַן.

The Gemara replies: **Lest you say: Since** *Shema* **includes** the acceptance of the yoke of **the kingdom of Heaven,** perhaps women are obligated in its recitation despite the fact that it is a time-bound, positive mitzva. Therefore, the mishna **teaches us** that, nevertheless, women are exempt.

"וּמִן הַתְּפִלִּין" פְּשִׁיטָא! – מַהוּ דְּתֵימָא: הוֹאִיל וְאִתְקַשׁ לִמְזוּזָה – קָמַשְׁמַע לַן.

We also learned in the mishna that women are exempt **from phylacteries.** The Gemara asks: That is **obvious** as well. The donning of phylacteries is only in effect at particular times; during the day but not at night, on weekdays but not on Shabbat or Festivals. The Gemara replies: **Lest you say: Since** the mitzva of phylacteries **is juxtaposed** in the Torah **to** the mitzva of ***mezuza*,** as it is written: "And you shall bind them as a sign upon your hands and they shall be frontlets between your eyes" (Deuteronomy 6:8), followed by: "And you shall write them upon the door posts of your house and on your gates" (Deuteronomy 6:9), just as women are obligated in the mitzva of *mezuza*, so too they are obligated in the mitzva of phylacteries. Therefore, the mishna **teaches us** that nevertheless, women are exempt.

"וְחַיָּיבִין בִּתְפִלָּה" דְּרַחֲמֵי נִינְהוּ. – מַהוּ דְּתֵימָא: הוֹאִיל וּכְתִיב בָּהּ "עֶרֶב וָבֹקֶר וְצָהֳרַיִם", כְּמִצְוַת עֲשֵׂה שֶׁהַזְּמַן גְּרָמָא דָּמֵי – קָמַשְׁמַע לָן.

We also learned in the mishna that women, slaves, and children are **obligated in prayer.** The Gemara explains that, although the mitzva of prayer is only in effect at particular times, which would lead to the conclusion that women are exempt, nevertheless, since prayer **is** supplication for **mercy** and women also require divine mercy, they are obligated. However, **lest you say: Since** regarding prayer it is **written: "Evening and morning and afternoon** I pray and cry aloud and He hears my voice" (Psalms 55:18), perhaps prayer should be **considered a time-bound, positive mitzva** and women would be exempt, the mishna **teaches us** that, fundamentally, the mitzva of prayer is not time-bound and, therefore, everyone is obligated.

"וּבִמְזוּזָה" פְּשִׁיטָא! – מַהוּ דְּתֵימָא: הוֹאִיל וְאִתְקַשׁ לְתַלְמוּד תּוֹרָה – קָמַשְׁמַע לָן.

We also learned in the mishna that women are obligated in the mitzva of *mezuza.* The Gemara asks: That too is **obvious.** Why would they be exempt from fulfilling this obligation, it is a positive mitzva that is not time-bound? The Gemara replies: **Lest you say: Since** the mitzva of *mezuza* **is juxtaposed** in the Torah to the mitzva of **Torah study** (Deuteronomy 11:19–20), just as women are exempt from Torah study, so too they are exempt from the mitzva of *mezuza.* Therefore, the mishna explicitly **teaches us** that they are obligated.

"וּבְבִרְכַּת הַמָּזוֹן" פְּשִׁיטָא! – מַהוּ דְּתֵימָא: הוֹאִיל וּכְתִיב "בְּתֵת ה׳ לָכֶם בָּעֶרֶב בָּשָׂר לֶאֱכֹל וְלֶחֶם בַּבֹּקֶר לִשְׂבֹּעַ", כְּמִצְוַת עֲשֵׂה שֶׁהַזְּמַן גְּרָמָא דָּמֵי – קָמַשְׁמַע לָן.

We also learned in the mishna that women are obligated to recite the **Grace after Meals.** The Gemara asks: That too is **obvious.** The Gemara replies: **Lest you say: Since it is written: "When the Lord shall give you meat to eat in the evening and bread in the morning to the full"** (Exodus 16:8), one might conclude that the Torah established fixed times for the meals and, consequently, for the mitzva of Grace after Meals and, therefore, it **is considered a time-bound, positive mitzva,** exempting women from its recitation. Therefore, the mishna **teaches us** that women are obligated.

אָמַר רַב אַדָּא בַּר אַהֲבָה: נָשִׁים חַיָּיבוֹת בְּקִדּוּשׁ הַיּוֹם דְּבַר תּוֹרָה. – אַמַּאי? מִצְוַת עֲשֵׂה שֶׁהַזְּמַן גְּרָמָא הוּא, וְכָל מִצְוַת עֲשֵׂה שֶׁהַזְּמַן גְּרָמָא נָשִׁים פְּטוּרוֹת! – אָמַר אַבַּיֵי: מִדְּרַבָּנַן.

**Rav Adda bar Ahava**[P] **said: Women are obligated to** recite **the sanctification of the** Shabbat **day** [***kiddush***][H] **by Torah law.** The Gemara asks: **Why?** *Kiddush* is a **time-bound, positive mitzva, and women are exempt** from **all time-bound, positive mitzvot. Abaye said:** Indeed, women are obligated to recite *kiddush* **by rabbinic,** but not by Torah **law.**

אֲמַר לֵיהּ רָבָא: וְהָא "דְּבַר תּוֹרָה" קָאָמַר! וְעוֹד, כָּל מִצְוֹת עֲשֵׂה נְחַיְּיבִינְהוּ מִדְּרַבָּנַן!

**Rava said to** Abaye: There are two refutations to your explanation. First, Rav Adda bar Ahava said that women are obligated to recite *kiddush* **by Torah law, and, furthermore,** the very explanation is difficult to understand. If the Sages do indeed institute ordinances in these circumstances, **let us obligate them** to fulfill **all** time-bound, **positive mitzvot by rabbinic law,** even though they are exempt by Torah law.

אֶלָּא אָמַר רָבָא: אָמַר קְרָא "זָכוֹר" "וְשָׁמוֹר" – כָּל שֶׁיֶּשְׁנוֹ בִּשְׁמִירָה יֶשְׁנוֹ בִּזְכִירָה, וְהָנֵי נָשֵׁי, הוֹאִיל וְאִיתְנְהוּ בִּשְׁמִירָה – אִיתְנְהוּ בִּזְכִירָה.

**Rather, Rava said:** This has a unique explanation. In the Ten Commandments in the book of Exodus, **the verse said: "Remember** Shabbat and sanctify it" (Exodus 20:8), while in the book of Deuteronomy it is said: **"Observe** Shabbat and sanctify it" (Deuteronomy 5:12). From these two variants we can deduce that **anyone included in** the obligation to **observe** Shabbat by avoiding its desecration, **is** also **included in** the mitzva to **remember** Shabbat by reciting *kiddush.* **Since these women are included in** the mitzva **to observe** Shabbat, as there is no distinction between men and women in the obligation to observe prohibitions in general and to refrain from the desecration of Shabbat in particular, so too **are they included in** the mitzva of **remembering** Shabbat.

אֲמַר לֵיהּ רָבִינָא לְרָבָא: נָשִׁים בְּבִרְכַּת הַמָּזוֹן, דְּאוֹרַיְיתָא אוֹ דְּרַבָּנַן? לְמַאי נָפְקָא מִינַּהּ – לְאַפּוֹקֵי רַבִּים יְדֵי חוֹבָתָן. אִי אָמְרַתְּ (בִּשְׁלָמָא) דְּאוֹרַיְיתָא – אָתֵי דְּאוֹרַיְיתָא וּמַפֵּיק דְּאוֹרַיְיתָא, אֶלָּא אִי אָמְרַתְּ דְּרַבָּנַן – הָוֵי "שֶׁאֵינוֹ מְחוּיָּיב בַּדָּבָר", וְכָל שֶׁאֵינוֹ מְחוּיָּיב בַּדָּבָר – אֵינוֹ מוֹצִיא אֶת הָרַבִּים יְדֵי חוֹבָתָן. מַאי?

**Ravina said to Rava:** We learned in the mishna that **women** are obligated in the mitzva of **Grace after Meals.** However, are they obligated **by Torah law** or merely **by rabbinic law? What difference does it make** whether it is by Torah or rabbinic law? The difference is regarding her ability **to fulfill the obligation of others** when reciting the blessing on their behalf. **Granted, if you say that** their obligation **is by Torah law,** one whose obligation **is by Torah law can come and fulfill the obligation** of others who are obligated **by Torah law. However, if you say** that their obligation is **by rabbinic law,** then from the perspective of Torah law, women **are** considered to be **one who is not obligated, and** the general principle is that **one who is not obligated** to fulfill a particular mitzva[H] **cannot fulfill the obligations of the many** in that mitzva. Therefore, it is important to know **what** is the resolution of this dilemma.[H]

**PERSONALITIES**

**Rav Adda bar Ahava – רַב אַדָּא בַּר אַהֲבָה:** A Babylonian *amora,* Rav Adda bar Ahava was among those who spanned the first and second generations of *amora'im.*

Looking at the various talmudic sources related to Rav Adda bar Ahava, it becomes clear that there were at least two, perhaps three, Sages referred to by that name. It appears that the reference in our Gemara is to the first and greatest Sage to go by that name. Rav Adda bar Ahava was one of Rav's greatest students; however, both Rav and Shmuel appreciated the extent of his righteousness and piety, and would rely on his merit in their belief that they would come to no harm. Future generations came to cite him as exemplifying behavior reflecting awe of Heaven. The Talmud tells of his modesty and the painstaking care he took with regard to the honor of Heaven, of his teachers, and of his fellows man.

It appears the calculation of the Hebrew calendar, referred to as *tekufat* Rav Adda, is named for this first Rav Adda, and, although Shmuel established his own calculation, Rav Adda's was far more accurate and now serves as the foundation for calculating the Jewish calendar.

**HALAKHA**

**Women are obligated in the sanctification of the Shabbat day [*kiddush*] – נָשִׁים חַיָּיבוֹת בְּקִדּוּשׁ:** Women are obligated to recite *kiddush* on Shabbat (*Rambam Sefer HaMadda, Hilkhot Avodat Kokhavim* 12:3; *Shulḥan Arukh, Oraḥ Ḥayyim* 271:2).

**One who is not obligated to fulfill a particular mitzva – שֶׁאֵינוֹ מְחוּיָּיב בַּדָּבָר:** One who is not obligated by Torah law to fulfill a specific mitzva cannot fulfill the obligation for someone obligated to fulfill that mitzva by Torah law with his blessing (Rambam *Sefer Ahava, Hilkhot Tefillin UMezuza VeSefer Torah* 1:11).

**The essence of women's obligation to recite Grace after Meals – מַהוּת חִיּוּב נָשִׁים בְּבִרְכַּת הַמָּזוֹן:** There is uncertainty as to whether the obligation of women to recite Grace after Meals is by Torah or rabbinic law. The dilemma raised in the Gemara remains unresolved and the ruling reached is consistent with the ruling in all cases of unresolved dilemmas. Therefore, women cannot fulfill the obligation for others obligated by Torah law in the mitzva of Grace after Meals (*Magen Avraham*; *Rambam Sefer Ahava, Hilkhot Berakhot* 5:15–16; *Shulḥan Arukh, Oraḥ Ḥayyim* 186:1).

## HALAKHA

**A son may recite a blessing on behalf of his father** – **בֵּן מְבָרֵךְ לְאָבִיו**: A minor can fulfill the obligation of an adult to recite Grace after Meals if the adult did not eat enough to leave him satisfied (Rambam *Sefer Ahava, Hilkhot Berakhot* 5:15–16; *Shulḥan Arukh, Oraḥ Ḥayyim* 186:2).

**One who experienced a seminal emission with regard to the blessing of the Torah** – **בַּעַל קֶרִי בְּבִרְכּוֹת הַתּוֹרָה**: Based on the ordinance instituted by Ezra, one who experienced a seminal emission is prohibited from engaging in Torah study, praying, and reciting *Shema* until he immerses himself. However, in subsequent generations that ordinance was repealed and one who experienced a seminal emission was permitted to engage in all those activities without immersion or bathing in nine *kav* of water. That remains the prevalent custom. Nevertheless, one who chooses to immerse himself is praiseworthy. He must, however, make certain that, by doing so, he does not let the time for *Shema* or prayer pass or miss the opportunity to participate in communal prayer (Rambam *Sefer Ahava, Hilkhot Keriat Shema* 4:8; *Shulḥan Arukh, Oraḥ Ḥayyim* 88:1).

**Contemplation is tantamount to speech** – **הִרְהוּר כְּדִבּוּר דָּמֵי**: The halakhic authorities disagreed whether or not contemplation is tantamount to speech, and, if it is, in what instances. The *ge'onim* ruled in accordance with the opinion of Rav Ḥisda that contemplation is not tantamount to speech as that seems to be the opinion upon which the discourse in the Gemara was predicated. Others ruled that contemplation is tantamount to speech only after the fact, particularly if one mouths the words, even if he does so inaudibly, according to the ruling of the Rambam. Similarly, in exigent circumstances, one fulfills his obligation with contemplation (*Shulḥan Arukh, Oraḥ Ḥayyim* 62:3–4).

## NOTES

**One whose obligation is by rabbinic law can come and fulfill the obligation of another whose obligation is by rabbinic law** – **אָתֵי דְּרַבָּנַן וּמַפֵּיק דְּרַבָּנַן**: In this *halakha* and in the homiletic interpretation of Rav Avira, a certain insight into rabbinic measures is provided. For all intents and purposes, there are two categories of mitzvot: mitzvot by Torah law and mitzvot by rabbinic law. However, here, it is clear that mitzvot by rabbinic law are an independent system in which there are specific obligations, i.e., mitzvot, as well as people obligated to fulfill them, who do not enter into the framework of mitzvot by Torah law.

**Yet You show favor to Israel** – **וַהֲלֹא אַתָּה נוֹשֵׂא פָּנִים לְיִשְׂרָאֵל**: The Rashbam notes that according to the literal meaning there is a distinction between *nesiat panim leYisrael* in the sense of showing favor to Israel, and *nesiat penei Yisrael*, in the sense of God rendering judgment in their favor (*Tosefot Rabbeinu Yehuda HaḤasid*).

**Ezra's ordinances** – **תַּקָּנַת עֶזְרָא**: The Gemara (*Bava Kama* 82a) cites a tradition with regard to the ten ordinances instituted by Ezra in order to enhance fulfillment of both mitzvot by Torah law and ancient customs. The emphasis in all the ordinances was enhancing the sanctity in the daily existence of the people. By Torah law, one who experienced a seminal emission is ritually impure and prohibited from eating *teruma* and consecrated foods. In his ordinance, Ezra instituted that the individual must purify himself before praying or engaging in Torah study. Although the ordinance was repealed several generations later, it remained the custom in many communities as well as a custom of the pious throughout the generations.

תָּא שְׁמַע, בֶּאֱמֶת אָמְרוּ: בֵּן מְבָרֵךְ לְאָבִיו, וְעֶבֶד מְבָרֵךְ לְרַבּוֹ, וְאִשָּׁה מְבָרֶכֶת לְבַעְלָהּ; אֲבָל אָמְרוּ חֲכָמִים: תָּבֹא מְאֵרָה לְאָדָם שֶׁאִשְׁתּוֹ וּבָנָיו מְבָרְכִין לוֹ.

Come and hear from what was taught in a *baraita*: **Actually they said** that **a son may recite a blessing** on behalf of **his father,**[H] **and a slave may recite a blessing** on behalf of **his master, and a woman may recite a blessing** on behalf of **her husband, but the Sages said: May a curse come to a man** who, due to his ignorance, requires **his wife and children to recite a blessing on his behalf.**

אִי אָמְרַתְּ בִּשְׁלָמָא דְּאוֹרָיְיתָא – אָתֵי דְּאוֹרָיְיתָא וּמַפֵּיק דְּאוֹרָיְיתָא, אֶלָּא אִי אָמְרַתְּ דְּרַבָּנַן – אָתֵי דְּרַבָּנַן וּמַפֵּיק דְּאוֹרָיְיתָא?

From here we may infer: **Granted, if you say that** their obligation **is by Torah law,** one whose obligation **is by Torah law can come and fulfill the obligation** of others who are obligated **by Torah law. However, if you say** that their obligation is **by rabbinic law,** can one who is obligated **by rabbinic law, come and fulfill the obligation** of one whose obligation is **by Torah law?**

וּלְטַעְמִיךְ, קָטָן בַּר חִיּוּבָא הוּא? – אֶלָּא, הָכָא בְּמַאי עָסְקִינַן – כְּגוֹן שֶׁאָכַל שִׁיעוּרָא דְּרַבָּנַן, דְּאָתֵי דְּרַבָּנַן וּמַפֵּיק דְּרַבָּנַן.

The Gemara challenges this proof: **And according to your reasoning,** is **a minor obligated** by Torah law to perform mitzvot? Everyone agrees that a minor is exempt by Torah law, yet here the *baraita* said that he may recite a blessing on behalf of his father. There must be another way to explain the *baraita*. **With what we are dealing here? With a case where** his father **ate** a quantity of food that did not satisfy his hunger, a **measure** for which one is only obligated **by rabbinic law** to recite Grace after Meals. In that case, one whose obligation **is by rabbinic law can come and fulfill the obligation** of another whose obligation **is by rabbinic law.**[N]

דָּרַשׁ רַב עֲוִירָא, זִמְנִין אֲמַר לַהּ מִשְּׁמֵיהּ דְּרַבִּי אַמֵּי וְזִמְנִין אֲמַר לַהּ מִשְּׁמֵיהּ דְּרַבִּי אַסִּי: אָמְרוּ מַלְאֲכֵי הַשָּׁרֵת לִפְנֵי הַקָּדוֹשׁ בָּרוּךְ הוּא: רִבּוֹנוֹ שֶׁל עוֹלָם, כָּתוּב בְּתוֹרָתְךָ ״אֲשֶׁר לֹא יִשָּׂא פָנִים וְלֹא יִקַּח שֹׁחַד״, וַהֲלֹא אַתָּה נוֹשֵׂא פָּנִים לְיִשְׂרָאֵל, דִּכְתִיב: ״יִשָּׂא ה׳ פָּנָיו אֵלֶיךָ״. אָמַר לָהֶם: וְכִי לֹא אֶשָּׂא פָּנִים לְיִשְׂרָאֵל? שֶׁכָּתַבְתִּי לָהֶם בַּתּוֹרָה: ״וְאָכַלְתָּ וְשָׂבָעְתָּ וּבֵרַכְתָּ אֶת ה׳ אֱלֹהֶיךָ״, וְהֵם מְדַקְדְּקִים [עַל] עַצְמָם עַד כַּזַּיִת וְעַד כַּבֵּיצָה.

After citing the *halakha* that one who eats a quantity of food that does not satisfy his hunger is obligated by rabbinic law to recite Grace after Meals, the Gemara cites a related homiletic interpretation. **Rav Avira taught, sometimes he said it in the name of Rabbi Ami, and sometimes he said it in the name of** Rabbi Asi: **The ministering angels said before the Holy One, Blessed be He: Master of the Universe, in Your Torah it is written:** "The great, mighty and awesome God **who favors no one and takes no bribe"** (Deuteronomy 10:17), **yet You,** nevertheless, **show favor to Israel,**[N] **as it is written: "The Lord shall show favor to you** and give you peace" (Numbers 6:26). **He replied to them: And how can I not show favor to Israel, as I wrote for them in the Torah: "And you shall eat and be satisfied, and bless the Lord your God"** (Deuteronomy 8:10), meaning that there is no obligation to bless the Lord until one is satiated; **yet they are exacting with themselves** to recite Grace after Meals even if they have eaten **as much as an olive-bulk or an egg-bulk.** Since they go beyond the requirements of the law, they are worthy of favor.

מתני׳ בַּעַל קֶרִי מְהַרְהֵר בְּלִבּוֹ וְאֵינוֹ מְבָרֵךְ לֹא לְפָנֶיהָ וְלֹא לְאַחֲרֶיהָ; וְעַל הַמָּזוֹן מְבָרֵךְ לְאַחֲרָיו וְאֵינוֹ מְבָרֵךְ לְפָנָיו. רַבִּי יְהוּדָה אוֹמֵר: מְבָרֵךְ לִפְנֵיהֶם וּלְאַחֲרֵיהֶם.

**MISHNA** Ezra the Scribe decreed that one who is ritually impure because of a seminal emission may not engage in matters of Torah until he has immersed in a ritual bath and purified himself. This *halakha* was accepted over the course of many generations; however, many disputes arose with regard to the Torah matters to which it applies.[N] Regarding this, the mishna says: If the time for the recitation of *Shema* arrived and **one** is impure due to a **seminal emission,**[H] he may **contemplate** *Shema* **in his heart, but neither recites the blessings preceding** *Shema*, **nor the blessings following it. Over food** which, after partaking, one is obligated by Torah law to recite a blessing, **one recites a blessing afterward, but one does not recite a blessing beforehand,** because the blessing recited prior to eating is a requirement by rabbinic law. **And** in all of these instances **Rabbi Yehuda says: He recites a blessing beforehand and thereafter** in both the case of *Shema* and in the case of food.

גמ׳ אָמַר רָבִינָא, זֹאת אוֹמֶרֶת: הִרְהוּר כְּדִבּוּר דָּמֵי. דְּאִי סָלְקָא דַּעְתָּךְ לָאו כְּדִבּוּר דָּמֵי, לָמָּה מְהַרְהֵר?

**GEMARA** **Ravina said: That is to say,** from the mishna that **contemplation is tantamount to speech.**[H] **As if it would enter your mind that it is not tantamount to speech,** then **why** does one who is impure because of a seminal emission **contemplate?** It must be that it is tantamount to speech.

אֶלָּא מַאי הִרְהוּר כְּדִבּוּר דָּמֵי, יוֹצִיא בִּשְׂפָתָיו!

The Gemara rejects this: **But what** are you saying, that **contemplation is tantamount to speech?** Then, if one who is impure because of a seminal emission is permitted to contemplate, why does he not **utter** the words **with his lips?**

כִּדְאַשְׁכְּחַן בְּסִינַי.

The Gemara answers: **As we found at** Mount **Sinai.** There one who had sexual relations with a woman was required to immerse himself before receiving the Torah, which was spoken and not merely contemplated. Here, too, it was decreed that one who was impure due to a seminal emission may not recite matters of Torah out loud until he immerses himself.

וְרַב חִסְדָּא אָמַר: הִרְהוּר לָאו כְּדִבּוּר דָּמֵי. דְּאִי סָלְקָא דַעְתָּךְ הִרְהוּר כְּדִבּוּר דָּמֵי – יוֹצִיא בִּשְׂפָתָיו!

**And Rav Ḥisda said** that the opposite conclusion should be drawn from the mishna: **Contemplation is not tantamount to speech, as if it would enter your mind** that **contemplation is tantamount to speech,** then one who is impure because of a seminal emission should *ab initio*, **utter** *Shema* **with his lips.**

אֶלָּא מַאי – הִרְהוּר לָאו כְּדִבּוּר דָּמֵי, לָמָּה מְהַרְהֵר? – אָמַר רַבִּי אֶלְעָזָר: כְּדֵי שֶׁלֹּא יְהוּ כָּל הָעוֹלָם עוֹסְקִין בּוֹ וְהוּא יוֹשֵׁב וּבָטֵל.

The Gemara challenges this argument: **But what** are you saying, that **contemplation is not tantamount to speech?** If so, **why does he contemplate? Rabbi Elazar said: So that** a situation **will not** arise **where everyone is engaged in** reciting *Shema* **and he sits idly** by.

וְנִגְרוֹס בְּפִרְקָא אַחֲרִינָא! – אָמַר רַב אַדָּא בַּר אַהֲבָה: בְּדָבָר שֶׁהַצִּבּוּר עוֹסְקִין בּוֹ.

The Gemara asks: If that is the only purpose, **let him study another chapter** and not specifically *Shema* or one of the blessings. **Rav Adda bar Ahava said:** It is fitting that one engage **in a matter in which the community is engaged.**



וַהֲרֵי תְּפִלָּה דְּדָבָר שֶׁהַצִּבּוּר עֲסוּקִין בּוֹ, וּתְנַן: הָיָה עוֹמֵד בִּתְפִלָּה וְנִזְכַּר שֶׁהוּא בַּעַל קֶרִי – לֹא יַפְסִיק אֶלָּא יְקַצֵּר, טַעְמָא דְּאַתְחֵיל, הָא לָא אַתְחֵיל – לֹא יַתְחִיל!

The Gemara challenges: **And prayer,** which is also **a matter in which the community is engaged, and we learned** in the mishna: **One who was standing in prayer and remembered that he is one** who experienced **a seminal emission** and did not yet immerse himself **should not interrupt** his prayer, **rather he should abridge it.** The Gemara infers: **The reason is because he** already **began** to pray; **however, if he did not** yet **begin,** then **he should not begin,** even by means of contemplation.

שָׁאנֵי תְּפִלָּה, דְּלֵית בָּהּ מַלְכוּת שָׁמַיִם. וַהֲרֵי בִּרְכַּת הַמָּזוֹן לְאַחֲרָיו, דְּלֵית בָּהּ מַלְכוּת שָׁמַיִם, וּתְנַן: עַל הַמָּזוֹן מְבָרֵךְ לְאַחֲרָיו וְאֵינוֹ מְבָרֵךְ לְפָנָיו! אֶלָּא: קְרִיאַת שְׁמַע וּבִרְכַּת הַמָּזוֹן – דְּאוֹרָיְיתָא, וּתְפִלָּה – דְּרַבָּנַן.

The Gemara responds: **Prayer is different** in **that it does not contain** the acceptance of the yoke of **the kingdom of Heaven.** The Gemara rejects this: **And Grace after Meals does not contain** the acceptance of the yoke of **the kingdom of Heaven, and** yet **we learned** in the mishna: **Over food, one recites a blessing afterward, but does not recite a blessing beforehand. Rather,** the differences must be explained otherwise: **The recitation of** ***Shema*** **and Grace after Meals** are both mitzvot **by Torah law, while prayer** is only **by rabbinic law.** Therefore, one who is impure need not pray.

אָמַר רַב יְהוּדָה: מִנַּיִן לְבִרְכַּת הַמָּזוֹן לְאַחֲרֶיהָ מִן הַתּוֹרָה – שֶׁנֶּאֱמַר: ״וְאָכַלְתָּ וְשָׂבָעְתָּ וּבֵרַכְתָּ״.

**Rav Yehuda said: From where is** the mitzva **by Torah law** to recite **Grace after Meals,** derived? **As it is stated: "And you shall eat and be satisfied and bless the Lord your God"** (Deuteronomy 8:10).

מִנַּיִן לְבִרְכַּת הַתּוֹרָה לְפָנֶיהָ מִן הַתּוֹרָה – שֶׁנֶּאֱמַר: ״כִּי שֵׁם ה׳ אֶקְרָא הָבוּ גֹדֶל לֵאלֹהֵינוּ״.

And **from where is** the mitzva **by Torah law** to recite **the blessing over the Torah before it** is read, derived? **As it is stated: "When I proclaim the Lord's name, give glory to our God"** (Deuteronomy 32:3), meaning that before one proclaims the Lord's name by reading the Torah, he must give glory to God.

אָמַר רַבִּי יוֹחָנָן: לָמַדְנוּ בִּרְכַּת הַתּוֹרָה לְאַחֲרֶיהָ מִן בִּרְכַּת הַמָּזוֹן מִקַּל וָחוֹמֶר, וּבִרְכַּת הַמָּזוֹן לְפָנֶיהָ מִן בִּרְכַּת הַתּוֹרָה מִקַּל וָחוֹמֶר; בִּרְכַּת הַתּוֹרָה לְאַחֲרֶיהָ מִן בִּרְכַּת הַמָּזוֹן מִקַּל וָחוֹמֶר: וּמָה מָזוֹן שֶׁאֵין טָעוּן לְפָנָיו – טָעוּן לְאַחֲרָיו, תּוֹרָה שֶׁטְּעוּנָה לְפָנֶיהָ – אֵינוֹ דִּין שֶׁטְּעוּנָה לְאַחֲרֶיהָ; וּבִרְכַּת הַמָּזוֹן לְפָנֶיהָ מִן בִּרְכַּת הַתּוֹרָה מִקַּל וָחוֹמֶר: וּמָה תּוֹרָה שֶׁאֵין טְעוּנָה לְאַחֲרֶיהָ – טְעוּנָה לְפָנֶיהָ, מָזוֹן שֶׁהוּא טָעוּן לְאַחֲרָיו – אֵינוֹ דִּין שֶׁיְּהֵא טָעוּן לְפָנָיו.

**Rabbi Yoḥanan said: We derived** that one must recite **the blessing over the Torah after** it is read **from Grace after Meals** by means of an ***a fortiori*** **inference.**[N] **And** we derive the obligation to recite **a blessing before** partaking of **food** from **the blessing over the Torah** by means of an ***a fortiori*** **inference. The blessing over the Torah after** it is read **from Grace after Meals** by means of an ***a fortiori*** **inference: Food, which does not require a blessing beforehand** by Torah law, **requires a blessing afterward; Torah, which requires** a blessing **beforehand, is it not right that it requires** a blessing **afterward? And** similarly: **The blessing before** partaking of **food** from **the blessing over the Torah** by means of an ***a fortiori*** **inference: Torah, which requires no** blessing **afterward** by Torah law, **requires** a blessing **beforehand; food, which requires** a blessing **afterward, is it not right that it requires** a blessing **beforehand?**

NOTES

**Deriving the blessing over the Torah after it is read from Grace after Meals by means of an *a fortiori* inference** – לִימּוּד בִּרְכַּת הַתּוֹרָה וּבִרְכַּת הַמָּזוֹן מִקַּל וָחוֹמֶר: The *a fortiori* inference is a form of logical proof. In this example, there are two *halakhot* with regard to which there is incomplete information. The attempt is to prove that each can help fill in the missing details of the other. However, this comparative proof is based on the tacit presumption that one *halakha* is consistently more stringent than the other and consequently an *a fortiori* inference can be drawn between them. Refutation of that inference is accomplished by demonstrating that the two *halakhot* are not actually comparable and that there are inconsistencies in terms of their relative stringency and leniency. Although the refutation does not prove that the conclusions reached are incorrect, it does invalidate the means used to arrive at those conclusions.

אִיכָּא לְמִפְרַךְ: מָה לְמָזוֹן – שֶׁכֵּן נֶהֱנֶה, וּמָה לְתוֹרָה – שֶׁכֵּן חַיֵּי עוֹלָם! וְעוֹד, תְּנַן: עַל הַמָּזוֹן מְבָרֵךְ לְאַחֲרָיו וְאֵינוֹ מְבָרֵךְ לְפָנָיו! תְּיוּבְתָּא.

The Gemara notes: The logic of this *a fortiori* inference **can be refuted: What** is true with regard **to food, where one derives pleasure** from eating,[N] is not true with regard to matters which offer no bodily pleasure. Therefore, the blessing over the Torah cannot be derived from the blessing over food. **And** similarly: **What** is true with regard to **Torah, that** provides **eternal life** to those who engage in its study, is not true with regard to matters that do not provide eternal life. Therefore, the blessing before partaking of food cannot be derived from the blessing over the Torah. **Furthermore, we learned** in the mishna: **Over food,** one who is impure due to a seminal emission **recites a blessing afterward, but does not recite a blessing beforehand.** The mishna does not derive the blessing recited before a meal from the blessing recited over Torah. Consequently, this is a **conclusive refutation** of Rabbi Yoḥanan's statement.

אָמַר רַב יְהוּדָה סָפֵק קָרָא קְרִיאַת שְׁמַע סָפֵק לֹא קָרָא – אֵינוֹ חוֹזֵר וְקוֹרֵא, סָפֵק אָמַר "אֱמֶת וְיַצִּיב", סָפֵק לֹא אָמַר – חוֹזֵר וְאוֹמֵר "אֱמֶת וְיַצִּיב". מַאי טַעְמָא – קְרִיאַת שְׁמַע דְּרַבָּנַן, "אֱמֶת וְיַצִּיב" דְּאוֹרָיְיתָא. –

**Rav Yehuda said:** One who is **uncertain whether he recited *Shema* or whether he did not recite** it **does not recite it again.** However, one who is **uncertain whether he recited: True and Firm** [***emet veyatziv***], the blessing that follows *Shema* in the morning, **must recite *emet veyatziv* again. What is the reason** for this? In his opinion, the obligation to recite ***Shema*** is only **by rabbinic law.** His ruling follows the principle that in cases of uncertainty involving rabbinic law, the ruling is lenient and he need not repeat it. However, since ***emet veyatziv*** is primarily a commemoration of the exodus from Egypt, it is a mitzva **by Torah law,**[N] and, in cases of uncertainty involving Torah law, the ruling is stringent and he must repeat it.

מְתִיב רַב יוֹסֵף: "וּבְשָׁכְבְּךָ וּבְקוּמֶךָ"! – אֲמַר לֵיהּ אַבָּיֵי: הַהוּא בְּדִבְרֵי תוֹרָה כְּתִיב.

**Rav Yosef raises an objection:** How can you say that the obligation to recite *Shema* is only by rabbinic law when it is explicitly written: "And you shall recite them to your children and speak of them when you sit in your home and when you walk by the way, **when you lie down and when you rise"** (Deuteronomy 6:7)? **Abaye said to him: That** verse **was written with regard to matters of Torah.** One need not interpret the verse in the conventional manner, as obligating the recitation of *Shema*, but rather as referring to the general obligation to study Torah.

תְּנַן: בַּעַל קֶרִי מְהַרְהֵר בְּלִבּוֹ וְאֵינוֹ מְבָרֵךְ לֹא לְפָנֶיהָ וְלֹא לְאַחֲרֶיהָ, וְעַל הַמָּזוֹן – מְבָרֵךְ לְאַחֲרָיו וְאֵינוֹ מְבָרֵךְ לְפָנָיו.

From here, the Gemara attempts to resolve this issue by citing proof from the mishna. **We learned** in the mishna: **One who experienced a seminal emission** may **contemplate** *Shema* **in his heart, but neither recites the blessings preceding** *Shema*, **nor the blessings thereafter. Over food** which, after partaking, one is obligated by Torah law to recite a blessing, **one recites a blessing thereafter, but not beforehand.**

וְאִי סָלְקָא דַּעְתָּךְ "אֱמֶת וְיַצִּיב" דְּאוֹרָיְיתָא – לְבָרוּךְ לְאַחֲרֶיהָ!

**And if it would enter your mind** that the obligation to recite ***emet veyatziv* is by Torah law, let him recite the blessing after** *Shema*. Since he does not recite the blessing, apparently, he is exempt.

מַאי טַעְמָא מְבָרֵךְ – אִי מִשּׁוּם יְצִיאַת מִצְרַיִם – הָא אַדְכַּר לֵיהּ בִּקְרִיאַת שְׁמַע.

The Gemara refutes this: **What is the reason that he recites** *emet veyatziv*? **If** it is **because** it deals primarily with **the exodus from Egypt, wasn't it** already **mentioned in the recitation of *Shema*,** in the portion of the ritual fringes?

וְנֵימָא הָא וְלָא לִבְעֵי הָא! – קְרִיאַת שְׁמַע עֲדִיפָא, דְּאִית בַּהּ תַּרְתֵּי.

The Gemara challenges: **And let him say this,** *emet veyatziv*, **and he will not need** to recite **that,** *Shema*. The Gemara responds: While one may commemorate the exodus from Egypt in either *Shema* or *emet veyatziv*, ***Shema* is preferable as it contains two** elements, both a commemoration of the exodus and an acceptance of the yoke of the kingdom of Heaven.

וְרַבִּי אֶלְעָזָר אָמַר: סָפֵק קָרָא קְרִיאַת שְׁמַע סָפֵק לֹא קָרָא – חוֹזֵר וְקוֹרֵא קְרִיאַת שְׁמַע, סָפֵק הִתְפַּלֵּל סָפֵק לֹא הִתְפַּלֵּל – אֵינוֹ חוֹזֵר וּמִתְפַּלֵּל. וְרַבִּי יוֹחָנָן אָמַר: וּלְוַאי שֶׁיִּתְפַּלֵּל אָדָם כׇּל הַיּוֹם כּוּלּוֹ.

**And Rabbi Elazar said** a different opinion: One who is **uncertain whether he recited *Shema***[H] or **whether he did not recite *Shema*, must recite *Shema* again.**[N] According to his opinion, there is a mitzva by Torah law to recite *Shema*. However, if one is **uncertain whether he prayed**[H] **or whether he did not pray, he does not pray again,** as the obligation to pray is by rabbinic law. **And Rabbi Yoḥanan said:** He must pray again; **if only a person would pray throughout the entire day.**[NH]

## NOTES

**What is true with regard to food, where one derives pleasure from eating – מָה לְמָזוֹן – שֶׁכֵּן נֶהֱנֶה:** The distinction between food and Torah is not an arbitrary one and can be understood on a more profound level. The Gemara stated: What is true with regard to food, where one derives pleasure from eating, etc. Because that pleasure remains with him after the meal, it is reasonable that one would be required to recite a blessing after eating. And, the Gemara stated: What is true with regard to Torah that provides eternal life, etc. Therefore, one would be required to prepare himself beforehand, by reciting a blessing (*Shitta Mekubbetzet*).

***Emet veyatziv* is a mitzva by Torah law – "אֱמֶת וְיַצִּיב" דְּאוֹרָיְיתָא:** This does not mean that the formula of *emet veyatziv* is by Torah law; rather it means that commemorating the exodus from Egypt, which is a central theme in *emet veyatziv*, is a mitzva by Torah law (*Talmidei Rabbeinu Yona*). One does not fulfill any mitzva of commemoration by reciting *Shema*, other than the commemoration of the exodus from Egypt in the third paragraph. Consequently, one who recited the third paragraph of *Shema* is no longer obligated by Torah law to recite *emet veyatziv*.

**One who is uncertain whether or not he recited *Shema* recites it again – סָפֵק קָרָא קְרִיאַת שְׁמַע – חוֹזֵר:** Some hold that Rabbi Elazar's opinion need not rely on the opinion that the reciting *Shema* is an obligation by Torah law. Even if the obligation is only by rabbinic law, it warrants repetition because it includes the acceptance of the yoke of the Kingdom of Heaven (*Tosefot HaRosh*).

**If only a person would pray throughout the entire day – וּלְוַאי שֶׁיִּתְפַּלֵּל אָדָם כׇּל הַיּוֹם כּוּלּוֹ:** This statement is based on a specific understanding of the essence of prayer, and the *halakha* combines the statements of Rabbi Yoḥanan and Shmuel. If prayers are really based on the sacrifices then there is clearly no room for an added prayer, as that would be tantamount to adding a sacrifice that is not required (Rif, *Tosefot Rabbi Yitzḥak*). That is, indeed, why there can be no voluntary communal prayer. However, introducing a novel element to the prayer transforms the prayer into a type of free-will offering, which can be offered at any time in addition to the required daily sacrifices. Therefore, the *halakha*, based on the opinion of Rav Hai Gaon, is that one may only add prayers through introduction of a new element.

## HALAKHA

**One who is uncertain whether or not he recited *Shema* – סָפֵק קָרָא קְרִיאַת שְׁמַע:** If one is uncertain whether or not he recited *Shema*, he must recite it again along with its accompanying blessings, because reciting *Shema* is an obligation by Torah law. The *halakha* is in accordance with the opinion of Rabbi Elazar, as the bulk of the *mishnayot*, *baraitot*, and statements in the Gemara are in accordance with his opinion (Rambam *Sefer Ahava, Hilkhot Keriat Shema* 2:13; *Shulḥan Arukh, Oraḥ Ḥayyim*, 67).

**One who is uncertain whether or not he prayed – סָפֵק הִתְפַּלֵּל:** One who is uncertain whether or not he prayed must pray again and is not required to introduce a new element to his prayer. When doing so, he stipulates: If I did not pray then, this prayer will fulfill my obligation; however, if I already prayed, this will be an added prayer (*Magen Avraham*). The *halakha* is in accordance with the opinion of Rabbi Yoḥanan who said: If only a person would pray throughout the entire day. Although prayer is not a Torah obligation, one who is uncertain whether or not he prayed may introduce a new element to his prayer and pray, as Rav Yehuda does not really disagree with Rabbi Yoḥanan (Rambam *Sefer Ahava, Hilkhot Tefilla* 10:6; *Shulḥan Arukh, Oraḥ Ḥayyim* 107:1).

**If only a person would pray throughout the entire day – וּלְוַאי שֶׁיִּתְפַּלֵּל אָדָם כׇּל הַיּוֹם כּוּלּוֹ:** One is always permitted to recite a voluntary prayer, as long as he introduces a new element to that prayer, as per the opinion of Rabbi Yoḥanan (Rambam *Sefer Ahava, Hilkhot Tefilla* 10:6, *Shulḥan Arukh, Oraḥ Ḥayyim* 107:1).

וְאָמַר רַב יְהוּדָה אָמַר שְׁמוּאֵל: הָיָה עוֹמֵד בִּתְפִלָּה וְנִזְכַּר שֶׁהִתְפַּלֵּל – פּוֹסֵק, וַאֲפִילּוּ בְּאֶמְצַע בְּרָכָה. – אִינִי? וְהָאָמַר רַב נַחְמָן: כִּי הֲוֵינַן בֵּי רַבָּה בַּר אֲבוּהּ, בְּעַן מִינֵּיהּ, הָנֵי בְּנֵי בֵּי רַב דְּטָעוּ וּמַדְכְּרִי דְּחוֹל בְּשַׁבָּת, מַהוּ שֶׁיִּגְמְרוּ? וַאֲמַר לַן: גּוֹמְרִין כׇּל אוֹתָהּ בְּרָכָה!

**And Rav Yehuda said** that **Shmuel said: One who was standing in prayer and remembered that he** already **prayed**[H] **must interrupt** his prayer, **even in the middle of a blessing.** The Gemara challenges this: **Is that so? Didn't Rav Naḥman say: When we were in the school of Rabba bar Avuh we raised a dilemma before him: Those students in the school of Rav** who **mistakenly recited** a blessing from the **weekday** *Amida* **on Shabbat,**[H] **what is** the ruling with regards to **completing** the weekday prayer? **And** Rabba bar Avuh **said to us:** The ruling is that **one must complete that entire blessing.** How then did Rav Yehuda say that one must interrupt his prayer even in the middle of a blessing?

הָכִי הָשְׁתָּא! הָתָם – גַּבְרָא בַּר חִיּוּבָא הוּא, וְרַבָּנַן הוּא דְּלָא אַטְרְחוּהוּ מִשּׁוּם כְּבוֹד שַׁבָּת, אֲבָל הָכָא – הָא צַלֵּי לֵיהּ.

The Gemara rejects this: **How can you compare** the two cases? **There,** on Shabbat, **the individual is one who is obligated** and should actually recite all eighteen blessings, **and it is the Sages who did not impose upon him**[N] **in deference to Shabbat** and instituted an abridged formula. **But here, didn't he** already **pray?** Therefore he can stop, even in the middle of a blessing.

וְאָמַר רַב יְהוּדָה אָמַר שְׁמוּאֵל: הִתְפַּלֵּל וְנִכְנַס לְבֵית הַכְּנֶסֶת וּמָצָא צִבּוּר שֶׁמִּתְפַּלְּלִין, אִם יָכוֹל לְחַדֵּשׁ בָּהּ דָּבָר – יַחֲזוֹר וְיִתְפַּלֵּל, וְאִם לָאו – אַל יַחֲזוֹר וְיִתְפַּלֵּל.

**And Rav Yehuda said** that **Shmuel said:** One who already **prayed, and** then **enters a synagogue to find a congregation** standing and **praying,**[H] **if he is able to introduce a new element,** an expression or request, into his prayer, **he may pray again, and if not, he may not pray again.**

וּצְרִיכָא: דְּאִי אַשְׁמְעִינַן קַמַּיְיתָא, הָנֵי מִילֵּי – יָחִיד וְיָחִיד,

The Gemara notes: This concept is identical to Shmuel's previous statement regarding one who already prayed that he need not pray again. Nevertheless, both statements are **necessary. If he had taught us the first** *halakha,* we would have said that **applies only** to a case involving **an individual** who prayed **and an individual** who began to repeat the prayer,

Perek **III**
Daf **21** Amud **b**

אוֹ צִבּוּר וְצִבּוּר, אֲבָל יָחִיד לְגַבֵּי צִבּוּר כְּמַאן דְּלָא צַלֵּי דָּמֵי – קָמַשְׁמַע לַן; וְאִי אַשְׁמְעִינַן הָכָא – מִשּׁוּם דְּלָא אַתְחִיל בָּהּ, אֲבָל הָתָם דְּאַתְחִיל בָּהּ, אֵימָא לָא – צְרִיכָא.

**or** a case where he prayed as part of **a congregation and** began to repeat it as part of **a congregation; however,** in a case where he initially prayed by himself and subsequently joined the congregation at the venue where it was praying, we might have said that **an individual vis-à-vis the congregation is** considered **as one who has not prayed.** Therefore, **he taught us** that in this case, too, one may not repeat the prayer. **And,** on the other hand, **if he had taught us here** only with regard to one who entered a synagogue, we would have thought that the reason he may not pray again is **because he did not** yet **begin** to recite the prayer, **but there, in the case where he** already **began** to recite the prayer, **say** that this is **not** the case and he may continue to repeat the prayer. Therefore, both statements are **necessary.**

אָמַר רַב הוּנָא: הַנִּכְנָס לְבֵית הַכְּנֶסֶת וּמָצָא צִבּוּר שֶׁמִּתְפַּלְּלִין, אִם יָכוֹל לְהַתְחִיל וְלִגְמוֹר עַד שֶׁלֹּא יַגִּיעַ שְׁלִיחַ צִבּוּר לְ״מוֹדִים״ – יִתְפַּלֵּל, וְאִם לָאו – אַל יִתְפַּלֵּל; רַבִּי יְהוֹשֻׁעַ בֶּן לֵוִי אָמַר: אִם יָכוֹל לְהַתְחִיל וְלִגְמוֹר עַד שֶׁלֹּא יַגִּיעַ שְׁלִיחַ צִבּוּר לִקְדוּשָּׁה – יִתְפַּלֵּל, וְאִם לָאו – אַל יִתְפַּלֵּל.

**Rav Huna said: One who** did not yet pray and **enters a synagogue and found that the congregation is** in the midst of **reciting the** *Amida* **prayer,**[H] **if he is able to begin and complete** his own prayer **before the prayer leader reaches** the blessing of **thanksgiving** [***modim***], **he should** begin to **pray, and, if not, he should not** begin to **pray. Rabbi Yehoshua ben Levi said: If he is able to begin and complete** his prayer **before the prayer leader reaches sanctification** [***kedusha***],[N] **then he should** begin to **pray. If not, then he should not** begin to **pray.**

HALAKHA

**One who was standing in prayer and remembered that he already prayed – הָיָה עוֹמֵד בִּתְפִלָּה וְנִזְכַּר שֶׁהִתְפַּלֵּל:** One who began praying under the mistaken assumption that he had not yet prayed, and then realized that he had, stops praying immediately, even if he is in the middle of a blessing and even if he is able to introduce a new element to his prayer. The *halakha* is in accordance with the opinion of Rav Yehuda because Rabbi Yoḥanan's statement refers only to situations where one is aware that he is praying an added, rather than a mandatory prayer. One is certainly not permitted to recite two mandatory prayers (*Shulḥan Arukh, Oraḥ Ḥayyim* 107:1).

**Who mistakenly recited a blessing from the weekday *Amida* on Shabbat – דְּטָעוּ וּמַדְכְּרִי דְּחוֹל בְּשַׁבָּת:** One who was reciting the morning, afternoon, or evening prayer on Shabbat and mistakenly began to recite a blessing from the corresponding weekday *Amida*, completes the blessing that he began and then continues with the Shabbat prayer, in accordance with the opinion of Rabba bar Avuh. If one began to recite a weekday blessing during the additional prayer, some say that he does the same as he does in the rest of the Shabbat prayers. Others say that he stops immediately and continues with the additional prayer. The later decisors of *halakha* ruled in accordance with the latter opinion to avoid a possible blessing in vain (*Mishna Berura*; Rambam *Sefer Ahava, Hilkhot Tefilla* 10:7; *Shulḥan Arukh, Oraḥ Ḥayyim* 268:2).

**One who already prayed and then enters a synagogue to find a congregation standing and praying – הִתְפַּלֵּל וְנִכְנַס לְבֵית הַכְּנֶסֶת וּמָצָא צִבּוּר שֶׁמִּתְפַּלְּלִין:** One who already prayed, enters a synagogue and finds the congregation praying, is permitted to recite another prayer with them if he is able to introduce a new element to it, in accordance with the opinion of Rabbi Yehuda (see Rambam *Sefer Ahava, Hilkhot Tefilla* 1:9, and *Shulḥan Arukh, Oraḥ Ḥayyim* 107:1).

NOTES

**And it is the Sages who did not impose upon him – וְרַבָּנַן הוּא דְּלָא אַטְרְחוּהוּ:** According to this opinion, Shabbat prayer is an abbreviated version of the weekday prayer, and therefore one who recites the weekday *Amida* on Shabbat and includes mention of Shabbat therein, has, for all intents and purposes, arrived at the essence of the prayer. Consequently, some hold that one who mistakenly begins a weekday blessing in the additional prayer on Shabbat stops immediately, as there is no connection between weekday blessings and the additional prayer (Ra'avad).

HALAKHA

**One who enters a synagogue and found the congregation reciting the *Amida* prayer – הַנִּכְנָס לְבֵית הַכְּנֶסֶת וּמָצָא צִבּוּר שֶׁמִּתְפַּלְּלִין וכו׳:** One who enters a synagogue and finds the congregation reciting the *Amida* prayer, if he is able to conclude his prayer before the prayer leader recites *kedusha* or *kaddish*, he may begin to pray. If not, he should wait until after the prayer leader recites *kedusha* or *kaddish* before beginning his prayer, as long as by doing so, the deadline for reciting that prayer does not pass. The *halakha* was ruled in accordance with the opinion of Rabbi Yehoshua ben Levi, who was greater than Rav Huna. In addition, the statement of Rav Adda bar Ahava and the talmudic discussion support his opinion. However, if he entered the synagogue after *kedusha*, if he is able to conclude his prayer before the prayer leader begins the blessing of thanksgiving, he may begin to pray, as, with regard to that case, there is no dispute between Rabbi Yehoshua ben Levi and Rav Huna (Rambam *Sefer Ahava, Hilkhot Tefilla* 10:16, *Shulḥan Arukh, Oraḥ Ḥayyim* 109:1).

NOTES

***Kedusha* – קְדוּשָּׁה:** Generally, the term *kedusha* refers to the sanctification recited in the prayer leader's repetition of the *Amida* prayer. However, there are additional passages that fall under that rubric, e.g., the sanctification recited in the first blessing accompanying *Shema* in the morning as well as the sanctification included in the prayer: "A Redeemer will come to Zion [*uva leTziyyon*]," recited at the conclusion of the service. The *ge'onim* debated whether an individual is permitted to recite those passages. Furthermore, there were those who asserted that the *kedusha* in the *Amida* prayer, since it is merely a series of verses, is not considered a sacred matter and may be recited by an individual (*Tosefot Rabbi Yehuda HaḤasid, Tosefot HaRosh*).

בְּמַאי קָא מִפַּלְגִי? מָר סָבַר: יָחִיד אוֹמֵר קְדוּשָּׁה; וּמָר סָבַר: אֵין יָחִיד אוֹמֵר קְדוּשָּׁה.

The Gemara clarifies: **With regard to what do they disagree?** The basis for their dispute is that one **Sage,** Rav Huna, **holds: An individual** is permitted to **recite *kedusha*** on his own, so he need not insist on reciting it along with the prayer leader; **and** the other **Sage,** Rabbi Yehoshua ben Levi, **holds** that **an individual may not recite *kedusha*** alone, and, therefore he is required to complete his prayer before the communal prayer leader reaches *kedusha*.

וְכֵן אָמַר רַב אַדָּא בַּר אַהֲבָה: מִנַּיִן שֶׁאֵין הַיָּחִיד אוֹמֵר קְדוּשָּׁה – שֶׁנֶּאֱמַר: ״וְנִקְדַּשְׁתִּי בְּתוֹךְ בְּנֵי יִשְׂרָאֵל״ – כָּל דָּבָר שֶׁבִּקְדוּשָּׁה לֹא יְהֵא פָּחוֹת מֵעֲשָׂרָה.

**Similarly, Rav Adda bar Ahava stated,** in accordance with the second opinion: **From where is it derived that an individual may not recite *kedusha*** alone? **As it is stated: "And I shall be hallowed among the children of Israel"** (Leviticus 22:32), **any expression of sanctity may not be** recited in a quorum of **fewer than ten** men.[H]

מַאי מַשְׁמַע? דְּתָנֵי רַבְּנַאי אֲחוּהּ דְּרַבִּי חִיָּיא בַּר אַבָּא: אַתְיָא ״תּוֹךְ״ ״תּוֹךְ״. כְּתִיב הָכָא: ״וְנִקְדַּשְׁתִּי בְּתוֹךְ בְּנֵי יִשְׂרָאֵל״ וּכְתִיב הָתָם: ״הִבָּדְלוּ מִתּוֹךְ הָעֵדָה הַזֹּאת״, מַה לְּהַלָּן עֲשָׂרָה, אַף כָּאן עֲשָׂרָה.

The Gemara asks: **How is this inferred** from that verse? The Gemara responds: This must be understood in light of a *baraita*, **which was taught by Rabbenai, the brother of Rabbi Ḥiyya bar Abba: It is inferred** by means of a verbal analogy [*gezera shava*] between the words **among, among.**[N] **Here it is written: "And I shall be hallowed among the children of Israel," and there,** regarding Korah's congregation, **it is written "Separate yourselves from among this congregation"** (Numbers 16:21). **Just as there** among connotes **ten, so too here,** among connotes **ten.** The connotation of ten associated with the word among written in the portion of Korah is, in turn, derived by means of another verbal analogy between the word congregation written there and the word congregation written in reference to the ten spies who slandered Eretz Yisrael: "How long shall I bear with this evil congregation?" (Numbers 14:27). Consequently, among the congregation there must be at least ten.

וּדְכוּלֵּי עָלְמָא מִיהַת מִפְסַק לָא פָּסֵיק.

**And,** in any case, **everyone** agrees that **one may not interrupt** his prayer in order to respond to *kedusha*.

אִיבַּעְיָא לְהוּ: מַהוּ לְהַפְסִיק לְ״יְהֵא שְׁמוֹ הַגָּדוֹל מְבוֹרָךְ״? כִּי אֲתָא רַב דִּימִי אָמַר, רַבִּי יְהוּדָה וְרַבִּי שִׁמְעוֹן תַּלְמִידֵי דְּרַבִּי יוֹחָנָן אָמְרִי: לַכֹּל אֵין מַפְסִיקִין, חוּץ מִן ״יְהֵא שְׁמוֹ הַגָּדוֹל מְבוֹרָךְ״, שֶׁאֲפִילּוּ עוֹסֵק בְּמַעֲשֵׂה מֶרְכָּבָה – פּוֹסֵק. וְלֵית הִלְכְתָא כְּוָתֵיהּ.

However, **a dilemma was raised** before the Sages of the yeshiva: **What is** the ruling? Is one permitted **to interrupt**[H] his prayer in order **to** recite: **"May His great name be blessed"** in *kaddish*? **When Rav Dimi came** from Eretz Yisrael to Babylonia, **he said: Rabbi Yehuda and Rabbi Shimon, disciples of Rabbi Yoḥanan, said: One may not interrupt** his prayer **for anything, except for: "May His great name be blessed," as even** if one was **engaged in** the exalted study of the **Act of the** Divine **Chariot** [*Ma'aseh Merkava*] (see Ezekiel 1) **he stops** to recite it. However, the Gemara concludes: **The *halakha* is not in accordance with his** opinion.[N]

״רַבִּי יְהוּדָה אוֹמֵר, מְבָרֵךְ לִפְנֵיהֶם וּלְאַחֲרֵיהֶם״. לְמֵימְרָא דְּקָסָבַר רַבִּי יְהוּדָה בַּעַל קֶרִי מוּתָּר בְּדִבְרֵי תוֹרָה? וְהָאָמַר רַבִּי יְהוֹשֻׁעַ בֶּן לֵוִי: מִנַּיִן לְבַעַל קֶרִי שֶׁאָסוּר בְּדִבְרֵי תוֹרָה – שֶׁנֶּאֱמַר: ״וְהוֹדַעְתָּם לְבָנֶיךָ וְלִבְנֵי בָנֶיךָ״, וְסָמֵיךְ לֵיהּ: ״יוֹם אֲשֶׁר עָמַדְתָּ וגו׳״ – מַה לְּהַלָּן בַּעֲלֵי קְרָיִין אֲסוּרִין, אַף כָּאן – בַּעֲלֵי קְרָיִין אֲסוּרִין!

We learned in the mishna that **Rabbi Yehuda says** with regard to one who experiences a seminal emission; **he recites a blessing beforehand and afterward** in both the case of *Shema* and in the case of food. The Gemara asks: **Is that to say that Rabbi Yehuda holds that one who experienced a seminal emission is permitted** to engage **in matters of Torah? Didn't Rabbi Yehoshua ben Levi say: From where** in the Torah is it derived **that one who experiences a seminal emission is prohibited from** engaging **in matters of Torah?**[N] **As it is stated:** "Just take heed and guard your soul diligently lest you forget the things your eyes have seen, and lest they depart from your heart, for all the days of your life, **and you shall impart them to your children and your children's children"** (Deuteronomy 4:9), from which we derive, among other things, the obligation to study Torah. **And, juxtaposed to it,** is the verse: **"The day that you stood** before the Lord your God at Horeb" (Deuteronomy 4:10). This juxtaposition teaches us that **just as below,** at the revelation at Mount Sinai, **those who experienced a seminal emission were prohibited** and were commanded to refrain from relations with their wives and immerse themselves, **so too here,** throughout the generations, **those who experience a seminal emission are prohibited** from engaging in Torah study.

וְכִי תֵּימָא: רַבִּי יְהוּדָה לָא דָּרֵישׁ סְמוּכִים, וְהָאָמַר רַב יוֹסֵף: אֲפִילּוּ מַאן דְּלָא דָּרֵישׁ סְמוּכִים בְּכָל הַתּוֹרָה – בְּמִשְׁנֵה תוֹרָה דָּרֵישׁ. דְּהָא רַבִּי יְהוּדָה לָא דָּרֵישׁ סְמוּכִין בְּכָל הַתּוֹרָה כּוּלָּהּ, וּבְמִשְׁנֵה תוֹרָה דָּרֵישׁ.

**And if you say that Rabbi Yehuda does not derive homiletic interpretations from juxtaposed** verses, **didn't Rav Yosef** already **say: Even one who does not derive homiletic interpretations from juxtaposed** verses throughout **the entire Torah,** nevertheless, **derives them in Deuteronomy [*Mishne Torah*],**[N] **as Rabbi Yehuda does not derive homiletic interpretations from juxtaposed** verses **throughout the entire Torah and he does derive them in *Mishne Torah*.**

### HALAKHA

**Any expression of sanctity may not be recited in a quorum of fewer than ten men – כָּל דָּבָר שֶׁבִּקְדוּשָּׁה לֹא יְהֵא פָּחוֹת מֵעֲשָׂרָה:** All matters of sanctity, e.g., *barekhu*, *kaddish*, and *kedusha* are only recited in the presence of ten men who have reached majority (Rambam *Sefer Ahava, Hilkhot Tefilla* 8:6, *Shulḥan Arukh, Oraḥ Ḥayyim* 55:1).

**What is the ruling? Is one permitted to interrupt, etc. – מַהוּ לְהַפְסִיק וכו׳:** It is prohibited to interrupt the *Amida* prayer for any sacred matter. However, if one hears *kaddish* he must remain silent during the recitation of the passage: May His great name be blessed for ever and time, as well as during the *barekhu* and *kedusha* prayers and he must focus his heart on the communal prayer leader as he recites them (*Shulḥan Arukh, Oraḥ Ḥayyim* 104:7).

### NOTES

**Among, among – ״תּוֹךְ״ ״תּוֹךְ״:** This verbal analogy appears in greater detail in parallel sources, while here, the essence of the proof is cited. Nevertheless, the question is: What is the meaning of among? How many people must be present in order for one of them to be characterized as being among them? It is derived indirectly from the verses until the conclusion is reached that even ten people are enough for that purpose.

**The *halakha* is not in accordance with his opinion – וְלֵית הִלְכְתָא כְּוָתֵיהּ:** From here it was derived that one who is engaged in prayer does not respond with any other praise or sanctification. This is illustrated by the following parable: A king ordered two people to perform different tasks, each must engage in performing his own task and neither should neglect his own task to perform the task of the other (*Ba'al Halakhot Gedolot*, *ge'onim*).

**From where in the Torah is it derived that one who experiences a seminal emission is prohibited from engaging in matters of Torah? – מִנַּיִן לְבַעַל קֶרִי שֶׁאָסוּר בְּדִבְרֵי תוֹרָה:** The question was posed: The immersion of one who experienced a seminal emission is a rabbinic ordinance instituted by Ezra. Why is the Gemara challenging Rabbi Yehuda's opinion from Rabbi Yehoshua ben Levi's statement as if it was by Torah law? The answer is: Since, based on Ezra's ordinance, the question is legitimate, the Gemara was not insistent on phrasing it with precision and posed the question utilizing the allusion of Rabbi Yehoshua ben Levi (*Shitta Mekubbetzet*). Furthermore, the Gemara below explains the entire matter differently (*Tosefot Rabbi Yehuda HaḤasid*).

**He derives them in Deuteronomy [*Mishne Torah*] – בְּמִשְׁנֵה תוֹרָה דָּרֵישׁ:** The reason is: Although the sanctity of Deuteronomy is equal to the sanctity of the other books of the Torah, it consists of Moses recapitulating that which was previously stated. Certainly, it was not repeated in vain. Moses' juxtapositions and combinations are significant and *halakha* may be derived from them (*Shitta Mekubbetzet*).

ובכל התורה כולה מנא לן דלא דריש - דתניא, בן עזאי אומר: נאמר "מכשפה לא תחיה" ונאמר "כל שוכב עם בהמה מות יומת", סמכו ענין לו, לומר: מה שוכב עם בהמה בסקילה - אף מכשפה נמי בסקילה;

**And from where do we derive** that Rabbi Yehuda **does not derive homiletic interpretations** from juxtaposed verses **throughout the entire Torah? As it was taught** in a *baraita* with regard to the punishment of a sorceress, **ben Azzai**[P] **says: It is stated: "You shall not allow a sorceress to live"** (Exodus 22:17), although the manner of her execution is not specified, **and it is stated: "Whoever lies with a beast shall surely be put to death"** (Exodus 22:18). The fact that the Torah **juxtaposed this matter to that** was **to say: Just as one who lies with a beast** is executed **by stoning** (see Leviticus 20), **so too a sorceress** is executed **by stoning.**

אמר ליה רבי יהודה: וכי מפני שסמכו ענין לו נוציא לזה לסקילה? אלא: אוב וידעוני בכלל כל המכשפים היו, ולמה יצאו - להקיש להן, ולומר לך: מה אוב וידעוני בסקילה - אף מכשפה בסקילה.

With regard to this proof **Rabbi Yehuda said to him: And does** the fact **that** the Torah **juxtaposed this matter to that warrant taking** this person **out to be stoned?** Should he be sentenced to the most severe of the death penalties on that basis **Rather,** the source is: **Mediums and wizards were included among all sorcerers. And why were they singled out**[B] from the rest, in the verse: "And a man or a woman who is a medium or a wizard shall surely be put to death; they shall stone them with stones, their blood is upon them" (Leviticus 20:27)? In order to **draw an analogy to them and say to you: Just as a medium and a wizard** are executed **by stoning, so too is a sorceress**[H] executed **by stoning.**

ובמשנה תורה מנא לן דדריש - דתניא, רבי אליעזר אומר: נושא אדם אנוסת אביו ומפותת אביו, אנוסת בנו ומפותת בנו.

**And from where do we derive** that Rabbi Yehuda **derives homiletic interpretations** from juxtaposed verses **in *Mishne Torah*? As it was taught** in another *baraita*: **Rabbi Eliezer said that a man** may **wed** a woman **raped by his father and** one **seduced by his father;** a woman **raped by his son and** one **seduced by his son.**[H] Though one is prohibited by Torah law from marrying the wife of his father or the wife of his son, this prohibition does not apply to a woman raped or seduced by them.

רבי יהודה אוסר באנוסת אביו ובמפותת אביו. ואמר רב גידל אמר רב: מאי טעמא דרבי יהודה, דכתיב "לא יקח איש את אשת אביו ולא יגלה (את) כנף אביו" - כנף שראה אביו לא יגלה.

**And Rabbi Yehuda prohibits** him from marrying **a woman raped by his father and a woman seduced by his father. And Rav Giddel said** that **Rav said: What is the reason for Rabbi Yehuda's** opinion? **As it is written: "A man shall not take his father's wife, and shall not uncover his father's skirt"** (Deuteronomy 23:1). The last expression, "and shall not uncover his father's skirt," implies that: **A skirt that has been seen by his father,** i.e., any woman who has had sexual relations with his father, **may not be uncovered** by his son, i.e., his son may not marry her.

וממאי דבאנוסת אביו כתיב - דסמיך ליה: "ונתן האיש השוכב עמה וגו'"!

**And from where** do we know **that** the verse **is written with regard to a woman raped by his father? As** the previous section, **juxtaposed to it,** deals with the laws of rape: **"And the man who lay with her must give** her father fifty shekels…because he has violated her" (Deuteronomy 22:29).

אמרי: אין, במשנה תורה דריש והני סמוכין מבעי ליה לאידך דרבי יהושע בן לוי, דאמר רבי יהושע בן לוי: כל המלמד לבנו תורה - מעלה עליו הכתוב כאילו קבלה מהר חורב שנאמר "והודעתם לבניך ולבני בניך", וכתיב בתריה: "יום אשר עמדת לפני ה' אלהיך בחורב".

At any rate, we see that in Deuteronomy, Rabbi Yehuda derives homiletic interpretations from juxtaposed verses. Why does he fail to derive that one who experiences a seminal emission is prohibited from engaging in matters of Torah from the juxtaposition of the verses? **They replied: Indeed, in *Mishne Torah*** Rabbi Yehuda **does derive homiletic interpretations** from the juxtaposition of verses, **but** he requires **these juxtaposed verses** in order **to** derive **another** statement **of Rabbi Yehoshua ben Levi, as Rabbi Yehoshua ben Levi said: One who teaches his son Torah, the verse ascribes to him** credit **as if he received** the Torah **from Mount Horeb. As it is stated: "And you shall impart them to your children and your children's children"** (Deuteronomy 4:9) **after which it is written: "The day that you stood before the Lord your God at Horeb."** Therefore, Rabbi Yehuda cannot derive from that same juxtaposition a prohibition banning one who experienced a seminal emission from engaging in matters of Torah.

תנן: זב שראה קרי, ונדה שפלטה שכבת זרע, המשמשת וראתה דם צריכין טבילה; ורבי יהודה פוטר.

**We learned** in a mishna that **a *zav* who experienced a seminal emission, and a menstruating woman who discharged semen, and a woman who engaged in intercourse** with her husband **and she saw** menstrual **blood,** all of whom are ritually impure for at least seven days due to the severity of their impurity, nevertheless **require ritual immersion** in order to purify themselves from the impurity of the seminal emission before they may engage in matters of Torah. **And Rabbi Yehuda exempts** them from immersion.

**PERSONALITIES**

Ben Azzai – בן עזאי: Ben Azzai is Shimon ben Azzai, one of the *tanna'im* in Yavne. Shimon ben Azzai was never ordained, which is why he is called by his name alone, without a title. He is usually referred to simply as ben Azzai. He was considered one of the outstanding Sages and his wisdom was celebrated for many generations. Apparently, he did not study Torah in his youth until he met Rabbi Akiva's daughter. She promised to marry him if he studied Torah. Consequently, he went to study with Rabbi Yehoshua and Rabbi Yishmael and was the primary student and even a disciple-colleague of Rabbi Akiva, whom he considered to be the preeminent Sage of his generation in Israel. It is unclear whether he never married, or whether he married Rabbi Akiva's daughter and left her a short time later due to his overwhelming desire to study Torah. He completely devoted himself to the study of Torah, as can be seen in the mishna in *Sota*, which says: Since ben Azzai died, there are no more diligent people. His statements can be found in the Mishna, in *baraitot* and in the Gemara dealing with both *halakha* and *aggada*. Apparently, he had several disciples in Tiberias, his city of residence. Ben Azzai engaged in the study of esoterica and is one of the four who entered the mystical orchard. The *baraita* in tractate *Ḥagiga* says that he peeked and died. The verse: "Precious in the sight of the Lord is the death of His saints" (Psalms 116:15), was quoted in reference to his death.

**BACKGROUND**

Why were they singled out – למה יצאו: This is an instance of one of the thirteen hermeneutic principles through which the Torah is interpreted: When a particular case, already included in the general category, is expressly mentioned to teach something new, that special provision applies to all other cases included in the general category. Here, included in the general category are all of the various kinds of sorcerers; explicitly specified are the mediums and wizards who are mentioned in their own verse. The verse that teaches that they are punished by stoning was expressly mentioned not only to teach about their punishment, but rather to illuminate the general category, i.e., the punishment for all sorcerers.

**HALAKHA**

**The legal status of a sorceress – דין מכשפה:** A sorcerer who performed actual sorcery is executed by stoning. One who merely creates the impression of sorcery is punished with lashes of rebellion (Rambam *Sefer HaMadda, Hilkhot Avodat Kokhavim* 11:15).

**A man may wed a woman raped by his father and one seduced by his father; a woman raped by his son and one seduced by his son – נושא אדם אנוסת אביו ומפותת אביו אנוסת בנו ומפותת בנו:** This is because the Torah only prohibited a woman married to his father or his son and not a woman with whom they had promiscuous relations (Rambam), as per the opinion of the Rabbis in their dispute with the individual opinion of Rabbi Yehuda (Rambam *Sefer Kedusha, Hilkhot Issurei Bia* 2:13; *Shulḥan Arukh, Even HaEzer* 15:5).

**BACKGROUND**

In order to convey the far-reaching nature of the opinion of the Rabbis – לְהוֹדִיעֲךָ כֹּחָן דְּרַבָּנַן: Since the statements of the Sages are deemed to be as concise and precise as possible, the expectation is that a dispute will be framed in a manner that will facilitate a more profound understanding of the different opinions. Therefore, one may not ascribe a broader scope to a given opinion beyond that which was expressed. At times, however, the disagreement is framed in a manner that does not, in fact, elucidate the entire scope of possibilities in the position of one of the parties to the dispute. That is the case when it is framed in a manner that demonstrates the far-reaching nature of the position of the other party to the dispute. In our case, that is the opinion of the Rabbis, who are stringent.

עַד כָּאן לֹא פָּטַר רַבִּי יְהוּדָה אֶלָּא בְּזָב שֶׁרָאָה קֶרִי – דְּמֵעִיקָּרָא לָאו בַּר טְבִילָה הוּא, אֲבָל בַּעַל קֶרִי גְּרֵידָא מְחַיֵּיב!

However, **Rabbi Yehuda only exempted** from immersion in the case **of a** ***zav*** **who experienced a seminal emission, who was unfit to immerse himself from the outset,** as even after immersion he would remain impure with the seven-day impurity of the *zav*. **But,** in the case of **one who experienced a seminal emission alone,** with no concurrent impurity, even Rabbi Yehuda **requires** immersion before he may engage in Torah matters.

וְכִי תֵּימָא, הוּא הַדִּין דַּאֲפִילּוּ בַּעַל קֶרִי גְּרֵידָא נַמִי פָּטַר רַבִּי יְהוּדָה; וְהַאי דְּקָא מִפַּלְגִי בְּזָב שֶׁרָאָה קֶרִי – לְהוֹדִיעֲךָ כֹּחָן דְּרַבָּנַן, אֵימָא סֵיפָא: הַמְשַׁמֶּשֶׁת וְרָאֲתָה דָּם צְרִיכָה טְבִילָה,

**And if you say: The same is true even** in the case of **one who experienced a seminal emission alone,** that **Rabbi Yehuda also exempts** him from immersion, **and the fact that they disagree** in the case of **a** ***zav*** **who experienced a seminal emission** and not in the case of a person who experienced a seminal emission alone **is in order to convey the far-reaching** nature of the opinion **of the Rabbis,**[B] who require immersion even in this case. If so, **say the last case** of that same mishna: **A woman who was engaged in intercourse and she saw** menstrual **blood requires immersion.**

לְמַאן קָתָנֵי לַהּ? אִילֵימָא לְרַבָּנַן – פְּשִׁיטָא! הַשְׁתָּא וּמַה זָּב שֶׁרָאָה קֶרִי דְּמֵעִיקָּרָא לָאו בַּר טְבִילָה הוּא – מְחַיְּיבִי רַבָּנַן, הַמְשַׁמֶּשֶׁת וְרָאֲתָה דָּם, דְּמֵעִיקָּרָא בַּת טְבִילָה הִיא – לֹא כׇּל שֶׁכֵּן! אֶלָּא לָאו רַבִּי יְהוּדָה הִיא, וְדַוְקָא קָתָנֵי לַהּ

The Gemara seeks to clarify: **In accordance with whose** opinion **was this** case in the mishna **taught? If you say** that it is in accordance with the opinion of **the Rabbis, that is obvious; if** in the case of **a** ***zav*** **who experienced a seminal emission who was unfit to immerse himself from the outset** when he experienced the seminal emission, **the Rabbis** nevertheless **require immersion, all the more so** wouldn't they require immersion for a **woman who engaged in intercourse and** only then **saw blood,** who **was fit to immerse herself from the outset,** when she came into contact with the seminal emission of her husband? **Rather, isn't this Rabbi Yehuda's** opinion, **and** this case **was taught specifically** in order to teach

Perek **III**
Daf **22** Amud **a**

מְשַׁמֶּשֶׁת וְרָאֲתָה נִדָּה אֵינָהּ צְרִיכָה טְבִילָה, אֲבָל בַּעַל קֶרִי גְּרֵידָא – מְחַיֵּיב! לֹא תֵּימָא 'מְבָרֵךְ' אֶלָּא 'מְהַרְהֵר'.

that **a woman who engaged in intercourse and saw menstrual** blood **is not required to immerse herself, but one who experienced a seminal emission alone,** with no concurrent impurity, **is required to do so?** If so we must interpret Rabbi Yehuda's statement in the mishna that one recites a blessing both beforehand and thereafter as follows: **Do not say** that one **recites a blessing** orally, but rather he means that **one contemplates** those blessings in his heart.

וּמִי אִית לֵיהּ לְרַבִּי יְהוּדָה הִרְהוּר? וְהָתַנְיָא: בַּעַל קֶרִי שֶׁאֵין לוֹ מַיִם לִטְבּוֹל – קוֹרֵא קְרִיאַת שְׁמַע, וְאֵינוֹ מְבָרֵךְ לֹא לְפָנֶיהָ וְלֹא לְאַחֲרֶיהָ, וְאוֹכֵל פִּתּוֹ וּמְבָרֵךְ לְאַחֲרֶיהָ וְאֵינוֹ מְבָרֵךְ לְפָנֶיהָ, אֲבָל מְהַרְהֵר בְּלִבּוֹ וְאֵינוֹ מוֹצִיא בִּשְׂפָתָיו, דִּבְרֵי רַבִּי מֵאִיר. רַבִּי יְהוּדָה אוֹמֵר: בֵּין כָּךְ וּבֵין כָּךְ מוֹצִיא בִּשְׂפָתָיו.

The Gemara challenges this explanation: **And does Rabbi Yehuda maintain that** there is validity to **contemplating** in his heart? **Wasn't it taught** in a *baraita*: **One who experienced a seminal emission and who has no water to immerse** and purify himself **recites** ***Shema*** **and neither recites the blessings** of *Shema* **beforehand nor thereafter?** And when **he eats his bread, he recites the blessing thereafter,** Grace after Meals, **but does not recite the blessing:** Who brings forth bread from the earth, **beforehand. However** in the instances where he may not recite the blessing, **he contemplates it in his heart rather than utter** it **with his lips,** this is **the statement of Rabbi Meir.** However **Rabbi Yehuda says: In either case, he utters** all of the blessings **with his lips.** Rabbi Yehuda does not consider contemplating the blessings in his heart a solution and permits them to be recited.

אָמַר רַב נַחְמָן בַּר יִצְחָק: עֲשָׂאָן רַבִּי יְהוּדָה כְּהִלְכוֹת דֶּרֶךְ אֶרֶץ.

**Rav Naḥman bar Yitzḥak said:** Rabbi Yehuda's statement in the mishna should be interpreted in another way. **Rabbi Yehuda rendered** the blessings **like** ***Hilkhot Derekh Eretz,*** which according to some Sages were not considered to be in the same category as all other matters of Torah and therefore one is permitted to engage in their study even after having experienced a seminal emission.

דְּתַנְיָא: ״וְהוֹדַעְתָּם לְבָנֶיךָ וְלִבְנֵי בָנֶיךָ״, וּכְתִיב בָּתְרֵיהּ ״יוֹם אֲשֶׁר עָמַדְתָּ לִפְנֵי ה׳ אֱלֹהֶיךָ בְּחוֹרֵב״, מָה לְהַלָּן בְּאֵימָה וּבְיִרְאָה וּבִרְתֵת וּבְזִיעַ אַף כָּאן בְּאֵימָה וּבְיִרְאָה וּבִרְתֵת וּבְזִיעַ;

**As it was taught** in a *baraita*: It is written: **"And you shall impart them to your children and your children's children"** (Deuteronomy 4:9), **and it is written thereafter: "The day that you stood before the Lord your God at Horeb"** (Deuteronomy 4:10). **Just as below,** the Revelation at Sinai was **in reverence, fear, quaking, and trembling, so too here,** in every generation, Torah must be studied with a sense of **reverence, fear, quaking, and trembling.**

מִכָּאן אָמְרוּ: הַזָּבִים וְהַמְצוֹרָעִים וּבָאִין עַל נִדּוֹת – מוּתָּרִים לִקְרוֹת בַּתּוֹרָה וּבַנְּבִיאִים וּבַכְּתוּבִים, לִשְׁנוֹת בְּמִשְׁנָה וּגְמָרָא וּבַהֲלָכוֹת וּבַאֲגָדוֹת, אֲבָל בַּעֲלֵי קְרָיִין אֲסוּרִים;

**From here** the Sages **stated:** ***Zavim*, lepers, and those who engaged in intercourse with menstruating women,** despite their severe impurity, **are permitted to read the Torah, Prophets, and Writings, and to study Mishna and Gemara and *halakhot* and *aggada*. However, those who experienced a seminal emission are prohibited** from doing so.[H] The reason for this distinction is that the cases of severe impurity are caused by ailment or other circumstances beyond his control and, as a result, they do not necessarily preclude a sense of reverence and awe as he studies Torah. This, however, is not the case with regard to impurity resulting from a seminal emission, which usually comes about due to frivolity and a lack of reverence and awe. Therefore, it is inappropriate for one who experiences a seminal emission to engage in matters of in Torah.

רַבִּי יוֹסֵי אוֹמֵר: שׁוֹנֶה הוּא בִּרְגִילִיּוֹת וּבִלְבַד שֶׁלֹּא יַצִּיעַ אֶת הַמִּשְׁנָה; רַבִּי יוֹנָתָן בֶּן יוֹסֵף אוֹמֵר: מַצִּיעַ הוּא אֶת הַמִּשְׁנָה וְאֵינוֹ מַצִּיעַ אֶת הַגְּמָרָא; רַבִּי נָתָן בֶּן אֲבִישָׁלוֹם אוֹמֵר: אַף מַצִּיעַ אֶת הַגְּמָרָא וּבִלְבַד שֶׁלֹּא יֹאמַר אַזְכָּרוֹת שֶׁבּוֹ; רַבִּי יוֹחָנָן הַסַּנְדְּלָר תַּלְמִידוֹ שֶׁל רַבִּי עֲקִיבָא מִשּׁוּם רַבִּי עֲקִיבָא אוֹמֵר: לֹא יִכָּנֵס לַמִּדְרָשׁ כָּל עִיקָּר, וְאָמְרִי לַהּ: לֹא יִכָּנֵס לְבֵית הַמִּדְרָשׁ כָּל עִיקָּר; רַבִּי יְהוּדָה אוֹמֵר: שׁוֹנֶה הוּא בְּהִלְכוֹת דֶּרֶךְ אֶרֶץ.

However, there are many opinions concerning the precise parameters of the Torah matters prohibited by this decree. **Rabbi Yosei says:** One who experiences a seminal emission **studies *mishnayot*** that he is **accustomed** to study,[N] **as long as he does not expound upon a** new **mishna** to study it in depth. **Rabbi Yonatan ben Yosef says: He expounds upon the mishna but he does not expound upon the Gemara,** which is the in-depth analysis of the Torah. **Rabbi Natan ben Avishalom says: He may even expound upon the Gemara, as long as he does not utter** the **mentions** of God's name **therein. Rabbi Yoḥanan the Cobbler, Rabbi Akiva's student, says in the name of Rabbi Akiva:** One who experiences a seminal emission **may not enter into homiletic interpretation** [*midrash*] of verses **at all. Some say** that he says: **He may not enter the study hall** [*beit hamidrash*] **at all. Rabbi Yehuda says: He may study** only ***Hilkhot Derekh Eretz*.** In terms of the problem raised above, apparently Rabbi Yehuda considers the legal status of the blessings to be parallel to the legal status of *Hilkhot Derekh Eretz*, and therefore one may utter them orally.

מַעֲשֶׂה בְּרַבִּי יְהוּדָה שֶׁרָאָה קֶרִי וְהָיָה מְהַלֵּךְ עַל גַּב הַנָּהָר. אָמְרוּ לוֹ תַּלְמִידָיו: רַבֵּינוּ, שְׁנֵה לָנוּ פֶּרֶק אֶחָד בְּהִלְכוֹת דֶּרֶךְ אֶרֶץ! יָרַד וְטָבַל וְשָׁנָה לָהֶם. אָמְרוּ לוֹ: לֹא כָּךְ לִמַּדְתָּנוּ רַבֵּינוּ: שׁוֹנֶה הוּא בְּהִלְכוֹת דֶּרֶךְ אֶרֶץ? אָמַר לָהֶם: אַף עַל פִּי שֶׁמֵּיקֵל אֲנִי עַל אֲחֵרִים, מַחְמִיר אֲנִי עַל עַצְמִי.

The Gemara relates **an incident involving Rabbi Yehuda** himself, who **experienced a seminal emission and was walking along the riverbank** with his disciples. **His disciples said to him: Rabbi, teach us a chapter from *Hilkhot Derekh Eretz*,** as he maintained that even in a state of impurity, it is permitted. **He descended and immersed himself** in the river **and taught them** *Hilkhot Derekh Eretz*. **They said to him: Did you not teach us, our teacher, that he may study *Hilkhot Derekh Eretz*? He said to them: Although I am lenient with others,** and allow them to study it without immersion, **I am stringent with myself.**[N]

תַּנְיָא, רַבִּי יְהוּדָה בֶּן בְּתֵירָא הָיָה אוֹמֵר: אֵין דִּבְרֵי תוֹרָה מְקַבְּלִין טוּמְאָה. מַעֲשֶׂה בְּתַלְמִיד אֶחָד שֶׁהָיָה מְגַמְגֵּם לְמַעְלָה מֵרַבִּי יְהוּדָה בֶּן בְּתֵירָא. אָמַר לֵיהּ: בְּנִי, פְּתַח פִּיךָ וְיָאִירוּ דְּבָרֶיךָ; שֶׁאֵין דִּבְרֵי תוֹרָה מְקַבְּלִין טוּמְאָה שֶׁנֶּאֱמַר "הֲלֹא כֹה דְבָרִי כָּאֵשׁ נְאֻם ה'" מָה אֵשׁ אֵינוֹ מְקַבֵּל טוּמְאָה אַף דִּבְרֵי תוֹרָה אֵינָן מְקַבְּלִין טוּמְאָה.

Further elaborating on the issue of Torah study while in a state of impurity, **it was taught** in a *baraita* that **Rabbi Yehuda ben Beteira**[P] **would say: Matters of Torah do not become ritually impure**[N] and therefore one who is impure is permitted to engage in Torah study. He implemented this *halakha* in practice. The Gemara relates **an incident involving a student who was** reciting *mishnayot* and *baraitot* **hesitantly before** the study hall of **Rabbi Yehuda ben Beteira.** The student experienced a seminal emission, and when he was asked to recite he did so in a rushed, uneven manner, as he did not want to utter the words of Torah explicitly. Rabbi Yehuda **said to him: My son, open your mouth and let your words illuminate, as matters of Torah do not become ritually impure, as it is stated: "Is not my word like fire, says the Lord"** (Jeremiah 23:29). **Just as fire does not become ritually impure, so too matters of Torah do not become ritually impure.**

אָמַר מָר: מַצִּיעַ אֶת הַמִּשְׁנָה וְאֵינוֹ מַצִּיעַ אֶת הַגְּמָרָא. מְסַיַּיע לֵיהּ לְרַבִּי אֶלְעַאי; דְּאָמַר רַבִּי אֶלְעַאי אָמַר רַבִּי אַחָא בַּר יַעֲקֹב מִשּׁוּם רַבֵּינוּ: הֲלָכָה, מַצִּיעַ אֶת הַמִּשְׁנָה וְאֵינוֹ מַצִּיעַ אֶת הַגְּמָרָא. כְּתַנָּאֵי: מַצִּיעַ אֶת הַמִּשְׁנָה וְאֵינוֹ מַצִּיעַ אֶת הַגְּמָרָא, דִּבְרֵי רַבִּי מֵאִיר; רַבִּי יְהוּדָה בֶּן גַּמְלִיאֵל אוֹמֵר מִשּׁוּם רַבִּי חֲנִינָא בֶּן גַּמְלִיאֵל: זֶה וָזֶה אָסוּר; וְאָמְרִי לַהּ: זֶה וָזֶה מוּתָּר.

In this *baraita* **the Master said** that one who is impure because of a seminal emission **expounds upon the mishna but does not expound upon the Gemara.** The Gemara notes: This statement **supports** the opinion of **Rabbi El'ai,**[P] as **Rabbi El'ai said** that **Rabbi Aḥa bar Ya'akov said in the name of Rabbeinu,** Rav: **The** *halakha* is that one who experienced a seminal emission **may expound upon the mishna but may not expound upon the Gemara.** This dispute **is parallel a tannaitic** dispute, as it was taught: One who experienced a seminal emission **expounds upon the mishna but does not expound upon the Gemara;** that is **the statement of Rabbi Meir. Rabbi Yehuda ben Gamliel says in the name of Rabbi Ḥanina ben Gamliel:** Both **this and that are prohibited. And some say** that he said: Both **this and that are permitted.**

## HALAKHA

*Zavim* and lepers…are permitted to read the Torah…But those who experienced a seminal emission are prohibited from doing so – הַזָּבִים וְהַמְצוֹרָעִים...מוּתָּרִים לִקְרוֹת בַּתּוֹרָה...אֲבָל בַּעֲלֵי קְרָיִין אֲסוּרִים: Everyone who is ritually impure is permitted to read the Torah, recite *Shema*, and pray, except for those who experienced a seminal emission, as Ezra decreed that they are prohibited to do so until they immerse in a ritual bath. However, in subsequent generations that ordinance was repealed and one who experienced a seminal emission was permitted to engage in all those activities without immersion or bathing in nine *kav* of water. That remains the prevalent custom (Rambam *Sefer Ahava*, *Hilkhot Keriat Shema* 4:8; *Shulḥan Arukh*, *Oraḥ Ḥayyim* 88).

## NOTES

He studies the *mishnayot* that he is accustomed to study – שׁוֹנֶה הוּא בִּרְגִילִיּוֹת: Some interpret this to refer to those *misnnayot* with which everyone is familiar, such as Ethics of the Fathers or those recited as part of the portion of the daily offering (Rav Sa'adia Gaon), and expound a mishna means that he may not explain it to others (*Arukh*).

I am stringent with myself – מַחְמִיר אֲנִי עַל עַצְמִי: Rabbi Yehuda followed the path of those Sages, who, although they ruled leniently with regard to a particular *halakha* and instructed the public accordingly, they did not rely upon that leniency themselves and, in doing so, at times, placed themselves in danger. They did so because they held their colleagues and their opinions in such high regard.

Matters of Torah do not become ritually impure – אֵין דִּבְרֵי תוֹרָה מְקַבְּלִין טוּמְאָה: This statement does not contradict the prohibition against reciting matters of Torah in a filthy place. The distinction is that ritual impurity is intangible and is experienced intellectually. Since the words of God are like fire, they do not become ritually impure. However, filth offends the senses and creates a clear impression that one is in a despicable place. Uttering matters of Torah there would fall under the rubric of: "For he has shown contempt for the word of the Lord" (Numbers 15:31; *Kesef Mishne*).

## PERSONALITIES

Rabbi Yehuda ben Beteira – רַבִּי יְהוּדָה בֶּן בְּתֵירָא: The Benei Beteira family produced renowned Sages over several generations. Some members of the family served as *Nasi* during the time of Hillel, but transferred the position to him.

It is almost certain that there were two Sages named Yehuda ben Beteira. The second may have been the grandson of the first. Both lived in the city of Netzivin in Babylonia: one, while the Temple was still standing, and the second at the end of the tannaitic period. The Rabbi Yehuda ben Beteira whose teaching is cited here is most likely the second one. He was one of the greatest Torah scholars of his age and organized the study of Torah throughout Babylonia before the great yeshivas were established. He was venerated by the Sages of Eretz Yisrael.

Rabbi El'ai – רַבִּי אֶלְעַאי: This page cites two Sages named Rabbi El'ai. The first, the Rabbi El'ai who makes a statement in the name of Rabbi Aḥa bar Ya'akov, was an *amora* in Eretz Yisrael during the generation of Rabbi Yoḥanan's students. The Rabbi El'ai who makes a statement with regard to the first shearing is the *tanna* Rabbi El'ai the Elder, a student of Rabbi Eliezer the Great, ben Hyrcanus, and father of the famous *tanna* Rabbi Yehuda ben El'ai.

מַאן דְּאָמַר זֶה וָזֶה אָסוּר – כְּרַבִּי יוֹחָנָן הַסַּנְדְּלָר, מַאן דְּאָמַר זֶה וָזֶה מוּתָּר – כְּרַבִּי יְהוּדָה בֶּן בְּתֵירָא.

Comparing these opinions: **The one who said** that both **this and that are prohibited** holds **in accordance with** the opinion of **Rabbi Yoḥanan the Cobbler; the one who said** that both **this and that are permitted** holds **in accordance with** the opinion of **Rabbi Yehuda ben Beteira.**

אָמַר רַב נַחְמָן בַּר יִצְחָק נָהוּג עָלְמָא כְּהָנֵי תְּלָת סָבֵי: כְּרַבִּי אֶלְעַאי בְּרֵאשִׁית הַגֵּז, כְּרַבִּי יֹאשִׁיָּה בִּכְלָאִים, כְּרַבִּי יְהוּדָה בֶּן בְּתֵירָא בְּדִבְרֵי תוֹרָה.

Summarizing the *halakha*, **Rav Naḥman bar Yitzḥak said: The universally** accepted **practice is in accordance with** the opinions of **these three elders: In accordance with** the opinion of **Rabbi El'ai with regard to** the *halakhot* of **the first shearing,**[H] **in accordance with** the opinion of **Rabbi Yoshiya with regard to** the laws of prohibited **diverse kinds,** and **in accordance with** the opinion of **Rabbi Yehuda ben Beteira with regard to matters of Torah.**

כְּרַבִּי אֶלְעַאי בְּרֵאשִׁית הַגֵּז – דְּתַנְיָא, רַבִּי אֶלְעַאי אוֹמֵר: רֵאשִׁית הַגֵּז אֵינוֹ נוֹהֵג אֶלָּא בָּאָרֶץ.

The Gemara elaborates: **In accordance with** the opinion of **Rabbi El'ai with regard to the first shearing, as it was taught** in a *baraita* that **Rabbi El'ai says:** The obligation to set aside **the first shearing** from the sheep for the priest **is only practiced in Eretz** Yisrael and not in the Diaspora, and that is the accepted practice.

כְּרַבִּי יֹאשִׁיָּה בִּכְלָאִים – כְּדִכְתִיב: ״לֹא תִזְרַע [כַּרְמְךָ] כִּלְאָיִם״, רַבִּי יֹאשִׁיָּה אוֹמֵר: לְעוֹלָם אֵינוֹ חַיָּיב עַד שֶׁיִּזְרַע חִטָּה וּשְׂעוֹרָה וְחַרְצָן בְּמַפּוֹלֶת יָד.

**In accordance with** the opinion of **Rabbi Yoshiya with regard to diverse kinds, as it is written: "You shall not sow your vineyard with diverse kinds"** (Deuteronomy 22:9).[H] **Rabbi Yoshiya says:** This means that **one** who sows diverse kinds **is not liable** by Torah law **until he sows wheat and barley and a** grape **pit with a single hand motion,** meaning that while sowing in the vineyard he violates the prohibition of diverse kinds that applies to seeds and to the vineyard simultaneously.

כְּרַבִּי יְהוּדָה בֶּן בְּתֵירָא בְּדִבְרֵי תוֹרָה, דְּתַנְיָא, רַבִּי יְהוּדָה בֶּן בְּתֵירָא אוֹמֵר: אֵין דִּבְרֵי תוֹרָה מְקַבְּלִין טוּמְאָה.

**In accordance with Rabbi Yehuda ben Beteira with regard to** one who experiences a seminal emission is permitted to engage in **matters of Torah, as it was taught** in a *baraita* that **Rabbi Yehuda ben Beteira says: Matters of Torah do not become ritually impure.**[H]

כִּי אֲתָא זְעֵירִי, אֲמַר: בַּטְּלוּהָ לִטְבִילוּתָא, וְאָמְרִי לַהּ: בַּטְּלוּהָ לִנְטִילוּתָא. מַאן דְּאָמַר ״בַּטְּלוּהָ לִטְבִילוּתָא״ – כְּרַבִּי יְהוּדָה בֶּן בְּתֵירָא. מַאן דְּאָמַר ״בַּטְּלוּהָ לִנְטִילוּתָא״ – כִּי הָא דְּרַב חִסְדָּא לַיֵּיט אַמַּאן דִּמְהַדַּר אַמַּיָּא בְּעִידַּן צְלוֹתָא.

And the Gemara relates: **When Ze'iri came** from Eretz Yisrael to Babylonia, **he** succinctly capsulated this *halakha* and **said: They abolished ritual immersion,**[N] **and some say that** he said: **They abolished ritual washing of the hands.** The Gemara explains: **The one who says** that **they abolished immersion** holds in accordance with the opinion of **Rabbi Yehuda ben Beteira** that one who experienced a seminal emission is not required to immerse. **And the one who says** that **they abolished washing of the hands** holds **in accordance with that which Rav Ḥisda cursed one who** goes out of his way **to seek water at the time of prayer.**

תָּנוּ רַבָּנַן: בַּעַל קֶרִי שֶׁנָּתְנוּ עָלָיו תִּשְׁעָה קַבִּין מַיִם – טָהוֹר; נַחוּם אִישׁ גַּם זוֹ לְחָשָׁהּ לְרַבִּי עֲקִיבָא, וְרַבִּי עֲקִיבָא לְחָשָׁהּ לְבֶן עַזַּאי, וּבֶן עַזַּאי יָצָא וּשְׁנָאָהּ לְתַלְמִידָיו בַּשּׁוּק. פְּלִיגִי בָּהּ תְּרֵי אֲמוֹרָאֵי בְּמַעֲרָבָא, רַבִּי יוֹסֵי בַּר אָבִין וְרַבִּי יוֹסֵי בַּר זְבִידָא: חַד תָּנֵי ׳שְׁנָאָהּ׳ וְחַד תָּנֵי ׳לְחָשָׁהּ׳.

**The Sages taught** in a *baraita*: **One who experienced a seminal emission who had nine** *kav* of drawn **water poured over him,** that is sufficient to render him **ritually pure** and he need not immerse himself in a ritual bath. The Gemara relates: **Naḥum of Gam Zo whispered** this *halakha* to **Rabbi Akiva, and Rabbi Akiva whispered it**[N] to his student **ben Azzai, and ben Azzai went out and taught it to his students** publicly **in the marketplace. Two** *amora'im* **in Eretz Yisrael, Rabbi Yosei bar Avin and Rabbi Yosei bar Zevida, disagreed** as to the correct version of the conclusion of the incident. **One taught:** Ben Azzai **taught it** to his students in the market. **And the other taught: Ben Azzai** also **whispered it** to his students.

מַאן דְּתָנֵי ׳שְׁנָאָהּ׳ מִשּׁוּם בִּטּוּל תּוֹרָה, וּמִשּׁוּם בִּטּוּל פְּרִיָּה וּרְבִיָּה. וּמַאן דְּתָנֵי ׳לְחָשָׁהּ׳ – שֶׁלֹּא יְהוּ תַּלְמִידֵי חֲכָמִים מְצוּיִים אֵצֶל נְשׁוֹתֵיהֶם כְּתַרְנְגוֹלִים.

The Gemara explains the rationale behind the two versions of this incident. **The** Sage **who taught** that ben Azzai **taught** the law openly in the market held that the leniency was **due to** concern that the *halakhot* requiring ritual immersion would promote **dereliction** in the study **of Torah.** The ruling of Rabbi Yehuda ben Beteira eases the way for an individual who experienced a seminal emission to study Torah. This was **also due to** concern that the *halakhot* requiring ritual immersion would promote **the suspension of procreation,** as one might abstain from marital relations to avoid the immersion required thereafter. **And the** Sage, **who taught** that ben Azzai only **whispered** this *halakha* to his students, held that he did so **in order that Torah scholars would not be with their wives like roosters.**[H] If the purification process was that simple, Torah scholars would engage in sexual activity constantly, which would distract them from their studies.

### HALAKHA

**The first shearing – רֵאשִׁית הַגֵּז:** The mitzva of the first shearing is in effect in all generations, whether or not the Temple is intact. However, it is only in effect in Eretz Yisrael as per the opinion of Rabbi El'ai. Some say that, by Torah law, it is in effect outside of Eretz Yisrael as well, but the custom is not in accordance with that opinion (Rema; Rambam *Sefer Zera'im, Hilkhot Bikkurim* 10:1; *Shulḥan Arukh, Yoreh De'a* 333:1).

**Diverse kinds in a vineyard – כִּלְאַיִם בַּכֶּרֶם:** One is liable for lashes for sowing diverse kinds in a vineyard only if he sowed wheat, barley, and a grape seed, or two species of vegetable and a grape seed, or a vegetable, a grain, and a grape seed, in a single motion. Sowing other diverse kinds of seeds together is prohibited only by rabbinic law, in accordance with the opinion of Rabbi Yoshiya (Rambam *Sefer Zera'im, Hilkhot Kilayim* 5:2, *Hilkhot Bikkurim* 8:13; *Shulḥan Arukh, Yoreh De'a* 296:1–2).

**Matters of Torah do not become ritually impure – אֵין דִּבְרֵי תוֹרָה מְקַבְּלִין טוּמְאָה:** Matters of Torah do not become ritually impure and nowadays everyone is permitted to study Torah and touch sacred objects even if he is ritually impure, in accordance with the opinion of Rabbi Yehuda ben Beteira (Rambam *Sefer Ahava, Hilkhot Keriat Shema* 4:8, *Hilkhot Tefilla* 4:5, *Hilkhot Tefillin Sefer Torah UMezuza* 10:8; *Shulḥan Arukh, Oraḥ Ḥayyim* 88, *Yoreh De'a* 282:9).

**So that Torah scholars would not be with their wives constantly, like roosters – שֶׁלֹּא יְהוּ תַּלְמִידֵי חֲכָמִים מְצוּיִים אֵצֶל נְשׁוֹתֵיהֶם כְּתַרְנְגוֹלִים:** It is inappropriate for a Torah scholar to overindulge in conjugal relations with his wife. The conjugal rights of the wife of a Torah scholar are once a week, on Shabbat eve (Rambam *Sefer HaMadda, Hilkhot De'ot* 5:4, *Sefer Ahava, Hilkhot Tefilla* 4:4; *Shulḥan Arukh, Oraḥ Ḥayyim* 240:1, *Even HaEzer* 25:2).

### NOTES

**They abolished ritual immersion – בַּטְּלוּהָ לִטְבִילוּתָא:** According to most commentaries, (Rambam, Ra'avad, *Shitta Mekubbetzet, Talmidei Rabbeinu Yona*), they could do so because Ezra's ordinance did not gain acceptance throughout Israel. The principle is that any ordinance that did not gain acceptance, even if it was instituted by Torah giants, may be overturned by later generations; even by a court of lower stature than the one that instituted it in the first place. Indeed, the ordinance was repealed for several reasons. It led to dereliction in the study of Torah and it discouraged procreation. Therefore, it only remained as a custom to enhance sanctity (*Me'iri*).

**Whispered it – לְחָשָׁהּ:** With regard to several *halakhot*, the Gemara says: This is the *halakha*, but a public ruling is not issued. If an individual poses the question, he is answered in accordance with the *halakha*. There are other *halakhot* which are not shared with individuals either and they remain the exclusive purview of the Torah scholars familiar with it.

אָמַר רַבִּי יַנַּאי: שָׁמַעְתִּי שֶׁמְּקִילִּין בָּהּ וְשָׁמַעְתִּי שֶׁמַּחְמִירִין בָּהּ, וְכׇל הַמַּחְמִיר בָּהּ עַל עַצְמוֹ מַאֲרִיכִין לוֹ יָמָיו וּשְׁנוֹתָיו.

With regard to this ritual immersion, **Rabbi Yannai said: I heard that there are those who are lenient with regard to it and I have heard that there are those who are stringent with regard to it.**[N] The *halakha* in this matter was never conclusively established **and anyone who** accepts **upon himself to be stringent with regard to it, they prolong for him his days and years.**[H]

אָמַר רַבִּי יְהוֹשֻׁעַ בֶּן לֵוִי: מָה טִיבָן שֶׁל טוֹבְלֵי שַׁחֲרִין? – מָה טִיבָן? הָא אִיהוּ דְּאָמַר: בַּעַל קֶרִי אָסוּר בְּדִבְרֵי תוֹרָה! – הָכִי קָאָמַר: מָה טִיבָן בְּאַרְבָּעִים סְאָה? אֶפְשָׁר בְּתִשְׁעָה קַבִּין, מָה טִיבָן בִּטְבִילָה? אֶפְשָׁר בִּנְתִינָה!

The Gemara relates that **Rabbi Yehoshua ben Levi said: What is the essence of those who immerse themselves in the morning?**[B] The Gemara retorts: How can one ask **what is their essence? Isn't he** the one **who said** that **one who experiences a seminal emission is prohibited from** engaging in **matters of Torah** and is required to immerse himself in the morning? Rather, **this is** what **he** meant to **say: What is the essence of** immersion in a ritual bath of **forty *se'a*** of water when **it is possible** to purify oneself **with nine *kav*?** Furthermore, **what is the essence of immersion** when **it is** also **possible** to purify oneself by **pouring** water?

אָמַר רַבִּי חֲנִינָא: גֶּדֶר גָּדוֹל גָּדְרוּ בָּהּ, דְּתַנְיָא: מַעֲשֶׂה בְּאֶחָד שֶׁתָּבַע אִשָּׁה לִדְבַר עֲבֵירָה. אָמְרָה לוֹ: רֵיקָא! יֵשׁ לְךָ אַרְבָּעִים סְאָה שֶׁאַתָּה טוֹבֵל בָּהֶן? מִיָּד פֵּירַשׁ.

Regarding this, **Rabbi Ḥanina said: They established a massive fence** protecting one from sinning with their decree that one must immerse himself in forty *se'a* of water. **As it was taught** in a *baraita*: There was **an incident involving one who solicited a woman to** commit **a sinful act. She said to him: Good-for-nothing. Do you have forty *se'a* in which to immerse** and purify **yourself** afterwards? He **immediately desisted.** The obligation to immerse oneself caused individuals to refrain from transgression.

אָמַר לְהוּ רַב הוּנָא לְרַבָּנַן: רַבּוֹתַי, מִפְּנֵי מָה אַתֶּם מְזַלְזְלִין בִּטְבִילָה זוֹ? אִי מִשּׁוּם צִינָּה, אֶפְשָׁר בַּמֶּרְחֲצָאוֹת!

**Rav Huna said to the Sages: Gentlemen, why do you disdain this immersion? If it is because** it is difficult for you to immerse in the **cold** waters of the ritual bath, **it is possible** to purify oneself by immersing oneself in the heated **bathhouses,** which are unfit for immersion for other forms of ritual impurity but are fit for immersion in this case.

אָמַר לֵיהּ רַב חִסְדָּא: וְכִי יֵשׁ טְבִילָה בְּחַמִּין? אָמַר לֵיהּ: רַב אַדָּא בַּר אַהֲבָה קָאֵי כְּוָותָךְ.

**Rabbi Ḥisda said to him: Is there ritual immersion in hot water?**[N] Rav Huna **said to him:** Indeed, doubts with regard to the fitness of baths have been raised, and **Rav Adda bar Ahava holds in accordance with your** opinion. Nevertheless, I remain convinced that it is permitted.

רַבִּי זֵירָא הֲוָה יָתֵיב בְּאַגְנָא דְּמַיָּא בֵּי מַסּוּתָא. אָמַר לֵיהּ לְשַׁמָּעֵיהּ: זִיל וְאַיְיתִי לִי תִּשְׁעָה קַבִּין וּשְׁדֵי עִלָּוַאי. אָמַר לֵיהּ רַבִּי חִיָּיא בַּר אַבָּא: לָמָּה לֵיהּ לְמָר כּוּלֵּי הַאי? וְהָא יָתֵיב בְּגַוַּויְיהוּ! אָמַר לֵיהּ: כְּאַרְבָּעִים סְאָה; מָה אַרְבָּעִים סְאָה בִּטְבִילָה וְלֹא בִּנְתִינָה אַף תִּשְׁעָה קַבִּין בִּנְתִינָה וְלֹא בִּטְבִילָה.

The Gemara relates: **Rabbi Zeira was sitting in a tub of water in the bathhouse. He said to his attendant: Go and get nine *kav*** of water **and pour it over me** so that I may purify myself from the impurity caused by a seminal emission. **Rabbi Ḥiyya bar Abba said to him: Why does my master** require **all of this? Aren't you seated in** at least nine *kav* of water in the tub. **He said to him:** The law of nine *kav* **parallels** the law of **forty *se'a*,** in that their *halakhot* are exclusive. **Just as forty *se'a*** can only purify an individual through **immersion and not through pouring, so too nine *kav*** can only purify one who experienced a seminal emission **through pouring**[H] **and not through immersion.**

רַב נַחְמָן תַּקֵּן חַצְבָּא בַּת תִּשְׁעָה קַבִּין. כִּי אֲתָא רַב דִּימִי אָמַר, רַבִּי עֲקִיבָא וְרַבִּי יְהוּדָה גְּלוֹסְטְרָא אָמְרוּ: לֹא שָׁנוּ אֶלָּא לְחוֹלֶה לְאוֹנְסוֹ, אֲבָל לְחוֹלֶה הַמַּרְגִּיל אַרְבָּעִים סְאָה.

The Gemara relates that **Rav Naḥman prepared a jug** with a capacity **of nine *kav*** so that his students could pour water over themselves and become pure. **When Rav Dimi came** from Eretz Yisrael to Babylonia, **he said: Rabbi Akiva and Rabbi Yehuda Gelostera**[L] **said:** The *halakha* that one who experienced a seminal emission can be purified by pouring nine *kav* **was only taught for a sick person** who experienced the emission **involuntarily. However, a sick person** who experienced a **normal** seminal emission[N] in the course of marital relations, is required to immerse himself in **forty *se'a*.**

אָמַר רַב יוֹסֵף: אִתְּבַר חַצְבֵיהּ דְּרַב נַחְמָן. כִּי אֲתָא רָבִין אָמַר: בְּאוּשָׁא הֲוָה עוּבְדָּא

**Rav Yosef said:** In that case, **Rav Naḥman's jug is broken,** meaning it is no longer of any use, as few people fall into the category of sick people who experienced seminal emissions. Nevertheless, **when Ravin came** from Eretz Yisrael to Babylonia **he said: In Usha there was an incident**

NOTES

**I heard that there are those who are lenient with regard to it and I have heard that there are those who are stringent with regard to it** – **שָׁמַעְתִּי שֶׁמְּקִילִּין בָּהּ וְשָׁמַעְתִּי שֶׁמַּחְמִירִין בָּהּ**: There are several interpretations of this statement. Some explained that lenient means that they do not require immersion but suffice with pouring nine *kav* of water and stringent means that they require immersion (*Shitta Mekubbetzet*). Others explained that lenient means immersion in a bath containing forty *se'a* and stringent means immersion in a full-fledged ritual bath (*Ba'al Halakhot Gedolot*).

**Immersion in hot water** – **טְבִילָה בְּחַמִּין**: The problem with bathhouses is not with the issue of immersion in hot water, as there are numerous methods to heat the water of the ritual bath while keeping it fit for immersion. The problem is that the water in bathhouses is drawn water, which is not fit for immersion at all. Therefore, they wondered whether or not immersion in hot water is appropriate (*Penei Yehoshua*).

**One who experienced a normal seminal emission** – **הַמַּרְגִּיל**: Some interpret this expression as a euphemism for conjugal relations with a woman based on the verse: "And she uncovered his feet [*margelotav*] and laid herself down" (Ruth 3:7; see Rav Sa'adia Gaon).

HALAKHA

**Anyone who accepts upon himself to be stringent with regard to this, they prolong for him his days and years** – **כׇּל הַמַּחְמִיר בָּהּ עַל עַצְמוֹ מַאֲרִיכִין לוֹ יָמָיו וּשְׁנוֹתָיו**: Even though the basic *halakha* is that one who experiences a seminal emission is not required to immerse himself, nevertheless, one who is stringent is praiseworthy as per the statement of Rabbi Yannai (*Tur, Oraḥ Ḥayyim* 241).

**Nine *kav* only through pouring** – **תִּשְׁעָה קַבִּין בִּנְתִינָה**: One who seeks to purify himself from the ritual impurity of a seminal emission by pouring nine *kav* of water must pour it on his back all at once as per the opinion of Rav Ḥisda (*Beit Yosef* on *Tur Oraḥ Ḥayyim* 88).

BACKGROUND

**Those who immerse themselves in the morning** – **טוֹבְלֵי שַׁחֲרִית**: Those mentioned here as immersing in the morning may have once comprised a clearly defined group who deviated from the path established by the Sages in different ways.

At the end of the *Tosefta* for tractate *Yadayim* we find the following: Those who immerse in the morning said: We rail against you Pharisees, for you recite the Name of God in a state of impurity. They replied: We rail against you who immerse in the morning, for you recite the Name in an impure body. Apparently, those who immersed in the morning considered themselves separate from the Pharisee Sages of Israel. Indeed, some theorize that this refers to an Essene cult that was particularly strict with regard to the laws of purity and whose members stringently purified themselves after seminal emissions by immersing in an actual ritual bath.

LANGUAGE

**Gelostera** – **גְּלוֹסְטְרָא**: The source of this word is from the Greek κλεῖστρον, *kleistron*, or from the Latin claustrum, both of which mean bolt or lock. The Sages used it to refer to a specific type of bolt. It seems here that it should be read *gelustara'a*, which is how it appears in other versions and manuscripts. In Aramaic, this refers to the individual who fashions bolts and the nickname was thus given to this Sage who worked as a locksmith. Many nicknames were similarly given to Sages based on their unique professions.

**HALAKHA**

The immersion of one who is impure because of a seminal emission – טְבִילַת בַּעַל קֶרִי: Although Ezra's ordinance was annulled, there are many communities where the custom remains for one who experienced a seminal emission to immerse himself before prayer. They hold that Ezra's ordinance was only repealed with regard to Torah study, not prayer (See Rambam *Sefer Ahava*, *Hilkhot Tefilla* 4:5–6).

**BACKGROUND**

*Kav* – קַב: This is a basic unit of measurement from which many other small units are derived. It is equivalent to one-sixth of a *se'a* or 24 egg-bulks.

Forty *se'a* – אַרְבָּעִים סְאָה: A *se'a* is one-thirtieth of a *kor* or the equivalent of 144 egg-bulks. Forty *se'a* are the equivalent of 80 *hin* or 5,760 egg-bulks. This is the minimum amount of water required for a ritual bath. A container large enough to hold 40 *se'a* or more is no longer considered to be a utensil, but rather, a building of sorts. This has ramifications in areas of *halakha* like ritual impurity and prohibited labor on Shabbat. The 40 *se'a* measure is the basis of all modern calculations of the various measures of volume. The Talmud tells us that the dimensions of a ritual bath must be 3 cubits by 1 cubit, and that its volume must be 40 *se'a*. Consequently, according to the Na'e scale, a ritual bath must contain 332 ℓ of water (87 US gal), and, according to the Ḥazon Ish, 573 ℓ (151 US gal).

בְּקִילְעָא דְּרַב אוֹשַׁעְיָא, אֲתוּ וּשְׁאַלוּ לְרַב אַסִי, אֲמַר לְהוּ: לֹא שָׁנוּ אֶלָּא לְחוֹלֶה הַמַּרְגִּיל, אֲבָל לְחוֹלֶה לְאוֹנְסוֹ פָּטוּר מִכְּלוּם. אֲמַר רַב יוֹסֵף: אִצְטְמִיד חַצְבֵיהּ דְּרַב נַחְמָן.

that this problem was raised **in Rav Oshaya's chamber,** and **they came and asked Rav Asi. He said to them: They only stated** the obligation to pour water over one who is impure because of a seminal emission **with regard to a sick person who experienced a normal** seminal emission, **but a sick person who experienced an involuntary** seminal emission is clearly **exempt from anything** and requires no immersion whatsoever. **Rav Yosef said:** In that case, **Rav Naḥman's jug is rejoined,** meaning that it is effective with regard to purification.

מִכְּדֵי כּוּלְּהוּ אֲמוֹרָאֵי וְתַנָּאֵי בְּדְעֶזְרָא קָמִיפַּלְגִי, וְנֶחֱזֵי עֶזְרָא הֵיכִי תַּקֵּן!

Up to now, discussion has focused on various problems pertaining to the laws of immersion as they concern one whose impurity is due to seminal emission. The Gemara asks: **Since all of the *amora'im* and *tanna'im* disagree with regard to** the decree of Ezra, **let us examine how Ezra instituted** this ordinance, as this is not an uncommon circumstance and we can see how they conducted themselves.

אֲמַר אַבַּיֵי: עֶזְרָא תַּקֵּן לְבָרִיא הַמַּרְגִּיל אַרְבָּעִים סְאָה, וּבָרִיא לְאוֹנְסוֹ – תִּשְׁעָה קַבִּין. וַאֲתוּ אֲמוֹרָאֵי וּפְלִיגִי בְּחוֹלֶה; מָר סָבַר: חוֹלֶה הַמַּרְגִּיל כְּבָרִיא הַמַּרְגִּיל, וְחוֹלֶה לְאוֹנְסוֹ כְּבָרִיא לְאוֹנְסוֹ; וּמָר סָבַר: חוֹלֶה הַמַּרְגִּיל כְּבָרִיא לְאוֹנְסוֹ, וְחוֹלֶה לְאוֹנְסוֹ פָּטוּר מִכְּלוּם.

**Abaye said: Ezra** did not institute a sweeping ordinance concerning every case of one who experienced a seminal emission; rather, he **instituted** only that **a healthy person who experienced a normal** seminal emission is required to immerse himself in **forty *se'a*, while for a healthy person** who experienced an **involuntary** seminal emission, **nine *kav*** are sufficient.[H] **And the *amora'im* came and disagreed with regard to a sick person. One Sage held** that **a sick person who experienced a normal** seminal emission is considered **like a healthy person who experienced a normal** seminal emission, **while a sick person** who experienced an **involuntary** seminal emission is considered **like a healthy person** who experienced an **involuntary** seminal emission. **However, another Sage maintained** that **a sick person who experienced a normal** seminal emission is considered **like a healthy person** who experienced an **involuntary** seminal emission, and consequently requires only that nine *kav* be poured over him, **while a sick person** who experienced an **involuntary** seminal emission **is exempt from any** form of immersion or purification.

אֲמַר רָבָא: נְהִי דְּתַקֵּן עֶזְרָא טְבִילָה, נְתִינָה מִי תַּקֵּן? וְהָאָמַר מָר: עֶזְרָא תַּקֵּן טְבִילָה לְבַעֲלֵי קְרָיִין! אֶלָּא אֲמַר רָבָא: עֶזְרָא תַּקֵּן טְבִילָה לְבָרִיא הַמַּרְגִּיל אַרְבָּעִים סְאָה. וַאֲתוּ רַבָּנַן וְהִתְקִינוּ לְבָרִיא לְאוֹנְסוֹ תִּשְׁעָה קַבִּין. וַאֲתוּ אֲמוֹרָאֵי וְקָא מִיפַּלְגִי בְּחוֹלֶה; מָר סָבַר: חוֹלֶה הַמַּרְגִּיל כְּבָרִיא הַמַּרְגִּיל, וְחוֹלֶה לְאוֹנְסוֹ כְּבָרִיא לְאוֹנְסוֹ; וּמָר סָבַר: לְבָרִיא הַמַּרְגִּיל אַרְבָּעִים סְאָה וְחוֹלֶה הַמַּרְגִּיל כְּבָרִיא לְאוֹנְסוֹ, תִּשְׁעָה קַבִּין, אֲבָל לְחוֹלֶה לְאוֹנְסוֹ – פָּטוּר מִכְּלוּם.

**Rava said: Although Ezra instituted immersion** for one who experienced a seminal emission, **did he institute the pouring** of nine *kav*?[B] **Didn't the Master say** that we have a tradition that **Ezra** only **instituted immersion for those who experienced a seminal emission? Rather, Rava said:** We must explain that the diverse opinions developed after Ezra's decree. **Ezra** himself **instituted immersion in forty *se'a*[B]** only **for a healthy person who experienced a normal** seminal emission. **And the Sages came and instituted that a healthy person who experienced an involuntary** seminal emission should have **nine *kav*** poured over him. **And** then **the *amora'im* came and disagreed** with regard to **a sick person; one Sage held** that **a sick person who experienced a normal** seminal emission is considered **like a healthy person who experienced a normal** seminal emission, **while a sick person** who experienced an **involuntary** seminal emission is considered **like a healthy person** who experienced an **involuntary** seminal emission, **another Sage maintained** that only **a healthy person who experienced a normal** seminal emission is required to immerse himself in **forty *se'a* while a sick person who experienced a normal** seminal emission is considered **like a healthy person** who experienced an **involuntary** seminal emission, requiring only **nine *kav*. But a sick person** who experienced an **involuntary** seminal emission **is exempt from any** form of immersion or purification.

אֲמַר רָבָא: הִלְכְתָא, בָּרִיא הַמַּרְגִּיל וְחוֹלֶה הַמַּרְגִּיל – אַרְבָּעִים סְאָה, וּבָרִיא לְאוֹנְסוֹ – תִּשְׁעָה קַבִּין, אֲבָל לְחוֹלֶה לְאוֹנְסוֹ – פָּטוּר מִכְּלוּם.

**Rava stated** that **the** halakhic ruling is in accordance with the first opinion: **A healthy person** who experienced **a normal** seminal emission **and a sick person** who experienced **a normal** seminal emission require **forty *se'a*, while a healthy person** who experienced **an involuntary** seminal emission suffices with **nine *kav*. But a sick person** who experienced an **involuntary** seminal emission **is exempt from** undergoing **any** rite of purification.

תָּנוּ רַבָּנַן: בַּעַל קֶרִי שֶׁנָּתְנוּ עָלָיו תִּשְׁעָה קַבִּין מַיִם – טָהוֹר; בַּמֶּה דְּבָרִים אֲמוּרִים – לְעַצְמוֹ, אֲבָל לַאֲחֵרִים – אַרְבָּעִים סְאָה; רַבִּי יְהוּדָה אוֹמֵר: אַרְבָּעִים סְאָה מִכׇּל מָקוֹם.

**The Sages taught** in a *Tosefta*: **One who experienced a seminal emission and had nine *kav* of** drawn **water poured over him is ritually pure. In what** case **is this statement said?** In a case involving Torah study **for himself, but** in order to purify himself that he may teach Torah **to others,** he must immerse himself in **forty *se'a*. Rabbi Yehuda says: Forty *se'a*** is required for purification **in any case.**

רַבִּי יוֹחָנָן וְרַבִּי יְהוֹשֻׁעַ בֶּן לֵוִי וְרַבִּי אֶלְעָזָר וְרַבִּי יוֹסֵי בְּרַבִּי חֲנִינָא, חַד מֵהַאי זוּגָא וְחַד מֵהַאי זוּגָא אַרֵישָׁא. חַד אָמַר: הָא דְּאָמְרַתְּ ״בַּמֶּה דְּבָרִים אֲמוּרִים לְעַצְמוֹ אֲבָל לַאֲחֵרִים אַרְבָּעִים סְאָה״ – לֹא שָׁנוּ אֶלָּא לְחוֹלֶה הַמַּרְגִּיל, אֲבָל לְחוֹלֶה לְאוֹנְסוֹ – תִּשְׁעָה קַבִּין; וְחַד אָמַר: כֹּל לַאֲחֵרִים – אֲפִילּוּ חוֹלֶה לְאוֹנְסוֹ – עַד דְּאִיכָּא אַרְבָּעִים סְאָה.

With regard to this issue, a dispute arose between **Rabbi Yoḥanan and Rabbi Yehoshua ben Levi, and Rabbi Elazar and Rabbi Yosei, son of Rabbi Ḥanina. One** member **of this pair**[N] **and one** member **of that pair** disagreed **with regard to the first clause** of the *Tosefta*. **One said: That which you said: In what** case **is this statement said?** In a case involving Torah study **for himself, but** in order to purify himself that he may teach Torah **to others,** he must immerse himself in **forty *se'a*,** was **only taught regarding a sick person who experienced a normal** seminal emission, **but for a sick person** who experienced an **involuntary** seminal emission, **nine *kav*** is sufficient even for teaching others. **And one said** that **anyone** who teaches **others, even** if he was **sick** and experienced an **involuntary** seminal emission, is not considered pure **until there are forty *se'a*.**

וְחַד מֵהַאי זוּגָא וְחַד מֵהַאי זוּגָא אַסֵּיפָא. חַד אָמַר: הָא דְּאָמַר רַבִּי יְהוּדָה ״אַרְבָּעִים סְאָה מִכׇּל מָקוֹם״ – לֹא שָׁנוּ אֶלָּא בְּקַרְקַע, אֲבָל בְּכֵלִים – לֹא; וְחַד אָמַר: אֲפִילּוּ בְּכֵלִים נָמֵי.

**And one** member **of this pair and one** member **of that pair** disagreed **with regard to the latter clause** of the *Tosefta*. **One said: That which Rabbi Yehuda said: Forty *se'a* in any case, was only taught when** the water is in **the ground,** in accordance with the Torah law of ritual bath,[N] **but not** if it was collected **in vessels. And one said: Even** forty *se'a* collected **in vessels** are sufficient for purification.

בִּשְׁלָמָא לְמַאן דַּאֲמַר אֲפִילּוּ בְּכֵלִים – הַיְינוּ דְּקָתָנֵי: ״רַבִּי יְהוּדָה אוֹמֵר אַרְבָּעִים סְאָה מִכׇּל מָקוֹם״. אֶלָּא לְמַאן דַּאֲמַר ״בְּקַרְקַע – אִין, בְּכֵלִים – לָא״ ״מִכׇּל מָקוֹם״ לְאֵתוֹיֵי מַאי?

The Gemara clarifies this problem: **Granted, according to the one who said** that forty *se'a* purifies **even in vessels. That is** why the *Tosefta* **taught: Rabbi Yehuda says: Forty *se'a* in any case. However,** according to **the one who said** that Rabbi Yehuda's opinion is that forty *se'a* **in the ground, yes,** it purifies, but **in vessels, no,** it does not purify, **what** does the expression **in any case** come **to include?**

לְאֵתוֹיֵי מַיִם שְׁאוּבִין.

The Gemara explains: In any case comes **to include drawn water,**[N] as Rabbi Yehuda permits immersion in forty *se'a* of water collected in the ground even if the water was drawn by human hand.

רַב פָּפָּא וְרַב הוּנָא בְּרֵיהּ דְּרַב יְהוֹשֻׁעַ וְרָבָא (בְּרַבִּי) בַּר שְׁמוּאֵל כְּרִיכוּ רִיפְתָּא בַּהֲדֵי הֲדָדֵי. אֲמַר לְהוּ רַב פָּפָּא: הַבוּ לִי לְדִידִי לְבָרוֹךְ, דִּנְפוּל עִילָּוַאי תִּשְׁעָה קַבִּין. אֲמַר לְהוּ רָבָא (בְּרַבִּי) [בַּר] שְׁמוּאֵל, תְּנֵינָא: בַּמֶּה דְּבָרִים אֲמוּרִים – לְעַצְמוֹ, אֲבָל לַאֲחֵרִים – אַרְבָּעִים סְאָה; אֶלָּא, הַבוּ לִי לְדִידִי לְבָרוֹךְ, דִּנְפוּל עִילָּוַאי אַרְבָּעִים סְאָה. אֲמַר לְהוּ רַב הוּנָא: הַבוּ לִי לְדִידִי לְבָרוֹךְ, דְּלֵיכָּא עִילָּוַאי לָא הַאי וְלָא הַאי.

The Gemara relates that **Rav Pappa and Rav Huna, son of Rav Yehoshua, and Rava bar Shmuel ate bread together. Rav Pappa said to them: Allow me to recite** Grace after Meals for the group, as I am ritually pure because **nine *kav*** of water **fell upon me;** in other words, he poured it over himself. **Rava bar Shmuel said to them: We learned, in what** case **is this statement** that nine *kav* purify, **said?** In a case involving Torah study **for himself. But,** in order to purify himself that he may teach Torah **to others,** and by extension to fulfill the obligation of others, he must immerse himself in **forty *se'a*.**[N] **Rather, allow me to recite** Grace after Meals for the group, **as forty *se'a*** of water **fell upon me;** in other words, I immersed myself in a ritual bath. **Rav Huna said to them: Allow me to recite** Grace after Meals for the group, **as I have** had **neither this nor that upon me** because I remained ritually pure.

רַב חָמָא טָבֵיל בְּמַעֲלֵי יוֹמָא דְּפִסְחָא לְהוֹצִיא רַבִּים יְדֵי חוֹבָתָן. וְלֵית הִלְכְתָא כְּוָותֵיהּ.

It is also said that **Rav Ḥama would immerse himself on Passover eve in order to fulfill the obligations of the masses.** However the Gemara concludes: **The *halakha* is not in accordance with his** opinion that distinguishes between the purification for oneself and purification for the sake of others.

מַתְנִי׳ הָיָה עוֹמֵד בַּתְּפִלָּה וְנִזְכַּר שֶׁהוּא בַּעַל קֶרִי – לֹא יַפְסִיק, אֶלָּא יְקַצֵּר.

**MISHNA** This mishna contains various statements with regard to individuals with different types of ritual impurity as well as the need to distance oneself from filth and impurity. **One who was standing in prayer and he recalled that he experienced a seminal emission,** and according to this opinion he is prohibited from praying, should **not interrupt** his prayer, **rather he should abridge** each individual blessing.

## NOTES

**One member of this pair – חַד מֵהַאי זוּגָא:** In other words, Rabbi Yoḥanan and Rabbi Yehoshua ben Levi constitute one pair. Although they were not members of the same generation, there was a personal connection between them and there are numerous disputes between them. The second pair is Rabbi Elazar and Rabbi Yosei son of Rabbi Ḥanina, who were both students of Rabbi Yoḥanan. In these matters, it was specifically the Sages from different pairs that disagreed with each other (*Arukh* based on Rabbeinu Ḥananel).

**Ritual bath – מִקְוֶה:** Regarding that which purifies an individual, the Torah states: "Only a spring or a pit wherein water collects [*mikve mayyim*] will be pure" (Leviticus 11:36). The Sages established the minimum quantity of water in a ritual bath capable of purifying an individual at forty *se'a*. The water must gather by itself. Not only does water drawn by hand fail to purify, in certain circumstances it can disqualify a ritual bath previously fit to purify. The Sages only permitted immersion in drawn water in certain cases where one is impure by rabbinic law.

**To include drawn water – לְאֵתוֹיֵי מַיִם שְׁאוּבִין:** Immersion in drawn water was permitted only to enable those who experienced a seminal emission to engage in matters of Torah. Since their impurity is not very severe, the Sages were lenient as to their purification. This is explicitly stated in the mishna (*Mikvaot* 5:1).

**To others, forty *se'a* – לַאֲחֵרִים – אַרְבָּעִים סְאָה:** The reason for the stringency with regard to teaching Torah to others is due to the fact that the prohibition for those who experienced a seminal emission to engage in Torah matters is derived by means of allusion from the revelation at Sinai, where the Torah was transmitted to the masses (*Tosefot HaRosh*, *Shitta Mekubbetzet*). That was why Rav Ḥama immersed himself in order to fulfill the obligations of the many at the Passover seder. Although he was not teaching them Torah, many people were there (Rav Natronai).

## BACKGROUND

**Soaking water** – מֵי הַמִּשְׁרָה: Flax cultivation was widespread throughout Israel at the time of the Mishna, and nearly every household would process the flax necessary to meet its own needs. The linen fiber was extracted from the flax by breaking it up and retting it in vats or pools of water and allowing it to soak until the outer husks would rot away revealing the fibers ready to be processed. This is why soaking water is often cited as an example of foul-smelling, stagnant water present in many homes.

**Urine flowing on his knees** – מַיִם שׁוֹתְתִין עַל בִּרְכָּיו: Both the anus and the urethra are controlled by muscles, which, in the course of the maturation process, one learns to control and relax when necessary. At the same time, there are situations of sudden fear or pain that can cause one to lose control over those muscles and lead to a spontaneous release of urine or excrement.

## NOTES

**The sacrifice of the wicked is an abomination** – זֶבַח רְשָׁעִים תּוֹעֵבָה: Some explain that this is an excerpt from a different verse in Proverbs: "The sacrifice of the wicked is an abomination to the Lord; but the prayer of the upright is His delight" (Proverbs 15:8; see *Siftei Ḥakhamim*).

יָרַד לִטְבּוֹל, אִם יָכוֹל לַעֲלוֹת וּלְהִתְכַּסּוֹת וְלִקְרוֹת עַד שֶׁלֹּא תֵּהֵא הָנֵץ הַחַמָּה – יַעֲלֶה וְיִתְכַּסֶּה וְיִקְרָא, וְאִם לָאו – יִתְכַּסֶּה בַּמַּיִם וְיִקְרָא; וְלֹא יִתְכַּסֶּה לֹא בַּמַּיִם הָרָעִים וְלֹא בְּמֵי הַמִּשְׁרָה, עַד שֶׁיַּטִּיל לְתוֹכָן מַיִם. וְכַמָּה יַרְחִיק מֵהֶן וּמִן הַצּוֹאָה – אַרְבַּע אַמּוֹת.

They stated a general principle: **One who descended to immerse himself,**[H] **if he is able to ascend, cover himself** with a garment, **and recite** the morning *Shema* **before sunrise, he should ascend, cover himself, and recite** *Shema*, **and if not,** he should **cover himself in the water and recite** *Shema* **there. He may not, however, cover himself in either foul water, or water** in which flax was **soaked,**[B] **until he pours** other **water into it. And** in general, **how far must one distance** himself **from** urine **and feces** in order to recite *Shema*? At least **four cubits.**

גמ׳ תָּנוּ רַבָּנַן: הָיָה עוֹמֵד בִּתְפִלָּה וְנִזְכַּר שֶׁהוּא בַּעַל קֶרִי – לֹא יַפְסִיק אֶלָּא יְקַצֵּר. הָיָה קוֹרֵא בַּתּוֹרָה וְנִזְכַּר שֶׁהוּא בַּעַל קֶרִי – אֵינוֹ מַפְסִיק וְעוֹלֶה, אֶלָּא מְגַמְגֵּם וְקוֹרֵא; רַבִּי מֵאִיר אוֹמֵר: אֵין בַּעַל קֶרִי רַשַּׁאי לִקְרוֹת בַּתּוֹרָה יוֹתֵר מִשְּׁלֹשָׁה פְּסוּקִים.

**GEMARA** A *baraita* further elaborates on the first *halakha* in the mishna. **The Sages taught: One who was standing in prayer and he recalled that he** had **experienced a seminal emission,** should **not interrupt** his prayer. **Rather, he should abridge. One who was reading the Torah and recalled that he experienced a seminal emission, does not interrupt** his reading, **but rather reads quickly** with less than perfect diction. **Rabbi Meir** disagrees and **says: One who experienced a seminal emission is not permitted to read more than three verses in the Torah,** as one may read no fewer than three verses in the Torah. After he completes three verses, he must stop and let someone else continue.

תַּנְיָא אִידָךְ: הָיָה עוֹמֵד בִּתְפִלָּה וְרָאָה צוֹאָה כְּנֶגְדּוֹ – מְהַלֵּךְ לְפָנָיו עַד שֶׁיִּזְרְקֶנָּה לַאֲחוֹרָיו אַרְבַּע אַמּוֹת. וְהָתַנְיָא: לְצִדְדִין! – לָא קַשְׁיָא: הָא – דְּאֶפְשָׁר, הָא – דְּלָא אֶפְשָׁר.

**It was taught in another** *baraita*: **One who was standing in prayer and he saw feces before him**[H] **must walk forward until he has placed it four cubits behind him.** The Gemara challenges this: **Wasn't it taught** in another *baraita* that it is sufficient if he distances himself four cubits **to the side?** The Gemara resolves this contradiction: **This is not difficult,** as **that** *baraita* which taught that it must be four cubits behind him, is referring to a case **where it is possible** for him to advance that distance, **while that** *baraita* which taught that he may distance himself four cubits to the side, is referring to a case **where it is not possible** to advance four cubits, in which case he must at least step to the side.

הָיָה מִתְפַּלֵּל וּמָצָא צוֹאָה בִּמְקוֹמוֹ, אָמַר רַבָּה: אַף עַל פִּי שֶׁחָטָא – תְּפִלָּתוֹ תְּפִלָּה. מַתְקִיף לַהּ רָבָא: וְהָא ״זֶבַח רְשָׁעִים תּוֹעֵבָה״! אֶלָּא אָמַר רָבָא: הוֹאִיל וְחָטָא, אַף עַל פִּי שֶׁהִתְפַּלֵּל – תְּפִלָּתוֹ תּוֹעֵבָה.

The Gemara cites another *halakha*: **One who was praying and** later **found feces in the place** where he prayed,[H] **Rabba said: Although he committed a transgression** in his failure to examine that venue to determine if it was worthy of prayer (*Tosafot*), **his prayer is a** valid **prayer** and he fulfilled his obligation. **Rava strongly objects to** his statement: **Isn't** it stated: **"The sacrifice of the wicked is an abomination,**[N] the more so as he offers it in depravity" (Proverbs 21:27), from which we derive that a mitzva performed inappropriately is no mitzva at all? Consequently, the fact that he did not pay proper attention invalidates his prayer. **Rather, Rava said: Because** this person **committed a transgression, although he prayed, his prayer is an abomination** and he must pray again.

תָּנוּ רַבָּנַן: הָיָה עוֹמֵד בִּתְפִלָּה וּמַיִם שׁוֹתְתִין עַל בִּרְכָּיו – פּוֹסֵק עַד שֶׁיִּכְלוּ הַמַּיִם, וְחוֹזֵר וּמִתְפַּלֵּל. לְהֵיכָן חוֹזֵר? רַב חִסְדָּא וְרַב הַמְנוּנָא, חַד אָמַר: חוֹזֵר לָרֹאשׁ; וְחַד אָמַר: לַמָּקוֹם שֶׁפָּסַק.

**The Sages taught** in a *baraita*: **One who was standing in prayer when,** for some reason, **urine is flowing on his knees,**[BH] **he must interrupt** his prayer **until the urine ceases, and then resume praying.** The Gemara, asks: **To where** in the prayer **does he return** when he resumes his prayer? **Rav Ḥisda and Rav Hamnuna** disagreed; **one said: He must return to the beginning** of the prayer, **and the other said:** He must return **to the point where he stopped.**

לֵימָא בְּהָא קָמִיפַּלְגִי,

The Gemara notes: **Let us say** that **they disagree about this:**

## HALAKHA

**One who was standing in prayer and he recalled that he experienced a seminal emission…one who descended to immerse himself, etc.** – ...הָיָה עוֹמֵד בִּתְפִלָּה וְנִזְכַּר שֶׁהוּא בַּעַל קֶרִי – יָרַד לִטְבּוֹל וכו׳: One who is in the ritual bath immersing himself when the time to recite *Shema* arrives, covers himself in the water and recites *Shema*. This applies only when the water is at least slightly murky and obscures view of his nakedness; however, not when the water is foul, in accordance with the mishna (Rambam *Sefer Ahava, Hilkhot Keriat Shema* 2:7).

**One who was standing in prayer when he saw feces before him** – הָיָה מִתְפַּלֵּל וְרָאָה צוֹאָה כְּנֶגְדּוֹ: One who is reciting *Shema* or praying and sees feces before him must walk forward until it is four cubits behind him. If he is unable to walk forward four cubits, he moves to the side. If he is in the middle of the *Amida* prayer, turns his head aside (*Magen Avraham*), and then continues where he interrupted his reciting of *Shema* or his prayer, in accordance with the *baraita* (Rambam *Sefer Ahava, Hilkhot Tefilla* 4:9; *Shulḥan Arukh, Oraḥ Ḥayyim* 81:2).

**One who was praying and later found feces in the place where he prayed** – הָיָה מִתְפַּלֵּל וּמָצָא צוֹאָה בִּמְקוֹמוֹ: One who prayed or recited *Shema* in a place where there was room for concern that feces were present, and indeed later discovered feces there, distances himself from that area and repeats the entire prayer in accordance with the opinion of Rava, who challenged Rabba's ruling and whose opinion was adopted (Rambam *Sefer Ahava, Hilkhot Tefilla* 4:9; *Shulḥan Arukh, Oraḥ Ḥayyim* 76:8).

**One who was standing in prayer when, for some reason, urine is flowing on his knees** – הָיָה עוֹמֵד בִּתְפִלָּה וּמַיִם שׁוֹתְתִין עַל בִּרְכָּיו: One who recites *Shema*, and the same is true with regard to the *Amida* prayer (*Peri Megadim*), and his urine began to flow must suspend his recitation until the flow stops and then start his prayer again, as per the opinion of Rava (Rambam *Sefer Ahava, Hilkhot Tefilla* 4:13; *Shulḥan Arukh, Oraḥ Ḥayyim* 76, 78).

מָר סָבַר: אִם שָׁהָה כְּדֵי לִגְמוֹר אֶת כּוּלָּהּ – חוֹזֵר לָרֹאשׁ; וּמָר סָבַר: לְמָקוֹם שֶׁפָּסַק.

One Sage held that, as a rule, if one interrupted his prayer and **delayed** continuing his prayer for an interval **sufficient to complete the entire** prayer,[H] **he returns to the beginning** of the prayer. **And** one **Sage held:** He returns **to the place** in the prayer **where he stopped.**

אֲמַר רַב אַשִׁי: הַאי "אִם שָׁהָה"? "אִם לֹא שָׁהָה" מִיבָּעֵי לֵיהּ! – אֶלָּא, דְּכוּלֵּי עָלְמָא אִם שָׁהָה כְּדֵי לִגְמוֹר אֶת כּוּלָּהּ – חוֹזֵר לָרֹאשׁ, וְהָתָם בִּדְלָא שָׁהָה קָמִיפַּלְגִי; דְּמָר סָבַר: גַּבְרָא דְּחוּיָא הוּא, וְאֵין רָאוּי, וְאֵין תְּפִלָּתוֹ תְּפִלָּה; וּמָר סָבַר: גַּבְרָא חַזְיָא הוּא, וּתְפִלָּתוֹ תְּפִלָּה.

Rejecting this possibility, **Rav Ashi said:** If that was the point of their dispute, they should not have simply issued a ruling in a case: **If he delayed.** They **should have** also addressed a case **if he did not delay** as well as discussing the length of the delay. **Rather, everyone,** both Rav Ḥisda and Rav Hamnuna, **agrees that if one delayed** continuing his prayer for an interval **sufficient to complete the entire** prayer, **he returns to the beginning** of the prayer. **And there,** in the dispute under discussion, **they disagreed with regard to one who did not delay** that long. The dispute deals with his particular predicament. **As** one **Sage held: He is a man** who is **disqualified and unfit, and his prayer is not a** valid **prayer;** therefore he must repeat it in its entirety. **And one Sage held: He is a man who is fit and his prayer is** a valid **prayer.**

תָּנוּ רַבָּנַן: הַנִּצְרָךְ לִנְקָבָיו – אַל יִתְפַּלֵּל, וְאִם הִתְפַּלֵּל – תְּפִלָּתוֹ תּוֹעֵבָה. אָמַר רַב זְבִיד וְאִיתֵּימָא רַב יְהוּדָה: לֹא שָׁנוּ אֶלָּא שֶׁאֵינוֹ יָכוֹל לִשְׁהוֹת בְּעַצְמוֹ, אֲבָל אִם יָכוֹל לִשְׁהוֹת בְּעַצְמוֹ – תְּפִלָּתוֹ תְּפִלָּה.

**The Sages taught** in a *baraita*: **One who needs to relieve himself may not pray,**[HN] **and if he prayed, his prayer is an abomination. Rav Zevid and some say Rav Yehuda said** in qualifying this statement: **They only taught** this *halakha* in a case where **one cannot restrain himself. But, if he can restrain himself, his prayer is a** valid **prayer** as he is not tarnished by his need to relieve himself.

וְעַד כַּמָּה? – אָמַר רַב שֵׁשֶׁת: עַד פַּרְסָה. אִיכָּא דְּמַתְנֵי לָהּ אַמַּתְנִיתָא: בַּמֶּה דְּבָרִים אֲמוּרִים – כְּשֶׁאֵין יָכוֹל לַעֲמוֹד עַל עַצְמוֹ, אֲבָל אִם יָכוֹל לַעֲמוֹד עַל עַצְמוֹ – תְּפִלָּתוֹ תְּפִלָּה. וְעַד כַּמָּה? אֲמַר רַב זְבִיד: עַד פַּרְסָה.

The Gemara asks: **And** for **how long** must he be able to restrain himself? **Rav Sheshet said:** For **as long as** it takes to walk **one parasang.**[B] **Some teach this** *halakha* directly **on** what was taught in **the** *baraita*: **In what** case **is this statement said? Where he is unable to restrain himself, but if he is able to restrain himself, his prayer is a** valid **prayer. And for how long? Rav Zevid said:** For as **long as** it takes to walk **one parasang.**

אָמַר רַבִּי שְׁמוּאֵל בַּר נַחְמָנִי אָמַר רַבִּי יוֹנָתָן: הַנִּצְרָךְ לִנְקָבָיו הֲרֵי זֶה לֹא יִתְפַּלֵּל, מִשּׁוּם שֶׁנֶּאֱמַר: "הִכּוֹן לִקְרַאת אֱלֹהֶיךָ יִשְׂרָאֵל".

**Rabbi Shmuel bar Naḥmani said** that **Rabbi Yonatan said: One who needs to relieve himself may not pray, because it is stated: "Prepare to greet your God, O Israel"** (Amos 4:12), and one must clear his mind of all distractions to prepare to receive the Lord during prayer.

וְאָמַר רַבִּי שְׁמוּאֵל בַּר נַחְמָנִי אָמַר רַבִּי יוֹנָתָן: מַאי דִּכְתִיב "שְׁמוֹר רַגְלְךָ כַּאֲשֶׁר תֵּלֵךְ אֶל בֵּית הָאֱלֹהִים", שְׁמוֹר עַצְמְךָ שֶׁלֹּא תֶּחֱטָא, וְאִם תֶּחֱטָא – הָבֵא קָרְבָּן לְפָנַי. "וְקָרוֹב לִשְׁמֹעַ דִּבְרֵי חֲכָמִים", אָמַר רָבָא: הֱוֵי קָרוֹב לִשְׁמוֹעַ דִּבְרֵי חֲכָמִים שֶׁאִם חוֹטְאִים מְבִיאִים קָרְבָּן וְעוֹשִׂים תְּשׁוּבָה. "מִתֵּת הַכְּסִילִים זָבַח" – אַל תְּהִי כַּכְּסִילִים שֶׁחוֹטְאִים וּמְבִיאִים קָרְבָּן וְאֵין עוֹשִׂים תְּשׁוּבָה.

In this context, the Gemara cites an additional statement, which **Rabbi Shmuel bar Naḥmani said** that **Rabbi Yonatan said: What is the meaning of that which is written: "Guard your foot**[N] **when you go to the house of God,** and prepare to listen; it is better than when fools offer sacrifices, as they know not to do evil" (Ecclesiastes 4:17)? It means: When you enter the house of the Lord, **guard yourself from transgression, and if you commit a transgression, bring a sacrifice before Me** in atonement. The verse continues: **"And draw near and listen to the words of the wise." Rava said: Be prepared to hearken to the words of the wise, who, if they commit a transgression, they bring a sacrifice and repent.** He interprets the next part of the verse: **"It is better than when fools give sacrifices,"** that **one should not act like the fools who commit a transgression and bring a sacrifice but do not repent.**

"כִּי אֵינָם יוֹדְעִים לַעֲשׂוֹת רָע", אִי הָכִי צַדִּיקִים נִינְהוּ! אֶלָּא, אַל תְּהִי כַּכְּסִילִים שֶׁחוֹטְאִים וּמְבִיאִים קָרְבָּן, וְאֵינָם יוֹדְעִים אִם עַל הַטּוֹבָה הֵם מְבִיאִים אִם עַל הָרָעָה הֵם מְבִיאִים. אָמַר הַקָּדוֹשׁ בָּרוּךְ הוּא: בֵּין טוֹב לְרַע אֵינָן מַבְחִינִים, וְהֵם מְבִיאִים קָרְבָּן לְפָנַי?

Regarding the end of the verse: **"As they know not to do evil,"**[N] the Gemara asks: **If so, they are righteous. Rather** it must be understood: **Do not be like the fools who commit a transgression and bring a sacrifice, but are unaware whether they are bringing it** as a thanks-offering **for the good,** or as an offering of atonement **for the evil.** This is the meaning of the verse: "As they know not to do evil"; they know not if and when their actions are evil. With regard to those individuals, **the Holy One, Blessed be He, said: They cannot distinguish between good and evil and yet they bring a sacrifice before me?**

**HALAKHA**

**If one delayed for an interval sufficient to complete the entire prayer – אִם שָׁהָה כְּדֵי לִגְמוֹר אֶת כּוּלָּהּ וכו׳:** One who interrupted his prayer or recitation of *Shema* long enough to have completed the entire prayer, even if the interval passed in silence, must repeat the prayer or *Shema* from the beginning. One who interrupted for a shorter period must return to the point in the prayer where he paused, in accordance with the opinion of Rav Ashi. In the case of prayer, that interval is defined as the beginning of that particular blessing. However, the first three and last three blessings are each considered one indivisible unit. Consequently, one who paused during any of the first three blessings must return to the beginning of the *Amida* prayer and one who paused during any of the three final blessings must return to the blessing of the Temple service [*retze*] (Rambam *Sefer Ahava, Hilkhot Tefilla* 4:13; *Shulḥan Arukh, Oraḥ Ḥayyim* 104:5).

**One who needs to relieve himself may not pray – הַנִּצְרָךְ לִנְקָבָיו אַל יִתְפַּלֵּל:** If he did pray, his prayer is an abomination and he is required repeat his prayer. However, if he is capable of restraining himself for the time it takes to walk a parasang, he fulfilled his obligation. If the end of the period when that prayer may be recited is imminent, he is permitted to pray under those circumstances (*Magen Avraham*, in accordance with the conclusion of Rav Zevid; Rambam *Sefer Ahava, Hilkhot Tefilla* 4:10; *Shulḥan Arukh, Oraḥ Ḥayyim* 92:1, 3).

**NOTES**

**One who needs to relieve himself may not pray – הַנִּצְרָךְ לִנְקָבָיו אַל יִתְפַּלֵּל:** He may not pray for two reasons: First, he is distracted and unable to concentrate on his prayer; and because one who needs to relieve himself is considered filthy and unfit to pray.

**Guard your foot – שְׁמוֹר רַגְלְךָ:** The word foot is used here as a euphemism for defecating as in the verse: "He is covering his feet" (Judges 3:24).

**As they know not to do evil – כִּי אֵינָם יוֹדְעִים לַעֲשׂוֹת רָע:** Here, the word to do [*la'asot*] is interpreted as it appears in the verse: "Nor did he trim [*asa*] his beard" (II Samuel 19:25), where it means to fix or arrange. Here too, *la'asot* evil means to reform it and make it better (Rav Ya'akov Emden). And the phrase: They are unaware whether they are bringing it as a thanks-offering for the good, or as an offering of atonement for the evil, means that, although they are bringing an offering, they believe that the sin had no effect, as the sacrifice fixes everything (*Tosefot Rabbi Yehuda HaḤasid*).

**BACKGROUND**

**As long as it takes to walk one parasang – הִילּוּךְ פַּרְסָה:** The determination of the length of time necessary to walk a parasang is connected to the disagreement with regard to the basic unit of measurement, the time necessary to walk a talmudic *mil*. The talmudic *mil* is a unit of distance related to, but not identical with, the Roman mile, from which it received its name. One *mil* is equal to 2,000 cubits, 960 m (1,049 yd) according to Na'e, or 1,150 m (1,258 yd) according to the Ḥazon Ish. The fundamental problem lies in the method used to determine a person's regular walking pace. According to the various opinions, the time it takes to walk a parasang is either one hour and twelve minutes or one hour and thirty-six minutes.

רַב אַשִׁי וְאִיתֵימָא רַבִּי חֲנִינָא בַּר פַּפָּא אָמַר: שְׁמוֹר נְקָבֶיךָ בְּשָׁעָה שֶׁאַתָּה עוֹמֵד בִּתְפִלָּה לְפָנַי.

**Rav Ashi and some say Rabbi Ḥanina bar Pappa said: Mind your orifices when you stand before me in prayer.**

תָּנוּ רַבָּנַן: הַנִּכְנָס לְבֵית הַכִּסֵּא – חוֹלֵץ תְּפִילָּיו בְּרִחוּק אַרְבַּע אַמּוֹת, וְנִכְנָס. אָמַר רַב אַחָא בַּר רַב הוּנָא אָמַר רַב שֵׁשֶׁת: לֹא שָׁנוּ אֶלָּא בֵּית הַכִּסֵּא קָבוּעַ, אֲבָל בֵּית הַכִּסֵּא עֲרַאי – חוֹלֵץ וְנִפְנֶה לְאַלְתַּר. וּכְשֶׁהוּא יוֹצֵא – מַרְחִיק אַרְבַּע אַמּוֹת וּמַנִּיחָן, מִפְּנֵי שֶׁעֲשָׂאוֹ בֵּית הַכִּסֵּא קָבוּעַ.

**The Sages taught: One who enters a bathroom**[H] **must remove his phylacteries**[H] **at a distance of four cubits and enter. Rav Aḥa bar Rav Huna said that Rav Sheshet said: This was only taught** with regard to one entering **a regular bathroom, but** one who enters **a makeshift bathroom may remove** his phylacteries and **defecate immediately. But when one exits** from a makeshift bathroom, **he must distance himself four cubits** before **donning** his phylacteries because **he has** now **rendered** that place **a regular bathroom.**

אִיבַּעֲיָא לְהוּ: מַהוּ שֶׁיִּכָּנֵס אָדָם בִּתְפִילִּין לְבֵית הַכִּסֵּא קָבוּעַ לְהַשְׁתִּין מַיִם? רָבִינָא שָׁרֵי, רַב אַדָּא בַּר מַתָּנָא אָסַר. אֲתוּ שַׁיְילוּהּ לְרָבָא, אֲמַר לְהוּ: אָסוּר, חָיְישִׁינַן שֶׁמָּא יִפָּנֶה בָּהֶן; וְאָמְרִי לָהּ: שֶׁמָּא יָפִיחַ בָּהֶן.

**A dilemma was raised** before the Sages in the yeshiva: **What is** the *halakha*; may **one enter a regular bathroom wearing his phylacteries in order to urinate?** The Sages disagreed: **Ravina permitted** to do so while **Rav Adda bar Mattana prohibited** it. **They came** and **asked this of Rava. He said to them: It is forbidden** because **we are concerned lest he will** come to **defecate with them** still on. **Others say** that this *halakha* is because we are concerned that, since he is already in the bathroom, he **might** forget that his phylacteries are on his head and **will break wind with them** still on him.

תַּנְיָא אִידָךְ: הַנִּכְנָס לְבֵית הַכִּסֵּא קָבוּעַ – חוֹלֵץ תְּפִילָּיו בְּרִחוּק אַרְבַּע אַמּוֹת, וּמַנִּיחָן בַּחַלּוֹן הַסָּמוּךְ לִרְשׁוּת הָרַבִּים וְנִכְנָס, וּכְשֶׁהוּא יוֹצֵא – מַרְחִיק אַרְבַּע אַמּוֹת וּמַנִּיחָן, דִּבְרֵי בֵּית שַׁמַּאי. וּבֵית הִלֵּל אוֹמְרִים: אוֹחֲזָן בְּיָדוֹ וְנִכְנָס; רַבִּי עֲקִיבָא אוֹמֵר: אוֹחֲזָן בְּבִגְדוֹ וְנִכְנָס.

**It was taught in another** *baraita*: **One who enters a regular bathroom must remove his phylacteries at a distance of four cubits, place them in the window** in the wall of the bathroom **adjacent to the public domain, and then enter. And when he exits, he must distance** himself **four cubits before donning them.** This is **the statement of Beit Shammai. Beit Hillel say:** He must remove his phylacteries but **he holds them in his hand and enters. Rabbi Akiva says: He holds them in his garment and enters.**

בְּבִגְדוֹ סָלְקָא דַּעְתָּךְ? זִימְנִין מִישְׁתְּלֵי לְהוּ וְנָפְלִי! אֶלָּא אֵימָא: אוֹחֲזָן בְּבִגְדוֹ וּבְיָדוֹ וְנִכְנָס,

The Gemara wonders: **Does it enter your mind** to say **in his garment?** There is room for concern because **sometimes he forgets them and** they **fall. Rather, say: He holds them with his garment and in his hand and enters** the bathroom. He holds the phylacteries in his hand and covers it with the garment.

וּמַנִּיחָם בַּחוֹרִין הַסְּמוּכִים לְבֵית הַכִּסֵּא; וְלֹא יַנִּיחֵם בַּחוֹרִין הַסְּמוּכִים לִרְשׁוּת הָרַבִּים, שֶׁמָּא יִטְּלוּ אוֹתָם עוֹבְרֵי דְּרָכִים וְיָבֹא לִידֵי חֲשָׁד.

It was established in the *baraita*: **And** if there is room to place them, **he places them in the holes adjacent to the bathroom, but he does not place them in the holes adjacent to the public domain, lest** the phylacteries **will be taken by passersby and he will come to be suspect.**

וּמַעֲשֶׂה בְּתַלְמִיד אֶחָד שֶׁהִנִּיחַ תְּפִילָּיו בַּחוֹרִין הַסְּמוּכִים לִרְשׁוּת הָרַבִּים, וּבָאת זוֹנָה אַחַת וּנְטָלָתַן, וּבָאת לְבֵית הַמִּדְרָשׁ וְאָמְרָה: רְאוּ מַה נָּתַן לִי פְּלוֹנִי בִּשְׂכָרִי! כֵּיוָן שֶׁשָּׁמַע אוֹתוֹ תַּלְמִיד כָּךְ, עָלָה לְרֹאשׁ הַגַּג וְנָפַל וּמֵת. בְּאוֹתָהּ שָׁעָה הִתְקִינוּ שֶׁיְּהֵא אוֹחֲזָן בְּבִגְדוֹ וּבְיָדוֹ וְנִכְנָס.

**And an incident** occurred **involving a student who placed his phylacteries in the holes adjacent to the public domain, and a prostitute passed by and took** the phylacteries. **She came to the study hall and said: See what so-and-so gave me as my payment.**[N] **When that student heard this, he ascended to the rooftop and fell and died. At that moment they instituted that one should hold them with his garment and in his hand and enter** to avoid situations of that kind.

תָּנוּ רַבָּנַן: בָּרִאשׁוֹנָה הָיוּ מַנִּיחִין תְּפִילִּין בַּחוֹרִין הַסְּמוּכִים לְבֵית הַכִּסֵּא, וּבָאִין עַכְבָּרִים וְנוֹטְלִין אוֹתָן. הִתְקִינוּ שֶׁיְּהוּ מַנִּיחִין אוֹתָן בַּחַלּוֹנוֹת הַסְּמוּכוֹת לִרְשׁוּת הָרַבִּים, וּבָאִין עוֹבְרֵי דְּרָכִים וְנוֹטְלִין אוֹתָן; הִתְקִינוּ שֶׁיְּהֵא אוֹחֲזָן בְּיָדוֹ וְנִכְנָס.

**The Sages taught** in a *baraita* on this topic: **At first, they would place the phylacteries in the holes adjacent to the bathroom and mice would come and take them** or gnaw upon them. Therefore, **they instituted that they should place them in the holes adjacent to the public domain,** where there were no mice. However, **passersby would come and take the** phylacteries. Ultimately, **they instituted that one should hold** the phylacteries **in his hand and enter.**

אָמַר רַבִּי מְיָאשָׁא בְּרֵיהּ דְּרַבִּי יְהוֹשֻׁעַ בֶּן לֵוִי: הֲלָכָה, גּוֹלְלָן כְּמִין סֵפֶר וְאוֹחֲזָן בִּימִינוֹ כְּנֶגֶד לִבּוֹ. אָמַר רַב יוֹסֵף בַּר מַנְיוּמִי אָמַר רַב נַחְמָן: וּבִלְבַד שֶׁלֹּא תְּהֵא רְצוּעָה יוֹצֵאת מִתַּחַת יָדוֹ טֶפַח.

On this topic, **Rabbi Meyasha, son of Rabbi Yehoshua ben Levi said: The** *halakha* in this case **is that one rolls up** the phylacteries in their straps **like a scroll,**[B] **and holds them in his hand opposite his heart. Rav Yosef bar Manyumi said that Rav Naḥman said:** This is **provided that the strap** of the phylacteries **does not emerge** more than **a handbreadth below his hand.**

**HALAKHA**

**One who enters a bathroom, etc. – הַנִּכְנָס לְבֵית הַכִּסֵּא וכו׳:** One who wishes to enter a bathroom but has no safe place to leave his phylacteries, should remove them at a distance of four cubits from the bathroom, wind their straps, cover them with his garment, hold them opposite his heart, and only then enter. He should make certain that the straps are not dangling from his hand. When he emerges, he should distance himself four cubits before donning them again (Rambam *Sefer Ahava, Hilkhot Tefillin UMezuza VeSefer Torah* 4:17; *Shulḥan Arukh, Oraḥ Ḥayyim* 43:5).

**Phylacteries in the bathroom – תְּפִילִּין בְּבֵית הַכִּסֵּא:** One may not defecate while phylacteries are on his head, nor may he enter a bathroom under those circumstances. As per the conclusion of Rava (Rambam *Sefer Ahava, Hilkhot Tefillin UMezuza VeSefer Torah* 4:17; *Shulḥan Arukh, Oraḥ Ḥayyim* 43:1).

**NOTES**

**See what so-and-so gave me as my payment – רְאוּ מַה נָּתַן לִי פְּלוֹנִי בִּשְׂכָרִי:** Apparently, the student was searching everywhere for his phylacteries. The prostitute who took them did not want to be accused of theft, so she brought them to the study hall and claimed that he gave them to her as her payment (Rav Ya'akov Emden).

**BACKGROUND**

**Rolls up the phylacteries in their straps like a scroll – גּוֹלְלָן כְּמִין סֵפֶר:** One of the manners in which the head phylacteries are rolled, probably the method called in the Gemara: Like a scroll.

Phylacteries of the head

אָמַר רַבִּי יַעֲקֹב בַּר אַחָא אָמַר רַבִּי זֵירָא: לֹא שָׁנוּ אֶלָּא שֶׁיֵּשׁ שָׁהוּת בַּיּוֹם לִלְבְּשָׁן, אֲבָל אֵין שָׁהוּת בַּיּוֹם לִלְבְּשָׁן – עוֹשֶׂה לָהֶן כְּמִין כִּיס טֶפַח, וּמַנִּיחָן.

**Rabbi Ya'akov bar Aḥa said** that **Rabbi Zeira said: It was only taught** that one rolls up his phylacteries when there is still time left **in the day to don them. If there is not time** left **in the day to don them** before nightfall, when phylacteries are not donned, **he makes a one-handbreadth pouch of sorts for them and he places them** in it.

אָמַר רַבָּה בַּר בַּר חָנָה אָמַר רַבִּי יוֹחָנָן: בַּיּוֹם – גּוֹלְלָן כְּמִין סֵפֶר וּמַנִּיחָן בְּיָדוֹ כְּנֶגֶד לִבּוֹ, וּבַלַּיְלָה – עוֹשֶׂה לָהֶן כְּמִין כִּיס טֶפַח, וּמַנִּיחָן.

Similarly, **Rabba bar bar Ḥana said** that **Rabbi Yoḥanan said: During the day one rolls up** the phylacteries **like a scroll and places them in his hand opposite his heart, and at night he makes a one-handbreadth pouch of sorts for them and he places them** in it.

אָמַר אַבָּיֵי: לֹא שָׁנוּ אֶלָּא בִּכְלִי שֶׁהוּא כֵּלְיָין, אֲבָל בִּכְלִי שֶׁאֵינוֹ כֵּלְיָין – אֲפִילּוּ פָּחוֹת מִטֶּפַח.

**Abaye said: They only taught** that it must be a one-handbreadth pouch **with regard to a vessel that is** the phylacteries' regular **vessel,**[NH] **but in a vessel that is not their** regular **vessel,** he may place the phylacteries in it, **even** if it is **less than a handbreadth.**

אָמַר מָר זוּטְרָא וְאִיתֵּימָא רַב אָשֵׁי: תֵּדַע, שֶׁהֲרֵי פַּכִּין קְטַנִּים מַצִּילִין בְּאֹהֶל הַמֵּת.

**Mar Zutra and, some say, Rav Ashi, said** as proof for that distinction: The laws of impurity state that only a space of at least a handbreadth can serve as a barrier to prevent the spread of impurity imparted by a corpse. Nevertheless, **small** sealed **vessels** less than a handbreadth in size **protect** their contents from ritual impurity even if they are inside **a tent over a corpse.** This proves that even a space smaller than a handbreadth can serve as a barrier before impurity.

אָמַר רַבָּה בַּר בַּר חָנָה: כִּי הֲוָה אָזְלִינַן בָּתְרֵיהּ דְּרַבִּי יוֹחָנָן, כִּי הֲוָה בָּעֵי לְמֵיעַל לְבֵית הַכִּסֵּא, כִּי הֲוָה נָקֵיט סִפְרָא דְּאַגַּדְתָּא – הֲוָה יָהֵיב לַן, כִּי הֲוָה נָקֵיט תְּפִילִּין – לָא הֲוָה יָהֵיב לַן, אֲמַר: הוֹאִיל וְשָׁרוּנְהוּ רַבָּנַן –

**Rabba bar bar Ḥana said: When we would walk after Rabbi Yoḥanan,** we would see **that when he sought to enter the bathroom while holding a book of *aggada*,**[B] **he would give** it **to us. When he was holding phylacteries, he would not give** them **to us,** as **he said: Since the Sages permitted** to hold **them,**

NOTES

A vessel that is their regular vessel – בִּכְלִי שֶׁהוּא כֵּלְיָין: The basis for this distinction is that a vessel that is designated for phylacteries is no longer considered a separate entity, but rather as ancillary to the phylacteries. Consequently, a small vessel designated for use with phylacteries is subsumed and does not constitute a barrier. However, if the vessel is larger than a handbreadth, since the space of a handbreadth is considered a substantial area in and of itself, it is not considered ancillary to the object inside it (*Shitta Mekubbetzet*).

HALAKHA

They only taught this with regard to a vessel that is the phylacteries' regular vessel – לֹא שָׁנוּ אֶלָּא בִּכְלִי שֶׁהוּא כֵּלְיָין: The pouch in which he places his phylacteries, if it was designed for that purpose, must be at least one handbreadth in size in order to permit him to enter the bathroom carrying it. For other purposes, even a smaller pouch is sufficient, as per the opinion of Abaye (Rambam *Sefer Ahava, Hilkhot Tefillin UMezuza VeSefer Torah* 4:19; *Shulḥan Arukh, Oraḥ Ḥayyim* 43:6).

BACKGROUND

Book of *aggada* – סִפְרָא דְּאַגַּדְתָּא: While the prohibition against committing the Oral Torah to writing was still in force several generations after the codification of the Mishna, the Sages would write down various notes for themselves. They were especially lenient with regard to aggadic books. The Gemara tells of several *amora'im* who would carry aggadic books which they frequently perused, while halakhic books were not common at all.

Perek **III**
Daf **23** Amud **b**

נִינְטְרַן. אָמַר רָבָא: כִּי הֲוָה אָזְלִינַן בָּתְרֵיהּ דְּרַב נַחְמָן, כִּי הֲוָה נָקֵיט סִפְרָא דְּאַגַּדְתָּא – יָהֵיב לַן, כִּי הֲוָה נָקֵיט תְּפִילִּין – לָא יָהֵיב לַן, אֲמַר: הוֹאִיל וְשָׁרוּנְהוּ רַבָּנַן – נִינְטְרַן.

**they will protect me.** Although there were people on hand to whom he could have handed the phylacteries, he kept them to protect himself from danger. **Rava said: When we would walk after Rabbi Naḥman,** we would see that **when he was holding a book of *aggada*, he would give** it **to us. When he was holding phylacteries, he would not give** them **to us,** as **he said: Since the Sages permitted** to hold **them, they will protect me.**

תָּנוּ רַבָּנַן: לֹא יֹאחַז אָדָם תְּפִילִּין בְּיָדוֹ וְסֵפֶר תּוֹרָה בִּזְרוֹעוֹ וְיִתְפַּלֵּל, וְלֹא יַשְׁתִּין בָּהֶן מַיִם, וְלֹא יִישַׁן בָּהֶן לֹא שֵׁינַת קֶבַע וְלֹא שֵׁינַת עֲרַאי. אָמַר שְׁמוּאֵל: סַכִּין, וּמָעוֹת, וּקְעָרָה, וְכִכָּר הֲרֵי אֵלּוּ כַּיּוֹצֵא בָּהֶן.

**The Sages taught: One may not hold phylacteries in his hand** or **a Torah scroll in his arm and pray,**[H] because his concern that the phylacteries or Torah scroll might fall will distract him from his prayer. **And** so too, with regard to sacred objects, **one may not urinate with them** in his hands **and may not sleep with them**[N] in his hands, **neither a deep sleep nor** even **a brief nap. Shmuel said:** Not only should one holding phylacteries refrain from prayer, but one holding **a knife, money, a bowl,** or a **loaf** of bread **have a similar** status in that his concern that they might fall will distract him from his prayer.

אָמַר רָבָא אָמַר רַב שֵׁשֶׁת: לֵית הִלְכְתָא כִּי הָא מַתְנִיתָא – דְּבֵית שַׁמַּאי הִיא. דְּאִי בֵּית הִלֵּל – הַשְׁתָּא בֵּית הַכִּסֵּא קָבוּעַ שָׁרֵי, בֵּית הַכִּסֵּא עֲרַאי מִיבַּעְיָא?!

**Rava said** that **Rav Sheshet said: The *halakha* is not in accordance with this *baraita*, because it** in accordance with the opinion of **Beit Shammai. As if** it was in accordance with the opinion of **Beit Hillel, now** Beit Hillel **permitted** to hold phylacteries in his hand when he defecates in a regular bathroom, **is it necessary** to say that it is permitted when he urinates in a **makeshift bathroom?**

HALAKHA

One may not hold phylacteries in his hand or a Torah scroll in his arm and pray – לֹא יֹאחַז אָדָם תְּפִילִּין בְּיָדוֹ וְסֵפֶר תּוֹרָה בִּזְרוֹעוֹ וְיִתְפַּלֵּל: One is prohibited from holding phylacteries or a Torah scroll in his hand while praying. The same is true when reciting *Shema* and *Pesukei DeZimra* (*Peri Megadim*). One must also refrain from holding a bowl or money or any other object of value, as his concern lest they fall and be damaged will distract him from praying properly (Rambam *Sefer Ahava, Hilkhot Tefilla* 5:5; *Shulḥan Arukh, Oraḥ Ḥayyim* 96:1).

NOTES

And may not sleep with them – וְלֹא יִישַׁן בָּהֶן: The reason is that they might fall off in his sleep (Rabbi Akiva Eiger and see *Sukka* 26b). The Vilna Gaon assumed that Rashi understood it that way.

## BACKGROUND

**Refutation and *halakha* – תְּיוּבְתָּא וְהִלְכָתָא:** The difference between *kashya*, a difficulty or contradiction, and *teyuvta*, a conclusive refutation, is that *kashya* with regard to a particular opinion does not disqualify that opinion; it merely poses a difficulty. *Teyuvta*, however, conclusively refutes and disqualifies that opinion. This is the case particularly where we encounter the phrase: This is a conclusive refutation…Indeed, this is a conclusive refutation. However, there do exist rare cases in which a particular *halakha* remains in place despite the existence of a conclusive refutation contradicting it. From here we learn that when there is an explanation in support of an *amora*, a refutation from a *baraita* does not necessarily prove it incorrect (Rabbi Betzalel Ronsburg).

**Bathroom – בֵּית הַכִּסֵּא:** There were very few places where bathrooms were actually indoors. In most places, people relieved themselves in empty lots, e.g., the municipal garbage dump. At night, it was possible to find a closer place for that purpose. However, during the day, because of numerous passersby, one was forced to find a spot that was a considerable distance beyond the city limits.

מֵיתִיבִי: "דְּבָרִים שֶׁהִתַּרְתִּי לְךָ כָּאן, אָסַרְתִּי לְךָ כָּאן", מַאי לָאו תְּפִילִּין? אִי אָמְרַתְּ בִּשְׁלָמָא בֵּית הִלֵּל – "הִתַּרְתִּי לְךָ כָּאן" – קָבוּעַ, "אָסַרְתִּי לְךָ כָּאן" – בֵּית הַכִּסֵּא עֲרַאי. אֶלָּא אִי אָמְרַתְּ בֵּית שַׁמַּאי – הָא לֹא שָׁרוּ וְלֹא מִידֵּי!

The Gemara **raised an objection** based on the second part of the *baraita*, where it was taught: **Matters which I permitted you** to do **here, I prohibited you** from doing **there.** In other words, there are matters that were permitted in a regular bathroom and not in a makeshift bathroom. **What, is it not** referring to **phylacteries? Granted, if you say** that the prohibition against urinating while wearing phylacteries is in accordance with the opinion of **Beit Hillel,** then we would understand the *baraita* as follows: Matters which **I permitted you** to do **here,** to hold phylacteries in a regular bathroom, **I have prohibited you** from doing **there,** in the **makeshift bathroom. But if you hold** that this *baraita* is in accordance with the opinion of **Beit Shammai, they did not permit anything** in a regular bathroom. What, then, is the meaning of matters which I permitted you to do here?

כִּי תַּנְיָא הַהִיא לְעִנְיַן טֶפַח וְטִפְחַיִים. דְּתַנְיָא חֲדָא: כְּשֶׁהוּא נִפְנֶה – מְגַלֶּה לַאֲחוֹרָיו טֶפַח וּלְפָנָיו טְפָחַיִים. וְתַנְיָא אִידָךְ: לַאֲחוֹרָיו טֶפַח, וּלְפָנָיו וְלֹא כְּלוּם!

This challenge is rejected by the Gemara, which explains: **When that** *baraita* **was taught** it was not in reference to phylacteries, but **with regard to the matter of one handbreadth and two handbreadths.** As is **it was taught in one** *baraita*: **When one relieves himself, he** must maintain modesty and **bare a single handbreadth** of his flesh **behind him and two handbreadths before him. And it was taught in another** *baraita*: One may only bare **a single handbreadth behind him and nothing before him.**

מַאי לָאו אִידִי וְאִידִי בְּאִישׁ, וְלֹא קַשְׁיָא: כָּאן לִגְדוֹלִים, כָּאן לִקְטַנִּים.

**What, are not** both **this** *baraita* **and that** one referring to **a male, and** the apparent contradiction between the two *baraitot* **is not difficult,** as **here** the *baraita* that states that one may bare a handbreadth behind him and nothing before him is referring to **defecation, while here,** the other *baraita* that states that one may bare a handbreadth behind him and two handbreadths before him is referring to **urination.** Accordingly, despite the fact that one may bare two handbreadths before him when urinating in a makeshift bathroom, matters that I have permitted you to do here, one may bare nothing before him when defecating in an established bathroom, I have prohibited you from doing there.

וְתִסְבְּרָא?! אִי בִּקְטַנִּים לַאֲחוֹרָיו טֶפַח לָמָּה לִי?! אֶלָּא, אִידִי וְאִידִי בִּגְדוֹלִים, וְלֹא קַשְׁיָא: הָא בְּאִישׁ, הָא בְּאִשָּׁה.

The Gemara immediately rejects this explanation: **And** how **can you understand** it that way? Can you accept that explanation? **If** that *baraita* is referring to **urination, why do I need to** bare **a handbreadth behind him? Rather,** both **this** *baraita* **and that** one are referring to **defecation and** the apparent contradiction between the two *baraitot* **is not difficult,** as **this** *baraita* that states that one may bare two handbreadths before him is referring **to a man,** who must bare before him to facilitate urination, while **this** other *baraita* that states that one may bare nothing before him is referring **to a woman,** who need not bare anything before her in order to urinate.

אִי הָכִי, הָא דְּקָתָנֵי עֲלַהּ: "וְזֶהוּ קַל וָחוֹמֶר שֶׁאֵין עָלָיו תְּשׁוּבָה", מַאי "אֵין עָלָיו תְּשׁוּבָה"? דַּרְכָּא דְּמִלְּתָא הָכִי אִיתָא! אֶלָּא לָאו – תְּפִילִּין, וּתְיוּבְתָּא דְּרָבָא אָמַר רַב שֵׁשֶׁת,

The Gemara challenges this: **If so, then that which was taught with regard** to this *halakha* in the *baraita*: **This is an *a fortiori* inference that cannot be rebutted,** meaning that even though logically it would have been appropriate to be stricter in the case of defecating in a regular bathroom than in the case of urinating in a makeshift bathroom, that is not the ruling. According to the distinction suggested above, **what** is **cannot be rebutted? That is the nature of the matter;** men and women need to bare themselves differently. **Rather,** is the *baraita* which states: Matters which I permitted you to do here, I prohibited you from doing there, **not** referring to **phylacteries?** And the *a fortiori* inference that cannot be rebutted is similarly referring to phylacteries. This is a **conclusive refutation** of that which **Rava said** that **Rav Sheshet said** that the *baraita* is not referring to phylacteries.

תְּיוּבְתָּא.

The Gemara concludes: Indeed, it is a **conclusive refutation.**[B]

מִכָּל מָקוֹם קַשְׁיָא: הַשְׁתָּא בֵּית הַכִּסֵּא קָבוּעַ שָׁרֵי, בֵּית הַכִּסֵּא עֲרַאי לֹא כָּל שֶׁכֵּן?!

The Gemara asks: **Nevertheless, it** remains **difficult: Now,** holding phylacteries in his hand when he defecates in a **regular bathroom**[B] **is permitted; all the more so** that it is permitted when he urinates in **a makeshift bathroom.**

הָכִי קָאָמַר: בֵּית הַכִּסֵּא קָבוּעַ דְּלֵיכָּא נִיצוֹצוֹת – שָׁרֵי, בֵּית הַכִּסֵּא עֲרַאי דְּאִיכָּא נִיצוֹצוֹת – אָסְרִי.

The Gemara explains: **It says as follows:** When defecating in **a regular bathroom, where** one sits **there are no drops** of urine on one's clothes or shoes, he need not dirty his hands to clean his garment, and therefore one is **permitted** to hold phylacteries in his hand. However, in **a makeshift bathroom, where** one stands, and **there are** ricocheting **drops** which he may touch with his hand, **it is prohibited.**

אִי הָכִי, אַמַּאי ״אֵין עָלָיו תְּשׁוּבָה״? תְּשׁוּבָה מְעַלַּיְתָא הִיא!

The Gemara challenges: **If so, then why** was it referred to as an *a fortiori* inference that "**cannot be refuted**"? This seems **an excellent refutation** that explains the distinction.

הָכִי קָאָמַר: הָא מִילְּתָא תֵּיתֵי לַהּ בְּתוֹרַת טַעְמָא וְלָא תֵּיתֵי לַהּ בְּקַל וָחוֹמֶר, דְּאִי אָתְיָא לַהּ בְּתוֹרַת קַל וָחוֹמֶר – זֶהוּ קַל וָחוֹמֶר שֶׁאֵין עָלָיו תְּשׁוּבָה.

The Gemara explains that **it says as follows: Derive this matter based on the reason** mentioned above that due to different circumstances the ruling is different. **Do not derive it by means of an *a fortiori* inference, as** if you were **to derive it by means of an *a fortiori* inference, it would** certainly **be an *a fortiori* inference that cannot be rebutted.**

תָּנוּ רַבָּנַן: הָרוֹצֶה לִיכָּנֵס לִסְעוּדַּת קֶבַע – מְהַלֵּךְ עֲשָׂרָה פְּעָמִים אַרְבַּע אַמּוֹת, אוֹ אַרְבָּעָה פְּעָמִים עֶשֶׂר אַמּוֹת וְיִפָּנֶה, וְאַחַר כָּךְ נִכְנָס.

**The Sages taught: One who wishes to enter** and partake of **a regular meal**[H] that will last for some time, **paces** a distance of **four cubits ten times, or ten cubits four times,** in order to expedite the movement of the bowels, and **defecates.** Only **then may he enter** and partake of the meal. That way he spares himself the unpleasantness of being forced to leave in the middle of the meal.

אָמַר רַבִּי יִצְחָק: הַנִּכְנָס לִסְעוּדַּת קֶבַע – חוֹלֵץ תְּפִילָּיו וְאַחַר כָּךְ נִכְנָס. וּפְלִיגָא דְּרַבִּי חִיָּיא, דְּאָמַר רַבִּי חִיָּיא: מַנִּיחָן עַל שֻׁלְחָנוֹ, וְכֵן הָדוּר לוֹ.

On this same subject, **Rabbi Yitzḥak said: One who partakes of a regular meal removes his phylacteries and then enters,** as it is inappropriate to partake in a meal where there is frivolity while wearing phylacteries. **And** this statement **disputes** the statement **of Rabbi Ḥiyya, as Rabbi Ḥiyya said:** During a formal meal **one places** his phylacteries **on his table, and it is admirable for him** to do **so** in order that they will be available to don immediately if he so desires.

וְעַד אֵימַת? אָמַר רַב נַחְמָן בַּר יִצְחָק: עַד זְמַן בְּרָכָה.

The Gemara asks: **And until when** in the meal must he refrain from wearing phylacteries? **Rav Naḥman bar Yitzḥak said: Until the time of the recitation of the blessing** of Grace after Meals.

תָּנֵי חֲדָא: צוֹרֵר אָדָם תְּפִילָּיו עִם מְעוֹתָיו בְּאַפְרַקְסוּתוֹ, וְתַנְיָא אִידָּךְ: לֹא יָצוּר!

**It was taught** in **one** *baraita*: **One may bundle his phylacteries with his money in his head covering** [*apraksuto*],[L] **and it was taught in another** *baraita*: **One may not bundle** phylacteries and money together.

לָא קַשְׁיָא: הָא – דְּאַזְמְנֵיהּ, הָא – דְּלָא אַזְמְנֵיהּ. דְּאָמַר רַב חִסְדָּא: הַאי סוּדָרָא תְּפִילִּין דְּאַזְמְנֵיהּ לְמֵיצַר בֵּיהּ תְּפִילִּין, צַר בֵּיהּ תְּפִילִּין – אָסוּר לְמֵיצַר בֵּיהּ פְּשִׁיטֵי, אַזְמְנֵיהּ וְלָא צַר בֵּיהּ, צַר בֵּיהּ וְלָא אַזְמְנֵיהּ – שְׁרֵי לְמֵיצַר בֵּיהּ זוּזֵי.

The Gemara explains: **This is not difficult,** as one must distinguish and say that **this** *baraita*, which prohibits bundling phylacteries and money together, refers to a case where the vessel **was designated** for use with phylacteries, while **this** *baraita*, which permits one to do so, refers to a case where the vessel **was not designated** for that purpose. As **Rav Ḥisda said:** With regard to **this cloth** used with **phylacteries that one designated to bundle phylacteries in it,** if one already **bundled phylacteries in it then it is prohibited to bundle coins**[B] **in it,** but if he only **designated it** for that purpose, **but did not yet bundle** phylacteries **in it,** or **if he bundled** phylacteries **in it** but did **not** originally **designate it** for that purpose, then **it is permitted to bundle money in it.**

וּלְאַבָּיֵי, דְּאָמַר הַזְמָנָה מִילְּתָא הִיא, אַזְמְנֵיהּ אַף עַל גַּב דְּלָא צַר בֵּיהּ. צַר בֵּיהּ, אִי אַזְמְנֵיהּ – אֲסִיר, אִי לָא אַזְמְנֵיהּ – לָא.

**And according to Abaye, who said** that **designation is significant,** as Abaye holds that all relevant *halakhot* apply to an object designated for a specific purpose, whether or not it has been already used for that purpose, the *halakha* is: **If he designated** the cloth, **even if he did not bundle** phylacteries **in it,** he is prohibited from bundling money in it. However, if **he bundled** phylacteries **in it, if he designated** the cloth for that particular use, **it is prohibited** to bundle money in it, but **if he did not designate it, no,** it is not prohibited.

בְּעָא מִינֵּיהּ רַב יוֹסֵף בְּרֵיהּ דְּרַב נְחוּנְיָא מֵרַב יְהוּדָה: מַהוּ שֶׁיַּנִּיחַ אָדָם תְּפִילָּיו תַּחַת מְרַאֲשׁוֹתָיו? תַּחַת מַרְגְּלוֹתָיו לָא קָא מִיבַּעְיָא לִי – שֶׁנּוֹהֵג בָּהֶן מִנְהַג בִּזָּיוֹן, כִּי קָא מִיבַּעְיָא לִי – תַּחַת מְרַאֲשׁוֹתָיו, מַאי? – אָמַר לֵיהּ, הָכִי אָמַר שְׁמוּאֵל: מוּתָּר, אֲפִילּוּ אִשְׁתּוֹ עִמּוֹ.

**Rav Yosef, son of Rav Neḥunya, raised a dilemma before Rav Yehuda: What is the** *halakha*; may **a man place his phylacteries** in his bed, **under his head** while he sleeps? He himself explains: With regard to whether or not one may place them **under his feet, I have no dilemma, as that would be treating them in a deprecating manner** and is certainly prohibited. **My dilemma is** whether or not one may place them **under his head; what is** the *halakha* in that case? Rav Yehuda **said to him, Shmuel said as follows: It is permitted, even** if his **wife is with him** in his bed.

מֵיתִיבֵי: לֹא יַנִּיחַ אָדָם תְּפִילָּיו תַּחַת מַרְגְּלוֹתָיו מִפְּנֵי שֶׁנּוֹהֵג בָּהֶם דֶּרֶךְ בִּזָּיוֹן, אֲבָל מַנִּיחָם תַּחַת מְרַאֲשׁוֹתָיו. וְאִם הָיְתָה אִשְׁתּוֹ עִמּוֹ – אָסוּר. הָיָה מָקוֹם שֶׁגָּבוֹהַּ שְׁלֹשָׁה טְפָחִים אוֹ נָמוּךְ שְׁלֹשָׁה טְפָחִים – מוּתָּר.

The Gemara **raises an objection** based on what was taught in a *baraita*: **A man may not place his phylacteries under his feet, as** in doing so, **he treats them in a deprecating manner, but he may place them under his head. And if his wife was with him, it is prohibited** even to place it under his head. **If there was a place** where he could place the phylacteries **three handbreadths above or three handbreadths below** his head **it is permissible,** as that space is sufficient for the phylacteries to be considered in a separate place.

תְּיוּבְתָּא דִּשְׁמוּאֵל! תְּיוּבְתָּא.

**This is a conclusive refutation of Shmuel's** statement. The Gemara concludes: Indeed, it is **a conclusive refutation.**

אָמַר רָבָא: אַף עַל גַּב דְּתַנְיָא תְּיוּבְתָּא דִּשְׁמוּאֵל – הִלְכְתָא כְּוָותֵיהּ. מַאי טַעְמָא?

**Rava said: Although** a *baraita* **was taught** that constitutes **a conclusive refutation of Shmuel, the** *halakha* **is in accordance with his** opinion in this matter. **What is the reason** for this?

### HALAKHA

**One who wishes to partake of a regular meal – הָרוֹצֶה לִיכָּנֵס לִסְעוּדַּת קֶבַע מְהַלֵּךְ וכו׳:** It is common courtesy that before beginning a meal one should ascertain whether or not he needs to relieve himself. If he does, he should see to it beforehand, as per the *baraita* (Rambam *Sefer HaMadda, Hilkhot De'ot* 4:2).

### LANGUAGE

**Head covering [*apraksuto*] – אַפְּרַקְסוּתוֹ:** The commentators disagree over the exact meaning of *apraksuto*. Some say that it is a type of scarf that covers the head with fringes dangling down on both sides in which objects might sometimes be wrapped (Rashi). However, according to the *ge'onim*, *apraksuto* refers to a broad, shawl-like undergarment generally worn beneath an outer cloak, and in which it was possible to fold pockets for storage.

The source of the word is most likely the Greek ἐπικάρσιον, *epikarsion*, meaning a gown or garment. Indeed, it is often written as it would sound in Greek or Syrian *afkaresot*.

### BACKGROUND

**Coins – פְּשִׁיטֵי:** Some explain this term literally as referring to simple copper coins. Others tied this word to the Middle Persian pišīz, meaning small coin, *peruta*.

**NOTES**

Whatever offers more protection is preferable – כָּל לְנַטּוּרִינְהוּ טְפֵי עָדִיף: This reason, in and of itself, would not be sufficient to allow Shmuel to dispute the ruling of the *baraita*. Rather, Shmuel relied on a different *baraita* in which it was taught that phylacteries may be brought into a regular bathroom. The priority placed on protecting the phylacteries led the Gemara to adopt Shmuel's opinion in this matter (*Penei Yehoshua*).

To teach us the practical *halakha* – וּלְאַגְמוֹרַן הֲלָכָה לְמַעֲשֶׂה: The general principle taught in the Gemara (*Bava Batra* 130b) is that practical *halakha* can neither be determined based on teaching alone nor based on observing the action of an authority. It can only be determined based on teaching applied to a practical situation. Therefore, it would not have been sufficient for Rava to teach this ruling in the classroom. He needed to illustrate to his students that this teaching was also put into practice.

**HALAKHA**

He would place them on a bench and spread a cloth over them – מַנַּח לְהוּ אַשְׁרְשִׁיפָא וּפָרֵיס סוּדָרָא עִילָוַיְיהוּ: One may not engage in conjugal relations with phylacteries in the room. If they are in the room, he must cover them with two vessels, the outermost of which must not be its regular container. One is permitted to place the phylacteries in a box and spread a garment over it, as that is considered to be two vessels (*Shulḥan Arukh, Oraḥ Ḥayyim* 240:6).

Two individuals sleeping in a single bed – שְׁנַיִם שֶׁיְּשֵׁנִים בְּמִטָּה אַחַת: In order to recite *Shema*, two unclothed individuals sharing a single blanket must have a garment from the waist down to serve as a barrier between them (Rambam *Sefer Ahava, Hilkhot Keriat Shema* 3:18; *Shulḥan Arukh, Oraḥ Ḥayyim* 73:1).

Even if his wife is with him – אִשְׁתּוֹ עִמּוֹ: One whose wife is in bed with him may turn his head and recite *Shema* in accordance with the opinions of Shmuel and Rav Yosef. Some require a garment to serve as a barrier between them, and it is proper to do so (Rambam *Sefer Ahava, Hilkhot Keriat Shema* 3:18; *Shulḥan Arukh, Oraḥ Ḥayyim* 73:2).

כָּל לְנַטּוּרִינְהוּ טְפֵי עָדִיף. וְהֵיכָא מַנַּח לְהוּ? – אָמַר רַבִּי יִרְמְיָה: בֵּין כַּר לְכֶסֶת, שֶׁלֹּא כְּנֶגֶד רֹאשׁוֹ.

Because **whatever** offers more **protection is preferable**[N] even at the cost of deprecation. **And where** under his head **does he place them? Rabbi Yirmeya said:** He places them **between the pillow and the mattress, not** directly **aligned with his head** but rather a bit to the side.

וְהָא תָּנֵי רַבִּי חִיָּיא: מַנִּיחָן בְּכוֹבַע תַּחַת מְרַאֲשׁוֹתָיו! דְּמַפֵּיק לֵיהּ לְמוּרְשָׁא כּוֹבַע לְבַר.

The Gemara asks: **Didn't Rabbi Ḥiyya teach a** *baraita* that in that case **he places them in a pouch** used for phylacteries, directly **under his head?** The Gemara replies: He does so in a manner **that the bulge** in the **pouch,** where the phylacteries are, **protrudes out** and is not beneath his head.

בַּר קַפָּרָא צָיֵיר לְהוּ בְּכִילְּתָא וּמַפֵּיק לְמוּרְשֵׁהוֹן לְבַר. רַב שֵׁישָׁא בְּרֵיהּ דְּרַב אִידִי מַנַּח לְהוּ אַשְׁרְשִׁיפָא וּפָרֵיס סוּדָרָא עִילָוַיְיהוּ.

On this note, the Gemara relates that **Bar Kappara would tie them in** his **bed curtain and project their bulge outward. Rav Sheisha son of Rav Idi, would place them on a bench and spread a cloth over them.**[H]

אָמַר רַב הַמְנוּנָא בְּרֵיהּ דְּרַב יוֹסֵף: זִמְנָא חֲדָא הֲוָה קָאֵימְנָא קַמֵּיהּ דְּרָבָא וְאָמַר לִי: זִיל אַיְיתִי לִי תְּפִילִּין. וְאַשְׁכַּחְתִּינְהוּ בֵּין כַּר לְכֶסֶת, שֶׁלֹּא כְּנֶגֶד רֹאשׁוֹ, וַהֲוָה יָדַעְנָא דְּיוֹם טְבִילָה הֲוָה, וּלְאַגְמוֹרַן הֲלָכָה לְמַעֲשֶׂה הוּא דַּעֲבַד.

**Rav Hamnuna, son of Rav Yosef, said: I was once standing before Rava and he told me: Go** and **bring me** my **phylacteries. And I found them** in his bed, **between the mattress and the pillow, not aligned with his head. And I knew** that **it was the day** of his wife's **immersion** in the ritual bath for purification from the ritual impurity of a menstruating woman, and he certainly engaged in marital relations in order to fulfill the mitzva, **and he did so,** he sent me to bring him his phylacteries, **to teach us the practical *halakha***[N] in that case.

בְּעִי מִינֵּיהּ רַב יוֹסֵף בְּרֵיהּ דְּרַב נְחוּנְיָא מֵרַב יְהוּדָה: שְׁנַיִם שֶׁיְּשֵׁנִים בְּמִטָּה אַחַת, מַהוּ שֶׁזֶּה יַחֲזִיר פָּנָיו וְיִקְרָא קְרִיאַת שְׁמַע, וְזֶה יַחֲזִיר פָּנָיו וְיִקְרָא קְרִיאַת שְׁמַע? אָמַר לֵיהּ הָכִי אָמַר שְׁמוּאֵל: וַאֲפִילּוּ אִשְׁתּוֹ עִמּוֹ.

**Rav Yosef, son of Rav Neḥunya,** who raised a dilemma above **raised a dilemma before Rav Yehuda: Two individuals sleeping in a single bed,**[H] given that it was standard practice to sleep without clothing, **what is the** *halakha*; is it permissible **for this one to turn his head** aside **and recite *Shema* and for that** one **turns his head and recites *Shema*;** or is it prohibited because they are unclothed and are considered unfit to recite *Shema* even though they are covered with a blanket? **He said to him: Shmuel said as follows:** This is permitted **even if his wife** is in bed **with him.**[H]

מַתְקִיף לַהּ רַב יוֹסֵף: אִשְׁתּוֹ וְלֹא מִיבַּעְיָא אַחֵר?! אַדְּרַבָּה! אִשְׁתּוֹ כְּגוּפוֹ, אַחֵר לָאו כְּגוּפוֹ!

**Rav Yosef strongly objects to** this response: You say that he is permitted to recite *Shema* in bed with **his wife, and needless to** say he is permitted to do so when in bed with **another. On the contrary,** since **his wife is like his own flesh,** and he will not have lustful thoughts of her, it is permitted; **another is not like his own flesh** and it is prohibited.

מֵיתִיבֵי: שְׁנַיִם שֶׁיְּשֵׁנִים בְּמִטָּה אַחַת – זֶה מַחֲזִיר פָּנָיו וְקוֹרֵא, וְזֶה מַחֲזִיר פָּנָיו וְקוֹרֵא. וְתַנְיָא אַחֲרִיתִי: הַיָּשֵׁן בְּמִטָּה, וּבָנָיו וּבְנֵי בֵיתוֹ בְּצִדּוֹ – הֲרֵי זֶה לֹא יִקְרָא קְרִיאַת שְׁמַע אֶלָּא אִם כֵּן הָיְתָה טַלִּית מַפְסֶקֶת בֵּינֵיהֶן. וְאִם הָיוּ בָּנָיו וּבְנֵי בֵיתוֹ קְטַנִּים – מוּתָּר.

The Gemara **raises an objection** to this from the resolution of an apparent contradiction between two *baraitot*. It was taught in one *baraita*: **Two** unclothed **individuals who are sleeping in a single bed, this one turns his head** aside **and recites** *Shema* **and that** one **turns his head** aside **and recites** *Shema*. **And it was taught in another** *baraita*: **One who is sleeping in bed and his** unclothed **children and members of his household are beside him, may not recite *Shema* unless a garment separates between them. If his children and the members of his household were minors, it is permitted** to recite *Shema* even without a garment separating between them.

בִּשְׁלָמָא לְרַב יוֹסֵף לָא קַשְׁיָא: הָא – אִשְׁתּוֹ, וְהָא – בְּאַחֵר. אֶלָּא לִשְׁמוּאֵל קַשְׁיָא!

**Granted, according to Rav Yosef,** the apparent contradiction between the two *baraitot* **is not difficult,** as **this** *baraita* is referring to a case **where his wife** is in the bed with him, **while this** other *baraita* is referring to a case **where another** person is in bed with him and there is concern lest he will have lustful thoughts. **However, according to Shmuel,** who permits one to recite *Shema* regardless of who is in bed with him, **it is** indeed **difficult.** How would he interpret the *baraita* that prohibits?

אָמַר לָךְ שְׁמוּאֵל: לְרַב יוֹסֵף מִי נִיחָא?! וְהָתַנְיָא: הָיָה יָשֵׁן בְּמִטָּה, וּבָנָיו וּבְנֵי בֵיתוֹ בְּמִטָּה – לֹא יִקְרָא קְרִיאַת שְׁמַע אֶלָּא אִם כֵּן הָיְתָה טַלִּיתוֹ מַפְסֶקֶת בֵּינֵיהֶן! אֶלָּא מַאי אִית לָךְ לְמֵימַר – אִשְׁתּוֹ לְרַב יוֹסֵף תַּנָּאֵי הִיא, לְדִידִי נַמִי תַּנָּאֵי הִיא.

The Gemara replies: **Shmuel** could have **said to you: And according to Rav Yosef's** opinion, **does it** work out **well? Wasn't it taught** in that same *baraita* that **one who is sleeping in bed and his children and members of his household are beside him, may not recite *Shema* unless a garment separates between them?** Doesn't Rav Yosef hold that his wife is like his own flesh and no separation is necessary? **Rather, what have you to say** in response? **Rav Yosef holds that there is a tannaitic** dispute in the case of **one's wife; I, too, hold that it is a tannaitic** dispute, and I accept the ruling of one of the *baraitot*.

אָמַר מָר: "זֶה מַחֲזִיר פָּנָיו וְקוֹרֵא קְרִיאַת שְׁמַע". וְהָא אִיכָּא עֲגָבוֹת! מְסַיַּיע לֵיהּ לְרַב הוּנָא, דְּאָמַר רַב הוּנָא: עֲגָבוֹת אֵין בָּהֶם מִשּׁוּם עֶרְוָה. לֵימָא מְסַיַּיע לֵיהּ לְרַב הוּנָא: הָאִשָּׁה יוֹשֶׁבֶת וְקוֹצָה לָהּ חַלָּתָהּ עֲרוּמָּה מִפְּנֵי שֶׁיְּכוֹלָה לְכַסּוֹת פָּנֶיהָ בַּקַּרְקַע, אֲבָל לֹא הָאִישׁ.

The Gemara reverts to clarify something mentioned above. **The Master said** in a *baraita*: **This one turns his head** aside **and recites *Shema*.** The Gemara notes a difficulty: **Aren't there** bare **buttocks?** This **supports** the opinion of **Rav Huna, as Rav Huna said: Buttocks do not constitute nakedness.**[H] **Let us say** that the following mishna **supports Rav Huna's** opinion: **A woman sits and separates her *halla* naked,** despite the fact that she must recite a blessing over the separation of the *halla*, **because she can cover her face,** a euphemism for her genitals, **in the ground, but a male,** whose genitals are not covered when he sits, may **not** do so. The mishna teaches that exposed buttocks do not constitute nakedness.

תַּרְגְּמָהּ רַב נַחְמָן בַּר יִצְחָק: כְּגוֹן שֶׁהָיוּ פָּנֶיהָ טוּחוֹת בַּקַּרְקַע.

**Rav Naḥman bar Yitzḥak interpreted** the mishna as referring to **a case where her face,** genitals, **was completely covered in the ground** such that her posterior was covered by the ground. Therefore, proof for Rav Huna's opinion cannot be brought from this mishna.

אָמַר מָר: "אִם הָיוּ בָּנָיו וּבְנֵי בֵיתוֹ קְטַנִּים – מוּתָּר". וְעַד כַּמָּה? – אָמַר רַב חִסְדָּא: תִּינוֹקֶת בַּת שָׁלֹשׁ שָׁנִים וְיוֹם אֶחָד, וְתִינוֹק בֶּן תֵּשַׁע שָׁנִים וְיוֹם אֶחָד. אִיכָּא דְּאָמְרִי: תִּינוֹקֶת בַּת אַחַת עֶשְׂרֵה שָׁנָה וְיוֹם אֶחָד, וְתִינוֹק בֶּן שְׁתֵּים עֶשְׂרֵה שָׁנָה וְיוֹם אֶחָד, אִידִי וְאִידִי עַד כְּדֵי "שָׁדַיִם נָכֹנוּ וּשְׂעָרֵךְ צִמֵּחַ".

**The Master said** in a *baraita*: **If his children and the members of his household were minors,**[H] even though they are unclothed, **it is permitted** to recite *Shema* even without a garment separating between them. The Gemara asks: **Until what** age is one still considered a minor? **Rav Ḥisda said: A girl** until she is **three years and one day old, and a boy** until **he is nine years and one day old,** for these are the ages from which a sexual act in which they participate is considered a sexual act. **Some say: A girl eleven years and one day old and a boy of twelve years and one day old,** as that is the age at which they are considered adults in this regard. This age is only approximate, as the age of majority for both **this,** the boy, **and that,** the girl, is **at** the onset of puberty in accordance with the verse: **"Your breasts were formed and your hair was grown"** (Ezekiel 16:7).

אָמַר לֵיהּ רַב כָּהֲנָא לְרַב אַשִׁי: הָתָם אָמַר רָבָא: אַף עַל גַּב דִּתְיוּבְתָּא דִּשְׁמוּאֵל, הִלְכְתָא כְּוָותֵיהּ דִּשְׁמוּאֵל. הָכָא מַאי? אָמַר לֵיהּ: אַטּוּ כּוּלְּהוּ בְּחַדָא מַחְתָּא מַחְתִינְהוּ?! אֶלָּא: הֵיכָא דְּאִיתְּמַר אִיתְּמַר, וְהֵיכָא דְּלָא אִיתְּמַר לָא אִיתְּמַר.

**Rav Kahana said to Rav Ashi: There,** with regard to the law of phylacteries, **Rava said: Despite a conclusive refutation** of the opinion **of Shmuel, the *halakha* is in accordance with** the opinion **of Shmuel. Here, what** is the ruling?[N] **He said to him: Were all of them woven in the same** act of **weaving?** Are there no distinctions between different cases? **Rather, where it is stated, it is stated, and where it is not stated, it is not stated,** and there is no comparison.

אָמַר לֵיהּ רַב מָרִי לְרַב פָּפָּא: שֵׂעָר יוֹצֵא בְּבִגְדוֹ מַהוּ? קְרָא עֲלֵיהּ: שֵׂעָר, שֵׂעָר.

**Rav Mari said to Rav Pappa:** Does it constitute nakedness **if one's** pubic **hair protruded from his garment?** Rav Pappa said **about him: A hair, a hair.**[N] You are splitting hairs and being pedantic over trivialities.

אָמַר ר' יִצְחָק: טֶפַח בְּאִשָּׁה עֶרְוָה. לְמַאי? אִילֵימָא לְאִסְתַּכּוֹלֵי בַּהּ, וְהָא אָמַר רַב שֵׁשֶׁת: לָמָּה מָנָה הַכָּתוּב תַּכְשִׁיטִין שֶׁבַּחוּץ עִם תַּכְשִׁיטִין שֶׁבִּפְנִים? לוֹמַר לָךְ: כׇּל הַמִּסְתַּכֵּל בְּאֶצְבַּע קְטַנָּה שֶׁל אִשָּׁה, כְּאִילּוּ מִסְתַּכֵּל בִּמְקוֹם הַתּוֹרֶף!

**Rabbi Yitzḥak stated: An** exposed **handbreadth in a woman** constitutes **nakedness.** The Gemara asks: Regarding **which** *halakha* was this said? **If you say** that it comes to prohibit **looking at** an exposed handbreadth in **her, didn't Rav Sheshet say: Why did the verse enumerate** "anklets and bracelets, rings, earrings and girdles" (Numbers 31:50), **jewelry that is** worn **externally,** over her clothing, e.g., bracelets, **together with jewelry** worn **internally,** beneath her clothing, near her nakedness, e.g., girdles? This was **to tell you: Anyone who gazes upon a woman's little finger**[H] is considered **as if he gazed upon her** naked **genitals,** for if his intentions are impure, it makes no difference where he looks or how much is exposed; even less than a handbreadth.

אֶלָּא: בְּאִשְׁתּוֹ, וְלִקְרִיאַת שְׁמַע.

**Rather,** it is referring even to **his wife, with regard to** the **recitation of *Shema*.** One may not recite *Shema* before an exposed handbreadth of his wife.

### HALAKHA

**Buttocks do not constitute nakedness – עֲגָבוֹת אֵין בָּהֶם מִשּׁוּם עֶרְוָה:** The halakhic decisors disagree whether or not to adopt Rav Huna's opinion that exposed buttocks do not constitute nakedness. Some accept his opinion (Rashba, *Magen Avraham*), while others reject it because it is not corroborated by the *baraita* (*Beit Yosef*, Vilna Gaon; see *Magen Avraham* on *Shulḥan Arukh, Oraḥ Ḥayyim* 73:2).

**If his children and members of his household were minors – אִם הָיוּ בָּנָיו וּבְנֵי בֵיתוֹ קְטַנִּים:** Regarding the recitation of *Shema* by one who was sleeping on the same bed with his unclothed children; if the boys were under the age of twelve and the girls under the age of eleven, it is permitted. If the boys were between twelve and thirteen and the girls between eleven and twelve, if they have two pubic hairs it is prohibited, and if not, it is permitted. Beyond those ages, it is prohibited. The *halakha* is ruled in accordance with the second version of Rav Ḥisda's statement (Rambam *Sefer Ahava, Hilkhot Keriat Shema* 3:19; *Shulḥan Arukh, Oraḥ Ḥayyim* 73:4).

**Anyone who gazes upon a woman's little finger – הַמִּסְתַּכֵּל בְּאֶצְבַּע קְטַנָּה שֶׁל אִשָּׁה:** One is prohibited from gazing for sensual pleasure upon a woman to whom he is not married. Even gazing upon her finger is prohibited. One who does so for his enjoyment is liable to receive rabbinically ordained lashes for rebelliousness (Rambam *Sefer Kedusha, Hilkhot Issurei Bia* 21:2; *Shulḥan Arukh, Even HaEzer* 21:1).

### NOTES

**Despite a conclusive refutation of Shmuel, the law is in accordance with him…Here, what is the ruling – אַף עַל גַּב דִּתְיוּבְתָּא דִּשְׁמוּאֵל, הִלְכְתָא כְּוָותֵיהּ...הָכָא מַאי:** The question of whether the *halakha* will be ruled in accordance with Shmuel even after he was refuted seems odd. However, since the nature of the *halakhot* regarding phylacteries and the recitation of *Shema* are similar, one might have presumed that since it was ruled in accordance with Shmuel with regard to *tefillin*, the same would be true here (*Tosefot Rabbeinu Yehuda HaḤasid*).

**A hair, a hair – שֵׂעָר, שֵׂעָר:** Meaning, ultimately it is hair and not flesh (*Rabbeinu Tam*).

אָמַר רַב חִסְדָּא: שׁוֹק בְּאִשָּׁה עֶרְוָה, שֶׁנֶּאֱמַר: "גַּלִּי שׁוֹק עִבְרִי נְהָרוֹת", וּכְתִיב "תִּגָּל עֶרְוָתֵךְ וְגַם תֵּרָאֶה חֶרְפָּתֵךְ". אָמַר שְׁמוּאֵל: קוֹל בְּאִשָּׁה עֶרְוָה, שֶׁנֶּאֱמַר: "כִּי קוֹלֵךְ עָרֵב וּמַרְאֵךְ נָאוֶה". אָמַר רַב שֵׁשֶׁת: שֵׂעָר בְּאִשָּׁה עֶרְוָה, שֶׁנֶּאֱמַר: "שַׂעְרֵךְ כְּעֵדֶר הָעִזִּים".

Along these lines, **Rav Ḥisda said:** Even **a woman's** exposed **leg is** considered **nakedness, as it is stated: "Uncover the leg and pass through the rivers"** (Isaiah 47:2), **and it is written** in the following verse: **"Your nakedness shall be revealed and your shame shall be seen"** (Isaiah 47:3). **Shmuel** further **stated: A woman's** singing **voice is** considered **nakedness,**[NH] which he derives from the praise accorded a woman's voice, **as it is stated: "Sweet is your voice and your countenance is alluring"** (Song of Songs 2:14). Similarly, **Rav Sheshet stated:** Even **a woman's hair is** considered **nakedness,**[H] for it too is praised, **as it is written: "Your hair is like a flock of goats,** trailing down from Mount Gilead" (Song of Songs 4:1).

אָמַר רַבִּי חֲנִינָא: אֲנִי רָאִיתִי אֶת רַבִּי שֶׁתָּלָה תְּפִילָּיו. מֵיתִיבִי: הַתּוֹלֶה תְּפִילָּיו יִתָּלוּ לוֹ חַיָּיו!

The Gemara resumes its discussion of phylacteries. **Rabbi Ḥanina said: I saw Rabbi** Yehuda HaNasi **hang his phylacteries.** The Gemara **raises an objection:** It was taught in a *baraita* that **one who hangs his phylacteries**[H] **will have his life hang** in the balance.

דּוֹרְשֵׁי חֲמוּרוֹת אָמְרוּ: "וְהָיוּ חַיֶּיךָ תְּלֻאִים לְךָ מִנֶּגֶד" – זֶה הַתּוֹלֶה תְּפִילָּיו!

Moreover, **the Symbolic Interpreters** of the Torah **said** that the verse: **"And your life shall hang in doubt before you [*minneged*]"** (Deuteronomy 28:66),[N] that is the punishment of **one who hangs his phylacteries.**

לָא קַשְׁיָא, הָא – בִּרְצוּעָה, הָא – בְּקְצִיצָה.

The Gemara replies: This apparent contradiction **is not difficult, as this** *baraita*, which condemns one who hangs his phylacteries, refers to one who hangs them **by the strap,** allowing the leather boxes into which the parchment is placed to dangle in a deprecating way, which is certainly prohibited. **That** *baraita*, which relates that Rabbi Yehuda HaNasi would hang his phylacteries and that it is clearly permitted, refers to when one hangs them **from the box** with the straps dangling.

וְאִיבָּעֵית אֵימָא: לָא שְׁנָא רְצוּעָה וְלָא שְׁנָא קְצִיצָה – אָסוּר, וְכִי תָּלָה רַבִּי – בְּכִיסְתָּא תָּלָה.

**And if you wish, say** another explanation instead: **There is no difference** whether he hangs the phylacteries from the **strap and there is no difference** whether he hangs the phylacteries from **the box;** both **are prohibited. And when Rabbi** Yehuda HaNasi **hung** his phylacteries, **he hung them in** their **pouch.**

אִי הָכִי, מַאי לְמֵימְרָא? – מַהוּ דְּתֵימָא: תִּיבָּעֵי הַנָּחָה כְּסֵפֶר תּוֹרָה, קָא מַשְׁמַע לָן.

The Gemara asks: **If so, what** is the purpose **to relate** that incident? The Gemara replies: **Lest you say** that phylacteries **would require placement** atop a surface, as is the custom with **a Torah scroll.** Therefore, **it teaches us** that this is unnecessary.

וְאָמַר רַבִּי חֲנִינָא: אֲנִי רָאִיתִי אֶת רַבִּי שֶׁגִּיהֵק וּפִיהֵק, וְנִתְעַטֵּשׁ, וְרָק

Since Rabbi Ḥanina related a story involving Rabbi Yehuda HaNasi, the Gemara cites another such story. **Rabbi Ḥanina said: I saw Rabbi** Yehuda HaNasi, while he was praying, **belch, yawn, sneeze, spit,**

#### NOTES

**A woman's singing voice is considered nakedness – קוֹל בְּאִשָּׁה עֶרְוָה:** The commentators and *poskim* delve into the specifics of this issue to determine the practical application of this statement. Some argue that it merely warns us to act modestly, and that it is inappropriate for a woman to expose certain parts of her body or to sing publicly. Others maintain that "nakedness" refers here strictly to the context of the recitation of the *Shema* and prayer, meaning that this is included in the category of "nakedness" regarding settings where one is forbidden to recite the *Shema* (see *Tosefot Rabbeinu Yehuda HaḤasid* and *Tosefot HaRosh*).

**"And your life shall hang in doubt [*minneged*]" – "וְהָיוּ חַיֶּיךָ תְּלֻאִים לְךָ מִנֶּגֶד":** Some commentators emphasize the homiletic interpretation of the phrase "And your life shall hang in doubt" by reading *minneged* to mean "from afar," and thus the sustenance of one who makes light of phylacteries will be kept at a distance from him (*Talmidei Rabbeinu Yona*). Alternately, *minneged* can mean measure-for-measure (*midda keneged midda*), such that one who hangs his phylacteries will suffer correspondingly, and his life will be hung in doubt (Rabbi Elazar Moshe Horowitz).

#### HALAKHA

**A woman's singing voice is considered nakedness – קוֹל בְּאִשָּׁה עֶרְוָה:** The sound of a woman's singing voice is considered nakedness, and a man may not hear the voice of a woman singing while reciting *Shema*, even the voice of his own wife. However, he is permitted to hear a voice to which he is accustomed and which he knows will not arouse in him lustful thoughts, even while reciting *Shema* (Rema; Rambam *Sefer Kedusha, Hilkhot Issurei Bia* 21:2; *Shulḥan Arukh, Oraḥ Ḥayyim* 75:3, *Even HaEzer* 21:1).

**A woman's hair is considered nakedness – שֵׂעָר בְּאִשָּׁה עֶרְוָה:** Hair that a woman (in most Jewish communities this applies only to a married woman) would normally cover is considered nakedness when exposed, and one is prohibited from reciting *Shema* with it in his sight, whether it is the hair of his wife or that of another woman (Rema; Rambam *Sefer Kedusha, Hilkhot Issurei Bia* 21:2; *Shulḥan Arukh, Oraḥ Ḥayyim* 75:1–2).

**One who hangs his phylacteries – הַתּוֹלֶה תְּפִילָּיו:** One is prohibited from hanging phylacteries, whether he suspends them by their boxes with the straps hanging down or by their straps with the boxes hanging down. One is permitted to hang the pouch in which they are stored, in accordance with both versions of the statement in the Gemara (Rambam *Sefer Ahava, Hilkhot Tefillin Mezuza VeSefer Torah* 4:9; *Shulḥan Arukh, Oraḥ Ḥayyim* 40:1).

Perek **III**
Daf **24** Amud **b**

וּמְמַשְׁמֵשׁ בְּבִגְדוֹ, אֲבָל לֹא הָיָה מִתְעַטֵּף, וּכְשֶׁהוּא מְפַהֵק – הָיָה מַנִּיחַ יָדוֹ עַל סַנְטֵרוֹ.

**and** if he was stung by a louse, he may **feel** for it and remove it **with his garment,**[H] **but he would not wrap himself** in his prayer shawl[H] if it fell during prayer. **And when he would yawn he would place his hand on his chin**[L] so that his open mouth would not be visible.

מֵיתִיבִי: הַמַּשְׁמִיעַ קוֹלוֹ בִּתְפִלָּתוֹ – הֲרֵי זֶה מִקְּטַנֵּי אֲמָנָה. הַמַּגְבִּיהַּ קוֹלוֹ בִּתְפִלָּתוֹ – הֲרֵי זֶה מִנְּבִיאֵי הַשֶּׁקֶר,

The Gemara **raises an objection** based on a *baraita*: **One who sounds his voice during his** *Amida* **prayer is among those of little faith,** as he seems to believe that the Lord cannot hear his prayer when it is uttered silently. **One who raises his voice during prayer** is considered to be **among the false prophets,** as they too were wont to cry out and shout to their gods.

מְגַהֵק וּמְפַהֵק – הֲרֵי זֶה מִגַּסֵּי הָרוּחַ. הַמִּתְעַטֵּשׁ בִּתְפִלָּתוֹ – סִימָן רַע לוֹ, וְיֵשׁ אוֹמְרִים: נִיכָּר שֶׁהוּא מְכוֹעָר. הָרָק בִּתְפִלָּתוֹ – כְּאִילּוּ רָק בִּפְנֵי הַמֶּלֶךְ!

Furthermore, one who **belches and yawns** while praying **is surely among the uncouth. One who sneezes during his prayer, for him it is a bad omen. And some say: It is clear that he is repulsive.** Also, **one who spits during prayer, it is tantamount to spitting in the face of the king.** In light of all this, how could Rabbi Yehuda HaNasi have done all that while praying?

#### HALAKHA

**And feel and remove it with his garment – וּמְמַשְׁמֵשׁ בְּבִגְדוֹ:** One who has a louse on his garment while reciting the *Amida* prayer may use his garment to remove it; however, he may not remove it with his hand (*Shulḥan Arukh, Oraḥ Ḥayyim* 97:3).

**But he would not wrap himself in his prayer shawl – אֲבָל לֹא הָיָה מִתְעַטֵּף:** If one's prayer shawl fell entirely off of him, he may not lift it and wrap himself in it during the *Amida* prayer, as that would constitute an interruption. If it fell partially off of him, he is permitted to adjust it (*Tosafot*; *Shulḥan Arukh, Oraḥ Ḥayyim* 97:4).

#### LANGUAGE

**Chin [*santer*] – סַנְטֵר:** In this context, there are two possible explanations of this word. According to the standard translation it is from the Greek ἀνθερεών *anthereon*, meaning chin. However, the *ge'onim*, Rabbeinu Ḥananel and, apparently, the Rambam explain that it means hips, from the Aramaic *satar*, meaning side. It is inappropriate to stand that way in prayer as it conveys levity and arrogance.

בִּשְׁלָמָא מְגַהֵק וּמְפַהֵק לָא קַשְׁיָא: כָּאן – לְאוֹנְסוֹ, כָּאן – לִרְצוֹנוֹ, אֶלָּא מִתְעַטֵּשׁ אַמִּתְעַטֵּשׁ קַשְׁיָא!

The Gemara explains: **Granted,** with regard to **one who belches and yawns, it is not difficult: Here,** in the case where Rabbi Yehuda HaNasi did so, **it was involuntary** and therefore permissible; **here,** where it is considered uncouth, is in a case where **it is deliberate.** However, the contradiction **between sneezing** in the case where Rabbi Yehuda HaNasi did so **and sneezing** where it is considered a bad omen **is difficult.**

מִתְעַטֵּשׁ אַמִּתְעַטֵּשׁ נַמִּי לָא קַשְׁיָא: כָּאן – מִלְמַעְלָה, כָּאן – מִלְּמַטָּה; דְּאָמַר רַב זֵירָא: הָא מִילְּתָא אִבְלַעָא לִי בֵּי רַב הַמְנוּנָא, וּתְקִילָא לִי כִּי כּוּלֵּי תַּלְמוּדַאי: הַמִּתְעַטֵּשׁ בִּתְפִלָּתוֹ – סִימָן יָפֶה לוֹ, כְּשֵׁם שֶׁעוֹשִׂים לוֹ נַחַת רוּחַ מִלְּמַטָּה, כָּךְ עוֹשִׂים לוֹ נַחַת רוּחַ מִלְמַעְלָה.

The Gemara responds: The contradiction **between sneezing** in one case **and sneezing** in the other case **is also not difficult: Here,** in the case of Rabbi Yehuda HaNasi, it is referring to sneezing **from above,** his nose; **here,** where it is a bad omen, is referring to sneezing **from below,** flatulence. **As Rav Zeira said: In the school of Rav Hamnuna I absorbed this matter** in passing, **and it is equal** in significance **to all the rest of my learning: One who sneezes in the midst of prayer, it is a good omen for him. Just as** the sneeze soothes his irritation, **giving him pleasure below,** it is a sign that **they are similarly giving him pleasure above.** Since Rav Zeira sneezed often, he was extremely pleased to hear this.

אֶלָּא רָק אָרָק קַשְׁיָא! – רָק אָרָק נַמִּי לָא קַשְׁיָא: אֶפְשָׁר כִּדְרַב יְהוּדָה; דְּאָמַר רַב יְהוּדָה: הָיָה עוֹמֵד בִּתְפִילָּה וְנִזְדַּמֵּן לוֹ רוֹק – מַבְלִיעוֹ בְּטַלִּיתוֹ, וְאִם טַלִּית נָאֶה הוּא – מַבְלִיעוֹ בְּאַפַּרְקְסוּתוֹ. רָבִינָא הֲוָה קָאֵי אֲחוֹרֵי רַב אָשֵׁי, נִזְדַּמֵּן לוֹ רוֹק, פַּתְקֵיהּ לַאֲחוֹרֵיהּ. אָמַר לֵיהּ: לָא סְבַר לַהּ מָר לְהָא דְּרַב יְהוּדָה ״מַבְלִיעוֹ בְּאַפַּרְקְסוּתוֹ״?! – אָמַר לֵיהּ: אֲנָא אֲנִינָא דַּעְתַּאי.

**However,** The contradiction **between spitting** in the case where Rabbi Yehuda HaNasi did so **and spitting** where it is deemed tantamount to spitting in the face of the king **is difficult.** The Gemara replies: The contradiction **between spitting** in one case **and spitting** in the other case **is also not difficult,** as **it is possible** to resolve it **in accordance with** the opinion of **Rav Yehuda,** as **Rav Yehuda said: One who was standing in prayer, and saliva happened** to accumulate in **his** mouth,[H] **he absorbs it in his garment. And if it was a fine garment** and he does not want it to become sullied, **he may cover it up in his head covering.** That way, one is permitted to spit. The Gemara relates: **Ravina was standing behind Rav Ashi** during prayer when **saliva happened** to accumulate in **his** mouth, **so he discharged it behind him.** Rav Ashi **said to him:** And **does the Master not hold** in accordance with **that** statement of **Rav Yehuda, who said** that **one absorbs it in his head covering? He said to him: I am delicate,** and the mere knowledge that there is spittle in my head covering disturbs my prayer.

הַמַּשְׁמִיעַ קוֹלוֹ בִּתְפִלָּתוֹ הֲרֵי זֶה מִקְּטַנֵּי אֲמָנָה. אָמַר רַב הוּנָא: לֹא שָׁנוּ אֶלָּא שֶׁיָּכוֹל לְכַוֵּין אֶת לִבּוֹ בְּלַחַשׁ, אֲבָל אֵין יָכוֹל לְכַוֵּין אֶת לִבּוֹ בְּלַחַשׁ – מוּתָּר; וְהָנֵי מִילֵּי – בְּיָחִיד, אֲבָל בְּצִיבּוּר – אָתֵי לְמִיטְרַד צִיבּוּרָא.

It was taught in a *baraita*: **One who sounds his voice during his** *Amida* **prayer is among those of little faith. Rav Huna said: This was only taught** in a case **where one is able to focus his heart** while praying silently, **but** if he **is unable to focus his heart** while praying **silently, he is permitted** to sound his voice. **This applies only to** one praying **alone,** but when he is praying **in a congregation** his voice **will come to disturb the congregation** and it is prohibited.

רַבִּי אַבָּא הֲוָה קָא מִשְׁתַּמֵּיט מִינֵּיהּ דְּרַב יְהוּדָה, דַּהֲוָה קָא בָּעֵי לְמֵיסַק לְאַרְעָא דְיִשְׂרָאֵל, דְּאָמַר רַב יְהוּדָה: כׇּל הָעוֹלֶה מִבָּבֶל לְאֶרֶץ יִשְׂרָאֵל עוֹבֵר בַּעֲשֵׂה, שֶׁנֶּאֱמַר: ״בָּבֶלָה יוּבָאוּ וְשָׁמָּה יִהְיוּ עַד יוֹם פׇּקְדִי אוֹתָם נְאֻם ה׳״. אָמַר: אֵיזִיל וְאֶשְׁמַע מִינֵּיהּ מִילְּתָא מִבֵּית וַועֲדָא, וַהֲדַר אֵפּוֹק.

The Gemara relates that **Rabbi Abba was avoiding** being seen **by** his teacher **Rav Yehuda,** as Rabbi Abba **sought to ascend to Eretz Yisrael** and his teacher disapproved, **as Rav Yehuda said: Anyone who ascends from Babylonia to Eretz Yisrael**[N] **transgresses a positive commandment, as it is stated: "They shall be taken to Babylonia and there they shall remain until the day that I recall them, said the Lord"** (Jeremiah 27:22). Rabbi Abba did not want to discuss his desire to emigrate with Rav Yehuda. Nevertheless **he said: I will go and hear something from him at the hall** where the Sages **assemble,** without being seen, **and afterwards I will leave** Babylonia.

אֲזַל אַשְׁכְּחֵיהּ לְתַנָּא דְּקָתָנֵי קַמֵּיהּ דְּרַב יְהוּדָה: הָיָה עוֹמֵד בִּתְפִלָּה וְנִתְעַטֵּשׁ – מַמְתִּין עַד שֶׁיִּכְלֶה הָרוּחַ וְחוֹזֵר וּמִתְפַּלֵּל; אִיכָּא דְּאָמְרִי: הָיָה עוֹמֵד בִּתְפִלָּה וּבִיקֵּשׁ לְהִתְעַטֵּשׁ – מַרְחִיק לַאֲחָרָיו אַרְבַּע אַמּוֹת, וּמִתְעַטֵּשׁ, וּמַמְתִּין עַד שֶׁיִּכְלֶה הָרוּחַ, וְחוֹזֵר וּמִתְפַּלֵּל; וְאוֹמֵר: ״רִבּוֹנוֹ שֶׁל עוֹלָם, יְצַרְתָּנוּ נְקָבִים נְקָבִים חֲלוּלִים חֲלוּלִים, גָּלוּי וְיָדוּעַ לְפָנֶיךָ חֶרְפָּתֵנוּ וּכְלִימָּתֵנוּ בְּחַיֵּינוּ, וּבְאַחֲרִיתֵנוּ רִמָּה וְתוֹלֵעָה״; וּמַתְחִיל מִמָּקוֹם שֶׁפָּסַק.

**He went and found the** *tanna,* who recites the tannaitic sources before the study hall, **reciting** the following *baraita* **before Rav Yehuda: One who was standing in prayer and sneezed** from below[H] **waits until the odor dissipates and resumes praying. Some say: One who was standing in prayer when he felt the need to sneeze** from below, **retreats four cubits, sneezes, waits until the odor dissipates and resumes praying. And** before resuming his prayer, **he says: Master of the universe, You have formed us with many orifices and cavities; our disgrace and shame in life are clear and evident before You, as is our destiny with maggots and worms,** and so we should not be judged harshly. **And he resumes** his prayer **from where he stopped.**[H]

### HALAKHA

**One who was standing in prayer, and saliva happened to accumulate in his mouth – הָיָה עוֹמֵד בִּתְפִילָּה וְנִזְדַּמֵּן לוֹ רוֹק:** It is prohibited to spit while praying. If saliva nevertheless accumulates, he should absorb it in his garment. If he is delicate, he should spit it behind him in accordance with the custom of Ravina (Rambam *Sefer Ahava, Hilkhot Tefilla* 4:11; *Shulḥan Arukh, Oraḥ Ḥayyim* 97:2).

**One who was standing in prayer and sneezed from below – הָיָה עוֹמֵד בִּתְפִלָּה וְנִתְעַטֵּשׁ:** One who was standing in prayer and broke wind must wait until the odor dissipates and only then resume his prayer from the point that he stopped. If one feels that he is about to break wind, he distances himself four cubits from where he was standing, and after breaking wind waits until the odor dissipates before reciting: Master of the universe, You have formed us with many orifices and cavities; our disgrace and shame in life are clear and evident before You, as is our destiny with maggots and worms. Only then does he return to the place that he had been standing and resume his prayer. The Rema notes that this applies specifically to one who is praying at home; however, one praying in public need neither distance himself nor recite Master of the universe, etc., as that would exacerbate his embarrassment. Rather, the custom is that he waits until the odor dissipates and resumes his prayer (Rambam *Sefer Ahava, Hilkhot Tefilla* 4:11–12; *Shulḥan Arukh, Oraḥ Ḥayyim* 103:1–2 and in the comment of the Rema).

**Manners during prayer – נִימּוּס בִּשְׁעַת הַתְּפִילָּה:** It is prohibited to belch or yawn while praying. If one yawns involuntarily, he covers his mouth with his hand. He should not place his hand on his chin as that is the conceit of the arrogant (in accordance with the Rif's explanation of the Gemara; *Shulḥan Arukh, Oraḥ Ḥayyim* 97:1 and the comment of the Rema).

### NOTES

**Anyone who ascends from Babylonia to Eretz Yisrael – כׇּל הָעוֹלֶה מִבָּבֶל לְאֶרֶץ יִשְׂרָאֵל:** Apparently even according to Rav Yehuda this prohibition, which is unique to Babylonia, does not apply while the Temple is standing, for then there is clearly a mitzva to immigrate to the land of Israel and fulfill the mitzvot that are connected with the land of Israel, as did Hillel the Elder. However, Rav Yehuda maintained that after the destruction of the Temple it was forbidden to leave Babylonia (Rabbi Yosef Ḥanina Meizlish).

### NOTES

**The approaches of Rav Huna and Rav Ḥisda – שִׁיטַת רַב הוּנָא וְרַב חִסְדָּא:** The differences in approach between Rav Huna and Rav Ḥisda appear to parallel those that were stated above with regard to their disagreement about prayer in the place of nakedness or filth. According to Rav Huna, cleanliness of the mouth is paramount. As a result, if one's mouth is covered it is acceptable. Rav Ḥisda, however, citing the verse: "All of my bones shall say," prohibits reciting *Shema* when the body is in a filthy place (*Kehillat Ya'akov*).

### HALAKHA

**A Torah scholar is prohibited from standing in a place of filth – תַּלְמִיד חָכָם אָסוּר לוֹ לַעֲמוֹד בִּמְקוֹם הַטִּנּוֹפֶת:** One may not engage in matters of Torah in a filthy place. Therefore, a Torah scholar, whose mind is always contemplating matters of Torah, may not stand there (*Shulḥan Arukh, Yoreh De'a* 246:26 in the comment of the Rema).

**One is permitted to contemplate matters of Torah everywhere, except… – בְּכָל מָקוֹם מוּתָּר לְהַרְהֵר בְּדִבְרֵי תוֹרָה חוּץ וכו׳:** One is prohibited from even contemplating matters of Torah in the bathroom or bathhouse, or in any filthy place in which there is feces and the like (Rambam *Sefer Ahava, Hilkhot Keriat Shema* 3:4; *Shulḥan Arukh, Oraḥ Ḥayyim* 85:2).

**One who was walking in filthy alleyways may not recite *Shema* – הָיָה מְהַלֵּךְ בִּמְבוֹאוֹת הַמְטוּנָּפוֹת לֹא יִקְרָא קְרִיאַת שְׁמַע:** One is prohibited from reciting *Shema* in a filthy alleyway. If one must pass through a place of that sort while reciting *Shema*, he pauses and only resumes reciting it after emerging from the alleyway. Some say that when he emerges, he must recite it from the beginning (Rema). Even though Rav Huna was more prominent than Rav Ḥisda, the *halakha* is ruled in accordance with Rav Ḥisda's more stringent opinion since most of the amoraic statements cited in the Gemara were based upon it (Rambam *Sefer Ahava, Hilkhot Keriat Shema* 3:14; *Shulḥan Arukh, Oraḥ Ḥayyim* 85:1).

### BACKGROUND

**Bathhouse – בֵּית הַמֶּרְחָץ:**

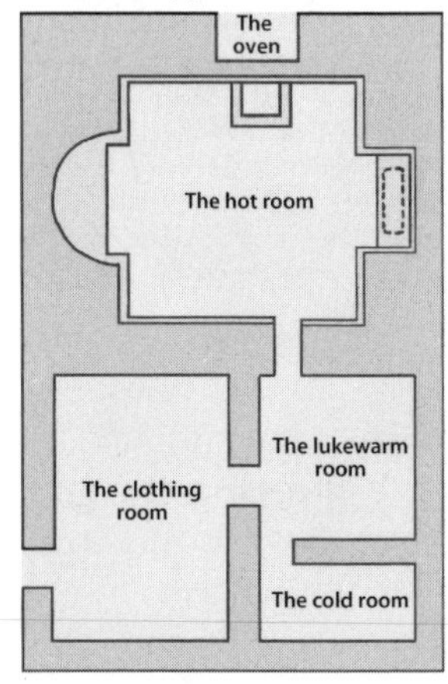


Diagram of a typical bathhouse from the mishnaic period

---

אָמַר לֵיהּ: אִילּוּ לֹא בָּאתִי אֶלָּא לִשְׁמוֹעַ דָּבָר זֶה – דַּיִּי.

Rabbi Abba **said to him: Had I only come** to the assembly of the Sages **to hear this teaching, it would have been sufficient for me.**

תָּנוּ רַבָּנַן: הָיָה יָשֵׁן בְּטַלִּיתוֹ וְאֵינוֹ יָכוֹל לְהוֹצִיא אֶת רֹאשׁוֹ מִפְּנֵי הַצִּנָּה – חוֹצֵץ בְּטַלִּיתוֹ עַל צַוָּארוֹ וְקוֹרֵא קְרִיאַת שְׁמַע. וְיֵשׁ אוֹמְרִים: עַל לִבּוֹ.

**The Sages taught:** One who **was sleeping** unclothed, but was covered **with his garment, and he is unable to stick his head out** from under the garment **because of the cold,** may **form a barrier with his garment at his neck and recite *Shema*** in bed. **And some say:** He must form a barrier with his garment **at his heart.**

וְתַנָּא קַמָּא – הֲרֵי לִבּוֹ רוֹאֶה אֶת הָעֶרְוָה! קָסָבַר: לִבּוֹ רוֹאֶה אֶת הָעֶרְוָה מוּתָּר.

The Gemara asks: **And** according to **the first *tanna*,** shouldn't he be prohibited from reciting *Shema* because **his heart sees** his **nakedness,** as there is no barrier between them? The Gemara responds: Indeed, the first *tanna* **holds that** when **one's heart sees** his **nakedness, it is permitted** to recite *Shema*, and a barrier is only necessary to separate between his mouth and his nakedness.

אָמַר רַב הוּנָא אָמַר רַבִּי יוֹחָנָן: הָיָה מְהַלֵּךְ בַּמְּבוֹאוֹת הַמְטוּנָּפוֹת – מַנִּיחַ יָדוֹ עַל פִּיו וְקוֹרֵא קְרִיאַת שְׁמַע. אָמַר לֵיהּ רַב חִסְדָּא: הָאֱלֹהִים! אִם אֲמָרָהּ לִי רַבִּי יוֹחָנָן בְּפוּמֵיהּ – לֹא צָיֵיתְנָא לֵיהּ.

**Rav Huna said** that **Rabbi Yoḥanan said: One who was walking in alleyways filthy** with human excrement and he must recite *Shema*, **he places his hand over his mouth and recites *Shema*. Rav Ḥisda said to him: By God!** Even **if Rabbi Yoḥanan had said it to me** directly, **with his own mouth, I would not have obeyed him.**[N]

אִיכָּא דְּאָמְרִי, אָמַר רַבָּה בַּר בַּר חָנָה אָמַר רַבִּי יְהוֹשֻׁעַ בֶּן לֵוִי: הָיָה מְהַלֵּךְ בַּמְּבוֹאוֹת הַמְטוּנָּפוֹת – מַנִּיחַ יָדוֹ עַל פִּיו וְקוֹרֵא קְרִיאַת שְׁמַע. אָמַר לֵיהּ רַב חִסְדָּא: הָאֱלֹהִים! אִם אֲמָרָהּ לִי רַבִּי יְהוֹשֻׁעַ בֶּן לֵוִי בְּפוּמֵיהּ – לֹא צָיֵיתְנָא לֵיהּ.

**Some say** this *halakha*: **Rabba bar bar Ḥana said** that **Rabbi Yehoshua ben Levi said: One who was walking in alleyways filthy** with human excrement and he must recite *Shema*, **he places his hand over his mouth and recites *Shema*. Rav Ḥisda said to him: By God!** Even **if Rabbi Yehoshua ben Levi had said it to me** directly, **with his own mouth, I would not have obeyed him.**

וּמִי אָמַר רַב הוּנָא הָכִי? וְהָאָמַר רַב הוּנָא: תַּלְמִיד חָכָם אָסוּר לוֹ לַעֲמוֹד בִּמְקוֹם הַטִּנּוֹפֶת – לְפִי שֶׁאִי אֶפְשָׁר לוֹ לַעֲמוֹד בְּלִי הִרְהוּר תּוֹרָה! לָא קַשְׁיָא, כָּאן – בְּעוֹמֵד, כָּאן – בִּמְהַלֵּךְ.

The Gemara challenges this: **Did Rav Huna** really **say that? Didn't Rav Huna say: A Torah scholar is prohibited from standing in a place of filth,**[H] **as he is unable to stand without contemplating Torah,** and uttering *Shema* orally is graver than mere contemplation. The Gemara responds: This **is not difficult; here,** Rav Huna prohibited contemplating Torah **in** a case where one is **standing** in a place of filth, while **here** he permitted to recite *Shema* **in** a case where one is **walking** through a place of filth.

וּמִי אָמַר רַבִּי יוֹחָנָן הָכִי? וְהָאָמַר רַבָּה בַּר בַּר חָנָה אָמַר רַבִּי יוֹחָנָן: בְּכָל מָקוֹם מוּתָּר לְהַרְהֵר בְּדִבְרֵי תוֹרָה – חוּץ מִבֵּית הַמֶּרְחָץ וּמִבֵּית הַכִּסֵּא. וְכִי תֵּימָא, הָכָא נַמִי, כָּאן בְּעוֹמֵד כָּאן בִּמְהַלֵּךְ; אִינִי?! וְהָא רַבִּי אַבָּהוּ הֲוָה קָא אָזֵיל בַּתְרֵיהּ דְּרַבִּי יוֹחָנָן, וַהֲוָה קָא קָרֵי קְרִיאַת שְׁמַע, כִּי מְטָא בַּמְּבוֹאוֹת הַמְטוּנָּפוֹת אִשְׁתִּיק. אָמַר לֵיהּ לְרַבִּי יוֹחָנָן: לְהֵיכָן אַהֲדַר? אָמַר לֵיהּ: אִם שָׁהִיתָ כְּדֵי לִגְמוֹר אֶת כּוּלָּהּ – חֲזוֹר לָרֹאשׁ!

The Gemara asks: **Did Rabbi Yoḥanan** really **say that? Didn't Rabba bar bar Ḥana say** that **Rabbi Yoḥanan said: One is permitted to contemplate matters of Torah everywhere, except**[H] **the bathhouse**[B] **and the bathroom?** Consequently, it is prohibited to even contemplate Torah in a place of filth. **And if you say: Here, too,** there is a distinction between the two cases, **here,** Rabbi Yoḥanan prohibited contemplating Torah **in** a case where one is **standing; here,** Rabbi Yoḥanan permitted to recite *Shema* **in** a case where one is **walking, is that so? Wasn't Rabbi Abbahu walking after Rabbi Yoḥanan and reciting *Shema*,** and **when he reached a filthy alleyway he fell silent** and stopped reciting *Shema*. When they emerged, Rabbi Abbahu **said to Rabbi Yoḥanan: To where** in *Shema* **should I return** and resume reciting it? Rabbi Yoḥanan **said to him: If you delayed** continuing *Shema* for an interval **sufficient to complete the entire** *Shema*, **return to the beginning** and recite it from there. From the fact that Rabbi Yoḥanan did not admonish him for interrupting his recitation, apparently he, too, prohibits reciting *Shema* while walking through a filthy alleyway.

הָכִי קָאָמַר לֵיהּ: לְדִידִי – לָא סְבִירָא לִי, לְדִידָךְ דִּסְבִירָא לָךְ – אִם שָׁהִיתָ כְּדֵי לִגְמוֹר אֶת כּוּלָּהּ חֲזוֹר לָרֹאשׁ.

The Gemara responds: This is not a proof, as **he says to him as follows: I do not hold** that one must interrupt the recitation of *Shema* in this case, but **for you, who holds** that one must, **if you delayed** *Shema* for an interval **sufficient to complete the entire** *Shema*, **return to the beginning** and recite it from there.

תַּנְיָא כְּוָתֵיהּ דְּרַב הוּנָא, תַּנְיָא כְּוָתֵיהּ דְּרַב חִסְדָּא. תַּנְיָא כְּוָתֵיהּ דְּרַב הוּנָא: הַמְהַלֵּךְ בַּמְּבוֹאוֹת הַמְטוּנָּפוֹת – מַנִּיחַ יָדוֹ עַל פִּיו וְיִקְרָא קְרִיאַת שְׁמַע. תַּנְיָא כְּוָתֵיהּ דְּרַב חִסְדָּא: הָיָה מְהַלֵּךְ בַּמְּבוֹאוֹת הַמְטוּנָּפוֹת – לֹא יִקְרָא קְרִיאַת שְׁמַע; וְלֹא עוֹד אֶלָּא שֶׁאִם הָיָה קוֹרֵא וּבָא – פּוֹסֵק.

The Gemara cites tannaitic sources to corroborate both the lenient and the stringent opinions. **It was taught** in a *baraita* **in accordance with** the opinion of **Rav Huna: One who was walking in filthy alleyways places his hand over his mouth and recites *Shema*. It was taught** in a *baraita* **in accordance with** the opinion of **Rav Ḥisda: One who was walking in filthy alleyways may not recite *Shema*.**[H] **Furthermore, if he was in the course of reciting** *Shema* when he reached a filthy alleyway, **he stops** his recitation at that point.

לֹא פָּסַק מַאי? – אָמַר רַבִּי מְיָאשָׁה בַּר בְּרֵיהּ דְּרַבִּי יְהוֹשֻׁעַ בֶּן לֵוִי: עָלָיו הַכָּתוּב אוֹמֵר "וְגַם אֲנִי נָתַתִּי לָהֶם חֻקִּים לֹא טוֹבִים וּמִשְׁפָּטִים לֹא יִחְיוּ בָּהֶם".

The Gemara asks: If **one did not stop**, what is his status? **Rabbi Meyasha, son of the son of Rabbi Yehoshua ben Levi,**[P] **said: Of him the verse says: "Moreover, I gave them statutes that were not good and laws by which they could not live"** (Ezekiel 20:25), as in this case following these statutes and laws led to sin, not to mitzva.

רַב אַסִּי אָמַר: "הוֹי מֹשְׁכֵי הֶעָוֹן בְּחַבְלֵי הַשָּׁוְא". רַב אַדָּא בַּר אַהֲבָה אָמַר מֵהָכָא: "כִּי דְבַר ה' בָּזָה".

**Rav Asi said** that this is derived from the verse: **"Woe to those who draw iniquity with cords of vanity"** (Isaiah 5:18), meaning that this man brings sin upon himself for naught. **Rav Adda bar Ahava said** it is derived **from here: "For he has shown contempt for the word of the Lord"** (Numbers 15:31), meaning that uttering God's word in a place of filth shows contempt for the Lord.

וְאִם פָּסַק מַה שְּׂכָרוֹ? אָמַר רַבִּי אַבָּהוּ עָלָיו הַכָּתוּב אוֹמֵר: "וּבַדָּבָר הַזֶּה תַּאֲרִיכוּ יָמִים".

The Gemara asks: **And if he stopped** his recitation, **what is his reward? Rabbi Abbahu said: Of him the verse says: "And it is through this matter that you will prolong your days"** (Deuteronomy 32:47), meaning that by being careful with one's speech one merits longevity.

אָמַר רַב הוּנָא: הָיְתָה טַלִּיתוֹ חֲגוּרָה לוֹ עַל מָתְנָיו – מוּתָּר לִקְרוֹת קְרִיאַת שְׁמַע. תַּנְיָא נַמִי הָכִי: הָיְתָה טַלִּיתוֹ, שֶׁל בֶּגֶד וְשֶׁל עוֹר וְשֶׁל שַׂק, חֲגוּרָה עַל מָתְנָיו – מוּתָּר לִקְרוֹת קְרִיאַת שְׁמַע;

**Rav Huna said: One** whose **garment was tied around his waist,** even if he was bare above the waist, **is permitted to recite *Shema*.** Indeed, **that** opinion **was also taught** in a *baraita*: **One** whose **garment** made **of cloth, of leather, of sack**[N] or of any other material **was strapped around his waist, he is permitted to recite *Shema*.**

**PERSONALITIES**

Rabbi Meyasha, son of the son of Rabbi Yehoshua ben Levi – רַבִּי מְיָאשָׁה בַּר בְּרֵיהּ דְּרַבִּי יְהוֹשֻׁעַ בֶּן לֵוִי: Based on his age and the Sages with whom he associated, apparently, Rabbi Meyasha was among the students of Rabbi Yoḥanan; however, he clearly learned most of his Torah from his grandfather, in whose name he often cites his teachings. Rabbi Meyasha did not live a long life, as he died during his grandfather's lifetime after a protracted illness. It is precisely the fact that so young a scholar was privileged to have halakhic statements cited in his name in both the Babylonian and the Jerusalem Talmuds as well as in midrashic literature that underscores his greatness.

**NOTES**

A garment of cloth, of leather, of sack – שֶׁל בֶּגֶד וְשֶׁל עוֹר וְשֶׁל שַׂק: This list begins with an ordinary garment, moves on to leather which is also appropriate, and ends with sackcloth, which is only barely considered suitable human clothing, in which, nevertheless, one is permitted to recite *Shema* (*Adderet Eliyahu*).

Perek **III**
Daf **25** Amud **a**

אֲבָל לִתְפִלָּה – עַד שֶׁיְּכַסֶּה אֶת לִבּוֹ.

**However, for prayer,** one may not recite it **until he covers his heart,** because in prayer he addresses God directly and he must dress accordingly.[H]

וְאָמַר רַב הוּנָא: שָׁכַח וְנִכְנַס בִּתְפִילִּין לְבֵית הַכִּסֵּא – מַנִּיחַ יָדוֹ עֲלֵיהֶן עַד שֶׁיִּגְמוֹר. עַד שֶׁיִּגְמוֹר סָלְקָא דַּעְתָּךְ?! – אֶלָּא כִּדְאָמַר רַב נַחְמָן בַּר יִצְחָק: עַד שֶׁיִּגְמוֹר עַמּוּד רִאשׁוֹן. וְלִפְסוֹק לְאַלְתַּר וְלֵיקוּם! – מִשּׁוּם דְּרַבָּן שִׁמְעוֹן בֶּן גַּמְלִיאֵל. דְּתַנְיָא, רַבָּן שִׁמְעוֹן בֶּן גַּמְלִיאֵל אוֹמֵר: עַמּוּד הַחוֹזֵר מֵבִיא אֶת הָאָדָם לִידֵי הִדְרוֹקָן, סִילּוֹן הַחוֹזֵר – מֵבִיא אֶת הָאָדָם לִידֵי יֵרָקוֹן.

**And Rav Huna said: One** who **forgot and entered the bathroom while donning phylacteries**[H] **places his hand on them until he finishes.** The Gemara wonders: **Does it enter your mind** that he can do so **until he is finished? Rather, as Rav Naḥman bar Yitzḥak said: Until he finishes** discharging **the first mass** of feces, at which point he can step out and remove his phylacteries. The Gemara asks: **Let him stop immediately** when he realizes that he is donning phylacteries **and stand** and step out. The Gemara replies: He cannot do so **because of** the statement of **Rabban Shimon ben Gamliel. As it was taught** in a *baraita*: **A mass** of feces **that is held back** without having been discharged **causes a person** to suffer **from dropsy** [*hidrokan*], **while a stream** of urine **that is held back causes a person** to suffer **from jaundice** [*yerakon*]. Since there is potential danger, the Sages did not require him to step out.

אִתְּמַר: צוֹאָה עַל בְּשָׂרוֹ, אוֹ יָדוֹ מוּנַּחַת בְּבֵית הַכִּסֵּא; רַב הוּנָא אָמַר: מוּתָּר לִקְרוֹת קְרִיאַת שְׁמַע; רַב חִסְדָּא אָמַר: אָסוּר לִקְרוֹת קְרִיאַת שְׁמַע. אָמַר רָבָא: מַאי טַעְמָא דְּרַב הוּנָא – דִּכְתִיב "כֹּל הַנְּשָׁמָה תְּהַלֵּל יָהּ הַלְלוּיָהּ".

**It was stated** that the Sages disagreed with regard to one who had **fecal matter on his skin**[H] or whose **hand,** but not the rest of his body, **was placed inside the bathroom.** Under those circumstances, **Rav Huna said:** He is **permitted to recite *Shema*. Rav Ḥisda said: He is prohibited from reciting *Shema*. Rava said: What is the reason for Rav Huna's** opinion? **As it is written: "Let every soul** [*neshama*] **praise the Lord; Halleluya"** (Psalms 150:6), which he interprets as "Let everything that has breath" [*neshima*]. As long as the mouth with which one recites praise is in a place of purity, the location of the other limbs of his body is irrelevant.

וְרַב חִסְדָּא אָמַר: אָסוּר לִקְרוֹת קְרִיאַת שְׁמַע. מַאי טַעְמָא דְּרַב חִסְדָּא – דִּכְתִיב "כָּל עַצְמוֹתַי תֹּאמַרְנָה ה' מִי כָמוֹךָ".

**And Rav Ḥisda said: He is prohibited from reciting *Shema*. What is the reason for Rav Ḥisda's** opinion? **As it is written: "All of my bones shall say: Lord, who is like You"** (Psalms 35:10). Since this praise is undertaken with one's entire body, he may not recite *Shema* even if just one limb is not appropriately clean.

**HALAKHA**

For prayer until he covers his heart – לִתְפִלָּה עַד שֶׁיְּכַסֶּה אֶת לִבּוֹ: One who has a garment strapped around his waist, even if it covers his nakedness and serves as a barrier between his nakedness and his heart, is prohibited from praying until he covers his entire body (*Mishna Berura*). If he failed to cover himself or, due to circumstances beyond his control, he had nothing with which to cover himself, and he nevertheless prayed, he fulfilled his obligation because his nakedness was covered (Rambam *Sefer Ahava, Hilkhot Tefilla* 4:7; *Shulḥan Arukh, Oraḥ Ḥayyim* 74:6, 91:1).

One who forgot and entered the bathroom while donning phylacteries – שָׁכַח וְנִכְנַס בִּתְפִילִּין לְבֵית הַכִּסֵּא: One who forgot that his phylacteries were on his head and began to defecate, covers them with his hand until he has passed the first mass of feces, after which he must emerge and remove them before returning to the bathroom. He dons his phylacteries only after cleaning himself (Rambam *Sefer Ahava, Hilkhot Tefillin Mezuza VeSefer Torah* 4:20; *Shulḥan Arukh, Oraḥ Ḥayyim* 43:8).

One who had fecal matter on his skin – צוֹאָה עַל בְּשָׂרוֹ: With regard to one who has fecal matter on his skin and seeks to recite *Shema*, there is a dispute between the authorities. Some ruled that he is permitted to do so as per the opinion of Rav Huna (Rif, Rosh, Rabbeinu Yona) and some ruled that it is prohibited as per the opinion of Rav Ḥisda (Rambam, *Or Zarua*). Even those who ruled leniently only did so if the fecal matter was covered and gave off no foul odor. One should adopt the more stringent ruling in all but exigent circumstances (Rambam *Sefer Ahava, Hilkhot Keriat Shema* 3:11; *Shulḥan Arukh, Oraḥ Ḥayyim* 76:4).

אִתְּמַר: רֵיחַ רַע שֶׁיֵּשׁ לוֹ עִיקָּר, רַב הוּנָא אָמַר: מַרְחִיק אַרְבַּע אַמּוֹת וְקוֹרֵא קְרִיאַת שְׁמַע; וְרַב חִסְדָּא אָמַר: מַרְחִיק אַרְבַּע אַמּוֹת מִמָּקוֹם שֶׁפָּסַק הָרֵיחַ, וְקוֹרֵא קְרִיאַת שְׁמַע.

**It was said** that the Sages disagreed over a similar issue: What is the legal status of **a foul odor that** emanates from a visible **source?**[H] **Rav Huna said: He distances himself four cubits** from the source of the odor **and recites *Shema*. And Rav Ḥisda said:** The source is irrelevant; **he distances himself four cubits from the place that the odor ceased and recites *Shema*.**

תַּנְיָא כְּוָתֵיהּ דְּרַב חִסְדָּא: לֹא יִקְרָא אָדָם קְרִיאַת שְׁמַע, לֹא כְּנֶגֶד צוֹאַת אָדָם וְלֹא כְּנֶגֶד צוֹאַת כְּלָבִים, וְלֹא כְּנֶגֶד צוֹאַת חֲזִירִים, וְלֹא כְּנֶגֶד צוֹאַת תַּרְנְגוֹלִים, וְלֹא כְּנֶגֶד צוֹאַת אַשְׁפָּה שֶׁרֵיחָהּ רַע; וְאִם הָיָה מָקוֹם גָּבוֹהַּ עֲשָׂרָה טְפָחִים אוֹ נָמוּךְ עֲשָׂרָה טְפָחִים – יוֹשֵׁב בְּצִדּוֹ וְקוֹרֵא קְרִיאַת שְׁמַע, וְאִם לָאו – מַרְחִיק מִמֶּנּוּ מְלוֹא עֵינָיו; וְכֵן לִתְפִלָּה. רֵיחַ רַע שֶׁיֵּשׁ לוֹ עִיקָּר – מַרְחִיק אַרְבַּע אַמּוֹת מִמְּקוֹם הָרֵיחַ, וְקוֹרֵא קְרִיאַת שְׁמַע.

The Gemara notes that **it was taught in** a *baraita* **in accordance with** the opinion of **Rav Ḥisda: A person may not recite *Shema* opposite human excrement, dog excrement, pig excrement,**[H] **chicken excrement, a foul-smelling dung-heap**[H] or anything repulsive. **However, if** the filth **were in a place ten handbreadths above**[H] **or ten handbreadths below** him, **he may sit alongside it and recite *Shema*,** as a height disparity of ten handbreadths renders it a separate domain. **And if** the filth were **not** ten handbreadths above or below him, **he must distance himself** until it remains beyond **his range of vision. And the same is true of prayer.**[H] However, from **a foul odor with** a visible **source, he distances himself four cubits from the place** that **the odor** ceased **and recites *Shema*.**

אָמַר רָבָא, לֵית הִלְכְתָא כִּי הָא מַתְנִיתָא בְּכָל הָנֵי שְׁמַעְתָּתָא אֶלָּא כִּי הָא דְּתַנְיָא: לֹא יִקְרָא אָדָם קְרִיאַת שְׁמַע לֹא כְּנֶגֶד צוֹאַת אָדָם וְלֹא כְּנֶגֶד צוֹאַת חֲזִירִים וְלֹא כְּנֶגֶד צוֹאַת כְּלָבִים בִּזְמַן שֶׁנָּתַן עוֹרוֹת לְתוֹכָן.

**Rava said: The *halakha* is not in accordance with this *baraita* in all of these rulings,** but **rather in accordance with that which was taught** in another *baraita*: **One may neither recite *Shema* opposite human excrement** under all circumstances, **nor opposite pig excrement, nor opposite dog excrement into which skins had been placed** for tanning, but other materials do not defile the venue of prayer.

בָּעוּ מִינֵּיהּ מֵרַב שֵׁשֶׁת: רֵיחַ רַע שֶׁאֵין לוֹ עִיקָּר מַהוּ? אָמַר לְהוּ: אֲתוּ חֲזוּ הָנֵי צִיפֵּי דְּבֵי רַב, דְּהָנֵי גָּנוּ וְהָנֵי גָּרְסִי. וְהָנֵי מִילֵּי – בְּדִבְרֵי תוֹרָה, אֲבָל בִּקְרִיאַת שְׁמַע – לֹא; וְדִבְרֵי תוֹרָה נַמִּי לֹא אֲמָרָן אֶלָּא דְּחַבְרֵיהּ, אֲבָל דִּידֵיהּ – לֹא.

**They raised a dilemma before Rav Sheshet: What is** the legal status of **a foul odor that has no** visible **source,**[H] e.g., flatulence? **He said to them: Come and see these mats in the study hall, as these** students **are sleeping** on them **and these** other students **are studying,** and they are not concerned about foul odors. **However, this only applies to Torah study** because there is no alternative, **but not to the recitation of *Shema*. And with regard to Torah study we said** that it is permitted **only** when the odor originated **with another, but not** when it originated **with himself.**

אִתְּמַר, צוֹאָה עוֹבֶרֶת; אַבַּיֵי אָמַר: מוּתָּר לִקְרוֹת קְרִיאַת שְׁמַע; רָבָא אָמַר: אָסוּר לִקְרוֹת קְרִיאַת שְׁמַע.

**It was stated** that the Sages disagreed over a parallel issue: What is the law with regard to **feces passing**[H] before him, being moved from place to place? **Abaye stated: One is permitted to recite *Shema*** opposite it, **while Rava said: One is forbidden to recite *Shema*** opposite it.

אָמַר אַבַּיֵי: מְנָא אָמִינָא לָהּ – דִּתְנַן: הַטָּמֵא עוֹמֵד תַּחַת הָאִילָן וְהַטָּהוֹר עוֹבֵר – טָמֵא, טָהוֹר עוֹמֵד תַּחַת הָאִילָן וְטָמֵא עוֹבֵר – טָהוֹר, וְאִם עָמַד – טָמֵא; וְכֵן בְּאֶבֶן הַמְנוּגַּעַת.

**Abaye said: From where do I say this** *halakha*? I say this on the basis of what **we learned** in a mishna: One who is afflicted with biblical leprosy renders the area beneath any covering under which he is located ritually impure. In a case where **the ritually impure** leper **is standing under** the branches of **a tree and a ritually pure** person **passes** under the branches of that same tree, the pure person **is** rendered **impure,** as the entire area under that covering is impure. However, if the **pure person is standing under the tree and the impure** leper **passes,**[HN] **he** remains **pure. And if** the leper **stopped** under the tree, the pure person is immediately rendered **impure. The same is true with regard to a stone afflicted** with biblical leprosy (see Leviticus 14), in that if it is merely being moved from place to place, it does not cause impurity. The upshot is that impurity is only disseminated in all directions when the source of the impurity is stationary.

וְרָבָא אָמַר לָךְ: הָתָם – בִּקְבִיעוּתָא תַּלְיָא מִילְּתָא, דִּכְתִיב: "בָּדָד יֵשֵׁב מִחוּץ לַמַּחֲנֶה מוֹשָׁבוֹ", הָכָא: "וְהָיָה מַחֲנֶיךָ קָדוֹשׁ" אָמַר רַחֲמָנָא, וְהָא לֵיכָּא.

**And Rava** could have **said to you: There,** in the case of leprosy, **it is contingent upon the permanence** of the place, **as** with regard to the leper **it is written: "He shall dwell alone; outside the camp shall his dwelling be"** (Leviticus 13:46). His impurity is in his permanent dwelling-place. **Here,** with regard to the obligation to distance oneself from something repulsive, **the Torah stated** the principle: **"And your camp shall be holy"** (Deuteronomy 23:15), **and there is no** holiness in those circumstances.

## HALAKHA

**A foul odor that has a source – רֵיחַ רַע שֶׁיֵּשׁ לוֹ עִיקָּר:** One who seeks to recite *Shema* must distance himself four cubits from the source of a foul odor. If he is still able to smell the odor, he must distance himself until he can no longer smell the foul odor, in accordance with the opinion of Rav Ḥisda, which is supported by the *baraita* (Rambam *Sefer Ahava, Hilkhot Keriat Shema* 3:12 and in the comment of the Ra'avad, who cites Rav Hai Gaon and disagrees with the Rambam).

**Dog excrement, pig excrement – צוֹאַת כְּלָבִים...חֲזִירִים:** The excrement of dogs and pigs; if one used them in processing animal skins or if they give off a foul odor, one must distance himself from them as he does from human excrement. If not, it is unnecessary, as per the *baraita* cited by Rava (Rambam *Sefer Ahava, Hilkhot Keriat Shema* 3:6; *Shulḥan Arukh, Oraḥ Ḥayyim* 79:4).

**A foul-smelling dung-heap – צוֹאַת אַשְׁפָּה שֶׁרֵיחָהּ רַע:** One is prohibited from reciting *Shema* opposite a foul-smelling dung-heap, in accordance with the *baraita* (*Shulḥan Arukh, Oraḥ Ḥayyim* 76:7).

**If the filth were in a place ten handbreadths above – הָיָה מָקוֹם גָּבוֹהַּ עֲשָׂרָה טְפָחִים:** If the excrement was ten handbreadths above or below the place where one was located, if it gave off no odor, according to the *Tur* who disagrees with Rabbeinu Yona, he is permitted to recite *Shema* there; as per the *baraita*. Some say that it is permitted even if it gave off a foul odor as the ten handbreadths are significant in terms of the odor as well. There are disputes with regard to other details as well; some say that in addition to being ten handbreadths above or below, it must rest on a surface that is four square handbreadths, which constitutes an independent domain (Rambam, *Eliyahu Rabba, Baḥ, Magen Avraham*) and others are lenient in that regard (Taz). There is also a dispute whether or not he is permitted to recite *Shema* in a case where the excrement is visible. Some hold that he may do so only in a case where it is not visible (Rashba; Rambam *Sefer Ahava, Hilkhot Keriat Shema* 3:9; *Shulḥan Arukh, Oraḥ Ḥayyim* 79:2).

**And the same is true of prayer – וְכֵן לִתְפִלָּה:** A place where one may not recite *Shema* one is also prohibited from reciting the *Amida* prayer (Rambam *Sefer Ahava, Hilkhot Tefilla* 4:8; *Shulḥan Arukh, Oraḥ Ḥayyim* 90:26).

**A foul odor that has no visible source – רֵיחַ רַע שֶׁאֵין לוֹ עִיקָּר:** One who broke wind and emitted a foul odor is prohibited from reciting *Shema* and studying Torah until the odor has dissipated. If the odor was emitted by another person, he is permitted to study Torah but prohibited to recite *Shema*, in accordance with the opinion of Rav Sheshet (Rambam *Sefer Ahava, Hilkhot Keriat Shema* 3:14).

**Feces passing – צוֹאָה עוֹבֶרֶת:** If excrement or a pig, even if it emerged from a river, was passing before him, one may not recite *Shema*. Some say that as long as it passes at a distance of four cubits, he may recite *Shema* (Rambam *Sefer Ahava, Hilkhot Keriat Shema* 3:13; *Shulḥan Arukh, Oraḥ Ḥayyim* 76:3).

**Ritual impurity passing – טוּמְאָה עוֹבֶרֶת:** If there was ritual impurity imparted by a leper under a tree and a ritually pure person passed under the tree, he becomes ritually impure. If a person was standing under a tree and the ritual impurity passed under that tree, he does not become ritually impure. If the ritual impurity came to a stop under the tree, he becomes ritually impure (Rambam, *Sefer Tahara, Hilkhot Tumat Tzara'at* 10:12).

## NOTES

**Ritual impurity passing – טוּמְאָה עוֹבֶרֶת:** The laws concerning this type of ritual impurity are relevant to the impurity of the dead and the impurity of the leper as well. With regard to those impurities, in addition to being imparted by touch, it is also spread by means of a tent, i.e., a corpse or leper that is underneath an awning or a tent, the impurity fills that space. The related *halakhot* are quite detailed, in tractate *Oholot* and elsewhere, and include the requirement that the impurity is stable. If the source of impurity is not standing in one place, it does not impart impurity of the tent (see Rashi).

אָמַר רַב פָּפָּא: פִּי חֲזִיר כְּצוֹאָה עוֹבֶרֶת דָּמֵי. פְּשִׁיטָא! – לָא צְרִיכָא, אַף עַל גַּב דִּסְלֵיק מִנַּהֲרָא.

On this topic **Rav Pappa said: The mouth of a pig is like passing feces.** The Gemara asks: **That is obvious.** The Gemara replies: **No,** this *halakha* is only **necessary** to teach that **even though** the pig **emerged from the river** and one might assume that its mouth was thereby cleansed, it never becomes completely clean.

אָמַר רַב יְהוּדָה: סָפֵק צוֹאָה – אֲסוּרָה; סָפֵק מֵי רַגְלַיִם – מוּתָּרִים. אִיכָּא דְּאָמְרִי, אָמַר רַב יְהוּדָה: סָפֵק צוֹאָה, בַּבַּיִת – מוּתֶּרֶת, בָּאַשְׁפָּה – אֲסוּרָה; סָפֵק מֵי רַגְלַיִם – אֲפִילּוּ בָּאַשְׁפָּה נַמִי מוּתָּרִין.

**Rav Yehuda said:** If there is **uncertainty** as to the presence of **feces,** e.g., whether something is or is not feces, and therefore whether or not one is permitted to utter sacred matters in its presence, **it is prohibited** to do so. However, if there is **uncertainty** as to the presence of **urine,**[H] **it is permitted** to do so. **Some say** an alternative version of this. **Rav Yehuda said:** If there is **uncertainty** as to the presence of **feces, in the home** one may assume that there is no feces present and **it is permitted** to speak sacred matters, but if there is doubt as to the presences of feces **in the dung-heap** it is **forbidden** to do so. If there is **uncertainty** as to the presence of **urine,** however, **even in the dung-heap it is permitted** to do so.

סָבַר לָהּ כִּי הָא דְּרַב הַמְנוּנָא, דְּאָמַר רַב הַמְנוּנָא: לֹא אָסְרָה תּוֹרָה אֶלָּא כְּנֶגֶד עַמּוּד בִּלְבַד,

**He holds in accordance with that which Rav Hamnuna** said, as **Rav Hamnuna said: The Torah prohibited** the utterance of sacred matters **only opposite the stream** of urine.

וּכְדְרַבִּי יוֹנָתָן. דְּרַבִּי יוֹנָתָן רָמֵי: כְּתִיב "וְיָד תִּהְיֶה לְךָ מִחוּץ לַמַּחֲנֶה וְיָצָאתָ שָׁמָּה חוּץ", וּכְתִיב: "וְיָתֵד תִּהְיֶה לְךָ וגו׳ וְכִסִּיתָ אֶת צֵאָתֶךָ"!

**And in accordance with** the opinion of **Rabbi Yonatan, as Rabbi Yonatan** raised a **contradiction** between two verses: On the one hand **it is written: "You shall also have a place outside the camp, to which you will go"** (Deuteronomy 23:13), meaning that one must exit the camp before attending to his bodily needs but there is no obligation to cover it; **and it is written** in another verse: **"And you shall have a spade** among your weapons; and when you ease yourself outside, you shall dig with it, and turn back **and cover your excrement"** (Deuteronomy 23:14), indicating a clear obligation to conceal one's excrement.

הָא כֵּיצַד – כָּאן בִּגְדוֹלִים, כָּאן בִּקְטַנִּים; אַלְמָא: קְטַנִּים לֹא אָסְרָה תּוֹרָה אֶלָּא כְּנֶגֶד עַמּוּד בִּלְבַד. הָא נְפוּל לְאַרְעָא – שָׁרֵי, וְרַבָּנַן הוּא דִּגְזוּר בְּהוּ, וְכִי גְּזוּר בְּהוּ רַבָּנַן – בְּוַדָּאָן, אֲבָל בִּסְפֵקָן לֹא גְּזוּר.

He resolves this contradiction: **How is this** resolved? **Here,** where one is required to conceal his bodily needs, **it refers to feces; here,** where there is no requirement to conceal his bodily needs, **it refers to urine. Consequently,** with regard to **urine,** reciting *Shema* **was only prohibited by Torah law opposite the stream** of urine, **but once it has fallen to the ground, it is permitted. And the Sages are those who issued a decree with regard to** urine. **And when they issued a decree, it was only in** a case of **their certain** presence, **but in** a case of **their uncertain** presence, **they did not issue a decree.**

וּבְוַדָּאָן עַד כַּמָּה? אָמַר רַב יְהוּדָה אָמַר שְׁמוּאֵל: כׇּל זְמַן שֶׁמְּטַפְּחִין; וְכֵן אָמַר רַבָּה בַּר בַּר חָנָה אָמַר רַבִּי יוֹחָנָן: כׇּל זְמַן שֶׁמְּטַפְּחִין; וְכֵן אָמַר עוּלָּא: כׇּל זְמַן שֶׁמְּטַפְּחִין. גְּנִיבָא מִשְּׁמֵיהּ דְּרַב אָמַר: כׇּל זְמַן שֶׁרִשּׁוּמָן נִיכָּר.

The Gemara asks: **In a case of the certain** presence of urine, **until when** and in what state does its presence preclude one from uttering sacred matters? **Rav Yehuda said** that **Shmuel said: As long as it** is wet enough to **moisten** the hands of one who touches it. **And so too Rabba bar bar Ḥana said** that **Rabbi Yoḥanan said: As long as it moistens. And so too Ulla said: As long as it moistens. Geniva**[P] **in the name of Rav said:** It is forbidden **as long as its mark is apparent** on the ground.

אָמַר רַב יוֹסֵף: שְׁרָא לֵיהּ מָרֵיהּ לִגְנִיבָא! הַשְׁתָּא צוֹאָה, אָמַר רַב יְהוּדָה אָמַר רַב: כֵּיוָן שֶׁקָּרְמוּ פָּנֶיהָ מוּתָּר, מֵי רַגְלַיִם מִיבַּעְיָא?!

**Rav Yosef said: May** God, **his Master, forgive Geniva,**[B] as Rav could have said no such thing. **Now,** in the case of **feces, Rav Yehuda said** that **Rav said: Once its surface has** dried sufficiently to form a **crust, one is permitted** to utter sacred matters opposite it; **is it necessary** to say that opposite **urine** it is permitted once it dries?

אָמַר לֵיהּ אַבָּיֵי: מַאי חָזֵית דְּסָמְכַתְּ אַהָא – סְמוֹךְ אַהָא! דְּאָמַר רַבָּה בַּר רַב הוּנָא אָמַר רַב: צוֹאָה, אֲפִילּוּ כְּחֶרֶס – אֲסוּרָה.

**Abaye said to him: What did you see that** led you to rely **on that** *halakha*? **Rely on this** *halakha*; **as Rabba bar Rav Huna said** that **Rav said:** Uttering sacred matters opposite **feces, even** if it is as dry **as earthenware, is prohibited.**

וְהֵיכִי דָּמֵי צוֹאָה כְּחֶרֶס? אָמַר רַבָּה בַּר בַּר חָנָה אָמַר רַבִּי יוֹחָנָן: כׇּל זְמַן שֶׁזּוֹרְקָהּ וְאֵינָהּ נִפְרֶכֶת; וְאִיכָּא דְּאָמְרִי: כׇּל זְמַן שֶׁגּוֹלְלָהּ וְאֵינָהּ נִפְרֶכֶת.

The Gemara asks: **What are the circumstances of** feces **like earthenware? Rabba bar bar Ḥana said** that **Rabbi Yoḥanan said: As long as one throws it and it does not crumble,** it is still considered moist. **And some say: As long as one** can **roll it** from place to place **and it does not crumble.**

אָמַר רָבִינָא: הֲוָה קָאֵימְנָא קַמֵּיהּ דְּרַב יְהוּדָה מִדִּיפְתִּי, חֲזָא צוֹאָה, אָמַר לִי: עַיֵּין אִי קָרְמוּ פָּנֶיהָ אִי לָא. אִיכָּא דְּאָמְרִי, הָכִי אָמַר לֵיהּ: עַיֵּין אִי מִפַּלְאֵי אַפְלוּיֵי.

**Ravina said: I was standing before Rav Yehuda of Difti** when **he saw feces. He said to me: Examine** it and see **whether or not its surface has** dried sufficiently to form a **crust. Some say** that **he said to him as follows: Examine** it and see **if it is cracked,** as only then is it considered dry.

## HALAKHA

**Uncertainty as to the presence of feces… uncertainty as to the presence of urine –** **סָפֵק צוֹאָה...סָפֵק מֵי רַגְלַיִם:** If there is uncertainty with regard to the presence of feces, if he is in the house, he may recite *Shema*, if he is in the dung-heap, he may not recite *Shema*. If there is uncertainty with regard to the presence of urine, he may recite *Shema* everywhere, as the Sages did not issue a decree in that case (Rambam *Sefer Ahava, Hilkhot Keriat Shema* 3:15; *Shulḥan Arukh, Oraḥ Ḥayyim* 76:7).

## PERSONALITIES

**Geniva – גְּנִיבָא:** A member of the first and second generations of *amora'im* in Babylonia, Geniva was one of the more colorful characters of the era. A Sage of great stature, he was often visited in his home by the *amora*, Rav, in whose name he cited many of his Torah statements. The second generation of *amora'im* treated his teachings with respect. While Geniva was a wealthy and powerful man, at the same time he was quarrelsome and contentious. Though the details of the incident are unclear, it is known that he had a serious dispute with the Exilarch at the time, Mar Ukva, and it was only by virtue of Mar Ukva's moderation and judiciousness that the affair did not come before the Persian authorities. Ultimately, Geniva was charged with another offense, perhaps plotting against the crown, and was sentenced to death by the authorities. The Sages of the following (third) generation cite his teachings, always appreciating his Torah while disapproving of his conduct.

## BACKGROUND

**May his Master forgive him – שְׁרָא לֵיהּ מָרֵיהּ:** Though this expression does not outwardly convey an element of condemnation, it still hints to the serious reprobation of a Sage whose statements or actions are inappropriate. It has been said that when God's name is desecrated through a Sage's actions, it is said of that Sage: May his Master forgive him.

## HALAKHA

**Feces as dry as earthenware** – צוֹאָה כְּחֶרֶס: Excrement that dried to the extent that it crumbles when it is rolled, assumes the legal status of dust. Some say that it assumes that legal status only if it crumbles when it is thrown, as per the second, more stringent, version of Rabbi Yoḥanan's statement (Rambam *Sefer Ahava, Hilkhot Keriat Shema* 3:7; *Shulḥan Arukh, Oraḥ Ḥayyim* 82:1).

**And urine, as long as it moistens** – וּמֵי רַגְלַיִם כָּל זְמַן שֶׁמַּטְפִּיחִין: It is prohibited to recite *Shema* opposite urine that was absorbed into the ground but remained moist. This is only true if it remained moist enough to moisten another object (Rema; Rambam *Sefer Ahava, Hilkhot Keriat Shema* 3:7; *Shulḥan Arukh, Oraḥ Ḥayyim* 82:2).

## BACKGROUND

**No inference can be deduced from this** – מֵהָא לֵיכָּא לְמִשְׁמַע מִינָּהּ: This expression, found throughout the Gemara, concludes the refutation of an inference [*diyuk*]. Inference in the Gemara is a method of interpretation used to draw conclusions from tannaitic sources. According to this method, inferences may be drawn not only from what is explicitly stated in a mishna or *baraita*, but also from what is left unsaid. The rejection of the inference is effected by illustrating that another part of the same mishna or *baraita* can lead to the opposite conclusion. In that case the Gemara concludes: No inference can be deduced from this, indicating that this mishna or *baraita* was not composed in a manner that lends itself to drawing conclusions by means of inference. Rather, it is to be accepted as written, without reading anything further into it.

מַאי הָוֵי עֲלַהּ? אִתְּמַר: צוֹאָה כְּחֶרֶס; אַמֵּימָר אָמַר: אֲסוּרָה; וּמָר זוּטְרָא אָמַר: מוּתֶּרֶת. אָמַר רָבָא, הִלְכְתָא: צוֹאָה כְּחֶרֶס אֲסוּרָה, וּמֵי רַגְלַיִם כָּל זְמַן שֶׁמַּטְפִּיחִין.

Since several opinions were expressed on the subject, the Gemara asks: **What** halakhic conclusion was reached **about this? It was stated** that the *halakha* is subject to dispute: Reciting sacred matters opposite **feces** as dry **as earthenware;**[H] **Ameimar said: It is prohibited, and Mar Zutra said: It is permitted. Rava said** that **the** *halakha* is: Opposite **feces** as dry **as earthenware it is prohibited, and** opposite **urine,** it is prohibited **as long as it moistens.**[H]

מֵיתִיבֵי: מֵי רַגְלַיִם כָּל זְמַן שֶׁמַּטְפִּיחִין – אֲסוּרִין, נִבְלְעוּ אוֹ יָבְשׁוּ – מוּתָּרִים; מַאי לָאו "נִבְלְעוּ" דּוּמְיָא "דְּיָבְשׁוּ", מַה יָּבְשׁוּ – דְּאֵין רִשּׁוּמָן נִיכָּר, אַף נִבְלְעוּ – דְּאֵין רִשּׁוּמָן נִיכָּר, הָא רִשּׁוּמָן נִיכָּר – אָסוּר, אַף עַל גַּב דְּאֵין מַטְפִּיחִין!

The Gemara **raises an objection** based on what was taught in a *baraita*: **Urine, as long as it moistens it is prohibited. If it was absorbed** into the ground **or dried** in place, **it is permitted. What, is** urine that was **absorbed not similar** to urine that **dried? Just as when it dries its mark is no** longer **apparent, so too when it is absorbed, its mark is no** longer **apparent** and then it is permissible. **But** when **its mark is apparent, it is prohibited, even though it no longer moistens.**

וּלְטַעֲמִיךְ, אֵימָא רֵישָׁא: כָּל זְמַן שֶׁמַּטְפִּיחִין הוּא דְּאָסוּר, הָא רִשּׁוּמָן נִיכָּר – שָׁרֵי! – אֶלָּא: מֵהָא לֵיכָּא לְמִשְׁמַע מִינָּהּ.

The Gemara raises a difficulty to counter this: **And according to your reasoning, say the first clause: As long as it moistens it is prohibited,** from which one can infer: **But if** it does not moisten, but **its mark is apparent, it is permitted. Rather, no** inference beyond its basic meaning **can be deduced from this**[B] *baraita*, as the inferences are contradictory.

לֵימָא כְּתַנָּאֵי: כְּלִי שֶׁנִּשְׁפְּכוּ מִמֶּנּוּ מֵי רַגְלַיִם – אָסוּר לִקְרוֹת קְרִיאַת שְׁמַע כְּנֶגְדּוֹ, וּמֵי רַגְלַיִם עַצְמָן שֶׁנִּשְׁפְּכוּ, נִבְלְעוּ – מוּתָּר, לֹא נִבְלְעוּ – אָסוּר. רַבִּי יוֹסֵי אוֹמֵר: כָּל זְמַן שֶׁמַּטְפִּיחִין.

The Gemara notes: **Let us say** that this is **parallel to a** dispute between **the** *tanna'im*, as it was taught a *baraita*: **It is forbidden to recite** ***Shema*** **opposite a vessel from which urine was poured. However, the urine itself that was poured,** if it **was absorbed it is permitted;** if it **was not absorbed, it is prohibited. Rabbi Yosei** disagrees and **says:** It is prohibited **as long as it moistens.**

מַאי "נִבְלְעוּ" וּמַאי "לֹא נִבְלְעוּ" דְּקָאָמַר תַּנָּא קַמָּא? אִילֵימָא נִבְלְעוּ – דְּאֵין מַטְפִּיחִין, לֹא נִבְלְעוּ – דְּמַטְפִּיחִין, וַאֲתָא רַבִּי יוֹסֵי לְמֵימַר: כָּל זְמַן שֶׁמַּטְפִּיחִין הוּא דְּאָסוּר, הָא רִשּׁוּמָן נִיכָּר שָׁרֵי – הַיְינוּ תַּנָּא קַמָּא! אֶלָּא "נִבְלְעוּ" – דְּאֵין רִשּׁוּמָן נִיכָּר, "לֹא נִבְלְעוּ" – דְּרִשּׁוּמָן נִיכָּר. וַאֲתָא רַבִּי יוֹסֵי לְמֵימַר: כָּל זְמַן שֶׁמַּטְפִּיחִין הוּא דְּאָסוּר, הָא רִשּׁוּמָן נִיכָּר – שָׁרֵי!

The Gemara clarifies this dispute: **What is** the meaning of **absorbed and not absorbed in what the first** ***tanna*** **says? If you say** that **absorbed** means that it **does not moisten and not absorbed** means that it **moistens, and Rabbi Yosei came to say: As long as it moistens it is prohibited, but** if there is no moisture but its **mark is apparent, it is permitted.** If so, **that is** identical to the opinion of the **first** ***tanna*** and there is no dispute at all. **Rather, absorbed** means that **its mark is not apparent** and **not absorbed** means that **its mark is apparent. And Rabbi Yosei came to say: As long as it moistens, it is prohibited, but** if there is no moisture but its **mark is apparent, it is permitted,** in which case the dispute in our Gemara is parallel to this tannaitic dispute.

לֹא, דְּכוּלֵּי עָלְמָא כָּל זְמַן שֶׁמַּטְפִּיחִין הוּא דְּאָסוּר, הָא רִשּׁוּמָן נִיכָּר – שָׁרֵי

The Gemara states that it is not necessarily parallel: **No, everyone,** both *tanna'im*, agrees that **as long as it moistens, it is prohibited,** and if there is no moisture but its **mark is apparent, it is permitted.**

Perek **III**
Daf **25** Amud **b**

וְהָכָא, בְּטוֹפֵחַ עַל מְנָת לְהַטְפִּיחַ אִיכָּא בֵּינַיְיהוּ.

**And here, the difference between them is** in a case **where it is moist enough to moisten** other things. According to the first *tanna* the prohibition is only in effect when the urine is moist enough to moisten other objects, while according to Rabbi Yosei it applies as long as the urine itself is moist, even if it is not moist enough to moisten other objects.

"יָרַד לִטְבּוֹל אִם יָכוֹל לַעֲלוֹת כו'". לֵימָא תְּנָא סְתָמָא כְּרַבִּי אֱלִיעֶזֶר, דְּאָמַר: עַד הָנֵץ הַחַמָּה!

We learned in a mishna that **one who descended to immerse himself** due to a seminal emission must calculate, **whether or not he is able to ascend,** cover himself with a garment and recite the morning *Shema* before sunrise. The Gemara asks: **Let us say** that Rabbi Yehuda HaNasi **taught** this in the **unattributed** mishna **in accordance with** the opinion of **Rabbi Eliezer, who said:** One may recite *Shema* **until sunrise.**

אֲפִילּוּ תֵּימָא רַבִּי יְהוֹשֻׁעַ, וְדִלְמָא כְּוָתִיקִין; דְּאָמַר רַבִּי יוֹחָנָן: וָתִיקִין הָיוּ גּוֹמְרִין אוֹתָהּ עִם הָנֵץ הַחַמָּה.

The Gemara immediately rejects this assumption: **Even if you say** that the mishna is in accordance with the opinion of **Rabbi Yehoshua,** who disagrees with Rabbi Eliezer and holds that one may recite the morning *Shema* until the third hour of the day, **and perhaps** the *halakha* in the mishna was directed toward those whose practice was **in accordance with** the custom of the ***vatikin***,[L] pious individuals who were scrupulous in their performance of mitzvot, with regard to whom **Rabbi Yoḥanan said: The *vatikin* would conclude** the recitation of *Shema* **with sunrise.**

"וְאִם לָאו יִתְכַּסֶּה בַּמַּיִם וְיִקְרָא". וַהֲרֵי לִבּוֹ רוֹאֶה אֶת הָעֶרְוָה!

We learned in the mishna: **And if** one calculates that he will **not** be able to ascend and cover himself with a garment in time to recite *Shema*, he should **cover himself in the water and recite** *Shema* there. The Gemara asks: How can one recite *Shema* with his head above water? **His heart sees** his **nakedness** as there is no barrier between them.

אָמַר רַבִּי אֶלְעָזָר, וְאִי תֵּימָא רַבִּי אַחָא בַּר אַבָּא בַּר אַחָא מִשּׁוּם רַבֵּינוּ: בְּמַיִם עֲכוּרִין שָׁנוּ, דְּדָמוּ כְּאַרְעָא סְמִיכְתָּא, שֶׁלֹּא יִרְאֶה לִבּוֹ עֶרְוָתוֹ.

Regarding this **Rabbi Elazar said, and some say** it was **Rabbi Aḥa bar Abba bar Aḥa in the name of Rabbeinu,** Rav: **This was taught with regard to murky water,**[H] **which** is considered to be **like solid earth.** Therefore, it constitutes a barrier so that **his heart does not see** his **nakedness.**

תָּנוּ רַבָּנַן: מַיִם צְלוּלִין – יֵשֵׁב בָּהֶן עַד צַוָּארוֹ וְקוֹרֵא; וְיֵשׁ אוֹמְרִים: עוֹכְרָן בְּרַגְלוֹ.

On this same topic, **the Sages taught** in a *baraita*: If one was in **clear water, he should sit in it up to his neck and recite *Shema*. And some say: He sullies** the water **with his foot.**

וְתַנָּא קַמָּא – וַהֲרֵי לִבּוֹ רוֹאֶה אֶת הָעֶרְוָה! – קָסָבַר: לִבּוֹ רוֹאֶה אֶת הָעֶרְוָה – מוּתָּר. וַהֲרֵי עֲקֵבוֹ רוֹאֶה אֶת הָעֶרְוָה! – קָסָבַר: עֲקֵבוֹ רוֹאֶה אֶת הָעֶרְוָה – מוּתָּר.

The Gemara asks: **And** according to **the first *tanna* doesn't his heart see** his **nakedness** through the clear water? The Gemara replies: **He holds** that even if **his heart sees** his **nakedness, it is permitted** to recite *Shema*. The Gemara continues and asks: **But** in the clear water, **doesn't his heel see** his **nakedness?** The Gemara replies: Here too, the first *tanna* **holds** that in a case where **his heel sees** his **nakedness**[H] it is **permitted.**

אִתְּמַר: עֲקֵבוֹ רוֹאֶה אֶת הָעֶרְוָה – מוּתָּר. נוֹגֵעַ, אַבַּיֵי אָמַר: אָסוּר, וְרָבָא אָמַר: מוּתָּר. רַב זְבִיד מַתְנֵי לַהּ לְהָא שְׁמַעְתָּא הָכִי. רַב חִינָּנָא בְּרֵיהּ דְּרַב אִיקָא מַתְנֵי לַהּ הָכִי: נוֹגֵעַ – דִּבְרֵי הַכֹּל אָסוּר; רוֹאֶה, אַבַּיֵי אָמַר: אָסוּר, רָבָא אָמַר: מוּתָּר, לֹא נִתְּנָה תּוֹרָה לְמַלְאֲכֵי הַשָּׁרֵת. וְהִלְכְתָא: נוֹגֵעַ – אָסוּר, רוֹאֶה – מוּתָּר.

The Gemara notes, **it was stated:** If **one's heel sees** his **nakedness it is permitted.** However, what is the *halakha* in a case where his heel **touches** his nakedness? May one in that circumstance recite *Shema* or not? **Abaye said: It is prohibited, and Rava said: It is permitted.** The Gemara notes: **Rav Zevid taught this *halakha* in that manner. Rav Ḥinnana, son of Rav Ika, taught it as follows:** In a case where his heel **touches** his nakedness, **everyone agrees that it is prohibited.** Their dispute is with regard to a case where his heel **sees** his nakedness. **Abaye said: It is prohibited, and Rava said: It is permitted; the Torah was not given to the ministering angels,** and a person, who, as opposed to a ministering angel, has genitals, cannot avoid this. **And the *halakha*** is that if his heel **touches** his nakedness **it is prohibited,** but if it merely **sees** his nakedness, **it is permitted.**

אָמַר רָבָא: צוֹאָה בַּעֲשָׁשִׁית – מוּתָּר לִקְרוֹת קְרִיאַת שְׁמַע כְּנֶגְדָּהּ, עֶרְוָה בַּעֲשָׁשִׁית – אָסוּר לִקְרוֹת קְרִיאַת שְׁמַע כְּנֶגְדָּהּ. צוֹאָה בַּעֲשָׁשִׁית מוּתָּר לִקְרוֹת קְרִיאַת שְׁמַע כְּנֶגְדָּהּ – דְּצוֹאָה בְּכִיסּוּי תַּלְיָא מִילְּתָא, וְהָא מִיכַּסְיָא; עֶרְוָה בַּעֲשָׁשִׁית אָסוּר לִקְרוֹת קְרִיאַת שְׁמַע כְּנֶגְדָּהּ "וְלֹא יִרְאֶה בְךָ עֶרְוַת דָּבָר" אָמַר רַחֲמָנָא, וְהָא קָמִיתַּחְזְיָא.

**Rava said: Opposite feces** covered only **by** a **lantern**-like covering,[H] which is transparent, **it is permitted to recite *Shema*.** But **opposite nakedness** covered only **by** a **lantern**-like covering,[H] **it is prohibited to recite *Shema*. Opposite feces in a lantern, it is permitted to recite *Shema*** because with regard to **feces,** the ability to recite *Shema* **is contingent upon covering,** as it is said: "And cover your excrement" (Deuteronomy 23:14), **and** although it is visible, **it is covered.** On the other hand, **opposite nakedness** covered only **by** a **lantern**-like covering, **it is prohibited to recite *Shema*; the Torah said: "And no indecent thing shall be seen in you"** (Deuteronomy 23:15), **and** here **it is seen.**

אָמַר אַבַּיֵי: צוֹאָה כָּל שֶׁהוּ – מְבַטְּלָהּ בְּרוֹק; אָמַר רָבָא: וּבְרוֹק עָבֶה. אָמַר רָבָא: צוֹאָה בְּגוּמָא – מַנִּיחַ סַנְדָּלוֹ עָלֶיהָ וְקוֹרֵא קְרִיאַת שְׁמַע. בָּעֵא מָר בְּרֵיהּ דְּרָבִינָא: צוֹאָה דְּבוּקָה בְּסַנְדָּלוֹ מַאי? תֵּיקוּ.

**Abaye said: A small amount of feces may be nullified with spittle,** and as long as it is covered, it is permitted to recite *Shema*. **Rava said:** This applies specifically when it is **thick spittle. Rava said: Feces in a hole** in the ground, **he places his sandal over** the hole to cover **it and recites *Shema*. Mar, son of Ravina, raised a dilemma: What** is the *halakha* in a case where **feces is stuck to his sandal?**[H] Perhaps he would be considered filthy in that case? **Let** this dilemma **stand** unresolved.

### LANGUAGE

*Vatikin* – **וָתִיקִין**: The origin of this word, used often by the Sages, is unknown and its meaning is unclear. Some say that the word is of Semitic origin while others maintain that it is from Greek. If it is indeed from Greek, then it likely comes from the word **ἠθικός**, *ethikos*, meaning ethics, in the sense of God-fearing. Some argue that it comes from the Arabic وثيق, *wathīq*, meaning strong or brave, or alternatively, hidden, in which case *vatikin* would mean modest ones. Based on the translation of the word in the book of Ben Sira, apparently, the word meant wise or experienced.

### HALAKHA

**This was taught with regard to murky water – בְּמַיִם עֲכוּרִין שָׁנוּ:** One is permitted to recite *Shema* when his body is submerged in murky water, in accordance with the Gemara's interpretation of the mishna (Rambam *Sefer Ahava, Hilkhot Keriat Shema* 2:7; *Shulḥan Arukh, Oraḥ Ḥayyim* 74:2).

**His heel sees his nakedness – עֲקֵבוֹ רוֹאֶה אֶת הָעֶרְוָה:** If any of one's limbs, the heel being only one example (Rabbeinu Yona, Rosh), is exposed to his nakedness, one is permitted to recite the *Shema*. If it is in contact with his or another's nakedness, it is prohibited (Rambam *Sefer Ahava, Hilkhot Keriat Shema* 3:17; *Shulḥan Arukh, Oraḥ Ḥayyim* 74:5).

**Feces covered by a lantern-like covering – צוֹאָה בַּעֲשָׁשִׁית:** One may recite *Shema* opposite covered fecal matter, even if the covering is transparent, as long as it emits no foul odor. Opposite fecal matter that emits a foul odor, even if it is covered, it is prohibited to recite *Shema* (Rambam *Sefer Ahava, Hilkhot Keriat Shema* 3:10; *Shulḥan Arukh, Oraḥ Ḥayyim* 76:1).

**Nakedness covered by a lantern-like covering – עֶרְוָה בַּעֲשָׁשִׁית:** It is prohibited to recite *Shema* opposite anything considered nakedness with a transparent covering (Rambam *Sefer Ahava, Hilkhot Keriat Shema* 3:16; *Shulḥan Arukh, Oraḥ Ḥayyim* 75:5).

**Feces stuck to his sandal – צוֹאָה דְּבוּקָה בְּסַנְדָּלוֹ:** It is prohibited to recite *Shema* opposite someone with fecal matter stuck to his sandal. This dilemma was not resolved in the Gemara and the *halakha* is in accordance with the stringent opinion (Rambam *Sefer Ahava, Hilkhot Keriat Shema* 3:11; *Shulḥan Arukh, Oraḥ Ḥayyim* 76:2).

## NOTES

A naked gentile – **גּוֹי עָרוֹם**: This problem stems from uncertainty regarding the basis of the prohibition of nakedness itself. Is the indecency of nakedness associated specifically with the holiness of Israel, just as, biblically, most laws of ritual impurity, leprosy, *zav*, and the like apply only to Jews, or is it associated with the very image of the human being? Consequently, it was necessary to specify that an unclothed gentile, too, is considered nakedness.

## HALAKHA

A naked gentile – **גּוֹי עָרוֹם**: One may not recite *Shema* opposite the nakedness of a gentile, which constitutes full-fledged nakedness in every sense, in accordance with the opinion of Rabbi Yehuda (Rambam *Sefer Ahava, Hilkhot Keriat Shema* 3:16; *Shulḥan Arukh, Oraḥ Ḥayyim* 75:4).

A chamber pot used for excrement or urine – **גְּרַף שֶׁל רְעִי וְעָבִיט שֶׁל מֵי רַגְלַיִם**: One must distance himself from a chamber pot of excrement or urine just as he distances himself from fecal matter, i.e., until it is beyond his range of vision before him and four cubits beyond the point where the odor ceases behind him (*Mishna Berura*). This applies even if it is empty and even if it was cleaned inside and out (*Mishna Berura*), and even if it was filled with water. This applies specifically to chamber pots made of wood or clay, but with regard to those made of metal or glass, if they were washed it is permitted, as long as it produces no odor (Rambam *Sefer Ahava, Hilkhot Keriat Shema* 3:12; *Shulḥan Arukh, Oraḥ Ḥayyim* 87:1).

אָמַר רַב יְהוּדָה: גּוֹי עָרוֹם – אָסוּר לִקְרוֹת קְרִיאַת שְׁמַע כְּנֶגְדּוֹ. מַאי אִירְיָא גּוֹי, אֲפִילּוּ יִשְׂרָאֵל נַמִּי! – יִשְׂרָאֵל – פְּשִׁיטָא לֵיהּ דְּאָסוּר, אֶלָּא גּוֹי אִיצְטְרִיכָא לֵיהּ; מַהוּ דְּתֵימָא: הוֹאִיל וּכְתִיב בְּהוּ ״אֲשֶׁר בְּשַׂר חֲמוֹרִים בְּשָׂרָם״, אֵימָא כַּחֲמוֹר בְּעָלְמָא הוּא – קָא מַשְׁמַע לָן: דְּאִינְהוּ נַמִּי אִיקְּרוּ עֶרְוָה, דִּכְתִיב ״וְעֶרְוַת אֲבִיהֶם לֹא רָאוּ״.

**Rav Yehuda said: Opposite a naked gentile,**[NH] **it is forbidden to recite *Shema*.** The Gemara asks: **Why did** the Gemara discuss **particularly** the case of **a gentile? Even with regard to a Jew** it is **also** prohibited. The Gemara replies: Opposite the nakedness of **a Jew, it is obvious** that it is **prohibited; however,** opposite the nakedness of **a gentile, it was necessary for him** to say. **Lest you say** that **since it is written about** gentiles: **"Their flesh is the flesh of donkeys"** (Ezekiel 23:20), **say** that his nakedness **is like** that of **a mere donkey** and does not constitute nakedness. The Gemara **taught us that their** nakedness **is also considered nakedness, as it is written** regarding the sons of Noah: **"And their father's nakedness they did not see"** (Genesis 9:23). Although Noah predated Abraham and was consequently not Jewish, his nakedness is mentioned.

״וְלֹא יִתְכַּסֶּה לֹא בְּמַיִם הָרָעִים וְלֹא בְּמֵי הַמִּשְׁרָה עַד שֶׁיַּטִּיל לְתוֹכָן מַיִם״. וְכַמָּה מַיָּא רָמֵי וְאָזֵיל? אֶלָּא הָכִי קָאָמַר: לֹא יִתְכַּסֶּה לֹא בְּמַיִם הָרָעִים וְלֹא בְּמֵי הַמִּשְׁרָה כְּלָל; וּמֵי רַגְלַיִם – עַד שֶׁיַּטִּיל לְתוֹכָן מַיִם, וְיִקְרָא.

And we learned in the mishna: **And** one who needs to recite *Shema* **may not cover himself with either foul water or water** in which flax was **soaked until he pours** other **water into it.** The Gemara asks: **How much water does he continue to pour** in order to render them a permissible covering. If he is covering himself in water in which flax was soaked, it must be a considerable amount of water, requiring at least an equally considerable amount of water to neutralize it. **Rather, this what it says: One may neither cover himself with foul water nor water** in which flax was **soaked at all; and urine,** which is considered repugnant, **until he adds** clean **water to it, and** only then **he may** recite *Shema*.

תָּנוּ רַבָּנַן: כַּמָּה יַטִּיל לְתוֹכָן מַיִם – כָּל שֶׁהוּא; רַבִּי זַכַּאי אוֹמֵר: רְבִיעִית.

**The Sages taught** a related disagreement in a *baraita*: **How much water must one add** in order **to** nullify urine? **Any quantity** is sufficient. **Rabbi Zakkai says:** One must add a **quarter** of a *log*.

אָמַר רַב נַחְמָן: מַחֲלוֹקֶת – לְבַסּוֹף, אֲבָל בַּתְּחִילָּה – כָּל שֶׁהֵן;

**Rav Naḥman said:** This **dispute** is with regard to a case where the urine is already in a vessel, and **afterward** one seeks to nullify it. **However,** if the clean water was in a vessel **at the beginning,** before the urine, each drop of urine is nullified as it enters the vessel and therefore **any amount** of clean water in the vessel is sufficient.

וְרַב יוֹסֵף אָמַר: מַחֲלוֹקֶת – לְכַתְּחִילָּה, אֲבָל לְבַסּוֹף – דִּבְרֵי הַכֹּל רְבִיעִית. אֲמַר לֵיהּ רַב יוֹסֵף לְשַׁמָּעֵיהּ: אַיְיתִי לִי רְבִיעִיתָא דְּמַיָּא, כְּרַבִּי זַכַּאי.

**And Rav Yosef said:** This **dispute** is with regard to the amount of water necessary to have in the vessel **at the beginning,** before the urine. **However, afterward, everyone agrees** that **a quarter** of a *log* is required. The Gemara relates: **Rav Yosef said to his servant** at the beginning: **Bring me a quarter** of a *log* **of water, in accordance with** the opinion of **Rabbi Zakkai.**

תָּנוּ רַבָּנַן: גְּרַף שֶׁל רְעִי וְעָבִיט שֶׁל מֵי רַגְלַיִם – אָסוּר לִקְרוֹת קְרִיאַת שְׁמַע כְּנֶגְדָּן, וְאַף עַל פִּי שֶׁאֵין בָּהֶן כְּלוּם, וּמֵי רַגְלַיִם עַצְמָן – עַד שֶׁיַּטִּיל לְתוֹכָן מַיִם. וְכַמָּה יַטִּיל לְתוֹכָן מַיִם? כָּל שֶׁהוּא; רַבִּי זַכַּאי אוֹמֵר: רְבִיעִית. בֵּין לִפְנֵי הַמִּטָּה בֵּין לְאַחַר הַמִּטָּה; רַבָּן שִׁמְעוֹן בֶּן גַּמְלִיאֵל אוֹמֵר: לְאַחַר הַמִּטָּה – קוֹרֵא, לִפְנֵי הַמִּטָּה – אֵינוֹ קוֹרֵא, אֲבָל מַרְחִיק הוּא אַרְבַּע אַמּוֹת וְקוֹרֵא; רַבִּי שִׁמְעוֹן בֶּן אֶלְעָזָר אוֹמֵר: אֲפִילּוּ בַּיִת מֵאָה אַמָּה – לֹא יִקְרָא עַד שֶׁיּוֹצִיאֵם, אוֹ שֶׁיַּנִּיחֵם תַּחַת הַמִּטָּה.

**The Sages taught** an elaboration of this point in the *Tosefta*: **Opposite a chamber pot** used for **excrement or urine,**[H] **it is prohibited to recite *Shema*, even if there is nothing in it,** as it is always considered filthy. **Opposite urine itself,** one may not recite *Shema* **until he pours water into it. And how much water must he pour into it? Any quantity. Rabbi Zakkai says: A quarter** of a *log*. That is the ruling **both** when it is **before the bed and** when it is **behind the bed. Rabban Shimon ben Gamliel says:** When it is **behind the bed, one may recite** *Shema*, but when it is **before the bed, one may not recite** *Shema*, **but he** must **distance himself four cubits and** only then **recite** *Shema*. **Rabbi Shimon ben Elazar** is even more strict, **saying: Even in a house one hundred cubits** in size, **one may not recite** *Shema* **until he removes it or places it beneath the bed.**

אִיבַּעְיָא לְהוּ: הֵיכִי קָאָמַר אַחַר הַמִּטָּה – קוֹרֵא מִיָּד, לִפְנֵי הַמִּטָּה – מַרְחִיק אַרְבַּע אַמּוֹת וְקוֹרֵא; אוֹ דִּילְמָא הָכִי קָאָמַר: לְאַחַר הַמִּטָּה – מַרְחִיק אַרְבַּע אַמּוֹת וְקוֹרֵא, לִפְנֵי הַמִּטָּה – אֵינוֹ קוֹרֵא כְּלָל?

**A dilemma was raised** before students at the yeshiva: **How does** Rabban Shimon ben Gamliel **state** this *halakha*? What did he mean? Did he mean that if the chamber pot is **behind the bed, he recites** *Shema* **immediately; before the bed, he distances himself four cubits and recites? Or perhaps he states the following:** If the chamber pot is **behind the bed, he distances himself four cubits and then recites** *Shema*, but if it is **before the bed he may not recite** *Shema* **at all?**

תָּא שְׁמַע, דְּתַנְיָא רַבִּי שִׁמְעוֹן בֶּן אֶלְעָזָר אוֹמֵר: אַחַר הַמִּטָּה – קוֹרֵא מִיָּד, לִפְנֵי הַמִּטָּה – מַרְחִיק אַרְבַּע אַמּוֹת; רַבָּן שִׁמְעוֹן בֶּן גַּמְלִיאֵל אוֹמֵר: אֲפִילּוּ בַּיִת מֵאָה אַמָּה – לֹא יִקְרָא עַד שֶׁיּוֹצִיאֵם אוֹ שֶׁיַּנִּיחֵם תַּחַת הַמִּטָּה.

In order to resolve this dilemma, the Gemara cites proof. **Come** and **hear** that **it was taught** in a *baraita*: **Rabbi Shimon ben Elazar says:** If it is **behind the bed he recites** *Shema* **immediately; before the bed, he distances himself four cubits. Rabban Shimon ben Gamliel says: Even** in a large **house of one hundred cubits one may not recite** *Shema* **until he removes it or places it beneath the bed.** Thus we see from this *baraita* that if the vessel is obstructed by the bed he may recite *Shema* immediately.

בְּעַיִין אִיפְּשִׁיטָא לָן, מַתְנְיָיתָא קַשְׁיָין אַהֲדָדֵי! – אֵיפוֹךְ בָּתְרַיְיתָא.

The Gemara notes: **Our dilemma has been resolved,** but **the** *baraitot* **contradict each other.** The statements made in the name of Rabban Shimon ben Gamliel in one *baraita* were made in the name of Rabbi Shimon ben Elazar in the other. The Gemara resolves the contradiction: **Reverse** the **latter** *baraita* and say that the names of the *tanna'im* were attached to the wrong opinions.

מַה חָזֵית דְּאַפְכַתְּ בָּתְרַיְיתָא? אֵיפוֹךְ קַמַּיְיתָא!

This solution is difficult: **What did you see** that led you to **reverse** the **latter** *baraita*? **Reverse the first** one.

מַאן שָׁמְעַתְּ לֵיהּ דְּאָמַר: כּוּלֵּיהּ בַּיִת כְּאַרְבַּע אַמּוֹת דָּמֵי – רַבִּי שִׁמְעוֹן בֶּן אֶלְעָזָר הִיא.

The Gemara proves that the latter *baraita* should be reversed in accordance with the opinions expressed by these Sages in general. **Who did you hear** that **said that an entire house is considered like four cubits? It is Rabbi Shimon ben Elazar,** who expressed that opinion in the *halakhot* of *eiruv* (Rav Nissim). Consequently, it is reasonable to posit that this would also be his opinion with regard to these *halakhot*, and the *baraita* was reversed accordingly.

אָמַר רַב יוֹסֵף, בְּעַאי מִינֵּיהּ מֵרַב הוּנָא: מִטָּה פָּחוֹת מִשְּׁלֹשָׁה – פְּשִׁיטָא לִי דִּכְלָבוּד – דָּמֵי; שְׁלֹשָׁה אַרְבָּעָה, חֲמִשָּׁה, שִׁשָּׁה, שִׁבְעָה, שְׁמוֹנָה, תִּשְׁעָה, מַהוּ? אָמַר לֵיהּ: לָא יָדַעְנָא. עֲשָׂרָה, וַדַּאי לָא מִיבַּעְיָא לִי. אָמַר אַבָּיֵי: שַׁפִּיר עֲבַדְתְּ דְּלָא אִיבַּעְיָא לָךְ, כָּל עֲשָׂרָה רְשׁוּתָא אַחֲרִיתִי הִיא.

**Rav Yosef said: I raised a dilemma before Rav Huna: It is obvious to me that a bed** under which there is a space of **less than three** handbreadths **is considered connected** [*lavud*][B] to the ground as if the void beneath it does not exist, as *halakha* considers a void of less than three handbreadths as sealed. What, then, is the dilemma? **What is** the *halakha* if that space is **three, four, five, six, seven, eight** or **nine** handbreadths? **He said to him: I do not know.** However, with regard to a space greater than **ten** handbreadths **I certainly have no dilemma,** as it is clear that this space is considered a separate domain. **Abaye said** to him: **You did well that you did not have a dilemma,** as the *halakha* is that **any** space **ten**[N] handbreadths high **is a separate domain.**

אָמַר רָבָא, הִלְכְתָא: פָּחוֹת מִשְּׁלֹשָׁה – כְּלָבוּד דָּמֵי, עֲשָׂרָה – רְשׁוּתָא אַחֲרִיתִי הִיא, מִשְּׁלֹשָׁה עַד עֲשָׂרָה – הַיְינוּ דִּבְעָא מִינֵּיהּ רַב יוֹסֵף מֵרַב הוּנָא וְלָא פְּשַׁט לֵיהּ. אָמַר רַב: הֲלָכָה כְּרַבִּי שִׁמְעוֹן בֶּן אֶלְעָזָר; וְכֵן אָמַר בָּאלִי אָמַר רַב יַעֲקֹב בְּרָהּ בַּת שְׁמוּאֵל: הֲלָכָה כְּרַבִּי שִׁמְעוֹן בֶּן אֶלְעָזָר; וְרָבָא אָמַר: אֵין הֲלָכָה כְּרַבִּי שִׁמְעוֹן בֶּן אֶלְעָזָר.

**Rava** summarized and **said: The** ***halakha*** **is that less than three** handbreadths **is considered connected** and it is permitted to recite *Shema*. **Ten** handbreadths **is a separate domain. Three to ten** handbreadths is the case with regard to which **Rav Yosef raised a dilemma before Rav Huna,** and Rav Huna **did not resolve it for him. Rav said: The** ***halakha*** **is in accordance with** the opinion of **Rabbi Shimon ben Elazar. And, so too,** the Sage **Bali said** that **Rav Ya'akov, son of Shmuel's daughter, said: The** ***halakha*** **is in accordance with** the opinion of **Rabbi Shimon ben Elazar. And Rava said: The** ***halakha*** **is not is in accordance with** the opinion of **Rabbi Shimon ben Elazar.**

רַב אַחַאי אִיעֲסַק לֵיהּ לִבְרֵיהּ בֵּי רַב יִצְחָק בַּר שְׁמוּאֵל בַּר מָרְתָא, עַיְּילֵיהּ לְחוּפָּה וְלָא הֲוָה מִסְתַּיְּיעָא מִילְּתָא. אֲזַל בָּתְרֵיהּ לְעַיּוֹנֵי, חֲזָא סֵפֶר תּוֹרָה דְּמַנְּחָא. אָמַר לְהוּ: אִיכּוּ הַשְׁתָּא לָא אֲתַאי סַכַּנְתּוּן לִבְרִי! דְּתַנְיָא: בַּיִת שֶׁיֵּשׁ בּוֹ סֵפֶר תּוֹרָה אוֹ תְּפִילִּין – אָסוּר לְשַׁמֵּשׁ בּוֹ אֶת הַמִּטָּה עַד שֶׁיּוֹצִיאֵם אוֹ שֶׁיַּנִּיחֵם כְּלִי בְּתוֹךְ כְּלִי.

The Gemara relates: **Rav Aḥai arranged for his son** to marry into **the family of Rav Yitzḥak bar Shmuel bar Marta. He led him to enter the wedding canopy** for the wedding ceremony, **but he was unsuccessful** in his attempts to consummate the marriage. Rav Aḥai **followed him to examine** possible causes of the problem and **he saw a Torah scroll placed** there. **He said to them: Had I not come now, you would have endangered** the life of **my son. As it was taught** in a *baraita*: **In a room in which there is a Torah scroll or phylacteries, it is forbidden to engage in conjugal relations**[H] **until he takes them out** of the room **or places them in a vessel inside a** second **vessel.**

אָמַר אַבָּיֵי: לֹא שָׁנוּ אֶלָּא בִּכְלִי שֶׁאֵינוֹ כְּלְיָין, אֲבָל בִּכְלִי שֶׁהוּא כְּלְיָין – אֲפִילּוּ עֲשָׂרָה מָאנֵי כְּחַד מָאנָא דָּמֵי. אָמַר רָבָא: גְּלִימָא

**Abaye said: They only taught** that a vessel inside a second vessel is sufficient **when the vessel is not their,** the Torah scroll's or the phylacteries', regular **vessel. But a vessel that is their** regular **vessel, even ten vessels are considered as one vessel,** and the Torah or phylacteries must be covered in another vessel not typically used for that purpose. **Rava said: A cloak**

**BACKGROUND**

Connected [*lavud*] – לָבוּד: A *halakha* transmitted to Moses from Sinai stating that two solid surfaces are considered as connected if the gap between them is less than three handbreadths. This *halakha* is applicable with regard to the establishment of Shabbat boundaries and the construction of a *sukka*.

**NOTES**

Less than three…ten – פָּחוֹת מִשְּׁלֹשָׁה...עֲשָׂרָה וכו׳: Two basic measurements are established here: A space of less than three handbreadths is considered as if it were connected, so any void smaller than this is not considered a separate domain with regard to practical demarcation of limits and boundaries. Ten handbreadths, however, establishes not only a significant separation, but a separate domain in and of itself. Since their beds were covered along the sides, anything less than three handbreadths is considered connected, while more than ten is considered a separate room (*Tosefot Rabbeinu Yitzḥak* based on the *ge'onim*).

**HALAKHA**

**In a room in which there is a Torah scroll or phylacteries, it is forbidden to engage in conjugal relations – בַּיִת שֶׁיֵּשׁ בּוֹ סֵפֶר תּוֹרָה אוֹ תְּפִילִּין אָסוּר לְשַׁמֵּשׁ בּוֹ אֶת הַמִּטָּה:** One is prohibited from engaging in conjugal relations in a room in which there is a Torah scroll, phylacteries, or other sacred objects or holy books until one covers them in one vessel inside another vessel (Rambam *Sefer Ahava, Hilkhot Tefillin Mezuza VeSefer Torah* 4:24; *Shulḥan Arukh, Oraḥ Ḥayyim* 40:2; 240:6).

**HALAKHA**

**For a Torah scroll, one must erect a partition – סֵפֶר תּוֹרָה צָרִיךְ לַעֲשׂוֹת לוֹ מְחִיצָה:** One who wishes to engage in conjugal relations must erect a partition ten handbreadths high between his bed and Torah scrolls or Bibles. If there is another room, he should move the sacred items there (Rambam *Sefer Ahava, Hilkhot Tefillin Mezuza VeSefer Torah* 10:7; *Shulḥan Arukh, Oraḥ Ḥayyim* 240:6).

**How far must one distance himself from urine and from feces… – כַּמָּה יַרְחִיק מֵהֶן וּמִן הַצּוֹאָה:** A person standing alongside excrement or foul water and wishes to recite *Shema*, if they are before him, he must distance himself until they are out of his sight. If they are behind him, he must distance himself four cubits beyond the point where the odor can no longer be sensed. Only then may he recite *Shema* (Rambam *Sefer Ahava, Hilkhot Keriat Shema* 3:8; *Shulḥan Arukh, Oraḥ Ḥayyim* 79:1).

**Distancing oneself from the bathroom – הַרְחָקָה מִבֵּית הַכִּסֵּא:** One may not recite *Shema* opposite a bathroom that has already been used, even if it is clean. He must distance himself from it as he would from excrement. If there are walls and it does not give off a foul odor, one may recite *Shema* adjacent to it (Rambam *Sefer Ahava, Hilkhot Keriat Shema* 3:2; *Shulḥan Arukh, Oraḥ Ḥayyim* 83:1).

**One who designated the structure for use as a bathroom – הִזְמִינוֹ לְבֵית הַכִּסֵּא:** It is prohibited to recite *Shema* inside a place that was designated for use as a bathroom even if it has not yet been used for that purpose. However, one may recite *Shema* opposite it, as mere designation does not disqualify the site to that extent (Rambam *Sefer Ahava, Hilkhot Keriat Shema* 3:3; *Shulḥan Arukh, Oraḥ Ḥayyim* 83:2).

**These Persian bathrooms…are considered as sealed – הָנֵי בָּתֵּי כִסְאֵי דְּפַרְסָאֵי...כִּסְתוּמִין דָּמוּ:** A bathroom from which the excrement and the urine reach a distance of four cubits by means of a pipe or a canal has the legal status of a sealed bathroom and if there is no foul odor, one may recite *Shema* opposite it (*Shulḥan Arukh, Oraḥ Ḥayyim* 83:4).

אַקְמִטְרָא – כִּכְלִי בְּתוֹךְ כְּלִי דָּמֵי. אָמַר רַבִּי יְהוֹשֻׁעַ בֶּן לֵוִי: סֵפֶר תּוֹרָה – צָרִיךְ לַעֲשׂוֹת לוֹ מְחִיצָה עֲשָׂרָה. מָר זוּטְרָא אִיקְּלַע לְבֵי רַב אַשִׁי, חַזְיֵיהּ לְדוּכְתֵּיהּ דְּמָר בַּר רַב אַשִׁי דְּמַנַּח בֵּיהּ סֵפֶר תּוֹרָה וְעָבֵיד לֵיהּ מְחִיצָה עֲשָׂרָה. אָמַר לֵיהּ: כְּמַאן – כְּרַבִּי יְהוֹשֻׁעַ בֶּן לֵוִי? אֵימַר דַּאֲמַר רַבִּי יְהוֹשֻׁעַ בֶּן לֵוִי – דְּלֵית לֵיהּ בֵּיתָא אַחֲרִינָא, מָר הָא אִית לֵיהּ בֵּיתָא אַחֲרִינָא! אָמַר לֵיהּ: לָאו אַדַּעְתַּאי.

**atop a chest is like a vessel within a vessel.** On a similar note, **Rabbi Yehoshua ben Levi said:** One who wishes to engage in marital relations in a room in which there is **a Torah scroll, must erect a partition**[H] **ten** handbreadths high. The Gemara relates: **Mar Zutra happened** to come **to the house of Rav Ashi** and **he saw** that **in the** bed **chamber of** his son **Mar bar Rav Ashi, there was a Torah scroll, and** a **partition of ten** handbreadths **had been erected for it. He said to him: In accordance with whose** opinion did you do this? Is it **in accordance with** the opinion of **Rabbi Yehoshua ben Levi? Say** that **Rabbi Yehoshua ben Levi said** this only as a makeshift solution in exigent situations, when **he has no other room** in which to place it, but **don't** you, **Master, have another room** where you could place the Torah scroll? **He said to him:** Indeed, **that** did **not** enter **my mind.**

״כַּמָּה יַרְחִיק מֵהֶן וּמִן הַצּוֹאָה – אַרְבַּע אַמּוֹת״. אָמַר רָבָא אָמַר רַב סְחוֹרָה אָמַר רַב הוּנָא: לֹא שָׁנוּ אֶלָּא לַאֲחוֹרָיו, אֲבָל לְפָנָיו – מַרְחִיק מְלֹא עֵינָיו, וְכֵן לִתְפִלָּה.

We learned in the mishna: **And, how far must one distance himself from urine and from feces**[H] in order to recite *Shema*? **Four cubits. Rava said** that **Rav Seḥora said** that **Rav Huna said: They only taught** that it is sufficient to distance oneself four cubits when the feces are **behind him, but** if they are **before him he must distance himself** to the point that it is **no longer within his range of vision;** and the *halakha* **is the same** for **prayer.**

אִינִי?! וְהָא אָמַר רַפְרָם בַּר פַּפָּא אָמַר רַב חִסְדָּא: עוֹמֵד אָדָם כְּנֶגֶד בֵּית הַכִּסֵּא וּמִתְפַּלֵּל! – הָכָא בְּמַאי עָסְקִינַן – בְּבֵית הַכִּסֵּא שֶׁאֵין בּוֹ צוֹאָה.

The Gemara challenges this: **Is that so? Didn't Rafram bar Pappa say** that **Rav Ḥisda said: One may stand opposite a bathroom**[H] **and pray.** The Gemara resolves this contradiction: **With what are we dealing here? With a bathroom that has no feces,** and therefore there is no need to distance himself to that extent.

אִינִי?! וְהָאֲמַר רַב יוֹסֵף בַּר חֲנִינָא: בֵּית הַכִּסֵּא שֶׁאָמְרוּ – אַף עַל פִּי שֶׁאֵין בּוֹ צוֹאָה, וּבֵית הַמֶּרְחָץ שֶׁאָמְרוּ – אַף עַל פִּי שֶׁאֵין בּוֹ אָדָם! אֶלָּא, הָכָא בְּמַאי עָסְקִינַן: בַּחֲדַתִּי.

The Gemara asks again: **Is that so? Didn't Rav Yosef bar Ḥanina say: The bathroom to which** the Sages **referred** in all of the *halakhot* of distancing oneself was **even** one **in which there were no feces, and the bathhouse to which** the Sages **referred** in all of the *halakhot* of uttering sacred matters, was **even** one **in which there was no** naked **person. Rather, with what are we dealing here?** We are dealing **with a new** structure, built as a bathroom but not yet used for that purpose.

וְהָא מִיבָּעֵי לֵיהּ לְרָבִינָא: הִזְמִינוֹ לְבֵית הַכִּסֵּא מַהוּ, יֵשׁ זִימּוּן אוֹ אֵין זִימּוּן? – כִּי קָא מִיבָּעֵי לֵיהּ לְרָבִינָא – לְמֵיקַם עֲלֵיהּ לְצַלּוֹיֵי בְּגַוֵּיהּ, אֲבָל כְּנֶגְדּוֹ – לֹא.

The Gemara asks: **Wasn't this** already **raised as a dilemma** by **Ravina: One who designated** the structure for use **as a bathroom,**[H] **what is its** legal status? Is **designation** effective **or is designation not** effective? The Gemara replies: **When Ravina raised the dilemma,** it was whether or not one may **stand and pray inside it, but** he had **no** dilemma whether or **not one may pray opposite it.**

אָמַר רָבָא: הָנֵי בָּתֵּי כִסְאֵי דְּפַרְסָאֵי, אַף עַל גַּב דְּאִית בְּהוּ צוֹאָה – כִּסְתוּמִין דָּמוּ.

**Rava said: These Persian bathrooms, even though they contain feces, they are considered as sealed,**[H] as they are constructed on an incline so the feces will roll out of the bathroom underground.

מתני׳ זָב שֶׁרָאָה קֶרִי, וְנִדָּה שֶׁפָּלְטָה שִׁכְבַת זֶרַע, וְהַמְשַׁמֶּשֶׁת שֶׁרָאֲתָה נִדָּה – צְרִיכִין טְבִילָה, וְרַבִּי יְהוּדָה פּוֹטֵר.

**MISHNA** Continuing the earlier discussion of the *halakhot* of immersion for Torah study and prayer for one who experienced a seminal emission, the mishna discusses a case where individuals who were already impure with a severe form of ritual impurity are exposed to the impurity of a seminal emission as well. They are required to immerse themselves and purify themselves of the impurity of the seminal emission even though they remain impure due to the more severe impurity. Consequently, even a ***zav***, whose impurity lasts at least seven days, **who experienced a seminal emission,** for which, were he not a *zav*, he would be impure for only one day; a **menstruating woman who discharged semen,** despite the fact that she is already impure with a severe impurity unaffected by her immersion; **and** a woman **who engaged in conjugal relations** with her husband **and** later **saw menstrual blood,** all **require immersion. And Rabbi Yehuda exempts** them from immersion.

גמ׳ אִיבַּעְיָא לְהוּ: בַּעַל קֶרִי שֶׁרָאָה זִיבָה, לְרַבִּי יְהוּדָה מַהוּ? כִּי פָּטַר רַבִּי יְהוּדָה הָתָם בְּזָב שֶׁרָאָה קֶרִי – דְּמֵעִיקָּרָא לָאו בַּר טְבִילָה הוּא, אֲבָל בַּעַל קֶרִי שֶׁרָאָה זִיבָה, דְּמֵעִיקָּרָא בַּר טְבִילָה הוּא – מְחַיֵּיב, אוֹ דִּילְמָא לָא שְׁנָא?

**GEMARA** **A dilemma was raised before** the students of the yeshiva: **One who experienced a seminal emission** and was therefore required to immerse himself, who later **saw a discharge** that rendered him a ***zav*; according to Rabbi Yehuda, what is the his legal status?** The Gemara explains the sides of the dilemma: **When,** in our mishna, **Rabbi Yehuda exempted a *zav* who saw a seminal emission** from immersion, that **was because from the outset he was not fit for immersion,** as the immersion would not be effective in purifying him from the impurity of a *zav*; **however, one who experienced a seminal emission,** who later **saw a discharge** that rendered him a ***zav*,** who **was fit for immersion** and only later became impure with the severe impurity of a *zav*, would Rabbi Yehuda **require** immersion? **Or perhaps there is no difference** and he is exempt from immersion in both cases?

תָּא שְׁמַע: הַמְשַׁמֶּשֶׁת וְרָאֲתָה נִדָּה צְרִיכָה טְבִילָה, וְרַבִּי יְהוּדָה פּוֹטֵר. וְהָא מְשַׁמֶּשֶׁת וְרָאֲתָה נִדָּה כְּבַעַל קֶרִי שֶׁרָאָה זִיבָה דָּמְיָא, וְקָא פָּטַר רַבִּי יְהוּדָה – שְׁמַע מִינָּהּ. תָּנֵי רַבִּי חִיָּיא בְּהֶדְיָא: בַּעַל קֶרִי שֶׁרָאָה זִיבָה – צָרִיךְ טְבִילָה, וְרַבִּי יְהוּדָה פּוֹטֵר.

In order to resolve this dilemma, **come** and **hear** the last case of the mishna: A woman **who engaged in conjugal relations** with her husband **and** later **saw menstrual blood requires immersion. And Rabbi Yehuda exempts** them from immersion. **Isn't the** woman **who engaged in conjugal relations** with her husband **and** later **saw menstrual blood like one who experienced a seminal emission,** who later **saw a discharge** that rendered him a ***zav*,** as in both cases there is a less severe ritual impurity followed by a more severe impurity; **and** nevertheless, **Rabbi Yehuda exempts. Conclude from this** that Rabbi Yehuda does not distinguish between the cases. And indeed, **Rabbi Ḥiyya explicitly taught: One who experienced a seminal emission** who later **saw a discharge** that rendered him a ***zav* requires immersion, and Rabbi Yehuda exempts.**

הדרן עלך מי שמתו

# Summary of **Perek III**

Several problems were addressed in this chapter. Primary among them is how the recitation of *Shema* requires one to distance himself from anything disgusting, filthy, or ritually impure. However, other related halakhic and aggadic matters were also cited.

In this chapter, *halakhot* were articulated with regard to the extent that dealing with burial of the dead exempts one from the obligation to recite *Shema*, and the guiding principles were clarified. It became clear that the basis of the myriad *halakhot* regarding respect for the dead is the comprehensive principle of maintaining human dignity. Due to that principle, several mitzvot are superseded due to both respect for the dead and human dignity. Several times in this chapter it was emphasized that the deceased should be treated like a person, and that his body is inexorably tied to his eternal soul.

Another fundamental discussion in this chapter dealt with the ordinance of Ezra, which prohibits one who experienced a seminal emission from engaging in Torah study and prayer until he immerses himself and becomes ritually pure. This ordinance had considerable influence on the life of the Jewish people for several generations, and many of the Sages sought to clarify its practical ramifications. It never achieved widespread acceptance among the Jewish people, and the Sages agreed to abrogate it. Nevertheless, the ordinance remains in effect, even today, as a custom of the pious.

In addition, there was considerable discussion devoted to the need to distance oneself from exposed nakedness while reciting *Shema* and praying. In this case, the reference is to exposed nakedness in its broadest sense, which includes not only exposure of the specific parts of the body usually associated with that term, but also all body parts that are usually covered. In practice, one must avoid exposure to any potentially alluring sights while reciting *Shema* and praying.

With regard to that issue, as well as with regard to avoiding exposure to filth, some of the Sages expressed stringent opinions that called for extreme measures to ensure total separation. However the guiding principle is: The Torah was not given to ministering angels. Exaggerated caution is difficult to implement and is even liable to cause people to distance themselves from Torah. Consequently, the *halakha* adopted moderate standards of cleanliness and modesty.

# Introduction to **Perek IV**

*Now his windows were open in his upper chamber toward Jerusalem and he kneeled upon his knees three times a day, and prayed, and gave thanks before his God, as he had done before.*

(Daniel 6:11)

The primary focus of this chapter is the *Amida* prayer, also called *Shemoneh Esreh* (Eighteen), which was the number of blessings originally instituted in the weekday prayer. It is recited on weekdays, on Shabbat, and on Festivals. The fundamental question is: What is the source of the *Amida* prayer? Is it tied to *Shema*, the course of a person's daily life, the days that turn into night and vice-versa? Or is the primary element its connection to the sacred service performed in the Temple, serving as a substitute form of worship since its destruction? This dilemma, manifest in the dispute amongst the Sages whether prayer was instituted by the Patriarchs or established parallel to the daily offerings in the Temple, touches upon the different characteristics of prayer and serves as a basis for the halakhic questions discussed in this chapter.

Clearly, there is a consensus that beyond the essential obligation to pray, the source of which was subject to dispute, the various prayers must be recited at fixed times. It is, then, necessary to ascertain the parameters of those times: When is the earliest and latest time that each prayer can be recited? This is relevant to the morning prayer, which is parallel to the daily offering sacrificed early in the morning when the Temple stood, and to the afternoon prayer, which is parallel to the daily offering sacrificed in the afternoon.

This close connection between the prayers and the communal offerings was already observed in practice when the Temple stood, as the people would recite a communal prayer together with the sacrifice of the offering. Consequently, there are two prayers that enjoy unique status in the context of this discussion: The additional prayer and the evening prayer.

The additional prayer was clearly instituted parallel to the offering; there is no other possible explanation. Therefore, its status and the parameters of the time that it may be recited are clearer. Yet specifically for that reason, there is room to consider whether or not this prayer, like the sacrifice after which it was modeled, is a matter exclusively for the community. The question is: May it only be recited in the framework of communal prayer; or, perhaps, may the additional prayer be recited even individually?

The opposite problem exists with regard to the evening prayer. Since this prayer is not directly parallel to a specific offering, it does not have a set time like the other prayers. On the other hand, in terms of its essence as a prayer recited at night, tied to the changes from day to night and to *Shema* of the day and the night, there is room to stipulate a set time and a fixed obligation as in the case of the other prayers.

The dispute between the Sages regarding this issue, whose far-reaching consequences will be related in this chapter, constitutes a manifestation of another aspect of the fundamental question: What is the obligation of prayer? Is the primary obligation to recite the prayer communally, with the devotional aspect of prayer secondary in importance? Or, perhaps, the essence of prayer is turning to God, and the primary obligation is in its devotional aspect and the desire to draw closer to God.

Between these two approaches, which differ with regard to the fundamental understanding of communal prayer, the more specific questions raised in this chapter are resolved.

מתני׳ תְּפִלַּת הַשַּׁחַר עַד חֲצוֹת, רַבִּי יְהוּדָה אוֹמֵר: עַד אַרְבַּע שָׁעוֹת. תְּפִלַּת הַמִּנְחָה עַד הָעֶרֶב; רַבִּי יְהוּדָה אוֹמֵר: עַד פְּלַג הַמִּנְחָה.

**MISHNA** This mishna determines the times beyond which the different prayers may not be recited. According to the Rabbis, **the morning prayer** may be recited **until noon. Rabbi Yehuda says:** It may be recited only **until four hours** after sunrise.[NH] According to the Rabbis, **the afternoon prayer** may be recited **until the evening. Rabbi Yehuda says:** It may be recited only **until the midpoint of the afternoon [*pelag hamin*ḥ*a*]**,[L] i.e., the midpoint of the period that begins with the sacrifice of the daily afternoon offering and ends at nightfall, which is the end of the afternoon.

תְּפִלַּת הָעֶרֶב אֵין לָהּ קֶבַע; וְשֶׁל מוּסָפִים כָּל הַיּוֹם, רַבִּי יְהוּדָה אוֹמֵר: עַד שֶׁבַע שָׁעוֹת.

**The evening prayer** may be recited throughout the night and **is not fixed** to a specific hour. According to the Rabbis, **the additional prayer** may be recited **all day. Rabbi Yehuda says:** It may be recited only **until seven hours** after sunrise.

גמ׳ וּרְמִינְהוּ: מִצְוָתָהּ עִם הָנֵץ הַחַמָּה, כְּדֵי שֶׁיִּסְמוֹךְ גְּאוּלָּה לִתְפִלָּה וְנִמְצָא מִתְפַּלֵּל בַּיּוֹם!

**GEMARA** We learned in the mishna that the morning prayer may be recited only until a few hours into the day. The Gemara **raises a contradiction** based on what was taught in a *baraita*: **The mitzva** is to recite the morning *Shema* **with sunrise** so that **he will juxtapose redemption,** which is mentioned in the blessings following *Shema,* **to the** *Amida* **prayer,** which is recited immediately after sunrise, and **find** himself **praying in the daytime.** Clearly, the time to recite the morning prayer is immediately after sunrise.

כִּי תַּנְיָא הַהִיא – לַוָּתִיקִין, דְּאָמַר רַבִּי יוֹחָנָן: וָתִיקִין הָיוּ גּוֹמְרִים אוֹתָהּ עִם הָנֵץ הַחַמָּה.

The Gemara responds: This *baraita* does not establish a binding *halakha.* Rather, it **taught that** rule specifically **with regard to those who are scrupulous in fulfillment of mitzvot [*vatikin*]. As Rabbi Yoḥanan said:** ***Vatikin*** **would finish** reciting the morning *Shema* **with sunrise,** but those who are not *vatikin* may recite their prayers later.

וְכוּלֵּי עָלְמָא עַד חֲצוֹת וְתוּ לָא? וְהָאָמַר רַב מָרִי בְּרֵיהּ דְּרַב הוּנָא בְּרֵיהּ דְּרַבִּי יִרְמְיָה בַּר אַבָּא אָמַר רַבִּי יוֹחָנָן: טָעָה וְלֹא הִתְפַּלֵּל עַרְבִית – מִתְפַּלֵּל בְּשַׁחֲרִית שְׁתַּיִם, שַׁחֲרִית – מִתְפַּלֵּל בְּמִנְחָה שְׁתַּיִם!

The Gemara asks: **Does everyone** hold that one may recite the morning prayer only **until noon and no later? Didn't Rav Mari, son of Rav Huna, son of Rabbi Yirmeya bar Abba, say that Rabbi Yoḥanan said: One who erred and did not recite the evening prayer,**[H] **prays in the morning prayer two** *Amida* prayers; one who erred and did not recite **the morning prayer, prays in the afternoon prayer two** *Amida* prayers? Apparently, the morning prayer may be recited until the evening, at least in the event that he forgot to recite it in the morning.

כּוּלֵּי יוֹמָא מְצַלֵּי וְאָזֵיל, עַד חֲצוֹת – יָהֲבִי לֵיהּ שְׂכַר תְּפִלָּה בִּזְמַנָּהּ, מִכָּאן וְאֵילָךְ – שְׂכַר תְּפִלָּה יָהֲבִי לֵיהּ, שְׂכַר תְּפִלָּה בִּזְמַנָּהּ – לָא יָהֲבִי לֵיהּ.

The Gemara answers: Indeed, **one may continue praying for the entire day.** However, if he prayed **until noon, they give him a reward for** reciting the **prayer at its** appointed **time.** If he prayed **from there on, they give him a reward for** reciting the **prayer. They do not give him a reward for** reciting the **prayer at its** appointed **time.**

אִיבַּעְיָא לְהוּ: טָעָה וְלֹא הִתְפַּלֵּל מִנְחָה, מַהוּ שֶׁיִּתְפַּלֵּל עַרְבִית שְׁתַּיִם? אִם תִּמְצָא לוֹמַר טָעָה וְלֹא הִתְפַּלֵּל עַרְבִית מִתְפַּלֵּל שַׁחֲרִית שְׁתַּיִם – מִשּׁוּם דְּחַד יוֹמָא הוּא, דִּכְתִיב ״וַיְהִי עֶרֶב וַיְהִי בֹקֶר יוֹם אֶחָד,״ אֲבָל הָכָא – תְּפִלָּה בִּמְקוֹם קָרְבָּן הִיא וְכֵיוָן דַּעֲבַר יוֹמוֹ בָּטֵל קָרְבָּנוֹ; אוֹ דִּילְמָא, כֵּיוָן דִּצְלוֹתָא רַחֲמֵי הִיא – כָּל אֵימַת דְּבָעֵי מְצַלֵּי וְאָזֵיל?

On the topic of one who forgot to pray and seeks to compensate for the prayer that he missed, **a dilemma was raised before them** in the study hall: **One who erred and did not recite the afternoon prayer, what is** the ruling? May he **recite** in **the evening prayer two** *Amida* prayers? The Gemara articulates the sides of the dilemma: **If you say** that **one who erred and did not pray the evening prayer prays in the morning prayer two** *Amida* prayers, perhaps that is **because** the evening and the morning are both part of **one day, as it is written: "And there was evening and there was morning, one day"** (Genesis 1:5); the evening and the following morning constitute a single unit. **But here,** in the case under discussion, perhaps **prayer is in place of sacrifice.** Since in the case of sacrifice we say, **since its day passed, his sacrifice is invalid**[N] and there is no way to compensate for the missed opportunity, the same should be true for prayer. **Or, perhaps, since prayer is supplication, any time that one wishes, he may continue to pray?**

**NOTES**

**The time for the morning prayer – זְמַן תְּפִלַּת הַשַּׁחַר:** Based on an allusion from the verse: "Evening and morning and at noon will I pray and cry aloud" (Psalms 55:18), it is derived that one is obligated to pray three times daily. The dispute with regard to the morning prayer is: Until what time is it considered morning (*She'iltot*)?

**And since its day passed, his sacrifice is invalid – וְכֵיוָן דַּעֲבַר יוֹמוֹ בָּטֵל קָרְבָּנוֹ:** From the verse: "To bring forth a fire-offering to the Lord, a burnt-offering and a meal-offering, a slaughtered sacrifice and libations, that of each day on its day" (Leviticus 23:37), it is derived that a particular day's offering is not acceptable on another day (Maharshal).

**HALAKHA**

**The end of the time for the morning prayer – סוֹף זְמַן תְּפִלַּת הַשַּׁחַר:** The period during which the morning prayer may be recited lasts until the end of the fourth hour or one-third of the day, as per the opinion of Rabbi Yehuda, since the Gemara ruled in accordance with his opinion. Nevertheless, some of the authorities (Rif, Rosh) established that one who failed to pray before that time may, after the fact, pray until midday. The fact that one is not yet permitted to recite the afternoon prayer at that time proves that there is still room to recite the morning prayer (Rambam *Sefer Ahava, Hilkhot Tefilla* 3:1; *Shulḥan Arukh, Oraḥ Ḥayyim* 89:1).

**One who erred and did not recite the evening prayer – טָעָה וְלֹא הִתְפַּלֵּל עַרְבִית:** One who erred or one who, due to circumstances beyond his control, failed to recite the *Amida* prayer at the appropriate time, may compensate for his failure after reciting the following prayer. However, one may not recite the compensatory prayer on its own, as per the Rashba. This *halakha* is in accordance with the statement of Rabbi Yoḥanan, which was universally accepted. There is no distinction between the various prayers. Even if the prayer that he missed was the afternoon prayer, he may compensate for it by reciting the evening prayer twice. The principle: Since its day passed, his sacrifice is invalid, does not apply here (Rambam *Sefer Ahava, Hilkhot Tefilla* 3:8–9; *Shulḥan Arukh, Oraḥ Ḥayyim* 108:1–2, 234:2).

**LANGUAGE**

**The midpoint of the afternoon [*pelag hamin*ḥ*a*] – פְּלַג הַמִּנְחָה:** This is based on the biblical term *bein ha'arbayim*. In rabbinic literature, this refers to the time between two definitions of evening. One definition of evening is the time that the sun begins to tend westward, which begins a half-hour after noon, six-and-a-half hours into the day. Absolute evening is sunset. *Bein ha'arbayim* is the midpoint between these two evenings. Here there is another sense of evening, the time when the daily evening offering is sacrificed. This is approximately halfway between noon and sunset, nine-and a half hours into the day. Based on that definition of evening, *bein ha'arbayim* is the midpoint between that time and sunset. The Gemara refers to this as the second midpoint of *minḥa*.

**HALAKHA**

**One intentionally failed to recite the prayer – שֶׁבִּטֵּל בְּמֵזִיד:** One who intentionally did not pray may not compensate for the missed prayer. If he wishes to recite a voluntary prayer he may do so, even without introducing a novel element to his prayer (Rambam *Sefer Ahava, Hilkhot Tefilla* 3:8; *Shulḥan Arukh, Oraḥ Ḥayyim* 108:7).

תָּא שְׁמַע: דְּאָמַר רַב הוּנָא בַּר יְהוּדָה אָמַר רַבִּי יִצְחָק אָמַר רַבִּי יוֹחָנָן: טָעָה וְלֹא הִתְפַּלֵּל מִנְחָה – מִתְפַּלֵּל עַרְבִית שְׁתַּיִם, וְאֵין בָּזֶה מִשּׁוּם ״עָבַר יוֹמוֹ בָּטֵל קָרְבָּנוֹ.״

**Come and hear** a resolution to this dilemma from that **which Rav Huna bar Yehuda said** that **Rabbi Yitzḥak said** that **Rabbi Yoḥanan said: One who erred and did not recite the afternoon prayer, prays in the evening prayer two** *Amida* **prayers and there is no element of: Its day passed, his sacrifice is invalid.**

מֵיתִיבֵי: ״מְעֻוָּת לֹא יוּכַל לִתְקֹן וְחֶסְרוֹן לֹא יוּכַל לְהִמָּנוֹת״; ״מְעֻוָּת לֹא יוּכַל לִתְקֹן״ – זֶה שֶׁבִּטֵּל קְרִיאַת שְׁמַע שֶׁל עַרְבִית וּקְרִיאַת שְׁמַע שֶׁל שַׁחֲרִית, אוֹ תְּפִלָּה שֶׁל עַרְבִית, אוֹ תְּפִלָּה שֶׁל שַׁחֲרִית; ״וְחֶסְרוֹן לֹא יוּכַל לְהִמָּנוֹת״ – זֶה שֶׁנִּמְנוּ חֲבֵירָיו לִדְבַר מִצְוָה וְלֹא נִמְנָה עִמָּהֶם!

With regard to the possibility to compensate for a prayer that he failed to recite at its appointed time, the Gemara **raises an objection** based on what was taught in a *baraita*. The meaning of the verse: **"That which is crooked cannot be made straight; and that which is wanting cannot be numbered"** (Ecclesiastes 1:15), is as follows: **That which is crooked cannot be made straight** refers to **one who omitted the evening** ***Shema*** **and the morning** ***Shema,*** **or the evening prayer, or the morning prayer. And that which is wanting cannot be numbered** [***lehimanot***] refers to **one whose friends reached a consensus** [***nimnu***] to perform **a mitzva and he was not part of their consensus** [***nimnu***] and, consequently, he missed his opportunity to join them in performance of the mitzva. This *baraita* clearly states that there is no way to compensate for a missed prayer.

אָמַר רַבִּי יִצְחָק אָמַר רַבִּי יוֹחָנָן: הָכָא בְּמַאי עָסְקִינַן – שֶׁבִּטֵּל בְּמֵזִיד.

To resolve this difficulty, **Rabbi Yitzḥak said** that **Rabbi Yoḥanan said: With what are we dealing here** in this *baraita*? We are dealing with a case where one **intentionally failed** to recite the prayer.[H] Only then he has no remedy. However, one who failed to pray due to error can compensate for the missed prayer by reciting the next prayer twice.

אָמַר רַב אָשֵׁי: דַּיְקָא נַמֵי דְּקָתָנֵי ״בִּטֵּל,״ וְלָא קָתָנֵי ״טָעָה״ – שְׁמַע מִינַּהּ.

**Rav Ashi said:** The language of the *baraita* **is also precise as it teaches omitted and did not teach erred.** This indicates that the *halakha* is different in the case of error. The Gemara concludes: Indeed, **learn from this.**

Perek **IV**
Daf **26** Amud **b**

**HALAKHA**

**One who erred and did not recite the afternoon prayer on the eve of Shabbat – טָעָה וְלֹא הִתְפַּלֵּל מִנְחָה בְּעֶרֶב שַׁבָּת:** One who erred and did not recite the afternoon prayer on Shabbat eve recites the Shabbat evening prayer twice; the first, to fulfill his obligation to recite the Shabbat evening prayer and the second to compensate for the afternoon prayer (Rambam *Sefer Ahava, Hilkhot Tefilla* 10:15; *Shulḥan Arukh, Oraḥ Ḥayyim* 108:9).

**One who erred and did not recite the afternoon prayer on Shabbat – טָעָה וְלֹא הִתְפַּלֵּל מִנְחָה בְּשַׁבָּת:** One who erred and did not recite the afternoon prayer on Shabbat recites the weekday evening prayer twice at the conclusion of Shabbat; the first to fulfill his obligation to recite the weekday evening prayer and the second to compensate for the Shabbat afternoon prayer. He recites *havdala* during the first evening prayer, in the fourth blessing: Who graciously grants knowledge. He may not recite *havdala* in the compensatory prayer. If he recites *havdala* in the second prayer and not the first, he did not fulfill his obligation to compensate for his missed prayer and must pray again (Rambam *Sefer Ahava, Hilkhot Tefilla* 10:15; *Shulḥan Arukh, Oraḥ Ḥayyim* 108:10).

תָּנוּ רַבָּנַן: טָעָה וְלֹא הִתְפַּלֵּל מִנְחָה בְּעֶרֶב שַׁבָּת – מִתְפַּלֵּל בְּלֵיל שַׁבָּת שְׁתַּיִם, טָעָה וְלֹא הִתְפַּלֵּל מִנְחָה בְּשַׁבָּת – מִתְפַּלֵּל בְּמוֹצָאֵי שַׁבָּת שְׁתַּיִם. מַבְדִּיל בָּרִאשׁוֹנָה וְאֵינוֹ מַבְדִּיל בַּשְּׁנִיָּה, וְאִם הִבְדִּיל בַּשְּׁנִיָּה וְלֹא הִבְדִּיל בָּרִאשׁוֹנָה – שְׁנִיָּה עָלְתָה לוֹ, רִאשׁוֹנָה לֹא עָלְתָה לוֹ.

On a similar note, **the Sages taught** in a *baraita*: **One who erred and did not recite the afternoon prayer on the eve of Shabbat,**[H] **prays in** the evening prayer **two** *Amida* prayers **on Shabbat evening. One who erred and did not recite the afternoon prayer on Shabbat,**[H] **recites two** *Amida* prayers in the evening prayer **at the conclusion of Shabbat. He recites** ***havdala*** [the prayer of **distinction**] between the sanctity of Shabbat and the profanity of the week by reciting: You have graced us, etc., in the fourth blessing of the *Amida,* which is: Who graciously grants knowledge, **in the first** prayer, as it is the actual evening prayer **but he does not recite** ***havdala*** **in the second** prayer, which is in place of the afternoon prayer. Moreover, **if he recited** ***havdala*** **in the second** prayer **and did not recite** ***havdala*** **in the first, the second prayer fulfilled his** obligation, the **first one did not fulfill his** obligation.

לֵימָא, דְּכֵיוָן דְּלָא אַבְדֵּיל בְּקַמַּיְיתָא כְּמַאן דְּלָא צַלֵּי דָּמֵי וּמְהַדְּרִינַן לֵיהּ?

The Gemara comments: **Is that to say** that **since he did not recite** ***havdala*** **in the first** prayer, he is **as one who did not pray and we require him to return** to the beginning of the prayer and repeat it? If so, the conclusion is that one who fails to recite *havdala* in the prayer must repeat that prayer.

וּרְמִינְהוּ: טָעָה וְלֹא הִזְכִּיר גְּבוּרוֹת גְּשָׁמִים בִּתְחִיַּית הַמֵּתִים וּשְׁאֵלָה בְּבִרְכַּת הַשָּׁנִים – מַחֲזִירִין אוֹתוֹ, הַבְדָּלָה בְּחוֹנֵן הַדַּעַת – אֵין מַחֲזִירִין אוֹתוֹ, מִפְּנֵי שֶׁיָּכוֹל לְאוֹמְרָהּ עַל הַכּוֹס! – קַשְׁיָא.

The Gemara **raises a contradiction** to the above conclusion from the *Tosefta*: **One who erred and did not mention the might of the rains:**[H] He makes the wind blow and rain fall **in** the second blessing of the *Amida*, the blessing on **the revival of the dead, and** one who erred and failed to recite **the request** for rain **in** the ninth blessing of the *Amida*, **the blessing of the years,**[H] **we require him to return** to the beginning of the prayer and repeat it. However, one who erred and failed to recite ***havdala*** **in** the blessing: **Who graciously grants knowledge,**[H] **we do not require him to return** to the beginning of the prayer and repeat it, **as he can recite** *havdala* **over the cup** of wine, independent of his prayer. This contradiction was not resolved and remains **difficult.**

אִיתְּמַר, רַבִּי יוֹסֵי בְּרַבִּי חֲנִינָא אָמַר: תְּפִלּוֹת אָבוֹת תִּקְּנוּם; רַבִּי יְהוֹשֻׁעַ בֶּן לֵוִי אָמַר: תְּפִלּוֹת כְּנֶגֶד תְּמִידִין תִּקְּנוּם.

The dispute between the Rabbis and Rabbi Yehuda with regard to the times beyond which the different prayers may not be recited is rooted in a profound disagreement, also manifest in a later amoraic dispute. **It was stated: Rabbi Yosei, son of Rabbi Ḥanina, said:** The practice of praying three times daily is ancient, albeit not in its present form; **prayers were instituted by the Patriarchs.** However, **Rabbi Yehoshua ben Levi said** that the **prayers were instituted based on the daily offerings**[HB] sacrificed in the Holy Temple, and the prayers parallel the offerings, in terms of both time and characteristics.

תַּנְיָא כְּוָותֵיהּ דְּרַבִּי יוֹסֵי בְּרַבִּי חֲנִינָא, וְתַנְיָא כְּוָותֵיהּ דְּרַבִּי יְהוֹשֻׁעַ בֶּן לֵוִי. תַּנְיָא כְּוָותֵיהּ דְּרַבִּי יוֹסֵי בְּרַבִּי חֲנִינָא: אַבְרָהָם תִּקֵּן תְּפִלַּת שַׁחֲרִית – שֶׁנֶּאֱמַר ״וַיַּשְׁכֵּם אַבְרָהָם בַּבֹּקֶר אֶל הַמָּקוֹם אֲשֶׁר עָמַד שָׁם,״ וְאֵין עֲמִידָה אֶלָּא תְּפִלָּה, שֶׁנֶּאֱמַר ״וַיַּעֲמֹד פִּינְחָס וַיְפַלֵּל״;

The Gemara comments: **It was taught** in a *baraita* **in accordance with** the opinion of **Rabbi Yosei, son of Rabbi Ḥanina, and it was taught** in a *baraita* **in accordance with** the opinion of **Rabbi Yehoshua ben Levi.** The Gemara elaborates: **It was taught** in a *baraita* **in accordance with** the opinion of **Rabbi Yosei, son of Rabbi Ḥanina: Abraham instituted the morning prayer, as it is stated** when Abraham came to look out over Sodom the day after he had prayed on its behalf: **"And Abraham rose early in the morning to the place where he had stood** before the Lord" (Genesis 19:27), **and** from the context as well as the language utilized in the verse, the verb **standing** means **nothing other than prayer,** as this language is used to describe Pinehas' prayer after the plague, **as it is stated: "And Pinehas stood up and prayed** and the plague ended" (Psalms 106:30). Clearly, Abraham was accustomed to stand in prayer in the morning.

יִצְחָק תִּקֵּן תְּפִלַּת מִנְחָה – שֶׁנֶּאֱמַר ״וַיֵּצֵא יִצְחָק לָשׂוּחַ בַּשָּׂדֶה לִפְנוֹת עָרֶב,״ וְאֵין שִׂיחָה אֶלָּא תְּפִלָּה, שֶׁנֶּאֱמַר ״תְּפִלָּה לְעָנִי כִי יַעֲטֹף וְלִפְנֵי ה׳ יִשְׁפֹּךְ שִׂיחוֹ״;

**Isaac instituted the afternoon prayer, as it is stated: "And Isaac went out to converse** [*lasuaḥ*] **in the field toward evening"** (Genesis 24:63), **and conversation** means **nothing other than prayer, as it is stated: "A prayer of the afflicted when he is faint and pours out his complaint** [*siḥo*] **before the Lord"** (Psalms 102:1). Obviously, Isaac was the first to pray as evening approached, at the time of the afternoon prayer.

יַעֲקֹב תִּקֵּן תְּפִלַּת עַרְבִית – שֶׁנֶּאֱמַר: ״וַיִּפְגַּע בַּמָּקוֹם וַיָּלֶן שָׁם,״ וְאֵין פְּגִיעָה אֶלָּא תְּפִלָּה, שֶׁנֶּאֱמַר ״וְאַתָּה אַל תִּתְפַּלֵּל בְּעַד הָעָם הַזֶּה וְאַל תִּשָּׂא בַעֲדָם רִנָּה וּתְפִלָּה וְאַל תִּפְגַּע בִּי.״

**Jacob instituted the evening prayer, as it is stated: "And he encountered** [*vayifga*] **the place and he slept there** for the sun had set" (Genesis 28:11). The word **encounter** means **nothing other than prayer, as it is stated** when God spoke to Jeremiah: **"And you, do not pray on behalf of this nation and do not raise on their behalf song and prayer, and do not encounter** [*tifga*] **Me** for I do not hear you" (Jeremiah 7:16). Jacob prayed during the evening, after the sun had set.

וְתַנְיָא כְּוָותֵיהּ דְּרַבִּי יְהוֹשֻׁעַ בֶּן לֵוִי: מִפְּנֵי מָה אָמְרוּ תְּפִלַּת הַשַּׁחַר עַד חֲצוֹת – שֶׁהֲרֵי תָּמִיד שֶׁל שַׁחַר קָרֵב וְהוֹלֵךְ עַד חֲצוֹת; וְרַבִּי יְהוּדָה אוֹמֵר: עַד אַרְבַּע שָׁעוֹת, שֶׁהֲרֵי תָּמִיד שֶׁל שַׁחַר קָרֵב וְהוֹלֵךְ עַד אַרְבַּע שָׁעוֹת.

**And it was taught** in a *baraita* **in accordance with** the opinion of **Rabbi Yehoshua ben Levi** that the laws of prayer are based on the laws of the daily offerings: **Why did** the Rabbis **say** that **the morning prayer** may be recited **until noon? Because,** although the **daily morning offering** is typically brought early in the morning, it may be **sacrificed until noon. And Rabbi Yehuda says:** My opinion, that the morning prayer may be recited **until four hours** into the day, is **because the daily morning offering is sacrificed until four hours.**

וּמִפְּנֵי מָה אָמְרוּ תְּפִלַּת הַמִּנְחָה עַד הָעֶרֶב – שֶׁהֲרֵי תָּמִיד שֶׁל בֵּין הָעַרְבַּיִם קָרֵב וְהוֹלֵךְ עַד הָעֶרֶב; רַבִּי יְהוּדָה אוֹמֵר: עַד פְּלַג הַמִּנְחָה, שֶׁהֲרֵי תָּמִיד שֶׁל בֵּין הָעַרְבַּיִם קָרֵב וְהוֹלֵךְ עַד פְּלַג הַמִּנְחָה.

**And why did** the Rabbis **say** that **the afternoon prayer** may be recited **until the evening? Because the daily afternoon offering is sacrificed until the evening. Rabbi Yehuda says** that **the afternoon prayer** may be recited only **until the midpoint of the afternoon because,** according to his opinion, **the daily afternoon offering is sacrificed until the midpoint of the afternoon.**

וּמִפְּנֵי מָה אָמְרוּ תְּפִלַּת הָעֶרֶב אֵין לָהּ קֶבַע – שֶׁהֲרֵי אֵבָרִים וּפְדָרִים שֶׁלֹּא נִתְעַכְּלוּ מִבָּעֶרֶב קְרֵבִים וְהוֹלְכִים כָּל הַלַּיְלָה;

**And why did they say** that **the evening prayer is not fixed? Because** the burning of the **limbs and fats** of the offerings that were **not consumed** by the fire on the altar **until the evening.** They remained on the altar and were **offered continuously** throughout **the entire night.**

**HALAKHA**

**One who erred and did not mention the might of the rains** – **טָעָה וְלֹא הִזְכִּיר גְּבוּרוֹת גְּשָׁמִים**: One who neglected to recite: He makes the winds blow and the rain fall, in the blessing: Who revives the dead; in the winter, he is required to repeat the *Amida* prayer, in accordance with the uncontested *Tosefta*. However, if he mentioned: He causes the dew to fall, he is not required to repeat the *Amida* prayer (Rambam *Sefer Ahava, Hilkhot Tefilla* 10:8; *Shulḥan Arukh, Oraḥ Ḥayyim* 114:5).

**One who erred and did not mention the request for rain in the blessing of the years** – **טָעָה וְלֹא הִזְכִּיר...וּשְׁאֵלָה בְּבִרְכַּת הַשָּׁנִים**: One who erroneously did not recite the request for rain in the blessing of the years during the winter, is required to repeat the *Amida* prayer even if he recited a request for dew (Rambam *Sefer Ahava, Hilkhot Tefilla* 10:9; *Shulḥan Arukh, Oraḥ Ḥayyim* 117:4).

**One who erred and failed to recite *havdala* in the blessing: Who graciously grants knowledge** – **טָעָה וְלֹא הִזְכִּיר... הַבְדָּלָה בְּחוֹנֵן הַדַּעַת**: One who neglected to recite *havdala* in the blessing: Who graciously grants knowledge, in the evening prayer at the conclusion of Shabbat, need not repeat the *Amida* prayer because he has the opportunity to recite it on a cup of wine (Rambam *Sefer Ahava, Hilkhot Tefilla* 10:14; *Shulḥan Arukh, Oraḥ Ḥayyim* 294:1).

**Prayers were instituted based on the daily offerings** – **תְּפִלּוֹת כְּנֶגֶד תְּמִידִין תִּקְּנוּם**: Ultimately, it was determined that the Sages instituted prayer based on the daily offerings. Consequently, several elements that apply to the *halakhot* of offerings apply to prayer as well, i.e., establishing a fixed place to pray, the capacity of improper thought to invalidate prayer, etc. Although the Talmud cites proof in support of both amoraic opinions, since the Gemara raised a challenge to the opinion of Rabbi Yosei son of Rabbi Ḥanina from the *baraita* supporting the opinion of Rabbi Yehoshua ben Levi, apparently that is the preferred opinion (*Kesef Mishne*, who disagrees with *Leḥem Mishne*; Rambam *Sefer Ahava, Hilkhot Tefilla* 1:5–6).

**BACKGROUND**

**Prayers were instituted based on the daily offerings** – **תְּפִלּוֹת כְּנֶגֶד תְּמִידִין תִּקְּנוּם**: Some explain that this means that prayers were instituted by the Sages after the destruction of the Temple to replace the offerings. However, these prayers were already extant throughout the Second Temple era with virtually the same formula that was instituted later, with certain known differences. Furthermore, there were already synagogues at that time, some even in close proximity to the Temple. The dispute in this case is whether the prayers were instituted to parallel the offerings, or whether the prayers have an independent source, unrelated to the Temple Service.

HALAKHA

*Minḥa gedola* – מִנְחָה גְּדוֹלָה: The period of *minḥa gedola* begins six-and-a-half hours into the day, half an hour after midday. The authorities disagree whether one may only recite the afternoon prayer at that point after the fact (Rambam) or whether even *ab initio* one is permitted to pray then (*Tur*). The conclusion is that, when the need arises, one is permitted to pray during the *minḥa gedola* period even though the ideal time to recite the afternoon prayer is during the period of *minḥa ketana*, which lasts from nine-and-a-half hours into the day until sunset (Rambam *Sefer Ahava, Hilkhot Tefilla* 3:3–4; *Shulḥan Arukh, Oraḥ Ḥayyim* 234:1).

BACKGROUNDS

Until and including – עַד וְעַד בִּכְלָל: The dilemma raised here is a fundamental problem in delineating halakhic parameters. Parallel dilemmas are raised in other cases to determine the application of halakhic parameters and to establish whether there is a set principle with regard to their application or whether each instance is handled individually.

וּמִפְּנֵי מָה אָמְרוּ שֶׁל מוּסָפִין כָּל הַיּוֹם – שֶׁהֲרֵי קָרְבַּן שֶׁל מוּסָפִין קָרֵב כָּל הַיּוֹם; רַבִּי יְהוּדָה אוֹמֵר: עַד שֶׁבַע שָׁעוֹת, שֶׁהֲרֵי קָרְבַּן מוּסָף קָרֵב וְהוֹלֵךְ עַד שֶׁבַע שָׁעוֹת.

**And why did** the Rabbis **say** that **the additional prayer** may be recited **all day? Because the additional offering is brought** throughout **the entire day.** However, **Rabbi Yehuda says** that **the additional prayer** may be recited **until the seventh hour** of the day, **because the additional offering is sacrificed until the seventh hour.**

וְאֵיזוֹ הִיא מִנְחָה גְּדוֹלָה – מִשֵּׁשׁ שָׁעוֹת וּמֶחֱצָה וּלְמַעְלָה; וְאֵיזוֹ הִיא מִנְחָה קְטַנָּה – מִתֵּשַׁע שָׁעוֹת וּמֶחֱצָה וּלְמַעְלָה.

The *baraita* continues and states that there are two times for the afternoon prayer. Greater, earlier *minḥa* [*minḥa gedola*] and lesser, later *minḥa* [*minḥa ketana*]. The Gemara clarifies the difference between them: **Which is *minḥa gedola*?**[H] **From six-and-a-half hours** after sunrise **and on,** which is a half an hour after noon and on. It is the earliest time that the daily afternoon offering may be sacrificed, as in the case on the eve of Passover that occurs on Shabbat. **Which is *minḥa ketana*? From nine-and-a-half hours and on,** which is the standard time that the daily afternoon offering is sacrificed.

אִיבַּעְיָא לְהוּ: רַבִּי יְהוּדָה פְּלַג מִנְחָה קַמָּא קָאָמַר, אוֹ פְּלַג מִנְחָה אַחֲרוֹנָה קָאָמַר? תָּא שְׁמַע: דְּתַנְיָא, רַבִּי יְהוּדָה אוֹמֵר: פְּלַג הַמִּנְחָה אַחֲרוֹנָה אָמְרוּ, וְהִיא אַחַת עֶשְׂרֵה שָׁעוֹת חָסֵר רְבִיעַ.

On that note, **a dilemma was raised before them: Rabbi Yehuda,** who holds that the afternoon prayer may be recited only until the midpoint of the afternoon, does **he say the midpoint of the first *minḥa*,** *minḥa gedola*? **Or,** does **he say the midpoint of the last *minḥa*? Come and hear** an explicit resolution to this dilemma: **As it was taught** in a *baraita*, **Rabbi Yehuda says: They said the midpoint of the last *minḥa*, and that is eleven hours minus a quarter** of an hour after sunrise, i.e., an hour-and-a-quarter hours before sunset.

נֵימָא תֶּיהֱוֵי תְּיוּבְתֵּיהּ דְּרַבִּי יוֹסֵי בְּרַבִּי חֲנִינָא! אָמַר לָךְ רַבִּי יוֹסֵי בְּרַבִּי חֲנִינָא: לְעוֹלָם אֵימָא לָךְ תְּפִלּוֹת אָבוֹת תִּקְּנוּם, וְאַסְמְכִינְהוּ רַבָּנַן אַקָּרְבָּנוֹת. דְּאִי לָא תֵּימָא הָכִי – תְּפִלַּת מוּסָף לְרַבִּי יוֹסֵי בְּרַבִּי חֲנִינָא מַאן תִּקְּנָהּ? אֶלָּא: תְּפִלּוֹת אָבוֹת תִּקְּנוּם, וְאַסְמְכִינְהוּ רַבָּנַן אַקָּרְבָּנוֹת.

In any case, it is clear that according to this *baraita* the *halakhot* of prayer are based on the Temple offerings. The Gemara suggests: **Let us say that this is a conclusive refutation of** the opinion of **Rabbi Yosei, son of Rabbi Ḥanina,** who held that the forefathers instituted the prayers. **Rabbi Yosei, son of Rabbi Ḥanina,** could have **said to you: Actually, I will say to you** that **the Patriarchs instituted the prayers and the Sages based** the times and characteristics of prayer **on the Temple offerings,** even though they do not stem from the same source. **As, if you do not say so,** that even Rabbi Yosei, son of Rabbi Ḥanina, would agree that the laws of offerings and those of prayers are related, **then, according to Rabbi Yosei, son of Rabbi Ḥanina, who instituted the additional prayer?** It is not one of the prayers instituted by the forefathers. **Rather,** even according to Rabbi Yosei, son of Rabbi Ḥanina, **the prayers were instituted by the Patriarchs and the Sages based them** on the laws of the **offerings.**

רַבִּי יְהוּדָה אוֹמֵר: עַד אַרְבַּע שָׁעוֹת. אִיבַּעְיָא לְהוּ: עַד וְעַד בִּכְלָל, אוֹ דִּילְמָא, עַד וְלֹא עַד בִּכְלָל? תָּא שְׁמַע, רַבִּי יְהוּדָה אוֹמֵר: עַד פְּלַג הַמִּנְחָה. אִי אָמְרַתְּ בִּשְׁלָמָא עַד וְלֹא עַד בִּכְלָל – הַיְינוּ דְּאִיכָּא בֵּין רַבִּי יְהוּדָה לְרַבָּנַן, אֶלָּא אִי אָמְרַתְּ עַד וְעַד בִּכְלָל – רַבִּי יְהוּדָה

We learned in the mishna that **Rabbi Yehuda says:** The morning prayer may be recited **until four hours** of the day. **A dilemma was raised before** the yeshiva students: When Rabbi Yehuda says **until,** does he mean **until and including**[B] the fourth hour, **or, perhaps** when he says **"until"** he means **until and not including,** in which case one may not pray during the fourth hour? **Come and hear** a resolution to this dilemma based on the mishna. **Rabbi Yehuda says:** The afternoon prayer may be recited only **until the midpoint of the afternoon.** Now, **granted, if you say** that **until** means **until and not including, then there is** a difference **between** the opinion of **Rabbi Yehuda and** the opinion of **the Rabbis. However, if you say** that **until** means **until and including,** then the opinion of **Rabbi Yehuda**



הַיְינוּ רַבָּנַן!

**is** identical to the opinion of **the Rabbis,** as the end of the period that begins with the midpoint of the afternoon is sunset.

אֶלָּא מַאי? עַד וְלֹא עַד בִּכְלָל – אֵימָא סֵיפָא: וְשֶׁל מוּסָפִין כָּל הַיּוֹם, רַבִּי יְהוּדָה אוֹמֵר: עַד שֶׁבַע שָׁעוֹת; וְתַנְיָא: הָיוּ לְפָנָיו שְׁתֵּי תְּפִלּוֹת, אַחַת שֶׁל מוּסָף, וְאַחַת שֶׁל מִנְחָה – מִתְפַּלֵּל שֶׁל מִנְחָה וְאַחַר כָּךְ שֶׁל מוּסָף, שֶׁזּוֹ תְּדִירָה וְזוֹ אֵינָהּ תְּדִירָה; רַבִּי יְהוּדָה אוֹמֵר: מִתְפַּלֵּל שֶׁל מוּסָף וְאַחַר כָּךְ שֶׁל מִנְחָה, שֶׁזּוֹ עוֹבֶרֶת וְזוֹ אֵינָהּ עוֹבֶרֶת.

The Gemara immediately rejects this proof: **Rather, what** is the alternative? That **until** means **until and not including?** It remains problematic. **Say the latter clause** of the mishna: **The additional prayer** may be recited **all day. Rabbi Yehuda says:** It may be recited **until the seven hours. And it was taught** in a *baraita*: **If** the obligation to recite **two prayers was before him, one the additional prayer and one the afternoon prayer, he prays the afternoon prayer** first **and the additional prayer thereafter,** because **this,** the afternoon prayer, **is** recited on a **frequent** basis, **and that,** the additional prayer, **is** recited on a relatively **infrequent** basis as it is only recited on Shabbat, the New Moon, and Festivals. The principle states: When a frequent practice and an infrequent practice clash, the frequent practice takes precedence over the infrequent practice. **Rabbi Yehuda says: He recites the additional prayer** first **and the afternoon prayer thereafter,** because the time to recite **this, the additional prayer,** will soon **elapse, and this,** the time to recite **the afternoon prayer,** will **not** soon **elapse,** as one may recite it until the midpoint of the afternoon.

אִי אָמְרַתְּ בִּשְׁלָמָא עַד וְעַד בִּכְלָל – הַיְינוּ דְּמַשְׁכַּחַתְּ לְהוּ שְׁתֵּי תְּפִלּוֹת בַּהֲדֵי הֲדָדֵי; אֶלָּא אִי אָמְרַתְּ עַד וְלֹא עַד בִּכְלָל – הֵיכִי מַשְׁכַּחַתְּ לְהוּ שְׁתֵּי תְּפִלּוֹת בַּהֲדֵי הֲדָדֵי? כֵּיוָן דְּאָתְיָא לַהּ שֶׁל מִנְחָה אָזְלָא לַהּ שֶׁל מוּסָפִין!

The relevant point is: **Granted, if you say** that **until** means **until and including, that is how you can find** a situation where the times to recite **two prayers,** the afternoon prayer and the additional prayer, **overlap. But if you say** that **until** means **until and not including,** and that until seven hours means until the beginning of the seventh hour, noon, then **how can you find** a situation where the times to recite **two prayers overlap? Once** the time to recite **the afternoon prayer,** a half hour past noon, **has arrived,** the time to recite **the additional prayer** is already **gone?**

אֶלָּא מַאי, עַד וְעַד בִּכְלָל? קַשְׁיָא רֵישָׁא: מַאי אִיכָּא בֵּין רַבִּי יְהוּדָה לְרַבָּנַן? – מִי סָבְרַתְּ דְּהַאי "פְּלַג מִנְחָה" פְּלַג אַחֲרוֹנָה קָאָמַר?! פְּלַג רִאשׁוֹנָה קָאָמַר, וְהָכִי קָאָמַר: אֵימַת נָפֵיק פְּלַג רִאשׁוֹנָה וְעָיֵיל פְּלַג אַחֲרוֹנָה? מִכִּי נָפְקֵי אַחַת עֶשְׂרֵה שָׁעוֹת חָסֵר רְבִיעַ.

**Rather, what** is the alternative? That **until** means **until and including?** Then **the first clause** of the mishna **is difficult,** as explained above with regard to the midpoint of the afternoon: **What is** the halakhic difference **between** the opinion of **Rabbi Yehuda and** the opinion of **the Rabbis?** The Gemara answers: **Do you think that** when **this midpoint of the afternoon** was mentioned it was **speaking of** the period following **the midpoint, the last** part of the afternoon, from an hour-and-a-quarter before sunset until sunset? This was not the intention. Rather, it was **speaking of** the period prior to **the midpoint, the first** part of the afternoon, which, as explained above, is from nine-and-a-half hours after sunrise until an hour-and-a-quarter before sunset. Consequently, until the midpoint of the afternoon means until the end of the first half of that afternoon period. **And this is what he is saying: When does the first half leave and the second half enter? From when eleven hours minus a quarter have passed** since sunrise. Rabbi Yehuda's use of the term until always means until and including.

אָמַר רַב נַחְמָן: אַף אֲנַן נַמִּי תָּנֵינָא,

Practically speaking, this means that, according to Rabbi Yehuda, it is permissible to recite the morning prayer until the end of the fourth hour. In support of this **Rav Naḥman said: We, too, learned** this in a mishna:

רַבִּי יְהוּדָה בֶּן בָּבָא הֵעִיד חֲמִשָּׁה דְּבָרִים: שֶׁמְּמָאֲנִין אֶת הַקְּטַנָּה, וְשֶׁמַּשִּׂיאִין אֶת הָאִשָּׁה עַל פִּי עֵד אֶחָד, וְעַל תַּרְנְגוֹל שֶׁנִּסְקַל בִּירוּשָׁלַיִם עַל שֶׁהָרַג אֶת הַנֶּפֶשׁ, וְעַל יַיִן בֶּן אַרְבָּעִים יוֹם שֶׁנִּתְנַסֵּךְ עַל גַּבֵּי הַמִּזְבֵּחַ, וְעַל תָּמִיד שֶׁל שַׁחַר שֶׁקָּרַב בְּאַרְבַּע שָׁעוֹת;

**Rabbi Yehuda ben Bava testified** about **five matters of** *halakha*:

When an orphan girl, who was married off by her mother or brother before reaching the age of majority, reaches the age of majority, she may refuse to continue living with her husband and thereby retroactively annul their marriage. Normally, marriage refusals are discouraged. However, in specific instances where it is clear that if the marriage were to remain in effect it would engender problems related to levirate marriage and *ḥalitza*, Rabbi Yehuda ben Bava testified that **one may persuade the minor girl to refuse**[H] to continue living with her husband, thereby resolving the complications involved in this case.

**And** he testified **that one may** allow **a woman** who, after hearing of her husband's death, seeks to remarry, **to marry based on** the testimony **one witness,**[H] as opposed to the two witnesses required for other testimonies of the Torah.

**And** he testified **about a rooster that was stoned**[H] to death **in Jerusalem for killing a person,** in order to teach that the Torah law (Exodus 21:28) which requires the stoning of an ox that killed a person, applies to other animals as well.

**And** he testified **about forty-day-old wine that was** used for **libation on the altar.**[H]

**And** he testified **about** the **daily morning offering that was sacrificed at four hours**[H] of the day.

שְׁמַע מִינַּהּ: "עַד" וְ"עַד" בִּכְלָל, שְׁמַע מִינַּהּ.

**Learn from this** final testimony, which is in accordance with the opinion of Rabbi Yehuda, that **until** means **until and including.** The Gemara concludes: Indeed, **learn from this.**

אָמַר רַב כָּהֲנָא: הֲלָכָה כְּרַבִּי יְהוּדָה, הוֹאִיל וּתְנַן בִּבְחִירְתָּא כְּוָותֵיהּ.

Based on this mishna, **Rav Kahana said: The** ***halakha*** **is in accordance with** the opinion of **Rabbi Yehuda since we learned** in a mishna in the **preferred** tractate, *Eduyyot*,[N] **in accordance with his** opinion. Since the *halakha* is ruled in accordance with all of the *mishnayot* in *Eduyyot*, the opinion of a *tanna* who rules in accordance with the opinion of Rabbi Yehuda in that mishna means that the *halakha* is in accordance with that opinion.

"וְעַל תָּמִיד שֶׁל שַׁחַר שֶׁקָּרַב בְּאַרְבַּע שָׁעוֹת." מַאן תְּנָא לְהָא, דִּתְנַן: "וְחַם הַשֶּׁמֶשׁ וְנָמָס" – בְּאַרְבַּע שָׁעוֹת.

**And about** the **daily morning offering that was sacrificed at four hours.** Based on this, the Gemara attempts to identify **the *tanna* who taught that which we learned** in the mishna about the manna that fell for the children of Israel in the desert: "And they gathered it morning by morning, each according to what he eats, **and when the sun grew hot it melted"** (Exodus 16:21); that took place **four hours** into the day.

## HALAKHA

**One may persuade the minor girl to refuse – שֶׁמְּמָאֲנִין אֶת הַקְּטַנָּה:** Two brothers were married to two sisters who were orphaned from their father. One of the sisters, who passed the age of majority, was betrothed to her husband of her own volition, and her marriage was by Torah law. The other sister was a minor and her brother agreed to her betrothal *in loco parentis*, and, consequently, her marriage was by rabbinic law. If the husband of the older sister died, his brother would be obligated to enter into a levirate marriage with the older sister. However, he would be forbidden to do so by the prohibition of marrying two sisters. In this case, based on the testimony of Rabbi Yehuda ben Bava, they persuade the younger sister to opt out of her marriage by means of the rite of refusal, enabling her husband to enter into a levirate marriage with the older sister (Rambam *Sefer Nashim, Hilkhot Yibbum VeḤalitza* 7:15; *Shulḥan Arukh, Even HaEzer* 175:11).

**One may allow a woman to marry based on one witness – וְשֶׁמַּשִּׂיאִין אֶת הָאִשָּׁה עַל פִּי עֵד אֶחָד:** If a woman's husband traveled to a distant venue, and one witness from that venue came and testified that he died, she may remarry based on that testimony. In all cases, the requirement is to have the testimony of two witnesses. However, since the information in this case is likely to be confirmed or contradicted, the assumption is that the woman would not remarry unless she was certain that the testimony was true. The Sages were lenient and accepted the testimony in order to save the woman from the never-ending status of a deserted wife (Rambam *Sefer Nashim, Hilkhot Gerushin* 12:15; *Shulḥan Arukh, Even HaEzer* 17:3).

**And about a rooster that was stoned – וְעַל תַּרְנְגוֹל שֶׁנִּסְקַל:** Any animal or bird that kills a person is put to death by stoning (Rambam *Sefer Nezikin, Hilkhot Nizkei Mamon* 10:2).

**Forty-day-old wine that was used for libation on the altar – יַיִן בֶּן אַרְבָּעִים יוֹם שֶׁנִּתְנַסֵּךְ עַל גַּבֵּי הַמִּזְבֵּחַ:** When forty days pass from the time the wine emerged from the wine press, it may be offered on the altar as a libation (Rambam *Sefer Avoda, Hilkhot Issurei Mizbe'aḥ* 6:9).

**The daily morning offering that was sacrificed at four hours – תָּמִיד שֶׁל שַׁחַר שֶׁקָּרַב בְּאַרְבַּע שָׁעוֹת:** Although the daily morning offering was sacrificed before sunrise, in exigent circumstances, it may be sacrificed until the end of the fourth hour of the day (Rambam *Sefer Avoda, Hilkhot Temidin UMusafin* 1:2).

## NOTES

**We also learned this in the preferred tractate, *Eduyyot* – וּתְנַן בִּבְחִירְתָּא (מַסֶּכֶת עֵדִיּוֹת):** This tractate includes numerous testimonies attested to by the Sages before their colleagues with regard to established *halakhot* that they heard and unique situations that they witnessed. In addition, this tractate contains other accepted *halakhot*. Apparently, there is an additional meaning of the name of the tractate, a variation on the word *idit*, which is the term used in *halakha* for the highest quality land. This tractate is the highest quality tractate in terms of its halakhic authority.

אַתָּה אוֹמֵר בְּאַרְבַּע שָׁעוֹת, אוֹ אֵינוֹ אֶלָּא בְּשֵׁשׁ שָׁעוֹת?! כְּשֶׁהוּא אוֹמֵר: ״כְּחֹם הַיּוֹם״ – הֲרֵי שֵׁשׁ שָׁעוֹת אָמוּר, הָא מָה אֲנִי מְקַיֵּים ״וְחַם הַשֶּׁמֶשׁ וְנָמָס״ – בְּאַרְבַּע שָׁעוֹת. מַנִּי? לֹא רַבִּי יְהוּדָה וְלֹא רַבָּנַן! אִי רַבִּי יְהוּדָה עַד אַרְבַּע שָׁעוֹת נַמִּי צַפְרָא הוּא, אִי רַבָּנַן – עַד חֲצוֹת נַמִּי צַפְרָא הוּא!

The Gemara asks: Do **you say** that the time when the sun grew hot was **at four hours, or** perhaps **it was only at six hours** of the day? **When** the verse **says: "In the heat of the day"** (Genesis 18:1), **six hours is** already **mentioned** in the Torah as the heat of the day. **How, then, do I establish** the verse: **"And when the sun grew hot it melted"**? This must refer to an earlier time, **at four hours. Who** is the *tanna* of this mishna? It is **neither Rabbi Yehuda nor the Sages. If** it was in accordance with the opinion of **Rabbi Yehuda, until four hours is also** considered **morning,** as he holds that the daily morning offering may still be sacrificed then, while here it says that in the morning the manna was gathered and it melted after the morning. **If** it was in accordance with the opinion of **the Rabbis, until noon is also** considered **morning,** since, according to the Sages, the daily morning offering could be sacrificed until noon. Apparently, this is an entirely new position.

אִי בָּעֵית אֵימָא: רַבִּי יְהוּדָה, אִי בָּעֵית אֵימָא: רַבָּנַן. אִי בָּעֵית אֵימָא רַבָּנַן – אָמַר קְרָא: ״בַּבֹּקֶר בַּבֹּקֶר״ – חַלְּקֵהוּ לִשְׁנֵי בְקָרִים; וְאִי בָּעֵית אֵימָא רַבִּי יְהוּדָה, הַאי בֹּקֶר יְתֵירָא – לְהַקְדִּים לוֹ שָׁעָה אַחַת. דְּכוּלֵּי עָלְמָא מִיהָא ״וְחַם הַשֶּׁמֶשׁ וְנָמָס״ בְּאַרְבַּע שָׁעוֹת,

The Gemara responds: **If you wish, say** that the mishna is in accordance with the opinion of **Rabbi Yehuda,** and **if you wish, say** instead that the mishna is in accordance with the opinion of **the Rabbis.** The Gemara explains: **If you wish, say** in accordance with the opinion of **the Rabbis. The verse states: Morning by morning, divide it into two mornings.** Morning, according to the Rabbis, lasts until noon. The repetition of the term morning in the Torah indicates that the period when the manna was gathered ended at the conclusion of the first half of the morning, i.e., the end of the third hour. **And if you wish, say** instead in accordance with the opinion of **Rabbi Yehuda,** who would say that: **This extra morning** in the phrase morning by morning comes to **make** the end of the period when the manna was gathered **an hour earlier.** In any event, **everyone agrees** that the verse, **And when the sun grew hot it melted,** refers to **four hours** of the day.

מַאי מַשְׁמַע? אָמַר רַבִּי אַחָא בַּר יַעֲקֹב, אָמַר קְרָא: ״וְחַם הַשֶּׁמֶשׁ וְנָמָס,״ אֵיזוֹ הִיא שָׁעָה שֶׁהַשֶּׁמֶשׁ חַם וְהַצֵּל צוֹנֵן? הֱוֵי אוֹמֵר בְּאַרְבַּע שָׁעוֹת.

The Gemara asks: **From where is the inference** drawn that this is the meaning of the verse? **Rabbi Aḥa bar Ya'akov said: The verse states: "When the sun grew hot it melted." Which is the hour that the sun is hot but the shade** remains **cool,** before the heat of the day, when even the shade is hot? **You must say at four hours.**

״תְּפִלַּת הַמִּנְחָה עַד הָעֶרֶב וכו׳.״ אָמַר לֵיהּ רַב חִסְדָּא לְרַב יִצְחָק: הָתָם אָמַר רַב כָּהֲנָא ״הֲלָכָה כְּרַבִּי יְהוּדָה הוֹאִיל וּתְנַן בִּבְחִירְתָּא כְּוָותֵיהּ,״ הָכָא מַאי? אִישְׁתִּיק וְלֹא אָמַר לֵיהּ וְלֹא מִידֵּי. אָמַר רַב חִסְדָּא: נֶחֱזֵי אֲנַן, מִדְּרַב מְצַלֵּי שֶׁל שַׁבָּת בְּעֶרֶב שַׁבָּת מִבְּעוֹד יוֹם – שְׁמַע מִינַּהּ הֲלָכָה כְּרַבִּי יְהוּדָה.

We learned in the mishna: The Rabbis hold that **the afternoon prayer** may be recited **until the evening.** Rabbi Yehuda says: It may be recited only until the midpoint of the afternoon. **Rav Ḥisda said to Rav Yitzḥak: There,** with regard to the morning prayer, **Rav Kahana said: The *halakha* is in accordance with** the opinion of **Rabbi Yehuda, since we learned** in a mishna in the **preferred** tractate, *Eduyyot*, **in accordance with his** opinion. **Here, what** is the ruling? **He was silent and said nothing to him,** as he was familiar with no established ruling in this matter. **Rav Ḥisda said: Let us see** and try to resolve this ourselves **from** the fact **that Rav prayed** the **Shabbat** prayers on the eve of Shabbat **while it was still day. Learn from this** that **the *halakha* is in accordance with** the opinion of **Rabbi Yehuda,** and the time for the afternoon prayer ends at the midpoint of the afternoon, after which time one may recite the evening prayer.

אַדְּרַבָּה, מִדְּרַב הוּנָא וְרַבָּנַן לֹא הֲווּ מְצַלּוּ עַד אוּרְתָּא, שְׁמַע מִינַּהּ אֵין הֲלָכָה כְּרַבִּי יְהוּדָה! הַשְׁתָּא דְּלֹא אִתְּמַר הִלְכְתָא לֹא כְּמָר וְלֹא כְּמָר, דַּעֲבַד כְּמָר – עֲבַד, וְדַעֲבַד כְּמָר – עֲבַד.

The Gemara immediately rejects the proof based on Rav's practice: **On the contrary, from** the fact **that Rav Huna and the Sages,** students of Rav **would not pray until evening, learn from that** that **the *halakha* is not in accordance with** the opinion of **Rabbi Yehuda.** The Gemara concludes: **Now that the *halakha* was stated neither in accordance with** the opinion of this **Sage nor in accordance with** the opinion of that **Sage, one who acted in accordance with** the opinion of this **Sage has acted** legitimately **and one who acted in accordance with** the opinion of that **Sage has acted** legitimately,[H] as this *halakha* is left to the decision of each individual.

רַב אִיקְלַע לְבֵי גְּנִיבָא וְצַלֵּי שֶׁל שַׁבָּת בְּעֶרֶב שַׁבָּת, וַהֲוָה מְצַלֵּי רַבִּי יִרְמְיָה בַּר אַבָּא לַאֲחוֹרֵי דְּרַב, וְסַיֵּים רַב וְלֹא פַּסְקֵיהּ לִצְלוֹתֵיהּ דְּרַבִּי יִרְמְיָה. שְׁמַע מִינַּהּ תְּלָת: שְׁמַע מִינַּהּ מִתְפַּלֵּל אָדָם שֶׁל שַׁבָּת בְּעֶרֶב שַׁבָּת, וּשְׁמַע מִינַּהּ מִתְפַּלֵּל תַּלְמִיד אֲחוֹרֵי רַבּוֹ, וּשְׁמַע מִינַּהּ אָסוּר לַעֲבוֹר כְּנֶגֶד הַמִּתְפַּלְּלִין.

The Gemara relates: **Rav happened by the house of** the Sage, **Geniva, and he prayed** the **Shabbat** prayer **on the eve of Shabbat** before nightfall.[H] **Rabbi Yirmeya bar Abba**[P] **was praying behind Rav, and Rav finished** his prayer **but did not** take three steps back and **interrupt the prayer** of **Rabbi Yirmeya. Derive from this** incident **three** *halakhot*: **Derive from this** that **one may pray the Shabbat** prayer **on the eve of Shabbat** before nightfall. **And derive from this that a student** may **pray behind his rabbi. And derive from this** that it is **prohibited to pass before those who are praying.**[H]

## HALAKHA

**One who acted in accordance with the opinion of this Sage has acted legitimately, and one who acted in accordance with the opinion of that Sage has acted legitimately – דַּעֲבַד כְּמָר עֲבַד, וְדַעֲבַד כְּמָר עֲבַד:** In the Gemara, the dispute between Rabbi Yehuda and the Rabbis with regard to the time beyond which one may not recite the afternoon prayer, until the evening or until the midpoint of *minḥa*, was not resolved. Therefore, the Gemara concluded that each individual has license to conduct himself as he pleases, and whichever option he chooses, he fulfills his obligation. However, once he chooses, he is required to continue conducting himself in accordance with that choice. Therefore, if he recites the afternoon prayer after the midpoint of *minḥa*, he may not recite the evening prayer until the evening. If he plans on reciting the evening prayer after the midpoint of *minḥa* before sunset, he must recite the afternoon prayer before the midpoint of *minḥa*. The generally accepted custom is that the afternoon prayer may be recited until sunset (Rambam *Sefer Ahava, Hilkhot Tefilla* 3:4; *Shulḥan Arukh, Oraḥ Ḥayyim* 233:1).

**One may recite the Shabbat prayer on the eve of Shabbat before nightfall – מִתְפַּלֵּל אָדָם שֶׁל שַׁבָּת בְּעֶרֶב שַׁבָּת:** One is permitted to pray the Shabbat evening prayer before nightfall and assume all of the customs of Shabbat, i.e., *kiddush* and the Shabbat meal, at that time. This is based on the opinion of Rabbi Yehuda with regard to the afternoon prayer, that one may always recite the evening prayer before nightfall. Even if one does not always conduct himself in accordance with this opinion, in deference to Shabbat the Sages were lenient and allowed him to do so on Shabbat eve (Rambam *Sefer Ahava, Hilkhot Tefilla* 3:7; *Shulḥan Arukh, Oraḥ Ḥayyim* 267:2).

**It is prohibited to pass before those who are praying – אָסוּר לַעֲבוֹר כְּנֶגֶד הַמִּתְפַּלְּלִין:** One may not pass within four cubits before another who is praying. However, one may pass adjacent to one who is praying if he is alongside and not before him. The *Zohar* on the portion of *Ḥayyei Sara* makes no distinction and prohibits passing within four cubits on all sides of one who is praying (Rambam *Sefer Ahava, Hilkhot Tefilla* 5:6; *Shulḥan Arukh, Oraḥ Ḥayyim* 102:4).

## PERSONALITIES

**Rabbi Yirmeya bar Abba – רַבִּי יִרְמְיָה בַּר אַבָּא:** A first and second generation Babylonian *amora*, Rabbi Yirmeya bar Abba was one of the first Sages to study under Rav after the latter's arrival in Babylonia. As Rabbi Yirmeya bar Abba was already a scholar in his own right, he came to Rav primarily to learn the Torah of Eretz Yisrael. Rav knew Rabbi Yirmeya bar Abba's family and considered his father, Abba, among the greatest penitents of all time. Rabbi Yirmeya bar Abba is among the most prominent promulgators of Rav's teachings, and many Sages from both Babylonia and Eretz Yisrael studied with him. His son, Rav Huna, was one of the Sages, as were his son-in-law, Rav Huna bar Ḥiyya, and his daughter's son, Levi ben Rav Huna bar Ḥiyya.

מְסַיַּיע לֵיהּ לְרַבִּי יְהוֹשֻׁעַ בֶּן לֵוִי, דְּאָמַר רַבִּי יְהוֹשֻׁעַ בֶּן לֵוִי: אָסוּר לַעֲבוֹר כְּנֶגֶד הַמִּתְפַּלְּלִין. – אִינִי?! וְהָא רַבִּי אַמֵּי וְרַבִּי אַסִּי חָלְפִי! – רַבִּי אַמֵּי וְרַבִּי אַסִּי חוּץ לְאַרְבַּע אַמּוֹת הוּא דְּחָלְפִי.

The Gemara responds: This **supports** the opinion of **Rabbi Yehoshua ben Levi, as Rabbi Yehoshua ben Levi said: It is prohibited to pass before those who are praying.** The Gemara asks: **Is that so? Didn't Rabbi Ami and Rabbi Asi pass** before those who were praying? The Gemara responds: **Rabbi Ami and Rabbi Asi** were **beyond four cubits** from those who were praying **when they passed.**

וְרַבִּי יִרְמְיָה הֵיכִי עֲבֵיד הָכִי? וְהָא אָמַר רַב יְהוּדָה אָמַר רַב: לְעוֹלָם אַל יִתְפַּלֵּל אָדָם

One particular detail was surprising: **How did Rabbi Yirmeya act that way** and pray behind Rav? **Didn't Rav Yehuda say** that **Rav said: A person should never pray**

Perek **IV**
Daf **27** Amud **b**

לֹא כְּנֶגֶד רַבּוֹ וְלֹא אֲחוֹרֵי רַבּוֹ;

directly **in front of his rabbi,** presumptuously indicating that he is his rabbi's equal, **and behind his rabbi**[H] as it creates the impression that he is bowing to him (*Tosafot*)?

וְתַנְיָא, רַבִּי אֱלִיעֶזֶר אוֹמֵר: הַמִּתְפַּלֵּל אֲחוֹרֵי רַבּוֹ, וְהַנּוֹתֵן שָׁלוֹם לְרַבּוֹ, וְהַמַּחֲזִיר שָׁלוֹם לְרַבּוֹ, וְהַחוֹלֵק עַל יְשִׁיבָתוֹ שֶׁל רַבּוֹ, וְהָאוֹמֵר דָּבָר שֶׁלֹּא שָׁמַע מִפִּי רַבּוֹ – גּוֹרֵם לַשְּׁכִינָה שֶׁתִּסְתַּלֵּק מִיִּשְׂרָאֵל!

**And it was taught** in a *baraita*, in a more extreme manner, as **Rabbi Eliezer says: One who prays behind his rabbi and one who greets his rabbi**[HN] without waiting for his rabbi to greet him first, **one who returns his rabbi's greeting** without saying: Greetings to you, rabbi, **one who rivals his rabbi's yeshiva,**[H] i.e., establishes a yeshiva of his own and teaches during his rabbi's lifetime without his consent (Rambam), **and one who says something** in the name of his rabbi **which he did not hear directly from his rabbi,**[HN] **causes the Divine Presence to withdraw from Israel.**

שָׁאנֵי רַבִּי יִרְמְיָה בַּר אַבָּא, דְּתַלְמִיד חָבֵר הֲוָה. וְהַיְינוּ דְּקָאָמַר לֵיהּ רַבִּי יִרְמְיָה בַּר אַבָּא לְרַב: ״מִי בְּדַלְתְּ?״ אָמַר לֵיהּ: אִין, בְּדֵילְנָא, וְלָא אָמַר, ״מִי בָּדֵיל מָר.״

With regard to Rabbi Yirmeya's conduct, the Gemara explains that **Rabbi Yirmeya bar Abba is different,** as he was not a mere student of Rav. Rather, he **was a disciple-colleague**[HN] and was, therefore, permitted to act that way. **And that is why** on one occasion, when Rav prayed the Shabbat prayer early, **Rabbi Yirmeya bar Abba asked him: Did you distance yourself** from labor and accept the sanctity of Shabbat? **Rav said to him: Yes, I distanced myself. And** Rabbi Yirmeya **did not say to him: Did the Master distance himself,** as would have been appropriate had he merely been Rav's student.

וּמִי בָּדֵיל?! וְהָאָמַר רַבִּי אָבִין פַּעַם אַחַת הִתְפַּלֵּל רַבִּי שֶׁל שַׁבָּת בְּעֶרֶב שַׁבָּת, וְנִכְנַס לַמֶּרְחָץ וְיָצָא וְשָׁנָה לָן פִּרְקִין וַעֲדַיִין לֹא חָשְׁכָה! אָמַר רָבָא: הַהוּא דְּנִכְנַס לְהָזִיעַ, וְקוֹדֶם גְּזֵירָה הֲוָה.

Although Rav replied that he distanced himself from labor, **did he** indeed need to **distance himself** from labor? **Didn't Rabbi Avin say: Once Rabbi** Yehuda HaNasi **prayed** the **Shabbat** prayer **on the eve of Shabbat** before nightfall. **He** then **entered the bathhouse and emerged and taught us our chapters** that we had learned, **and it was not yet dark. Rava said: That** is a case where he had **entered** the bathhouse **to perspire, and it was before the** Sages issued a **decree** prohibiting perspiring in a bathhouse on Shabbat.

אִינִי?! וְהָא אַבָּיֵי שְׁרָא לֵיהּ לְרַב דִּימִי בַּר לִיוָאֵי לְכַבְרוּיֵי סַלֵּי!

The Gemara asks: **Is that so,** that he was required to refrain from labor? **Didn't Abaye permit Rav Dimi bar Liva'ei to fumigate baskets with sulfur** even though he had already recited the Shabbat prayer, indicating that it is permitted to perform labor even after the Shabbat prayer?

הַהוּא טָעוּתָא הֲוַאי.

The Gemara responds: **That was an error,**[H] as Rav Dimi did not intend to begin Shabbat early. It was a cloudy day and he mistakenly thought that the sun had set and that was why he prayed. Consequently, even though he prayed, the Shabbat prayer did not obligate him to conduct himself in accordance with the sanctity of Shabbat and he was allowed to perform labor even after his prayer.

**HALAKHA**

**A person should never pray…and behind his rabbi – אַל יִתְפַּלֵּל אָדָם... וְלֹא אֲחוֹרֵי רַבּוֹ:** A student may not pray directly behind his rabbi, before him, or alongside him, within four cubits. Beyond four cubits, it is considered a separate domain and, therefore, is permitted. Some say that this applies only when they are praying as individuals, but when praying with a congregation, if that is the regular seating arrangement, it is not a problem. Even though it is preferable to avoid doing so, the custom is to allow it (Rambam *Sefer HaMadda, Hilkhot Talmud Torah* 5:6; *Shulḥan Arukh, Oraḥ Ḥayyim* 90:24 and in the comment of the Rema).

**One who greets his rabbi – וְהַנּוֹתֵן שָׁלוֹם לְרַבּוֹ:** A student may not greet his rabbi in the manner that he greets others. He must bow before him and say: Greetings to you, my rabbi. If the rabbi greeted him, he should reply: Greetings to you, my rabbi, my teacher, as per the statement of Rabbi Eliezer here, as the prohibition to greet his rabbi is limited to when he does not greet him with the requisite respect. Some say that a student may not greet his rabbi at all (Jerusalem Talmud; Rambam *Sefer HaMadda, Hilkhot Talmud Torah* 5:5; *Shulḥan Arukh, Yoreh De'a* 242:16 and in the comment of the Rema).

**One who rivals his rabbi's yeshiva – וְהַחוֹלֵק עַל יְשִׁיבָתוֹ שֶׁל רַבּוֹ:** Entering into a dispute with one's rabbi is tantamount to entering into a dispute with the Divine Presence. What is the definition of one who enters into a dispute with his rabbi? It is one who establishes, in his rabbi's lifetime, a rival study hall where he teaches without the permission of his rabbi (Rambam *Sefer HaMadda, Hilkhot Talmud Torah* 5:1–2; *Shulḥan Arukh, Yoreh De'a* 242:2).

**One who says something which he did not hear directly from his rabbi – וְהָאוֹמֵר דָּבָר שֶׁלֹּא שָׁמַע מִפִּי רַבּוֹ:** A student may not make an unattributed statement that he did not hear from his rabbi, as others are liable to mistakenly assume that he heard it from his rabbi. When making a statement from another source, he must attribute it to that source (Rambam *Sefer HaMadda, Hilkhot Talmud Torah* 5:9; *Shulḥan Arukh, Yoreh De'a* 242:24, see the comment of the *Shakh*).

**He was a disciple-colleague – דְּתַלְמִיד חָבֵר הֲוָה:** A disciple-colleague may pray behind his rabbi. However, even a disciple-colleague may not pray before him (Rambam *Sefer HaMadda, Hilkhot Talmud Torah* 5:9; *Shulḥan Arukh, Oraḥ Ḥayyim* 90:25).

**Accepting Shabbat by mistake – קַבָּלַת שַׁבָּת בְּטָעוּת:** An individual who inadvertently began Shabbat before its designated time and lit candles and recited the Shabbat evening prayer before realizing his error, may perform labor that is prohibited on Shabbat until Shabbat begins. At that time, he must repeat the evening prayer. However, a community that inadvertently began Shabbat before its designated time, and prayed after the midpoint of *minḥa*, need not pray again. With regard to performance of labor prohibited on Shabbat, some permit it as their acceptance of Shabbat was inadvertent. Others distinguish between those members of the community who lit Shabbat candles, for whom labor is prohibited, and those who did not light candles, for whom it is permitted (*Magen Avraham*). Others rule in accordance with this opinion *ab initio*, but not after the fact (*Shulḥan Arukh HaRav; Shulḥan Arukh, Oraḥ Ḥayyim* 263:14).

**NOTES**

**One who greets his rabbi – וְהַנּוֹתֵן שָׁלוֹם לְרַבּוֹ:** Various explanations were suggested for this *halakha*. According to Rashi, it prohibits a student from greeting his rabbi in the same manner in which he greets others. He should address him with greater deference. Others say that this prohibits a student from addressing his rabbi at all; he must wait until the rabbi addresses him (*Talmidei Rabbeinu Yona*). Apparently, the practice in Babylonia was different from the practice in Eretz Yisrael (see tractate *Shekalim*).

**One who says something which he did not hear directly from his rabbi – וְהָאוֹמֵר דָּבָר שֶׁלֹּא שָׁמַע מִפִּי רַבּוֹ:** In certain cases, Sages allowed themselves to make statements that they did not hear from their rabbi. They saw an educational need to place emphasis on different aspects, which superseded any concern with regard to precision in quoting their mentors.

**He was a disciple-colleague – דְּתַלְמִיד חָבֵר הֲוָה:** This refers to a student whose growth in Torah stature ultimately rendered him his teacher's colleague. Nevertheless, he continued to treat him with the deference accorded to a mentor. Sometimes this term refers to a younger individual who, due to his lack of experience, still relies on his teacher's oral traditions, but does not require his teacher's explanations of those traditions.

**PERSONALITIES**

**Avidan – אֲבִידָן:** Also referred to as Avdan, his name is an abbreviated version of the name Abba Yudan. He was a student of Rabbi Yehuda HaNasi, with whom he had a close relationship and he often served as the one who repeated and disseminated Rabbi Yehuda HaNasi's lectures. Therefore, he was able to transmit many teachings in the name of Rabbi Yehuda HaNasi of which other Sages were unaware. Considered to be one of the last *tanna'im*, Avidan was widely recognized as a wise and pious man. A series of tragic events befell him near the end of his life, when he was afflicted with leprosy and his two sons drowned. The Sages saw this as divine punishment for insulting Rabbi Yishmael son of Rabbi Yosei, although that, too, was performed in his zeal to defend his rabbi's honor. Isolated statements are cited in his name in the Talmud and midrash.

**HALAKHA**

***Kiddush* while it is still day – קִדּוּשׁ מִבְּעוֹד יוֹם:** One who began Shabbat before its designated time may recite *kiddush* and eat the Shabbat meal before dark, as per the statement that Rav Naḥman said that Shmuel said, in accordance with which the Gemara ruled. Some say that he must extend the meal until after dark and make certain to eat at least an olive-bulk past dark, so that it will be considered a meal eaten on Shabbat, as it is stated: "Eat that today; for today is Shabbat unto the Lord" (Exodus 16:25). *Ab initio*, one should adopt that stringency (*Mishna Berura*; Rambam *Sefer Ahava, Hilkhot Tefilla* 3:7, *Sefer Zemanim, Hilkhot Shabbat* 29:11; *Shulḥan Arukh, Oraḥ Ḥayyim* 267:2).

**One prays the evening prayer of the conclusion of Shabbat on Shabbat and recites *havdala* over the cup of wine – מִתְפַּלֵּל אָדָם שֶׁל מוֹצָאֵי שַׁבָּת בְּשַׁבָּת, וְאוֹמֵר הַבְדָּלָה עַל הַכּוֹס:** This is only done in exigent circumstances or when it is necessary to facilitate the performance of a mitzva. Then one is permitted to recite the evening prayer of the conclusion of Shabbat on Shabbat and to recite *havdala* over a cup of wine. However, one does not recite the blessing over the candle or perform prohibited labor until nightfall. In regular circumstances, there is no need to end Shabbat hastily, especially because many hold in accordance with the ruling of the *Tur* that one may not recite the evening prayer, *Arvit*, until dark (Rambam *Sefer Ahava, Hilkhot Tefilla* 3:7, *Sefer Zemanim, Hilkhot Shabbat* 29:11; *Shulḥan Arukh, Oraḥ Ḥayyim* 293:3).

**The evening prayer is optional – תְּפִלַּת עַרְבִית רְשׁוּת:** The evening prayer is optional, as per the opinion of Rabbi Yehoshua in his dispute with Rabban Gamliel; and the opinion of Rava in his dispute with Abaye. This is in accordance with the accepted halakhic principle. Although it is optional, there is still a mitzva to recite this prayer and it should not be missed. The Rif writes that now that all of Israel has accepted upon themselves to recite the evening prayer, it has become obligatory like the morning and afternoon prayers (Rambam *Sefer Ahava, Hilkhot Tefilla* 1:6, 3:6–7, 9:9; *Tur, Oraḥ Ḥayyim* 235).

וְטָעוּתָא מִי הָדְרָא?! וְהָא אָמַר אֲבִידָן: פַּעַם אַחַת נִתְקַשְּׁרוּ שָׁמַיִם בְּעָבִים, כִּסְבוּרִים הָעָם לוֹמַר חֲשֵׁכָה הוּא, נִכְנְסוּ לְבֵית הַכְּנֶסֶת וְהִתְפַּלְּלוּ שֶׁל מוֹצָאֵי שַׁבָּת בְּשַׁבָּת, וְנִתְפַּזְּרוּ הֶעָבִים וְזָרְחָה הַחַמָּה,

The Gemara goes on to ask: **Can a mistake be reversed,** enabling one to conduct himself as if he had not prayed? **Didn't Avidan,**[P] a student of Rabbi Yehuda HaNasi, **say: Once the sky became overcast,** leading **the people to think that it was** the **dark** of night; **they entered the synagogue and recited the** evening **prayer of the conclusion of Shabbat on Shabbat. And** later, **the clouds cleared and the sun shone,** indicating that it was still day.

וּבָאוּ וְשָׁאֲלוּ אֶת רַבִּי, וְאָמַר: הוֹאִיל וְהִתְפַּלְּלוּ – הִתְפַּלְּלוּ! – שָׁאנֵי צִבּוּר, דְּלָא מַטְרְחִינַן לְהוּ.

**And they came and asked Rabbi** Yehuda HaNasi what they should do, **and he said: Since they have prayed, they have prayed,** and they need not pray again. Although they prayed erroneously, their mistake is not reversible and what was done remains. The Gemara responds: **A community is different** in **that we do not burden them** to pray again.

אָמַר רַבִּי חִיָּיא בַּר אָבִין: רַב צַלֵּי שֶׁל שַׁבָּת בְּעֶרֶב שַׁבָּת, רַבִּי יֹאשִׁיָּה מְצַלֵּי שֶׁל מוֹצָאֵי שַׁבָּת בְּשַׁבָּת. רַב צַלֵּי שֶׁל שַׁבָּת בְּעֶרֶב שַׁבָּת. אוֹמֵר קְדוּשָּׁה עַל הַכּוֹס, אוֹ אֵינוֹ אוֹמֵר קְדוּשָּׁה עַל הַכּוֹס? תָּא שְׁמַע: דְּאָמַר רַב נַחְמָן אָמַר שְׁמוּאֵל: מִתְפַּלֵּל אָדָם שֶׁל שַׁבָּת בְּעֶרֶב שַׁבָּת וְאוֹמֵר קְדוּשָּׁה עַל הַכּוֹס. וְהִלְכְתָא כְּוָותֵיהּ.

The Gemara continues to discuss the possibility of reciting the evening prayer early, even on Shabbat. **Rabbi Ḥiyya bar Avin said: Rav prayed** the **Shabbat** prayer **on the eve of Shabbat** before nightfall. **Rabbi Yoshiya would pray the** evening **prayer of the conclusion of Shabbat on Shabbat.** With regard to the fact that **Rav prayed** the **Shabbat** prayer **on the eve of Shabbat** before nightfall, the dilemma is raised: In those cases, did **he recite *kiddush* over the cup** of wine, **or did he not recite *kiddush* over the cup** of wine before the stars emerged? **Come and hear** a resolution to this, as **Rav Naḥman said** that **Shmuel said: One prays** the **Shabbat** prayer **on the eve of Shabbat** before nightfall **and recites *kiddush* over the cup** of wine.[H] **And the *halakha* is in accordance with his** ruling.

רַבִּי יֹאשִׁיָּה מְצַלֵּי שֶׁל מוֹצָאֵי שַׁבָּת בְּשַׁבָּת. אוֹמֵר הַבְדָּלָה עַל הַכּוֹס אוֹ אֵינוֹ אוֹמֵר הַבְדָּלָה עַל הַכּוֹס? תָּא שְׁמַע דְּאָמַר רַב יְהוּדָה אָמַר שְׁמוּאֵל: מִתְפַּלֵּל אָדָם שֶׁל מוֹצָאֵי שַׁבָּת בְּשַׁבָּת, וְאוֹמֵר הַבְדָּלָה עַל הַכּוֹס.

A similar dilemma was raised concerning the fact that **Rabbi Yoshiya would pray the** evening **prayer of the conclusion of Shabbat on Shabbat:** After praying, while it is still Shabbat, **does he recite *havdala* over the cup** of wine **or does one not recite *havdala* over the cup** of wine? **Come and hear** a resolution to this, as **Rav Yehuda said** that **Shmuel said: One prays the** evening **prayer of the conclusion of Shabbat on Shabbat and recites *havdala* over the cup** of wine.[H]

אָמַר רַבִּי זֵירָא אָמַר רַבִּי אַסִּי אָמַר רַבִּי אֶלְעָזָר אָמַר רַבִּי חֲנִינָא אָמַר רַב: בְּצַד עַמּוּד זֶה הִתְפַּלֵּל רַבִּי יִשְׁמָעֵאל בְּרַבִּי יוֹסֵי שֶׁל שַׁבָּת בְּעֶרֶב שַׁבָּת.

**Rabbi Zeira said** that **Rabbi Asi said** that **Rabbi Elazar said** that **Rabbi Ḥanina said** that **Rav said: Alongside this** specific **pillar** before me, **Rabbi Yishmael, son of Rabbi Yosei, prayed** the **Shabbat** prayer **on the eve of Shabbat** before nightfall.

כִּי אֲתָא עוּלָּא, אָמַר: בְּצַד תְּמָרָה הֲוָה וְלֹא בְּצַד עַמּוּד הֲוָה, וְלֹא רַבִּי יִשְׁמָעֵאל בְּרַבִּי יוֹסֵי הֲוָה אֶלָּא רַבִּי אֶלְעָזָר בְּרַבִּי יוֹסֵי הֲוָה, וְלֹא שֶׁל שַׁבָּת בְּעֶרֶב שַׁבָּת הֲוָה אֶלָּא שֶׁל מוֹצָאֵי שַׁבָּת בְּשַׁבָּת הֲוָה.

**But when Ulla came** from the Eretz Yisrael to Babylonia, he related a different version of this story. **He said** that he had heard: This transpired **beside a palm tree, not beside a pillar, and it was not Rabbi Yishmael, son of Rabbi Yosei, but** it was **Rabbi Elazar son of Rabbi Yosei, and it was not** the **Shabbat** prayer **on Shabbat eve** before nightfall, **rather** it was the **prayer of the conclusion of Shabbat on Shabbat.**

"תְּפִלַּת הָעֶרֶב אֵין לָהּ קֶבַע." מַאי "אֵין לָהּ קֶבַע?" אִילֵימָא דְּאִי בָּעֵי מְצַלֵּי כּוּלֵּיהּ לֵילְיָא – לִיתְנֵי תְּפִלַּת הָעֶרֶב כׇּל הַלַּיְלָה! אֶלָּא מַאי "אֵין לָהּ קֶבַע?"

We learned in the mishna: **The evening prayer** may be recited throughout the night and **is not fixed** to a specific hour. The Gemara asks: **What is the meaning of is not fixed? If you say that if** one **wishes, he may pray throughout the night,** then **let the** mishna **teach: The evening prayer** may be recited **throughout the night. Rather, what is** the meaning of **not fixed?**

כְּמַאן דְּאָמַר: תְּפִלַּת עַרְבִית רְשׁוּת. דְּאָמַר רַב יְהוּדָה אָמַר שְׁמוּאֵל: תְּפִלַּת עַרְבִית, רַבָּן גַּמְלִיאֵל אוֹמֵר: חוֹבָה, רַבִּי יְהוֹשֻׁעַ אוֹמֵר: רְשׁוּת. אָמַר אַבָּיֵי: הֲלָכָה כְּדִבְרֵי הָאוֹמֵר חוֹבָה. וְרָבָא אָמַר: הֲלָכָה כְּדִבְרֵי הָאוֹמֵר רְשׁוּת.

It is **in accordance with** the opinion of **the one who said: The evening prayer is optional. As Rav Yehuda said** that **Shmuel said** with regard to **the evening prayer. Rabban Gamliel says:** It is **obligatory. Rabbi Yehoshua says:** It is **optional. Abaye said: The *halakha* is in accordance with the statement of the one who said** The evening prayer is **obligatory. Rava said: The *halakha* is in accordance with the statement of the one who said:** The evening prayer is **optional.**[H]

תָּנוּ רַבָּנַן: מַעֲשֶׂה בְּתַלְמִיד אֶחָד שֶׁבָּא לִפְנֵי רַבִּי יְהוֹשֻׁעַ, אָמַר לוֹ: תְּפִלַּת עַרְבִית רְשׁוּת אוֹ חוֹבָה? אָמַר לֵיהּ: רְשׁוּת.

**The Sages taught:** There was **an incident involving a student who came before Rabbi Yehoshua.** The student **said to him: Is the evening prayer optional or obligatory?** Rabbi Yehoshua **said to him: Optional.**

בָּא לִפְנֵי רַבָּן גַּמְלִיאֵל, אָמַר לוֹ: תְּפִלַּת עַרְבִית רְשׁוּת אוֹ חוֹבָה? אָמַר לוֹ: חוֹבָה. אָמַר לוֹ: וַהֲלֹא רַבִּי יְהוֹשֻׁעַ אָמַר לִי רְשׁוּת! אָמַר לוֹ: הַמְתֵּן עַד שֶׁיִּכָּנְסוּ בַּעֲלֵי תְרִיסִין לְבֵית הַמִּדְרָשׁ.

The same student **came before Rabban Gamliel and said to him: Is the evening prayer optional or obligatory?** Rabban Gamliel **said to him: Obligatory.** The student **said to** Rabban Gamliel: **But didn't Rabbi Yehoshua tell me** that the evening prayer is **optional?** Rabban Gamliel **said to** the student: **Wait until the "masters of the shields,"**[L] a reference to the Torah scholars who battle in the war of Torah, **enter the study hall,** at which point we will discuss this issue.

כְּשֶׁנִּכְנְסוּ בַּעֲלֵי תְרִיסִין, עָמַד הַשּׁוֹאֵל וְשָׁאַל: תְּפִלַּת עַרְבִית רְשׁוּת אוֹ חוֹבָה? אָמַר לוֹ רַבָּן גַּמְלִיאֵל: חוֹבָה. אָמַר לָהֶם רַבָּן גַּמְלִיאֵל לַחֲכָמִים: כְּלוּם יֵשׁ אָדָם שֶׁחוֹלֵק בְּדָבָר זֶה? אָמַר לֵיהּ רַבִּי יְהוֹשֻׁעַ: לָאו. אָמַר לוֹ: וַהֲלֹא מִשְּׁמְךָ אָמְרוּ לִי רְשׁוּת!

**When the masters of the shields entered, the questioner stood** before everyone present **and asked: Is the evening prayer optional or obligatory? Rabban Gamliel said to him: Obligatory.** In order to ascertain whether or not Rabbi Yehoshua still maintained his opinion, **Rabban Gamliel said to** the Sages: **Is there any person who disputes this matter? Rabbi Yehoshua said to him: No,** no one disagrees. In deference to the *Nasi*, he did not wish to argue with him publicly (*Tziyyun LeNefesh Ḥayya*). Rabban Gamliel **said to** Rabbi Yehoshua: **But was it not in your name that they told me** that the evening prayer is **optional?**

אָמַר לֵיהּ: יְהוֹשֻׁעַ, עֲמוֹד עַל רַגְלֶיךָ וְיָעִידוּ בְּךָ! עָמַד רַבִּי יְהוֹשֻׁעַ עַל רַגְלָיו וְאָמַר: אִלְמָלֵא אֲנִי חַי וְהוּא מֵת – יָכוֹל הַחַי לְהַכְחִישׁ אֶת הַמֵּת, וְעַכְשָׁיו שֶׁאֲנִי חַי וְהוּא חַי – הֵיאַךְ יָכוֹל הַחַי לְהַכְחִישׁ אֶת הַחַי?

Rabban Gamliel **said to** Rabbi Yehoshua: **Yehoshua, stand on your feet and they will testify against you. Rabbi Yehoshua stood on his feet and said: If I were alive and** the student **were dead, the living can contradict the dead,** and I could deny issuing that ruling. **Now that I am alive and he is alive, how can the living contradict the living?** I have no choice but to admit that I said it.

הָיָה רַבָּן גַּמְלִיאֵל יוֹשֵׁב וְדוֹרֵשׁ, וְרַבִּי יְהוֹשֻׁעַ עוֹמֵד עַל רַגְלָיו, עַד שֶׁרִנְּנוּ כָּל הָעָם וְאָמְרוּ לְחוּצְפִּית הַתּוּרְגְּמָן: עֲמוֹד! וְעָמַד.

In the meantime, **Rabban Gamliel,** as the *Nasi*, **was sitting and lecturing, and Rabbi Yehoshua** all the while **was standing on his feet,** because Rabban Gamliel did not instruct him to sit. He remained standing in deference to the *Nasi*. This continued for some time, **until** it aroused great resentment against Rabban Gamliel, and **all of the people** assembled began **murmuring and said to Ḥutzpit the disseminator:**[P] **Stop** conveying Rabban Gamliel's lecture. **And he stopped.**

אָמְרִי: עַד כַּמָּה נְצַעֲרֵיהּ וְנֵיזִיל? בְּרֹאשׁ הַשָּׁנָה אֶשְׁתָּקַד צַעֲרֵיהּ, בִּבְכוֹרוֹת בְּמַעֲשֶׂה דְּרַבִּי צָדוֹק צַעֲרֵיהּ, הָכָא נַמִּי צַעֲרֵיהּ, תָּא וְנַעַבְרֵיהּ!

The Gemara relates that in their murmuring **they said: How long will** Rabban Gamliel **continue afflicting him? Last year on Rosh HaShana, he afflicted him;** Rabban Gamliel ordered Rabbi Yehoshua to come to him carrying his staff and bag, on the day on which Yom Kippur occurred, according to Rabbi Yehoshua's calculations. **Regarding the firstborn, in the incident** involving the question **of Rabbi Tzadok, he afflicted him** just as he did now, and forced him to remain standing as punishment for his failure to defend his differing opinion. **Here too, he is afflicting him. Let us remove him** from his position as *Nasi*.

מַאן נוֹקִים לֵיהּ? נוֹקְמֵיהּ לְרַבִּי יְהוֹשֻׁעַ? בַּעַל מַעֲשֶׂה הוּא; נוֹקְמֵיהּ לְרַבִּי עֲקִיבָא? דִּילְמָא עָנֵישׁ לֵיהּ, דְּלֵית לֵיהּ זְכוּת אָבוֹת;

It was so agreed, but the question arose: **Who shall we establish** in his place? Shall we **establish Rabbi Yehoshua** in his place? The Sages rejected that option because Rabbi Yehoshua **was party to the incident**[N] for which Rabban Gamliel was deposed. Appointing him would be extremely upsetting for Rabban Gamliel. Shall we **establish Rabbi Akiva** in his place? The Sages rejected that option because Rabbi Akiva, who descended from a family of converts, would be vulnerable. **Perhaps** due to Rabban Gamliel's resentment he **would** cause **him** to be divinely **punished as he lacks the merit of his ancestors** to protect him.

אֶלָּא נוֹקְמֵיהּ לְרַבִּי אֶלְעָזָר בֶּן עֲזַרְיָה, דְּהוּא חָכָם וְהוּא עָשִׁיר וְהוּא עֲשִׂירִי לְעֶזְרָא. הוּא חָכָם – דְּאִי מַקְשֵׁי לֵיהּ מְפָרֵק לֵיהּ, וְהוּא עָשִׁיר – דְּאִי אִית לֵיהּ לְפַלּוּחֵי לְבֵי קֵיסָר אַף הוּא אֵיזִיל וּפְלַח, וְהוּא עֲשִׂירִי לְעֶזְרָא – דְּאִית לֵיהּ זְכוּת אָבוֹת וְלָא מָצֵי עָנֵישׁ לֵיהּ. אֲתוּ וַאֲמַרוּ לֵיהּ: נִיחָא לֵיהּ לְמָר דְּלֶיהֱוֵי רֵישׁ מְתִיבְתָּא? אֲמַר לְהוּ: אֵיזִיל וְאִימְלִיךְ בְּאֱינָשֵׁי בֵיתִי. אֲזַל וְאִמְלִיךְ בִּדְבֵיתְהוּ. אֲמַרָה לֵיהּ:

**Rather,** suggested the Sages, **let us establish Rabbi Elazar ben Azarya** in his place, his outstanding characteristics set him apart from the other candidates. **He is wise, rich, and a tenth** generation descendant **of Ezra.** The Gemara explains: **He is wise, so if** Rabban Gamliel raises a **challenge** in matters of Torah, **he will answer it** and not be embarrassed. **And he is rich, so if the need** arises **to pay homage to the Caesar's court** and serve as a representative of Israel to lobby and negotiate, he has sufficient wealth to cover the costs of the long journeys, taxes, and gifts, so **he too is able to go and pay homage. And he is** a **tenth** generation descendant **of Ezra, so he has the merit of his ancestors, and** Rabban Gamliel **will be unable to** cause **him** to be **punished. They came and said to him: Would the Master consent to being the Head of the Yeshiva? He said to them: I will go and consult with my household. He went and consulted with his wife. She said to him:**

**LANGUAGE**

Shields [*terisin*] – תְּרִיסִין: From the Greek θυρεός, *thureos*, meaning large shield. Keepers of the shield are the ones who hold those shields, i.e., warriors.

**PERSONALITIES**

Ḥutzpit the disseminator – חוּצְפִּית הַתּוּרְגְּמָן: Rabbi Ḥutzpit, one of the Sages of the Mishna (see *Shevi'it* ch. 10) is known as Rabban Gamliel's *turgeman*. That position entailed more than merely repeating the Sage's lecture aloud. He also expanded upon the concise, cryptic statements made by that Sage in the course of the lecture. Because of his skill in explaining Rabban Gamliel's lectures, Rabbi Ḥutzpit was called: The mouth that produced pearls. We know nothing else about him, except that he died as one of the ten martyrs at the hands of the Roman empire.

**NOTES**

Rabbi Yehoshua was party to the incident – רַבִּי יְהוֹשֻׁעַ בַּעַל מַעֲשֶׂה הוּא: Some explained that Rabbi Yehoshua was not appointed because that would have created the impression that he initiated the dispute as a ploy to be appointed *Nasi* (Maharsha).

**PERSONALITIES**

Rabbi Elazar ben Azarya – רַבִּי אֶלְעָזָר בֶּן עֲזַרְיָה: One of the most significant *tanna'im* in the generation following the destruction of the Temple, Rabbi Elazar ben Azarya descended from a family of great wisdom, distinguished lineage, and wealth. His father, Azarya, was also a Torah scholar and an extremely wealthy man. He supported his brother Shimon, one of the Sages, who is, therefore, referred to as Shimon brother of Azarya. Rabbi Elazar ben Azarya's family were priests, descended from Ezra the Scribe, and there are traditions that tell of similarities between them. Some conjecture that Rabbi Eliezer was Rabbi Elazar ben Azarya's mentor.

Rabbi Yehoshua – רַבִּי יְהוֹשֻׁעַ: This is Rabbi Yehoshua ben Ḥananya the Levite, one of the leading Sages in the generation following the destruction of the Second Temple. He had served as one of the Levite singers in the Temple. After its destruction, he was among the students who went with their primary teacher, Rabban Yoḥanan ben Zakkai, to Yavne. Unlike his colleague Rabbi Eliezer, Rabbi Yehoshua completely adhered to the approach of his teacher and of Beit Hillel.

**HALAKHA**

An Ammonite and a Moabite – עַמּוֹנִי וּמוֹאָבִי: Those who dwell in contemporary lands of Ammon and Moab, i.e., Jordan, do not have the legal status of Ammonites and Moabites, and converts from those areas may enter the congregation of Israel in accordance with the opinion of Rabbi Yehoshua (Rambam *Sefer Kedusha, Hilkhot Issurei Bia* 12:25; *Shulḥan Arukh, Even HaEzer* 4:10).

**BACKGROUND**

Everything that parts from a group parts from the majority – כָּל דְּפָרֵישׁ מֵרוּבָּא פָּרֵישׁ: This principle applies to many dilemmas with regard to the laws of prohibited and permitted mixtures. One may only rely on this principle in specific cases. In other words, the object must have spontaneously emerged from a mixture whose proportions are known. That is not the case when the object remains in the mixture. In that case, the sample is flawed and there is room for concern that the object in question is not really from the majority component. Then the principle is: Anything that is fixed, i.e., remains in the mixture, is considered an evenly balanced uncertainty and the object is not attributed to the majority.

דִּלְמָא מַעַבְרִין לָךְ? אָמַר לַהּ: לִשְׁתַּמֵּשׁ אֱינָשׁ יוֹמָא חֲדָא בְּכַסָּא דְּמוֹקְרָא, וּלְמָחָר לִיתְּבַר. אָמְרָה לֵיהּ: לֵית לָךְ חִיוָּרְתָּא. הַהוּא יוֹמָא בַּר תְּמָנֵי סְרֵי שְׁנֵי הֲוָה, אִתְרְחִישׁ לֵיהּ נִיסָּא וְאַהְדַּרוּ לֵיהּ תְּמָנֵי סְרֵי דָּרֵי חִיוָּרְתָּא. הַיְינוּ דְּקָאָמַר רַבִּי אֶלְעָזָר בֶּן עֲזַרְיָה: הֲרֵי אֲנִי "כְּבֶן" שִׁבְעִים שָׁנָה, וְלֹא "בֶּן" שִׁבְעִים שָׁנָה.

There is room for concern. **Perhaps they will remove you** from office just as they removed Rabban Gamliel. **He said to her,** based on the folk saying: **Let a person use an expensive goblet one day and let it break tomorrow.** In other words, one should take advantage of an opportunity that presents itself and he need not concern himself whether or not it will last. **She said to him: You have no white** hair, and it is inappropriate for one so young to head the Sages. The Gemara relates: **That day, he was eighteen years old, a miracle transpired for him and eighteen rows of hair turned white.** The Gemara comments: **That** explains **that which Rabbi Elazar ben Azarya**[P] **said: I am as one who is seventy years old and he did not say: I am seventy years old,** because he looked older than he actually was.

תָּנָא: אוֹתוֹ הַיּוֹם סִלְּקוּהוּ לְשׁוֹמֵר הַפֶּתַח וְנִתְּנָה לָהֶם רְשׁוּת לַתַּלְמִידִים לִיכָּנֵס. שֶׁהָיָה רַבָּן גַּמְלִיאֵל מַכְרִיז וְאוֹמֵר: כָּל תַּלְמִיד שֶׁאֵין תּוֹכוֹ כְּבָרוֹ – לֹא יִכָּנֵס לְבֵית הַמִּדְרָשׁ.

**It was taught: On that day** that they removed Rabban Gamliel from his position and appointed Rabbi Elazar ben Azarya in his place, there was also a fundamental change in the general approach of the study hall as **they dismissed the guard at the door and permission was granted to the students to enter.** Instead of Rabban Gamliel's selective approach that asserted that the students must be screened before accepting them into the study hall, the new approach asserted that anyone who seeks to study should be given opportunity to do so. **As Rabban Gamliel would proclaim and say: Any student whose inside,** his thoughts and feelings, **are not like his outside,** i.e., his conduct and his character traits are lacking, **will not enter the study hall.**

הַהוּא יוֹמָא אִתּוֹסְפוּ כַּמָּה סַפְסְלֵי. אָמַר רַבִּי יוֹחָנָן: פְּלִיגִי בָּהּ אַבָּא יוֹסֵף בֶּן דּוֹסְתַּאי וְרַבָּנַן, חַד אָמַר: אִתּוֹסְפוּ אַרְבַּע מְאָה סַפְסְלֵי; וְחַד אָמַר: שְׁבַע מְאָה סַפְסְלֵי. הֲוָה קָא חָלְשָׁה דַּעְתֵּיהּ דְּרַבָּן גַּמְלִיאֵל, אָמַר: דִּלְמָא חַס וְשָׁלוֹם מָנַעְתִּי תּוֹרָה מִיִּשְׂרָאֵל. אַחְזוּ לֵיהּ בְּחֶלְמֵיהּ חַצְבֵי חִיוָּרֵי דְּמַלְיָין קִטְמָא. וְלָא הִיא, הַהִיא לְיַתּוֹבֵי דַּעְתֵּיהּ הוּא דְּאַחְזוּ לֵיהּ.

The Gemara relates: **On that day several benches were added** to the study hall to accommodate the numerous students. **Rabbi Yoḥanan said: Abba Yosef ben Dostai and the Rabbis disputed this** matter. **One said: Four hundred benches were added** to the study hall. **And one said: Seven hundred benches were added** to the study hall. When he saw the tremendous growth in the number of students, **Rabban Gamliel was disheartened. He said: Perhaps, Heaven forbid, I prevented Israel from** engaging in **Torah** study. **They showed him in his dream white jugs filled with ashes** alluding to the fact that the additional students were worthless idlers. The Gemara comments: **That is not** the case, but **that** dream **was shown to him to ease his mind** so that he would not feel bad.

תָּנָא: עֵדֻיּוֹת בּוֹ בַּיּוֹם נִשְׁנֵית, וְכָל הֵיכָא דְּאָמְרִינַן "בּוֹ בַּיּוֹם" – הַהוּא יוֹמָא הֲוָה. וְלֹא הָיְתָה הֲלָכָה שֶׁהָיְתָה תְּלוּיָה בְּבֵית הַמִּדְרָשׁ שֶׁלֹּא פֵּירְשׁוּהָ. וְאַף רַבָּן גַּמְלִיאֵל לֹא מָנַע עַצְמוֹ מִבֵּית הַמִּדְרָשׁ אֲפִילּוּ שָׁעָה אַחַת,

**It was taught:** There is a tradition that tractate *Eduyyot* **was taught that day. And everywhere** in the Mishna or in a *baraita* **that they say: On that day, it is** referring to **that day. There was no** ***halakha*** **whose ruling was pending in the study hall that they did not explain** and arrive at a practical halakhic conclusion. **And even Rabban Gamliel did not avoid the study hall for even one moment,** as he held no grudge against those who removed him from office and he participated in the halakhic discourse in the study hall as one of the Sages.

דִּתְנַן: בּוֹ בַּיּוֹם בָּא יְהוּדָה גֵּר עַמּוֹנִי לִפְנֵיהֶם בְּבֵית הַמִּדְרָשׁ, אָמַר לָהֶם: מָה אֲנִי לָבֹא בַּקָּהָל?

**As we learned** in a mishna: **On that day, Yehuda, the Ammonite convert came before** the students in the study hall **and he said to them: What is my** legal status in terms of **entering into the congregation** of Israel, i.e., to marry a Jewish woman?

אָמַר לוֹ רַבָּן גַּמְלִיאֵל: אָסוּר אַתָּה לָבֹא בַּקָּהָל. אָמַר לוֹ רַבִּי יְהוֹשֻׁעַ: מוּתָּר אַתָּה לָבֹא בַּקָּהָל. אָמַר לוֹ רַבָּן גַּמְלִיאֵל: וַהֲלֹא כְּבָר נֶאֱמַר: "לֹא יָבֹא עַמּוֹנִי וּמוֹאָבִי בִּקְהַל ה'"! אָמַר לוֹ רַבִּי יְהוֹשֻׁעַ: וְכִי עַמּוֹן וּמוֹאָב בִּמְקוֹמָן הֵן יוֹשְׁבִין?! כְּבָר עָלָה סַנְחֵרִיב מֶלֶךְ אַשּׁוּר וּבִלְבֵּל אֶת כָּל הָאוּמּוֹת, שֶׁנֶּאֱמַר: "וְאָסִיר גְּבֻלוֹת עַמִּים וַעֲתוּדוֹתֵיהֶם שׁוֹשֵׂתִי וְאוֹרִיד כַּבִּיר יוֹשְׁבִים," וְכָל דְּפָרֵישׁ – מֵרוּבָּא פָּרֵישׁ.

**Rabban Gamliel said to him: You are forbidden to enter into the congregation. Rabbi Yehoshua**[P] **said to him: You are permitted to enter into the congregation. Rabban Gamliel said to** Rabbi Yehoshua: **Wasn't it already stated: "An Ammonite and a Moabite**[H] **shall not enter into the congregation of the Lord;** even to the tenth generation shall none of them enter into the congregation of the Lord forever" (Deuteronomy 23:4)? How can you permit him to enter the congregation? **Rabbi Yehoshua said to** Rabban Gamliel: **Do Ammon and Moab reside in their place? Sennacherib already came and** through his policy of population transfer, **scrambled all the nations** and settled other nations in place of Ammon. Consequently, the current residents of Ammon and Moab are not ethnic Ammonites and Moabites, **as it is stated in** reference to Sennacherib: **"I have removed the bounds of the peoples, and have robbed their treasures, and have brought down as one mighty the inhabitants"** (Isaiah 10:13). **And** although it is conceivable that this particular convert is an ethnic Ammonite, nevertheless, there is no need for concern due to the halakhic principle: **Anything that parts** from a group **parts from the majority,**[B] and the assumption is that he is from the majority of nations whose members are permitted to enter the congregation.

אָמַר לוֹ רַבָּן גַּמְלִיאֵל: וַהֲלֹא כְּבָר נֶאֱמַר: ״וְאַחֲרֵי כֵן אָשִׁיב אֶת שְׁבוּת בְּנֵי עַמּוֹן נְאֻם ה׳״ – וּכְבָר שָׁבוּ.

**Rabban Gamliel said to** Rabbi Yehoshua: **But wasn't it already stated: "But afterward I will bring back the captivity of the children of Ammon, says the Lord"** (Jeremiah 49:6) **and they have already returned** to their land? Therefore, he is an ethnic Ammonite and he may not convert.

אָמַר לוֹ רַבִּי יְהוֹשֻׁעַ: וַהֲלֹא כְּבָר נֶאֱמַר: ״וְשַׁבְתִּי אֶת שְׁבוּת עַמִּי יִשְׂרָאֵל״ – וַעֲדַיִין לֹא שָׁבוּ. מִיָּד הִתִּירוּהוּ לָבֹא בַּקָּהָל.

**Rabbi Yehoshua said to** Rabban Gamliel: That is no proof. **Wasn't it already stated** in another prophecy: **"And I will turn the captivity of My people Israel** and they shall build the waste cities, and inhabit them; and they shall plant vineyards, and drink the wine thereof; they shall also make gardens, and eat the fruit of them" (Amos 9:14), **and they have not yet returned?** In rendering the ruling, only proven facts may be taken into consideration. **They immediately permitted him to enter the congregation.** This proves that Rabban Gamliel did not absent himself from the study hall that day and participated in the halakhic discourse.

אָמַר רַבָּן גַּמְלִיאֵל: הוֹאִיל וְהָכִי הֲוָה, אֵיזִיל וְאֲפַיְּיסֵיהּ לְרַבִּי יְהוֹשֻׁעַ. כִּי מְטָא לְבֵיתֵיהּ, חַזְיִנְהוּ לְאַשִׁיָּתָא דְּבֵיתֵיהּ דְּמַשְׁחֲרָן. אָמַר לֵיהּ: מִכּוֹתְלֵי בֵּיתְךָ אַתָּה נִיכָּר שֶׁפֶּחָמִי אַתָּה. אָמַר לוֹ: אוֹי לוֹ לַדּוֹר שֶׁאַתָּה פַּרְנָסוֹ, שֶׁאִי אַתָּה יוֹדֵעַ בְּצַעֲרָן שֶׁל תַּלְמִידֵי חֲכָמִים בַּמֶּה הֵם מִתְפַּרְנְסִים וּבַמֶּה הֵם נִזּוֹנִים.

**Rabban Gamliel said** to himself: **Since this is** the situation,[N] that the people are following Rabbi Yehoshua, apparently he was right. Therefore, it would be appropriate for me to **go and appease Rabbi Yehoshua. When he reached** Rabbi Yehoshua's **house, he saw** that **the walls of his house were black.** Rabban Gamliel **said to** Rabbi Yehoshua in wonderment: **From the walls of your house it is apparent that you are a blacksmith,**[N] as until then he had no idea that Rabbi Yehoshua was forced to engage in that arduous trade in order to make a living. Rabbi Yehoshua **said to him: Woe unto a generation that you are its leader as you are unaware of the difficulties of Torah scholars, how they make a living and how they feed themselves.**

אָמַר לוֹ: נַעֲנֵיתִי לָךְ, מְחוֹל לִי! לֹא אַשְׁגַּח בֵּיהּ. עֲשֵׂה בִּשְׁבִיל כְּבוֹד אַבָּא! פַּיֵּיס.

Rabban Gamliel **said to him: I insulted you, forgive me.** Rabbi Yehoshua **paid him no attention** and did not forgive him. He asked him again: **Do it in deference to my father,** Rabban Shimon ben Gamliel, who was one of the leaders of Israel at the time of the destruction of the Temple. **He was appeased.**

אָמְרוּ: מַאן נֵיזִיל וְלֵימָא לְהוּ לְרַבָּנַן? אָמַר לְהוּ הַהוּא כּוֹבֵס: אֲנָא אָזֵילְנָא. שְׁלַח לְהוּ רַבִּי יְהוֹשֻׁעַ לְבֵי מִדְרְשָׁא: מַאן דְּלָבֵישׁ מַדָּא יִלְבַּשׁ מַדָּא, וּמַאן דְּלָא לָבֵישׁ מַדָּא יֵימַר לֵיהּ לְמַאן דְּלָבֵישׁ מַדָּא ״שְׁלַח מַדָּךְ וַאֲנָא אֶלְבְּשֵׁיהּ?״! אָמַר לְהוּ רַבִּי עֲקִיבָא לְרַבָּנַן: טְרוֹקוּ גַּלֵּי, דְּלָא לֵיתוֹ עַבְדֵי דְּרַבָּן גַּמְלִיאֵל וּלְצַעֲרוּ לְרַבָּנַן.

Now that Rabbi Yehoshua was no longer offended, it was only natural that Rabban Gamliel would be restored to his position. **They said: Who will go and inform the Sages?** Apparently, they were not eager to carry out the mission that would undo the previous actions and remove Rabbi Elazar ben Azarya from his position as *Nasi*. **This launderer said to them: I will go. Rabbi Yehoshua sent to** the Sages **to the study hall: The one who wears the uniform will** continue to **wear the uniform,** the original *Nasi* will remain in his position so that **the one who did not wear the uniform will** not **say to the one who wears the uniform, remove your uniform and I will wear it.** Apparently, the Sages believed that this emissary was dispatched at the initiative of Rabban Gamliel and they ignored him. **Rabbi Akiva said to the Sages: Lock the gates so that Rabban Gamliel's servants will not come and disturb the Sages.**

אָמַר רַבִּי יְהוֹשֻׁעַ: מוּטָב דְּאֵיקוּם וְאֵיזִיל אֲנָא לְגַבַּיְיהוּ. אֲתָא, טְרַף אַבָּבָא. אָמַר לְהוּ: מַזֶּה בֶּן מַזֶּה יַזֶּה, וְשֶׁאֵינוֹ לֹא מַזֶּה וְלֹא בֶּן מַזֶּה יֹאמַר לְמַזֶּה בֶּן מַזֶּה: מֵימֶיךָ מֵי מְעָרָה וְאֶפְרְךָ אֵפֶר מִקְלֶה? אָמַר לוֹ רַבִּי עֲקִיבָא: רַבִּי יְהוֹשֻׁעַ, נִתְפַּיַּיסְתָּ? כְּלוּם עָשִׂינוּ אֶלָּא בִּשְׁבִיל כְּבוֹדְךָ! לְמָחָר אֲנִי וְאַתָּה נַשְׁכִּים לְפִתְחוֹ.

When he heard what happened, **Rabbi Yehoshua said: It is best if I go to them. He came and knocked on the door. He said to them** with a slight variation: **One who sprinkles** pure water on those who are ritually impure, **son of one who sprinkles** water **shall** continue **to sprinkle** water. And it is inappropriate that he who is **neither one who sprinkles nor son of one who sprinkles will say to one who sprinkles son of one who sprinkles: Your water is cave water** and not the running water required to purify one exposed to ritual impurity imparted by a corpse **and your ashes are burnt ashes** and not the ashes of a red heifer. **Rabbi Akiva said to him: Rabbi Yehoshua, have you been appeased? Everything we did was to** defend **your honor.** If you have forgiven him, none of us is opposed. **Early tomorrow you and I will go to** Rabban Gamliel's **doorway** and offer to restore him to his position as *Nasi*.

### NOTES

**Since this is the situation – הוֹאִיל וְהָכִי הֲוָה:** Rabban Gamliel's reaction is based on the premise that until a *halakha* was voted on in the study hall and adopted as final, the extent to which it represents the truth cannot be determined. Once the Sages arrive at a decision with regard to a specific issue, it is deemed to be absolute truth. The fact that Rabbi Yehoshua was right became clear by means of the conclusive determination of the *halakha*.

**From the walls of your house it is apparent that you are a blacksmith – מִכּוֹתְלֵי בֵּיתְךָ אַתָּה נִיכָּר שֶׁפֶּחָמִי אַתָּה:** Rabbi Yehoshua's actual profession is unclear. Some interpret the word *peḥami* as coal worker, i.e., one who makes charcoal from wood. Others interpret it as blacksmith, a conclusion supported by the Jerusalem Talmud which states that Rabbi Yehoshua manufactured needles.

## HALAKHA

**And the additional prayer all day – וְשֶׁל מוּסָפִין כָּל הַיּוֹם:** *Ab initio*, the time to recite the additional prayer extends through the end of the seventh hour. One who recites it later than that is called negligent. Nevertheless, one who recites the additional prayer later fulfills his obligation, as the time to recite it is all day, as per the opinion of the Rabbis (Rambam *Sefer Ahava*, *Hilkhot Tefilla* 3:5; *Shulḥan Arukh*, *Oraḥ Ḥayyim* 286:1).

## NOTES

**Is called negligent – נִקְרָא פּוֹשֵׁעַ:** The Hebrew word *poshe'a* can refer either to a transgressor, who commits a *pesha*, *a transgression*, or to one who is negligent, who is guilty of *peshia*, negligence. As one is within his rights to recite the additional prayer all day, referring to him as a transgressor is a bit extreme. Rabbi Akiva Eiger in *Gilyon HaShas* refers to the Gemara below on 43b where one who arrives last to the study hall is similarly called a *poshe'a*. Rashi there defines it as one who is lazy, which seems more in line with negligence than transgression. It is conceivable that the determination whether it is negligence or transgression depends on the definition of the term, is called. If it refers to an objective pronouncement, he has certainly not transgressed any *halakha*. On the other hand, if it refers to the subjective judgment of onlookers, it is certainly possible that they would conclude that one who postpones reciting the additional prayer and comes last to the study hall is also a transgressor.

אָמְרִי: הֵיכִי נַעֲבֵיד? נַעַבְרֵיהּ – גְּמִירִי: מַעֲלִין בַּקֹּדֶשׁ וְאֵין מוֹרִידִין! נִדְרוֹשׁ מָר חֲדָא שַׁבְּתָא וּמָר חֲדָא שַׁבְּתָא – אָתֵי לְקַנְאוּיֵי! אֶלָּא: לִדְרוֹשׁ רַבָּן גַּמְלִיאֵל תְּלָתָא שַׁבְּתֵי, וְרַבִּי אֶלְעָזָר בֶּן עֲזַרְיָה חֲדָא שַׁבְּתָא. וְהַיְינוּ דְּאָמַר מָר: שַׁבָּת שֶׁל מִי הָיְתָה – שֶׁל רַבִּי אֶלְעָזָר בֶּן עֲזַרְיָה הָיְתָה. וְאוֹתוֹ תַּלְמִיד – רַבִּי שִׁמְעוֹן בֶּן יוֹחַאי הֲוָה.

The question arose what to do with Rabbi Elazar ben Azarya? **They said: What shall we do? Remove him** from his position. That is inappropriate as we **learned** a *halakha* through tradition: One **elevates** to a higher level of **sanctity and does not downgrade.** Therefore, one who was the *Nasi* of the Sanhedrin cannot be demoted. **Let one Sage lecture one week and the other Sage one week, they will come to be jealous** one of another, as they will be forced to appoint one as the acting head of the Sanhedrin. **Rather, Rabban Gamliel will lecture three weeks and Rabbi Elazar ben Azarya** will lecture as head of the yeshiva **one week.** That arrangement was adopted **and that is** the explanation of the exchange in tractate *Ḥagiga*: **Whose week was it? It was the week of Rabbi Elazar ben Azarya.** One final detail: **That student** who asked the original question that sparked this entire incident **was Rabbi Shimon ben Yoḥai.**

״וְשֶׁל מוּסָפִין כָּל הַיּוֹם.״ אָמַר רַבִּי יוֹחָנָן: וְנִקְרָא פּוֹשֵׁעַ.

We learned in the mishna: **And the additional prayer** may be recited **all day.**[H] **Rabbi Yoḥanan said:** Nevertheless, **one** who postpones his prayer excessively **is called negligent.**[N]

תָּנוּ רַבָּנַן: הָיוּ לְפָנָיו שְׁתֵּי תְפִלּוֹת, אַחַת שֶׁל מִנְחָה וְאַחַת שֶׁל מוּסָף – מִתְפַּלֵּל שֶׁל מִנְחָה וְאַחַר כָּךְ מִתְפַּלֵּל שֶׁל מוּסָף, שֶׁזּוֹ תְּדִירָה וְזוֹ אֵינָהּ תְּדִירָה. רַבִּי יְהוּדָה אוֹמֵר: מִתְפַּלֵּל שֶׁל מוּסָף וְאַחַר כָּךְ מִתְפַּלֵּל שֶׁל מִנְחָה, שֶׁזּוֹ מִצְוָה עוֹבֶרֶת וְזוֹ מִצְוָה שֶׁאֵינָהּ עוֹבֶרֶת. אָמַר רַבִּי יוֹחָנָן, הֲלָכָה: מִתְפַּלֵּל שֶׁל מִנְחָה וְאַחַר כָּךְ מִתְפַּלֵּל שֶׁל מוּסָף.

**The Rabbis taught** in a *baraita*: **If** the obligation to recite **two prayers was before him, one, the additional prayer and one, the afternoon prayer, he recites the afternoon prayer** first **and the additional prayer thereafter,** because **this,** the afternoon prayer, **is** recited on a **frequent** basis, **and this one,** the additional prayer, is recited on a relatively **infrequent** basis. **Rabbi Yehuda says: He recites the additional prayer** first **and the afternoon prayer thereafter,** because **this, the additional prayer, is a mitzva** whose time soon **elapses,** as it may only be recited until the seventh hour **and this, the afternoon prayer, is a mitzva** whose time does **not** soon **elapse** as one may recite it until the midpoint of the afternoon. **Rabbi Yoḥanan said: The *halakha*** is that **he recites the afternoon prayer** first **and the additional prayer thereafter,** in accordance with the opinion of the Rabbis.

רַבִּי זֵירָא כִּי הֲוָה חָלֵישׁ מִגִּירְסֵיהּ, הֲוָה אָזֵיל וְיָתֵיב אַפִּתְחָא דְּבֵי רַבִּי נָתָן בַּר טוֹבִי, אָמַר: כִּי חָלְפִי רַבָּנַן אֵיקוּם מִקַּמַּיְיהוּ וְאֶקַּבֵּל אַגְרָא. נְפַק אֲתָא רַבִּי נָתָן בַּר טוֹבִי, אָמַר לֵיהּ: מַאן אָמַר הֲלָכָה בֵּי מִדְרְשָׁא? אָמַר לֵיהּ, הָכִי אָמַר רַבִּי יוֹחָנָן: אֵין הֲלָכָה כְּרַבִּי יְהוּדָה דְּאָמַר: מִתְפַּלֵּל אָדָם שֶׁל מוּסָף וְאַחַר כָּךְ מִתְפַּלֵּל שֶׁל מִנְחָה.

The Gemara cites additional sources relating to this issue: **When Rabbi Zeira would tire of his studies, he would go and sit in the doorway of Rabbi Natan bar Tovi's study hall. He said** to himself: **When the** entering and exiting **Sages pass, I will rise before them and be rewarded** for the mitzva of honoring Torah scholars. **Rabbi Natan bar Tovi** himself **emerged and came** to where Rabbi Zeira was seated. Rabbi Zeira **said to him: Who** just **stated a *halakha* in the study hall?** Rabbi Natan bar Tovi **said to him: Rabbi Yoḥanan** just **said as follows: The *halakha* is not in accordance with** the opinion of **Rabbi Yehuda who said: He recites the additional prayer** first **and the afternoon prayer thereafter.**

אָמַר לֵיהּ: רַבִּי יוֹחָנָן אֲמָרָהּ?! אָמַר לֵיהּ: אִין. תְּנָא מִינֵּיהּ אַרְבְּעִין זִמְנִין. אָמַר לֵיהּ: חֲדָא הִיא לָךְ, אוֹ חֲדַת הִיא לָךְ? אָמַר לֵיהּ: חֲדַת הִיא לִי, מִשּׁוּם דִּמְסַפְּקָא לִי בְּרַבִּי יְהוֹשֻׁעַ בֶּן לֵוִי.

Rabbi Zeira **said to him:** Did **Rabbi Yoḥanan** himself **say** this *halakha*? Rabbi Natan **said to him: Yes. He learned** this statement **from him forty times,** etching it into his memory. Rabbi Natan **said to him:** Is this *halakha* so dear to you because **it is singular for you,** as it is the only *halakha* that you learned in the name of Rabbi Yoḥanan, **or is it new to you,** as you were previously unaware of this ruling? Rabbi Zeira **said to him:** It is somewhat **new to me, as I was uncertain** whether this *halakha* was said in the name of Rabbi Yoḥanan or in the name of **Rabbi Yehoshua ben Levi.** Now it is clear to me that this *halakha* is in the name of Rabbi Yoḥanan.

אָמַר רַבִּי יְהוֹשֻׁעַ בֶּן לֵוִי: כׇּל הַמִּתְפַּלֵּל תְּפִלָּה שֶׁל מוּסָפִין לְאַחַר שֶׁבַע שָׁעוֹת לְרַבִּי יְהוּדָה, עָלָיו הַכָּתוּב אוֹמֵר: ״נוּגֵי מִמּוֹעֵד אָסַפְתִּי מִמֵּךְ הָיוּ.״ מַאי מַשְׁמַע דְּהַאי ״נוּגֵי״ לִישָּׁנָא דִּתְבָרָא הוּא? כִּדְמְתַרְגֵּם רַב יוֹסֵף: ״תַּבְרָא אָתֵי עַל שַׂנְאֵיהוֹן דְּבֵית יִשְׂרָאֵל עַל דְּאַחַרוּ זִמְנֵי מוֹעֲדַיָּא דִּבִירוּשְׁלַיִם.״

**Rabbi Yehoshua ben Levi said:** With regard to **anyone who recites the additional prayer after seven hours** of the day, **according to Rabbi Yehuda, the verse states: "Those who are destroyed [*nugei*] far from the Festivals, I shall gather from you,** they who carried for you the burden of insult" (Zephaniah 3:18). **From where** may it **be inferred that *nugei* is an expression of destruction? As Rav Yosef translated** the verse into Aramaic: **Destruction comes upon the enemies of the house of Israel,** a euphemism for Israel itself, **for they have delayed the times of the Festivals in Jerusalem.** This proves both that *nugei* means destruction and that destruction comes upon those who fail to fulfill a mitzva at its appointed time.

אָמַר רַבִּי אֶלְעָזָר: כׇּל הַמִּתְפַּלֵּל תְּפִלָּה שֶׁל שַׁחֲרִית לְאַחַר אַרְבַּע שָׁעוֹת לְרַבִּי יְהוּדָה, עָלָיו הַכָּתוּב אוֹמֵר: ״נוּגֵי מִמּוֹעֵד אָסַפְתִּי מִמֵּךְ הָיוּ.״ מַאי מַשְׁמַע דְּהַאי ״נוּגֵי״ לִישָּׁנָא דְּצַעֲרָא הוּא? דִּכְתִיב: ״דָּלְפָה נַפְשִׁי מִתּוּגָה.״ רַב נַחְמָן בַּר יִצְחָק אָמַר, מֵהָכָא: ״בְּתוּלֹתֶיהָ נּוּגוֹת וְהִיא מַר לָהּ.״

Similarly, **Rabbi Elazar said: Regarding anyone who recites the morning prayer after four hours** of the day, **according to Rabbi Yehuda, the verse states: "Those who are in sorrow [*nugei*] far from the Festivals, I shall gather from you,** they who carried for you the burden of insult" (Zephaniah 3:18). **From where** may it **be inferred that *nugei* is an expression of sorrow? As it is written: "My soul drips in sorrow [*tuga*]"** (Psalms 119:28). **Rav Naḥman bar Yitzḥak said:** The proof that *nugei* indicates suffering is **from here: "Her virgins are sorrowed [*nugot*] and she is embittered"** (Lamentations 1:4).

רב אַוְיָא חֲלַשׁ וְלָא אֲתָא לְפִרְקָא דְּרַב יוֹסֵף. לְמָחָר כִּי אֲתָא, בְּעָא אַבַּיֵּי לְאַנּוּחֵי דַּעְתֵּיהּ דְּרַב יוֹסֵף. אֲמַר לֵיהּ: מַאי טַעְמָא לָא אֲתָא מָר לְפִרְקָא? אֲמַר לֵיהּ: דַּהֲוָה חֲלִישׁ לִבַּאי וְלָא מָצֵינָא. אֲמַר לֵיהּ: אַמַּאי לָא טְעַמְתְּ מִידֵּי וְאָתֵית? אֲמַר לֵיהּ: לָא סָבַר לַהּ מָר לְהָא דְּרַב הוּנָא? דְּאָמַר רַב הוּנָא: אָסוּר לוֹ לְאָדָם שֶׁיִּטְעוֹם כְּלוּם קוֹדֶם שֶׁיִּתְפַּלֵּל תְּפִלַּת הַמּוּסָפִין! – אֲמַר לֵיהּ: אִיבָּעֵי לֵיהּ לְמָר לְצַלּוֹיֵי צְלוֹתָא דְּמוּסָפֵי בְּיָחִיד, וְלִטְעוֹם מִידֵּי וְלֵיתֵי! – אֲמַר לֵיהּ: וְלָא סָבַר לַהּ מָר לְהָא דְּאָמַר רַבִּי יוֹחָנָן: אָסוּר לוֹ לְאָדָם שֶׁיַּקְדִּים תְּפִלָּתוֹ לִתְפִלַּת הַצִּבּוּר?! – אֲמַר לֵיהּ: לָאו אִתְּמַר עֲלַהּ: אָמַר רַבִּי אַבָּא: בְּצִבּוּר שָׁנוּ?!

After mentioning until when the additional prayer may be recited, the Gemara relates: **Rav Avya was ill and did not come to Rav Yosef's Shabbat lecture. When** Rav Avya **came the following day, Abaye sought to placate Rav Yosef,** and through a series of questions and answers sought to make clear to him that Rav Avya's failure to attend the lecture was not a display of contempt for Rav Yosef.

To this end, he asked him: **Why did the Master not attend the Shabbat lecture?**

Rav Avya **said to him: Because my heart was faint and I was unable** to attend.

Abaye **said to him: Why did you not eat something and come?**

Rav Avya **said to him:** Does **the Master not hold** in accordance with **that** statement **of Rav Huna? As Rav Huna said: A person may not taste anything before he recites the additional prayer.**[H]

Abaye **said to him: My Master should have recited the additional prayer individually, eaten something, and** then **come** to the lecture.

Rav Avya **said to him:** Does **my Master not hold** in accordance with **that** statement **of Rabbi Yoḥanan: A person may not recite his** individual **prayer prior to the communal prayer?**[H]

Abaye **said to him:** Was **it not stated regarding this** *halakha*, **Rabbi Abba said: They taught** this **in a communal** setting?

In other words, only one who is part of a congregation is prohibited from praying alone prior to the prayer of the congregation. Even though Rav Avya was incorrect, the reason for his failure to attend the lecture was clarified through this discussion.

וְלֵית הִלְכְתָא; לָא כְּרַב הוּנָא וְלָא כְּרַבִּי יְהוֹשֻׁעַ בֶּן לֵוִי; כְּרַב הוּנָא – הָא דַּאֲמַרַן, כְּרַבִּי יְהוֹשֻׁעַ בֶּן לֵוִי – דְּאָמַר רַבִּי יְהוֹשֻׁעַ בֶּן לֵוִי: כֵּיוָן שֶׁהִגִּיעַ זְמַן תְּפִלַּת מִנְחָה, אָסוּר לוֹ לְאָדָם שֶׁיִּטְעוֹם כְּלוּם קוֹדֶם שֶׁיִּתְפַּלֵּל תְּפִלַּת הַמִּנְחָה.

**And** the Gemara summarizes: **The** ***halakha*** **is neither in accordance with** the statement of **Rav Huna nor in accordance with** the statement of **Rabbi Yehoshua ben Levi.** The Gemara explains: It is not **in accordance with** the statement of **Rav Huna, as we said** above with regard to the prohibition to eat prior to the additional prayer. It is not **in accordance with** the statement of **Rabbi Yehoshua ben Levi, as Rabbi Yehoshua ben Levi said: Once the time** to recite **the afternoon prayer has arrived, a person may not taste anything before he recites the afternoon prayer.**[H]

מתני׳ רַבִּי נְחוּנְיָא בֶּן הַקָּנָה הָיָה מִתְפַּלֵּל בִּכְנִיסָתוֹ לְבֵית הַמִּדְרָשׁ וּבִיצִיאָתוֹ תְּפִלָּה קְצָרָה. אָמְרוּ לוֹ: מָה מָקוֹם לִתְפִלָּה זוֹ? אָמַר לָהֶם: בִּכְנִיסָתִי אֲנִי מִתְפַּלֵּל שֶׁלֹּא יֶאֱרַע דָּבָר תַּקָּלָה עַל יָדִי, וּבִיצִיאָתִי אֲנִי נוֹתֵן הוֹדָאָה עַל חֶלְקִי.

**MISHNA** In addition to the *halakhot* relating to the fixed prayers, the Gemara relates: **Rabbi Neḥunya ben Hakana would recite a brief prayer upon his entrance into the study hall and upon his exit. They said to him:** The study hall is not a dangerous place that would warrant a prayer when entering and exiting, so **what room is there for this prayer? He said to them: Upon my entrance, I pray that no mishap will transpire** caused **by me** in the study hall. **And upon my exit, I give thanks for my portion.**

גמ׳ תָּנוּ רַבָּנַן: בִּכְנִיסָתוֹ מַהוּ אוֹמֵר? יְהִי רָצוֹן מִלְּפָנֶיךָ ה׳ אֱלֹהַי שֶׁלֹּא יֶאֱרַע דְּבַר תַּקָּלָה עַל יָדִי, וְלֹא אֶכָּשֵׁל בִּדְבַר הֲלָכָה וְיִשְׂמְחוּ בִּי חֲבֵרַי, וְלֹא אוֹמַר עַל טָמֵא טָהוֹר וְלֹא עַל טָהוֹר טָמֵא, וְלֹא יִכָּשְׁלוּ חֲבֵרַי בִּדְבַר הֲלָכָה וְאֶשְׂמַח בָּהֶם.

**GEMARA** **The Sages taught** in a *baraita* the complete formula of Rabbi Neḥunya ben Hakana's prayer: **Upon his entrance, what does he say? May it be Your will, Lord my God, that no mishap** in determining the *halakha* **transpires** caused **by me, and that I not fail in any matter of** ***halakha***, **and that my colleagues,** who together with me engage in clarifying the *halakha*, **will rejoice in me.** He specified: **And that I will neither declare pure that which is impure, nor declare impure that which is pure and that my colleagues will not fail in any matter of** ***halakha***, **and that I will rejoice in them.**

בִּיצִיאָתוֹ מַהוּ אוֹמֵר? מוֹדֶה אֲנִי לְפָנֶיךָ ה׳ אֱלֹהַי שֶׁשַּׂמְתָּ חֶלְקִי מִיּוֹשְׁבֵי בֵּית הַמִּדְרָשׁ וְלֹא שַׂמְתָּ חֶלְקִי מִיּוֹשְׁבֵי קְרָנוֹת, שֶׁאֲנִי מַשְׁכִּים וְהֵם מַשְׁכִּימִים – אֲנִי מַשְׁכִּים לְדִבְרֵי תוֹרָה וְהֵם מַשְׁכִּימִים לִדְבָרִים בְּטֵלִים, אֲנִי עָמֵל וְהֵם עֲמֵלִים – אֲנִי עָמֵל וּמְקַבֵּל שָׂכָר וְהֵם עֲמֵלִים וְאֵינָם מְקַבְּלִים שָׂכָר, אֲנִי רָץ וְהֵם רָצִים – אֲנִי רָץ לְחַיֵּי הָעוֹלָם הַבָּא וְהֵם רָצִים לִבְאֵר שַׁחַת.

**Upon his exit, what did he say? I give thanks before You, Lord my God, that You have placed my lot among those who sit in the study hall, and that you have not given me my portion among those who sit** idly **on street corners. I rise early, and they rise early. I rise early** to pursue **matters of Torah, and they rise early** to pursue **frivolous matters. I toil and they toil. I toil and receive a reward, and they toil and do not receive a reward. I run and they run.**[N] **I run to the life of the World-to-Come and they run to the pit of destruction.**

### HALAKHA

**Tasting before the additional prayer – טְעִימָה קוֹדֶם מוּסָף:** One is permitted to taste a small amount of food, such as fruit or even bread, before the additional prayer, provided it is less than an egg-bulk. An actual meal, though, is prohibited. Some hold that this is prohibited by law (*Taz* according to medieval commentaries), while others hold that it is merely custom (*Baḥ* and *Magen Avraham*; *Shulḥan Arukh*, *Oraḥ Ḥayyim* 286:3).

**A person may not recite his individual prayer prior to the communal prayer – אָסוּר לוֹ לְאָדָם שֶׁיַּקְדִּים תְּפִלָּתוֹ לִתְפִלַּת הַצִּבּוּר:** One praying as part of a congregation may not recite his individual prayer before the rest of the congregation begins to pray, unless the designated time for prayer is passing and the congregation is extending the service by adding liturgy or for some other reason. This is in accordance with the conclusion in our Gemara based on the statement by Rabbi Yoḥanan (Rambam *Sefer Ahava, Hilkhot Tefilla* 10:16; *Shulḥan Arukh, Oraḥ Ḥayyim* 90:10).

**Tasting before the afternoon prayer – טְעִימָה קוֹדֶם מִנְחָה:** One is permitted to eat fruit or even bread prior to the afternoon prayer, provided it is less than a egg-bulk. An actual meal, however, is prohibited (*Shulḥan Arukh, Oraḥ Ḥayyim* 232:2–3).

### NOTES

**I run and they run – אֲנִי רָץ וְהֵם רָצִים:** In the course of one's life, everyone moves rapidly towards death. One engaged in Torah study runs toward life in the World-to-Come, while those engaged in idle pursuits run to the pit of destruction (*Talmidei Rabbeinu Yona*).

תָּנוּ רַבָּנַן: כְּשֶׁחָלָה רַבִּי אֱלִיעֶזֶר, נִכְנְסוּ תַּלְמִידָיו לְבַקְּרוֹ. אָמְרוּ לוֹ: רַבֵּינוּ, לַמְּדֵנוּ אוֹרְחוֹת חַיִּים וְנִזְכֶּה בָּהֶן לְחַיֵּי הָעוֹלָם הַבָּא.

On a similar note, the Gemara recounts related stories with different approaches. **The Sages taught: When Rabbi Eliezer fell ill, his students entered to visit him. They said to him: Teach us paths of life,** guidelines by which to live, **and we will thereby merit the life of the World-to-Come.**

אָמַר לָהֶם: הִזָּהֲרוּ בִּכְבוֹד חַבְרֵיכֶם, וּמִנְעוּ בְּנֵיכֶם מִן הַהִגָּיוֹן, וְהוֹשִׁיבוּם בֵּין בִּרְכֵּי תַּלְמִידֵי חֲכָמִים, וּכְשֶׁאַתֶּם מִתְפַּלְּלִים – דְּעוּ לִפְנֵי מִי אַתֶּם עוֹמְדִים, וּבִשְׁבִיל כָּךְ תִּזְכּוּ לְחַיֵּי הָעוֹלָם הַבָּא.

**He said to them: Be vigilant in the honor of your counterparts and prevent your children from logic** when studying verses that tend toward heresy (*ge'onim*),[N] **and place** your children, while they are still young, **between the knees of Torah scholars, and when you pray, know before Whom you stand. For doing that, you will merit the life of the World-to-Come.**

וּכְשֶׁחָלָה רַבִּי יוֹחָנָן בֶּן זַכַּאי, נִכְנְסוּ תַּלְמִידָיו לְבַקְּרוֹ. כֵּיוָן שֶׁרָאָה אוֹתָם הִתְחִיל לִבְכּוֹת. אָמְרוּ לוֹ תַּלְמִידָיו: נֵר יִשְׂרָאֵל, עַמּוּד הַיְמִינִי, פַּטִּישׁ הֶחָזָק, מִפְּנֵי מָה אַתָּה בּוֹכֶה?

A similar story is told about Rabbi Eliezer's mentor, Rabban Yoḥanan ben Zakkai:[P] When **Rabbi Yoḥanan ben Zakkai fell ill his students entered to visit him. When he saw them, he began to cry.**[N] **His students said to him: Lamp of Israel, the right pillar, the mighty hammer,** the man whose life's work is the foundation of the future of the Jewish people, **for what** reason **are you crying?** With a life as complete as yours, what is upsetting you?

אָמַר לָהֶם: אִילּוּ לִפְנֵי מֶלֶךְ בָּשָׂר וָדָם הָיוּ מוֹלִיכִין אוֹתִי, שֶׁהַיּוֹם כָּאן וּמָחָר בַּקֶּבֶר, שֶׁאִם כּוֹעֵס עָלַי – אֵין כַּעֲסוֹ כַּעַס עוֹלָם, וְאִם אוֹסְרֵנִי – אֵין אִיסּוּרוֹ אִיסּוּר עוֹלָם, וְאִם מְמִיתֵנִי – אֵין מִיתָתוֹ מִיתַת עוֹלָם, וַאֲנִי יָכוֹל לְפַיְּיסוֹ בִּדְבָרִים וּלְשַׁחֲדוֹ בְּמָמוֹן – אַף עַל פִּי כֵן הָיִיתִי בּוֹכֶה; וְעַכְשָׁיו שֶׁמּוֹלִיכִים אוֹתִי לִפְנֵי מֶלֶךְ מַלְכֵי הַמְּלָכִים הַקָּדוֹשׁ בָּרוּךְ הוּא, שֶׁהוּא חַי וְקַיָּים לְעוֹלָם וּלְעוֹלְמֵי עוֹלָמִים, שֶׁאִם כּוֹעֵס עָלַי – כַּעֲסוֹ כַּעַס עוֹלָם, וְאִם אוֹסְרֵנִי – אִיסּוּרוֹ אִיסּוּר עוֹלָם, וְאִם מְמִיתֵנִי – מִיתָתוֹ מִיתַת עוֹלָם, וְאֵינִי יָכוֹל לְפַיְּיסוֹ בִּדְבָרִים וְלֹא לְשַׁחֲדוֹ בְּמָמוֹן; וְלֹא עוֹד, אֶלָּא שֶׁיֵּשׁ לְפָנַי שְׁנֵי דְרָכִים, אַחַת שֶׁל גַּן עֵדֶן וְאַחַת שֶׁל גֵּיהִנָּם, וְאֵינִי יוֹדֵעַ בְּאֵיזוֹ מוֹלִיכִים אוֹתִי – וְלֹא אֶבְכֶּה?!

**He said to them:** I cry in fear of heavenly judgment, as the judgment of the heavenly court is unlike the judgment of man. **If they were leading me before a flesh and blood king** whose life is temporal **who is here today and** dead **in the grave tomorrow; if he is angry with me, his anger is not eternal** and, consequently, his punishment is not eternal; **if he incarcerates me, his incarceration is not an eternal incarceration,** as I might maintain my hope that I would ultimately be freed. **If he kills me, his killing is not for eternity,** as there is life after any death that he might decree. Moreover, **I am able to appease him with words** and even **bribe him with money,** and **even so I would cry** when standing before royal judgment. **Now that they are leading me before the supreme King of Kings, the Holy One, Blessed be He, Who lives and endures forever and all time; if He is angry with me, His anger is eternal; if He incarcerates me His incarceration is an eternal incarceration; and if He kills me His killing is for eternity. I am unable to appease Him with words and bribe him with money. Moreover, but I have two paths before me, one of the Garden of Eden and one of Gehenna, and I do not know on which they are leading me; and will I not cry?**

אָמְרוּ לוֹ: רַבֵּינוּ, בָּרְכֵנוּ! אָמַר לָהֶם: יְהִי רָצוֹן שֶׁתְּהֵא מוֹרָא שָׁמַיִם עֲלֵיכֶם כְּמוֹרָא בָּשָׂר וָדָם. אָמְרוּ לוֹ תַּלְמִידָיו: עַד כָּאן?! – אָמַר לָהֶם: וּלְוַאי! תֵּדְעוּ, כְּשֶׁאָדָם עוֹבֵר עֲבֵירָה אוֹמֵר: "שֶׁלֹּא יִרְאֵנִי אָדָם."

His students **said to him: Our teacher, bless us. He said to them: May it be** His **will that the fear of Heaven shall be upon you like the fear of flesh and blood. His students** were puzzled **and said: To that point** and not beyond? Shouldn't one fear God more? **He said to them: Would that** a person achieve that level of fear. **Know that when one commits a transgression, he says** to himself: I hope **that no man will see me.** If one was as concerned about avoiding shame before God as he is before man, he would never sin.

בִּשְׁעַת פְּטִירָתוֹ, אָמַר לָהֶם: פַּנּוּ כֵּלִים מִפְּנֵי הַטּוּמְאָה, וְהָכִינוּ כִּסֵּא לְחִזְקִיָּהוּ מֶלֶךְ יְהוּדָה שֶׁבָּא.

The Gemara relates that **at the time of his death,** immediately beforehand, **he said to them: Remove the vessels** from the house and take them outside **due to the ritual impurity** that will be imparted by my corpse, which they would otherwise contract. **And prepare a chair for Hezekiah, the King of Judea, who is coming**[N] from the upper world to accompany me.

מתני׳ רַבָּן גַּמְלִיאֵל אוֹמֵר: בְּכָל יוֹם וָיוֹם מִתְפַּלֵּל אָדָם שְׁמוֹנֶה עֶשְׂרֵה. רַבִּי יְהוֹשֻׁעַ אוֹמֵר: מֵעֵין שְׁמוֹנֶה עֶשְׂרֵה. רַבִּי עֲקִיבָא אוֹמֵר: אִם שְׁגוּרָה תְּפִלָּתוֹ בְּפִיו – מִתְפַּלֵּל שְׁמוֹנֶה עֶשְׂרֵה, וְאִם לָאו – מֵעֵין שְׁמוֹנֶה עֶשְׂרֵה.

**MISHNA** The mishna cites a dispute with regard to the obligation to recite the *Amida* prayer, also known as *Shemoneh Esreh*, the prayer of eighteen blessings, or simply as *tefilla*, prayer. **Rabban Gamliel says: Each and every day a person recites the** prayer of **eighteen blessings. Rabbi Yehoshua says:** A short prayer is sufficient, and one only recites **an abridged** version of the prayer of **eighteen blessings. Rabbi Akiva says** an intermediate opinion: **If he is fluent in his prayer, he recites the** prayer of **eighteen blessings, and if not,** he need only recite **an abridged** version of the prayer of **eighteen blessings.**[H]

רַבִּי אֱלִיעֶזֶר אוֹמֵר: הָעוֹשֶׂה תְּפִלָּתוֹ קֶבַע אֵין תְּפִלָּתוֹ תַּחֲנוּנִים.

**Rabbi Eliezer says: One whose prayer is fixed, his prayer is not supplication** and is flawed. The Gemara will clarify the halakhic implications of this flaw.

### NOTES

**And prevent your children from logic when studying verses that tend toward heresy – וּמִנְעוּ בְּנֵיכֶם מִן הַהִגָּיוֹן:** Many explanations were suggested for this phrase. According to Rashi, it means that one should prevent his children from studying Bible in general. Some say that it refers specifically to when the children merely study the Bible without understanding it. For this reason, they should be seated at the knee of a Torah scholar who will teach them the meaning of the text (*HaKotev*). Others explained that one should prevent children from studying the philosophical discipline of logic (Rav Hai Gaon). Yet others held that it means that one should prevent them from studying the Bible in a way that is not in accordance with the interpretation of the Sages (*Arukh*).

**He began to cry – הִתְחִיל לִבְכּוֹת:** Some say that he cried in order to enhance his students' fear of divine judgment and to spur them on to engage more fervently in Torah and mitzvot (*HaKotev*, *Ḥefetz Hashem*).

**Prepare a chair for Hezekiah, the King of Judea, who is coming – וְהָכִינוּ כִּסֵּא לְחִזְקִיָּהוּ מֶלֶךְ יְהוּדָה שֶׁבָּא:** Some say that it was specifically Hezekiah who appeared to Rabban Yoḥanan because he was one of his descendants (Rav Sa'adia Gaon). Others say that Hezekiah appeared because Rabban Yoḥanan, like Hezekiah before him, brought about an increase in the Torah study among the Jews (see Proverbs 25:1). This may also be interpreted symbolically. Hezekiah, as the representative of the royal House of David, was declaring that there is no anger over the fact that Rabbi Yoḥanan filled the position of *Nasi* in place of the descendants of Beit Hillel who were descendants of the House of David. It was also an allusion to the fact that the position of *Nasi*, the throne represented by the chair, would be restored to a descendant of the House of David, Rabban Gamliel (*Tziyyun LeNefesh Ḥayya*). Others interpret the appearance of King Hezekiah as a message that, although Hezekiah did not surrender when Assyria laid siege to Jerusalem, he approved of Rabban Yoḥanan's concessions to Roman rule as timely, and that is why he came to accompany him (Rabbi Y. A. Herzog).

### PERSONALITIES

**Rabban Yoḥanan ben Zakkai – רַבָּן יוֹחָנָן בֶּן זַכַּאי:** *Nasi* of the Sanhedrin following the destruction of the Temple, Rabban Yoḥanan ben Zakkai was among the greatest leaders of Israel of any generation. A priest, Rabban Yoḥanan ben Zakkai was one of the youngest students of Hillel the Elder. He led Israel for many years of his long life. Prior to the destruction of the Temple he lived in Beror Ḥayil, afterwards he moved to the city of Arev.

### HALAKHA

**If he is fluent in his prayer, he recites the prayer of eighteen blessings, and if not, he need only recite an abridged version of the prayer of eighteen blessings – אִם שְׁגוּרָה תְּפִלָּתוֹ בְּפִיו – מִתְפַּלֵּל שְׁמוֹנֶה עֶשְׂרֵה וְאִם לָאו מֵעֵין שְׁמוֹנֶה עֶשְׂרֵה:** One who stands in prayer and is fluent in the prayer is required to recite the entire *Amida* prayer. This is in accordance with Rabbi Akiva, who adopts the compromise position between the other two opinions. The *halakha* is generally ruled in accordance with his opinion. Only in exigent circumstances, i.e., when the time is passing or when traveling, may one recite the first three blessings of the *Amida* prayer, followed by *havinenu*, followed by the final three blessings. Even if it turns out that he does have time later to recite the entire *Amida* prayer, he need not do so (Rambam *Sefer Ahava*, *Hilkhot Tefilla* 2:2; *Shulḥan Arukh*, *Oraḥ Ḥayyim* 110:1).

רַבִּי יְהוֹשֻׁעַ אוֹמֵר: הַהוֹלֵךְ בִּמְקוֹם סַכָּנָה מִתְפַּלֵּל תְּפִלָּה קְצָרָה, וְאוֹמֵר: ״הוֹשַׁע ה׳ אֶת עַמְּךָ אֶת שְׁאֵרִית יִשְׂרָאֵל, בְּכׇל פָּרָשַׁת הָעִבּוּר יִהְיוּ צׇרְכֵיהֶם לְפָנֶיךָ, בָּרוּךְ אַתָּה ה׳ שׁוֹמֵעַ תְּפִלָּה.

**Rabbi Yehoshua says: One who** cannot recite a complete prayer because he **is walking in a place of danger, recites a brief prayer and says: Redeem, Lord, Your people, the remnant of Israel, at every transition** [*parashat ha'ibur*], the meaning of which will be discussed in the Gemara. **May their needs be before You. Blessed are You, Lord, Who listens to prayer.**

הָיָה רוֹכֵב עַל הַחֲמוֹר – יֵרֵד וְיִתְפַּלֵּל, וְאִם אֵינוֹ יָכוֹל לֵירֵד – יַחֲזִיר אֶת פָּנָיו, וְאִם אֵינוֹ יָכוֹל לְהַחֲזִיר אֶת פָּנָיו – יְכַוֵּין אֶת לִבּוֹ כְּנֶגֶד בֵּית קׇדְשֵׁי הַקֳּדָשִׁים. הָיָה מְהַלֵּךְ בִּסְפִינָה אוֹ בְּאַסְדָּא – יְכַוֵּין אֶת לִבּוֹ כְּנֶגֶד בֵּית קׇדְשֵׁי הַקֳּדָשִׁים.

While praying, one must face toward the direction of the Holy Temple. **One who was riding on a donkey should dismount and pray** calmly. **If he is unable to dismount, he should turn his face** toward the direction of the Temple. **If he is unable to turn his face,** it is sufficient that **he focus his heart opposite the Holy of Holies.** Similarly, **one who was traveling in a ship or on a raft** [*asda*][B] and is unable to turn and face in the direction of Jerusalem, **should focus his heart opposite the Holy of Holies.**

גמ׳ הָנֵי שְׁמוֹנֶה עֶשְׂרֵה כְּנֶגֶד מִי?

**GEMARA** Since the mishna deals with the fundamental obligation to recite the *Amida* prayer, the Gemara seeks to resolve fundamental problems pertaining to this prayer. **Corresponding to what were these eighteen** blessings instituted?[N] When the *Shemoneh Esreh* was instituted by the Sages, on what did they base the number of blessings?

אָמַר רַבִּי הִלֵּל בְּרֵיהּ דְּרַבִּי שְׁמוּאֵל בַּר נַחְמָנִי: כְּנֶגֶד שְׁמוֹנֶה עֶשְׂרֵה אַזְכָּרוֹת שֶׁאָמַר דָּוִד בְּ״הָבוּ לַה׳ בְּנֵי אֵלִים.״ רַב יוֹסֵף אָמַר: כְּנֶגֶד שְׁמוֹנֶה עֶשְׂרֵה אַזְכָּרוֹת שֶׁבִּקְרִיאַת שְׁמַע. אָמַר רַבִּי תַּנְחוּם אָמַר רַבִּי יְהוֹשֻׁעַ בֶּן לֵוִי: כְּנֶגֶד שְׁמוֹנֶה עֶשְׂרֵה חוּלְיוֹת שֶׁבַּשִּׁדְרָה.

**Rabbi Hillel, son of Rabbi Shmuel bar Naḥmani, said: Corresponding to the eighteen mentions of God's name** that King **David said** in the psalm: **"Give unto the Lord, O you sons of might"** (Psalms 29). **Rav Yosef said: Corresponding to the eighteen mentions of God's name in *Shema*. Rabbi Tanḥum said** that **Rabbi Yehoshua ben Levi said: Corresponding to the eighteen vertebrae in the spine** beneath the ribs.

וְאָמַר רַבִּי תַּנְחוּם אָמַר רַבִּי יְהוֹשֻׁעַ בֶּן לֵוִי: הַמִּתְפַּלֵּל צָרִיךְ שֶׁיִּכְרַע עַד שֶׁיִּתְפַּקְּקוּ כׇּל חוּלְיוֹת שֶׁבַּשִּׁדְרָה;

Since Rabbi Yehoshua ben Levi's opinion based the *Amida* prayer on the spinal vertebrae, the Gemara cites another statement of his that connects the two: **Rabbi Tanḥum said** that **Rabbi Yehoshua ben Levi said:** In those blessings where one is required to bow, **one who prays must bow**[H] **until all the vertebrae in the spine protrude.**

עוּלָּא אָמַר: עַד כְּדֵי שֶׁיִּרְאֶה אִיסָּר כְּנֶגֶד לִבּוֹ; רַבִּי חֲנִינָא אָמַר: כֵּיוָן שֶׁנִּעְנַע רֹאשׁוֹ שׁוּב אֵינוֹ צָרִיךְ. אָמַר רָבָא: וְהוּא – דִּמְצַעֵר נַפְשֵׁיהּ וּמֶחֱזֵי כְּמַאן דְּכָרַע.

Establishing a different indicator to determine when he has bowed sufficiently, **Ulla said:** Until **he can see a small coin** [*issar*],[B] on the ground before him **opposite his heart**[N] (Rav Hai Gaon). **Rabbi Ḥanina said:** There is room for leniency; **once he moves his head** forward, **he need not** bow any further. **Rava said: But that** applies only if **he is exerting himself** when doing so, **and he appears like one who is bowing.** However, if he is able, he should bow further.

הָנֵי תְּמָנֵי סְרֵי, תְּשַׁסְרֵי הָוְיָין!

Until now, the prayer of eighteen blessings has been discussed as if it was axiomatic. The Gemara wonders: Are **these eighteen** blessings? **They are nineteen.**

אָמַר רַבִּי לֵוִי: בִּרְכַּת הַמִּינִים בְּיַבְנֶה תִּקְנוּהָ. כְּנֶגֶד מִי תִּקְנוּהָ?

**Rabbi Levi said: The blessing of the heretics,** which curses informers, **was instituted in Yavne** and is not included in the original tally of blessings. Nevertheless, since the number of blessings corresponds to various allusions, the Gemara attempts to clarify: **Corresponding to what was** this nineteenth blessing **instituted?**

אָמַר רַבִּי לֵוִי: לְרַבִּי הִלֵּל בְּרֵיהּ דְּרַבִּי שְׁמוּאֵל בַּר נַחְמָנִי – כְּנֶגֶד ״אֵל הַכָּבוֹד הִרְעִים,״ לְרַב יוֹסֵף – כְּנֶגֶד ״אֶחָד״ שֶׁבִּקְרִיאַת שְׁמַע; לְרַבִּי תַּנְחוּם אָמַר רַבִּי יְהוֹשֻׁעַ בֶּן לֵוִי – כְּנֶגֶד חוּלְיָא קְטַנָּה שֶׁבַּשִּׁדְרָה.

**Rabbi Levi said: According to Rabbi Hillel, son of Rabbi Shmuel bar Naḥmani,** who said that the eighteen blessings correspond to the eighteen mentions of God's name that King David said in the psalm, the nineteenth blessing **corresponds to** a reference to God in that psalm, where a name other than the tetragrammaton was used: **"The God of glory thunders"** (Psalms 29:3). **According to Rav Yosef,** who said that the eighteen blessings correspond to the eighteen mentions of God's name in *Shema*, the additional blessing **corresponds to** the word **one that is in *Shema*.** Although it is not the tetragrammaton, it expresses the essence of faith in God. **According to** what **Rabbi Tanḥum** said that **Rabbi Yehoshua ben Levi said,** that the eighteen blessings correspond to the eighteen vertebrae in the spine, the additional blessing **corresponds to the small vertebra that is** at the bottom **of the spine.**

**BACKGROUND**

Raft [*asda*] – אַסְדָּא:

Babylonian raft from the First Temple period

*Issar* – אִיסָּר: The *issar* was one of the smallest coins, although a *peruta* was worth only an eighth of an *issar*, and was typically made of copper. The size of an *issar* is often used as a gauge of measurement in the Talmud.

Two sides of an *issar*

**NOTES**

**Corresponding to what were these eighteen blessings instituted** – הָנֵי שְׁמוֹנֶה עֶשְׂרֵה כְּנֶגֶד מִי: The Gemara was impelled to search for a source for eighteen blessings, as it elsewhere condemned excessive praise of God. Therefore, it cites an allusion to show that there is a solid foundation for this practice (*Penei Yehoshua*). The Jerusalem Talmud added: These blessings correspond to the eighteen times that Abraham, Isaac, and Jacob are mentioned in a single verse, and the eighteen mitzvot commanded in the construction of the Sanctuary.

**Until he can see an *issar* opposite his heart** – כְּדֵי שֶׁיִּרְאֶה אִיסָּר כְּנֶגֶד לִבּוֹ: There are several interpretations of this phrase. Rashi explains that when one bends over, there will be a wrinkle of flesh the size of an *issar* near his heart. Others explained that one standing opposite an individual who is bowing will be able to see no more than the size of an *issar* next to his heart (Rashi as quoted by *Talmidei Rabbeinu Yona*).

**HALAKHA**

**One who prays must bow, etc.** – הַמִּתְפַּלֵּל צָרִיךְ שֶׁיִּכְרַע וכו׳: In those blessings of the *Amida* prayer in which one is required to bow, he must do so until the vertebrae in the spine protrude. He should not bend so low that his head is level with his belt, as that appears arrogant. One who is sick or elderly may lower his head in a manner that makes it obvious that he wishes to bow (Rambam *Sefer Ahava*, *Hilkhot Tefilla* 5:12; *Shulḥan Arukh*, *Oraḥ Ḥayyim* 113:4–5).

תָּנוּ רַבָּנַן: שִׁמְעוֹן הַפַּקּוֹלִי הִסְדִּיר שְׁמוֹנֶה עֶשְׂרֵה בְּרָכוֹת לִפְנֵי רַבָּן גַּמְלִיאֵל עַל הַסֵּדֶר בְּיַבְנֶה. אָמַר לָהֶם רַבָּן גַּמְלִיאֵל לַחֲכָמִים: כְּלוּם יֵשׁ אָדָם שֶׁיּוֹדֵעַ לְתַקֵּן בִּרְכַּת הַמִּינִים? עָמַד שְׁמוּאֵל הַקָּטָן וְתִקְּנָהּ,

In light of the previous mention of the blessing of the heretics, the Gemara explains how this blessing was instituted: **The Sages taught: Shimon HaPakuli**[L] **arranged** the **eighteen blessings,** already extant during the period of the Great Assembly, **before Rabban Gamliel,** the *Nasi* of the Sanhedrin, **in order**[N] **in Yavne.** Due to prevailing circumstances, there was a need to institute a new blessing directed against the heretics. **Rabban Gamliel said to the Sages: Is there any person who knows to institute the blessing of the heretics,** a blessing directed against the Sadducees? **Shmuel HaKatan,** who was one of the most pious men of that generation, **stood and instituted it.**

לְשָׁנָה אַחֶרֶת שְׁכָחָהּ.

The Gemara relates: **The next year,** when Shmuel HaKatan served as the prayer leader, **he forgot** that blessing,

**LANGUAGE**

**HaPakuli** – הַפַּקּוֹלִי: Shimon HaPakuli was referred to as such because of his profession, for he worked with bundles. φάκελος, *fakelos,* is Greek for a bundle of wood.

**NOTES**

**Arranged…in order** – הִסְדִּיר...עַל הַסֵּדֶר: Although the members of the Great Assembly instituted the formulas of the individual blessings, each individual recited only those blessings relevant to him (*Talmidei Rabbeinu Yona*). Alternatively, perhaps there was no definite order to the blessings (*Ḥefetz Hashem*), and Shimon HaPakuli came and established a definite order. "Arranged…in order," indicates that one who failed to recite the *Amida* prayer in that order did not fulfill his obligation (*Alfasi Zuta*).

## Perek **IV**
## Daf **29** Amud **a**

וְהִשְׁקִיף בָּהּ שְׁתַּיִם וְשָׁלֹשׁ שָׁעוֹת וְלֹא הֶעֱלוּהוּ.

**and scrutinized it,** in an attempt to remember the blessing for **two or three hours, and they did not remove him** from serving as prayer leader.

אַמַּאי לֹא הֶעֱלוּהוּ? וְהָאָמַר רַב יְהוּדָה אָמַר רַב: טָעָה בְּכָל הַבְּרָכוֹת כּוּלָּן – אֵין מַעֲלִין אוֹתוֹ, בְּבִרְכַּת הַמִּינִים – מַעֲלִין אוֹתוֹ, חָיְישִׁינַן שֶׁמָּא מִין הוּא!

The Gemara asks: **Why did they not remove him? Didn't Rav Yehuda say** that **Rav said:** One who was serving as the prayer leader before the congregation and **erred in** reciting **any of the blessings,**[H] **they do not remove him** from serving as the prayer leader. However, one who erred while reciting **the blessing of the heretics they remove him,** as **we suspect that perhaps he is a heretic** and intentionally omitted the blessing to avoid cursing himself. Why, then, did they not remove Shmuel HaKatan?[P]

שָׁאנֵי שְׁמוּאֵל הַקָּטָן, דְּאִיהוּ תִּקְּנָהּ.

The Gemara answers: **Shmuel HaKatan is different because he instituted** this blessing and there is no suspicion of him.

וְנֵיחוּשׁ דִּלְמָא הֲדַר בֵּיהּ! אָמַר אַבַּיֵי, גְּמִירִי: טָבָא לָא הָוֵי בִּישָׁא.

The Gemara continues: **Let us suspect** that **perhaps he reconsidered** and, although he had been righteous, he had a change of heart? **Abaye said: We learned** through tradition that a **good** person **does not become wicked.**

וְלָא?! וְהָכְתִיב "וּבְשׁוּב צַדִּיק מִצִּדְקָתוֹ וְעָשָׂה עָוֶל"! הַהוּא רָשָׁע מֵעִיקָּרוֹ, אֲבָל צַדִּיק מֵעִיקָּרוֹ – לֹא.

The Gemara challenges this: **And** does he **not** become wicked? **Isn't it** explicitly **written: "And when the righteous one returns from his righteousness and does wicked** like all of the abominations that the wicked one has done, will he live? All of the righteous deeds that he has done will not be remembered given the treachery that he has carried out, and in his sin that he has transgressed, for these he shall die" (Ezekiel 18:24)? Abaye responds: **That** verse refers to a righteous individual who was **initially wicked**[N] and repented, but ultimately returned to his evil ways. **However, one who is initially righteous** does **not** become wicked.

וְלֹא?! וְהָא תְּנַן: אַל תַּאֲמִין בְּעַצְמְךָ עַד יוֹם מוֹתְךָ, שֶׁהֲרֵי יוֹחָנָן כֹּהֵן גָּדוֹל שִׁמֵּשׁ בִּכְהוּנָּה גְּדוֹלָה שְׁמוֹנִים שָׁנָה וּלְבַסּוֹף נַעֲשָׂה צְדוֹקִי!

The Gemara asks: **And** does he **not** become wicked? **Didn't we learn** in a mishna: **Do not be sure of yourself until the day you die, as Yoḥanan the High Priest served in the High Priesthood for eighty years and ultimately became a Sadducee.** Even one who is outstanding in his righteousness can become a heretic.

אָמַר אַבַּיֵי: הוּא יַנַּאי הוּא יוֹחָנָן. רָבָא אָמַר: יַנַּאי לְחוּד וְיוֹחָנָן לְחוּד, יַנַּאי – רָשָׁע מֵעִיקָּרוֹ, וְיוֹחָנָן – צַדִּיק מֵעִיקָּרוֹ. הָנִיחָא לְאַבַּיֵי, אֶלָּא לְרָבָא קַשְׁיָא!

**Abaye responded: He is Yannai he is Yoḥanan.**[N] In other words, from its inception, the entire Hasmonean dynasty had the same positive attitude toward the Sadducees, and there was no distinction between Yoḥanan Hyrcanus and Alexander Yannai. Yoḥanan the High Priest had Sadducee leanings from the outset. **Rava said: Yannai is distinct and Yoḥanan is distinct.** They did not share the same position in this regard. **Yannai was wicked from the outset and Yoḥanan was righteous from the outset.** If so, **it works out well according to Abaye's** opinion; **however, according to Rava's** opinion, **it is difficult.** How could Yoḥanan, a righteous individual, have changed and turned wicked?

**HALAKHA**

**One who erred in reciting any of the blessings** – טָעָה בְּכָל הַבְּרָכוֹת: A communal prayer leader who inadvertently omits a blessing, or even several blessings (*Taz, Perisha*) in the *Amida* prayer, is not replaced. Rather, they wait a while and jog his memory, and he then he resumes his prayer from the blessing that he omitted. One who skips the blessing of the heretics is replaced immediately. However, if he began reciting that blessing and only then erred, he need not be replaced. With regard to other blessings, if he omitted them intentionally, he is immediately replaced (*Mishna Berura*; Rambam *Sefer Ahava, Hilkhot Tefilla* 10:3; *Shulḥan Arukh, Oraḥ Ḥayyim* 126:1).

**PERSONALITIES**

**Shmuel HaKatan** – שְׁמוּאֵל הַקָּטָן: One of the *tanna'im* from the era of the destruction of the Temple, Shmuel HaKatan [The Small] was among the outstanding pious men of his generation and was well known for his humility and love of humanity. The Gemara relates that a Heavenly Voice emerged and proclaimed that he was among those worthy of divine inspiration, though his generation was not worthy. Indeed, the Gemara also relates prophecies that he uttered at the time of his death.

**NOTES**

**Righteous individual who was initially wicked** – רָשָׁע מֵעִיקָּרוֹ: Some find evidence for this interpretation from the language of the verse: "And when the righteous one returns from his righteousness." In other words, he is reverting to his previous condition (Mahari).

**He is Yannai he is Yoḥanan** – הוּא יַנַּאי הוּא יוֹחָנָן: This dispute with regard to Yannai and Yoḥanan alludes to the general assessment of the entire royal house of the Hasmoneans. In this passage, Yoḥanan the High Priest symbolizes all the Hasmonean kings who served as High Priests for approximately eighty years. Ultimately, the degree to which they distanced themselves from the Pharisee tradition and drew closer to the Sadducee tradition became more and more evident, culminating in the reign of Alexander Yannai. The dispute here focuses on whether their dynasty was flawed from its inception or whether it deteriorated over time.

אָמַר לָךְ רָבָא: צַדִּיק מֵעִיקָּרוֹ נָמֵי, דִּלְמָא הָדַר בֵּיהּ. אִי הָכִי, אַמַּאי לֹא אַסְּקוּהוּ?

The Gemara responds: **Rava** could have **said to you:** There is **also** room for concern **that one who is righteous from the outset will perhaps reconsider** and turn wicked, as was the case with Yoḥanan the High Priest. **If so,** the original question is difficult: **Why did they not remove** Shmuel HaKatan from serving as the prayer leader?

שָׁאנֵי שְׁמוּאֵל הַקָּטָן דְּאַתְחֵיל בַּהּ. דְּאָמַר רַב יְהוּדָה אָמַר רַב, וְאִיתֵּימָא רַבִּי יְהוֹשֻׁעַ בֶּן לֵוִי: לֹא שָׁנוּ אֶלָּא שֶׁלֹּא הִתְחִיל בָּהּ, אֲבָל הִתְחִיל בָּהּ - גּוֹמְרָהּ.

The Gemara answers: The case of **Shmuel HaKatan is different, as he began** reciting the blessing of the heretics and while reciting it he became confused and forgot the end of the blessing. Consequently, he was not suspected of heretical leanings. Indeed, **Rav Yehuda said** that **Rav, and some say** that **Rabbi Yehoshua ben Levi, said: They only taught** that one who errs while reciting the blessing of the heretics is removed in a case **where he did not begin** reciting **it. But** if he **began** reciting **it,** then we allow him to collect his thoughts **and finish** reciting **it.**

הָנֵי שֶׁבַע דְּשַׁבְּתָא כְּנֶגֶד מִי? אָמַר רַבִּי חֲלַפְתָּא בֶּן שָׁאוּל: כְּנֶגֶד שִׁבְעָה קוֹלוֹת שֶׁאָמַר דָּוִד עַל הַמַּיִם.

To this point, the Gemara discussed allusions to the nineteen blessings that constitute the weekday *Amida* prayer. The Gemara asks: **Corresponding to what** were **these seven** blessings **of the Shabbat** *Amida* prayer instituted? The Gemara answers: **Rabbi Ḥalafta ben Shaul said: Corresponding to the seven "voices" which David mentioned on the waters;** in other words, the seven times that "the voice of God" is mentioned in Psalms 29, which served as the source for the weekday prayer.

הָנֵי תֵּשַׁע דְּרֹאשׁ הַשָּׁנָה כְּנֶגֶד מִי? אָמַר רַבִּי יִצְחָק דְּמִן קַרְטִיגְנִין: כְּנֶגֶד תִּשְׁעָה אַזְכָּרוֹת שֶׁאָמְרָה חַנָּה בִּתְפִלָּתָהּ, דְּאָמַר מָר: בְּרֹאשׁ הַשָּׁנָה נִפְקְדָה שָׂרָה רָחֵל וְחַנָּה.

The Gemara asks further: **Corresponding to what** were **these nine** blessings **of the Rosh HaShana** additional prayer instituted? **Rabbi Yitzḥak of Kartignin said:** They **correspond to the nine mentions of God's name that Hannah said in her prayer** (1 Samuel 2:10). The connection between Hannah's prayer and Rosh HaShana is based on what **the Master said: On Rosh HaShana, Sarah, Rachel, and Hannah were remembered** and the divine decree that they would conceive their sons was issued.

הָנֵי עֶשְׂרִים וְאַרְבַּע דְּתַעֲנִיתָא כְּנֶגֶד מִי? אָמַר רַבִּי חֶלְבּוֹ: כְּנֶגֶד עֶשְׂרִים וְאַרְבַּע רְנָנוֹת שֶׁאָמַר שְׁלֹמֹה בְּשָׁעָה שֶׁהִכְנִיס אָרוֹן לְבֵית קָדְשֵׁי הַקֳּדָשִׁים. אִי הָכִי, כָּל יוֹמָא נָמֵי נֵמְרִינְהוּ! אֵימַת אֲמָרִינְהוּ שְׁלֹמֹה - בְּיוֹמָא דְּרַחֲמֵי, אֲנַן נָמֵי בְּיוֹמָא דְּרַחֲמֵי אָמְרִי לְהוּ.

The Gemara continues: **Corresponding to what** were **these twenty-four** blessings **of the** *Amida* prayer of **the fast** days instituted? **Rabbi Ḥelbo said:** They **correspond to the twenty-four "songs" that Solomon said when he brought the ark into the Holy of Holies** during the dedication of the Temple, as there are twenty-four expressions of song, prayer, and supplication there (1 Kings 8). The Gemara asks: **If so, then let us say these** twenty-four blessing **every day.** The Gemara answers: **When did Solomon say them? On a day** of supplication for **mercy. We, too, say them on a day of** supplication for **mercy.**

"רַבִּי יְהוֹשֻׁעַ אוֹמֵר מֵעֵין שְׁמוֹנֶה עֶשְׂרֵה." מַאי מֵעֵין שְׁמוֹנֶה עֶשְׂרֵה? רַב אָמַר: מֵעֵין כָּל בְּרָכָה וּבְרָכָה, וּשְׁמוּאֵל אָמַר: "הֲבִינֵנוּ ה׳ אֱלֹהֵינוּ לָדַעַת דְּרָכֶיךָ, וּמוֹל אֶת לְבָבֵנוּ לְיִרְאָתֶךָ, וְתִסְלַח לָנוּ לִהְיוֹת גְּאוּלִים, וְרַחֲקֵנוּ מִמַּכְאוֹבֵינוּ, וְדַשְּׁנֵנוּ בִּנְאוֹת אַרְצֶךָ, וּנְפוּצוֹתֵינוּ מֵאַרְבַּע תְּקַבֵּץ, וְהַתּוֹעִים עַל דַּעְתְּךָ יִשָּׁפֵטוּ, וְעַל הָרְשָׁעִים תָּנִיף יָדֶיךָ, וְיִשְׂמְחוּ צַדִּיקִים בְּבִנְיַן עִירֶךָ וּבְתִקּוּן הֵיכָלֶךָ וּבִצְמִיחַת קֶרֶן לְדָוִד עַבְדֶּךָ וּבַעֲרִיכַת נֵר לְבֶן יִשַׁי מְשִׁיחֶךָ, טֶרֶם נִקְרָא אַתָּה תַעֲנֶה, בָּרוּךְ אַתָּה ה׳ שׁוֹמֵעַ תְּפִלָּה."

We learned in the mishna that **Rabbi Yehoshua says** that each day one recites **an abridged** version of the prayer of **eighteen blessings.** The Gemara asks: **What** is the **abridged** version of the prayer of **eighteen blessings?** There are different opinions. **Rav said:** One recites **an abridged** version **of each and every blessing. Shmuel said:** An abridged version of the prayer of eighteen blessings refers to a blessing composed specifically to be recited in place of the thirteen middle blessings. It contains references to each of the thirteen middle blessings. The formula for that blessing is: **Grant us understanding, Lord our God, to know Your ways, and sensitize our hearts so that we may revere You, and forgive us so that we may be redeemed, and keep us far from our suffering, and satisfy us with the pastures of Your land, and gather our scattered** people **from the four** corners of the earth, **and those who go astray shall be judged according to Your will, and raise Your hand against the wicked, and may the righteous rejoice in the rebuilding of Your city, and the restoration of Your Sanctuary, and in the flourishing of Your servant David, and in establishing a light for Your Messiah, son of Yishai. Before we call, may You answer. Blessed are You, Lord, Who listens to prayer."**

לָיֵיט עֲלַהּ אַבָּיֵי אַמַּאן דִּמְצַלֵּי "הֲבִינֵנוּ."

Although Shmuel mentioned this abridged prayer, **Abaye would curse anyone**[N] **who recited** the prayer: **Grant us understanding,** as he held that one may recite it only in exigent circumstances (Rabbi Ḥananel, *Me'iri*).

NOTES

**Would curse anyone** – לָיֵיט עֲלַהּ: This means that Abaye disapproved of this custom and would harshly criticize those who followed it. This is the meaning of this phrase throughout the Talmud.

HALAKHA

One may recite: Grant us understanding throughout the entire year, except for – כָּל הַשָּׁנָה כּוּלָּהּ מִתְפַּלֵּל אָדָם הֲבִינֵנוּ חוּץ: One does not recite: Grant us understanding, during the rainy season because one must include the request for rain, which does not appear in the formula of the blessing. Similarly, one does not recite: Grant us understanding at the conclusion of Shabbat, because *havdala* does not appear in the formula of the blessing. Others explain that it may not be recited at the conclusion of Shabbat because it is liable to create the mistaken impression that the *halakha* is in accordance with the opinion of Rabbi Akiva. Some are uncertain whether or not, in exigent circumstances, i.e., if the time to recite the prayer is passing, one would be permitted to recite: Grant us understanding at the conclusion of Shabbat, even though it does not include *havdala* (Rabbi Akiva Eiger). The *Biur Halakha* rules that it is permitted (Rambam *Sefer Ahava*, *Hilkhot Tefilla* 2:4; *Shulḥan Arukh*, *Oraḥ Ḥayyim* 110:1).

One who erred and did not recite the request for rain in the blessing of the years – טָעָה...שְׁאֵלָה בְּבִרְכַּת הַשָּׁנִים: If he failed to request rain in the blessing of the years, he recites the request in the blessing: Who listens to prayer. If he only realized his omission after completing that blessing, but prior to beginning the blessing of Temple service: Find favor, he immediately recites the request for rain and then continues with the following blessing. If he began the next blessing but has not yet completed the *Amida* prayer, he returns to the blessing of the years and continues from there. However, if he completed the *Amida* prayer, he must repeat the prayer from the beginning. That is the conclusion of the Gemara according to the Rif and the Rambam (Rambam *Sefer Ahava*, *Hilkhot Tefilla* 10:9; *Shulḥan Arukh*, *Oraḥ Ḥayyim* 117:5).

PERSONALITIES

Rav Beivai bar Abaye – רַב בֵּיבַי בַּר אַבַּיֵי: Rav Beivai was a fifth generation Babylonian *amora* and apparently the son of Abaye, Rava's friend and colleague. There is no available information with regard to the identity of his teachers. Presumably, he studied with his father and the other Sages of the previous generation. He engaged in halakhic discussions primarily with Rav Pappa and Rav Huna, son of Rav Yehoshua. Apparently, he lived in Pumbedita and worked with his father as a farmer. His statements appear throughout the Talmud, although he never headed his own yeshiva. Rav Beivai engaged in the study of esoterica and many of his statements in that area are found in the Talmud.

אָמַר רַב נַחְמָן אָמַר שְׁמוּאֵל: כָּל הַשָּׁנָה כּוּלָּהּ מִתְפַּלֵּל אָדָם "הֲבִינֵנוּ," חוּץ מִמּוֹצָאֵי שַׁבָּת וּמִמּוֹצָאֵי יָמִים טוֹבִים, מִפְּנֵי שֶׁצָּרִיךְ לוֹמַר הַבְדָּלָה בְּ"חוֹנֵן הַדַּעַת."

The Gemara further restricts the occasions when one may recite the abridged prayer. **Rav Naḥman said** that **Shmuel said: One may recite: Grant us understanding throughout the entire year, except for**[H] in the **evening** prayer **or at the conclusion of Shabbat and at the conclusion of Festivals, because he must recite** the prayer of **distinction [*havdala*]** in the blessing: **Who graciously grants knowledge.**

מַתְקִיף לַהּ רַבָּה בַּר שְׁמוּאֵל: וְנֵימְרַהּ בְּרָכָה רְבִיעִית בִּפְנֵי עַצְמָהּ! מִי לָא תְּנַן, רַבִּי עֲקִיבָא אוֹמֵר: אוֹמְרָהּ בְּרָכָה רְבִיעִית בִּפְנֵי עַצְמָהּ; רַבִּי אֱלִיעֶזֶר אוֹמֵר: בְּהוֹדָאָה!

**Rabba bar Shmuel strongly objects to this:** After reciting the three initial blessings, **let us say *havdala* as an independent fourth blessing,** and afterwards recite the prayer of **Grant us understanding.** This is feasible. **Didn't we learn** in a mishna that **Rabbi Akiva says: He says *havdala* as an independent fourth blessing? Rabbi Eliezer says:** He says *havdala* **in** the blessing of **thanksgiving.**

אַטּוּ כָּל הַשָּׁנָה כּוּלָּהּ מִי עָבְדִינַן כְּרַבִּי עֲקִיבָא, דְּהַשְׁתָּא נַמִי נַעֲבֵיד?! כָּל הַשָּׁנָה כּוּלָּהּ מַאי טַעְמָא לָא עָבְדִינַן כְּרַבִּי עֲקִיבָא – תְּמָנֵי סְרֵי תַּקּוּן, תְּשַׁסְרֵי לָא תַּקּוּן; הָכָא נַמִי – שְׁבַע תַּקּוּן, תְּמָנֵי לָא תַּקּוּן.

The Gemara responds: **Do we practice in accordance with** the opinion of **Rabbi Akiva throughout the entire year** regarding this issue, **that we will also practice** this way **now? Throughout the entire year, what is the reason that we do not practice in accordance with** the opinion of **Rabbi Akiva?** Because **they instituted eighteen** blessings, **they did not institute nineteen. Here too, they instituted seven** blessings, **they did not institute eight.** Therefore, the possibility to recite *havdala* as an independent fourth blessing is rejected.

מַתְקִיף לַהּ מָר זוּטְרָא: וְנִכְלְלַהּ מִכְּלָל "הֲבִינֵנוּ ה' אֱלֹהֵינוּ הַמַּבְדִּיל בֵּין קֹדֶשׁ לְחוֹל"! קַשְׁיָא.

**Mar Zutra strongly objects to this: Let us include *havdala*** in the **framework** of the abridged blessing: **Grant us understanding, Lord our God, Who distinguishes between sacred and profane.** No response was offered to this objection, and it remains **difficult.**

אָמַר רַב בֵּיבַי בַּר אַבַּיֵי: כָּל הַשָּׁנָה כּוּלָּהּ מִתְפַּלֵּל אָדָם "הֲבִינֵנוּ" חוּץ מִימוֹת הַגְּשָׁמִים, מִפְּנֵי שֶׁצָּרִיךְ לוֹמַר שְׁאֵלָה בְּבִרְכַּת הַשָּׁנִים. מַתְקִיף לַהּ מָר זוּטְרָא: וְנִכְלְלַהּ מִכְּלָל "וְדַשְּׁנֵנוּ בִּנְאוֹת אַרְצֶךָ וְתֵן טַל וּמָטָר"!

**Rav Beivai bar Abaye**[P] **said:** There is an additional restriction that applies to the abridged prayer. **One may recite Grant us understanding throughout the entire year, except during the rainy season, because he must recite the request** for rain **in the blessing of the years. Mar Zutra strongly objects to this: Let us include** the request for rain in the **framework** of the abridged blessing: **And satisfy us with the pastures of Your land, and grant dew and rain.**

אָתֵי לְאִטְרוּדֵי. אִי הָכִי, הַבְדָּלָה בְּ"חוֹנֵן הַדַּעַת" נַמִי אָתֵי לְאִטְרוּדֵי!

The Gemara responds: That is unfeasible, as he will **become confused** by introducing a new element to the standard formula of the blessing. The Gemara asks: **If so,** by introducing ***havdala* in** the framework of the abridged blessing in the section alluding to the blessing, **Who graciously grants knowledge,** he will **also become confused.** Why did the Gemara fail to respond to Mar Zutra's strong objection with regard to *havdala* in that manner?

אָמְרִי: הָתָם כֵּיוָן דְּאָתְיָא בִּתְחִלַּת צְלוֹתָא – לָא מִטְרִיד, הָכָא כֵּיוָן דְּאָתְיָא בְּאֶמְצַע צְלוֹתָא – מִטְרִיד.

The Gemara answers: **They say** that these cases are different: **There,** regarding *havdala,* **since** the introduction of the new element **comes at the beginning of the prayer, he will not** become **confused. Here, since** the request for rain **comes in the middle of the prayer, he will** become **confused.**

מַתְקִיף לַהּ רַב אַשִׁי: וְנֵימְרַהּ בְּ"שׁוֹמֵעַ תְּפִלָּה"! דְּאָמַר רַבִּי תַּנְחוּם אָמַר רַב אַסִי: טָעָה וְלֹא הִזְכִּיר גְּבוּרוֹת גְּשָׁמִים בִּתְחִיַּית הַמֵּתִים – מַחֲזִירִין אוֹתוֹ, שְׁאֵלָה בְּבִרְכַּת הַשָּׁנִים – אֵין מַחֲזִירִין אוֹתוֹ, מִפְּנֵי שֶׁיָּכוֹל לְאוֹמְרָהּ בְּ"שׁוֹמֵעַ תְּפִלָּה," וְהַבְדָּלָה בְּ"חוֹנֵן הַדַּעַת" – אֵין מַחֲזִירִין אוֹתוֹ, מִפְּנֵי שֶׁיָּכוֹל לְאוֹמְרָהּ עַל הַכּוֹס! – טָעָה שָׁאנֵי.

**Rav Ashi strongly objects to this:** If so, **let us say** the request for rain **in** the framework of the abridged blessing in the section alluding to the blessing **Who listens to prayer. As Rabbi Tanḥum said** that **Rav Asi said: One who erred and did not mention the might of the rains** in the blessing on **the revival of the dead, we require him to return** to the beginning of the prayer and repeat it. However, one who erred and failed to recite **the request** for rain **in** the ninth blessing of the *Amida,* **the blessing of the years,**[H] **we do not require him to return** to the beginning of the prayer and repeat it **because he can recite it in** the blessing **Who listens to prayer. And** one who erred and failed to recite ***havdala* in** the blessing **Who graciously grants knowledge, we do not require him to return** to the beginning of the prayer and repeat it, **as he can recite** *havdala* **over the cup** of wine. One can ask for rain in the blessing Who listens to prayer, and, consequently, can introduce it at the end of the abridged blessing without becoming confused. The Gemara responds: **One who erred is different,** and only then does he have the option to ask for rain in the blessing Who listens to prayer. *Ab initio,* the request for rain may not be inserted there.

גּוּפָא, אָמַר רַבִּי תַּנְחוּם אָמַר רַב אַסִי: טָעָה וְלֹא הִזְכִּיר גְּבוּרוֹת גְּשָׁמִים בִּתְחִיַּית הַמֵּתִים – מַחֲזִירִין אוֹתוֹ, שְׁאֵלָה בְּבִרְכַּת הַשָּׁנִים – אֵין מַחֲזִירִין אוֹתוֹ, מִפְּנֵי שֶׁיָּכוֹל לְאוֹמְרָהּ בְּ"שׁוֹמֵעַ תְּפִלָּה," וְהַבְדָּלָה בְּ"חוֹנֵן הַדַּעַת" – אֵין מַחֲזִירִין אוֹתוֹ, מִפְּנֵי שֶׁיָּכוֹל לְאוֹמְרָהּ עַל הַכּוֹס.

The statement that Rabbi Tanḥum said that Rav Asi said was incidental to the previous discussion. The Gemara attempts to understand **the matter itself. Rabbi Tanḥum said** that **Rav Asi said: One who erred and did not mention the might of the rains** in the blessing on **the revival of the dead, we require him to return** to the beginning of the prayer and repeat it. However, one who erred and failed to recite **the request** for rain **in the blessing of the years, we do not require him to return** to the beginning of the prayer and repeat it **because he can recite it in** the blessing **Who listens to prayer. And** one who erred and failed to recite ***havdala*** **in** the blessing **Who graciously grants knowledge, we do not require him to return** to the beginning of the prayer and repeat it, **as he can recite** *havdala* **over the cup** of wine.

מֵיתִיבֵי: טָעָה וְלֹא הִזְכִּיר גְּבוּרוֹת גְּשָׁמִים בִּתְחִיַּית הַמֵּתִים – מַחֲזִירִין אוֹתוֹ, שְׁאֵלָה בְּבִרְכַּת הַשָּׁנִים – מַחֲזִירִין אוֹתוֹ, וְהַבְדָּלָה בְּ"חוֹנֵן הַדַּעַת" – אֵין מַחֲזִירִין אוֹתוֹ, מִפְּנֵי שֶׁיָּכוֹל לְאוֹמְרָהּ עַל הַכּוֹס!

The Gemara **raised an objection** based on what was taught in the *Tosefta*: **One who erred and did not mention the might of the rains** in the blessing on **the revival of the dead, we require him to return** to the beginning of the prayer and repeat it. One who erred and failed to recite **the request** for rain **in the blessing of the years, we require him to return** to the beginning of the prayer and repeat it. However, one who erred and failed to recite ***havdala*** **in** the blessing **Who graciously grants knowledge, we do not require him to return** to the beginning of the prayer and repeat it, **as he can recite** *havdala* **over the cup** of wine. The *Tosefta* contradicts the statement of Rabbi Tanḥum with regard to one who erred and failed to recite the request for rain in the blessing of the years.

לָא קַשְׁיָא: הָא בְּיָחִיד, הָא בְּצִבּוּר.

The Gemara responds: **This is not difficult. This** case, where we require him to return to the beginning of the prayer and repeat it, refers to a situation where he is praying **as an individual.** While **that** case, where we do not require him to return to the beginning of the prayer and repeat it, refers to a situation where he is praying **as** part of **a congregation.**

בְּצִבּוּר מַאי טַעְמָא לֹא – מִשּׁוּם דְּשָׁמְעָהּ מִשְּׁלִיחַ צִבּוּר, אִי הָכִי, הַאי "מִפְּנֵי שֶׁיָּכוֹל לְאוֹמְרָהּ בְּשׁוֹמֵעַ תְּפִילָּה" – "מִפְּנֵי שֶׁשּׁוֹמֵעַ מִשְּׁלִיחַ צִיבּוּר" מִיבָּעֵי לֵיהּ!

The Gemara raises a difficulty: When praying **as** part of **a congregation, what is the reason** that he need **not** need return to the beginning of the prayer and repeat it? **Because** he can fulfill his obligation **when he hears it from the communal prayer leader** in the repetition of the *Amida* prayer. **If so,** Rabbi Tanḥum's formulation is imprecise. **That** which he said that he need not return to the beginning of the prayer and repeat it **because he can recite it in** the blessing: **Who listens to prayer, should have been: Because he hears it from the communal prayer leader.** This proves that the attempt to rebuff the challenge from the *Tosefta* to Rabbi Tanḥum was incorrect.

אֶלָּא, אִידִי וְאִידִי בְּיָחִיד, וְלָא קַשְׁיָא: הָא – דְּאִדְּכַר קוֹדֶם "שׁוֹמֵעַ תְּפִלָּה,"

Rather, both **this** statement of Rabbi Tanḥum **and that** statement in the *Tosefta* refer to one praying **as an individual, and it is,** nevertheless, **not difficult. This** case, where we do not require him to return to the beginning of the prayer and repeat it, refers to a case where **he recalls** his error **before** he reaches the blessing: **Who listens to prayer,** in which case he can ask for rain in that blessing.

Perek **IV**
Daf **29** Amud **b**

הָא – דְּאִדְּכַר בָּתַר "שׁוֹמֵעַ תְּפִלָּה."

**This** case, where we require him to return to the beginning of the prayer and repeat it, refers to a situation where **he recalls his error after** he reaches the blessing: **Who listens to prayer,** in which case the option of asking for rain in that blessing no longer exists and he must return to the beginning of the prayer.

## HALAKHA

**One who erred and did not mention the New Moon – טָעָה וְלֹא הִזְכִּיר שֶׁל רֹאשׁ חֹדֶשׁ:** If one forgot to recite: May there rise and come, in the morning or afternoon prayers on the New Moon, he does the following: If he realized his omission before beginning the following blessing of thanksgiving, even if he concluded the blessing of Temple service: And may our eyes witness, he recites it there. If he began the blessing of thanksgiving but did not yet complete the *Amida* prayer, he returns to the blessing of Temple service. If he realizes his omission only after concluding the *Amida* prayer, he repeats the *Amida* from the beginning. If he completed the *Amida* prayer but has not yet moved his feet, or has not yet completed the supplications that he always recites at the end of his prayer, he returns to the blessing of Temple service. If one forgot to recite: May there rise and come, in the evening prayer, whether it is a one-day or two-day New Moon, he need not repeat the *Amida* prayer (Rambam *Sefer Ahava, Hilkhot Tefilla* 10:10; *Shulḥan Arukh, Oraḥ Ḥayyim* 422:1).

## NOTES

**Prayer which is fixed and prayer which is supplication – קֶבַע וְתַחֲנוּנִים:** The difference between the opinions of Rabbi Ya'akov bar Idi and the Rabbis is as follows. According to Rabbi Ya'akov bar Idi, the emphasis is on one's intent and inner devotion. According to the Sages, the demand is merely that one turn to God with an expression of supplication (Rabbi Ḥananel).

**אָמַר רַבִּי תַּנְחוּם אָמַר רַב אַסִי אָמַר רַבִּי יְהוֹשֻׁעַ בֶּן לֵוִי: טָעָה וְלֹא הִזְכִּיר שֶׁל רֹאשׁ חֹדֶשׁ בַּעֲבוֹדָה – חוֹזֵר לַעֲבוֹדָה, נִזְכַּר בְּהוֹדָאָה – חוֹזֵר לַעֲבוֹדָה. בְּ״שִׂים שָׁלוֹם״ – חוֹזֵר לַעֲבוֹדָה, וְאִם סִיֵּים – חוֹזֵר לָרֹאשׁ.**

On a similar note, the Gemara cites an additional statement of Rabbi Tanḥum. **Rabbi Tanḥum said** that **Rav Asi said** that **Rabbi Yehoshua ben Levi said: One who erred and did not mention the New Moon,**[H] the addition: May there rise and come [*ya'aleh veyavo*] **in the** blessing of Temple **service**, the seventeenth blessing in the *Amida* prayer, **he returns to the** blessing of Temple **service.** So too, if he **remembers during** the blessing of **thanksgiving, he returns to the** blessing of Temple **service.** If he remembers in the blessing: **Grant peace, he returns to the** blessing of Temple **service. If** he remembers after he **completed** the *Amida* prayer, **he returns to the beginning** of the prayer.

**אָמַר רַב פַּפָּא בְּרֵיהּ דְּרַב אַחָא בַּר אַדָּא: הָא דַּאֲמַרַן ״סִיֵּים חוֹזֵר לָרֹאשׁ״ – לֹא אֲמַרַן אֶלָּא שֶׁעָקַר רַגְלָיו, אֲבָל לֹא עָקַר רַגְלָיו – חוֹזֵר לָעֲבוֹדָה.**

**Rav Pappa son of Rav Aḥa bar Adda said: That which we said** that if he already **finished** the *Amida* prayer **he returns to the beginning, we only said** that in a case **where he** already **moved his feet** from where he stood in prayer. **However,** if he **did not** yet **move his feet, he** need only **return to the** blessing of Temple **service,** and include the addition for the New Moon therein.

**אֲמַר לֵיהּ: מְנָא לָךְ הָא? אֲמַר לֵיהּ: מֵאַבָּא מָרִי שְׁמִיעַ לִי, וְאַבָּא מָרִי מֵרַב.**

**He said to him: From where do you** derive **this** *halakha*? **He said to him: My father my teacher told** it to **me and my father my teacher** heard it **from Rav.**

**אָמַר רַב נַחְמָן בַּר יִצְחָק: הָא דַּאֲמַרַן ״עָקַר רַגְלָיו חוֹזֵר לָרֹאשׁ״ – לֹא אֲמַרַן אֶלָּא שֶׁאֵינוֹ רָגִיל לוֹמַר תַּחֲנוּנִים אַחַר תְּפִלָּתוֹ, אֲבָל רָגִיל לוֹמַר תַּחֲנוּנִים אַחַר תְּפִלָּתוֹ – חוֹזֵר לַעֲבוֹדָה.**

On a similar note, **Rav Naḥman bar Yitzḥak said: That which we said** that if he already **moved his feet he returns to the beginning, we only said** that in a case **where he is unaccustomed to reciting** additional **supplications after his prayer. However,** if **he is accustomed to reciting supplications after his prayer,** and while reciting them he remembers that he omitted mention of the New Moon from his prayer, **he** need only **return to the** blessing of Temple **service,** and he includes the addition for the New Moon therein.

**אִיכָּא דְּאָמְרִי, אָמַר רַב נַחְמָן בַּר יִצְחָק: הָא דַּאֲמַרַן כִּי לֹא עָקַר רַגְלָיו חוֹזֵר לָעֲבוֹדָה – לָא אֲמַרַן אֶלָּא שֶׁרָגִיל לוֹמַר תַּחֲנוּנִים אַחַר תְּפִלָּתוֹ, אֲבָל אִם אֵינוֹ רָגִיל לוֹמַר תַּחֲנוּנִים אַחַר תְּפִלָּתוֹ – חוֹזֵר לָרֹאשׁ.**

**Some say, Rav Naḥman bar Yitzḥak said: That which we said** that if he **did not** yet **move his feet, he** need only **return to the** blessing of Temple **service, we only said** that in a case **where he is accustomed to reciting** additional **supplications after his prayer. However,** if **he is unaccustomed to reciting supplications after his prayer, he must return to the beginning of the prayer,** as it is considered as if he already completed it.

**״רַבִּי אֱלִיעֶזֶר אוֹמֵר: כָּל הָעוֹשֶׂה תְּפִלָּתוֹ קֶבַע״ וְכוּ׳. מַאי ״קֶבַע?״ אָמַר רַבִּי יַעֲקֹב בַּר אִידִי אָמַר רַבִּי אוֹשַׁעְיָא: כָּל שֶׁתְּפִלָּתוֹ דּוֹמָה עָלָיו כְּמַשּׂוֹי; וְרַבָּנַן אָמְרִי: כָּל מִי שֶׁאֵינוֹ אוֹמְרָהּ בִּלְשׁוֹן תַּחֲנוּנִים; רַבָּה וְרַב יוֹסֵף דְּאָמְרִי תַּרְוַיְיהוּ: כָּל שֶׁאֵינוֹ יָכוֹל לְחַדֵּשׁ בָּהּ דָּבָר.**

We learned in the mishna that **Rabbi Eliezer says: One whose prayer is fixed, his prayer is not supplication.** The Gemara asks: **What is** the meaning of **fixed** in this context? **Rabbi Ya'akov bar Idi said** that **Rabbi Oshaya said:** It means **anyone for whom his prayer is like a burden upon him,** from which he seeks to be quickly unburdened. **The Rabbis say:** This refers to **anyone who does not recite** prayer **in the language of supplication,** but as a standardized recitation without emotion. **Rabba and Rav Yosef both said:** It refers to **anyone unable to introduce** a novel **element**, i.e., something personal reflecting his personal needs, to his prayer, and only recites the standard formula.[N]

**אָמַר רַבִּי זֵירָא: אֲנָא יָכֵילְנָא לְחַדּוּשֵׁי בָּהּ מִילְּתָא, וּמִסְתְּפֵינָא דִּלְמָא מִטְרִידְנָא.**

**Rabbi Zeira said: I could introduce** a novel **element** in every prayer, but **I am afraid that perhaps I will** become **confused.** Consequently, there is no room to require the masses to introduce a novel element into their prayers.

**אַבַּיֵי בַּר אָבִין וְרַבִּי חֲנִינָא בַּר אָבִין דְּאָמְרִי תַּרְוַיְיהוּ: כָּל שֶׁאֵין מִתְפַּלֵּל עִם דִּמְדּוּמֵי חַמָּה, דְּאָמַר רַבִּי חִיָּיא בַּר אַבָּא אָמַר רַבִּי יוֹחָנָן: מִצְוָה לְהִתְפַּלֵּל עִם דִּמְדּוּמֵי חַמָּה; וְאָמַר רַבִּי זֵירָא: מַאי קְרָאָה – ״יִירָאוּךָ עִם שָׁמֶשׁ וְלִפְנֵי יָרֵחַ דּוֹר דּוֹרִים.״ לָיְיטִי עֲלַהּ בְּמַעְרְבָא אַמַּאן דִּמְצַלֵּי עִם דִּמְדּוּמֵי חַמָּה, מַאי טַעְמָא? דִּלְמָא מִיטְּרְפָא לֵיהּ שַׁעְתָּא.**

The brothers, **Abaye bar Avin and Rabbi Ḥanina bar Avin, both said:** One whose prayer is fixed refers to **anyone who does not** make the effort to **pray with the reddening of the sun,** just after sunrise and just before sunset, which are auspicious times for prayer. As **Rabbi Ḥiyya bar Abba said** that **Rabbi Yoḥanan said: It is a mitzva to pray with the reddening of the sun. And Rabbi Zeira said: What is the verse** that alludes to this? **"Let them fear You with the sun and before the moon, generation after generation"** (Psalms 72:5). Prayer, the manifestation of the fear of God, should be undertaken adjacent to sunrise and sunset. Nevertheless, **in the West,** Eretz Yisrael, **they cursed one who prays with the reddening of the sun,** adjacent to sunset. **What is the reason? Perhaps,** due to preoccupation, he will become **confused about the hour** and the time for prayer will pass.

״רַבִּי יְהוֹשֻׁעַ אוֹמֵר: הַמְהַלֵּךְ בִּמְקוֹם סַכָּנָה מִתְפַּלֵּל תְּפִלָּה קְצָרָה וכו׳ בְּכָל פָּרָשַׁת הָעִבּוּר.״ מַאי ״פָּרָשַׁת הָעִבּוּר״? אָמַר רַב חִסְדָּא אָמַר מָר עוּקְבָא: אֲפִילּוּ בְּשָׁעָה שֶׁאַתָּה מִתְמַלֵּא עֲלֵיהֶם עֶבְרָה כְּאִשָּׁה עוּבָּרָה – יִהְיוּ כָּל צָרְכֵיהֶם לְפָנֶיךָ. אִיכָּא דְּאָמְרִי, אָמַר רַב חִסְדָּא אָמַר מָר עוּקְבָא: אֲפִילּוּ בְּשָׁעָה שֶׁהֵם עוֹבְרִים עַל דִּבְרֵי תוֹרָה – יִהְיוּ כָּל צָרְכֵיהֶם לְפָנֶיךָ.

We learned in the mishna that **Rabbi Yehoshua says: One who is walking in a place of danger, recites a brief prayer… at *parashat ha'ibur*.** The Gemara asks: **What is the meaning of *parashat ha'ibur*? Rav Ḥisda**[P] **said that Mar Ukva said:** This can be interpreted in a manner underscoring two connotations of the term *ibur*: **Even at a time when You are as filled with anger [*evra*], towards them, as a pregnant woman [*ubara*], may all of their needs be before You. Some say** a different version of what **Rav Ḥisda said that Mar Ukva said: Even when they violate [*ovrim*] the commandments of the Torah, may all of their needs be before You.**

תָּנוּ רַבָּנַן: הַמְהַלֵּךְ בִּמְקוֹם גְּדוּדֵי חַיָּה וְלִסְטִים מִתְפַּלֵּל תְּפִלָּה קְצָרָה. וְאֵיזוֹ הִיא תְּפִלָּה קְצָרָה? רַבִּי אֱלִיעֶזֶר אוֹמֵר: ״עֲשֵׂה רְצוֹנְךָ בַּשָּׁמַיִם מִמַּעַל, וְתֵן נַחַת רוּחַ לִירֵאֶיךָ מִתַּחַת, וְהַטּוֹב בְּעֵינֶיךָ עֲשֵׂה, בָּרוּךְ אַתָּה ה׳ שׁוֹמֵעַ תְּפִלָּה״.

One formula for the prayer recited in places of danger is cited in the mishna. Additional formulas are cited in the *Tosefta*. **The Sages taught: One who walks in a place where there are groups of wild beasts and robbers recites an abbreviated prayer.**[H] **Which is an abbreviated prayer? Rabbi Eliezer says, "Carry out Your will in the heavens above, and give peace of mind to those who fear You below, and perform that which is good in Your eyes. Blessed are You, Lord, Who listens to prayer."**

רַבִּי יְהוֹשֻׁעַ אוֹמֵר: ״שְׁמַע שַׁוְעַת עַמְּךָ יִשְׂרָאֵל וַעֲשֵׂה מְהֵרָה בַּקָּשָׁתָם, בָּרוּךְ אַתָּה ה׳ שׁוֹמֵעַ תְּפִלָּה״.

**Rabbi Yehoshua says** that he recites: **Hear the cry of Your nation, Israel, and quickly fulfill their request. Blessed are You, Lord, Who listens to prayer.**

רַבִּי אֶלְעָזָר בְּרַבִּי צָדוֹק אוֹמֵר: ״שְׁמַע צַעֲקַת עַמְּךָ יִשְׂרָאֵל וַעֲשֵׂה מְהֵרָה בַּקָּשָׁתָם, בָּרוּךְ אַתָּה ה׳ שׁוֹמֵעַ תְּפִלָּה״.

**Rabbi Eliezer, son of Rabbi Tzadok says** that he recites: **Hear the shout of Your nation, Israel, and quickly fulfill their request. Blessed are You, Lord, Who listens to prayer.**

אֲחֵרִים אוֹמְרִים: ״צָרְכֵי עַמְּךָ יִשְׂרָאֵל מְרוּבִּין וְדַעְתָּם קְצָרָה, יְהִי רָצוֹן מִלְּפָנֶיךָ ה׳ אֱלֹהֵינוּ שֶׁתִּתֵּן לְכָל אֶחָד וְאֶחָד כְּדֵי פַּרְנָסָתוֹ וּלְכָל גְּוִיָּה וּגְוִיָּה דֵּי מַחְסוֹרָהּ, בָּרוּךְ אַתָּה ה׳ שׁוֹמֵעַ תְּפִלָּה״.

***Aḥerim* say** that he recites: **The needs of Your nation, Israel, are many and their intelligence is limited,** and, consequently, they are unable to effectively articulate their thoughts in prayer (Maharsha). So **may it be Your will, Lord our God, to provide each and every one with his necessary sustenance, and to each and every body all that it lacks. Blessed are You, Lord, Who listens to prayer.**

אָמַר רַב הוּנָא: הֲלָכָה כַּאֲחֵרִים.

**Rav Huna said: The *halakha*** with regard to the version of the prayer recited in a place of danger **is in accordance with** the opinion of ***Aḥerim*.**

אָמַר לֵיהּ אֵלִיָּהוּ לְרַב יְהוּדָה אֲחוּהַ דְּרַב סָלָא חֲסִידָא: לָא תִּרְתַּח וְלָא תֶּחֱטֵי, לָא תִּרְוֵי וְלָא תֶּחֱטֵי, וּכְשֶׁאַתָּה יוֹצֵא לַדֶּרֶךְ – הִמָּלֵךְ בְּקוֹנְךָ וָצֵא. מַאי ״הִמָּלֵךְ בְּקוֹנְךָ וָצֵא״? אָמַר רַבִּי יַעֲקֹב אָמַר רַב חִסְדָּא: זוֹ תְּפִלַּת הַדֶּרֶךְ. וְאָמַר רַבִּי יַעֲקֹב אָמַר רַב חִסְדָּא: כָּל הַיּוֹצֵא לַדֶּרֶךְ צָרִיךְ לְהִתְפַּלֵּל תְּפִלַּת הַדֶּרֶךְ.

On the topic of prayers recited while traveling and in times of danger, the Gemara discusses the traveler's prayer. When he appeared to him, **Elijah** the Prophet **said to Rav Yehuda brother of Rav Sala Ḥasida: Do not get angry and you will not sin. Do not get drunk and you will not sin. And when you set out on a journey, consult with your Creator, and then set out. Rabbi Ya'akov said** that **Rav Ḥisda said: That is the traveler's prayer.**[H] **And Rabbi Ya'akov said** that **Rav Ḥisda said:** It is not only good advice, but established *halakha* that **anyone who sets out on a journey must recite the traveler's prayer** prior to embarking on his journey.

מַאי תְּפִלַּת הַדֶּרֶךְ? ״יְהִי רָצוֹן מִלְּפָנֶיךָ ה׳ אֱלֹהַי, שֶׁתּוֹלִיכֵנִי לְשָׁלוֹם וְתַצְעִידֵנִי לְשָׁלוֹם וְתִסְמְכֵנִי לְשָׁלוֹם, וְתַצִּילֵנִי מִכַּף כָּל אוֹיֵב וְאוֹרֵב בַּדֶּרֶךְ, וְתִשְׁלַח בְּרָכָה בְּמַעֲשֵׂי יָדַי, וְתִתְּנֵנִי לְחֵן לְחֶסֶד וּלְרַחֲמִים בְּעֵינֶיךָ וּבְעֵינֵי כָל רוֹאַי, בָּרוּךְ אַתָּה ה׳ שׁוֹמֵעַ תְּפִלָּה״.

The Gemara asks: **What is** the formula for **the traveler's prayer?** The Gemara answers: **May it be Your will, Lord my God, to lead me to peace, direct my steps to peace, and guide me to peace, and rescue me from the hands of any enemy or ambush along the way, and send blessing to the work of my hands, and let me find grace, kindness, and compassion in Your eyes and in the eyes of all who see me. Blessed are You, Lord, Who hears prayer.**

אָמַר אַבָּיֵי: לְעוֹלָם

**Abaye said: At all times**



לִישַׁתֵּף אֱינָשׁ נַפְשֵׁיהּ בַּהֲדֵי צִבּוּרָא. הֵיכִי נֵימָא? – ״יְהִי רָצוֹן מִלְּפָנֶיךָ ה׳ אֱלֹהֵינוּ שֶׁתּוֹלִיכֵנוּ לְשָׁלוֹם וכו׳.

**a person should associate himself with the congregation** and should not pray for himself alone. **How should he say it? May it be Your will, Lord our God, that You lead us to peace, etc.,** in the plural.

#### PERSONALITIES

Rav Ḥisda – רַב חִסְדָּא: One of the greatest second generation Babylonian *amora'im*, Rav Ḥisda, a priest, was one of Rav's younger students. After Rav's death, he remained a disciple-colleague of Rav's student, Rav Huna. Throughout his life, Rav Ḥisda showed great affection for the teachings of Rav, and constantly tried to learn additional matters of Torah in his name. Although he was poor as a youth, he became wealthy and lived most of his life in comfort. He was very generous toward his fellow man. He was devoted to his students, his sons, and his daughters, guiding them along the straight and narrow in both spiritual and worldly matters.

#### HALAKHA

**One who walks in a place where there are groups of wild beasts and robbers recites an abbreviated prayer – הַמְהַלֵּךְ בִּמְקוֹם גְּדוּדֵי חַיָּה וְלִסְטִים מִתְפַּלֵּל תְּפִלָּה קְצָרָה:** When walking in a dangerous place, one recites an abbreviated prayer. The formula is in accordance with the opinion of *Aḥerim:* The needs of Your nation, Israel, are many, etc., as per the ruling of Rav Huna. However, if one arrives at a safe haven before the time for prayer has passed, he recites the standard *Amida* prayer. If he was unable to recite the standard *Amida* prayer, his legal status is equal to one who forgot to pray and he compensates for the missed prayer after completing the next *Amida* prayer (Rambam *Sefer Ahava, Hilkhot Tefilla* 4:19; *Shulḥan Arukh, Oraḥ Ḥayyim* 110:4 in the comment of the Rema).

**The traveler's prayer – תְּפִלַּת הַדֶּרֶךְ:** One who sets out on a journey recites May it be Your will, as formulated in the Gemara. It is recited in the plural as per the ruling of Abaye (see *Beit Yosef*; Rambam *Sefer Ahava, Hilkhot Berakhot* 10:25; *Shulḥan Arukh, Oraḥ Ḥayyim* 110:4).

אֵימַת מְצַלֵּי? – אָמַר רַבִּי יַעֲקֹב אָמַר רַב חִסְדָּא: מִשָּׁעָה שֶׁמְּהַלֵּךְ בַּדֶּרֶךְ. עַד כַּמָּה? – אָמַר רַבִּי יַעֲקֹב אָמַר רַב חִסְדָּא: עַד פַּרְסָה. וְהֵיכִי מְצַלֵּי לַהּ? – רַב חִסְדָּא אָמַר: מְעוּמָּד; רַב שֵׁשֶׁת אָמַר: אֲפִילּוּ מְהַלֵּךְ.

The Gemara discusses specific details pertaining to this prayer. **When does one pray? Rabbi Ya'akov said** that **Rav Ḥisda said: From when one sets out on his journey,**[H] and not before. **How long** must one's planned journey be in order to require him to recite this prayer (*Ba'al Halakhot Gedolot*)? **Rabbi Ya'akov said** that **Rav Ḥisda said: At least a parasang.**[H] **How does he recite** this prayer? **Rav Ḥisda said:** Only while **standing** in one place. **Rav Sheshet said: Even walking**[H] or sitting.

רַב חִסְדָּא וְרַב שֵׁשֶׁת הֲווּ קָאָזְלִי בְּאוֹרְחָא, קָם רַב חִסְדָּא וְקָא מְצַלֵּי. אֲמַר לֵיהּ רַב שֵׁשֶׁת לְשַׁמָּעֵיהּ: מַאי קָא עָבֵיד רַב חִסְדָּא? אֲמַר לֵיהּ: קָאֵי וּמְצַלֵּי. אֲמַר לֵיהּ: אוֹקְמָן נַמִי לְדִידִי וַאֲצַלֵּי, מִהְיוֹת טוֹב אַל תִּקָּרֵא רַע.

The Gemara relates: **Rav Ḥisda and Rav Sheshet were walking along the path, Rav Ḥisda stood and recited** the traveler's prayer. Since he was blind and did not see his colleague, **Rav Sheshet asked his servant: What is Rav Ḥisda doing** now? His servant **said to him: He is standing and praying.** Rav Sheshet **said to** his servant: **Stand me up as well and I will pray.** Even though Rav Sheshet held that there is no need to stand during this prayer, nevertheless: **From being good, do not be called wicked.** In other words, one should do better if he is able. Rav Sheshet said that one is not required to stop and stand. He did not say that it is preferable to walk or sit. Since standing in this case required no special effort on his part, as Rav Ḥisda had stopped to stand and pray anyway, why insist on sitting?

מַאי אִיכָּא בֵּין "הֲבִינֵנוּ" לִתְפִלָּה קְצָרָה? – הֲבִינֵנוּ – בָּעֵי לְצַלּוּיֵי שָׁלֹשׁ קַמַּיְיתָא וְשָׁלֹשׁ בַּתְרַיְיתָא, וְכִי מָטֵי לְבֵיתֵיהּ לָא בָּעֵי לְמֶהְדַּר לְצַלּוּיֵי; בִּתְפִלָּה קְצָרָה – לָא בָּעֵי לְצַלּוּיֵי לֹא שָׁלֹשׁ קַמַּיְיתָא וְלֹא שָׁלֹשׁ בַּתְרַיְיתָא, וְכִי מָטֵי לְבֵיתֵיהּ בָּעֵי לְמֶהְדַּר לְצַלּוּיֵי.

The mishna mentioned both a brief prayer recited in times of danger and an abridged prayer, with regard to which there was a dispute between the *tanna'im*. The Gemara asks: **What is** the practical halakhic difference between the abridged prayer: **Grant us understanding and the brief prayer** recited in times of danger? The Gemara answers: One who recites: **Grant us understanding is required to recite the first three** blessings **and the last three** blessings of the *Amida* prayer, **and when he reaches his home, he need not pray again.** One who recites **the brief prayer,** however, **need recite neither the first three** blessings **nor the last three** blessings of the *Amida* prayer. **However, when he reaches his home, he must pray again.** Grant us understanding has the legal status of the *Amida* prayer, despite its brevity, while the brief prayer is merely recited in place of the *Amida* prayer in exigent circumstances.

וְהִלְכְתָא: הֲבִינֵנוּ – מְעוּמָּד, תְּפִלָּה קְצָרָה – בֵּין מְעוּמָּד בֵּין מְהַלֵּךְ.

**The** ***halakha*** **is: Grant us understanding,** as mentioned above, has the legal status of the *Amida* prayer, and must therefore be recited while **standing.**[H] **The brief prayer,** since it does not have that status, may be recited **whether** one is **standing or whether** one is **walking.**[H]

"הָיָה רוֹכֵב עַל הַחֲמוֹר" וכו׳. תָּנוּ רַבָּנַן: הָיָה רוֹכֵב עַל הַחֲמוֹר וְהִגִּיעַ זְמַן תְּפִלָּה, אִם יֵשׁ לוֹ מִי שֶׁיֹּאחֵז אֶת חֲמוֹרוֹ – יֵרֵד לְמַטָּה וְיִתְפַּלֵּל, וְאִם לָאו – יֵשֵׁב בִּמְקוֹמוֹ וְיִתְפַּלֵּל; רַבִּי אוֹמֵר: בֵּין כָּךְ וּבֵין כָּךְ – יֵשֵׁב בִּמְקוֹמוֹ וְיִתְפַּלֵּל, לְפִי שֶׁאֵין דַּעְתּוֹ מְיוּשֶּׁבֶת עָלָיו.

We learned in the mishna: **One who was riding on a donkey**[H] should dismount and pray. Only in exigent circumstances may he pray while riding, focusing his heart toward Jerusalem and the Holy of Holies. **The Sages taught** in a *Tosefta*: **One who was riding on a donkey and the time for prayer arrived, if he has someone to hold** onto **the donkey, he should dismount and pray. If not, he should sit in his place** atop the donkey **and pray. Rabbi** Yehuda HaNasi **says: In any case,** whether or not there is someone to hold onto the donkey, **he should sit in his place** atop the donkey **and pray, as his mind will not be calm.** Since he is hurrying to arrive at his destination, the need to dismount the donkey, stand in prayer, and remount the donkey would delay his journey, and the delay is likely to interfere with his concentration during prayer.

אָמַר רָבָא וְאִיתֵּימָא רַבִּי יְהוֹשֻׁעַ בֶּן לֵוִי: הֲלָכָה כְּרַבִּי.

**Rava, and some say Rabbi Yehoshua ben Levi, said:** The ***halakha*** here **is in accordance with** the opinion of **Rabbi** Yehuda HaNasi.

תָּנוּ רַבָּנַן: סוּמָא וּמִי שֶׁאֵינוֹ יָכוֹל לְכַוֵּין אֶת הָרוּחוֹת – יְכַוֵּין לִבּוֹ כְּנֶגֶד אָבִיו שֶׁבַּשָּׁמַיִם, שֶׁנֶּאֱמַר: "וְהִתְפַּלְלוּ אֶל ה׳";

**The Sages taught** in a *Tosefta*: **A blind person and one who is unable to approximate the directions** and, therefore, is unable to face Jerusalem in order to pray, **may focus his heart towards his Father in Heaven, as it is stated: "And they shall pray to the Lord"** (I Kings 8:44).

### HALAKHA

**From when one sets out on his journey** – מִשָּׁעָה שֶׁמְּהַלֵּךְ בַּדֶּרֶךְ: The traveler's prayer is recited as soon as one sets out on his journey, i.e., when he leaves the city (*Eliyahu Rabba, Peri Megadim*). Some say that it is recited when one decides to set out on the journey (*Taz*). *Ab initio*, one should conduct oneself in accordance with the opinion of *Eliyahu Rabba* (*Shulḥan Arukh HaRav, Mishna Berura; Shulḥan Arukh, Oraḥ Ḥayyim* 110:7).

**At least a parasang** – עַד פַּרְסָה: One does not recite the traveler's prayer unless he plans on traveling at least a parasang. If his plan is to travel a shorter distance, he should recite the prayer without a blessing. *Ab initio*, he should recite the prayer in the first parasang of his journey (*Shulḥan Arukh, Oraḥ Ḥayyim* 110:7 and in the comment of the Rema).

**The traveler's prayer while walking** – תְּפִלַּת הַדֶּרֶךְ בִּמְהַלֵּךְ: In this case, Rav Sheshet conducted himself according to the opinion of Rav Ḥisda. Because of this, the medieval commentaries disagreed whether to rule in accordance with the opinion of Rav Sheshet, which is the general rule in his dispute with Rav Ḥisda, or in accordance with the opinion of Rav Ḥisda. Ultimately, the ruling was as follows: *Ab initio*, one should stand in one place and recite the traveler's prayer. However, if one is riding an animal, he need not dismount. If possible, though, he should stop the animal and then recite the prayer (*Shulḥan Arukh, Oraḥ Ḥayyim* 110:4).

**Grant us understanding while standing** – הֲבִינֵנוּ מְעוּמָּד: One recites the abridged version of the *Amida* prayer: Grant us understanding, in the same manner that he recites the standard *Amida* prayer, standing (*Shulḥan Arukh, Oraḥ Ḥayyim* 110:1).

**The brief prayer whether one is standing or whether one is walking** – תְּפִלָּה קְצָרָה בֵּין מְעוּמָּד בֵּין מְהַלֵּךְ: When one is allowed to recite a brief prayer because he is walking in a place where he is threatened by bands of wild animals or highwaymen, he may continue walking as he recites it (Rambam *Sefer Ahava, Hilkhot Tefilla* 4:19; *Shulḥan Arukh, Oraḥ Ḥayyim* 110:3).

**One who was riding on a donkey** – הָיָה רוֹכֵב עַל הַחֲמוֹר: One who is riding on a donkey need not dismount in order to pray, even if there is someone available to hold the donkey, as per the opinion of Rabbi Yehoshua ben Levi and the conclusion of the Gemara (Rambam *Sefer Ahava, Hilkhot Tefilla* 5:2; *Shulḥan Arukh, Oraḥ Ḥayyim* 94:4).

הָיָה עוֹמֵד בְּחוּץ לָאָרֶץ – יְכַוֵּין אֶת לִבּוֹ כְּנֶגֶד אֶרֶץ יִשְׂרָאֵל, שֶׁנֶּאֱמַר: "וְהִתְפַּלְלוּ אֵלֶיךָ דֶּרֶךְ אַרְצָם"; הָיָה עוֹמֵד בְּאֶרֶץ יִשְׂרָאֵל – יְכַוֵּין אֶת לִבּוֹ כְּנֶגֶד יְרוּשָׁלַיִם, שֶׁנֶּאֱמַר: "וְהִתְפַּלְלוּ אֶל ה' דֶּרֶךְ הָעִיר אֲשֶׁר בָּחַרְתָּ"; הָיָה עוֹמֵד בִּירוּשָׁלַיִם – יְכַוֵּין אֶת לִבּוֹ כְּנֶגֶד בֵּית הַמִּקְדָּשׁ, שֶׁנֶּאֱמַר: "וְהִתְפַּלְלוּ אֶל הַבַּיִת הַזֶּה"; הָיָה עוֹמֵד בְּבֵית הַמִּקְדָּשׁ – יְכַוֵּין אֶת לִבּוֹ כְּנֶגֶד בֵּית קָדְשֵׁי הַקֳּדָשִׁים, שֶׁנֶּאֱמַר: "וְהִתְפַּלְלוּ אֶל הַמָּקוֹם הַזֶּה"; הָיָה עוֹמֵד בְּבֵית קָדְשֵׁי הַקֳּדָשִׁים – יְכַוֵּין אֶת לִבּוֹ כְּנֶגֶד בֵּית הַכַּפֹּרֶת; הָיָה עוֹמֵד אֲחוֹרֵי בֵית הַכַּפֹּרֶת – יִרְאֶה עַצְמוֹ כְּאִילּוּ לִפְנֵי הַכַּפֹּרֶת; נִמְצָא: עוֹמֵד בְּמִזְרָח – מַחֲזִיר פָּנָיו לַמַּעֲרָב, בְּמַעֲרָב – מַחֲזִיר פָּנָיו לַמִּזְרָח, בַּדָּרוֹם – מַחֲזִיר פָּנָיו לַצָּפוֹן, בַּצָּפוֹן – מַחֲזִיר פָּנָיו לַדָּרוֹם; נִמְצְאוּ כָל יִשְׂרָאֵל מְכַוְּונִין אֶת לִבָּם לְמָקוֹם אֶחָד.

אָמַר רַבִּי אָבִין, וְאִיתֵּימָא רַבִּי אֲבִינָא: מַאי קְרָאָה – "כְּמִגְדַּל דָּוִיד צַוָּארֵךְ בָּנוּי לְתַלְפִּיּוֹת", תֵּל שֶׁכָּל פִּיּוֹת פּוֹנִים בּוֹ.

אֲבוּהּ דִּשְׁמוּאֵל וְלֵוִי, כִּי הֲווֹ בָּעוּ לְמִיפַּק לְאוֹרְחָא הֲווֹ מַקְדְּמִי וּמְצַלּוּ, וְכִי הֲוָה מָטֵי זְמַן קְרִיאַת שְׁמַע קָרוּ.

כְּמַאן – כִּי הַאי תַּנָּא – דְּתַנְיָא: הַשְׁכִּים לָצֵאת לַדֶּרֶךְ – מְבִיאִין לוֹ שׁוֹפָר וְתוֹקֵעַ, לוּלָב וּמְנַעְנֵעַ, מְגִילָּה וְקוֹרֵא בָהּ, וּכְשֶׁיַּגִּיעַ זְמַן קְרִיאַת שְׁמַע קוֹרֵא. הַשְׁכִּים לֵישֵׁב בְּקָרוֹן אוֹ בִּסְפִינָה – מִתְפַּלֵּל, וּכְשֶׁיַּגִּיעַ זְמַן קְרִיאַת שְׁמַע קוֹרֵא;

רַבִּי שִׁמְעוֹן בֶּן אֶלְעָזָר אוֹמֵר: בֵּין כָּךְ וּבֵין כָּךְ קוֹרֵא קְרִיאַת שְׁמַע וּמִתְפַּלֵּל, כְּדֵי שֶׁיִּסְמוֹךְ גְּאוּלָּה לִתְפִלָּה.

בְּמַאי קָמִיפַּלְגִי? – מָר סָבַר: תְּפִלָּה מְעוּמָּד עָדִיף, וּמָר סָבַר: מִסְמַךְ גְּאוּלָּה לִתְפִלָּה עָדִיף.

מָרֵימָר וּמָר זוּטְרָא הֲווֹ מְכַנְּפִי בֵּי עַשְׂרָה בְּשַׁבְּתָא דְרִגְלָא וּמְצַלּוּ, וַהֲדַר נָפְקִי לְפִרְקָא.

רַב אַשִׁי מְצַלֵּי בַּהֲדֵי צִבּוּרָא בְּיָחִיד מְיוּשָׁב, כִּי הֲוָה אָתֵי לְבֵיתֵיהּ הֲדַר וּמְצַלֵּי מְעוּמָּד. אָמְרִי לֵיהּ רַבָּנַן: וְלַעֲבֵיד מָר כִּמְרֵימָר וּמָר זוּטְרָא! – אָמַר לְהוּ: טְרִיחָא לִי מִלְּתָא. – וְלַעֲבֵיד מָר כְּאֲבוּהּ דִּשְׁמוּאֵל וְלֵוִי! – אָמַר לְהוּ: לֹא חֲזֵינָא לְהוּ לְרַבָּנַן קַשִׁישֵׁי מִינַּן דְּעָבְדִי הָכִי.

---

One who was standing in prayer **in the Diaspora, should focus his heart toward Eretz Yisrael,** as it is stated: "And they shall pray to You by way of their land" which You have given to their fathers (I Kings 8:48).

One who was standing **in Eretz Yisrael, should focus his heart toward Jerusalem,** as it is stated: "And they shall pray to the Lord by way of the city that You have chosen" (I Kings 8:44).

One who was standing **in Jerusalem, should focus his heart toward the Temple,** as it is stated: "And they shall pray toward this house" (II Chronicles 6:32).

One who was standing **in the Temple, should focus his heart toward the Holy of Holies,** as it is stated: "And they shall pray toward this place" (I Kings 8:35).

One who was standing **in the Holy of Holies, should focus his heart toward the seat of the ark-cover** [*kapporet*], atop the ark, the dwelling place of God's glory.

One who was standing **behind the seat of the ark-cover, should visualize himself as if standing before the ark-cover** and turn toward it.

**Consequently,** one **standing** in prayer **in the East turns to face west,** and one standing **in the West, turns to face east.** One standing **in the South, turns to face north,** and one standing **in the North, turns to face south;** **all of** the people of **Israel** find themselves **focusing their hearts toward one place,** the Holy of Holies in the Temple.[H]

An allusion to this is found in what **Rabbi Avin, and some say Rabbi Avina,** said: What verse alludes **to this?** "Your neck is like the **Tower of David, built with turrets** [*talpiyyot*], one thousand shields hang from it, all of the armor of the mighty" (Song of Songs 4:4). He interprets the word *talpiyyot* as the hill [*tel*] toward which all mouths [*piyyot*] turn, i.e., the Temple Mount.

With regard to prayer while traveling, the Gemara relates: **When Shmuel's father and Levi wanted to set out on a journey** in the morning, **they would pray early** before sunrise. **When,** during their journey, **the time to recite** *Shema* **would arrive, they recited it.**

The Gemara asks: **In accordance with whose** opinion did they do this? **In accordance with this** *tanna*, **as it was taught** in the *Tosefta*: **One who rose early to set out on his path**[H] before the time to recite *Shema* arrives, **they bring him a** *shofar* **and he sounds it,** if it was Rosh HaShana; **a** *lulav* **and he takes it** on *Sukkot*; **a megilla,** the Scroll of Esther, **and he reads it** on Purim; **and when the time comes to recite** *Shema*, **he recites it.** So too, **one who rose early to sit in a wagon or in a boat prays, and when the time comes to recite** *Shema*, **he recites it.**

**Rabbi Shimon ben Elazar, says: In either case,** it is preferable to **recite** *Shema* **and** then **pray** the *Amida* prayer in the wagon **so that he will juxtapose redemption and prayer.**

The Gemara explains: **Regarding what do they disagree?** The Gemara answers: **This Sage,** the first *tanna*, **holds that** prayer while **standing is preferable.** Therefore, one should pray earlier, at home, while standing. **This Sage,** Rabbi Shimon ben Elazar, **holds** that the **juxtaposition of redemption and prayer is preferable,** even if in doing so one is unable to stand while praying.

On a similar note, the Gemara cites additional circumstances where Sages were forced to make exceptional arrangements to pray: **Mareimar and Mar Zutra would gather ten** people **on the Shabbat of the festival and pray, and set out to deliver their lecture** [*pirka*]. Due to the crowds that gathered to hear the lectures of the Sages on the festival, they were unable to pray at the proper time, so they were forced to pray earlier.

In similar circumstances, **Rav Ashi would pray with the congregation individually while seated,** so that they would not notice that he was praying. Afterwards, **when he would come to his house, he would pray again** while **standing** in order to pray without distraction. **The Sages said to him: The Master should do as Mareimar and Mar Zutra do,** i.e., gather a prayer quorum at home to pray before the lecture. **He said to them: It is burdensome to me** to delay the lecture so much. The Sages **said to him: The Master should do as Shmuel's father and Levi did** and pray before sunrise. **He said to them: I have not seen Sages older than us do that,** indicating that this is not the accepted *halakha*.

**Turning in prayer –** הַפְנָיָה בַּתְּפִלָּה: Everyone faces the Holy of Holies in Jerusalem while praying, i.e., those west of Jerusalem turn east, etc. If one cannot determine the direction of Jerusalem, it does not prevent him from praying, and he may suffice with focusing his heart toward heaven (Rambam *Sefer Ahava*, *Hilkhot Tefilla* 5:3; *Shulḥan Arukh*, *Oraḥ Ḥayyim* 94:1, 3).

**One who rose early to set out on his path –** הַמַּשְׁכִּים לַדֶּרֶךְ: In exigent circumstances, e.g., one needs to set out on a journey early, he may pray any time after dawn at home, standing. When the time to recite *Shema* arrives, he recites it in the course of the journey, as per the opinion of the first *tanna*, even though he does not juxtapose redemption with prayer. These days, the custom is to wait and recite both *Shema* and the *Amida* prayer in the course of the journey (*Mishna Berura*). Since, as a rule, we are unable to muster proper intent while praying, it is preferable to juxtapose redemption and prayer (*Shulḥan Arukh HaRav*; *Shulḥan Arukh*, *Oraḥ Ḥayyim* 89:8).

## NOTES

The additional prayer is only recited in a city where there is a quorum of ten [*hever ir*] – אֵין תְּפִלַּת הַמּוּסָפִין אֶלָּא בְּחֶבֶר עִיר: This is because the additional prayer is not one of personal requests and supplication. Rather, it is praise of God modeled after the sacrificial offerings. It is only appropriate to recite this communal praise in the framework of a congregation (*Talmidei Rabbeinu Yona*).

## BACKGROUND

*Ḥever ir* – חֶבֶר עִיר: According to most commentaries, the *ḥever ir* is a type of city council on which the leading Sages sat, either in official capacities or just as religious leaders. The *ge'onim*, and Rashi in certain places, translate the word *ḥaver* as outstanding Torah scholar. The *ḥaver* was the leader or chief rabbi of the city and the congregation generally prayed with him. According to this interpretation, the additional prayer was only recited in the leader's presence.

## HALAKHA

The additional prayer is recited…with a *ḥever ir* or without a *ḥever ir* – תְּפִלַּת הַמּוּסָפִין...בְּחֶבֶר עִיר וְשֶׁלֹּא בְּחֶבֶר עִיר: Each individual is required to recite the additional prayer, whether or not there is a quorum of ten in the city, as per the opinion of the Rabbis in their dispute with Rabbi Elazar ben Azarya (*Shulḥan Arukh, Oraḥ Ḥayyim* 286:2).

מתני׳ רַבִּי אֶלְעָזָר בֶּן עֲזַרְיָה אוֹמֵר: אֵין תְּפִלַּת הַמּוּסָפִין אֶלָּא בְּחֶבֶר עִיר, וַחֲכָמִים אוֹמְרִים: בְּחֶבֶר עִיר וְשֶׁלֹּא בְּחֶבֶר עִיר; רַבִּי יְהוּדָה אוֹמֵר מִשְּׁמוֹ: כָּל מָקוֹם שֶׁיֵּשׁ שָׁם חֶבֶר עִיר – יָחִיד פָּטוּר מִתְּפִלַּת הַמּוּסָפִין.

**MISHNA** **Rabbi Elazar ben Azarya says: The additional prayer is only** recited **in a city where there is a quorum of ten** [***ḥever ir***].[NB] **The Rabbis say:** One may recite the additional prayer **with a *ḥever ir* or without a *ḥever ir*.**[H] **Rabbi Yehuda says** another opinion **in his name,** the name of Rabbi Elazar ben Azarya: **Any place where there is a *ḥever ir*, an individual is** completely **exempt from** reciting **the additional prayer.**

גמ׳ רַבִּי יְהוּדָה הַיְינוּ תַּנָּא קַמָּא! אִיכָּא בֵּינַיְיהוּ: יָחִיד שֶׁלֹּא בְּחֶבֶר עִיר; תַּנָּא קַמָּא סָבַר: פָּטוּר, וְרַבִּי יְהוּדָה סָבַר: חַיָּיב.

**GEMARA** There is no apparent difference between the opinion of Rabbi Elazar ben Azarya and the opinion cited in his name by Rabbi Yehuda. The Gemara asks: **Rabbi Yehuda's** opinion **is** identical to the opinion of Rabbi Elazar ben Azarya cited by **the first *tanna*.** The Gemara answers: **There is a** practical halakhic difference **between them:** The case of **an individual who is not in** a place where there is **a *ḥever ir*.** In other words, in a place where there is not a prayer quorum of ten people, the **first *tanna* holds** that Rabbi Elazar ben Azarya's opinion is that the **individual is exempt** from reciting the additional prayer, as it was only instituted to be recited with a quorum. **And Rabbi Yehuda holds** that Rabbi Elazar ben Azarya's opinion is that the individual is **obligated** to recite the additional prayer, as he is only exempt in a place where there is a prayer quorum, and, therefore, a communal prayer leader fulfills his obligation.

אָמַר רַב הוּנָא בַּר חִינָּנָא אָמַר רַב חִיָּיא בַּר רַב: הֲלָכָה כְּרַבִּי יְהוּדָה שֶׁאָמַר מִשּׁוּם רַבִּי אֶלְעָזָר בֶּן עֲזַרְיָה. אָמַר לֵיהּ רַב חִיָּיא בַּר אָבִין: שַׁפִּיר קָאָמְרַתְּ, דְּאָמַר שְׁמוּאֵל: מִיּוֹמַי לָא מְצַלֵּינָא צְלוֹתָא דְּמוּסָפִין בְּיָחִיד

**Rav Huna bar Ḥinnana said** that **Ḥiyya bar Rav said: The *halakha* is in accordance with** the opinion of **Rabbi Yehuda, who said** it **in the name of** his mentor, **Rabbi Elazar ben Azarya. Rav Ḥiyya bar Avin said to him: You have spoken well,** as proven by what **Shmuel said: In all my days I have never prayed the additional prayer as an individual**

Perek **IV**
Daf **30** Amud **b**

## LANGUAGE

Army [*pulmusa*] – פּוּלְמוּסָא: From the Greek πόλεμος, *polemos*, meaning war.

## PERSONALITIES

Rabbi Ḥanina Kara, the Bible expert – רַבִּי חֲנִינָא קָרָא: A second generation *amora* in Eretz Yisrael, Rabbi Ḥanina was a disciple of Rabbi Ḥanina bar Ḥama, Rabbi Ḥanina the Great, and Rabbi Yannai. Apparently, Rabbi Ḥanina not only taught young children, but was also a Bible expert, which is why he was called *Kara*. He is mentioned in the Talmud and the midrash in discussions with his two teachers, both on matters relating to his work and also on other halakhic matters.

בִּנְהַרְדְּעָא, לְבַר מֵהַהוּא יוֹמָא דַּאֲתָא פּוּלְמוּסָא דְּמַלְכָּא לְמָתָא וְאִטְרִידוּ רַבָּנַן וְלָא צַלּוֹ, וְצַלֵּי לִי בְּיָחִיד, וַהֲוַאי יָחִיד שֶׁלֹּא בְּחֶבֶר עִיר.

**in** Nehardeʼa, where there is always a prayer quorum, **except for the day when the king's army** [***pulmusa***][L] **came to the city, and the Sages were preoccupied and did not pray** communally, **and I prayed as an individual, and I was an individual** who was **not** praying **in a prayer quorum.** Shmuel's conduct was in accordance with the opinion of Rabbi Yehuda in this matter.

יָתֵיב רַבִּי חֲנִינָא קָרָא קַמֵּיהּ דְּרַבִּי יַנַּאי, וְיָתֵיב וְקָאָמַר: הֲלָכָה כְּרַבִּי יְהוּדָה שֶׁאָמַר מִשּׁוּם רַבִּי אֶלְעָזָר בֶּן עֲזַרְיָה. אָמַר לֵיהּ: פּוּק קְרָא קְרָאֵיךְ לְבָרָא! דְּאֵין הֲלָכָה כְּרַבִּי יְהוּדָה שֶׁאָמַר מִשּׁוּם רַבִּי אֶלְעָזָר בֶּן עֲזַרְיָה.

Yet this opinion was not universally accepted. The Gemara relates: **Rabbi Ḥanina Kara,** the Bible expert,[P] **sat before Rabbi Yannai, and he sat and he said: The *halakha* is in accordance with** the opinion of **Rabbi Yehuda who said** it **in the name of Rabbi Elazar ben Azarya.** Rabbi Yannai **said to him: Go and read your verses outside,** as that *halakha* is not accepted by the Sages in the study hall, and it belongs outside, **as the *halakha* is not in accordance with** the opinion of **Rabbi Yehuda who said** it **in the name of Rabbi Elazar ben Azarya.**

אָמַר רַבִּי יוֹחָנָן: אֲנִי רָאִיתִי אֶת רַבִּי יַנַּאי דְּצַלֵּי וַהֲדַר צַלֵּי. אָמַר לֵיהּ רַבִּי יִרְמְיָה לְרַבִּי זֵירָא: וְדִילְמָא מֵעִיקָּרָא לָא כַּוֵּון דַּעְתֵּיהּ, וּלְבַסּוֹף כַּוֵּון דַּעְתֵּיהּ? אָמַר לֵיהּ: חֲזִי מַאן גַּבְרָא רַבָּה דְּקָמַסְהֵיד עֲלֵיהּ!

**Rabbi Yoḥanan said: I saw Rabbi Yannai, who prayed and then prayed again.** Presumably, his first prayer was the morning prayer and his second prayer was the additional prayer. Apparently, he does not hold in accordance with the opinion of Rabbi Elazar ben Azarya. Rather, he holds that even when not part of a prayer quorum, an individual must recite the additional prayer. Later on, when this story was related in the study hall, **Rabbi Yirmeya said to** his teacher, **Rabbi Zeira:** What proof is there that the second prayer was the additional prayer? **Perhaps initially he did not focus his mind** on his prayer **and ultimately he focused his mind,** i.e., he repeated the morning prayer in order to do so with proper concentration. Rabbi Zeira **said to him: Look at who the great man is who is testifying about him.** Rabbi Yoḥanan certainly observed carefully before relating what he witnessed.

רַבִּי אַמִי וְרַבִּי אַסִי אַף עַל גַּב דַּהֲווּ לְהוּ תְּלֵיסַר בֵּי כְּנִישָׁתָא בְּטַבֶרְיָא, לָא הָווּ מְצַלּוּ אֶלָּא בֵּינֵי עַמּוּדֵי הֵיכָא דַּהֲווּ גָּרְסִי.

Regarding prayers of the Sages, the Gemara further relates that, **although there were thirteen synagogues in Tiberias, Rabbi Ami and Rabbi Asi would only pray between the columns**[N] **where they studied,**[H] as prayer is beloved in the eyes of God, specifically in a place of Torah.

אִיתְּמַר, רַב יִצְחָק בַּר אַבְדִּימִי מִשּׁוּם רַבֵּינוּ אָמַר: הֲלָכָה כְּרַבִּי יְהוּדָה שֶׁאָמַר מִשּׁוּם רַבִּי אֶלְעָזָר בֶּן עֲזַרְיָה. רַבִּי חִיָּיא בַּר אַבָּא צַלֵּי וַהֲדַר צַלֵּי. אֲמַר לֵיהּ רַבִּי זֵירָא: מַאי טַעְמָא עָבֵיד מָר הָכִי? אִילֵימָא מִשּׁוּם דְּלָא כַּוֵּין מָר דַּעְתֵּיהּ – וְהָאָמַר רַבִּי אֱלִיעֶזֶר: לְעוֹלָם יָמוֹד אָדָם אֶת עַצְמוֹ, אִם יָכוֹל לְכַוֵּין אֶת לִבּוֹ – יִתְפַּלֵּל, וְאִם לָאו – אַל יִתְפַּלֵּל! – אֶלָּא דְּלָא אַדְכַּר מָר דְּרֵישׁ יַרְחָא,

**It was stated: Rav Yitzḥak bar Avdimi in the name of Rabbeinu, Rav, said: The *halakha* is in accordance with** the opinion of **Rabbi Yehuda who said it in the name of Rabbi Elazar ben Azarya.** The Gemara relates: **Rabbi Ḥiyya bar Abba prayed** and then **prayed again. Rav Zeira said to him: Why did the Master do this? If you say because the Master did not focus his mind** the first time, **didn't Rabbi Eliezer say: One must always evaluate himself** before he prays? **If he is able to focus his heart** on prayer, **he should pray, but if not,** if he is unable to do so, **he should not pray.**[H] Apparently, that was not the reason that he prayed twice. **Rather,** because **my Master did not mention the New Moon** in his prayer, so he prayed again.

וְהָתַנְיָא: טָעָה וְלֹא הִזְכִּיר שֶׁל רֹאשׁ חֹדֶשׁ בְּעַרְבִית – אֵין מַחֲזִירִין אוֹתוֹ מִפְּנֵי שֶׁיָּכוֹל לְאוֹמְרָהּ בְּשַׁחֲרִית, בְּשַׁחֲרִית – אֵין מַחֲזִירִין אוֹתוֹ מִפְּנֵי שֶׁיָּכוֹל לְאוֹמְרָהּ בְּמוּסָפִין, בְּמוּסָפִין – אֵין מַחֲזִירִין אוֹתוֹ מִפְּנֵי שֶׁיָּכוֹל לְאוֹמְרָהּ בְּמִנְחָה!

The Gemara asks: **Wasn't it taught** in a *baraita*: **One who erred and did not mention the New Moon in the evening prayer,**[H] **we do not require him to return** to the beginning of the prayer and repeat it, **because he can recite it in the morning prayer.** One who erred and did not mention the New Moon **in the morning prayer, we do not require him to return** to the beginning of the prayer and repeat it, **because he can recite it in the additional prayer.** One who erred and did not mention the New Moon **in the additional prayer, we do not require him to return** to the beginning of the prayer and repeat it, **because he can recite it in the afternoon prayer?** Omitting mention of the New Moon does not require one to repeat the *Amida* prayer. Consequently, that was not the reason that Rabbi Ḥiyya bar Abba prayed a second time.

אֲמַר לֵיהּ: לָאו אִיתְּמַר עֲלַהּ, אָמַר רַבִּי יוֹחָנָן, בְּצִבּוּר שָׁנוּ.

Rabbi Ḥiyya bar Abba **said to him: Wasn't it stated about that** *baraita* that **Rabbi Yoḥanan said: They taught** this *baraita* specifically with regard to prayer **in a communal** framework?[H] However, an individual who fails to mention the New Moon is required to pray again? That is why Rabbi Ḥiyya bar Abba prayed twice.

כַּמָּה יִשְׁהֶה בֵּין תְּפִלָּה לִתְפִלָּה? רַב הוּנָא וְרַב חִסְדָּא, חַד אָמַר: כְּדֵי שֶׁתִּתְחוֹנֵן דַּעְתּוֹ עָלָיו; וְחַד אָמַר: כְּדֵי שֶׁתִּתְחוֹלֵל דַּעְתּוֹ עָלָיו.

Stemming from the discussion about individuals who recite two prayers consecutively, the Gemara asks: **How long should one wait between** the first **prayer and** the second **prayer?**[H] **Rav Huna and Rav Ḥisda** agreed about this in principle, but they formulated their opinions differently (Rashi). **One said** that an individual must wait long enough **so that his mind will be in a pleading** mode [*tithonen*], enabling him to recite the second prayer as a plea. **One of them said:** Long enough **so that his mind will be in a beseeching** mode [*titholel*], enabling him to beseech God in his second prayer.

מַאן דְּאָמַר כְּדֵי שֶׁתִּתְחוֹנֵן דַּעְתּוֹ עָלָיו – דִּכְתִיב: "וָאֶתְחַנַּן אֶל ה'"; וּמַאן דְּאָמַר כְּדֵי שֶׁתִּתְחוֹלֵל דַּעְתּוֹ עָלָיו – דִּכְתִיב: "וַיְחַל מֹשֶׁה".

The Gemara points out that both Rav Huna and Rav Ḥisda based their positions on the prayers of Moses. **The one who said: So that his mind will be in a pleading** mode [*tithonen*], **as it is written: "And I pleaded [*va'ethanan*] before the Lord"** (Deuteronomy 3:23). **And the one who said: So that his mind will be in a beseeching** mode [*titholel*] **as it is written: "And Moses besought [*vayeḥal*] the Lord"** (Exodus 32:11).

אָמַר רַב עָנָן אָמַר רַב: טָעָה וְלֹא הִזְכִּיר שֶׁל רֹאשׁ חֹדֶשׁ עַרְבִית – אֵין מַחֲזִירִין אוֹתוֹ, לְפִי שֶׁאֵין בֵּית דִּין מְקַדְּשִׁין אֶת הַחֹדֶשׁ אֶלָּא בַּיּוֹם.

The Gemara resumes the above discussion with regard to omission of the mention of the New Moon in the *Amida* prayer. **Rav Anan said** that **Rav said: One who erred and did not mention the New Moon in the evening prayer, we do not require him to return** to the beginning of the prayer and repeat it, **because the court only sanctifies the new month by day,** and the prayer of the New Moon, which parallels the court's sanctification of the new month, belongs in the daytime prayer.

## NOTES

**Between the columns** – **בֵּינֵי עַמּוּדֵי**: Some say that this is repeated here to teach us that they would even recite the additional prayer between the columns, as they held that there is no need for a quorum of ten (*Penei Yehoshua*).

## HALAKHA

**Would only pray…where they studied** – **לָא הָווּ מְצַלּוּ אֶלָּא...הֵיכָא דַּהֲווּ גָּרְסִי**: A permanent study hall is more sacred than a synagogue. Therefore, assuming that one prays with a prayer quorum, it is a greater mitzva to pray in the study hall than in the synagogue, as per the custom of Rabbi Ami and Rabbi Asi. Some say that, even without a prayer quorum, it is preferable to pray in the study hall (Rambam *Sefer Ahava*, *Hilkhot Tefilla* 8:3; *Shulḥan Arukh*, *Oraḥ Ḥayyim* 90:18; and in the comment of the Rema).

**Intent during prayer** – **כַּוָּונָה בִּתְפִילָּה**: While praying, one must focus his heart on the meaning of the words (*Mishna Berura*), at least during the first blessing of the *Amida* prayer, the blessing of the Patriarchs. If he was unable to muster the proper intent, he is required to repeat the prayer. However, these days, one does not repeat the *Amida* prayer for lack of proper intent, as it is safe to assume that he will not muster the requisite intent the second time either (Rambam *Sefer Ahava*, *Hilkhot Tefilla* 4:15; *Shulḥan Arukh*, *Oraḥ Ḥayyim* 101:1 and in the comment of the Rema).

**One who erred and did not mention the New Moon in the evening prayer** – **טָעָה וְלֹא הִזְכִּיר שֶׁל רֹאשׁ חֹדֶשׁ עַרְבִית**: One who erred and did not say: May there rise and come, in the evening prayer on the New Moon, whether it is a one-day or two-day New Moon, is not required to repeat the prayer, as per the opinion of Rav Ashi and the conclusion of the Gemara (Rambam *Sefer Ahava*, *Hilkhot Tefilla* 10:11; *Shulḥan Arukh*, *Oraḥ Ḥayyim* 422:1).

**A prayer leader who did not mention: May there rise and come** – **שְׁלִיחַ צִיבּוּר שֶׁלֹּא הִזְכִּיר יַעֲלֶה וְיָבוֹא**: If a prayer leader forgot to recite May there rise and come in the repetition of the morning prayer and already completed his prayer, he need not repeat the prayer because he is going to mention the New Moon in the additional prayer, as per the opinion of Rabbi Yoḥanan. If he realizes the omission before completing his prayer, he returns to the blessing of Temple service and recites: May there rise and come (*Shulḥan Arukh*, *Oraḥ Ḥayyim* 126:3).

**How long should one wait between the first prayer and the second prayer** – **כַּמָּה יִשְׁהֶה בֵּין תְּפִלָּה לִתְפִלָּה**: If one must recite two prayers at the same time, e.g., the morning prayer and the additional prayer, or the a prayer along with a compensatory prayer, one must wait a period of time sufficient to walk four cubits (Jerusalem Talmud) between the two prayers in order to settle his mind so that he may focus on pleading before God, as there is no halakhic difference between the two expressions in the Gemara: *tithonen* and *titholel* (Rambam *Sefer Ahava*, *Hilkhot Tefilla* 10:15; *Shulḥan Arukh*, *Oraḥ Ḥayyim* 105).

אָמַר אַמֵימָר: מִסְתַּבְּרָא מִילְּתָא דְּרַב בְּחֹדֶשׁ מָלֵא, אֲבָל בְּחֹדֶשׁ חָסֵר – מַחֲזִירִין אוֹתוֹ.

**Ameimar said: Rav's statement is reasonable in a full month,** i.e., a month in which there are two potential days of the New Moon, the thirtieth day of the previous month and the first day of the new month. If one neglected to mention the New Moon on the night of the thirtieth, we do not require him to return to the beginning of the prayer and repeat it, because he can mention it the next night, which is the night of the first of the new month, which is the primary day of the New Moon. **But in a short month** of twenty-nine days, followed by one day of the New Moon, **we require him to return** to the beginning of the prayer and repeat it, even in the evening prayer.

אָמַר לֵיהּ רַב אַשִׁי לְאַמֵימָר: מִכְּדִי רַב טַעְמָא קָאָמַר, מַה לִּי חָסֵר וּמַה לִּי מָלֵא! אֶלָּא, לָא שְׁנָא.

**Rav Ashi said to Ameimar: Since Rav states a reason** for his statement, **what** difference **is** there **to me** if the month is **short, and what** difference **is** there **to me** if it is **full? Rather, there is no difference.** Rav based his opinion on the parallel drawn between the sanctification of the month and the mention of the New Moon in the *Amida* prayer; the sanctification of the month is not relevant at night.

הדרן עלך תפלת השחר

# Summary of **Perek IV**

Many of the fundamental dilemmas raised in this chapter remained unresolved in the Gemara. Even where the Gemara did reach a conclusion, the conclusion did not always remain throughout the generations, as rulings in favor of one opinion were changed to favor the other. Consequently, many of the *halakhot* remain unresolved even today.

A decision was reached with regard to the time of the morning prayer; this lasts until the end of the fourth hour of the day. However, with regard to the time of the afternoon prayer, the *tanna'im* disagreed whether it extends until the evening or until the midpoint of *minḥa*, an hour and a quarter before the evening. No clear halakhic ruling was reached regarding this issue. The Gemara's conclusion is: One who practices in accordance with this Sage has fulfilled his obligation, and one who practices in accordance with that Sage has fulfilled his obligation. In other words, the decision remains in the hands of each individual. This lack of clarity blurs the distinction between the times of the afternoon and evening prayers as well as the boundary between the weekday and Shabbat prayers, which are recited during this time frame.

Another problem resolved in the Gemara concerns the evening prayer. In the dispute over this issue, which led to the temporary dismissal of the *Nasi*, the ruling was that the evening prayer is optional. Nevertheless, the custom adopted by the Jewish people throughout the generations was to treat the evening prayer as an obligation.

On a similar note, there were two conflicting approaches to the obligation to recite the *Amida* prayer. One approach favored a fixed daily prayer, while the other advocated a prayer whose essence was primarily devotional; any time that a person was unable to pray with all his heart, he would pray an abridged prayer or even not pray at all. The halakhic conclusion took the middle ground. However, fundamentally, even Rabbi Akiva's opinion, which was adopted, accepts the principle that prayer and the language of the prayer are not a fixed obligation; rather, prayer reflects the individual's circumstances and state of mind at the time.

Sages throughout Jewish history conducted themselves in this manner. Nevertheless, here too the custom adopted by the Jewish people corresponds with the first opinion that one must always recite the complete *Amida* prayer, even when he is incapable of praying with all his heart.

With regard to the additional prayer, the ruling was that the obligation to recite this prayer is incumbent even upon an individual praying alone, separate from the community.

Ultimately, it seems that the ruling accepted throughout the Jewish people is based on the approach that "the prayers were instituted parallel to the daily offerings in the Temple." At the same time, there is room for individual devotional prayer, which is not included in the framework of communal prayer.

# Introduction to **Perek V**

Chapter Four dealt primarily with clarifying the framework for prayer, i.e., establishing the times of the fixed prayers and defining the circumstances in which an individual is exempt from prayer. The primary focus of Chapter Five is the content of the prayer, the details within this framework. While the previous chapter discussed the individual's obligation to engage in the act of prayer, this chapter focuses on elucidating the spiritual demands, namely, the requisite and desired approach to prayer. In particular, the chapter deals with how one approaches prayer; what elements are required, permitted, or prohibited to introduce into the prayer formula; and what prayer is capable of accomplishing. Despite the legalistic manner in which the Gemara deals with issues, the *halakha* is very closely tied to the philosophical questions involved.

There are various methods of preparation for prayer, such as adopting an approach of gravity, studying Torah, or engaging in performance of a mitzva and experiencing the joy associated with that performance. More than an expression of difference of opinion, these constitute a variety of complementary approaches to different aspects of prayer: Petition and submission, the joy of thanksgiving and the gravity of contemplation. The many aggadic passages in this chapter shed light on these different aspects of prayer.

Even the additions to the daily prayers hold significance. Prayer is a specific framework that expresses particular approaches to supplication and perspectives on faith. A person may not introduce elements to prayer indiscriminately. This was especially significant at a time when there were various deviant sects very close to traditional Judaism, who secretly sought to introduce their deviant ideas into the accepted prayer formula. On the other hand, there are specific elements that one must emphasize and include in his requests. It was vital to determine the most significant, general needs that may and even must be incorporated into the various blessings, such as the request for rain, emphasis of the sanctity of the Festivals, and recitation of *havdala* between the sacred and the profane.

Although at times one is required to include additions to the standard prayer formula, it is incumbent upon the individual to ensure that he is not swept away in a wave of enthusiasm that might lead him to introduce elements to his prayer that deviate from the fundamental tenets of Judaism.

Prayer places numerous demands upon one engaged in it. Primary among them is the requirement that one achieve a sense of absolute self-negation as he stands before his Maker. Nevertheless, the Gemara also alludes to and elaborates upon the reward of one who prays and God's response to those who call out to Him with all their heart.

מתני׳ אֵין עוֹמְדִין לְהִתְפַּלֵּל אֶלָּא מִתּוֹךְ כּוֹבֶד רֹאשׁ. חֲסִידִים הָרִאשׁוֹנִים הָיוּ שׁוֹהִין שָׁעָה אַחַת וּמִתְפַּלְּלִין, כְּדֵי שֶׁיְּכַוְּונוּ לִבָּם לַאֲבִיהֶם שֶׁבַּשָּׁמַיִם. אֲפִילּוּ הַמֶּלֶךְ שׁוֹאֵל בִּשְׁלוֹמוֹ לֹא יְשִׁיבֶנּוּ, וַאֲפִילּוּ נָחָשׁ כָּרוּךְ עַל עֲקֵבוֹ לֹא יַפְסִיק.

**MISHNA** **One** may **only stand** and begin to pray **from** an approach of **gravity** and submission.[H] There is a tradition that **the early** generations of **pious** men **would wait one hour,** in order to reach the solemn frame of mind appropriate for prayer, **and then pray, so that they would focus their hearts toward their Father in Heaven.** Standing in prayer is standing before God and, as such, **even if the king greets him, he should not respond to him; and even if a snake is wrapped on his heel, he should not interrupt** his prayer.

גמ׳ מְנָא הָנֵי מִילֵּי? אָמַר רַבִּי אֶלְעָזָר דְּאָמַר קְרָא: ״וְהִיא מָרַת נָפֶשׁ״.

**GEMARA** We learned in the mishna that prayer should be undertaken in an atmosphere of gravity. The Gemara asks: **From where are these matters** derived? Rabbi Elazar said: They are derived from the verses describing the prayer of Hannah, mother of Samuel, **as the verse states: "And she felt bitterness of soul,** and she prayed to the Lord and she wept and wept" (I Samuel 1:10).

מִמַּאי? דִּילְמָא חַנָּה שָׁאנֵי, דַּהֲוַה מְרִירָא לִבָּא טוּבָא!

The Gemara rejects this proof: **From what** does that conclusion ensue? **Perhaps Hannah is different,** as her **heart was extremely embittered,** her prayer was embittered as well. This does not prove that everyone must pray in that frame of mind.

אֶלָּא אָמַר רַבִּי יוֹסֵי בְּרַבִּי חֲנִינָא מֵהָכָא: ״וַאֲנִי בְּרֹב חַסְדְּךָ אָבוֹא בֵיתֶךָ אֶשְׁתַּחֲוֶה אֶל הֵיכַל קָדְשְׁךָ בְּיִרְאָתֶךָ״.

**Rather, Rabbi Yosei, son of Rabbi Ḥanina, said,** it can be proved **from here,** as David said: **"But as for me, by Your abundant lovingkindness I will enter Your house, at Your Holy Temple I will bow in reverence for You"** (Psalms 5:8). **Entering into prayer like entering the Holy Temple must be performed reverentially.**

מִמַּאי, דִּילְמָא דָּוִד שָׁאנֵי, דַּהֲוָה מְצַעֵר נַפְשֵׁיהּ בְּרַחֲמֵי טוּבָא! – אֶלָּא אָמַר רַבִּי יְהוֹשֻׁעַ בֶּן לֵוִי מֵהָכָא ״הִשְׁתַּחֲווּ לַה׳ בְּהַדְרַת קֹדֶשׁ״, אַל תִּקְרֵי ״בְּהַדְרַת״ אֶלָּא ״בְּחֶרְדַּת״.

The Gemara rejects this proof as well: **From what** does that conclusion ensue? **Perhaps David is different, as he would excessively afflict himself in prayer** in order to atone for his transgression with Bathsheba. Consequently, his cannot serve as a paradigm for proper conduct in prayer. **Rather, Rabbi Yehoshua ben Levi said,** it can be derived **from here,** from this verse that David said, not about his own worship, but about worship of God in general: "Give, unto the Lord, the honor of His name, **bow to the Lord in the beauty of holiness** [***behadrat kodesh***]" (Psalms 29:2). **Do not read: In the beauty of** [***behadrat***] holiness. **Rather** read: **In trembling of** [***beḥerdat***] holiness; one must enter into prayer from an atmosphere of gravity engendered by sanctity.

מִמַּאי? דִּילְמָא לְעוֹלָם אֵימָא לָךְ הַדְרַת מַמָּשׁ, כִּי הָא דְּרַב יְהוּדָה הֲוָה מְצַיֵּין נַפְשֵׁיהּ וַהֲדַר מְצַלֵּי! – אֶלָּא אָמַר רַב נַחְמָן בַּר יִצְחָק מֵהָכָא ״עִבְדוּ אֶת ה׳ בְּיִרְאָה וְגִילוּ בִּרְעָדָה״.

The Gemara rejects this too: **From what** does that conclusion ensue? **Perhaps, actually I would say to you** that it should be read as it is written: **Specifically, "in the beauty,"** and it means that one should pray in beautiful clothing, **as in the case of Rav Yehuda who would adorn himself and then pray.**[H] Rav Yehuda believed that one who comes before the King must wear his most beautiful clothing. The Gemara has yet to find a source for the *halakha* that one must approach prayer from an atmosphere of gravity. **Rather, Rav Naḥman bar Yitzḥak said** it can be derived **from here,** from this verse: **"Serve the Lord in fear and rejoice with trembling"** (Psalms 2:11).

מַאי ״וְגִילוּ בִּרְעָדָה״? אָמַר רַב אַדָּא בַּר מַתָּנָא אָמַר רַבָּה: בִּמְקוֹם גִּילָה שָׁם תְּהֵא רְעָדָה.

Having cited this verse from Psalms, the Gemara asks: **What is** the meaning of **rejoice with trembling? Rav Adda bar Mattana said** that **Rabba said:** One may not experience unbridled joy; even **where there is rejoicing, there should be trembling.**

אַבַּיֵּי הֲוָה יָתֵיב קַמֵּיהּ דְּרַבָּה, חַזְיֵיהּ דַּהֲוָה קָא בָדַח טוּבָא, אָמַר: ״וְגִילוּ בִּרְעָדָה״ כְּתִיב!

On that note, the Gemara relates: **Abaye was sitting before** his teacher **Rabba,** and Rabba **saw that he was excessively joyful. He said** to Abaye: **It is written: Rejoice with trembling,** one's joy should not be unrestrained.

**HALAKHA**

**One may only stand and begin to pray from an approach of gravity and submission – אֵין עוֹמְדִין אֶלָּא מִתּוֹךְ כּוֹבֶד רֹאשׁ:** One may stand to pray only from an atmosphere of awe and submission. He must not pray from a mood of laughter or lightheartedness, idle chatter or anger, but from a feeling of joy (Rambam *Sefer Ahava, Hilkhot Tefilla* 4:16, 18; *Shulḥan Arukh, Oraḥ Ḥayyim* 93:2).

**Who would adorn himself and then pray – הֲוָה מְצַיֵּין נַפְשֵׁיהּ וַהֲדַר מְצַלֵּי:** The Sages and their students only prayed when clothed appropriately. The Rema writes that in periods of calm, one should dress in fine clothing while praying; in wrathful times one should clasp one hand in the other while praying, like a servant standing before his master (Rambam *Sefer Ahava, Hilkhot Tefilla* 5:5; *Shulḥan Arukh, Oraḥ Ḥayyim* 91:6).

NOTES

I am donning phylacteries – אֲנָא תְּפִילִּין מַנַּחְנָא: Some explain this response to mean that he is joyful because he is wearing phylacteries, and therefore joy is permitted (*HaKotev*). Others interpret this based on a tradition that due to an illness, Rabba was unable to don phylacteries earlier, and he was overjoyed to finally be privileged to perform this mitzva (*Talmidei Rabbeinu Yona*).

אָמַר לֵיהּ: אֲנָא תְּפִילִּין מַנַּחְנָא.

Abaye **said to him:** It is permissible for me because **I am donning phylacteries**[N] now and as long as they are upon me they ensure that the fear of God is upon me.

רַבִּי יִרְמְיָה הֲוָה יָתֵיב קַמֵּיהּ דְּרַבִּי זֵירָא, חַזְיֵיהּ דַּהֲוָה קָא בָּדַח טוּבָא, אָמַר לֵיהּ, ״בְּכָל עֶצֶב יִהְיֶה מוֹתָר״ כְּתִיב!

Similarly, the Gemara relates that **Rabbi Yirmeya was sitting before Rabbi Zeira. He saw that Rabbi Yirmeya was excessively joyful. He said to him: It is written: "In all sorrow there is profit"** (Proverbs 14:23); sorrow is appropriate, not excessive joy.

אָמַר לֵיהּ: אֲנָא תְּפִילִּין מַנַּחְנָא.

Rabbi Yirmeya **said to him:** It is permissible for me because **I am donning phylacteries.**

מָר בְּרֵיהּ דְּרָבִינָא עֲבַד הִילּוּלָא לִבְרֵיהּ, חֲזַנְהוּ לְרַבָּנַן דַּהֲווּ קָבָדְחִי טוּבָא,

On a similar note, the Gemara relates: **Mar, son of Ravina, made a wedding** feast **for his son and he saw the Sages, who were excessively joyous.**

Perek **V**
Daf **31** Amud **a**

BACKGROUND

A cup of valuable white glass – כָּסָא דְּזוּגִיתָא:

Glass vessels from the talmudic period

אַיְיתִי כָּסָא דְּמוֹקְרָא, בַּת אַרְבַּע מְאָה זוּזֵי, וּתְבַר קַמַּיְיהוּ, וְאַעֲצִיבוּ.

**He brought a valuable cup**[B] **worth four hundred** ***zuz*** **and broke it before them and they became sad.**

רַב אָשֵׁי עֲבַד הִילּוּלָא לִבְרֵיהּ, חֲזַנְהוּ לְרַבָּנַן דַּהֲווּ קָא בָּדְחִי טוּבָא, אַיְיתִי כָּסָא דְּזוּגִיתָא חִיוָּרְתָּא וּתְבַר קַמַּיְיהוּ, וְאַעֲצִיבוּ.

The Gemara also relates: **Rav Ashi made a wedding** feast **for his son and he saw the Sages, who were excessively joyous. He brought a cup of** extremely valuable **white glass and broke it before them, and they became sad.**

אֲמַרוּ לֵיהּ רַבָּנַן לְרַב הַמְנוּנָא זוּטִי בְּהִלּוּלָא דְּמָר בְּרֵיהּ דְּרָבִינָא: לִישְׁרֵי לַן מָר! – אֲמַר לְהוּ: וַי לַן דְּמָיְתִינַן, וַי לַן דְּמָיְתִינַן! אָמְרִי לֵיהּ: אֲנַן מָה נַעֲנֵי בַּתְרָךְ? – אֲמַר לְהוּ: הֵי תּוֹרָה וְהֵי מִצְוָה דְּמַגְנוּ עֲלַן?

Similarly, the Gemara relates: **The Sages said to Rav Hamnuna Zuti at the wedding** feast **of Mar, son of Ravina: Let the Master sing for us.** Since he believed that the merriment had become excessive, **he said to them,** singing: **Woe unto us, for we shall die, woe unto us, for we shall die.**[N] **They said to him: What shall we respond after you?** What is the chorus of the song? **He said to them,** you should respond: **Where is Torah and where is mitzva that protect us?**

NOTES

Woe unto us, for we shall die – וַי לַן דְּמָיְתִינַן: Some explain the relevance of this to a wedding as follows: As a person is destined to die and does not exist eternally as an individual, he must bring offspring into the world and perpetuate the existence of humankind (*Yoḥasin*).

One is forbidden to fill his mouth with mirth in this world – אָסוּר לְאָדָם שֶׁיְּמַלֵּא שְׂחוֹק פִּיו בָּעוֹלָם הַזֶּה: Some explain that this prohibition is not due to mourning over the destruction of the Temple; rather, it is prohibited because excessive frivolity leads one to become insensitive to transgression and distracts him from pursuing the fulfillment of the will of God (*Talmidei Rabbeinu Yona, Shitta Mekubbetzet*).

אָמַר רַבִּי יוֹחָנָן מִשּׁוּם רַבִּי שִׁמְעוֹן בֶּן יוֹחַאי: אָסוּר לְאָדָם שֶׁיְּמַלֵּא שְׂחוֹק פִּיו בָּעוֹלָם הַזֶּה, שֶׁנֶּאֱמַר: ״אָז יִמָּלֵא שְׂחוֹק פִּינוּ וּלְשׁוֹנֵנוּ רִנָּה״, אֵימָתַי – בִּזְמַן שֶׁ״יֹּאמְרוּ בַגּוֹיִם הִגְדִּיל ה׳ לַעֲשׂוֹת עִם אֵלֶּה״. אָמְרוּ עָלָיו עַל רֵישׁ לָקִישׁ, שֶׁמִּיָּמָיו לֹא מִלֵּא שְׂחוֹק פִּיו בָּעוֹלָם הַזֶּה מִכִּי שְׁמָעַהּ מֵרַבִּי יוֹחָנָן רַבֵּיהּ.

In a similar vein, **Rabbi Yoḥanan said in the name of Rabbi Shimon ben Yoḥai: One is forbidden to fill his mouth with mirth in this world,**[NH] as long as we are in exile (*ge'onim*), **as it is stated:** "When the Lord returns the captivity of Zion we will be as dreamers" (Psalms 126:1). Only **"then will our mouths fill with laughter and our lips with song"** (Psalms 126:2). **When** will that joyous era arrive? When **"they will say among nations, the Lord has done great things with these"** (Psalms 126:2). **They said about Reish Lakish that throughout his life he did not fill his mouth with laughter in this world once he heard this** statement **from his teacher, Rabbi Yoḥanan.**

HALAKHA

One is forbidden to fill his mouth with mirth in this world – אָסוּר שֶׁיְּמַלֵּא שְׂחוֹק פִּיו בָּעוֹלָם הַזֶּה: One may not fill his mouth with laughter in this world. Some say that it is because it will lead him to fail to fulfill the mitzvot. Others say that frivolity leads to sin (see *Magen Avraham* and *Taz*; *Shulḥan Arukh, Oraḥ Ḥayyim* 560:5).

One may neither stand and begin to pray from judgment nor from a matter of *halakha* – אֵין עוֹמְדִין לְהִתְפַּלֵּל לֹא מִתּוֹךְ דִּין, וְלֹא מִתּוֹךְ דְּבַר הֲלָכָה: One may not stand to pray immediately following a trial or an involved halakhic discourse (Rambam *Sefer Ahava, Hilkhot Tefilla* 4:18; *Shulḥan Arukh, Oraḥ Ḥayyim* 93:3).

תָּנוּ רַבָּנַן: אֵין עוֹמְדִין לְהִתְפַּלֵּל לֹא מִתּוֹךְ דִּין, וְלֹא מִתּוֹךְ דְּבַר הֲלָכָה, אֶלָּא מִתּוֹךְ הֲלָכָה פְּסוּקָה.

We learned in the mishna that it is appropriate to stand and begin to pray from an atmosphere of gravity. Regarding this **the Sages taught: One** may **neither stand** and begin to pray directly **from** involvement in **judgment nor** directly **from** deliberation over the ruling in a **matter of** ***halakha***,[H] as his preoccupation with the judgment or the halakhic ruling will distract him from prayer. **Rather** it is appropriate to pray directly **from** involvement in the study of **a** universally accepted **conclusive** ***halakha*** that leaves no room for further deliberation and will not distract him during prayer.

וְהֵיכִי דָּמֵי הֲלָכָה פְּסוּקָה?

**And** the Gemara asks: **What is an example** of **a conclusive** ***halakha*?**

אָמַר אַבָּיֵי: כִּי הָא דְּרַבִּי זֵירָא, דְּאָמַר רַבִּי זֵירָא: בְּנוֹת יִשְׂרָאֵל הֶחְמִירוּ עַל עַצְמָן שֶׁאֲפִילּוּ רוֹאוֹת טִיפַּת דָּם כְּחַרְדָּל – יוֹשְׁבוֹת עָלֶיהָ שִׁבְעָה נְקִיִּים.

The Gemara offers several examples: **Abaye said:** One **like this** *halakha* **of Rabbi Zeira, as Rabbi Zeira said: The daughters of Israel were stringent with themselves;** to the extent **that even if they see a drop of blood corresponding to** the size of **a mustard** seed **she sits seven clean** days **for it.**[H] By Torah law, a woman who witnesses the emission of blood during the eleven days following her fixed menstrual period is not considered a menstruating woman;[B] rather she immerses herself and is purified the next day. However, the women of Israel accepted the stringency upon themselves that if they see any blood whatsoever, they act as it if were the blood of a *zava*,[B] which obligates her to count seven more clean days before becoming ritually pure (see Leviticus 15:25).

רָבָא אָמַר: כִּי הָא דְּרַב הוֹשַׁעְיָא, דְּאָמַר רַב הוֹשַׁעְיָא: מַעֲרִים אָדָם עַל תְּבוּאָתוֹ וּמַכְנִיסָהּ בְּמוֹץ שֶׁלָּהּ, כְּדֵי שֶׁתְּהֵא בְּהֶמְתּוֹ אוֹכֶלֶת וּפְטוּרָה מִן הַמַּעֲשֵׂר.

Citing an additional example of a conclusive *halakha*, **Rava said:** One **like this** *halakha* **of Rav Hoshaya, as Rav Hoshaya said: A person may employ artifice** to circumvent obligations[N] incumbent **upon** him in dealing with **his grain and bring it into** the courtyard **in its chaff**[H] **so that his animal will eat** from it, **and** the grain **is exempt** from **tithes.** *Halakha* dictates that one is obligated to tithe grain that has been threshed and piled, regardless of the ultimate purpose for which the grain was intended. By Torah law, one is exempt from tithing grain that was not threshed and is therefore still in its chaff. By rabbinic law, one is prohibited from eating this grain in the framework of a meal. Feeding animals is permitted without first tithing that grain.

וְאִיבָּעֵית אֵימָא: כִּי הָא דְּרַב הוּנָא, דְּאָמַר רַב הוּנָא אָמַר רַבִּי זְעֵירָא: הַמַּקִּיז דָּם בִּבְהֵמַת קָדָשִׁים – אָסוּר בַּהֲנָאָה וּמוֹעֲלִין בּוֹ.

**And if you wish, say** instead yet another example of a conclusive *halakha*, which is the recommended prelude to prayer. One **like this** *halakha* **of Rav Huna,** as **Rav Huna said** that **Rabbi Zeira said: One who lets blood from a consecrated animal**[H] that was consecrated as a sacrifice; deriving **benefit** from that blood **is prohibited.** Although blood of an offering that was sprinkled on the altar is not considered Temple property, nevertheless, deriving benefit from the blood of a living, consecrated animal is considered prohibited use of Temple property. In so doing, **one misuses** property consecrated to the Temple, and as in any other case of misusing Temple property, if he did so unwittingly, he is liable to bring a guilt-offering.

רַבָּנַן עָבְדִי כְּמַתְנִיתִין, רַב אַשִׁי עָבֵיד כְּבָרַיְיתָא.

It is related that **the Sages acted in accordance with** the opinion of **our mishna** and rose to pray from an atmosphere of gravity; **Rav Ashi acted in accordance with** the opinion of **the** ***baraita*** and preceded his prayer with a conclusive *halakha*.

תָּנוּ רַבָּנַן: אֵין עוֹמְדִין לְהִתְפַּלֵּל לֹא מִתּוֹךְ עַצְבוּת, וְלֹא מִתּוֹךְ עַצְלוּת, וְלֹא מִתּוֹךְ שְׂחוֹק, וְלֹא מִתּוֹךְ שִׂיחָה, וְלֹא מִתּוֹךְ קַלּוּת רֹאשׁ, וְלֹא מִתּוֹךְ דְּבָרִים בְּטֵלִים – אֶלָּא מִתּוֹךְ שִׂמְחָה שֶׁל מִצְוָה.

On the topic of proper preparation for prayer, **the Sages taught: One may neither stand to pray from** an atmosphere of **sorrow**[H] **nor** an atmosphere of **laziness, nor** an atmosphere of **laughter, nor** an atmosphere of **conversation, nor** an atmosphere of **frivolity, nor** an atmosphere of **purposeless matters. Rather,** one should approach prayer **from** an atmosphere imbued with **the joy of a mitzva.**

## HALAKHA

**Even if they see a drop of blood corresponding to the size of a mustard seed, she sits seven clean days for it – שֶׁאֲפִילּוּ רוֹאוֹת טִיפַּת דָּם כְּחַרְדָּל יוֹשְׁבוֹת עָלֶיהָ שִׁבְעָה נְקִיִּים:** If a woman discovers that a drop of blood emerged from her womb, even if she did not feel it emerge, based on this rabbinic decree, she must wait seven clean days before purifying herself (Rambam *Sefer Kedusha, Hilkhot Issurei Bia* 11:4; *Shulḥan Arukh, Yoreh De'a* 183).

**A person may employ artifice in dealing with his grain and bring it into the courtyard in its chaff – מַעֲרִים אָדָם עַל תְּבוּאָתוֹ וּמַכְנִיסָהּ בְּמוֹץ שֶׁלָּהּ:** One is permitted to bring grain into his courtyard while it is still mixed with chaff, in order to feed it to his animal. He is then exempt from tithing it, even if he subsequently winnows it a little bit at a time for personal use (Rambam *Sefer Zera'im, Hilkhot Ma'aser* 3:6; *Shulḥan Arukh, Yoreh De'a* 331:84).

**One who lets blood from a consecrated animal – הַמַּקִּיז דָּם בִּבְהֵמַת קָדָשִׁים:** It is forbidden to benefit from blood let from an animal that has been consecrated. One who does so is guilty of misuse of property consecrated to the Temple (Rambam *Sefer Avoda, Hilkhot Me'ila* 2:11).

**One may neither stand to pray from an atmosphere of sorrow, etc. – אֵין עוֹמְדִין לְהִתְפַּלֵּל לֹא מִתּוֹךְ עַצְבוּת וכו׳:** One may only stand to pray from an atmosphere of reverence and subservience; not one of laughter, frivolity, idle conversation, or anger. He must also approach his prayer with joy (Rambam *Sefer Ahava, Hilkhot Tefilla* 4:16; *Shulḥan Arukh, Oraḥ Ḥayyim* 93:2). This is in accordance with Rav Ashi and the *baraita* (see the *Baḥ*; Rambam *Sefer Ahava, Hilkhot Tefilla* 4:18; *Shulḥan Arukh, Oraḥ Ḥayyim* 93:2–3).

## NOTES

**A person may employ artifice to circumvent obligations – מַעֲרִים אָדָם:** Several examples exist in *halakha* where one is permitted to employ artifice in this manner. The common denominator in all of these cases is that the artifice is not an attempt to circumvent the essence of the halakhic ruling by Torah law, but rather to prevent a derivative prohibition. In this case, essentially, animal food is exempt from tithing. However, once it has been threshed, technically, *halakha* requires it to be tithed. Therefore, the artifice here is a permitted action undertaken to resolve a technical difficulty that arose.

## BACKGROUND

**menstruating woman – נִדָּה:** By Torah law, a woman is ritually impure for seven days after the onset of her menstrual bleeding. On the eve of the eighth day, she immerses herself in a spring or ritual bath to purify herself. According to Torah law, a menstruating woman may purify herself on the eighth day, even if she had been bleeding for the entire seven-day period. The Talmud, however, states that women themselves adopted a stringency, and consequently, any woman who experiences uterine bleeding is required to wait seven days without any bleeding before immersion in the ritual bath. From the beginning of her period, until she immerses herself, she renders both people and objects with which she comes into contact, or people who carry her even without making contact, ritually impure. Similarly, a man who has sexual intercourse with a menstruating woman becomes ritually impure for seven days.

***Zava* – זָבָה:** A woman who experiences a flow of menstrual-type blood on three consecutive days during a time of the month when she is not due to experience menstrual bleeding. The first secretion makes her ritually impure, but until the third secretion her status is that of a woman who keeps watch a day for a day, and she is not subject to all the halakhic rulings of a *zava*. After experiencing bleeding on the third day, the woman is considered a *zava* and is obligated to bring a sacrifice as part of her purification process. A *zava* imparts ritual impurity in the same way as a *zav*. In addition, a man who engages in sexual relations with her becomes a primary source of ritual impurity and imparts ritual impurity to others.

## NOTES

From involvement in a matter of *halakha* – מִתּוֹךְ דְּבַר הֲלָכָה: The parallel passage in the Jerusalem Talmud adds that one who engages in tending to communal needs before prayer has the same legal status as one who is involved in a matter of *halakha*.

So that, consequently, he will remember him – שֶׁמִּתּוֹךְ כָּךְ זוֹכְרֵהוּ: Some explain this as: So that he will remember it. When remembering parting from his colleague, he will always be reminded of this *halakha* (*Alfasi Zuta*).

An indication of this matter – סִימָן לַדָּבָר: The Gemara does not say: A proof for this, but rather: An indication, because in the verse it is not phrased as a command or instruction, but merely as a statement; if one focuses his heart, his prayer is accepted (*Shitta Mekubbetzet*).

Bows and prostrations – כְּרִיעוֹת וְהִשְׁתַּחֲוָיוֹת: The commentaries dispute whether these bows and prostrations were part of his *Amida* prayer, or whether they were an addition to that prayer. Some explain that he bowed after completing the standard prayer (Rashba, *Me'iri*, HaRav Rabbeinu Yosef), so that this would not contradict the *halakhot* requiring one to stand while praying. Others explained that, in fact, all this took place during the *Amida* prayer itself, as per the simple understanding of the Gemara (*Tosafot*, *Tosefot Rabbeinu Yehuda HaḤasid*).

A house with windows – בַּיִת שֶׁיֵּשׁ בּוֹ חַלּוֹנוֹת: Some explain that this is so one will be able to see the expanses and the sky (Rashi), and others say that the windows were necessary to further illuminate the synagogue as light has a salutary effect and facilitates one's focus on his prayer (*Talmidei Rabbeinu Yona*).

## HALAKHA

When he would pray with the congregation he would shorten his prayer and go up – כְּשֶׁהָיָה מִתְפַּלֵּל עִם הַצִּיבּוּר הָיָה מְקַצֵּר וְעוֹלֶה: It is inappropriate for a communal prayer leader to prolong his prayer and thereby burden the congregation. He should conduct himself in accordance with the conduct of Rabbi Akiva (Rambam *Sefer Ahava*, *Hilkhot Tefilla* 6:2; *Shulḥan Arukh*, *Oraḥ Ḥayyim* 53:11).

One should always pray in a house with windows – לְעוֹלָם יִתְפַּלֵּל אָדָם בְּבַיִת שֶׁיֵּשׁ בּוֹ חַלּוֹנוֹת: It is appropriate for a synagogue to have windows facing Jerusalem, so that congregants will face them while praying. It is preferable for a synagogue to have twelve windows (*Zohar*, *Vayak-hel*; Rambam *Sefer Ahava*, *Hilkhot Tefilla* 5:6; *Shulḥan Arukh*, *Oraḥ Ḥayyim* 90:4).

וְכֵן לֹא יִפָּטֵר אָדָם מֵחֲבֵרוֹ לֹא מִתּוֹךְ שִׂיחָה, וְלֹא מִתּוֹךְ שְׂחוֹק, וְלֹא מִתּוֹךְ קַלּוּת רֹאשׁ, וְלֹא מִתּוֹךְ דְּבָרִים בְּטֵלִים – אֶלָּא מִתּוֹךְ דְּבַר הֲלָכָה, שֶׁכֵּן מָצִינוּ בַּנְּבִיאִים הָרִאשׁוֹנִים שֶׁסִּיְּימוּ דִּבְרֵיהֶם בְּדִבְרֵי שֶׁבַח וְתַנְחוּמִים.

**Similarly, a person should neither take leave of another from** an atmosphere of **conversation, nor from** an atmosphere of **laughter, nor from** an atmosphere of **frivolity, nor from** an atmosphere of **purposeless matters. Rather,** one should take leave of another **from** involvement in a **matter of *halakha*.**[N] **As we found in** the books of the Bible dealing with **the early prophets, that they would conclude their talks with words of praise and consolation.**

וְכֵן תָּנָא מָרִי בַּר בְּרֵיהּ דְּרַב הוּנָא בְּרֵיהּ דְּרַבִּי יִרְמְיָה בַּר אַבָּא: אַל יִפָּטֵר אָדָם מֵחֲבֵירוֹ אֶלָּא מִתּוֹךְ דְּבַר הֲלָכָה, שֶׁמִּתּוֹךְ כָּךְ זוֹכְרֵהוּ.

**And so Mari, the grandson of Rav Huna, son of Rabbi Yirmeya bar Abba, taught in a *baraita*: One should only take leave of another from** involvement in a **matter of *halakha*, so that, consequently, he will remember him;**[N] whenever he recalls the one from whom he took leave he will think well of him because of the new *halakha* that he taught him (*Eliyahu Zuta*).

כִּי הָא דְּרַב כָּהֲנָא אַלְוְיֵיהּ לְרַב שִׁימִי בַּר אַשִׁי מִפּוּם נַהֲרָא עַד בֵּי צִנְיָתָא דְּבָבֶל, כִּי מְטָא לְהָתָם, אֲמַר לֵיהּ: מָר, וַדַּאי דְּאָמְרִי אִינָשֵׁי: הָנֵי צִנְיָתָא דְּבָבֶל אִיתְנְהוּ מֵאָדָם הָרִאשׁוֹן וְעַד הַשְׁתָּא?

As in the incident related by the Gemara **that Rav Kahana accompanied Rav Shimi bar Ashi from** the town of **Pum Nahara to the palm grove** in **Babylonia. When he arrived there,** Rav Kahana **said to** Rav Shimi bar Ashi: **Master, what is meant by that which people say: These palm trees** of **Babylonia have been** in this place from the time of **Adam the first** man **until now?**

אֲמַר לֵיהּ: אַדְכַּרְתַּן מִילְּתָא דְּרַבִּי יוֹסֵי בְּרַבִּי חֲנִינָא, דְּאָמַר רַבִּי יוֹסֵי בְּרַבִּי חֲנִינָא: מַאי דִּכְתִיב ״בְּאֶרֶץ אֲשֶׁר לֹא עָבַר בָּהּ אִישׁ וְלֹא יָשַׁב אָדָם שָׁם״, וְכִי מֵאַחַר דְּלֹא עָבַר הֵיאַךְ יָשַׁב? אֶלָּא לוֹמַר לְךָ: כָּל אֶרֶץ שֶׁגָּזַר עָלֶיהָ אָדָם הָרִאשׁוֹן לְיִשּׁוּב – נִתְיַשְּׁבָה, וְכָל אֶרֶץ שֶׁלֹּא גָּזַר עָלֶיהָ אָדָם הָרִאשׁוֹן לְיִשּׁוּב – לֹא נִתְיַשְּׁבָה.

Rav Shimi bar Ashi **said to him: You reminded me of something that Rabbi Yosei, son of Rabbi Ḥanina,** said, **as Rabbi Yosei, son of Rabbi Ḥanina, said: What is** the meaning of **that which is written: "In a land through which no man has passed and where no person [*adam*] has settled"** (Jeremiah 2:6)? This verse is difficult; **since it is** a land through which **no** person **has passed, how** could anyone **have settled** there permanently? The statement that "no person has settled there" is redundant. **Rather,** this verse comes **to teach** that **every land through which Adam the first** man passed and **decreed that it would be settled was settled, and every land** through **which** Adam passed and **decreed that it would not be settled was not settled.** Based on this, what people say is true, and the palm trees of Babylonia are from the time of Adam, meaning that from the time of Adam this land was decreed to be suitable for growing palm trees (*Me'iri*). The Gemara cited an example of how one who parts from another with Torah learns something new.

רַב מָרְדֳּכַי אַלְוְיֵיהּ לְרַב שִׁימִי בַּר אַשִׁי מֵהַגְרוֹנְיָא וְעַד בֵּי כֵּיפֵי, וְאָמְרִי לַהּ: עַד בֵּי דּוּרָא.

Having mentioned the mitzva for a student to accompany his Rabbi, the Gemara relates that **Rav Mordekhai accompanied** his mentor, **Rav Shimi bar Ashi,** a great distance, **from** the city of **Hagronya to Bei Keifei; and some say** that he accompanied from Hagronya **to Bei Dura.**

תָּנוּ רַבָּנַן: הַמִּתְפַּלֵּל צָרִיךְ שֶׁיְּכַוֵּין אֶת לִבּוֹ לַשָּׁמַיִם. אַבָּא שָׁאוּל אוֹמֵר, סִימָן לַדָּבָר: ״תָּכִין לִבָּם תַּקְשִׁיב אָזְנֶךָ״.

Returning to the topic of preparation for prayer, **the Sages taught** in the *Tosefta*: **One who prays must focus his heart toward Heaven. Abba Shaul says: An indication of** the importance of this **matter**[N] is stated in the verse: "The desire of the humble You have heard, Lord; **direct their hearts, Your ear will listen"** (Psalms 10:17). In other words, if one focuses his heart in prayer as a result of God directing his heart, his prayer will be accepted as God's ear will listen.

תַּנְיָא, אָמַר רַבִּי יְהוּדָה: כָּךְ הָיָה מִנְהָגוֹ שֶׁל רַבִּי עֲקִיבָא, כְּשֶׁהָיָה מִתְפַּלֵּל עִם הַצִּיבּוּר – הָיָה מְקַצֵּר וְעוֹלֶה, מִפְּנֵי טוֹרַח צִבּוּר, וּכְשֶׁהָיָה מִתְפַּלֵּל בֵּינוֹ לְבֵין עַצְמוֹ – אָדָם מַנִּיחוֹ בְּזָוִית זוֹ וּמוֹצְאוֹ בְּזָוִית אַחֶרֶת, וְכָל כָּךְ לָמָּה – מִפְּנֵי כְּרִיעוֹת וְהִשְׁתַּחֲוָיוֹת.

With regard to one's intent during prayer, **it was taught** in a *baraita* that **Rabbi Yehuda said: This was the custom of Rabbi Akiva, when he would pray with the congregation he would shorten** his prayer **and go up,**[H] **due to** his desire to avoid being an **encumbrance on the congregation** by making them wait for him to finish his prayer. **But when he prayed by himself** he would extend his prayers to an extent that a **person would leave** Rabbi Akiva alone **in one corner** of the study hall **and** later **find him** still praying **in another corner. And why** would Rabbi Akiva move about **so much? Because of his bows and prostrations.**[N] Rabbi Akiva's enthusiasm in prayer was so great, that as a result of his bows and prostrations, he would unwittingly move from one corner to the other (Rav Hai Gaon).

אָמַר רַבִּי חִיָּיא בַּר אַבָּא: לְעוֹלָם יִתְפַּלֵּל אָדָם בְּבַיִת שֶׁיֵּשׁ בּוֹ חַלּוֹנוֹת, שֶׁנֶּאֱמַר: ״וְכַוִּין פְּתִיחָן לֵיהּ״ וגו׳.

Many *halakhot* are derived from evoking the prayers of biblical characters. **Rabbi Ḥiyya bar Abba said: One should always pray in a house with windows,**[NH] **as it is stated** regarding Daniel: "And when Daniel knew that the writing was signed, he went to his house. In his attic **there were open windows** facing Jerusalem, and three times a day he knelt upon his knees and prayed and gave thanks before his God, just as he had done before" (Daniel 6:11).

יָכוֹל יִתְפַּלֵּל אָדָם כָּל הַיּוֹם כּוּלּוֹ – כְּבָר מְפוֹרָשׁ עַל יְדֵי דָנִיֵּאל: ״וְזִמְנִין תְּלָתָא״ וגו׳.

In the *Tosefta*, additional *halakhot* were derived from Daniel's prayer. I **might have thought that one could pray** as many times as he wishes **throughout the entire day; it has already been articulated by Daniel,** with regard to whom it is stated: **"And three times** a day he knelt upon his knees and prayed." This teaches that there are fixed prayers.

יָכוֹל מִשֶּׁבָּא לַגּוֹלָה הוּחַלָּה? – כְּבָר נֶאֱמַר: ״דִּי הוּא עָבֵד מִן קַדְמַת דְּנָא״.

**I might have thought that this** practice of fixed prayer **began** only **when he came to** the Babylonian **exile;**[N] **it was stated:** "Just **as he had done before."**

יָכוֹל יִתְפַּלֵּל אָדָם לְכָל רוּחַ שֶׁיִּרְצֶה? – תַּלְמוּד לוֹמַר ״(לָקֳבֵל) נֶגֶד יְרוּשְׁלֶם״.

Further, I **might have** thought **that one may pray** facing **any direction he wishes; the verse states:** The appropriate direction for prayer is **"facing Jerusalem."**

יָכוֹל יְהֵא כּוֹלְלָן בְּבַת אַחַת – כְּבָר מְפוֹרָשׁ עַל יְדֵי דָוִד, דִּכְתִיב: ״עֶרֶב וָבֹקֶר וְצָהֳרַיִם״ וגו׳.

Daniel does not describe how these three prayers are distributed during the day. I **might have** thought **that one may include all** three prayers **at one time; it has already been articulated by David** that one may not do so, **as it is written: "Evening and morning and noon,** I pray and cry aloud and He hears my voice" (Psalms 55:18).

יָכוֹל יַשְׁמִיעַ קוֹלוֹ בִּתְפִלָּתוֹ? – כְּבָר מְפוֹרָשׁ עַל יְדֵי חַנָּה, שֶׁנֶּאֱמַר: ״וְקוֹלָהּ לֹא יִשָּׁמֵעַ״.

Furthermore, **I might have** thought **that one may make his voice heard in his** *Amida* **prayer; it has already been articulated by Hannah** in her prayer, **as it is stated:** "And Hannah spoke in her heart, only her lips moved **and her voice could not be heard"** (1 Samuel 1:13).

יָכוֹל יִשְׁאַל אָדָם צְרָכָיו וְאַחַר כָּךְ יִתְפַּלֵּל? – כְּבָר מְפוֹרָשׁ עַל יְדֵי שְׁלֹמֹה, שֶׁנֶּאֱמַר: ״לִשְׁמֹעַ אֶל הָרִנָּה וְאֶל הַתְּפִלָּה״, ״רִנָּה״ – זוֹ תְּפִלָּה, ״תְּפִלָּה״ – זוֹ בַּקָּשָׁה. אֵין אוֹמֵר דְּבַר בַּקָּשָׁה אַחַר אֱמֶת וְיַצִּיב, אֲבָל אַחַר הַתְּפִלָּה – אֲפִילּוּ כְּסֵדֶר וִדּוּי שֶׁל יוֹם הַכִּפּוּרִים אוֹמֵר.

*Halakhot* regarding the order of the prayers were also learned from the prayers of biblical characters. I **might have** thought **that one should request his own needs first, and afterwards recite prayers** of thanksgiving and praise; **it has already been articulated by Solomon** that this is not so, as in Solomon's prayer at the dedication of the Holy Temple **it is stated: "To hear the song and the prayer** that Your servant prays before You today" (1 Kings 8:28). In this verse, **song is prayer** in the sense of thanks and praise, and **prayer is** one's **request** of his personal needs. Therefore, one who is praying **does not speak matters of request after** he began to recite *emet veyatziv* prior to the *Amida* prayer, which is the essence of prayer. Rather, he begins with praise in the first three blessings of the *Amida* prayer, and only thereafter does he include requests for his needs. **But after the** *Amida* **prayer** there is no limit. If he desires to recite **even the equivalent of the order of the confession**[B] **of Yom Kippur,** he may **recite** it.

אִיתְּמַר נַמִי, אָמַר רַב חִיָּיא בַּר אַשִׁי אָמַר רַב: אַף עַל פִּי שֶׁאָמְרוּ שׁוֹאֵל אָדָם צְרָכָיו בְּ״שׁוֹמֵעַ תְּפִלָּה״, אִם בָּא לוֹמַר אַחַר תְּפִלָּתוֹ אֲפִילּוּ כְּסֵדֶר שֶׁל יוֹם הַכִּפּוּרִים – אוֹמֵר.

This **was also stated** by an *amora*; **Rav Ḥiyya bar Ashi said** that **Rav said: Although** the Sages **said** that **one requests his** personal **needs in** the blessing: **Who listens to prayer,** that is with regard to one who wishes to do so as part of the *Amida* prayer. **If he comes** to add **and recite** additional requests **after** completing **his** *Amida* **prayer, even** if his personal requests are **the equivalent of the order of the confession of Yom Kippur,** he may **recite** them.[H]

אָמַר רַב הַמְנוּנָא: כַּמָּה הִלְכְתָא גַּבְרְוָותָא אִיכָּא לְמִשְׁמַע מֵהָנֵי קְרָאֵי דְּחַנָּה: ״וְחַנָּה הִיא מְדַבֶּרֶת עַל לִבָּהּ״ – מִכָּאן לַמִּתְפַּלֵּל צָרִיךְ שֶׁיְּכַוֵּין לִבּוֹ. ״רַק שְׂפָתֶיהָ נָעוֹת״ – מִכָּאן לַמִּתְפַּלֵּל שֶׁיַּחְתּוֹךְ בִּשְׂפָתָיו. ״וְקוֹלָהּ לֹא יִשָּׁמֵעַ״ – מִכָּאן, שֶׁאָסוּר לְהַגְבִּיהַּ קוֹלוֹ בִּתְפִלָּתוֹ. ״וַיַּחְשְׁבֶהָ עֵלִי לְשִׁכֹּרָה״ – מִכָּאן שֶׁשִּׁכּוֹר אָסוּר לְהִתְפַּלֵּל.

**Rav Hamnuna said: How many significant** *halakhot* **can be derived from these verses** of the prayer **of Hannah?** As it says: "And Hannah spoke in her heart, only her lips moved and her voice could not be heard, so Eli thought her to be drunk" (1 Samuel 1:13). The Gemara elaborates: **From** that which is stated **here: "And Hannah spoke in her heart,"** the *halakha* that **one who prays must focus his heart** on his prayer is derived. And **from** that which is stated **here: "Only her lips moved,"** the *halakha* that **one who prays must enunciate** the words **with his lips,** not only contemplate them in his heart, is derived.[H] **From** that which is written **here: "And her voice could not be heard,"** the *halakha* that **one is forbidden to raise his voice in his** *Amida* **prayer** as it must be recited silently. **From** the continuation of the verse **here: "So Eli thought her to be drunk,"** the *halakha* that **a drunk person is forbidden to pray.**[H] That is why he rebuked her.

״וַיֹּאמֶר אֵלֶיהָ עֵלִי עַד מָתַי תִּשְׁתַּכָּרִין״ וגו׳ – אָמַר רַבִּי אֶלְעָזָר: מִכָּאן, לָרוֹאֶה בַּחֲבֵרוֹ

On the subject of Eli's rebuke of Hannah, as it is stated: **"And Eli said to her: How long will you remain drunk?** Remove your wine from yourself" (1 Samuel 1:14); **Rabbi Elazar said: From here** the *halakha* that **one who sees in another**

## NOTES

**This began when he came to exile – מִשֶּׁבָּא לַגּוֹלָה הוּחַלָּה:** Some interpret the word *huḥala* not as began but rather as fell ill. In other words, lest you say that before he was exiled, Daniel prayed more and only in exile did he fall ill and was forced to curtail his prayer (Maharshal).

## BACKGROUND

**Confession – וִדּוּי:** This is an essential part of the process of repentance. The Torah obligates a person who has sinned to confess his sin (see Numbers 5:6–7). This confession, in which the sinner acknowledges and expresses regret for his sin, is made by him alone in private. In certain circumstances, however, where the sin involved has become public knowledge, a public confession is required. In many communities, the confessional prayer is recited every weekday. The Yom Kippur service includes many prayers and petitions for atonement, and the extended confessional prayer: For the sin…is recited several times during the course of the day. The confessional prayer was also recited by a person bringing a sin-offering, a guilt-offering, or a free-will burnt-offering as he placed his hands on the head of the sacrifice.

## HALAKHA

**Request during prayer – בַּקָּשָׁה בִּתְפִלָּה:** One may add personal requests related to the topic of the blessing in the thirteen middle blessings of request and may add any request in the final blessing of the thirteen: Who listens to prayer. At the end of the *Amida* prayer, one may introduce any prayer he chooses, both before and after he recites the verse: May…find favor (Rambam *Sefer Ahava, Hilkhot Tefilla* 6:2;. *Shulḥan Arukh, Oraḥ Ḥayyim* 119:1).

**From here the *halakha* that one who prays must enunciate the words with his lips is derived – מִכָּאן לַמִּתְפַּלֵּל שֶׁיַּחְתּוֹךְ בִּשְׂפָתָיו:** One may not merely contemplate his prayer; he must mouth the words. However, one may not pray out loud unless he is alone and is unable otherwise to concentrate on his prayer. When praying with a congregation, one may not pray audibly in order to avoid distracting those praying beside him (Rambam *Sefer Ahava, Hilkhot Tefilla* 5:9; *Shulḥan Arukh, Oraḥ Ḥayyim* 101:2).

**From here the *halakha* that a drunk person is forbidden to pray – מִכָּאן,שֶׁשִּׁכּוֹר אָסוּר לְהִתְפַּלֵּל:** One who drank a quarter of a *log* of wine may not pray until he becomes sober. One who drank more than a quarter of a *log* and already prayed, if he is sufficiently sober to be capable of speaking before a king, his prayer is valid. If not, his prayer is an abomination and he must repeat it when sober. There are distinctions between various levels of intoxication explicated elsewhere in the Talmud (Rambam *Sefer Ahava, Hilkhot Tefilla* 4:17; *Shulḥan Arukh, Oraḥ Ḥayyim* 99:1).

דָּבָר שֶׁאֵינוֹ הָגוּן צָרִיךְ לְהוֹכִיחוֹ. ״וַתַּעַן חַנָּה וַתֹּאמֶר לֹא אֲדֹנִי״ אָמַר עוּלָּא וְאִיתֵּימָא רַבִּי יוֹסֵי בְּרַבִּי חֲנִינָא, אָמְרָה לֵיהּ: לֹא אָדוֹן אַתָּה בְּדָבָר זֶה, וְלֹא רוּחַ הַקּוֹדֶשׁ שׁוֹרָה עָלֶיךָ, שֶׁאַתָּה חוֹשְׁדֵנִי בְּדָבָר זֶה.

**an unseemly matter, he must reprimand him,** is derived.[H] **"And Hannah answered and she said no, my master,** I am a woman of sorrowful spirit, and I have drunk neither wine nor liquor, but I pour out my soul before the Lord" (1 Samuel 1:15). Regarding the words: "No, my master," **Ulla, and some say Rabbi Yosei, son of Rabbi Ḥanina, said** that **she said to him,** in an allusion: **With regard to this matter, you are not a master, and the Divine Spirit does not rest upon you, as you** falsely **suspect me of this.**

אִיכָּא דְּאָמְרִי, הָכִי אָמְרָה לֵיהּ: לֹא אָדוֹן אַתָּה, לָאו אִיכָּא שְׁכִינָה וְרוּחַ הַקּוֹדֶשׁ גַּבָּךְ, שֶׁדַּנְתַּנִי לְכַף חוֹבָה וְלֹא דַּנְתַּנִי לְכַף זְכוּת, מִי לֹא יָדַעְתְּ דְּאִשָּׁה קְשַׁת רוּחַ אָנֹכִי?!

**Some say** another version of her response. **She said to him,** questioning: **Aren't you a master? Aren't the Divine Presence and Divine Spirit with you that you judged me to be guilty, and you did not judge me to be innocent? Didn't you know that I am a woman of distressed spirit?**

״וְיַיִן וְשֵׁכָר לֹא שָׁתִיתִי״ – אָמַר רַבִּי אֶלְעָזָר: מִכָּאן, לַנֶּחְשָׁד בְּדָבָר שֶׁאֵין בּוֹ שֶׁצָּרִיךְ לְהוֹדִיעוֹ.

With regard to Hannah's explanation that **"I have drunk neither wine nor liquor," Rabbi Elazar**[P] **said: From here** the *halakha* is derived **that one who is suspected of something of which he is not** guilty cannot suffice merely with the personal knowledge of his innocence, but **must inform** the one who suspects him that he is innocent and clear himself of suspicion.

״אַל תִּתֵּן אֶת אֲמָתְךָ לִפְנֵי בַּת בְּלִיַּעַל״ – אָמַר רַבִּי אֶלְעָזָר: מִכָּאן, לְשִׁכּוֹר שֶׁמִּתְפַּלֵּל כְּאִילּוּ עוֹבֵד עֲבוֹדָה זָרָה, כְּתִיב הָכָא ״לִפְנֵי בַּת בְּלִיַּעַל״, וּכְתִיב הָתָם ״יָצְאוּ אֲנָשִׁים בְּנֵי בְלִיַּעַל מִקִּרְבֶּךָ״, מָה לְהַלָּן עֲבוֹדָה זָרָה, אַף כָּאן – עֲבוֹדָה זָרָה.

**"Do not take your maidservant as a wicked woman** [*bat beliya'al*], for out of the abundance of my complaint and anger have I spoken until now" (1 Samuel 1:16). **Rabbi Elazar said: From here the** *halakha* **that when a drunk person prays it is as if he engaged in idol worship** is derived[N] **as it is written here** that Hannah, suspected of praying while drunk, defends herself and says: "Do not take your maidservant **as a** ***bat beliya'al*****"**; and **it is written there** with regard to a city that has been instigated to engage in idol worship: ***"Benei beliya'al*** **have gone out from your midst** and have lured the inhabitants of their city, saying let us go and serve other gods which we have not known" (Deuteronomy 13:14). By means of this verbal analogy it is derived: **Just as there,** in the case of the idolatrous city, the term *beliya'al* indicates **idol worship, so too here,** in the case of one who prays drunk, *beliya'al* indicates **idol worship.**

״וַיַּעַן עֵלִי וַיֹּאמֶר לְכִי לְשָׁלוֹם״ – אָמַר רַבִּי אֶלְעָזָר: מִכָּאן, לַחוֹשֵׁד אֶת חֲבֵרוֹ בְּדָבָר שֶׁאֵין בּוֹ שֶׁצָּרִיךְ לְפַיְּיסוֹ; וְלֹא עוֹד, אֶלָּא שֶׁצָּרִיךְ לְבָרְכוֹ, שֶׁנֶּאֱמַר: ״וֵאלֹהֵי יִשְׂרָאֵל יִתֵּן אֶת שֵׁלָתֵךְ״.

The verse continues: **"And Eli answered and said: May you go in peace"** (1 Samuel 1:17). **Rabbi Elazar said: From here** the *halakha* is derived **that one who suspects another of something that he has not** done, **he must appease him. Moreover,** the one who suspected him **must bless him,** as Eli continued and offered Hannah a blessing, **as it is stated: "And may the God of Israel grant your request** that you have asked of Him" (1 Samuel 1:17).

״וַתִּדֹּר נֶדֶר וַתֹּאמַר ה׳ צְבָאוֹת״, אָמַר רַבִּי אֶלְעָזָר: מִיּוֹם שֶׁבָּרָא הַקָּדוֹשׁ בָּרוּךְ הוּא אֶת עוֹלָמוֹ, לֹא הָיָה אָדָם שֶׁקְּרָאוֹ לְהַקָּדוֹשׁ בָּרוּךְ הוּא ״צְבָאוֹת״, עַד שֶׁבָּאתָה חַנָּה וּקְרָאַתּוֹ ״צְבָאוֹת״;

Incidental to this discussion of Hannah's prayer, the Gemara explores related topics. In her prayer, Hannah said: **"And she swore an oath and said, Lord of Hosts** [***Tzeva'ot***] if You will indeed look upon the affliction of Your maidservant and remember me and not forget Your maidservant and will give Your maidservant a male child, I will give him to the Lord all the days of his life, and there shall be no razor come upon his head" (1 Samuel 1:11). **Rabbi Elazar said: From the day that the Holy One, Blessed be He created His world, there was no person who called the Holy One, Blessed be He, Lord of Hosts until Hannah came and called Him Lord of Hosts.** This is the first time in the Bible that God is referred to by this name.

אָמְרָה חַנָּה לִפְנֵי הַקָּדוֹשׁ בָּרוּךְ הוּא: רִבּוֹנוֹ שֶׁל עוֹלָם, מִכׇּל צִבְאֵי צְבָאוֹת שֶׁבָּרָאתָ בְּעוֹלָמְךָ קָשֶׁה בְּעֵינֶיךָ שֶׁתִּתֵּן לִי בֵּן אֶחָד?!

Rabbi Elazar explains that **Hannah said before the Holy One, Blessed be He: Master of the Universe,** are You not the Lord of the Hosts, and **of all of the hosts and hosts** of creations **that You created in Your world, is it difficult in Your eyes to grant me one son?**

**HALAKHA**

**From here the** ***halakha*** **that one who sees in another an unseemly matter, he must reprimand him, is derived –** מִכָּאן, לָרוֹאֶה בַּחֲבֵרוֹ דָּבָר שֶׁאֵינוֹ הָגוּן צָרִיךְ לְהוֹכִיחוֹ: One who sees that another has sinned or is heading in that direction, it is a mitzva to direct him back to the straight and narrow and inform him that he is hurting himself with his wicked actions, even if he did not explicitly violate a Torah prohibition (Rambam *Sefer HaMadda, Hilkhot De'ot* 6:7).

**PERSONALITIES**

**Rabbi Elazar –** רַבִּי אֶלְעָזָר: In the Gemara, citations of Rabbi Elazar, with no patronymic, refer to Rabbi Elazar ben Pedat, a second-generation, Eretz Yisrael *amora*. He was born in Babylonia, where he was a student of both Rav and Shmuel. In his youth, he immigrated to Eretz Yisrael, where he married. In Eretz Yisrael, he became the primary student of Rabbi Yoḥanan. The connection between them was so close that at times, the Gemara raises a contradiction between the statement of one and the statement of the other, under the assumption that it was unlikely that they would hold different opinions in matters of *halakha*.

**NOTES**

**From here the** ***halakha*** **that when a drunk person prays it is as if he engaged in idol worship is derived –** מִכָּאן, לְשִׁכּוֹר שֶׁמִּתְפַּלֵּל כְּאִילּוּ עוֹבֵד עֲבוֹדָה זָרָה: Drunkenness causes confusion. One who stands in prayer drunk is liable to conjure false images in his conception of the Divine. That is the essence of idolatry (Rashba).

מָשָׁל לְמָה הַדָּבָר דּוֹמֶה – לְמֶלֶךְ בָּשָׂר וָדָם שֶׁעָשָׂה סְעוּדָה לַעֲבָדָיו, בָּא עָנִי אֶחָד וְעָמַד עַל הַפֶּתַח, אָמַר לָהֶם: תְּנוּ לִי פְּרוּסָה אַחַת! וְלֹא הִשְׁגִּיחוּ עָלָיו; דָּחַק וְנִכְנַס אֵצֶל הַמֶּלֶךְ. אָמַר לוֹ: אֲדוֹנִי הַמֶּלֶךְ, מִכׇּל סְעוּדָה שֶׁעָשִׂיתָ קָשֶׁה בְּעֵינֶיךָ לִיתֵּן לִי פְּרוּסָה אַחַת?!

The Gemara suggests **a parable: To what is this similar?** It is similar to a **flesh and blood king who made a feast for his servants. A poor person came and stood at the door. He said to them: Give me one slice** of bread! **And they paid him no attention. He pushed and entered before the king. He said to him: My lord, the King, from this entire feast that you have prepared, is it so difficult in your eyes to give me a single slice** of bread?

״אִם רָאֹה תִרְאֶה״, אָמַר רַבִּי אֶלְעָזָר: אָמְרָה חַנָּה לִפְנֵי הַקָּדוֹשׁ בָּרוּךְ הוּא: רִבּוֹנוֹ שֶׁל עוֹלָם, אִם ״רָאֹה״ – מוּטָב, וְאִם לָאו – ״תִּרְאֶה״,

As for the double language in the verse, **"if you will look upon [*im ra'o tireh*]," Rabbi Elazar said: Hannah said before the Holy One, Blessed be He: Master of the Universe, if You will look upon [*ra'o*]** me now, **fine, and if not,** in any case **You will see [*tireh*].**

אֵלֵךְ וְאֶסְתַּתֵּר בִּפְנֵי אֶלְקָנָה בַּעְלִי, וְכֵיוָן דְּמִסְתַּתַּרְנָא מַשְׁקוּ לִי מֵי סוֹטָה, וְאִי אַתָּה עוֹשֶׂה תּוֹרָתְךָ פַּלַּסְתֵּר, שֶׁנֶּאֱמַר: ״וְנִקְּתָה וְנִזְרְעָה זָרַע״.

What was Hannah threatening? She said: **I will go and seclude myself** with another man **before Elkana, my husband. Since I secluded myself, they will force me to drink the *sota*[B] water** to determine whether or not I have committed adultery. I will be found innocent, **and since You will not make Your Torah false [*pelaster*],[L]** I will bear children. With regards to a woman who is falsely suspected of adultery and drank the *sota* water, the Torah **says:** "And if the woman was not defiled, but was pure, then **she shall be acquitted and she shall conceive"** (Numbers 5:28).

הָנִיחָא לְמַאן דְּאָמַר אִם הָיְתָה עֲקָרָה נִפְקֶדֶת – שַׁפִּיר, אֶלָּא לְמַאן דְּאָמַר אִם הָיְתָה יוֹלֶדֶת בְּצַעַר – יוֹלֶדֶת בְּרֶיוַח, נְקֵבוֹת – יוֹלֶדֶת זְכָרִים, שְׁחוֹרִים – יוֹלֶדֶת לְבָנִים, קְצָרִים – יוֹלֶדֶת אֲרוּכִים, מַאי אִיכָּא לְמֵימַר?

However, Rabbi Elazar's opinion **works out well** according **to the one who said** that the verse means: **If she were barren, she will be remembered** by God and granted children. **But** according **to the one who said** that the verse means that childbearing will be easier and more successful, i.e., **if she had** previously **given birth with pain,** she now **gives birth with ease,** or if she had previously given birth to **daughters,** she now **gives birth to sons,** or if she had previously given birth to **black** children, considered to be unattractive, she now **gives birth to fair** children, or if she had previously given birth to **short,** weak children, she **gives birth to tall,** strong children, **what can be said?**

דְּתַנְיָא: ״וְנִקְּתָה וְנִזְרְעָה זָרַע״ – מְלַמֵּד, שֶׁאִם הָיְתָה עֲקָרָה נִפְקֶדֶת, דִּבְרֵי רַבִּי יִשְׁמָעֵאל; אָמַר לֵיהּ רַבִּי עֲקִיבָא: אִם כֵּן, יֵלְכוּ כׇּל הָעֲקָרוֹת כּוּלָּן וְיִסְתַּתְּרוּ, וְזוֹ שֶׁלֹּא קִלְקְלָה נִפְקֶדֶת! אֶלָּא מְלַמֵּד שֶׁאִם הָיְתָה יוֹלֶדֶת בְּצַעַר – יוֹלֶדֶת בְּרֶיוַח, קְצָרִים – יוֹלֶדֶת אֲרוּכִים, שְׁחוֹרִים – יוֹלֶדֶת לְבָנִים, אֶחָד – יוֹלֶדֶת שְׁנַיִם.

**As it was taught** in a *baraita* that the *tanna'im* disputed the interpretation of the verse in Numbers: **"Then she shall be acquitted and she shall conceive" teaches that if she was barren, she will be remembered** by God and granted children; this is **the statement of Rabbi Yishmael. Rabbi Akiva said to him: If so, all barren women will go and seclude themselves** with men who are not their husbands, **and any** woman **who did not** commit the **sin** of adultery **will be remembered** by God and granted children. **Rather,** the verse **teaches** that this is merely a promise for greater ease in childbirth; **if she has** previously **given birth with pain,** she now **gives birth with ease,** if she has previously given birth to **short** children, she **gives birth to tall** children, if she has previously given birth to **black** children, she now **gives birth to fair** children, if she has previously given birth to **one** child, she now **gives birth to two** children.

מַאי ״אִם רָאֹה תִרְאֶה״ – דִּבְּרָה תּוֹרָה כִּלְשׁוֹן בְּנֵי אָדָם.

According to Rabbi Akiva's explanation, **what** is derived from the double language uttered by Hannah: ***Im ra'o tireh*? The Torah spoke in the language of men,** meaning that this double language is not extraordinary and nothing may be derived from it. It is common biblical vernacular.

״בָּעֳנִי אֲמָתֶךָ״, ״אַל תִּשְׁכַּח אֶת אֲמָתֶךָ״ ״וְנָתַתָּה לַאֲמָתְךָ״.

In the oath/prayer uttered by Hannah, she refers to herself as "Your servant" [*amatekha*] three times: **"The affliction of Your maidservant…** and **not forget Your maidservant and will give Your maidservant"** (1 Samuel 1:11).

אָמַר רַבִּי יוֹסֵי בְּרַבִּי חֲנִינָא: שָׁלֹשׁ אֲמָתוֹת הַלָּלוּ לָמָּה – אָמְרָה חַנָּה לִפְנֵי הַקָּדוֹשׁ בָּרוּךְ הוּא: רִבּוֹנוֹ שֶׁל עוֹלָם, שְׁלֹשָׁה בִּדְקֵי מִיתָה בָּרָאתָ בָּאִשָּׁה, וְאָמְרִי לַהּ: שְׁלֹשָׁה דִּבְקֵי מִיתָה, וְאֵלּוּ הֵן: נִדָּה וְחַלָּה וְהַדְלָקַת הַנֵּר, כְּלוּם עָבַרְתִּי עַל אַחַת מֵהֶן?!

**Rabbi Yosei, son of Rabbi Ḥanina, said: Why** are **these three maidservants [*amatot*]** cited in the verse? They are cited to teach that **Hannah said before the Holy One, Blessed be He: Master of the Universe, You have created three crucibles** potentially leading to **death[N] in a woman,** where she is particularly vulnerable. Alternatively, **some say:** Master of the Universe, You have created **three accelerants of death** in a woman. **They are** mitzvot that, as a rule, pertain to women: Observing the *halakhot* of **a menstruating woman,** separating ***ḥalla*** from dough, **and lighting** Shabbat **candles. Have I ever violated one of them?** Hannah attests to her status as God's maidservant [*ama*]. The reference to these three mitzvot is drawn from the etymological similarity between *amatekha*, your maidservant, and *mita*, death.

### BACKGROUND

**Sota – סוֹטָה:** The Torah describes the procedure governing such a woman (Numbers 5:11–31): First, her husband warns her in the presence of witnesses against being alone together with a specific man about whom he is suspicious. If she disobeys this warning and is observed alone with that man (even though there is no concrete evidence that she actually committed adultery), she and her husband can no longer live together as man and wife until she has undergone the following ordeal to determine whether she has committed adultery. The woman (accompanied by her husband and two Torah scholars) is taken to the Temple in Jerusalem and forced by the priests to stand in a public place while holding the special meal-offering that she is required to bring. There she is again questioned about her behavior. If she continues to protest her fidelity and takes an oath to that effect, a scroll is brought and the curses of the *sota* mentioned in the Torah passage cited above are written on it. If she does not admit that she has committed adultery, the scroll is submerged in a clay vessel filled with water taken from the Temple basin and some earth from the Temple floor, and the scroll's writing is dissolved in the water. She is then forced to drink that water. If the husband's allegation is true, in the words of the Torah, "her belly shall swell and her thigh shall fall away" (Numbers 5:27), until ultimately she dies from the water's curse. If she is innocent, the water will bring her blessing and she is permitted to resume normal marital relations with her husband.

### LANGUAGE

**False [*pelaster*] – פַּלַּסְתֵּר:** The source of this word is the Greek πλάστης, *plastès*, meaning a molder, a modeler; metaphorically, in this context, it means false.

### NOTES

**Three crucibles potentially leading to death – שְׁלֹשָׁה בִּדְקֵי מִיתָה:** The source for this is the mishna in tractate *Shabbat* (31b) that states that for failure to fulfill these mitzvot women are punished. Various explanations were suggested why these three mitzvot were particularly emphasized. Some hold that the reason is because it is women who generally have the opportunity to engage in their performance. Another explanation ties each of these mitzvot to Eve's sin with the tree of knowledge, and each alludes to and symbolizes one of the consequences of that transgression (*Shabbat* 32a).

"וְנָתַתָּה לַאֲמָתְךָ זֶרַע אֲנָשִׁים".

Later in her prayer, Hannah says: **"And You will grant Your servant an offspring of men."**

מַאי "זֶרַע אֲנָשִׁים"? אָמַר רַב: גַּבְרָא בְּגוּבְרִין; וּשְׁמוּאֵל אָמַר: זֶרַע שֶׁמּוֹשֵׁחַ שְׁנֵי אֲנָשִׁים, וּמַאן אִינּוּן – שָׁאוּל וְדָוִד; וְרַבִּי יוֹחָנָן אָמַר: זֶרַע שֶׁשָּׁקוּל כִּשְׁנֵי אֲנָשִׁים, וּמַאן אִינּוּן – מֹשֶׁה וְאַהֲרֹן, שֶׁנֶּאֱמַר: "מֹשֶׁה וְאַהֲרֹן בְּכֹהֲנָיו וּשְׁמוּאֵל בְּקֹרְאֵי שְׁמוֹ"; וְרַבָּנַן אָמְרִי: "זֶרַע אֲנָשִׁים" – זֶרַע שֶׁמּוּבְלָע בֵּין אֲנָשִׁים.

The Gemara asks: **What is** the meaning of **"an offspring of men"? Rav said:** Hannah prayed for **a man among men,** a son who would be outstanding and exceptional. **And Shmuel said:** This expression means **an offspring who will anoint two men** to royalty. **And who were they? Saul and David. And Rabbi Yoḥanan said:** Hannah prayed that she would bear **an offspring who** would be **the equiva-lent of two** of the world's greatest **men. And who were they? Moses and Aaron. As it is stated: "Moses and Aaron among His priests and Samuel among those who call His name"** (Psalms 99:6). In this verse, Hannah's son, Samuel, is equated to Moses and Aaron **And the Rabbis say: "An offspring of men":** Hannah prayed for **an offspring who would be inconspicuous among men,** that he would not stand out in any way.

כִּי אֲתָא רַב דִּימִי, אָמַר: לֹא אָרוֹךְ וְלֹא גּוּץ, וְלֹא קָטָן וְלֹא אַלָּם, וְלֹא צָחוֹר וְלֹא גִּיחוֹר, וְלֹא חָכָם וְלֹא טִפֵּשׁ.

The Gemara relates: **When Rav Dimi came** from Eretz Yisrael to Babylonia, **he said** in explanation: Hannah prayed that her son would not be conspicuous among men; **neither too tall nor too short; neither too small nor too fat; neither too white nor too red; neither too smart nor too stupid.**

"אֲנִי הָאִשָּׁה הַנִּצֶּבֶת עִמְּכָה בָּזֶה" אָמַר רַבִּי יְהוֹשֻׁעַ בֶּן לֵוִי: מִכָּאן, שֶׁאָסוּר לֵישֵׁב בְּתוֹךְ אַרְבַּע אַמּוֹת שֶׁל תְּפִלָּה.

When Hannah came to the Temple with her son Samuel, she told Eli: "My lord, as your soul lives, my lord, **I am the woman who stood here with you** to pray to the Lord" (1 Samuel 1:26). **Rabbi Yehoshua ben Levi said: From here** the *halakha* **that it is forbidden to sit within four cubits of** one who is **praying** is derived.[H] As the verse says: "Who stood here with you," indicating that Eli stood alongside Hannah because she was praying.

"אֶל הַנַּעַר הַזֶּה הִתְפַּלָּלְתִּי" – אָמַר רַבִּי אֶלְעָזָר: שְׁמוּאֵל מוֹרֶה הֲלָכָה לִפְנֵי רַבּוֹ הָיָה, שֶׁנֶּאֱמַר: "וַיִּשְׁחֲטוּ אֶת הַפָּר וַיָּבִיאוּ אֶת הַנַּעַר אֶל עֵלִי", מִשּׁוּם דְּ"וַיִּשְׁחֲטוּ אֶת הַפָּר" הֵבִיאוּ הַנַּעַר אֶל עֵלִי?!

Additionally, Hannah's emphasis in speaking to Eli, **"for this youth I prayed"** (1 Samuel 1:27), indicates that she came to protect him from danger. As **Rabbi Elazar said: Samuel was** one who **taught** ***halakha*** **in the presence of his teacher.**[N] Hannah wanted to pray that he not be punished by death at the hand of Heaven for his transgression, **as it is stated: "And they slaughtered the cow and they brought the youth to Eli"** (1 Samuel 1:25). This verse is puzzling **Because they slaughtered the cow,** therefore, **they brought the youth to Eli?** What does one have to do with the next?

אֶלָּא, אָמַר לְהוּ עֵלִי: קִרְאוּ כֹּהֵן, לֵיתֵי וְלִשְׁחוֹט. חֲזִינְהוּ שְׁמוּאֵל דְּהָווּ מְהַדְּרִי בָּתַר כֹּהֵן לְמִישְׁחַט, אָמַר לְהוּ: לָמָּה לְכוּ לְאַהֲדוּרֵי בָּתַר כֹּהֵן לְמִישְׁחַט? שְׁחִיטָה בְּזָר כְּשֵׁרָה! אַיְיתוּהוּ לְקַמֵּיהּ דְּעֵלִי, אָמַר לֵיהּ: מְנָא לָךְ הָא? אָמַר לֵיהּ: מִי כְּתִיב "וְשָׁחַט הַכֹּהֵן"?! "וְהִקְרִיבוּ הַכֹּהֲנִים" כְּתִיב! מִקַּבָּלָה וְאֵילָךְ מִצְוַת כְּהוּנָּה; מִכָּאן לִשְׁחִיטָה שֶׁכְּשֵׁרָה בְּזָר.

**Rather,** this is what happened: **Eli said to** those who brought the offering: **Call a priest; he will come and slaughter** the offering **Samuel saw them looking for a priest to slaughter** the animal. **He said to them: Why do you** need **to look for a priest to slaughter** it **Slaughter** of an offering performed **by a non-priest is valid.**[H] **They brought him before Eli** to clarify his statement. Eli **said to him: How do you know this?** Samuel **said to him: Is it written** in the Torah: **And the priest shall slaughter** indicating that the offering may only be slaughtered by a priest? **It is written: "And the priest shall offer,"** only **from** the stage of **receiving** the blood in the bowl **and onward is it a mitzva** incumbent upon **priests** alone. **From here** the *halakha* that **slaughter by a non-priest is acceptable** is derived.

אָמַר לֵיהּ: מֵימָר שַׁפִּיר קָא אָמְרַתְּ, מִיהוּ, מוֹרֶה הֲלָכָה בִּפְנֵי רַבְּךָ אַתְּ – וְכָל הַמּוֹרֶה הֲלָכָה בִּפְנֵי רַבּוֹ חַיָּיב מִיתָה. אֲתַיָא חַנָּה וְקָא צָוְוחָה קַמֵּיהּ: "אֲנִי הָאִשָּׁה הַנִּצֶּבֶת עִמְּכָה בָּזֶה" וגו'. אָמַר לָהּ: שִׁבְקִי לִי דְּאַעַנְשֵׁיהּ, וּבָעֵינָא רַחֲמֵי וְיָהֵיב לָךְ רַבָּא מִינֵּיהּ. אָמְרָה לֵיהּ: "אֶל הַנַּעַר הַזֶּה הִתְפַּלָּלְתִּי".

Eli **said to** Samuel: **You have spoken well** and your statement is correct, but **nevertheless, you are** one who **issued a halakhic ruling in the presence of your teacher, and anyone who issues a halakhic ruling in the presence of his teacher,** even if the particular *halakha* is correct, **is liable for death**[H] at the hand of Heaven for showing contempt for his teacher. **Hannah came and shouted before him "I am the woman who stood here with you** to pray to the Lord;" do not punish the child who was born of my prayers. **He said to her: Let me punish him, and I will pray** for mercy, that the Holy One, Blessed be He, **will grant you** a son who will be **greater than this** one. **She said to him: "For this youth I prayed"** and I want no other.

## HALAKHA

**From here the *halakha* that it is forbidden to sit within four cubits of one who is praying is derived – מִכָּאן, שֶׁאָסוּר לֵישֵׁב בְּתוֹךְ אַרְבַּע אַמּוֹת שֶׁל תְּפִלָּה:** One may not sit within four cubits on any side of one who is praying, as per the opinion of Rabbi Yehoshua ben Levi cited here. If one is himself engaged in Torah study or prayer, it is permitted, as in that case he does not appear to be displaying contempt for the prayer of the person beside him (*Shulḥan Arukh HaRav*; Rambam *Sefer Ahava, Hilkhot Tefilla* 5:6; *Shulḥan Arukh, Oraḥ Ḥayyim* 102:1).

**Slaughter by a non-priest is valid – שְׁחִיטָה בְּזָר כְּשֵׁרָה:** Non-priests are permitted to slaughter consecrated animals and even sacrifices of the most sacred order. This is true with regard to both individual and communal offerings (Rambam *Sefer Avoda, Hilkhot Biat HaMikdash* 9:6, *Sefer Avoda, Hilkhot Ma'aseh HaKorbanot* 5:1, *Sefer Avoda, Hilkhot Pesulei HaMukdashim* 1:1).

**Anyone who issues a halakhic ruling in the presence of his teacher is liable for death – הַמּוֹרֶה הֲלָכָה בִּפְנֵי רַבּוֹ חַיָּיב מִיתָה:** One is always forbidden to teach *halakha* in the presence of his teacher, and one who does so is punished by death at the hand of Heaven. One who is a distance of at least twelve *mil* from his teacher, a distance derived in tractate *Sanhedrin* from the size of Israelite camp in the desert, and someone happens to ask him a question, he may answer. However, he is forbidden to establish himself as a halakhic authority until his teacher dies or has given him permission to issue halakhic rulings. If one is within three parasangs, twelve *mil*, of his teacher, even with his permission he may issue rulings (Rema). Some say that one who issues halakhic rulings within twelve *mil* of his teacher is liable to receive the death penalty. Beyond twelve *mil*, although he is prohibited from doing so, he is exempt from receiving the death penalty (Rambam *Sefer HaMadda, Hilkhot Talmud Torah* 5:2–3; *Shulḥan Arukh, Yoreh De'a* 242:4 and in the Rema).

## NOTES

**Samuel was one who taught *halakha* in the presence of his teacher – שְׁמוּאֵל מוֹרֶה הֲלָכָה לִפְנֵי רַבּוֹ הָיָה:** This did not transpire when Samuel was first brought to the Tabernacle, but on one of the Festivals after he was already grown (*ge'onim*).

"וְחַנָּה הִיא מְדַבֶּרֶת עַל לִבָּהּ" אָמַר רַבִּי אֶלְעָזָר מִשּׁוּם רַבִּי יוֹסֵי בֶּן זִמְרָא: עַל עִסְקֵי לִבָּהּ. אָמְרָה לְפָנָיו: רִבּוֹנוֹ שֶׁל עוֹלָם, כָּל מַה שֶּׁבָּרָאתָ בְּאִשָּׁה לֹא בָּרָאתָ דָּבָר אֶחָד לְבַטָּלָה, עֵינַיִם לִרְאוֹת, וְאׇזְנַיִם לִשְׁמוֹעַ, חוֹטֶם לְהָרִיחַ, פֶּה לְדַבֵּר, יָדַיִם לַעֲשׂוֹת בָּהֶם מְלָאכָה, רַגְלַיִם לְהַלֵּךְ בָּהֶן, דַּדִּים לְהָנִיק בָּהֶן; דַּדִּים הַלָּלוּ שֶׁנָּתַתָּ עַל לִבִּי לָמָּה, לֹא לְהָנִיק בָּהֶן?! תֵּן לִי בֵּן וְאָנִיק בָּהֶן.

The Gemara continues to deal with Hannah's prayer. It is said: **"And Hannah spoke on her heart."** Several interpretations are offered to explain her use of the phrase "on her heart" instead of the common phrase to her heart (Maharsha). **Rabbi Elazar said in the name of Rabbi Yosei ben Zimra:** Hannah spoke to God **concerning matters of her heart. She said before Him: Master of the Universe,** of all the organs **You created in a woman, You have not created one in vain.** Every organ fulfills its purpose; **eyes to see, ears to hear, a nose to smell, a mouth to speak, hands with which to perform labor, feet with which to walk, breasts with which to nurse.** If so, **these breasts that You placed upon my heart, to what** purpose did You place them? Was it **not** in order **to nurse with them? Grant me a son and I will nurse with them.**

וְאָמַר רַבִּי אֶלְעָזָר מִשּׁוּם רַבִּי יוֹסֵי בֶּן זִמְרָא: כׇּל הַיּוֹשֵׁב בְּתַעֲנִית בְּשַׁבָּת – קוֹרְעִים לוֹ גְּזַר דִּינוֹ שֶׁל שִׁבְעִים שָׁנָה, וְאַף עַל פִּי כֵן חוֹזְרִין וְנִפְרָעִין מִמֶּנּוּ דִּין עוֹנֶג שַׁבָּת.

Tangentially, the Gemara also cites an additional statement that **Rabbi Elazar said in the name of Rabbi Yosei ben Zimra: Anyone who sits** in observance of a **fast on Shabbat,**[NH] his merit is great and **they tear up** and repeal **his sentence of seventy years;** because everyone is enjoying himself and a feast is prepared, it is more difficult to fast on Shabbat than on any other day. **Nevertheless, they then hold him accountable** for failing to fulfill **the *halakha* of delight of Shabbat.**

מַאי תַּקַּנְתֵּיהּ? אֲמַר רַב נַחְמָן בַּר יִצְחָק: לֵיתִיב תַּעֲנִיתָא לְתַעֲנִיתָא.

The Gemara asks: **What is his remedy** to atone and avoid punishment? **Rav Naḥman bar Yitzḥak said: He must sit** in observance of another **fast** on a weekday to atone **for the fast** on Shabbat.

וְאָמַר רַבִּי אֶלְעָזָר: חַנָּה הֵטִיחָה דְּבָרִים כְּלַפֵּי מַעְלָה, שֶׁנֶּאֱמַר: "וַתִּתְפַּלֵּל עַל ה׳" – מְלַמֵּד, שֶׁהֵטִיחָה דְּבָרִים כְּלַפֵּי מַעְלָה.

After explaining the uncommon expression, on her heart, the Gemara cites an additional statement in the matter of Hannah. **And Rabbi Elazar said: Hannah spoke impertinently toward** God **on High. As it is stated: "And she prayed onto the Lord,"** as opposed to the common phrase: To the Lord. This **teaches that she spoke impertinently toward on High.**

וְאָמַר רַבִּי אֶלְעָזָר: אֵלִיָּהוּ הֵטִיחַ דְּבָרִים כְּלַפֵּי מַעְלָה, שֶׁנֶּאֱמַר: "וְאַתָּה הֲסִבֹּתָ אֶת לִבָּם אֲחֹרַנִּית". אָמַר רַבִּי שְׁמוּאֵל בַּר רַבִּי יִצְחָק: מִנַּיִן שֶׁחָזַר הַקָּדוֹשׁ בָּרוּךְ הוּא וְהוֹדָה לוֹ לְאֵלִיָּהוּ?

**And** on a similar note, **Rabbi Elazar said** that **Elijah spoke impertinently toward** God **on High** as well in his prayer at Mount Carmel, **as it is stated:** "Answer me, Lord, answer me, that this people will know that You are the Lord, God, **and You have turned their hearts backward"** (I Kings 18:37), claiming that God caused Israel to sin. On this topic, **Rabbi Shmuel bar Rabbi Yitzḥak said: From where do we know that the Holy One, Blessed be He, ultimately conceded to Elijah** that he was correct?

Perek **V**
Daf **32** Amud **a**

דִּכְתִיב: "וַאֲשֶׁר הֲרֵעֹתִי".

**As it is written** in a future prophecy: "In that day, says the Lord, I will assemble the lame, and I will gather those who are abandoned and **those with whom I have dealt in wickedness"** (Micah 4:6). God states that He caused Israel to act wickedly.

אָמַר רַבִּי חָמָא בְּרַבִּי חֲנִינָא: אִלְמָלֵא שָׁלֹשׁ מִקְרָאוֹת הַלָּלוּ – נִתְמוֹטְטוּ רַגְלֵיהֶם שֶׁל שׂוֹנְאֵי יִשְׂרָאֵל:

Similarly, **Rabbi Ḥama, son of Rabbi Ḥanina, said: Had it not been for these three verses, the legs of the enemies of Israel,** a euphemism for Israel itself, **would have collapsed,** as Israel would have been unable to withstand God's judgment.

חַד, דִּכְתִיב: "וַאֲשֶׁר הֲרֵעֹתִי", וְחַד, דִּכְתִיב "הִנֵּה כַחֹמֶר בְּיַד הַיּוֹצֵר כֵּן אַתֶּם בְּיָדִי בֵּית יִשְׂרָאֵל"; וְחַד, דִּכְתִיב: "וַהֲסִרֹתִי אֶת לֵב הָאֶבֶן מִבְּשַׂרְכֶם וְנָתַתִּי לָכֶם לֵב בָּשָׂר".

**One** is the verse just mentioned in which **it is written: "Those whom I have dealt in wickedness." And one** is the verse in which **it is written: "Behold, like clay in the potter's hand, so are you in My hand, house of Israel"** (Jeremiah 18:6). **And one** is the verse in which **it is written:** "And I will give you a new heart and a new spirit I will place within you, **and I will remove the heart of stone from your flesh and I will give you a heart of flesh"** (Ezekiel 36:26). These three verses indicate that God influences a person's decisions, and therefore one does not have sole responsibility for his actions.

**NOTES**

**Anyone who sits in observance of a fast on Shabbat – הַיּוֹשֵׁב בְּתַעֲנִית בְּשַׁבָּת:** Opinions differ as to whether this refers specifically to a fast that one fasts after experiencing a bad dream the night before, in order to repent and thereby prevent the actualization of that dream, which, according to the *ge'onim*, is permitted on Shabbat, or whether it is saying that even in other specific cases, one is permitted to fast on Shabbat in order to repent (see Rashba).

**HALAKHA**

**Anyone who sits in observance of a fast on Shabbat – הַיּוֹשֵׁב בְּתַעֲנִית בְּשַׁבָּת:** It is generally prohibited to fast on Shabbat beyond the sixth hour of the day, noon, although one may fast on Shabbat after having a bad dream. That is because through fasting, the decree against him will be repealed and the depression caused by the dream will dissipate, contributing to his sense of enjoyment on Shabbat. Nevertheless, one who does so must fast again on a weekday to atone for fasting on Shabbat and negating the primary mitzva of enjoyment on Shabbat (Rambam *Sefer Zemanim, Hilkhot Shabbat* 30:12, *Sefer Zemanim, Hilkhot Ta'anit* 1:12; *Shulḥan Arukh, Oraḥ Ḥayyim* 288:1, 4).

רַב פַּפָּא אָמַר, מֵהָכָא: ״וְאֶת רוּחִי אֶתֵּן בְּקִרְבְּכֶם וְעָשִׂיתִי אֵת אֲשֶׁר בְּחֻקַּי תֵּלֵכוּ״.

**Rav Pappa said** there is a clearer proof **from here: "And I will place My spirit within you and I will cause you to walk in My statutes,** and you will observe My decrees and do them" (Ezekiel 36:27).

וְאָמַר רַבִּי אֶלְעָזָר: מֹשֶׁה הֵטִיחַ דְּבָרִים כְּלַפֵּי מַעְלָה, שֶׁנֶּאֱמַר: ״וַיִּתְפַּלֵּל מֹשֶׁה אֶל ה׳״, אַל תִּקְרֵי ״אֶל״ ה׳ אֶלָּא ״עַל״ ה׳,

**And Rabbi Elazar said: Moses** also **spoke impertinently toward** God **on High, as it is stated** in the verse following the sin of those who murmured against God in the desert: **"And Moses prayed to the Lord** and the fire subsided" (Numbers 11:2), and this verse is interpreted homiletically: **Do not read to [*el*] the Lord,** but rather **onto [*al*] the Lord,**[N] which indicates that he spoke impertinently.

שֶׁכֵּן דְּבֵי רַבִּי אֱלִיעֶזֶר בֶּן יַעֲקֹב קוֹרִין לְאַלְפִּי״ן עַיְינִי״ן וּלְעַיְינִי״ן אַלְפִּי״ן.

The Gemara explains the basis for this interpretation: **As** the Sages **of the school of Rabbi Eliezer ben Ya'akov would** indiscriminately **read *alef* as *ayin* and *ayin* as *alef*** and in this case transforming *el* into *al*.[L]

דְּבֵי רַבִּי יַנַּאי אָמְרִי, מֵהָכָא: ״וְדִי זָהָב״,

The Sages of **the school of Rabbi Yannai,** however, **say** proof that Moses spoke impertinently toward God on High is derived **from here,** Moses' rebuke at the beginning of Deuteronomy: **"And Di Zahav"** (Deuteronomy 1:1). This is an entry in a list of places where Moses had spoken to Israel. As there was no place encountered by that name, it is interpreted as an allusion to another matter.

מַאי ״וְדִי זָהָב״? אָמְרִי דְּבֵי רַבִּי יַנַּאי, כָּךְ אָמַר מֹשֶׁה לִפְנֵי הַקָּדוֹשׁ בָּרוּךְ הוּא: רִבּוֹנוֹ שֶׁל עוֹלָם, בִּשְׁבִיל כֶּסֶף וְזָהָב שֶׁהִשְׁפַּעְתָּ לָהֶם לְיִשְׂרָאֵל עַד שֶׁאָמְרוּ דַּי – הוּא גָּרַם שֶׁעָשׂוּ אֶת הָעֵגֶל.

We must clarify: **What is** the meaning of **and Di Zahav?** The Sages of **the school of Rabbi Yannai said**[B] **that Moses said the following before the Holy One, Blessed be He,** to atone for Israel after the sin of the Golden Calf: **Master of the Universe, because of the gold and silver that you lavished upon Israel** during the exodus from Egypt **until they said enough [*dai*];** it was this wealth **that caused** Israel **to make the** Golden **Calf.**

אָמְרִי דְּבֵי רַבִּי יַנַּאי: אֵין אֲרִי נוֹהֵם מִתּוֹךְ קוּפָּה שֶׁל תֶּבֶן אֶלָּא מִתּוֹךְ קוּפָּה שֶׁל בָּשָׂר.

Establishing a general moral principle, the Sages **the school of Rabbi Yannai said: A lion does not roar** standing **over a basket of straw** from which he derives no pleasure, **but** he roars standing **over a basket of meat,** as he only roars when satiated.

אָמַר רַבִּי אוֹשַׁעְיָא: מָשָׁל, לְאָדָם שֶׁהָיְתָה לוֹ פָּרָה כְּחוּשָׁה וּבַעֲלַת אֵבָרִים, הֶאֱכִילָהּ כַּרְשִׁינִין וְהָיְתָה מְבַעֶטֶת בּוֹ. אָמַר לָהּ: מִי גָּרַם לִיךְ שֶׁתְּהֵא מְבַעֶטֶת בִּי – אֶלָּא כַּרְשִׁינִין שֶׁהֶאֱכַלְתִּיךְ.

Similarly, **Rabbi Oshaya said:** This is **comparable to a person who had a lean, but large-limbed cow.** At one point, **he fed it lupines** a choice food, **and** soon thereafter the cow **was kicking him. He said to** the cow: **Who caused you** to begin **kicking me if not the lupines I fed you?** Here, too, the sin was caused by an abundance of good.

אָמַר רַבִּי חִיָּיא בַּר אַבָּא אָמַר רַבִּי יוֹחָנָן: מָשָׁל, לְאָדָם אֶחָד שֶׁהָיָה לוֹ בֵּן, הִרְחִיצוֹ וְסָכוֹ, וְהֶאֱכִילוֹ וְהִשְׁקָהוּ, וְתָלָה לוֹ כִּיס עַל צַוָּארוֹ, וְהוֹשִׁיבוֹ עַל פֶּתַח שֶׁל זוֹנוֹת, מַה יַּעֲשֶׂה אוֹתוֹ הַבֵּן שֶׁלֹּא יֶחֱטָא?!

The Gemara offers another analogy: **Rabbi Ḥiyya bar Abba said** that **Rabbi Yoḥanan said:** This is **comparable to a person who had a son; he bathed him and anointed him** with oil, **fed him and gave him drink, and hung a purse** of money **around his neck** Then, he **brought** his son **to the entrance of a brothel. What could the son do to avoid sinning?**

אָמַר רַב אַחָא בְּרֵיהּ דְּרַב הוּנָא אָמַר רַב שֵׁשֶׁת: הַיְינוּ דְּאָמְרִי אֱינָשֵׁי ״מְלֵי כְּרֵסֵיהּ זְנֵי בִּישֵׁי״, שֶׁנֶּאֱמַר: ״כְּמַרְעִיתָם וַיִּשְׂבָּעוּ שָׂבְעוּ וַיָּרָם לִבָּם עַל כֵּן שְׁכֵחוּנִי״; רַב נַחְמָן אָמַר, מֵהָכָא: ״וְרָם לְבָבֶךָ וְשָׁכַחְתָּ אֶת ה׳״; וְרַבָּנַן אָמְרִי, מֵהָכָא: ״וְאָכַל וְשָׂבַע וְדָשֵׁן וּפָנָה״;

On a similar note, **Rav Aḥa, son of Rav Huna, said** that **Rav Sheshet said: That is what people say** in a popular maxim: **Filling his stomach is a type of sin, as it is stated: "When they were fed and became full they were sated, and their hearts were lifted and they have forgotten Me"** (Hosea 13:6). **Rav Naḥman said:** This principle is derived not from the verse in Hosea, but **from here: "And your heart is lifted and you forget the Lord"** (Deuteronomy 8:14). **And the Rabbis say** that this principle is derived **from here: "And they will have eaten and been sated and fattened, and they will turn** to other gods" (Deuteronomy 31:20).

וְאִי בָּעֵית אֵימָא, מֵהָכָא: ״וַיִּשְׁמַן יְשׁוּרוּן וַיִּבְעָט״. אָמַר רַבִּי שְׁמוּאֵל בַּר נַחְמָנִי אָמַר רַבִּי יוֹנָתָן: מִנַּיִן שֶׁחָזַר הַקָּדוֹשׁ בָּרוּךְ הוּא וְהוֹדָה לוֹ לְמֹשֶׁה – שֶׁנֶּאֱמַר: ״וְכֶסֶף הִרְבֵּיתִי לָהֶם וְזָהָב עָשׂוּ לַבַּעַל״.

**And if you wish, say** instead that it is derived **from here: "And Jeshurun grew fat and kicked"** (Deuteronomy 32:15). **Rabbi Shmuel bar Naḥmani said** that **Rabbi Yonatan said: From where** in the Torah is it derived that **the Holy One, Blessed be He,** ultimately **conceded to Moses** that the reason for the sin of the Golden Calf was indeed the riches lavished upon Israel? **As it is stated "And I gave them an abundance of silver and gold, which they used for the Ba'al"** (Hosea 2:10).

**NOTES**

**Do not read to [*el*] the Lord, but rather onto [*al*] the Lord – אַל תִּקְרֵי ״אֶל״ ה׳ אֶלָּא ״עַל״ ה׳:** The verse is interpreted in this manner because of its unusual formulation. The verse states that Moses prayed to the Lord, but the content of his prayer is not mentioned. Therefore, to the Lord is interpreted as onto the Lord, i.e., Moses became angry and spoke impertinently (*Penei Yehoshua*).

**LANGUAGE**

***Alef* into *ayin* – אַלְפִּי״ן עַיְינִי״ן:** Interchange of guttural letters was very common in the Galilee. Nearly all guttural letters were obscured and swallowed when pronounced in this region, and were all ultimately pronounced the same. Some Sages utilize these interchanges, some of which appear in the Bible in certain roots, in the homiletic interpretation of the verses. The interchange of the *heh* and *ḥet* was most common; however *alef* and *ayin* were also interchanged. This was done not only by those in the study hall of Rabbi Eliezer ben Ya'akov, but also according to the approach of Rabbi Meir.

**BACKGROUND**

**The Sages of the school of Rabbi…said – אָמְרִי דְּבֵי רַבִּי...:** This unique expression is rooted in the practice of those generations. During the lifetimes of prominent Sages, the Sages' students would bond and form a close-knit community. During the particular teacher's lifetime, and often after his death as well, the Sages of a particular school would continue studying Torah together according to the approach espoused by their teacher. In the period of the *tanna'im*, this phenomenon was expressed with the phrase: It was taught in the school of Rabbi… in the sense that the *halakha* was taught in the study hall of a particular Sage. In the period of the *amora'im* or with regard to matters not incorporated in the Mishna, the phrase: The Sages of the school of Rabbi…said, was employed.

"וַיְדַבֵּר ה׳ אֶל מֹשֶׁה לֵךְ רֵד", מַאי "לֵךְ רֵד"? אָמַר רַבִּי אֶלְעָזָר, אָמַר לוֹ הַקָּדוֹשׁ בָּרוּךְ הוּא לְמֹשֶׁה: מֹשֶׁה, רֵד מִגְּדוּלָּתְךָ! כְּלוּם נָתַתִּי לְךָ גְּדוּלָּה אֶלָּא בִּשְׁבִיל יִשְׂרָאֵל, וְעַכְשָׁיו יִשְׂרָאֵל חָטְאוּ – אַתָּה לָמָּה לִי? מִיָּד תָּשַׁשׁ כּוֹחוֹ שֶׁל מֹשֶׁה, וְלֹא הָיָה לוֹ כֹּחַ לְדַבֵּר. וְכֵיוָן שֶׁאָמַר: "הֶרֶף מִמֶּנִּי וְאַשְׁמִידֵם" אָמַר מֹשֶׁה: דָּבָר זֶה תָּלוּי בִּי – מִיָּד עָמַד וְנִתְחַזֵּק בִּתְפִלָּה וּבִקֵּשׁ רַחֲמִים.

The Gemara elaborates upon additional aspects of the sin of the Golden Calf. It is stated: **"And the Lord said to Moses: Go and descend,** for your people whom you have lifted out of the land of Egypt have been corrupted" (Exodus 32:7). **What is the meaning of "go and descend"? Rabbi Elazar said: The Holy One, Blessed be He, said to Moses: Moses, descend from your greatness.**[N] **Isn't it only for the sake of Israel,** so that you may serve as an emissary, **that I granted you prominence; and now that Israel has sinned, why do I** need **you?** There is no need for an emissary. **Immediately, Moses' strength waned and he was powerless to speak** in defense of Israel. **And once** God **said** to Moses: **"Leave Me be, that I may destroy them"** (Deuteronomy 9:19), **Moses said** to himself: If God is telling me to let Him be, it must be because **this matter is dependent upon me. Immediately Moses stood and was strengthened in prayer, and asked** that God have **mercy** on the nation of Israel and forgive them for their transgression.

מָשָׁל, לְמֶלֶךְ שֶׁכָּעַס עַל בְּנוֹ וְהָיָה מַכֵּהוּ מַכָּה גְּדוֹלָה, וְהָיָה אוֹהֲבוֹ יוֹשֵׁב לְפָנָיו וּמִתְיָרֵא לוֹמַר לוֹ דָּבָר. אָמַר הַמֶּלֶךְ: אִלְמָלֵא אוֹהֲבִי זֶה שֶׁיּוֹשֵׁב לְפָנַי הֲרַגְתִּיךָ! אָמַר: דָּבָר זֶה תָּלוּי בִּי – מִיָּד עָמַד וְהִצִּילוֹ.

The Gemara says: This is **comparable to a king who became angry at his son** who had sinned against him, **and beat him,** administering a **severe beating.** At that moment, **a well-wisher** of the king **was sitting before him** and witnessed the entire event, **and was afraid to say anything to** the king about the excessive beating. Meanwhile, **the king said** to his son: **Were it not for this well-wisher of mine who is sitting before me, I would have killed you.** Upon hearing this, the king's friend **said** to himself: This is clearly a sign that **this matter,** rescuing the son from the hands of his father, **is dependent upon me. Immediately he stood and rescued him** from the king.

"וְעַתָּה הַנִּיחָה לִּי וְיִחַר אַפִּי בָהֶם וַאֲכַלֵּם וְאֶעֱשֶׂה אוֹתְךָ לְגוֹי גָּדוֹל" וגו׳ – אָמַר רַבִּי אַבָּהוּ: אִלְמָלֵא מִקְרָא כָּתוּב אִי אֶפְשָׁר לְאוֹמְרוֹ; מְלַמֵּד, שֶׁתְּפָסוֹ מֹשֶׁה לְהַקָּדוֹשׁ בָּרוּךְ הוּא כְּאָדָם שֶׁהוּא תּוֹפֵס אֶת חֲבֵירוֹ בְּבִגְדוֹ, וְאָמַר לְפָנָיו: רִבּוֹנוֹ שֶׁל עוֹלָם, אֵין אֲנִי מַנִּיחֲךָ עַד שֶׁתִּמְחוֹל וְתִסְלַח לָהֶם.

In an additional aspect of the sin of the Golden Calf, God told Moses: **"Now leave Me be, that My wrath will be enraged against them and I will consume them; and I will make of you a great nation"** (Exodus 32:10). Explaining this verse, **Rabbi Abbahu said: Were the verse not written** in this manner, **it would be impossible to utter** it, in deference to God. The phrase: Leave Me be, **teaches that Moses grabbed the Holy One, Blessed be He, as a person who grabs his friend by his garment** would, **and he said before Him: Master of the Universe, I will not leave You be until You forgive and pardon them.**

"וְאֶעֱשֶׂה אוֹתְךָ לְגוֹי גָּדוֹל" וגו׳ – אָמַר רַבִּי אֶלְעָזָר, אָמַר מֹשֶׁה לִפְנֵי הַקָּדוֹשׁ בָּרוּךְ הוּא: רִבּוֹנוֹ שֶׁל עוֹלָם, וּמָה כִּסֵּא שֶׁל שָׁלֹשׁ רַגְלַיִם אֵינוֹ יָכוֹל לַעֲמוֹד לְפָנֶיךָ בִּשְׁעַת כַּעַסְךָ, כִּסֵּא שֶׁל רֶגֶל אֶחָד עַל אַחַת כַּמָּה וְכַמָּה!

In the same verse, God promised Moses: **"And I will make of you a great nation."** What was Moses' response? **Rabbi Elazar said: Moses said before the Holy One, Blessed be He: Master of the Universe, if a chair with three legs,** the collective merit of the three forefathers, **is unable to stand before You in Your moment of wrath, all the more so** that **a chair with one leg,** my merit alone, will be unable to withstand your wrath.

וְלֹא עוֹד אֶלָּא שֶׁיֵּשׁ בִּי בּוֹשֶׁת פָּנִים מֵאֲבוֹתַי. עַכְשָׁיו יֹאמְרוּ: רְאוּ פַּרְנָס שֶׁהֶעֱמִיד עֲלֵיהֶם, בִּקֵּשׁ גְּדוּלָּה לְעַצְמוֹ וְלֹא בִּקֵּשׁ עֲלֵיהֶם רַחֲמִים.

**Moreover, but I have** a sense of **shame before my forefathers. Now** they will **say: See** this **leader that** God **placed over** Israel. **He requested greatness for himself but did not pray for** God to have **mercy upon them** in their troubled time.

"וַיְחַל מֹשֶׁה אֶת פְּנֵי ה׳" – אָמַר רַבִּי אֶלְעָזָר: מְלַמֵּד שֶׁעָמַד מֹשֶׁה בִּתְפִלָּה לִפְנֵי הַקָּדוֹשׁ בָּרוּךְ הוּא עַד שֶׁהֶחֱלָהוּ; וְרָבָא אָמַר: עַד שֶׁהֵפֵר לוֹ נִדְרוֹ, כְּתִיב הָכָא "וַיְחַל" וּכְתִיב הָתָם "לֹא יַחֵל דְּבָרוֹ", וְאָמַר מָר: הוּא אֵינוֹ מֵיחֵל אֲבָל אֲחֵרִים מְחַלִּין לוֹ.

The Torah continues: **"And Moses beseeched [*vayḥal*] before the Lord"** (Exodus 32:11). Many interpretations were given for this uncommon term, *vayḥal*: **Rabbi Elazar said:** It **teaches that Moses stood in prayer before the Holy One, Blessed be He, until it made him ill [*heḥelahu*]** from overexertion. **And Rava said:** Moses stood in prayer **until he nullified His vow,** as the term *vayḥal* alludes to nullification of an oath. **Here it is written *vayḥal*, and there** referring to vows, **it is written: "He shall not nullify [*lo yaḥel*] his word"** (Numbers 30:3). **And** with regard to vows, **the Master said: He** who vowed **cannot nullify** his vow, **but others,** the court, **can nullify** his vow **for him.** Here, it is as if Moses nullified the Lord's vow to destroy Israel.

וּשְׁמוּאֵל אָמַר: מְלַמֵּד שֶׁמָּסַר עַצְמוֹ לְמִיתָה עֲלֵיהֶם, שֶׁנֶּאֱמַר: "וְאִם אַיִן מְחֵנִי נָא מִסִּפְרְךָ".

**And Shmuel said:** The term *vayḥal* **teaches that** Moses **gave his life,** from the term *ḥalal*, a dead person, **for** Israel, **as it is stated: "And if not, erase me, please, from Your book"** (Exodus 32:32).

אָמַר רָבָא אָמַר רַב יִצְחָק: מְלַמֵּד שֶׁהֶחֱלָה עֲלֵיהֶם מִדַּת רַחֲמִים.

**Rava,** also interpreting this verse, **said** that **Rav Yitzḥak said:** The term *vayḥal* **teaches that he caused the Divine Attribute of Mercy to take effect [*heḥela*] upon them.**

**NOTES**

**Go and descend…descend from your greatness – לֵךְ רֵד...רֵד מִגְּדוּלָּתְךָ:** The phrase, go and descend, is not interpreted as a command to literally descend the mountain, but as a symbolic expression. As God did not tell Moses what to do once he descended the mountain, apparently, this is a statement removing Moses from his position of prominence (Maharsha). Indeed, that seems to be the case, as, after commanding him to descend, God continued to speak to Moses, indicating that go and descend referred to descent from prominence, not from the mountain (*Tziyyun LeNefesh Ḥayya*).

## NOTES

**His strength weakened like a female – תָּשַׁשׁ כֹּחוֹ כִּנְקֵבָה:** God's ability is one of the manifestations of His essence. Consequently, when it appears that God is incapable of performing a certain action, it is ostensibly due to a diminution in His power; His strength weakened like a female. Therefore, when God forgave the people in response to Moses' prayers, it was affirmation that the Lord does, in fact, maintain and rule all worlds. That is the subtext of God's reaction: You have given Me life with your words (Rav Nissim Gaon, Rashba).

וְרַבָּנָן אָמְרִי: מְלַמֵּד שֶׁאָמַר מֹשֶׁה לִפְנֵי הַקָּדוֹשׁ בָּרוּךְ הוּא: רִבּוֹנוֹ שֶׁל עוֹלָם, חוּלִּין הוּא לְךָ מֵעֲשׂוֹת כַּדָּבָר הַזֶּה.

**And the Rabbis say** that this term constitutes the essence of Moses' claim: **It teaches that Moses said before the Holy One Blessed be He: It is a sacrilege [*ḥullin*] for You to do something like this.**

"וַיְחַל מֹשֶׁה אֶת פְּנֵי ה׳". תַּנְיָא, רַבִּי אֱלִיעֶזֶר הַגָּדוֹל אוֹמֵר: מְלַמֵּד שֶׁעָמַד מֹשֶׁה בִּתְפִלָּה לִפְנֵי הַקָּדוֹשׁ בָּרוּךְ הוּא עַד שֶׁאֲחָזַתּוּ אֲחִילוּ. מַאי אֲחִילוּ? אָמַר רַבִּי אֶלְעָזָר: אֵשׁ שֶׁל עֲצָמוֹת. מַאי אֵשׁ שֶׁל עֲצָמוֹת? אָמַר אַבָּיֵי: אֶשְׁתָּא דְּגַרְמֵי.

And another interpretation of the verse, **"And Moses beseeched [*vayḥal*] before the Lord." It was taught** in a *baraita*: **Rabbi Eliezer the Great says: This** term **teaches that Moses stood in prayer until he was overcome by *aḥilu*.** Even the Sages were unfamiliar with this term. Therefore, the Gemara asks: **What is** the meaning of ***aḥilu*? Rabbi Elazar,** an *amora* of Eretz Yisrael, **said** that *aḥilu* **is fire in the bones.** However, this expression was familiar in Eretz Yisrael but not in Babylonia. They asked in Babylonia: **What is** the disease that they called **fire of the bones? Abaye said** that is a disease known in Babylonia as ***eshta degarmei***, which in Aramaic means **fire of the bones;** in other words, a fever.

"זְכֹר לְאַבְרָהָם לְיִצְחָק וּלְיִשְׂרָאֵל עֲבָדֶיךָ אֲשֶׁר נִשְׁבַּעְתָּ לָהֶם בָּךְ". מַאי "בָּךְ" – אָמַר רַבִּי אֶלְעָזָר: אָמַר מֹשֶׁה לִפְנֵי הַקָּדוֹשׁ בָּרוּךְ הוּא: רִבּוֹנוֹ שֶׁל עוֹלָם, אִלְמָלֵא נִשְׁבַּעְתָּ לָהֶם בַּשָּׁמַיִם וּבָאָרֶץ הָיִיתִי אוֹמֵר: כְּשֵׁם שֶׁשָּׁמַיִם וָאָרֶץ בְּטֵלִים – כָּךְ שְׁבוּעָתְךָ בְּטֵלָה. וְעַכְשָׁיו שֶׁנִּשְׁבַּעְתָּ לָהֶם בְּשִׁמְךָ הַגָּדוֹל, מָה שִׁמְךָ הַגָּדוֹל חַי וְקַיָּים לְעוֹלָם וּלְעוֹלְמֵי עוֹלָמִים – כָּךְ שְׁבוּעָתְךָ קַיֶּימֶת לְעוֹלָם וּלְעוֹלְמֵי עוֹלָמִים.

As Moses continues his prayer, he says: **"Remember Abraham, Isaac and Israel Your servants, to whom You swore in Your name"** (Exodus 32:13). **What is** the meaning of **in Your name? Rabbi Elazar said: Moses said before the Holy One, Blessed be He: Master of the Universe, had You sworn to them by the heavens and the earth, I would say: Just as the heavens and the earth will** ultimately **be no more, so too Your oath will be null and void. Now that You swore to them by Your great name, just as Your name lives and stands for all eternity, so too does Your oath live and stand for all eternity.**

"וַתְּדַבֵּר אֲלֵיהֶם אַרְבֶּה אֶת זַרְעֲכֶם כְּכוֹכְבֵי הַשָּׁמַיִם וְכָל הָאָרֶץ הַזֹּאת אֲשֶׁר אָמַרְתִּי". הַאי "אֲשֶׁר אָמַרְתִּי"? "אֲשֶׁר אָמַרְתָּ" מִיבְּעֵי לֵיהּ!

In this verse, Moses continues: **"And You said to them: I will make your offspring as numerous as the stars of heaven, and all this land of which I have spoken** I will give to your offspring that they shall inherit it forever." The Gemara clarifies a puzzling phrase in this verse **That** phrase **of which I have spoken, it should** have said: **Of which You have spoken,** as Moses is referring to God's promise to the forefathers.

אָמַר רַבִּי אֶלְעָזָר: עַד כָּאן דִּבְרֵי תַלְמִיד, מִכָּאן וְאֵילָךְ – דִּבְרֵי הָרַב. וְרַבִּי שְׁמוּאֵל בַּר נַחְמָנִי אָמַר: אֵלּוּ וָאֵלּוּ דִּבְרֵי תַלְמִיד, אֶלָּא כָּךְ אָמַר מֹשֶׁה לִפְנֵי הַקָּדוֹשׁ בָּרוּךְ הוּא: רִבּוֹנוֹ שֶׁל עוֹלָם, דְּבָרִים שֶׁאָמַרְתָּ לִי "לֵךְ אֱמוֹר לָהֶם לְיִשְׂרָאֵל" בִּשְׁמִי, הָלַכְתִּי וְאָמַרְתִּי לָהֶם בִּשְׁמְךָ, עַכְשָׁיו מָה אֲנִי אוֹמֵר לָהֶם?

**Rabbi Elazar said: To this** point, the verse cites **the words of the student,** Moses; **from this point,** and all this land of which I have spoken, the verse cites **the words of the Master,** God. **And Rabbi Shmuel bar Naḥmani said: These and those are the words of the student;** Moses spoke the entire verse. **Rather, Moses said before the Holy One, Blessed be He: Master of the Universe, those matters which You told me to go and say to Israel in My name, I went and told** it **to them in Your name.** I have already told Israel of God's promise to the forefathers. **Now what do I say to them?**

"מִבִּלְתִּי יְכֹלֶת ה׳", "יָכוֹל ה׳" מִיבְּעֵי לֵיהּ!

The Gemara moves to a discussion of additional prayers offered by Moses. Moses said that if God fails to bring the Jewish people into Eretz Yisrael, the nations of the world will say: **"The Lord did not have the ability [*yekholet*]** to bring this people into the land which He swore to them, and He killed them in the desert" (Numbers 14:16). The Gemara examines this verse closely: The verse should not have utilized the term *yekholet*, an abstract feminine noun, but rather, **it should have said: "The Lord** was not **able [*yakhol*],"** a masculine verb.

אָמַר רַבִּי אֶלְעָזָר, אָמַר מֹשֶׁה לִפְנֵי הַקָּדוֹשׁ בָּרוּךְ הוּא: רִבּוֹנוֹ שֶׁל עוֹלָם, עַכְשָׁיו יֹאמְרוּ אוּמּוֹת הָעוֹלָם: תָּשַׁשׁ כֹּחוֹ כִּנְקֵבָה וְאֵינוֹ יָכוֹל לְהַצִּיל. אָמַר הַקָּדוֹשׁ בָּרוּךְ הוּא לְמֹשֶׁה: וַהֲלֹא כְּבָר רָאוּ נִסִּים וּגְבוּרוֹת שֶׁעָשִׂיתִי לָהֶם עַל הַיָּם! – אָמַר לְפָנָיו: רִבּוֹנוֹ שֶׁל עוֹלָם, עֲדַיִין יֵשׁ לָהֶם לוֹמַר: לְמֶלֶךְ אֶחָד – יָכוֹל לַעֲמוֹד, לִשְׁלֹשִׁים וְאֶחָד מְלָכִים – אֵינוֹ יָכוֹל לַעֲמוֹד.

**Rabbi Elazar said: Moses** phrased it that way because he **said before the Holy One, Blessed be He: Master of the Universe, now the nations of the world will say that His strength weakened like a female**[N] **and He is unable to rescue** the nation of Israel. **The Holy One Blessed be He, said to Moses: And did** the nations of the world **not already see the miracles and the mighty** acts **that I performed on behalf of** Israel **at the Red Sea?** Moses **said before Him: Master of the Universe, they can still say:** The Lord **can stand up to a single king** like Pharaoh and defeat him, but **He is unable stand** up **to the thirty-one kings** in the land of Canaan.

אָמַר רַבִּי יוֹחָנָן: מִנַּיִן שֶׁחָזַר הַקָּדוֹשׁ בָּרוּךְ הוּא וְהוֹדָה לוֹ לְמֹשֶׁה – שֶׁנֶּאֱמַר: "וַיֹּאמֶר ה׳ סָלַחְתִּי כִּדְבָרֶךָ". תָּנֵי דְּבֵי רַבִּי יִשְׁמָעֵאל: כִּדְבָרֶיךָ עֲתִידִים אוּמּוֹת הָעוֹלָם לוֹמַר כֵּן.

**Rabbi Yoḥanan said: From where** is it derived that **the Holy One Blessed be He, ultimately conceded to Moses? As it is said: "And the Lord said: I have forgiven according to your word"** (Numbers 14:20). The Sages **of the school of Rabbi Yishmael taught: According to your word,** it will be, as indeed **in the future the nations of the world will say this.**

אַשְׁרֵי תַּלְמִיד שֶׁרַבּוֹ מוֹדֶה לוֹ.

The Gemara concludes: **Happy is the student whose teacher concedes to him** as the Lord conceded to Moses.

״וְאוּלָם חַי אָנִי״. אָמַר רָבָא אָמַר רַב יִצְחָק: מְלַמֵּד, שֶׁאָמַר לוֹ הַקָּדוֹשׁ בָּרוּךְ הוּא לְמֹשֶׁה: מֹשֶׁה, הֶחֱיִיתַנִי בִּדְבָרֶיךָ.

Explaining the next verse, **"Nevertheless, as I live,** and the glory of the Lord fills the entire world" (Numbers 14:21), **Rava said** that **Rav Yitzḥak said:** This **teaches** that **the Holy One, Blessed be He, said to Moses: Moses, you have given Me life with your words.** I am happy that on account of your arguments, I will forgive Israel.

דָּרַשׁ רַבִּי שִׂמְלַאי: לְעוֹלָם יְסַדֵּר אָדָם שִׁבְחוֹ שֶׁל הַקָּדוֹשׁ בָּרוּךְ הוּא וְאַחַר כָּךְ יִתְפַּלֵּל. מְנָלַן – מִמֹּשֶׁה, דִּכְתִיב: ״וָאֶתְחַנַּן אֶל ה׳ בָּעֵת הַהִיא״; וּכְתִיב ״ה׳ אֱלֹהִים אַתָּה הַחִלּוֹתָ לְהַרְאוֹת אֶת עַבְדְּךָ אֶת גָּדְלְךָ וְאֶת יָדְךָ הַחֲזָקָה אֲשֶׁר מִי אֵל בַּשָּׁמַיִם וּבָאָרֶץ אֲשֶׁר יַעֲשֶׂה כְמַעֲשֶׂיךָ וְכִגְבוּרוֹתֶיךָ״, וּכְתִיב בָּתְרֵיהּ ״אֶעְבְּרָה נָּא וְאֶרְאֶה אֶת הָאָרֶץ הַטּוֹבָה וגו׳״.

Based on Moses' prayers, **Rabbi Simlai taught: One should always set forth praise of the Holy One, Blessed be He, and then pray** for his own needs.[H] **From where do we** derive that one should conduct himself in this manner? **From Moses, as it is written** in his prayer: **"And I beseeched the Lord at that time"** (Deuteronomy 3:23). **And** immediately afterward in his prayer, **it is written: "Lord, God, You have begun to show Your servant Your greatness and Your strong hand, for what God is there in the heavens or on earth who can perform deeds such as Yours and Your might"** (Deuteronomy 3:24)? Here, Moses began with praise of God, **and** it is only **thereafter** that **it is written: "Please, let me pass over and see the good land** that is beyond the Jordan, that good hill country and the Lebanon" (Deuteronomy 3:25). Only after his praise did Moses make his personal request.

סִימָן: מַעֲשִׂי״ם, צְדָקָ״ה, קָרְבָּ״ן, כֹּהֵ״ן, תַּעֲנִי״ת, מִנְעָ״ל, בַּרְזֶ״ל.

The Gemara prefaces the next discourse with **a mnemonic symbol:**[B] **Deeds, charity, offering, priest, fast, shoe, iron.**

**HALAKHA**

One should always set forth praise of the Holy One, Blessed be He, and then pray for his own needs – לְעוֹלָם יְסַדֵּר אָדָם שִׁבְחוֹ שֶׁל הַקָּדוֹשׁ בָּרוּךְ הוּא וְאַחַר כָּךְ יִתְפַּלֵּל: One who prays must first praise God, and only then request his own needs. All prayers are formulated in that manner (Rambam *Sefer Ahava*, *Hilkhot Tefilla* 1:2).

**BACKGROUND**

A mnemonic symbol – סִימָן: Because the Talmud was studied orally for many generations, mnemonic devices were necessary to remember a series of *halakhot* and the order in which they were taught.



אָמַר רַבִּי אֶלְעָזָר: גְּדוֹלָה תְּפִלָּה יוֹתֵר מִמַּעֲשִׂים טוֹבִים. שֶׁאֵין לְךָ גָּדוֹל בְּמַעֲשִׂים טוֹבִים יוֹתֵר מִמֹּשֶׁה רַבֵּינוּ, אַף עַל פִּי כֵן לֹא נַעֲנָה אֶלָּא בִּתְפִלָּה, שֶׁנֶּאֱמַר: ״אַל תּוֹסֶף דַּבֵּר אֵלַי״, וְסָמִיךְ לֵיהּ ״עֲלֵה רֹאשׁ הַפִּסְגָּה״.

**Rabbi Elazar said:** This story proves that **prayer is greater than good deeds** without prayer (*Tosafot*), as **there was none greater in** the performance of **good deeds than Moses our teacher; nevertheless, his request was granted,** albeit in a limited manner, in his request to enter Eretz Yisrael, **only through prayer,** when God permitted him to climb the mountain and look out over the land. **As,** initially **it is stated: "Speak no more to Me," juxtaposed to which is: "Go up to the summit of the mountain."**

וְאָמַר רַבִּי אֶלְעָזָר: גְּדוֹלָה תַּעֲנִית יוֹתֵר מִן הַצְּדָקָה. מַאי טַעְמָא – זֶה בְּגוּפוֹ וְזֶה בְּמָמוֹנוֹ.

After comparing and contrasting prayer and good deeds, the Gemara explores another comparison. **Rabbi Elazar said: A fast is greater than charity. What is the reason** that fasting is greater? Because a fast **is** a mitzva performed **with one's body** as he afflicts himself, **while** charity **is** performed only **with one's money.**

וְאָמַר רַבִּי אֶלְעָזָר: גְּדוֹלָה תְּפִלָּה יוֹתֵר מִן הַקָּרְבָּנוֹת, שֶׁנֶּאֱמַר ״לָמָּה לִּי רֹב זִבְחֵיכֶם״, וּכְתִיב ״וּבְפָרִשְׂכֶם כַּפֵּיכֶם״.

In another comparison, **Rabbi Elazar said: Prayer is greater than sacrifices, as it is stated: "To what purpose is the multitude of your sacrifices to Me,** says the Lord. I am full of the burnt-offerings of rams and the fat of fed beasts; I do not desire the blood of bulls and sheep and goats" (Isaiah 1:11). **And** several verses later **it is written: "And when you spread forth your hands** I will hide My eyes from you, and even if you increase your prayer, I will not hear; your hands are full of blood" (Isaiah 1:15). Not only Israel's sacrifices, but even their prayers, which are on a higher spiritual level, will not be accepted.

אָמַר רַבִּי יוֹחָנָן: כָּל כֹּהֵן שֶׁהָרַג אֶת הַנֶּפֶשׁ לֹא יִשָּׂא אֶת כַּפָּיו, שֶׁנֶּאֱמַר ״יְדֵיכֶם דָּמִים מָלֵאוּ״.

Speaking of that verse in Isaiah, the Gemara cites that **Rabbi Yoḥanan said: Any priest who killed a person**[H] **may not lift his hands** in the Priestly Blessing[B] **as it is stated:** "And when you spread forth your hands I will hide My eyes from you… **your hands are full of blood."** Here we see that the Priestly Blessing, performed with hands spread forth, is not accepted when performed by priests whose "hands are full of blood."

**HALAKHA**

A priest who killed a person – כֹּהֵן שֶׁהָרַג אֶת הַנֶּפֶשׁ: A priest who killed a person, even unwittingly, may not recite the Priestly Blessing. If he did so under duress, he is permitted to recite it (*Be'er Heitev*). Some say that even if he repents, the prohibition remains in effect, while others are lenient and allow him to recite the Priestly Blessing after repenting (Rema; Rambam *Sefer Ahava*, *Hilkhot Tefilla* 15:3; *Shulḥan Arukh*, *Oraḥ Ḥayyim* 128:35).

**BACKGROUND**

The Priestly Blessing – בִּרְכַּת כֹּהֲנִים: The three verses of blessing (Numbers 6:24–26) with which the priests bless the congregation in the synagogue. The Priestly Blessing is recited between the blessings of thanksgiving and peace, the final two blessings in the repetition of the *Amida* prayer. As the priests turn to face the congregation to recite the Priestly Blessing, they first recite a blessing acknowledging the holiness of the priestly line and their responsibility to bless the people in a spirit of love. While reciting the Priestly Blessing, the priests lift their hands according to the traditional rite (known as *nesiat kappayim*). In most places in Eretz Yisrael, the Priestly Blessing is recited by the priests during the repetition of every morning and additional prayer. In the Diaspora, however, there is a long established Ashkenazi practice of reciting it only during the additional prayer on Festivals.

וְאָמַר רַבִּי אֶלְעָזָר: מִיּוֹם שֶׁחָרַב בֵּית הַמִּקְדָּשׁ נִנְעֲלוּ שַׁעֲרֵי תְפִלָּה, שֶׁנֶּאֱמַר: ״גַּם כִּי אֶזְעַק וַאֲשַׁוֵּעַ שָׂתַם תְּפִלָּתִי״, וְאַף עַל פִּי שֶׁשַּׁעֲרֵי תְּפִילָּה נִנְעֲלוּ שַׁעֲרֵי דִמְעָה לֹא נִנְעֲלוּ, שֶׁנֶּאֱמַר: ״שִׁמְעָה תְפִלָּתִי ה׳ וְשַׁוְעָתִי הַאֲזִינָה אֶל דִּמְעָתִי אַל תֶּחֱרַשׁ״.

On the subject of prayer, **Rabbi Elazar also said: Since the day the Temple was destroyed the gates of prayer were locked** and prayer is not accepted as it once was, **as it is said** in lamentation of the Temple's destruction: **"Though I plead and call out, He shuts out my prayer"** (Lamentations 3:8). Yet, **despite** the fact **that the gates of prayer were locked** with the destruction of the Temple, **the gates of tears were not locked,** and one who cries before God may rest assured that his prayers will be answered, **as it is stated: "Hear my prayer, Lord, and give ear to my pleading, keep not silence at my tears"** (Psalms 39:13). Since this prayer is a request that God should pay heed to the tears of one who is praying, he is certain that at least the gates of tears are not locked.

רָבָא לֹא גָּזַר תַּעֲנִיתָא בְּיוֹמָא דְעֵיבָא מִשּׁוּם שֶׁנֶּאֱמַר ״סַכֹּתָה בֶעָנָן לָךְ מֵעֲבוֹר תְּפִלָּה״.

With regard to the locking of the gates of prayer, the Gemara relates that **Rava did not decree a fast on a cloudy day because it is stated: "You have covered Yourself in a cloud, through which prayer cannot pass"** (Lamentations 3:44). The verse indicates that clouds are a bad omen, indicating that God has averted His face (Rav Hai Gaon).

וְאָמַר רַבִּי אֶלְעָזָר: מִיּוֹם שֶׁחָרַב בֵּית הַמִּקְדָּשׁ נִפְסְקָה חוֹמַת בַּרְזֶל בֵּין יִשְׂרָאֵל לַאֲבִיהֶם שֶׁבַּשָּׁמַיִם, שֶׁנֶּאֱמַר ״וְאַתָּה קַח לְךָ מַחֲבַת בַּרְזֶל וְנָתַתָּה אוֹתָהּ קִיר בַּרְזֶל בֵּינְךָ וּבֵין הָעִיר״.

**And Rabbi Elazar said: Since the day the Temple was destroyed an iron wall separates Israel from their Father in heaven, as it is stated** to the prophet Ezekiel, instructing him to symbolize that separation: **"And take for yourself an iron griddle, and set it as an iron wall between yourself and the city…** it will be a sign for the house of Israel" (Ezekiel 4:3).

אָמַר רַבִּי חָנִין אָמַר רַבִּי חֲנִינָא: כָּל הַמַּאֲרִיךְ בִּתְפִלָּתוֹ אֵין תְּפִלָּתוֹ חוֹזֶרֶת רֵיקָם. מְנָא לָן – מִמֹּשֶׁה רַבֵּינוּ, שֶׁנֶּאֱמַר: ״וָאֶתְפַּלֵּל אֶל ה׳״, וּכְתִיב בַּתְרֵיהּ: ״וַיִּשְׁמַע ה׳ אֵלַי גַּם בַּפַּעַם הַהִיא״.

The Gemara cites other statements in praise of prayer: **Rabbi Ḥanin said** that **Rabbi Ḥanina said: Anyone who prolongs his prayer is** assured that **his prayer does not return unanswered;** it will surely be accepted. **From where do we** derive this? **From Moses our teacher, as it is stated** that Moses said: "So I fell down before the Lord the forty days and forty nights that I fell down; **and I prayed to the Lord"** (Deuteronomy 9:26–27), **and it is written thereafter: "And the Lord heard me that time as well,** the Lord would not destroy you" (Deuteronomy 10:10).

אִינִי?! וְהָא אָמַר רַבִּי חִיָּיא בַּר אַבָּא אָמַר רַבִּי יוֹחָנָן: כָּל הַמַּאֲרִיךְ בִּתְפִלָּתוֹ וּמְעַיֵּין בָּהּ – סוֹף בָּא לִידֵי כְּאֵב לֵב, שֶׁנֶּאֱמַר: ״תּוֹחֶלֶת מְמֻשָּׁכָה מַחֲלָה לֵב״, מַאי תַּקַּנְתֵּיהּ – יַעֲסוֹק בַּתּוֹרָה, שֶׁנֶּאֱמַר: ״וְעֵץ חַיִּים תַּאֲוָה בָאָה״, וְאֵין עֵץ חַיִּים אֶלָּא תּוֹרָה, שֶׁנֶּאֱמַר: ״עֵץ חַיִּים הִיא לַמַּחֲזִיקִים בָּהּ״! – לָא קַשְׁיָא, הָא – דְּמַאֲרִיךְ וּמְעַיֵּין בָּהּ, הָא – דְּמַאֲרִיךְ וְלָא מְעַיֵּין בָּהּ.

The Gemara raises an objection: **Is that so? Didn't Rabbi Ḥiyya bar Abba** say that **Rabbi Yoḥanan said: Anyone who prolongs his prayer and expects it to be answered, will ultimately come to heartache,** as it will not be answered. **As it is stated: "Hope deferred makes the heart sick"** (Proverbs 13:12). **And what is the remedy** for one afflicted with that illness? He should **engage in Torah** study, **as it is stated: "But desire fulfilled is the tree of life"** (Proverbs 13:12), **and tree of life is nothing other than Torah, as it is stated: "It is a tree of life to those who hold fast to it,** and those who support it are joyous" (Proverbs 3:18). This is **not difficult. This,** Rabbi Ḥiyya bar Abba's statement that one will suffer heartache refers to one **who prolongs** his prayer **and expects it to be answered; that,** Rabbi Ḥanin's statement that one who prolongs his prayer is praiseworthy refers to **one who prolongs his prayer and** does **not expect it to be answered.**

אָמַר רַבִּי חָמָא בְּרַבִּי חֲנִינָא: אִם רָאָה אָדָם שֶׁהִתְפַּלֵּל וְלֹא נַעֲנָה יַחֲזוֹר וְיִתְפַּלֵּל, שֶׁנֶּאֱמַר: ״קַוֵּה אֶל ה׳ חֲזַק וְיַאֲמֵץ לִבֶּךָ וְקַוֵּה אֶל ה׳״.

On a similar note, **Rabbi Ḥama, son of Rabbi Ḥanina, said: A person who prayed and saw that he was not answered,** should **pray again, as it is stated: "Hope in the Lord, strengthen yourself, let your heart take courage, and hope in the Lord"** (Psalms 27:14). One should turn to God with hope, and if necessary turn to God again with hope.

תָּנוּ רַבָּנַן, אַרְבָּעָה צְרִיכִין חִזּוּק, וְאֵלּוּ הֵן: תּוֹרָה, וּמַעֲשִׂים טוֹבִים, תְּפִלָּה וְדֶרֶךְ אֶרֶץ.

Connected to the emphasis on the need to bolster one's effort in prayer, the Gemara notes that **the Sages taught** in a *baraita*: **Four** things **require bolstering,** constant effort to improve, **and they are: Torah, good deeds, prayer, and occupation.**

תּוֹרָה וּמַעֲשִׂים טוֹבִים מִנַּיִן – שֶׁנֶּאֱמַר ״רַק חֲזַק וֶאֱמַץ מְאֹד לִשְׁמֹר וְלַעֲשׂוֹת כְּכָל הַתּוֹרָה״. ״חֲזַק״ – בַּתּוֹרָה, ״וֶאֱמַץ״ – בְּמַעֲשִׂים טוֹבִים.

For each of these, a biblical proof is cited: **From where** is it derived that **Torah and good deeds** require bolstering? **As it is stated** in the instruction to Joshua: **"Only be strong and be extremely courageous, observe and do all of the Torah** that Moses My servant commanded you; do not deviate to the right or to the left, that you may succeed wherever you go" (Joshua 1:7). In this verse, observe refers to Torah study and do refers to good deeds (Maharsha); the apparently repetitive language is not extraneous. The Gemara derives: **Be strong in Torah and be courageous in good deeds.**

תְּפִלָּה מִנַּיִן – שֶׁנֶּאֱמַר "קַוֵּה אֶל ה' חֲזַק וְיַאֲמֵץ לִבֶּךָ וְקַוֵּה אֶל ה'"; 

**From where** is it derived that **prayer** requires bolstering? **As it is said: "Hope in the Lord, strengthen yourself, let your heart take courage, and hope in the Lord."**

דֶּרֶךְ אֶרֶץ מִנַּיִן – שֶׁנֶּאֱמַר "חֲזַק וְנִתְחַזַּק בְּעַד עַמֵּנוּ" וגו'.

**From where** is it derived that **occupation** requires bolstering? **As it is stated: "Be strong and we will be strong for the sake of our nation** and for the cities of our God" (II Samuel 10:12). All of one's labor requires bolstering.

"וַתֹּאמֶר צִיּוֹן עֲזָבַנִי ה' וַה' שְׁכֵחָנִי". הַיְינוּ עֲזוּבָה הַיְינוּ שְׁכוּחָה! אָמַר רֵישׁ לָקִישׁ, אָמְרָה כְּנֶסֶת יִשְׂרָאֵל לִפְנֵי הַקָּדוֹשׁ בָּרוּךְ הוּא: רִבּוֹנוֹ שֶׁל עוֹלָם, אָדָם נוֹשֵׂא אִשָּׁה עַל אִשְׁתּוֹ רִאשׁוֹנָה – זוֹכֵר מַעֲשֵׂה הָרִאשׁוֹנָה, אַתָּה עֲזַבְתַּנִי וּשְׁכַחְתַּנִי.

The Gemara cites a midrash on the following verse from Isaiah, relating to the sin of the Golden Calf and Moses' supplication for forgiveness: **"But Zion said: The Lord has forsaken me and the Lord has forgotten me.** Can a woman forget her suckling baby, that she would not have compassion for the child of her womb? These may forget, but you I will not forget" (Isaiah 49:14–15). The Gemara seeks to clarify: **Forsaken is the same as forgotten.** They are synonymous; why repeat the same idea twice? **Reish Lakish said: The community of Israel said before the Holy One, Blessed be He: Master of the Universe,** even when **a man marries** a second **wife after his first wife, he** certainly **recalls the deeds of his first** wife. Yet **You have** not only **forsaken me,** but You have **forgotten me** as well.

אָמַר לָהּ הַקָּדוֹשׁ בָּרוּךְ הוּא: בִּתִּי, שְׁנֵים עָשָׂר מַזָּלוֹת בָּרָאתִי בָּרָקִיעַ וְעַל כָּל מַזָּל וּמַזָּל בָּרָאתִי לוֹ שְׁלֹשִׁים חַיִל וְעַל כָּל חַיִל וְחַיִל בָּרָאתִי לוֹ שְׁלֹשִׁים לִגְיוֹן, וְעַל כָּל לִגְיוֹן וְלִגְיוֹן בָּרָאתִי לוֹ שְׁלֹשִׁים רַהֲטוֹן, וְעַל כָּל רַהֲטוֹן וְרַהֲטוֹן בָּרָאתִי לוֹ שְׁלֹשִׁים קַרְטוֹן, וְעַל כָּל קַרְטוֹן וְקַרְטוֹן בָּרָאתִי לוֹ שְׁלֹשִׁים גַּסְטְרָא, וְעַל כָּל גַּסְטְרָא וְגַסְטְרָא תָּלִיתִי בּוֹ שְׁלֹשׁ מֵאוֹת וְשִׁשִּׁים וַחֲמִשָּׁה אַלְפֵי רִבּוֹא כּוֹכָבִים כְּנֶגֶד יְמוֹת הַחַמָּה – וְכוּלָּן לֹא בָּרָאתִי אֶלָּא בִּשְׁבִילֵךְ, וְאַתְּ אָמַרְתְּ עֲזַבְתַּנִי וּשְׁכַחְתַּנִי?!

**The Holy One, Blessed be He, said to** Israel: **My daughter, I created twelve constellations in the firmament,**[B] **and for each and every constellation I have created thirty armies, and for each and every army I have created thirty legions** [*ligyon*],[L] **and for each and every legion I have created thirty infantry division leaders** [*rahaton*],[L] **and for each and every infantry division leader I have created thirty military camp leaders** [*karton*],[L] **and for each and every military camp leader I have created thirty leaders of forts** [*gastera*],[L] **and on each and every leader of a fort I have hung three hundred and sixty-five thousand stars corresponding to the days of the solar year. And all of them I have created only for your sake; and you said** the Lord **has forsaken me and** the Lord **has forgotten me?**

"הֲתִשְׁכַּח אִשָּׁה עוּלָהּ", אָמַר הַקָּדוֹשׁ בָּרוּךְ הוּא: כְּלוּם אֶשְׁכַּח עוֹלוֹת אֵילִים וּפִטְרֵי רְחָמִים שֶׁהִקְרַבְתְּ לְפָנַי בַּמִּדְבָּר?! אָמְרָה לְפָנָיו: רִבּוֹנוֹ שֶׁל עוֹלָם, הוֹאִיל וְאֵין שִׁכְחָה לִפְנֵי כִּסֵּא כְבוֹדְךָ שֶׁמָּא לֹא תִּשְׁכַּח לִי מַעֲשֵׂה הָעֵגֶל? – אָמַר לָהּ: "גַּם אֵלֶּה תִשְׁכַּחְנָה".

The verse goes on to say: **"Can a woman forget her suckling baby,** that she would not have compassion for the child of her womb? These may forget, but you I will not forget." The meaning of this verse is that **the Holy One, Blessed be He, said** to the community of Israel: **Have I forgotten the ram offerings and firstborn animals that you offered before Me in the desert?** The community of Israel **replied to Him: Master of the Universe, since there is no forgetfulness before the Throne of Your Glory, perhaps you will not forget my sin of the Golden Calf?** God **responded to** Israel: **"These** [*elu*] **too shall be forgotten."** "These" is a reference to the sin of the Golden Calf, regarding which Israel said: "These [*elu*] are your gods."

אָמְרָה לְפָנָיו: רִבּוֹנוֹ שֶׁל עוֹלָם, הוֹאִיל וְיֵשׁ שִׁכְחָה לִפְנֵי כִּסֵּא כְבוֹדֶךָ, שֶׁמָּא תִּשְׁכַּח לִי מַעֲשֵׂה סִינַי? – אָמַר לָהּ: "וְאָנֹכִי לֹא אֶשְׁכָּחֵךְ".

The community of Israel **said before Him: Master of the Universe, since there is forgetfulness before the Throne of Your Glory, perhaps You will** also **forget the events** revolving around the revelation at **Sinai?** God **said to** Israel: **I** [*anokhi*] **will not forget you** the revelation at Sinai, which began with: "I [*anokhi*] am the Lord your God."

וְהַיְינוּ דְּאָמַר רַבִּי אֶלְעָזָר אָמַר רַב אוֹשַׁעְיָא: מַאי דִּכְתִיב "גַּם אֵלֶּה תִשְׁכַּחְנָה" – זֶה מַעֲשֵׂה הָעֵגֶל, "וְאָנֹכִי לֹא אֶשְׁכָּחֵךְ" – זֶה מַעֲשֵׂה סִינַי.

The Gemara notes: **That is** what **Rabbi Elazar said** that **Rav Oshaya said: What is** the meaning of that which is **written: "These too will be forgotten"? That is the sin of the Golden Calf.** And what is the meaning of **I will not forget you? Those are the events** that transpired at **Sinai.**

"חֲסִידִים הָרִאשׁוֹנִים הָיוּ שׁוֹהִין שָׁעָה אַחַת".

We learned in the mishna that **the early** generations of **pious** men **would wait one hour** in order to achieve the solemn frame of mind appropriate for prayer.

מְנָא הָנֵי מִילֵּי? אָמַר רַבִּי יְהוֹשֻׁעַ בֶּן לֵוִי: אָמַר קְרָא "אַשְׁרֵי יוֹשְׁבֵי בֵיתֶךָ".

The Gemara asks: **From where are these matters** derived? **Rabbi Yehoshua ben Levi said:** This is alluded to when **the verse states: "Happy are those who dwell in Your House"** (Psalms 84:5), immediately after which it is said: "They will yet praise You, Selah."

**BACKGROUND**

**Constellations in the firmament – צְבָא הַשָּׁמַיִם:** The list of constellations and stars and their details is based on the imagery of the various units of the Roman army. One must take into account that the specific order appears differently in different versions of the Talmud, and the meaning of the various terms cannot be easily determined.

**LANGUAGE**

**Legion [*ligyon*] – לִגְיוֹן:** Based on the Latin legio/legionis. It is a legion, the largest Roman unit.

**Infantry division leader [*rahaton*] – רַהֲטוֹן:** The source of this word is unclear. Some attribute it to the Greek ἀριθμός, *arithmos*, which is literally translated as number and refers to a military unit of indeterminate size, perhaps part of a fortification. The structure of the Roman army consisted of armies, which were divided into one or more legions and their auxiliary forces. The legion, which numbered between three and six thousand soldiers, was divided into ten divisions, which were further divided into up to six camps. The Gemara's description of the heavenly hosts is influenced by the division of the large armies at the time.

**Military camp leader [*karton*] – קַרְטוֹן:** This word is based on the Latin cohors/cohortis, meaning a military unit.

**Leaders of forts [*gastera*] – גַּסְטְרָא:** This term is based on the Latin castra, meaning a (military) camp.

וְאָמַר רַבִּי יְהוֹשֻׁעַ בֶּן לֵוִי: הַמִּתְפַּלֵּל צָרִיךְ לִשְׁהוֹת שָׁעָה אַחַת אַחַר תְּפִלָּתוֹ, שֶׁנֶּאֱמַר: ״אַךְ צַדִּיקִים יוֹדוּ לִשְׁמֶךָ יֵשְׁבוּ יְשָׁרִים אֶת פָּנֶיךָ״.

**And Rabbi Yehoshua ben Levi said: One who prays must** also **wait one hour after his prayer, as it is stated: "Surely the righteous will give thanks unto Your name, the upright will sit before You"** (Psalms 140:14), meaning that after thanking God through prayer, one should stay and sit before Him.

תַּנְיָא נַמִּי הָכִי: הַמִּתְפַּלֵּל צָרִיךְ שֶׁיִּשְׁהֶא שָׁעָה אַחַת קוֹדֶם תְּפִלָּתוֹ, וְשָׁעָה אַחַת אַחַר תְּפִלָּתוֹ. קוֹדֶם תְּפִלָּתוֹ מִנַּיִן – שֶׁנֶּאֱמַר: ״אַשְׁרֵי יוֹשְׁבֵי בֵיתֶךָ״. לְאַחַר תְּפִלָּתוֹ מִנַּיִן – דִּכְתִיב ״אַךְ צַדִּיקִים יוֹדוּ לִשְׁמֶךָ יֵשְׁבוּ יְשָׁרִים אֶת פָּנֶיךָ״.

That opinion **was also taught** in a *baraita*: **One who prays must wait one hour before his prayer and one hour after his prayer.**[NH] **From where** is it derived that one must wait one hour **before his prayer? As it is stated: "Happy are those who dwell in Your House." And from where** is it derived that one must stay one hour **after his prayer? As it is written: "Surely the righteous will give thanks unto Your name, the upright will sit before You."**

תָּנוּ רַבָּנַן: חֲסִידִים הָרִאשׁוֹנִים הָיוּ שׁוֹהִין שָׁעָה אַחַת וּמִתְפַּלְּלִין שָׁעָה אַחַת וְחוֹזְרִין וְשׁוֹהִין שָׁעָה אַחַת. וְכִי מֵאַחַר שֶׁשּׁוֹהִין תֵּשַׁע שָׁעוֹת בַּיּוֹם בִּתְפִלָּה, תּוֹרָתָן הֵיאַךְ מִשְׁתַּמֶּרֶת, וּמְלַאכְתָּם הֵיאַךְ נַעֲשֵׂית?

**The Sages taught** in a *baraita* with regard to waiting before and after prayer: **The the early** generations of **pious** men **would wait one hour, pray one hour, then wait one hour again.** This raises the question: **Since** the early pious men **would spend nine hours per day** engaged either **in prayer** or the requisite waiting periods before and after prayer, three hours each for the morning, afternoon, and evening prayers, **how is their Torah preserved?** There was little time remaining to review their studies. **And how was their work accomplished?**

אֶלָּא מִתּוֹךְ שֶׁחֲסִידִים הֵם – תּוֹרָתָם מִשְׁתַּמֶּרֶת, וּמְלַאכְתָּן מִתְבָּרֶכֶת.

The Gemara answers: **Rather, because they were pious** they merited that **their Torah is preserved and their work is blessed.**

״אֲפִילּוּ הַמֶּלֶךְ שׁוֹאֵל בִּשְׁלוֹמוֹ לֹא יְשִׁיבֶנּוּ״.

Additionally, we learned in the mishna: **Even if the king greets him** while he is praying, **he should not respond to him**[H] as one may not interrupt his prayer.

אָמַר רַב יוֹסֵף: לֹא שָׁנוּ אֶלָּא לְמַלְכֵי יִשְׂרָאֵל, אֲבָל לְמַלְכֵי אוּמּוֹת הָעוֹלָם פּוֹסֵק.

In limiting application of this principle, **Rav Yosef said: They only taught** this mishna **with regard to kings of Israel,** as a Jewish king would understand that the individual did not fail to respond to his greeting due to disrespect for the king. **However, with regard to kings of the nations of the world, he interrupts** his prayer and responds to their greeting due to the potential danger.

מֵיתִיבֵי: הַמִּתְפַּלֵּל וְרָאָה אַנָּס בָּא כְּנֶגְדּוֹ, רָאָה קָרוֹן בָּא כְּנֶגְדּוֹ – לֹא יְהֵא מַפְסִיק אֶלָּא מְקַצֵּר וְעוֹלֶה!

The Gemara **raised an objection** to Rav Yosef's statement: **One who is praying and saw a violent person,** feared by all, **coming toward him, or a carriage coming toward him**[H] and he is in the way, **he should not stop** his prayer **but rather abridge it and move** out of the way.

לָא קַשְׁיָא: הָא – דְּאֶפְשָׁר לְקַצֵּר יְקַצֵּר, וְאִם לָאו – פּוֹסֵק.

The Gemara responds: This is **not difficult.** Rather, **this** that teaches to abridge one's prayer rather than stopping, refers to a case **where it is possible to abridge** his prayer and complete it in time, in which case he **should abridge** it. **And if** it is **not** a situation where he can abridge his prayer, **he interrupts** his prayer.

תָּנוּ רַבָּנַן: מַעֲשֶׂה בְּחָסִיד אֶחָד שֶׁהָיָה מִתְפַּלֵּל בַּדֶּרֶךְ, בָּא הֶגְמוֹן אֶחָד וְנָתַן לוֹ שָׁלוֹם וְלֹא הֶחֱזִיר לוֹ שָׁלוֹם. הִמְתִּין לוֹ עַד שֶׁסִּיֵּים תְּפִלָּתוֹ. לְאַחַר שֶׁסִּיֵּים תְּפִלָּתוֹ, אָמַר לוֹ: רֵיקָא, וַהֲלֹא כָּתוּב בְּתוֹרַתְכֶם ״רַק הִשָּׁמֶר לְךָ וּשְׁמֹר נַפְשְׁךָ״, וּכְתִיב ״וְנִשְׁמַרְתֶּם מְאֹד לְנַפְשֹׁתֵיכֶם״. כְּשֶׁנָּתַתִּי לְךָ שָׁלוֹם לָמָּה לֹא הֶחֱזַרְתָּ לִי שָׁלוֹם? אִם הָיִיתִי חוֹתֵךְ רֹאשְׁךָ בְּסַיִיף, מִי הָיָה תּוֹבֵעַ אֶת דָּמְךָ מִיָּדִי?!

**The Sages taught:** There was a related **incident, involving a particular pious man who was praying** while traveling **along his path** when **an officer** [*hegmon*][L] **came and greeted him.** The pious man did not pause from his prayer **and did not respond with a greeting.**[N] The officer **waited for him until he finished his prayer.**

**After he finished his prayer,** the officer **said him:** You **good for nothing.** You endangered yourself; I could have killed you.

**Isn't it written in your Torah: "Take utmost care and guard yourself diligently"** (Deuteronomy 4:9)?[N]

**And it is also written: "Take therefore good heed unto yourselves"** (Deuteronomy 4:15)? Why did you ignore the danger to your life?

**When I greeted you, why did you not respond with a greeting? Were I to sever your head with a sword, who would hold me accountable for your** spilled **blood?**

אָמַר לוֹ: הַמְתֵּן לִי עַד שֶׁאֲפַיֶּיסְךָ בִּדְבָרִים. אָמַר לוֹ: אִילּוּ הָיִיתָ עוֹמֵד לִפְנֵי מֶלֶךְ בָּשָׂר וָדָם, וּבָא חֲבֵרְךָ וְנָתַן לְךָ שָׁלוֹם – הָיִיתָ

The pious man **said to him: Wait for me until I will appease you with** my **words.**

**He said to him: Had you been standing before a flesh and blood king and your friend came and greeted you,** would you

## NOTES

One who prays must wait one hour before his prayer…after his prayer – הַמִּתְפַּלֵּל צָרִיךְ שֶׁיִּשְׁהֶא שָׁעָה אַחַת קוֹדֶם תְּפִלָּתוֹ...אַחַר תְּפִלָּתוֹ: Waiting before prayer is in order to prepare for prayer and the brief waiting period after prayer is to avoid the impression that he is eager to flee. Because the prayer of the early generations of pious men was so intense, they required a full hour of preparation beforehand and a full hour thereafter to ease their return to mundane activities.

An incident, involving a particular pious man…and did not respond with a greeting – ...מַעֲשֶׂה בְּחָסִיד אֶחָד וְלֹא הֶחֱזִיר לוֹ שָׁלוֹם: The commentaries ask why the pious man did not act in accordance with the *halakha* and interrupt his prayer and respond to the greeting due to the danger. They answer that because the officer offered his greeting and even waited for him, the pious man knew that the officer would accept his explanation and apology afterward (*Taz, Tziyyun LeNefesh Ḥayya*).

Take utmost care and guard yourself diligently – וְנִשְׁמַרְתֶּם מְאֹד לְנַפְשֹׁתֵיכֶם: Though this verse is often utilized as a warning to avoid danger, that is not its plain meaning. It is actually a section of a verse that warns one to stay away from idolatry. Nonetheless, as an allusion, the Sages used it for this purpose (Maharsha).

## HALAKHA

One who prays must wait one hour before his prayer…after his prayer – הַמִּתְפַּלֵּל צָרִיךְ שֶׁיִּשְׁהֶא שָׁעָה אַחַת קוֹדֶם תְּפִלָּתוֹ...אַחַר תְּפִלָּתוֹ: One should wait one hour before prayer to focus his heart on the Holy One, Blessed be He, and one should also wait after prayer to avoid the impression that it is burdensome to him. The early generations of pious men would wait a full hour; however, for most people, a short time, e.g., the time that it takes to walk the length of two doorways that was taught at the beginning of this tractate, is sufficient (*Magen Avraham*; Rambam *Sefer Ahava*, *Hilkhot Tefilla* 4:16; *Shulḥan Arukh*, *Oraḥ Ḥayyim* 93:1).

Even if the king greets him, he should not respond to him – אֲפִילּוּ הַמֶּלֶךְ שׁוֹאֵל בִּשְׁלוֹמוֹ לֹא יְשִׁיבֶנּוּ: One who is in the midst of the *Amida* prayer should not interrupt his prayer to show deference to anyone; even to a king of Israel. If it is a non-Jewish king or a violent person (*Be'er Heitev*) one is permitted to interrupt his prayer. If possible, though, it is preferable to move out of the way or to abbreviate one's prayer instead (Rambam *Sefer Ahava*, *Hilkhot Tefilla* 6:9; *Shulḥan Arukh*, *Oraḥ Ḥayyim* 104:1).

One who is praying and saw a violent person, feared by all, coming toward him, or a carriage coming toward him – הַמִּתְפַּלֵּל וְרָאָה אַנָּס בָּא כְּנֶגְדּוֹ, רָאָה קָרוֹן בָּא כְּנֶגְדּוֹ: One who is standing and praying on the road and sees a carriage or some other hindrance approaching, he should move out of the way rather than interrupt his prayer (Rambam *Sefer Ahava*, *Hilkhot Tefilla* 6:9; *Shulḥan Arukh*, *Oraḥ Ḥayyim* 104:2).

## LANGUAGE

Officer [*hegmon*] – הֶגְמוֹן: From the Greek ἡγεμών, *hegemon*, this term originally referred to an army commander, and was later used to refer to a governor or a minister in general. The Talmud utilizes this term in the civil, not the military sense.

מַחֲזִיר לוֹ?! – אָמַר לוֹ: לָאו. וְאִם הָיִיתָ מַחֲזִיר לוֹ, מָה הָיוּ עוֹשִׂים לְךָ? – אָמַר לוֹ: הָיוּ חוֹתְכִים אֶת רֹאשִׁי בְּסַיִיף. – אָמַר לוֹ: וַהֲלֹא דְּבָרִים קַל וָחוֹמֶר; וּמָה אַתָּה שֶׁהָיִיתָ עוֹמֵד לִפְנֵי מֶלֶךְ בָּשָׂר וָדָם שֶׁהַיּוֹם כָּאן וּמָחָר בַּקֶּבֶר – כָּךְ; אֲנִי שֶׁהָיִיתִי עוֹמֵד לִפְנֵי מֶלֶךְ מַלְכֵי הַמְּלָכִים הַקָּדוֹשׁ בָּרוּךְ הוּא, שֶׁהוּא חַי וְקַיָּים לָעַד וּלְעוֹלְמֵי עוֹלָמִים – עַל אַחַת כַּמָּה וְכַמָּה!

**return** his greeting?
The officer **said to him: No.**
The pious man continued: **And if you would** greet **him, what would they do to you?**
The officer **said to him: They would cut** off **my head with a sword.**
The pious man **said to him: Isn't this matter an *a fortiori* inference? You who were standing before a king of flesh and blood,**
of whom your fear is limited **because today he is here but tomorrow he is in the grave,**
would have reacted in **that** way;
**I, who was standing** and praying **before the Supreme King of kings, the Holy One, Blessed be He,**
**Who lives and endures for all eternity,**
**all the more so** that I could not pause to respond to someone's greeting.

מִיָּד נִתְפַּיֵּיס אוֹתוֹ הֶגְמוֹן, וְנִפְטַר אוֹתוֹ חָסִיד לְבֵיתוֹ לְשָׁלוֹם.

When he heard this, **the officer was immediately appeased and the pious man returned home in peace.**

״אֲפִילּוּ נָחָשׁ כָּרוּךְ עַל עֲקֵבוֹ לֹא יַפְסִיק״. אָמַר רַב שֵׁשֶׁת: לֹא שָׁנוּ אֶלָּא נָחָשׁ, אֲבָל עַקְרָב – פּוֹסֵק.

We learned in the mishna that **even if a snake is wrapped around his heel, he may not interrupt** his prayer. In limiting application of this principle, **Rav Sheshet said: They only taught** this mishna **with regard to a snake,** as if one does not attack the snake it will not bite him. **But** if **a scorpion**[H] approaches an individual while he is praying, **he stops,** as the scorpion is liable to sting him even if he does not disturb it.

מֵיתִיבֵי: נָפַל לְגוֹב אֲרָיוֹת אֵין מְעִידִין עָלָיו שֶׁמֵּת, נָפַל לַחֲפִירָה מְלֵאָה נְחָשִׁים וְעַקְרַבִּים – מְעִידִין עָלָיו שֶׁמֵּת!

The Gemara **raises an objection** based on what was taught in a *Tosefta*: Those who saw one **fall into a lions' den** but did not see what happened to him thereafter, **do not testify that he died.** Their testimony is not accepted by the court as proof that he has died as it is possible that the lions did not eat him. However, those who saw one **fall into a pit of snakes and scorpions,**[H] **testify that he died** as surely the snakes bit him.

שָׁאנֵי הָתָם, דְּאַגַּב אִיצְצָא מַזְּקִי.

The Gemara responds: This is not difficult. **There,** in the case of one who falls into a pit of snakes, it **is different, as due to the pressure** of his falling on top of them, the snakes **will harm him,** but a snake who is not touched will not bite.

אָמַר רַבִּי יִצְחָק: רָאָה שְׁוָורִים פּוֹסֵק, דְּתָנֵי רַב הוֹשַׁעְיָה: מַרְחִיקִין מִשּׁוֹר תָּם חֲמִשִּׁים אַמָּה, וּמִשּׁוֹר מוּעָד – כִּמְלוֹא עֵינָיו.

The Gemara cites another *halakha* stating that he must interrupt his prayer in a case of certain danger. **Rabbi Yitzḥak said: One who saw oxen**[H] coming toward him, **he interrupts** his prayer, **as Rav Hoshaya taught: One distances himself fifty cubits from an innocuous ox [*shor tam*],**[B] an ox with no history of causing damage with the intent to injure, **and from a forewarned ox [*shor muad*],**[B] an ox whose owner was forewarned because his ox has gored three times already, one distances himself until it is beyond **eyeshot.**

תָּנָא מִשְּׁמֵיהּ דְּרַבִּי מֵאִיר: רֵישׁ תּוֹרָא בְּדִקּוּלָא – סְלֵיק לְאִגָּרָא, וּשְׁדֵי דַּרְגָּא מִתּוּתָךְ. אָמַר שְׁמוּאֵל: הָנֵי מִילֵּי – בְּשׁוֹר שָׁחוֹר וּבְיוֹמֵי נִיסָן, מִפְּנֵי שֶׁהַשָּׂטָן מְרַקֵּד לוֹ בֵּין קַרְנָיו.

It was **taught in the name of Rabbi Meir:** While **the head of the ox is** still **in the basket** and he is busy eating, **go up on the roof and kick the ladder out from underneath you. Shmuel said: This applies only with regard to a black ox,**[B] **and during the days of Nisan, because** that species of ox is particularly dangerous, and during that time of year **Satan dances between its horns.**

**BACKGROUND**

**Innocuous ox [*shor tam*]– שׁוֹר תָּם:** An animal that is not known to cause damage with the intent to injure. The first three times an animal causes damage of this nature, its owner is only required to pay half the damage it has caused. Afterwards it becomes a dangerous forewarned animal, an animal with a history of causing injury. The owner of a forewarned animal is required to pay for all the damage it causes. An animal can be considered innocuous with regard to certain kinds of damage and forewarned with regard to others. For example, an ox that has a history of goring other oxen is still considered innocuous with regard to goring humans. Similarly, if it is established that the animal causes injury only on certain days, for example, on Shabbat and Festivals, it may be considered forewarned on those days alone and innocuous during the rest of the week. An animal that is forewarned can regain status as innocuous if, on three separate occasions, animals that it was accustomed to attacking passed by and it refrained from attacking them.

**Forewarned ox [*shor muad*] – שׁוֹר מוּעָד:** In its more limited sense, this expression is used to refer to an ox whose owner has been forewarned, i.e., an ox that has gored three times. If an ox causes damage by goring, or, in general, any animal causes malicious damage, the first three times that it does so, the owner is liable for only half of the resulting damage. If, however, the ox gores a fourth time, and the owner was officially notified that it had gored three times previously, the animal is considered forewarned, and the owner must pay in full for the resulting damage.

**HALAKHA**

**Even if a snake is wrapped around his heel… a scorpion – נָחָשׁ כָּרוּךְ עַל עֲקֵבוֹ...עַקְרָב:** One who was standing in prayer and a snake wrapped itself around his ankle, he should not interrupt his prayer to tell someone else to remove the snake (*Mishna Berura*). If he sees that the snake is agitated and primed for attack, he stops his prayer (Jerusalem Talmud). However, in the case of a scorpion, which is deadly (*Magen Avraham*), one always stops his prayer (Rambam *Sefer Ahava, Hilkhot Tefilla* 6:9; *Shulḥan Arukh, Oraḥ Ḥayyim* 104:3).

**One who fell into a lions' den…snakes and scorpions – נָפַל לְגוֹב אֲרָיוֹת...נְחָשִׁים וְעַקְרַבִּים:** Based on witnessing someone fall into a lions' den, one cannot testify that he is dead, as perhaps they did not harm him. However, if he witnessed him fall into a pit of snakes and scorpions, he can testify that he is dead, as due to the pressure of his falling on top of them they certainly harmed him and he died (Rambam *Sefer Nashim, Hilkhot Gerushin* 13:17; *Shulḥan Arukh, Even HaEzer* 17:29).

**One who saw oxen – רָאָה שְׁוָורִים:** One who is standing in prayer and sees an ox approaching stops his prayer and distances himself from the ox. If the local oxen are known to be benign, he need not distance himself (*Shulḥan Arukh, Oraḥ Ḥayyim* 104:4).

**BACKGROUND**

**Black ox – שׁוֹר שָׁחוֹר:** The ox referenced here may be the buffalo. It is very similar to common cattle, and is distinguishable by its strength, size, dark color, the shape of its horns, and the extended period during which it remains in the water. It is indigenous to Asia, and is used primarily as a work animal. Though mild-mannered around those who tend to it, it can be very dangerous to strangers and many have died as a result of its attacks.

Black ox

תָּנוּ רַבָּנַן: מַעֲשֶׂה בְּמָקוֹם אֶחָד שֶׁהָיָה עָרוֹד וְהָיָה מַזִּיק אֶת הַבְּרִיּוֹת, בָּאוּ וְהוֹדִיעוּ לוֹ לְרַבִּי חֲנִינָא בֶּן דּוֹסָא. אָמַר לָהֶם: הַרְאוּ לִי אֶת חוֹרוֹ! הֶרְאוּהוּ אֶת חוֹרוֹ, נָתַן עֲקֵבוֹ עַל פִּי הַחוֹר, יָצָא וּנְשָׁכוֹ וּמֵת אוֹתוֹ עָרוֹד.

With regard to the praise for one who prays and need not fear even a snake, **the Sages taught:** There was **an incident in one place where an** ***arvad***[B] **was harming the people. They came and told Rabbi Ḥanina ben Dosa** and asked for his help. **He told them: Show me** the **hole of the** ***arvad***. **They showed him its hole. He placed his heel over the mouth of the hole and the** ***arvad*** **came out and bit him, and died.**

נְטָלוֹ עַל כְּתֵפוֹ וֶהֱבִיאוֹ לְבֵית הַמִּדְרָשׁ. אָמַר לָהֶם: רְאוּ בָּנַי, אֵין עָרוֹד מֵמִית אֶלָּא הַחֵטְא מֵמִית.

Rabbi Ḥanina ben Dosa **placed** the *arvad* **over his shoulder and brought it to the study hall. He said to** those assembled there: **See, my sons, it is not** the ***arvad*** **that kills** a person, **rather transgression kills** a person. The *arvad* has no power over one who is free of transgression.

בְּאוֹתָהּ שָׁעָה אָמְרוּ: אוֹי לוֹ לְאָדָם שֶׁפָּגַע בּוֹ עָרוֹד, וְאוֹי לוֹ לְעָרוֹד שֶׁפָּגַע בּוֹ רַבִּי חֲנִינָא בֶּן דּוֹסָא.

**At that moment** the Sages **said: Woe unto the person who was attacked by an** ***arvad*** **and woe unto the** ***arvad*** **that was attacked by Rabbi Ḥanina ben Dosa.**

מתני׳ מַזְכִּירִין גְּבוּרוֹת גְּשָׁמִים בִּתְחִיַּית הַמֵּתִים וּשְׁאֵלָה בְּבִרְכַּת הַשָּׁנִים, וְהַבְדָּלָה בְּחוֹנֵן הַדַּעַת; רַבִּי עֲקִיבָא אוֹמֵר: אוֹמְרָהּ בְּרָכָה רְבִיעִית בִּפְנֵי עַצְמָהּ; רַבִּי אֱלִיעֶזֶר אוֹמֵר: בְּהוֹדָאָה.

**MISHNA** This mishna speaks of additions to the standard formula of the *Amida* prayer and the blessings in which they are incorporated. **One mentions the might of the rains** and recites: He makes the wind blow and the rain fall, **in** the second blessing of the *Amida* prayer, the blessing of **the revival of the dead.**[H] **And the request** for rain: And grant dew and rain as a blessing, **in** the ninth blessing of the *Amida* prayer, **the blessing of the years.**[H] **And the prayer of distinction** [***havdala***], between the holy and the profane recited in the evening prayer following Shabbat and festivals, **in** the fourth blessing of the *Amida* prayer: **Who graciously grants knowledge.**[H] **Rabbi Akiva says:** *Havdala* **is recited** as **an independent fourth blessing. Rabbi Eliezer says** that it is recited **in** the seventeenth blessing of the *Amida* prayer, the blessing of **thanksgiving.**

גמ׳ ״מַזְכִּירִין גְּבוּרוֹת גְּשָׁמִים״. מַאי טַעְמָא?

**GEMARA** We learned in the mishna that **one mentions the might of the rains** in the second blessing of the *Amida* prayer, the blessing of the revival of the dead. The Gemara asks: **What is the reason** that the might of the rains is mentioned specifically in that blessing?

אָמַר רַב יוֹסֵף: מִתּוֹךְ שֶׁשְּׁקוּלָה כִּתְחִיַּית הַמֵּתִים, לְפִיכָךְ קְבָעוּהָ בִּתְחִיַּית הַמֵּתִים.

**Rav Yosef said: Because** the might of the rains **is equivalent to the resurrection of the dead,** as rain revives new life in the plant world (Jerusalem Talmud).

״וּשְׁאֵלָה בְּבִרְכַּת הַשָּׁנִים״. מַאי טַעְמָא?

**And** we also learned in the mishna that the **request** for rain is added to **the blessing of the years.** Here, too, the Gemara asks: **What is the reason** that the request for rain is recited specifically in that blessing?

אָמַר רַב יוֹסֵף: מִתּוֹךְ שֶׁהִיא פַּרְנָסָה, לְפִיכָךְ קְבָעוּהָ בְּבִרְכַּת פַּרְנָסָה.

**Rav Yosef said: Because** rain is a component of **sustenance, therefore it was inserted in the blessing of sustenance** as part of our request for bountiful sustenance.

״הַבְדָּלָה בְּחוֹנֵן הַדַּעַת״. מַאי טַעְמָא?

We also learned in the mishna that ***havdala***, distinguishing between Shabbat and the weekdays, is added **in** the blessing of: **Who graciously grants knowledge.** Here too the Gemara asks: **What is the reason** that *havdala* is recited specifically in that blessing?

אָמַר רַב יוֹסֵף: מִתּוֹךְ שֶׁהִיא חָכְמָה, קְבָעוּהָ בְּבִרְכַּת חָכְמָה; וְרַבָּנַן אָמְרִי: מִתּוֹךְ שֶׁהִיא חוֹל, לְפִיכָךְ קְבָעוּהָ בְּבִרְכַּת חוֹל.

**Rav Yosef said:** *Havdala* is recited in that blessing **because it** requires **wisdom** to distinguish between two entities, **they established it in the blessing of wisdom. The Rabbis say** a different reason: **Because** *havdala* **is** the distinction between the sacred and the **profane,** the Sages **established it in the blessing of weekdays.** The first three blessings of the *Amida* prayer are recited both on weekdays and on Shabbat and Festivals. The blessing: Who graciously grants knowledge, is the first of the blessings recited exclusively during the week.

אָמַר רַב אַמִי: גְּדוֹלָה דֵּעָה שֶׁנִּתְּנָה בִּתְחִלַּת בְּרָכָה שֶׁל חוֹל.

Having mentioned the blessing of wisdom, the Gemara cites that which **Rav Ami said** with regard to knowledge: **Great is knowledge that was placed at the beginning of the weekday blessings;** an indication of its significance.

**BACKGROUND**

*Arvad* – עָרוֹד: Based on the descriptions in the Gemara, apparently the *arvad* is a type of snake or perhaps a large, very dangerous reptile. In parallel discussions in the Jerusalem Talmud, the *arvad* is called a *ḥavarbar*. Some identify this as the black snake or a snake of the *coluber* genus, which, although not poisonous, is very aggressive and bites.

Caspian whipsnake

**HALAKHA**

**One mentions the might of the rains in the blessing of the revival of the dead** – מַזְכִּירִין גְּבוּרוֹת גְּשָׁמִים בִּתְחִיַּית הַמֵּתִים: During the rainy season one mentions rain in the second blessing of the *Amida* prayer, the blessing of Divine Might (Rambam *Sefer Ahava, Hilkhot Tefilla* 2:15; *Shulḥan Arukh, Oraḥ Ḥayyim* 114:1).

**The request for rain is recited in the blessing of the years** – וּשְׁאֵלָה בְּבִרְכַּת הַשָּׁנִים: During the rainy season, which in Eretz Yisrael begins on the seventh of Marḥeshvan and outside of Israel, sixty days after the Tishrei, or autumnal, equinox, the request for rain is inserted in the blessing of the years, the ninth blessing of the *Amida* prayer (Rambam *Sefer Ahava, Hilkhot Tefilla* 2:16; *Shulḥan Arukh, Oraḥ Ḥayyim* 117:1).

**And** ***havdala*** **in the blessing: Who graciously grants knowledge** – וְהַבְדָּלָה בְּחוֹנֵן הַדַּעַת: One recites *havdala* at the conclusion of Shabbat and Festivals in the blessing: Who graciously grants knowledge, in the evening prayer. This is in accordance with the unattributed opinion in the mishna and the conclusion of the Gemara (Rambam *Sefer Ahava, Hilkhot Tefilla* 2:4; *Shulḥan Arukh, Oraḥ Ḥayyim* 294:1).

וְאָמַר רַב אַמִי: גְּדוֹלָה דֵּעָה שֶׁנִּתְּנָה בֵּין שְׁתֵּי אוֹתִיּוֹת, שֶׁנֶּאֱמַר: ״כִּי אֵל דֵּעוֹת ה׳״. וְכָל מִי שֶׁאֵין בּוֹ דֵּעָה אָסוּר לְרַחֵם עָלָיו, שֶׁנֶּאֱמַר: ״כִּי לֹא עַם בִּינוֹת הוּא עַל כֵּן לֹא יְרַחֲמֶנּוּ עוֹשֵׂהוּ״.

**And Rav Ami said** in praise of knowledge: **Great is knowledge that was placed between two letters,** two names of God, **as it is stated: "For God of knowledge is the Lord"** (1 Samuel 2:3). **And** since knowledge is regarded so highly, **anyone without knowledge,**[N] **it is forbidden to have compassion upon him, as it is stated: "For they are a people of no wisdom, so their Creator will have no compassion upon them** and their Creator will not be gracious unto them" (Isaiah 27:11). If God shows no mercy for those who lack wisdom, all the more so should people refrain from doing so.

אָמַר רַבִּי אֶלְעָזָר: גָּדוֹל מִקְדָּשׁ שֶׁנִּתַּן בֵּין שְׁתֵּי אוֹתִיּוֹת, שֶׁנֶּאֱמַר: ״פָּעַלְתָּ ה׳ מִקְּדָשׁ ה׳״.

Similarly, **Rabbi Elazar said: Great is the Holy Temple,** as it too **was placed between two letters,** two names of God, **as it is stated:** "The place in which to dwell which **You have made, Lord, the Temple, Lord,** which Your hands have prepared" (Exodus 15:17).

וְאָמַר רַבִּי אֶלְעָזָר: כָּל אָדָם שֶׁיֵּשׁ בּוֹ דֵּעָה – כְּאִילּוּ נִבְנָה בֵּית הַמִּקְדָּשׁ בְּיָמָיו; דֵּעָה נִתְּנָה בֵּין שְׁתֵּי אוֹתִיּוֹת, מִקְדָּשׁ נִתַּן בֵּין שְׁתֵּי אוֹתִיּוֹת.

Noting the parallel between these two ideas, **Rabbi Elazar** added **and said: Anyone with knowledge,** it is **as if the Holy Temple was built in his days;**[N] **knowledge was placed between two letters** and **the Temple was placed between two letters,** signifying that they stand together.

מַתְקִיף לָהּ רַב אַחָא קַרְחִינָאָה: אֶלָּא מֵעַתָּה, גְּדוֹלָה נְקָמָה שֶׁנִּתְּנָה בֵּין שְׁתֵּי אוֹתִיּוֹת, שֶׁנֶּאֱמַר: ״אֵל נְקָמוֹת ה׳״!

**Rav Aḥa Karḥina'a strongly objects to this** approach that being placed between two names of God accords significance: **However, if so,** the same should hold true for vengeance. **Great is revenge that was placed between two letters, as it is stated: "God of vengeance, Lord,** God of vengeance shine forth" (Psalms 94:1).

אָמַר לֵיהּ: אִין, בְּמִילְּתַהּ מִיהָא גְּדוֹלָה הִיא. וְהַיְינוּ דְּאָמַר עוּלָּא: שְׁתֵּי נְקָמוֹת הַלָּלוּ לָמָּה? אַחַת לְטוֹבָה וְאַחַת לְרָעָה, לְטוֹבָה – דִּכְתִיב: ״הוֹפִיעַ מֵהַר פָּארָן״, לְרָעָה – דִּכְתִיב: ״אֵל נְקָמוֹת ה׳ אֵל נְקָמוֹת הוֹפִיעַ״.

**He said to him: Yes. At least in its place,** in the appropriate context, **it is great.** At times it is necessary. **That is that which Ulla said: Why** are **these two vengeances** mentioned in a single verse? **One for good and one for evil.** Vengeance **for good, as it is written: "He shined forth from Mount Paran"** (Deuteronomy 33:2) with regard to God's vengeance against the wicked; vengeance **for evil, as it is written: "God of vengeance, Lord, God of vengeance shine forth"** with regard to the punishment of Israel.

״רַבִּי עֲקִיבָא אוֹמֵר אוֹמְרָהּ בְּרָכָה רְבִיעִית״ כו׳.

A tannaitic dispute is cited in the mishna with regard to the appropriate blessing in which to recite *havdala* within the *Amida* prayer. **Rabbi Akiva says:** *Havdala* **is recited** as an independent **fourth blessing.** Rabbi Eliezer says that it is recited in the seventeenth blessing of the *Amida* prayer, the blessing of thanksgiving. The first *tanna* says that it is recited in the fourth blessing of the *Amida* prayer: Who graciously grants knowledge.

אָמַר לֵיהּ רַב שֶׁמֶן בַּר אַבָּא לְרַבִּי יוֹחָנָן: מִכְּדִי אַנְשֵׁי כְּנֶסֶת הַגְּדוֹלָה תִּקְּנוּ לָהֶם לְיִשְׂרָאֵל, בְּרָכוֹת וּתְפִלּוֹת קְדוּשּׁוֹת וְהַבְדָּלוֹת, נֶחֱזֵי הֵיכָן תַּקּוּן.

Regarding this, **Rav Shemen,** Shimon, **bar Abba said to Rabbi Yoḥanan: Now, since** the eighteen blessings of the *Amida* prayer and the other prayer formulas for prayer **were instituted for Israel by the members of the Great Assembly** just like all the other **blessings and prayers, sanctifications and *havdalot*; let us see where** in the *Amida* prayer the members of the Great Assembly **instituted**[N] to recite *havdala.*

אָמַר לֵיהּ: בַּתְּחִילָּה קְבָעוּהָ בַּתְּפִלָּה, הֶעֱשִׁירוּ – קְבָעוּהָ עַל הַכּוֹס, הֶעֱנוּ – חֲזָרוּ וּקְבָעוּהָ בַּתְּפִלָּה, וְהֵם אָמְרוּ: הַמַּבְדִּיל בַּתְּפִלָּה צָרִיךְ שֶׁיַּבְדִּיל עַל הַכּוֹס.

Rabbi Yoḥanan replied that that would be impossible, as the customs associated with *havdala* went through several stages. **He said to him: Initially,** during the difficult, early years of the Second Temple, **they established** that *havdala* is to be recited **in the** *Amida* **prayer.** Subsequently, when the people **became wealthy, they established** that *havdala* is to be recited **over the cup** of wine. When the people **became impoverished, they again established** that **it** was to be recited **in the** *Amida* **prayer. And they said: One who recites *havdala* in the** *Amida* **prayer must,** if he is able (*Shitta Mekubbetzet, Me'iri*), **recite *havdala* over the cup**[H] of wine as well. Due to all these changes, it was not clear when exactly *havdala* was to be recited.

אִיתְּמַר נַמִי, אָמַר רַבִּי חִיָּיא בַּר אַבָּא אָמַר רַבִּי יוֹחָנָן: אַנְשֵׁי כְּנֶסֶת הַגְּדוֹלָה תִּקְּנוּ לָהֶם לְיִשְׂרָאֵל בְּרָכוֹת וּתְפִלּוֹת קְדוּשּׁוֹת וְהַבְדָּלוֹת. בַּתְּחִלָּה קְבָעוּהָ בַּתְּפִלָּה, הֶעֱשִׁירוּ – קְבָעוּהָ עַל הַכּוֹס, חָזְרוּ וְהֶעֱנוּ – קְבָעוּהָ בַּתְּפִלָּה, וְהֵם אָמְרוּ: הַמַּבְדִּיל בַּתְּפִלָּה צָרִיךְ שֶׁיַּבְדִּיל עַל הַכּוֹס.

**It was also stated: Rabbi Ḥiyya bar Abba said** that **Rabbi Yoḥanan said: The members of the Great Assembly established for Israel blessings and prayers, sanctifications and *havdalot*. Initially, they established** that *havdala* is to be recited **in the** *Amida* **prayer.** Subsequently, when the people **became wealthy, they established** that *havdala* is to be recited **over the cup** of wine. When the people **again became impoverished, they established** that **it** was to be recited **in the** *Amida* **prayer. And they said: One who recites *havdala* in the** *Amida* **prayer must recite *havdala* over the cup** of wine as well.

**NOTES**

**Anyone without knowledge – מִי שֶׁאֵין בּוֹ דֵּעָה:** Knowledge in this context does not refer specifically to intellectual capability, but rather to one's fundamental ability to conduct himself and live in accordance with that capability. That is why the Gemara relates so harshly to one without knowledge, as by failing to realize his potential, he negates his own essence. Every creature that maintains his fundamental essence deserves compassion; one without knowledge negates the very justification of his existence (Maharsha).

**Anyone with knowledge, it is as if the Holy Temple was built in his days – כָּל אָדָם שֶׁיֵּשׁ בּוֹ דֵּעָה – כְּאִילּוּ נִבְנָה בֵּית הַמִּקְדָּשׁ בְּיָמָיו:** The Sages already established that one who engages in the study of the laws of the burnt-offering it is as if he sacrificed a burnt-offering. Therefore, anyone with knowledge can achieve ultimate closeness to God, which is the purpose of the Temple and the service performed therein. Consequently, it is as if the Temple was built in his days (*Torat HaOla* of the Rema).

**Let us see where the members of the Great Assembly instituted it – נֶחֱזֵי הֵיכָן תַּקּוּן:** This suggestion is not raised on every occasion. It is only relevant with regard to those ordinances that everyone performs on a regular basis and there is no danger that it will be forgotten or mistaken (*Tosafot*).

**HALAKHA**

**One who recites *havdala* in the *Amida* prayer must recite *havdala* over the cup – הַמַּבְדִּיל בַּתְּפִלָּה, צָרִיךְ שֶׁיַּבְדִּיל עַל הַכּוֹס:** One who recited *havdala* in the *Amida* prayer must repeat *havdala* over a cup of wine (Rambam *Sefer Ahava, Hilkhot Tefilla* 2:12; *Shulḥan Arukh, Oraḥ Ḥayyim* 294:1).

אִיתְּמַר נַמִי, רַבָּה וְרַב יוֹסֵף דְּאָמְרִי תַּרְוַיְיהוּ: הַמַּבְדִּיל בַּתְּפִלָּה צָרִיךְ שֶׁיַּבְדִּיל עַל הַכּוֹס.

**It was also stated: Rabba and Rav Yosef who both said: One who recites *havdala* in the *Amida* prayer must recite *havdala* over the cup** of wine as well.

אָמַר רָבָא, וּמוֹתְבִינַן אַשְּׁמַעְתִּין: טָעָה וְלֹא הִזְכִּיר גְּבוּרוֹת גְּשָׁמִים בִּתְחִיַּית הַמֵּתִים וּשְׁאֵלָה בְּבִרְכַּת הַשָּׁנִים – מַחֲזִירִין אוֹתוֹ, וְהַבְדָּלָה בְּחוֹנֵן הַדַּעַת – אֵין מַחֲזִירִין אוֹתוֹ, מִפְּנֵי שֶׁיָּכוֹל לְאוֹמְרָהּ עַל הַכּוֹס!

**Rava said: We raise an objection to our *halakha*** based on what was taught in a *Tosefta*: **One who erred and did not mention the might of the rains in** the second blessing in the *Amida*, the blessing on **the revival of the dead,**[H] **and** one who erred and failed to recite **the request** for rain **in** the ninth blessing of the *Amida*, **the blessing of the years,**[H] **we require him to return** to the beginning of the prayer and repeat it. However, one who erred and failed to recite ***havdala* in** the blessing: **Who graciously grants knowledge,**[H] **we do not require him to return** to the beginning of the prayer and repeat it, **as he can recite *havdala* over the cup** of wine. Apparently, *havdala* over the cup of wine is optional, not obligatory, at it says because he can recite and not that he must.

לָא תֵּימָא "מִפְּנֵי שֶׁיָּכוֹל לְאוֹמְרָהּ עַל הַכּוֹס", אֶלָּא אֵימָא "מִפְּנֵי שֶׁאוֹמְרָהּ עַל הַכּוֹס".

The Gemara answers: **Do not say** as it appears in the *Tosefta*: **Because he can recite *havdala* over the cup** of wine. **Rather, say: Because he recites *havdala* over the cup** of wine.

אִיתְּמַר נַמִי, אָמַר רַבִּי בִּנְיָמִין בַּר יֶפֶת: שָׁאַל רַבִּי יוֹסֵי אֶת רַבִּי יוֹחָנָן בְּצַיְדָּן, וְאָמְרִי לַהּ, רַבִּי שִׁמְעוֹן בֶּן יַעֲקֹב דְּמִן צוֹר אֶת רַבִּי יוֹחָנָן, וַאֲנָא שְׁמַעִית: הַמַּבְדִּיל בַּתְּפִלָּה, צָרִיךְ שֶׁיַּבְדִּיל עַל הַכּוֹס אוֹ לֹא? וְאָמַר לֵיהּ: צָרִיךְ שֶׁיַּבְדִּיל עַל הַכּוֹס.

Proof that one must recite *havdala* over the cup of wine as well as in the *Amida* prayer **was also stated: Rabbi Binyamin bar Yefet said** that **Rabbi Yosei asked Rabbi Yoḥanan in Sidon, and some say that Rabbi Shimon ben Ya'akov from** the city of **Tyre** asked **Rabbi Yoḥanan, and I,** Binyamin bar Yefet, **heard: One who** already **recited *havdala* in the *Amida* prayer, must he recite *havdala* over the cup** of wine **or not? And** Rabbi Yoḥanan **said to him: He must recite *havdala* over the cup.**

אִיבַּעְיָא לְהוּ: הַמַּבְדִּיל עַל הַכּוֹס, מַהוּ שֶׁיַּבְדִּיל בַּתְּפִלָּה?

Having clarified the question whether one who recited *havdala* during the *Amida* prayer must also recite *havdala* over the cup of wine, **a dilemma was raised before** the Sages: **One who** already **recited *havdala* over the cup** of wine, **what is** the ruling as far as his obligation **to recite *havdala* in the *Amida* prayer** is concerned?

אָמַר רַב נַחְמָן בַּר יִצְחָק, קַל וָחוֹמֶר מִתְּפִלָּה: וּמַה תְּפִלָּה דְּעִיקַּר תַּקַּנְתָּא הִיא – אָמְרִי: הַמַּבְדִּיל בַּתְּפִלָּה צָרִיךְ שֶׁיַּבְדִּיל עַל הַכּוֹס; הַמַּבְדִּיל עַל הַכּוֹס, דְּלָאו עִיקַּר תַּקַּנְתָּא הִיא – לֹא כָּל שֶׁכֵּן?!

**Rav Naḥman bar Yitzḥak said:** This can be derived ***a fortiori* from** the established *halakha* regarding *havdala* in **the *Amida* prayer. Just as** *havdala* in **the *Amida* prayer, which is** where **the principal ordinance** to recite *havdala* was instituted, the Sages **said** that it is not sufficient and **one who recited *havdala* in the *Amida* prayer must recite *havdala* over the cup** of wine as well, **all the more so** that **one who recited *havdala* over the cup** of wine, **which is not** where **the principal ordinance** to recite *havdala* was instituted, but was merely a later addition, did not fulfill his obligation and must recite *havdala* in the *Amida* prayer.

תָּנֵי רַב אַחָא אֲרִיכָא קַמֵּיהּ דְּרַב חִינָּנָא: הַמַּבְדִּיל בַּתְּפִלָּה מְשׁוּבָּח יוֹתֵר מִמִּי שֶׁיַּבְדִּיל עַל הַכּוֹס, וְאִם הִבְדִּיל בָּזוֹ וּבָזוֹ – יָנוּחוּ לוֹ בְּרָכוֹת עַל רֹאשׁוֹ.

**Rabbi Aḥa Arikha, the tall, taught** a *baraita* **before Rav Ḥinnana: One who recited *havdala* in the *Amida* prayer** is **more praiseworthy than one who recites it over the cup** of wine, **and if he recited *havdala* in this,** the *Amida* prayer, **and that,** over the cup of wine, **may blessings rest upon his head.**

הָא גּוּפָא קַשְׁיָא! אָמְרַתְּ, הַמַּבְדִּיל בַּתְּפִלָּה מְשׁוּבָּח יוֹתֵר מִמִּי שֶׁיַּבְדִּיל עַל הַכּוֹס, אַלְמָא: תְּפִלָּה לְחוּדַהּ סַגִּי, וַהֲדַר תָּנֵי: אִם הִבְדִּיל בָּזוֹ וּבָזוֹ – יָנוּחוּ לוֹ בְּרָכוֹת עַל רֹאשׁוֹ, וְכֵיוָן דְּנָפֵיק לֵיהּ בַּחֲדָא – אִפְּטַר, וְהָוְיָא בְּרָכָה שֶׁאֵינָהּ צְרִיכָה; וְאָמַר רַב וְאִיתֵּימָא רֵישׁ לָקִישׁ, וְאָמְרִי לַהּ רַבִּי יוֹחָנָן וְרֵישׁ לָקִישׁ דְּאָמְרִי תַּרְוַיְיהוּ: כָּל הַמְבָרֵךְ בְּרָכָה שֶׁאֵינָהּ צְרִיכָה – עוֹבֵר מִשּׁוּם: "לֹא תִשָּׂא"!

**This** *baraita* **is** apparently **self-contradictory.** On the one hand, **you said that one who recites *havdala* in the *Amida* prayer** is **more praiseworthy than one who recites *havdala* over the cup** of wine, indicating that reciting *havdala* in **the *Amida* prayer alone is sufficient. And then it is taught: If one recited *havdala* in this,** the *Amida* prayer, **and that,** over the cup of wine, **may blessings rest upon his head. And since he fulfilled** his obligation to recite *havdala* **with one,** he is **exempt, and** the additional recitation of *havdala* over the cup of wine **is an unnecessary blessing. And Rav, and some say Reish Lakish, and** still others **say Rabbi Yoḥanan and Reish Lakish both said: Anyone who recites an unnecessary blessing**[H] **violates** the biblical prohibition: **"Do not take** the name of the Lord your God in vain" (Exodus 20:6).

אֶלָּא, אֵימָא הָכִי: אִם הִבְדִּיל בָּזוֹ וְלֹא הִבְדִּיל בָּזוֹ – יָנוּחוּ לוֹ בְּרָכוֹת עַל רֹאשׁוֹ.

**Rather,** emend this *baraita* **and say as follows: If one recited *havdala* in this and not in that, may blessings rest upon his head.**

בְּעָא מִינֵּיהּ רַב חִסְדָּא מֵרַב שֵׁשֶׁת: טָעָה בָּזוֹ וּבָזוֹ, מַהוּ? אָמַר לֵיהּ: טָעָה בָּזוֹ וּבָזוֹ – חוֹזֵר לָרֹאשׁ.

**Rav Ḥisda asked Rav Sheshet** with regard to these blessings: If **one erred** in *havdala* both **in this and in that, what is** the ruling? Rav Sheshet **said to him: One who erred in this,** the *Amida* prayer, **and that,** over the cup of wine,[H] **returns to the beginning** of both the *Amida* prayer and the *havdala* over the cup of wine.

## HALAKHA

One who erred and did not mention the might of the rains in the blessing on the revival of the dead – טָעָה וְלֹא הִזְכִּיר גְּבוּרוֹת גְּשָׁמִים בִּתְחִיַּית הַמֵּתִים: One who forgot to mention: He makes the wind blow and the rain fall, in the blessing of the revival of the dead during the winter, we require him to return to the beginning of the prayer and repeat it. However, if he mentioned: He causes the dew to fall, we do not require him to return to the beginning of the prayer and repeat it (Rambam *Sefer Ahava, Hilkhot Tefilla* 10:8; *Shulḥan Arukh, Oraḥ Ḥayyim* 114:5).

One who erred and did not mention…the request for rain in the blessing of the years – טָעָה וְלֹא הִזְכִּיר...וּשְׁאֵלָה בְּבִרְכַּת הַשָּׁנִים: One who erred and did not request rain in the blessing of the years during the winter, we do not require him to return to the beginning of the prayer and repeat it, even if he requested dew, as per the unattributed opinion in the Gemara (Rambam *Sefer Ahava, Hilkhot Tefilla* 10:9; *Shulḥan Arukh, Oraḥ Ḥayyim* 117:4).

One who erred and did not mention…*havdala* in the blessing: Who graciously grants knowledge – טָעָה וְלֹא הִזְכִּיר...וְהַבְדָּלָה בְּחוֹנֵן הַדַּעַת: One who failed to recite *havdala* in the blessing: Who graciously grants knowledge, in the evening prayer at the conclusion of Shabbat and Festivals need not repeat the prayer, because he is required to recite *havdala* over a cup of wine (Rambam *Sefer Ahava, Hilkhot Tefilla* 10:14; *Shulḥan Arukh, Oraḥ Ḥayyim* 294:1).

One who recites an unnecessary blessing – הַמְבָרֵךְ בְּרָכָה שֶׁאֵינָהּ צְרִיכָה: One who recites an unnecessary blessing, e.g., one who recited a blessing during a meal over food that was already exempted by the blessing: Who brings forth bread from the earth, is considered, by rabbinic law (*Magen Avraham*), as if he took God's name in vain. One must avoid reciting two blessings when one will suffice (Rambam *Sefer Ahava, Hilkhot Berakhot* 1:15; *Shulḥan Arukh, Oraḥ Ḥayyim* 215:4 and see 206:6).

One who erred in this, the *Amida* prayer, and that, over the cup of wine – טָעָה בָּזוֹ וּבָזוֹ: One who failed to recite *havdala* in the *Amida* prayer and later ate before reciting *havdala* over the cup of wine, must repeat the evening *Amida* prayer and recite *havdala* in the fourth blessing. Since eating was an action that he was not permitted to perform, he is referred to as one who erred (*Talmidei Rabbeinu Yona*; *Shulḥan Arukh, Oraḥ Ḥayyim* 294:1).

אָמַר לֵיהּ רָבִינָא לְרָבָא: הִלְכְתָא מַאי? – אָמַר לֵיהּ: כִּי קִידּוּשׁ, מָה קִידּוּשׁ אַף עַל גַּב דִּמְקַדֵּשׁ בִּצְלוֹתָא מְקַדֵּשׁ אַכָּסָא, אַף הַבְדָּלָה נַמִּי – אַף עַל גַּב דְּמַבְדִּיל בִּצְלוֹתָא מַבְדִּיל אַכָּסָא.

There are conflicting opinions with regard to reciting *havdala* over the cup of wine after reciting it in the *Amida* prayer. One opinion holds that it is appropriate to recite *havdala* a second time, while the other holds that it is prohibited. **Ravina said to Rava: What is the *halakha*?** Rava **said to him:** The *halakha* in the case of *havdala* is **like** the *halakha* in the case of **kiddush. Just as** in the case of **kiddush, although one recited *kiddush* in the** *Amida* **prayer** he must, nevertheless, **recite *kiddush*** again **over the cup** of wine, **so too with *havdala*, although one recited *havdala* in the** *Amida* **prayer** he must **recite *havdala*** again **over the cup** of wine.

״רַבִּי אֱלִיעֶזֶר אוֹמֵר: בְּהוֹדָאָה״.

The mishna states that **Rabbi Eliezer says:** It is recited **in** the seventeenth blessing of the *Amida* prayer, the blessing of **thanksgiving.**

רַבִּי זֵירָא הֲוָה רְכִיב חֲמָרָא, הֲוָה קָא שָׁקִיל וְאָזֵיל רַבִּי חִיָּיא בַּר אָבִין בַּתְרֵיהּ. אָמַר לֵיהּ, וַדַּאי דְּאָמְרִיתוּ מִשְּׁמֵיהּ דְּרַבִּי יוֹחָנָן: הֲלָכָה כְּרַבִּי אֱלִיעֶזֶר בְּיוֹם טוֹב שֶׁחָל לִהְיוֹת אַחַר הַשַּׁבָּת? – אָמַר לֵיהּ: אִין.

The Gemara cites the conclusion with regard to this *halakha* by relating a story: **Rabbi Zeira was riding a donkey** while **Rabbi Ḥiyya bar Avin was coming and walking after him. He said to him: Is it true that you said in the name of Rabbi Yoḥanan** that the ***halakha* is in accordance with** the opinion of **Rabbi Eliezer** in the case of **a Festival that occurs** directly **after Shabbat?** Since in that case, one cannot recite *havdala* in the blessing of Who graciously grants knowledge, as it is not included in the *Amida* prayer on the Festival, there is no alternative but to adopt Rabbi Eliezer's ruling. **He said to him: Yes.**

הֲלָכָה – מִכְּלָל דִּפְלִיגִי!

The Gemara wonders: Saying that the ***halakha*** is in accordance with the opinion of Rabbi Eliezer, **indicates that** his peers **dispute** his opinion. Where do we find that dispute?

וְלָא פְּלִיגִי?! וְהָא פְּלִיגִי רַבָּנַן!

The Gemara rejects this: **And don't they dispute** his opinion? **Don't the Rabbis dispute** his opinion, as, in their opinion the blessing of *havdala* is recited in the blessing: Who graciously grants knowledge?

אֵימַר דִּפְלִיגִי רַבָּנַן – בִּשְׁאָר יְמוֹת הַשָּׁנָה, בְּיוֹם טוֹב שֶׁחָל לִהְיוֹת אַחַר הַשַּׁבָּת מִי פְּלִיגִי?

The Gemara replies: **Say that the Rabbis dispute** Rabbi Eliezer's opinion **during the rest of the days of the year,** when the option to recite *havdala* in the blessing: Who graciously grants knowledge exists, but **in the case of a Festival that occurs** directly **after Shabbat, do they dispute** his opinion? The Rabbis would agree with him in that case.

וְהָא פָּלֵיג רַבִּי עֲקִיבָא!

The Gemara continues: **Doesn't Rabbi Akiva dispute** his opinion? He holds that *havdala* is recited as an independent fourth blessing, in which case there is a dispute.

אַטּוּ כָּל הַשָּׁנָה כּוּלָּהּ מִי עָבְדִינַן כְּרַבִּי עֲקִיבָא, דְּהַשְׁתָּא נֵיקוּ וְנַעֲבֵיד כְּוָותֵיהּ?! כָּל הַשָּׁנָה כּוּלָּהּ מַאי טַעְמָא לָא עָבְדִינַן כְּרַבִּי עֲקִיבָא? – דִּתְמָנֵי סְרֵי תַּקּוּן, תְּשַׁסְרֵי לָא תַּקּוּן, הָכָא נַמִּי – שֶׁבַע תַּקּוּן, תְּמָנֵי לָא תַּקּוּן!

The Gemara responds: **Is that to say that throughout the entire year we act in accordance with** the opinion of **Rabbi Akiva** in this matter, **so that now,** on a Festival that occurs directly after Shabbat, **we will stand and act in accordance with** his opinion? **What is the reason that throughout the whole, entire year, we do not act in accordance with** the opinion of **Rabbi Akiva? Because** the Sages **instituted eighteen** blessings, **they did not institute nineteen** blessings. **Here, too,** the Sages **instituted seven** blessings, **they did not institute eight** blessings. Therefore, Rabbi Akiva's opinion is not taken into consideration in this case.

אָמַר לֵיהּ: לָאו ״הֲלָכָה״ אִתְּמַר, אֶלָּא ״מַטִּין״ אִתְּמַר.

In response to these questions, Rabbi Zeira **said to him** that **it was not** that **the *halakha*** is in accordance with the opinion of Rabbi Eliezer **that was stated** in the name of Rabbi Yoḥanan, from which one could infer that there was in fact a dispute; rather it was that one is **inclined**[N] to favor the opinion of Rabbi Eliezer **that was stated** in the name of Rabbi Yoḥanan.

דְּאִתְּמַר, רַבִּי יִצְחָק בַּר אַבְדִּימִי אָמַר מִשּׁוּם רַבֵּינוּ: הֲלָכָה, וְאָמְרִי לָהּ: מַטִּין.

As indeed **it was stated** that there is a dispute among the Sages in this matter. **Rav Yitzḥak bar Avdimi said in the name of Rabbeinu,** Rav: **The *halakha*** is in accordance with the opinion of Rabbi Eliezer. **And some say this** statement: One is **inclined** to favor of the opinion of Rabbi Eliezer.

**NOTES**

*Halakha*...inclined – הֲלָכָה...מַטִּין: In this matter, there are various manners in which a specific opinion might be adopted as *halakha*. When it is established that the *halakha* is in accordance with a particular opinion, the *halakha* is disseminated to the public as conclusive. When it is established merely that the *halakha* is inclined in favor of a particular opinion, it is not disseminated to the general public. However, if an individual asks, the answer provided is in accordance with this ruling. A third manner in which an opinion might be adopted is by saying that the opinion of one of the Sages seems to be the *halakha*. On the one hand, the *halakha* has not been established in accordance with his opinion. On the other hand, one who conducts himself in accordance with that opinion is neither reprimanded nor encouraged.

רַבִּי יוֹחָנָן אָמַר: מוֹדִים; וְרַבִּי חִיָּיא בַּר אַבָּא אָמַר: נִרְאִין.

**Rabbi Yoḥanan said** that there is no dispute here, and the Rabbis **agree** with Rabbi Eliezer. **And Rabbi Ḥiyya bar Abba said** that it was established that Rabbi Eliezer's opinion **appears** to be correct.

אָמַר רַבִּי זֵירָא: נְקוֹט דְּרַבִּי חִיָּיא בַּר אַבָּא בִּידָךְ, דְּדַיֵּיק וּגְמַר שְׁמַעְתָּא מִפּוּמָּא דְּמָרָהּ שַׁפִּיר כְּרַחֲבָא דְּפוּמְבְּדִיתָא.

With regard to this difference of opinion **Rabbi Zeira said: Take this** statement of **Rabbi Ḥiyya bar Abba in your hand, as he is scrupulous and he learned the *halakha* well from the mouth of its originator, like** the Sage **Raḥava**[N] from the city **Pumbedita.** Raḥava was famous for the precision with which he would transmit material that he learned from his teacher.

דְּאָמַר רַחֲבָא אָמַר רַבִּי יְהוּדָה: הַר הַבַּיִת סְטָיו כָּפוּל הָיָה, וְהָיָה סְטָיו לִפְנִים מִסְּטָיו.

The Gemara cites an example: **Raḥava said** that **Rabbi Yehuda said: The Temple Mount was a double *stav*,**[L] **and there was a *stav* within a *stav*.** Here Raḥava used his Rabbi's language in describing the structure of the Temple and the rows of columns it contained, a row within a row; but he did not employ the common term *itzteba*, portico, but rather *stav*, as he heard it from his Rabbi.

אָמַר רַב יוֹסֵף: אֲנָא לָא הַאי יָדַעְנָא וְלָא הַאי יָדַעְנָא, אֶלָּא מִדְּרַב וּשְׁמוּאֵל יָדַעְנָא דְּתַקִּינוּ לַן מַרְגָּנִיתָא בְּבָבֶל:

**Rav Yosef said** the conclusive *halakha* on this topic: **I don't know this and I don't know that, but I do know from** the statements of **Rav and Shmuel they have instituted a pearl for us in Babylonia.** They established a version that combines the first blessing of the Festival with the formula of *havdala*, parallel to the opinion of the Rabbis who include *havdala* in the first blessing that follows the first three blessings. They instituted to recite:

וַתּוֹדִיעֵנוּ ה׳ אֱלֹהֵינוּ אֶת מִשְׁפְּטֵי צִדְקֶךָ וַתְּלַמְּדֵנוּ לַעֲשׂוֹת חֻקֵּי רְצוֹנֶךָ, וַתַּנְחִילֵנוּ זְמַנֵּי שָׂשׂוֹן וְחַגֵּי נְדָבָה וַתּוֹרִישֵׁנוּ קְדוּשַּׁת שַׁבָּת וּכְבוֹד מוֹעֵד וַחֲגִיגַת הָרֶגֶל, בֵּין קְדוּשַּׁת שַׁבָּת לִקְדוּשַּׁת יוֹם טוֹב הִבְדַּלְתָּ וְאֶת יוֹם הַשְּׁבִיעִי מִשֵּׁשֶׁת יְמֵי הַמַּעֲשֶׂה קִדַּשְׁתָּ, הִבְדַּלְתָּ וְקִדַּשְׁתָּ אֶת עַמְּךָ יִשְׂרָאֵל בִּקְדוּשָּׁתֶךָ, וַתִּתֶּן לָנוּ וכו׳.

**You have made known to us,[H] Lord our God, Your righteous laws, and taught us to perform Your will's decrees.**
**You have given us as our heritage seasons of joy and Festivals of voluntary offerings.**
**You have given us as our heritage the holiness of Shabbat, the glory of the festival and the festive offerings of the Pilgrim Festivals.**
**You have distinguished between the holiness of Shabbat and the holiness of the Festival,**
**and have made the seventh day holy over the six days of work.**
**You have distinguished and sanctified Your people Israel with Your holiness,**
**And You have given us, etc.**

מתני׳ הָאוֹמֵר ״עַל קַן צִפּוֹר יַגִּיעוּ רַחֲמֶיךָ״ וְ״עַל טוֹב יִזָּכֵר שְׁמֶךָ״, ״מוֹדִים מוֹדִים״ – מְשַׁתְּקִין אוֹתוֹ.

MISHNA Concluding the laws of prayer in this tractate, the mishna raises several prayer-related matters. This mishna speaks of certain innovations in the prayer formula that warrant the silencing of a communal prayer leader who attempts to introduce them in his prayers, as their content tends toward heresy. **One who recites** in his supplication: Just as **Your mercy is extended to a bird's nest,**[H] as You have commanded us to send away the mother before taking her chicks or eggs (Deuteronomy 22:6–7), so too extend Your mercy to us; **and** one who recites: **May Your name be mentioned with the good** or one who recites: **We give thanks, we give thanks**[H] twice, they **silence him.**

גמ׳ בִּשְׁלָמָא ״מוֹדִים מוֹדִים״ מְשַׁתְּקִין אוֹתוֹ – מִשּׁוּם דְּמֶיחֱזֵי כִּשְׁתֵּי רְשׁוּיוֹת, וְ״עַל טוֹב יִזָּכֵר שְׁמֶךָ״ – נַמִי מַשְׁמַע עַל הַטּוֹבָה וְלֹא עַל הָרָעָה, וּתְנַן: חַיָּיב אָדָם לְבָרֵךְ עַל הָרָעָה כְּשֵׁם שֶׁמְּבָרֵךְ עַל הַטּוֹבָה. אֶלָּא ״עַל קַן צִפּוֹר יַגִּיעוּ רַחֲמֶיךָ״ מַאי טַעְמָא?

GEMARA Our mishna cited three instances where the communal prayer leader is silenced. The Gemara clarifies: **Granted,** they silence one who repeats: **We give thanks, we give thanks, as it appears like** he is acknowledging and praying to **two authorities. And** granted that **they also silence** one who says: **May Your name be mentioned with the good,** as **clearly** he is thanking God only **for the good and not for the bad, and we learned** in a mishna: **One is required to bless** God **for the bad**[H] **just as he blesses** Him **for the good. However,** in the case of one who recites: Just as **Your mercy is extended to a bird's nest, why** do they silence him?

פְּלִיגִי בַּהּ תְּרֵי אֲמוֹרָאֵי בְּמַעְרְבָא, רַבִּי יוֹסֵי בַּר אָבִין וְרַבִּי יוֹסֵי בַּר זְבִידָא; חַד אָמַר: מִפְּנֵי שֶׁמַּטִּיל קִנְאָה בְּמַעֲשֵׂה בְרֵאשִׁית, וְחַד אָמַר: מִפְּנֵי שֶׁעוֹשֶׂה מִדּוֹתָיו שֶׁל הַקָּדוֹשׁ בָּרוּךְ הוּא רַחֲמִים, וְאֵינָן אֶלָּא גְּזֵרוֹת.

**Two *amora'im* in Eretz Yisrael disputed this** question; **Rabbi Yosei bar Avin and Rabbi Yosei bar Zevida; one said** that this was **because he engenders jealousy among God's creations,** as it appears as though he is protesting the fact that the Lord favored one creature over all others. **And one said** that this was **because he transforms the attributes of the Holy One, Blessed be He, into** expressions of **mercy,**[N] **when they are nothing but decrees** of the King that must be fulfilled without inquiring into the reasons behind them.

## NOTES

**As he is scrupulous…like Raḥava – דְּדַיֵּיק...כְּרַחֲבָא:** Various interpretations were suggested in explanation of Raḥava's unique precision. Some *ge'onim* explain that Raḥava was uncertain whether he heard the statement in the name of Rabbi Yehuda, the *tanna*, or Rav Yehuda, the *amora*, and he therefore repeated the statement in a manner that included them both. Others reject this (Rabbeinu Ḥananel, Rashi) and say that he repeated what he learned from his teacher verbatim.

**He transforms the attributes of the Holy One, Blessed be He, into mercy – שֶׁעוֹשֶׂה מִדּוֹתָיו שֶׁל הַקָּדוֹשׁ בָּרוּךְ הוּא רַחֲמִים, וְאֵינָן אֶלָּא גְּזֵרוֹת:** The Rambam explains that compassion is not the reason for this mitzva, as if that was the case, God would have prohibited slaughtering animals for food. Although in midrash, this mitzva is interpreted as a manifestation of compassion, it should be understood as guidance for man to act with compassion toward creatures, not as an indication of God's compassion on those creatures (Ramban on the Torah).

## LANGUAGE

**Colonnade [*stav*] – סְטָיו:** From the Greek στοά, *stoa*, meaning a roofed row of columns, *stav* refers to a row of columns that is attached to a building. The Gemara refers to a double *stav*; two rows of columns.

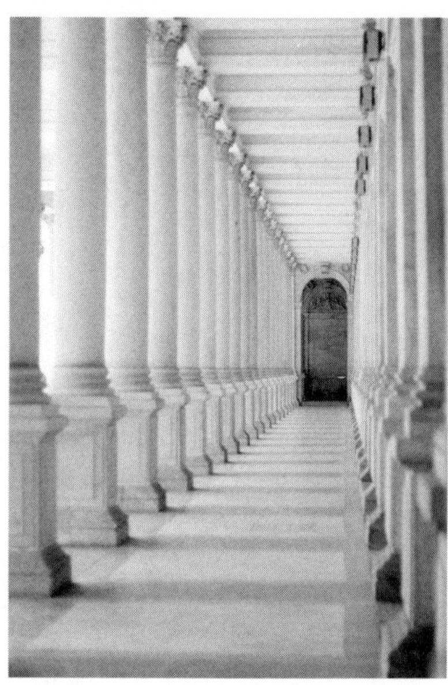

Colonnade

## HALAKHA

**The *havdala* of: And You have made known to us, etc. – הַבְדָּלַת וַתּוֹדִיעֵנוּ:** According to Rav Yosef's conclusion, the addition to the evening prayer on Festivals that occur at the conclusion of Shabbat: And You have made known to us, is the accepted formula for *havdala* on that occasion (Rambam *Sefer Ahava, Hilkhot Tefilla* 2:12; *Shulḥan Arukh, Oraḥ Ḥayyim* 491:2).

**One who recites: Just as Your mercy is extended to a bird's nest… – הָאוֹמֵר עַל קַן צִפּוֹר וכו׳:** Those who hear one who recites in his prayer: Just as Your mercy is extended to a bird's nest or a similar formula, should silence him, as per our mishna (Rambam *Sefer Ahava, Hilkhot Tefilla* 9:6).

**One who recites: We give thanks, we give thanks – הָאוֹמֵר מוֹדִים מוֹדִים:** Those who hear one who recites: We give thanks, we give thanks, should silence him, as per our mishna (Rambam *Sefer Ahava, Hilkhot Tefilla* 9:4; *Shulḥan Arukh, Oraḥ Ḥayyim* 121:2).

**One is required to bless God for the bad, etc. … – חַיָּיב אָדָם לְבָרֵךְ עַל הָרָעָה וכו׳:** One is required to bless God for the bad that befalls him with devotion and enthusiasm just as he does when good befalls him (Rambam *Sefer Ahava, Hilkhot Berakhot* 10:3; *Shulḥan Arukh, Oraḥ Ḥayyim* 222:2).

הַהוּא דְּנָחֵית קַמֵּיהּ דְּרַבָּה, וַאֲמַר: אַתָּה חַסְתָּ עַל קַן צִפּוֹר, אַתָּה חוּס וְרַחֵם עָלֵינוּ. אָמַר רַבָּה: כַּמָּה יָדַע הַאי צוּרְבָא מֵרַבָּנַן לְרַצּוֹיֵי לְמָרֵיהּ! – אֲמַר לֵיהּ אַבָּיֵי: וְהָא ״מְשַׁתְּקִין אוֹתוֹ״ תְּנַן!

The Gemara relates that **a particular** individual **descended before the ark** as prayer leader **in the presence of Rabba, and said** in his prayers: **You have shown mercy to the bird's nest, now have mercy and pity upon us. Rabba said: How much does this Torah scholar know to appease** the Lord, **his Master. Abaye said to him: Didn't we learn** in a mishna that **they silence him?**

וְרַבָּה נַמִי – לְחַדּוּדֵי אַבָּיֵי הוּא דְּבָעֵי.

The Gemara explains: **And Rabba too** held in accordance with this mishna but merely acted this way because **he wanted to hone Abaye's** intellect. Rabba did not make his statement to praise the scholar, but simply to test his nephew, Abaye, and to encourage him to articulate what he knows about that mishna.

הַהוּא דְּנָחֵית קַמֵּיהּ דְּרַבִּי חֲנִינָא, אָמַר: הָאֵל הַגָּדוֹל הַגִּבּוֹר וְהַנּוֹרָא וְהָאַדִּיר וְהָעִזּוּז וְהַיָּראוּי הֶחָזָק וְהָאַמִּיץ וְהַוַּדַּאי וְהַנִּכְבָּד.

With regard to additions to prayers formulated by the Sages, The Gemara relates that **a particular** individual **descended before the ark** as prayer leader **in the presence of Rabbi Ḥanina.** He extended his prayer and **said: God, the great, mighty, awesome, powerful, mighty, awe-inspiring, strong, fearless, steadfast and honored.**

הִמְתִּין לוֹ עַד דְּסַיֵּים, כִּי סַיֵּים אָמַר לֵיהּ: סַיֵּימְתִּינְהוּ לְכוּלְּהוּ שִׁבְחֵי דְּמָרָךְ?! לָמָּה לִי כּוּלֵּי הַאי? אֲנַן הָנֵי תְּלָת דְּאָמְרִינַן – אִי לָאו דְּאָמְרִינְהוּ מֹשֶׁה רַבֵּנוּ בְּאוֹרַיְיתָא, וַאֲתוֹ אַנְשֵׁי כְנֶסֶת הַגְּדוֹלָה וְתַקְּנִינְהוּ בִּתְפִלָּה – לָא הֲוֵינַן יָכְולִין לְמֵימַר לְהוּ, וְאַתְּ אָמְרַתְּ כּוּלֵּי הַאי וְאָזְלַתְּ! מָשָׁל, לְמֶלֶךְ בָּשָׂר וָדָם שֶׁהָיוּ לוֹ אֶלֶף אֲלָפִים דִּינְרֵי זָהָב, וְהָיוּ מְקַלְּסִין אוֹתוֹ בְּשֶׁל כֶּסֶף, וַהֲלֹא גְּנַאי הוּא לוֹ!

Rabbi Ḥanina **waited for him until he completed** his prayer. **When he finished,** Rabbi Ḥanina **asked him: Have you concluded all of the praises of your Master? Why do I need all of this** superfluous praise?[H] **Even these three** praises **that we recite:** The great, mighty and awesome, **had Moses our teacher not said them in the Torah and had the members of the Great Assembly not come and incorporated them into the** *Amida* prayer, **we would not be permitted to recite them. And you went on and recited all of these. It is comparable to a king who possessed many thousands of golden dinars, yet they were praising him for silver** ones.[BN] **Isn't that deprecatory?** All of the praises we could possibly lavish upon the Lord are nothing but a few silver dinars relative to many thousands of gold dinars. Reciting a litany of praise does not enhance God's honor.

וְאָמַר רַבִּי חֲנִינָא: הַכֹּל בִּידֵי שָׁמַיִם – חוּץ מִיִּרְאַת שָׁמַיִם, שֶׁנֶּאֱמַר: ״וְעַתָּה יִשְׂרָאֵל מָה ה׳ אֱלֹהֶיךָ שׁוֹאֵל מֵעִמָּךְ כִּי אִם לְיִרְאָה״.

Tangentially, the Gemara cites an additional statement by Rabbi Ḥanina concerning principles of faith. **And Rabbi Ḥanina said: Everything is in the hands of Heaven, except for fear of Heaven.** Man has free will to serve God or not, **as it is stated: "And now Israel, what does the Lord your God ask of you other than to fear** the Lord your God, to walk in all of His ways, to love Him and to serve the Lord your God with all your heart and with all your soul" (Deuteronomy 10:12). The Lord asks man to perform these matters because ultimately, the choice is his hands.

אַטּוּ יִרְאַת שָׁמַיִם מִילְּתָא זוּטַרְתָּא הִיא?! וְהָאָמַר רַבִּי חֲנִינָא מִשּׁוּם רַבִּי שִׁמְעוֹן בֶּן יוֹחַי: אֵין לוֹ לְהַקָּדוֹשׁ בָּרוּךְ הוּא בְּבֵית גְּנָזָיו אֶלָּא אוֹצָר שֶׁל יִרְאַת שָׁמַיִם, שֶׁנֶּאֱמַר: ״יִרְאַת ה׳ הִיא אוֹצָרוֹ״!

The verse says: What does the Lord your God ask of you other than to fear the Lord your God. The Gemara asks: **Is fear of Heaven a minor matter** that it can be presented as if God is not asking anything significant? **Didn't Rabbi Ḥanina say in the name of Rabbi Shimon ben Yoḥai: The Holy One, Blessed be He, has nothing in his treasury other than a treasure of fear of Heaven, as it is stated: "Fear of the Lord is his treasure"** (Isaiah 33:6). The Lord values and treasures fear of Heaven over all else.

אִין, לְגַבֵּי מֹשֶׁה מִילְּתָא זוּטַרְתָּא הִיא. דְּאָמַר רַבִּי חֲנִינָא: מָשָׁל, לְאָדָם שֶׁמְּבַקְּשִׁים מִמֶּנּוּ כְּלִי גָּדוֹל וְיֵשׁ לוֹ – דּוֹמֶה עָלָיו כִּכְלִי קָטָן, קָטָן וְאֵין לוֹ – דּוֹמֶה עָלָיו כִּכְלִי גָּדוֹל.

The Gemara responds: **Indeed, for Moses** fear of Heaven **is a minor matter. As Rabbi Ḥanina stated: It is comparable to one who is asked for a large vessel and he has** one, **it seems to him like a small vessel** because he owns it. However, one who is asked for just a **small** vessel and he does not have one, **it seems to him like a large vessel.** Therefore, Moses could say: What does the Lord your God ask of you other than to fear, because in his eyes it was a minor matter.

״מוֹדִים מוֹדִים – מְשַׁתְּקִין אוֹתוֹ״.

We learned in the mishna if one repeats: **We give thanks, we give thanks, they silence him.**

אָמַר רַבִּי זֵירָא: כָּל הָאוֹמֵר ״שְׁמַע״ ״שְׁמַע״ – כְּאוֹמֵר ״מוֹדִים מוֹדִים״ דָּמֵי.

**Rabbi Zeira said: One who** repeats himself while reciting *Shema* and **says: Listen Israel, Listen Israel**[H] **is like one who says: We give thanks, we give thanks.**

מֵיתִיבֵי: הַקּוֹרֵא אֶת שְׁמַע וְכוֹפְלָהּ – הֲרֵי זֶה מְגוּנֶּה. מְגוּנֶּה הוּא דַּהֲוֵי, שַׁתּוֹקֵי לָא מְשַׁתְּקִינַן לֵיהּ!

The Gemara **raises an objection:** It was taught in a *baraita*: **One who recites** ***Shema*** **and repeats it, it is reprehensible.** One may infer: **It is reprehensible, but they do not silence him.**

### HALAKHA

**Adding praises – מוֹסִיפִים בִּשְׁבָחִים:** One may not add to the praises of God that were incorporated into the formula of the *Amida* prayer, for the reasons enumerated by Rabbi Ḥanina in the Gemara. However in personal, private pleas, one is permitted to do so (*Tur* in the name of the Tosafist, Rabbeinu Yitzḥak; Rambam *Sefer Ahava, Hilkhot Tefilla* 9:7; *Shulḥan Arukh, Oraḥ Ḥayyim* 113:9).

**One who says: Listen…Listen – הָאוֹמֵר ״שְׁמַע״ ״שְׁמַע״:** There is a dispute whether this prohibition applies to the repetition of the word *Shema* (*Ba'al Halakhot Gedolot*, Rabbeinu Ḥananel) or to the repetition of the entire verse (Rashi). The *halakha* ruled in accordance with both opinions, and one may not repeat the word or the verse, except in a congregation, in which case repetition is permitted in specific cases (Jerusalem Talmud, *Baḥ*; Rambam *Sefer Ahava, Hilkhot Keriat Shema* 2:11; *Shulḥan Arukh, Oraḥ Ḥayyim* 61:9).

### BACKGROUND

**Dinars of gold and silver – דִּינְרֵי זָהָב...כֶּסֶף:** In talmudic times the average proportion between gold dinars to silver was 25:1, so the difference in their relative value was significant.

Dinars of gold (Nero)

Dinars of silver (Vespasian)

### NOTES

**Dinars of gold and silver – דִּינְרֵי זָהָב...כֶּסֶף:** The Rambam explains that the problem was not that he brought too few dinars, but that the praise does not reach the heights of the One being praised at all, as silver dinars of are qualitatively inferior to gold dinars. Similarly, the praises that people lavish on God do not relate to His level of perfection at all. According to the Ritva's explanation, the rhetorical question: Isn't that deprecatory, refers to the person praying, whose praise indicates his lack of understanding of the King's greatness.

לָא קַשְׁיָא: הָא – דְּאָמַר מִילְּתָא מִילְּתָא וְתָנֵי לַהּ, וְהָא – דְּאָמַר פְּסוּקָא פְּסוּקָא וְתָנֵי לֵיהּ.

The Gemara answers: **This is not difficult; this** case, where although it is reprehensible when one repeats *Shema*, they do not silence him, is referring to **one who recites and repeats each individual word** as he says it. In so doing he ruins the recitation of *Shema*. However, **this** case, where Rabbi Zeira holds that one who repeats *Shema* they silence him, refers to **one who recites and repeats an entire verse,** as it appears that he is worshiping separate authorities.

אָמַר לֵיהּ רַב פַּפָּא לְאַבַּיֵי: וְדִילְמָא מֵעִיקָּרָא לָא כַּוֵּון דַּעְתֵּיהּ, וּלְבַסּוֹף כַּוֵּון דַּעְתֵּיהּ?

**Rav Pappa said to Abaye** with regard to this *halakha*: **And perhaps initially he did not focus his attention** on the recitation of *Shema*, so he repeated it **and ultimately he focused his attention** as he recited it the second time?

אָמַר לֵיהּ:

Abaye **said to him:**

Perek **V**
Daf **34** Amud **a**

חַבְרוּתָא כְּלַפֵּי שְׁמַיָּא מִי אִיכָּא?! אִי לָא כַּוֵּון דַּעְתֵּיהּ מֵעִיקָּרָא – מָחֵינַן לֵיהּ בְּמַרְזַפְתָּא דְּנַפָּחָא עַד דִּמְכַוֵּין דַּעְתֵּיהּ.

**Can one have** that degree of **familiarity with Heaven,**[N] to the extent that he can take his words lightly and say them however he likes? **If he did not focus his attention initially, we beat him with a blacksmith's hammer**[B] **until he focuses his attention,** as conduct of that sort is unacceptable.

מתני׳ (הָאוֹמֵר: יְבָרְכוּךָ טוֹבִים – הֲרֵי זֶה דַּרְכֵי מִינוּת). הָעוֹבֵר לִפְנֵי הַתֵּיבָה וְטָעָה – יַעֲבוֹר אַחֵר תַּחְתָּיו, וְלֹא יְהֵא סַרְבָן בְּאוֹתָהּ שָׁעָה. מֵהֵיכָן הוּא מַתְחִיל? מִתְּחִלַּת הַבְּרָכָה שֶׁטָּעָה זֶה.

**MISHNA** This mishna and the next one deal with the communal prayer leader. (**If one says: "May the good bless You," this is a path of heresy.**)[N] **One who is passing before the ark,** as prayer leader, **and erred,**[H] **another should** immediately **pass in his place, and at that moment,** this replacement **should not refuse** in the interest of courtesy. The *Amida* prayer was interrupted and he should replace him as quickly as possible. **From where does** the replacement **commence? From the beginning of the blessing in which** the former **had erred.**

הָעוֹבֵר לִפְנֵי הַתֵּיבָה לֹא יַעֲנֶה ״אָמֵן״ אַחַר הַכֹּהֲנִים מִפְּנֵי הַטֵּירוּף, וְאִם אֵין שָׁם כֹּהֵן אֶלָּא הוּא – לֹא יִשָּׂא אֶת כַּפָּיו. וְאִם הַבְטָחָתוֹ שֶׁהוּא נוֹשֵׂא אֶת כַּפָּיו וְחוֹזֵר לִתְפִלָּתוֹ – רַשַּׁאי.

In order to prevent the prayer leader from erring in his prayer, it was said that **one who passes before the ark should not respond amen after the** blessing of the **priests,**[H] **because of** potential **confusion.** Since the mishna is describing a situation in which he was praying without a prayer book, responding amen would interrupt the order of the prayer and potentially lead him to begin a different blessing. For this reason, even **if there is no priest other than** the communal prayer leader,[H] **he does not lift his hands** to bless the people, lest he become confused. **And,** however, **if he is certain that he can lift his hands and resume his prayer** without becoming confused, **he is permitted** to recite the blessing.

**NOTES**

Can one have familiarity with Heaven – חַבְרוּתָא כְּלַפֵּי שְׁמַיָּא מִי אִיכָּא: Apparently this applies specifically to one who repeats a section of the prayer aloud, as he thereby shows that the first time that he recited it he did so with contempt and without focus. However, if one failed to muster the appropriate intent the first time, there is nothing wrong with repeating it silently (*Tal Torah*).

If one says: May the good bless You, this is a path of heresy – הָאוֹמֵר יְבָרְכוּךָ טוֹבִים הֲרֵי זֶה דַּרְכֵי מִינוּת: The heresy here lies in the fact that by saying: May the good bless You, one intimates that the wicked have a different god, indicating a belief in two entities (Rashba, based on the Jerusalem Talmud). Some explain an additional problem in that formula, as one is supposed to include both the good and the wicked in his prayers and not leave the wicked isolated (Rashba).

**BACKGROUND**

A blacksmith's hammer – מַרְזַפְתָּא דְּנַפָּחָא:

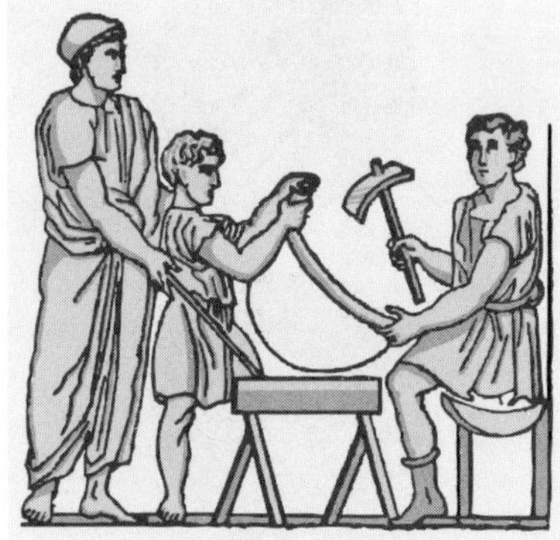

Blacksmith striking with the hammer in his hand, from a Byzantine ivory relief

**HALAKHA**

One who is passing before the ark, as prayer leader, and erred – הָעוֹבֵר לִפְנֵי הַתֵּיבָה וְטָעָה: If a communal prayer leader errs in his prayer and is unable to resume his prayer, another replaces him and, in that circumstance, should not refuse for reasons of propriety. He begins at the beginning of the blessing where his predecessor erred (Rambam *Sefer Ahava*, *Hilkhot Tefilla* 10:3; *Shulḥan Arukh*, *Oraḥ Ḥayyim* 126:2, *Oraḥ Ḥayyim* 53:17).

One who passes before the ark should not answer amen after the blessing of the priests – הָעוֹבֵר לִפְנֵי הַתֵּיבָה לֹא יַעֲנֶה אָמֵן אַחַר הַכֹּהֲנִים: A communal prayer leader may not answer amen after the priests. In our generation, opinions differ as to whether the concern for potential confusion applies to a prayer leader praying from a prayer book as well (*Magen Avraham*, *Taz*; Rambam *Sefer Ahava*, *Hilkhot Nesiat Kappayim* 14:5; *Shulḥan Arukh*, *Oraḥ Ḥayyim* 128:19).

If there is no priest other than him, etc. – וְאִם אֵין שָׁם כֹּהֵן אֶלָּא הוּא וכו׳: Although we learned that a prayer leader who is a priest should not recite the Priestly Blessing due to concern for potential confusion, in our generation when everyone prays from a prayer book, this is not a concern; everyone has the legal status of one who is certain that he will resume his prayer without error (*Magen Abraham*; Rambam *Sefer Ahava*, *Hilkhot Nesi'at Kappayim* 15:10; *Shulḥan Arukh*, *Oraḥ Ḥayyim* 128:20).

גמ׳ תָּנוּ רַבָּנַן: הָעוֹבֵר לִפְנֵי הַתֵּיבָה – צָרִיךְ לְסָרֵב, וְאִם אֵינוֹ מְסָרֵב – דּוֹמֶה לְתַבְשִׁיל שֶׁאֵין בּוֹ מֶלַח, וְאִם מְסָרֵב יוֹתֵר מִדַּאי – דּוֹמֶה לְתַבְשִׁיל שֶׁהִקְדִּיחַתּוּ מֶלַח. כֵּיצַד הוּא עוֹשֶׂה – פַּעַם רִאשׁוֹנָה יְסָרֵב, שְׁנִיָּה מְהַבְהֵב, שְׁלִישִׁית – פּוֹשֵׁט אֶת רַגְלָיו וְיוֹרֵד.

**GEMARA** The mishna teaches that one who replaces a communal prayer leader who erred in the middle of the *Amida* prayer should not refuse when approached. The Gemara cites the general *halakha* with regard to proper conduct when one is approached to serve as prayer leader. **The Sages taught** in a *baraita*: One who is approached **to pass before the ark** to serve as prayer leader, for the sake of propriety **should refuse,**[H] to avoid creating the impression that he is too eager. **And if he does not refuse,** but jumps at the opportunity, **he is like cooked food without salt,** which is to say that he acts in bad taste. **However, if he refuses too much** this is similarly inappropriate, as **he is like cooked food that was ruined by** too much **salt. So how should he act?** The appropriate conduct when approached to serve as communal prayer leader is as follows: When approached **the first time, one should refuse; the second** time, one should **vacillate** like a wick that has just begun to catch a flame but is not yet burning; and **the third** time, **he should stretch his legs and descend** before the ark.

תָּנוּ רַבָּנַן: שְׁלֹשָׁה רוּבָּן קָשֶׁה וּמִיעוּטָן יָפֶה, וְאֵלּוּ הֵן: שְׂאוֹר, וּמֶלַח, וְסַרְבָנוּת.

On this note, the Gemara cites that which **the Sages taught** in a *baraita*: There are **three** things that **are harmful in excess but are beneficial when used sparingly.** They are: **Leavening** in dough, **salt** in a cooked dish **and refusal** for the sake of propriety.

אָמַר רַב הוּנָא: טָעָה בְּשָׁלֹשׁ רִאשׁוֹנוֹת – חוֹזֵר לָרֹאשׁ, בְּאֶמְצָעִיּוֹת – חוֹזֵר לְ״אַתָּה חוֹנֵן״, בָּאַחֲרוֹנוֹת – חוֹזֵר לַ״עֲבוֹדָה״;

The mishna states that when one replaces the communal prayer leader, he commences from the beginning of the blessing in which the former had erred. However that is not universally true, as **Rav Huna said:** One who **erred in** any of **the first three** blessings **he must return to the beginning** of the *Amida* prayer because the first three blessing comprise a single entity. Likewise, if one **erred in** any of **the** thirteen **middle** blessings, **he returns to** the blessing of: **You grace** humanity, the first of the middle blessings. If one erred **in** any of the three **final** blessings, **he must return to the** blessing of **Temple service,** which is the first of the final blessings.[H]

וְרַב אַסִּי אָמַר: אֶמְצָעִיּוֹת אֵין לָהֶן סֵדֶר.

**And Rav Asi** disputes one aspect of Rav Huna's opinion, as **he said: The middle** blessings **have no** set **order.** If one erred in any of them he may insert it at whatever point he becomes aware of his error.

מְתִיב רַב שֵׁשֶׁת: ״מֵהֵיכָן הוּא חוֹזֵר – מִתְּחִלַּת הַבְּרָכָה שֶׁטָּעָה זֶה״, תְּיוּבְתָּא דְּרַב הוּנָא!

**Rav Sheshet raised an objection** based on a *baraita*: **From where does he** commence **repetition** of the *Amida* prayer? He commences **from the beginning of the blessing in which** the former **had erred.** If so, this is **a conclusive refutation of Rav Huna's** opinion, as Rav Huna said that if one erred in one of the middle blessings, he returns to the beginning of the middle blessings, not to the beginning of that particular blessing.

אָמַר לָךְ רַב הוּנָא: אֶמְצָעִיּוֹת – כּוּלְּהוּ חֲדָא בִּרְכְתָא נִינְהוּ.

**Rav Huna** could have **said to you: The middle** blessings **are all** considered **one blessing;** commencing from the beginning of the blessing means returning to the beginning of the middle blessings.

אָמַר רַב יְהוּדָה: לְעוֹלָם אַל יִשְׁאַל אָדָם צְרָכָיו לֹא בְּשָׁלֹשׁ רִאשׁוֹנוֹת, וְלֹא בְּשָׁלֹשׁ אַחֲרוֹנוֹת, אֶלָּא בְּאֶמְצָעִיּוֹת. דְּאָמַר רַבִּי חֲנִינָא: רִאשׁוֹנוֹת – דּוֹמֶה לְעֶבֶד שֶׁמְּסַדֵּר שֶׁבַח לִפְנֵי רַבּוֹ, אֶמְצָעִיּוֹת – דּוֹמֶה לְעֶבֶד שֶׁמְּבַקֵּשׁ פְּרָס מֵרַבּוֹ, אַחֲרוֹנוֹת – דּוֹמֶה לְעֶבֶד שֶׁקִּבֵּל פְּרָס מֵרַבּוֹ וְנִפְטָר וְהוֹלֵךְ לוֹ.

**Rav Yehuda said:** There is an additional distinction between the various sections of the *Amida* prayer: **One must never request his** own **needs in the first three**[H] **or in the last three** blessings; **rather,** he should do so **in the middle** blessings. **As Rabbi Ḥanina said:** During the **first** three blessings, he **is like a servant who arranges praise before his master;** during the **middle** blessings, he **is like a servant who requests a reward from his master;** during the **final** three blessings, one **is like a servant who** already **received a reward from his master and is taking his leave and departing.**

תָּנוּ רַבָּנַן: מַעֲשֶׂה בְּתַלְמִיד אֶחָד שֶׁיָּרַד לִפְנֵי הַתֵּיבָה בִּפְנֵי רַבִּי אֱלִיעֶזֶר וְהָיָה מַאֲרִיךְ יוֹתֵר מִדַּאי. אָמְרוּ לוֹ תַּלְמִידָיו: כַּמָּה אַרְכָן הוּא זֶה! – אָמַר לָהֶם: כְּלוּם מַאֲרִיךְ יוֹתֵר מִמֹּשֶׁה רַבֵּינוּ?! דִּכְתִיב בֵּיהּ: ״אֵת אַרְבָּעִים הַיּוֹם וְאֶת אַרְבָּעִים הַלַּיְלָה״ וגו׳.

Continuing on the subject of prayer, **the Sages taught:** There was **an incident where one student descended** to serve as prayer leader **before the ark in the presence of Rabbi Eliezer, and he was excessively prolonging his prayer. His students** complained and **said to him: How long-winded he is. He said to them: Is** this student **prolonging** his prayer any more **than Moses our teacher** did? **As about** Moses **it is written:** "And I prostrated myself before the Lord **for the forty days and forty nights** that I prostrated myself" (Deuteronomy 9:25). There is no limit to the duration of a prayer.

### HALAKHA

**One who is approached to pass before the ark should refuse – הָעוֹבֵר לִפְנֵי הַתֵּיבָה – צָרִיךְ לְסָרֵב וכו׳:** One who is approached to serve as prayer leader should initially refuse for reasons of propriety. This applies specifically to a case where the individual is not the regular prayer leader (*Shulḥan Arukh, Oraḥ Ḥayyim* 53:16).

**One who errs in his prayer – הַטּוֹעֶה בִּתְפִלָּתוֹ:** If one erred in his prayer, i.e., he skipped a blessing; if he did so in the first three blessings, he must return to the beginning of the *Amida* prayer. If he erred in the final three blessings he returns to the beginning of the blessing of Temple service. If he erred in the middle blessings, contrary to Rashi's opinion, the Rif and the Rashbam explained and the Rambam and the Ra'avad concurred that he returns to the beginning of that particular blessing and continues in order, in accordance with the opinion of Rav Asi (Rambam *Sefer Ahava, Hilkhot Tefilla* 10:1, 4; *Shulḥan Arukh, Oraḥ Ḥayyim* 119:3).

**One must never request his own needs in the first three, etc. – לְעוֹלָם אַל יִשְׁאַל אָדָם צְרָכָיו לֹא בְּשָׁלֹשׁ רִאשׁוֹנוֹת וכו׳:** One may only request his personal needs in the thirteen middle blessings, not during the first three or last three blessings, as per the opinion of Rav Yehuda (Rambam *Sefer Ahava, Hilkhot Tefilla* 1:4, 6:3; *Shulḥan Arukh, Oraḥ Ḥayyim* 112:1).

HALAKHA

**These are the blessings in which a person bows** – **אֵלּוּ בְּרָכוֹת שֶׁאָדָם שׁוֹחֶה בָּהֶן**: During the *Amida* prayer, one bows at the beginning and end of the blessing of Patriarchs and at the beginning and end of the blessing of thanksgiving. One who bows beyond that, we prevent him from doing so. One who bows in the middle of blessings, the custom is not to prevent him from doing so (*Magen Avraham*; Rambam *Sefer Ahava*, *Hilkhot Tefilla* 5:10; *Shulḥan Arukh*, *Oraḥ Ḥayyim* 113:1).

LANGUAGE

**Ordinary person [*hedyot*]** – **הֶדְיוֹט**: This word comes from the Greek ἰδιώτης *idiotès* and means a common person, one of the masses. The Sages use the term to refer to a typical person who has no outstanding qualities. This term refers to a commoner as opposed to a king or an ordinary priest as opposed to a High Priest. It may also refer to one who engages in labor in which he is not expert.

שׁוּב מַעֲשֶׂה בְּתַלְמִיד אֶחָד שֶׁיָּרַד לִפְנֵי הַתֵּיבָה בִּפְנֵי רַבִּי אֱלִיעֶזֶר וְהָיָה מְקַצֵּר יוֹתֵר מִדַּאי. אָמְרוּ לוֹ תַּלְמִידָיו: כַּמָּה קַצְרָן הוּא זֶה! אָמַר לָהֶם: כְּלוּם מְקַצֵּר יוֹתֵר מִמֹּשֶׁה רַבֵּינוּ?! דִּכְתִיב: ״אֵל נָא רְפָא נָא לָהּ״.

There was **again an incident where one student descended** to serve as prayer leader **before the ark in the presence of Rabbi Eliezer, and he was excessively abbreviating his prayer. His students** protested **and said to him: How brief is his** prayer. **He said to them: Is he abbreviating** his prayer **any more than Moses our teacher** did? **As it is written** with regard to the prayer Moses recited imploring God to cure Miriam of her leprosy: "And Moses cried out to the Lord, saying: '**Please, God, heal her, please**'" (Numbers 12:13). This student's prayer was certainly no briefer than the few words recited by Moses.

אָמַר רַבִּי יַעֲקֹב אָמַר רַב חִסְדָּא: כָּל הַמְבַקֵּשׁ רַחֲמִים עַל חֲבֵירוֹ אֵין צָרִיךְ לְהַזְכִּיר שְׁמוֹ, שֶׁנֶּאֱמַר: ״אֵל נָא רְפָא נָא לָהּ״, וְלָא קָמַדְכַּר שְׁמָהּ דְּמִרְיָם.

Having mentioned Moses' prayer for Miriam, the Gemara cites what **Rabbi Ya'akov said** that **Rav Ḥisda said: Anyone who requests mercy on** behalf of **another need not mention his name, as it is stated: "Please, God, heal her, please," and he did not mention Miriam's name.**

תָּנוּ רַבָּנַן: אֵלּוּ בְּרָכוֹת שֶׁאָדָם שׁוֹחֶה בָּהֶן: בְּאָבוֹת תְּחִלָּה וָסוֹף, בְּהוֹדָאָה תְּחִלָּה וָסוֹף, וְאִם בָּא לָשׁוּחַ בְּסוֹף כָּל בְּרָכָה וּבְרָכָה וּבִתְחִלַּת כָּל בְּרָכָה וּבְרָכָה – מְלַמְּדִין אוֹתוֹ שֶׁלֹּא יִשְׁחֶה.

**The Sages taught** in a *Tosefta*: **These** are the **blessings** in the *Amida* prayer **in which a person bows:**[H] **In** the first blessing, the blessing of the **Patriarchs,** one bows **at the beginning and the end; in** the blessing of **thanksgiving,** one bows **at the beginning and the end; and if one seeks to bow at the end of each and every blessing and at the beginning of each and every blessing, they teach him not to bow** so as not to go beyond the ordinance instituted by the Sages.

אָמַר רַבִּי שִׁמְעוֹן בֶּן פָּזִי אָמַר רַבִּי יְהוֹשֻׁעַ בֶּן לֵוִי מִשּׁוּם בַּר קַפָּרָא: הֶדְיוֹט – כְּמוֹ שֶׁאָמַרְנוּ.

**Rabbi Shimon ben Pazi said** that **Rabbi Yehoshua ben Levi said in the name of** the *tanna* **bar Kappara: An ordinary** person [*hedyot*],[L] conducts himself **as we said;** he bows at the beginning and the end of the blessings of Patriarchs and thanksgiving and is admonished if he seeks to bow at the beginning and end of the other blessings.

Perek **V**
Daf **34** Amud **b**

HALAKHA

**The bows of a king and a High Priest** – **כְּרִיעוֹת מֶלֶךְ וְכֹהֵן גָּדוֹל**: A High Priest bows at the beginning and end of each blessing, according to the Rambam, based on a variant reading of the Gemara to which he had access (*Kesef Mishne*). Alternatively, that was his ruling as a compromise between the differing opinions in the Gemara (*Leḥem Mishne*). The king bows when he begins reciting the *Amida* prayer and stands upright when he concludes (Rambam *Sefer Ahava*, *Hilkhot Tefilla* 5:10).

**Bowing [*kidda*]…kneeling [*keria*]…prostrating [*hishtaḥava'a*]** – **קִידָּה...כְּרִיעָה...הִשְׁתַּחֲוָאָה**: Whenever *keria* is mentioned it refers to kneeling upon one's knees; *kidda* refers to bowing one's head; *hishtaḥava'a* refers to spreading out one's hands and legs (Rambam *Sefer Ahava*, *Hilkhot Tefilla* 5:13).

**How does one lower his head** – **נְפִילַת אַפַּיִם כֵּיצַד**: One who lowers his head leans to the side, as per the custom of Abaye and Rava. When one has phylacteries on his arm he leans to the right side and when he does not have phylacteries he leans to the left (*Baḥ*; Rambam *Sefer Ahava*, *Hilkhot Tefilla* 5:14, 9:5; *Shulḥan Arukh*, *Oraḥ Ḥayyim* 131:1).

כֹּהֵן גָּדוֹל – בְּסוֹף כָּל בְּרָכָה וּבְרָכָה, וְהַמֶּלֶךְ – תְּחִלַּת כָּל בְּרָכָה וּבְרָכָה וְסוֹף כָּל בְּרָכָה וּבְרָכָה.

It is appropriate, though, for **a High Priest** to bow **at the end of each and every blessing; and** for **a king** to bow **at the beginning of each and every blessing and at the end of each and every blessing.**[H] This is because the more lofty one's status, the more important it is to demonstrate his subservience to God.

אָמַר רַבִּי יִצְחָק בַּר נַחְמָנִי, לְדִידִי מִפָּרְשָׁא לִי מִינֵּיהּ דְּרַבִּי יְהוֹשֻׁעַ בֶּן לֵוִי: הֶדְיוֹט – כְּמוֹ שֶׁאָמַרְנוּ, כֹּהֵן גָּדוֹל – תְּחִלַּת כָּל בְּרָכָה וּבְרָכָה, הַמֶּלֶךְ – כֵּיוָן שֶׁכָּרַע, שׁוּב אֵינוֹ זוֹקֵף, שֶׁנֶּאֱמַר: ״וַיְהִי כְּכַלּוֹת שְׁלֹמֹה לְהִתְפַּלֵּל וגו׳ קָם מִלִּפְנֵי מִזְבַּח ה׳ מִכְּרֹעַ עַל בִּרְכָּיו״.

**Rabbi Yitzḥak bar Naḥmani said: It was explained to me** directly **from Rabbi Yehoshua ben Levi** himself differently: **An ordinary** person, conducts himself **as we said; a High Priest** bows at **the beginning of each and every blessing; the king, once he has bowed** at the beginning of the first blessing, **does not rise** until he concludes the entire prayer, **as it is stated: "And it was that when Solomon finished praying** all of his prayer to the Lord, **he rose from before the altar of the Lord, from kneeling upon his knees** with his hands spread forth toward the heavens" (1 Kings 8:54).

תָּנוּ רַבָּנַן: קִידָּה – עַל אַפַּיִם, שֶׁנֶּאֱמַר: ״וַתִּקֹּד בַּת שֶׁבַע אַפַּיִם אֶרֶץ״, כְּרִיעָה – עַל בִּרְכַּיִם, שֶׁנֶּאֱמַר: ״מִכְּרֹעַ עַל בִּרְכָּיו״, הִשְׁתַּחֲוָאָה – זוֹ פִּשּׁוּט יָדַיִם וְרַגְלַיִם, שֶׁנֶּאֱמַר: ״הֲבוֹא נָבוֹא אֲנִי וְאִמְּךָ וְאַחֶיךָ לְהִשְׁתַּחֲוֹת לְךָ אָרְצָה״.

Having mentioned Solomon bowing, the Gemara distinguishes between various types of bowing. **The Sages taught** in a *baraita*: The term ***kidda*** means bowing **upon** one's **face,** with his face toward the ground, **as it is stated: "Then Bathsheba bowed [*vatikod*] with her face to the ground"** (1 Kings 1:31). ***Keria*** means bowing **upon one's knees,** as regarding Solomon **it is stated:** He finished praying and **"he rose from before the altar of the Lord, from kneeling [*mikkeroa*] upon his knees."** Finally, ***hishtaḥava'a***,[H] **that is** bowing with **one's hands and legs spread** in total submission, **as it is stated** in Jacob's question to Joseph in response to his dream: **"Shall we, I and your mother and your brothers, come and bow down [*lehishtaḥavot*] to you to the ground?"** (Genesis 37:10).

אָמַר רַב חִיָּיא בְּרֵיהּ דְּרַב הוּנָא: חֲזֵינָא לְהוּ אַבַּיֵּי וְרָבָא דְּמַצְלוּ אַצְלוּיֵי.

On the topic of bowing, **Rav Ḥiyya, son of Rav Huna, said: I saw Abaye and Rava, who would lean** their heads[H] and not actually prostrate themselves on the ground.

תָּנֵי חֲדָא: הַכּוֹרֵעַ בְּהוֹדָאָה הֲרֵי זֶה מְשׁוּבָּח; וְתַנְיָא אִידָךְ: הֲרֵי זֶה מְגוּנֶּה!

The Gemara asks: **One** *baraita* **taught: One who bows in the** blessing of **thanksgiving, it is praiseworthy. And it was taught in another** *baraita*: One who bows in the blessing of thanksgiving, **it is reprehensible.** These *baraitot* are contradictory.

לָא קַשְׁיָא: הָא – בַּתְּחִלָּה, הָא – לְבַסּוֹף.

The Gemara reconciles these two *baraitot*: This is **not difficult; this** *baraita*, which praises one who bows in the blessing of thanksgiving, refers to one who bows **at the beginning** of the blessing. **This** *baraita*, which condemns one who bows in the blessing of thanksgiving, refers to one who bows **at the end** of the blessing.

רָבָא כָּרַע בְּהוֹדָאָה תְּחִלָּה וָסוֹף. אָמְרִי לֵיהּ רַבָּנַן: אַמַּאי קָא עָבֵיד מָר הָכִי? – אָמַר לְהוּ: חֲזֵינָא לְרַב נַחְמָן דְּכָרַע, וַחֲזֵינָא לֵיהּ לְרַב שֵׁשֶׁת דְּקָא עָבֵד הָכִי.

**Rava bowed in** the blessing of **thanksgiving,**[N] both **beginning and end. The Sages said to him: Why does our master do this? He said to them: I saw Rav Naḥman who bowed** in the blessing of thanksgiving, **and I saw Rav Sheshet who did so** as well.

וְהָתַנְיָא: הַכּוֹרֵעַ בְּהוֹדָאָה הֲרֵי זֶה מְגוּנֶּה!

**But wasn't it taught** in a *baraita* that **one who bows in thanksgiving, it is reprehensible?**

הַהִיא – בְּהוֹדָאָה שֶׁבְּהַלֵּל.

Rava explained: **That** *baraita* refers to one who bows **in the thanksgiving** that is **in** ***hallel,*** when one recites: Give thanks to the Lord. Then, bowing is inappropriate.

וְהָתַנְיָא: הַכּוֹרֵעַ בְּהוֹדָאָה וּבְהוֹדָאָה שֶׁל הַלֵּל הֲרֵי זֶה מְגוּנֶּה!

The Sages continue to question Rava's conduct: **But wasn't it taught** explicitly in a *baraita*: **One who bows in thanksgiving or in thanksgiving of** ***hallel,*** **it is reprehensible?** The term thanksgiving unqualified does not refer to thanksgiving of *hallel*; it obviously refers to the blessing of thanksgiving recited in the *Amida* prayer. One who bows in either, it is reprehensible.

כִּי תַּנְיָא הַהִיא – בְּהוֹדָאָה דְּבִרְכַּת הַמָּזוֹן.

The Gemara rejects this challenge as well: **When that** *baraita* **was taught,** it was in reference to the blessing of **thanksgiving,** the second blessing recited **in Grace after Meals:** We thank You.

מתני׳ הַמִּתְפַּלֵּל וְטָעָה – סִימָן רַע לוֹ, וְאִם שְׁלִיחַ צִבּוּר הוּא – סִימָן רַע לְשׁוֹלְחָיו, מִפְּנֵי שֶׁשְּׁלוּחוֹ שֶׁל אָדָם כְּמוֹתוֹ. אָמְרוּ עָלָיו עַל רַבִּי חֲנִינָא בֶּן דּוֹסָא, שֶׁהָיָה מִתְפַּלֵּל עַל הַחוֹלִים וְאוֹמֵר: ״זֶה חַי וְזֶה מֵת״. אָמְרוּ לוֹ: מִנַּיִן אַתָּה יוֹדֵעַ? אָמַר לָהֶם: אִם שְׁגוּרָה תְּפִלָּתִי בְּפִי – יוֹדֵעַ אֲנִי שֶׁהוּא מְקוּבָּל, וְאִם לָאו – יוֹדֵעַ אֲנִי שֶׁהוּא מְטוֹרָף.

**MISHNA** Concluding its discussion of the *halakhot* of prayer, the mishna discusses less practical aspects of prayer. **One who prays and** realizes that he **erred** in his prayer, it is **a bad omen for him;** it indicates to him that his prayer was not accepted. **And if he** who erred **is the communal prayer leader,** it is **a bad omen for those who sent him, because a person's agent** has legal status **equivalent to his own.** On a similar note, **they said about Rabbi Ḥanina ben Dosa**[P] **that he would pray on** behalf of **the sick and** immediately after his prayer he would **say: This** one shall recover from his illness and **live and this** one shall **die.** When **they said to him: From where do you know? He said to them: If my prayer is fluent in my mouth** as I recite it and there are no errors, **I know that** my prayer **is accepted. And if not, I know that** my prayer **is rejected.**

גמ׳ אַהֵיָא?

**GEMARA** We learned in the mishna that if one errs in his prayer it is a bad omen. The Gemara asks: **In which blessing** is an error a bad omen?

אָמַר רַב חִיָּיא אָמַר רַב סַפְרָא מִשּׁוּם חַד דְּבֵי רַבִּי: בְּאָבוֹת.

**Rabbi Ḥiyya said** that **Rav Safra said in the name of one of the** Sages of the **school of Rabbi** Yehuda HaNasi: An error is a bad omen **in** the first blessing of the *Amida* prayer, the blessing of **Patriarchs.**"[N]

אִיכָּא דְּמַתְנֵי לַהּ אַבָּרַיְיתָא: הַמִּתְפַּלֵּל צָרִיךְ שֶׁיְּכַוֵּין אֶת לִבּוֹ בְּכוּלָּן, וְאִם אֵינוֹ יָכוֹל לְכַוֵּין בְּכוּלָּן – יְכַוֵּין אֶת לִבּוֹ בְּאַחַת;

**Some teach** that **this** statement was made **on a** ***baraita*** referring to another topic. It was taught in a *baraita*: **One who prays must focus his heart**[H] **in all** of the blessings. **And if he is unable to focus** his heart **in all of them, he should focus his heart** at least **in one.**

אָמַר רַבִּי חִיָּיא אָמַר רַב סַפְרָא מִשּׁוּם חַד דְּבֵי רַבִּי: בְּאָבוֹת.

Regarding this *baraita*, **Rabbi Ḥiyya said** that **Rav Safra said in the name of one of the** Sages of the **school of Rabbi** Yehuda HaNasi: **In** one refers to the blessing of **Patriarchs.**

NOTES

**Rava bowed in the blessing of thanksgiving – רָבָא כָּרַע בְּהוֹדָאָה:** Some say that this does not refer to the blessing of thanksgiving in the silent *Amida* prayer; rather, it refers to the blessing of thanksgiving recited by the congregation during the repetition of the *Amida* prayer [*modim derabbanan*]. According to this interpretation, there is no contradiction between the different sources (Ra'avad, *Tosefot HaRosh*).

**In the blessing of the Patriarchs – בְּאָבוֹת:** The preeminent status of this blessing stems from its juxtaposition with redemption, from the fact that it begins and ends with a blessing and that it includes mention of several of God's names (Maharsha).

PERSONALITIES

**Rabbi Ḥanina ben Dosa – רַבִּי חֲנִינָא בֶּן דּוֹסָא:** A *tanna* who lived at the end of the Second Temple period, Rabbi Ḥanina ben Dosa was a disciple of Rabban Yoḥanan ben Zakkai. However, he is best known as the performer of miraculous acts, a righteous man whose prayers were always heard on high. The Talmud is replete with stories of miracles that took place for him and those close to him. He was indigent and earned a very meager living. He is the paradigm of a full-fledged righteous man who received no reward in this world. In tractate *Avot*, several of his moral/ethical teachings are cited, which underscore the primacy of the fear of Heaven and the need for mutual affection in interpersonal relationships.

HALAKHA

**One who prays must focus his heart, etc. – הַמִּתְפַּלֵּל צָרִיךְ שֶׁיְּכַוֵּין אֶת לִבּוֹ וכו׳:** Ideally one should focus his heart throughout the entire prayer. However, after the fact, even if he failed to focus his attention, he fulfilled his obligation. Nonetheless, if one failed to have intention during the blessing of Patriarchs, he did not fulfill his obligation and must repeat the prayer. In our times, however, one does not repeat the *Amida* prayer due to lack of requisite intent (Rema; Rambam *Sefer Ahava, Hilkhot Tefilla* 10:1; *Shulḥan Arukh, Oraḥ Ḥayyim* 101:1).

"אָמְרוּ עָלָיו עַל רַבִּי חֲנִינָא" וכו׳. מְנָא הָנֵי מִילֵּי? אָמַר רַבִּי יְהוֹשֻׁעַ בֶּן לֵוִי, דְּאָמַר קְרָא: "בּוֹרֵא נִיב שְׂפָתַיִם שָׁלוֹם שָׁלוֹם לָרָחוֹק וְלַקָּרוֹב אָמַר ה׳ וּרְפָאתִיו".

We learned in the mishna: **They said about Rabbi Ḥanina** ben Dosa that the indication whether or not his prayer was accepted was whether the prayer was fluent in his mouth as he recited it. The Gemara asks: **From where are these matters,** that this is an accurate indication of whether or not his prayer was accepted, derived? **Rabbi Yehoshua ben Levi said: As the verse stated: "The Lord that creates the expression of the lips**[N] **says, Peace, peace, to him that is far off and to him that is near; and I will heal him"** (Isaiah 57:19). It can be inferred from this verse that if speech of the lips, fluent speech, is granted to one who prays, it indicates that his prayer on behalf of the ill has been accepted and I will heal him, that person will be healed.

אָמַר רַבִּי חִיָּיא בַּר אַבָּא אָמַר רַבִּי יוֹחָנָן: כׇּל הַנְּבִיאִים כּוּלָּן לֹא נִתְנַבְּאוּ אֶלָּא לְמַשִּׂיא בִּתּוֹ לְתַלְמִיד חָכָם וּלְעוֹשֶׂה פְּרַקְמַטְיָא לְתַלְמִיד חָכָם, וּלְמְהַנֶּה תַּלְמִיד חָכָם מִנְּכָסָיו, אֲבָל תַּלְמִידֵי חֲכָמִים עַצְמָן – "עַיִן לֹא רָאָתָה אֱלֹהִים זוּלָתְךָ יַעֲשֶׂה לִמְחַכֵּה לוֹ".

In conclusion of this discussion, the Gemara cites that which **Rabbi Ḥiyya bar Abba said** that **Rabbi Yoḥanan said** with regard to the reward of the righteous: **All the prophets only prophesied** in their prophecies of consolation, **with regard to one who** values wisdom and therefore **marries his daughter to a Torah scholar and to one who conducts business** [*perakmatya*][L] **on behalf of a Torah scholar as well as to one who** utilizes his wealth **to benefit a Torah scholar** in some other way. **However,** the prophets did not describe the extent of the reward for **Torah scholars themselves,** whose reward is not quantifiable as it is stated: "And from of old they have not heard, they have not lent an ear, **no eye has seen it, God, aside from You, who will do for those who await Him"** (Isaiah 64:3).

וְאָמַר רַבִּי חִיָּיא בַּר אַבָּא אָמַר רַבִּי יוֹחָנָן: כׇּל הַנְּבִיאִים כּוּלָּן לֹא נִתְנַבְּאוּ אֶלָּא לִימוֹת הַמָּשִׁיחַ, אֲבָל לָעוֹלָם הַבָּא – "עַיִן לֹא רָאָתָה אֱלֹהִים זוּלָתְךָ".

**And Rabbi Ḥiyya bar Abba said** that **Rabbi Yoḥanan said: All the prophets only prophesied** with regard to the change in world order in the end of days **with regard to the days of the Messiah. However, with regard to the World-to-Come,** which exists on a higher level, it is stated: **"No eye has seen it, God, aside from You."**[H]

וּפְלִיגָא דִּשְׁמוּאֵל, דְּאָמַר שְׁמוּאֵל: אֵין בֵּין הָעוֹלָם הַזֶּה לִימוֹת הַמָּשִׁיחַ אֶלָּא שִׁעְבּוּד מַלְכֻיּוֹת בִּלְבַד. שֶׁנֶּאֱמַר: "כִּי לֹא יֶחְדַּל אֶבְיוֹן מִקֶּרֶב הָאָרֶץ".

**And** the Gemara notes that this statement **disagrees with** the opinion of **Shmuel, as Shmuel said: The only** difference **between this world and the days of the Messiah**[H] is with regard to **servitude to** foreign **kingdoms alone.** While in the days of the Messiah, Israel will be independent and free from enslavement to foreign powers, the world order will remain otherwise unchanged, **as it is stated: "For the poor shall not cease from the land"** (Deuteronomy 15:11), which indicates that the ways of the world are set and unchanging.

וְאָמַר רַבִּי חִיָּיא בַּר אַבָּא אָמַר רַבִּי יוֹחָנָן: כׇּל הַנְּבִיאִים כּוּלָּן לֹא נִתְנַבְּאוּ אֶלָּא לְבַעֲלֵי תְשׁוּבָה, אֲבָל צַדִּיקִים גְּמוּרִים – "עַיִן לֹא רָאָתָה אֱלֹהִים זוּלָתְךָ".

**And Rabbi Ḥiyya bar Abba said** that **Rabbi Yoḥanan said: All of the prophets only prophesied** their prophecies of consolation **with regard to penitents but with regard to the full-fledged righteous** it is stated: **"No eye has seen it, God, aside from You."**

וּפְלִיגָא דְּרַבִּי אֲבָהוּ, דְּאָמַר רַבִּי אֲבָהוּ: מָקוֹם שֶׁבַּעֲלֵי תְשׁוּבָה עוֹמְדִין – צַדִּיקִים גְּמוּרִים אֵינָם עוֹמְדִין, שֶׁנֶּאֱמַר: "שָׁלוֹם שָׁלוֹם לָרָחוֹק וְלַקָּרוֹב". לָרָחוֹק בְּרֵישָׁא וַהֲדַר לַקָּרוֹב.

**And** the Gemara notes that **this** statement **disagrees with** the opinion of **Rabbi Abbahu** who holds that penitents are superior to the righteous. **As Rabbi Abbahu said: In the place where penitents stand, even the full-fledged righteous do not stand,**[H] **as it is stated: "Peace, peace upon him who is far and him who is near."** Peace and greeting is extended first to **him who is far,** the penitent, **and** only **thereafter** is peace extended to **him who is near,** the full-fledged righteous.

וְרַבִּי יוֹחָנָן אָמַר לָךְ: מַאי "רָחוֹק" – שֶׁהָיָה רָחוֹק מִדְּבַר עֲבֵירָה מֵעִיקָּרָא, וּמַאי קָרוֹב – שֶׁהָיָה קָרוֹב לִדְבַר עֲבֵירָה, וְנִתְרַחֵק מִמֶּנּוּ הָשְׁתָּא.

**And Rabbi Yoḥanan** could have **said to you: What is** the meaning of **him who is far?** This refers to the full-fledged righteous **who was distant from an act of transgression from the outset,** and to whom peace is extended first. **What is** meant by **him who is near?** This refers to the penitent **who was close to an act of transgression but has now distanced** himself **from it,** and to whom peace is extended only after it has been extended to him who has been righteous from the outset.

מַאי "עַיִן לֹא רָאָתָה"? אָמַר רַבִּי יְהוֹשֻׁעַ בֶּן לֵוִי: זֶה יַיִן הַמְשׁוּמָּר בַּעֲנָבָיו מִשֵּׁשֶׁת יְמֵי בְרֵאשִׁית; רַבִּי שְׁמוּאֵל בַּר נַחְמָנִי אָמַר: זֶה עֵדֶן שֶׁלֹּא שָׁלְטָה בּוֹ עֵין כׇּל בְּרִיָּה.

Earlier, Rabbi Yoḥanan said that there is a reward referred to in the verse: "No eye has seen it." The Gemara asks: **What is** this reward about which it is said: **"No eye has seen it"? Rabbi Yehoshua ben Levi said: That is the wine that has been preserved**[N] **in its grapes since the six days of creation** and which no eye has ever seen. **Rabbi Shmuel bar Naḥmani said: That is Eden, which no creature's eye has ever surveyed.**

## NOTES

**The Lord that creates the expression of the lips** – בּוֹרֵא נִיב שְׂפָתַיִם: Several possibilities were raised with regard to how this idea is derived from this verse. Rashi interprets *borei*, creator, as *bari*, healthy or strong. When one's lips utter the prayer assertively it is a fortuitous omen for the one on whose behalf prayer is being recited. Some say that one sees that the product [*tenuva*] of his lips is being expressed with ease (Rabbeinu Ḥananel). Others interpret *borei* as deriving from the term *berirut*, clarity. When one's speech is clear, it is successful (*Shitta Mekubbetzet*). Additionally, the verse continues "The Lord that creates the expression of the lips…peace." When the speech of the lips emerges peacefully, it is successful (Maharsha).

**Wine that has been preserved** – יַיִן הַמְשׁוּמָּר: The metaphor chosen to symbolize the ultimate reward as wine. Just as wine causes the heart to rejoice and helps one forget his troubles, so too, the ultimate joy with which the righteous will be rewarded will be unmitigated by any suffering or worries. The Sages described this wine as having been preserved in its grapes in Eden, as, since the creation of the world there has never been a period of pure unadulterated joy. That is the reward of the righteous (Rashba).

## LANGUAGE

**Business** [*perakmatya*] – פְּרַקְמַטְיָא: This term comes from the Greek πραγματεία, *pragmateia*, meaning conduct of business or trade.

## HALAKHA

**All the prophets only prophesied with regard to the days of the Messiah. However, with regard to the World-to-Come, it is stated: "No eye has seen it, God, aside from You"** – כׇּל הַנְּבִיאִים כּוּלָּן לֹא נִתְנַבְּאוּ אֶלָּא לִימוֹת הַמָּשִׁיחַ, אֲבָל לָעוֹלָם הַבָּא עַיִן לֹא רָאָתָה אֱלֹהִים זוּלָתְךָ: Rabbi Yoḥanan's statement is accepted as *halakha*; the goodness of the World-to-Come is beyond the purview of human comprehension, and those rewards described by the prophets refer only to the days of the Messiah in this world (Rambam *Sefer HaMadda*, *Hilkhot Teshuva* 8:7).

**The days of the Messiah** – יְמוֹת הַמָּשִׁיחַ: Although different statements appear with regard to this issue, the ruling is that Messianic times will not necessarily herald a change in the world order. Primarily, the Messianic era will feature the restoration of the kingdom of Israel in a state guided by Torah law (Rambam *Sefer HaMadda*, *Hilkhot Teshuva* 9:2, *Sefer Shofetim*, *Hilkhot Melakhim* 12:2).

**In the place where penitents stand, even the full-fledged righteous do not stand** – מָקוֹם שֶׁבַּעֲלֵי תְשׁוּבָה עוֹמְדִין צַדִּיקִים גְּמוּרִים אֵינָם עוֹמְדִין: The virtue of the penitent is greater than that of the full-fledged righteous, in accordance with the opinion of Rabbi Abbahu (Rambam *Sefer HaMadda*, *Hilkhot Teshuva* 7:4).

שֶׁמָּא תֹּאמַר, אָדָם הָרִאשׁוֹן הֵיכָן הָיָה? – בַּגַּן.

**Lest you will say: Where was Adam the first** man? Wasn't he there and didn't he survey Eden? The Gemara responds: Adam was only **in the Garden** of Eden, not in Eden itself.

וְשֶׁמָּא תֹּאמַר: הוּא גַּן, הוּא עֵדֶן – תַּלְמוּד לוֹמַר: "וְנָהָר יוֹצֵא מֵעֵדֶן לְהַשְׁקוֹת אֶת הַגָּן", גַּן לְחוּד וְעֵדֶן לְחוּד.

**And lest you will say: It is the Garden and it is Eden;** two names describing the same place. That is not the case, as **the verse states: "And a river went out from Eden to water the Garden"** (Genesis 2:10). Obviously, the **Garden** exists **on its own and Eden** exists **on its own.**

תָּנוּ רַבָּנַן: מַעֲשֶׂה שֶׁחָלָה בְּנוֹ שֶׁל רַבָּן גַּמְלִיאֵל, שִׁגֵּר שְׁנֵי תַלְמִידֵי חֲכָמִים אֵצֶל רַבִּי חֲנִינָא בֶּן דּוֹסָא לְבַקֵּשׁ עָלָיו רַחֲמִים. כֵּיוָן שֶׁרָאָה אוֹתָם עָלָה לַעֲלִיָּיה וּבִקֵּשׁ עָלָיו רַחֲמִים. בִּירִידָתוֹ, אָמַר לָהֶם: לְכוּ – שֶׁחֲלָצַתּוּ חַמָּה. אָמְרוּ לוֹ: וְכִי נָבִיא אַתָּה?! אָמַר לָהֶן: לֹא נָבִיא אָנֹכִי וְלֹא בֶן נָבִיא אָנֹכִי, אֶלָּא כָּךְ מְקוּבְּלַנִי: אִם שְׁגוּרָה תְּפִלָּתִי בְּפִי – יוֹדֵעַ אֲנִי שֶׁהוּא מְקוּבָּל, וְאִם לָאו – יוֹדֵעַ אֲנִי שֶׁהוּא מְטוֹרָף. יָשְׁבוּ וְכָתְבוּ וְכִוְּונוּ אוֹתָהּ שָׁעָה. וּכְשֶׁבָּאוּ אֵצֶל רַבָּן גַּמְלִיאֵל, אָמַר לָהֶן: הָעֲבוֹדָה! לֹא חִסַּרְתֶּם וְלֹא הוֹתַרְתֶּם אֶלָּא כָּךְ הָיָה מַעֲשֶׂה, בְּאוֹתָהּ שָׁעָה שֶׁחֲלָצַתּוּ חַמָּה וְשָׁאַל לָנוּ מַיִם לִשְׁתּוֹת.

Having mentioned Rabbi Ḥanina ben Dosa in our mishna, the Gemara proceeds to further praise the efficacy of his prayer: **The Sages taught:** There was **an incident where Rabban Gamliel's son fell ill.** Rabban Gamliel **dispatched two scholars to Rabbi Ḥanina ben Dosa to pray for mercy** and healing **on his behalf. When** Rabbi Ḥanina ben Dosa **saw them** approaching, **he went up to the attic** on the roof of his house **and prayed for mercy on his behalf. Upon his descent, he said to** the messengers: You may **go** and return to Rabban Gamliel, **as the fever has already left** his son and he has been healed. The messengers **asked him:** How do you know? **Are you a prophet? He replied to them: I am neither a prophet nor son of a prophet** (see Amos 7:14), **but I have received** a tradition with regard to **this** indication: **If my prayer is fluent in my mouth** as I recite it and there are no errors, **I know that** my prayer **is accepted. And if not, I know that** my prayer **is rejected.** The Gemara relates that these messengers **sat and wrote and approximated that** precise **moment** when Rabbi Ḥanina ben Dosa told them this. **When they came before Rabban Gamliel** and related all that had happened and showed him what they had written, Rabban Gamliel **said to them:** I swear **by the Temple service** that in the time you wrote **you were neither earlier or later; rather, this is how the event** transpired: Precisely at that moment **his fever broke and he asked us for water to drink.**

וְשׁוּב מַעֲשֶׂה בְּרַבִּי חֲנִינָא בֶּן דּוֹסָא שֶׁהָלַךְ לִלְמוֹד תּוֹרָה אֵצֶל רַבִּי יוֹחָנָן בֶּן זַכַּאי, וְחָלָה בְּנוֹ שֶׁל רַבִּי יוֹחָנָן בֶּן זַכַּאי. אָמַר לוֹ: חֲנִינָא בְּנִי, בַּקֵּשׁ עָלָיו רַחֲמִים וְיִחְיֶה. הִנִּיחַ רֹאשׁוֹ בֵּין בִּרְכָּיו וּבִקֵּשׁ עָלָיו רַחֲמִים – וְחָיָה. אָמַר רַבִּי יוֹחָנָן בֶּן זַכַּאי: אִלְמָלֵי הֵטִיחַ בֶּן זַכַּאי אֶת רֹאשׁוֹ בֵּין בִּרְכָּיו כָּל הַיּוֹם כּוּלּוֹ – לֹא הָיוּ מַשְׁגִּיחִים עָלָיו. אָמְרָה לוֹ אִשְׁתּוֹ: וְכִי חֲנִינָא גָּדוֹל מִמְּךָ?! אָמַר לָהּ: לָאו, אֶלָּא הוּא דּוֹמֶה כְּעֶבֶד לִפְנֵי הַמֶּלֶךְ, וַאֲנִי דּוֹמֶה כְּשַׂר לִפְנֵי הַמֶּלֶךְ.

**And** there was **another incident** involving **Rabbi Ḥanina ben Dosa, who went to study Torah before Rabbi Yoḥanan ben Zakkai, and Rabbi Yoḥanan's son fell ill. He said to him: Ḥanina, my son, pray for mercy on behalf of** my son **so that he will live. Rabbi Ḥanina ben Dosa placed his head between his knees** in order to meditate **and prayed for mercy upon his behalf, and** Rabbi Yoḥanan ben Zakkai's son **lived. Rabbi Yoḥanan ben Zakkai said** about himself: **Had ben Zakkai stuck his head between his knees throughout the entire day, they would have paid him no attention. His wife said to him: And is Ḥanina greater than you? He replied to her: No, but** his prayer is better received than my own because **he is like a servant before the King,**[N] and as such he is able to enter before the King and make various requests at all times. **I,** on the other hand, **am like a minister before the King,** and I can enter only when invited and can make requests only with regard to especially significant matters.

וְאָמַר רַבִּי חִיָּיא בַּר אַבָּא אָמַר רַבִּי יוֹחָנָן: אַל יִתְפַּלֵּל אָדָם אֶלָּא בְּבַיִת שֶׁיֵּשׁ שָׁם חַלּוֹנוֹת, שֶׁנֶּאֱמַר: "וְכַוִּין פְּתִיחָן לֵיהּ בְּעִלִּיתֵהּ (לָקֳבֵל) נֶגֶד יְרוּשְׁלֶם."

**And** on the topic of prayer, **Rabbi Ḥiyya bar Abba said** that **Rabbi Yoḥanan said: One may only pray in a house with windows,**[N] as then he can see the heavens and focus his heart, **as it is stated** with regard to Daniel's prayer: "In his attic **there were open windows facing** Jerusalem" (Daniel 6:11).

אָמַר רַב כָּהֲנָא: חֲצִיף עֲלַי מַאן דִּמְצַלֵּי בְּבִקְעָתָא.

With regard to the appropriate place to pray, **Rav Kahana said: I consider impudent one who prays in a field.**[H]

וְאָמַר רַב כָּהֲנָא: חֲצִיף עֲלַי מַאן דִּמְפָרֵשׁ חֶטְאֵיהּ, שֶׁנֶּאֱמַר: "אַשְׁרֵי נְשׂוּי פֶּשַׁע כְּסוּי חֲטָאָה".

Employing parallel language, **Rav Kahana also said: I consider impudent one who specifies his transgression,**[H] **as it is stated: "Happy is he whose iniquity is forgiven, whose transgression is covered over"** (Psalms 32:1); one who conceals his transgressions indicates that he is ashamed of them, and due to his shame he will be forgiven.

הדרן עלך אין עומדין

## NOTES

**Like a servant before the King – כְּעֶבֶד לִפְנֵי הַמֶּלֶךְ:** Rabban Yoḥanan ben Zakkai sought to express that the acceptance of Rabbi Ḥanina's prayer was because his devotion to God was greater, although his Torah knowledge was not (*Or Hashem* of Rabbi Ḥisdai Crescas). The parable is explained that the minister, specifically because he is engaged in more significant undertakings, cannot raise his own personal problems or the problems of others before the king (see *HaKotev*).

**One may only pray in a house with windows – אַל יִתְפַּלֵּל אָדָם אֶלָּא בְּבַיִת שֶׁיֵּשׁ שָׁם חַלּוֹנוֹת:** Some say, based on the verse cited, that this was not to illuminate the room, but rather to symbolize the connection between one praying and the site of the Temple in Jerusalem (*Talmidei Rabbeinu Yona*), or to represent the direct path open to heaven (Maharsha).

## HALAKHA

**I consider impudent one who prays in a field – חֲצִיף עֲלַי מַאן דִּמְצַלֵּי בְּבִקְעָתָא:** One should not pray where there are no walls, as one experiences awe of the God in an enclosed place more than he does in an open one. Some say that this restriction applies specifically to a place where people pass regularly (*Magen Avraham*; *Shulḥan Arukh, Oraḥ Ḥayyim* 90:5).

**I consider impudent one who specifies his transgression – חֲצִיף עֲלַי מַאן דִּמְפָרֵשׁ חֶטְאֵיהּ:** The fundamental question whether it is appropriate to specify one's transgression appears in tractate *Yoma* (87a), and is the subject of a dispute among *tanna'im* and *amora'im*. They conclude that there is a distinction between those transgressions which are public, which may be specified (*Magen Avraham*), and those which are private. Similarly, there is a distinction between one who confesses with no one else present, in which case it is permitted (see *Beit Yosef*), and one who confesses in the presence of others (Rambam *Sefer HaMadda*, *Hilkhot Teshuva* 2:5; *Shulḥan Arukh, Oraḥ Ḥayyim* 607:2).

# Summary of **Perek V**

Chapter Five contains discussions of ideas, mostly aggadic in nature, relating to the essence of prayer and its general role. Nevertheless, the *aggada* sections do not deal solely with the abstract and the sublime; they have practical halakhic ramifications in determining the appropriate manner of prayer.

Two discussions constitute the bulk of the chapter. The first deals with an individual's approach to prayer; the second relates to permitted and prohibited additions to the prayer formula.

Discussion of the individual's approach to prayer, which appears at the beginning and the end of the chapter, establishes the need for absolute concentration on the prayer. The mitzva of prayer, as opposed to the mitzva to recite *Shema*, is not by Torah law. However, since the essence of prayer is the intent of the heart one must concentrate on his prayer with all his might. Only a clear and present danger to one's life exempts him from this absolute demand. Because of the obligation to concentrate in this manner, any error or slip of the tongue in the course of prayer renders it seriously flawed, which is disgraceful for the prayer leader and for those who sent him.

Most of the *halakhot* in this chapter deal with additions to the established prayers. At the same time, not all of the changes are discussed in this chapter. They appear in the prayer book, which details the additions and changes introduced on Shabbat, Festivals, and other days of a unique nature. Furthermore, any of the issues that relate to changes in the prayers are discussed throughout the Talmud in different contexts: The prayers for rain in tractate *Ta'anit*; the additions on Shabbat, the New Moon, and Hanukka in tractate *Shabbat*; and so on.

However, as *Tosafot* explains, the *halakhot* here can be seen as fundamental principles that serve as the basis for more detailed discussions in other tractates. In this chapter, only the general framework is presented: These types of additions to prayer exist, and they are to be recited at the appropriate times. The discussions in this chapter do not reach a clear conclusion even with regard to inappropriate additions. These include those that undermine the style of prayer, e.g., unnecessary repetition, or those that compromise the fundamental tenets of the Torah, e.g., additions that are liable to appear heretical. These issues are discussed in greater detail in other tractates.

# Introduction to **Perek VI**

The origins of blessings of enjoyment, which are recited before partaking of any kind of pleasure, are ancient. Chapter Six seeks to clarify the details of these blessings, but not to establish the essential obligation to recite them. Consequently, the fundamental issue throughout the chapter is the question of parameters and definitions. What do these blessings include? Which blessings are appropriate for which items?

From a practical perspective, blessings of enjoyment can be divided into two categories: Blessings recited over food and drink, and blessings recited over fragrances. Within each category, some blessings are more general, while others are more specific. Most of the discussions revolve around determining the parameters of each blessing.

Blessings over food range from the general to the particular, from general blessings recited over different types of food to blessings recited over very specific items. The most comprehensive blessing: By whose word all things came to be, is applicable to all foods. The blessings over the fruit of the earth are more detailed and include a separate blessing for fruit of the trees. Within this category, there is an even more specific blessing over wine: Who creates fruit of the vine.

Within the category of fruit of the earth, there is also a specific blessing for cooked grains: Who creates the various kinds of nourishment, and there is even a blessing recited exclusively over bread: Who brings forth bread from the earth.

These are merely preliminary determinations. The criteria for defining the objects of the blessings must also be established. What constitutes fruit of the tree and fruit of the ground, for these purposes? What is considered a cooked food and what, exactly, is bread? Although some foods clearly fall into a specific category, there are many food items whose categorization is less obvious and whose blessing must be determined. Consequently, most of the discussion in this chapter focuses upon the categorization of these borderline items. There is one underlying principle common to all of these deliberations: A more specific blessing is preferable. The higher the quality and the more extensive the processing of the food item, the more specific and exceptional the blessing. Therefore, the discussion is an attempt to delineate those parameters and to determine the quality and degree of processing of each item.

The discussion of blessings over fragrances is similar with regard to the categorization and the relative level of sophistication of each substance.

Only toward the chapter's end does the Gemara begin a fundamental discussion of the blessings recited after eating. This is a prelude to the detailed analysis of the blessing mandated by Torah law, Grace after Meals, which appears in Chapter Seven.

מתני׳ כֵּיצַד מְבָרְכִין עַל הַפֵּירוֹת? עַל פֵּירוֹת הָאִילָן הוּא אוֹמֵר: ״בּוֹרֵא פְּרִי הָעֵץ״, חוּץ מִן הַיַּיִן, שֶׁעַל הַיַּיִן הוּא אוֹמֵר: ״בּוֹרֵא פְּרִי הַגָּפֶן״; וְעַל פֵּירוֹת הָאָרֶץ הוּא אוֹמֵר: ״בּוֹרֵא פְּרִי הָאֲדָמָה״, חוּץ מִן הַפַּת, שֶׁעַל הַפַּת הוּא אוֹמֵר: ״הַמּוֹצִיא לֶחֶם מִן הָאָרֶץ״; וְעַל הַיְּרָקוֹת הוּא אוֹמֵר: ״בּוֹרֵא פְּרִי הָאֲדָמָה״, רַבִּי יְהוּדָה אוֹמֵר: ״בּוֹרֵא מִינֵי דְשָׁאִים״.

**MISHNA** This mishna discusses the blessings recited over various foods. **How does one recite a blessing**[N] **over fruits?**[N] **Over** different **fruits** that grow on a **tree**[H] **one recites: Who creates fruit of the tree, with the exception of wine.** Although wine is produced from fruit of the tree, due to its significance, it's blessing differs from other fruits of the tree. **Over wine one recites: Who creates fruit of the vine. Over fruits** that grow from **the earth, one recites: Who creates fruit of the ground, with the exception of bread.** Bread, too, is significant and its blessing differs from other fruits of the ground, **as over bread one recites: Who brings forth bread from the earth.**[H] **Over** herbs and leafy **vegetables**[HB] **one recites: Who creates fruit of the ground. Rabbi Yehuda says** that there is room to distinguish between fruits that grow from the earth, herbs, and leafy vegetables. Although they are all fruit of the ground, since they have different qualities, the blessing on the latter is: **Who creates various kinds of herbs.**

גמ׳ מְנָא הָנֵי מִילֵּי? דְּתָנוּ רַבָּנַן: ״קֹדֶשׁ הִלּוּלִים לַה׳״ – מְלַמֵּד שֶׁטְּעוּנִים בְּרָכָה לִפְנֵיהֶם וּלְאַחֲרֵיהֶם. מִכָּאן אָמַר רַבִּי עֲקִיבָא: אָסוּר לְאָדָם שֶׁיִּטְעוֹם כְּלוּם קוֹדֶם שֶׁיְּבָרֵךְ,

**GEMARA** Concerning the fundamental basis for blessings, the Gemara asks: **From where are these matters,** the obligation to recite a blessing before eating, derived? The Gemara answers: **As the Sages taught** in the *Sifra*: With regard to saplings, it is stated that in their fourth year their fruit will be: **"…sanctified for praises before the Lord"** (Leviticus 19:24). This verse **teaches** that **they require** praise of God in the form of a **blessing** both **beforehand and thereafter,** as the verse says praises in the plural. **From here, Rabbi Akiva said: A person is forbidden to taste anything before he recites a blessing,** as without reciting praise over food, it has the status of a consecrated item, from which one is forbidden to derive pleasure.

וְהַאי ״קֹדֶשׁ הִלּוּלִים״ לְהָכִי הוּא דַּאֲתָא?! הַאי מִיבָּעֵי לֵיהּ, חַד: דַּאֲמַר רַחֲמָנָא – אַחֲלֵיהּ וַהֲדַר אַכְלֵיהּ; וְאִידָךְ: דָּבָר הַטָּעוּן שִׁירָה – טָעוּן חִלּוּל, וְשֶׁאֵינוֹ טָעוּן שִׁירָה – אֵין טָעוּן חִלּוּל, וְכִדְרַבִּי שְׁמוּאֵל בַּר נַחְמָנִי אָמַר רַבִּי יוֹנָתָן; דְּאָמַר רַבִּי שְׁמוּאֵל בַּר נַחְמָנִי אָמַר רַבִּי יוֹנָתָן: מִנַּיִן שֶׁאֵין אוֹמְרִים שִׁירָה אֶלָּא עַל הַיַּיִן – שֶׁנֶּאֱמַר: ״וַתֹּאמֶר לָהֶם הַגֶּפֶן הֶחֳדַלְתִּי אֶת תִּירוֹשִׁי הַמְשַׂמֵּחַ אֱלֹהִים וַאֲנָשִׁים״, אִם אֲנָשִׁים מְשַׂמֵּחַ – אֱלֹהִים בַּמֶּה מְשַׂמֵּחַ? מִכָּאן, שֶׁאֵין אוֹמְרִים שִׁירָה אֶלָּא עַל הַיַּיִן!

The Gemara asks: **And did this** verse: **"Sanctified for praises," come for that** purpose? **This** verse **is necessary** to derive other matters. **One** being **that the Merciful One said: Redeem it and then eat it.** This midrash interprets *hillul,* praise, as *ḥillul,* redemption.[N] **And the other** matter derived from this verse is: **An object which** is offered upon the altar and **requires a song** of praise when it is offered, as is the case with the libation of wine, **requires redemption. And that which does not require a song** of praise, all other fruits, **does not require redemption. And** this is **in accordance with** the opinion that **Rabbi Shmuel bar Naḥmani said** that **Rabbi Yonatan said, as Rabbi Shmuel bar Naḥmani said** that **Rabbi Yonatan said: From where** is it derived that **one only recites a song** of praise in the Temple **over the** libation of **wine** on the altar? **As it is stated: "And the vine replied: Should I leave my wine, which gladdens God and man,** and go and wave above the trees?" (Judges 9:13). **If** wine **gladdens people, in what** way **does it gladden God?** Rather, derive **from here that one only recites a song** of praise **over wine,**[H] as wine gladdens God when offered as part of the service in the Temple.In any case, other *halakhot* have been derived from this verse. From where, then, is the requirement to recite blessings derived?

### HALAKHA

**Over fruits that grow on a tree – עַל פֵּירוֹת הָאִילָן:** Over fruits that grow on a tree and their significant products one recites: Who creates fruit of the tree (Rambam *Sefer Ahava, Hilkhot Berakhot* 8:1; *Shulḥan Arukh, Oraḥ Ḥayyim* 202:1).

**As over bread one recites: Who brings forth bread from the earth – שֶׁעַל הַפַּת הוּא אוֹמֵר: הַמּוֹצִיא לֶחֶם מִן הָאָרֶץ:** Over bread one recites: Who brings forth bread from the earth (Rambam *Sefer Ahava, Hilkhot Berakhot* 3:2; *Shulḥan Arukh, Oraḥ Ḥayyim* 167:2).

**Over fruits of the earth…and over vegetables – עַל פֵּירוֹת הָאָרֶץ...וְעַל הַיְּרָקוֹת:** Over fruits that grow from the earth, their products, with the exception of bread, and vegetables, one recites: Who creates fruit of the ground (Rambam *Sefer Ahava, Hilkhot Berakhot* 8:1; *Shulḥan Arukh, Oraḥ Ḥayyim* 203:1, 205:1).

**That one only recites a song of praise over wine – שֶׁאֵין אוֹמְרִים שִׁירָה אֶלָּא עַל הַיַּיִן:** The songs of praise that accompanied the sacrifice of communal offerings in the Temple were recited as the libation associated with that offering was poured on the altar (Rambam *Sefer Avoda, Hilkhot Kelei HaMikdash* 3:2).

### BACKGROUND

**Vegetables and leafy greens – יְרָקוֹת וּדְשָׁאִים:** In the language of the Sages there are three fundamental types of fruits of the ground, not including fruit: Vegetables, greens and seeds. Vegetables are those plants whose edible portion is their fruit, e.g., zucchini and gourds. Greens are those plants whose green leaves are eaten, e.g., lettuce and cabbage. And those fruits of the ground whose seeds are eaten are referred to as such, e.g., legumes. Rabbi Yehuda seeks to assign a different blessing to each of these types.

### NOTES

**How does one recite a blessing – כֵּיצַד מְבָרְכִין:** The early commentaries wondered why the mishna begins discussing the details of the *halakhot* of blessings without first ascertaining that there is a requirement to recite a blessing. *Tosafot* explain that, as we find in the Gemara, there is a logical reason that one should recite a blessing, and therefore the mishna does not discuss it. Some explained that the mishna here relies on what was stated in the third chapter, that an acute mourner does not recite blessings (*Tosafot, Tosefot Rabbeinu Yehuda HaḤasid*); or on the mishna in the first chapter, which discusses short and long blessings (*Talmidei Rabbeinu Yona*). This is the conclusion; however, the original suggestion of the Gemara was that there is a Torah source for blessings (*Tziyyun LeNefesh Ḥayya*) and the Gemara sought a Torah source.

**The fruits – הַפֵּירוֹת:** The mishna deals with the significant, general blessings and in that context, fruits refers to all food items. Animals are also referred to in certain places as fruits of the earth (*Tziyyun LeNefesh Ḥayya*). Therefore, more specific blessings, e.g., Who creates the various kinds of nourishment, were not included in the mishna (*Penei Yehoshua*).

***Hillulim* – *ḥillulim* – הִלּוּלִים חִלּוּלִים:** This homiletic interpretation is based on the common interchange of the letters *heh* and *ḥet*. The similar pronunciation of these letters reached almost complete identity in the Galilee. The Jerusalem Talmud, which was formulated in the Galilee, offers even more far-reaching homiletic interpretations based on this interchange. Nevertheless, the Ra'avad explains that in this case the interchange of letters was not necessary as a basis for the interpretation; as it is stated in the Torah that one redeems [*ḥillul*] his vineyard (Deuteronomy 20:6), and the praise [*hillul*] is simultaneous to the redemption, as prior to redemption, one may not eat the fruit (Rashba).

**BACKGROUND**

**Fourth-year sapling – נֶטַע רְבָעִי:** Fruit growing on a tree during the first three years after it was planted is called *orla* and may not be eaten, nor may any other benefit be derived from it. Fruit that grows during the following year, the fourth year after the tree was planted, has the legal status equivalent to that of second tithe. It must be taken to Jerusalem and eaten there. If it cannot be taken to Jerusalem, it is redeemed and the redemption money is taken to Jerusalem, where it must be spent on food and drink. As long as the Temple was standing, the Sages instituted that anyone living a single day's journey from Jerusalem was prohibited from redeeming his fourth-year grapes. He was required to take them to Jerusalem in order to adorn the streets of Jerusalem with fruit (*Beitza* 5a). Nowadays, fourth-year produce still must be redeemed, albeit for a nominal sum rather than its real value, since the redemption money is no longer taken to Jerusalem.

**Fourth-year grapevine – כֶּרֶם רְבָעִי:** During the fourth year after the vine was planted, the grapes have the legal status equivalent to that of second tithe. They must be taken to Jerusalem and eaten in a state of ritual purity, or must be redeemed and the money taken to Jerusalem and spent on food or drink. There is a dispute in the Talmud whether this *halakha* applies to fruits other than grapes.

**Small, incomplete clusters of grapes – עוֹלְלוֹת:** This refers to clusters of grapes without a central stalk, or clusters on which the grapes do not hang down one upon the other. The Torah prohibits gathering these incompletely formed clusters of grapes (Leviticus 19:20; see also Deuteronomy 24:21). They must be left for the poor. The Sages differed as to whether this law applies to an entire vineyard that grew in this manner.

הָנִיחָא לְמַאן דְּתָנֵי "נֶטַע רְבָעִי", אֶלָּא לְמַאן דְּתָנֵי "כֶּרֶם רְבָעִי" מַאי אִיכָּא לְמֵימַר? דְּאִתְּמַר: רַבִּי חִיָּיא וְרַבִּי שִׁמְעוֹן בְּרַבִּי, חַד תָּנֵי: "כֶּרֶם רְבָעִי", וְחַד תָּנֵי: "נֶטַע רְבָעִי"!

Indeed, **this** works out **well according to the one who taught,** as a rule: **A fourth-year sapling**[B] in the *mishnayot* dealing with the prohibition to eat fruits produced during the first three years of a tree's existence and the sanctity of the fruit produced in its fourth year; as, in his opinion, fourth-year fruits that grow on all trees must be redeemed. **However, according to the one who taught,** as a rule: **A fourth-year grapevine,**[B] **what can be said?** Indeed, he derives the *halakha* that only wine that is accompanied by a song of praise requires redemption, from the interpretation of *hillul* as *ḥillul*. **As it was stated: Rabbi Ḥiyya and Rabbi Shimon, son of Rabbi** Yehuda HaNasi, **one taught** these *mishnayot* using the term: **A fourth-year grapevine, and one taught** using the term: **A fourth-year sapling.**

וּלְמַאן דְּתָנֵי "כֶּרֶם רְבָעִי" – הָנִיחָא אִי יָלֵיף גְּזֵרָה שָׁוָה, דְּתַנְיָא: רַבִּי אוֹמֵר, נֶאֱמַר כָּאן: "לְהוֹסִיף לָכֶם תְּבוּאָתוֹ", וְנֶאֱמַר לְהַלָּן: "וּתְבוּאַת הַכָּרֶם" – מָה לְהַלָּן כֶּרֶם אַף כָּאן כֶּרֶם. אִיַּיתַּר לֵיהּ חַד "הִלּוּל" לִבְרָכָה;

**And according to the one who taught: A fourth year grapevine, this** works out **well if he derives** this matter **from a verbal analogy** [*gezera shava*], and therefore need not derive this *halakha* from the term *hillulim*. **As it was taught** in a *baraita* that **Rabbi** Yehuda HaNasi **said: It is stated here** with regard to the laws of the prohibition of fruit for the tree's first three years: "But in the fifth year you may eat its fruit, **so that it may increase your produce** [*tevuato*]; I am the Lord your God" (Leviticus 19:25). **And it is stated below,** with regard to the laws of diverse kinds: "You shall not sow your vineyard with two kinds of seed, lest the growth of the seed that you have sown be forfeited **with the produce** [*utevuat*] **of the vineyard**" (Deuteronomy 22:9). Based on a verbal analogy, it can be derived **Just as below,** with regard to the laws of diverse kinds, the produce is that which grows in **vineyards; so too, here,** with regard to the *halakhot* of the fruits of a sapling, the produce is that which grows in **vineyards.** Consequently, according to the one who holds this verbal analogy, **one extra *hillul*** remains from which to derive **the blessing.** Since he derives that the laws of fourth-year saplings apply only to grapes from the verbal analogy, he can derive the requirement to recite blessings before partaking of food from the word *hillulim*.

וְאִי לָא יָלֵיף גְּזֵרָה שָׁוָה – בְּרָכָה מְנָא לֵיהּ? וְאִי נַמִי יָלֵיף גְּזֵרָה שָׁוָה – אַשְׁכְּחַן לְאַחֲרָיו, לְפָנָיו מִנַּיִן!

**And if he does not derive** this *halakha* by means of **a verbal analogy,** he must derive this *halakha* from the term *hillulim*, in which case, **from where does he derive** the mitzva **to recite a blessing** before partaking of food? **And even if he derives** this *halakha* by means of **a verbal analogy, we found** a source for the obligation to recite a blessing **after** eating, similar to the obligation stated in the verse: "And you will eat and be satisfied and then you shall bless." However, **from where** is it derived that there is an obligation to recite a blessing **beforehand?** From one *hillul*, the fundamental *halakha* of redemption of fourth-year saplings is derived.

הָא לָא קַשְׁיָא, דְּאָתְיָא בְּקַל וָחוֹמֶר: כְּשֶׁהוּא שָׂבֵעַ מְבָרֵךְ – כְּשֶׁהוּא רָעֵב לֹא כׇּל שֶׁכֵּן?

The Gemara answers this: This is **not difficult, as it** may be **derived by means of an *a fortiori* inference: If when he is satiated,** after eating, **he is** obligated to **recite a blessing** over food, **when he is hungry,** before eating, **all the more so** that he is obligated to recite a blessing over food.

אַשְׁכְּחַן כֶּרֶם, שְׁאָר מִינִין מִנַּיִן?

The Gemara comments: In that way, **we found** a source for the obligation to recite a blessing over the produce of **vineyards,** but **from where** is it derived with regard to **other types of** produce?

דְּיָלֵיף מִכֶּרֶם, מָה כֶּרֶם דָּבָר שֶׁנֶּהֱנֶה וְטָעוּן בְּרָכָה – אַף כׇּל דָּבָר שֶׁנֶּהֱנֶה טָעוּן בְּרָכָה.

The Gemara responds: **It is derived** by means of the hermeneutic principle What do we find, **from** the produce of a **vineyard: Just as** the fruit of the **vineyard is an item** from **which one derives benefit and it requires a blessing, so too, any item** from **which one derives benefit, requires a blessing.**

אִיכָּא לְמִפְרַךְ: מָה לְכֶרֶם שֶׁכֵּן חַיָּיב בְּעוֹלְלוֹת!

The Gemara rejects this proof: **This** derivation **can be refuted,** as a vineyard is unique: **What** is unique about a **vineyard, that it is obligated in** the mitzva requiring to give **small, incomplete clusters of grapes** [*olelot*][B] to the poor? That is a stringency that does not apply to other fruits. Perhaps the blessing is also a stringency that applies only to grapes.

קָמָה תּוֹכִיחַ. מָה לְקָמָה – שֶׁכֵּן חַיֶּיבֶת בְּחַלָּה!

The Gemara answers: In that case, **standing grain can prove** that the *halakha* of *olelot* is not a factor in the obligation to recite a blessing. One is obligated by Torah law to recite a blessing after eating bread, even though the *halakha* of *olelot* does not apply to grain. The Gemara rejects this proof **What** is unique about **ripe grain, that it is obligated in** the mitzva of separating ***ḥalla*** from the dough? That is a stringency that does not apply to other foods. Perhaps the blessing is also a stringency that applies only to grain.

כֶּרֶם יוֹכִיחַ. וְחָזַר הַדִּין: לֹא רְאִי זֶה כִּרְאִי זֶה וְלֹא רְאִי זֶה כִּרְאִי זֶה, הַצַּד הַשָּׁוֶה שֶׁבָּהֶן – דָּבָר שֶׁנֶּהֱנֶה וְטָעוּן בְּרָכָה, אַף כָּל דָּבָר שֶׁנֶּהֱנֶה טָעוּן בְּרָכָה.

The Gemara responds: In that regard, **vineyards can prove** that the *halakha* of *ḥalla* is not a factor in the obligation to recite a blessing. In summary: **And the derivation has reverted** to its starting point. However, at this point the *halakha* is derived from a combination of the two sources: **The aspect of this is not like the aspect of that,**[B] **and the aspect of that is not like the aspect of this; the common denominator is:** Both are **items** from **which one derives benefit and** each **requires a blessing.** A general principle may be derived: **So too, any item** from **which one derives benefit, requires a blessing.**

מַה לְהַצַּד הַשָּׁוֶה שֶׁבָּהֶן – שֶׁכֵּן יֵשׁ בּוֹ צַד מִזְבֵּחַ! וְאָתֵי נַמִּי זַיִת דְּאִית בֵּיהּ צַד מִזְבֵּחַ.

Again, the Gemara objects: **What** is unique about **the common denominator** between grapes and grain that prevents utilizing it as a paradigm for other food items? Grapes and grain **have an aspect** of being offered upon the **altar,** and perhaps that is the reason that they require blessings. Based on that reasoning, although all other food items cannot be derived from the common denominator, **an olive may also be derived as it too has an aspect** of being offered upon the **altar,** as olive oil is one of the components of a meal offering.

וְזַיִת מִצַּד מִזְבֵּחַ אָתֵי?! וְהָא בְּהֶדְיָא כְּתִיב בֵּיהּ כֶּרֶם, דִּכְתִיב: ״וַיַּבְעֵר מִגָּדִישׁ וְעַד קָמָה וְעַד כֶּרֶם זָיִת״! אָמַר רַב פָּפָּא: ״כֶּרֶם זַיִת״ – אִיקְּרִי, ״כֶּרֶם״ סְתָמָא – לָא אִיקְּרִי.

The Gemara questions this point: **Is an olive derived from** the fact that it **has an aspect** of being offered upon the **altar? Isn't it written explicitly with regard to** the olive **listed** that the orchard in which it grows is called ***kerem*****; as it is written: "And burnt up from the shocks and the standing grain and the olive yards [*kerem zayit*]"** (Judges 15:5)? Just as the orchard in which grapes grow is called *kerem*, and grapes require a blessing, the olive also grows in a *kerem* and should require a blessing. **Rav Pappa said:** Nevertheless, an analogy may not be drawn between the two; where the olive grows **is called** ***kerem zayit*****, it is not called** ***kerem*** **unmodified,** which is a term reserved for grapevines.

מִכָּל מָקוֹם קַשְׁיָא: מַה לְהַצַּד הַשָּׁוֶה שֶׁבָּהֶן – שֶׁכֵּן יֵשׁ בָּהֶן צַד מִזְבֵּחַ! אֶלָּא: דְּיָלֵיף לָהּ מִשִּׁבְעַת הַמִּינִין – מַה שִּׁבְעַת הַמִּינִין דָּבָר שֶׁנֶּהֱנֶה וְטָעוּן בְּרָכָה, אַף כָּל דָּבָר שֶׁנֶּהֱנֶה טָעוּן בְּרָכָה.

The Gemara returns to the issue at hand, noting that **in any case, it is difficult: What** is unique about **the common denominator** between grapes and grain? That they **possess an aspect** of being offered upon the **altar. Rather, it is derived from** the obligation to recite a blessing **upon the seven species.**[B] After the verse speaks of the seven species, it states: "And you will eat and be satisfied and then you shall bless." This is a paradigm for all other foods, that they too require a blessing: **Just as the seven species are items** from **which one derives benefit and require a blessing, any item** from **which one derives benefit, requires a blessing.**

מַה לְשִׁבְעַת הַמִּינִין שֶׁכֵּן חַיָּיבִין בְּבִכּוּרִים! וְעוֹד: הָתִינַח לְאַחֲרָיו, לְפָנָיו מְנַיִן?

Again, the Gemara rejects this: **What** is unique **about the seven species? That one is obligated in** the mitzva **of first fruits.** However, other produce with regard to which one is not obligated in the mitzva of first fruits, from where is it derived that they require a blessing? **Furthermore,** even if the seven species can serve as a paradigm, **this** works out **well** with regard to the blessing **thereafter;** but **from where** is the obligation to recite a blessing **beforehand** derived?

הָא לָא קַשְׁיָא; דְּאָתֵי בְּקַל וָחוֹמֶר: כְּשֶׁהוּא שָׂבֵעַ מְבָרֵךְ – כְּשֶׁהוּא רָעֵב לֹא כָּל שֶׁכֵּן.

The Gemara responds to the question: This is **not difficult, as it** may be **derived by means of an** ***a fortiori*** **inference: If when he is satiated,** after eating, **he** is obligated to **recite a blessing** over food, **when he is hungry,** before eating, **all the more so** he is obligated to recite a blessing over food.

וּלְמַאן דְּתָנֵי ״נֶטַע רְבָעִי״ – הָא תִּינַח כָּל דָּבָר נְטִיעָה, דְּלָאו בַּר נְטִיעָה, כְּגוֹן בָּשָׂר בֵּיצִים וְדָגִים, מְנָא לֵיהּ? – אֶלָּא, סְבָרָא הוּא: אָסוּר לוֹ לְאָדָם שֶׁיֵּהָנֶה מִן הָעוֹלָם הַזֶּה בְּלֹא בְּרָכָה.

In any case, this is not an absolute proof. Furthermore, even **according to the one who taught: A fourth-year grapevine** in all the relevant *mishnayot*, **it** works out **well** with regard to **everything that can be planted,** that one is obligated to recite a blessing. However, with regard to **items that cannot be planted, such as meat, eggs, and fish, from where does he** derive the *halakha* that one is obligated to recite a blessing? **Rather,** all previous attempts at deriving this *halakha* are rejected. The fundamental obligation to recite a blessing over food is founded on **reason: One is forbidden to derive benefit from this world without a blessing.**[H]

## BACKGROUND

**The aspect of this is not like the aspect of that – לֹא רְאִי זֶה כִּרְאִי זֶה:** In this discussion, a special form of halakhic exegesis appears in its entirety. The fundamental structure is that of an analogy or an interpretation based on induction. One case is used as a precedent for a series of similar cases. That analogy can be contested by demonstrating a specific difference between the primary case and the others. The response to that challenge is to cite an additional case, where the same *halakha* applies and this difference does not exist. If there is then a challenge citing a specific difference between the second case and the others, the Gemara will state: The aspect of this is not like the aspect of that, and the aspect of that is not like the aspect of this. In other words, the Gemara will attempt to use both cases together in order to prove its argument, by illustrating that there is no significance to the differences between each of those cases and the others. This proof can also be repudiated if it is demonstrated that there exists a specific characteristic common to the two source cases different from all the others.

**The seven species – שִׁבְעַת הַמִּינִים:** The seven species are seven agricultural products, two grains and five fruits, listed in the Torah as being those products for which Eretz Yisrael was praised. The seven species are wheat, barley, grapes, figs, pomegranates, olive oil, and date honey (Deuteronomy 8:8).

## HALAKHA

**One is forbidden to derive benefit from this world without a blessing – אָסוּר לוֹ לְאָדָם שֶׁיֵּהָנֶה מִן הָעוֹלָם הַזֶּה בְּלֹא בְּרָכָה:** One is required by rabbinic law to recite a blessing before eating even a minuscule amount of food. The *a fortiori* inference cited by the Gemara is not accepted as a Torah source for the blessing (*Kesef Mishne*). The Gemara accepts the reasoning that one recites a blessing over anything from which he derives benefit (*Tosafot* and Rosh; Rambam *Sefer Ahava, Hilkhot Tefilla* 1:2; *Shulḥan Arukh, Oraḥ Ḥayyim* 210:1).

תָּנוּ רַבָּנַן: אָסוּר לוֹ לָאָדָם שֶׁיֵּהָנֶה מִן הָעוֹלָם הַזֶּה בְּלֹא בְּרָכָה, וְכׇל הַנֶּהֱנֶה מִן הָעוֹלָם הַזֶּה בְּלֹא בְּרָכָה – מָעַל. מַאי תַּקַּנְתֵּיהּ – יֵלֵךְ אֵצֶל חָכָם.

**The Sages taught** in a *Tosefta*: **One is forbidden to derive benefit from this world,** which is the property of God, **without** reciting a **blessing** beforehand. **And anyone who derives benefit from this world without a blessing,** it is as if he is guilty of **misuse** of a consecrated object. The Gemara adds: **What is his remedy? He should go to a Sage.**

יֵלֵךְ אֵצֶל חָכָם – מַאי עָבֵיד לֵיהּ?! הָא עֲבַד לֵיהּ אִיסּוּרָא! – אֶלָּא אָמַר רָבָא: יֵלֵךְ אֵצֶל חָכָם מֵעִיקָּרָא וִילַמְּדֶנּוּ בְּרָכוֹת, כְּדֵי שֶׁלֹּא יָבֹא לִידֵי מְעִילָה.

The Gemara is puzzled: **He should go to a Sage; what will he do to him?** How can the Sage help after **he has already violated a prohibition?** Rather, Rava **said,** this is how it should be understood: **He should go to a Sage initially,** in his youth, **and** the Sage **will teach him blessings, so that he will not come to** be guilty of this type of **misuse** of a consecrated object in the future.

אָמַר רַב יְהוּדָה אָמַר שְׁמוּאֵל: כׇּל הַנֶּהֱנֶה מִן הָעוֹלָם הַזֶּה בְּלֹא בְּרָכָה – כְּאִילּוּ נֶהֱנֶה מִקׇּדְשֵׁי שָׁמַיִם, שֶׁנֶּאֱמַר: ״לַה׳ הָאָרֶץ וּמְלוֹאָהּ״. רַבִּי לֵוִי רָמֵי: כְּתִיב ״לַה׳ הָאָרֶץ וּמְלוֹאָהּ״, וּכְתִיב: ״הַשָּׁמַיִם שָׁמַיִם לַה׳ וְהָאָרֶץ נָתַן לִבְנֵי אָדָם״! לָא קַשְׁיָא, כָּאן – קוֹדֶם בְּרָכָה,

Similarly, **Rav Yehuda said** that **Shmuel said: One who derives benefit from this world without a blessing, it is as if he enjoyed objects consecrated to the heavens, as it is stated: "The earth and all it contains is the Lord's,** the world and all those who live in it (Psalms 24:1). Rabbi Levi expressed this concept differently. **Rabbi Levi raised a contradiction: It is written: "The earth and all it contains is the Lord's," and it is written** elsewhere: **"The heavens are the Lord's and the earth He has given over to mankind"** (Psalms 115:16). There is clearly a contradiction with regard to whom the earth belongs. He himself resolves the contradiction: This is **not difficult. Here,** the verse that says that the earth is the Lord's refers to the situation **before a blessing** is recited,

Perek **VI**
Daf **35** Amud **b**

כָּאן לְאַחַר בְּרָכָה.

and **here,** where it says that He gave the earth to mankind refers to **after a blessing** is recited.

אָמַר רַבִּי חֲנִינָא בַּר פָּפָּא: כׇּל הַנֶּהֱנֶה מִן הָעוֹלָם הַזֶּה בְּלֹא בְּרָכָה כְּאִילּוּ גּוֹזֵל לְהַקָּדוֹשׁ בָּרוּךְ הוּא וּכְנֶסֶת יִשְׂרָאֵל, שֶׁנֶּאֱמַר: ״גּוֹזֵל אָבִיו וְאִמּוֹ וְאוֹמֵר אֵין פָּשַׁע חָבֵר הוּא לְאִישׁ מַשְׁחִית״; וְאֵין אָבִיו אֶלָּא הַקָּדוֹשׁ בָּרוּךְ הוּא, שֶׁנֶּאֱמַר: ״הֲלֹא הוּא אָבִיךָ קָּנֶךָ״; וְאֵין אִמּוֹ אֶלָּא כְּנֶסֶת יִשְׂרָאֵל, שֶׁנֶּאֱמַר: ״שְׁמַע בְּנִי מוּסַר אָבִיךָ וְאַל תִּטֹּשׁ תּוֹרַת אִמֶּךָ״.

**Rabbi Ḥanina bar Pappa said: Anyone who derives benefit from this world without a blessing, it is as if he stole from God and the community of Israel, as it is stated: "Whoever robs his father and his mother and says: It is no transgression, he is the companion of a destroyer"** (Proverbs 28:24).[N] The phrase, **his father, refers to none other than God, as it is stated: "Is He not your Father Who created you,** Who made you and established you" (Deuteronomy 32:6). The phrase **his mother refers to none other than the community of Israel, as it is stated: "Hear, my son, the discipline of your father and do not forsake the Torah of your mother"** (Proverbs 1:8). The mention of the Torah as emanating from the mouth of the mother apparently means that your mother is the community of Israel.

מַאי ״חָבֵר הוּא לְאִישׁ מַשְׁחִית״? אָמַר רַבִּי חֲנִינָא בַּר פָּפָּא: חָבֵר הוּא לְיָרָבְעָם בֶּן נְבָט שֶׁהִשְׁחִית אֶת יִשְׂרָאֵל לַאֲבִיהֶם שֶׁבַּשָּׁמַיִם.

**What** is the meaning of the continuation of the verse: **He is the companion of a destroyer? Rabbi Ḥanina bar Pappa said:** He is a **companion of Jeroboam ben Nevat, who corrupted Israel before their Father in heaven** by sinning and causing others to sin.

רַבִּי חֲנִינָא בַּר פָּפָּא רָמֵי: כְּתִיב ״וְלָקַחְתִּי דְגָנִי בְּעִתּוֹ״ וגו׳, וּכְתִיב: ״וְאָסַפְתָּ דְגָנֶךָ״ וגו׳!

On a similar note, the Gemara cites that **Rabbi Ḥanina bar Pappa raised a contradiction: It is written, "I will take back My grain**[N] **at its time** and wine in its season" (Hosea 2:11), **and it is written: "And you shall gather your grain,** your wine and your oil" (Deuteronomy 11:14). To whom does the grain belong: To God, or to the people?

לָא קַשְׁיָא: כָּאן בִּזְמַן שֶׁיִּשְׂרָאֵל עוֹשִׂין רְצוֹנוֹ שֶׁל מָקוֹם, כָּאן בִּזְמַן שֶׁאֵין יִשְׂרָאֵל עוֹשִׂין רְצוֹנוֹ שֶׁל מָקוֹם.

The Gemara responds: This is **not difficult. Here,** where God promises Israel that they will gather their grain, the verse refers to **a time when they perform God's will. Here,** where the verse indicates that the grain belongs to God, it refers to **a time when they do not perform God's will,** as then He will take back the grain, demonstrating that it belongs to Him.

**NOTES**

As if he stole from God…robs his father and mother – כְּאִילּוּ גּוֹזֵל לְהַקָּדוֹשׁ בָּרוּךְ הוּא...אָבִיו וְאִמּוֹ: There are several explanations as to why the verse, "Whoever robs his father and mother…he is the companion of a destroyer," was diverted from its simple sense, and interpreted in a manner that broadens its meaning beyond the nuclear family to encompass a much more significant scope. The allusion here is from the verse, "Do not forsake the Torah of your mother," in which the phrase "the Torah of your mother" refers to the Torah of the entire Jewish community.

I will take back My grain – וְלָקַחְתִּי דְגָנִי: Some explained that the difference between this verse and the verse, "And you shall gather your grain," is with regard to the question, to whom does the grain belong. The verse in Hosea refers to the grain as the property of God, while the verse in Deuteronomy refers to the grain as belonging to man. This parallels what was stated above with regard to the verse, "The heavens are the Lord's" (Rav Yoshiya Pinto).

תָּנוּ רַבָּנַן: ״וְאָסַפְתָּ דְגָנֶךָ״ – מָה תַּלְמוּ לוֹמַר – לְפִי שֶׁנֶּאֱמַר: ״לֹא יָמוּשׁ סֵפֶר הַתּוֹרָה הַזֶּה מִפִּיךָ״, יָכוֹל דְּבָרִים כִּכְתָבָן? תַּלְמוּ לוֹמַר: ״וְאָסַפְתָּ דְגָנֶךָ״ – הַנְהֵג בָּהֶן מִנְהַג דֶּרֶךְ אֶרֶץ, דִּבְרֵי רַבִּי יִשְׁמָעֵאל;

**The Sages taught: What** is the meaning of that which **the verse states: "And you shall gather your grain"? Because it is stated: "This Torah shall not depart from your mouths,** and you shall contemplate in it day and night" (Joshua 1:8), **I might** have thought **that these matters are** to be understood **as they are written;** one is to literally spend his days immersed exclusively in Torah study. Therefore, **the verse states: "And you shall gather your grain,** your wine and your oil," **assume in their** regard, **the way of the world;** set aside time not only for Torah, but also for work. This is **the statement of Rabbi Yishmael.**

רַבִּי שִׁמְעוֹן בֶּן יוֹחַאי אוֹמֵר: אֶפְשָׁר אָדָ חוֹרֵשׁ בִּשְׁעַת חֲרִישָׁה, וְזוֹרֵעַ בִּשְׁעַת זְרִיעָה וְקוֹצֵר בִּשְׁעַת קְצִירָה, וְדָשׁ בִּשְׁעַת דִּישָׁה וְזוֹרֶה בִּשְׁעַת הָרוּחַ, תּוֹרָה מַה תְּהֵא עָלֶיהָ אֶלָּא: בִּזְמַן שֶׁיִּשְׂרָאֵל עוֹשִׂין רְצוֹנוֹ שֶׁ מָקוֹם – מְלַאכְתָּן נַעֲשֵׂית עַל יְדֵי אֲחֵרִים שֶׁנֶּאֱמַר: ״וְעָמְדוּ זָרִים וְרָעוּ צֹאנְכֶם״ וגו׳ וּבִזְמַן שֶׁאֵין יִשְׂרָאֵל עוֹשִׂין רְצוֹנוֹ שֶׁ מָקוֹם – מְלַאכְתָּן נַעֲשֵׂית עַל יְדֵי עַצְמָן שֶׁנֶּאֱמַר: ״וְאָסַפְתָּ דְגָנֶךָ״; וְלֹא עוֹד, אֶלָּא שֶׁמְּלֶאכֶת אֲחֵרִים נַעֲשֵׂית עַל יָדָן, שֶׁנֶּאֱמַר ״וְעָבַדְתָּ אֶת אוֹיִבֶךָ״ וגו׳.

**Rabbi Shimon ben Yoḥai says: Is it possible that a person plows in the plowing season and sows in the sowing season and harvests in the harvest season and threshes in the threshing season and winnows in the windy season,** as grain is separated from the chaff by means of the wind, and is constantly busy; **what will become of Torah? Rather,** one must dedicate himself exclusively to Torah at the expense of other endeavors; as **when Israel performs God's will, their work is performed by others, as it is stated: "And strangers will stand and feed your flocks,** and foreigners will be your plowmen and your vinedressers" (Isaiah 61:5). **When Israel does not perform God's will, their work is performed by them** themselves, as it is stated: **"And you shall gather your grain." Moreover,** if Israel fails to perform God's will, **others' work will be performed by them, as it is stated: "You shall serve your enemy** whom God shall send against you, in hunger, in thirst, in nakedness and in want of all things" (Deuteronomy 28:48).[H]

אָמַר אַבַּיֵי: הַרְבֵּה עָשׂוּ כְּרַבִּי יִשְׁמָעֵאל וְעָלְתָה בְּיָדָן, כְּרַבִּי שִׁמְעוֹן בֶּן יוֹחַי – וְלֹ עָלְתָה בְּיָדָן.

Summing up this dispute, **Abaye said:** Although there is room for both opinions, **many have acted in accordance with** the opinion of **Rabbi Yishmael,** and combined working for a living and learning Torah, **and** although they engaged in activities other than the study of Torah, **were successful** in their Torah study. **Many have acted in accordance with** the opinion of **Rabbi Shimon ben Yoḥai and were not successful** in their Torah study. They were ultimately forced to abandon their Torah study altogether.

אָמַר לְהוּ רָבָא לְרַבָּנַן: בְּמָטוּתָא מִינַּייכ בְּיוֹמֵי נִיסָן וּבְיוֹמֵי תִשְׁרֵי לָא תִּתַחְזוּ קַמַּאי, כִּ הֵיכִי דְּלָא תִּטַּרְדוּ בִּמְזוֹנַייכוּ כּוּלָּא שַׁתָּא.

Similarly, **Rava said to the Sages** who would attend his study hall: **I implore you; during** the months of **Nisan and Tishrei,** the crucial agricultural periods, **do not appear before me.** Engage in your agricultural work then **so that you will not be preoccupied with your sustenance all year.**

אָמַר רַבָּה בַּר בַּר חָנָה אָמַר רַבִּי יוֹחָנָן מִשּׁוּ רַבִּי יְהוּדָה בְּרַבִּי אֶלְעַאי: בֹּא וּרְאֵה שֶׁלֹּ כְּדוֹרוֹת הָרִאשׁוֹנִים דּוֹרוֹת הָאַחֲרוֹנִים, דּוֹרוֹ הָרִאשׁוֹנִים עָשׂוּ תּוֹרָתָן קֶבַע וּמְלַאכְתָּ עֲרַאי – זוֹ וָזוֹ נִתְקַיְּימָה בְּיָדָן, דּוֹרוֹ הָאַחֲרוֹנִים שֶׁעָשׂוּ מְלַאכְתָּן קֶבַע וְתוֹרָתָ עֲרַאי – זוֹ וָזוֹ לֹא נִתְקַיְּימָה בְּיָדָן.

Summarizing these statements, **Rabba bar bar Ḥana said** that **Rabbi Yoḥanan said in the name of** the *tanna* **Rabbi Yehuda, son of Rabbi El'ai: Come and see that the latter generations are not like the earlier generations;** rather they are their inferiors. **The earlier generations made their Torah permanent and their work occasional,** and **this,** Torah study, **and that,** their work, **were successful for them.** However, **the latter generations who made their work permanent and their Torah occasional, neither this nor that was successful for them.**

וְאָמַר רַבָּה בַּר בַּר חָנָה אָמַר רַבִּי יוֹחָ מִשּׁוּם רַבִּי יְהוּדָה בְּרַבִּי אֶלְעַאי: בֹּא וּרְאֵ שֶׁלֹּא כְּדוֹרוֹת הָרִאשׁוֹנִים דּוֹרוֹת הָאַחֲרוֹנִים דּוֹרוֹת הָרִאשׁוֹנִים הָיוּ מַכְנִיסִין פֵּירוֹתֵיהֶן דֶּרֶ טְרַקְסְמוֹן – כְּדֵי לְחַיְּיבָן בְּמַעֲשֵׂר, דּוֹרוֹ הָאַחֲרוֹנִים מַכְנִיסִין פֵּירוֹתֵיהֶן דֶּרֶךְ גַּגּוֹ דֶּרֶךְ חֲצֵרוֹת דֶּרֶךְ קַרְפֵּיפוֹת – כְּדֵי לְפָטְ מִן הַמַּעֲשֵׂר; דְּאָמַר רַבִּי יַנַּאי: אֵין הַטֶּבֶ מִתְחַיֵּיב בְּמַעֲשֵׂר עַד שֶׁיִּרְאֶה פְּנֵי הַבַּיִ שֶׁנֶּאֱמַר: ״בִּעַרְתִּי הַקֹּדֶשׁ מִן הַבַּיִת״;

Along these lines, **Rabba bar bar Ḥana said** that **Rabbi Yoḥanan said in the name of Rabbi Yehuda, son of Rabbi El'ai: Come and see that the latter generations are not like the earlier generations.** In the **earlier generations,** people **would bring their fruits into their courtyards through the main gate in order to obligate them in tithes.** However, **the latter generations bring their fruits through roofs, through courtyards and through enclosed courtyards,** avoiding the main gate **in order to exempt them from** the mitzva of **tithing. As Rabbi Yannai said: Untithed produce is not obligated in** the mitzva of **tithing until it sees the front of the house** through which people enter and exit, and it is brought into the house that way **as it is stated** in the formula of the confession of the tithes: **"I have removed the consecrated from the house"** (Deuteronomy 26:13), as the obligation to tithe produce whose purpose has not yet been designated takes effect only when it is brought into the house.

וְרַבִּי יוֹחָנָן אָמַר: אֲפִילּוּ חָצֵר קוֹבַעַת שֶׁנֶּאֱמַר: ״וְאָכְלוּ בִשְׁעָרֶיךָ וְשָׂבֵעוּ״.

**And Rabbi Yoḥanan said: Even** bringing it into the **courtyard determines** its status as having completed the production process and obligates the produce to be tithed, **as it is written** in the confession of the tithes: "And I have given to the Levite, the stranger, the orphan and the widow, **and they shall eat in your gates and be satisfied"** (Deuteronomy 26:12).

**HALAKHA**

**Torah and labor – תּוֹרָה וּמְלָאכָה:** The Sages said that in addition to learning Torah, one should engage in labor to support himself (*Magen Avraham*). Any Torah that is not accompanied by labor is null and void and leads to transgression, as poverty will ultimately lead him to stray from observance of God's will. Nevertheless, one must be careful to make Torah his priority, and labor secondary. Then he will be successful at both (Rambam *Sefer HaMadda, Hilkhot Talmud Torah* 3:7; *Shulḥan Arukh, Oraḥ Ḥayyim* 156:1).

״חוּץ מִן הַיַּיִן״ וכו׳. מַאי שְׁנָא יַיִן? אִילֵימָא מִשּׁוּם דְּאִשְׁתַּנִּי לְעִלּוּיָא, אִשְׁתַּנִּי לִבְרָכָה? וַהֲרֵי שֶׁמֶן, דְּאִשְׁתַּנִּי לְעִלּוּיָא וְלָא אִשְׁתַּנִּי לִבְרָכָה! דְּאָמַר רַב יְהוּדָה אָמַר שְׁמוּאֵל, וְכֵן אָמַר רַבִּי יִצְחָק אָמַר רַבִּי יוֹחָנָן: שֶׁמֶן זַיִת מְבָרְכִין עָלָיו ״בּוֹרֵא פְּרִי הָעֵץ״!

We learned in our mishna: Over fruits that grow on a tree one recites: Who creates fruit of the tree, **with the exception of wine** that even though it originates from fruit of the tree, a separate blessing was established for it: Who creates the fruit of the vine. The Gemara asks: **What is different** about **wine,** that a separate blessing was established for it? **If you say that because the fruit changed for the better** into wine therefore, **the blessing changed.** Olive **oil changed for the better and** nevertheless, **its blessing did not change. As Rabbi Yehuda said** that **Shmuel said, and so too Rabbi Yitzḥak said** that **Rabbi Yoḥanan said: Over olive oil, one recites: Who creates fruit of the tree,**[H] just as he does over the fruit itself.

אָמְרִי: הָתָם מִשּׁוּם דְּלָא אֶפְשָׁר, הֵיכִי נְבָרֵיךְ? נְבָרֵיךְ ״בּוֹרֵא פְּרִי הַזַּיִת״ – פֵּירָא גּוּפֵיהּ ״זַיִת״ אִקְּרִי.

The Sages **said: There,** in the case of oil, **it is because it is impossible** to find an appropriate blessing, as **how shall we recite the blessing? If we recite the blessing: Who creates fruit of the olive, the fruit itself is called olive** and that is what was created. The oil is a man-made product of that fruit, rendering that formula inappropriate. Similarly reciting a formula parallel to the blessing on wine: Who creates the fruit of the vine, is inappropriate as the grapes themselves are the fruit that was created, as opposed to oil which was not.

וּנְבָרֵיךְ עֲלֵיהּ ״בּוֹרֵא פְּרִי עֵץ זַיִת״! – אֶלָּא אָמַר מָר זוּטְרָא: חַמְרָא – זַיְין, מִשְׁחָא – לָא זַיְין.

The Gemara challenges: Nevertheless, it is still possible to formulate a blessing, **as we may recite the blessing: Who creates fruit of the olive tree,** which would be parallel to the blessing recited over wine. **Rather Mar Zutra offered** a different rationale: The reason that no separate blessing was established over oil is because, as opposed to **wine** that **nourishes, oil does not nourish.**

וּמִשְׁחָא לָא זַיְין?! וְהָתְנַן: הַנּוֹדֵר מִן הַמָּזוֹן, מוּתָּר בְּמַיִם וּבְמֶלַח, וְהָוֵינַן בָּהּ: מַיִם וּמֶלַח הוּא דְּלָא אִקְּרִי מָזוֹן, הָא כׇּל מִילֵּי אִקְּרִי מָזוֹן,

The Gemara asks: **And oil does not nourish? Didn't we learn** in a mishna: **One who vows that nourishment** is forbidden to him[H] **is permitted** to eat **water and salt,** as they are not considered nourishment. **And we discussed this** *halakha*: By inference, **water and salt are not considered nourishment, but all** other edible **items are considered nourishment.**

נֵימָא תֶּיהֱוֵי תְּיוּבְתָּא דְּרַב וּשְׁמוּאֵל, דְּאָמְרִי: אֵין מְבָרְכִין ״בּוֹרֵא מִינֵי מְזוֹנוֹת״ אֶלָּא בַּחֲמֵשֶׁת הַמִּינִין בִּלְבַד! וְאָמַר רַב הוּנָא: בְּאוֹמֵר ״כׇּל הַזָּן עָלַי״;

**Let us say that this is a conclusive refutation of Rav and Shmuel, who said: One only recites: Who creates various kinds of nourishment over the five species** of grain **alone,** as they alone are considered nourishing. **And Rav Huna said** as a solution that this mishna referred to a case **where** he vows **and says: Anything that nourishes** is prohibited **to me.** That formula includes anything that is at all nourishing and therefore only water and salt are excluded. Olive oil is not excluded.

אַלְמָא מִשְׁחָא זַיְין! – אֶלָּא: חַמְרָא סָעֵיד, וּמִשְׁחָא לָא סָעֵיד. – וְחַמְרָא מִי סָעֵיד?! וְהָא רָבָא הֲוָה שָׁתֵי חַמְרָא כׇּל מַעֲלֵי יוֹמָא דְּפִסְחָא כִּי הֵיכִי דְּנִגְרְרֵיהּ לְלִבֵּיהּ וְנֵיכוּל מַצָּה טְפֵי! – טוּבָא גָּרֵיר, פּוּרְתָּא סָעֵיד.

**Apparently, oil nourishes. Rather,** there is another distinction between wine and oil: **Wine satisfies, oil does not satisfy.** Wine not only nourishes, but it is also filling. The Gemara asks: **And does wine satisfy? Wouldn't Rava drink wine all** day on **the eve of Passover**[H] **in order to stimulate his heart,** i.e., whet his appetite **so that he might eat more** *matza* at the seder? Wine does not satisfy, it whets the appetite. The Gemara answers: **A lot** of wine **stimulates, a little satisfies.**

וּמִי סָעֵיד כְּלָל?! וְהָכְתִיב: ״וְיַיִן יְשַׂמַּח לְבַב אֱנוֹשׁ וְלֶחֶם לְבַב אֱנוֹשׁ יִסְעָד״ וגו׳ נַהֲמָא הוּא דְּסָעֵיד, חַמְרָא לָא סָעֵיד! – אֶלָּא: חַמְרָא אִית בֵּיהּ תַּרְתֵּי – סָעֵיד וּמְשַׂמַּח, נַהֲמָא – מִסְעַד סָעֵיד, שַׂמּוֹחֵי לָא מְשַׂמַּח.

Again, the Gemara asks: **Does** wine **satisfy at all? Isn't it written: "Wine gladdens the heart of man,** making the face brighter than oil, **and bread fills man's heart"** (Psalms 104:15); **bread is that which satisfies, wine does not satisfy. Rather,** this verse is not a proof; **wine has two** advantages, **it satisfies and gladdens. Bread,** however, **satisfies but does not gladden.**

אִי הָכִי נְבָרֵיךְ עֲלֵיהּ שָׁלֹשׁ בְּרָכוֹת! לָא קָבְעִי אֱינָשֵׁי סְעוּדָּתַיְיהוּ עִלָּוֵיהּ.

Since wine possesses all of these virtues, the Gemara asks: **If so, let us recite** the **three blessings** of Grace after Meals **over it** after drinking just as we do after eating bread. The Gemara answers: **People do not base their meals on** wine.

אֲמַר לֵיהּ רַב נַחְמָן בַּר יִצְחָק לְרָבָא: אִי קְבַע עִלָּוֵיהּ סְעוּדָּתֵיהּ מַאי? אֲמַר לֵיהּ: לִכְשֶׁיָּבֹא אֵלִיָּהוּ וְיֹאמַר אִי הָוֵי קְבִיעוּתָא, הַשְׁתָּא מִיהָא בָּטְלָה דַּעְתּוֹ אֵצֶל כׇּל אָדָם.

**Rav Naḥman bar Yitzḥak said to Rava: If one based his meal on it, what is the** ruling? Must he recite the Grace after Meals as he does after bread? He replied: **When Elijah comes**[B] **and says** whether or not **it can serve as the basis** for a meal, this will be resolved. **Nevertheless, now** until then, **his intention is** rendered **irrelevant**[B] **by** the opinions of **all other men** and he is not required to recite the complete Grace after Meals.

**HALAKHA**

**Over olive oil, one recites: Who creates fruit of the tree – שֶׁמֶן זַיִת מְבָרְכִין עָלָיו וכו׳:** One who drinks plain olive oil does not recite any blessing, as it is harmful. If he eats it with bread, he does not recite a blessing, as the blessing recited over the bread exempts it. If one drank it mixed with beet juice [*anigeron*] for medicinal purposes, e.g., because he has a sore throat, then the oil is primary and he recites: Who creates fruit of the tree. If he is not drinking it for medicinal purposes, but for his enjoyment alone, then the *anigeron* is primary and he recites: By whose word all things came to be, and thereby exempts the olive oil (Rambam *Sefer Ahava, Hilkhot Berakhot* 8:2; *Shulḥan Arukh, Oraḥ Ḥayyim* 202:4).

**One who vows that nourishment is forbidden to him – הַנּוֹדֵר מִן הַמָּזוֹן:** One who vowed that all nourishment is forbidden to him is prohibited from eating anything made of the five species of grain. However, if he vowed that anything that nourishes is forbidden to him, he is prohibited from eating anything other than salt and salt water (*Shulḥan Arukh, Yoreh De'a* 217:19).

**Wouldn't Rava drink wine all day on the eve of Passover – הֲוָה שָׁתֵי חַמְרָא כׇּל מַעֲלֵי יוֹמָא דְּפִסְחָא:** One is permitted to drink wine on the eve of Passover, as long as he drinks a lot, as per Rava's custom (*Shulḥan Arukh, Oraḥ Ḥayyim* 471:1).

**BACKGROUND**

**When Elijah comes – לִכְשֶׁיָּבֹא אֵלִיָּהוּ:** When Elijah comes, is a standard concept that appears in *halakha* with specific applications. It originates in the book of Ezra where an uncertainty is left unresolved "until there arose a priest with *Urim veTummim*" (2:63). Elijah does not come to establish new *halakhot*, but to resolve uncertainties that arose due to the lack of sufficient evidence to fully resolve the dilemma.

**His intention is rendered irrelevant – בָּטְלָה דַּעְתּוֹ:** When a person does something that people do not generally do, or he does so in a manner that is uncommon, he is described as one whose opinion is irrelevant. His action is considered aberrant and incomplete, even if he does so on a regular basis.

גּוּפָא: אָמַר רַב יְהוּדָה אָמַר שְׁמוּאֵל, וְכֵן אָמַר רַבִּי יִצְחָק אָמַר רַבִּי יוֹחָנָן: שֶׁמֶן זַיִת מְבָרְכִין עָלָיו ״בּוֹרֵא פְּרִי הָעֵץ״. הֵיכִי דָּמֵי? אִילֵימָא דְּקָא שָׁתֵי לֵיהּ מִשְׁתֶּה – אַוזּוּקֵי מַזִּיק לֵיהּ! דְּתַנְיָא: הַשּׁוֹתֶה שֶׁמֶן שֶׁל תְּרוּמָה – מְשַׁלֵּם אֶת הַקֶּרֶן וְאֵינוֹ מְשַׁלֵּם אֶת הַחוֹמֶשׁ, הַסָּךְ שֶׁמֶן שֶׁל תְּרוּמָה – מְשַׁלֵּם אֶת הַקֶּרֶן וּמְשַׁלֵּם אֶת הַחוֹמֶשׁ!

Previously, the Gemara cited the *halakha* that one recites the blessing: Who creates fruit of the tree, over olive oil. The Gemara discusses **the matter itself. Rav Yehuda said** that **Shmuel said, and so too Rabbi Yitzḥak said** that **Rabbi Yoḥanan said: One recites the blessing: Who creates fruit of the tree, over olive oil** just as he does over the fruit itself. **What are the circumstances? If you say that he drank it** plain, **it causes damage to** the drinker.[N] **As it was taught** in a *baraita*: **One who drinks oil of *teruma*,**[H] while unaware that it was *teruma*, **pays the principal and does not pay** the additional **fifth** which is the typical penalty for unintentional misuse of consecrated property, as in that case the individual is considered to have only damaged consecrated property without deriving benefit from it. **One who anoints** his body **with the oil of *teruma* pays the principal and pays the fifth,** as he derived benefit from it. Apparently, one who drinks oil derives no benefit and it even causes him damage.

אֶלָּא: דְּקָא אָכִיל לֵיהּ עַל יְדֵי פַּת. אִי הָכִי, הָוְיָא לֵיהּ פַּת עִיקָּר וְהוּא טָפֵל; וּתְנַן, זֶה הַכְּלָל: כֹּל שֶׁהוּא עִיקָּר וְעִמּוֹ טְפֵלָה – מְבָרֵךְ עַל הָעִיקָּר וּפוֹטֵר אֶת הַטְּפֵלָה! אֶלָּא: דְּקָא שָׁתֵי לֵיהּ עַל יְדֵי אַנִיגְרוֹן; דַּאֲמַר רַבָּה בַּר שְׁמוּאֵל: אַנִיגְרוֹן – מַיָּא דְּסִלְקָא, אַנְסִיגְרוֹן – מַיָּא

**Rather,** it is referring to a case where **he eats** the oil **by** dipping **bread** into it. **If so,** the **bread is primary and** the oil **secondary, and we learned** in a mishna: **This is the principle: Any** food **that is primary, and** is eaten **with** food that is **secondary,**[H] **one recites a blessing over the primary** food, and that blessing **exempts the secondary** from the requirement to recite a blessing before eating it. A blessing need only be recited over the bread, not over the oil. **Rather,** it is referring to a case **where he is drinking it by means of an *anigeron*, as Rabba bar Shmuel said: *Anigeron*[L] is water** in which a **beet** was boiled, ***ansigeron*[L]** is **the water**

Perek **VI**
Daf **36** Amud **a**

דְּכוּלְּהוּ שָׁלְקֵי.

in which **all boiled** vegetables were boiled. A certain amount of oil is added to *anigeron*.

אִם כֵּן, הָוֵה לֵיהּ אַנִיגְרוֹן עִיקָּר וְשֶׁמֶן טָפֵל. וּתְנַן, זֶה הַכְּלָל: כֹּל שֶׁהוּא עִיקָּר וְעִמּוֹ טְפֵלָה – מְבָרֵךְ עַל הָעִיקָּר וּפוֹטֵר אֶת הַטְּפֵלָה!

However, **if so,** here too, ***anigeron* is primary**[H] **and oil is secondary, and we learned** in a mishna: **This is the principle: Any** food **that is primary, and** it is eaten **with** food that is **secondary, one recites a blessing over the primary** food, and that blessing **exempts the secondary** from the requirement to recite a blessing before eating it. One need recite a blessing only over the *anigeron*.

הָכָא בְּמַאי עָסְקִינַן – בְּחוֹשֵׁשׁ בִּגְרוֹנוֹ. דְּתַנְיָא: הַחוֹשֵׁשׁ בִּגְרוֹנוֹ – לֹא יְעַרְעֶנּוּ בְּשֶׁמֶן תְּחִלָּה בְּשַׁבָּת, אֲבָל נוֹתֵן שֶׁמֶן הַרְבֵּה לְתוֹךְ אַנִיגְרוֹן וּבוֹלֵעַ.

The Gemara reconciles: **With what are we dealing here?** With **one who has a sore throat,** which he is treating with oil. **As it was taught** in a *baraita*: **One who has a sore throat should not,** ***ab initio***, **gargle oil on Shabbat**[H] for medicinal purposes, as doing so would violate the decree prohibiting the use of medicine on Shabbat. **However, he may,** even *ab initio*, **add a large amount of oil to the *anigeron* and swallow it.** Since it is common practice to swallow oil either alone or with a secondary ingredient like *anigeron* for medicinal purposes, in this case one recites: Who creates fruit of the tree.

פְּשִׁיטָא! – מַהוּ דְּתֵימָא; כֵּיוָן דִּלְרְפוּאָה קָא מְכַוֵּין – לָא לִבָרֵיךְ עֲלֵיהּ כְּלָל, קָא מַשְׁמַע לָן: כֵּיוָן דְּאִית לֵיהּ הֲנָאָה מִינֵּיהּ בָּעֵי בָּרוֹכֵי.

The Gemara challenges: **This is obvious** that one must recite a blessing. The Gemara responds: **Lest you say: Since he intends** to use it **for medicinal** purposes, **let him not recite a blessing over it at all,** as one does not recite a blessing before taking medicine. Therefore, **it teaches us** that, **since he derived pleasure from it,**[H] **he must recite a blessing** over it.

קִמְחָא דְחִיטֵּי – רַב יְהוּדָה אָמַר ״בּוֹרֵא פְּרִי הָאֲדָמָה״; וְרַב נַחְמָן אָמַר ״שֶׁהַכֹּל נִהְיָה בִּדְבָרוֹ״.

The Gemara clarifies: If one was eating plain **wheat flour,**[H] what blessing would he recite? **Rav Yehuda said** that one recites: **Who creates fruit of the ground, and Rav Naḥman said** that one recites: **By Whose word all things came to be.**

### NOTES

**It causes damage to the drinker – אַוזּוּקֵי מַזִּיק לֵיהּ:** One does not recite a blessing over self-inflicted injury, as a blessing is praise of God for His benevolence, and we do not offer thanks for damage (*Derush VeḤiddush*). Some explain this slightly differently, that one who drinks oil is not considered to be drinking the oil, but rather to be damaging the oil (*Alfei Menashe*).

### HALAKHA

**One who drinks oil of *teruma* – הַשּׁוֹתֶה שֶׁמֶן שֶׁל תְּרוּמָה:** One who drinks oil of *teruma* pays the principal and does not pay the additional fifth (Rambam *Sefer Zera'im*, *Hilkhot Teruma* 10:11).

**Any food that is primary, and is eaten with food that is secondary – כֹּל שֶׁהוּא עִיקָּר וְעִמּוֹ טְפֵלָה:** This applies when one food is the primary component of a meal and is eaten together with another food that is secondary. In addition, this applies both in cases where the foods are mixed and in cases where they are eaten separately but at the same time. Both before the meal and thereafter, one recites a blessing over the primary food and, thereby, exempts the secondary food (Rambam *Sefer Ahava*, *Hilkhot Berakhot* 3:5; *Shulḥan Arukh*, *Oraḥ Ḥayyim* 204:12).

### LANGUAGE

***Anigeron* – אַנִיגְרוֹן:** From the Greek οἰνόγαρον, *oinogaron*, meaning wine mixed with oil.

***Ansigeron* – אַנְסִיגְרוֹן:** Based on parallel texts and manuscripts, apparently the proper reading is *akhsigeron* from the Greek ὀξύγαρον, *oxugaron*, meaning wine vinegar into which small fish and various other food items are mixed.

### HALAKHA

***Anigeron* is primary – הָוֵה לֵיהּ אַנִיגְרוֹן עִיקָּר:** One who drinks oil mixed with beet juice for his own pleasure recites: By whose word all things came to be, because the beet juice is the primary ingredient. One who is suffering from a sore throat and drinks it for medicinal purposes, since the oil is then the primary ingredient, recites: Who creates fruits of the tree (Rambam *Sefer Ahava*, *Hilkhot Berakhot* 8:2; *Shulḥan Arukh*, *Oraḥ Ḥayyim* 202:4).

**One who has a sore throat…on Shabbat – הַחוֹשֵׁשׁ בִּגְרוֹנוֹ...בְּשַׁבָּת:** One who has a sore throat may not drink oil and keep it in his mouth, even if it is mixed with beet juice. However, he is permitted to swallow the oil. If it happens to alleviate his pain, that is fine. Some, however, prohibit doing so (*Baḥ*). In practice, it depends on the local custom at the time. When and where healthy people do not drink oil in that manner, it is prohibited (Rambam *Sefer Zemanim*, *Hilkhot Shabbat* 21:24; *Shulḥan Arukh*, *Oraḥ Ḥayyim* 328:32).

**Since he derived pleasure from it – כֵּיוָן דְּאִית לֵיהּ הֲנָאָה מִינֵּיהּ:** One must recite a blessing over medicine whose pleasant taste he enjoys (*Shulḥan Arukh*, *Oraḥ Ḥayyim* 204:8).

**Wheat flour – קִמְחָא דְחִיטֵּי:** Over wheat flour, whether finely ground or only partially ground, that tastes like wheat, one recites: By Whose word all things came to be, as per the opinion of Rav Naḥman, as eating flour is unusual (Rif). This is the opinion upon which the subsequent talmudic discussion is based (Rambam *Sefer Ahava*, *Hilkhot Berakhot* 3:2; *Shulḥan Arukh*, *Oraḥ Ḥayyim* 208:5).

אָמַר לֵיהּ רָבָא לְרַב נַחְמָן: לָא תִּפְלוֹג עֲלֵיהּ דְּרַב יְהוּדָה, דְּרַבִּי יוֹחָנָן וּשְׁמוּאֵל קָיְימִי כְּוָותֵיהּ; דְּאָמַר רַב יְהוּדָה אָמַר שְׁמוּאֵל, וְכֵן אָמַר רַבִּי יִצְחָק אָמַר רַבִּי יוֹחָנָן: שֶׁמֶן זַיִת – מְבָרְכִין עָלָיו ״בּוֹרֵא פְּרִי הָעֵץ״; אַלְמָא: אַף עַל גַּב דְּאִשְׁתַּנִּי – בְּמִלְּתֵיהּ קָאֵי; הָא נַמִי, אַף עַל גַּב דְּאִשְׁתַּנִּי – בְּמִלְּתֵיהּ קָאֵי.

**Rava said to Rav Naḥman: Do not disagree with Rav Yehuda, as Rabbi Yoḥanan and Shmuel hold in accordance with his** opinion, even though they addressed another topic. **As Rav Yehuda said** that **Shmuel said, and so too Rabbi Yitzḥak said** that **Rabbi Yoḥanan said: One recites the blessing: Who creates fruit of the tree, over olive oil. Consequently, even though** the olive **has changed** into olive oil, **the formula** of the blessing **remains as it was. This too, even though** the wheat **has changed** into flour, its blessing **remains as it was:** Who creates fruit of the ground.

מִי דָּמֵי! הָתָם – לֵית לֵיהּ עִלּוּיָא אַחֲרִינָא, הָכָא – אִית לֵיהּ עִלּוּיָא אַחֲרִינָא בְּפַת.

The Gemara responds: **Is it comparable? There,** the olive oil **has no** potential for **additional enhancement,** while **here,** the flour **has the** potential for **additional enhancement as bread.** Since oil is the olive's finished product, one should recite the same blessing over it as over the tree itself. Wheat flour, on the other hand, is used to bake bread, so the flour is a raw material for which neither the blessing over wheat nor the blessing over bread is appropriate. Only the blessing: By Whose word all things came to be is appropriate.

וְכִי אִית לֵיהּ עִלּוּיָא אַחֲרִינָא לָא מְבָרְכִינַן עֲלֵיהּ ״בּוֹרֵא פְּרִי הָאֲדָמָה״ אֶלָּא ״שֶׁהַכֹּל״?! וְהָא אָמַר רַבִּי זֵירָא אָמַר רַב מַתָּנָא אָמַר שְׁמוּאֵל: אַקְּרָא חַיָּיא וְקִמְחָא דִּשְׂעָרֵי מְבָרְכִינַן עֲלַיְיהוּ ״שֶׁהַכֹּל נִהְיָה בִּדְבָרוֹ״, מַאי לָאו, דְּחִיטֵּי – ״בּוֹרֵא פְּרִי הָאֲדָמָה״!

The Gemara asks: **When it has no** potential for **additional enhancement, one does not recite: Who creates fruit of the ground; rather** one recites: By Whose word **all things** came to be? **Didn't Rabbi Zeira say** that **Rav Mattana said** that **Shmuel said: Over a raw gourd**[B] **and over barley flour,**[H] **one recites the blessing: By Whose word all things came to be. What, is that not to say that over wheat** flour one recites: **Who creates fruit of the ground?** Over barley flour, which people do not typically eat, it is appropriate to recite: By Whose word all things came to be. Over wheat flour, it is appropriate to recite: Who creates fruit of the ground.

לָא, דְּחִיטֵּי נַמִי, ״שֶׁהַכֹּל נִהְיָה בִּדְבָרוֹ״.

This argument is rejected: **No,** one **also** recites: **By Whose word all things came to be,** over **wheat** flour.

וְלַשְׁמְעִינַן דְּחִיטֵּי וְכָל שֶׁכֵּן דִּשְׂעָרֵי!

The Gemara asks: **Then let** the Sages **teach us** that this *halakha* applies **with regard to wheat flour, and all the more so regarding barley** flour as well.

אִי אַשְׁמְעִינַן דְּחִיטֵּי – הֲוָה אָמִינָא: הָנֵי מִילֵּי דְּחִיטֵּי, אֲבָל דִּשְׂעָרֵי לָא לְבָרֵיךְ עֲלֵיהּ כְּלָל – קָא מַשְׁמַע לַן.

The Gemara responds: It was necessary to teach us that one must recite a blessing even before eating barley flour. **Had** the Sages **taught us** this *halakha* with regard to **wheat, I would have said: This applies** only with regard to **wheat** flour, **but** over **barley** flour, **let one not recite a blessing at all.** Therefore, **it teaches us** that one recites a blessing over barley flour.

וּמִי גָּרַע מִמֶּלַח וְזָמִית?! דִּתְנַן: עַל הַמֶּלַח וְעַל הַזָּמִית אוֹמֵר: ״שֶׁהַכֹּל נִהְיָה בִּדְבָרוֹ״! אִיצְטְרִיךְ, סָלְקָא דַּעְתָּךְ אָמִינָא: מֶלַח וְזָמִית – עֲבִיד אֱינָשׁ דְּשָׁדֵי לְפוּמֵיהּ, אֲבָל קִמְחָא דִּשְׂעָרֵי, הוֹאִיל וְקָשֶׁה לְקוּקְיָאנֵי – לָא לְבָרֵיךְ עֲלֵיהּ כְּלָל; קָא מַשְׁמַע לַן: כֵּיוָן דְּאִית לֵיהּ הֲנָאָה מִינֵּיהּ – בָּעֵי בָּרוֹכֵי.

The Gemara challenges this explanation. How could one have considered that possibility? **Is it inferior to salt and salt water [*zamit*]?**[HL] **As we learned** in a mishna that **over salt and salt water one recites: By Whose word all things came to be,** and all the more so it should be recited over barley flour. This question is rejected: Nevertheless, **it was necessary** to teach the *halakha* regarding barley flour, as **it might enter your mind to say:** Although **one** occasionally **places salt or salt water into his mouth, barley flour, which** is damaging to one who eats it **and causes intestinal worms, let one recite no blessing over it at all.** Therefore, **it teaches us, since one derives pleasure from it, he must recite a blessing.**

קוֹרָא – רַב יְהוּדָה אָמַר: ״בּוֹרֵא פְּרִי הָאֲדָמָה״; וּשְׁמוּאֵל אָמַר: ״שֶׁהַכֹּל נִהְיָה בִּדְבָרוֹ״.

Another dispute over the appropriate blessing is with regard to the **heart of palm [*kura*],**[H] which is a thin membrane covering young palm branches that was often eaten. **Rav Yehuda said** that one should recite: **Who creates fruit of the ground.** And **Shmuel,** Rav Yehuda's teacher **said** that one should recite: **By Whose word all things came to be.**

רַב יְהוּדָה אָמַר ״בּוֹרֵא פְּרִי הָאֲדָמָה״ – פֵּירָא הוּא, וּשְׁמוּאֵל אָמַר ״שֶׁהַכֹּל נִהְיָה בִּדְבָרוֹ״ – הוֹאִיל וְסוֹפוֹ לְהַקְשׁוֹת.

**Rav Yehuda said: Who creates fruit of the ground; it is a fruit. And Shmuel said: By Whose word all things came to be, since it will ultimately harden** and it is considered part of the tree, not a fruit.

אָמַר לֵיהּ שְׁמוּאֵל לְרַב יְהוּדָה: שִׁינָּנָא! כְּוָותָךְ מִסְתַּבְּרָא, דְּהָא צְנוֹן סוֹפוֹ לְהַקְשׁוֹת וּמְבָרְכִינַן עֲלֵיהּ ״בּוֹרֵא פְּרִי הָאֲדָמָה״. וְלָא הִיא, צְנוֹן נָטְעֵי אֱינָשֵׁי אַדַּעְתָּא דְּפוּגְלָא, דִּקְלָא – לָא נָטְעֵי אֱינָשֵׁי אַדַּעְתָּא דְּקוּרָא.

**Shmuel said to Rav Yehuda: *Shinnana*.**[B] **It is reasonable** to rule **in accordance with your** opinion,[N] as **a radish ultimately hardens** if left in the ground; nevertheless, one who eats it while it is soft **recites over it: Who creates fruit of the ground.** In any case, despite this praise, the Gemara states: **That is not so; people plant a radish with the soft** radish **in mind.** However, **people do not plant palm trees with the heart of palm in mind** and therefore it cannot be considered a fruit.

### BACKGROUND

**Gourd – קְרָא:** The gourd is trellised on branches and its fruits hang down. Also called the bottle gourd or *Lagenaria vulgaris*, the *kera* is a leafy summer vegetable of the gourd family. Usually, it grows extended on the ground, but at times it is trellised on trees. The greenish-white gourd produced by the plant is sizeable (40–50 cm long and 25–30 cm wide) and shaped like a jug or a bottle. The young fruit is generally eaten cooked and its seeds are eaten as dessert.

Trellised gourd

***Shinnana* – שִׁינָּנָא:** According to Rashi and others, *shinnana* means sharp or witty, and reflects the degree to which Shmuel respected his primary student. The *ge'onim*, however, explain that according to oral tradition, *shinnana* means big-toothed, and was a nickname for Rav Yehuda based on his appearance.

### HALAKHA

**Over a raw gourd and over barley flour – אַקְּרָא חַיָּיא וְקִמְחָא דִּשְׂעָרֵי:** One recites: By Whose word all things came to be, before eating a raw gourd and barley flour (Rambam *Sefer Ahava, Hilkhot Berakhot* 3:2; *Shulḥan Arukh, Oraḥ Ḥayyim* 204:1).

**Over salt and over salt water – עַל הַמֶּלַח וְעַל הַזָּמִית:** Over salt and salt water, one recites: By whose word all things came to be (Rambam *Sefer Ahava, Hilkhot Berakhot* 8:4; *Shulḥan Arukh, Oraḥ Ḥayyim* 204:1).

**Heart of palm – קוֹרָא:** A heart of palm is the soft branch that grows on the palm tree each year. One recites over it: By Whose word all things came to be, as per Shmuel, whose opinion is the basis for the discussion in the Gemara, despite the fact that he praised Rav Yehuda's opinion (Rambam *Sefer Ahava, Hilkhot Berakhot* 8:4; *Shulḥan Arukh, Oraḥ Ḥayyim* 204:1).

### LANGUAGE

**Salt water [*zamit*] – זָמִית:** From the Greek ζωμός, *zomos,* meaning soup or brine.

### NOTES

**It is reasonable to rule in accordance with your opinion – כְּוָותָךְ מִסְתַּבְּרָא:** Similar expressions of praise are found uttered by Sages with regard to positions contrary to their own. Nonetheless, it is conceivable that the one uttering the praise did not necessarily adopt that opinion. Every halakhic determination is based upon certain fundamental elements, clarified in the Gemara, from which a halakhic ruling emerges. There are often several considerations that lead to a particular conclusion. An expression of approval for one consideration, will not necessarily change one's opinion. In this case, Shmuel holds that the blessing is determined based upon the primary objective in planting the tree, and Rav Yehuda holds that the blessing is determined based upon its fitness for consumption. The proof for Rav Yehuda's opinion is ultimately rejected in favor of a more compelling principle.

וְכָל הֵיכָא דְּלָא נָטְעֵי אֱינָשֵׁי אַדַּעְתָּא דְּהָכִי – לָא מְבָרְכִינַן עֲלֵיהּ?! וַהֲרֵי צָלָף, דְּנָטְעֵי אֱינָשֵׁי אַדַּעְתָּא דְּפִרְחָא, וּתְנַן: עַל מִינֵי נִצְפָּה עַל הֶעָלִין וְעַל הַתְּמָרוֹת אוֹמֵר: "בּוֹרֵא פְּרִי הָאֲדָמָה", וְעַל הָאֶבְיוֹנוֹת וְעַל הַקַּפְרִיסִין אוֹמֵר: "בּוֹרֵא פְּרִי הָעֵץ"!

In response to this, the Gemara asks: **And whenever people do not plant with that** result **in mind, one does not recite a blessing over it?** What of the **caper-bush**[BH] **that people plant with their fruit in mind, and we learned** in a mishna **that with regard to the parts of the caper-bush [*nitzpa*], over the leaves and young fronds, one recites: Who creates fruit of the ground, and over the berries and buds he recites: Who creates fruit of the tree.** This indicates that even over leaves and various other parts of the tree that are secondary to the fruit, the blessing is: Who creates fruit of the ground, and not: By Whose word all things came to be.

אָמַר רַב נַחְמָן בַּר יִצְחָק: צָלָף – נָטְעֵי אֱינָשֵׁי אַדַּעְתָּא דְּשׁוּתָא, דִּקְלָא – לָא נָטְעֵי אֱינָשֵׁי אַדַּעְתָּא דְּקוּרָא. וְאַף עַל גַּב דְּקַלְּסֵיהּ שְׁמוּאֵל לְרַב יְהוּדָה, הִלְכְתָא כְּוָותֵיהּ דִּשְׁמוּאֵל.

**Rav Naḥman bar Yitzḥak said** that there is still a difference: **Caper-bushes, people plant** them **with** their **leaves in mind; palm trees, people do not plant** them **with** the **heart of palm in mind.** Therefore, no proof may be brought from the *halakha* in the case of the caper-bush to the *halakha* in the case of the of the palm. The Gemara concludes: **Although Shmuel praised Rav Yehuda, the *halakha* is in accordance with** the opinion of **Shmuel.**

אָמַר רַב יְהוּדָה אָמַר רַב: צָלָף שֶׁל עָרְלָה בְּחוּצָה לָאָרֶץ – זוֹרֵק אֶת הָאֶבְיוֹנוֹת וְאוֹכֵל אֶת הַקַּפְרִיסִין. לְמֵימְרָא, דְּאֶבְיוֹנוֹת פֵּירֵי וְקַפְרִיסִין לָאו פֵּירֵי?! וּרְמִינְהוּ: עַל מִינֵי נִצְפָּה עַל הֶעָלִים וְעַל הַתְּמָרוֹת אוֹמֵר "בּוֹרֵא פְּרִי הָאֲדָמָה", וְעַל הָאֶבְיוֹנוֹת וְעַל הַקַּפְרִיסִין אוֹמֵר "בּוֹרֵא פְּרִי הָעֵץ"!

Incidental to this discussion, the Gemara cites an additional *halakha* concerning the caper-bush. **Rav Yehuda said** that **Rav said: A caper-bush during the first three years of its growth [*orla*]**[H] **outside of Eretz** Yisrael, when its fruits are prohibited by rabbinic and not Torah law, **one throws out the berries,** the primary fruit, **but eats the buds.** The Gemara raises the question: **Is that to say that the berries are fruit** of the caper, **and the bud is not fruit? The Gemara raises a contradiction** from what we learned in the mishna cited above: **With regard to the parts of the caper-bush [*nitzpa*], over the leaves and young fronds, one recites: Who creates fruit of the ground, and over the berries, and buds he recites: Who creates fruit of the tree.** Obviously, the buds are also considered the fruit of the caper-bush.

הוּא דְּאָמַר כְּרַבִּי עֲקִיבָא; דִּתְנַן, רַבִּי אֱלִיעֶזֶר אוֹמֵר: צָלָף – מִתְעַשֵּׂר תְּמָרוֹת וְאֶבְיוֹנוֹת וְקַפְרִיסִין. רַבִּי עֲקִיבָא אוֹמֵר: אֵין מִתְעַשֵּׂר אֶלָּא אֶבְיוֹנוֹת בִּלְבַד, מִפְּנֵי שֶׁהוּא פְּרִי.

The Gemara responds: Rav's **statement is in accordance with** the opinion of **Rabbi Akiva, as we learned** in a mishna that **Rabbi Eliezer says: A caper-bush is tithed**[H] **from** its component parts, **its young fronds, berries and buds,** as all these are considered its fruit. **And Rabbi Akiva says: Only the berries alone are tithed, because it** alone **is** considered **fruit.** It was in accordance with this opinion, that Rav prohibited only the eating of the berries during the caper-bush's years of *orla*.

וְנֵימָא: "הֲלָכָה כְּרַבִּי עֲקִיבָא"! – אִי אָמַר הֲלָכָה כְּרַבִּי עֲקִיבָא, הֲוָה אָמִינָא – אֲפִילּוּ בָּאָרֶץ, קָא מַשְׁמַע לַן: כָּל הַמֵּיקֵל בָּאָרֶץ – הֲלָכָה כְּמוֹתוֹ בְּחוּצָה לָאָרֶץ, אֲבָל בָּאָרֶץ לֹא.

The Gemara asks: If this is the case, why did Rav issue what seemed to be an independent ruling regarding *orla*? **He should have** simply **said: The *halakha* is in accordance with** the opinion of **Rabbi Akiva,** from which we could have drawn a practical halakhic conclusion regarding *orla* as well. The Gemara responds: **Had Rav said: The *halakha* is in accordance with** the opinion of **Rabbi Akiva, I would have said** that the *halakha* is in accordance with his opinion **even in Eretz** Yisrael. Therefore, **he teaches us** by stating the entire *halakha*, that there is a principle: **Anyone who is lenient** in a dispute with regard to the *halakhot* of *orla* **in Eretz** Yisrael,[N] **the *halakha* is in accordance with his** opinion **outside of Eretz** Yisrael, **but not in Eretz** Yisrael.

### HALAKHA

**Caper-bush – צָלָף:** One recites: Who creates fruits of the ground, over the leaves, young fronds, and even the buds of the caper-bush. With regard to the buds, we rely on the discussion in the Gemara that concludes that the buds are not part of the fruit. However, one recites: Who creates fruits of the tree, over the berries, as they are the fruit of the caper-bush (Rambam *Sefer Ahava, Hilkhot Berakhot* 8:6; *Shulḥan Arukh, Oraḥ Ḥayyim* 202:6).

**A caper-bush during the first three years of its growth [*orla*] – צָלָף שֶׁל עָרְלָה:** In Eretz Yisrael, the berries, buds, and young fronds are all prohibited due to *orla*, since they are all edible. Outside of Eretz Yisrael, since the most lenient opinions regarding the laws of *orla* in Eretz Yisrael are applied, only the berries of the caper bush are prohibited (Rambam *Sefer Zera'im, Hilkhot Ma'aser Sheni VeNeta Revai* 10:3; *Shulḥan Arukh, Oraḥ Ḥayyim* 202:6, *Yoreh De'a* 294:3).

**A caper-bush is tithed – צָלָף מִתְעַשֵּׂר:** Only the berries of the caper-bush need to be tithed, unless he planted it with the express intention of eating the fronds (Rambam *Sefer Zera'im, Hilkhot Terumot* 2:4).

### NOTES

**Anyone who is lenient in Eretz Yisrael – כָּל הַמֵּיקֵל בָּאָרֶץ:** The principle is that if one is lenient with regard to certain *halakhot* in Eretz Yisrael, the *halakha* is in accordance with his opinion outside of Eretz Yisrael. This is based upon the principle that in cases of uncertainty in matters of rabbinic legislation, one is lenient. According to most opinions, the obligation to fulfill land-based mitzvot outside of Eretz Yisrael is by rabbinic law and, therefore, one should be lenient in every dispute. This is true all the more so when it is based on two rabbinic pronouncements, where a rabbinic decree is issued with regard to a rabbinic ordinance.

### BACKGROUND

**Caper-bush – צָלָף:** The most common species of caper-bush in Israel is the thorny caper-bush (*Capparis spinosa*), a thorny, deciduous bush growing to a height of a meter and a half. Its rounded leaves range in color from purple to green. There is a pair of thorns alongside each leaf. The caper-bush has large white flowers, approximately 6 cm in diameter, with purple stamens.

The buds of the caper-bush, the *kaprisin,* from the Greek **κάππαρις**, *capparis*, meaning caper-bush or fruit of the caper-bush, are the buds of flowers that have not yet bloomed. These buds are pickled and eaten.

These buds open into new flowers on a daily basis, are then pollinated and wither on that same day. The ripe fruit, or berries of the caper-bush, the *avyona*, is similar in shape to a date or small squash, and grows to 6 cm.

In the Mediterranean region, e.g., in Provence and Greece, the caper-bush is grown primarily for its pickled buds.

The young fronds are apparently the caper-bush's young, purple-green branches and their leaves, which in ancient times were pickled and eaten. They are called *shuta* in Aramaic.

Botanically, the fruit of the caper-bush is the berry, which is generally eaten pickled, even today.

Caper-bush

Buds and the flower of the caper-bush

Fruit of the caper-bush

וְנֵימָא: הֲלָכָה כְּרַבִּי עֲקִיבָא בְּחוּצָה לָאָרֶץ, דְּכָל הַמֵּיקֵל בָּאָרֶץ – הֲלָכָה כְּמוֹתוֹ בְּחוּצָה לָאָרֶץ! – אִי אָמַר הָכִי, הֲוָה אָמֵינָא: הָנֵי מִילֵּי – גַּבֵּי מַעְשַׂר אִילָן, דְּבָאָרֶץ גּוּפָא מִדְּרַבָּנַן, אֲבָל גַּבֵּי עׇרְלָה דְּבָאָרֶץ מִדְּאוֹרָיְיתָא – אֵימָא בְּחוּצָה לָאָרֶץ נָמֵי נִגְזוֹר, קָא מַשְׁמַע לַן.

The Gemara questions this: If so, then **let** Rav **say: The *halakha* is in accordance with** the opinion of **Rabbi Akiva outside of Eretz** Yisrael **as anyone who is lenient** in a dispute with regard to the *halakhot* of *orla* **in Eretz** Yisrael, **the *halakha* is in accordance with his** opinion **outside of Eretz** Yisrael. The Gemara answers: **Had he said that, I would have said: That only applies with regard to the tithing of trees** which even **in Eretz** Yisrael **itself is an obligation by rabbinic law; but with regard to *orla*,** which is prohibited **in Eretz** Yisrael **by Torah law, say that we should issue a decree** prohibiting *orla* **even outside of Eretz** Yisrael. Therefore, **he teaches us** that even with regard to *orla* the *halakha* is in accordance with the opinion of Rabbi Akiva.

רָבִינָא אַשְׁכְּחֵיהּ לְמָר בַּר רַב אַשִׁי דְּקָא זָרֵיק אֲבִיּוֹנוֹת וְקָאָכֵיל קַפְרִיסִין. אָמַר לֵיהּ: מַאי דַּעְתָּךְ – כְּרַבִּי עֲקִיבָא דְּמֵיקֵל, וְלַעֲבֵיד מָר כְּבֵית שַׁמַּאי דְּמַקִּילִי טְפֵי! דִּתְנַן: צָלָף, בֵּית שַׁמַּאי אוֹמְרִים: כִּלְאַיִם בַּכֶּרֶם, וּבֵית הִלֵּל אוֹמְרִים: אֵין כִּלְאַיִם בַּכֶּרֶם, אֵלּוּ וָאֵלּוּ מוֹדִים שֶׁחַיָּיב בְּעׇרְלָה.

On this topic, the Gemara relates: **Ravina found Mar bar Rav Ashi throwing away the berries and eating the buds** of an *orla* caper-bush. Ravina **said to** Mar bar Rav Ashi: **What is your opinion,** that you are eating the buds? If it is **in accordance with** the opinion of **Rabbi Akiva, who is lenient, then you should act in accordance with** the opinion of **Beit Shammai, who are even more lenient. As we learned** in a mishna with regard to the laws of forbidden mixtures of diverse kinds that **Beit Shammai say: A caper-bush is** considered **a diverse kind in the vineyard,** as it is included in the prohibition against planting vegetables in a vineyard. **Beit Hillel say:** A caper-bush is **not** considered **a diverse kind in a vineyard.** Nevertheless, **these and those,** Beit Shammai and Beit Hillel, **agree** that the caper-bush is **obligated in** the prohibition of ***orla.***

הָא גּוּפָא קַשְׁיָא! אָמְרַתְּ צָלָף, בֵּית שַׁמַּאי אוֹמְרִים: כִּלְאַיִם בַּכֶּרֶם, אַלְמָא מִין יָרָק הוּא, וַהֲדַר תָּנֵי: אֵלּוּ וָאֵלּוּ מוֹדִים שֶׁחַיָּיב בְּעׇרְלָה, אַלְמָא מִין אִילָן הוּא!

Before dealing with the problem posed by Ravina to Mar bar Rav Ashi the Gemara notes an internal contradiction in this mishna. **This mishna itself is problematic: You said that Beit Shammai say: A caper-bush is** considered **a diverse kind in a vineyard;**[H] **apparently,** they hold that **it is a type of vegetable** bush, **and then you taught: These and those,** Beit Shammai and Beit Hillel, **agree** that the caper-bush is **obligated in** the prohibition of ***orla*; apparently, it is a type of tree.**

הָא לָא קַשְׁיָא; בֵּית שַׁמַּאי סְפוּקֵי מְסַפְּקָא לְהוּ, וְעָבְדִי הָכָא לְחוּמְרָא וְהָכָא לְחוּמְרָא. מִכׇּל מָקוֹם, לְבֵית שַׁמַּאי הֲוָה לֵיהּ סְפֵק עׇרְלָה, וּתְנַן: סְפֵק עׇרְלָה בְּאֶרֶץ יִשְׂרָאֵל – אָסוּר, וּבְסוּרְיָא – מוּתָּר, וּבְחוּצָה לָאָרֶץ – יוֹרֵד

The Gemara responds: This is **not difficult; Beit Shammai are uncertain** whether the caper-bush is a vegetable bush or a tree, **and here,** regarding diverse kinds, **they act stringently and here,** regarding *orla*, **they act stringently. In any case, according to Beit Shammai** the caper-bush has the status of **uncertain *orla*,** and **we learned** the consensus *halakha* in a mishna: **Uncertain *orla***[H] **in Eretz Yisrael is forbidden to eat, and in Syria it is permitted,** and we are not concerned about its uncertain status.[N] **Outside of Eretz** Yisrael, the gentile owner of a field **may go down** into his field

### HALAKHA

A caper-bush…in a vineyard – צָלָף...בַּכֶּרֶם: The caper-bush is considered a tree and therefore may be planted in a vineyard, as per the opinion of Beit Hillel (Rambam *Sefer Zera'im, Hilkhot Kilayim* 5:20; *Shulḥan Arukh, Yoreh De'a* 296:15).

Uncertain *orla* – סְפֵק עׇרְלָה: A vineyard, in which there are both *orla* vines and permissible vines and the owner sells grapes from that vineyard; in Eretz Yisrael, one may not eat those grapes. In Syria, however, one is permitted to purchase grapes from the owner of that vineyard as long as he does not know that they are from that vineyard; assuming, of course, that he owns additional vineyards. Outside of Eretz Yisrael and Syria, even if he knows that the grapes are from that vineyard, the grapes are permitted, as long as he did not see that the grapes were picked from the *orla* trees. Grapes from a vineyard outside of Eretz Yisrael, with regard to which there is uncertainty whether or not the vines are *orla*, are certainly permitted, in accordance with the mishna in *Orla* (Rambam *Sefer Kedusha, Hilkhot Ma'akhalot Assurot* 10:11; *Shulḥan Arukh, Yoreh De'a* 294:9).

### NOTES

Eretz Yisrael and Syria – אֶרֶץ יִשְׂרָאֵל וְסוּרְיָא: In the context of land-based mitzvot, there exists an intermediate domain that is neither considered as Eretz Yisrael nor as outside of Eretz Yisrael, i.e., Syria. Halakhically, Syria constitutes the land conquered by King David in Aram. Had these conquests taken place after the conquest of the entire Eretz Yisrael in the promised borders, Syria would have been annexed and considered halakhically as an integral part of Eretz Yisrael. However, since these conquests took place before the conquest was complete, they were only temporarily considered part of Eretz Yisrael. Furthermore, there was no concentrated Jewish settlement there after the return to Zion from Babylonia. Therefore, Syria remained a halakhically intermediate domain.

Perek **VI**
Daf **36** Amud **b**

וְלוֹקֵחַ, וּבִלְבַד שֶׁלֹּא יִרְאֶנּוּ לוֹקֵט!

**and take** from the *orla* fruit, and **as long as** the Jew **does not see him gather** it, he may purchase the fruit from the gentile. If so, then outside of Eretz Yisrael, one may act in accordance with the opinion of Beit Shammai who hold that the caper-bush has the status of uncertain *orla*, and eat even the berries without apprehension.

רַבִּי עֲקִיבָא בִּמְקוֹם רַבִּי אֱלִיעֶזֶר עָבְדִינַן כְּוָתֵיהּ, וּבֵית שַׁמַּאי בִּמְקוֹם בֵּית הִלֵּל אֵינָהּ מִשְׁנָה.

The Gemara answers: The general rule that outside of Eretz Yisrael one acts in accordance with the lenient opinion in a dispute within Eretz Yisrael applies when **Rabbi Akiva** expresses a more lenient opinion **in place of Rabbi Eliezer,** and **we act in accordance with his** opinion. **And** however, when **Beit Shammai** express an opinion **where Beit Hillel** disagree, their opinion is considered as if it were **not** in the **mishna,**[B] and is completely disregarded.

וְתִיפּוֹק לֵיהּ דְּנַעֲשָׂה שׁוֹמֵר לַפְּרִי, וְרַחֲמָנָא אָמַר: ״וַעֲרַלְתֶּם עׇרְלָתוֹ אֶת פִּרְיוֹ״ – אֶת הַטָּפֵל לְפִרְיוֹ, וּמַאי נִיהוּ – שׁוֹמֵר לַפְּרִי!

The Gemara approaches this matter from a different perspective: **Let us derive** the *halakha* that buds are included in the prohibition of *orla* from the fact that the bud **serves as protection for the fruit,**[N] **and the Torah says:** "When you enter the land and plant any tree for food **you shall regard its fruit [*et piryo*] as *orla*"** (Leviticus 19:23), and *et piryo* is interpreted to mean **that which is secondary to the fruit. What is that? That** section of the plant **which is protection for the fruit.** The buds should be prohibited as *orla*, since they protect the fruit.

### BACKGROUND

When Beit Shammai express an opinion where Beit Hillel disagree, their opinion is considered as if it were not in the mishna – בֵּית שַׁמַּאי בִּמְקוֹם בֵּית הִלֵּל אֵינָהּ מִשְׁנָה: The reason for this rejection is that, in general, a tannaitic dispute is a disagreement with regard to details, and the decision is reached based on the judgment of the Sages of that particular generation. Consequently, the opinion that was not accepted was also not completely rejected. This is not the case when Beit Shammai articulate an opinion fundamentally different than the opinion of Beit Hillel. When that position is rejected, there is no room for further discussion.

### NOTES

Protection for the fruit – שׁוֹמֵר לַפְּרִי: In the framework of the laws of ritual impurity of foods, the Sages dealt with different aspects of the precise determination of what constitutes food as well as determining which parts that, in and of themselves, are not edible that can nevertheless be considered as food. In general, there are two concepts: Handle and protection. The handle is not food but is used in order to hold the fruit. Protection is deemed as fruit, since the fruit cannot survive for any length of time without it.

אָמַר רָבָא: הֵיכָא אָמְרִינַן דְּנַעֲשָׂה שׁוֹמֵר לַפְּרִי – הֵיכָא דְּאִיתֵיהּ בֵּין בְּתָלוּשׁ בֵּין בִּמְחוּבָּר, הָכָא – בִּמְחוּבָּר אִיתֵיהּ, בְּתָלוּשׁ לֵיתֵיהּ.

**Rava said: Where do we say** that a section of the plant **becomes protection for the fruit?** That is specifically **when it exists both when** the fruit **is detached** from the tree **and when it is** still **connected** to the tree. However, **here, it exists when** the fruit **is connected** to the tree, **but when it is detached it does not,** and since the protection falls off of the fruit when it is picked, it is no longer considered protection.

אֵיתִיבֵיהּ אַבָּיֵי: פִּיטְמָא שֶׁל רִמּוֹן מִצְטָרֶפֶת, וְהַנֵּץ שֶׁלּוֹ אֵין מִצְטָרֵף; מִדְּקָאָמַר ״הַנֵּץ שֶׁלּוֹ אֵין מִצְטָרֵף״, אַלְמָא דְּלָאו אוֹכֶל הוּא, וּתְנַן גַּבֵּי עָרְלָה: קְלִיפֵּי רִמּוֹן וְהַנֵּץ שֶׁלּוֹ, קְלִיפֵּי אֱגוֹזִים וְהַגַּרְעִינִין – חַיָּיבִין בְּעָרְלָה!

**Abaye raised a challenge** based on what we learned with regard to the *halakhot* of ritual impurity: **The crown of a pomegranate joins** together with the pomegranate as a unified entity with regard to calculating the requisite size in order to become ritually impure.[H] **And its flower,**[B] however, **does not join** together with the pomegranate in that calculation. **From the fact that it says** that **the pomegranate's flower does not join, consequently** the flower is secondary to the fruit and **is not** considered **food. And we learned** in a mishna regarding the laws of *orla*: **The rinds of a pomegranate and its flower, nutshells, and pits** of all kinds, **are** all **obligated in** the prohibition of ***orla***. This indicates that the criteria dictating what is considered protection of a fruit and what is considered the fruit itself with regard to ritual impurity, are not the same criteria used with regard to *orla*, as is illustrated by the case of the pomegranate flower. Therefore, even if the buds are not regarded as protecting the fruit with regard to ritual impurity, they may still be considered fruit with regard to *orla*.

אֶלָּא אָמַר רָבָא: הֵיכָא אָמְרִינַן דְּנַעֲשָׂה לְהוּ שׁוֹמֵר לְפֵירֵי – הֵיכָא דְּאִיתֵיהּ בִּשְׁעַת גְּמַר פֵּירָא, הַאי קַפְרֵס לֵיתֵיהּ בִּשְׁעַת גְּמַר פֵּירָא.

**Rather, Rava said** another explanation: **Where do we say** that a section of the plant **becomes protection for the fruit? Where it exists when the fruit is ripe. This bud does not exist when the fruit is ripe,** because it falls off beforehand.

אִינִי?! וְהָאֲמַר רַב נַחְמָן אָמַר רַבָּה בַּר אֲבוּהּ: הָנֵי מַתְחַלֵי דְּעָרְלָה – אֲסִירִי, הוֹאִיל וְנַעֲשׂוּ שׁוֹמֵר לְפֵירֵי; וְשׁוֹמֵר לְפֵירֵי אֵימַת הָוֵי – בְּכוּפְרָא, וְקָא קָרֵי לֵיהּ שׁוֹמֵר לְפֵירֵי!

The Gemara challenges this explanation as well: **Is that so? Didn't Rav Naḥman** say that **Rabba bar Avuh said: Those *orla* date coverings are prohibited, because they became protection for the fruit.**[H] **And when do** these coverings serve as **protection for the fruit? When the fruit is still young; and he,** nevertheless, **calls them protection for the fruit.** This indicates that in order to be considered protection for the fruit it need not remain until the fruit is fully ripened. The question remains: Why are the buds not accorded the same status as the berries of the caper-bush?

רַב נַחְמָן סְבַר לַהּ כְּרַבִּי יוֹסֵי; דִּתְנַן, רַבִּי יוֹסֵי אוֹמֵר: סְמָדַר – אָסוּר מִפְּנֵי שֶׁהוּא פְּרִי, וּפְלִיגִי רַבָּנַן עֲלֵיהּ.

The Gemara explains that **Rav Naḥman held** in accordance with the opinion of **Rabbi Yosei, as we learned** in a mishna that **Rabbi Yosei says: The grape-bud,**[H] i.e., a cluster of grapes in its earliest stage, immediately after the flowers dropped from the vine, **is prohibited** due to *orla*, **because it is** already considered **a fruit.** According to this opinion, even the date coverings that exist in the earliest stage of the ripening process are nevertheless considered protection for the fruit and prohibited due to *orla*. **The Rabbis disagree with him,** explaining that fruit at that stage is not considered fruit; and, therefore, the date coverings and caper-bush buds are not considered protection for the fruit and are not prohibited due to *orla*.

מַתְקִיף לַהּ רַב שִׁימִי מִנְּהַרְדְּעָא: וּבִשְׁאָר אִילָנֵי מִי פְּלִיגִי רַבָּנַן עֲלֵיהּ?! וְהָתְנַן: מֵאֵימָתַי אֵין קוֹצְצִין אֶת הָאִילָנוֹת בַּשְּׁבִיעִית? בֵּית שַׁמַּאי אוֹמְרִים: כָּל הָאִילָנוֹת מִשֶּׁיּוֹצִיאוּ; וּבֵית הִלֵּל אוֹמְרִים: הֶחָרוּבִין מִשֶּׁיְּשַׁרְשְׁרוּ, וְהַגְּפָנִים מִשֶּׁיְּגָרְעוּ וְהַזֵּיתִים מִשֶּׁיָּנִיצוּ, וּשְׁאָר כָּל הָאִילָנוֹת – מִשֶּׁיּוֹצִיאוּ;

**Rav Shimi of Neharde'a strongly objects to this *halakha*: Do the Rabbis disagree with** the opinion of Rabbi Yosei **with regard to** the fruits **of all other trees** besides grapes, that even in the very first stage of ripening, they are considered fruit? **Didn't we learn** in a mishna: With regard to fruit, which grows during the Sabbatical year, the Torah says: "And the Shabbat of the land shall be to you for eating" (Leviticus 25:6). The Sages inferred, for eating, and not for loss. Because one is prohibited from discarding fruit grown during the Sabbatical year, the question is raised: **From when may one no** longer **cut trees during the Sabbatical year** as he thereby damages the fruit? **Beit Shammai say: All trees, from when** the blossoms fall off and **fruit** begins to **emerge** in its earliest stage. **And Beit Hillel say:** There is a distinction between different types of trees. **Carob trees** may not be cut **from when they** form **chains** of carobs,[H] **vines** may not be cut ***misheyegaru***, explained below, **olives from when they blossom, and all other trees from when** fruit **emerges.**

## BACKGROUND

**The crown of a pomegranate and its flower – רִמּוֹן וָנֵץ:** The flower [*netz*] of the pomegranate is a name given to the stamens found in the crown of the fruit. The flower, which is a type of cover for the crown is not considered part of the pomegranate at all. However, that is not the case with regard to the crown itself, as its removal is liable to cause substantial damage to the pomegranate, to the point that it will fall from the tree.

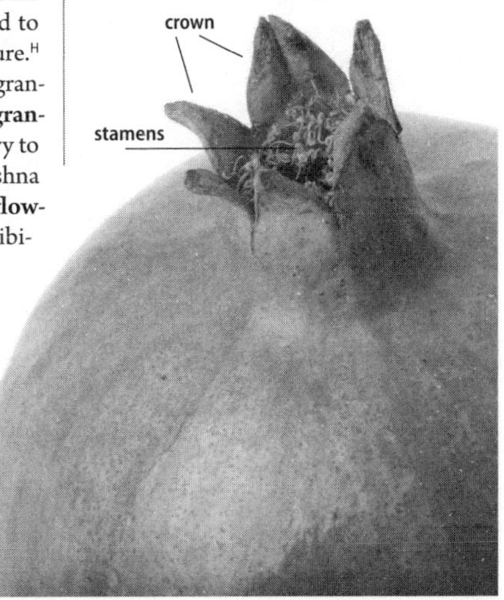

Pomegranate

## HALAKHA

**Parts of a pomegranate that join together, with regard to calculating the requisite size in order to become ritually impure – צֵירוּף חֶלְקֵי הָרִימּוֹן לְשִׁיעוּר לְעִנְיַן טוּמְאָה:** With regard to the ritual impurity of food, the crown of the pomegranate joins together with the pomegranate in calculating the requisite measure, but its flower does not (Rambam *Sefer Tahara, Hilkhot Tumat Okhelin* 5:21).

**A protector of the fruit with regard to *orla* – שׁוֹמֵר לַפְּרִי לְעִנְיַן עָרְלָה:** The peels that protect a fruit, as well as pits and blossoms, have the same legal status as the fruit with regard to *orla* (*Shulḥan Arukh, Yoreh De'a* 294:1).

**Grape-bud – סְמָדַר:** The grape-bud does not have the legal status of a fruit with regard to *orla* and fourth-year produce (Rambam *Sefer Zera'im, Hilkhot Ma'aser Sheni VeNeta Reva'i* 9:13; *Shulḥan Arukh, Yoreh De'a* 294:1).

**Carob trees from when they form chains of carobs – הֶחָרוּבִין מִשֶּׁיְּשַׁרְשְׁרוּ:** The prohibition to destroy fruits of the Sabbatical year applies to carobs when they form chains, as per the opinion of Beit Hillel. This leads to the conclusion that, at that stage, they are considered fruits and one recites over them: Who creates fruit of the tree (Rema). Others say that one cannot derive the *halakha* with regard to the appropriate blessing from the *halakha* with regard to the Sabbatical year. The *Magen Avraham* ruled that one recites: Who creates fruit of the ground, due to the uncertainty. If they have a bitter taste, one recites no blessing at all (*Mishna Berura*; Rambam *Sefer Zera'im, Hilkhot Shemitta VeYovel* 5:18; *Shulḥan Arukh, Oraḥ Ḥayyim* 202:2).

HALAKHA

**The blessing over peppers – בִּרְכַּת פִּלְפְּלִים:** One does not recite a blessing over dry peppers, as they are not usually eaten. Over damp, fresh peppers one recites: Who creates fruit of the ground, as they are only eaten dry in mixtures with other foods (*Magen Avraham*; Rambam *Sefer Ahava, Hilkhot Berakhot* 8:7; *Shulḥan Arukh, Oraḥ Ḥayyim* 202:2, 16, 18).

**One who chews peppers on Yom Kippur – כָּס פִּלְפְּלֵי בְּיוֹמָא דְכִפּוּרֵי:** One who eats dried peppers or ginger on Yom Kippur is not liable, as that is not the way they are usually eaten. One is liable for eating damp, fresh peppers (Rambam *Sefer Ahava, Hilkhot Berakhot* 8:7, *Sefer Zemanim, Hilkhot Shevitat Asor* 2:6; *Shulḥan Arukh, Oraḥ Ḥayyim* 202:2, 16, 18).

**The blessing over ginger – בִּרְכַּת זַנְגְּבִיל:** Over fresh ginger consumed for one's enjoyment, one recites: Who creates fruit of the ground. Dry ginger is exempt from a blessing, in accordance with the opinion of Rava (Rambam *Sefer Ahava, Hilkhot Berakhot* 8:7; *Shulḥan Arukh, Oraḥ Ḥayyim* 202:16, 18).

BACKGROUND

**Ginger – זַנְגְּבִילָא:** Ginger is the rhizome of the plant *Zingiber officinale* from the *Zingiberaccae* family. Ginger is a perennial plant with annual leafy stems, which grows to approximately 1 m (3–4 ft) in height. It produces clusters of white and pink flower buds that bloom into yellow flowers. Originally from India, it spread to neighboring countries as well. Dried ginger roots are used as a spice in baking and in the production of wines and other alcoholic beverages.

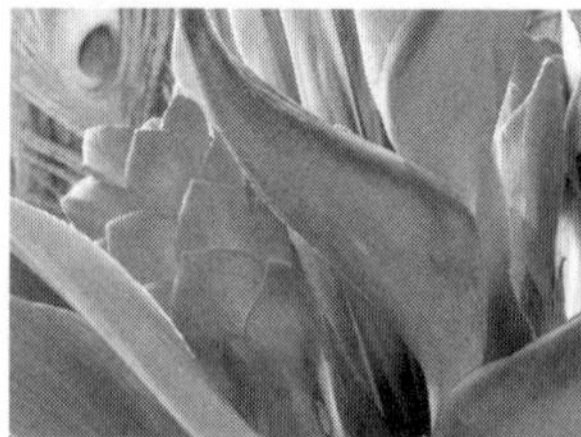

Ginger plant

וְאָמַר רַב אַסִי: הוּא בּוֹסֶר, הוּא גָּרוּעַ, הוּא פּוֹל הַלָּבָן. פּוֹל הַלָּבָן סָלְקָא דַעְתָּךְ?! אֶלָּא אֵימָא: שִׁיעוּרוֹ כְּפוֹל הַלָּבָן. מַאן שָׁמְעַתְּ לֵיהּ דְּאָמַר: בּוֹסֶר – אִין, סְמָדַר – לָא, רַבָּנַן, וְקָתָנֵי: שְׁאָר כָּל הָאִילָנוֹת מִשֶּׁיּוֹצִיאוּ!

**And Rav Asi said:** *Sheyegaru* in our mishna is to be understood: **It is an unripe grape, it is a grape kernel, it is a white bean.** Before this is even explained, the Gemara expresses its astonishment: **Does it enter your mind** that the grape is, at any stage, **a white bean? Rather, say: Its size,** that of an unripe grape, is equivalent to the size **of a white bean.** In any case, **whom did you hear that said: An unripe grape, yes,** is considered fruit, while **a grape-bud, no,** is not considered fruit? Wasn't it **the Rabbis** who disagree with Rabbi Yosei, **and it is taught** that, according to these Sages, one is forbidden to cut **all other trees from when** fruit **emerges.** This indicates that even they agree that from the very beginning of the ripening process, the fruit is forbidden due to *orla*. The question remains: Why are the buds permitted?

אֶלָּא אָמַר רָבָא: הֵיכָא אָמְרִינַן דְּהָוֵי שׁוֹמֵר לִפְרִי – הֵיכָא דְּכִי שָׁקְלַתְּ לֵיהּ לְשׁוֹמֵר מָיֵית פֵּירָא, הָכָא – כִּי שָׁקְלַתְּ לֵיהּ לָא מָיֵית פֵּירָא.

**Rather, Rava said** a different explanation: **Where do we say** that a section of the plant **becomes protection for the fruit? Where if you remove the protection, the fruit dies. Here,** in the case of the caper-bush, **when you remove** the bud, **the fruit does not die.**

הֲוָה עוּבְדָּא וְשַׁקְלוּהּ לְנֵץ דְּרִמּוֹנָא – וְיָבֵשׁ רִמּוֹנָא, וְשַׁקְלוּהּ לְפִרְחָא דְּבִיטִיתָא – וְאִיקַּיֵּים בִּיטִיתָא.

In fact, **there was an incident and they removed the flower of a pomegranate, and the pomegranate withered. And they removed the flower of the fruit of a caper-bush and the fruit of the caper-bush survived.** Therefore, buds are not considered protection for the fruit.

וְהִלְכְתָא כְּמָר בַּר רַב אַשִׁי, דְּזָרֵיק אֶת הָאֶבְיוֹנוֹת וְאָכֵיל אֶת הַקַּפְרִיסִין. וּמִדִּלְגַבֵּי עָרְלָה לָאו פֵּירָא נִינְהוּ – לְגַבֵּי בְּרָכוֹת נַמִּי לָאו פֵּירָא נִינְהוּ, וְלָא מְבָרְכִינַן עֲלֵיהּ ״בּוֹרֵא פְּרִי הָעֵץ״, אֶלָּא ״בּוֹרֵא פְּרִי הָאֲדָמָה״.

The Gemara concludes: **The *halakha* is in accordance with** the opinion of **Mar bar Rav Ashi, who discarded the berries and ate the buds. And since they are not** considered **fruit with regard to *orla*, they are also not** considered **fruit with regard to blessings, and one does not recite over them: Who creates fruit of the tree, but rather: Who creates fruit of the ground.**

פִּלְפְּלֵי – רַב שֵׁשֶׁת אָמַר: ״שֶׁהַכֹּל״; רָבָא אָמַר: לָא כְּלוּם. וְאָזְדָא רָבָא לְטַעְמֵיהּ, דְּאָמַר רָבָא: כָּס פִּלְפְּלֵי בְּיוֹמָא דְכִפּוּרֵי – פָּטוּר, כָּס זַנְגְּבִילָא בְּיוֹמָא דְכִפּוּרֵי – פָּטוּר.

The question arose with regard to the blessing over **peppers.**[H] **Rav Sheshet said:** One who eats peppers must recite: **By Whose word all things came to be. Rava said: One** need **not recite** a blessing **at all.** This is consistent with Rava's opinion that eating peppers is not considered eating, **as Rava said: One who chews on peppers on Yom Kippur**[H] **is exempt, one who chews on ginger**[B] **on Yom Kippur is exempt.** Eating sharp spices is an uncommon practice, and is therefore not considered to be eating, which is prohibited by Torah law on Yom Kippur.

מֵיתִיבֵי: הָיָה רַבִּי מֵאִיר אוֹמֵר, מִמַּשְׁמַע שֶׁנֶּאֱמַר: ״וַעֲרַלְתֶּם עָרְלָתוֹ אֶת פִּרְיוֹ״, אֵינִי יוֹדֵעַ שֶׁעֵץ מַאֲכָל הוּא?! אֶלָּא מַה תַּלְמוּד לוֹמַר ״עֵץ מַאֲכָל״ – לְהָבִיא עֵץ שֶׁטַּעַם עֵצוֹ וּפִרְיוֹ שָׁוֶה, וְאֵיזֶהוּ – זֶה הַפִּלְפְּלִין, לְלַמֶּדְךָ שֶׁהַפִּלְפְּלִין חַיָּיבִין בְּעָרְלָה, וּלְלַמֶּדְךָ שֶׁאֵין אֶרֶץ יִשְׂרָאֵל חֲסֵרָה כְּלוּם, שֶׁנֶּאֱמַר: ״אֶרֶץ אֲשֶׁר לֹא בְמִסְכֵּנֻת תֹּאכַל בָּהּ לֶחֶם לֹא תֶחְסַר כֹּל בָּהּ״!

**The Gemara raised an objection** to this based on what was taught in a *baraita*, that regarding the verse: "When you enter the land and plant any tree for food you shall regard its fruit as *orla*" (Leviticus 19:23), **Rabbi Meir would say: By inference from that which is stated: "You shall regard its fruit as *orla*," don't I know that it is** referring to **a tree** that produces **food? Rather,** for what purpose **does the verse state: "Any tree for food"? To include a tree whose wood and fruit have the same taste. And which tree is this? This is the pepper** tree. **And** this comes **to teach you that the peppers,** and even the wood portions, are edible and are therefore **obligated in** the prohibition of ***orla*, and to teach that Eretz Yisrael lacks nothing, as it is stated: "A land where you shall eat bread without scarceness, you shall lack nothing"** (Deuteronomy 8:9). **Obviously,** peppers are fit for consumption.

לָא קַשְׁיָא: הָא בְּרַטִּיבְתָּא, הָא בְּיַבֶּשְׁתָּא.

The Gemara responds: This is **not difficult,** as there is a distinction between two different cases. **This,** where Rabbi Meir spoke of peppers fit for consumption, **is** referring to a case **when it is damp** and fresh; **and this,** where chewing on pepper is not considered eating on Yom Kippur and does not require a blessing, **is** referring to a case **when it is dry.**

אָמְרִי לֵיהּ רַבָּנַן לְמָרֵימָר: כָּס זַנְגְּבִילָא בְּיוֹמָא דְכִפּוּרֵי – פָּטוּר. וְהָא אָמַר רָבָא: הַאי הֶמַּלְתָּא דְּאָתְיָא מִבֵּי הִנְדּוּאֵי – שְׁרֵיָא, וּמְבָרְכִינַן עֲלֶיהָ ״בּוֹרֵא פְּרִי הָאֲדָמָה״! לָא קַשְׁיָא: הָא בְּרַטִּיבְתָּא, הָא בְּיַבֶּשְׁתָּא.

With regard to this discussion of chewing pepper on Yom Kippur, the Gemara cites what **the Sages said to Mareimar:** Why **is one who chews ginger on Yom Kippur exempt? Didn't Rava say: One is permitted** to eat **the ginger that comes from India, and over it, one recites: Who creates fruit of the ground.**[H] With regard to blessing, it is considered edible; therefore, with regard to chewing on Yom Kippur it should be considered edible as well. The Gemara responds: This is **not difficult. This,** where a blessing is recited, **is** referring to a case **when it is damp** and fresh; **this,** where no blessing is recited, **is** referring to a case **when it is dry.**

חֲבִיץ קְדֵרָה, וְכֵן דַּיְיסָא; רַב יְהוּדָה אָמַר: "שֶׁהַכֹּל נִהְיָה בִּדְבָרוֹ"; רַב כָּהֲנָא אָמַר: "בּוֹרֵא מִינֵי מְזוֹנוֹת". בְּדַיְיסָא גְּרֵידָא כּוּלֵּי עָלְמָא לָא פְּלִיגִי דְּ"בוֹרֵא מִינֵי מְזוֹנוֹת", כִּי פְּלִיגִי – בְּדַיְיסָא כְּעֵין חֲבִיץ קְדֵרָה, רַב יְהוּדָה אָמַר: "שֶׁהַכֹּל" – סָבַר דּוּבְשָׁא עִיקָּר; רַב כָּהֲנָא אָמַר: "בּוֹרֵא מִינֵי מְזוֹנוֹת" – סָבַר סְמִידָא עִיקָּר. אָמַר רַב יוֹסֵף: כְּוָותֵיהּ דְּרַב כָּהֲנָא מִסְתַּבְּרָא, דְּרַב וּשְׁמוּאֵל דְּאָמְרִי תַּרְוַיְיהוּ: כָּל שֶׁיֵּשׁ בּוֹ מֵחֲמֵשֶׁת הַמִּינִין מְבָרְכִין עָלָיו "בּוֹרֵא מִינֵי מְזוֹנוֹת".

The Gemara cites a similar dispute with regard to the blessing be recited over *ḥavitz*, a dish consisting of flour, oil, and honey cooked in a **pot as well as pounded grain.**[H] **Rav Yehuda said** that one recites: **By Whose word all things came to be. Rav Kahana said** that one recites: **Who creates the various kinds of nourishment.** The Gemara explains: **With regard to pounded grain alone, everyone agrees that one recites: Who creates the various kinds of nourishment. When they argue, it is with regard to pounded grain** mixed with honey, **in the manner of a** ***ḥavitz*** cooked in a **pot. Rav Yehuda said** that one recites: By Whose word **all things** came to be, as he **held that the honey is primary,** and on honey one recites: By Whose word all things came to be. **Rav Kahana said** that one recites: **Who creates the various kinds of nourishment,** as **he held that the flour,** as is the case with all products produced from grain, **is primary,** and therefore one recites: Who creates the various kinds of nourishment. **Rav Yosef said: It is reasonable** to say **in accordance with** the opinion of **Rav Kahana, as Rav and Shmuel both said: Anything that has of the five species** of grain **in it, one recites over it: Who creates the various kinds of nourishment,**[N] even if it is mixed with other ingredients.

גּוּפָא, רַב וּשְׁמוּאֵל דְּאָמְרִי תַּרְוַיְיהוּ: כָּל שֶׁיֵּשׁ בּוֹ מֵחֲמֵשֶׁת הַמִּינִין מְבָרְכִין עָלָיו "בּוֹרֵא מִינֵי מְזוֹנוֹת"; וְאִיתְּמַר נַמִי, רַב וּשְׁמוּאֵל דְּאָמְרִי תַּרְוַיְיהוּ: כָּל שֶׁהוּא מֵחֲמֵשֶׁת הַמִּינִין מְבָרְכִין עָלָיו "בּוֹרֵא מִינֵי מְזוֹנוֹת".

With regard to the *halakha* of the blessing recited over the five species of grain, the Gemara clarifies **the matter itself. Rav and Shmuel both said: Anything that has of the five species** of grain **in it, one recites over it: Who creates the various kinds of nourishment.** Elsewhere, **it was stated** that **Rav and Shmuel both said: Anything that is from the five species** of grain, **one recites over it: Who creates the various kinds of nourishment.** This is problematic, as these statements appear redundant.

וּצְרִיכָא: דְּאִי אַשְׁמְעִינַן "כָּל שֶׁהוּא" – הֲוָה אָמִינָא מִשּׁוּם דְּאִיתֵיהּ בְּעֵינֵיהּ, אֲבָל עַל יְדֵי תַּעֲרוֹבוֹת – לֹא,

The Gemara explains: Both statements are **necessary,** as **had he taught us** only: **Anything that is** from the five species of grain, one recites over it: Who creates the various kinds of nourishment, **I would have said** that is **because** the grain **is in its pure,** unadulterated form, **but** if one eats it **in** the context of **a mixture, no,** one does not recite: Who creates the various kinds of nourishment.

Perek **VI**
Daf **37** Amud **a**

קָא מַשְׁמַע לַן, "כָּל שֶׁיֵּשׁ בּוֹ". וְאִי אַשְׁמְעִינַן "כָּל שֶׁיֵּשׁ בּוֹ", הֲוָה אָמִינָא כָּל שֶׁיֵּשׁ בּוֹ חֲמֵשֶׁת הַמִּינִים – אִין, אֲבָל אוֹרֶז וְדוֹחַן – לָא, מִשּׁוּם דְּעַל יְדֵי תַּעֲרוֹבֶת; אֲבָל אִיתֵיהּ בְּעֵינֵיהּ – נֵימָא אֲפִילּוּ אוֹרֶז וְדוֹחַן נַמִי מְבָרְכִין עָלָיו "בּוֹרֵא מִינֵי מְזוֹנוֹת". קָא מַשְׁמַע לַן: כָּל שֶׁהוּא מֵחֲמֵשֶׁת הַמִּינִים הוּא דִּמְבָרְכִין עָלָיו "בּוֹרֵא מִינֵי מְזוֹנוֹת"; לְאַפּוּקֵי אוֹרֶז וְדוֹחַן, דַּאֲפִילּוּ אִיתֵיהּ בְּעֵינֵיהּ – לָא מְבָרְכִינַן "בּוֹרֵא מִינֵי מְזוֹנוֹת".

Therefore, **he teaches us: Anything that has** of the five species of grain **in it,** even if it is in the context of a mixture with other ingredients. **And had he taught us** only: **Anything that has** of the five species of grain **in it, I would have said** that specifically over **anything that has** of the five species of grain **in it, yes,** one recites: Who creates the various kinds of nourishment, even if it is in the context of a mixture with other ingredients. **However,** over anything that has **rice**[B] **and millet**[B] in it, **no,** one does not recite: Who creates the various kinds of nourishment, **because** one is eating **it in** the context of **a mixture. However,** if the rice or millet **is in its pure,** unadulterated form, **say** that **even over rice and millet one recites: Who creates the various kinds of nourishment,** because they, too, are types of grain.[B] Therefore, **he teaches us** specifically: **Anything that is from the five species** of grain, **one recites over it: Who creates the various kinds of nourishment, to the exclusion of rice and millet,** over **which, even in its pure,** unadulterated form, **one does not recite: Who creates the various kinds of nourishment.**

**HALAKHA**

**Over pounded grain – בְּדַיְיסָא:** Over any food containing one of the five species of grain, even if they are not the primary ingredient, one recites: Who creates the various kinds of nourishment, in accordance with the opinions of Rav and Shmuel (Rambam *Sefer Ahava, Hilkhot Berakhot* 3:4; *Shulḥan Arukh, Oraḥ Ḥayyim* 208:2, 9).

**NOTES**

**Anything that has of the five species of grain in it, one recites over it: Who creates the various kinds of nourishment – כָּל שֶׁיֵּשׁ בּוֹ מֵחֲמֵשֶׁת הַמִּינִין מְבָרְכִין עָלָיו בּוֹרֵא מִינֵי מְזוֹנוֹת:** The defining characteristics of the food over which this blessing is recited can be explained in two ways: One is that their significance stems from the fact that they are among the seven species for which Israel is praised, as spelt is considered a type of wheat and oats and rye are considered types of barley. Another explanation is that they are more nourishing than other foods. The discussion with regard to the inclusion of rice and millet in this category is based upon, among other considerations, the question: What is the central consideration in determining the criteria for reciting: Who creates the various kinds of nourishment (*Penei Yehoshua*).

**BACKGROUND**

**Rice – אוֹרֶז:** Rice, *Oryza savita*, is an annual grass from the grain family, which grows to a height of approximately 1 m. It grows predominantly in marshland and in irrigated fields during the summer. Rice seeds have yellowish shells, though there are red varieties as well. It is indigenous to the Far East; however, it was brought to Eretz Yisrael prior to the mishnaic period. Rice is used primarily for cereal, and due its lack of adhesiveness, it is difficult to make it into bread. Nevertheless, they would bake rice bread or mix it with other grains and bake bread.

Rice

**Millet [*doḥan*] – דּוֹחַן:** Among the early commentaries, there are various opinions with regard to the identity of *doḥan*. The standard identity is *Panicum miliaceum*, a type of millet from the grain family. It is a perennial grass that reaches a height of 1–1.5 m. Its flowers are long, weighty, and cylindrical, and its small seeds (2–3 mm) are yellow. It was often used for animal feed or cereal, though at times it was mixed with other grains to make bread.

Millet

**Types of grain – מִינֵי דָּגָן:** There is much that we do not know about the division into species in the Mishna and the Talmud and many distinctions are unclear. Nevertheless, there is a botanical distinction somewhat parallel to the Gemara's definition of the species of grains. Within the grain family, there is a distinction between the *Panicoidae* family that includes millet, rice, and corn, among others, which the Talmud does not consider grain; and the *Pooidae* family, which includes the five species of grain.

**The blessing over rice – בִּרְכַּת אוֹרֶז:** Before eating uncooked rice, one recites: Who creates fruit of the ground, and thereafter: Who creates the many forms of life. If he boiled it to the point that it is mashed (Rema), or ground it and baked it into bread, he recites beforehand: Who creates the various forms of nourishment, and thereafter: Who creates the many forms of life, as per the Gemara's conclusion, contrary to the opinions of Rav and Shmuel. In a mixture of rice and grain, its status is determined by the majority component. Due to the dispute between Rashi and Tosafot with regard to what is orez, translated here as rice, some hold that the blessing to be recited over modern-day rice today is: By whose word all things came to be (Mishna Berura; Rambam Sefer Ahava, Hilkhot Berakhot 3:10; Shulḥan Arukh, Oraḥ Ḥayyim 208:7).

**The blessing over millet – בִּרְכַּת דּוֹחַן:** Before eating millet bread or cooked millet, one recites: By Whose word all things came to be, as with regard to millet, the Gemara adopted the opinions of Rav and Shmuel (Rambam Sefer Ahava, Hilkhot Berakhot 3:4; Shulḥan Arukh, Oraḥ Ḥayyim 208:8).

**A cooked dish made of the five species of grain – תַּבְשִׁיל מֵחֲמֵשֶׁת הַמִּינִים:** Before eating dishes made of the five species of grain, one recites: Who creates the various forms of nourishment, and thereafter, the one blessing abridged from the three blessings of Grace after Meals (Rambam Sefer Ahava, Hilkhot Berakhot 3:4; Shulḥan Arukh, Oraḥ Ḥayyim 208:2).

**Rice on Passover – אוֹרֶז בְּפֶסַח:** The prohibition of leaven on Passover does not apply to rice, and one does not fulfill his obligation on the eve of Passover with unleavened rice bread. Some prohibit eating rice on Passover based on a decree due to the concern lest actual leaven is mixed with the rice or lest people may mistakenly believe that it is leaven (Tur, Hagahot Maimoniyot, Mordekhai), and one should not diverge from observance of that decree. That is the custom in the Ashkenazic communities (Rema; Rambam Sefer Zemanim, Hilkhot Ḥametz UMatza 5:1; Shulḥan Arukh, Oraḥ Ḥayyim 453:1).

**One who chews wheat – הַכּוֹסֵס אֶת הַחִטָּה:** One who chews wheat or any other grain (Magen Avraham) that was uncooked or roasted, if the kernels are intact and they are, at least occasionally, eaten in that form, beforehand one recites: Who creates fruit of the ground, and thereafter: Who creates the many forms of life. Tosafot was uncertain whether or not the blessing thereafter is one blessing abridged from the three blessings of Grace after Meals. Therefore, the Rema wrote that one should only eat it in the framework of a meal and exempt it from a blessing thereafter with Grace after Meals. If he eats it outside the framework of a meal, he recites: Who creates the many forms of life, thereafter (Magen Avraham: Rambam Sefer Ahava, Hilkhot Berakhot 3:2; Shulḥan Arukh, Oraḥ Ḥayyim 208:4).

**If he ground the wheat, baked it, and cooked the bread – טְחָנָהּ אֲפָאָהּ וּבִשְּׁלָהּ:** A loaf of bread that was broken into pieces and cooked, if the pieces are the size of an olive-bulk, even if it does not have the appearance of bread, one recites beforehand: Who brings forth bread from the earth, and Grace after Meals thereafter. If the pieces are smaller than an olive-bulk, even if it has the appearance of bread, beforehand one recites: Who creates the various forms of nourishment, and the one blessing abridged from the three blessings of Grace after Meals thereafter (Rambam Sefer Ahava, Hilkhot Berakhot 3:8; Shulḥan Arukh, Oraḥ Ḥayyim 168:10).

**Wheat kernels crushed into three parts [teraggis] – טְרָגִיס:** From the Greek τράγος, tragos, meaning hulled grain, groats, used for porridge.

**Wheat kernels crushed into four parts [zariz] – זְרִיז; wheat kernels crushed into five parts [arsan] – עַרְסָן:** According to Rav Sa'adia Gaon these are types of shredded barley, just as terragis is crushed wheat. This appears to be its meaning based on Nedarim 41b.

---

וְאוֹרֶז וְדוֹחַן לָא מְבָרְכִינַן ״בּוֹרֵא מִינֵי מְזוֹנוֹת״?! וְהָתַנְיָא: הֵבִיאוּ לְפָנָיו פַּת אוֹרֶז וּפַת דּוֹחַן – מְבָרֵךְ עָלָיו תְּחִלָּה וָסוֹף כְּמַעֲשֵׂה קְדֵרָה; וְגַבֵּי מַעֲשֵׂה קְדֵרָה תַּנְיָא: בַּתְּחִלָּה מְבָרֵךְ עָלָיו ״בּוֹרֵא מִינֵי מְזוֹנוֹת״, וּלְבַסּוֹף מְבָרֵךְ עָלָיו בְּרָכָה אַחַת מֵעֵין שָׁלֹשׁ!

כְּמַעֲשֵׂה קְדֵרָה, וְלֹא כְּמַעֲשֵׂה קְדֵרָה; כְּמַעֲשֵׂה קְדֵרָה – דִּמְבָרְכִין עָלָיו תְּחִלָּה וָסוֹף; וְלֹא כְּמַעֲשֵׂה קְדֵרָה, דְּאִילּוּ בְּמַעֲשֵׂה קְדֵרָה – בַּתְּחִלָּה ״בּוֹרֵא מִינֵי מְזוֹנוֹת״, וּלְבַסּוֹף בְּרָכָה מֵעֵין שָׁלֹשׁ, וְאִילּוּ הָכָא, בַּתְּחִלָּה מְבָרֵךְ עָלָיו ״שֶׁהַכֹּל נִהְיָה בִּדְבָרוֹ״, וּלְבַסּוֹף ״בּוֹרֵא נְפָשׁוֹת רַבּוֹת וְחֶסְרוֹנָן עַל כָּל מַה שֶּׁבָּרָאתָ״.

וְאוֹרֶז לָאו מַעֲשֵׂה קְדֵרָה הוּא? וְהָתַנְיָא, אֵלּוּ הֵן מַעֲשֵׂה קְדֵרָה: חִילְקָא, טְרָגִיס, סוֹלֶת, זְרִיז, וְעַרְסָן, וְאוֹרֶז!

הָא מַנִּי – רַבִּי יוֹחָנָן בֶּן נוּרִי הִיא; דְּתַנְיָא, רַבִּי יוֹחָנָן בֶּן נוּרִי אוֹמֵר: אוֹרֶז מִין דָּגָן הוּא, וְחַיָּיבִין עַל חִמּוּצוֹ כָּרֵת, וְאָדָם יוֹצֵא בּוֹ יְדֵי חוֹבָתוֹ בְּפֶסַח; אֲבָל רַבָּנַן לָא.

וְרַבָּנַן לָא?! וְהָתַנְיָא: הַכּוֹסֵס אֶת הַחִטָּה מְבָרֵךְ עָלֶיהָ ״בּוֹרֵא פְּרִי הָאֲדָמָה״; טְחָנָהּ אֲפָאָהּ וּבִשְּׁלָהּ, בִּזְמַן שֶׁהַפְּרוּסוֹת קַיָּימוֹת – בַּתְּחִלָּה מְבָרֵךְ עָלֶיהָ ״הַמּוֹצִיא לֶחֶם מִן הָאָרֶץ״, וּלְבַסּוֹף מְבָרֵךְ עָלֶיהָ שָׁלֹשׁ בְּרָכוֹת, אִם אֵין הַפְּרוּסוֹת קַיָּימוֹת – בַּתְּחִלָּה מְבָרֵךְ עָלֶיהָ ״בּוֹרֵא מִינֵי מְזוֹנוֹת״, וּלְבַסּוֹף מְבָרֵךְ עָלֶיהָ בְּרָכָה אַחַת מֵעֵין שָׁלֹשׁ;

הַכּוֹסֵס אֶת הָאוֹרֶז מְבָרֵךְ עָלָיו ״בּוֹרֵא פְּרִי הָאֲדָמָה״; טְחָנוֹ אֲפָאוֹ וּבִשְּׁלוֹ, אַף עַל פִּי שֶׁהַפְּרוּסוֹת קַיָּימוֹת – בַּתְּחִלָּה מְבָרֵךְ עָלָיו ״בּוֹרֵא מִינֵי מְזוֹנוֹת״, וּלְבַסּוֹף מְבָרֵךְ עָלָיו בְּרָכָה אַחַת מֵעֵין שָׁלֹשׁ.

---

With regard to the previous conclusion, the Gemara asks: **And over rice and millet we do not recite: Who creates the various kinds of nourishment? But wasn't it taught** in a baraita: **If they brought before him rice**[H] **bread or millet**[H] **bread, he recites the blessing over it both** before and after, as he would recite the blessing over **a cooked dish** containing dough from the five species of the grain. **And with regard to a cooked dish,**[H] it was taught in a baraita: **At the start, one recites: Who creates the various kinds of nourishment, and at the end, one recites one blessing abridged from the** three blessings of Grace after Meals [al hamiḥya]. Apparently, one recites: Who creates the various kinds of nourishment, over rice and millet.

The Gemara rejects this proof: Indeed, rice or millet is **like a cooked dish, and is not like a cooked dish** in every sense. The Gemara elaborates: It is considered **like a cooked dish** in that **one recites a blessing over it both at the beginning and the end. And it is unlike a cooked dish** in that **over a cooked dish, at the start, one recites: Who creates the various kinds of nourishment, and at the end, one recites one blessing abridged from the three blessings of Grace after Meals; whereas here, over rice, at the start, one recites: By Whose word all things came to be, and at the end, one recites: Who creates the many forms of life and their needs for all that You have created.**

The Gemara challenges: **And rice is not a cooked dish? Wasn't it taught** in a baraita that **these are cooked dishes: Wheat kernels split into two parts, wheat kernels crushed into three parts [teraggis],**[L] **flour, wheat kernels crushed into four parts [zariz], wheat kernels crushed into five parts [arsan]**[L] **and rice?** Apparently, rice is considered a cooked dish like crushed wheat.

The Gemara responds: **Whose opinion is reflected in this** baraita? **It is Rabbi Yoḥanan ben Nuri's opinion, as it was taught** in a baraita: **Rabbi Yoḥanan ben Nuri says: Rice is a type of grain** in every respect and, therefore, **one is liable to death by karet if it leavens** on Passover and he eats it intentionally. **And a person** who ate matza baked from rice flour **fulfills his obligation on Passover;**[H] however, according to **the Rabbis, no,** rice is not in the category of a cooked dish.

The Gemara challenges this: **And the Rabbis** hold that rice is **not** considered a cooked dish? **Wasn't it taught** in a Tosefta: **One who chews wheat**[H] **recites: Who creates fruit of the ground. However, if he ground** the wheat, **baked it, and cooked** the bread,[H] there is a distinction between two situations: **When the slices are intact** and did not dissolve in the boiling process, **at the start one recites: Who brings forth bread from the earth, and at the end one recites the three blessings** of Grace after Meals, as he does after eating bread **When the slices** dissolved in the course of the boiling process and **are not intact, then at the start one recites: Who creates the various kinds of nourishment, and at the end one recites one blessing abridged from the three blessings** of Grace after Meals.

**One who chews rice recites: Who creates fruit of the ground. If one ground it, baked it, and then cooked it, even though the pieces are intact, at the start one recites: Who creates the various kinds of nourishment, and at the end one recites one blessing abridged from the three blessings** of Grace after Meals.

מַנִּי? אִילֵימָא רַבִּי יוֹחָנָן בֶּן נוּרִי הִיא, דְּאָמַר ״אוֹרֶז מִין דָּגָן הוּא״ – ״הַמּוֹצִיא לֶחֶם מִן הָאָרֶץ״ וְשָׁלֹשׁ בְּרָכוֹת בָּעֵי בָּרוֹכֵי!

The Gemara discusses this *Tosefta*: **Whose** opinion is reflected in **this** *Tosefta*? **If you say that** it is the opinion of **Rabbi Yoḥanan ben Nuri who said** that **rice is a type of grain,** it should have said that one must recite: **Who brings forth bread from the earth,** beforehand **and** the **three blessings** of Grace after Meals thereafter, as he does after eating bread.

אֶלָּא לָאו – רַבָּנַן הִיא, וּתְיוּבְתָּא דְּרַב וּשְׁמוּאֵל!

**Rather, isn't it** the opinion of **the Rabbis,** who hold that rice is not a type of grain, but nevertheless hold that over rice one recites: Who creates the various kinds of nourishment? If so, this is a **conclusive refutation of** the opinion of **Rav and Shmuel.**

תְּיוּבְתָּא.

The Gemara comments: Indeed, this **is a conclusive refutation** of their opinion.

אָמַר מָר: הַכּוֹסֵס אֶת הַחִטָּה מְבָרֵךְ עָלֶיהָ ״בּוֹרֵא פְּרִי הָאֲדָמָה״. וְהָתַנְיָא: ״בּוֹרֵא מִינֵי זְרָעִים״! – לָא קַשְׁיָא: הָא רַבִּי יְהוּדָה, וְהָא רַבָּנַן; דִּתְנַן, וְעַל יְרָקוֹת אוֹמֵר: ״בּוֹרֵא פְּרִי הָאֲדָמָה״; רַבִּי יְהוּדָה אוֹמֵר: ״בּוֹרֵא מִינֵי דְשָׁאִים״.

Above, it was taught in the *Tosefta* that **the Master said: One who chews wheat recites: Who creates fruit of the ground.** The Gemara challenges: **Wasn't it taught** in a *baraita* that one who chews wheat recites: **Who creates various kinds of seeds?** The Gemara resolves the problem: This is **not difficult,** as it is the subject of a tannaitic dispute. **This** opinion, that one must recite: Who creates various kinds of seeds, is the opinion of **Rabbi Yehuda, and this** opinion, that one must recite: Who creates fruit of the ground, is the opinion of the **Rabbis. As we learned** in our mishna: **Over** herbs and leafy **vegetables one recites: Who creates fruit of the ground. Rabbi Yehuda says: Who creates various kinds of herbs.** Rabbi Yehuda designates specific blessings for every type of plant, and he certainly distinguishes between vegetables in general and seeds.

אָמַר מָר: הַכּוֹסֵס אֶת הָאוֹרֶז – מְבָרֵךְ עָלָיו ״בּוֹרֵא פְּרִי הָאֲדָמָה״, טְחָנוֹ אֲפָאוֹ וּבִשְּׁלוֹ, אַף עַל פִּי שֶׁהַפְּרוּסוֹת קַיָּימוֹת – בַּתְּחִלָּה מְבָרֵךְ עָלָיו ״בּוֹרֵא מִינֵי מְזוֹנוֹת״, וּלְבַסּוֹף בְּרָכָה אַחַת מֵעֵין שָׁלֹשׁ.

It was taught in the same *Tosefta* that **the Master said: One who chews rice recites: Who creates fruit of the ground. If one ground it, baked it and then cooked it, even though the pieces are intact, at the start one recites: Who creates the various kinds of nourishment, and at the end one recites one blessing abridged from** the **three** blessings of Grace after Meals.

וְהָתַנְיָא: לְבַסּוֹף וְלֹא כְלוּם! – אָמַר רַב שֵׁשֶׁת: לָא קַשְׁיָא: הָא רַבָּן גַּמְלִיאֵל וְהָא רַבָּנַן. דְּתַנְיָא, זֶה הַכְּלָל: כֹּל שֶׁהוּא מִשִּׁבְעַת הַמִּינִים, רַבָּן גַּמְלִיאֵל אוֹמֵר: שָׁלֹשׁ בְּרָכוֹת, וַחֲכָמִים אוֹמְרִים: בְּרָכָה אַחַת מֵעֵין שָׁלֹשׁ.

The Gemara raises the challenge: **Wasn't it taught** in a *baraita* that in that case, **at the end** one need **not** recite **any** of the blessings recited over the fruits of Eretz Yisrael, but rather: Who creates the many forms of life. **Rav Sheshet said:** This is **not difficult,** as this is the subject of a tannaitic dispute. **This,** that one recites one blessing abridged from the three blessings of Grace after Meals, is the opinion of **Rabban Gamliel. This,** that one need only recite: Who creates the many forms of life, is the opinion of the **Rabbis. As it was taught** in a *Tosefta* that **this is the principle: Anything that is from the seven species** of grain and fruits for which Eretz Yisrael is praised, **Rabban Gamliel says:** Afterwards, one recites the **three blessings** of the Grace after Meals. **And the Rabbis say: One blessing abridged from** the **three** blessings of Grace after Meals is sufficient.

וּמַעֲשֶׂה בְּרַבָּן גַּמְלִיאֵל וְהַזְּקֵנִים שֶׁהָיוּ מְסוּבִּין בַּעֲלִיָּיה בִּירִיחוֹ, וְהֵבִיאוּ לִפְנֵיהֶם כּוֹתָבוֹת וְאָכְלוּ, וְנָתַן רַבָּן גַּמְלִיאֵל רְשׁוּת לְרַבִּי עֲקִיבָא לְבָרֵךְ. קָפַץ וּבֵרֵךְ רַבִּי עֲקִיבָא בְּרָכָה אַחַת מֵעֵין שָׁלֹשׁ. אָמַר לֵיהּ רַבָּן גַּמְלִיאֵל: עֲקִיבָא, עַד מָתַי אַתָּה מַכְנִיס רֹאשְׁךָ בֵּין הַמַּחֲלוֹקֶת! אָמַר לוֹ: רַבֵּינוּ, אַף עַל פִּי שֶׁאַתָּה אוֹמֵר כֵּן וַחֲבֵרֶיךָ אוֹמְרִים כֵּן, לִמַּדְתָּנוּ רַבֵּינוּ: יָחִיד וְרַבִּים הֲלָכָה כְּרַבִּים.

The Gemara relates: **And** there was an **incident involving Rabban Gamliel and the Sages who were sitting in an upper floor in Jericho and they brought dates before them and they ate. And** afterwards, **Rabban Gamliel gave Rabbi Akiva permission to recite the blessing. Rabbi Akiva hurried and recited**[N] **one blessing abridged from** the **three** blessings of Grace after Meals. **Rabban Gamliel said: Akiva, until when will you** continue to **stick your head into the dispute**[N] among the Sages with regard to what you did? Rabbi Akiva **said to him: Our teacher, even though you say this while your colleagues** disagree and **say that, you taught us, our teacher,**[N] the general principle that guides resolution of halakhic disputes: In a dispute between **an individual and the many, the *halakha* is in accordance with** the opinion of **the many.** Although you are the *Nasi*, it is appropriate to act in accordance with the opinion of the many.

רַבִּי יְהוּדָה אוֹמֵר מִשְּׁמוֹ: כֹּל שֶׁהוּא מִשִּׁבְעַת הַמִּינִים

The Gemara records a variation on the dispute between Rabban Gamliel and the Rabbis: **Rabbi Yehuda says in his name,** the name of Rabbi Akiva. With regard to **anything that is from the seven species**

NOTES

**Hurried and recited – קָפַץ וּבֵרֵךְ:** Some explain that he rushed to recite a blessing hastily, as in deference to Rabban Gamliel, he did not want to argue with him. Therefore, he recited the blessing quickly, as once he reached the point in the blessing where he mentioned the name of God, they would not force him to repeat or alter his blessing (*Tziyyun LeNefesh Ḥayya*).

**Stick your head into the dispute – מַכְנִיס רֹאשְׁךָ בֵּין הַמַּחֲלוֹקֶת:** Presumably, even had he acted in accordance with the opinion of Rabban Gamliel, he would have stuck his head into the dispute. Rather, the explanation is that everyone agrees that Grace after Meals exempts even food items over which one recites the one blessing abridged from the three blessings of Grace after Meals, and therefore Rabban Gamliel thought it would have been preferable to recite the blessing in a manner in which he fulfills his obligation according to all opinions (*Ḥefetz Hashem*).

**You taught us, our teacher – לִמַּדְתָּנוּ רַבֵּינוּ:** This statement should be understood as a colloquial phrase, and does not necessarily indicate that Rabbi Akiva in fact learned this *halakha* from Rabban Gamliel. The Sages taught, however, that when a student makes a comment with regard to a *halakha* that was forgotten by his Rabbi or one greater than he, it is proper etiquette to employ the phrase: You taught us, our teacher.

**HALAKHA**

**This cooked dish which contains pieces of bread – חֲבִיצָא:** Over pieces of uncooked bread that was prepared in milk, honey, or the like, if the pieces are the size of an olive-bulk, even if it does not have the appearance of bread, one recites beforehand: Who brings forth bread from the earth, and Grace after Meals thereafter. If the pieces are smaller than an olive-bulk, even if it has the appearance of bread, beforehand, one recites: Who creates the various kinds of nourishment, and the one blessing abridged from the three blessings of Grace after Meals thereafter, in accordance with the opinions of Rabba and Rav Sheshet (Rambam *Sefer Ahava, Hilkhot Berakhot* 3:4; *Shulḥan Arukh, Oraḥ Ḥayyim* 168:10).

**The first time the priest would stand and offer meal-offerings – הָיָה עוֹמֵד וּמַקְרִיב מְנָחוֹת וכו׳:** One who sacrifices a meal-offering from the new crop recites: Who has given us life, sustained us and brought us to this time. That is the ruling of the Rambam, who disagrees with the interpretation of Rashi and *Tosafot* (Rambam *Sefer Avoda, Hilkhot Temidin UMusafin* 7:18).

**And all of the meal-offerings, he crumbles them into pieces the size of an olive-bulk – וְכוּלָּן פּוֹתְתָן כַּזַּיִת:** The meal-offerings must be divided into smaller pieces after they are made, each of which should be the size of an olive-bulk, but the offering is valid even if the pieces are smaller (Rambam *Sefer Avoda, Hilkhot Ma'aseh HaKorbanot* 13:10).

**NOTES**

**The priest would stand and offer meal-offerings – הָיָה עוֹמֵד וּמַקְרִיב מְנָחוֹת:** Several explanations were suggested for this matter, especially with regard to the identity of the priest involved (see Rashi, *Tosafot*, and *Me'iri*), and some explain that it refers to a priest who offers the *omer* meal-offering and the first-fruits meal-offering, upon which he recites: Who has given us life, sustained us, and brought us to this time (*Adderet Eliyahu*).

וְלֹא מִין דָּגָן הוּא, אוֹ מִין דָּגָן וְלֹא עֲשָׂאוֹ פַּת, רַבָּן גַּמְלִיאֵל אוֹמֵר: שָׁלֹשׁ בְּרָכוֹת, וַחֲכָמִים אוֹמְרִים: בְּרָכָה אַחַת; כֹּל שֶׁאֵינוֹ לֹא מִשִּׁבְעַת הַמִּינִין וְלֹא מִין דָּגָן, כְּגוֹן פַּת אוֹרֶז וְדוֹחַן – רַבָּן גַּמְלִיאֵל אוֹמֵר: בְּרָכָה אַחַת מֵעֵין שָׁלֹשׁ, וַחֲכָמִים אוֹמְרִים: וְלֹא כְלוּם.

**and is not a species of grain,** but one of the fruits, **or which is a species of grain and has not been made into bread,** there is a dispute. **Rabban Gamliel says** that one recites the **three blessings** of the Grace after Meals **and the Rabbis say** that one recites **a single blessing. And** over **anything that is neither one of the seven species nor a species of grain, such as rice bread or millet bread, Rabban Gamliel says** that after eating, one recites **one blessing abridged from** the **three** blessings of Grace after Meals, **and the Rabbis say** that one need **not** recite **any** blessing, i.e. Grace after Meals or one blessing abridged from three, but instead he recites: Who creates the many forms of life. If so, the *Tosefta*, which says that after rice one recites one blessing abridged from three, is in accordance with Rabbi Yehuda's version of Rabban Gamliel's opinion.

בְּמַאי אוֹקִימְתָּא – כְּרַבָּן גַּמְלִיאֵל, אֵימָא סֵיפָא דְּרֵישָׁא: אִם אֵין הַפְּרוּסוֹת קַיָּימוֹת – בַּתְּחִלָּה מְבָרֵךְ עָלֶיהָ ״בּוֹרֵא מִינֵי מְזוֹנוֹת״, וּלְבַסּוֹף מְבָרֵךְ עָלֶיהָ בְּרָכָה אַחַת מֵעֵין שָׁלֹשׁ, מַנִּי? אִי רַבָּן גַּמְלִיאֵל – הַשְׁתָּא אַכּוֹתָבוֹת וְאַדַּיְיסָא אָמַר רַבָּן גַּמְלִיאֵל שָׁלֹשׁ בְּרָכוֹת, אִם אֵין הַפְּרוּסוֹת קַיָּימוֹת מִיבַּעְיָא?!

The Gemara challenges: **How did you establish** the *Tosefta*? **In accordance with** the opinion of **Rabban Gamliel. Say the latter clause of the first** section of this *Tosefta*, which states that even over wheat bread, **when the slices are not intact,** then **at the start one recites: Who creates the various kinds of nourishment, and at the end one recites one blessing abridged from** the **three** blessings of Grace after Meals. **Whose** opinion is reflected in that section of the *Tosefta*? **If** it is the opinion of **Rabban Gamliel, now** if over **dates and pounded wheat, Rabban Gamliel said** that one recites the **three blessings** of Grace after Meals, in a case **where the slices** of bread **are not intact, is it necessary** to say that one recites Grace after Meals?

אֶלָּא פְּשִׁיטָא – רַבָּנַן, אִי הָכִי קַשְׁיָא דְּרַבָּנַן אַדְּרַבָּנַן! אֶלָּא, לְעוֹלָם רַבָּנַן, וּתְנֵי גַּבֵּי אוֹרֶז: וּלְבַסּוֹף אֵינוֹ מְבָרֵךְ עָלָיו וְלֹא כְלוּם.

**Rather, it is clear** that the *Tosefta* is in accordance with the opinion of **the Rabbis. If so, there is a contradiction between** one opinion of **the Rabbis and** a second opinion of **the Rabbis.** The Gemara resolves the contradiction: **Rather, actually,** the *Tosefta* is in accordance with the opinion of **the Rabbis and** emend the text **and teach with regard to rice: At the end one does not recite any blessing,** consistent with their opinion in the *baraita*.

אָמַר רָבָא: הַאי רִיהֲטָא דְּחַקְלָאֵי דְּמַפְּשִׁי בֵּיהּ קִמְחָא – מְבָרֵךְ ״בּוֹרֵא מִינֵי מְזוֹנוֹת״. מַאי טַעְמָא – דִּסְמִידָא עִיקָּר. דִּמְחוֹזָא, דְּלָא מַפְּשִׁי בֵּיהּ קִמְחָא – מְבָרֵךְ עָלָיו ״שֶׁהַכֹּל נִהְיָה בִּדְבָרוֹ״. מַאי טַעְמָא – דּוּבְשָׁא עִיקָּר. וַהֲדַר אָמַר רָבָא: אִידֵּי וְאִידֵּי ״בּוֹרֵא מִינֵי מְזוֹנוֹת״; דְּרַב וּשְׁמוּאֵל דְּאָמְרִי תַּרְוַיְיהוּ: כֹּל שֶׁיֵּשׁ בּוֹ מֵחֲמֵשֶׁת הַמִּינִים מְבָרְכִין עָלָיו ״בּוֹרֵא מִינֵי מְזוֹנוֹת״.

With regard to the blessings recited over various types of porridge, **Rava said:** Over **the farmer's mixture of flour and honey to which they add** extra **flour, one recites: Who creates the various kinds of nourishment What is the reason?** Because **the flour is** the **primary** ingredient in the mixture. Over this same dish, however, when it is prepared in the manner that it is prepared in **Meḥoza** where **they do not add** extra **flour, one recites: By Whose word all things came to be. What is the reason?** Because in that dish, **the honey is** the **primary** ingredient. **And Rava reconsidered and said:** Over **both this,** the mixture of the farmers, and **that,** the mixture of Meḥoza, one recites: **Who creates the various kinds of nourishment. As Rav and Shmuel both said: Anything that is from the five species** of grain, **one recites over it: Who creates the various kinds of nourishment.**

אָמַר רַב יוֹסֵף: הַאי חֲבִיצָא דְּאִית בֵּיהּ פֵּרוּרִין כַּזַּיִת – בַּתְּחִלָּה מְבָרֵךְ עָלָיו ״הַמּוֹצִיא לֶחֶם מִן הָאָרֶץ״, וּלְבַסּוֹף מְבָרֵךְ עָלָיו שָׁלֹשׁ בְּרָכוֹת; דְּלֵית בֵּיהּ פֵּרוּרִין כַּזַּיִת – בַּתְּחִלָּה מְבָרֵךְ עָלָיו ״בּוֹרֵא מִינֵי מְזוֹנוֹת״, וּלְבַסּוֹף בְּרָכָה אַחַת מֵעֵין שָׁלֹשׁ.

**Rav Yosef said:** Over **this cooked dish, which contains pieces** of bread[H] that are the size of **an olive-bulk, at the start one recites: Who brings forth bread from the earth, and afterward one recites** the **three blessings** of Grace after Meals as he would over bread. Over that same cooked dish, **which does not contain pieces** of bread that are the size of **an olive bulk, at the start one recites: Who creates the various kinds of nourishment, and at the end one recites one blessing abridged from** the **three** blessings of Grace after Meals, as he would over a cooked dish.

אָמַר רַב יוֹסֵף: מְנָא אָמִינָא לַהּ – דְּתַנְיָא: הָיָה עוֹמֵד וּמַקְרִיב מְנָחוֹת בִּירוּשָׁלַיִם, אוֹמֵר: בָּרוּךְ שֶׁהֶחֱיָינוּ וְקִיְּמָנוּ וְהִגִּיעָנוּ לַזְּמַן הַזֶּה; נְטָלָן לְאָכְלָן – מְבָרֵךְ ״הַמּוֹצִיא לֶחֶם מִן הָאָרֶץ״, וְתָנֵי עֲלַהּ: וְכוּלָּן פּוֹתְתָן כַּזַּיִת.

**And Rav Yosef said: From where do I say this** *halakha*? **As it was taught** in a *baraita*: The first time the priest **would stand and offer meal-offerings**[NH] **in Jerusalem, he would recite: Who has given us life, sustained us, and brought us to this time,** as it is the first time that he fulfilled the mitzva of offering that sacrifice (Rashi). **When he would take** the meal offerings in order **to eat them, he would recite: Who brings forth bread from the earth. And it was taught on the** topic of meal-offerings: **And all of the** meal-offerings, **he crumbles** them into pieces, approximately the size of an **olive-bulk.**[H] This proves that over bread crumbs the size of an olive-bulk, one recites: Who brings forth bread from the earth.

אָמַר לֵיהּ אַבַּיֵי: אֶלָּא מֵעַתָּה, לְתַנָּא דְּבֵי רַבִּי יִשְׁמָעֵאל דְּאָמַר, "פּוֹרְכָן עַד שֶׁמַּחֲזִירָן לְסָלְתָּן", הָכִי נַמִי דְּלָא בָּעֵי בָּרוֹכֵי "הַמּוֹצִיא לֶחֶם מִן הָאָרֶץ"?! וְכִי תֵּימָא הָכִי נַמִי, וְהָתַנְיָא: לָקַט מִכּוּלָּן כְּזַיִת וַאֲכָלָן, אִם חָמֵץ הוּא – עָנוּשׁ כָּרֵת, וְאִם מַצָּה הוּא – אָדָם יוֹצֵא בּוֹ יְדֵי חוֹבָתוֹ בְּפֶסַח!

**Abaye said to** Rav Yosef: **But** if what you say is **so, then now, according to the *tanna* of the school of Rabbi Yishmael** who **said** with regard to meal-offerings: **He crushes them until he restores them to** the form that they were when **they were flour,** would you say that **so too,** in that case, **he need not recite: Who brings forth bread from the earth? And if you say** that **that is so,** that one does not recite: Who brings forth bread from the earth, over these meal-offerings, **wasn't it taught** in a *baraita*: **One who gathered an olive-bulk** sized portion **from all of** the crumbs of the meal-offerings **and ate them, if it was** an offering of **leavened bread** like that of a thanks-offering, if he ate them on Passover he is **punishable by *karet*. If** it was an offering **of unleavened bread, one fulfills his obligation** to eat *matza* **on Passover.** This illustrates that bread crumbs, regardless of their size, are always considered bread.

הָכָא בְּמַאי עָסְקִינַן – בְּשֶׁעֲרָסָן, אִי הָכִי, אֵימָא סֵיפָא: וְהוּא שֶׁאֲכָלָן בִּכְדֵי אֲכִילַת פְּרָס, וְאִי בְּשֶׁעֲרָסָן – הַאי "שֶׁאֲכָלָן"?! "שֶׁאֲכָלוֹ" מִיבְּעֵי לֵיהּ!

Rav Yosef answered that this is not the case, and one does not recite a blessing over bread crumbs as he would over actual bread. Rather, **with what are we dealing here?** With a case **where** one mixed the bread crumbs with water **and compacted them** into a single mass. The Gemara challenges this: **If so, say the latter clause,** in which we learn that **this case** of one who eats the crumbs speaks specifically about **when he ate them,** all of the crumbs that constitute the size of an olive-bulk **in the time it takes to eat a half-loaf of bread. And if** it is referring to a case where **one compacted them** into a single mass, **that** expression: **When he ate them,** is inappropriate. **When he ate it, is what it needed** to say, as it is a single loaf.

אֶלָּא הָכָא בְּמַאי עָסְקִינַן – בְּבָא מִלֶּחֶם גָּדוֹל.

**Rather,** it can be explained in another way: **With what are we dealing here?** With a case **where** each of the crumbs **came from a large** loaf of **bread** over which one is obligated to recite: Who brings forth bread from the earth. Over crumbs that were never part of a loaf of bread large enough to require this blessing, however, one need only recite: Who brings forth bread from the earth, if they are at least the size of an olive-bulk.

מַאי הֲוָה עֲלַהּ? אָמַר רַב שֵׁשֶׁת: הַאי חֲבִיצָא, אַף עַל גַּב דְּלֵית בֵּיהּ פֵּירוּרִין כְּזַיִת – מְבָרֵךְ עֲלָיו "הַמּוֹצִיא לֶחֶם מִן הָאָרֶץ". אָמַר רָבָא: וְהוּא דְּאִיכָּא עֲלֵיהּ תּוֹרִיתָא דְּנַהֲמָא.

Since all of the proofs for and against this opinion were rejected, the Gemara asks: **What** conclusion **was** reached **about** this *halakha*? **Rav Sheshet said:** Over **this cooked dish, which contains** bread **crumbs, even though it does not contain crumbs** the size **of an olive-bulk, one recites: Who brings forth bread from the earth. Rava said: This is** specifically in a case where the crumbs still **have the appearance of bread** and did not dissolve completely.

טְרוֹקְנִין חַיָּיבִין בְּחַלָּה. וְכִי אֲתָא רָבִין אָמַר רַבִּי יוֹחָנָן: טְרוֹקְנִין פְּטוּרִין מִן הַחַלָּה. מַאי טְרוֹקְנִין? אָמַר אַבַּיֵי: כּוּבָּא דְּאַרְעָא.

Another issue concerned ***terokanin,***[HL] with regard to which it was said that **they are obligated in** the mitzva to separate ***ḥalla,***[H] meaning that *terokanin* have the halakhic status of bread. **And, when Ravin came** from Eretz Yisrael to Babylonia, **he said** that **Rabbi Yoḥanan said: *Terokanin* are exempt from** the mitzva to separate ***ḥalla.*** The Gemara asks: **What are *terokanin*? Abaye said:** *Terokanin* are made of a watery mixture of flour and water roasted in a **cavity** in a stove **in the ground** and is not actually bread.

וְאָמַר אַבַּיֵי: טְרִיתָא פְּטוּרָה מִן הַחַלָּה. מַאי טְרִיתָא? אִיכָּא דְּאָמְרִי: גָּבִיל מְרַתַּח, וְאִיכָּא דְּאָמְרִי: נַהֲמָא דְּהִנְדְּקָא; וְאִיכָּא דְּאָמְרִי: לֶחֶם הֶעָשׂוּי לְכוּתָּח.

**And Abaye said: *Terita***[HL] **is exempt from** the mitzva to separate ***ḥalla.*** The Gemara asks: **What** is ***terita***? There are several opinions: **Some say,** it is flour and water **kneaded** that is poured onto a **boiling** hot stove.[N] **And some say,** it is **bread from India,**[N] made from dough wrapped around a skewer and covered with oil or eggs before baking. **And some say,** it is **bread made for *kutaḥ*,**[HB] bread baked in an unusual manner so that it would become extremely leavened and could be used as an ingredient in the Babylonian spice, *kutaḥ*.

תָּנֵי רַבִּי חִיָּיא: לֶחֶם הֶעָשׂוּי לְכוּתָּח פָּטוּר מִן הַחַלָּה. וְהָא תַּנְיָא: חַיָּיב בְּחַלָּה! הָתָם כְּדְקָתָנֵי טַעְמָא, רַבִּי יְהוּדָה אוֹמֵר: מַעֲשֶׂיהָ מוֹכִיחִין עָלֶיהָ, עֲשָׂאָן

And similarly, **Rabbi Ḥiyya taught: Bread made for *kutaḥ***; one **is exempt from** the mitzva to separate ***ḥalla.*** The Gemara asks: **Wasn't it taught** in a *baraita* that one **is obligated in** the mitzva to separate ***ḥalla*** from bread made for *kutaḥ*? The Gemara answers: **There, as the reason was taught** that **Rabbi Yehuda says:** There is a distinction between different types of bread made for *kutaḥ*, as **the actions** taken in **its** preparation **prove** the purpose for which **it** was made. **If he made them**

## HALAKHA

*Terokanin* – **טְרוֹקְנִין**: These are baked goods made of a watery combination of flour and water, which are baked in a cavity in the stove (*Magen Avraham*). Beforehand one recites: Who creates the various kinds of nourishment, and the one blessing abridged from the three blessings of Grace after Meals thereafter. If he based his meal on *terokanin*, one recites beforehand: Who brings forth bread from the earth, and Grace after Meals thereafter (Rambam *Sefer Zera'im, Hilkhot Bikkurim* 6:12; *Shulḥan Arukh, Oraḥ Ḥayyim* 168:15).

***Terokanin* are obligated in the mitzva to separate *ḥalla*** – **טְרוֹקְנִין חַיָּיבִין בְּחַלָּה**: One is required to separate *ḥalla* from the dough from which *terokanin* are baked (Rambam *Sefer Zera'im, Hilkhot Bikkurim* 6:14; *Shulḥan Arukh, Yoreh De'a* 329:5).

***Terita*** – **טְרִיתָא**: Before eating baked goods prepared and baked differently from bread, e.g., *terita* and Indian bread, one recites: Who creates the various kinds of nourishment, even if he based his meal upon them. Some hold that if he based his meal upon them, he recites: Who brings forth bread from the earth (*Tur*), and the *Magen Avraham* ruled that this is the practical *halakha* (Rambam *Sefer Zera'im, Hilkhot Bikkurim* 6:12; *Shulḥan Arukh, Oraḥ Ḥayyim* 168:15–16).

**Bread made for *kutaḥ*** – **לֶחֶם הֶעָשׂוּי לְכוּתָּח**: If bread was made for *kutaḥ* and it is obvious from the manner in which it was prepared that this was its purpose, he is exempt from the obligation to separate *ḥalla* as per the opinion of Rav Yehuda. The same is true with regard to *terita*. If he prepared it in the standard manner in which bread is prepared, he is obligated to separate *ḥalla* (Rambam *Sefer Zera'im, Hilkhot Bikkurim* 6:14; *Shulḥan Arukh, Yoreh De'a* 329:5).

## LANGUAGE

*Terokanin* – **טְרוֹקְנִין**: Perhaps from the Greek **τρωκτά**, *trokta*, meaning food items and fruits eaten for dessert.

*Terita* – **טְרִיתָא**: Some identify its source in the Latin panis tortus, meaning pretzel; and others estimate that it is from the Middle Iranian tarīt, meaning bread made for soaking in milk or soup, parallel to bread made for *kutaḥ*.

## NOTES

**It is flour and water kneaded that is poured onto a boiling hot stove** – **גָּבִיל מְרַתַּח**: The version in the Rif is: Boiling dough [*meratah gavil*], meaning flour poured into boiling water which cooks in that water (Rav Hai Gaon, *Talmidei Rabbeinu Yona*).

**Bread from India** – **נַהֲמָא דְּהִנְדְּקָא**: Some explain this name as a reference to a method of baking common in India (Rashash and see *Arukh*). Others hold that this was not made as food at all; rather, it was used by women for decorative purposes (*Talmidei Rabbeinu Yona, Me'iri*).

## BACKGROUND

*Kutaḥ* – **כּוּתָּח**: The *kutaḥ* or the *kutḥa* (in Syriac, *kudḥa*) was a typical Babylonian spice made from whey, salt, and bread that fermented to the verge of moldering. This spice was extremely sharp to the point where it could be eaten only by the Babylonians who were accustomed to eating it. In the mishna, it is referred to as the Babylonian *kutaḥ*.

כְּעָבִין – חַיָּיבִין, כְּלִמּוּדִין – פְּטוּרִים. אֲמַר לֵיהּ אַבָּיֵי לְרַב יוֹסֵף: הַאי כּוּבָּא דְּאַרְעָא מַאי מְבָרְכִין עֲלֵיהּ? אֲמַר לֵיהּ: מִי סָבְרַתְּ נַהֲמָא הוּא?! גּוּבְלָא בְּעָלְמָא הוּא וּמְבָרְכִין עֲלֵיהּ ״בּוֹרֵא מִינֵי מְזוֹנוֹת״.

**thick** [*ke'avin*],[L] so that they appear like loaves of bread, **they are obligated** in *ḥalla*, and if he shaped them **like boards** [*kelimmudin*],[L] **they are exempt,** since they will certainly only be used for *kutaḥ*. **Abaye said to Rav Yosef: What blessing is recited over the dough of the ground?** Rav Yosef **said to him: Do you think that it is bread? It is merely kneaded** dough, **and** just like over all other cooked grains, **one recites over it the blessing: Who creates the various kinds of nourishment.**

מָר זוּטְרָא קְבַע סְעוּדְתֵּיהּ עֲלֵיהּ, וּבָרֵיךְ עֲלֵיהּ, ״הַמּוֹצִיא לֶחֶם מִן הָאָרֶץ״ וְשָׁלֹשׁ בְּרָכוֹת.

**Mar Zutra based his meal on this** dough, and **he recited: Who brings forth bread from the earth,** beforehand and the **three blessings** of Grace after Meals thereafter. Since he based his meal on it, he considered it to be bread.

אָמַר מָר בַּר רַב אַשִׁי: וְאָדָם יוֹצֵא בָּהֶן יְדֵי חוֹבָתוֹ בְּפֶסַח, מַאי טַעְמָא – ״לֶחֶם עוֹנִי״ קָרֵינַן בֵּיהּ.

**Mar bar Rav Ashi said:** With these types of bread, **a person fulfills his obligation** to eat *matza* **on Passover. What is the reason?** Because **we call it bread of affliction,** and in that sense, it is in the category of *matza*.

וְאָמַר מָר בַּר רַב אַשִׁי: הַאי דּוּבְשָׁא דְּתַמְרֵי מְבָרְכִין עֲלֵיהּ ״שֶׁהַכֹּל נִהְיָה בִּדְבָרוֹ״. מַאי טַעְמָא? – זֵיעָה בְּעָלְמָא הוּא.

**And** with regard to blessings, **Mar bar Rav Ashi said: Over this date honey**[HN] **one recites: By Whose word all things came to be. What is the reason** that one does not recite: Who creates fruit of the tree, as he does over the date itself? Because date honey is not the essence of the fruit, but **merely moisture** that drips from the ripe fruit.

כְּמַאן? כִּי הַאי תַּנָּא, דְּתְנַן: דְּבַשׁ תְּמָרִים, וְיֵין תַּפּוּחִים, וְחוֹמֶץ סִפְוָנִיּוֹת, וּשְׁאָר מֵי פֵּירוֹת שֶׁל תְּרוּמָה – רַבִּי אֱלִיעֶזֶר מְחַיֵּיב קֶרֶן וְחוֹמֶשׁ, וְרַבִּי יְהוֹשֻׁעַ פּוֹטֵר.

**In accordance with whose** opinion does he recite that blessing? **In accordance with** the opinion of **this** *tanna*, **as we learned** in a mishna: If a non-priest ate **date honey, apple wine or vinegar made from grapes of autumn** that grow stunted at the end of the season and are unfit for wine production, **or** any **other** type of **juice** made **from fruits of** *teruma*,[H] **Rabbi Eliezer obligates** him to repay **the principal and** an additional **fifth** as a penalty for misuse of consecrated items. **And Rabbi Yehoshua exempts** him from payment, because he holds that these are byproducts of the fruit and do not have the status of the fruit itself. Mar bar Rav Ashi's ruling with regard to blessings was based on Rabbi Yehoshua's ruling with regard to *teruma*.

אֲמַר לֵיהּ הַהוּא מֵרַבָּנַן לְרָבָא: טְרִימָא מַהוּ? לָא הֲוָה אַדַּעְתֵּיהּ דְּרָבָא מַאי קָאָמַר לֵיהּ. יָתֵיב רָבִינָא קַמֵּיהּ דְּרָבָא, אֲמַר לֵיהּ: דְּשׁוּמְשְׁמֵי קָא אָמְרַתְּ, אוֹ דְּקוּרְטְמֵי קָא אָמְרַתְּ, אוֹ דְּפוּרְצְנֵי קָא אָמְרַתְּ?

**One of the Sages said to Rava: What is** the *halakha* with regard to *terima*?[L] **Rava** was unfamiliar with the term *terima* and **did not understand what he was saying to him. Ravina sat before Rava and said to** the student who had posed the question to Rava: In posing the question, are **you speaking of sesame** *terima* **or** are **you speaking of safflower**[B] *terima* **or** are **you speaking of grape-pits** *terima*?

## HALAKHA

Date honey – דּוּבְשָׁא דְּתַמְרֵי: Before eating date honey one recites: By Whose word all things came to be (Rambam *Sefer Ahava, Hilkhot Berakhot* 3:9; *Shulḥan Arukh, Oraḥ Ḥayyim* 202:8).

Date honey…of *teruma* – דְּבַשׁ תְּמָרִים...שֶׁל תְּרוּמָה: One may not extract liquids from *teruma* fruits with the exception of olives and grapes, as per the opinion of Rav Asi. A non-priest who drinks that extract is exempt from payment as the ruling is in accordance with the opinion of Rabbi Yehoshua in disputes with Rabbi Eliezer (Rambam *Sefer Zera'im, Hilkhot Terumot* 11:2).

## NOTES

Date honey – דּוּבְשָׁא דְּתַמְרֵי: Some wondered with regard to the Gemara's description of date honey as mere moisture, given that the Torah refers to the date itself as honey. Rav Hai Gaon explained that the Gemara refers to dates that were pickled and boiled in order to extract their honey, while the Torah describes the honey that drips from the date on its own, over which one recites: Who creates fruit of the tree.

## BACKGROUND

Safflower – קוּרְטְמֵי: The safflower, *Carthamus tinctorius*, is an annual, cultivated, vascular plant, which grows to a height of 80 cm and is found in arid regions. Its leaves are elongated and thorny, and its flowers have an orange tinge. Its petals are used in dyeing fabrics and food coloring. Oil is extracted from its seeds, even today.

Safflower plant

## LANGUAGE

Thick [*ke'avin*] – כְּעָבִין: There is a variant reading, *ke'akhin*, which some explain as snakelike; in other words, long narrow strips that evoke a snake (*Ma'adanei Melekh*). Others explain that it is from the Arabic كعك, or the Persian kāk, meaning a loaf of bread, particularly one that is spiced.

Like boards [*kelimmudin*] – כְּלִמּוּדִין: Some explain that it means like a novice, who is not so careful in shaping the loaf (*Arukh*).

*Terima* – טְרִימָא: From the Greek τρῖμμα, *trimma*, meaning a beverage made from roasted grain and crushed fruit. Because it was a Greek word, Rava, who was an Aramaic speaking Babylonian, did not ascertain its meaning until he identified its Babylonian equivalent, *ḥashilata*.

אַדְּהָכִי וְהָכִי אַסְקָהּ רָבָא לְדַעְתֵּיהּ, אֲמַר לֵיהּ: חֲשִׁילָתָא וַדַּאי קָא אָמְרַתְּ, וְאַדְכַּרְתַּן מִלְּתָא הָא דַּאֲמַר רַב אַסִי: הַאי תַּמְרֵי שֶׁל תְּרוּמָה – מוּתָּר לַעֲשׂוֹת מֵהֶן טְרִימָא, וְאָסוּר לַעֲשׂוֹת מֵהֶן שֵׁכָר. וְהִלְכְתָא: תַּמְרֵי וְעַבְדִינְהוּ טְרִימָא – מְבָרְכִין עֲלַוַיְיהוּ "בּוֹרֵא פְּרִי הָעֵץ". מַאי טַעְמָא – בְּמִלְּתַיְיהוּ קַיְימֵי כִּדְמֵעִיקָּרָא.

Meanwhile, **Rava comprehended** the meaning of the term **and said to** the Sage: **Certainly, you are speaking of pressed** items, **and you reminded me of a matter that Rav Asi said: Those dates of *teruma*; one is permitted** to press them in order **to make *terima*,** because the dates maintain their form, **and one is forbidden to make** date **beer** from them, as in so doing the dates are damaged and it is forbidden to damage *teruma*. The Gemara concludes: The *halakha* is that **over dates** that were **made into *terima*,**[H] **one recites: Who creates fruit of the tree. What is the reason?** Because **they remain in their original state.**

שְׁתִיתָא, רַב אָמַר: "שֶׁהַכֹּל נִהְיָה בִּדְבָרוֹ", וּשְׁמוּאֵל אָמַר: "בּוֹרֵא מִינֵי מְזוֹנוֹת".

The Gemara raises another question with regard to the blessing recited on **roasted barley to which honey or vinegar was added** [*shetita*].[H] **Rav said** that one recites: **By Whose word all things came to be; and Shmuel said** that one recites: **Who creates the various kinds of nourishment.**

אָמַר רַב חִסְדָּא: וְלָא פְּלִיגִי, הָא בְּעָבָה הָא בְּרַכָּה; עָבָה – לַאֲכִילָה עָבְדִי לַהּ, רַכָּה – לִרְפוּאָה קָא עָבְדִי לַהּ.

**Rav Ḥisda said: And they do not disagree,** as each is referring to a different case. **This,** where Shmuel said that one recites: Who creates the various kinds of nourishment, **is in** a case where the mixture is **thick,** while **this,** where Rav said that one recites: By Whose word all things came to be, **is in** a case where the mixture is **thin.** When it is **thick, he made it as food;** therefore one recites a blessing just as he would over any food made from the five species of grain. When it is **thin, he made it as medicine,** therefore one only recites: By Whose word all things came to be.

מְתִיב רַב יוֹסֵף: וְשָׁוִין, שֶׁבּוֹחֲשִׁין אֶת הַשְּׁתוּת בְּשַׁבָּת וְשׁוֹתִין זֵיתוֹם הַמִּצְרִי; וְאִי סָלְקָא דַּעְתָּךְ לִרְפוּאָה קָא מְכַוֵּין, רְפוּאָה בְּשַׁבָּת מִי שָׁרֵי?!

With regard to the assumption that this mixture is essentially medicinal, **Rav Yosef raised a challenge** from the laws of Shabbat: **And they agree that one may mix *shetita* on Shabbat**[H] **and drink Egyptian beer** [***zitom haMitzri***],[L] which contains a mixture of a pungent spice in flour. **And if it enters your mind** to say that when one prepares *shetita*, **his intention is for medicinal** purposes, **is medicine permitted on Shabbat?**[N]

אֲמַר לֵיהּ אַבָּיֵי: וְאַתְּ לָא תִּסְבְּרָא?! וְהָא תְּנַן: כָּל הָאוֹכָלִין אוֹכֵל אָדָם לִרְפוּאָה בְּשַׁבָּת, וְכָל הַמַּשְׁקִין שׁוֹתֶה! אֶלָּא מָה אִית לָךְ לְמֵימַר? – גַּבְרָא לַאֲכִילָה קָא מְכַוֵּין, הָכִי נַמִּי – גַּבְרָא לַאֲכִילָה קָא מְכַוֵּין.

**Abaye said to** Rav Yosef: **Do you not hold** that to be true? **Didn't we learn** in a mishna: **All foods** that are commonly eaten; **a person may eat** them **for medicinal** purposes **on Shabbat,**[H] **and all drinks** that are not designated for medicinal purposes, a person may **drink** them for medicinal purposes on Shabbat. **But what can you say** in explaining that ruling? **The man's intention** is for the purpose of **eating;** here **too,** when he mixes the *shetita*, **the man's intention is** for the purpose of **eating.**

לִישָּׁנָא אַחֲרִינָא: אֶלָּא מָה אִית לָךְ לְמֵימַר – גַּבְרָא לַאֲכִילָה קָא מְכַוֵּין וּרְפוּאָה מִמֵּילָא קָא הָוְיָא, הָכִי נַמִּי – לַאֲכִילָה קָא מְכַוֵּין וּרְפוּאָה מִמֵּילָא קָא הָוְיָא.

The Gemara cites **another version** of what was taught above: **But what can you say** in explaining that ruling? **The man's intention is for** the purpose of **eating and the cure comes about on its own;** here **too, the man's intention is for** the purpose of **eating and the cure comes about on its own.** Ostensibly, after proving that it is permissible to drink the *shetita* on Shabbat, it is clearly a type of food over which one is required to recite a blessing. If so, it is difficult to understand the need for Rav and Shmuel to point out that one is required to recite a blessing over it.

וּצְרִיכָא דְּרַב וּשְׁמוּאֵל: דְּאִי מֵהַאי – הֲוָה אָמֵינָא לַאֲכִילָה קָא מְכַוֵּין וּרְפוּאָה מִמֵּילָא קָא הָוְיָא; אֲבָל הָכָא, כֵּיוָן דְּלְכַתְּחִילָּה לִרְפוּאָה קָא מְכַוֵּין, לָא לִבָרֵיךְ עֲלָוַיהּ כְּלָל – קָא מַשְׁמַע לַן: כֵּיוָן דְּאִית לֵיהּ הֲנָאָה מִינֵּיהּ, בָּעֵי בָּרוֹכֵי.

Therefore the Gemara says: **And** the statement **of Rav and Shmuel is necessary, as if** the *halakha* had been derived solely **from this** mishna that permits drinking *shetita* on Shabbat, **I would have said:** This applies specifically when **one's intention is for** the purpose of **eating and the cure comes about on its own. Here, however, since from the outset, his intention** in eating the *shetita* **is for** the purpose of **medicine;** just as one recites no blessing when he ingests medicine, **let him recite no blessing over** the *shetita* **at all.** Therefore, Rav and Shmuel **taught us** that here, **since he derives pleasure from** eating **it,** he **is required to recite a blessing.**

HALAKHA

Dates that were made into *terima* – תַּמְרֵי וְעַבְדִינְהוּ טְרִימָא: Before eating mashed dates, one recites: Who creates fruit of the tree, in accordance with the opinion of Rava (Rambam *Sefer Ahava*, *Hilkhot Berakhot* 3:9; *Shulḥan Arukh*, *Oraḥ Ḥayyim* 202:8).

Roasted barley to which honey or vinegar was added [*shetita*] – שְׁתִיתָא: Before consuming a thick liquid mixed with grain, one recites: Who creates the various kinds of nourishment, and then one blessing abridged from the three blessings of Grace after Meals thereafter. If the mixture is watery, beforehand one recites: By Whose word all things came to be, and thereafter: Who creates the many forms of life (Rambam *Sefer Ahava*, *Hilkhot Berakhot* 3:3; *Shulḥan Arukh*, *Oraḥ Ḥayyim* 208:6).

That one may mix *shetita* on Shabbat – שֶׁבּוֹחֲשִׁין אֶת הַשְּׁתוּת בְּשַׁבָּת: It is permitted to mix *shetita* with vinegar on Shabbat; however, one should change the manner in which it is normally prepared by adding the vinegar to the flour rather than vice-versa (Rambam *Sefer Zemanin*, *Hilkhot Shabbat* 21:33; *Shulḥan Arukh*, *Oraḥ Ḥayyim* 321:14).

Foods for medicinal purposes on Shabbat – מַאֲכָלֵי מַרְפֵּא בְּשַׁבָּת: On Shabbat, for medicinal purposes, one is permitted to consume foods normally eaten by the healthy people as per the determination of the Gemara here and in tractate *Shabbat* (Rambam *Sefer Zemanim*, *Hilkhot Shabbat* 21:22; *Shulḥan Arukh*, *Oraḥ Ḥayyim* 328:37).

LANGUAGE

Egyptian beer [*zitom haMitzri*] – זֵיתוֹם הַמִּצְרִי: From the Greek ζῦθος, *zuthos*, or the Latin zythum, meaning a kind of beer made from barley, a kind of malt-liquor. According to the talmudic depiction, it is made from one-third barley, one-third safflower, and one-third salt.

NOTES

Medicine on Shabbat – רְפוּאָה בְּשַׁבָּת: The Sages decreed that one may only use medicine on Shabbat in life-threatening circumstances or instances of grave danger. Consequently, they prohibited all curative actions, especially preparing and taking medicine. In tractate *Shabbat*, there is a discussion with regard to various foods and whether they should be considered as food that may be eaten on Shabbat, even by those deriving medicinal benefit; or whether they are prohibited, because their primary use is medicinal, which is prohibited by rabbinic decree.

## NOTES

**What does one recite *hamotzi*…*motzi* – מָה הוּא אוֹמֵר הַמּוֹצִיא...מוֹצִיא**: This dispute is based on the grammatical determination of the precise nature of the intermediate tense in Hebrew. Should it be considered a verb, which is restricted to a certain tense, or an adjective? The dispute is with regard to how to underscore the perpetual aspect God's role in the preparation of bread (*Ḥokhmat Mano'aḥ*).

״שֶׁעַל הַפַּת הוּא אוֹמֵר הַמּוֹצִיא״ וכו׳. תָּנוּ רַבָּנַן: מָה הוּא אוֹמֵר? ״הַמּוֹצִיא לֶחֶם מִן הָאָרֶץ״, רַבִּי נְחֶמְיָה אוֹמֵר: ״מוֹצִיא לֶחֶם מִן הָאָרֶץ״. אָמַר רָבָא: בְּ״מוֹצִיא״ כּוּלֵּי עָלְמָא לָא פְּלִיגִי דְּאַפֵּיק מַשְׁמַע, דִּכְתִיב: ״אֵל מוֹצִיאָם מִמִּצְרַיִם״, כִּי פְּלִיגִי – בְּ״הַמּוֹצִיא״; רַבָּנַן סָבְרִי: ״הַמּוֹצִיא״ – דְּאַפֵּיק מַשְׁמַע, דִּכְתִיב: ״הַמּוֹצִיא לְךָ מַיִם מִצּוּר הַחַלָּמִישׁ״; וְרַבִּי נְחֶמְיָה סָבַר: ״הַמּוֹצִיא״ – דְּמַפֵּיק מַשְׁמַע, שֶׁנֶּאֱמַר: ״הַמּוֹצִיא אֶתְכֶם מִתַּחַת סִבְלוֹת מִצְרָיִם״.

We learned in the mishna **that over bread one recites: Who brings forth bread from the earth. The Sages taught** in a *baraita*: **What does** one who eats bread **recite** before eating? **Who brings forth [*hamotzi*] bread from the earth. Rabbi Neḥemya says** that the blessing is phrased: **Who brought forth [*motzi*] bread from the earth.**[N] **Rava said: Everyone agrees that** the term ***motzi* means brought,** in the past tense, **as it is written: "God who brought them forth [*motziam*] from Egypt** is for them like the horns of the wild ox" (Numbers 23:22). **When do they disagree? With regard to** the term ***hamotzi*, as the Rabbis hold** that ***hamotzi* means** that God **brought forth,** in the past tense, **as it is written: "Who brought forth [*hamotzi*] for you water from a rock of flint"** (Deuteronomy 8:15), which depicts a past event. **Rabbi Neḥemya holds** that the term ***hamotzi* means** that God **brings forth** in the present tense, **as it is stated** in Moses' prophecy to the Jewish people in Egypt: "And you will know that I am the Lord your God **who is bringing you forth [*hamotzi*] from under the burdens of Egypt"** (Exodus 6:7). Since, in that context, *hamotzi* is used with regard to an event transpiring in the present or possibly even one that will transpire in the future, it is inappropriate to include this term in a blessing referencing the past.

וְרַבָּנַן? – הַהוּא, הָכִי קָאָמַר לְהוּ קוּדְשָׁא בְּרִיךְ הוּא לְיִשְׂרָאֵל: כַּד מַפֵּיקְנָא לְכוּ עֲבִידְנָא לְכוּ מִלְּתָא כִּי הֵיכִי דְּיָדְעִיתוּ דַּאֲנָא הוּא דְּאַפֵּיקִית יָתְכוֹן מִמִּצְרַיִם, דִּכְתִיב: ״וִידַעְתֶּם כִּי אֲנִי ה׳ אֱלֹהֵיכֶם הַמּוֹצִיא״.

**And the Rabbis,** how do they respond to that proof? The Sages interpret **that** verse to mean that **the Holy one, Blessed be He, said to Israel as follows: When I bring you forth, I will perform something for you that you will know that I am the one who brought you forth from Egypt, as it is written: "And you will know that I am the Lord your God who brought you forth [*hamotzi*]"**; in this verse, too, *hamotzi* refers to the past.

מִשְׁתַּבְּחִין לֵיהּ רַבָּנַן לְרַבִּי זֵירָא [אֶת] בַּר רַב זְבִיד אֲחוּהּ דְּרַבִּי שְׁמוּאֵל בַּר רַב זְבִיד דְּאָדָם גָּדוֹל הוּא, וּבָקִי בִּבְרָכוֹת הוּא. אָמַר לָהֶם: לִכְשֶׁיָּבֹא לְיֶדְכֶם הֲבִיאוּהוּ לְיָדִי. זִמְנָא חֲדָא אִיקְּלַע לְגַבֵּיהּ, אַפִּיקוּ לֵיהּ רִיפְתָּא, פְּתַח וַאֲמַר ״מוֹצִיא״. אָמַר: זֶה הוּא שֶׁאוֹמְרִים עָלָיו דְּאָדָם גָּדוֹל הוּא וּבָקִי בִּבְרָכוֹת הוּא?! בִּשְׁלָמָא אִי אֲמַר ״הַמּוֹצִיא״ –

On that note, the Gemara relates: **The Sages would praise son of Rav Zevid, brother of Rabbi Shmuel bar Rav Zevid to Rabbi Zeira, that he is a great man and he is expert in blessings.** Rabbi Zeira **said to** the Sages: **When he comes to you, bring him to me** so that I can meet him. **One day he happened** to come **before him. They brought out bread** to the guest, **he began and recited: Who brought forth [*motzi*] bread from the earth.** Rabbi Zeira grew annoyed **and said: This is he of whom they say that he is a great man and expert in blessings? Granted, had he recited: *Hamotzi,***

Perek **VI**
Daf **38** Amud **b**

## HALAKHA

**And the *halakha* is *hamotzi* – וְהִלְכְתָא הַמּוֹצִיא**: The formula of the blessing recited before eating bread is *hamotzi*, although one fulfills his obligation if he recites *motzi* (*Mishna Berura*), in accordance with the opinion of the Rabbis and the ruling of the Gemara (Rambam *Sefer Ahava, Hilkhot Berakhot* 3:2; *Shulḥan Arukh, Oraḥ Ḥayyim* 167:2).

אַשְׁמְעִינַן טַעְמָא, וְאַשְׁמְעִינַן דְּהִלְכְתָא כְּרַבָּנַן; אֶלָּא דַּאֲמַר ״מוֹצִיא״ מַאי קָא מַשְׁמַע לַן? – וְאִיהוּ דַּעֲבַד – לְאַפּוֹקֵי נַפְשֵׁיהּ מִפְּלוּגְתָּא.

I would have understood that **he** thereby **taught us the meaning** of the verse: "Who brought you forth from Egypt," **and he** thereby **taught us that the *halakha* is in accordance with** the opinion of **the Rabbis. However, what did he teach us by reciting *motzi*?** Everyone agrees that one fulfills his obligation when reciting *motzi*. The Gemara explains: The son of Rav Zevid **did this** in order **to preclude himself from** taking sides in **the dispute.** He preferred to phrase his blessing in a manner appropriate according to all opinions, rather than teach a novel concept, which is not universally accepted.

וְהִלְכְתָא: ״הַמּוֹצִיא לֶחֶם מִן הָאָרֶץ״, דְּקַיְימָא לַן כְּרַבָּנַן, דְּאָמְרִי: דְּאַפֵּיק מַשְׁמַע.

The Gemara concludes: **And the *halakha*** is that one recites: **Who brings forth [*hamotzi*]**[H] **bread from the earth, as we hold in accordance with** the opinion of **the Rabbis who say** that it also means: Who brought forth.

"וְעַל הַיְּרָקוֹת אוֹמֵר" וכו׳. קָתָנֵי יְרָקוֹת דּוּמְיָא דְּפַת – מָה פַּת שֶׁנִּשְׁתַּנָּה עַל יְדֵי הָאוּר, אַף יְרָקוֹת נַמִּי שֶׁנִּשְׁתַּנּוּ עַל יְדֵי הָאוּר. אָמַר רַבְּנַאי מִשְּׁמֵיהּ דְּאַבָּיֵי, זֹאת אוֹמֶרֶת: שְׁלָקוֹת מְבָרְכִין עֲלֵיהֶן "בּוֹרֵא פְּרִי הָאֲדָמָה". מִמַּאי – מִדְּקָתָנֵי יְרָקוֹת דּוּמְיָא דְּפַת.

We learned in the mishna that **over vegetables one recites:** Who creates fruits of the ground. The Gemara comments: The mishna **taught vegetables** together with, and therefore **similar to, bread,** and from this analogy one may infer: **Just as bread** is food **that was transformed by fire, so too vegetables** retain the blessing: Who creates fruits of the ground, after they **have been transformed by fire. Rabbenai said in the name of** Abaye: **This means** that **over boiled vegetables**[H] **one recites: Who creates fruits of the ground. From where** is this matter inferred? From the fact that the mishna **taught vegetables similar to bread.**

דָּרַשׁ רַב חִסְדָּא מִשּׁוּם רַבֵּינוּ, וּמַנּוּ – רַב: שְׁלָקוֹת מְבָרְכִין עֲלֵיהֶם "בּוֹרֵא פְּרִי הָאֲדָמָה"; וְרַבּוֹתֵינוּ הַיּוֹרְדִין מֵאֶרֶץ יִשְׂרָאֵל, וּמַנּוּ – עוּלָּא מִשְּׁמֵיהּ דְּרַבִּי יוֹחָנָן אָמַר: שְׁלָקוֹת מְבָרְכִין עֲלֵיהֶן "שֶׁהַכֹּל נִהְיָה בִּדְבָרוֹ"; וַאֲנִי אוֹמֵר: כָּל שֶׁתְּחִלָּתוֹ "בּוֹרֵא פְּרִי הָאֲדָמָה", שְׁלָקוֹ – "שֶׁהַכֹּל נִהְיָה בִּדְבָרוֹ"; וְכָל שֶׁתְּחִלָּתוֹ "שֶׁהַכֹּל נִהְיָה בִּדְבָרוֹ", שְׁלָקוֹ – "בּוֹרֵא פְּרִי הָאֲדָמָה".

**Rav Ḥisda taught in the name of Rabbeinu; and** the Gemara remarks incidentally: **Who is** Rabbeinu? **Rav. Over boiled vegetables one recites: Who creates fruit of the ground. And our Rabbis who descended from Eretz Yisrael,** and again the Gemara explains: **And who is** the Sage with this title? **Ulla said in the name of Rabbi Yoḥanan: Over boiled vegetables one recites: By whose word all things came to be,** since after they are boiled, they are no longer the same as they were before. Expressing his own opinion, Rav Ḥisda said: **And I say** that there is an intermediate opinion: **Any** vegetable that, when eaten **in its original** uncooked state, one recites: **Who creates fruit of the ground,** when he **boiled it,** he recites: **By whose word all things came to be,** as boiling damages it qualitatively. **And any** vegetable that when eaten **in its original** uncooked state, one recites: **By whose word all things came to be,** because it is not typically eaten raw, when he **boiled it,** he recites: **Who creates fruit of the ground.**

בִּשְׁלָמָא כֹּל שֶׁתְּחִלָּתוֹ "שֶׁהַכֹּל נִהְיָה בִּדְבָרוֹ" שְׁלָקוֹ "בּוֹרֵא פְּרִי הָאֲדָמָה" – מַשְׁכַּחַתְּ לָהּ בְּכַרְבָּא וְסִלְקָא וְקָרָא; אֶלָּא כֹּל שֶׁתְּחִלָּתוֹ "בּוֹרֵא פְּרִי הָאֲדָמָה", שְׁלָקוֹ – "שֶׁהַכֹּל", הֵיכִי מַשְׁכַּחַתְּ לָהּ? אָמַר רַב נַחְמָן בַּר יִצְחָק: מַשְׁכַּחַתְּ לָהּ בְּתוּמֵי וְכַרָתֵי.

The Gemara asks: **Granted, any** vegetable that, when eaten **in its original** uncooked state, one recites: **By whose word all things came to be,** when he **boiled it,** he recites: **Who creates fruit of the ground,** as **you** can **find** several vegetables, e.g., **cabbage, chard,**[B] **and pumpkin** which are virtually inedible raw, and boiling renders it edible. **However,** under **what** circumstances can **you find** a case where **any** vegetable that when eaten **in its original** uncooked state, one recites: **Who creates fruit of the ground,** when he **boiled it,** he recites: **By whose word all things came to be,** as boiling damages the vegetable qualitatively? **Rav Naḥman bar Yitzḥak said: You** can **find it** in the case of **garlic and leeks.**

דָּרַשׁ רַב נַחְמָן מִשּׁוּם רַבֵּינוּ, וּמַנּוּ – שְׁמוּאֵל: שְׁלָקוֹת מְבָרְכִין עֲלֵיהֶם "בּוֹרֵא פְּרִי הָאֲדָמָה"; וַחֲבֵרֵינוּ הַיּוֹרְדִים מֵאֶרֶץ יִשְׂרָאֵל, וּמַנּוּ – עוּלָּא, מִשְּׁמֵיהּ דְּרַבִּי יוֹחָנָן אָמַר: שְׁלָקוֹת מְבָרְכִין עֲלֵיהֶן "שֶׁהַכֹּל נִהְיָה בִּדְבָרוֹ";

**Rav Naḥman taught in the name of Rabbeinu; and who is** Rabbeinu? **Shmuel: Over boiled vegetables one recites: Who creates fruit of the ground. And our colleagues**[N] **who descended from Eretz Yisrael; and who is** the Sage with this title? **Ulla said in the name of Rabbi Yoḥanan: Over boiled vegetables, one recites: By whose word all things came to be.**

וַאֲנִי אוֹמֵר: בְּמַחֲלוֹקֶת שְׁנוּיָה. דְּתַנְיָא: יוֹצְאִין בְּרָקִיק הַשָּׁרוּי וּבִמְבוּשָּׁל שֶׁלֹּא נִמּוֹחַ, דִּבְרֵי רַבִּי מֵאִיר, וְרַבִּי יוֹסֵי אוֹמֵר: יוֹצְאִים בְּרָקִיק הַשָּׁרוּי, אֲבָל לֹא בִּמְבוּשָּׁל, אַף עַל פִּי שֶׁלֹּא נִמּוֹחַ.

Rav Naḥman remarked: **I say this** is dependent upon and **taught** as a tannaitic **dispute, as it was taught** in a *baraita* with regard to the *halakhot* of *matza* on Passover: **One fulfills the** mitzva of *matza* **with a wafer soaked** in water[H] or **with** one that is **boiled** as long that **it did not dissolve;** this is **the statement of Rabbi Meir. And Rabbi Yosei says: One fulfills the** mitzva of *matza* **with a soaked wafer but not with** one that is **boiled even if it did not dissolve.** Rav Naḥman concludes that this dispute with regard to boiled *matza* reflects a larger dispute with regard to boiling in general, whether or not it diminishes the flavor of that which is boiled.

וְלָא הִיא, דְּכוּלֵּי עָלְמָא – שְׁלָקוֹת מְבָרְכִין עֲלֵיהֶן "בּוֹרֵא פְּרִי הָאֲדָמָה", וְעַד כָּאן לָא קָאָמַר רַבִּי יוֹסֵי הָתָם – אֶלָּא מִשּׁוּם דְּבָעֵינַן טַעַם מַצָּה וְלֵיכָּא, אֲבָל הָכָא – אֲפִילּוּ רַבִּי יוֹסֵי מוֹדֶה.

This approach is rejected by the Gemara: **That is not so; as everyone agrees that over boiled vegetables one recites: Who creates fruit of the ground. Rabbi Yosei only said** the *halakha*, that one fulfills his obligation of *matza* if it is soaked but not if it is boiled, **there, because** in order to fulfill the mitzva, **we require** the **taste of** *matza*,[N] **and it is lacking. However, here, even Rabbi Yosei agrees** that boiling vegetables does not damage it qualitatively.

## HALAKHA

**Boiled vegetables – שְׁלָקוֹת:** Before eating a boiled vegetable which is eaten both raw and cooked, one always recites: Who creates fruit of the ground. Before eating a vegetable normally eaten raw, if it is cooked, one recites: By whose word all things came to be. Before eating a vegetable only eaten cooked, when it is cooked, one recites: Who creates fruit of the ground, and when raw: By whose word all things came to be, in accordance with the ruling of Rav Ḥisda (Rambam *Sefer Ahava, Hilkhot Berakhot* 8:3; *Shulḥan Arukh, Oraḥ Ḥayyim* 205:1).

**A soaked wafer on Passover – רָקִיק שָׁרוּי בְּפֶסַח:** One fulfills his obligation, after-the-fact, on the eve of Passover with unleavened bread soaked in water, i.e., in the case of an elderly or sick person (*Magen Avraham*; Rambam *Sefer Zemanim, Hilkhot Ḥametz UMatza* 6:6. *Shulḥan Arukh, Oraḥ Ḥayyim* 461:4).

## BACKGROUND

**Chard – סִלְקָא:** The *Beta vulgaris cicla* is an annual garden beet plant from the Chenopod family, which reaches a height of 15–30 cm. Chard leaves are eaten cooked and taste like spinach. The plant continues to grow after its leaves are pruned. Nowadays, its leaves are also used as birdfeed.

Chard

## NOTES

**And our Rabbis who descended from Eretz Yisrael… And our colleagues – ...רַבּוֹתֵינוּ הַיּוֹרְדִין מֵאֶרֶץ יִשְׂרָאֵל וַחֲבֵרֵינוּ וכו׳:** Both expressions, our Rabbis who descended from Eretz Yisrael and our colleagues who descended from Eretz Yisrael, refer to Ulla. Rav Ḥisda, due to his humility, referred to him as our Rabbis; and Rav Naḥman, the father-in-law of the Exilarch and a judge, who considered himself Ulla's equal, referred to him as our colleagues.

**The taste of *matza* – טַעַם מַצָּה:** Although there is no obligation to taste a specific unleavened bread flavor (see the *Me'iri*), however, when it is boiled, it is no longer considered bread of affliction, as it has the taste of rich unleavened bread and one cannot fulfill his obligation with it (*Talmidei Rabbeinu Yona, Tosefot HaRosh*).

אָמַר רַבִּי חִיָּיא בַּר אַבָּא אָמַר רַבִּי יוֹחָנָן: שְׁלָקוֹת מְבָרְכִין עֲלֵיהֶם ״בּוֹרֵא פְּרִי הָאֲדָמָה״, וְרַבִּי בִּנְיָמִין בַּר יֶפֶת אָמַר רַבִּי יוֹחָנָן: שְׁלָקוֹת מְבָרְכִין עֲלֵיהֶם ״שֶׁהַכֹּל נִהְיָה בִּדְבָרוֹ״. אָמַר רַב נַחְמָן בַּר יִצְחָק: קָבַע עוּלָּא לְשַׁבַּשְׁתֵּיהּ כְּרַבִּי בִּנְיָמִין בַּר יֶפֶת.

Ulla's statement in the name of Rabbi Yoḥanan with regard to boiled vegetables was cited above. The Gemara cites two conflicting traditions with regard to Rabbi Yoḥanan's statement. **Rabbi Ḥiyya bar Abba said** that **Rabbi Yoḥanan said: Over boiled vegetables, one recites: Who creates fruit of the ground, and Rabbi Binyamin bar Yefet said** that **Rabbi Yoḥanan said: Over boiled vegetables, one recites: By whose word all things came to be.** Commenting on this, **Rav Naḥman bar Yitzḥak said: Ulla established his error in accordance with** the opinion of **Rabbi Binyamin bar Yefet,** which conflicted with the prevailing opinion among the Sages in Babylonia.

תָּהֵי בָּהּ רַבִּי זֵירָא: וְכִי מָה עִנְיַן רַבִּי בִּנְיָמִין בַּר יֶפֶת אֵצֶל רַבִּי חִיָּיא בַּר אַבָּא? רַבִּי חִיָּיא בַּר אַבָּא – דָּיֵיק וְגָמִיר שְׁמַעְתָּא מֵרַבִּי יוֹחָנָן רַבֵּיהּ, וְרַבִּי בִּנְיָמִין בַּר יֶפֶת – לָא דָּיֵיק; וְעוֹד, רַבִּי חִיָּיא בַּר אַבָּא כָּל תְּלָתִין יוֹמִין מְהַדַּר תַּלְמוּדֵיהּ קַמֵּיהּ דְּרַבִּי יוֹחָנָן רַבֵּיהּ, וְרַבִּי בִּנְיָמִין בַּר יֶפֶת לָא מְהַדַּר; וְעוֹד, בַּר מִן דֵּין וּבַר מִן דֵּין, דְּהַהוּא תּוּרְמְסָא דְּשָׁלְקִי לֵיהּ שְׁבַע זִמְנִין בְּקִדֵּרָה וְאָכְלִי לֵיהּ בְּקִנּוּחַ סְעוּדָה, אָתוּ וּשְׁאַלוּ לְרַבִּי יוֹחָנָן, וַאֲמַר לְהוּ: מְבָרְכִין עֲלָוֵיהּ ״בּוֹרֵא פְּרִי הָאֲדָמָה״;

**Rabbi Zeira wondered** with regard to Ulla's approach: **What is the matter of Rabbi Binyamin bar Yefet**[N] doing in the same discussion **with Rabbi Ḥiyya bar Abba? Rabbi Ḥiyya bar Abba was meticulous and learned the** ***halakha*** **from Rabbi Yoḥanan, his teacher; and Rabbi Binyamin bar Yefet was not meticulous. Furthermore, every thirty days, Rabbi Ḥiyya bar Abba reviews his studies**[N] **before Rabbi Yoḥanan, his teacher, while Rabbi Binyamin bar Yefet does not review** his studies. **Furthermore, aside from these** reasons concerning the difference between a wise and meticulous student like Rabbi Ḥiyya bar Abba and a student like Rabbi Binyamin bar Yefet, one can also bring proof from the custom of Rabbi Yoḥanan, as **the lupin**[B] **is boiled seven times in a pot and eaten as dessert** at the end of a **meal. They came and asked Rabbi Yoḥanan** with regard to the blessing to be recited over this lupin, **and he said to them: One recites over it: Who creates fruit of the ground,** indicating that one recites that blessing over boiled vegetables.

וְעוֹד, אָמַר רַבִּי חִיָּיא בַּר אַבָּא: אֲנִי רָאִיתִי אֶת רַבִּי יוֹחָנָן שֶׁאָכַל זַיִת מָלִיחַ וּבֵירֵךְ עָלָיו תְּחִלָּה וָסוֹף. אִי אָמְרַתְּ בִּשְׁלָמָא שְׁלָקוֹת בְּמִילְּתַיְיהוּ קָיְימִי – בִּתְחִלָּה מְבָרֵךְ עָלָיו ״בּוֹרֵא פְּרִי הָעֵץ״, וּלְבַסּוֹף מְבָרֵךְ עָלָיו בְּרָכָה אַחַת מֵעֵין שָׁלֹשׁ, אֶלָּא אִי אָמְרַתְּ שְׁלָקוֹת לָאו בְּמִילְּתַיְיהוּ קָיְימִי, בִּשְׁלָמָא בִּתְחִלָּה מְבָרֵךְ עָלָיו ״שֶׁהַכֹּל נִהְיָה בִּדְבָרוֹ״, אֶלָּא לְבַסּוֹף מַאי מְבָרֵךְ?

**Furthermore, Rabbi Ḥiyya bar Abba said: I saw Rabbi Yoḥanan eat a salted olive,** which, halakhically, is considered cooked, **and he recited a blessing over it both before and after. Granted, if you say** that **boiled vegetables remain in their original state** and that cooking does not qualitatively damage them, then certainly **at the start one recites over it: Who creates fruit of the tree, and at the end one recites over it one blessing abridged from** the **three** blessings of Grace after Meals, just as he would over any of the seven species for which Eretz Yisrael was praised. **However, if you say** that **boiled vegetables do not remain in their original state, granted, at the start, one recites: By whose word all things came to be. However, at the end, what blessing does he recite?** There are several opinions that hold that no blessing is recited after eating something whose initial blessing was: By whose word all things came to be.

דִּילְמָא: ״בּוֹרֵא נְפָשׁוֹת רַבּוֹת וְחֶסְרוֹנָן עַל כָּל מַה שֶּׁבָּרָא״.

The Gemara rejects this: That is no proof, as **perhaps** Rabbi Yoḥanan held that on items over which at the start one recites: By whose word all things came to be, at the end he recites: **Who creates the many forms of life and their needs, for all that You have created.**

מֵתִיב רַב יִצְחָק בַּר שְׁמוּאֵל: יְרָקוֹת שֶׁאָדָם יוֹצֵא בָּהֶן יְדֵי חוֹבָתוֹ בְּפֶסַח – יוֹצֵא בָּהֶן וּבְקֶלַח שֶׁלָּהֶן, אֲבָל לֹא כְּבוּשִׁין וְלֹא שְׁלוּקִין וְלֹא מְבוּשָּׁלִין; וְאִי סָלְקָא דַּעְתָּךְ בְּמִילְּתַיְיהוּ קָאֵי – שְׁלוּקִין אַמַּאי לֹא?

**Rabbi Yitzḥak bar Shmuel raised an objection** to the ruling that over both boiled vegetables and raw vegetables one recites the same blessing, from a *baraita* concerning the *halakhot* of eating bitter herbs on Passover: **Vegetables with which one may fulfill his obligation** in the mitzva of bitter herbs **on Passover,**[H] **one fulfills** his obligation **with** both the vegetables **themselves as well as with their stalks. However,** one may **neither** fulfill his obligation **with pickled** vegetables, **nor with boiled** vegetables **nor with cooked** vegetables. **And if it would enter your mind** that **they remain in their original state, why are boiled** vegetables not fit for use in fulfilling the mitzva of bitter herbs?

שָׁאנֵי הָתָם, דְּבָעֵינַן טַעַם מָרוֹר – וְלֵיכָּא.

The Gemara answers: **It is different there,** as even if we assert that boiled vegetables remain in their original state, **we require the taste of bitter herbs, and it is lacking.** There is no proof that boiling damages the vegetable qualitatively.

אָמַר לֵיהּ רַבִּי יִרְמְיָה לְרַבִּי זֵירָא: רַבִּי יוֹחָנָן הֵיכִי מְבָרֵךְ עַל זַיִת מָלִיחַ? כֵּיוָן דִּשְׁקִילָא לְגַרְעִינֵיהּ

The Gemara related above that Rabbi Yoḥanan recited a blessing over a salted olive. With regard to this story, **Rabbi Yirmeya said to Rabbi Zeira: How did Rabbi Yoḥanan recite a blessing over a salted olive** after he ate it? **Since the pit was removed,** i.e., he did not eat it,

## NOTES

What is the matter of Rabbi Binyamin bar Yefet – מָה עִנְיַן רַבִּי בִּנְיָמִין בַּר יֶפֶת: Rabbi Zeira's astonishment was explained in several manners. Some saw it merely as an expression of surprise: How could those in the study hall have the same approach to these two versions when the difference in their reliability is so significant? Others explain that Rabbi Zeira's difficulty has halakhic ramifications. Since according to Rabbi Naḥman bar Yitzḥak, Ulla relied upon Rabbi Binyamin bar Yefet's statement, Rabbi Zeira said that it is inconceivable that Ulla would have relied on a statement contrary to the statement of Rabbi Ḥiyya bar Abba. Therefore, Rabbi Yoḥanan must have made his statements with regard to two different cases, which supports the statement of Rav Ḥisda, who posited a similar distinction (Rashba).

Reviews his studies – מְהַדַּר תַּלְמוּדֵיהּ: Rabbi Ḥiyya bar Abba would summarize before Rabbi Yoḥanan the material that he learned from him, in order to ascertain whether he accurately understood Rabbi Yoḥanan's opinions in all those areas.

## BACKGROUND

Lupin – תּוּרְמְסָא: Lupin is a name common to several plants from the legume family and from the *faboideae* sub-family. The cultivated lupin, *lupinus termis*, and the yellow lupin, *lupinus luteus*, are the most common forms of the plant.

These plants, which grow to a height of approximately 1 m, have leaves divided into several leaflets. Their flowers are light blue or yellow with small seeds (8 mm for the yellow lupin and 15 mm for the cultivated lupin) that grow in pods. Due to the presence of certain alkaloids, their natural flavor is bitter. In order to eat them, they are soaked, rinsed, and soaked again; alternatively, only the seeds are soaked. Even today, boiled lupin seeds are sold as a dessert, though the plant is generally utilized for animal feed or fertilizer.

Cultivated lupin

## HALAKHA

Bitter herbs on Passover – מָרוֹר בְּפֶסַח: All vegetables suitable for use in fulfilling the mitzva of bitter herbs, both their leaves, when damp and fresh, and their stalks, whether dry or damp, may be used. However, one does not fulfill his obligation if they were cooked, pickled, or lost their flavor (Rambam *Sefer Zemanim, Hilkhot Ḥametz UMatza* 7:13. *Shulḥan Arukh, Oraḥ Ḥayyim* 473:5).

בְּצַר לֵיהּ שִׁיעוּרָא!

**it lacks the** requisite **measure?**[H] The smallest quantity of food that is considered eating is the size of an olive-bulk, and an olive with its pit removed is smaller than that.

אָמַר לֵיהּ: מִי סָבְרַתְּ כְּזַיִת גָּדוֹ בָּעֵינַן?! כְּזַיִת בֵּינוֹנִי בָּעֵינַן וְהָא אִיכָּא וְהַהוּא דְּאַיְיתוּ לְקַמֵּיהּ דְּרַבִּי יוֹחָנָן זַיִת גָּדוֹל הֲוָה, דְּאַף עַל גַּב דְּשָׁקְלוּ לְגַרְעִינוּתֵיהּ פַּשׁ לֵיהּ שִׁיעוּרָא.

**He said to him: Do you hold that we require a large olive** as the measure of food necessary in order to recite a blessing after eating? **We require a medium-sized olive and that** olive **was** that size, as the olive **that they brought before Rabbi Yoḥanan was a large olive. Even though they removed its pit, the** requisite **measure remained.**[H]

דִּתְנַן: זַיִת שֶׁאָמְרוּ – לֹא קָטָן וְלֹא גָּדוֹ אֶלָּא בֵּינוֹנִי, וְזֶהוּ אָגוּרִי. וְאָמַר רַבִּ אַבָּהוּ: לֹא אָגוּרִי שְׁמוֹ אֶלָּא אַבְרוּטִ שְׁמוֹ, וְאָמְרִי לָהּ: סַמְרוּסִי שְׁמוֹ, וְלָמָּ נִקְרָא שְׁמוֹ אָגוּרִי – שֶׁשַּׁמְנוֹ אָגוּ בְּתוֹכוֹ.

The Gemara cites a proof that the halakhic measure of an olive is not based on a large olive **as we learned** in a mishna: **The olive of which** the Sages **spoke** with regard to the halakhic measures is **neither small nor large, but medium, and that** olive **is called *aguri*. And Rabbi Abbahu said: The name** of that genus of olives **is not *aguri*, but its name is *avruti*, and some say** that **its name is *samrusi*.**[L] **And why,** then, **is it called *aguri*? Because its oil is accumulated [*agur*] inside it.**

נֵימָא כְּתַנָּאֵי, דְּהָנְהוּ תְּרֵי תַּלְמִידֵ דְּהָווּ יָתְבֵי קַמֵּיהּ דְּבַר קַפָּרָא, הֵבִיא לְפָנָיו כְּרוּב וְדוּרְמַסְקִין וּפַרְגִּיּוֹת, נָתַ בַּר קַפָּרָא רְשׁוּת לְאֶחָד מֵהֶן לְבָרֵךְ, קָפַץ וּבֵרֵךְ עַל הַפַּרְגִּיּוֹת, לִגְלֵג עָלָי חֲבֵירוֹ. כָּעַס בַּר קַפָּרָא, אָמַר: לֹא עַ הַמְבָרֵךְ אֲנִי כּוֹעֵס אֶלָּא עַל הַמְלַגְלֵ אֲנִי כּוֹעֵס; אִם חֲבֵירְךָ דּוֹמֶה כְּמִ שֶׁלֹּא טָעַם טַעַם בָּשָׂר מֵעוֹלָם – אַתָּה עַל מָה לִגְלַגְתָּ עָלָיו?! חָזַר וְאָמַ לֹא עַל הַמְלַגְלֵג אֲנִי כּוֹעֵס אֶלָּא עַ הַמְבָרֵךְ אֲנִי כּוֹעֵס. וְאָמַר: אִם חָכְמָה אֵין כָּאן, זְקֵנָה אֵין כָּאן?!

With regard to the appropriate blessing over boiled vegetables: **Let us say** that this dispute **is parallel** to a dispute between the *tanna'im*, as the Gemara relates: **Two students were sitting before bar Kappara when** cooked **cabbage,** cooked Damascene **plums**[B] **and pullets were set before him. Bar Kappara gave one of** the students **permission to recite a blessing.**[N] **He hurried and recited a blessing over the pullets** and **his counterpart ridiculed him** for gluttonously reciting the blessing that should have been recited later, first. **Bar Kappara became angry** with both of them, **he said: I am not angry with the one who recited the blessing, but at the one who ridiculed** him. **If your counterpart is like one who never tasted the flavor of meat** and was therefore partial to the pullet, and hurriedly ate it, **why did you ridicule him?** Bar Kappara **continued and said** to the second student: **I am not upset at the one who ridiculed** him, **rather** it is **with the one who recited the blessing that I am angry. And he said: If there is no wisdom here, is there no elder here?** If you are uncertain which blessing to recite first, couldn't you have asked me, as I am an elder?

תָּנָא: וּשְׁנֵיהֶם לֹא הוֹצִיאוּ שְׁנָתָן.

The Gemara concludes that **it was taught: And both of them did not** live **out his year.** Due to bar Kappara's anger they were punished, and both died within the year.

מַאי לָאו בְּהָא קָא מִיפַּלְגִי; דִּמְבָרֵךְ סָבַר: שְׁלָקוֹת וּפַרְגִּיּוֹת "שֶׁהַכֹּל נִהְיָה בִּדְבָרוֹ", הִלְכָּךְ חָבִיב עָדִיף; וּמְלַגְלֵג סָבַר: שְׁלָקוֹת – "בּוֹרֵא פְּרִי הָאֲדָמָה" פַּרְגִּיּוֹת – "שֶׁהַכֹּל נִהְיָה בִּדְבָרוֹ" הִלְכָּךְ פֵּירָא עָדִיף!

The Gemara attempts to infer from this story to the topic at hand: **What? Is it not that they disagreed with regard to the following?** The **one who recited the blessing** over the pullet first **held** that the blessing to be recited over both **boiled vegetables and pullet** is: **By whose word all things came to be, and, therefore,** that which **he prefers** takes **precedence** and is eaten first. The **one who ridiculed** him **held** that over **boiled vegetables** one recites: **Who creates fruit of the ground,** and over **pullet** one recites: **By whose word all things came to be, and, therefore, the fruit** takes **precedence,**[H] as its blessing is more specific and therefore more significant.

**HALAKHA**

**The requisite measure for a final blessing – שִׁיעוּר לִבְרָכָה אַחֲרוֹנָה:** One does not recite a blessing after eating if he ate less than an olive-bulk of bread or any other food. Some maintain that after eating an entity, e.g., an olive with its pit, one recites a final blessing. Therefore, one should not eat less than an olive-bulk of any entity, in accordance with the Jerusalem Talmud (Rambam *Sefer Ahava, Hilkhot Berakhot* 1:1 *Shulḥan Arukh, Oraḥ Ḥayyim* 210:1).

**The measure of an olive-bulk – שִׁעוּר כְּזַיִת:** One who eats any food prohibited by Torah law, is liable for punishment, whether lashes, *karet,* or death at the hands of Heaven, if he ate the measure of a medium olive-bulk. There are different opinions with regard to the relative size of that olive; some say it is the equivalent of one-half of an egg-bulk (*Shulḥan Arukh*, and see *Magen Avraham*). Others say, one-third of an egg-bulk (Rambam). The later commentaries ruled that with regard to foods that one is required to eat by Torah law, e.g., unleavened bread at the seder on Passover, one must eat at least one-half of an egg-bulk. With regard to foods that one is required to eat by rabbinic law, e.g., bitter herbs at the seder on Passover, after the fact, one fulfills his obligation even if he only consumed one-third of an egg-bulk (*Sha'arei Teshuva*; Rambam *Sefer Kedusha, Hilkhot Ma'akhalot Assurot* 14:1; *Shulḥan Arukh, Oraḥ Ḥayyim* 486).

**The fruit takes precedence – פֵּירָא עָדִיף:** If one has two kinds of food before him, one of which has a more significant blessing, for example: Who creates fruit of the tree, or: Who creates fruit of the ground, as opposed to: By whose word all things came to be, one should recite the more significant blessing first, even if he prefers the other food (*Magen Avraham*; *Shulḥan Arukh, Oraḥ Ḥayyim* 211:3).

**LANGUAGE**

*Avruti, samrusi* – **אַבְרוּטִי, סַמְרוּסִי:** The source of these words and their meaning are uncertain and even their correct pronunciation is unclear. There are variant readings, *avursi* or *avruci*. It might be possible to tie the word to an Iranian precursor. The Greek word ωραιος, *averius*, has the same meaning: Ripe.

The term *samrusi* might come from the Greek ἡμίωραιος, *hemioraios*. When it appears with the Latin prefix semi, half, it means half-ripe. Nevertheless, all of these explanations are speculative.

**BACKGROUND**

**Damascene plums – דּוּרְמַסְקִין:** These are a species of plum indigenous to Damascus, *Prunus domestica var. damascena*. Even today, these are black or yellow, spherical or ovule, hair-covered fruit, up to 3 cm in diameter that grow on trees or shrubs with white flowers and wide, coarse leaves. Because of halakhic difficulties (see *Tosafot*), Rashi determines that this term refers to a vegetable. Nevertheless, it is possible that they are speaking of cooked plums, over which one might recite: Who creates fruit of the ground.

Branch and fruit of the Damascene plum

**NOTES**

**Bar Kappara gave one of the students permission to recite a blessing – נָתַן בַּר קַפָּרָא רְשׁוּת לְאֶחָד מֵהֶן לְבָרֵךְ:** The early commentaries wondered why each of them did not recite a blessing for himself, as there is no *zimmun* with regard to fruit. They explained that with regard to the blessing before eating, it is permissible to do so (*Tosafot*, Rashba). They continued that bar Kappara himself only wished to eat the secondary portion, and therefore he asked one of his students to recite the blessing over the primary food in his place (*Penei Yehoshua*). In the Jerusalem Talmud they commented on this incident: Two people are gone, i.e., dead, and we still do not know what to do in this case (see Rashba).

BACKGROUND

**Turnip – לִפְתָּא:** *Brassica rapa*, the modern-day rapeseed, is a garden vegetable from the mustard and cabbage family, *Cruciferae*. Its dark, thick, generally spherical roots are eaten, primarily boiled.

Turnip

**Dill – שֶׁבֶת:** *Anethum graveolens* is an annual or biennial herb from the *Apiaceaa* family. Reaching a height of 50–80 cm, and bearing small, yellow flowers, the dill plant and its thread-like leaves have a unique scent. These leaves are used as a spice and often used for pickling zucchini, or cooked in soup. Oil is extracted from the seeds and in the past was used for medicinal purposes. In the time of the Mishna, dill was common in herb-gardens. Today, it is grown in gardens on a limited basis and grows wild in different places.

Dill

לָא, דְּכוּלֵּי עָלְמָא שְׁלָקוֹת וּפַרְגִּיוֹת "שֶׁהַכֹּל נִהְיָה בִּדְבָרוֹ", וְהָכָא בְּהַאי סְבָרָא קָא מִיפַּלְגִי: מָר סָבַר: חָבִיב עָדִיף, וּמָר סָבַר: כְּרוּב עָדִיף, דְּזַיֵּין.

The Gemara rejects this explanation: **No, everyone agrees** that over **boiled vegetables and pullet** one recites: **By whose word all things came to be, and here they argue over this:** This Sage, who recited the blessing, **held that** the food which is **preferred takes precedence** and one recites a blessing over it first, **and the Sage** who ridiculed him **held: Cabbage takes precedence, as it nourishes.**

אָמַר רַבִּי זֵירָא, כִּי הֲוֵינַן בֵּי רַב הוּנָא אָמַר לָן: הָנֵי גַּרְגְּלִידֵי דְּלִפְתָּא, פַּרְמִינְהוּ פְּרִימָא רַבָּא – "בּוֹרֵא פְּרִי הָאֲדָמָה", פְּרִימָא זוּטָא – "שֶׁהַכֹּל נִהְיָה בִּדְבָרוֹ". וְכִי אֲתָאן לְבֵי רַב יְהוּדָה אָמַר לָן: אִידִי וְאִידִי "בּוֹרֵא פְּרִי הָאֲדָמָה", וְהָא דְּפַרְמִינְהוּ טְפֵי – כִּי הֵיכִי דְּנִמְתִּיק טַעְמֵיהּ.

**Rabbi Zeira said: When we were in the study hall of Rav Huna he said to us: These turnip heads,**[B] if **one cut them extensively** into small pieces, he recites over them: **Who creates fruit of the ground,** because by doing so, he enhanced their flavor. If he **cut them slightly** into large slices, he recites over them: **By whose word all things came to be. And when we came to the study hall of Rav Yehuda he said to us:** Over both **these,** small pieces, **and those,** large slices, one recites: **Who creates fruit of the ground, and the fact that he cut them extensively was in order to sweeten its flavor.**[H]

אָמַר רַב אַשִׁי, כִּי הֲוֵינַן בֵּי רַב כָּהֲנָא אָמַר לָן: תַּבְשִׁילָא דְּסִלְקָא דְּלָא מַפְשׁוּ בָּהּ קִמְחָא – "בּוֹרֵא פְּרִי הָאֲדָמָה", דְּלִפְתָּא, דְּמַפְשׁוּ בָּהּ קִמְחָא טְפֵי – "בּוֹרֵא מִינֵי מְזוֹנוֹת"; וַהֲדַר אָמַר: אִידִי וְאִידִי "בּוֹרֵא פְּרִי הָאֲדָמָה", וְהַאי דְּשַׁדֵי בָּהּ קִמְחָא טְפֵי – לְדַבּוֹקֵי בְּעָלְמָא עַבְדִי לָהּ.

On a similar note, **Rav Ashi said: When we were in the study hall of Rav Kahana, he said to us:** Over **a cooked dish of beets to which they,** typically, **do not add** a **significant** amount of **flour** one recites: **Who creates fruit of the ground.** Over **a cooked dish of turnips to which they,** typically, **add** a **more significant** amount of **flour,** one recites: **Who creates the various types of nourishment. And** Rav Kahana **reconsidered** his previous statement and said: Over both **these,** beets, **and those,** turnips, one recites: **Who creates fruit of the ground, and the fact that they threw extra flour in** with the turnips, **they did so merely** so the components of the cooked dish would **stick together.** The primary ingredient in the dish remains the turnips, not the flour.[H]

אָמַר רַב חִסְדָּא: תַּבְשִׁיל שֶׁל תְּרָדִין – יָפֶה לַלֵּב וְטוֹב לָעֵינַיִם, וְכָל שֶׁכֵּן לִבְנֵי מֵעַיִם. אָמַר אַבָּיֵי: וְהוּא דְּיָתֵיב אַבֵּי תְפֵי וְעָבֵיד "תּוּךְ תּוּךְ".

Tangential to this mention of a turnip dish, **Rav Ḥisda** added, **and said: A cooked dish of beets is beneficial for the heart, good for the eyes and all the more so, for the intestines. Abaye said: That** is specifically when the dish **sits on the stove and makes a *tukh tukh*** sound, i.e., it boils.

אָמַר רַב פַּפָּא: פְּשִׁיטָא לִי, מַיָּא דְּסִלְקָא – כְּסִלְקָא, וּמַיָּא דְּלִפְתָּא – כְּלִפְתָּא, וּמַיָּא דְּכוּלְּהוּ שְׁלָקֵי – כְּכוּלְּהוּ שְׁלָקֵי. בָּעֵי רַב פַּפָּא: מַיָּא דְּשִׁיבְתָא מַאי, לְמַתּוֹקֵי טַעְמָא עָבְדִי, אוֹ לְעַבּוֹרֵי זוּהֲמָא עָבְדִי לָהּ?

**Rav Pappa said: It is clear to me** that **beet water,** water in which beets were boiled, **has** the same status **as beets, and turnip water has** the same status **turnips, and the water** in which **all boiled vegetables**[H] were boiled **has** the same status **as all boiled vegetables.** However, **Rav Pappa raised a dilemma: What** is the status of **water** in which **dill**[B] was boiled? **Do they use** dill **to sweeten the taste, or do they use it to remove** residual **filth?** If the dill was added to flavor the food then the water in which it was boiled should be treated like water in which any other vegetable was boiled. However, if the dill was added merely absorb the residue of the soup, then there was never any intention to flavor the dish and one should not recite a blessing over it.

תָּא שְׁמַע: הַשֶּׁבֶת, מִשֶּׁנָּתְנָה טַעַם בַּקְּדֵרָה – אֵין בָּהּ מִשּׁוּם תְּרוּמָה וְאֵינָהּ מְטַמְּאָה טוּמְאַת אוֹכָלִים. שְׁמַע מִינַּהּ: לְמַתּוֹקֵי טַעְמָא עָבְדִי לָהּ, שְׁמַע מִינַּהּ.

**Come and hear** a resolution to this dilemma from what we learned in a mishna in the tractate *Okatzin*: **Dill,**[H] **once it has** already **given** its **flavor in the pot,** no longer has any value and **is no** longer **subject to** the *halakhot* of *teruma* **and** since it is no longer considered food, **it can no** longer become impure with **the ritual impurity of food. Learn from this** that **they used dill to sweeten the taste.** The Gemara concludes: Indeed, **learn from this.**

HALAKHA

**Vegetable slices – חֲתִיכוֹת יָרָק:** With regard to a vegetable that was cut into small pieces, if it maintains its identity and form (*Mishna Berura*), its blessing remains the same (*Shulḥan Arukh, Oraḥ Ḥayyim* 205:4).

**A cooked dish of vegetables and flour – תַּבְשִׁיל יָרָק וְקֶמַח:** Before eating vegetables to which flour was added for purposes of consistency, one recites: Who creates fruit of the ground, as he does over vegetables, in accordance with the opinion of Rav Kahana (Rambam *Sefer Ahava, Hilkhot Berakhot* 83:11; *Shulḥan Arukh, Oraḥ Ḥayyim* 208:2).

**Vegetable water – מֵי יְרָקוֹת:** Before eating soup made from vegetables that are typically eaten with their broth, if he cooked them with the intention to eat the vegetables as well, he recites: Who creates fruit of the ground, in accordance with the opinion of Rav Pappa (Rambam *Sefer Ahava, Hilkhot Berakhot* 8:4; *Shulḥan Arukh, Oraḥ Ḥayyim* 205:2).

**Dill – הַשֶּׁבֶת:** Once dill was cooked and flavored the food with which it was cooked, it no longer has the legal status of food as far as the *halakhot* of ritual impurity and *teruma* are concerned (Rambam *Sefer Zera'im, Hilkhot Teruma* 15:12, *Sefer Tahara, Hilkhot Tumat Okhelin* 1:7).

אָמַר רַב חִיָּיא בַּר אַשִׁי: פַּת צְנוּמָה בַּקְּעָרָה מְבָרְכִין עָלֶיהָ ״הַמּוֹצִיא״. וּפְלִיגָא דְּרַבִּי חִיָּיא, דְּאָמַר רַבִּי חִיָּיא: צָרִיךְ שֶׁתִּכְלֶה בְּרָכָה עִם הַפַּת.

**Rav Ḥiyya bar Ashi said: Over dry bread** that was placed **in a bowl** to soak,[N] **one recites: Who brings forth** bread from the earth, even if there is another loaf of bread before him, as it is considered bread in every respect. This *halakha* **disagrees with** the opinion of **Rabbi Ḥiyya, as Rabbi Ḥiyya said: The blessing must conclude with** the beginning of the breaking of **the** loaf of **bread.** The dried bread had already been sliced and separated from the loaf.

מַתְקִיף לַהּ רָבָא: מַאי שְׁנָא צְנוּמָה דְּלָא – מִשּׁוּם דְּכִי כַּלְיָא בְּרָכָה אַפְּרוּסָה קָא כַּלְיָא; עַל הַפַּת נַמִי, כִּי קָא גָּמְרָה – אַפְּרוּסָה גָּמְרָה!

**Rava strongly objects to this** assumption: **What is different about dried bread, that** one does **not** recite: Who brings forth bread from the earth, over it, **because when the blessing concludes, it concludes on a slice?** In a case where he recites a blessing **on** a loaf of **bread as well, when he completes** the blessing, **he completes it on a slice,** as one cuts the bread before the blessing.

Perek **VI**
Daf **39** Amud **b**

אֶלָּא אָמַר רָבָא: מְבָרֵךְ וְאַחַר כָּךְ בּוֹצֵעַ.

**Rather, Rava said:** When breaking bread, one **recites the blessing** over the complete loaf **and** only **afterwards, he breaks it.**[H]

נְהַרְדְּעֵי עָבְדִי כְּרַבִּי חִיָּיא, וְרַבָּנַן עָבְדִי כְּרָבָא. אָמַר רָבִינָא, אָמְרָה לִי אֵם: אֲבוּךְ עָבֵיד כְּרַבִּי חִיָּיא, דְּאָמַר רַבִּי חִיָּיא: צָרִיךְ שֶׁתִּכְלֶה בְּרָכָה עִם הַפַּת, וְרַבָּנַן עָבְדִי כְּרָבָא. וְהִלְכְתָא כְּרָבָא, דְּאָמַר: מְבָרֵךְ וְאַחַר כָּךְ בּוֹצֵעַ.

The Gemara relates: The Sages **of Neharde'a acted in accordance with** the opinion of **Rabbi Ḥiyya** and would recite the blessing as they were breaking the bread and conclude the blessing as he finished breaking off the piece of bread. **And the Rabbis acted in accordance with** the opinion of **Rava** and would recite the blessing before breaking the bread. **Ravina said: My mother told me: Your father acted in accordance with** the opinion of **Rabbi Ḥiyya, as Rabbi Ḥiyya said: The blessing must conclude with** the beginning of the breaking of **the** loaf of **bread. And the Rabbis acted in accordance with** the opinion of **Rava.** The Gemara concludes: **The *halakha* is in accordance with** the opinion of **Rava,** who **said** one **recites the blessing** over the complete loaf **and** only **afterwards he breaks it.**

אִיתְּמַר, הֵבִיאוּ לִפְנֵיהֶם פְּתִיתִין וּשְׁלֵמִין; אָמַר רַב הוּנָא: מְבָרֵךְ עַל הַפְּתִיתִין וּפוֹטֵר אֶת הַשְּׁלֵמִין, וְרַבִּי יוֹחָנָן אָמַר: שְׁלֵמָה מִצְוָה מִן הַמּוּבְחָר, אֲבָל פְּרוּסָה שֶׁל חִטִּין וּשְׁלֵמָה מִן הַשְּׂעוֹרִין – דִּבְרֵי הַכֹּל מְבָרֵךְ עַל הַפְּרוּסָה שֶׁל חִטִּין וּפוֹטֵר אֶת הַשְּׁלֵמָה שֶׁל שְׂעוֹרִין.

**It was stated** that there was an amoraic dispute with regard to whether to recite the blessing over a whole loaf of bread or to recite it over a piece of bread: If **they brought pieces and whole** loaves[N] of bread **before** those partaking of a meal, **Rav Huna said: One** may **recite the blessing over the pieces and** with that blessing **exempts the whole** loaves as well. **Rabbi Yoḥanan said: The optimal manner** in which to fulfill **the mitzva** is to recite the blessing over the **whole** loaf. **However,** if the **piece**[H] **was of wheat** bread **and the whole** loaf **was of barley** bread, **everyone agrees** that **one recites a blessing over the piece of wheat** bread. Although it is a piece of bread, it is nevertheless of superior quality, **and** in so doing **one exempts the whole** loaf **of barley** bread.

אָמַר רַבִּי יִרְמְיָה בַּר אַבָּא: כְּתַנָּאֵי; תּוֹרְמִין בָּצָל קָטָן שָׁלֵם אֲבָל לֹא חֲצִי בָּצָל גָּדוֹל. רַבִּי יְהוּדָה אוֹמֵר: לֹא כִּי, אֶלָּא חֲצִי בָצָל גָּדוֹל. מַאי לָאו בְּהָא קָמִיפַּלְגִי, דְּמָר סָבַר: חָשׁוּב עָדִיף, וּמָר סָבַר שָׁלֵם עָדִיף!

**Rabbi Yirmeya bar Abba said** that the dispute between Rav Huna and Rabbi Yoḥanan is **parallel** to a **tannaitic** dispute with regard to the *halakhot* of *teruma*. We learned: Even though the onions from which the *teruma* must be separated are divided equally between the two, **one separates *teruma* from a whole small onion**[H] **but not from half of a large onion. Rabbi Yehuda says: No, rather,** he separates *teruma* from **half of a large onion. What, is it not that they disagree over this** point, **that** one **Sage,** Rabbi Yehuda, **held** that the **more significant takes precedence;** therefore half of a large onion which is of superior quality is preferable, **and** the first *tanna* **held** that the **whole** item **takes precedence?**

הֵיכָא דְּאִיכָּא כֹּהֵן – כּוּלֵּי עָלְמָא לָא פְּלִיגִי דְּחָשׁוּב עָדִיף, כִּי פְּלִיגִי – דְּלֵיכָּא כֹּהֵן. דִּתְנַן: כָּל מָקוֹם שֶׁיֵּשׁ כֹּהֵן – תּוֹרֵם מִן הַיָּפֶה, וְכָל מָקוֹם שֶׁאֵין כֹּהֵן – תּוֹרֵם מִן הַמִּתְקַיֵּים, רַבִּי יְהוּדָה אוֹמֵר: אֵין תּוֹרֵם אֶלָּא מִן הַיָּפֶה.

The Gemara rejects this comparison: **Where there is a priest** who can immediately take the *teruma* from him, **everyone agrees** that **more significant takes precedence. When they disagree** is in a case **where there is no priest** there, **as we learned** in a mishna: **Everywhere that there is a priest, one separates *teruma* from the best,**[H] **and whenever there is no priest, one separates *teruma* from that which will endure,** so that when a priest ultimately receives it, he will be able to derive benefit from it. **Rabbi Yehuda says: One** always **separates *teruma* only from the best,** even though it is not the longest-lasting.

**NOTES**

**Over dry bread that was placed in a bowl to soak – פַּת צְנוּמָה בַּקְּעָרָה:** The difficulty with this *halakha* is in determining to which case it refers. Is it referring to a case where the bread stands alone, and one may recite: Who brings forth bread from the earth, over it? Or does it refer to a case where it is together with other loaves, and one must choose to prefer it or equate the two (*Tosafot*)? Therefore, some explain that this refers not to a situation that already occurred; but, rather, to teach that *ab initio* one may take bread, crumble it, soak it, and only then recite the blessing: Who brings forth bread from the earth. He need not recite the blessing when cutting the slice from the loaf (see *Tosefot HaRosh*, *Ḥiddushei HaRamban*, and *Alfei Menashe*).

**HALAKHA**

**Blessing and breaking bread – בְּרָכָה וּבְצִיעָה עַל הַפַּת:** One recites a blessing over a whole loaf of bread. However, one begins to slice from the loaf only to the extent that the piece is still attached to the loaf and if he lifts the slice, the entire loaf will be lifted with it. Only then does he recite the blessing. After reciting the blessing, he separates the piece from the loaf and eats it, in accordance with the opinion of Rava (Rambam *Sefer Ahava, Hilkhot Berakhot* 7:2; *Shulḥan Arukh, Oraḥ Ḥayyim* 167:1).

**A whole loaf…a piece – שְׁלֵמָה...פְּרוּסָה:** When one has a whole loaf of unrefined bread and a slice of refined bread before him, he recites a blessing over the whole loaf, even if it is made of coarse flour. If it was a wheat slice and a barley loaf, he places the slice beneath the loaf and breaks from both at once, in accordance with the opinion of Rabbi Yoḥanan (Rambam *Sefer Ahava, Hilkhot Berakhot* 7:4; *Shulḥan Arukh, Oraḥ Ḥayyim* 167:1).

**One separates *teruma* from a whole small onion – תּוֹרְמִין בָּצָל קָטָן שָׁלֵם:** It is preferable to separate a whole small onion as *teruma*, rather than from a partial onion, even if it is large, as per the unattributed mishna (Rambam *Sefer Zera'im, Hilkhot Terumot* 5:2).

**One separates *teruma* from the best – תּוֹרֵם מִן הַיָּפֶה:** One separates *teruma* from the highest quality produce. However, if there is no priest available and there is concern that the fruits may spoil, one separates *teruma* from produce that is more durable, as per the unattributed mishna (Rambam *Sefer Zera'im, Hilkhot Terumot* 5:1).

**NOTES**

**Pieces and whole loaves – פְּתִיתִין וּשְׁלֵמִין:** Rabbi Yoḥanan's opinion that one recites a blessing over whole loaves because they are more esthetic is understandable. However, Rav Huna's opinion must be explained, as well. Several commentaries assert that Rav Huna did not give preference to the pieces; he simply equated them to the whole loaves. He said that they only take precedence if they are larger (Rashi). Others explain that since the pieces are already sliced, they can be eaten immediately, and pleasure from them is instantaneous. It is preferable to recite a blessing over them, rather than the whole loaves, which one must slice before enjoying them (Rav Hai Gaon, Rashba).

אָמַר רַב נַחְמָן בַּר יִצְחָק: וִירֵא שָׁמַיִם יוֹצֵא יְדֵי שְׁנֵיהֶן, וּמַנּוּ? מָר בְּרֵיהּ דְּרָבִינָא. דְּמָר בְּרֵיהּ דְּרָבִינָא מַנִּיחַ פְּרוּסָה בְּתוֹךְ הַשְּׁלֵמָה וּבוֹצֵעַ.

With regard to the dispute between Rabbi Yoḥanan and Rav Huna, **Rav Naḥman bar Yitzḥak said: A God-fearing individual fulfills both. And who is this** God-fearing person? **Mar, son of Ravina,**[P] as the Gemara relates that **Mar, son of Ravina,** would **place the piece inside the** whole **loaf and break** them together.

תָּנֵי תַּנָּא קַמֵּיהּ דְּרַב נַחְמָן בַּר יִצְחָק: מַנִּיחַ הַפְּרוּסָה בְּתוֹךְ הַשְּׁלֵמָה וּבוֹצֵעַ וּמְבָרֵךְ. אָמַר לֵיהּ: מַה שְּׁמָךְ? אָמַר לֵיהּ: שַׁלְמָן. אָמַר לֵיהּ: שָׁלוֹם אַתָּה וּשְׁלֵמָה מִשְׁנָתְךָ, שֶׁשַּׂמְתָּ שָׁלוֹם בֵּין הַתַּלְמִידִים.

Similarly, the Gemara relates that **the *tanna* recited** a *baraita* **before Rav Naḥman bar Yitzḥak: One places the piece inside the whole** loaf, then **breaks** the bread **and recites a blessing.** Rav Naḥman **said to him: What is your name? He answered: Shalman.** Rav Naḥman **replied** with a pun: **You are peace** [*shalom*] **and** the **teaching** that **you** recited **is complete** [*shelema*] as by means of this *baraita* the disputing opinions are reconciled and **you established peace among students.**

אָמַר רַב פַּפָּא: הַכֹּל מוֹדִים בְּפֶסַח שֶׁמַּנִּיחַ פְּרוּסָה בְּתוֹךְ שְׁלֵמָה וּבוֹצֵעַ. מַאי טַעְמָא – ״לֶחֶם עֹנִי״ כְּתִיב.

This resolution is reinforced in a unique case, as **Rav Pappa said: Everyone agrees that** while fulfilling the mitzva of eating *matza* **on Passover, one places the piece inside the whole and breaks.**[NH] **What is the reason?** With regard to *matza* the phrase **"Bread of affliction"** (Deuteronomy 16:3) **is written,** and the poor typically eat their bread in pieces. Therefore, eating *matza* on Passover evening, the broken *matza* is also significant.

אָמַר רַבִּי אַבָּא: וּבְשַׁבָּת חַיָּיב אָדָם לִבְצוֹעַ עַל שְׁתֵּי כִּכָּרוֹת. מַאי טַעְמָא – ״לֶחֶם מִשְׁנֶה״ כְּתִיב.

In connection to the various *halakhot* with regard to breaking bread, especially on Festivals, the Gemara cites another *halakha*. **Rabbi Abba said: And on Shabbat one is obligated to break** bread for the meal **over two loaves. What is the reason?** Because in the Torah portion that discusses gathering manna on Friday for Shabbat, the phrase: **"Twice as much bread"** (Exodus 16:22) **is written.** To commemorate this, Shabbat meals are based on two loaves of bread.

אָמַר רַב אַשִׁי: חֲזֵינָא לֵיהּ לְרַב כָּהֲנָא דְּנָקֵיט תַּרְתֵּי וּבָצַע חֲדָא. רַבִּי זֵירָא הֲוָה בָּצַע אַכּוּלָּא שֵׁירוּתָא. אָמַר לֵיהּ רָבִינָא לְרַב אַשִׁי: וְהָא קָא מִתְחֲזֵי כִּרְעַבְתָנוּתָא! אָמַר [לֵיהּ]: כֵּיוָן דְּכָל יוֹמָא לָא קָעָבֵיד הָכִי, וְהָאִידָּנָא קָא עָבֵיד – לָא מִתְחֲזֵי כִּרְעַבְתָנוּתָא.

With regard to the manner in which these two loaves are to be broken, **Rav Ashi said: I saw Rav Kahana who would take two** loaves **and break one.**[H] **Rabbi Zeira would break** off one large piece from the loaf, and eat from it **for the entire** Shabbat **meal.**[NH] **Ravina said to Rav Ashi** about this: **Doesn't it appear gluttonous** for one to break off so large a piece? Rav Ashi **said to him: Since every** other **day** he **does not do so, and today he does, it does not appear gluttonous,** but rather in deference to the mitzva of the Shabbat meals.

רַב אַמִי וְרַב אַסִי כִּי הֲוָה מִתְרְמֵי לְהוּ רִיפְתָּא דְּעֵרוּבָא מְבָרְכִין עֲלֵיהּ ״הַמּוֹצִיא לֶחֶם מִן הָאָרֶץ״, אָמְרִי: הוֹאִיל וְאִתְעֲבִיד בֵּיהּ מִצְוָה חֲדָא – נַעֲבֵיד בֵּיהּ מִצְוָה אַחֲרִיתִי.

With regard to eating on Shabbat, the Gemara relates: **Rav Ami and Rav Asi, when the** opportunity to use **the bread of the *eiruv***[NH] in the Shabbat meal **would present itself,** they would **recite: Who brings forth bread from the earth over it. They said** in explanation: **Since one mitzva was performed with it, we will perform another mitzva with it.**

## PERSONALITIES

**Mar, son of Ravina – מָר בְּרֵיהּ דְּרָבִינָא:** He was one of the outstanding, fourth-generation, Babylonian *amora'im* and the son of the first Sage by the name of Ravina. He was renowned in the Talmud as an extremely God-fearing individual and from his conduct, proper behavior for a God-fearing individual was derived. He was extremely vigilant in avoiding any matter that involved a diminution in the appropriate deference to God or excessive levity. He was extremely careful in his choice of words in order to avoid any possibility of affronting his rabbis. He studied primarily before Rav Naḥman bar Yitzḥak, as a disciple-colleague. The Talmud relates that he left halakhic notes that served as the basis for discussion in subsequent generations.

## NOTES

**Everyone agrees that on Passover, one places the piece inside the whole and breaks – הַכֹּל מוֹדִים בְּפֶסַח שֶׁמַּנִּיחַ פְּרוּסָה בְּתוֹךְ שְׁלֵמָה וּבוֹצֵעַ:** Some maintain that unlike all other festivals, on Passover, one may break the piece rather then the whole because of the verse: "Bread of affliction" (Rav Hai Gaon and others). Nevertheless, already in the geonic period, the custom was to take a whole loaf of unleavened bread together with the piece (*Seder Rav Amram*); the whole loaf in honor of the festival, as it is more respectful to recite a blessing over a whole loaf, and the piece as bread of affliction (*Talmidei Rabbeinu Yona*). The custom today is to take two whole loaves of unleavened bread and a piece.

**Rabbi Zeira would break off one large piece from the loaf, and eat from it for the entire Shabbat meal – רַבִּי זֵירָא הֲוָה בָּצַע אַכּוּלָּא שֵׁירוּתָא:** Rashi understands this to mean that Rabbi Zeira would break off one large piece. Others explain that he would break all of the loaves before him, in honor of Shabbat (Rashba, *Shitta Mekubbetzet*).

**The bread of the *eiruv* – רִיפְתָּא דְּעֵרוּבָא:** There are different opinions with regard to which *eiruv* the Gemara is referring; some said the joining of the courtyards (Rashi) and others said the joining of the cooked dishes (*Me'iri*).

## HALAKHA

**Everyone agrees that on Passover, one places the piece, etc. – הַכֹּל מוֹדִים בְּפֶסַח שֶׁמַּנִּיחַ פְּרוּסָה וכו׳:** On Passover, one places the slice beneath the whole and he breaks them both, as per the opinion of Rav Pappa (Rambam *Sefer Zemanim, Hilkhot Ḥametz UMatza* 8:6; *Shulḥan Arukh, Oraḥ Ḥayyim* 475:1).

**Who would take two loaves and break one – דְּנָקֵיט תַּרְתֵּי וּבָצַע חֲדָא:** On Shabbat, one holds the two loaves and breaks one of them, as per the custom of Rav Kahana. The authorities disagreed, however, which loaf to slice. According to the *Shulḥan Arukh*, on weekdays one holds one loaf over the other while reciting the blessing, and he breaks the bottom one. At the meals on Shabbat and festival evenings, however, one breaks the top loaf, based on *kabbala* (Rema). The custom of the *Baḥ* was to break the top one while the Maharshal would break both. The *Magen Avraham* ruled that practically speaking, during *kiddush*, one should place one loaf atop the other, and while reciting: Who brings forth bread from the earth, he takes the top loaf and places it on the bottom, and then breaks it (Rambam *Sefer Zemanim, Hilkhot Shabbat* 30:9; *Shulḥan Arukh, Oraḥ Ḥayyim* 274:1).

**Would break off one large piece from the loaf, and eat from it for the entire Shabbat meal – הֲוָה בָּצַע אַכּוּלָּא שֵׁירוּתָא:** It is a mitzva to break off a large piece that will last throughout the meal, as per the custom of Rabbi Zeira (Rambam *Sefer Ahava, Hilkhot Berakhot* 7:3; *Shulḥan Arukh, Oraḥ Ḥayyim* 274:2).

**The bread of the *eiruv* – רִיפְתָּא דְּעֵרוּבָא:** It is customary to use the loaf of the *eiruv*, used for either the joining of the courtyards or the joining of the cooked dishes, as one of the two loaves in the Shabbat morning meal (*Shulḥan Arukh, Oraḥ Ḥayyim* 394:2 in the comment of the Rema).

אָמַר רַב: ״טוֹל בְּרוֹךְ, טוֹל בְּרוֹךְ״ – אֵינוֹ צָרִיךְ לְבָרֵךְ, ״הָבֵא מֶלַח, הָבֵא לִפְתָּן״ – צָרִיךְ לְבָרֵךְ; וְרַבִּי יוֹחָנָן אָמַר: אֲפִילּוּ ״הָבִיאוּ מֶלַח, הָבִיאוּ לִפְתָּן״ – נַמִּי אֵינוֹ צָרִיךְ לְבָרֵךְ; ״גַּבֵּיל לְתוֹרֵי גַּבֵּיל לְתוֹרֵי״ – צָרִיךְ לְבָרֵךְ; וְרַב שֵׁשֶׁת אָמַר: אֲפִילּוּ ״גַּבֵּיל לְתוֹרֵי״ נַמִּי אֵינוֹ צָרִיךְ לְבָרֵךְ, דְּאָמַר רַב יְהוּדָה אָמַר רַב: אָסוּר לְאָדָם שֶׁיֹּאכַל קוֹדֶם שֶׁיִּתֵּן מַאֲכָל לִבְהֶמְתּוֹ, שֶׁנֶּאֱמַר: ״וְנָתַתִּי עֵשֶׂב בְּשָׂדְךָ לִבְהֶמְתֶּךָ״ וַהֲדַר ״וְאָכַלְתָּ וְשָׂבָעְתָּ״.

Continuing to discuss the *halakhot* of breaking bread, **Rav said:** One who broke bread, and before eating it, offered a piece to another, and said: **Take it and recite a blessing, take** it and **recite a blessing,**[N] **need not recite the blessing** a second time, because that is considered to have been for the purpose of the blessing. If, however, he said: **Bring salt or bring relish, he must recite the blessing** a second time, as that is considered an interruption between the blessing and eating the bread. **And Rabbi Yoḥanan said: Even** if he said: **Bring salt** or **bring relish,** it is not considered an interruption **and he need not recite the blessing** a second time. Only if he said: **Mix** the food **for the oxen, mix** the food **for the oxen,** it is considered an interruption **and he is required to recite the blessing** a second time.[H] **And Rav Sheshet said: Even** if he said: **Mix for the oxen, he need not recite a blessing** a second time, as that is also considered to be for the purpose of the blessing, **as Rav Yehuda said** that **Rav said: One is prohibited from eating before feeding his animals,**[H] **as it is stated: "And I will give grass in your fields for your animals"** first **and** only **then: "And you shall eat and be satisfied"** (Deuteronomy 11:15). In the verse, preparation of food for one's cattle precedes preparation of his own food. Consequently, it is considered part of the preparation for one's own meal.

אָמַר רָבָא בַּר שְׁמוּאֵל מִשּׁוּם רַבִּי חִיָּיא: אֵין הַבּוֹצֵעַ רַשַּׁאי לִבְצוֹעַ עַד שֶׁיָּבִיאוּ מֶלַח אוֹ לִפְתָּן לִפְנֵי כָּל אֶחָד וְאֶחָד. רָבָא בַּר שְׁמוּאֵל אִקְּלַע לְבֵי רֵישׁ גָּלוּתָא, אַפִּיקוּ לֵיהּ רִיפְתָּא וּבְצַע לְהֶדְיָא. אָמְרוּ לֵיהּ: הֲדַר מָר מִשְּׁמַעְתֵּיהּ? אָמַר לְהוּ: לֵית דֵּין צְרִיךְ בְּשַׁשׁ.

**Rava bar Shmuel said in the name of Rabbi Ḥiyya: One who breaks** bread **is not permitted to break** it **until they bring salt**[NH] **or relish before each and every one** seated at the table. However, the Gemara relates that **Rava bar Shmuel** himself **happened** to come **to the House of the Exilarch. They brought him bread, which he immediately broke,** without waiting for them to bring salt or relish. **They said to him: Did the Master reconsider his halakhic** ruling? **He said to them:** Although poor quality bread requires salt in order to give the bread flavor, and therefore one must wait before breaking bread, **this** refined bread served in the House of the Exilarch needs no salt, and **does not require waiting.**

וְאָמַר רָבָא בַּר שְׁמוּאֵל מִשּׁוּם רַבִּי חִיָּיא: אֵין מֵי רַגְלַיִם כָּלִים אֶלָּא בִּישִׁיבָה. אָמַר רַב כָּהֲנָא: וּבֶעָפָר תִּיחוּחַ אֲפִילּוּ בַּעֲמִידָה; וְאִי לֵיכָּא עֲפַר תִּיחוּחַ – יַעֲמוֹד בְּמָקוֹם גָּבוֹהַּ וְיַשְׁתִּין לְמָקוֹם מִדְרוֹן.

**And Rava bar Shmuel said in the name of Rabbi Ḥiyya: Urine only completely** leaves the body[H] if one urinates **seated,** as, otherwise, due to concern that drops of urine will drip onto his clothes, he attempts to conclude prematurely. **Rav Kahana said: Over loose soil** which absorbs the urine, one is not concerned that it will splash on him; therefore, **even when standing** the urine leaves his body. **And if there is no loose soil** there is another way to prevent the urine from splashing on his clothes while standing. **Stand on an elevated place and urinate down an inclined plane.**

וְאָמַר רָבָא בַּר שְׁמוּאֵל מִשְּׁמֵיהּ דְּרַבִּי חִיָּיא: אַחַר כָּל אֲכִילָתְךָ אֱכוֹל מֶלַח, וְאַחַר כָּל שְׁתִיָּיתְךָ שְׁתֵה מַיִם, וְאִי אַתָּה נִזּוֹק. תַּנְיָא נַמִּי הָכִי: אַחַר כָּל אֲכִילָתְךָ אֱכוֹל מֶלַח, וְאַחַר כָּל שְׁתִיָּיתְךָ שְׁתֵה מַיִם, וְאִי אַתָּה נִזּוֹק. תַּנְיָא אִידָךְ: אָכַל כָּל מַאֲכָל וְלֹא אָכַל מֶלַח, שָׁתָה כָּל מַשְׁקִין וְלֹא שָׁתָה מַיִם, בַּיּוֹם – יִדְאַג מִרֵיחַ הַפֶּה, וּבַלַּיְלָה – יִדְאַג מִפְּנֵי אַסְכָּרָה.

**And Rava bar Shmuel said** the following advice **in the name of Rabbi Ḥiyya: After all eating, eat salt and after all drinking, drink water and you will not be harmed. That was also taught** in a *baraita*: **After all eating, eat salt and after all drinking, drink water and you will not be harmed. It was taught** in **another** *baraita*: **If one ate any food and did not eat salt** afterward, or **if he drank any liquid and did not drink water** afterward, **during the day, he should be concerned about bad breath, and at night he should be concerned about diphtheria.**

תָּנוּ רַבָּנַן: הַמְּקַפֶּה אֲכִילָתוֹ בְּמַיִם – אֵינוֹ בָּא לִידֵי חוֹלִי מֵעַיִם. וְכַמָּה? אָמַר רַב חִסְדָּא: קִיתוֹן לְפַת.

On the topic of health, the Gemara cites that **the Sages taught** in a *baraita*: **One who inundates his food with water,** i.e., one who drinks a great deal of water, **will not come to suffer** from **intestinal illness.** The Gemara asks: **And how much** water? **Rav Ḥisda said: One jug** [***kiton***][L] **per loaf.**

אָמַר רַב מָרִי אָמַר רַבִּי יוֹחָנָן: הָרָגִיל בַּעֲדָשִׁים אַחַת לִשְׁלֹשִׁים יוֹם – מוֹנֵעַ אַסְכָּרָה מִתּוֹךְ בֵּיתוֹ. אֲבָל כָּל יוֹמָא, לָא. מַאי טַעְמָא – מִשּׁוּם דְּקָשֶׁה לְרֵיחַ הַפֶּה.

**Rav Mari said** that **Rabbi Yoḥanan said: One who is accustomed** to eat **lentils once in thirty days prevents diphtheria from** afflicting **his house.** The Gemara comments: **However,** one should **not** eat lentils **every day. What is the reason? Because it is deleterious** in that it causes **bad breath.**

## NOTES

**Take it and recite a blessing, take it and recite a blessing** – טוֹל בְּרוֹךְ, טוֹל בְּרוֹךְ: Apparently, the duplication comes to teach us that even if he unnecessarily repeated the instructions, since it was for the purpose of eating, it is not considered an interruption (*Tal Torah*).

**One who breaks bread is not permitted to break it until they bring salt** – אֵין הַבּוֹצֵעַ רַשַּׁאי לִבְצוֹעַ עַד שֶׁיָּבִיאוּ מֶלַח: The simple reason is that the salt is necessary in order to give the food some taste, and consequently, refined bread does not require salt. Some explained based on the Gemara's statement that a person's table is like an altar; one must place salt on the table, just as salt is placed on the altar (*ge'onim*). Additionally, salt serves as a reminder of the "eternal covenant of salt" (Numbers 18:19) between God and the Jewish people and protects the Jewish people from its detractors (Rosh).

## HALAKHA

**An interruption between blessing and eating** – הַפְסָקָה בֵּין בְּרָכָה וַאֲכִילָה: *Ab initio*, one may not interrupt between reciting the blessing and eating, with either speech or even prolonged silence, and if he spoke, he must repeat the blessing. Nevertheless, if his interruption was for the purpose of eating, he need not repeat his blessing. In that sense, even if one said: Feed the animals, it is considered for the purpose of eating. This is in accordance with the opinion of Rav Sheshet who is the latest of the *amora'im* cited, and the *halakha* is in accordance with the latest opinion (Rambam *Sefer Ahava, Hilkhot Berakhot*, 1:8; *Shulḥan Arukh, Oraḥ Ḥayyim* 167:6).

**One is prohibited from eating before feeding his animals** – אָסוּר לְאָדָם שֶׁיֹּאכַל קוֹדֶם שֶׁיִּתֵּן מַאֲכָל לִבְהֶמְתּוֹ: It is a mitzva to feed one's animals and slaves before he eats, in accordance with the opinion of Rav Yehuda (Rambam *Sefer Kinyan, Hilkhot Avadim* 9:8; *Sefer Mitzvot Gadol*, Positive Commandments 87).

**One who breaks bread is not permitted to break it until they bring salt** – אֵין הַבּוֹצֵעַ רַשַּׁאי לִבְצוֹעַ עַד שֶׁיָּבִיאוּ מֶלַח: One may not break bread until he has salt or relish before him. If he has refined bread, or if it is seasoned, or if he eats it dry, it does not require salt. If he so chooses, he may eat it without salt (Rabbeinu Ḥananel; Rambam *Sefer Ahava, Hilkhot Berakhot*, 7:3; *Shulḥan Arukh, Oraḥ Ḥayyim* 167:5).

**Urine only completely leaves the body** – אֵין מֵי רַגְלַיִם כָּלִים: A man should not urinate when standing unless he is standing at the high end of an inclined plane or if he urinates into soft dirt (Rambam *Sefer Ahava, Hilkhot Tefillin UMezuza VeSefer Torah* 4:18; *Shulḥan Arukh, Oraḥ Ḥayyim* 3:13).

## LANGUAGE

**Jug [*kiton*]** – קִיתוֹן: From the Greek κώθων, *koton*, meaning a vessel used for drinking or a saucer.

וְאָמַר רַב מָרִי אָמַר רַבִּי יוֹחָנָן: הָרָגִיל בְּחַרְדָּל אַחַת לִשְׁלֹשִׁים יוֹם – מוֹנֵעַ חֳלָאִים מִתּוֹךְ בֵּיתוֹ, אֲבָל כָּל יוֹמָא, לָא. מַאי טַעְמָא – מִשּׁוּם דְּקָשֶׁה לְחוּלְשָׁא דְּלִבָּא.

**And Rav Mari said** that **Rabbi Yoḥanan said: One who is accustomed** to eat **mustard once in thirty days prevents illnesses from** afflicting **his house.** The Gemara comments: **However,** one should **not** eat mustard **every day. What is the reason? Because it is deleterious** in that it causes **weakness of the heart.**

אָמַר רַב חִיָּיא בַּר אַשִׁי אָמַר רַב: הָרָגִיל בְּדָגִים קְטַנִּים אֵינוֹ בָּא לִידֵי חוֹלִי מֵעַיִם; וְלֹא עוֹד אֶלָּא שֶׁדָּגִים קְטַנִּים מַפְרִין וּמַרְבִּין וּמַבְרִין כָּל גּוּפוֹ שֶׁל אָדָם.

Another health recommendation: **Rabbi Ḥiyya bar Ashi said** that **Rav said: One who is accustomed** to eat **small fish will not come to suffer** from **intestinal illness. Moreover,** eating **small fish causes one's entire body to flourish, to grow, and to be healthy.**

אָמַר רַבִּי חָמָא בְּרַבִּי חֲנִינָא: הָרָגִיל בְּקֶצַח אֵינוֹ בָּא לִידֵי כְּאֵב לֵב. מֵיתִיבֵי, רַבָּן שִׁמְעוֹן בֶּן גַּמְלִיאֵל אוֹמֵר: קֶצַח – אֶחָד מִשִּׁשִּׁים סַמְּנֵי הַמָּוֶת הוּא, וְהַיָּשֵׁן לְמִזְרַח גָּרְנוֹ – דָּמוֹ בְּרֹאשׁוֹ! לָא קַשְׁיָא: הָא בְּרֵיחוֹ, הָא בְּטַעְמוֹ. אִימֵּיהּ דְּרַבִּי יִרְמְיָה אָפְיָא לֵיהּ רִיפְתָּא, וּמְדַבְּקָא לֵיהּ וּמְקַלְּפָא לֵיהּ.

**Rabbi Ḥama, son of Rabbi Ḥanina, said: One who is accustomed** to eat **black cumin,**[B] a medicine for the heart, **will not come to suffer** from **heart pain. The Gemara raises an objection: Rabban Shimon ben Gamliel says: Black cumin is one of sixty deadly drugs, and** therefore **one who sleeps to the east of its storage** area, where its odor wafts with the westerly wind, responsibility for **his blood is on his** own **head.** The Gemara responds: This is **not difficult, as this,** where Rabban Shimon ben Gamliel said that black cumin is harmful, refers to **its odor,** whereas **this,** where Rabbi Ḥama, son of Rabbi Ḥanina, said that it is beneficial for the heart, refers only to **its taste.** And the Gemara relates: **The mother of Rabbi Yirmeya would bake him bread and would stick** black cumin **to it** so its taste would be absorbed, **and she would peel it** off, so that its odor would not harm him.

״רַבִּי יְהוּדָה אוֹמֵר: בּוֹרֵא מִינֵי דְשָׁאִים״. אָמַר רַבִּי זֵירָא וְאִיתֵּימָא רַבִּי חִינָּנָא בַּר פַּפָּא: אֵין הֲלָכָה כְּרַבִּי יְהוּדָה. וְאָמַר רַבִּי זֵירָא וְאִיתֵּימָא רַבִּי חִינָּנָא בַּר פַּפָּא: מַאי טַעְמָא דְּרַבִּי יְהוּדָה – אָמַר קְרָא: ״בָּרוּךְ ה׳ יוֹם יוֹם״, וְכִי בַּיּוֹם מְבָרְכִין אוֹתוֹ וּבַלַּיְלָה אֵין מְבָרְכִין אוֹתוֹ?! אֶלָּא לוֹמַר לְךָ: כָּל יוֹם וָיוֹם תֵּן לוֹ מֵעֵין בִּרְכוֹתָיו; הָכָא נַמִי, כָּל מִין וּמִין תֵּן לוֹ מֵעֵין בִּרְכוֹתָיו.

We learned in the mishna that **Rabbi Yehuda says** that one recites over herbs and leafy greens: **Who creates various kinds of herbs. Rabbi Zeira, and some say Rabbi Ḥinnana bar Pappa, said: The** ***halakha*** **is not in accordance with** the opinion of **Rabbi Yehuda.**[HN] **And Rabbi Zeira, and some say Rabbi Ḥinnana bar Pappa, said: What is the reason for Rabbi Yehuda's** opinion? **The verse says: "Blessed is the Lord, day by day"** (Psalms 68:20).[N] The question arises: **Is it so that one blesses Him by day and does not bless Him at night? Rather,** the verse comes **to tell you: Each and every day, give the Lord** the appropriate **blessings** for that day. **Here too,** with regard to the blessings recited over food, for **each and every type** of food, **give the** Lord the appropriate blessings for that food.

וְאָמַר רַבִּי זֵירָא וְאִיתֵּימָא רַבִּי חִינָּנָא בַּר פַּפָּא: בּוֹא וּרְאֵה שֶׁלֹּא כְּמִדַּת הַקָּדוֹשׁ בָּרוּךְ הוּא מִדַּת בָּשָׂר וָדָם: מִדַּת בָּשָׂר וָדָם – כְּלִי רֵיקָן מַחֲזִיק, מָלֵא אֵינוֹ מַחֲזִיק; אֲבָל הַקָּדוֹשׁ בָּרוּךְ הוּא אֵינוֹ כֵּן – מָלֵא מַחֲזִיק, רֵיקָן אֵינוֹ מַחֲזִיק, שֶׁנֶּאֱמַר: ״וַיֹּאמֶר אִם שָׁמוֹעַ תִּשְׁמַע״, ״אִם שָׁמוֹעַ״ – תִּשְׁמַע, וְאִם לָאו – לֹא תִשְׁמַע. דָּבָר אַחֵר: ״אִם שָׁמוֹעַ״ בְּיָשָׁן – ״תִּשְׁמַע״ בְּחָדָשׁ, וְאִם יִפְנֶה לְבָבְךָ – שׁוּב לֹא תִשְׁמַע.

**And Rabbi Zeira, and some say Rabbi Ḥinnana bar Pappa said: Come and see that the attribute of flesh and blood is unlike the attribute of the Holy One, Blessed be He. The attribute of flesh and blood is** that **an empty vessel holds** that which is placed within it, while **a full** vessel **does not hold** it. **The attribute of the Holy One, Blessed be He,** however, **is not so,** as if God adds to a person who is **a full vessel** in terms of knowledge or good attributes, he will **hold** it; a person who is **an empty** vessel **will not hold** it. This is alluded to by the verse where **it is said: "And He said, if you will surely listen** [*shamo'a tishma*] to the voice of the Lord your God and do what is right in His eyes" (Exodus 15:26). This verse is interpreted homiletically: **If you listen** [*shamo'a*] in the present, **you will listen** [*tishma*] in the future as well; **and if not, you will not listen. Alternatively: If you listened** [*shamo'a*] **to the old,** you review what you already learned, then **you will listen** [*tishma*] **to the new** as well. But **if you turn your heart away, you will no longer be able to hear.**

BACKGROUND

**Black cumin** – קֶצַח: *Nigella*, from the *Ranunculaceae* family, is an annual plant that grows to a height of 30 cm and beyond. The leaves of the black cumin plant are cut into short lobes. The plant has blue flowers that grow to a circumference of 3 cm and bloom in early spring. Its black, nearly triangular seeds, which are found in a five-sectioned sheath, are only 2–3 mm in both width and length, with up to 500 seeds weighing a single gram. Used today as a spice, black cumin was used in the past for medicinal purposes. Black cumin contains an etheric oil as well as melanthin, a glycoside similar to saponin. Twenty grams of black cumin seed can induce vomiting and miscarriage, and melanthin, even in a concentration of two parts per thousand, kills animals.

Garden variety black cumin

HALAKHA

**The blessing over vegetables** – בִּרְכַּת הַיְּרָקוֹת: Before eating vegetables, raw or cooked, when they are normally eaten in both forms (*Mishna Berura*), one recites: Who creates fruit of the ground (Rambam *Sefer Ahava, Hilkhot Berakhot*, 8:1; *Shulḥan Arukh, Oraḥ Ḥayyim* 205:1).

NOTES

**The *halakha* is not in accordance with the opinion of Rabbi Yehuda** – אֵין הֲלָכָה כְּרַבִּי יְהוּדָה: Some have a variant reading in this Gemara: The *halakha* is in accordance with the opinion of Rabbi Yehuda, according to which several difficulties are resolved, e.g., the contradiction between the conclusion here and the contradictory conclusion reached in the tractate *Sukka* (*Or Zarua, Alfei Menashe*). Nevertheless, according to our version, the commentaries explained that it was necessary for the Gemara to emphasize that the *halakha* is not in accordance with Rabbi Yehuda, even though his is an individual opinion. There is a compelling rationale for his opinion, and we would have been liable to rule in accordance with his opinion (*Penei Yehoshua*).

**Blessed is the Lord, day by day** – בָּרוּךְ ה׳ יוֹם יוֹם: The derivation here is not from the distinction between day and night, but rather from the repetition: Day by day, from which it is understood that one is required to bless the Lord with the blessing unique to that day (Rav Yoshiya Pinto, Maharsha).

מתני׳ בֵּירַךְ עַל פֵּירוֹת הָאִילָן ״בּוֹרֵא פְּרִי הָאֲדָמָה״ – יָצָא, וְעַל פֵּירוֹת הָאָרֶץ ״בּוֹרֵא פְּרִי הָעֵץ״ – לֹא יָצָא. וְעַל כּוּלָּם, אִם אָמַר ״שֶׁהַכֹּל נִהְיָה בִּדְבָרוֹ״ – יָצָא.

**MISHNA** This mishna discusses how, after the fact, a more general blessing exempts one from the obligation to recite a more specific one. **One who recited: Who creates fruit of the ground, over fruit of the tree, fulfilled** his obligation. One who recited: **Who creates fruit of the tree, over fruits of the earth, did not fulfill** his obligation. **And over all** food items, **one who recited: By whose word all things came to be, fulfilled** his obligation.[H]

גמ׳ מַאן תַּנָּא דְּעִיקַּר אִילָן אַרְעָא הִיא? אָמַר רַב נַחְמָן בַּר יִצְחָק: רַבִּי יְהוּדָה הִיא, דִּתְנַן: יָבֵשׁ הַמַּעְיָן וְנִקְצַץ הָאִילָן – מֵבִיא וְאֵינוֹ קוֹרֵא; רַבִּי יְהוּדָה אוֹמֵר: מֵבִיא וְקוֹרֵא.

**GEMARA** The Gemara begins by ascertaining: **Who is the *tanna*** that holds that **the primary** factor in the growth **of a tree is the earth,** and therefore one may recite: Who creates fruit of the ground, over fruits of the tree fulfills his obligation? **Rav Naḥman bar Yitzḥak said:** That is the opinion of **Rabbi Yehuda, as we learned** in a mishna dealing with the *halakhot* of first fruits: If, after one picked the first fruits from his field, **the spring dried up and the tree** upon which the fruit grew **was chopped** down,[H] **he brings** the first fruits to the Temple but **does not read** the accompanying praise. The tree or spring, which were the primary components of the growth of the fruit, no longer exist and he cannot recite the passage thanking God for "the good land." **Rabbi Yehuda says: He brings** the first fruits **and reads** the accompanying praise, as the land is the primary factor in the growth of the tree, and the tree itself is merely an extension of the land. Even after the tree is felled, the land remains intact. Similarly, with regard to blessings, the *halakha* maintains that fruit of the tree is considered to be fruit of the ground, as well.

״עַל פֵּירוֹת הָאָרֶץ״ וכו׳. פְּשִׁיטָא! – אָמַר רַב נַחְמָן בַּר יִצְחָק: לֹא נִצְרְכָה אֶלָּא לְרַבִּי יְהוּדָה דְּאָמַר ״חִטָּה מִין אִילָן הִיא״; דְּתַנְיָא: אִילָן שֶׁאָכַל מִמֶּנּוּ אָדָם הָרִאשׁוֹן, רַבִּי מֵאִיר אוֹמֵר: גֶּפֶן הָיָה, שֶׁאֵין לְךָ דָּבָר שֶׁמֵּבִיא יְלָלָה עַל הָאָדָם אֶלָּא יַיִן, שֶׁנֶּאֱמַר: ״וַיֵּשְׁתְּ מִן הַיַּיִן וַיִּשְׁכָּר״; רַבִּי נְחֶמְיָה אוֹמֵר: תְּאֵנָה הָיְתָה, שֶׁבְּדָבָר שֶׁנִּתְקַלְקְלוּ בּוֹ נִתַּקְּנוּ, שֶׁנֶּאֱמַר ״וַיִּתְפְּרוּ עֲלֵה תְאֵנָה״; רַבִּי יְהוּדָה אוֹמֵר: חִטָּה הָיְתָה, שֶׁאֵין הַתִּינוֹק יוֹדֵעַ לִקְרוֹת אַבָּא וְאִמָּא עַד שֶׁיִּטְעוֹם טַעַם דָּגָן.

We learned in the mishna: One who recited: Who creates fruit of the tree, **over fruits of the earth,** did not fulfill his obligation. The Gemara asks: **That is obvious,** as fruits of the earth do not fall under the rubric of trees. **Rav Naḥman bar Yitzḥak said:** This ruling in the mishna **is only necessary according to** the opinion of **Rabbi Yehuda,** who **said** in another context that **wheat is a type of tree,**[B] **as we learned** in a *baraita*: **The tree from which Adam, the first** man, **ate, Rabbi Meir says: It was a vine, as nothing brings wailing** and trouble **upon man** even today **other than wine,** as **it is stated** with regard to Noah: **"And he drank from the wine and became drunk"** (Genesis 9:21). **Rabbi Neḥemya says: It was a fig** tree, **as with the object with which they were corrupted** and sinned **they were rehabilitated, as it is stated: "And they sewed together fig leaves** and made for themselves loincloths" (Genesis 3:7). They must have taken the leaves from the tree closest at hand, the Tree of Knowledge. **Rabbi Yehuda says: It was wheat, as,** even today, **the child does not know how to call** his **father and mother until he tastes the taste of grain.**

סָלְקָא דַּעְתָּךְ אָמִינָא, הוֹאִיל וְאָמַר רַבִּי יְהוּדָה חִטָּה מִין אִילָן הִיא, לִיבָרֵךְ עֲלֵיהּ ״בּוֹרֵא פְּרִי הָעֵץ״ – קָא מַשְׁמַע לָן: הֵיכָא מְבָרְכִינַן ״בּוֹרֵא פְּרִי הָעֵץ״ – הֵיכָא דְּכִי שָׁקְלַתְּ לֵיהּ לְפֵירֵיהּ אִיתֵיהּ לְגַוְוזָא וַהֲדַר מַפֵּיק,

Based on this, **it might have entered your mind to say, since Rabbi Yehuda said** that **wheat is a type of tree, one should recite over it: Who creates fruit of the tree.** Therefore, the mishna **taught us** that with regard to blessings, the principle is different. **Where does one recite: Who creates fruit of the tree?**[H] Only in a case **where, when you take the fruit, the branch remains and again produces** fruit.



אֲבָל הֵיכָא דְּכִי שָׁקְלַתְּ לֵיהּ לְפֵירֵי לֵיתֵיהּ לְגַוְוזָא דַּהֲדַר מַפֵּיק – לֹא מְבָרְכִינַן עֲלֵיהּ ״בּוֹרֵא פְּרִי הָעֵץ״ אֶלָּא ״בּוֹרֵא פְּרִי הָאֲדָמָה״.

**However,** in a situation **where, when you take the fruit, the branch does not remain and again produce** fruit, **we do not recite the blessing: Who creates fruit of the tree, but rather: Who creates fruit of the ground.**

״וְעַל כּוּלָּן אִם אָמַר שֶׁהַכֹּל״ וכו׳. אִתְּמַר, רַב הוּנָא אָמַר: חוּץ מִן הַפַּת וּמִן הַיַּיִן; וְרַבִּי יוֹחָנָן אָמַר: אֲפִילּוּ פַּת וְיַיִן.

We learned in the mishna: **And on all** food items, **if he recited:** By whose word **all things** came to be, he fulfilled his obligation. **It was stated** that the *amora'im* disputed the precise explanation of the mishna. **Rav Huna said:** This *halakha* applies to all foods **except for bread and wine.** Since they have special blessings, one does not fulfill his obligation by reciting the general blessing: By whose word all things came to be. **And Rabbi Yoḥanan said:** One fulfills his obligation with the blessing: By whose word all things came to be,[H] **even** over **bread and wine.**[N]

**HALAKHA**

**An incorrect blessing – שִׁינּוּי בִּבְרָכוֹת:** If one mistakenly recited: Who creates fruit of the ground, over the fruit of a tree, he fulfilled his obligation. However, if one recited: Who creates fruit of the tree, over fruit of the ground, he did not. After the fact, if one mistakenly recited: By whose word all things came to be, he fulfilled his obligation, in accordance with our mishna (Rambam *Sefer Ahava, Hilkhot Berakhot* 8:10; *Shulḥan Arukh, Oraḥ Ḥayyim* 206:1).

**The spring dried up and the tree was chopped down – יָבֵשׁ הַמַּעְיָן וְנִקְצַץ הָאִילָן:** If he separated his first fruits and subsequently, the spring from which the field was irrigated dried up, or the tree on which the fruits grew died, he brings the first fruits but does not read the accompanying Torah portion (Rambam *Sefer Zera'im, Hilkhot Bikkurim* 4:12).

**Where does one recite: Who creates fruit of the tree – הֵיכָא מְבָרְכִינַן בּוֹרֵא פְּרִי הָעֵץ:** One recites: Who creates fruit of the tree, over fruits that grow on trees whose leaves grow from the tree itself, and its trunk remains intact. However, if the leaves emerge from its roots, it has the legal status of fruit of the ground. There are different opinions with regard to which fruits fall into which category based on conflicting interpretations of the Gemara (*Shulḥan Arukh, Oraḥ Ḥayyim* 203:2).

**BACKGROUND**

**Wheat is a type of tree – חִטָּה מִין אִילָן:** Clearly, wheat is not at all like a tree. However, within the *Poaceae* family, to which wheat belongs, there are several very large plants, which, structurally, are not fundamentally different from wheat. For example, giant bamboo looks like a tree in every respect.

**HALAKHA**

**The effectiveness of: By whose word all things came to be – תּוֹקֶף בִּרְכַּת שֶׁהַכֹּל:** After the fact, one who recited: By whose word all things came to be, over any food item, including bread and wine, fulfilled his obligation. This is based on the principle that in disputes with Rav Huna, the *halakha* is in accordance with the opinion of Rabbi Yoḥanan (Rambam *Sefer Ahava, Hilkhot Berakhot* 8:10; *Shulḥan Arukh, Oraḥ Ḥayyim* 167:10).

**NOTES**

**Bread and wine – פַּת וְיַיִן:** Bread and wine are unique among foods as no other food has an exclusive blessing. Even the specific blessing: Who creates fruit of the tree, is recited over several types of fruit. Consequently, one could say that one who does not recite the exclusive blessing over bread and wine, it is as if he did not recite a blessing at all (Rashash).

נֵימָא כְּתַנָּאֵי: רָאָה פַּת וְאָמַר ״כַּמָּה נָאָה פַּת זוֹ בָּרוּךְ הַמָּקוֹם שֶׁבְּרָאָהּ״ – יָצָא. רָאָה תְּאֵנָה וְאָמַר: ״כַּמָּה נָאָה תְּאֵנָה זוֹ בָּרוּךְ הַמָּקוֹם שֶׁבְּרָאָהּ״ – יָצָא, דִּבְרֵי רַבִּי מֵאִיר; רַבִּי יוֹסֵי אוֹמֵר: כָּל הַמְשַׁנֶּה מִמַּטְבֵּעַ שֶׁטָּבְעוּ חֲכָמִים בִּבְרָכוֹת – לֹא יָצָא יְדֵי חוֹבָתוֹ. נֵימָא, רַב הוּנָא דְּאָמַר כְּרַבִּי יוֹסֵי, וְרַבִּי יוֹחָנָן דְּאָמַר כְּרַבִּי מֵאִיר!

The Gemara remarks: **Let us say** that this dispute is **parallel to a tannaitic** dispute found elsewhere, as it was taught in a *Tosefta*: One who **saw bread and said: How pleasant is this bread, blessed is the Omnipresent Who created it, fulfilled** his obligation to recite a blessing. **One who saw a date and said: How pleasant is this date, blessed is the Omnipresent Who created it, fulfilled** his obligation. This is **the statement of Rabbi Meir. Rabbi Yosei says: One who deviates from the formula coined by the Sages in blessings,**[H] **did not fulfill his obligation.** If so, **let us say** that **Rav Huna,** who **said** that one who recites: By whose word all things came to be, over bread or wine, did not fulfill his obligation, holds **in accordance with** the opinion of **Rabbi Yosei; and Rabbi Yoḥanan,** who **said** that one who recites: By whose word all things came to be, over bread or wine fulfills his obligation, holds **in accordance with** the opinion of **Rabbi Meir.**

אָמַר לָךְ רַב הוּנָא: אֲנָא דַּאֲמַרִי אֲפִילּוּ לְרַבִּי מֵאִיר; עַד כָּאן לָא קָאָמַר רַבִּי מֵאִיר הָתָם – אֶלָּא הֵיכָא דְּקָא מַדְכַּר שְׁמֵיהּ דְּפַת, אֲבָל הֵיכָא דְּלָא קָא מַדְכַּר שְׁמֵיהּ דְּפַת – אֲפִילּוּ רַבִּי מֵאִיר מוֹדֶה.

The Gemara rejects this: **Rav Huna** could have **said to you: I said** my statement, **even** in accordance with the opinion of **Rabbi Meir,** as **Rabbi Meir only stated** his opinion, that one who alters the formula of the blessing fulfills his obligation, **there, where** the individual explicitly **mentions the term bread** in his blessing, **but where he does not mention** the **term bread, even Rabbi Meir agrees** that he did not fulfill his obligation.

וְרַבִּי יוֹחָנָן אָמַר לָךְ: אֲנָא דַּאֲמַרִי אֲפִילּוּ לְרַבִּי יוֹסֵי, עַד כָּאן לֹא קָאָמַר רַבִּי יוֹסֵי הָתָם – אֶלָּא מִשּׁוּם דְּקָאָמַר בְּרָכָה דְּלָא תַּקִּינוּ רַבָּנַן, אֲבָל אָמַר ״שֶׁהַכֹּל נִהְיָה בִּדְבָרוֹ״ דְּתַקִּינוּ רַבָּנַן – אֲפִילּוּ רַבִּי יוֹסֵי מוֹדֶה.

**And Rabbi Yoḥanan** could have **said to you: I said** my statement **even** in accordance with the opinion of **Rabbi Yosei,** as **Rabbi Yosei only stated** his opinion, that one who alters the formula of the blessing does not fulfill his obligation, **there, because he recited a blessing that was not instituted by the Sages; however, if he recited: By whose word all things came to be, which was instituted by the Sages, even Rabbi Yosei agrees** that, after the fact, he fulfilled his obligation to recite a blessing.

בִּנְיָמִין רָעֲיָא כְּרַךְ רִיפְתָּא וַאֲמַר: ״בְּרִיךְ מָרֵיהּ דְּהַאי פִּיתָּא״. אָמַר רַב: יָצָא. וְהָאָמַר רַב: כָּל בְּרָכָה שֶׁאֵין בָּהּ הַזְכָּרַת הַשֵּׁם אֵינָהּ בְּרָכָה! – דַּאֲמַר: ״בְּרִיךְ רַחֲמָנָא מָרֵיהּ דְּהַאי פִּיתָּא״.

Regarding blessings that do not conform to the formula instituted by the Sages, the Gemara relates that **Binyamin the shepherd ate bread and** afterward **recited** in Aramaic: **Blessed is the Master of this bread. Rav said,** he thereby **fulfilled** his obligation to recite a blessing. The Gemara objects: **But didn't Rav** himself **say: Any blessing that does not contain mention of God's name is not** considered a **blessing?** The Gemara emends the formula of his blessing. **He said: Blessed is the All-Merciful, Master of this bread.**[H]

וְהָא בָּעֵינַן שָׁלֹשׁ בְּרָכוֹת! מַאי ״יָצָא״ דְּקָאָמַר רַב – נַמִי, יָצָא יְדֵי בְּרָכָה רִאשׁוֹנָה.

The Gemara asks: **But don't we require three blessings** in Grace after Meals? How did he fulfill his obligation with one sentence? The Gemara explains: **What is: Fulfills his obligation, that Rav also said? He fulfills** the obligation **of the first** of the three **blessings,** and must recite two more to fulfill his obligation completely.

מַאי קָמַשְׁמַע לָן – אַף עַל גַּב דַּאֲמָרָהּ בִּלְשׁוֹן חוֹל,

The Gemara asks: **What is he teaching us?** The Gemara answers: **Although he recited** the blessing **in a secular language,**[H] other than Hebrew, he fulfilled his obligation.

תְּנֵינָא, ״וְאֵלּוּ נֶאֱמָרִים בְּכָל לָשׁוֹן: פָּרָשַׁת סוֹטָה, וִידּוּי מַעֲשֵׂר, קְרִיאַת שְׁמַע, וּתְפִלָּה, וּבִרְכַּת הַמָּזוֹן״! אִצְטְרִיךְ, סָלְקָא דַּעְתָּךְ אָמִינָא; הָנֵי מִילֵּי – דַּאֲמָרָהּ בִּלְשׁוֹן חוֹל כִּי הֵיכִי דְּתַקִּינוּ רַבָּנַן בִּלְשׁוֹן קֹדֶשׁ, אֲבָל לֹא אֲמָרָהּ בִּלְשׁוֹן חוֹל כִּי הֵיכִי דְּתַקִּינוּ רַבָּנַן בִּלְשׁוֹן קֹדֶשׁ, אֵימָא לָא – קָא מַשְׁמַע לָן.

This remains difficult, as **we** already **learned** this in a mishna in *Sota*: **And these are recited in any language** that one understands: **The portion of** the swearing of the *sota*, the **confession** of the **tithes**[B] when a homeowner declares that he has given all *teruma* and tithes appropriately, **the recitation of** ***Shema*****, and the** *Amida* **prayer and Grace after Meals.** If Grace after Meals is clearly on the list of matters that may be recited in any language, what did Rav teach us? The Gemara answers: Rav's ruling with regard to Binyamin the Shepherd **is necessary, as it might have entered your mind to say: This,** the permission to recite Grace after Meals in any language, **applies only** to a case where one **recited it in a secular language, just as it was instituted by the Sages in the holy tongue. However,** in a case **where** one **did not recite** the blessing **in a secular language, just as it was instituted by the Sages in the holy tongue, say** that **no,** he did **not** fulfill his obligation. Therefore, Rav **teaches us** that, after the fact, not only is the language not an impediment to fulfillment of his obligation to recite a blessing, the formula is not an impediment either.

**HALAKHA**

One who deviates from the formula coined by the Sages in blessings – הַמְשַׁנֶּה מִמַּטְבֵּעַ שֶׁטָּבְעוּ חֲכָמִים בִּבְרָכוֹת: Although it is inappropriate to deviate from the formula of a blessing as established by the Sages, if one included the essential components of a blessing, i.e., God's name and sovereignty, one fulfills his obligation (Rambam *Sefer Ahava, Hilkhot Berakhot* 1:5).

Blessed is the All-Merciful, Master of this bread – בְּרִיךְ רַחֲמָנָא מָרֵיהּ דְּהַאי פִּיתָּא: One who recited a blessing with the formula: Blessed is the All-Merciful, Master of this bread, before eating bread, he fulfilled his obligation to recite: Who brings forth bread from the earth. If he recited it after eating bread, he fulfilled his obligation to recite the first blessing of Grace after Meals, in accordance with the opinion of Rav (*Shulḥan Arukh, Oraḥ Ḥayyim* 167:10, 187:1).

Although he recited in a secular language – דַּאֲמָרָהּ בִּלְשׁוֹן חוֹל: One may recite a blessing in any language, although it should be a precise translation of the formula established by the Sages (Rambam *Sefer Ahava, Hilkhot Berakhot* 1:6).

**BACKGROUND**

The confession of tithes – וִידּוּי מַעֲשֵׂר: This declaration was made on the last day of Passover in the fourth and seventh years of the Sabbatical cycle. It states that one's obligations with regard to *teruma* and the tithing of his produce were properly fulfilled. The text of this declaration is in Deuteronomy 26:13–15. During the Second Temple period, Yoḥanan the High Priest discontinued the practice of reciting this declaration due to concern that since agricultural *halakhot* were not being properly observed, many of those making the declaration would not be speaking the truth.

גּוּפָא, אָמַר רַב: כָּל בְּרָכָה שֶׁאֵין בָּהּ הַזְכָּרַת הַשֵּׁם – אֵינָהּ בְּרָכָה. וְרַבִּי יוֹחָנָן אָמַר: כָּל בְּרָכָה שֶׁאֵין בָּהּ מַלְכוּת – אֵינָהּ בְּרָכָה. אָמַר אַבַּיֵי: כְּוָותֵיהּ דְּרַב מִסְתַּבְּרָא, דְּתַנְיָא: ״לֹא עָבַרְתִּי מִמִּצְוֹתֶיךָ וְלֹא שָׁכָחְתִּי״. ״לֹא עָבַרְתִּי״ – מִלְּבָרֶכְךָ, ״וְלֹא שָׁכָחְתִּי״ – מִלְּהַזְכִּיר שִׁמְךָ עָלָיו, וְאִילּוּ מַלְכוּת לָא קָתָנֵי.

The Gemara considers **the matter** of Rav's opinion **itself** and cites the fundamental dispute in that regard. **Rav said: Any blessing that does not contain mention of God's name is not** considered a **blessing. And Rabbi Yoḥanan said: Any blessing that does not contain mention of** God's **sovereignty**[H] **is not** considered a **blessing. Abaye said: It stands to reason in accordance with** the opinion of **Rav, as it was taught** in a *Tosefta*: In the confession of the tithes, one recites, **"I did not transgress your mitzvot and I did not forget"** (Deuteronomy 26:13). The meaning of phrase, **I did not transgress,** is that I did not refrain **from blessing You** when separating tithes; and the meaning of the phrase, **and I did not forget,** is that I did not forget **to mention Your name in** the blessing recited **over it. However, this** *baraita* **did not teach** that one must mention God's **sovereignty** in the blessing.

וְרַבִּי יוֹחָנָן – תְּנִי ״וְלֹא שָׁכָחְתִּי״ מִלְּהַזְכִּיר שִׁמְךָ וּמַלְכוּתְךָ עָלָיו.

**And Rabbi Yoḥanan** would say: **Emend** the *baraita*: **And I did not forget to mention Your name and Your sovereignty in** the blessing recited **over it;**[N] indicating that one must mention both God's name and God's sovereignty.

מתני׳ וְעַל דָּבָר שֶׁאֵין גִּדּוּלוֹ מִן הָאָרֶץ אוֹמֵר: ״שֶׁהַכֹּל נִהְיָה בִּדְבָרוֹ״. עַל הַחוֹמֶץ וְעַל הַנּוֹבְלוֹת וְעַל הַגּוֹבַאי אוֹמֵר: ״שֶׁהַכֹּל נִהְיָה בִּדְבָרוֹ״; רַבִּי יְהוּדָה אוֹמֵר: כָּל שֶׁהוּא מִין קְלָלָה אֵין מְבָרְכִין עָלָיו.

**MISHNA And over** a food **item whose growth is not from the ground, one recites: By whose word all things came to be.** And **over vinegar,** wine that fermented and spoiled, **and over** ***novelot,***[H] dates that spoiled, **and over locusts, one recites: By whose word all things came to be. Rabbi Yehuda says:** Over **any** food item **that is a type** resulting from a **curse, one does not recite a blessing over it** at all. None of the items listed exist under normal conditions, and they come about as the result of a curse.

הָיוּ לְפָנָיו מִינִין הַרְבֵּה, רַבִּי יְהוּדָה אוֹמֵר: אִם יֵשׁ בֵּינֵיהֶן מִין שִׁבְעָה – עָלָיו הוּא מְבָרֵךְ; וַחֲכָמִים אוֹמְרִים: מְבָרֵךְ עַל אֵיזֶה מֵהֶן שֶׁיִּרְצֶה.

On a different note: If there were **many types** of food **before him,** over which food should he recite a blessing first? **Rabbi Yehuda says: If there is one of the seven species** for which Eretz Yisrael was praised **among them, he recites** the first **blessing over it. And the Rabbis say: He recites a blessing over whichever of them he wants.**

גמ׳ תָּנוּ רַבָּנַן: עַל דָּבָר שֶׁאֵין גִּדּוּלוֹ מִן הָאָרֶץ, כְּגוֹן: בְּשַׂר בְּהֵמוֹת חַיּוֹת וְעוֹפוֹת וְדָגִים, אוֹמֵר ״שֶׁהַכֹּל נִהְיָה בִּדְבָרוֹ״; עַל הֶחָלָב וְעַל הַבֵּיצִים וְעַל הַגְּבִינָה אוֹמֵר ״שֶׁהַכֹּל״; עַל הַפַּת שֶׁעִפְּשָׁה, וְעַל הַיַּיִן שֶׁהִקְרִים, וְעַל הַתַּבְשִׁיל שֶׁעָבַר צוּרָתוֹ אוֹמֵר ״שֶׁהַכֹּל״; עַל הַמֶּלַח וְעַל הַזָּמִית וְעַל כְּמֵהִין וּפִטְרִיּוֹת אוֹמֵר ״שֶׁהַכֹּל״. לְמֵימְרָא, דִּכְמֵהִין וּפִטְרִיּוֹת לָאו גִּדּוּלֵי קַרְקַע נִינְהוּ?! וְהָתַנְיָא: הַנּוֹדֵר מִפֵּירוֹת הָאָרֶץ – אָסוּר בְּפֵירוֹת הָאָרֶץ וּמוּתָּר בִּכְמֵהִין וּפִטְרִיּוֹת, וְאִם אָמַר ״כָּל גִּדּוּלֵי קַרְקַע עָלַי״ – אָסוּר אַף בִּכְמֵהִין וּפִטְרִיּוֹת!

**GEMARA The Sages taught: Over a** food **item whose growth is not from the earth, for example, meat from domesticated animals,**[N] **non-domesticated animals, and fowl and fish, one recites: By whose word all things came to be.** So too, **over milk, and over eggs, and over cheese, one recites:** By whose word **all things** came to be. This is not only true with regard to items that come from animals, but **over moldy bread, and over wine that fermented slightly, and over a cooked dish that spoiled,**[H] **one recites: By whose word all things came to be,** because the designated blessing is inappropriate for food that is partially spoiled. Similarly, **over salt and over brine, and over truffles and mushrooms,**[B] **one recites: By whose word all things came to be.** The Gemara asks: **Is this to say** that **truffles and mushrooms are not** items **that grow from the ground? Wasn't it taught** in a *baraita*: **One who vows** not to eat **from the fruit of the earth**[H] **is forbidden** to eat all **fruit of the earth;** however, he **is permitted** to eat **truffles and mushrooms.** And **if he said: All** items **that grow from the ground** are forbidden **to me, he is forbidden** to eat **even truffles and mushrooms.** Apparently, truffles and mushrooms are items that grow from the ground.

אָמַר אַבַּיֵי: מִירְבָּא רָבוּ מֵאַרְעָא, מִינְקֵי לָא יָנְקֵי מֵאַרְעָא.

**Abaye said:** With regard **to growth, they grow from the earth,** but with regard **to sustenance, they do not draw sustenance from the earth.**

וְהָא ״עַל דָּבָר שֶׁאֵין גִּדּוּלוֹ מִן הָאָרֶץ״ קָתָנֵי! – תְּנִי: עַל דָּבָר שֶׁאֵין יוֹנֵק מִן הָאָרֶץ.

The Gemara asks: Why is that distinction significant? **Wasn't it taught: Over** a food **item whose growth is not from the ground** one recites the blessing: By whose word all things came to be? Even according to Abaye, mushrooms grow from the ground. The Gemara answers: **Emend** the mishna to read: **Over** a food **item that does not draw sustenance from the ground,** one recites: By whose word all things came to be. Consequently, even over mushrooms one recites: By whose word all things came to be.

## HALAKHA

**Any blessing that does not contain mention of God's sovereignty – כָּל בְּרָכָה שֶׁאֵין בָּהּ מַלְכוּת:** Every blessing must contain mention of God's name and His sovereignty over the world, in accordance with the opinion of Rabbi Yoḥanan. The Gemara generally rules in accordance with his opinion in disputes with Rav (Rambam *Sefer Ahava, Hilkhot Berakhot* 1:10; *Shulḥan Arukh, Oraḥ Ḥayyim* 167:10).

**Over vinegar and over** ***novelot*** **– עַל הַחוֹמֶץ וְעַל הַנּוֹבְלוֹת:** Before eating vinegar, *novelot*, and locusts, one recites: By whose word all things came to be, as per the unattributed mishna (Rambam *Sefer Ahava, Hilkhot Berakhot* 8:8; *Shulḥan Arukh, Oraḥ Ḥayyim* 204:1).

**Over moldy bread, and over wine that fermented slightly, and over a cooked dish that spoiled – הַפַּת שֶׁעִפְּשָׁה...תַּבְשִׁיל שֶׁעָבַר צוּרָתוֹ:** Over a dish that is slightly spoiled, as well as all other foods that spoiled only slightly and remain edible, one recites: By whose word all things came to be (Rambam *Sefer Ahava, Hilkhot Berakhot* 8:8; *Shulḥan Arukh, Oraḥ Ḥayyim* 204:1).

**One who vows not to eat from the fruit of the earth – הַנּוֹדֵר מִפֵּירוֹת הָאָרֶץ:** One who vows that all fruits of the earth are forbidden to him, is prohibited from eating all fruits and vegetables and is permitted to eat truffles and mushrooms. If he vowed that all items that grow from the ground are forbidden to him, they, too, are prohibited (Rambam *Sefer Hafla'a, Hilkhot Nedarim* 9:11; *Shulḥan Arukh, Yoreh De'a* 217:23).

## NOTES

**Emend the** ***baraita*****: And I did not forget to mention Your name and Your sovereignty in the blessing recited over it – תְּנִי וְלֹא שָׁכַחְתִּי מִלְּהַזְכִּיר שִׁמְךָ וּמַלְכוּתְךָ עָלָיו:** Apparently, in the version of the Gemara before *Tosafot*, this question and answer do not appear. However, even according to the version of the Gemara before us, it is not an emendation of the text of the *Sifrei*. Rather, it is a logical assumption that, in that context, there was no need to enumerate, in detail, all of the elements that must be included in the blessing on that occasion.

**Meat from domesticated animals, etc. – בְּשַׂר בְּהֵמוֹת וכו׳:** The list in the *baraita* is somewhat surprising because it lists the meat products and mentions the blessing, and then lists the milk products and mentions the blessing. Why not list them all together? The explanation is that, apparently, the author of the *baraita* heard this basic *halakha* from several different teachers who cited different lists. He combined all of the examples, as he heard them, into one *baraita* (Rashba).

## BACKGROUND

**Mushrooms – פִּטְרִיּוֹת:** *Fungi*, which also include truffles, are a subsystem of plants within the *Thallophta* system.

All of the thousands of types of mushrooms lack chlorophyll, and, consequently, are incapable of photosynthesis. Therefore, they are unable to assimilate non-organic material. Mushrooms, even when they are in the ground, do not draw sustenance from it, but rather from decomposing organic material within the ground. There are mushrooms that exist symbiotically with other plants and are capable of taking in nitrogen and transferring it by means of mycorrhiza to the host plant.

Mushrooms consist of thin strands that branch out into a braid called mycelium, which is the body of the mushroom, and through which its nutrients are absorbed. From that mycelium in the ground, the fruit itself, which contains the reproductive organs of the mushroom, emerges. The fruit is usually large and conspicuous, and that is the part of the mushroom that is consumed (see Truffles, 47a, p. 303).

## HALAKHA

*Novelot* – נוֹבְלוֹת: These are dates that were scorched by the heat of the sun and their blessing is: By whose word all things came to be, as per the second version cited by the Gemara. There was no dispute with regard to this. Over dates that fell from the tree before they were ripe, one also recites: By Whose word all things came to be (*Magen Avraham* in the name of the *Baḥ*; *Shulḥan Arukh, Oraḥ Ḥayyim* 202:9, 204:1).

Are lenient with regard to *demai* – הַקַּלִּין שֶׁבַּדְּמַאי: Fruits which are typically ownerless, e.g., *shittin*, *novelot*, etc., do not acquire *demai* status (Rambam, *Sefer Zera'im, Hilkhot Ma'aser* 13:1).

## NOTES

Are lenient with regard to *demai* – הַקַּלִּין שֶׁבַּדְּמַאי: The *halakhot* of *demai* are unique, as according to the Gemara's conclusion, the obligation to tithe *demai* is not the result of genuine uncertainty as to whether the produce was tithed. Rather, it is virtually certain that they were tithed. As for these fruits, with regard to which the Sages are lenient with regard to *demai*, some (Rambam based on the Jerusalem Talmud) hold that they are exempt from *demai* not because they were tithed by an *am ha'aretz*, but because they are generally ownerless property. The Babylonian Talmud disagrees.

״וְעַל הַנּוֹבְלוֹת״. מַאי נוֹבְלוֹת? רַבִּי זֵירָא וְרַבִּי אִילְעָא, חַד אָמַר: בּוּשְׁלֵי כַּמְרָא. וְחַד אָמַר: תַּמְרֵי דְזִיקָא.

We learned in the mishna that **over *novelot*** one recites: By whose word all things came to be. The Gemara asks: **What are *novelot*?**[H] The Gemara responds that the *amora'im* **Rabbi Zeira and Rabbi Il'a** disputed this. **One said** that the term refers to dates that, due to extreme conditions, were **burned by the heat** of the sun and ripened prematurely. **And one said** that they are **dates** that fell from the tree because **of the wind.**

תְּנַן, רַבִּי יְהוּדָה אוֹמֵר: כׇּל שֶׁהוּא מִין קְלָלָה אֵין מְבָרְכִין עָלָיו; בִּשְׁלָמָא לְמַאן דַּאֲמַר בּוּשְׁלֵי כַּמְרָא – הַיְינוּ דְּקָרֵי לֵיהּ מִין קְלָלָה, אֶלָּא לְמַאן דַּאֲמַר תַּמְרֵי דְזִיקָא – מַאי מִין קְלָלָה?

**We learned** later in the mishna that **Rabbi Yehuda says:** Over **any** food item **that is a type** resulting from a **curse, one does not recite a blessing over it** at all. **Granted, according to the one who said** that *novelot* are dates **burned by the heat** of the sun, **that is** the reason **that** he **considers them a type of curse; however, according to the one who said** that *novelot* are **dates that** fell because **of the wind, what** is the reason that it is considered a **type of curse?** Dates that fell from the tree are no worse than other dates.

אַשְּׁאָרָא.

The Gemara reconciles: Rabbi Yehuda's statement was **about the rest,** the vinegar and locusts, not about the *novelot*.

אִיכָּא דְאָמְרִי: בִּשְׁלָמָא לְמַאן דַּאֲמַר בּוּשְׁלֵי כַּמְרָא – הַיְינוּ דִּמְבָרְכִינַן עֲלַיְיהוּ ״שֶׁהַכֹּל״; אֶלָּא לְמַאן דְּאָמַר תַּמְרֵי דְזִיקָא ״שֶׁהַכֹּל״?! ״בּוֹרֵא פְּרִי הָעֵץ״ מִבָּעֵי לֵיהּ לְבָרוֹכֵי!

**Some say** that the Gemara raised the question differently: **Granted, according to the one who said** that *novelot* are dates **burned by the heat** of the sun, **that is** the reason **that we recite over them: By whose word all things came to be,** as they are of inferior quality. **However, to the one who said** that *novelot* are **dates that** fell because **of the wind,** should we recite over them: By whose word all things came to be? **We should recite: Who creates fruit of the tree.**

אֶלָּא: בְּנוֹבְלוֹת סְתָמָא – כּוּלֵּי עָלְמָא לָא פְּלִיגִי דְּבוּשְׁלֵי כַּמְרָא נִינְהוּ, כִּי פְּלִיגִי – בְּנוֹבְלוֹת תְּמָרָה. דִּתְנַן: הַקַּלִּין שֶׁבַּדְּמַאי: הַשִּׁיתִין, וְהָרִימִין, וְהָעוּזְרָדִין, בְּנוֹת שׁוּחַ, וּבְנוֹת שִׁקְמָה, וְגוּפְנִין, וְנִצְפָּה, וְנוֹבְלוֹת תְּמָרָה.

**Rather,** the conclusion is, **with regard to *novelot* unmodified, everyone agrees that they are** dates that were **burned by the heat** of the sun. **When they argue,** it is **with regard to** those dates known as ***novelot temara,* as we learned** in a mishna concerning the laws of doubtfully tithed produce [*demai*]: Although, under normal circumstances, fruits that come into one's possession by means of an *am ha'aretz* must be tithed due to concern lest the *am ha'aretz* failed to do so, the following fruits of inferior quality are **lenient with regard to *demai***[NH] and one need not tithe them: ***Shittin,***[B] ***rimin,***[B] ***uzradin,***[B] ***benot shuaḥ, benot shikma,***[B] ***gufnin, nitzpa,* and *novelot temara.***

שִׁיתִין – אָמַר רַבָּה בַּר בַּר חָנָה אָמַר רַבִּי יוֹחָנָן: מִין תְּאֵנִים, רִימִין – כַּנְדֵי; הָעוּזְרָדִין – טוּלְשֵׁי; בְּנוֹת שׁוּחַ – אָמַר רַבָּה בַּר בַּר חָנָה אָמַר רַבִּי יוֹחָנָן: תְּאֵינֵי חִיוָּרָתָא; בְּנוֹת שִׁקְמָה – אָמַר רַבָּה בַּר בַּר חָנָה אָמַר רַבִּי יוֹחָנָן: דּוּבְלֵי. גּוּפְנִין – שִׁילְהֵי גּוּפְנֵי; נִצְפָּה – פִּרְחָה. נוֹבְלוֹת תְּמָרָה – רַבִּי אִילְעָא וְרַבִּי זֵירָא, חַד אָמַר: בּוּשְׁלֵי כַּמְרָא, וְחַד אָמַר: תַּמְרֵי דְזִיקָא.

The Gemara identifies these plants. ***Shittin,* Rabba bar bar Ḥana said** that **Rabbi Yoḥanan said:** They are **a type** of **figs. *Rimin*** are **lote. *Uzradin*** are **crabapples. *Benot shuaḥ,* Rabba bar bar Ḥana said** that **Rabbi Yoḥanan said:** They are **white dates. *Benot shikma,* Rabba bar bar Ḥana said** that **Rabbi Yoḥanan said:** They are **the fruit of the sycamore tree. *Gufnin*** are **the last grapes** which remain on the tree at the end of the season. ***Nitzpa*** are the **fruit of the caper-bush. *Novelot temara,* Rabbi Il'a and Rabbi Zeira** disagreed. **One said** that they are dates **burned by the heat** of the sun, **and one said** that they are **dates** that fell because **of the wind.**

## BACKGROUND

*Shittin* – שִׁיתִין: In many places, the fig tree produces two cycles of unripe fruit: During the winter or early spring, either before the leaves have begun to reemerge or beneath the leaves. Most of these fruit never ripen, and are shed when the summer figs begin to bloom. These *shittin* were eaten with salt, but because they would fall on their own, they were considered ownerless property, and, therefore, exempt from *demai*.

*Shittin*

*Rimin* – רִימִין: Seemingly, *rimin* are the fruit of the *Ziziphus lotus*, also called the jujube, from the *Rhamnaceae* family. This thorny, deciduous shrub that grows to a height of 1.5 m, has many tangled, purplish leaves (approximately 1.5 cm) with visible veins. At the base of each green-yellow leaf is a pair of thorns. The fruit of this plant is a small, yellowish, edible sphere (less than 1 cm), which is generally picked from the wild bushes that grow in ownerless areas in valleys and mountainsides.

*Rimin*

*Uzradin* – עוּזְרָדִין: *Crataegus azarolus*, also known as the hawthorn, is a member of the *Rosaceae* family.

This is a thorny, deciduous shrub which can grow anywhere from 2–4 m, and sometimes reaches 8 m, the size of a tree. It grows in mountainous regions, especially around Jerusalem. It blooms in the spring, forming small clusters of white flowers. The small (1–1.5 cm), red or orange fruit of the *uzrad*, which contains two or three pits, is similar in both its appearance and its sour taste to a crabapple. While generally found in the wild, some raise and cultivate these plants.

*Uzradin*

*Benot shikma* – בְּנוֹת שִׁקְמָה: These are the fruits of the *Ficus sycamorus* from the *Moraceae* or mulberry family. This refers to fruits that grow on the sycamore that were not cultivated by human hand in order to enhance the quality of the produce. Due to their small size and tastelessness, they are not considered the primary product of the tree and are exempt from the *halakhot* of *demai*.

Fruits of the sycamore tree

בִּשְׁלָמָא לְמַאן דְּאָמַר בּוּשְׁלֵי כְּמָרָא הַיְינוּ דְּקָתָנֵי הַקִּלִּין שֶׁבִּדְמַאי — סְפֵק הוּא דְּפָטוּר, הָא וַדַּאן חַיָּיב; אֶלָּא לְמַאן דְּאָמַר תְּמָרֵי דְּזִיקָא, וַדַּאי חַיָּיב?! הֶפְקֵרָא נִינְהוּ!

**Here too, the Gemara asks: Granted, according to the one who** said that *novelot* are dates **burned by the heat** of the sun, **that is the** reason **that it was taught** concerning them: Their *halakhot* are lenient with regard to *demai*, meaning that it is **those** with regard to which there is **uncertainty** whether or not they were tithed **that are exempt** from being tithed. Those with regard to which there is **certainty** that they were not tithed, **one is obligated** to tithe those dates. **However, according to the one who** said that *novelot* are dates felled because **of the wind, this is difficult: Those** regarding which there is **certainty** that they were not tithed, **one is obligated? They are ownerless,** and ownerless produce is exempt from the requirement to tithe.

הָכָא בְּמַאי עָסְקִינַן — שֶׁעֲשָׂאָן גּוֹרֶן דְּאָמַר רַבִּי יִצְחָק אָמַר רַבִּי יוֹחָנָן מִשּׁוּם רַבִּי אֱלִיעֶזֶר בֶּן יַעֲקֹב: הַלֶּקֶט וְהַשִּׁכְחָה וְהַפֵּאָה שֶׁעֲשָׂאָן גּוֹרֶן הוּקְבְּעוּ לְמַעֲשֵׂר.

**The Gemara responds: With what are we dealing here?** With a case where he gathered the dates that fell because of the wind and **made them into a pile, like a pile of threshed grain,** signifying that the produce is a finished product. **As Rabbi Yitzḥak said that Rabbi Yoḥanan said in the name of Rabbi Eliezer ben Ya'akov:** Even gifts to the poor such as **gleanings, forgotten sheaves, and** produce of **the corners,**[H] which are normally exempt from tithes, if a poor person gathered them and **made them into a pile of threshed grain,** by rabbinic law **they were rendered** obligated in **tithes.** In that case, only *demai* would be exempt from tithes.

אִיכָּא דְּאָמְרִי:

**Some say** that the discussion was as follows:

---

**Perek VI**
**Daf 41 Amud a**

בִּשְׁלָמָא לְמַאן דְּאָמַר תְּמָרֵי דְּזִיקָא הַיְינוּ דְּהָכָא דְּהָכָא קָרֵי לַהּ "נוֹבְלוֹת" סְתָמָא וְהָתָם קָרֵי לַהּ "תְּמָרָה", אֶלָּא לְמַאן דְּאָמַר בּוּשְׁלֵי כְּמָרָא — נִתְנֵי אִיד וְאִיד "נוֹבְלוֹת תְּמָרָה" אוֹ אִידֵי וְאִידֵי "נוֹבְלוֹת" סְתָמָא! — קַשְׁיָא.

**Granted, according to the one who** said that *novelot temara* are dates **felled by the wind, that is why here,** when our mishna speaks of ruined dates, **it calls them** *novelot*, unmodified and there, when it speaks of those that fell because of the wind, **it calls them** *novelot temara*. **However, according to the one who** said that *novelot temara* are dates **burned by the heat** of the sun,[B] **it should have taught** in **this** mishna here and that, the mishna in tractate *Demai*, *novelot temara*; or taught in **this** and that *novelot*, **unmodified.** The use of different terms indicates that the *mishnayot* are discussing different items. No answer was found to this question, and the Gemara notes that indeed, according to the one who said that *novelot temara* are dates burned by the heat of the sun, **it is difficult.**

"הָיוּ לְפָנָיו מִינִין הַרְבֵּה" וְכוּ'. אָמַר עוּלָּא: מַחֲלוֹקֶת בְּשֶׁבִּרְכוֹתֵיהֶן שָׁווֹת דְּרַבִּי יְהוּדָה סָבַר: מִין שִׁבְעָה עֲדִיף וְרַבָּנַן סָבְרִי: מִין חָבִיב עֲדִיף, אֲבָל בְּשֶׁאֵין בִּרְכוֹתֵיהֶן שָׁווֹת — דִּבְרֵי הַכֹּל מְבָרֵךְ עַל זֶה וְחוֹזֵר וּמְבָרֵךְ עַל זֶה.

**The mishna cited a dispute with regard to the order in which one is** supposed to recite the blessings when **there were many types** of **food before him.**[H] Rabbi Yehuda says: If there is one of the seven species for which Eretz Yisrael was praised among them, he recites the first blessing over it. And the Rabbis say: He recites a blessing over whichever of them he wants. **Ulla said: This dispute is** specifically in a case **where the blessings** to be recited over each type of food **are the same,** as in that case **Rabbi Yehuda holds: The type of the seven** species **takes precedence,** and the Rabbis hold: **The preferred type takes precedence,** and a blessing is recited over it first. **However, when their blessings are not the same, everyone agrees that one must recite a blessing over this** type of food **and then recite another blessing over that,** ensuring that the appropriate blessing is recited over each type of food.

מֵיתִיבֵי: הָיוּ לְפָנָיו צְנוֹן וְזַיִת — מְבָרֵךְ עַל הַצְּנוֹן וּפוֹטֵר אֶת הַזַּיִת! — הָכָא בְּמַאי עָסְקִינַן — כְּשֶׁהַצְּנוֹן עִקָּר.

**The Gemara raises an objection** to this based on what was taught in a *baraita*: If **a radish and an olive were before him, he recites a blessing over the radish and exempts the olive** from the requirement of a blessing, although their blessings are different. The Gemara answers: **With what are we dealing here?** With a case **where the radish is the primary** component for the one partaking of them, and the olive serves only to temper the taste of the radish. Therefore, he need recite a blessing only over the radish.

**HALAKHA**

Tithes from gleanings, forgotten sheaves, and produce of the corners – מַעֲשֵׂר בְּלֶקֶט שִׁכְחָה וּפֵאָה: Gleanings, forgotten sheaves, and produce of the corners are exempt from tithes. However, if one gathered them into a pile of threshed grain, they are obligated in tithes by rabbinic decree, in accordance with the opinion of Rabbi Eliezer ben Ya'akov (Rambam, Sefer Zera'im, Hilkhot Terumot 2:9).

**BACKGROUND**

Dates burned by the heat of the sun – בּוּשְׁלֵי כְּמָרָא: According to Rashi, these are dates burned by the heat of the sun. The ge'onim explain that this refers to dates that do not ripen fully on the tree and remain unripe. Therefore, various measures are taken to artificially ripen the fruit, among them warming the dates on the ground. Consequently, they are called bushlei, meaning ripened by, kamra, burying and heating.

**HALAKHA**

There were many types of food before him – הָיוּ לְפָנָיו מִינִין הַרְבֵּה וכו': There are two opinions about the halakhic ruling in this case. According to one opinion (Rosh), the halakha is in accordance with the opinion of Rabbi Yehuda, as explained in the Gemara: With regard to fruits which require the same blessing, one recites a blessing over the item which is one of the seven species, as in that case Rabbi Yehuda agrees with the Rabbis (Taz); and if none of the food items is one of the seven species, one recites a blessing over whichever he prefers or whichever he likes better. According to the second opinion (Rambam), the halakha is in accordance with the opinion of the Rabbis, and one recites a blessing over that which he likes better first, and if he likes them both the same, he recites a blessing over that which is of the seven species first. The halakhic conclusion is unclear. Some prefer the first opinion (Mishna Berura). Others hold that one may decide to conduct himself in accordance with whichever position he prefers (Shulhan Arukh HaRav based on the Taz; Rambam Sefer Ahava, Hilkhot Berakhot 8:13; Shulhan Arukh, Oraḥ Ḥayyim 211:1).

אִי הָכִי, אֵימָא סֵיפָא; רַבִּי יְהוּדָה אוֹמֵר: מְבָרֵךְ עַל הַזַּיִת, שֶׁהַזַּיִת מִמִּין שִׁבְעָה; לֵית לֵיהּ לְרַבִּי יְהוּדָה הָא דִּתְנַן: כֹּל שֶׁהוּא עִיקָּר וְעִמּוֹ טְפֵלָה – מְבָרֵךְ עַל הָעִיקָּר וּפוֹטֵר אֶת הַטְּפֵלָה?! וְכִי תֵּימָא הָכִי נַמִּי דְּלֵית לֵיהּ, וְהָתַנְיָא: רַבִּי יְהוּדָה אוֹמֵר, אִם מֵחֲמַת צְנוֹן בָּא הַזַּיִת – מְבָרֵךְ עַל הַצְּנוֹן וּפוֹטֵר אֶת הַזַּיִת!

The Gemara continues and asks: **If so, say the latter clause** of the *baraita* where **Rabbi Yehuda says: One recites a blessing over the olive, as the olive is a type of the seven** species. **Does Rabbi Yehuda not accept that** principle **which we learned** in a mishna: Any food **that is primary, and** is eaten **with** food that is **secondary, one recites a blessing over the primary** food, and that blessing **exempts the secondary** from the requirement to recite a blessing before eating it? **And if you say: Indeed, he does not hold** that the primary food exempts the secondary, **wasn't it taught** in a *baraita*: **Rabbi Yehuda says: If** it is **due to the radish** that **the olive comes, one recites a blessing over the radish**[B] **and exempts the olive.**[B] If so, the dispute whether to recite a blessing over the radish or the olive must be in a case where the radish is not primary. This is an apparent contradiction of Ulla's statement.

לְעוֹלָם בִּצְנוֹן עִיקָּר עָסְקִינַן, וְכִי פְּלִיגִי רַבִּי יְהוּדָה וְרַבָּנַן – בְּמִילְּתָא אַחֲרִיתִי פְּלִיגִי, וְחַסּוֹרֵי מְחַסְּרָא וְהָכִי קָתָנֵי: הָיוּ לְפָנָיו צְנוֹן וְזַיִת – מְבָרֵךְ עַל הַצְּנוֹן וּפוֹטֵר אֶת הַזַּיִת. בַּמֶּה דְּבָרִים אֲמוּרִים – כְּשֶׁהַצְּנוֹן עִיקָּר, אֲבָל אֵין הַצְּנוֹן עִיקָּר – דִּבְרֵי הַכֹּל מְבָרֵךְ עַל זֶה וְחוֹזֵר וּמְבָרֵךְ עַל זֶה; וּשְׁנֵי מִינִין בְּעָלְמָא שֶׁבִּרְכוֹתֵיהֶן שָׁווֹת – מְבָרֵךְ עַל אֵיזֶה מֵהֶן שֶׁיִּרְצֶה. רַבִּי יְהוּדָה אוֹמֵר: מְבָרֵךְ עַל הַזַּיִת, שֶׁהַזַּיִת מִמִּין שִׁבְעָה.

The Gemara responds: **Actually, we are dealing with** a case where the **radish** is the **primary** component of the meal, **and when Rabbi Yehuda and the Rabbis disagree, it is with regard to a different case that they disagree, and this** *baraita* **is incomplete and it teaches the following:** If **a radish and an olive were before him, he recites a blessing over the radish and exempts the olive. In what** circumstances **does this apply?** Specifically **when the radish is primary, but when the radish is not primary, everyone agrees that one recites** the appropriate **blessing over this** one **and then he again recites** the appropriate **blessing over that** one. However, **in general,** if **two types of food whose blessings are identical** were before him, **he recites a blessing over whichever of them that he wants. Rabbi Yehuda says: He recites a blessing over the olive, as the olive is a type of the seven** species.

פְּלִיגִי בָּהּ רַבִּי אַמִי וְרַבִּי יִצְחָק נַפָּחָא; חַד אָמַר מַחֲלוֹקֶת בְּשֶׁבִּרְכוֹתֵיהֶן שָׁווֹת, דְּרַבִּי יְהוּדָה סָבַר: מִין שִׁבְעָה עָדִיף, וְרַבָּנַן סָבְרִי: מִין חָבִיב עָדִיף, אֲבָל בְּשֶׁאֵין בִּרְכוֹתֵיהֶן שָׁווֹת – דִּבְרֵי הַכֹּל מְבָרֵךְ עַל זֶה וְחוֹזֵר וּמְבָרֵךְ עַל זֶה; וְחַד אָמַר: אַף בְּשֶׁאֵין בִּרְכוֹתֵיהֶן שָׁווֹת נַמִּי מַחֲלוֹקֶת.

**Rabbi Ami and Rabbi Yitzḥak Nappaḥa disagreed with regard to** this subject. **One said:** The **dispute** is in a case **where their blessings are identical,** as **Rabbi Yehuda held:** A **type of the seven species takes precedence** and the blessing is recited over it first. **And the Rabbis held: The preferred type takes precedence,** and a blessing is recited over it first; **however, when their blessings are not identical, everyone agrees that one recites** the appropriate **blessing over this** one **and then he again recites** the appropriate **blessing over that** one. **And one said: Even when their blessings are not identical,** there is **also** a **dispute.**

בִּשְׁלָמָא לְמַאן דְּאָמַר בְּשֶׁבִּרְכוֹתֵיהֶן שָׁווֹת מַחֲלוֹקֶת – שַׁפִּיר, אֶלָּא לְמַאן דְּאָמַר בְּשֶׁאֵין בִּרְכוֹתֵיהֶן שָׁווֹת פְּלִיגִי – בְּמַאי פְּלִיגִי? – אָמַר רַבִּי יִרְמְיָה: לְהַקְדִּים.

The Gemara discusses this: **Granted, according to the one who said** that the **dispute** is **in** a case **where their blessings are identical, it works out well. However, according to the one who says** that **they disagree in** a case **where their blessings are not identical,** then **about what do they disagree?** One mus recite two blessings in any case. **Rabbi Yirmeya said:** They disagree with regard to which blessing **precedes** the other.

דְּאָמַר רַב יוֹסֵף וְאִיתֵּימָא רַבִּי יִצְחָק: כֹּל הַמּוּקְדָּם בְּפָסוּק זֶה מוּקְדָּם לִבְרָכָה, שֶׁנֶּאֱמַר: ״אֶרֶץ חִטָּה וּשְׂעֹרָה וְגֶפֶן וּתְאֵנָה וְרִמּוֹן אֶרֶץ זֵית שֶׁמֶן וּדְבָשׁ״.

**As Rav Yosef, and some say Rabbi Yitzḥak, said: Each** food whose significance is manifest in that it **precedes** the others **in this verse,** which sings the praises of Eretz Yisrael, **takes precedence** over the others **in terms of blessing** as well, **as it is stated: "A land of wheat**[B] **and barley,**[B] **vines, figs**[B] **and pomegranates, a land of olive oil and honey"** (Deuteronomy 8:8).

וּפְלִיגָא דְּרַבִּי חָנָן, דְּאָמַר רַבִּי חָנָן: כָּל הַפָּסוּק כּוּלּוֹ לְשִׁיעוּרִין נֶאֱמַר.

The Gemara notes: And this opinion **disagrees** with the opinion **of Rabbi Ḥanan. As Rabbi Ḥanan said: The entire verse was stated for** the purpose of teaching **measures** with regard to different *halakhot* in the Torah.

## HALAKHA

**Each food that precedes the others in this verse, takes precedence in terms of blessing – כָּל הַמּוּקְדָּם בְּפָסוּק זֶה מוּקְדָּם לִבְרָכָה:** According to all opinions, when there is no preference for one of the food items in terms of the significance of the blessing, nor in terms of the fact that he likes one better, one recites the blessing over the food item enumerated earlier in the verse first (Rambam *Sefer Ahava, Hilkhot Berakhot* 8:13; *Shulḥan Arukh, Oraḥ Ḥayyim* 211:4).

## BACKGROUND

**Radish – צְנוֹן:** The radish, *Raphanus sativus*, is an edible root of the *Brassicaceae* family that was domesticated in pre-Roman times. Radishes are grown and eaten throughout the world. There are numerous varieties of radishes, varying in size, color, and duration of cultivation time. Some radishes are grown for their seeds. Oilseed radishes, as the name implies, are grown for oil production.

**Olive – זַיִת:** The olive, *Olea europaea*, is a species of small tree in the *Oleaceae* family, native to the coastal areas of the eastern Mediterranean Basin, the adjoining coastal areas of southeastern Europe, western Asia, northern Africa, as well as northern Iran at the southern end of the Caspian Sea. The olive was one of the three main elements in Israelite cuisine. Olive oil was used not only for food and for cooking, but also for lighting, sacrificial offerings, ointment, and anointment for priestly and royal office.

**Wheat – חִטָּה:** Wheat, *Triticum spp.*, is a cereal grain. It is originally from the Fertile Crescent region of the Near East, but is now cultivated worldwide. Globally, wheat is the leading source of vegetable protein in human food, having higher protein content than corn or rice, the other major cereals. In terms of total food production, it is currently second only to rice in terms of human consumption.

**Barley – שְׂעֹרָה:** Cultivated barley is a cereal grain of the genus *Hordeum*. Cultivated barley descended from wild barley, *Hordeum spontaneum*, which still grows wild in the Middle East. Cultivated barley is an annual plant, but there are many other perennial species. It is utilized as a major animal fodder, as base malt for beer and certain distilled beverages, and as a component of various health foods. It is used in soups and stews, and in barley bread in various cultures.

The ancient Israelites cultivated both wheat and barley. These two grains are mentioned first in the biblical list of the seven species for which Eretz Yisrael was praised. Their significance as food in ancient Israelite cuisine is also seen in the celebration of the barley harvest at the festival of *Shavuot*, and the wheat harvest at the festival of *Sukkot*.

**Figs – תְּאֵנָה:** The common fig, *Ficus carica*, is a deciduous tree reaching heights up to 6 m (19 ft) in the *Ficus* genus from the *Moraceae* family. It is a temperate species native to the Middle East. Figs were cultivated throughout Eretz Yisrael and fresh and dried figs were part of the daily diet. A common way of preparing dried figs was to chop them and press them into a cake. Figs are frequently mentioned in the Bible (see for example, I Samuel 25:18, I Samuel 30:12, and I Chronicles 12:41).

"חִטָּה" – דִּתְנַן: הַנִּכְנָס לְבַיִת הַמְנוּגָּע וְכֵלָיו עַל כְּתֵפָיו וְסַנְדָּלָיו וְטַבְּעוֹתָיו בְּיָדָיו – הוּא וְהֵן טְמֵאִין מִיָּד; הָיָה לָבוּשׁ כֵּלָיו, וְסַנְדָּלָיו בְּרַגְלָיו, וְטַבְּעוֹתָיו בְּאֶצְבְּעוֹתָיו – הוּא טָמֵא מִיָּד, וְהֵן טְהוֹרִין עַד שֶׁיִּשְׁהֶא בִּכְדֵי אֲכִילַת פְּרָס, פַּת חִטִּין וְלֹא פַּת שְׂעוֹרִין, מֵיסֵב וְאוֹכְלָן בְּלִפְתָּן.

**Wheat** was mentioned as the basis for calculating the time required for one to become ritually impure by entering a house afflicted with leprosy, **as we learned** in a mishna: **One who enters a house afflicted** with leprosy of the house[H] (see Leviticus 14:33–53) **with his clothes** resting **on his shoulders, and his sandals and his rings are in his hands,** both **he and they,** the clothes, sandals, and rings, **immediately** become **ritually impure.**[N] However, if **he was dressed in his clothes, and his sandals were on his feet and his rings on his fingers, he immediately becomes ritually impure** upon entering the house, **but they,** the clothes, sandals, and rings, **remain pure until he stays** in the house **long enough to eat half a loaf** of bread.[B] This calculation is made with **wheat bread,** which takes less time to eat, **and not** with **barley bread,** and with one who is **reclining and eating** the bread **with a relish,** which hastens the eating. There is, then, a Torah measurement that is connected specifically to wheat.

"שְׂעוֹרָה" – דִּתְנַן: עֶצֶם כִּשְׂעוֹרָה מְטַמֵּא בְּמַגָּע וּבְמַשָּׂא, וְאֵינוֹ מְטַמֵּא בְּאֹהֶל.

**Barley** is also used as the basis for a measure, **as we learned** in a mishna: **A bone** from a corpse that is the size **of** a grain of **barley**[H] **imparts ritual impurity through contact and by being carried,** but **it does not impart impurity** by means **of a tent,** i.e., if the bone was inside a house, it does not defile all of the articles in the house.

"גֶּפֶן" – כְּדֵי רְבִיעִית יַיִן לְנָזִיר. "תְּאֵנָה" – כִּגְרוֹגֶרֶת לְהוֹצָאַת שַׁבָּת. "רִמּוֹן" – כִּדְתְנַן: כָּל כְּלֵי בַעֲלֵי בָתִּים

The halakhic measure determined by **vines** is **the quantity of a quarter** ***log*** **of wine**[H] **for a Nazirite** and not the wine equivalent of a quarter *log* of water, which is a slightly different measure. **Figs** serve as the basis for the measure of **a dried fig-bulk,** typically the smallest unit of food for which someone will be held liable **for carrying out on Shabbat**[H] from one domain to another. **Pomegranates** teach us a particular measurement as well, **as we learned** in a mishna: **All** ritually impure wooden **utensils belonging to** ordinary **homeowners** become pure through breaking the utensil,

Perek **VI**
Daf **41** Amud **b**

שִׁיעוּרָן כְּרִמּוֹנִים.

as an impure vessel loses its status as a vessel and consequently its impurity when it can no longer be used, if they have holes **the size of pomegranates.**

"אֶרֶץ זֵית שֶׁמֶן" – אָמַר רַבִּי יוֹסֵי בְּרַבִּי חֲנִינָא: אֶרֶץ שֶׁכָּל שִׁיעוּרֶיהָ כְּזֵיתִים. כָּל שִׁיעוּרֶיהָ סָלְקָא דַּעְתָּךְ?! וְהָא אִיכָּא הָנָךְ דַּאֲמַרַן! אֶלָּא: אֶרֶץ שֶׁרוֹב שִׁיעוּרֶיהָ כְּזֵיתִים.

**A land of olive oil: Rabbi Yosei, son of Rabbi Ḥanina, said** that the verse should be expounded as follows: **A land, all of whose measures are** the size of **olives.** The Gemara poses a question: **Can it enter your mind** that it is a land **all of whose measures** are the size of olives? **Aren't there those** measures **that we mentioned** above, which are not the size of olives? **Rather, say: A land, most of whose measures are** the size of **olives,** as most of the measures relating to forbidden foods and other matters are the size of olives.

"דְּבַשׁ" – כַּכּוֹתֶבֶת הַגַּסָּה בְּיוֹם הַכִּפּוּרִים. וְאִידָּךְ? הָנֵי שִׁיעוּרִין בְּהֶדְיָא מִי כְּתִיבִי?! אֶלָּא מִדְּרַבָּנַן וּקְרָא אַסְמַכְתָּא בְּעָלְמָא.

**Honey,** i.e., dates from which date honey is extracted, also alludes to a measurement. With regard to Yom Kippur, one is only liable if he eats the equivalent **of a large date**[B] **on Yom Kippur.**[H] The Gemara asks: **And** what will **the other** *amora*, who interpreted the verse as referring to the *halakhot* of precedence in blessings, say with regard to this midrash? The Gemara responds: **Are these measures written explicitly** in the Torah? **Rather,** they are **by rabbinic** law, **and the verse** is **a mere support,**[N] an allusion to these measures.

**HALAKHA**

**One who enters a house afflicted with leprosy of the house** – הַנִּכְנָס לְבַיִת הַמְנוּגָּע: One who enters a house afflicted with leprosy becomes ritually impure immediately. With regard to his clothing: If he was carrying them, they, too, become ritually impure immediately. If he was wearing them, they only become ritually impure if he remained in the house long enough to eat half a loaf of bread (Rambam *Sefer Tahara, Hilkhot Tumat Tzara'at* 5:6–7).

**A bone the size of a grain of barley** – עֶצֶם כִּשְׂעוֹרָה: A bone the size of a grain of barley, or larger, transmits ritual impurity by means of contact and by being carried, but not by means of a tent, as per the unattributed mishna (Rambam *Sefer Tahara, Hilkhot Tumat Met* 3:2).

**The quantity of a quarter** ***log*** **of wine** – כְּדֵי רְבִיעִית יַיִן: A Nazirite who drank a quarter of a *log* of wine or any other product of the vine is punished with lashes as per the mishna (Rambam *Sefer Hafla'a, Hilkhot Nezirut* 5:2).

**A dried fig-bulk for carrying out on Shabbat** – כִּגְרוֹגֶרֶת לְהוֹצָאַת שַׁבָּת: The quantity of most foods forbidden by Torah law to be carried from one domain to another on Shabbat is the measure of a dried fig-bulk (Rambam *Sefer Zemanim, Hilkhot Shabbat* 18:1).

**NOTES**

**Ritual impurity of a house afflicted with leprosy** – טוּמְאַת בַּיִת הַמְנוּגָּע: From the verse: "And one who enters the house during the days when it is closed up shall be impure until evening" (Leviticus 14:46), it is derived that one who enters that house becomes impure but his clothes do not. The following verse, however, states: "One who lies in the house shall wash his clothing and one who eats in the house shall wash his clothing" (Leviticus 14:47), indicating that under those circumstances, his clothes become ritually impure as well. The Sages concluded that the clothes of one who stays in the house for a certain period of time ,one who lies, become ritually impure. In determining the duration of that period of time, the Sages adopted the measure of: One who eats in the house, which they defined as the time it takes for one who reclines to eat half a loaf of wheat bread with relish.

**BACKGROUND**

**Eating half a loaf of bread** – אֲכִילַת פְּרָס: The time that it takes to consume half a loaf of bread serves as a gauge in many areas of *halakha*. Later authorities debate the basis of this tannaitic dispute; whether a half-loaf is the size of three or four egg-bulks. Opinions varied with regard to the amount of time represented by this measure, especially with regard to foods whose time of consumption is not uniform. Opinions regarding the duration of this period of time, range from three to nine minutes.

**BACKGROUND**

**Date** – תָּמָר: The date palm *Phoenix dactylifera* is a palm in the *Phoenix* genus, cultivated for its edible sweet fruit. It is a medium-sized tree, 15–25 m tall, growing singly or forming a clump with several stems from a single root system. The leaves are 3–5 m long, the full span of the crown ranges from 6–10 m.

Dates were eaten fresh or dried, but were used mostly boiled into a thick, durable syrup called date honey and used as a sweetener. The honey in the biblical reference of a "land flowing with milk and honey" (see Exodus 3:8 for example), is date honey.

**HALAKHA**

**The equivalent of a large date on Yom Kippur** – כַּכּוֹתֶבֶת הַגַּסָּה בְּיוֹם הַכִּפּוּרִים: The quantity of food for which one is liable on Yom Kippur is an amount the size of a large date-bulk, which is slightly smaller than an egg-bulk (Rambam *Sefer Zemanim, Hilkhot Shevitat Asor* 2:1; *Shulḥan Arukh, Oraḥ Ḥayyim* 612:1).

**NOTES**

**A mere support** – אַסְמַכְתָּא בְּעָלְמָא: Apparently, according to the conclusion of the Gemara, even Rabbi Ḥanan holds that this verse was not stated with regard to measurements. The measurements are a *halakha* transmitted to Moses from Sinai, and the use of the verse in this context is merely for mnemonic purposes and as a support (see Rabbi Eliyahu Mizraḥi).

רַב חִסְדָּא וְרַב הַמְנוּנָא הֲווּ יָתְבִי בִּסְעוּדְתָא, אַיְיתוּ לְקַמַּיְיהוּ תַּמְרֵי וְרִמּוֹנֵי, שָׁקַל רַב הַמְנוּנָא בְּרֵיךְ אַתַּמְרֵי בְּרֵישָׁא. אֲמַר לֵיהּ רַב חִסְדָּא: לָא סְבִירָא לֵיהּ מָר לְהָא דְּאָמַר רַב יוֹסֵף וְאִיתֵּימָא רַבִּי יִצְחָק: כֹּל הַמּוּקְדָּם בְּפָסוּק זֶה קוֹדֵם לִבְרָכָה?!

With regard to the *halakhot* of precedence in blessings, the Gemara relates: **Rav Ḥisda and Rav Hamnuna were sitting at a meal. They brought dates and pomegranates before them. Rav Hamnuna took and recited a blessing over the dates first. Rav Ḥisda said to him:** Does **the Master not hold that** *halakha* **which Rav Yosef, and some say Rabbi Yitzḥak, said: Each** food that **precedes** the others **in this verse, precedes** the others **in terms of blessing as well?** The pomegranate precedes the date in that verse.

אֲמַר לֵיהּ: זֶה שֵׁנִי לְ״אֶרֶץ״, וְזֶה חֲמִישִׁי לְ״אֶרֶץ״. – אֲמַר לֵיהּ: מַאן יְהֵיב לָן נִגְרֵי דְּפַרְזְלָא וְנִשְׁמְעִינָךְ.

Rav Hamnuna **said to him: This,** the date, **is** mentioned **second to** the word **land,**[H] in the verse: "A land of olive oil and honey," just after the olive, **and this,** the pomegranate, is **fifth to the word land.** Rav Ḥisda **said to him** admiringly: **Who will give us iron legs that we may serve you** and constantly hear from you novel ideas.

אִיתְּמַר: הֵבִיאוּ לִפְנֵיהֶם תְּאֵנִים וַעֲנָבִים בְּתוֹךְ הַסְּעוּדָה; אָמַר רַב הוּנָא: טְעוּנִים בְּרָכָה לִפְנֵיהֶם וְאֵין טְעוּנִים בְּרָכָה לְאַחֲרֵיהֶם. וְכֵן אָמַר רַב נַחְמָן: טְעוּנִים בְּרָכָה לִפְנֵיהֶם וְאֵין טְעוּנִים בְּרָכָה לְאַחֲרֵיהֶם; וְרַב שֵׁשֶׁת אָמַר: טְעוּנִין בְּרָכָה בֵּין לִפְנֵיהֶם בֵּין לְאַחֲרֵיהֶם, שֶׁאֵין לְךָ דָּבָר שֶׁטָּעוּן בְּרָכָה לְפָנָיו וְאֵין טָעוּן בְּרָכָה לְאַחֲרָיו אֶלָּא פַּת הַבָּאָה בְּכִסָּנִין בִּלְבַד. וּפְלִיגָא דְּרַבִּי חִיָּיא, דְּאָמַר רַבִּי חִיָּיא: פַּת פּוֹטֶרֶת כׇּל מִינֵי מַאֲכָל, וְיַיִן פּוֹטֵר כׇּל מִינֵי מַשְׁקִים.

**It was stated: If they brought figs and grapes before them during a meal,** what blessings need to be recited? **Rav Huna said: They require a blessing before** eating **them, and do not require a blessing after** eating **them,** as Grace after Meals exempts them. **And so too, Rav Naḥman said: They require a blessing before** eating **them and do not require a blessing after** eating **them. And Rav Sheshet said: They require a blessing both before** eating **them and after** eating **them,** even if he ate them during the meal, **as you have nothing which requires a blessing before** eating **it and does not require a blessing after** eating **it,** because it is exempted by Grace after Meals, **except bread,** a sweetened and spiced pastry, **that comes as dessert,** as it, too, is a type of bread. The statements of both Rav Huna and Rav Sheshet **disagree with** the opinion **of Rabbi Ḥiyya,**[PN] **as Rabbi Ḥiyya said: Bread exempts all the types of food** that one eats after it, **and wine exempts all types of drinks** that one drink after it,[H] and one need not recite a blessing either before or after eating them.

אָמַר רַב פַּפָּא, הִלְכְתָא: דְּבָרִים הַבָּאִים מֵחֲמַת הַסְּעוּדָה בְּתוֹךְ הַסְּעוּדָה – אֵין טְעוּנִים בְּרָכָה לֹא לִפְנֵיהֶם וְלֹא לְאַחֲרֵיהֶם, וְשֶׁלֹּא מֵחֲמַת הַסְּעוּדָה בְּתוֹךְ הַסְּעוּדָה – טְעוּנִים בְּרָכָה לִפְנֵיהֶם וְאֵין טְעוּנִים בְּרָכָה לְאַחֲרֵיהֶם; לְאַחַר הַסְּעוּדָה – טְעוּנִים בְּרָכָה בֵּין לִפְנֵיהֶם בֵּין לְאַחֲרֵיהֶם.

Summarizing, **Rav Pappa said** that **the** *halakha* is: Food **items that come due to the meal,**[HN] which are eaten together with the bread as part of the meal, **during the meal, neither require a blessing before** eating **them nor after** eating **them,** as they are considered secondary to the bread. **And** food items like fruit, **that do not come due to the meal,** as part of the meal, but may be brought **during the meal, require a blessing before** eating **them and do not require a blessing after** eating **them.** If they come **after the meal, they require a blessing both before** eating **them and after** eating **them.**

שָׁאֲלוּ אֶת בֶּן זוֹמָא, מִפְּנֵי מָה אָמְרוּ: דְּבָרִים הַבָּאִים מֵחֲמַת הַסְּעוּדָה בְּתוֹךְ הַסְּעוּדָה אֵינָם טְעוּנִים בְּרָכָה לֹא לִפְנֵיהֶם וְלֹא לְאַחֲרֵיהֶם? אָמַר לָהֶם: הוֹאִיל וּפַת פּוֹטַרְתָּן. אִי הָכִי, יַיִן נָמֵי נִפְטְרֵיהּ פַּת! – שָׁאנֵי יַיִן,

The Gemara relates that the students **asked Ben Zoma: Why did** the Sages **say** that food **items that come due to the meal during the meal, neither require a blessing before** eating **them nor after** eating **them? He said to them: Because bread exempts them.** They asked: **If so, bread should also exempt wine.** Yet, one recites a blessing over wine during the meal. The Gemara responds: **Wine is different,**[H]

PERSONALITIES

**Rabbi Ḥiyya** – רַבִּי חִיָּיא: Rabbi Ḥiyya ben Abba from the city of Kafri in Babylonia was among the last *tanna'im*, a colleague-disciple of Rabbi Yehuda HaNasi.

Rabbi Ḥiyya descended from a family of distinguished lineage that traced its ancestry back to King David and produced many Sages. While he was still in Babylonia, Rabbi Ḥiyya was considered a Torah luminary. When he ascended to Eretz Yisrael from Babylonia with his family, some, engaging in hyperbole, said that the Torah was about to be forgotten until he came from Babylonia and reestablished it. When he came to Eretz Yisrael, he became a disciple and a colleague of Rabbi Yehuda HaNasi, with whom he had a very close relationship. He was especially close to Rabbi's son, Shimon, who was also his business partner. Rabbi Ḥiyya was among the prominent Torah scholars in his generation and was the right-hand man of his nephew, Rav, who, although he was known as the Rabbi of all Israel, received certain traditions from Rabbi Ḥiyya. In addition to his prominence as a Torah scholar, Rabbi Ḥiyya was outstanding in his piety, as reflected in several anecdotes throughout the Talmud.

His most significant project was the redaction he did together with his own colleague-disciple, Rabbi Oshaya, of an anthology of external *mishnayot* to complement the Mishna redacted by Rabbi Yehuda HaNasi. Their anthology was considered to be most authoritative, to the point that it was said that any *baraita* that was not reviewed by them is unfit to enter the study hall. Some believe that he edited the *Tosefta*.

Apparently, upon his arrival in Eretz Yisrael, he received financial support from the house of the *Nasi*; however, his primary livelihood was from international trade, primarily of silk. He had twin daughters, Pazi and Tavi, who were the matriarchs of significant families of Torah scholars. He also had twin sons, Yehuda, the son-in-law of Rabbi Yannai, and Ḥizkiya. Both were among the leading Torah scholars in the transitional generation between *tanna'im* and *amora'im*, and they apparently replaced him at the head of his private yeshiva in the city of his residence, Tiberias.

All of the students of Rabbi Yehuda HaNasi were his friends, and he was even close with the *tanna* Rabbi Shimon ben Ḥalafta. The younger students of Rabbi Yehuda HaNasi, Rabbi Ḥanina, Rabbi Oshaya, Rabbi Yannai, and others, studied Torah from him and were, to a certain degree, his students as well. His brothers' sons, Rabba bar Ḥana, and above all, the great *amora*, Rav, were his primary disciples. He also appears as a central character in the *Zohar*.

Rabbi Ḥiyya was buried in Tiberias and later his two sons were buried beside him.

HALAKHA

**This is second to the word land** – זֶה שֵׁנִי לְ״אֶרֶץ״ וכו׳: One recites a blessing first over the species most closely following the word "land" both times that it appears in the verse that enumerates the seven species. This principle does not apply to dishes of cooked grain or wine, as they have their own blessings and take precedence (Rema; Rambam *Sefer Ahava*, *Hilkhot Berakhot* 8:13; *Shulḥan Arukh*, *Oraḥ Ḥayyim* 211:4).

**Wine exempts all types of drinks that one drinks after it** – וְיַיִן פּוֹטֵר כׇּל מִינֵי מַשְׁקִים: The blessing over wine exempts all other drinks from the requirement to recite a blessing either before or after drinking them. This is true for drinks which he had in mind (*Shulḥan Arukh HaRav*) or drinks which were before him (*Be'er Heitev*) when he recited the blessing before drinking (*Shulḥan Arukh*, *Oraḥ Ḥayyim* 174:2).

**Food items that come due to the meal** – דְּבָרִים הַבָּאִים מֵחֲמַת הַסְּעוּדָה: Foods which are eaten as integral parts of a meal, e.g., cooked dishes, require no blessing at all. Fruits and the like, which are supplementary to the meal, require a blessing before eating them. If one decided to conclude his meal and to eat fruit before reciting Grace after Meals, he must recite a blessing both before and after eating the fruit in accordance with the opinion of Rav Pappa (Rambam *Sefer Ahava*, *Hilkhot Berakhot* 4:11; *Shulḥan Arukh*, *Oraḥ Ḥayyim* 177:1–2).

**Wine is different** – שָׁאנֵי יַיִן וכו׳: Wine, even if one drinks it during the meal, requires a separate blessing (*Shulḥan Arukh*, *Oraḥ Ḥayyim* 174:1, 7).

NOTES

**Disagree with the opinion of Rabbi Ḥiyya** – וּפְלִיגָא דְּרַבִּי חִיָּיא: The *amora'im* disagree with Rabbi Ḥiyya, despite the fact that he appears throughout the Talmud as a *tanna*, because Rabbi Ḥiyya lived during the last generation of *tanna'im*. Consequently, he is sometimes considered a *tanna* and sometimes an *amora*. This is supported by the fact that the *halakha* is ruled in accordance with those statements made by Rabbi Ḥiyya as a *tanna*, i.e., Rabbi Ḥiyya taught, while his comments as an *amora*, i.e., Rabbi Ḥiyya said, have the same authority as any other early *amora*.

**Food items that come due to the meal** – דְּבָרִים הַבָּאִים מֵחֲמַת הַסְּעוּדָה: The authorities discussed this issue and its explanation at great length. According to Rav Hai Gaon, the various approaches to the topic stem from the question: What is the meaning of the phrase, that come due to the meal? Does it mean that only those foods that people regularly eat as part of a meal are exempted by the blessing over bread? Alternatively, can it be interpreted that anything served due to this particular meal is exempted by the blessing over bread?

דּוֹגֵם בְּרָכָה לְעַצְמוֹ.

**as it causes a blessing itself.**[N] It is so significant, that one recites a blessing over it together with other blessings like *kiddush* and *havdala*, even though he does not particularly want to drink it. During a meal too, a blessing is recited over the wine and it is not exempted by the blessing over the bread.

רַב הוּנָא אֲכַל תְּלֵיסַר רִיפְתֵּי בְּנֵי תְּלָתָא תְּלָתָא בְּקַבָּא וְלָא בָּרֵיךְ. אֲמַר לֵיהּ רַב נַחְמָן: עֲדֵי כַּפְנָא! אֶלָּא: כֹּל שֶׁאֲחֵרִים קוֹבְעִים עָלָיו סְעוּדָּה צָרִיךְ לְבָרֵךְ.

As the Gemara mentioned bread that comes as dessert,[B] it now relates that **Rav Huna ate thirteen** substantially sized, sweetened **loaves, three** loaves **per** *kav* of flour, **and he did not recite** Grace after Meals[N] because they were not genuine bread. **Rav Naḥman said to him: That is hunger.**[N] One does not typically eat that much merely as dessert. **Rather, over anything which** is substantial enough to satiate and **others base a meal** upon it,[H] **one must recite** Grace after Meals.

רַב יְהוּדָה הֲוָה עָסֵיק לֵיהּ לִבְרֵיהּ בֵּי רַב יְהוּדָה בַּר חֲבִיבָא, אַיְיתוּ לְקַמַּיְיהוּ פַּת הַבָּאָה בְּכִסָּנִין. כִּי אֲתָא, שְׁמַעִינְהוּ דְּקָא מְבָרְכִי ״הַמּוֹצִיא״. אֲמַר לְהוּ: מַאי ״צִיצִי״ דְּקָא שָׁמַעְנָא? דִּילְמָא ״הַמּוֹצִיא לֶחֶם מִן הָאָרֶץ״ קָא מְבָרְכִיתוּ?! – אָמְרִי לֵיהּ: אִין, דְּתַנְיָא רַבִּי מוֹנָא אָמַר מִשּׁוּם רַבִּי יְהוּדָה: פַּת הַבָּאָה בְּכִסָּנִין מְבָרְכִין עָלֶיהָ ״הַמּוֹצִיא״ וְאָמַר שְׁמוּאֵל: הֲלָכָה כְּרַבִּי מוֹנָא.

The Gemara also relates: **Rav Yehuda was engaged** in preparations for **his son's** wedding **at the house of Rav Yehuda bar Ḥaviva when they brought bread that comes as dessert**[H] **before them. When it arrived, he heard them reciting: Who brings forth** bread from the earth. **He said to them: What is this** ***tzitzi*** **sound that I hear? Perhaps you are reciting: Who brings forth bread from the earth? They said to him: Yes,** indeed, **as it was taught** in a *baraita*: **Rabbi Mona said in the name of Rabbi Yehuda: Over bread that comes as dessert, one recites: Who brings forth** bread from the earth. **And Shmuel said: The** ***halakha*** **is in accordance with** the opinion of **Rabbi Mona.**

אֲמַר לְהוּ: אֵין הֲלָכָה כְּרַבִּי מוֹנָא אִתְּמַר. אָמְרִי לֵיהּ: וְהָא מָר הוּא דַּאֲמַר מִשְּׁמֵיהּ דִּשְׁמוּאֵל, לַחְמָנִיּוֹת – מְעָרְבִין בָּהֶן וּמְבָרְכִין עֲלֵיהֶן ״הַמּוֹצִיא״! – שָׁאנֵי הָתָם דְּקָבַע סְעוּדָּתֵיהּ עֲלַיְיהוּ, אֲבָל הֵיכָא דְּלָא קָבַע סְעוּדָּתֵיהּ עֲלַיְיהוּ – לָא.

Rav Yehuda **said to them:** You are mistaken. Actually, **it was stated** that Shmuel said: **The** ***halakha*** **is not in accordance with** the opinion of **Rabbi Mona. They said to him: But aren't you, Master, the one who said in the name of Shmuel** with regard to **wafers:**[H] **One may establish an** ***eiruv***, the joining of courtyards, to permit carrying in a shared courtyard and the joining of cooked foods, to permit cooking on a festival for Shabbat, **with them and recite over them: Who brings forth** bread from the earth. Why is that the blessing over those wafers? They too are sweetened bread that comes as dessert. He answered them: **It is different there as he based his meal upon them, but here, where one did not base his meal upon them, no,** he does not recite: Who brings forth bread from the earth.

רַב פַּפָּא אִיקְּלַע לְבֵי רַב הוּנָא בְּרֵיהּ דְּרַב נָתָן, בָּתַר דִּגְמַר סְעוּדָּתַיְיהוּ אַיְיתוּ לְקַמַּיְיהוּ מִידֵּי לְמֵיכַל, שְׁקַל רַב פַּפָּא וְקָא אָכֵיל. אָמְרִי לֵיהּ: לָא סְבִר לָהּ מָר ״גָּמַר אָסוּר מִלֶּאֱכוֹל״?! אֲמַר לְהוּ: סַלֵּק אִתְּמַר.

The Gemara relates: **Rav Pappa happened** to come **to the house of Rav Huna, son of Rav Natan. After they finished their meal, they brought before them something to eat. Rav Pappa took** this food item **and ate** it without reciting a blessing. **They said to him:** Do you, **Master, not hold** that once **one finished** his meal **he is forbidden to eat** again without reciting a blessing? **He said to them** that in the correct version of that *halakha*, **it is stated: Removed.** One need recite a second blessing only when eating after the table was removed from before him.

**BACKGROUND**

**Bread that comes as dessert – כִּסָּנִין:** The precise meaning of *kissanin*, translated here as bread that comes as dessert, is unclear. The *ge'onim* and early commentaries disputed this issue. According to Rav Hai Gaon, *kissanin* are a type of toast-like dried bread, seasoned or unseasoned, and which was eaten for dessert. Rabbeinu Ḥananel explained that they are pockets of dough filled with sugar, almonds, and nuts, and baked, and eaten as a delicacy during the meal. Others maintain that they are types of delicacies made from toasted wheat, almonds, and other nuts, that are served for dessert.

The origin of the term itself is also unclear. Some believe that it is derived from *kasses*, to gnaw, or *kis*, pocket. Others believe that it is from the Persian or Greek.

**HALAKHA**

**Over anything which is substantial enough to satiate and others base a meal upon it – כָּל שֶׁאֲחֵרִים קוֹבְעִים עָלָיו סְעוּדָּה:** One who ate baked items other than bread, from the five species of grain, in an amount upon which others regularly base a meal, is obligated to recite Grace after Meals. This is in accordance with the opinion of Rav Naḥman (Rambam *Sefer Ahava, Hilkhot Berakhot* 3:9; *Shulḥan Arukh, Oraḥ Ḥayyim* 168:6).

**Bread that comes as dessert – פַּת הַבָּאָה בְּכִסָּנִין:** Over bread that comes as dessert, one does not recite: Who brings forth bread from the earth, as per the opinion of Rav Yehuda, as the *halakha* is not ruled in accordance with the opinion of Rabbi Mona. With regard to the meaning of the term, bread that comes as dessert, many opinions were articulated. The later commentaries are unclear as to the precise definition. Therefore, one must adopt the stringency to eat food items that might fall into this category, exclusively within the framework of a meal (*Shulḥan Arukh HaRav*; *Mishna Berura*; Rambam, *Sefer Ahava, Hilkhot Berakhot* 3:9; *Shulḥan Arukh, Oraḥ Ḥayyim* 186:7).

**Wafers – לַחְמָנִיּוֹת:** Over types of pastries made from a watery dough, even if it was not mixed with honey or the like, one recites: Who creates the various kinds of nourishment (*Shulḥan Arukh, Oraḥ Ḥayyim* 186:6, 8).

**NOTES**

**s it causes a blessing itself – דּוֹגֵם בְּרָכָה לְעַצְמוֹ:** Rashi's expla- ation is that wine is unique because one recites a blessing over together with other blessings like *kiddush* and *havdala*. Others xplained that it is more significant than other beverages as an xclusive blessing was designated for it (Rabbeinu Ḥananel). Yet thers explain that not only does it have an exclusive blessing, ut that blessing includes mention of the vine itself, while in e blessing over other fruits, the name of the particular tree is ot mentioned (Rashbam).

**av Huna ate…and did not recite Grace after Meals – רַב הוּנָא אֲכַל...וְלָא בָּרֵיךְ:** Several expalnations were suggested for this matter. Some explained that the rationale behind Rav Huna's conduct is unknown (*ge'onim*). Others explained that since it was not a fixed meal, he did not recite Grace after Meals, but he recited one blessing abridged from the three blessings of Grace after Meals (*Talmidei Rabbeinu Yona*); or that he did not even recite the abridged blessing because the spices were the primary component (*Penei Yehoshua*). Yet others explained that Rav Huna ate actual bread but did not recite a blessing beforehand because he experienced a seminal emission, and since the blessing is required by rabbinic law, he held that he should not utter God's name (*Tziyyun LeNefesh Ḥayya* and see *Melo HaRo'im*).

**That is hunger – עֲדֵי כַּפְנָא:** Various explanations were suggested for this matter and there are several versions of the text, as well. Some explained: Is the Master still hungry after eating all that? Certainly he is required to recite a blessing (*Talmidei Rabbeinu Yona*). Others explained: How will he be able to withstand famine if that is the way he is accustomed to eat (Rav Sa'adia Gaon)? Alternatively: By eating that way, he causes famine (*ge'onim*).

רָבָא וְרַבִּי זֵירָא אִיקְּלַעוּ לְבֵי רֵישׁ גָּלוּתָא, לְבָתַר דְּסַלִּיקוּ תַּכָּא מִקַּמַּיְיהוּ שְׁדַרוּ לְהוּ רִיסְתְּנָא מִבֵּי רֵישׁ גָּלוּתָא, רָבָא אֲכֵיל וְרַבִּי זֵירָא לֹא אֲכֵיל. אֲמַר לֵיהּ: לָא סְבַר לָהּ מָר ״סִלֵּק אָסוּר מִלֶּאֱכוֹל״?! – אֲמַר לֵיהּ: אֲנַן אַתַּכָּא דְּרֵישׁ גָּלוּתָא סָמְכִינַן.

Similarly, the Gemara relates: **Rava and Rabbi Zeira happened to** come **to the house of the Exilarch. After** the meal, **when they removed the table from before them, a portion** [*ristena*][L] **of** food **was sent to them from the house of the Exilarch. Rava ate** it **and Rabbi Zeira did not eat** it. Rabbi Zeira **said to** Rava: Do you, **Master, not hold** that once the table was **removed, he is forbidden to eat?** Rava **said to him: We are dependent upon the table of the Exilarch,**[H] and so long as he has not completed his meal, his guests have not completed their meals either.

אֲמַר רַב: הָרָגִיל בְּשֶׁמֶן – שֶׁמֶן מְעַכְּבוֹ. אֲמַר רַב אַשִׁי, כִּי הֲוֵינַן בֵּי רַב כָּהֲנָא אֲמַר לָן: כְּגוֹן אֲנַן דִּרְגִילִינַן בְּמִשְׁחָא – מִשְׁחָא מְעַכְּבָא לָן. וְלֵית הִלְכְתָא כְּכָל הָנֵי שְׁמַעְתָּתָא, אֶלָּא כִּי הָא דְּאָמַר רַבִּי חִיָּיא בַּר אַשִׁי אָמַר רַב, שָׁלֹשׁ תְּכִיפוֹת הֵן: תֵּכֶף לִסְמִיכָה שְׁחִיטָה, תֵּכֶף לִגְאוּלָּה תְּפִלָּה, תֵּכֶף לִנְטִילַת יָדַיִם בְּרָכָה.

**Rav said: One who is accustomed to** applying fragrant **oil** to his hands after meals, failure to apply that **oil delays** the end of **his meal** and he is not considered to have finished his meal and is not required to recite a blessing before continuing to eat. Similarly, **Rav Ashi said: When we were in the house of Rav Kahana, he said to us: We, for example, who are accustomed to oil,** failure to apply that **oil delays** the end of the meal **for us.** Nevertheless, the Gemara concludes: **And the *halakha* is not in accordance with all of these statements** and the end of the meal is not determined by those factors. **Rather, it is** determined by **that which Rabbi Ḥiyya bar Ashi said** that **Rav said: There are three** pairs that **immediately** follow each other:[N] **Immediately** following **placing hands** on the head of a sacrifice, is its **slaughter;**[H] **immediately** following the blessing of **redemption** recited after *Shema*, is the *Amida* **prayer;**[H] and **immediately** following the ritual **washing of the hands** after a meal, is **the blessing of** Grace after Meals.[NH]

אָמַר אַבַּיֵי, אַף אָנוּ נֹאמַר: תֵּכֶף לְתַלְמִידֵי חֲכָמִים בְּרָכָה, שֶׁנֶּאֱמַר: ״וַיְבָרְכֵנִי ה׳ בִּגְלָלֶךָ״. אִיבָּעֵית אֵימָא מֵהָכָא, שֶׁנֶּאֱמַר: ״וַיְבָרֶךְ ה׳ אֶת בֵּית הַמִּצְרִי בִּגְלַל יוֹסֵף״.

**Abaye said** that on a similar note, **we too will say: Immediately** following the entrance of **Torah scholars** into a house, a **blessing** rests upon that house, **as it is stated** with regard to Laban and Jacob: **"The Lord has blessed me because of you"** (Genesis 30:27). **If you wish, say** instead, that the proof is **from here, as it is stated:** "And it was from when he placed him in charge of his house and over all that he owned, **the Lord blessed the house of the Egyptian on account of Joseph"** (Genesis 39:5).

מתני׳ בֵּרֵךְ עַל הַיַּיִן שֶׁלִּפְנֵי הַמָּזוֹן – פָּטַר אֶת הַיַּיִן שֶׁלְּאַחַר הַמָּזוֹן, בֵּרֵךְ עַל הַפַּרְפֶּרֶת שֶׁלִּפְנֵי הַמָּזוֹן – פָּטַר אֶת הַפַּרְפֶּרֶת שֶׁלְּאַחַר הַמָּזוֹן, בֵּרֵךְ עַל הַפַּת – פָּטַר אֶת הַפַּרְפֶּרֶת, עַל הַפַּרְפֶּרֶת – לֹא פָּטַר אֶת הַפַּת; בֵּית שַׁמַּאי אוֹמְרִים: אַף לֹא מַעֲשֵׂה קְדֵרָה.

**MISHNA** This mishna explains those cases and those circumstances in which blessings recited over particular foods exempt other foods at the meal from the requirement to recite a blessing over them. **One who recited a blessing over the wine that** one drank **before the meal,**[H] with that blessing **he exempted the wine that** he drinks **after the meal.** Similarly, **one who recited a blessing over the appetizers**[H] **that** one ate **before the meal,** with that blessing **he exempted the appetizers that** he eats **after the meal. One who recited a blessing over the bread exempted the appetizers,** as they are considered secondary to the bread. However, one who recited a blessing **over the appetizers did not exempt the bread. Beit Shammai say:** The blessing recited over the appetizers **did not exempt even a cooked dish** that he eats during the meal.

הָיוּ יוֹשְׁבִין – כׇּל אֶחָד מְבָרֵךְ לְעַצְמוֹ, הֵסֵבּוּ – אֶחָד מְבָרֵךְ לְכוּלָּן.

An additional *halakha* is cited: If several people **were sitting** to eat, not in the framework of a joint meal, **each recites a blessing for himself. If they were reclined** on divans to eat, which renders it a joint meal, **one recites a blessing on behalf of them all.**

## LANGUAGE

A portion [*ristena*] – רִיסְתְּנָא: Based on the Gemara on 50a, apparently the correct version of the word is *distena*, from the Persian, although there is uncertainty with regard to the source word. It is apparently connected to the Persian dast, meaning hand. The plural, dastān, means handful; perhaps, it is because they would give guests a gift that size.

## NOTES

**There are three pairs that immediately follow each other** – שָׁלֹשׁ תְּכִיפוֹת הֵן: The Jerusalem Talmud cites textual allusions to each of these: Immediately following placing hands on the head of a sacrifice, is its slaughter, as it is stated: "And he shall lay his hands…and slaughter" (Leviticus 3:13). Immediately following the blessing of redemption recited after *Shema*, is the *Amida* prayer, as it is stated: "God is my rock and my redemption" (Psalms 19:15), and juxtaposed to it is the verse: "God will answer you on a day of sorrow" (Psalms 20:2). Immediately following the ritual washing of the hands after a meal, is the blessing of Grace after Meals, as it is stated: "Lift up your hands to the sanctuary, and bless the Lord" (Psalms 134:2). Some wondered why the list does not include: Immediately following the ritual washing of the hands, is the meal? They answered that the reason is because there is no biblical allusion to it (*Shitta Mekubbetzet*), or that it is an explicit mishna that needs no repetition (*Mitzpe Eitan*).

**Immediately following the ritual washing of the hands after a meal, is the blessing of Grace after Meals** – תֵּכֶף לִנְטִילַת יָדַיִם בְּרָכָה: Apparently, the Gemara here is referring to the final waters, the ritual washing of the hands after the meal followed immediately by Grace after Meals, but from the Jerusalem Talmud it appears that this is actually referring to washing hands before the meal.

## HALAKHA

**We are dependent upon the table of the Exilarch** – אֲנַן אַתַּכָּא דְּרֵישׁ גָּלוּתָא סָמְכִינַן: One who was eating at the table of a host may continue eating even if he thought to recite Grace after Meals, as the duration of his meal is dependent on the host, in accordance with the opinion of Rava (*Shulḥan Arukh, Oraḥ Ḥayyim* 179:2).

**Immediately following placing hands is slaughter** – תֵּכֶף לִסְמִיכָה שְׁחִיטָה: One must juxtapose the slaughter of a sacrifice to the laying of hands upon its head as much as possible (Rambam *Sefer Avoda, Hilkhot Ma'aseh HaKorbanot* 3:12).

**Immediately following redemption is prayer** – תֵּכֶף לִגְאוּלָּה תְּפִלָּה: One may not interrupt between the blessing: Who redeemed Israel, and the start of the *Amida* prayer (Rambam *Sefer Ahava, Hilkhot Tefilla* 7:17; *Shulḥan Arukh, Oraḥ Ḥayyim* 111:1).

**Immediately following the ritual washing of the hands after a meal, is the blessing of Grace after Meals** – תֵּכֶף לִנְטִילַת יָדַיִם בְּרָכָה: Once one washed his hands with the final waters, he may not eat until after he recites Grace after Meals (Rambam *Sefer Ahava, Hilkhot Berakhot* 6:20; *Shulḥan Arukh, Oraḥ Ḥayyim* 179:1).

**One who recited a blessing over the wine that one drank before the meal** – בֵּרֵךְ עַל הַיַּיִן שֶׁלִּפְנֵי הַמָּזוֹן: One who recites a blessing over wine before the meal exempts the wine after the meal from a blessing (Rambam *Sefer Ahava, Hilkhot Berakhot* 4:12; *Shulḥan Arukh, Oraḥ Ḥayyim* 174:4).

**One who recited a blessing over the appetizers** – בֵּרֵךְ עַל הַפַּרְפֶּרֶת: The blessing over bread exempts all appetizers whose blessing is: Who creates the various kinds of nourishment; however, the blessing on those appetizers does not exempt the bread, as per the mishna (*Tur, Oraḥ Ḥayyim* 176).

בָּא לָהֶם יַיִן בְּתוֹךְ הַמָּזוֹן – כׇּל אֶחָד וְאֶחָד מְבָרֵךְ לְעַצְמוֹ. אַחַר הַמָּזוֹן – אֶחָד מְבָרֵךְ לְכוּלָּם, וְהוּא אוֹמֵר עַל הַמּוּגְמָר, וְאַף עַל פִּי שֶׁאֵין מְבִיאִין אֶת הַמּוּגְמָר אֶלָּא לְאַחַר סְעוּדָּה.

Additionally: If **wine came before them during the meal, each and every** diner **recites a blessing** over the wine **for himself.** If the wine came **after the meal,**[H] **one recites a blessing on behalf of them all. And he,** who recited the blessing over the wine, also **says** the blessing **over the incense** [*mugmar*],[B] **although they only bring the incense** to the diners **after the meal.**

גמ׳ אָמַר רַבָּה בַּר בַּר חָנָה אָמַר רַבִּי יוֹחָנָן: לֹא שָׁנוּ אֶלָּא בְּשַׁבָּתוֹת וְיָמִים טוֹבִים הוֹאִיל וְאָדָם קוֹבֵעַ סְעוּדָּתוֹ עַל הַיַּיִן, אֲבָל בִּשְׁאָר יְמוֹת הַשָּׁנָה – מְבָרֵךְ עַל כׇּל כּוֹס וְכוֹס.

**GEMARA** With regard to the mishna's statement that wine that precedes a meal exempts wine that follows a meal, **Rabba bar bar Ḥana said** that **Rabbi Yoḥanan said: This** ***halakha* was only taught with regard to Shabbat and Festivals, since,** because one can continue drinking at his leisure, **one bases his meal on the wine. However, during the rest of the days of the year,** one who drinks wine at a meal **recites a blessing over each and every cup,** as his original intention was not to drink a lot.

אִתְּמַר נַמִי, אָמַר רַבָּה בַּר מָרִי אָמַר רַבִּי יְהוֹשֻׁעַ בֶּן לֵוִי: לֹא שָׁנוּ אֶלָּא בְּשַׁבָּתוֹת וְיָמִים טוֹבִים, וּבְשָׁעָה שֶׁאָדָם יוֹצֵא מִבֵּית הַמֶּרְחָץ, וּבִשְׁעַת הַקָּזַת דָּם, הוֹאִיל וְאָדָם קוֹבֵעַ סְעוּדָּתוֹ עַל הַיַּיִן, אֲבָל בִּשְׁאָר יְמוֹת הַשָּׁנָה – מְבָרֵךְ עַל כׇּל כּוֹס וְכוֹס.

**It was also stated: Rabba bar Mari said** that **Rabbi Yehoshua ben Levi said: This was only taught** in the mishna **with regard to Shabbat and Festivals, and when a person emerges** tired **from the bathhouse,** and wishes to eat and rest, **and during bloodletting,** after which one tends to drink a lot, **since** on these occasions **one** typically **bases his meal on wine. However, during the rest of the days of the year,** one who drinks wine at a meal **recites a blessing over each and every cup.**

רַבָּה בַּר מָרִי אִיקְּלַע לְבֵי רָבָא בְּחוֹל, חַזְיֵיהּ דְּבָרֵיךְ לִפְנֵי הַמָּזוֹן וַהֲדַר בָּרֵיךְ לְאַחַר הַמָּזוֹן, אֲמַר לֵיהּ: יִישַׁר, וְכֵן אָמַר רַבִּי יְהוֹשֻׁעַ בֶּן לֵוִי.

The Gemara relates that **Rabba bar Mari happened** to come **to the house of Rava during the week. He saw him recite a blessing** over wine **before the meal, and again recite a blessing** on the wine **after the meal. He said to him: Well done. And so too, Rabbi Yehoshua ben Levi said** that this was proper conduct.

רַב יִצְחָק בַּר יוֹסֵף אִיקְּלַע לְבֵי אַבָּיֵי בְּיוֹם טוֹב, חַזְיֵיהּ דְּבָרֵיךְ אַכׇּל כָּסָא וְכָסָא. אֲמַר לֵיהּ: לָא סָבַר לַהּ מָר לְהָא דְּרַבִּי יְהוֹשֻׁעַ בֶּן לֵוִי?! – אֲמַר לֵיהּ: נִמְלַךְ אֲנָא.

The Gemara also relates: **Rabbi Yitzḥak bar Yosef happened** to come **to the house of Abaye on a Festival. He saw that he recited a blessing over each and every cup** of wine. Rabbi Yitzḥak **said to him:** Does the **Master not hold** in accordance with **that** ***halakha*** **of Rabbi Yehoshua ben Levi,** who said that one blessing is sufficient? Abaye **said to him:** My original intention was not to base my meal upon wine and with each cup **I change my mind** and decide to drink it. Even Rabbi Yehoshua ben Levi would agree that under those circumstances, one must recite a blessing over each and every cup.

אִיבַּעְיָא לְהוּ: בָּא לָהֶם יַיִן בְּתוֹךְ הַמָּזוֹן, מַהוּ שֶׁיִּפְטוֹר אֶת הַיַּיִן שֶׁלְּאַחַר הַמָּזוֹן? אִם תִּמְצֵי לוֹמַר ״בֵּרַךְ עַל הַיַּיִן שֶׁלִּפְנֵי הַמָּזוֹן פּוֹטֵר אֶת הַיַּיִן שֶׁלְּאַחַר הַמָּזוֹן״ – מִשּׁוּם דְּזֶה לִשְׁתּוֹת וְזֶה לִשְׁתּוֹת, אֲבָל הָכָא דְּזֶה לִשְׁתּוֹת וְזֶה לִשְׁרוֹת – לָא; אוֹ דִּילְמָא לָא שְׁנָא?

**A dilemma was raised before** the Sages: If **wine came out to them during the meal, what is** the *halakha* with regard to **exempting the wine after the meal** from a blessing? The dilemma is as follows: **If you say: One who recited a blessing over the wine that** one drank **before the meal,** with that blessing **he exempted the wine that** he drinks **after the meal,** perhaps that **is because** the purpose of drinking **this,** wine before the meal, **is to drink, and that,** wine after the meal, **is to drink** for its own sake. **However, here, where** the purpose of drinking **this,** the wine after the meal, **is to drink and that,** the wine during the meal, **is to moisten**[H] the food and to facilitate its consumption, **no.** The blessing on one cannot exempt the other. **Or perhaps there is no difference,** and all drinking is considered the same.

רַב אָמַר: פּוֹטֵר, וְרַב כָּהֲנָא אָמַר: אֵינוֹ פּוֹטֵר. רַב נַחְמָן אָמַר: פּוֹטֵר, וְרַב שֵׁשֶׁת אָמַר: אֵינוֹ פּוֹטֵר. רַב הוּנָא וְרַב יְהוּדָה וְכׇל תַּלְמִידֵי דְּרַב אָמְרִי: אֵינוֹ פּוֹטֵר. אֵיתִיבֵיהּ רָבָא לְרַב נַחְמָן: בָּא לָהֶם יַיִן בְּתוֹךְ הַמָּזוֹן – כׇּל אֶחָד וְאֶחָד מְבָרֵךְ לְעַצְמוֹ לְאַחַר הַמָּזוֹן – אֶחָד מְבָרֵךְ לְכוּלָּם! אֲמַר לֵיהּ, הָכִי קָאָמַר: אִם לֹא בָּא לָהֶם יַיִן בְּתוֹךְ הַמָּזוֹן אֶלָּא לְאַחַר הַמָּזוֹן – אֶחָד מְבָרֵךְ לְכוּלָּם.

Opinions differed: **Rav said: It exempts, and Rav Kahana said: It does not exempt. Rav Naḥman said: It exempts, and Rav Sheshet said: It does not exempt. Rav Huna and Rav Yehuda and all the students of Rav said: It does not exempt. Rava raised an objection to Rav Naḥman** from our mishna: **If wine came before them during the meal, each and every** diner **recites a blessing** over the wine **for himself.** If the wine came **after the meal, one recites a blessing on behalf of them all.** Apparently, even though they recited a blessing over wine during the course of the meal, they must recite a blessing over the wine after the meal as well. Rav Naḥman **said to him:** The mishna **says as follows:** There are two independent cases. The second case is: **If wine did not come before them during the meal, but only after the meal, one recites a blessing on behalf of them all.**

**HALAKHA**

**If wine came before them during the meal… after the meal** – בָּא לָהֶם יַיִן בְּתוֹךְ הַמָּזוֹן...אַחַר הַמָּזוֹן: Over wine during the meal, each individual recites a blessing for himself; after the meal, one recites a blessing on behalf of them all (Rambam *Sefer Ahava, Hilkhot Berakhot* 7:6 *Shulḥan Arukh, Oraḥ Ḥayyim* 174:8).

**This is to drink and that is to moisten** – דְּזֶה לִשְׁתּוֹת וְזֶה לִשְׁרוֹת: Nowadays, when it is customary to continue eating until Grace after Meals, the blessing on wine during a meal exempts wine that one drinks after the meal (*Magen Avraham, Taz; Shulḥan Arukh, Oraḥ Ḥayyim* 174:4–5).

**BACKGROUND**

**Incense** [*mugmar*] – מוּגְמָר: This is incense that was brought out at the end of a meal in order to freshen the house. It was also commonly used to scent clothing. The origin of the word seems to be the Aramaic *gumra*, meaning coal. The incense was placed on the coals to release it into the air.

Earthenware vessel for incense

NOTES

**Clarification of Beit Shammai's opinion** – בֵּרוּר דַּעַת בֵּית שַׁמַּאי: Ordinarily, when the Gemara seeks to clarify the opinion of Beit Shammai, it raises the question: Are we trying to understand Beit Shammai's reasoning? In virtually all cases, the *halakha* is in accordance with the opinion of Beit Hillel when there is a disagreement between them. In this case, however, it is clear that understanding the opinion of Beit Shammai will shed light on Beit Hillel's opinion as well, and that is why the Gemara chose to analyze it (*Me'iri*).

**They sat…they reclined** – יָשְׁבוּ...הֵסֵבּוּ: Some explain that the term, they reclined [*heisevu*], both here and elsewhere, is related to the word circle [*sivuv*], meaning that those reclining sat around a table or surrounding the surface where the food was placed (*ge'onim*, *Tosefot Rabbeinu Yehuda HaḤasid*). Based on that interpretation, individuals surrounding the bread, even when not reclining in the literal sense, are considered to have dined together, and one may recite a blessing on behalf of the others.

HALAKHA

**But it did exempt a cooked dish** – אֲבָל מַעֲשֵׂה קְדֵרָה פָּטַר וכו׳: The blessing over an appetizer: Who creates the various kinds of nourishment, exempts cooked grain dishes; and the blessing over cooked grain dishes exempts those appetizers. That is how the Rambam resolved the unresolved dilemma in the Gemara (Rambam *Sefer Ahava*, *Hilkhot Berakhot* 4:6; *Shulḥan Arukh*, *Oraḥ Ḥayyim* 176:1).

**Let us go and eat in such-and-such a place** – נֵיזִיל וְנֵיכוּל לַחְמָא בְּדוּךְ פְּלָן: Designating a particular place to eat together is considered as establishing a communal meal even without reclining (Rambam *Sefer Ahava*, *Hilkhot Berakhot* 1:12; *Shulḥan Arukh*, *Oraḥ Ḥayyim* 167:11).

"בֵּרַךְ עַל הַפַּת – פָּטַר אֶת הַפַּרְפֶּרֶת, עַל הַפַּרְפֶּרֶת – לֹא פָּטַר אֶת הַפַּת; בֵּית שַׁמַּאי אוֹמְרִים: אַף לֹא מַעֲשֵׂה קְדֵרָה".

We learned in the mishna: **One who recited a blessing over the bread exempted the appetizers,** as they are considered secondary to the bread. However, one who recited a blessing **over the appetizers did not exempt the bread. Beit Shammai say:** The blessing recited over the appetizers **did not exempt even a cooked dish** that he eats during the meal.

אִיבַּעְיָא לְהוּ: בֵּית שַׁמַּאי אַרֵישָׁא פְּלִיגִי, אוֹ דִּילְמָא אַסֵּיפָא פְּלִיגִי? דְּקָאָמַר תַּנָּא קַמָּא: בֵּרַךְ עַל הַפַּת פָּטַר אֶת הַפַּרְפֶּרֶת וְכׇל שֶׁכֵּן מַעֲשֵׂה קְדֵרָה, וְאָתוּ בֵּית שַׁמַּאי לְמֵימַר: לֹא מִבַּעְיָא פַּרְפֶּרֶת – דְּלָא פָּטְרָה לְהוּ פַּת, אֶלָּא אֲפִילּוּ מַעֲשֵׂה קְדֵרָה – נָמֵי לָא פָּטְרָה; אוֹ דִּילְמָא אַסֵּיפָא פְּלִיגִי, דְּקָתָנֵי: בֵּרַךְ עַל הַפַּרְפֶּרֶת לֹא פָּטַר אֶת הַפַּת, פַּת הוּא דְּלָא פָּטַר, אֲבָל מַעֲשֵׂה קְדֵרָה – פָּטַר. וְאָתוּ בֵּית שַׁמַּאי לְמֵימַר: וַאֲפִילּוּ מַעֲשֵׂה קְדֵרָה נָמֵי לֹא פָּטַר

With regard to this case, **a dilemma was raised before** the Sages: Do **Beit Shammai**[N] **disagree with the first clause** in the mishna **or with the latter clause,** as it may be explained in both ways? It can be understood that **the first *tanna* says: One who recited a blessing over the bread exempted the appetizers and all the more so** it exempted **a cooked dish. And Beit Shammai come to say: It goes without saying that** the blessing over **bread does not exempt appetizers;** as the blessing over bread **does not even exempt a cooked dish. Or perhaps they disagree with the latter clause, as it was taught: One who recited a blessing over the appetizers did not exempt the bread.** By inference, the blessing **did not exempt bread, but it did exempt a cooked dish.**[H] **And Beit Shammai come to say** that the blessing over the appetizers **did not exempt even a cooked dish.**

תֵּיקוּ.

The Gemara concludes: **Let it stand,** as this dilemma remains unresolved.

"הָיוּ יוֹשְׁבִין כׇּל אֶחָד וְאֶחָד" כו׳. הֵסֵבּוּ – אִין, לֹא הֵסֵבּוּ – לָא. וּרְמִינְהוּ: עֲשָׂרָה שֶׁהָיוּ הוֹלְכִים בַּדֶּרֶךְ, אַף עַל פִּי שֶׁכּוּלָּם אוֹכְלִים מִכִּכָּר אֶחָד – כׇּל אֶחָד וְאֶחָד מְבָרֵךְ לְעַצְמוֹ; יָשְׁבוּ לֶאֱכוֹל, אַף עַל פִּי שֶׁכׇּל אֶחָד וְאֶחָד אוֹכֵל מִכִּכָּרוֹ – אֶחָד מְבָרֵךְ לְכוּלָּם. קָתָנֵי "יָשְׁבוּ", אַף עַל פִּי שֶׁלֹּא הֵסֵבּוּ!

The mishna distinguished between a case where several people **were sitting** to eat, which is not a joint meal, **and each and every** diner recites a blessing for himself; and a case where they were reclined on divans, which renders it a joint meal, and one recites a blessing on behalf of all of them. The Gemara infers: If **they reclined, yes,** it is considered a joint meal; if **they did not recline, no. And** the Gemara **raises a contradiction: Ten** people **who were walking on the road, even if they are all eating from one loaf, each and every one recites a blessing for himself. If they sat to eat, even if each and every one is eating from his own loaf, one recites a blessing on behalf of them all** as it is considered a joint meal. In any case, **it was taught: If they sat** to eat, **even though they did not recline.**[N] Apparently, sitting together is enough to render it a joint meal and reclining is not required.

אָמַר רַב נַחְמָן בַּר יִצְחָק, כְּגוֹן דְּאָמְרִי: נֵיזִיל וְנֵיכוּל לַחְמָא בְּדוּךְ פְּלָן.

**Rav Naḥman bar Yitzḥak said:** With regard to those walking along the road, it was **in a case where they said: Let us go and eat in such-and-such a place.**[H] Since they designated a specific location to eat together in advance, it is considered a joint meal.

כִּי נָח נַפְשֵׁיהּ דְּרַב, אֲזַלוּ תַּלְמִידָיו בָּתְרֵיהּ. כִּי הֲדַרִי, אָמְרִי: נֵיזִיל וְנֵיכוּל לַחְמָא אַנַּהַר דַּנָּק. בָּתַר דִּכְרַכִי יָתְבִי וְקָא מִיבַּעְיָא לְהוּ: הֵסֵבּוּ דַּוְקָא תְּנַן, אֲבָל יָשְׁבוּ – לָא, אוֹ דִּילְמָא כֵּיוָן דְּאָמְרִי נֵיזִיל וְנֵיכוּל רִיפְתָּא בְּדוּכְתָּא פְּלָנִיתָא – כִּי הֵסֵבּוּ דָּמֵי? לָא הֲוָה בִּידַיְיהוּ.

On a similar note, the Gemara relates: **When Rav died, his students went after his** casket to the city where he was to be buried. **When they returned, they said: Let us go and eat bread on the** banks of **the Dannak River. After they ate, they sat, and raised a dilemma: Did we learn** in the mishna **specifically** if they **reclined,** it is considered a joint meal; **however,** if they merely **sat** together, **no,** it is not considered a joint meal? **Or perhaps, since they said: Let us go and eat in such-and-such a place,** it is considered **as if they reclined? It was not within their capability** to resolve this dilemma.

קָם רַב אַדָּא בַּר אַהֲבָה

**Rav Adda bar Ahava stood,**

Perek **VI**
Daf **43** Amud **a**

NOTES

**And reversed his cloak, so that his tear was behind him** – אַהְדַּר קְרָעֵיהּ לַאֲחוֹרֵיהּ: Just as one rends his garment at the death of close relatives, one rends his garment over the death of his teacher. The tear is made in the front of the garment where it is visible. Obviously, Rav's students rent their garments at Rav's funeral; however, to express the added sense of mourning, Rav Adda reversed his garment and rent his garment in a different place.

אַהְדַּר קְרָעֵיהּ לַאֲחוֹרֵיהּ, וּקְרַע קְרִיעָה אַחֲרִינָא. אֲמַר: נָח נַפְשֵׁיהּ דְּרַב וּבִרְכַּת מְזוֹנָא לָא גְּמִירִנַן! עַד דַּאֲתָא הַהוּא סָבָא, רְמָא לְהוּ מַתְנִיתִין אַבָּרַיְיתָא וְשַׁנֵּי לְהוּ: כֵּיוָן דְּאָמְרִי נֵיזִיל וְנֵיכוּל לַחְמָא בְּדוּךְ פְּלָן – כְּהֵסֵבּוּ דָּמֵי.

and **reversed** his cloak, so that **his tear** which he had rent in mourning of Rav was **behind him,**[N] **and** in mourning, **he rent another tear** in his garment. **He said: Rav is dead, and we have not** yet **learned** the *halakhot* of the **Grace after Meals. Until, this elder came and raised a contradiction** from **the mishna to the *baraita*,** as cited above, **and he resolved it for them: Since they said: Let us go and eat in such-and-such a place,** it is considered **as if they reclined.**

"הֵסֵבּוּ – אֶחָד מְבָרֵךְ". אָמַר רַב: לֹא שָׁנוּ אֶלָּא פַּת דִּבְעֵי הֲסִבָּה, אֲבָל יַיִן לֹא בָּעֵי הֲסִבָּה. וְרַבִּי יוֹחָנָן אָמַר: אֲפִילּוּ יַיִן נַמִי בָּעֵי הֲסִבָּה.

We learned in the mishna: **If they were reclined, one recites a blessing** on behalf of them all. **Rav said: This** *halakha* **was only taught** with regard to **bread that** it **requires reclining** to enable one to recite a blessing on behalf of them all. **However, wine does not require reclining. And Rabbi Yoḥanan said: Even wine requires reclining as well.**

אִיכָּא דְּאָמְרִי, אָמַר רַב: לֹא שָׁנוּ אֶלָּא פַּת – דִּמְהַנְּיָא לֵיהּ הֲסִבָּה, אֲבָל יַיִן – לֹא מְהַנְּיָא לֵיהּ הֲסִבָּה. וְרַבִּי יוֹחָנָן אָמַר: אֲפִילּוּ יַיִן נַמִי מְהַנְּיָא לֵיהּ הֲסִבָּה.

**Some say** that **Rav said:** The mishna **only taught that reclining is effective** and enables one to recite a blessing on behalf of them all, with regard to a group eating **bread. However,** with regard to a group drinking **wine, reclining is ineffective** and each individual must recite a blessing for himself. **And Rabbi Yoḥanan said: Even** with regard to **wine, reclining is effective.**

מֵיתִיבִי: כֵּיצַד סֵדֶר הֲסִבָּה? אוֹרְחִין נִכְנָסִין וְיוֹשְׁבִין עַל גַּבֵּי סַפְסָלִין וְעַל גַּבֵּי קָתֶדְרָאוֹת עַד שֶׁיִּכָּנְסוּ כּוּלָּם. הֵבִיאוּ לָהֶם מַיִם כׇּל אֶחָד וְאֶחָד נוֹטֵל יָדוֹ אַחַת, בָּא לָהֶם יַיִן – כׇּל אֶחָד וְאֶחָד מְבָרֵךְ לְעַצְמוֹ; עָלוּ וְהֵסֵבּוּ וּבָא לָהֶם מַיִם, אַף עַל פִּי שֶׁכׇּל אֶחָד וְאֶחָד נָטַל יָדוֹ אַחַת – חוֹזֵר וְנוֹטֵל שְׁתֵּי יָדָיו. בָּא לָהֶם יַיִן, אַף עַל פִּי שֶׁכׇּל אֶחָד וְאֶחָד בֵּרֵךְ לְעַצְמוֹ – אֶחָד מְבָרֵךְ לְכוּלָּם.

The Gemara **raises an objection** based on a *Tosefta*: **What is the order of reclining**[N] at a meal? The **guests enter and sit upon benches and chairs** [*katedraot*][L] **until all are assembled.** Afterward, **they brought them water and each and every one washes one hand**[N] in which to hold the cup of wine. When **wine came before them** prior to the meal, **each and every one recites a blessing** over the wine **for himself.** Then, when **they entered and reclined** on the divans for the meal itself, **and water came before them, despite** the fact **that each and every one** already **washed one hand, they wash both hands again** prior to the meal, so that they will be able to eat with both hands. If **wine came before them** during the meal, **despite** the fact **that each and every one** already **recited a blessing for himself, one recites a blessing on behalf of them all.**

לְהָאֵיךְ לִישָּׁנָא דְּאָמַר רַב: לֹא שָׁנוּ אֶלָּא פַּת דִּבְעֵי הֲסִבָּה, אֲבָל יַיִן לֹא בָּעֵי הֲסִבָּה – קַשְׁיָא רֵישָׁא!

If so, **according to that version** that **Rav said: This** *halakha* **was only taught** with regard to **bread that** it **requires reclining** to enable one to recite a blessing on behalf of them all. **However, wine does not require reclining; the first clause** of the *Tosefta*, which taught that each guest recites a blessing over the wine for himself, **is difficult.**

שָׁאנֵי אוֹרְחִין דְּדַעְתַּיְיהוּ לְמִיעְקַר.

The Gemara answers: **Guests are different, as** when they are sitting in the hall prior to the meal, **their intention is to leave** and enter the dining room. Therefore, while there, their drinking together is not considered a joint meal.

וּלְהָאֵיךְ לִישָּׁנָא דְּאָמַר רַב: לֹא שָׁנוּ אֶלָּא פַּת דִּמְהַנְּיָא לֵיהּ הֲסִבָּה, אֲבָל יַיִן לֹא מְהַנְּיָא לֵיהּ הֲסִבָּה – קַשְׁיָא סֵיפָא!

**And according to the version** that **Rav said:** The mishna **only taught that reclining is effective** and enables one to recite a blessing on behalf of them all, with regard to a group eating **bread. However,** with regard to a group drinking **wine, reclining is ineffective** and each individual must recite a blessing for himself; **the latter clause** of the *Tosefta*, which taught that when drinking wine when reclining, one recites a blessing on behalf of all, **is difficult.**

שָׁאנֵי הָתָם, דְּמִגּוֹ דְּקָא מְהַנְּיָא לֵיהּ הֲסִבָּה לְפַת, מְהַנְּיָא לֵיהּ הֲסִבָּה לְיַיִן.

The Gemara responds: **There it is different, as since reclining is effective** and enables one to recite a blessing on behalf of them all **for bread, reclining is effective for wine** as well.

"בָּא לָהֶם יַיִן בְּתוֹךְ הַמָּזוֹן". שָׁאֲלוּ אֶת בֶּן זוֹמָא: מִפְּנֵי מָה אָמְרוּ "בָּא לָהֶם יַיִן בְּתוֹךְ הַמָּזוֹן – כׇּל אֶחָד וְאֶחָד מְבָרֵךְ לְעַצְמוֹ, לְאַחַר הַמָּזוֹן – אֶחָד מְבָרֵךְ לְכוּלָּם"? – אָמַר לָהֶם: הוֹאִיל וְאֵין בֵּית הַבְּלִיעָה פָּנוּי.

We learned in the mishna: If **wine came before them during the meal,** each and every diner recites a blessing over the wine for himself. If the wine came after the meal, one recites a blessing on behalf of them all. The *Tosefta* relates: **They asked Ben Zoma: Why did** the Sages **say:** If **wine came before them during the meal, each and every** diner **recites a blessing** over the wine **for himself;** but if the wine came **after the meal, one recites a blessing on behalf of them all? He said to them:** This is **because** while eating, **the throat is not available.**[N] If one recites a blessing on behalf of them all, he would be forced to wait until they all had finished eating and readied themselves to drink the wine together (*Tosafot*). To prevent imposing upon them, the Sages ruled that there is no need to recite the blessing together.

"וְהוּא אוֹמֵר עַל הַמּוּגְמָר" כו'. מִדְּקָתָנֵי "וְהוּא אוֹמֵר עַל הַמּוּגְמָר", מִכְּלָל דְּאִיכָּא עָדִיף מִינֵּיהּ, וְאַמַּאי?

We learned in the mishna: **And he,** who recited the blessing over the wine, also **says** the blessing **over the incense** [*mugmar*]. The Gemara asks: **From the fact that it was taught: And he says** the blessing **over the incense, it may be inferred** that although **there is** someone who should **take precedence over him,** to recite the blessing. Who is that individual and **why** should he take precedence?

## NOTES

**Reclining – הֲסִבָּה:** In talmudic times, the custom was to partake of significant meals while reclining, not sitting upright. This was the custom of the wealthy, free men, who had the ability to leisurely relax and carry on conversations during the meal.

**Washes one hand – נוֹטֵל יָדוֹ אַחַת:** Although the Sages said that one who washes his hands before eating fruit counts himself among the arrogant, that refers to a case where he does it as a mitzva. Here he washes his hands in the interest of cleanliness and, therefore, it is not a problem (*Tosefot Rav Yehuda HaḤasid*).

**Because the throat is not available – הוֹאִיל וְאֵין בֵּית הַבְּלִיעָה פָּנוּי:** The reason is that, in answering amen, he would endanger himself by talking while eating. That is the reason according to the Jerusalem Talmud (*Talmidei Rabbeinu Yona* and others). Others explain that since everyone is eating and their throats are not available, it is not the time to drink. Although there are those who drink while eating, the Sages made no distinction between cases, and maintain that since it is not the time to drink, it is inappropriate to institute a blessing at that time (*Shitta Mekubbetzet*).

## LANGUAGE

**Chairs [*katedraot*] – קָתֶדְרָאוֹת:** From the Greek καθέδρα, *cathedra*, meaning chair or seat.

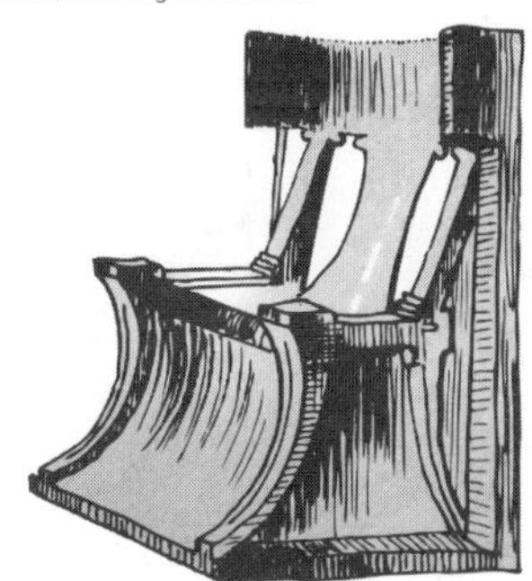

Chair from the talmudic era

## BACKGROUND

**Musk – מוּשְׁק:** Musk has a powerful odor. Some used it as a perfume by itself, although it is more commonly the dominant component of several fragrances used in manufacturing perfumes. Musk is extracted from the excretions of various animals, although historically, it was primarily collected from a pocket in which the glandular secretions of the male musk deer accumulate. The musk deer is the *Moschus moschiferus*, a hornless, deer-like animal that grows to a height of 60 cm. Some associate musk with the biblical myrrh.

Siberian musk deer

**Balsam – אֲפַרְסְמוֹן:** The balsam is likely the *Commiphora opobalsamum*, also known as *Commiphora gileadensis*, from the *Burseraceae* family, known in English as Balm of Gilead or Balsam of Mecca. This is not to be confused with the Balm of Gilead found in other parts of the world that is made from the resin of a different tree, the balsam poplar. The balsam is a short bush or tree of 3–5 m with thin branches, many small leaves, and small white flowers. The highest quality perfume is derived from the resin that drips slowly from the edges of the stalks in small droplets, though the perfume is generally extracted by boiling the branches. This perfume is also used medicinally, as well as in incense and as a fragrant oil. Apparently, this is the *tzori* mentioned among the incense oils used in the Temple. During the Second Temple period, the choicest balsam trees grew in the Jericho valley, and it was considered worth its weight in gold. That is why it merited its own special blessing: Who creates oil of our land. Later, areas where the balsam was grown were considered the private property of the Emperor. This explains the phrase: The balsam of the house of Caesar.

A balsam tree and its fruit

הוֹאִיל וְהוּא נָטַל יָדָיו תְּחִלָּה בָּאַחֲרוֹנָה.

The Gemara responds: The one who washed his hands first **since he washed his hands first after** the meal, prior to Grace after Meals, he should have been the one to recite the blessing over the incense.

מְסַיַּיע לֵיהּ לְרַב, דְּאָמַר רַב חִיָּיא בַּר אַשִׁי אָמַר רַב: הַנּוֹטֵל יָדָיו תְּחִלָּה בָּאַחֲרוֹנָה – הוּא מְזוּמָּן לִבְרָכָה. רַב וְרַבִּי חִיָּיא הֲווּ יָתְבִי קַמֵּיהּ דְּרַבִּי בִּסְעוּדָּתָא. אָמַר לֵיהּ רַבִּי לְרַב: קוּם מְשִׁי יְדָךְ! חַזְיֵיהּ דַּהֲוָה מְרַתֵּת, אָמַר לֵיהּ רַבִּי חִיָּיא בַּר פַּחְתֵי! עַיֵּין בְּבִרְכַּת מְזוֹנָא קָאָמַר לָךְ.

The Gemara comments: This **supports** the opinion **of Rav as Rav Ḥiyya bar Ashi said** that **Rav said: He who washes his hands first after** the meal **is designated to recite the blessing** of Grace after Meals.[H] The Gemara relates: **Rav and Rabbi Ḥiyya were seated before Rabbi Yehuda HaNasi at a meal. Rabbi** Yehuda HaNasi **said to Rav: Stand and wash your hands.** Rabbi Ḥiyya **saw** that Rav **was trembling,** as Rav thought that Rabbi was criticizing him for eating too much or for having dirty hands. **Rabbi Ḥiyya said** to Rav: **Son of noblemen, he is saying to you to review Grace after Meals.** As you will be the one reciting Grace after Meals, he told you to wash your hands first.

אָמַר רַבִּי זֵירָא אָמַר רָבָא בַּר יִרְמְיָה: מֵאֵימָתַי מְבָרְכִין עַל הָרֵיחַ – מִשֶּׁתַּעֲלֶה תִּמַּרְתּוֹ. אָמַר לֵיהּ רַבִּי זֵירָא לְרָבָא בַּר יִרְמְיָה: וְהָא לָא קָא אָרַח! – אָמַר לֵיהּ: וּלְטַעֲמִיךְ ״הַמּוֹצִיא לֶחֶם מִן הָאָרֶץ״ דִּמְבָרֵךְ – וְהָא לָא אֲכַל! אֶלָּא – דַּעְתֵּיהּ לְמֵיכַל, הָכָא נַמִי דַּעְתֵּיהּ לְאָרוֹחֵי.

Having mentioned the blessing over incense, the Gemara proceeds to discuss various *halakhot* that deal with blessings recited over scents. **Rabbi Zeira said** that **Rava bar Yirmeya said: From when does one recite the blessing over the scent** of incense?[NH] **From when its column** of smoke **rises** after the incense has been placed upon the coals. **Rabbi Zeira said to Rava bar Yirmeya: But** at that point, **he has not** yet **smelled it.** Rava bar Yirmeya **said to him: And according to your reasoning,** the blessing: **Who brings forth bread from the earth, that one recites** before eating bread at that point, **he has not yet eaten** from it. **Rather,** in that case, one recites the blessing when **he intends to eat; here too, he intends to smell.**

אָמַר רַבִּי חִיָּיא בְּרֵיהּ דְּאַבָּא בַּר נַחְמָנִי אָמַר רַב חִסְדָּא אָמַר רַב, וְאָמְרִי לַהּ אָמַר רַב חִסְדָּא אָמַר זְעֵירִי: כָּל הַמּוּגְמָרוֹת מְבָרְכִין עֲלֵיהֶן ״בּוֹרֵא עֲצֵי בְשָׂמִים״, חוּץ מִמּוּשְׁק שֶׁמִּן חַיָּה הוּא, שֶׁמְּבָרְכִין עָלָיו ״בּוֹרֵא מִינֵי בְשָׂמִים״.

**Rabbi Ḥiyya, son of Abba bar Naḥmani, said** that **Rav Ḥisda said** that **Rav said, and some say that Rav Ḥisda said** that **Ze'iri said: Over all the incense one recites:**[H] **Who creates fragrant trees, except for musk,**[HB] which **is** extracted **from a living creature,** and over which **one recites: Who creates various spices.**

מֵיתִיבֵי: אֵין מְבָרְכִין ״בּוֹרֵא עֲצֵי בְשָׂמִים״ אֶלָּא עַל אֲפַרְסְמוֹן שֶׁל בֵּית רַבִּי, וְעַל אֲפַרְסְמוֹן שֶׁל בֵּית קֵיסָר, וְעַל הַהֲדַס שֶׁבְּכָל מָקוֹם!

**The Gemara raises an objection** based on what was taught in a *baraita*: **One only recites: Who creates fragrant trees over the balsam**[NB] **from the house of Rabbi** Yehuda HaNasi, **and over balsam from the house of Caesar and over myrtle everywhere.** According to the previous statement one recites that blessing over all types of incense.

תְּיוּבְתָּא.

The Gemara comments: Indeed, it is a **conclusive refutation.**

## HALAKHA

**He who washes his hands first after the meal is designated to recite the blessing of Grace after Meals – הַנּוֹטֵל יָדָיו תְּחִלָּה בָּאַחֲרוֹנָה הוּא מְזוּמָּן לִבְרָכָה:** The one who leads the reciting of Grace after Meals is first to wash his hands with the final waters (Rambam *Sefer Ahava, Hilkhot Berakhot* 7:12; *Shulḥan Arukh, Oraḥ Ḥayyim* 181:6).

**From when does one recite the blessing over the scent of incense – מֵאֵימָתַי מְבָרְכִין עַל הָרֵיחַ:** One recites a blessing over incense when the column of smoke rises (Rambam *Sefer Ahava, Hilkhot Berakhot* 9:2; *Shulḥan Arukh, Oraḥ Ḥayyim* 216:12).

**Over all the incense one recites – כָּל הַמּוּגְמָרוֹת מְבָרְכִין עֲלֵיהֶן וכו׳:** One recites the same blessing over incense that he recites over the material from which the incense was prepared (Rambam *Sefer Ahava, Hilkhot Berakhot* 9:2; *Shulḥan Arukh, Oraḥ Ḥayyim* 216:13).

**Except for musk – חוּץ מִמּוּשְׁק:** Over a fragrance not produced from plants, one recites: Who creates various spices, as in the case of musk in the Gemara (Rambam *Sefer Ahava, Hilkhot Berakhot* 9:1; *Shulḥan Arukh, Oraḥ Ḥayyim* 216:2).

## NOTES

**From when does one recite the blessing over the scent of incense – מֵאֵימָתַי מְבָרְכִין עַל הָרֵיחַ:** Many commentaries wondered why this question is raised specifically with regard to smell. All blessings are recited prior to deriving pleasure from the subject of the blessing. Some explained that this case is different, because the fragrance has not yet been produced, and it will only emerge by means of an action that he will perform. Add that to the fact that he will only derive pleasure later, and there is room to posit that he should recite the blessing later. That is why the response was from the blessing: Who brings forth bread from the earth, which is also recited before the bread is broken, meaning that he must break the bread and eat it between the blessing and deriving pleasure (*Adderet Eliyahu, Tziyyun LeNefesh Ḥayya*).

**One only recites: Who creates fragrant trees, over the balsam – אֵין מְבָרְכִין בּוֹרֵא עֲצֵי בְשָׂמִים אֶלָּא עַל אֲפַרְסְמוֹן:** There are those who explain that balsam was accorded its own blessing because it grows specifically in Eretz Yisrael, and its blessing includes praise of the land (*Talmidei Rabbeinu Yona*). Others explain that it was accorded its own blessing because its smell is extremely pleasant and one senses it even when the balsam is still on the tree and not only after the oil has been extracted from it (*ge'onim*).

אָמַר לֵיהּ רַב חִסְדָּא לְרַב יִצְחָק: הַאי מִשְׁחָא דַּאֲפַרְסְמוֹן מַאי מְבָרְכִין עֲלֵיהּ? – אָמַר לֵיהּ, הָכִי אָמַר רַב יְהוּדָה: "בּוֹרֵא שֶׁמֶן אַרְצֵנוּ". אָמַר לֵיהּ: בַּר מִינֵּיהּ דְּרַב יְהוּדָה דַּחֲבִיבָא לֵיהּ אֶרֶץ יִשְׂרָאֵל, לְכוּלֵּי עָלְמָא מַאי?

אָמַר לֵיהּ: הָכִי אָמַר רַבִּי יוֹחָנָן: "בּוֹרֵא שֶׁמֶן עָרֵב".

אָמַר רַב אַדָּא בַּר אַהֲבָה: הַאי כְּשַׁרְתָּא מְבָרְכִין עֲלֵיהּ "בּוֹרֵא עֲצֵי בְשָׂמִים", אֲבָל מִשְׁחָא כְּבִישָׁא – לָא; וְרַב כָּהֲנָא אָמַר: אֲפִילּוּ מִשְׁחָא כְּבִישָׁא, אֲבָל מִשְׁחָא טְחִינָא – לָא; נְהַרְדְּעֵי אָמְרִי: אֲפִילּוּ מִשְׁחָא טְחִינָא.

Rav Ḥisda said to Rav Yitzḥak: This balsam oil, what blessing does one recite over it?[H] Rav Yitzḥak said to him, this is what Rav Yehuda said: One recites: **Who creates the oil of our land,** as balsam only grew in Eretz Yisrael, in the Jordan valley. Rav Ḥisda **said to him: Except for Rav Yehuda, for whom Eretz Yisrael was** extremely **beloved** and who therefore mentioned it in his blessing, **what** blessing does **everyone** else recite over balsam oil?

He said to him: This is what Rabbi Yoḥanan said: One recites: **Who creates pleasant oil.**

Rav Adda bar Ahava said: Over costus, a spice, one recites: Who creates fragrant trees, but over oil that was pressed with spices to absorb their scents, no, one does not recite that blessing. And Rav Kahana said: Even over oil pressed with spices, one recites: Who creates fragrant trees, but not over oil into which spices were ground. The Sages of Neharde'a say: Even over oil into which spices were ground, which is of even lower quality, one recites this blessing.

אָמַר רַב גִּידֵּל אָמַר רַב: הַאי סַמְלַק מְבָרְכִין עֲלֵיהּ "בּוֹרֵא עֲצֵי בְשָׂמִים". אָמַר רַב חֲנַנְאֵל אָמַר רַב: הָנֵי חִלְפֵי דְּיַמָּא מְבָרְכִין עֲלַיְיהוּ "בּוֹרֵא עֲצֵי בְשָׂמִים". אָמַר מָר זוּטְרָא: מַאי קְרָאָה? "וְהִיא הֶעֱלָתַם הַגָּגָה וַתִּטְמְנֵם בְּפִשְׁתֵּי הָעֵץ".

Rav Giddel said that Rav said: Over this jasmine [simlak],[B] one recites: Who creates fragrant trees. Rav Ḥananel said that Rav said: Over these spikenards,[B] which grow next to the sea, one recites: Who creates fragrant trees. Mar Zutra said: What is the verse from which we derive that even a plant with soft stalks can be called a tree? From the verse: **"She had taken them up to the roof and hidden them under the trees of flax"** (Joshua 2:6); evidently, even stalks of flax are called "trees."

רַב מְשַׁרְשְׁיָא אָמַר: הַאי נַרְקוֹם דְּגִינּוּנִיתָא מְבָרְכִין עֲלֵיהּ "בּוֹרֵא עֲצֵי בְשָׂמִים", דְּדַבְרָא – "בּוֹרֵא עִשְׂבֵי בְשָׂמִים". אָמַר רַב שֵׁשֶׁת: הָנֵי סִיגְלֵי מְבָרְכִין עֲלַיְיהוּ "בּוֹרֵא עִשְׂבֵי בְשָׂמִים". אָמַר מָר זוּטְרָא: הַאי מַאן דְּמוֹרַח בְּאֶתְרוֹגָא אוֹ בְּחַבּוּשָׁא אוֹמֵר "בָּרוּךְ שֶׁנָּתַן רֵיחַ טוֹב בַּפֵּירוֹת".

Rav Mesharshiya said: Over this garden daffodil[B] one recites: Who creates fragrant trees, while over a wild daffodil that grows in the field, one recites: Who creates fragrant plants. Rav Sheshet said: Over fragrant violets[B] one recites: Who creates fragrant plants. Mar Zutra said: One who smells a citron [etrog] or a quince[B] recites: Blessed…who gave pleasant fragrance in fruits.[H]

### HALAKHA

This balsam oil, what blessing does one recite over it – הַאי מִשְׁחָא דַּאֲפַרְסְמוֹן מַאי מְבָרְכִין עֲלֵיהּ: Over balsam oil one recites: Who creates pleasant oil, as per the opinion of Rabbi Yohanan (Rambam Sefer Ahava, Hilkhot Berakhot 9:3; Shulḥan Arukh, Oraḥ Ḥayyim 216:4).

### HALAKHA

One who smells a citron or a quince – הַאי מַאן דְּמוֹרַח בְּאֶתְרוֹגָא אוֹ בְּחַבּוּשָׁא: One recites: Who gives pleasant fragrance in fruits, when smelling the fragrance of edible fruit (Rambam Sefer Ahava, Hilkhot Berakhot 9:1; Shulḥan Arukh, Oraḥ Ḥayyim 216:2).

### BACKGROUND

**Jasmine – סַמְלַק:** According to Rashi's description of the structure of the leaves, this is likely the *Jasmin fruticans*, one of the varieties of jasmine.

**Spikenards – חִלְפֵי דְּיַמָּא:** *Cymbopogon schoenanthus* or *Andropogon schoenanthus*, also known as camel grass, fever grass, and West Indian lemon grass, is a perennial plant from the *Poaceae* family that grows to a height of 60 cm. It grows primarily in arid areas and is an important source of food for camels. Oil is extracted from its pleasantly scented leaves in order to produce medicine and perfume.

**Daffodil – נַרְקוֹם דְּגִינּוּנִיתָא:** In the Talmud, the term *narkom* or *narkos*, based on various sources, refers to the daffodil, from the Greek νάρκισσος, *narkissos*. The common daffodil, *Narcissus tazetta* from the *Amaryllidaccae* family is an onion-shaped plant that grows wild throughout Eretz Yisrael. Its flat leaves reach a length of 54 cm. Its fragrant flowers are arranged up to ten on one stalk. The flower has a circumference of 3 cm. Its sepals are white and its corona is yellow. Daffodils are grown even today for decorative purposes.

**Violets – סִיגְלֵי:** *Viola odorata* from the *Violaceae* family, is an annual decorative plant whose leaves are concentrated in a rosette at its base. It reaches a height of 51 cm. In the spring, it blooms with fragrant purple flowers. In modern times, it is used primarily for decorative purposes.

**Quince – חַבּוּשָׁא:** *Cydnia vulgaris* is a fruit tree from the *Rosaceaea* family. It is also called *parish* and *ispargal* in the Mishna. It is a deciduous fruit tree that reaches a height of 5 m and in certain circumstances even higher. Its leaves are wide and long ovules, reaching 9 cm. Its large flowers are pink or white. Its yellow fruit is round or pear-shaped. In most of the species, the fruit is covered with a thin, gray, hair-like substance. The fruit is hard. With cooking it softens and has a good taste and smell. Consequently, its primary use is in fruit soups and compotes. Nowadays, the quince is grown in Eretz Yisrael.

Jasmine

Spikenards


Daffodil

Fragrant violet

Quince

NOTES

**From where is it derived that one recites a blessing over scent** – **מִנַּיִן שֶׁמְּבָרְכִין עַל הָרֵיחַ**: Ostensibly, scent is included in the general concept that one is forbidden to derive benefit from this world without reciting a blessing. Therefore, the question is, why was it necessary to cite a special derivation in this case? Rashi in tractate *Nidda* explains that since the benefit derived from smell is less substantial than other physical pleasures, no blessing should be necessary. Others explain that since deriving benefit from this world without reciting a blessing is likened to misusing consecrated property; with regard to those laws, smell is considered inconsequential. Therefore, no blessing is necessary (*Tziyyun LeNefesh Ḥayya*). Others contend that since enjoying a fragrance does not fundamentally compromise the integrity of the object, it is not self-evident that a blessing is required (Rabbi Elazar Moshe Horowitz).

אָמַר רַב יְהוּדָה: הַאי מַאן דְּנָפֵיק בְּיוֹמֵי נִיסָן וְחָזֵי אִילָנֵי דְּקָא מְלַבְלְבֵי, אוֹמֵר: בָּרוּךְ שֶׁלֹּא חִיסֵּר בְּעוֹלָמוֹ כְּלוּם וּבָרָא בּוֹ בְּרִיּוֹת טוֹבוֹת וְאִילָנוֹת טוֹבוֹת לְהִתְנָאוֹת בָּהֵן בְּנֵי אָדָם. אָמַר רַב זוּטְרָא בַּר טוֹבִיָּה אָמַר רַב: מִנַּיִן שֶׁמְּבָרְכִין עַל הָרֵיחַ – שֶׁנֶּאֱמַר: ״כֹּל הַנְּשָׁמָה תְּהַלֵּל יָהּ״, אֵיזֶהוּ דָּבָר שֶׁהַנְּשָׁמָה נֶהֱנֵית מִמֶּנּוּ וְאֵין הַגּוּף נֶהֱנֶה מִמֶּנּוּ – הֱוֵי אוֹמֵר: זֶה הָרֵיחַ.

On a related topic, the Gemara cites that **Rav Yehuda said: One who goes out during Nisan and sees trees that are blossoming recites:**[H] **Blessed… who has withheld nothing from His world, and has created in it beautiful creatures and trees for human beings to enjoy. Rav Zutra bar Toviya said** that **Rav said: From where** is it derived **that one recites a blessing over scent?**[N] **As it is stated: "Let every soul praise the Lord"** (Psalms 150:6). He explains the verse: **What is it from which the soul derives benefit and the body does not derive benefit from it? You must say: That is scent.** Even over items from which only the soul derives benefit, one must recite a blessing and praise God.

וְאָמַר רַב זוּטְרָא בַּר טוֹבִיָּה אָמַר רַב: עֲתִידִים בַּחוּרֵי יִשְׂרָאֵל שֶׁיִּתְּנוּ רֵיחַ טוֹב כַּלְּבָנוֹן, שֶׁנֶּאֱמַר: ״יֵלְכוּ יוֹנְקוֹתָיו וִיהִי כַזַּיִת הוֹדוֹ וְרֵיחַ לוֹ כַּלְּבָנוֹן״.

**And Rav Zutra bar Toviya said** that **Rav said: The young men of Israel are destined to emit a sweet scent as the Lebanon, as it is stated: "His branches shall spread and his beauty will be as the olive tree, and his fragrance as Lebanon"** (Hosea 14:7).

וְאָמַר רַב זוּטְרָא בַּר טוֹבִיָּה אָמַר רַב, מַאי דִּכְתִיב: ״אֶת הַכֹּל עָשָׂה יָפֶה בְעִתּוֹ״ מְלַמֵּד, שֶׁכׇּל אֶחָד וְאֶחָד יִפָּה לוֹ הַקָּדוֹשׁ בָּרוּךְ הוּא אוּמָנָתוֹ בְּפָנָיו.

**And Rav Zutra bar Toviya said** that **Rav said: What is** the meaning of **that which is written: "He has made everything beautiful in its time,** and he has placed the world in their heart, yet so man cannot find out the work that God has done from the beginning even to the end" (Ecclesiastes 3:11)? This **teaches that each and every individual, God has made his work pleasant for him in his own eyes.** In that way, each individual will be satisfied with his work, enabling the world to function properly.

אָמַר רַב פַּפָּא, הַיְינוּ דְּאָמְרִי אֱינָשֵׁי: תְּלֵה לֵיהּ קוֹרָא לְדָבָר אַחֵר – וְאִיהוּ דִּידֵיהּ עָבֵיד.

**Rav Pappa said: This is** the proverb **that people say: Hang a heart of palm on a pig, and he will** continue **to perform his** standard activities. Although hearts of palm are a delicacy, a pig will roll it in the mud as is his wont. Every creature has its own particular tastes, and one cannot draw conclusions with regard to one based on the standards of another.

וְאָמַר רַב זוּטְרָא בַּר טוֹבִיָּה אָמַר רַב: אֲבוּקָה כִּשְׁנַיִם, וְיָרֵחַ כִּשְׁלֹשָׁה. אִיבַּעְיָא לְהוּ: אֲבוּקָה כִּשְׁנַיִם בַּהֲדֵי דִּידֵיהּ, אוֹ דִּילְמָא אֲבוּקָה כִּשְׁנַיִם לְבַר מִדִּידֵיהּ? – תָּא שְׁמַע: וְיָרֵחַ כִּשְׁלֹשָׁה. אִי אָמְרַתְּ בִּשְׁלָמָא בַּהֲדֵי דִּידֵיהּ – שַׁפִּיר, אֶלָּא אִי אָמְרַתְּ לְבַר מִדִּידֵיהּ – אַרְבָּעָה לָמָּה לִי? וְהָאָמַר מָר: לְאֶחָד – נִרְאֶה וּמַזִּיק, לִשְׁנַיִם – נִרְאֶה וְאֵינוֹ מַזִּיק, לִשְׁלֹשָׁה – אֵינוֹ נִרְאֶה כׇּל עִיקָּר! אֶלָּא לָאו שְׁמַע מִינַּהּ אֲבוּקָה כִּשְׁנַיִם בַּהֲדֵי דִּידֵיהּ, שְׁמַע מִינַּהּ.

**And Rav Zutra bar Toviya said** that **Rav said:** For one walking on a dark path, if he has **a torch** in his hand, **it is like two** were walking on that path **and** the light of the **moon is like three.** The Gemara **raises a dilemma: Is a torch like two including** the one carrying the torch **or perhaps a torch is like two besides him** for a total of three? **Come and hear** a proof from that which Rav said: **And the moon is like three. Granted, if you say** three **including him,** it works out **well. However, if you say** three **besides him, why do I need four,** what purpose do they serve? **Didn't the Master say: To one** walking alone, a demon **can be seen and cause** him **harm. To two** people, a demon can be seen **and** does not **cause** them **harm. To three** people, **it cannot be seen at all** Four people are no better than three. **Rather, can't we learn from this** that **a torch is like two,** means two **including him.** The Gemara comments: Indeed, **conclude from this.**

וְאָמַר רַב זוּטְרָא בַּר טוֹבִיָּה אָמַר רַב, וְאָמְרִי לַהּ אָמַר רַב חָנָא בַּר בִּיזְנָא אָמַר רַבִּי שִׁמְעוֹן חֲסִידָא, וְאָמְרִי לַהּ אָמַר רַבִּי יוֹחָנָן מִשּׁוּם רַבִּי שִׁמְעוֹן בֶּן יוֹחַי: נוֹחַ לוֹ לְאָדָם שֶׁיַּפִּיל עַצְמוֹ לְתוֹךְ כִּבְשַׁן הָאֵשׁ וְאַל יַלְבִּין פְּנֵי חֲבֵרוֹ בָּרַבִּים. מְנָלַן – מִתָּמָר, שֶׁנֶּאֱמַר: ״הִיא מוּצֵאת״ וגו׳.

**And Rav Zutra bar Toviya said** that **Rav said; and some say Rav Ḥana bar Bizna said** that **Rabbi Shimon Ḥasida said; and some say Rabbi Yoḥanan said in the name of Rabbi Shimon ben Yoḥai: It is preferable,** from an ethical perspective, **for one to throw himself into a fiery furnace rather than humiliate another in public.**[H] **From where do we** derive this? **From Tamar,** the daughter-in-law of Judah, when she was taken out to be burned, **as it is stated: "As she was brought forth,** she sent to her father-in-law, saying I am pregnant by the man to whom these belong, and she said examine these, to whom does this seal, cord and staff belong?" (Genesis 38:25). Despite her dire situation, she did not reveal that she was pregnant with Judah's child; rather, she left the decision to him, to avoid humiliating him in public.

HALAKHA

**One who goes out during Nisan and sees trees that are blossoming recites** – **הַאי מַאן דְּנָפֵיק בְּיוֹמֵי נִיסָן וְחָזֵי אִילָנֵי דְּקָא מְלַבְלְבֵי, אוֹמֵר וכו׳**: One who sees fruit trees in blossom during the season of Nisan, spanning the months of Adar, Nisan, and Iyar (*Be'er Heitev*), recites: Blessed…who has withheld nothing from His world, and has created in it beautiful creatures and trees for human beings to enjoy. One recites the blessing only once a year, and if, before he recites the blessing, the fruits on the tree have already grown, he may no longer recite it that year (Rambam *Sefer Ahava, Hilkhot Berakhot* 10:13; *Shulḥan Arukh, Oraḥ Ḥayyim* 226:1)

**It is preferable, from an ethical perspective, for one to throw himself into a fiery furnace rather than humiliate another in public** – **נוֹחַ לוֹ לְאָדָם שֶׁיַּפִּיל עַצְמוֹ לְתוֹךְ כִּבְשַׁן הָאֵשׁ וְאַל יַלְבִּין פְּנֵי חֲבֵרוֹ בָּרַבִּים**: It is forbidden to publicly embarrass another. One must make every effort to avoid doing so, as one who commits that transgression has no share in the World-to-Come (Rambam *Sefer HaMadda, Hilkhot De'ot* 6:8).

תָּנוּ רַבָּנַן: הֵבִיאוּ לְפָנָיו שֶׁמֶן וַהֲדַס, בֵּית שַׁמַּאי אוֹמְרִים: מְבָרֵךְ עַל הַשֶּׁמֶן וְאַחַר כָּךְ מְבָרֵךְ עַל הַהֲדַס; וּבֵית הִלֵּל אוֹמְרִים: מְבָרֵךְ עַל הַהֲדַס וְאַחַר כָּךְ מְבָרֵךְ עַל הַשֶּׁמֶן. אָמַר רַבָּן גַּמְלִיאֵל: אֲנִי אַכְרִיעַ. שֶׁמֶן – זָכִינוּ לְרֵיחוֹ וְזָכִינוּ לְסִיכָתוֹ, הֲדַס – לְרֵיחוֹ זָכִינוּ, לְסִיכָתוֹ לֹא זָכִינוּ. אָמַר רַבִּי יוֹחָנָן: הֲלָכָה כְּדִבְרֵי הַמַּכְרִיעַ.

**The Sages taught: If they brought before him** both scented **oil and a myrtle** branch,[HB] **Beit Shammai say: One recites a blessing over the oil first and over the myrtle** branch **thereafter. And Beit Hillel say: One recites a blessing over the myrtle** branch first **and over the oil thereafter. Rabban Gamliel said: I will decide**[N] this dispute in favor of the opinion of Beit Shammai, that one should recite a blessing over the oil first, as it is more significant. With regard to **oil; we are privileged** to enjoy **its fragrance and we are privileged** to enjoy it by **anointing** ourselves with **it.** With regard to the **myrtle** branch; **we are privileged** to enjoy **its fragrance, we are not privileged** to enjoy it by **anointing** ourselves with **it. Rabbi Yoḥanan said: The *halakha* is in accordance with** the opinion of **the decisor,** Rabban Gamliel.

רַב פָּפָּא אִיקְּלַע לְבֵי רַב הוּנָא בְּרֵיהּ דְּרַב אִיקָא, אַיְיתוֹ לְקַמַּיְיהוּ שֶׁמֶן וַהֲדַס, שְׁקַל רַב פָּפָּא בָּרֵיךְ אַהֲדַס בְּרֵישָׁא וַהֲדַר בָּרֵיךְ אַשֶּׁמֶן. אֲמַר לֵיהּ: לָא סָבַר לַהּ מָר הֲלָכָה כְּדִבְרֵי הַמַּכְרִיעַ?! – אֲמַר לֵיהּ, הָכִי אָמַר רָבָא: הֲלָכָה כְּבֵית הִלֵּל. וְלָא הִיא, לְאִשְׁתַּמּוֹטֵי נַפְשֵׁיהּ הוּא דַּעֲבַד.

The Gemara relates: **Rav Pappa happened** to come **to the house of Rav Huna, son of Rav Ika. They brought before him** both scented **oil and a myrtle** branch. **Rav Pappa took and recited a blessing** over the **myrtle branch first and then recited a blessing** over the **oil.** Rav Huna **said to him:** And **does the Master not hold** that **the *halakha* is in accordance** with the opinion of **the decisor?** If so, you should have recited a blessing over the oil first. Rav Pappa said: **Rava said the following: The *halakha* is in accordance with** the opinion of **Beit Hillel.** The Gemara comments: **That is not so,** as Rava did not issue that ruling. **Rather, Rav Pappa did** this **in order to extricate himself**[N] from an unpleasant situation and justify his conduct.

תָּנוּ רַבָּנַן: הֵבִיאוּ לִפְנֵיהֶם שֶׁמֶן וְיַיִן, בֵּית שַׁמַּאי אוֹמְרִים: אוֹחֵז הַשֶּׁמֶן בִּימִינוֹ וְאֶת הַיַּיִן בִּשְׂמֹאלוֹ, מְבָרֵךְ עַל הַשֶּׁמֶן וְחוֹזֵר וּמְבָרֵךְ עַל הַיַּיִן; בֵּית הִלֵּל אוֹמְרִים: אוֹחֵז אֶת הַיַּיִן בִּימִינוֹ וְאֶת הַשֶּׁמֶן בִּשְׂמֹאלוֹ, מְבָרֵךְ עַל הַיַּיִן וְחוֹזֵר וּמְבָרֵךְ עַל הַשֶּׁמֶן. וְטָחוֹ בְּרֹאשׁ הַשַּׁמָּשׁ, וְאִם שַׁמָּשׁ תַּלְמִיד חָכָם הוּא – טָחוֹ בַּכּוֹתֶל, מִפְּנֵי שֶׁגְּנַאי לְתַלְמִיד חָכָם לָצֵאת לַשּׁוּק כְּשֶׁהוּא מְבוּשָּׂם.

**Our Sages taught** in a *baraita*: If **they brought before them** both scented **oil and wine,**[H] **Beit Shammai say: He grasps the oil in his right** hand, since he recites a blessing over the oil first, **and the wine in his left** hand. **He recites a blessing over the oil and then he recites a blessing over the wine. Beit Hillel say** the opposite: **He grasps the wine in his right** hand **and the oil in his left** hand. **He recites a blessing over the wine and then he recites a blessing over the oil. And** after he has recited a blessing over the oil and anointed his hands with it, **he smears** it **on the head of the servant** so that his hands will not remain perfumed. **And if the servant is a Torah scholar,**[N] **he smears** the oil **on the wall, as it is unbecoming for a Torah scholar to go out perfumed into the marketplace.**

תָּנוּ רַבָּנַן: שִׁשָּׁה דְּבָרִים גְּנַאי לוֹ לְתַלְמִיד חָכָם: אַל יֵצֵא כְּשֶׁהוּא מְבוּשָּׂם לַשּׁוּק, וְאַל יֵצֵא יְחִידִי בַּלַּיְלָה, וְאַל יֵצֵא בְּמִנְעָלִים הַמְטוּלָּאִים, וְאַל יְסַפֵּר עִם אִשָּׁה בַּשּׁוּק, וְאַל יָסֵב בַּחֲבוּרָה שֶׁל עַמֵּי הָאָרֶץ, וְאַל יִכָּנֵס בָּאַחֲרוֹנָה לְבֵית הַמִּדְרָשׁ; וְיֵשׁ אוֹמְרִים: אַף לֹא יַפְסִיעַ פְּסִיעָה גַּסָּה, וְאַל יְהַלֵּךְ בְּקוֹמָה זְקוּפָה.

Tangential to the mention of conduct unbecoming a Torah scholar, **the Sages taught** in a *baraita*: **Six things are disgraceful for a Torah scholar:**[NH] **He may not go out perfumed into the marketplace; he may not go out** of his house **alone at night; he may not go out** wearing **patched shoes; he may not converse with a woman in the marketplace; he may not recline** and participate in a meal **in the company of ignoramuses; and he may not be the last to enter the study hall. And some say** that **he may not take long strides and he may not walk with an upright posture.**

## HALAKHA

**If they brought before him both scented oil and a myrtle branch – הֵבִיאוּ לְפָנָיו שֶׁמֶן וַהֲדַס:** One before whom a myrtle branch and scented oil were brought, if their blessings are the same, recites the blessing on the myrtle branch and exempts the oil, in accordance with the opinion of Beit Hillel and Rav Pappa, as proof based on an action is decisive. Even though the Gemara said: And that is not so, that was only in terms of the attribution to Rava, not in terms of the *halakha* (Rambam *Sefer Ahava, Hilkhot Berakhot* 9:3; *Shulḥan Arukh, Oraḥ Ḥayyim* 216:12).

**If they brought before them both scented oil and wine – הֵבִיאוּ לִפְנֵיהֶם שֶׁמֶן וְיַיִן:** One before whom wine and scented oil were brought, takes the wine in his right hand and recites the blessing over it and then recites the blessing over the oil (Rambam, *Sefer Ahava, Hilkhot Berakhot* 7:14; *Shulḥan Arukh, Oraḥ Ḥayyim* 206:4).

**Six things are disgraceful for a Torah scholar – שִׁשָּׁה דְּבָרִים גְּנַאי לוֹ לְתַלְמִיד חָכָם וכו׳:** A Torah scholar may not go out in public when he or his clothes are perfumed because of suspicion of homosexual acts. He may not even go out in public with his hair perfumed, as the ruling is in accordance with the stringent opinion (*Kesef Mishne*). If he spread perfume on his body due to an odor or filth, it is permitted. Similarly, a Torah scholar may not go out alone at night unless he has a standing appointment to go and study every night at the same time. He may not wear patched shoes with a patch upon a patch during the summer, but during the rainy season it is permitted, if he cannot afford better shoes. A Torah scholar must be vigilant with every action that he takes so that others will not speak ill or be suspicious of him. For that reason, he should not converse with a woman in public or sit in the company of ignoramuses. In the interest of propriety, he should neither run in public nor walk with an upright posture (Rambam *Sefer HaMadda, Hilkhot De'ot* 5:2, 7, 8, 9).

## BACKGROUND

**Myrtle branch – הֲדַס:** The common myrtle *Myrtus communis L.* is widespread in the Mediterranean region and is commonly cultivated. The leaves give off an aromatic and refreshing smell somewhat reminiscent of myrrh or eucalyptus; the taste is very intense, quite disagreeable, and strongly bitter.

Myrtle branches

## NOTES

**Rabban Gamliel said I will decide [*akhria*] – אָמַר רַבָּן גַּמְלִיאֵל: אֲנִי אַכְרִיעַ:** The meaning of the concept of *makhria* here is different from its typical meaning in the Talmud. Normally, the *makhria* is one whose opinion is a compromise between the two previously stated opinions. Here, however, Rabban Gamliel decides entirely in accordance with the opinion of Beit Shammai. Some attempt to explain that, here too, it is a compromise position. Beit Shammai and Beit Hillel disagreed with regard to both refined oil spread on the body and oil made for fragrance. Rabban Gamliel ruled that one recites a blessing over oil that is spread on the body but not oil made for fragrance, which differs from both opinions (*Tziyyun LeNefesh Ḥayya*).

**In order to extricate himself – לְאִשְׁתַּמּוֹטֵי נַפְשֵׁיהּ הוּא דַּעֲבַד:** Many wondered how Rav Pappa could say something untrue, especially when others could learn an incorrect *halakha* based on his statement. Furthermore, many authorities rule in accordance with his opinion. They explain Rav Pappa's statement slightly differently. In this case, he ruled against Rabbi Yoḥanan's opinion, in accordance with the opinion of Beit Hillel. Since he did not want to take credit for this ruling, in an act of humility he attributed the ruling to his teacher, Rava (Responsa of Rav Menaḥem Azarya MiFano). Others explain that, as stated above, the use of the term *makhria* with regard to the opinion of Rabban Gamliel is unconventional. The principle that the *halakha* is in accordance with the opinion of the *makhria* refers to a compromise opinion. Rava explicitly ruled in *Bava Metzia* that this principle does not apply in cases like this one. Therefore, the *halakha* should be in accordance with the opinion of Beit Hillel, and Rav Pappa relied upon this ruling. The Gemara merely notes that Rava's statement refers to another topic and was not explicitly stated with regard to the dispute in our Gemara (*Tziyyun LeNefesh Ḥayya* and *Penei Yehoshua*).

**And if the servant is a Torah scholar – וְאִם שַׁמָּשׁ תַּלְמִיד חָכָם הוּא וכו׳:** Some explain that if the servant is a Torah scholar it is inappropriate to wipe the oil on his head and he must wipe his hands on something else. It is inappropriate for a Torah scholar to go perfumed in public (*Melo HaRo'im*).

**Six things are disgraceful for a Torah scholar – שִׁשָּׁה דְּבָרִים גְּנַאי לוֹ לְתַלְמִיד חָכָם:** The number comes to emphasize that the other things, introduced with the phrase: And some say, are disgraceful for all (*Alfasi Zuta*). These things were enumerated because, even though they are not prohibited actions, Torah scholars may not perform them so as not to be suspected of inappropriate conduct (*Ḥefetz Hashem*).

״אַל יֵצֵא כְּשֶׁהוּא מְבוּשָּׂם לַשּׁוּק״ – אָמַר רַבִּי אַבָּא בְּרֵיהּ דְּרַבִּי חִיָּיא בַּר אַבָּא אָמַר רַבִּי יוֹחָנָן: בְּמָקוֹם שֶׁחֲשׁוּדִים עַל מִשְׁכַּב זָכוּר. אָמַר רַב שֵׁשֶׁת: לָא אֲמַרַן אֶלָּא בְּבִגְדוֹ, אֲבָל בְּגוּפוֹ – זֵיעָה מַעַבְרָא לֵיהּ. אָמַר רַב פַּפָּא: וּשְׂעָרוֹ כְּבִגְדוֹ דָּמֵי; וְאָמְרִי לָהּ, כְּגוּפוֹ דָּמֵי.

The Gemara elaborates on the statements of the *baraita*. **He may not go out perfumed into the marketplace; Rabbi Abba, son of Rabbi Ḥiyya bar Abba, said** that **Rabbi Yoḥanan said:** This prohibition only applies **in a place where they are suspected of homosexuality.** One who goes out into the marketplace perfumed, will arouse suspicion. **Rav Sheshet said: We only said this with regard to his clothing** that was perfumed, **but with regard to his body,** it is permitted, as **his sweat causes the fragrance to dissipate. Rav Pappa said:** In this regard, **his hair is** considered **like his clothing. And some say: His hair is** considered **like his body.**

״וְאַל יֵצֵא יְחִידִי בַּלַּיְלָה״ – מִשּׁוּם חֲשָׁדָא, וְלָא אֲמַרַן אֶלָּא דְּלָא קְבִיעַ לֵיהּ עִידָּנָא, אֲבָל קְבִיעַ לֵיהּ עִידָּנָא – מֵידַע יְדִיעַ דִּלְעִידָּנֵיהּ קָא אָזֵיל.

**He may not go out** of his house **alone at night because of suspicion** of promiscuity. **And** therefore **this was only** prohibited **if he does not have a set time** during the night to study with his teacher, **but** if **he has a set time,** everyone **knows that he is going to** study with his teacher at **his set time,** and they will not be suspicious of him.

״וְאַל יֵצֵא בְּמִנְעָלִים הַמְטוּלָּאִים״ – מְסַיַּיע לֵיהּ לְרַבִּי חִיָּיא בַּר אַבָּא, דְּאָמַר רַבִּי חִיָּיא בַּר אַבָּא: גְּנַאי הוּא לְתַלְמִיד חָכָם שֶׁיֵּצֵא בְּמִנְעָלִים הַמְטוּלָּאִים. אִינִי?! וְהָא רַבִּי חִיָּיא בַּר אַבָּא נָפֵיק! – אָמַר מָר זוּטְרָא בְּרֵיהּ דְּרַב נַחְמָן: בִּטְלַאי עַל גַּבֵּי טְלַאי. וְלָא אֲמַרַן אֶלָּא בְּפַנְתָּא, אֲבָל בְּגִילְדָּא – לֵית לָן בָּהּ; וּבְפַנְתָּא לָא אֲמַרַן אֶלָּא בְּאוֹרְחָא אֲבָל בְּבֵיתָא – לֵית לָן בָּהּ; וְלָא אֲמַרַן אֶלָּא בִּימוֹת הַחַמָּה, אֲבָל בִּימוֹת הַגְּשָׁמִים – לֵית לָן בָּהּ.

**He may not go out** wearing **patched shoes.** This **supports** the statement of **Rabbi Ḥiyya bar Abba, as Rabbi Ḥiyya bar Abba said: It is disgraceful for a Torah scholar to go out** wearing **patched shoes.** The Gemara challenges: **Is that so? Didn't Rabbi Ḥiyya bar Abba** himself **go out** wearing patched shoes? **Mar Zutra, son of Rav Naḥman, said:** It is only prohibited when the shoe has **a patch upon a patch. And we only said this with regard to** patches on **the upper** part of the shoe **but** if the patch is **on the sole, this does not** apply. **And with regard to** patches on **the upper** part of the shoe, **we only said this** when he is out **on the road, but in his house, we need not** be concerned. **And we only said this with regard to the summer** when the patches would be visible to all, **but during the rainy season,** when the mud obscures the view of the patches, **we need not** be concerned.

״וְאַל יְסַפֵּר עִם אִשָּׁה בַּשּׁוּק״ – אָמַר רַב חִסְדָּא: וַאֲפִילּוּ הִיא אִשְׁתּוֹ. תַּנְיָא נַמִי הָכִי: אֲפִילּוּ הִיא אִשְׁתּוֹ, וַאֲפִילּוּ הִיא בִּתּוֹ, וַאֲפִילּוּ הִיא אֲחוֹתוֹ – לְפִי שֶׁאֵין הַכֹּל בְּקִיאִין בִּקְרוֹבוֹתָיו.

**He may not converse with a woman in the marketplace. Rav Ḥisda said: Even if she is his wife. This was also taught** in a *baraita*: One may not converse with a woman in the market, **even if she is his wife, even if she is his daughter and even if she is his sister,** for **not everyone is well-versed in** the identity of **his female relatives** and they will suspect that he is talking to women who are not his relatives.

״וְאַל יָסֵב בַּחֲבוּרָה שֶׁל עַמֵּי הָאָרֶץ״ – מַאי טַעְמָא? – דִּילְמָא אָתֵי לְאִמְשׁוֹכֵי בַּתְרַיְיהוּ.

**He may not recline** and participate in a meal **in the company of ignoramuses.** The Gemara explains: **What is the reason? Perhaps he will be drawn after them** and emulate them.

״וְאַל יִכָּנֵס אַחֲרוֹנָה לְבֵית הַמִּדְרָשׁ״ – מִשּׁוּם דְּקָרוּ לֵיהּ פּוֹשֵׁעַ.

**He may not be the last to enter the study hall.** The Gemara explains: **Because they** will **call him negligent,** in other words, careless and lazy.

וְיֵשׁ אוֹמְרִים: ״אַף לֹא יַפְסִיעַ פְּסִיעָה גַּסָּה״ – דְּאָמַר מָר: פְּסִיעָה גַּסָּה נוֹטֶלֶת אֶחָד מֵחֲמֵשׁ מֵאוֹת מִמְּאוֹר עֵינָיו שֶׁל אָדָם. מַאי תַּקַּנְתֵּיהּ? – לְהַדְרֵיהּ בְּקִדּוּשָׁא דְּבֵי שִׁמְשֵׁי.

**And some say he may not take long strides, as the Master said: A long stride takes** away **one five-hundredth of a person's eyesight.** The Gemara asks: **What is his remedy** if he took long strides? The Gemara responds: **He can restore it** by drinking the wine of ***kiddush* on** Shabbat **eve.**

״וְאַל יְהַלֵּךְ בְּקוֹמָה זְקוּפָה״ – דְּאָמַר מָר: הַמְהַלֵּךְ בְּקוֹמָה זְקוּפָה אֲפִילּוּ אַרְבַּע אַמּוֹת, כְּאִילּוּ דּוֹחֵק רַגְלֵי שְׁכִינָה, דִּכְתִיב: ״מְלֹא כָל הָאָרֶץ כְּבוֹדוֹ״.

**And he may not walk with an upright posture,** but slightly bowed, **as the Master said: One who walks with an upright posture** and in an arrogant manner, **even four cubits,** it is **as if he is pushing away the feet of the Divine Presence,** as **it is written: "The entire world is full of His glory"** (Isaiah 6:3). One who walks in an arrogant way shows a lack of regard for the glory and honor of God that is surrounding him, and thereby chases God from that place.

מתני׳ הֵבִיאוּ לְפָנָיו מָלִיחַ תְּחִלָּה וּפַת עִמּוֹ – מְבָרֵךְ עַל הַמָּלִיחַ וּפוֹטֵר אֶת הַפַּת, שֶׁהַפַּת טְפֵלָה לוֹ. זֶה הַכְּלָל: כָּל שֶׁהוּא עִיקָּר וְעִמּוֹ טְפֵלָה – מְבָרֵךְ עַל הָעִיקָּר וּפוֹטֵר אֶת הַטְּפֵלָה.

**MISHNA** If they brought salted food before him to eat first and bread with it,[H] he recites a blessing over the salted food and thereby exempts the bread, because the salted food is primary while the bread is secondary to it. This is the principle: Any food that is primary and a secondary food is with it,[N] one recites a blessing over the primary and, in so doing, exempts the secondary from its own blessing.

גמ׳ וּמִי אִיכָּא מִידִי דְּהָוֵי מָלִיחַ עִיקָּר וּפַת טְפֵלָה?! אָמַר רַב אַחָא בְּרֵיהּ דְּרַב עַוִירָא אָמַר רַב אַשִׁי: בְּאוֹכְלֵי פֵּירוֹת גְּנוֹסַר שָׁנוּ.

**GEMARA** The Gemara asks: **And is there a** circumstance **where salted food is primary and bread is secondary?** Generally, no meal has a salted food item as its primary component. **Rav Aḥa, son of Rav Avira, said** that **Rav Ashi said:** This *halakha* **was taught with regard to those who eat fruits of Genosar,**[N] which are extremely sweet and which would be eaten along with salted foods in order to temper this sweetness. They would eat bread along with those salted foods.

אָמַר רַבָּה בַּר בַּר חָנָה: כִּי הֲוָה אָזְלִינַן בָּתְרֵיהּ דְּרַבִּי יוֹחָנָן לְמֵיכַל פֵּירוֹת גְּנוֹסַר, כִּי הָוֵינַן בֵּי מְאָה – מְנַקְּטִינַן לֵיהּ לְכָל חַד וְחַד עַשְׂרָה עַשְׂרָה, וְכִי הָוֵינַן בֵּי עַשְׂרָה – מְנַקְּטִינַן לֵיהּ כָּל חַד וְחַד מְאָה מְאָה, וְכָל מְאָה מִינַּיְיהוּ הֲוָה מַחֲזֵיק לְהוּ צַנָּא בַּר תְּלָתָא סָאוֵי וְאָכֵיל לְהוּ וּמִשְׁתַּבַּע דְּלָא טָעֵים זִיוּנָא. זִיוּנָא סָלְקָא דַּעְתָּךְ?! אֶלָּא אֵימָא: מְזוֹנָא.

On a related note, the Gemara employs hyperbole in praising the fruits of Genosar. **Rabba bar bar Ḥana said: When we would go after Rabbi Yoḥanan to eat fruits of Genosar,**[B] **when we were one hundred** people together, **each and every one of us would bring him ten** fruits, **and when we were ten** people together, **each and every one of us would bring him one hundred** fruits, **and every hundred of** the fruits **would** require a **basket of three *se'a* to hold them.** Rabbi Yoḥanan would **eat them** all, **and** was prepared **to swear**[N] **that he had not tasted** any **food.** The Gemara asks: **Does it enter your mind** that he claimed that **he had not tasted** any **food? Rather, say** that he had not tasted any **sustenance.** Due to their delicious taste, he was still not satiated.

רַבִּי אַבָּהוּ אָכֵיל עַד דַּהֲוָה שָׁרֵיק לֵיהּ דּוּדְבָא מֵאַפּוּתֵיהּ; וְרַב אַמִי וְרַב אַסִי הָווּ אָכְלִי עַד דִּנְתוּר מַזַּיְיהוּ. רַבִּי שִׁמְעוֹן בֶּן לָקִישׁ הֲוָה אָכֵיל עַד דְּמָרֵיד, וַאֲמַר לְהוּ רַבִּי יוֹחָנָן לִדְבֵי נְשִׂיאָה, וַהֲוָה מְשַׁדֵּר לֵיהּ רַבִּי יְהוּדָה נְשִׂיאָה בַּאלוּשֵׁי אַבָּתְרֵיהּ וּמַיְיתִי לֵיהּ לְבֵיתֵיהּ.

The Gemara continues to wax hyperbolic: **Rabbi Abbahu ate** fruits of Genosar **until** the sweet, lush fruits made his skin so slippery that **a fly would slip from his forehead. And Rav Ami and Rav Asi would eat** them **until their hair fell out. Rabbi Shimon ben Lakish would eat** them **until he became confused. And** then **Rabbi Yoḥanan would tell the household of the *Nasi*** about his condition **and Rabbi Yehuda Nesia would send the authorities after him and** they **would take him to his house.**

כִּי אֲתָא רַב דִּימִי, אָמַר: עִיר אַחַת הָיְתָה לוֹ לְיַנַּאי הַמֶּלֶךְ בְּהַר הַמֶּלֶךְ, שֶׁהָיוּ מוֹצִיאִים מִמֶּנָּה שִׁשִּׁים רִבּוֹא סִפְלֵי טָרִית לְקוֹצְצֵי תְאֵנִים מֵעֶרֶב שַׁבָּת לְעֶרֶב שַׁבָּת.

On a similar note, the Gemara relates: **When Rav Dimi came** from Eretz Yisrael to Babylonia **he said: King Yannai had a city on the King's Mountain, from which they would take six-hundred thousand bowls of sardines**[B] **for those cutting figs** off the trees during the course of the week **from Shabbat eve to Shabbat eve.** There were so many workers, and the fruit was so sweet, that they needed such a vast quantity of salted fish to enable them to continue with their work.

כִּי אֲתָא רָבִין, אָמַר: אִילָן אֶחָד הָיָה לוֹ לְיַנַּאי הַמֶּלֶךְ בְּהַר הַמֶּלֶךְ, שֶׁהָיוּ מוֹרִידִים מִמֶּנּוּ אַרְבָּעִים סְאָה גּוֹזָלוֹת מִשָּׁלֹשׁ בְּרִיכוֹת בַּחֹדֶשׁ. כִּי אֲתָא רַבִּי יִצְחָק, אָמַר: עִיר אַחַת הָיְתָה בְּאֶרֶץ יִשְׂרָאֵל וְגוּפְנִית שְׁמָהּ, שֶׁהָיוּ בָּהּ שְׁמֹנִים זוּגוֹת אַחִים כֹּהֲנִים נְשׂוּאִים לִשְׁמֹנִים זוּגוֹת אֲחָיוֹת כֹּהֲנוֹת. וּבְדַקוּ רַבָּנַן מִסּוּרָא וְעַד נְהַרְדְּעָא, וְלָא אַשְׁכְּחוּ בַּר מִבְּנָתֵיהּ דְּרַב חִסְדָּא דַּהֲווּ נְסִיבָן לְרָמִי בַּר חָמָא וּלְמָר עוּקְבָא בַּר חָמָא, וְאַף עַל גַּב דְּאִינְהִי הָווּ כָּהֲנָתָא – אִינְהוּ לָא הָווּ כָּהֲנֵי.

On the subject of the King's Mountain and Eretz Yisrael, **when Rav Dimi came** from Eretz Yisrael to Babylonia, **he said: King Yannai had a tree on the King's Mountain from which they would remove forty *se'a* of pigeons from three broods each month. When Rabbi Yitzḥak came** from Eretz Yisrael to Babylonia **he said: There was a city in Eretz Yisrael named Gufnit, in which there were eighty pairs of brothers who were priests, married to eighty pairs of sisters, who were all from priestly** families. **And** to assess the frequency of that phenomenon, the Gemara relates: **The Sages checked from Sura to Neharde'a, and with the exception of the daughters of Rav Ḥisda, who were married to Rami bar Ḥama and** his brother **Mar Ukva bar Ḥama, they could not find** a similar case. **And,** even in the case that they found, **although they,** the sisters, **were** the daughters **of a priest, they,** the brothers **were not priests.** Throughout virtually the entire country of Babylonia, they could not find a similar circumstance.

### HALAKHA

**If they brought salted food before him to eat first and bread with it** – הֵבִיאוּ לְפָנָיו מָלִיחַ תְּחִלָּה וּפַת עִמּוֹ: One who is eating salted food as the primary component of his meal, and eats bread along with it, recites a blessing over the salted food and exempts the bread, in accordance with our mishna (Rambam *Sefer Ahava, Hilkhot Berakhot* 3:5; *Shulḥan Arukh, Oraḥ Ḥayyim* 212:1).

### NOTES

**Any food that is primary and a secondary food is with it** – כָּל שֶׁהוּא עִיקָּר וְעִמּוֹ טְפֵלָה: This mishna comes primarily to teach that it is conceivable that even bread, the most significant food as far as blessings are concerned, can be considered secondary to another food (*Talmidei Rabbeinu Yona, Tosefot Rabbeinu Yehuda HaḤasid* and others). The formulation of the principle comes to teach that even in a case where the primary and secondary foods are not actually eaten together, the primary still exempts the secondary (*Alfasi Zuta*).

**With regard to those who eat fruits of Genosar** – בְּאוֹכְלֵי פֵּירוֹת גְּנוֹסַר: Some explain that the fig juice causes one's lips to hurt and only salted foods allay that pain (*ge'onim*).

**And was prepared to swear...** – וּמִשְׁתַּבַּע וכו׳: This does not mean that Rabbi Yoḥanan would have actually taken an oath that he did not eat. Rather, it is an expression employing poetic license saying that it was as if he had not eaten and was still hungry (*Sefer Ḥasidim*).

### BACKGROUND

**Genosar** – גְּנוֹסַר: Genosar is the name of a beautiful valley that stretches along the western shore of the Sea of Galilee, north of Tiberias.

Josephus describes the area as follows: "Its nature is wonderful as well as its beauty; its soil is so fruitful that all sorts of trees can grow upon it, and the inhabitants accordingly plant all sorts of trees there; for the temper of the air is so well mixed, that it agrees very well with those several sorts, particularly walnuts, which require the coldest air, flourish there in vast plenty; there are palm trees also, which grow best in hot air; fig trees also and olives grow near them, which yet require an air that is more temperate. It supplies men with the principal fruits, with grapes and figs continually during ten months of the year and the rest of the fruits as they become ripe together through the whole year; for besides the good temperature of the air, it is also watered from a most fertile fountain" (Wars of the Jews, Book III, 10:8).

**Sardines** – טָרִית: The *Sardinella* is a common species of fish indigenous to the Mediterranean in great numbers, which are often eaten salted. They are among the items for which the shores of Eretz Yisrael were praised.

One of the types of sardine, the spotted-fin sardine

## HALAKHA

**One who ate grapes and figs and pomegranates – אָכַל עֲנָבִים וּתְאֵנִים וְרִמּוֹנִים:** Over the five species of fruit for which Eretz Yisrael was praised, grapes, figs, pomegranates, olives, and dates, one recites beforehand: Who creates fruit of the tree, before eating; and one blessing abridged from the three blessings of Grace after Meals, thereafter. The formula for the conclusion of the blessing after eating fruit from Eretz Yisrael is: For the land and for its fruit, while the conclusion of the blessing after eating fruit from outside of Eretz Yisrael is: For the land and for the fruit. This is in accordance with the opinion of the Rabbis and the conclusion of the Gemara (Rambam *Sefer Ahava, Hilkhot Berakhot* 8:1, 14; *Shulḥan Arukh, Oraḥ Ḥayyim* 208:1, 10).

## BACKGROUND

**Five species of grain – חֲמֵשֶׁת מִינֵי דָגָן:** These are the varieties of seed to which the *halakhot* relating to agricultural produce in Eretz Yisrael apply. The Mishna lists the five species as *ḥittim, se'orim, kusmin, shibbolet shu'al,* and *shifon* (*Ḥalla* 1:1), which are commonly, albeit inaccurately, translated as wheat, barley, spelt, oats, and rye. All five species grew in Eretz Yisrael in ancient times. Neither oats nor rye grew there then.

The five species of grain are referred to in talmudic literature by the generic names *tevu'a* (*Ḥalla* 1:2) and *dagan*, i.e., grain. The precise identity of the five species is difficult to determine. Professor Yehuda Feliks maintains that three of the five are species of the *Triticum* genus, wheat, and identifies *ḥittim* as durum wheat, used primarily for bread (*Triticum durumand vulgare*); *kusmin* as rice wheat (*Triticum dicoccum*); *shifon* as spelt wheat (*Triticum spelta*); the other two species are of the *Horedeum* genus, barley; *se'orim* are six- and four-rowed barley (*Hordeumsativum* and *vulgare*); and *shibbolet shu'al* is two-rowed barley (*Hordeum distichum*).

אָמַר רַב: כָּל סְעוּדָה שֶׁאֵין בָּהּ מֶלַח אֵינָהּ סְעוּדָה. אָמַר רַבִּי חִיָּיא בַּר אַבָּא אָמַר רַבִּי יוֹחָנָן: כָּל סְעוּדָה שֶׁאֵין בָּהּ שָׁרִיף אֵינָהּ סְעוּדָה.

On the topic of salted food, **Rav said: Any meal in which there is no salt is not** considered **a meal. Rabbi Ḥiyya bar Abba said** that **Rabbi Yoḥanan said: Any meal in which there is no** cooked item with **gravy** (Rashi) **is not** considered **a meal.**

מתני׳ אָכַל עֲנָבִים וּתְאֵנִים וְרִמּוֹנִים – מְבָרֵךְ אַחֲרֵיהֶם שָׁלֹשׁ בְּרָכוֹת, דִּבְרֵי רַבָּן גַּמְלִיאֵל. וַחֲכָמִים אוֹמְרִים: בְּרָכָה אַחַת מֵעֵין שָׁלֹשׁ. רַבִּי עֲקִיבָא אוֹמֵר: אֲפִילּוּ אָכַל שֶׁלֶק וְהוּא מְזוֹנוֹ – מְבָרֵךְ עָלָיו שָׁלֹשׁ בְּרָכוֹת. הַשּׁוֹתֶה מַיִם לִצְמָאוֹ – מְבָרֵךְ "שֶׁהַכֹּל נִהְיָה בִּדְבָרוֹ"; רַבִּי טַרְפוֹן אוֹמֵר: "בּוֹרֵא נְפָשׁוֹת רַבּוֹת וְחֶסְרוֹנָן".

**MISHNA** **One who ate** from the fruit for which Eretz Yisrael was praised, **grapes and figs and pomegranates,**[H] **recites** the **three blessings** of Grace after Meals, as he would after eating bread; this is **the statement of Rabban Gamliel. And the Rabbis say:** One need only recite **one blessing abridged from** the **three** blessings of Grace after Meals. **Rabbi Akiva says:** The three blessings of Grace after Meals are not restricted to bread; rather, **even if one ate boiled vegetables, but it is** his primary **sustenance, he recites** the **three blessings** of Grace after Meals. Additionally: **One who drinks water** to quench **his thirst recites: By whose word all things came to be. Rabbi Tarfon says:** He recites: **Who creates the many forms of life and their needs.**

גמ׳ מַאי טַעְמָא דְּרַבָּן גַּמְלִיאֵל? – דִּכְתִיב: "אֶרֶץ חִטָּה וּשְׂעֹרָה" וגו׳, וּכְתִיב: "אֶרֶץ אֲשֶׁר לֹא בְמִסְכֵּנֻת תֹּאכַל בָּהּ לֶחֶם" וגו׳, וּכְתִיב: "וְאָכַלְתָּ וְשָׂבָעְתָּ וּבֵרַכְתָּ אֶת ה׳ אֱלֹהֶיךָ".

**GEMARA** The Gemara asks: **What is the reason** for the opinion **of Rabban Gamliel?** The Gemara responds: **As it is written** in the verse that deals in praise of Eretz Yisrael: **"A land of wheat and barley,** vines, figs, and pomegranates, a land of olive oil and honey" (Deuteronomy 8:8), **and it is written: "A land in which you will eat bread without scarcity"** (Deuteronomy 8:9), **and it is written: "And you will eat and be satisfied and then you shall bless the Lord your God** for the good land He has given you" (Deuteronomy 8:10). Rabban Gamliel concludes from here that the fruits for which Eretz Yisrael was praised are included in the mitzva to recite a blessing after eating. Since that Torah portion alludes to three blessings, fruit also requires three blessings.

וְרַבָּנַן? – "אֶרֶץ" הִפְסִיק הָעִנְיָן. וְרַבָּן גַּמְלִיאֵל נַמִי, "אֶרֶץ" הִפְסִיק הָעִנְיָן! – הַהוּא מִבְּעֵי לֵיהּ לְמַעוֹטֵי הַכּוֹסֵס אֶת הַחִטָּה.

**And** what do **the Rabbis** hold? The verse: **"A land** in which you will eat bread without scarcity," **concluded** discussion of **that matter,** and the mitzva: "You will eat and be satisfied and then you shall bless," applies only to bread. **And** if so, according to **Rabban Gamliel as well, doesn't "land" conclude** discussion of **that matter? Rather, that** verse **is necessary** in order **to exclude one who chews** raw **wheat** from the obligation to recite Grace after Meals. Even according to Rabban Gamliel, it does not have the legal status of bread.

אָמַר רַבִּי יַעֲקֹב בַּר אִידִי אָמַר רַבִּי חֲנִינָא: כָּל שֶׁהוּא מֵחֲמֵשֶׁת הַמִּינִין – בַּתְּחִלָּה מְבָרֵךְ עָלָיו "בּוֹרֵא מִינֵי מְזוֹנוֹת", וּלְבַסּוֹף בְּרָכָה אַחַת מֵעֵין שָׁלֹשׁ.

**Rabbi Ya'akov bar Idi said** that **Rabbi Ḥanina said: Anything that is from the five species** of grain,[B] **at the start, one recites over it: Who creates the various kinds of nourishment, and at the end one blessing abridged from** the **three** blessings of Grace after Meals

אָמַר רַבָּה בַּר מָרִי אָמַר רַבִּי יְהוֹשֻׁעַ בֶּן לֵוִי: כֹּל שֶׁהוּא מִשִּׁבְעַת הַמִּינִין – בַּתְּחִלָּה מְבָרֵךְ "בּוֹרֵא פְּרִי הָעֵץ" וּלְבַסּוֹף בְּרָכָה אַחַת מֵעֵין שָׁלֹשׁ.

**Rabba bar Mari said** that **Rabbi Yehoshua ben Levi said: Anything that is from the seven species** for which the Eretz Yisrael was praised, **at the start, one recites over it: Who creates fruit of the tree, and** afterward and **at the end, one blessing abridged from** the **three** blessings of Grace after Meals.

אָמַר לֵיהּ אַבַּיֵי לְרַב דִּימִי: מַאי נִיהוּ בְּרָכָה אַחַת מֵעֵין שָׁלֹשׁ? – אָמַר לֵיהּ: אַפֵּירֵי דְעֵץ – "עַל הָעֵץ וְעַל פְּרִי הָעֵץ וְעַל תְּנוּבַת הַשָּׂדֶה וְעַל אֶרֶץ חֶמְדָּה טוֹבָה וּרְחָבָה שֶׁהִנְחַלְתָּ לַאֲבוֹתֵינוּ לֶאֱכוֹל מִפִּרְיָהּ וְלִשְׂבּוֹעַ מִטּוּבָהּ, רַחֵם ה׳ אֱלֹהֵינוּ עַל יִשְׂרָאֵל עַמֶּךָ וְעַל יְרוּשָׁלַיִם עִירֶךָ וְעַל מִקְדָּשְׁךָ וְעַל מִזְבַּחֲךָ וְתִבְנֶה יְרוּשָׁלַיִם עִיר קָדְשְׁךָ בִּמְהֵרָה בְיָמֵינוּ וְהַעֲלֵנוּ לְתוֹכָהּ וְשַׂמְּחֵנוּ בָּהּ כִּי אַתָּה טוֹב וּמֵטִיב לַכֹּל".

**Abaye said to Rav Dimi: What is the** formula of **one blessing abridged from** the **three** blessings of Grace after Meals? He said to him: **Over fruits of a tree one recites:**

**For the tree and the fruit of the tree,**
**and for the produce of the field,**
**and for the desirable, good and spacious land that you gave as heritage to our ancestors**
**that they might eat of its fruit and be satisfied with its goodness.**
**Have compassion, Lord our God,**
**upon Israel Your people and upon Jerusalem Your city,**
**and upon Your Temple and upon Your altar.**
**May You rebuild Jerusalem, Your holy city, swiftly in our time,**
**and may You bring us back there rejoicing in it**
**as You are good and do good to all.**

דַּחֲמֵשֶׁת הַמִּינִין – "עַל הַמִּחְיָה וְעַל הַכַּלְכָּלָה וְעַל תְּנוּבַת הַשָּׂדֶה" כו׳ וְחוֹתֵם "עַל הָאָרֶץ וְעַל הַמִּחְיָה".

After eating products baked from one of the **five species** of grain, one recites: **For the nourishment and sustenance and for the produce of the field, and he concludes: For the land and for the nourishment.**

מֵיחָתֵם בְּמַאי חָתֵים? כִּי אֲתָא רַב דִּימִי אֲמַר: רַב חָתֵים בְּרֹאשׁ חֹדֶשׁ "בָּרוּךְ מְקַדֵּשׁ יִשְׂרָאֵל וְרָאשֵׁי חֳדָשִׁים". הָכָא מַאי?

However, the question was raised: In terms of **conclusion, with what does he conclude** the blessing?[N] As one does not conclude a blessing with two themes, with which of the themes should he conclude the blessing? **When Rav Dimi came** from Eretz Yisrael to Babylonia **he said: Rav** would **conclude** the blessing **on the New Moon: Blessed…Who sanctifies Israel and the New Moons.** Apparently, one can conclude a blessing with two themes. **What** does one recite **here?**

רַב חִסְדָּא אָמַר: "עַל הָאָרֶץ וְעַל פֵּירוֹתֶיהָ"; וְרַבִּי יוֹחָנָן אָמַר: "עַל הָאָרֶץ וְעַל הַפֵּירוֹת". אָמַר רַב עַמְרָם: וְלָא פְּלִיגִי, הָא – לָן, וְהָא – לְהוּ.

**Rav Ḥisda said: For the land and for its fruits. Rabbi Yoḥanan said: For the land and for the fruits. Rav Amram said: They do not disagree;** rather, **this** blessing, for its fruits, is **for us,** in Babylonia, **and this** blessing, for the fruits, is for **them,** in Eretz Yisrael.

מַתְקִיף לָהּ רַב נַחְמָן בַּר יִצְחָק: אִינְהוּ אָכְלִי וַאֲנַן מְבָרְכִין?! אֶלָּא אֵיפוּךְ: רַב חִסְדָּא אָמַר: "עַל הָאָרֶץ וְעַל הַפֵּירוֹת"; רַבִּי יוֹחָנָן אָמַר: "עַל הָאָרֶץ וְעַל פֵּירוֹתֶיהָ".

**Rav Naḥman bar Yitzḥak strongly objects: They,** in Eretz Yisrael, **eat and we,** in Babylonia, **recite a blessing?** How can we, residents of Babylonia, recite a blessing for the fruits of Eretz Yisrael while eating the fruits of Babylonia? **Rather, reverse** the opinions: **Rav Ḥisda said: For the land and for the fruits, and Rabbi Yoḥanan said: For the land and for its fruits.**

---

NOTES

**The conclusion of one blessing abridged from the three blessings of Grace after Meals – חֲתִימַת בְּרָכָה מֵעֵין שָׁלֹשׁ:** The question with regard to the conclusion of the blessing relates to the order of that conclusion. Not only is it problematic to conclude a blessing with two components, the issue, which component to recite first. also arises. Based on the content of the blessing, fruit should be mentioned first. Based on the natural order, the earth produces the fruit, so the earth should be recited first. Therefore, they used the example of the blessing on the New Moon, which concludes: Who sanctifies Israel and the New Moons. Even though Israel was not mentioned in the blessing, in the conclusion of the blessing Israel should be mentioned first because they sanctify the New Moon. The same is true with regard to mentioning the land prior to the fruits.

---

Perek **VI**
Daf **44** Amud **b**

אָמַר רַב יִצְחָק בַּר אַבְדִּימִי מִשּׁוּם רַבֵּינוּ: עַל הַבֵּיעָא וְעַל מִינֵי קוּפְרָא בִּתְחִלָּה מְבָרֵךְ "שֶׁהַכֹּל" וּלְבַסּוֹף "בּוֹרֵא נְפָשׁוֹת רַבּוֹת" וכו׳. אֲבָל יַרְקָא – לָא; וְרַבִּי יִצְחָק אָמַר: אֲפִילּוּ יַרְקָא, אֲבָל מַיָּא – לָא; וְרַב פָּפָּא אָמַר: אֲפִילּוּ מַיָּא.

**Rav Yitzḥak bar Avdimi said in the name of Rabbeinu,** Rav: **Over the egg and types of meat** [*kupra*],[L] **at the start, one recites: By Whose word all things came to be, and at the end: Who creates the many forms of life.**[H] **However,** after eating **vegetables, no,** one does not recite a blessing at all. **Rabbi Yitzḥak said: Even** after eating **vegetables** one recites a blessing; **but** after drinking **water, no,** one does not recite a blessing at all. **And Rav Pappa said: Even** after drinking **water** one must recite a blessing.

מָר זוּטְרָא עֲבִיד כְּרַב יִצְחָק בַּר אַבְדִּימִי, וְרַב שִׁימִי בַּר אַשִׁי עָבֵיד כְּרַבִּי יִצְחָק, וְסִימָנָךְ: חַד כִּתְרֵי וּתְרֵי כְּחַד.

**Mar Zutra acted in accordance with** the opinion of **Rabbi Yitzḥak bar Avdimi** and did not recite a blessing after eating vegetables, while **Rav Shimi bar Ashi acted in accordance with** the opinion of **Rabbi Yitzḥak** and recited a blessing after eating vegetables. **And a mnemonic** by which to remember which Sage acted in accordance with which: **One like two, and two like one.** In other words, Mar Zutra, who is known only by his name and not by his patronymic, acted in accordance with Rav Yitzḥak bar Avdimi who is known by both his name and his patronymic. Rav Shimi bar Ashi, who is known by both his names, followed the opinion of Rabbi Yitzḥak, who is known only by his first name.[N]

אָמַר רַב אַשִׁי: אֲנָא, זִמְנָא דְּכִי מִדְּכַרְנָא עֲבֵידְנָא כְּכוּלְּהוּ.

On this topic, **Rav Ashi said: At times when I remember,**[N] **I act in accordance with** the opinions of **all of them** and recite a blessing even after drinking water.

תְּנַן: כָּל שֶׁטָּעוּן בְּרָכָה לְאַחֲרָיו טָעוּן בְּרָכָה לְפָנָיו, וְיֵשׁ שֶׁטָּעוּן בְּרָכָה לְפָנָיו וְאֵין טָעוּן בְּרָכָה לְאַחֲרָיו. בִּשְׁלָמָא לְרַב יִצְחָק בַּר אַבְדִּימִי – לְאַפּוֹקֵי יַרְקָא, לְרַבִּי יִצְחָק – לְאַפּוֹקֵי מַיָּא, אֶלָּא לְרַב פָּפָּא לְאַפּוֹקֵי מַאי?

**We learned** in a mishna: **Anything that requires a blessing thereafter requires a blessing beforehand; and there are** items **that require a blessing beforehand and do not require a blessing thereafter.** If so, **granted, according to Rav Yitzḥak bar Avdimi's** opinion, it **excludes vegetables** from the requirement to recite a blessing thereafter. And, granted, **according to Rabbi Yitzḥak's** opinion as well, it **excludes water** from the requirement to recite a blessing thereafter. **However, according to Rav Pappa's opinion, what does it exclude?** What food requires a blessing before eating but does not require a blessing after eating?

לְאַפּוֹקֵי מִצְוֹת.

The Gemara answers: It comes **to exclude mitzvot,** as one recites a blessing before performing a mitzva, but not thereafter.

וְלִבְנֵי מַעַרְבָא דְּבָתַר דְּמַסְּלְקֵי תְּפִילַּיְיהוּ מְבָרְכִי "אֲשֶׁר קִדְּשָׁנוּ בְּמִצְוֹתָיו וְצִוָּנוּ לִשְׁמוֹר חֻקָּיו" – לְאַפּוֹקֵי מַאי?

The Gemara challenges: **And for the residents of the West,** Eretz Yisrael, **who, after they remove their phylacteries, recite: Who has made us holy through His mitzvot and commanded us to keep His laws,**[N] **what** does the *halakha* in the mishna **come to exclude?**

---

LANGUAGE

**Meat** [*kupra*] **– קוּפְרָא:** Apparently, the correct reading here is *kupeda*, from the Greek κοπάδιον, *kopadion*, perhaps via Syriac, meaning a piece of meat.

HALAKHA

**The obligation to recite the blessing: Who creates the many forms of life – חוֹבַת בִּרְכַּת בּוֹרֵא נְפָשׁוֹת:** After eating anything over which one recites beforehand: By Whose word all things came to be, as well as fruits of trees that are not among the seven species, and vegetables, one recites: Who creates the many forms of life and their needs. This is in accordance with the opinion of Rav Ashi, who was a late *amora* (Rambam *Sefer Ahava*, *Hilkhot Berakhot* 8:1; *Shulḥan Arukh*, *Oraḥ Ḥayyim* 204:1, 7).

NOTES

**The obligation to recite a blessing afterward – חוֹבַת בְּרָכָה אַחֲרוֹנָה:** Several explanations were offered as to why it is more obvious that one is required to recite a blessing before eating certain foods than it is to recite a blessing thereafter. Some explain that the blessings recited after eating are derived from the verse in the Torah that enumerates the seven species. Therefore, it is unclear whether or not the obligation extends to other foods (*Penei Yehoshua*). Others suggest that, after eating, one recites a blessing over the lingering taste of the food; but water, for example, has no lingering taste (*Tosefot Rabbeinu Yehuda HaḤasid*).

**At times when I remember – זִמְנָא דְּכִי מִדְּכַרְנָא:** Some explain this as follows: If Rav Ashi forgot to recite a blessing before drinking water, even if he had almost finished drinking, he would recite the blessing on the water. When he finished, he would recite the final blessing, even though it seems redundant (*Tal Torah*).

**To keep His laws – לִשְׁמוֹר חֻקָּיו:** It seems that the blessing: To keep His statutes, was a type of concluding blessing recited by an individual after completing the performance of a mitzva, offering praise and thanks for the fact that one had the privilege to fulfill God's will (Ramban in tractate *Nidda*).

## HALAKHA

To exclude fragrances – לְאַפּוֹקֵי רֵיחָנֵי: There is no blessing recited after smelling a fragrance (*Shulḥan Arukh, Oraḥ Ḥayyim* 216:1).

## BACKGROUND

Leeks – כְּרֵישִׁין: *Allium porrum*, is an edible vegetable botanically related to onion and garlic. Its long, flat leaves, ranging in length from 5–30 cm, form a kind of stalk. Today leeks are used as a spice in cooking soup or meat. In the East, however, leeks are still eaten uncooked. Some commentators state that the *ḥatzir* included among the foods mentioned with nostalgia by those who left Egypt (Numbers 11:5) is the leek, which was a common garden vegetable in ancient Egypt.

Leek

Cabbage – כְּרוּב: Cabbage is a popular cultivar of the species *Brassica oleracea Linne* (*Capitata* Group) of the *Brassicaceae* (or *Cruciferae*) family and is a leafy green vegetable. It is a herbaceous, biennial, dicotyledonous flowering plant, distinguished by a short stem upon which there is crowded a mass of leaves, usually green but in some varieties red or purplish. While immature, it forms a characteristic compact, globular cluster known as a head of cabbage. Cabbage is an excellent source of vitamin C. It also contains significant amounts of glutamine, an amino acid that has anti-inflammatory properties.

Cabbage

לְאַפּוֹקֵי רֵיחָנֵי.

The Gemara responds: It serves **to exclude** types of **fragrances.**[H] Everyone agrees that no blessing is recited after smelling them.

אָמַר רַבִּי יַנַּאי אָמַר רַבִּי: כֹּל שֶׁהוּא כְּבֵיצָה – בֵּיצָה טוֹבָה מִמֶּנּוּ. כִּי אֲתָא רָבִין אֲמַר: טָבָא בֵּיעֲתָא מְגוּלְגַּלְתָּא מִשִּׁיתָּא קַיְיסֵי סוּלְתָּא. כִּי אֲתָא רַב דִּימִי אֲמַר: טָבָא בֵּיעֲתָא מְגוּלְגַּלְתָּא מִשִּׁיתָּא, מְטוּיְתָא מֵאַרְבַּע, מְבוּשַּׁלְתָּא – כֹּל שֶׁהוּא כְּבֵיצָה בֵּיצָה טוֹבָה הֵימֶנּוּ, לְבַר מִבִּשְׂרָא.

Since the blessing recited over an egg was mentioned, the Gemara cites what **Rabbi Yannai said** that **Rabbi** Yehuda HaNasi **said: Anything that is an egg's equivalent** in volume, **an egg is superior to it.** Similarly, **when Ravin came** from Eretz Yisrael to Babylonia **he said: A lightly cooked egg is better than six** ***log*** **of fine flour.** Similarly, **when Rav Dimi came** from Eretz Yisrael to Babylonia **he said: A lightly cooked egg is better than six** *log* of fine flour, a **roasted** egg is better than **four,** and with regard to a **cooked** egg, they said: **Anything that is an egg's equivalent, an egg is superior to it.**

״רַבִּי עֲקִיבָא אוֹמֵר: אֲפִילּוּ אָכַל שֶׁלֶק״ כּוּ׳. וּמִי אִיכָּא מִידֵּי דַּהֲוָה שֶׁלֶק מְזוֹנֵי?! אָמַר רַב אָשֵׁי: בְּקֶלַח שֶׁל כְּרוּב שָׁנוּ.

We learned in the mishna that **Rabbi Akiva says: Even** if **one ate boiled vegetables, but it is his** primary **sustenance, he recites** the **three blessings** of Grace after Meals, as he would after eating bread. The Gemara asks: **And is there a** vegetable **where in its boiled** state **it is** primary **sustenance? Rav Ashi said: This was taught** with regard to **a cabbage stalk,** which is nourishing.

תָּנוּ רַבָּנַן: טְחוֹל – יָפֶה לַשִּׁינַּיִם וְקָשֶׁה לִבְנֵי מֵעַיִם, כְּרֵישִׁין – קָשִׁין לַשִּׁינַּיִם וְיָפִין לִבְנֵי מֵעַיִם. כָּל יָרָק חַי מוֹרִיק, וְכָל קָטָן מַקְטִין, וְכָל נֶפֶשׁ מֵשִׁיב אֶת הַנֶּפֶשׁ, וְכָל קָרוֹב לַנֶּפֶשׁ מֵשִׁיב אֶת הַנֶּפֶשׁ. כְּרוּב לְמָזוֹן וּתְרָדִין לִרְפוּאָה, אוֹי לוֹ לַבַּיִת שֶׁהַלֶּפֶת עוֹבֶרֶת בְּתוֹכוֹ.

Similarly, **the Sages taught** in a *baraita* dealing with types of sustenance: Meat of the **spleen is beneficial for the teeth and harmful for the intestines. Leeks,**[B] however, **are harmful for the teeth and beneficial for the intestines.** They also said that **all raw vegetables** turn one's face **pale.** Generally speaking, **anything small** that has not yet reached its full size is harmful and **impedes growth, and any living creature** eaten whole, e.g., a fully grown fish, **restores the soul. And anything close to the soul restores the soul. Cabbage**[B] **is for nourishment and beets for healing. Woe unto the house through which the turnip passes,** for it is extremely harmful.

אָמַר מָר: טְחוֹל – יָפֶה לַשִּׁינַּיִם וְקָשֶׁה לִבְנֵי מֵעַיִם. מַאי תַּקַּנְתֵּיהּ? – נִלְעֲסֵיהּ וְנִשְׁדְּיֵיהּ.

**The Master said** in a *baraita*: **The spleen is beneficial for the teeth and harmful for the intestines.** The Gemara asks: **What is its remedy?** The Gemara responds: **One should chew it,** spit it out, **and throw it away.**

כְּרֵישִׁין – קָשִׁין לַשִּׁינַּיִם וְיָפִין לִבְנֵי מֵעַיִם. מַאי תַּקַּנְתֵּיהּ? – לִשְׁלְקִינְהוּ וְנִבְלְעִינְהוּ.

**Leeks are harmful for the teeth and beneficial for the intestines.** The Gemara asks: **What is its remedy?** The Gemara responds: **One should boil them and swallow them** without chewing.

כָּל יָרָק חַי מוֹרִיק. אָמַר רַבִּי יִצְחָק: בִּסְעוּדָה רִאשׁוֹנָה שֶׁל אַחַר הַקָּזָה.

**All raw vegetables** turn one's face **pale. Rabbi Yitzḥak said:** It refers here **to the first meal after bloodletting,** when a person should eat more substantial food.

וְאָמַר רַבִּי יִצְחָק: כָּל הָאוֹכֵל יָרָק קוֹדֶם אַרְבַּע שָׁעוֹת – אָסוּר לְסַפֵּר הֵימֶנּוּ. מַאי טַעְמָא? מִשּׁוּם רֵיחָא. וְאָמַר רַבִּי יִצְחָק: אָסוּר לְאָדָם שֶׁיֹּאכַל יָרָק חַי קוֹדֶם אַרְבַּע שָׁעוֹת.

**And Rabbi Yitzḥak said: Anyone who eats vegetables before four hours** of the day, **it is forbidden to speak with him.** The Gemara asks: **What is the reason?** The Gemara explains: This is **because the smell** of vegetables from his mouth bothers others who have not yet eaten. **And** in general, **Rabbi Yitzḥak said: It is forbidden to eat raw vegetables before four hours** of the day.

אַמֵימָר וּמָר זוּטְרָא וְרַב אָשֵׁי הֲווּ יָתְבִי, אַיְיתוּ קַמַּיְיהוּ יָרָק חַי קוֹדֶם אַרְבַּע שָׁעוֹת, אַמֵימָר וְרַב אָשֵׁי אֲכוּל וּמָר זוּטְרָא לָא אֲכַל. אָמְרוּ לֵיהּ: מַאי דַּעְתִּיךְ – דְּאָמַר רַבִּי יִצְחָק: כָּל הָאוֹכֵל יָרָק קוֹדֶם אַרְבַּע שָׁעוֹת אָסוּר לְסַפֵּר הֵימֶנּוּ, מִשּׁוּם רֵיחָא – וְהָא אֲנַן דְּקָא אָכְלִינַן וְקָא מִשְׁתָּעֵית בַּהֲדַן!

The Gemara relates that **Ameimar, Mar Zutra, and Rav Ashi were sitting. They brought raw vegetables before them before four hours** of the day. **Ameimar and Rav Ashi ate and Mar Zutra did not eat. They said to him: What is your thinking** that led you not to eat? Was it because **Rabbi Yitzḥak said: Anyone who eats vegetables before four hours** of the day, **it is forbidden to speak with him because of the smell? Aren't we eating and you are** nevertheless **speaking with us?**

אֲמַר לְהוּ: אֲנָא כְּאִידַּךְ דְּרַבִּי יִצְחָק סְבִירָא לִי, דְּאָמַר רַבִּי יִצְחָק: אָסוּר לְאָדָם שֶׁיֹּאכַל יָרָק חַי קוֹדֶם אַרְבַּע שָׁעוֹת.

**He said to them: I hold in accordance with the other** *halakha* of **Rabbi Yitzḥak, as Rabbi Yitzḥak said** simply: **It is forbidden to eat raw vegetables before four hours** of the day.

כָּל קָטָן מַקְטִין. אָמַר רַב חִסְדָּא: אֲפִילּוּ גַּדְיָא בַּר זוּזָא. וְלָא אֲמַרַן אֶלָּא דְּלֵית בֵּיהּ רִבְעָא, אֲבָל אִית בֵּיהּ רִבְעָא – לֵית לַן בַּהּ.

**Anything small impedes growth. Rav Ḥisda said:** This applies **even to a small goat,** worth a ***zuz***. Although the goat is worth a *zuz*, it is still small. **And we only said** this with regard **to** a goat that **has not** reached **one fourth** of its ultimate size. **But** if **it has** reached **one fourth** of its ultimate size, **we need not** be concerned.

כָּל נֶפֶשׁ מֵשִׁיב נֶפֶשׁ. אָמַר רַב פָּפָּא: אֲפִילּוּ גִּילְדָּנֵי דְּבֵי גִּילֵי.

**And any living creature** eaten whole **restores the soul. Rav Pappa said:** This includes **even small fish** that grow **among the reeds,**[B] as even a small creature is beneficial if it reached its full size.

כָּל הַקָּרוֹב לַנֶּפֶשׁ מֵשִׁיב אֶת הַנֶּפֶשׁ; אָמַר רַב אַחָא בַּר יַעֲקֹב: עוּנְקָא. אָמַר לֵיהּ רָבָא לְשַׁמָּעֵיהּ: כִּי מַיְיתִית לִי אוּמְצָא דְּבִשְׂרָא, טְרַח וְאַיְיתִי לִי מֵהֵיכָא דְּמִקָּרַב לְבֵי בָּרוּךְ.

**Anything close to the soul**[N] **restores the soul. Rav Aḥa bar Ya'akov said:** This refers to the **neck,** which is close to the animal's vital organs. The Gemara relates that **Rava said to his servant: When you bring me a piece of meat, make an effort to bring me** a piece **from the place of the blessing,** the neck, where the animal was slaughtered and the slaughterer recited a blessing over the ritual slaughter.

כְּרוּב לְמָזוֹן וּתְרָדִין לִרְפוּאָה. כְּרוּב, לְמָזוֹן אִין וְלִרְפוּאָה לָא?! וְהָא תַּנְיָא: שִׁשָּׁה דְּבָרִים מְרַפְּאִין אֶת הַחוֹלֶה מֵחָלְיוֹ וּרְפוּאָתָן רְפוּאָה, וְאֵלּוּ הֵן: כְּרוּב, וּתְרָדִין, וּמֵי סִיסִין, דְּבַשׁ, וְקֵיבָה, וְהֶרֶת, וְיוֹתֶרֶת הַכָּבֵד! אֶלָּא אֵימָא: כְּרוּב אַף לְמָזוֹן.

**Cabbage for nourishment and beets for healing.** The Gemara asks: Is **cabbage** good **for nourishment and not for healing? Wasn't it taught** in a *baraita*: **Six things cure the ill person of his disease**[N] **and their cure is an** effective **cure, and these are: Cabbage, beets, chamomile**[B] **water, honey, stomach, *heret*, and liver.** Evidently, cabbage is also good for healing. The Gemara responds: **Rather, say: Cabbage is even for sustenance** and all the more so for healing, which is not the case with beets.

אוֹי לוֹ לַבַּיִת שֶׁהַלֶּפֶת עוֹבֶרֶת בְּתוֹכוֹ. אִינִי?! וְהָא אָמַר לֵיהּ רַב לְשַׁמָּעֵיהּ: כִּי חָזֵית לִיפְתָּא בְּשׁוּקָא – לָא תֵּימָא לִי: בְּמַאי כָּרְכַתְּ רִיפְתָּא!

**Woe unto the house through which the turnip passes,** as it is extremely damaging. The Gemara asks: **Is that so? Didn't Rav say to his servant: When you see a turnip in the market, do not ask me with what will you eat your bread today?** Buy the turnip and bring it for the meal. Apparently, the turnip is a significant and appropriate food.

אָמַר אַבַּיֵי: מִבְּלִי בָּשָׂר; וְרָבָא אָמַר: מִבְּלִי יַיִן. אִיתְּמַר, רַב אָמַר: מִבְּלִי בָּשָׂר; וּשְׁמוּאֵל אָמַר: מִבְּלִי עֵצִים; וְרַבִּי יוֹחָנָן אָמַר: מִבְּלִי יַיִן.

**Abaye said:** The turnip is harmful only when it is eaten **without meat. And Rava said: Without wine. It was stated** that **Rav said:** The turnip is harmful when it is eaten **without meat. And Shmuel said: Without wood,** meaning when it is not properly cooked. **And Rabbi Yoḥanan said: Without wine.**

אָמַר לֵיהּ רָבָא לְרַב פָּפָּא: סוּדָנִי, אֲנַן תָּבְרִינַן לַהּ בְּבִשְׂרָא וְחַמְרָא, אַתּוּן דְּלָא נְפִישׁ לְכוּ חַמְרָא – בְּמַאי תָּבְרִיתוּ לַהּ? – אָמַר לֵיהּ: בְּצִיבֵי. כִּי הָא דְּבֵיתְהוּ דְּרַב פָּפָּא בָּתַר דִּמְבַשְּׁלָא לַהּ – תָּבְרָא לַהּ בִּתְמָנָן אוּפֵי פָּרְסָיָיתָא.

Along the same lines, **Rava said to Rav Pappa: Farmer** (*ge'onim*) **we break** the harmful aspects of the turnip **with meat and wine. You, who do not have a lot of wine, with what do you break its** harmful aspects? Rav Pappa **said to him: With wood. As that** is what **Rav Pappa's wife** would do. **After she cooked** the turnip, **she would break it with eighty pieces** of wood **from a palm tree.**

תָּנוּ רַבָּנַן: דָּג קָטָן מָלִיחַ פְּעָמִים שֶׁהוּא מֵמִית – בְּשִׁבְעָה, בְּשִׁבְעָה עָשָׂר, וּבְעֶשְׂרִים וְשִׁבְעָה; וְאָמְרִי לַהּ: בְּעֶשְׂרִים וּשְׁלֹשָׁה. וְלָא אֲמַרַן אֶלָּא בְּמָטוּי וְלָא מָטוּי, אֲבָל מָטוּי שַׁפִּיר – לֵית לַן בַּהּ; וּדְלָא מָטוּי שַׁפִּיר לָא אֲמַרַן אֶלָּא דְּלָא שָׁתָה בָּתְרֵיהּ שִׁכְרָא, אֲבָל שָׁתָה בָּתְרֵיהּ שִׁכְרָא לֵית לַן בַּהּ.

On the topic of foods, the Gemara cites what **the Sages taught** in a *baraita*: **A small salted fish sometimes kills,** specifically **seven** days, **seventeen** days, **and twenty-seven** days after it was salted. **And some say: Twenty-three. And we only said this when it is roasted and not roasted** well, **but** when it is **roasted well, we need not** be concerned. **And when it is not roasted well, we only said this when one does not drink beer thereafter; however,** when **one drinks beer thereafter, we need not** be concerned.

"וְהַשּׁוֹתֶה מַיִם לִצְמָאוֹ" וכו׳. לְאַפּוֹקֵי מַאי? – אָמַר רַב אִידִי בַּר אָבִין: לְאַפּוֹקֵי לְמַאן

We learned in the mishna that the *tanna'im* disagreed with regard to one who **drinks water** to quench **his thirst.**[H] The Gemara asks: **What does** this emphasis on his thirst come **to exclude? Rav Idi bar Avin said:** It comes **to exclude one**

**BACKGROUND**

Small fish that grow among the reeds – גִּילְדָּנֵי דְּבֵי גִּילֵי: Apparently, these small fish, which live among the reeds, are a species of toothcarp, *Cyprinodon*. They grow to only a few centimeters in length and, unlike regular carp, have mouths full of teeth.

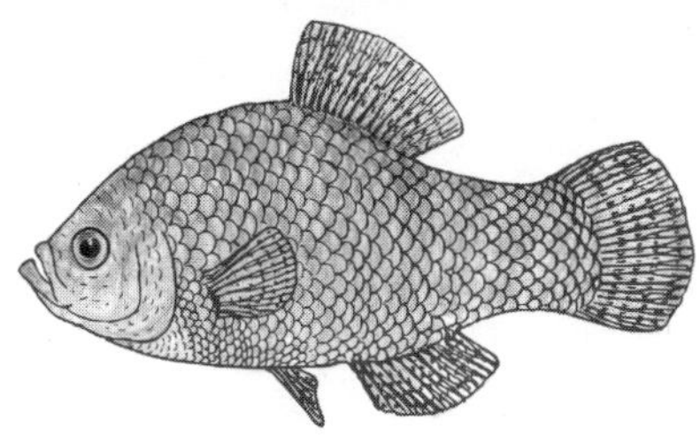

Toothcarp

Chamomile – סִיסִין: According to the *ge'onim*, these are the *Matricaria chamomilla*, from the *Asteraceae* family, which grow wild in Eretz Yisrael even today. They are annual, fragrant plants whose leaves split into multiple lobes. The flowers are arranged in a circle, such that the sepals are white and the petals are yellow. This plant is still used medicinally. It is prepared as a tea to aid with digestive problems and colds as well as to treat various external wounds.

Chamomile plant in bloom

**NOTES**

Anything close to the soul – כָּל הַקָּרוֹב לַנֶּפֶשׁ: Close to the place that the soul leaves the body, i.e., the neck. This is the sense of the verse, "Because the blood is the soul" (Deuteronomy 12:23, see Maharsha).

Six things cure the ill of his disease – שִׁשָּׁה דְּבָרִים מְרַפְּאִין אֶת הַחוֹלֶה מֵחָלְיוֹ: These six items were enumerated because they are foods that even healthy people eat. The *baraita* came to teach that they have medicinal value (*ge'onim*).

**HALAKHA**

One who drinks water to quench his thirst – וְהַשּׁוֹתֶה מַיִם לִצְמָאוֹ וכו׳: One who drinks water to quench his thirst recites a blessing beforehand. One who drinks water to facilitate swallowing the food in his throat does not recite a blessing (*Shulḥan Arukh*, *Oraḥ Ḥayyim* 204:7).

דַּחֲנַקְתֵּיהּ אוּמְצָא.

**who was choked by a piece of meat** and drank water in order to wash it down. He need not recite a blessing.

רַבִּי טַרְפוֹן אוֹמֵר: ״בּוֹרֵא נְפָשׁוֹת רַבּוֹת וְחֶסְרוֹנָן״. אֲמַר לֵיהּ רָבָא בַּר רַב חָנָן לְאַבַּיֵי, וְאָמְרִי לַהּ לְרַב יוֹסֵף: הִלְכְתָא מַאי? – אֲמַר לֵיהּ: פּוּק חֲזִי מַאי עַמָּא דָּבַר.

We learned in the mishna that **Rabbi Tarfon says:** Over water one recites:[H] **Who creates the many forms of life and their needs. Rava bar Rav Ḥanan said to Abaye, and some say to Rav Yosef: What is the *halakha*[N]** in this dispute? **He said to him: Go out and observe what the people are doing** and act accordingly.

הדרן עלך כיצד מברכין

## HALAKHA

**Blessing over water** – בִּרְכַּת הַמַּיִם: Before drinking water, one recites: By Whose word all things came to be, and thereafter: Who creates the many forms of life and their needs, in accordance with the common custom of the people (*Shulḥan Arukh, Oraḥ Ḥayyim*, 204:7).

## NOTES

**What is the *halakha*** – הִלְכְתָא מַאי: This question was asked because Rabbi Tarfon's rationale is logical. Therefore, it was unclear whether the principle that the *halakha* is in accordance with the majority would apply in this matter (*Tosefot Rabbeinu Yehuda HaḤasid*).

# Summary of **Perek VI**

This chapter is devoted to a detailed discussion of one issue: Determining the parameters of the various items over which there is a requirement to recite blessings of enjoyment before partaking of them. This analysis, by its very nature, deals with numerous details and specific, defined questions.

The approach of the *tanna*, Rabbi Yehuda, and the other Sages who subscribed to his opinion seeks to increase the number of specific blessings and assign each food type, or limited group of food types, its own specific blessing. By contrast, the Rabbis ruled in favor of establishing a comprehensive system of blessings that progresses from the general to the specific.

Among the general distinctions in this chapter, the most central is the distinction between foods which do not grow in the ground, over which one recites: By Whose word all things came to be, and those which do grow in the ground. Within the latter category, there is a further distinction between fruits over which one recites: Who creates fruit of the ground, and those over which one recites: Who creates fruit of the tree. Furthermore, the Gemara arrives at a definition of the foods over which one recites: Who creates the various kinds of nourishment, i.e., various foods made from grains. A distinction is made between these foods and bread, which is made from the unadulterated five species of grain baked in the form of bread, over which one recites: Who brings forth bread from the earth.

Similarly, a general principle was established with regard to the *halakhot* of final blessings: If one is obligated to recite a blessing prior to eating a food item, then there is an obligation to recite a blessing thereafter as well. Although conclusions with regard to final blessings are only reached in the following chapter, the basis for these conclusions is established here.

# Introduction to **Perek VII**

*For the Lord your God is bringing you to a good land: a land with brooks of water, fountains and depths, springing forth in valleys and hills; a land of wheat and barley, vines and fig-trees and pomegranates, a land of olive oil and honey; a land in which you will eat bread without scarcity, you will lack nothing in it, a land whose stones are iron, and out of whose hills you will dig copper. You will eat and be satisfied, and bless the Lord, your God, for the good land He has given you.*

(Deuteronomy 8:7–10)

After the blessings of enjoyment were discussed in the previous chapter, this chapter is devoted to the blessing recited after the meal, Grace after Meals. This blessing is unique and more significant than the blessings of enjoyment as it is a mitzva by Torah law. Its component parts are also longer and more numerous than the formula of the blessings of enjoyment, and its *halakhot* are also numerous. Therefore, an entire chapter was devoted to it; it is the central theme of Chapter Seven, around which all of its myriad topics revolve.

Although there was also a discussion of Grace after Meals in the previous chapter, there it dealt with the question: What are the foods that obligate one to recite Grace after Meals? This chapter deals primarily with the prayer aspect of Grace after Meals. It also deals with the practical ramifications of the principle, which was accorded the authority of *halakha*, that blessings should not be recited over items that have been corrupted from a moral standpoint. The verse: "The covetous one who recites a blessing has blasphemed the Lord" (Psalms 10:3, according to the interpretation of one of the Sages), alludes to that fact and it is clear that reciting a blessing over any food whose consumption is prohibited is not a mitzva but quite the contrary. It is necessary to determine with regard to which food items these prohibitions apply.

Grace after Meals is fundamentally a blessing over the meal, as it is stated: "You will eat, and be satisfied, and bless the Lord." As one often dines in the company of others, the Gemara deals with various questions with regard to the procedure through which people dining may unite by means of the blessing of *zimmun*. The *zimmun* is a special blessing recited when several individuals happen to dine together. In this chapter, questions with regard to the number of people required to generate a *zimmun*, the essence of the connection between them in its formation and in its dissolution, and the formula of the *zimmun* blessing in various groupings are raised.

The *zimmun* blessing is also pivotal in the discussion of another fundamental issue addressed in this chapter. Apparently, *zimmun* is a component of Grace after Meals. Beyond the obligation to recite the *zimmun* and the fact that it is an integral component of Grace after Meals when the requisite forum is present, the Gemara must still ascertain the fundamental components of the obligation to recite the rest of Grace after Meals: What are the fundamental components of the basic obligation? Are all four blessings that comprise Grace after Meals of equal significance? How and in what circumstances may one abridge or omit any of them?

מתני׳ שְׁלֹשָׁה שֶׁאָכְלוּ כְּאַחַת חַיָּיבִין לְזַמֵּן. אָכַל דְּמַאי, וּמַעֲשֵׂר רִאשׁוֹן שֶׁנִּטְּלָה תְּרוּמָתוֹ, מַעֲשֵׂר שֵׁנִי וְהֶקְדֵּשׁ שֶׁנִּפְדּוּ, וְהַשַּׁמָּשׁ שֶׁאָכַל כַּזַּיִת, וְהַכּוּתִי – מְזַמְּנִין עָלָיו.

**MISHNA** This mishna sets out the essential *halakhot* pertaining to the invitation to recite Grace after Meals after a joint meal [*zimmun*]: **Three** people **who ate as one are required to form a *zimmun***[HB] and recite Grace after Meals.[B] If, among the diners, **one ate doubtfully tithed**[B] produce [***demai***],[B] **and first tithe**[B] **from which its *teruma***[B] **was** already **taken,**[H] or **second tithe,**[B] **and consecrated food that were redeemed** and therefore permitted to be eaten; **and** even **the waiter** who served the meal to the diners and **who ate** at least **an olive-bulk**[H] from the meal, **and the Samaritan [*Kuti*]**[B] who ate with two others at a meal; each of these people is included among the three **to obligate** those with whom they ate **in a *zimmun*.**[H]

## HALAKHA

**Three people who ate as one are required to form a *zimmun* – שְׁלֹשָׁה שֶׁאָכְלוּ כְּאַחַת חַיָּיבִין לְזַמֵּן:** Three who ate together are required to form a *zimmun* prior to reciting Grace after Meals (Rambam *Sefer Ahava*, *Hilkhot Berakhot* 5:2; *Shulḥan Arukh*, *Oraḥ Ḥayyim* 192:1).

**One ate doubtfully tithed produce [*demai*], and first tithe from which its *teruma* was already taken – אָכַל דְּמַאי וּמַעֲשֵׂר רִאשׁוֹן שֶׁנִּטְּלָה תְּרוּמָתוֹ:** One who eats *demai* or first tithe from which *teruma* was taken, even if it was taken improperly, as stated in the Gemara, or second tithe or consecrated property that were redeemed, may be included in a *zimmun* (Rambam *Sefer Ahava*, *Hilkhot Berakhot* 1:20).

**A waiter who ate an olive-bulk – וְהַשַּׁמָּשׁ שֶׁאָכַל כַּזַּיִת:** If a waiter ate an olive-bulk, he may be included in a *zimmun*. If not, he may not be included in a *zimmun* (*Shulḥan Arukh*, *Oraḥ Ḥayyim* 199:1).

**And the Samaritan [*Kuti*] obligates those with whom he ate in a *zimmun* – וְהַכּוּתִי מְזַמְּנִין עָלָיו:** Although the mishna permitted the inclusion of a *Kuti* in a *zimmun*, later generations in the Mishna and Talmud decreed that *Kutim* are like gentiles and cannot participate in any ritual act (Rif; Rosh; *Shulḥan Arukh*, *Oraḥ Ḥayyim* 199:2).

## BACKGROUND

***Zimmun* – זִמּוּן:** An introductory blessing to Grace after Meals, recited whenever at least three people eat together. Three men are required to recite this blessing; three women may recite the blessing. Women and men may not form a quorum of three together.

**Grace after Meals – בִּרְכַּת הַמָּזוֹן:** The blessing ordained in the Torah (Deuteronomy 8:10) to be recited after eating food. The Torah obligation to recite a blessing after food applies only to a meal that satisfies one's hunger, but the Sages require a person to say Grace after Meals after eating more than an olive-bulk of bread. The original structure of Grace after Meals contained three blessings: Who feeds all; the blessing of the land; Who builds Jerusalem. A fourth: Who is good and does good, was added later. It is not certain whether women are required by Torah law to recite Grace after Meals, but they are certainly required to do so by rabbinic ordinance. When three men eat together, Grace after Meals is preceded by an invitation [*zimmun*] to the participants in the meal to join together to recite Grace after Meals. Passages mentioning the sanctity of the day on Shabbat, Festivals, and other special occasions are added to Grace after Meals, as are petitionary prayers, according to local custom.

**Tithes – מַעַשְׂרוֹת:** Certain portions of agricultural produce are designated by Torah law for special purposes. According to most opinions, only grain, wine, and olive oil are required by Torah law to be tithed. By rabbinic decree, however, any food that grows from the ground must be tithed. There are three main tithes: First tithe, second tithe, and poor-man's tithe. These tithes are separated from produce after they ripen and are brought into the house. Ownerless produce is exempt from tithes, and therefore no tithes are taken during the Sabbatical year when all food growing from the ground is deemed ownerless. Similarly, food eaten in the course of a casual, incidental meal, i.e., eaten straight from the tree, need not be tithed. Most of the laws of tithes are described in tractate *Ma'asrot*.

**Doubtfully tithed produce [*demai*] – דְּמַאי:** *Demai* is produce, or food made from produce, which was purchased from a person who may not have separated the various tithes as required by *halakha*. The literal meaning of the word *demai* is suspicion, i.e., produce about which there is a suspicion that tithes were not properly taken from it. In the Second Temple period, the Sages decreed that this produce should be considered as having uncertain status, even though the owner claimed that he separated the tithes. Therefore, the buyer of this produce must tithe it himself. Nevertheless, since it was probable that the produce was in fact tithed, certain leniencies were permitted with regard to eating and using doubtfully tithed produce.

**First tithe – מַעֲשֵׂר רִאשׁוֹן:** After *teruma*, the portion of the crop given to the priests, is separated, one-tenth of the remaining produce is given to the Levites. This produce is called first tithe. The owner is permitted to give first tithe to any Levite he chooses. A Levite who received first tithe is required to set aside one-tenth of this tithe as *teruma* of the tithe and give it to a priest. The remaining first tithe, after the Levite set aside the *teruma* of the tithe, remains the Levite's property. It has no sanctity, and may be eaten by anyone. Produce from which first tithe was not set aside has the legal status of untithed produce, and may not be eaten. Since not everyone was conscientious about setting aside first tithe, the Sages instituted that one must separate this tithe from doubtfully tithed produce as well. in that case, however, it is not given to a Levite.

***Teruma* – תְּרוּמָה:** Whenever the term *teruma* appears without qualification, it refers to *teruma gedola*. Deuteronomy 18:4 commands: "The first fruit of your grain, of your wine, and of your oil" be given to the priest (see also Numbers 18:12). The Sages extended the scope of this commandment to include all produce. This commandment applies only in Eretz Yisrael. After the first fruits have been separated, a certain portion of the produce must be separated for priests. The Torah does not specify the amount of *teruma* that must be separated; one may theoretically fulfill one's obligation by giving even a single kernel of grain from an entire crop. The Sages established a measure: One-fortieth for a generous gift, one-fiftieth for an average gift, and one-sixtieth for a miserly gift. A person should not separate the other tithes until he separates *teruma*. *Teruma* is considered sacred and may only be eaten by a priest and his household while they are in a state of ritual purity (see Leviticus 22:9–15). To emphasize that state of ritual purity, the Sages obligated the priests to wash their hands before partaking of it. This is the source for the practice of washing the hands before eating. A ritually impure priest or a non-priest who eats *teruma* is subject to the penalty of death at the hand of Heaven. If *teruma* becomes ritually impure, it may no longer be eaten and must be burned. Nevertheless, it remains the property of the priest and he may benefit from its burning. Nowadays, *teruma* is not given to the priests because they have no definite proof of their priestly lineage. Nevertheless, the obligation to separate *teruma* remains; however, only a small portion of the produce is separated.

**Second tithe – מַעֲשֵׂר שֵׁנִי:** This is a tithe that is set aside after the *teruma* is given to the priests and the first tithe is given to the Levites. Second tithe is separated during the first, second, fourth, and fifth years of the Sabbatical cycle. After second tithe is set aside, it is brought to Jerusalem to be eaten there by its owner. If the journey to Jerusalem is too long and it would be difficult to transport all of the second tithe there, or if the produce became ritually impure, it could be redeemed for an equivalent sum of money. If the owner redeems his own produce, he is required to add one-fifth of its value. This redemption money is brought to Jerusalem, where it is spent on food. Second tithe can only be redeemed with minted coins bearing an imprint; unstamped coins and promissory notes cannot be used. Today, second tithe is still redeemed, but for a nominal sum, since in the absence of the Temple it is no longer brought to Jerusalem. The laws of second tithe are discussed in tractate *Ma'aser Sheni*.

**Samaritan [*Kuti*] – כּוּתִי:** They are the descendants of the nations displaced by Sennacherib, King of Assyria, and brought to settle in Eretz Yisrael. Eventually, they accepted upon themselves several mitzvot (II Kings 17). At the beginning of the Second Temple period, during the times of Ezra and Nehemiah, relations between the Samaritans and the Jews deteriorated. Later, the Samaritans established a center of worship on Mount Gerizim, establishing the sanctity of that mountain as one of the Ten Commandments. Consequently, the possibility that their blessings and prayers, although somewhat similar to the Jewish liturgy, might conclude in a manner antithetical to Judaism, was a very real one. Some generations of Jewish Sages recognized Samaritans as half-Jews. They went so far as to say: In the mitzvot that the Samaritans adopted, they are extremely exacting in their fulfillment, even more than the Jews are. Ultimately, as the Samaritans continued to distance themselves from the Jewish people in virtually every regard, they were accorded the legal status of gentiles.

אָכַל טֶבֶל, וּמַעֲשֵׂר רִאשׁוֹן שֶׁלֹּא נִטְּלָה תְּרוּמָתוֹ, וּמַעֲשֵׂר שֵׁנִי וְהֶקְדֵּשׁ שֶׁלֹּא נִפְדּוּ, וְהַשַּׁמָּשׁ שֶׁאָכַל פָּחוֹת מִכַּזַּיִת, וְהַנָּכְרִי – אֵין מְזַמְּנִין עָלָיו. נָשִׁים וַעֲבָדִים וּקְטַנִּים אֵין מְזַמְּנִין עֲלֵיהֶן. עַד כַּמָּה מְזַמְּנִין? עַד כַּזַּיִת; רַבִּי יְהוּדָה אוֹמֵר: עַד כַּבֵּיצָה.

However, **one who ate untithed produce** [***tevel***],[NHB] **and first tithe from which its *teruma* was not separated, and second tithe, and consecrated food that were not redeemed, and the waiter who did not eat an olive-bulk, and the gentile**[H] who ate with two Jews, none of these people is included among the three **to obligate** those with whom they ate **in a *zimmun*. Women, slaves, and minors**[H] **do not obligate** those with whom they ate **in a *zimmun*. How much** must one eat **to obligate** those with whom he ate **in a *zimmun*?**[H] **An olive-bulk** of food suffices to obligate those with whom they ate in a *zimmun*. **Rabbi Yehuda says: An egg-bulk** is the minimum measure to obligate those with whom they ate in a *zimmun*.

גמ׳ מְנָא הָנֵי מִילֵּי? אָמַר רַב אַסִּי: דְּאָמַר קְרָא ״גַּדְּלוּ לַה׳ אִתִּי וּנְרוֹמְמָה שְׁמוֹ יַחְדָּו״. רַבִּי אַבָּהוּ אָמַר מֵהָכָא: ״כִּי שֵׁם ה׳ אֶקְרָא הָבוּ גֹדֶל לֵאלֹהֵינוּ״.

**GEMARA** With regard to the basic mitzva of *zimmun*, the Gemara asks: **From where are these matters** derived, that after a meal in which three diners participated, a *zimmun* must be recited? **Rav Asi said: As the verse states: "Praise God**[N] **with me, and we will exalt His name together"** (Psalms 34:4), i.e., the one reciting the blessing turns to at least two others to praise God together. **Rabbi Abbahu said:** The source of the mitzva of *zimmun* is derived **from** the verse **here: "When I call the Name of the Lord, give** [plural] **praise to our God"** (Deuteronomy 32:3).

אָמַר רַב חָנָן בַּר אַבָּא: מִנַּיִן לָעוֹנֶה אָמֵן שֶׁלֹּא יַגְבִּיהַּ קוֹלוֹ יוֹתֵר מִן הַמְבָרֵךְ – שֶׁנֶּאֱמַר: ״גַּדְּלוּ לַה׳ אִתִּי וּנְרוֹמְמָה שְׁמוֹ יַחְדָּו״.

Having mentioned these verses, the Gemara cites related matters. **Rav Ḥanan bar Abba said: From where** is it derived **that one who answers amen should not raise his voice louder than the one reciting the blessing?**[H] **As it is stated: "Praise God with me, and we will exalt His Name together"**; together and not with the respondent raising his voice louder than the one reciting the blessing.

אָמַר רַבִּי שִׁמְעוֹן בֶּן פָּזִי: מִנַּיִן שֶׁאֵין הַמְתַרְגֵּם רַשַּׁאי לְהַגְבִּיהַּ קוֹלוֹ יוֹתֵר מִן הַקּוֹרֵא – שֶׁנֶּאֱמַר: ״מֹשֶׁה יְדַבֵּר וְהָאֱלֹהִים יַעֲנֶנּוּ בְקוֹל״; שֶׁאֵין תַּלְמוּד לוֹמַר ״בְּקוֹל״, וּמַה תַּלְמוּד לוֹמַר ״בְּקוֹל״ – בְּקוֹלוֹ שֶׁל מֹשֶׁה.

Similarly, **Rabbi Shimon ben Pazi said: From where** is it derived **that the translator**[B] who translated the public Torah reading into Aramaic **is not permitted to raise his voice louder than the reader?**[N] **As it is stated: "Moses spoke, and God responded in a voice"** (Exodus 19:19). This verse requires further consideration, as **there is no need for the verse to state: In a voice.** The phrase, in a voice, adds nothing. Rather, to **what** purpose **did the verse state: In a voice? In Moses' voice** i.e., in a voice no louder than Moses' voice. This verse instructs subsequent generations that Torah readers and translators should keep their voices at an equal volume just as Moses transmitted God's word to the people and their voices were equal in volume.

תַּנְיָא נַמִי הָכִי: אֵין הַמְתַרְגֵּם רַשַּׁאי לְהַגְבִּיהַּ קוֹלוֹ יוֹתֵר מִן הַקּוֹרֵא, וְאִם אִי אֶפְשָׁר לַמְתַרְגֵּם לְהַגְבִּיהַּ קוֹלוֹ כְּנֶגֶד הַקּוֹרֵא – יְמַעֵךְ הַקּוֹרֵא קוֹלוֹ וְיִקְרָא.

**This was also taught** in a *baraita*: **The translator is not permitted to raise his voice louder than the reader.** The converse is also true; **and if the translator cannot raise his voice to match** that of **the reader, the reader should lower his voice and read.**

אִתְּמַר: שְׁנַיִם שֶׁאָכְלוּ כְּאַחַת; פְּלִיגִי רַב וְרַבִּי יוֹחָנָן, חַד אָמַר: אִם רָצוּ לְזַמֵּן מְזַמְּנִין; וְחַד אָמַר: אִם רָצוּ לְזַמֵּן – אֵין מְזַמְּנִין.

The mishna rules that three who ate as one are required to join together and recite Grace after Meals. The Gemara discusses this *halakha* further: **It was stated: Two who ate as one**[N] and wish to join together in a *zimmun* although they are under no obligation, are they permitted to do so? **Rav and Rabbi Yoḥanan disagreed: One said: If they wanted to join together, they may form a *zimmun*. The other said:** Even **if they wanted to join together, they may not form a *zimmun*.**

**NOTES**

**One who ate untithed produce** – **אָכַל טֶבֶל**: Authorities disagree whether or not one who ate untithed produce, or anything else prohibited by Torah law, is obligated to recite Grace after Meals. It is clear from the mishna that a *zimmun* cannot be formed based on one who ate untithed produce, as his eating is not considered significant and individuals do not form a group for that purpose. The Rambam holds that no blessing should be recited over prohibited food, regarding which it is said: "He has blasphemed God" (Psalms 10:3), whereas the Ra'avad holds that he should nevertheless recite a blessing since he has derived benefit from this world, and one who derives benefit is obligated to recite a blessing.

**Praise God** – **גַּדְּלוּ לַה׳**: From the fact that the verse states, "Praise God with me," and not merely, "Let us praise and exalt," we derive not only the number of people that constitute a *zimmun* but also the manner in which the *zimmun* is performed; one turns to the others and tells them to join him in blessing God (*Tosefot Rabbi Yehuda HaḤasid*, *Tosefot HaRosh*).

**The translator…the reader** – **הַמְתַרְגֵּם...הַקּוֹרֵא**: This means that the reader and the translator must speak in the same voice; neither louder than the other. Consequently, the reader may also not raise his voice louder than the translator. That is the halakhic ruling. The Gemara formulated the *halakha* in this way simply because the order is that reader reads first, and the translator must then calibrate his voice to the volume of the reader's voice. Proof is cited from Moses, as Moses spoke first and God responded in the same voice (*Ḥefetz Hashem*). The problem with regard to the apparently unrelated proof-text that is cited in the Gemara is thereby resolved (see *Tosafot*, Maharsha, and others).

**Two who ate as one** – **שְׁנַיִם שֶׁאָכְלוּ כְּאַחַת**: The Jerusalem Talmud links this dispute to the dispute with regard to whether or not two individuals who sit in judgment constitute a court. In that case, too, the fundamental question is whether the halakhic unit of three is to be understood as an absolute minimum required by the *halakha* or as an *ab initio* recommendation.

**HALAKHA**

**One who ate untithed produce** – **אָכַל טֶבֶל**: One who eats untithed produce or other prohibited food, even if the prohibition is merely by rabbinic law, does not recite a blessing and is not included in a *zimmun* (Rambam *Sefer Ahava*, *Hilkhot Berakhot* 1:19; *Shulḥan Arukh*, *Oraḥ Ḥayyim* 196:1).

**And the gentile, etc.** – **וְהַנָּכְרִי וכו׳**: A gentile cannot be included in a *zimmun* (Rambam *Sefer Ahava*, *Hilkhot Berakhot* 5:7; *Shulḥan Arukh*, *Oraḥ Ḥayyim* 199:4).

**Women, slaves, and minors** – **נָשִׁים וַעֲבָדִים וּקְטַנִּים**: Women, slaves, and minors do not combine to form a *zimmun*; however, members of each group may form a *zimmun* by themselves. Three women who sat at a meal together may form a *zimmun*. Similarly, three slaves or three minors who sat together at a meal may form a *zimmun*; however, women, slaves, and minors may not combine to form a *zimmun* together, due to concern for the promiscuity of slaves (Rambam *Sefer Ahava*, *Hilkhot Berakhot* 5:7; *Shulḥan Arukh*, *Oraḥ Ḥayyim* 199:6).

**How much must one eat to obligate those with whom he ate in a *zimmun*** – **עַד כַּמָּה מְזַמְּנִין**: One may not include someone who ate less than an olive-bulk in a *zimmun* and recite Grace after Meals with him, in accordance with the opinion of the Rabbis (Rambam *Sefer Ahava*, *Hilkhot Berakhot* 5:8; *Shulḥan Arukh*, *Oraḥ Ḥayyim* 196:4).

**From where is it derived that one who answers amen should not raise his voice louder than the one reciting the blessing** – **מִנַּיִן לָעוֹנֶה אָמֵן שֶׁלֹּא יַגְבִּיהַּ קוֹלוֹ וכו׳**: One who answers amen should not raise his voice louder than the one reciting the blessing (Rambam *Sefer Ahava*, *Hilkhot Berakhot* 1:14; *Shulḥan Arukh*, *Oraḥ Ḥayyim* 124:12).

**BACKGROUND**

**Untithed produce** – **טֶבֶל**: This is produce from which *teruma* and tithes have not been separated. The Torah prohibits the consumption of untithed produce. One who eats untithed produce is punished by death at the hand of Heaven. However, once the tithes were separated, even though they were not yet given to those for whom they are designated, the produce no longer has the status of untithed produce and it may be eaten.

**Translator** – **מְתַרְגֵּם**: In mishnaic and talmudic times, in later generations in many Jewish communities, and in Yemenite communities even today, it was customary to translate the Torah reading into the *lingua franca*. The Torah reader would recite a verse and the translator, based on an accepted translation, would interpret the meaning of the verse. The Aramaic translation of the Torah by Onkelos was formulated first and foremost for this purpose.

תְּנַן: שְׁלֹשָׁה שֶׁאָכְלוּ כְּאַחַת חַיָּיבִין לְזַמֵּן
שְׁלֹשָׁה – אִין, שְׁנַיִם – לָא!

The Gemara cites a proof from what **we learned** in our mishna: **Three who ate as one are required to join together** and recite Grace after Meals. By inference: **Three, yes,** they form a *zimmun*; **two, no,** they do not form a *zimmun*. This contradicts the opinion that holds that two individuals who wish to form a *zimmun* may do so.

הָתָם חוֹבָה, הָכָא רְשׁוּת.

The Gemara answers: There is no proof from the mishna, as **there,** the mishna discussed an **obligatory** *zimmun*; **here,** the *amora'im* disagree with regard to an **optional** *zimmun*.

תָּא שְׁמַע: שְׁלֹשָׁה שֶׁאָכְלוּ כְּאַחַת – חַיָּיבִין לְזַמֵּן וְאֵין רַשָּׁאִין לֵיחָלֵק; שְׁלֹשָׁה אִין, שְׁנַיִם לָא!

The Gemara cites an additional proof. **Come and hear: Three who ate as one are required to join together** and recite Grace after Meals **and may not disperse**[H] to recite Grace after Meals individually. Apparently, **three, yes,** they form a *zimmun*; **two, no,** they do not form a *zimmun*. If a *zimmun* was possible with two people, three people would not be forbidden to disperse, as even if one recited Grace after Meals alone, the remaining two would constitute a *zimmun*.

שָׁאנֵי הָתָם, דִּקְבַעוּ לְהוּ בְּחוֹבָה מֵעִיקָּרָא.

The Gemara rejects this proof: **It is different there,** in the case of a group of three who dispersed, because **from the outset, they established themselves as** a group of three who were **obligated** to form a *zimmun*. Consequently, they are not permitted to forego an obligatory *zimmun* in favor of an optional one.

תָּא שְׁמַע: הַשַּׁמָּשׁ שֶׁהָיָה מְשַׁמֵּשׁ עַל הַשְּׁנַיִם – הֲרֵי זֶה אוֹכֵל עִמָּהֶם אַף עַל פִּי שֶׁלֹּא נָתְנוּ לוֹ רְשׁוּת, הָיָה מְשַׁמֵּשׁ עַל הַשְּׁלֹשָׁה – הֲרֵי זֶה אֵינוֹ אוֹכֵל עִמָּהֶם אֶלָּא אִם כֵּן נָתְנוּ לוֹ רְשׁוּת!

The Gemara cites an additional proof. **Come and hear,** based on what was taught in a *baraita*: **A waiter who was serving**[H] **two people eats with them, although they did not give him permission** to do so, because he will thereby be eligible to join them in a *zimmun*. If a waiter **was serving three** people, **he may not eat with them unless they gave him permission** to do so. Evidently, two may not form a *zimmun*. If that were the case, the waiter would require permission even when serving two people.

שָׁאנֵי הָתָם,

The Gemara responds: **It is different there,**

**HALAKHA**

**Three…may not disperse – ...שְׁלוֹשָׁה וְאֵין רַשָּׁאִין לֵיחָלֵק:** Three who ate together may not divide to recite Grace after Meals and thereby negate the mitzva of *zimmun* (Rambam *Sefer Ahava, Hilkhot Berakhot* 5:10; *Shulḥan Arukh, Oraḥ Ḥayyim* 193:1).

**A waiter who was serving – הַשַּׁמָּשׁ שֶׁהָיָה מְשַׁמֵּשׁ:** It is a mitzva for two people who ate together to seek a third person to include in a *zimmun*. Therefore, if a waiter was serving two others, he may eat even without express permission from the diners, since presumably they want him to join them in a *zimmun*. If a waiter serves three others, however, he must ask their permission before eating (*Shulḥan Arukh, Oraḥ Ḥayyim* 170:21).

Perek **VII**
Daf **45** Amud **b**

דְּנִיחָא לְהוּ דְּמִקְבַּע לְהוּ בְּחוֹבָה מֵעִיקָּרָא.

in the case of a waiter, **because from the outset, they prefer to establish** their *zimmun* **as an obligation** rather than as an option.

תָּא שְׁמַע: נָשִׁים מְזַמְּנוֹת לְעַצְמָן וַעֲבָדִים מְזַמְּנִים לְעַצְמָן, נָשִׁים וַעֲבָדִים וּקְטַנִּים אִם רָצוּ לְזַמֵּן – אֵין מְזַמְּנִין; (וְהָא נָשִׁים אֲפִילּוּ מֵאָה) וְהָא מֵאָה נָשֵׁי כִּתְרֵי גַּבְרֵי דָּמְיָין, וְקָתָנֵי: נָשִׁים מְזַמְּנוֹת לְעַצְמָן וַעֲבָדִים מְזַמְּנִין לְעַצְמָן!

The Gemara cites yet another proof. **Come and hear: Women form a *zimmun* for themselves**[H] **and slaves form a *zimmun* for themselves;** however, **women, slaves, and minors,** even **if they wish to form a *zimmun*** together, **they may not form a *zimmun*. Aren't one hundred women** considered **the equivalent of two men,**[N] in that they cannot constitute a prayer quorum, and yet they may form a *zimmun*? Apparently, like women, two men can form a *zimmun* on their own.

שָׁאנֵי הָתָם, דְּאִיכָּא דֵּעוֹת.

The Gemara rejects this: **There it is different because,** although women cannot constitute a prayer quorum, since **there are** three individual **minds,** i.e., people, three women can fulfill the verse: "Praise God with me, and we will exalt His name together." Two men cannot.

אִי הָכִי אֵימָא סֵיפָא: נָשִׁים וַעֲבָדִים אִם רָצוּ לְזַמֵּן אֵין מְזַמְּנִין, אַמַּאי לָא? וְהָא אִיכָּא דֵּעוֹת!

The Gemara objects: **If so, say the latter clause** of this *baraita*: **Women and slaves, if they wish to form a *zimmun*, they may not form a *zimmun*. Why not? Aren't** they individual **minds,** which should enable the collective praise of God?

שָׁאנֵי הָתָם – מִשּׁוּם פְּרִיצוּתָא.

The Gemara responds: That is not the reason that women and slaves were prohibited from forming a *zimmun* together. Rather, **it is different there,** as the Sages were concerned with regard to women and slaves joining together **due to promiscuity.**

תִּסְתַּיֵּים דְּרַב דְּאָמַר ״אִם רָצוּ לְזַמֵּן אֵין מְזַמְּנִין״. דְּאָמַר רַב דִּימִי בַּר יוֹסֵף אָמַר רַב: שְׁלֹשָׁה שֶׁאָכְלוּ כְּאַחַת וְיָצָא אֶחָד מֵהֶם לַשּׁוּק – קוֹרִין לוֹ וּמְזַמְּנִין עָלָיו, טַעְמָא – דְּקוֹרִין לוֹ, הָא לָא קוֹרִין לוֹ – לָא!

In the dispute between Rav and Rabbi Yoḥanan, it is unclear which *amora* held which opinion. The Gemara seeks to resolve this: **Conclude that Rav** is the one who **said: If they wanted to join together, they may not form a *zimmun*. As Rav Dimi bar Yosef said** that **Rav said: Three** people **who ate as one and one of them went out to the marketplace, they call him and include him in the *zimmun*.**[N] **The reason is because they call him;** by inference, **if they do not call him, no,** they cannot form a *zimmun*.

**HALAKHA**

**Women form a *zimmun* for themselves – נָשִׁים מְזַמְּנוֹת לְעַצְמָן:** Women are permitted to form a *zimmun* when they are by themselves, as may slaves. However, women and slaves may not form a *zimmun* together (Rambam *Sefer Ahava, Hilkhot Berakhot* 5:7; *Shulḥan Arukh, Oraḥ Ḥayyim* 199:6).

**NOTES**

**One hundred women are considered the equivalent of two men – מֵאָה נָשֵׁי כִּתְרֵי גַּבְרֵי:** Elsewhere, the Gemara states that one hundred women are the equivalent of one man (*Yevamot* 117a). With regard to other areas, no number of women is considered significant. However, because *zimmun* is dependent upon on the number of people, it inconceivable that several women would be considered as one (Rabbi Zvi Hirsch Ḥayot; see *Tosafot*).

**They call him and include him in the *zimmun* – קוֹרִאין לוֹ וּמְזַמְּנִין עָלָיו:** This *halakha*, which permits inclusion of a third person in a *zimmun* from wherever he is located, was restricted (*ge'onim*) to a situation where he hears the voices of those reciting the blessing and is willing to rejoin them (Rabbeinu Ḥananel).

שָׁאנֵי הָתָם, דְּאִקְּבַעוּ לְהוּ בְּחוֹבָה מֵעִיקָּרָא.

The Gemara rejects this proof: **It is different there,** in the case of three who ate together and one of them left, because **from the outset, they established themselves as** a group of three who were **obligated** to form a *zimmun*. That is why they need to call him and include him in their *zimmun*.

אֶלָּא, תִּסְתַּיֵּים דְּרַבִּי יוֹחָנָן הוּא דְּאָמַר ״אִם רָצוּ לְזַמֵּן – אֵין מְזַמְּנִין״. דְּאָמַר רַבָּה בַּר בַּר חָנָה אָמַר רַבִּי יוֹחָנָן: שְׁנַיִם שֶׁאָכְלוּ כְּאַחַת – אֶחָד מֵהֶן יוֹצֵא בְּבִרְכַּת חֲבֵירוֹ.

The Gemara now attempts to prove the opposite: **Rather, conclude that Rabbi Yoḥanan is the one who said: If they wanted to join together they may not form a *zimmun*,** as **Rabba bar bar Ḥana said** that **Rabbi Yoḥanan said: Two** people **who ate as one, one fulfills his obligation** to recite a blessing **with the** recitation of the **blessing of the other.**

וְהָוֵינַן בַּהּ; מַאי קָא מַשְׁמַע לַן? תְּנֵינָא: שָׁמַע וְלֹא עָנָה – יָצָא! וְאָמַר רַבִּי זֵירָא: לוֹמַר שֶׁאֵין בִּרְכַּת הַזִּימּוּן בֵּינֵיהֶם, תִּסְתַּיֵּים.

The Gemara comments: **And we discussed it** in an attempt to clarify the *halakha*. **What is he teaching us? We** already **learned this** *halakha* explicitly: **One who heard** a blessing **and did not respond,**[H] nevertheless **he fulfilled** his obligation **And Rabbi Zeira said:** Rabbi Yoḥanan's statement teaches us that **there is no blessing of *zimmun* among them.** Indeed **conclude** that Rabbi Yoḥanan is the *amora* who held that two may not form a *zimmun*.

אֲמַר לֵיהּ רָבָא בַּר רַב הוּנָא לְרַב הוּנָא: וְהָא רַבָּנַן דְּאָתוּ מִמַּעַרְבָא אָמְרִי: אִם רָצוּ לְזַמֵּן – מְזַמְּנִין, מַאי לָאו דִּשְׁמִיעַ לְהוּ מֵרַבִּי יוֹחָנָן? – לָא, דִּשְׁמִיעַ לְהוּ מֵרַב מִקַּמֵּי דְּנָחֵית לְבָבֶל.

With regard to this, **Rava bar Rav Huna said to** his father **Rav Huna: Didn't the Sages who came from the West,** from Eretz Yisrael, **say that** two individuals who ate together, **if they wanted to join together, they may form a *zimmun*? What, is it not that they heard** it **from Rabbi Yoḥanan,** who was from Eretz Yisrael? Rav Huna answered: **No,** this is not a proof, as it is possible **that they heard** this *halakha* **from Rav before he** left Eretz Yisrael and **descended to Babylonia.**

גּוּפָא, אָמַר רַב דִּימִי בַּר יוֹסֵף אָמַר רַב: שְׁלֹשָׁה שֶׁאָכְלוּ כְּאַחַת וְיָצָא אֶחָד מֵהֶם לַשּׁוּק – קוֹרְאִין לוֹ וּמְזַמְּנִין עָלָיו. אָמַר אַבַּיֵי: וְהוּא דְּקָרוּ לֵיהּ וְעָנֵי.

The Gemara now explains **the matter** of Rav's statement **itself: Rav Dimi bar Yosef said** that **Rav said: Three** people **who ate as one and one of them went out**[H] **to the marketplace, they call him and include him in the *zimmun*,** even if he is not beside them. And **Abaye said: This is only** in a case **that they call him and he responds,** but if he too far away to answer he cannot be included.

אָמַר מָר זוּטְרָא: וְלָא אֲמָרַן אֶלָּא בִּשְׁלֹשָׁה, אֲבָל בַּעֲשָׂרָה – עַד דְּנֵיתֵי.

**Mar Zutra said: We only said** this, that it is sufficient to hear and answer **with regard to** a *zimmun* of **three; but, with regard to** a quorum of **ten,**[H] they may not form a *zimmun* which includes mention of God's name **until** the one who left **comes** and sits with them.

מַתְקִיף לָהּ רַב אָשֵׁי: אַדְּרַבָּא, אִיפְּכָא מִסְתַּבְּרָא! תִּשְׁעָה – נִרְאִין כַּעֲשָׂרָה, שְׁנַיִם אֵין נִרְאִין כִּשְׁלֹשָׁה!

**Rav Ashi strongly objects to this: On the contrary, the opposite is more reasonable. Nine** people who ate together **appear like ten,** so even if one is missing, the quorum does not seem to be incomplete. **Two** people who ate together **do not appear like three,** so it would be reasonable to require the actual presence of the third.

וְהִלְכְתָא כְּמָר זוּטְרָא. מַאי טַעְמָא – כֵּיוָן דִּבְעֵי לְאַדְכּוּרֵי שֵׁם שָׁמַיִם, בְּצִיר מֵעֲשָׂרָה לָאו אוֹרַח אַרְעָא.

The Gemara concludes: **And the *halakha* is in accordance with the** opinion of **Mar Zutra. What is the reason? Because it is inappropriate to invoke God's name** with **fewer than ten** people present. Since a *zimmun* of ten includes mention of God's name, all ten must be present.

אָמַר אַבַּיֵי, נְקִיטִינַן: שְׁנַיִם שֶׁאָכְלוּ כְּאַחַת – מִצְוָה לֵיחָלֵק. תַּנְיָא נָמֵי הָכִי: שְׁנַיִם שֶׁאָכְלוּ כְּאַחַת – מִצְוָה לֵיחָלֵק; בַּמֶּה דְּבָרִים אֲמוּרִים – כְּשֶׁשְּׁנֵיהֶם סוֹפְרִים, אֲבָל אֶחָד סוֹפֵר וְאֶחָד בּוּר – סוֹפֵר מְבָרֵךְ, וּבוּר יוֹצֵא.

With regard to the *halakhot* of *zimmun*, **Abaye said** that **we have a tradition: Two** people **who ate as one,**[NH] **it is a mitzva** for them **to separate** and for each to recite a blessing for himself. **This was also taught** in a *baraita*: **Two** people **who ate as one, it is a mitzva** for them **to separate**. The *baraita*, however, adds: **In what** case **are these matters stated?** Specifically **when both** individuals **are learned people** [*soferim*][B] and capable of reciting prayers and blessings. **However,** if **one of them was a learned person and the other an ignoramus, the learned person recites the blessing** and **the ignoramus thereby fulfills** his obligation.

אָמַר רָבָא, הָא מִילְּתָא אֲמַרִיתָא אֲנָא, וְאִיתְּמַרָה מִשְּׁמֵיהּ דְּרַבִּי זֵירָא כְּוָותִי: שְׁלֹשָׁה שֶׁאָכְלוּ כְּאַחַת – אֶחָד מַפְסִיק לִשְׁנַיִם וְאֵין שְׁנַיִם מַפְסִיקִין לְאֶחָד.

**Rava said: This is a statement that I said and it was stated in the name of Rabbi Zeira in accordance with my** opinion: **Three** people **who ate as one** but did not conclude their meals together, **one interrupts** his meal in order **to** join the other **two**[H] in a *zimmun*, **but two do not interrupt** their meal **to** join the other **one** in a *zimmun*.

וְלָא?! וְהָא רַב פָּפָּא אַפְסֵיק לֵיהּ לְאַבָּא מָר בְּרֵיהּ, אִיהוּ וְחַד! שָׁאנֵי רַב פָּפָּא דִּלְפָנִים מִשּׁוּרַת הַדִּין הוּא דַּעֲבַד.

The Gemara challenges: **And** do two really **not** interrupt their meal to join the other one in a *zimmun*? **Didn't Rav Pappa interrupt** his meal **to** enable **Abba Mar, his son,** to recite the *zimmun* blessing; and, in that case, it was Rav Pappa **and one** other person? The Gemara responds: The case **of Rav Pappa is different,** as he **acted beyond the letter of the law.**

**HALAKHA**

**One who heard a blessing and did not respond – שָׁמַע וְלֹא עָנָה:** One who heard a blessing recited by another who had in mind to fulfill his obligation and he, too, intended to fulfill his obligation with that blessing, fulfilled his obligation even if he did not respond (Rambam *Sefer Ahava, Hilkhot Berakhot* 1:11; *Shulḥan Arukh, Oraḥ Ḥayyim* 213:2).

**Three who ate as one and one of them went out – שְׁלֹשָׁה שֶׁאָכְלוּ כְּאַחַת וְיָצָא:** If three ate as one and one of them left, they call him to tell him that they want to recite the *zimmun* and he joins with them even though he is not there (Rambam *Sefer Ahava, Hilkhot Berakhot* 5:13; *Shulḥan Arukh, Oraḥ Ḥayyim* 194:2).

**One of ten – אֶחָד מֵעֲשָׂרָה:** If one member of a group of ten left, they may not invoke God's name in their *zimmun* unless they are together, as per the Gemara's conclusion in accordance with the opinion of Mar Zutra (Rambam *Sefer Ahava, Hilkhot Berakhot* 5:13; *Shulḥan Arukh, Oraḥ Ḥayyim* 194:2).

**Two who ate as one – שְׁנַיִם שֶׁאָכְלוּ כְּאַחַת:** Two who ate together should each recite Grace after Meals on their own. If one of them does not know how to recite Grace after Meals, the other should recite it aloud and fulfill the obligation on the other's behalf (Rambam *Sefer Ahava, Hilkhot Berakhot* 5:15; *Shulḥan Arukh, Oraḥ Ḥayyim* 193:1).

**One interrupts his meal in order to join the other two – אֶחָד מַפְסִיק לִשְׁנַיִם:** Three people who ate together, if two of them so desire, the third must interrupt his meal and join them in a *zimmun*. However, two need not interrupt their meal to join one in a *zimmun* (Rambam *Sefer Ahava, Hilkhot Berakhot* 7:6; *Shulḥan Arukh, Oraḥ Ḥayyim* 200:1).

**NOTES**

**We have a tradition: Two people who ate as one – נְקִיטִינַן שְׁנַיִם שֶׁאָכְלוּ וכו׳:** Ostensibly, Abaye's statement is a halakhic ruling in accordance with the opinion of Rabbi Yoḥanan that two may not form a *zimmun*. However, this is difficult: Why did he not simply state that the *halakha* is in accordance with the opinion of Rabbi Yoḥanan? Perhaps, even though they issued the same ruling, their rationales are different. Rabbi Yoḥanan holds that two cannot form a *zimmun* under any circumstances. Abaye's reasoning is that when there is no obligation to form a *zimmun*, it is preferable for each to recite the blessing himself (see Rashba and *Tziyyun LeNefesh Ḥayya*).

**BACKGROUND**

**Learned people [*soferim*] – סוֹפְרִים:** Literally, scribes or counters, this is a term often used in reference to the Sages. *Halakhot* that are by rabbinic law are often referred to as *midivrei soferim*. Tractate *Kiddushin* (30a) states: This is why the Sages of the earlier generations were called *soferim*, because they would count all the letters of the Torah. In *Berakhot*, the term refers to one sufficiently learned to recite Grace after Meals by himself.

יהודה בר מרימר ומר בר רב אשי ורב אחא מדיפתי כרכי ריפתא בהדי הדדי לא הוה בהו חד דהוה מופלג מחבריה לברוכי להו; יתבי וקא מיבעיא להו הא דתנן: שלשה שאכלו כאחת חייבי לזמן – הני מילי היכא דאיכא אדם גדול, אבל היכא דכי הדדי נינהו – חלוק ברכות עדיף.

The Gemara relates that three Sages, **Yehuda bar Mareimar,**[P] **Mar bar Rav Ashi and Rav Aḥa of Difti ate bread together. None among them was greater than the other** in either age or wisdom, rendering him the obvious choice to **recite the blessing on their behalf. They sat down and raised a dilemma: That which we learned** in our mishna: **Three** people **who ate as one are required to join together** and recite Grace after Meals, does **that apply only when there is a great man**[N] among them, **but where they are on a par with each other,** perhaps **separating** and reciting independent **blessings is preferable?**

בריך איניש לנפשיה, אתו לקמיה דמרימר, אמר להו: ידי ברכה – יצאתם ידי זימון – לא יצאתם. וכי תימרו ניהדר ונזמן – אין זימון למפרע.

Indeed, that is what they did, and **each person recited the blessing for himself.**[H] Later, **they came before Mareimar** to ask him if they had acted correctly. Mareimar **said to them:** Although **you fulfilled your** obligation to recite a **blessing** over your food, **you did not fulfill** your obligation to form a *zimmun*. **And if you say: Let us go back and form a *zimmun*, there is no retroactive *zimmun*.** Once the blessing over the meal has been recited, one can no longer recite the *zimmun*.

בא ומצאן כשהן מברכים, מהו אומר אחריהם? רב זביד אמר: "ברוך ומבורך" רב פפא אמר: עונה אמן.

The Gemara discusses another question: **One who came and found them reciting the *zimmun* blessing, what does he say after them**[H] in response to the *zimmun*. **Rav Zevid said** that he says: **Blessed** is He **and blessed** is His Name for ever and all time (*Tosafot*). **Rav Pappa said: He answers amen.**

ולא פליגי: הא דאשכחינהו דקא אמרי "נברך", והא דאשכחינהו דקא אמרי "ברוך"; אשכחינהו דקא אמרי "נברך" - אומר "ברוך ומבורך", אשכחינהו דקא אמרי "ברוך" – עונה אמן.

The Gemara explains that Rav Zevid and Rav Pappa **do not disagree. This is** in a case **where he found them saying: Let us bless; and that is** in a case **where he found them saying: Blessed be.** The Gemara specifies: **Where he found them saying: Let us bless, he says: Blessed** is He **and blessed** is His Name for ever and all time; **where he found them saying: Blessed be, he answers amen.**

תני חדא: העונה אמן אחר ברכותיו הרי זה משובח, ותניא אידך: הרי זה מגונה!

A similar explanation resolves a difficulty in a related topic. **One *baraita* taught: One who answers amen after his own blessings,**[NH] **it is praiseworthy. Another *baraita* taught: It is reprehensible.**

לא קשיא: הא – ב"בונה ירושלים", הא - בשאר ברכות.

The Gemara resolves this apparent contradiction: This is **not difficult. This,** where the first *baraita* says that it is praiseworthy to answer amen after his own blessing, **is in the blessing: Who builds Jerusalem; this,** where the second *baraita* deems it offensive, **is in other blessings.**

אביי עני ליה בקלא כי היכי דלשמע פועלים וליקומו, ד"הטוב והמטיב" לא דאורייתא. רב אשי עני ליה בלחישא כי היכי דלא נזלזלו ב"הטוב והמטיב".

The Gemara relates: **Abaye would answer** amen **aloud** after reciting the blessing: Who builds Jerusalem, **so the workers would hear and stand** to return to work, **as** the ensuing blessing: **Who is good and does good, is not** required **by Torah law,** so the laborers working for the homeowner need not recite it. **Rav Ashi,** on the other hand, would **answer** amen **in a whisper,**[H] **so that** those who heard him **would not relate to** the blessing: **Who is good and does good, with contempt.**

## PERSONALITIES

**Mareimar – מרימר:** Mareimar was a sixth-generation Babylonian *amora*. Although we do not know much about his personality, it is known that Mareimar was a colleague-disciple of Mar Zutra and a friend of Rav Ashi. Apparently, he was a resident of Sura and the Sages of Sura would follow his instructions. Apparently, the last Sage named Ravina was his primary student.

After Rav Ashi's death, although not immediately, Mareimar is said to have taken his place as head of the yeshiva in Sura and he and Ravina together continued redacting the Talmud. It is possible that the prefix Mar before his name is an indication that he was affiliated with the family of the Exilarch.

Mareimar's son, Rav Yehuda bar Mareimar, was an important Sage in the following generation.

## NOTES

**When there is a great man – דאיכא אדם גדול:** This notion that a *zimmun* is initiated only by a great man is based on the verses cited as proof-texts for *zimmun*. King David said, "Praise God with me," and, "When I call the Name of God," is a quote from Moses. That is why the Gemara surmised that a *zimmun* is only significant when a great man invites those present to join (*Tosefot Rabbi Yehuda HaḤasid*).

**One who answers amen after his own blessings – העונה אמן אחר ברכותיו:** One who answers amen after his own blessings is considered reprehensible or a fool for various reasons. Some say that by answering amen he interrupts between the blessing and the object of the blessing (Rav Yehudai Gaon, cited in the Rashba). Others say that saying amen is tantamount to declaring that he has completed reciting praise. When he immediately recites another blessing, he negates that declaration (*Talmidei Rabbeinu Yona*).

## HALAKHA

**Three who separated – שלשה שנפרדו:** Three who ate together and recited Grace after Meals individually may no longer form a *zimmun* (*Shulḥan Arukh, Oraḥ Ḥayyim* 194:1).

**One who came and found them reciting the *zimmun* blessing, what does he say after them – בא ומצאן שהן מברכים מהו אומר אחריהן:** One who did not eat, but found himself among a group of people who were forming a *zimmun*, if he heard the one leading the *zimmun* say: Let us bless, he responds: Blessed is He and blessed is His name. If he entered while they were responding he should answer amen (Rambam *Sefer Ahava, Hilkhot Berakhot* 5:17; *Shulḥan Arukh, Oraḥ Ḥayyim* 198:1).

**One who answers amen after his own blessings – העונה אמן אחר ברכותיו:** Halakhic authorities disagree whether one answers amen after his own blessing only following the blessing: Who builds Jerusalem (*Tosafot*) or also at the conclusion of any series of blessings (*ge'onim*, Rambam). Customs differ accordingly. The Ashkenazi custom is to answer amen only after the blessing: Who builds Jerusalem. The Sephardic custom is to do so after any series of blessings (Rambam *Sefer Ahava, Hilkhot Berakhot* 1:16; *Shulḥan Arukh, Oraḥ Ḥayyim* 188:1, 215:1).

**He would answer in a whisper – עני ליה בלחישה:** There is no consensus among halakhic authorities whether or not when one answers amen after the blessing: Who builds Jerusalem, he should do so out loud. Some distinguish between various circumstances, explaining that one should not reprimand those who conduct themselves in accordance with Abaye's opinion (*Taz*; *Shulḥan Arukh, Oraḥ Ḥayyim* 188:2).

רַבִּי זֵירָא חֲלַשׁ, עַל לְגַבֵּיהּ רַבִּי אַבָּהוּ, קַבֵּיל עֲלֵיהּ: אִי מִתְפַּח קְטִינָא חֲרִיךְ שָׁקֵי – עָבֵידְנָא יוֹמָא טָבָא לְרַבָּנַן. אִתְפַּח, עֲבַד סְעוּדְתָא לְכוּלְּהוּ רַבָּנַן. כִּי מְטָא לְמִשְׁרֵי, אָמַר לֵיהּ לְרַבִּי זֵירָא: לִישְׁרֵי לַן מָר! – אָמַר לֵיהּ: לָא סְבַר לַהּ מָר לְהָא דְּרַבִּי יוֹחָנָן דְּאָמַר: בַּעַל הַבַּיִת בּוֹצֵעַ? שְׁרָא לְהוּ.

The Gemara recounts: **Rabbi Zeira**[P] **took ill. Rabbi Abbahu went to visit him and resolved: If the little man with the scorched legs,** a nickname for Rabbi Zeira, **is cured, I will make a festival,** a feast **for the Sages.** Rabbi Zeira **was cured** and Rabbi Abbahu **made a feast for all the Sages. When it came time to break** bread, Rabbi Abbahu **said to Rabbi Zeira: Master,** please **break** bread **for us.** Rabbi Zeira **said to him: Doesn't the Master hold** in accordance with **that** *halakha* **of Rabbi Yoḥanan, who said: The host breaks** bread? Rabbi Abbahu **broke** bread **for them.**[N]

כִּי מְטָא לְבָרוּכֵי, אָמַר לֵיהּ: נִבְרֵיךְ לַן מָר! – אָמַר לֵיהּ: לָא סְבַר לַהּ מָר לְהָא דְּרַב הוּנָא דְּמִן בָּבֶל דְּאָמַר: בּוֹצֵעַ מְבָרֵךְ?

**When** the time **came to recite the blessing,** Rabbi Abbahu **said to** Rabbi Zeira: **Master, recite** Grace after Meals **on our behalf.** Rabbi Zeira **said to him: Doesn't the Master hold** in accordance with **that** *halakha* **of Rabbi Huna of Babylonia, who said: He who breaks** bread **recites** Grace after Meals?

וְאִיהוּ כְּמַאן סְבִירָא לֵיהּ?

The Gemara asks: **And in accordance with whose** opinion **does** Rabbi Abbahu **hold** that he asked Rabbi Zeira to recite Grace after Meals?

כִּי הָא דְּאָמַר רַבִּי יוֹחָנָן מִשּׁוּם רַבִּי שִׁמְעוֹן בֶּן יוֹחַי: בַּעַל הַבַּיִת בּוֹצֵעַ וְאוֹרֵחַ מְבָרֵךְ, בַּעַל הַבַּיִת בּוֹצֵעַ – כְּדֵי שֶׁיִּבְצַע בְּעַיִן יָפָה, וְאוֹרֵחַ מְבָרֵךְ – כְּדֵי שֶׁיְּבָרֵךְ בַּעַל הַבַּיִת.

The Gemara answers: Rabbi Abbahu holds in accordance with that *halakha* **that Rabbi Yoḥanan said in the name of Rabbi Shimon ben Yoḥai: The host breaks bread**[H] **and a guest recites** Grace after Meals.[H] **The host breaks** bread **so that he will break** bread **generously,** whereas a guest might be embarrassed to break a large piece for himself and other guests; **and the guest recites** Grace after Meals **so that he may bless the host** in the course of reciting Grace after Meals, as the Gemara proceeds to explain.

מַאי מְבָרֵךְ – "יְהִי רָצוֹן שֶׁלֹּא יֵבוֹשׁ בַּעַל הַבַּיִת בָּעוֹלָם הַזֶּה וְלֹא יִכָּלֵם לָעוֹלָם הַבָּא";

**What is** the formula of the blessing with which the guest **blesses** his host?

**May it be Your will that the master of the house shall not suffer shame in this world, nor humiliation in the World-to-Come.**

וְרַבִּי מוֹסִיף בָּהּ דְּבָרִים: "וְיַצְלַח מְאֹד בְּכָל נְכָסָיו, וִיהִיוּ נְכָסָיו וּנְכָסֵינוּ מוּצְלָחִים וּקְרוֹבִים לָעִיר, וְאַל יִשְׁלוֹט שָׂטָן לֹא בְּמַעֲשֵׂי יָדָיו וְלֹא בְּמַעֲשֵׂי יָדֵינוּ, וְאַל יִזְדַּקֵּר לֹא לְפָנָיו וְלֹא לְפָנֵינוּ שׁוּם דְּבַר הִרְהוּר חֵטְא וַעֲבֵירָה וְעָוֹן מֵעַתָּה וְעַד עוֹלָם".

**Rabbi** Yehuda HaNasi **added to it elements** pertaining to material success:

**And may he be very successful with all his possessions,**
**and may his possessions and our possessions be successful and near the city,**
**and may Satan control neither his deeds nor our deeds,**
**and may no thought of sin, iniquity, or transgression stand before him or before us**
**from now and for evermore.**

עַד הֵיכָן בִּרְכַּת הַזִּמּוּן?

The Gemara asks: **Until where** does **the** ***zimmun*** **blessing**[N] extend?[H]

רַב נַחְמָן אָמַר: עַד "נְבָרֵךְ"; וְרַב שֵׁשֶׁת אָמַר: עַד "הַזָּן".

**Rav Naḥman says:** The blessing extends only **until: Let us bless. Rav Sheshet says** that the *zimmun* blessing extends **until** the end of the first blessing of Grace after Meals: **Who feeds** all.

**NOTES**

**Rabbi Abbahu's opinion** – דַּעַת רַבִּי אַבָּהוּ: Some explained that by inviting Rabbi Zeira to break bread, Rabbi Abbahu sought to honor him. He did not seek to assert that that is the *halakha*. For precisely that reason, Rabbi Zeira refused, as both agreed that the host breaks bread (*Tosefot Rabbi Yehuda HaHasid, Ḥefetz Hashem*).

**The *zimmun* blessing** – בִּרְכַּת הַזִּמּוּן: Were the *zimmun* blessing an independent blessing, like all blessings it would require mention of God's Name and God's sovereignty. However, according to the Jerusalem Talmud, apparently, a blessing that is not recited on a regular basis and only on occasion, i.e., when three people ate together, is not considered a full-fledged blessing and does not require mention of God's Name and God's sovereignty. Similarly, the laws of juxtaposed blessings do not apply to blessings of that type (see *Temim De'im* of the Ra'avad).

**HALAKHA**

**The host breaks bread** – בַּעַל הַבַּיִת בּוֹצֵעַ: The host breaks bread, in accordance with the opinion of Rabbi Yoḥanan. Some accord the honor to the greatest among those assembled (*Magen Avraham*; Rambam *Sefer Ahava, Hilkhot Berakhot* 7:2; *Shulḥan Arukh, Oraḥ Ḥayyim* 167:14).

**And a guest recites Grace after Meals** – וְאוֹרֵחַ מְבָרֵךְ: Grace after Meals is recited by a guest, in accordance with the opinion of Rabbi Shimon bar Yoḥai (Rambam *Sefer Ahava, Hilkhot Berakhot* 7:2; *Shulḥan Arukh, Oraḥ Ḥayyim* 201:1).

**Until where does the *zimmun* blessing extend** – עַד הֵיכָן בִּרְכַּת הַזִּימּוּן: If one interrupts his meal to form a *zimmun* with the other diners who completed their meals, the authorities disagree whether the *halakha* is in accordance with the opinion of Rav Naḥman, and he must wait until the one leading the *zimmun* says: Let us bless (Rif, Rambam, *Shulḥan Arukh*), or in accordance with the opinion of Rav Sheshet, and he must wait until the leader recites: Who feeds all (*Halakhot Gedolot, Tosafot, Tur*; Rambam *Sefer Ahava, Hilkhot Berakhot* 5:2; *Shulḥan Arukh, Oraḥ Ḥayyim* 200:2 and the comment of the Rema).

**PERSONALITIES**

**Rabbi Zeira** – רַבִּי זֵירָא: Born in Babylonia, Rabbi Zeira, known in the Jerusalem Talmud as Rabbi Ze'ira, became one of the great third-generation Eretz Yisrael *amora'im*. His father was a Persian government tax collector; however, he was praised as one of the few who filled that position properly. When Rabbi Zeira ascended to Eretz Yisrael, he decided to identify completely with the Torah of Eretz Yisrael. The Gemara relates that he fasted one hundred fasts in order to forget the Torah that he studied in Babylonia.

Rabbi Zeira was famous for his sharp intellect and was the author of incisive *halakhot*. He was also known as an extremely God-fearing man. There are several stories related to his distinction in that area. He did not even want to be ordained with the title Rabbi, due to his modesty. It was only after he was told that with that ordination comes atonement for his sins that he relented.

The Gemara related that he fasted one hundred additional fasts so that the fire of Gehenna would not harm him, and he would test himself by entering a fiery furnace. On one occasion, his legs were scorched, and from then on he was called: The little man with the scorched legs.

He was a contemporary of Rav Ḥisda, Rav Sheshet, and Rabba in Babylonia and of the disciples of Rabbi Yoḥanan in Eretz Yisrael, and he engaged in extensive halakhic discourse with them. Apparently, he was a flax merchant in Eretz Yisrael and it is conceivable that he had occasion in the course of his business to return to Babylonia several times.

The text of the beginning of Rabbi Zeira's eulogy is preserved in the Talmud: The land of Shinar, Babylonia, conceived and gave birth; the land of splendor, Eretz Yisrael, raised her plaything. Woe unto her, said Reket, Tiberias, for she has lost her beloved vessel.

He had a son, Rabbi Ahava, who was a Sage in the following generation.

נֵימָא כְּתַנָּאֵי; דְּתָנֵי חֲדָא: בִּרְכַּת הַמָּזוֹן שְׁנַיִם וּשְׁלֹשָׁה; וְתַנְיָא אִידָךְ: שְׁלֹשָׁה וְאַרְבָּעָה סָבְרוּהָ, דְּכוּלֵּי עָלְמָא "הַטּוֹב וְהַמֵּטִיב" לָאו דְּאוֹרַיְיתָא הִיא; מַאי לָאו בְּהָא קָמִיפַּלְגִי, מַאן דְּאָמַר "שְׁתַּיִם וְשָׁלֹשׁ" – קָסָבַר עַד "הַזָּן", וּמַאן דְּאָמַר שָׁלֹשׁ וְאַרְבַּע – קָסָבַר עַד "נְבָרֵךְ"!

The Gemara proposes: **Let us say** that this amoraic dispute **is parallel to** a dispute **between the** ***tanna'im*****. As one** ***baraita*** **taught: Grace after Meals** is **two and three**[H] blessings, **and another** ***baraita*** **taught: Grace after Meals** is **three and four** blessings. In attempting to understand these conflicting *baraitot*, the Sages **assumed that everyone** agrees that the blessing: **Who is good and does good,** the fourth blessing of Grace after Meals, **is not** required **by Torah law. What** then? **Is it not that they disagree about this: The one who said** that Grace after Meals is **two and three** blessings **holds that the** ***zimmun*** **blessing extends until** the end of the blessing: **Who feeds** all? If there is a *zimmun*, three blessings are recited; if there is no *zimmun*, only two blessings are recited, since the blessing: **Who feeds** all, is not recited. **And the one who said** that Grace after Meals is **three and four** blessings **holds** that the *zimmun* blessing extends only **until: Let us bless,** and includes no part of Grace after Meals itself. If there is a *zimmun*, four blessings are recited, the three blessing of Grace after Meals plus the blessing of the *zimmun*, while if there is not, only three blessings are recited.

לָא, רַב נַחְמָן מְתָרֵץ לְטַעְמֵיהּ וְרַב שֵׁשֶׁת מְתָרֵץ לְטַעְמֵיהּ.

This explanation distinguishing between the *baraitot* is rejected: **No; Rav Naḥman explains in accordance with his reasoning and Rav Sheshet explains in accordance with his reasoning.**

רַב נַחְמָן מְתָרֵץ לְטַעְמֵיהּ; דְּכוּלֵּי עָלְמָא עַד "נְבָרֵךְ", מַאן דְּאָמַר: "שָׁלֹשׁ וְאַרְבַּע" – שַׁפִּיר וּמַאן דְּאָמַר "שְׁתַּיִם וְשָׁלֹשׁ" – אָמַר לָךְ: הָכָא בְּבִרְכַּת פּוֹעֲלִים עָסְקִינַן, דְּאָמַר מָר: פּוֹתֵחַ בְּ"הַזָּן" וְכוֹלֵל "בּוֹנֵה יְרוּשָׁלַיִם" בְּבִרְכַּת הָאָרֶץ.

**Rav Naḥman explains in accordance with his reasoning; everyone** agrees that the *zimmun* blessing extends only **until Let us bless.** According to **the one who said** that Grace after Meals is **three and four** blessings, this works out **well. And the one who said** that Grace after Meals is **two and three** blessings could have **said to you: Here we are dealing with the blessing recited by laborers, as the Master said** that when a laborer is working, he is permitted to abridge Grace after Meals, and **he begins with** the blessing: **Who feeds** all, **and includes** the third blessing: **Who builds Jerusalem, in** the context of the second blessing, **the blessing of the land.**

רַב שֵׁשֶׁת מְתָרֵץ לְטַעְמֵיהּ; דְּכוּלֵּי עָלְמָא עַד "הַזָּן", מַאן דְּאָמַר שְׁתַּיִם וְשָׁלֹשׁ – שַׁפִּיר, וּמַאן דְּאָמַר שָׁלֹשׁ וְאַרְבַּע – קָסָבַר: "הַטּוֹב וְהַמֵּטִיב" דְּאוֹרַיְיתָא הִיא.

**Rav Sheshet explains in accordance with his reasoning; everyone** agrees that the *zimmun* blessing extends **until** the end of the blessing: **Who feeds** all. According to **the one who said** that Grace after Meals is **two and three** blessings, this works out **well; and the one who said** that Grace after Meals is **three and four** blessings **holds** that the blessing: **Who is good and does good, is** required **by Torah law.**

אָמַר רַב יוֹסֵף: תֵּדַע דְּ"הַטּוֹב וְהַמֵּטִיב" לָאו דְּאוֹרַיְיתָא – שֶׁהֲרֵי פּוֹעֲלִים עוֹקְרִים אוֹתָהּ.

With regard to the matter of the blessing: Who is good and does good, **Rav Yosef said: Know** that the blessing: **Who is good and does good, is not** required **by Torah law, as laborers** who recite Grace after Meals at work **eliminate it.** If it can be eliminated, it could not be a Torah obligation.

אָמַר רַב יִצְחָק בַּר שְׁמוּאֵל בַּר מָרְתָא מִשְּׁמֵיהּ דְּרַב: תֵּדַע דְּ"הַטּוֹב וְהַמֵּטִיב" לָאו דְּאוֹרַיְיתָא – שֶׁהֲרֵי פּוֹתֵחַ בָּהּ בְּ"בָרוּךְ" וְאֵין חוֹתֵם בָּהּ בְּ"בָרוּךְ". כִּדְתַנְיָא: כׇּל הַבְּרָכוֹת כּוּלָּן פּוֹתֵחַ בָּהֶן בְּ"בָרוּךְ" וְחוֹתֵם בָּהֶן בְּ"בָרוּךְ" חוּץ מִבִּרְכַּת הַפֵּירוֹת, וּבִרְכַּת הַמִּצְוֹת, וּבְרָכָה הַסְּמוּכָה לַחֲבֶרְתָּהּ, וּבְרָכָה אַחֲרוֹנָה שֶׁבִּקְרִיאַת שְׁמַע; יֵשׁ מֵהֶן שֶׁפּוֹתֵחַ בָּהֶן בְּ"בָרוּךְ" וְאֵין חוֹתֵם בְּ"בָרוּךְ",

**Rav Yitzḥak bar Shmuel bar Marta said** another proof **in the name of Rav: Know** that the blessing: **Who is good and does good, is not** required **by Torah law,** as one who recites it **begins** to recite it **with: Blessed, but does not conclude reciting it with: Blessed.** This is the formula in all comparable blessings, **as it was taught** in a *baraita*: **All blessings,** one **begins** to recite **them with: Blessed, and concludes** reciting **them with: Blessed, except for blessings over fruit, blessings over mitzvot,**[N] **a blessing that is juxtaposed to another** blessing,[N] **and the final blessing after** ***Shema*****. There are among these** blessings **those that** one who recites it **begins** to recite it **with: Blessed, but does not conclude reciting it with: Blessed;**

Perek **VII**
Daf **46** Amud **b**

וְיֵשׁ מֵהֶן שֶׁחוֹתֵם בָּהֶן בְּ"בָרוּךְ" וְאֵין פּוֹתֵחַ בְּ"בָרוּךְ". וְ"הַטּוֹב וְהַמֵּטִיב" פּוֹתֵחַ בְּ"בָרוּךְ" וְאֵין חוֹתֵם בְּ"בָרוּךְ", מִכְּלָל דִּבְרָכָה בִּפְנֵי עַצְמָהּ הִיא.

**and there are among these** blessings **that** one who recites it **concludes** reciting it **with: Blessed, but does not begin** reciting it **with: Blessed.** The blessing: **Who is good and does good,** one who recites it **begins** to recite it **with: Blessed, but does not conclude** reciting it **with: Blessed.** This proves **by inference that it is an independent blessing.**

HALAKHA

**Grace after Meals is two and three blessings** – בִּרְכַּת הַמָּזוֹן שְׁנַיִם וּשְׁלֹשָׁה: The *halakha* is in accordance with the interpretation of *Tosafot*. If three people who ate together and each knows only one of the blessings, each recites the blessing that he knows. However, one who knows only part of a blessing may not recite it (*Shulḥan Arukh*, *Oraḥ Ḥayyim* 194:3).

NOTES

**Blessings over fruit, blessings over mitzvot** – בִּרְכַּת הַפֵּירוֹת וּבִרְכַּת הַמִּצְוֹת: Generally speaking, the blessings recited over food or before performance of a mitzva are short blessings with a single theme. They contain neither pleas nor requests. As such, it is sufficient to open with: Blessed. More lengthy, complex blessings, e.g., *kiddush* on Shabbat, which must include praise of God's creation, or the blessings prior to reciting *Shema*, which include a petition on behalf of the Jewish people, must both open and close with words of praise to the Almighty (Rashi; Rashbam *Pesaḥim* 104a).

**A blessing that is juxtaposed to another blessing** – בְּרָכָה הַסְּמוּכָה לַחֲבֶרְתָּהּ: Lengthy blessings ordinarily open and close with: Blessed. However, when there is a series of blessings that follow one another, e.g., the eighteen blessings of the *Amida* prayer and the blessings of Grace after Meals, the first blessing opens with: Blessed, while the subsequent blessings do not. That is either because the opening of the first blessing in the series is considered as providing an opening for all of the blessings in the series (Rashi; Rashbam *Pesaḥim* 104b) or because the closing: Blessed of the previous blessing serves as an opening for the blessing that follows (*Tosafot*).

### HALAKHA

**Grace after Meals of a mourner** – בִּרְכַּת הַמָּזוֹן לְאָבֵל: In a house of mourning, one adds to the fourth blessing: The true Judge, Who judges, etc., in accordance with the custom of Mar Zutra (Rambam *Sefer Ahava, Hilkhot Berakhot* 2:8; *Shulḥan Arukh, Oraḥ Ḥayyim* 189:2, *Yoreh De'a* 379:1).

### BACKGROUND

**The order of reclining** – סֵדֶר הַסֵּבָּה:

**Persian Custom**

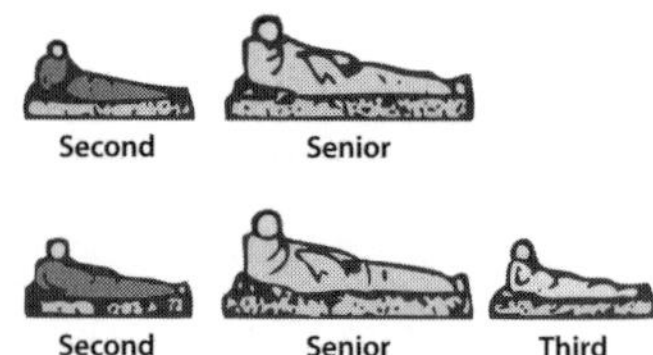


**Jewish Custom**

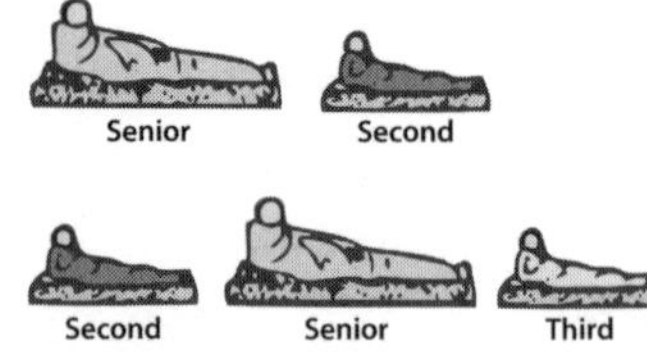


Diagram of the different manners of the order of reclining based on the version of the *baraita* according to Rashi's version. According to the version cited in *Tosafot*, when there are three people, the second is below and not above the greatest person present.

וְאָמַר רַב נַחְמָן בַּר יִצְחָק: תֵּדַע דְּ״הַטּוֹב וְהַמֵּטִיב״ לָאו דְּאוֹרַיְיתָא – שֶׁהֲרֵי עוֹקְרִין אוֹתָהּ בְּבֵית הָאָבֵל. כִּדְתַנְיָא: מַה הֵם אוֹמְרִים בְּבֵית הָאָבֵל? ״בָּרוּךְ הַטּוֹב וְהַמֵּטִיב״; רַבִּי עֲקִיבָא אוֹמֵר: ״בָּרוּךְ דַּיַּין הָאֱמֶת״.

And Rav Naḥman bar Yitzḥak said: Know that the blessing: Who is good and does good, is not required by Torah law, as it is eliminated in the house of the mourner, as it was taught in a *baraita* according to the opinion of Rabbi Akiva: What do they say in the house of the mourner?[H] Blessed…Who is good and does good. Rabbi Akiva says: Blessed…the true Judge.

״הַטּוֹב וְהַמֵּטִיב״ אִין, ״דַּיַּין אֱמֶת״ לָא?! – אֶלָּא אֵימָא: אַף ״הַטּוֹב וְהַמֵּטִיב״.

The first opinion in the *baraita* is challenged: Who is good and does good, yes, it is recited in the house of the mourner, the true Judge, no, it is not recited? Rather, say: Who is good and does good, is recited as well.

מָר זוּטְרָא אִיקְּלַע לְבֵי רַב אַשִׁי, אִיתְרַע בֵּיהּ מִלְּתָא, פְּתַח וּבְרִיךְ: הַטּוֹב וְהַמֵּטִיב, אֵל אֱמֶת דַּיַּין אֱמֶת, שׁוֹפֵט בְּצֶדֶק, לוֹקֵחַ בְּמִשְׁפָּט, וְשַׁלִּיט בְּעוֹלָמוֹ לַעֲשׂוֹת בּוֹ כִּרְצוֹנוֹ כִּי כָל דְּרָכָיו מִשְׁפָּט, שֶׁהַכֹּל שֶׁלּוֹ וַאֲנַחְנוּ עַמּוֹ וַעֲבָדָיו, וּבַכֹּל אֲנַחְנוּ חַיָּיבִים לְהוֹדוֹת לוֹ וּלְבָרְכוֹ, גּוֹדֵר פְּרָצוֹת בְּיִשְׂרָאֵל הוּא יִגְדּוֹר אֶת הַפִּרְצָה הַזֹּאת בְּיִשְׂרָאֵל לְחַיִּים.

The Gemara recounts: Mar Zutra happened to come to Rav Ashi's home when an incident of mourning befell Rav Ashi. Mar Zutra began a combined blessing and recited:

**Who is good and does good,**
**God of truth, the true Judge,**
**Who judges with righteousness, takes away with justice,**
**and is the ruler of His world to do in it as He wills,**
**as all His ways are just,**
**that all is His and we are His people and His servants,**
**and in everything we are obligated to thank Him and bless Him,**
**Who repairs the breaches in Israel,**
**He will repair this breach in Israel for life.**

Mar Zutra included both: Who is good and does good, as well as mourning and acceptance of divine justice.

לְהֵיכָן הוּא חוֹזֵר? רַב זְבִיד מִשְּׁמֵיהּ דְּאַבַּיֵּי אָמַר: חוֹזֵר לָרֹאשׁ, וְרַבָּנַן אָמְרִי: לַמָּקוֹם שֶׁפָּסַק. וְהִלְכְתָא: לַמָּקוֹם שֶׁפָּסַק.

Returning to the original topic, it was mentioned above that one interrupts his meal to form a *zimmun* with two others who finished eating. The question is raised: **To where does he return**[N] when he finishes his own meal and must begin to recite his own Grace after Meals? **Rav Zevid in the name of Abaye said: He returns to the beginning** and recites the entire Grace after Meals. **And the Rabbis say: He returns to the place that he stopped. And the *halakha* is: He returns to the place that he stopped,** i.e., to the beginning of the second blessing.

אָמַר לֵיהּ רֵישׁ גָּלוּתָא לְרַב שֵׁשֶׁת: אַף עַל גַּב דְּרַבָּנַן קַשִּׁישֵׁי אַתּוּן, פַּרְסָאֵי בְּצָרְכֵי סְעוּדָה בְּקִיאֵי מִינַּיְיכוּ, בִּזְמַן שֶׁהֵן שְׁתֵּי מִטּוֹת – גָּדוֹל מֵסֵב בָּרֹאשׁ וְשֵׁנִי לוֹ לְמַעְלָה הֵימֶנּוּ, וּבִזְמַן שֶׁהֵם שָׁלֹשׁ – גָּדוֹל מֵסֵב בָּאֶמְצַע, שֵׁנִי לוֹ לְמַעְלָה הֵימֶנּוּ, שְׁלִישִׁי לוֹ לְמַטָּה הֵימֶנּוּ.

On the topic of meals, the Gemara relates the following: **The Exilarch said to Rav Sheshet: Although you are elderly Sages, the Persians are more expert than you with regard to the required** etiquette at **meals.** The Persian custom is that **when there are two divans** on which they would recline, **the greater** of the two people **reclines first and the** person **second to him** in importance reclines on the divan **above him,** alongside his head. **When there are three** divans, **the greatest** of the three **reclines** on the middle divan, **the one second to him** in importance reclines on the divan **above him, and the one third to him** in importance reclines on the divan **below** the greatest of the three.[B]

אָמַר לֵיהּ: וְכִי בָּעֵי אִישְׁתַּעוּיֵי בַּהֲדֵיהּ, מִתְרֵיץ תָּרוֹצֵי וְיָתֵיב וּמִשְׁתָּעֵי בַּהֲדֵיהּ! – אָמַר לֵיהּ: שָׁאנֵי פַּרְסָאֵי דְּמַחֲוֵי לֵיהּ בְּמָחוֹג.

Rav Sheshet **said to** the Exilarch that the custom is flawed. **If the** greater **wishes to speak with** the one second to him in importance who is reclining above his head, **he must straighten up and sit and** only then will he be able to **speak to him.** The Exilarch **answered: The Persians are different, as they signal** and communicate **with** hand **gestures,** especially during mealtimes, so there is no need to sit up.

מַיִם רִאשׁוֹנִים מֵהֵיכָן מַתְחִילִין? אָמַר לֵיהּ: מִן הַגָּדוֹל.

Rav Sheshet asked the Exilarch about the Persian practice with regard to **the first waters.** When washing hands before the meal, **from where do they begin?** The Exilarch **said to him: They begin from the greatest.**[N]

### NOTES

**To where does he return** – לְהֵיכָן הוּא חוֹזֵר: Since the Gemara does not elaborate with regard to what matter this question is directed, there is room to interpret it in different manners. Some explain that it refers to one who joined the *zimmun* and waited for others to complete their blessing before resuming his meal. Alternatively, it refers to three who ate and one of them left (*Tosafot*). Others say that it refers to Grace after Meals in the house of mourning, i.e., after inserting the passage to comfort the mourners, from where do they resume Grace after Meals (*ge'onim*)?

**From where do they begin…They begin from the greatest** – מֵהֵיכָן מַתְחִילִין...מִן הַגָּדוֹל: The reference here is not to the greatest of those reclining, but rather to the one who will recite Grace after Meals for the others, as is clear from the continuation of the Gemara.

יֵשֵׁב גָּדוֹל וְיִשְׁמוֹר יָדָיו עַד שֶׁנּוֹטְלִי כּוּלָּן?! – אָמַר לֵיהּ: לְאַלְתַּר מַיְיתוּ תַּכָּא קַמֵּיהּ.

Rav Sheshet asked: If that is so, **should the greatest** person present **sit and keep his hands clean** and wait until **everyone has washed** so that they may all be served? The Exilarch **said to him: They bring him his table** [*takka*][LB] **immediately,** as the custom was that each person ate at his own private table, and they brought the table before the greatest person present immediately after he washed so that he need not wait for the others.

מַיִם אַחֲרוֹנִים מֵהֵיכָן מַתְחִילִין? – אָמַר לֵיהּ: מִן הַקָּטָן.

Rav Sheshet asked the Exilarch about the Persian practice with regard to **the final waters.** When washing hands after the meal, **from where do they begin?** The Exilarch **said to him: They begin with the least significant** of the attendees.

וְגָדוֹל יָתֵיב וְיָדָיו מְזוּהָמוֹת עַד שֶׁנּוֹטְלִי כּוּלָּן?! אָמַר לֵיהּ: לָא מְסַלְּקִי תַּכָּא מִקַּמֵּיהּ עַד דְּנִימְטֵי מַיָּא לְגַבֵּיהּ.

Rav Sheshet said: If so, **should the greatest** person present **sit with dirty hands until everyone washes** his hands? The Exilarch **said to him: They do not remove the table from before him until the water reaches him;** he can continue eating while the others are washing.

אָמַר רַב שֵׁשֶׁת: אֲנָא מַתְנִיתָא יָדַעְנָא, דְּתַנְיָא, כֵּיצַד סֵדֶר הֲסִבָּה? בִּזְמַן שֶׁהֵן שְׁתֵּי מִטּוֹת – גָּדוֹל מֵסֵב בָּרֹאשׁ וְשֵׁנִי לוֹ לְמַטָּה הֵימֶנּוּ. בִּזְמַן שֶׁהֵן שָׁלֹשׁ מִטּוֹת – גָּדוֹל מֵסֵב בָּרֹאשׁ, שֵׁנִי לוֹ לְמַעְלָה הֵימֶנּוּ, שְׁלִישִׁי לוֹ לְמַטָּה הֵימֶנּוּ. מַיִם הָרִאשׁוֹנִים מַתְחִילִין מִן הַגָּדוֹל, מַיִם אַחֲרוֹנִים, בִּזְמַן שֶׁהֵן חֲמִשָּׁה – מַתְחִילִין מִן הַגָּדוֹל, וּבִזְמַן שֶׁהֵן מֵאָה – מַתְחִילִין מִן הַקָּטָן עַד שֶׁמַּגִּיעִין אֵצֶל חֲמִשָּׁה, וְחוֹזְרִין וּמַתְחִילִין מִן הַגָּדוֹל וּלְמָקוֹם שֶׁמַּיִם אַחֲרוֹנִים חוֹזְרִין – לְשָׁם בְּרָכָה חוֹזֶרֶת.

**Rav Sheshet said:** In terms of conduct at a meal, **I know a *baraita*, as it was taught: What is the order of reclining?**[H] **When there are two divans** on which they would recline, **the greater** of the two people **reclines first, and the** person **second to him** in importance reclines on the divan **below him. When there are three divans, the greatest** of the three **reclines first,** on the middle divan, **the one second to him** in importance reclines on the divan **above him, and the one third to him** in importance reclines on the divan **below** the greatest of the three. **The first waters**[H] before the meal, **they begin with the greatest** person present. **The final waters;**[H] **when they are five** people, **they begin with the greatest** person present. **When they are** more than that, even **one hundred, they begin** the final waters **with the least significant** of the attendees **until they reach the five greatest** present, at which point **they return and begin with the greatest** present. **And to the place that the final waters return the blessing also reverts,** and the greatest present, the first among the final five to wash his hands, recites Grace after Meals.

מְסַיַּיע לֵיהּ לְרַב, דְּאָמַר רַבִּי חִיָּיא בַּר אַשִׁי אָמַר רַב: כָּל הַנּוֹטֵל יָדָיו בָּאַחֲרוֹנָה תְּחִלָּה – הוּא מְזוּמָּן לִבְרָכָה.

**This** *baraita* **supports** the opinion of **Rav, as Rabbi Ḥiyya bar Ashi said** that **Rav said: Whoever washes his hands first at the end** of the meal **is designated to** recite **the blessing** of Grace after Meals.

רַב וְרַבִּי חִיָּיא הֲווּ יָתְבִי בִּסְעוּדְתָא קַמֵּיהּ דְּרַבִּי. אָמַר לֵיהּ רַבִּי לְרַב: קוּם מְשִׁי יְדָךְ. חַזְיֵיהּ דְּקָא מְרַתֵּת, אָמַר לֵיהּ: בַּר פַּחְתֵּי, עַיֵּין בְּבִרְכַּת מְזוֹנָא קָאָמַר לָךְ.

Similarly, the Gemara relates: **Rav and Rabbi Ḥiyya were seated at a meal before Rabbi** Yehuda HaNasi. **Rabbi** Yehuda HaNasi **said to Rav: Stand, wash your hands.** Rabbi Ḥiyya **saw that** Rav **was trembling** in fear that perhaps he had conducted himself improperly during the meal and therefore had to wash his hands. Rabbi Ḥiyya **said to him: Son of noblemen, he is saying to you to review Grace after Meals,** as the first to wash his hands after the meal is honored with leading the blessing.

תָּנוּ רַבָּנַן: אֵין מְכַבְּדִין – לֹא בִּדְרָכִים, וְלֹא בִּגְשָׁרִים,

The Gemara continues to discuss the topic of washing after a meal. **The Sages taught:** Although it is customary to defer to greater people, nevertheless, **one shows deference neither on roads**[NH] **nor on bridges,**

**BACKGROUND**

Table – תַּכָּא:

Drawing taken from an earthenware bowl, a rendering of an individual reclining on a divan and eating. Next to him is the small table.

**LANGUAGE**

Table [*takka*] – תַּכָּא: From the Greek θᾶκος, *takos* meaning chair, seat.

**HALAKHA**

**The order of reclining – סֵדֶר הֲסִבָּה:** The order of reclining at a meal is in accordance with the *baraita* cited by Rav Sheshet (Rambam *Sefer Ahava, Hilkhot Berakhot* 7:1).

**The first waters – מַיִם הָרִאשׁוֹנִים:** The greatest person present washes his hands with the first waters first. The custom of the Rosh was that the greatest washed his hands last in order to avoid interruption and speaking between washing and reciting the blessing, and many adopted his custom (*Baḥ* and *Taz*; Rambam *Sefer Ahava, Hilkhot Berakhot* 7:1; *Shulḥan Arukh, Oraḥ Ḥayyim* 165:2).

**Final waters – מַיִם אַחֲרוֹנִים:** If there are five or fewer people, the individual reciting Grace after Meals washes first. If there are more than five people, they begin from the least significant person present and wash in the order in which they are seated. One does not defer to the other until only five remain who did not yet wash their hands. When only five people remain, the person reciting Grace after Meals is the first among them to wash his hands (Rambam *Sefer Ahava, Hilkhot Berakhot* 7:12; *Shulḥan Arukh, Oraḥ Ḥayyim* 181:6).

**One shows deference neither on roads, etc. – אֵין מְכַבְּדִין לֹא בִּדְרָכִים וכו׳:** Deference is only shown to a greater individual by allowing him to enter first in a doorway fit for a *mezuza* (*Shulḥan Arukh, Yoreh De'a* 242:17 in the Rema).

**NOTES**

**One shows deference neither on roads, etc. – אֵין מְכַבְּדִין לֹא בִּדְרָכִים וכו׳:** If deference was shown on roads, it would cause people to lose valuable work time as well as impede those who are in a hurry to pass. Similarly, deference is not shown on bridges because of potential danger. With regard to dirty hands, deference is not shown because of the unpleasantness of waiting with dirty hands and because one might forget and fail to wash them (*Me'iri, Ḥefetz Hashem*).

Nor with regard to dirty hands – לֹא בְּיָדַיִם מְזֹהֲמוֹת: One does not defer to his superior by allowing him to wash his hands first at the end of a meal. The one reciting Grace after Meals washes his hands first to enable him to review the blessing that he is about to recite (Vilna Gaon; Rambam *Sefer Ahava, Hilkhot Berakhot* 7:12; *Shulḥan Arukh, Oraḥ Ḥayyim* 181:6).

Those reclining at a meal may not eat anything until the one breaking bread has tasted the bread – אֵין הַמְסֻבִּין רַשָּׁאִין לֶאֱכֹל כְּלוּם: Participants in a meal may eat nothing until the one who breaks bread has tasted the bread (Rambam *Sefer Ahava, Hilkhot Berakhot* 7:5; *Shulḥan Arukh, Oraḥ Ḥayyim* 167:15).

Two people who are eating from a single dish must wait for each other – שְׁנַיִם מַמְתִּינִין זֶה לָזֶה בִּקְעָרָה: Two people who are eating from a single dish must wait for each other; but, if there are three, two need not wait for the third (Rambam *Sefer Ahava, Hilkhot Berakhot* 7:6; *Shulḥan Arukh, Oraḥ Ḥayyim* 170:2).

The one who breaks bread extends his hand – הַבּוֹצֵעַ הוּא פּוֹשֵׁט יָדוֹ: The one who breaks bread takes from it first, although he may defer to others (Rambam *Sefer Ahava, Hilkhot Berakhot* 7:5; *Shulḥan Arukh, Oraḥ Ḥayyim* 167:17).

The one who breaks bread may not break the bread until amen has ended – אֵין הַבּוֹצֵעַ רַשָּׁאי לִבְצוֹעַ עַד שֶׁיְכַלֶּה אָמֵן: The one who breaks bread may not do so until the majority of those responding have answered amen, in accordance with the opinion of Rav Ḥisda (Rambam *Sefer Ahava, Hilkhot Berakhot* 7:5; *Shulḥan Arukh, Oraḥ Ḥayyim* 167:16).

Ravin – רָבִין: This refers to Rabbi Avin, a third generation Eretz Yisrael *amora*.

Ravin was one of the younger students of Rabbi Yoḥanan and was often found studying from Rabbi Yoḥanan's more prominent students. Apparently, he was a merchant by trade, and served as an emissary to transmit the Torah of Eretz Yisrael to the Babylonian Sages. Rabbi Avin was considered a prominent student and a perfectionist who transmitted the teachings of his Rabbi, primarily Rabbi Yoḥanan, very precisely. His arrival is often mentioned after the arrival of Rav Dimi, and the *halakha* is generally in accordance with his opinion. Although the Babylonian Sages respected the Torah that he transmitted, they did not consider him a particularly great scholar. Nevertheless, his statements appear frequently in both the Babylonian and Jerusalem Talmud, where he is called Rabbi Bon. His considerable level of sanctity is described there.

Two Sages by this name appear in the Talmud. The second Rabbi Avin was the son of the first Rabbi Avin, who died prior to the birth of his son.

וְלֹא בְּיָדַיִם מְזֹהֲמוֹת.

רָבִין וְאַבַּיֵי הֲווּ קָא אָזְלֵי בְּאוֹרְחָא, קַדְמֵיהּ חֲמָרֵיהּ דְּרָבִין לְדְאַבַּיֵי, וְלָא אֲמַר לֵיהּ ״נֵיזִיל מָר״. אֲמַר: מִדְּסָלֵיק הַאי מֵרַבָּנָן מִמַּעְרְבָא גַּס לֵיהּ דַּעְתֵּיהּ. כִּי מְטָא לְפִתְחָא דְבֵי כְנִישְׁתָּא, אֲמַר לֵיהּ: נֵיעַל מָר. אֲמַר לֵיהּ: וְעַד הַשְׁתָּא לָאו מָר אֲנָא?! – אֲמַר לֵיהּ, הָכִי אָמַר רַבִּי יוֹחָנָן: אֵין מְכַבְּדִין אֶלָּא בְּפֶתַח שֶׁיֵּשׁ בָּהּ מְזוּזָה.

דְּאִית בָּהּ מְזוּזָה – אִין, דְּלֵית בָּהּ מְזוּזָה – לָא, אֶלָּא מֵעַתָּה, בֵּית הַכְּנֶסֶת וּבֵית הַמִּדְרָשׁ דְּלֵית בְּהוּ מְזוּזָה, הָכִי נַמִי דְּאֵין מְכַבְּדִין?! אֶלָּא אֵימָא: בְּפֶתַח הָרָאוּי לִמְזוּזָה.

אֲמַר רַב יְהוּדָה בְּרֵיהּ דְרַב שְׁמוּאֵל בַּר שֵׁילָת מִשְּׁמֵיהּ דְרַב: אֵין הַמְסֻבִּין רַשָּׁאִין לֶאֱכֹל כְּלוּם עַד שֶׁיִּטְעוֹם הַבּוֹצֵעַ. יָתֵיב רַב סָפְרָא וְקָאֲמַר: לִטְעוֹם אִיתְּמַר.

לְמַאי נָפְקָא מִינַּהּ – שֶׁחַיָּיב אָדָם לוֹמַר בִּלְשׁוֹן רַבּוֹ.

תָּנוּ רַבָּנַן: שְׁנַיִם מַמְתִּינִין זֶה לָזֶה בִּקְעָרָה, שְׁלֹשָׁה אֵין מַמְתִּינִין, הַבּוֹצֵעַ הוּא פּוֹשֵׁט יָדוֹ תְּחִלָּה, וְאִם בָּא לַחֲלוֹק כָּבוֹד לְרַבּוֹ אוֹ לְמִי שֶׁגָּדוֹל הֵימֶנּוּ – הָרְשׁוּת בְּיָדוֹ.

רַבָּה בַּר בַּר חָנָה הֲוָה עָסֵיק לֵיהּ לִבְרֵיהּ בֵּי רַב שְׁמוּאֵל בַּר רַב קְטִינָא, קַדֵּים וְיָתֵיב וְקָמַתְנֵי לֵיהּ לִבְרֵיהּ: אֵין הַבּוֹצֵעַ רַשָּׁאי לִבְצוֹעַ עַד שֶׁיְכַלֶּה אָמֵן מִפִּי הָעוֹנִים. רַב חִסְדָּא אֲמַר: מִפִּי רוֹב הָעוֹנִים.

אֲמַר לוֹ רָמִי בַּר חָמָא: מַאי שְׁנָא רוּבָּא – דְּאַכַּתִּי לָא כַּלְיָא בְּרָכָה, מִיעוּטָא נַמִי לָא כַּלְיָא בְּרָכָה!

אֲמַר לֵיהּ: שֶׁאֲנִי אוֹמֵר, כָּל הָעוֹנֶה אָמֵן יוֹתֵר מִדַּאי אֵינוֹ אֶלָּא טוֹעֶה.

nor with regard to **dirty hands,**[H] i.e., with regard to washing hands at the end of a meal.

The Gemara recounts: **Ravin**[P] **and Abaye were traveling along the road** on donkeys. **Ravin's donkey preceded** Abaye's and Ravin **did not say** to Abaye: Let the Master go first. Abaye **said to himself: Ever since this one of the Sages,** Ravin, **ascended from the West,** Eretz Yisrael, **he has become arrogant. When they reached the door of the synagogue,** Ravin **said to** Abaye: **Let the Master enter** first. Abaye **said to him: Until now was I not Master?** Why do you only begin deferring to me now but did not do so while we were traveling? Ravin **said to him: Rabbi Yoḥanan said the following: One only defers** to those greater than he **at a doorway that has a mezuza,** as only there is it appropriate to allow him to go first.

The Gemara challenges: A doorway **that has a mezuza, yes,** one defers; a doorway **that does not have a mezuza, no,** one does not defer? **If so, a synagogue or study hall that has no mezuza, there too, does one not defer** at their doorways? **Rather, say** that this is the principle: One only shows deference **at a doorway** where it is worthy **of affixing a mezuza,** but not on a road or a bridge.

The Gemara continues with the subject of deferring to one's superior during a meal: **Rav Yehuda, son of Rav Shmuel bar Sheilat, said in the name of Rav: Those reclining** at a meal **may not eat anything until the one breaking bread has tasted** the bread.[H] **Rav Safra sat and said:** May not **taste, was stated** by Rav, and not: May not eat.

The Gemara asks: **What difference does it make** whether Rav said taste or eat? The Gemara explains that there is no difference and that Rav Safra's insistence teaches that **one must say** what he was taught in the precise **language** employed **by his teacher** without altering a single detail.

The Gemara continues to discuss the subject of honors during a meal. **The Sages taught: Two people** who are eating **from a single dish must wait for each other,**[H] but if there are **three,** everyone eats when he wishes and **they need not wait for** each other. Generally, **the one who breaks bread extends his hand**[H] to take food **first,** but **if he wishes to defer to his teacher or to one who is greater** than he, **he has permission** to do so.

The Gemara relates: **Rabba bar bar Ḥana engaged in** preparations **for his son's wedding in the house of Rav Shmuel bar Rav Ketina.** He arrived early and sat and taught his son the *halakhot* of meals: **The one who breaks bread may not break** the bread **until amen has ended**[H] from the mouths of those responding. **Rav Ḥisda said:** One need only wait until amen has ended **from the mouths of the majority of those responding.**

**Rami bar Ḥama said to him: What is different** regarding the **majority** that one must wait until their amen ends before proceeding? **That until then, the blessing has not yet concluded.** If so, when the amen of **the minority** has not yet ended **as well, the blessing has not yet concluded.** Why doesn't the one breaking bread need to wait in that case?

**Rav Ḥisda said to him: Because I say** that **anyone who answers** an **amen** of **excessive** duration **is merely mistaken.**

תָּנוּ רַבָּנַן: אֵין עוֹנִין לֹא אָמֵן חֲטוּפָה וְלֹא אָמֵן קְטוּפָה, וְלֹא אָמֵן יְתוֹמָה וְלֹא יִזְרוֹק בְּרָכָה מִפִּיו.

With regard to answering amen, **the Sages taught: One should not respond** with **an abbreviated [*ḥatufa*] amen,**[H] in which the first syllable is not properly enunciated, **and a truncated [*ketufa*] amen,** in which the second syllable is not properly enunciated, **and an orphaned [*yetoma*] amen,**[N] in which the respondent is unaware of the blessing to which he is responding. Similarly, **one should not** quickly and indifferently **discharge a blessing from his mouth.**

בֶּן עַזַּאי אוֹמֵר: כׇּל הָעוֹנֶה אָמֵ[ן] יְתוֹמָה – יִהְיוּ בָּנָיו יְתוֹמִים, חֲטוּפָה – יִתְחַטְּפוּ יָמָיו, קְטוּפָה – יִתְקַטְּפוּ יָמָיו וְכׇל הַמַּאֲרִיךְ בְּאָמֵן – מַאֲרִיכִין ל[וֹ] יָמָיו וּשְׁנוֹתָיו.

**Ben Azzai says: Anyone who recites an orphaned amen, his children will be orphaned;** one who recites an **abbreviated** amen, **his days will be abbreviated** and incomplete; one who recites **a truncated** amen, **his days will be truncated. One who extends his amen, they will extend his days and years for him.** Nonetheless, one should not prolong it extensively.

רַב וּשְׁמוּאֵל הֲווּ יָתְבִי בִּסְעוּדְתָא אֲתָא רַב שִׁימִי בַּר חִיָּיא הֲוָ[ה] קָמְסַרְהֵב וְאָכֵיל. אָמַר לֵיהּ רַב: מַ[אי] דַּעְתָּךְ – לְאִיצְטָרוּפֵי בַּהֲדָן? אֲנַ[ן] אֲכֵילְנָא לָן! – אֲמַר לֵיהּ שְׁמוּאֵל: אִ[י] מַיְיתוּ לִי אַרְדִּילָיָא, וְגוֹזָלַיָּא לְאַבָּא – מִי לָא אָכְלִינַן?!

Returning to matters of *zimmun*, the Gemara relates: **Rav and Shmuel were sitting at a meal** when, much later, **Rav Shimi bar Ḥiyya arrived and was hurrying and eating. Rav said to him: What is your thinking?** Are you rushing in order **to join together with us** for a *zimmun*? **We have already eaten** and finished **our** meal before you arrived. **Shmuel said to** Rav: We have not really finished our meal, as **if they brought me truffles**[B] **or a young pigeon for Abba,** Rav, **wouldn't we eat it?** Since we would still eat, we have not yet finished our meal and Rabbi Shimi bar Ḥiyya can join us in the *zimmun*.[H]

תַּלְמִידֵי דְּרַב הֲווּ יָתְבִי בִּסְעוּדְתָא [עָ]עַל רַב אַחָא. אָמְרִי: אֲתָא גַּבְרָא רַבָּ[ה] דִּמְבָרֵךְ לָן. אֲמַר לְהוּ: מִי סָבְרִית[וּ] דְּגָדוֹל מְבָרֵךְ?! עִיקָּר שֶׁבִּסְעוּדָ[ה] מְבָרֵךְ. וְהִלְכְתָא: גָּדוֹל מְבָרֵךְ, אַ[ף] עַל גַּב דַּאֲתָא לְבַסּוֹף.

**Rav's students were seated at a meal** when **Rav Aḥa entered.** The students **said: A great man has come who can recite the blessing on our behalf.** Rav Aḥa **said to them: Do you think that the greatest recites the blessing?** That is not so. Rather, one of **the main** participants who was present from the beginning **of the meal recites the blessing.** The Gemara concludes: **The *halakha*,** however, **is that the greatest** person present **recites the blessing,**[H] **even if he arrived at the end** of the meal.

״אָכַל דְּמַאי״ וכו׳. הָא לָא חֲזֵי לֵיהּ! כֵּיוָן דְּאִי בָּעֵי – מַפְקַר לְהוּ לְנִכְסֵי[הּ] וְהָוֵי עָנִי, וְחָזֵי לֵיהּ, דִּתְנַן: מַאֲכִילִין אֶ[ת] הָעֲנִיִּים דְּמַאי וְאֶת הָאַכְסַנְיָא דְּמַא[י] וְאָמַר רַב הוּנָא: תָּנָא, בֵּית שַׁמַּא[י] אוֹמְרִים: אֵין מַאֲכִילִין אֶת הָעֲנִיִּי[ם] וְאֶת הָאַכְסַנְיָא דְּמַאי.

In the mishna, we learned that if, among the diners, **one ate doubtfully tithed produce [*demai*],**[N] he is included among the three to obligate those with whom he ate in a *zimmun*. The Gemara raises an objection: **But *demai* is not fit for his** consumption. He is forbidden to eat *demai*. The Gemara responds: He may recite Grace after Meals over it **because, if he wants, he could declare all of his property ownerless [*hefker*]**[B] **and he would be a pauper,** in which case the *demai* would be **fit for his** consumption. **As we learned** in a mishna: **One may feed the impoverished *demai***[H] **and one may feed soldiers [*akhsania*],**[L] whose support is imposed upon the residents of the city, ***demai*. And Rav Huna said: It was taught** in a *baraita* that **Beit Shammai say: One may not feed the impoverished and soldiers *demai*.**

### NOTES

**Amen – אָמֵן:** Several explanations were given for the various types of amen. Some explained *ḥatufa* as answering amen before the one reciting the blessing completed the blessing (*Arukh*). Some explained *ketufa* as one who stops in the middle of the word or slurred in between blessings (Rav Sa'adia Gaon). Some explained *yetoma* as amen answered long after the blessing was recited (*Arukh*).

**Doubtfully tithed produce [*demai*] – דְּמַאי:** *Demai* is produce that was purchased from an *am ha'aretz*, and, therefore, there is room for uncertainty whether or not it was tithed. The Gemara explains that this is not an actual uncertainty, but merely a concern, as most *amei ha'aretz* tithe. Due to that concern, anyone who purchases doubtfully tithed produce is required to tithe a second time. However, because it is merely due to a concern, the Sages were lenient in exigent circumstances, i.e., for the poor or to feed an army garrison, and permitted the use of *demai*.

### BACKGROUND

**Truffles – אַרְדִּילָיָא:** Truffles (*Tuberaceae*) are a unique family of fungi in that they remain underground in their entirety, even their fruit. Their fruit looks like a slightly rounded bulb, and may be black, brown, or off-white. They are generally 3–5 cm in diameter, although they can grow up to 10 cm, and the weight of a large truffle can reach as much as a kilogram.

Truffles are revealed when the ground above them cracks or by animals trained for that purpose. Most young truffles are edible and are considered a delicacy.

Truffles

**Ownerless property [*hefker*] – הֶפְקֵר:** When declaring an object ownerless, one must totally renounce his ownership of the property in question. He may not cede ownership in favor of certain people, thereby enabling them to acquire it, while denying others the opportunity to do so. According to some authorities it is necessary to renounce one's ownership of property in the presence of at least three people. Other authorities maintain that even a private statement is sufficient. Certain property is deemed ownerless by Torah law, e.g., produce that grows in the Sabbatical Year. Property belonging to a convert who dies without heirs is also ownerless. There is no obligation to tithe the produce that is ownerless.

### LANGUAGE

**Soldiers [*akhsania*] – אַכְסַנְיָא:** This word comes from the Greek ξενία, *xenia*, meaning for foreigners or to foreigners. It is a reference to a place that served as lodging for foreigners. Some understood the word to be synonymous with the Greek ὀψωνία, *opsonia*, meaning supply of food for the army.

### HALAKHA

**[O]ne should not respond with an abbreviated [*ḥatufa*] [a]men, etc. – אֵין עוֹנִים לֹא אָמֵן חֲטוּפָה וכו׳:** One must not answer amen hurriedly or while unaware of the blessing to which he is responding. Neither should he excessively prolong his answer of amen, in accordance with the statement [of] the *baraita* and the opinion of Rav Ḥisda. (Rambam *Sefer [A]hava, Hilkhot Tefilla* 1:14; *Shulḥan Arukh, Oraḥ Ḥayyim* 124:8).

**[T]o what point can a third join – עַד מָתַי מִצְטָרֵף שְׁלִישִׁי:** If two individuals ate a meal together and a third came to eat with them, as long as the two are willing to eat more, the third may join them for a *zimmun*, in accordance with the opinion of Shmuel (Rambam *Sefer Ahava, Hilkhot Berakhot* 5:9; *Shulḥan Arukh, Oraḥ Ḥayyim* 197:1).

**The greatest recites the blessing – גָּדוֹל מְבָרֵךְ:** The greatest member of the group recites Grace after Meals, even if he arrived at the end (Rambam *Sefer Ahava, Hilkhot Berakhot* 7:12; *Shulḥan Arukh, Oraḥ Ḥayyim* 201:1).

**One may feed the impoverished *demai*, etc. – מַאֲכִילִין אֶת הָעֲנִיִּים דְּמַאי וכו׳:** It is permissible to feed *demai* to the poor and to short-term guests (Rambam, based on the Jerusalem Talmud), as well as to an army garrison (Rambam *Sefer Zera'im, Hilkhot Terumot* 10:11).

״מַעֲשֵׂר רִאשׁוֹן שֶׁנִּטְּלָה תְּרוּמָתוֹ״. פְּשִׁיטָא! לָא צְרִיכָא אֶלָּא שֶׁהִקְדִּימוֹ בְּשִׁבֳּלִים, וְהִפְרִישׁ מִמֶּנּוּ תְּרוּמַת מַעֲשֵׂר וְלֹא הִפְרִישׁ מִמֶּנּוּ תְּרוּמָה גְּדוֹלָה; וְכִדְרַבִּי אַבָּהוּ, דְּאָמַר רַבִּי אַבָּהוּ אָמַר רֵישׁ לָקִישׁ: מַעֲשֵׂר רִאשׁוֹן שֶׁהִקְדִּימוֹ בְּשִׁבֳּלִים – פָּטוּר מִתְּרוּמָה גְּדוֹלָה, שֶׁנֶּאֱמַר: ״וַהֲרֵמֹתֶם מִמֶּנּוּ תְּרוּמַת ה׳ מַעֲשֵׂר מִן הַמַּעֲשֵׂר״ – מַעֲשֵׂר מִן הַמַּעֲשֵׂר אָמַרְתִּי לְךָ, וְלֹא תְּרוּמָה גְּדוֹלָה וּתְרוּמַת מַעֲשֵׂר מִן הַמַּעֲשֵׂר

We learned in the mishna: If, among the diners, one ate **first tithe from which its *teruma* was** already **taken,**[N] he may be included in a *zimmun*. The Gemara remarks: **It is obvious** that if the *teruma* was already taken there is no problem. Why was it necessary for the mishna to teach that one can join a *zimmun*? The Gemara explains: **It was only necessary** to teach this *halakha* **in a case** where the Levite **preceded** the priest while the grain was still **on the stalks,**[H] **and he separated the *teruma* of the tithes** but **did not separate the *teruma gedola*.** *Teruma gedola* was not separated from the tithe that was eaten by the Levite. Although this should not be done *ab initio*, after the fact it is permitted, and one who eats first tithe produce under these circumstances may be included in a *zimmun*. **And** this is **in accordance with** the opinion of **Rabbi Abbahu, as Rabbi Abbahu said** that **Reish Lakish said: First tithe** in which the Levite **preceded** the priest while the grain was still **on the stalks**[H] **is exempt from *teruma gedola*, as it is stated: "And you shall set apart from it a gift for the Lord, even a tenth part of the tithe"** (Numbers 18:26). This verse **teaches** that the Levite is obligated to set apart **a tenth part of the tithe,** i.e., the *teruma* of the tithe **and not *teruma gedola* and the *teruma* of the tithe.**

אָמַר לֵיהּ רַב פַּפָּא לְאַבַּיֵי: אִי הָכִי, אֲפִילּוּ הִקְדִּימוֹ בִּכְרִי נָמֵי! אֲמַר לֵיהּ: עָלֶיךָ אָמַר קְרָא

**Rav Pappa said to Abaye: If so, even if** the Levite **preceded** the priest after the kernels of grain were removed from the stalks and placed **in a pile,** the Levite should not have to separate *teruma gedola*. Abaye **said to him: With regard to your** claim, **the verse stated:**

### NOTES

**Separation of *teruma* and tithes** – הַפְרָשׁוֹת תְּרוּמָה וּמַעֲשֵׂר: The proper way to separate *teruma* and tithes is as follows: Generally, these gifts are not separated until after the produce has bees harvested, threshed and gathered into piles. The *teruma gedola*, given to the priest, is separated first. The average gift, as determined by the Rabbis, is one-fiftieth of the crop. Next, one-tenth of the remaining heap is separated as the first tithe and given to the Levite. The Levite himself must tithe his portion for the priest as the *teruma* of the tithe, which has the legal status of *teruma*. Next, an additional tithe is separated, the second tithe. This must be brought to Jerusalem and eaten there by its owners, or exchanged for its value in coins which must then be spent on food in Jerusalem. During the third and sixth years of the Sabbatical cycle, the poor-man's tithe is given to the Jewish poor in lieu of the second tithe.

### HALAKHA

**That he preceded the priest while the grain was still on the stalks** – שֶׁהִקְדִּימוֹ בְּשִׁבֳּלִים: If a Levite took the tithe while the grain was still on the stalks, once the *teruma* of the tithe was separated, it may be eaten and a blessing may be recited over it (Rambam *Sefer Ahava*, *Hilkhot Berakhot* 1:20).

**First tithe in which the Levite preceded the priest while the grain was still on the stalks** – מַעֲשֵׂר רִאשׁוֹן שֶׁהִקְדִּימוֹ בְּשִׁבֳּלִים: If a Levite took the tithe while the grain was still on the stalks, he is required to separate *teruma* of the tithe from it, but not *teruma gedola*, in accordance with the opinion of Rabbi Abbahu (Rambam *Sefer Zera'im*, *Hilkhot Terumot* 3:13).

Perek **VII**
Daf **47** Amud **b**

״מִכֹּל מַעְשְׂרֹתֵיכֶם תָּרִימוּ״. וּמָה רָאִיתָ? הַאי אִידְּגַן וְהַאי לָא אִידְּגַן.

**"From all of that is given to you, you shall set apart** that which is the Lord's *teruma*" (Numbers 18:29). God's *teruma*, *teruma gedola* must be taken from all of the Levites' gifts. The Gemara asks: **And what did you see**[N] that led you to require *teruma gedola* from first tithe that was taken from grain in piles and not from first tithe that was taken from grain on stalks? Abaye answers: **This,** after it was threshed and placed into piles, is completely processed and **has become grain, and that,** which remained on the stalk, **did not** yet **become grain.** The verse regarding *teruma gedola* states: "The first of your grain" (Deuteronomy 18:4), is given to the priest. Once it is considered grain, the right of the priest takes effect and the Levite is required to separate *teruma gedola*.

״מַעֲשֵׂר שֵׁנִי וְהֶקְדֵּשׁ שֶׁנִּפְדּוּ״. פְּשִׁיטָא! הָכָא בְּמַאי עָסְקִינַן – כְּגוֹן שֶׁנָּתַן אֶת הַקֶּרֶן וְלֹא נָתַן אֶת הַחוֹמֶשׁ, וְהָא קָא מַשְׁמַע לָן: דְּאֵין חוֹמֶשׁ מְעַכֵּב.

The mishna states that if, among the diners, one ate **second tithe and consecrated food that were redeemed,**[H] he may be included in a *zimmun*. The Gemara remarks: **It is obvious** that if these items were redeemed that one could participate in a *zimmun*. The Gemara responds: **With what are we dealing here?** We are dealing with **a case** where the consecrated property was not completely redeemed, i.e., **where one gave** payment for **the principal,** the value of the tithe, **but he did not give** payment for **the fifth** that he must add when redeeming items that he consecrated; **and the** mishna **teaches us** that failure to add **the fifth does not invalidate** the redemption.

״הַשַּׁמָּשׁ שֶׁאָכַל כַּזַּיִת״ פְּשִׁיטָא! מַהוּ דְּתֵימָא שַׁמָּשׁ לָא קָבַע – קָא מַשְׁמַע לָן.

We learned in the mishna: **The waiter who ate** at least **an olive bulk** from the meal may join in a *zimmun*. The Gemara remarks: **It is obvious.** Why was it necessary for the mishna to teach this *halakha*? The Gemara answers: **Lest you say that the waiter** who stands and serves the diners **did not establish** himself as a participant in the meal and, therefore, cannot join the *zimmun*, the mishna **teaches us** that even the waiter is considered to have established himself as a participant in the meal.

### NOTES

**And what did you see** – וּמָה רָאִיתָ: This question is the standard formula when two verses or *halakhot*, whose details were not elucidated, are explained. One verse is applied to one case while the second is assigned to a second case. The Gemara then asks: What did you see that led you to distinguish between these cases and explain the verses in that manner? You could have just as easily posited the reverse? Here the question is asked because the one who preceded the priest while the grain remained on the stalks is more deserving of penalty because he is certain that *teruma* has yet to be separated, whereas the Levite who precedes the priest while the grain is already in a pile could have assumed that the owner already separated *teruma* (*Tosefot HaRosh*).

### HALAKHA

**Second tithe and consecrated food that were redeemed** – מַעֲשֵׂר שֵׁנִי וְהֶקְדֵּשׁ שֶׁנִּפְדּוּ: One is permitted to recite blessings over and eat consecrated items or second tithe produce that were redeemed for their value in coins even before he adds the required one-fifth of its value (Rambam *Sefer Ahava*, *Hilkhot Berakhot* 1:20).

״וְהַכּוּתִי מְזַמְּנִין עָלָיו״. אַמַּאי? לֹא יְהֵ
אֶלָּא עַם הָאָרֶץ, וְתַנְיָא: אֵין מְזַמְּנִין עַל עַ
הָאָרֶץ!

The mishna states that a **Samaritan [*Kuti*] may be included in a *zimmun*.** The Gemara asks: **Why?** Even if you consider him a member of the Jewish people, **let him be merely an *am ha'aretz*,**[B] one who is not scrupulous in matters of ritual purity and tithes, **and it was taught** in a *baraita*: **An *am ha'aretz* may not be included in a *zimmun*.**[H]

אַבַּיֵי אָמַר: בְּכוּתִי חָבֵר. רָבָא אָמַר: אֲפִי
תֵּימָא בְּכוּתִי עַם הָאָרֶץ, וְהָכָא בְּעַם הָאָרֶ
דְּרַבָּנַן דִּפְלִיגִי עֲלֵיהּ דְּרַבִּי מֵאִיר עָסְקִינַ
דְּתַנְיָא: אֵיזֶהוּ עַם הָאָרֶץ? כָּל שֶׁאֵינוֹ אוֹכֵ
חוּלָּיו בְּטָהֳרָה, דִּבְרֵי רַבִּי מֵאִיר; וַחֲכָמִי
אוֹמְרִים: כָּל שֶׁאֵינוֹ מְעַשֵּׂר פֵּירוֹתָיו כָּרָאוּ
וְהָנֵי כּוּתָאֵי – עַשּׂוּרֵי מְעַשְּׂרִי כַּדְחָזֵי, דִּבְמַא
דִּכְתִיב בְּאוֹרַיְיתָא מִזְהַר זְהִירִי דַּאֲמַר מָ
כָּל מִצְוָה שֶׁהֶחֱזִיקוּ בָּהּ כּוּתִים – הַרְבֵּ
מְדַקְדְּקִין בָּהּ, יוֹתֵר מִיִּשְׂרָאֵל.

The Gemara offers several answers: **Abaye said:** The mishna is referring to a ***Kuti* who is a *ḥaver*,** one who is scrupulous in those areas. **Rava said: Even if you say** that the mishna refers to a ***Kuti*** who is an ***am ha'aretz*, and here** the prohibition to include an *am ha'aretz* in a *zimmun* refers to an *am ha'aretz* as defined by **the Rabbis who disagree with Rabbi Meir, as it was taught** in a *baraita*: **Who is an *am ha'aretz*? Anyone who does not eat non-sacred food in** a state of **ritual purity.** This is **the statement of Rabbi Meir. And the Rabbis say:** An *am ha'aretz* is **anyone who does not appropriately tithe his produce. And these *Kutim* tithe** their produce **appropriately, as they are scrupulous with regard to that which is written in the Torah, as the Master said: Any mitzva that the *Kutim* embraced** and accepted upon themselves, **they** are even **more exacting in its** observance **than Jews.**

תָּנוּ רַבָּנַן: אֵיזֶהוּ עַם הָאָרֶץ? כָּל שֶׁאֵינוֹ קוֹרֵ
קְרִיאַת שְׁמַע עַרְבִית וְשַׁחֲרִית, דִּבְרֵי רַבִּ
אֱלִיעֶזֶר, רַבִּי יְהוֹשֻׁעַ אוֹמֵר: כָּל שֶׁאֵינוֹ מַנִּי
תְּפִילִּין, בֶּן עַזַּאי אוֹמֵר: כָּל שֶׁאֵין לוֹ צִיצִיו
בְּבִגְדוֹ, רַבִּי נָתָן אוֹמֵר: כָּל שֶׁאֵין מְזוּזָה עַ
פִּתְחוֹ, רַבִּי נָתָן בַּר יוֹסֵף אוֹמֵר: כָּל שֶׁיֵּשׁ 
בָּנִים וְאֵינוֹ מְגַדְּלָם לְתַלְמוּד תּוֹרָה, אֲחֵרִי
אוֹמְרִים: אֲפִילּוּ קָרָא וְשָׁנָה וְלֹא שִׁמֵּ
תַּלְמִידֵי חֲכָמִים הֲרֵי זֶה עַם הָאָרֶץ. אָמַ
רַב הוּנָא: הֲלָכָה כַּאֲחֵרִים.

The Gemara cites a *baraita* with additional opinions with regard to the defining characteristics of an *am ha'aretz*: **The Sages taught: Who is an *am ha'aretz*? One who does not recite *Shema* in the evening and morning. Rabbi Yehoshua says:** An *am ha'aretz* is **one who does not don phylacteries. Ben Azzai says:** An *am ha'aretz* is **one who does not have ritual fringes on his garment. Rabbi Natan says:** An *am ha'aretz* is **one who does not have a *mezuza* on his doorway. Rabbi Natan bar Yosef says:** An *am ha'aretz* is **one who has children but** who does not want them to study Torah, so he **does not raise them to** engage in **Torah study. *Aḥerim* say: Even if one read the Bible and studied Mishna and did not serve Torah scholars** to learn from them the meaning of the Torah that he studied, **that is an *am ha'aretz*. Rav Huna said: The *halakha* is in accordance with** the opinion of ***Aḥerim*.**

רָמִי בַּר חָמָא לֹא אַזְמִין עֲלֵיהּ דְּרַב מְנַשְׁיָ
בַּר תַּחְלִיפָא דְּתָנֵי סִיפְרָא וְסִפְרֵי וְהִלְכְתָ
כִּי נָח נַפְשֵׁיהּ דְּרָמִי בַּר חָמָא, אָמַר רָבָא: לָ
נָח נַפְשֵׁיהּ דְּרָמִי בַּר חָמָא אֶלָּא דְּלָא אַזְמִ
אַרַב מְנַשְׁיָא בַּר תַּחְלִיפָא. וְהָתַנְיָא, אֲחֵרִי
אוֹמְרִים: אֲפִילּוּ קָרָא וְשָׁנָה וְלֹא שִׁמֵּ
תַּלְמִידֵי חֲכָמִים הֲרֵי זֶה עַם הָאָרֶץ! שָׁא
רַב מְנַשְׁיָא בַּר תַּחְלִיפָא דִּמְשַׁמַּע לְהוּ לְרַבָּ
וְרָמִי בַּר חָמָא הוּא דְּלָא דַּק אַבַּתְרֵיהּ. לִישָּׁ
אַחֲרִינָא: דְּשָׁמַע שְׁמַעֲתָא מִפּוּמַּיְיהוּ דְּרַבָּ
וְגָרֵיס לְהוּ – כְּצוּרְבָא מֵרַבָּנַן דָּמֵי.

The Gemara relates: **Rami bar Ḥama did not include Rav Menashya bar Taḥlifa, who studied *Sifra*, *Sifrei*, and *halakhot*, in a *zimmun*** because he had merely studied and did not serve Torah scholars. **When Rami bar Ḥama passed away, Rava said: Rami bar Ḥama died only because he did not include Rabbi Menashya bar Taḥlifa in a *zimmun*.** The Gemara asks: **Was it not taught** in a *baraita*: ***Aḥerim* say: Even if one read the Bible and studied mishna and did not serve Torah scholars, that is an *am ha'aretz*?** Why, then, was Rami bar Ḥama punished? The Gemara answers: **Rav Menashya bar Taḥlifa is different, as he served the Sages. And it was Rami bar Ḥama who was not precise** in his efforts to check **after him** to ascertain his actions. **Another version** of the Gemara's answer: Anyone **who hears *halakhot* from the mouths of Sages and studies them is considered a Torah scholar.**

״אָכַל טֶבֶל וּמַעֲשֵׂר״ וכו׳. טֶבֶל – פְּשִׁיטָא
לָא צְרִיכָא – בְּטֶבֶל טָבוּל מִדְּרַבָּנַן. הֵיכִ
דָּמֵי – בְּעָצִיץ שֶׁאֵינוֹ נָקוּב.

The mishna states that **one who ate untithed produce and** first **tithe** etc. is not included in a *zimmun*. The Gemara remarks: **It is obvious** as one is forbidden to eat untithed produce. The Gemara responds: **It was only necessary** to teach this *halakha* with regard to a case where it is only considered **untithed produce by rabbinic law,** although by Torah law it was permitted. **What are the circumstances?** Where the produce grew **in an unperforated flowerpot,** as anything grown disconnected from the ground is not considered produce of the ground and is exempt by Torah law from tithing. It is only by rabbinic law that it is considered untithed.

״מַעֲשֵׂר רִאשׁוֹן״ כו׳. פְּשִׁיטָא! לָא צְרִיכָא
כְּגוֹן שֶׁהִקְדִּימוֹ בִּכְרִי. מַהוּ דְּתֵימָא: כִּדְאָמַ
לֵיהּ רַב פַּפָּא לְאַבַּיֵי – קָא מַשְׁמַע לָן, כִּדְשָׁ
לֵיהּ.

We learned in the mishna that one who ate **first tithe** from which its *teruma* was not separated may not be included in a *zimmun*. The Gemara remarks: **It is obvious.** The Gemara responds: **It was only necessary** for the mishna to teach this with regard to a case **where** the Levite **preceded** the priest after the kernels of grain were placed **in a pile. Lest you say as Rav Pappa said to Abaye,** that in that case, too, the produce should be exempt from the obligation to separate *teruma gedola*, the *tanna* of the mishna **teaches us as** Abaye **responded** to Rav Pappa, that there is a difference between the case when the grain was on the stalks and the case when the grain was in a pile.

**BACKGROUND**

**Am ha'aretz – עַם הָאָרֶץ:** The term *am ha'aretz*, literally, people of the land, already appears in the books of Ezra and Nehemiah as a term reserved for gentiles, not Jews. At a later stage, *am ha'aretz* became a derogatory epithet for a Jew who acts like a gentile. Fundamentally, an *am ha'aretz* is not just one ignorant of Torah, who might be called an ignoramus or fool [*boor*], but one who actually behaves in a non-Jewish manner. It is clear from this *baraita* that *am ha'aretz* is not a clearly defined concept. There are many opinions with regard to characterizing an *am ha'aretz*. They range from the opinion that the term refers to one who does not serve Torah scholars and learn from them to the opinion that the term refers to one with no Torah, no Mishna and no manners. According to the first opinion, many learned people are included in this category. According to the second opinion, an *am ha'aretz* is the basest of individuals to whom the most derogatory epithets are generally applied. The common application of the term is to one devoid of spirituality, with no profession or occupation, no education, and no connection to Torah and mitzvot.

However, in the talmudic era, and even more so in later times, the situation changed in two respects. First, while there remained many who were uneducated, the *am ha'aretz* in its most extreme form disappeared, as even simple Jews upheld Torah and mitzvot to the best of their ability. Secondly, to avoid causing rifts among the nation in exile and in their wanderings, the *halakhot* restricting inclusion of most types of *am ha'aretz* were repealed.

**HALAKHA**

**An *am ha'aretz* may not be included in a *zimmun* – אֵין מְזַמְּנִין עַל עַם הָאָרֶץ:** Nowadays, even a full-fledged *am ha'aretz* may be included in a *zimmun* so as not to cause divisiveness within the Jewish people (*Tosafot*). Only one who has excluded himself from the community of Israel may not be included in a *zimmun* (*Magen Avraham*; *Shulḥan Arukh*, *Oraḥ Ḥayyim* 199:3).

LANGUAGE

Unminted coin [*asimon*] – אֲסִימוֹן: From the Greek ἄσημον, *asèmon*, meaning a coin not stamped with any particular form.

Unminted coin

NOTES

The laws of the second tithe – דִּין מַעֲשֵׂר שֵׁנִי: The second tithe must be taken to Jerusalem and eaten there. However, because fruit may rot along the way, the Torah permitted one to sell that tithe, take the money to Jerusalem, and use that money to purchase food to eat there. Based on the interpretation cited in the Gemara here, the second tithe may be exchanged only for coins.

HALAKHA

Inclusion of a convert in a *zimmun* – צֵירוּף גֵּר לְזִימּוּן: Until the proselyte immerses, he may not be included in a *zimmun* (*Shulḥan Arukh*, *Yoreh De'a* 268:4).

Acceptance of a convert – קַבָּלַת גֵּר: After the convert is circumcised and heals, he is immersed in a ritual bath and thereby becomes a full-fledged Jew. In Temple times, the conversion was not complete until the convert brought an animal or two birds as a burnt-offering. Even if the convert later reverts to his previous faith, his conversion to Judaism remains in effect and he has the legal status of an apostate Jew. The Torah explicitly commands Jews to provide a convert with all his needs, to love him, and not to torment him by reminding him of his past (Rambam *Sefer Kedusha*, *Hilkhot Issurei Bia* 13:6; *Shulḥan Arukh*, *Yoreh De'a* 268:2).

One who frees his slave – הַמְשַׁחְרֵר עַבְדּוֹ: One who frees his Canaanite slave violates a positive mitzva, though he is permitted to do so to facilitate the fulfillment of a mitzva (Rambam *Sefer Kinyan*, *Hilkhot Avadim* 9:6; *Shulḥan Arukh*, *Yoreh De'a* 267:79).

״מַעֲשֵׂר שֵׁנִי״ וכו׳. פְּשִׁיטָא! לָא צְרִיכָא שֶׁנִּפְדּוּ וְלֹא נִפְדּוּ כְּהִלְכָתָן; מַעֲשֵׂר שֵׁנִי – כְּגוֹן שֶׁפְּדָאוֹ עַל גַּבֵּי אֲסִימוֹן, וְרַחֲמָנָא אָמַר: ״וְצַרְתָּ הַכֶּסֶף בְּיָדְךָ״ – כֶּסֶף שֶׁיֵּשׁ (לוֹ) עָלָיו צוּרָה, הֶקְדֵּשׁ – שֶׁחִלְּלוֹ עַל גַּבֵּי קַרְקַע וְלֹא פְּדָאוֹ בְּכֶסֶף, וְרַחֲמָנָא אָמַר: ״וְנָתַן הַכֶּסֶף וְקָם לוֹ״.

We also learned in the mishna that if one ate **second tithe** and consecrated food that had not been redeemed, he may not be included in a *zimmun*. The Gemara remarks: **It is obvious?** Why was it necessary for the mishna to teach this *halakha*? The Gemara responds: **It was only necessary** for the mishna to teach this *halakha* with regard to a case **where they were redeemed, but not redeemed properly, i.e., second tithe that was redeemed with an unminted coin** [***asimon***],[L] a silver bullion that had not been engraved. **And the Torah says: "And bind up** [***vetzarta***] **the money in your hand"** (Deuteronomy 14:25), which the Sages interpreted as follows: *Vetzarta* refers to **money that has a form** [***tzura***] engraved **upon it. Consecrated property;** in a case **where he redeemed it** by exchanging it **for land instead of money, and the Torah states: "He will give the money and it will be assured to him"** (Leviticus 27:19).[N]

״וְהַשַּׁמָּשׁ שֶׁאָכַל פָּחוֹת מִכַּזַּיִת״. פְּשִׁיטָא! אַיְּידֵי דִּתְנָא רֵישָׁא ״כַּזַּיִת״, תְּנָא סֵיפָא ״פָּחוֹת מִכַּזַּיִת״.

The mishna states that **a waiter who ate less than an olive-bulk** may not join a *zimmun*. The Gemara remarks: **It is obvious.** Why was it necessary for the mishna to teach this *halakha*? The Gemara answers: **Since the first clause** of the mishna **taught** the *halakha* with regard to a waiter who ate **an olive-bulk, the latter clause taught** the *halakha* with regard to a waiter who ate **less than an olive-bulk.** Although it is obvious, in the interest of arriving at a similar formulation in the two parts of the mishna, it was included.

״וְהַנָּכְרִי אֵין מְזַמְּנִין עָלָיו״. פְּשִׁיטָא! הָכָא בְּמַאי עָסְקִינַן – בְּגֵר שֶׁמָּל וְלֹא טָבַל, דְּאָמַר רַבִּי זֵירָא אָמַר רַבִּי יוֹחָנָן: לְעוֹלָם אֵינוֹ גֵּר עַד שֶׁיָּמוּל וְיִטְבּוֹל, וְכַמָּה דְּלָא טְבַל גּוֹי הוּא.

The mishna further states that **a gentile is not included in a *zimmun*.** The Gemara remarks: **It is obvious.** Why was it necessary for the mishna to teach this *halakha*? The Gemara answers: **With what are we dealing here?** We are dealing **with** a case of **a convert**[H] **who was circumcised but** did **not** yet **immerse** himself in a ritual bath, **as Rabbi Zeira said** that **Rabbi Yoḥanan said: One is never** considered **a proselyte until he is circumcised and immerses** himself. **As long as he did not immerse** himself, **he is a gentile.**[H]

״נָשִׁים וַעֲבָדִים וּקְטַנִּים אֵין מְזַמְּנִין עֲלֵיהֶן״. אָמַר רַבִּי יוֹסֵי: קָטָן הַמּוּטָל בַּעֲרִיסָה מְזַמְּנִין עָלָיו.

We also learned in the mishna that **women, slaves, and minors are not included in a *zimmun*. Rabbi Yosei said: A minor lying in a cradle is included in a *zimmun*.**

וְהָא תְּנַן: נָשִׁים וַעֲבָדִים וּקְטַנִּים אֵין מְזַמְּנִין עֲלֵיהֶם!

The Gemara objects: **Didn't we learn** in the mishna **that women, slaves, and minors are not included in a *zimmun*?**

הוּא דְּאָמַר כְּרַבִּי יְהוֹשֻׁעַ בֶּן לֵוִי, דְּאָמַר רַבִּי יְהוֹשֻׁעַ בֶּן לֵוִי: אַף עַל פִּי שֶׁאָמְרוּ קָטָן הַמּוּטָל בַּעֲרִיסָה אֵין מְזַמְּנִין עָלָיו – אֲבָל עוֹשִׂין אוֹתוֹ סְנִיף לַעֲשָׂרָה.

The Gemara responds: Rabbi Yosei **stated** his opinion **in accordance with** the opinion of **Rabbi Yehoshua ben Levi, as Rabbi Yehoshua ben Levi said: Although a minor lying in a cradle is not included in a *zimmun*, one may make him an adjunct to** complete an assembly of **ten** people, enabling them to invoke God's name in a *zimmun*.

וְאָמַר רַבִּי יְהוֹשֻׁעַ בֶּן לֵוִי: תִּשְׁעָה וְעֶבֶד מִצְטָרְפִין. מֵיתִיבֵי: מַעֲשֶׂה בְּרַבִּי אֱלִיעֶזֶר שֶׁנִּכְנַס לְבֵית הַכְּנֶסֶת וְלֹא מָצָא עֲשָׂרָה, וְשִׁחְרֵר עַבְדּוֹ וְהִשְׁלִימוֹ לַעֲשָׂרָה. שִׁחְרֵר – אִין, לֹא שִׁחְרֵר – לָא! תְּרֵי אִיצְטְרִיכוּ, שִׁחְרֵר חַד וְנָפֵיק בְּחַד.

On the subject of completing a *zimmun*, **Rabbi Yehoshua ben Levi said: Nine** Jews **and a slave join together** to form a *zimmun* of ten. The Gemara **raises an objection:** There was an **incident involving Rabbi Eliezer, who entered a synagogue and did not find** a quorum of **ten, and he liberated his slave and he completed the** quorum of **ten.** From this we may infer that if he **freed** his slave, **yes,** he may join the quorum of ten, but if he **did not free** him, **no,** he may not join the quorum of ten. The Gemara responds: In that case, **two were required** to complete the quorum; Rabbi Eliezer **freed one and fulfilled his obligation with** another **one,** who completed the quorum of ten without being freed.

וְהֵיכִי עָבֵיד הָכִי? וְהָאָמַר רַב יְהוּדָה: כׇּל הַמְשַׁחְרֵר עַבְדּוֹ עוֹבֵר בַּעֲשֵׂה, שֶׁנֶּאֱמַר: ״לְעֹלָם בָּהֶם תַּעֲבֹדוּ״! לִדְבַר מִצְוָה שָׁאנֵי. מִצְוָה הַבָּאָה בַּעֲבֵירָה הִיא! מִצְוָה דְּרַבִּים שָׁאנֵי.

With regard to this incident, the Gemara asks: **How did he do that? Didn't Rav Yehuda say: Anyone who frees his** Canaanite **slave violates a positive mitzva, as it is stated** with regard to Canaanite slaves: "You will keep them as an inheritance for your children after you, to hold as a possession; **they will serve as bondsmen for you forever"** (Leviticus 25:46)? How, then, could Rabbi Eliezer have freed his slave? The Gemara answers: The case of **a mitzva is different.** The Gemara asks: **It is a mitzva that comes through a transgression,** and a mitzva fulfilled in that manner is inherently flawed. The Gemara responds: **A mitzva** that benefits **the many is different,** and one may free his slave for that purpose.

וְאָמַר רַבִּי יְהוֹשֻׁעַ בֶּן לֵוִי: לְעוֹלָם יַשְׁכִּים אָדָם לְבֵית הַכְּנֶסֶת כְּדֵי שֶׁיִּזְכֶּה וְיִמָּנֶה עִם עֲשָׂרָה הָרִאשׁוֹנִים שֶׁאֲפִילּוּ מֵאָה בָּאִים אַחֲרָיו – קִבֵּל עָלָיו שְׂכַר כּוּלָּם. שְׂכַר כּוּלָּם – סָלְקָא דַּעְתָּךְ?! אֶלָּא אֵימָא: נוֹתְנִין לוֹ שָׂכָר כְּנֶגֶד כּוּלָּם.

In praise of a quorum of ten, the Gemara states that **Rabbi Yehoshua ben Levi said: One should always rise early** to go **to the synagogue**[H] **in order to have the privilege and be counted among the first ten** to complete the quorum, **as even if one hundred** people **arrive after him, he receives the reward of them all,** as they are all joining that initial quorum. The Gemara is perplexed: **Does it enter your mind** that he receives **the reward of them all?** Why should he take away their reward? **Rather,** emend the statement and **say: He receives a reward equivalent to** the reward of **them all.**

אָמַר רַב הוּנָא: תִּשְׁעָה וְאָרוֹן מִצְטָרְפִין. אֲמַר לֵיהּ רַב נַחְמָן: וְאָרוֹן גַּבְרָא הוּא?! – אֶלָּא אָמַר רַב הוּנָא: תִּשְׁעָה נִרְאִין כַּעֲשָׂרָה מִצְטָרְפִין. אָמְרִי לַהּ: כִּי מְכַנְּפִי, וְאָמְרִי לַהּ: כִּי מְבַדְּרִי.

With regard to the laws of joining a quorum, **Rav Huna said: Nine plus an ark** in which the Torah scrolls are stored **join** to form a quorum of ten.[N] **Rav Naḥman said to him: Is an ark a man,** that it may be counted in the quorum of ten? **Rather, Rav Huna said: Nine who appear like ten may join together.** There was disagreement over this: **Some said this** *halakha* as follows: Nine appear like ten **when they are gathered. And some said this** *halakha* as follows: Nine appear like ten **when they are scattered,** the disagreement being which formation creates the impression of a greater number of individuals.

אָמַר רַב אַמֵּי: שְׁנַיִם וְשַׁבָּת מִצְטָרְפִין. אֲמַר לֵיהּ רַב נַחְמָן: וְשַׁבָּת גַּבְרָא הוּא?! – אֶלָּא אָמַר רַבִּי אַמֵּי: שְׁנֵי תַלְמִידֵי חֲכָמִים הַמְחַדְּדִין זֶה אֶת זֶה בַּהֲלָכָה מִצְטָרְפִין. מַחְוֵי רַב חִסְדָּא: כְּגוֹן אֲנָא וְרַב שֵׁשֶׁת. מַחְוֵי רַב שֵׁשֶׁת: כְּגוֹן אֲנָא וְרַב חִסְדָּא.

Similarly, **Rav Ami said: Two** people **and Shabbat join** to form a *zimmun.* **Rav Naḥman said to him: Is Shabbat a person,** that it may be counted in a *zimmun*? **Rather, Rav Ami said: Two Torah scholars who hone each other's** intellect **in halakhic** discourse **join together** and are considered three. The Gemara relates: **Rav Ḥisda pointed** to an example of two such Torah scholars who hone each other's intellect: **For example, me and Rav Sheshet.** Similarly, **Rav Sheshet pointed: For example, me and Rav Ḥisda.**

אָמַר רַבִּי יוֹחָנָן: קָטָן פּוֹרֵחַ מְזַמְּנִין עָלָיו. תַּנְיָא נַמִּי הָכִי: קָטָן שֶׁהֵבִיא שְׁתֵּי שְׂעָרוֹת מְזַמְּנִין עָלָיו, וְשֶׁלֹּא הֵבִיא שְׁתֵּי שְׂעָרוֹת – אֵין מְזַמְּנִין עָלָיו, וְאֵין מְדַקְדְּקִין בְּקָטָן. הָא גוּפָא קַשְׁיָא! אָמְרַתְּ: הֵבִיא שְׁתֵּי שְׂעָרוֹת – אִין, לֹא הֵבִיא – לָא, וַהֲדַר תָּנֵי: אֵין מְדַקְדְּקִין בְּקָטָן, לְאַתּוּיֵי מַאי? לָאו

With regard to a minor's inclusion in a *zimmun,* **Rabbi Yoḥanan said: A mature minor,** i.e., one who is still a minor in terms of age, but is displaying signs of puberty, **is included in a *zimmun*.** **That** opinion **was also taught** in a *baraita*: **A minor who grew two** pubic **hairs,** a sign of puberty, **is included in a *zimmun*; and one who did not grow two hairs is not included in a *zimmun*. And one is not exacting with regard to a minor.** The Gemara comments: **This** *baraita* **itself is difficult. You said that** a minor **who grew two hairs, yes,** he is included, **one who did not grow** two hairs, **no,** he is not included, **and then it taught that one is not exacting with regard to a minor. What** does this last clause come **to include? Is it not**

#### HALAKHA

**One should always rise early to go to the synagogue – לְעוֹלָם יַשְׁכִּים אָדָם לְבֵית הַכְּנֶסֶת:** One must make an effort to be among the first ten to arrive at the synagogue for prayer (Rambam *Sefer Ahava, Hilkhot Tefilla* 8:1; *Shulḥan Arukh, Oraḥ Ḥayyim* 90:14).

#### NOTES

**Nine plus an ark may join together – תִּשְׁעָה וְאָרוֹן מִצְטָרְפִין:** Many have questioned this formulation as well as the explanation subsequently offered by the Gemara, which is, ostensibly, completely different from the initial statement. The idea of nine plus an ark was explained as referring to an ark with a Torah scroll inside it, and we know that with regard to certain matters, e.g., declaring a leap year, a child holding a Torah scroll was counted to complete a quorum in exigent circumstances. Consequently, there was room to consider that he could also be counted to complete a prayer quorum. Some explain that this ark is none other than the Ark of the Covenant that was in the Holy Temple, with regard to which the Gemara says (*Bava Batra* 99a) that although it was visible from all sides, it did not occupy space. So too here, the tenth person will be like that Ark, i.e., he seems to be there although he is not (*Kol Eliyahu*). Some related to the words *aron* and Shabbat as acronyms: *Alef, resh, vav, nun* standing for *eḥad ro'e ve'eino nir'e,* meaning, "one who sees but is not seen"; *shin, bet, tav* standing for *sheneihem benei Torah,* meaning, "both are Torah scholars."

Perek **VII**
Daf **48** Amud **a**

לְאַתּוּיֵי קָטָן פּוֹרֵחַ.

**to include a mature minor?** Explain the *baraita* as follows: A minor who grew two hairs is included in a *zimmun,* and we are not exacting with regard to a minor to ascertain whether or not he has reached the age of majority.

וְלֵית הִלְכְתָא כְּכׇל הָנֵי שְׁמַעְתָּתָא, אֶלָּא כִּי הָא דְּאָמַר רַב נַחְמָן: קָטָן הַיּוֹדֵעַ לְמִי מְבָרְכִין – מְזַמְּנִין עָלָיו.

The Gemara concludes: **The *halakha* is not in accordance with all of these statements. Rather,** the *halakha* **is in accordance with this** statement **that Rav Naḥman said: A minor who knows to Whom one recites a blessing**[H] **is included in a *zimmun*.**

#### HALAKHA

**A minor who knows to Whom one recites a blessing – קָטָן הַיּוֹדֵעַ לְמִי מְבָרְכִין:** A minor who knows to Whom one recites Grace after Meals may be included in a *zimmun* if he has reached a more advanced stage of childhood; some say approximately the age of seven (*Be'er Heitev*) and others say approximately the age of nine (*Magen Avraham*). In practice, some are stringent and limit participation in a *zimmun* to those who have reached majority (Rambam *Sefer Ahava, Hilkhot Berakhot* 5:7; *Shulḥan Arukh, Oraḥ Ḥayyim* 199:10, and the comment of the Rema).

אביי ורבא הוו יתבי קמיה דרבה, אמר להו רבה: למי מברכין? אמרי ליה: לרחמנא. – ורחמנא היכא יתיב? רבא אחוי לשמי טללא, אביי נפק לברא אחוי כלפי שמיא. אמר להו רבה: תרוייכו רבנן הויתו. היינו דאמרי אינשי: בוצין בוצין מקטפיה ידיע.

The Gemara relates that **Abaye and Rava,** when they were children, **were seated before Rabba. Rabba said to them: To whom does one recite blessings? They said to him: To God, the All Merciful.** Rabba asked them: **And where does the All-Merciful reside? Rava pointed to the ceiling. Abaye went outside and pointed toward the heaven. Rabba said to them: You will both become Sages. It is as the popular saying goes: A cucumber**[B] **can be recognized from its blossoming** stage. Similarly, a great person can be recognized even from a young age.

אמר רב יהודה בריה דרב שמואל בר שילת משמיה דרב: תשעה אכלו דגן ואחד אכל ירק – מצטרפין. אמר רבי זירא, בעאי מיניה מרב יהודה: שמונה מהו? שבעה מהו? – אמר ליה: לא שנא. ששה ודאי לא מבעיא לי. אמר ליה רבי ירמיה: שפיר עבדת דלא איבעיא לך, התם טעמא מאי – משום דאיכא רובא, הכא נמי – איכא רובא. ואיהו סבר: רובא דמינכר בעינן.

**Rav Yehuda, son of Rav Shmuel bar Sheilat, said in the name of Rav: If nine ate grain and one ate vegetables, they join and** form a *zimmun* of ten. **Rabbi Zeira said: I raised a dilemma before Rav Yehuda: What is** the ruling if **eight** ate grain and two ate vegetables? May they join together? **What is** the ruling if **seven** ate grain?[H] **He said to him: There is no difference. I certainly**[N] **had no dilemma with regard to six,** as it was clear to me that six are insufficient to warrant a *zimmun*. **Rabbi Yirmeya said to him: You did well that you had no dilemma** with regard to six, but for the opposite reason. **There,** in the case of seven or eight, **what is the reason** that they form a *zimmun* of ten? **Because there is a majority** of those dining who ate grain. **Here too, there is a majority.** Rabbi Zeira, however, **held: We require an obvious majority.** Therefore, contrary to the opinion of Rabbi Yirmeya, it was clear to him that six who ate grain are insufficient to form a *zimmun*.

ינאי מלכא ומלכתא כריכו ריפתא בהדי הדדי, ומדקטל להו לרבנן – לא הוה ליה איניש לברוכי להו. אמר לה לדביתהו: מאן יהיב לן גברא דמברך לן? אמרה ליה: אשתבע לי דאי מייתינא לך גברא – דלא מצערת ליה. אשתבע לה. אייתיתיה לשמעון בן שטח אחוה, אותביה בין דידיה לדידה. אמר ליה: חזית כמה יקרא עבדינא לך! – אמר ליה: לאו את קא מוקרת לי, אלא אורייתא היא דמוקרא לי, דכתיב ״סלסלה ותרוממך תכבדך כי תחבקנה״. אמר לה: קא חזית דלא מקבל מרות!

The Gemara relates: **King Yannai and the queen ate bread together. And since** Yannai **executed the Sages, there was no one to recite the** Grace after Meals **blessing on their behalf.**[N] **He said to his wife: Who will provide us** with **a man to recite the blessing on our behalf? She said to him: Swear to me that if I bring you such a man, you will not harass him. He swore, and she brought her brother, Shimon ben Shataḥ. She sat him between** the King's throne **and hers.** The King **said to him: Do you see how much honor I am according you? He responded:** It is **not you who honors me; rather, the Torah honors me, as it is written: "Extol her and she will exalt you;**[N] **she will bring you to honor when you embrace her"** (Proverbs 4:8). Yannai **said to** his wife: **You see that he does not accept authority.**

יהבו ליה כסא לברוכי. אמר היכי אבריך – ״ברוך שאכל ינאי וחביריו משלו״? שתייה לההוא כסא. יהבו ליה כסא אחרינא ובריך.

**They gave** Shimon ben Shataḥ **a cup** of wine **over which to recite** Grace after Meals. **He said: How shall I recite the blessing?** Shall I say: **Blessed is He from Whom Yannai and his companions have eaten?** I have not eaten anything. **He drank that cup** of wine. **They gave him another cup, and he recited the** Grace after Meals **blessing.** By drinking the first cup he joined the other diners and was therefore eligible to recite Grace after Meals on their behalf.

אמר רבי אבא בריה דרבי חייא בר אבא (אמר רבי יוחנן): שמעון בן שטח דעבד – לגרמיה הוא דעבד, דהכי אמר רבי חייא בר אבא אמר רבי יוחנן: לעולם אינו מוציא את הרבים ידי חובתן עד שיאכל כזית דגן.

With regard to this story, **Rabbi Abba, son of Rabbi Ḥiyya bar Abba, said** (that **Rabbi Yoḥanan said**)**: That which Shimon ben Shataḥ did,** reciting Grace after Meals on their behalf, **he did on his own,**[N] and not in accordance with the accepted *halakha*, as **Rabbi Ḥiyya bar Abba said** that **Rabbi Yoḥanan said** as follows: **One** who recites Grace after Meals **cannot fulfill the obligation of others** to recite it **until he eats an olive-bulk of grain.**

BACKGROUND

**Cucumber – בוצין:** *Butzin* is the Aramaic name for the hairy cucumber, *Cucumis chate (Cucumis sativus var. chate)*, a summer vegetable of the *Cucurbitaceae* family, and a species of gourd, erroneously called *melafefon* in modern Hebrew. The fruit is long (up to 80 cm) and narrow (about 3 cm) and is bent or twisted. Its skin is bright green, spotted with darker green, and is covered with small hairs. The fruit may be eaten raw or cooked.

Apparently, the meaning of the folk saying: *Butzin* can be recognized its blossoming, or from their stem according to a variant text, is as follows: Upon the emergence of the blossom, one can distinguish between the fruitless male flower and the female flower.

The flower of the common cucumber
A. The female flower at whose base the emerging fruit is visible
B. The fruitless male flower

HALAKHA

**Joining to form a *zimmun* – צירוף לזימון:** Seven men who ate bread and three who tasted some other food may join together to form a *zimmun* of ten, in accordance with Rabbi Zeira's opinion that an obvious majority is required (Rambam *Sefer Ahava, Hilkhot Berakhot* 5:8; *Shulḥan Arukh, Oraḥ Ḥayyim* 197:2).

NOTES

**Certainly – ודאי:** Early commentaries explained that *vav, dalet, alef, yod* is an acronym for *ve'arba'a okhlu yerek*, meaning and four ate vegetables (*Kesef Mishne*).

**There was no one to recite the Grace after Meals blessing on their behalf – לא הוה ליה איניש לברוכי:** This does not mean that no one was familiar with the blessing, but that they sought a great man who could bless them. Since the king had killed all of the Sages, there was no one worthy to bless them (*Etz Yosef*).

**Extol her and she will exalt you – סלסלה ותרוממך:** In variant readings of this Gemara, including in the manuscripts before the *ge'onim*, the verse quoted by Shimon ben Shataḥ was: "Extol her and she will exalt you, and your seat will be amongst princes," which is more appropriate for the case at hand, since he was seated between the king and queen. This verse does not appear in Scripture, and its source is the book of Ben Sira. Although this work was not canonized by the Sages, neither was it rejected outright, and its salient verses are cited.

**He did on his own – לגרמיה הוא דעבד:** Some interpret this to mean that he acted for himself, to fulfill his own obligation. Fulfilling the obligations of the others at the meal did not concern him, as they were the Sadducee associates of King Yannai, who do not care to recite the blessing in accordance with rabbinic ordinances. For that reason, he was not concerned with discharging their obligations. However, one who wishes fulfill the obligation of another with his blessing must conduct himself differently (Rabbeinu Ḥananel).

מֵיתִיבִי, רַבָּן שִׁמְעוֹן בֶּן גַּמְלִיאֵל אוֹמֵר: עָלָה וְהֵסֵיב עִמָּהֶם, אֲפִילּוּ לֹא טָבַל עִמָּהֶם אֶלָּא בְּצִיר, וְלֹא אָכַל עִמָּהֶם אֶלָּא גְּרוֹגֶרֶת אַחַת – מְצָרְפָן!

אִיצְטָרוֹפֵי מִצְטָרֵף, אֲבָל לְהוֹצִיא אֶת הָרַבִּים יְדֵי חוֹבָתָן – עַד שֶׁיֹּאכַל כַּזַּיִת דָּגָן.

אִיתְּמַר נַמֵּי, אָמַר רַב חָנָא בַּר יְהוּדָה מִשְּׁמֵיהּ דְּרָבָא: אֲפִילּוּ לֹא

**Perek VII / Daf 48 Amud b**

טָבַל עִמָּהֶם אֶלָּא בְּצִיר, וְלֹא אָכַל עִמָּהֶם אֶלָּא גְּרוֹגֶרֶת אַחַת – מְצָרְפָן, וּלְהוֹצִיא אֶת הָרַבִּים יְדֵי חוֹבָתָן – אֵינוֹ מוֹצִיא עַד שֶׁיֹּאכַל כַּזַּיִת דָּגָן. אָמַר רַב חָנָא בַּר יְהוּדָה מִשְּׁמֵיהּ דְּרָבָא הִלְכְתָא: אָכַל עָלֶה יָרָק וְשָׁתָה כּוֹס שֶׁל יַיִן – מְצָרְפָן, לְהוֹצִיא – אֵינוֹ מוֹצִיא עַד שֶׁיֹּאכַל כַּזַּיִת דָּגָן.

אָמַר רַב נַחְמָן: מֹשֶׁה תִּקֵּן לְיִשְׂרָאֵל בִּרְכַּת "הַזָּן" בְּשָׁעָה שֶׁיָּרַד לָהֶם מָן. יְהוֹשֻׁעַ תִּקֵּן לָהֶם בִּרְכַּת הָאָרֶץ כֵּיוָן שֶׁנִּכְנְסוּ לָאָרֶץ. דָּוִד וּשְׁלֹמֹה תִּקְּנוּ "בּוֹנֵה יְרוּשָׁלַיִם". דָּוִד תִּקֵּן "עַל יִשְׂרָאֵל עַמֶּךָ וְעַל יְרוּשָׁלַיִם עִירֶךָ", וּשְׁלֹמֹה תִּקֵּן "עַל הַבַּיִת הַגָּדוֹל וְהַקָּדוֹשׁ". "הַטּוֹב וְהַמֵּטִיב" בְּיַבְנֶה תִּקְּנוּהָ כְּנֶגֶד הֲרוּגֵי בֵּיתָר. דְּאָמַר רַב מַתְנָא: אוֹתוֹ הַיּוֹם שֶׁנִּיתְּנוּ הֲרוּגֵי בֵּיתָר לִקְבוּרָה תִּקְּנוּ בְּיַבְנֶה "הַטּוֹב וְהַמֵּטִיב", "הַטּוֹב" – שֶׁלֹּא הִסְרִיחוּ, "וְהַמֵּטִיב" – שֶׁנִּיתְּנוּ לִקְבוּרָה.

תָּנוּ רַבָּנַן, סֵדֶר בִּרְכַּת הַמָּזוֹן כָּךְ הִיא: בְּרָכָה רִאשׁוֹנָה – בִּרְכַּת "הַזָּן", שְׁנִיָּה – בִּרְכַּת הָאָרֶץ, שְׁלִישִׁית – בּוֹנֵה יְרוּשָׁלַיִם, רְבִיעִית – "הַטּוֹב וְהַמֵּטִיב", וּבְשַׁבָּת – מַתְחִיל בְּנֶחָמָה וּמְסַיֵּים בְּנֶחָמָה, וְאוֹמֵר קְדוּשַּׁת הַיּוֹם בָּאֶמְצַע; רַבִּי אֱלִיעֶזֶר אוֹמֵר: רָצָה לְאוֹמְרָהּ בְּנֶחָמָה – אוֹמְרָהּ, בְּבִרְכַּת הָאָרֶץ – אוֹמְרָהּ בִּבְרָכָה שֶׁתִּקְּנוּ חֲכָמִים בְּיַבְנֶה – אוֹמְרָהּ; וַחֲכָמִים אוֹמְרִים: אֵינוֹ אוֹמְרָהּ אֶלָּא בְּנֶחָמָה בִּלְבַד.

---

The Gemara **raises an objection** based on what was taught in a *baraita*: **Rabban Shimon ben Gamliel says:**[N] **One who entered and reclined together** with those who were dining, **even if he only dipped with them** a small bit of food **in spicy brine** that was before them **and ate with them only a single dry fig, he joins them.** This *baraita* demonstrates that one need not necessarily eat grain to recite Grace after Meals on their behalf.

The Gemara responds: Indeed, **he joins them,** but he cannot **satisfy the obligation of the many**[H] unless he has eaten an olive-bulk of grain.

Similarly, this *halakha* **was also stated: Rav Ḥana bar Yehuda said in the name of Rava: Even if he only**

dipped with them a small bit of food **in brine and ate with them only a single dry fig, he joins them. And to satisfy the obligation of the many, he does not satisfy their obligation until he eats an olive-bulk of grain.** Rabbi Ḥana bar Yehuda said in the name of Rava that the *halakha* is: **If one ate a vegetable leaf and drank a cup of wine, he joins** the diners. However, **to satisfy** the obligation of others, **he does not satisfy their obligation until he eats an olive-bulk of grain.**

With regard to the origins of the four blessings of Grace after Meals, **Rav Naḥman said:**

**Moses instituted for Israel**[N] the first blessing of: **Who feeds** all, **when the manna descended for them** and they needed to thank God.

**Joshua instituted the blessing of the land when they entered Eretz Yisrael.**

**David and Solomon instituted** the third blessing: **Who builds Jerusalem,** in the following manner:

**David instituted "…on Israel Your people and on Jerusalem Your city…"** as he conquered the city,

**and Solomon instituted "…on the great and Holy Temple…"** as he was the one who built the Temple.

**They** instituted the blessing: **Who is good and does good, at Yavne**[N] in reference to the slain Jews of the city of **Beitar** at the culmination of the bar Kokheva rebellion. They were ultimately brought to burial after a period during which Hadrian refused to permit their burial. **As Rav Mattana said: On the same day that the slain of Beitar were brought to burial, they instituted the blessing: Who is good and does good, at Yavne. Who is good,** thanking God that the corpses **did not decompose** while awaiting burial, **and does good,** thanking God **that they were** ultimately **brought to burial.**

On the topic of the blessings of Grace after Meals, the Gemara adds that **the Sages taught** in a *baraita* that **the order of Grace after Meals**[H] **is as follows: The first blessing is the blessing of: Who feeds** all; **the second is the blessing of the land; the third is: Who builds Jerusalem; and the fourth is: Who is good and does good. On Shabbat one begins**[H] the third blessing **with consolation and ends with consolation and mentions the sanctity of the day** with mention of Shabbat **in the middle. Rabbi Eliezer says: If one** wishes to recite the supplement for the sanctity of Shabbat in **the blessing of consolation:** Who builds Jerusalem, **he recites it** there; **in the blessing of the land, he recites it there; in the blessing instituted by the Sages at Yavne,** Who is good and does good, **he recites it there. And the Rabbis say: He may only recite** the mention of the sanctity of Shabbat in the context of **the blessing of consolation.**

---

NOTES

**The Gemara raises an objection: Rabban Shimon ben Gamliel says, etc. – מֵיתִיבִי רַבָּן שִׁמְעוֹן בֶּן גַּמְלִיאֵל אוֹמֵר וכו׳:** This objection is not raised from the statement of Rabban Shimon ben Gamliel against Shimon ben Shataḥ, as not only are Rabban Shimon ben Gamliel and Shimon ben Shataḥ both *tanna'im*, Shimon ben Shataḥ preceded Rabban Shimon ben Gamliel and was greater than him. Rather, this objection is to the opinion that Shimon ben Shataḥ acted on his own, against the opinion of the Rabbis. Therefore, the Gemara sought to cite an opinion similar to that of Shimon ben Shataḥ. The objection is to the statement of the *amora'im* (*Tziyyun LeNefesh Ḥayya*).

HALAKHA

**To satisfy the obligation of the many – לְהוֹצִיא אֶת הָרַבִּים יְדֵי חוֹבָתָן:** One who ate an olive-bulk of grain may satisfy the obligation of others who are unable to recite the blessing, even if they ate enough to be satiated (*Shulḥan Arukh, Oraḥ Ḥayyim* 197:4).

NOTES

**Moses instituted for Israel, etc. – מֹשֶׁה תִּקֵּן לְיִשְׂרָאֵל וכו׳:** Based on the proofs cited below, apparently the first three blessings are by Torah law. If so, how is it that they were not recited until the days of David and Solomon? They explain that the basis and fundamental essence of the blessings are alluded to in the Torah, but the formulae of the blessings were instituted over time by those Jewish luminaries (Rashba).

**Who is good and does good, at Yavne – הַטּוֹב וְהַמֵּטִיב בְּיַבְנֶה:** According to the explanation that the blessing: Who is good and does good, was instituted to commemorate the burial of those massacred at Beitar, the question arises: Why was it incorporated into Grace after Meals? Some explain that since Grace after Meals is, in its entirety, thanksgiving to God, the Sages added an additional expression of thanksgiving (*Talmidei Rabbeinu Yona*). Moreover, since there was a tradition that after the massacre at Beitar there would be no Jewish independence until the messianic era, they juxtaposed the commemoration of Beitar adjacent to the blessing: Who builds Jerusalem (Jerusalem Talmud). Some explain that this sad event was incorporated into Grace after Meals so that there would not be excessive joy, and to introduce a bit of sadness into joyous occasions (*Me'iri*).

HALAKHA

**The order of Grace after Meals – סֵדֶר בִּרְכַּת הַמָּזוֹן:** The order of Grace after Meals is: Who feeds all, the blessing of the land, Who builds Jerusalem, and Who is good and does good (Rambam *Sefer Ahava, Hilkhot Berakhot* 2:1; Tur, *Oraḥ Ḥayyim* 187).

**On Shabbat one begins, etc. – וּבְשַׁבָּת מַתְחִיל וכו׳:** On Shabbat, one begins and ends the third blessing with consolation and mentions the sanctity of the day: Favor and strengthen us, in the middle (Rambam *Sefer Ahava, Hilkhot Berakhot* 2:5; *Shulḥan Arukh, Oraḥ Ḥayyim* 188:4–5).

## NOTES

**The blessing before eating – בְּרָכָה שֶׁלִּפְנֵי הַמָּזוֹן:** Even though this *baraita* cites *a fortiori* inferences indicating that the blessing prior to eating is by Torah law, that is not the accepted *halakha*. The *a fortiori* inference was already refuted at the beginning of the sixth chapter. Therefore, the halakhic conclusion remains that the obligation to recite a blessing prior to eating is merely by rabbinic law (*Shitta Mekubbetzet*).

## BACKGROUND

**Yavne – יַבְנֶה:** Yavne is an ancient city mentioned in the Bible. Apparently, it is the city Yavne'el, located in the tribal lands of Judah. It was a Philistine city for many years, and it is listed as one on the cities whose walls were breached by King Uziyya of Judea.

Yavne is located a bit more than a kilometer from the Mediterranean coast, due west of Jerusalem. It was conquered by Vespasian during the campaign to quash the Great Revolt that culminated in the destruction of the Second Temple. Apparently, several Sages who did not support the revolt settled there. When Rabban Yoḥanan ben Zakkai joined them, Yavne became the spiritual center of Eretz Yisrael and the seat of the Sanhedrin for many years, apparently until the bar Kokheva rebellion. The main yeshiva there was called the vineyard in Yavne [*kerem beYavne*].

חֲכָמִים הַיְינוּ תַּנָּא קַמָּא! אִיכָּא בֵּינַיְיהוּ דִּיעֲבַד.

The Gemara remarks: **The** opinion of the **Rabbis is** identical with the opinion of **the first** ***tanna***. Both opinions hold that the mention of Shabbat is in the third blessing. The Gemara responds: **The difference between** the opinion of the Rabbis and the opinion of the first *tanna* is with regard to **after the fact.** They both agree that *ab initio*, Shabbat should be mentioned in the third blessing. If, though, one inadvertently mentioned Shabbat in one of the other blessings mentioned by Rabbi Eliezer, the first *tanna* holds that he fulfilled his obligation and the Rabbis emphasize that it may only be recited in the blessing of consolation.

תָּנוּ רַבָּנַן: מִנַּיִן לְבִרְכַּת הַמָּזוֹן מִן הַתּוֹרָה? שֶׁנֶּאֱמַר: "וְאָכַלְתָּ וְשָׂבָעְתָּ וּבֵרַכְתָּ" – זוֹ בִּרְכַּת הַזָּן, "אֶת ה' אֱלֹהֶיךָ" – זוֹ בִּרְכַּת הַזִּמּוּן, "עַל הָאָרֶץ" – זוֹ בִּרְכַּת הָאָרֶץ, "הַטּוֹבָה" – זוֹ בּוֹנֵה יְרוּשָׁלַיִם, וְכֵן הוּא אוֹמֵר: "הָהָר הַטּוֹב הַזֶּה וְהַלְּבָנוֹן", "אֲשֶׁר נָתַן לָךְ" – זוֹ הַטּוֹב וְהַמֵּטִיב. אֵין לִי אֶלָּא לְאַחֲרָיו, לְפָנָיו מִנַּיִן? אָמַרְתָּ קַל וָחוֹמֶר, כְּשֶׁהוּא שָׂבֵעַ מְבָרֵךְ – כְּשֶׁהוּא רָעֵב לֹא כׇּל שֶׁכֵּן?

**The Sages taught** in a *Tosefta*: **From where** is it derived that **Grace after Meals is from the Torah? As it is stated: "And you shall eat and be satisfied, and you shall bless** the Lord, your God, for the good land that He has given you" (Deuteronomy 8:10). The Gemara explains: **And you shall bless, that is the blessing of: Who feeds all. The Lord, your God, that is the** ***zimmun*** **blessing** in which God's name is invoked. **For the land, that is the blessing of the land; good that is** the blessing: **Who builds Jerusalem, and it also says: "This good mountain and Lebanon"** (Deuteronomy 3:25), which is interpreted homiletically as referring to Jerusalem and the Temple. **That He gave you, that is: Who is good and does good.** However, **I only have** a Torah source for blessings **after** eating, i.e., Grace after Meals. **From where** is it derived that one is obligated to recite blessings **before** eating?[N] **You said** that it can be derived through **an** ***a fortiori*** **inference: When one is satisfied, he** is obligated to **recite a blessing** and thank God for food; **when he is hungry, all the more so** that he should recite a blessing to offer thanks for the food he will eat.

רַבִּי אוֹמֵר: [אֵינוֹ צָרִיךְ], "וְאָכַלְתָּ וְשָׂבָעְתָּ וּבֵרַכְתָּ" – זוֹ בִּרְכַּת הַזָּן, אֲבָל בִּרְכַּת הַזִּמּוּן – מִ"גַּדְּלוּ לַה' אִתִּי" נָפְקָא, "עַל הָאָרֶץ" – זוֹ בִּרְכַּת הָאָרֶץ, "הַטּוֹבָה" – זוֹ בּוֹנֵה יְרוּשָׁלַיִם, וְכֵן הוּא אוֹמֵר "הָהָר הַטּוֹב הַזֶּה וְהַלְּבָנוֹן", "הַטּוֹב וְהַמֵּטִיב" – בְּיַבְנֶה תִּקְנוּהָ. אֵין לִי אֶלָּא לְאַחֲרָיו, לְפָנָיו מִנַּיִן? תַּלְמוּד לוֹמַר: "אֲשֶׁר נָתַן לָךְ" – מִשֶּׁנְּתָנוֹ לָךְ.

**Rabbi** Yehuda HaNasi **says: It is not necessary** to interpret the verse this way; rather, it should be understood in a slightly different manner as follows: **"And you shall eat and be satisfied, and you shall bless, that is the blessing of: Who feeds** all; **however, the** ***zimmun*** **blessing is derived** from the verse: **"Praise God with me** and we will exalt His name together" (Psalms 34:3). He continues: **For the land, that is the blessing of the land. Good, that is** the blessing: **Who builds Jerusalem, and it also says: This good mountain and Lebanon. They instituted** the blessing: **Who is good and does good, at Yavne**[B] and as such, it has no biblical source. However, **I only have** a Torah source for blessings **after** eating, i.e., Grace after Meals. **From where** is it derived that one is obligated to recite blessings **before** eating? **The verse states: That he gave you.** A blessing must be recited over food **from** the moment that God **gave it to you,** not only afterward.

רַבִּי יִצְחָק אוֹמֵר: אֵינוֹ צָרִיךְ, הֲרֵי הוּא אוֹמֵר "וּבֵרַךְ אֶת לַחְמְךָ וְאֶת מֵימֶיךָ", אַל תִּקְרֵי "וּבֵרַךְ" אֶלָּא "וּבָרֵךְ", וְאֵימָתַי קְרוּי לֶחֶם – קוֹדֶם שֶׁיֹּאכְלֶנּוּ.

**Rabbi Yitzḥak says:** That source for the obligation to recite a blessing beforehand **is not necessary, as it says: "And He will bless your bread and your water"** (Exodus 23:25); **do not read: And He will bless** [*uveirakh*], **rather: And you will bless** [*uvareikh*]. **And when is it called bread? Before it is eaten.**

רַבִּי נָתָן אוֹמֵר: אֵינוֹ צָרִיךְ, הֲרֵי הוּא אוֹמֵר: "כְּבֹאֲכֶם הָעִיר כֵּן תִּמְצְאוּן אֹתוֹ בְּטֶרֶם יַעֲלֶה הַבָּמָתָה לֶאֱכֹל כִּי לֹא יֹאכַל הָעָם עַד בֹּאוֹ כִּי הוּא יְבָרֵךְ הַזֶּבַח אַחֲרֵי כֵן יֹאכְלוּ הַקְּרֻאִים".

**Rabbi Natan says:** That source for the obligation to recite a blessing beforehand **is not necessary, as it says** when the maidens told Saul: **"As soon you come into the city, find him right away, before he goes up to the high place to eat; for the people will not eat until he comes, because he will bless the sacrifice; and afterwards all those who are invited will eat;** now go, for you shall find him at this time of day" (I Samuel 9:13). A blessing recited prior to eating is explicitly mentioned in that verse.

וְכׇל כָּךְ לָמָּה? לְפִי שֶׁהַנָּשִׁים דַּבְּרָנִיּוֹת הֵן. וּשְׁמוּאֵל אָמַר: כְּדֵי לְהִסְתַּכֵּל בְּיׇפְיוֹ שֶׁל שָׁאוּל, דִּכְתִיב: "מִשִּׁכְמוֹ וָמַעְלָה גָּבֹהַּ מִכׇּל הָעָם". וְרַבִּי יוֹחָנָן אָמַר: לְפִי שֶׁאֵין מַלְכוּת נוֹגַעַת בַּחֲבֶרְתָּהּ אֲפִילּוּ כִּמְלֹא נִימָא.

Tangentially, the Gemara asks: **Why** did these maidens go on **so expansively** while speaking to Saul? **It is because women are chatterers. And Shmuel said** a different reason: They spoke expansively **in order to gaze upon Saul's beauty** longer, **as it is written** about him: "An excellent young man; no one among the Israelites was better than he; **he was taller than the people from the shoulders up"** (I Samuel 9:2). **Rabbi Yoḥanan said** that their expansiveness was initiated by God because **one sovereignty does not overlap with its counterpart even one hairbreadth.** Saul's coronation was delayed so that Samuel's leadership would not be curtailed.

וְאֵין לִי אֶלָּא בִּרְכַּת הַמָּזוֹן, בִּרְכַּת הַתּוֹרָה מִנַּיִן? אָמַר רַבִּי יִשְׁמָעֵאל: קַל וָחוֹמֶר, עַל חַיֵּי שָׁעָה מְבָרֵךְ – עַל חַיֵּי עוֹלָם הַבָּא לֹא כׇּל שֶׁכֵּן? רַבִּי חִיָּיא בַּר נַחְמָנִי תַּלְמִידוֹ שֶׁל רַבִּי יִשְׁמָעֵאל אוֹמֵר מִשּׁוּם רַבִּי יִשְׁמָעֵאל: אֵינוֹ צָרִיךְ, הֲרֵי הוּא אוֹמֵר: ״עַל הָאָרֶץ הַטּוֹבָה אֲשֶׁר נָתַן לָךְ״, וּלְהַלָּן הוּא אוֹמֵר: ״וְאֶתְּנָה לְךָ אֶת לֻחֹת הָאֶבֶן וְהַתּוֹרָה וְהַמִּצְוָה״ וגו׳.

The *baraita* with regard to Grace after Meals continues: **I only have a** Torah source for **Grace after Meals. From where** is the obligation to recite **the blessing of the Torah** derived? Several answers are offered: **Rabbi Yishmael said:** It is derived through **an *a fortiori* inference** from Grace after Meals: **Over** food, which is an aspect of **temporal life, one recites a blessing, all the more so** one recites a blessing over the Torah, which is **eternal life. Rabbi Ḥiyya bar Naḥmani,** the **student of Rabbi Yishmael, says in the name of Rabbi Yishmael: This** *a fortiori* inference **is not necessary,** as this *halakha* can be derived from the same verse from which Grace after Meals is derived, **as it states: "For the good land that He gave [*natan*] you," and below,** with regard to the Torah, **it says: "And I will give [*ve'etna*] you the stone tablets, and the Torah and the mitzva,** which I have written, that you may teach them" (Exodus 24:12). Here, just as giving with regard to the good land requires a blessing, giving with regard to the Torah requires a blessing.

רַבִּי מֵאִיר אוֹמֵר: וּמִנַּיִן שֶׁכְּשֵׁם שֶׁמְּבָרֵךְ עַל הַטּוֹבָה כָּךְ מְבָרֵךְ עַל הָרָעָה? תַּלְמוּד לוֹמַר: ״אֲשֶׁר נָתַן לְךָ ה׳ אֱלֹהֶיךָ״ – דַּיָּינְךָ, בְּכׇל דִּין שֶׁדָּנְךָ, בֵּין מִדָּה טוֹבָה וּבֵין מִדָּה פּוּרְעָנוּת.

Concerning this verse, **Rabbi Meir says: From where** is it derived that **just as one recites a blessing over the good** that befalls him **he recites a blessing over the bad? The verse states: "That the Lord, your God gave you."** "Your God" is a reference to the attribute of divine justice; **your Judge, in whatever judgment that He judges you, whether it is a positive measure of goodness or a measure of calamity.**

רַבִּי יְהוּדָה בֶּן בְּתֵירָא אוֹמֵר: אֵינוֹ צָרִיךְ, הֲרֵי הוּא אוֹמֵר: ״טוֹבָה״. ״הַטּוֹבָה״; ״טוֹבָה״ – זוֹ תּוֹרָה, וְכֵן הוּא אוֹמֵר: ״כִּי לֶקַח טוֹב נָתַתִּי לָכֶם״. ״הַטּוֹבָה״ – זוֹ בִּנְיַן יְרוּשָׁלַיִם, וְכֵן הוּא אוֹמֵר ״הָהָר הַטּוֹב הַזֶּה וְהַלְּבָנוֹן״.

**Rabbi Yehuda ben Beteira says:** Proof for a blessing over the Torah from a different verse **is not necessary, as it says:** "For the good [*hatova*] land." Two different matters are derived from different aspects of the word *hatova*: ***Tova,* that is Torah, as it says: "For I have given you good [*tov*] teachings,** do not forsake My Torah" (Proverbs 4:2); ***hatova,* that is the building of Jerusalem, as it says: "This good mountain [*hatov*] and Lebanon."**

תַּנְיָא, רַבִּי אֱלִיעֶזֶר אוֹמֵר: כׇּל שֶׁלֹּא אָמַר ״אֶרֶץ חֶמְדָּה טוֹבָה וּרְחָבָה״ בְּבִרְכַּת הָאָרֶץ, וּ״מַלְכוּת בֵּית דָּוִד״ בְּבוֹנֵה יְרוּשָׁלַיִם – לֹא יָצָא יְדֵי חוֹבָתוֹ; נַחוּם הַזָּקֵן אוֹמֵר: צָרִיךְ שֶׁיַּזְכִּיר בָּהּ בְּרִית. רַבִּי יוֹסֵי אוֹמֵר: צָרִיךְ שֶׁיַּזְכִּיר בָּהּ תּוֹרָה. פְּלִימוֹ אוֹמֵר: צָרִיךְ שֶׁיַּקְדִּים בְּרִית לְתוֹרָה, שֶׁזּוֹ נִתְּנָה בְּשָׁלֹשׁ בְּרִיתוֹת,

With regard to the formula of Grace after Meals, the Gemara continues: **It was taught** in a *baraita*: **Rabbi Eliezer says: Anyone who did not say: A desirable,[H] good, and spacious land in the blessing of the land, and** who did not mention **the royal house of David in** the blessing: **Who builds Jerusalem, did not fulfill his obligation. Naḥum the Elder says: One must mention the covenant** of circumcision **in the** blessing of the land. **Rabbi Yosei says: One must mention the Torah in** the blessing of the land. **Pelimu,** one of the last *tanna'im*, **says: He must** make mention of the **covenant** of circumcision **preceding** mention of the **Torah,[H] as this,** the Torah, **was given** to the Jewish people **with three covenants,[N]**

## HALAKHA

**Anyone who did not say: A desirable, etc. – כׇּל שֶׁלֹּא אָמַר אֶרֶץ חֶמְדָּה וכו׳:** In Grace after Meals, one must mention: A desirable, good, and spacious land, the Davidic dynasty, the covenant, and the Torah. As far as the manner in which they are to be mentioned is concerned, there is an ancient Sephardic custom to say: Land, covenant, and Torah followed by: For Your covenant… Some suffice with a single mention of these themes (Rosh, the Ashkenazic custom; *Tur, Oraḥ Ḥayyim* 187).

**He must make mention of the covenant of circumcision preceding mention of the Torah – מַקְדִּים בְּרִית לְתוֹרָה:** When reciting Grace after Meals, mention of the covenant of circumcision precedes mention of the Torah, in accordance with the opinion of Pelimu (Rambam *Sefer Ahava, Hilkhot Berakhot* 2:3; *Shulḥan Arukh, Oraḥ Ḥayyim* 187:3).

## NOTES

**As this was given with three covenants – שֶׁזּוֹ נִתְּנָה בְּשָׁלֹשׁ בְּרִיתוֹת:** Various opinions exist with regard to the essence of the three covenants with which the Torah was given. Some explain that this refers to the three covenants mentioned in the verses: "These are the words of the covenant that God commanded Moses to make with the children of Israel in the land of Moab, aside from the covenant which He made with them at Horeb" (Deuteronomy 28:69), and, "to bring you into the covenant of the Lord, your God…" (Deuteronomy 29:11). There were three covenants; one in Horeb, one in the plains of Moab, and one mentioned in the Torah portion of *Nitzavim* (Rambam; Ran; *Talmidei Rabbeinu Yona*). Others say that this is actually a reference to the three times the word covenant is mentioned in the framework of the giving of the Torah at Sinai: "Behold, I effect a covenant" (Exodus 34:10), "I have effected a covenant with you" (Exodus 34:27), and "the words of the covenant, the Ten Commandments" (Exodus 34:28; see Rav Hai Gaon).

Perek **VII**
Daf **49** Amud **a**

וְזוֹ נִתְּנָה בִּשְׁלֹשׁ עֶשְׂרֵה בְּרִיתוֹת.

**and that,** the covenant of circumcision, **was given with thirteen covenants,** as the word *brit*, covenant, appears thirteen times in the portion dealing with the circumcision of Abraham (Genesis 17:1–14).

רַבִּי אַבָּא אוֹמֵר: צָרִיךְ שֶׁיֹּאמַר בָּהּ הוֹדָאָה תְּחִלָּה וָסוֹף, וְהַפּוֹחֵת – לֹא יִפְחוֹת מֵאַחַת, וְכׇל הַפּוֹחֵת מֵאַחַת הֲרֵי זֶה מְגוּנֶּה.

**Rabbi Abba says: One must mention thanks** in the blessing of thanksgiving in Grace after Meals **at the beginning and the end[H]** of the blessing. **And one who decreases** the number of expressions of thanksgiving **may not decrease** their number **to fewer than one, and if anyone decreases** their number **to fewer than one, it is reprehensible.**

וְכׇל הַחוֹתֵם ״מַנְחִיל אֲרָצוֹת״ בְּבִרְכַּת הָאָרֶץ, וּ״מוֹשִׁיעַ אֶת יִשְׂרָאֵל״ בְּ״בוֹנֵה יְרוּשָׁלַיִם״ – הֲרֵי זֶה בּוּר, וְכׇל שֶׁאֵינוֹ אוֹמֵר ״בְּרִית וְתוֹרָה״ בְּבִרְכַּת הָאָרֶץ וּ״מַלְכוּת בֵּית דָּוִד״ בְּבוֹנֵה יְרוּשָׁלַיִם – לֹא יָצָא יְדֵי חוֹבָתוֹ.

The Gemara added that the conclusions of the blessing of the land and the blessing: Who builds Jerusalem, may also not be changed. **Anyone who concludes the blessing of the land: Who bequeaths lands[N] and** concludes **the blessing: Who builds Jerusalem,** with the formula: **Who redeems Israel, is an ignoramus,** as he thereby corrupts the intention of the blessing. **And anyone who does not mention covenant and Torah[H] in the blessing of the land and the royal house of David in** the blessing: **Who builds Jerusalem, did not fulfill his obligation.**

## HALAKHA

**One must mention thanks at the beginning and the end – הוֹדָאָה תְּחִלָּה וָסוֹף:** One should mention thanks at the beginning and the end of this blessing over food. One must mention thanks at least once (Rambam *Sefer Ahava, Hilkhot Berakhot* 2:3; *Tur, Oraḥ Ḥayyim* 187).

**Anyone who does not mention covenant and Torah – כׇּל שֶׁאֵינוֹ אוֹמֵר בְּרִית וְתוֹרָה:** One who does not mention covenant, Torah, and the Davidic dynasty in Grace after Meals did not fulfill his obligation. Some exempted women from mentioning covenant and Torah (Rema), while others obligated them to mention it (*Magen Avraham*; Rambam *Sefer Ahava, Hilkhot Berakhot* 2:4; *Shulḥan Arukh, Oraḥ Ḥayyim* 187:3–4, 187:3).

## NOTES

**Who bequeaths lands – מַנְחִיל אֲרָצוֹת:** The problem with this expression is that it indicates that there is no special gratitude for Eretz Yisrael, which is the purpose of the blessing, as God bequeaths lands to other nations as well. He thereby corrupts the purpose of the blessing (*Beit Yosef, Oraḥ Ḥayyim* 187).

## NOTES

**Requires mention of God's sovereignty – צְרִיכָה מַלְכוּת:** Some also explain why sovereignty is not mentioned in the blessing: Who builds Jerusalem. Since the primary theme of this blessing is the Davidic dynasty, it is not in keeping with the deference due God to mention God's sovereignty and human sovereignty together (*Talmidei Rabbeinu Yona*).

**Levi raised an objection to the opinion of Rabbi Yehuda HaNasi – אֵיתִיבֵיהּ לֵוִי לְרַבִּי וכו׳:** It seems superfluous for Levi to raise an objection from both: Who sanctifies Israel and the seasons, and: Who sanctifies Israel and the New Moon, as the same response is appropriate for both. However, there is room to distinguish between the objections. New Moons, as opposed to Festivals, are not solely dependent on the determination of the court, as the New Moon is determined by the appearance of the new moon, which is determined by God. There are even some *tanna'im* who hold that the court need not play a role in the sanctification of the New Moon. Therefore, it is conceivable that the sanctity of Israel and the sanctity of the New Moon are two distinct matters (*Tziyyun LeNefesh Ḥayya*; see Rabbi Elazar Moshe Horowitz).

## BACKGROUND

**Exilarch – רֵישׁ גָּלוּתָא:** The Exilarch, who descended from the House of David, was recognized by the Jews as the heir to the scepter of Judah and entrusted with broad official powers. He was the leader of the Jews of the Persian Empire and their representative to the authorities, who regarded him as a member of a royal dynasty. Consequently, he enjoyed a lofty position within the Persian court. During various periods, he was considered third in the royal hierarchy. He was responsible for the collection of a major portion of the government taxes and could appoint leaders and judges whose powers included the imposition of corporal, and sometimes capital, punishment. Adjacent to the Exilarch's home was a special rabbinical court appointed by him to deal with cases involving money and, in particular, property. He also seems to have had the authority to make certain appointments throughout the country, though most of them were made in consultation with the heads of the great academies. The Exilarchs themselves were referred to in the Talmud by the honorific title *Mar* before or after their name, and were devoted to the Torah. Some of them were, indeed, significant scholars in their own right.

מְסַיֵּיעַ לֵיהּ לְרַבִּי אִילְעָא, דְּאָמַר רַבִּי אִילְעָא אָמַר רַבִּי יַעֲקֹב בַּר אַחָא מִשּׁוּם רַבֵּינוּ: כֹּל שֶׁלֹּא אָמַר ״בְּרִית וְתוֹרָה״ בְּבִרְכַּת הָאָרֶץ וּ״מַלְכוּת בֵּית דָּוִד״ בְּבוֹנֵה יְרוּשָׁלַיִם – לֹא יָצָא יְדֵי חוֹבָתוֹ.

The Gemara notes: **This** *baraita* **supports** the opinion of **Rabbi Il'a, as Rabbi Il'a said** that **Rabbi Ya'akov bar Aḥa said in the name of Rabbeinu,** Rabbi Yehuda HaNasi: **Anyone who did not mention covenant and Torah in the blessing of the land and the royal house of David in** the blessing: **Who builds Jerusalem, did not fulfill his obligation.**

פְּלִיגִי בַּהּ אַבָּא יוֹסֵי בֶּן דּוֹסְתַּאי וְרַבָּנַן, חַד אָמַר: ״הַטּוֹב וְהַמֵּטִיב״ צְרִיכָה מַלְכוּת, וְחַד אָמַר: אֵינָהּ צְרִיכָה מַלְכוּת; מַאן דְּאָמַר ״צְרִיכָה מַלְכוּת״ – קָסָבַר: דְּרַבָּנַן, וּמַאן דְּאָמַר ״אֵינָהּ צְרִיכָה מַלְכוּת״ – קָסָבַר: דְּאוֹרַיְיתָא.

**Abba Yosei ben Dostai and the Rabbis disagreed** whether or not God's sovereignty must be invoked in the blessing: Who is good and does good. **One said: Who is good and does good, requires** mention of God's **sovereignty,**[N] **and one said: It does not require** mention of God's **sovereignty.** The Gemara explains: **The one who said that it requires** mention of God's **sovereignty holds that** this blessing was instituted **by the Sages,** so it is not a continuation of the previous blessings. As an independent blessing, God's sovereignty must be mentioned. **The one who said that it does not require** mention of God's **sovereignty holds that** the obligation to recite this blessing **is by Torah law.** Therefore, it is a continuation of the previous blessings.

תָּנוּ רַבָּנַן: מַהוּ חוֹתֵם? בְּ״בִנְיַן יְרוּשָׁלַיִם״; רַבִּי יוֹסֵי בְּרַבִּי יְהוּדָה אוֹמֵר: ״מוֹשִׁיעַ יִשְׂרָאֵל״. ״מוֹשִׁיעַ יִשְׂרָאֵל״ – אִין, ״בִּנְיַן יְרוּשָׁלַיִם״ – לָא?! – אֶלָּא אֵימָא: אַף ״מוֹשִׁיעַ יִשְׂרָאֵל״.

**The Sages taught** in a *baraita*: With **what** formula **does he conclude** the third blessing of Grace after Meals? He concludes it **with: The building of Jerusalem. Rabbi Yosei son of Rabbi Yehuda says:** He concludes it with: **Who redeems Israel.** This is perplexing: Is that to say that with: **Who redeems Israel, yes,** he concludes the blessing; with: **The building of Jerusalem, no,** he does not conclude the blessing? The Gemara responds: **Rather, say** that Rabbi Yosei son of Rabbi Yehuda said the following: One who recites the blessing concludes either with: The building of Jerusalem, **or even** with: **Who redeems Israel.**

רַבָּה בַּר רַב הוּנָא אִיקְּלַע לְבֵי רֵישׁ גָּלוּתָא, פְּתַח בַּחֲדָא וְסַיֵּים בְּתַרְתֵּי. אָמַר רַב חִסְדָּא: גְּבוּרְתָּא לְמֶחְתַּם בְּתַרְתֵּי! וְהָתַנְיָא, רַבִּי אוֹמֵר: אֵין חוֹתְמִין בִּשְׁתַּיִם!

The Gemara recounts: **Rabba bar Rav Huna happened** to come **to the house of the Exilarch.**[B] While reciting the blessing: Who builds Jerusalem in Grace after Meals, **he opened with one** theme: Have compassion on Jerusalem, **and concluded with two** themes: Both the building of Jerusalem and Who redeems Israel. **Rav Ḥisda said** derisively: It takes **great fortitude to conclude with two** themes. How could you conclude with two themes? **Wasn't it taught** in a *baraita* that **Rabbi** Yehuda HaNasi **says: One may not conclude with two** themes? Each blessing has its own particular ending.

גּוּפָא, רַבִּי אוֹמֵר: אֵין חוֹתְמִין בִּשְׁתַּיִם. אֵיתִיבֵיהּ לֵוִי לְרַבִּי: ״עַל הָאָרֶץ וְעַל הַמָּזוֹן״! – אֶרֶץ דְּמַפְּקָא מָזוֹן. ״עַל הָאָרֶץ וְעַל הַפֵּירוֹת״! – אֶרֶץ דְּמַפְּקָא פֵּירוֹת;

The Gemara discusses **the matter itself: Rabbi** Yehuda HaNasi **says: One may not conclude with two** themes. **Levi,** his student, **raised an objection to** the opinion of **Rabbi** Yehuda HaNasi[N] based on the standard conclusions of various blessings. The second blessing of Grace after Meals concludes: **For the land and for the food.** Rabbi Yehuda HaNasi explained that the conclusion to that blessing is actually a single theme: **The land that produces food.** Levi raised a similar objection from the blessing that concludes: **For the land and for the fruit.** Rabbi Yehuda HaNasi explained that there, too, it means: **The land that produces fruit.**

״מְקַדֵּשׁ יִשְׂרָאֵל וְהַזְּמַנִּים״! – יִשְׂרָאֵל דְּקַדְּשִׁינְהוּ לִזְמַנִּים; ״מְקַדֵּשׁ יִשְׂרָאֵל וְרָאשֵׁי חֳדָשִׁים״! – יִשְׂרָאֵל דְּקַדְּשִׁינְהוּ לְרָאשֵׁי חֳדָשִׁים;

Levi cited two other blessings: **Who sanctifies Israel and the seasons.** It means: **Who sanctifies Israel, who sanctify the seasons. Who sanctifies Israel and the New Moon.** It means: **Who sanctifies Israel, who sanctify the New Moons.**

״מְקַדֵּשׁ הַשַּׁבָּת וְיִשְׂרָאֵל וְהַזְּמַנִּים״! – חוּץ מִזּוֹ.

Levi cited an additional blessing that concludes with two themes, the blessing recited when Shabbat coincides with a Festival: **Who sanctifies Shabbat, Israel, and the seasons.** Rabbi Yehuda HaNasi answered: **Except for that** one.

וּמַאי שְׁנָא? – הָכָא – חֲדָא הִיא, הָתָם – תַּרְתֵּי, כָּל חֲדָא וַחֲדָא בְּאַפֵּי נַפְשָׁהּ.

The Gemara asks: **What is different** about this blessing? The Gemara answers: **Here,** the blessing thanks God **for one** matter, the sanctity of the day. However, **there,** in the conclusion of the third blessing of Grace after Meals, the building of Jerusalem and redemption of Israel are **two** themes, and **each one is distinct** from the other.

וְטַעְמָא מַאי אֵין חוֹתְמִין בִּשְׁתַּיִם – לְפִי שֶׁאֵין עוֹשִׂין מִצְוֹת חֲבִילוֹת חֲבִילוֹת.

The Gemara asks: **And what is the reason that one does not conclude** a blessing **with two** themes? The Gemara responds: **Because** there is a general principle: **One does not perform mitzvot in bundles;** rather, each mitzva must have its own blessing.

מַאי הָוֵי עֲלַהּ?

The Gemara has yet to arrive at a clear conclusion regarding the conclusion of the third blessing of Grace after Meals. The Gemara asks: **What** conclusion was reached **about it?**

אָמַר רַב שֵׁשֶׁת: פָּתַח בְּ״רַחֵם עַל עַמְּךָ יִשְׂרָאֵל״ חוֹתֵם בְּ״מוֹשִׁיעַ יִשְׂרָאֵל״, פָּתַח בְּ״רַחֵם עַל יְרוּשָׁלַיִם״ – חוֹתֵם בְּ״בוֹנֵה יְרוּשָׁלַיִם״. וְרַב נַחְמָן אָמַר: אֲפִילּוּ פָּתַח בְּ״רַחֵם עַל יִשְׂרָאֵל״ חוֹתֵם בְּ״בוֹנֵה יְרוּשָׁלַיִם״, מִשּׁוּם שֶׁנֶּאֱמַר: ״בּוֹנֵה יְרוּשָׁלַיִם ה׳ נִדְחֵי יִשְׂרָאֵל יְכַנֵּס״, אֵימָתַי ״בּוֹנֵה יְרוּשָׁלַיִם ה׳״ – בִּזְמַן שֶׁ״נִּדְחֵי יִשְׂרָאֵל יְכַנֵּס״.

**Rav Sheshet said:** If **he opened with: Have compassion on Your people, Israel,** mentioning redemption of Israel at the start, **he concludes with: Who redeems Israel;** if **he opened with: Have compassion on Jerusalem, he concludes with: Who builds Jerusalem. Rav Naḥman said: Even if he opened with: Have compassion on Israel,**[H] **he concludes with: Who builds Jerusalem, because it is stated: "The Lord builds Jerusalem; He gathers in the exiles of Israel"** (Psalms 147:2). This verse is interpreted to mean: **When does God build Jerusalem? When He gathers in the exiles of Israel.** The rebuilding of Jerusalem symbolizes Israel's redemption.

אָמַר לֵיהּ רַבִּי זֵירָא לְרַב חִסְדָּא: נֵיתֵי מָר וְנִתְנֵי! – אָמַר לֵיהּ: בִּרְכַּת מְזוֹנָא לָא גְּמִירְנָא וְתַנּוּיֵי מַתְנֵינָא?! – אָמַר לֵיהּ: מַאי הַאי? – אָמַר לֵיהּ: דְּאִקְלַעִי לְבֵי רֵישׁ גָּלוּתָא וּבָרֵיכִי בִּרְכַּת מְזוֹנָא, וְזַקְפַּי רַב שֵׁשֶׁת לְקוֹעֵיהּ עֲלַי כְּחִוְיָא. – וְאַמַּאי? – דְּלָא אֲמַרִי לָא בְּרִית וְלָא תּוֹרָה וְלָא מַלְכוּת. – וְאַמַּאי לָא אֲמַרְתְּ? – כִּדְרַב חֲנַנְאֵל אָמַר רַב, דְּאָמַר רַב חֲנַנְאֵל אָמַר רַב: לֹא אָמַר בְּרִית וְתוֹרָה וּמַלְכוּת – יָצָא. בְּרִית – לְפִי שֶׁאֵינָהּ בְּנָשִׁים, תּוֹרָה וּמַלְכוּת – לְפִי שֶׁאֵינָן לֹא בְּנָשִׁים וְלֹא בַּעֲבָדִים. – וְאַתְּ שְׁבַקְתְּ כָּל הָנֵי תַּנָּאֵי וְאָמוֹרָאֵי וַעֲבַדְתְּ כְּרַב!

On a similar topic, the Gemara relates: **Rabbi Zeira said to Rav Ḥisda: Let the Master come and teach** Mishna. **He responded: I have not yet learned Grace after Meals, and I will teach Mishna? He responded: What is this?** Why do you say that you have not yet learned Grace after Meals? **He said to him: I happened** to come **to the house of the Exilarch and recited Grace after Meals, and Rav Sheshet stiffened his neck over me like a snake,**[B] i.e., he got angry and challenged me. Rabbi Zeira asked: **And why** did Rav Sheshet become angry with you? He answered: **I did not mention covenant, Torah, or sovereignty** in Grace after Meals. Rabbi Zeira wondered: **And why did you not mention** those themes? He answered that he did so **in accordance with** the opinion that **Rav Ḥananel** said that **Rav**[P] **said, as Rav Ḥananel said** that **Rav said: If one does not mention covenant, Torah or sovereignty** in Grace after Meals, **he** nevertheless **fulfilled** his obligation because these themes are not applicable to all of Israel. **Covenant does not apply to women; Torah and sovereignty apply neither to women nor to slaves.** Rabbi Zeira said to him: Rav Sheshet should have been angry with you. **And you abandoned all of these *tanna'im* and *amora'im*** who disagree with him, **and followed Rav?** Evidently, many *tanna'im* and *amora'im* hold that covenant, Torah, and sovereignty must be mentioned in the second blessing of Grace after Meals.[N]

אָמַר רַבָּה בַּר בַּר חָנָה אָמַר רַבִּי יוֹחָנָן: ״הַטּוֹב וְהַמֵּטִיב״ צְרִיכָה מַלְכוּת. מַאי קָא מַשְׁמַע לַן? – כָּל בְּרָכָה שֶׁאֵין בָּהּ מַלְכוּת לֹא שְׁמָהּ בְּרָכָה, וְהָא אֲמָרָהּ רַבִּי יוֹחָנָן חֲדָא זִימְנָא! – אָמַר רַבִּי זֵירָא: לוֹמַר שֶׁצְּרִיכָה שְׁתֵּי מַלְכֻיּוֹת, חֲדָא דִּידַהּ, וַחֲדָא דְּ״בוֹנֵה יְרוּשָׁלַיִם״.

**Rabba bar bar Ḥana said** that **Rabbi Yoḥanan said:** The blessing: **Who is good and does good, requires** mention of God's **sovereignty.**[H] The Gemara asks: **What is he teaching us** that we did not already know? If you say that he is teaching us that **any blessing that does not contain mention of** God's **sovereignty is not** considered a **blessing, didn't Rabbi Yoḥanan already say** that *halakha* **once? Rabbi Zeira said:** Rabba bar bar Ḥana **is saying that** the blessing: Who is good and does good, **requires two** mentions of **sovereignty, one for itself and one for** the blessing: **Who builds Jerusalem.**

## HALAKHA

**He opened with: Have compassion on Israel – פָּתַח בְּרַחֵם עַל יִשְׂרָאֵל:** One opens the third blessing with: Have compassion on Israel and concludes it with: Who builds Jerusalem, in accordance with the opinion of Rav Naḥman (Rambam *Sefer Ahava, Hilkhot Berakhot* 2:4; *Shulḥan Arukh, Oraḥ Ḥayyim* 188:4).

**Who is good and does good requires mention of God's sovereignty – הַטּוֹב וְהַמֵּטִיב צְרִיכָה מַלְכוּת:** Beyond the requisite mention of sovereignty, it is mentioned two additional times in this blessing, in accordance with the opinion of Rav Pappa (Rambam *Sefer Ahava, Hilkhot Berakhot* 2:7; *Shulḥan Arukh, Oraḥ Ḥayyim* 189:1).

## BACKGROUND

**Rav Sheshet stiffened his neck over me like a snake – רַב שֵׁשֶׁת לְקוֹעֵיהּ עֲלַי כְּחִוְיָא:** Several snakes indigenous to Eretz Yisrael and Babylonia are capable of straightening their necks as a threatening gesture or in attack. One such snake is the venomous Egyptian cobra. *Naja hae.*

A cobra stiffening its neck

## NOTES

**Rav Ḥisda's blessing – בִּרְכָתוֹ שֶׁל רַב חִסְדָּא:** Many questioned why Rav Ḥisda recited Grace after Meals without mentioning covenant, Torah, and sovereignty, contrary to the virtually unanimous opinion of the Sages. Even if Rav Ḥananel permitted this after the fact, he did not prescribe to do so *ab initio*. Some explain that Rav Ḥisda inadvertently neglected to mention covenant, Torah, and sovereignty. Once he did so, he did not return to mention it (*Penei Yehoshua*). Others explain that there were women and slaves reclining at that table, and he sought to recite a formula appropriate for all present (*Tziyyun LeNefesh Ḥayya*). Alternatively, he held that because women and slaves do not mention covenant and sovereignty, men should not mention them either to ensure a universally uniform formula for Grace after Meals (Rashba).

## PERSONALITIES

**Rav – רַב:** Rav Abba ben Ivu was the greatest of the first generation of Babylonian *amora'im*. Rav was born in Babylonia to a distinguished family that produced many Sages and traced its lineage back to King David. Rav moved to Eretz Yisrael with his uncle, Rabbi Ḥiyya, studied Torah primarily with Rabbi Yehuda HaNasi and his uncle, and became a member of Rabbi Yehuda HaNasi's court. Rav remained in Eretz Yisrael for a period, but later returned to Babylonia and settled there. Although Torah centers existed in Babylonia, in Hutzal and Neharde'a, prior to Rav's return, Rav founded a large academy in Sura and raised the level of scholarship to rival that of Eretz Yisrael. After some time, he was recognized as the leading Torah Sage in Babylonia, and ultimately in Eretz Yisrael as well.

Because Rav engaged in halakhic discourse with the last of the *tanna'im*, the Gemara established a principle: Rav is a *tanna* and disputes, i.e., Rav's status was akin to that of a *tanna* in the sense that his statements may not be challenged from a *baraita* because he too is considered a *tanna* in that sense. Therefore, according to a geonic tradition, if Rav or Rabbi Abba is mentioned in a *baraita*, it is understood to refer to Rav. On this *amud*, the *tanna* Rabbi Abba is mentioned three times.

Rav and his students accomplished a great deal in various areas. Halakhic midrash, especially the *Sifra*, were edited in his school. Additionally, Rav instituted the Rosh HaShana liturgy, the shofar blasts of the school of Rav, and other prayers.

Shmuel was his close friend and adversary in matters of *halakha*. Their arguments, the disputes of Rav and Shmuel, appear throughout the Talmud. The *halakha* is in accordance with the opinion of Rav in ritual matters and with the opinion of Shmuel in monetary matters.

Over the course of many years, Rav engaged in large-scale commerce together with the family of Rabbi Ḥiyya, and was wealthy throughout his life. Apparently, after he became head of the school in Sura, his son, Ivu, managed his affairs.

Beyond his prominence as a Torah scholar, he was universally lauded for his great piety and humility, and was cited as a model for the ideal behavior of a great personage. After his death, the people continued to venerate him and dirt from his grave was used as a talisman to heal illnesses.

Rav lived a long life and had many disciples. Essentially, all of the Sages of the following generation were his students, and statements in his name constitute a significant portion of the Babylonian Talmud. His most prominent students were Rav Ḥisda and Rav Hamnuna.

Rav had at least two sons: Ivu and Ḥiyya. Ḥiyya bar Rav was also a Sage, and his son, Shimi bar Ḥiyya, who studied under his grandfather, was an important Sage as well. Rav married into the family of the Exilarch, and Ravna Neḥemya and Ravna Ukva were Sages descended from the Exilarch who were Rav's daughter's sons.

אִי הָכִי, נִבְעֵי תְּלָת – חֲדָא דִּידָהּ, וַחֲדָא דְּ״בוֹנֵה יְרוּשָׁלַיִם״ וַחֲדָא דְּבִרְכַּת הָאָרֶץ! – אֶלָּא, בִּרְכַּת הָאָרֶץ מַאי טַעְמָא לָא? – מִשּׁוּם דַּהֲוַיָא לַהּ בְּרָכָה הַסְּמוּכָה לַחֲבֶרְתָּהּ, ״בּוֹנֵה יְרוּשָׁלַיִם״ נַמִי לָא תִּבְעֵי דַּהֲוָיָא לַהּ בְּרָכָה הַסְּמוּכָה לַחֲבֶרְתָּהּ!

The Gemara asks: **If so,** that God's sovereignty must be mentioned a second time in the blessing: Who is good and does good, to compensate for the fact that it was not mentioned in the blessing: Who builds Jerusalem, **it should require three** mentions; **one of its own, one for** the blessing: **Who builds Jerusalem, and one for the blessing of the land,** in which sovereignty is also not mentioned. **Rather,** in **the blessing of the land, what is the reason** that sovereignty is **not** mentioned? **Because it is a blessing juxtaposed to another** preceding blessing. **Who builds Jerusalem, should also not require** its own mention of God's sovereignty, **as it is a blessing juxtaposed to another** preceding blessing.

הוּא הַדִּין דַּאֲפִילּוּ ״בּוֹנֵה יְרוּשָׁלַיִם״ נַמִי לָא בָּעְיָא, אַיְּידֵי דַּאֲמַר מַלְכוּת בֵּית דָּוִד – לָאו אוֹרַח אַרְעָא דְּלָא אֲמַר מַלְכוּת שָׁמַיִם. רַב פָּפָּא אָמַר, הָכִי קָאָמַר: צְרִיכָה שְׁתֵּי מַלְכֻיּוֹת לְבַר מִדִּידָהּ.

The Gemara responds: **The same is true even** with regard to the blessing: **Who builds Jerusalem,** that it **does not require** mention of sovereignty. However, **since he mentioned royal house of David** in the blessing, **it would not be proper** if **he did not mention God's sovereignty** as well. On the other hand, **Rav Pappa said:** The blessing: Who is good and does good, **requires two** mentions of **sovereignty besides its own;** one to compensate for its lack of mention in the blessing: Who builds Jerusalem, and one for the blessing of the land.

יָתֵיב רַבִּי זֵירָא אֲחוֹרֵי דְּרַב גִּידֵּל, וְיָתֵיב רַב גִּידֵּל קַמֵּיהּ דְּרַב הוּנָא וְיָתֵיב וְקָאָמַר: טָעָה וְלֹא הִזְכִּיר שֶׁל שַׁבָּת, אוֹמֵר: ״בָּרוּךְ שֶׁנָּתַן שַׁבָּתוֹת לִמְנוּחָה לְעַמּוֹ יִשְׂרָאֵל בְּאַהֲבָה לְאוֹת וְלִבְרִית, בָּרוּךְ מְקַדֵּשׁ הַשַּׁבָּת״. אֲמַר לֵיהּ: מַאן אֲמָרָהּ? – רַב.

The Gemara recounts: **Rabbi Zeira sat behind**[B] **Rav Giddel** in the study hall, **and Rav Giddel sat before Rav Huna, and he sat and he said: One who erred and did not mention** the formula **for Shabbat** in Grace after Meals, **says** the following abridged version instead: **Blessed…Who gave *Shabbatot* for rest to His people Israel with love, as a sign and a covenant; Blessed…Who sanctifies the Shabbat.** Rav Huna **said to him: Who said** this *halakha*? He answered: **Rav.**

הֲדַר יָתֵיב וְקָאָמַר: טָעָה וְלֹא הִזְכִּיר שֶׁל יוֹם טוֹב אוֹמֵר: ״בָּרוּךְ שֶׁנָּתַן יָמִים טוֹבִים לְעַמּוֹ יִשְׂרָאֵל לְשִׂמְחָה וּלְזִכָּרוֹן, בָּרוּךְ מְקַדֵּשׁ יִשְׂרָאֵל וְהַזְּמַנִּים״. אֲמַר לֵיהּ: מַאן אֲמָרָהּ? – רַב.

**Again** Rav Giddel **sat and said: One who erred and did not mention** the formula **for Festivals**[H] in Grace after Meals, **says: "Blessed…Who gave Festivals to His people Israel for joy and for commemoration; Blessed…Who sanctifies Israel and the seasons.** Rav Huna **said to him: Who said** this *halakha*? He answered: **Rav**

הֲדַר יָתֵיב וְקָאָמַר: טָעָה וְלֹא הִזְכִּיר שֶׁל רֹאשׁ חוֹדֶשׁ אוֹמֵר: ״בָּרוּךְ שֶׁנָּתַן רָאשֵׁי חֳדָשִׁים לְעַמּוֹ יִשְׂרָאֵל לְזִכָּרוֹן״, וְלָא יָדַעְנָא – אִי אֲמַר בַּהּ ״שִׂמְחָה״ אִי לָא אֲמַר בַּהּ ״שִׂמְחָה״, אִי חָתֵים בַּהּ אִי לָא חָתֵים בַּהּ, אִי דִּידֵיהּ אִי דְּרַבֵּיהּ.

**Again** Rav Giddel **sat and said: If one erred and did not mention the New Moon,**[H] **he says: "Blessed…Who gave the New Moon to His people Israel for commemoration.** Rabbi Zeira, who related this incident, said: **I do not know whether he mentioned joy in** the formula **or whether he did not mention joy, whether he concluded this** formula **with a blessing** as he did in the parallel formulas for Shabbat and Festivals **or if he did not conclude it** with a blessing; **and whether this** *halakha* **is his or whether it is his teacher** Rav's statement.

גִּידֵּל בַּר מַנְיוֹמֵי הֲוָה קָאֵי קַמֵּיהּ דְּרַב נַחְמָן, טָעָה רַב נַחְמָן

The Gemara relates: **Giddel bar Manyumi was standing before Rav Naḥman, Rav Naḥman erred** and did not mention the special formula for Shabbat in Grace after Meals,

BACKGROUND

**Sat behind** – **יָתֵיב אֲחוֹרֵי:** Among the earlier generations, it was customary for Torah scholars to sit before their masters in a particular order, with the most prominent students in the first rows and the lesser students behind them.

Especially when there was no *amora* in the study hall to transmit the lecture to all present, a significant portion of the time was dedicated to discussions between the Rabbi and the more prominent students, those seated in the front row. Younger students would ask older students for explanations of the Rabbi's statements or pose questions to them that they dared not pose to the Rabbi directly.

HALAKHA

**One who erred and did not mention Shabbat…the Festivals** – **טָעָה וְלֹא הִזְכִּיר שֶׁל שַׁבָּת...שֶׁל יוֹם טוֹב:** One who forgot to mention Shabbat in Grace after Meals must recite a brief, independent blessing. Similarly, if one forgot to recite the special formula for the Festival, he must recite a brief blessing devoted to the sanctity of the Festival (Rambam *Sefer Ahava, Hilkhot Berakhot* 2:12; *Shulḥan Arukh, Oraḥ Ḥayyim* 188:6).

**One who erred and did not mention the New Moon** – **טָעָה וְלֹא הִזְכִּיר שֶׁל רֹאשׁ חֹדֶשׁ:** If one did not recite the special formula for the New Moon, he recites a brief blessing; however, he does not conclude the blessing with God's name, as the matter remained unresolved in the Gemara, and with regard to uncertain blessings there is no leniency when the potential invocation of God's name in vain is involved (Rambam *Sefer Ahava, Hilkhot Berakhot* 2:13; *Shulḥan Arukh, Oraḥ Ḥayyim* 188:7).

Perek **VII**
Daf **49** Amud **b**

וְהָדַר לְרֵישָׁא. אֲמַר לֵיהּ: מַאי טַעְמָא עָבֵיד מָר הָכִי? אֲמַר לֵיהּ, דְּאָמַר רַבִּי שֵׁילָא אָמַר רַב: טָעָה – חוֹזֵר לָרֹאשׁ.

**and he returned to the beginning** of Grace after Meals and repeated it. Giddel bar Manyumi **said to** Rav Naḥman: **Why did the master act in that manner? He said: As Rabbi Sheila said** that **Rav said: If one erred, he returns to the beginning.**

וְהָא אָמַר רַב הוּנָא אָמַר רַב: טָעָה – אוֹמֵר: ״בָּרוּךְ שֶׁנָּתַן״! אֲמַר לֵיהּ: לָאו אִיתְּמַר עֲלַהּ, אָמַר רַב מְנַשְּׁיָא בַּר תַּחְלִיפָא אָמַר רַב: לֹא שָׁנוּ אֶלָּא שֶׁלֹּא פָּתַח בְּ״הַטּוֹב וְהַמֵּטִיב״, אֲבָל פָּתַח בְּ״הַטּוֹב וְהַמֵּטִיב״ – חוֹזֵר לָרֹאשׁ.

Giddel bar Manyumi challenged: **Didn't Rav Huna say** that **Rav said: If one erred, he recites: Blessed…Who gave?** Rav Naḥman **said to him: Wasn't it stated about this** that **Rabbi Menashya bar Taḥlifa said** that **Rav said: They only taught that** one recites the short blessing in a case where **he did not** yet **begin** reciting: **Who is good and does good; however, if he** already **began** reciting: **Who is good and does good, he must return to the beginning** of Grace after Meals?

אָמַר רַב אִידִי בַּר אָבִין אָמַר רַב עַמְרָם אָמַר רַב נַחְמָן אָמַר שְׁמוּאֵל: טָעָה וְלֹא הִזְכִּיר שֶׁל רֹאשׁ חֹדֶשׁ בַּתְּפִלָּה – מַחֲזִירִין אוֹתוֹ, בְּבִרְכַּת הַמָּזוֹן – אֵין מַחֲזִירִין אוֹתוֹ.

**Rav Idi bar Avin said** that **Rav Amram said** that **Rav Naḥman said** that **Shmuel said: If one erred and did not mention the** formula for the **New Moon in his** ***Amida*** **prayer, we require him to return** to the beginning of the prayer and repeat it. However, if one erred and forgot to mention the New Moon **in Grace after Meals, we do not require him to return** to the beginning and repeat it.

אֲמַר לֵיהּ רַב אָבִין לְרַב עַמְרָם: מַאי שְׁנָא תְּפִלָּה וּמַאי שְׁנָא בִּרְכַּת הַמָּזוֹן? – אֲמַר לֵיהּ: אַף לְדִידִי קַשְׁיָא לִי, וּשְׁאֵילְתֵּיהּ לְרַב נַחְמָן, וַאֲמַר לִי: מִינֵּיהּ דְּמָר שְׁמוּאֵל לָא שְׁמִיעַ לִי, אֶלָּא נֶחֱזֵי אֲנַן, תְּפִלָּה דְּחוֹבָה הִיא – מַחֲזִירִין אוֹתוֹ; בִּרְכַּת מְזוֹנָא, דְּאִי בָּעֵי אָכֵיל אִי בָּעֵי לָא אָכֵיל – אֵין מַחֲזִירִין אוֹתוֹ.

**Rav Avin said to Rav Amram** about this: **What is the difference between** the *Amida* **prayer and Grace after Meals? He said to him: That** question **was also difficult for me and I asked Rav Naḥman** about **it, and he said to me: I did not hear** the reason **from Mar Shmuel** himself, **but let us see** if we can analyze it ourselves. For the *Amida* **prayer, which is an obligation, we require him to return** to the beginning of the prayer and repeat it. For **Grace after Meals, which** is not an obligation, as **if he wants** to eat, **he eats and if he wants** not to eat, **he does not eat, we do not require him to return** to the beginning and repeat it. Grace after Meals is not a full-fledged obligation; it is dependent upon eating, which is optional. Consequently, failure to mention the New Moon in Grace after Meals is not a source of concern.

אֶלָּא מֵעַתָּה, שַׁבָּתוֹת וְיָמִים טוֹבִים דְּלָא סַגִּי דְּלָא אָכֵיל, הָכִי נַמִי דְּאִי טָעֵי הָדַר! – אֲמַר לֵיהּ: אִין, דַּאֲמַר רַבִּי שֵׁילָא אָמַר רַב: טָעָה – חוֹזֵר לָרֹאשׁ. וְהָא אָמַר רַב הוּנָא אָמַר רַב: טָעָה – אוֹמֵר "בָּרוּךְ שֶׁנָּתַן"! לָאו אִיתְּמַר עֲלַהּ: לֹא שָׁנוּ אֶלָּא שֶׁלֹּא פָּתַח בְּ"הַטּוֹב וְהַמֵּטִיב", אֲבָל פָּתַח בְּ"הַטּוֹב וְהַמֵּטִיב" – חוֹזֵר לָרֹאשׁ.

The Gemara asks: **If so, on Shabbatot and Festivals,** when there is a mitzva to eat and **when it is not possible to refrain from eating,**[N] there **too, if he erred** and failed to mention them in Grace after Meals, would you say that **he must return** to the beginning and repeat it? **He said: Yes. As Rabbi Sheila said** that **Rav said: If one erred, he returns to the beginning** of Grace after Meals. The Gemara asks: **Didn't Rav Huna say** that **Rav said: If one erred, he recites: Blessed…Who gave?** The Gemara rejects this: **Wasn't it stated about this: They only taught that** one recites the short blessing in a case where **he did not** yet **begin** reciting: **Who is good and does good; however,** if **he** already **began** reciting: **Who is good and does good,**[H] **he must return to the beginning** of Grace after Meals.

"עַד כַּמָּה מְזַמְּנִין" וכו׳.

There is a dispute in the mishna: **How much** must one eat **to obligate** those with whom they ate **in a** ***zimmun***? An olive-bulk; Rabbi Yehuda says: An egg-bulk.

לְמֵימְרָא, דְּרַבִּי מֵאִיר חָשֵׁיב לֵיהּ כְּזַיִת וְרַבִּי יְהוּדָה כְּבֵיצָה – וְהָא אִיפְּכָא שָׁמְעִינַן לְהוּ! דִּתְנַן: וְכֵן מִי שֶׁיָּצָא מִירוּשָׁלַיִם וְנִזְכַּר שֶׁהָיָה בְּיָדוֹ בְּשַׂר קֹדֶשׁ, אִם עָבַר צוֹפִים – שׂוֹרְפוֹ בִּמְקוֹמוֹ, וְאִם לָאו – חוֹזֵר וְשׂוֹרְפוֹ לִפְנֵי הַבִּירָה מֵעֲצֵי הַמַּעֲרָכָה.

The Gemara asks: **Is that to say that Rabbi Meir considers an olive-bulk significant and Rabbi Yehuda considers an egg-bulk significant? Didn't we hear them** say **the opposite** elsewhere? **As we learned** in a mishna: **And similarly, one who left Jerusalem and remembered that there was consecrated meat in his hand,**[H] which may not be removed from Jerusalem, **if he passed** Mount **Scopus,** or anywhere that is a comparable distance from the Temple Mount, **he burns** the sanctified meat **at the site** where **he** is located; **and if** he has **not** yet traveled that distance, **he must return to burn it before the Temple with the wood of the arrangement** that was designated for burning consecrated items that were disqualified.

עַד כַּמָּה הֵם חוֹזְרִים? רַבִּי מֵאִיר אוֹמֵר: זֶה וָזֶה בִּכְבֵיצָה; וְרַבִּי יְהוּדָה אוֹמֵר: זֶה וָזֶה בִּכְזַיִת!

The Gemara asks: **How much** meat must be in their possession in order to obligate **them to return? Rabbi Meir says:** One must return **for an egg-bulk of this,** sanctified meat, **and that,** leaven mentioned there previously. **And Rabbi Yehuda says:** One must return **for an olive-bulk of this and that.** Their opinions there seem to contradict their opinions in our mishna.

אָמַר רַבִּי יוֹחָנָן: מוּחְלֶפֶת הַשִּׁיטָה. אַבָּיֵי אָמַר: לְעוֹלָם לָא תֵּיפוּךְ, הָכָא בִּקְרָאֵי פְּלִיגִי, רַבִּי מֵאִיר סָבַר: "וְאָכַלְתָּ" – זוֹ אֲכִילָה, "וְשָׂבָעְתָּ" – זוֹ שְׁתִיָּה, וַאֲכִילָה בִּכְזַיִת. וְרַבִּי יְהוּדָה סָבַר: "וְאָכַלְתָּ וְשָׂבָעְתָּ" – אֲכִילָה שֶׁיֵּשׁ בָּהּ שְׂבִיעָה, וְאֵיזוֹ זוֹ – כְּבֵיצָה.

To resolve this contradiction, **Rabbi Yoḥanan said: The opinions are reversed** in one of these sources and must be emended. **Abaye said: Actually do not reverse** them. **Here,** with regard to *zimmun*, **they disagree with regard to** the interpretation of **verses. Rabbi Meir holds: "And you shall eat," that is eating; "and be satisfied," that is drinking** after eating. The *halakha* is in accordance with the standard halakhic principle that **eating** is defined as the consumption of **an olive-bulk. And Rabbi Yehuda holds: "And you shall eat and be satisfied,"**[N] refers to **eating that includes satisfaction. And what is** considered eating with satisfaction? The consumption of **an egg-bulk.**

### HALAKHA

**He already began reciting: Who is good and does good – פָּתַח בְּ״הַטּוֹב וְהַמֵּטִיב״:** One who failed to mention the sanctity of the day on Shabbat or a Festival in Grace after Meals and already began to recite: Who is good and does good, returns to the beginning of Grace after Meals. One who failed to mention the New Moon or the Festival on the intermediate days of the Festival, need not return (Rambam *Sefer Ahava, Hilkhot Berakhot* 2:12–13; *Shulḥan Arukh, Oraḥ Ḥayyim* 188:6–7).

**One who left Jerusalem and remembered that there was consecrated meat in his hand – מִי שֶׁיָּצָא מִירוּשָׁלַיִם וְנִזְכַּר שֶׁהָיָה בְּיָדוֹ בְּשַׂר קֹדֶשׁ:** If one forgot and left Jerusalem with at least an olive-bulk of sanctified meat, as the *halakha* is in accordance with Rabbi Yehuda, he must return to Jerusalem and burn it in front of the Temple. If he has already passed Mount Scopus, he burns it where he is (Rambam *Sefer Avoda, Hilkhot Pesulei HaMukdashim* 19:8).

### NOTES

**On Shabbatot and Festivals, when it is not possible to refrain from eating – שַׁבָּתוֹת וְיָמִים טוֹבִים דְּלָא סַגִּי דְּלָא אָכֵיל:** It is forbidden to fast on Shabbat and on the three pilgrimage Festivals. From the verses that describe how the manna was collected for Shabbat (Exodus 16:15), the Sages derive that there is a requirement to eat three meals. Eating these meals on Shabbat fulfills the requirement of enjoyment [*oneg*] on Shabbat (see Isaiah 58:13). There is a requirement to rejoice [*simḥa*] on the Festival (Deuteronomy 16:14), which is interpreted as including an obligation to eat two meals. Although it is also forbidden to fast on the New Moon, there is no requirement to eat a full meal with bread.

**And you shall eat and be satisfied – וְאָכַלְתָּ וְשָׂבָעְתָּ:** Virtually all commentaries emphasize that neither Rabbi Yehuda nor Rabbi Meir hold that the *halakha* is actually derived from this verse; it is merely an allusion. According to both opinions, the sense of satisfaction resulting from eating is transient rather than complete satisfaction. Rabbi Meir asserts that eating without drinking is unpleasant, and only after the diner drinks does he have a sense of satisfaction. According to Rabbi Yehuda, based on our tradition (*Yoma* 86a), an egg-bulk fills the entire throat and provides a sense of satisfaction known as the satisfaction of the throat (see Rabbi Ya'akov Emden and *Shibbolei HaLeket*).

## NOTES

**The dispute between Rabbi Meir and Rabbi Yehuda** – מַחְלוֹקֶת רַבִּי מֵאִיר וְרַבִּי יְהוּדָה: According to Abaye, the dispute between Rabbi Yehuda and Rabbi Meir is based on the determination of the measure of halakhic significance in each context. Apparently, with regard to consecrated foods, as opposed to most other areas of *halakha*, there are two different measures. While the minimum measure of the prohibition to eat consecrated meat is an olive-bulk, it cannot become ritually impure if it is less than an egg-bulk. Because there are these two measures, there is room to dispute which of them is the determining measure for other areas of *halakha*, e.g., the requirement to return to Jerusalem to burn meat that one inadvertently took with him.

**Both in a group of ten…** – אֶחָד עֲשָׂרָה וכו׳: Some interpret this expression to mean that one invokes God's name in any *zimmun* in which anywhere between ten and ten thousand men participate, although there are differences in the formula based on the number, i.e., one hundred, one thousand, etc. The Gemara interprets this phrase differently (*Shenot Eliyahu*; see *Hagahot HaRashash*).

**Shmuel said: One should never exclude himself from the collective** – לְעוֹלָם אַל יוֹצִיא אָדָם אֶת עַצְמוֹ מִן הַכְּלָל: The Jerusalem Talmud points out that whenever the prayer leader calls upon others to praise God by reciting: Bless [*barekhu*], as is common practice when called up to the Torah as well as in other places in prayer, by definition the leader is excluding himself from the community. The rationale for this practice is that by concluding: Bless the Lord, with: The Blessed One, he is effectively joining the community in blessing God (*Tosafot*).

## HALAKHA

**The formula of the *zimmun*** – נוּסַח הַזִּימּוּן: Three people dining together recite: Let us bless. Four or more recite: Bless. Ten or more dining together recite: Let us bless our God. The *halakha* is in accordance with the opinion of Rabbi Akiva that there is no distinction between ten and more than ten (Rambam *Sefer Ahava, Hilkhot Berakhot* 5:2, 4; *Shulḥan Arukh, Oraḥ Ḥayyim* 192:1).

הָתָם – בִּסְבָרָא פְּלִיגִי, רַבִּי מֵאִיר סָבַר: חֲזָרָתוֹ כְּטוּמְאָתוֹ – מָה טוּמְאָתוֹ בִּכְבֵיצָה, אַף חֲזָרָתוֹ בִּכְבֵיצָה; וְרַבִּי יְהוּדָה סָבַר: חֲזָרָתוֹ כְּאִיסּוּרוֹ – מָה אִיסּוּרוֹ בִּכְזַיִת, אַף חֲזָרָתוֹ בִּכְזַיִת.

On the other hand, **there,** in the case of leaven and sanctified foods **they disagree** not with regard to the interpretation of verses, but **with regard to logical reasoning. Rabbi Meir holds:** The requirement to **return** consecrated food **is analogous to its ritual impurity, and just as its** susceptibility to **ritual impurity is** only when it is the size of an **egg-bulk, so too,** the requirement to **return it is** only when it is the size of an **egg-bulk. And Rabbi Yehuda holds** The requirement to **return** consecrated food **is analogous to its prohibition, and just as its prohibition is** only when it is the size of an **olive-bulk, so too,** the requirement to **return it is** only when it is the size of an **olive-bulk.**[N]

מתני׳ כֵּיצַד מְזַמְּנִין? בִּשְׁלֹשָׁה – אוֹמֵר: ״נְבָרֵךְ״, בִּשְׁלֹשָׁה וָהוּא – אוֹמֵר: ״בָּרְכוּ״.

**MISHNA** The mishna delineates distinctions in the *halakhot* of the *zimmun* blessing, based on the number of people present. **How does one recite the *zimmun*? In** a group of **three** people, the one reciting the *zimmun* **says: Let us bless** the One from Whose food we have eaten. **In** a group of **three** people **and him,** the one reciting the *zimmun* **says: Bless** the One from Whose food we have eaten, as even without him there are enough people to recite the *zimmun.*

בַּעֲשָׂרָה – אוֹמֵר: ״נְבָרֵךְ אֱלֹהֵינוּ״, בַּעֲשָׂרָה וָהוּא – אוֹמֵר: ״בָּרְכוּ״; אֶחָד עֲשָׂרָה וְאֶחָד עֲשָׂרָה רִבּוֹא.

With the increase in the number of participants, the blessing is more complex. **In** a group of **ten** people, the one reciting the *zimmun* **says Let us bless our God. In** a group of **ten** people **and him,** the one reciting the *zimmun* **says: Bless** our God. This formula is recited **both** in a group of **ten**[N] **and in** a group of **one hundred thousand.**

בְּמֵאָה – הוּא אוֹמֵר: ״נְבָרֵךְ ה׳ אֱלֹהֵינוּ״. בְּמֵאָה וָהוּא – אוֹמֵר: ״בָּרְכוּ״, וּבְאֶלֶף – הוּא אוֹמֵר: ״נְבָרֵךְ לַה׳ אֱלֹהֵינוּ אֱלֹהֵי יִשְׂרָאֵל״, בְּאֶלֶף וָהוּא – אוֹמֵר: ״בָּרְכוּ״, בְּרִבּוֹא – אוֹמֵר: ״נְבָרֵךְ לַה׳ אֱלֹהֵינוּ אֱלֹהֵי יִשְׂרָאֵל אֱלֹהֵי צְבָאוֹת יוֹשֵׁב הַכְּרוּבִים עַל הַמָּזוֹן שֶׁאָכַלְנוּ״, בְּרִבּוֹא וָהוּא – אוֹמֵר: ״בָּרְכוּ״,

**In** a group of **one hundred** people, the one reciting the *zimmun* **says Let us bless the Lord our God. In** a group of **one hundred** people **and him,** the one reciting the *zimmun* **says: Bless** the Lord our God. **In** a group of **one thousand** people, the one reciting the *zimmun* **says: Let us bless the Lord our God, the God of Israel. In** a group of **one thousand** people **and him, he says: Bless** the Lord our God the God of Israel. **In** a group of **ten thousand** people, the one reciting the *zimmun* **says: Let us bless the Lord our God, the God of Israel, the God of Hosts, Who sits upon the cherubs, for the food that we have eaten. In** a group of **ten thousand** people **and him** the one reciting the *zimmun* **says: Bless** the Lord our God, the God of Israel, the God of Hosts, Who sits upon the cherubs, for the food that we have eaten.

כְּעִנְיָן שֶׁהוּא מְבָרֵךְ כָּךְ עוֹנִים אַחֲרָיו: ״בָּרוּךְ ה׳ אֱלֹהֵינוּ אֱלֹהֵי יִשְׂרָאֵל אֱלֹהֵי צְבָאוֹת יוֹשֵׁב הַכְּרוּבִים עַל הַמָּזוֹן שֶׁאָכַלְנוּ״.

The principle is that **just as he recites the blessing, so too** those present **recite in response: Blessed be the Lord our God, the God of Israel, the God of Hosts, Who sits upon the cherubs, for the food that we have eaten.**

רַבִּי יוֹסֵי הַגְּלִילִי אוֹמֵר: לְפִי רוֹב הַקָּהָל הֵם מְבָרְכִים, שֶׁנֶּאֱמַר: ״בְּמַקְהֵלוֹת בָּרְכוּ אֱלֹהִים ה׳ מִמְּקוֹר יִשְׂרָאֵל״. אָמַר רַבִּי עֲקִיבָא: מָה מָצִינוּ בְּבֵית הַכְּנֶסֶת – אֶחָד מְרוּבִּים וְאֶחָד מוּעָטִים אוֹמֵר ״בָּרְכוּ אֶת ה׳״. רַבִּי יִשְׁמָעֵאל אוֹמֵר: ״בָּרְכוּ אֶת ה׳ הַמְבוֹרָךְ״.

On a similar note, **Rabbi Yosei HaGelili says: According to the size of the crowd, they recite the blessing, as it is stated: "Bless you God in full assemblies, even the Lord, you who are from the fountain of Israel"** (Psalms 68:27). **Rabbi Akiva said** that there are no distinctions based on the size of the crowd: **What do we find in the synagogue? Both** when there are **many and** when there are **few** as long as there is a quorum of ten, the prayer leader **says: Bless** [*barekhu*] **the Lord. Rabbi Yishmael said** that in the synagogue one recites: **Bless the Lord the blessed One.**[H]

גמ׳ אָמַר שְׁמוּאֵל: לְעוֹלָם אַל יוֹצִיא אָדָם אֶת עַצְמוֹ מִן הַכְּלָל.

**GEMARA** **Shmuel said: One should never exclude himself from the collective.**[N]

תְּנַן: בִּשְׁלֹשָׁה וָהוּא – אוֹמֵר: ״בָּרְכוּ״!

The Gemara raises a challenge from what **we learned** in our mishna **In** a group of **three** people **and him,** the one reciting the *zimmun* **says: Bless** the One from Whose food we have eaten. He thereby excludes himself from the collective.

אֵימָא:

The Gemara answers: **Say** that the meaning of the mishna is:

אַף "בָּרְכוּ", וּמִכָּל מָקוֹם "נְבָרֵךְ" עָדִיף. דְּאָמַר רַב אַדָּא בַּר אַהֲבָה: אָמְרִי בֵּי רַב, תְּנֵינָא: שִׁשָּׁה נֶחֱלָקִין עַד עֲשָׂרָה;

He may **even** say: **Bless; nevertheless: Let us bless, is preferable as Rav Adda bar Ahava said** that **they said in the school of Rav: We learned:** A group of **six to ten** people may **divide** into two groups, each forming its own *zimmun*. However, a group of ten, which invokes God's name in the *zimmun*, may not divide into two groups as that would negate the opportunity to invoke God's name.

אִי אָמְרַתְּ בִּשְׁלָמָא "נְבָרֵךְ" עָדִיף – מִשּׁוּם הָכִי נֶחֱלָקִין, אֶלָּא אִי אָמְרַתְּ "בָּרְכוּ" עָדִיף – אַמַּאי נֶחֱלָקִין? אֶלָּא לָאו שְׁמַע מִינַּהּ "נְבָרֵךְ" עָדִיף – שְׁמַע מִינַּהּ.

The Gemara proceeds: **Granted, if you say: Let us bless is preferable, that is why** six people who ate together may **divide** into two groups. **However, if you say: Bless is preferable, why** are they permitted to **divide** into two groups? Neither group would be able to say: Bless. **Rather, mustn't one conclude from this: Let us bless is preferable** as the one reciting the *zimmun* does not exclude himself from the group? The Gemara sums up the discussion: Indeed, **conclude from this** that that is the case.

תַּנְיָא נַמִי הָכִי: בֵּין שֶׁאָמַר "בָּרְכוּ" בֵּין שֶׁאָמַר "נְבָרֵךְ" אֵין תּוֹפְסִין אוֹתוֹ עַל כָּךְ, וְהַנַּקְדָנִין תּוֹפְסִין אוֹתוֹ עַל כָּךְ. וּמִבִּרְכוֹתָיו שֶׁל אָדָם נִיכָּר אִם תַּלְמִיד חָכָם הוּא אִם לָאו. כֵּיצַד? רַבִּי אוֹמֵר: "וּבְטוּבוֹ" – הֲרֵי זֶה תַּלְמִיד חָכָם, "וּמִטּוּבוֹ" – הֲרֵי זֶה בּוּר.

**That was also taught** in the *Tosefta*: **Both** if **he said: Bless, and** if **he said: Let us bless, we do not reprimand him for** doing **so; and the punctilious reprimand him for** doing **so. And** the Gemara says: As a rule, **from** the style of **one's blessings it is obvious whether or not he is a Torah scholar. How so?** For example, **Rabbi** Yehuda HaNasi **says:** In a *zimmun*, one who recites: Blessed be the One from Whose food we have eaten **and by Whose goodness** we live, **he is a Torah scholar.** However, one who recites: Blessed be the One from Whose food we have eaten **and from Whose goodness** we live, **he is an ignoramus,**[NH] as that expression insinuates that only some of God's goodness was bestowed upon him, which is tantamount to a denial of God's lovingkindness.

אָמַר לֵיהּ אַבָּיֵי לְרַב דִּימִי: וְהָכְתִיב "וּמִבִּרְכָתְךָ יְבֹרַךְ אֶת בֵּית עַבְדְּךָ לְעוֹלָם"! בִּשְׁאֵלָה שָׁאנֵי. בִּשְׁאֵלָה נַמִי, הָכְתִיב "הַרְחֶב פִּיךָ וַאֲמַלְאֵהוּ"! הַהוּא בְּדִבְרֵי תוֹרָה כְּתִיב.

**Abaye said to Rav Dimi: Isn't it written** that King David articulated his prayer in that manner: "Be pleased, therefore, to bless Your servant's house, that it abide before You forever; for You, Lord God, have spoken. **And from Your blessing may Your servant's house be blessed forever**" (II Samuel 7:29). David said: From Your blessing. The Gemara answers: **In** a case of **request it is different,** as it is inappropriate to demand the full bounty of God's blessing. The Gemara questions this: **In** a case of **request, too, is it not written** that a request for the full bounty of God's blessing is granted: **"Open your mouth wide, that I will fill it"** (Psalms 81:11)? What one receives corresponds to what he requests. The Gemara answered: **That** verse **is written with regard to matters of Torah,** where it is wholly appropriate to make excessive requests.

תַּנְיָא, רַבִּי אוֹמֵר: "בְּטוּבוֹ חָיִינוּ" – הֲרֵי זֶה תַּלְמִיד חָכָם, "חַיִּים" – הֲרֵי זֶה בּוּר. נְהַרְבְּלָאֵי מַתְנוּ אִיפְּכָא, וְלֵית הִילְכְתָא כִּנְהַרְבְּלָאֵי.

On the topic of the *zimmun* formula, **it was taught** in a *baraita*: **Rabbi** Yehuda HaNasi **says:** One who recites in a *zimmun*: **And by His goodness we live, he is a Torah scholar.** However, one who recites: And by His goodness **they live, he is a fool,** as he excluded himself from the collective. The Sages **of Neharbela**[B] **taught the opposite.** In their opinion, they live is preferable because it is a more inclusive formula, whereas, we live is more limited and personal. Nonetheless, the Gemara concludes: **The** ***halakha*** **is not in accordance with** the opinion of the Sages **of Neharbela.**

אָמַר רַבִּי יוֹחָנָן: "נְבָרֵךְ שֶׁאָכַלְנוּ מִשֶּׁלּוֹ" – הֲרֵי זֶה תַּלְמִיד חָכָם, "לְמִי שֶׁאָכַלְנוּ מִשֶּׁלּוֹ" – הֲרֵי זֶה בּוּר.

On a similar note, **Rabbi Yoḥanan said:** One who recites in a *zimmun*: **Let us bless the One Whose food we have eaten, he is a Torah scholar.** However, one who recites: Let us bless **to Him from Whose food we have eaten,**[N] **he is an ignoramus,** as it appears that the blessing is directed to the host of the meal.

אָמַר לֵיהּ רַב אַחָא בְּרֵיהּ דְּרָבָא לְרַב אָשֵׁי: וְהָא אָמְרִינַן "לְמִי שֶׁעָשָׂה לַאֲבוֹתֵינוּ וְלָנוּ אֶת כָּל הַנִּסִּים הָאֵלּוּ"! אָמַר לֵיהּ: הָתָם מוֹכְחָא מִילְּתָא, מַאן עָבֵיד נִיסֵּי – קוּדְשָׁא בְּרִיךְ הוּא.

**Rabbi Aḥa the son of Rava** questioned this and **said to Rav Ashi: Don't we say** during the Passover seder: **To He Who performed all of these miracles for our ancestors and for us,** using the expression: To He Who? Rav Ashi **said to him: There,** in the case of miracles performed for our ancestors and for us, **it is self-evident** that the blessing refers to God. **Who performs miracles? The Holy One, blessed be He.** In the case of food, however, it is not self-evident, as the host of the meal also provided the food that was eaten.

**NOTES**

**And from Whose goodness we live, he is an ignoramus – וּמִטּוּבוֹ הֲרֵי זֶה בּוּר:** Rashi explains that he is an ignoramus because he appears to be limiting God's generosity. Maharsha suggests that this expression appears to state that when God shares His bounty with human beings He diminishes Himself. The statement: By Whose goodness we live, on the other hand, indicates that even when He gives to others, God diminishes nothing of himself. This helps explain the continuation of the Gemara: In a case of request it is different, since making a request in no way implies that God is diminished.

**To Him from Whose food we have eaten – לְמִי שֶׁאָכַלְנוּ מִשֶּׁלּוֹ:** Had he said simply: That we have eaten from his food, it would have been clear that he is referring to God, since everyone eats His food. However, by saying: To him whose food we have eaten, he appears to be blessing a particular person, the host who provided the food (*Talmidei Rabbeinu Yona*).

**HALAKHA**

**Deviation from the formula instituted by the Sages in blessings – שִׁינּוּי מִמַּטְבֵּעַ שֶׁקָּבְעוּ חֲכָמִים בִּבְרָכוֹת:** One may not deviate from the formula instituted by the Sages in blessings. One who makes a change in any of the details enumerated by the Sages, which constitutes a change in content, is a fool (*Shulḥan Arukh, Oraḥ Ḥayyim* 192:1).

**BACKGROUND**

**Sages of Neharbela – נְהַרְבְּלָאֵי:** The city of Naharbela may have been along the Baal (Bel, Bil) River in Babylonia.

It is explained in tractate *Sanhedrin* that the head of the Sages of that city was Rami (Rav Ami) bar Berukhi, and that the phrase: Of Neharbela taught, refers primarily to him. However, other than the fact that he was from Neharbela, nothing is known about him.

## NOTES

**The synagogue and Grace after Meals – בֵּית הַכְּנֶסֶת וּבִרְכַּת הַמָּזוֹן:** When there are ten men in the synagogue, the name of the Lord [*Hashem*] is invoked, but in Grace after Meals one only mentions: Our God [*Elokeinu*]. This is because a synagogue is a place designated for sanctity and is an appropriate place to invoke God's name, which is not the case with regard to the place where one eats (*Shitta Mekubbetzet*).

**From where is it derived that even fetuses in their mother's womb recited the song at the Red Sea – מִנַּיִן שֶׁאֲפִילּוּ עוּבָּרִין שֶׁבִּמְעֵי אִמָּן אָמְרוּ שִׁירָה עַל הַיָּם:** It is entirely appropriate for fetuses in the womb to recite song, as it is said that an angel teaches the fetus the Torah in its entirety while *in utero* (*Iyyun Ya'akov*).

## HALAKHA

**We would recite the Grace after Meals blessing in groups of three – מְבָרְכִינַן שְׁלֹשָׁה שְׁלֹשָׁה:** In a situation where it is impossible to hear the leader of the *zimmun* due to the size of the crowd, the people should divide themselves into smaller groups of ten and recite the *zimmun*. If the host will object, they may even divide into less conspicuous groups of three as they did in the house of the Exilarch (*Shulḥan Arukh, Oraḥ Ḥayyim* 193:1 in the comment of the Rema).

אָמַר רַבִּי יוֹחָנָן: ״בָּרוּךְ שֶׁאָכַלְנוּ מִשֶּׁלּוֹ״ – הֲרֵי זֶה תַּלְמִיד חָכָם, ״עַל הַמָּזוֹן שֶׁאָכַלְנוּ״ – הֲרֵי זֶה בּוּר.

**Rabbi Yoḥanan said** with regard to the formula of the *zimmun* that one who recites in a *zimmun*: **Blessed be the One from Whose food we have eaten, he is a Torah scholar.** However, one who recites: **For the food we have eaten, he is an ignoramus,** as it appears that he is blessing the host of the meal. If he was blessing God, why would he restrict the blessing to food (*Tosafot*)?

אָמַר רַב הוּנָא בְּרֵיהּ דְּרַב יְהוֹשֻׁעַ: לֹא אָמְרָן אֶלָּא בִּשְׁלֹשָׁה, דְּלֵיכָּא שֵׁם שָׁמַיִם, אֲבָל בַּעֲשָׂרָה דְּאִיכָּא שֵׁם שָׁמַיִם – מוֹכְחָא מִילְּתָא, כִּדְתְנַן: כָּעִנְיָן שֶׁהוּא מְבָרֵךְ כָּךְ עוֹנִין אַחֲרָיו: ״בָּרוּךְ ה׳ אֱלֹהֵי יִשְׂרָאֵל אֱלֹהֵי הַצְּבָאוֹת יוֹשֵׁב הַכְּרוּבִים עַל הַמָּזוֹן שֶׁאָכַלְנוּ״.

**Rav Huna, son of Rav Yehoshua said: We only said** this *halakha* **with regard to** a *zimmun* **of three, where there is no** mention of **God's name.** In a *zimmun* of **ten, however, where there is** mention of **God's name, it is self-evident** to whom the blessing refers, **as we learned** in our mishna: **Just as he recites the blessing, so too** do those present **recite in response: Blessed be the Lord our God, the God of Israel, the God of Hosts, Who sits upon the cherubs, for the food that we have eaten.**

״אֶחָד עֲשָׂרָה, וְאֶחָד עֲשָׂרָה רִבּוֹא״. הָא גּוּפָא קַשְׁיָא! אָמְרַתְּ: אֶחָד עֲשָׂרָה וְאֶחָד עֲשָׂרָה רִבּוֹא – אַלְמָא כִּי הֲדָדֵי נִינְהוּ, וַהֲדַר קָתָנֵי: בְּמֵאָה אוֹמֵר, בְּאֶלֶף אוֹמֵר, בְּרִבּוֹא אוֹמֵר!

We learned in our mishna with regard to the formula of *zimmun*: This formula is recited **both** in a group of **ten and in** a group of **one hundred thousand.** The Gemara raises an objection: **The** mishna **itself is difficult.** On one hand, **you said:** This formula is recited **both** in a group of **ten and in** a group of **one hundred thousand; consequently,** the two cases **are the same.** On the other hand, **it is then taught: In** a group of **one hundred** people, the one reciting the *zimmun* **says; in** a group of **one thousand** people, the one reciting the *zimmun* **says; in** a group of **ten thousand** people, the one reciting the *zimmun* **says.** Evidently, the formula depends on the number of people.

אָמַר רַב יוֹסֵף, לָא קַשְׁיָא: הָא רַבִּי יוֹסֵי הַגְּלִילִי, הָא רַבִּי עֲקִיבָא; דִּתְנַן, רַבִּי יוֹסֵי הַגְּלִילִי אוֹמֵר: לְפִי רוֹב הַקָּהָל הֵם מְבָרְכִין, שֶׁנֶּאֱמַר: ״בְּמַקְהֵלוֹת בָּרְכוּ אֱלֹהִים״. ״אָמַר רַבִּי עֲקִיבָא, מָה מָצִינוּ בְּבֵית הַכְּנֶסֶת״ וכו׳.

**Rav Yosef said:** This is **not difficult,** as these two statements are the opinions of different Sages. **This is** the opinion of **Rabbi Yosei HaGelili, and that is** the opinion of **Rabbi Akiva. As we learned** in our mishna: **Rabbi Yosei HaGelili says: According to the size of the crowd, they recite the blessing, as it is stated: "Bless you God in full assemblies,** even the Lord, you who are from the fountain of Israel" (Psalms 68:27). We also learned in our mishna that **Rabbi Akiva said** that there are no distinctions based on the size of the crowd: **What do we find in the synagogue?**[N] Both when there are many and when there are few, as long as there is a quorum of ten the prayer leader says: Bless the Lord. In the case of Grace after Meals as well, the formula remains the same regardless of the number of people participating in the *zimmun*.

וְרַבִּי עֲקִיבָא, הַאי קְרָא דְּרַבִּי יוֹסֵי הַגְּלִילִי מַאי עָבֵיד לֵיהּ? מִיבְּעֵי לֵיהּ לְכִדְתַנְיָא; הָיָה רַבִּי מֵאִיר אוֹמֵר: מִנַּיִן שֶׁאֲפִילּוּ עוּבָּרִין שֶׁבִּמְעֵי אִמָּן אָמְרוּ שִׁירָה עַל הַיָּם – שֶׁנֶּאֱמַר: ״בְּמַקְהֵלוֹת בָּרְכוּ אֱלֹהִים ה׳ מִמְּקוֹר יִשְׂרָאֵל״. וְאִידָּךְ? – מִ״מְּקוֹר״ נָפְקָא.

The Gemara asks: **And Rabbi Akiva, what does he do with that verse** cited by **Rabbi Yosei HaGelili?** The Gemara answers: **He needs it to** derive **that which was taught** in a *baraita*: **Rabbi Meir says: From where** is it derived **that even fetuses in their mother's womb recited** the **song at the** Red **Sea?**[N] **As it is stated** in the chapter of Psalms that describes the exodus from Egypt: **"In assemblies, bless God, the Lord, from the source of Israel,"** and fetuses are included in these assemblies. The Gemara asks: **And** from where does **the other** Sage, Rabbi Yosei HaGelili derive the matter of the singing of the fetuses? The Gemara answers: **He derives** it **from the source** of Israel, which he interprets as an allusion to the womb.

אָמַר רָבָא: הֲלָכָה כְּרַבִּי עֲקִיבָא. רָבִינָא וְרַב חָמָא בַּר בּוּזִי אִקְלְעוּ לְבֵי רֵישׁ גָּלוּתָא, קָם רַב חָמָא וְקָא מְהַדַּר אַבֵּי מְאָה. אָמַר לֵיהּ רָבִינָא: לָא צְרִיכַתְּ, הָכִי אָמַר רָבָא: הֲלָכָה כְּרַבִּי עֲקִיבָא.

**Rava said: The** ***halakha*** **is in accordance with** the opinion of **Rabbi Akiva.** The Gemara recounts that **Ravina and Rav Ḥama bar Buzi happened** to come **to** a banquet at **the house of the Exilarch.** At the end of the meal, **Rav Ḥama rose and was seeking** to gather a group of **one hundred** participants in the meal so that the *zimmun* for one hundred could be recited. **Ravina said to him: You need not** do so, as **Rava declared the following: The** ***halakha*** **is in accordance with** the opinion of **Rabbi Akiva** and the formula remains the same regardless of the number of people participating in the *zimmun*, as long as there are at least ten.

אָמַר רָבָא: כִּי אָכְלִינַן רִפְתָּא בֵּי רֵישׁ גָּלוּתָא מְבָרְכִינַן שְׁלֹשָׁה שְׁלֹשָׁה. וְלִיבָרְכוּ עֲשָׂרָה עֲשָׂרָה! – שָׁמַע רֵישׁ גָּלוּתָא וְאִיקְפַּד. – וְנֵיפְקוּ בְּבִרְכְתָא דְּרֵישׁ גָּלוּתָא! – אַיְּידֵי דְּהָווּ כּוּלֵּי עָלְמָא לָא שָׁמְעִי.

The Gemara discusses Rava's conduct at meals at the house of the Exilarch. **Rava said: When we would eat bread at the house of the Exilarch, we would recite the** Grace after Meals **blessing in groups of three.**[H] The Gemara asks: **Let them recite the blessing in groups of ten.** The Gemara answers: Then **the Exilarch would hear and become angry** upon seeing a large group of Sages reciting Grace after Meals before he completed his meal. The Gemara asks: **Why could they not satisfy their obligation with the Exilarch's blessing?** The Gemara answers: **Since everyone is making noise, they do not hear** and would not fulfill their obligation.

אָמַר רַבָּה תּוֹסְפָאָה: הָנֵי שְׁלֹשָׁה דִּכְרַכִי רִפְתָּא בַּהֲדֵי הֲדָדֵי, וְקָדֵים חַד מִינַּיְיהוּ וּבָרֵיךְ לְדַעְתֵּיהּ, אִינּוּן נָפְקִין בְּזִמּוּן דִּידֵיהּ, אִיהוּ לָא נָפֵיק בְּזִמּוּן דִּידְהוּ, לְפִי שֶׁאֵין זִמּוּן לְמַפְרֵעַ.

**Rabba Tosefa'a said: These three** people, **who break bread together and one of them went ahead and recited** Grace after Meals **on his own** without a *zimmun*, **they,** the other two diners, **fulfill** their obligation **with his** participation in their ***zimmun*****; he,** however, **does not fulfill** his obligation **with** his participation in **their *zimmun* because there is no retroactive *zimmun*,**[H] and once he recited his blessing, participating in the *zimmun* accomplishes nothing for him.

"רַבִּי יִשְׁמָעֵאל אוֹמֵר". רַפְרָם בַּר פַּפָּא אִקְלַע לְבֵי כְנִישְׁתָּא דַּאֲבֵי גִיבַר, קָם קְרָא בְּסִפְרָא וְאָמַר: "בָּרְכוּ אֶת ה'", וְאִשְׁתִּיק וְלָא אָמַר "הַמְבוֹרָךְ". אַוְּושׁוּ כּוּלֵּי עָלְמָא: "בָּרְכוּ אֶת ה' הַמְבוֹרָךְ"! אָמַר רָבָא: פַּתְיָא אוּכָּמָא, בַּהֲדֵי פְּלוּגְתָּא לְמָה לָךְ! וְעוֹד: הָא נָהוּג עָלְמָא כְּרַבִּי יִשְׁמָעֵאל.

The mishna states that Rabbi Akiva holds that in the synagogue, one recites: Bless the Lord, while **Rabbi Yishmael said** that he recites: **Bless the Lord the blessed One. Rafram bar Pappa happened** to come **to the synagogue of Abei Givar when he rose to read from the** Torah **scroll and recited: Bless the Lord, and was silent, and did not recite: The blessed One.** Because Rafram bar Pappa followed the principle that the *halakha* is in accordance with the opinion of Rabbi Akiva,[H] and those present were not accustomed to that ruling, **everyone** in the synagogue **cried out: Bless the Lord the blessed One. Rava said** to Rafram bar Pappa: **You black pot,** a fond nickname for a Torah scholar who invests great effort in Torah study and worship of God, **why are you** involving yourself **in this** tannaitic **dispute?** Although Rabbi Akiva and Rabbi Yishmael disagree, Rabbi Yishmael's formula, in which Rabbi Akiva's formula is included, is acceptable to both. **Furthermore, standard practice is in accordance with** the opinion of **Rabbi Yishmael.**

מתני׳ שְׁלֹשָׁה שֶׁאָכְלוּ כְּאַחַת – אֵינָן רַשָּׁאִין לֵיחָלֵק, וְכֵן אַרְבָּעָה וְכֵן חֲמִשָּׁה; שִׁשָּׁה – נֶחְלָקִין, עַד עֲשָׂרָה; וַעֲשָׂרָה – אֵין נֶחְלָקִין, עַד עֶשְׂרִים.

**MISHNA** **Three** people **who ate as one are not permitted to divide**[H] and recite Grace after Meals individually; rather, they recite the *zimmun* together. **And the same** is true of **four** who ate together, **and the same** is true of **five.** However, a group of **six, up to** but not including **ten** people who ate as one, **may divide** into two groups, each reciting its own *zimmun*. **And** a group of **ten may not divide** into two groups **until there are twenty** people present. The general principle is that a group may not divide unless the smaller groups will be able to recite the same *zimmun* formula that the whole group would have recited.

שְׁתֵּי חֲבוּרוֹת שֶׁהָיוּ אוֹכְלוֹת בְּבַיִת אֶחָד, בִּזְמַן שֶׁמִּקְצָתָן רוֹאִין אֵלּוּ אֶת אֵלּוּ – הֲרֵי אֵלּוּ מִצְטָרְפִין לְזִמּוּן, וְאִם לָאו – אֵלּוּ מְזַמְּנִין לְעַצְמָן וְאֵלּוּ מְזַמְּנִין לְעַצְמָן.

The mishna states a *halakha* with regard to two groups joining together: **Two groups that were eating in one house, when some** members of each group **can see each other, they may combine to** form a ***zimmun*****.**[H] **And if not, these recite a *zimmun* for themselves and those recite a *zimmun* for themselves.**

אֵין מְבָרְכִין עַל הַיַּיִן עַד שֶׁיִּתֵּן לְתוֹכוֹ מַיִם, דִּבְרֵי רַבִּי אֱלִיעֶזֶר; וַחֲכָמִים אוֹמְרִים: מְבָרְכִין.

The mishna also speaks of the blessing over wine: **One does not recite a blessing over wine until he adds water to it,** that is **the statement of Rabbi Eliezer.** Undiluted wine is too strong to drink and a blessing is inappropriate. **And the Rabbis say:** Since it is possible to drink undiluted wine, one **recites a blessing over it.**

גמ׳ מַאי קָא מַשְׁמַע לַן? תְּנֵינָא חֲדָא זִימְנָא: שְׁלֹשָׁה שֶׁאָכְלוּ כְּאַחַת חַיָּיבִין לְזַמֵּן!

**GEMARA** At the beginning of the mishna, we learned that three people who ate together may not disperse. The Gemara asks: **What does this** mishna **teach us? We** already **learned this once: Three** people **who ate as one are required to form a *zimmun*.**

הָא קָא מַשְׁמַע לַן, כִּי הָא דְּאָמַר רַבִּי אַבָּא אָמַר שְׁמוּאֵל: שְׁלֹשָׁה שֶׁיָּשְׁבוּ לֶאֱכוֹל כְּאַחַת וַעֲדַיִן לֹא אָכְלוּ – אֵינָן רַשָּׁאִין לֵיחָלֵק.

The Gemara answers: **This teaches us that** *halakha* **which Rabbi Abba said** that **Shmuel said: Three** individuals **who sat to eat as one,**[H] **and they have not yet begun to eat,** nevertheless, **they are not permitted to divide** and recite Grace after Meals individually.

לִישָּׁנָא אַחֲרִינָא: אָמַר רַבִּי אַבָּא אָמַר שְׁמוּאֵל, הָכִי קָתָנֵי: שְׁלֹשָׁה שֶׁיָּשְׁבוּ לֶאֱכוֹל כְּאַחַת, אַף עַל פִּי שֶׁכָּל אֶחָד וְאֶחָד אוֹכֵל מִכִּכָּרוֹ – אֵינָן רַשָּׁאִין לֵיחָלֵק. אִי נַמִי: כִּי הָא דְּרַב הוּנָא, דְּאָמַר רַב הוּנָא: שְׁלֹשָׁה שֶׁבָּאוּ מִשָּׁלֹשׁ חֲבוּרוֹת – אֵינָן רַשָּׁאִין לֵיחָלֵק.

The Gemara cites **another version: Rabbi Abba said** that **Shmuel said** that **this is what** the mishna **teaches: Three** individuals **who sat to eat as one, even though** they do not share a meal, but **each and every one** of them **eats from his own loaf, they** are considered a single group in terms of *zimmun*, and **are not permitted to divide. Alternatively,** perhaps the mishna comes to teach **that** *halakha* **of Rav Huna, as Rav Huna said: Three** individuals **who came from three** different **groups**[NH] and sat together to continue their meals also form a *zimmun* and **are not permitted to divide.**

**HALAKHA**

**Retroactive *zimmun* – זִמּוּן לְמַפְרֵעַ:** If three individuals ate as one and one of them recited Grace after Meals on his own before the others, the remaining two may include him in their *zimmun*, although he does not fulfill his own obligation as there is no retroactive *zimmun*, i.e., after he already recited Grace after Meals (Rambam *Sefer Ahava, Hilkhot Berakhot* 5:14; *Shulḥan Arukh, Oraḥ Ḥayyim* 194:1).

**The *halakha* is in accordance with the opinion of Rabbi Akiva – הֲלָכָה כְּרַבִּי עֲקִיבָא:** Although Rava ruled in accordance with the opinion of Rabbi Akiva that the formula: Bless the Lord, is recited, the universal practice since the time of the Gemara is to recite: Bless the Lord Who is Blessed, as one thereby satisfies all tannaitic opinions (Rambam *Sefer Ahava, Hilkhot Tefilla* 9:1; *Shulḥan Arukh, Oraḥ Ḥayyim* 57:1).

**Three people who ate as one are not permitted to divide – שְׁלֹשָׁה שֶׁאָכְלוּ כְּאַחַת אֵינָן רַשָּׁאִין לֵיחָלֵק וכו׳:** A group of up to five people dining together may not divide into smaller groups. From six to ten, they may divide into groups of at least three each. Similarly, a group of between ten and nineteen people may not divide into smaller groups; however, from twenty and beyond, they may divide into groups of at least ten each (Rambam *Sefer Ahava, Hilkhot Berakhot* 5:10; *Shulḥan Arukh, Oraḥ Ḥayyim* 193:1).

**Combining groups to form a *zimmun* – צֵירוּף חֲבוּרוֹת לְזִמּוּן:** If two groups are in the same house, or even if they are in separate houses but can see each other (Jerusalem Talmud, *Talmidei Rabbeinu Yona*, Rosh), they may combine for a *zimmun* (Rambam *Sefer Ahava, Hilkhot Berakhot* 5:12; *Shulḥan Arukh, Oraḥ Ḥayyim* 195:1).

**Three who sat to eat as one – שְׁלֹשָׁה שֶׁיָּשְׁבוּ לֶאֱכוֹל כְּאַחַת:** If three sat to eat, even if each is eating from his own loaf and even if they did not yet eat an olive-bulk, they may not divide as per the opinion of Shmuel (Rambam *Sefer Ahava, Hilkhot Berakhot* 5:10; *Shulḥan Arukh, Oraḥ Ḥayyim* 193:4).

**Three who came from three groups – שְׁלֹשָׁה שֶׁבָּאוּ מִשָּׁלֹשׁ חֲבוּרוֹת:** Three people who came from three different groups of three each may not divide. However, if their original groups included them in their *zimmun*, even if they did not recite the *zimmun*, they may no longer form a *zimmun*. Similarly, if the original groups were comprised of four individuals each, and those who remained recited the *zimmun* before this new group was constituted, the obligation to recite a *zimmun* has left them. These two cases are according to the two explanations of this statement (Rambam *Sefer Ahava, Hilkhot Berakhot* 5:11; *Shulḥan Arukh, Oraḥ Ḥayyim* 193:5).

**NOTES**

**Three who came from three groups – שְׁלֹשָׁה שֶׁבָּאוּ מִשָּׁלֹשׁ חֲבוּרוֹת:** This *halakha* was explained in a manner that deviates from the interpretation common to most commentaries. According to this opinion, three who came from three different groups are not permitted to divide and leave their original groups; but rather, they must return to their original groups and participate in the *zimmun* there. However, if they already formed their own *zimmun*, although they acted improperly, their obligation to rejoin their original groups to form a *zimmun* is eliminated (Rav Hai Gaon).

אָמַר רַב חִסְדָּא: וְהוּא – שֶׁבָּאוּ מִשָּׁלֹשׁ חֲבוּרוֹת שֶׁל שְׁלֹשָׁה בְּנֵי אָדָם.

**Rav Ḥisda said: And that** is only the *halakha* in a case where the three individuals **came from three groups of three people** each, so that each original group was independently obligated to recite the *zimmun*, and that obligation never lapsed.

אָמַר רָבָא:

**Rava** qualified this, and **said:**



וְלָא אֲמָרַן – אֶלָּא דְּלָא אַקְדִּימוּ הָנָךְ וְאַזְמוּן עֲלַיְיהוּ בְּדוּכְתַּיְיהוּ, אֲבָל אַזְמוּן עֲלַיְיהוּ בְּדוּכְתַּיְיהוּ – פָּרַח זִימּוּן מִינַּיְיהוּ.

**We only said** this *halakha* in a case **where those** members of the previous groups **did not include them in the *zimmun* in their** original **place, but in a case where they included them in the *zimmun* in their** original **place,**[N] **their** obligation to participate in a ***zimmun* has left them.** The obligation incumbent upon these three individuals to form a *zimmun* stems from their obligation to form a *zimmun* with the members of their original groups. If their groups already included them in a *zimmun*, their obligation as individuals has lapsed and they can no longer form another *zimmun*.

אָמַר רָבָא: מְנָא אָמֵינָא לַהּ? דִּתְנַן: מִטָּה שֶׁנִּגְנְבָה חֶצְיָהּ, אוֹ שֶׁאָבְדָה חֶצְיָהּ, אוֹ שֶׁחֲלָקוּהָ אַחִין אוֹ שׁוּתָּפִין – טְהוֹרָה. הֶחֱזִירוּהָ – מְקַבֶּלֶת טוּמְאָה מִכָּאן וּלְהַבָּא.

In order to explain the general principle contained in this halakhic ruling, **Rava said: From where do I** derive to **say this** *halakha*? **As we learned** in a mishna: **A** ritually impure **bed, half of which was stolen**[NH] **or half of which was lost, or it was divided by brothers** after they inherited it from their father, or was divided by **partners, it is ritually pure.** This is true with regard to any ritually impure utensil that was broken or divided; it is no longer a utensil and is therefore ritually pure. However, **if they restored it** and reattached the parts, **it is susceptible to ritual impurity from here on.**

מִכָּאן וּלְהַבָּא – אִין, לְמַפְרֵעַ – לָא, אַלְמָא: כֵּיוָן דִּפַלְגוּהָ פָּרַח לַהּ טוּמְאָה מִינַּהּ, הָכָא נַמִי: כֵּיוָן דְּאַזְמוּן עֲלַיְיהוּ – פָּרַח זִימּוּן מִינַּיְיהוּ.

Rava infers: **From here on, yes,** it is susceptible to ritual impurity, **retroactively, no,** it does not reassume its previous status of ritual impurity. **Apparently, once they divided it, the ritual impurity left it.** Although it was restored, it does not reassume its previous status of ritual impurity. **Here, too, once they included them in the *zimmun*, their** obligation **left them** and they do not reassume their previous obligation.

"שְׁתֵּי חֲבוּרוֹת" וכו׳. תָּנָא: אִם יֵשׁ שַׁמָּשׁ בֵּינֵיהֶם – שַׁמָּשׁ מְצָרְפָן.

The mishna explained the circumstances in which **two groups** that were eating in one house may combine to form a *zimmun*. The Gemara adds: **It was taught: If there is a** common **waiter among them,** serving both groups, **the waiter joins them** into a single group,[H] even if they cannot see each other.

"אֵין מְבָרְכִין עַל הַיַּיִן". תָּנוּ רַבָּנַן: יַיִן, עַד שֶׁלֹּא נָתַן לְתוֹכוֹ מַיִם – אֵין מְבָרְכִין עָלָיו "בּוֹרֵא פְּרִי הַגֶּפֶן" אֶלָּא "בּוֹרֵא פְּרִי הָעֵץ" וְנוֹטְלִין מִמֶּנּוּ לַיָּדַיִם, מִשֶּׁנָּתַן לְתוֹכוֹ מַיִם – מְבָרְכִין עָלָיו "בּוֹרֵא פְּרִי הַגֶּפֶן" וְאֵין נוֹטְלִין מִמֶּנּוּ לַיָּדַיִם, דִּבְרֵי רַבִּי אֱלִיעֶזֶר; וַחֲכָמִים אוֹמְרִים: בֵּין כָּךְ וּבֵין כָּךְ מְבָרְכִין עָלָיו "בּוֹרֵא פְּרִי הַגֶּפֶן" וְאֵין נוֹטְלִין הֵימֶנּוּ לַיָּדַיִם.

In the mishna, we learned: **One does not recite a blessing over wine** until he adds water to it, that is the statement of Rabbi Eliezer. And the Rabbis say: One recites a blessing over it. Regarding this, **the Sages taught** in the *Tosefta*: **Over wine,**[H] **until he added water to it, one does not recite: Who creates fruit of the vine; rather,** he recites: **Who creates fruit of the tree,** as it is merely fruit juice and not wine. Moreover, since it is not halakhically considered wine, **one** ritually **washes his hands with it. Once he added water to it,** however, it is considered wine, and **one recites over it: Who creates fruit of the vine, and one does not** ritually **wash his hands with it,** that is **the statement of Rabbi Eliezer. The Rabbis say: In either case,** whether water has been added or not, it is considered wine for all intents and purposes, and **one recites over it: Who creates fruit of the vine, and one may not** ritually **wash his hands from it.**[NH]

## NOTES

**They included them in the *zimmun* in their original place** – וְאַזְמוּן עֲלַיְיהוּ בְּדוּכְתַּיְיהוּ: There are two primary opinions with regard to the understanding of this statement. Some explain that these individuals were each originally members of groups of three people. They had not yet finished eating or had left in the middle of their meal, so the other two members of the group recited a *zimmun* which included the third member (Ra'avad; see Rashi). Others hold that there was a larger group of four or more, and these individuals, who had been part of the group, left. The rest of the group formed a *zimmun* without them (Ramban; *Talmidei Rabbeinu Yona*). The language: They included them in the *zimmun*, supports the former explanation, whereas the analogy to the bed supports the latter explanation.

**A bed, half of which was stolen** – מִטָּה שֶׁנִּגְנְבָה חֶצְיָהּ וכו׳: One of the foundations of the *halakhot* of ritual impurity is that a broken vessel cannot become ritually impure. Therefore, when the bed was disassembled, the ritual impurity was eliminated. The connection to the discussion in the Gemara is that even if the bed is reassembled from its original parts, it is considered as if it had never been ritually impure at all. In general, the conclusion is that, according to *halakha*, if an entity that was disassembled into its component parts, those parts no longer retain identity with that entity, and each is treated as an independent object.

**And one may not ritually wash his hands from it** – וְאֵין נוֹטְלִין הֵימֶנּוּ לַיָּדַיִם: Rashi's commentary indicates that he understands that, according to Rabbi Eliezer, one may wash his hands before a meal with undiluted wine. This explanation is difficult on many levels. While it is possible to resolve the difficulties, the Ra'avad's explanation that this refers to using wine to wash his hands to clean them, and not for ritual purity, is preferable. Therefore, undiluted wine, which is not that significant, may be used to clean one's hands. Once diluted, however, it is significant and may not be used for that purpose (see Rashba).

## HALAKHA

**A bed, half of which was stolen** – מִטָּה שֶׁנִּגְנְבָה חֶצְיָהּ וכו׳: A ritually impure bed that was inherited by two brothers and divided, or half of which was stolen, becomes ritually pure (Rambam *Sefer Tahara*, *Hilkhot Kelim* 26:12).

**The waiter joins them into a single group** – שַׁמָּשׁ מְצָרְפָן: If two groups that cannot see each other share a common waiter, the waiter joins them into a single group and they can form a *zimmun* together, if that was their original intention (Jerusalem Talmud; Rambam *Sefer Ahava*, *Hilkhot Berakhot* 5:12; *Shulḥan Arukh*, *Oraḥ Ḥayyim* 195:1).

**The blessing over wine** – בִּרְכַּת הַיַּיִן: One recites: Who creates fruit of the vine, over wine, whether or not it is diluted, as per the opinion of the Rabbis (*Shulḥan Arukh*, *Oraḥ Ḥayyim* 202:1).

**And one may not ritually wash his hands from it** – וְאֵין נוֹטְלִין הֵימֶנּוּ לַיָּדַיִם: Some authorities rule that washing one's hands before a meal may only be performed with water (Rashi), while others say that one could do so with wine, if not for the fact that it shows contempt for the food (Rashba). Ultimately, it depends upon the interpretation of the opinion of the Rabbis (Maharshal; Vilna Gaon; Rambam *Sefer Ahava*, *Hilkhot Berakhot* 7:9; *Shulḥan Arukh*, *Oraḥ Ḥayyim* 160:12).

כְּמַאן אָזְלָא הָא דְּאָמַר שְׁמוּאֵל: עוֹשֶׂה אָדָם כָּל צְרָכָיו בַּפַּת, כְּמַאן? כְּרַבִּי אֱלִיעֶזֶר.

**In accordance with whose** opinion **is that** *halakha* **which Shmuel said: A person may perform all his needs with bread?** He may use it for purposes other than food, and he need not be concerned that he is treating the food contemptuously. **In accordance with whose** opinion among the tannaitic opinions cited above? The Gemara answers: It is **in accordance with** the opinion of **Rabbi Eliezer,**[N] who permits one to wash his hands with undiluted wine.

אָמַר רַבִּי יוֹסֵי בְּרַבִּי חֲנִינָא: מוֹדִים חֲכָמִים לְרַבִּי אֱלִיעֶזֶר בְּכוֹס שֶׁל בְּרָכָה, שֶׁאֵין מְבָרְכִין עָלָיו עַד שֶׁיִּתֵּן לְתוֹכוֹ מַיִם. מַאי טַעְמָא? – אָמַר רַב אוֹשַׁעְיָא: בָּעֵינַן מִצְוָה מִן הַמּוּבְחָר.

**Rabbi Yosei bar Rabbi Ḥanina said: The Rabbis agree with Rabbi Eliezer with regard to a cup of blessing,** e.g., the cup of wine over which Grace after Meals is recited, **that one does not recite a blessing over it until he adds water to it. What is the reason? Rav Oshaya said: We require** that **a mitzva be** performed **in the best** possible manner.

וְרַבָּנַן – לְמַאי חֲזֵי? – אָמַר רַבִּי זֵירָא: חֲזֵי לְקוֹרְיְיטֵי.

With regard the issue of wine itself, the Gemara asks: **And according to the Rabbis, for what is** undiluted wine, which is virtually undrinkable, **fit? Rabbi Zeira said:** It is good **for *koraiytei*,**[L] a medicinal drink made of wine and oil.

תָּנוּ רַבָּנַן, אַרְבָּעָה דְּבָרִים נֶאֶמְרוּ בַּפַּת: אֵין מַנִּיחִין בָּשָׂר חַי עַל הַפַּת, וְאֵין מַעֲבִירִין כּוֹס מָלֵא עַל הַפַּת, וְאֵין זוֹרְקִין אֶת הַפַּת, וְאֵין סוֹמְכִין אֶת הַקְּעָרָה בַּפַּת.

The Gemara continues to discuss the topic of using food. **The Sages taught: Four things were said with regard to bread: One may not place raw meat on bread** so the blood will not drip onto the bread and render it inedible; **and one may not pass a full cup** of wine **over bread** lest the wine drip on it and ruin the bread; **and one may not throw bread; and one may not prop up a dish with** a piece of **bread.** The basis for these laws is the need to treat bread with respect.

אֲמֵימָר וּמָר זוּטְרָא וְרַב אַשִׁי כָּרְכוּ רִיפְתָּא בַּהֲדֵי הֲדָדֵי אַיְיתִי לְקַמַּיְיהוּ תַּמְרֵי וְרִמּוֹנֵי, שְׁקַל מָר זוּטְרָא פְּתַק לְקַמֵּיהּ דְּרַב אַשִׁי דִּסְתְּנָא, אֲמַר לֵיהּ: לָא סְבַר לָהּ מָר לְהָא דְּתַנְיָא: אֵין זוֹרְקִין אֶת הָאוֹכָלִין?! – הַהִיא – בְּפַת תַּנְיָא. – וְהָתַנְיָא: כְּשֵׁם שֶׁאֵין זוֹרְקִין אֶת הַפַּת כָּךְ אֵין זוֹרְקִין אֶת הָאוֹכָלִין! – אֲמַר לֵיהּ, וְהָתַנְיָא: אַף עַל פִּי שֶׁאֵין זוֹרְקִין אֶת הַפַּת אֲבָל זוֹרְקִין אֶת הָאוֹכָלִין!

The Gemara recounts: **Ameimar, Mar Zutra**[P] **and Rav Ashi ate bread together when they brought dates and pomegranates before them. Mar Zutra took** fruit **and threw a portion before Rav Ashi.** Rav Ashi was astounded and **said to him:** Does **the Master not hold with that which was taught** in a *baraita*: **One may not throw food?**[N] He responded: **That was taught with regard to bread,** not other foods. Rav Ashi challenged him again: **Wasn't it taught** in a *baraita*: **Just as one may not throw bread, so too one may not throw** other **foods?** Mar Zutra **said to him: Wasn't** the opposite **taught** in another *baraita*: **Although one may not throw bread, he may throw** other **foods?**

אֶלָּא לָא קַשְׁיָא: הָא – בְּמִידֵי דִּמְמָאִיס, הָא – בְּמִידֵי דְּלָא מְמָאִיס.

**Rather,** that is **not difficult,** as the two *baraitot* address two different cases. **This** *baraita*, in which it is taught that one may not throw other foods, refers to a food **item that becomes disgusting** when thrown, whereas **that** *baraita*, in which it is taught that one may throw other foods, refers to a food **item that does not become disgusting** when thrown.[H]

תָּנוּ רַבָּנַן: מַמְשִׁיכִין יַיִן בְּצִנּוֹרוֹת לִפְנֵי חָתָן וְלִפְנֵי כַּלָּה, וְזוֹרְקִין לִפְנֵיהֶם קְלָיוֹת וֶאֱגוֹזִים בִּימוֹת הַחַמָּה אֲבָל לֹא בִּימוֹת הַגְּשָׁמִים, אֲבָל לֹא גְּלוּסְקָאוֹת – לֹא בִּימוֹת הַחַמָּה וְלֹא בִּימוֹת הַגְּשָׁמִים.

Similarly, **the Sages taught: One may draw wine through pipes**[H] **before a bride and groom** as a blessed omen, and one may **throw roasted grain and nuts before them in the summer, but not in the rainy season,** as in the summer they can be retrieved and eaten, which is not the case in the rainy season. **But one may not throw cakes, neither in the summer nor in the rainy season.**

אָמַר רַב יְהוּדָה: שָׁכַח וְהִכְנִיס אוֹכָלִין לְתוֹךְ פִּיו בְּלֹא בְּרָכָה – מְסַלְּקָן לְצַד אֶחָד וּמְבָרֵךְ.

**Rav Yehuda said: If one forgot and put food** items **in his mouth without** reciting **a blessing, he moves them to one side** of his mouth **and recites the blessing.**

תַּנְיָא חֲדָא: בּוֹלְעָן; וְתַנְיָא אִידָךְ: פּוֹלְטָן; וְתַנְיָא אִידָךְ: מְסַלְּקָן!

The Gemara notes that there are three *baraitot* on this topic: **It was taught** in **one** *baraita*: **He swallows them. It was taught** in **another** *baraita*: **He spits them out. Another** *baraita* **taught: He moves them** to the side of his mouth.

לָא קַשְׁיָא: הָא דְּתַנְיָא בּוֹלְעָן – בְּמַשְׁקִין, וְהָא דְּתַנְיָא פּוֹלְטָן – בְּמִידֵי דְּלָא מְמָאִיס, וְהָא דְּתַנְיָא מְסַלְּקָן – בְּמִידֵי דִּמְמָאִיס.

The Gemara explains: That is **not difficult,** as each *baraita* addresses a different case. **This** *baraita* **in which it was taught: He swallows them** refers **to liquids,**[N] as there is no alternative. **This** *baraita* **in which it was taught: He spits them out,** refers to a food **item that does not become disgusting** and if he removes it from his mouth he can subsequently eat it. **This** *baraita* **in which it was taught: He moves them** to the side of his mouth, refers to **a** food **item that becomes disgusting,** in which case it is sufficient to move it to the side.[H]

### NOTES

In accordance with whose opinion? In accordance with the opinion of Rabbi Eliezer – כְּמַאן? כְּרַבִּי אֱלִיעֶזֶר: It can be explained that Shmuel's opinion is not only in accordance with the opinion of Rabbi Eliezer. It is possible to reconcile his opinion with the opinion of the Rabbis who disagree with Rabbi Eliezer. Nevertheless, Shmuel articulated his opinion according to the opinion of Rabbi Eliezer because the conclusion emerges more clearly from his opinion (Rashba; see *Tosafot*).

One may not throw food – אֵין זוֹרְקִין אֶת הָאוֹכָלִין: It appears that the Rosh explains that one may not throw cakes at all, not because they become disgusting, but in deference to bread, as throwing bread is always considered disrespectful whether or not it spoils (*Beit Yosef*). The reason that it is prohibited to treat food with contempt is because it is tantamount to denying the beneficence of God, Who provides one with food (*HaBoneh*).

He swallows them, refers to liquids – בּוֹלְעָן בְּמַשְׁקִין: The reason that one swallows liquids without reciting a blessing is because the liquid in his mouth is no longer considered food as no one else would drink it. Once it loses that status, it cannot regain it (Rabbeinu Ḥananel).

### LANGUAGE

*Koraiytei* – קוֹרְיְיטֵי: This word may be from the Greek καρυῶτις, *karuotis*, a type of nut-shaped date. Apparently they mixed it with various liquids, e.g., strong wine, and used it for medicinal purposes.

### PERSONALITIES

Mar Zutra – מָר זוּטְרָא: A colleague of Rav Ashi, Mar Zutra was one of the leading Sages of his generation. He was a disciple-colleague of his teachers, Rav Pappa and Rav Naḥman bar Yitzḥak.

Beyond his greatness in *halakha* and *aggada*, Mar Zutra was noted as a preacher and his homiletic interpretations are cited throughout the Talmud. He apparently held an official position as the scholar and preacher of the House of the Exilarch. Late in his life, he was appointed head of the yeshiva of Pumbedita.

Meetings between Mar Zutra, Ameimar, and Rav Ashi are frequently mentioned in the Talmud, and some of these meetings may well have been formal conferences of the leaders of Babylonian Jewry of that generation.

### HALAKHA

Using food – שִׁימּוּשׁ בְּאוֹכָלִין: Food may be utilized for any purpose, so long as it does not thereby become too disgusting to be eaten. Throwing bread is forbidden under any circumstances because it constitutes a display of contempt for this significant food (*Bayit Ḥadash, Magen Avraham*; Rambam *Sefer Ahava, Hilkhot Berakhot* 7:9; *Shulḥan Arukh, Oraḥ Ḥayyim* 171:1).

One may draw wine through pipes, etc. – מַמְשִׁיכִין יַיִן בְּצִנּוֹרוֹת וכו׳: Even during celebrations, one may not throw food that will thereby become disgusting and unfit for consumption. One may draw wine through pipes if the wine can later be used (Rambam *Sefer Ahava, Hilkhot Berakhot* 7:9; *Shulḥan Arukh, Oraḥ Ḥayyim* 171:4).

Food that he put in his mouth – אוֹכָלִין שֶׁהִכְנִיס לְפִיו: If one put food or drink into his mouth without reciting a blessing and is able to remove the food without it becoming disgusting, he should do so and recite a blessing. If not, he should move the food to the side of his mouth and recite the blessing. Liquids may be swallowed (Rambam *Sefer Ahava, Hilkhot Berakhot* 8:12; *Shulḥan Arukh, Oraḥ Ḥayyim* 172:1–2).

**HALAKHA**

One who ate and drank and did not recite a blessing – מִי שֶׁאָכַל וְשָׁתָה וְלֹא בֵּרַךְ: One who ate and recalled that he did not recite a blessing does not recite a blessing. Some authorities (Ra'avad) explain otherwise and hold that he is obligated to recite a blessing. Some adopt a stringency in that case and eat additional food over which they recite a blessing (*Magen Avraham*; Rambam *Sefer Ahava, Hilkhot Berakhot* 4:2; *Shulḥan Arukh, Oraḥ Ḥayyim* 176:8).

One who immersed and emerged, as he emerges he recites: Blessed – טָבַל וְעָלָה, אוֹמֵר בַּעֲלִיָּיתוֹ: בָּרוּךְ וכו׳: One recites a blessing over immersion as he emerges from the water (Rambam *Sefer Ahava, Hilkhot Berakhot* 11:7; *Shulḥan Arukh, Yoreh De'a* 268:2).

**LANGUAGE**

*Asparagus* – אַסְפָּרָגוֹס: This word comes from the Greek ἀσπάραγος, *asparagos*. It is a type of cabbage soaked in wine, or some other liquor, into which ground medicines were mixed. According to the descriptions in early medical texts, this drink was used to induce bowel movement. Drinking too much, however, causes serious harm.

**BACKGROUND**

*Konam* – קוֹנָם: An entire tractate in the Talmud, tractate *Nedarim*, explains the validity and effectiveness of various types of vows and the differences between them. In order to avoid inadvertently consecrating items, various terms were coined for taking vows. One of them is *konam*, which is a substitute for the word sacrifice [*korban*], meaning, this item will be forbidden to me like a sacrifice. One of the manners in which a vow can be dissolved is by showing the one who took the vow that his vow was predicated on a fundamental error.

בְּמִידֵי דְּלָא מְמָאִיס נַמִי, לְסַלְּקִינְהוּ לְצַד אֶחָד וְלִיבָרֵךְ! תַּרְגְּמָא רַב יִצְחָק קַסְקְסָאָה קַמֵּיהּ דְּרַבִּי יוֹסֵי בַּר אָבִין מִשְּׁמֵיהּ דְּרַבִּי יוֹחָנָן; מִשּׁוּם שֶׁנֶּאֱמַר "יִמָּלֵא פִי תְּהִלָּתֶךָ".

The Gemara asks: **With regard to a** food **item that does not become disgusting as well, let him shift it to the side and recite the blessing.** Why need he spit it out? **Rav Yitzḥak Kaskesa'a explained before Rabbi Yosei bar Avin, in the name of Rabbi Yoḥanan:** One spits it out **because it is stated: "My mouth will be filled with Your praise"** (Psalms 71:8), meaning that one should recite God's praises with his entire mouth, not merely half.

בְּעוֹ מִינֵּיהּ מֵרַב חִסְדָּא: מִי שֶׁאָכַל וְשָׁתָה וְלֹא בֵּרַךְ – מַהוּ שֶׁיַּחְזוֹר וִיבָרֵךְ? – אֲמַר לְהוּ: מִי שֶׁאָכַל שׁוּם וְרֵיחוֹ נוֹדֵף, יַחְזוֹר וְיֹאכַל שׁוּם אַחֵר כְּדֵי שֶׁיְּהֵא רֵיחוֹ נוֹדֵף?!

**They raised a dilemma before Rav Ḥisda: One who ate and drank and did not recite a blessing,**[H] **what is** the ruling? Does he **return and recite** the blessing that he should have recited beforehand before he continues eating or not? In response, Rav Ḥisda **said to them** an analogy: Should **one who ate garlic and the odor** on **his** breath **smells return and eat another garlic so that the odor** on **his** breath **will smell?** That is to say, one must recite a blessing. Should one who committed a transgression and failed to recite a blessing before eating, remedy his situation by continuing to eat without reciting a blessing (*Talmidei Rabbeinu Yona*)?

אָמַר רָבִינָא: הִלְכָּךְ, אֲפִילּוּ גָּמַר סְעוּדָתוֹ יַחְזוֹר וִיבָרֵךְ, דְּתַנְיָא: טָבַל וְעָלָה, אוֹמֵר בַּעֲלִיָּיתוֹ: בָּרוּךְ אֲשֶׁר קִדְּשָׁנוּ בְּמִצְוֹתָיו וְצִוָּנוּ עַל הַטְּבִילָה.

**Ravina said: Therefore, even if one finished his meal, he must return and recite a blessing.** He cites a proof, **as it was taught** in a *baraita* with regard to the laws of immersion: **One** who was ritually impure **who immersed** himself in a ritual bath **and emerged, as he emerges he recites: Blessed**[H] **...Who has made us holy through His mitzvot and has commanded us about ritual immersion.** Evidently, in certain cases, one may recite the blessing after completing the act.

וְלָא הִיא, הָתָם – מֵעִיקָּרָא גַּבְרָא לָא חֲזֵי, הָכָא – מֵעִיקָּרָא גַּבְרָא חֲזֵי, וְהוֹאִיל וְאִידְּחֵי אִידְּחֵי.

The Gemara rejects the parallel between the cases: **That is not so,** as **there,** in the case of immersion, **initially,** before he immersed himself, **the man was unfit** to recite the blessing because he was ritually impure; **here,** in the case where one did not recite a blessing before eating, **initially he was fit** to recite the blessing, **and since** he did not recite the blessing before he ate and he concluded his meal **and is, therefore, excluded** from reciting the blessing, he is completely **excluded** and has no way to remedy the situation.

תָּנוּ רַבָּנַן: אַסְפָּרָגוֹס – יָפֶה לַלֵּב וְטוֹב לָעֵינַיִם וְכׇל שֶׁכֵּן לִבְנֵי מֵעַיִם, וְהָרָגִיל בּוֹ – יָפֶה לְכׇל גּוּפוֹ, וְהַמִּשְׁתַּכֵּר הֵימֶנּוּ – קָשֶׁה לְכׇל גּוּפוֹ.

Tangential to the laws concerning wine that the Gemara cited earlier, **the Sages taught: *Asparagus*,**[L] wine or other alcoholic beverages that they were accustomed to drink early in the morning before eating, **is agreeable for the heart and beneficial for the eyes, and all the more so for the intestines. And** in extolling the virtues of this drink, the Gemara says: **One who is accustomed to** drink it, **it is agreeable for his entire body.** However, one must be careful, as **one who** drinks excessively and **becomes drunk, it is harmful for his entire body.**

מִדְּקָתָנֵי יָפֶה לַלֵּב, מִכְּלָל דִּבְחַמְרָא עָסְקִינַן, וְקָתָנֵי: וְכׇל שֶׁכֵּן לִבְנֵי מֵעַיִם, וְהָתַנְיָא: לל״ע״ט יָפֶה לְרמ״ת קָשֶׁה!

The Gemara discusses this: **From the fact that it was taught** that *asparagus* is **agreeable for the heart,** it may be inferred that **we are dealing with** *asparagus* made from **wine,** which is known to be agreeable for the heart. **And we learned: And all the more so,** *asparagus* is **beneficial for the intestines. Wasn't it taught** in a *baraita*: **For** *L-E-T*, which is an acronym for *lev*, heart; *einayim*, eyes; *teḥol*, spleen, **it is beneficial,** but **for** *R-M-T*, *rosh*, head; *me'ayim* intestines; *taḥtoniot*, hemorrhoids, **it is harmful.** Apparently, *asparagus* is harmful for one's intestines.

כִּי תַּנְיָא הַהִיא – בִּמְיוּשָּׁן, כְּדִתְנַן: קוֹנָם יַיִן שֶׁאֲנִי טוֹעֵם, שֶׁהַיַּיִן קָשֶׁה לִבְנֵי מֵעַיִם, אָמְרוּ לוֹ: וַהֲלֹא מְיוּשָּׁן יָפֶה הוּא לִבְנֵי מֵעַיִם, וְשָׁתַק – אָסוּר בְּחָדָשׁ וּמוּתָּר בִּמְיוּשָּׁן, שְׁמַע מִינַּהּ.

The Gemara responds: **That** *baraita*, in which **it was taught** that *asparagus* is beneficial to one's intestines, refers to *asparagus* made **with old wine. As we learned** in the mishna concerning the laws of vows that one who vowed: **Wine is *konam***[B] **for me to taste because it is harmful to the intestines, and** those who heard him **said to him: But isn't old** wine **beneficial to the intestines? If he was silent** and did not argue the point, he is **forbidden** to drink **new** wine because of his vow, **but he is permitted** to drink **old** wine. **Conclude from this** that old wine is beneficial for the intestines.

תנו רבנן ששה דברים נאמרו באספרגוס: אין שותין אותו אלא כשהוא חי ומלא, מקבלו בימין ושותהו בשמאל, ואין משיחין אחריו, ואין מפסיקין בו, ואין מחזירין אותו אלא למי שנתנו לו ורק אחריו, ואין סומכין אותו אלא במינו.

**The Sages taught: Six things were said with regard to *asparagus*: One only drinks it undiluted and** from **a full** cup; **he receives it** from the attendant **in his right** hand **and drinks it with** his **left** hand; **one should not converse after** drinking it **and one does not stop** while drinking **it,** but should drink it all at once; **one only returns it to** the one **who gave it to him; and he spits after** drinking **it; and one may only supplement it with its own kind,** meaning that after drinking *asparagus,* one should only eat something that is used to make similar beverages, e.g., dates after date beer, etc.

והתניא: אין סומכין אותו אלא בפת! – לא קשיא הא בדחמרא, הא בדשכרא.

The Gemara challenges: **Wasn't it taught** in a *baraita* that **one may only supplement** *asparagus* **with bread?** The Gemara responds: That is **not difficult. This** *baraita,* in which it was taught that one supplements it with bread, refers to *asparagus* made **of wine,** while **that** *baraita,* in which it was taught that one supplements it, refers to *asparagus* made **of beer.**

תני חדא: ללע״ט יפה לרמ״ת קשה, ותניא אידך: לרמ״ת יפה ללע״ט קשה! – לא קשיא; הא בדחמרא, הא בדשכרא.

**It was taught** in **one** *baraita* that *asparagus* **is beneficial for *L-E-T*,** heart, eyes, and spleen, **and harmful for *R-M-T*,** head, intestines, and hemorrhoids. **And it was taught** in **another** *baraita* that *asparagus* **is beneficial for *R-M-T*,** head, intestines, and hemorrhoids, **and harmful for *L-E-T*,** heart, eyes, and spleen. The Gemara responds: That is **not difficult. This** *baraita,* in which it was taught that *asparagus* is beneficial for *L-E-T,* refers to *asparagus* made **of wine,** while **that** *baraita,* in which it was taught that *asparagus* is harmful for *L-E-T,* refers to *asparagus* made **of beer.**

תני חדא: רק אחריו לוקה, ותניא אידך: לא רק אחריו לוקה! – לא קשיא: הא בדחמרא, הא בדשכרא.

The Gemara resolves a contradiction between two other *baraitot* in the same manner. **It was taught** in **one** *baraita* that **if he spit after** drinking *asparagus,* he **suffers** an illness. **And it was taught** in **another** *baraita* that **if he did not spit after** drinking *asparagus,* he **suffers** an illness. The Gemara responds: That is **not difficult. This** *baraita,* in which it was taught that if he spit after drinking it he **suffers** an illness, refers to *asparagus* made **of wine,** while **that** *baraita,* in which it was taught that if he did not spit he suffers an illness, refers to *asparagus* made **of beer.**

אמר רב אשי: השתא דאמרת לא רק אחריו לוקה – מימיו נזרקין אפילו בפני המלך.

**Rav Ashi said: Now** that **you said** that **if he did not spit after** drinking it he **suffers** an illness, **its water,** the saliva in his mouth after drinking *asparagus,* may be expelled **even** when standing **before the king,** as failure to do so will endanger him.

אמר רבי ישמעאל בן אלישע, שלשה דברים סח לי סוריאל שר הפנים: אל תטול חלוקך בשחרית מיד השמש ותלבש; ואל תטול ידיך ממי שלא נטל ידיו; ואל תחזיר כוס אספרגוס אלא למי שנתנו לך, מפני שתכספית, ואמרי לה: אסתלגנית של מלאכי חבלה מצפין לו לאדם ואומרים: אימתי יבא אדם לידי אחד מדברים הללו וילכד.

**Rabbi Yishmael ben Elisha said: Suriel, the** heavenly **ministering** angel **of the Divine Presence, told me three things**[N] from on high: **Do not take your cloak in the morning from the hand of your servant and wear it; do not** ritually **wash your hands from one who has not** ritually **washed his own hands;**[H] **and only return a cup of *asparagus* to the one who gave it to you.** Why is this? **Because a band of demons and some say a band of angels of destruction** lie **in wait for a person and say: When will a person encounter one of these circumstances and be captured?**

אמר רבי יהושע בן לוי, שלשה דברים סח לי מלאך המות: אל תטול חלוקך שחרית מיד השמש ותלבש; ואל תטול ידיך ממי שלא נטל ידיו; ואל תעמוד לפני הנשים בשעה שחוזרות מן המת, מפני שאני מרקד ובא לפניהן וחרבי בידי ויש לי רשות לחבל.

Similarly, the Gemara relates that **Rabbi Yehoshua ben Levi said: The Angel of Death told me three things: Do not take your cloak in the morning from the hand of your servant and wear it; do not** ritually **wash your hands from one who has not** ritually **washed** his own **hands; and do not stand before the women when they return from** the burial of **the deceased, because I dance and come before them and my sword is in hand, and I have license to destroy.**

ואי פגע מאי תקנתיה? – לינשוף מדוכתיה ארבע אמות, אי איכא נהרא – ליעבריה, ואי איכא דרכא אחרינא – ליזיל בה, ואי איכא גודא ליקו אחורא, ואי לא – ליהדר אפיה ולימא ״ויאמר ה׳ אל השטן יגער ה׳ בך״ וגו׳ עד דחלפי מיניה.

The Gemara asks: **And if one encounters** women returning from a funeral, **what is his remedy?** The Gemara answers: **Let him jump four cubits from where he stands; if there is a river, let him cross it; if there is another path, let him go down it; if there is a wall, let him stand behind it; and if not, he should turn his face around and recite** the verse: **"And the Lord said to the Satan: The Lord rebukes you,** Satan, the Lord that has chosen Jerusalem rebukes you; is not this man a brand plucked from the fire?" (Zechariah 3:2), **until they pass him.**

NOTES

Rabbi Yishmael ben Elisha said: Suriel, the heavenly ministering angel of the Divine Presence, told me three things – אמר רבי ישמעאל: בן אלישע שלשה דברים סח לי סוריאל שר הפנים: Rashi explains that Suriel is an angel who is significant enough to serve before the King. We find that Rabbi Yishmael ben Elisha interacted with the Divine Presence when he entered the Holy of Holies, and he was asked to bless God (see above, 7a, p. 39). It is likely that on one such occasion the angel warned him about the various destructive forces that lie in wait to injure or even kill a man (Maharsha).

HALAKHA

**Do not ritually wash your hands from one who has not ritually washed his own hands** – אל תטול ידיך ממי שלא נטל ידיו: One may not have his hands washed in the morning by another who did not yet wash his own hands. Some hold that the same holds true with regard to washing before eating (*Taz*; *Shulḥan Arukh, Oraḥ Ḥayyim* 4:11).

## HALAKHA

**Rinsing, washing, undiluted, and full – הֲדָחָה, שְׁטִיפָה, חַי, וּמָלֵא:** The cup of blessing must be rinsed inside and washed outside. First, one pours pure wine into the cup, and only then does he dilute it with water. This is the custom in accordance with the second explanation of Rashi, that one must pour directly from the vessel in which the wine was stored. After he dilutes the wine, the cup should be filled to the brim. According to the kabbalists, one should accustom himself to observe all ten customs outlined by Rabbi Zeira (*Magen Avraham*; *Shulḥan Arukh*, *Oraḥ Ḥayyim* 183:1–2).

**He takes it in his two hands – נוֹטְלוֹ בִּשְׁתֵּי יָדָיו:** One must raise the cup with both hands in a display of affection for the mitzva (*Shulḥan Arukh*, *Oraḥ Ḥayyim* 183:4).

אָמַר רַבִּי זֵירָא אָמַר רַבִּי אַבָּהוּ, וְאָמְרִי לַהּ בְּמַתְנִיתָא תָּנָא, עֲשָׂרָה דְּבָרִים נֶאֶמְרוּ בְּכוֹס שֶׁל בְּרָכָה: טָעוּן הֲדָחָה, וּשְׁטִיפָה, חַי, וּמָלֵא, עִיטּוּר, וְעִיטּוּף, נוֹטְלוֹ בִּשְׁתֵּי יָדָיו, וְנוֹתְנוֹ בְּיָמִין, וּמַגְבִּיהוֹ מִן הַקַּרְקַע טֶפַח, וְנוֹתֵן עֵינָיו בּוֹ; וְיֵשׁ אוֹמְרִים: אַף מְשַׁגְּרוֹ בְּמַתָּנָה לְאַנְשֵׁי בֵּיתוֹ.

**Rabbi Zeira said** that **Rabbi Abbahu said, and some say that this** *halakha* **was taught in a** *baraita*: **Ten things were said with regard to a cup of blessing,**[N] e.g., the cup of wine over which Grace after Meals is recited: **It requires rinsing and washing;** it must be **undiluted**[N] wine, **and full;** it requires **adorning and wrapping; he takes it in his two hands and places it in his right** hand, **and he lifts it** at least **one handbreadth from the ground, and** when reciting the blessing **he fixes his eyes upon it. And some say: He also sends it as a gift to members of his household.**

אָמַר רַבִּי יוֹחָנָן, אָנוּ אֵין לָנוּ אֶלָּא אַרְבָּעָה בִּלְבַד: הֲדָחָה, שְׁטִיפָה, חַי, וּמָלֵא. תָּנָא: הֲדָחָה מִבִּפְנִים וּשְׁטִיפָה מִבַּחוּץ.

**Rabbi Yoḥanan said: We only have**[N] **four** of those ten things: **Rinsing, washing,** the wine must be **undiluted, and** the cup must be **full.**[H] In explanation, **it was taught: Rinsing is from the inside** of the cup, **and washing is from the outside** of the cup.

אָמַר רַבִּי יוֹחָנָן: כׇּל הַמְבָרֵךְ עַל כּוֹס מָלֵא – נוֹתְנִין לוֹ נַחֲלָה בְּלִי מְצָרִים, שֶׁנֶּאֱמַר: ״וּמָלֵא בִּרְכַּת ה׳ יָם וְדָרוֹם יְרָשָׁה״. רַבִּי יוֹסֵי בַּר חֲנִינָא אוֹמֵר: זוֹכֶה וְנוֹחֵל שְׁנֵי עוֹלָמִים, הָעוֹלָם הַזֶּה וְהָעוֹלָם הַבָּא.

**Rabbi Yoḥanan said: Anyone who recites a blessing over a full cup, they give him a boundless inheritance,**[N] **as it is stated: "And full of the blessing of the Lord, possess the sea and the south** (Deuteronomy 33:23), indicating that one whose cup is full will receive God's blessing and will inherit from all sides. **Rabbi Yosei bar Ḥanina says: He merits and inherits two worlds, this world and the World-to-Come.**

״עִיטּוּר״ – רַב יְהוּדָה מְעַטְּרֵהוּ בְּתַלְמִידִים, רַב חִסְדָּא מְעַטֵּר לֵיהּ בְּנַטְלֵי. אָמַר רַבִּי חָנָן: וּבְחַי. אָמַר רַב שֵׁשֶׁת: וּבְבִרְכַּת הָאָרֶץ.

The Gemara continues explaining the ten things said with regard to the cup of blessing: The Sages would **adorn** the cup of blessing in different ways. **Rav Yehuda** would **adorn it with students,** as when he recited the blessing he would surround himself with students to accord honor to the blessing. **Rav Ḥisda,** however, would **adorn it with** other **cups;** he would surround the cup of blessing with other cups. **Rabbi Ḥanan said: And** specifically **with undiluted** wine. **Rav Sheshet said: And in the blessing of the land.**

״עִיטּוּף״ – רַב פַּפָּא מִעַטֵּף וְיָתֵיב, רַב אַסִּי פָּרֵיס סוּדָרָא עַל רֵישֵׁיהּ.

The Sages also had different customs with regard to **wrapping. Rav Pappa** would **wrap** himself in his prayer shawl **and sit** and recite Grace after Meals. **Rav Asi spread a cloth on his head** as an sign of respect.

״נוֹטְלוֹ בִּשְׁתֵּי יָדָיו״ – אָמַר רַבִּי חִינָּנָא בַּר פַּפָּא: מַאי קְרָאָה – ״שְׂאוּ יְדֵיכֶם קֹדֶשׁ וּבָרְכוּ אֶת ה׳״.

With regard to what was said that **he takes it in his two hands,**[H] **Rabbi Ḥinnana bar Pappa said: What is the verse** that proves this? As it is stated: **"Lift your hands in holiness and bless the Lord** (Psalms 134:2).

״וְנוֹתְנוֹ לְיָמִין״. אָמַר רַבִּי חִיָּיא בַּר אַבָּא אָמַר רַבִּי יוֹחָנָן, רִאשׁוֹנִים שָׁאֲלוּ: שְׂמֹאל מַהוּ שֶׁתְּסַיֵּיעַ לְיָמִין? אָמַר רַב אַשִׁי: הוֹאִיל וְרִאשׁוֹנִים אִיבַּעְיָא לְהוּ וְלָא אִיפְּשַׁט לְהוּ,

As for what was said after he takes it in his two hands: **And he places it in his right** hand, **Rabbi Ḥiyya bar Abba said** that **Rabbi Yoḥanan said: The early** Sages **asked: What is** the ruling, may **the left** hand **assist the right** when taking the cup? **Rav Ashi said: Since the early** Sages **raised this dilemma and it was not resolved for them,**

## NOTES

**Ten things were said with regard to a cup of blessing – עֲשָׂרָה דְּבָרִים נֶאֶמְרוּ בְּכוֹס שֶׁל בְּרָכָה:** All of these ten things are done in order to raise the level of holiness and purity associated with a cup of blessing.

Rinsing and washing; so that it should be clean and pure within and without.

Undiluted; to indicate the complete, living truth expressed in his blessing.

Full; to show that there is nothing lacking in one's faith.

Adorning; for the crown that is one's own.

Wrapping; wrapping oneself in a prayer shawl is appropriate preparation for encountering God, as it indicates awe of Heaven.

He takes it in his two hands and places it in his right; he takes it in his left hand, symbolizing justice, and places it in his right hand, symbolizing mercy, indicating that God's mercy should overcome His justice.

He lifts it one handbreadth from the ground; lifting it towards Heaven represents the cup of salvation (see Psalms 116:13).

He fixes his eyes upon it; by focusing on the cup, he attempts to ensure these ideas will be on his mind as he recites the blessing.

He also sends it as a gift to members of his household; sharing generously, representing the prayer that God should be generous with us as well (Maharsha).

**Undiluted – חַי:** Many explanations were suggested for this term. Some interpret it as undiluted wine (Rashi), or wine that was brought whole from the barrel (another explanation in Rashi), or that it is clear (Rav Sa'adia Gaon), or that the cup was whole (*Talmidei Rabbeinu Yona*). Most commentaries accept Rabbeinu Tam's explanation that this refers to wine that is partially diluted and that is diluted a second time while reciting the blessing (Rashba, *Tosefot HaRosh*).

**We only have – אָנוּ אֵין לָנוּ וכו׳:** Everyone agrees that Rabbi Yoḥanan does not negate all of the other customs mentioned with regard to the cup of blessing. Some say that Rabbi Yoḥanan sought to emphasize that these four in particular are not only *ab initio* requirements, but also invalidate the cup of blessing after the fact (*Talmidei Rabbeinu Yona*). Others explained that Rabbi Yoḥanan is simply saying that before learning this *baraita* only these four practices were customary (*Hefetz Hashem*).

**Anyone who recites a blessing over a full cup, they give him a boundless inheritance – כׇּל הַמְבָרֵךְ עַל כּוֹס מָלֵא נוֹתְנִין לוֹ נַחֲלָה בְּלִי מְצָרִים:** The fact that these individuals merit a boundless inheritance is derived from the verse: "Possess the sea and the south [*yam vedarom*]," as in the absence of additional boundaries to the north and the east, the reference is to a boundless inheritance (Rav Sa'adia Gaon). The commentaries questioned how Rabbi Yosei the son of Rabbi Ḥanina derives that one who recites a blessing over a full cup merits a place in the World-to-Come. Some explain that this follows the earlier passage: If one merits a boundless inheritance in this world, that is merely the fruits of the mitzva. The essential reward of this mitzva, and indeed any mitzva, is the World-to-Come (*Talmidei Rabbeinu Yona*; see *Tosefot HaRosh*). Others explain this in light of an allusion from the previous verse: *Yam* is an allusion to *yom*, day, this day, as in this world. *Darom* is a allusion to *dar rom*, dwell on high, the World-to-Come (Rav Sa'adia Gaon).

אֲנַן נַעֲבֵד לְחוּמְרָא.

**we will act stringently**[H] and not assist the right hand with the left.

״וּמַגְבִּיהוֹ מִן הַקַּרְקַע טֶפַח״ – אָמַר רַב אַחָא בְּרַבִּי חֲנִינָא: מַאי קְרָאָה – ״כּוֹס יְשׁוּעוֹת אֶשָּׂא וּבְשֵׁם ה׳ אֶקְרָא״.

**And he lifts it** at least **one handbreadth from the ground.**[H] **Rav Aḥa bar Ya'akov said: What is the verse** that proves this? **"I will lift the cup of salvation and upon the name of the Lord I will call"** (Psalms 116:13).

״וְנוֹתֵן עֵינָיו בּוֹ״ – כִּי הֵיכִי דְּלָא נֵיסַח דַּעְתֵּיהּ מִינֵּיהּ.

**And he fixes his eyes upon** the cup; **so that his attention will not be distracted from it.**

״וּמְשַׁגְּרוֹ לְאַנְשֵׁי בֵיתוֹ בְּמַתָּנָה״ – כִּי הֵיכִי דְּתִתְבָּרֵךְ דְּבֵיתְהוּ.

**And he sends it as a gift to members of his household;**[H] **so that his wife will be blessed.**

עוּלָּא אִקְלַע לְבֵי רַב נַחְמָן, כְּרַךְ רִיפְתָּא, בְּרִיךְ בִּרְכַּת מְזוֹנָא, יְהַב לֵיהּ כָּסָא דְבִרְכְתָא לְרַב נַחְמָן. אֲמַר לֵיהּ רַב נַחְמָן: לִישַׁדַּר מָר כָּסָא דְבִרְכְתָא לְיַלְתָּא. אֲמַר לֵיהּ, הָכִי אָמַר רַבִּי יוֹחָנָן: אֵין פְּרִי בִטְנָהּ שֶׁל אִשָּׁה מִתְבָּרֵךְ אֶלָּא מִפְּרִי בִטְנוֹ שֶׁל אִישׁ, שֶׁנֶּאֱמַר: ״וּבֵרַךְ פְּרִי בִטְנְךָ״ – ״פְּרִי בִטְנָהּ״ לֹא נֶאֱמַר אֶלָּא ״פְּרִי בִטְנְךָ״.

The Gemara relates: **Ulla happened** to come **to the house of Rav Naḥman. He ate bread, recited Grace after Meals, and gave the cup of blessing to Rav Naḥman. Rav Naḥman said to him: Master, please send the cup of blessing to Yalta,**[P] my wife. Ulla **responded to him:** There is no need, **as Rabbi Yoḥanan said as follows: The fruit of a woman's body is blessed only from the fruit of a man's body, as it is stated:** "And He will love you, and bless you, and make you numerous, **and He will bless the fruit of your body"** (Deuteronomy 7:13). The Gemara infers: "He will bless **the fruit of her body" was not stated. Rather,** "He will bless **the fruit of your** [masculine singular] **body."** For his wife to be blessed with children, it is sufficient to give the cup to Rav Naḥman.

תַּנְיָא נָמֵי הָכִי, רַבִּי נָתָן אוֹמֵר: מִנַּיִן שֶׁאֵין פְּרִי בִטְנָהּ שֶׁל אִשָּׁה מִתְבָּרֵךְ אֶלָּא מִפְּרִי בִטְנוֹ שֶׁל אִישׁ – שֶׁנֶּאֱמַר: ״וּבֵרַךְ פְּרִי בִטְנְךָ״ – ״פְּרִי בִטְנָהּ״ לֹא נֶאֱמַר אֶלָּא ״פְּרִי בִטְנְךָ״.

**That** opinion **was also taught** in a *baraita*: **Rabbi Natan says: From where** is it derived **that the fruit of a woman's body is only blessed from the fruit of a man's body? As it is stated: And He will bless the fruit of your body;** He will bless **the fruit of her body was not stated. Rather,** He will bless **the fruit of your body.**

אַדְּהָכִי שְׁמַעָה יַלְתָּא, קָמָה בְּזִיהֲרָא וְעָלְתָה לְבֵי חַמְרָא וּתְבַרָא אַרְבַּע מְאָה דַּנֵּי דְחַמְרָא. אֲמַר לֵיהּ רַב נַחְמָן: נְשַׁדַּר לַהּ מָר כָּסָא אַחֲרִינָא, שְׁלַח לַהּ: כָּל הַאי נַבְגָּא דְבִרְכְתָא הִיא. שְׁלַחָה לֵיהּ: מִמַּהֲדוּרֵי מִילֵּי וּמִסְמַרְטוּטֵי כַּלְמֵי.

The Gemara relates that **meanwhile Yalta heard** Ulla's refusal to send her the cup of blessing. Yalta was the daughter of the Exilarch and was accustomed to being treated with deference, so **she arose in a rage, entered the wine-storage, and broke four hundred barrels of wine.** Afterward, **Rav Naḥman said to** Ulla: **Let the Master send her another cup.** Ulla **sent** Yalta a different cup with a message saying that **all** of the wine in **this barrel is** wine **of blessing;**[N] although you did not drink from the cup of blessing itself, you may at least drink from the barrel from which the cup of blessing was poured. **She sent him** a stinging response: **From itinerant** peddlers, Ulla traveled regularly from Eretz Yisrael to Babylonia and back, come meaningless **words, and from rags** come **lice.**

אָמַר רַב אַסִּי: אֵין מְסִיחִין עַל כּוֹס שֶׁל בְּרָכָה. וְאָמַר רַב אַסִּי: אֵין מְבָרְכִין עַל כּוֹס שֶׁל פּוּרְעָנוּת. מַאי כּוֹס שֶׁל פּוּרְעָנוּת? אָמַר רַב נַחְמָן בַּר יִצְחָק: כּוֹס שֵׁנִי. תַּנְיָא נָמֵי הָכִי: הַשּׁוֹתֶה כְּפָלַיִם לֹא יְבָרֵךְ, מִשּׁוּם שֶׁנֶּאֱמַר ״הִכּוֹן לִקְרַאת אֱלֹהֶיךָ יִשְׂרָאֵל״ – וְהַאי לָא מִתַּקַּן.

**Rav Asi said: One may not speak over a cup of blessing**[H] from the moment he takes it in his hand until he drinks it. **And Rav Asi said: One may not recite a blessing over a cup of punishment.** The Gemara clarifies: **What is a cup of punishment? Rav Naḥman bar Yitzḥak said: A second cup. That** opinion **was also taught** in a *baraita*: **One who drinks in pairs should not recite a blessing, because it is stated: "Prepare to meet your God, O Israel"** (Amos 4:12). One must be well-prepared in order to stand before his Creator, **and this** person who drank two cups of wine **is not prepared,** as drinking an even number of cups of wine is dangerous due to demons.

אָמַר רַבִּי אַבָּהוּ, וְאָמְרִי לַהּ בְּמַתְנִיתָא תָּנָא: הָאוֹכֵל וּמְהַלֵּךְ – מְבָרֵךְ מְעוּמָּד, וּכְשֶׁהוּא אוֹכֵל מְעוּמָּד – מְבָרֵךְ מְיוּשָּׁב, וּכְשֶׁהוּא מֵיסֵב וְאוֹכֵל – יוֹשֵׁב וּמְבָרֵךְ. וְהִלְכְתָא: בְּכוּלְּהוּ יוֹשֵׁב וּמְבָרֵךְ.

הדרן עלך שלשה שאכלו

In concluding the *halakhot* of blessings, the Gemara cites that **Rabbi Abbahu said, and some say it was taught in a *baraita*: One who eats and walks, recites the blessing** of Grace after Meals **standing** in one place, **and one who eats standing, recites the blessing** while **seated, and one who eats reclining** on a divan **sits and** then **recites the blessing. And the *halakha* is: In all of these cases one sits and** then **recites the blessing.**[H]

**HALAKHA**

**We will act stringently – אֲנַן נַעֲבֵד לְחוּמְרָא:** One takes the cup of blessing in the right hand alone, without the support of the left hand (*Shulḥan Arukh, Oraḥ Ḥayyim* 183:4).

**And he lifts it at least one handbreadth from the ground – וּמַגְבִּיהוֹ מִן הַקַּרְקַע טֶפַח:** The cup of blessing must be raised one handbreadth above the surface on which it rests (Jerusalem Talmud), and one fixes his eyes upon the cup (*Shulḥan Arukh, Oraḥ Ḥayyim* 183:4).

**And he sends it…to members of his household – וּמְשַׁגְּרוֹ לְאַנְשֵׁי בֵיתוֹ:** One must give wine from the cup of blessing to his wife, in accordance with the opinion of Rav Naḥman (*Shulḥan Arukh, Oraḥ Ḥayyim* 183:4 in the comment of the Rema).

**One may not speak over a cup of blessing – אֵין מְסִיחִין עַל כּוֹס שֶׁל בְּרָכָה:** The one reciting the blessing may not speak from the time he takes the cup of blessing until he recites the blessing. Some hold (*Talmidei Rabbeinu Yona*) that the others present at the meal are likewise prohibited to speak (Rambam *Sefer Ahava, Hilkhot Berakhot* 7:15; *Shulḥan Arukh, Oraḥ Ḥayyim* 183:6).

**In all of these cases one sits and then recites the blessing – בְּכוּלְּהוּ יוֹשֵׁב וּמְבָרֵךְ:** Regardless of the manner in which one eats, he recites Grace after Meals seated, unless he was walking and eating (Rambam *Sefer Ahava, Hilkhot Berakhot* 4:1; *Shulḥan Arukh, Oraḥ Ḥayyim* 183:9, 11).

**PERSONALITIES**

**Yalta – יַלְתָּא:** The wife of Rav Naḥman, Yalta was the daughter of the Exilarch.

Yalta is mentioned several times throughout the Talmud, and various exchanges between her, Rav Naḥman, and the other Sages of her generation are recorded. As can be seen here, Yalta was assertive in her opinions and had a strong sense of self-importance. If we consider that to a large extent, Rav Naḥman's status as the head of the court and as a judge with the authority of the Exilarch was dependent upon his marriage, we can understand why Yalta was insulted by Ulla's remark that seemingly belittled Yalta's role.

The Gemara also relates certain matters that Yalta was permitted to do out of respect for her position as a member of the Exilarch's family. It also relates that she asked many questions that illustrated her extensive Torah knowledge.

Although she had a quick temper and was self-important due to her position, she did not refrain from approaching Sages and asking them questions. She even went out of her way to offer them assistance in times of need.

Yalta's name ultimately became a virtual appellation for a rich and spoiled woman.

Opinions with regard to the origin of her name differ. Some believe that is short for Ayalta (Ayala) or Ya'alta. In the Mandaic language, an Aramaic dialect, *yalta* means a young girl, which is perhaps the source of her name.

**NOTES**

**This barrel is of blessing – נַבְגָּא דְבִרְכְתָא:** Some explained that this barrel includes the entire series of cups drunk along with the cup of blessing. Others held that the various cups with which cup of blessing is adorned are called the barrel of blessing (*ge'onim*).

# Summary of **Perek VII**

This chapter dealt with the halakhic determination that any meal in which several people were established as part of the group partaking of that meal requires a *zimmun*. Due to the significance of this mitzva, members of that group are forbidden to separate and recite Grace after Meals individually.

With regard to the details of the *halakhot* of *zimmun*, although there were Sages who sought to add to the details of the *zimmun* formula, the conclusion reached in this chapter was that in terms of the number of participants there are but two formulas: The standard formula recited in a quorum of three diners and the formula that includes invocation of the name of God when there are ten or more diners.

Due to the affinity of the *zimmun* blessing to communal prayer, which requires a quorum of ten men, it is understandable why women were totally or at least to a large extent, exempted from it.

Although various Sages sought to integrate the *zimmun* blessing and Grace after Meals into one cohesive unit, ultimately they remained separate. Grace after Meals is a distinct unit comprised of four blessings even when it is not preceded by a *zimmun*.

Within Grace after Meals, opinions differ whether the four blessings: Who feeds all, the blessing of the land, Who builds Jerusalem, and Who is good and does good, are all of equal standing. Some of the Sages held that all of the blessings are alluded to in the Torah. However, the conclusion reached was that the fourth blessing: Who is good and does good, is a rabbinic addition and the obligation to recite it is not on a par with the obligation to recite the first three blessings. Although their establishment and formulation developed over the course of many generations, their source is the Torah itself.

Although the halakhic ruling is that in certain circumstances one may abridge or alter the formula of those blessings, their essence and certain key concepts, i.e., land, Torah, covenant, and life, are always required.

A totally different area that was clarified in the course of the discussions with regard to the *zimmun* blessing relates to foods that have an element of prohibition associated with them, over which it is inappropriate to recite a blessing or to form a *zimmun*. There are various details involved in distinguishing between the food items; however, fundamentally the Sages arrived at the following division: Over those items where required gifts were not separated or a required action was not performed but nevertheless there is no prohibition to derive pleasure from them, one may recite a blessing. However, over those items where the failure to separate the gifts or perform the action results in a prohibition to derive pleasure from them, one may neither recite Grace after Meals nor the *zimmun* blessing.

# Introduction to **Perek VIII**

Grace after Meals, and even more so the *zimmun* blessing, lend an element of worship and prayer to every meal. However, even the meal itself is not merely an exercise in eating, but it contains a wide-ranging collection of laws of precedence with regard to the various food items consumed in the course of a meal.

By the letter of the law, one is not required to avoid ritual impurity, other than when dealing with consecrated items or entering the Temple. However, the nation's elite, *ḥaverim* and Torah scholars, were always vigilant in their observance of the *halakhot* of ritual impurity and observed a standard of purity equal to that observed by priests. The plethora of *halakhot* associated with ritual purity and impurity and the preponderance of rabbinic decrees in that area created a situation where it was necessary to be especially vigilant during every meal in order to avoid both becoming ritually impure himself and making the food ritually impure. Special care was required with regard to liquids, as by rabbinic decree, they become ritually impure by means of contact with any impurity and they then render impure all objects with which they subsequently come into contact. In fact, both Beit Shammai and Beit Hillel seek to minimize as much as possible the potential of a person or food items becoming ritually impure in the course of a meal.

Although most of the disputes cited in the mishna in this chapter deal with purity and impurity, there is a discussion in the Gemara with regard to the order of the blessings recited at the conclusion of Shabbat. Although the *halakhot* of Shabbat per se have no direct connection to tractate *Berakhot*, since the procedure for remembering the day and acknowledging its sanctity at its outset and at its conclusion: "Remember the Sabbath day to keep it holy" (Exodus 20:7), involves various blessings of enjoyment, e.g., blessings on wine, spices, etc., that is their connection to tractate *Berakhot*.

The special blessing recited over light at the conclusion of Shabbat and Yom Kippur is unlike all other blessings of enjoyment. Although, on the one hand, one derives a modicum of pleasure from the light, due to other considerations, it falls into the category of the blessings discussed in the ninth chapter, blessings of praise and thanksgiving. A person recites the blessing over the very existence of light and not over any direct pleasure or benefit derived from it. Indeed, this dual characteristic stands at the center of the talmudic discussion surrounding the blessing over light.

מתני׳ אֵלּוּ דְּבָרִים שֶׁבֵּין בֵּית שַׁמַּאי וּבֵין בֵּית הִלֵּל בִּסְעוּדָה: בֵּית שַׁמַּאי אוֹמְרִים, מְבָרֵךְ עַל הַיּוֹם וְאַחַר כָּךְ מְבָרֵךְ עַל הַיַּיִן, וּבֵית הִלֵּל אוֹמְרִים: מְבָרֵךְ עַל הַיַּיִן וְאַחַר כָּךְ מְבָרֵךְ עַל הַיּוֹם.

**MISHNA** These are the **matters** of dispute **between Beit Shammai and Beit Hillel with regard to** the *halakhot* of **a meal:** One dispute concerns the order of blessings in *kiddush*. **Beit Shammai say:** When one recites *kiddush* over wine, **one recites a blessing over the** sanctification of the **day and recites a blessing over the wine thereafter. And Beit Hillel say: One recites a blessing over the wine and recites a blessing over the day thereafter.**[H]

בֵּית שַׁמַּאי אוֹמְרִים: נוֹטְלִין לַיָּדַיִם וְאַחַר כָּךְ מוֹזְגִין אֶת הַכּוֹס, וּבֵית הִלֵּל אוֹמְרִים: מוֹזְגִין אֶת הַכּוֹס וְאַחַר כָּךְ נוֹטְלִין לַיָּדַיִם.

Similarly, Beit Hillel and Beit Shammai disagree with regard to drinking wine before a meal. **Beit Shammai say: One washes his hands and mixes** water with the wine in **the cup thereafter, and Beit Hillel say: One mixes** water with the wine in **the cup and** only **washes his hands thereafter.** The basis of this particular dispute is with regard to the laws of ritual purity, as the Gemara will explain below.

בֵּית שַׁמַּאי אוֹמְרִים: מְקַנֵּחַ יָדָיו בַּמַּפָּה וּמַנִּיחָהּ עַל הַשּׁוּלְחָן, וּבֵית הִלֵּל אוֹמְרִים: עַל הַכֶּסֶת.

Also with regard to the laws of ritual purity, **Beit Shammai say:** After washing, **one dries his hands with a cloth and places it on the table. And Beit Hillel say:** One places it **on the cushion** upon which he is sitting.

בֵּית שַׁמַּאי אוֹמְרִים: מְכַבְּדִין אֶת הַבַּיִת וְאַחַר כָּךְ נוֹטְלִין לַיָּדַיִם, וּבֵית הִלֵּל אוֹמְרִים: נוֹטְלִין לַיָּדַיִם וְאַחַר כָּךְ מְכַבְּדִין אֶת הַבַּיִת.

Similarly, **Beit Shammai say: One sweeps the** area of the **house** where the meal took place **and he washes his hands** with the final waters before Grace after Meals **thereafter. And Beit Hillel say: One washes his hands and sweeps the house thereafter.**

בֵּית שַׁמַּאי אוֹמְרִים: נֵר וּמָזוֹן בְּשָׂמִים וְהַבְדָּלָה וּבֵית הִלֵּל אוֹמְרִים: נֵר וּבְשָׂמִים מָזוֹן וְהַבְדָּלָה.

Just as they dispute the order of the blessings in *kiddush*, they dispute the order of the blessings in *havdala*. If a meal continued until the conclusion of Shabbat, **Beit Shammai say:** One recites the blessing over the **candle,** then the Grace after **Meals** blessing, then the blessing over the **spices,** and finally the blessing of ***havdala*. And Beit Hillel say:** The order is **candle, spices,** Grace after **Meals, and *havdala*.**

בֵּית שַׁמַּאי אוֹמְרִים: ״שֶׁבָּרָא מְאוֹר הָאֵשׁ״ וּבֵית הִלֵּל אוֹמְרִים: ״בּוֹרֵא מְאוֹרֵי הָאֵשׁ״.

With regard to the blessing over the candle, **Beit Shammai say: Who created [*bara*] the light of fire. And Beit Hillel say: Who creates [*boreh*] the lights of fire.**[H]

אֵין מְבָרְכִין לֹא עַל הַנֵּר וְלֹא עַל הַבְּשָׂמִים שֶׁל גּוֹיִם וְלֹא עַל הַנֵּר וְלֹא עַל הַבְּשָׂמִים שֶׁל מֵתִים וְלֹא עַל הַנֵּר וְלֹא עַל הַבְּשָׂמִים שֶׁל עֲבוֹדָה זָרָה. וְאֵין מְבָרְכִין עַל הַנֵּר עַד שֶׁיֵּאוֹתוּ לְאוֹרוֹ.

**One may neither recite a blessing over the candle nor over the spices of gentiles, nor over the candle nor the spices** designated to pay respects **to the dead, nor over the candle nor the spices of idolatry.**[H] The mishna cites another *halakha* with regard to the blessing over the candle: **And one does not recite the blessing over the candle until he derives benefit from its light.**

מִי שֶׁאָכַל וְשָׁכַח וְלֹא בֵּירֵךְ, בֵּית שַׁמַּאי אוֹמְרִים: יַחֲזוֹר לִמְקוֹמוֹ וִיבָרֵךְ, וּבֵית הִלֵּל אוֹמְרִים: יְבָרֵךְ בַּמָּקוֹם שֶׁנִּזְכַּר. וְעַד מָתַי מְבָרֵךְ? עַד כְּדֵי שֶׁיִּתְעַכֵּל הַמָּזוֹן שֶׁבְּמֵעָיו.

The mishna cites an additional dispute: **One who ate and forgot and did not recite a blessing; Beit Shammai say: He returns to the place** where he ate **and recites the blessing. Beit Hillel say:** That is unnecessary. **He recites the blessing at the place** where **he remembered.** Both agree, however, that there is a limit with regard to how long after eating one may recite Grace after Meals. **And until when does he recite the blessing? Until the food is digested in his intestines.**

בָּא לָהֶן יַיִן אַחַר הַמָּזוֹן, אִם אֵין שָׁם אֶלָּא אוֹתוֹ כּוֹס – בֵּית שַׁמַּאי אוֹמְרִים: מְבָרֵךְ עַל הַיַּיִן וְאַחַר כָּךְ מְבָרֵךְ עַל הַמָּזוֹן, וּבֵית הִלֵּל אוֹמְרִים מְבָרֵךְ עַל הַמָּזוֹן וְאַחַר כָּךְ מְבָרֵךְ עַל הַיַּיִן.

**Wine came before** the diners **after the meal;**[H] **if only that cup** of wine **is there, Beit Shammai say: One recites a blessing over the wine and recites a blessing over the food,** Grace after Meals, **thereafter. And Beit Hillel say: One recites a blessing over the food and recites a blessing over the wine thereafter.**

וְעוֹנִין אָמֵן אַחַר יִשְׂרָאֵל הַמְבָרֵךְ, וְאֵין עוֹנִין אָמֵן אַחַר כּוּתִי הַמְבָרֵךְ, עַד שֶׁיִּשְׁמַע כׇּל הַבְּרָכָה כּוּלָּהּ.

**And one answers amen after a Jew who recites a blessing**[H] even if he did not hear the entire blessing, **and one does not answer amen after a Samaritan [*Kuti*] who recites a blessing until he hears the whole blessing in its entirety,** as perhaps the *Kuti* introduced an element inconsistent with the Jewish faith in that section of the blessing that he did not hear.

**HALAKHA**

**One recites a blessing over the wine and recites a blessing over the day thereafter – מְבָרֵךְ עַל הַיַּיִן וְאַחַר כָּךְ מְבָרֵךְ עַל הַיּוֹם:** In *kiddush*, one recites the blessing over the wine first and recites *kiddush* to sanctify the day thereafter, in accordance with the opinion of Beit Hillel (Rambam *Sefer Zemanim*, *Hilkhot Shabbat* 29:6–7; *Shulḥan Arukh*, *Oraḥ Ḥayyim* 271:10).

**The blessing over the light in *havdala* – בִּרְכַּת הַמָּאוֹר בְּהַבְדָּלָה:** One recites: Who creates the lights of the fire, over the light of *havdala*, in accordance with the opinion of Beit Hillel (*Shulḥan Arukh*, *Oraḥ Ḥayyim* 298:1).

**One may neither recite a blessing…over the candle nor over the spices of idolatry – אֵין מְבָרְכִין...וְלֹא עַל הַנֵּר וְלֹא עַל הַבְּשָׂמִים שֶׁל עֲבוֹדָה זָרָה וכו׳:** One may not recite a blessing over spices that were not intended for their scent, e.g., fragrances to neutralize the odor of the dead or those of a bathroom. Nor may one recite a blessing over spices of idolatry. One may neither recite a blessing over the light of idolatry nor over the light of a party of gentiles. One may neither recite a blessing over a candle lit due to respect, e.g., a candle for the dead, nor over a candle lit by a gentile on Shabbat (Rambam *Sefer Ahava*, *Hilkhot Berakhot* 9:8–9; *Sefer Zemanim*, *Hilkhot Shabbat* 29:25; *Shulḥan Arukh*, *Oraḥ Ḥayyim* 217:2, 5–6, 298:12).

**Wine came before the diners after the meal – בָּא לָהֶן יַיִן אַחַר הַמָּזוֹן:** One recites Grace after Meals first and the blessing over the wine thereafter, in accordance with the opinion of Beit Hillel (Rambam *Sefer Ahava*, *Hilkhot Berakhot* 7:14; *Shulḥan Arukh*, *Oraḥ Ḥayyim* 174:3).

**And one answers amen after a Jew who recites a blessing – וְעוֹנִין אָמֵן אַחַר יִשְׂרָאֵל הַמְבָרֵךְ:** One who hears the end of a blessing recited by a Jew answers amen. One who hears an entire blessing recited by a gentile may also answer amen (*Taz*), as his intention is certainly to bless Heaven (*Magen Avraham*, based on the Rema *Oraḥ Ḥayyim* 156); some disagree (*Baḥ*; Rambam *Sefer Ahava*, *Hilkhot Berakhot* 1:13; *Shulḥan Arukh*, *Oraḥ Ḥayyim* 215:2).

## NOTES

**What is alternatively** – מַאי דָּבָר אַחֵר: Even though Beit Shammai also cite two reasons, the Gemara does not find it noteworthy, since Beit Shammai did not explicitly introduce the second reason with the term alternatively. The term, alternatively, emphasizes that it is an additional reason not stated previously. Beit Shammai's two statements can be understood as two aspects of a single reason (*Shitta Mekubbetzet*; Rabbi Elazar Moshe Horowitz).

## BACKGROUND

**The frequent takes precedence** – תָּדִיר קוֹדֵם: Since reality dictates that two actions cannot be performed simultaneously and one action must precede another, several principles were established to determine the order in which they should be performed. This is especially prevalent in the area of sacrifices, each of which contains a host of intricate details, which must be executed. There are additional criteria, other than frequency, which determine precedence with regard to sacrifices, e.g., significance, primary status, and others. Those principles are applied to other areas of *halakha* where similar problems of precedence arise.

גמ׳ תָּנוּ רַבָּנַן, דְּבָרִים שֶׁבֵּין בֵּית שַׁמַּאי וּבֵית הִלֵּל בַּסְּעוּדָה: בֵּית שַׁמַּאי אוֹמְרִים, מְבָרֵךְ עַל הַיּוֹם וְאַחַר כָּךְ מְבָרֵךְ עַל הַיַּיִן, שֶׁהַיּוֹם גּוֹרֵם לַיַּיִן שֶׁיָּבֹא וּכְבָר קִדֵּשׁ הַיּוֹם וַעֲדַיִין יַיִן לֹא בָּא;

**GEMARA** **The Sages taught** in a *Tosefta*: These are the **matters** of dispute **between Beit Shammai and Beit Hillel with regard to** the *halakhot* of **a meal: Beit Shammai say:** When one recites *kiddush* over wine, **one recites a blessing over the** sanctification of the **day and recites a blessing over the wine thereafter as the day causes the wine to come** before the meal. And Beit Shammai offer an additional reason: **The day has** already **been sanctified and the wine has not yet come.** Since Shabbat was sanctified first, it should likewise be mentioned first.

וּבֵית הִלֵּל אוֹמְרִים: מְבָרֵךְ עַל הַיַּיִן וְאַחַר כָּךְ מְבָרֵךְ עַל הַיּוֹם, שֶׁהַיַּיִן גּוֹרֵם לִקְדוּשָּׁה שֶׁתֵּאָמֵר. דָּבָר אַחֵר: בִּרְכַּת הַיַּיִן תְּדִירָה וּבִרְכַּת הַיּוֹם אֵינָהּ תְּדִירָה. תָּדִיר וְשֶׁאֵינוֹ תָּדִיר – תָּדִיר קוֹדֵם. וַהֲלָכָה כְּדִבְרֵי בֵית הִלֵּל.

**And Beit Hillel say: One recites a blessing over the wine and recites a blessing over the day thereafter,** because **the wine causes the sanctification to be recited.** Were there no wine, *kiddush* would not be recited. **Alternatively,** Beit Hillel say: **The blessing over wine is** recited **frequently, and the blessing over the day is not** recited **frequently,** and there is a general principle: When **a frequent** practice and **an infrequent** practice clash, **the frequent practice takes precedence** over the infrequent practice. The *Tosefta* concludes: **The *halakha* is in accordance with the statement of Beit Hillel.**

מַאי ״דָּבָר אַחֵר״? – וְכִי תֵּימָא הָתָם תַּרְתֵּי וְהָכָא חֲדָא – הָכִי נַמִי תַּרְתֵּי נִינְהוּ: בִּרְכַּת הַיַּיִן תְּדִירָה וּבִרְכַּת הַיּוֹם אֵינָהּ תְּדִירָה, תָּדִיר וְשֶׁאֵינוֹ תָּדִיר – תָּדִיר קוֹדֵם.

The Gemara asks: **What is alternatively?**[N] Why did Beit Hillel cite an additional reason? The Gemara responds: **And if you say** that **there** Beit Shammai cite **two** reasons, **and here** Beit Hillel offer only **one**, therefore Beit Hillel said **they are two** reasons **here as well: The blessing over wine is** recited **frequently and the blessing over the day is not** recited **frequently.** When **a frequent** practice and **an infrequent** practice clash, **the frequent** practice **takes precedence**[B] over the infrequent practice.

״וַהֲלָכָה כְּדִבְרֵי בֵית הִלֵּל״ – פְּשִׁיטָא! דְּהָא נָפְקָא בַּת קוֹל!

It was taught in the *Tosefta*: **The *halakha* is in accordance with the statement of Beit Hillel.** The Gemara remarks: **It is obvious, as a Heavenly Voice emerged** and proclaimed that the *halakha* is always in accordance with the opinion of Beit Hillel. Why did the *Tosefta* tell us here that the *halakha* is in accordance with their opinion?

אִיבָּעֵית אֵימָא: קוֹדֶם בַּת קוֹל, וְאִיבָּעֵית אֵימָא: לְאַחַר בַּת קוֹל,

The Gemara offers two answers: **If you wish, say** that this *Tosefta* was taught **before the Heavenly Voice** emerged and proclaimed that general principle. **And if you wish, say** instead, that this *Tosefta* was indeed taught **after the Heavenly Voice** emerged,

Perek **VIII**
Daf **52** Amud **a**

## NOTES

**One disregards a Heavenly Voice** – אֵין מַשְׁגִּיחִין בְּבַת קוֹל: Rabbi Yehoshua did not intend to say that one disregards a Heavenly Voice in all circumstances. Rather, it is disregarded in matters of *halakha*. Rabbi Yehoshua invoked this principle (*Bava Metzia* 59b) as a corollary of the principle: The Torah is not in heaven (Deuteronomy 30:12). On that basis, any supernatural determinations that run contrary to the rabbinic interpretation of the Torah are not authoritative, as that authority is the exclusive purview of the earthly court (see Rambam *Hilkhot Yesodei HaTorah*, with regard to prophecy).

וְרַבִּי יְהוֹשֻׁעַ הִיא, דְּאָמַר: אֵין מַשְׁגִּיחִין בְּבַת קוֹל.

**and** this *Tosefta* **is** in accordance with the opinion of **Rabbi Yehoshua who said,** with regard to the Heavenly Voice that emerged and proclaimed that the *halakha* is in accordance with the opinion of Rabbi Eliezer in the case of the oven of *akhnai* (*Bava Metzia* 59b), that **one disregards a Heavenly Voice.**[N] Just as he disregarded the Heavenly Voice in his dispute with Rabbi Eliezer, so too, one disregards the Heavenly Voice that proclaimed that the *halakha* is in accordance with the opinion of Beit Hillel.

וְסָבְרִי בֵּית שַׁמַּאי דְּבִרְכַּת הַיּוֹם עֲדִיפָא?! וְהָתַנְיָא: הַנִּכְנָס לְבֵיתוֹ בְּמוֹצָאֵי שַׁבָּת – מְבָרֵךְ עַל הַיַּיִן וְעַל הַמָּאוֹר וְעַל הַבְּשָׂמִים וְאַחַר כָּךְ אוֹמֵר הַבְדָּלָה, וְאִם אֵין לוֹ אֶלָּא כּוֹס אֶחָד – מַנִּיחוֹ לְאַחַר הַמָּזוֹן וּמְשַׁלְשְׁלָן כּוּלָּן לְאַחֲרָיו!

As to the substance of these statements, the Gemara asks: **Do Beit Shammai hold** that **the blessing over the day takes precedence? Wasn't it taught** in a *baraita*: **One who enters his house at the conclusion of Shabbat recites a blessing over the wine,** then over **the candle,** then over **the spices, and recites *havdala* thereafter? And if he has only one cup** of wine, **he leaves it for after the** last Shabbat **meal and arranges all** of the blessings: Grace after Meals, the blessings of *havdala* and the blessing over wine **together thereafter.** Evidently, the blessing over wine precedes the primary *havdala* blessing.

וְהָא, מִמַּאי דְּבֵית שַׁמַּאי הִיא, דִּלְמָא בֵּית הִלֵּל הִיא?

The Gemara asks: **And this** *baraita*, **from where** is it ascertained **that it is** in accordance with the opinion of **Beit Shammai? Perhaps it is** in accordance with the opinion of **Beit Hillel.** Beit Shammai's opinion cannot be challenged with an unattributed *baraita*.

לא סלקא דעתך, דקתני מאור ואח[ר] כך בשמים, ומאן שמעת ליה דאית ליה האי סברא – בית שמאי; דתניא אמר רבי יהודה: לא נחלקו בית שמאי ובית הלל על המזון שבתחלה ועל הבדלה שהיא בסוף, על מה נחלקו? על המאור ועל הבשמים – בית שמאי אומרים: מאור ואחר כך בשמים, ובית הלל אומרים: בשמים ואחר כך מאור.

The Gemara responds: **It cannot enter your mind** that this *baraita* is in accordance with the opinion of Beit Hillel, **as it was taught** at the beginning of the *baraita*: **Light** and **spices thereafter. And who, did you hear, adopts that reasoning? Beit Shammai. As it was taught** in a *Tosefta* that **Rabbi Yehuda said: Beit Shammai and Beit Hillel did not dispute that** Grace after **Meals** is recited **first and that *havdala*** **is recited last. With regard to what did they disagree?** With regard to the blessings recited in the middle of *havdala*, the blessings **over the light and over the spices.**[N] **Beit Shammai say: Light and spices thereafter; and Beit Hillel say: Spices and light thereafter.** Therefore, the *baraita*, where it is taught that the blessing over the candle precedes the blessing over the spices, must be according to Beit Shammai and it says that wine precedes *havdala*.

וממאי דבית שמאי היא ואליבא דרבי יהודה, דילמא בית הלל היא ואליבא דרבי מאיר?

The Gemara presents another challenge: **And from where** do you ascertain **that this** *baraita* **is** the opinion of **Beit Shammai in accordance with** the interpretation of **Rabbi Yehuda? Perhaps it is** the opinion of **Beit Hillel in accordance with** the interpretation of **Rabbi Meir.**

לא סלקא דעתך, דקתני הכ[א] במתניתין: בית שמאי אומרים, נ[ר] ומזון בשמים והבדלה, ובית הל[ל] אומרים: נר ובשמים מזון והבדלה והתם בברייתא קתני: אם אין ל[ו] אלא כוס אחד – מניחו לאחר המזו[ן] ומשלשלן כולן לאחריו, שמע מינ[ה] דבית שמאי היא ואליבא דרב[י] יהודה.

The Gemara responds: **It cannot enter your mind** that this *baraita* is the opinion of Beit Hillel in accordance with the interpretation of Rabbi Meir. **As it was taught here in the mishna,** which like all unattributed *mishnayot* is in accordance with the opinion of Rabbi Meir: **Beit Shammai say:** One recites the blessing over the **candle,** then the Grace after **Meals** blessing, then the blessing over the **spices,** and finally the blessing of ***havdala*. And Beit Hillel say:** The order is **candle, spices,** Grace after **Meals, and *havdala*. And there, in the *baraita*, it was taught: And if he has only one cup** of wine, **he leaves it for after the** last Shabbat **meal and arranges all** of the blessings: Grace after Meals, the blessings of *havdala*, and the blessing over wine **together thereafter.** According to the *baraita*, all of the blessings follow Grace after Meals. Since the *baraita* and the mishna do not correspond, **conclude from here** that the *baraita* **is** the opinion of **Beit Shammai, in accordance with** the interpretation of **Rabbi Yehuda.**

ומכל מקום קשיא! קא סברי בי[ת] שמאי: שאני עיולי יומא מאפוק[י] יומא, עיולי יומא – כמה דמקדמינ[ן] ליה עדיף, אפוקי יומא – כמ[ה] דמאחרינן ליה עדיף, כי היכי דל[א] להוי עלן כמשוי.

**And, nevertheless,** after the Gemara has proven that the *baraita* corresponds to the opinion of Beit Shammai as interpreted by Rabbi Yehuda, the contradiction between Beit Shammai's statement in the *baraita* and their statement in the *Tosefta* **is difficult.** The Gemara responds: **Beit Shammai hold** that **the arrival of the day** of Shabbat or a Festival **is different from the departure of the day.** As with regard to **the arrival of the day, the more that we can advance it, the better;** with regard to **the departure of the day, the more we postpone it, the better, so that** Shabbat **should not be like a burden to us.** Consequently, although Beit Shammai situate *kiddush* before the blessing over the wine, they agree that one should recite *havdala* after the blessing over the wine.

וסברי בית שמאי ברכת המזו[ן] טעונה כוס?! והא תנן: בא להם י[ין] לאחר המזון, אם אין שם אלא או[תו] כוס – בית שמאי אומרים: מברך ע[ל] היין ואחר כך מברך על המזון. מא[י] לאו דמברך עילויה ושתי ליה! לא[,] דמברך עילויה ומנח ליה.

The above discussion referred to Beit Shammai's opinion with regard to Grace after Meals recited over a cup of wine. The Gemara poses the question: **And do Beit Shammai hold** that **Grace after Meals requires a cup** of wine? **Didn't we learn** in the mishna: **Wine came before** the diners **after the meal; if only that cup** of wine **is there, Beit Shammai say: One recites a blessing over the wine and recites a blessing over the food,** Grace after Meals, **thereafter. What? Is it not that he recites a blessing over** the wine **and drinks it,** leaving Grace after Meals without wine? The Gemara rejects this: **No.** The mishna means that **he recites a blessing over** the cup of wine **and leaves it** to drink from it after Grace after Meals.

והאמר מר: המברך צרי[ך] שיטעום! – דטעים ליה. והאמר מ[ר] טעמו – פגמו! – דטעים ליה בידיה.

The Gemara raises a difficulty: **Didn't the Master say** that **one who recites a blessing is required to taste?** The Gemara answers: Indeed, this refers to a case **where he tasted it.** The Gemara raises a difficulty: **Didn't the Master say** that one who **tasted** the cup of wine **disqualified it**[H] and it is no longer suitable to be used for a cup of blessing? The Gemara answers: This does not refer to a case where he drank the wine; but rather, where **he tasted it with his hand** or poured a bit into another cup and drank from it.

NOTES

**The dispute over the order of *havdala* – המחלוקת בסדר ההבדלה:** According to Beit Shammai's opinion, one first recites a blessing over the candle, as the benefit from it is immediate. That is followed by the blessing over the benefit he derives from the meal and the spices, whose fragrance he enjoyed last. Finally, he recites the blessing of *havdala* itself. Beit Hillel links spices to honoring Shabbat as their fragrance raises the spirits of the person saddened by the conclusion of Shabbat. Therefore, the blessing over the spices is juxtaposed to the blessing over the candle (*Talmidei Rabbeinu Yona; Tosefot Rabbi Yehuda HaḤasid*).

HALAKHA

**One who tasted the cup of wine disqualified it – טעמו פגמו:** If one tasted even a minute quantity (*Mishna Berura*) from the cup of wine accompanying *kiddush*, *havdala*, or Grace after Meals, the contents of the cup are disqualified for use as a cup of blessing. One who merely poured some of the wine from the cup into his hand or into a separate vessel and drank it did not disqualify the cup (Rambam *Sefer Zemanim, Hilkhot Shabbat* 29:16; *Shulḥan Arukh, Oraḥ Ḥayyim* 182:3).

וְהָאָמַר מָר: כּוֹס שֶׁל בְּרָכָה צָרִיךְ שִׁיעוּר, וְהָא קָא פָּחֵית לֵיהּ מִשִּׁיעוּרֵיהּ – דְּנָפִישׁ לֵיהּ טְפֵי מִשִּׁיעוּרֵיהּ.

The Gemara raises a difficulty: **Didn't the Master say: A cup o blessing requires** a minimum **measure** of wine? By drinking th wine, **doesn't he diminish** the cup **from** containing **its** minimun **measure?** The Gemara answers: This refers to a case where **the cu contained more than the** required **measure** of wine.

וְהָא, "אִם אֵין שָׁם אֶלָּא אוֹתוֹ כּוֹס" קָתָנֵי! – תְּרֵי לָא הָוֵי, וּמֵחַד נָפִישׁ.

The Gemara asks: **Wasn't it taught** explicitly: **If he has only on cup** of wine? If there is more than the required measure of wine, h does not have only one cup. The Gemara responds: Indeed, **ther are not two** cups, **but** there is **more than one.**

וְהָא תָּנֵי רַבִּי חִיָּיא, בֵּית שַׁמַּאי אוֹמְרִים: מְבָרֵךְ עַל הַיַּיִן וְשׁוֹתֵהוּ, וְאַחַר כָּךְ מְבָרֵךְ בִּרְכַּת הַמָּזוֹן! – אֶלָּא: תְּרֵי תַּנָּאֵי וְאַלִּיבָּא דְּבֵית שַׁמַּאי.

The Gemara raises another difficulty: **Didn't Rabbi Ḥiyya teach i** a *baraita* that **Beit Shammai say: He recites a blessing over th wine and drinks it, and recites Grace after Meals thereafter?** Ev dently, according to Beit Shammai, wine is not required for Grac after Meals. **Rather,** it must be that **two** ***tanna'im*** hold **in acco dance with Beit Shammai** and differ with regard to their opinion

"בֵּית שַׁמַּאי אוֹמְרִים" וכו'.

We learned in our mishna that Beit Shammai and Beit Hillel di agree over whether the washing of the hands or mixing water wit the wine takes precedence. **Beit Shammai say:** One washes hi hands and mixes water with the wine in the cup thereafter, and Be Hillel say: One mixes water with the wine in the cup and onl washes his hands thereafter.

תָּנוּ רַבָּנַן, בֵּית שַׁמַּאי אוֹמְרִים: נוֹטְלִין לַיָּדַיִם וְאַחַר כָּךְ מוֹזְגִין אֶת הַכּוֹס, שֶׁאִם אַתָּה אוֹמֵר מוֹזְגִין אֶת הַכּוֹס תְּחִלָּה – גְּזֵרָה שֶׁמָּא יִטַּמְּאוּ מַשְׁקִין שֶׁאֲחוֹרֵי הַכּוֹס מֵחֲמַת יָדָיו, וְיַחְזְרוּ וִיטַמְּאוּ אֶת הַכּוֹס.

**The Sages taught** a *Tosefta* where this issue is discussed in greate detail: **Beit Shammai say: One washes** his **hands and mixes wate** with the wine **in the cup thereafter, as if you say** that **one mixe water** with the wine **in the cup first,** his hands will remain ritual impure, as the Sages **decreed** that unwashed hands have secon degree ritual impurity[B] status as if they touched something rendere ritually impure by a creeping animal.[B] Consequently, there is roo for concern that **the liquid that** inevitably drips **on the outside o the cup might become ritually impure due to his hands, and** thos liquids **will in turn render the cup ritually impure.**[N] Consequent Beit Shammai said that the hands must be washed first in order t prevent that result.

וְלִיטַמּוּ יָדַיִם לַכּוֹס!

The Gemara asks: If the concern is with regard to ritual impurity t the cup, why mention the liquids on the outside of the cup? **Let hi hands render the cup ritually impure** directly.

יָדַיִם שְׁנִיּוֹת הֵן, וְאֵין שֵׁנִי עוֹשֶׂה שְׁלִישִׁי בְּחוּלִּין אֶלָּא עַל יְדֵי מַשְׁקִין.

The Gemara answers: **Hands have second** degree ritual impurit status, **and** there is a general halakhic principle that an object c **second** degree ritual impurity status **cannot confer third** degre ritual impurity status **upon non-sacred items,**[H] as opposed to *ter ma* or consecrated food, **except by means of liquids.** By rabbini decree, liquids that come into contact with second degree ritu impurity assume first degree ritual impurity status and, consequent can render non-sacred items impure.

וּבֵית הִלֵּל אוֹמְרִים: מוֹזְגִין אֶת הַכּוֹס וְאַחַר כָּךְ נוֹטְלִין לַיָּדַיִם, שֶׁאִם אַתָּה אוֹמֵר נוֹטְלִין לַיָּדַיִם תְּחִלָּה, גְּזֵרָה שֶׁמָּא יִטַּמְּאוּ מַשְׁקִין שֶׁבַּיָּדַיִם מֵחֲמַת הַכּוֹס, וְיַחְזְרוּ וִיטַמְּאוּ אֶת הַיָּדַיִם.

**And Beit Hillel say: One mixes water** with the wine **in the cup an** only **washes** his **hands thereafter, as if you say** that **one washes h hands first,** there is **a decree lest the liquid** from the outside of th cup that dampened **one's hands will be rendered ritually impur due to the cup** which is liable to be impure, **and** the liquid **will i turn render his hands ritually impure.**

וְנִיטַמֵּי כּוֹס לַיָּדַיִם! – אֵין כְּלִי מְטַמֵּא אָדָם.

The Gemara asks: **Let the cup render** his **hands ritually impur** directly, without any liquid? The Gemara responds that, accordin to a general principle in the *halakhot* of ritual impurity, **a vessel doe not render a person ritually impure.**[H] The cup alone does n render his hands ritually impure.

וְנִיטַמֵּי לְמַשְׁקִין שֶׁבְּתוֹכוֹ! – הָכָא בִּכְלִי שֶׁנִּטַמְּאוּ אֲחוֹרָיו בְּמַשְׁקִין עָסְקִינַן, דְּתוֹכוֹ טָהוֹר וְגַבּוֹ טָמֵא. דִּתְנַן: כְּלִי שֶׁנִּטַמְּאוּ אֲחוֹרָיו בְּמַשְׁקִין – אֲחוֹרָיו טְמֵאִים,

The Gemara asks: If the back of the cup is ritually impure, **let render the liquids that are within** the cup **ritually impure?** Th Gemara answers: **Here we are dealing with a vessel** that only **th outside of which has been rendered ritually impure by liquids** by rabbinic law and not by Torah law. In that case, **the inside** of th cup **is pure and the outside is impure. As we learned** in a mishn **A vessel whose outer side is rendered ritually impure by liqui** only **the outer side** of the vessel **is impure,**

## BACKGROUND

**Second degree ritual impurity – שֵׁנִי לְטוּמְאָה:** Something that became ritually impure by contact with an object with first degree ritual impurity status. Ritually impure food of the second degree is called disqualified. It can confer third degree ritual impurity status to *teruma* and sacrificial foods. Any liquids that come in contact with an object with second degree ritual impurity status themselves assume first degree status. The Sages decreed that certain items, such as sacred books and unwashed hands, have second degree ritual impurity status.

**A creeping animal – שֶׁרֶץ:** This term generally refers to rodents, lizards, insects, or any other small creature that crawls. Ritual impurity is imparted by the carcasses of eight creeping animals (Leviticus 11:29–30). The Talmud often refers to these eight creatures with the term creeping animal, without any further description. The Sages stated that the smallest of these eight animals was at least the size of a lentil-bulk at birth. Therefore, one only contracts ritual impurity if he comes into contact with a piece of the carcass of a creeping animal that is no smaller than that. Moreover, one is liable to receive lashes for eating a lentil-bulk of that type of animal.

## NOTES

**The laws of ritual impurity – דִּינֵי הַטּוּמְאָה:** The *halakhot* of ritual purity and impurity are among the most complex of Torah laws (*Shabbat* 31a; see Rashi). However, there are certain fundamental principles that apply universally. Most items that are impure by Torah law, i.e., a dead creeping animal, the carcass of an animal, a leper, and a *zav*, are primary sources of ritual impurity and render any person or vessel with which they come into contact ritually impure. A person, vessel, or food which comes into contact with a primary source of ritual impurity becomes a secondary source of ritual impurity and assumes first degree ritual impurity status. The item most sensitive to becoming ritually impure is consecrated meat, which may assume even fourth degree ritual impurity status. *Teruma* can assume no lower than third degree status and non-sacred items can assume no lower than second decree status. An item that becomes ritually impure but cannot render other items impure is deemed invalid or disqualified, not impure. To this basic system, the Sages added numerous decrees. One is: Liquids that become ritually impure always assume first degree ritual impurity status. This was a decree due to liquids of a *zav* (see *Shabbat* 14b; *Bekhorot* 38a). Any food item that comes into contact with a ritually impure liquid assumes at least second degree status.

## HALAKHA

**An object of second degree ritual impurity status cannot confer third degree ritual impurity status upon non-sacred items – וְאֵין שֵׁנִי עוֹשֶׂה שְׁלִישִׁי בְּחוּלִּין:** In a case of non-sacred items, as opposed to *teruma* or consecrated foods, an object of second degree ritual impurity status is itself simply invalid and, consequently, cannot render anything else ritually impure. The Sages decreed, however, that if an object of second degree ritual impurity status came into contact with liquid, the liquid assumes first degree ritual impurity status (Rambam *Sefer Tahara, Hilkhot She'ar Avot HaTumot* 11:2; 7:5).

**A vessel does not render a person ritually impure – אֵין כְּלִי מְטַמֵּא אָדָם:** A vessel of first degree ritual impurity status cannot render a person ritually impure. It can, though, render his hands ritually impure only until the first joint (Rambam *Sefer Tahara, Hilkhot She'ar Avot HaTumot* 8:1).

**A vessel, the outside of which has been rendered ritually impure by liquids – כְּלִי שֶׁנִּטַמְּאוּ אֲחוֹרָיו בְּמַשְׁקִין:** If the outside of a vessel came into contact with ritually impure liquids, only that portion assumes second degree ritual impurity status; however, the inside of the vessel does become ritually impure for use with consecrated items (Rambam *Sefer Tahara, Hilkhot She'ar Avot HaTumot* 7:3; *Hilkhot Kelim* 13:4).

תּוֹכוֹ וְאוֹגְנוֹ וְאָזְנוֹ וְיָדָיו טְהוֹרִין, נִטְמָ תּוֹכוֹ – נִטְמָא כּוּלּוֹ.

**while its inner side, and its rim,** the edge of the vessel that protrudes outwards, **and its ear**-shaped handle,[B] **and its** straight **handles** are **pure.** However, if **the inside** of the vessel **became ritually impure, it is all ritually impure.**

בְּמַאי קָא מִיפַּלְגִי?

Although the decrees of Beit Hillel and Beit Shammai are different, they are based on realistic contingencies and on concerns shared by both parties. The Gemara seeks to clarify: **With regard to what do they disagree?** What is the crux of their dispute?

בֵּית שַׁמַּאי סָבְרִי: אָסוּר לְהִשְׁתַּמֵּ בִּכְלִי שֶׁנִּטְמְאוּ אֲחוֹרָיו בְּמַשְׁקִין, גְּזֵרָ מִשּׁוּם נִיצוֹצוֹת, וְלֵיכָּא לְמִגְזַר שֶׁמָּ יִטָּמְאוּ הַמַּשְׁקִין שֶׁבַּיָּדַיִם בַּכּוֹס;

The Gemara explains: **Beit Shammai hold: It is prohibited to use a vessel the outer side of which has been rendered ritually impure by liquids.** This prohibition stems from **a decree** of the Sages, due to concern **for drips** of liquid that would fall from inside the vessel to its outer side, as those drips themselves would be rendered ritually impure by virtue of their contact with the outer side of the vessel. **And** Beit Shammai hold that **there is no** reason to **issue a decree** due to the concern of Beit Hillel **lest the liquid on one's hands will be rendered ritually impure by the cup, as** Beit Shammai hold that the use of a vessel of that kind is prohibited.

וּבֵית הִלֵּל סָבְרִי: מוּתָּר לְהִשְׁתַּמֵּ בִּכְלִי שֶׁנִּטְמְאוּ אֲחוֹרָיו בְּמַשְׁקִין, אָמְרִ נִיצוֹצוֹת לָא שְׁכִיחִי, וְאִיכָּא לְמֵיחַ שֶׁמָּא יִטָּמְאוּ מַשְׁקִין שֶׁבַּיָּדַיִם מֵחֲמַ הַכּוֹס.

**And Beit Hillel hold: One is permitted to use a vessel the outer side of which has been rendered ritually impure by liquid,** as they **say: Drips are uncommon,** and decrees are not issued on the basis of an uncommon case. Because Beit Hillel permit the use of a vessel of that kind, **there is concern lest the liquid on one's hands will be rendered ritually impure due to the cup.**

דָּבָר אַחֵר: תֵּכֶף לִנְטִילַת יָדַיִם סְעוּדָה.

**Alternatively,** Beit Hillel hold that one mixes the water with the wine in the cup and then washes his hands due to the principle: **Immediately** after **the washing of the hands** comes **the meal.**[H] Therefore, he mixes the water and wine in the cup, then he washes his hands, and then he immediately proceeds to the meal.

מַאי דָּבָר אַחֵר? – הָכִי קָאָמְרִי לְהוּ בֵּי הִלֵּל לְבֵית שַׁמַּאי: לְדִידְכוּ דְּאָמְרִיתּ "אָסוּר לְהִשְׁתַּמֵּשׁ בִּכְלִי שֶׁאֲחוֹרָ טְמֵאִין" דְּגָזְרִינַן מִשּׁוּם נִיצוֹצוֹת, אֲפִי הָכִי – הָא עֲדִיפָא, דְּתֵכֶף לִנְטִילַת יָדַ סְעוּדָה.

The Gemara asks: **What** is the point of Beit Hillel adding: **Alternatively?** The Gemara answers: **Beit Hillel said to Beit Shammai as follows:** Even **according to you, who said** that **it is prohibited to use a vessel the outer side of which is ritually impure as we issued a decree due to** concern for **drips, even so,** our opinion **is preferable** to yours, as our opinion adheres to the principle: **Immediately** after **the washing of the hands** comes **the meal.**

בֵּית שַׁמַּאי אוֹמְרִים, מְקַנֵּחַ וכו׳.

We learned in the mishna that Beit Hillel and Beit Shammai disagree over where the cloth that one used to dry his hands should be placed. **Beit Shammai say:** After washing, **one dries** his hands with a cloth and places it on the table. And Beit Hillel say: One places it on the cushion upon which he is sitting.

תָּנוּ רַבָּנַן, בֵּית שַׁמַּאי אוֹמְרִים: מְקַנֵּ יָדָיו בְּמַפָּה וּמַנִּיחָהּ עַל הַשֻּׁלְחָן, שֶׁאִ אַתָּה אוֹמֵר עַל הַכֶּסֶת – גְּזֵרָה שֶׁמָּ יִטָּמְאוּ מַשְׁקִין שֶׁבְּמַפָּה מֵחֲמַת הַכֶּסֶ וְיַחְזְרוּ וִיטַמְּאוּ אֶת הַיָּדַיִם.

In a *Tosefta*, **the Sages taught** in greater detail: **Beit Shammai say:** After washing, **one dries his hands with a cloth and places it on the table, as if you say** that he should place the cloth **on the cushion,** there is room to issue a **decree lest the liquids on the cloth,** which is wet because he used it to dry his hands, **become ritually impure due to** their contact **with the cushion, and** the liquids **would in turn render the hands** of anyone who touches the towel **ritually impure.**

וְנִטַמְּיֵיהּ כֶּסֶת לְמַפָּה! – אֵין כְּלִי מְטַמֵּ כְּלִי.

The Gemara asks: Even without the liquid, **let the cushion render the towel ritually impure** directly? The Gemara answers: There is a principle: **A vessel does not render** another **vessel ritually impure.**

וְנִטַמְּיֵיהּ כֶּסֶת לְגַבְרָא גּוּפֵיהּ! – אֵין כְּ מְטַמֵּא אָדָם.

The Gemara asks: **Let the cushion render the man** sitting upon it **ritually impure.** The Gemara answers: There, too, there is a general principle: **A vessel does not render a person ritually impure.**

וּבֵית הִלֵּל אוֹמְרִים: עַל הַכֶּסֶת, שֶׁאִ אַתָּה אוֹמֵר עַל הַשֻּׁלְחָן, גְּזֵרָה שֶׁמָּ יִטָּמְאוּ מַשְׁקִין שֶׁבְּמַפָּה מֵחֲמַת הַשּׁוּלְחָ וְיַחְזְרוּ וִיטַמְּאוּ אֶת הָאוֹכָלִין.

**And Beit Hillel say:** One places it **on the cushion** upon which he is sitting, **as if you say** that he should place it **on the table,** there is room to issue a **decree lest the liquids on the towel might be rendered ritually impure** by their contact **with the table,** and those liquids **in turn will render the food** placed on the table **ritually impure.**

**BACKGROUND**

Rim and ear-shaped handle – אוֹגֶן וְאוֹזֶן:

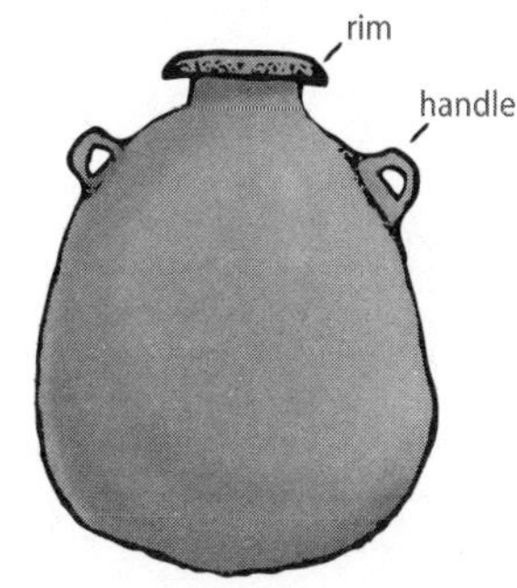


Jug from the talmudic period

**HALAKHA**

**Immediately after the washing of the hands comes the meal – תֵּכֶף לִנְטִילַת יָדַיִם סְעוּדָה:** Authorities disagree whether or not one must be careful to avoid a pause between washing one's hands and reciting: Who brings forth bread from the earth. Some say that one must refrain from pausing (*Tur*, based on the Jerusalem Talmud), others hold that it is not necessary (Rif; Rambam). It is preferable to refrain from pausing. The duration of a pause between washing and reciting the blessing over bread that would constitute an interruption is the time it takes to walk twenty-two cubits (*Shulḥan Arukh, Oraḥ Ḥayyim* 166:1 and the comment of the Rema).

וּלְטַמֵּא שֻׁלְחָן לָאוֹכָלִין שֶׁבְּתוֹכוֹ! – הָכָא בְּשֻׁלְחָן שֵׁנִי עָסְקִינַן, וְאֵין שֵׁנִי עוֹשֶׂה שְׁלִישִׁי בְּחוּלִּין אֶלָּא עַל יְדֵי מַשְׁקִין.

The Gemara asks: **Let the table render the food upon it ritually impure** directly. The Gemara explains: **Here we are dealing with a table** that has **second** degree ritual impurity status, and an object of **second** degree ritual impurity status **can only confer third** degree ritual impurity status **upon non-sacred items by means of liquids.** By rabbinic decree, liquids that come into contact with second degree ritual impurity assume first degree ritual impurity status and, consequently, can render non-sacred items impure.

בְּמַאי קָמִיפַּלְגִי? – בֵּית שַׁמַּאי סָבְרִי: אָסוּר לְהִשְׁתַּמֵּשׁ בְּשֻׁלְחָן שֵׁנִי, גְּזֵרָה מִשּׁוּם אוֹכְלֵי תְרוּמָה;

The Gemara seeks to clarify: **With regard to what do they disagree?** The Gemara answers: The basis of their dispute is that **Beit Shammai hold: It is prohibited to use a table** that has **second** degree ritual impurity status for purposes of eating because of **a decree due to those who eat *teruma*.** A table with that status renders *teruma* ritually impure through contact. To prevent priests who partake of *teruma* from unwittingly eating off a table of that sort, a decree was issued prohibiting its use even with non-sacred food.

וּבֵית הִלֵּל סָבְרִי: מוּתָּר לְהִשְׁתַּמֵּשׁ בְּשֻׁלְחָן שֵׁנִי, אוֹכְלֵי תְרוּמָה זְרִיזִין הֵם.

**And Beit Hillel hold: It is permitted to use a table** that has **second** degree ritual impurity status, and we are not concerned about the priests. As **those who eat *teruma* are vigilant**[N] and would ascertain the status of a table before eating.

דָּבָר אַחֵר: אֵין נְטִילַת יָדַיִם לְחוּלִּין מִן הַתּוֹרָה.

**Alternatively,** Beit Hillel hold that **there is no** requirement of **washing of the hands for non-sacred items by Torah law.**[N]

מַאי דָּבָר אַחֵר? – הָכִי קָאָמְרִי לְהוּ בֵּית הִלֵּל לְבֵית שַׁמַּאי: וְכִי תֵּימְרוּ מַאי שְׁנָא גַּבֵּי אוֹכָלִין דְּחָיְישִׁינַן, וּמַאי שְׁנָא גַּבֵּי יָדַיִם דְּלָא חָיְישִׁינַן – אֲפִילּוּ הָכִי הָא עֲדִיפָא, דְּאֵין נְטִילַת יָדַיִם לְחוּלִּין מִן הַתּוֹרָה. מוּטָב שֶׁיִּטַּמְּאוּ יָדַיִם דְּלֵית לְהוּ עִיקָּר מִדְּאוֹרָיְיתָא – וְאַל יִטַּמְּאוּ אוֹכָלִים דְּאִית לְהוּ עִיקָּר מִדְּאוֹרָיְיתָא.

The Gemara asks: **What is** the point of Beit Hillel adding the additional reason introduced with: **Alternatively?** The Gemara answers: **Beit Hillel said to Beit Shammai as follows: And if you say, what is the difference with regard to food that we are concerned** that it might be rendered ritually impure by the cloth on the table; **and what is the difference with regard to hands that we are not concerned** that they might be rendered ritually impure by the cloth placed on the cushion? Beit Hillel continue: We can respond that **even so, this is preferable,** as **there is no** requirement of **washing of the hands for non-sacred items by Torah law. It is preferable that hands,** whose impurity **has no basis in Torah law, will become ritually impure** with second degree ritual impurity status, **and food,** whose impurity **has a basis in Torah law, will not become ritually impure.**

״בֵּית שַׁמַּאי אוֹמְרִים, מְכַבְּדִין״ וכו׳.

We learned in the mishna that Beit Hillel and Beit Shammai disagree over whether cleaning the place where one ate or washing one's hands should be performed first after the meal. **Beit Shammai say: One sweeps the** area of the **house** where the meal took place **and he washes his hands** with the final waters **thereafter. And Beit Hillel say: One washes his hands and sweeps the house thereafter.**

תָּנוּ רַבָּנַן, בֵּית שַׁמַּאי אוֹמְרִים: מְכַבְּדִין אֶת הַבַּיִת וְאַחַר כָּךְ נוֹטְלִין לַיָּדַיִם, שֶׁאִם אַתָּה אוֹמֵר ״נוֹטְלִין לַיָּדַיִם תְּחִלָּה״, נִמְצָא אַתָּה מַפְסִיד אֶת הָאוֹכָלִין. אֲבָל נְטִילַת יָדַיִם לְבֵית שַׁמַּאי תְּחִלָּה – לָא סְבִירָא לְהוּ, מַאי טַעְמָא – מִשּׁוּם פֵּירוּרִין.

**The Sages taught** in a *Tosefta* where this issue is discussed in greater detail: **Beit Shammai say: One sweeps the** area of the **house** where the meal took place **and washes his hands thereafter,**[H] **as if you say that one washes his hands first,** the water is liable to splash on the remaining crumbs and **you will have ruined the food. But Beit Shammai do not hold that the washing of the hands is first. What is the reason? Due to** concern, lest the **crumbs** will be made disgusting.

וּבֵית הִלֵּל אוֹמְרִים: אִם שַׁמָּשׁ תַּלְמִיד חָכָם הוּא, נוֹטֵל פֵּירוּרִין שֶׁיֵּשׁ בָּהֶם כְּזַיִת וּמַנִּיחַ פֵּירוּרִין שֶׁאֵין בָּהֶן כְּזַיִת.

**And Beit Hillel say: If the attendant is a Torah scholar,** he **removes the crumbs that are an olive-bulk** from the table at the end of the meal **and leaves** only **crumbs that are not an olive-bulk,** as food that is less than an olive-bulk is not considered food and there is no prohibition to ruin it.

מְסַיֵּיעַ לֵיהּ לְרַבִּי יוֹחָנָן, דְּאָמַר רַבִּי יוֹחָנָן: פֵּירוּרִין שֶׁאֵין בָּהֶם כְּזַיִת מוּתָּר לְאַבְּדָן בְּיָד.

This **supports** the opinion of **Rabbi Yoḥanan, as Rabbi Yoḥanan said: Crumbs that are less than an olive-bulk** in size, **one may destroy them with his hand** without violating the prohibition against ruining food.

בְּמַאי קָמִיפַּלְגִי? בֵּית הִלֵּל סָבְרִי: אָסוּר לְהִשְׁתַּמֵּשׁ בְּשַׁמָּשׁ עַם הָאָרֶץ; וּבֵית שַׁמַּאי סָבְרִי: מוּתָּר לְהִשְׁתַּמֵּשׁ בְּשַׁמָּשׁ עַם הָאָרֶץ.

Here too the Gemara poses the question: **With regard to what do they disagree?** The Gemara answers: The basis of their argument is that **Beit Hillel hold: One is forbidden to use** the services of **a waiter** who is an ***am ha'aretz*.**[N] Therefore, there is no room for concern that food will be ruined as only crumbs remain on the table. **And Beit Shammai hold: One is permitted to use** the services of **an attendant** who is an ***am ha'aretz*.** Food will remain on the table and, therefore, there is room for concern that food will be ruined. The solution is to clean the food off the table and only then wash one's hands.

## NOTES

**Those who eat *teruma* are vigilant – אוֹכְלֵי תְרוּמָה זְרִיזִין הֵם:** This expression is stated both in reference to priests and to those who sacrifice the Paschal lamb. The implication is that because of their awareness that they are engaged in sacred activities, those individuals are vigilant with regard to every detail. There is thus no concern that they might err due to negligence or laziness.

**Washing of the hands for non-sacred items by Torah law – נְטִילַת יָדַיִם לְחוּלִּין מִן הַתּוֹרָה:** Washing hands before eating *teruma* is also not a requirement by Torah law, as by Torah law, there is no concept of partial ritual impurity restricted to a single part of the body, e.g., hands. This statement can be understood as follows, based on the Jerusalem Talmud: There is no requirement to wash one's hands in any circumstance by Torah law, and there is no requirement to wash one's hands before eating non-sacred items at all (see *Hagahot Ben Arye*).

**A waiter who is an *am ha'aretz* – שַׁמָּשׁ עַם הָאָרֶץ:** Some explain that if the waiter is an *am ha'aretz*, once the homeowner of the house leaves the table the waiter will dispose of all the crumbs, including those that are the size of an olive-bulk. Therefore, it is preferable for the homeowner to sweep away the crumbs himself in an appropriate manner (*ge'onim*).

## HALAKHA

**One sweeps the house and washes his hands thereafter – מְכַבְּדִין אֶת הַבַּיִת וְאַחַר כָּךְ נוֹטְלִין לַיָּדַיִם:** One sweeps the house and washes his hands thereafter, in accordance with the opinion of Rav Huna. Nowadays, when the custom is not to remove the table from before the diner, there is no need to insist upon the order in which those acts are performed (Rambam *Sefer Ahava*, *Hilkhot Berakhot* 7:11; *Shulḥan Arukh*, *Oraḥ Ḥayyim* 180:3).

אָמַר רַבִּי יוֹסֵי בַּר חֲנִינָא אָמַר רַב הוּנָא בְּכוּלֵּיהּ פִּרְקִין הֲלָכָה כְּבֵית הִלֵּל, בַּר מֵהָא דַּהֲלָכָה כְּבֵית שַׁמַּאי. וְרַבִּי אוֹשַׁעְיָא מַתְנֵי אִיפְּכָא, וּבְהָא נַמִּי הֲלָכָה כְּבֵית הִלֵּל.

**Rabbi Yosei bar Ḥanina said that Rav Huna said: In our entire chapter, the *halakha* is in accordance with** the opinion of **Beit Hillel, except for this** case, **where the *halakha* is in accordance with** the opinion of **Beit Shammai. And Rabbi Oshaya would teach the opposite** and reverse the opinions of Beit Hillel and Beit Shammai as they appear in our mishna, **and in this** case **as well, the *halakha* is in accordance with** the opinion of **Beit Hillel.**

״בֵּית שַׁמַּאי אוֹמְרִים, נֵר וּמָזוֹן״ וכו׳.

We learned in the mishna that **Beit Shammai say:** One recites the blessing over the **candle,** then the Grace after **Meals** blessing, then the blessing over the spices, and finally the blessing of *havdala*. And Beit Hillel say: The order is candle, spices, Grace after Meals, and *havdala*.

רַב הוּנָא בַּר יְהוּדָה אִיקְּלַע לְבֵי רָבָא, חַזְיֵיהּ לְרָבָא דְּבָרֵיךְ אַבְּשָׂמִים בְּרֵישָׁא. אֲמַר לֵיהּ: מִכְּדִי בֵּית שַׁמַּאי וּבֵית הִלֵּל אַמָּאוֹר לָא פְּלִיגִי; דְּתַנְיָא, בֵּית שַׁמַּאי אוֹמְרִים: נֵר וּמָזוֹן בְּשָׂמִים וְהַבְדָּלָה. וּבֵית הִלֵּל אוֹמְרִים: נֵר וּבְשָׂמִים מָזוֹן וְהַבְדָּלָה!

The Gemara relates that **Rav Huna bar Yehuda happened** to come **to Rava's house. He saw that Rava recited a blessing over the spices first.** Rav Huna bar Yehuda **said to him: Now since Beit Hillel and Beit Shammai do not disagree with regard to** the blessing over **light, as we learned** in our mishna that **Beit Shammai say:** One recites the blessing over the **candle,** then the Grace after **Meals** blessing, then the blessing over the **spices,** and finally the blessing of ***havdala*. And Beit Hillel say:** The order is **candle, and spices,** Grace after **Meals,** and ***havdala*,**[H] why did you recite the blessing over the spices first?

עָנֵי רָבָא בַּתְרֵיהּ: זוֹ דִּבְרֵי רַבִּי מֵאִיר, אֲבָל רַבִּי יְהוּדָה אוֹמֵר: לֹא נֶחְלְקוּ בֵּית שַׁמַּאי וּבֵית הִלֵּל עַל הַמָּזוֹן שֶׁהוּא בַּתְּחִילָּה וְעַל הַבְדָּלָה שֶׁהִיא בַּסּוֹף. עַל מָה נֶחְלְקוּ – עַל הַמָּאוֹר וְעַל הַבְּשָׂמִים, שֶׁבֵּית שַׁמַּאי אוֹמְרִים: עַל הַמָּאוֹר וְאַחַר כָּךְ בְּשָׂמִים, וּבֵית הִלֵּל אוֹמְרִים: בְּשָׂמִים וְאַחַר כָּךְ מָאוֹר.

**Rava answered after him:** Indeed, **that is the statement of Rabbi Meir. However, Rabbi Yehuda says** in a *baraita* that **Beit Hillel and Beit Shammai neither disagree with regard to** Grace after **Meals that it is** recited **first, nor with regard to *havdala*, which is** recited **last. With regard to what do they disagree?** They disagree **with regard to the light and the spices. Beit Shammai say:** One recites a blessing **over light and over spices thereafter, and Beit Hillel say:** One recites a blessing **over spices and over light thereafter.**

וְאָמַר רַבִּי יוֹחָנָן: נָהֲגוּ הָעָם כְּבֵית הִלֵּל אַלִּיבָּא דְּרַבִּי יְהוּדָה.

**And Rabbi Yoḥanan said: The people were accustomed** to conduct themselves **in accordance with** the opinion of **Beit Hillel according to** the interpretation of **Rabbi Yehuda.** The blessing over the spices is recited first.

״בֵּית שַׁמַּאי אוֹמְרִים, שֶׁבָּרָא״ כו׳.

The mishna cited a dispute between Beit Hillel and Beit Shammai with regard to the formula of the blessing over fire in *havdala*. **Beit Shammai say: Who created [*bara*]** the light of fire. And Beit Hillel say: Who creates [*boreh*] the lights of fire.

אָמַר רָבָא: בְּ״בָרָא״ כּוּלֵּי עָלְמָא לָא פְּלִיגִי דְּבָרָא מַשְׁמַע, כִּי פְּלִיגִי בְּ״בוֹרֵא״, בֵּית שַׁמַּאי סָבְרִי: בּוֹרֵא – דַּעֲתִיד לְמִבְרָא; וּבֵית הִלֵּל סָבְרִי: ״בּוֹרֵא״ נַמִּי דִּבְרָא מַשְׁמַע.

Regarding this, Rava says: **With regard** to the word ***bara*, everyone agrees that it means created** in the past. **Where they disagree is with regard to** the word *boreh*. **Beit Shammai hold: *Boreh*** means that God **will create in the future, and Beit Hillel hold: *Boreh* also means that He has created** in the past.

מְתִיב רַב יוֹסֵף: ״יוֹצֵר אוֹר וּבוֹרֵא חֹשֶׁךְ״, ״יוֹצֵר הָרִים וּבוֹרֵא רוּחַ״, ״בּוֹרֵא הַשָּׁמַיִם וְנוֹטֵיהֶם״! אֶלָּא אָמַר רַב יוֹסֵף: בְּ״בָרָא״ וּ״בוֹרֵא״ כּוּלֵּי עָלְמָא לָא פְּלִיגִי דִּבְרָא מַשְׁמַע. כִּי פְּלִיגִי – בְּ״מָאוֹר״ וּ״מְאוֹרֵי״; דְּבֵית שַׁמַּאי סָבְרִי: חֲדָא נְהוֹרָא אִיכָּא בְּנוּרָא, וּבֵית הִלֵּל סָבְרִי: טוּבָא נְהוֹרֵי אִיכָּא בְּנוּרָא. תַּנְיָא נַמִּי הָכִי, אָמְרוּ לָהֶם בֵּית הִלֵּל לְבֵית שַׁמַּאי: הַרְבֵּה מְאוֹרוֹת יֵשׁ בָּאוּר.

**Rav Yosef raised an objection:** How can there be a dispute over the meaning of the word *boreh*? In the following verses it is clear that it refers to acts of creation in the past: **"Who forms light and creates [*boreh*] darkness"** (Isaiah 45:7), **"Who forms mountains and creates [*boreh*] wind"** (Amos 4:13), or **"Who creates [*boreh*] the heavens and stretches them out"** (Isaiah 42:5). **Rather, said Rav Yosef: With regard to both *bara* and *boreh*, everyone agrees that** they **mean created. Where they disagree is with regard to the light** of the fire or **the lights** of the fire.[H] **As Beit Shammai hold** that **there is one light in a fire, and Beit Hillel hold** that **there are many lights in a fire,**[N] as a flame consists of red, green, and white light. **That was also taught** in a *baraita*: **Beit Hillel said to Beit Shammai: There are many lights in the fire.**

אֵין מְבָרְכִין כו׳. בִּשְׁלָמָא נֵר – מִשּׁוּם דְּלֹא שָׁבַת, אֶלָּא בְּשָׂמִים מַה טַּעַם לֹא?

We learned in the mishna that **one may neither recite a blessing** over the candle nor over the spices of gentiles. The Gemara asks: **Granted,** the prohibition against the recitation of a blessing over **a candle** of gentiles in *havdala*, as the flame of the candle **did not rest.** Because it was burning during Shabbat, one should not recite a blessing over it at the conclusion of Shabbat. **However, what is the reason that** one may **not** recite a blessing over **spices** of gentiles?

HALAKHA

**Candle, and spices, Grace after Meals, and *havdala* – נֵר וּבְשָׂמִים מָזוֹן וְהַבְדָּלָה:** The halakhic ruling is that one recites a blessing over the spices first and over the candle thereafter, in accordance with the opinion of Rabbi Yoḥanan (Rambam *Sefer Zemanim, Hilkhot Shabbat* 29:24; *Shulḥan Arukh, Oraḥ Ḥayyim* 296:1).

**Where they disagree is with regard to the light of the fire or the lights of the fire – כִּי פְּלִיגִי בְּמָאוֹר וּמְאוֹרֵי:** One recites: Who creates the lights of the fire, in accordance with the opinion of Beit Hillel (Rambam *Sefer Zemanim, Hilkhot Shabbat* 29:24; *Shulḥan Arukh, Oraḥ Ḥayyim* 298:1).

NOTES

**There is one light in a fire…there are many lights in a fire – חֲדָא נְהוֹרָא אִיכָּא בְּנוּרָא...טוּבָא נְהוֹרֵי אִיכָּא בְּנוּרָא:** Some explain that according to Beit Hillel, light does not have merely one use, but many different uses (Ra'avad). Others explain that according to Beit Shammai, one recites a blessing only over the basic light, whereas Beit Hillel hold that one recites a blessing over all its component parts (*Shenot Eliyahu*).

אָמַר רַב יְהוּדָה אָמַר רַב: הָכָא בְּמִסִּבַּת גּוֹיִם עָסְקִינַן, מִפְּנֵי שֶׁסְּתָם מְסִבַּת גּוֹיִם לַעֲבוֹדָה זָרָה הִיא.

**Rav Yehuda said** that **Rav said: Here we are dealing with a part** arranged by **gentiles** and the spices used at that party were prohibite because **the parties of gentiles are generally** devoted **to idolatry.**

הָא מִדְּקָתָנֵי סֵיפָא: אֵין מְבָרְכִין לֹא עַל הַנֵּר וְלֹא עַל הַבְּשָׂמִים שֶׁל עֲבוֹדָה זָרָה, מִכְּלָל דְּרֵישָׁא לָאו בַּעֲבוֹדָה זָרָה עָסְקִינַן!

The Gemara asks: **But from that which was taught in the latter claus** of the mishna: **One may neither recite a blessing over the candl nor over the spices of idolatry,** infer **by implication** that in **the firs clause** of our mishna **we are not dealing with idolatry?** There mus be a different reason why the spices of gentiles are prohibited.

אָמַר רַבִּי חֲנִינָא מִסּוּרָא: "מַה טַּעַם" קָאָמַר, מַה טַּעַם אֵין מְבָרְכִין עַל הַנֵּר וְלֹא עַל הַבְּשָׂמִים שֶׁל גּוֹיִם – מִפְּנֵי שֶׁסְּתָם מְסִבַּת גּוֹיִם לַעֲבוֹדָה זָרָה.

**Rabbi Ḥanina of Sura said:** These two *halakhot* are complementar and the mishna **states** the *halakha* employing the style of: **What i the reason.** The mishna should be understood as follows: **What i the reason that one may neither recite a blessing over the candl nor over the spices of gentiles?**[H] **Because the parties of gentiles ar generally** devoted **to idolatry** and one may neither recite a blessin over the candle nor over the spices of idolatry.

תָּנוּ רַבָּנַן: אוֹר שֶׁשָּׁבַת מְבָרְכִין עָלָיו, וְשֶׁלֹּא שָׁבַת – אֵין מְבָרְכִין עָלָיו. מַאי שָׁבַת וּמַאי לֹא שָׁבַת?

**The Sages taught** in a *baraita*: **Over light that rested,**[N] **one may recit a blessing** in *havdala*, **and over** light **that did not rest, one may no recite a blessing.** The Gemara asks: **What is** meant by **rested, an what is** meant by **did not rest?**

HALAKHA

**Nor over the spices of gentiles – וְלֹא עַל הַבְּשָׂמִים שֶׁל נָכְרִים:** One may not recite a blessing over the scent of spices from parties of gentiles, as those parties are presumably to celebrate idolatry (Rambam *Sefer Zemanim, Hilkhot Shabbat* 29:25, *Sefer Ahava, Hilkhot Berakhot* 9:9; *Shulḥan Arukh, Oraḥ Ḥayyim* 297:2).

NOTES

**Light that rested – אוֹר שֶׁשָּׁבַת:** The blessing recited over the candle at the conclusion of Shabbat is specifically over the change that took place; previously he did not have the option to kindle a fire due to the sanctity of Shabbat, and now he is permitted to use it. Consequently, even though as far as the gentile is concerned there is no prohibition to kindle a fire on Shabbat, the light he possesses is a Shabbat light to which the prohibition of Shabbat never applied. Therefore, at the conclusion of Shabbat, no change has taken place in its status. By the same token, a flame that burned on Shabbat in accordance with all the strictures and limitations of Shabbat is considered a light that rested.



אִי נֵימָא, לֹא שָׁבַת מֵחֲמַת מְלָאכָה אֲפִילּוּ מִמְּלָאכָה דְּהֶתֵּירָא – וְהָתַנְיָא: אוֹר שֶׁל חַיָּה וְשֶׁל חוֹלֶה מְבָרְכִין עָלָיו!

**If we say** that did not rest means that **it did not rest from labor, eve from labor that is permitted? Wasn't it taught** in a *baraita* that **ove light** that was kindled on Shabbat **for a woman giving birth or** dangerously **ill person,**[H] for whom one is permitted to perform pr hibited labor on Shabbat, **one may recite a blessing** during *havdal* at the conclusion of Shabbat?

אֲמַר רַב נַחְמָן בַּר יִצְחָק: מַאי שָׁבַת – שֶׁשָּׁבַת מֵחֲמַת מְלֶאכֶת עֲבֵירָה, תַּנְיָא נַמִּי הָכִי: עֲשָׁשִׁית שֶׁהָיְתָה דּוֹלֶקֶת וְהוֹלֶכֶת כָּל הַיּוֹם כּוּלּוֹ – לְמוֹצָאֵי שַׁבָּת מְבָרְכִין עָלֶיהָ.

**Rav Naḥman bar Yitzḥak said: What is** meant by **rested?** Light tha **rested from labor of transgression** on Shabbat. However, if the ligh burned for the entire Shabbat or was kindled on Shabbat in a permi sible manner, one may recite a blessing over it. **That** *halakha* **was als taught** in a *baraita*: **A lantern**[B] **that was continuously burnin throughout the entire day** of Shabbat, **one may recite a blessing ov it at the conclusion of Shabbat.**

תָּנוּ רַבָּנַן: גּוֹי שֶׁהִדְלִיק מִיִּשְׂרָאֵל וְיִשְׂרָאֵל שֶׁהִדְלִיק מִגּוֹי – מְבָרְכִין עָלָיו, גּוֹי מִגּוֹי – אֵין מְבָרְכִין עָלָיו.

**The Sages taught** in a *baraita*: **A gentile who lit** a candle **from** candle that was in the possession **of a Jew**[H] **or if a Jew lit** a candle **fro a gentile, one may recite a blessing over it** at the conclusion of Sha bat. However, **if a gentile** lit a candle **from a gentile, one may n recite a blessing over it.**

מַאי שְׁנָא גּוֹי מִגּוֹי דְּלָא – מִשּׁוּם דְּלָא שָׁבַת, אִי הָכִי יִשְׂרָאֵל מִגּוֹי נַמִּי, הָא לָא שָׁבַת!

The Gemara asks: **What is different** about a candle that **a gentile l from a gentile, that** one may **not** recite a blessing over it? **Becaus** the light **did not rest** on Shabbat. **If so,** the light of **a Jew** who lit candle **from a gentile also did not rest** on Shabbat.

וְכִי תֵּימָא, הָךְ אִיסּוּרָא אֲזַל לֵיהּ וְהָא אַחֲרִינָא הוּא וּבִידָא דְּיִשְׂרָאֵל קָא מִתְיַלְּדָא – אֶלָּא הָא דְּתַנְיָא: הַמּוֹצִיא שַׁלְהֶבֶת לִרְשׁוּת הָרַבִּים חַיָּיב, אַמַּאי חַיָּיב? מַה שֶּׁעָקַר לֹא הִנִּיחַ וּמַה שֶּׁהִנִּיחַ לֹא עָקַר!

**And if you say** that **this prohibited** flame **has gone and this** flame a new and **different** one which **came into being in the possession a Jew,** as a flame is not a concrete, static object, but rather it co stantly recreates itself; **however, this** *halakha* **that was taught** in *Tosefta* in tractate *Shabbat* states: **One who carries out a flame** fro the private **to the public domain** on Shabbat **is liable** for carrying o from one domain to another. If the flame is constantly recreating its **why is he liable? That** flame **which he lifted** from the private doma **he did not place** in the public domain **and that which he placed h did not lift.** One is only liable for carrying out on Shabbat if he lifte an object from one domain and placed that same object in anoth domain. Since one who carries out a flame on Shabbat is consider liable, evidently, despite any change that it may undergo, the flame essentially considered a single entity.

HALAKHA

**Light for a woman giving birth or an ill person – אוֹר שֶׁל חַיָּה וְשֶׁל חוֹלֶה:** If light was kindled on Shabbat for a woman giving birth or a dangerously ill person, even if kindled by a Jew (*Magen Avraham*), one may recite a blessing over it at the conclusion of Shabbat, as per the *baraita* (Rambam *Sefer Zemanim, Hilkhot Shabbat* 29:27; *Shulḥan Arukh, Oraḥ Ḥayyim* 298:5).

**A gentile…from a Jew – נָכְרִי...מִיִּשְׂרָאֵל:** If a gentile lit a candle from the candle of a Jew or if a Jew lit a candle from the candle of a gentile, one may recite a blessing over the light at the conclusion of Shabbat. However, if a gentile lit a candle from the candle of another gentile, one may not recite a blessing over it (Rambam *Sefer Zemanim, Hilkhot Shabbat* 29:26; *Shulḥan Arukh, Oraḥ Ḥayyim* 298:6).

BACKGROUND

**Lantern – עֲשָׁשִׁית:**

Lantern

אֶלָּא: לְעוֹלָם דְּאִיסּוּרָא נַמִּי אִיתֵיה וְכִי קָא מְבָרֵךְ – אַתּוֹסֶפְתָּא דְּהֶתֵּירָא קָא מְבָרֵךְ. אִי הָכִי, גּוֹי מִגּוֹי נַמִּי!

**Rather, actually that prohibited** flame **is also extant, and when one recites the blessing, he recites the blessing over the permitted addition** to that flame. The Gemara asks: **If so,** even if **a gentile** lit a candle **from a gentile as well,** the flame should be considered essentially new; one should be able to recite a blessing over the addition.

אִין הָכִי נַמִּי, גְּזֵירָה מִשּׁוּם גּוֹי רִאשׁוֹן וְעַמּוּד רִאשׁוֹן.

The Gemara answers: **Yes, it is indeed so.** Fundamentally, there is no reason to prohibit doing so. However, the Sages issued **a decree because of the first gentile,** who did not light the flame from another gentile, **and the first pillar** of flame that was kindled on Shabbat. Consequently, they prohibited all somewhat similar cases, including when a gentile lights a flame from another gentile.

תָּנוּ רַבָּנַן: הָיָה מְהַלֵּךְ חוּץ לַכְּרַךְ וְרָאָה אוּר, אִם רוֹב גּוֹיִם – אֵינוֹ מְבָרֵךְ, אִם רוֹב יִשְׂרָאֵל – מְבָרֵךְ.

**The Sages taught** in a *baraita*: **If one was walking outside the city, saw fire** there, and wanted to recite the blessing over it as part of *havdala*, **if the** city has a **majority of gentiles he may not recite the blessing** over the fire, but **if** the city has a **majority of Jews, he may recite the blessing.**[H]

הָא גּוּפָא קַשְׁיָא! אָמַרְתְּ: אִם רוֹב גּוֹיִם – אֵינוֹ מְבָרֵךְ, הָא מֶחֱצָה עַל מֶחֱצָה – מְבָרֵךְ; וַהֲדַר תָּנֵי: אִם רוֹב יִשְׂרָאֵל – מְבָרֵךְ, הָא מֶחֱצָה עַל מֶחֱצָה – אֵינוֹ מְבָרֵךְ!

The Gemara notes: **The matter itself is difficult** in this *baraita*. **You said** in the *baraita* that if the town has a **majority of gentiles he may not recite the blessing.** By inference, if the town population was **half** gentiles **and half** Jews, **one may recite a blessing. And then you teach** that **if** the town has a **majority of Jews, he may recite the blessing.** By inference, if the town population was **half** gentiles **and half** Jews, **one may not recite a blessing.** The inferences from two sections of the *baraita* are contradictory.

בְּדִין הוּא דַּאֲפִילּוּ מֶחֱצָה עַל מֶחֱצָה נַמִּי מְבָרֵךְ, וְאַיְּידֵי דִּתְנָא רֵישָׁא "רוֹב נׇכְרִים" – תְּנָא סֵיפָא "רוֹב יִשְׂרָאֵל".

The Gemara responds: **By right,** the *baraita* should have taught that **even** if the town population was **half** gentiles **and half** Jews, **one may recite a blessing,** but **since in the first clause it taught: The majority of gentiles, in the latter clause it** used the same expression and **taught: The majority of Jews.**

תָּנוּ רַבָּנַן: הָיָה מְהַלֵּךְ חוּץ לַכְּרַךְ וְרָאָה תִּינוֹק וַאֲבוּקָה בְּיָדוֹ, בּוֹדֵק אַחֲרָיו, אִם יִשְׂרָאֵל הוּא – מְבָרֵךְ, אִם נׇכְרִי הוּא – אֵינוֹ מְבָרֵךְ.

And **the Sages taught: One who was walking outside the city** at the conclusion of Shabbat **and saw a child with a torch**[B] **in his hand, he** must **check after his** background. **If** the child **is a Jew, he may recite a blessing** over this flame, **but if** the child **is a gentile, he may not recite a blessing** over it.

מַאי אִירְיָא תִּינוֹק, אֲפִילּוּ גָּדוֹל נַמִּי!

The Gemara asks: **Why was it taught** specifically with regard to **a child? Even if he were an adult,** one would **also** need to investigate whether he was a Jew or a gentile in order to determine whether or not he may recite a blessing over the torch.

אָמַר רַב יְהוּדָה אָמַר רַב: הָכָא בִּסְמוּךְ לִשְׁקִיעַת הַחַמָּה עָסְקִינַן, גָּדוֹל – מוֹכְחָא מִילְּתָא דְּוַדַּאי נׇכְרִי הוּא, תִּינוֹק – אֵימַר יִשְׂרָאֵל הוּא אִקְּרִי וְנָקֵיט.

**Rav Yehuda said** that **Rav said: Here we are dealing with** a case where, although it was the conclusion of Shabbat, it was still **soon after sunset.** Therefore, in the case of **an adult, it is self-evident that he is a gentile,** as a Jew would not be so quick to take fire in his hand immediately after Shabbat. In the case of **a child,** however, **say that** perhaps **he is a Jew** and **it happened that he took** the torch.

תָּנוּ רַבָּנַן: הָיָה מְהַלֵּךְ חוּץ לַכְּרַךְ וְרָאָה אוּר, אִם עָבֶה כְּפִי הַכִּבְשָׁן – מְבָרֵךְ עָלָיו, וְאִם לָאו – אֵינוֹ מְבָרֵךְ עָלָיו.

And **the Sages taught: One who was walking outside the city** at the conclusion of Shabbat **and saw a fire, if** the fire is at least **as thick as the opening of a furnace, one may recite a blessing over it,** as a fire of that kind is kindled for the light it produces as well. **And if** it is **not** at least that thick, **one may not recite a blessing over it.**

תָּנֵי חֲדָא: אוּר שֶׁל כִּבְשָׁן מְבָרְכִין עָלָיו, וְתַנְיָא אִידָךְ: אֵין מְבָרְכִין עָלָיו!

**It was taught** in **one** *baraita*: During *havdala*, **one may recite a blessing over the fire of a furnace;**[NH] **and it was taught** in **another** *baraita*: **One may not recite a blessing over** the fire of a furnace. There is an apparent contradiction between the *baraitot*.

לָא קַשְׁיָא; הָא – בִּתְחִלָּה, הָא – לְבַסּוֹף.

The Gemara responds: This is **not difficult,** as **this** *baraita* which prohibits reciting the blessing is speaking **at the beginning** when the furnace was just kindled and the fire is designated solely to heat the objects in the furnace; **that** *baraita,* which permits reciting the blessing, is speaking **at the end,** when the fire is no longer needed to heat the objects in the furnace, and its light is used for other purposes.

תָּנֵי חֲדָא: אוּר שֶׁל תַּנּוּר וְשֶׁל כִּירַיִם מְבָרְכִין עָלָיו, וְתַנְיָא אִידָךְ: אֵין מְבָרְכִין עָלָיו!

The Gemara cites a similar contradiction between *baraitot*: **It was taught** in **one** *baraita*: During *havdala,* **one may recite a blessing over the fire of an oven or a stove; and it was taught** in **another** *baraita*: **One may not recite a blessing over it.**

**HALAKHA**

**If the city has a majority of Jews, he may recite the blessing – אִם רוֹב יִשְׂרָאֵל מְבָרֵךְ:** If one was walking outside a city at the conclusion of Shabbat and saw its lights, and if the majority, or at least half, of its residents are Jews, he may recite a blessing. If the majority are gentiles, he may not (Rambam *Sefer Zemanim, Hilkhot Shabbat* 29:26; *Shulḥan Arukh, Oraḥ Ḥayyim* 298:7).

**The fire of a furnace – אוּר שֶׁל כִּבְשָׁן:** One may not recite a blessing over fire emerging from a furnace at the beginning of the process of burning bricks, as it is not for the purpose of light at that stage. After the bricks have been burned, it is for the purpose of light and one may recite a blessing over it (Rambam *Sefer Zemanim, Hilkhot Shabbat* 29:26; *Shulḥan Arukh, Oraḥ Ḥayyim* 298:10).

**BACKGROUND**

Torch – אֲבוּקָה:

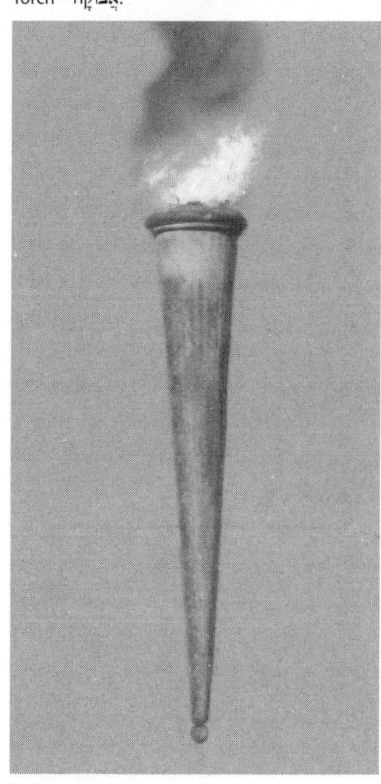

Torch from the biblical era

**NOTES**

**The fire of a furnace – אוּר שֶׁל כִּבְשָׁן:** Some explain this differently: When the fire is first lit in the furnace, one may not recite a blessing over it because there is a lot of smoke and its light is not bright. Later, however, as the fire continues to burn, the smoke subsides and one may recite a blessing over it (Rav Hai Gaon). Others explain that this refers specifically to the conclusion of Shabbat just after nightfall and reverse the ruling. One who sees the fire at its early stages may recite a blessing as it was certainly kindled after Shabbat concluded. However, if the fire is at a later stage, one may not recite a blessing over it as it was clearly kindled on Shabbat (*Me'iri*; *Shitta Mekubbetzet*).

לָא קַשְׁיָא: הָא בִּתְחִלָּה, הָא לְבַסּוֹף.

The Gemara responds: This is **not difficult,** as a similar distinction between the *baraitot* may be suggested. **This** *baraita,* which prohibits reciting the blessing, is speaking **at the beginning,** when the oven or stove was just kindled and the fire is designated solely to heat the objects on the stove or in the oven; **that** *baraita,* which permits reciting the blessing, is speaking **at the end,** when the fire is no longer needed to heat the objects on the stove or in the oven and its light is used for other purposes.

תָּנֵי חֲדָא: אוֹר שֶׁל בֵּית הַכְּנֶסֶת וְשֶׁל בֵּית הַמִּדְרָשׁ מְבָרְכִין עָלָיו, וְתַנְיָא אִידָךְ: אֵין מְבָרְכִין עָלָיו!

The Gemara cites another contradiction: **It was taught** in **one** *baraita*: During *havdala,* **one may recite a blessing over the light of a synagogue or a study hall;**[H] **and it was taught** in **another** *baraita*: **One may not recite a blessing over it.**

לָא קַשְׁיָא: הָא – דְּאִיכָּא אָדָם חָשׁוּב, הָא – דְּלֵיכָּא אָדָם חָשׁוּב.

The Gemara responds: This is **not difficult,** as **this** *baraita,* which prohibits reciting the blessing, is speaking in a case **where there is an important person**[N] in the synagogue and the fire is kindled in his honor and not to provide light; **that** *baraita,* which permits reciting the blessing, is speaking in a case **where there is no important person** present and the fire is kindled to provide light.

וְאִי בָּעֵית אֵימָא: הָא וְהָא דְּאִיכָּא אָדָם חָשׁוּב, וְלָא קַשְׁיָא: הָא דְּאִיכָּא חַזָּנָא, הָא דְּלֵיכָּא חַזָּנָא,

**And if you wish, say** instead that **this** *baraita* and **that** *baraita* are speaking in a case **where there is an important person** present in the synagogue, **and** this is **not difficult** because the contradiction can be resolved as follows: **This** *baraita,* which permits reciting the blessing, is speaking in a case **where there is a caretaker**[B] in the synagogue who uses the light; **that** *baraita,* which prohibits reciting the blessing, is speaking in a case **where there is no caretaker** and the light is kindled for purposes of honor.

וְאִי בָּעֵית אֵימָא: הָא וְהָא דְּאִיכָּא חַזָּנָא, וְלָא קַשְׁיָא: הָא דְּאִיכָּא סֶהֲרָא, וְהָא דְּלֵיכָּא סֶהֲרָא.

**And if you wish, say** instead that **this** *baraita* **and that** *baraita* are both referring to a case **where there is a caretaker** present in the synagogue **and** this is **not difficult** because the contradiction can be resolved as follows: **This** *baraita,* which prohibits reciting the blessing, is speaking in a case **where there is moonlight,** so the caretaker did not light the fire to provide light as the moonlight is sufficient; **that** *baraita,* which permits reciting the blessing, is speaking in a case **where there is no moonlight,** and the caretaker lights the fire to provide light.

תָּנוּ רַבָּנַן: הָיוּ יוֹשְׁבִין בְּבֵית הַמִּדְרָשׁ וְהֵבִיאוּ אוּר לִפְנֵיהֶם. בֵּית שַׁמַּאי אוֹמְרִים: כָּל אֶחָד וְאֶחָד מְבָרֵךְ לְעַצְמוֹ; וּבֵית הִלֵּל אוֹמְרִים: אֶחָד מְבָרֵךְ לְכוּלָּן, מִשּׁוּם שֶׁנֶּאֱמַר: ״בְּרׇב עָם הַדְרַת מֶלֶךְ״.

**The Sages taught** in a *baraita*: **People were seated in the study hall and they brought fire before them** at the conclusion of Shabbat. **Beit Shammai say: Each and every individual recites a blessing for himself; and Beit Hillel say: One recites a blessing on behalf of everyone**[HN] and the others answer amen. Beit Hillel's reasoning is **as it is stated: "The splendor of the King is in the multitude of the people"** (Proverbs 14:28). When everyone joins together to hear the blessing the name of God is glorified.

בִּשְׁלָמָא בֵּית הִלֵּל מְפָרְשִׁי טַעְמָא, אֶלָּא בֵּית שַׁמַּאי מַאי טַעְמָא? – קָסָבְרִי: מִפְּנֵי בִּיטּוּל בֵּית הַמִּדְרָשׁ.

The Gemara asks: **Granted, Beit Hillel,** they **explain** their **reasoning but what is the reason** for the opinion **of Beit Shammai** to prohibit reciting the blessing communally? The Gemara answers: **They hold** that it is prohibited **due to** the fact that it will lead to **suspension of** study in **the study hall.** Waiting for someone to recite the blessing will interrupt Torah study for several minutes.

תַּנְיָא נַמִי הָכִי: שֶׁל בֵּית רַבָּן גַּמְלִיאֵל לֹא הָיוּ אוֹמְרִים ״מַרְפֵּא״ בְּבֵית הַמִּדְרָשׁ מִפְּנֵי בִּיטּוּל בֵּית הַמִּדְרָשׁ.

**This** concern for disrupting Torah study **was also taught** in a *baraita*: The members of **the house of Rabban Gamliel would not say good health**[H] when someone sneezed **in the study hall, due to** the fact that it would lead to **suspension of** study in **the study hall.**

״אֵין מְבָרְכִין לֹא עַל הַנֵּר וְלֹא עַל הַבְּשָׂמִים שֶׁל מֵתִים״. מַאי טַעְמָא? נֵר – לְכָבוֹד הוּא דַּעֲבִידָא, בְּשָׂמִים – לַעֲבוּרֵי רֵיחָא הוּא דַּעֲבִידִי.

We learned in the mishna: **One may neither recite a blessing over the candle nor over the spices** designated to honor **the dead.**[H] The Gemara explains: **What is the reason?** Because a **candle** of the dead is **kindled for** the purpose of **honoring** the dead, not for light; **the spices** are **to neutralize the** bad **odor,**[H] not for their pleasant fragrance.

אָמַר רַב יְהוּדָה אָמַר רַב: כׇּל שֶׁמּוֹצִיאִין לְפָנָיו בַּיּוֹם וּבַלַּיְלָה אֵין מְבָרְכִין עָלָיו, וְכֹל שֶׁאֵין מוֹצִיאִין לְפָנָיו אֶלָּא בַּלַּיְלָה – מְבָרְכִין עָלָיו.

And **Rav Yehuda said** that **Rav said:** Any deceased **before whom** a candle **is taken out** both **by day and by night,** it is evident that the candle is for the purpose of honoring the deceased; therefore, **one may not recite a blessing over it. And any** deceased **before whom** a candle **is taken out only by night,** it is evident that the purpose of the candle is for its light alone, and **one may recite a blessing over it.**

## HALAKHA

**The light of a synagogue or a study hall** – אוֹר שֶׁל בֵּית הַכְּנֶסֶת וְשֶׁל בֵּית הַמִּדְרָשׁ: There are differing opinions with regard to this issue. Some say that if an important person is present in the synagogue, one may recite a blessing as the light is for his needs (*Tosafot*). Others say the opposite. Some ruled in accordance with the first opinion (*Shulḥan Arukh HaRav*). If a caretaker was eating there, it is permitted. But if the light of the moon was shining there, one may not recite a blessing over the light of the synagogue. In general, if the lights were for the sake of illumination rather than honor, one is permitted to recite a blessing (Rambam *Sefer Zemanim, Hilkhot Shabbat* 29:26; *Shulḥan Arukh, Oraḥ Ḥayyim* 298:11).

**One recites a blessing on behalf of everyone** – אֶחָד מְבָרֵךְ לְכוּלָּן: One recites the blessing over light on behalf of everyone present, in accordance with the opinion of Beit Hillel (*Shulḥan Arukh, Oraḥ Ḥayyim* 298:14).

**Would not say good health** – לֹא הָיוּ אוֹמְרִים מַרְפֵּא: One should discuss only Torah matters in the study hall. Consequently, even saying good health to one who sneezed is prohibited. Some were lenient in this regard in later generations, as people became less vigilant in avoiding other matters in the study hall (*Shakh*; Rambam *Sefer HaMadda, Hilkhot Talmud Torah* 4:9; *Shulḥan Arukh, Yoreh De'a* 246:17).

**One may neither recite a blessing over the candle…of the dead** – אֵין מְבָרְכִין לֹא עַל הַנֵּר...שֶׁל מֵתִים: Over light kindled to honor the dead, even during the day, one may not recite a blessing. Over any light kindled for the sake of illumination, however, one may recite a blessing (*Shulḥan Arukh, Oraḥ Ḥayyim* 298:12).

**Spices made to neutralize the bad odor** – בְּשָׂמִים הָעֲשׂוּיִים לְמְנוֹעַ רֵיחַ: Over spices intended to neutralize bad odors, one may not recite a blessing (Rambam *Sefer Ahava, Hilkhot Berakhot* 9:8; *Shulḥan Arukh, Oraḥ Ḥayyim* 217:2).

## NOTES

**Where there is an important person** – דְּאִיכָּא אָדָם חָשׁוּב: Some explain: If an important person is present in the synagogue, the fire was clearly kindled to provide light. If not, the light is to honor the synagogue and one may not recite a blessing over it (Rabbeinu Ḥananel, *ge'onim*).

**One recites a blessing on behalf of everyone** – אֶחָד מְבָרֵךְ לְכוּלָּן: Ostensibly, wouldn't it be preferable for each one to recite his own blessing as is the case with regard to Grace after Meals? Since the blessing over the candle is not a blessing over pleasure or benefit derived, but rather a blessing of thanks to God for creating this phenomenon, blessings of thanksgiving are best recited in multitudes of people, as then it is much more obvious (*Penei Yehoshua*).

## BACKGROUND

**Caretaker** – חַזָּנָא: This is the synagogue caretaker, the person charged with organizing and cleaning the synagogue and performing similar duties. He would sometimes reside in the synagogue, which was generally out of town, in order to better perform his tasks. The use of the term *ḥazzan* in the sense of communal prayer leader is a much later development.

אָמַר רַב הוּנָא: בְּשָׂמִים שֶׁל בֵּית הַכִּסֵּא, וְשֶׁמֶן הָעָשׂוּי לְהַעֲבִיר אֶת הַזּוּהֲמָא – אֵין מְבָרְכִין עָלָיו.

Similarly, **Rav Huna said: Over spices** used to deodorize **the bathroom and** fragrant **oil** intended **to remove filth, one may not recite a blessing** as they are not used for their pleasant fragrance.

לְמֵימְרָא, דְּכָל הֵיכָא דְּלָאו לְרֵיחָא עֲבִידָא לָא מְבָרְכִין עִלָּוֵיהּ, מֵתִיבִי: הַנִּכְנָס לַחֲנוּתוֹ שֶׁל בַּשָּׂם וְהֵרִיחַ רֵיחַ, אֲפִילּוּ יָשַׁב שָׁם כׇּל הַיּוֹם כּוּלּוֹ – אֵינוֹ מְבָרֵךְ אֶלָּא פַּעַם אֶחָד, נִכְנָס וְיָצָא, נִכְנָס וְיָצָא – מְבָרֵךְ עַל כׇּל פַּעַם וּפַעַם; וְהָא הָכָא דְּלָאו לְרֵיחָא הוּא דַּעֲבִידָא וְקָמְבָרֵךְ!

The Gemara asks: **Is that to say** that any case **where it is not used for** its pleasant **fragrance, one may not recite a blessing over it?** The Gemara **raises an objection** based on the *Tosefta*: **One who enters the store of a perfumer,**[H] **and smelled a fragrance, even if he sat there throughout the entire day, he only recites a blessing once.** However, **if one entered and exited, entered and exited, he recites a blessing on each and every occasion. Isn't** it a case **here, where** the spices **are not intended for fragrance,** as they are not used to improve the scent in the store, **and,** nevertheless, **one recites a blessing?**

אִין, לְרֵיחָא נַמִי הוּא דַּעֲבִידָא, כִּי הֵיכִי דְּנֵירְחוּ אֱינָשֵׁי וְנֵיתוּ וְנִזְבּוּן מִינֵּיהּ.

The Gemara responds: **Yes,** in this case the spices **are also intended for fragrance;** they are used to generate a scent in the store **so that people will smell** them **and come and purchase from him.**

תָּנוּ רַבָּנַן: הָיָה מְהַלֵּךְ חוּץ לַכְּרַךְ וְהֵרִיחַ רֵיחַ, אִם רוֹב נׇכְרִים – אֵינוֹ מְבָרֵךְ, אִם רוֹב יִשְׂרָאֵל – מְבָרֵךְ. רַבִּי יוֹסֵי אוֹמֵר: אֲפִילּוּ רוֹב יִשְׂרָאֵל נַמִי אֵינוֹ מְבָרֵךְ, מִפְּנֵי שֶׁבְּנוֹת יִשְׂרָאֵל מְקַטְּרוֹת לִכְשָׁפִים.

**The Sages taught** in a *baraita*: **One who was walking outside a city and smelled a scent; if the majority** of the town's residents **are gentiles he may not recite a blessing** over the scent, but **if the majority are Jews, he may recite a blessing. Rabbi Yosei says: Even if the majority are Jews, one may not recite a blessing,** as **the daughters of Israel burn incense to witchcraft** and the spices were certainly made for witchcraft, not for their fragrance.

אַטּוּ כּוּלְּהוּ לִכְשָׁפִים מְקַטְּרָן?! – הָוֵה לַהּ מִיעוּטָא לִכְשָׁפִים, וּמִיעוּטָא נַמִי לְגַמֵּר אֶת הַכֵּלִים, אִשְׁתַּכַּח רוּבָּא דְּלָאו לְרֵיחָא עָבִיד, וְכׇל רוּבָּא דְּלָאו לְרֵיחָא עָבִיד – לָא מְבָרֵךְ.

The Gemara asks: **Is that to say that they all burn incense to witchcraft?** Rather, **there is a minority** of people who burn incense **to witchcraft, and a** different **minority** who burn spices in order **to perfume** their **garments with incense.**[H] **A majority,** therefore, exists that **does not use it for fragrance, and in a case where the majority does not use it for fragrance, one does not recite a blessing.**

אָמַר רַבִּי חִיָּיא בַּר אַבָּא אָמַר רַבִּי יוֹחָנָן: הַמְהַלֵּךְ בְּעַרְבֵי שַׁבָּתוֹת בִּטְבֶרְיָא וּבְמוֹצָאֵי שַׁבָּתוֹת בְּצִפּוֹרִי וְהֵרִיחַ רֵיחַ – אֵינוֹ מְבָרֵךְ, מִפְּנֵי שֶׁחֶזְקָתוֹ אֵינוֹ עָשׂוּי אֶלָּא לְגַמֵּר בּוֹ אֶת הַכֵּלִים.

Similarly, **Rabbi Ḥiyya bar Abba said** that **Rabbi Yoḥanan said: One who walks on Shabbat eve in Tiberias**[B] **or at the conclusion of Shabbat in Tzippori,**[B] **and smelled the scent** of incense **may not recite a blessing, as the presumption is** that **it was intended to perfume garments.**

תָּנוּ רַבָּנַן: הָיָה מְהַלֵּךְ בְּשׁוּק שֶׁל עֲבוֹדָה זָרָה, נִתְרַצָּה לְהָרִיחַ – הֲרֵי זֶה חוֹטֵא.

On a related note, the Gemara cites the following: **The Sages taught** in a *baraita*: **One who was walking in the marketplace of idolators and willingly smelled** the incense wafting there, **he is a sinner,** as he should not have the intention to smell it.

Perek **VIII**
Daf **53** Amud **b**

״וְאֵין מְבָרְכִין עַל הַנֵּר עַד שֶׁיֵּאוֹתוּ״.

We learned in the mishna: **And one does not recite the blessing over the candle until he derives benefit** from its light.

אָמַר רַב יְהוּדָה אָמַר רַב: לֹא ״יֵאוֹתוּ״ יֵאוֹתוּ מַמָּשׁ אֶלָּא: כֹּל שֶׁאִילּוּ עוֹמֵד בְּקָרוֹב וּמִשְׁתַּמֵּשׁ לְאוֹרָהּ וַאֲפִילּוּ בְּרִיחוּק מָקוֹם. וְכֵן אָמַר רַב אָשֵׁי: בְּרִיחוּק מָקוֹם שָׁנִינוּ.

**Rav Yehuda said** that **Rav said: Benefit does not** mean that the one reciting the blessing must have **actually benefited** from the light of the candle. **Rather, as long as one could stand close** to the candle **and utilize its light,** anyone who sees it may recite a blessing over it, **even if** he is standing **at a distance. And similarly, Rav Ashi said: We learned** this *halakha*, that one may recite a blessing over the light of a candle even with regard to those standing **in a place that is distant.**

מֵיתִיבִי: הָיְתָה לוֹ נֵר טְמוּנָה בְּחֵיקוֹ אוֹ בְּפָנָס, אוֹ שֶׁרָאָה שַׁלְהֶבֶת וְלֹא נִשְׁתַּמֵּשׁ לְאוֹרָהּ, אוֹ נִשְׁתַּמֵּשׁ לְאוֹרָהּ וְלֹא רָאָה שַׁלְהֶבֶת – אֵינוֹ מְבָרֵךְ עַד שֶׁיִּרְאֶה שַׁלְהֶבֶת וְיִשְׁתַּמֵּשׁ לְאוֹרָהּ;

The Gemara **raises an objection** from a *Tosefta*: **One who had a candle hidden in his lap** or placed **inside an opaque lamp,**[H] **or if he saw a flame and did not utilize its light, or if he utilized its light and did not see a flame, may not recite a blessing until he** both **sees the flame and utilizes its light.**

**HALAKHA**

**One who enters the store of a perfumer – הַנִּכְנָס לַחֲנוּתוֹ שֶׁל בַּשָּׂם:** One who enters the store of a perfumer recites: Who creates types of spices. If one exits the store with no intention to return and reenters several times, he recites a blessing each time he enters (Rambam *Sefer Ahava, Hilkhot Berakhot* 9:5; *Shulḥan Arukh, Oraḥ Ḥayyim* 217:1).

**Incense to perfume garments – רֵיחַ לְמוּגְמָר:** One does not recite a blessing over incense used to perfume garments (Rambam *Sefer Ahava, Hilkhot Berakhot* 9:8; *Shulḥan Arukh, Oraḥ Ḥayyim* 217:3).

**BACKGROUND**

**Tiberias – טְבֶרְיָא:** The city of Tiberias was founded in the year 21 CE by Herod Antipas and was named for the Roman emperor, Tiberius. However, the city was constructed upon the ruins of an ancient settlement, which, according to most opinions, was the biblical city of Rakkat (Joshua 19:35). There is a discussion among the Sages with regard to the graves located there, which led to a prohibition against priests living there.

**Tzippori – צִפּוֹרִי:** Tzippori is located in central Lower Galilee. It was destroyed after the death of Herod, but was later reconstructed in great splendor. At the conclusion of the tannaitic period, concurrent with the development and growth of the Jewish settlement in the Galilee, the city rose in prominence. Rabbi Yehuda HaNasi moved there and transferred the seat of the Sanhedrin there as well, transforming the city into a Torah center for an extended period. During the period that the Jerusalem Talmud was redacted, Tzippori continued to be a significant urban center in Lower Galilee.

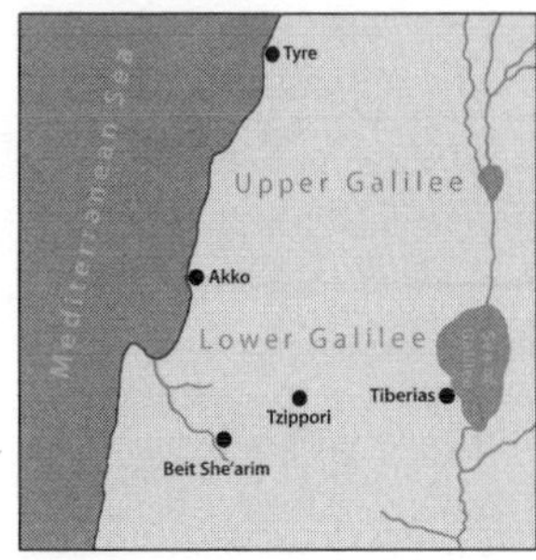

Map of Galilee

**HALAKHA**

**One who had a candle hidden in his lap or placed inside an opaque lamp, etc. – הָיְתָה לוֹ נֵר טְמוּנָה בְּחֵיקוֹ אוֹ בְּפָנָס וכו׳:** One may not recite a blessing over a light until he sees it and can make use of its light, e.g., to distinguish between two coins (*Mishna Berura*). Consequently, if the light was placed in one's lap or inside a lamp creating a situation where the flame cannot be seen but the light can be used, or if the flame can be seen but the light cannot be used, one may not recite: Who creates the lights of the fire, in accordance with the conclusion of the Gemara (*Shulḥan Arukh, Oraḥ Ḥayyim* 298:15).

LANGUAGE

*Pundeyon* – פּוּנְדְּיוֹן: This refers to a coin worth two *issarim*; in Latin, dupondius.

BACKGROUND

*Pundeyon* – פּוּנְדְּיוֹן:

*Pundeyon* of the Roman emperor Tiberius

A coin of Tiberias – מַטְבֵּעַ שֶׁל טְבֶרְיָה:

Tiberias coins on which the name of the city was written

A coin of Tzippori – מַטְבֵּעַ שֶׁל צִפּוֹרִי:

Tzippori coin on which the name of the town was written, from the reign of the Roman emperor Trajan

בִּשְׁלָמָא מִשְׁתַּמֵּשׁ לְאוֹרָהּ וְלֹא רָאָה שַׁלְהֶבֶת – מַשְׁכַּחַתְּ לַהּ דְּקָיְימָא בְּקֶרֶן זָוִית, אֶלָּא רָאָה שַׁלְהֶבֶת וְלֹא נִשְׁתַּמֵּשׁ לְאוֹרָהּ הֵיכִי מַשְׁכַּחַתְּ לַהּ, לָאו דְּמִרַחֲקָא?

The Gemara first clarifies the content of the *Tosefta* itself: **Granted,** a case where one **utilizes its light and did not see a flame, can be found where** the flame **is situated** around **a corner,** illuminating the area but hidden from his view. But **how can** a case where one **saw a flame and did not utilize its light be found? Is it not** referring to a case **where one is distant?** Apparently, one must actually utilize the flame; merely having the potential to utilize it is not sufficient.

לָא, כְּגוֹן דְּעָמְיָא וְאָזְלָא.

The Gemara rejects this: **No.** This refers to **a case where** the flame is **gradually dimming.** One sees the flame, but is unable to utilize its light.

תָּנוּ רַבָּנַן: גֶּחָלִים לוֹחֲשׁוֹת – מְבָרְכִין עֲלֵיהֶן, אוֹמְמוֹת – אֵין מְבָרְכִין עֲלֵיהֶן. הֵיכִי דָּמֵי לוֹחֲשׁוֹת? – אָמַר רַב חִסְדָּא: כֹּל שֶׁאִילּוּ מַכְנִיס לְתוֹכָן קֵיסָם וְדוֹלֶקֶת מֵאֵילֶיהָ.

**The Sages taught** in a *baraita*: **One may recite a blessing over smoldering coals**[H] just as he does over a candle; however, **over dimming** [*omemot*] coals, **one may not recite a blessing.** The Gemara asks: **What are the circumstances of smoldering coals? Rav Ḥisda said:** Smoldering coals are **any** coals **that, if one places a wood chip among them, it ignites on its own** without fanning the flame.

אִיבַּעְיָא לְהוּ: אוֹמְמוֹת אוֹ עוֹמְמוֹת?

With regard to the wording of the *baraita*, the Gemara **raises a dilemma:** Does the *baraita* say *omemot* beginning with an *alef*, or *omemot* beginning with an *ayin*?

תָּא שְׁמַע, דְּאָמַר רַב חִסְדָּא בַּר אַבְדִּימִי: ״אֲרָזִים לֹא עֲמָמֻהוּ בְּגַן אֱלֹהִים״.

**Come and hear** a resolution, **as Rav Ḥisda bar Avdimi said:** The correct version is *omemot* beginning with an *ayin*, as it is stated: **"The cedars in the garden of God could not dim it** [*amamuhu*]" (Ezekiel 31:8).

וְרָבָא אָמַר: ״אוֹתוֹ״ מַמָּשׁ.

**And** with regard to the question whether or not one must actually benefit from the flame's light in order to recite a blessing, **Rava said:** When the mishna said **benefit,** it meant that he must **actually** derive benefit from the light.

וְכַמָּה? אָמַר עוּלָּא: כְּדֵי שֶׁיַּכִּיר בֵּין אִיסָּר לְפוּנְדְּיוֹן; חִזְקִיָּה אָמַר: כְּדֵי שֶׁיַּכִּיר בֵּין מְלוּזְמָא שֶׁל טְבֶרְיָא לִמְלוּזְמָא שֶׁל צִפּוֹרִי.

The Gemara asks: **And how** adjacent must one be in order to be considered to have derived benefit from the flame? **Ulla said: So that he can distinguish between an** *issar* **and a** *pundeyon*,[LB] two coins of the period. **Ḥizkiya said: So that he can distinguish between a weight** used in **Tiberias**[B] **and a weight** used in **Tzippori,**[B] which were slightly different.

רַב יְהוּדָה מְבָרֵךְ אַדְּבֵי אַדָּא דַּיָּילָא. רָבָא מְבָרֵךְ אַדְּבֵי גּוּרְיָא בַּר חָמָא. אַבָּיֵי מְבָרֵךְ אַדְּבֵי בַּר אֲבוּהּ.

The Gemara relates that the *amora'im* conducted themselves in accordance with their above-stated opinions. At the conclusion of Shabbat, **Rav Yehuda** would **recite a blessing over** the light **of the house of Adda, the servant,** which was far from his house. **Rava** would **recite a blessing over** the light **of the house of Gurya bar Ḥama,** which was adjacent to his house. **Abaye** would **recite a blessing over** the light **of the house of bar Avuh.**

אָמַר רַב יְהוּדָה אָמַר רַב: אֵין מְחַזְּרִין עַל הָאוּר כְּדֶרֶךְ שֶׁמְּחַזְּרִים עַל הַמִּצְוֹת. אָמַר רַבִּי זֵירָא: מֵרֵישׁ הֲוָה מְהַדַּרְנָא, כֵּיוָן דִּשְׁמַעְנָא לְהָא דְּרַב יְהוּדָה אָמַר רַב – אֲנָא נָמֵי לָא מְהַדַּרְנָא, אֶלָּא אִי מִקְּלַע לִי מִמֵּילָא – מְבָרֵיכְנָא.

**Rav Yehuda said** that **Rav said** a general halakhic principle: **One need not seek out light**[HN] at the conclusion of Shabbat **in the manner that one seeks out** other **mitzvot.** If no flame is available over which to recite a blessing, it does not prevent one from reciting *havdala*. And **Rav Zeira said: Initially I would seek out** light, **once I heard this** *halakha* that **Rav Yehuda said** that **Rav said, I too do not seek out** light. **However, if** a candle **happens** to become available **to me, I recite a blessing** over it.

HALAKHA

**Smoldering coals** – גֶּחָלִים לוֹחֲשׁוֹת: One may recite a blessing over the light of smoldering coals (Rambam *Sefer Zemanim, Hilkhot Shabbat* 29:26; *Shulḥan Arukh, Oraḥ Ḥayyim* 298:9).

**One need not seek out light** – אֵין מְחַזְּרִין עַל הָאוּר: There is no obligation to seek out a light in order to recite the blessing during *havdala* at the conclusion of Shabbat, in accordance with the opinion of Rav Yehuda (Rambam *Sefer Zemanim, Hilkhot Shabbat* 29:26; *Shulḥan Arukh, Oraḥ Ḥayyim* 298:1).

NOTES

**One need not seek out light** – אֵין מְחַזְּרִין עַל הָאוּר: This is because the blessing recited over the candle is merely to commemorate the creation of the first light; it is neither a fixed blessing of thanksgiving nor is it a genuine blessing made over pleasure or benefit derived. Therefore, it is secondary to the *havdala* blessing (*Tosefot Rabbi Yehuda HaḤasid*; *Tosefot HaRosh*).

"מִי שֶׁאָכַל" וכו׳. אָמַר רַב זְבִיד וְאִיתֵּימָא רַב דִּימִי בַּר אַבָּא: מַחֲלוֹקֶת בְּשָׁכַח, אֲבָל בְּמֵזִיד – דִּבְרֵי הַכֹּל יַחֲזוֹר לִמְקוֹמוֹ וִיבָרֵךְ.

Our mishna cited a dispute regarding **one who ate** and forgot and did not recite a blessing;[H] Beit Shammai say: He returns to the place where he ate and recites the blessing. Beit Hillel say: That is unnecessary. He recites the blessing at the place where he remembered. **Rav Zevid said and some say Rav Dimi bar Abba** said: This **dispute is** only with regard to a case **where one forgot** to recite the blessing, **but** if he did so **intentionally, everyone agrees that he must return to** the **place** where **he** ate **and recite a blessing.**

פְּשִׁיטָא, "וְשָׁכַח" תְּנַן!

The Gemara asks: **This is obvious. We learned** in the mishna: **And forgot,** not if he did so intentionally.

מַהוּ דְּתֵימָא: הוּא הַדִּין אֲפִילּוּ בְּמֵזִיד, וְהַאי דְּקָתָנֵי "וְשָׁכַח" – לְהוֹדִיעֲךָ כֹּחָן דְּבֵית שַׁמַּאי, קָמַשְׁמַע לָן.

The Gemara explains: **Lest you say** that **the same is true,** that Beit Hillel permit one to recite a blessing without returning to the place where he ate, **even** in a case where he **willfully** did not recite a blessing, **and that which was taught: And forgot, is to convey the far-reaching** nature **of** the opinion of **Beit Shammai,**[N] who require him to return to the place where he ate even if he forgot, Rav Zevid **teaches us** that there is no disagreement in that case.

תַּנְיָא, אָמְרוּ לָהֶם בֵּית הִלֵּל לְבֵית שַׁמַּאי: לְדִבְרֵיכֶם מִי שֶׁאָכַל בְּרֹאשׁ הַבִּירָה וְשָׁכַח וְיָרַד וְלֹא בֵּרַךְ, יַחֲזוֹר לְרֹאשׁ הַבִּירָה וִיבָרֵךְ?! – אָמְרוּ לָהֶן בֵּית שַׁמַּאי לְבֵית הִלֵּל: לְדִבְרֵיכֶם, מִי שֶׁשָּׁכַח אַרְנָקִי בְּרֹאשׁ הַבִּירָה, לֹא יַעֲלֶה וְיִטְּלֶנָּה?! לִכְבוֹד עַצְמוֹ הוּא עוֹלֶה – לִכְבוֹד שָׁמַיִם לֹא כׇּל שֶׁכֵּן?

**It was taught** in a *baraita* that **Beit Hillel said to Beit Shammai: According to your statement, one who ate atop** the Temple Mount, **God's chosen place of residence, and forgot and descended without reciting a blessing, must he return to the top of** the Temple Mount, **God's chosen place of residence, to recite a blessing? Beit Shammai said to Beit Hillel:** Why not? **And according to your statement, one who forgot his purse atop** the Temple Mount, **God's chosen place of residence, would he not ascend to retrieve it? If one ascends in deference to his own** needs, **all the more so** he should ascend **in deference to Heaven.**

הָנְהוּ תְּרֵי תַּלְמִידֵי, חַד עֲבֵיד בְּשׁוֹגֵג כְּבֵית שַׁמַּאי – וְאַשְׁכַּח אַרְנְקָא דְּדַהֲבָא, וְחַד עֲבֵיד בְּמֵזִיד כְּבֵית הִלֵּל – וְאַכְלֵיהּ אַרְיָא.

The Gemara relates: There were **these two students** who ate and did not recite a blessing. **One of them did so unwittingly,** and, **in accordance with** the opinion of **Beit Shammai,** returned to where he ate,**and found a purse of gold. One of them did so intentionally,** and, **in accordance with** the opinion of **Beit Hillel,** albeit in circumstances where they agree with Beit Shammai, did not return **and a lion ate him.**

רַבָּה בַּר בַּר חָנָה הֲוָה קָאָזֵל בְּשַׁיַּירְתָּא, אֲכַל וְאִשְׁתְּלִי וְלָא בָּרֵיךְ; אֲמַר: הֵיכִי אַעֲבֵיד? אִי אָמֵינָא לְהוּ "אַנְשַׁאי לְבָרֵךְ" – אָמְרוּ לִי: בָּרֵיךְ, כׇּל הֵיכָא דִּמְבָרְכַתְּ לְרַחֲמָנָא מְבָרְכַתְּ. מוּטָב דְּאָמֵינָא לְהוּ אַנְשַׁאי יוֹנָה דְּדַהֲבָא. אֲמַר לְהוּ: אַנְטְרוּ לִי, דְּאַנְשַׁאי יוֹנָה דְּדַהֲבָא. אָזֵיל וּבָרֵיךְ וְאַשְׁכַּח יוֹנָה דְּדַהֲבָא,

The Gemara further relates: **Rabba bar bar Ḥana was once traveling with a caravan. He ate and forgot and did not recite a blessing. He said** to himself: **What shall I do? If I say to them: I forgot to recite a blessing, they** will **say to me to recite a blessing** here, as **wherever you recite a blessing, you recite a blessing to God.** It is **better that I say to them: I forgot a golden dove.** Then they will wait for me while I retrieve it. **He said to them: Wait for me, as I forgot a golden dove. He went and recited a blessing and found a golden dove.**

וּמַאי שְׁנָא יוֹנָה – דִּמְתִילִי כְּנֶסֶת יִשְׂרָאֵל לְיוֹנָה, דִּכְתִיב "כַּנְפֵי יוֹנָה נֶחְפָּה בַכֶּסֶף וְאֶבְרוֹתֶיהָ בִּירַקְרַק חָרוּץ" מַה יּוֹנָה אֵינָהּ נִיצּוֹלֶת אֶלָּא בִּכְנָפֶיהָ, אַף יִשְׂרָאֵל אֵין נִיצּוֹלִין אֶלָּא בְּמִצְוֹת.

The Gemara asks: **What is different** about a **dove,** that he specifically said that that was the object that he forgot? The Gemara answers: **Because the community of Israel is likened to a dove, as it is written: "The wings of a dove, covered in silver, and its pinions with the shimmer of gold"** (Psalms 68:14). The Gemara explains the parable: **Just as a dove is saved** from its enemies **only by its wings, so too, Israel is saved only by** the merit of the **mitzvot.**

"עַד אֵימָתַי הוּא" וכו׳.

We learned in the mishna: **And until when does he** recite the blessing? Until the food is digested in his intestines.

כַּמָּה שִׁיעוּר עִכּוּל? – אָמַר רַבִּי יוֹחָנָן: כׇּל זְמַן שֶׁאֵינוֹ רָעֵב וְרֵישׁ לָקִישׁ אָמַר: כׇּל זְמַן שֶׁיִּצְמָא מֵחֲמַת אֲכִילָתוֹ.

The Gemara asks: **What is the duration of digestion?**[H] **Rabbi Yoḥanan said:** As long as **he is not** yet **hungry** again. **And Reish Lakish said: As long as he is thirsty due to his eating.**

אֲמַר לֵיהּ רַב יֵימַר בַּר שְׁלַמְיָא לְמָר זוּטְרָא, וְאָמְרִי לַהּ רַב יֵימַר בַּר שֵׁיזָבִי לְמָר זוּטְרָא: מִי אֲמַר רֵישׁ לָקִישׁ הָכִי? וְהָאָמַר רַב אַמִּי אָמַר רֵישׁ לָקִישׁ: כַּמָּה שִׁיעוּר עִכּוּל – כְּדֵי לְהַלֵּךְ אַרְבַּע מִילִין!

**Rav Yeimar bar Shelamya said to Mar Zutra, and some say** that it was **Rav Yeimar bar Sheizevi** who said to **Mar Zutra: Did Reish Lakish say that? Didn't Rav Ami say** that **Reish Lakish said: What is the duration of digestion? As long as** it takes **to walk four** *mil*?

**HALAKHA**

One who ate and forgot and did not recite a blessing – אָכַל וְלֹא בֵּרַךְ: The authorities disagree with regard to the conclusions that result from this *halakha*. Some say that one who erred and failed to recite a blessing need not return, but one who did so intentionally must return. If he did not return, he fulfilled his obligation after-the-fact (Rambam). Others say that even one who erred and failed to recite a blessing must return, although, if he did not return, he nevertheless fulfilled his obligation. One who did so intentionally and did not return did not fulfill his obligation (Rosh). The consensus is that one must return, although if he did not and recited a blessing elsewhere, he fulfilled his obligation (*Magen Avraham; Taz; Be'er Heitev; Shulḥan Arukh HaRav*; Rambam *Sefer Ahava, Hilkhot Berakhot* 4:1; *Shulḥan Arukh, Oraḥ Ḥayyim* 184:1).

The duration of digestion – שִׁיעוּר עִכּוּל: One may recite Grace after Meals until the food is digested in his intestines. Authorities disagree with regard to the duration of digestion. Some say that after a sizable meal it is until one becomes hungry again, in accordance with the opinion of Rabbi Yoḥanan, and after a meager meal it is the length of time it takes to walk four *mil*, as Rabbi Yoḥanan and Reish Lakish did not dispute that point (*Taz*). Others are more stringent and hold that after a meager meal one must recite a blessing immediately (*Magen Avraham*; Rambam *Sefer Ahava, Hilkhot Berakhot* 2:14; *Shulḥan Arukh, Oraḥ Ḥayyim* 184:5).

**NOTES**

To convey the far-reaching nature of the opinion of Beit Shammai – לְהוֹדִיעֲךָ כֹּחָן דְּבֵית שַׁמַּאי: It would have been equally pertinent to convey the far-reaching nature of the opinion of Beit Hillel, especially as that would underscore the lenient, rather than the stringent, opinion. However, since the practical *halakha* in this case is in accordance with the opinion of Beit Shammai, as even Beit Hillel agreed that one who wishes to conduct himself in accordance with the opinion of Beit Shammai is praiseworthy, the Gemara sought to clarify their opinion (*Ḥefetz Hashem*).

לָא קַשְׁיָא: כָּאן בַּאֲכִילָה מְרוּבָּה, כָּאן בַּאֲכִילָה מוּעֶטֶת.

The Gemara answers: This is **not difficult. Here,** where Reish Lakish said the duration is as long as it takes to walk four *mil,* is **in** a case where he ate **a sizable meal, here,** where Reish Lakish said the duration is as long as he remains thirsty, is **in** a case where he ate **a meager meal.**

״בָּא לָהֶן יַיִן״ וכו׳.

We learned in the mishna a tannaitic dispute with regard to a case where **wine came before** the diners after the meal, and we also learned in the mishna that one answers amen after a Jew recites a blessing even if he did not hear the entire blessing.

לְמֵימְרָא, דְּיִשְׂרָאֵל אַף עַל גַּב דְּלָא שָׁמַע כּוּלָּהּ בְּרָכָה עוֹנֶה, וְכִי לָא שָׁמַע הֵיכִי נָפֵיק!

The Gemara asks: **Is that to say that** if **a Jew** recites a blessing, **even though** one **did not hear the entire blessing, he responds** amen? **If he did not hear** the entire blessing, **how did he fulfill** his obligation?

אָמַר חִיָּיא בַּר רַב: בְּשֶׁלֹּא אָכַל עִמָּהֶן. וְכֵן אָמַר רַב נַחְמָן אָמַר רַבָּה בַּר אֲבוּהּ: בְּשֶׁלֹּא אָכַל עִמָּהֶן. אָמַר לֵיהּ רַב לְחִיָּיא בְּרֵיהּ: בְּרִי, חֲטוֹף וּבָרֵיךְ. וְכֵן אֲמַר רַב הוּנָא לְרַבָּה בְּרֵיהּ: חֲטוֹף וּבָרֵיךְ.

**Ḥiyya bar Rav said:** This is not a case where one seeks to fulfill his obligation by responding amen; rather, it is a case **where he did not eat with them** yet still wishes to answer amen to their blessing. **And so Rav Naḥman said** that **Rabba bar Avuh said:** It is a case **where he did not eat with them.** The Gemara relates: **Rav said to his son Ḥiyya: My son, seize** the opportunity **and recite a blessing** quickly.[H] **And similarly Rav Huna said to his son, Rabba, seize** the opportunity **and recite a blessing.**

לְמֵימְרָא, דִּמְבָרֵךְ עֲדִיף מִמַּאן דְּעָנֵי אָמֵן, וְהָתַנְיָא, רַבִּי יוֹסֵי אוֹמֵר: גָּדוֹל הָעוֹנֶה אָמֵן יוֹתֵר מִן הַמְבָרֵךְ!

The Gemara asks: **Is that to say that one who recites a blessing is preferable to one who answers amen? Wasn't it taught** in a *baraita* that **Rabbi Yosei says:** The reward of **the one who answers amen is greater**[N] **than** the reward of **the one who recites the blessing?**

אָמַר לֵיהּ רַבִּי נְהוֹרָאי: הַשָּׁמַיִם! כֵּן הוּא; תֵּדַע, שֶׁהֲרֵי גּוּלְיָירִין יוֹרְדִין וּמִתְגָּרִין בַּמִּלְחָמָה וְגִבּוֹרִים יוֹרְדִין וּמְנַצְּחִין.

**Rabbi Nehorai said to him: By Heavens,** an oath in the name of God, **it is so. Know** that this is true, **as the military assistants** [*gulyarin*][L] **descend to the** battlefield **and initiate the war and the mighty descend and prevail.** The amen that follows a blessing is compared to the mighty who join the war after the assistants, illustrating that answering amen is more significant than reciting the initial blessing.

תַּנָּאֵי הִיא, דְּתַנְיָא: אֶחָד הַמְבָרֵךְ וְאֶחָד הָעוֹנֶה אָמֵן בְּמַשְׁמָע, אֶלָּא שֶׁמְּמַהֲרִין לַמְבָרֵךְ יוֹתֵר מִן הָעוֹנֶה אָמֵן.

The Gemara responds: This is subject to **a tannaitic dispute, as it was taught** in a *baraita*: **Both the one who recites a blessing and the one who answers** amen **are included** among those who "stand up and bless" (Nehemiah 9:5), but **they hurry to** reward, i.e., **the one who recites the blessing, more than** they hurry to reward, i.e., **the one who answers amen.**

בָּעֵי מִינֵּיהּ שְׁמוּאֵל מֵרַב: מַהוּ לַעֲנוֹת אָמֵן אַחַר תִּינוֹקוֹת שֶׁל בֵּית רַבָּן? – אֲמַר לֵיהּ: אַחַר הַכֹּל עוֹנִין אָמֵן חוּץ מִתִּינוֹקוֹת שֶׁל בֵּית רַבָּן הוֹאִיל וּלְהִתְלַמֵּד עֲשׂוּיִין. וְהָנֵי מִילֵּי בִּדְלָא עִידָּן מִפְטַרַיְיהוּ, אֲבָל בְּעִידָּן מִפְטְרַיְיהוּ – עוֹנִין.

**Shmuel raised a dilemma before Rav: What is** the *halakha* with regard to **answering amen after** the blessings of **schoolchildren? Rav said to him: One answers amen following everyone** whom we hear recite a blessing, **except for schoolchildren,**[H] **as they** recite blessings merely in order **to learn** them, not as expressions of thanksgiving. **This applies** specifically **at a time when they are not fulfilling their obligation** with the recitation of the blessing, but are simply learning. **However, at a time when they are fulfilling their obligation** through the recitation of a blessing, **one answers** amen after their blessing.

תָּנוּ רַבָּנַן: שֶׁמֶן מְעַכֵּב אֶת הַבְּרָכָה, דִּבְרֵי רַבִּי זִילַאי; רַבִּי זִיוַאי אוֹמֵר: אֵינוֹ מְעַכֵּב; רַב אַחָא אוֹמֵר: שֶׁמֶן טוֹב מְעַכֵּב; רַבִּי זוּהֲמַאי אוֹמֵר: כְּשֵׁם שֶׁמְּזוֹהָם פָּסוּל לַעֲבוֹדָה – כָּךְ יָדַיִם מְזוֹהָמוֹת פְּסוּלוֹת לִבְרָכָה.

**The Sages taught** in a *baraita*: If one does not have **oil** to spread on and cleanse his hands after eating, this **prevents** him from reciting **the** Grace after Meals **blessing;** this is **the statement of Rabbi Zilai. Rabbi Zivai**[P] **says:** Lack of that **oil does not prevent one** from reciting Grace after Meals. **Rav Aḥa says:** Lack of **fine oil prevents one** from reciting Grace after Meals. One must wait until he rubs oil on his hands. **Rav Zuhamai says: Just as one who is filthy is unfit for Temple service,**[N] **so too are filthy hands unfit for** reciting **the** Grace after Meals **blessing.**

אֲמַר רַב נַחְמָן בַּר יִצְחָק: אֲנָא לָא זִילַאי וְלָא זִיוַאי וְלָא זוּהֲמַאי יָדַעְנָא, אֶלָּא מַתְנִיתָא יָדַעְנָא; דְּאָמַר רַב יְהוּדָה אָמַר רַב, וְאָמְרִי לַהּ בְּמַתְנִיתָא תָּנָא: ״וְהִתְקַדִּשְׁתֶּם״ – אֵלּוּ מַיִם רִאשׁוֹנִים, ״וִהְיִיתֶם קְדֹשִׁים״ – אֵלּוּ מַיִם אַחֲרוֹנִים, ״כִּי קָדוֹשׁ״ – זֶה שֶׁמֶן, ״אֲנִי ה׳ אֱלֹהֵיכֶם״ – זוֹ בְּרָכָה.

**Rav Naḥman bar Yitzḥak said** of this: **I do not know of Zilai or Zivai or Zuhamai; rather, I know a *baraita*, as Rav Yehuda said** that **Rav said, and some say** that it was **taught in a *baraita*:** It is stated: "And you shall sanctify yourselves, and you shall be holy, for holy am I, the Lord your God" (Leviticus 20:26). With regard to this verse, the Sages said: **And you shall sanctify yourselves, these are the first waters** with which one washes his hands before the meal; **and you shall be holy, these are the final waters;**[NH] **for holy, this is oil** which one spreads on his hands; **am I, the Lord your God, this is** the Grace after Meals **blessing.**

הדרן עלך אלו דברים

## HALAKHA

**Seize the opportunity and recite a blessing – חֲטוֹף וּבָרֵיךְ:** It is appropriate to make an effort to be given the cup of blessing in order to lead the *zimmun* before Grace after Meals, as per Rav Huna's advice to his son (*Shulḥan Arukh, Oraḥ Ḥayyim* 201:4).

**One answers amen following everyone whom we hear recite a blessing, except for schoolchildren – אַחַר הַכֹּל עוֹנִין אָמֵן חוּץ מִתִּינוֹקוֹת:** If one hears a blessing recited by any Jewish person, although he did not hear the entire blessing and although he is not obligated to recite that blessing, he must answer amen. However, one does not answer amen after blessings recited by children who are just learning to recite blessings. However, when children recite blessings which they are obligated to recite, one answers amen (Rambam *Sefer Ahava, Hilkhot Berakhot* 1:13; *Shulḥan Arukh, Oraḥ Ḥayyim* 215:2–3).

**Final waters – מַיִם אַחֲרוֹנִים:** Washing one's hands with final waters is required. Some say that in a place where there is no Sodomite salt one need not insist on final waters (*Tosafot*), and that is a common custom (*Magen Avraham*). According to the kabbalists, one should insist upon washing with final waters (Rambam *Sefer Ahava, Hilkhot Berakhot* 7:11–12; *Shulḥan Arukh, Oraḥ Ḥayyim* 181:1).

## NOTES

**The one who answers amen is greater – גָּדוֹל הָעוֹנֶה אָמֵן:** Some explain that the reward of one who answers amen is greater because he thereby completes the mitzva (*Tosefot HaRosh*).

**One who is filthy is unfit for Temple service – שֶׁמְּזוֹהָם פָּסוּל לַעֲבוֹדָה:** This refers to a filthy animal that is unfit as a sacrifice to God because it emits a bad odor.

**And you shall be holy, these are the final waters – וִהְיִיתֶם קְדֹשִׁים אֵלּוּ מַיִם אַחֲרוֹנִים:** This indicates that washing hands with the final waters is a mitzva due to sanctity, while other sources indicate that it is obligatory because of the danger posed by Sodomite salt, which is harmful to the eyes. Some explain that both reasons are correct; even when there is no danger from Sodomite salt, the mitzva remains (*Rabbanei Tzarfat*). Others explain that the mitzva due to sanctity applies to the one reciting the blessing, while the other diners, for whom the only reason is the Sodomite salt, may wait and wash their hands after reciting Grace after Meals (*She'iltot DeRav Aḥai; Talmidei Rabbeinu Yona*).

## LANGUAGE

**Military assistants [*gulyarin*] – גּוּלְיָירִין:** The meaning of this word and its origin are unclear. Some say that it is from the Latin galearius, meaning a soldier's servant. Others claim that it is from Greek. In any case, its imagery is based on the strategy of ancient armies, which, at the outset, dispatched light regiments to harass the enemy, after which they would deploy heavy battalions comprised of legions of mighty warriors who would determine the outcome of the battle.

## PERSONALITIES

**Rabbi Zilai, Rabbi Zivai – רַבִּי זִילַאי, רַבִּי זִיוַאי:** The strange names of these Sages, along with the fact that they do not appear in any other sources, leads one to conjecture that Zivai, Zilai, and Zuhamai are nicknames rather than the actual names of these individuals. It seems that certain Sages who only stated a single well-known *halakha* came to be known by that *halakha*. The *halakha* concerning disqualification due to filth, *zohama*, led to its author being called Rav Zuhamai. Apparently, that is the case with regard to Zilai and Zivai as well (Rabbi Tzvi Hirsch Ḥayyot).

# Summary of **Perek VIII**

This chapter reviewed two sets of problems based on disputes between Beit Shammai and Beit Hillel with regard to meal protocol.

The first set of problems dealt primarily with the *halakhot* of precedence in various components of a meal. These *halakhot* are tied to comprehensive halakhic frameworks associated primarily with the *halakhot* of sacrifices and ritual purity and impurity. As usual, the *halakha* was ruled in accordance with the opinion of Beit Hillel in all of these cases, with one exception. There too, due to variant readings, the ruling is not unequivocally in accordance with Beit Shammai. Although the considerations of both Beit Shammai and Beit Hillel are substantially similar, i.e., distancing oneself from all ritual impurity, both impurity of people and impurity of vessels, it can be said that Beit Hillel's primary emphasis is on distancing oneself from ritual impurity by Torah law, even if that entails a certain lack of vigilance vis-à-vis other forms of ritual impurity.

Another dispute, with regard to the order in which various blessings are recited, especially those associated with *kiddush* and *havdala*, was not conclusively resolved in this chapter. Its conclusive resolution with regard to its most complex circumstance, i.e., a Festival that begins at the conclusion of Shabbat when *kiddush* and *havdala* converge, can be found in tractate *Pesaḥim*, where the definitive order of the blessings is: Wine, *kiddush*, candle, *havdala*, and Who has given us life, etc.

Another set of problems discussed in great detail in this chapter is the blessing of *havdala* and the accompanying blessing over light. These blessings were highlighted because they constitute a basis for both blessings recited prior to fulfilling mitzvot and blessings of praise and thanksgiving, which are discussed in Chapter Nine. Among the significant halakhic conclusions drawn with regard to this matter is the fact that one may recite the blessings only over spices and candles that were specifically designated for that purpose. One may neither recite the blessings over incidental fragrances and lights nor over those that have an element of prohibition.

# Introduction to **Perek IX**

In this chapter, which concludes tractate *Berakhot*, many different types of blessings are discussed. Despite the differences between these blessings, there are fundamental issues common to all of these blessings that fuse them into a single unit.

The blessings in this chapter are neither blessings of enjoyment nor blessings over mitzvot. A significant number of them constitute the independent category of blessings of thanksgiving for God's beneficence.

In addition to the blessings of thanksgiving, there are several other blessings that do not fall into this category. Nevertheless, all those blessings share a common denominator. They all instruct us that anything that deviates from the norm obligates one to recite a blessing, be it a permanent fixture in nature, e.g., mountains and seas; natural phenomena, e.g., thunder and lightning; unique creatures; or events of extreme benevolence, e.g., miracles or tragic events. The significance of these blessings is the acknowledgement that everything in this world is the work of God. We offer thanks for His goodness and miracles and accept the tragedies and disasters.

Fundamentally, these blessings are not expressions of thanks. Rather, they are declarations of a faith-based approach that the Creator directs and supervises everything. Consequently, everything that transpires in the world should be tied to the understanding that "it is the Lord that does all these things" (Isaiah 45:7).

The blessings recited over unique phenomena come to underscore God's involvement in every mundane occurrence as well. The epitome of this approach is the incorporation of God's name into the standard greeting exchanged when people meet. Although one might consider the introduction of God's name into routine exchanges as belittling His greatness, because of the rationale implicit in the verse: "It is time to work for the Lord; they have made void Your Torah" (Psalms 119:126), attributing everything in the world to God was made top priority.

The vast topic of dreams and their interpretation, which arises in this chapter incidentally, is based upon the same fundamental perception that there is nothing in our existence that is meaningless. One must seek meaning and significance in even ethereal matters like dreams. Once meaning is ascertained, it should serve as a road map to guide the dreamer along the path of his life.

This mishna, which includes all of this chapter's *mishnayot*, contains a series of blessings and *halakhot* that are not recited at specific times, but rather in response to various experiences and events.

מתני׳ הָרוֹאֶה מָקוֹם שֶׁנַּעֲשׂוּ בּוֹ נִסִּים לְיִשְׂרָאֵל, אוֹמֵר: ״בָּרוּךְ... שֶׁעָשָׂה נִסִּים לַאֲבוֹתֵינוּ בַּמָּקוֹם הַזֶּה״. מָקוֹם שֶׁנֶּעֶקְרָה מִמֶּנּוּ עֲבוֹדָה זָרָה, אוֹמֵר ״בָּרוּךְ... שֶׁעָקַר עֲבוֹדָה זָרָה מֵאַרְצֵנוּ״.

**MISHNA** **One who sees a place where miracles occurred on Israel's behalf recites: Blessed**[H]**... Who performed miracles for our forefathers in this place.** One who sees **a place from which idolatry was eradicated recites: Blessed... Who eradicated idolatry from our land.**

עַל הַזִּיקִין, וְעַל הַזְּוָעוֹת, וְעַל הָרְעָמִים, וְעַל הָרוּחוֹת, וְעַל הַבְּרָקִים אוֹמֵר: ״בָּרוּךְ... שֶׁכֹּחוֹ וּגְבוּרָתוֹ מָלֵא עוֹלָם״. עַל הֶהָרִים וְעַל הַגְּבָעוֹת וְעַל הַיַּמִּים, וְעַל הַנְּהָרוֹת, וְעַל הַמִּדְבָּרוֹת אוֹמֵר ״בָּרוּךְ... עוֹשֵׂה בְרֵאשִׁית״. רַבִּי יְהוּדָה אוֹמֵר: הָרוֹאֶה אֶת הַיָּם הַגָּדוֹל אוֹמֵר: ״בָּרוּךְ שֶׁעָשָׂה אֶת הַיָּם הַגָּדוֹל״, בִּזְמַן שֶׁרוֹאֵהוּ לִפְרָקִים.

One who sees conspicuous natural occurrences recites a blessing. **For *zikin* and *zeva'ot*,** which the Gemara will discuss below, **for thunder,** gale force **winds, and lightning,** manifestations of the power of the Creator, one **recites: Blessed... Whose strength and power fill the world. For** extraordinary (Rambam) **mountains, hills, seas, rivers, and deserts, one recites: Blessed... Author of creation.**[NH] Consistent with his opinion that a separate blessing should be instituted for each individual species, **Rabbi Yehuda says: One who sees the great sea**[H] **recites** a special blessing: **Blessed... Who made the great sea.** As with all blessings of this type, one only recites it **when he sees** the sea **intermittently,**[H] not on a regular basis.

עַל הַגְּשָׁמִים, וְעַל בְּשׂוֹרוֹת טוֹבוֹת, אוֹמֵר ״בָּרוּךְ הַטּוֹב וְהַמֵּטִיב״. עַל בְּשׂוֹרוֹת רָעוֹת אוֹמֵר: ״בָּרוּךְ דַּיַּין הָאֱמֶת״. בָּנָה בַּיִת חָדָשׁ וְקָנָה כֵּלִים חֲדָשִׁים, אוֹמֵר: ״בָּרוּךְ... שֶׁהֶחֱיָינוּ וְקִיְּמָנוּ וְהִגִּיעָנוּ לַזְּמַן הַזֶּה״. מְבָרֵךְ עַל הָרָעָה מֵעֵין עַל הַטּוֹבָה, וְעַל הַטּוֹבָה מֵעֵין עַל הָרָעָה.

**For rain and** other **good tidings, one recites** the special blessing: **Blessed... Who is good and Who does good.** Even **for bad tidings,**[H] **one recites** a special blessing: **Blessed... the true Judge.** Similarly, when **one built a new house or purchased new vessels, he recites: Blessed... Who has given us life, sustained us, and brought us to this time.** The mishna articulates a general principle: **One recites a blessing for the bad** that befalls him **just as** he does **for the good.** In other words, one recites the appropriate blessing for the trouble that he is experiencing at present despite the fact that it may conceal some positive element in the future. **Similarly,** one must recite a blessing for **the good** that befalls him **just as for the bad.**

וְהַצּוֹעֵק לְשֶׁעָבַר – הֲרֵי זוֹ תְּפִלַּת שָׁוְא; הָיְתָה אִשְׁתּוֹ מְעוּבֶּרֶת, וְאוֹמֵר: ״יְהִי רָצוֹן שֶׁתֵּלֵד אִשְׁתִּי זָכָר״ – הֲרֵי זוֹ תְּפִלַּת שָׁוְא; הָיָה בָּא בַּדֶּרֶךְ וְשָׁמַע קוֹל צְוָחָה בָּעִיר, וְאוֹמֵר: ״יְהִי רָצוֹן שֶׁלֹּא תְּהֵא בְּתוֹךְ בֵּיתִי״ – הֲרֵי זוֹ תְּפִלַּת שָׁוְא.

The mishna states: **And one who cries out over the past** in an attempt to change that which has already occurred, **it is a vain prayer.** For example, **one whose wife was pregnant and he says: May it be** God's **will that my wife will give birth to a male child, it is a vain prayer.** Or **one who was walking on the path** home **and he heard the sound of a scream in the city, and he says: May it be** God's **will that** this scream **will not be from my house, it is a vain prayer.** In both cases, the event already occurred.

הַנִּכְנָס לִכְרַךְ מִתְפַּלֵּל שְׁתַּיִם, אַחַת בִּכְנִיסָתוֹ וְאַחַת בִּיצִיאָתוֹ; בֶּן עַזַּאי אוֹמֵר: אַרְבַּע, שְׁתַּיִם בִּכְנִיסָתוֹ וּשְׁתַּיִם בִּיצִיאָתוֹ, נוֹתֵן הוֹדָאָה עַל שֶׁעָבַר וְצוֹעֵק עַל הֶעָתִיד.

The Sages also said: **One who enters a large city,** the Gemara explains below that this is in a case where entering the city is dangerous, **recites two prayers: One upon his entrance,** that he may enter in peace, **and one upon his exit,** that he may leave in peace. **Ben Azzai says:** He recites **four** prayers, **two upon his entrance and two upon his exit.** In addition to praying that he may enter and depart in peace, he **gives thanks for the past and cries out** in prayer **for the future.**

חַיָּיב אָדָם לְבָרֵךְ עַל הָרָעָה כְּשֵׁם שֶׁמְּבָרֵךְ עַל הַטּוֹבָה, שֶׁנֶּאֱמַר: ״וְאָהַבְתָּ אֵת ה׳ אֱלֹהֶיךָ בְּכָל לְבָבְךָ״ וגו׳. ״בְּכָל לְבָבְךָ״ – בִּשְׁנֵי יְצָרֶיךָ, בְּיֵצֶר טוֹב וּבְיֵצֶר הָרָע; ״וּבְכָל נַפְשְׁךָ״ – אֲפִילּוּ הוּא נוֹטֵל אֶת נַפְשְׁךָ, ״וּבְכָל מְאֹדֶךָ״ – בְּכָל מָמוֹנְךָ. דָּבָר אַחֵר: ״בְּכָל מְאֹדֶךָ״ – בְּכָל מִדָּה וּמִדָּה שֶׁהוּא מוֹדֵד לְךָ הֱוֵי מוֹדֶה לוֹ.

The mishna articulates a general principle: **One is obligated to recite a blessing for the bad** that befalls him **just as he recites a blessing for the good** that befalls him, **as it is stated: "And you shall love the Lord your God with all your heart,** with all your soul, and with all your might" (Deuteronomy 6:5). The mishna explains this verse as follows: **"With all your heart"** means **with your two inclinations,**[N] **with your good inclination and your evil inclination,** both of which must be subjugated to the love of God. **With all your soul** means **even if God takes your soul. "And with all your might"** means **with all your money,** as money is referred to in the Bible as might. **Alternatively,** it may be explained that **"with all your might"** means **with every measure that He metes out to you;** whether it is good or troublesome, **thank Him.**

## HALAKHA

**One who sees a place where miracles occurred on Israel's behalf recites: Blessed, etc. – הָרוֹאֶה מָקוֹם שֶׁנַּעֲשׂוּ בּוֹ נִסִּים לְיִשְׂרָאֵל, אוֹמֵר: בָּרוּךְ וכו׳:** One who sees a place where miracles were performed on Israel's behalf recites: Blessed... Who performed miracles, etc. This blessing, like all other blessings recited over a sight, requires invocation of God's name and His sovereignty (Rambam *Sefer Ahava, Hilkhot Berakhot* 10:9; *Shulḥan Arukh, Oraḥ Ḥayyim* 218:1).

**Blessed...Author of creation – בָּרוּךְ...עוֹשֵׂה בְרֵאשִׁית:** One who sees mountains, hills, seas, rivers, or deserts recites: Blessed... Author of creation (Rambam *Sefer Ahava, Hilkhot Berakhot* 10:15; *Shulḥan Arukh, Oraḥ Ḥayyim* 228:1).

**One who sees the great sea – הָרוֹאֶה אֶת הַיָּם הַגָּדוֹל:** One who sees the great sea, a reference to the Mediterranean Sea, though some say it refers to an ocean (*Leḥem Ḥamudot, Magen Avraham*) recites: Blessed... Who makes the great sea (*Tur*). Some say that he recites the blessing in the past tense: Who made the great sea, in accordance with the opinion of Rav Yehuda (Rambam *Sefer Ahava, Hilkhot Berakhot* 10:15; *Shulḥan Arukh, Oraḥ Ḥayyim* 228:1).

**When he sees it intermittently – בִּזְמַן שֶׁרוֹאֵהוּ לִפְרָקִים:** Just as with all blessings recited over sight, one recites the blessing over the sea only if he did not see it for thirty days. The day that he saw it last and the day that he sees it now are not included in the tally (*Mishna Berura*; Rambam *Sefer Ahava, Hilkhot Berakhot* 10:15; *Shulḥan Arukh, Oraḥ Ḥayyim* 218:3, 224:13).

**For bad tidings – עַל בְּשׂוֹרוֹת רָעוֹת:** Over bad tidings, whether they are bad for him or for others (*Biur Halakha*), one recites: Blessed is the true Judge (Rambam *Sefer Ahava, Hilkhot Berakhot* 10:3; *Shulḥan Arukh, Oraḥ Ḥayyim* 222, 2).

## NOTES

**Blessed...Author of creation – בָּרוּךְ...עוֹשֵׂה בְרֵאשִׁית:** Since some of these phenomena, e.g., thunder and lightning, are formed anew each time, the formula of the blessing is in the present tense (*Tziyyun LeNefesh Ḥayya*).

**With your two inclinations – בִּשְׁנֵי יְצָרֶיךָ:** One fulfills the will of his Creator with his good inclination and combats the evil inclination to subdue it, thereby worshipping God with both inclinations (*Talmidei Rabbeinu Yona*).

לֹא יָקֵל אָדָם אֶת רֹאשׁוֹ כְּנֶגֶד שַׁעַר הַמִּזְרָח, שֶׁהוּא מְכֻוָּן כְּנֶגֶד בֵּית קׇדְשֵׁי הַקֳּדָשִׁים. וְלֹא יִכָּנֵס לְהַר הַבַּיִת בְּמַקְלוֹ, וּבְמִנְעָלוֹ, וּבְפוּנְדָּתוֹ, וּבְאָבָק שֶׁעַל רַגְלָיו, וְלֹא יַעֲשֶׂנּוּ קַפַּנְדַּרְיָא; וּרְקִיקָה – מִקַּל וָחוֹמֶר.

The mishna teaches several Temple-related *halakhot*. **One may not act irreverently** or conduct himself flippantly **opposite the eastern gate** of the Temple Mount, **which is aligned opposite the Holy of Holies.** In deference to the Temple, one **may not enter the Temple Mount with his staff, his shoes, his money belt [*punda*],**[L] or even **the dust on his feet. One may not make** the Temple **a shortcut** to pass through it, **and through an *a fortiori* inference,** all the more so **one may not spit** on the Temple Mount.

כׇּל חוֹתְמֵי בְּרָכוֹת שֶׁבַּמִּקְדָּשׁ הָיוּ אוֹמְרִים: "עַד הָעוֹלָם". מִשֶּׁקִּלְקְלוּ הַצְּדוֹקִים וְאָמְרוּ אֵין עוֹלָם אֶלָּא אֶחָד – הִתְקִינוּ שֶׁיְּהוּ אוֹמְרִים: "מִן הָעוֹלָם וְעַד הָעוֹלָם".

The mishna relates: **At the conclusion of all blessings** recited **in the Temple, those** reciting the blessing **would say:** Blessed are You Lord, God of Israel, **until everlasting [*haolam*],** the world. But **when the Sadducees**[B] **strayed and declared** that **there is but one world** and there is no World-to-Come, the Sages **instituted that** at the conclusion of the blessing **one recites: From everlasting [*haolam*] to everlasting [*haolam*].**

וְהִתְקִינוּ שֶׁיְּהֵא אָדָם שׁוֹאֵל אֶת שְׁלוֹם חֲבֵרוֹ בַּשֵּׁם, שֶׁנֶּאֱמַר: "וְהִנֵּה בֹעַז בָּא מִבֵּית לֶחֶם וַיֹּאמֶר לַקּוֹצְרִים: ה׳ עִמָּכֶם, וַיֹּאמְרוּ לוֹ: יְבָרֶכְךָ ה׳"; וְאוֹמֵר: "ה׳ עִמְּךָ גִּבּוֹר הֶחָיִל"; וְאוֹמֵר: "אַל תָּבוּז כִּי זָקְנָה אִמֶּךָ"; וְאוֹמֵר: "עֵת לַעֲשׂוֹת לַה׳ הֵפֵרוּ תּוֹרָתֶךָ". רַבִּי נָתָן אוֹמֵר: הֵפֵרוּ תּוֹרָתֶךָ מִשּׁוּם עֵת לַעֲשׂוֹת לַה׳.

The Sages also **instituted that one should greet another in the name** of God,[N] i.e., one should mention God's name in his greeting, **as it is stated: "And presently Boaz came from Bethlehem and said to the harvesters, The Lord is with you, and they said to him, May the Lord bless you"** (Ruth 2:4). **And it says:** "And the angel of God appeared to him **and said to him, God is with you, mighty man of valor"** (Judges 6:12). **And it says: "And despise not your mother when she is old"** (Proverbs 23:22), i.e. one must not neglect customs which he inherits. **And** lest you say that mentioning God's name is prohibited, **it says: "It is time to work for the Lord; they have made void Your Torah"** (Psalms 119:126), i.e., it is occasionally necessary to negate biblical precepts in order to perform God's will, and greeting another is certainly God's will. **Rabbi Natan says** another interpretation of the verse: **"Make void Your Torah" because "it is the time to work for the Lord,"**[N] i.e., occasionally it is necessary to negate biblical precepts in order to bolster the Torah.

גמ׳ מְנָא הָנֵי מִילֵּי? אָמַר רַבִּי יוֹחָנָן, דְּאָמַר קְרָא: "וַיֹּאמֶר יִתְרוֹ בָּרוּךְ ה׳ אֲשֶׁר הִצִּיל" וגו׳.

**GEMARA** With regard to the obligation to recite a blessing for a miracle, the Gemara asks: **From where are these matters** derived?[N] **Rabbi Yoḥanan said: The verse states: "And Jethro said: Blessed be the Lord, Who delivered** you out of the hand of the Egyptians, and out of the hand of Pharaoh; Who delivered the people from under the hand of the Egyptians" (Exodus 18:10); a blessing is recited for a miracle.

אַנִּיסָּא דְּרַבִּים מְבָרְכִינַן, אַנִּיסָּא דְּיָחִיד לָא מְבָרְכִינַן?! וְהָא הַהוּא גַּבְרָא דַּהֲוָה קָא אָזֵיל בְּעֵבַר יְמִינָא, נְפַל עֲלֵיהּ אַרְיָא, אִתְעֲבִיד לֵיהּ נִיסָּא וְאִיתְּצַל מִינֵּיהּ; אֲתָא לְקַמֵּיהּ דְּרָבָא, וַאֲמַר לֵיהּ: כׇּל אֵימַת דְּמָטֵית לְהָתָם – בָּרֵיךְ "בָּרוּךְ... שֶׁעָשָׂה לִי נֵס בַּמָּקוֹם הַזֶּה"!

The Gemara asks: **For a miracle** that occurs for the **multitudes we recite a blessing,** but **for a miracle** that befalls **an individual** person **we do not recite a blessing? Wasn't** there an incident where **a certain man was walking along the right side** of the Euphrates River when **a lion attacked him, a miracle was performed for him, and he was rescued? He came before Rava who said to him: Every time that you arrive there,** to the site of the miracle, **recite the blessing, "Blessed...Who performed a miracle for me in this place."**

וּמָר בְּרֵיהּ דְּרָבִינָא הֲוָה קָאָזֵיל בְּפַקְתָּא דַּעֲרָבוֹת וּצְחָא לְמַיָּא, אִתְעֲבִיד לֵיהּ נִיסָּא אִיבְּרִי לֵיהּ עֵינָא דְמַיָּא וְאִישְׁתִּי.

**And** once when **Mar, son of Ravina, was walking in a valley of willows**[B] and was **thirsty for water, a miracle was performed for him** and **a spring of water was created for him, and he drank.**

**LANGUAGE**

**Money belt [*punda*] – פּוּנְדָּה:** The source of this word, which occasionally appears as *apunda*, is the Latin funda, meaning a belt pack, a money belt or Greek φοῦνδα, *funda*, meaning belt or pocket. A *punda* is a hollow belt with a pocket for money, thereby it serves as both a belt and a wallet.

**BACKGROUND**

**Sadducees and Boethusians – צְדוֹקִים וּבַיְיתוֹסִים:** These were heterodox sects during the Second Temple period. These sects did not accept the Oral Torah at all, and they interpreted the Written Torah in their own way. Several customs were introduced during the Second Temple period in order to help the Sadducees understand the error of their ways, i.e., to underscore the differences between normative practice and theirs, and to underscore the fact that the *halakha* ignores their opinions. Among these innovations were: Having the High Priest take an oath before entering the Holy of Holies on Yom Kippur and requiring other witnesses to testify to the reliability of the witnesses to the New Moon.

**Valley of willows – פַּקְתָּא דַּעֲרָבוֹת:** This valley is well known in the Talmud as a desert, apparently, along the route taken by caravans. There was no drinking water there, and only in certain isolated places were there people selling water brought from the rivers. In addition, it was a place prone to attacks by highwaymen.

**NOTES**

**One should greet another in the name of God – שֶׁיְּהֵא אָדָם שׁוֹאֵל אֶת שְׁלוֹם חֲבֵרוֹ בַּשֵּׁם:** Some explain that the greeting: Shalom, is included in this category. Since the Sages said that Shalom is one of God's names, one who greets another with Shalom greets him with the name of God (*Arukh*).

**Rabbi Natan says: "Make void Your Torah" because "it is the time to work for the Lord" – רַבִּי נָתָן אוֹמֵר: הֵפֵרוּ תּוֹרָתֶךָ מִשּׁוּם עֵת לַעֲשׂוֹת לַה׳:** Some explain that Rabbi Natan did not seek to add anything to the mishna. However, since this is the end of the chapter and of the tractate, and in most tractates there is an attempt to end on a positive note. Therefore, he reversed the order of the verse so that tractate *Berakhot* would end with: It is the time to work for the Lord (Rabbi Zekharya Stern).

**From where are these matters derived – מְנָא הָנֵי מִילֵּי:** Rashi has a variant, simpler reading of this question. However, the question remains: All of these blessings were instituted by the Sages. Why, then, does the Gemara seek Torah support for them? There is still room to say that there is no reason for one to recite a blessing over a miracle that was performed on behalf of another, as he himself did not derive any benefit from that miracle. Therefore, evidence is cited from Jethro, who recited a blessing under those circumstances (*Tziyyun LeNefesh Ḥayya*).

וְתוּ, זִמְנָא חֲדָא הֲוָה קָאָזֵיל בְּרִסְתְּקָא דִּמְחוֹזָא וּנְפַל עֲלֵיהּ גַּמְלָא פְּרִיצָא, אִיתְפְּרַקָא לֵיהּ אָשִׁיתָא, עַל לְגַוָּהּ; כִּי מְטָא לַעֲרָבוֹת, בָּרִיךְ: בָּרוּךְ... שֶׁעָשָׂה לִי נֵס בַּעֲרָבוֹת וּבְגָמָל, כִּי מְטָא לְרִסְתְּקָא דִּמְחוֹזָא, בָּרִיךְ: בָּרוּךְ... שֶׁעָשָׂה לִי נֵס בְּגָמָל וּבַעֲרָבוֹת! – אָמְרִי: אַנִּיסָּא דְּרַבִּים כּוּלֵּי עָלְמָא מִיחַיְּיבִי לְבָרוֹכֵי, אַנִּיסָּא דְּיָחִיד – אִיהוּ חַיָּיב לְבָרוֹכֵי.

**Furthermore, once** when Mar, son of Ravina, **was walking in the marketplace** *[risteka]*[L] **of Meḥoza and a wild camel** *[gamla peritza]*[L] **attacked him. The wall cracked open, he went inside it,** and he was rescued. Ever since, **when he came to the reeds he recited: Blessed…Who performed a miracle for me in the reeds**[N] **and with the camel.** And, **when he came to the marketplace of Meḥoza he recited: Blessed…Who performed a miracle for me with the camel and in the reeds,** indicating that one recites a blessing even for a miracle that occurs to an individual. The Sages **say: On a miracle** performed on behalf **of the multitudes, everyone is obligated to recite a blessing;**[H] **on a miracle** performed on behalf **of an individual,** only the individual **is obligated to recite a blessing.**[H]

תָּנוּ רַבָּנַן: הָרוֹאֶה מַעְבְּרוֹת הַיָּם, וּמַעְבְּרוֹת הַיַּרְדֵּן, מַעְבְּרוֹת נַחֲלֵי אַרְנוֹן, אַבְנֵי אֶלְגָּבִישׁ בְּמוֹרַד בֵּית חוֹרוֹן, וְאֶבֶן שֶׁבִּקֵּשׁ לִזְרוֹק עוֹג מֶלֶךְ הַבָּשָׁן עַל יִשְׂרָאֵל, וְאֶבֶן שֶׁיָּשַׁב עָלֶיהָ מֹשֶׁה בְּשָׁעָה שֶׁעָשָׂה יְהוֹשֻׁעַ מִלְחָמָה בַּעֲמָלֵק, וְאִשְׁתּוֹ שֶׁל לוֹט, וְחוֹמַת יְרִיחוֹ שֶׁנִּבְלְעָה בִּמְקוֹמָהּ – עַל כּוּלָּן צָרִיךְ שֶׁיִּתֵּן הוֹדָאָה וָשֶׁבַח לִפְנֵי הַמָּקוֹם.

**The Sages taught** in a *baraita* a list of places where one is required to recite a blessing due to miracles that were performed there: **One who sees the crossings of the** Red **Sea,** where Israel crossed; **and the crossings of the Jordan;**[H] **and the crossings of the streams of Arnon; the hailstones of Elgavish on the descent of Beit Ḥoron; the rock that Og, King of Bashan, sought to hurl upon Israel; and the rock upon which Moses sat when Joshua waged war against Amalek; and Lot's wife; and the wall of Jericho that was swallowed up in its place. On all of these** miracles **one must give thanks and offer praise before God.**

בִּשְׁלָמָא מַעְבְּרוֹת הַיָּם, דִּכְתִיב: "וַיָּבֹאוּ בְנֵי יִשְׂרָאֵל בְּתוֹךְ הַיָּם בַּיַּבָּשָׁה"; מַעְבְּרוֹת הַיַּרְדֵּן, דִּכְתִיב: "וַיַּעַמְדוּ הַכֹּהֲנִים נֹשְׂאֵי הָאָרוֹן בְּרִית ה׳ בֶּחָרָבָה בְּתוֹךְ הַיַּרְדֵּן הָכֵן וְכָל יִשְׂרָאֵל עֹבְרִים בֶּחָרָבָה עַד אֲשֶׁר תַּמּוּ כָּל הַגּוֹי לַעֲבוֹר אֶת הַיַּרְדֵּן".

The Gemara elaborates: **Granted,** the miracles at **the crossings of the sea** are recorded explicitly in the Torah, **as it is stated: "And the Israelites went into the sea on dry ground** and the water was a wall for them on their right and on their left" (Exodus 14:22). So too, the miracle at **the crossings of the Jordan, as it is stated: "The priests who bore the ark of God's covenant stood on dry land within the Jordan, while all Israel crossed on dry land until the entire nation finished crossing the Jordan"** (Joshua 3:17).

אֶלָּא מַעְבְּרוֹת נַחֲלֵי אַרְנוֹן מְנָלַן? – דִּכְתִיב: "עַל כֵּן יֵאָמַר בְּסֵפֶר מִלְחֲמוֹת ה׳ אֶת וָהֵב בְּסוּפָה" וגו׳; תָּנָא: "אֶת וָהֵב בְּסוּפָה" – שְׁנֵי מְצוֹרָעִים הָיוּ דַּהֲווֹ מְהַלְּכִין בְּסוֹף מַחֲנֵה יִשְׂרָאֵל, כִּי הָווּ קָא חָלְפִי יִשְׂרָאֵל אָתוּ אֱמוֹרָאֵי

**However, from where do we** derive the miracle that occurred at **the crossing of the streams of Arnon? As it is stated:** "Wherefore it is said in the Book of the Wars of the Lord: *Vahev* in *Sufa*, and the valleys of Arnon. And the slope of the valleys that incline toward the seat of Ar, and lean upon the border of Moab" (Numbers 21:14–15). It was **taught:** ***"Vahev in Sufa"*; there were two lepers,** one named Et and the second named Hev, **who were walking at the rear of the camp of Israel. As Israel passed, the Emorites came**

Perek **IX**
Daf **54** Amud **b**

עָבְדִי לְהוֹן נְקִירוֹתָא וְטָשׁוּ בְּהוֹן, אָמְרִי: כִּי חָלְפִי יִשְׂרָאֵל הָכָא נִקְטְלִינוּן, וְלָא הָווּ יָדְעִי דַּאֲרוֹן הֲוָה מַסְגֵּי קַמַּיְיהוּ דְּיִשְׂרָאֵל וַהֲוָה מֵמִיךְ לְהוּ טוּרֵי מִקַּמַּיְיהוּ; כֵּיוָן דַּאֲתָא אָרוֹן, אִדַּבְּקוּ טוּרֵי בַּהֲדֵי הֲדָדֵי וְקַטְלִינוּן, וּנְחַת דְּמַיְיהוּ לְנַחֲלֵי אַרְנוֹן. כִּי אָתוּ אֶת וָהֵב, חֲזוּ דְּמָא דְּקָא נָפֵיק מִבֵּינֵי טוּרֵי, אָתוּ וְאָמְרִי לְהוּ לְיִשְׂרָאֵל וַאֲמַרוּ שִׁירָה, הַיְינוּ דִּכְתִיב: "וְאֶשֶׁד הַנְּחָלִים אֲשֶׁר נָטָה לְשֶׁבֶת עָר וְנִשְׁעַן לִגְבוּל מוֹאָב."

**and prepared caves for themselves and they hid in them. They said: When Israel passes here we will kill them. And they did not know** that the **Ark** of the Covenant **preceded** the children of **Israel and would flatten mountains before them. When** the **Ark came, the mountains adhered one to another and killed them; and their blood** flowed **down to the streams of Arnon. When Et and Hev,** the lepers, **arrived, they saw the blood that was emerging from between the mountains, and they came and told Israel** what had happened. Israel **recited** a **song** of praise, **as it is stated: "And at the cascade of the brooks that goes down to the dwelling of Ar, and lies upon the border of Moab"** (Numbers 21:15). This refers to the cascade of the brooks where the mountain, which had once been a valley, spread out in the direction of the mountain in Ar, in Moab.

אַבְנֵי אֶלְגָּבִישׁ – מַאי אַבְנֵי אֶלְגָּבִישׁ?

Among the sites enumerated in the mishna where one is obligated to recite a blessing in recognition of the miracles that occurred there, was the site of **the hailstones of Elgavish.** The Gemara asks: **What** are the **hailstones of Elgavish?**

**LANGUAGE**

Marketplace [*risteka*] – רִסְתְּקָא: From the Iranian rastak, meaning a straight line. In talmudic times, it was used to mean district or village. Here it refers to a row of stores or the fence surrounding them.

Wild camel [*gamla peritza*] – גַּמְלָא פְּרִיצָא: Rav Sa'adia Gaon explains here, and so it seems from the context, that this refers to a camel in heat. During their rutting period, camels run wild and pose a danger to all who encounter them.

**NOTES**

**Who performed a miracle for me in the reeds – שֶׁעָשָׂה לִי נֵס בַּעֲרָבוֹת:** He mentioned the place but not the miracle. The miracle was, in essence, performed to the place with the appearance of the spring. Remnants of the spring remained there as well (*Hagahot* of Rabbi Neḥemya Beirakh).

**HALAKHA**

**For a miracle that was performed on behalf of the multitudes, everyone is obligated to recite a blessing – אַנִּיסָּא דְּרַבִּים כּוּלֵּי עָלְמָא מִיחַיְּיבִי לְבָרוֹכֵי:** For a miracle that was performed for the entire Jewish people, or at least the majority thereof, everyone is required to recite a blessing. If it was performed for only a segment of the Jewish people, only those for whom the miracle was performed recite a blessing (*Mishna Berura*; Rambam *Sefer Ahava, Hilkhot Berakhot* 10:9; *Shulḥan Arukh, Oraḥ Ḥayyim* 218:2).

**For a miracle that was performed on behalf of an individual, only the individual is obligated to recite a blessing – אַנִּיסָּא דְּיָחִיד אִיהוּ חַיָּיב לְבָרוֹכֵי:** Upon arriving at a place where a miracle was performed for him, one recites a blessing for his miracle. All his progeny must also recite a blessing for this miracle. His children recite: Who performed a miracle for my father; his descendants recite: Who performed a miracle for my father's father, or: Who performed a miracle for my ancestors (*Mishna Berura*). He must include in the blessing all miracles that were performed for him in other places; in accordance with the opinion of Ravina (Rambam *Sefer Ahava, Hilkhot Berakhot* 10:9; *Shulḥan Arukh, Oraḥ Ḥayyim* 218:4–5).

**One who sees the crossings of the Red Sea and the crossings of the Jordan, etc. – הָרוֹאֶה מַעְבְּרוֹת הַיָּם, וּמַעְבְּרוֹת הַיַּרְדֵּן וכו׳:** One who sees a place where miracles were performed for Israel, i.e., the crossings of the sea and the Jordan and the rest of the places that miracles were performed for the people of Israel at various times, recites: Blessed…Who performed miracles for our forefathers in this place (*Shulḥan Arukh, Oraḥ Ḥayyim* 218:1).

The rock that Og, King of Bashan, sought to throw upon Israel – אֶבֶן שֶׁבִּקֵּשׁ עוֹג מֶלֶךְ הַבָּשָׁן לִזְרוֹק עַל יִשְׂרָאֵל: Almost all commentators explain this by means of allusion and esoterica, as this story is aggadic and not historical. One approach suggests that Moses was concerned that Og had unique merit in his favor due to his interaction with Abraham (see tractate Nidda 61a); that is represented by the mountain that was as wide as the entire camp of Israel. The merit of Israel, who are likened to grasshoppers (Numbers ch. 13), succeeds in perforating this mountain. According to this aggada, the story of the killing of Og can be understood as joining the merit of Moses, ten cubits is an exaggeration, with the merit of the nation, the axe, and the merit of the forefathers, Moses' leap, in order to kill Og (Rashba). An additional approach suggests that a mountain is a common metaphor for the evil inclination (see the end of Tractate Sota), and Og wanted to corrupt Israel just as Balak did, which is alluded to by the mountain he wished to throw upon them. In this case, Israel's merit saved them from being corrupted (Darash Moshe).

**HALAKHA**

Over Lot – עַל לוֹט: One who sees Lot's wife, the pillar of salt, recites a blessing both for the miracle that was performed for her and for the miracle that was performed for Lot, her husband. Over Lot's wife, one recites: Blessed…the true Judge, while over Lot: Blessed…Who remembers the righteous (Shulḥan Arukh, Oraḥ Ḥayyim 218:8).

תָּנָא: אֲבָנִים שֶׁעָמְדוּ עַל גַּב אִישׁ וְיָרְדוּ עַל גַּב אִישׁ; עָמְדוּ עַל גַּב אִישׁ – זֶה מֹשֶׁה, דִּכְתִיב: "וְהָאִישׁ מֹשֶׁה עָנָו מְאֹד", וּכְתִיב: "וַיַּחְדְּלוּ הַקֹּלוֹת וְהַבָּרָד וּמָטָר לֹא נִתַּךְ אָרְצָה". יָרְדוּ עַל גַּב אִישׁ – זֶה יְהוֹשֻׁעַ, דִּכְתִיב: "קַח לְךָ אֶת יְהוֹשֻׁעַ בִּן נוּן אִישׁ אֲשֶׁר רוּחַ בּוֹ", וּכְתִיב: "וַיְהִי בְּנֻסָם מִפְּנֵי בְּנֵי יִשְׂרָאֵל הֵם בְּמוֹרַד בֵּית חוֹרֹן וַה' הִשְׁלִיךְ עֲלֵיהֶם אֲבָנִים גְּדֹלוֹת".

אֶבֶן שֶׁבִּקֵּשׁ עוֹג מֶלֶךְ הַבָּשָׁן לִזְרוֹק עַל יִשְׂרָאֵל – גְּמָרָא גְּמִירִי לָהּ. אֲמַר: מַחֲנֶה יִשְׂרָאֵל כַּמָּה הָוֵי – תְּלָתָא פַּרְסֵי, אֵיזִיל וְאֵיעֲקַר טוּרָא בַּר תְּלָתָא פַּרְסֵי וְאֵישַׁדֵּי עֲלַיְיהוּ וְאִיקַטְלִינְהוּ. אֲזַל עֲקַר טוּרָא בַּר תְּלָתָא פַּרְסֵי וְאַיְיתֵיהּ עַל רֵישֵׁיהּ, וְאַיְיתֵי קוּדְשָׁא בְּרִיךְ הוּא עֲלֵיהּ קַמְצֵי וּנְקַבוּהַ וְנָחֵית בְּצַוָּארֵיהּ;

הֲוָה בָּעֵי לְמִשְׁלְפָהּ, מִשְׁכִי שִׁינֵּיהּ לְהַאי גִּיסָא וּלְהַאי גִּיסָא וְלָא מָצֵי לְמִשְׁלְפָהּ, וְהַיְינוּ דִּכְתִיב: "שִׁנֵּי רְשָׁעִים שִׁבַּרְתָּ"; וְכִדְרַבִּי שִׁמְעוֹן בֶּן לָקִישׁ, דְּאָמַר רַבִּי שִׁמְעוֹן בֶּן לָקִישׁ: מַאי דִּכְתִיב "שִׁנֵּי רְשָׁעִים שִׁבַּרְתָּ" – אַל תִּקְרֵי "שִׁבַּרְתָּ" אֶלָּא "שִׁרְבַּבְתָּ".

מֹשֶׁה כַּמָּה הֲוָה – עֶשֶׂר אַמּוֹת, שְׁקֵיל נַרְגָּא בַּר עֶשֶׂר אַמִּין שְׁוָר עֶשֶׂר אַמִּין, וּמְחֵיהּ בְּקַרְסוּלֵּיהּ וְקַטְלֵיהּ.

וְאֶבֶן שֶׁיָּשַׁב עָלֶיהָ מֹשֶׁה – דִּכְתִיב: "וִידֵי מֹשֶׁה כְּבֵדִים וַיִּקְחוּ אֶבֶן וַיָּשִׂימוּ תַחְתָּיו וַיֵּשֶׁב עָלֶיהָ".

וְאִשְׁתּוֹ שֶׁל לוֹט – שֶׁנֶּאֱמַר: "וַתַּבֵּט אִשְׁתּוֹ מֵאַחֲרָיו וַתְּהִי נְצִיב מֶלַח". וְחוֹמַת יְרִיחוֹ שֶׁנִּבְלְעָה – דִּכְתִיב: "וַתִּפֹּל הַחוֹמָה תַּחְתֶּיהָ".

בִּשְׁלָמָא כּוּלְּהוּ – נִיסָּא, אֶלָּא אִשְׁתּוֹ שֶׁל לוֹט, פּוּרְעֲנוּתָא הוּא! – דַּאֲמַר "בָּרוּךְ... דַּיַּין הָאֱמֶת".

וְהָא "הוֹדָאָה וְשֶׁבַח" קָתָנֵי! – תְּנֵי: עַל לוֹט וְעַל אִשְׁתּוֹ מְבָרְכִים שְׁתַּיִם, עַל אִשְׁתּוֹ אוֹמֵר: "בָּרוּךְ... דַּיַּין הָאֱמֶת", וְעַל לוֹט אוֹמֵר: "בָּרוּךְ... זוֹכֵר אֶת הַצַּדִּיקִים". אָמַר רַבִּי יוֹחָנָן: אֲפִילּוּ בִּשְׁעַת כַּעֲסוֹ שֶׁל הַקָּדוֹשׁ בָּרוּךְ הוּא זוֹכֵר אֶת הַצַּדִּיקִים, שֶׁנֶּאֱמַר: "וַיְהִי בְּשַׁחֵת אֱלֹהִים אֶת עָרֵי הַכִּכָּר וַיִּזְכֹּר אֱלֹהִים אֶת אַבְרָהָם וַיְשַׁלַּח אֶת לוֹט מִתּוֹךְ הַהֲפֵכָה" וְגו'.

It is taught in the midrash: They are the stones that remained suspended in the air and did not fall because of [al gav] a man [ish] and they fell down because of [al gav] a man [ish]. The Gemara explains: They remained suspended because of a man; that is Moses, whom the verse refers to as a man, as it is written: "And the man Moses was very modest" (Numbers 12:3), and it is written: "And Moses went out of the city from Pharaoh, and spread forth his hands unto the Lord; the thunders and hail ceased, and the rain was not poured upon the earth" (Exodus 9:33). Moses' hailstones remained suspended. And the stones descended because of a man; that is Joshua, who was also called man, as it is written: "Take Joshua the son of Nun, a man in whom is spirit" (Numbers 27:18). And it is written that when Joshua and his people waged war against the army of the Emorite kings, God told him not to fear them because God would deliver them into his hands; and indeed, they died by means of these stones: "As they fled from before Israel, while they were at the descent of Beit Ḥoron, that the Lord cast down great stones from heaven upon them unto Azeka, and they died; they were more who died with the hailstones than they whom the children of Israel slew by sword" (Joshua 10:11).

With regard to the **rock that Og, King of Bashan, sought to throw upon Israel,**[N] there is no biblical reference, but rather **a tradition was transmitted.** The Gemara relates that Og said: **How** large **is the camp of Israel? It is three parasangs. I will go and uproot a mountain three parasangs** long **and I will hurl it upon them and kill them. He went, uprooted a mountain three parasangs** long, **and brought it on his head. And The Holy One, Blessed be He, brought grasshoppers upon it and they pierced** the peak of **the mountain and it fell on his neck.**

**Og wanted to remove it** from his head; **his teeth were extended to one side** of his head **and to the other and he was unable to** remove it. **And that is what is written: "You break the teeth of the wicked"** (Psalms 3:8). **And this is in accordance with** the homiletic interpretation of **Rabbi Shimon Ben Lakish, as Rabbi Shimon Ben Lakish said: What is the meaning of that which is written: "You break the teeth of the wicked"? Do not read it as: You break [shibarta], but rather as: You lengthened [shirbavta].**

The story concludes: **How tall was Moses? He was ten cubits** tall. **He took an axe ten cubits long, jumped up ten cubits, and struck Og in the ankle and killed him.**

One must recite a blessing when he sees the **rock upon which Moses sat, as it is written: "But Moses' hands were heavy; and they took a stone and put it under him, and he sat thereon"** (Exodus 17:12).

And one must recite a blessing upon seeing **Lot's wife, as it is stated: "But his wife looked back from behind him, and she became a pillar of salt"** (Genesis 19:26). **And the wall of Jericho that was swallowed, as it is written: "And the wall fell down flat"** (Joshua 6:20).

The Gemara asks: **Granted,** that one recites a blessing on **all of these.** They **are miracles; however, Lot's wife is a tragedy.** Why recite a blessing on a tragedy? The Gemara answers: **One who** sees that place **recites: Blessed…the true Judge.**

The Gemara asks: **But** the baraita teaches that for all of these one must give **thanks and offer praise?** The Gemara answers: The language of the mishna should be emended **and teach: Over Lot**[H] **and his wife one recites two blessings. Over his wife he recites: Blessed…the true Judge, and on Lot he recites: Blessed…Who remembers the righteous. As Rabbi Yoḥanan said: From the story of Lot it is possible to learn that even during a time of wrath of the Holy One, Blessed be He, He remembers the righteous, as it is stated: "And it came to pass, when God destroyed the cities of the plain, that God remembered Abraham and sent Lot out of the midst of the overthrow, when He overthrew the cities in which Lot dwelt"** (Genesis 19:29).

וְחוֹמַת יְרִיחוֹ שֶׁנִּבְלְעָה – וְחוֹמַת יְרִיחוֹ נִבְלְעָה? וְהָא נָפְלָה! שֶׁנֶּאֱמַר: ״וַיְהִי כִּשְׁמֹעַ הָעָם אֶת קוֹל הַשּׁוֹפָר וַיָּרִיעוּ הָעָם תְּרוּעָה גְדוֹלָה, וַתִּפֹּל הַחוֹמָה תַּחְתֶּיהָ!״ כֵּיוָן דִּפְוּתְיָהּ וְרוּמָהּ כִּי הֲדָדֵי נִינְהוּ, מִשּׁוּם הָכִי אִבְלַעָה בְּלוּעֵי.

The mishna also taught that we recite a blessing for **the wall of Jericho that was swallowed** up in its place. The Gemara asks: **Were the walls of Jericho swallowed up** into the ground? **Didn't they fall, as it is stated: "And it came to pass, when the people heard the sound of the shofar, that the people shouted with a great shout, and the wall fell down flat"** (Joshua 6:20)? The Gemara explains: **Since the width and height** of the walls **were equal to one another, therefore, they were swallowed.** Had they merely fallen it would have had no effect, as their width was equal to their height.

אָמַר רַב יְהוּדָה אָמַר רַב: אַרְבָּעָה צְרִיכִין לְהוֹדוֹת – יוֹרְדֵי הַיָּם, הוֹלְכֵי מִדְבָּרוֹת, וּמִי שֶׁהָיָה חוֹלֶה וְנִתְרַפֵּא, וּמִי שֶׁהָיָה חָבוּשׁ בְּבֵית הָאֲסוּרִים וְיָצָא.

**Rav Yehuda said** that **Rav said: Four must** offer **thanks**[NH] to God with a thanks-offering and a special blessing. They are: **Seafarers, those who walk in the desert, and one who was ill and recovered, and one who was incarcerated in prison**[N] **and went out.** All of these appear in the verses of a psalm (Psalms 107).

יוֹרְדֵי הַיָּם מְנָלַן – ״יוֹרְדֵי הַיָּם בָּאֳנִיּוֹת וגו׳ הֵמָּה רָאוּ מַעֲשֵׂי ה׳״, וְאוֹמֵר: ״וַיַּעֲמֵד רוּחַ סְעָרָה יַעֲלוּ שָׁמַיִם יֵרְדוּ תְהוֹמוֹת״, וְאוֹמֵר: ״יָחוֹגּוּ וְיָנוּעוּ כַּשִּׁכּוֹר״, וְאוֹמֵר: ״וַיִּצְעֲקוּ אֶל ה׳ בַּצַּר לָהֶם וּמִמְּצוּקֹתֵיהֶם יוֹצִיאֵם״, וְאוֹמֵר: ״יָקֵם סְעָרָה לִדְמָמָה״, וְאוֹמֵר: ״וַיִּשְׂמְחוּ כִי יִשְׁתֹּקוּ״, וְאוֹמֵר: ״יוֹדוּ לַה׳ חַסְדּוֹ וְנִפְלְאוֹתָיו לִבְנֵי אָדָם״.

The Gemara elaborates: **From where do we** derive that **seafarers** are required to thank God?

**"They who go down to the sea in ships,** who do business in great waters; **they see the works of the Lord"** (Psalms 107:23–24).

**And it says: "For He commands and raises the stormy wind** which lifts up the waves thereof.

**They mount up to the heaven, they go down again to the depths:** their soul is melted because of trouble" (Psalms 107:25–26).

**And it says: "They reel to and fro, and stagger like a drunken man,** and are at their wits' end."

**And it says** immediately thereafter: **"Then they cry unto the Lord in their trouble, and He brings them out of their distress"** (Psalms 107:28).

**And it says: "He makes the storm calm,** so the waves thereof are still" (Psalms 107:29),

**and it says: "Then are they glad because they be quiet;** so He brings them unto their desired haven" (Psalms 107:30),

**and it says: "They are grateful to God for His loving-kindness and His wonders for mankind"** (Psalms 107:31).

הוֹלְכֵי מִדְבָּרוֹת מְנָלַן – דִּכְתִיב: ״תָּעוּ בַמִּדְבָּר בִּישִׁימוֹן דָּרֶךְ עִיר מוֹשָׁב לֹא מָצָאוּ וַיִּצְעֲקוּ אֶל ה׳ וַיַּדְרִיכֵם בְּדֶרֶךְ יְשָׁרָה״, ״יוֹדוּ לַה׳ חַסְדּוֹ״.

The Gemara asks: **From where do we** derive that **those who walk in the desert** are required to thank God? The Gemara answers:

**As it is written** in the same psalm:

**"They wandered in the wilderness in a solitary way; they found no city in which to dwell"** (Psalms 107:4),

**"And then they cried unto the Lord** in their trouble, and He delivered them out of their distresses.

**And He led them forth by the right way"** (Psalms 107:6–7).

After God guides them on the right way, it is said: **"They are grateful to God for His goodness"** (Psalms 107:8).

מִי שֶׁחָלָה וְנִתְרַפֵּא – דִּכְתִיב: ״אֱוִלִים מִדֶּרֶךְ פִּשְׁעָם וּמֵעֲוֺנֹתֵיהֶם יִתְעַנּוּ כָּל אֹכֶל תְּתַעֵב נַפְשָׁם״ וגו׳, ״וַיִּזְעֲקוּ אֶל ה׳ בַּצַּר לָהֶם״ וגו׳, ״יִשְׁלַח דְּבָרוֹ וְיִרְפָּאֵם״ וגו׳, ״יוֹדוּ לַה׳ חַסְדּוֹ״.

That **one who was ill and recovered** must offer thanks is derived, **as it is written:**

**"Fools, because of their transgression and because of their iniquities, are afflicted.**

**Their soul abhors all manner of meat** and they draw near unto the gates of death" (Psalms 107:17–18),

and: **"Then they cry unto the Lord in their trouble,** and He saves them from their distress" (Psalms 107:19),

and then: **"He sent His word and healed them,** and delivered them from their destructions" (Psalms 107:20).

After they are healed: **"They are grateful to God for His goodness"** (Psalms 107:21).

## NOTES

**Four must offer thanks – אַרְבָּעָה צְרִיכִין לְהוֹדוֹת:** The order here is different from the order of the verses. In Psalms they were enumerated according to frequency; the most frequent appearing first. Here they are enumerated according to the danger presented by each; the most dangerous listed first (Rav Hai Gaon).

Based on those verses, it would appear that only those who encountered difficulty or danger, e.g., a sea traveler who encountered a storm or a traveler in the desert who lost his way, would be obligated to offer thanks. Others argue that this obligation is incumbent upon anyone who undergoes one of these experiences, whether or not he encountered an actual threat. Some suggest that beyond these four experiences, one who encounters and survives any danger is obligated to offer thanks, as well, and those enumerated in the verses and the Gemara are simply common occurrences. Others disagree and rule that they may recite the blessing on a voluntary basis but are not obligated to do so (*Me'iri*).

**One who was incarcerated in prison – מִי שֶׁהָיָה חָבוּשׁ בְּבֵית הָאֲסוּרִים:** According to Rav Hai Gaon, the obligation to express thanks upon release from prison is incumbent upon anyone who was incarcerated, even if it was for purely financial matters, e.g., outstanding debts or failure to pay taxes. Others hold that the obligation applies only if he was imprisoned for capital crimes (*Magen Avraham*). Others hold that the ruling is based on conditions in the prison.

## HALAKHA

**Four must offer thanks – אַרְבָּעָה צְרִיכִין לְהוֹדוֹת:** Those who go to sea and successfully reach their destination, those who walk in the desert and arrive at a settlement, a sick person who was healed, and one who was in prison and was released must offer thanks with the blessing: Blessed…Who bestows goodness on the unworthy, Who has bestowed on me much good. Those who hear respond: May He Who bestowed much good on you continue to bestow on you much good, Selah (Rambam *Sefer Ahava, Hilkhot Berakhot* 10:8; *Shulhan Arukh, Orah Hayyim* 219:1–2).

## HALAKHA

**And he must offer thanks before ten people – וּצְרִיךְ לְאוֹדוֹיֵי קַמֵּי עַשְׂרָה:** One offers thanks for a miracle in the presence of ten people, two of whom must be Sages who have studied *halakha* (*Magen Avraham*). It is customary to recite this blessing in the synagogue after the Torah reading. Even if there are not ten people, one is obligated to recite the blessing (Rambam *Sefer Ahava, Hilkhot Berakhot* 10:8; *Shulḥan Arukh, Oraḥ Ḥayyim* 219:3).

**You have exempted me from offering thanks – פַּטַרְתּוּן יָתִי מִלְּאוֹדוֹיֵי:** If one recites a blessing for a miracle that befell someone else and the individual for whom the miracle was performed heard the entire blessing, intended to fulfill his obligation (*Mishna Berura*), and answered amen, he is exempt from offering any further thanks. The authorities imposed certain restrictions with regard to the ability of one to recite this blessing on another's behalf (see *Magen Avraham, Taz*; *Shulḥan Arukh, Oraḥ Ḥayyim* 219:4).

## NOTES

**You have exempted me from offering thanks – פַּטַרְתּוּן יָתִי מִלְּאוֹדוֹיֵי:** Some suggest that they did so intentionally so that Rav Yehuda would not be inconvenienced. Furthermore, so that he would not need to recite the formula: Blessed…Who bestows goodness on the unworthy, publicly in the synagogue because it contains an element of self-deprecation (*Iyyun Ya'akov*).

מִי שֶׁהָיָה חָבוּשׁ בְּבֵית הָאֲסוּרִין מְנָלַן – דִּכְתִיב: ״יֹשְׁבֵי חֹשֶׁךְ וְצַלְמָוֶת״ וגו׳, ״כִּי הִמְרוּ אִמְרֵי אֵל״ וגו׳, וְאוֹמֵר: ״וַיַּכְנַע בֶּעָמָל לִבָּם״ וגו׳, וְאוֹמֵר: ״וַיִּזְעֲקוּ אֶל ה׳ בַּצַּר לָהֶם״, וְאוֹמֵר: ״יוֹצִיאֵם מֵחֹשֶׁךְ וְצַלְמָוֶת״ וגו׳, וְאוֹמֵר: ״יוֹדוּ לַה׳ חַסְדּוֹ״.

**From where** do we derive that **one who was incarcerated in prison** must offer thanks?
**As it is written: "Such as sit in darkness and in the shadow of death,** bound in affliction and iron.
**Because they rebelled against the words of God** and scorned the counsel of the most High" (Psalms 107:10–11).
**And it says: "Therefore He brought down their heart with labor;** they fell down, and there was none to help" (Psalms 107:12),
**and it says: "Then they cried unto the Lord in their trouble,** and He saved them from their distresses" (Psalms 107:13),
**and it says: "He brought them out of darkness and the shadow of death,**
and broke their shackles" (Psalms 107:14).
**And** after God takes them out from that darkness and shadow of death, **it says: "They are grateful to God for His goodness."**

מַאי מְבָרֵךְ? – אָמַר רַב יְהוּדָה: ״בָּרוּךְ... גּוֹמֵל חֲסָדִים טוֹבִים״. אַבַּיֵי אָמַר: וּצְרִיךְ לְאוֹדוֹיֵי קַמֵּי עַשְׂרָה, דִּכְתִיב: ״וִירוֹמְמוּהוּ בִּקְהַל עָם״ וגו׳. מָר זוּטְרָא אָמַר: וּתְרֵין מִינַּיְיהוּ רַבָּנַן, שֶׁנֶּאֱמַר: ״וּבְמוֹשַׁב זְקֵנִים יְהַלְלוּהוּ״.

The Gemara asks: **What blessing** does he **recite? Rav Yehuda said: Blessed is…Who bestows acts of loving-kindness. Abaye said: And he must** offer **thanks before ten** people,[H] **as it is written** in the same chapter: **"Let them exalt Him also in the congregation of the people** and praise Him in the assembly of the elders" (Psalms 107:32), and congregation indicates a group of at least ten. **Mar Zutra said: Two of them** must be **Sages, as it is stated** there: **"And praise Him in the assembly of elders."** These elders are the Sages, and the use of the plural indicates a minimum of two.

מַתְקִיף לַהּ רַב אַשִׁי: וְאֵימָא כּוּלְּהוּ רַבָּנַן! – מִי כְּתִיב ״בִּקְהַל זְקֵנִים״?! ״בִּקְהַל עָם״ כְּתִיב. – וְאֵימָא: בֵּי עַשְׂרָה שְׁאָר עַמָּא, וּתְרֵי רַבָּנַן! – קַשְׁיָא.

**Rav Ashi strongly objects to this: Say** that **all of them** must be **Sages.** The Gemara rejects this: **Is it written: In the congregation of elders? In the congregation of the people is written;** and the Sages are among them. Yet there is still room to object: **Say** that **ten** are from **the rest of the people,** and in addition there must be **two Sages.** No satisfactory answer was found, and the question remains **difficult,** although the *halakha* was not rejected.

רַב יְהוּדָה חֲלַשׁ וְאִתְפַּח, עַל לְגַבֵּיהּ רַב חָנָא בַּגְדָּתָאָה וְרַבָּנַן, אָמְרִי לֵיהּ: בְּרִיךְ רַחֲמָנָא דִּיהַבָךְ נִיהֲלַן וְלָא יְהַבָךְ לְעַפְרָא. אָמַר לְהוּ: פַּטַרְתּוּן יָתִי מִלְּאוֹדוֹיֵי.

The Gemara relates: **Rav Yehuda fell sick and recovered, Rav Ḥana of Baghdad and the Sages entered to visit him. They said to him: Blessed is God Who gave you to us and did not give you to the dust. He said to them: You have exempted me from** offering **thanks,**[HN] as your statement fulfilled my obligation to recite a blessing.

וְהָא אָמַר אַבַּיֵי: בָּעֵי אוֹדוֹיֵי בְּאַפֵּי עַשְׂרָה! – דַּהֲווּ בֵּי עַשְׂרָה. וְהָא אִיהוּ לָא קָא מוֹדֶה! – לָא צְרִיךְ, דְּעָנֵי בָּתְרַיְיהוּ אָמֵן.

The Gemara asks: **But didn't Abaye say** that **one must offer thanks before ten?** The Gemara answers: **There were ten** people there when the Sages blessed God in Rav Yehuda's presence. The Gemara raises another difficulty: **But** Rav Yehuda **did not offer thanks** himself; others offered thanks on his behalf. The Gemara answers: **He did not need** to recite it himself **as he answered amen after their** blessing. Answering amen after a blessing is tantamount to reciting the blessing himself.

אָמַר רַב יְהוּדָה: שְׁלֹשָׁה צְרִיכִין שִׁימּוּר, וְאֵלּוּ הֵן: חוֹלֶה, חָתָן, וְכַלָּה. בְּמַתְנִיתָא תָּנָא: חוֹלֶה, חַיָּה, חָתָן, וְכַלָּה. וְיֵשׁ אוֹמְרִים: אַף אָבֵל. וְיֵשׁ אוֹמְרִים: אַף תַּלְמִידֵי חֲכָמִים בַּלַּיְלָה.

Incidental to Rav Yehuda's earlier statement, which organized several cases into a single category, the Gemara cites similar statements of his. **Rav Yehuda said: Three require protection** from harm: **A sick person, a bridegroom, and a bride. It was taught in a *baraita*: A sick person, a woman in childbirth, a bridegroom, and a bride** require protection from harm. **And some say: Even a mourner. And some say: Even Torah scholars at night.** Those whose thoughts are focused elsewhere or are in a weakened physical state require protection.

וְאָמַר רַב יְהוּדָה, שְׁלֹשָׁה דְּבָרִים הַמַּאֲרִיךְ בָּהֶן מַאֲרִיכִין יָמָיו וּשְׁנוֹתָיו שֶׁל אָדָם: הַמַּאֲרִיךְ בִּתְפִלָּתוֹ, וְהַמַּאֲרִיךְ עַל שֻׁלְחָנוֹ, וְהַמַּאֲרִיךְ בְּבֵית הַכִּסֵּא.

**And Rav Yehuda said: There are three matters which,** when **one who prolongs their** duration, **they extend a person's days and years.** They are: **One who prolongs his prayer, one who prolongs his** mealtime at the **table, and one who prolongs** his time in **the bathroom.**

וְהַמַּאֲרִיךְ בִּתְפִלָּתוֹ, מַעַלְיוּתָא הִיא?! וְהָאָמַר רַבִּי חִיָּיא בַּר אַבָּא אָמַר רַבִּי יוֹחָנָן:

The Gemara asks: **And one who prolongs his prayer; is that a virtue? Didn't Rabbi Ḥiyya bar Abba say that Rabbi Yoḥanan said:**

כָּל הַמַּאֲרִיךְ בִּתְפִלָּתוֹ וּמְעַיֵּין בָּהּ סוֹף בָּא לִידֵי כְּאֵב לֵב, שֶׁנֶּאֱמַר: ״תּוֹחֶלֶת מְמֻשָּׁכָה מַחֲלָה לֵב״. וְאָמַר רַבִּי יִצְחָק: שְׁלֹשָׁה דְּבָרִים מַזְכִּירִים עֲוֹנוֹתָיו שֶׁל אָדָם, וְאֵלּוּ הֵן: קִיר נָטוּי, וְעִיּוּן תְּפִלָּה, וּמוֹסֵר דִּין עַל חֲבֵירוֹ לַשָּׁמַיִם!

**Anyone who prolongs his prayer and expects it** to be answered,[H] **will ultimately come to heartache, as it is stated: "Hope deferred makes the heart sick"** (Proverbs 13:12). Similarly, **Rabbi Yitzḥak said: Three matters evoke a person's sins, and they are:** Endangering oneself by sitting or standing next to an **inclined wall** that is about to collapse, **expecting prayer** to be accepted, as that leads to an assessment of his status and merit, **and passing a case against another**[N] **to Heaven,** as praying for Heaven to pass judgment on another person causes one's own deeds to be examined and compared with the deeds of that other person. This proves that prolonging prayer is a fault.

הָא לָא קַשְׁיָא, הָא – דִּמְעַיֵּין בָּהּ, הָא – דְּלָא מְעַיֵּין בָּהּ. וְהֵיכִי עָבֵיד – דְּמַפִּישׁ בְּרַחֲמֵי.

The Gemara resolves the apparent contradiction: This is **not difficult. This,** where we learned that prolonging prayer is undesirable, refers to a situation when one **expects** his prayer to be accepted, **while this,** where Rav Yehuda says that prolonging prayer prolongs one's life, refers to a situation where one does **not expect** his prayer to be accepted. **How does he** prolong his prayer? By **increasing** his **supplication.**

וְהַמַּאֲרִיךְ עַל שֻׁלְחָנוֹ – דִּלְמָא אָתֵי עַנְיָא וְיָהֵיב לֵיהּ, דִּכְתִיב: ״הַמִּזְבֵּחַ עֵץ שָׁלוֹשׁ אַמּוֹת גָּבֹהַּ״, וּכְתִיב: ״וַיְדַבֵּר אֵלַי זֶה הַשֻּׁלְחָן אֲשֶׁר לִפְנֵי ה׳״, פָּתַח בְּמִזְבֵּחַ וְסִיֵּים בְּשֻׁלְחָן! רַבִּי יוֹחָנָן וְרַבִּי אֶלְעָזָר דְּאָמְרִי תַּרְוַיְיהוּ: כָּל זְמַן שֶׁבֵּית הַמִּקְדָּשׁ קַיָּים – מִזְבֵּחַ מְכַפֵּר עַל יִשְׂרָאֵל, וְעַכְשָׁיו – שֻׁלְחָנוֹ שֶׁל אָדָם מְכַפֵּר עָלָיו.

As for the virtue of **prolonging one's** mealtime at the **table,** which Rav Yehuda mentioned, the Gemara explains: **Perhaps a poor person will come** during the meal and the host will be in a position to **give him** food immediately, without forcing the poor person to wait. The Sages elsewhere praised a person who acts appropriately at a meal, **as it is written: "The altar, three cubits high** and the length thereof, two cubits, was of wood, and so the corners thereof; the length thereof, and the walls thereof, were also of wood" (Ezekiel 41:22), **and it is written** in the continuation of that verse: **"And he said unto me: This is the table that is before the Lord."** The language of this verse is difficult, as it **begins with the altar and concludes with the table.** Rather, **Rabbi Yoḥanan and Rabbi Elazar both say: As long as the Temple stood, the altar atoned for Israel's** transgressions. **Now that it is destroyed, a person's table atones for his** transgressions.

וְהַמַּאֲרִיךְ בְּבֵית הַכִּסֵּא מַעַלְיוּתָא הִיא?! וְהָתַנְיָא, עֲשָׂרָה דְּבָרִים מְבִיאִין אֶת הָאָדָם לִידֵי תַחְתּוֹנִיּוֹת: הָאוֹכֵל עֲלֵי קָנִים, וַעֲלֵי גְּפָנִים, וְלוּלְבֵי גְּפָנִים, וּמוֹרִיגֵי בְהֵמָה, וְשִׁדְרוֹ שֶׁל דָּג, וְדָג מָלִיחַ שֶׁאֵינוֹ מְבוּשָּׁל כָּל צָרְכּוֹ, וְהַשּׁוֹתֶה שִׁמְרֵי יַיִן, וְהַמְקַנֵּחַ בְּסִיד וּבַחַרְסִית, וְהַמְקַנֵּחַ בִּצְרוֹר שֶׁקִּנַּח בּוֹ חֲבֵירוֹ, וְיֵשׁ אוֹמְרִים: אַף הַתּוֹלֶה עַצְמוֹ בְּבֵית הַכִּסֵּא יוֹתֵר מִדַּאי!

With regard to what Rav Yehuda said in praise of **one who prolongs** his time **in the bathroom,** the Gemara asks: **Is that a virtue? Wasn't it taught** in a *baraita*: **Ten things bring a person to** suffer from **hemorrhoids: One who eats the leaves of bulrushes, grape leaves, tendrils of grapevines, the palate and tongue of an animal,** as well as any other part of the animal which is not smooth and which has protrusions, **the spine of a fish, a salty fish that is not fully cooked, and one who drinks wine dregs, and one who wipes himself with lime and clay,** the materials from which earthenware is made, **and one who wipes himself with a stone with which another** person **wiped himself. And some say: One who suspends himself too much in the bathroom as well.** This proves that prolonging one's time in the bathroom is harmful.

לָא קַשְׁיָא, הָא – דְּמַאֲרִיךְ וְתָלֵי, הָא – דְּמַאֲרִיךְ וְלָא תָּלֵי.

The Gemara responds: This is **not difficult. This** *baraita,* which teaches that doing so is harmful, refers to where **one prolongs** his time there **and suspends** himself, while **this** statement of Rav Yehuda refers to where **one prolongs** his time there **and does not suspend** himself.

כִּי הָא דַּאֲמַרָה לֵיהּ הַהִיא מַטְרוֹנִיתָא לְרַבִּי יְהוּדָה בְּרַבִּי אֶלְעַאי: פָּנֶיךָ דּוֹמִים לְמְגַדְּלֵי חֲזִירִים וּלְמַלְוֵי בְּרִבִּית. – אֲמַר לַהּ: הֵימְנוּתָא! לְדִידִי תַּרְוַיְיהוּ אֲסִירָן; אֶלָּא, עֶשְׂרִים וְאַרְבָּעָה בֵּית הַכִּסֵּא אִיכָּא מֵאוּשְׁפִּיזַאי לְבֵי מִדְרְשָׁא, דְּכִי אָזֵילְנָא בָּדֵיקְנָא נַפְשַׁאי בְּכוּלְּהוּ.

The Gemara relates the benefits of prolonging one's time in the bathroom. **Like that** incident **when a matron** [*matronita*][L] **said to Rabbi Yehuda son of Rabbi El'ai: Your face is** fat and full, **like the** faces of **pig farmers and usurers** who do not work hard and who make a plentiful living. **He said to her: Honestly, those two** occupations **are prohibited to me; rather,** why is it that my face is nice? Because **there are twenty-four bathrooms between my lodging and the study hall, and when I walk** I stop and **examine myself in all of them.**

## HALAKHA

**Anyone who prolongs his prayer and expects it to be answered – הַמַּאֲרִיךְ בִּתְפִלָּתוֹ וּמְעַיֵּין בָּהּ:** One should not expect that because he prayed with conviction God must fulfill his request. On the contrary, doing so evokes his sins. Rather, he should approach his prayer with the thought that even though he is poor and contemptible, he requests that the Creator grant his request in His abundant loving-kindness for His creations (*Shulḥan Arukh, Oraḥ Ḥayyim* 98:5).

## NOTES

**And passing a case against another – וּמוֹסֵר דִּין עַל חֲבֵירוֹ:** This refers specifically to a case where there is a court of law capable of adjudicating the case. If one foregoes the court, it appears that he is so confident that his merit will guarantee that his request will be granted. Therefore, the heavenly court closely examines his deeds (*Tosefot Rabbi Yehuda HaḤasid*).

## LANGUAGE

**Matron** [*matronita*] **– מַטְרוֹנִיתָא:** This is the Aramaic form of the Latin word matrona, meaning woman; particularly an important woman.

וְאָמַר רַב יְהוּדָה, שְׁלֹשָׁה דְּבָרִים מְקַצְּרִים יָמָיו וּשְׁנוֹתָיו שֶׁל אָדָם: מִי שֶׁנּוֹתְנִין לוֹ סֵפֶר תּוֹרָה לִקְרוֹת וְאֵינוֹ קוֹרֵא, כּוֹס שֶׁל בְּרָכָה לְבָרֵךְ וְאֵינוֹ מְבָרֵךְ, וְהַמַּנְהִיג עַצְמוֹ בְּרַבָּנוּת.

And Rav Yehuda said: **Three things curtail a person's days and years: One who is** invited and **given the Torah scroll to read and he does not read,** one who is given **a cup of blessing over which to recite a blessing and he does not recite a blessing,**[H] **and one who conducts himself with** an air of **superiority.**[N]

סֵפֶר תּוֹרָה לִקְרוֹת וְאֵינוֹ קוֹרֵא – דִּכְתִיב: ״כִּי הוּא חַיֶּיךָ וְאֹרֶךְ יָמֶיךָ״. כּוֹס שֶׁל בְּרָכָה לְבָרֵךְ וְאֵינוֹ מְבָרֵךְ – דִּכְתִיב: ״וַאֲבָרְכָה מְבָרְכֶיךָ״. וְהַמַּנְהִיג עַצְמוֹ בְּרַבָּנוּת – דְּאָמַר רַבִּי חָמָא בַּר חֲנִינָא: מִפְּנֵי מָה מֵת יוֹסֵף קוֹדֶם לְאֶחָיו – מִפְּנֵי שֶׁהִנְהִיג עַצְמוֹ בְּרַבָּנוּת.

The Gemara details the biblical sources for these cases: One who is given the **Torah scroll to read and he does not read, as it is written** of the Torah: **"It is your life and the length of your days"** (Deuteronomy 30:20). **A cup of blessing over which to recite a blessing and he does not recite a blessing, as it is written: "I will bless them that bless you"** (Genesis 12:3); one who blesses is blessed and one who does not bless does not merit a blessing. **And** with regard to **one who conducts himself with** an air of **superiority, as Rabbi Ḥama, son of Rabbi Ḥanina, said: Why did Joseph die before his brothers,** as evidenced by the order in the verse: "And Joseph died, and all his brethren, and all that generation" (Exodus 1:6)? **Because he conducted himself with** an air of **superiority,** and those who did not serve in a leadership role lived on after he died.

וְאָמַר רַב יְהוּדָה אָמַר רַב, שְׁלֹשָׁה צְרִיכִים רַחֲמִים: מֶלֶךְ טוֹב, שָׁנָה טוֹבָה, וַחֲלוֹם טוֹב. מֶלֶךְ טוֹב – דִּכְתִיב: ״פַּלְגֵי מַיִם לֵב מֶלֶךְ בְּיַד ה׳״. שָׁנָה טוֹבָה – דִּכְתִיב: ״תָּמִיד עֵינֵי ה׳ אֱלֹהֶיךָ בָּהּ מֵרֵאשִׁית הַשָּׁנָה וְעַד אַחֲרִית שָׁנָה״. חֲלוֹם טוֹב – דִּכְתִיב ״וְתַחֲלִימֵנִי וּתְחַיֵּינִי״.

**Rav Yehuda said in the name of Rav: Three** matters **require** a plea for **mercy**[N] to bring them about: **A good king, a good year, and a good dream.** These three, kings, years, and dreams, are all bestowed by God and one must pray that they should be positive and constructive. The Gemara enumerates the sources for these cases: **A good king, as it is written: "The king's heart is in the hand of the Lord as the watercourses:** He turns it whithersoever He will" (Proverbs 21:1). A **good year, as it is written: "The eyes of the Lord, thy God are always upon it, from the beginning of the year even unto the end of the year"** (Deuteronomy 11:12). And a **good dream, as it is written:** "O Lord by these things men live, and altogether therein is the life of my spirit; wherefore **You will recover me [*vataḥlimeni*], and make me to live"** (Isaiah 38:16). Due to their apparent etymological similarity, the word *taḥlimeni* is interpreted as deriving from the word *ḥalom*, dream.

אָמַר רַבִּי יוֹחָנָן: שְׁלֹשָׁה דְּבָרִים מַכְרִיז עֲלֵיהֶם הַקָּדוֹשׁ בָּרוּךְ הוּא בְּעַצְמוֹ, וְאֵלּוּ הֵן: רָעָב, וְשׂוֹבַע, וּפַרְנָס טוֹב. רָעָב – דִּכְתִיב: ״כִּי קָרָא ה׳ לָרָעָב״ וגו׳, שׂוֹבַע – דִּכְתִיב: ״וְקָרָאתִי אֶל הַדָּגָן וְהִרְבֵּיתִי אֹתוֹ״, פַּרְנָס טוֹב – דִּכְתִיב: ״וַיֹּאמֶר ה׳ אֶל מֹשֶׁה לֵאמֹר רְאֵה קָרָאתִי בְשֵׁם בְּצַלְאֵל״ וגו׳.

Similarly, **Rabbi Yoḥanan said: Three matters are proclaimed by the Holy One, Blessed be He, Himself: Famine, plenty, and a good leader.**[N] The Gemara enumerates the sources for these cases: **Famine, as it is written: "For the Lord has called for a famine;** and it shall also come upon the land seven years" (II Kings 8:1). **Plenty, as it is written: "And I will call for the grain and will increase it, and lay no famine upon you"** (Ezekiel 36:29). And **a good leader, as it is written: "And the Lord spoke unto Moses, saying: See I have called by name Bezalel,** son of Uri, son of Hur, of the tribe of Judah" (Exodus 31:1–2).

אָמַר רַבִּי יִצְחָק: אֵין מַעֲמִידִין פַּרְנָס עַל הַצִּבּוּר אֶלָּא אִם כֵּן נִמְלָכִים בַּצִּבּוּר, שֶׁנֶּאֱמַר: ״רְאוּ קָרָא ה׳ בְּשֵׁם בְּצַלְאֵל״. אָמַר לוֹ הַקָּדוֹשׁ בָּרוּךְ הוּא לְמֹשֶׁה: מֹשֶׁה, הָגוּן עָלֶיךָ בְּצַלְאֵל? אָמַר לוֹ: רִבּוֹנוֹ שֶׁל עוֹלָם, אִם לְפָנֶיךָ הָגוּן – לְפָנַי לֹא כׇּל שֶׁכֵּן? אָמַר לוֹ: אַף עַל פִּי כֵן, לֵךְ אֱמוֹר לָהֶם. הָלַךְ וְאָמַר לָהֶם לְיִשְׂרָאֵל: הָגוּן עֲלֵיכֶם בְּצַלְאֵל? אָמְרוּ לוֹ: אִם לִפְנֵי הַקָּדוֹשׁ בָּרוּךְ הוּא וּלְפָנֶיךָ הוּא הָגוּן – לְפָנֵינוּ לֹא כׇּל שֶׁכֵּן!

With regard to Bezalel's appointment, **Rabbi Yitzḥak said: One may only appoint a leader over a community if he consults with the community**[N] and they agree to the appointment, **as it is stated:** "And Moses said unto the children of Israel: **See, the Lord has called by name Bezalel,** son of Uri, son of Hur, of the tribe of Judah" (Exodus 35:30). **The Lord said to Moses: Moses, is Bezalel** a **suitable** appointment in **your** eyes? Moses **said to Him: Master of the universe, if he is a suitable** appointment in **Your** eyes, **then all the more so** in **my** eyes. The Holy One, Blessed be He, **said to him: Nevertheless go and tell** Israel and ask their opinion. Moses **went and said to Israel: Is Bezalel suitable** in **your** eyes? **They said to him: If he is suitable** in the eyes **of the Holy One, Blessed be He, and** in **your** eyes, **all the more so** he is suitable in **our** eyes.

אָמַר רַבִּי שְׁמוּאֵל בַּר נַחְמָנִי אָמַר רַבִּי יוֹנָתָן: בְּצַלְאֵל עַל שֵׁם חׇכְמָתוֹ נִקְרָא. בְּשָׁעָה שֶׁאָמַר לוֹ הַקָּדוֹשׁ בָּרוּךְ הוּא לְמֹשֶׁה: לֵךְ אֱמוֹר לוֹ לִבְצַלְאֵל עֲשֵׂה לִי מִשְׁכָּן אָרוֹן וְכֵלִים, הָלַךְ מֹשֶׁה וְהָפַךְ, וְאָמַר לוֹ: עֲשֵׂה אָרוֹן וְכֵלִים וּמִשְׁכָּן. אָמַר לוֹ: מֹשֶׁה רַבֵּינוּ, מִנְהָגוֹ שֶׁל עוֹלָם – אָדָם בּוֹנֶה בַּיִת וְאַחַר כָּךְ מַכְנִיס לְתוֹכוֹ כֵּלִים, וְאַתָּה אוֹמֵר: עֲשֵׂה לִי אָרוֹן וְכֵלִים וּמִשְׁכָּן! כֵּלִים שֶׁאֲנִי עוֹשֶׂה – לְהֵיכָן אַכְנִיסֵם? שֶׁמָּא כָּךְ אָמַר לְךָ הַקָּדוֹשׁ בָּרוּךְ הוּא: עֲשֵׂה מִשְׁכָּן אָרוֹן וְכֵלִים. אָמַר לוֹ: שֶׁמָּא בְּצֵל אֵל הָיִיתָ וְיָדַעְתָּ!

**Rabbi Shmuel bar Naḥmani said** that **Rabbi Yonatan said: Bezalel was called** by that name **on account of his wisdom. When the Holy One, Blessed be He, said to Moses: Go say to Bezalel, "Make a tabernacle, an ark, and vessels"** (see Exodus 31:7–11), **Moses went and reversed** the order **and told** Bezalel: **"Make an ark, and vessels, and a tabernacle"** (see Exodus 25–26). **He said to** Moses: **Moses, our teacher, the** standard **practice** throughout the **world** is that **a person builds a house and** only **afterward places the vessels** in the house, **and you say to me: Make an ark, and vessels, and a tabernacle.** If I do so in the order you have commanded, **the vessels that I make, where shall I put them? Perhaps God told you the following: "Make a tabernacle, ark, and vessels"** (see Exodus 36). Moses **said to** Bezalel: **Perhaps you were in God's shadow [*betzel El*], and you knew** precisely what He said. You intuited God's commands just as He stated them, as if you were there.

**HALAKHA**

**A cup of blessing over which to recite a blessing and he does not recite a blessing** – כּוֹס שֶׁל בְּרָכָה לְבָרֵךְ וְאֵינוֹ מְבָרֵךְ: It is inappropriate for a guest to refuse the offer of the cup of blessing to recite the blessing (*Magen Avraham*). The life of one who refuses is, God forbid, cut short (*Shulḥan Arukh, Oraḥ Ḥayyim* 201:3).

**NOTES**

**And one who conducts himself with an air of superiority** – וְהַמַּנְהִיג עַצְמוֹ בְּרַבָּנוּת: Stating that one who conducts himself with an air of superiority will find his days and years curtailed appears to contradict other places in the Gemara where a Rabbi is implored to present himself in an authoritative manner. The Maharsha suggests that there is a distinction between one elected or appointed as a community leader, who must act with assertiveness, and one who conducts himself with an air of superiority without the agreement and support of the community.

**Three require mercy** – שְׁלֹשָׁה צְרִיכִים רַחֲמִים: This is mentioned so that one will be certain to pray for mercy at all times for these matters, and to teach that it is effective to pray for mercy in these cases (*Tosefot Rabbi Yehuda HaḤasid*). Some explained that one should pray for mercy in these areas even if they are already in place or have already occurred, lest they change for the worse (*Tziyyun LeNefesh Ḥayya*).

**Three matters are proclaimed by the Holy One, Blessed be He, Himself: Famine, plenty, and a good leader** – אָמַר רַבִּי יוֹחָנָן: שְׁלֹשָׁה דְּבָרִים מַכְרִיז עֲלֵיהֶם הַקָּדוֹשׁ בָּרוּךְ הוּא בְּעַצְמוֹ, וְאֵלּוּ הֵן: רָעָב, וְשׂוֹבַע, וּפַרְנָס טוֹב: An example of this is Joseph's interpretation of Pharaoh's dreams (Genesis 41). Joseph tells Pharaoh: "What God is about to do He has declared unto Pharaoh" (Genesis 41:25). He then explains that God informed Pharaoh by means of his dreams of famine, plenty, and the need to appoint a good leader to oversee collection and distribution of the food (*Iyyun Ya'akov*).

**One may only appoint a leader over a community if he consults with the community** – אֵין מַעֲמִידִין פַּרְנָס עַל הַצִּבּוּר אֶלָּא אִם כֵּן נִמְלָכִים בַּצִּבּוּר: The reason that this consultation is essential is because if there is communal agreement with regard to the appointment, the leader's decisions will more likely be accepted and followed. This is also the basis for establishing courts in matters of litigation. Each side chooses one judge and the third judge is chosen by both parties. Both Rashi and *Tosafot* (*Sanhedrin* 23a) explain that this method of selection is employed so that the litigants will more readily accept the decisions of the court (*Etz Yosef*).

אָמַר רַב יְהוּדָה אָמַר רַב: יוֹדֵעַ הָיָה בְּצַלְאֵל לִצְרֵף אוֹתִיּוֹת שֶׁנִּבְרְאוּ בָּהֶן שָׁמַיִם וָאָרֶץ, כְּתִיב הָכָא: "וַיְמַלֵּא אֹתוֹ רוּחַ אֱלֹהִים בְּחָכְמָה וּבִתְבוּנָה וּבְדַעַת", וּכְתִיב הָתָם "ה' בְּחָכְמָה יָסַד אָרֶץ כּוֹנֵן שָׁמַיִם בִּתְבוּנָה" וּכְתִיב: "בְּדַעְתּוֹ תְּהוֹמוֹת נִבְקָעוּ".

**Rav Yehuda said** that **Rav said: Bezalel knew** how **to join** the **letters with which heaven and earth were created.** From where do we derive this? **It is written here** in praise of Bezalel: **"And I have filled him with the spirit of God, in wisdom, and in understanding, and in knowledge,** and in all manner of workmanship" (Exodus 31:3); **and it is written there** with regard to creation of heaven and earth: **"The Lord, by wisdom, founded the earth; by understanding He established the heavens"** (Proverbs 3:19), **and it is written: "By His knowledge the depths were broken up and the skies drop down the dew"** (Proverbs 3:20). We see that wisdom, understanding, and knowledge, the qualities with which the heavens and earth were created, are all found in Bezalel.

אָמַר רַבִּי יוֹחָנָן: אֵין הַקָּדוֹשׁ בָּרוּךְ הוּא נוֹתֵן חָכְמָה אֶלָּא לְמִי שֶׁיֵּשׁ בּוֹ חָכְמָה, שֶׁנֶּאֱמַר "יָהֵב חָכְמְתָא לְחַכִּימִין וּמַנְדְּעָא לְיָדְעֵי בִינָה". שְׁמַע רַב תַּחֲלִיפָא בַּר מַעַרְבָא וְאַמְרָהּ קַמֵּיהּ דְּרַבִּי אַבָּהוּ, אֲמַר לֵיהּ: אַתּוּן מֵהָתָם מַתְנִיתוּ לַהּ, אֲנַן מֵהָכָא מַתְנִינַן לַהּ - דִּכְתִיב: "וּבְלֵב כָּל חֲכַם לֵב נָתַתִּי חָכְמָה".

On a similar note, **Rabbi Yoḥanan said: The Holy One, Blessed be He, only grants wisdom to one who** already **possesses wisdom, as it is stated: "He gives wisdom unto the wise, and knowledge to they who know understanding"** (Daniel 2:21). **Rav Taḥalifa, from the West,** Eretz Yisrael, **heard** this **and repeated it before Rabbi Abbahu.** Rabbi Abbahu **said to him: You learned** proof for this idea **from there; we learn it from here: As it is written** in praise of the builders of the Tabernacle: **"And in the hearts of all who are wise-hearted I have placed wisdom"** (Exodus 31:6).

אָמַר רַב חִסְדָּא: כָּל חֲלוֹם וְלֹא טְוָות. וְאָמַר רַב חִסְדָּא: חֶלְמָא דְּלָא מְפַשַּׁר - כְּאִגַּרְתָּא דְּלָא מִקַּרְיָא. וְאָמַר רַב חִסְדָּא: לָא חֶלְמָא טָבָא מִקַּיַּים כּוּלֵּיהּ, וְלָא חֶלְמָא בִּישָׁא מִקַּיַּים כּוּלֵּיהּ. וְאָמַר רַב חִסְדָּא: חֶלְמָא בִּישָׁא עָדִיף מֵחֶלְמָא טָבָא. וְאָמַר רַב חִסְדָּא: חֶלְמָא בִּישָׁא - עַצִיבוּתֵיהּ מִסְתַּיֵּיהּ, חֶלְמָא טָבָא - חֶדְוֵויהּ מִסְתַּיֵּיהּ. אָמַר רַב יוֹסֵף: חֶלְמָא טָבָא - אֲפִילּוּ לְדִידִי בְּדִיחוּתֵיהּ מַפַּכְחָא לֵיהּ. וְאָמַר רַב חִסְדָּא: חֶלְמָא בִּישָׁא קָשֶׁה מִנַּגְדָּא, שֶׁנֶּאֱמַר: "וְהָאֱלֹהִים עָשָׂה שֶׁיִּרְאוּ מִלְּפָנָיו". וְאָמַר רַבָּה בַּר בַּר חָנָה אָמַר רַבִּי יוֹחָנָן: זֶה חֲלוֹם רַע.

Related to what was stated above, that one should pray for a good dream, the Gemara cites additional maxims concerning dreams and their interpretation. **Rav Ḥisda said:** One should see **any dream, and not a fast.**[N] In other words, any dream is preferable to a dream during a fast. **And Rav Ḥisda said: A dream not interpreted is like a letter not read.** As long as it is not interpreted it cannot be fulfilled; the interpretation of a dream creates its meaning. **And Rav Ḥisda said: A good dream is not entirely fulfilled and a bad dream is not entirely fulfilled. And Rav Ḥisda said: A bad dream is preferable to a good dream,** as a bad dream causes one to feel remorse and to repent. **And Rav Ḥisda said: A bad dream, his sadness is enough for him; a good dream, his joy is enough for him.** This means that the sadness or joy engendered by the dream renders the actual fulfillment of the dream superfluous. Similarly, **Rav Yosef said: Even for me, the joy of a good dream negates it.** Even Rav Yosef, who was blind and ill, derived such pleasure from a good dream that it was never actually realized. **And Rav Ḥisda said: A bad dream is worse than lashes, as it is stated: "God has so made it, that men should fear before Him"** (Ecclesiastes 3:14), **and Rabba bar bar Ḥana said** that **Rabbi Yoḥanan said: That is a bad dream** that causes man to fear.

"הַנָּבִיא אֲשֶׁר אִתּוֹ חֲלוֹם יְסַפֵּר חֲלוֹם וַאֲשֶׁר דְּבָרִי אִתּוֹ יְדַבֵּר דְּבָרִי אֱמֶת מַה לַתֶּבֶן אֶת הַבָּר נְאֻם ה'", וְכִי מָה עִנְיַן בָּר וְתֶבֶן אֵצֶל חֲלוֹם? אֶלָּא אָמַר רַבִּי יוֹחָנָן מִשּׁוּם רַבִּי שִׁמְעוֹן בֶּן יוֹחַי: כְּשֵׁם שֶׁאִי אֶפְשָׁר לַבָּר בְּלֹא תֶבֶן - כָּךְ אִי אֶפְשָׁר לַחֲלוֹם בְּלֹא דְּבָרִים בְּטֵלִים.

With regard to the verse: **"The prophet that has a dream, let him tell a dream; and he that has My word, let him speak My word faithfully. What has the straw to do with the grain? says the Lord"** (Jeremiah 23:28), the Gemara asks: **What do straw and grain have to do with a dream? Rather, Rabbi Yoḥanan said in the name of Rabbi Shimon bar Yoḥai: Just as it is impossible for the grain to grow without straw, so too it is impossible to dream without idle matters.** Even a dream that will be fulfilled in the future contains some element of nonsense.

אָמַר רַבִּי בֶּרֶכְיָה: חֲלוֹם, אַף עַל פִּי שֶׁמִּקְצָתוֹ מִתְקַיֵּים - כּוּלּוֹ אֵינוֹ מִתְקַיֵּים, מְנָא לַן - מִיּוֹסֵף, דִּכְתִיב: "וְהִנֵּה הַשֶּׁמֶשׁ וְהַיָּרֵחַ" וגו'.

On a similar note, **Rabbi Berekhya said: Even though part of a dream is fulfilled, all of it is not fulfilled. From where do we** derive this? **From** the story of **Joseph's** dream, **as it is written:** "And he said: Behold, I have dreamed yet a dream: **and, behold, the sun and the moon**

Perek **IX**
Daf **55** Amud **b**

וְהַהִיא שַׁעְתָּא אִמֵּיהּ לָא הֲוָת.

and eleven stars bowed down to me" (Genesis 37:9), **and at that time his mother was no longer** alive. According to the interpretation of the dream, the moon symbolizes Joseph's mother. Even this dream that was ultimately fulfilled contained an element that was not fulfilled.

**NOTES**

**Any dream, and not a fast – כָּל חֲלוֹם וְלֹא טְוָות:** Some explain that every dream has meaning except for a dream that one dreams during a fast, as while afflicted in the midst of a fast one will certainly experience bad dreams (*Arukh*, *Tosefot Rabbi Yehuda HaḤasid*). Some explain that the Gemara means that any dream, even a bad one, is preferable to fasting (Rav Sa'adia Gaon). The commentaries are reluctant to interpret Rav Ḥisda's statement according to its simple meaning, i.e., one should never fast in response to a dream, as it is Rav Ḥisda himself who teaches (*Shabbat* 11a) that if one experiences a bad dream it is advantageous to fast that very same day (*Iyyun Ya'akov*).

אָמַר רַבִּי לֵוִי: לְעוֹלָם יְצַפֶּה אָדָם לַחֲלוֹם טוֹב עַד עֶשְׂרִים וּשְׁתַּיִם שָׁנָה. מְנָלַן – מִיּוֹסֵף, דִּכְתִיב: ״אֵלֶּה תֹּלְדוֹת יַעֲקֹב יוֹסֵף בֶּן שְׁבַע עֶשְׂרֵה שָׁנָה״ וגו׳, וּכְתִיב: ״וְיוֹסֵף בֶּן שְׁלֹשִׁים שָׁנָה בְּעָמְדוֹ לִפְנֵי פַּרְעֹה״ וגו׳. מִן שִׁבְסְרֵי עַד תְּלָתִין כַּמָּה הָוֵי – תְּלָת סְרֵי, וְשַׁב דְּשָׂבְעָא וְתַרְתֵּי דְּכַפְנָא – הָא עֶשְׂרִים וּשְׁתַּיִם.

From the same source, **Rabbi Levi said: One should always anticipate** fulfillment of a **good dream up to twenty-two years** after the dream. **From where do we** derive this? **From Joseph, as it is written** in the story of Joseph's dream: **"These are the generations of Jacob. Joseph, being seventeen years old,** was feeding the flock with his brethren" (Genesis 37:2); **and it is written: "And Joseph was thirty years old when he stood before Pharaoh** King of Egypt" (Genesis 41:46). **From seventeen to thirty how many** years **are they? Thirteen;** and add **seven years of plenty and two of famine;** the total is **twenty-two** and only then was the dream fulfilled when his brothers came and bowed down to him.

אָמַר רַב הוּנָא: לְאָדָם טוֹב אֵין מַרְאִין לוֹ חֲלוֹם טוֹב, וּלְאָדָם רַע אֵין מַרְאִין לוֹ חֲלוֹם רַע.

**Rav Huna said: A good person is not shown a good dream**[N] **and a wicked person is not shown a bad dream;** rather, a good person is punished for his relatively few transgressions with bad dreams and a wicked person is rewarded for his relatively few merits with good dreams.

תַּנְיָא נַמִי הָכִי: כָּל שְׁנוֹתָיו שֶׁל דָּוִד לֹא רָאָה חֲלוֹם טוֹב, וְכָל שְׁנוֹתָיו שֶׁל אֲחִיתוֹפֶל לֹא רָאָה חֲלוֹם רַע.

**That was also taught** in a *baraita*: **All of** King **David's life he never saw a good dream, and all of Ahitophel's life he never saw a bad dream.**

וְהָכְתִיב: ״לֹא תְאֻנֶּה אֵלֶיךָ רָעָה״, וְאָמַר רַב חִסְדָּא אָמַר רַב יִרְמְיָה בַּר אַבָּא: שֶׁלֹּא יַבְהִילוּךָ לֹא חֲלוֹמוֹת רָעִים וְלֹא הִרְהוּרִים רָעִים, ״וְנֶגַע לֹא יִקְרַב בְּאָהֳלֶךָ״ – שֶׁלֹּא תִּמְצָא אִשְׁתְּךָ סָפֵק נִדָּה בְּשָׁעָה שֶׁאַתָּה בָּא מִן הַדֶּרֶךְ! – אֶלָּא: אִיהוּ לָא חֲזֵי לֵיהּ, אַחֲרִינֵי חָזוּ לֵיהּ.

The Gemara raises a difficulty: **Is it not written: "No evil shall befall you,** neither shall any plague come near your tent" (Psalms 91:10)? **And Rav Ḥisda said** that **Rav Yirmeya bar Abba said** in explanation of that verse: This means **that you will be frightened neither by bad dreams nor by evil thoughts. Neither shall any plague come near your tent** means **that you will never find your wife** with the **uncertain** status of a **menstruating woman when you return from a journey.** This proves that it is impossible that a righteous person will experience bad dreams throughout his life. **Rather,** one might say that **he does not see** bad dreams; **others see** bad dreams about him.

וְכִי לָא חָזֵי אִיהוּ מַעֲלְיוּתָא הוּא?! וְהָאָמַר רַבִּי זְעֵירָא: כָּל הַלָּן שִׁבְעָה יָמִים בְּלֹא חֲלוֹם נִקְרָא רַע, שֶׁנֶּאֱמַר: ״וְשָׂבֵעַ יָלִין בַּל יִפָּקֶד רָע״, אַל תִּקְרֵי ״שָׂבֵעַ״ אֶלָּא ״שֶׁבַע״! – אֶלָּא הָכִי קָאָמַר: דַּחֲזָא וְלָא יָדַע מַאי חֲזָא.

The Gemara asks: **And when he does not see** a dream, **is that a virtue? Didn't Rabbi Zeira say: Anyone who sleeps seven days without a dream is called evil,**[N] as it indicates that God does not wish to appear to him even in that indirect manner. Allusion to this is, **as it is stated: "And he that has it shall lie satisfied** [*vesave'a*], **he shall not be visited with evil"** (Proverbs 19:23). The Sages said: **Do not read** it as **satisfied** [*vesave'a*], **rather** read it as **seven** [*vesheva*], which is an allusion to the fact that one who sleeps seven times and does not experience a dream is considered evil. **Rather,** one must say that David saw dreams **and the** *baraita* **says as follows:** David certainly **saw** dreams, **but he did not understand**[N] what he saw.

אָמַר רַב הוּנָא בַּר אַמֵּי אָמַר רַבִּי פְּדָת אָמַר רַבִּי יוֹחָנָן: הָרוֹאֶה חֲלוֹם וְנַפְשׁוֹ עֲגוּמָה יֵלֵךְ וְיִפְתְּרֶנּוּ בִּפְנֵי שְׁלֹשָׁה. יִפְתְּרֶנּוּ?! וְהָאָמַר רַב חִסְדָּא: חֶלְמָא דְּלָא מְפַשַּׁר כְּאִגַּרְתָּא דְּלָא מְקַרְיָא! – אֶלָּא אֵימָא: יְטִיבֶנּוּ בִּפְנֵי שְׁלֹשָׁה. לַיְתֵי תְּלָתָא וְלֵימָא לְהוּ: חֶלְמָא טָבָא חֲזַאי. וְלֵימְרוּ לֵיהּ הָנָךְ: טָבָא הוּא, וְטָבָא לֶיהֱוֵי, רַחֲמָנָא לְשַׁוְּיֵיהּ לְטַב. שֶׁבַע זִימְנִין לִגְזְרוּ עֲלָךְ מִן שְׁמַיָּא דְּלֶהֱוֵי טָבָא, וְיֶהֱוֵי טָבָא. וְלֵימְרוּ שָׁלֹשׁ הֲפוּכוֹת, וְשָׁלֹשׁ פְּדוּיוֹת, וְשָׁלֹשׁ שְׁלוֹמוֹת.

**Rav Huna bar Ami said** that **Rabbi Pedat said** that **Rabbi Yoḥanan said: One who sees a dream** from which **his soul is distraught,**[H] **should go and** have **it interpreted before three.** The Gemara is surprised by this: **Interpreted? Didn't Rav Ḥisda say: A dream not interpreted is like a letter not read?** If one is concerned about a dream, why would he actively promote its fulfillment? **Rather, say** as follows: **He should better it before three.** He should **bring three** people and say to them: **I saw a good dream. And they** should **say to him: It is good, and let it be good,** may **God make it good.** May they **decree upon you from heaven seven times that it will be good, and it will be good.** Afterwards **they recite three** verses of **transformation** from bad to good, **three** verses of **redemption, and three** verses which mention **peace.**

שָׁלֹשׁ הֲפוּכוֹת – ״הָפַכְתָּ מִסְפְּדִי לְמָחוֹל לִי פִּתַּחְתָּ שַׂקִּי וַתְּאַזְּרֵנִי שִׂמְחָה״, ״אָז תִּשְׂמַח בְּתוּלָה בְּמָחוֹל וּבַחֻרִים וּזְקֵנִים יַחְדָּו וְהָפַכְתִּי אֶבְלָם לְשָׂשׂוֹן״ וגו׳, ״וְלֹא אָבָה ה׳ אֱלֹהֶיךָ לִשְׁמֹעַ אֶל בִּלְעָם וַיַּהֲפֹךְ״ וגו׳.

The Gemara elaborates: **Three transformations:**

**"You transformed my mourning into dancing;**
**You loosed my sackcloth, and girded me with gladness"** (Psalms 30:12);

**"Then shall the virgin rejoice in the dance, and the young men and the old together;**
**for I will transform their mourning into joy, and will comfort them and make them rejoice from their sorrow"** (Jeremiah 31:12);

and: **"Nevertheless the Lord your God would not hearken unto Balaam;**
**but the Lord your God transformed the curse into a blessing unto you"** (Deuteronomy 23:6).

## NOTES

**A good person is not shown a good dream** – לְאָדָם טוֹב אֵין מַרְאִין לוֹ חֲלוֹם טוֹב: Since the purpose of a dream is to cause a person to repent, a good person is shown a bad dream to facilitate his repentance. A bad person is shown good dreams as part of his punishment, since his repentance is not desired (*HaKotev*). Even though there are cases where good dreams were experienced by good people, i.e., Joseph, that is when seeing the dream plays a role in its realization (*Tziyyun LeNefesh Ḥayya*).

**Anyone who sleeps seven days without a dream is called evil** – כָּל הַלָּן שִׁבְעָה יָמִים בְּלֹא חֲלוֹם נִקְרָא רַע: The idea that going without a dream for an extended period happens to the evil can be explained by understanding that dreams are an expression of the subconscious thoughts of a person during the day, as the Gemara derives from the book of Daniel (2:29). It is clear that every person has inappropriate thoughts that they regret. Even people who carry out wicked deeds usually regret their actions and want to repent. Many dreams are an unconscious manifestation of these thoughts. Consequently, one who has no dreams for seven days must have performed some evil deed and did not even consider repenting (*Iyyun Ya'akov*).

**Saw but he did not understand** – חֲזָא וְלָא יָדַע: Some explain that this refers to one who sees a dream and remembers it, yet does not understand its meaning, as it has no apparent meaning whatsoever (*Ḥefetz Hashem*).

## HALAKHA

**One who sees a dream from which his soul is distraught** – הָרוֹאֶה חֲלוֹם וְנַפְשׁוֹ עֲגוּמָה: One who experiences a dream and his soul is distraught, even if its meaning is not evil (*Mishna Berura*), should come before three of his friends in the morning and recite the formula for bettering a dream (*Shulḥan Arukh, Oraḥ Ḥayyim* 220:1).

שָׁלֹשׁ פְּדוּיוֹת – דִּכְתִיב: "פָּדָה בְשָׁלוֹם נַפְשִׁי מִקְּרָב לִי" וגו', "וּפְדוּיֵי ה' יְשֻׁבוּן" וגו', "וַיֹּאמֶר הָעָם אֶל שָׁאוּל הֲיוֹנָתָן יָמוּת אֲשֶׁר עָשָׂה הַיְשׁוּעָה" וגו'.

**And three redemptions, as it is written:**
"**He has redeemed my soul in peace so that none came near me;** for they were many that strove with me" (Psalms 55:19);
"**The redeemed of the Lord shall return,** and come with singing unto Zion, and everlasting joy shall be upon their heads;
they shall obtain gladness and joy, and sorrow and sighing shall flee away" (Isaiah 35:10);
and: "**The people said to Saul: Shall Jonathan die, who has wrought this great salvation** in Israel?
So the people rescued Jonathan, that he died not" (1 Samuel 14:45).

שָׁלֹשׁ שְׁלוֹמוֹת – דִּכְתִיב: "בּוֹרֵא נִיב שְׂפָתָיִם שָׁלוֹם שָׁלוֹם לָרָחוֹק וְלַקָּרוֹב אָמַר ה' וּרְפָאתִיו", "וְרוּחַ לָבְשָׁה אֶת עֲמָשַׂי" וגו', "וַאֲמַרְתֶּם כֹּה לֶחָי וְאַתָּה שָׁלוֹם וּבֵיתְךָ שָׁלוֹם" וגו'.

**And three** mentions of **peace, as it is written:**
"**Peace, peace, to him that is far off and to him that is near, says the Lord that creates the expression of the lips; and I will heal him**" (Isaiah 57:19);
"**Then the spirit clothed Amasai,** who was chief of the captains: Yours are we, David, and on your side, you son of Yishai;
**peace, peace be unto you, and peace be to your helpers**" (1 Chronicles 12:19);
and: "**Thus you shall say: All hail and peace be both unto you,**
**and peace be to your house,** and peace be unto all that you have" (1 Samuel 25:6).

אַמֵימָר וּמָר זוּטְרָא וְרַב אַשִׁי הֲווּ יָתְבִי בַּהֲדֵי הֲדָדֵי, אָמְרִי: כָּל חַד וְחַד מִינַּן לֵימָא מִלְּתָא דְּלָא שְׁמִיעַ לֵיהּ לְחַבְרֵיהּ. פָּתַח חַד מִינַּיְיהוּ וַאֲמַר: הַאי מַאן דַּחֲזָא חֶלְמָא וְלָא יָדַע מַאי חֲזָא, לֵיקוּם קַמֵּי כָּהֲנֵי בְּעִידָּנָא דְּפָרְסִי יְדַיְיהוּ, וְלֵימָא הָכִי: רִבּוֹנוֹ שֶׁל עוֹלָם, אֲנִי שֶׁלָּךְ וַחֲלוֹמוֹתַי שֶׁלָּךְ, חֲלוֹם חָלַמְתִּי וְאֵינִי יוֹדֵעַ מַה הוּא, בֵּין שֶׁחָלַמְתִּי אֲנִי לְעַצְמִי וּבֵין שֶׁחָלְמוּ לִי חֲבֵירַי וּבֵין שֶׁחָלַמְתִּי עַל אֲחֵרִים, אִם טוֹבִים הֵם – חַזְּקֵם וְאַמְּצֵם כַּחֲלוֹמוֹתָיו שֶׁל יוֹסֵף, וְאִם צְרִיכִים רְפוּאָה – רְפָאֵם כְּמֵי מָרָה עַל יְדֵי מֹשֶׁה רַבֵּינוּ, וּכְמִרְיָם מִצָּרַעְתָּהּ, וּכְחִזְקִיָּה מֵחָלְיוֹ, וּכְמֵי יְרִיחוֹ עַל יְדֵי אֱלִישָׁע. וּכְשֵׁם שֶׁהָפַכְתָּ קִלְלַת בִּלְעָם הָרָשָׁע לִבְרָכָה – כֵּן הֲפוֹךְ כָּל חֲלוֹמוֹתַי עָלַי לְטוֹבָה. וּמְסַיֵּים בַּהֲדֵי כָּהֲנֵי, דְּעָנֵי צִבּוּרָא אָמֵן. וְאִי לָא – לֵימָא הָכִי: "אַדִּיר בַּמָּרוֹם שׁוֹכֵן בִּגְבוּרָה, אַתָּה שָׁלוֹם וְשִׁמְךָ שָׁלוֹם, יְהִי רָצוֹן מִלְּפָנֶיךָ שֶׁתָּשִׂים עָלֵינוּ שָׁלוֹם".

The Gemara relates: **Ameimar**[P] **and Mar Zutra and Rav Ashi were sitting together. They said: Let each and every one of us say something that the other has not heard. One of them began and said: One who saw a dream and does not know what he saw**[HN] **should stand before the priests when they lift their hands** during the Priestly Blessing **and say the following:**
**Master of the Universe, I am Yours and my dreams are Yours,**
**I dreamed a dream and I do not know what it is.**
**Whether I have dreamed of myself, whether my friends have dreamed of me or whether I have dreamed of others,**
**if** the dreams **are good, strengthen them and reinforce them like the dreams of Joseph.**
**And if** the dreams **require healing,**
**heal them like the** bitter **waters of Mara by Moses our teacher, and like Miriam from her leprosy,**
**and like Hezekiah from his illness, and like the** bitter **waters of Jericho by Elisha.**
**And just as You transformed the curse of Balaam the wicked into a blessing,**
**so transform all of my dreams for me for the best.**
**And** he should **complete** his prayer **together with the priests so the congregation responds amen** both to the blessing of the priests and to his individual request. **And if** he is **not** able to recite this entire formula, **he should say:**
**Majestic One on high, Who dwells in power,**
**You are peace and Your name is peace.**
**May it be Your will that You bestow upon us peace.**

פָּתַח אִידָךְ וַאֲמַר: הַאי מַאן דְּעָיֵיל לְמָתָא וְדָחֵיל מֵעֵינָא בִּישָׁא, לִנְקוֹט זַקְפָּא דִּידֵיהּ דִּימִינֵיהּ בִּידָא דִּשְׂמָאלֵיהּ, וְזַקְפָּא דִּידֵיהּ דִּשְׂמָאלֵיהּ בִּידָא דִּימִינֵיהּ, וְלֵימָא הָכִי: אֲנָא פְּלוֹנִי בַּר פְּלוֹנִי מִזַּרְעָא דְּיוֹסֵף קָאָתֵינָא דְּלָא שָׁלְטָא בֵּיהּ עֵינָא בִּישָׁא, שֶׁנֶּאֱמַר: "בֵּן פֹּרָת יוֹסֵף בֵּן פֹּרָת עֲלֵי עָיִן" וגו', אַל תִּקְרֵי "עֲלֵי עָיִן" אֶלָּא "עוֹלֵי עַיִן". רַבִּי יוֹסֵי בְּרַבִּי חֲנִינָא אָמַר מֵהָכָא: "וְיִדְגּוּ לָרֹב בְּקֶרֶב הָאָרֶץ". מָה דָּגִים שֶׁבַּיָּם מַיִם מְכַסִּים עֲלֵיהֶם וְאֵין עַיִן רָעָה שׁוֹלֶטֶת בָּהֶם, אַף זַרְעוֹ שֶׁל יוֹסֵף אֵין עַיִן רָעָה שׁוֹלֶטֶת בָּהֶם. וְאִי דָּחֵיל מֵעֵינָא בִּישָׁא דִּילֵיהּ – לֶיחֱזֵי אַטַּרְפָּא דִּנְחִירֵיהּ דִּשְׂמָאלֵיהּ.

**Another began and said: One who enters a city and fears the evil eye**[N] should **hold the thumb** [***zekafa***][L] **of his right hand in his left hand and the thumb of his left hand in his right hand and recite the following: I, so-and-so son of so-and-so, come from the descendants of Joseph,** over whom **the evil eye has no dominion, as it is stated: "Joseph is a fruitful vine, a fruitful vine by a fountain** [***alei ayin***]; its branches run over the wall" (Genesis 49:22). **Do not read** it as ***alei ayin***; **but rather,** read it as ***olei ayin***, who rise above the eye and the evil eye has no dominion over him. **Rabbi Yosei, son of Rabbi Ḥanina, said:** Derive it **from here,** from what is stated in Jacob's blessing of Joseph's sons: **"And let them grow like fish into a multitude in the midst of the earth"** (Genesis 48:16): **Just as fish in the sea are covered by water and the evil eye has no dominion over them** as they cannot be seen, **so too the offspring of Joseph, the evil eye has no dominion over them. And if he is concerned about his own evil eye,** lest it damage others, he should **look at the side of his left nostril.**

## PERSONALITIES

Ameimar – אַמֵימָר: Ameimar was one of the most prominent of the fifth and sixth generation Babylonian *amora'im*. He was born and raised in Neharde'a, where he studied and taught Torah. He also, apparently, learned Torah from the Sages in Pumbedita. The Sages whose statements he quotes were primarily fifth generation Babylonian *amora'im*, disciples of Abaye and Rava. Various sources indicate that he served as a rabbi and a judge in Neharde'a and instituted ordinances there. However, his influence and authority were significant in other places too, e.g., Meḥoza. The most prominent Sages of the subsequent generation, among them, Rav Ashi, learned Torah from him and appeared before his court. We know that he had at least one son, named Mar, who learned Torah from Rav Ashi, even during Ameimar's lifetime.

## HALAKHA

**One who saw a dream and does not know what he saw – הַאי מַאן דַּחֲזָא חֶלְמָא וְלָא יָדַע מַאי חֲזָא:** One who experienced a dream and is concerned because he does not know what it was should recite the formula of the prayer set forth in the Gemara during the Priestly Blessing. He should so so specifically on the day after the night when he saw the dream (*Magen Avraham*). In places where priests do not recite the Priestly Blessing, he should recite this formula while the prayer leader recites the final blessing of the *Amida* prayer, the blessing of peace (*Shulḥan Arukh, Oraḥ Ḥayyim* 130:1).

## NOTES

**One who saw a dream and does not know what he saw – הַאי מַאן דַּחֲזָא חֶלְמָא וְלָא יָדַע מַאי חֲזָא:** One approach understands that this statement refers to someone who does not know whether the dream that he saw was good or bad. This approach suggests that, in addition to reciting the formula for bettering a dream, he should also recite this prayer during the Priestly Blessing (*Eliya Rabba*). The Maharsha suggests that only one who saw a disturbing dream recites the formula for bettering a dream. The prayer recited during the Priestly Blessing is recited only by one who wakes up upset by his dream but has no recollection of its content.

**One who fears the evil eye – הַמִּתְיָירֵא מֵעַיִן הָרַע:** Some explain this figuratively: If one enters a strange place and fears that the local population, motivated by hatred and jealousy, will harm him, it is preferable that he hold his left hand in his right, etc., i.e., do nothing, to avoid provoking an altercation. Conversely, if one fears that he poses a threat to others, he should look at his nose, i.e., focus exclusively on his own affairs and not on others (*Beit Ya'akov*).

## LANGUAGE

**Thumb** [***zekafa***] **– זַקְפָּא:** According to the *ge'onim*, *zekafa* here means sleeve. Thus the implication is that one should place his hand into the sleeve of his garment and do nothing.

NOTES

**All dreams follow the mouth** – **כָּל הַחֲלוֹמוֹת הוֹלְכִים אַחַר הַפֶּה**: Numerous explanations were suggested for this statement, especially in light of the subsequent stories related in the Gemara. Early commentaries explained that an interpreter of dreams who deciphers dreams accurately is one of those unique people capable of bringing good or evil upon the one seeking the interpretation (*Tosefot Rabbi Yehuda HaḤasid, She'elot UTeshuvot min HaShamayim*). Others explained that this is like the symbolic acts of the prophets, whose explicit interpretations enhance and facilitate the dream's coming true (*Iyei HaYam*). Others explained that dreams follow the mouth of the dreamer in the sense that what he ate earlier or what he said will affect his dreams. Others explained that interpretation of dreams and the guidance of the dreamer are dependent upon whether the interpreter interprets the dream in a manner that will cause the dreamer to repent or in some other way (*HaKotev*).

פָּתַח אִידַּךְ וַאֲמַר: הַאי מַאן דַּחֲלִישׁ, יוֹמָא קַמָּא – לָא לְגַלֵּי כִּי הֵיכִי דְּלָא לִתְרַע מַזָּלֵיהּ, מִכָּאן וְאֵילָךְ – לְגַלֵּי. כִּי הָא דְּרָבָא, כִּי הֲוָה חָלֵישׁ – יוֹמָא קַמָּא לָא מְגַלֵּי, מִכָּאן וְאֵילָךְ אָמַר לֵיהּ לְשַׁמָּעֵיהּ, פּוּק אַכְרִיז: רָבָא חָלֵשׁ. מַאן דְּרָחֵים לִי – לִבְעֵי עֲלַי רַחֲמֵי, וּמַאן דְּסָנֵי לִי – לֶחְדֵי לִי, וּכְתִיב ״בִּנְפֹל אוֹיִבְךָ אַל תִּשְׂמָח וּבִכָּשְׁלוֹ אַל יָגֵל לִבֶּךָ פֶּן יִרְאֶה ה׳ וְרַע בְּעֵינָיו וְהֵשִׁיב מֵעָלָיו אַפּוֹ״.

**Another began and said: One who is sick should not reveal** it **on the first day** of his illness **so that his luck should not suffer; from there on** he may **reveal** it. **Like that which Rava** does **when he falls ill; on the first day he does not reveal it, from there on he says to his servant: Go out and announce: Rava is sick. Those who love me will pray** that God have **mercy on me and those who hate me will rejoice** over **my** distress. **And it is written: "Rejoice not when your enemy falls, and let not your heart be glad when he stumbles; lest the Lord see it, and it displease Him, and He turn away His wrath from him"** (Proverbs 24:17–18). The joy of my enemy over my distress will also assist my healing.

שְׁמוּאֵל כִּי הֲוָה חָזֵי חֶלְמָא בִּישָׁא אָמַר: ״וַחֲלֹמוֹת הַשָּׁוְא יְדַבֵּרוּ״. כִּי הֲוָה חָזֵי חֶלְמָא טָבָא אָמַר: וְכִי הַחֲלוֹמוֹת הַשָּׁוְא יְדַבֵּרוּ? וְהָכְתִיב: ״בַּחֲלוֹם אֲדַבֶּר בּוֹ״.

The Gemara relates: **Shmuel, when he would see a bad dream** would **say: "And the dreams speak falsely"** (Zechariah 10:2). **When he would see a good dream,** he would **say: And do dreams speak falsely? Isn't it written: "I speak with him in a dream"** (Numbers 12:6)?

רָבָא רָמֵי: כְּתִיב ״בַּחֲלוֹם אֲדַבֶּר בּוֹ״, וּכְתִיב ״וַחֲלֹמוֹת הַשָּׁוְא יְדַבֵּרוּ!״ – לָא קַשְׁיָא, כָּאן – עַל יְדֵי מַלְאָךְ, כָּאן – עַל יְדֵי שֵׁד.

**Rava raised a contradiction** between these verses: On the one hand **it is written: "I speak with him in a dream"; and** on the other hand **it is written: "And the dreams speak falsely."** The Gemara resolves this contradiction: This is **not difficult** because there are two types of dreams. **Here,** the verse, "I speak with him in a dream," refers to dreams that come **by means of an angel; here,** the verse, "And the dreams speak falsely," refers to dreams that come **by means of a demon.**

אָמַר רַבִּי בִּיזְנָא בַּר זַבְדָּא אָמַר רַבִּי עֲקִיבָא אָמַר רַבִּי פַּנְדָּא אָמַר רַב נַחוּם אָמַר רַבִּי בִּירַיִם מִשּׁוּם זָקֵן אֶחָד, וּמַנּוּ – רַבִּי בְּנָאָה: עֶשְׂרִים וְאַרְבָּעָה פּוֹתְרֵי חֲלוֹמוֹת הָיוּ בִּירוּשָׁלַיִם, פַּעַם אַחַת חָלַמְתִּי חֲלוֹם וְהָלַכְתִּי אֵצֶל כּוּלָּם, וּמַה שֶּׁפָּתַר לִי זֶה לֹא פָּתַר לִי זֶה – וְכוּלָּם, נִתְקַיְּימוּ בִּי, לְקַיֵּים מַה שֶּׁנֶּאֱמַר: כָּל הַחֲלוֹמוֹת הוֹלְכִים אַחַר הַפֶּה.

In a long chain of those transmitting this statement, it is said that **Rabbi Bizna bar Zavda said** that **Rabbi Akiva said** that **Rabbi Panda said** that **Rav Naḥum said** that **Rabbi Birayim said in the name of one elder, and who is he, Rabbi Bena'a: There were twenty-four interpreters of dreams in Jerusalem. One time, I dreamed a dream and went to each of them** to interpret it. **What one interpreted for me the other did not interpret for me, and** nevertheless, **all of** the interpretations **were realized in me, to fulfill that which is stated: All dreams follow the mouth**[N] of the interpreter.

אַטּוּ ״כָּל הַחֲלוֹמוֹת הוֹלְכִים אַחַר הַפֶּה״ קְרָא הוּא?! – אִין, וְכִדְרַבִּי אֶלְעָזָר, דְּאָמַר רַבִּי אֶלְעָזָר: מִנַּיִן שֶׁכָּל הַחֲלוֹמוֹת הוֹלְכִין אַחַר הַפֶּה – שֶׁנֶּאֱמַר: ״וַיְהִי כַּאֲשֶׁר פָּתַר לָנוּ כֵּן הָיָה״. אָמַר רָבָא: וְהוּא דִּמְפַשַּׁר לֵיהּ מֵעֵין חֶלְמֵיהּ, שֶׁנֶּאֱמַר: ״אִישׁ כַּחֲלֹמוֹ פָּתָר״.

The Gemara asks: **Is that to say that all dreams follow the mouth is a verse** cited as corroboration? The Gemara responds: **Yes, and in accordance with** the opinion of **Rabbi Elazar, as Rabbi Elazar said: From where** is it derived **that all dreams follow the mouth** of the interpreter? **As it is stated** in the story of the dreams of Pharaoh's two ministers. The butler and the baker said to Pharaoh: **"And it came to pass, as he interpreted to us, so it was"** (Genesis 41:13). **Rava said,** one must attach a caveat to this: **This is only** in a case where **it is interpreted for him** in a manner **akin to the dream** where the interpretation is relevant to the dream, **as it is stated** in the story of Joseph's interpretation of the dreams of Pharaoh's two ministers: **"Each man according to his dream he did interpret"** (Genesis 41:12).

״וַיַּרְא שַׂר הָאֹפִים״ – מְנָא יָדַע? אָמַר רַבִּי אֶלְעָזָר: מְלַמֵּד שֶׁכָּל אֶחָד וְאֶחָד הֶרְאוּהוּ חֲלוֹמוֹ וּפִתְרוֹן חֲלוֹמוֹ שֶׁל חֲבֵירוֹ.

With regard to Joseph's interpretation of these dreams, the Gemara asks, it is written: **"The baker saw** that the interpretation was good" (Genesis 40:16); **from where did** the baker **know** that the interpretation was good? **Rabbi Elazar said:** This **teaches that each** of them **was shown his dream and the interpretation of the other's dream.** That is how he knew that it was the correct interpretation.

אָמַר רַבִּי יוֹחָנָן: הִשְׁכִּים וְנָפַל לוֹ פָּסוּק לְתוֹךְ פִּיו – הֲרֵי זוֹ נְבוּאָה קְטַנָּה.

With regard to the veracity of dreams, **Rabbi Yoḥanan said: One who awakened** in the morning **and a** specific **verse happens into his mouth, it is a minor prophecy** and an indication that the content of the verse will be fulfilled.

וְאָמַר רַבִּי יוֹחָנָן, שְׁלֹשָׁה חֲלוֹמוֹת מִתְקַיְּימִין: חֲלוֹם שֶׁל שַׁחֲרִית, וַחֲלוֹם שֶׁחָלַם לוֹ חֲבֵירוֹ, וַחֲלוֹם שֶׁנִּפְתַּר בְּתוֹךְ חֲלוֹם. וְיֵשׁ אוֹמֵר: אַף חֲלוֹם שֶׁנִּשְׁנָה, שֶׁנֶּאֱמַר ״וְעַל הִשָּׁנוֹת הַחֲלוֹם״ וגו׳.

**Rabbi Yoḥanan also said: Three dreams are fulfilled: A dream of the morning, a dream that one's fellow dreamed about him, and a dream that is interpreted within a dream. And some say that a dream that is repeated** several times is also fulfilled, **as it is stated: "And for that the dream was doubled** unto Pharaoh twice, it is because the thing is established by God, and God will shortly bring it to pass" (Genesis 41:32).

אָמַר רַבִּי שְׁמוּאֵל בַּר נַחְמָנִי אָמַ
רַבִּי יוֹנָתָן: אֵין מַרְאִין לוֹ לְאָדָם אֶלָּ
מֵהִרְהוּרֵי לִבּוֹ, שֶׁנֶּאֱמַר: ״אַנְתְּ מַלְכָּא
רַעְיוֹנָךְ עַל מִשְׁכְּבָךְ סְלִקוּ״, וְאִיבָּעֵיו
אֵימָא מֵהָכָא: ״וְרַעְיוֹנֵי לִבְבָךְ תִּנְדַּע״
אָמַר רָבָא: תֵּדַע, דְּלָא מַחֲווּ לֵיהּ לְאֵינָ
לָא דִּקְלָא דְּדַהֲבָא, וְלָא פִּילָא דְּעָיֵי
בְּקוֹפָא דְּמַחְטָא.

**Rabbi Shmuel bar Naḥmani said** that **Rabbi Yonatan said: A person is only is shown** in his dream **the thoughts of his heart** when he was awake, as evidenced by what Daniel said to Nebuchadnezzar, **as it is stated: "As for you, O king, your thoughts came upon your bed,** what should come to pass hereafter" (Daniel 2:29). **And if you wish, say** instead that it is derived **from here,** a related verse: **"And that you may know the thoughts of your** heart" (Daniel 2:30). How will you know the thoughts of your heart? By their being revealed to you in a dream. **Rava said: Know** that this is the case, **for one is neither shown a golden palm tree nor an elephant** going through **the eye of a needle** in a dream. In other words, dreams only contain images that enter a person's mind.

Perek **IX**
Daf **56** Amud **a**

אָמַר לֵיהּ קֵיסָר לְרַבִּי יְהוֹשֻׁעַ בְּרַבִּ
חֲנַנְיָא: אָמְרִיתוּ דְּחָכְמִיתוּ טוּבָא, אֵימָ
לִי מַאי חָזֵינָא בְּחֶלְמַאי! אָמַר לֵיהּ: חָזֵיו
דִּמְשַׁחֲרֵי לָךְ פָּרְסָאֵי וְגָרְבִי בָּךְ, וְרָעֵי בָּ
שִׁקְצֵי בְּחוּטְרָא דְּדַהֲבָא. הִרְהֵר כּוּלֵּי
יוֹמָא, וּלְאוּרְתָּא חֲזָא. אָמַר לֵיהּ שָׁבוֹ
מַלְכָּא לִשְׁמוּאֵל: אָמְרִיתוּ דְּחָכְמִי
טוּבָא, אֵימָא לִי מַאי חָזֵינָא בְּחֶלְמָא
אָמַר לֵיהּ: חָזֵית דְּאָתוּ רוֹמָאֵי וְשָׁבוּ לָךְ
וְטָחֲנִי בָּךְ קַשְׁיָיתָא בְּרֵחְיָיא דְּדַהֲבָא
הִרְהֵר כּוּלֵּיהּ יוֹמָא וּלְאוּרְתָּא חֲזָא.

On a similar note, the Gemara relates that the Roman **emperor said to Rabbi Yehoshua, son of Rabbi Ḥananya: You** Jews **say that you are extremely wise.** If that is so, **tell me what I will see in my dream.** Rabbi Yehoshua **said to him: You will see the Persians capture you, and enslave you, and force you to herd unclean animals with a golden staff. He thought the entire day** about the images described to him by Rabbi Yehoshua **and that night he saw** it in his dream. **King Shapur**[P] of Persia **said to Shmuel: You** Jews **say that you are extremely wise.** If that is so, **tell me what I will see in my dream. Shmuel said to him: You will see the Romans come and take you into captivity** and force you **to grind date pits in mills of gold. He thought the entire day** about the images described to him by Shmuel, **and that night he saw** it in his dream.

בַּר הַדְיָא מְפַשֵּׁר חֶלְמֵי הֲוָה, מַאן דְּיָהֵי
לֵיהּ אַגְרָא – מְפַשֵּׁר לֵיהּ לְמַעַלְיוּתָא
וּמַאן דְּלָא יָהֵיב לֵיהּ אַגְרָא – מְפַשֵּׁ
לֵיהּ לִגְרִיעוּתָא. אַבַּיֵּי וְרָבָא חֲזוֹ חֶלְמָא
אַבַּיֵּי יְהֵיב לֵיהּ זוּזָא וְרָבָא לָא יְהֵיב לֵי
אָמְרִי לֵיהּ: אַקְרִינַן בְּחֶלְמִין ״שׁוֹרְךָ טָבוּ
לְעֵינֶיךָ״ וגו׳. לְרָבָא אָמַר לֵיהּ: פָּסֵי
עִסְקָךְ וְלָא אֲהַנֵּי לָךְ לְמֵיכַל מֵעוּצְבָּ
דְּלִבָּךְ, לְאַבַּיֵּי אָמַר לֵיהּ: מַרְוַוח עִסְקָךְ
וְלָא אֲהַנֵּי לָךְ לְמֵיכַל מֵחֶדְוָא דְּלִבָּךְ.

The Gemara relates: **Bar Haddaya was an interpreter of dreams.** For **one who gave him a fee, he would interpret** the dream **favorably, and for one who did not give him a fee, he would interpret** the dream **unfavorably.** The Gemara relates: There was an incident in which both **Abaye and Rava saw an** identical **dream**[N] and they asked bar Haddaya to interpret it. **Abaye gave him money** and paid his fee, **while Rava did not give him** money. **They said to him:** The verse: **"Your ox shall be slain before your eyes** and you shall not eat thereof" (Deuteronomy 28:31) **was read to us in our dream. He** interpreted their dream and **to Rava he said: Your business will be lost and you will derive no pleasure from eating because of the** extreme **sadness of your heart. To Abaye he said: Your business will profit and you will be unable to eat due to the joy in your heart.**

אָמְרִי לֵיהּ: אַקְרִינַן ״בָּנִים וּבָנוֹת תּוֹלִיד
וגו׳, לְרָבָא – אֲמַר לֵיהּ כְּבִישׁוּתֵי
לְאַבַּיֵּי אָמַר לֵיהּ: בְּנָךְ וּבְנָתָךְ נְפִישׁ
וּמִינַּסְבָן בְּנָתָךְ לְעָלְמָא, וּמְדַמְיָין בְּאַפ
כִּדְקָא אָזְלָן בִּשְׁבְיָה.

**They said to him:** The verse, **"You shall beget sons and daughters, but they shall not be yours; for they shall go into captivity"** (Deuteronomy 28:41), **was read to us** in our dream. He interpreted their dreams, and **to Rava he said** its literal, **adverse** sense. **To Abaye he said: Your sons and daughters will be numerous, and your daughters will be married to outsiders and it will seem to you as if they were taken in captivity.**

אַקְרְיָין ״בָּנֶיךָ וּבְנֹתֶיךָ נְתֻנִים לְעַ
אַחֵר״, לְאַבַּיֵּי אָמַר לֵיהּ: בְּנָךְ וּבְנָתָ
נְפִישִׁין, אַתְּ אָמְרַתְּ לְקָרִיבָךְ, וְהִי
אָמְרָה לְקָרִיבָהּ, וְאַכְפָּה לָךְ וְיָהֲבַ
לְהוּן לְקָרִיבָהּ, דַּהֲוֵי כְּעַם אַחֵר. לְרָבָ
אָמַר לֵיהּ: דְּבֵיתְהוּ שְׁכִיבָא, וְאָתוּ בְּנֵ
וּבְנָתֵיהּ לִידֵי אִיתְּתָא אַחֲרִיתִי, דְּאָמַ
רָבָא אָמַר רַבִּי יִרְמְיָה בַּר אַבָּא אָמַ
רַב: מַאי דִּכְתִיב ״בָּנֶיךָ וּבְנֹתֶיךָ נְתֻנִ
לְעַם אַחֵר״ – זוֹ אֵשֶׁת הָאָב.

They said to him: **The verse: "Your sons and your daughters shall be given unto another people"** (Deuteronomy 28:32), **was read to us** in our dream. **To Abaye he said: Your sons and daughters will be numerous. You say,** that they should marry **your relatives and** your wife **says** that they should marry **her relatives and she will impose** her will **upon you and they will be given** in marriage **to her relatives, which is like another nation** as far as you are concerned. **To Rava he said: Your wife will die and your sons and daughters will come into the hands of another woman. As Rava said** that **Rabbi Yirmeya bar Abba said** that **Rav said: What is** the meaning of **that which is written** in the verse: **"Your sons and your daughters shall be given unto another people"? This** refers to **the father's wife,** the stepmother.

**PERSONALITIES**

**King Shapur – שָׁבוֹר מַלְכָּא:** *Shavor Malka* is the Persian King Shapur I (3901–3932; 141–172 CE), the second ruler of the Sassanid dynasty. He was one of the great Persian kings who expanded the borders of the kingdom. He waged several wars against the Romans and conquered extensive territory from them, reaching as far as Syria. He even managed to take the Roman Emperor Valerianus into captivity. However, he did not always win his wars and was defeated by the Romans in several battles. Unlike most of the kings of that dynasty, he was tolerant of other religions. The Gemara relates at length his close relationship with the Jews and how he valued and appreciated Jewish customs. On several occasions the Talmud recounts his friendship with the *amora* Shmuel.

Image of King Shapur I on a coin from his reign

**NOTES**

**Abaye and Rava saw a dream – אַבַּיֵּי וְרָבָא חֲזוֹ חֶלְמָא:** Apparently, these stories did not all take place at the same time; rather, over the course of many years. Similarly, their interpretations were not realized until much time elapsed. Apparently, Rava did not accept bar Haddaya's interpretations, as he believed that dreams have intrinsic meaning and that they may or may not be realized, independent of their interpretation. At first, Rava did not notice that all of the interpretations were one-sided. He realized it only much later when he saw them realized. Rava assumed that those dreams that were realized immediately, e.g., the *vav* of *peter ḥamor*, were coincidences, or that bar Haddaya had seen his phylacteries beforehand (Rav Ya'akov Emden).

## PERSONALITIES

**Abaye – אַבַּיֵי:** One of the outstanding Sages of the Talmud, Abaye was a fourth generation Babylonian *amora*. He lost both of his parents at an early age and was raised in the house of his uncle, Rabba. Some say that his real name was Naḥmani or Kilil and Abaye was just a nickname. Although his uncle was a priest and the head of the yeshiva, he lived in poverty, as did Abaye. He was the primary student of his uncle and of Rav Yosef. After Rav Yosef's death, Abaye succeeded him as the head of the yeshiva in Pumbedita. In addition to his prominence as a Torah scholar, he was known for his righteousness and his acts of kindness.

His exchanges and halakhic arguments with his uncle and, even more so, with Rav Yosef, can be found throughout the Talmud. However, his disputes with his colleague Rava are especially significant. Their disputes, known as the discussions of Abaye and Rava, are examples of profound and edifying disputes and are among the foundations of the Babylonian Talmud. In these disputes, with few exceptions, the *halakha* is ruled in accordance with the opinion of Rava.

## BACKGROUND

**Lettuce – חַסָּא:** The Mishna and the Gemara speak of lettuce known as Arabic lettuce, خس, which is different from the European variety in several respects.

The long, large lettuce leaves form a type of head, 30–51 cm, filled with wrinkles and folds. These leaves are tasty, sweet in the language of the Sages, and the lettuce is grown primarily for those leaves. However, when the reproductive stage of the plant begins, a long, woody stalk is formed from which small, bitter leaves grow.

It is for this reason that lettuce can serve as an omen for good and prosperity as well as an omen for bitterness.

Lettuce, called *ḥazzeret* in Hebrew (*Lactuca sativa var. longifolia*), a leafy winter vegetable

אַקְרִינַן בְּחֶלְמִין ״לֵךְ אֱכֹל בְּשִׂמְחָה לַחְמֶךָ״, לְאַבַּיֵי אֲמַר לֵיהּ: מַרְוַוח עִסְקָךְ, וְאָכְלַתְּ וְשָׁתֵית וְקָרֵית פְּסוּקָא מֵחֶדְוָא דְּלִבָּךְ. לְרָבָא אֲמַר לֵיהּ: פָּסֵיד עִסְקָךְ, טָבְחַתְּ וְלָא אָכְלַתְּ וְשָׁתֵית וְקָרֵית לְפַכּוּחֵי פַּחְדָּךְ.

They said to him: The verse: **"Go your way, eat your bread with joy,** and drink your wine with a merry heart" (Ecclesiastes 9:7), **was read to us in our dream. To Abaye**[P] **he said: Your business will profit and you will eat and drink and read the verse out of the joy of your heart. To Rava he said: Your business will be lost, you will slaughter but not eat, you will drink** wine and **read** passages from the Bible in order **to allay your fears.**

אַקְרִינַן ״זֶרַע רַב תּוֹצִיא הַשָּׂדֶה״, לְאַבַּיֵי אֲמַר לֵיהּ מֵרֵישֵׁיהּ, לְרָבָא אֲמַר לֵיהּ מִסֵּיפֵיהּ.

They said to him: The verse: **"You shall carry much seed out into the field,** and shall gather little in; for the locust shall consume it" (Deuteronomy 28:38), **was read to us** in our dream. **To Abaye he said from the beginning** of the verse, that he will enjoy an abundant harvest. **To Rava he said from the end** of the verse, that his harvest will be destroyed.

אַקְרִינַן ״זֵיתִים יִהְיוּ לְךָ בְּכָל גְּבוּלֶךָ״ וגו׳, לְאַבַּיֵי אֲמַר לֵיהּ מֵרֵישֵׁיהּ, לְרָבָא אֲמַר לֵיהּ מִסֵּיפֵיהּ.

They said to him: The verse: **"You shall have olive-trees throughout all your borders,** but you shall not anoint yourself with the oil; for your olives shall drop off" (Deuteronomy 28:40), **was read to us** in our dream. And again, **to Abaye he said from the beginning** of the verse. **To Rava he said from the end** of the verse.

אַקְרִינַן ״וְרָאוּ כָּל עַמֵּי הָאָרֶץ״ וגו׳, לְאַבַּיֵי אֲמַר לֵיהּ: נְפַק לָךְ שְׁמָא דְּרֵישׁ מְתִיבְתָּא הָוֵית, אֵימְתָךְ נָפְלַת בְּעָלְמָא. לְרָבָא אֲמַר לֵיהּ: בֵּי גַנְזֵי דְּמַלְכָּא אִתְּבַר, וּמִתְפַּסְתְּ בְּגַנָּבֵי, וְדָיְינִי כּוּלֵּי עָלְמָא קַל וָחוֹמֶר מִינָּךְ. לְמָחָר אִתְּבַר בֵּי גַנְזָא דְּמַלְכָּא, וְאָתוּ וְתָפְשִׂי לֵיהּ לְרָבָא.

They said to him: The verse: **"All the peoples of the earth shall see** that the name of the Lord is called upon you; and they shall be afraid of you" (Deuteronomy 28:10), **was read to us** in our dream. **To Abaye he said: Your name will become well-known as head of the yeshiva, and you will be feared by all. To Rava he said: The king's treasury was broken** into **and you will be apprehended as a thief, and everyone will draw an *a fortiori* inference from you:** If Rava who is wealthy and of distinguished lineage can be arrested on charges of theft, what will become of the rest of us? Indeed, **the next day, the king's treasury was burglarized, and they came and apprehended Rava.**

אָמְרִי לֵיהּ: חֲזַן חַסָּא עַל פּוּם דָּנֵי. לְאַבַּיֵי אֲמַר לֵיהּ: עֵיף עִסְקָךְ כְּחַסָּא, לְרָבָא אֲמַר לֵיהּ: מָרִיר עִסְקָךְ כִּי חַסָּא.

Abaye and Rava **said to him: We saw lettuce**[B] **on the mouth of the barrels. To Abaye he said: Your business will double like lettuce** whose leaves are wide and wrinkled. **To Rava he said: Your work will be bitter like a lettuce** stalk.

אָמְרִי לֵיהּ: חֲזַן בִּשְׂרָא עַל פּוּם דָּנֵי. לְאַבַּיֵי אֲמַר לֵיהּ: בָּסֵים חַמְרָךְ וְאָתוּ כּוּלֵּי עָלְמָא לְמִזְבַּן בִּשְׂרָא וְחַמְרָא מִינָּךְ. לְרָבָא אֲמַר לֵיהּ: תָּקֵיף חַמְרָךְ, וְאָתוּ כּוּלֵּי עָלְמָא לְמִזְבַּן בִּשְׂרָא לְמֵיכַל בֵּיהּ.

**They said to him: We saw meat on the mouth of barrels. To Abaye he said: Your wine will be sweet and everyone will come to buy meat and wine from you. To Rava he said: Your wine will spoil, and everyone will go to buy meat in order to eat with it,** to dip the meat in your vinegar.

אָמְרִי לֵיהּ: חֲזַן חָבִיתָא דְּתָלֵי בְּדִיקְלָא, לְאַבַּיֵי אֲמַר לֵיהּ: מִדַּלֵּי עִסְקָךְ כְּדִיקְלָא. לְרָבָא אֲמַר לֵיהּ: חָלֵי עִסְקָךְ כְּתַמְרֵי.

**They said to him: We saw a barrel hanging from a palm tree. To Abaye he said: Your business will rise like a palm tree. To Rava he said: Your work will be sweet like dates** which are very cheap in Babylonia, indicating that you will be compelled to sell your merchandise at a cheap price.

אָמְרִי לֵיהּ: חֲזַן רוּמָּנָא דְּקָדְחִי אַפּוּם דָּנֵי, לְאַבַּיֵי אֲמַר לֵיהּ: עַשֵּׁיק עִסְקָךְ כְּרוּמָּנָא. לְרָבָא אֲמַר לֵיהּ: קָאוֵי עִסְקָךְ כְּרוּמָּנָא.

**They said to him: We saw a pomegranate taking root on the mouth of barrels. To Abaye he said: Your business will increase in value like a pomegranate. To Rava he said: Your work will go sour like a pomegranate.**

אָמְרִי לֵיהּ: חֲזַן חָבִיתָא דִּנְפַל לְבֵירָא, לְאַבַּיֵי אֲמַר לֵיהּ: מִתְבָּעֵי עִסְקָךְ, כְּדַאֲמַר ״נְפַל פִּתָּא בְּבֵירָא וְלָא אִשְׁתַּכַּח״. לְרָבָא אֲמַר לֵיהּ: פָּסֵיד עִסְקָךְ וְשָׁדְיָא לֵיהּ לְבֵירָא.

**They said to him: We saw a barrel fall into a pit. To Abaye he said: Your merchandise will be in demand** as the adage says: **Bread falls in a pit and is not found.** In other words, everyone will seek your wares and they will not find them due to increased demand. **To Rava he said: Your merchandise will be ruined and you will throw it** away **into a pit.**

אָמְרִי לֵיהּ: חֲזֵינַן בַּר חֲמָרָא דְּקָאֵי אַאִיסַדַן וְנוֹעֵר, לְאַבַּיֵי אֲמַר לֵיהּ: מַלְכָּא הָוֵית, וְקָאֵי אָמוֹרָא עֲלָךְ. לְרָבָא אֲמַר לֵיהּ: פֶּטֶר חֲמוֹר גְּהִיט מִתְּפִילָּךְ. אֲמַר לֵיהּ: לְדִידִי חָזֵי לִי וְאִיתֵיהּ! – אֲמַר לֵיהּ: וָא״ו דְּ״פֶטֶר חֲמוֹר״ וַדַּאי גְּהִיט מִתְּפִילָּךְ.

**They said to him: We saw a donkey-foal standing near our heads, braying. To Abaye he said: You will be a king,** that is to say, **head of the yeshiva, and an interpreter will stand near you** to repeat your teachings to the masses out loud. **To Rava he said:** I see the words ***peter ḥamor*, first-born donkey, erased from your phylacteries.** Rava **said to him: I myself saw it and it is there.** Bar Haddaya **said to him:** The letter ***vav* of** the word ***peter ḥamor* is certainly erased from your phylacteries.**

Turnip-heads [gargelidei] – גַּרְגְּלִידֵי: From the Greek γογγυλίδιον, goggulidion, meaning a round turnip-head.

House [appadna] – אַפַּדְנָא: The source of this word is Persian and during the Achaemenid period it denoted the king's palace. The word, whose original form was apadana, entered the Aramaic language early (Daniel 11:45) and was adopted in other languages as well.

לְסוֹף אֲזַל רָבָא לְחוּדֵיהּ לְגַבֵּיהּ, אֲמַר לֵיהּ: חֲזַאי דַּשָּׁא בָרַיְיתָא דִּנְפַל, אֲמַר לֵיהּ: אִשְׁתְּךָ שָׁכְבָא. אֲמַר לֵיהּ: חֲזַאי כָּכֵי וְשִׁנֵּי דִּנְתוּר, אֲמַר לֵיהּ: בְּנָךְ וּבְנָתָךְ שָׁכְבָן. אֲמַר לֵיהּ: חֲזַאי תַּרְתֵּי יוֹנֵי דְּפָרְחָן אֲמַר לֵיהּ: תְּרֵי נְשֵׁי מְגָרְשַׁת. אֲמַר לֵיהּ: חֲזַאי תְּרֵי גַּרְגְּלִידֵי דְּלִפְתָּא, אֲמַר לֵיהּ: תְּרֵין קוּלְפֵי בָלְעַת. אֲזַל רָבָא הַהוּא יוֹמָא וְיָתֵיב בֵּי מִדְרָשָׁא כּוּלֵּיהּ יוֹמָא אַשְׁכַּח הָנֵי תְּרֵי סַגִּי נַהוֹרֵי דַּהֲווֹ קָמִנְצוּ בַּהֲדֵי הֲדָדֵי, אֲזַל רָבָא לְפָרוֹקִינְהוּ – וּמְחוּהוּ לְרָבָא תְּרֵי דְּלוּ לְמִמְחְיֵיהּ אַחֲרִיתִי, אֲמַר: מִסְתַּאי, אֲמַר: תְּרֵין חֲזַאי.

Ultimately, Rava went to bar Haddaya **alone**. Rava said to him: I saw the outer door of my house fall. Bar Haddaya **said to him: Your wife will die,** as she is the one who protects the house. Rava said to him: I saw my front and back teeth fall out. He said to him: Your sons and daughters will die. Rava **said to** him: I saw two doves that were flying. He said to him: You will divorce two women. Rava said to him: I saw two turnip-heads [gargelidei]. He said to him: You will receive two blows **with a club** shaped like a turnip. **That same day Rava went and sat in the study hall the entire day.** He discovered these two blind people who were fighting with each other. Rava went to separate them and they struck Rava two blows. When they raised their staffs to strike him an additional blow, he said: That is **enough for me, I only saw two.**

לְסוֹף אֲתָא רָבָא וְיָהֵיב לֵיהּ אַגְרָא, אֲמַר לֵיהּ: חֲזַאי אַשִׁיתָא דִּנְפַל. אֲמַר לֵיהּ: נְכָסִים בְּלָא מֵצָרִים קָנֵית. אֲמַר לֵיהּ: חֲזַאי אַפַּדְנָא דְּאַבָּיֵי דִּנְפַל וְכַסְיָין אַבְקֵיהּ. אֲמַר לֵיהּ: אַבָּיֵי שָׁכֵיב וּמְתִיבְתֵּיהּ אָתְיָא לְגַבָּךְ. אֲמַר לֵיהּ: חֲזַאי אַפַּדְנָא דִּידִי דִּנְפִיל, וְאָתוּ כּוּלֵּי עָלְמָא שָׁקֵיל לְבִינָתָא לְבִינָתָא, אֲמַר לֵיהּ: שְׁמַעֲתָתַךְ מִבַּדְּרָן בְּעָלְמָא. אֲמַר לֵיהּ: חֲזַאי דְּאִבְקַע רֵישִׁי וּנְתַר מוֹקְרִי. אֲמַר לֵיהּ: אוּדְרָא מִבֵּי סָדְיָא נָפֵיק אֲמַר לֵיהּ: אַקְרְיוּן הַלֵּל הַמִּצְרָאָה בְּחֶלְמָא, אֲמַר לֵיהּ: נִיסָּא מִתְרַחֲשֵׁי לָךְ.

Ultimately, Rava came and gave him, bar Haddaya, a fee. And then Rava, said to him: I saw my wall fall. Bar Haddaya **said to** him: You will acquire property without limits. Rava said to him: I saw Abaye's house [appadna] fall and its dust covered me. Bar Haddaya said to him: Abaye will die and his yeshiva will come to you. Rava said to him: I saw my house fall, and everyone came and took the bricks. He said to him: **Your teachings will be disseminated throughout the world.** Rava said to him: I saw that my head split and my brain fell out. He said to him: **A feather will fall out of the pillow** near your head. Rava said to him: **The Egyptian hallel,** the hallel that celebrates the Exodus, **was read to me in a dream.** He said to him: **Miracles will be performed for you.**

הֲוָה קָא אָזֵיל בַּהֲדֵיהּ בְּאַרְבָּא, אֲמַר: בַּהֲדֵי גַּבְרָא דְּמִתְרַחֲשׁ לֵיהּ נִיסָּא לְמָה לִי? בַּהֲדֵי דְּקָא סָלֵיק נְפַל סִיפְרָא מִינֵּיהּ, אַשְׁכְּחֵיהּ רָבָא וַחֲזָא דַּהֲוָה כְּתִיב בֵּיהּ: כָּל הַחֲלוֹמוֹת הוֹלְכִין אַחַר הַפֶּה. אֲמַר: רָשָׁע בְּדִידָךְ קַיְימָא וְצַעֲרַתָּן כּוּלֵּי הַאי! כּוּלְּהוּ מָחֵילְנָא לָךְ, בַּר מִבְּרַתֵּיהּ דְּרַב חִסְדָּא. יְהֵא רַעֲוָא דְּלִמַּסֵּר הַהוּא גַּבְרָא לִידֵי דְמַלְכוּתָא דְּלָא מְרַחֲמוּ עֲלֵיהּ.

Bar Haddaya **was going with** Rava **on a ship;** bar Haddaya **said: Why am I going with a person for whom miracles will be performed,** lest the miracle will be that the ship will sink and he alone will be saved. As bar Haddaya **was climbing** onto the ship **a book fell from him.** Rava found it **and saw: All dreams follow the mouth,** written therein. He said to bar Haddaya: **Scoundrel.** It was dependent **on you, and you caused me** so much suffering. **I forgive you for everything except for the daughter of Rav Ḥisda,** Rava's wife, whom bar Haddaya predicted would die. **May it be** Your **will that this man be delivered into the hands of a kingdom that has no compassion on him.**

אֲמַר: מַאי אַעֲבִיד? גְּמִירִי: דִּקְלָלַת חָכָם אֲפִילּוּ בְּחִנָּם הִיא בָּאָה, וְכׇל שֶׁכֵּן רָבָא דְּבְדִינָא קָא לָיֵיט. אֲמַר: אֵיקוּם וְאִיגְלִי, דְּאָמַר מָר: גָּלוּת מְכַפֶּרֶת עָוֹן.

Bar Haddaya **said to himself: What will I do? We learned** through tradition **that the curse of a Sage,** even if baseless, **comes true? And all the more so in the case of Rava,** as he **cursed me justifiably.** He said to himself: **I will get up and go into exile, as the Master said: Exile atones for transgression.**

קָם גְּלִי לְבֵי רוֹמָאֵי, אֲזַל יָתֵיב אַפִּתְחָא דְּרֵישׁ טוּרְזִינָא דְמַלְכָּא. רֵישׁ טוּרְזִינָא חֲזָא חֶלְמָא, אֲמַר לֵיהּ: חֲזַאי חֶלְמָא דְּעַיֵּיל מַחְטָא בְּאֶצְבַּעְתִּי, אֲמַר לֵיהּ: הַב לִי זוּזָא! וְלָא יְהַב לֵיהּ, לָא אֲמַר לֵיהּ וְלָא מִידֵּי. אֲמַר לֵיהּ: חֲזַאי דִּנְפַל תַּכְלָא בִּתְרֵי אֶצְבְּעָתִי, אֲמַר לֵיהּ: הַב לִי זוּזָא! וְלָא יְהַב לֵיהּ וְלָא אֲמַר לֵיהּ. אֲמַר לֵיהּ: חֲזַאי דִּנְפַל תַּכְלָא בְּכוּלֵּיהּ יְדָא, אֲמַר לֵיהּ: נְפַל תַּכְלָא בְּכוּלְּהוּ שִׁירָאֵי. שְׁמַע בֵּי מַלְכָּא וְאַתְיוּהּ לְרֵישׁ טוּרְזִינָא, קָא קָטְלִי לֵיהּ אֲמַר לְהוּ: אֲנָא אַמַּאי? אַיְיתוּ לְהַאי דַּהֲוָה יָדַע וְלָא אֲמַר! אַיְיתוּהוּ בַּר הַדַּיָא, אֲמְרִי לֵיהּ: אַמְּטוּל זוּזָא דִּידָךְ חֲרַבוּ

He arose and exiled himself to the seat of the Roman government. He went and sat by the entrance, where **the keeper of the king's wardrobe** stood. **The wardrobe guard dreamed a dream.** He said to bar Haddaya: **I saw in the dream that a needle pierced my finger.** Bar Haddaya **said to him: Give me a zuz.** He did not give him the coin so bar Haddaya **said nothing to him. Again,** the guard **said to him: I saw a worm that fell between my two fingers,** eating them. Bar Haddaya **said to him: Give me a zuz.** He did not give him the coin, **so** bar Haddaya said nothing to him. **Again,** the guard **said to him: I saw that a worm fell upon my entire hand,** eating it. Bar Haddaya **said to him: A worm fell** upon and ate **all the silk garments. They** heard of this **in the king's palace and they brought the wardrobe keeper and were** in the process of **executing him. He said to them: Why me? Bring the one who knew and did not say** the information that he knew. **They brought** bar Haddaya and **said to him: Because of your zuz,** ruin came upon

שִׁירָאֵי דְּמַלְכָּא! כְּפִיתוּ תְּרֵין אַרְזֵי בְּחַבְלָא, אַסּוּר חַד כַּרְעֵיהּ לְחַד אַרְזָא וְחַד כַּרְעֵיהּ לְחַד אַרְזָא, וְשָׁרוּ לְחַבְלָא עַד דְּאִצְטְלִיק רֵישֵׁיהּ, אֲזַל כָּל חַד וְחַד וְקָם אַדּוּכְתֵּיהּ וְאִצְטְלִיק וּנְפַל בִּתְרֵין.

**the king's silk** garments. **They tied two cedar** trees together **with a rope and tied one of his legs to one cedar and one of his legs to** the other **cedar and they released the rope until his head split open. Each** tree **went back and stood in its place and** bar Haddaya **split and fell** completely split **in two.**

שָׁאַל בֶּן דָּמָא בֶּן אֲחוֹתוֹ שֶׁל רַבִּי יִשְׁמָעֵאל אֶת רַבִּי יִשְׁמָעֵאל: רָאִיתִי שְׁנֵי לְחָיַי שֶׁנָּשְׁרוּ. אָמַר: שְׁנֵי גְּדוּדֵי רוֹמִי יָעֲצוּ עָלֶיךָ רָעָה, וּמֵתוּ.

The Gemara relates a story with regard to a Sage who interpreted dreams: Rabbi Yishmael. **Ben Dama, son of Rabbi Yishmael's sister, asked** his uncle, **Rabbi Yishmael: I saw** in a dream that **my two cheeks fell off.** What does my dream mean? Rabbi Yishmael **said to him: Two Roman battalions spoke ill of you, and they died.** Cheeks symbolize a mouth that speaks evil.

אֲמַר לֵיהּ בַּר קַפָּרָא לְרַבִּי: רָאִיתִי חוֹטְמִי שֶׁנָּשַׁר, אֲמַר לֵיהּ: חֲרוֹן אַף נִסְתַּלֵּק מִמְּךָ. אֲמַר לֵיהּ: רָאִיתִי שְׁנֵי יָדַי שֶׁנֶּחְתְּכוּ, אֲמַר לֵיהּ: לֹא תִּצְטָרֵךְ לְמַעֲשֵׂה יָדֶיךָ. אֲמַר לֵיהּ: אֲרָאִיתִי שְׁנֵי רַגְלַי שֶׁנִּקְטְעוּ, אֲמַר לֵיהּ: עַל סוּס אַתָּה רוֹכֵב. חֲזַאי דְּאָמְרִי לִי: בַּאֲדָר מִיתַת וְנִיסָן לָא חָזֵית, אֲמַר לֵיהּ: בְּאַדְרוּתָא מִיתַת, וְלָא אָתֵית לִידֵי נִסָּיוֹן.

Similarly, the Gemara relates: **Bar Kappara said to Rabbi** Yehuda HaNasi: **I saw** in a dream that **my nose fell off,** what is the meaning of my dream? **He said to him:** This is an allusion that **anger** [*ḥaron af*] that had been directed against you **has been removed from you.** Bar Kappara **said to him: I saw** in a dream that **my two hands were cut off.** Rabbi **said to him:** This dream means that **you will not require the labor of your hands,** as you will be rich and you will have considerable means without effort. Bar Kappara **said to him: I saw my two legs were cut off.** Rabbi Yehuda HaNasi **said: You are riding a horse.** He said to him: **I saw that** they were saying **to me that in** the month of **Adar I will die and I will not see Nisan He said to him: You will die in glory** [*adruta*][N] **and you will not be brought to temptation** [*nissayon*].

אֲמַר לֵיהּ הַהוּא מִינָא לְרַבִּי יִשְׁמָעֵאל: רָאִיתִי שֶׁאֲנִי מַשְׁקֶה שֶׁמֶן לַזֵּיתִים, אֲמַר לֵיהּ: בָּא עַל אִמּוֹ. אֲמַר לֵיהּ: חֲזַאי דְּקָטֵיף לִי כּוֹכָבָא, אֲמַר לֵיהּ: בַּר יִשְׂרָאֵל גְּנַבְתְּ. אֲמַר לֵיהּ: חֲזַאי דִּבְלַעְתִּי לְכוֹכָבָא. אֲמַר לֵיהּ: בַּר יִשְׂרָאֵל זַבִּנְתֵּיהּ, וְאָכְלַתְּ לִדְמֵיהּ. אֲמַר לֵיהּ: חֲזַאי עֵינַי דְּנָשְׁקָן אַהֲדָדֵי, אֲמַר לֵיהּ: בָּא עַל אֲחוֹתוֹ. אֲמַר לֵיהּ: חֲזַאי דְּנָשְׁקִי סִיהֲרָא, אֲמַר לֵיהּ: בָּא עַל אֵשֶׁת יִשְׂרָאֵל. אֲמַר לֵיהּ: חֲזַאי דְּדָרֵיכְנָא בְּטוּנָא דְּאָסָא, אֲמַר לֵיהּ: בָּא עַל נַעֲרָה הַמְאוֹרָסָה. אֲמַר לֵיהּ: חֲזַאי טוּנָא מֵעִילָּאִי וְהוּא מִתַּתַּאי, אֲמַר לֵיהּ: מִשְׁכָּבְךָ הָפוּךְ. אֲמַר לֵיהּ: חֲזַאי עוֹרְבֵי דְּהָדְרִי לְפוּרְיֵיהּ, אֲמַר לֵיהּ: אִשְׁתְּךָ זָנְתָה מֵאֲנָשִׁים הַרְבֵּה. אֲמַר לֵיהּ: חֲזַאי יוֹנֵי דְּהָדְרִי לְפוּרְיֵיהּ, אֲמַר לֵיהּ: נָשִׁים הַרְבֵּה טִמֵּאתָ. אֲמַר לֵיהּ: חֲזַאי דְּנָקֵיט תְּרֵי יוֹנֵי וּפַרְחָן, אֲמַר לֵיהּ: תַּרְתֵּי נָשֵׁי נְסַבְתְּ וּפְטַרְתִּינוּן בְּלֹא גֵּט.

The Gemara relates a different case of dream interpretation: **A certain heretic said to Rabbi Yishmael: I saw** in my dream **that I was irrigating olives with** olive **oil.** What is the interpretation of my dream? **He said to him:** It is a sign that **you had relations with your mother,** as oil comes from the olive, and he is returning the oil to the olives. That heretic **said to Rabbi Yishmael: I saw that I was plucking a star. He said to him: You kidnapped an Israelite man,** as Israel is likened to the stars.[N] The heretic **said to him: I saw that I swallowed a star. He said to him: You sold the Israelite man** whom you kidnapped **and spent the money** that you received from the sale. The heretic **said to him: I saw my eyes kissing one another. He said to him: You had relations with your sister** as siblings are like two eyes. The heretic **said to him: I saw myself kissing the moon. He said to him: You slept with an Israelite woman,** who is likened to the moon. **He said to him: I saw that I was treading in the shade of a myrtle tree. He said to him: You slept with a betrothed young woman,** as it was customary to make a canopy of myrtle for the betrothal. **He said to him: I saw that the shade was above me, and** the tree **was below me. He said to him: Your bed is upside-down,** your relations with the betrothed woman were unnatural. **He said to him: I saw ravens circling my bed. He said to him: Your wife committed adultery with many men. He said to him: I saw doves circling around my bed. He said to him: You defiled many women. He said to him: I saw that I was holding two doves and** they were **flying. He said to him: You married two women and dismissed them** from your house **without a divorce.**

אֲמַר לֵיהּ: חֲזַאי דְּקָלֵיפְנָא בֵּיעֵי, אֲמַר לֵיהּ: שָׁכְבֵי קָא מְשַׁלַּחַת. אֲמַר לֵיהּ: כּוּלְּהוּ אִיתְנְהוּ בִּי, בַּר מֵהָא דְּלֵיתֵיהּ! אַדְּהָכִי וְהָכִי אָתְיָא הַאי אִיתְּתָא, וַאֲמַרָה לֵיהּ: הַאי גְּלִימָא דִּמְכַסָּא – דְּגַבְרָא פְּלוֹנִי הוּא, דְּמִית וְאַשְׁלַחְתֵּיהּ.

**He said to him: I saw myself peeling eggs. He said to him: You stripped dead people,** because an egg is eaten at the meal of comfort after burying the dead. The same heretic **said to him: Everything** you have interpreted **is true, with the exception of this one,** the last interpretation, **which is not true. Meanwhile, this woman came and said to him: This cloak that you are wearing** belongs **to such-and-such a man, who died and whom you stripped** of his clothing.

אֲמַר לֵיהּ: חֲזַאי דְּאָמְרִי לִי: שְׁבַק לָךְ אֲבוּךְ נִכְסֵי בְּקַפּוֹדְקִיָא. אֲמַר לֵיהּ: אִית לָךְ נִכְסֵי בְּקַפּוֹדְקִיָא? אֲמַר לֵיהּ: לָאו. אֲזַל אֲבוּךְ לְקַפּוֹדְקִיָא? אֲמַר לֵיהּ: לָאו. – אִם כֵּן, קַפָּא – כְּשׁוּרָא, דִּיקָא – עַשְׂרָה, זִיל חֲזִי קַפָּא דְּרֵישׁ עַשְׂרָה, שֶׁהִיא מְלֵאָה זוּזֵי, אֲזַל אַשְׁכַּח שֶׁהִיא מְלֵאָה זוּזֵי.

**He said to** Rabbi Yishmael: **I saw that they said to me** in a dream: **Your father left you property in Cappadocia.** Rabbi Yishmael **said to him: Do you have property in Cappadocia?** The heretic **said to him: No. Did your father** ever **go to Cappadocia?** The heretic **said to him: No.** Rabbi Yishmael **said to him: If so,** it must be understood as follows: ***Kappa*** in Greek means **beam;** ***deka***[L] means **ten. Go look at the tenth beam** in your house and you will find **that it is full of coins. He went and found that it was full of coins.**

NOTES

**You will die in glory** [*adruta*] – **בְּאַדְרוּתָא מִיתַת**: Some interpret *mitat* not as death, but as coming, from the Aramaic *ata*. In other words, you will come in glory (Rashash).

**The connection between Israel and the stars** – **הַקֶּשֶׁר בֵּין יִשְׂרָאֵל לַכּוֹכָבִים**: Israel is likened to the stars in the Book of Daniel where it is stated: "And some of the host and of the stars it cast down to the ground" (Daniel 8:10). This is interpreted to mean that God "shall destroy they who are mighty and the people of the saints" (Daniel 8:24; and see Rav Ya'akov Emden).

LANGUAGE

*Kappa deka* – **קַפָּא דִּיקָא**: The double meaning of the name Cappadocia, which is the state of Καππαδοκία, Kappadokia, in Asia Minor, is apparently as follows: *Kappa* means beam, which is *kora* in Aramaic. Some associated this word with the Greek κάππα, *kappa*, meaning a crooked pole (*Mosaf HaArukh*). This supports Rashi's comment with regard to the use of the Greek word *kappa*. Indeed, its meaning in Aramaic is beam. The Greek δέκα, *deka*, means ten. Therefore, Cappadocia is understood to mean the tenth beam.

אָמַר רַבִּי חֲנִינָא: הָרוֹאֶה בְּאֵר בַּחֲלוֹם – רוֹאֶה שָׁלוֹם, שֶׁנֶּאֱמַר ״וַיַּחְפְּרוּ עַבְדֵי יִצְחָק בַּנָּחַל וַיִּמְצְאוּ שָׁם בְּאֵר מַיִם חַיִּים״. רַבִּי נָתָן אוֹמֵר מָצָא תּוֹרָה, שֶׁנֶּאֱמַר: ״כִּי מֹצְאִי מָצָא חַיִּים״, וּכְתִיב הָכָא: ״בְּאֵר מַיִם חַיִּים״. רָבָא אָמַר: חַיִּים מַמָּשׁ.

The Gemara continues dealing with interpretations of the details of dreams: **Rabbi Ḥanina said: One who sees a well in a dream sees peace, as it is said: "And Isaac's servants dug in the valley and found there a well of living water"** (Genesis 26:19), and ultimately there was peace. **Rabbi Natan says:** One who sees a well in his dream it is a symbol that **he has found Torah,** as the well symbolizes Torah. **As it is stated** with regard to the Torah: **"For whoever finds me finds life"** (Proverbs 8:35), **and it is written here: "A well of living water,"** and we see that a well is linked to Torah as both are associated with life. **Rava said:** The well in the dream symbolizes **actual life.**

אָמַר רַבִּי חָנָן, שָׁלֹשׁ שְׁלוֹמוֹת הֵן נָהָר, צִפּוֹר, וּקְדֵרָה. נָהָר – דִּכְתִיב ״הִנְנִי נֹטֶה אֵלֶיהָ כְּנָהָר שָׁלוֹם״ צִפּוֹר – דִּכְתִיב: ״כְּצִפֳּרִים עָפוֹת כֵּן יָגֵן ה׳ צְבָאוֹת״ וגו׳, קְדֵרָה – דִּכְתִיב ״ה׳ תִּשְׁפֹּת שָׁלוֹם לָנוּ״. אָמַר רַבִּי חֲנִינָא: וּבִקְדֵרָה שֶׁאֵין בָּהּ בָּשָׂר שָׁנִינוּ ״וּפָרְשׂוּ כַּאֲשֶׁר בַּסִּיר וּכְבָשָׂר בְּתוֹךְ קַלָּחַת״.

**Rabbi Ḥanan said: There are three** items seen in dreams that are indications of **peace: A river, a bird and a pot.** The Gemara elaborates: **A river, as it is written: "I will extend peace to her like a river"** (Isaiah 66:12); **a bird, as it is written: "As birds hovering, so will the Lord of hosts protect Jerusalem"** (Isaiah 31:5); and **a pot, as it is written: "Lord, You will establish [*tishpot*] peace for us"** (Isaiah 26:12). Peace is likened to a pot which is placed [*shafat*] on the fire. **And Rabbi Ḥanina said: We learned** that a pot in a dream is a sign of peace **with regard to a pot that does not have meat in it,** as a pot that has meat in it symbolizes calamity, as it is stated: **"Yea, they chop them in pieces, as that which is in the pot, and as flesh within the cauldron"** (Micah 3:3).

אָמַר רַבִּי יְהוֹשֻׁעַ בֶּן לֵוִי: הָרוֹאֶה נָהָר בַּחֲלוֹם יַשְׁכִּים וְיֹאמַר ״הִנְנִי נֹטֶה אֵלֶיהָ כְּנָהָר שָׁלוֹם״, קוֹדֶם שֶׁיְּקַדְּמֶנּוּ פָּסוּק אַחֵר – ״כִּי יָבוֹא כַנָּהָר צָר״ הָרוֹאֶה צִפּוֹר בַּחֲלוֹם יַשְׁכִּים וְיֹאמַר ״כְּצִפֳּרִים עָפוֹת כֵּן יָגֵן״ וגו׳, קוֹדֶם שֶׁיְּקַדְּמֶנּוּ פָּסוּק אַחֵר – ״כְּצִפּוֹר נוֹדֶדֶת מִן קִנָּהּ״ וגו׳. הָרוֹאֶה קְדֵרָה בַּחֲלוֹם יַשְׁכִּים וְיֹאמַר ״ה׳ תִּשְׁפֹּת שָׁלוֹם לָנוּ״, קוֹדֶם שֶׁיְּקַדְּמֶנּוּ פָּסוּק אַחֵר – ״שְׁפֹת הַסִּיר שְׁפֹת״.

Since rivers, birds, and pots have ambiguous connotations, it is recommended that someone who sees them in a dream recite a verse that interprets the dream positively. **Rabbi Yehoshua ben Levi said:** One who sees something in a dream that may be interpreted ambiguously should quickly recite an appropriate verse suggestive of a positive interpretation. For example, **one who sees a river in a dream** should **rise early** and **recite: "I will extend peace to her like a river," before a different verse,** with a negative connotation, **can precede it** in becoming reality: **"For distress will come in like a river"** (Isaiah 59:19). **One who sees a bird in a dream** should **rise early and recite: "As birds hovering, so will the Lord of hosts protect Jerusalem," before a different verse,** with a negative connotation, **can precede it** in becoming reality: **"As a bird that wanders from her nest,** so is a man that wanders from his place" (Proverbs 27:8). **One who sees a pot in a dream** should **rise early and recite: "Lord, You will establish peace for us," before a different verse,** which concludes with a wrathful prophecy, **can precede it** in becoming reality: **"Set on the pot, set it on"** (Ezekiel 24:3).

הָרוֹאֶה עֲנָבִים בַּחֲלוֹם יַשְׁכִּים וְיֹאמַר ״כַּעֲנָבִים בַּמִּדְבָּר״, קוֹדֶם שֶׁיְּקַדְּמֶנּוּ פָּסוּק אַחֵר – ״עֲנָבֵמוֹ עִנְּבֵי רוֹשׁ״ הָרוֹאֶה הַר בַּחֲלוֹם יַשְׁכִּים וְיֹאמַר ״מַה נָּאווּ עַל הֶהָרִים רַגְלֵי מְבַשֵּׂר״ קוֹדֶם שֶׁיְּקַדְּמֶנּוּ פָּסוּק אַחֵר – ״עַל הֶהָרִים אֶשָּׂא בְכִי וָנֶהִי״.

Similarly, **one who sees grapes in a dream** should **rise early and recite:** "I found Israel **like grapes in the wilderness"** (Hosea 9:10), **before a different verse,** with a negative connotation, **can precede it** in becoming reality: **"Their grapes are grapes of gall,** their clusters are bitter" (Deuteronomy 32:32). **One who sees a mountain in a dream** should **rise early and recite: "How beautiful upon the mountains are the feet of the messenger** of good tidings, that announces peace, the harbinger of good tidings, that announces salvation" (Isaiah 52:7), **before a different verse,** with a negative connotation, **can precede it** in becoming reality: **"For the mountains will I take up a weeping and wailing"** (Jeremiah 9:9).

הָרוֹאֶה שׁוֹפָר בַּחֲלוֹם יַשְׁכִּים וְיֹאמַר ״וְהָיָה בַּיּוֹם הַהוּא יִתָּקַע בְּשׁוֹפָר גָּדוֹל״, קוֹדֶם שֶׁיְּקַדְּמֶנּוּ פָּסוּק אַחֵר ״תִּקְעוּ שׁוֹפָר בַּגִּבְעָה״.

**One who sees a *shofar*[B] in a dream** should **rise early and recite: "And it shall come to pass in that day, that a great *shofar* shall be sounded;** and they shall come that were lost in the land of Assyria, and they that were dispersed in the land of Egypt" (Isaiah 27:13), **before a different verse,** in which the *shofar* is a symbol of war, **can precede it** in becoming reality: **"Blow you the horn [*shofar*] in Giva"** (Hosea 5:8).

הָרוֹאֶה כֶּלֶב בַּחֲלוֹם יַשְׁכִּים וְיֹאמַר ״וּלְכֹל בְּנֵי יִשְׂרָאֵל לֹא יֶחֱרַץ כֶּלֶב לְשֹׁנוֹ״, קוֹדֶם שֶׁיְּקַדְּמֶנּוּ פָּסוּק אַחֵר ״וְהַכְּלָבִים עַזֵּי נֶפֶשׁ״. הָרוֹאֶה אֲרִי בַּחֲלוֹם יַשְׁכִּים וְיֹאמַר ״אַרְיֵה שָׁאָג מִי לֹא יִירָא״, קוֹדֶם שֶׁיְּקַדְּמֶנּוּ פָּסוּק אַחֵר – ״עָלָה אַרְיֵה מִסֻּבְּכוֹ״.

**One who sees a dog in a dream** should **rise early and recite: "But against any of the children of Israel shall not a dog whet his tongue"** (Exodus 11:7), **before a different verse,** with a negative connotation, **can precede it** in becoming reality: **"Yea, the dogs are greedy"** (Isaiah 56:11). **One who sees a lion[B] in a dream** should **rise early and recite: "The lion has roared, who will not fear?** The Lord God has spoken, who can but prophesy?" (Amos 3:8), **before a different verse,** with a negative connotation, **can precede it** in becoming reality: **"A lion is gone up from his thicket,** and a destroyer of nations is set out, gone forth from his place" (Jeremiah 4:7).

### BACKGROUND

***Shofar* – שׁוֹפָר:** The *shofar* is sounded on Rosh HaShana (Leviticus 23:24). It is also used to proclaim the Jubilee Year (Leviticus 25:9) and for other ritual purposes. Only an animal horn that is naturally hollow, e.g., that of a ram, a goat, or an antelope, may be used for this purpose. A solid horn and the horn of a cow are unacceptable. In the Temple it was customary to use the horn of a mountain goat.

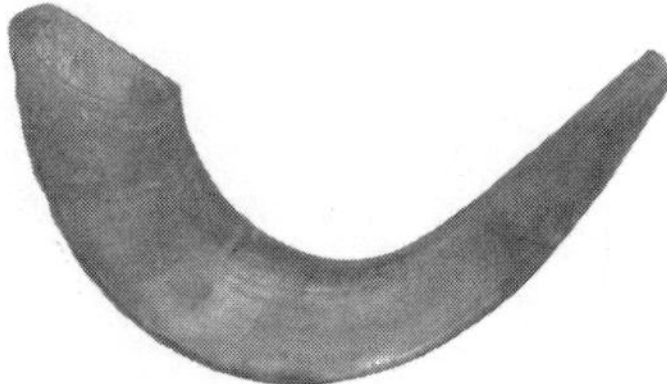

*Shofar*

**Lion – אֲרִי:** The lion, *Panthera leo*, is one of the four largest cats in the *Panthera* genus and a member of the family *Felidae*. With some males exceeding 250 kg (550 lb), it is second only to the tiger in the cat family in terms of size. Lions spend much of their time resting and are inactive approximately 20 hours per day. Although lions can be active at any time, their activity generally peaks after dusk, when they engage in socializing and grooming. Intermittent bursts of activity follow throughout the night hours until dawn, when hunting most often takes place.

Lions have an array of facial expressions and body postures that are very communicative. Their repertoire of vocalizations is also large. Lions tend to roar in a very characteristic manner, starting with a few deep, long roars that trail off into a series of shorter ones. They most often roar at night. The sound, which can be heard from a distance of 8 km (5 mi), is used to announce the lion's presence. Lions have the loudest roar of any large cat.

Lion

## BACKGROUND

**Heart of palm** [*kura*] – **קוּרָא**: The flavorful, white, upper part of the trunk of the date palm is considered a delicacy, which in talmudic times would be boiled or fried. In Babylonia, the heart of palm was greatly valued because, in addition to having a good taste, it was quite rare. Once the upper part is cut off, the tree no longer grows. Consequently, the heart of palm was only removed from superfluous male trees, which do not produce fruit, or trees that were going to be cut down due to overcrowding.

Heart of palm is at the top of the trunk of a date-palm, the treetop from which the tree grows and develops

## NOTES

**A pumpkin is only shown to one who fears Heaven** – **אֵין מַרְאִין דְּלוּעִין אֶלָּא לְמִי שֶׁהוּא יְרֵא שָׁמַיִם**: Some explain that pumpkins are among the largest fruits, yet rather than growing tall, they remain on the ground. This is similar to those who fear Heaven, who are humble and self-deprecating (Rav Nissim Gaon).

הָרוֹאֶה תִּגְלַחַת בַּחֲלוֹם יַשְׁכִּים וְיֹאמַר ״וַיְגַלַּח וַיְחַלֵּף שִׂמְלֹתָיו״, קוֹדֶם שֶׁיַּקְדְּמֶנּוּ פָּסוּק אַחֵר – ״כִּי אִם גֻּלַּחְתִּי וְסָר מִמֶּנִּי כֹחִי״. הָרוֹאֶה בְּאֵר בַּחֲלוֹם יַשְׁכִּים וְיֹאמַר ״בְּאֵר מַיִם חַיִּים״, קוֹדֶם שֶׁיַּקְדְּמֶנּוּ פָּסוּק אַחֵר – ״כְּהָקִיר בַּיִר מֵימֶיהָ״. הָרוֹאֶה קָנֶה בַּחֲלוֹם יַשְׁכִּים וְיֹאמַר ״קָנֶה רָצוּץ לֹא יִשְׁבּוֹר״, קוֹדֶם שֶׁיַּקְדְּמֶנּוּ פָּסוּק אַחֵר – ״הִנֵּה בָטַחְתָּ לְּךָ עַל מִשְׁעֶנֶת הַקָּנֶה הָרָצוּץ״.

**One who sees a shave in a dream** should **rise early and recite** "**And he shaved himself, and changed his raiment**" (Genesis 41:14), which was said with regard to Joseph when he left prison and rose to greatness, **before a different verse,** with a negative connotation, **can precede it** in becoming reality: "**If I be shaven then my strength will go from me, and I shall become weak**" (Judges 16:17). **One who sees a well in a dream** should **rise early and recite:** "**A well of living waters**" (Song of Songs 4:15) **before a different verse,** with a negative connotation, **can precede it** in becoming reality: "**As a cistern wells with her water** so it wells in its wickedness" (Jeremiah 6:7). **One who sees a reed in a dream** should **rise early and recite:** "**A bruised reed shall he not break**" (Isaiah 42:3), in praise of the Messiah, **before a different verse,** with a negative connotation, **can precede it** in becoming reality: "**Now, behold, you trust upon the staff of this bruised reed**" (II Kings 18:21), which is a disparaging depiction of Egypt.

תָּנוּ רַבָּנַן: הָרוֹאֶה קָנֶה בַּחֲלוֹם – יְצַפֶּה לְחָכְמָה, שֶׁנֶּאֱמַר: ״קְנֵה חָכְמָה״, קָנִים – יְצַפֶּה לְבִינָה, שֶׁנֶּאֱמַר: ״וּבְכָל קִנְיָנְךָ קְנֵה בִינָה״. אָמַר רַבִּי זֵירָא: קָרָא, קוּרָא, קִירָא, קַנְיָא – כּוּלְּהוּ מַעְלוּ לְחֶלְמָא. תַּנְיָא: אֵין מַרְאִין דְּלוּעִין אֶלָּא לְמִי שֶׁהוּא יְרֵא שָׁמַיִם בְּכָל כֹּחוֹ.

**The Sages teach: One who sees a reed** [*kaneh*] **in a dream should expect wisdom, as it is stated:** "**Get** [*kene*] **wisdom**" (Proverbs 4:7). One who sees several **reeds** [*kanim*] **should expect understanding, as it said:** "**Yea, with all your acquisition** [*kinyanekha*] **acquire understanding**" (Proverbs 4:7). **Rabbi Zeira said: Pumpkin** [*kara*], **heart of palm** [*kura*],[B] **wax** [*kira*] **and reed** [*kanya*], **are all advantageous when one dreams about** them. **It was taught** in a *baraita*: **A pumpkin is only shown** in a dream **to one who fears Heaven**[N] **with all his might,** because pumpkins [*delu'im*] are interpreted as an acronym for *dalu einai lamarom*, "My eyes were raised on high" (Isaiah 38:14).

הָרוֹאֶה שׁוֹר בַּחֲלוֹם יַשְׁכִּים וְיֹאמַר ״בְּכוֹר שׁוֹרוֹ הָדָר לוֹ״, קוֹדֶם שֶׁיַּקְדְּמֶנּוּ פָּסוּק אַחֵר – ״כִּי יִגַּח שׁוֹר אֶת אִישׁ״.

**One who sees an ox in a dream,** should **rise early and recite** "**His firstling bullock, majesty is his**" (Deuteronomy 33:17), **before a different verse,** with a negative connotation, **can precede it** in becoming reality: "**And if an ox gore a man**" (Exodus 21:28).

תָּנוּ רַבָּנַן, חֲמִשָּׁה דְּבָרִים נֶאֶמְרוּ בַּשּׁוֹר: הָאוֹכֵל מִבְּשָׂרוֹ – מִתְעַשֵּׁר, נְגָחוֹ – הָוְיָין לֵיהּ בָּנִים שֶׁמְּנַגְּחִים בַּתּוֹרָה, נְשָׁכוֹ – יִסּוּרִין בָּאִים עָלָיו, בְּעָטוֹ – דֶּרֶךְ רְחוֹקָה נִזְדַּמְּנָה לוֹ, רְכָבוֹ – עוֹלֶה לִגְדוּלָּה.

**The Sages taught** in a *baraita*: **Five matters are said** about dreams with regard to **the ox.** One who dreams that **he ate from its flesh will become wealthy.** One who dreams that it **gored him will have sons** who are Torah scholars, **who gore** each other **in an** attempt to better understand **Torah.** One who dreams that **it bit him, suffering is coming to him.** One who dreams that **it kicked him will be required to travel a great distance in the future.** One who dreams that **he was riding it,** it is a sign that he will **rise to greatness.**

וְהָתַנְיָא: רְכָבוֹ – מֵת! – לָא קַשְׁיָא; הָא – דְּרָכֵיב הוּא לְתוֹרָא, הָא – דְּרָכֵיב תּוֹרָא לְדִידֵיהּ.

The Gemara challenges: **Wasn't it taught** in a *baraita* that one who dreams that **he was riding it,** it is a sign that he will **die?** The Gemara responds: This is **not difficult. This,** which taught that he will rise to greatness, refers to a case where he saw **that he was riding the ox, while this,** which taught that it is a sign of his imminent death, refers to a case where he saw **that the ox was riding him.**

הָרוֹאֶה חֲמוֹר בַּחֲלוֹם – יְצַפֶּה לִישׁוּעָה, שֶׁנֶּאֱמַר: ״הִנֵּה מַלְכֵּךְ יָבוֹא לָךְ צַדִּיק וְנוֹשָׁע הוּא עָנִי וְרֹכֵב עַל חֲמוֹר״. הָרוֹאֶה חָתוּל בַּחֲלוֹם, בְּאַתְרָא דְּקָרוּ לֵיהּ שׁוּנְרָא – נַעֲשֵׂית לוֹ שִׁירָה נָאָה, שִׁינְרָא – נַעֲשָׂה לוֹ שִׁינּוּי רַע. הָרוֹאֶה עֲנָבִים בַּחֲלוֹם, לְבָנוֹת, בֵּין בִּזְמַנָּן וּבֵין שֶׁלֹּא בִּזְמַנָּן – יָפוֹת, שְׁחוֹרוֹת, בִּזְמַנָּן – יָפוֹת, שֶׁלֹּא בִּזְמַנָּן – רָעוֹת. הָרוֹאֶה סוּס לָבָן בַּחֲלוֹם, בֵּין בְּנַחַת בֵּין בִּרְדוּף – יָפֶה לוֹ, אָדוֹם, בְּנַחַת – יָפֶה, בִּרְדוּף – קָשֶׁה.

**One who sees a donkey in a dream should anticipate salvation, as it is said:** "**Behold, your king comes unto you; he is triumphant, and victorious, lowly, and riding upon a donkey**" (Zechariah 9:9). **One who sees a cat in a dream in a place where** in Aramaic **they call it** ***shunra*****, a nice song** [*shira na'a*] **will be composed for him.** If he sees a cat in a place where they call cat ***shinra*****, it is a sign that he will undergo a change for the worse** [*shinui ra*]. **One who sees grapes in a dream** and they were **white** or light colored, regardless of **whether** it was **in their season or not in their season, it is a good** sign. One who sees **black** grapes **in their season, it is a good** omen. However, one who sees black grapes when it was **not in their season, it is a bad** omen. **One who sees a white horse in a dream,** regardless of **whether** the horse was **walking or running, it is a good** omen **for him.** One who sees a **red** horse **walking, it is a good** omen; **running, it is a bad** omen.

הָרוֹאֶה יִשְׁמָעֵאל בַּחֲלוֹם – תְּפִלָּתוֹ נִשְׁמַעַת, וְדַוְקָא יִשְׁמָעֵאל בֶּן אַבְרָהָם אֲבָל טַיָּיעָא בְּעָלְמָא – לָא. הָרוֹאֶה גָּמָל בַּחֲלוֹם – מִיתָה נִקְנְסָה לוֹ מִן הַשָּׁמַיִם וְהִצִּילוּהוּ מִמֶּנָּה. אָמַר רַבִּי חָמָא בְּרַבִּי חֲנִינָא: מַאי קְרָאָה – "וְאָנֹכִי אֵרֵד עִמְּךָ מִצְרַיְמָה וְאָנֹכִי אַעַלְךָ גַם עָלֹה". רַב נַחְמָן בַּר יִצְחָק אָמַר מֵהָכָא: "גַּם ה׳ הֶעֱבִיר חַטָּאתְךָ לֹא תָמוּת".

The Gemara says: **One who sees Ishmael in a dream,** it is an omen that **his prayer** will be **heard,** just as Ishmael's prayer was heard. The Gemara notes: This refers **specifically** to where one saw **Ishmael, son of Abraham,** but **not** if one saw **a random Arab. One who sees a camel** [*gamal*] **in a dream,** it is an omen that **death was decreed upon him from heaven but he was spared. Rabbi Ḥama, son of Rabbi Ḥanina, said: What verse** alludes to this? **"I will go down with you into Egypt; and I will also surely bring you up again** [*gam alo*]**"** (Genesis 56:4), the acronym for which is *gamal.* **Rav Naḥman bar Yitzḥak said:** The source for this is **from here,** another verse: **"The Lord also** [*gam*] **has put away your sin;**[N] **you shall not die"** (II Samuel 12:13).

הָרוֹאֶה פִּינְחָס בַּחֲלוֹם – פֶּלֶא נַעֲשָׂה לוֹ, הָרוֹאֶה פִּיל בַּחֲלוֹם – פְּלָאוֹת נַעֲשׂוּ לוֹ, פִּילִים – פִּלְאֵי פְלָאוֹת נַעֲשׂוּ לוֹ.

**One who sees Pinehas in a dream,** it is an omen **that a miracle will be performed on his behalf,** just as miracles were performed for Pinehas. **One who sees an elephant**[B] [*pil*] **in a dream** it is an omen that **miracles** [*pelaot*] **will be performed for him.** One who sees multiple **elephants** in a dream, **miracles upon miracles will be performed for him.**

וְהָתַנְיָא: כָּל מִינֵי חַיּוֹת יָפִין לַחֲלוֹם חוּץ מִן הַפִּיל וּמִן הַקּוֹף! – לָא קַשְׁיָא,

The Gemara asks: **Was it not taught** in a *baraita*: **All species of animals are good** omens **in a dream, with the exception of an elephant and a monkey?** The Gemara answers: This is **not difficult.**

### NOTES

**One who sees a camel [*gamal*]…"The Lord also [*gam*] has put away your sin" – הָרוֹאֶה גָּמָל...גַּם ה׳ הֶעֱבִיר חַטָּאתְךָ:** Some explain that in the words *gam Hashem* are an allusion to the Greek letter *gamma* (Γ, γ), to which the Sages refer as *gam,* which corresponds to the Hebrew letter *gimmel.* Even its shape is somewhat similar to the hump of a camel (Maharsha).

### BACKGROUND

**Elephant – פִּיל:** Elephants are large land mammals in the *Elephantidae* family. Elephants are the largest living land animals on Earth today. The elephant's gestation period is 22 months, the longest of any land animal. At birth, an elephant calf typically weighs 105 kilograms (230 lb). Elephants typically live for 50 to 70 years.

Elephant

Perek **IX**
Daf **57** Amud **a**

הָא – דִּמְסָרַג, הָא – דְּלָא מְסָרַג. הָרוֹאֶה הוּנָא בַּחֲלוֹם – נֵס נַעֲשָׂה לוֹ. חֲנִינָא חֲנַנְיָא יוֹחָנָן – נִסֵּי נִסִּים נַעֲשׂוּ לוֹ. הָרוֹאֶה הֶסְפֵּד בַּחֲלוֹם – מִן הַשָּׁמַיִם חָסוּ עָלָיו וּפְדָאוּהוּ. וְהָנֵי מִילֵּי – בִּכְתָבָא.

**This** opinion, that seeing an elephant is a good omen, refers to a case where one saw **it saddled, while this** opinion, that it is a bad omen, refers to a case where the elephant **is not saddled. One who sees** a man named **Huna in a dream,** it is a sign that **a miracle will be performed for him,** because the letter *nun* in the name Huna represents the word *nes,* miracle. One who sees a man named **Ḥanina, Ḥananya, or Yoḥanan,** it is a sign that **many miracles will be performed for him,** since the letter *nun* appears twice in those names. One who sees **a eulogy in a dream,** it is a sign that **the heavens had mercy upon him, and spared him** from a divine death sentence and there will be no need to eulogize him in reality. The Gemara restricts this statement and says that **this only applies** if he saw the eulogy **written** and not yet delivered.

הָעוֹנֶה "יְהֵא שְׁמֵיהּ רַבָּא מְבָרַךְ" מוּבְטָח לוֹ שֶׁהוּא בֶּן הָעוֹלָם הַבָּא. הַקּוֹרֵא קְרִיאַת שְׁמַע – רָאוּי שֶׁתִּשְׁרֶה עָלָיו שְׁכִינָה, אֶלָּא שֶׁאֵין דּוֹרוֹ זַכַּאי לְכָךְ.

**One who answers** in a dream: **May His great name be blessed** from *kaddish* **is assured that he is one** who has a place in **the World-to-Come. One** who sees himself **reciting *Shema*** in a dream **is worthy of having the Divine Presence rest upon him, but his generation is unworthy,** and, therefore, the Divine Presence does not actually rest upon him.

הַמַּנִּיחַ תְּפִילִּין בַּחֲלוֹם – יְצַפֶּה לִגְדוּלָּה, שֶׁנֶּאֱמַר: "וְרָאוּ כָּל עַמֵּי הָאָרֶץ כִּי שֵׁם ה׳ נִקְרָא עָלֶיךָ" וגו׳ וְתַנְיָא, רַבִּי אֱלִיעֶזֶר הַגָּדוֹל אוֹמֵר: אֵלּוּ תְּפִילִּין שֶׁבָּרֹאשׁ. הַמִּתְפַּלֵּל בַּחֲלוֹם סִימָן יָפֶה לוֹ, וְהָנֵי מִילֵּי – דְּלָא סַיֵּים.

**One who** sees himself **don phylacteries in a dream should anticipate greatness, as it is stated: "And all the peoples of the earth shall see that the name of the Lord is called upon you;** and they shall be afraid of you" (Deuteronomy 28:10). **And it was taught** in a *baraita* that **Rabbi Eliezer the Great says: That the Name of the Lord is called upon you, refers to phylacteries of the head,** as they represent God's name upon man. **One who** sees himself **pray in a dream,** it is **an auspicious omen.** However, the Gemara adds a caveat and says: **This only applies** in a case where he saw in the dream that he **had not** yet **finished** his prayer and is therefore still close to God. If, in the dream, he had already finished his prayer, it is not an omen.

**NOTES**

A vine branch [*soreka*], he should anticipate the Messiah – שׂוֹרֵקָה יְצַפֶּה לְמָשִׁיחַ: Some add an allusion from the verse: "I will hiss [*eshreka*] for them, and gather them" (Zechariah 10:8), as *eshreka* has a sound similar to *soreka* (Rav Ya'akov Emden).

הַבָּא עַל אִמּוֹ בַּחֲלוֹם – יְצַפֶּה לְבִינָה, שֶׁנֶּאֱמַר: "כִּי אִם לַבִּינָה תִקְרָא". הַבָּא עַל נַעֲרָה מְאוֹרָסָה – יְצַפֶּה לְתוֹרָה, שֶׁנֶּאֱמַר: "תּוֹרָה צִוָּה לָנוּ מֹשֶׁה מוֹרָשָׁה קְהִלַּת יַעֲקֹב", אַל תִּקְרֵי "מוֹרָשָׁה" אֶלָּא מְאוֹרָשָׂה. הַבָּא עַל אֲחוֹתוֹ בַּחֲלוֹם – יְצַפֶּה לְחָכְמָה, שֶׁנֶּאֱמַר: "אֱמֹר לַחָכְמָה אֲחֹתִי אָתְּ". הַבָּא עַל אֵשֶׁת אִישׁ בַּחֲלוֹם – מוּבְטָח לוֹ שֶׁהוּא בֶּן הָעוֹלָם הַבָּא, וְהָנֵי מִילֵּי – דְּלָא יָדַע לָהּ וְלָא הִרְהֵר בָּהּ מֵאוּרְתָּא.

**One who sees** that **he had relations with his mother** [*em*] **in a dream, he should anticipate** attaining **understanding, as it is stated: "Yea if** [*im*] **you call for understanding"** (Proverbs 2:3), and in this homiletic interpretation *im* is considered to be the equivalent of *em*. **One who sees** that he **had relations with a betrothed young woman** in a dream, **he should anticipate Torah, as it is stated: "Moses commanded us Torah, an inheritance** [*morasha*] **of the congregation of Jacob"** (Deuteronomy 33:4). **Do not read** it as *morasha*; **rather,** read it as *me'orasa*, **betrothed. One who** sees that he **had relations with his sister in a dream, should anticipate wisdom, as it is stated: "Say unto wisdom: You are my sister"** (Proverbs 7:4). **One who** sees that **he had relations with a married woman in a dream is assured that he is one** who has a place in **the World-to-Come.** He receives his place as well as that of another person in the Garden of Eden, as the married woman represents a portion belonging to someone else. However, the Gemara adds a caveat and says: **This only applies** in a case where **he did not know her and was not thinking about her that evening;** rather, he saw an unidentified woman in his dream by chance.

אָמַר רַבִּי חִיָּיא בַּר אַבָּא: הָרוֹאֶה חִטִּים בַּחֲלוֹם – רָאָה שָׁלוֹם, שֶׁנֶּאֱמַר: "הַשָּׂם גְּבוּלֵךְ שָׁלוֹם חֵלֶב חִטִּים יַשְׂבִּיעֵךְ". הָרוֹאֶה שְׂעוֹרִים בַּחֲלוֹם – סָרוּ עֲוֹנוֹתָיו, שֶׁנֶּאֱמַר: "וְסָר עֲוֹנֶךָ וְחַטָּאתְךָ תְּכֻפָּר". אָמַר רַבִּי זֵירָא: אֲנָא לָא סְלֵקִי מִבָּבֶל לְאֶרֶץ יִשְׂרָאֵל עַד דַּחֲזַאי שַׂעֲרֵי בְּחֶלְמָא.

**Rabbi Ḥiyya bar Abba said: One who sees wheat in a dream has seen peace, as it is stated: "He makes your borders peace; He gives you in plenty the fat of wheat"** (Psalms 147:14). And **one who sees barley** [*se'orim*] **in a dream** has received a sign that **his iniquities are taken away, as it is stated: "And your iniquity is taken away** [*vesar avonekh*], **and your sin expiated"** (Isaiah 6:7); *se'orim* is an acronym for *sar avon*. **Rabbi Zeira said: I did not ascend from Babylonia to Eretz Yisrael until I saw barley in my dream.**

הָרוֹאֶה גֶּפֶן טְעוּנָה בַּחֲלוֹם – אֵין אִשְׁתּוֹ מַפֶּלֶת נְפָלִים, שֶׁנֶּאֱמַר: "אֶשְׁתְּךָ כְּגֶפֶן פֹּרִיָּה". שׂוֹרֵקָה – יְצַפֶּה לְמָשִׁיחַ, שֶׁנֶּאֱמַר: "אֹסְרִי לַגֶּפֶן עִירֹה, וְלַשֹּׂרֵקָה בְּנִי אֲתֹנוֹ".

**One who sees a vine laden** with grapes **in a dream,** it is an omen that **his wife will not miscarry, as it is stated: "Your wife shall be as a fruitful vine,** in the innermost parts of your house" (Psalms 128:3). One who sees a planted **vine branch** in a dream **should anticipate the Messiah,**[N] **as it is stated: "Binding his foal unto the vine and his donkey's colt unto the vine branch"** (Genesis 49:11).

הָרוֹאֶה תְּאֵנָה בַּחֲלוֹם – תּוֹרָתוֹ מִשְׁתַּמֶּרֶת בְּקִרְבּוֹ, שֶׁנֶּאֱמַר: "נֹצֵר תְּאֵנָה יֹאכַל פִּרְיָהּ". הָרוֹאֶה רִמּוֹנִים בַּחֲלוֹם, זוּטְרֵי – פָּרֵי עִסְקֵיהּ כְּרִמּוֹנָא, רַבְרְבֵי – רָבֵי עִסְקֵיהּ כְּרִמּוֹנָא. פַּלְגֵי, אִם תַּלְמִיד חָכָם הוּא – יְצַפֶּה לְתוֹרָה, שֶׁנֶּאֱמַר: "אַשְׁקְךָ מִיַּיִן הָרֶקַח מֵעֲסִיס רִמֹּנִי", וְאִם עַם הָאָרֶץ הוּא – יְצַפֶּה לְמִצְוֹת, שֶׁנֶּאֱמַר: "כְּפֶלַח הָרִמּוֹן רַקָּתֵךְ". מַאי "רַקָּתֵךְ" – אֲפִילּוּ רֵיקָנִין שֶׁבָּךְ מְלֵאִים מִצְוֹת כָּרִמּוֹן.

**One who sees a fig tree in a dream,** it is a sign that **his Torah is preserved within him, as it is stated: "One who keeps the fig tree shall eat the fruit thereof"** (Proverbs 27:18). **One who sees pomegranates in a dream,** if they were **small, his business will flourish like the seeds of** the **pomegranate,** which are numerous; and if they were **large, his business will increase like a pomegranate.** One who saw **slices of pomegranates** in his dream, **if he is a Torah scholar he should anticipate Torah, as it is stated: "I would cause you to drink of spiced wine, of the juice of my pomegranate"** (Song of Songs 8:2), which is traditionally understood as an allusion to Torah. **And if** the dreamer **is an ignoramus, he should anticipate mitzvot,** as it is stated: **"Your temples are like a split pomegranate"** (Song of Songs 4:3). As the Gemara previously interpreted homiletically, **What is** the meaning of the word **"Your temples** [*rakatekh*]**"? Even the most ignorant** [*reikanin*] among you, Israel, **are full of mitzvot like a pomegranate.**

הָרוֹאֶה זֵיתִים בַּחֲלוֹם, זוּטְרֵי – פָּרֵי וְרָבֵי וְקָאֵי עִסְקֵיהּ כְּזֵיתִים, וְהָנֵי מִילֵּי – פֵּרֵי, אֲבָל אִילָנֵי – הָוְיָין לֵיהּ בָּנִים מְרוּבִּין, שֶׁנֶּאֱמַר: "בָּנֶיךָ כִּשְׁתִלֵי זֵיתִים" וגו'. אִיכָּא דְּאָמְרִי: הָרוֹאֶה זַיִת בַּחֲלוֹם – שֵׁם טוֹב יוֹצֵא לוֹ, שֶׁנֶּאֱמַר: "זַיִת רַעֲנָן יְפֵה פְרִי תֹאַר קָרָא ה' שְׁמֵךְ". הָרוֹאֶה שֶׁמֶן זַיִת בַּחֲלוֹם – יְצַפֶּה לִמְאוֹר תּוֹרָה, שֶׁנֶּאֱמַר: "וְיִקְחוּ אֵלֶיךָ שֶׁמֶן זַיִת זָךְ". הָרוֹאֶה תְּמָרִים בַּחֲלוֹם – תַּמּוּ עֲוֹנוֹתָיו, שֶׁנֶּאֱמַר: "תַּם עֲוֹנֵךְ בַּת צִיּוֹן".

**One who sees olives in a dream,** and they were **small,** it is a sign that **his business will flourish, increase and be durable like olives.** However, the Gemara adds a caveat, saying that **this applies only** when he sees the **fruit** of an olive tree; **but,** one who sees olive **trees,** it is a sign that **he will have many children, as it is stated: "Your children like olive plants,** round about your table" (Psalms 128:3). **Some say that one who sees an olive tree in a dream,** it is a sign that a **good reputation will spread for him, as it is stated:** "The Lord called your name **a leafy olive tree, fair with goodly fruit"** (Jeremiah 11:16). **One who sees olive oil in a dream should anticipate the light of Torah, as it is stated: "That they bring unto you pure olive oil** beaten for the light" (Exodus 27:20). **One who sees palm trees** [*temarim*] **in a dream** has seen a sign that **his transgressions have ceased, as it is stated: "Your iniquity is finished, O daughter of Zion"** (Lamentations 4:22), as the Gemara likens *temara*, date, to *tam ra*, evil has ceased.

אָמַר רַב יוֹסֵף: הָרוֹאֶה עֵז בַּחֲלוֹם – שָׁנָה מִתְבָּרֶכֶת לוֹ, עִזִּים – שָׁנִים מִתְבָּרְכוֹת לוֹ, שֶׁנֶּאֱמַר: ״וְדֵי חֲלֵב עִזִּים לְלַחְמְךָ״. הָרוֹאֶה הֲדַס בַּחֲלוֹם – נְכָסָיו מַצְלִיחִין לוֹ, וְאִם אֵין לוֹ נְכָסִים – יְרוּשָּׁה נוֹפֶלֶת לוֹ מִמָּקוֹם אַחֵר. אָמַר עוּלָּא, וְאָמְרִי לָהּ בְּמַתְנִיתָא תְּנָא: וְהוּא דַּחֲזָא בְּכַנַּיְיהוּ. הָרוֹאֶה אֶתְרוֹג בַּחֲלוֹם – הָדוּר הוּא לִפְנֵי קוֹנוֹ, שֶׁנֶּאֱמַר: ״פְּרִי עֵץ הָדָר כַּפֹּת תְּמָרִים״. הָרוֹאֶה לוּלָב בַּחֲלוֹם – אֵין לוֹ אֶלָּא לֵב אֶחָד לְאָבִיו שֶׁבַּשָּׁמַיִם.

**Rav Yosef says: One who sees a goat in a dream,** it is a sign that **his year will be blessed;** one who sees **goats, his years will be blessed, as it is stated: "And there will be goats' milk enough for your food,** for the food of your household; and sustenance for your maidens" (Proverbs 27:27). **One who sees myrtle in a dream,** it is a sign that **his property will be successful. And if he does not** own **property,** it is a sign that **he will receive an inheritance. Ulla said, and some say it was taught in a** ***baraita*****:** This applies exclusively to a case **where he saw** them **on their stem. One who sees a citron** [***etrog***] **in a dream** has seen a sign that **he is honored** [***hadur***] **before his Creator, as it is stated** with regard to the citron: **"The fruit of goodly trees** [***hadar***]**, branches of palm trees"** (Leviticus 23:40). **One who sees a palm branch** [***lulav***] **in a dream,** it is a sign that **he has but one heart for his Father in heaven.** *Lulav* is interpreted homiletically as *lo lev*, he has a heart.

הָרוֹאֶה אַוָּוז בַּחֲלוֹם – יְצַפֶּה לְחָכְמָה שֶׁנֶּאֱמַר: ״חָכְמוֹת בַּחוּץ תָּרֹנָּה״. וְהַבָּא עָלֶיהָ – הָוֵי רֹאשׁ יְשִׁיבָה. אָמַר רַב אַשִׁי: אֲנִי רְאִיתִיהָ וּבָאתִי עָלֶיהָ, וְסַלְקִיר לִגְדוּלָּה.

**One who sees a goose in a dream should anticipate wisdom, as it is stated: "Wisdoms cry aloud in the streets,**[N] she utters her voice in the broad places" (Proverbs 1:20); geese tend to sound their voices. One who dreams that **he has relations with** the goose **will become head of the yeshiva. Rav Ashi said: I saw** a goose and **had relations with it** in my dream **and I ascended to greatness** and became head of the yeshiva.

הָרוֹאֶה תַּרְנְגוֹל בַּחֲלוֹם – יְצַפֶּה לְבֵן זָכָר, תַּרְנְגוֹלִים – יְצַפֶּה לְבָנִים זְכָרִים. תַּרְנְגוֹלֶת – יְצַפֶּה לְתַרְבִּיצָה נָאָה וְגִילָה. הָרוֹאֶה בֵּיצִים בַּחֲלוֹם – תְּלוּיָה בַּקָּשָׁתוֹ, נִשְׁתַּבְּרוּ – נַעֲשֵׂית בַּקָּשָׁתוֹ, וְכֵן אֱגוֹזִים וְכֵן קִשּׁוּאִים, וְכֵן כׇּל כְּלֵי זְכוּכִית, וְכֵן כׇּל הַנִּשְׁבָּרִים כָּאֵלּוּ.

**One who sees a rooster in a dream** should anticipate **a male child.** One who sees multiple **roosters should expect male children.** One who sees **a hen** [***tarnegolet***] **should anticipate a beautiful garden and** reason to **rejoice** [***tarbitza na'a vegila***], as *tarnegolet* is interpreted as an acronym for *tarbitza na'a vegila*. **One who sees eggs in a dream,** it is a sign that **his request is pending,** as egg in Aramaic is *beya*, which is similar to the term for request. If one saw that the eggs **broke,** it is a sign that **his request** has already been **granted,** as that which was hidden inside the shell was revealed. **The same is true of nuts, and the same is true of cucumbers, and the same is true of all glass vessels, and the same is true of anything similarly fragile** that broke in his dream, it is a sign that his request was granted.

הַנִּכְנָס לִכְרַךְ – נַעֲשׂוּ לוֹ חֲפָצָיו, שֶׁנֶּאֱמַר ״וַיַּנְחֵם אֶל מְחוֹז חֶפְצָם״. הַמְגַלֵּחַ רֹאשׁ בַּחֲלוֹם – סִימָן יָפֶה לוֹ, רֹאשׁוֹ וּזְקָנוֹ – לוֹ וּלְכׇל מִשְׁפַּחְתּוֹ.

**One** who dreams that **he entered a city,** it is a sign that **his desires will be fulfilled, as it is stated: "And He led them unto their desired haven"** (Psalms 107:30). **One who shaves his head in a dream, it is a good omen for him,** as the removal of undesired hairs is a sign of renewal and greatness. If he **shaved his head and his beard** in a dream, it is a good omen **for him and his entire family.**

הַיּוֹשֵׁב בַּעֲרֵיבָה קְטַנָּה – שֵׁם טוֹב יוֹצֵא לוֹ, בַּעֲרֵיבָה גְּדוֹלָה – לוֹ וּלְכׇל מִשְׁפַּחְתּוֹ. וְהָנֵי מִילֵּי – דְּמִדַּלְיָא דַּלּוּיֵי.

**One who sits in a small boat** in a dream, it is a sign that **a good reputation will spread for him.** If he sees himself sitting **in a large boat** in a dream, **a good reputation will spread for him and his entire family.** The Gemara notes that **this only applies** where **the boat was floating high** on the waves.

הַנִּפְנֶה בַּחֲלוֹם – סִימָן יָפֶה לוֹ, שֶׁנֶּאֱמַר ״מִהַר צֹעֶה לְהִפָּתֵחַ״, וְהָנֵי מִילֵּי – דְּלָא קִנַּח.

**One who defecates** in a dream, **it is a good omen for him, as it is stated: "He that is bent down shall speedily be loosed;** and he shall not go down dying into the pit, neither shall his bread fail" (Isaiah 51:14). The Gemara notes that **this only applies** where **he does not wipe** and get his hands dirty.

הָעוֹלֶה לַגַּג בַּחֲלוֹם – עוֹלֶה לִגְדוּלָּה, יָרַד – יוֹרֵד מִגְּדוּלָּתוֹ. אַבַּיֵי וְרָבָא דְּאָמְרִי תַּרְוַויְיהוּ: כֵּיוָן שֶׁעָלָה – עָלָה. הַקּוֹרֵעַ בְּגָדָיו בַּחֲלוֹם – קוֹרְעִים לוֹ גְּזַר דִּינוֹ. הָעוֹמֵד עָרוֹם בַּחֲלוֹם, בְּבָבֶל – עוֹמֵד בְּלֹא חֵטְא, בְּאֶרֶץ יִשְׂרָאֵל – עָרוֹם בְּלֹא מִצְוֹת. הַנִּתְפָּס לְסַרְדְּיוֹט – שְׁמִירָה נַעֲשֵׂית לוֹ, נְתָנוּהוּ בְּקוֹלָר – הוֹסִיפוּ לוֹ שְׁמִירָה עַל שְׁמִירָתוֹ, וְהָנֵי מִילֵּי – בְּקוֹלָר אֲבָל חַבְלָא בְּעָלְמָא – לָא.

**One who climbs up to the roof in a dream,** it is a sign that **he will ascend to greatness.** If, after he climbed up, **he climbed** back **down,** it is a sign that he **will descend from** the **greatness he** achieved. **Abaye and Rava both said: Once one ascended** to the roof in his dream, **he ascended,** and even if he dreams that he descended, it remains a good omen for him. **One who rips his clothing in a dream,** it is a sign that they **rip up his sentence. One who stands naked in Babylonia in a dream,** it is a sign that **he stands free of transgression.** Although living outside Israel is itself a transgression, his nakedness symbolizes that he has been absolved of that sin. If one dreamed that he stood naked **in Eretz Yisrael,** it is a sign that he is **naked without mitzvot. One** who dreams that **he was apprehended** and guarded **by a soldier** [***sardeyot***]**,**[L] it is a sign that **protection was provided him** by heaven. If he sees that **he is wearing a neck chain** [***kolar***]**,**[L] it is a sign that **they have increased his level of protection.** However, the Gemara notes that **this only applies** to a case where his neck was placed **in a neck chain; if** his neck was **simply** placed in **a noose, it does not** indicate heavenly protection.

NOTES

One who sees a goose in a dream… "Wisdoms cry aloud in the streets" – הָרוֹאֶה אַוָּוז בַּחֲלוֹם...חָכְמוֹת בַּחוּץ תָּרֹנָּה: Some explain this based on numerology [*gematria*]. Since: "Wisdom (*hokhma*)… hath hewn out her seven pillars" (Proverbs 9:1), and the plural (*hokhmot*) indicates fourteen pillars. The word goose, *avaz*, (*alef* = 1; *vav* = 6; *zayin* = 7) also has a numerological value of fourteen (Rav Sa'adia Gaon).

LANGUAGE

Soldier [*sardeyot*] – סַרְדְּיוֹט: From the Greek στρατιώτης, *stratiotès*, meaning soldier.

Neck chain [*kolar*] – קוֹלָר: From the Latin collare, it is a chain placed around the neck of prisoners or animals.

Roman prisoner's neck chain

Roman collared slaves

## BACKGROUND

**Drum** – **טַבְלָא**: This is a small hand held drum or tambourine. This explains the talmudic expression: To hang a drum, as this drum could be hung on various objects and beaten.

Drum from the talmudic era

**Bloodletting** – **הַקָּזַת דָּם**: Bloodletting involves spilling small quantities of blood. It was used both as a cure and as a general preventive therapy that was believed to keep a person healthy. Bloodletting was based on an ancient system of medicine in which blood and other bodily fluid were considered to be humors, the proper balance of which was believed to maintain health. It was the most common medical practice performed by doctors on both humans and animals from antiquity through the late 19th century, a period of almost two millennia. Today it is well established that bloodletting is not effective for most diseases. The only remaining condition for which it is used is *Polycythemia vera*, a disease in which the body produces too many red blood cells. Among the symptoms of this illness are bleeding gums, excessive bleeding from ordinary cuts and bruises, and a reddish color of the skin.

הַנִּכְנָס לַאֲגַם בַּחֲלוֹם – נַעֲשֶׂה רֹאשׁ יְשִׁיבָה, לְיַעַר – נַעֲשֶׂה רֹאשׁ לִבְנֵי כַלָּה.

**One who enters a marsh in a dream,** it is a sign that **he will become head of a yeshiva,** as he appears to be standing alone with all the bulrushes, large and small, surrounding him like the head of a yeshiva, around whom all the students gather. One who dreams that he entered **a forest** and sees only large trees around him, it is a sign that he **will be made head of** only **the advanced students** [*kalla*] where he will explain the lessons only to the outstanding students in the yeshiva, each of whom is himself a great tree, set apart from the others.

רַב פַּפָּא וְרַב הוּנָא בְּרֵיהּ דְּרַב יְהוֹשֻׁעַ חֲזוּ חֶלְמָא, רַב פַּפָּא דְּעָיֵיל לְאַגְמָא – נַעֲשָׂה רֹאשׁ יְשִׁיבָה, רַב הוּנָא בְּרֵיהּ דְּרַב יְהוֹשֻׁעַ דְּעָיֵיל לְיַעַר – נַעֲשָׂה רֹאשׁ לִבְנֵי כַלָּה. אִיכָּא דְּאָמְרִי: תַּרְוַיְיהוּ לְאַגְמָא עָיְילִי, אֶלָּא רַב פַּפָּא דְּתָלֵי טַבְלָא – נַעֲשָׂה רֹאשׁ יְשִׁיבָה, רַב הוּנָא בְּרֵיהּ דְּרַב יְהוֹשֻׁעַ דְּלָא תָּלֵי טַבְלָא – נַעֲשָׂה רֹאשׁ לִבְנֵי כַלָּה. אָמַר רַב אָשֵׁי: אֲנָא עָיְילִית לְאַגְמָא, וּתְלַאי טַבְלָא וּנְבַחִי בָּהּ נְבוּחֵי.

The Gemara relates: **Rav Pappa and Rav Huna, son of Rav Yehoshua,** each **saw a dream: Rav Pappa,** who saw **that he entered a marsh** in his dream, **was appointed head of a yeshiva. Rav Huna, son of Rav Yehoshua,** who saw **that he entered a forest** in his dream, **was appointed head of the advanced students. Some say that both of them** dreamed that **they entered a marsh,** but **Rav Pappa,** who dreamed **that a drum**[B] **hung** from his neck, **was appointed head of the yeshiva,** as banging a drum symbolizes the head of a yeshiva who sounds his voice in public. **Rav Huna, son of Rav Yehoshua,** who **did not** dream **that a drum hung around** his neck, was only **appointed head of the advanced students. Rav Ashi said:** I dreamed that **I entered a marsh and hung a drum and beat it,** and Rav Ashi became head of the yeshiva.

תָּנֵי תַּנָּא קַמֵּיהּ דְּרַב נַחְמָן בַּר יִצְחָק: הַמַּקִּיז דָּם בַּחֲלוֹם – עֲוֹנוֹתָיו מְחוּלִין לוֹ.

The *tanna* who recited *mishnayot* **before Rav Naḥman bar Yitzḥak taught: One who lets blood in a dream,** it is a sign that **his transgressions have been forgiven,** because red, the color of blood, is a metaphor for sin: "Though your sins be as scarlet… though they be red like crimson" (Isaiah 1:18). Consequently, bloodletting[B] can symbolize transgressions leaving him.

וְהָתַנְיָא: עֲוֹנוֹתָיו סְדוּרִין לוֹ! מַאי סְדוּרִין – סְדוּרִין לִימָּחֵל.

The Gemara asks: **Was it not taught** in a *baraita*: One who sees that he is letting-blood in a dream, it is a sign that **his transgressions are enumerated before him?** The Gemara answers: **What** is meant by **enumerated?** This means that they are **enumerated to be forgiven.**

תָּנֵי תַּנָּא קַמֵּיהּ דְּרַב שֵׁשֶׁת: הָרוֹאֶה נָחָשׁ בַּחֲלוֹם – פַּרְנָסָתוֹ מְזוּמֶּנֶת לוֹ, נְשָׁכוֹ – נִכְפְּלָה לוֹ, הֲרָגוֹ – אָבְדָה פַּרְנָסָתוֹ. אֲמַר לֵיהּ רַב שֵׁשֶׁת: כׇּל שֶׁכֵּן שֶׁנִּכְפְּלָה פַּרְנָסָתוֹ! וְלָא הִיא, רַב שֵׁשֶׁת הוּא דַּחֲזָא חִוְיָא בְּחֶלְמֵיהּ וְקַטְלֵיהּ.

The *tanna* who recited *mishnayot* **before Rav Sheshet taught: One who sees a snake in a dream,** it is a sign that **his livelihood is accessible to him** just as dust is readily accessible to a snake. If one saw that the snake **bit him** in his dream, it is a sign that his livelihood **will double. If he killed** the snake, it is a sign that **he will lose his livelihood. Rav Sheshet said to** the *tanna*: On the contrary, if one dreamed that he killed the snake it is a sign that **all the more so his livelihood will double.** The Gemara remarks: **But that is not so. Rav Sheshet saw a snake in his dream and killed it,** so he sought to interpret his dream positively.

תָּנֵי תַּנָּא קַמֵּיהּ דְּרַבִּי יוֹחָנָן: כׇּל מִינֵי מַשְׁקִין יָפִין לַחֲלוֹם חוּץ מִן הַיַּיִן, יֵשׁ שׁוֹתֵהוּ וְטוֹב לוֹ, וְיֵשׁ שׁוֹתֵהוּ וְרַע לוֹ; יֵשׁ שׁוֹתֵהוּ וְטוֹב לוֹ – שֶׁנֶּאֱמַר: ״וְיַיִן יְשַׂמַּח לְבַב אֱנוֹשׁ״, וְיֵשׁ שׁוֹתֵהוּ וְרַע לוֹ – שֶׁנֶּאֱמַר: ״תְּנוּ שֵׁכָר לְאוֹבֵד וְיַיִן לְמָרֵי נָפֶשׁ״.

The *tanna* who recited *mishnayot* **before Rabbi Yoḥanan taught: One who sees any kind of drink in a dream it is a good** omen **except for wine,** as **there is** one **who drinks it** in a dream **and it is** a **good** omen **for him, and there is** one **who drinks it** in a dream **and it is a bad** omen **for him.** The Gemara elaborates: **There is** one **who drinks** wine **and it is a good** omen **for him, as it is stated: "And wine that makes glad the heart of man"** (Psalms 104:15), **and there is** one **who drinks it** in a dream **and it is a bad** omen **for him, as it is stated: "Give strong drink unto him that is ready to perish, and wine unto the bitter in soul"** (Proverbs 31:6).

אָמַר לֵיהּ רַבִּי יוֹחָנָן לְתַנָּא, תְּנִי: תַּלְמִיד חָכָם לְעוֹלָם טוֹב לוֹ, שֶׁנֶּאֱמַר ״לְכוּ לַחֲמוּ בְלַחְמִי וּשְׁתוּ בְּיַיִן מָסָכְתִּי״.

**Rabbi Yoḥanan said to the** *tanna:* You should **teach** that for a **Torah scholar,** a dream of wine is **always** a **good** omen, **as it is stated: "Come, eat of my bread and drink of the wine which I have mingled"** (Proverbs 9:5).

אָמַר רַבִּי יוֹחָנָן: הִשְׁכִּים וְנָפַל פָּסוּק לְת פִּיו – הֲרֵי זֶה נְבוּאָה קְטַנָּה. תָּנוּ רַבָּ שְׁלֹשָׁה מְלָכִים הֵם: הָרוֹאֶה דָּוִד בַּחֲלוֹם יְצַפֶּה לַחֲסִידוּת, שְׁלֹמֹה – יְצַפֶּה לְחָכְמָ אַחְאָב – יִדְאַג מִן הַפּוּרְעָנוּת.

**Rabbi Yoḥanan said: One who awakened** in the morning and **a verse** immediately **falls into his mouth,** it is **a minor prophecy. The Sages taught: There are three kings** whose appearance in a dream is significant. **One who sees David in a dream should expect piety;** one who sees **Solomon should expect wisdom;** and one who sees **Ahab**[N] **should be concerned about calamity.**

שְׁלֹשָׁה נְבִיאִים הֵם: הָרוֹאֶה סֵפֶר מְלָכִים יְצַפֶּה לִגְדוּלָּה, יְחֶזְקֵאל – יְצַפֶּה לְחָכְמָ יְשַׁעְיָה – יְצַפֶּה לְנֶחָמָה, יִרְמְיָה – יִדְ מִן הַפּוּרְעָנוּת.

There are also **three books of Prophets** whose appearance in a dream is meaningful: **One who sees the book of Kings should anticipate greatness,** royalty; one who sees the book of **Ezekiel should anticipate wisdom,** as the configuration of the Divine Chariot is described therein; one who sees the book of **Isaiah should anticipate consolation;** and one who sees the book of **Jeremiah should be concerned about calamity,** because Jeremiah prophesied extensively of impending calamity.

שְׁלֹשָׁה כְּתוּבִים גְּדוֹלִים הֵם: הָרוֹאֶה סֵ תְּהִלִּים – יְצַפֶּה לַחֲסִידוּת, מִשְׁלֵי – יְצַפֶּ לְחָכְמָה, אִיּוֹב – יִדְאַג מִן הַפּוּרְעָנוּת.

Similarly, there are **three great** books of **Writings** whose appearance in a dream has particular significance: **One who sees the book of Psalms should anticipate piety;** one who sees the book of **Proverbs should anticipate wisdom;** one who sees the book of **Job should be concerned about calamity.**

שְׁלֹשָׁה כְּתוּבִים קְטַנִּים הֵם: הָרוֹאֶ שִׁיר הַשִּׁירִים בַּחֲלוֹם – יְצַפֶּה לַחֲסִידוּ קֹהֶלֶת – יְצַפֶּה לְחָכְמָה, קִינוֹת – יִדְ מִן הַפּוּרְעָנוּת. הָרוֹאֶה מְגִלַּת אֶסְתֵּר – נַעֲשָׂה לוֹ.

**There are** also **three minor** books of **Writings** whose appearance in a dream is significant: **One who sees Song of Songs in a dream should anticipate piety,** as it describes God's love for Israel; one who sees **Ecclesiastes should anticipate wisdom;** one who sees **Lamentations should be concerned about calamity;** and **one who sees the scroll of Esther,** it is a sign that **a miracle will be performed on his behalf.**

שְׁלֹשָׁה חֲכָמִים הֵם: הָרוֹאֶה רַ בַּחֲלוֹם – יְצַפֶּה לְחָכְמָה, רַבִּי אֶלְעָזָר עֲזַרְיָה – יְצַפֶּה לַעֲשִׁירוּת, רַבִּי יִשְׁמָעֵאל אֱלִישָׁע – יִדְאַג מִן הַפּוּרְעָנוּת.

**There are three Sages** whose appearance in a dream is significant: **One who sees Rabbi** Yehuda HaNasi **in a dream should anticipate wisdom;** one who sees **Rabbi Elazar ben Azarya should anticipate wealth,** as he was particularly wealthy; and one who sees **Rabbi Yishmael ben Elisha**[P] **should be concerned about calamity,** as he was one of the ten martyrs executed by the Romans.

שְׁלֹשָׁה תַּלְמִידֵי חֲכָמִים הֵם: הָרוֹאֶ בֶּן עַזַּאי בַּחֲלוֹם – יְצַפֶּה לַחֲסִידוּת, זוֹמָא – יְצַפֶּה לְחָכְמָה, אַחֵר – יִדְאַג הַפּוּרְעָנוּת.

There are **three Torah scholars** who, despite their greatness in Torah, were never given the title Rabbi, and whose appearance in a dream is significant: **One who sees Ben Azzai in a dream should anticipate piety;** one who sees **Ben Zoma should anticipate wisdom;** and one who sees ***Aḥer*,**[P] Elisha ben Avuya, **should be concerned about calamity,** as he strayed from the path of righteousness.

כָּל מִינֵי חַיּוֹת יָפוֹת לַחֲלוֹם, חוּץ מִן הַפִּ וְהַקּוֹף וְהַקִּפּוֹד. וְהָאָמַר מָר: הָרוֹאֶה פִּ בַּחֲלוֹם – פֶּלֶא נַעֲשָׂה לוֹ! – לָא קַשְׁיָ הָא – דִּמְסַרַג, הָא – דְּלָא מְסַרַג.

The Gemara says: **All types of animals are auspicious** signs **for a dream except for an elephant, a monkey and a long-tailed ape.** The Gemara asks: **Didn't the Master say: A miracle will be performed for one who sees an elephant in a dream?** The Gemara answers: This is **not difficult. This** statement that a vision of an elephant is a good omen refers to a case **where it is saddled,** while **this** statement that it is not a good omen refers to a case **where it is not saddled.**

### NOTES

**One who sees David…Solomon…Ahab – הָרוֹאֶה דָּוִד...שְׁלֹמֹה...אַחְאָב:** Each of these three kings distinguished himself in his own way during his reign (see tractate *Megilla* ch. 1). Ahab, however, was singled out over all other kings because of the double calamity he suffered: He died in war and is enumerated among those who have no place in the World-to-Come (*Tziyyun LeNefesh Ḥayya*).

### PERSONALITIES

**Rabbi Yishmael ben Elisha – רַבִּי יִשְׁמָעֵאל בֶּן אֱלִישָׁע:** Rabbi Yishmael ben Elisha the first, whose son and daughter were taken into captivity, is the one called Rabbi Yishmael High Priest. He served as High Priest at the end of the Second Temple period and was renowned for his piety. The Talmud describes the vision that he saw when serving in the Holy of Holies. In addition, a kabbalistic work, *Pirkei Heikhalot*, is attributed to him. Since he was one of the prominent leaders of the people after the destruction of Jerusalem, he was apprehended by the Romans, together with his close friend, the *Nasi*, Rabban Shimon ben Gamliel the first. He was tortured to death by the Romans. His death is depicted in the liturgical prayer: These I shall remember [*Ele Ezkera*], recited in many communities on Yom Kippur, as well as in one of the *kinot* recited on the Ninth of Av.

Rabbi Yishmael ben Elisha's grandson, Yishmael ben Elisha the second, is the Rabbi Yishmael widely quoted in the Mishna and the Talmud. As related in the Gemara, he, too, was taken into captivity, and was redeemed by Rabbi Yehoshua for a significant ransom. He then became a student of Rabbi Yehoshua and one of the prominent speakers in Yavne. He was a friend of Rabbi Akiva, with whom he engaged in many disputes. Each established a significant halakhic-exegetical schools of thought. The thirteen hermeneutic principles of the Torah, as articulated by Rabbi Yishmael, are the foundations of midrash and *halakha*. Many of his Torah statements are attributed to him in the Mishna and very many of his opinions appear in the Gemara under the general rubric: The school of Rabbi Yishmael taught. The Sages of the following generation studied with him and Rabbi Yoshiya and Rabbi Yonatan were his primary students.

Apparently, he died before the bar Kokheva revolt. His sons and daughters are mentioned in the Gemara and it is possible that the *tanna*, Rabbi Eliezer, son of Rabbi Yishmael, was his son.

***Aḥer* – אַחֵר:** Elisha ben Avuya was born in Jerusalem at the end of the Second Temple period. His was one of the most prominent and wealthiest families in Jerusalem. However, as related in the Jerusalem Talmud, they were influenced by foreign culture and did not have particularly close ties to Judaism. Due to certain extraordinary events, Elisha received an intensive Jewish education and his prodigious talents catapulted him to rank as one of the most prominent Sages of his time. At the same time, even as he frequented the study hall, he had ties to the various forms of Greek culture and took interest in and read heretical literature. Elisha ben Avuya left Judaism completely. In addition to the explanation in tractate *Ḥagiga*, attributing this to his entrance into the mystical orchard, there are several alternative explanations for this decision. Specifically, Elisha ben Avuya experienced severe emotional upheaval in his life, resulting, perhaps, from the oppression during the reign of Hadrian. Several sources indicate that he did not merely violate Torah prohibitions, he went so far as to collaborate with the Romans against his fellow Jews and various acts of cruelty were attributed to him. That explains the hostility towards him that was still palpable two generations later, during the tenure of Rabbi Yehuda HaNasi. Rabbi Meir was, apparently, the only contemporary Sage who continued to maintain ties with him and even studied Torah from him, which prompted criticism of Rabbi Meir himself. Beyond the hostility that lasted for generations, there was the sense of pain and sorrow over a Sage of his prominence who abandoned the path of Torah. In addition, there is the sense that *Aḥer* himself was also miserable over his rebellion and abandonment of Judaism, but he was simply unable to muster the strength to return after having gone so far in embracing the path of evil. That is why his Torah statements remain in the Talmud, an ethical pronouncement of his appears in tractate *Avot*, and in *Avot DeRabbi Natan*, an entire chapter is devoted to his Torah statements.

According to the standard version of the Babylonian Talmud, the *tanna* Rabbi Ya'akov was his daughter's son.

## NOTES

All kinds of colors are auspicious for a dream, except for sky-blue [*tekhelet*] – כָּל מִינֵי צִבְעוֹנִין יָפִין לַחֲלוֹם, חוּץ מִן הַתְּכֵלֶת: Some explain that the word for sky-blue [*tekhelet*] is similar to the word for end [*takhlit*], and for that reason it is a bad omen (Rav Ya'akov Emden).

## BACKGROUND

An eagle-owl, and an owl – קַרְיָא וְקִפּוּפָא: These birds, whose appearance in dreams is troubling, are nocturnal, and because of their strange facial features they are considered ominous omens for the dreamer. Opinions differ as to their precise identity, and it is only possible to conjecture, based on different translations, that the reference is to the birds listed below.

Eagle-owl – אוֹחַ

*Bubo bubo aharonil* – This bird, which may be the *karya*, is a large nocturnal bird with a wingspan of 24 cm.

Owl – כּוֹס

*Athene noctua* – A small nocturnal bird

Barn owl – תִּנְשֶׁמֶת

*Strix flammea* – This bird, which may be the *kipufa*, is a large, nocturnal bird that is more than 33 cm long.

## LANGUAGE

*Kurferai* – קוּרְפְּרַאי: According to the version of the text before us, *kurferai* is a bird, apparently a nocturnal bird of prey, identified by some as the *Brachyotis palustris*. According to the Munich manuscript, however, *kurferai* is a type of vermin, and according to Rashi it is a blind mole rat, *Spalax typhus*. Seeing it in a dream is considered an ominous omen because of its blindness and strange appearance.

כָּל מִינֵי מַתֶּכֶת יָפִין לַחֲלוֹם, חוּץ מִמָּר, פָּסֵל וְקַרְדּוֹם, וְהָנֵי מִילֵּי – דַּחֲזָנְהוּ בְּקַתַּיְיהוּ. כָּל מִינֵי פֵּירוֹת יָפִין לַחֲלוֹם, חוּץ מִפַּגֵּי תְמָרָה. כָּל מִינֵי יְרָקוֹת יָפִין לַחֲלוֹם, חוּץ מֵרָאשֵׁי לְפָתוֹת. וְהָאָמַר רַב: לֹא אִיעַתַּרִי עַד דַּחֲזַאי רָאשֵׁי לְפָתוֹת! – כִּי חֲזָא – בְּכַנַּיְיהוּ חֲזָא. כָּל מִינֵי צִבְעוֹנִין יָפִין לַחֲלוֹם, חוּץ מִן הַתְּכֵלֶת. כָּל מִינֵי עוֹפוֹת יָפִין לַחֲלוֹם, חוּץ מִן קַרְיָא וְקִפּוּפָא וְקוּרְפְּרַאי.

Similarly, the Gemara says: **All types of metal** utensils **are ausp**icious signs **for a dream, except for a hoe, a chisel, and an axe,** as these are instruments of destruction. The Gemara notes that th**is applies** specifically **when they are seen on their handles. On** a similar note, the Gemara says: **All kinds of fruit are auspiciou**s signs **for a dream except for unripe dates. All kinds of vegetable**s **are auspicious** signs **for a dream except for turnip heads. Th**e Gemara challenges: **Didn't Rav say: I did not become wealth**y **until I saw turnip heads** in my dream? Apparently turnip heads ar**e** a good omen. The Gemara responds: **When Rav saw** them, **he sa**w **them on their stems;** if one sees turnip heads already picked, it is a bad omen. Similarly, **all kinds of colors are auspicious** signs **for** a **dream, except for sky-blue** [*tekhelet*].[N] **All kinds of birds are au**spicious signs in a dream **except for an eagle-owl, and an owl,**[B] **an**d **a *kurferai*,**[L] all of which are nocturnal and have strange and frightening appearances.

(הַגּוּ״ף הַגּוּ״ף מֵעֵי״ן מְשִׁיבִי״ן וּמַרְחִיבִי״ן, סִימָן).

The words: **The body, the body, microcosm, ease,** and **comfort ar**e **mnemonics** for matters that the Gemara will discuss, each of whic**h** represents a list with shared qualities, similar to the lists cited abov**e**.

שְׁלֹשָׁה נִכְנָסִין לַגּוּף וְאֵין הַגּוּף נֶהֱנֶה מֵהֶן: גּוּדְגְּדָנִיּוֹת, וְכַפְנִיּוֹת, וּפַגֵּי תְמָרָה. שְׁלֹשָׁה אֵין נִכְנָסִין לַגּוּף וְהַגּוּף נֶהֱנֶה מֵהֶן; אֵלּוּ הֵן: רְחִיצָה, וְסִיכָה, וְתַשְׁמִישׁ. שְׁלֹשָׁה מֵעֵין הָעוֹלָם הַבָּא, אֵלּוּ הֵן: שַׁבָּת, שֶׁמֶשׁ, וְתַשְׁמִישׁ.

The Gemara says: **Three** food items **enter the body** yet **the bo**dy **does not benefit from them: Cherries, bad dates, and unrip**e **dates.** In contrast: **Three** matters **do not enter the body** yet **th**e **body benefits from them, and they are: Washing, anointing, an**d **usage** [*tashmish*], commonly used as a euphemism for conjug**al** relations. **Three** matters **are microcosms of the World-to-Com**e **and they are: Sabbath, the sun and usage.**

תַּשְׁמִישׁ דְּמַאי? אִילֵימָא תַּשְׁמִישׁ הַמִּטָּה – הָא מַכְחֵשׁ כָּחֵישׁ! – אֶלָּא: תַּשְׁמִישׁ נְקָבִים.

The Gemara asks: **Usage of what** benefits the body and is a micr**o**cosm of the World-to-Come? **If you say** that it refers to **conjug**al **relations, doesn't that weaken** the body? **Rather,** it refers to **usag**e **of his orifices,** relieving oneself.

שְׁלֹשָׁה מְשִׁיבִין דַּעְתּוֹ שֶׁל אָדָם, אֵלּוּ הֵן: קוֹל וּמַרְאֶה וָרֵיחַ. שְׁלֹשָׁה מַרְחִיבִין דַּעְתּוֹ שֶׁל אָדָם, אֵלּוּ הֵן: דִּירָה נָאָה, וְאִשָּׁה נָאָה, וְכֵלִים נָאִים.

**Three** matters **ease one's mind, and they are: Voice, sight, an**d **smell,** when they are pleasant and aesthetic. **Three** matters **give** a **person comfort, and they are: A beautiful abode, a beautiful wi**fe **and beautiful vessels.**

(חֲמִשָּׁ״ה וְשִׁשָּׁ״ה וַעֲשָׂרָ״ה סִימָן). חֲמִשָּׁה אֶחָד מִשִּׁשִּׁים, אֵלּוּ הֵן: אֵשׁ, דְּבַשׁ, וְשַׁבָּת, וְשֵׁינָה, וַחֲלוֹם. אֵשׁ – אֶחָד מִשִּׁשִּׁים לַגֵּיהִנָּם, דְּבַשׁ – אֶחָד מִשִּׁשִּׁים לַמָּן, שַׁבָּת – אֶחָד מִשִּׁשִּׁים לָעוֹלָם הַבָּא, שֵׁינָה – אֶחָד מִשִּׁשִּׁים לְמִיתָה, חֲלוֹם – אֶחָד מִשִּׁשִּׁים לִנְבוּאָה.

The numbers **five, six, and ten are mnemonics** for the categories t**hat** follow. The Gemara says: There are **five** matters in our world whic**h** are **one-sixtieth** of their most extreme manifestations. **They ar**e: **Fire, honey, Shabbat, sleep, and a dream.** The Gemara elaborate**s:** Our **fire** is **one-sixtieth of** the fire of **Gehenna; honey is one-six**ti**eth of manna; Shabbat is one-sixtieth of the World-to-Com**e; **sleep is one-sixtieth of death;** and **a dream is one-sixtieth** of **prophecy.**

שִׁשָּׁה דְּבָרִים סִימָן יָפֶה לַחוֹלֶה, אֵלּוּ הֵן: עִטּוּשׁ, זִיעָה, שִׁלְשׁוּל, קֶרִי, וְשֵׁינָה, וַחֲלוֹם. עִטּוּשׁ – דִּכְתִיב ״עֲטִישׁוֹתָיו תָּהֶל אוֹר״, זִיעָה – דִּכְתִיב ״בְּזֵעַת אַפֶּיךָ תֹּאכַל לֶחֶם״, שִׁלְשׁוּל – דִּכְתִיב ״מִהַר צֹעֶה לְהִפָּתֵחַ וְלֹא יָמוּת לַשַּׁחַת״, קֶרִי – דִּכְתִיב ״יִרְאֶה זֶרַע יַאֲרִיךְ יָמִים״, שֵׁינָה – דִּכְתִיב ״יָשַׁנְתִּי אָז יָנוּחַ לִי״, חֲלוֹם – דִּכְתִיב ״וַתַּחֲלִימֵנִי וְהַחֲיֵנִי״.

Similarly: **Six matters are good omens for the sick: Sneezin**g, **sweating, diarrhea, a seminal emission, sleep, and a dream.** The**y** are all alluded to in Scripture: **Sneezing, as it is written: "His snee**z**es flash forth light"** (Job 41:10), indicating that by means o**f a** sneeze one comes to see the light of the world. **Sweat, as it is wr**it**ten: "In the sweat of your face shall you eat bread"** (Genesis 3:1**9**). **Diarrhea, as it is written: "He that is bent down shall speedily b**e **loosed; and he shall not go down dying into the pit"** (Isaiah 51:14). **A seminal emission, as it is written: "That he might see his see**d**,** **prolong his days"** (Isaiah 53:10). **Sleep, as it is written: "I shou**ld **have slept; then had I been at rest"** (Job 3:13). **A dream, as it** is **written: "Wherefore You recover me** [***vataḥalimeni***]**, and ma**k**e** **me to live"** (Isaiah 38:16); *vataḥalimeni* is interpreted as etym**o**logically similar to *ḥalom*, dream.

שִׁשָּׁה דְּבָרִים מְרַפְּאִין אֶת הַחוֹלֶה מֵחָלְיוֹ וּרְפוּאָתוֹ רְפוּאָה, אֵלּוּ הֵן: כְּרוּב, וּתְרָדִין, וְסִיסִין יְבֵשִׁין, וְקֵיבָה, וְהֶרֶת, וְיוֹתֶרֶת הַכָּבֵד, וְיֵשׁ אוֹמְרִים: אַף דָּגִים קְטַנִּים. וְלֹא עוֹד אֶלָּא, שֶׁדָּגִים קְטַנִּים מַפְרִין וּמַבְרִין כָּל גּוּפוֹ שֶׁל אָדָם.

Similarly: **Six matters cure a sick person from his illness, and th**eir **cure is** an effective **cure. They are: Cabbage, beets, dried foley,** a medicinal plant, **the stomach, the placenta, and the diaphragm** of an animal. **Some say** that **small fish** also possess these qualiti**es.** **Furthermore, small fish cause one's entire body to flourish an**d **become healthy.**

עֲשָׂרָה דְּבָרִים מַחֲזִירִין אֶת הַחוֹלֶה לְחָלְיוֹ, וְחָלְיוֹ קָשֶׁה, אֵלּוּ הֵן: בְּשַׂר שׁוֹר, בָּשָׂר שָׁמֵן, בְּשַׂר צָלִי בְּשַׂר צִפֳּרִים, וּבֵיצָה צְלוּיָה, וְתִגְלַחַת, וְשַׁחֲלַיִם וְהֶחָלָב, וְהַגְּבִינָה, וְהַמֶּרְחָץ, וְיֵשׁ אוֹמְרִים: אַף אֱגוֹזִים, וְיֵשׁ אוֹמְרִים: אַף קִשּׁוּאִים.

In contrast, **there are ten matters that** cause a sick person who has recovered to suffer a **relapse of his illness, and his illness is** even more **severe, and they are:** Eating **ox meat,** eating **fatty meat** in general, eating **roasted meat,** eating **poultry,** eating **a roasted egg, shaving,** eating **cress,** drinking **milk,** eating **cheese, and** bathing in a **bathhouse. And some say** eating **nuts, and some say even** eating **cucumbers.**

תָּנָא דְּבֵי רַבִּי יִשְׁמָעֵאל: לָמָּה נִקְרָא שְׁמָם "קִשּׁוּאִים" – מִפְּנֵי שֶׁהֵן קָשִׁין לַגּוּף כַּחֲרָבוֹת. אִינִי? וְהָכְתִיב "וַיֹּאמֶר ה' לָהּ שְׁנֵי גוֹיִם בְּבִטְנֵךְ" אַל תִּקְרֵי "גוֹיִם" אֶלָּא "גֵּיִים", וְאָמַר רַב יְהוּדָה אָמַר רַב: אֵלּוּ אַנְטוֹנִינוֹס וְרַבִּי, שֶׁלֹּא פָּסְקוּ מִשֻּׁלְחָנָם לֹא צְנוֹן וְלֹא חֲזֶרֶת וְלֹא קִשּׁוּאִים לֹא בִּימוֹת הַחַמָּה וְלֹא בִּימוֹת הַגְּשָׁמִים!

It was **taught** in the **school of Rabbi Yishmael: Why are they called cucumbers** [*kishu'im*]? **Because they are as harmful** [*kashim*] **to the body as swords.** The Gemara asks: **Is that really so? Is it not written: "And the Lord said unto her: Two nations** [*goyim*] **are in your womb"** (Genesis 25:23) and the Gemara says: **Do not read** it as *goyim*, **rather** read it as *gayim*, **proud ones. And Rav Yehuda said** that **Rav said:** This verse was fulfilled in **these** two great individuals who descended from Rebecca: **Antoninus and Rabbi** Yehuda HaNasi, **whose tables,** because of their wealth, **never lacked for radish, lettuce or cucumbers, neither in summer nor in the rainy season.** Apparently, cucumbers are good and are even a delicacy of kings.

לָא קַשְׁיָא, הָא – בְּרַבְרְבֵי, הָא – בְּזוּטְרֵי.

The Gemara resolves: This is **not difficult. This** that says they is harmful to the body refers **to large ones,** while **this** that says they were always served on the table of Rabbi Yehuda HaNasi and Antoninus refers **to small ones.**

תָּנוּ רַבָּנַן: מֵת בַּבַּיִת – שָׁלוֹם בַּבַּיִת, אָכַל וְשָׁתָה בַּבַּיִת – סִימָן יָפֶה לַבַּיִת, נָטַל כֵּלִים מִן הַבַּיִת – סִימָן רַע לַבַּיִת. תַּרְגְּמָא רַב פַּפָּא בִּמְסָאנָא וְסַנְדְּלָא. כֹּל דְּשָׁקֵיל שְׁכָבָא מַעַלְיָא בַּר מִמְּסָאנָא וְסַנְדְּלָא, כֹּל דְּיָהֵיב שְׁכָבָא מַעַלְיָא בַּר מֵעַפְרָא וְחַרְדְּלָא.

With regard to dreams, **the Sages taught:** One who dreams that he sees a **corpse in his house,** it is a sign of **peace in his house.** If the corpse **ate and drank in the house, it is good omen for the house.** If the corpse **removed vessels from the house, it is a bad omen for the house,** as it suggests that the corpse is taking someone from the house with him. **Rav Pappa explained** this only if the dream was **with regard to a shoe and a sandal,** as that indicates that someone from the house is going to embark on a long journey. As the Sages said: **Everything** that **a corpse takes** in a dream is a **good** omen **except a shoe and a sandal; everything that a corpse gives** in a dream is a **good** omen **except dust and mustard,** which looks like dust, as they portend burial.

"מְקוֹם שֶׁנֶּעֶקְרָה מִמֶּנּוּ עֲבוֹדָה זָרָה". תָּנוּ רַבָּנַן: הָרוֹאֶה מַרְקוּלִיס, אוֹמֵר: "בָּרוּךְ שֶׁנָּתַן אֶרֶךְ אַפַּיִם לְעוֹבְרֵי רְצוֹנוֹ". מָקוֹם שֶׁנֶּעֶקְרָה מִמֶּנּוּ עֲבוֹדָה זָרָה אוֹמֵר: "בָּרוּךְ שֶׁעָקַר עֲבוֹדָה זָרָה מֵאַרְצֵנוּ, וּכְשֵׁם שֶׁנֶּעֶקְרָה מִמָּקוֹם זֶה כֵּן תֵּעָקֵר מִכָּל מְקוֹמוֹת יִשְׂרָאֵל, וְהָשֵׁב לֵב עוֹבְדֵיהֶם לְעָבְדֶךָ". וּבְחוּץ לָאָרֶץ אֵין צָרִיךְ לוֹמַר "וְהָשֵׁב לֵב עוֹבְדֵיהֶם לְעָבְדֶךָ" – מִפְּנֵי שֶׁרוּבָּהּ גּוֹיִם. רַבִּי שִׁמְעוֹן בֶּן אֶלְעָזָר אוֹמֵר: אַף בְּחוּץ לָאָרֶץ צָרִיךְ לוֹמַר כֵּן, מִפְּנֵי שֶׁעֲתִידִים לְהִתְגַּיֵּיר, שֶׁנֶּאֱמַר "אָז אֶהְפֹּךְ אֶל עַמִּים שָׂפָה בְרוּרָה".

We learned in the mishna that one who sees **a place from which idolatry was eradicated** should recite the blessing: Blessed…Who eradicated idolatry from our land. On this topic **the Sages taught** in the *Tosefta*: **One who sees** the idol called **Mercury** [*Markulis*][NH] **recites: Blessed…who has shown patience to those who violate His will,** as each day new rocks would be thrown upon the pile constructed in Mercury' honor (*Tosafot*). One who sees **a place from which idolatry was eradicated**[H] **should recite: Blessed…Who eradicated idolatry from our land. And just as it was eradicated from this place, so too may it be eradicated from all places of Israel, and restore the hearts of their worshippers to worship You. Outside of Eretz** Yisrael, **one need not recite: And restore the hearts of their worshippers to worship You, since it is predominantly populated by gentiles. Rabbi Shimon ben Elazar says: Even outside of Eretz** Yisrael **one is required to recite that** formula **because** in the end of days all nations **will convert, as it is stated: "For then will I turn to the peoples a pure language,** that they may all call upon the Name of the Lord, to serve Him with one consent" (Zephaniah 3:9).

דָּרֵשׁ רַב הַמְנוּנָא: הָרוֹאֶה בָּבֶל הָרְשָׁעָה צָרִיךְ לְבָרֵךְ חָמֵשׁ בְּרָכוֹת; רָאָה בָּבֶל אוֹמֵר "בָּרוּךְ שֶׁהֶחֱרִיב בָּבֶל הָרְשָׁעָה"; רָאָה בֵּיתוֹ שֶׁל נְבוּכַדְנֶצַּר אוֹמֵר: "בָּרוּךְ שֶׁהֶחֱרִיב בֵּיתוֹ שֶׁל נְבוּכַדְנֶצַּר הָרָשָׁע"; רָאָה גּוֹב שֶׁל אֲרָיוֹת אוֹ כִּבְשַׁן הָאֵשׁ אוֹמֵר: "בָּרוּךְ שֶׁעָשָׂה נִסִּים לַאֲבוֹתֵינוּ בַּמָּקוֹם הַזֶּה"; רָאָה מַרְקוּלִיס אוֹמֵר "בָּרוּךְ שֶׁנָּתַן אֶרֶךְ אַפַּיִם לְעוֹבְרֵי רְצוֹנוֹ"; רָאָה מָקוֹם שֶׁנּוֹטְלִין מִמֶּנּוּ עָפָר אוֹמֵר: "בָּרוּךְ אוֹמֵר וְעוֹשֶׂה גּוֹזֵר וּמְקַיֵּים".

The Gemara goes on to discuss special blessings instituted by the Sages to be recited upon seeing extraordinary sights. **Rav Hamnuna taught: One who sees the wicked Babylonia must recite five blessings.**[H] The Gemara elaborates:

**One who saw** the ruins of **Babylonia, recites: Blessed…Who destroyed the wicked Babylonia.**

**One who saw** the ruins of **Nebuchadnezzar's house, recites: Blessed…Who destroyed the house of wicked Nebuchadnezzar.**

**One who saw the lion's den** into which Daniel was thrown (see Daniel ch. 6) **or the furnace** into which Hananiah, Mishael, and Azariah **were thrown** (see Daniel ch. 3), **recites: Blessed…Who performed miracles for our ancestors in this place.**

**One who saw Mercury, recites: Blessed…Who has shown patience to those who violate His will.**

**One who saw a place from which earth is taken,** as over the generations earth was taken from certain places and used as fertilizer or for construction in the surrounding areas, **recites: Blessed…Who speaks and acts, decrees and fulfills.**

**NOTES**

**One who sees Mercury [*Markulis*] – הָרוֹאֶה מַרְקוּלִיס:** *Markulis* is the name by which the Sages referred to the Roman god Mercury, who was the Roman version of the Greek god Hermes. Among the various roles attributed to him was patron of the roads and journeys. Therefore, idols of him were often placed at the entrance to roadways, usually incomplete, symbolic images. Travelers would place stones before these idols and at times, a pile of stones would serve to symbolize the god himself. Each passerby would place a stone as an offering to him. Some explain that because each idol-worshipper would throw a rock upon the pile, each rock represented an individual idol-worshipper. Therefore, one may include in the blessing: And may the hearts of their worshippers be restored to worship You (*Ḥefetz Hashem*). Others explain that this illustrates that although this form of idolatry is a demeaning form of worship, one nevertheless recites a blessing upon seeing it (Rav Ya'akov Emden).

**HALAKHA**

**One who sees Mercury [*Markulis*] – הָרוֹאֶה מַרְקוּלִיס:** One who sees idolatry recites the blessing: Blessed…Who has shown patience to those who violate His will. This blessing should not be recited more than once in thirty days (Rambam *Sefer Ahava, Hilkhot Berakhot* 10:9; *Shulḥan Arukh, Oraḥ Ḥayyim* 224:1).

**A place from which idolatry was eradicated – מָקוֹם שֶׁנֶּעֶקְרָה מִמֶּנּוּ עֲבוֹדַת כּוֹכָבִים:** One who sees a place in Eretz Yisrael from which idolatry was eradicated recites: Blessed…Who eradicated idolatry from our land. Outside of Eretz Yisrael, one recites: Who eradicated idolatry from this place. In both cases, one concludes: Just as you eradicated it from this place, so too may it be eradicated from all places and may the hearts of their worshippers be restored to worship You, in accordance with the opinion of Rabbi Shimon ben Elazar (Rambam *Sefer Ahava, Hilkhot Berakhot* 10:9; *Shulḥan Arukh, Oraḥ Ḥayyim* 224:2).

**The blessings of Babylonia – בִּרְכוֹת בָּבֶל:** One who sees wicked Babylonia recites: Blessed…Who destroyed the wicked Babylonia. One who sees the ruins of Nebuchadnezzar's house recites: Blessed…Who destroyed the house of wicked Nebuchadnezzar. One who sees the lion's den into which Daniel was thrown or the furnace that was stoked for Ḥananya, Mishael, and Azarya, recites: Blessed…Who performed miracles for the righteous in this place (*Shulḥan Arukh, Oraḥ Ḥayyim* 224:3).

**NOTES**

The curse of Babylonia – קִלְלַת בָּבֶל: Some say the soil of Babylonia was used to produce mortar (see Rashi). This is alluded to by the etymological similarity between the word *vetetetiha*, and I will sweep it, and the word *tit*, mortar (*Talmidei Rabbeinu Yona*).

רָבָא כִּי הֲוָה חָזֵי חֲמָרֵי דְּשָׁקְלִי עַפְרָא, טָרֵיף לְהוּ יְדָא עַל גַּבַּיְיהוּ וַאֲמַר: רְהוּטוּ צַדִּיקֵי לְמֶעְבַּד רְעוּתָא דְּמָרַיְיכוּ. מָר בְּרֵיהּ דְּרָבִינָא כִּי הֲוָה מָטֵי לְבָבֶל, הֲוָה שָׁקֵיל עַפְרָא בְּסוּדָרֵיהּ וְשָׁדֵי לְבָרָא, לְקַיֵּים מַה שֶּׁנֶּאֱמַר: ״וְטֵאטֵאתִיהָ בְּמַטְאֲטֵא הַשְׁמֵד״. אָמַר רַב אַשִׁי: אֲנָא הָא דְּרַב הַמְנוּנָא לָא שְׁמִיעַ לִי, אֶלָּא מִדַּעְתַּאי בָּרֵיכְתִּינְהוּ לְכוּלְּהוּ.

The Gemara relates that **when Rava would see donkeys carrying earth** from Babylonia, **he would slap their backs with his hand and say to them: Run, righteous ones, and fulfill the will of your Master. When Mar, son of Ravina, would arrive in Babylonia he would take earth in his kerchief and throw it outside, to fulfill that which is said: "And I will sweep it with the broom of destruction"** (Isaiah 14:23).[N] **Rav Ashi said: I never heard the** statement of **Rav Hamnuna,** that one who sees Babylonia the wicked must recite five blessings. **However, based on my independent reasoning, I recited all of the blessings.**

Perek **IX**
Daf **58** Amud **a**

**NOTES**

When Babylonia was cursed, its neighbors were cursed along with it. When Samaria was cursed, its neighbors were blessed – נִתְקַלְּלָה בָּבֶל נִתְקַלְּלוּ שְׁכֵנֶיהָ, נִתְקַלְּלָה שׁוֹמְרוֹן נִתְבָּרְכוּ שְׁכֵנֶיהָ: It is well known that when Babylonia or similar countries are punished, it is because the country has reached an intolerable level of corruption and evil. Their punishment does nothing to alter that status. In contrast, punishment meted out to the people of Israel cleanses them of their sins, after which they are without sin. Rabbi Yirmeya's first statement is based on the rabbinic dictum: Woe to the wicked, woe to his neighbor, as even after receiving its punishment, Babylonia is still held responsible for its wickedness. Samaria, on the other hand, is purified of its sins after receiving punishment, which has a salutary effect on its neighbors, as well, as the Sages teach: Good for the righteous, good for his neighbor (*Anaf Yosef*).

**HALAKHA**

One who sees multitudes of Israel – הָרוֹאֶה אוֹכְלוֹסֵי יִשְׂרָאֵל: One who sees six hundred thousand Jews recites the blessing: Blessed…Who knows all secrets (Rambam *Sefer Ahava, Hilkhot Berakhot*, 10:11; *Shulḥan Arukh, Oraḥ Ḥayyim* 224:5).

**LANGUAGE**

Multitude [*okhlosa*] – אוֹכְלוֹסָא: From the Greek ὄχλος, *okhlos*, meaning multitude.

Loaves [*geluskaot*] – גְּלוּסְקָאוֹת: From the Greek κόλλιξ, *kollix*, meaning loaf of bread or roll.

אָמַר רַבִּי יִרְמְיָה בֶּן אֶלְעָזָר: נִתְקַלְּלָה בָּבֶל – נִתְקַלְּלוּ שְׁכֵנֶיהָ, נִתְקַלְּלָה שׁוֹמְרוֹן – נִתְבָּרְכוּ שְׁכֵנֶיהָ. נִתְקַלְּלָה בָּבֶל נִתְקַלְּלוּ שְׁכֵנֶיהָ, דִּכְתִיב: ״וְשַׂמְתִּיהָ לְמוֹרַשׁ קִפֹּד וְאַגְמֵי מָיִם״. נִתְקַלְּלָה שׁוֹמְרוֹן נִתְבָּרְכוּ שְׁכֵנֶיהָ, דִּכְתִיב: ״וְשַׂמְתִּי שֹׁמְרוֹן לְעִי הַשָּׂדֶה לְמַטָּעֵי כָרֶם״ וגו׳.

With regard to Babylonia, the Gemara cites what **Rabbi Yirmeya ben Elazar said:** When **Babylonia was cursed, its neighbors were cursed** along with it. When **Samaria was cursed, its neighbors were blessed.** When **Babylonia was cursed its neighbors were cursed** along with it, **as it is written: "I will also make it a possession for the bittern,** a wading bird, **and pools of water"** (Isaiah 14:23); not only will it be destroyed, but the site will become a habitat for destructive, environmentally harmful creatures. When **Samaria was cursed,** however, **its neighbors were blessed, as it is written: "Therefore I will make Samaria a heap in the field, a place for the planting of vineyards"** (Micah 1:6); although destroyed, it will serve a beneficial purpose.

וְאָמַר רַב הַמְנוּנָא: הָרוֹאֶה אוֹכְלוֹסֵי יִשְׂרָאֵל, אוֹמֵר: ״בָּרוּךְ חֲכַם הָרָזִים״. אוֹכְלוֹסֵי גוֹיִם אוֹמֵר: ״בּוֹשָׁה אִמְּכֶם״ וגו׳.

**And Rav Hamnuna said: One who sees multitudes of Israel,**[H] six hundred thousand Jews, **recites: Blessed…Who knows all secrets.** One who sees **multitudes of gentiles recites: "Your mother shall be sore ashamed,** she that bore you shall be confounded; behold, the hindermost of the nations shall be a wilderness, a dry land, and a desert" (Jeremiah 50:12).

תָּנוּ רַבָּנַן: הָרוֹאֶה אוֹכְלוֹסֵי יִשְׂרָאֵל אוֹמֵר: ״בָּרוּךְ חֲכַם הָרָזִים״. שֶׁאֵין דַּעְתָּם דּוֹמָה זֶה לָזֶה, וְאֵין פַּרְצוּפֵיהֶן דּוֹמִים זֶה לָזֶה. בֶּן זוֹמָא רָאָה אוֹכְלוֹסָא עַל גַּב מַעֲלָה בְּהַר הַבַּיִת, אָמַר: ״בָּרוּךְ חֲכַם הָרָזִים״, וּ״בָרוּךְ שֶׁבָּרָא כׇּל אֵלּוּ לְשַׁמְּשֵׁנִי״.

**The Sages taught** in a *Tosefta*: **One who sees multitudes of Israel recites: Blessed…Who knows all secrets.** Why is this? He sees a whole nation **whose minds are unlike each other and whose faces are unlike each other,** and He Who knows all secrets, God, knows what is in each of their hearts. The Gemara relates: **Ben Zoma once saw a multitude [*okhlosa*]**[L] **of Israel** while standing **on a stair on the Temple Mount.** He immediately **recited: Blessed…Who knows all secrets and Blessed…Who created all these to serve me.**

הוּא הָיָה אוֹמֵר: כַּמָּה יְגִיעוֹת יָגַע אָדָם הָרִאשׁוֹן עַד שֶׁמָּצָא פַּת לֶאֱכוֹל: חָרַשׁ, וְזָרַע, וְקָצַר, וְעִמֵּר, וְדָשׁ, וְזָרָה, וּבֵרַר, וְטָחַן, וְהִרְקִיד, וְלָשׁ, וְאָפָה, וְאַחַר כָּךְ אָכַל, וַאֲנִי מַשְׁכִּים וּמוֹצֵא כׇּל אֵלּוּ מְתוּקָּנִין לְפָנַי. וְכַמָּה יְגִיעוֹת יָגַע אָדָם הָרִאשׁוֹן עַד שֶׁמָּצָא בֶּגֶד לִלְבּוֹשׁ: גָּזַז וְלִבֵּן וְנִפֵּץ וְטָוָה וְאָרַג, וְאַחַר כָּךְ מָצָא בֶּגֶד לִלְבּוֹשׁ, וַאֲנִי מַשְׁכִּים וּמוֹצֵא כׇּל אֵלֶּה מְתוּקָּנִים לְפָנַי. כׇּל אוּמּוֹת שׁוֹקְדוֹת וּבָאוֹת לְפֶתַח בֵּיתִי, וַאֲנִי מַשְׁכִּים וּמוֹצֵא כׇּל אֵלּוּ לְפָנַי.

Explaining his custom, **he would say: How much effort did Adam the first** man **exert before he found bread to eat:** He **plowed, sowed, reaped, sheaved, threshed, winnowed** in the wind, **separated the** grain from the chaff, **ground** the grain into flour, **sifted, kneaded, and baked and** only **thereafter he ate. And I,** on the other hand, **wake up and find all of these prepared for me.** Human society employs a division of labor, and each individual benefits from the service of the entire world. Similarly, **how much effort did Adam the first** man **exert before he found a garment to wear?** He **sheared, laundered, combed, spun and wove, and** only **thereafter he found a garment to wear. And I,** on the other hand, **wake up and find all of these prepared for me.** Members of **all nations,** merchants and craftsmen, **diligently come to the entrance of my home, and I wake up and find all of these before me.**

הוּא הָיָה אוֹמֵר: אוֹרֵחַ טוֹב מַהוּ אוֹמֵר – כַּמָּה טְרָחוֹת טָרַח בַּעַל הַבַּיִת בִּשְׁבִילִי, כַּמָּה בָּשָׂר הֵבִיא לְפָנַי, כַּמָּה יַיִן הֵבִיא לְפָנַי, כַּמָּה גְלוּסְקָאוֹת הֵבִיא לְפָנַי, וְכׇל מַה שֶּׁטָּרַח – לֹא טָרַח אֶלָּא בִּשְׁבִילִי. אֲבָל אוֹרֵחַ רַע מַהוּ אוֹמֵר – מַה טּוֹרַח טָרַח בַּעַל הַבַּיִת זֶה? פַּת אַחַת אָכַלְתִּי, חֲתִיכָה אַחַת אָכַלְתִּי, כּוֹס אֶחָד שָׁתִיתִי, כׇּל טוֹרַח שֶׁטָּרַח בַּעַל הַבַּיִת זֶה – לֹא טָרַח אֶלָּא בִּשְׁבִיל אִשְׁתּוֹ וּבָנָיו.

Ben Zoma **would say: A good guest, what does he say? How much effort did the host expend on my behalf, how much meat did the host bring before me. How much wine did he bring before me. How many loaves [*geluskaot*]**[L] **did he bring before me. All the effort that he expended, he expended only for me. However, a bad guest, what does he say? What effort did the host expend? I ate only one piece of bread, I ate** only **one piece of meat** and **I drank** only **one cup of wine. All the effort that the home owner expended he only expended on behalf of his wife and children.**

עַל אוֹרֵחַ טוֹב מַהוּ אוֹמֵר – "זְכֹר כִּי תַשְׂגִּיא פָעֳלוֹ
אֲשֶׁר שֹׁרְרוּ אֲנָשִׁים". עַל אוֹרֵחַ רָע כְּתִיב – "לָכֵן
יְרֵאוּהוּ אֲנָשִׁים" וגו'.

**With regard to a good guest, what does he say? "Remember that you magnify his work, whereof men have sung"** (Job 36:24); he praises and acknowledges those who helped him. **With regard to a bad guest it is written: "Men do therefore fear him;** he regards not any who are wise of heart" (Job 37:24).

"וְהָאִישׁ בִּימֵי שָׁאוּל זָקֵן בָּא בַאֲנָשִׁים", אָמַר רָבָא
וְאִיתֵּימָא רַב זְבִיד וְאִיתֵּימָא רַב אוֹשַׁעְיָא: זֶה יִשַׁי
אֲבִי דָוִד שֶׁיָּצָא בְּאוֹכְלוֹסָא, וְנִכְנַס בְּאוֹכְלוֹסָא
וְדָרַשׁ בְּאוֹכְלוֹסָא. אָמַר עוּלָּא: נְקִיטִינַן – אֵין
אוֹכְלוֹסָא בְּבָבֶל. תָּנָא: אֵין אוֹכְלוֹסָא פְּחוּתָה
מִשִּׁשִּׁים רִבּוֹא.

On the topic of multitudes, the Gemara cites another verse: **"And the man in the days of Saul was old, and came among men"** (I Samuel 17:12). **Rava, and some say Rav Zevid, and some say Rav Oshaya, said:** This refers to **Yishai, father of David, who** always **went out with multitudes, and entered with multitudes, and taught Torah with multitudes. Ulla said: We hold there is no multitude in Babylonia.**[N] The Sage **taught: A multitude is no fewer than six hundred thousand** people.

תָּנוּ רַבָּנַן: הָרוֹאֶה חַכְמֵי יִשְׂרָאֵל אוֹמֵר: "בָּרוּךְ
שֶׁחָלַק מֵחָכְמָתוֹ לִירֵאָיו", חַכְמֵי אוּמּוֹת הָעוֹלָם
אוֹמֵר: "בָּרוּךְ שֶׁנָּתַן מֵחָכְמָתוֹ לְבָשָׂר וָדָם". הָרוֹאֶה
מַלְכֵי יִשְׂרָאֵל אוֹמֵר: "בָּרוּךְ שֶׁחָלַק מִכְּבוֹדוֹ
לִירֵאָיו", מַלְכֵי אוּמּוֹת הָעוֹלָם – אוֹמֵר: "בָּרוּךְ
שֶׁנָּתַן מִכְּבוֹדוֹ לְבָשָׂר וָדָם".

**The Sages taught: One who sees the Sages of Israel recites: Blessed…Who has shared of His wisdom with those who revere Him.** One who sees **Sages of the nations of the world**[H] **recites: Blessed…Who has given**[N] **of His wisdom to flesh and blood.**[N] **One who sees kings of Israel recites: Blessed…Who has shared of His glory with those who revere Him.** One who sees **kings of the** other **nations of the world**[H] **recites: Blessed…Who has given of His glory to flesh and blood.**

אָמַר רַבִּי יוֹחָנָן: לְעוֹלָם יִשְׁתַּדֵּל אָדָם לָרוּץ לִקְרַאת
מַלְכֵי יִשְׂרָאֵל, וְלֹא לִקְרַאת מַלְכֵי יִשְׂרָאֵל בִּלְבַד
אֶלָּא אֲפִילּוּ לִקְרַאת מַלְכֵי אוּמּוֹת הָעוֹלָם, שֶׁאִם
יִזְכֶּה – יַבְחִין בֵּין מַלְכֵי יִשְׂרָאֵל לְמַלְכֵי אוּמּוֹת
הָעוֹלָם.

**Rabbi Yoḥanan said: One should always strive to run toward kings of Israel** to greet them. **And not only** should he run **toward kings of Israel, but also toward kings of the nations of the world, so that if he will be privileged** to witnesses the glory of the Messiah (Rashi) and the World-to-Come, **he will distinguish between the kings of Israel and the kings of the nations of the world.**

רַב שֵׁשֶׁת סַגִּי נְהוֹר הֲוָה, הֲווּ קָאָזְלִי כּוּלֵּי עָלְמָא
לְקַבּוּלֵי אַפֵּי מַלְכָּא, וְקָם אֲזַל בַּהֲדַיְיהוּ רַב שֵׁשֶׁת.
אַשְׁכְּחֵיהּ הַהוּא מִינָא אֲמַר לֵיהּ: חַצְבֵי לְנַהֲרָא
כַּגְנֵי לַיָּיא?! אֲמַר לֵיהּ: תָּא חֲזִי דְּיָדַעְנָא טְפֵי מִינָּךְ.
חֲלַף גּוּנְדָּא קַמַּיְיתָא, כִּי קָא אָוְושָׁא אֲמַר לֵיהּ
הַהוּא מִינָא: אָתָא מַלְכָּא. אֲמַר לֵיהּ רַב שֵׁשֶׁת:
לָא קָאָתֵי. חֲלַף גּוּנְדָּא תִּנְיָינָא, כִּי קָא אָוְושָׁא
אֲמַר לֵיהּ הַהוּא מִינָא: הַשְׁתָּא קָא אָתֵי מַלְכָּא.
אֲמַר לֵיהּ רַב שֵׁשֶׁת: לָא קָא אָתֵי מַלְכָּא. חֲלַף
תְּלִיתָאֵי, כִּי קָא שָׁתְקָא, אֲמַר לֵיהּ רַב שֵׁשֶׁת: וַדַּאי
הַשְׁתָּא אָתֵי מַלְכָּא.

The Gemara relates: **Rav Sheshet**[P] **was blind. Everyone was going to greet the king and Rav Sheshet stood up and went along with them. This heretic found him** there **and said to him:** The intact **jugs go to the river, where do the broken** jugs **go?** Why is a blind person going to see the king? Rav Sheshet **said to him: Come see that I know more than you do. The first troop passed,** and **when the noise grew louder, this heretic said to him: The king is coming. Rav Sheshet said to him:** The king **is not coming. The second troop passed,** and **when the noise grew louder, this heretic said to him: Now the king is coming. Rav Sheshet said to him: The king is not coming. The third** troop **passed,** and **when there was silence, Rav Sheshet said to him: Certainly now the king is coming.**

אֲמַר לֵיהּ הַהוּא מִינָא: מְנָא לָךְ הָא? אֲמַר לֵיהּ:
דְּמַלְכוּתָא דְּאַרְעָא כְּעֵין מַלְכוּתָא דִּרְקִיעָא.
דִּכְתִיב "צֵא וְעָמַדְתָּ בָהָר לִפְנֵי ה' וְהִנֵּה ה' עֹבֵר
וְרוּחַ גְּדוֹלָה וְחָזָק מְפָרֵק הָרִים וּמְשַׁבֵּר סְלָעִים לִפְנֵי
ה' לֹא בָרוּחַ ה' וְאַחַר הָרוּחַ רַעַשׁ לֹא בָרַעַשׁ ה'
וְאַחַר הָרַעַשׁ אֵשׁ לֹא בָאֵשׁ ה' וְאַחַר הָאֵשׁ קוֹל
דְּמָמָה דַקָּה".

**This heretic said to him: How do you know this?** Rav Sheshet **said to him: Royalty on earth is like royalty in the heavens, as it is written** with regard to God's revelation to Elijah the Prophet on Mount Horeb:

**"And He said: Go forth, and stand upon the mount before the Lord.**
**And, behold, the Lord passed by, and a great and strong wind rent the mountains, and broke in pieces the rocks before the Lord;**
**but the Lord was not in the wind;**
**and after the wind an earthquake;**
**but the Lord was not in the earthquake;**
**and after the earthquake a fire;**
**but the Lord was not in the fire;**
**and after the fire a still small voice.**
And it was so, when Elijah heard it, that he wrapped his face in his mantle and went out, and stood in the entrance of the cave" (I Kings 19:11–13). God's revelation was specifically at the moment of silence.

## NOTES

**There is no multitude in Babylonia – אֵין אוֹכְלוֹסָא בְּבָבֶל:** Some explain that even if there was a multitude, numerically, in Babylonia, one would still not recite this blessing because it was formulated specifically as praise for when one sees that number of Jews in Eretz Yisrael (*Beit Yosef* according to the Rambam; see *Ma'adanei Yom Tov*).

**Who has shared…Who has given – שֶׁחָלַק…שֶׁנָּתַן:** According to most authorities, there is a difference between the formula of the blessing for a Jew: Who has shared [*ḥalak*], and that recited for a non-Jew: Who has given [*natan*]. There are various explanations for this distinction. Some say that the blessing for a Jew, *ḥalak*, is based on the verse: "For the portion [*ḥelek*] of the Lord is His people" (Deuteronomy 32:9), which is not the case with regard to other nations (*Beit Yosef*). Others explain that the phrase, has shared, indicates an ongoing connection with God as a recipient of His beneficence at all times. This is not the case with the formula of the phrase, has given, which indicates that the connection was subsequently severed (Abudarham). Others explain that it is impossible to ever complete one's study of Torah, so the verb *ḥalak* implies that no matter how much one studies, it will always remain but a portion [*ḥelek*] of the whole (Rabbi Mordekhai Yaffe).

**To flesh and blood – לְבָשָׂר וָדָם:** The formula of the blessing for non-Jews in standard editions of the Talmud is *livriyotav*, to His creations, rather than *levasar vadam*, to flesh and blood. The censor made this change to soften the contrast between: Those who revere him, which is the formula of the blessing recited for Jews, emphasizing their connection with God, and: Flesh and blood, which indicates no such connection. The formula: To His creations, indicates that non-Jews have a connection with God as well.

## PERSONALITIES

**Rav Sheshet – רַב שֵׁשֶׁת:** A prominent third generation Babylonian *amora*, Rav Sheshet was the primary student of Rav Huna, even though he also served and studied under the rest of the Sages of that generation. Even in his generation Rav Sheshet was famous for his unsurpassed expertise in *baraitot*. Due to his comprehensive familiarity with even the most obscure areas of Oral Law, he was nicknamed Sinai. Many of the Sages of the generation came to study from him as they knew that his teachings were always based on early sources.

In his later years Rav Sheshet became blind, but remained involved in all aspects of life and was a frequent visitor to the house of the Exilarch. He was characteristically extremely forceful, hard as steel, and did not defer even to eminent world leaders.

Apparently, Rav Sheshet was a garment merchant who earned enough to live comfortably.

## HALAKHA

**One who sees the Sages of Israel…Sages of nations of the world – הָרוֹאֶה חַכְמֵי יִשְׂרָאֵל…חַכְמֵי אוּמּוֹת הָעוֹלָם:** One who sees Sages of Israel recites: Blessed…Who has shared of His wisdom with those who revere Him. One who sees great Sages of other nations, who are prominent in disciplines of general wisdom, e.g., the sciences (*Magen Avraham*), recites: Who has given of His wisdom to flesh and blood (Rambam *Sefer Ahava, Hilkhot Berakhot* 10:11; *Shulḥan Arukh, Oraḥ Ḥayyim* 224:6–7).

**One who sees kings of Israel…kings of the nations of the world – הָרוֹאֶה מַלְכֵי יִשְׂרָאֵל…מַלְכֵי אוּמּוֹת הָעוֹלָם:** One who sees kings of Israel recites: Blessed…Who has shared of His glory with those who revere Him. One who sees kings of other nations recites: Who has given of His glory to flesh and blood (Rambam *Sefer Ahava, Hilkhot Berakhot* 10:11; *Shulḥan Arukh, Oraḥ Ḥayyim* 224:8).

## PERSONALITIES

**Rabbi Sheila – רבי שילא:** Rabbi Sheila was one of the first Babylonian *amora'im*. After the death of Rabbi Yehuda HaNasi, Rabbi Sheila was the spiritual leader of the Jewish community in Babylonia. He was the *Reish Sidra*, the head of the yeshiva of sorts, in the most important yeshiva there. Apparently, he lived in Neharde'a. Even the prominent *amora* Shmuel was officially subject to his authority.

When Rav arrived in Babylonia, Rav Sheila did not recognize his greatness and used him as a disseminator of his lectures. However, after he discovered his identity, he treated him with great respect and even accepted his authority. Rav, though, did not want to insult Rav Sheila, so he moved to Sura and opened his own yeshiva.

Apparently, Rav Sheila's yeshiva continued to function for a period after his death and many traditions that emerged from that study hall appear in the Gemara.

Many disputes between Rav and Rabbi Sheila appear in the Gemara, and various halakhic rulings are cited in his name.

## NOTES

**Who had relations with a gentile woman – דבעל נכרית:** Though the punishment for having relations with a non-Jewish woman is not delineated in the Torah, the absolute condemnation of this deed is explicit in Numbers (ch. 25) in the context of Israel's transgression with the Midianite women. The conclusion drawn from the Torah there is: One who has relations with a gentile woman, zealots attack him. Therefore, one committing this sin would be punished in different ways, depending on the gravity of the context in which it was committed.

**The punishment of an informer – עונשו של מלשין:** Informers are among those with no place in the World-to-Come and are not afforded the protection of the law. Until recent generations, they were sentenced to death by Jewish courts based on the tenet: One who comes to kill you, kill him first. The informer constitutes a severe threat to the entire Jewish community, so at times, standard judicial procedure is suspended and he is sentenced to death.

## LANGUAGE

**Authority [*harmana*] – הרמנא:** This word is similar to the Middle Parthian hramān. It is related in origin to the Middle Persian framān, meaning command.

**Messenger [*peristaka*] – פריסתקא:** From Persian, meaning messenger or delegate. It appears in Middle Persian as frēstak, which was borrowed by other languages (as in Ezra 4:9, *afarsattekhaye*).

כי אתא מלכא, פתח רב ששת וקא מברך ליה. אמר ליה ההוא מינא: למאן דלא חזית ליה קא מברכת?! ומאי הוי עליה דההוא מינא? איכא דאמרי: חברוהי כחלינהו לעיניה, ואיכא דאמרי: רב ששת נתן עיניו בו, ונעשה גל של עצמות.

**When the king came, Rav Sheshet began to bless him. The heretic** mockingly **said to him: Do you bless someone you do not see?** The Gemara asks: **And what ultimately happened to this heretic? Some say** that his **friends gouged out his eyes, and some say** that **Rav Sheshet fixed his gaze upon him, and** the heretic **became a pile of bones.**

רבי שילא נגדיה לההוא גברא דבעל גויה. אזל אכל ביה קורצי בי מלכא, אמר: איכא חד גברא ביהודאי דקא דיין דינא בלא הרמנא דמלכא. שדר עליה פריסתקא, כי אתא אמרי ליה: מאי טעמא נגדתיה להאי? אמר להו: דבא על חמרתא. אמרי ליה: אית לך סהדי? אמר להו: אין. אתא אליהו, אדמי ליה כאיניש, ואסהיד. אמרי ליה: אי הכי בר קטלא הוא! – אמר להו: אנן מיומא דגלינן מארעין לית לן רשותא למקטל, אתון – מאי דבעיתון עבידו ביה.

As for the connection between divine and earthly royalty, the Gemara cites another story: **Rabbi Sheila**[P] ordered that **a man who had relations with a gentile woman**[NH] be **flogged.** That man **went to inform the king and said: There is one man among the Jews who renders judgment without the king's authority [*harmana*].**[L] The king **sent a messenger [*peristaka*]**[L] **for** Rabbi Sheila to bring him to trial. **When** Rabbi Sheila **came, they said to him: Why did you** order **flogging for this man? He said to them:** Because **he had relations with a female donkey.** According to Persian law this was an extremely heinous crime, so **they said to him: Do you have witnesses** that he did so? **He replied: Yes,** and **Elijah** the prophet **came and appeared as a person and testified. They said to** Rabbi Sheila: **If so, he is liable for the death penalty;** why did you not sentence him to death? **He replied: Since the day we were exiled from our land we do not have the authority to execute, but you, do with him as you wish.**

עד דמעייני ביה בדינא, פתח רבי שילא ואמר: "לך ה׳ הגדלה והגבורה" וגו׳. אמרי ליה: מאי קאמרת? אמר להו: הכי קאמינא – בריך רחמנא דיהיב מלכותא בארעא כעין מלכותא דרקיעא, ויהב לכו שולטנא ורחמי דינא. אמרו: חביבא עליה יקרא דמלכותא כולי האי! יהבי ליה קולפא, אמרו ליה: דון דינא.

As they **considered the sentence,** Rabbi Sheila praised God for saving him from danger: **"Yours, O Lord, is the greatness, power,** glory, triumph, and majesty; for all that is in heaven and on earth is Yours; Yours is the kingdom O Lord, and You are exalted as head above all" (I Chronicles 29:11). **They asked him: What did you say? He told them: This is what I said: Blessed is Merciful One who grants kingdom on earth** that is a **microcosm of the kingdom in heaven, and granted you dominion and love of justice. They said to him:** Indeed, the **honor of royalty is so dear to you. They gave him a staff** to symbolize his license to sit in judgment and **said to him: Judge.**

כי הוה נפיק, אמר ליה ההוא גברא: עביד רחמנא ניסא לשקרי הכי?! – אמר ליה: רשע! לאו חמרי איקרו? דכתיב "אשר בשר חמורים בשרם". חזייה דקאזיל למימרא להו דקרינהו חמרי, אמר: האי רודף הוא, והתורה אמרה: אם בא להרגך – השכם להרגו, מחייה בקולפא וקטליה.

**As he was leaving, that man said to** Rabbi Sheila: **Does God perform such miracles for liars? He replied: Scoundrel! Aren't** gentiles **called donkeys? As it is written: "Whose flesh is as the flesh of donkeys"** (Ezekiel 23:20). Rabbi Sheila **saw that he was going to tell** the Persian authorities **that he called them donkeys. He said:** This man has the legal status of **a pursuer.** He seeks to have me killed. **And the Torah said: If one comes to kill you, kill him first. He struck him with the staff and killed him.**[N]

## HALAKHA

**Who had relations with a gentile woman – דבעל נכרית:** One who had promiscuous relations with a gentile woman on a single occasion is liable for violating the rabbinic prohibitions against having relations with a gentile woman and with a promiscuous woman, for which he receives lashes of rebelliousness. If he entered into a long-term promiscuous relationship with her, he thereby violated the rabbinic decree that deems him in violation of the prohibitions forbidding having relations with a menstruating woman, a maidservant, a gentile woman and a promiscuous woman. If he has relations with her within the framework of marriage, he is punished with lashes for violating Torah law, although some dispute this (Rambam *Sefer Kedusha, Hilkhot Issurei Bia* 12:2; *Shulḥan Arukh, Even HaEzer* 16 and in the comment of the Rema).

אָמַר: הוֹאִיל וְאִתְעֲבִיד לִי נִיסָּא בְּהַא
קְרָא – דָּרְשִׁינָא לֵיהּ: "לְךָ ה' הַגְּדֻלָּה" –
מַעֲשֵׂה בְרֵאשִׁית, וְכֵן הוּא אוֹמֵר: "עֹשֶׂה
גְדֹלוֹת עַד אֵין חֵקֶר". "וְהַגְּבוּרָה" –
יְצִיאַת מִצְרַיִם, שֶׁנֶּאֱמַר "וַיַּרְא יִשְׂרָאֵ
אֶת הַיָּד הַגְּדֹלָה" וגו'. "וְהַתִּפְאֶרֶת" –
חַמָּה וּלְבָנָה שֶׁעָמְדוּ לוֹ לִיהוֹשֻׁעַ, שֶׁנֶּאֱמַ
"וַיִּדֹּם הַשֶּׁמֶשׁ וְיָרֵחַ עָמָד" וגו'. "וְהַנֵּצַח" –
זוֹ מַפַּלְתָּה שֶׁל רוֹמִי, וְכֵן הוּא אוֹמֵר "וְי
נִצְחָם עַל בְּגָדַי" וגו'. "וְהַהוֹד" – זוֹ מִלְחֶמֶ
נַחֲלֵי אַרְנוֹן, שֶׁנֶּאֱמַר "עַל כֵּן יֵאָמַר בְּסֵפֶ
מִלְחֲמֹת ה' אֶת וָהֵב בְּסוּפָה" וגו'. "כִּי כֹ
בַּשָּׁמַיִם וּבָאָרֶץ" – זוֹ מִלְחֶמֶת סִיסְרָא
שֶׁנֶּאֱמַר "מִן שָׁמַיִם נִלְחָמוּ הַכּוֹכָבִי
מִמְּסִלּוֹתָם" וגו'. "לְךָ ה' הַמַּמְלָכָה" –
מִלְחֶמֶת עֲמָלֵק, וְכֵן הוּא אוֹמֵר: "כִּי יָ
עַל כֵּס יָהּ". "וְהַמִּתְנַשֵּׂא" – זוֹ מִלְחֶמֶת גּ
וּמָגוֹג, וְכֵן הוּא אוֹמֵר: "הִנְנִי אֵלֶיךָ גּוֹג נְשִׂיא
רֹאשׁ מֶשֶׁךְ וְתֻבָל". "לְכֹל לְרֹאשׁ" – אָמַ
רַב חָנָן בַּר רָבָא אָמַר רַבִּי יוֹחָנָן: אֲפִילּ
רֵישׁ גַּרְגִּיתָא מִן שְׁמַיָּא מַנּוּ לֵיהּ.

Rabbi Sheila **said: Since a miracle was performed on my behalf with this verse** that I cited, **I will interpret it homiletically: Yours, O Lord, is the greatness; that is the act of creation, and so it says: "Who does great things past finding out"** (Job 9:10);
**And the power; that is the exodus from Egypt, as it is stated: "And Israel saw the great work** which the Lord did to the **Egyptians"** (Exodus 14:31);
**And the glory; that is the sun and the moon that stood still for Joshua, as it is stated: "And the sun stood still, and the moon stayed,** until the nation had avenged themselves of their enemies" (Joshua 10:13);
**And the triumph; that is the downfall of Rome, and so it says** describing the downfall of Edom, whom the Sages identified as the forefather of Rome: **"Their lifeblood is dashed against My garments** and I have stained all My raiment" (Isaiah 63:3);
**And the majesty; this is the war of the valleys of Arnon, as it is stated: "Wherefore it is said in the book of the Wars of the Lord: Vahev in Sufa,** and the valleys of Arnon" (Numbers 21:14);
**For all that is in the heaven and in the earth is Yours; this is the war of Sisera, as it is stated: "They fought from heaven, the stars in their courses** fought against Sisera" (Judges 5:20).
**Yours is the kingdom, O Lord; this is the war of Amalek, and so it** says: "And he said: **The hand upon the throne of the Lord:** the Lord will have war with Amalek from generation to generation" (Exodus 17:16), as then God will sit on His throne.
**And you are exalted; this is the war of Gog and Magog, and so it says: "I am against you, O Gog, the chief prince of Meshekh and Tubal"** (Ezekiel 38:3); and:
**As head above all; Rav Ḥanan bar Rava said** that **Rabbi Yoḥanan said:** All leadership and authority, **even** the most insignificant, the **one responsible for distributing water, is appointed by heaven.**

בְּמַתְנִיתָא תָּנָא מִשְּׁמֵיהּ דְּרַבִּי עֲקִיבָא
"לְךָ ה' הַגְּדֻלָּה" – זוֹ קְרִיעַת יַ
סוּף, "וְהַגְּבוּרָה" – זוֹ מַכַּת בְּכוֹרוֹת
"וְהַתִּפְאֶרֶת" – זוֹ מַתַּן תּוֹרָה, "וְהַנֵּצַח" –
זוֹ יְרוּשָׁלַיִם, "וְהַהוֹד" – זוֹ בֵּית הַמִּקְדָּשׁ.

**It was taught in a *baraita* in the name of Rabbi Akiva:**
**Yours, O Lord, is the greatness; this is the splitting of the Red Sea;**
**the power; this is the plague of the firstborn;**
**the glory; this is the giving of the Torah;**
**the triumph; this is Jerusalem;**
and **the majesty; this is the Temple.**

Perek **IX**
Daf **58** Amud **b**

תָּנוּ רַבָּנַן: הָרוֹאֶה בָּתֵּי יִשְׂרָאֵל, בְּיִשּׁוּבָ
אוֹמֵר: "בָּרוּךְ מַצִּיב גְּבוּל אַלְמָנָה"
בְּחוּרְבָּנָן אוֹמֵר: "בָּרוּךְ דַּיַּין הָאֱמֶת". בָּתֵּ
אוּמּוֹת הָעוֹלָם, בְּיִשּׁוּבָן אוֹמֵר: "בֵּית גֵּאִים
יִסַּח ה'", בְּחוּרְבָּנָן אוֹמֵר: "אֵל נְקָמוֹת ה
אֵל נְקָמוֹת הוֹפִיעַ".

**The Sages taught: One who sees the houses of Israel**[H] **inhabited** and tranquil **recites: Blessed…Who establishes the border of the widow.** One who sees them **in ruins he recites: Blessed…the true Judge.** One who sees **the houses of the nations of the world**[H] **inhabited recites: "The Lord will destroy the house of the proud,** but He will establish the border of the widow" (Proverbs 15:25). **And** if he sees them **in ruins he recites: "God of vengeance, Lord, God of vengeance, shine forth"** (Psalms 94:1).

עוּלָּא וְרַב חִסְדָּא הֲווּ קָא אָזְלִי בְּאוֹרְחָא
כִּי מְטוֹ אַפִּתְחָא דְּבֵי רַב חָנָא בַּר חֲנִילַאי
נְגַד רַב חִסְדָּא וְאִתְנַח. אֲמַר לֵיהּ עוּלָּא
אַמַּאי קָא מִתְנַחֵת? וְהָאָמַר רַב: אֲנָחָה
שׁוֹבֶרֶת חֲצִי גּוּפוֹ שֶׁל אָדָם, שֶׁנֶּאֱמַר
"וְאַתָּה בֶן אָדָם הֵאָנַח בְּשִׁבְרוֹן מָתְנַיִם
וגו'", וְרַבִּי יוֹחָנָן אָמַר: אַף כָּל גּוּפוֹ שֶׁל אָדָם
שֶׁנֶּאֱמַר: "וְהָיָה כִּי יֹאמְרוּ אֵלֶיךָ עַל מָה
אַתָּה נֶאֱנָח וְאָמַרְתָּ אֶל שְׁמוּעָה כִּי בָאָה
וְנָמֵס כָּל לֵב" וגו'!

The Gemara relates that **Ulla**[P] **and Rav Ḥisda were once walking along the road when they came upon the doorway of the house of Rav Ḥana bar Ḥanilai. Rav Ḥisda groaned and sighed. Ulla asked him: Why are you sighing? Didn't Rav say: Sighing breaks half of one's body? As it is stated: "Sigh, therefore, you son of man; with the breaking of your loins"** (Ezekiel 21:11); sighing breaks a person down to his loins. **And Rabbi Yoḥanan said** that sighing breaks **even** one's **entire body, as it is stated: "And it shall be, when they say unto you: Why are you sighing? That you shall say: Because of the tidings, for it comes; and every heart shall melt,** and all hands shall be slack, and every spirit shall be faint, and all knees shall drip with water" (Ezekiel 21:12).

**HALAKHA**

**One who sees the houses of Israel – הָרוֹאֶה בָּתֵּי יִשְׂרָאֵל:** One who sees the houses of Israel inhabited recites: Blessed…Who establishes the border of the widow. Upon seeing them in ruins, he recites: Blessed…the true Judge. Some say that this applies only in Eretz Yisrael (*Magen Avraham*), while others say that this applies only to synagogues (Maharshal, based on the Rif; Rambam *Sefer Ahava, Hilkhot Berakhot* 10:10; *Shulḥan Arukh, Oraḥ Ḥayyim* 224:10).

**One who sees…the houses of the nations of the world – בָּתֵּי אוּמּוֹת הָעוֹלָם:** One who sees the houses of gentiles inhabited recites: The Lord will destroy the house of the proud. Upon seeing them in ruins, he recites: God of vengeance, Lord, God of vengeance, shine forth. Rashi explains that this refers to their private homes, inhabited in serenity, tranquility and prosperity. The Rif maintains that this refers to their houses of worship (*Taz* and *Be'er Hetev*, based on the Rif; Rambam *Sefer Ahava, Hilkhot Berakhot* 10:19; *Shulḥan Arukh, Oraḥ Ḥayyim* 224:11).

**PERSONALITIES**

**Ulla – עוּלָּא:** Ulla bar Yishmael was an *amora* and one of the most important emissaries from Eretz Yisrael to Babylonia.

Ulla was one of Rabbi Yoḥanan's students who regularly brought the Torah of Eretz Yisrael to Babylonia. He would return to Eretz Yisrael and transmit the innovations of the Babylonian Sages.

Ulla journeyed often and would travel from place to place to teach Torah, which is why Yalta called him an itinerant peddler. The Babylonian Sages held him in high regard and the second generation Babylonian *amora'im* treated him with great respect. Rav Ḥisda referred to him as: Our Rabbi who comes from Eretz Yisrael, and Rav Yehuda sent his son to Ulla to learn practical *halakha*. In the Jerusalem Talmud, he is normally referred to as Ulla bar Yishmael or Ulla the descender. Many *halakhot* are cited in his name, and many of the Sages of the succeeding generation were his students.

We know nothing of his private life. The *amora*, Rabba bar Ulla, may have been his son. We know that he died during one of his journeys to Babylonia and was brought back to Eretz Yisrael for burial.

אֲמַר לֵיהּ: הֵיכִי לָא אֶתְנַח? בֵּיתָא דַּהֲווֹ בָּהּ שִׁיתִּין אַפְיָיתָא בִּימָמָא וְשִׁיתִּין אַפְיָיתָא בְּלֵילְיָא, וְאָפְיָין לְכָל מַאן דִּצְרִיךְ. וְלָא שְׁקַל יְדָא מִן כִּיסָא, דִּסְבַר: דִּילְמָא אָתֵי עָנִי בַּר טוֹבִים, וְאַדְּמָטוּ לֵיהּ לְכִיסָא קָא מִכְסִיף. וְתוּ, הָווּ פְּתִיחִין לֵיהּ אַרְבַּע בָּבֵי לְאַרְבַּע רוּחָתָא דְּעָלְמָא, וְכָל דַּהֲוָה עָיֵיל כְּפֵין נָפֵיק כִּי שָׂבַע. וְהָווּ שָׁדוּ לֵיהּ חִטֵּי וְשַׂעֲרֵי בִּשְׁנֵי בַּצּוֹרֶת אַבְּרַאי, דְּכָל מַאן דִּכְסִיפָא מִילְּתָא לְמִשְׁקַל בִּימָמָא אָתֵי וְשָׁקֵיל בְּלֵילְיָא. הָשְׁתָּא נְפַל בְּתִלָּא, וְלָא אֶתְנַח?!

Rav Ḥisda **said to** Ulla: **How can I not sigh?** We see **this house wher**[e] **there were sixty cooks during the day and sixty cooks at night wh**[o] **would cook for anyone in need, and** Rav Ḥana **never removed his han**[d] **from his pocket** because he **thought: Perhaps a well-born poor perso**[n] might **come and** in the time that passed **until he put his hand in hi**[s] **pocket** to give him charity, the poor person **would be embarrasse**[d]. **Moreover,** that house had **four doors open in all four directions, an**[d] **anyone who entered hungry left satiated. And they would scatter whea**[t] **and barley outside during years of drought** so that **anyone who wa**[s] **embarrassed to take** the grain **during the day could come and take** it **a**[t] **night. Now** that the house **has fallen in ruins,** how can **I not sigh?**

אֲמַר לֵיהּ, הָכִי אָמַר רַבִּי יוֹחָנָן: מִיּוֹם שֶׁחָרַב בֵּית הַמִּקְדָּשׁ נִגְזְרָה גְּזֵירָה עַל בָּתֵּיהֶן שֶׁל צַדִּיקִים שֶׁיֶּחֱרְבוּ, שֶׁנֶּאֱמַר: ״בְּאָזְנָי ה׳ צְבָאוֹת אִם לֹא בָּתִּים רַבִּים לְשַׁמָּה יִהְיוּ גְּדֹלִים וְטוֹבִים מֵאֵין יוֹשֵׁב״. וְאָמַר רַבִּי יוֹחָנָן: עָתִיד הַקָּדוֹשׁ בָּרוּךְ הוּא לְהַחֲזִירָן לְיִשּׁוּבָן, שֶׁנֶּאֱמַר: ״שִׁיר הַמַּעֲלוֹת לְדָוִד הַבֹּטְחִים בַּה׳ כְּהַר צִיּוֹן״, מָה הַר צִיּוֹן עָתִיד הַקָּדוֹשׁ בָּרוּךְ הוּא לְהַחֲזִירוֹ לְיִשּׁוּבוֹ, אַף בָּתֵּיהֶן שֶׁל צַדִּיקִים עָתִיד הַקָּדוֹשׁ בָּרוּךְ הוּא לְהַחֲזִירָן לְיִשּׁוּבָן. חַזְיֵיהּ דְּלָא מְיַישַּׁב דַּעְתֵּיהּ, אֲמַר לֵיהּ: דַּיּוֹ לָעֶבֶד שֶׁיְּהֵא כְּרַבּוֹ.

Ulla **said to** Rav Ḥisda: You have nothing about which to sigh, as **Rabb**[i] **Yoḥanan said as follows: From the day that the Temple was destroye**[d] **a decree was issued upon the houses of the righteous that they woul**[d] **be destroyed, as it is stated: "In mine ears said the Lord of hosts: Of truth many houses shall be desolate, even great and fair, without i**[n]**habitant"** (Isaiah 5:9). **And Rabbi Yoḥanan said:** In the **future,** in th[e] end of days, **the Holy One, Blessed be He, will restore them to thei**[r] original locations and their **inhabited state, as it is stated: "A Song o**[f] **Ascents of David.**[N] **They who trust in the Lord are as Mount Zio**[n]" which cannot be moved but abides forever" (Psalms 125:1). From thi[s] verse one may infer that **just as in the future the Holy One, Blessed b**[e] **He, will restore Mount Zion to its inhabited state, so too, in the futur**[e] **the Holy One, Blessed be He, will restore the houses of the righteou**[s] **to their inhabited state,** so you have no reason to sigh. **Seeing that h**[e] **was still not satisfied,** Ulla **said to him: It is enough for a servant to b**[e] **like his master.** Since God leaves His home, the Holy Temple, in ruin[s] one should not be distraught over the destruction of the houses of th[e] righteous.

תָּנוּ רַבָּנַן: הָרוֹאֶה קִבְרֵי יִשְׂרָאֵל אוֹמֵר: ״בָּרוּךְ אֲשֶׁר יָצַר אֶתְכֶם בַּדִּין, וְזָן אֶתְכֶם בַּדִּין, וְכִלְכֵּל אֶתְכֶם בַּדִּין, וְאָסַף אֶתְכֶם בַּדִּין, וְעָתִיד לַהֲקִימְכֶם בַּדִּין״. מָר בְּרֵיהּ דְּרָבִינָא מְסַיֵּים בָּהּ מִשְּׁמֵיהּ דְּרַב נַחְמָן: ״וְיוֹדֵעַ מִסְפַּר כּוּלְּכֶם, וְהוּא עָתִיד לְהַחֲיוֹתְכֶם וּלְקַיֵּים אֶתְכֶם, בָּרוּךְ מְחַיֵּה הַמֵּתִים״. קִבְרֵי גּוֹיִם אוֹמֵר: ״בּוֹשָׁה אִמְּכֶם״ וגו׳.

**The Sages taught** in a *baraita*: **One who sees graves of Israel recites:**
**Blessed…Who formed you in judgment,**
**and Who nourished you in judgment,**
**and Who sustained you in judgment,**
**and collected** your soul **in judgment,**
**and in the future will raise you** from the dead **in judgment.**
And **Mar, son of Ravina, concludes** the formula of this blessing **in th**[e] **name of Rav Naḥman:**
**And Who knows the number of you all,**
**and Who in the future will restore you to life and sustain you.**
**Blessed…Who revives the dead.**
One who sees **graves of gentiles**[H] **recites: "Your mother shall be sor**[e] **ashamed,** she who bore you shall be confounded; behold, the hin[d]ermost of the nations shall be a wilderness, a dry land, and a deser[t]" (Jeremiah 50:12).

אָמַר רַבִּי יְהוֹשֻׁעַ בֶּן לֵוִי: הָרוֹאֶה אֶת חֲבֵירוֹ לְאַחַר שְׁלֹשִׁים יוֹם אוֹמֵר: ״בָּרוּךְ שֶׁהֶחֱיָינוּ וְקִיְּימָנוּ וְהִגִּיעָנוּ לַזְּמַן הַזֶּה״, לְאַחַר שְׁנֵים עָשָׂר חֹדֶשׁ אוֹמֵר: ״בָּרוּךְ מְחַיֵּה הַמֵּתִים״. אָמַר רַב: אֵין הַמֵּת מִשְׁתַּכֵּחַ מִן הַלֵּב אֶלָּא לְאַחַר שְׁנֵים עָשָׂר חֹדֶשׁ, שֶׁנֶּאֱמַר: ״נִשְׁכַּחְתִּי כְּמֵת מִלֵּב הָיִיתִי כִּכְלִי אוֹבֵד״.

**Rabbi Yehoshua ben Levi said: One who sees his friend after thirt**[y] **days**[N] have passed since last seeing him **recites: Blessed…Who ha**[s] **given us life, sustained us and brought us to this time.** One who see[s] his friend **after twelve months**[HN] **recites: Blessed…Who revives th**[e] **dead.** As **Rav said: A dead person is only forgotten from the heart afte**[r] **twelve months** have elapsed, **as it is stated: "I am forgotten as a dea**[d] **man out of mind; I am like a lost vessel"** (Psalms 31:13), and with regar[d] to the laws of lost objects, it is human nature to despair of recovering [a] lost object after twelve months (see *Bava Metzia* 28a).

**NOTES**

A Song of Ascents of David – שִׁיר הַמַּעֲלוֹת לְדָוִד: In most editions, the Talmud quotes this verse as: "A Song of Ascents of David," even though in the standard text of the Bible the words "of David" do not appear. It is not uncommon to find minor discrepancies when the Sages of the Talmud quote biblical verses. This phenomenon has been attributed by some to the nature of the Talmud, which was transmitted orally for several generations before it was committed to writing. In *Ein Ya'akov*, the introductory phrase is omitted from Rabbi Yoḥanan's statement, which begins: They who trust in the Lord.

One who sees his friend after thirty days – הָרוֹאֶה אֶת חֲבֵירוֹ לְאַחַר שְׁלֹשִׁים יוֹם: *Tosafot* and the Rosh both write that this applies only to one who is especially close to the person he meets and he is not merely an acquaintance. In a responsum, the Rashba notes that there is no difference between men and women; in either case, this *halakha* applies (*Etz Yosef*).

One who sees his friend after twelve months – לְאַחַר שְׁנֵים עָשָׂר חֹדֶשׁ: One explanation for the obligation to recite this blessing is the fact that on every Rosh HaShana and Yom Kippur all mankind is judged. If a full year has passed since the last time these two individuals met, obviously, each has been tried and lived. An appropriate reaction to meeting someone who has survived that ordeal is to recite: Blessed…Who revives the dead (Maharsha).

**HALAKHA**

One who sees graves of Israel…graves of gentiles – הָרוֹאֶה קִבְרֵי יִשְׂרָאֵל...קִבְרֵי נָכְרִים: One who sees graves of Israel recites: Blessed…Who formed you in judgment, etc. This is recited only upon seeing several graves, but over a single grave one does not recite a blessing (*Mishna Berura*). One who sees a grave of gentiles recites: Your mother shall be sore ashamed (Rambam *Sefer Ahava, Hilkhot Berakhot* 10:10; *Shulḥan Arukh, Oraḥ Ḥayyim* 224:12).

One who sees his friend after thirty days…after twelve months – הָרוֹאֶה אֶת חֲבֵירוֹ לְאַחַר שְׁלֹשִׁים יוֹם...לְאַחַר שְׁנֵים עָשָׂר חֹדֶשׁ: One who is happy upo[n] meeting a friend after having not seen him for thirty days recites: Blessed… Who has given us life, etc. If he sees him after twelve months, he recite[s] Blessed…Who revives the dead (Rambam *Sefer Ahava, Hilkhot Berakho*[t] 10:2; *Shulḥan Arukh, Oraḥ Ḥayyim* 225:1).

רַב פַּפָּא וְרַב הוּנָא בְּרֵיהּ דְּרַב יְהוֹשֻׁעַ הֲווֹ קָאָזְלִי בְּאוֹרְחָא, פְּגַעוּ בֵּיהּ בְּרַב חֲנִינָא בְּרֵיהּ דְּרַב אִיקָא, אֲמַרוּ לֵיהּ: בַּהֲדֵי דַּחֲזֵינָךְ בְּרֵיכִינַן עֲלָךְ תַּרְתֵּי: ״בָּרוּךְ אֲשֶׁר חָלַק מֵחָכְמָתוֹ לִירֵאָיו״ וְ״שֶׁהֶחֱיָינוּ״. אֲמַר לְהוּ: אֲנָא נַמִי, כֵּיוָן דַּחֲזֵיתִינְכוּ חֲשַׁבְתִּינְכוּ עִלָּוַאי כְּשִׁיתִּין רִבְוָון בֵּית יִשְׂרָאֵל, וּבְרֵכִינָא עֲלַיְיכוּ תְּלָתָא, הָנָךְ תַּרְתֵּי וּ״בָרוּךְ חֲכַם הָרָזִים״. אֲמַרוּ לֵיהּ: חֲכִימַת כּוּלֵּי הַאי?! יַהֲבוּ בֵּיהּ עֵינַיְיהוּ וְשָׁכֵיב.

The Gemara relates: **Rav Pappa and Rav Huna, son of Rav Yehoshua, were once walking along the road when they met Rav Ḥanina the son of Rav Ika. They said to him: When we saw you we recited two blessings over** meeting **you: Blessed…Who has given of His wisdom to those who revere Him, and: Who has given us life…** as they had not seen him in over a month. **He said to them: I too, once I saw you, considered you in my eyes as** equivalent to **six hundred thousand** of the **house of Israel, and I recited three blessings over you. I recited those two** that you recited, as well as: **Blessed…Who knows all secrets,** which is the blessing recited upon seeing six hundred thousand Israelites. **They said to him: Are you all that clever?**[N] **They fixed their gaze upon him and he died.**

אָמַר רַבִּי יְהוֹשֻׁעַ בֶּן לֵוִי: הָרוֹאֶה אֶת הַבַּהֲקָנִים אוֹמֵר: ״בָּרוּךְ מְשַׁנֶּה הַבְּרִיּוֹת״. מֵיתִיבֵי: רָאָה אֶת הַכּוּשִׁי וְאֶת הַגִּיחוֹר וְאֶת הַלַּוְוקָן וְאֶת הַקִּפֵּחַ וְאֶת הַנַּנָּס וְאֶת הַדַּרְנִיקוֹס אוֹמֵר: ״בָּרוּךְ מְשַׁנֶּה אֶת הַבְּרִיּוֹת״. אֶת הַקִּטֵּעַ וְאֶת הַסּוּמָא וְאֶת פְּתוּיֵי הָרֹאשׁ וְאֶת הַחִגֵּר וְאֶת הַמּוּכֶּה שְׁחִין וְאֶת הַבַּהֲקָנִים אוֹמֵר: ״בָּרוּךְ דַּיַּין אֱמֶת!״

The Gemara continues to discuss the obligation to recite a blessing over unusual phenomena. **Rabbi Yehoshua ben Levi said: One who sees spotted people recites: Blessed…Who makes creatures different.**[NH] The Gemara **raises a challenge: One who saw a person with** unusually **black skin, a person with** unusually **red skin, a person with** unusually **white skin** [*lavkan*],[L] **an** unusually **tall and thin person, a dwarf, or one with warts** [*darnikos*] **recites: Blessed…Who makes creatures different.** However, one who sees **an amputee, a blind person, a flat-headed person, a lame person, one afflicted with boils, or spotted people recites: Blessed…the true Judge,** not: Who makes creatures different.

לָא קַשְׁיָא, הָא – מִמְּעֵי אִמּוֹ, הָא – בָּתַר דְּאִיתְיְלִיד. דַּיְקָא נַמִי, דְּקָתָנֵי דּוּמְיָא דְּקִטֵּעַ, שְׁמַע מִינַּהּ.

The Gemara answers: This is **not difficult. This,** where Rabbi Yehoshua ben Levi says to recite: Who makes creatures different, refers to a case where the individual was spotted **from** when he was **in his mother's womb,** since birth. While **this,** where one recites: The true Judge, refers to a case where the individual only became spotted **after he was born.** The Gemara remarks: The language of the *baraita* **is also precise** as it draws a parallel to other cases, as **it taught** that a spotted person is **similar to an amputee,** which, in general, is a handicap incurred after birth. The Gemara concludes: Indeed, **conclude from this.**

תָּנוּ רַבָּנַן: הָרוֹאֶה פִּיל קוֹף וְקַפּוֹף אוֹמֵר: ״בָּרוּךְ מְשַׁנֶּה אֶת הַבְּרִיּוֹת״. רָאָה בְּרִיּוֹת טוֹבוֹת וְאִילָנוֹת טוֹבוֹת אוֹמֵר: ״בָּרוּךְ שֶׁכָּכָה לוֹ בְּעוֹלָמוֹ״.

**The Sages taught: One who sees an elephant, a monkey, or a vulture** (Rashi) **recites: Blessed…Who makes creatures different. One who saw beautiful** or otherwise outstanding **creatures** or **beautiful trees**[H] **recites: Blessed…Who has such things in His world.**

״עַל הַזִּיקִין״ – מַאי זִיקִין? אָמַר שְׁמוּאֵל: כּוֹכְבָא דְּשָׁבִיט. וְאָמַר שְׁמוּאֵל: נְהִירִין לִי שְׁבִילֵי דִשְׁמַיָּא כִּשְׁבִילֵי דִּנְהַרְדְּעָא, לְבַר מִכּוֹכְבָא דְּשָׁבִיט דְּלָא יָדַעְנָא מַאי נִיהוּ. וּגְמִירִי דְּלָא עָבַר כְּסִלָא, וְאִי עָבַר כְּסִלָא – חָרֵב עָלְמָא. וְהָא קָא חָזֵינַן דַּעֲבַר! – זִיוֵיהּ הוּא דַּעֲבַר, וּמִתְחֲזֵי כִּדְעָבַר אִיהוּ. רַב הוּנָא בְּרֵיהּ דְּרַב יְהוֹשֻׁעַ אָמַר: וִילוֹן הוּא דְּמִקְרַע, דְּמִגַּלְגַּל וּמַחֲזֵי נְהוֹרָא דִּרְקִיעַ. רַב אָשֵׁי אָמַר: כּוֹכְבָא הוּא דְּעָקַר מֵהַאי גִּיסָא דִּכְסִלָא, וְחָזֵי לֵיהּ חַבְרֵיהּ מֵהָךְ גִּיסָא וּמִבְעִית, וּמֶחֱזֵי כְּמַאן דַּעֲבַר.

We learned in the mishna that **over *zikin*,** one recites: Whose strength and power fill the world. The Gemara asks: **What are *zikin*? Shmuel said: A comet.**[H] **Shmuel also said: The paths of the sky are as clear to me as the paths** of my city, **Neharde'a, except for comets, that I do not know what they are. And we learn** through tradition **that a comet does not pass the Orion** constellation, **and if it does pass Orion, the world will be destroyed.** The Gemara asks: **Don't we see that** comets **pass** Orion? The Gemara rejects this: **The aura** of the comet **passes** Orion **and it appears as though** the comet itself **passes. Rav Huna, son of Rav Yehoshua, said** a different answer: It is merely that ***vilon***, one of the firmaments, **rips and furls and the light of** the next **firmament is seen,** and this appears like a comet. **Rav Ashi said** another explanation: It is not a comet that passes Orion, but a **star that is uprooted from one side of Orion, and another** star, **from the other side** of Orion, **sees it and gets startled** and shudders, **and appears as if it is passing.**

**NOTES**

Are you all that clever – חֲכִימַת כּוּלֵּי הַאי: The blessing, Blessed…Who knows all secrets, is intended to bless the greatness of God, Who knows what is in the minds of all, even the most outstanding Sages. Discerning who is the Sage worthy of having that blessing recited also requires outstanding wisdom (Ramban; *Tziyyun LeNefesh Ḥayya*).

Blessed…Who makes creatures different – בָּרוּךְ מְשַׁנֶּה הַבְּרִיּוֹת: This blessing is recited upon seeing an elephant or a monkey; although they have a certain resemblance to man, they are nevertheless very different (*Me'iri*).

**LANGUAGE**

One with unusually white skin [*lavkan*] – לַוְוקָן: From the Greek λευκόν, *leukon*, meaning pallid.

**HALAKHA**

Different creatures – בְּרִיּוֹת מְשׁוּנּוֹת: One who sees people or animals whose form and appearance were strange from birth recites: Blessed…Who makes creatures different. If the unusual appearance was caused by injury and was not from birth, such as if one's hand was amputated, he recites: Blessed…the true Judge. Some say that one should not recite this blessing unless it is a person for whom he feels pity, but for a gentile afflicted in this way he does not recite the blessing. One recites this blessing only once. Some say that one recites another blessing if thirty days have elapsed between sightings. Others determined that after thirty days one should recite the blessing without invoking God's name and His Sovereignty (*Mishna Berura*; Rambam *Sefer Ahava, Hilkhot Berakhot* 10:12; *Shulḥan Arukh, Oraḥ Ḥayyim* 225:8–9).

One who saw beautiful creatures or beautiful trees – רָאָה בְּרִיּוֹת טוֹבוֹת וְאִילָנוֹת טוֹבוֹת: One who sees exceptionally beautiful people, animals, or trees recites: Blessed…Who has such things in His world. One does not recite this blessing a second time unless he sees something even more beautiful (Rambam *Sefer Ahava, Hilkhot Berakhot* 10:13; *Shulḥan Arukh, Oraḥ Ḥayyim* 225:10).

A comet – כּוֹכְבָא דְּשָׁבִיט: One who sees a comet recites: Blessed…Who has such things in His world. One does not recite this blessing a second time the same night even if he sees another comet (Rambam *Sefer Ahava, Hilkhot Berakhot* 10:14; *Shulḥan Arukh, Oraḥ Ḥayyim* 227:1).

**BACKGROUND**

**The constellation Scorpio – עַקְרַבָּא:** The stars of Scorpio are all adjacent to the Milky Way, but the tail of Scorpio, referred to by the Sages as the River of Fire, is located within the perimeter of the Milky Way.

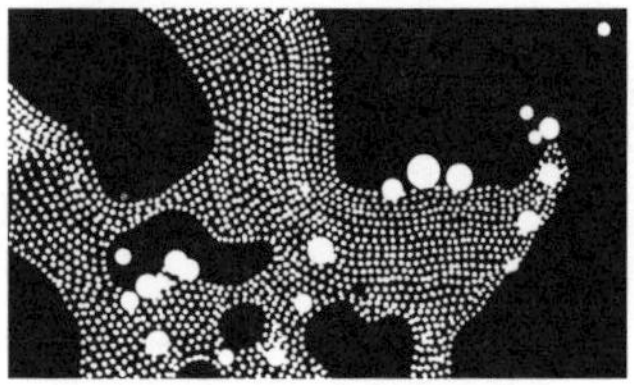

Schematic drawing of Scorpio and the Milky Way

**Pleiades – כִּימָה:** *Kima* is traditionally associated with Pleiades. The naked eye generally discerns only six stars in this system; with a telescope, however, a much greater number are visible. It is not known how Shmuel knew about the large number of stars in Pleiades, as even the sharpest eye is capable of discerning no more than seven.

The constellation Pleiades, based on a telescopic photograph

שְׁמוּאֵל רָמֵי: כְּתִיב ״עֹשֶׂה עָשׁ כְּסִיל וְכִימָה״, וּכְתִיב ״עֹשֵׂה כִימָה וּכְסִיל״. הָא כֵּיצַד: אִלְמָלֵא חַמָּה שֶׁל כְּסִיל – לֹא נִתְקַיֵּים עוֹלָם מִפְּנֵי צִינָּה שֶׁל כִּימָה, וְאִלְמָלֵא צִינָּה שֶׁל כִּימָה – לֹא נִתְקַיֵּים עוֹלָם מִפְּנֵי חַמָּה שֶׁל כְּסִיל.

On the subject of stars, the Gemara notes that **Shmuel raised a contradiction** between the implications of two verses with regard to constellations. On the one hand **it is written: "Who makes Ursa Major, Orion, and Pleiades,** and the chambers of the south" (Job 9:9); Orion precedes Pleiades. **And** on the other hand **it is written: "He Who makes Pleiades and Orion"** (Amos 5:8); Pleiades precedes Orion. **So how is** this reconciled? The Gemara replies: **Were it not for Orion's heat, the universe could not exist because of the cold of Pleiades;** and conversely, **were it not for the cold of Pleiades, the universe could not exist because of the heat of Orion.**

וּגְמִירִי, אִי לָאו עוּקְצָא דְעַקְרַבָּא דְּמַנַּח בִּנְהַר דִּינוּר – כָּל מַאן דַּהֲוָה טָרֵיק לֵיהּ עַקְרַבָּא לָא הֲוָה חַיֵּי. וְהַיְינוּ דְּקָאָמַר לֵיהּ רַחֲמָנָא לְאִיּוֹב: ״הַתְקַשֵּׁר מַעֲדַנּוֹת כִּימָה אוֹ מֹשְׁכוֹת כְּסִיל תְּפַתֵּחַ״.

**And we learned** a tradition that **if the tail of** the constellation **Scorpio**[B] did **not** rest **in the River of Fire, anyone stung by a scorpion would not survive. And that is what the All-Merciful said to Job** of the relationship between heat and cold among the stars: **"Can you bind the chains of the Pleiades or loosen the bands of Orion?"** (Job 38:31); God alternates intensifying the power of different constellations in order to raise or lower the temperature.

מַאי כִּימָה? אָמַר שְׁמוּאֵל: כְּמֵאָה כֹּכְבֵי. אָמְרִי לָהּ דְּמִכַּנְּפֵי, וְאָמְרִי לָהּ דְּמִבַּדְּרָן.

With regard to Pleiades, the Gemara asks: **What is Pleiades [*Kima*]?**[B] Why is it called by that name? **Shmuel said:** Because it is **approximately a hundred [*keme'a*] stars,** as that is the number of stars in that constellation; **some say that** they are **concentrated and some say that** they are **dispersed.**

מַאי עָשׁ? אָמַר רַב יְהוּדָה: יוּתָא. מַאי יוּתָא? אָמְרִי לַהּ: זְנַב טָלֶה, וְאָמְרִי לַהּ: רֵישָׁא דְעֶגְלָא. וּמִסְתַּבְּרָא כְּמַאן דְּאָמַר זְנַב טָלֶה, דִּכְתִיב: ״וְעַיִשׁ עַל בָּנֶיהָ תַנְחֵם״. אַלְמָא חַסְרָה, וּמִתְחֲזְיָא

With regard to the verse: "Who makes Ursa Major, Orion, and Pleiades" (Job 9:9), the Gemara asks: **What is Ursa Major [*Ash*]? Rav Yehuda said:** It is the star called ***Yota.*** This name was unfamiliar as well, so the Gemara asks: **What is *Yota*?** There is disagreement; **some say** that *Yota* is the group of stars comprising the **tail of Aries, while others say** that *Yota* belongs to **the head of Taurus.** The Gemara concludes: **And it stands to reason in accordance with the** opinion of the **one who said** that *Yota* is the group of stars comprising the **tail of Aries, as it is written: "Or can you guide Ursa** Major **with her sons?"** (Job 38:32); **apparently it was incomplete and** the tail **appears**

Perek **IX**
Daf **59** Amud **a**

**BACKGROUND**

**Ursa Major and Pleiades – עַיִשׁ וְכִימָה:** There are many problems with regard to the identities of the various stars and the explanations of their details. Apparently, Ursa Major [*Yota*] is the largest star in Taurus, called *el Davran*, meaning the late one or the one that lags behind, as it appears to follow the Pleiades star system. This star is called the eye of the ox, because it is a part of the head of the calf or ox. However, it can also be viewed as a tail, following far behind Aries that precedes it. The movement is from left to right, so that Ursa Major (*Yota*) follows Aries and the stars of Pleiades.

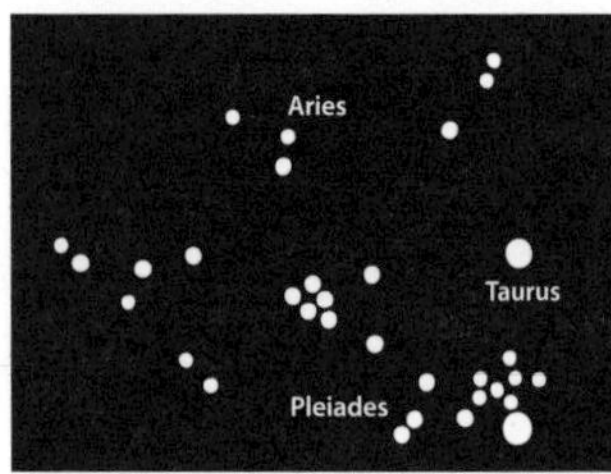


Aries, Taurus, and Pleiades

כְּטַרְפָּא דְּטָרֵיף. וְהַאי דְּאָזְלָא בָּתְרַהּ – דְּאָמְרָה לַהּ: הַב לִי בְּנַי! שֶׁבְּשָׁעָה שֶׁהַקָּדוֹשׁ בָּרוּךְ הוּא בִּקֵּשׁ לְהָבִיא מַבּוּל לָעוֹלָם, נָטַל שְׁנֵי כּוֹכָבִים מִכִּימָה וְהֵבִיא מַבּוּל לָעוֹלָם, וּכְשֶׁבִּקֵּשׁ לְסָתְמָהּ – נָטַל שְׁנֵי כּוֹכָבִים מֵעַיִשׁ וּסְתָמָהּ.

**as if it was appended** onto it. The Gemara explains: **And the fact that** Ursa Major **follows** Pleiades,[B] it is as if Ursa Major **is saying** to Pleiades: **Give me** back **my children,** my two stars. As it is related: **When the Holy One, Blessed be He, sought to bring a flood into the world, He took two stars from Pleiades and brought the flood upon the world. And** afterward, **when He wished to fill** the void, **He took two stars from Ursa Major and filled** the void with them. Consequently, the constellation of Ursa Major attempts to persuade Pleiades, seeking to get its stars back.

וְלִיהַדַר לַהּ? – אֵין הַבּוֹר מִתְמַלֵּא מֵחוּלְיָתוֹ, אִי נַמִּי: אֵין קָטֵיגוֹר נַעֲשֶׂה סָנֵיגוֹר.

The Gemara asks: **And return it,** why did the Holy One, Blessed be He not restore the original two stars to Pleiades? The Gemara answers: **A pit cannot be filled by its own earth;** when a pit is excavated, the earth that was excavated from it is insufficient to refill it. **Alternatively,** one could say that **a prosecutor cannot become an advocate;** since these stars caused the flood it is not appropriate that they facilitate the end of the flood.

וְלִיבְרֵי לַהּ תְּרֵי כֹּכְבֵי אַחֲרִינֵי! – ״אֵין כָּל חָדָשׁ תַּחַת הַשָּׁמֶשׁ״. אָמַר רַב נַחְמָן: עָתִיד הַקָּדוֹשׁ בָּרוּךְ הוּא לְהַחֲזִירָן לַהּ, שֶׁנֶּאֱמַר: ״וְעַיִשׁ עַל בָּנֶיהָ תַנְחֵם״.

The Gemara argues: **Then** God should have **created two other** new **stars** for Pleiades. The Gemara responds: **"There is nothing new under the sun"** (Ecclesiastes 1:9). **Rav Naḥman said:** In the **future, the Holy One, Blessed be He, will restore** those same stars **to** Ursa Major, **as it is stated: "Or can you guide [*tanḥem*] Ursa** Major **with her sons?"** (Job 38:32), which is interpreted homiletically in the sense of consolation [*tanḥumim*] apparently due to the restoration of those stars.

״וְעַל הַזְּוָעוֹת״. מַאי זְוָעוֹת? אֲמַר רַב קְטִינָא: גּוֹהָא. רַב קְטִינָא הֲוָה קָאָזֵיל בְּאוֹרְחָא, כִּי מְטָא אַפִּתְחָא דְּבֵי אוֹבָא טַמְיָא גְּנַח גּוֹהָא. אֲמַר: מִי יָדַע אוֹבָא טַמְיָא הַאי גּוֹהָא מַהוּ? רְמָא לֵיהּ קָלָא: קְטִינָא קְטִינָא, אַמַּאי לָא יָדַעְנָא? בְּשָׁעָה שֶׁהַקָּדוֹשׁ בָּרוּךְ הוּא זוֹכֵר אֶת בָּנָיו שֶׁשְּׁרוּיִים בְּצַעַר בֵּין אוּמּוֹת הָעוֹלָם מוֹרִיד שְׁתֵּי דְמָעוֹת לַיָּם הַגָּדוֹל, וְקוֹלוֹ נִשְׁמָע מִסּוֹף הָעוֹלָם וְעַד סוֹפוֹ, וְהַיְינוּ גּוֹהָא.

**And** we learned in the mishna that **over *zeva'ot*** one recites the blessing: Whose strength and power fill the world. The Gemara asks: **What are *zeva'ot*? Rav Ketina said: An earthquake.**[N] The Gemara relates: **Rav Ketina was once walking along the road when he came to the entrance of the house of a necromancer and an earthquake rumbled. He said: Does this necromancer know what is this earthquake?** The necromancer **raised his voice** and said: **Ketina, Ketina, why would I not know?** Certainly this earthquake occurred because **when the Holy One, Blessed be He, remembers His children who are suffering among the nations of the world, He sheds two tears into the great sea.**[N] **The sound** of their reverberation **is heard from one end of the earth to the other. And that is an earthquake.**

אֲמַר רַב קְטִינָא: אוֹבָא טַמְיָא כַּדִּיב הוּא, וּמִילֵּיהּ כַּדִּיבִין. אִי הָכִי – גּוֹהָא גּוֹהָא מִיבָּעֵי לֵיהּ! וְלָא הִיא, גּוֹהָא גּוֹהָא עָבֵיד, וְהַאי דְּלָא אוֹדֵי לֵיהּ – כִּי הֵיכִי דְּלָא לִיטְעֵי כּוּלֵּי עָלְמָא אֲבַתְרֵיהּ.

**Rav Ketina said: The necromancer is a liar and his statements are lies. If so, it would necessitate an earthquake** followed by another **earthquake,** one for each tear. The Gemara remarks: **That is not so,** as it indeed **causes an earthquake** followed by another **earthquake; and the fact** that Rav Ketina **did not admit that** the necromancer was correct was **so that everyone would not mistakenly follow him.**

וְרַב קְטִינָא דִּידֵיהּ אֲמַר: סוֹפֵק כַּפָּיו, שֶׁנֶּאֱמַר: ״וְגַם אֲנִי אַכֶּה כַפִּי אֶל כַּפִּי וַהֲנִיחֹתִי חֲמָתִי״. רַבִּי נָתָן אוֹמֵר: אֲנָחָה מִתְאַנֵּחַ, שֶׁנֶּאֱמַר: ״וַהֲנִיחֹתִי חֲמָתִי בָּם וְהִנֶּחָמְתִּי״. וְרַבָּנַן אָמְרִי: בּוֹעֵט בָּרָקִיעַ, שֶׁנֶּאֱמַר: ״הֵידָד כְּדֹרְכִים יַעֲנֶה אֶל כָּל יֹשְׁבֵי הָאָרֶץ״. רַב אַחָא בַּר יַעֲקֹב אָמַר: דּוֹחֵק אֶת רַגְלָיו תַּחַת כִּסֵּא הַכָּבוֹד, שֶׁנֶּאֱמַר: ״כֹּה אָמַר ה׳ הַשָּׁמַיִם כִּסְאִי וְהָאָרֶץ הֲדֹם רַגְלָי״.

**Rav Ketina also stated his own** explanation for the earthquake: Because God **claps His hands** together in anger, **as it is stated: "I will also smite My hands together and I will satisfy My fury;** I, the Lord, have spoken it" (Ezekiel 21:22). **Rabbi Natan says:** The earthquake is caused because God **sighs** over the dire straits in which Israel finds itself, **as it is stated:** "Thus shall My anger spend itself, **and I will satisfy My fury upon them, and I will be eased"** (Ezekiel 5:13). **And the Rabbis say:** An earthquake is caused when God **kicks the firmament,** causing a rumbling, **as it is stated:** "The Lord roars from on high, from His holy dwelling He makes His voice heard. He roars mightily over His dwelling place, **He cries out like those who tread grapes, against all the inhabitants of the earth"** (Jeremiah 25:30). **Rav Aḥa bar Ya'akov said:** An earthquake is caused when God **forces His feet beneath the throne of glory** and the world quakes, **as it is stated: "The heaven is My throne, and the earth is My footstool"** (Isaiah 66:1).

״וְעַל הָרְעָמִים״. מַאי רְעָמִים? אֲמַר שְׁמוּאֵל: עֲנָנֵי בְּגַלְגְּלָא, שֶׁנֶּאֱמַר: ״קוֹל רַעַמְךָ בַּגַּלְגַּל הֵאִירוּ בְרָקִים תֵּבֵל רָגְזָה וַתִּרְעַשׁ הָאָרֶץ״. וְרַבָּנַן אָמְרִי: עֲנָנֵי דְּשָׁפְכִי מַיָּא לַהֲדָדֵי, שֶׁנֶּאֱמַר: ״לְקוֹל תִּתּוֹ הֲמוֹן מַיִם בַּשָּׁמַיִם״. רַב אַחָא בַּר יַעֲקֹב אֲמַר: בַּרְקָא תַּקִּיפָא דְּבָרֵיק בַּעֲנָנָא, וּמְתַבַּר גִּזִיזֵי דְּבַרְדָּא. רַב אַשִׁי אֲמַר: עֲנָנֵי חַלְחוּלֵי מְחַלְחֲלֵי, וְאָתֵי זִיקָא וּמְנַשֵּׁב אַפּוּמַיְיהוּ, וְדָמֵי כְּזִיקָא עַל פּוּם דָּנֵי. וּמִסְתַּבְּרָא כְּרַב אַחָא בַּר יַעֲקֹב – דְּבָרֵיק בַּרְקָא וּמְנַהֲמֵי עֲנָנֵי, וְאָתֵי מִטְרָא.

We **also** learned in the mishna that **over thunder** one recites: Whose strength and power fill the world.[H] The Gemara asks: **What** causes **thunder? Shmuel said:** When the **clouds** located **in the curvature** of the firmament collide with the firmament itself, they produce this sound, **as it is stated: "The voice of Your thunder was in the whirlwind; the lightning lighted up the world; the earth trembled and shook"** (Psalms 77:19). **And the Rabbis say:** Thunder is the sound of **clouds pouring water into one another, as it is stated: "At the sound of His giving a multitude of waters in the heavens"** (Jeremiah 10:13). **Rav Aḥa bar Ya'akov said:** Thunder is caused by **a powerful lightning bolt that flashes in the cloud and shatters the hailstones. Rav Ashi said:** Because the **clouds are hollow, and when the wind comes and blows across their mouths,** it sounds like **wind blowing in the mouth of a jug.** The Gemara concludes: **And it stands to reason in accordance with** the opinion of **Rav Aḥa bar Ya'akov; as lightning flashes, the clouds rumble, and the rain comes.**

״וְעַל הָרוּחוֹת״. מַאי רוּחוֹת? אֲמַר אַבַּיֵּי: זַעֲפָא. וַאֲמַר אַבַּיֵּי: גְּמִירִי, דְּזַעֲפָא בְּלֵילְיָא לָא הָוֵי. וְהָא קָא חָזֵינַן דְּהָוֵי! – הַהוּא דְּאַתְחוּלֵי בִּימָמָא. וַאֲמַר אַבַּיֵּי: גְּמִירִי, דְּזַעֲפָא תַּרְתֵּי שָׁעֵי לָא קָאֵי, לְקַיֵּים מַה שֶּׁנֶּאֱמַר: ״לֹא תָקוּם פַּעֲמַיִם צָרָה״. – וְהָא קָא חָזֵינַן דְּקָאֵי! – דְּמַפְסִיק בֵּינֵי בֵּינֵי.

We **also** learned in the mishna **that over wind** one recites the blessing: Whose strength and power fill the world. The Gemara asks: **What are** these **winds? Abaye said:** These are **gale force winds. Abaye said: We learned** through tradition **that there are no gale force winds at night.** The Gemara asks: **Don't we see that there are** gale force winds at night? The Gemara answers: **This** gale force wind that blows at night does not begin blowing at night; rather, it **begins** blowing **during the day. And Abaye said: We learned** through tradition **that a gale force wind does not last two hours, to fulfill that which is stated: "Trouble shall not rise up a second time"** (Nahum 1:9). The Gemara asks: **Don't we see that it does last** longer than two hours? The Gemara answers: Actually, it does not last longer than two hours. The fact that we sense that it does last longer is due to cases where it does not blow uninterruptedly, but **it** briefly **stops in between.**

**NOTES**

**An earthquake – גּוֹהָא:** All early talmudic commentaries hold that these explanations of how earthquakes develop are to be understood as symbolism and esoterica. Essentially, this underscores that the relationship between God and Israel is at the basis of all phenomena in the world, and therefore natural phenomena in the world always have some connection to that relationship. An earthquake is an expression of God's pain over the destruction of the Temple. The Sages disagree only with regard to finding a verse that appropriately articulates this concept (Rav Hai Gaon, Rav Nissim Gaon, Rabbeinu Ḥananel).

**When the Holy One, Blessed be He, remembers His children who are suffering among the nations of the world, He sheds two tears into the great sea – בְּשָׁעָה שֶׁהַקָּדוֹשׁ בָּרוּךְ הוּא זוֹכֵר אֶת בָּנָיו שֶׁשְּׁרוּיִים בְּצַעַר בֵּין אוּמּוֹת הָעוֹלָם מוֹרִיד שְׁתֵּי דְמָעוֹת לַיָּם הַגָּדוֹל:** According to Rav Nissim Gaon, it is essential to underscore that, unquestionably, there is no room for comparison between God and a human being. He neither laughs, nor cries, nor sighs, nor sheds tears. Rather, the aggadic portions of the Talmud must be understood as metaphors and must not be taken literally. The explanations offered by Rav Ketina and the other Sages should be understood as statements that point to the unique connection that exists between God and the Jewish people. Due to the significance of the Jewish people in His eyes, the different natural phenomena should be viewed as signs to inform the Jewish people that God is anxious and concerned about their fate in exile (*HaKotev*).

**HALAKHA**

**God's might in nature – גְּבוּרוֹת ה׳ בַּטֶּבַע:** Over earthquakes [*zeva'ot*], thunder, strong winds and lightning one recites: Whose strength and power fill the world. If one so chooses, he may instead recite: Author of creation. The custom is to recite: Whose strength and power, over thunder, and: Author of creation, over lightning (*Mishna Berura*; Rambam *Sefer Ahava, Hilkhot Berakhot* 10:14; *Shulḥan Arukh, Oraḥ Ḥayyim* 227:1).

## NOTES

**Straighten the crookedness of the heart** – לִפְשׁוֹט עַקְמוּמִית שֶׁבַּלֵּב: Some say that one who has crookedness in his heart will fear thunder, whereas one who trusts in God has nothing to fear. Therefore, the sound of thunder helps one focus exclusively on his obligations to God (*Kashot Meyushav*).

## BACKGROUND

**Rainbow** – קֶשֶׁת: A rainbow is an optical and meteorological phenomenon that causes a spectrum of light to appear in the sky when the sun shines on droplets of moisture in the Earth's atmosphere. It takes the form of a multicolored arc.

Rainbow

## HALAKHA

**The blessing over a rainbow** – בִּרְכַּת הַקֶּשֶׁת: Each time one sees a rainbow in a cloud, even if he sees it multiple times within thirty days (*Magen Avraham*), he recites: Blessed…Who remembers the covenant, is faithful (and is faithful, Rambam; *Tur*) to His covenant and fulfills His word, in accordance with the opinion of Rav Pappa (Rambam *Sefer Ahava, Hilkhot Berakhot* 10:16; *Shulḥan Arukh, Oraḥ Ḥayyim* 229:1).

**Over mountains and hills** – עַל הֶהָרִים וְעַל הַגְּבָעוֹת: Over conspicuously shaped (Rambam) mountains and hills one recites: Author of creation (*Shulḥan Arukh, Oraḥ Ḥayyim* 228:1, 3).

וְעַל הַבְּרָקִים אוֹמֵר ״בָּרוּךְ שֶׁכֹּחוֹ וּגְבוּרָתוֹ מָלֵא עוֹלָם״. מַאי בְּרָקִים? אֲמַר רָבָא: בְּרָקָא. וַאֲמַר רָבָא: בְּרָקָא יְחִידָאָה, וּבְרָקָא חִיוָּרָא, וּבְרָקָא יְרוֹקְתָא, וַעֲנָנֵי דְּסָלְקָן בְּקֶרֶן מַעֲרָבִית וְאָתְיָין מִקֶּרֶן דְּרוֹמִית, וְתַרְתֵּי עֲנָנֵי דְּסָלְקָן חֲדָא לְאַפֵּי חֲבֶרְתָּהּ – כּוּלְּהוּ קַשְׁיָין.

We **also** learned in the mishna that **over lightning one recites: Blessed… Whose strength and power fill the world.** The Gemara asks: **What is** this **lightning? Rava said: A bright light. And Rava said: A single** bolt of **lightning, white lightning, green lightning, clouds that rise in the western corner and come from the southern corner, and two clouds that rise with one facing the other are all** signs of **trouble.**

לְמַאי נַפְקָא מִינָּהּ – לְמִבְעֵי רַחֲמֵי. וְהָנֵי מִילֵּי – בְּלֵילְיָא, אֲבָל בְּצַפְרָא לֵית בְּהוּ מְשָׁשָׁא.

The Gemara asks: **What practical difference** is there in the knowledge that they are signs of trouble? The Gemara answers: So that we may **pray for God's mercy,** that they cause us no harm. The Gemara remarks that **this only applies** when these phenomena appear **at night. In the morning, however, they are insignificant.**

אֲמַר רַבִּי שְׁמוּאֵל בַּר יִצְחָק: הָנֵי עֲנָנֵי דְּצַפְרָא לֵית בְּהוּ מְשָׁשָׁא, דִּכְתִיב: ״וְחַסְדְּכֶם כַּעֲנַן בֹּקֶר״ וגו׳. אֲמַר לֵיהּ רַב פַּפָּא לְאַבַּיֵי, הָא אָמְרִי אֱינָשֵׁי: כַּד מִפְתַּח בָּבֵי מִיטְרָא, בַּר חַמָּרָא, מוֹךְ שַׂקִּיךְ וּגְנִי! – לָא קַשְׁיָא, הָא – דִּקְטַר בְּעֵיבָא, הָא – דִּקְטַר בַּעֲנָנֵי.

**Rabbi Shmuel bar Yitzḥak said: Morning clouds** dissipate immediately so they **have no substance, as it is written: "For your goodness is as a morning cloud,** and as the dew that early passes away" (Hosea 6:4). With regard to this, **Rav Pappa said to Abaye: But** don't **people say** the maxim: **If there is rain when people open their doors** in the morning, **donkey-driver, fold your sack and go to sleep,** as rain will continue to fall all day. Apparently morning clouds indicate that there will be rain all day. The Gemara responds: This is **not difficult,** as **this,** that suggests that there will be considerable rain, refers to a case where the sky is **covered with thick clouds,** while **this** opinion, where Rabbi Shmuel bar Yitzḥak said that morning clouds have no substance and will not produce much rain, refers to a case where the sky is **covered with flimsy clouds** which will certainly pass.

אָמַר רַבִּי אֲלֶכְּסַנְדְּרִי אָמַר רַבִּי יְהוֹשֻׁעַ בֶּן לֵוִי: לֹא נִבְרְאוּ רְעָמִים אֶלָּא לִפְשׁוֹט עַקְמוּמִית שֶׁבַּלֵּב, שֶׁנֶּאֱמַר: ״וְהָאֱלֹהִים עָשָׂה שֶׁיִּרְאוּ מִלְּפָנָיו״. וְאָמַר רַבִּי אֲלֶכְּסַנְדְּרִי אָמַר רַבִּי יְהוֹשֻׁעַ בֶּן לֵוִי: הָרוֹאֶה אֶת הַקֶּשֶׁת בֶּעָנָן צָרִיךְ שֶׁיִּפּוֹל עַל פָּנָיו, שֶׁנֶּאֱמַר: ״כְּמַרְאֵה הַקֶּשֶׁת אֲשֶׁר יִהְיֶה בֶעָנָן וגו׳ וָאֶרְאֶה וָאֶפֹּל עַל פָּנַי״, לָיְיטִי עֲלָהּ בְּמַעֲרָבָא, מִשּׁוּם דְּמֶחֱזֵי כְּמַאן דְּסָגֵיד לְקַשְׁתָּא. אֲבָל בָּרוֹכֵי וַדַּאי מְבָרֵךְ. מַאי מְבָרֵךְ – ״בָּרוּךְ זוֹכֵר הַבְּרִית״. בְּמַתְנִיתָא תָּנָא, רַבִּי יִשְׁמָעֵאל בְּנוֹ שֶׁל רַבִּי יוֹחָנָן בֶּן בְּרוֹקָא אוֹמֵר: ״נֶאֱמָן בִּבְרִיתוֹ וְקַיָּים בְּמַאֲמָרוֹ״. אֲמַר רַב פַּפָּא: הִלְכָּךְ נֵימְרִינְהוּ לְתַרְוַיְיהוּ ״בָּרוּךְ זוֹכֵר הַבְּרִית וְנֶאֱמָן בִּבְרִיתוֹ וְקַיָּים בְּמַאֲמָרוֹ״.

**Rabbi Alexandri said** that **Rabbi Yehoshua ben Levi said: Thunder was created only** to impose fear and **straighten the crookedness of the heart,**[N] **as it is stated: "And God has so made it, that men should fear before Him"** (Ecclesiastes 3:14). **And Rabbi Alexandri said** that **Rabbi Yehoshua ben Levi said: One who sees a rainbow**[B] **in a cloud must fall upon his face, as it is stated: "As the appearance of the bow that is in the cloud** in the day of rain, so was the appearance of the brightness round about. This was the appearance of the likeness of the glory of the Lord. **And when I saw it, I fell upon my face"** (Ezekiel 1:28). The colors of the rainbow symbolize the glory of God and one may not stare at them. Yet, **in the West,** Eretz Yisrael, **they would curse** one who fell upon his face when seeing a rainbow **because it appears as one who is bowing to the rainbow.** As far as **blessing** is concerned, **however,** all agree that **one certainly recites a blessing. What** blessing **does one recite? Blessed.. Who remembers the covenant** with Noah.[H] **It was taught in a *baraita*** that **Rabbi Yishmael, son of Rabbi Yoḥanan ben Beroka, says** that the blessing is: Blessed…**Who is faithful to His covenant and fulfills His word. Rav Pappa said: Therefore we will say them both** combined: **Blessed…Who remembers the covenant and is faithful to His covenant and fulfills His word.**

״עַל הֶהָרִים וְעַל הַגְּבָעוֹת״. אַטּוּ כָּל הָנֵי דַּאֲמַרַן עַד הָשְׁתָּא, לָאו מַעֲשֵׂה בְרֵאשִׁית נִינְהוּ? וְהָכְתִיב: ״בְּרָקִים לַמָּטָר עָשָׂה״! – אֲמַר אַבַּיֵי: כְּרוֹךְ וּתְנִי. רָבָא אֲמַר: הָתָם מְבָרֵךְ תַּרְתֵּי, ״בָּרוּךְ שֶׁכֹּחוֹ מָלֵא עוֹלָם״, וְ״עוֹשֶׂה מַעֲשֵׂה בְרֵאשִׁית״, הָכָא – ״עוֹשֶׂה מַעֲשֵׂה בְרֵאשִׁית״ אִיכָּא, ״שֶׁכֹּחוֹ מָלֵא עוֹלָם״ – לֵיכָּא.

We learned in the mishna that **over mountains and hills**[H] one recites: Blessed…Author of creation. The Gemara asks: **Is that to say that all those that we mentioned until now,** such as lightning, **are not acts of creation?** Among God's praise for creation of the world and forming the mountains, **is it not** also **written: "He makes lightning for the rain"** (Psalms 135:7)? **Abaye said: Combine** the two statements and **teach that** in all the cases in our mishna, one recites these two blessings. **Rava said: There,** over lightning and thunder, **one recites two** blessings: **Blessed.. Whose power fills the world,** and: **Author of creation. Here,** however, over mountains and hills, **one** recites the blessing: **Author of creation,** but **need not** recite: **Whose power fills the world.**

אָמַר רַבִּי יְהוֹשֻׁעַ בֶּן לֵוִי: הָרוֹאֶה רָקִיעַ בְּטָהֳרָתָהּ אוֹמֵר: ״בָּרוּךְ עוֹשֶׂה בְרֵאשִׁית״. אֵימָתַי? אֲמַר אַבַּיֵי: כִּי אֲתָא מִטְרָא כּוּלֵּי לֵילְיָא, וּבְצַפְרָא אֲתָא אִסְתְּנָא, וּמְגַלְיָא לְהוּ לִשְׁמַיָּא.

**Rabbi Yehoshua ben Levi said: One who sees the firmament in its purity recites: Blessed…Author of creation.** The Gemara asks: **When** does the firmament appear in its purity? **Abaye said: When rain** falls **all night and in the morning a northern wind blows, exposing the heavens.**

וּפְלִיגִי דְּרַפְרָם בַּר פַּפָּא אָמַר רַב חִסְדָּא, דְּאָמַר רַפְרָם בַּר פַּפָּא אָמַר רַב חִסְדָּא: מִיּוֹם שֶׁחָרַב בֵּית הַמִּקְדָּשׁ לֹא נִרְאֵית רָקִיעַ בְּטָהֳרָתָהּ, שֶׁנֶּאֱמַר: ״אַלְבִּישׁ שָׁמַיִם קַדְרוּת וְשַׂק אָשִׂים כְּסוּתָם״.

The Gemara notes: **And** in this they **disagree with Rafram bar Pappa** who said that **Rav Ḥisda said,** as **Rafram bar Pappa said** that **Rav Ḥisda said: Since the day the Temple was destroyed the firmament has not been seen in its purity, as it is said: "I clothe the heavens with blackness and I make sackcloth their covering"** (Isaiah 50:3).

תָּנוּ רַבָּנַן: הָרוֹאֶה חַמָּה בִּתְקוּפָתָהּ, לְבָנָה בִּגְבוּרָתָהּ, וְכוֹכָבִים בִּמְסִילוֹתָם, וּמַזָּלוֹת כְּסִדְרָן, אוֹמֵר: ״בָּרוּךְ עוֹשֶׂה בְרֵאשִׁית״ וְאֵימַת הָוֵי? – אֲמַר אַבַּיֵי: כָּל עֶשְׂרִים וּשְׁמוֹנֶה שְׁנִין, וַהֲדַר מַחֲזוֹר וְנָפְלָה תְּקוּפַת נִיסָן בְּשַׁבְּתַאי בְּאוֹרְתָא דִּתְלָת נַגְהֵי אַרְבַּע.

**The Sages taught: One who sees the sun in** the beginning **of its cycle,**[HB] **the moon in its might,**[B] **the planets in their orbit, or the signs of the zodiac** aligned **in their order recites: Blessed…Author of creation.** The Gemara asks: **And when is it** that the sun is at the beginning of its cycle? **Abaye said: Every twenty-eight years** when the **cycle** is complete and **returns** to its genesis, **and the Nisan,** vernal, **equinox,** when the spring days and nights are of equal length, **falls within** the constellation of **Saturn on the night of the third and eve of the fourth** day of the week, as then their arrangement returns to be as it was when the constellations were first placed in the heavens.

״רַבִּי יְהוּדָה אוֹמֵר: הָרוֹאֶה הַיָּם״ וכו׳ ״לִפְרָקִים״ עַד כַּמָּה? אָמַר רָמִי בַּר אַבָּא אָמַר רַב יִצְחָק: עַד שְׁלֹשִׁים יוֹם.

We learned in the mishna that **Rabbi Yehuda said: One who sees the great sea** intermittently **recites:** Blessed…Who has made the great sea. The Gemara asks: **How much** is **intermittently? Rami bar Abba said** that **Rav Yitzḥak said: Thirty days.**

וְאָמַר רָמִי בַּר אַבָּא אָמַר רַב יִצְחָק: הָרוֹאֶה פְּרָת אַגִּשְׁרָא דְּבָבֶל אוֹמֵר: ״בָּרוּךְ עוֹשֶׂה בְרֵאשִׁית״. וְהָאִידָּנָא דְּשַׁנְיוּהּ פָּרְסָאֵי – מִבֵּי שָׁבוֹר וּלְעֵיל, רַב יוֹסֵף אָמַר: מֵאִיהִי דְּקִירָא וּלְעֵיל. וַאֲמַר רָמִי בַּר אַבָּא: הָרוֹאֶה דִּגְלַת אַגִּשְׁרָא דְּשַׁבִּיסְתָּנָא אוֹמֵר: ״בָּרוּךְ עוֹשֶׂה בְרֵאשִׁית״.

**And Rami bar Abba said** that **Rav Yitzḥak said: One who sees the Euphrates River near the bridge of Babylonia recites: Blessed…Author of creation.** The Gemara adds: **And now that the Persians have rerouted**[H] the course of the river, one only recites the blessing **from Beit Shavor upriver.** Downriver, it no longer flows as it did at creation, so there one does not recite the blessing: Author of creation. **Rav Yosef said:** One only recites the blessing **from Ihi Dekira upriver. And Rami bar Abba said: One who sees the Tigris on the bridge of Shabistana**[B] **recites: Blessed…Author of creation.**

מַאי ״חִדֶּקֶל״? – אָמַר רַב אַשִׁי: שֶׁמֵּימָיו חַדִּין וְקַלִּין. מַאי ״פְּרָת״ – שֶׁמֵּימָיו פָּרִין וְרָבִין.

The Gemara proceeds to explain the names of these rivers. **What is** the source of the name *Ḥidekel* [Tigris]? **Rav Ashi said:** Its name is an acronym derived from the fact that **its waters are sharp** [*ḥadin*] **and light** [*kalin*] and therefore good for drinking. **What** is the source of the name *Perat* [Euphrates]? It is so named **because its waters are fruitful** [*parin*] **and multiply** [*ravin*]; there are many fish in it.

וַאֲמַר רָבָא: הַאי דַּחֲרִיפֵי בְּנֵי מְחוֹזָא – מִשּׁוּם דְּשָׁתוּ מַיָּא דְּדִגְלַת, הַאי דְּגִיחוֹרִי – מִשּׁוּם דִּמְשַׁמְּשֵׁי בִּימָמָא, וְהַאי דְּנָיְידֵי עֵינַיְיהוּ – מִשּׁוּם דְּדָיְירוּ בְּבַיִת אָפֵל.

As for the Tigris River, **Rava said: The inhabitants** of the city **Meḥoza**[B] **are sharp because they drink the water of the Tigris; they are red because they engage in** conjugal **relations in the daytime; and their eyes move** constantly **because they live in dark houses.**

״עַל הַגְּשָׁמִים״ כו׳. וְעַל הַגְּשָׁמִים ״הַטּוֹב וְהַמֵּטִיב״ מְבָרֵךְ?! וְהָאָמַר רַבִּי אַבָּהוּ, וְאָמְרִי לָהּ בְּמַתְנִיתָא תָּנָא: מֵאֵימָתַי מְבָרְכִין עַל הַגְּשָׁמִים – מִשֶּׁיֵּצֵא חָתָן לִקְרַאת כַּלָּה.

We learned in our mishna that **over rain** one recites the blessing: Blessed…Who is good and does good. The Gemara asks: **And over rain** does **one** really **recite the blessing: Who is good and does good? Didn't Rabbi Abbahu say, and some say it was taught in a** *baraita*: **From when does one recite the blessing on rain?**[H] **From when the groom went out to meet the bride.** In other words, there are puddles of water on the ground. The groom, meaning the raindrops from above, cause the bride, meaning the water below, to splash.

**HALAKHA**

**One who sees the sun in its cycle – הָרוֹאֶה חַמָּה בִּתְקוּפָתָהּ:** This occurs every twenty-eight years, when the beginning of the season of Nisan, spring, is in the constellation of Saturn on the eve of the fourth day of the week. One recites: Blessed…Author of creation. One recites the blessing at sunrise (Rif). If one failed to do so at sunrise, he may recite the blessing until three hours of the day have passed. Some later commentaries wrote that one may even recite the full blessing, invoking the name of God and His Sovereignty, as late as noon (Rambam *Sefer Ahava, Hilkhot Berakhot* 10:18; *Shulḥan Arukh, Oraḥ Ḥayyim* 229:2).

**Now that the Persians have rerouted – וְהָאִידָּנָא דְּשַׁנְיוּהּ פָּרְסָאֵי:** One does not recite: Author of creation when seeing rivers where they have been rerouted by man (*Shulḥan Arukh, Oraḥ Ḥayyim* 228:2).

**From when does one recite the blessing on rain – מֵאֵימָתַי מְבָרְכִין עַל הַגְּשָׁמִים:** If a drought is afflicting the community at large and rain falls, one recites a blessing despite the fact that the rain was not sufficient to be considered a significant rainfall [*revia*]. One does not recite the blessing unless it rained enough that the drops falling can cause the puddles on the ground to bubble (Rambam *Sefer Ahava, Hilkhot Berakhot* 10:6; *Shulḥan Arukh, Oraḥ Ḥayyim* 221:1).

**BACKGROUND**

**Meḥoza – מְחוֹזָא:** A city on the Tigris located near the Malka River. It was a large commercial city and most of its inhabitants were Jews. Unlike most other Jewish communities, Meḥoza's Jews generally earned their living from commerce. Jews from different countries lived in Meḥoza, and many converts lived there as well. After Neharde'a was destroyed in 259 CE, its yeshiva moved to Meḥoza. Meḥoza became the Torah center of leading scholars such as Rav Naḥman, Rav Sheshet, Rava (who later became head of the yeshiva in Meḥoza), Ameimar, and Rav Kahana (Rav Ashi's teacher). After Abaye's death, c. 338 CE, the yeshiva in Pumbedita, then headed by Rava, also moved to Meḥoza for a period of time.

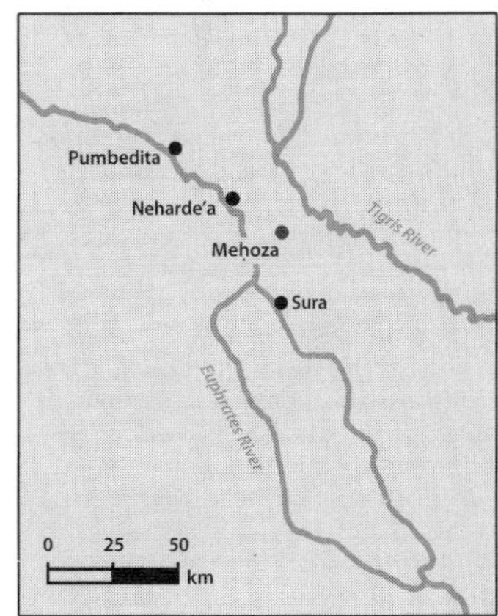


Map of central Babylonia

**BACKGROUND**

**The sun in its cycle – חַמָּה בִּתְקוּפָתָהּ:** According to an approximate calculation of the solar year, based on Shmuel's reckoning of the seasons, a year is three hundred and sixty-five days and six hours long. Based on this, each of the four seasons lasts ninety-one days and seven and a half hours. Since ninety-one days are exactly thirteen weeks, each season begins seven and a half hours later than the previous one. After four years, a small cycle, the season begins at the same hour of the day, though five days later in the week. Only after twenty-eight years does the season begin on the same day of the week at the same hour. Therefore, when one divides the number of years since creation by twenty-eight, he arrives at the number of large cycles of the sun that have passed. Since each day has the name of a specific constellation, according to the cycle of seven planets, the beginning of the night of the fourth day of the week, the day of the creation of the heavenly lights, is called the hour of Saturn.

**The moon in its might – לְבָנָה בִּגְבוּרָתָהּ:** Some explain that this refers to the end of the month, when the moon is located opposite Aries, which is considered the beginning of the Zodiac cycle. Similarly, when the rest of the stars are located in that position, one recites the blessing over the beginning of their cycle.

**The bridge of Shabistana – גִּשְׁרָא דְּשַׁבִּיסְתָּנָא:** The source of the word Shabistana is the Persian šabestān meaning night dwelling. According to ancient tradition there was a bridge and dam that was closed at night and obstructed the flow of the water there (Rav Sa'adia Gaon).

מַאי מְבָרְכִין? אָמַר רַב יְהוּדָה: ״מוֹדִים אֲנַחְנוּ לָךְ עַל כׇּל טִפָּה וְטִפָּה שֶׁהוֹרַדְתָּ לָנוּ״, וְרַבִּי יוֹחָנָן מְסַיֵּים בָּהּ הָכִי: ״אִילּוּ פִינוּ מָלֵא שִׁירָה כַּיָּם וכו׳ אֵין אֲנַחְנוּ מַסְפִּיקִין לְהוֹדוֹת לְךָ ה׳ אֱלֹהֵינוּ... עַד ׳תִשְׁתַּחֲוֶה׳, בָּרוּךְ אַתָּה ה׳ רוֹב הַהוֹדָאוֹת״.

The Gemara asks: **What blessing does one recite? Rav Yehuda said:** The formula of the blessing is: **We thank You for each and every drop that You have made fall for us. And Rav Yoḥanan concludes** the blessing as follows: **If our mouths were as full of song as the sea…we could not sufficiently praise You O Lord our God,** and he continues with the formula of *nishmat* that is recited on Shabbat morning, **until: Shall bow** before You. **Blessed are You, O Lord,** to Whom **abundant thanksgivings** are offered.[H]

״רוֹב הַהוֹדָאוֹת״ וְלָא ״כׇּל הַהוֹדָאוֹת״?! – אָמַר רָבָא: אֵימָא ״הָאֵל הַהוֹדָאוֹת״. אָמַר רַב פָּפָּא: הִלְכָּךְ נֵימְרִינְהוּ לְתַרְוַיְיהוּ ״רוֹב הַהוֹדָאוֹת״ וְ״הָאֵל הַהוֹדָאוֹת״.

The Gemara asks: Does the blessing say: **Abundant thanksgivings, and not: All thanksgivings?** Certainly all thanksgivings are due to God. **Rava said:** Emend the formula of the blessing and **say: The God of thanksgivings. Rav Pappa said: Therefore, we will recite them both: Abundant thanksgivings, and: The God of thanksgivings.**[N]

וְאֶלָּא קַשְׁיָא! – לָא קַשְׁיָא, הָא – דִּשְׁמַע מִשְׁמַע, הָא – דַּחֲזָא מֵחֲזֵי.

**However, it is** still **difficult,** as apparently the blessing for rain is not: Who is good and does good, as it appears in our mishna. The Gemara responds: This is **not difficult. This,** which we learned in our mishna, that one recites: Who is good and does good, refers to a case **where one heard** that rain fell. **This,** where we learned that one recites: We thank You, etc., refers to a case **where one saw** the rain fall.

דִּשְׁמַע מִשְׁמַע – הַיְינוּ בְּשׂוֹרוֹת טוֹבוֹת, וּתְנַן: עַל בְּשׂוֹרוֹת טוֹבוֹת אוֹמֵר: ״בָּרוּךְ הַטּוֹב וְהַמֵּטִיב״!

The Gemara asks: **One heard** that the rain fell; **that is** a case of **good tidings. And we learned** in the mishna **that upon** hearing **good tidings one recites: Who is good and does good.** Therefore, there is no reason for the mishna to mention rain separately.

אֶלָּא אִידִי וְאִידִי דַּחֲזֵי מֵחֲזֵי, וְלָא קַשְׁיָא, הָא – דַּאֲתָא פּוּרְתָּא, הָא – דַּאֲתָא טוּבָא. וְאִיבָּעֵית אֵימָא: הָא וְהָא דַּאֲתָא טוּבָא, וְלָא קַשְׁיָא, הָא – דְּאִית לֵיהּ אַרְעָא, הָא – דְּלֵית לֵיהּ אַרְעָא.

**Rather,** the difficulty can be otherwise resolved: **This,** Rabbi Abbahu's statement, **and that,** the mishna, both refer to a case where one saw the rain fall, **and** this is **not difficult. This,** Rabbi Abbahu's statement that one recites We thank You, etc., **refers to** a case **where a little** rain **fell,** while **that,** the mishna which says that one recites: Who is good and does good refers to a case **where a lot** of rain **fell. And if you wish, say** instead that **this and that** refer to cases **where a lot** of rain **fell,** and this is **not difficult. This,** the mishna, **refers to** a case **where one owns land,** while **that,** Rabbi Abbahu's statement that one recites: We thank You, etc., **refers to** a case **where one does not own land,** so the rain does not benefit him directly.

אִית לֵיהּ אַרְעָא ״הַטּוֹב וְהַמֵּטִיב״ מְבָרֵךְ?! וְהָא תְּנַן: בָּנָה בַּיִת חָדָשׁ וְקָנָה כֵּלִים חֲדָשִׁים אוֹמֵר: ״בָּרוּךְ... שֶׁהֶחֱיָינוּ... וְהִגִּיעָנוּ לַזְּמַן הַזֶּה״, שֶׁלּוֹ וְשֶׁל אֲחֵרִים אוֹמֵר: ״הַטּוֹב וְהַמֵּטִיב״!

The Gemara asks: **One who owns land recites: Who is good and does good? Didn't we learn** in the mishna: **One who built a new house or purchased new vessels recites: Blessed…Who has given us life…and brought us to this time.** However, if the land belonged **to him and others** in partnership, **he recites: Who is good and does good?** For rain falling onto land that one owns exclusively, he recites: Who has given us life and not: Who is good and does good.

לָא קַשְׁיָא, הָא – דְּאִית לֵיהּ שׁוּתָּפוּת, הָא – דְּלֵית לֵיהּ שׁוּתָּפוּת, וְהָתַנְיָא: קִצּוּרוֹ שֶׁל דָּבָר, עַל שֶׁלּוֹ הוּא אוֹמֵר: ״בָּרוּךְ... שֶׁהֶחֱיָינוּ וְקִיְּימָנוּ״, עַל שֶׁלּוֹ וְעַל שֶׁל חֲבֵירוֹ אוֹמֵר: ״בָּרוּךְ הַטּוֹב וְהַמֵּטִיב״.

The Gemara answers: This is **not difficult. This,** the mishna where we learned that one recites: Who is good and does good, **refers to** a case **where one** owns his land **in partnership** with another; **that,** Rabbi Abbahu's statement that one recites: Who has given us life, **refers to** a case **where one** owns the land exclusively and **does not have a partnership. And** indeed, this *halakha* **was taught** in a *baraita*: **The gist of the matter is, for** that which **is** exclusively **his, he recites: Blessed…Who has given us life and sustained us; for** that which **belongs to him and to another** in partnership, **he recites: Who is good and does good.**[H]

וְכׇל הֵיכָא דְּלֵית לַאֲחֲרִינָא בַּהֲדֵיהּ לָא מְבָרֵךְ ״הַטּוֹב וְהַמֵּטִיב״?! – וְהָתַנְיָא, אָמְרוּ לֵיהּ: יָלְדָה אִשְׁתּוֹ זָכָר, אוֹמֵר ״בָּרוּךְ הַטּוֹב וְהַמֵּטִיב״! – הָתָם נָמֵי, דְּאִיכָּא אִשְׁתּוֹ בַּהֲדֵיהּ, דְּנִיחָא לַהּ בְּזָכָר.

The Gemara challenges this principle: **And in every case where others are not with him, one does not recite: Who is good and does good? Wasn't it taught** in a *baraita*: **If they told him that his wife gave birth to a male,**[H] **he recites: Who is good and does good?** The Gemara responds: **There too, his wife is with him, as she is also happy that a male** child was born.

תָּא שְׁמַע: מֵת אָבִיו וְהוּא יוֹרְשׁוֹ, בַּתְּחִלָּה אוֹמֵר: ״בָּרוּךְ דַּיַּין הָאֱמֶת״, וּלְבַסּוֹף הוּא אוֹמֵר: ״בָּרוּךְ הַטּוֹב וְהַמֵּטִיב״! – הָתָם נָמֵי, דְּאִיכָּא אַחֵי דְּקָא יָרְתִי בַּהֲדֵיהּ.

The Gemara challenges further: **Come and hear** a contradiction from what was taught in a *baraita*: One whose **father died and he is his heir,**[H] **initially recites: Blessed…the true Judge,** upon hearing of his father's death, **and ultimately,** upon receiving his inheritance, **he recites: Blessed…Who is good and does good.** Despite the fact that the son alone benefits, he nevertheless recites: Who is good and does good. The Gemara responds: **There, too,** it refers to a case **where he has brothers who inherit along with him.**

## HALAKHA

**The blessing for rain – בִּרְכַּת הַגְּשָׁמִים:** If one does not own a field and sees rain falling, he recites: We thank You, and concludes with: God of abundant thanksgivings, in accordance with the opinion of Rav Pappa. If one owns a field, he recites: Who has given us life, etc. If one owns a field in partnership, he recites: Who is good and does good. Some say that he recites the blessing even if he did not see the rain falling, but merely was told that it fell (Rambam *Sefer Ahava, Hilkhot Berakhot* 10:5; *Shulḥan Arukh, Oraḥ Ḥayyim* 221:2, and in the Rema).

**For that which is exclusively his…Who has given us life…For that which belongs to him and to another…Who is good and does good – עַל שֶׁלּוֹ...שֶׁהֶחֱיָינוּ...עַל שֶׁלּוֹ וְעַל שֶׁל חֲבֵירוֹ...הַטּוֹב וְהַמֵּטִיב:** If one hears from a reliable source (*Magen Avraham*) good tidings that benefit him alone, one recites: Who has given us life, etc. If one's partners also benefit from these good tidings, he recites: Who is good and does good (Rambam *Sefer Ahava, Hilkhot Berakhot* 10:7; *Shulḥan Arukh, Oraḥ Ḥayyim* 222:1).

**His wife gave birth to a male – יָלְדָה אִשְׁתּוֹ זָכָר:** If one's wife gave birth to a son, both he and his wife recite: Who is good and does good (*Shulḥan Arukh, Oraḥ Ḥayyim* 223:1).

**One whose father died and he is his heir – מֵת אָבִיו וְהוּא יוֹרְשׁוֹ:** If one's father died, he recites: Blessed…the true Judge. If his father owned property and he was his heir, he recites two blessings. First, over the death he recites: The true Judge; then he recites the blessing for the inheritance. If he is the sole heir, over the inheritance he recites: Who has given us life, etc. If there were additional heirs, he recites: Who is good and does good (Rambam *Sefer Ahava, Hilkhot Berakhot* 10:7; *Shulḥan Arukh, Oraḥ Ḥayyim* 223:2).

## NOTES

**Therefore, we will recite them both: Abundant thanksgivings, and: The God of thanksgivings – הִלְכָּךְ נֵימְרִינְהוּ לְתַרְוַיְיהוּ רוֹב הַהוֹדָאוֹת וְהָאֵל הַהוֹדָאוֹת:** Several explanations are offered for Rav Pappa's statement: Therefore, we will recite them both. Some explain that he intended to combine the formula of Rabbi Yoḥanan's blessing with the formula of Rava's blessing (see *Me'iri*). According to the version of our Gemara, Rav Pappa only calls for the combination of the conclusions of the blessings. Apparently, the term *rov* should be interpreted neither as most nor as all. Rather, it is an abstract praise of God; He is the object of multiple expressions of thanksgiving. However, because it could be misunderstood as meaning most and not all, and because even: The God of thanksgivings could be misunderstood to imply the existence of another god who is the object of more thanksgivings, Rav Pappa combines the two formulas to emphasize the appropriate interpretation (Ramban *Milḥamot Hashem*; Rabbeinu Aharon HaLevi; *Talmidei Rabbeinu Yona; see Ma'adanei Yom Tov*).

תָּא שְׁמַע: שִׁינּוּי יַיִן אֵינוֹ צָרִיךְ לְבָרֵךְ, שִׁינּוּי מָקוֹם צָרִיךְ לְבָרֵךְ. וְאָמַר רַבִּי יוֹסֵף בַּר אַבָּא אָמַר רַבִּי יוֹחָנָן: אַף עַל פִּי שֶׁאָמְרוּ "שִׁינּוּי יַיִן אֵינוֹ צָרִיךְ לְבָרֵךְ", אֲבָל אוֹמֵר "בָּרוּךְ הַטּוֹב וְהַמֵּטִיב!" – הָתָם נַמִּי דְּאִיכָּא בְּנֵי חֲבוּרָה דְּשָׁתוּ בַּהֲדֵיהּ.

The Gemara cites an additional challenge: **Come and hear** a contradiction based on what was taught in a *baraita*: In the case of **a change in** the type of **wine**[HN] during a meal, **one need not recite the blessing:** Who creates fruit of the vine, a second time. However, in the case of **a change in place, one must recite a** second **blessing**[H] over the wine. **And Rabbi Yosef bar Abba said that Rabbi Yoḥanan said: Although** the Sages **said that** in the case of **a change in** the type of **wine one need not recite** a second **blessing** over the wine, **he does recite: Blessed…Who is good and does good.** The Gemara responds: **There, too,** it refers to a case where he is not alone, but where **members of the group are drinking with him.**

"בָּנָה בַּיִת חָדָשׁ וְקָנָה כֵּלִים חֲדָשִׁים" וכו׳ אָמַר רַב הוּנָא: לֹא שָׁנוּ אֶלָּא שֶׁאֵין לוֹ כַּיּוֹצֵא בָּהֶן, אֲבָל יֵשׁ לוֹ כַּיּוֹצֵא בָּהֶן – אֵינוֹ צָרִיךְ לְבָרֵךְ. וְרַבִּי יוֹחָנָן אָמַר: אֲפִילּוּ יֵשׁ לוֹ כַּיּוֹצֵא בָּהֶן צָרִיךְ לְבָרֵךְ.

We learned in the mishna: One who **built a new house or purchased new vessels**[H] recites: Blessed…Who has given us life, sustained us and brought us to this time. With regard to this blessing, **Rav Huna said: They only taught** that one recites: Who has given us life, upon purchasing a new vessel when **he does not** already **have something similar,** i.e., something he inherited. **However, if he** already **has something similar he need not recite a blessing,** as it is not new to him. **Rabbi Yoḥanan said: Even if one** already **has something similar** that he inherited, **he must recite a blessing** because he never before purchased a vessel of that kind.

Perek **IX**
Daf **60** Amud **a**

מִכְּלָל דִּכִי קָנָה וְחָזַר וְקָנָה – דִּבְרֵי הַכֹּל אֵין צָרִיךְ לְבָרֵךְ.

The Gemara deduces: This proves **by inference that if he purchases** a new object **and then purchases** a similar object, **everyone agrees that he is not required to recite a blessing,** as he has already recited a blessing over the purchase of that type of item.

וְאִיכָּא דְּאָמְרִי, אָמַר רַב הוּנָא: לֹא שָׁנוּ אֶלָּא שֶׁלֹּא קָנָה וְחָזַר וְקָנָה, אֲבָל קָנָה וְחָזַר וְקָנָה – אֵין צָרִיךְ לְבָרֵךְ. וְרַבִּי יוֹחָנָן אָמַר אֲפִילּוּ קָנָה חָזַר וְקָנָה – צָרִיךְ לְבָרֵךְ. מִכְּלָל דִּכִי יֵשׁ לוֹ וְקָנָה – דִּבְרֵי הַכֹּל צָרִיךְ לְבָרֵךְ.

**Some say** a different version of this dispute: **Rav Huna said: They only taught** that one recites the blessing: Who has given us life, on a new vessel **if he did not purchase** that item in the past **and purchased** the item now, for the first time. **However, if he purchased** that item in the past **and purchased** the item **again, he need not recite a blessing. And Rabbi Yoḥanan said: Even if one purchased** that item in the past **and purchased** a similar item **again, he must recite a blessing.** This proves **by inference that if one** already **has** a vessel **and** then **purchased** similar vessels, **everyone agrees that he must recite a blessing.**

מֵיתִיבֵי: בָּנָה בַּיִת חָדָשׁ וְאֵין לוֹ כַּיּוֹצֵא בּוֹ, קָנָה כֵּלִים חֲדָשִׁים וְאֵין לוֹ כַּיּוֹצֵא בָּהֶם – צָרִיךְ לְבָרֵךְ, יֵשׁ לוֹ כַּיּוֹצֵא בָּהֶם – אֵין צָרִיךְ לְבָרֵךְ, דִּבְרֵי רַבִּי מֵאִיר. רַבִּי יְהוּדָה אוֹמֵר בֵּין כָּךְ וּבֵין כָּךְ – צָרִיךְ לְבָרֵךְ.

The Gemara **raises an objection** based on what was taught in a *baraita*: One who **built a new house and does not** already **own a similar** house, **or purchased new vessels and does not** already **own similar** vessels, **must recite a blessing.** However, if **he** already **owns a similar** one, **he need not recite a blessing,** this is **the statement of Rabbi Meir. Rabbi Yehuda,** on the other hand, **says: In either case, he must recite a blessing.**

בִּשְׁלָמָא לְלִישָּׁנָא קַמָּא, רַב הוּנָא – כְּרַבִּי מֵאִיר, וְרַבִּי יוֹחָנָן – כְּרַבִּי יְהוּדָה, אֶלָּא לְלִישָּׁנָא בַּתְרָא, בִּשְׁלָמָא רַב הוּנָא – כְּרַבִּי יְהוּדָה, אֶלָּא רַבִּי יוֹחָנָן, דַּאֲמַר כְּמַאן? לֹא כְּרַבִּי מֵאִיר וְלֹא כְּרַבִּי יְהוּדָה!

The Gemara asks: **Granted, according to the first version** of the dispute between Rav Huna and Rabbi Yoḥanan, one could say that **Rav Huna** holds **in accordance with** the opinion of **Rabbi Meir, and** that **Rabbi Yoḥanan** holds **in accordance with** the opinion of **Rabbi Yehuda. However, according to the latter version** of the dispute, **granted, Rav Huna** holds **in accordance with** the opinion of **Rabbi Yehuda, but in accordance with whose** opinion **did Rabbi Yoḥanan state** his opinion? His statement **is neither in accordance with** the opinion of **Rabbi Meir nor in accordance with** the opinion of **Rabbi Yehuda.**

אָמַר לָךְ רַבִּי יוֹחָנָן: הוּא הַדִּין דִּלְרַבִּי יְהוּדָה, קָנָה וְחָזַר וְקָנָה – נַמִּי צָרִיךְ לְבָרֵךְ, וְהָא דְּקָא מִיפַּלְגִי בְּיֵשׁ לוֹ וְקָנָה – לְהוֹדִיעֲךָ כֹּחוֹ דְּרַבִּי מֵאִיר, דַּאֲפִילּוּ קָנָה וְיֵשׁ לוֹ – אֵין צָרִיךְ לְבָרֵךְ, וְכָל שֶׁכֵּן קָנָה וְחָזַר וְקָנָה, דְּאֵין צָרִיךְ לְבָרֵךְ.

The Gemara responds: **Rabbi Yoḥanan** could have **said to you: The same is true according to Rabbi Yehuda's** opinion; in a case where **one has purchased** an item in the past **and purchased** a similar item **again, he must recite a blessing.** The fact **that they** only **disagreed with regard to** a case **where he** already **owned** similar vessels **and he purchased** new ones does not indicate that this is their only disagreement. The dispute was presented in this way **to convey the far-reaching nature of Rabbi Meir's** opinion; **even** in a case where **one purchased** an item **while owning a** similar item, **he need not recite a blessing; all the more so** in a case where **he purchased** an item **and then purchased** a similar item **again, he need not recite a blessing.**

**HALAKHA**

**A change in wine – שִׁינּוּי יַיִן:** Over a new type of wine that was served during a meal, one recites: Who is good and does good, but there is no need to repeat: Who creates fruit of the vine (Rambam *Sefer Ahava, Hilkhot Berakhot* 4:9; *Shulḥan Arukh, Oraḥ Ḥayyim* 175:1).

**A change in place, one must recite a blessing – שִׁינּוּי מָקוֹם צָרִיךְ לְבָרֵךְ:** One who began eating in one house, stopped in the middle of his meal and went to another house; even if he plans to return to the first house immediately and not linger in the second house at all, he is obligated to recite Grace after Meals before he leaves, recite a new blessing when he returns to continue his meal, and then recite Grace after Meals again (*Shulḥan Arukh* based on the Rambam). Others say that if some of the diners remained in their seats, he need not recite a blessing before continuing his meal (Rema, based on *Tosafot*). That is the Ashkenazic custom (*Shulḥan Arukh HaRav, Mishna Berura*; Rambam *Sefer Ahava, Hilkhot Berakhot* 4:3; *Shulḥan Arukh, Oraḥ Ḥayyim* 178:1–2 and the Rema).

**One who built a new house or purchased new vessels – בָּנָה בַּיִת חָדָשׁ וְקָנָה כֵּלִים חֲדָשִׁים:** One who built or purchased (*Mishna Berura*) a new house or new vessels or clothing (*Magen Avraham*) for himself, even if he had already purchased or inherited similar vessels in the past, if they are vessels that cause people joy, everyone in accordance with his standing in society (*Mishna Berura*), recites: Who has given us life, etc. The vessels need not necessarily be new; the ruling is the same with regard to old vessels as long as they are new to him and he never owned anything similar in the past. This is in accordance with Rabbi Yoḥanan, as the *halakha* is in accordance with his opinion in disputes with Rav Huna, and in accordance with the last version of their dispute (*Kesef Mishne*; Rambam *Sefer Ahava, Hilkhot Berakhot* 10:1; *Shulḥan Arukh, Oraḥ Ḥayyim* 223:3).

**NOTES**

**A change in wine – שִׁינּוּי יַיִן:** Some explain that one recites: Who is good and does good specifically over a change in the type of wine and not over a change in the type of bread, because the process of production of bread is completed by man, while production of wine is completed by Heaven (*ge'onim*). Others explain that it is because wine gladdens the heart while bread does not (Rosh).

NOTES

**The strength of leniency is preferable** – כֹּחַ דְּהֶתֵּירָא עָדִיף לֵיהּ: Some argue that the opposite should be true. Every blessing involves invocation of God's name; a Sage who requires a blessing, should be considered to hold the lenient view, as he is not concerned that it might entail invocation of God's name in vain (see *Kesef Mishne, Hilkhot Berakhot* ch. 10). Others explain that because reciting: Who has given us life, is in fulfillment of one's obligation to praise God for His greatness, even if one is not obligated to recite the blessing, he may do so. Consequently, one who holds that the blessing need not be recited adopts the more lenient position (*Tziyyun LeNefesh Ḥayya*).

**One does not mention miraculous acts** – אֵין מַזְכִּירִין מַעֲשֵׂה נִסִּים: Though miracles do occur, one should not request that the laws of nature be altered on his behalf (*Ḥefetz Hashem*).

HALAKHA

**One recites a blessing for the bad that befalls him just as he does for the good, and for the good just as he does for the bad** – מְבָרֵךְ עַל הָרָעָה מֵעֵין עַל הַטּוֹבָה וְעַל הַטּוֹבָה מֵעֵין עַל הָרָעָה: One recites a blessing in accordance with the present reality, not in accordance with the way he predicts the situation will develop in the future. Therefore, one recites the appropriate blessing for the moment: The true Judge, even though it might be beneficial in the future. Similarly, one recites: Who has given us life, etc., or: Who is good and does good, even though harm is liable to result from the phenomenon over which he is reciting the blessing (Rambam *Sefer Ahava, Hilkhot Berakhot* 10:4; *Shulḥan Arukh, Oraḥ Ḥayyim* 222:4).

**A vain prayer** – תְּפִלַּת שָׁוְא: One is forbidden to pray for a certain outcome after the event has already occurred, even though he does not know what happened and how it happened. This refers, for example, to one who prays forty days or more after conception that his wife will give birth to a male child (Rambam *Sefer Ahava, Hilkhot Berakhot* 10:22; *Shulḥan Arukh, Oraḥ Ḥayyim* 230:1).

וְלִיפַלְגוּ בְּקָנָה וְחָזַר וְקָנָה דְּאֵין צָרִיךְ לְבָרֵךְ, לְהוֹדִיעֲךָ כֹּחוֹ דְּרַבִּי יְהוּדָה! – כֹּחַ דְּהֶתֵּירָא עָדִיף לֵיהּ.

The Gemara asks: **And** if that is the reason for presenting the dispute in this manner, **let them disagree with regard to** a case **where one purchased** an item in the past **and** then **purchased** a similar item **again,** where according to Rabbi Meir **one need not recite a blessing, in order to convey the far-reaching nature of Rabbi Yehuda's** opinion; as Rabbi Yehuda requires a blessing in that case. The Gemara responds: The Gemara preferred the version before us in order to demonstrate the extent to which Rabbi Meir was lenient in not requiring a blessing because **the strength of leniency is preferable.**[N]

״מְבָרֵךְ עַל הָרָעָה״ כו׳.

We learned in the mishna: **One recites a blessing for the bad** that befalls him just as he does for the good.[H] This is to say that one recites the blessing appropriate for the present situation even if it is bad, despite the fact that it may develop into a positive situation in the future.

הֵיכִי דָּמֵי? – כְּגוֹן דִּשְׁקַל בִּדְקָא בְּאַרְעֵיהּ, אַף עַל גַּב דְּטָבָא הִיא לְדִידֵיהּ, דְּמַסְּקָא אַרְעָא שִׂירְטוֹן וְשָׁבְחָא – הָשְׁתָּא מִיהָא רָעָה הִיא.

The Gemara asks: **What are the circumstances?** The Gemara explains: **In a case where a dam was breached** and water flowed **onto one's land despite** the fact **that this will** ultimately **be beneficial for him, for his land will be covered with sediment** from the flowing water **which will enhance** the quality of his soil, **it is** nonetheless **bad at present.**

״וְעַל הַטּוֹבָה״ כו׳.

One must recite a blessing **for the good** that befalls him just as for the bad.

הֵיכִי דָּמֵי? – כְּגוֹן דְּאַשְׁכַּח מְצִיאָה, אַף עַל גַּב דְּרָעָה הִיא לְדִידֵיהּ, דְּאִי שָׁמַע בָּהּ מַלְכָּא שָׁקֵיל לָהּ מִינֵּיהּ – הָשְׁתָּא מִיהָא טוֹבָה הִיא.

The Gemara asks: **What are the circumstances?** The Gemara explains: **In a case where one found a lost object, despite** the fact **that it is** ultimately **bad for him** because **if the king heard about it, he would** certainly **take it from him.** At that time, the law deemed all found objects the property of the king's treasury and one who did not report such an object would be punished. Nevertheless, **it is favorable at present.**

״הָיְתָה אִשְׁתּוֹ מְעוּבֶּרֶת וְאָמַר יְהִי רָצוֹן שֶׁתֵּלֵד כו׳ הֲרֵי זוֹ תְּפִלַּת שָׁוְא״.

We learned in the mishna: **One whose wife was pregnant and he said May it be** God's **will that** my wife **will give birth** to a male child, **it is a vain prayer.**[H]

וְלָא מְהַנֵּי רַחֲמֵי?! מְתִיב רַב יוֹסֵף: ״וְאַחַר יָלְדָה בַּת וַתִּקְרָא אֶת שְׁמָהּ דִּינָה״. מַאי ״וְאַחַר״? אָמַר רַב: לְאַחַר שֶׁדָּנָה לֵאָה דִּין בְּעַצְמָהּ וְאָמְרָה: שְׁנֵים עָשָׂר שְׁבָטִים עֲתִידִין לָצֵאת מִיַּעֲקֹב, שִׁשָּׁה יָצְאוּ מִמֶּנִּי, וְאַרְבָּעָה מִן הַשְּׁפָחוֹת – הֲרֵי עֲשָׂרָה, אִם זֶה זָכָר – לֹא תְּהֵא אֲחוֹתִי רָחֵל כְּאַחַת הַשְּׁפָחוֹת! מִיָּד נֶהֶפְכָה לְבַת, שֶׁנֶּאֱמַר: ״וַתִּקְרָא אֶת שְׁמָהּ דִּינָה״! – אֵין מַזְכִּירִין מַעֲשֵׂה נִסִּים.

**Is a prayer** in that case **ineffective? Rav Yosef raises an objection** based on a *baraita*: It is stated: **"And afterwards she bore a daughter, and called her name Dina"** (Genesis 30:21). The Gemara asks: **What is** meant by the addition of the word: **Afterwards?** What does the verse seek to convey by emphasizing that after the birth of Zebulun she gave birth to Dina? **Rav said: After Leah passed judgment on herself and said: Twelve tribes are destined to descend from Jacob, six came from me and four from the maidservants, that is ten,** and **if this** fetus **is male, my sister** Rachel **will not** even **be** the equivalent **of one the maidservants; immediately** the fetus **was transformed into a daughter, as it is stated: And she called her name Dina;** meaning she named her after her judgment [*din*]. The Gemara rejects this: **One does not mention miraculous acts**[N] to teach general *halakha*.

וְאִיבָּעֵית אֵימָא: מַעֲשֵׂה דְּלֵאָה – בְּתוֹךְ אַרְבָּעִים יוֹם הֲוָה. כְּדְתַנְיָא: שְׁלֹשָׁה יָמִים הָרִאשׁוֹנִים – יְבַקֵּשׁ אָדָם רַחֲמִים שֶׁלֹּא יַסְרִיחַ, מִשְּׁלֹשָׁה וְעַד אַרְבָּעִים – יְבַקֵּשׁ רַחֲמִים שֶׁיְּהֵא זָכָר, מֵאַרְבָּעִים יוֹם וְעַד שְׁלֹשָׁה חֳדָשִׁים – יְבַקֵּשׁ רַחֲמִים שֶׁלֹּא יְהֵא סַנְדָּל, מִשְּׁלֹשָׁה חֳדָשִׁים וְעַד שִׁשָּׁה – יְבַקֵּשׁ רַחֲמִים שֶׁלֹּא יְהֵא נֵפֶל, מִשִּׁשָּׁה וְעַד תִּשְׁעָה – יְבַקֵּשׁ רַחֲמִים שֶׁיֵּצֵא בְּשָׁלוֹם.

The Gemara introduces an alternative explanation: **And if you wish, say** instead that the **story of Leah** and her prayer with regard to the fetus **was within forty days** of conception. **As it was taught** in a *baraita*: During **the first three days** after intercourse, **one should pray that** the seed **not putrefy,** that it will fertilize the egg and develop into a fetus. **From the third** day **until the fortieth, one should pray that it will be male. From the fortieth** day **until three months, one should pray that it will not be** deformed, in the shape of a **flat fish,** as when the fetus does not develop it assumes a shape somewhat similar to a flat sandal fish. **From the third month until the sixth, one should pray that it will not be stillborn.** And **from the sixth** month **until the ninth, one should pray that it will be emerge safely.** Therefore, during the first forty days from conception, one may still pray to affect the gender of the fetus.

וּמִי מְהַנֵּי רַחֲמֵי? וְהָאָמַר רַב יִצְחָק בְּרֵיהּ דְּרַב אַמֵּי: אִישׁ מַזְרִיעַ תְּחִלָּה – יוֹלֶדֶת נְקֵבָה, אִשָּׁה מַזְרַעַת תְּחִלָּה – יוֹלֶדֶת זָכָר, שֶׁנֶּאֱמַר: ״אִשָּׁה כִּי תַזְרִיעַ וְיָלְדָה זָכָר״! – הָכָא בְּמַאי עָסְקִינַן – כְּגוֹן שֶׁהִזְרִיעוּ שְׁנֵיהֶם בְּבַת אַחַת.

The Gemara asks: **Is prayer effective** for that purpose? **Didn't Rav Yitzḥak son of Rav Ami, say:** The tradition teaches that the gender of the fetus is determined at the moment of conception. If the **man emits seed first,** his wife **gives birth to a female;** if the **woman emits seed first, she gives birth to a male, as it is stated: "When a woman emitted seed and bore a male"** (Leviticus 12:2). The Gemara answers: **With what are we dealing here?** We are dealing **with a case where they both emit seed simultaneously.** In that case, the gender is undetermined and prayer may be effectual.

"הָיָה בָא בַדֶּרֶךְ".

We learned in the mishna: **One who was walking along the way** and heard a scream from the city, and says: May it be God's will that this scream will not be from my house, it is a vain prayer.

תָּנוּ רַבָּנַן, מַעֲשֶׂה בְּהִלֵּל הַזָּקֵן שֶׁהָיָה בָא בַדֶּרֶךְ וְשָׁמַע קוֹל צְוָחָה בָּעִיר, אָמַר: מוּבְטָח אֲנִי שֶׁאֵין זֶה בְּתוֹךְ בֵּיתִי. וְעָלָיו הַכָּתוּב אוֹמֵר: "מִשְּׁמוּעָה רָעָה לֹא יִירָא נָכוֹן לִבּוֹ בָּטֻחַ בַּה'". אָמַר רָבָא: כָּל הֵיכִי דְּדָרְשַׁתְּ לְהַאי קְרָא, מֵרֵישֵׁיהּ לְסֵיפֵיהּ – מִדְּרִישׁ, מִסֵּיפֵיהּ לְרֵישֵׁיהּ – מִדְּרִישׁ. מֵרֵישֵׁיהּ לְסֵיפֵיהּ מִדְּרִישׁ: "מִשְּׁמוּעָה רָעָה לֹא יִירָא", מָה טַעַם "נָכוֹן לִבּוֹ בָּטֻחַ בַּה'". מִסֵּיפֵיהּ לְרֵישֵׁיהּ מִדְּרִישׁ: "נָכוֹן לִבּוֹ בָּטֻחַ בַּה'" – "מִשְּׁמוּעָה רָעָה לֹא יִירָא".

**The Sages taught: There was an incident involving Hillel the Elder, who was coming on the road when he heard a scream in the city. He said: I am certain that** the scream **is not** coming **from my house. And of him, the verse says: "He shall not be afraid of evil tidings; his heart is steadfast, trusting in the Lord"** (Psalms 112:7). **Rava said: Any way that you interpret this verse,** its meaning is clear. **It** can be **interpreted from beginning to end**[N] or **it** can be **interpreted from end to beginning.** The Gemara explains: **It** can be **interpreted from beginning to end: Why is** it that: **He shall not be afraid of evil tidings?** Because **his heart is steadfast, trusting in the Lord.** The Gemara continues: **And it** can be **interpreted from end to beginning:** One whose **heart is steadfast, trusting in the Lord** is a person who **shall not be afraid of evil tidings.**

הַהוּא תַּלְמִידָא דַּהֲוָה קָא אָזֵיל בָּתְרֵיהּ דְּרַבִּי יִשְׁמָעֵאל בְּרַבִּי יוֹסֵי בְּשׁוּקָא דְּצִיּוֹן. חַזְיֵיהּ דְּקָא מְפַחֵיד, אֲמַר לֵיהּ: חַטָּאָה אַתְּ, דִּכְתִיב: "פָּחֲדוּ בְצִיּוֹן חַטָּאִים". אֲמַר לֵיהּ: וְהָכְתִיב "אַשְׁרֵי אָדָם מְפַחֵד תָּמִיד"! – אֲמַר לֵיהּ: הַהוּא בְּדִבְרֵי תוֹרָה כְּתִיב.

The Gemara relates: **This student was once walking after Rabbi Yishmael, son of Rabbi Yosei, in the marketplace of Zion.** Rabbi Yishmael **saw that** the student **was afraid. He said to him: You are a sinner, as it is written: "The transgressors in Zion are afraid,** trembling has seized the ungodly" (Isaiah 33:14). The student **replied: And is it not written: "Happy is the man that fears always"** (Proverbs 28:14)? Rabbi Yishmael **said to him: That** verse **is written with regard to matters of Torah,** that one should be afraid lest he forget them. For everything else, one must trust in God.

יְהוּדָה בַּר נָתָן הֲוָה שָׁקֵיל וְאָזֵיל בָּתְרֵיהּ דְּרַב הַמְנוּנָא, אִתְנַח. אֲמַר לֵיהּ: יִסּוּרִים בָּעֵי הַהוּא גַּבְרָא לְאֵתוּיֵי אַנַּפְשֵׁיהּ?! דִּכְתִיב "כִּי פַחַד פָּחַדְתִּי וַיֶּאֱתָיֵנִי וַאֲשֶׁר יָגֹרְתִּי יָבֹא לִי". – וְהָא כְּתִיב: "אַשְׁרֵי אָדָם מְפַחֵד תָּמִיד"! – הַהוּא בְּדִבְרֵי תוֹרָה כְּתִיב.

In a similar vein, the Gemara relates: **Yehuda bar Natan was coming and going after Rav Hamnuna.**[P] Yehuda bar Natan **sighed;** Rav Hamnuna **said to him: Do you wish to bring suffering upon yourself; as it is stated: "For that which I did fear is come upon me, and that which I was afraid of has overtaken me"** (Job 3:25)? He responded: **Is it not said: "Happy is the man who fears always"?** Rav Hamnuna answered: **That** verse **is written with regard to matters of Torah.**

"הַנִּכְנָס לִכְרַךְ".

**We learned** in the mishna: **One who enters a large city**[H] recites two prayers; Ben Azzai says he recites four prayers.

תָּנוּ רַבָּנַן, בִּכְנִיסָתוֹ מַהוּ אוֹמֵר: "יְהִי רָצוֹן מִלְּפָנֶיךָ ה' אֱלֹהַי שֶׁתַּכְנִיסֵנִי לִכְרַךְ זֶה לְשָׁלוֹם". נִכְנַס, אוֹמֵר: "מוֹדֶה אֲנִי לְפָנֶיךָ ה' אֱלֹהַי שֶׁהִכְנַסְתַּנִי לִכְרַךְ זֶה לְשָׁלוֹם". בִּקֵּשׁ לָצֵאת, אוֹמֵר: "יְהִי רָצוֹן מִלְּפָנֶיךָ ה' אֱלֹהַי וֵאלֹהֵי אֲבוֹתַי שֶׁתּוֹצִיאֵנִי מִכְּרַךְ זֶה לְשָׁלוֹם". יָצָא, אוֹמֵר: "מוֹדֶה אֲנִי לְפָנֶיךָ ה' אֱלֹהַי שֶׁהוֹצֵאתַנִי מִכְּרַךְ זֶה לְשָׁלוֹם, וּכְשֵׁם שֶׁהוֹצֵאתַנִי לְשָׁלוֹם כָּךְ תּוֹלִיכֵנִי לְשָׁלוֹם, וְתִסְמְכֵנִי לְשָׁלוֹם, וְתַצְעִידֵנִי לְשָׁלוֹם, וְתַצִּילֵנִי מִכַּף כָּל אוֹיֵב וְאוֹרֵב בַּדֶּרֶךְ".

**The Sages taught** the details of Ben Azzai's teaching in a *baraita*: **Upon his entrance** to the city **what does he recite?**

**May it be Your will, O Lord my God, that You bring me into this city to peace.**

After **he entered** the city, **he recites: I thank You, O Lord my God, that You brought me into this city to peace.**

When he **seeks to leave** the city, **he recites: May it be Your will, O Lord my God and God of my ancestors, that You take me out of this city to peace.**

After **he left, he recites: I give thanks before You, O Lord my God, that You took me out of this city to peace;**

**and just as You took me out to peace,**

**so too lead me to peace, support me to peace, direct my steps to peace,**

**and rescue me from the hand of any enemy or** those **lying in ambush along the way.**

אָמַר רַב מַתָּנָא: לֹא שָׁנוּ אֶלָּא בִּכְרַךְ שֶׁאֵין דָּנִין וְהוֹרְגִין בּוֹ, אֲבָל בִּכְרַךְ שֶׁדָּנִין וְהוֹרְגִין בּוֹ – לֵית לַן בַּהּ.

**Rav Mattana said: This was taught only with regard to a city where** criminals **are not tried and executed,** as in a place like that he may be killed without trial. **However, in a city where** criminals **are tried and executed,** these prayers **do not apply,** as if one is not guilty he will not be harmed.

אִיכָּא דְּאָמְרִי, אָמַר רַב מַתָּנָא: אֲפִילּוּ בִּכְרַךְ שֶׁדָּנִין וְהוֹרְגִין בּוֹ, זִימְנִין דְּלָא מִתְרְמֵי לֵיהּ אִינִישׁ דְּיָלֵיף לֵיהּ זְכוּתָא.

**Some say** that **Rav Mattana said** the opposite: **Even in a city where** criminals **are tried and executed** one must pray for mercy, **as sometimes he may not encounter a person who will plead in his favor.**

NOTES

**From beginning to end – מֵרֵישֵׁיהּ לְסֵיפֵיהּ:** According to Rashi, there is no significant difference in the interpretation of the verse whether it is interpreted from beginning to end or from end to beginning. Therefore, many ask why Rava found it necessary to make this point. One suggestion is that when read from beginning to end, the verse is interpreted as a promise; one will need not fear evil tidings if his heart relies on God. Read from the end to the beginning, the verse is interpreted as a statement of fact, as in the case of Hillel; one who relies on God does not fear bad tidings (Ra'avad, Rashba).

PERSONALITIES

**Rav Hamnuna – רַב הַמְנוּנָא:** Rav Hamnuna was a second generation Babylonian *amora* and a student of Rav. There was another *amora* named Rav Hamnuna in the following generation who was also associated with Rav, although he was primarily a student of Rav Ḥisda. This Rav Hamnuna was one of the students of Rav who stayed in his study hall and perpetuated the tradition of the school of Rav and the Elders of the School of Rav. Although he was affiliated with Rav Huna and accepted his halakhic authority, Rav Hamnuna was the head of a yeshiva in his own right and taught many of the outstanding Sages of the next generation, among them Rabbi Zeira and Rav Yosef.

HALAKHA

**One who enters a large city – הַנִּכְנָס לִכְרַךְ:** Before entering a city whose rulers falsely accuse people of crimes, one should recite: May it be Your will, O Lord my God, that You bring me into this city to peace. Having entered the city, he recites: I thank You, O Lord my God that You brought me into this city to peace. Upon leaving the city in peace, one recites: I give thanks before You, O Lord my God, that You took me out of this city to peace; and just as You took me out to peace, so too lead me to peace, etc. (Rambam *Sefer Ahava, Hilkhot Berakhot* 10:25; *Shulḥan Arukh, Oraḥ Ḥayyim* 230:1).

## BACKGROUND

**Bathhouse** – מֶרְחָץ: The collapse of one of the bathhouse walls was liable to cause boiling water or extremely hot air to be released, endangering the lives of those in the bathhouse.

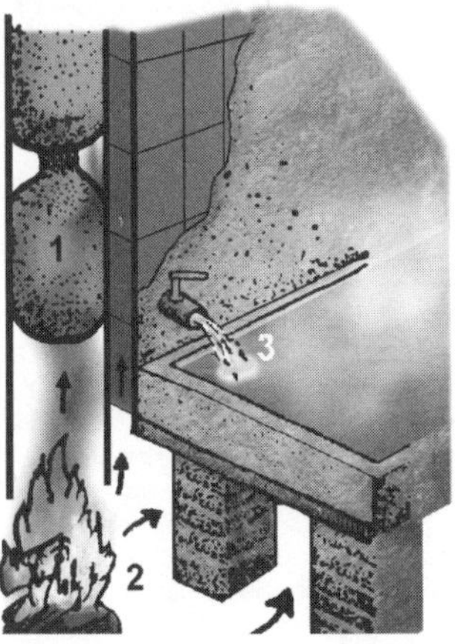


Sketch of a Roman bathhouse from the time of the Mishna. The bathhouse consisted of several component parts:

1. Water tanks. Boiling water was in the lower tank while cold water could be added to the upper tank.
2. A fire from which hot air would pass through conduits in the floor and warm the room.
3. The bathing area.

Ruins of a Roman bathhouse

## NOTES

**From here we derive that permission is granted to a doctor to heal** – מִכָּאן שֶׁנִּיתְּנָה רְשׁוּת לָרוֹפֵא לְרַפְּאוֹת: In the time of the Mishna, heretical groups maintained that one is prohibited from interfering in matters that are in God's purview by engaging in healing. Some explained that a specific Torah source is necessary to permit one to heal illnesses that are not caused by man, as in so doing he acts contrary to God's will. Others explained that the emphasis of this verse is that doctors are permitted to heal and to accept payment for their services. One might have thought that since he is engaged in the mitzva of saving lives, he may not accept payment. The verse teaches that he may (*Tosefot Rabbeinu Yehuda HaḤasid; Tosefot HaRosh*).

תָּנוּ רַבָּנַן, הַנִּכְנָס לְבֵית הַמֶּרְחָץ, אוֹמֵר: ״יְהִי רָצוֹן מִלְּפָנֶיךָ ה׳ אֱלֹהַי שֶׁתַּצִּילֵנִי מִזֶּה וְכַיּוֹצֵא בּוֹ, וְאַל יֶאֱרַע בִּי דְּבַר קַלְקָלָה וְעָוֹן, וְאִם יֶאֱרַע בִּי דְּבַר קַלְקָלָה וְעָוֹן – תְּהֵא מִיתָתִי כַּפָּרָה לְכָל עֲוֹנוֹתַי״.

**The Sages taught: One who enters a** Roman **bathhouse,**[HB] where a fire burns beneath the pool of water used for bathing, and where there is the risk of collapse, **says:**

**May it be Your will, O Lord my God, that you save me from this and similar** matters,

**and do not let ruin or iniquity befall me,**

**and if ruin or iniquity does befall me, let my death be atonement for all of my transgressions.**

אֲמַר אַבַּיֵי: לָא לֵימָא אֱינָשׁ הָכִי, דְּלָא לִפְתַּח פּוּמֵיהּ לַשָּׂטָן; דַּאֲמַר רֵישׁ לָקִישׁ וְכֵן תָּנָא מִשְּׁמֵיהּ דְּרַב יוֹסֵי: לְעוֹלָם אַל יִפְתַּח אָדָם פִּיו לַשָּׂטָן.

**Abaye said: One should not say:** If ruin befalls me, **so as not to open his mouth to Satan** and provoke him. **As Rabbi Shimon ben Lakish said and as it was taught** in a *baraita* **in the name of Rabbi Yosei: One should never open his mouth to Satan** by raising, at his own initiative, the possibility of mishap or death.

אֲמַר רַב יוֹסֵף: מַאי קְרָאָה – דִּכְתִיב ״כִּמְעַט כִּסְדֹם הָיִינוּ לַעֲמֹרָה דָּמִינוּ״ מַאי אַהְדַּר לְהוּ נָבִיא – ״שִׁמְעוּ דְבַר ה׳ קְצִינֵי סְדֹם״ וגו׳.

**Rav Yosef said: What is the verse** that alludes to this? **As it is written: "We should have almost been as Sodom, we should have been like unto Gomorrah"** (Isaiah 1:9), after which **what did** the prophet **reply to them? "Hear the word of the Lord, rulers of Sodom;** give ear unto the law of our God, people of Gomorrah" (Isaiah 1:10). After the analogy to Sodom was raised, it was realized.

כִּי נָפֵיק מַאי אוֹמֵר? אָמַר רַב אַחָא: ״מוֹדֶה אֲנִי לְפָנֶיךָ ה׳ שֶׁהִצַּלְתַּנִי מִן הָאוּר״.

Returning to the subject of the Roman bathhouse, the Gemara asks: **When he emerges** from the bathhouse, **what does he say? Rav Aḥa said: I give thanks to You, Lord, that You saved me from the fire.**

רַבִּי אַבָּהוּ עַל לְבֵי בָנֵי, אִפְּחִית בֵּי בָנֵי מִתּוּתֵיהּ, אִתְרְחִישׁ לֵיהּ נִיסָּא קָם עַל עַמּוּדָא שְׁזֵיב מְאָה וְחַד גַּבְרֵי בְּחַד אֶבְרֵיהּ, אֲמַר: הַיְינוּ דְּרַב אַחָא.

The Gemara relates: **Rabbi Abbahu entered a bathhouse when the bathhouse** floor **collapsed beneath him and a miracle transpired on his behalf. He stood on a pillar and saved one hundred and one men with one arm.** He held one or two people in his arm, with others holding on them and so on, so that all were saved. **He said: This is** confirmation of the statement **of Rav Aḥa,** who said that one should offer thanks upon leaving the bathhouse safely.

דַּאֲמַר רַב אַחָא: הַנִּכְנָס לְהַקִּיז דָּם אוֹמֵר: ״יְהִי רָצוֹן מִלְּפָנֶיךָ ה׳ אֱלֹהַי שֶׁיְּהֵא עֵסֶק זֶה לִי לִרְפוּאָה וּתְרַפְּאֵנִי, כִּי אֵל רוֹפֵא נֶאֱמָן אַתָּה וּרְפוּאָתְךָ אֱמֶת, לְפִי שֶׁאֵין דַּרְכָּן שֶׁל בְּנֵי אָדָם לְרַפְּאוֹת אֶלָּא שֶׁנָּהֲגוּ״.

**As Rav Aḥa said: One who enters to let blood**[H] **says:**

**May it be Your will, O Lord my God,**

**that this enterprise be for healing and that You should heal me.**

**As You are a faithful God of healing and Your healing is truth.**

**Because it is not the way of people to heal, but they have become accustomed.**

Rav Aḥa is saying that people should not practice medicine as they lack the ability to heal; rather, healing should be left to God.

אֲמַר אַבַּיֵי: לָא לֵימָא אֱינָשׁ הָכִי, דְּתָנֵי דְּבֵי רַבִּי יִשְׁמָעֵאל: ״וְרַפֹּא יְרַפֵּא״ – מִכָּאן שֶׁנִּיתְּנָה רְשׁוּת לָרוֹפֵא לְרַפְּאוֹת.

**Abaye** responded and **said: One should not say this,** as it was **taught** in **the school of Rabbi Yishmael** that from the verse, **"And shall cause him to be thoroughly healed"** (Exodus 21:19), **from here** we derive **that permission is granted to a doctor to heal.**[NH] The practice of medicine is in accordance with the will of God.

כִּי קָאֵי מַאי אוֹמֵר? – אָמַר רַב אַחָא: ״בָּרוּךְ רוֹפֵא חִנָּם״.

As for bloodletting, the Gemara asks: **When one stands** after having let blood, **what does he say? Rav Aḥa said:** He recites in gratitude: **Blessed…Who heals without payment.**

## HALAKHA

**One who enters a bathhouse** – הַנִּכְנָס לְבֵית הַמֶּרְחָץ: In the time of the Gemara, one who entered a bathhouse, which was heated from below, recited upon entering: May it be Your will, O Lord my God, that You bring me in peace, and take me out in peace, and save me from this and similar fires at the end of days. Having left in peace, one would recite: I thank You, O Lord my God, that You saved me from this fire. Nowadays these prayers are not recited, as bathhouses are not particularly dangerous (*Magen Avraham; Taz*; Rambam *Sefer Ahava, Hilkhot Berakhot* 10:20; *Shulḥan Arukh, Oraḥ Ḥayyim* 230:3).

**One who enters to let blood** – הַנִּכְנָס לְהַקִּיז דָּם: One who enters to let blood or receive any medical treatment (*Magen Avraham*) recites upon entering: May it be Your will, O Lord my God, that this enterprise heal me, as You heal without payment. After treatment one recites: Blessed…Who heals the sick. Some say that this blessing should be recited with the invocation of God's name and His Sovereignty (*Beit Yosef; Taz*). Others say that this is not the prevalent custom (*Peri Megadim*). Yet others say that one invokes God's name and His Sovereignty only in the case of a particularly dangerous procedure (*Be'er Hetev*; Rambam *Sefer Ahava, Hilkhot Berakhot* 10:21; *Shulḥan Arukh, Oraḥ Ḥayyim* 230:4).

**From here we derive that permission is granted to a doctor to heal** – מִכָּאן שֶׁנִּיתְּנָה רְשׁוּת לָרוֹפֵא לְרַפְּאוֹת: Permission is granted to a doctor to heal, and it is a mitzva to do so. One who refrains from healing, even if there is another doctor available, is a murderer (*Shulḥan Arukh, Yoreh De'a* 336:1).

הַנִּכְנָס לְבֵית הַכִּסֵּא אוֹמֵר: ״הִתְכַּבְּדוּ מְכוּבָּדִים קְדוֹשִׁים מְשָׁרְתֵי עֶלְיוֹן, תְּנוּ כָבוֹד לֵאלֹהֵי יִשְׂרָאֵל, הַרְפּוּ מִמֶּנִּי עַד שֶׁאֶכָּנֵס וְאֶעֱשֶׂה רְצוֹנִי וְאָבֹא אֲלֵיכֶם״. אָמַר אַבַּיֵּי: לָא לֵימָא אִינִישׁ הָכִי, דִּלְמָא שָׁבְקִי לֵיהּ וְאָזְלִי. אֶלָּא לֵימָא: ״שִׁמְרוּנִי שִׁמְרוּנִי, עִזְרוּנִי עִזְרוּנִי, סַמְּכוּנִי סַמְּכוּנִי, הַמְתִּינוּ לִי הַמְתִּינוּ לִי, עַד שֶׁאֶכָּנֵס וְאֵצֵא, שֶׁכֵּן דַּרְכָּן שֶׁל בְּנֵי אָדָם״. כִּי נָפֵיק אוֹמֵר: ״בָּרוּךְ אֲשֶׁר יָצַר אֶת הָאָדָם בְּחָכְמָה, וּבָרָא בוֹ נְקָבִים נְקָבִים חֲלוּלִים חֲלוּלִים גָּלוּי וְיָדוּעַ לִפְנֵי כִסֵּא כְבוֹדֶךָ שֶׁאִם יִפָּתֵחַ אֶחָד מֵהֶם אוֹ אִם יִסָּתֵם אֶחָד מֵהֶם אִי אֶפְשָׁר לַעֲמוֹד לְפָנֶיךָ״.

**One who enters a bathroom**[H] **says** to the angels who accompany him at all times:
**Be honored, honorable holy ones, servants of** the One **on High, give honor to the God of Israel,**
**leave me until I enter and do my will and come** back **to you.**
**Abaye said: A person should not say this, lest they abandon him and go. Rather he should say:**
**Guard me, guard me,**
**help me, help me,**
**support me, support me,**
**wait for me, wait for me until I enter and come out, as this is the way of man.**
**Upon exiting, one says:**
**Blessed...Who formed man in wisdom,**
**and created in him many orifices and cavities.**
**It is revealed and known before the throne of Your glory**
**that were one of them to be ruptured or blocked, it would be impossible to survive and stand before You.**

מַאי חָתֵים? – אָמַר רַב: ״רוֹפֵא חוֹלִים״. אָמַר שְׁמוּאֵל: קָא שַׁוְינְהוּ אַבָּא לְכוּלֵּי עָלְמָא קְצִירֵי! אֶלָּא: ״רוֹפֵא כׇל בָּשָׂר״. רַב שֵׁשֶׁת אָמַר: ״מַפְלִיא לַעֲשׂוֹת״. אָמַר רַב פָּפָּא: הִלְכָּךְ נִמְרִינְהוּ לְתַרְוַיְיהוּ ״רוֹפֵא כׇל בָּשָׂר וּמַפְלִיא לַעֲשׂוֹת״.

The Gemara asks: With **what** should one **conclude** this blessing? **Rav said:** One should conclude: Blessed... **Healer of the sick. Shmuel said: Abba,** Rav, **has rendered everyone sick. Rather,** one should say: **Healer of all flesh. Rav Sheshet said:** One should conclude: **Who performs wondrous deeds. Rav Pappa said: Therefore, let us say them both: Healer of all flesh, Who performs wondrous deeds.**[H]

הַנִּכְנָס לִישַׁן עַל מִטָּתוֹ אוֹמֵר מִ״שְּׁמַע יִשְׂרָאֵל״ עַד ״וְהָיָה אִם שָׁמוֹעַ״. וְאוֹמֵר: ״בָּרוּךְ הַמַּפִּיל חֶבְלֵי שֵׁינָה עַל עֵינַי וּתְנוּמָה עַל עַפְעַפַּי וּמֵאִיר לְאִישׁוֹן בַּת עַיִן. יְהִי רָצוֹן מִלְּפָנֶיךָ ה׳ אֱלֹהַי שֶׁתַּשְׁכִּיבֵנִי לְשָׁלוֹם וְתֵן חֶלְקִי בְּתוֹרָתֶךָ, וְתַרְגִּילֵנִי לִידֵי מִצְוָה, וְאַל תַּרְגִּילֵנִי לִידֵי עֲבֵירָה, וְאַל תְּבִיאֵנִי לִידֵי חֵטְא, וְלֹא לִידֵי עָוֹן, וְלֹא לִידֵי נִסָּיוֹן, וְלֹא לִידֵי בִזָּיוֹן, וְיִשְׁלוֹט בִּי יֵצֶר טוֹב וְאַל יִשְׁלוֹט בִּי יֵצֶר הָרָע, וְתַצִּילֵנִי מִפֶּגַע רָע וּמֵחֳלָאִים רָעִים, וְאַל יְבַהֲלוּנִי חֲלוֹמוֹת רָעִים וְהִרְהוּרִים רָעִים, וּתְהֵא מִטָּתִי שְׁלֵמָה לְפָנֶיךָ, וְהָאֵר עֵינַי פֶּן אִישַׁן הַמָּוֶת, בָּרוּךְ אַתָּה ה׳ הַמֵּאִיר לָעוֹלָם כּוּלּוֹ בִּכְבוֹדוֹ״.

The Gemara proceeds to cite additional blessings recited as part of one's daily routine. **One who enters to sleep on his bed**[H] **recites** *Shema* in his bed **from** ***Shema Yisrael*** **to** ***VeHaya Im Shamoa.*** **Then he recites:**
**Blessed...Who makes the bands of sleep fall upon my eyes and slumber upon my eyelids,**
**and illuminates the pupil of the eye.**
**May it be Your will, O Lord my God,**
**that You make me lie down in peace and give me my portion in Your Torah,**
**accustom me to mitzvot and do not accustom me to transgression,**
**lead me not into error, nor into iniquity, nor into temptation nor into disgrace.**
**May the good inclination have dominion over me**
**and may the evil inclination not have dominion over me.**
**Save me from an evil mishap and evil diseases.**
**Let neither bad dreams nor troubling thoughts disturb me.**
**May my bed be flawless before You,** that my progeny should not be flawed.
**Enlighten my eyes** in the morning **lest I sleep** the sleep of **death,** never to awaken.
**Blessed are You, O Lord, Who gives light to the whole world in His glory.**

כִּי מִתְּעַר אוֹמֵר: ״אֱלֹהַי, נְשָׁמָה שֶׁנָּתַתָּ בִּי טְהוֹרָה, אַתָּה יְצַרְתָּהּ בִּי, אַתָּה נְפַחְתָּהּ בִּי, וְאַתָּה מְשַׁמְּרָהּ בְּקִרְבִּי, וְאַתָּה עָתִיד לִיטְּלָהּ מִמֶּנִּי וּלְהַחֲזִירָהּ בִּי לֶעָתִיד לָבֹא. כׇּל זְמַן שֶׁהַנְּשָׁמָה בְּקִרְבִּי מוֹדֶה אֲנִי לְפָנֶיךָ ה׳ אֱלֹהַי וֵאלֹהֵי אֲבוֹתַי, רִבּוֹן כׇּל הָעוֹלָמִים אֲדוֹן כׇּל הַנְּשָׁמוֹת, בָּרוּךְ אַתָּה ה׳ הַמַּחֲזִיר נְשָׁמוֹת לִפְגָרִים מֵתִים״.

**When one awakens, he recites:**
**My God, the soul**[H] **You have placed within me is pure.**
**You formed it within me,**
**You breathed it into me,**
**and You guard it while it is within me.**
**One day You will take it from me and restore it within me in the time to come.**
**As long as the soul is within me, I thank You,**
**O Lord my God and God of my ancestors, Master of all worlds, Lord of all souls.**
**Blessed are You, O Lord, who restores souls to lifeless bodies.**

**HALAKHA**

**One who enters a bathroom – הַנִּכְנָס לְבֵית הַכִּסֵּא:** Though no longer customary (*Beit Yosef*), in previous generations one would recite: Be honored, honorable holy ones... guard me. Today, we do not consider ourselves so righteous that angels would accompany us (*Taz*; Rambam *Sefer Ahava, Hilkhot Tefilla* 7:5; *Shulḥan Arukh, Oraḥ Ḥayyim* 3:1).

**Therefore, let us say them both: Healer of all flesh, Who performs wondrous deeds – הִלְכָּךְ נִמְרִינְהוּ לְתַרְוַיְיהוּ רוֹפֵא כׇל בָּשָׂר וּמַפְלִיא לַעֲשׂוֹת:** The blessing concludes: Healer of all flesh, Who performs wondrous deeds, in accordance with the opinion of Rav Pappa (Rambam *Sefer Ahava, Hilkhot Tefilla* 7:5; *Shulḥan Arukh, Oraḥ Ḥayyim* 6:1).

**One who enters to sleep on his bed – הַנִּכְנָס לִישַׁן עַל מִטָּתוֹ:** When one goes to sleep, he should recite at least the first section of *Shema*, though the custom is to recite all three sections (*Magen Avraham*) along with the blessing: Who makes the bands of sleep...(Rambam *Sefer Ahava, Hilkhot Tefilla* 7:1–2; *Shulḥan Arukh, Oraḥ Ḥayyim* 239:1).

**When one awakens, he recites: My God, the soul, etc. – כִּי מִתְּעַר אוֹמֵר: ״אֱלֹהַי נְשָׁמָה וכו׳״:** When one awakens from sleep, he recites: My God, the soul, etc. (Rambam *Sefer Ahava, Hilkhot Tefilla* 7:3; *Shulḥan Arukh, Oraḥ Ḥayyim* 46:1).

כִּי שָׁמַע קוֹל תַּרְנְגוֹלָא לֵימָא: "בָּרוּךְ אֲשֶׁר נָתַן לַשֶּׂכְוִי בִינָה לְהַבְחִין בֵּין יוֹם וּבֵין לַיְלָה". כִּי פָּתַח עֵינֵיהּ לֵימָא: "בָּרוּךְ פּוֹקֵחַ עִוְרִים". כִּי תָּרֵיץ וְיָתֵיב לֵימָא: "בָּרוּךְ מַתִּיר אֲסוּרִים". כִּי לָבֵישׁ לֵימָא: "בָּרוּךְ מַלְבִּישׁ עֲרוּמִּים". כִּי זָקֵיף לֵימָא: "בָּרוּךְ זוֹקֵף כְּפוּפִים". כִּי נָחֵית לְאַרְעָא לֵימָא: "בָּרוּךְ רוֹקַע הָאָרֶץ עַל הַמָּיִם". כִּי מַסְגֵּי לֵימָא: "בָּרוּךְ הַמֵּכִין מִצְעֲדֵי גָבֶר". כִּי סַיֵּים מְסָאנֵיהּ לֵימָא: "בָּרוּךְ שֶׁעָשָׂה לִי כָּל צְרָכַי". כִּי אָסַר הֶמְיָינֵיהּ לֵימָא: "בָּרוּךְ אוֹזֵר יִשְׂרָאֵל בִּגְבוּרָה". כִּי פָּרֵיס סוּדָרָא עַל רֵישֵׁיהּ לֵימָא: "בָּרוּךְ עוֹטֵר יִשְׂרָאֵל בְּתִפְאָרָה".

**Upon hearing the sound of the rooster, one should recite: Blessed…Who gave the heart [*sekhvi*] understanding**[N] **to distinguish between day and night.**

**Upon opening his eyes, one should recite: Blessed…Who gives sight to the blind.**

**Upon sitting up straight, one should recite: Blessed…Who sets captives free.**

**Upon dressing, one should recite: Blessed…Who clothes the naked,** as they would sleep unclothed.

**Upon standing up straight, one should recite: Blessed…Who raises those bowed down.**

**Upon descending** from one's bed **to the ground, one should recite: Blessed… Who spreads the earth above the waters,** in thanksgiving for the creation of solid ground upon which to walk.

**Upon walking, one should recite: Blessed…Who makes firm the steps of man.**

**Upon putting on his shoes, one should recite: Blessed…Who has provided me with all I need,** as shoes are a basic necessity.

**Upon putting on his belt, one should recite: Blessed…Who girds Israel with strength.**

**Upon spreading a shawl upon his head, one should recite: Blessed…Who crowns Israel with glory.**[H]

כִּי מִעַטַּף בְּצִיצִית לֵימָא: "בָּרוּךְ אֲשֶׁר קִדְּשָׁנוּ בְּמִצְוֹתָיו וְצִוָּנוּ לְהִתְעַטֵּף בַּצִּיצִית". כִּי מַנַּח תְּפִילִּין אַדְּרָעֵיהּ לֵימָא: "בָּרוּךְ אֲשֶׁר קִדְּשָׁנוּ בְּמִצְוֹתָיו וְצִוָּנוּ לְהָנִיחַ תְּפִילִּין". אַרֵישֵׁיהּ לֵימָא: "בָּרוּךְ אֲשֶׁר קִדְּשָׁנוּ בְּמִצְוֹתָיו וְצִוָּנוּ עַל מִצְוַת תְּפִילִּין". כִּי מָשֵׁי יְדֵיהּ לֵימָא: "בָּרוּךְ אֲשֶׁר קִדְּשָׁנוּ בְּמִצְוֹתָיו וְצִוָּנוּ עַל נְטִילַת יָדַיִם". כִּי מָשֵׁי אַפֵּיהּ לֵימָא: בָּרוּךְ הַמַּעֲבִיר חֶבְלֵי שֵׁינָה מֵעֵינַי וּתְנוּמָה מֵעַפְעַפַּי, וִיהִי רָצוֹן מִלְּפָנֶיךָ ה׳ אֱלֹהַי שֶׁתַּרְגִּילֵנִי בְּתוֹרָתֶךָ וְדַבְּקֵנִי בְּמִצְוֹתֶיךָ, וְאַל תְּבִיאֵנִי לֹא לִידֵי חֵטְא וְלֹא לִידֵי עָוֹן וְלֹא לִידֵי נִסָּיוֹן וְלֹא לִידֵי בִזָּיוֹן, וְכוֹף אֶת יִצְרִי לְהִשְׁתַּעְבֵּד לָךְ, וְרַחֲקֵנִי מֵאָדָם רַע וּמֵחָבֵר רַע, וְדַבְּקֵנִי בְּיֵצֶר טוֹב וּבְחָבֵר טוֹב בְּעוֹלָמְךָ, וּתְנֵנִי הַיּוֹם וּבְכָל יוֹם לְחֵן וּלְחֶסֶד וּלְרַחֲמִים בְּעֵינֶיךָ וּבְעֵינֵי כָל רוֹאַי, וְתִגְמְלֵנִי חֲסָדִים טוֹבִים, בָּרוּךְ אַתָּה ה׳ גּוֹמֵל חֲסָדִים טוֹבִים לְעַמּוֹ יִשְׂרָאֵל".

**Upon wrapping himself in ritual fringes,**[H] **one should recite: Blessed…Who has made us holy through His commandments and has commanded us to wrap ourselves in** a garment with **ritual fringes.**

**Upon donning his phylacteries**[H] **on his arm, one should recite: Blessed… Who has made us holy through His commandments and has commanded us to don phylacteries.**

Upon donning phylacteries **on his head one should recite: Blessed…Who has made us holy through His commandments and has commanded us with regard to the mitzva of phylacteries.**

**Upon** ritually **washing his hands: Blessed…Who has made us holy through His commandments and has commanded us with regard to the washing of the hands.**

**Upon washing his face, one recites: Blessed…Who removes the bands of sleep from my eyes and slumber from my eyelids.**

**And may it be Your will, O Lord my God, to accustom me in Your Torah,**
**attach me to Your mitzvot, and lead me not into transgression,**
**nor into error, nor into iniquity, nor into temptation nor into disgrace.**
**Bend my** evil **inclination to be subservient to You,**
**and distance me from an evil person and an evil acquaintance.**
**Help me attach myself to the good inclination and to a good friend in Your world.**
**Grant me, today and every day, grace, loving-kindness, and compassion in Your eyes and the eyes of all who see me,**
**and bestow loving-kindness upon me.**
**Blessed are You, O Lord, Who bestows loving-kindness on His people, Israel**

## NOTES

**Who gave the heart [*sekhvi*] understanding – אֲשֶׁר נָתַן לַשֶּׂכְוִי:** The primary meaning of *sekhvi* is heart, and the blessing refers to one's heart being imbued with understanding, as it appears in the verse: "Or who has given understanding to the heart [*sekhvi*]" (Job 38:36). In any case, because in certain places a rooster was called *sekhvi*, and because one rises and distinguishes between day and night with the cries of a rooster, the blessing was formulated in this manner (Rosh).

## HALAKHA

**Blessings of thanksgiving in the morning – בִּרְכוֹת הוֹדָאָה בַּשַּׁחַר:** Early in the morning, upon hearing the rooster crow, one recites: Who gave the heart understanding. Upon donning his outer garments (*Mishna Berura*), one recites: Who clothes the naked. While passing his hands over his eyes with a cloth (*Magen Avraham*), one recites: Who gives sight to the blind. Upon sitting, one recites: Who sets captives free. Upon standing up straight, one recites: Who raises those bowed down. Upon placing his feet upon the ground, one recites: Who spreads the earth above the waters. Upon putting on his shoes, one recites: Who has provided me with all I need. Upon walking, one recites: Who makes firm the steps of man. Others say to recite: Who made firm the footsteps of man (*HaAguda*) and that is the custom (*Magen Avraham*). Upon putting on his belt, one recites: Who girds Israel with strength. The *Beit Yosef* in the name of the Ra'avad says that one recites that blessing when he ties the sash separating his heart from his nakedness; the *Mishna Berura* says that he recites it when putting on his pants. Upon placing his hat or scarf upon his head, one recites: Who crowns Israel with glory. Upon washing his hands, one recites: Regarding the washing of the hands. Upon washing his face, he recites: Who removes the bands of sleep from my eyes, etc., and: May it be Your will…Blessed…Who bestows loving-kindness on His people, Israel. One does not answer amen after reciting: Who removes the bands of sleep from my eyes, until the conclusion of the blessing: Who bestows loving-kindness on His people, Israel, as it is all one blessing.

Nowadays, both because our hands are ritually unclean and because people are ignorant of the *halakhot*, the custom is to recite all of the blessings in the synagogue (Rambam *Sefer Ahava, Hilkhot Tefilla* 7:4; *Shulḥan Arukh, Oraḥ Ḥayyim* 46:1–2).

**Upon wrapping himself in ritual fringes – כִּי מִעַטַּף בְּצִיצִית:** When wrapping himself in a garment with ritual fringes, he recites: To wrap ourselves in ritual fringes. Authorities disagree regarding whether one recites: In ritual fringes [*betzitzit*] (*Levush*; *Mishna Berura*) or: In the ritual fringes [*batzitzit*] (*Baḥ*, *Be'er Hetev*, and *Maḥzik Berakha*; Rambam *Sefer Ahava, Hilkhot Tzitzit* 3:8; *Shulḥan Arukh, Oraḥ Ḥayyim* 8:5).

**Upon donning his phylacteries – כִּי מַנַּח תְּפִילִּין:** When one dons phylacteries, he first dons the phylacteries of the arm and then the phylacteries of the head. When placing the phylacteries upon his arm, before tightening the strap (*Mishna Berura*), one recites: To don phylacteries. Immediately thereafter, one begins to don the phylacteries of the head, with the one blessing recited over both. Only if he spoke, or delayed a significant amount of time (*Mishna Berura*), between donning the phylacteries of the arm and the head does one recite a separate blessing over the phylacteries of the head: Regarding the mitzva of phylacteries (Rif, Rambam, Rashi, Rashba, *Shulḥan Arukh HaRav*). Others maintain that one is always obligated to recite the second blessing, even if there was no interruption between the phylacteries of the arm and the phylacteries of the head (Rema); this is the Ashkenazic custom. Nevertheless, after the second blessing it is preferable to recite: Blessed be the name of God's glorious kingdom forever and ever, due to concern that the blessing may be in vain (*Mishna Berura*; Mahari ben Ḥaviv, *Agur*; Rambam *Sefer Ahava, Hilkhot Tefillin* 4:4; *Shulḥan Arukh, Oraḥ Ḥayyim* 25:5, 9, and in the comment of the Rema).

"חַיָּיב אָדָם לְבָרֵךְ" כו׳. מַאי "חַיָּיב לְבָרֵךְ עַל הָרָעָה כְּשֵׁם שֶׁמְּבָרֵךְ עַל הַטּוֹבָה"?! – אִילֵּימָא: כְּשֵׁם שֶׁמְּבָרֵךְ עַל הַטּוֹבָה "הַטּוֹב וְהַמֵּטִיב", כָּךְ מְבָרֵךְ עַל הָרָעָה "הַטּוֹב וְהַמֵּטִיב". – וְהָתְנַן: עַל בְּשׂוֹרוֹת טוֹבוֹת אוֹמֵר "הַטּוֹב וְהַמֵּטִיב", עַל בְּשׂוֹרוֹת רָעוֹת אוֹמֵר "בָּרוּךְ דַּיַּין הָאֱמֶת"! – אָמַר רָבָא: לֹא נִצְרְכָה אֶלָּא לְקַבּוֹלִינְהוּ בְּשִׂמְחָה.

We learned in the mishna: **One is obligated to recite a blessing** for the bad that befalls him just as he recites a blessing for the good that befalls him. The Gemara asks: **What** does it mean: **One is obligated to recite a blessing for the bad just as for the good?**[N] **If we say** this means that **just as one recites a blessing for a positive event** with the formula: **Who is good and does good, so too one recites a blessing for a calamity** with the formula: **Who is good and does good, didn't we learn** in our mishna that **over good tidings one recites: Who is good and does good,** while **over bad tidings one recites: Blessed...the true Judge?** Rather, **Rava said:** The mishna's statement **was only necessary** to instruct us **to accept** bad tidings **with** the same **joy**[H] with which we accept good tidings, not to instruct with regard to which blessing to recite.

אָמַר רַב אַחָא מִשּׁוּם רַבִּי לֵוִי: מַאי קְרָא – "חֶסֶד וּמִשְׁפָּט אָשִׁירָה לְךָ ה׳ אֲזַמֵּרָה", אִם חֶסֶד – אָשִׁירָה, וְאִם מִשְׁפָּט – אָשִׁירָה.

**Rav Aḥa said in the name of Rabbi Levi: What** is the **verse** that alludes to this? **"I will sing of loving-kindness and justice; unto You, O Lord, will I sing praises"** (Psalms 101:1). Rav Aḥa explains: **If** it is **loving-kindness, I will sing, and if** it is **justice, I will sing.** I will thank God in song for the bad just as for the good.

רַבִּי שְׁמוּאֵל בַּר נַחְמָנִי אָמַר מֵהָכָא: "בַּה׳ אֲהַלֵּל דָּבָר בֵּאלֹהִים אֲהַלֵּל דָּבָר"; "בַּה׳ אֲהַלֵּל דָּבָר" – זוֹ מִדָּה טוֹבָה, "בֵּאלֹהִים אֲהַלֵּל דָּבָר" – זוֹ מִדַּת פּוּרְעָנוּת.

**Rabbi Shmuel bar Naḥmani said:** The proof is **from here,** as it is stated: **"In God, I will praise His word; in the Lord, I will praise His word"** (Psalms 56:11). The Gemara explains that **In God, I will praise His word; that is** the revelation of God's **attribute of benevolence,** while: **In the Lord, I will praise His word; that is the attribute of suffering;** even if God brings suffering to bear upon me, I will still praise Him.

רַבִּי תַּנְחוּם אָמַר מֵהָכָא: "כּוֹס יְשׁוּעוֹת אֶשָּׂא וּבְשֵׁם ה׳ אֶקְרָא", "צָרָה וְיָגוֹן אֶמְצָא וּבְשֵׁם ה׳ אֶקְרָא".

**Rabbi Tanḥum said:** The proof is **from here,** as it is stated: **"I will lift up the cup of salvation and call upon the name of the Lord"** (Psalms 116:13), and: **"I found trouble and sorrow, but I called upon the name of the Lord"** (Psalms 116:3–4).

וְרַבָּנַן אָמְרִי מֵהָכָא: "ה׳ נָתַן וַה׳ לָקָח יְהִי שֵׁם ה׳ מְבֹרָךְ".

**And the Rabbis said:** The proof is **from here,** as it is stated: **"The Lord has given and the Lord has taken away; blessed be the name of the Lord"** (Job 1:21).

אָמַר רַב הוּנָא אָמַר רַב מִשּׁוּם רַבִּי מֵאִיר, וְכֵן תָּנָא מִשְּׁמֵיהּ דְּרַבִּי עֲקִיבָא: לְעוֹלָם יְהֵא אָדָם רָגִיל לוֹמַר "כָּל דְּעָבֵיד רַחֲמָנָא לְטַב עָבֵיד".

**Rav Huna said** that **Rav said** that **Rabbi Meir said; and so it was taught** in a *baraita* **in the name of Rabbi Akiva: One must always accustom oneself to say:**[H] **Everything that God does, He does for the best.**

כִּי הָא, דְּרַבִּי עֲקִיבָא דַּהֲוָה קָאָזֵיל בְּאוֹרְחָא, מְטָא לְהַהִיא מָתָא, בְּעָא אוּשְׁפִּיזָא וְלָא יָהֲבִי לֵיהּ. אֲמַר: "כָּל דְּעָבֵיד רַחֲמָנָא לְטָב". אֲזַל וּבָת בְּדַבְרָא, וַהֲוָה בַּהֲדֵיהּ תַּרְנְגוֹלָא וַחֲמָרָא וּשְׁרָגָא. אֲתָא זִיקָא כַּבְיֵיהּ לִשְׁרָגָא, אֲתָא שׁוּנְרָא אַכְלֵיהּ לְתַרְנְגוֹלָא, אֲתָא אַרְיֵה אַכְלֵיהּ לַחֲמָרָא. אֲמַר: כָּל דְּעָבֵיד רַחֲמָנָא לְטָב. בֵּיהּ בְּלֵילְיָא אֲתָא גַּיְיסָא, שַׁבְיֵיהּ לְמָתָא. אֲמַר לְהוּ: לָאו אָמְרִי לְכוּ "כָּל מַה שֶּׁעוֹשֶׂה הַקָּדוֹשׁ בָּרוּךְ הוּא

The Gemara relates: **Like this** incident, **when Rabbi Akiva was walking along the road and came to a certain city, he inquired about lodging and they did not give him** any. **He said: Everything that God does, He does for the best. He went and slept in a field, and he had with him a rooster, a donkey and a candle. A** gust of **wind came and extinguished the candle; a cat came and ate the rooster; and a lion came and ate the donkey. He said: Everything that God does, He does for the best. That night, an army came and took the city into captivity.** It turned out that Rabbi Akiva alone, who was not in the city and had no lit candle, noisy rooster or donkey to give away his location, was saved. **He said to them: Didn't I tell you? Everything that God does,**

Perek **IX**
Daf **61** Amud **a**

הַכֹּל לְטוֹבָה!

**He does for the best.**

וְאָמַר רַב הוּנָא אָמַר רַב מִשּׁוּם רַבִּי מֵאִיר: לְעוֹלָם יִהְיוּ דְּבָרָיו שֶׁל אָדָם מוּעָטִין לִפְנֵי הַקָּדוֹשׁ בָּרוּךְ הוּא, שֶׁנֶּאֱמַר: "אַל תְּבַהֵל עַל פִּיךָ וְלִבְּךָ אַל יְמַהֵר לְהוֹצִיא דָבָר לִפְנֵי הָאֱלֹהִים כִּי הָאֱלֹהִים בַּשָּׁמַיִם וְאַתָּה עַל הָאָרֶץ עַל כֵּן יִהְיוּ דְבָרֶיךָ מְעַטִּים".

**And Rav Huna said** that **Rav said in the name of Rabbi Meir: One's words should always be few before the Holy One, Blessed be He, as it is stated: "Be not rash with your mouth and let not your heart be hasty to utter a word before God; for God is in heaven, and you upon earth. Therefore, let your words be few"** (Ecclesiastes 5:1).

NOTES

**One is obligated to recite a blessing for the bad just as for the good** – חַיָּיב לְבָרֵךְ עַל הָרָעָה כְּשֵׁם שֶׁמְּבָרֵךְ עַל הַטּוֹבָה: The Gemara's assumption that one should recite: Who is good and does good, for a calamity seems surprising. However, one could assert that a person reciting a blessing for a calamity believes in essence that it is not absolute evil, but a manifestation of God's goodness to encourage him to reassess his life's direction (*Talmidei Rabbeinu Yona*). Consequently, it is conceivable that one would recite: Who is good and does good, even over a calamity.

HALAKHA

**To accept them with joy** – לְקַבּוֹלִינְהוּ בְּשִׂמְחָה: One is obligated to recite a blessing over a calamity that befalls him with the same dedication of mind and eagerness of spirit as when he joyfully recites a blessing over a favorable event (Rambam *Sefer Ahava, Hilkhot Berakhot* 10:3; *Shulḥan Arukh, Oraḥ Ḥayyim* 222:3).

**One must always accustom oneself to say** – לְעוֹלָם יְהֵא אָדָם רָגִיל לוֹמַר וכו׳: One must accustom oneself to say: Everything that God does, He does for the best (*Shulḥan Arukh, Oraḥ Ḥayyim* 230:5).

LANGUAGE

Two faces [*du partzufin*] – דּוּ פַּרְצוּפִין: *Du* from the Greek δύ', *du* or δύο, *duo*, meaning two; *partzuf* from the Greek πρόσωπον, *prosopon*, meaning mask or cover for the face. In Hebrew, this term is a synonym for face.

NOTES

**Face…tail** – פַּרְצוּף...זָנָב: In the Gemara in *Ketubot* (8a), in the context of seeking to explain a dispute, the possibility is raised that they disagree with regard to whether there was one or there were two creations of man. Most commentaries tie that dispute to the question in our Gemara, whether man was created with one face and the woman was subsequently an independent creation, or whether he was created with two faces and the creation of Eve was merely the separation the two faces from each other, i.e., not a creation at all. Another possible explanation of the dispute is based on the opinion in our Gemara: At first, the thought entered His mind to create two, but ultimately only one was created. On that basis, the dispute can be explained as a disagreement: Which is the determining factor, thought or action? Rabbeinu Ḥananel explains that the one who says that there were two creations holds that originally man and woman were created as independent entities. The first woman fled and, therefore, Eve was created a second time from man.

**Tail** – זָנָב: The the word tail, here and in several other places in the Talmud, refers to an appendage, unlike the object to which it is attached in appearance or size (*Arukh*). Some explain tail here as a limb of secondary importance, as a tail is to a body (Rashba).

דָּרֵשׁ רַב נַחְמָן בַּר רַב חִסְדָּא: מַאי דִּכְתִיב ״וַיִּיצֶר ה׳ אֱלֹהִים אֶת הָאָדָם״ בִּשְׁנֵי יוּ״דִין – שְׁנֵי יְצָרִים בָּרָא הַקָּדוֹשׁ בָּרוּךְ הוּא, אֶחָד יֵצֶר טוֹב וְאֶחָד יֵצֶר רָע.

**Rav Naḥman bar Rav Ḥisda interpreted homiletically: What is the meaning of that which is written: "Then the Lord God formed [*vayyitzer*] man"** (Genesis 2:7), **with a double *yod*?** This double *yod* alludes to that fact that **the Holy One, Blessed be He, created two inclinations; one a good inclination and one an evil inclination.**

מַתְקִיף לַהּ רַב נַחְמָן בַּר יִצְחָק: אֶלָּא מֵעַתָּה, בְּהֵמָה דְּלָא כְּתִיב בַּהּ ״וַיִּיצֶר״ – לֵית לַהּ יִצְרָא?! וְהָא קָא חָזֵינַן דְּמַזְּקָא וְנָשְׁכָא וּבָעֲטָא! אֶלָּא כִּדְרַבִּי שִׁמְעוֹן בֶּן פָּזִי, דְּאָמַר רַבִּי שִׁמְעוֹן בֶּן פָּזִי: אוֹי לִי מִיּוֹצְרִי וְאוֹי לִי מִיִּצְרִי.

**Rav Naḥman bar Yitzḥak strongly objects to this: If that is so,** does **an animal, with regard to whom *vayyitzer* is not written** with a double *yod*, **not have an inclination? Don't we see that it causes damage and bites and kicks? Rather,** interpret the double *yod* homiletically, **in accordance with** the opinion of **Rabbi Shimon ben Pazi, as Rabbi Shimon ben Pazi said:** This alludes to the difficulty of human life; **woe unto me from my Creator [*yotzri*] and woe unto me from my inclination [*yitzri*].** If one opts to follow either his Creator or his inclination woe unto him from the other.

אִי נַמִי: כִּדְרַבִּי יִרְמְיָה בֶּן אֶלְעָזָר, דְּאָמַר רַבִּי יִרְמְיָה בֶּן אֶלְעָזָר: דּוּ פַּרְצוּפִין בָּרָא הַקָּדוֹשׁ בָּרוּךְ הוּא בְּאָדָם הָרִאשׁוֹן, שֶׁנֶּאֱמַר: ״אָחוֹר וָקֶדֶם צַרְתָּנִי״.

**Alternatively,** this duplication in the language of creation can be explained **in accordance with** the statement of **Rabbi Yirmeya ben Elazar as Rabbi Yirmeya ben Elazar said: The Holy One, Blessed be He created two faces [*du partzufin*]**[L] **on Adam the first** man; he was created both male and female in a single body, **as it is stated: "You have formed me [*tzartani*] behind and before"** (Psalms 139:5); *tzartani* is derived from the word *tzura* [face]. God formed two faces on a single creation, back and front.

״וַיִּבֶן ה׳ אֱלֹהִים אֶת הַצֵּלָע״,

It is stated: **"And the *tzela* which the Lord, God,** had taken from the man, **He made** a woman, and brought her unto the man" (Genesis 2:22)

רַב וּשְׁמוּאֵל; חַד אָמַר: פַּרְצוּף, וְחַד אָמַר: זָנָב,

**Rav and Shmuel** disagree over the meaning of the word *tzela*: **One said:** It means **face.** Eve was originally one face or side of Adam. **And one said:** It means **tail,**[N] which he explains to mean that the *tzela* was an appendage, i.e., one of the ribs in Adam's chest.

בִּשְׁלָמָא לְמַאן דְּאָמַר ״פַּרְצוּף״ – הַיְינוּ דִּכְתִיב ״אָחוֹר וָקֶדֶם צַרְתָּנִי״, אֶלָּא לְמַאן דְּאָמַר ״זָנָב״, מַאי ״אָחוֹר וָקֶדֶם צַרְתָּנִי״? – כִּדְרַבִּי אַמִי, דְּאָמַר רַבִּי אַמִי: ״אָחוֹר״ לְמַעֲשֵׂה בְרֵאשִׁית ״וָקֶדֶם״ לְפוּרְעָנוּת.

The Gemara analyzes this dispute: **Granted,** according **to the one who said** that *tzela* means **face; that is why it is written: "You have formed me [*tzartani*] behind and before." However,** according **to the one who said** that *tzela* means **tail,**[N] **what is** meant by the verse: **"You have formed me [*tzartani*] behind and before"?** The Gemara answers: It can be explained **in accordance with** the opinion of **Rabbi Ami, as Rabbi Ami said: Behind** means Adam was created at the end of **the act of creation; and before** means that he was first **for punishment.**

בִּשְׁלָמָא ״אָחוֹר לְמַעֲשֵׂה בְרֵאשִׁית״ – דְּלָא אִברִי עַד מַעֲלֵי שַׁבְּתָא, אֶלָּא ״וָקֶדֶם לְפוּרְעָנוּת״ פּוּרְעָנוּת דְּמַאי? אִילֵימָא פּוּרְעָנוּת דְּנָחָשׁ – וְהָתַנְיָא, רַבִּי אוֹמֵר: בִּגְדוּלָּה מַתְחִילִין מִן הַגָּדוֹל, וּבִקְלָלָה מַתְחִילִין מִן הַקָּטָן.

The Gemara asks: **Granted,** Adam was **behind,** or last, **in the act of creation,** meaning that **he was not created until** the sixth day, **Shabbat eve; however, before,** or first, **for punishment,** to **what punishment** does this refer? **If you say** that he was first **for punishment** in the wake of the episode with **the snake, wasn't it taught** in a *baraita* that, with regard to punishment, **Rabbi** Yehuda HaNasi **says: In** conferring **honor, one begins with the greatest; in cursing, one begins with the least significant.**

בִּגְדוּלָּה מַתְחִילִין מִן הַגָּדוֹל – דִּכְתִיב: ״וַיְדַבֵּר מֹשֶׁה אֶל אַהֲרֹן וְאֶל אֶלְעָזָר וְאֶל אִיתָמָר בָּנָיו הַנּוֹתָרִים קְחוּ״ וגו׳. בִּקְלָלָה מַתְחִילִין מִן הַקָּטָן – בַּתְּחִלָּה נִתְקַלֵּל נָחָשׁ, וּלְבַסּוֹף נִתְקַלְּלָה חַוָּה, וּלְבַסּוֹף נִתְקַלֵּל אָדָם!

The Gemara explains: **In** conferring **honor, one begins with the greatest, as it is written: "And Moses said unto Aaron, and Elazar and Itamar, his remaining sons: Take** the meal-offering that remains" (Leviticus 10:12). Aaron, who was the greatest among those involved, is mentioned first. And **in cursing, one begins with the least significant** as **first** the **snake was cursed, then Eve was cursed, and ultimately Adam** himself **was cursed.** The punishment did not begin with Adam.

אֶלָּא פּוּרְעָנוּת דְּמַבּוּל, דִּכְתִיב: ״וַיִּמַח אֶת כׇּל הַיְקוּם אֲשֶׁר עַל פְּנֵי הָאֲדָמָה מֵאָדָם וְעַד בְּהֵמָה״, בְּרֵישָׁא אָדָם וַהֲדַר בְּהֵמָה.

**Rather,** this refers to **the punishment of the flood, as it is written: "And He blotted out every living substance which was upon the face of the ground, both man and cattle,** creeping things and fowl of the heaven" (Genesis 7:23); the punishment **began with man, then the animals,** and ultimately all the other creatures.

בִּשְׁלָמָא לְמַאן דְּאָמַר פַּרְצוּף – הַיְינוּ דִּכְתִיב ״וַיִּיצֶר״ בִּשְׁנֵי יוּ״דִין, אֶלָּא לְמַאן דְּאָמַר זָנָב, מַאי ״וַיִּיצֶר״?

Returning to interpretation of *vayyitzer*, the Gemara asks: **Granted according to the one who said** that Eve was originally a **face** or side of Adam; **that is why it is written *vayyitzer*,** with a double *yod*, which allude to the two formations. **However, according to the one who said** that she was a **tail,** or appendage, of Adam, **what is** conveyed by spelling ***vayyitzer*** with a double *yod*?

כְּדְרַבִּי שִׁמְעוֹן בֶּן פָּזִי, דְּאָמַר רַבִּי שִׁמְעוֹן בֶּן פָּזִי: אוֹי לִי מִיּוֹצְרִי אוֹי לִי מִיִּצְרִי.

The Gemara responds: This is interpreted homiletically **in accordance with** the opinion of **Rabbi Shimon ben Pazi, as Rabbi Shimon ben Pazi said:** This comes to emphasize that which a person says to himself in every circumstance: **Woe unto me from my Creator and woe unto me from my inclination.**

בִּשְׁלָמָא לְמַאן דְּאָמַר פַּרְצוּף – הַיְינוּ דִּכְתִיב "זָכָר וּנְקֵבָה בְּרָאָם", אֶלָּא לְמַאן דְּאָמַר זָנָב – מַאי "זָכָר וּנְקֵבָה בְּרָאָם"? כִּדְרַבִּי אַבָּהוּ, דְּרַבִּי אַבָּהוּ רָמֵי: כְּתִיב "זָכָר וּנְקֵבָה בְּרָאָם", וּכְתִיב "כִּי בְּצֶלֶם אֱלֹהִים עָשָׂה אֶת הָאָדָם"! הָא כֵּיצַד – בַּתְּחִלָּה עָלָה בְּמַחְשָׁבָה לִבְרֹאת שְׁנַיִם, וּלְבַסּוֹף לֹא נִבְרָא אֶלָּא אֶחָד.

**Granted, according to the one who said** that Eve was a **face, that is** why **it is written: "Male and female, He created them"** (Genesis 5:2). **However, according to the one who said** that Eve was a **tail, what is** the meaning of the verse: **"Male and female, He created them"?** The Gemara answers: It can be explained in accordance with the opinion of **Rabbi Abbahu.** As **Rabbi Abbahu raised a contradiction** between the verses: On the one hand **it is written: "Male and female, He created them," and** on the other hand **it is written: "For in the image of God He made man"** (Genesis 9:6), indicating that man was created alone. **How, then,** does he resolve the contradiction? **At first, the thought entered** God's mind **to create two, and ultimately, only one was** actually **created.**

בִּשְׁלָמָא לְמַאן דְּאָמַר "פַּרְצוּף" – הַיְינוּ דִּכְתִיב "וַיִּסְגֹּר בָּשָׂר תַּחְתֶּנָּה", אֶלָּא לְמַאן דְּאָמַר "זָנָב", מַאי "וַיִּסְגֹּר בָּשָׂר תַּחְתֶּנָּה"? – אָמַר רַבִּי יִרְמְיָה וְאִיתֵּימָא רַב זְבִיד וְאִיתֵּימָא רַב נַחְמָן בַּר יִצְחָק: לֹא נִצְרְכָה אֶלָּא לִמְקוֹם חֲתָךְ.

The Gemara asks: **Granted, according to the one who said** that Eve was a **face, that is** why **it is written:** "And He took one of his sides **and closed up the place with flesh in its place"** (Genesis 2:21), as it was necessary to close the side that was open. **However, according to the one who said** that Eve was originally a **tail, what is** meant by the verse: **"And closed up the place with flesh in its place"? Rabbi Yirmeya said, and some say Rav Zevid** said, **and some say Rav Naḥman bar Yitzḥak** said: **It was necessary** to say that **only with regard to the place of the incision.**

בִּשְׁלָמָא לְמַאן דְּאָמַר "זָנָב" – הַיְינוּ דִּכְתִיב "וַיִּבֶן", אֶלָּא לְמַאן דְּאָמַר "פַּרְצוּף", מַאי "וַיִּבֶן"?

The Gemara challenges the other opinion: **Granted, according to the one** who said that Eve was a **tail, that is** why **it is written: "And** the Lord God **built** the *tzela*" (Genesis 2:22); it was a completely new building. **However, according to the one who said** that Eve was a complete **face** or side, **what is** the meaning of: **"And He built"?** What needed to be built?

לְכִדְרַבִּי שִׁמְעוֹן בֶּן מְנַסְיָא, דְּדָרַשׁ רַבִּי שִׁמְעוֹן בֶּן מְנַסְיָא: מַאי דִּכְתִיב "וַיִּבֶן ה׳ אֶת הַצֵּלָע" – מְלַמֵּד שֶׁקִּלְּעָהּ הַקָּדוֹשׁ בָּרוּךְ הוּא לְחַוָּה וֶהֱבִיאָהּ לְאָדָם הָרִאשׁוֹן, שֶׁכֵּן בִּכְרַכֵּי הַיָּם קוֹרִין לְקְלִיעֲתָא בְּנָיְיתָא.

The Gemara responds: This must be interpreted homiletically, **in accordance with** the opinion of **Rabbi Shimon ben Menasya, as Rabbi Shimon ben Menasya interpreted homiletically: What is** the meaning of **that which is written: "And the Lord God built the *tzela*"?** This verse **teaches that the Holy One, Blessed be He, braided Eve's** hair, **and** then **brought her to Adam, as in the coastal towns, they call braiding** hair, **building.**

דָּבָר אַחֵר: "וַיִּבֶן", אָמַר רַב חִסְדָּא, וְאָמְרִי לַהּ בְּמַתְנִיתָא תָּנָא: מְלַמֵּד שֶׁבְּנָאָהּ הַקָּדוֹשׁ בָּרוּךְ הוּא לְחַוָּה כְּבִנְיַן אוֹצָר, מָה אוֹצָר זֶה קָצָר מִלְמַעְלָה וְרָחָב מִלְּמַטָּה, כְּדֵי לְקַבֵּל אֶת הַפֵּירוֹת – אַף אִשָּׁה קְצָרָה מִלְמַעְלָה וּרְחָבָה מִלְּמַטָּה, כְּדֵי לְקַבֵּל אֶת הַוָּלָד.

**Alternatively,** the verse: **And He built,** could be understood as a description of her basic shape, as **Rav Ḥisda said, and some say that it is taught in a *baraita*:** This verse **teaches that the Holy One, Blessed be He, built Eve like the structure of a storehouse. Just as a storehouse is** built **narrow on top and wide on the bottom, in order to hold produce** without collapsing; **so too a woman** is created **narrow on top and wide on the bottom, in order to hold the fetus.**

"וַיְבִאֶהָ אֶל הָאָדָם", אָמַר רַבִּי יִרְמְיָה בֶּן אֶלְעָזָר: מְלַמֵּד שֶׁנַּעֲשָׂה הַקָּדוֹשׁ בָּרוּךְ הוּא שׁוֹשְׁבִין לְאָדָם הָרִאשׁוֹן; מִכָּאן לִמְּדָה תּוֹרָה דֶּרֶךְ אֶרֶץ שֶׁיַּחֲזוֹר גָּדוֹל עִם קָטָן בְּשׁוֹשְׁבִינוּת, וְאַל יֵרַע לוֹ.

With regard to the verse: **"And brought her unto the man"** (Genesis 2:22), **Rabbi Yirmeya ben Elazar said:** This verse **teaches that the Holy One, Blessed be He, was Adam the first** man's **best man. From here, the Torah taught that it is a desired mode of behavior for a greater individual to seek out a lesser individual to** assist him and **serve as his best man.**[B] The greater individual should help the lesser **and should not feel badly** about it, that it might be beneath his dignity.

וּלְמַאן דְּאָמַר "פַּרְצוּף", הֵי מִינַּיְיהוּ סַגִּי בְּרֵישָׁא? אָמַר רַב נַחְמָן בַּר יִצְחָק: מִסְתַּבְּרָא דְּגַבְרָא סַגִּי בְּרֵישָׁא, דְּתַנְיָא: לֹא יְהַלֵּךְ אָדָם אֲחוֹרֵי אִשָּׁה בַּדֶּרֶךְ וַאֲפִילּוּ אִשְׁתּוֹ, נִזְדַּמְּנָה לוֹ עַל הַגֶּשֶׁר – יְסַלְּקֶנָּה לִצְדָדִין, וְכָל הָעוֹבֵר אֲחוֹרֵי אִשָּׁה בַּנָּהָר – אֵין לוֹ חֵלֶק לָעוֹלָם הַבָּא.

The Gemara asks: **And according to the one who said** that Eve was a **face** or side of Adam, **which one of them walked in front? Rav Naḥman bar Yitzḥak said: It is reasonable** to say **that the man walked in front, as it was taught** in a *baraita*: **A man should not walk behind a woman**[H] **on a path,** as he will look at her constantly. **And even if one's wife happens upon him along a bridge, he should** walk quickly in order to **move her to** his **side** so that she will not walk before him. **And anyone who walks behind a woman in a river** in order to see her exposed skin when she lifts her clothing as she passes through the water **has no portion in the World-to-Come.**

**BACKGROUND**

**Best man – שׁוֹשְׁבִינוּת:** The best man [*shushvin*] is the groom's friend and companion. Unlike weddings today, in which the best man simply accompanies the groom to the wedding canopy, in the times of the Mishna and Gemara, the best man would see to all of the groom's needs and even prepare a special banquet in his honor. The relationship between the best man and the groom was particularly close and the term came to mean friendship in general. There is a legal element to this relationship, as the groom is obligated to return the favor and serve as best man when his best man gets married.

**HALAKHA**

**A man should not walk behind a woman – לֹא יְהַלֵּךְ אָדָם אֲחוֹרֵי אִשָּׁה:** A man should not walk close behind a woman, lest he have improper thoughts. One who finds himself in that situation should speed up and pass her (Rambam *Sefer Kedusha, Hilkhot Issurei Bia* 21:22; *Shulḥan Arukh, Even HaEzer* 21:1).

## NOTES

**And Elkana walked after his wife** – וַיֵּלֶךְ אֶלְקָנָה אַחֲרֵי אִשְׁתּוֹ: Many have noted that there is no such verse in the Bible. The *ge'onim* commented that in the villages there were teachers of Talmud who were not experts in Bible and who often misquoted verses. Similarly, the Sages received ancient traditions that continued to be transmitted despite the fact that they were inconsistent with the traditional text of the Bible. Finally, Sages would combine verses and cite them as if they were a single verse (see *Tosafot* at the beginning of *Eruvin* and *Tosafot* in the first chapter of *Sanhedrin* with regard to the term *totafot*). In our case, the Maharshal raises the possibility that Elkana was the Levite husband of the concubine in Giva, with regard to whom it is stated that he walked after his wife (see Judges 19:3). However, the Maharshal himself has doubts with regard to this explanation. Finally, this quote may be a reworking of the language of the verse: "And Elkana went to Rama to [*al*] his house" (I Samuel 2:11). The word *al* here has a different connotation, like its meaning in the verse: "And the men came after [*al*] the women" (Exodus 35:22). Consequently, the verse states that Elkana walked after his house, i.e., his wife (Maharsha).

**Behind a lion and not behind a woman, behind a woman and not behind idolatry** – אֲחוֹרֵי אֲרִי וְלֹא אֲחוֹרֵי אִשָּׁה, אֲחוֹרֵי אִשָּׁה וְלֹא אֲחוֹרֵי עֲבוֹדָה זָרָה: To understand this order, one should note that King David, who smote the lion, sinned as a result of looking at a woman. Therefore, being behind a woman is more perilous than being behind a lion. The Sages already said that it is more difficult to distance oneself from idolatry than from other transgressions. However, it is conceivable that one who worships idolatry also acknowledges God's existence; one who fails to pray in the synagogue, however, indicates that he has no connection to God whatsoever (*Iyyun Ya'akov*, Maharsha).

**The evil inclination is like a fly…like a type of wheat** – יֵצֶר הָרַע דּוֹמֶה לִזְבוּב...כְּמִין חִטָּה: Rav and Shmuel each liken the evil inclination to something that, despite its minuscule size, has the capacity to cause great damage, e.g., wheat that leavens and rises. The difference between their opinions is that according to Rav, the evil inclination is flawed from the outset, like a fly, while according to Shmuel, it is not intrinsically evil when properly channeled (*Iyyun Ya'akov*).

## HALAKHA

**And not behind a synagogue** – וְלֹא אֲחוֹרֵי בֵּית הַכְּנֶסֶת: One is prohibited from walking past the entrance of a synagogue while the congregation is praying, even during the verses of praise and *Shema*, which precede the *Amida* prayer (*Mishna Berura*). If one is carrying a load or wearing phylacteries, if there is another synagogue in the city, if the synagogue has an additional entrance on another side of the building, or if one is riding an animal, he is permitted to do so, as in those cases others will not suspect him of having engaged in a public display of disregard for the synagogue (Rambam *Sefer Ahava*, *Hilkhot Tefilla* 6:1; *Shulḥan Arukh*, *Oraḥ Ḥayyim* 90:8).

תָּנוּ רַבָּנַן: הַמַּרְצֶה מָעוֹת לְאִשָּׁה מִיָּדוֹ לְיָדָהּ כְּדֵי לְהִסְתַּכֵּל בָּהּ – אֲפִילּוּ יֵשׁ בְּיָדוֹ תּוֹרָה וּמַעֲשִׂים טוֹבִים כְּמֹשֶׁה רַבֵּינוּ – לֹא יִנָּקֶה מִדִּינָהּ שֶׁל גֵּיהִנָּם, שֶׁנֶּאֱמַר ״יָד לְיָד לֹא יִנָּקֶה רָע״ – לֹא יִנָּקֶה מִדִּינָהּ שֶׁל גֵּיהִנָּם.

**The Sages taught: One who counts money for a woman from his hand to her hand in order to look upon her, even if he has accumulated Torah and good deeds like Moses our teacher, he will not be absolved from the punishment of Gehenna, as it is stated: "Hand to hand, the evil man shall not go unpunished"** (Proverbs 11:21); one who hands money from his hand to her hand, even if he received the Torah from God's hand to his own, like Moses, **he will not be absolved from the punishment of Gehenna,** which is called evil.

אָמַר רַב נַחְמָן: מָנוֹחַ עַם הָאָרֶץ הָיָה, דִּכְתִיב ״וַיֵּלֶךְ מָנוֹחַ אַחֲרֵי אִשְׁתּוֹ״.

**Rav Naḥman said:** From the following verse we know that Samson's father, **Manoah, was an ignoramus, as it is written: "And Manoah.. went after his wife"** (Judges 13:11).

מַתְקִיף לַהּ רַב נַחְמָן בַּר יִצְחָק: אֶלָּא מֵעַתָּה גַּבֵּי אֶלְקָנָה, דִּכְתִיב ״וַיֵּלֶךְ אֶלְקָנָה אַחֲרֵי אִשְׁתּוֹ״, וְגַבֵּי אֱלִישָׁע דִּכְתִיב ״וַיָּקָם וַיֵּלֶךְ אַחֲרֶיהָ״, הָכִי נָמֵי אַחֲרֶיהָ מַמָּשׁ?! אֶלָּא – אַחֲרֵי דְּבָרֶיהָ וְאַחֲרֵי עֲצָתָהּ, הָכָא נָמֵי – אַחֲרֵי דְּבָרֶיהָ וְאַחֲרֵי עֲצָתָהּ.

**Rav Naḥman bar Yitzḥak strongly objects to this: If that is so** that you understand the verse literally, what do you say about the verse **with regard to Elkana,** the father of the prophet Samuel, **as it is written: "And Elkana walked after his wife,"**[N] and what of the verse **with regard to** the prophet **Elisha, as it is written: "And he arose and followed her"** (II Kings 4:30)? **Does** this verse **mean** that he **literally walked after her? Rather,** certainly this verse means that **he followed her words and advice.** If so, then the verse concerning Manoah may be similarly interpreted; he followed his wife's advice and guidance and did not literally walk behind her.

אָמַר רַב אַשִׁי: וּלְמַאי דְּקָאָמַר רַב נַחְמָן מָנוֹחַ עַם הָאָרֶץ הָיָה – אֲפִילּוּ בֵּי רַב נָמֵי לָא קְרָא, שֶׁנֶּאֱמַר: ״וַתָּקָם רִבְקָה וְנַעֲרֹתֶיהָ וַתִּרְכַּבְנָה עַל הַגְּמַלִּים וַתֵּלַכְנָה אַחֲרֵי הָאִישׁ״, וְלֹא לִפְנֵי הָאִישׁ.

**Rav Ashi said: And according to what Rav Naḥman said,** that **Manoah was an ignoramus; he did not even** learn to **read** the basic Torah stories that even children learn **in school, as it is stated: "Rebecca arose, and her damsels, and they rode upon the camels, and followed the man"** (Genesis 24:61); they followed him and did **not** walk **before the man.**

אָמַר רַבִּי יוֹחָנָן: אֲחוֹרֵי אֲרִי וְלֹא אֲחוֹרֵי אִשָּׁה, אֲחוֹרֵי אִשָּׁה – וְלֹא אֲחוֹרֵי עֲבוֹדָה זָרָה, אֲחוֹרֵי עֲבוֹדָה זָרָה – וְלֹא אֲחוֹרֵי בֵּית הַכְּנֶסֶת בְּשָׁעָה שֶׁהַצִּבּוּר מִתְפַּלְּלִין.

On this topic, **Rabbi Yoḥanan said:** It is preferable to walk **behind a lion and not behind a woman,** and preferable to walk **behind a woman and not behind idolatry,**[N] for then it will appear as if he is accompanying the idolatry. It is preferable to walk **behind idolatry and not behind a synagogue**[H] **when the congregation is praying,** as he appears to separate himself from the community in that he does not wish to join them in prayer.

וְלָא אֲמַרַן אֶלָּא דְּלָא דָּרֵי מִידֵּי, וְאִי דָּרֵי מִידֵּי – לֵית לַן בַּהּ, וְלָא אֲמַרַן אֶלָּא דְּלֵיכָּא פִּתְחָא אַחֲרִינָא וְאִי אִיכָּא פִּתְחָא אַחֲרִינָא – לֵית לַן בַּהּ, וְלָא אֲמַרַן אֶלָּא דְּלָא רְכִיב חֲמָרָא, אֲבָל רְכִיב חֲמָרָא – לֵית לַן בַּהּ, וְלָא אֲמַרַן אֶלָּא דְּלָא מַנַּח תְּפִילִּין, אֲבָל מַנַּח תְּפִילִּין – לֵית לַן בַּהּ.

This last *halakha* has numerous caveats: **And we only said** this **in a case where he is not carrying something, and if he is carrying something, this does not apply,** as everyone will understand why he did not enter the synagogue. **And we only said** this **in a case where there is no other entrance** to the synagogue, **and if there is another entrance, this does not apply. And we only said** this **in a case where he is not riding a donkey, and if he is riding a donkey, this does not apply. And we only said** this **in a case where he is not donning phylacteries, but if he is donning phylacteries, this does not apply.**

אָמַר רַב: יֵצֶר הָרַע דּוֹמֶה לִזְבוּב, וְיוֹשֵׁב בֵּין שְׁנֵי מִפְתְּחֵי הַלֵּב, שֶׁנֶּאֱמַר: ״זְבוּבֵי מָוֶת יַבְאִישׁ יַבִּיעַ שֶׁמֶן רוֹקֵחַ״. וּשְׁמוּאֵל אָמַר: כְּמִין חִטָּה הוּא דּוֹמֶה, שֶׁנֶּאֱמַר: ״לַפֶּתַח חַטָּאת רוֹבֵץ״.

**Rav said: The evil inclination is like a fly and it sits between the two entrances of the heart, as it is stated: "Dead flies make the ointment of the perfumer fetid and putrid"** (Ecclesiastes 10:1). **And Shmuel said:** The evil inclination **is like a type of wheat,**[N] **as it is stated: "Transgression [*ḥatat*] couches at the door"** (Genesis 4:7); *ḥatat* is interpreted homiletically as related to *ḥitta*, wheat.

תָּנוּ רַבָּנַן: שְׁתֵּי כְלָיוֹת יֵשׁ בּוֹ בָּאָדָם, אַחַת יוֹעַצְתּוֹ לְטוֹבָה וְאַחַת יוֹעַצְתּוֹ לְרָעָה. וּמִסְתַּבְּרָא דְּטוֹבָה לִימִינוֹ וְרָעָה לִשְׂמֹאלוֹ, דִּכְתִיב: ״לֵב חָכָם לִימִינוֹ וְלֵב כְּסִיל לִשְׂמֹאלוֹ״.

**The Sages taught** in a *baraita*: **A person has two kidneys; one advises him to do good and one advises him to do evil. And it stands to reason** that the one advising him to do **good is to his right and** the one that advises him to do **evil is to his left, as it is written: "A wise man's understanding is at his right hand, but a fool's understanding is at his left"** (Ecclesiastes 10:2).

תָּנוּ רַבָּנַן: כְּלָיוֹת יוֹעֲצוֹת, לֵב מֵבִין, לָשׁוֹן מְחַתֵּךְ, פֶּה גּוֹמֵר, וֶשֶׁט מַכְנִיס וּמוֹצִיא כׇּל מִינֵי מַאֲכָל, קָנֶה מוֹצִיא קוֹל

Tangential to the subject of kidneys, the Gemara cites that which **the Sages taught** in a *baraita* with regard to the roles of various organs: **The kidneys advise, the heart understands, the tongue shapes** the sounds that emerges from the mouth, the **mouth completes** the shaping of the voice, the **esophagus takes in and lets out all kinds of food** the **trachea produces the voice,**

רֵיאָה שׁוֹאֶבֶת כׇּל מִינֵי מַשְׁקִין, כָּבֵד כּוֹעֵס, מָרָה זוֹרֶקֶת בּוֹ טִפָּה וּמַנִּיחָתוֹ, טְחוֹל שׂוֹחֵק, קׇרְקְבָן טוֹחֵן, קֵיבָה יְשֵׁנָה, אַף נֵעוֹר. נֵעוֹר הַיָּשֵׁן, יָשֵׁן הַנֵּעוֹר – נִמּוֹק וְהוֹלֵךְ לוֹ. תָּנָא: אִם שְׁנֵיהֶם יְשֵׁנִים אוֹ שְׁנֵיהֶם נְעוֹרִים – מִיָּד מֵת.

and the **lungs draw all kinds of liquids,** the **liver becomes angry,** the **gall** bladder **injects a drop** of gall **into** the liver and **allays** anger, the **spleen laughs,**[N] the **maw grinds** the food, and the **stomach** brings **sleep,** the **nose awakens.** If they reversed roles such that **the** organ which brings on **sleep** were to **awaken,** or **the** organ which **awakens** were to bring on **sleep,** the individual **would gradually deteriorate. It was taught: If both** bring on **sleep or both awaken,** the person **immediately dies.**

תַּנְיָא, רַבִּי יוֹסֵי הַגְּלִילִי אוֹמֵר: צַדִּיקִים יֵצֶר טוֹב שׁוֹפְטָן, שֶׁנֶּאֱמַר: ״וְלִבִּי חָלַל בְּקִרְבִּי״. רְשָׁעִים – יֵצֶר רַע שׁוֹפְטָן, שֶׁנֶּאֱמַר: ״נְאֻם פֶּשַׁע לָרָשָׁע בְּקֶרֶב לִבִּי אֵין פַּחַד אֱלֹהִים לְנֶגֶד עֵינָיו״. בֵּינוֹנִים – זֶה וָזֶה שׁוֹפְטָן, שֶׁנֶּאֱמַר: ״יַעֲמֹד לִימִין אֶבְיוֹן לְהוֹשִׁיעַ מִשֹּׁפְטֵי נַפְשׁוֹ״.

With regard to one's inclinations, **it was taught** in a *baraita* that **Rabbi Yosei HaGelili says: The good inclination rules**[N] **the righteous, as it is stated: "And my heart is dead within me"** (Psalms 109:22); the evil inclination has been completely banished from his heart. The **evil inclination rules the wicked, as it is stated: "Transgression speaks to the wicked, there is no fear of God before his eyes"** (Psalms 36:2). **Middling people are ruled by both** the good and evil inclinations, **as it is stated: "Because He stands at the right hand of the needy, to save him from them that rule his soul"** (Psalms 109:31).

אָמַר רַבָּה: כְּגוֹן אָנוּ בֵּינוֹנִים. אָמַר לֵיהּ אַבָּיֵי: לָא שָׁבֵיק מָר חַיֵּי לְכׇל בְּרִיָּה!

**Rabba said:** People **like us** are **middling. Abaye,** his student and nephew, **said to him:** If **the Master** claims that he is merely middling, he **does not leave** room for **any creature to live.** If a person like you is middling, what of the rest of us?

וְאָמַר רָבָא: לָא אִיבְרִי עָלְמָא אֶלָּא לִרְשִׁיעֵי גְּמוּרֵי אוֹ לְצַדִּיקֵי גְּמוּרֵי. אָמַר רָבָא: לֵידַע אִינִישׁ בְּנַפְשֵׁיהּ אִם צַדִּיק גָּמוּר הוּא אִם לָאו. אָמַר רַב: לָא אִיבְרִי עָלְמָא אֶלָּא לְאַחְאָב בֶּן עׇמְרִי וּלְרַבִּי חֲנִינָא בֶּן דּוֹסָא. לְאַחְאָב בֶּן עׇמְרִי – הָעוֹלָם הַזֶּה, וּלְרַבִּי חֲנִינָא בֶּן דּוֹסָא – הָעוֹלָם הַבָּא.

**And Rava said: The world was created only for** the sake of **the full-fledged wicked or the full-fledged righteous;**[N] others do not live complete lives in either world. **Rava said: One should know of himself whether or not he is completely righteous,** as if he is not completely righteous, he knows that his life will be a life of suffering. **Rav said: The world was only created for** the wicked **Ahab ben Omri and for Rabbi Ḥanina ben Dosa.** The Gemara explains: For **Ahab ben Omri, this world** was created, as he has no place in the World-to-Come, **and** for **Rabbi Ḥanina ben Dosa, the World-to-Come** was created.

״וְאָהַבְתָּ אֵת ה׳ אֱלֹהֶיךָ״. תַּנְיָא, רַבִּי אֱלִיעֶזֶר אוֹמֵר: אִם נֶאֱמַר ״בְּכׇל נַפְשְׁךָ״, לָמָּה נֶאֱמַר ״בְּכׇל מְאֹדֶךָ״? וְאִם נֶאֱמַר ״בְּכׇל מְאֹדֶךָ״, לָמָּה נֶאֱמַר ״בְּכׇל נַפְשְׁךָ״? אֶלָּא: אִם יֵשׁ לְךָ אָדָם שֶׁגּוּפוֹ חָבִיב עָלָיו מִמָּמוֹנוֹ – לְכָךְ נֶאֱמַר ״בְּכׇל נַפְשְׁךָ״, וְאִם יֵשׁ לְךָ אָדָם שֶׁמָּמוֹנוֹ חָבִיב עָלָיו מִגּוּפוֹ – לְכָךְ נֶאֱמַר ״בְּכׇל מְאֹדֶךָ״. רַבִּי עֲקִיבָא אוֹמֵר: ״בְּכׇל נַפְשְׁךָ״ אֲפִילּוּ נוֹטֵל אֶת נַפְשְׁךָ.

We learned in our mishna the explanation of the verse: **"And you shall love the Lord your God** with all your heart and all your soul and all your might" (Deuteronomy 6:5). This was elaborated upon when **it was taught** in a *baraita*: **Rabbi Eliezer**[P] **says: If it is stated: "With all your soul," why does it state: "With all your might"?** Conversely, **if it stated: "With all your might," why does it state: "With all your soul"? Rather,** this means that **if one's body is dearer to him than his property, therefore it is stated: "With all your soul";** one must give his soul in sanctification of God. **And if one's money is dearer to him than his body, therefore it is stated: "With all your might";** with all your assets. **Rabbi Akiva says: "With all your soul"** means: **Even if** God **takes your soul.**

תָּנוּ רַבָּנַן: פַּעַם אַחַת גָּזְרָה מַלְכוּת הָרְשָׁעָה שֶׁלֹּא יַעַסְקוּ יִשְׂרָאֵל בַּתּוֹרָה, בָּא פַּפּוּס בֶּן יְהוּדָה וּמְצָאוֹ לְרַבִּי עֲקִיבָא שֶׁהָיָה מַקְהִיל קְהִלּוֹת בָּרַבִּים וְעוֹסֵק בַּתּוֹרָה. אָמַר לֵיהּ: עֲקִיבָא, אִי אַתָּה מִתְיָרֵא מִפְּנֵי מַלְכוּת?

The Gemara relates at length how Rabbi Akiva fulfilled these directives. **The Sages taught: One time,** after the bar Kokheva rebellion, **the evil empire** of Rome **decreed that Israel may not engage in** the study and practice of **Torah. Pappos ben Yehuda came and found Rabbi Akiva, who was convening assemblies in public and engaging in Torah** study. Pappos **said to him: Akiva, are you not afraid of the empire?**

### PERSONALITIES

**Rabbi Eliezer – רַבִּי אֱלִיעֶזֶר:** When the name Rabbi Eliezer occurs in the Talmud without a patronymic, it refers to Rabbi Eliezer ben Hyrcanus, also known as Rabbi Eliezer the Great, who was one of the leading Sages in the period after the destruction of the Second Temple.

Rabbi Eliezer was born to a wealthy family of Levites who traced their lineage back to Moses. Rabbi Eliezer began studying Torah late in life, but quickly became an outstanding disciple of Rabban Yoḥanan ben Zakkai. Indeed, Rabban Yoḥanan remarked: If all the Sages of Israel were on one side of a scale and Eliezer ben Hyrcanus on the other, he would outweigh them all.

Rabbi Eliezer was blessed with a remarkable memory. All his life he attempted, in his Torah study and his halakhic rulings, to follow the traditions of his Rabbis without adding to them. Nevertheless, although he was the primary student of Rabban Yoḥanan ben Zakkai, who was a disciple of Beit Hillel, he was considered one who tended towards the views of Bet Shammai. Rabbi Eliezer's close friend, Rabbi Yehoshua ben Ḥananya, completely followed the views of Beit Hillel, and many fundamental halakhic disputes between these Sages are recorded in the Mishna.

Because of his staunch and unflinching adherence to tradition, Rabbi Eliezer was unwilling to accede to the majority view when his own views were based on tradition. Indeed, Rabbi Eliezer's conduct generated so much tension among the Sages that Rabban Gamliel, who was the brother of his wife, Ima Shalom, was forced to excommunicate him to prevent controversy from proliferating. This ban was lifted only after Rabbi Eliezer's death. All of the Sages of the next generation were Rabbi Eliezer's students, most prominent among them Rabbi Akiva. Rabbi Eliezer's son, Hyrcanus, was also one of the Sages.

### NOTES

**The spleen laughs [*soḥek*] – טְחוֹל שׂוֹחֵק:** Some spell the word with a *shin*, *shoḥek*, meaning grinds. They understand this to mean that the spleen also plays a role in crushing and grinding the food one eats (Rabbi Eliezer ben Yoel HaLevi).

**The good inclination rules them [*shofetan*] – יֵצֶר טוֹב שׁוֹפְטָן:** Some explain the word *shofet* to mean leads or rules, indicating that the good inclination alone rules the righteous. Others explain that one is judged according to his actions, and the righteous, who have only the good inclination, are judged by it, while the wicked are judged by the evil inclination, which incites and rages (Rabbi Yoshiya Pinto, Maharsha).

**The world was created only for the full-fledged wicked or the full-fledged righteous – לָא אִיבְרִי עָלְמָא אֶלָּא לִרְשִׁיעֵי גְּמוּרֵי אוֹ לְצַדִּיקֵי גְּמוּרֵי:** Though there have been righteous people who derived pleasure from this world, e.g., the Patriarchs and the righteous kings, this was unrelated to reward, but rather resulted from their unique destinies and manifestations of God's loving kindness (Rav Ya'akov Emden).

NOTES

All my days I have been troubled, etc. – כָּל יָמַי הָיִיתִי מִצְטַעֵר וכו׳: In other sources it is related that Rabbi Akiva had a look of joy on his face while being tortured. His students asked him not about the act of self-sacrifice itself, as all of Israel is commanded in this respect, but, rather about the willing acceptance of his suffering. He explained that he rejoiced at the opportunity to fulfill this mitzva completely.

BACKGROUND

The Eastern Gate – שַׁעַר הַמִּזְרָח:

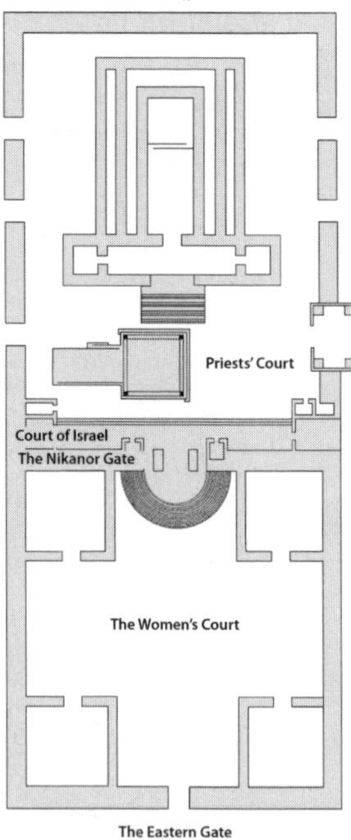


Diagram of the Temple Mount and the Temple

Mount Scopus [*Tzofim*] – צוֹפִים: There is a dispute among the Sages whether *Tzofim* refers to a specific place adjacent to Jerusalem or whether it is merely a term used to describe any place from which Jerusalem is visible. Even among those who hold that it refers to a specific place, there is a dispute. Some hold that it refers to Mount Scopus, while others identify it as the modern Shuafat, located on the road heading north out of Jerusalem.

אָמַר לוֹ: אֶמְשׁוֹל לְךָ מָשָׁל, לְמָה הַדָּבָר דּוֹמֶה – לְשׁוּעָל שֶׁהָיָה מְהַלֵּךְ עַל גַּב הַנָּהָר, וְרָאָה דָּגִים שֶׁהָיוּ מִתְקַבְּצִים מִמָּקוֹם לְמָקוֹם, אָמַר לָהֶם: מִפְּנֵי מָה אַתֶּם בּוֹרְחִים? אָמְרוּ לוֹ: מִפְּנֵי רְשָׁתוֹת שֶׁמְּבִיאִין עָלֵינוּ בְּנֵי אָדָם. אָמַר לָהֶם: רְצוֹנְכֶם שֶׁתַּעֲלוּ לַיַּבָּשָׁה, וְנָדוּר אֲנִי וְאַתֶּם כְּשֵׁם שֶׁדָּרוּ אֲבוֹתַי עִם אֲבוֹתֵיכֶם? אָמְרוּ לוֹ: אַתָּה הוּא שֶׁאוֹמְרִים עָלֶיךָ פִּקֵּחַ שֶׁבַּחַיּוֹת?! לֹא פִּקֵּחַ אַתָּה, אֶלָּא טִפֵּשׁ אַתָּה! וּמַה בִּמְקוֹם חִיּוּתֵנוּ אָנוּ מִתְיָירְאִין, בִּמְקוֹם מִיתָתֵנוּ עַל אַחַת כַּמָּה וְכַמָּה! אַף אֲנַחְנוּ, עַכְשָׁיו שֶׁאָנוּ יוֹשְׁבִים וְעוֹסְקִים בַּתּוֹרָה, שֶׁכָּתוּב בָּהּ: ״כִּי הוּא חַיֶּיךָ וְאֹרֶךְ יָמֶיךָ״ – כָּךְ, אִם אָנוּ הוֹלְכִים וּמְבַטְּלִים מִמֶּנָּה – עַל אַחַת כַּמָּה וְכַמָּה!

Rabbi Akiva **answered him: I will relate a parable. To what can thi be compared?** It is like **a fox walking along a riverbank when h sees fish gathering** and fleeing **from place to place.**

The fox **said to them: From what are you fleeing?**

**They said to him:** We are fleeing **from the nets that people ca upon us.**

**He said to them: Do you wish to come up onto dry land, and we wi reside together just as my ancestors resided with your ancestor**

The fish **said to him: You are the one of whom they say, he is th cleverest of animals? You are not clever; you are a fool. If we ar afraid in** the water, **our** natural **habitat** which gives us **life,** then i **a habitat** that causes our **death, all the more so.**

The moral is: **So too, we** Jews, **now that we sit and engage in Tora** study, **about which it is written: "For that is your life, and th length of your days"** (Deuteronomy 30:20), we fear the empir **to this extent; if we proceed to sit idle from its** study, as its aba donment is the habitat that causes our death, **all the more so** wi we fear the empire.

אָמְרוּ: לֹא הָיוּ יָמִים מוּעָטִים עַד שֶׁתְּפָסוּהוּ לְרַבִּי עֲקִיבָא וַחֲבָשׁוּהוּ בְּבֵית הָאֲסוּרִים, וְתָפְסוּ לְפַפּוֹס בֶּן יְהוּדָה וַחֲבָשׁוּהוּ אֶצְלוֹ. אָמַר לוֹ: פַּפּוֹס! מִי הֱבִיאֲךָ לְכָאן? אֲמַר לֵיהּ: אַשְׁרֶיךָ רַבִּי עֲקִיבָא שֶׁנִּתְפַּסְתָּ עַל דִּבְרֵי תוֹרָה, אוֹי לוֹ לְפַפּוֹס שֶׁנִּתְפַּס עַל דְּבָרִים בְּטֵלִים.

The Sages **said: Not a few days passed until they seized Rabbi Akiv and incarcerated him in prison, and seized Pappos ben Yehuda an incarcerated him alongside him.** Rabbi Akiva **said to him: Pappo who brought you here?** Pappos **replied: Happy are you, Rabb Akiva, for you were arrested on** the charge of engaging in **Tora** study. **Woe unto Pappos who was seized on** the charge of engagin in **idle matters.**

בְּשָׁעָה שֶׁהוֹצִיאוּ אֶת רַבִּי עֲקִיבָא לַהֲרִיגָה זְמַן קְרִיאַת שְׁמַע הָיָה, וְהָיוּ סוֹרְקִים אֶת בְּשָׂרוֹ בְּמַסְרְקוֹת שֶׁל בַּרְזֶל, וְהָיָה מְקַבֵּל עָלָיו עוֹל מַלְכוּת שָׁמַיִם. אָמְרוּ לוֹ תַּלְמִידָיו: רַבֵּינוּ, עַד כָּאן?! אָמַר לָהֶם: כָּל יָמַי הָיִיתִי מִצְטַעֵר עַל פָּסוּק זֶה ״בְּכָל נַפְשְׁךָ״ – אֲפִילּוּ נוֹטֵל אֶת נִשְׁמָתְךָ, אָמַרְתִּי: מָתַי יָבֹא לְיָדִי וַאֲקַיְּימֶנּוּ, וְעַכְשָׁיו שֶׁבָּא לְיָדִי לֹא אֲקַיְּימֶנּוּ?! הָיָה מַאֲרִיךְ בְּ״אֶחָד״ עַד שֶׁיָּצְתָה נִשְׁמָתוֹ בְּ״אֶחָד״. יָצְתָה בַּת קוֹל וְאָמְרָה: אַשְׁרֶיךָ רַבִּי עֲקִיבָא שֶׁיָּצְאָה נִשְׁמָתְךָ בְּ״אֶחָד״.

The Gemara relates: **When they took Rabbi Akiva out to be execu ed, it was time for the recitation of *Shema*. And they were rakin his flesh with iron combs, and he was** reciting *Shema*, thereby a **cepting upon himself the yoke of Heaven. His students said to hir Our teacher, even now,** as you suffer, you recite *Shema*? **He said t them: All my days I have been troubled**[N] **by the verse: With all you soul,** meaning: **Even if God takes your soul.**[H] **I said** to myself: **Whe will the** opportunity **be afforded me to fulfill this** verse? **Now tha it has been afforded me, shall I not fulfill it? He prolonged** his u tering of the word: **One, until his soul left** his body as he uttered hi final word: **One. A voice descended** from heaven **and said: Happ are you, Rabbi Akiva, that your soul left** your body **as you uttere One.**

אָמְרוּ מַלְאֲכֵי הַשָּׁרֵת לִפְנֵי הַקָּדוֹשׁ בָּרוּךְ הוּא: זוֹ תּוֹרָה וְזוֹ שְׂכָרָהּ? ״מִמְתִים יָדְךָ ה׳ מִמְתִים״ וגו׳! – אָמַר לָהֶם ״חֶלְקָם בַּחַיִּים״. יָצְתָה בַּת קוֹל וְאָמְרָה: אַשְׁרֶיךָ רַבִּי עֲקִיבָא שֶׁאַתָּה מְזוּמָּן לְחַיֵּי הָעוֹלָם הַבָּא.

**The ministering angels said before the Holy One, Blessed be H This is Torah and this its reward?** As it is stated: **"From death, b Your hand, O Lord, from death** of the world" (Psalms 17:14); You hand, God, kills and does not save. God **said** the end of the verse t the ministering angels: **"Whose portion is in this life."** And then **Heavenly Voice emerged and said: Happy are you, Rabbi Akiva, a you are destined for life in the World-to-Come,** as your portion i already in eternal life.

״לֹא יָקֵל אָדָם אֶת רֹאשׁוֹ כְּנֶגֶד שַׁעַר הַמִּזְרָח שֶׁהוּא מְכוּוָּן כְּנֶגֶד בֵּית קׇדְשֵׁי הַקֳּדָשִׁים״ וכו׳. אָמַר רַב יְהוּדָה אָמַר רַב: לֹא אָמְרוּ אֶלָּא מִן הַצּוֹפִים וְלִפְנִים, וּבְרוֹאֶה. אִיתְּמַר נַמִי, אָמַר רַבִּי אַבָּא בְּרֵיהּ דְּרַבִּי חִיָּיא בַּר אַבָּא, הָכִי אָמַר רַבִּי יוֹחָנָן: לֹא אָמְרוּ אֶלָּא מִן הַצּוֹפִים וְלִפְנִים, וּבְרוֹאֶה, וּבְשֶׁאֵין גָּדֵר, וּבִזְמַן שֶׁהַשְּׁכִינָה שׁוֹרָה.

We learned in the mishna that **one may not act irreverently opposit the Eastern Gate,**[BH] **which is aligned with the Holy of Holies.** Lir iting this *halakha*, **Rav Yehuda said** that **Rav said: They only said** th *halakha* with regard to irreverent behavior **from Mount Scopu** [*Tzofim*][B] **and within,**[H] **and** specifically areas from where **one can se** the Temple. **It is also stated: Rabbi Abba, son of Rabbi Ḥiyya ba Abba, said: Rabbi Yoḥanan said the following: They only said** thi *halakha* with regard to Mount **Scopus and within,** when **one can se and when there is no fence** obstructing his view, **and when the D vine Presence is resting** there, i.e., when the Temple is standing.

HALAKHA

Even if God takes your soul – אֲפִילּוּ נוֹטֵל אֶת נִשְׁמָתְךָ: There are three severe transgressions for which one is obligated to sacrifice his life rather than commit them: Idol worship, murder, and licentiousness (Rambam *Sefer HaMadda*, *Hilkhot Yesodei HaTorah* 5:7).

One may not act irreverently opposite the Eastern Gate – לֹא יָקֵל אָדָם אֶת רֹאשׁוֹ כְּנֶגֶד שַׁעַר הַמִּזְרָח: One is forbidden to act irreverently opposite the Eastern Gate and the Nikanor Gate, which is the eastern gate of the Temple courtyard, because they are aligned with the Holy of Holi (Rambam *Sefer Avoda*, *Hilkhot Beit HaBeḥira* 7:5).

From Mount Scopus and within – מִן הַצּוֹפִים וְלִפְנִים: During the Temp era, it was prohibited to act irreverently anywhere closer to the Temp than Mount Scopus, if the Temple could be seen from there, and the was no obstructing barrier (Rambam *Sefer Avoda*, *Hilkhot Beit HaBeḥi* 7:8).

תָּנוּ רַבָּנַן: הַנִּפְנֶה בִּיהוּדָה לֹא יִפָּנֶה מִזְרָח וּמַעֲרָב אֶלָּא צָפוֹן וְדָרוֹם, וּבַגָּלִיל לֹא יִפָּנֶה אֶלָּא מִזְרָח וּמַעֲרָב. וְרַבִּי יוֹסֵי מַתִּיר, שֶׁהָיָה רַבִּי יוֹסֵי אוֹמֵר: לֹא אָסְרוּ אֶלָּא בְּרוֹאֶה, וּבְמָקוֹם שֶׁאֵין שָׁם גָּדֵר וּבִזְמַן שֶׁהַשְּׁכִינָה שׁוֹרָה. וַחֲכָמִים אוֹסְרִים.

In this context, **the Sages taught: One who defecates in Judea should not defecate** when facing **east and west,**[H] for then he is facing Jerusalem; **rather** he should do so **facing north and south. But in the Galilee** which is north of Jerusalem, **one should only defecate** facing **east and west. Rabbi Yosei permits** doing so, **as Rabbi Yosei was wont to say: They only prohibited** doing so when **one can see** the Temple, **where there is no fence, and when the Divine Presence is resting** there. **And the Rabbis prohibit** doing so.

חֲכָמִים הַיְינוּ תַּנָּא קַמָּא! – אִיכָּא בֵּינַיְיהוּ צְדָדִין.

The Gemara argues: But the opinion of the **Rabbis,** who prohibit this, **is** identical to that of the **first** anonymous ***tanna,*** who also prohibits doing so. The Gemara replies: The practical difference **between them is** with regard to **the sides,** i.e., a place in Judea that is not directly east or west of Jerusalem, or a place in the Galilee that is not directly north of Jerusalem. According to the first *tanna*, it is prohibited; according to the Rabbis, it is permitted.

תַּנְיָא אִידָךְ: הַנִּפְנֶה בִּיהוּדָה לֹא יִפָּנֶה מִזְרָח וּמַעֲרָב אֶלָּא צָפוֹן וְדָרוֹם, וּבַגָּלִיל – צָפוֹן וְדָרוֹם אָסוּר, מִזְרָח וּמַעֲרָב מוּתָּר. וְרַבִּי יוֹסֵי מַתִּיר, שֶׁהָיָה רַבִּי יוֹסֵי אוֹמֵר: לֹא אָסְרוּ אֶלָּא בְּרוֹאֶה. רַבִּי יְהוּדָה אוֹמֵר: בִּזְמַן שֶׁבֵּית הַמִּקְדָּשׁ קַיָּים אָסוּר, בִּזְמַן שֶׁאֵין בֵּית הַמִּקְדָּשׁ קַיָּים – מוּתָּר. רַבִּי עֲקִיבָא אוֹסֵר בְּכׇל מָקוֹם.

**It was taught** in **another** *baraita*: **One who defecates in Judea should not defecate** when facing **east and west; rather,** he should only do so facing **north and south. And in the Galilee,** defecating while facing **north and south is prohibited,** while **east and west is permitted. And Rabbi Yosei permitted** doing so, **as Rabbi Yosei was wont to say: They only prohibited** doing so when **one can see** the Temple. **Rabbi Yehuda says: When the Temple is standing, it is prohibited,** but **when the Temple is not standing, it is permitted.** The Gemara adds that **Rabbi Akiva prohibits** defecating **anywhere** while facing east and west.

רַבִּי עֲקִיבָא הַיְינוּ תַּנָּא קַמָּא! – אִיכָּא בֵּינַיְיהוּ חוּץ לָאָרֶץ.

The Gemara challenges this: **Rabbi Akiva's** position **is identical to** that of **the first,** anonymous ***tanna,*** who also prohibits doing so. The Gemara responds: The practical difference **between them** is with regard to places **outside of Eretz** Yisrael, as according to Rabbi Akiva, even outside of Eretz Yisrael, defecating while facing east and west is prohibited.

רַבָּה הֲווּ שָׁדְיָין לֵיהּ לִבְנֵי מִזְרָח וּמַעֲרָב, אֲזַל אַבַּיֵּי שַׁדְנְהוּ צָפוֹן וְדָרוֹם, עָל רַבָּה תְּרַצְנְהוּ. אֲמַר: מַאן הַאי דְּקָמְצַעֵר לִי? אֲנָא כְּרַבִּי עֲקִיבָא סְבִירָא לִי, דְּאָמַר: בְּכׇל מָקוֹם אָסוּר.

The Gemara relates that in **Rabba's** bathroom, **the bricks were placed east and west** in order to ensure that he would defecate facing north and south. **Abaye went** and **placed them north and south,** to test if Rabba was particular about their direction or if they had simply been placed east and west incidentally. **Rabba entered** and **fixed them. He said: Who is the one that is upsetting me? I hold in accordance with** the opinion of **Rabbi Akiva, who said: It is prohibited everywhere.**

Perek **IX**
Daf **62** Amud **a**

תַּנְיָא, אָמַר רַבִּי עֲקִיבָא: פַּעַם אַחַת נִכְנַסְתִּי אַחַר רַבִּי יְהוֹשֻׁעַ לְבֵית הַכִּסֵּא, וְלָמַדְתִּי מִמֶּנּוּ שְׁלֹשָׁה דְּבָרִים: לָמַדְתִּי שֶׁאֵין נִפְנִין מִזְרָח וּמַעֲרָב אֶלָּא צָפוֹן וְדָרוֹם, וְלָמַדְתִּי שֶׁאֵין נִפְרָעִין מְעוּמָּד אֶלָּא מְיוּשָּׁב, וְלָמַדְתִּי שֶׁאֵין מְקַנְּחִין בְּיָמִין אֶלָּא בִּשְׂמֹאל. אָמַר לֵיהּ בֶּן עַזַּאי: עַד כָּאן הֵעַזְתָּ פָּנֶיךָ בְּרַבְּךָ! – אָמַר לֵיהּ: תּוֹרָה הִיא וְלִלְמוֹד אֲנִי צָרִיךְ.

**It was taught** in a *baraita* in tractate *Derekh Eretz* that **Rabbi Akiva said: I once entered the bathroom after** my teacher **Rabbi Yehoshua, and I learned three things from** observing **his** behavior: **I learned that one should not defecate** while facing **east and west, but rather** while facing **north and south; I learned that one should not uncover himself** while **standing,**[H] **but** while **sitting,** in the interest of modesty; **and I learned that one should not wipe with his right** hand,[HN] **but with his left. Ben Azzai,** a student of Rabbi Akiva, **said to him: You were impertinent to your teacher to that extent** that you observed that much? **He replied: It is Torah, and I must learn.**[N]

תַּנְיָא, בֶּן עַזַּאי אוֹמֵר: פַּעַם אַחַת נִכְנַסְתִּי אַחַר רַבִּי עֲקִיבָא לְבֵית הַכִּסֵּא, וְלָמַדְתִּי מִמֶּנּוּ שְׁלֹשָׁה דְּבָרִים: לָמַדְתִּי שֶׁאֵין נִפְנִין מִזְרָח וּמַעֲרָב אֶלָּא צָפוֹן וְדָרוֹם, וְלָמַדְתִּי שֶׁאֵין נִפְרָעִין מְעוּמָּד אֶלָּא מְיוּשָּׁב, וְלָמַדְתִּי שֶׁאֵין מְקַנְּחִין בְּיָמִין אֶלָּא בִּשְׂמֹאל. אָמַר לוֹ רַבִּי יְהוּדָה: עַד כָּאן הֵעַזְתָּ פָּנֶיךָ בְּרַבְּךָ?! – אָמַר לוֹ: תּוֹרָה הִיא וְלִלְמוֹד אֲנִי צָרִיךְ.

Similarly, **we learned** in a *baraita*: **Ben Azzai said: I once entered a bathroom after Rabbi Akiva, and I learned three things from** observing **his** behavior: **I learned that one should not defecate** while facing **east and west, but rather** while facing **north and south; I learned that one should not uncover himself** while **standing, but** while **sitting; and I learned that one should not wipe with his right** hand, **but with his left. Rabbi Yehuda said to him: You were impertinent to your teacher to that extent? He replied: It is Torah, and I must learn.**

**HALAKHA**

**East and west** – **מִזְרָח וּמַעֲרָב**: It is prohibited to defecate in an exposed place without barriers facing east-west, so as not to show contempt for the Divine Presence, which rests in the west, and because the Temple is located to the west. This *halakha* also applies outside of Eretz Yisrael, in accordance with the opinion of Rabbi Akiva (Rambam *Sefer Avoda, Hilkhot Beit HaBeḥira* 7:9; *Shulḥan Arukh, Oraḥ Ḥayyim* 3:5).

**HALAKHA**

**One should not uncover himself while standing** – **שֶׁאֵין נִפְרָעִין מְעוּמָּד**: One who needs to relieve himself should not expose himself while standing, but only after he sits, in the interest of modesty. (Rambam *Sefer HaMadda, Hilkhot De'ot* 5:6; *Shulḥan Arukh, Oraḥ Ḥayyim* 3:2).

**One should not wipe with his right hand** – **שֶׁאֵין מְקַנְּחִין בְּיָמִין**: One should not wipe himself with his right hand, but rather with his left, for the reasons enumerated in the Gemara (Rambam *Sefer HaMadda, Hilkhot De'ot* 5:6; *Shulḥan Arukh, Oraḥ Ḥayyim* 3:10).

**NOTES**

**And I learned that one should not wipe with his right hand** – **וְלָמַדְתִּי שֶׁאֵין מְקַנְּחִין בְּיָמִין**: All the reasons cited here are relevant, but as a rule, great respect is accorded the right side. It is associated with good, and one must attempt to avoid performing disgraceful activities with that hand (*HaBoneh*).

**It is Torah, and I must learn** – **תּוֹרָה הִיא וְלִלְמוֹד אֲנִי צָרִיךְ**: If the question arises: Why, in all of these cases, did the disciple not simply ask his rabbi as to the proper way to conduct himself in these situations? The answer is that he wanted a practical rather than a theoretical answer, and he thought that the ideal manner to learn the practical *halakha* is to watch his mentor in action (Maharsha). The essence of the matter is that Torah encompasses all facets of life. Even in areas considered personal and private, a great person must conduct himself in accordance with the Torah, so that others may learn from him.

PERSONALITIES

**Rav Kahana – רַב כָּהֲנָא:** There were several Sages with this name. Here, the reference is to Rav Kahana, disciple-colleague of Rav. Rav Kahana was born in Babylonia during the first generation of *amora'im*. When Rav came to Babylonia, Rav Kahana became his student. Despite his young age, Rav Kahana was already a Torah luminary who aquired Rav's traditions, but not his logical reasoning.

In defending his Rabbi's honor, Rav Kahana ran afoul of the Persian government and was forced into exile to Eretz Yisrael, where he lived for a certain period, during which he studied Torah from its Sages. Rabbi Shimon ben Lakish, a Sage in Eretz Yisrael, praised him, saying: A lion ascended from Babylonia. The rest of the Sages of that generation agreed with that assessment, and in the Jerusalem Talmud his name is usually cited simply as Kahana. Rav Kahana later returned to Babylonia. Apparently, towards the end of his life, he returned to Eretz Yisrael.

Rav Kahana's greatness was acknowledged by subsequent generations and his teachings were considered authoritative, to the extent that they were used to challenge amoraic opinions, as if they were tannaitic statements. Even Rabbi Yoḥanan considered Rav Kahana to be sharper than he. Rabbi Yoḥanan treated him as his teacher, often deferentially quoting Torah that he learned from him.

HALAKHA

**Where one may defecate – הֵיכָן נִפְנִין:** Behind a fence, one may defecate immediately, in accordance with the statement of Ulla. In an open field, one may do so as long as others cannot see him exposed. This is in accordance with the opinion of Rav Ashi, the latest *amora* cited, who expressed an opinion on this matter. Some commentaries explained that he only disagreed with Ulla with regard to that particular detail (*Beit Yosef*; Rambam *Sefer HaMadda, Hilkhot De'ot* 5:6; *Shulḥan Arukh, Oraḥ Ḥayyim* 3:8).

**Preserving the purity of the olive press – שְׁמִירַת טָהֳרַת בֵּית הַבַּד:** One who employs *amei ha'aretz* and seeks to produce wine in ritual purity, must have them immerse in a ritual bath in his presence before beginning to work. If they go to defecate and were not obscured from his eyes, they remain ritually pure. If he was unable to see them, however, they are presumed to have become ritually impure, in accordance with the mishna in *Teharot* (Rambam *Sefer Tahara, Hilkhot Metamei Mishkav UMoshav* 13:2).

רַב כָּהֲנָא עַל, גְּנָא תּוּתֵיהּ פּוּרְיֵיהּ דְּרַב. שְׁמָעֵיהּ דְּשָׂח וְשָׂחַק וְעָשָׂה צְרָכָיו, אֲמַר לֵיהּ: דָּמֵי פּוּמֵיהּ דְּאַבָּא כִּדְלָא שָׂרֵיף תַּבְשִׁילָא! אֲמַר לוֹ: כָּהֲנָא, הָכָא אַתְּ? פּוּק, דְּלָאו אוֹרַח אַרְעָא. אֲמַר לוֹ: תּוֹרָה הִיא וְלִלְמוֹד אֲנִי צָרִיךְ.

On a similar note, the Gemara relates that **Rav Kahana**[P] **entered and lay beneath Rav's bed. He heard** Rav **chatting and laughing** with his wife, **and seeing to his needs,** i.e., having relations with her. Rav Kahana **said to** Rav: **The mouth of Abba,** Rav, **is like** one whom **has never eaten a cooked dish,** i.e., his behavior was lustful. Rav **said to him: Kahana, you are here? Leave, as this is an undesirable mode of behavior.** Rav Kahana **said to him: It is Torah, and I must learn.**

מִפְּנֵי מָה אֵין מְקַנְּחִין בְּיָמִין אֶלָּא בִּשְׂמֹאל? אָמַר רָבָא: מִפְּנֵי שֶׁהַתּוֹרָה נִיתְּנָה בְּיָמִין, שֶׁנֶּאֱמַר: ״מִימִינוֹ אֵשׁ דָּת לָמוֹ״. רַבָּה בַּר בַּר חָנָה אָמַר: מִפְּנֵי שֶׁהִיא קְרוֹבָה לַפֶּה. וְרַבִּי שִׁמְעוֹן בֶּן לָקִישׁ אָמַר: מִפְּנֵי שֶׁקּוֹשֵׁר בָּהּ תְּפִילִּין. רַב נַחְמָן בַּר יִצְחָק אָמַר: מִפְּנֵי שֶׁמַּרְאֶה בָּהּ טַעֲמֵי תוֹרָה.

The Gemara asks: **Why must one not wipe** himself **with his right** hand **but with his left? Rava said: Because the Torah was given with the right** hand, **as it is stated: "At His right hand was a fiery law unto them"** (Deuteronomy 33:2). **Rabba bar bar Ḥana said: Because** the right hand **is close to the mouth,** i.e., people eat with the right hand. **And Rabbi Shimon ben Lakish said: Because one ties the phylacteries** onto his left hand **with** his right hand. **Rav Naḥman bar Yitzḥak said: Because one points to the** cantillation **notes of the Torah with** his right hand.

כְּתַנָּאֵי, רַבִּי אֱלִיעֶזֶר אוֹמֵר: מִפְּנֵי שֶׁאוֹכֵל בָּהּ. רַבִּי יְהוֹשֻׁעַ אוֹמֵר: מִפְּנֵי שֶׁכּוֹתֵב בָּהּ. רַבִּי עֲקִיבָא אוֹמֵר: מִפְּנֵי שֶׁמַּרְאֶה בָּהּ טַעֲמֵי תוֹרָה.

The Gemara notes that this is **parallel to a tannaitic** dispute: **Rabbi Eliezer says:** One is forbidden to wipe himself with his right hand **because he eats with it. Rabbi Yehoshua says: Because he writes with it. Rabbi Akiva says: Because he points to the notes of the Torah with it.**

אָמַר רַבִּי תַּנְחוּם בַּר חֲנִילַאי: כׇּל הַצָּנוּעַ בְּבֵית הַכִּסֵּא נִצּוֹל מִשְּׁלֹשָׁה דְּבָרִים: מִן הַנְּחָשִׁים, וּמִן הָעֲקְרַבִּים, וּמִן הַמַּזִּיקִין. וְיֵשׁ אוֹמְרִים: אַף חֲלוֹמוֹתָיו מְיוּשָּׁבִים עָלָיו.

**Rabbi Tanḥum bar Ḥanilai said: Anyone who is modest in the bathroom will be saved from three things: From snakes, from scorpions, and from demons. And some say** that **even his dreams will be settling for him.**

הַהוּא בֵּית הַכִּסֵּא דַּהֲוָה בִּטְבֶרְיָא, כִּי הָווּ עָיְילִי בֵּיהּ בֵּי תְרֵי אֲפִילּוּ בִּימָמָא מִתַּזְּקִי. רַבִּי אַמִי וְרַבִּי אַסִי הָווּ עָיְילִי בֵּיהּ חַד וְחַד לְחוּדֵיהּ וְלָא מִתַּזְּקִי. אָמְרִי לְהוּ רַבָּנַן: לָא מִסְתַּפִּיתוּ? – אָמְרִי לְהוּ: אֲנַן קַבָּלָה גְּמִירִינַן, קַבָּלָה דְּבֵית הַכִּסֵּא – צְנִיעוּתָא וּשְׁתִיקוּתָא, קַבָּלָה דְּיִסּוּרֵי – שְׁתִיקוּתָא וּמִבְּעֵי רַחֲמֵי.

The Gemara relates: **There was a particular bathroom in** the city of **Tiberias, where, when two would enter it, even during the day, they would be harmed** by demons. When **Rabbi Ami and Rabbi Asi would each enter alone, they were not harmed. The Sages said to them: Aren't you afraid?** Rabbi Ami and Rabbi Asi **said to them: We have learned** through tradition: The **tradition** to avoid danger in the bathroom is to conduct oneself with **modesty and silence. The tradition** to end **suffering** is with **silence and prayer.**

אַבָּיֵי מְרַבְּיָא לֵיהּ אִמֵּיהּ אִמְּרָא לְמֵיעַל בַּהֲדֵיהּ לְבֵית הַכִּסֵּא. וּלְרַבְּיָא לֵיהּ גַּדְיָא! – שָׂעִיר בְּשָׂעִיר מִיחֲלַף.

Because fear of demons in bathrooms was pervasive, the Gemara relates: **Abaye's mother raised a lamb to accompany him to the bathroom.** The Gemara objects: She should have **raised a goat for him.** The Gemara responds: **A goat** could be **interchanged with a goat-demon.** Since both the demon and the goat are called *sa'ir*, they were afraid to bring a goat to a place frequented by demons.

רָבָא, מִקַּמֵּי דַּהֲוָה רֵישָׁא – מְקַרְקְשָׁא לֵיהּ בַּת רַב חִסְדָּא אַמְגוּזָא בְּלַקְנָא, בָּתַר דִּמְלַךְ – עָבְדָא לֵיהּ כַּוְּותָא, וּמַנְחָא לֵיהּ יָדָא אַרֵישֵׁיהּ.

**Before Rava became the head of the yeshiva,** his wife, **the daughter of Rav Ḥisda, would rattle a nut in a copper vessel for him.** This was in order to fend off demons when he was in the bathroom. **After** he was chosen to **preside** as head of the yeshiva, he required an additional degree of protection, so **she constructed a window for him,** opposite where he would defecate, **and placed her hand upon his head.**

אָמַר עוּלָּא: אֲחוֹרֵי הַגָּדֵר – נִפְנֶה מִיָּד, וּבְבִקְעָה – כׇּל זְמַן שֶׁמִּתְעַטֵּשׁ וְאֵין חֲבֵרוֹ שׁוֹמֵעַ. אִיסִּי בַּר נָתָן מַתְנֵי הָכִי, אֲחוֹרֵי הַגָּדֵר – כׇּל זְמַן שֶׁמִּתְעַטֵּשׁ וְאֵין חֲבֵרוֹ שׁוֹמֵעַ, וּבְבִקְעָה – כׇּל זְמַן שֶׁאֵין חֲבֵרוֹ רוֹאֵהוּ.

With regard to where one may or may not go to defecate,[H] **Ulla said: Behind a fence, one** need not distance himself from people and may **defecate immediately. In a valley** or open field, one must distance himself **sufficiently so that if he passes wind, no one will hear him. Isi bar Natan taught as follows: Behind a fence** one must distance himself **sufficiently so that if he passes wind another does not hear him, and in a valley,** one must distance himself **sufficiently so that no one can see him.**

מֵיתִיבֵי: יוֹצְאִין מִפֶּתַח בֵּית הַבַּד וְנִפְנִין לַאֲחוֹרֵי הַגָּדֵר וְהֵן טְהוֹרִין!

The Gemara **raises an objection** based on what we learned in a mishna in *Teharot*: Physical laborers, who usually fall into the category of *am ha'aretz* and are not generally cautious with regard to the laws of ritual purity, **exit from the entrance of the olive press, defecate behind the fence, and are ritually pure.**[H] There is no reason to be concerned that they might become impure in the interim. This indicates that a greater distance is unnecessary.

בְּטָהֳרוֹת הֵקֵלּוּ.

The Gemara responds: **With regard to** the laws of **ritual purity, they were lenient.** To ensure maintenance of purity, they were lenient and did not require a greater distance.

תָּא שְׁמַע: כַּמָּה יַרְחִיקוּ וְיִהְיוּ טְהוֹרִין – כְּדֵי שֶׁיְּהֵא רוֹאֵהוּ! – שָׁאנֵי אוֹכְלֵי טְהָרוֹת, דְּאַקִּילוּ בְּהוּ רַבָּנַן.

**Come and hear** from what we learned: **How far** may workers **distance themselves, and** the fruit and oil **will** remain **pure?**[N] They may distance themselves only **so far that he** still **sees him.** This contradicts the opinion of Isi bar Natan, who required them to distance themselves sufficiently that they may not be seen. The Gemara responds: Those **who eat in purity are different, as the Sages were lenient with them.**

רַב אַשִׁי אָמַר: מַאי "כׇּל זְמַן שֶׁאֵין חֲבֵרוֹ רוֹאֶה" דְּקָאָמַר אִיסִי בַּר נָתָן – כׇּל זְמַן שֶׁאֵין חֲבֵרוֹ רוֹאֶה אֶת פֵּרוּעוֹ, אֲבָל לְדִידֵיהּ חָזֵי לֵיהּ.

**Rav Ashi said: What is** the meaning of: **So long as another does not see him, which** was the standard that **Isi bar Natan said? Sufficient that another person cannot see his nakedness, although he does see him.**

הַהוּא סַפְדָּנָא דִּנְחֵית קַמֵּיהּ דְּרַב נַחְמָן, אָמַר: הַאי צָנוּעַ בְּאוֹרְחוֹתָיו הֲוָה. אָמַר לֵיהּ רַב נַחְמָן: אַתְּ עַיֵּילְתְּ בַּהֲדֵיהּ לְבֵית הַכִּסֵּא, וִידַעַתְּ אִי צָנוּעַ אִי לָא? דְּתַנְיָא: אֵין קוֹרִין צָנוּעַ – אֶלָּא לְמִי שֶׁצָּנוּעַ בְּבֵית הַכִּסֵּא.

The Gemara relates: **There was a particular eulogizer who went** to eulogize an important person **in the presence of Rav Naḥman.** Of the deceased, **he said: This man was modest in his ways. Rav Naḥman said to him: Did you go to the bathroom with him and know whether or not he was modest? As we learned** in a *baraita*: **One can only describe as modest one who is modest** even **in the bathroom,** when no one else is there.

וְרַב נַחְמָן, מַאי נָפְקָא לֵיהּ מִינֵּיהּ? – מִשּׁוּם דְּתַנְיָא: כְּשֵׁם שֶׁנִּפְרָעִין מִן הַמֵּתִים – כָּךְ נִפְרָעִין מִן הַסַּפְדָּנִין וּמִן הָעוֹנִין אַחֲרֵיהֶן.

The Gemara asks: **And what difference** did it make **to Rav Naḥman,** that he was so insistent upon the details of whether or not this man was modest? The Gemara answers: **Because it was taught** in a *baraita*: **Just as the deceased are punished, so too are the eulogizers**[H] **and those who answer after them.** The deceased are punished for transgressions committed in their lifetimes. The eulogizers and those who answer are punished for accepting the attribution of virtues that the deceased did not possess.

תָּנוּ רַבָּנַן: אֵיזֶהוּ צָנוּעַ – זֶה הַנִּפְנֶה בַּלַּיְלָה בְּמָקוֹם שֶׁנִּפְנֶה בַּיּוֹם.

**The Sages taught** in a *baraita*: **Who is a modest person? One who defecates at night where he defecates during the day,** i.e., who distances himself at night, in order to relieve himself, no less than he distances himself during the day.

אִינִי?! וְהָאָמַר רַב יְהוּדָה אָמַר רַב: לְעוֹלָם יַנְהִיג אָדָם אֶת עַצְמוֹ שַׁחֲרִית וְעַרְבִית, כְּדֵי שֶׁלֹּא יְהֵא צָרִיךְ לְהִתְרַחֵק. וְתוּ, רָבָא בִּימָמָא הֲוָה אָזֵיל עַד מִיל, וּבְלֵילְיָא אָמַר לֵיהּ לְשַׁמָּעֵיהּ: פַּנּוּ לִי דּוּכְתָּא בִּרְחוֹבָא דְּמָתָא. וְכֵן אָמַר לֵיהּ רַבִּי זֵירָא לְשַׁמָּעֵיהּ: חֲזִי מַאן דְּאִיכָּא אֲחוֹרֵי בֵּי חַבְרַיָּא, דְּבָעֵינָא לְמִפְנֵי! – לָא תֵּימָא "בְּמָקוֹם" אֶלָּא אֵימָא "כְּדֶרֶךְ שֶׁנִּפְנֶה בַּיּוֹם".

The Gemara challenges: **Is that so? Didn't Rav Yehuda say** that **Rav said: One must always accustom himself** to defecate **in the morning and at night,** when it is dark, **so that he will not need to distance himself? Moreover, during the day, Rava would go up to a** *mil* outside the city, **and at night he would tell his servant: Clear a place for me in the city street. And so too, Rabbi Zeira told his servant: See who is behind the study hall, as I need to defecate.** These Sages did not defecate at night in the same place where they defecated during the day. **Rather,** emend the statement and **say** as follows: **In the manner that one defecates during the day,**[H] i.e. he should conduct himself at night with the same degree of modesty with which he removes his clothing when defecating during the day.

רַב אַשִׁי אָמַר: אֲפִילּוּ תֵּימָא "בְּמָקוֹם" – לָא נִצְרְכָה אֶלָּא לְקֶרֶן זָוִית.

**Rav Ashi said: Even if you say** that the text can remain as it was: **Where he defecates during the day,** it was **only necessary in** the case of **a corner,** where one may conceal himself. In the interest of modesty, he should go around the corner at night, just as he does during the day.

גּוּפָא, אָמַר רַב יְהוּדָה אָמַר רַב: לְעוֹלָם יַנְהִיג אָדָם אֶת עַצְמוֹ שַׁחֲרִית וְעַרְבִית, כְּדֵי שֶׁלֹּא יְהֵא צָרִיךְ לְהִתְרַחֵק.

The Gemara discusses **the matter itself. Rav Yehuda said** that **Rav said: One must always accustom himself** to defecate early **in the morning and** late **at night so that he will not need to distance himself.**

תַּנְיָא נַמִי הָכִי, בֶּן עַזַּאי אוֹמֵר: הַשְׁכֵּם וָצֵא, הַעֲרֵב וָצֵא, כְּדֵי שֶׁלֹּא תִּתְרַחֵק. מַשְׁמֵשׁ וְשֵׁב, וְאַל תֵּשֵׁב וּתְמַשְׁמֵשׁ, שֶׁכׇּל הַיּוֹשֵׁב וּמְמַשְׁמֵשׁ – אֲפִילּוּ עוֹשִׂין כְּשָׁפִים בְּאַסְפַּמְיָא – בָּאִין עָלָיו.

**That** opinion **was also taught** in a *baraita*: **Ben Azzai said: Rise early** in the morning **and go** defecate, wait for **evening and go** defecate, **so that you will not** need to **distance yourself.** He also said: **Touch** around the anus first to assist in the opening of orifices **and then sit; do not sit and** then **touch, for anyone who sits and** then **touches, even if sorcery is performed in** a distant place like **Aspamia,**[L] the sorcery **will come upon him.**

וְאִי אִנְשִׁי וְיָתֵיב וְאַחַר כָּךְ מְשַׁמֵּשׁ, מַאי תַּקַּנְתֵּיהּ? – כִּי קָאֵי לֵימָא הָכִי: לָא לִי לָא לִי, לָא תַּחִים וְלָא תַּחְתִּים, לָא הָנֵי וְלָא מֵהָנֵי, לָא חַרְשֵׁי דְּחַרְשָׁא וְלָא חַרְשֵׁי דְּחַרַשְׁתָּא.

The Gemara says: **And if one forgets and sits and then touches, what is his remedy? When** he **stands,** he should **recite the following** incantation: **Not for me, not for me, neither** *taḥim* **nor** *taḥtim*, types of sorcery, **neither these nor from these, neither the sorcery of a sorcerer nor the sorcery of a sorceress.**

**NOTES**

**How far may workers distance themselves, and the fruit and oil will remain pure – כַּמָּה יַרְחִיקוּ וְיִהְיוּ טְהוֹרִין:** Generally, *amei ha'aretz* were assumed to be lax in their observance of the laws of ritual purity, and as a rule were not considered ritually pure, as there is no Torah requirement for one to be pure except when eating *teruma* and consecrated items. As a result, when workers who were *amei ha'aretz* would operate an olive press, they were supervised to ensure that they, and, consequently, the oil, would not become ritually impure.

**HALAKHA**

**So too are the eulogizers punished – כָּךְ נִפְרָעִין מִן הַסַּפְדָּנִין:** One who eulogizes the dead is prohibited from exaggerating excessively in praise of the deceased. Rather, one should mention his actual good qualities and embellish them a bit. He should not praise the deceased for qualities that he did not possess at all. If the deceased had no positive qualities, none should be mentioned. One who makes unfounded statements or extreme exaggerations in praise of the deceased brings punishment upon both himself and the deceased (*Shulḥan Arukh, Yoreh De'a* 344:1).

**In the manner that one defecates during the day – כְּדֶרֶךְ שֶׁנִּפְנֶה בַּיּוֹם:** When relieving himself at night, one should expose himself no more than he does during the day, in the interest of modesty (Rambam *Sefer HaMadda, Hilkhot De'ot* 5:6; *Shulḥan Arukh, Oraḥ Ḥayyim* 3:12).

**LANGUAGE**

**Aspamia – אַסְפַּמְיָא:** Ἰσπανία is the Greek name for Spain. Due to its distance from Eretz Yisrael and Babylonia, and with travel conditions being what they were, the word Aspamia is used to refer to a very distant place at the ends of the earth.

תַּנְיָא, בֶּן עַזַּאי אוֹמֵר: עַל כׇּל מִשְׁכָּב שְׁכַב – חוּץ מִן הַקַּרְקַע, עַל כׇּל מוֹשָׁב שֵׁב – חוּץ מִן הַקּוֹרָה. אָמַר שְׁמוּאֵל: שֵׁינָה בְּעַמּוּד הַשַּׁחַר – כְּאִסְטְמָא לְפַרְזְלָא, יְצִיאָה בְּעַמּוּד הַשַּׁחַר – כְּאִסְטְמָא לְפַרְזְלָא.

Continuing with the subject of health, **it was taught** in a *baraita*: **Ben Azzai says: On all beds, lie, except for the ground. On all seats, sit, except for a beam,** lest you fall off. **Shmuel said: Sleeping at dawn**[N] is as effective **as forging** [*istema*][L] is **to iron. A** bowel **movement at dawn** is as beneficial **as forging** is **to iron.**

בַּר קַפָּרָא הֲוָה מְזַבֵּן מִילֵּי בְּדִינָרֵי: עַד דְּכָפְנַתְּ – אֱכוֹל, עַד דְּצָחֵית – שְׁתִי, עַד דְּרָתְחָא קִדְרָךְ – שְׁפוֹךְ. קַרְנָא קָרְיָא בְּרוֹמִי – בַּר מְזַבֵּין תְּאֵנֵי, תְּאֵנֵי דַּאֲבוּךְ זַבֵּין!

Similarly, the Gemara relates: **Bar Kappara would sell sayings for dinars;**[N] he would express his ideas in brief maxims.[N] For example: **If you are hungry, eat;** do not delay eating, as the hunger may pass and your food will be of no benefit. So too, **if you are thirsty, drink; while the pot is still boiling, pour it** out before it cools off. This is a metaphor for relieving oneself. Bar Kappara also said: **When the horn is sounded in Rome,** signifying that there is demand for figs in the Roman market, **son of a fig seller, sell your father's figs,** even without his permission, so as not to miss the opportunity.

אָמַר לְהוּ אַבָּיֵי לְרַבָּנַן: כִּי עָיְילִיתוּ בִּשְׁבִילֵי דִּמְחוֹזָא לְמִיפַּק בֵּיהּ בְּחַקְלָא, לָא תֶּחֱזוּ לָא לְהָךְ גִּיסָא וְלָא לְהָךְ גִּיסָא, דִּלְמָא יָתְבִי נָשֵׁי וְלָאו אוֹרַח אַרְעָא לְאִסְתַּכּוֹלֵי בְּהוּ.

**Abaye said to the Sages: When you enter the paths of** the city of **Meḥoza in order to go out** and defecate **in a field, look neither to one side nor to the other, as perhaps women are sitting there and it is improper to look at them.**

רַב סָפְרָא עָל לְבֵית הַכִּסֵּא, אֲתָא רַבִּי אַבָּא נְחַר לֵיהּ אַבָּבָא, אֲמַר לֵיהּ: לֵיעוּל מָר! בָּתַר דִּנְפַק, אֲמַר לֵיהּ: עַד הַשְׁתָּא לָא עָיְילַתְּ לְשֵׂעִיר, וְגָמְרַתְּ לָךְ מִילֵּי דְשֵׂעִיר?! לָאו הָכִי תְּנַן: מְדוּרָה הָיְתָה שָׁם, וּבֵית הַכִּסֵּא שֶׁל כָּבוֹד, וְזֶה הָיָה כְּבוֹדוֹ: מְצָאוֹ נָעוּל – בְּיָדוּעַ שֶׁיֵּשׁ שָׁם אָדָם, מְצָאוֹ פָּתוּחַ – בְּיָדוּעַ שֶׁאֵין שָׁם אָדָם, אַלְמָא: לָאו אוֹרַח אַרְעָא הוּא!

The Gemara relates: **Rav Safra once entered a bathroom** when **Rabbi Abba came along.** To determine if he could enter, Rabbi Abba **coughed next to the door.** Rav Safra **said to him: Enter, master. When he came out, Rabbi Abba said to him: Until now, you never entered Seir,** the land of the Edomites, who are not strict in their practice of modesty, **and** yet **you** already **learned the** customs **of Seir? Didn't we learn** in the mishna concerning the Temple: **There was a fire** next to the ritual bath, **and a bathroom of honor. And this was its honor: If one found it locked, it was known that someone was inside; if he found it open, it was known that no one was inside.** Speaking in the bathroom **is not a desired mode of behavior.**

וְהוּא סָבַר: מְסוּכָּן הוּא, דְּתַנְיָא, רַבָּן שִׁמְעוֹן בֶּן גַּמְלִיאֵל אוֹמֵר: עַמּוּד הַחוֹזֵר – מֵבִיא אֶת הָאָדָם לִידֵי הַדְרוֹקָן. סִילוֹן הַחוֹזֵר – מֵבִיא אֶת הָאָדָם לִידֵי יֵרָקוֹן.

The Gemara explains the opinion of Rav Safra, who told Rabbi Abba that he could enter while in the bathroom: Rav Safra **held that it was dangerous** for Rabbi Abba. If he waited and was uncertain whether or not he could enter, he would endanger himself. **As it was taught** in a *baraita*: **Rabbi Shimon ben Gamliel says: A column** of feces **that is held back** because one cannot relieve himself **causes dropsy** [***hidrokan***].[L] **A stream** [***silon***][L] of urine **that is held back causes jaundice.**

רַבִּי אֶלְעָזָר עָל לְבֵית הַכִּסֵּא, אֲתָא הַהוּא רוֹמָאָה דַּחְקֵיהּ, קָם רַבִּי אֶלְעָזָר וּנְפַק. אֲתָא דְּרָקוֹנָא שְׁמַטֵיהּ לְכַרְכְּשֵׁיהּ, קָרֵי עֲלֵיהּ רַבִּי אֶלְעָזָר: ״וְאֶתֵּן אָדָם תַּחְתֶּיךָ״ אַל תִּקְרֵי ״אָדָם״ אֶלָּא אֱדוֹם.

The Gemara relates that **Rabbi Elazar entered a bathroom. This Roman came and pushed him** away. **Rabbi Elazar stood and left,** and **a serpent**[B] **came and ripped out the intestines** of the Roman. **Rabbi Elazar recited the following verse about** the Roman: **"Therefore I will give man** [***adam***] **for you"** (Isaiah 43:4); **do not read it as *adam*, but rather read** it **as Edom,** meaning a Roman.

״וְאָמַר לַהֲרׇגְךָ וַתָּחׇס עָלֶיךָ״,

With regard to modesty in a bathroom, the Gemara cites an additional biblical allusion. When David found Saul in the cave and spared him, tearing the corner of his coat, he said to him: "Behold this day, your eyes have seen how the Lord has delivered you today into my hand in the cave, **and he said to kill you; and you spared you"** (I Samuel 24:10).

**NOTES**

**Sleeping [*sheina*] at dawn – שֵׁינָה בְּעַמּוּד הַשַּׁחַר:** Some explain *sheina* in this context to mean urine [*sheten*]. The advantages of that interpretation are: It parallels the following statement with regard to a bowel movement at dawn; and it avoids the contradiction between praise of sleep in the morning here and the critical pronouncements of the Sages with regard to sleep in the morning elsewhere (*Musaf HaArukh*, and see Rav Hai Gaon and Maharsha).

**Would sell sayings for dinars – מְזַבֵּן מִילֵּי בְּדִינָרֵי:** Some interpret this expression symbolically to mean that bar Kappara spoke very little. Others say that he would literally charge a fee for his sayings (*ge'onim*).

**The sayings of bar Kappara – פִּתְגָּמֵי בַּר קַפָּרָא:** These sayings are different expressions of a single concept: One should not miss an opportunity, for then all is lost. This is also true with regard to the pot; if the pot boils over, the water overflows, and is lost. These sayings apply equally to both one's material life and one's spiritual life (*Arukh; ge'onim*).

**Entered Seir – עָיְילַתְּ לְשֵׂעִיר:** Some explain that the inhabitants of Seir, the Edomites, were immodest; several people would sit in the bathroom together. Others say that this is an allusion to the demon, Seir; you became immodest like a demon in the bathroom (Rav Sa'adia Gaon).

**LANGUAGE**

**Forging [*istema*] – אִסְטְמָא:** Apparently from the Greek στόμωμα, *stomoma,* meaning steel.

**Dropsy [*hidrokan*] – הַדְרוֹקָן:** From the Greek ὑδρωπικός, *udropikos,* and ὑδρωπικόν, *udropikon,* which describe a condition where one's limbs become swollen and filled with water.

**Stream [*silon*] – סִילוֹן:** From the Greek σωλήν, *solèn,* meaning hose or drainpipe. That is why this word then became the term for the stream that passes through the pipe or through any other round opening.

**BACKGROUND**

**Serpent – דְּרָקוֹנָא:** The creature that ripped out the intestines of the Roman appears to have been a large desert reptile of the *varanidae* family, perhaps a desert monitor, *Varanus griseus*. It grows to a meter length, is extremely daring, and attacks much larger creatures, biting and shaking its prey into submission.

Large desert serpent

"ואמר?!" "ואמרתי" מיבעי ליה! "ותחס?!" "וחסתי" מיבעי ליה! – אמר רבי אלעזר, אמר לו דוד לשאול מן התורה – בן הריגה אתה, שהרי רודף אתה והתורה אמרה: בא להרגך השכם להרגו. אלא צניעות שהיתה בך – היא חסה עליך,

The Gemara asks: Why does the verse say: **And he said? It should** say: **And I said.** Why does the verse say: **And you spared? It should** say: **And I spared.** Rather, **Rabbi Elazar said: David said to Saul: By Torah law, you should be killed, as you are a pursuer** who seeks to kill me, **and the Torah says: If one comes to kill you, kill him first. But it was the modesty that you displayed that spared you.**

ומאי היא – דכתיב: "ויבא אל גדרות הצאן על הדרך ושם מערה ויבא שאול להסך את רגליו". תנא: גדר לפנים מן גדר, ומערה לפנים ממערה. "להסך" – אמר רבי אלעזר: מלמד שסיכך עצמו כסוכה.

**And what is this** modesty? **As it is written: "And he came to the sheepcotes by the way, where there was a cave, and Saul went in to cover his feet,** to defecate. Now David and his men were sitting in the innermost parts of the cave" (I Samuel 24:3). **It was taught** that the Sages said: **There was a fence within a fence, and a cave within a cave,** and Saul entered to defecate in the interest of modesty. With regard to the use of the term, **to cover** his feet, **Rabbi Elazar said:** This **teaches that,** even there, **he covered himself** with his garment **like a *sukka*.**

"ויקם דוד ויכרת את כנף המעיל אשר לשאול בלט" אמר רבי יוסי ברבי חנינא: כל המבזה את הבגדים סוף אינו נהנה מהם, שנאמר: "והמלך דוד זקן בא בימים ויכסהו בבגדים ולא יחם לו".

The Gemara continues with a homiletic interpretation of the verse: **"Then David arose, and cut off the corner of Saul's robe privily"** (I Samuel 24:4). **Rabbi Yosei, son of Rabbi Ḥanina, said: Anyone who treats clothing with contempt,** like David who tore Saul's robe for no reason, will be punished in that **ultimately he will not benefit from** his garments, **as it is stated: "Now King David was old and stricken in years; and they covered him with clothes, but he could get no heat"** (I Kings 1:1).

"אם ה׳ הסיתך בי ירח מנחה", אמר רבי אלעזר אמר ליה הקדוש ברוך הוא לדוד: "מסית" קרית לי? הרי אני מכשילך בדבר שאפילו תינוקות ש בית רבן יודעים אותו, דכתיב: "כי תשא את ראש בני ישראל לפקדיהם ונתנו איש כפר נפשו" וגו מיד "ויעמד שטן על ישראל", וכתיב: "ויסת את דו בהם לאמר לך מנה את ישראל". וכיון דמנינהו ל שקל מינייהו כופר, דכתיב: "ויתן ה׳ דבר בישרא מהבקר ועד עת מועד".

As for David's statement to Saul: **"If it be the Lord that has incited you against me, let Him accept an offering"** (I Samuel 26:19), **Rabbi Elazar said** that **the Holy One, Blessed be He, said to David: Do you call Me an inciter?** In retribution, **I will cause you to fail in a matter that even schoolchildren know, as it is written: "When you take the sum of the children of Israel,[H] according to their number, then shall they give every man a ransom for his soul** unto the Lord, when you number them; that there be no plague among them, when you number them" (Exodus 30:12). **Immediately** after God said this to David, **"Satan stood up against Israel** and incited David to number Israel" (I Chronicles 21:1). Moreover, **it is written:** "And again the anger of the Lord was kindled against Israel, **and He incited David against them, saying: Go, number Israel and Judea"** (II Samuel 24:1). The proportional response to David's calling God an inciter was that He incited David. **And when he counted them, he did not take a ransom from them,** and he was punished, **as it is written: "So the Lord sent a pestilence upon Israel from the morning even to the appointed time"** (II Samuel 24:15).

מאי "עת מועד?" – אמר שמואל סבא חתניה דרב חנינא משמיה דרבי חנינא: משעת שחיטת התמי עד שעת זריקתו. רבי יוחנן אמר: עד חצות ממש.

The Gemara asks: **What** is the meaning of **the appointed time? Shmuel the elder, father-in-law of Rabbi Ḥanina, said in the name of Rabbi Ḥanina:** It means **from when the daily offering is slaughtered until when** its blood **is sprinkled. Rabbi Yoḥanan said:** It means **precisely until noon.**

"ויאמר למלאך המשחית בעם רב", אמר רב אלעזר, אמר ליה הקדוש ברוך הוא למלאך: טו לי רב שבהם, שיש בו ליפרע מהם כמה חובו באותה שעה מת אבישי בן צרויה ששקול כרוב של סנהדרין.

It is also stated there: "The Lord repented Him of the evil **and said to the angel that destroyed the many** [*rav*] **people:** It is enough; now stay your hand" (II Samuel 24:16). Explaining the meaning of the word *rav*, **Rabbi Elazar said** that **the Holy One, Blessed be He, said to the angel: Take for me a great one** [*rav*] **from among them, who is worthy of defraying several** of Israel's **debts.** As a result, **at that moment Avishai ben Tzeruya, who was equivalent to the majority of the Sanhedrin, died.** His death atoned for the entire nation.

"ובהשחית ראה ה׳ וינחם", מאי ראה?

On a parallel note, it is said: **"The Lord beheld, and He repented him** of the evil" (I Chronicles 21:15). The Gemara asks: **What did the Lord behold?**

אמר רב: ראה יעקב אבינו, דכתיב: "ויאמר יעק כאשר ראם". ושמואל אמר: אפרו של יצחק רא שנאמר: "אלהים יראה לו השה".

**Rav said: He saw** and remembered **the patriarch, Jacob,** about whom the term seeing is used: **"And Jacob said when he saw them** [*ra'am*]: This is God's camp" (Genesis 32:3). **And Shmuel said: He saw** and remembered **Isaac's ashes,[N] as it is said** in the portion of the binding of Isaac: **"God will provide** [*yireh*] **Himself the lamb for a burnt-offering"** (Genesis 22:8).

## HALAKHA

**When you take the sum of the children of Israel – כי תשא את ראש בני ישראל:** According to the Gemara in *Yoma* (22b), the source prohibiting counting the Jewish people directly is the passage in Hosea (2:1): "And the children of Israel shall be as the sand of the sea, which will be neither measured nor counted," which is understood both as a blessing and a prohibition.

The Torah first alludes to the problem involved in counting Jews directly with the mitzva of the half-shekel: "When you take the sum of the children of Israel according to their counting, then each man will give atonement for his soul when you count them; then there will be no plague as you count them" (Exodus 30:12).

The Gemara derives from the actions of King Saul that there is a general prohibition against counting the people. Saul counted the people *batela'im* (I Samuel 15:4). The Sages understood this phrase to mean: With lambs. King Saul counted one lamb for each man instead of counting the men directly.

Even indirect counting is permitted only for the purpose of a mitzva. Otherwise, counting is prohibited. For this reason David was punished for arranging a census merely: "So that I may know the number of the people" (II Samuel 24:2). In contrast, he was not punished when he counted his soldiers, which is a necessary step in waging war (II Samuel 18:1).

This idea finds its way into everyday Jewish practice, where counting men for a prayer quorum is done indirectly (*Peri Ḥadash, Oraḥ Ḥayyim* 55).

## NOTES

**Isaac's ashes – אפרו של יצחק:** Isaac was not actually sacrificed as a burnt-offering. Nevertheless, because that was Abraham's intention, the ram that was sacrificed in his place is considered as if it was actually Isaac, and the ashes of the ram are considered the ashes of Isaac (Maharsha).

רַבִּי יִצְחָק נַפָּחָא אָמַר: כֶּסֶף כִּפּוּרִים רָאָה, שֶׁנֶּאֱמַר: ״וְלָקַחְתָּ אֶת כֶּסֶף הַכִּפּוּרִים מֵאֵת בְּנֵי יִשְׂרָאֵל״ וגו׳. רַבִּי יוֹחָנָן אָמַר: בֵּית הַמִּקְדָּשׁ רָאָה, דִּכְתִיב: ״בְּהַר ה׳ יֵרָאֶה״.

**Rabbi Yitzḥak Nappaḥa said: He saw the money of atone ment** that Israel gave when they were counted during the Exodus from Egypt, **as it is stated: "And you shall take the atonement money from the children of Israel,** and shal appoint it for the service of the tent of meeting, that it may be a memorial for the children of Israel before the Lord, tc make atonement for your souls" (Exodus 30:16). **Rabbi Yo ḥanan said: He saw the Temple, as it is written: "On the mount where the Lord is seen** [*yera'e*]**"** (Genesis 22:14).

פְּלִיגִי בָּהּ רַבִּי יַעֲקֹב בַּר אִידִי וְרַבִּי שְׁמוּאֵל בַּר נַחְמָנִי, חַד אָמַר: כֶּסֶף הַכִּפּוּרִים רָאָה, וְחַד אָמַר: בֵּית הַמִּקְדָּשׁ רָאָה. וּמִסְתַּבְּרָא כְּמַאן דְּאָמַר בֵּית הַמִּקְדָּשׁ רָאָה, שֶׁנֶּאֱמַר: ״אֲשֶׁר יֵאָמֵר הַיּוֹם בְּהַר ה׳ יֵרָאֶה״.

Additional *amora'im*, **Rabbi Ya'akov bar Idi and Rabb Shmuel bar Naḥmani, differed** in their opinions of wha God saw. **One said: He saw the money of atonement, anc one said: He saw the Temple, as it is stated:** "And Abrahan called the name of that place: The Lord will see; **as it is saic to this day: On the mount where the Lord is seen"** (Ger esis 22:14); generations later, they will recall the initial rev elation on Mount Moria, as the angel also appeared to Davic on this mountain.

״לֹא יִכָּנֵס אָדָם לְהַר הַבַּיִת בְּמַקְלוֹ״ וכו׳. מַאי קַפַּנְדַּרְיָא? אָמַר רָבָא: קַפַּנְדַּרְיָא כִּשְׁמָהּ. וְרַב חָנָא בַּר אַדָּא מִשְּׁמֵיהּ דְּרַב סָמָא בְּרֵיהּ דְּרַב מָרִי אָמַר: כְּמַאן דְּאָמַר אֱינָשׁ ״אַדְּמַקִּיפְנָא אַדָּרֵי – אֵיעוֹל בְּהָא״. אָמַר רַב נַחְמָן אָמַר רַבָּה בַּר אֲבוּהּ: הַנִּכְנָס לְבֵית הַכְּנֶסֶת עַל מְנָת שֶׁלֹּא לַעֲשׂוֹתוֹ קַפַּנְדַּרְיָא – מוּתָּר לַעֲשׂוֹתוֹ קַפַּנְדַּרְיָא.

We learned in the mishna that, in deference to the Templ **a person may not enter the Temple Mount with his staff** and his shoes. He may not make it a *kappandarya*. The Ge mara asks: **What** is the meaning of ***kappandarya*?**[L] **Rav said:** ***Kappandarya*, as its name** implies; a shortcut. **Ra Ḥana bar Adda in the name of Rav Sama, son of Rav Mar said:** One may interpret this as an acrostic, **as people say Instead of circumventing the rows** of houses [*ademakifn adarei*], **I will enter this** [*ei'ol beha*] one. **Rav Naḥman sai** that **Rabba bar Avuh said:** This *halakha* applies in a syn gogue as well. However, **one who enters a synagogue no** intending **to make it a shortcut**[H] **is permitted to make it shortcut** if he later changed his mind.

רַבִּי אַבָּהוּ אָמַר: אִם הָיָה שְׁבִיל מֵעִיקָּרוֹ – מוּתָּר. אָמַר רַבִּי חֶלְבּוֹ אָמַר רַב הוּנָא: הַנִּכְנָס לְבֵית הַכְּנֶסֶת לְהִתְפַּלֵּל – מוּתָּר לַעֲשׂוֹתוֹ קַפַּנְדַּרְיָא, שֶׁנֶּאֱמַר: ״וּבְבֹא עַם הָאָרֶץ לִפְנֵי ה׳ בַּמּוֹעֲדִים״ וגו׳.

Similarly, **Rabbi Abbahu said: If it was originally a pat** that passed through the site where the synagogue was erec ed, **one is permitted** to pass through, as the public right o passage is not negated by the construction of a synagogu **Rabbi Ḥelbo said** that **Rav Huna said: One who enters synagogue to pray is permitted to make it a shortcut, as i is stated: "But when the people of the land shall com before the Lord in the appointed seasons,** he that enter by way of the north gate to worship shall go forth by the wa of the south gate" (Ezekiel 46:9).

״וּרְקִיקָה מִקַּל וָחוֹמֶר״. אָמַר רַב בֵּיבַי אָמַר רַבִּי יְהוֹשֻׁעַ בֶּן לֵוִי: כׇּל הָרוֹקֵק בְּהַר הַבַּיִת בִּזְמַן הַזֶּה – כְּאִילּוּ רוֹקֵק בְּבָבַת עֵינוֹ, שֶׁנֶּאֱמַר: ״וְהָיוּ עֵינַי וְלִבִּי שָׁם כׇּל הַיָּמִים״.

We learned in the mishna that **spitting** on the Templ Mount is prohibited **through an *a fortiori* inference. Ra Beivai said** that **Rabbi Yehoshua ben Levi said: Anyon who spits on the Temple Mount,**[H] even **today, it is as if h spit in the pupil of** God's **eye, as it is stated: "And My eye and My heart shall be there perpetually"** (1 Kings 9:3).

אָמַר רָבָא: רְקִיקָה בְּבֵית הַכְּנֶסֶת – שְׁרֵיָא, מִידֵּי דַּהֲוָה אַמִּנְעָל. מָה מִנְעָל, בְּהַר הַבַּיִת – אָסוּר, בְּבֵית הַכְּנֶסֶת – מוּתָּר, אַף רְקִיקָה, בְּהַר הַבַּיִת – הוּא דְּאָסוּר, בְּבֵית הַכְּנֶסֶת – שָׁרֵי.

**Rava said: Spitting in a synagogue is permitted, just as i the case of shoes. Just as wearing shoes is prohibited o the Temple Mount** but **permitted in a synagogue, so, to spitting is prohibited on the Temple Mount** but **permitte in a synagogue.**

אָמַר לֵיהּ רַב פָּפָּא לְרָבָא, וְאָמְרִי לַהּ רָבִינָא לְרָבָא, וְאָמְרִי לַהּ רַב אַדָּא בַּר מַתָּנָא לְרָבָא: אַדְּיָלֵיף מִמִּנְעָל, נֵילַף מִקַּפַּנְדַּרְיָא!

**Rav Pappa said to Rava, and some say** that **Ravina said t Rava, and some say that Rav Adda bar Mattana said t Rava: Instead of deriving** this **from** the case of wearing **shoe, derive it from** the case of **a shortcut.** Just as a shortcu through a synagogue is prohibited, so too is spitting prohi ited.

## HALAKHA

**A person may not enter the Temple Mount with his staff, etc. – לֹא יִכָּנֵס אָדָם לְהַר הַבַּיִת בְּמַקְלוֹ וכו׳:** One may not enter the Temple Mount with a staff, shoes or a money belt, in deference to the Temple (Rambam *Sefer Avoda, Hilkhot Beit HaBeḥira* 7:2).

**A shortcut in the synagogue – קַפַּנְדַּרְיָא בְּבֵית הַכְּנֶסֶת:** If one's original intention, upon entering a synagogue, was not to use the synagogue as a shortcut, he is permitted to exit on the other side, using it as a shortcut. If the synagogue was constructed on a preexisting path, one may *ab initio* use it as a shortcut, regardless of intent. One who enters a synagogue in order to pray is permitted to exit on the other side, using it as a shortcut. Some (*Tur*) say this is a mitzva (Rambam *Sefer Ahava, Hilkhot Tefilla* 11:10; *Shulḥan Arukh, Oraḥ Ḥayyim* 151:5).

**Anyone who spits on the Temple Mount – הָרוֹקֵק בְּהַר הַבַּיִת:** One is obligated to conduct himself with a sense of awe and reverence vis-à-vis the Temple. This applies when the Temple is no longer standing, just as it did when it was intact. Therefore, one is forbidden to spit at the site of the Temple even today (Rambam *Sefer Avoda, Hilkhot Beit HaBeḥira* 7:7, and see 7:2).

## LANGUAGE

**Shortcut [*kappandarya*] – קַפַּנְדַּרְיָא:** From the Latin compendiaria meaning shortcut. Rava's statement: *Kappandarya* is as its name implies, meant that *kappandarya* should be understood according to its Latin meaning. Rav Ḥana bar Adda added an additional interpretation based on an acronym.

אֲמַר לֵיהּ: תַּנָּא יָלֵיף מִמִּנְעָל, וְאַתְּ אָמְרַתְּ מִקַּפַּנְדַּרְיָא! מַאי הִיא? דְּתַנְיָא: לֹא יִכָּנֵס אָדָם לְהַר הַבַּיִת לֹא בְּמַקְלוֹ שֶׁבְּיָדוֹ, וְלֹא בְּמִנְעָלוֹ שֶׁבְּרַגְלוֹ, וְלֹא בְּמָעוֹת הַצְּרוּרִין לוֹ בִּסְדִינוֹ, וּבְפוּנְדָּתוֹ מוּפְשֶׁלֶת לַאֲחוֹרָיו, וְלֹא יַעֲשֶׂנָּה קַפַּנְדַּרְיָא, וּרְקִיקָה מִקַּל וָחוֹמֶר מִמִּנְעָל, וּמַה מִּנְעָל שֶׁאֵין בּוֹ דֶּרֶךְ בִּזָּיוֹן אָמְרָה תּוֹרָה "שַׁל נְעָלֶיךָ מֵעַל רַגְלֶיךָ", רְקִיקָה שֶׁהִיא דֶּרֶךְ בִּזָּיוֹן – לֹא כׇּל שֶׁכֵּן.

Rava **said to him:** The ***tanna* derives** the prohibition of spitting **from** the case of **a shoe, and you say** that it should be derived **from** the case of **a shortcut?** The Gemara elaborates: **What is this** derivation from the case of a shoe? **As it was taught** in a *baraita*: **One may neither enter the Temple Mount with his staff in his hand, nor with his shoes on his feet, nor with money tied in his cloth and with his money-belt slung behind him, nor** should one **make it a shortcut. All the more so, spitting** is prohibited ***a fortiori* from** the *halakha* with regard to wearing **a shoe. Just as** with regard **to a shoe, which is generally not considered contemptuous, the Torah said: "Put off your shoes from off your feet, for the place upon which you stand is holy ground"** (Exodus 3:5), **all the more so spitting, which is considered contemptuous,** should be prohibited.

רַבִּי יוֹסֵי בַּר יְהוּדָה אוֹמֵר: אֵינוֹ צָרִיךְ, הֲרֵי הוּא אוֹמֵר "כִּי אֵין לָבוֹא אֶל שַׁעַר הַמֶּלֶךְ בִּלְבוּשׁ שָׂק", וַהֲלֹא דְּבָרִים קַל וָחוֹמֶר, וּמַה שַּׂק שֶׁאֵינוֹ מָאוּס לִפְנֵי בָּשָׂר וָדָם כָּךְ, רְקִיקָה שֶׁהִיא מְאוּסָה, לִפְנֵי מֶלֶךְ מַלְכֵי הַמְּלָכִים – לֹא כׇּל שֶׁכֵּן?

**Rabbi Yosei bar Yehuda, says: This** *a fortiori* inference **is unnecessary.** It could be otherwise derived. **It says: "For none may enter within the king's gate clothed with sackcloth"** (Esther 4:2). **This matter** can be inferred ***a fortiori*****: Just as sackcloth, which is** generally **not** considered **repulsive before** one who is **flesh and blood, is** forbidden within the king's gate, **all the more so spitting, which is repulsive,** should be forbidden **before the King of Kings.**

אֲמַר לֵיהּ, אֲנָא הָכִי קָאָמִינָא: נֵימָא הָכָא לְחוּמְרָא וְהָכָא לְחוּמְרָא,

The one who challenged him, Rav Pappa or Ravina, **said to Rava: I** intended to **say the following: Let us say, be stringent here,** with regard to the Temple Mount, **and be stringent here,** with regard to the synagogue,

Perek **IX**
Daf **63** Amud **a**

וְאֵימָא: הַר הַבַּיִת דְּאָסוּר בְּמִנְעָל – לֵילַף מִמִּנְעָל, אֲבָל בֵּית הַכְּנֶסֶת דִּשְׁרֵי בְּמִנְעָל, אַדְּיָלֵיף מִמִּנְעָל וּלְהֶיתֵּר – נֵילַף מִקַּפַּנְדַּרְיָא וּלְאִיסּוּר!

**and say** as follows: With regard to **the Temple Mount,** where one is **prohibited** from wearing **shoes, let us derive** the prohibition of spitting **from** the case of **shoes. However,** with regard to **a synagogue,** where one is **permitted** to wear **shoes, instead of deriving** the law with regard to spitting **from** the case of **shoes and permitting** it, **derive it from** the case of **a shortcut, and prohibit** it.

אֶלָּא אֲמַר רָבָא: כְּבֵיתוֹ. מָה בֵּיתוֹ, אַקַּפַּנְדַּרְיָא – קָפֵיד אִינִישׁ, אַרְקִיקָה וּמִנְעָל לָא קָפֵיד אִינִישׁ, אַף בֵּית הַכְּנֶסֶת, קַפַּנְדַּרְיָא הוּא דְּאָסוּר, רְקִיקָה וּמִנְעָל – שָׁרֵי.

**Rather, Rava said** a different reason: The synagogue is **like one's house. Just as one objects to** a person using **his house as a shortcut,** but **does not mind spitting and** wearing **shoes** therein, **so too** in the case of a **synagogue, a shortcut is prohibited** while **spitting and** wearing **shoes are permitted.**[H]

"כׇּל חוֹתְמֵי בְרָכוֹת שֶׁבַּמִּקְדָּשׁ" וכו'.

We learned in the mishna: **At the conclusion of all blessings** recited **in the Temple,** the one reciting the blessing would say: Blessed are You Lord, God of Israel, until everlasting.

כׇּל כָּךְ לָמָּה – לְפִי שֶׁאֵין עוֹנִין אָמֵן בַּמִּקְדָּשׁ. וּמִנַּיִן שֶׁאֵין עוֹנִין אָמֵן בַּמִּקְדָּשׁ – שֶׁנֶּאֱמַר "קוּמוּ בָּרְכוּ אֶת ה' אֱלֹהֵיכֶם מִן הָעוֹלָם עַד הָעוֹלָם". וְאוֹמֵר "וִיבָרְכוּ שֵׁם כְּבוֹדֶךָ וּמְרוֹמַם עַל כׇּל בְּרָכָה וּתְהִלָּה".

The Gemara explains: **Why** were they insistent upon this formula **to that extent? Because one does not answer amen in the Temple.**[H] Because there is a unique response to the blessings in the Temple, a unique formula for their conclusion was instituted. **From where** is it derived **that one does not answer amen in the Temple? As it is stated: "Stand up and bless the Lord, your God, from everlasting to everlasting"** (Nehemiah 9:5), which refers to the conclusion. **The verse** in Nehemiah **continues: "And let them say: Blessed be Your glorious name, that is exalted above all blessing and praise"** (Nehemiah 9:5). The response is exalted above other blessings.

יָכוֹל כׇּל הַבְּרָכוֹת כּוּלָּן תְּהֵא לָהֶן תְּהִלָּה אַחַת – תַּלְמוּד לוֹמַר: "וּמְרוֹמַם עַל כׇּל בְּרָכָה וּתְהִלָּה", עַל כׇּל בְּרָכָה וּבְרָכָה – תֵּן לוֹ תְּהִלָּה.

From the beginning of the verse, I **might** have thought that **all of the blessings there will have** only **a single** expression of **praise,** amen. Therefore, **the verse teaches: "That is exalted above all blessing and praise"; for every blessing,** a unique **praise is offered.** Therefore, the appropriate response to a blessing in the Temple is: Blessed are You Lord, God of Israel, from everlasting until everlasting.

"הִתְקִינוּ שֶׁיְּהֵא אָדָם שׁוֹאֵל בִּשְׁלוֹם חֲבֵירוֹ" וכו'. מַאי "וְאוֹמֵר"?

We learned in the mishna that the Sages **instituted that a person will greet another** with the name of God, and several biblical sources were cited. The Gemara asks: **Why** is it necessary for the mishna to cite all of those sources, introduced with the phrase: **And it says?** Why was the proof from Boaz's statement to the harvesters: The Lord is with you, insufficient?

**HALAKHA**

**Respect for a synagogue – כְּבוֹד בֵּית הַכְּנֶסֶת:** One is prohibited from using the synagogue as a shortcut. However, one is permitted to spit in it as long as he rubs the spit into the ground with his foot. This applies only on weekdays. On Shabbat, one may only place his shoe over it until it is absorbed into the ground (*Mishna Berura*). One is permitted to enter a synagogue wearing shoes (Rambam *Sefer Ahava, Hilkhot Tefilla* 11:8; *Shulḥan Arukh, Oraḥ Ḥayyim* 151:5–7).

**One does not answer amen in the Temple – שֶׁאֵין עוֹנִין אָמֵן בַּמִּקְדָּשׁ:** In the Temple, they would not answer amen after blessings. Therefore, on fast days, when the prayer leader reached the end of the first of six additional blessings and recited: He who answered Abraham, etc., he would continue: Blessed are You, Lord our God, God of Israel, from eternity to eternity. Blessed are You, Lord, the Redeemer of Israel. Those who heard would respond: Blessed be the name of His glorious kingdom, for ever and ever (Rambam *Sefer Zemanim, Hilkhot Ta'aniyot* 4:15).

וְכִי תֵּימָא: בֹּעַז מִדַּעְתֵּיהּ דְּנַפְשֵׁיהּ קָאָמַר – תָּא שְׁמַע "ה' עִמְּךָ גִּבּוֹר הֶחָיִל". וְכִי תֵּימָא: מַלְאָךְ הוּא דְּקָאָמַר לֵיהּ לְגִדְעוֹן – תָּא שְׁמַע "אַל תָּבוּז כִּי זָקְנָה אִמֶּךָ".

The Gemara explains: **And if you say: Boaz said this on his ow** and it proves nothing with regard to normative practice, **come an hear** a proof from the verse: **"The Lord is with you, mighty ma of valor"** (Judges 6:12). **And if you say** that **it was an angel wh said** this **to Gideon,** that perhaps this verse was the angel informin Gideon that the Lord is with him, but it is not the standard formu of a greeting, **come** and **hear** proof from the verse: **"And despis not**[N] **your mother when she is old"** (Proverbs 23:22); the custor of the nation's elders are an adequate source from which to deriv *halakha*.

וְאוֹמֵר: "עֵת לַעֲשׂוֹת לַה' הֵפֵרוּ תּוֹרָתֶךָ". אָמַר רָבָא: הַאי קְרָא מֵרֵישֵׁיהּ לְסֵיפֵיהּ מִדְּרִישׁ, מִסֵּיפֵיהּ לְרֵישֵׁיהּ מִדְּרִישׁ.

**And the verse states: "It is time to work for the Lord; they hav made void Your Torah"** (Psalms 119:126). Of this, **Rava said: Thi verse** can be **interpreted from beginning to end, and** can be **inte preted from end to beginning.**

מֵרֵישֵׁיהּ לְסֵיפֵיהּ מִדְּרִישׁ: "עֵת לַעֲשׂוֹת לַה'", מַאי טַעַם – מִשּׁוּם "הֵפֵרוּ תּוֹרָתֶךָ". מִסֵּיפֵיהּ לְרֵישֵׁיהּ מִדְּרִישׁ: "הֵפֵרוּ תּוֹרָתֶךָ" מַאי טַעְמָא – מִשּׁוּם "עֵת לַעֲשׂוֹת לַה'".

The Gemara elaborates: This verse can be **interpreted from begi ning to end: It is time to work for the Lord; what is the reasor Because they have made void Your Torah,** so it must be remedie Conversely, it can be **interpreted from end to beginning** as follow **They have made void Your Torah; what is the reason? Because is time to work for the Lord.** By means of violating the Torah, it possible to fundamentally rectify the situation.

תַּנְיָא, הִלֵּל הַזָּקֵן אוֹמֵר: בִּשְׁעַת הַמְכַנְּסִין – פַּזֵּר, בִּשְׁעַת הַמְפַזְּרִים – כַּנֵּס. וְאִם רָאִיתָ דּוֹר שֶׁהַתּוֹרָה חֲבִיבָה עָלָיו – פַּזֵּר, שֶׁנֶּאֱמַר: "יֵשׁ מְפַזֵּר וְנוֹסָף עוֹד", וְאִם רָאִיתָ דּוֹר שֶׁאֵין הַתּוֹרָה חֲבִיבָה עָלָיו – כַּנֵּס, שֶׁנֶּאֱמַר: "עֵת לַעֲשׂוֹת לַה' הֵפֵרוּ תּוֹרָתֶךָ".

With regard to this verse, **it was taught** in a *baraita* that **Hillel th Elder says: At the time of gathering,** if the Sages of the generatio see to it that the Torah remains the purview of the few, **disseminat** it to the public at large. **At the time of dissemination, gather,** an leave it to others to disseminate the Torah. **And if you see a ge eration for whom Torah is beloved, disseminate, as it is state "There is who scatters, and yet increases"** (Proverbs 11:24). Ho ever, **if you see a generation for whom Torah is not beloved, gat er;** do not cause the Torah to be disgraced, **as it is stated: "It is tim to work for the Lord; they have made void Your Torah."** Prever ing Torah study in that situation is a manifestation of work for th Lord.

דְּרַשׁ בַּר קַפָּרָא: זָלַת – קְבוֹץ קְנֵה מִינֵּהּ, בַּאֲתַר דְּלֵית גְּבַר – תַּמָּן הֱוֵי גְּבַר. אָמַר אַבָּיֵי, שְׁמַע מִינַּהּ: בַּאֲתַר דְּאִית גְּבַר – תַּמָּן לָא תֶּהֱוֵי גְּבַר.

On a similar note, **bar Kappara**[P] **taught:** If the price of the mercha dise has **declined, jump and purchase from it; and where there no man, there be a man;**[N] where there is no one to fill a particul role, accept that role upon yourself. **Abaye said: Infer from this** th **where there is a man, there do not be a man.**

פְּשִׁיטָא! – לָא נְצְרְכָה אֶלָּא בְּשֶׁשְּׁנֵיהֶם שָׁוִין.

The Gemara asks: Isn't Abaye's conclusion **obvious?** The Gema explains: **This** statement **is only necessary** in a case **where** there a **two who are equal.** Although you, too, are suited to fill that ro since another qualified person is already filling that role, allow hi to succeed.

דְּרַשׁ בַּר קַפָּרָא: אֵיזוֹהִי פָּרָשָׁה קְטַנָּה שֶׁכׇּל גּוּפֵי תוֹרָה תְּלוּיִן בָּהּ – "בְּכׇל דְּרָכֶיךָ דָעֵהוּ וְהוּא יְיַשֵּׁר אֹרְחֹתֶיךָ". אָמַר רָבָא: אֲפִילּוּ לִדְבַר עֲבֵירָה.

**Bar Kappara taught: Which is a brief passage upon which a fundamental** principles of **Torah are dependent? "In all your wa acknowledge Him, and He will direct your paths"** (Proverbs 3:6 **Rava said:** One must apply this principle **even to acts of transgre sion,** as even then one must adhere to God and refrain from sinnir excessively.

דְּרַשׁ בַּר קַפָּרָא: לְעוֹלָם יְלַמֵּד אָדָם אֶת בְּנוֹ אוּמָּנוּת נְקִיָּה וְקַלָּה. מַה הִיא? אָמַר רַב חִסְדָּא: מַחְטָא דְּתַלְמִיוּתָא.

**Bar Kappara taught: A person should always teach his child clean and simple craft.** The Gemara asks: **What** craft is considere clean and simple? **Rav Ḥisda said: Cutting precious stones.**

תַּנְיָא, רַבִּי אוֹמֵר: לְעוֹלָם אַל יַרְבֶּה אָדָם רֵעִים בְּתוֹךְ בֵּיתוֹ, שֶׁנֶּאֱמַר: "אִישׁ רֵעִים לְהִתְרוֹעֵעַ".

Several ethical tenets and guidelines for life **were taught** in a *b raita.* **Rabbi** Yehuda HaNasi **says: One should never have to many friends in his house,** i.e., people should not become acc tomed to being overly intimate in his house, **as it is stated: "The are friends that one has to his own hurt"** (Proverbs 18:24); or with friends of that kind will ultimately come to quarrel.

תַּנְיָא, רַבִּי אוֹמֵר: אַל יְמַנֶּה אָדָם אַפִּטְרוֹפּוֹס בְּתוֹךְ בֵּיתוֹ, שֶׁאִלְמָלֵי לֹא מִינָּה פּוֹטִיפַר אֶת יוֹסֵף אַפִּטְרוֹפּוֹס בְּתוֹךְ בֵּיתוֹ – לֹא בָּא לְאוֹתוֹ דָּבָר.

**It was taught** in a *baraita* that **Rabbi** Yehuda HaNasi **says: Do n appoint an administrator** [*apitropos*][L] **within your house, as ha Potiphar not appointed Joseph as administrator within his hous** Joseph **would not have come to that incident** involving him in legations of sexual impropriety.

## NOTES

**Despise not** – אַל תָּבוּז: Because one could argue that in the story of Gideon the blessing in God's name was said only by the angel, one must return to Boaz's statement. There is room to suggest that this custom is not binding, as it was established many generations earlier. Therefore, the Sages said: Despise not ancient customs, with the claim that your mother is elderly. Though one could posit that using God's name in this manner is contemptuous, the Sages teach: It is time to work for the Lord; they have made void Your Torah; it is preferable to mention God's name in this manner than to have it completely forgotten (Rabbi Yoshiya Pinto; *Maharsha*).

**Where there is no man, there be a man** – בַּאֲתַר דְּלֵית גְּבַר תַּמָּן הֱוֵי גְּבַר: This statement of bar Kappara appears to be a direct Aramaic translation of Hillel's pronouncement in the mishna in *Avot* (2:6): In a place where there are no men, strive to be a man. Why does bar Kappara repeat it, and why does Abaye choose to comment here, rather than on the mishna?

One approach suggests that the mishna refers to general communal situations, and Hillel requires someone who recognizes a lack of leadership to take charge, even at the expense of his personal Torah study. The context of bar Kappara's teaching indicates that he is talking about Torah leadership. A scholar who finds that there is no one to assume the mantle of leadership and to issue rulings in matters of *halakha*, should do so himself. With regard to that point, Abaye comments: When there is competent Torah leadership, one need not step forward (Maharsha).

## PERSONALITIES

**Bar Kappara** – בַּר קַפָּרָא: One of the Sages of the final generation of *tanna'im*, in the intermediate period between the *tanna'im* and *amora'im*, bar Kappara was a disciple of Rabbi Yehuda HaNasi and a friend of his son, Shimon. His first name may have been Shimon, although it is not clear from the sources.

Some believe that because of his renowned wisdom, he would literally sell his sayings for dinars. He would charge for his proverbs and guidance (*ge'onim*), and he was famous for his homilies and parables.

According to some sources, he was the son of Rabbi Elazar HaKappar. This is a possible explanation for the name bar Kappara, though, in the sources, their relationship is not sufficiently clear to make this determination.

Like other disciples of Rabbi Yehuda HaNasi, bar Kappara compiled anthologies of extra-mishnaic teachings, called: The Great *Mishnayot* of bar Kappara. In the Talmud, these *mishnayot* are cited with the introduction: *Tani* bar Kappara, meaning, bar Kappara taught.

Bar Kappara's primary student was his sister's son, Rabbi Yehuda bar Padda.

## LANGUAGE

**Administrator [*apitropos*]** – אַפִּטְרוֹפּוֹס: From the Greek ἐπίτροπος, *epitropos*, meaning appointee. This refers to the protector of those in his custody, and the like.

תַּנְיָא, רַבִּי אוֹמֵר: לָמָה נִסְמְכָה פָּרָשַׁת נָזִיר לְפָרָשַׁת סוֹטָה – לוֹמַר לְךָ שֶׁכָּל הָרוֹאֶה סוֹטָה בְּקִלְקוּלָהּ יַזִּיר עַצְמוֹ מִן הַיַּיִן.

It was taught in a *baraita*, **Rabbi** Yehuda HaNasi **says: Why is the portion of the Nazirite** (Numbers ch. 6) **juxtaposed with the portion of the** *sota* (Numbers ch. 5)? They are juxtaposed **to tell you that anyone who sees a** *sota* **in her disgrace,** her transgression, **should renounce wine,** as wine is one of the causes of that transgression.

אָמַר חִזְקִיָּה בְּרֵיהּ דְּרַבִּי פַּרְנָךְ אָמַר רַבִּי יוֹחָנָן: לָמָּה נִסְמְכָה פָּרָשַׁת סוֹטָה לְפָרָשַׁת תְּרוּמוֹת וּמַעְשְׂרוֹת – לוֹמַר לְךָ: כָּל שֶׁיֵּשׁ לוֹ תְּרוּמוֹת וּמַעְשְׂרוֹת וְאֵינוֹ נוֹתְנָן לַכֹּהֵן – סוֹף נִצְרָךְ לַכֹּהֵן עַל יְדֵי אִשְׁתּוֹ, שֶׁנֶּאֱמַר: "וְאִישׁ אֶת קֳדָשָׁיו לוֹ יִהְיוּ", וְסָמִיךְ לֵיהּ: "אִישׁ אִישׁ כִּי תִשְׂטֶה אִשְׁתּוֹ", וּכְתִיב: "וְהֵבִיא הָאִישׁ אֶת אִשְׁתּוֹ וְגוֹ'". וְלֹא עוֹד אֶלָּא – סוֹף שֶׁנִּצְרָךְ לָהֶן, שֶׁנֶּאֱמַר: "וְאִישׁ אֶת קֳדָשָׁיו לוֹ יִהְיוּ".

**Ḥizkiya, son of Rabbi Parnakh, said that Rabbi Yoḥanan said: Why is the portion of** *sota* **juxtaposed with the portion of** *terumot* **and tithes** (Numbers ch. 5)? They are juxtaposed **to tell you: Anyone who has** *terumot* **and tithes and does not give them to a priest,** will **ultimately require** the services **of a priest by means of his wife, as it is stated: "And every man's hallowed things shall be his"** (Numbers 5:10). This refers to one who keeps those hallowed items for himself. **To this** the Torah **juxtaposed: "If any man's wife go aside and act unfaithfully against him"** (Numbers 5:12). **And it is written: "Then shall the man bring his wife unto the priest"** (Numbers 5:15). **Moreover, ultimately** that man **will require** assistance from the tithe given to the poor, **as it is stated: "And every man's hallowed things shall be his"** (Numbers 5:10). He will himself need those very hallowed items that he was unwilling to give to others.

אָמַר רַב נַחְמָן בַּר יִצְחָק: וְאִם נָתַן – סוֹף מִתְעַשֵּׁר, שֶׁנֶּאֱמַר: "אִישׁ אֲשֶׁר יִתֵּן לַכֹּהֵן לוֹ יִהְיֶה" – לוֹ יִהְיֶה מָמוֹן הַרְבֵּה.

**Rav Naḥman bar Yitzḥak said: And if he gave them, ultimately he will become wealthy, as it is said: "Whatsoever any man gives the priest, it shall be his"** (Numbers 5:10); **much property shall be his.**

אָמַר רַב הוּנָא בַּר בְּרֶכְיָה מִשּׁוּם רַבִּי אֶלְעָזָר הַקַּפָּר: כָּל הַמְשַׁתֵּף שֵׁם שָׁמַיִם בְּצַעֲרוֹ – כּוֹפְלִין לוֹ פַּרְנָסָתוֹ, שֶׁנֶּאֱמַר: "וְהָיָה שַׁדַּי בְּצָרֶיךָ וְכֶסֶף תּוֹעָפוֹת לָךְ".

**Rav Huna bar Berekhya said in the name of Rabbi Elazar HaKappar: Anyone who includes the name of heaven in his distress,** i.e., who turns and prays to God in his time of trouble, **his livelihood will** ultimately **be doubled, as it is stated: "And the Almighty be your treasure, and precious** [*toafot*] **silver unto you"** (Job 22:25). If you include God in your trouble, your silver will be doubled. *Eif*, which in Aramaic means double, is etymologically similar to *toafot*.

רַבִּי שְׁמוּאֵל בַּר נַחְמָנִי אָמַר: פַּרְנָסָתוֹ מְעוֹפֶפֶת לוֹ כְּצִפּוֹר, שֶׁנֶּאֱמַר: "וְכֶסֶף תּוֹעָפוֹת לָךְ".

**Rabbi Shmuel bar Naḥmani said** a different explanation: This means that **his sustenance flies** [*meofefet*] **to him like a bird, as it is stated: "And precious silver** [*toafot*] **unto you."**

אָמַר רַבִּי טָבִי אָמַר רַבִּי יֹאשִׁיָּה: כָּל הַמְרַפֶּה עַצְמוֹ מִדִּבְרֵי תוֹרָה – אֵין בּוֹ כֹּחַ לַעֲמוֹד בְּיוֹם צָרָה, שֶׁנֶּאֱמַר: "הִתְרַפִּיתָ בְּיוֹם צָרָה צַר כֹּחֶכָה". אָמַר רַב אַמִי בַּר מַתְנָה אָמַר שְׁמוּאֵל: וַאֲפִילּוּ מִצְוָה אַחַת, שֶׁנֶּאֱמַר: "הִתְרַפִּיתָ" – מִכָּל מָקוֹם.

**Rabbi Tavi said in the name of Rabbi Yoshiya: Anyone who is lax in his** study of **matters of Torah will** ultimately **lack the strength to stand on a day of adversity, as it is stated: "If you faint in the day of adversity, your strength is small indeed"** (Proverbs 24:10). **Rav Ami bar Mattana said that Shmuel said: And even** if he was lax in the performance of **a single** mitzva, **as it is stated: If you faint;** this applies **in any case,** even in the case of a single mitzva.

אָמַר רַב סַפְרָא, רַבִּי אַבָּהוּ הֲוָה מִשְׁתָּעֵי: כְּשֶׁיָּרַד חֲנִינָא בֶּן אֲחִי רַבִּי יְהוֹשֻׁעַ לַגּוֹלָה הָיָה מְעַבֵּר שָׁנִים וְקוֹבֵעַ חֳדָשִׁים בְּחוּצָה לָאָרֶץ.

**Rav Safra said: Rabbi Abbahu would relate: When Ḥanina,[P] son of Rabbi Yehoshua's brother, went to the Diaspora,** Babylonia, **he would intercalate years[B] and establish months outside of Eretz** Yisrael.[N] Because Judaism in Eretz Yisrael had declined in the wake of the bar Kokheva rebellion, he considered it necessary to cultivate the Jewish community in Babylonia as the center of the Jewish people. Among other things, he intercalated the years and established the months even though the *halakha* restricts those activities to Eretz Yisrael.

שִׁגְּרוּ אַחֲרָיו שְׁנֵי תַלְמִידֵי חֲכָמִים, רַבִּי יוֹסֵי בֶּן כֵּיפַר וּבֶן בְּנוֹ שֶׁל זְכַרְיָה בֶּן קְבוּטָל. כֵּיוָן שֶׁרָאָה אוֹתָם, אָמַר לָהֶם: לָמָּה בָּאתֶם? אָמְרוּ לִי לִלְמוֹד תּוֹרָה בָּאנוּ. הִכְרִיז עֲלֵיהֶם: אֲנָשִׁים הַלָּלוּ גְּדוֹלֵי הַדּוֹר הֵם, וַאֲבוֹתֵיהֶם שִׁמְּשׁוּ בְּבֵית הַמִּקְדָּשׁ, כְּאוֹתָהּ שֶׁשָּׁנִינוּ: זְכַרְיָה בֶּן קְבוּטָל אוֹמֵר: הַרְבֵּה פְּעָמִים קָרִיתִי לְפָנָיו בְּסֵפֶר דָּנִיֵּאל.

Eventually, the Sages of Eretz Yisrael **sent two Torah scholars after him, Rabbi Yosei ben Keifar and the grandson of Zekharya ben Kevutal.** When **Ḥanina saw them, he asked them: Why did you come? They responded: We came to study Torah.** Since he saw his standing enhanced by the Sages of Eretz Yisrael coming to study Torah from him, **he proclaimed about them: These people are eminent** scholars **of our generation, and their fathers served in the Temple.** As we learned in tractate *Yoma*: **Zekharya ben Kevutal says: Many times I read before** the High Priest from **the book of Daniel** on the eve of Yom Kippur.

---

### PERSONALITIES

**Ḥanina (Ḥananya) – חֲנִינָא:** Rabbi Yehoshua ben Hananya's nephew, Ḥananya, was a member of the fourth generation of *tanna'im*. His primary teacher was his uncle, Rabbi Yehoshua, but he also studied Torah from other prominent Sages of that generation.

Apparently, Ḥananya visited Babylonia several times. However, with the outbreak of the bar Kokheva revolt, he settled there and established a Torah center; its influence was manifest in the rise in the level of Babylonian Torah study over the course of several generations. Since Eretz Yisrael remained desolate for several years after the revolt and most of its Sages were killed, Ḥananya remained one of the only prominent Sages in the world, leading him to intercalate years in Babylonia. It was only due to the resolute position of the Sages of Eretz Yisrael, and the opposition of the other Babylonian Sages, that he relented.

Ḥananya's statements do not appear in the Mishna, although they appear in many *baraitot*. There is a tradition that the prominent *amora* Shmuel was one of his descendants.

### BACKGROUND

**Intercalate years – מְעַבֵּר שָׁנִים:** The annual Jewish calendar follows a lunar cycle with twelve months of twenty-nine or thirty days. But it is also related to the solar calendar, because the Festivals must be observed in their appropriate seasons. In particular, Passover must be at the time of the barley harvest, and *Sukkot* at the time of the autumnal equinox. The solar year is slightly more than eleven days longer than the lunar year. To compensate for this difference, a thirteenth lunar month is occasionally added, following the month of Adar, and is called the Second Adar. During the period when the calendar was set each year by the Sanhedrin, the question of whether to add an extra month required a unique decision-making process. First, the matter was considered by three judges selected from the Sanhedrin. If they thought an additional month was necessary, two more judges were asked to join the deliberations. If this body also agreed, two more judges were added, bringing the total to seven. These judges would render the final decision. Among the factors the judges would consider, in addition to the need for the Festivals to fall in their appropriate seasons, were climatic conditions and whether the crops had ripened sufficiently. Since the fourth century CE, the Jewish calendar has operated on a fixed astronomical system using a nineteen-year cycle, correlating the lunar and solar calendars. Months are added in the 3rd, 6th, 8th, 11th, 14th, 17th, and 19th years of each cycle.

### NOTES

**He would intercalate years and establish months outside of Eretz Yisrael – הָיָה מְעַבֵּר שָׁנִים וְקוֹבֵעַ חֳדָשִׁים בְּחוּצָה לָאָרֶץ:** The significance of intercalating years is not merely that of one specific *halakha*. Because the times when the Festivals occur are determined by the intercalation of the years and the establishment of the months, for all intents and purposes, the existence of the Festivals and the very unity of the Jewish people is ultimately dependent upon intercalating the years. At that time, intercalation was based on special considerations calculated each year when the need arose, as until the fourth century CE leap years were not determined in advance. As a result, the place where the year was intercalated was viewed as the central authority of the entire Jewish people. This explains the resolute insistence by the Sages of Eretz Yisrael on their authority to determine this matter. Although Rabbi Akiva was not the only person to intercalate years outside of Eretz Yisrael, whenever it was undertaken, it was either due to exigent circumstances, when the authorities prohibited intercalating the years in Eretz Yisrael, or at the behest of the Sages of Eretz Yisrael.

**BACKGROUND**

**Establish months** – קוֹבֵעַ חֳדָשִׁים: The moon's monthly cycle is slightly more than twenty-nine-and-a-half days. In the Talmud, unless stated otherwise, a month is understood as having twenty-nine days. But it was, of course, frequently necessary to add an additional day to the month. During the long period in antiquity when the Hebrew calendar was established by the court based on the testimony of witnesses who saw the new moon, the addition of an extra day to a month was determined by their testimony. If the moon was sighted on the night after the twenty-ninth day of the month, the next day was the first day of the following month. If, however, the moon was not sighted that night, or if witnesses to the new moon did not appear in Jerusalem to testify the following day, an extra day was added to the previous month, making it thirty days long. In that case, both the thirtieth and the following day would be the days of the New Moon. Since the fourth century CE, the Jewish calendar has operated on a fixed astronomical system in which, generally, twenty-nine-day months and thirty-day months alternate.

התחיל הוא מטמא והם מטהרים, הוא אוסר והם מתירים. הכריז עליהם: אנשים הללו של שוא הם, של תהו הם. אמרו לו: כבר בנית – ואי אתה יכול לסתור, כבר גדרת – ואי אתה יכול לפרוץ.

These two scholars, however, began to dispute every decisio Ḥanina rendered in response to questions raised in the study ha **He** ruled it **impure and they** ruled it **pure; he prohibited** it an **they permitted** it. Eventually, **he proclaimed about them: Thes people are worthless. They are** good **for nothing** and they kno nothing. **They said to him: You have already built** up our name and glorified us; **you cannot** now **demolish. You have alread built a fence and you cannot break through it.**

אמר להם: מפני מה אני מטמא ואתם מטהרים, אני אוסר ואתם מתירים? – אמרו לו: מפני שאתה מעבר שנים וקובע חדשים בחוץ לארץ.

**He said to them: Why is it that** when **I** rule something **impur you** rule it **pure;** when **I prohibit** it, **you permit** it? **They said t him:** We do this **because you intercalate the years and establis the months outside of Eretz** Yisrael.

אמר להם: והלא עקיבא בן יוסף היה מעבר שנים וקובע חדשים בחוץ לארץ? – אמרו לו: הנח רבי עקיבא, שלא הניח כמותו בארץ ישראל. אמר להם: אף אני לא הנחתי כמותי בארץ ישראל. – אמרו לו: גדיים שהנחת נעשו תישים בעלי קרנים, והם שגרונו אצלך, וכן אמרו לנו: לכו ואמרו לו בשמנו: אם שומע – מוטב, ואם לאו – יהא בנדוי.

**He said to them: Didn't** Rabbi **Akiva ben Yosef** also **intercalat years and establish months**[B] **outside of Eretz** Yisrael? **They r plied to him: Leave** the case of **Rabbi Akiva, as,** when he left, **h did not leave behind anyone** as great in Torah **as he in Eret Yisrael.** Rabbi Ḥanina **said to them: I also did not leave behin anyone** as great **as me in Eretz Yisrael. They said to him: Th kids who you left behind have grown into goats with horn** they are greater than you are. **And they sent us to you, and thi is what they said to us: Go and tell him in our name: If he obey fine; and if** he does **not** obey, **he will be ostracized.**

Perek **IX**
Daf **63** Amud **b**

**HALAKHA**

**If a Sage ruled an item impure, his colleague is not permitted to rule it pure, etc.** – חָכָם שֶׁטִּמֵּא אֵין חֲבֵרוֹ רַשַּׁאי לְטַהֵר וכו׳: If a Sage issued a ruling to prohibit a particular case, once the ruling has been publicized, his colleague may not issue a contrary ruling based on his own reasoning. Even if the second Sage nevertheless issued a lenient ruling, the matter remains prohibited (Ra'avad, Rivash). Some say that this applies even when the second Sage is both more knowledgeable than the first and there is a greater number of members in his court than in the court of the Sage who issued the original, stringent ruling (Ra'avad, Rivash). However, others say that if the second Sage is greater, he may issue a contrary ruling (Moreinu HaRav Yosef Colon, Ran, Rabbeinu Yeruḥam). Either way, the second Sage is permitted to initiate deliberations with the first to convince him to reconsider his original ruling. Similarly, another Sage may issue a different halakhic ruling with regard to the same law, in a different case (Rema). However, if the second Sage has a clear tradition with regard to the *halakha* in question, and it is clear to him that the initial Sage was mistaken with regard to an established *halakha* or a matter that appears in a mishna, he may issue a contrary ruling (*Shulḥan Arukh, Yoreh De'a* 242:31).

**BACKGROUND**

**The vineyard in Yavne** – כֶּרֶם בְּיַבְנֶה: Apparently, the seat of the Sanhedrin in Yavne was called the vineyard in Yavne. According to an ancient tradition, the Sanhedrin was called a vineyard because when it was in session, the Sages themselves, along with their students, would sit in rows, like the rows of a vineyard (Jerusalem Talmud). The seat of the Sanhedrin may also have been located near vineyards, lending the name a double meaning.

ואמרו לאחינו שבגולה: אם שומעין – מוטב, ואם לאו – יעלו להר, אחיה יבנה מזבח, חנניה ינגן בכנור, ויכפרו כולם ויאמרו: אין להם חלק באלהי ישראל.

**And** in order to underscore this, **tell our brethren in exile: If the obey** the Sages of Eretz Yisrael to excommunicate Ḥanina, **fin and if** they do **not** obey us, it is as if they are seceding from th Jewish people. **They should climb a mountain; Aḥiya,** one of th leaders of the Babylonian Jewish community, **will build an alta Ḥananya,** son of Rabbi Yehoshua's brother, who was a Levite, **wi play the lute, and all will** proclaim **heresy and say that they hav no portion in the God of Israel.**

מיד געו כל העם בבכיה ואמרו: חס ושלום! יש לנו חלק באלהי ישראל.

This message had a profound impact on the people, and **immed ately the entire nation burst into tears, saying: God forbid. W do have a portion in the God of Israel.** They reconsidered the plans to establish Babylonia as the center of the Jewish people.

וכל כך למה? – משום שנאמר: ״כי מציון תצא תורה ודבר ה׳ מירושלים״.

The Gemara asks: **Why** did the Sages of Eretz Yisrael go **to th extent** to stop Ḥanina? The Gemara answers: **Because it is state "For out of Zion shall go forth the Torah, and the word of th Lord from Jerusalem"** (Isaiah 2:3).

בשלמא הוא מטהר והם מטמאין – לחומרא, אלא הוא מטמא והם מטהרין, היכי הוי? והא תניא: חכם שטמא – אין חברו רשאי לטהר, אסר – אין חברו רשאי להתיר! – קסברי: כי היכי דלא נגררו בתריה.

The Gemara considers the details of this event: **Granted,** Ḥanin would rule an item **pure and** the Sages from Eretz Yisrael woul rule it **impure;** they ruled **stringently. But** in a case where **h** ruled an item **impure and they** ruled it **pure, what are** the circu stances? How could they rule pure that which he ruled impur **Was it not taught** in a *baraita*: **If a Sage** ruled an item **impure, h colleague is not permitted** to rule it **pure;**[H] if he **prohibited** it, **h colleague may not permit** it? The Gemara explains: **They he** that they must do so in this case, **so that people would not b drawn after him;** due to the exigencies of the time they ove turned his rulings.

תנו רבנן: כשנכנסו רבותינו לכרם ביבנה היו שם רבי יהודה ורבי יוסי ורבי נחמיה ורבי אליעזר בנו של רבי יוסי הגלילי, פתחו כולם בכבוד אכסניא ודרשו.

**The Sages taught: When our Rabbis,** the Sages of the Mishn **entered the vineyard,** the academy, **in Yavne,**[B] **Rabbi Yehud Rabbi Yosei, Rabbi Neḥemya, and Rabbi Eliezer, son of Rabb Yosei HaGelili, were there** presiding over the Sages. **They a began** to speak **in honor of** their **hosts,** the local population ho ing them and their students as guests, **and they taught.**

פתח רבי יהודה ראש המדברים בכל מקו
בכבוד תורה ודרש: "ומשה יקח את האה
ונטה לו מחוץ למחנה", והלא דברים ק
וחומר, ומה ארון ה' שלא היה מרוחק אל
שנים עשר מיל אמרה תורה: "והיה כל מבק
ה' יצא אל אהל מועד", תלמידי חכמי
שהולכים מעיר לעיר וממדינה למדינה ללמו
תורה – על אחת כמה וכמה.

Rabbi Yehuda, head of the speakers[B] in every place, opened his speech in honor of Torah, and taught: It is stated: "Now Moses used to take the tent and pitch it outside the camp, far off from the camp; and he called it the Tent of Meeting. And it came to pass, that every seeker of God went out unto the Tent of Meeting, which was outside the camp" (Exodus 33:7). He said: **Isn't this an *a fortiori* inference? Just as the Torah says of the ark of God, which was only twelve *mil* from the camp: "Every seeker of God went out unto the Tent of Meeting"; all the more so** should **Torah scholars,** who wander great distances and **go from city to city and country to country to study Torah,** be called seekers of God.

"ודבר ה' אל משה פנים אל פנים". אמר רב
יצחק, אמר לו הקדוש ברוך הוא למשה
משה, אני ואתה נסביר פנים בהלכה. איכ
דאמרי, כך אמר לו הקדוש ברוך הוא למשה
כשם שאני הסברתי לך פנים – כך אתה הסב
פנים לישראל, והחזר האהל למקומו.

The Gemara continues: It is stated: **"And the Lord spoke unto Moses, face to face"** (Exodus 33:11). **Rabbi Yitzḥak said: The Holy One, Blessed be He, said to Moses: Moses, you and I will show cheerful faces in** the study of ***halakha*** to those who come to study. **Some say** that **the Holy One, Blessed be He, told Moses: Just as I showed you a cheerful face, so too you will show Israel a cheerful face and restore the tent to its place** in the camp.

"ושב אל המחנה" וגו'. אמר רבי אבה
אמר לו הקדוש ברוך הוא למשה: עכש
יאמרו הרב בכעס ותלמיד בכעס, ישרא
מה תהא עליהם? אם אתה מחזיר האה
למקומו – מוטב, ואם לאו – יהושע בן נ
תלמידך משרת תחתיך.

It is said: **"And he would return into the camp;** but his minister, Joshua bin-Nun, a young man, departed not out of the Tent" (Exodus 33:11). **Rabbi Abbahu said: The Holy One, Blessed be He, told Moses: Now,** they will say: **The Master,** God, **is angry and** the **student,** Moses, is also **angry, and what will happen to Israel?** Rather, you must restore the tent to its place among the people. **If you restore the tent to its place, fine; and if not, Joshua bin-Nun, your student,** will **serve** as Israel's leader **in your place.**

והיינו דכתיב: "ושב אל המחנה". אמר רבא
אף על פי כן לא יצא הדבר לבטלה, שנאמ
"ומשרתו יהושע בן נון נער לא ימיש מתו
האהל".

**And that is what is written: "And he would return into the camp;** but his minister, Joshua bin-Nun, a young man, departed not out of the Tent." **Rava said: Nevertheless,** though Moses obeyed and restored the tent, **the statement** written with regard to the role of Joshua **was not uttered for naught.** Joshua bin-Nun remained as deputy to Moses, and ultimately served in his place, as it is stated: **"But his minister, Joshua bin-Nun, a young man, departed not out of the Tent."**

ועוד פתח רבי יהודה בכבוד תורה ודר
"הסכת ושמע ישראל היום הזה נהיי
לעם". וכי אותו היום נתנה תורה לישרא
והלא אותו יום סוף ארבעים שנה היה! אל
ללמדך: שחביבה תורה על לומדיה בכל יו
ויום כיום שנתנה מהר סיני.

**And Rabbi Yehuda again began** to speak **in honor of Torah and taught:** When Moses took leave of Israel on his last day in this world, he said: **"Keep silence [*hasket*] and hear, Israel; this day you have become a people** unto the Lord your God" (Deuteronomy 27:9). This is surprising: **Was the Torah given to Israel on that day? Wasn't that day at the end of forty years** since the Torah was given? **Rather,** it comes **to teach that each and every day the Torah is as dear to those who study it, as** it was **on the day it was given from Mount Sinai.**

אמר רבי תנחום בריה דרבי חייא איש כפ
עכו: תדע, שהרי אדם קורא קריאת שמ
שחרית וערבית, וערב אחד אינו קורא – דומ
כמי שלא קרא קריאת שמע מעולם.

**Rabbi Tanḥum, son of Rabbi Ḥiyya, of the village of Akko, said: Know** that the Torah is indeed beloved, **as one who recites *Shema*, morning and evening,** for his entire life, and **does not recite it one evening, it is as if he never recited *Shema*.** He cannot compensate for what he missed.

"הסכת" – עשו כתות כתות ועסקו בתור
לפי שאין התורה נקנית אלא בחבורה. כדר
יוסי ברבי חנינא, דאמר רבי יוסי ברבי חנינ
מאי דכתיב "חרב אל הבדים ונאלו" – חר
על שונאיהם של תלמידי חכמים שיושבי
בד בבד ועוסקים בתורה. ולא עוד אל
שמטפשים, כתיב הכא "ונאלו", וכתיב הת
"אשר נואלנו". ולא עוד אלא שחוטאים
שנאמר "ואשר חטאנו".

The Gemara interprets the word ***hasket*** in this verse homiletically, as an acronym of the words *as*, make, and *kat*, group. **Form [*asu*] many groups [*kitot*] and study Torah, for the Torah is only acquired** through study **in a group.**[N] This is **in accordance with** the opinion of **Rabbi Yosei, son of Rabbi Ḥanina; as Rabbi Yosei, son of Rabbi Ḥanina, said: What is** the meaning of **that which is written: "A sword is upon the boasters [*habaddim*], and they shall become fools [*noalu*]"** (Jeremiah 50:36)? This verse can be interpreted homiletically: **A sword upon the enemies of Torah scholars,** a euphemism for the Torah scholars themselves, **who sit alone [*bad bevad*] and study Torah. And furthermore,** those who study alone **grow foolish,**[N] **as it is written here, *noalu*, and elsewhere it is written** that after Miriam was afflicted with leprosy, Aaron told Moses: **"For that we have done foolishly [*noalnu*]"** (Numbers 12:11). **And furthermore, they sin** due to that ignorance, **as** at the end of that same verse **it is stated:** "For that we have done foolishly, **and for that we have sinned."**

**BACKGROUND**

**Head of the speakers – ראש המדברים:** Though Rabbi Yehuda was never the *Nasi* of the Sanhedrin, this title was more than a mere honorific; it was a permanent appointment by the Roman government. Once the Roman authorities discovered his sympathetic attitude to their empire, they appointed him head of the Sages of Eretz Yisrael (see *Shabbat* 33b).

**NOTES**

**The Torah is only acquired in a group – אין התורה נקנית אלא בחבורה:** The Holy Torah is a Torah of life. It does not guide its followers towards a life of asceticism or a rejection of the wholesome pleasures of the world that can raise the spirits of an individual. Therefore, the Torah anticipates that those who walk in its path will be members of a community, whose support and encouragement will help facilitate their spiritual growth and development (*Ein Ayah*).

**Torah scholars who sit alone and study Torah…grow foolish – חכמים שיושבין בד בבד ועוסקין בתורה...מטפשין:** An essential aspect of a Torah scholar is the role that he plays in improving the world around him. To accomplish this, the scholar must develop an appreciation for opinions that are at variance with his own, both in the realm of *halakha* and in the realm of ethics. That kind of openness comes about only by means of group study, in the course of which one becomes accustomed to hearing opinions that are different from his own. When one chooses to limit debate and to remain secluded within his own closed community, he is unable to learn the ideas and thoughts of his peers and will consequently be unwilling to accept dissenting positions. Isolation inevitably leads to intractable disagreements and, ultimately, to bitter fights and arguments (*Ein Ayah*).

אִיבָּעֵית אֵימָא מֵהָכָא ״נוֹאֲלוּ שָׂרֵי צֹעַן״.

**If you wish, say** instead that it is derived **from here: "The princes of Tzoan are become fools [*noalu*]"** (Isaiah 19:13).

דָּבָר אַחֵר: ״הַסְכֵּת וּשְׁמַע יִשְׂרָאֵל״ – כַּתְּתוּ עַצְמְכֶם עַל דִּבְרֵי תוֹרָה, כִּדְאָמַר רֵישׁ לָקִישׁ. דְּאָמַר רֵישׁ לָקִישׁ: מִנַּיִן שֶׁאֵין דִּבְרֵי תוֹרָה מִתְקַיְּימִין אֶלָּא בְּמִי שֶׁמֵּמִית עַצְמוֹ עָלֶיהָ – שֶׁנֶּאֱמַר: ״זֹאת הַתּוֹרָה אָדָם כִּי יָמוּת בְּאֹהֶל״.

The Gemara offers **an alternative** explanation of this verse: **"Keep silence [*hasket*] and hear, Israel"; break [*kattetu*] yourselves over words of the Torah.** This is **in accordance with** the opinion **of Reish Lakish, as Reish Lakish said: From where** is it derived **that matters of Torah are only retained by one who kills himself over it?**[HN] **As it is stated: "This is the Torah: When one dies in a tent"** (Numbers 19:14); true Torah study demands the total devotion of one who is willing to dedicate his life in the tent of Torah.

דָּבָר אַחֵר: ״הַסְכֵּת וּשְׁמַע יִשְׂרָאֵל״ – הַס וְאַחַר כָּךְ כַּתֵּת. כִּדְרָבָא, דְּאָמַר רָבָא: לְעוֹלָם יִלְמוֹד אָדָם תּוֹרָה וְאַחַר כָּךְ יֶהְגֶּה.

The Gemara offers yet another **alternative explanation** of this verse: **"Keep silence [*hasket*] and hear, Israel"**; first **be silent [*has*]** and listen and **then** study intensively in order to **analyze [*kattet*]** and clarify the details. This is **in accordance with** the opinion of **Rava, as Rava said: One must always study Torah** and gain expertise in it, **and** only **then analyze** and delve into it.

אָמְרִי דְּבֵי רַבִּי יַנַּאי: מַאי דִּכְתִיב ״כִּי מִיץ חָלָב יוֹצִיא חֶמְאָה וּמִיץ אַף יוֹצִיא דָם וּמִיץ אַפַּיִם יוֹצִיא רִיב״,

**In the school of Rabbi Yannai they said: What is** the meaning **of that which is written: "For the churning of milk brings forth curd, and the wringing of the nose [*af*] brings forth blood, so the forcing of wrath [*appayim*] brings forth strife"** (Proverbs 30:33)?

בְּמִי אַתָּה מוֹצֵא חֶמְאָה שֶׁל תּוֹרָה – בְּמִי שֶׁמֵּקִיא חָלָב שֶׁיָּנַק מִשְּׁדֵי אִמּוֹ עָלֶיהָ.

With regard to the beginning of the verse: For the churning of milk brings forth curd; **in whom do you find the cream of Torah? With one who spits out the milk that he nursed from his mother's breasts over it;** one who struggles with all his might to study Torah.

״וּמִיץ אַף יוֹצִיא דָם״ – כׇּל תַּלְמִיד שֶׁכּוֹעֵס עָלָיו רַבּוֹ פַּעַם רִאשׁוֹנָה וְשׁוֹתֵק – זוֹכֶה לְהַבְחִין בֵּין דָּם טָמֵא לְדָם טָהוֹר.

With regard to: **And the wringing of the nose brings forth blood; any student whose rabbi is angry [*af*] with him the first time and he is silent** and does not react, **will merit** to be able **to distinguish between blood that is ritually impure and blood that is ritually pure.**

״וּמִיץ אַפַּיִם יוֹצִיא רִיב״, כׇּל תַּלְמִיד שֶׁכּוֹעֵס עָלָיו רַבּוֹ פַּעַם רִאשׁוֹנָה וּשְׁנִיָּה וְשׁוֹתֵק – זוֹכֶה לְהַבְחִין בֵּין דִּינֵי מָמוֹנוֹת לְדִינֵי נְפָשׁוֹת. דִּתְנַן, רַבִּי יִשְׁמָעֵאל אוֹמֵר: הָרוֹצֶה שֶׁיִּתְחַכֵּם יַעֲסוֹק בְּדִינֵי מָמוֹנוֹת, שֶׁאֵין לְךָ מִקְצוֹעַ בַּתּוֹרָה יוֹתֵר מֵהֶן, שֶׁהֵן כְּמַעְיָן נוֹבֵעַ.

As for: **And the forcing of wrath [*appayim*] brings forth strife; any student whose rabbi is angry with him for the first and second times,** *appayim* being the plural of *af*, **and he is silent, merits to distinguish between monetary cases,** strife, **and capital cases,** as that is the highest level of learning. **As we learned in** a mishna: **Rabbi Yishmael says: One who seeks to become wise should engage in monetary laws, as there is no greater discipline in Torah, as they are like a flowing well** in which innovations constantly spring forth.

אָמַר רַבִּי שְׁמוּאֵל בַּר נַחְמָנִי: מַאי דִּכְתִיב ״אִם נָבַלְתָּ בְהִתְנַשֵּׂא וְאִם זַמּוֹתָ יָד לְפֶה״ – כׇּל הַמְנַבֵּל עַצְמוֹ עַל דִּבְרֵי תוֹרָה – סוֹפוֹ לְהִתְנַשֵּׂא, וְאִם זָמַם – יָד לְפֶה.

Similarly, **Rabbi Shmuel bar Naḥmani said: What is** the meaning **of that which is written: "If you have done foolishly in lifting up yourself, or if you have planned devices [*zamota*], lay your hand over your mouth"** (Proverbs 30:32)? **Anyone who abases himself over matters of Torah,** asking questions despite the shame he feels for his ignorance, **will ultimately be exalted. And if he muzzles [*zamam*] himself** due to embarrassment, he will end up with his **hand over** his **mouth,** unable to answer.

פָּתַח רַבִּי נְחֶמְיָה בִּכְבוֹד אַכְסַנְיָא וְדָרַשׁ: מַאי דִּכְתִיב ״וַיֹּאמֶר שָׁאוּל אֶל הַקֵּינִי לְכוּ סֻרוּ רְדוּ מִתּוֹךְ עֲמָלֵקִי פֶּן אוֹסִפְךָ עִמּוֹ וְאַתָּה עָשִׂיתָה חֶסֶד עִם כׇּל בְּנֵי יִשְׂרָאֵל״, וַהֲלֹא דְּבָרִים קַל וָחוֹמֶר: וּמָה יִתְרוֹ שֶׁלֹּא קֵירֵב אֶת מֹשֶׁה אֶלָּא לִכְבוֹד עַצְמוֹ – כָּךְ, הַמְאָרֵחַ תַּלְמִיד חָכָם בְּתוֹךְ בֵּיתוֹ, וּמַאֲכִילוֹ וּמַשְׁקֵהוּ וּמְהַנֵּהוּ מִנְּכָסָיו – עַל אַחַת כַּמָּה וְכַמָּה.

The Gemara returns to the homilies offered by the Sages in the vineyard of Yavne. **Rabbi Neḥemya began** to speak **in honor of the hosts and taught: What is** the meaning of **that which is written: "And Saul said unto the Kenites: Go, depart, get you down from among the Amalekites lest I destroy you with them, for you showed kindness to all the Children of Israel when they came up out of Egypt"** (I Samuel 15:6)? **Isn't this an *a fortiori* inference: Just as Jethro,** the forbearer of the Kenite tribe, who **only befriended Moses for his own honor,**[N] is treated **in this way** and rewarded that his merit would protect his descendants; all **the more so** should **one who hosts a Torah scholar in his home providing him with food and drink and availing him of his possessions,** be rewarded with that protection.

## HALAKHA

**Matters of Torah are only retained by one who kills himself over it – שֶׁאֵין דִּבְרֵי תוֹרָה מִתְקַיְּימִין אֶלָּא בְּמִי שֶׁמֵּמִית עַצְמוֹ עָלֶיהָ:** The Torah is not retained by one who studies it nonchalantly or by one who studies in comfort. Rather, Torah is retained only by one who is willing to afflict himself in order to study, withholding sleep from his eyes and slumber from his eyelids (Rambam *Sefer HaMadda, Hilkhot Talmud Torah* 3:12; *Shulḥan Arukh, Yoreh De'a* 246:21).

## NOTES

**Matters of Torah are only retained by one who kills himself over it – אֵין דִּבְרֵי תוֹרָה מִתְקַיְּימִין אֶלָּא בְּמִי שֶׁמֵּמִית עַצְמוֹ עָלֶיהָ:** While educators often try to make Torah study easier because they believe that doing so will lead students to accumulate more information and Torah knowledge, their approach is fundamentally flawed. The significance of Torah education is qualitative, not quantitative. It is not the sheer volume of knowledge amassed; it is the quality of the Torah wisdom that is attained. Simplistic, facile methods of study do not facilitate deep understanding. That can only be achieved through hard work and serious effort (*Ein Ayah*).

**The good of Jethro – טוֹבַת יִתְרוֹ:** Rashi explains that the good deed performed by Jethro was that he hosted a meal for Moses and the elders of Israel in the desert. The Maharsha provides a more obvious explanation: Jethro's good deed was that he invited Moses into his home and gave him his daughter Zipporah as a wife, which he did only for his own benefit.

פָּתַח רַבִּי יוֹסֵי בִּכְבוֹד אַכְסַנְיָא וְדָרַשׁ: "לֹ
תְתַעֵב אֲדֹמִי כִּי אָחִיךָ הוּא לֹא תְתַע
מִצְרִי כִּי גֵר הָיִיתָ בְאַרְצוֹ", וַהֲלֹא דְּבָרִי
קַל וָחוֹמֶר: וּמָה מִצְרִיִּים שֶׁלֹּא קֵרְבוּ אֶ
יִשְׂרָאֵל אֶלָּא לְצוֹרֶךְ עַצְמָן, שֶׁנֶּאֱמַר "וְאִ
יָדַעְתָּ וְיֶשׁ בָּם אַנְשֵׁי חַיִל וְשַׂמְתָּם שָׂ
מִקְנֶה עַל אֲשֶׁר לִי" – כָּךְ, הַמְאָרֵחַ תַּלְמִי
חָכָם בְּתוֹךְ בֵּיתוֹ וּמַאֲכִילוֹ וּמַשְׁקֵד
וּמְהַנֵּהוּ מִנְּכָסָיו – עַל אַחַת כַּמָּה וְכַמָּה.

Rabbi Yosei began to speak **in honor of the hosts, and taught:** It is said: **"You shall not abhor an Edomite, for he is your brother; you shall not abhor an Egyptian, because you were a stranger in his land"** (Deuteronomy 23:8). **Isn't this an *a fortiori* inference: Just as the Egyptians, who only befriended Israel,** even when they hosted them, **for their own benefit,** as Pharaoh said to Joseph, **as it is stated: "And if you know any able men among them, then make them rulers over my cattle"** (Genesis 47:6), are treated **this way, all the more so** should **one who hosts a Torah scholar in his home, providing him with food and drink and availing him of his possessions** without concern for personal gain, be treated this way.

פָּתַח רַבִּי אֱלִיעֶזֶר בְּנוֹ שֶׁל רַבִּי יוֹסֵי הַגְּלִי
בִּכְבוֹד אַכְסַנְיָא וְדָרַשׁ: "וַיְבָרֶךְ ה׳ אֶ
עֹבֵד אֱדֹם הַגִּתִּי בַּעֲבוּר אֲרוֹן הָאֱלֹהִים
וַהֲלֹא דְּבָרִים קַל וָחוֹמֶר: וּמָה אָרוֹן שֶׁלֹּ
אָכַל וְשָׁתָה, אֶלָּא כִּבֵּד וְרִבֵּץ לְפָנָיו
כָּךְ, הַמְאָרֵחַ תַּלְמִיד חָכָם בְּתוֹךְ בֵּית
וּמַאֲכִילוֹ וּמַשְׁקֵהוּ וּמְהַנֵּהוּ מִנְּכָסָיו – עַ
אַחַת כַּמָּה וְכַמָּה.

**Rabbi Eliezer, son of Rabbi Yosei HaGelili,** began to speak **in honor of the hosts, and taught:** It is stated: **"The Lord has blessed the house of Oved-edom…because of the ark of God"** (II Samuel 6:12). **Isn't this an *a fortiori* inference: Just as** in reward for honoring **the ark, which neither ate nor drank, but before which** Oved-edom simply **swept and sprinkled** water to settle the dust, he was treated **this way** and merited a blessing, **all the more so** should **one who hosts a Torah scholar in his home, providing him with food and drink and availing him of his possessions** without concern for his personal gain, be rewarded with such a blessing.

מַאי הִיא בְּרָכָה שֶׁבֵּרְכוֹ? – אָמַר רַב יְהוּדָ
בַּר זְבִידָא: זוֹ חָמוֹת וּשְׁמוֹנֶה כַּלּוֹתֶי
שֶׁיָּלְדוּ שִׁשָּׁה שִׁשָּׁה בְּכֶרֶס אֶחָד,

The Gemara asks: **What is** that **blessing with which** Oved-edom **was blessed? Rav Yehuda bar Zevida said: This is Ḥamot and her eight daughters-in-law, each of whom bore six in a single womb,**[N]

## NOTES

**Six in a single womb – שִׁשָּׁה שִׁשָּׁה בְּכֶרֶס אֶחָד:** Some explain that this does not mean that they actually gave birth to sextuplets, but rather that each bore six sons. This appears to be the meaning of the verse (*Beit Ya'akov*).



שֶׁנֶּאֱמַר: "פְּעֻלְּתַי הַשְּׁמִינִי", וּכְתִיב "כִּ
בֵרְכוֹ אֱלֹהִים", "כָּל אֵלֶּה מִבְּנֵי עֹבֵ
אֱדֹם הֵמָּה וּבְנֵיהֶם וַאֲחֵיהֶם אִישׁ חַיִ
בַּכֹּחַ לַעֲבֹדָה שִׁשִּׁים וּשְׁנַיִם לְעֹבֵד אֱדֹם".

**as it is stated:** "And Oved-edom had **sons…Peulletai the eighth," and** in the continuation of the same verse **it is written: "For God blessed him"** (I Chronicles 26:4–5); apparently, these eight children were the blessing, as it is stated: **"All these were of the sons of Oved-edom; they and their sons and their brethren, able men in strength for the service; sixty-two of Oved-edom"** (I Chronicles 26:8). Each of the nine women gave birth to six sons, for a total of fifty-four. If one adds the original eight, there were sixty-two altogether.

אָמַר רַבִּי אָבִין הַלֵּוִי: כָּל הַדּוֹחֵק אֶ
הַשָּׁעָה – שָׁעָה דּוֹחַקְתּוֹ, וְכָל הַנִּדְחֶה מִפְּ
הַשָּׁעָה – שָׁעָה נִדְחֵית מִפָּנָיו,

**Rabbi Avin HaLevi said: If one forces the moment** and attempts to take advantage of an undeserved opportunity, the **moment forces him** and he is pushed aside. **If one yields to the moment** and relinquishes an opportunity that presents itself, the **moment yields to him.**

מִדְּרַבָּה וְרַב יוֹסֵף. דְּרַב יוֹסֵף סִינַי, וְרַבָּ
עוֹקֵר הָרִים. אִצְטְרִיכָא לְהוּ שַׁעְתָּא, שְׁלַ
לְהָתָם: סִינַי וְעוֹקֵר הָרִים, אֵיזֶה מֵהֶ
קוֹדֵם? שְׁלַחוּ לְהוּ: סִינַי קוֹדֵם, שֶׁהַכֹּ
צְרִיכִין לְמָרֵי חִטַּיָּא. אַף עַל פִּי כֵן לֹא קִבֵּ
עָלָיו רַב יוֹסֵף, דְּאָמְרִי לֵיהּ כַּלְדָּאֵי: מָלְכַ
תַּרְתֵּין שְׁנִין.

This may be derived **from** an incident involving **Rabba and Rav Yosef,**[N] **as Rav Yosef** was **Sinai,** extremely erudite, **and Rabba** was **one who uproots mountains,** extremely sharp. **The moment arrived when they were needed;** one of them was to be chosen as head of the yeshiva. **They sent** the following question **there,** to the Sages of Eretz Yisrael: **Which takes precedence, Sinai or one who uproots mountains? They sent to them** in response: **Sinai takes precedence,** for **everyone needs the owner of the wheat,** one who is expert in the sources. **Nevertheless, Rav Yosef did not accept** the appointment, **as the Chaldean**[N] astrologers **told him: You will preside** as head of the yeshiva for **two years.**

מְלַךְ רַבָּה עֶשְׂרִין וְתַרְתֵּין שְׁנִין, מְלַךְ רַ
יוֹסֵף תַּרְתֵּין שְׁנִין וּפַלְגָּא.

**Rabba presided** as head of the yeshiva for **twenty-two years.** After he died, **Rav Yosef presided** for **two and a half years.** Though he did not take advantage of the opportunity that presented itself, he ultimately fulfilled that for which he was destined.

כָּל הָנָךְ שְׁנֵי דִּמְלַךְ רַבָּה, אֲפִילּוּ אוּמָּנָ
לְבֵיתֵיהּ לָא קְרָא.

The Gemara relates that **all those years that Rabba presided,** Rav Yosef **did not even call a bloodletter to his home.** Rav Yosef did not assume even the slightest air of authority, and would go to seek out the bloodletter rather than call upon the bloodletter to accommodate him.

## NOTES

**Rabba and Rav Yosef – רַבָּה וְרַב יוֹסֵף:** When Rav Yehuda, who was the head of the yeshiva in Pumbedita, died, there were two qualified candidates to replace him: Rabba and Rav Yosef. Rabba, who was younger than Rav Yosef, was renowned for his sharp intellect, while Rav Yosef was renowned for his encyclopedic knowledge. Since there was uncertainty with regard to which of them should be chosen, they posed a fundamental question to the Sages of Eretz Yisrael: Which takes precedence, "Sinai" or one who uproots mountains? The answer that was received was that Sinai takes precedence. However, Rav Yosef, for reasons described in the Gemara, deferred, and during the twenty-two years that Rabba served as head of the yeshiva, Rav Yosef did not assume even the slightest air of authority. Only after Rabba's death, Rav Yosef assumed the position at the head of the yeshiva.

**Chaldeans – כַּלְדָּאֵי:** It is apparent from several places in the Talmud that the Chaldeans, or, as they are known in the book of Daniel (2:4), *Kasdim*, were sorcerers and magicians with whom the Torah prohibits consulting. However, the Chaldeans were the scientists of that era and their primary area of expertise was astrology, i.e., foretelling a person's future based on the stars. Although not everyone approved of consulting the Chaldeans (see *Tosafot*, *Shabbat* 156b), there is no real transgression in doing so, and it was not uncommon for Jewish men and women to seek their advice.

וְאָמַר רַבִּי אָבִין הַלֵּוִי: מַאי דִּכְתִיב "יַעַנְךָ ה׳ בְּיוֹם צָרָה יְשַׂגֶּבְךָ שֵׁם אֱלֹהֵי יַעֲקֹב", "אֱלֹהֵי יַעֲקֹב" וְלֹא אֱלֹהֵי אַבְרָהָם וְיִצְחָק – מִכָּאן לְבַעַל הַקּוֹרָה שֶׁיִּכָּנֵס בְּעָבְיָהּ שֶׁל קוֹרָה.

**And Rabbi Avin HaLevi said: What is** the meaning of **that whic is written: "The Lord will answer you on the day of distress;**[N] **th name of the God of Jacob set you upon high"** (Psalms 20:2)? Is God specifically **the God of Jacob and not the God of Abrahar and Isaac?** Rather, **from here** the general principle is derived: **On who owns a beam should approach** carrying **the thick portion c the beam.** A builder, carrying a beam in order to affix it in a buildin must calibrate it and measure carefully so that the thick part of th beam fits in its place; so too must Jacob, who fathered and raise the children who would become the people of Israel, continue t pray for them and complete the task of nation-building.

וְאָמַר רַבִּי אָבִין הַלֵּוִי: כָּל הַנֶּהֱנֶה מִסְּעוּדָה שֶׁתַּלְמִיד חָכָם שָׁרוּי בְּתוֹכָהּ כְּאִילּוּ נֶהֱנֶה מִזִּיו שְׁכִינָה, שֶׁנֶּאֱמַר: "וַיָּבֹא אַהֲרֹן וְכֹל זִקְנֵי יִשְׂרָאֵל לֶאֱכָל לֶחֶם עִם חֹתֵן מֹשֶׁה לִפְנֵי הָאֱלֹהִים". וְכִי לִפְנֵי אֱלֹהִים אָכְלוּ? וַהֲלֹא לִפְנֵי מֹשֶׁה אָכְלוּ!

**And Rabbi Avin HaLevi said: One who partakes of a meal a which a Torah scholar is present, it is as if he enjoyed the radiar splendor of the Divine Presence, as it is stated: "And Aaron cam and all the elders of Israel, to eat bread with Moses' father-in-la before God"** (Exodus 18:12). **Did they** actually **eat before God Didn't they eat before Moses?**

אֶלָּא לוֹמַר לְךָ: כָּל הַנֶּהֱנֶה מִסְּעוּדָה שֶׁתַּלְמִיד חָכָם שָׁרוּי בְּתוֹכָהּ – כְּאִילּוּ נֶהֱנֶה מִזִּיו שְׁכִינָה.

**Rather,** this verse comes **to tell you** that **one who partakes in meal at which a Torah scholar is present, it is as if he enjoyed th radiant splendor of the Divine Presence.**

וְאָמַר רַבִּי אָבִין הַלֵּוִי: הַנִּפְטָר מֵחֲבֵרוֹ אַל יֹאמַר לוֹ "לֵךְ בְּשָׁלוֹם", אֶלָּא "לֵךְ לְשָׁלוֹם". שֶׁהֲרֵי יִתְרוֹ שֶׁאָמַר לוֹ לְמֹשֶׁה "לֵךְ לְשָׁלוֹם" – עָלָה וְהִצְלִיחַ. דָּוִד שֶׁאָמַר לוֹ לְאַבְשָׁלוֹם "לֵךְ בְּשָׁלוֹם" – הָלַךְ וְנִתְלָה.

**And Rabbi Avin HaLevi said: One who takes leave from anothe should not say to him: Go in peace, but rather,** he should say: **G to peace.**[N] **As we see** that, on the one hand, **Jethro said to Mose "Go to peace"** (Exodus 4:18), and **Moses ascended and was su cessful.** On the other hand, **David said to** his son, **Absalom: "G in peace"** (II Samuel 15:9), and Absalom **went and was** ultimate **hanged.**

וְאָמַר רַבִּי אָבִין הַלֵּוִי: הַנִּפְטָר מִן הַמֵּת אַל יֹאמַר לוֹ "לֵךְ לְשָׁלוֹם" אֶלָּא "לֵךְ בְּשָׁלוֹם", שֶׁנֶּאֱמַר: "וְאַתָּה תָּבוֹא אֶל אֲבֹתֶיךָ בְּשָׁלוֹם".

**Rabbi Avin HaLevi also said: One who takes leave from a dea person should not say to him: Go to peace, but rather,** one shoul say: **Go in peace, as it is stated: "But you shall go to your father in peace"** (Genesis 15:15).

אָמַר רַבִּי לֵוִי בַּר חִיָּיא: הַיּוֹצֵא מִבֵּית הַכְּנֶסֶת וְנִכְנָס לְבֵית הַמִּדְרָשׁ וְעוֹסֵק בַּתּוֹרָה – זוֹכֶה וּמְקַבֵּל פְּנֵי שְׁכִינָה, שֶׁנֶּאֱמַר "יֵלְכוּ מֵחַיִל אֶל חָיִל יֵרָאֶה אֶל אֱלֹהִים בְּצִיּוֹן".

**Rabbi Levi bar Ḥiyya said: One who leaves the synagogue an** immediately **enters the study hall**[H] **and engages in Torah** study, **i privileged to receive the Divine Presence, as it is stated: "The go from strength to strength, every one of them appears befor God in Zion"** (Psalms 84:8); those who go from a place of pray to a place of Torah study are privileged to receive a divine revelatio in Zion.

אָמַר רַבִּי חִיָּיא בַּר אַשִׁי אָמַר רַב: תַּלְמִידֵי חֲכָמִים אֵין לָהֶם מְנוּחָה לֹא בָּעוֹלָם הַזֶּה וְלֹא בָּעוֹלָם הַבָּא, שֶׁנֶּאֱמַר: "יֵלְכוּ מֵחַיִל אֶל חָיִל יֵרָאֶה אֶל אֱלֹהִים בְּצִיּוֹן".

With regard to that same verse, **Rabbi Ḥiyya bar Ashi said** that **Ra said: Torah scholars have rest neither in this world nor in th World-to-Come,** as in both worlds they are constantly progressin **as it is stated: "They go from strength to strength, every one c them appears before God in Zion."**

אָמַר רַבִּי אֶלְעָזָר אָמַר רַבִּי חֲנִינָא: תַּלְמִידֵי חֲכָמִים מַרְבִּים שָׁלוֹם בָּעוֹלָם, שֶׁנֶּאֱמַר: "וְכָל בָּנַיִךְ לִמּוּדֵי ה׳ וְרַב שְׁלוֹם בָּנָיִךְ",

**Rabbi Elazar said** that **Rabbi Ḥanina said: Torah scholars i crease peace in the world, as it is said: "And all your childre [*banayikh*] shall be taught of the Lord, and great shall be th peace of your children"** (Isaiah 54:13). If all the children of Isra are taught of the Lord, there will be peace for all.

אַל תִּקְרֵי "בָּנָיִךְ" אֶלָּא "בּוֹנָיִךְ". "שָׁלוֹם רָב לְאֹהֲבֵי תוֹרָתֶךָ וְאֵין לָמוֹ מִכְשׁוֹל", "יְהִי שָׁלוֹם בְּחֵילֵךְ שַׁלְוָה בְּאַרְמְנוֹתָיִךְ", "לְמַעַן אַחַי וְרֵעָי אֲדַבְּרָה נָּא שָׁלוֹם בָּךְ", "לְמַעַן בֵּית ה׳ אֱלֹהֵינוּ אֲבַקְשָׁה טוֹב לָךְ", "ה׳ עֹז לְעַמּוֹ יִתֵּן ה׳ יְבָרֵךְ אֶת עַמּוֹ בַשָּׁלוֹם".

The Sages interpreted this verse homiletically: **Do not read you children [*banayikh*], but your builders [*bonayikh*].**[N] Torah scho ars are those who build peace for their generation. As it is state **"Those who love Your Torah have great peace; there is no stur bling block for them"** (Psalms 119:165); and **"May there be peac within your walls, prosperity within your palaces"** (Psalms 122:7 because: **"For the sake of my brothers and friends, I shall sa Peace be within you. For the sake of the House of the Lord, ou God, I will seek your good"** (Psalms 122:8–9), and **"May the Lor give strength to His people; the Lord will bless His people wit peace"** (Psalms 29:11).[N]

הדרן עלך הרואה
וסליקא לה מסכת ברכות

## NOTES

The Lord will answer you on the day of distress – יַעַנְךָ ה׳ בְּיוֹם צָרָה: The Maharshal explains that the phrasing of this passage is based on the biblical text, as Jacob said: "Unto God, who answered me in the day of my distress" (Genesis 35:3), and the psalmist said: "The Lord will answer you on the day of distress; the name of the God of Jacob set you upon high." Jacob employed that same language.

Go to peace – לֵךְ לְשָׁלוֹם: Some say that man's role in life is to seek perfection, and therefore one says to the living: Go to peace, meaning, perfect yourself. To the dead, one says: Go in peace, as that which one acquired during his lifetime remains with him (*HaKotev*). The Maharsha, however, explains this to mean that the only blessing suitable for the dead is that they be brought to their burial in peace. On the other hand, the living must confront challenges and problems every day, so they may be blessed to find peace wherever they go.

Your children [*banayikh*]...your builders [*bonayikh*] – בָּנַיִךְ...בּוֹנָיִךְ: Since the verse mentions your children twice, some explain it as an allusion that the sons will be the architects of peace (*Ḥefetz Hashem*).

Concluding the tractate on the topic of peace – סִיּוּם הַמַּסֶּכֶת בְּעִנְיַן הַשָּׁלוֹם: There is a principle among the Sages that one should conclude on a positive note. Therefore, they conclude tractate *Berakhot*, whose entire focus was upon blessings and prayers that unite the sublime world on high with the mundane world below, with the mention of Torah scholars. Torah scholars engage in the study of Torah and the fulfillment of mitzvot that unite the divine entourage on high with the entourage below.

## HALAKHA

One who leaves the synagogue and enters the study hall – הַיּוֹצֵא מִבֵּית הַכְּנֶסֶת וְנִכְנָס לְבֵית הַמִּדְרָשׁ: After praying, one should proceed to the study hall and study Torah for at least a little while (*Magen Avraham*). Even one who does not have the requisite skills to study Torah, should proceed to the study hall and stay there for a while or review some material with which he is familiar. He will thereby be rewarded for going there (Rema; *Shulḥan Arukh*, *Oraḥ Ḥayyim* 155:1).

# Summary of **Perek IX**

The bulk of this chapter discusses the numerous blessings, which are recited on different occasions. Among these blessings, some are more specific and are recited on rare occasions; and some are more general and are recited on many different occasions.

Among the more general blessings are: Who has given us life, and: Who is good and does good. These two blessings of thanksgiving are recited each time a person feels that something good has befallen him: A general event like rainfall; a private celebration like the birth of a son; joy over a new acquisition; or even the joy of meeting a friend. Detailed parameters were established in the *halakha* with regard to the time and manner in which these blessings are recited. Nevertheless, the personal feelings and considerations of the one reciting the blessing, who uses it to offer thanks to God, also play a role.

Another general blessing, which is recited over an entire series of events, is: The true Judge. This blessing is recited as a faith-based acceptance and justification in response to any event involving misfortune or tragedy. Based on the fundamental concept of the mishna, the Gemara emphasizes that not only is there an obligation to recite a blessing over tragic events, but that one should recite the blessing joyfully, motivated by the profound belief that everything the Holy One, Blessed be He does, He does for the best. God's judgment is a true judgment; even though it may not be obvious at present, it is, at its core, a manifestation of good.

In addition to general blessings, there are several blessings recited only in specific cases. For example: Over God's might in nature: Whose strength fills the world; over the wonders of creation in general: Author of creation; over strange creatures: Who makes creatures different. Some blessings are recited as an expression of sympathy, for example: The true Judge. Others express praise and thanksgiving, for example: Who created beautiful creatures. They all come to underscore that one should view every event and phenomenon encountered in the course of life as an act of God and a manifestation of His will.

This chapter also discusses the *halakhot* governing the obligation of one who recovers from illness or is extricated from danger. In addition to the halakhic discussions, the chapter also includes fundamental philosophical determinations with regard to the role of miracles, the essence of dreams, the power of prayer, and the general problem of good versus evil.

# Index of **Background**


א

אַבָּא – Abba...30

אֲבוּקָה – Torch...339

אוֹגֶן וְאוֹזֶן – Rim and ear-shaped handle...335

אוֹחַ – Eagle-owl...372

אִי בָּעֵית אֵימָא – If you wish, you could say instead...8

אִי מִכְּלָלָא מַאי – If based on an inference, what of it...76

אִיסָּר – *Issar*...187

אֲכִילַת פְּרָס – Eating half a loaf of bread...271

אַל תִּקְרֵי – Do not read...27

אָמַר מָר – The Master said...9

אָמְרִי אֱינָשֵׁי – People say...9

אָמְרִי דְּבֵי רַבִּי... – The Sages of the school of Rabbi... said...212

אַסְדָּא – Raft...187

אֲפַרְסְמוֹן – Balsam...278

אַרְבָּעִים סְאָה – Forty *se'a*...146

אַרְדִּילַיָא – Truffles...303

אֲרוֹנוֹת – Coffins...131

אֲרִי – Lion...365

ב

(בְּ)דִיעֲבַד – After the fact...101

בּוּצִין – Cucumber...308

בּוּשְׁלֵי כַּמְרָא – Dates burned by the heat of the sun...269

בָּטְלָה דַעְתּוֹ – His opinion is rendered irrelevant...242

בֵּית הַכִּסֵּא – Bathroom...152

בֵּית הַמֶּרְחָץ – Bathhouse...158

בֵּית הַפְּרָס – *Beit haperas*...130

בֵּית שַׁמַּאי בִּמְקוֹם בֵּית הִלֵּל אֵינָהּ מִשְׁנָה – When Beit Shammai express an opinion where Beit Hillel disagree, their opinion is considered as if it were not in the mishna...246

בְּמַאי קָא מִפַּלְגִי – With regard to what do they disagree...22

בְּנוֹת שִׁקְמָה – *Benot shikma*...268

בַּר אוֹרְיַאן – Son of Torah...79

בָּרַיְיתָא – *Baraita*...10

בִּרְכַּת הַמָּזוֹן – Grace after Meals...293

בִּרְכַּת כֹּהֲנִים – The Priestly Blessing...215

בָּתֵּי הַתְּפִילִּין – Phylacteries compartments...34

ג

גּוּבְתָא דְּכוּחְלָא – Tube of eyeshadow...125

גּוֹלְלָן כְּמִין סֵפֶר – Rolls up the phylacteries in their straps like a scroll...150

גִּילְדָּנֵי דְּבֵי גִילֵּי – Small fish that grow among the reeds...287

גְּמִירִי – They learned...82

גֵּנוֹסָר – Genosar...283

גִּשְׁרָא דְּשַׁבִּיסְתָּנָא – The bridge of Shabistana...383

ד

דּוּרְמַסְקִין – Damascene plums...259

דִּינָרֵי זָהָב...כֶּסֶף – Dinars of gold and silver...225

דְּמַאי – Doubtfully tithed produce [*demai*]...293

דְּרָקוֹנָא – Serpent...400

ה

הָא גּוּפָא קַשְׁיָא – This is contradictory...53

הַבּוֹר וְחוּלְיָתוֹ – The pit and its mouth...17

הֲדַס – Myrtle branch...281

הַהוּא סָבָא – A certain elder...51

הַכָּנָף פְּתִיל – *Hakanaf petil*...106

הַמְמוּנֶּה – The appointed one...75

הַקָּזַת דָּם – Bloodletting...370

ו

וְאֵין צָרִיךְ לוֹמַר – And, needless to say...94

וִדּוּי – Confession...207

וִידּוּי מַעֲשֵׂר – The confession of tithes...266

וּרְמִינְהוּ – The Gemara raises a contradiction...10

ז

זָבָה – *Zava*...205

זַיִת – Olive...270

זִמּוּן – *Zimmun*...293

זַנְגְּבִילָא – Ginger...248

זַקְפֵי לְקוֹעֵיה כְּחִוְיָא – Rav Sheshet stiffened his neck like a snake...313

ח

חֲבוּשָׁא – Quince...279

חָבֵר עִיר – *Ḥever ir*...196

חַד אָמַר...וְחַד אָמַר – One said...And one said...27

חַזָּנָא – Caretaker...340

חִטָּה – Wheat...270

חִטָּה מִין אִילָן – Wheat is a type of tree...265

חִיוְיָא – Snake...80

חִלְפֵי דְּיַמָּא – Spikenards...279

חַמָּה בִּתְקוּפָתָהּ – The sun in its cycle...383

חֲמֵשֶׁת מִינֵי דָגָן – Five species of grain...284

חָסָא – Lettuce...362

חַסּוּרֵי מִחַסְּרָא – The mishna is incomplete...94

ט

טֶבֶל – Untithed produce...294

טַבְלָא – Drum...370

טְבֶרְיָא – Tiberias...341

טוֹבְלֵי שַׁחֲרִית – Those who immerse in the morning...145

טָרִית – Sardines...283

י

יַבְנֶה – Yavne...310

יְרָקוֹת וּדְשָׁאִים – Vegetables and leafy greens...237

יָתֵיב אֲחוֹרֵי – Sat behind...314

כ

כַּוָּונָה – Intent...91

כּוּךְ לְמֵת – A grave for the dead...99

כִּי אֲתָא רַב דִּימִי – When Rav Dimi came...37

כִּימָה – Pleiades...380

כּוֹס – Owl...372

כּוּתָּח – *Kutaḥ*...253

כּוּתִי – Samaritan [*Kuti*]...293

כָּל דְּפָרֵישׁ מֵרוּבָּא פָּרֵישׁ – Everything that parts from a group parts from the majority...182

כַּלָּה – *Kalla*...32

כִּנּוֹר – Lyre...17

כָּסָא דְּזוּגִיתָא – A cup of valuable white glass...204

כִּסָּנִין – Bread that comes as dessert...273

כַּרְבַּלְתָּא דְּתַרְנְגוֹלָא – The crest of the rooster...40

כְּרוּב – Cabbage...286

כְּרוּם – *Kerum*...37

כְּרֵישִׁין – Leeks...286

כֶּרֶם בְּיַבְנֶה – The vineyard in Yavne...406

כֶּרֶם רְבָעִי – Fourth-year grapevine...238

כַּרְתִּי – Leek-green...59

# Index of **Background**


ל

לָא אֲמָרָן אֶלָּא – 16...This *halakha* was only said

לֹא רְאִי זֶה כִּרְאִי זֶה – The aspect of this is not like the aspect 239...of that

לָא שְׁמִיעַ לְהוּ – 10...They did not hear

לָאו בְּפֵירוּשׁ אִיתְּמַר אֶלָּא מִכְּלָלָא אִיתְּמַר – It was not said 54...explicitly; rather, it was stated based on inference

לָבוּד – 165...Connected [*lavud*]

לְבָנָה בִּגְבוּרָתָהּ – 383...The moon in its might

לְהוֹדִיעֲךָ כֹּחָן דְּרַבָּנַן – In order to convey the far-reaching 142...nature of the opinion of the Rabbis

לִכְשֶׁיָּבֹא אֵלִיָּהוּ – 242...When Elijah comes

לְכַתְּחִלָּה – 101...*Ab initio*

לָמָּה יָצְאוּ – 141...Why were they singled out

לִפְתָּא – 260...Turnip

מ

מַאי קְרָא – 18...From what verse is it derived

מֵהָא לֵיכָּא לְמִשְׁמַע מִינָּהּ – No inference can be deduced from 162...this

מוּגְמָר – 275...Incense [*mugmar*]

מוּשְׁק – 278...Musk

מְחוֹזָא – 383...Meḥoza

מַחֲצֶלֶת שֶׁל קָנִים – 124...A mat of reeds

מַטְבֵּעַ שֶׁל טְבֶרְיָה – 342...A coin of Tiberias

מַטְבֵּעַ שֶׁל צִפּוֹרִי – 342...A coin of Tzippori

מֵי גִּיחוֹן – 66...The waters of the Gihon

מֵי הַמִּשְׁרָה – 148...Soaking water

מַיִם שׁוֹתְתִין עַל בִּרְכָּיו – 148...Urine flowing on his knees

מִינָא – 40...Heretic

מִינֵי דָגָן – 249...Types of grain

מַמְזֵר – 45...*Mamzer*

מַסְרֵק – 125...Comb

מְעַבֵּר שָׁנִים – 405...Intercalate years

מַעֲלֶה עָלָיו הַכָּתוּב כְּאִילּוּ עֲשָׂאָהּ – The verse ascribes him credit 33...as if he performed the mitzva

מַעְרְבָא – 10...The West

מַעֲשֶׂה לִסְתּוֹר – 111...A story to contradict

מַעֲשֵׂר רִאשׁוֹן – 293...First tithe

מַעֲשֵׂר שֵׁנִי – 293...Second tithe

מַעַשְׂרוֹת – 293...Tithes

מַרְגְּלָא בְּפוּמֵּיהּ – 113...He was wont to say

מְרָזַפְתָּא דְּנַפְּחָא – 226...A blacksmith's hammer

מֶרְחָץ – 388...Bathhouse

מִשּׁוּם – 39...In the name of

מִשְׁמְרוֹת כְּהוּנָּה – 76...The priestly watches

מַתְנִיתִין – 10...Our mishna

מְתַרְגֵּם – 294...Translator

נ

נְגָעִים – 28...Leprosy

נִדָּה – 205...A menstruating woman

נְהַרְבְּלָאֵי – 317...Sages of Neharbela

נְהַרְדְּעָא – 77...Nehardea

נֶטַע רְבָעִי – 238...Fourth-year sapling

נָקוּד – 20...Dots

נַרְקוֹם דְּגִינוּנִיתָא – 279...Daffodil

ס

סֵדֶר הַסְּבָה – 300...The order of reclining

סוֹטָה – 209...*Sota*

סוֹפְרִים – 296...Learned people [*soferim*]

סוּרָא – 77...Sura

סִיגְלֵי – 279...Violets

סִימָן – 215...A mnemonic symbol

סִיסִין – 287...Chamomile

סֵיפָא – 8...Latter clause

סִלְקָא – 257...Chard

סְמָלָק – 279...Jasmine

סִפְרָא דְּאַגַּדְתָּא – 151...Book of *aggada*

סִפְרָא דְּבֵי רַב – 75...The *Sifra* of the school of Rav

ע

עַד וְעַד בִּכְלָל – 176...Until and including

עוּזְרְדִין – 268...*Uzradin*

עוֹלֵלוֹת – 238...Small, incomplete clusters of grapes

עַיִשׁ וְכִימָה – 380...Ursa Major and Pleiades

עַם הָאָרֶץ – 305...*Am ha'aretz*

עַמּוּד הַשַּׁחַר – 7...Dawn

עַמּוּד הַשַּׁחַר וְהָנֵץ הַחַמָּה – 53...Dawn and sunrise

עַקְרַבָּא – 380...The constellation Scorpio

עָרוֹד – 59...Wild donkey

עָרְוָד – 220...*Arvad*

עֲשָׁשִׁית – 338...Lantern

פ

פּוּנְדְּיוֹן – 342...*Pundeyon*

פִּטְרִיּוֹת – 267...Mushrooms

פִּיטוּרֵי – 49...Ropes

פִּיל – 367...Elephant

פַּקְתָּא דַּעֲרָבוֹת – 350...Valley of willows

פִּרְקָא – 36...Lecture

פְּשַׁטוּ לָהּ – 10...They resolved this

פְּשִׁיטָא – 77...Obviously

פְּשִׁיטֵי – 153...Coins

צ

צְבָא הַשָּׁמַיִם – 217...Constellations in the firmament

צְדוֹקִים וּבַיְיתוֹסִים – 350...Sadducees and Boethusians

צוֹפִים – 396...Mount Scopus [*Tzofim*]

צִיצִית – 82...Ritual fringes

צָלָף – 245...Caper-bush

צְנוֹן – 270...Radish

צִפּוֹרִי – 341...Tzippori

ק

קַב – 146...*Kav*

קְהָלָא קַדִּישָׁא – 60...The holy community

קוֹבֵעַ חֳדָשִׁים – 406...Establish months

קוֹנָם – 322...*Konam*

קוּרָא – 366...Heart of palm [*kura*]

קוֹרְטְמֵי – 254...Safflower

קַל וָחוֹמֶר – 27...An *a fortiori* inference

קֶצַח – 264...Black cumin

קְרָא – 244...Gourd

קַרְיָא וְקִפּוֹפָא – 372...An eagle-owl, and an owl

קֶשֶׁר שֶׁל תְּפִילִּין – 42...Knot of the phylacteries

קֶשֶׁת – 382...Rainbow

ר

רֹאשׁ הַמְדַבְּרִים – 407...Head of the speakers

רַבִּי יְהוּדָה אוֹמֵר עַד שֶׁיִּשְׁחוֹט אֶת הַוְּרִידִין – Rabbi Yehuda says 51...until he slaughters the jugular veins

רְבִיעִית – 96...Quarter of a *log*

רִימִין – 268...*Rimin*

רֵישׁ גָּלוּתָא – 312...Exilarch

רִמּוֹן וְנֵץ – 247...The crown of a pomegranate and its flower

# Index of **Background**

ש


239...The seven species – שִׁבְעַת הַמִּינִים

23...The enemies of Israel – שׂוֹנְאֵי יִשְׂרָאֵל

365...*Shofar* – שׁוֹפָר

219...Forewarned ox [*shor muad*] – שׁוֹר מוּעָד

219...Black ox – שׁוֹר שָׁחוֹר

219...Innocuous ox [*shor tam*] – שׁוֹר תָּם

393...Best man – שׁוֹשְׁבִינוּת

The placement of the phylacteries of the – שִׂימָה כְּנֶגֶד הַלֵּב
92...arm must be opposite the heart

244...*Shinnana* – שִׁינָּנָא

268...*Shittin* – שִׁיתִין

114...Divine Presence – שְׁכִינָה

334...Second degree ritual impurity – שֵׁנִי לְטוּמְאָה

48...Two doorways – שְׁנֵי פְּתָחִים

396...The Eastern Gate – שַׁעַר הַמִּזְרָח

270...Barley – שְׂעֹרָה

161...May his Master forgive him – שָׁרֵא לֵיהּ מָרֵיהּ

68...Stool – שְׁרַפְרַף

334...A creeping animal – שֶׁרֶץ


ת


270...Figs – תְּאֵנָה

332...The frequent takes precedence – תָּדִיר קוֹדֵם

258...Lupin – תּוּרְמְסָא

This refutation of the statement of – תְּיוּבְתָּא דְּרַב...תְּיוּבְתָּא
69...Rav X is a conclusive refutation

152...Refutation and *halakha* – תְּיוּבְתָּא וְהִלְכְתָא

301...Table – תַּכָּא

59...Sky-blue – תְּכֵלֶת

271...Date – תָּמָר

8...*Tanna* – תַּנָּא

19...It was taught – תָּנָא

95...The *tanna* of the school – תָּנָא דְּבֵי

128...The oven of *akhnai* – תַּנּוּרוֹ שֶׁל עַכְנַאי

A *tanna* taught before Rabbi – תָּנֵי תַּנָּא קַמֵּיהּ דְּרַבִּי יוֹחָנָן
27...Yoḥanan

9...It was taught in a *baraita* – תַּנְיָא

372...Barn owl – תִּנְשֶׁמֶת

Prayers were instituted based on – תְּפִלּוֹת כְּנֶגֶד תְּמִידִין תִּקְּנוּם
175...the daily offerings

293...*Teruma* – תְּרוּמָה

# Index of
# **Language**

## א

259...Avruti, samrusi – אַבְרוּטֵי, סַמְרוּסֵי
374...Multitude [okhlosa] – אוּכְלוֹסָא
18...Astrologers [itztagninim] – אִיצְטַגְנִינִים
67...An enclosed veranda [akhsadra] – אַכְסַדְרָה
303...Soldiers [akhsania] – אַכְסַנְיָא
212...Alef into ayin – אָלְפִין עֵיְינִין
243...Anigeron – אֲנִיגְרוֹן
243...Ansigeron – אַנְסִיגְרוֹן
110...Gatehouse [anpilon] – אַנְפִּילוֹן
400...Forging [istema] – אִסְטְמָא
109...Delicate [istenis] – אִסְטְנִיס
306...Unminted coin [asimon] – אֲסִימוֹן
399...Aspamia – אַסְפַּמְיָא
322...Asparagus – אַסְפַּרְגּוֹס
363...House [appadna] – אַפַּדְנָא
404...Administrator [apitropos] – אֲפּוֹטְרוֹפּוֹס
153...Head covering [apraksuto] – אִפְּרַקְסוּתוֹ
126...His skull [arneka demoḥei] – אַרְנְקָא דְמוֹחֵיה

## ב

36...House of mourning [bei tammaya] – בֵּי טַמְיָא
130...Beit haperas – בֵּית הַפְּרָס
93...Son of noblemen [bar paḥtei] – בַּר פַּחְתֵּי

## ג

344...Military assistants [gulyarin] – גּוּלְיָירִין
32...Seal [gushpanka] – גּוּשְׁפַּנְקָא
105...Verbal analogy [gezera shava] – גְּזֵרָה שָׁוָה
49...Gimatriya – גִּימַטְרִיָּא
145...Gelostera – גְּלוֹסְטְרָא
374...Loaves [geluskaot] – גְּלוּסְקָאוֹת
351...Wild camel [gamla peritza] – גַּמְלָא פְּרִיצָא
217...Leaders of forts [gastera] – גַּסְטְרָא
363...Turnip-heads [gargelidei] – גַּרְגְּלִידֵי

## ד

392...Two faces [du partzufin] – דּוּ פַּרְצוּפִין
127...Like them [dugma] – דּוּגְמָא
123...Saddlebag [disakaya] – דִּיסַקְיָא

## ה

218...Officer [hegmon] – הֶגְמוֹן
228...Ordinary person [hedyot] – הֶדְיוֹט
400...Dropsy [hidrokan] – הִידְרוֹקָן
188...HaPakuli – הַפָּקוּלִי
303...Ownerless property [hefker] – הֶפְקֵר
376...Authority [harmana] – הַרְמָנָא

## ו

163...Vatikin – וָתִיקִין

## ז

255...Egyptian beer [zitom haMitzri] – זִיתוֹם הַמִּצְרִי
244...Salt water [zamit] – זָמִית
359...Thumb [zekafa] – זְקָפָא
250...Wheat kernels crushed into four parts [zariz] – זָרִיז

## ח

34...Entity [ḥativa] – חֲטִיבָה

## ט

36...Arab [taya'a] – טַיָּיעָא
250...Wheat kernels crushed into three parts [teraggis] – טְרָגִיס
253...Terokanin – טְרוֹקָנִין
254...Terima – טְרִימָא
253...Terita – טְרִיתָא
110...Banquet hall [teraklin] – טְרַקְלִין

## כ

36...This is how [kadu bar] – כַּדּוּ בַּר
254...Like boards [kelimmudin] – כְּלִמּוּדִין
254...Thick [ke'avin] – כְּעָבִין

## ל

217...Legion [ligyon] – לִגְיוֹן
379...One with unusually white skin [lavkan] – לַוְקָן
70...Highwaymen [listim] – לִסְטִים

## מ

355...Matron [matronita] – מַטְרוֹנִיתָא
100...Mil – מִיל

## ס

224...Colonnade [stav] – סְטָיו
400...Stream [silon] – סִילוֹן
156...Chin [santer] – סַנְטֵר
369...Soldier [sardeyot] – סַרְדְּיוֹט

## ע

250...Wheat kernels crushed into five parts [arsan] – עַרְסָן

## פ

196...Army [pulmusa] – פּוּלְמוּסָא
350...Money belt [punda] – פּוּנְדָּה
342...Pundeyon – פּוּנְדְּיוֹן
173...The midpoint of the afternoon [pelag haminḥa] – פְּלַג הַמִּנְחָה
209...False [pelaster] – פְּלַסְתֵּר
112...Entourage [pamalia] – פָּמַלְיָא
124...Curtain [pargod] – פַּרְגּוֹד
376...Messenger [peristaka] – פְּרִיסְתָּקָא
100...Parasang [parsa] – פַּרְסָה
94...Lying [perakdan] – פְּרַקְדָּן
230...Business [perakmatya] – פְּרַקְמַטְיָא

## צ

100...Torah scholar [tzurva merabbanan] – צוּרְבָא מֵרַבָּנָן

## ק

369...Neck chain [kolar] – קוֹלָר
285...Meat [kupra] – קוּפְרָא
321...Koraiytei – קוֹרַיְיטֵי
372...Kurferai – קוּרְפְּרַאי
263...Jug [kiton] – קִיתוֹן
42...Countenance [kelaster] – קְלַסְתֵּר
364...Kappa deka – קַפָּא דִּיקָא
402...Shortcut [kappandarya] – קַפָּנְדַּרְיָא
217...Military camp leader [karton] – קַרְטוֹן
277...Chairs [katedraot] – קָתֶדְרָאוֹת

## ר

217...Infantry division leader [rahaton] – רַהֲטוֹן
274...A portion [ristena] – רִיסְתְּנָא
351...Marketplace [risteka] – רִסְתְּקָא

## ת

301...Table [takka] – תַּכָּא
181...Shields [terisin] – תְּרִיסִין

# Index of **Personalities**


**א**

180...Avidan – אַבִידָן
362...Abaye – אַבַּיֵי
371...*Aḥer* – אַחֵר
359...Ameimar – אַמֵימָר

**ב**

83...Ben Zoma – בֶּן זוֹמָא
141...Ben Azzai – בֶּן עַזַּאי
404...Bar Kappara – בַּר קַפָּרָא
61...Berurya – בְּרוּרְיָא

**ג**

161...Geniva – גְּנִיבָא

**ח**

181...Ḥutzpit the disseminator – חוּצְפִּית הַתּוּרְגְּמָן
98...Ḥiyya bar Rav – חִיָּיא בַּר רַב
405...Ḥanina (Ḥananya) – חֲנִינָא

**ט**

110...Tavi – טָבִי

**י**

325...Yalta – יַלְתָּא

**ל**

125...Levi and Rabbi Afes – לֵוִי וְרַבִּי אָפֵס

**מ**

262...Mar, son of Ravina – מָר בְּרֵיהּ דְּרָבִינָא
321...Mar Zutra – מָר זוּטְרָא
297...Mareimar – מָרֵימָר

**ע**

377...Ulla – עוּלָּא
127...Akavya ben Mahalalel – עֲקַבְיָא בֶּן מַהֲלַלְאֵל

**ר**

313...Rav – רַב
135...Rav Adda bar Ahava – רַב אַדָּא בַּר אַהֲבָה
190...Rav Beivai bar Abaye – רַב בֵּיבַי בַּר אַבַּיֵי
30...Rav Huna – רַב הוּנָא
387...Rav Hamnuna – רַב הַמְנוּנָא
193...Rav Ḥisda – רַב חִסְדָּא
72...Rav Yeḥezkel – רַב יְחֶזְקֵאל
398...Rav Kahana – רַב כָּהֲנָא
Rav Mari, son of the daughter of – רַב מָרִי בְּרָהּ דְּבַת שְׁמוּאֵל
108...Shmuel
112...Rav Safra – רַב סַפְרָא
375...Rav Sheshet – רַב שֵׁשֶׁת
395...Rabbi Eliezer – רַבִּי אֱלִיעֶזֶר
143...Rabbi El'ai – רַבִּי אֶלְעַאי
208...Rabbi Elazar – רַבִּי אֶלְעָזָר
182...Rabbi Elazar ben Azarya – רַבִּי אֶלְעָזָר בֶּן עֲזַרְיָה
344...Rabbi Zilai, Rabbi Zivai – רַבִּי זִילַאי, רַבִּי זִיוַאי
298...Rabbi Zeira – רַבִּי זֵירָא
272...Rabbi Ḥiyya – רַבִּי חִיָּיא
38...Rabbi Ḥelbo – רַבִּי חֶלְבּוֹ
229...Rabbi Ḥanina ben Dosa – רַבִּי חֲנִינָא בֶּן דּוֹסָא
196...Rabbi Ḥanina Kara, the Bible expert – רַבִּי חֲנִינָא קָרָא
92...Rabbi Yoshiya – רַבִּי יֹאשִׁיָּה
143...Rabbi Yehuda ben Beteira – רַבִּי יְהוּדָה בֶּן בְּתֵירָא
182...Rabbi Yehoshua – רַבִּי יְהוֹשֻׁעַ
22...Rabbi Yehoshua ben Levi – רַבִּי יְהוֹשֻׁעַ בֶּן לֵוִי
98...Rabbi Yehoshua ben Korḥa – רַבִּי יְהוֹשֻׁעַ בֶּן קָרְחָה
28...Rabbi Yoḥanan – רַבִּי יוֹחָנָן
96...Rabbi Yona – רַבִּי יוֹנָה
14...Rabbi Yosei – רַבִּי יוֹסֵי
178...Rabbi Yirmeya bar Abba – רַבִּי יִרְמְיָה בַּר אַבָּא
371...Rabbi Yishmael ben Elisha – רַבִּי יִשְׁמָעֵאל בֶּן אֱלִישָׁע
Rabbi Meyasha, son of – רַבִּי מְיָאשָׁה בַּר בְּרֵיהּ דְּרַבִּי יְהוֹשֻׁעַ בֶּן לֵוִי
159...the son of Rabbi Yehoshua ben Levi
15...Rabbi Natan – רַבִּי נָתָן
376...Rabbi Sheila – רַבִּי שֵׁילָא
43...Rabbi Shimon ben Yoḥai – רַבִּי שִׁמְעוֹן בֶּן יוֹחַי
25...Rabbi Shimon ben Lakish – רַבִּי שִׁמְעוֹן בֶּן לָקִישׁ
302...Ravin – רָבִין
7...Rabban Gamliel – רַבָּן גַּמְלִיאֵל
186...Rabban Yoḥanan ben Zakkai – רַבָּן יוֹחָנָן בֶּן זַכַּאי

**ש**

361...King Shapur – שָׁבוֹר מַלְכָּא
188...Shmuel HaKatan – שְׁמוּאֵל הַקָּטָן

**ת**

128...Theodosius – תּוֹדוֹס


# Image **Credits**

*The following* קדיש *requires the presence of a* מנין.

יִתְגַּדַּל וְיִתְקַדַּשׁ שְׁמֵהּ רַבָּא
בְּעָלְמָא דְּהוּא עָתִיד לְאִתְחַדָּתָא
וּלְאַחֲיָאָה מֵתַיָּא, וּלְאַסָּקָא יָתְהוֹן לְחַיֵּי עָלְמָא
וּלְמִבְנֵא קַרְתָּא דִירוּשְׁלֵם, וּלְשַׁכְלָלָא הֵיכְלֵהּ בְּגַוַּהּ
וּלְמֶעְקַר פֻּלְחָנָא נֻכְרָאָה מֵאַרְעָא
וְלַאֲתָבָא פֻּלְחָנָא דִשְׁמַיָּא לְאַתְרֵהּ
וְיַמְלִיךְ קֻדְשָׁא בְּרִיךְ הוּא בְּמַלְכוּתֵהּ וִיקָרֵהּ
(נוסח ספרד: וְיַצְמַח פּוּרְקָנֵהּ וִיקָרֵב מְשִׁיחֵהּ)
בְּחַיֵּיכוֹן וּבְיוֹמֵיכוֹן וּבְחַיֵּי דְכָל בֵּית יִשְׂרָאֵל
בַּעֲגָלָא וּבִזְמַן קָרִיב, וְאִמְרוּ אָמֵן.

יְהֵא שְׁמֵהּ רַבָּא מְבָרַךְ לְעָלַם וּלְעָלְמֵי עָלְמַיָּא.

יִתְבָּרַךְ וְיִשְׁתַּבַּח וְיִתְפָּאַר וְיִתְרוֹמַם וְיִתְנַשֵּׂא
וְיִתְהַדָּר וְיִתְעַלֶּה וְיִתְהַלָּל
שְׁמֵהּ דְּקֻדְשָׁא בְּרִיךְ הוּא
לְעֵלָּא מִן כָּל בִּרְכָתָא
/בעשרת ימי תשובה: לְעֵלָּא לְעֵלָּא מִכָּל בִּרְכָתָא/
וְשִׁירָתָא, תֻּשְׁבְּחָתָא וְנֶחֱמָתָא, דַּאֲמִירָן בְּעָלְמָא
וְאִמְרוּ אָמֵן. (קהל: אָמֵן)

עַל יִשְׂרָאֵל וְעַל רַבָּנָן
וְעַל תַּלְמִידֵיהוֹן וְעַל כָּל תַּלְמִידֵי תַלְמִידֵיהוֹן
וְעַל כָּל מָאן דְּעָסְקִין בְּאוֹרַיְתָא
דִּי בְּאַתְרָא (בארץ ישראל: קַדִּישָׁא) הָדֵין, וְדִי בְּכָל אֲתַר וַאֲתַר
יְהֵא לְהוֹן וּלְכוֹן שְׁלָמָא רַבָּא
חִנָּא וְחִסְדָּא, וְרַחֲמֵי, וְחַיֵּי אֲרִיכֵי, וּמְזוֹנֵי רְוִיחֵי
וּפֻרְקָנָא מִן קֳדָם אֲבוּהוֹן דִּי בִשְׁמַיָּא
וְאִמְרוּ אָמֵן.

יְהֵא שְׁלָמָא רַבָּא מִן שְׁמַיָּא
וְחַיִּים (טוֹבִים) עָלֵינוּ וְעַל כָּל יִשְׂרָאֵל
וְאִמְרוּ אָמֵן.

*Bow, take three steps back, as if taking leave of the Divine Presence, then bow, first left, then right, then center, while saying:*

עֹשֶׂה שָׁלוֹם/ בעשרת ימי תשובה: הַשָּׁלוֹם/ בִּמְרוֹמָיו
הוּא יַעֲשֶׂה בְרַחֲמָיו שָׁלוֹם, עָלֵינוּ וְעַל כָּל יִשְׂרָאֵל
וְאִמְרוּ אָמֵן.

*The following Kaddish requires the presence of a minyan.*

Magnified and sanctified may His great name be,
in the world that will in future be renewed,
reviving the dead and raising them up to eternal life.
He will rebuild the city of Jerusalem
and in it re-establish His Temple.
He will remove alien worship from the earth
and restore to its place the worship of Heaven.
Then the Holy One, blessed be He,
will reign in His sovereignty and splendor.
May it be in your lifetime and in your days,
(*Nusaḥ Sepharad:* make His salvation flourish,
and hasten His messiah,)
and in the lifetime of all the House of Israel,
swiftly and soon – and say: Amen.

May His great name be blessed for ever and all time.

Blessed and praised,
glorified and exalted,
raised and honored,
uplifted and lauded
be the name of the Holy One,
blessed be He,
beyond any blessing,
song, praise and consolation uttered in the world –
and say: Amen.

To Israel, to the teachers,
their disciples and their disciples' disciples,
and to all who engage in the study of Torah,
in this (*in Israel add:* holy) place or elsewhere,
may there come to them and you great peace,
grace, kindness and compassion,
long life, ample sustenance and deliverance,
from their Father in Heaven –
and say: Amen.

May there be great peace from heaven,
and (good) life for us and all Israel –
and say: Amen.

*Bow, take three steps back, as if taking leave of the Divine Presence, then bow, first left, then right, then center, while saying:*

May He who makes peace in His high places,
in His compassion make peace for us and all Israel –
and say: Amen.

*The following paragraph is recited three times:*

הַדְרָן עֲלָךְ מַסֶּכֶת בְּרָכוֹת וְהַדְרָךְ עֲלָן, דַּעְתָּן עֲלָךְ מַסֶּכֶת בְּרָכוֹת וְדַעְתָּךְ עֲלָן, לָא נִתְנְשֵׁי מִנָּךְ מַסֶּכֶת בְּרָכוֹת וְלָא תִתְנְשֵׁי מִנַּן, לָא בְּעָלְמָא הָדֵין וְלָא בְּעָלְמָא דְאָתֵי.

יְהִי רָצוֹן מִלְּפָנֶיךָ יהוה אֱלֹהֵינוּ וֵאלֹהֵי אֲבוֹתֵינוּ, שֶׁתְּהֵא תוֹרָתְךָ אֻמָּנוּתֵנוּ בָּעוֹלָם הַזֶּה, וּתְהֵא עִמָּנוּ לָעוֹלָם הַבָּא. חֲנִינָא בַּר פַּפָּא, רָמֵי בַּר פַּפָּא, נַחְמָן בַּר פַּפָּא, אֲחַאי בַּר פַּפָּא, אַבָּא מָרִי בַּר פַּפָּא, רַפְרַם בַּר פַּפָּא, רָכִישׁ בַּר פַּפָּא, סוּרְחָב בַּר פַּפָּא, אַדָּא בַּר פַּפָּא, דָּרוּ בַּר פַּפָּא.

הַעֲרֶב נָא יהוה אֱלֹהֵינוּ אֶת דִּבְרֵי תוֹרָתְךָ בְּפִינוּ וּבְפִי עַמְּךָ בֵּית יִשְׂרָאֵל, וְנִהְיֶה אֲנַחְנוּ וְצֶאֱצָאֵינוּ (וְצֶאֱצָאֵי צֶאֱצָאֵינוּ) וְצֶאֱצָאֵי עַמְּךָ בֵּית יִשְׂרָאֵל, כֻּלָּנוּ יוֹדְעֵי
שְׁמֶךָ וְלוֹמְדֵי תוֹרָתְךָ לִשְׁמָהּ. מֵאֹיְבַי תְּחַכְּמֵנִי מִצְוֹתֶךָ תהלים קיט
כִּי לְעוֹלָם הִיא־לִי: יְהִי־לִבִּי תָמִים בְּחֻקֶּיךָ לְמַעַן לֹא אֵבוֹשׁ: לְעוֹלָם לֹא־אֶשְׁכַּח פִּקּוּדֶיךָ כִּי־בָם חִיִּיתָנִי: בָּרוּךְ אַתָּה יהוה לַמְּדֵנִי חֻקֶּיךָ: אָמֵן אָמֵן אָמֵן סֶלָה וָעֶד.

מוֹדִים אֲנַחְנוּ לְפָנֶיךָ יהוה אֱלֹהֵינוּ וֵאלֹהֵי אֲבוֹתֵינוּ שֶׁשַּׂמְתָּ חֶלְקֵנוּ מִיּוֹשְׁבֵי בֵּית הַמִּדְרָשׁ, וְלֹא שַׂמְתָּ חֶלְקֵנוּ מִיּוֹשְׁבֵי קְרָנוֹת. שֶׁאָנוּ מַשְׁכִּימִים וְהֵם מַשְׁכִּימִים, אָנוּ מַשְׁכִּימִים לְדִבְרֵי תוֹרָה, וְהֵם מַשְׁכִּימִים לִדְבָרִים בְּטֵלִים. אָנוּ עֲמֵלִים וְהֵם עֲמֵלִים, אָנוּ עֲמֵלִים וּמְקַבְּלִים שָׂכָר, וְהֵם עֲמֵלִים וְאֵינָם מְקַבְּלִים שָׂכָר. אָנוּ רָצִים וְהֵם רָצִים, אָנוּ רָצִים לְחַיֵּי הָעוֹלָם הַבָּא, וְהֵם רָצִים לִבְאֵר
שַׁחַת, שֶׁנֶּאֱמַר: וְאַתָּה אֱלֹהִים תּוֹרִדֵם לִבְאֵר שַׁחַת תהלים נה
אַנְשֵׁי דָמִים וּמִרְמָה לֹא־יֶחֱצוּ יְמֵיהֶם וַאֲנִי אֶבְטַח־בָּךְ:

יְהִי רָצוֹן מִלְּפָנֶיךָ יהוה אֱלֹהַי, כְּשֵׁם שֶׁעֲזַרְתַּנִי לְסַיֵּם מַסֶּכֶת בְּרָכוֹת כֵּן תְּעַזְרֵנִי לְהַתְחִיל מַסֶּכְתּוֹת וּסְפָרִים אֲחֵרִים וּלְסַיְּמָם, לִלְמֹד וּלְלַמֵּד לִשְׁמֹר וְלַעֲשׂוֹת וּלְקַיֵּם אֶת כָּל דִּבְרֵי תַלְמוּד תּוֹרָתְךָ בְּאַהֲבָה, וּזְכוּת כָּל הַתַּנָּאִים וְאָמוֹרָאִים וְתַלְמִידֵי חֲכָמִים יַעֲמֹד לִי וּלְזַרְעִי שֶׁלֹּא תָמוּשׁ הַתּוֹרָה מִפִּי וּמִפִּי זַרְעִי וְזֶרַע זַרְעִי
עַד עוֹלָם, וְיִתְקַיֶּם בִּי: בְּהִתְהַלֶּכְךָ תַּנְחֶה אֹתָךְ בְּשָׁכְבְּךָ משלי ו
תִּשְׁמֹר עָלֶיךָ וַהֲקִיצוֹתָ הִיא תְשִׂיחֶךָ: כִּי־בִי יִרְבּוּ יָמֶיךָ משלי ט
וְיוֹסִיפוּ לְּךָ שְׁנוֹת חַיִּים: אֹרֶךְ יָמִים בִּימִינָהּ בִּשְׂמֹאולָהּ משלי ג
עֹשֶׁר וְכָבוֹד: יהוה עֹז לְעַמּוֹ יִתֵּן יהוה יְבָרֵךְ אֶת־עַמּוֹ תהלים כט
בַשָּׁלוֹם:

*The following paragraph is recited three times:*

הַדְרָן We shall return to you, tractate *Berakhot,* and your glory is upon us. Our thoughts are upon you, tractate *Berakhot,* and your thoughts are upon us. We will not be forgotten from you, tractate *Berakhot,* and you will not be forgotten from us; neither in this world nor in the World-to-Come.

יְהִי רָצוֹן May it be Your will, Lord our God and God of our ancestors, that Your Torah will be our avocation in this world and will accompany us to the World-to-Come. Ḥanina bar Pappa, Ramei bar Pappa, Naḥman bar Pappa, Aḥai bar Pappa, Abba Mari bar Pappa, Rafram bar Pappa, Rakhish bar Pappa, Surḥav bar Pappa, Adda bar Pappa, Daru bar Pappa.

הַעֲרֶב נָא Please, Lord our God, make the words of Your Torah sweet in our mouths and in the mouths of Your people, the house of Israel, so that we, our descendants (and their descendants), and the descendants of Your people, the house of Israel, may all know Your name and
study Your Torah for its own sake. Your commandments *Psalms 119*
make me wiser than my enemies, for they are ever with me. Let my heart be undivided in Your statutes, in order that I may not be put to shame. I will never forget Your precepts, for with them You have quickened me. Blessed are You, O Lord; teach me Your statutes. Amen, Amen, Amen, Selah, Forever.

מוֹדִים We give thanks before You, Lord Our God and God of our ancestors, that You have placed our lot among those who sit in the study hall and that you have not given us our portion among those who sit idly on street corners. We rise early and they rise early. We rise early to pursue matters of Torah and they rise early to pursue frivolous matters. We toil and they toil. We toil and receive a reward and they toil and do not receive a reward. We run and they run. We run to the life of the World-to-Come and they run to the pit of destruction,
as it is stated: But You, God, will bring them down into *Psalms 55*
the pit of destruction; men of blood and deceit shall not live out half their days; but as for me, I will trust in You.

יְהִי רָצוֹן May it be Your will, Lord my God, just as you have assisted me in completing tractate *Berakhot* so assist me to begin other tractates and books and conclude them to learn and to teach, to observe and to perform, and to fulfill all the teachings of Your Torah with love. And may the merit of all the *tanna'im* and *amora'im* and Torah scholars stand for me and my descendants so that the Torah will not move from my mouth and from the mouths of my descendants and the descendants of my
descendants forever. And may the verse: When you *Proverbs 6*
walk, it shall lead you, when you lie down, it shall watch over you; and when you awaken, it shall talk with you
be fulfilled in me. For in the Torah your days shall be *Proverbs 9*
multiplied, and the years of your life shall be increased.
Length of days is in her right hand; in her left hand are *Proverbs 3*
riches and honor. May the Lord give strength to His *Psalms 29*
people; the Lord will bless His people with peace.

# תלמוד בבלי
## ברכות

הוצאת קורן ירושלים

# מסכת ברכות


COMMENTARY BY

Rabbi Adin Even-Israel
(Steinsaltz)

EDITOR-IN-CHIEF

Rabbi Dr Tzvi Hersh Weinreb

SENIOR CONTENT EDITOR

Rabbi Dr Shalom Z Berger

MANAGING EDITOR

Rabbi Joshua Schreier


•


SHEFA FOUNDATION

KOREN PUBLISHERS JERUSALEM

מֵאֵימָתַי קוֹרִין אֶת שְׁמַע בְּעַרְבִין? – מִשָּׁעָה שֶׁהַכֹּהֲנִים נִכְנָסִים לֶאֱכוֹל בִּתְרוּמָתָן עַד סוֹף הָאַשְׁמוּרָה הָרִאשׁוֹנָה, דִּבְרֵי ר' אֱלִיעֶזֶר. וַחֲכָמִים אוֹמְרִים: עַד חֲצוֹת. רַבָּן גַּמְלִיאֵל אוֹמֵר: עַד שֶׁיַּעֲלֶה עַמּוּד הַשַּׁחַר. מַעֲשֶׂה וּבָאוּ בָנָיו מִבֵּית הַמִּשְׁתֶּה, אָמְרוּ לוֹ: לֹא קָרִינוּ אֶת שְׁמַע. –אָמַר לָהֶם: אִם לֹא עָלָה עַמּוּד הַשַּׁחַר חַיָּיבִין אַתֶּם לִקְרוֹת. וְלֹא זוֹ בִּלְבַד אָמְרוּ, אֶלָּא *כׇּל מַה שֶּׁאָמְרוּ חֲכָמִים "עַד חֲצוֹת" מִצְוָתָן עַד שֶׁיַּעֲלֶה עַמּוּד הַשַּׁחַר; *הֶקְטֵר חֲלָבִים וְאֵבָרִים מִצְוָתָן עַד שֶׁיַּעֲלֶה עַמּוּד הַשַּׁחַר, *וְכׇל הַנֶּאֱכָלִים לְיוֹם אֶחָד מִצְוָתָן עַד שֶׁיַּעֲלֶה עַמּוּד הַשַּׁחַר, א"כ, לָמָּה אָמְרוּ חֲכָמִים "עַד חֲצוֹת"? °כְּדֵי לְהַרְחִיק אָדָם מִן הָעֲבֵירָה.§ **גמ'** *תַּנָּא הֵיכָא קָאֵי דְּקָתָנֵי 'מֵאֵימָתַי'? וְתוּ, מַאי שְׁנָא (א) דְּתָנֵי בְּעַרְבִית בְּרֵישָׁא? לִתְנֵי דְּשַׁחֲרִית בְּרֵישָׁא! –תַּנָּא אַקְּרָא קָאֵי, *דִּכְתִיב °"בְּשׇׁכְבְּךָ וּבְקוּמֶךָ". וְהָכִי קָתָנֵי: זְמַן קְרִיאַת שְׁמַע דִּשְׁכִיבָה אֵימַת – מִשָּׁעָה שֶׁהַכֹּהֲנִים נִכְנָסִין לֶאֱכוֹל בִּתְרוּמָתָן. וְאִי בָּעֵית אֵימָא: יָלֵיף מִבְּרִיָּיתוֹ שֶׁל עוֹלָם, דִּכְתִיב °"וַיְהִי עֶרֶב וַיְהִי בֹקֶר יוֹם אֶחָד". אִי הָכִי, סֵיפָא דְּקָתָנֵי *"בַּשַּׁחַר מְבָרֵךְ שְׁתַּיִם לְפָנֶיהָ וְאַחַת לְאַחֲרֶיהָ, בָּעֶרֶב מְבָרֵךְ שְׁתַּיִם לְפָנֶיהָ וּשְׁתַּיִם לְאַחֲרֶיהָ" – לִתְנֵי דְּעַרְבִית בְּרֵישָׁא! – תַּנָּא פָּתַח בְּעַרְבִית וַהֲדַר תָּנֵי בְּשַׁחֲרִית, עַד דְּקָאֵי בְּשַׁחֲרִית – פָּרֵישׁ מִילֵּי דְּשַׁחֲרִית, וַהֲדַר פָּרֵישׁ מִילֵּי דְעַרְבִית.§ אָמַר מָר: "מִשָּׁעָה שֶׁהַכֹּהֲנִים נִכְנָסִים לֶאֱכוֹל בִּתְרוּמָתָן". מִכְּדִי, כֹּהֲנִים אֵימַת קָא אָכְלִי תְּרוּמָה – מִשְּׁעַת צֵאת הַכּוֹכָבִים, לִתְנֵי מִשְּׁעַת צֵאת הַכּוֹכָבִים! –מִלְּתָא אַגַּב אוֹרְחֵיהּ קָמַשְׁמַע לַן, כֹּהֲנִים אֵימַת קָא אָכְלִי בִּתְרוּמָה – מִשְּׁעַת צֵאת הַכּוֹכָבִים, וְהָא קָמַשְׁמַע לַן: *דְּכַפָּרָה לָא מְעַכְּבָא. כִּדְתַנְיָא: *°"וּבָא הַשֶּׁמֶשׁ וְטָהֵר" – בִּיאַת שִׁמְשׁוֹ מְעַכַּבְתּוֹ מִלֶּאֱכוֹל בִּתְרוּמָה וְאֵין כַּפָּרָתוֹ מְעַכַּבְתּוֹ מִלֶּאֱכוֹל בִּתְרוּמָה. *וּמִמַּאי דְּהַאי 'וּבָא הַשֶּׁמֶשׁ' בִּיאַת הַשֶּׁמֶשׁ, וְהַאי 'וְטָהֵר' טְהַר יוֹמָא, דִּילְמָא

(דברים ו) (בראשית א) (ויקרא כב)

**מֵאֵימָתַי** קוֹרִין אֶת שְׁמַע בְּעַרְבִין. מִשָּׁעָה שֶׁהַכֹּהֲנִים נִכְנָסִים לֶאֱכוֹל בִּתְרוּמָתָן. כֹּהֲנִים שֶׁנִּטְמְאוּ וְטָבְלוּ, וְהֶעֱרִיב שִׁמְשָׁן, וְהִגִּיעַ עִתָּם לֶאֱכוֹל בִּתְרוּמָה: עַד סוֹף הָאַשְׁמוּרָה הָרִאשׁוֹנָה. שְׁלִישׁ הַלַּיְלָה, כִּדְמְפָרֵשׁ בַּגְּמָרָא (דף ג.). וּמִשָּׁם וְאֵילָךְ עָבַר זְמַן, דְּלָא מִקְּרֵי תּוּ זְמַן שְׁכִיבָה, וְלָא קָרֵינַן בֵּיהּ "בְּשׇׁכְבְּךָ". וּמִקַּמֵּי הָכִי נָמֵי לָאו זְמַן שְׁכִיבָה, לְפִיכָךְ הַקּוֹרֵא קוֹדֶם לָכֵן – לֹא יָצָא יְדֵי חוֹבָתוֹ. אִם כֵּן לָמָּה קוֹרִין אוֹתָהּ בְּבֵית הַכְּנֶסֶת? – כְּדֵי לַעֲמוֹד בִּתְפִלָּה מִתּוֹךְ דִּבְרֵי תוֹרָה. וְהָכִי תַּנְיָא בבריי' בִּבְרָכוֹת יְרוּשַׁלְמִי. וּלְפִיכָךְ, חוֹבָה עָלֵינוּ לְקָרוֹתָהּ מִשֶּׁתֶּחְשַׁךְ. וּבִקְרִיאַת פָּרָשָׁה רִאשׁוֹנָה שֶׁאָדָם קוֹרֵא עַל מִטָּתוֹ – יָצָא: עַד שֶׁיַּעֲלֶה עַמּוּד הַשַּׁחַר. שֶׁכׇּל הַלַּיְלָה קָרוּי זְמַן שְׁכִיבָה: הֶקְטֵר חֲלָבִים וְאֵבָרִים. שֶׁל קׇרְבָּנוֹת שֶׁנִּזְרַק דָּמָן בַּיּוֹם: מִצְוָתָן. לְהַעֲלוֹת כׇּל הַלַּיְלָה, וְאֵינָן נִפְסָלִים בְּלִינָה עַד שֶׁיַּעֲלֶה עַמּוּד הַשַּׁחַר וְהֵן לְמַטָּה מִן הַמִּזְבֵּחַ, דִּכְתִיב "לֹא יָלִין לַבֹּקֶר" (שמות לד): חֲלָבִים. שֶׁל כׇּל קׇרְבָּנוֹת: אֵבָרִים. שֶׁל עוֹלָה: וְכׇל הַנֶּאֱכָלִים לְיוֹם אֶחָד. כְּגוֹן חַטָּאת וְאָשָׁם, וְכִבְשֵׂי עֲצֶרֶת, וּמְנָחוֹת וְתוֹדָה: מִצְוָתָן. זְמַן אֲכִילָתָן: עַד שֶׁיַּעֲלֶה עַמּוּד הַשַּׁחַר. וְהוּא מְבִיאָן לִהְיוֹת נוֹתָר, דִּכְתִיב בְּתוֹדָה: "לֹא יַנִּיחַ מִמֶּנּוּ עַד בֹּקֶר" (ויקרא ז), וְכֻלָּם מִתּוֹדָה יָלְמְדוּ: אִם כֵּן לָמָּה אָמְרוּ חֲכָמִים עַד חֲצוֹת. בִּקְרִיאַת שְׁמַע וּבַאֲכִילַת קָדָשִׁים: כְּדֵי לְהַרְחִיק אָדָם מִן הָעֲבֵירָה. וַאֲסָרוּם בַּאֲכִילָה קוֹדֶם זְמַנָּן, כְּדֵי שֶׁלֹּא יָבֹא לְאׇכְלָן לְאַחַר עַמּוּד הַשַּׁחַר וְיִתְחַיֵּיב כָּרֵת, וְכֵן בִּקְרִיאַת שְׁמַע – לְזָרֵז אֶת הָאָדָם, שֶׁלֹּא יֹאמַר: יֵשׁ לִי עוֹד שָׁהוּת, וּבְתוֹךְ כָּךְ יַעֲלֶה עַמּוּד הַשַּׁחַר וְעָבַר לוֹ הַזְּמַן. וְהֶקְטֵר חֲלָבִים דְּקָתָנֵי הָכָא לֹא אָמְרוּ בּוֹ חֲכָמִים "עַד חֲצוֹת" כְּלָל, וְלֹא נָקַט לְהוּ הָכָא אֶלָּא לְהוֹדִיעַ שֶׁכׇּל דָּבָר הַנּוֹהֵג בַּלַּיְלָה – כָּשֵׁר כׇּל הַלַּיְלָה. וְהָכִי נָמֵי תְּנַן בְּפֶרֶק שֵׁנִי דִּמְגִלָּה (דף כ:): כׇּל הַלַּיְלָה כָּשֵׁר לִקְצִירַת הָעוֹמֶר וּלְהֶקְטֵר חֲלָבִים וְאֵבָרִים: **גמ'** הֵיכָא קָאֵי. מֵהֵיכָא קָא סָלֵיק דְּתָנָא בֵּיהּ חוֹבַת קְרִיאַת שְׁמַע, שֶׁהִתְחִיל לִשְׁאוֹל כָּאן זְמַן הַקְּרִיאָה: אַקְּרָא קָאֵי. וְשָׁם לָמַד חוֹבַת הַקְּרִיאָה: וְאִיבָּעֵית אֵימָא. הָא דְּתָנָא עַרְבִין בְּרֵישָׁא יָלֵיף מִבְּרִיָּיתוֹ שֶׁל עוֹלָם: וַהֲדַר תָּנָא בְּשַׁחֲרִית. "מֵאֵימָתַי קוֹרִין אֶת שְׁמַע בְּשַׁחֲרִית": מִשְּׁעַת צֵאת הַכּוֹכָבִים. שֶׁהוּא גְּמַר בִּיאַת הַשֶּׁמֶשׁ – כִּדְיָלֵיף לְקַמָּן (עמוד ב): דִּילְמָא

**מאימתי** קורין וכו'. פי' רש"י: ואנן היכי קרינן מבעוד יום ואין אנו ממתינין לצאת הכוכבים. כדמפרש בגמ'? על כן פירש רש"י שקריאת שמע שעל המטה עיקר, והוא לאחר צאת הכוכבים. והכי איתא בירושלמי: אם קרא קודם לכן – לא יצא, ואם כן למה אנו מתפללין קריאת שמע בבית הכנסת – כדי לעמוד בתפלה מתוך דברי תורה. תימא לפירושו: והלא אין העולם רגילין לקרות סמוך לשכיבה אלא פרשה ראשונה (לקמן דף ס:), ואם כן – שלש פרשיות היה לו לקרות! ועוד קשה: דצריך לברך בקריאת שמע שתים לפניה ושתים לאחריה, בערבית. ועוד: דאותה קריאת שמע סמוך למטה אינה אלא בשביל המזיקין, כדאמר בסמוך (דף ה.), "ואם תלמיד חכם הוא אינו צריך". ועוד קשה: דא"כ פסקינן כרבי יהושע בן לוי דאמר תפלות באמצע תקנום. פי': באמצע – בין שני קריאת שמע, בין קריאת שמע של שחרית ובין ק"ש של ערבית. ואנן קיי"ל כר' יוחנן, דאמר לקמן (דף ד:): איזהו בן העולם הבא – זה הסומך גאולה של ערבית לתפלה. לכן פי' ר"ת: דאדרבה, קריאת שמע של בית הכנסת עיקר. ואם תאמר: היאך אנו קורין כל כך מבעוד יום? ויש לומר: דקיימא לן כרבי יהודה, דאמר בפרק "תפלת השחר" (דף כו.) דזמן תפלת מנחה עד פלג המנחה, דהיינו אחד עשר שעות פחות רביע. ומיד כשיכלה זמן המנחה – מתחיל זמן ערבית. ואם תאמר: היאך אנו מתפללין תפלת מנחה סמוך לחשכה ואפילו לאחר פלג המנחה? יש לומר: דקיימא לן כרבנן, דאמרי זמן תפלת המנחה עד הערב. ואמרינן לקמן (דף כז.): השתא דלא אתמר הלכתא לא כמר ולא כמר, דעבד כמר – עבד ודעבד כמר – עבד. מכל מקום קשיא: דהוי כתרי קולי דסתרן אהדדי; שהרי מאיזה טעם אנו מתפללין ערבית מיד לאחר פלג המנחה – משום דקיימא לן דשעת המנחה כלה כדברי רבי יהודה, ומיד הוי זמן ערבית, ובזמן התפלה עצמה לא קיימא לן כרבי יהודה אלא כרבנן! על כן אומר ר"י: דודאי קריאת שמע של בית הכנסת עיקר, ואנו שמתפללין ערבית מבעוד יום – סבירא לן כהני תנאי דגמרא, דאמרי משעה שקדש היום וגם משעה שבני אדם נכנסים להסב, דהיינו סעודת ע"ש, והיא היתה מבעוד יום, ומאותה שעה הוי זמן תפלה. וגם ראיה (לקמן כז:), דרב הוי מצלי של שבת בערב שבת, ומסתמא גם היה קורא קריאת שמע. מכל אותן הראיות משמע דקריאת שמע של בית הכנסת היא עיקר. והא דקאמר בירושלמי למה היו קורין בבהכ"נ וכו' – אומר ר"ת: שהיו רגילין לקרות ק"ש קודם תפלתם, כמו שאנו רגילין לומר 'אשרי' תחלה. ואותה ק"ש אינה אלא לעמוד בתפלה מתוך דברי תורה. ומכאן נראה: מי שקורא קריאת שמע על מטתו שאין לברך, וגם אינו צריך לקרות אלא פרשה ראשונה: **ליתני** דשחרית ברישא. כדאשכחן בתמיד, דכתיב של בוקר תחלה: **אי** הכי סיפא דקתני שחרית ברישא. אי אמרת בשלמא דסמיך אקרא ד"בשכבך" – א"כ אינו מקפיד קרא אלא אק"ש. אלא א"א דסמיך אקרא דברייתו של עולם – א"כ קפיד אכל מילי, א"כ סיפא דקתני וכו': **מברך** שתים לפניה וכו'. (ירושלמי) ושבע ברכות הוי כנגד "שבע ביום הללתיך" (תהלים קיט), ולא קא חשיב "יראו עינינו" דההיא ברכה תקנו רבנן כדי להמתין לחבריהם בבית הכנסת. ודוקא בבית הכנסת שלהם, שהיו עומדים בשדה והם מסוכנים מן המזיקים, אבל בבתי כנסיות שלנו אין צריכין להמתין לחבריהם אלא בלילה: **והא** קמ"ל דכפרה לא מעכבא. וא"ת: הא תנינא חדא זימנא (פ"ד) ומייתי לה בהערל (דף עד:) – העריב שמשו אוכל בתרומה? וי"ל: דרגילות של משניות לאשמועינן בקוצר אף למה שמפורש כבר*: דילמא

**א** א מיי' פ"א מהלכות ק"ש הלכה ט' סמ"ג עשין י"ח טור וש"ע או"ח סימן רל"ה סעיף א':

**ב** ב ג מיי' וסמ"ג שם טוש"ע שם סעיף ג':

**ג** ד מיי' פ"ד מהל' מעשה קרבנות הלכה ב' סמ"ג עשין (קכ"ו) [קפ"ט]:

**ד** ה מיי' פ"א שם הלכה ח' [סמ"ג שם]:

**ה** ו מיי' פ"א מהל' ק"ש הלכה ה' סמ"ג עשין י"ח טוש"ע או"ח סי' נ"ח וסי' רל"ה סעי' א':

**ו** ז מיי' פ"ז מהל' תמידות ה"ב [סמ"ג לאוין רנ"ו]:

## רב נסים גאון

**גמ' ובא** השמש וטהר ביאת שמשו מעכבתו מלאכול בתרומה. מכלל דהאי דכתב רחמנא (ויקרא כ"ב) ואחר יאכל מן הקדשים אינו מותר אלא בתרומה בלבד אבל דבר שהוא למעלה הימנה מן הקדשים אינו מותר לטמא לאוכלו לאחר ביאת השמש בלבד אלא אסור הוא כל אותה הלילה לאכול בקדשים עד שיבא היום ויביא כפרתו ואז יהא מותר בקדשים ואיתא מפרשא במסכת יבמות בפ' הערל (דף עד) והכי אמרי הא דתנן טבל ועלה אוכל במעשר העריב שמשו אוכל בתרומה הביא כפרתו אוכל בקדשים מנלן אמר רבא אמר רב חסדא ג' קראי כתיבי כתיב (ויקרא כ"ב) לא יאכל מן הקדשים כי אם רחץ בשרו במים תלה הדבר ברחיצה בלבד וכתי' (שם) ובא השמש וטהר [ואחר יאכל מן הקדשים] תלה הדבר גם בביאת השמש והיא שעת יציאת הכוכבים וכתיב (שם י"ב) וכפר עליה הכהן וטהרה תלה גמירו' הטהר גם בהקרבת קרבן ואלו המקראות היו נראין כסותרין זה את זה ולפי שאי אפשר להיות דברי הכתובין סותרין זה את זה כי כלם נכוחים למבין העתיקו לנו קדמונינו פירושם והעמידו לנו כל אחד ואחד מאלו המקראות בדבר שהוא מיוחד לו ואמרו הא כיצד כאן למעשר כאן לתרומה כאן לקדשים הפסוק הראשון שתלה בו הדבר ברחיצה בלבד הוא מיוחד למעשר והפסוק השני שצריכו לביאת השמש הוא מיוחד לתרומה אבל קדש המזבח אין מותר לו לאכלן אלא א"כ הביא הכפרה שהוא מתחייב בה ואז תהא כפרתו גמורה כדכתיב וכפר עליה הכהן וטהרה: ואני אפרש לך עיקר גדול שלמדונו רבותינו ז"ל כי אלו הג' דברים המעשר והתרומה והקדשים כל אחד ואחד יש לו יתרון ויש בו חומרא שהוא מיוחדת בו לזולתי חבירו ואע"פ ששלשתן קראן הכתוב קדשים. המעשר כבר נאמר בו (דברים כ"ו) בערתי הקדש מן הבית ויש בו חומרא שאין מותר לאכלו חוץ להביאו למקדש פודהו

לחומת ירושלים אלא חייבין הן בעליו לשאת אותו לשם ולאכלו שם כדכתיב (שם י"ב) לא תוכל לאכול בשעריך כי אם לפני ה' אלהיך תאכלנו וכתיב (שם) והבאתם שמה. ודבר שאין יכול בשווין (מאחרים) [לאחרים] ואם רצה ליטלו לעצמו יש עליו לתת שומתו ומוסיף חומש כדכתיב (ויקרא כ"ז) ואם גאל יגאל איש ממעשרו וגו' ויהיו דמיו שמורין אצלו עד עת עלותו לרגל מעלהו עמו לירושלים ומוציאו לשם במאכל ובמשתה כדכתיב (דברים י"ד) ונתתה הכסף בכל אשר תאוה נפשך. וחייב להתודות עליו כדכתיב בפרשת כי תכלה לעשר (שם כ"ו) ואמרת לפני ה' אלהיך ומפורש בספרי (פרשת כי תבא) ואמרת בכל לשון לפני ה' אלהיך זה וידוי מעשר ואסור לאוכלו באנינות ואם נטמא אסור באכילה והאוכלו חייב מלקות ומה שמן להדליקו בנר כדכתיב (שם) ולא בערתי ממנו בטמא ודרשינן ליה בין שאני טמא והוא טהור בין שאני טהור והוא טמא ומה שמשתייר ממנו לשנה הרביעית ושנה השביעית עד ערב יום טוב האחרון של [illegible]

*) [illegible]

מגילה פרק ב' דף כ:

מכילתא דר"י פ' בא פסחים סח: מגילה כ:

[תענית ב.]

[ועי' תוס' לקמן כא. ד"ה הכות ותו' סוטה לב: ד"ה ורבו]

לקמן יא.

## גליון הש"ס

**במתני'** כדי להרחיק עי' תוס' פסחים ק"כ ע"ב ד"ה אמר רבא. **בתוס'** מברך כו' כדי להמתין לחבריהם כו' עי' תוס' לקמן ד ע"ב ד"ה דאמר. ובתוס' לקמן כ"ז ע"ב ד"ה והלכתא ובמגילה כג ע"ב ד"ה ואין. **בהגהות** מוהרצ"ב אחר מלה מכל. וע"ע גיטין ל"ד ע"ב תוס' ד"ה אלמנה.

כלים פ"א נגעי' פרק י"ד ת"כ פ' אמור יבמות עד:

עיין גירסת הגאונים בספר המאור

## הגהות הב"ח

(א) גמ' מאי שנא דתני ערבית בריש':

[ועי' תוס' זבחי' כח. ד"ה אמר ותוס' מנחות נג. ד"ה הכל]

תורה אור

דילמא ביאת אורו הוא, ומאי 'וטהר' – טהר גברא! –אמר רבה בר רב שילא: א"כ לימא קרא 'ויטהר', מאי 'וטהר' – טהר יומא. כדאמרי אינשי "איערב שמשא ואדכי יומא". במערבא הא דרבה בר רב שילא לא שמיע להו, ובעו לה מיבעיא: האי 'ובא השמש' ביאת שמשו הוא, ומאי 'וטהר' – טהר יומא, או דילמא ביאת אורו הוא, ומאי 'וטהר' – טהר גברא? (א) והדר פשטו לה מברייתא, מדקתני בברייתא "סימן לדבר צאת הכוכבים" שמע מינה: ביאת שמשו הוא, ומאי 'וטהר' – טהר יומא.§ אמר מר: "משעה שהכהנים נכנסים לאכול בתרומתן". ורמינהו: "מאימתי קורין את שמע בערבין? משהעני נכנס לאכול פתו במלח, עד שעה שעומד ליפטר מתוך סעודתו". סיפא ודאי פליגא אמתניתין; רישא, מי לימא פליגי אמתני'? –לא, עני וכהן חד שיעורא הוא. ורמינהו: *"מאימתי מתחילין לקרות ק"ש בערבית? – משעה שבני אדם נכנסין לאכול פתן בערבי שבתות, דברי ר"מ. וחכמים אומרים: משעה שהכהנים זכאין לאכול בתרומתן, סימן לדבר צאת הכוכבים. ואע"פ שאין ראיה לדבר זכר לדבר, שנאמר °"ואנחנו עושים במלאכה והחצים מחזיקים ברמחים מעלות השחר עד צאת הכוכבים", ואומר °"והיו לנו הלילה משמר והיום מלאכה". *מאי 'ואומר'? – וכי תימא מכי ערבא שמשא לילייא הוא, ואינהו דמחשכי ומקדמי, ת"ש: "והיו לנו הלילה משמר והיום מלאכה". קא סלקא דעתך ד'עני' ו'בני אדם' חד שיעורא הוא, ואי אמרת 'עני' ו'כהן' חד שיעורא הוא – חכמים היינו רבי מאיר! אלא שמע מינה: עני שיעורא לחוד וכהן שיעורא לחוד! –לא, 'עני' ו'כהן' חד שיעורא הוא, ו'עני' ו'בני אדם' לאו חד שיעורא הוא. –ו'עני' ו'כהן' חד שיעורא הוא? ורמינהו: מאימתי מתחילין לקרות שמע בערבין? – משעה שקדש היום בערבי שבתות, דברי ר' אליעזר. רבי יהושע אומר: משעה שהכהנים מטוהרים לאכול בתרומתן. רבי מאיר אומר: משעה שהכהנים טובלין לאכול בתרומתן. אמר לו ר' יהודה: והלא כהנים מבעוד יום הם טובלים! ר' חנינא אומר: משעה שעני נכנס לאכול פתו במלח. ר' אחאי, ואמרי לה ר' אחא, אומר: משעה שרוב בני אדם נכנסין להסב. ואי אמרת 'עני' ו'כהן' חד שיעורא הוא – ר' חנינא היינו ר' יהושע! אלא לאו שמע מינה: שיעורא דעני לחוד, ושיעורא דכהן לחוד, שמע מינה. הי מינייהו מאוחר? – מסתברא דעני מאוחר, דאי אמרת ד'עני' מוקדם – ר' חנינא היינו ר' אליעזר. אלא לאו שמע מינה ד'עני' מאוחר, שמע מינה.§ אמר מר: "אמר ליה רבי יהודה: והלא כהנים מבעוד יום הם טובלים". שפיר קאמר ליה רבי יהודה לרבי מאיר! – ורבי מאיר, הכי קאמר ליה: מי סברת דאנא אבין השמשות דידך קא אמינא? אנא אבין השמשות דרבי יוסי קא אמינא. דאמר *רבי יוסי: בין השמשות כהרף עין. זה נכנס וזה יוצא ואי אפשר לעמוד עליו. קשיא

**דילמא ביאת אורו.** שיאור השמש ביום השמיני וטהר האיש עצמו בהבאת קרבנותיו, ואחר יאכל: **אם כן.** דהאי קרא 'וטהר' לשון לווי הוא, נימא קרא 'ויטהר', מאי 'וטהר': **אדכי.** לשון עבר, נתפנה מן העולם השמש: **מברייתא.** דקתני לקמן בשמעתין (ב) "משעה שהכהנים נכנסין לאכול בתרומתן, וראיה לדבר צאת הכוכבים", ש"מ: אין כפרתן מעכבתן: **משהעני.** שאין לו נר להדליק בסעודתו: **סיפא ודאי פליגא אמתני'.** דקתני הכא "עד שעה שעומד ליפטר מתוך הסעודה", והיינו לא כר' אליעזר ולא כרבנן ולא כרבן גמליאל, דדריש "ובשכבך" – תחלת זמן שכיבה, ובמתני' תנן "עד סוף האשמורה הראשונה": **עני וכהן.** עני – כל לילותיו, וכהן טמא לאכול בתרומה: **חד שיעורא הוא.** **צאת הכוכבים:** **בערבי שבתות.** ממהרין לסעודה, שהכל מוכן: **שאין ראיה לדבר.** שהיום כלה בצאת הכוכבים, זכר לדבר איכא: **דמחשבי.** ועושין מלאכה בלילה משקיעת החמה עד צאת הכוכבים: **ומקדמי.** ומשכימין, קודם היום, דאימא: יום לא הוי עד הנץ החמה, והם מקדימין מעלות השחר. דהוי כמו מהלך ה' מילין (פסחים דף צג:): **ת"ש והיה לנו הלילה משמר.** מדקאמר "והיום מלאכה" אלמא האי דעבר מעלות השחר עד צאת הכוכבים – יממא הוא. וזכר לדבר איכא, דכל עת מלאכה קורא הכתוב "יום": **קס"ד. רוב בני אדם** [א] היינו עניים, כלומר: בני אדם בערבי שבתות, ועניים בימות החול – חד שיעורא הוא: **משעה שקדש היום.** בערבי שבתות. היינו בין השמשות, ספק יום ספק לילה, וכיון דספק הוא – קדש היום מספק: **משעה שהכהנים טובלים.** היינו קודם בין השמשות, כדי שיהא להם קודם בין השמשות הערב שמש. והכי אמרינן ב"במה מדליקין" (דף לה.) דזמן הטבילה קודם בין השמשות מעט: **והלא כהנים מבעוד יום הם טובלים.** רבי יהודה לטעמיה, דאמר ב"במה מדליקין": *בין השמשות, כדי מהלך חצי מיל קודם צאת הכוכבים קרוי בין השמשות, והוי ספק. הלכך טבילה דמקמי הכי – מבעוד יום הוא, ולאו זמן שכיבה הוא. ולקמן מפרש מאי אהדר ליה רבי מאיר: **נכנסין להסב.** אית דאמרי בימות החול, ואית דאמרי בשבתות. מכל מקום מאוחר הוא (לכולם): **והי מינייהו מאוחר.** (לכולם) דעני או דכהן: ה"ג אי ס"ד דעני קודם ר' חנינא היינו ר' אליעזר: **בין השמשות דרבי יהודה** [ב] מהלך חצי מיל לפני צאת הכוכבים, ודרבי יוסי כהרף עין לפני צאת הכוכבים, ורבי מאיר כרבי יוסי ס"ל, וכי טביל מקמי הכי – סמוך לחשכה הוא, וזמן שכיבה קרינן ביה:

**דילמא** ביאת אורו הוא. פי' רש"י: עד שיזרח אורו של יום השמיני, ומאי 'וטהר' טהר גברא – שיטהר האיש בהבאת קרבנותיו. ותימא לפירושו: לפרוך אההיא ד"הערל" (דף עד:). דהעריב שמשו אוכל בתרומה וכו' מנלן דביאת שמשו הוא? ועוד: היכי מצי למימר דמיירי בזריחה? דאי בזריחה הוא – הוה מצי למכתב בקרא "וזרח השמש וטהר", כמו "ממזרח השמש" (במדבר כא). או לשון יציאה כמו "השמש יצא על הארץ" (בראשית יט), (ג) ונקט בקרא "ובא השמש" – אלמא דהיינו שקיעת החמה. ועוד: דבסמוך קא מבעיא ליה האי ובא השמש אי ביאת אורו הוא, ופשיט מברייתא "זכר לדבר וכו'" – תפשוט ממתניתין (דנגעים פי"ד): העריב שמשו אוכל בתרומה, אלמא דהיינו ביאת שמש! וי"ל דה"פ: ממאי דהאי "ובא השמש וטהר" – ביאת שמש הוא ממש, ומאי 'וטהר'–טהר יומא, דהיינו צאת הכוכבים, דילמא ביאת אורו הוא, דהיינו תחלתה של שקיעת החמה, והוא תחלת הכנסתה ברקיע ועדיין יש שהות ביום *חמש מילין עד צאת הכוכבים. ומאי 'וטהר' – טהר גברא. והשתא למתניתין ד"הערל" לא קשה מידי, דמצי למימר: (ד) העריב שמשו דהתם – היינו ביאת אורו, ואף מהתם לא תפשוט דהיינו צאת הכוכבים. משום הכי איצטריך לאתויי הכא הברייתא דצאת הכוכבים:

**אם כן** לימא קרא ויטהר. אף על גב דבכמה מקומות כתיב 'וטהר' – התם ליכא למיטעי, אבל הכא דליכא למיטעי – הוה ליה למכתב 'ויטהר': **משעה** שהעני נכנס לאכול פתו במלח. תימה, עני גופיה מתי יתפלל? דהא אמרת זמן אכילתו היינו זמן ק"ש, וכיון דהגיע זמן ק"ש אסור להתחיל בסעודה עד שיתפלל כרישא, כדתניא לקמן (דף ד:): "יקורא ק"ש ומתפלל ואוכל פתו ומברך, וכל העובר על דברי חכמים חייב מיתה"! ויש לומר דזמן תפלה הוי קודם לזמן סעודה, דלאו דוקא פורתא מעיקרא קאמר, שעד שיכינו לו סעודתו יקרא ויתפלל: **אע"פ** שאין ראיה לדבר. ראיה גמורה אינה, דהא לא מיירי התם לענין ק"ש: **ואי** קדים רבי חנינא היינו ר' אליעזר. ולא מצי למימר דעני קדים לקדוש היום, או קדוש היום קדים לשעורא דעני, דלא מסתברא לחלק כל כך בשעורי זמן שכיבה דכל זמנים הללו אית ביה: **אמר** ליה ר' יהודה והלא כהנים מבעוד יום הם טובלים. תימה מאי תיקשי ליה לנפשיה, שהרי פלג המנחה מבעוד יום היא, והוא אומר (לקמן דף כו.): מיד כשיעבור פלג המנחה הוי זמן תפלת ערבית! ויש לומר: דלדידיה לא קשיא, דלא דריש 'בשכבך ובקומך', אבל לרבנן דדרשי – קשיא, דלאו זמן שכיבה: קשיא

הכנענים כדכתב (ויקרא כ"ב) וכהן כי יקנה נפש ומפורש (יבמות ס"ו) מנין לכהן שנשא אשה ... עבדים שיאכלו בתרומה ת"ל וכהן כי יקנה נפש ומנין לאשתו שקנתה עבדים שיאכלו בתרומה ת"ל וכהן כי יקנה נפש קנין כספו קנין שקנה קנין אוכל ורשאי הכהן למוכרה לתרומה לכהן אחר לפי שהוא בכספו ואסור לאכלה בלא רחיצת ידים ואינה מותרת לטבול יום אלא עד צאת הכוכבים ואם נפל חלק אחד של תרומה לתוך צ"ט חלקים של חולין נאסר הכל לישראל ונעשה הכל כתרומה שאין לישראל היתר לאכלה ואינה מותרת אלא לכהן בלבד אבל אם נפל אחד של תרומה לתוך ק' של חולין מפרישו ממנו חלק אחד ונותנו לכהן והשאר מותר לישראל הרי אלו בתרומה מה שאין כן בבכורים (בכורים פרק ב' משנה א') התרומה והבכורים חייבין עליהן מיתה וחומש ואסורין לזרים ועולין בא' ומאה וטעונין רחיצת ידים והערב שמש הרי אלו בתרומה ובבכורים מה שאין כן במעשר. והתרומה' שישנן בקודש שהוא קרוי קרבן מפני שמקריבין ממנו אמוריו והלבונה על גבי המזבח ואם תהיה מחשבת כהן המקריבו באחת מהעבודה' הארבע שהן שחיטה וקבלה והולכה וזריקה אם מחשב בשחיטה לזרוק דמה או להקטיר אמוריה למחרת אותו היום או אם יחשב באחת הארבע העבודות לאכול הזמנה כזית בשר חוץ לזמנו נעשה אותו הזבח פיגול ונפסל במחשבה שחשב בשעת עבודה כדכתיב (ויקרא ז') לא יחשב לו פגול ודרשינן (זבחים דף כ"ט) במחשבה נפסל וכן מה שישתייר ממנו עד שיעבור העת והזמן הקצוב לו כבר נעשה נותר כדכתיב (ויקרא י"ט) ביום זבחכם יאכל וממחרת והנותר וגו' הפגול והנותר אם אכל אדם מהן כזית במזיד חייב כרת ובשוגג חייב חטאת כדתנן (כריתות פרק א') ל"ו כריתות בתורה ומהן האוכל חלב ודם ונותר ופגול על אלו חייבין על זדונן כרת ועל שגגתן חטאת וכן נמי האדם הטמא אם יאכל כזית מבשר הקדשים במזיד חייב כרת כדכתב' (ויקרא ז') והנפש אשר תאכל בשר מזבח השלמי' [וגו'] וטומאתו עליו ונכרתה' ואם בשוגג אבל חייב קרבן עולה ויורד היינו שאמר בו הכתוב (שם ה') ואם לא תשיג ידו וכל הקרבן שחלק בו הכתוב בין עשיר לעני נקרא עולה ויורד והחטאת המתחייבין בה על החלב ועל הדם והפגול והנותר וכלל המנויין במשנתנו הן חטאת קבועה אין דל בין עשיר שוין בה ואיתה לפירושיה קרבן עולה

ויורד המתחייבין בו טמא שאכל את הקודש בפרשת (ויקרא ה) ונפש כי תחטא ושמעה בפסוק שני ונפש אשר תגע בכל דבר טמא לפי שהשלים הענין בפסוק השלישי וכתיב ונעלם ממנו והוא ידע ואשם וכשאנו מעיינין באלו הפסוקים אנו רואין בהן זולתי זכרון הטומאה לא יותר ובכל דבר ידענו כי כל אדם מישראל אם הוא נוגע בדבר טמא אינו חייב אלא ליטהר בלבד ואין עליו חטא בזה הדבר ולא אשמה אלא אם כן עשה דבר שגורם לו אשמה ופשע שמתחייב עליו להתכפר בקרבן ולא מצינו בפשוטן של כתובים הללו כלום מזה הדבר אבל העתיקו לנו רבותינו ז"ל פירושן של דברים הללו וביררו והגידו לנו אי זו פשע הוא שחייב אותו הקרבן ההוא [illegible]



הגהות הב"ח

(א) גמ' והדר פשטו מברייתא: (ב) רש"י ד"ה מברייתא וכו' שהכהנים זכאין לאכול בתרומה סימן לדבר צאת: (ג) תוס' ד"ה דילמא וכו' על לא מדנקט בקרא ובא הש וכו' מברייתא סימן לד (ד) בא"ד העריב שמשו דהתם (היינו ביאת אורו תיבות אלו מוקפות בח"ב לבנה ונכתב בלדו היינו לאו דוקא שקיעת החמה:

גליון הש"ס

גמ' טהר יומא. [illegible] בהגהת [illegible]

הגהות הגר"א

[א] רש"י ד"ה קס"ד כו' היינו עניים. נ"ב [illegible] [ב] שם ד"ה בין השמשות מהלך חצי מיל. [illegible] (שבת ל"ד:)

נחמיה ד — שם — מגילה כ: — תוספתא ברכות פ"א — רש"א מ"ז — רש"ל מ"ז — שבת ל"ד ב' [נדה נ"ג.]

קשיא דר' מאיר אדר"מ! – תרי תנאי אליבא דר"מ. קשיא דר' אליעזר אדר' אליעזר! – תרי תנאי אליבא דר' אליעזר. ואב"א: רישא לאו ר' אליעזר היא.§ "עד סוף האשמורה".§ מאי קסבר ר' אליעזר? אי קסבר שלש משמרות הוי הלילה – לימא עד ארבע שעות! ואי קסבר ארבע משמרות הוי הלילה – לימא עד שלש שעות! –לעולם קסבר שלש משמרות הוי הלילה והא קמ"ל: דאיכא משמרות ברקיע ואיכא משמרות בארעא, דתניא: ר' אליעזר אומר: שלש משמרות הוי הלילה ועל כל משמר ומשמר יושב הקב"ה ושואג כארי, שנאמר: "ה' ממרום ישאג וממעון קדשו יתן קולו שאוג ישאג על נוהו", וסימן לדבר: משמרה ראשונה – חמור נוער, שניה – כלבים צועקים, שלישית – תינוק יונק משדי אמו ואשה מספרת עם בעלה. מאי קא חשיב ר' אליעזר? אי תחלת משמרות קא חשיב, תחלת משמרה ראשונה סימנא למה לי? אורתא הוא! אי סוף משמרות קא חשיב – סוף משמרה אחרונה למה לי סימנא? יממא הוא! –אלא: חשיב סוף משמרה ראשונה ותחלת משמרה אחרונה ואמצעית דאמצעיתא. ואב"א כולהו סוף משמרות קא חשיב, וכי תימא: אחרונה לא צריך, למאי נפקא מינה – למיקרי ק"ש למאן דגני בבית אפל ולא ידע זמן ק"ש אימת, כיון דאשה מספרת עם בעלה ותינוק יונק משדי אמו – ליקום וליקרי. אמר רב יצחק בר שמואל משמי' דרב: ג' משמרות הוי הלילה, ועל כל משמר ומשמר יושב הקב"ה ושואג כארי ואומר: אוי לבנים שבעונותיהם החרבתי את ביתי ושרפתי את היכלי והגליתים לבין אומות העולם.§ תניא, א"ר יוסי: פעם אחת הייתי מהלך בדרך, ונכנסתי לחורבה אחת מחורבות ירושלים להתפלל. בא אליהו זכור לטוב ושמר לי על הפתח (והמתין לי) עד שסיימתי תפלתי. לאחר שסיימתי תפלתי אמר לי: שלום עליך, רבי! ואמרתי לו: שלום עליך, רבי ומורי! ואמר לי: בני מפני מה נכנסת לחורבה זו? אמרתי לו: להתפלל. ואמר לי: היה לך להתפלל בדרך! ואמרתי לו: מתירא הייתי שמא יפסיקו בי *עוברי דרכים. ואמר לי: היה לך להתפלל תפלה קצרה. באותה שעה למדתי ממנו שלשה דברים: למדתי שאין נכנסין לחורבה, ולמדתי שמתפללין בדרך, ולמדתי שהמתפלל בדרך – מתפלל תפלה קצרה. ואמר לי: בני, מה קול שמעת בחורבה זו? ואמרתי לו: שמעתי בת *קול שמנהמת כיונה ואומרת: אוי לבנים שבעונותיהם החרבתי את ביתי ושרפתי את היכלי והגליתים לבין האומות. ואמר לי: חייך וחיי ראשך, לא שעה זו בלבד אומרת כך, אלא בכל יום ויום שלש פעמים אומרת כך; ולא זו בלבד, אלא בשעה שישראל נכנסין לבתי כנסיות ולבתי מדרשות ועונין "יהא *שמיה הגדול מבורך" הקב"ה מנענע ראשו ואומר: אשרי המלך שמקלסין אותו בביתו כך, מה לו לאב שהגלה את בניו, ואוי להם לבנים שגלו מעל שולחן אביהם.§ ת"ר, מפני שלשה דברים אין נכנסין לחורבה: מפני חשד, מפני המפולת ומפני המזיקין. "מפני חשד" – ותיפוק ליה משום מפולת!

בחדתי

**קשיא דרבי מאיר אדרבי מאיר.** לעיל אמר: משעה שבני אדם נכנסין לאכול פתן בערבי שבתות, והוא שעור מאוחר משל כהן, והכא אמר: משעת טבילה, שהיא קודם בין השמשות: **קשיא דר' אליעזר.** דברייתא, אדר' אליעזר דמתני': **ואב"א רישא.** דמתני': **לאו ר' אליעזר היא.** והא דקתני "דברי ר' אליעזר" – אסוף הזמן קאי, דקאמר עד סוף האשמורה הראשונה, ופליגי רבנן עליה, ואמרי "עד חצות". דר' אליעזר דריש 'בשכבך' – זמן התחלת שכיבה, שבני אדם הולכים לשכב, זה קודם וזה מאוחר. ורבנן דרשי – כל זמן שכיבה, דהיינו כל הלילה, אלא שעשו סייג לדבר ואמרו עד חצות. ור"ג לית ליה הסייג: **מאי קסבר כו'.** הוה ליה לומר זמן הנכר: **אי קסבר.** דפליגי תנאי לקמן בהא מלתא, איכא מאן דאמר: "ג' משמרות הוי הלילה", במשמרות עבודת המלאכים ושיר שלהם נחלק לשלש חלקים, ראשונה לכת אחת, שניה לכת אחרת, שלישית לכת שלישית. ואיכא מאן דאמר "ארבע משמרות הוי הלילה": **והא קמ"ל.** כשנתן לך סימן זמן הקריאה בסוף האשמורה ולא פי' לך סימן מפורש – למדך שיש היכר לכל אדם בדבר, כי היכי דאיכא ברקיע: **ישאג שאוג ישאג.** הרי ג': **ואשה מספרת עם בעלה.** כבר הגיע ליום, ובני אדם מתעוררים משינתן, והשוכבים יחד מספרים זה עם זה: **מאי קא חשיב.** סימנים הללו שנתן למשמרות הארץ, היכן נתנו, בתחלת האשמורות או בסופן: **אורתא הוא.** צאת הכוכבים: **ושמר.** והמתין. כמו: "לא יאמר אדם לחבירו שמור לי בלד ע"ג פלוני" (סנהדרין דף סג:). ובב"ק בפ' "החובל" (דף צ:): "שמרה עומדת על פתח חצרה". וכן: "ואביו שמר את הדבר" (בראשית לז), "שומר אמונים" (ישעיהו כו): **תפלה קצרה.** ["הביננו"], ולקמן מפרש לה בפ' "תפלת השחר" (דף כט.): **אשרי המלך שמקלסין אותו בביתו כך.** אשרי כל זמן שהיה קלוס זה בתוך בהמ"ק: **מפני חשד.** שלא יאמרו זונה מוכנת לו שם: **ומפני המפולת.** שחומת החורבה רעועה, ומסוכן הוא, פן תפול החומה עליו: **תיפוק ליה.** כלומר: למה לנו ג' טעמים לדבר א' – הרי די באחת מהן! אם לא בא ללמדך שיש שעות שאין הטעם הזה, וצריך להניח בשביל זה:

**קשיא** דר' מאיר אדר' מאיר. דלא מצי למימר בשעה שבני אדם נכנסין וכהן חד שעורא הוא. דאם כן – רבי מאיר היינו רבי אחאי, לפי' רש"י שפי': שרוב בני אדם נכנסין להסב, דהיינו בע"ש. *[וגאון כן](א) לא מסתברא למימר דבני אדם ממהרין כל כך בערבי שבתות כמו בזמן שהכהנים טובלין. דהיינו מעבוד יום קודם הערב שמש: **קשיא** דרבי אליעזר אדרבי אליעזר. דלא מצי למימר משקדש היום וכהנים נכנסין לאכול בתרומתן חד שעורא הוא. דא"כ – ר' אליעזר היינו ר' יהושע: **למאן** דגני בבית אפל. וא"ת: והלא רבי אליעזר בעי (לקמן ד' ט:) עד שיכיר בין תכלת לכרתי בק"ש של שחרית! וי"ל: מ"מ, כיון שידע מתי יעלה עמוד השחר, קודם שיקום ויזמן עצמו, כבר הגיע אותו עת: **היה** לך להתפלל תפלה קצרה. לכאורה משמע שאין זה 'הביננו'. דהא קא בעי לקמן (ד' ל.), מאי איכא בין 'הביננו' לתפלה קצרה? א"כ: לפי' הקונ' שפי' בכאן דהיינו 'הביננו' – קשה. אלא ע"כ היינו תפלה אחרינא, כדמפרש לקמן: *"צרכי עמך מרובים וכו'". וגם על זה קשה: דלקמן אמרינן שאין לומר תפלת של "צרכי עמך" אלא במקום סכנה. ורבי יוסי לא הוה במקום סכנה – פי' במקום לסטים, מדהשיב לו: שמא יפסיקו בי עוברי דרכים, ולא השיב: שמא יהרגוני לסטים. ונראה לי כפ"ה, תפלה קצרה דהכא היינו 'הביננו'. ואע"ג דלייט עלה אביי *אמאן דמתפלל 'הביננו' – היינו דוקא בעיר, אבל בשדה מותר. והא דאמרי' לקמן: "מאי איכא בין 'הביננו' לתפלה קצרה!" הכי קאמר: בין תפלה קצרה דאמר בפ' "תפלת השחר" (דף כט:), כגון "צרכי עמך וכו'". אבל ודאי תפלה קצרה דהכא צ"ל "הביננו": **ועונין** יהא שמיה הגדול מבורך. מכאן יש לסתור מה שפי' במחזור ויטרי: יהא שמיה רבא – שזו תפלה שאנו מתפללין שימלא שמו, כדכתיב (שמות יז) "כי יד על כס יה", שלא יהא שמו שלם וכסאו שלם עד שימחה זרעו של עמלק. ופירושו כך: יהא שמי"ה – שם יה רבא, כלומר: שאנו מתפללין שיהא שמו גדול ושלם, ומבורך לעולם – הוי תפלה אחרת, כלומ': ומבורך לעולם הבא. וזה לא נראה, מדקאמר הכא: יהא שמיה הגדול מבורך, משמע דתפלה אחת היא, ואינו רוצה לומר שיהא שמו גדול ושלם, אלא: יהא שמו הגדול מבורך. וגם מה שאומרים העולם: לכך אומרים קדיש בלשון ארמית – לפי שתפלה נאה ושבח גדול הוא, על כן נתקן בלשון תרגום *שלא יבינו המלאכים ויהיו מתקנאין בנו, וזה אינו נראה, שהרי כמה תפלות יפות שהם בלשון עברי! אלא נראה כדאמרינן בסוף סוטה (דף מט.): אין העולם מתקיים אלא אסדרא דקדושתא ואיהא שמיה רבא דבתר אגדתא, שהיו רגילין לומר קדיש אחר הדרשה, ושם היו עמי הארצות ולא היו מבינים כולם לשון הקודש, לכך תקנוהו בלשון תרגום שהיו הכל מבינים, שזה היה לשונם:

*גי' רש"ל. וכס"א גריס אי נמי

תורה אור

ירמיה כה

רש"ל

בכרי"ף ל"ג

ס"א יפסיקוני

קול הברה ועי' תוס' סנהדרין י"א. ד"ה בת קול

גי' רש"א שמו

הגהות הב"ח

(א) תוס' ד"ה קשיא דרבי מאיר וכו' דהיינו בע"ש א' נמי לא מסתברא.

גליון הש"ס

גמ' מפני חשד. עיין שבת כג:

ז א טוש"ע או"ח סימן א' סעיף ב ג:
ח ב טור או"ח סי' נ"ו:
ט ג מיי' פ"ה מהל' תפלה ה"ו ופי"ב מהל' רוצח ושמירת נפש הלכה ו' (סמ"ג עשין י"ט ועשין ע"ט) טוש"ע או"ח סימן צ' סעיף ו':

## רב נסים גאון

בתרומה *)ומעלת הקדש עדיפא מהתרומה שיש בו חיוב כרת והוא חמור יות' מהמיתה ואע"פ ששניהם בידי שמים כדאמרינן (בסוף) מסכת כריתות (דף כג) דהא איסור מעילה לר' קל במיתה וקדשים איסור חמור בכרת ואתי איסור מעילה דקיל וחייל אאיסור כרת דחמיר ואיתא נמי בהרב' מקומות מן התלמוד אנו מזכירין מהן מה שעלה בידינו במס' שבת בפ' במה מדליקין (דף כה) ובפסחים בפ' כל שעה (דף לג) ובחגיגה בפרק חומר בקודש (דף כה) וביבמות בפרק הערל (דף עג) ובשחיטת חולין (דף לא) בפרק השוחט אחד בעוף וכסדר הזה נמי אירע להיות דינם במעלות הטומאה כמו שתדע שהשרץ הוא אב הטומאה וכל מה שנגע בו מן החולין נקרא ראשון ומה שנגע בראשון נקרא שני והשני בחולין אינו מטמא שלישי ואינו פוסל ולפיכך קראתו המשנה פסול ולא קראהו טמא לפי שכל ולד טמא שאינו מטמא אחר פסול מיקרי וכל ולד טמא שמטמא אחר הוא שנקרא טמא וזה עיקר ראוי להיזהר בו וכך שנינו במס' טהרות (פ"ב מ"ג) הראשון שבחולין טמא ומטמא השני פסול ואינו מטמא ויש במקומות הרבה במשנה מה שמסייע לזה והיה ר' עקיבא סובר כי השני בחולין מטמא שלישי כדמפורש במס' סוטה (פרק כשם דף כז) אלא על אותה סתם המשנה שהזכרנו אנו סומכין ולא על דבריו של ר' עקיבא ואע"פ שכל התנאין שסוברין (באותו) [כאותו] הסתם מנאם במסכת סוטה (דף ל) והעמידם כולם בשיטה אחת וקיימא לן דכל מילתא דאקמוה רבנן בשיטה נפקא לה מהלכתא מיהו אין אנו תופסין זה העיקר אלא אם אין אנו מוצאין בתלמוד מה שדוחה אותו עיקר ומסייע דברי אותם התנאים שהעמדנום בשיטה והרי מצינו סיוע לאותם התנאים חדא בהדא מס' דברכות בפ' ואלו דברים (דף נב) דאמרינן הכא בשולחן שני עסקינן ואין שני עושה שלישי בחולין ובמס' חולין בפ' השוחט (דף לג) ידים שניות הן ואין שני עושה שלישי בחולין ובמס' יו"ט בפ' יו"ט שחל להיות ערב שבת (דף יח) אמרינן ולד הטומאה היכא משכחת לה גבי תרומה כהנים זריזין הן ובפסחים בפרק כל שעה (דף לד ועי' רש"י שם) אמרי כי האי גוונא ואיבעי תימא התם דנגעי בראשון דהוו להו אינהו שני ושני עושה שלישי בתרומה מכלל דבחולין אין שני עושה שלישי ובפרק (ו') [ד] דמס' טבול יום איתא בג' משניות מסודרות מפני [שהוא] שלישי ושלישי טהור בחולין והזכירו במס' נדה בפרק ראשון (דף ז) אחת מהן ואשכחן בתלמוד ארץ ישראל (ברכות פרק אין עומדין הלכה א') דעבודה להא מילתא דוגמא להילכתא פסיקאתא דגרסינן אבדן שאל לר' כמה מעלות לקודש א"ל ד'. כמה מעלות בתרומה א"ל ג'. וקאים מצלי כדי לעמוד להתפלל מתוך דבר תורה [illegible]

*) עיין רש"ל שם ודברי רבינו צריכין באור.

בחדתי. -ותיפוק ליה משום מזיקין -בתרי. -אי בתרי- חשד נמי ליכא! -בתרי ופריצי. "מפני המפולת" -ותיפוק ליה משום חשד ומזיקין! -בתרי וכשרי. "מפני המזיקין" - ותיפוק ליה מפני חשד ומפולת! -בחורבה חדתי, ובתרי וכשרי. -אי בתרי - מזיקין נמי ליכא! -במקומן חיישינן. ואב"א: לעולם בחד, ובחורבה חדתי דקאי בדברא, דהתם משום חשד ליכא, דהא אשה בדברא לא שכיחא, ומשום מזיקין איכא. *ת"ר: ארבע משמרות הוי הלילה, דברי רבי. ר' נתן אומר: שלש. מ"ט דר' נתן? דכתיב "ויבא גדעון ומאה איש אשר אתו בקצה המחנה ראש האשמרת התיכונה", תנא: אין תיכונה אלא שיש לפניה ולאחריה. ורבי? מאי תיכונה - אחת מן התיכונה שבתיכונות. ור' נתן? מי כתיב 'תיכונה שבתיכונות'?! 'תיכונה' כתיב. מ"ט דרבי? - א"ר זריקא א"ר אמי א"ר יהושע בן לוי: כתוב אחד אומר "חצות לילה אקום להודות לך על משפטי צדקך", וכתוב אחד אומר: "קדמו עיני אשמורות", הא כיצד? - ארבע משמרות הוי הלילה. ור' נתן? סבר לה כרבי יהושע, דתנן: ר' יהושע אומר: עד שלש שעות, שכן דרך מלכים לעמוד בשלש שעות: שית דליליא ותרתי דיממא, הוו להו שתי משמרות. רב אשי אמר: משמרה ופלגא נמי משמרות קרו להו. ואמר רבי זריקא אמר רבי אמי אמר רבי יהושע בן לוי: *אין אומרין בפני המת אלא דבריו של מת. אמר רבי אבא בר כהנא: לא אמרן אלא בדברי תורה, אבל מילי דעלמא לית לן בה. ואיכא דאמרי, אמר רבי אבא בר כהנא: לא אמרן אלא *[אפילו] בדברי תורה, וכ"ש מילי דעלמא. ודוד בפלגא דליליא הוה קאי? מאורתא הוה קאי! דכתיב: "קדמתי בנשף ואשועה", ומאי דהאי נשף אורתא הוא - דכתיב "בנשף בערב יום באישון לילה ואפלה"! אמר רב אושעיא אמר רבי אחא, הכי קאמר (דוד): מעולם לא עבר עלי חצות לילה בשינה. רבי זירא אמר: עד חצות לילה היה מתנמנם כסוס. מכאן ואילך היה מתגבר כארי. רב אשי אמר: עד חצות לילה היה עוסק בדברי תורה, מכאן ואילך בשירות ותשבחות. ונשף אורתא הוא? הא נשף צפרא הוא! דכתיב "ויכם דוד מהנשף ועד הערב למחרתם" מאי לאו מצפרא ועד ליליא! - לא, מאורתא ועד אורתא. - אי הכי, לכתוב "מהנשף ועד הנשף" או "מהערב ועד הערב"! - אלא אמר רבא: תרי נשפי הוו, נשף ליליא ואתי יממא, נשף יממא ואתי ליליא. ודוד מי הוה ידע פלגא דליליא אימת? השתא משה רבינו לא הוה ידע, דכתיב "כחצות הלילה אני יוצא בתוך מצרים", מאי 'כחצות'? אילימא דאמר ליה קודשא בריך הוא 'כחצות' - *מי איכא ספיקא קמי שמיא?! אלא דאמר ליה (למחר) *בחצות (כי השתא), ואתא איהו ואמר: כחצות, אלמא מספקא ליה - ודוד הוה ידע?! -דוד סימנא הוה ליה, *דאמר רב אחא בר ביזנא א"ר שמעון חסידא: כנור היה תלוי למעלה ממטתו של דוד, וכיון שהגיע חצות לילה בא רוח צפונית ונושבת בו ומנגן מאליו, מיד היה עומד ועוסק בתורה עד שעלה עמוד השחר. כיון שעלה עמוד השחר נכנסו חכמי ישראל אצלו, אמרו לו: אדונינו המלך, עמך ישראל צריכין פרנסה. אמר להם: לכו והתפרנסו זה מזה. אמרו לו: אין הקומץ משביע את הארי *ואין הבור מתמלא מחוליתו. *אמר להם: לכו ופשטו ידיכם בגדוד. מיד יועצים באחיתופל ונמלכין בסנהדרין, ושואלין באורים ותומים. אמר רב יוסף: מאי קרא? - (דכתיב) "ואחרי אחיתופל בניהו בן יהוידע ואביתר ושר צבא למלך יואב". אחיתופל - זה יועץ, וכה"א "ועצת אחיתופל אשר יעץ בימים ההם כאשר ישאל (איש) בדבר האלהים"; בניהו

בחדתי. שנפלה מחדש, שהחומה שלה נפלה, ועודנה בחזקתה: חשד נמי ליכא. (במסכת קידושין דף פ:): תנן: אבל אשה מתייחדת עם שני אנשים: בתרי ופריצי. דאמרינן התם: לא שנו אלא בכשרים: במקומן חיישינן. במקום שהם מצויין תדיר, חיישינן אפילו בתרי: בדברא. בשדה: קדמו עיני אשמורות. אלמא: חצות לילה שהיה דוד עומד - שתי משמרות יש בהם: ור' נתן. אמר לך: האי "קדמו עיני אשמורות" דקאמר דוד - קודמו לשאר מלכים קאמר, שדרכן לעמוד בשלש שעות ביום, בתחלת שעה שלישית: שית דליליא. חצות לילה הוי שש שעות: ותרתי דיממא. ששאר מלכים ישנים, הוו להו תרתי משמרות של שמונה שעות: אלא לדבר הלכה. אסור לספר לפניו, שהכל חייבין לספר בהן, והמת דומם והוה ליה "לועג לרש חרף עושהו" (משלי יז): אבל מילי דעלמא. שאין גנאי לו אם אין מתחרשין בהן - לית לן בה: מאורתא. מתחלת הלילה: בנשף בערב יום. בהעריב היום קרוי נשף: ה"ג. (א) קרא דחצות לילה: מעולם לא עבר עלי חצות לילה בשינה, שקודם לכן קיימי עומד: מתנמנם כסוס. עוסק בתורה כשהוא מתנמנם, כסוס הזה שאינו נרדם לעולם, אלא מתנמנם וגעור תמיד: בשירות ותשבחות. והכי מפרש בהכוא קרא "להודות לך" וגו': למחרתם. ליום מחרת של חניסם שם. ה"נ אי הכי לכתוב מהנשף ועד הנשף – אלא אמר רב אשי תרי נשפי הוו: נשף יממא. קפץ ועולה, כמו "לנשוף מדוכתיה" (מגילה דף ג.), וכמו "האי בוקא דאטמא דנשף מדוכתיה – טרפה" (חולין דף נד.): ואתא איהו ואמר 'כחצות'. לפי שלא היה יודע לכוין השעה ולהעמיד דבריו בשעת הסמוכה: כנור היה תלוי למעלה ממטתו. ופתחיו לצד צפון, כיון שהגיע חצות הלילה רוח צפונית מנשבת בו. דאמר מר (ב"ב דף כה.): ארבע רוחות מנשבות בכל יום ויום, שש שעות ראשונות של כל יום - מנשבת רוח מזרחית מהלוך החמה, [א] ושש אחרונות – רוח דרומית, ובתחלת הלילה רוח מערבית, ובחצות הלילה רוח צפונית(ב): אין הבור מתמלא מחוליתו. העוקר חוליא מבור כרוי וחוזר ומשליכו לתוכו – אין מתמלאת בכך. אף כאן, אם אין אתה מכין לעניים שבנו מזונות ממקום אחר אין אנו יכולין לפרנס משל עצמנו: יועצים באחיתופל. איזה הדרך ילכו, והיאך יפיבו מגן ומשחית, ועכסיסי מערב מלחמה: ונמלכין בסנהדרין. נוטלין מהם רשות, כדי שיתפללו עליהם: ושואלין באורים ותומים. אם יצליחו: ה"ג. מאי קרא ואחרי אחיתופל בניהו בן יהוידע ואביתר ושר צבא למלך יואב. אחיתופל זה יועץ: בניהו

במקומן חיישינן. פי': שידוע שרגילין שם המזיקין. והסיח לעיל לדברי ופריצי ליכא משום מזיקין - איירי בספק, שאין רגילין: אין אומרין בפני המת אלא דבריו של מת. ופסק *רב אלפס משום רב האי: דוקא דברי תורה, אבל דברים דעלמא - לית לן בה. ודוקא בארבע אמות שלו: רוח צפונית מנשבת. פי': לגדה. דהא אמרינן בפרק "לא יחפור" (ב"ב דף כה.) שהיא מנשבת עם כל אחד ואחד: *ואתא איהו ואמר כחצות. ואם תאמר: מכל מקום לימא "בחצות" כמו שאמרו לו מן השמים, דהא משה אמרו לו. וי"ל: שלא רצה לומר להם דבר שלא היה יכול להראות ולהוכיח, אם ישאלו לו: ואין הבור מתמלא מחוליתו. פירש רש"י: אם יחפור ויחזיר בו עפרו לא יהא מלא. *ותימה: דאין הנדון דומה לראיה, שהרי לא היה אומר להם אלא ליטול מן העשירים וליתן לעניים. אם היה מלוה ליטול מן העניים ולחזור וליתן להם - אז היה דומה למשל. ומפרש רבינו חננאל: מחוליתו - מנביעתו, כלומר: אין הבור המתמלא מן המים הנובעים בו. ובתוספתא יש: אין הבור מתמלא מחוליתו, אלא אם כן מושכין לו מים מגל אחר. ור"י פירש: שאם תחפור מגל זה ותניח מגל אחר לא תמלא. שמה שנותן כאן - חסר כאן. כמו כן, מה שנוטל מן העשירים - יתחסר מן העשירים:

עין משפט נר מצוה

י א מיי' פ"ג מהלכות אבילות הלכה ט' סמ"ג עשין דרבנן ב' טור וש"ע יו"ד סימן שמד סעיף יז:

רב נסים גאון

ליגע בכלום דבר מקדש המוכח עד שיביא הכפרה שהוא מתחייב בה ולכן אם נכנס למקדש משערי ניקנור ולפנים שהוא מחנה שכינה נתחייב כרת אם היה מזיד ואם היה שוגג בחטאת כדתנא בתוספ' (כלים פרק א') כל הטמאין שנכנסו משערי ניקנור ולפנים אפי' מחוסרי כפרה חייבין על זדונן כרת ועל שגגתן חטאת ובמשנה בתחלת טהרות (כלים פרק א' משנה ח') עזרת ישראל מקודשת ממנה שאין מחוסר כפורים נכנס לשם וחייבין עליה חטאת ובספרי (פרשת נשא) מפורש מפתח עזרה ולפנים מחנה שכינה ותניא בספרי *)טמא יהיה לרבות את הטבול יום עוד טומאתו בו לרבות מחוסר כפרה ואיתא בגזירות בפרק ג' מינין (דף מס' מכות דף ח) ולאחר שיביא הכפרה ויקריבנה הכהן כראוי והלכה ויכפר עליו כבר נגמרה לו טהרתו והותר לו לוכל בקדשי מזבח ולהכנס למחנה שכינה והיינו מעזרת ישראל ולפנים וכדאמר הכתוב (ויקרא יב) וכפר עליה הכהן וטהרה וכבר אמרו חכמים כי הוא חייב טבילה לאחר שמקריב כפרתו ואז יהא מותר לוכל בקדשים כדתנן בפרק חומר בקודש (חגיגה דף כ) וכו מחוסר כפורים צריכין טבילה לקודש אבל לא לתרומה ואמרינן בגמרא (שם דף כג) כיון דעד האידנא הוו אסירי למיכל בקודש אצרכינהו רבנן טבילה ואלו השמות שהן קריין לטמא כמו שהזכרנו איתנהו מסודרין במשנה בתחלת טהרות (כלים פרק א' משנה ה') מחוסר כפורים אסור בקודש ומותר בתרומה ובמעשר חזר להיות טבול יום אסור בקודש ובתרומה ומותר במעשר חזר להיות בעל קרי אסור בשלשתן ובמשנת נגעים בפרק י"ד (משנה ג') כבס בגדיו וטבל טהר מלטמא בשרץ והרי הוא טבול יום אוכל במעשר העריב שמשו אוכל בתרומה הביא כפרתו אוכל בקדשים והיינו מתני' שהזכרנו מקודם ובפסחים בפרק כל שעה (דף לה ע"ש) אמרינן העריב אין לא העריב לא אמאי הא טהור הוא אלא מעלה

הרי נתברר לנו עכשיו מכל אלו הראיות כי התרומה מעלתה למעלה מן המעשר והיא למטה מן הקדשים וכי זה שאמר הכתוב ובא השמש וטהר על השמש הוא חוזר ולא על האדם הטמא כלומר שיתפנו פני הרקיע מאורו של יום ויראו הכוכבים אותה העת היא תחלת הלילה וזהו עת שנתחייבנו בו בקריית שמע של ערבית וכל מי שקרא קריאת שמע קודם זה העת לא יצא ידי חובתו כדגרסי' בגמ' דבני מערבא (הלכה א') תני הקורא את שמע קודם לכן לא יצא ידי חובתו. חלוקתם של ר' יהודה ור' יוסי בבין השמשות שנויה היא בהא ברייתא דפרק במה מדליקין (דף לד) תנו רבנן בין השמשות מן היום ומן הלילה ספק כולו מן היום ספק כולו מן הלילה ומטילין אותו לחומרי שני ימים איזהו בין השמשות משתשקע החמה כל זמן שפני מזרח מאדימין הכסיף התחתון ולא הכסיף העליון בין השמשות הכסיף העליון והשוה לתחתון לילה דברי ר' יהודה ר' נחמיה אומר בין השמשות משתשקע החמה כדי הילוך חצי מיל ר' יוסי אומר בין השמשות כהרף עין זה נכנס וזה יוצא אי אפשר לעמוד עליו והכל שוין הן שהעת הנקרא בין השמשות ספק יום ספק לילה הוא אין יוצאין בו ידי חובת היום ולא ידי חובת הלילה כל המצות הנוהגות ביום אין יוצאין בהן בבין השמשות שאינו ודאי יום וכל המצות הנוהגות בלילה אין יוצאין בהן ידי חובה וכו' וגם הם שוין בטבילה שצריכה להיות בשעה שהוא יום ודאי שאין בה ספק (כדתנן) [כדתניא] (בפסחים דף ל ועוד) כל חייבי טבילות טבילתן ביום נדה ויולדת טבילתן בלילה לא יחלקו אלא בשעה שהיא בין השמשות אי זו היא וכמה שיעורא וסבר ר' יהודה כי מעת שקיעת החמה ועד שיסתלק זוהר מעל הארץ ויכסיף דמדומה מן הרקיע זהו בין השמשות שהוא ספק יום ספק לילה והטבילה צריכה להיות קודם זה העת לדעתו ור' יוסי חלק עליו ואמר כי זה העת שקרא אותו ר' יהודה בין השמשות יום הוא ודאי ואין בו ספק ומותר לטמא לטבול בו וכי בין השמשות שהוא ספק עת דחוק הוא למאד ושיעורו כהרף עין סמוך ליציאת הכוכבים דאמרינן (שבת דף לה) אמר רב יהודה אמר שמואל בין השמשות דר' יהודה לר' יוסי טובלין בו כהנים ואמרינן התם במס' נדה בפרק בא סימן התחתון (דף נג) האיך תנא סבר [illegible] בין השמשות דר' יהודה והדר מתחיל בין השמשות דר' יוסי והאי תנא סבר בין השמשות דר' יוסי מישך שייך בדר' יהודה ועל עיקר זו החלוקה שישנה ביניהם באו הדברים שבין ר' מאיר ור' יהודה בכאן כי ר' מאיר התיר לקרוא קריית שמע של ערבית משעה שהכהנים טובלין וכשהשיב עליו ר' יהודה לפי דעתו כי הטבילה אינה (אלא) לאחר שקיעת החמה כי אותו העת מתחילין בין השמשות להכנס ואינה לטבילה אלא קודם שקיעת החמה והאיך יוצאין באותו העת ידי חובתן מקריית שמע של ערבית ועדיין היום עומד אמר לו ר' מאיר אני איני סובר כדעתך בבין השמשות אלא כי העת שאתה קוריהו בין השמשות הוא אצלי אני**) ודאי יום שאין בו ספק ומותר לטבול בו ואני סובר בבין השמשות כדעתו של ר' יוסי שהוא כהרף עין ואי אפשר לעמוד עליו ואל תשיבני אתה מדרך הדעת שלך כי איני סובר כדבריך אלא כר' יוסי אני סובר ולפיכך אמרתי משעה שהכהנים טובלין ופסקינן הלכתא (שבת דף לה) כר' יהודה לענין שבת לחומרא וכר' יוסי לענין תרומה דלא אכלי כהני עד דנפיק בין השמשות דר' יוסי לחומרא נמי: (דף ג) **רבנן** מפני ג' דברים כו' ותיפוק לי משום מזיקין בתרי מכלל דתרי לא מזקי להו ואיתא מיפרשא בפרק כיצד מברכין על הפירות (דף מג) דתני לאחד נראה ומזיק לשנים נראה ואינו מזיק אלא אם כן יהיה אותו המקום קבוע למזיקין צריכין לחוש להם ואפי' בתרי כדאמרי' בדוכתא דקביעי חיישינן ומה שאמרו אי בתרי חשדא נמי ליכא זה הדבר בנוי על אותו העיקר שבמשנה בפרק עשרה יוחסין (קידושין דף פ') לא יתייחד איש אחד עם שתי נשים אבל אשה אחת מתייחדת עם שני אנשים והואיל (והשנים) [והן שנים] מותר להן להתייחד עם האשה כי החשד מסתלק מביניהן אלא אם כן היו פרוצים כי הפרוצין החשד קבוע הוא בהן ואפי' אם היו עשרה כדאמרי' (שם) אמר רב יהודה אמר שמואל לא שנו אלא בכשרים אבל בפרוצין אפילו עשרה נמי לא מעשה היה והוציאוה י' במטה ומזה העיקר אמרי' נמי הכא בתרי ופריצי: **ר' זירא** אמר עד חצות לילה

*) בספרי פ' חקת שלפנינו ליתא להאי ליקוט. **) פירושו כמו אלי.

מסורת הש"ס

שופטים ז; תהלים קיט; שם; תהלים קיט; משלי ז; ש"א ל; שמות יא; סנהדרין טז. כל הענין; ד"ה א כז; שמואל ב טז

לקמן דף ט: לקמן נח. גי' רי"ף ורש"ל [סוכה כו:] גיטין ו. לקמן נט. [פי' עפר שע"פ הבור מעפר שחופרין מן הבור אינו מתמלא עד שיוסיפו בו עפר אחר ערוך חליא]

הגהות הב"ח

(א) רש"י ד"ה ה"ג האי קרא דחצות: (ב) ד"ה כנור וכו' לפונית הסה"ד ואח"כ מ"ה ד"ה אין הקומץ [illegible]

גליון הש"ס

גמ' בתרי חשד נמי ליכא. [illegible] שם וכה"א ועצת אחיתופל. [illegible] תוס' ד"ה אין אומרין כו'. ודוקא בד' אמות שלו. [illegible]

הגהות הגר"א

[א] רש"י ד"ה כנור. [illegible]

בניהו בן יהוידע — זה סנהדרין, ואביתר — אלו אורים ותומים, וכן הוא אומר: °"ובניהו בן יהוידע על הכרתי ועל הפלתי"; ולמה נקרא שמם כרתי ופלתי? כרתי — שכורתים דבריהם, פלתי — שמופלאים בדבריהם;* ואח"כ "שר צבא למלך יואב". אמר רב יצחק בר אדא ואמרי לה אמר רב יצחק בריה דרב אידי: מאי קרא — °"עורה כבודי עורה הנבל וכנור אעירה שחר". רבי זירא אמר: משה לעולם הוה ידע, ודוד נמי הוה ידע. וכיון דדוד הוה ידע, כנור למה ליה? — לאתעורי משנתיה. וכיון דמשה הוה ידע, למה ליה למימר 'כחצות'? — משה קסבר: שמא יטעו אצטגניני פרעה ויאמרו משה בדאי הוא. דאמר מר: *למד לשונך לומר איני יודע, שמא תתבדה ותאחז. רב אשי אמר: בפלגא אורתא דתליסר נגהי ארבסר הוה קאי, והכי קאמר משה לישראל: אמר הקב"ה, למחר כחצות הלילה כי האידנא, אני יוצא בתוך מצרים.§ °"לדוד שמרה נפשי כי חסיד אני" — לוי ור' יצחק: חד אמר: כך אמר דוד לפני הקב"ה: רבונו של עולם! לא חסיד אני?! שכל מלכי מזרח ומערב ישנים עד שלש שעות, ואני °"חצות לילה אקום להודות לך". ואידך: כך אמר דוד לפני הקב"ה: רבונו של עולם, לא חסיד אני?! שכל מלכי מזרח ומערב יושבים אגודות אגודות בכבודם, ואני ידי מלוכלכות בדם ובשפיר ובשליא כדי לטהר אשה לבעלה. ולא עוד: אלא כל מה שאני עושה אני נמלך במפיבשת רבי, ואומר לו: מפיבשת רבי! יפה דנתי, יפה חייבתי? יפה זכיתי? יפה טהרתי? יפה טמאתי? ולא בושתי. א"ר יהושע בריה דרב אידי: מאי קרא — °"ואדברה בעדתיך נגד מלכים ולא אבוש". תנא: לא מפיבשת שמו אלא איש *בשת שמו, ולמה נקרא שמו מפיבשת? — שהיה מבייש פני דוד בהלכה. לפיכך זכה דוד ויצא ממנו כלאב. וא"ר יוחנן: לא כלאב שמו אלא דניאל שמו, ולמה נקרא שמו כלאב — שהיה מכלים פני מפיבשת בהלכה, ועליו אמר שלמה בחכמתו: °"בני אם חכם לבך ישמח לבי גם אני", ואומר: °"חכם בני ושמח לבי ואשיבה חרפי דבר". ודוד מי קרי לנפשיה חסיד?! והכתיב °"לולא האמנתי לראות בטוב ה' בארץ חיים" ותנא משמיה דרבי יוסי: למה נקוד על לולא? — אמר דוד לפני הקב"ה: רבש"ע! מובטח אני בך שאתה משלם שכר טוב לצדיקים לעתיד לבוא, אבל איני יודע אם יש לי חלק ביניהם אם לאו! — שמא יגרום החטא; *כדר' יעקב בר אידי, דר' יעקב בר אידי רמי, כתיב: °"והנה אנכי עמך ושמרתיך בכל אשר תלך" וכתיב °"ויירא יעקב מאד"! אמר: שמא יגרום החטא, *כדתניא: °"עד יעבר עמך ה' עד יעבר עם זו קנית"; "עד יעבר עמך ה'" — זו ביאה ראשונה, "עד יעבר עם זו קנית" — זו ביאה שניה; מכאן אמרו חכמים: ראוים היו ישראל ליעשות להם נס בימי עזרא כדרך שנעשה להם בימי יהושע בן נון, אלא שגרם החטא.§ "וחכ"א עד חצות". חכמים כמאן סבירא להו? אי כרבי אליעזר סבירא להו — לימרו כרבי אליעזר!

ואי

תורה אור

שמואל ב כ · תהלים נז · שם פו · שם קיט · שם · משלי כג · שם כז · תהלים כז · בראשית כח · שם לב · שמות טו

בניהו בן יהוידע זה סנהדרין. שהיה אב בית דין: וכן הוא אומר ובניהו בן יהוידע על הכרתי ועל הפלתי. ראשון וקודם להם, שבתחילה נוטלים רשות, ואח"כ שואלים אם יצליחו: ואביתר אלו אורים ותומים. שכל ימי דוד היה נשאל באביתר עד מלחמת אבשלום ששאל אביתר ולא עלתה לו, ושאל צדוק ועלתה לו, כדאמרי' ב"סדר עולם", ונסתלק אז מן הכהונה: שכורתים את דבריהם. שאומרים דברים קצובים וגמורים, שלא יפחתו ולא יוסיפו: שר צבא למלך יואב. להוליך אנשי המלחמה: מאי קרא. דכנור היה תלוי למעלה ממטתו ומעוררו: עורה כבודי. אל תתכבדי בשינה כשאר מלכים: אעירה שחר. שאר מלכים השחר מעוררן, ואני מעורר את השחר: שמא יטעו אצטגניני פרעה. אם אני יודע לכוין השעה — הם אינם יודעים לכוין השעה, וקודם שיגיע חצות יהו סבורים שהגיע, ועדיין לא באה המכה, ויאמרו: משה בדאי הוא. הלכך, טוב לאחוז לשון איני יודע: דאמר מר. במסכת דרך ארץ: ותאחז. תהא נאחז ונכשל בדבריך: תליסר נגהי ארבסר. ליל שעבר שלשה עשר (א) ולמחרת יגיע ארבעה עשר: ידי מלוכלכות בדם. שהנשים מראות לו דם נדה, אם טמא אם טהור, שיש מראות דם טהור באשה: ובשפיר. הוא עור הולד שהעצמות והגידים והבשר נצורים בתוכו. ויש שפיר שהאשה יושבת עליו ימי טומאה וימי טהרה, ואי זה — זה המרוקם, ובמס' נדה (דף כד ב) מפרש לה, ויש שפיר מלא מים ודם שאינו חשוב ולד לישב עליו טומאת יולדת וימי טהרתה: ובשליא. דתנן (שם כו.): אין שליא בלא ולד. והוא כמין לבוש שהולד שוכב בתוכה, וקורין ושטי"דור בלע"ז. ותניא (שם): אין שליא פחותה מטפח, ותחלתה כחוט של ערב וסופה כתורמוס. והיו מביאין אותה לפניו לראות אם יש בה כשיעור ואם עשויה כדת שליא — שנחזיקנה שהיה ולד בתוכה ונמוח, ותשב עליו ימי טומאה וטהרה, אם לאו: זכיתי וחייבתי. שייך בדיני ממונות ודיני נפשו': טמאתי וטהרתי. בהלכות טומאה וטהרה: מפיבושת. [מפי בושת], בדברי הלכה היוצאין מפיו היה בושת לדוד, שפעמים שהיה טועה והוא אומר לו: טעית: לפיכך. בזכות שהיה דוד מקטין עצמו — זכה ויצא ממנו כלאב: אלא דניאל שמו. במקום אחד אומר (שמואל ב ג) "ומשנהו כלאב לאביגיל אשת נבל" וגו', ובמקום אחר אומר "והשני דניאל לאביגיל", בדברי הימים (א ג): שהיה מכלים פני מפיבושת. כל אב — מכלים (ב) את הרב, שהיה אב בהוראות: לולא האמנתי לראות בטוב ה'.(ג) כבר טרדוני מיראתך, כמו שנאמר "כי גרשוני היום מהסתפח בנחלת ה' לאמר לך עבוד" וגו' (שמואל א כו): נקוד על לולא. לדרוש את הנקודה שהיא ממעטת את משמעות הכתוב, לומר שלא דבר ברור היה לו לראות בטוב ה'. 'לולא' לשון אם לא, כמו "לולי אלהי אבי וגו' היה לי" (בראשית לא): שמא יגרום החטא. תירוצא הוא: לעולם מוחזק בידו שהוא חסיד, וזה שספק בידו אם יראה בטוב ה' — לפי שהיה ירא שמא יחטא ויגרום החטא מלראות בטוב: ויירא יעקב. שמא אחר הבטחה חטאתי, וכדתניא, שהחטא גורם שאין ההבטחה מתקיימת: ביאה ראשונה. שבאו (ד) בימי יהושע: ביאה שנייה. כשעלו מגלות בבל בימי עזרא: ראויים היו(ה) ליעשות להם נס. לבוא ביד רמה: אלא שגרם החטא. ולא הלכו אלא ברשות כורש, וכל ימי מלכי פרס נשתעבדו להם, לכורש ולאחשורוש ולדריוש האחרון: חכמים כמאן סבירא להו. במשמעות "בשכבך" האמור בתורה: אי כר' אליעזר סבירא להו. דאית ליה: "בשכבך" — כל זמן שבני אדם עוסקין לילך ולשכב, זה מקדים וזה מאחר: לימרו(ו) כר' אליעזר. דאמר "סוף האשמורה הראשונה", דודאי כל שדעתו לישן כבר שכב וישן:

ואי

בניהו זה סנהדרין. מסברא אומר כן. אביתר אלו אורים ותומים וכן הוא אומר ובניהו בן יהוידע על הכרתי ועל הפלתי. כלומר: היה קודם להם, אם כן: אורים ותומים היו אחר בניהו. א"כ, אביתר שהוזכר אחר בניהו — היינו אורים ותומים, כך פירש רש"י. ותימא לפירושו: פשיטא דאביתר כהן היה בימי דוד, שלא היה כהן אחר, שכולם נהרגו בנוב עיר הכהנים, ולמה צריך ראיה עליה? ועוד, לגירסת הקונטרס "בניהו בן יהוידע" אין זה הפסוק בשום מקום! לכך (מפרש) [גריס] רבינו תם כדאי' (בדה"א כ"ז) *"ואחרי אחיתופל יהוידע בן בניהו" זה סנהדרין, וכן הוא אומר "ובניהו בן יהוידע על הכרתי ועל הפלתי", ופי' ר"ת: דכרתי ופלתי — היינו סנהדרין שכורתין דבריהם לאמתן, ופלתי — שמופלאים בהוראה, כמו מופלא שבבית דין. וא"ת: היכי פשיט יהוידע בן בניהו מבניהו בן יהוידע? וי"ל: דמסתמא ממלא מקום אביו היה, וכי היכי דאביו היה מסנהדרין — גם הוא היה מהם*:

וקורא

[וכ"ה בערוך ערך אחר]

[ועי' תוס' סנהדרין טז: ד"ה ואחרי]

ת הש"ס

ה נקרא שמם תומים אורים את דבריהם שמשלימים את ועי' ביומא עג:

י ארץ זוטא פ"ג

כמות דף עט. רס ר"ת אלא איש בעל שמו וע"ש]

סנהדרין דף לח:

ם וסוטה דף לו.

הות הב"ח

ד"ה תליסר וכו' ר של שלשה עשר יגיע ארבעה ב) ד"ה שהיה ו' מכלים את פני ד"ה לולא וכו' בארץ ישראל כבר (ד) ד"ה ביאה או לארץ בימי ה) ד"ה ראויים שראל ליעשות: לימא כר' אליעזר מר עד סוף:

## רב נסים גאון

יושב ומנמנם כסוס איתא במסכת סוכה בפ' הישן (דף כו) אמר רב אסור לאדם לישן ביום יותר משינת הסוס אמר אביי שינתיה דמר כדרב דרב כר' דר' כדוד מלך ישראל דדוד כדסוסיא דסוסי שיתין נישמי. הא דאמר (רב) [רב אחא] הכא אין הבור מתמלא מחוליתו מתפרשא לך מההיא דבפרק הרואה מקום (דף נט) דתניא בשעה שבקש הקב"ה להביא מבול לעולם נטל ב' כוכבים מכימה והביא מבול לעולם וכשבקש לסתמם נטל ב' כוכבים מעיש וסתמן ומדאקשינן וליסתמה בדידה ופרקינן אין הבור מתמלא מחוליתו שמעת מינה דהכין הוא פירושה שהבור אם תחזיר לתוכו העפר שניטלת ממנו אינו ממלא אותו אלא צריך להוסיף עפר אחר ולפיכך לא היו מספיקין כאן אותן ב' כוכבים שניטלו ממנה והוצרך ליטול ב' כוכבים מעיש לסתמן ולזה נתכוונו העם באמרם לדוד המלך אין הבור מתמלא מחוליתו תשובה לדבריו שאמר להם לכו התפרנסו זה מזה כלומר כי אין מספיק לנו מה שאנו נהנים זה מזה אלא צריכין אנו תוספת ממקום אחר מיד אמר להם לכו ופשטו ידיכם בגדוד:

18–20

**וקורא** קריאת שמע ומתפלל. מכאן משמע שמשעה שהגיע זמן קריאת שמע של לילה שאין לו לאכול סעודה עד שיקרא ק"ש ויתפלל ערבית: **דאמר** רבי יוחנן איזהו בן העוה"ב וכו'. ואנו שאומרים "יראו עינינו" ופסוקים אחרים אחר "השכיבנו". נראה, הואיל ותקינו להו רבנן – ה"ל כגאולה אריכתא, דתקינו לומר זה, שבתוך כך יתפלל חבירו גם הוא, ולא ילך מבהכ"נ עד שיגמור כל אחד תפלתו. וגם יש באותם פסוקים י"ח אזכרות כנגד י"ח ברכות ד"שמנה עשרה", ואגב שתקנו לומר אותם פסוקים תקנו לומר חתימה של "יראו עינינו". והלכה כר' יוחנן דברייתא מסייע ליה, וכן פסק ה"ג. ואם כן, יש ליזהר שלא לספר בין גאולה דערבית לשמנה עשרה. ומיהו, בסדר רב עמרם פי': מה שאנו אומרים קדיש בין גאולה לתפלת ערבית – לאשמעינן דלא בעינן מסמך גאולה דערבית לתפלה, משום דתפלת ערבית רשות. ולא נהירא, [דאם כן], ר' יוחנן סבירא ליה תפלת ערבית חובה, דפלוגתא היא *דרב ור' יוחנן, והלכה כר' יוחנן. ונכון להחמיר ולהזהר מלספר בינתים. ואי תימא: קשיא הלכתא אהלכתא, דקיימא לן תפלת ערבית רשות, והכא פסקינן כרבי יוחנן! צריך לומר: דאפילו אי סובר רבי יוחנן כרב דאמר רשות היא, מכל מקום מחייב לסמוך. אם כן – גם לנו יש לסמוך: הא

**ואי כרבן גמליאל סבירא להו.** דמשמע ליה "בשכבך" – כל זמן שבני אדם שוכבים, ויש בכלל הזה כל הלילה: **לימרו כר"ג. עד עמוד השחר:** מן העבירה. שמא יסמוך על שהות שיש לו, כדתניא: **קימעא.** מעט: **משום אונס שינה.** התוקפתו לעבור על דברי חכמים, הוזקקו להזהירו יותר: **ממאן דאמר.** לקמן, בפ' "תפלת השחר" (דף כז:): **אמר מר קורא ק"ש.** של ערבית תחלה ואח"כ מתפלל: **מסייע ליה לר' יוחנן.** דאמר ערבית נמי – ק"ש ואחר כך תפלה, *כדי שיסמוך גאולה לתפלה. ודלא כר' יהושע בן לוי דאמר תפלה ואחר כך ק"ש: **זה הסומך.** וכל שכן בשחרית, דעיקר גאולה במצרים בשחרית הוה, כדכתיב "ממחרת הפסח יצאו בני ישראל" (במדבר לג). וסמיכת גאולה לתפלה רמזה דוד בספר תהלים, דכתיב "ה' צורי וגואלי" (תהלים יט), וסמיך ליה "יענך ה' ביום צרה" (שם כ). ואמרי' בברכות ירושלמי (פ"א): מי שאינו סומך גאולה לתפלה למה הוא דומה – לאוהבו של מלך שבא ודפק על פתחו של מלך, יצא המלך ומצאו שהפליג – אף הוא הפליג. אלא יהיה אדם מקרב להקב"ה אליו, ומרצהו בתשבחות וקלוסין של יציאת מצרים, והוא מתקרב אליו, ובעודו קרוב אליו יש לו לתבוע צרכיו: **באמצע תקנום.** בין שני ק"ש תקנו כל תפלות של יום. דקא סבר: תפלת ערבית קודמת לק"ש: **גאולה מאורתא לא הוי.** הילכך: גאולה דאורתא לא חשיבא להדורי עלה סמיכת תפלה: **מה קימה ק"ש ואח"כ תפלה.** דבשחרית כולהו מודו דבעי מסמך: **שלש פעמים.** כנגד שלש תפלות: **דאית ביה תרתי.** דאתי באל"ף בי"ת, ויש בו שבח הכנת מזון לכל חי: **אפילו הכי.** אף על פי שהפסיק נו"ן מפני נפילה שבה, ולא חבה לרמזה – חזר ורמז סמיכת הנפילה תכף לה: **ויעף אלי.** בפריחה אחת, ולא הרגיע בינתים: **מועף ביעף.** שתי פריחות: **באחת.** בפריחה אחת: **אמרו בלבבכם.** אמרו מה שכתוב "על לבבך" (דברים ו): **על משכבכם.** שנאמר "בשכבך" (שם): **ודומו.** בשינה אחרי כן: ואם

תורה אור

ואי כרבן גמליאל סבירא להו – לימרו כרבן גמליאל! –לעולם כרבן גמליאל סבירא להו, והא דקא אמרי 'עד חצות' – כדי להרחיק את האדם מן העבירה. כדתניא: "חכמים עשו סייג לדבריהם, כדי שלא יהא אדם בא מן השדה בערב ואומר: אלך לביתי ואוכל קימעא ואשתה קימעא ואישן קימעא, ואח"כ אקרא ק"ש ואתפלל. וחוטפתו שינה ונמצא ישן כל הלילה; אבל אדם בא מן השדה בערב, נכנס לבית הכנסת, אם רגיל לקרות קורא, ואם רגיל לשנות שונה, וקורא ק"ש ומתפלל, ואוכל פתו ומברך; *וכל העובר על דברי חכמים חייב מיתה". מאי שנא בכל דוכתא דלא קתני 'חייב מיתה', ומאי שנא הכא דקתני 'חייב מיתה'? איבעית אימא: משום דאיכא אונס שינה; ואיבע"א: לאפוקי ממאן דאמר *תפלת ערבית רשות, קמ"ל דחובה.§ אמר מר: "קורא ק"ש ומתפלל". מסייע ליה לר' יוחנן, *דאמר ר' יוחנן: איזהו בן העולם הבא? – זה הסומך גאולה לתפלה של ערבית. רבי יהושע בן לוי אומר: תפלות באמצע תקנום. במאי קא מפלגי? *אי בעית אימא קרא, איבע"א סברא. איבע"א סברא, דר' יוחנן סבר: גאולה מאורתא נמי הוי, אלא גאולה מעלייתא לא הויא אלא עד צפרא; ור' יהושע בן לוי סבר: כיון דלא הויא אלא מצפרא, לא הויא גאולה מעלייתא. ואב"א קרא – ושניהם מקרא אחד דרשו, דכתיב: °"בשכבך ובקומך", ר' יוחנן סבר: מקיש שכיבה לקימה – מה קימה ק"ש ואח"כ תפלה, אף שכיבה נמי ק"ש ואח"כ תפלה; ר' יהושע בן לוי סבר: מקיש שכיבה לקימה – מה קימה ק"ש סמוך למטתו, אף שכיבה נמי ק"ש סמוך למטתו. מתיב מר בריה דרבינא: *בערב מברך שתים לפניה ושתים לאחריה; ואי אמרת בעי לסמוך, הא לא קא סמך גאולה לתפלה, דהא בעי למימר "השכיבנו"! אמרי: כיון דתקינו רבנן "השכיבנו", כגאולה אריכתא דמיא. דאי לא תימא הכי – שחרית היכי מצי סמיך? והא *אמר רבי יוחנן, בתחלה אומר: °"ה' שפתי תפתח", ולבסוף הוא אומר: °"יהיו לרצון אמרי פי"! אלא: התם כיון דתקינו רבנן למימר "ה' שפתי תפתח" – כתפלה אריכתא דמיא, הכא נמי, כיון דתקינו רבנן למימר "השכיבנו"– כגאולה אריכתא דמיא.§ אמר רבי אלעזר *א"ר אבינא: כל האומר °"תהלה לדוד" בכל יום שלש פעמים – מובטח לו שהוא בן העולם הבא. מאי טעמא? אילימא משום דאתיא באל"ף בי"ת – נימא °"אשרי תמימי דרך" דאתיא בתמניא *אפין! אלא משום דאית ביה °"פותח את ידך" נימא *"הלל הגדול" דכתיב ביה: °"נתן לחם לכל בשר"! – אלא: משום דאית ביה תרתי. אמר רבי יוחנן: מפני מה לא נאמר נו"ן באשרי? – מפני שיש בה מפלתן של שונאי ישראל, דכתיב: °"נפלה לא תוסיף קום בתולת ישראל". במערבא מתרצי לה הכי: "נפלה ולא תוסיף לנפול עוד קום בתולת ישראל". אמר רב נחמן בר יצחק: אפילו הכי(א) חזר דוד וסמכן ברוח הקדש, שנא' °"סומך ה' לכל הנופלים".§ א"ר אלעזר בר אבינא: גדול מה שנאמר במיכאל יותר ממה שנאמר בגבריאל, דאילו במיכאל כתי' °"ויעף אלי אחד מן השרפים", ואילו גבי גבריאל כתי': °"והאיש גבריאל אשר ראיתי בחזון בתחלה מעף ביעף וגו'". מאי משמע דהאי "אחד" מיכאל הוא? אמר ר' יוחנן: אתיא "אחד" "אחד", כתיב הכא "ויעף אלי אחד מן השרפים" וכתי' התם °"והנה מיכאל אחד (מן) השרים הראשונים בא לעזרני". תנא: מיכאל באחת, גבריאל בשתים, אליהו בארבע, ומלאך המות בשמנה, ובשעת המגפה באחת.§ א"ר יהושע בן לוי: אע"פ שקרא אדם ק"ש בביהכ"נ, מצוה לקרותו על מטתו. אמר רבי *יוסי: מאי קרא – °"רגזו ואל תחטאו אמרו בלבבכם על משכבכם ודמו סלה". אמר רב נחמן: אם

* נ"א אלפי"ן

דברים ו · תהלים נא · שם יט · שם קמה · שם קמה · שם קטו · עמוס ה · תהלים קמה · ישעיה ו · דניאל ט · שם י · תהלים ד

**עין משפט נר מצוה**

יא א מיי' פ"ו מהלכות תפלה הלכה ז טור ושו"ע או"ח סימן רלה סעיף ב:

יב ב מיי' פ"ז שם הלכה יח סמג עשין יט טור או"ח סימן רלו ושו"ע או"ח סימן רלו סעיף ב:

יג ג מיי' פ"ב שם הלכה ט (סמג שם) טור ושו"ע או"ח סי' קי"א סעיף א':

יד ד מיי' (וסמג) שם טוש"ע או"ח סימן קכב סעיף ב:

טו ה מיי' פ"ז שם הלכה יב סמג עשין יט טוש"ע או"ח סימן נא סעיף ז [ורב אלפס פ' אין עומדין דף כו א]:

טז ו מיי' פ"ז שם הלכה ב טוש"ע או"ח סימן רלט סעיף א:

עירובין כה.

[לקמן כז ב כפי שנדפס שם בלא הגליון וע"ע תוס' שם ד"ה והלכתא]

לקמן יא.

[בע"י וברב אלפס אי' בר אבינא וכזה נכון מהמאמר הסמוך וע"ל שם וא"ר אלעזר]

[נ"ל רב אסי או רב יוסף]

**רב נסים גאון**

**ואיבעית** אימא לאפוקי ממאן דאמר דתפלת ערבית רשות. מי הוא שאמר דתפלת ערבית רשות ר' יהושע הוא ואיתא בפרק תפלת השחר (דף כז) אמר רב יהודה אמר שמואל תפלת ערבית רבן גמליאל אומר חובה ר' יהושע אומר רשות.

ערכ"י ד' ל. ד"ה

**הגהות ד**

(א) גמ' חזר ד... ברכות הק

[לקמן כז ב שבת פז:]

לקמן דף ט:

[יבמות לה: קי ב"ב ח: ע. סנהדרין ל. שב ע"ב בתוס' זבר מנחות יג: ער תמורה ל:]

לקמן ט ב וע' ד"ה כיון

**גליון הש"ס** **בגמ'** וכל העובר על ד"ח. עירובין כ"א ע"ב ועי' רש"י סוטה ד ע"ב ד"ה נעקר ובתוס' שם: **שם** מאורתא נמי הוי. ע"ל ט ע"א: **שם** כיון דתקינו רבנן השכיבנו. עי' תשובת הרשב"א סימן נ"א: **שם** בכל יום ג"פ. בהרא"ש ליתא בטור וברוקח סימן ש"ך איתא לדוד בכל יום מובטח לו: **שם** מפני שיש בה מפלתן. עי' תשובת הרשב"א סימן מ"ע: **בהגהות** מהרי"ב אחר הס"ד והלכתא. וע"ע מגילה כ"ג ע"א תוס' ד"ה כיון:

ואם תלמיד חכם הוא. שרגיל במשנתו לחזור על גרסתו תמיד – דיו בכך: ירגיז יצר טוב. שיעשה מלחמה עם יצר הרע: ודומו סלה. יום הדומיה הוא יום המות, שהוא דומיה עולמית: זה מקרא. חומש, שמצוה לקרות בתורה: זו משנה. שיתעסקו במשנה: זה גמרא. סברת טעמי המשניות שממנו יוצאה הוראה. אבל המורים הוראה מן המשנה נקראו "מבלי העולם" במס' סוטה (דף כב.): כאילו אוחז חרב של שתי פיות בידו. להרוג את המזיקין: מאי משמע. (ב) דבקריאת שמע: התעיף עיניך בו. אם תכפל וסגרת עיניך בתורה (ג) היא משתכחת ממך: ובני רשף יגביהו עוף. העוף מסלקם ממך (ד): קטב מרירי. זה שם שד הצהרים במסכת פסחים (דף קיא:): ולחומי רשף. כתיב בין רעב למזיקין, נדרש לפניו ולאחריו – יסורין ומזיקין: אפילו תינוקות של בית רבן יודעים. שהתורה מגינה, שלמדין מספר חומש "אם שמוע תשמע כל המחלה אשר שמתי וגו'". ואפילו הקטנים שלא הגיעו לספר איוב, כבר למדו:

החשיתי מטוב. מן התורה: וכאבי נעכר. מכה עכורה: המוכר עצב. שפירש הימנו דבר חשוב כזה, ומתוך דוחקו מכרו: ושמח. שהרי הקב"ה מזהירם מלעזוב אותה ומשבחה לפניהם ב"לקח טוב" אחר שנתנה להם: פשפש ולא מצא. לא מצא עבירה בידו שבשבילה ראוין יסורין הללו לבא: אשרי הגבר אשר תיסרנו יה ומתורתך תלמדנו. שבשביל יסורין צריך אדם לבא לידי תלמוד תורה: יסורין של אהבה. הקב"ה מייסרו בעוה"ז בלא שום עון, כדי להרבות שכרו בעולם הבא יותר מכדי זכיותיו: וה' חפץ דכאו החלי. מי שהקב"ה חפץ בו, מחלהו ביסורין: אשם. קרבן: נפשו. מדעתו: דבר זה. שאשרי אדם אשר תיסרנו יה: מתורתך תלמדנו. כלומר: מתורתך אנו למדין אותו: נאמר ברית ביסורין דכתיב "אלה דברי הברית". אחר הקללות נאמר במשנה תורה: אף יסורין ממרקין כל עונותיו של אדם גרסי': ודרך חיים. חיי העוה"ב, הויין לו תוכחות מוסר לאדם:

תורה אור

אם תלמיד חכם הוא אין צריך. אמר אביי: אף תלמיד חכם מיבעי ליה למימר חד פסוקא דרחמי, כגון °"בידך אפקיד רוחי פדיתה אותי ה' אל אמת" (תהלים לא). § א"ר לוי בר חמא אמר ר"ש בן לקיש: לעולם ירגיז אדם יצר טוב על יצר הרע, שנא' °"רגזו ואל תחטאו" (שם ד). אם נצחו – מוטב, ואם לאו – יעסוק בתורה, שנאמר: "אמרו בלבבכם"; אם נצחו – מוטב, ואם לאו – יקרא קריאת שמע, שנאמר: "על משכבכם"; אם נצחו – מוטב, ואם לאו – יזכור לו יום המיתה, שנאמר: "ודמו סלה". וא"ר לוי בר חמא אמר ר' שמעון בן לקיש: מאי דכתיב °"ואתנה לך את לחת האבן והתורה והמצוה אשר כתבתי להורתם" (שמות כד) "לחת" – אלו עשרת הדברות, "תורה" – זה מקרא, "והמצוה" – זו משנה, "אשר כתבתי" – אלו נביאים וכתובים, "להורתם" זה תלמוד; *מלמד שכולם נתנו למשה מסיני. § א"ר יצחק: כל הקורא ק"ש על מטתו, כאלו אוחז חרב של שתי פיות בידו שנאמר °"רוממות אל בגרונם וחרב פיפיות בידם" (תהלים קמט). מאי משמע? אמר מר זוטרא ואיתימא רב אשי: מרישא דעניינא, דכתיב °"יעלזו חסידים בכבוד ירננו על משכבותם" (שם), וכתיב בתריה: "רוממות אל בגרונם וחרב פיפיות בידם". ואמר רבי יצחק: כל הקורא קריאת שמע על מטתו – מזיקין בדילין הימנו, שנאמר °"ובני רשף יגביהו עוף" (איוב ה); ואין 'עוף' אלא תורה, שנאמר: °"התעיף עיניך בו ואיננו" (משלי כג); ואין 'רשף' אלא מזיקין, שנאמר °"מזי רעב ולחמי רשף וקטב מרירי" (דברים לב). אמר רבי שמעון בן לקיש: כל העוסק בתורה יסורין בדילין הימנו, שנאמר: "ובני רשף יגביהו עוף"; ואין 'עוף' אלא תורה, שנאמר: "התעיף עיניך בו ואיננו"; ואין 'רשף' אלא יסורין, שנאמר: "מזי רעב ולחמי רשף". אמר ליה רבי יוחנן: *הא אפילו תינוקות של בית רבן יודעין אותו, שנאמר: °"ויאמר אם שמוע תשמע לקול ה' אלהיך והישר בעיניו תעשה והאזנת למצותיו ושמרת כל חקיו כל המחלה אשר שמתי במצרים לא אשים עליך כי אני ה' רופאך" (שמות טו)! אלא: כל שאפשר לו לעסוק בתורה ואינו עוסק – הקב"ה מביא עליו יסורין מכוערין ועוכרין אותו, שנא': °"נאלמתי דומיה החשיתי מטוב וכאבי נעכר" (תהלים לט). *ואין 'טוב' אלא תורה, שנאמר: °"כי לקח טוב נתתי לכם תורתי אל תעזובו" (משלי ד). אמר רבי זירא ואיתימא רבי חנינא בר פפא: בא וראה שלא כמדת הקב"ה מדת בשר ודם, מדת בשר ודם – אדם מוכר חפץ לחבירו, מוכר עצב ולוקח שמח; אבל הקב"ה אינו כן – נתן להם תורה לישראל ושמח, שנא': "כי לקח טוב נתתי לכם תורתי אל תעזובו". אמר רבא ואיתימא רב חסדא: אם רואה אדם שיסורין באין עליו – יפשפש במעשיו, שנא' °"נחפשה דרכינו ונחקורה *ונשובה עד ה'" (איכה ג); פשפש ולא מצא – יתלה בבטול תורה, שנאמר: °"אשרי הגבר אשר תיסרנו יה ומתורתך תלמדנו" (תהלים צד). ואם תלה ולא מצא – בידוע שיסורין של אהבה הם, שנאמר: °"כי את אשר יאהב ה' יוכיח" (משלי ג). אמר רבא אמר רב סחורה אמר רב הונא: כל שהקב"ה חפץ בו – מדכאו ביסורין, שנאמר: °"וה' חפץ דכאו החלי" (ישעיה נג); יכול אפילו לא קבלם מאהבה – תלמוד לומר °"אם תשים אשם נפשו" (שם שם), מה אשם לדעת – אף יסורין לדעת. ואם קבלם (א) מה שכרו – °"יראה זרע יאריך ימים" (שם); ולא עוד אלא שתלמודו מתקיים בידו, שנא': "וחפץ ה' בידו יצלח". פליגי בה רבי יעקב בר אידי ורבי אחא בר חנינא, חד אמר: אלו הם יסורין של אהבה – כל שאין בהן בטול תורה, שנאמר: "אשרי הגבר אשר תיסרנו יה ומתורתך תלמדנו"; וחד אמר: אלו הם יסורין של אהבה – כל שאין בהן בטול תפלה, שנאמר: °"ברוך אלהים אשר לא הסיר תפלתי וחסדו מאתי" (תהלים סו). אמר להו רבי אבא בריה דר' חייא בר אבא, הכי אמר *ר' חייא בר אבא א"ר יוחנן: אלו ואלו יסורין של אהבה הן, שנאמר: "כי את אשר יאהב ה' יוכיח"; אלא מה ת"ל "ומתורתך תלמדנו"? – אל תקרי *"תלמדנו" אלא 'תלמדנו'; דבר זה מתורתך תלמדנו; ק"ו משן ועין: מה שן ועין שהן אחד מאבריו של אדם – עבד יוצא בהן לחרות, יסורין שממרקין כל גופו של אדם – על אחת כמה וכמה, והיינו דרבי שמעון בן לקיש, דאמר רשב"ל: נאמר 'ברית' במלח ונאמר 'ברית' ביסורין; נאמר 'ברית' במלח, דכתיב °"ולא תשבית מלח ברית" (ויקרא ב), ונאמר 'ברית' ביסורין, דכתיב: °"אלה דברי הברית" (דברים כח). מה 'ברית' – האמור במלח – מלח ממתקת את הבשר, אף 'ברית' האמור ביסורין – יסורין ממרקין כל עונותיו של אדם. § *תניא, רבי שמעון בן יוחאי אומר: שלש מתנות טובות נתן הקדוש ברוך הוא לישראל, וכולן לא נתנן אלא ע"י יסורין. אלו הן: תורה וארץ ישראל והעולם הבא. תורה מנין – שנאמר: "אשרי הגבר אשר תיסרנו יה ומתורתך תלמדנו". ארץ ישראל – דכתיב °"כי כאשר ייסר איש את בנו ה' אלהיך מיסרך" (שם ח), וכתיב בתריה: "כי ה' אלהיך מביאך אל ארץ טובה". העולם הבא – דכתיב °"כי נר מצוה ותורה אור ודרך חיים תוכחות מוסר" (משלי ו). תני תנא קמיה דר' יוחנן: כל העוסק בתורה ובגמילות חסדים וקובר

[ג' מגילה יט ב]

כע. חולין פח:]

לקמן מח: ע"ז יט: מנחות נג: אבות פ"ו

י"ת בסגול אלא בצירי (ח"מ)

ס"פ יתרו וספרי פ' ואתחנן ע"ש

רב נסים גאון

מה אשם לדעת אף יסורין לדעת. כי הקרבנות אין מותר להקריבן אלא ברצון בעלים ולא בעל כורחן כדתניא (ערכין דף כא וס"כ) יקריב אותו מלמד שכופין אותו יכול בעל כורחו ת"ל לרצונו הא כיצד כופין עד שיאמר רוצה אני ואמרו עוד מנין למתעסק בקדשים שפסול וכו' לעכב מנין תלמוד לומר לרצונכם תזבחוהו (לרצונכם זבחו) לדעתכם זבחו ואיתא בשחיטת חולין בפ' הכל שוחטין (דף יג) ובמס' נדרים בפרק אין בין מודר הנאה מחברו (דף לה) איתא אמר ר' יוחנן הכל צריכין [דעת] חוץ ממחוסר כפרה:

ס"א פשפש ומצא יעשה תשובה שנאמר ונשובה

[ויתכן להיות הכי אמר אבא א"ר יוחנן אלו וכו' ועיין מו"ק דף כב.]

## הגהות הב"ח

(א) גמ' אם קבלם עליו מאהבה מה שכרו: (ב) רש"י ד"ה מאי משמע סמך דבקריאת שמע: (ג) ד"ה התעיף וכו' בתורה הס"ד ואח"כ מ"ה ואיננו היא משתכחת: (ד) ד"ה ובני רשף וכו' העוף מסלק ממך את בני רשף הס"ד:

וְקוֹבֵר אֶת בָּנָיו – מוֹחֲלִין לוֹ עַל כָּל עֲוֹנוֹתָיו. אֲמַר לֵיהּ רַבִּי יוֹחָנָן: בִּשְׁלָמָא תּוֹרָה וּגְמִילוּת חֲסָדִים – דִּכְתִיב: "בְּחֶסֶד וֶאֱמֶת יְכֻפַּר עָוֹן"; "חֶסֶד" – זוֹ גְּמִילוּת חֲסָדִים, שֶׁנֶּאֱמַר: "רֹדֵף צְדָקָה וָחָסֶד יִמְצָא חַיִּים צְדָקָה וְכָבוֹד", "אֱמֶת" – זוֹ תּוֹרָה, שֶׁנֶּאֱמַר: "אֱמֶת קְנֵה וְאַל תִּמְכֹּר"; אֶלָּא קוֹבֵר אֶת בָּנָיו – מְנַיִן? תָּנָא לֵיהּ הַהוּא סָבָא מִשּׁוּם ר' שִׁמְעוֹן בֶּן יוֹחַאי: אָתְיָא "עָוֹן", "עָוֹן", כְּתִיב הָכָא: "בְּחֶסֶד וֶאֱמֶת יְכֻפַּר עָוֹן", וּכְתִיב הָתָם "וּמְשַׁלֵּם עֲוֹן אָבוֹת אֶל חֵיק בְּנֵיהֶם". א"ר יוֹחָנָן: נְגָעִים וּבָנִים אֵינָן יִסּוּרִין שֶׁל אַהֲבָה. וּנְגָעִים לָא?! וְהָתַנְיָא: כָּל מִי שֶׁיֵּשׁ בּוֹ אֶחָד מֵאַרְבָּעָה מַרְאוֹת נְגָעִים הַלָּלוּ – אֵינָן אֶלָּא מִזְבַּח כַּפָּרָה! – מִזְבַּח כַּפָּרָה הָווּ, יִסּוּרִין שֶׁל אַהֲבָה לָא הָווּ. ואב"א: הָא לָן וְהָא לְהוּ. וְאִי בָּעֵית אֵימָא: הָא בְּצִנְעָא, הָא בְּפַרְהֶסְיָא. וּבָנִים לָא?! הֵיכִי דָּמֵי? אִילֵימָא דַּהֲווֹ לְהוּ וּמִתוּ – וְהָא א"ר יוֹחָנָן: דֵּין גַּרְמָא דַּעֲשִׂירָאָה בִּיר. אֶלָּא: הָא – דְּלָא הֲוָה לֵיהּ כְּלָל, וְהָא – דַּהֲווֹ לֵיהּ וּמִתוּ. רַבִּי חִיָּיא בַּר אַבָּא חֲלַשׁ, עָל לְגַבֵּיהּ ר' יוֹחָנָן. א"ל: חֲבִיבִין עָלֶיךָ יִסּוּרִין? א"ל: לָא הֵן וְלָא שְׂכָרָן. א"ל: הַב לִי יְדָךְ! יְהַב לֵיהּ יְדֵיהּ וְאוֹקְמֵיהּ. ר' יוֹחָנָן חֲלַשׁ, עָל לְגַבֵּיהּ ר' חֲנִינָא. א"ל: חֲבִיבִין עָלֶיךָ יִסּוּרִין? א"ל: לָא הֵן וְלָא שְׂכָרָן. א"ל: הַב לִי יְדָךְ! יְהַב לֵיהּ יְדֵיהּ (א) וְאוֹקְמֵיהּ. אַמַּאי? לוֹקִים ר' יוֹחָנָן לְנַפְשֵׁיהּ! – אָמְרֵי: אֵין חָבוּשׁ מַתִּיר עַצְמוֹ מִבֵּית הָאֲסוּרִים. רַבִּי אֶלְעָזָר חֲלַשׁ, עָל לְגַבֵּיהּ רַבִּי יוֹחָנָן. חֲזָא דַּהֲוָה קָא גָּנֵי בְּבֵית אָפֵל, גַּלְיֵיהּ לִדְרָעֵיהּ וּנְפַל נְהוֹרָא. חַזְיֵיהּ דַּהֲוָה קָא בָּכֵי ר' אֶלְעָזָר. א"ל: אַמַּאי קָא בָּכֵית? אִי מִשּׁוּם תּוֹרָה דְּלָא אַפֵּשְׁתְּ – שָׁנִינוּ: אֶחָד הַמַּרְבֶּה וְאֶחָד הַמַּמְעִיט וּבִלְבַד שֶׁיְּכַוֵּין לִבּוֹ לַשָּׁמַיִם! וְאִי מִשּׁוּם מְזוֹנֵי – לֹא כָּל אָדָם זוֹכֶה לִשְׁתֵּי שֻׁלְחָנוֹת! וְאִי מִשּׁוּם בְּנֵי – דֵּין גַּרְמָא דַּעֲשִׂירָאָה בִּיר. א"ל: לְהַאי שׁוּפְרָא דְּבָלֵי בְּעַפְרָא קָא בָּכֵינָא. א"ל: עַל דָּא וַדַּאי קָא בָּכֵית, וּבָכוּ תַּרְוַיְיהוּ. אַדְּהָכִי וְהָכִי, א"ל: חֲבִיבִין עָלֶיךָ יִסּוּרִין? א"ל: לָא הֵן וְלָא שְׂכָרָן. א"ל: הַב לִי יְדָךְ! יְהַב לֵיהּ יְדֵיהּ וְאוֹקְמֵיהּ. רַב הוּנָא תְּקִיפוּ לֵיהּ אַרְבַּע מְאָה דַּנֵּי דְּחַמְרָא, עָל לְגַבֵּיהּ רַב יְהוּדָה אֲחוּהּ דְּרַב סָלָא חֲסִידָא וְרַבָּנַן, וְאָמְרֵי לַהּ: רַב אַדָּא בַּר אַהֲבָה וְרַבָּנַן, וַאֲמַרוּ לֵיהּ: לְעַיֵּין מָר בְּמִילֵּיהּ. אֲמַר לְהוּ: וּמִי חֲשִׁידְנָא בְּעֵינַיְיכוּ?! אֲמַרוּ לֵיהּ: מִי חֲשִׁיד קֻבְּ"ה דְּעָבֵיד דִּינָא בְּלָא דִינָא?! אֲמַר לְהוּ: אִי אִיכָּא מָאן דִּשְׁמִיעַ עֲלַי מִלְּתָא – לֵימָא. אֲמַרוּ לֵיהּ: הָכִי שְׁמִיעַ לָן דְּלָא יָהֵיב מָר שְׁבִישָׁא לַאֲרִיסֵיהּ. אֲמַר לְהוּ: מִי קָא שָׁבֵיק לִי מִידֵּי מִינֵּיהּ? הָא קָא גָּנֵיב לֵיהּ כּוּלֵּיהּ! אָמְרוּ לֵיהּ: הַיְינוּ דְּאָמְרֵי אִינָשֵׁי: בָּתַר גַּנָּבָא גְּנוֹב, וְטַעְמָא טְעֵים. אֲמַר לְהוּ: קַבִּילְנָא עֲלַי דְּיָהֵיבְנָא לֵיהּ. אִיכָּא דְּאָמְרֵי: הֲדַר חַלָּא וַהֲוָה חַמְרָא; וְאִיכָּא דְּאָמְרֵי: אִייקַר חַלָּא וְאִיזְדַּבַּן בִּדְמֵי דְּחַמְרָא.§ תַּנְיָא, אַבָּא בִּנְיָמִין אוֹמֵר: עַל שְׁנֵי דְּבָרִים הָיִיתִי מִצְטַעֵר כָּל יָמַי – עַל תְּפִלָּתִי שֶׁתְּהֵא לִפְנֵי מִטָּתִי, וְעַל מִטָּתִי שֶׁתְּהֵא נְתוּנָה בֵּין צָפוֹן לְדָרוֹם. עַל תְּפִלָּתִי שֶׁתְּהֵא לִפְנֵי מִטָּתִי – מַאי "לִפְנֵי מִטָּתִי"? אִילֵימָא לִפְנֵי מִטָּתִי מַמָּשׁ – וְהָאָמַר רַב יְהוּדָה אָמַר רַב וְאִיתֵּימָא ריב"ל: מִנַּיִן לַמִּתְפַּלֵּל שֶׁלֹּא יְהֵא דָּבָר חוֹצֵץ בֵּינוֹ לְבֵין הַקִּיר – שֶׁנֶּאֱמַר: "וַיַּסֵּב חִזְקִיָּהוּ פָּנָיו אֶל הַקִּיר וַיִּתְפַּלֵּל". לָא תֵּימָא "לִפְנֵי מִטָּתִי", אֶלָּא אֵימָא: סָמוּךְ לְמִטָּתִי. "וְעַל מִטָּתִי שֶׁתְּהֵא נְתוּנָה בֵּין צָפוֹן לְדָרוֹם" – דא"ר חָמָא בְּרַבִּי חֲנִינָא אָמַר רַבִּי יִצְחָק: כָּל הַנּוֹתֵן מִטָּתוֹ בֵּין צָפוֹן לְדָרוֹם הָוְיָין לֵיהּ בָּנִים זְכָרִים, שֶׁנֶּאֱמַר: "וּצְפוּנְךָ תְּמַלֵּא בִטְנָם יִשְׂבְּעוּ בָנִים". רַב נַחְמָן בַּר יִצְחָק אָמַר: אַף אֵין אִשְׁתּוֹ מַפֶּלֶת נְפָלִים; כְּתִיב הָכָא: "וּצְפוּנְךָ תְּמַלֵּא בִטְנָם", וּכְתִיב הָתָם "וַיִּמְלְאוּ יָמֶיהָ לָלֶדֶת וְהִנֵּה תוֹמִים בְּבִטְנָהּ".§ תַּנְיָא, אַבָּא בִּנְיָמִין אוֹמֵר: שְׁנַיִם שֶׁנִּכְנְסוּ לְהִתְפַּלֵּל, וְקָדַם אֶחָד מֵהֶם לְהִתְפַּלֵּל וְלֹא הִמְתִּין אֶת חֲבֵרוֹ וְיָצָא – טוֹרְפִין לוֹ תְּפִלָּתוֹ בְּפָנָיו, שֶׁנֶּאֱמַר: "טֹרֵף נַפְשׁוֹ בְּאַפּוֹ הַלְמַעַנְךָ תֵּעָזַב אָרֶץ". וְלֹא עוֹד אֶלָּא שֶׁגּוֹרֵם לַשְּׁכִינָה שֶׁתִּסְתַּלֵּק מִיִּשְׂרָאֵל, שֶׁנֶּאֱמַר: "וְיֶעְתַּק צוּר מִמְּקֹמוֹ", וְאֵין 'צוּר' אֶלָּא הקב"ה, שֶׁנֶּאֱמַר: "צוּר יְלָדְךָ תֶּשִׁי". וְאִם הִמְתִּין לוֹ מַה שְּׂכָרוֹ?

אמר

(משלי כא; שם כג; ירמיה לב; ישעיה לח; תהלים יז; בראשית כה; איוב יח; דברים לב)

**רש"י**

וּבָנִים. קָא סָלְקָא דַעְתִּיךְ הַקּוֹבֵר אֶת בָּנָיו: אַרְבַּע מַרְאוֹת. שְׂאֵת וְתוֹלַדְתָּהּ, בַּהֶרֶת וְתוֹלַדְתָּהּ. בַּהֶרֶת עַזָּה – כַּשֶּׁלֶג, שְׁנִיָּה לָהּ – כְּסִיד הַהֵיכָל. שְׂאֵת כְּצֶמֶר לָבָן, שְׁנִיָּה לָהּ – כִּקְרוּם בֵּיצָה: הָא לָן וְהָא לְהוּ. בא"י שֶׁעָרֵי חוֹמָה מְקוּדָּשׁוֹת בָּהּ, וּמְצוֹרָע טָעוּן שִׁילּוּחַ חוּצָה לָהֶן – אֵינָן יִסּוּרִין שֶׁל אַהֲבָה(ב). בָּבֶל שֶׁאֵין טְעוּנִין שִׁילּוּחַ, וְהֵן מִזְבַּח כַּפָּרָה – הָווּ יִסּוּרִין שֶׁל אַהֲבָה: בְּצִנְעָא. תַּחַת בְּגָדָיו: דֵּין גַּרְמָא דַּעֲשִׂירָאָה בִּיר. זֶה עֶצֶם שֶׁל בֵּן עֲשִׂירִי, שֶׁמֵּת לוֹ: בִּיר. כְּמוֹ בַּר. וְגַר עֶצֶם פָּחוֹת מִכַּשְּׂעוֹרָה מִמֶּנּוּ (ג) בְּסוּדָרוֹ לְעָגְמַת נֶפֶשׁ. וְגַבְרָא רַבָּא כר"י לָא בָּאוּ לוֹ יִסּוּרִין שֶׁאֵינָן שֶׁל אַהֲבָה: דַּהֲווֹ לְהוּ בָּנִים וּמֵתוּ. הָווּ לְהוּ יִסּוּרִין שֶׁל אַהֲבָה, שֶׁהָאֲבֵלוּת מְכַפֶּרֶת עַל עֲוֹנוֹתָיו: גַּלְיֵיהּ. רַבִּי יוֹחָנָן לִדְרָעֵיהּ: וּנְפַל נְהוֹרָא. שֶׁהָיָה בְּשָׂרוֹ מַבְהִיק, שֶׁיָּפֶה הָיָה מְאֹד כִּדְאָמְרִינַן בב"מ בְּ"הַשּׂוֹכֵר אֶת הַפּוֹעֲלִים" (דף פד.): אִי מִשּׁוּם תּוֹרָה. שֶׁלֹּא לָמַדְתָּ הַרְבֵּה כִּרְצוֹנְךָ: אֶחָד הַמַּרְבֶּה וְאֶחָד הַמַּמְעִיט. לְעִנְיַן קָרְבָּנוֹת שְׁנוּיָה בִּשְׁלֹהֵי מְנָחוֹת (דף קי.): נֶאֱמַר בְּעוֹלַת בְּהֵמָה "רֵיחַ נִיחוֹחַ", וּבְמִנְחָה "רֵיחַ נִיחוֹחַ" לְלַמֶּדְךָ שֶׁאֶחָד הַמַּרְבֶּה וְכוּ': אִי מִשּׁוּם מְזוֹנֵי. שֶׁאֵינְךָ עָשִׁיר: עַל דָּא וַדַּאי קָא בָּכֵית. עַל זֶה וַדַּאי יֵשׁ לְךָ לִבְכּוֹת: דַּנֵּי. חָבִיּוֹת: תְּקִיפוּ. הֶחְמִיצוּ: לְעַיֵּין מָר בְּמִילֵּיהּ. יְפַשְׁפֵּשׁ בְּמַעֲשָׂיו: אִי אִיכָּא דִּשְׁמִיעַ עֲלַי מִילְּתָא לֵימָא. אִם יֵשׁ כָּאן שֶׁשָּׁמַע עָלַי דָּבָר שֶׁאֲנִי צָרִיךְ לַחֲזוֹר בִּי יוֹדִיעֵנִי: שְׁבִישָׁא. חֶלְקוֹ בִּזְמוֹרוֹת הַגֶּפֶן שֶׁחוֹתְכִין מֵהֶן בִּשְׁעַת הַזָּמִיר, וּתְנַן (ב"מ דף קג.): כְּשֵׁם שֶׁחוֹלְקִין בַּיַּיִן כָּךְ חוֹלְקִין בַּזְּמוֹרוֹת וּבַקָּנִים. "שָׂרִיגִים" מְתַרְגְּמִינַן "שְׁבִשִׁין" (בראשית מ): מִי שָׁבֵיק לִי מִידֵּי מִינֵּיהּ. וְכִי אֵינוֹ חָשׁוּד בְּעֵינֵיכֶם שֶׁהוּא גּוֹנֵב לִי הַרְבֵּה יוֹתֵר מֵחֶלְקוֹ: בָּתַר גַּנָּבָא גְּנוֹב כו'. הַגּוֹנֵב מִן הַגַּנָּב – אַף הוּא טוֹעֵם טַעַם גְּנֵבָה: סָמוּךְ לְמִטָּתִי. כָּל יָמַי נִזְהַרְתִּי שֶׁלֹּא לַעֲשׂוֹת מְלָאכָה וְשֶׁלֹּא לַעֲסוֹק בַּתּוֹרָה כְּשֶׁעָמַדְתִּי מִמִּטָּתִי עַד שֶׁאֶקְרָא ק"ש וְאֶתְפַּלֵּל: צָפוֹן לַדָּרוֹם. רֹאשָׁהּ וּמַרְגְּלוֹתֶיהָ, זֶה לַצָּפוֹן וְזֶה לַדָּרוֹם. וְנִרְאֶה בְּעֵינַי שֶׁהַשְּׁכִינָה בַּמִּזְרָח אוֹ בַּמַּעֲרָב, לְפִיכָךְ נָכוֹן לְהָסֵב דֶּרֶךְ תַּשְׁמִישׁ לְרוּחוֹת אֲחֵרוֹת: וּצְפוּנְךָ. לְשׁוֹן צָפוֹן, וְסֵיפֵיהּ דִּקְרָא "יִשְׂבְּעוּ בָנִים": תְּמַלֵּא בִטְנָם. תְּמַלֵּא יְמֵי הֵרָיוֹנָם: טוֹרֵף נַפְשׁוֹ בְּאַפּוֹ. לְךָ אוֹמֵר: אֲשֶׁר גָּרַמְתָּ לְךָ לִטְרוֹף אֶת נַפְשְׁךָ בְּפָנֶיךָ וּמַה הִיא הַנֶּפֶשׁ – זוֹ תְּפִלָּה, כְּמוֹ שֶׁנֶּאֱמַר "וָאֶשְׁפּוֹךְ אֶת נַפְשִׁי לִפְנֵי ה'" (ש"א א): הַלְמַעַנְךָ תֵּעָזַב אָרֶץ. וְכִי סָבוּר הָיִיתָ שֶׁבִּשְׁבִילְךָ שֶׁיָּצָאתָ,(ד) תִּסְתַּלֵּק הַשְּׁכִינָה וְיַעֲזוֹב אֶת חֲבֵירְךָ הַמִּתְפַּלֵּל לְפָנֶיהָ לוֹ:

**תוספות**

**הא** לן והא להו. פי' רש"י: לבני ארץ ישראל שצריכין שילוח חוץ לשלשה מחנות – לא הוו יסורין של אהבה. ותימה: דשילוח מחנות לא היה נוהג אלא בזמן שהיובל נוהג ובתי ערי חומה. ובימי האמוראין לא היה היובל נוהג, כדאמרינן במסכת גיטין (פ"ד דף לו.), והיאך היה מדבר ר' יוחנן מדבר שלא היה נוהג בימיו? וי"מ: הא לן והא להו – לענין טומאה. שנזהרין בא"י ולא בבבל: **והאמר** רבי יוחנן דין גרמא דעשיראה ביר. פי' רש"י: דלאדם חשוב כר' יוחנן מסתמא לא היו אלא יסורין של אהבה. ותימה: דהא מסיק דהיכא דלא הוו ליה בנים כלל לא הוו יסורין של אהבה, והרי כמה צדיקים שלא היו להם בנים!(ה) ואי משום בנות – ר' יוחנן נמי הוו ליה בנות, כפ' בתרא דקדושין (דף עא.) ונראה לפרש דהכי פריך: והאמר ר' יוחנן דין גרמא וכו', אלמא מדהוה רגיל לנחם אחרים בכך – ש"מ דהוו יסורין של אהבה. אבל אינו תלוי בכך, שהצדיקים עצמם פעמים מעונים ביסורין: *ה"ג **לא** כל אדם זוכה לשתי שלחנות. אבל אין לגרוס אין אדם זוכה דהא כמה צדיקים זוכין לשתי שלחנות כגון *רבי וכדאמרינן בפרק בתרא דהוריות (דף י:): **דינא** בלא דינא. הרבה צדיקים יש שלוקין בגופם ובממונם, אלא הם היו יודעים שלא היה נותן שבישא לאריסיה, והיו רוצים לרמוז לו שלא יעשה עוד: **שלא** יהא דבר חוצץ בינו לבין הקיר. אבל מלתא דקביעא כגון ארון ותיבה – אין זה הפסק. אבל מטה, נראה שאין זה קבוע: **אלא** אימא סמוך למטתי. שלא היה עושה מלאכה עד שיתפלל. ורש"י פירש: אפילו ללמוד, שאסור ללמוד קודם תפלה. ולא ידעתי מנא ליה. אבל ראיה דשרי ללמוד קודם דלקמן בפרק שני (דף יד ב) אמרינן דרב מקדים ומשי ידיה ומברך ומתני פרקיה וקרי ק"ש, כי מטא זמן ק"ש כו': **כל** הנותן מטתו בין צפון לדרום וכו'. ולא בין מזרח למערב, ודוקא כשישן עם אשתו, מפני שהשכינה מצויה בין מזרח למערב והיה הדבר גנאי לשכב אצל אשתו מפני התשמיש. וכן משמע, ומוכחי קראי: המתפלל

**עין משפט נר מצוה**

יז א מיי' פ"ז מהל' בית הבחירה הל' ט טוש"ע או"ח סי' ג' סעיף ו וכסימן ר"מ סעיף יז:

יח ב מיי' פ"ה מהלכות תפלה הלכה ו סמג עשין יט טוש"ע או"ח סימן צ סעיף כא:

יט ג מיימוני פ"ט שם הלכה ד טוש"ע או"ח סימן פ"ט סעיף ו:

[ע"ג ד ב תורה דכתיב כו']

כ ד מיי' פ"ט שם הלכה יא סמג עשין יט טוש"ע או"ח סימן צ סעיף טו:

[וכ"ה במס' דרך ארץ זוטא פ"ד]

[בבא מציעא פה א]

**רב נסים גאון**

דין גרמא דעשיראה ביר. פרשו רבי' שרירא ורבי' האיי חמודו ז"ל ר' יוחנן קבר י' בנים זכרים וכי העשירי שבהן נפל לתוך יורה גדולה שהיתה רותחת ריתוח קשה וחזק ונמס בשרו ונמק נטל ר' יוחנן עצם של אצבע קטנה שלו וצררה בסדינו והי' מנחם בה אחרים ואית דאמרי כי נשאר לן בן אחד ושמו ר' מתנה ושיגרו מארץ ישראל לבבל ללמוד תורה לפני שמואל:

**גליון הש"ס**

**תום'** ד"ה לא כו'. אין אדם זוכה כו'. עי' שבת דף נה ע"ב תוס' ד"ה ארבעה:

**מסורת הש"ס**

בערוך ערך גר' עצם שן הוה לי וכ"כ הרשב"ם וי"מ ביר סעיו לאבל

[לקמן מד. וש"נ

ב"ב דף קטז.

[נדרים ז: מנהל

[אלעזר]

[אלעזר]

לקמן ז. מנחות צו. יומא מב. שב

[ועיין תוס' נדי ולאמר]

**הגהות ה**

(א) גמ' ואוקמ... לא לוקים ר"י (ב) רש"י ד"ה ו... אהבה בבבל שא... שילוח הוו מזב... ויסורין של אהבה... דין גרמא וכו'... ממנו שאינו מטו... והיה נושאו קש... לעגמת: (ד) ד"ה... וכו' שילאת מב... חבירך תסתלק (ה) תוס' ד"ה וי... שלא הוו להם... יהושע לא מצינו... בנים ולא משו...

אמר ר' יוסי ברבי חנינא: זוכה לברכות הללו, שנאמר: "לוא הקשבת למצותי ויהי כנהר שלומך וצדקתך כגלי הים ויהי כחול זרעך וצאצאי מעיך וגו'". § תניא, אבא בנימין אומר: אלמלי נתנה רשות לעין לראות, אין כל בריה יכולה לעמוד מפני המזיקין. אמר אביי: אינהו נפישי מינן, וקיימי עלן כי כסלא לאוגיא. אמר רב הונא: כל חד וחד מינן, אלפא משמאליה ורבבתא מימיניה.* אמר רבא: האי דוחקא דהוי בכלה – מינייהו הוי; הני ברכי דשלהי – מנייהו;(א) הני מאני דרבנן דבלו – מחופיא דידהו; הני כרעי דמנקפן – מנייהו. האי מאן דבעי למידע להו – לייתי קיטמא נהילא ונהדר אפורייה, ובצפרא חזי כי כרעי דתרנגולא. האי מאן דבעי למחזינהו – ליתי שיליתא דשונרתא אוכמתא בת אוכמתא, בוכרתא בת בוכרתא, וליקליה בנורא ולשחקיה ולימלי עיניה מיניה, וחזי להו. ולשדייה בגובתא דפרזלא ולחתמיה בגושפנקא דפרזלא דילמא גנבי מיניה. ולחתום פומיה כי היכי דלא ליתזק. רב ביבי בר אביי עבד הכי חזא ואתזק. בעו רבנן רחמי עליה ואתסי. § תניא, אבא בנימין אומר: אין תפלה של אדם נשמעת אלא בבית הכנסת, שנאמר: "לשמוע אל הרנה ואל התפלה", במקום רנה שם תהא תפלה. אמר רבין בר רב אדא א"ר יצחק: מנין שהקב"ה מצוי בבית הכנסת, שנאמר: "אלהים נצב בעדת אל"; ומנין לעשרה שמתפללין ששכינה עמהם – שנאמר: "אלהים נצב בעדת אל"; *ומנין לשלשה שיושבין בדין ששכינה עמהם – שנאמר: "בקרב אלהים ישפוט"; ומנין לשנים שיושבים ועוסקין בתורה ששכינה עמהם – שנאמר: "אז נדברו יראי ה' איש אל רעהו ויקשב ה' וגו'". מאי "ולחושבי שמו"? *אמר רב אשי:(ב) חשב אדם לעשות מצוה ונאנס ולא עשאה – מעלה עליו הכתוב כאילו עשאה. ומנין שאפילו אחד שיושב ועוסק בתורה ששכינה עמו – שנאמר: "בכל המקום אשר אזכיר את שמי אבוא אליך וברכתיך". וכי מאחר דאפילו חד – תרי מבעיא?! – תרי מכתבן מלייהו בספר הזכרונות, חד לא מכתבן מליה בספר הזכרונות. וכי מאחר דאפי' תרי – תלתא מבעיא?! מהו דתימא: דינא שלמא בעלמא הוא, ולא אתיא שכינה – קמ"ל דדינא נמי היינו תורה. וכי מאחר דאפי' תלתא – עשרה מבעיא?! – עשרה קדמה שכינה ואתיא, תלתא – עד דיתבי. § א"ר אבין בר רב אדא א"ר יצחק: מנין שהקב"ה מניח תפילין – שנאמר: "נשבע ה' בימינו ובזרוע עזו", "בימינו" – זו תורה, שנאמר: "מימינו אש דת למו", "ובזרוע עזו" – אלו תפילין, שנאמר: "ה' עז לעמו יתן". ומנין שהתפילין עוז הם לישראל – דכתי': "וראו כל עמי הארץ כי שם ה' נקרא עליך ויראו ממך", *ותניא, ר' אליעזר הגדול אומר: אלו תפילין שבראש. א"ל רב נחמן בר יצחק לרב חייא בר אבין: הני תפילין דמרי עלמא מה כתיב בהו? א"ל: "ומי כעמך ישראל גוי אחד בארץ". ומי משתבח קוב"ה בשבחייהו דישראל?! אין, דכתיב: "את ה' האמרת היום" (וכתיב): "וה' האמירך היום". *אמר להם הקב"ה לישראל: אתם עשיתוני *חטיבה אחת בעולם, ואני אעשה אתכם חטיבה אחת בעולם; אתם עשיתוני חטיבה אחת בעולם, שנאמר: "שמע ישראל ה' אלהינו ה' אחד". ואני אעשה אתכם חטיבה אחת בעולם, שנאמר: "ומי כעמך ישראל גוי אחד בארץ". אמר ליה רב אחא בריה דרבא לרב אשי: תינח בחד ביתא, בשאר בתי מאי? – א"ל: "כי מי גוי גדול" "ומי גוי גדול" "אשריך ישראל" "או הנסה אלהים" "ולתתך עליון". – אי הכי נפישי להו טובי בתי! אלא "כי מי גוי גדול" "ומי גוי גדול" דדמיין להדדי – בחד ביתא, "אשריך ישראל" "ומי כעמך ישראל" – בחד ביתא, "או הנסה אלהים" – בחד ביתא, "ולתתך עליון" – בחד ביתא. וכולהו

ישעיה מח · תהלים פב · מלאכי ג · שמות כ · דברים לג · ישעיה סב · תהלים כט · דברים כח · דה"א יז · דברים כו · שם ו · שם ד · שם לג

**רש"י**

לוא הקשבת. לשון המתנה היא: למצותי. בשביל מצותי, אשר לויתי לגמול חסד: לראות. כל השדים העומדים לפניו: כי כסלא לאוגיא. כשורת חפירה המקפת האוגיא שעושין תחת הגפנים, כמו ששנינו: (מו"ק דף ג) אין עושין אוגיות לגפנים לאסוף שם מים להשקות הגפן. 'כסלא' הוא תלם של מענה המקפת סביב סביב את כל האוגיא, והגפן נטוע בתל, וגרסינן נדרים (דף ו ב) "הדין אוגיא להוי פאה": האי דוחקא דהוי בכלה. פעמים שבני אדם יושבים רווחים ביום השבת (ג) שבאין לשמוע דרשה, ודומה להם כיושבים דחוקים: הני ברכי דשלהי. ברכים עייפים: מאני דרבנן דבלו. בגדי התלמידים שבלים מהר, והם אינם בני מלאכה שיבלו בגדיהם: מחופיא דידהו. שאין המזיקים יושבין אצלם ומתחככים בהם. חופיא לשון "חופף ומספסף", (שבת דף נ:) פריי"ר בלע"ז: שליתא דשונרתא. שליית הולד של חתול נקבה: בוכרתא. הבכורה לאמה: בת בוכרתא. ואף אמה היתה בכורה: ולימלי עיניה מיניה. ישים מעט מעט בעיניו. כל לשון נתינה בעין קורהו בלשון גמרא לשון מלוי, לפי שמדבר מועט הוא מלא: גובתא דפרזלא. קנה חלול של ברזל: ולחתמיה. לקנה: בגושפנקא דפרזלא. בחותם של ברזל, דמזידי דלייר ומזיקין לית להו רשותא, כדאמרינן ב"כל הבשר" בשחיטת חולין (דף קה ב): במקום רנה. בבהכ"נ, ששם אומרים הצבור שירות ותשבחות בנעימת קול ערב: בעדת אל. בבית מועד שלו: ומנין לעשרה וכו'. עדה קרויה בעשרה, שנא' "עד מתי לעדה הרעה הזאת" (במדבר יד) – יצאו כלב ויהושע: בקרב אלהים ישפוט. ואין בית דין קרוים אלהים אלא בג', בפ"ק דסנהדרין (דף ג ב): ויקשב ה'. ממתין להם שם: אשר אזכיר את שמי. אשר יזכר שמי על (ז) מצותי ודברי: אבוא אליך. לשון יחיד הוא: מכתבן מלייהו. כדכתיב "ויכתב ספר זכרון לפניו" (סיפא דקרא): קדמה שכינה ואתיא. קודם שיהיו כל העשרה. נצב בעדת אל. מעיקרא משמע: עד דיתבי. כדכתיב "ישפוט" – בשעת המשפט: עוז לעמו. ומנין שהתפילין עוז הם לישראל – דכתיב "וראו וגו' ויראו ממך": מה כתיב בהו. בשלמא בתפילין דידן כתיב "שמע" (דברים ו) "והיה אם שמוע" (שם יא) "קדש לי כל בכור" (שמות יג) "והיה כי יביאך" (שם) פרשיות שנצטוו בהם לשום זכרון מצותיו של הקב"ה אות וזכרון להם לישראל, אלא בדידיה מאי כתיב בהו: האמרת. לשון חשיבות ושבח, כמו "יתאמרו כל פועלי און" (תהלים צד) – ישתבחו: בשאר בתי מאי (ה). שהרי ארבעה בתים הם: וכולהו

**תוספות**

*המתפלל ולא המתין את חבירו טורפין לו וכו'. פירש רבינו תם: דזה היה להם בבתי כנסיות שלהם שהיו בשדה, ולכך בלילה יש להמתין. והר"י היה מאחר תפלתו ומאריך עד שילאו כולם. ואם בתוך כך היה שום אדם בא בבית הכנסת היה מעיין בספר, עד שגמרו תפלתם. ונאה להחמיר אף לנו: כי כסלא לאוגיא. כעין תלמים המקיפין את הערוגה, כדאמרינן בריש נדרים (דף ו:): "הדין אוגיא להוי פאה": חד לא מכתבן מליה בספר הזכרונות. כלומר: עם אחרים. אבל בספר לבדו נכתבין, כדאמרינן "וכל מעשיך בספר נכתבין" (אבות פרק ב), כ"ש מדה טובה: אלו תפילין שבראש.(ו) לפי שיש בהן רוב שם של שדי, שהשי"ן כתובה בקמט שבבתים, והדלי"ת ברצועות. ותימא משבת פרק "במה מדליקין" (דף כח ב) דקאמר: מן המותר בפיך – ולא מפיק רצועות מתורת ה' בפיך! ועוד, דבפ' בתרא דמגילה (דף כו ב) קרי לרצועות תשמישי קדושה בעלמא! אלא י"ל: אלו תפילין שבראש – לפי שהן בגבהו של ראש ונראין, דשייך בהו "וראו". אבל תפילין של יד – מכוסין, דכתיב (שמות יג) "לך לאות על ידך" – ולא לאחרים לאות*: מי כעמך ישראל. זה שיסד הפייטן (ביום א' דפסח) "טוטפת כלילו גדלי": *אחורי בית הכנסת. פי' רש"י: כל פתחי בתי כנסיות היו למזרח ואחוריהם למערב, וזה המתפלל אחורי בית הכנסת ואינו מחזיר פניו לבהכ"נ נראה ככופר במי שהצבור מתפללין לפניו. ולא נהירא, דאדרבה במהדר אפיה לבית הכנסת מיחזי כשתי רשויות: שהקהל מתפללין למערב – והוא מתפלל כנגדם למזרח. ע"כ נראה: אחורי בהכ"נ – מי שהוא אחורי העם במזרח, והעם משתחוים למערב, ולהכי קאמר ולא מהדר אפיה כו'. ודוקא הם, שהיה מנהגם להתפלל למערב. אבל אנו מתפללים למזרח, שאנו במערבו של א"י. וכתיב "והתפללו אליך דרך ארצם" (מ"א ח). ונראה, כמו שפי' להם לצד מערב – יתפרש לנו לצד מזרח: שאלמלי

**עין משפט נר מצוה**

כא א מיי' פ"ח מהלכות תפלה הלכה א (סמג עשין יט) טור וש"ע או"ח סימן צ סעיף ט:

[ועי' תוס' שבת סב. ד"ה ש"ין ותוס' עירובין צז. ד"ה קשר ומגילה כו: ד"ה תשמישי ותוספות מנחות לה: ד"ה אלו]

**גליון הש"ס**

גמ' אין תפלתו של אדם כו'. עי' ע"ז ל ע"ב תוס' ד"ה כיון. ונרשם מכאן אלא עם הצבור: רש"י ד"ה ומנין לעשרה וכו' עדה כו'. לקמן כ"א ע"ב.

**מסורת הש"ס**

ול מצדך אלף מינך ס"א (וכ"ה בילקוט ובע"י)

**הגהות הב"ח**

(א) ... 

ת סוכה יג. ד"ה בכולן

ע"ש קדושין מ. ע"ש

נז. מנחות לה: סוטה יז. חולין פט.]

כב א מיי' פ"ה מהלכות תפלה הלכה ו סמג עשין יט טוש"ע או"ח סי' צ סעיף יט:
כג ב ג מיי' פ"ח שם הלכה ב ופכ"ד מהל' שבת הלכה ה סמג עשין יב יט טוש"ע או"ח סי' צ סעיף יב ובסי' ש"א סעיף א [רב אלפס כאן ובשבת פרק טו]:
כד ד טור וש"ע י"ד סי' שד"מ סעיף א [סמ"ג עשין יב]:
כה ה מיי' פ"ה מהלכות תפלה הלכה ו סמג עשין יט טוש"ע או"ח סימן צ סעיף ז:
כו ו טור או"ח סי' רלב:

וכולהו כתיבי באדרעיה.§ אמר רבין בר רב אדא אמר רבי יצחק: כל הרגיל לבא לבית הכנסת ולא בא יום אחד – הקב"ה משאיל בו, שנאמר: °"מי בכם ירא ה' שמע בקול עבדו אשר הלך חשכים ואין נגה לו";(א) אם לדבר מצוה הלך – נוגה לו, ואם לדבר הרשות הלך – אין נוגה לו. "יבטח בשם ה'", מאי טעמא – משום דהוה ליה לבטוח בשם ה' ולא בטח.§ אמר ר' יוחנן: בשעה שהקב"ה בא בבית הכנסת ולא מצא בה עשרה – °מיד הוא כועס, שנא': °"מדוע באתי ואין איש קראתי ואין עונה". א"ר חלבו אמר רב הונא: כל הקובע *מקום לתפלתו – אלהי אברהם בעזרו. וכשמת – אומרים לו: אי עניו, אי חסיד, מתלמידיו של אברהם אבינו! ואברהם אבינו מנא לן דקבע מקום? – דכתיב: °"וישכם אברהם בבקר אל המקום אשר עמד שם", *ואין עמידה אלא תפלה, שנאמר: °"ויעמוד פינחס ויפלל".§ *אמר רבי חלבו אמר רב הונא: היוצא מבית הכנסת אל יפסיע פסיעה גסה. אמר אביי: לא אמרן אלא למיפק, אבל למיעל – מצוה למרהט, שנא'(ב) °"נרדפה לדעת את ה'". אמר רבי זירא: מריש כי הוה חזינא להו לרבנן דקא רהטי לפרקא בשבתא, אמינא: קא מחליין(ג) רבנן שבתא. כיון דשמענא להא דרבי תנחום א"ר יהושע בן לוי: לעולם ירוץ אדם [א] לדבר הלכה ואפילו בשבת, שנא' °"אחרי ה' ילכו כאריה ישאג וגו'"(ד) אנא נמי רהיטנא.§ אמר ר' זירא: אגרא דפרקא – רהטא. אמר אביי: אגרא דכלה – דוחקא. אמר רבא: אגרא דשמעתא – סברא. אמר רב פפא: אגרא דבי *טמיא – שתיקותא. אמר מר זוטרא: אגרא דתעניתא – צדקתא. אמר רב ששת: אגרא דהספדא – דלויי. אמר רב אשי: אגרא דבי הלולי – מילי.§ אמר רב הונא: כל המתפלל אחורי בית הכנסת נקרא רשע, שנאמר: °"סביב רשעים יתהלכון". אמר אביי: לא אמרן אלא דלא מהדר אפיה לבי כנישתא, אבל מהדר אפיה לבי כנישתא – לית לן בה. ההוא גברא דקא *מצלי אחורי בי כנישתא ולא מהדר אפיה לבי כנישתא. חלף *אליהו, חזייה, אידמי ליה כטייעא. א"ל: כדו בר קיימת קמי מרך?! שלף ספסרא וקטליה. א"ל: ההוא מרבנן לרב ביבי בר אביי, ואמרי לה רב ביבי לרב נחמן בר יצחק: מאי °"כרם זלת לבני אדם"? – אמר ליה: אלו דברים שעומדים ברומו של עולם ובני אדם מזלזלין בהן. ר' יוחנן ור' אלעזר דאמרי תרוייהו: כיון שנצטרך אדם לבריות – פניו משתנות ככרום, שנאמר: "כרם זלת לבני אדם". מאי כרום? – כי אתא רב דימי אמר: עוף אחד יש בכרכי הים וכרום שמו, וכיון שחמה זורחת *מתהפך לכמה גוונין. ר' אמי ור' אסי דאמרי תרוייהו: כאלו נדון בשני דינים, אש ומים, שנאמר: °"הרכבת אנוש לראשנו באנו באש ובמים".§ ואמר רבי חלבו אמר רב הונא: לעולם יהא אדם זהיר בתפלת המנחה, שהרי אליהו לא נענה אלא בתפלת המנחה, שנאמר: °"ויהי בעלות המנחה ויגש אליהו הנביא ויאמר וגו'". *"ענני ה' ענני"; ענני – שתרד אש מן השמים, ועני – שלא יאמרו מעשה כשפים הם. ר' יוחנן אמר: אף בתפלת ערבית, שנאמר: °"תכון תפלתי קטרת לפניך משאת כפי מנחת ערב". רב נחמן בר יצחק אמר: אף תפלת שחרית, שנאמר: °"ה' בקר תשמע קולי בקר אערך לך ואצפה".§ וא"ר חלבו אמר רב הונא: כל הנהנה מסעודת חתן ואינו משמחו – עובר בחמשה קולות, שנאמר: °"קול ששון וקול שמחה קול חתן וקול כלה קול אומרים הודו את ה' צבאות". ואם משמחו מה שכרו? – אמר רבי יהושע בן לוי: זוכה לתורה שנתנה בחמשה קולות, שנאמר: °"ויהי ביום השלישי בהית הבקר ויהי קולות וברקים וענן כבד על ההר וקל שופר" וגו' "ויהי קול השפר" וגו' "והאלהים יעננו בקול". איני?! והא כתיב °"וכל העם רואים את הקולות"! –אותן קולות דקודם מתן תורה הוו. רבי אבהו אמר: כאילו הקריב תודה, שנאמר: °"מבאים תודה בית ה'". רב נחמן בר יצחק אמר: כאילו בנה אחת מחורבות ירושלים, שנאמר: °"כי אשיב את שבות הארץ כבראשונה אמר ה'".§ וא"ר חלבו אמר רב הונא: כל אדם שיש בו יראת שמים – דבריו נשמעין, שנאמר: °"סוף דבר הכל נשמע את האלהים ירא וגו'". מאי °"כי זה כל האדם"? *א"ר אלעזר: אמר הקב"ה: כל העולם כלו לא נברא אלא בשביל זה. רבי אבא בר כהנא אמר: שקול זה כנגד כל העולם כולו. *ר' שמעון בן עזאי אומר, ואמרי לה ר' שמעון בן זומא אומר: כל העולם כולו לא נברא אלא לצוות לזה.§ וא"ר חלבו אמר רב הונא: כל שיודע בחברו שהוא רגיל ליתן לו שלום – יקדים לו שלום, שנאמר: °"בקש שלום ורדפהו", ואם נתן לו ולא החזיר – נקרא גזלן, שנאמר: °"ואתם בערתם הכרם גזלת העני בבתיכם".§ אמר

ג (פינחס ויפלל)

מקורות בגליון: ישעיה נ; סס; ישעיה נ; בראשית יט; תהלים קו; הושע ו; סס יא; תהלים יב; [ע' תוס' עירובין יח: ד"ה ולא אחורי]; סס; ס"א עליו; סס סו; [לקמן ט:]; מלכים א יח; תהלים קמא; סס ה; ירמיה לג; שמות יט; סס כ; ירמיה לג; סס; קהלת יב; סס; תהלים לד; ישעיה ג

וכולהו כתיבי באדרעיה. כל הכתובים הללו כתובים בזרוע בבית אחד. שאותן של יד אינן אלא בית אחד, כדאמרינן במנחות (דף לד:) "וכל הפרשיות כתובות בו": משאיל בו. מה טיבו של פלוני, למה לא בא: ירא את ה'(ה). שהיה רגיל לבא אליו: אשר הלך חשכים ואין נוגה לו. אשר עתה הלך למקום חשך,(ו) אשר ימנע עצמו מלהשכים לפתחי: ואין עונה. שיעור שיכולו לענות דבר קדושה: אלהי אברהם. שקבע מקום לתפלתו: בעזרו. כדרך שהיה עוזר לאברהם: אל יפסיע פסיעה גסה. לפי שמראה בעצמו שעכוב בית הכנסת דומה עליו כמשוי: נרדפה. לשון מרוצה משמע, שהרודף רץ: לפרקא. לשמוע הדרשה: מחליין רבנן שבתא. דאמר מר (שבת ד' קיג:): אסור לפסוע פסיעה גסה בשבת, שנאמר "אם תשיב משבת רגלך": אגרא דפרקא. עיקר קבול שכר הרגלים לשמוע דרשה מפי חכם – היא שכר המרוצה, שהרי רובם אינם מבינים להעמיד גרסא ולומר שמועה מפי רבן לאחר זמן שיקבלו שכר למוד: אגרא דכלה. שבת שלפני הרגל, שהכל נאספין לשמוע הלכות הרגל: אגרא דשמעתא סברא. שהוא יגע וטורח ומחשב להבין טעמו של דבר: אגרא דתענית' צדקתא. שנותנין צדקה לערב לפרנסת העניים *שהתענו היום: דלויי. להרים קול בלשון נהי ועגמת נפש, שיבכו השומעים:

מילי. לשמח החתן בדברים: אחורי בית הכנסת. כל פתחי בית הכנסת היו במזרח וזכי תניא בתוספתא דמגילה (פרק ג): מעין מקדש ומשכן, פניהם למערב ואחוריהם למזרח. והמתפלל אחורי בית הכנסת ואינו מחזיר פניו לבית הכנסת נראה ככופר במי שהצבור מתפללין לפניו. והא דרב הונא מוקי לה לאביי(ז) בדלא מהדר אפיה לבי כנישתא: חלף ההוא טייעא. סוחר ערבי: כדו בר*. כדו = שתי, בר = רשות, כי הכי דאמרינן בתוספתא (ד' מה:) "הא דעיילי בבר": כרום זלות. סיפיה דקרא דלעיל: דברים שעומדים ברומו של עולם. כגון תפלה, שעולה למעלה: כיון שנצטרך אדם לבריות. הוא זל בעיניהם: לראשנו. להיות נושה בנו, דמתרגמינן "כנושה" (שמות כב) – כרשיא: עובר בחמשה קולות. מזלזל בחמשה קולות שבירך הקב"ה את ישראל: אותן קולות דקודם מתן תורה הוו. הנך קולות בתראי היינו הנך דאיירי בהו לעיל, וקאמר דנראין היו, ואע"פ שהקול אינו נראה – זה נראה: מביאים תודה בית ה'. כי אשיב את שבות וגו'. סיפיה דקרא דחמשה קולות דלעיל הוא: בשביל זה. שיברא זה: לצוות. של"וון בלע"ז: גזלת העני. והלא אף גזלת העשיר גזלה היא! אלא: גזלת העני שאין לו כלום לגזול ממנו, אלא שלא להשיב על שלומו:
ונענע

תורה אור

מסורת הש"ס: כשתי רשויות כעין יעקב; ע"ל ד"ז ע"ב; לקמן כו:; כ"א ואמר; בית אבל ו' עצמו' של מתו נט. רש"י ד"ה טמיא; ס"א ההוא טייע א"ל כדו' [ג' כדובר]

## הגהות הגר"א

[א] גמ' לדבר הלכה. נ"ב ג' הרי"ף והרא"ש מצוה:

## גליון הש"ס

גמ' מיד הוא כועס כו'. עי' בזוה"ק פרשת תרומה [ד' קל"א ע"א] ועי' בתשובת רשב"א סי' נ': שם כל הנהנה מסעודת חתן כו'. מג"א סימן קנ"ו:

[עי' סנהדרין דף לה. וברש"י שם]:

## הגהות הב"ח

(א) גמ' ואם לדבר מצוה: (ב) שם שנאמר ונדעה נרדפה: (ג) שם אמינא קא מחללין רבנן: (ד) שם כאריה ישאג כי הוא ישאג ויחרדו בנים מים אנא נמי רהיטנא: (ה) רש"י ד"ה ירא ה' כצ"ל ותיבת את נמחק: (ו) ד"ה אשר הלך וכו' חשך ומנע עצמו מלהשכים לביהכ"נ הס"ד: (ז) ד"ה אחורי וכו' מוקים לה אביי כצ"ל ואות למ"ד נמחק:

[שבת ל:]

[בשבת שם אית' שמעון בן עזאי ועי' ברטנורה רפ"ד דאבות ורש"י קדושין מט: ד"ה בן עזאי]

כז א מיי' פ"ה מהלכות דעות הלכה ז:
כח ב מיי' פ"י מה' יסודי התורה הלכה ד:

ונענע לי בראשו. כמודה בברכתי ועונה אמן: דעת בהמתו לא הוה ידע. במסכת ע"א מפרש לה, בפ"ק: מאי קרא. דאף הוי כרגע – דכתיב "כי רגע באפו חיים ברצונו": בתלת שעי קמייתא. באחד מרגעי תלת שעות ראשונות: שורייקי. טוי"ש בלע"ז: לצדיק לא טוב. לענוש את הצדיקים: מרדות אחת. לשון רדוי וקנטעה, שאדם שם על לבו מאליו: ורדפה את מאהביה וגו'. וכשמתחרטת שאין עוזר – משים על לבה לאמר: "אשובה אל אישי הראשון": תחת גערה במבין. תחת גערה שאדם מבין – טובה מהכות כסיל מאה. תחת הטעם למעלה תחת הת"ו ולא כמו "אל תירא ואל תחת" (דברים א) שטעמו בחי"ת, אלא למעלה תחת הת"ו ראשון, לומר שהוא שם דבר. שאי אפשר לפותרו לשון תפעל לומר: תכניע את האדם, אלא תכנע היא בעצמה. ולכך שיוה את נקודתה – לומר שהוא שם דבר: ג' דברים בקש משה ונתן לו. שהרי לסוף שאלתו כתיב: "גם את הדבר הזה אשר דברת אעשה": להודיעו דרכיו. מנהג מדת משפטיו, כגון: מפני מה צדיק וטוב לו, רשע ורע לו, צדיק ורע לו, רשע וטוב לו: את אשר אחון. את אשר יכמרו רחמי עליו לשעה, ואע"פ שאינו כדאי: כשרציתי. בסנה: לא רצית. שנא' "ויסתר משה פניו": ופליגא. דר' יהושע בן קרחה דשמעינן על כך, אדרבי שמואל שאמר: קבל שכר על זה: לקלסתר פנים. "כי קרן עור פניו": ותמונת ה' יביט. זה מראה אחוריים, כך שנוי' בספרי (פ' בהעלותך): קשר של תפילין. מאחוריו הוא, ואמרי' לעיל דהקב"ה מניח תפילין: חלני

תורה אור — ישעיה נו

א"ר יוחנן משום ר' יוסי:(א) מנין שהקב"ה מתפלל? שנאמר: °"והביאותים אל הר קדשי ושמחתים בבית תפלתי", 'תפלתם' לא נאמר אלא 'תפלתי', מכאן שהקב"ה מתפלל. מאי מצלי? אמר רב זוטרא בר טוביה אמר רב: יה"ר מלפני שיכבשו רחמי את כעסי, ויגולו רחמי על מדותי, ואתנהג עם בני במדת רחמים, ואכנס להם *לפנים משורת הדין. תניא, א"ר ישמעאל בן אלישע: פעם אחת נכנסתי להקטיר קטורת לפני ולפנים, וראיתי אכתריאל יה ה' צבאות שהוא יושב על כסא רם ונשא ואמר לי: ישמעאל בני, ברכני! – אמרתי לו: יה"ר מלפניך שיכבשו רחמיך את כעסך ויגולו רחמיך על מדותיך ותתנהג עם בניך במדת הרחמים ותכנס להם לפנים משורת הדין, ונענע לי בראשו.(ב) וקמ"ל *שלא תהא ברכת הדיוט קלה בעיניך.§ וא"ר יוחנן משום ר' יוסי: מנין שאין מרצין לו לאדם בשעת כעסו – דכתיב °"פני ילכו והנחתי לך"; אמר לו הקב"ה למשה: המתן לי עד שיעברו פנים של זעם ואניח לך. ומי איכא רתחא קמיה דקודשא בריך הוא?! –אין, *דתניא: °"ואל זועם בכל יום". וכמה זעמו? – רגע. וכמה רגע? – אחד *מחמשת רבוא ושמונת אלפים ושמונה מאות ושמנים ושמונה בשעה, וזו היא רגע, *ואין כל בריה יכולה לכוין אותה שעה, חוץ מבלעם הרשע, דכתיב ביה: °"ויודע דעת עליון". *השתא דעת בהמתו לא הוה ידע – דעת עליון הוה ידע?! אלא: מלמד, שהיה יודע לכוין אותה שעה שהקב"ה כועס בה, והיינו דאמר להו נביא לישראל: °"עמי זכר נא מה יעץ בלק מלך מואב וגו'". מאי °"למען דעת צדקות ה'"? א"ר אלעזר: אמר להם הקב"ה לישראל: דעו כמה צדקות עשיתי עמכם שלא כעסתי בימי בלעם הרשע, שאלמלי כעסתי – לא נשתייר משונאיהם של ישראל שריד ופליט; והיינו דקא"ל בלעם לבלק: °"מה אקב לא קבה אל ומה אזעם לא זעם ה'", מלמד, שכל אותן הימים לא זעם. וכמה זעמו? – רגע. וכמה רגע? – א"ר אבין ואיתימא רבי אבינא: רגע כמימריה. ומנא לן דרגע רתח? – שנא': °"כי רגע באפו חיים ברצונו". ואב"א, מהכא: °"חבי כמעט רגע עד יעבר זעם". ואימת רתח? אמר אביי: בהנך תלת שעי קמייתא, כי חיורא כרבלתא דתרנגולא וקאי אחד כרעא. כל שעתא ושעתא נמי קאי הכי! כל שעתא אית ביה שורייקי סומקי, בההיא שעתא לית ביה שורייקי סומקי. ההוא מינא דהוה בשבבותיה דר' יהושע בן לוי, הוה קא מצער ליה טובא בקראי. יומא חד שקל תרנגולא ואוקמיה בין כרעי' דערסא ועיין ביה, סבר: כי מטא ההיא שעתא אלטייה. כי מטא ההיא שעתא נייס. אמר: ש"מ לאו אורח ארעא למעבד הכי, °"ורחמיו על כל מעשיו" כתיב, וכתיב: °"גם ענוש לצדיק לא טוב". תנא משמיה דר' מאיר: בשעה שהחמה זורחת, וכל מלכי מזרח ומערב מניחים כתריהם בראשיהם ומשתחוים לחמה, מיד כועס הקב"ה.§ וא"ר יוחנן משום רבי יוסי: טובה מרדות אחת בלבו של אדם יותר מכמה מלקיות, שנא': °"ורדפה את מאהביה" וגו' "ואמרה אלכה ואשובה אל אישי הראשון כי טוב לי אז מעתה"; וריש לקיש אמר: יותר ממאה מלקיות, שנאמר: °"תחת גערה במבין מהכות כסיל מאה".§ וא"ר יוחנן משום ר' יוסי: שלשה דברים בקש משה מלפני הקב"ה ונתן לו; בקש שתשרה שכינה על ישראל ונתן לו; שנאמר: °"הלוא בלכתך עמנו", *בקש שלא תשרה שכינה על אומות העולם ונתן לו, שנאמר: °"ונפלינו אני ועמך", בקש להודיעו דרכיו של הקב"ה ונתן לו, שנא': °"הודיעני נא את דרכיך" אמר לפניו: רבש"ע! מפני מה יש צדיק וטוב לו ויש צדיק ורע לו, יש רשע וטוב לו ויש רשע ורע לו? אמר לו: משה צדיק וטוב לו – צדיק בן צדיק, צדיק ורע לו – צדיק בן רשע, רשע וטוב לו – רשע בן צדיק, רשע ורע לו – רשע בן רשע.§ אמר מר: צדיק וטוב לו – צדיק בן צדיק, צדיק ורע לו – צדיק בן רשע. איני? והא כתיב: °"פקד עון אבות על בנים", וכתיב: °"*ובנים לא יומתו על אבות" ורמינן *קראי אהדדי ומשנינן: לא קשיא, הא – כשאוחזין מעשה אבותיהם בידיהם, הא – כשאין אוחזין מעשה אבותיהם בידיהם! אלא, הכי קא"ל: צדיק וטוב לו – צדיק גמור, צדיק ורע לו – צדיק שאינו גמור, רשע וטוב לו – רשע שאינו גמור, רשע ורע לו – רשע גמור. ופליגא דר' מאיר, דא"ר מאיר: שתים נתנו לו ואחת לא נתנו לו, שנא': °"וחנתי את אשר אחן" – אע"פ שאינו הגון, – "ורחמתי את אשר ארחם" – אע"פ שאינו הגון. °"ויאמר לא תוכל לראות את פני", תנא משמיה דר' יהושע בן קרחה, כך א"ל הקב"ה למשה: כשרציתי לא רצית, עכשיו שאתה רוצה – איני רוצה. ופליגא דר' שמואל בר נחמני א"ר יונתן; דא"ר שמואל בר נחמני א"ר יונתן, בשכר שלש זכה לשלש: בשכר °"ויסתר משה פניו"–זכה לקלסתר פנים. בשכר "כי ירא"–זכה °"ויראו מגשת אליו", בשכר "מהביט"–זכה °"ותמנת ה' יביט".§ °"והסרתי את כפי וראית את אחרי" – *אמר רב חנא בר ביזנא א"ר שמעון חסידא: מלמד שהראה הקב"ה למשה קשר של תפילין.§ וא"ר יוחנן משום ר' יוסי: כל דבור ודבור שיצא מפי הקב"ה לטובה, אפי' על תנאי, לא חזר בו. מנא לן? ממשה רבינו שנא': °"הרף ממני ואשמידם" וגו' "ואעשה אותך לגוי עצום". אע"ג דבעא משה רחמי עלה דמלתא ובטלה אפ"ה אוקמה בזרעיה שנא' °"בני משה גרשום ואליעזר. ויהיו בני אליעזר רחביה הראש" וגו' "ובני רחביה רבו למעלה וגו'". ותני רב יוסף: למעלה מששים רבוא, אתיא 'רביה' 'רביה', כתיב הכא "רבו למעלה", וכתיב התם °"ובני ישראל פרו וישרצו וירבו".§

אמר

שאלמלי כעסתי לא נשתייר וכו'. ואם תאמר: מה היה יכול לומר בשעת רגע? יש לומר: כלם. אי נמי: מאחר שהיה מתחיל קללתו באותה שעה – היה מזיק אפילו לאחר כן: ההוא מינא דהוה בשבבותיה דריב"ל כו' לאו אורח ארעא. אף על גב דהמינים וכו' מורידין ולא מעלין. *היינו בידי אדם, אבל בידי שמים לאו אורח ארעא להעניש ולהטריחם ולהורגם בידי שמים שלא כדרך בני אדם. ואי גרסינן הכא גוי – ניחא, דקאמר התם: הגוי ורועי בהמה דקה – לא מעלין ולא מורידין*:
לא

[ע"ז כו:]
[ועיין תוס' ע"ז ד: ד"ה ק"מ לאו כו']

כתובות לג. בבא מציעא: ב"מ כז: [ל:] — מגילה קף טו. — דף ז. כל הענין — ב"ח שאין — במדבר כג — סנהדרין קה: מיכה ו — שם — במדבר כג — תהלים ל — ישעיה כו — תהלים קמה — משלי יז — הושע ב — משלי יז — שמות לג [ב"ב טו:] — שם שם — שם לד — דברים כד — כתובות כג. [ב"ב לג: וע"ז לו: ד"ה לכתוב] — שמות לג שם — במדבר יב שם ג — שמות לג — דברים ט — דה"א כג — שמות א

שמות לג

תהלים ז

יש גורסים שמונה רבוא ויותר נכון למחוק הרבוא כלל ולגרוס שמונת אלפים שמונה מאות ופ"ח שמכוון נגד פסוקי תורה

## רב נסים גאון

טובה מרדות אחת בלבו של אדם יותר מק' מלקיות שנא' (משלי יז) תחת גערה במבין. מכלל שהמבין הוא הלב וכי הגערה מהניא ביה טפי ממה דמהניא המלקות לגוף ובפרק הרואה (דף סא) אמרי' תנו רבנן לב מבין כליות יועצות: והא כתי' פוקד עון אבות על בנים וכתיב לא יומתו אבות על בנים ורמינן קראי אהדדי ומשנינן כאן שאוחזין מעשה אבותיהם בידיהם וכאן שאין אוחזין מעשה אבותיהם בידיהם עיקרה דהא רמיא ודהא שינוייה במס' סנהדרין (דף כז) בפרק דיני ממונות בגמרא זה בורר לו אחד:

סנהדרין כז:

במדבר יב

מנחות דף לה:

הגהות הב"ח

(א) גמ' משום ר' יוסי בן זמרא מנין שהקב"ה: (ב) שם בראשו וקמ"ל נ"ב ס"א מאי קמ"ל:

הגהות הב"ח

(א) גמ' שבא אברהם אבינו וקראו: (ב) שם אף כאן דוד כיון: (ג) רש"י ד"ה ואומר וכו' היום ואי אפשר:

גליון הש"ס

**גמ'** אפ"ה לא אקנא ביה כו'. עב"ב קכג ע"א וברש"א בח"א: **שם** אלא שמות. עי' שם קמג ע"ב תוד"ה שהיו: **שם** קינה לדוד מיבעי ליה. עיין בזוה"ק פרשה וילא ד"ה וירא והנה באר בשדה. למשני לחשיב דוד דקוב"ה סליק ליה חובוי להאי עלמא. כיון דחמא דהכא בהאי עלמא בעי למיגבי מיניה חדי תו דחמא כו': **שם** הא בצדיק גמור כו'. עי' זוה"ק ר"פ פינחס: **שם** שעה משחקת לו שאני כו'. מג"א ס"ס קנ"ו: **שם** גדולה שמושה כו'. עי' תוס' כתובות י"ז ע"א ד"ה מבטלין:

**לא** היה אדם שקראו אדון. וא"ת: והא כתיב "ברוך ה' אלהי שם" (בראשית ט)? וי"ל: דהתם אינו באל"ף דל"ת, שהוא לשון אדנות. וא"ת: אמאי לא מייתי קרא "אדני (אלהים) מה תתן לי" (שם טו), שהוא כתוב קודם? וי"ל: שהפרשיות לא נאמרו כסדר, ואין מוקדם ומאוחר בתורה, וזה הפסוק דבין הבתרים היה קודם לכן. וכן נ"ל ע"כ; שהרי אברהם היה בן שבעים שנה בברית בין הבתרים. "ואחר הדברים האלה" (שם) נאמר אחר מלחמת המלכים, כדפירש רש"י בפירוש חומש, ובמלחמת המלכים היה בן ע"ג שנים, שהרי כל הימים של סדום נ"ב שנים, כדאמרי' בפ"ק דשבת (דף יא). לא מהם י"ב שנים שעבדו את כדרלעומר וי"ג שנים של מרידה ונשאר מישובה כ"ו שנים שהיתה בשלוה. ובהפיכתה היה אברהם בן צ"ט שנה, שהרי היתה ההפיכה שנה אחת קודם שנולד יצחק, לא מהם ששה ועשרים שנה למפרע של שלוה – נמצא שבן ע"ג שנה היה במלחמת המלכים. אם כן היתה פרשת בין הבתרים קודם לפרשת "אחר הדברים" שלש שנים, ואותה פרשה מסיימת "ויחשבה לו לצדקה" – ולכך הביא אותו פסוק ד"במה אדע", שהוא מוקדם. ומזה מיישב רשב"ם דבמקום אחד משמע שהיה לילה, דכתיב "וספור הככבים" (בראשית טו) ובתר הכי כתי' "ויהי השמש לבוא" – משמע שהוא יום. אלא ודאי ש"מ דשני פרשיות הם, ולאו בבת אחת נאמרו, ואין מוקדם ומאוחר בתורה:

רב

אדני אלהים. כתוב באל"ף דל"ת: הפעם אודה את ה'. לפי שראתה ברוח הקודש שיעקב מעמיד שנים עשר שבטים ולו ארבע נשים, כיון שילדה בן רביעי הודית על חלקה שעלה יותר מן החשבון המגיע לה: ראו מה בין בני לבן חמי. על שם העתיד קראה שמו, כדאמרינן לקמן: שמא גרים. רות. המואביה, משום דאיירי בפירושי השמות נקט לה: למה רגשו גוים. מה תועלת להם? אלמא: דבר קל הוא בעיניו: מי שלבו נוקפו. הירא מעבירות שבידו: אומר כן. מפרש "אל תתחר במרעים"–אל תתקוטט, והוא אינו כן, אלא: אל תתחר במרעים–*להתחברות במעשיהם, לומר אעשה כן גם אני: ואומר אל יקנא לבך בחטאים כי אם ביראת ה' כל היום. (ג) *אפשר לומר: אל תתקוטט עם רשעים כי אם ביראת ה', יראי ה'? אלא על כרחך: אל יקנא לבך לעשות כמותן: יחילו. יצליחו. וחבירו "על כן לא יחיל טובו" (איוב כ): מרום משפטיך מנגדו. מסולקין דיניך ברחוק הימנו: יפיח בהם. בנפיחתו הוא דוחה אותם כקש: ושמתי מקום. סיפיה דקרא "ולא יוסיפו בני עולה לענותו": כתיב לענותו. בספר שמואל: וכתיב לכלותו. בדברי הימים (א יז): בתחלה. כשנבנה הבית נבנה על מנת שלא לענות עוד אויבים לישראל: ולבסוף. כשחטאו, נגזר עליהם ענוי, ותפלתם מגינה עליהם מן הכליון: לא יכילנא. תש כחי:

עת

תורה אור

א"ר יוחנן משום ר"ש בן יוחי: מיום שברא הקב"ה את העולם לא היה אדם שקראו להקב"ה אדון, עד שבא אברהם(א) וקראו אדון, שנאמר: "ויאמר אדני (אלהים) במה אדע כי אירשנה". אמר רב: אף דניאל לא נענה אלא בשביל אברהם, שנא': "ועתה שמע אלהינו אל תפלת עבדך ואל תחנוניו והאר פניך על מקדשך השמם למען אדני". 'למענך' מבעי ליה! אלא – למען אברהם שקראך אדון.§ וא"ר יוחנן משום ר"ש בן יוחי: מנין שאין מרצין לו לאדם בשעת כעסו? – שנאמר: "פני ילכו והנחותי לך".§ ואמר ר"י משום ר"ש בן יוחי: מיום שברא הקב"ה את עולמו לא היה אדם שהודה להקב"ה עד שבאתה לאה והודתו, שנאמר: "הפעם אודה את ה'".§ 'ראובן' – א"ר אלעזר: אמרה לאה: ראו מה בין בני לבן חמי; דאילו בן חמי, אע"ג דמדעתיה זבניה לבכירותיה, דכתיב "וימכר את בכרתו ליעקב" חזו מה כתיב ביה: "וישטם עשו את יעקב", וכתיב: "ויאמר הכי קרא שמו יעקב ויעקבני זה פעמים וגו'". ואילו בני, אע"ג דעל כרחיה שקליה יוסף לבכירותיה מניה, דכתיב: "ובחללו יצועי אביו נתנה בכרתו לבני יוסף" אפי' הכי לא אקנא ביה, דכתיב "וישמע ראובן ויצלהו מידם".§ "רות" – *מאי רות? א"ר יוחנן: שזכתה ויצא ממנה דוד שריוהו להקב"ה בשירות ותשבחות. מנא לן דשמא גרים? – אמר רבי *אליעזר: דאמר קרא: "לכו חזו מפעלות ה' אשר שם שמות בארץ", אל תקרי 'שמות' אלא 'שמות'.§ וא"ר יוחנן משום רבי שמעון בן יוחי: קשה תרבות רעה בתוך ביתו של אדם יותר ממלחמת גוג ומגוג, שנאמר: "מזמור לדוד בברחו מפני אבשלום בנו", וכתיב בתריה: "ה' מה רבו צרי רבים קמים עלי"; ואילו גבי מלחמת גוג ומגוג כתיב: "למה רגשו גוים ולאמים יהגו ריק", ואילו "מה רבו צרי" לא כתיב. "מזמור לדוד בברחו מפני אבשלום בנו", "מזמור לדוד"?! "קינה לדוד" מיבעי ליה! א"ר שמעון בן *אבישלום: משל למה הדבר דומה? – לאדם שיצא עליו שטר חוב, קודם שפרעו היה עצב, לאחר שפרעו שמח – אף כן(ב) דוד, כיון שאמר לו הקב"ה "הנני מקים עליך רעה מביתך" – היה עצב, אמר: שמא עבד או ממזר הוא דלא חייס עלי. כיון דחזא דאבשלום הוא שמח, משום הכי אמר 'מזמור'.§ *וא"ר יוחנן משום ר"ש בן יוחי: מותר להתגרות ברשעים בעולם הזה, שנאמר: "עזבי תורה יהללו רשע ושמרי תורה יתגרו בם". תניא נמי הכי, *רבי דוסתאי בר' מתון אומר: מותר להתגרות ברשעים בעוה"ז, שנא': "עזבי תורה יהללו רשע וגו'"; ואם לחשך אדם לומר: והא כתיב "אל תתחר במרעים אל תקנא בעשי עולה"! אמור לו: מי שלבו נוקפו אומר כן; אלא "אל תתחר במרעים" – להיות כמרעים, "אל תקנא בעשי עולה" – להיות כעושי עולה, ואומר: "אל יקנא לבך בחטאים כי אם ביראת ה' כל היום". איני?! והאמר ר' יצחק: אם ראית רשע שהשעה משחקת לו אל תתגרה בו, שנאמר: "יחילו דרכיו בכל עת"; ולא עוד אלא שזוכה בדין, שנאמר: "מרום משפטיך מנגדו", ולא עוד אלא שרואה בצריו, שנאמר: "כל צורריו יפיח בהם"! –לא קשיא: הא במילי דידיה, הא במילי דשמיא. ואיבעית אימא: הא והא במילי דשמיא, ולא קשיא: הא ברשע שהשעה משחקת לו, הא ברשע שאין השעה משחקת לו. ואב"א: הא והא ברשע שהשעה משחקת לו, ולא קשיא, הא בצדיק גמור, הא בצדיק שאינו גמור, *דאמר רב הונא: מאי דכתיב "למה תביט בוגדים תחריש בבלע רשע צדיק ממנו", וכי רשע בולע צדיק?! והא כתיב "ה' לא יעזבנו בידו", וכתיב: "לא יאנה לצדיק כל און"! –אלא: צדיק ממנו – בולע. צדיק גמור – אינו בולע. ואב"א: *שעה משחקת לו שאני.§ וא"ר יוחנן משום רבי שמעון בן יוחי: כל הקובע מקום *לתפלתו אויביו נופלים תחתיו, שנאמר: "ושמתי מקום לעמי לישראל ונטעתיו ושכן תחתיו ולא ירגז עוד ולא יסיפו בני עולה לענותו כאשר בראשונה". רב הונא רמי: כתיב "לענותו" וכתיב *"לכלותו" – בתחילה "לענותו" ולבסוף "לכלותו".§ וא"ר יוחנן משום רבי שמעון בן יוחי: גדולה שמושה של תורה יותר מלמודה, שנא': "פה אלישע בן שפט אשר יצק מים על ידי אליהו" "למד" לא נאמר אלא "יצק" – מלמד שגדולה שמושה יותר מלמודה.§ א"ל רבי יצחק לרב נחמן: מ"ט לא אתי מר לבי כנישתא לצלויי? אמר ליה: לא יכילנא. א"ל: לכנפי למר עשרה וליצלי. אמר ליה: טריחא לי מלתא. –ולימא ליה מר לשלוחא דצבורא, בעידנא דמצלי צבורא ליתי ולודעיה למר. א"ל: מאי כולי האי? א"ל: דאמר ר' יוחנן משום ר"ש בן יוחי,

מאי

בראשית טו | דניאל ט | שמות לג | בראשית כט | שם כה | שם כז | שם | דה"א ה | בראשית לז | תהלים מו | שם ג | שם ב | תהלים ג | שמואל ב יב | משלי כח | תהלים לז | משלי כג | תהלים י | שם | חבקוק א | תהלים לז | משלי יב | שמואל ב ז | מלכים ב ג

ס"א להתאוות | עי' בפרש"י שבת | ב"ב יד: ע"ש | נ"ל אלעזר | (ועי' תוס' יומא לח ב ותוספות כתובות קד ב ס"ה שני) | ד"א אמר סתם ברא דרחים על אבא | מגילה ו ב | מס' ד"א רבה פ | מגילה ו: ב"מ עא. | פי' על זה תמצא בע"י [וברש"ל] בילקוט תהלים תרמ"ט | נ"א לתורתו | בס' שבידינו כתיב לבלותו

**מאי דכתיב** [א] "ואני תפלתי לך ה' עת רצון"? – אימתי *עת רצון – בשעה שהצבור מתפללין. ר' יוסי ברבי חנינא אמר, מהכא: "כה אמר ה' בעת רצון עניתיך". ר' אחא ברבי חנינא אמר, מהכא: "הן אל כביר ולא ימאס", וכתיב: "פדה בשלום נפשי מקרב-לי כי ברבים היו עמדי". תניא נמי הכי, רבי נתן אומר: מנין שאין הקב"ה מואס בתפלתן של רבים, שנאמר: "הן אל כביר ולא ימאס", וכתיב: "פדה בשלום נפשי מקרב-לי וגו'". (ה) אמר הקב"ה כל העוסק בתורה ובגמילות חסדים ומתפלל עם הצבור – מעלה אני עליו כאילו פדאני, לי ולבני, מבין אומות העולם: אמר ר"ל: כל מי שיש לו בית הכנסת בעירו ואינו נכנס שם להתפלל – נקרא שכן רע, שנאמר: "כה אמר ה' על כל שכני הרעים הנגעים בנחלה אשר הנחלתי את עמי את ישראל"; ולא עוד אלא שגורם גלות לו ולבניו, שנא': "הנני נתשם מעל אדמתם ואת בית יהודה אתוש מתוכם". אמרו ליה לר' יוחנן: איכא סבי בבבל. תמה ואמר: "למען ירבו ימיכם וימי בניכם על האדמה" כתיב, אבל בחוצה לארץ לא! כיון דאמרי ליה: מקדמי ומחשכי לבי כנישתא, אמר: היינו דאהני להו. כדאמר ר' יהושע בן לוי לבניה: קדימו וחשיכו ועיילו לבי כנישתא, כי היכי דתורכו חיי. א"ר אחא ברבי חנינא: מאי קרא – "אשרי אדם שמע לי לשקד על דלתתי יום יום לשמור מזוזת פתחי", וכתיב בתריה: "כי מצאי מצא חיים". אמר רב חסדא: לעולם יכנס אדם שני פתחים בבית הכנסת. שני פתחים סלקא דעתך?!– אלא, אימא: שיעור שני פתחים, ואחר כך יתפלל.§ "על זאת יתפלל כל חסיד אליך לעת מצא", אמר ר' חנינא: "לעת מצא" – זו אשה, שנא': "מצא אשה מצא טוב". *במערבא, כי נסיב איניש איתתא, אמרי ליה הכי: מצא או מוצא? "מצא" – דכתיב "מצא אשה מצא טוב ויפק רצון מה'", "מוצא" דכתיב: "ומוצא אני מר ממות את האשה וגו'". ר' נתן אומר: "לעת מצא" – זו תורה, שנאמר: "כי מצאי מצא חיים וגו'". רב נחמן בר יצחק אמר: "לעת מצא" – זו מיתה, שנא': "למות תוצאות". תניא נמי הכי: תשע מאות ושלשה מיני מיתה נבראו בעולם, שנאמר: "למות תוצאות" – "תוצאות" בגימטריא הכי הוו. קשה שבכלן – אסכרא, ניחא שבכלן – נשיקה; אסכרא – דמיא כחיזרא בגבבא דעמרא דלאחורי נשרא, ואיכא דאמרי: כפיטורי בפי ושט. נשיקה דמיא כמשחל בניתא מחלבא. ר' יוחנן אמר: "לעת מצא" – זו קבורה. א"ר חנינא: מאי קרא – "השמחים אלי גיל ישישו כי ימצאו קבר". אמר רבה בר רב שילא, היינו דאמרי אינשי: ליבעי איניש רחמי אפילו עד זיבולא בתרייתא שלמא. מר זוטרא אמר: "לעת מצא" – זה בית הכסא. אמרי במערבא: הא דמר זוטרא עדיפא מכלהו: אמר ליה רבא לרפרם בר פפא: לימא לן מר מהני מילי מעלייתא דאמרת משמיה דרב חסדא במילי דבי כנישתא! אמר ליה, הכי אמר רב חסדא: מאי דכתי' "אהב ה' שערי ציון מכל משכנות יעקב" – אוהב ה' שערים המצויינים(ג) בהלכה יותר מבתי כנסיות ומבתי מדרשות. והיינו דאמר ר' חייא בר אמי משמיה דעולא: מיום שחרב בית המקדש אין לו להקב"ה בעולמו אלא ארבע אמות של הלכה בלבד. *ואמר אביי: מריש הוה גריסנא בגו ביתא ומצלינא בבי כנישתא, כיון דשמענא להא דאמר רבי חייא בר אמי משמיה דעולא: מיום שחרב בית המקדש אין לו להקב"ה בעולמו אלא ארבע אמות של הלכה בלבד – לא הוה מצלינא אלא היכא דגריסנא. *רבי אמי ורבי אסי אף על גב דהוו להו תליסר בי כנישתא בטבריא לא מצלו אלא ביני עמודי, היכא דהוו גרסי.§ ואמר רבי חייא בר אמי משמיה דעולא: גדול הנהנה מיגיעו(ג) יותר מירא שמים, דאילו גבי ירא שמים כתיב: "אשרי איש ירא את ה'", ואילו גבי נהנה מיגיעו כתיב: "יגיע כפיך כי תאכל אשריך וטוב לך" *"אשריך" בעולם הזה, "וטוב לך" לעולם הבא, ולגבי ירא שמים "וטוב לך" לא כתיב ביה.§ ואמר רבי חייא בר אמי משמיה דעולא: לעולם ידור אדם במקום רבו, שכל זמן ששמעי בן גרא קיים לא נשא שלמה את בת פרעה. והתניא: אל ידור! – לא קשיא: הא דכייף ליה, הא דלא כייף ליה.§ אמר רב הונא בר יהודה אמר רבי מנחם אמר ר' אמי: מאי דכתי' "ועוזבי ה' יכלו" – זה המניח ס"ת(ז) ויוצא. רבי אבהו נפיק בין גברא לגברא. בעי רב פפא: בין פסוקא לפסוקא מהו? תיקו. רב ששת מהדר אפיה וגרים, אמר: אנן בדידן ואינהו בדידהו.§ אמר רב הונא בר יהודה אמר רבי אמי: לעולם ישלים אדם פרשיותיו עם הצבור שנים מקרא ואחד תרגום ואפילו

---

**רש"י**

עת רצון: אלמא: יש שעה שהיא של רצון: כביר לא ימאס. תפלת רבים לא ימאס: מקרב לי. ממלחמות הבאות עלי: כי ברבים היו עמדי. שהתפללו עמי: פדה בשלום. זה שעוסק בדברי שלום, דהיינו תורה, דכתיב "וכל נתיבותיה שלום" (משלי ג). וכן גמילות חסדים נמי שלום הוא, שמתוך שגומל חסד בגופו לחבירו הוא מכיר שהוא אוהבו, ובא לידי אחוה ושלום: הנני נותשם מעל אדמתם. סיפיה דקרא הוא: מקדמי. שחרית: מחשכי. ערבית, כלומר, מאחרין בבית הכנסת: שיעור של שני פתחים. רוחב, יכנס לפנים, שלא ישב סמוך לפתח, דנראה עליו כמשוי עכוב בית הכנסת, ויהא מזומן סמוך לפתח לצאת: יתפלל לעת מצא. יתפלל שיהיו מלווין לו כשיפטר: לעת מצא זו מיתה. שימות במיתה יפה ונוחה: אסכרא. איסטר"אנגולמנט בלע"ז, שנחנק הגוף: כחיזרא בגבבא דעמרא דלאחורי נשרא. כענפי הסירים הנסבכים בגזית הצמר כשאדם מושך בחזקה ומשליך לאחור, שאי אפשר שלא ינתק הצמר עמהם: כפיטורי בפי ושט. יש אוקיינוס יש בו מקומות שאינו מקבל ברזל, ומחברין לוחי הספינה ע"י חבלים ועקלים שתוחבי' בנקביו, ותוקעין אותו בדוחק לפי שהם גסין כמדת הנקב: פיטורי. חבלים. דמתרגמינן "ופטורי ציצים" (מלכים א ו) – חטוטין: בפי ושט. הוא הנקב, שהוא עגול כפי ושט: כמשחל בניתא מחלבא. כמושך נימת שער מתוך החלב: זיבולא בתרייתא שלמא. שיהא לו שלום כל ימי חייו, ואף ביום קבורתו עד השלכת עפר האחרונה שבכיסוי קבורתו: זיבולא. פלא"ה בלע"ז: לעת מצא זה בית הכסא. שיהא דר במקום שיש בית הכסא סמוך לו. לפי שהיתה קרקע של בבל מלולת מים, ואין יכולין לחפור שם חפירות, והיו צריכין לצאת בשדות ולהתרחק מאד: המצויינים. ציון ואסיפת לבור: ביני עמודי. שבית המדרש נכון עליהם מלמעלה: שכל זמן ששמעי בן גרא קיים כו'. דסמוך למיתת שמעי כתיב "ויתחתן שלמה את פרעה" (מלכים א ג): הא דכייף ליה. אם כפוף הוא לרבו לקבל תוכחתו – ידור אצלו, ואם לאו – טוב להתרחק ממנו, ויהי שוגג ואל יהי מזיד: מהדר אפיה וגרים. משנתו, כשקורין בספר תורה: ישלים פרשיותיו. של כל שבת ושבת: ואפילו

---

**תוספות**

(ה) **רב** ששת מהדר אפיה וגרים. וא"ת: והא אמרינן בסוטה (פ"ז ד' לט.) מאי דכתי' "וכפתחו עמדו כל העם" (נחמיה ח) – כיון שנפתח ספר תורה אסור לספר אפי' בדבר הלכה! ויש לומר: התם איירי בקול רם, כדי שלא יבטלו קול קריאת התורה, והכא איירי בנחת. והאי דקא מהדר אפיה – רבותא משמע, אע"ג דמהדר אפיה, שנראה כמניח ספר תורה–שפיר דמי, והאי דאהדר אפיה–כדי שיכוון גרסתו. ורב אלפס (מגילה פ"ד) כתב דה"ג מפרשי: דוקא שיש שם עשרה אחריני, אז יכול ללמוד, אבל אין שם עשרה כי אם עמו – לא. והכא מיירי שהיו שם עשרה בלא הוא. ועוד תירץ האלפסי: שאני רב ששת שתורתו אומנתו הוא.(ו) ואנן מסתבר לן כי האי *תירוצא*: **שנים** מקרא ואחד תרגום. יש מפרשים: והוא הדין ללועזות בלע"ז שלהן הוי כמו תרגום

---

**עין משפט נר מצוה**

כט א מיי' פ"ח מהלכות תפלה הלכה ח' סמג עשין יט טוש"ע או"ח סימן צ סעיף ט:

ל ב מיי' שם וסמ"ג שם טוש"ע או"ח סימן צ סעיף יח:

לא ג מיי' שם הלכה ב וסמג שם טור שו"ע או"ח שם סעיף כ:

לב ד מיי' שם הלכה ג וסמג שם טוש"ע או"ח שם סעיף יט:

לג ה ו מיי' פי"ב שם הלכה ט סמג שם טוש"ע או"ח סימן קמ"ו סעיף א:

[וע' תוס' סוטה לט. ד"ה כיון]

לד ז [טור שם] ח מיי' שם סמ"ג שם טוש"ע שם סעיף ב [רב אלפס כאן ובפרק הקורא את המגילה דף רע"ג]:

לה ט מיי' פי"ג שם הלכה כה סמג שם טור ושו"ע או"ח סימן רפ"ה סעיף א:

**הגהות הגר"א**

[א] גמ' מאי דכתי' ואני. נ"ב גי' רי"ף ורא"ש אין תפלתו של אדם נשמעת אלא בבית הכנסת שנאמר ואני:

[יבמות סג:]

קהלת ז

**גליון הש"ס**

גמ' כל העוסק בתורה כו'. ברי"ף איתא ומנוי בבהכ"נ: שם לעולם ידור כו'. מג"א סימן תר"ח סק"ג: שם בין פסוקא לפסוקא כו'. עי' יומא ע ע"א בתי' ד"ה ולא מפני: רש"י ד"ה כמשחל כו' כמושך כו'. כי מן המים משיתהו שמות ב' (מתרגם מן מיא שחלתיה):

[מגילה כט. ועיין שם הוטב]

---

**הגהות הב"ח** (partially cut off at the right edge)

...פדה בשלום נפשי וגו' מאי פדה ...פי אמר הקב"ה: ...המצויינים שם ...ג) שם הגהה ...יותר: (ז) שם ...ת ס"ת כשהוא ...: (ה) תו' קודם ...ששת נ"ל ד"ה ...פתחים פירש ...שיעור ב' פתחים ...להכנס לבית ...שיעור רוחב ב' ...שם ח' אמות אבל ...מאחר שהוא יושב ...לי סמוך לפתח ...סמוך וכן אם ...הכנסת נר והיה ...עם בע"כ צריך ...ב וסמוך לפתח ...פי' שלא ימהר ...כשבא בבית ...לא ישב מעט כדי ...דעתו עליו שגם ...הגון להתחיל ...עליו כמשאוי: ...רב ששת וכו' ...הוא וכתב ואנן מסתבר:

...ע: תענית כז: ...סנהדרין סז.]

לקמן דף ל:

תהלים קכח שם קמח

[ע"ש חולין מד:]

ישעיה א

תוספות

תרגום שמפרש לפעמים. כי כמו שהתרגום מפרש לע"ה, כך הם מבינים מתוך הלע"ז. ולא נהירא, שהרי התרגום מפרש כמה שאין ללמוד מן העברי, כדאשכחן *בכמה דוכתי דאמר רב יוסף (מגילה ד' ג.): אלמלא תרגומא דהאי קרא לא ידענא מאי קאמר. ע"כ אין לומר בשום לשון פעם שלישית כי אם בלשון תרגום:

**ואפילו** עטרות ודיבון וכו'. פי' רש"י: אפי' עטרות ודיבון שאין בו תרגום, שצריך לקרותו שלשה פעמים בעברי. וקשה: אמאי נקט עטרות ודיבון, שיש לו מ"מ תרגום ירושלמי. היה לו לומר "ראובן ושמעון", או פסוקא אחרינא שאין בו תרגום כלל! ויש לומר: משום הכי נקט עטרות ודיבון, אע"ג שאין בו תרגום ידוע אלא תרגום ירושלמי, וצריך לקרות ג' פעמים העברי – מ"מ יותר טוב לקרות פעם שלישית בתרגום: **כאילו** מתענה תשיעי ועשירי. ה"פ: אם נצטווה להתענות יום ט'. והקשה רבינו שמואל ב"ר אהרן מינבי"ל: מאי קשיא ליה, והא כתיב "בראשון בארבעה עשר יום לחדש בערב תאכלו מצות" (שמות יב) ואותו ערב ר"ל ערב של ט"ו, הכא נמי נימא: מאי ערב – ערב של עשירי! ויש לומר דשאני התם, דכתיב "תאכלו" לבסוף, דמשמע הכי: בראשון בי"ד בלילה תאכלו מצות. אבל הכא כתיב "ועניתם" קודם "בערב", דמשמע ועניתם מיד ביום התשיעי: **ישלים** פרשיותיו עם הצבור. נראה דכל השבוע, מכיון דמתחילין לקרות הפרשה, דהיינו ממנחת שבת ואילך עד שבת הבאה, נקראת עם הצבור. ואע"ג דלענין גיטין לא נקרא קמי שבת אלא מרביעי ואילך (בפסחים דף קו.). [*וזמן השלמה, יש במדרש,(ב) ג' דברים צוה רבינו הקדוש לבניו בשעה שנפטר: שלא תאכלו לחם בשבת עד שתגמרו כל הפרשה, משמע דקודם אכילה צריך להשלימה. ומיהו, אם השלימה לאחר אכילה – שפיר דמי. מ"מ, מצוה מן המובחר קודם אכילה: **לא** לעולם ליליא הוא. תימה: אם כן לימא רבותא, שפעמים יש אדם קורא לאחר שיעלה עמוד השחר שני פעמים ויוצא בו משום שחרית ומשום ערבית! וי"ל דהכי קאמר: לעולם לילה הוא בשאר מצות דבעינן בהו יום, כמו תפילין וציצית. אבל גבי ק"ש – לא, הואיל ואיכא אינשי דקיימי בההיא שעתא – לאו זמן שכיבה הוא. והאי דנקט לאחר שיעלה עמוד השחר – לאו דוקא מיד הוא, דהא צריך להמתין לכל הפחות שיעורא דמתניתין (לקמן ט:) עד שיכיר בין תכלת *לכרתי:

לעולם

גמרא

תורה אור

וַאֲפִילּוּ: *°"עֲטָרוֹת וְדִיבֹן" (במדבר לב) שֶׁכׇּל הַמַּשְׁלִים פָּרָשִׁיּוֹתָיו עִם הַצִּבּוּר מַאֲרִיכִין לוֹ יָמָיו וּשְׁנוֹתָיו. רַב בֵּיבַי בַּר אַבַּיֵי סְבַר לְאַשְׁלוֹמִינְהוּ לְפָרָשִׁיָּיתָא *דְּכוּלָּא שַׁתָּא בְּמַעֲלֵי יוֹמָא דְכִפּוּרֵי. *תְּנָא לֵיהּ חִיָּיא בַּר רַב מִדִּפְתִּי: כְּתִיב °"וְעִנִּיתֶם אֶת נַפְשֹׁתֵיכֶם בְּתִשְׁעָה לַחֹדֶשׁ בָּעֶרֶב" (ויקרא כג), וְכִי בְּתִשְׁעָה מִתְעַנִּין? וַהֲלֹא בַּעֲשָׂרָה מִתְעַנִּין! אֶלָּא לוֹמַר לָךְ: כׇּל הָאוֹכֵל וְשׁוֹתֶה בַּתְּשִׁיעִי – מַעֲלֶה עָלָיו הַכָּתוּב כְּאִילּוּ מִתְעַנֶּה תְּשִׁיעִי וַעֲשִׂירִי. סְבַר לְאַקְדּוּמִינְהוּ, אֲמַר לֵיהּ הַהוּא סָבָא, תְּנֵינָא: וּבִלְבַד שֶׁלֹּא יַקְדִּים וְשֶׁלֹּא יְאַחֵר. כִּדְאָמַר לְהוּ ר' יְהוֹשֻׁעַ בֶּן לֵוִי לִבְנֵיהּ: אַשְׁלִימוּ פָּרָשִׁיּוֹתַיְיכוּ עִם הַצִּבּוּר שְׁנַיִם מִקְרָא וְאֶחָד תַּרְגּוּם, *וְהִזָּהֲרוּ בַּוְּרִידִין כְּרַבִּי יְהוּדָה, דִּתְנַן; *רַבִּי יְהוּדָה אוֹמֵר: עַד שֶׁיִּשְׁחוֹט אֶת הַוְּרִידִין; וְהִזָּהֲרוּ בְּזָקֵן שֶׁשָּׁכַח תַּלְמוּדוֹ מֵחֲמַת אוֹנְסוֹ, דְּאָמְרִינַן: *לוּחוֹת וְשִׁבְרֵי לוּחוֹת מוּנָּחוֹת בָּאָרוֹן.§ אֲמַר לְהוּ רָבָא לִבְנֵיהּ: כְּשֶׁאַתֶּם חוֹתְכִין בָּשָׂר – אַל תַּחְתְּכוּ עַל גַּב הַיָּד. אִיכָּא דְּאָמְרִי: מִשּׁוּם סַכָּנָה; וְאִיכָּא דְּאָמְרִי: מִשּׁוּם קִלְקוּל סְעוּדָה. וְאַל תֵּשְׁבוּ עַל מִטַּת אֲרַמִּית, וְאַל תַּעַבְרוּ אֲחוֹרֵי בֵית הַכְּנֶסֶת בְּשָׁעָה שֶׁהַצִּבּוּר מִתְפַּלְּלִין. *"וְאַל תֵּשְׁבוּ עַל מִטַּת אֲרַמִּית" – אִיכָּא דְּאָמְרִי: לָא תִּגְנוּ בְּלָא ק"ש; וְאִיכָּא דְּאָמְרִי דְּלָא תִנְסְבוּ גִּיּוֹרְתָּא; וְא"ד: אֲרַמִּית מַמָּשׁ, וּמִשּׁוּם מַעֲשֶׂה דְּרַב פָּפָּא. *דְּרַב פָּפָּא אֲזַל לְגַבֵּי אֲרַמִּית, הוֹצִיאָה לוֹ מִטָּה, אָמְרָה לוֹ: שֵׁב! אָמַר לָהּ: אֵינִי יוֹשֵׁב עַד שֶׁתַּגְבִּיהִי אֶת הַמִּטָּה; הִגְבִּיהָה אֶת הַמִּטָּה וּמָצְאוּ שָׁם תִּינוֹק מֵת. מִכָּאן אָמְרוּ חֲכָמִים: אָסוּר לֵישֵׁב עַל מִטַּת אֲרַמִּית. "וְאַל תַּעַבְרוּ אֲחוֹרֵי בֵית הַכְּנֶסֶת בְּשָׁעָה שֶׁהַצִּבּוּר מִתְפַּלְּלִין" – מְסַיֵּיעַ לֵיהּ לְרַבִּי יְהוֹשֻׁעַ בֶּן לֵוִי, דְּאָמַר ר' יְהוֹשֻׁעַ בֶּן לֵוִי: *אָסוּר לוֹ לְאָדָם שֶׁיַּעֲבוֹר אֲחוֹרֵי בֵית הַכְּנֶסֶת בְּשָׁעָה שֶׁהַצִּבּוּר מִתְפַּלְּלִין. אֲמַר אַבַּיֵי: וְלָא אֲמַרַן אֶלָּא דְּלֵיכָּא פִּתְחָא אַחֲרִינָא, אֲבָל אִיכָּא פִּתְחָא אַחֲרִינָא – לֵית לָן בָּהּ. וְלָא אֲמַרַן אֶלָּא דְּלֵיכָּא בֵּי כְנִישְׁתָּא אַחֲרִינָא, אֲבָל אִיכָּא בֵּי כְנִישְׁתָּא אַחֲרִינָא – לֵית לָן בָּהּ. וְלָא אֲמַרַן אֶלָּא דְּלָא דָּרֵי טוּנָא וְלָא רָהֵיט, וְלָא מַנַּח תְּפִילִּין, אֲבָל אִיכָּא חַד מֵהָנָךְ – לֵית לָן בָּהּ.§ תַּנְיָא אָמַר ר"ע: בִּשְׁלֹשָׁה דְּבָרִים אוֹהֵב אֲנִי אֶת הַמָּדִיִּים: כְּשֶׁחוֹתְכִין אֶת הַבָּשָׂר – אֵין חוֹתְכִין אֶלָּא עַל גַּבֵּי הַשּׁוּלְחָן, כְּשֶׁנּוֹשְׁקִין – אֵין נוֹשְׁקִין אֶלָּא עַל גַּב הַיָּד, וּכְשֶׁיּוֹעֲצִין – אֵין יוֹעֲצִין אֶלָּא בַּשָּׂדֶה. אֲמַר רַב אַדָּא בַּר אַהֲבָה: מַאי קְרָאָה – °"וַיִּשְׁלַח יַעֲקֹב וַיִּקְרָא לְרָחֵל וּלְלֵאָה הַשָּׂדֶה אֶל צֹאנוֹ" (בראשית לא).§ תַּנְיָא, אָמַר רַבָּן גַּמְלִיאֵל: בִּשְׁלֹשָׁה דְּבָרִים אוֹהֵב אֲנִי אֶת הַפַּרְסִיִּים: הֵן צְנוּעִין בַּאֲכִילָתָן, וּצְנוּעִין בְּבֵית הַכִּסֵּא, וּצְנוּעִין בְּדָבָר אַחֵר. °"אֲנִי צִוֵּיתִי לִמְקֻדָּשָׁי" (ישעיה יג). תָּנֵי רַב יוֹסֵף: אֵלּוּ הַפַּרְסִיִּים הַמְקוּדָּשִׁין וּמְזוּמָּנִין לְגֵיהִנָּם.§ "רַבָּן גַּמְלִיאֵל אוֹמֵר וכו'".§ אָמַר רַב יְהוּדָה אָמַר שְׁמוּאֵל: הֲלָכָה כר"ג. *תַּנְיָא, ר"ש בֶּן יוֹחַי אוֹמֵר: פְּעָמִים שֶׁאָדָם קוֹרֵא ק"ש שְׁתֵּי פְעָמִים בַּלַּיְלָה, אַחַת קוֹדֶם שֶׁיַּעֲלֶה עַמּוּד הַשַּׁחַר, וְאַחַת לְאַחַר שֶׁיַּעֲלֶה עַמּוּד הַשַּׁחַר, וְיוֹצֵא בָּהֶן יְדֵי חוֹבָתוֹ, אַחַת שֶׁל יוֹם וְאַחַת שֶׁל לַיְלָה. הָא גוּפָא קַשְׁיָא! אָמְרַתְּ "פְּעָמִים שֶׁאָדָם קוֹרֵא קְרִיַּת שְׁמַע שְׁתֵּי פְעָמִים בַּלַּיְלָה", אַלְמָא – לְאַחַר שֶׁיַּעֲלֶה עַמּוּד הַשַּׁחַר לֵילְיָא הוּא, וַהֲדַר תָּנֵי: "יוֹצֵא בָּהֶן יְדֵי חוֹבָתוֹ אַחַת שֶׁל יוֹם וְאַחַת שֶׁל לַיְלָה", אַלְמָא – יְמָמָא הוּא! – לָא, לְעוֹלָם לֵילְיָא הוּא, וְהָא דְּקָרֵי לֵיהּ יוֹם – דְּאִיכָּא אֱינָשֵׁי דְּקָיְימִי בְּהַהִיא שַׁעְתָּא. אָמַר רַב אַחָא בַּר חֲנִינָא אָמַר רַבִּי יְהוֹשֻׁעַ בֶּן לֵוִי: הֲלָכָה כְּרַבִּי שִׁמְעוֹן בֶּן יוֹחַי. אִיכָּא דְּמַתְנֵי לְהָא דְּרַב אַחָא בַּר חֲנִינָא אַהָא דְּתַנְיָא, רַבִּי שִׁמְעוֹן בֶּן יוֹחַי אוֹמֵר מִשּׁוּם ר' עֲקִיבָא: פְּעָמִים שֶׁאָדָם קוֹרֵא קְרִיַּת שְׁמַע שְׁתֵּי פְעָמִים בַּיּוֹם, אַחַת קוֹדֶם הָנֵץ הַחַמָּה וְאַחַת לְאַחַר הָנֵץ הַחַמָּה, וְיוֹצֵא בָּהֶן יְדֵי חוֹבָתוֹ, אַחַת שֶׁל יוֹם וְאַחַת שֶׁל לַיְלָה. הָא גוּפָא קַשְׁיָא! אָמְרַתְּ "פְּעָמִים שֶׁאָדָם קוֹרֵא ק"ש שְׁתֵּי פְעָמִים בַּיּוֹם", אַלְמָא – קוֹדֶם הָנֵץ הַחַמָּה יְמָמָא הוּא, וַהֲדַר תָּנֵי: "יוֹצֵא בָּהֶן יְדֵי חוֹבָתוֹ אַחַת שֶׁל יוֹם וְאַחַת שֶׁל לַיְלָה", אַלְמָא – לֵילְיָא הוּא!

לָא

רש"י

ואפי' עטרות ודיבון. שאין בו תרגום: מעלה עליו הכתוב כו'. והכי קאמר קרא: הכינו עצמכם בתשעה לחדש לענוי המחרת, והרי הוא בעיני כענוי היום: לאקדומינהו. לסדר כל הפרשיות בשבת אחת או בשתי שבתות: עד שישחוט את הורידין. כדי שיצא כל הדם. ולא אמר כן אלא בעוף, הואיל ולאו כולו כאחד: מחמת אונסו. שחלה, או שנטרד בדוחק מזונות, והזהרו בו לכבדו: שברי לוחות מונחות בארון. דכתיב (דברים י) "אשר שברת ושמתם בארון" – אף השברים משים בארון: משום סכנה. שלא יקוץ ידו: משום קלקול סעודה. אף בחבורה קטנה יצא דם וילכלך את המאכל וימאיס את המסובין: בלא ק"ש. שתהא מטתך דומה למטת ארמית: ארמית ממש. על מטת ארמית: מעשה דרב פפא. שאמרה לו: שב על המטה, והיה בנה מת מוטל עליה, והיתה רוצה להעליל עליו ולומר שישב עליו והרגו: אסור לעבור וכו'. שנראה כמבריח עצמו מפתח בית הכנסת שבמזרח: על גב היד. את יד חברו הוא נושק, ודרך חשיבות הוא זה, מפני סרוך: אלא בשדה. דאמרי אינשי: חזינא לכותל: בדבר אחר. תשמיש: אני צויתי למקודשי. במפלת בבל כתיב, אני צויתי את מלכי פרס (א) ומדי לבא ולהשחיתה: ליליא הוא. עד הנץ החמה: דקיימי בההיא שעתא. הלכך זמן ק"ש דיום הוא, דגבי קריאת שמע "ובקומך" כתיב, והא קיימי: והאי

עין משפט נר מצוה

לו א מיי' פ"ו מהלכות תפלה הלכה א סמג עשין יט טוש"ע או"ח סימן ל סעיף ח:

לז ב ג מיי' פ"א מהל' ק"ש הל' י יב סמג עשין יח טוש"ע או"ח סימן נח סעיף ג ד ה ובסימן רלה סעיף ד:

[גי' הערוך בערך כל הרכובי סבר לאשלומינהו לכלהו פרשייתא דכלה במעלי יומא דכפורי פי' הן שמנה פרשיות שקורין כל' שבתות שבאלול וכו' שבתות שבתשרי ומפני שהיה רב ביבי ערוך בתלמוד הכלה במס' כלה לא מצא פנאי להשלים כל פרשה בשבתה]

רב נסים גאון

**ואיכא** דאמרי משום ארמית ממש. ממעשה אמרי דרב פפא שהיה לרב פפא היתה לו מלוה אצל גוי אמר כיון שדחקו רב פפא לגבי במלוה שלו רצה הגוי לעשות לו עלילה במרמה כדי להנצל בה מן התביעה' שלו מה עשה נטל תינוק אחד קטן מת והשכיבו על מטה שלו וכסהו בבגדים כדי שלא ירגיש בו אדם ואמר לו לרב פפא בא עמי לביתי ואני נותן לך את שיש לך אצלי הלך אצלו ונכנס לביתו אמר לו הגוי שב לך על המטה נתן עיניו רב פפא בדברים שהיו על המטה קודם שישב עליה ומצא התינוק המת מוטמן בתוך הבגדים והרגיש הדברים שרצה להתעולל עליו עלילות ברשע ומאותה שעה אסרו חכמים לישב על מטה ארמית מפני כן וזה המעשה בקבלה הוא אצלי מרבי אדונינו הרב הקדוש רבנו חושיאל ריש בי רבנן ז"ל ולתחיה הוא וגם מצאתי אותו בתשו' הגאונים כמו כן:

[טוב להגיה ללבן]

מסורת הש"ס

[וקדושין דף מט. פסוק כלותרן] | ס"א דיבון שבסוף מסעי | פסחים קט"ו ר"ה דף ט. | [סנהדרין נו.] | חולין פ"ב דף כז. | ב"ב פ"ק דף י' נט. | פסחים קיב. | [וע"ש ברש"י המעשה בענין אחר גם בפי' רש"י] | לקמן דף סא. | תוספתא פ"א | [כל"ל וכ"ה בסמג עשין יט]

הגהות הב"ח

(א) רש"י ד"ה אני וכו' פרס לבא כל ומדי נמחק: (ב) ד"ה ישלים וכו' במדרש דברים:

לא, לעולם יממא הוא, והאי דקרו ליה ליליא – דאיכא אינשי דגנו בההיא שעתא. אמר רבי אחא ברבי חנינא אמר רבי יהושע בן לוי: הלכה כר"ש שאמר משום רבי עקיבא. אמר רבי זירא: ובלבד שלא יאמר "השכיבנו". כי אתא רב יצחק בר יוסף אמר: הא דרבי אחא ברבי חנינא אמר ריב"ל, *לאו בפירוש איתמר אלא מכללא איתמר. דההוא זוגא דרבנן דאשתכור בהלולא דבריה דר' יהושע בן לוי, אתו לקמיה דריב"ל, אמר: *כדאי הוא ר"ש לסמוך עליו בשעת הדחק.§ "מעשה שבאו בניו וכו'".§ ועד השתא לא שמיע להו הא דר"ג?! – הכי קאמרי ליה: רבנן פליגי עילווך – *ויחיד ורבים הלכה כרבים, או דלמא רבנן כוותך סבירא להו, והאי דקאמרי "עד חצות" – כדי להרחיק אדם מן העבירה? אמר להו: רבנן כוותי סבירא להו, וחייבין אתם. והאי דקאמרי "עד חצות" – כדי להרחיק אדם מן העבירה.§ "ולא זו בלבד אמרו אלא וכו'".§ ור"ג מי קאמר "עד חצות" דקתני "ולא זו בלבד(א) אמרו"? הכי קאמר להו ר"ג לבניה: אפילו לרבנן דקאמרי "עד חצות" – מצותה עד שיעלה עמוד השחר, והאי דקא אמרי "עד חצות" – כדי להרחיק אדם מן העבירה.§ "הקטר חלבים וכו'".§ *ואילו אכילת פסחים לא קתני. ורמינהי: ק"ש ערבית, והלל בלילי פסחים, ואכילת פסח – מצותן עד שיעלה עמוד השחר! אמר רב יוסף לא קשיא, הא – ר' אלעזר בן עזריה, הא – רבי עקיבא. *דתניא: °"ואכלו את (שמות יב)
הבשר בלילה הזה", רבי אלעזר בן עזריה אומר: נאמר כאן "בלילה הזה" ונאמר
להלן °"ועברתי בארץ מצרים בלילה הזה" – מה להלן עד חצות, אף כאן עד חצות. (שם)
אמר ליה ר' עקיבא: והלא כבר נאמר °"בחפזון" – עד שעת חפזון! א"כ מה תלמוד (שם)
לומר "בלילה" – יכול יהא נאכל כקדשים ביום, תלמוד לומר: "בלילה", בלילה הוא נאכל, ולא ביום. בשלמא לר' אלעזר בן עזריה דאית ליה גזירה שוה – איצטריך למכתב ליה "הזה", אלא לר' עקיבא – האי "הזה" מאי עביד ליה? – למעוטי לילה אחר הוא דאתא; סד"א הואיל ופסח קדשים קלים ושלמים קדשים קלים, מה שלמים נאכלין לשני ימים ולילה אחד – אף פסח נאכל שתי לילות במקום ב' ימים, ויהא נאכל לב' לילות ויום אחד קמ"ל "בלילה הזה" – בלילה הזה הוא נאכל, ואינו נאכל
בלילה אחר. ור' אלעזר בן עזריה? מ°"לא תותירו עד בקר" נפקא. ורבי עקיבא? – אי (שם)
מהתם הוה אמינא: מאי "בקר" – בקר שני. ורבי אלעזר? אמר לך: כל בקר – בקר
ראשון הוא. והני תנאי כהני תנאי, *דתניא: °"שם תזבח את הפסח בערב כבוא (דברים טז)
השמש מועד צאתך ממצרים". ר' אליעזר אומר: 'בערב' אתה זובח, ו'כבוא השמש' אתה אוכל, ו'מועד צאתך ממצרים' אתה שורף; רבי יהושע אומר: 'בערב' אתה זובח, 'כבוא השמש' אתה אוכל, ועד מתי אתה אוכל והולך – עד 'מועד צאתך ממצרים'. א"ר אבא: הכל מודים, כשנגאלו ישראל ממצרים – לא נגאלו אלא בערב,
שנאמר: °"הוציאך ה' אלהיך ממצרים לילה", וכשיצאו – לא יצאו אלא ביום, שנא' (שם)
°"ממחרת הפסח יצאו בני ישראל ביד רמה". על מה נחלקו – על שעת חפזון; ר' (במדבר לג)
אלעזר בן עזריה סבר: מאי חפזון – חפזון דמצרים, ורבי עקיבא סבר: מאי חפזון – חפזון דישראל. *תנ"ה: "הוציאך ה' אלהיך ממצרים לילה" – וכי בלילה יצאו? והלא לא יצאו אלא ביום, שנא': "ממחרת הפסח יצאו בני ישראל ביד רמה"! אלא: מלמד
שהתחילה להם גאולה מבערב.§ °"דבר נא באזני העם וגו'" – אמרי דבי ר' ינאי: (שמות יא)
*אין "נא" אלא לשון בקשה, אמר ליה הקב"ה למשה: בבקשה ממך, לך ואמור להם לישראל; בבקשה מכם, שאלו ממצרים כלי כסף וכלי זהב, שלא יאמר אותו

**רש"י**

והאי דקרו ליה ליליא. דקאמר: יוצא בו ק"ש של לילה: משום דאיכא דגנו. וקריאה ביה "ובשכבך": ובלבד שלא יאמר השכיבנו. הקורא ק"ש של לילה שחרית סמוך לעמוד השחר, לא יאמר "השכיבנו", שאין עוד זמן תחלת שכיבה אלא זמן סוף שכיבה: דאשתכור. וישנו ונרדמו עד לאחר עמוד השחר: בשעת הדחק. אבל שלא בשעת הדחק – לא: הכי קא אמרי ליה. לרבן גמליאל, ולא גרס "אלא": רבנן פליגי עילווך. כלומר: מי פליגי רבנן עלך, דהא דקאמרי עד חצות, דווקא קאמרי, דלא משמע להו "ובשכבך" – כל זמן שכיבה, אלא: כל זמן שדרך בני אדם להתעסק לילך ולשכב, ומיהו בהא פליגי אדרבי אליעזר, דאלו רבי אליעזר סבירא ליה זמן עסק שכיבה אינו אלא עד האשמורה הראשונה, ולרבנן עד חצות. ואת סבירא לך "ובשכבך" – כל זמן שבני אדם שוכבים, והיינו כל הלילה, ויחיד ורבים – הלכה כרבים: או דילמא כוותך סבירא להו. ומשמע להו "ובשכבך" – כל זמן שכיבה, והא דקאמרי "עד חצות" – הרחקה הוא, כדי לזרז. ומיהו, היכא דפשעים ולא קרא קודם חצות – עדיין זמן חיובא הוא, ומחייבי, ונפקי ידי ק"ש בזמנו: כוותי סבירא להו. ו"חייבין" אתם לקרות גרסינן, ולא גרסינן "מותרים", דאפילו שלא בזמנו (עמוד ב) תנן: הקורא מכאן ואילך לא הפסיד, כאדם הקורא בתורה: שעת חפזון. שנחפזו לצאת, והיינו עמוד השחר, כדכתיב "לא תצאו איש מפתח ביתו עד בקר" (שמות יב): יכול יהא נאכל. כשאר קדשים ביום שחיטתו, כדרך תודה שאף היא זמן אכילתה יום אחד, ואוכל והולך כל יום שחיטתה והלילה עד הבקר, (ב) כדין תודה, דכתיב "ביום קרבנו יאכל" (ויקרא ז): מה שלמים נאכלין לשני ימים ולילה אחד. שביניהם, דכתיב "ביום זבחכם יאכל וממחרת" (שם יט), אף פסח נמי, הואיל ואינו נאכל אלא בלילה נוקים שני לילות במקום שני ימים דשלמים, ויהא נאכל בשני לילות ויום אחד. לא שיאכלנו ביום, אלא שיהא שהות זמן שלא יפסל באכילה בשביל המתנת היום, ויאכלנו בלילה השנית – (ג) קמ"ל: שם תזבח את הפסח בערב כבוא השמש מועד צאתך ממצרים. הרי לך שלשה זמנים שאינם שוים. "בערב" – כי ינטו צללי ערב, היינו לאחר חצות, שנתקלקלה חמה מראש כל אדם ונטתה למערב; "כבוא השמש" – משתחשך; "מועד צאתך ממצרים" – בבקר. כילד יתקיימו כולם: 'בערב' – זמן שחיטה, 'כבוא השמש' – התחלת זמן אכילה, 'מועד צאתך' – זמן שריפה, כלומר: בבקר הוא נעשה נותר, שהגיע זמן שריפה, אלא לפי שאין שורפין קדשים ביום טוב ממתינין לו עד בקר שני: עד מתי אתה אוכל. היינו כר"ע. אבל לתנא קמא עד חצות לילה הוי זמן אכילה, ותו לא, דאי לא – מאי ביניייהו: הכל מודים. רבי עקיבא גופיה מודה שבלילה, מחצות ואילך, היתה שעת חפזון למצרים לשלחם מן הארץ, מערב נגאלו. נתנו להם רשות לצאת: חפזון דמצרים. מכת הבכורים, שעל ידם נחפזו למהר לשלחם: חפזון דישראל. לא שמעו להם לצאת עד בקר: אותו

**תוספות**

לעולם יממא הוא. ואם תאמר: ליתני שתי פעמים קודם הנץ החמה והוי רבותא טפי, דאפילו קודם הנץ הוי זמן דקריאת שמע של שחרית! וי"ל כדפרישנא: דהאי יממא – לענין שאר מצות. אבל לענין ק"ש, הואיל ואיכא אינשי דגנו – לאו זמן קימה הוא. ותימה: דקשיא דרבי עקיבא אדר' עקיבא, דהכא קאמר: אחר הנץ, ולקמן (עמוד ב) קאמר: משיכיר בין חמור לערוד, דהיינו אפילו קודם! וי"ל: דתרי תנאי אליבא דרבי עקיבא. אי נמי, יש לומר: יממא הוא – אפילו גבי קרית שמע, דהא זמן קימה הוא. והא דלא נקט ב' פעמים קודם הנץ – משום דבעי לאשמועינן שאינו יוצא בשל לילה אחר הנץ*: ובלבד שלא יאמר השכיבנו. פירש בקונטרס: מילתא דר"ש בן יוחי, דקורא קודם שיעלה עמוד השחר קאי. ונראה לי דלא ודאי זמן שכיבה הוא, ומאי למימר "השכיבנו". ועוד, דהוה ליה למימר אמאי דסליק מיניה! ופי' השר מקוצי: דקאי אקודם הנץ דסליק מיניה, ולכך קאמר דלא מצי למימר "השכיבנו" דלאו זמן שכיבה הוא, כיון שעלה כבר עמוד השחר, אפילו קודם הנץ: ר' אלעזר בן עזריה אומר נאמר כאן בלילה הזה וכו'. וא"ת: היכי מצי למימר רבי אלעזר בן עזריה עד חצות, והכתיב "לא תותירו ממנו עד בקר" (שמות יב), דמשמע – עד בקר מיהא מצי לאכלו! ויש לומר: דמאי למימר דהכי קאמר – לא תעשו דבר שיבא לידי נותר עד הבקר. שאם לא יהא נאכל עד חצות לא תוכל לאוכלו ולא לשורפו בלילה, כדקא אמרינן *"ביום אתה שורפו ואי אתה שורפו בלילה", ואם כן ישאר עד הבקר: אלא

**עין משפט נר מצוה**

לח א מיי' פ"א מהל' ק"ש הל' י' [סמ"ג עשין יח] טוש"ע או"ח סימן נח סעיף ד:
לט ב מיי' פ"ח מהל' קרבן פסח הל' יד:

**מסורת הש"ס**

[שבת מה. נדה ו. ט:]
[לעיל ג: יבמות מ. נדה ט:]
פסחים פט. ד"ה לאלתר
מגילה כא. מכילתא דר"י פרשה בא
ספרי פ' ראה
ספרי שם
[סנהדרין מג: פט.]
[לקמן יח: שבת כט. לט: קמה: עירובין מו. נז. יבמות מ: כתובות פ: ב"ק כ: ב"מ לו: ק"א. בבא בתרא מ: קכו. קכז. שבועות כא. חולין לג. נב. קיא: מנחות מ:]
[פסחים ג. זבחים נו:]

**הגהות הב"ח**

(א) גמ' ולא זו בלבד הכי קאמר כצ"ל ותיבת אמרו נמחק: (ב) רש"י ד"ה יכול יהא וכו' עד הבקר מן התורה דכתיב ביום: (ג) ד"ה מה שלמים וכו' בלילה השנית. נ"ב ולקמ"ל סוף פסחים דף ק"ך ע"ב הביא תחלה פי' רבינו דהכא ואח"כ כתב וי"ל ולי נראה שאף ביום שביניהם יאכל דהא לא בא למעט אלא יום שחיטתו שלפני לילה הראשון של פסח אבל מכאן ואילך יאכלנו עד עמוד השחר של ליל שני קמ"ל עכ"ל:

אותו צדיק: "ועבדום וענו אתם" – קיים בהם, "ואחרי כן יצאו ברכש גדול" – לא קיים בהם. אמרו לו: ולואי שנצא בעצמנו. משל לאדם שהיה חבוש בבית האסורים, והיו אומרים לו בני אדם: מוציאין אותך למחר מבית האסורין ונותנין לך ממון הרבה, ואומר להם: בבקשה מכם, הוציאוני היום ואיני מבקש כלום.§ "וישאלום". א"ר אמי: מלמד, שהשאילום בעל כרחם. איכא דאמרי: בעל כרחם דמצרים, וא"ד: בעל כרחם דישראל. מ"ד בעל כרחם דמצרים – דכתיב "ונות בית תחלק שלל"; מ"ד בעל כרחם דישראל – משום משוי. "וינצלו את מצרים". *א"ר אמי: מלמד שעשאוה כמצודה שאין בה דגן. ור"ל אמר: עשאוה כמצולה שאין בה דגים.§ "אהיה אשר אהיה". א"ל הקב"ה למשה: לך אמור להם לישראל: אני הייתי עמכם בשעבוד זה ואני אהיה עמכם בשעבוד מלכיות. אמר לפניו: רבש"ע! דיה לצרה בשעתה. א"ל הקב"ה: לך אמור להם "אהיה שלחני אליכם".§ *"ענני ה' ענני". א"ר אבהו: למה אמר אליהו "ענני" ב' פעמים? מלמד שאמר אליהו לפני הקב"ה: רבש"ע! 'ענני' – שתרד אש מן השמים ותאכל כל אשר על המזבח, ו'ענני' – שתסיח דעתם כדי שלא יאמרו מעשה כשפים הם, שנאמר: "ואתה הסבת את לבם אחורנית".§ **מתני'** *מאימתי קורין את שמע בשחרית? משיכיר בין תכלת ללבן. ר' אליעזר אומר: בין תכלת לכרתי. *(וגומרה) *עד הנץ (א) החמה. *ר' יהושע אומר: עד שלש שעות שכן דרך מלכים לעמוד בשלש שעות. *הקורא מכאן ואילך לא הפסיד, כאדם הקורא בתורה.§ **גמ'** מאי "בין תכלת ללבן"? אילימא בין גבבא דעמרא חיורא לגבבא דעמרא דתכלתא – הא בליליא נמי מידע ידעי! אלא: *בין תכלת שבה ללבן שבה. תניא, רבי מאיר אומר: משיכיר בין זאב לכלב; ר"ע אומר: בין חמור לערוד; *ואחרים אומרים: משיראה את חברו רחוק ד' אמות ויכירנו. אמר רב הונא: הלכה כאחרים. אמר אביי: לתפילין – כאחרים, לק"ש – כותיקין, *דאמר ר' יוחנן: ותיקין היו *גומרין אותה עם הנץ החמה. תניא נמי הכי: ותיקין היו גומרין אותה עם הנץ החמה, כדי שיסמוך גאולה לתפלה ונמצא מתפלל ביום. א"ר זירא: מאי קראה – "ייראוך עם שמש ולפני ירח דור דורים".§ העיד ר"י בן אליקים משום קהלא קדישא דבירושלים: כל הסומך גאולה לתפלה – אינו נזוק כל היום כולו. א"ר זירא: איני?! והא אנא סמכי ואיתזקי! א"ל: במאי איתזקת – דאמטיית אסא לבי מלכא; התם נמי מבעי לך למיהב אגרא למחזי אפי מלכא, דא"ר יוחנן: *לעולם ישתדל אדם לרוץ לקראת מלכי ישראל, ולא לקראת מלכי ישראל בלבד אלא אפילו לקראת מלכי אומות העולם, שאם יזכה – יבחין בין מלכי ישראל למלכי אומות העולם. אמר ליה רבי אלעא לעולא: כי עיילת להתם שאיל בשלמא דרב ברונא אחי במעמד כל החבורה, דאדם גדול הוא ושמח במצות: זימנא חדא סמך גאולה לתפלה ולא פסיק חוכא מפומיה כוליה יומא.§ היכי מצי סמיך? והא א"ר יוחנן: *בתחלה הוא אומר: "ה' שפתי תפתח" ולבסוף הוא אומר: "יהיו לרצון אמרי פי וגו'"! – אמר ר' אלעזר: תהא בתפלה של ערבית. -והא אמר ר' יוחנן: *איזהו בן העוה"ב – זהו הסומך גאולה של ערבית לתפלה של ערבית. -אלא א"ר אלעזר: תהא בתפלת המנחה. רב אשי אמר: אפי' תימא אכולהו, וכיון דקבעוה רבנן בתפלה – כתפלה אריכתא דמיא, דאי לא תימא הכי, *ערבית היכי מצי סמיך? והא בעי למימר השכיבנו! אלא, כיון דתקינו רבנן השכיבנו – כגאולה אריכתא דמיא, ה"נ, כיון דקבעוה רבנן בתפלה – כתפלה אריכתא דמיא.§ מכדי, האי "יהיו לרצון אמרי פי" – משמע לבסוף ומשמע מעיקרא – דבעינא למימר. מ"ט תקנוהו רבנן לאחר י"ח ברכות? לימרו מעיקרא! – א"ר יהודה בריה דר' שמעון בן פזי: הואיל ולא אמרו דוד אלא לאחר י"ח פרשיות, לפיכך תקינו רבנן לאחר י"ח ברכות. הני י"ח, י"ט הוין!-"אשרי האיש" ו"למה רגשו גוים" חדא פרשה היא. דאמר ר' יהודה בריה דרבי שמעון בן פזי: ק"ג פרשיות אמר דוד, ולא אמר "הללויה" עד שראה במפלתן של רשעים, שנאמר: "יתמו חטאים מן הארץ ורשעים עוד אינם ברכי נפשי את ה' הללויה". הני ק"ג, ק"ד הוין! אלא שמע מינה: "אשרי האיש" ו"למה רגשו גוים" חדא פרשה היא. דאמר ר' שמואל בר נחמני אמר רבי יוחנן:

כל

תורה אור: בראשית טו; שמות יב; תהלים סח; שמות יב; שם ג; שם; מ"א יח; שם; תהלים עב; שם; תהלים קד

אותו צדיק. אנכרים: כמצודה שאין בה דגן. דרך לציידי עופות לזרוק דגן תחת מצודות כדי שיבאו עופות וילכדון, וכשאין בה דגן אין עוף פונה אליה, כך ריקנו המצרים מכל ממונם. "וינצלו" – כתרגומו: ורוקינו: כמצולה שאין בה דגים. כמו מצולות ים, כלומר: בתוך התהום אין מצויין דגים, אלא על שפת הים היכא דאיכא מזון: דיה לצרה בשעתה. דיה לצרה שיתאוננו בה בשעה שתבא עליהם, למה תדאיבם עכשיו בבשורה קשה שתסיח דעתם. מלבא בלבם מזימה של רשע להכחישני ולומר: על ידי כשפים הבאתי האש הזאת: מתני' תכלת. ירוק הוא, וקרוב לצבע כרתי שקורין פוריי"ש: גמ' בין תכלת שבה ללבן שבה. גיזת צמר שצבעה תכלת, ויש בה מקומות שלא עלה שם הצבע יפה: ערוד. חמור הבר: לתפילין. להניח תפילין, שמצות הנחתן קודם קריאת שמע. בפ' שני (ד' יד:): ותיקין. אנשים ענוים ומחבבין מצוה: מתפלל ביום. דהנץ החמה לדברי הכל יום הוא: מאי קראה. דמצוה להתפלל עם הנץ החמה: דכתיב ייראוך עם שמש וגו'. מתי מתיראין ממך – כשמוראך מקבלים עליהם, דהיינו מלכות שמים שמקבלין עליהם בק"ש(ב): עם שמש. כלומר: כשהשמש יוצא, היינו עם הנץ החמה: ולפני ירח. אף תפלת המנחה מצותה עם דמדומי חמה: שאם יזכה. לעוה"ב לראות גדולתן של ישראל: יבחין. כמה הרבה גדולתן יותר על האומות עכשיו: תהא. הא דרבי יוחנן בתפלת ערבית, דלא חיישינן לסמוך גאולה לתפלה, דגאולה ביממא הואי: דא"ר יהודה בריה דר' שמעון. גרסי':

פתח

אלא בין תכלת ללבן שבה. פי' רש"י: צמר הצבוע תכלת ויש מקומות שלא עלה שם הצבע שפיר. וקשה, דאמרינן במנחות: (מג ב ושם) ראה מצוה זו שבה תלוי מצוה אחרת, ואיזו זו ק"ש. כדתנן עד שיכיר בין תכלת ללבן. ואי קאי אגיזת צמר, אינה תלויה בציצית! ועוד: בלילה נמי פעמים יכולין לראות צמר שאינו צבוע כדרכו! ע"כ יש לפרש: בין תכלת שבה – בציצית, שהיה קבוע בו תכלת וגם שני חוטין לבן, ועושין בו חוליא של תכלת וחוליא של לבן: **אחרים** אומרים עד שיראה חברו וכו'. בירושלמי: במה אנן קיימין, אי ברגיל – אפי' ברחוק טפי חכים ליה. ואי בשאינו רגיל – אפילו בקרוב נמי לא חכים ליה. תפתר ברגיל ואינו רגיל, כההיא אכסניא דאתי לקילין. וצריך לומר דהאי אחרים לאו ר' מאיר נינהו, דהא ר' מאיר איירי לעיל מינייהו*: **לק"ש** כותיקין. תימה: דלעיל פסקינן כמאן דמתיר לאחר עמוד השחר מיד, ולקמן פסקי' הלכה כר' יהושע דאמר עד ג' שעות, והכא פסק אביי שהוא בתרא ואמר כותיקין ומשמע דהכי הלכתא! וי"ל: דודאי זמן ק"ש מתחיל לאחר עמוד השחר, וזמנו עד ג' שעות, ומיהו – מצוה מן המובחר כותיקין, סמוך להנץ החמה כדי לסמוך גאולה לתפלה. ואפי' ותיקין נמי מודו לרבי יהושע, שאם לא קרא קודם הנץ החמה – דיכול לקרות עד שלש שעות, ועל זה אנו סומכין. וכן בפ' "מי שמתו" (דף כ"ב ב) דקאמר: בעל קרי שירד לטבול אם יכול לעלות ולקרות קודם הנץ וכו', ומסיק בגמרא (דף כ"ה ב): דילמא כר' יהושע וכותיקין. כלומר: מתני' דקתני קודם הנץ החמה – כותיקין. אלמא: ותיקין נמי מודו לר' יהושע שאין שעה עוברת עד שלש שעות. ומיהו, קשה: דאמרינן ביומא (דף לז. ושם): אף היא עשתה נברשת של זהב, כיון שהחמה זורחת היו נצוצות יוצאות הימנה, והיו יודעין שהגיע הנץ החמה, ובא זמן ק"ש של שחרית. ומוקי לה התם, בשאר עמא דירושלים – אלמא משמע דעיקר זמן ק"ש לאחר הנץ החמה, והא לא הוי כותיקין שהיו קורין קודם להנץ, סמוך להנץ! וי"ל: דאותו זמן הוקבע לצבור לפי שלא היו יכולין להקדים ולמהר כותיקין, כי רוב בני אדם אינם יכולין לכוון אותה שעה:

**כל** הסומך גאולה לתפלה אינו נזוק. וא"ת: והלא כל העולם סומכין גאולה לתפלה, ומאי רבותיה דרב ברונא דלא פסיק חוכא מפומיה? ויש לומר, דהכי קאמר: כל הסומך גאולה לתפלה כותיקין, שקורין ק"ש קודם הנץ ותפלה לאחר הנץ:

כל

**מ** א ב מיי' פ"א מהלכות ק"ש הלכה יא ופ"ד מהל' תפילין הלכה י סמג עשין יח טוש"ע או"ח סימן נח סעיף א' ובסי' פט סעיף א:

**מא** ג מיי' פ"ז מהלכות תפלה הלכה יז סמג עשין י"ט טוש"ע או"ח סימן סו סעיף ח וסי' קי"א סעיף א:

**מב** ד מיי' פ"ג מהל' אבל הלכה יד טור שו"ע או"ח סימן רכד סעיף ט [רב אלפס לקמן פרק הרואה דף מז:]:

**מג** ה [מיי' פ"ז מהל' תפלה הלכה יח] סמ"ג עשין יט טוש"ע או"ח סימן רלו סעיף ב:

[ע' תוס' סוטה יב. וע"ז סד:]

## הגהות הב"ח

(א) במשנה וגומרה עד הנץ. נ"ב ר"א הוא דקאמר לה עיין לקמן דף כ"ה ריש ע"ב: (ב) רש"י ד"ה ייראוך וכו' בק"ש. נכתב בלדו עי' לקמן דף כט ע"ב פי' רש"י ייראוך עם שמש זו תפלת יוצר היפך ממה שפי' כאן אק"ש:

[נ"א ל"ג עי' תוי"ט]

[עי' תוס' מנחות מג: ד"ה בין וכו' דלו פי' רש"י דהכא ופי' באופן אחר]

לקמן כה: כו.

תוספתא פ"א

## רב נסים גאון

**אחרים** אומרים כדי שיראה את חברו ברחוק ד' אמות ויכירנו. הא מילתא איתמר עלה בגמ' דבני מערבא מה אנן קיימין אם ברגיל אפי' ברחוק כמה חכים ליה ואי בשאינו רגיל אפי' קאים גביה לא חכים ליה אלא כאן אנו קיימין ברגיל ואינו רגיל כההוא דאזיל לאכסניא ואתי לקיצין: **העיד** (ר' שמעון) [ר"י] בן אליקים משום קהלה קדושה בגמ' דבני מערבא במס' דמעשר שני (ספ"ב הלכה ד') פרשו עדה קדושה ר' יוסי בן (משולם) [המשולם] ור' שמעון בן מנסיא ובמס' דיום טוב בפרק אין צדין (דף כז) גרסי' אמר ר' שמעון בן פזי אמר ר' יהושע בן לוי אמר ר' יוסי בן שאול אמר ר' משום קהלה קדושה שבירושלים *)ר' שמעון בן מנסיא וחבריו ובאגדתא דקהלת (פסוק רלה חיים) למה קורין אותן עדה קדושה שהיו משלשין את היום שליש לתפלה שליש לתורה שליש למלאכה ויש אומרים על שהיו יגעים בתורה בימות החורף ובמלאכה בימות הקיץ ר' יצחק בן אלעזר קרי לר' שמלאי ברקי עדה קדושה שהיו משלשין את היום ויש אומרים על שהיו יגעין בתורה וכו':

*) ע"ש בגמ' ורש"י וצ"ע.

פסחים קיט. [וע"ש ד"ה כמצודה]

[לעיל ו.]

[מנחות מג:]

[לקמן ד' כה:]

[לעיל דף ג:]

[פירש"י על זה תמצא י:]

תוספתא פ"א

[פי' קורחין עי' תוס' מז: ועי' תוס' יומא סוף ד"ה אמר אביי]

לקמן יט: נח.

לעיל ד:

ג"ז שם

שם

פָּתַח בְּאַשְׁרֵי וְסִיֵּים בְּאַשְׁרֵי. אַלְמָא חֲדָא הִיא, ד"אַשְׁרֵי כָּל חוֹסֵי בוֹ" סִיּוּמָא ד"לָמָּה רָגְשׁוּ גוֹיִם" הוּא: בִּרְיוֹנֵי. פָּרִיצִים: חַטָּאִים כְּתִיב. קְרֵי בֵּיהּ חֲטָאִים שֶׁיִּכְלֶה יֵצֶר הָרָע: שְׁפֵיל. הַשְׁפֵּיל עַצְמְךָ לְסוֹף הַמִּקְרָא. כָּל דָּבָר שֶׁהוּא בַּסּוֹף קָרוּי שִׁפּוּלוֹ שֶׁל דָּבָר: סְמוּכִים לָעַד לְעוֹלָם. בְּדִבְרֵי תוֹרָה כְּתִיב, [אַחֲרָיו] "נֶאֱמָנִים כָּל פִּקּוּדָיו" סְמוּכִים (ג) – סְמִיכַת כָּל פִּקּוּדָיו "עֲשׂוּיִם בֶּאֱמֶת וְיָשָׁר" וּלְצוֹרֶךְ, וְלֹא דָּבָר רֵק: כְּלוּם יֵשׁ עֶבֶד שֶׁמּוֹרֵד בְּרַבּוֹ. וְיָבֹא לְהַכְחִישׁ אֶת דִּבְרֵי הַנָּבִיא: אֱמוֹר לוֹ כְּלוּם יֵשׁ בֵּן כו'. וְהָא חָזֵינַן הָכָא דַּהֲוָה: הָכָא נַמִי הֲוָה. סוֹפֵיהּ לִהְיוֹת: וְאָמַר שִׁירָה. כְּנֶגֶד כּוּלָּם אָמַר שִׁירָה לִכְשֶׁשָּׁרְתָה רוּחַ הַקֹּדֶשׁ עָלָיו:

תורה אור

וְכָל קְרָבַי. עַל שֵׁם קִרְבֵי אִמּוֹ שֶׁדָּר בְּתוֹכָן: מַאי מַשְׁמַע. דְּעַל יוֹם הַמִּיתָה נֶאֱמַר: בֹּא וּרְאֵה וְכוּ'. הוּא סָבַר דְּהָכִי בָּעֵי: מַאי שְׁנָא קְרָבַיִם דְּנָקַט: חֲמִשָּׁה בָּרְכִי נַפְשִׁי. לְעֵיל חָשִׁיב לְהוּ: מַאי דִּכְתִיב מִי כְּהֶחָכָם וּמִי יוֹדֵעַ פֵּשֶׁר דָּבָר. מִשּׁוּם דְּאַיְירִי בְּסוֹפָהּ בִּסְמִיכַת גְּאוּלָּה לִתְפִלָּה נָקַט לֵיהּ: דְּאַשְׁכְּחַן דַּאֲזַל אֵלִיָּהוּ לְגַבֵּי אַחְאָב. דִּכְתִיב "וַיֵּלֶךְ אֵלִיָּהוּ לְהֵרָאוֹת אֶל אַחְאָב": יְהוֹרָם אֲזַל לְגַבֵּי אֱלִישָׁע. כְּשֶׁהָלְכוּ עַל מוֹאָב הוּא וִיהוֹשָׁפָט (במלכים ב ג). דְּמִתּוֹךְ שֶׁלֹּא הָיוּ הוֹלְכִים זֶה אֵצֶל זֶה לֹא הָיָה מוֹכִיחוֹ עַל שֶׁלֹּא נָשָׂא אִשָּׁה: כַּבְשֵׁי דְּרַחֲמָנָא. סְתָרִים דְּהקב"ה, כְּמוֹ "רֵישָׁא בְּכִבְשָׁא" (חולין ד' נג:) בְּהַטְמָנַת הָאֵפֶר: נִגְזְרָה גְּזֵרָה. שְׁמוּעוֹת: מְקוּבְּלַנִי מִבֵּית אֲבִי אַבָּא. דָּוִד, שֶׁרָאָה אֶת הַמַּלְאָךְ וְחַרְבּוֹ שְׁלוּפָה בְּיָדוֹ בְּסוֹף סֵפֶר שְׁמוּאֵל (ב כד), וְלֹא מָנַע עַצְמוֹ מִן הָרַחֲמִים:
חָבִי

כָּל פָּרָשָׁה שֶׁהָיְתָה חֲבִיבָה עַל דָּוִד, פָּתַח בָּהּ
בְּ"אַשְׁרֵי" וְסִיֵּים בָּהּ בְּ"אַשְׁרֵי"; פָּתַח בְּ"אַשְׁרֵי" –
תהלים א דִּכְתִיב, °"אַשְׁרֵי הָאִישׁ", וְסִיֵּים בְּ"אַשְׁרֵי" – דִּכְתִיב,
שם ב °"אַשְׁרֵי כָּל חוֹסֵי בוֹ".§ הָנְהוּ בִּרְיוֹנֵי דַּהֲווּ
בְּשִׁבָבוּתֵיהּ דר"מ וַהֲווּ קָא מְצַעֲרוּ לֵיהּ טוּבָא,
הֲוָה קָא בָּעֵי ר' מֵאִיר רַחֲמֵי עֲלַוַיְהוּ כִּי הֵיכִי
דְּלִימוּתוּ. אֲמַרָה לֵיהּ בְּרוּרְיָא דְּבֵיתְהוּ: מַאי דַּעְתָּךְ? –
שם קד מִשּׁוּם דִּכְתִיב: °"יִתַּמּוּ חַטָּאִים", מִי כְּתִיב 'חוֹטְאִים'?!
חַטָּאִים כְּתִיב! וְעוֹד, שְׁפִיל לְסֵיפֵיהּ דִּקְרָא: "וּרְשָׁעִים
עוֹד אֵינָם", כֵּיוָן דְּיִתַּמּוּ חַטָּאִים – וּרְשָׁעִים עוֹד אֵינָם? אֶלָּא, °בְּעֵי רַחֲמֵי עֲלַוַיְהוּ דְּלִהְדְּרוּ
בִּתְשׁוּבָה – "וּרְשָׁעִים עוֹד אֵינָם". בְּעָא רַחֲמֵי עֲלַוַיְהוּ וַהֲדַרוּ בִּתְשׁוּבָה. אֲמַר לָהּ הַהוּא
ישעיה נד מִינָא לִבְרוּרְיָא: כְּתִיב °"רָנִּי עֲקָרָה לֹא יָלָדָה" – מִשּׁוּם דְּלֹא יָלְדָה – רָנִּי?! אֲמַרָה לֵיהּ: שַׁטְיָא!
שְׁפִיל לְסֵיפֵיהּ דִּקְרָא, דִּכְתִיב: "כִּי רַבִּים בְּנֵי שׁוֹמֵמָה מִבְּנֵי בְעוּלָה אָמַר ה'"; *אֶלָּא
ילדה כצ"ל רש"ל מַאי "עֲקָרָה לֹא יָלָדָה" – רָנִּי כְּנֶסֶת יִשְׂרָאֵל שֶׁדּוֹמָה לְאִשָּׁה עֲקָרָה שֶׁלֹּא יָלְדָה בָּנִים
תהלים ג לְגֵיהִנָּם כְּוָתַיְיכוּ.§ א"ל: הַהוּא מִינָא לר' אַבָּהוּ, כְּתִיב °"מִזְמוֹר לְדָוִד בְּבָרְחוֹ מִפְּנֵי
שם נז אַבְשָׁלוֹם בְּנוֹ", וּכְתִיב °"לְדָוִד מִכְתָּם בְּבָרְחוֹ מִפְּנֵי שָׁאוּל בַּמְּעָרָה", הֵי מַעֲשֶׂה הֲוָה
בְּרֵישָׁא? מִכְּדֵי מַעֲשֵׂה שָׁאוּל הֲוָה בְּרֵישָׁא, – לִכְתּוֹב בְּרֵישָׁא! אֲמַר לֵיהּ: אַתּוּן דְּלָא
[דף ז. ע"ש] דָּרְשִׁיתוּן סְמוּכִין – קַשְׁיָא לְכוּ, אֲנַן דְּדָרְשִׁינַן סְמוּכִים – לָא קַשְׁיָא לַן. *דא"ר יוֹחָנָן:
תהלים קיא סְמוּכִין מִן הַתּוֹרָה מִנַּיִן – שֶׁנֶּאֱמַר: °"סְמוּכִים לָעַד לְעוֹלָם עֲשׂוּיִם בֶּאֱמֶת וְיָשָׁר". לָמָּה
נִסְמְכָה פָּרָשַׁת אַבְשָׁלוֹם לְפָרָשַׁת גּוֹג וּמָגוֹג – שֶׁאִם יֹאמַר לְךָ אָדָם: כְּלוּם יֵשׁ עֶבֶד שֶׁמּוֹרֵד בְּרַבּוֹ?! אַף אַתָּה אֱמוֹר לוֹ:
כְּלוּם יֵשׁ בֵּן שֶׁמּוֹרֵד בְּאָבִיו?! אֶלָּא – הֲוָה, הָכָא נַמִי – הֲוָה.§ אָמַר רִבִּי יוֹחָנָן מִשּׁוּם רַבִּי שִׁמְעוֹן בֶּן יוֹחַי, מַאי דִּכְתִיב:
משלי לא °"פִּיהָ פָּתְחָה בְחָכְמָה וְתוֹרַת חֶסֶד עַל לְשׁוֹנָהּ", כְּנֶגֶד מִי אָמַר שְׁלֹמֹה מִקְרָא זֶה? לֹא אֲמָרוֹ אֶלָּא כְּנֶגֶד דָּוִד
תהלים קג אָבִיו, שֶׁדָּר בַּחֲמִשָּׁה עוֹלָמִים וְאָמַר שִׁירָה; דָּר בִּמְעֵי אִמּוֹ וְאָמַר שִׁירָה, שֶׁנֶּאֱמַר: °"בָּרְכִי נַפְשִׁי אֶת ה' וְכָל קְרָבַי
שם אֶת שֵׁם קָדְשׁוֹ". יָצָא לַאֲוִיר הָעוֹלָם וְנִסְתַּכֵּל בְּכוֹכָבִים וּמַזָּלוֹת וְאָמַר שִׁירָה, שֶׁנֶּאֱמַר: °"בָּרְכוּ ה' מַלְאָכָיו גִּבֹּרֵי
כֹחַ עֹשֵׂי דְבָרוֹ לִשְׁמֹעַ בְּקוֹל דְּבָרוֹ בָּרְכוּ ה' כָּל צְבָאָיו וגו'". יָנַק מִשְּׁדֵי אִמּוֹ וְנִסְתַּכֵּל בְּדַדֶּיהָ וְאָמַר שִׁירָה, שֶׁנֶּאֱמַר:
שם °"בָּרְכִי נַפְשִׁי אֶת ה' וְאַל תִּשְׁכְּחִי כָּל גְּמוּלָיו". מַאי כָּל גְּמוּלָיו? אָמַר ר' אַבָּהוּ: שֶׁעָשָׂה לָהּ דַּדִּים בִּמְקוֹם בִּינָה. טַעְמָא
[נ"ל רב] מַאי? אָמַר (רַבִּי) יְהוּדָה: כְּדֵי שֶׁלֹּא יִסְתַּכֵּל בִּמְקוֹם עֶרְוָה; רַב מַתְנָא אָמַר: כְּדֵי שֶׁלֹּא יִינַק מִמְּקוֹם הַטִּנּוֹפֶת. רָאָה
תהלים קד בְּמַפַּלְתָּן שֶׁל רְשָׁעִים וְאָמַר שִׁירָה, שֶׁנֶּאֱמַר: °"יִתַּמּוּ חַטָּאִים מִן הָאָרֶץ וּרְשָׁעִים עוֹד אֵינָם בָּרְכִי נַפְשִׁי אֶת ה'
שם הַלְלוּיָהּ". נִסְתַּכֵּל בְּיוֹם הַמִּיתָה וְאָמַר שִׁירָה, שֶׁנֶּאֱמַר: °"בָּרְכִי נַפְשִׁי אֶת ה' ה' אֱלֹהַי גָּדַלְתָּ מְּאֹד הוֹד וְהָדָר לָבָשְׁתָּ".
שם מַאי מַשְׁמַע (א) דְּעַל יוֹם הַמִּיתָה נֶאֱמַר? אָמַר רַבָּה בַּר רַב שֵׁילָא: מִסֵּיפָא דְּעִנְיָינָא, דִּכְתִיב: °"תַּסְתִּיר פָּנֶיךָ יִבָּהֵלוּן תֹּסֵף
רוּחָם יִגְוָעוּן וגו'".§ רַב שִׁימִי בַּר עוּקְבָא וְאָמְרִי לַהּ מָר עוּקְבָא הֲוָה שְׁכִיחַ קַמֵּיהּ דר' שִׁמְעוֹן בֶּן פָּזִי, וַהֲוָה מְסַדֵּר אַגַּדְתָּא
שם קג קַמֵּיהּ דר' יְהוֹשֻׁעַ בֶּן לֵוִי; אֲמַר לֵיהּ: מַאי דִּכְתִיב °"בָּרְכִי נַפְשִׁי אֶת ה' וְכָל קְרָבַי אֶת שֵׁם קָדְשׁוֹ"? אֲמַר לֵיהּ: בֹּא וּרְאֵה
[מגילה יד. ע"ש] שֶׁלֹּא כְּמִדַּת הַקָּדוֹשׁ בָּרוּךְ הוּא מִדַּת בָּשָׂר וָדָם; *מִדַּת בָּשָׂר וָדָם – צָר צוּרָה עַל גַּבֵּי הַכּוֹתֶל וְאֵינוֹ יָכוֹל לְהַטִּיל
בָּהּ רוּחַ וּנְשָׁמָה, קְרָבַיִם וּבְנֵי מֵעַיִם; וְהקב"ה אֵינוֹ כֵּן, צָר צוּרָה בְּתוֹךְ צוּרָה וּמַטִּיל בָּהּ רוּחַ וּנְשָׁמָה, קְרָבַיִם וּבְנֵי
שמואל א ב מֵעַיִם. וְהַיְינוּ דַּאֲמַרָה חַנָּה: °"אֵין קָדוֹשׁ כַּה' כִּי אֵין בִּלְתֶּךָ וְאֵין צוּר כֵּאלֹהֵינוּ". מַאי "אֵין צוּר כֵּאלֹהֵינוּ"? – אֵין צַיָּיר
[ע"ש היטב] כֵּאלֹהֵינוּ. *מַאי "כִּי אֵין בִּלְתֶּךָ"? – אָמַר ר' יְהוּדָה בַּר מְנַסְיָא: אַל תִּקְרֵי "כִּי אֵין בִּלְתֶּךָ" אֶלָּא "אֵין לְבַלּוֹתֶךָ", שֶׁלֹּא כְּמִדַּת
הַקָּדוֹשׁ בָּרוּךְ הוּא מִדַּת בָּשָׂר וָדָם: מִדַּת בָּשָׂר וָדָם – מַעֲשֵׂה יָדָיו מְבַלִּין אוֹתוֹ, וְהקב"ה מְבַלֶּה מַעֲשָׂיו. א"ל: אֲנָא הָכִי
קָא אָמֵינָא לָךְ, הָנֵי חֲמִשָּׁה "בָּרְכִי נַפְשִׁי" כְּנֶגֶד מִי אֲמָרָן דָּוִד? – לֹא אֲמָרָן אֶלָּא כְּנֶגֶד הקב"ה וּכְנֶגֶד נְשָׁמָה. מָה הקב"ה
מָלֵא כָּל הָעוֹלָם – אַף נְשָׁמָה מְלֵאָה אֶת כָּל הַגּוּף; מָה הַקָּדוֹשׁ בָּרוּךְ הוּא רוֹאֶה וְאֵינוֹ נִרְאֶה – אַף נְשָׁמָה רוֹאָה וְאֵינָהּ
נִרְאֵית; מָה הקב"ה זָן אֶת כָּל הָעוֹלָם כֻּלּוֹ – אַף נְשָׁמָה זָנָה אֶת כָּל הַגּוּף; מָה הקב"ה טָהוֹר – אַף נְשָׁמָה טְהוֹרָה; מָה
הקב"ה יוֹשֵׁב בְּחַדְרֵי חֲדָרִים – אַף נְשָׁמָה יוֹשֶׁבֶת בְּחַדְרֵי חֲדָרִים; יָבֹא מִי שֶׁיֵּשׁ בּוֹ חֲמִשָּׁה דְבָרִים הַלָּלוּ וִישַׁבַּח לְמִי
קהלת ח שֶׁיֵּשׁ בּוֹ חֲמִשָּׁה דְבָרִים הַלָּלוּ.§ אָמַר רַב הַמְנוּנָא: מַאי דִּכְתִיב: °"מִי כְּהֶחָכָם וּמִי יוֹדֵעַ פֵּשֶׁר דָּבָר"? מִי כְּהַקָּדוֹשׁ
בָּרוּךְ הוּא שֶׁיּוֹדֵעַ לַעֲשׂוֹת פְּשָׁרָה בֵּין שְׁנֵי צַדִּיקִים, בֵּין חִזְקִיָּהוּ לִישַׁעְיָהוּ. חִזְקִיָּהוּ אָמַר: "לֵיתֵי יְשַׁעְיָהוּ גַּבָּאִי,
מלכים א יח דְּהָכִי אַשְׁכְּחַן בְּאֵלִיָּהוּ דַּאֲזַל לְגַבֵּי אַחְאָב, (שֶׁנֶּאֱמַר: °"וַיֵּלֶךְ אֵלִיָּהוּ לְהֵרָאוֹת אֶל אַחְאָב")". יְשַׁעְיָהוּ אָמַר: "לֵיתֵי חִזְקִיָּהוּ
גַּבַּאי, דְּהָכִי אַשְׁכְּחַן בִּיהוֹרָם בֶּן אַחְאָב דַּאֲזַל לְגַבֵּי אֱלִישָׁע". מֶה עָשָׂה הקב"ה – הֵבִיא יִסּוּרִים עַל חִזְקִיָּהוּ, וְאָמַר לוֹ
מלכים ב כ ישעיה לח לִישַׁעְיָהוּ: לֵךְ וּבַקֵּר אֶת הַחוֹלֶה; שֶׁנֶּאֱמַר: °"בַּיָּמִים הָהֵם חָלָה חִזְקִיָּהוּ לָמוּת וַיָּבֹא אֵלָיו יְשַׁעְיָהוּ בֶן אָמוֹץ הַנָּבִיא וַיֹּאמֶר
אֵלָיו: כֹּה אָמַר ה' (צְבָאוֹת) צַו לְבֵיתֶךָ כִּי מֵת אַתָּה וְלֹא תִחְיֶה וגו'". מַאי "כִּי מֵת אַתָּה וְלֹא תִחְיֶה" – "מֵת אַתָּה" – בָּעוֹלָם
הַזֶּה, "וְלֹא תִחְיֶה" – לָעוֹלָם הַבָּא. אֲמַר לֵיהּ: מַאי כּוּלֵּי הַאי? אֲמַר לֵיהּ: מִשּׁוּם דְּלָא עָסְקַתְּ בִּפְרִיָּה וּרְבִיָּה. א"ל: מִשּׁוּם דַּחֲזַאי
לִי בְּרוּחַ הַקֹּדֶשׁ °דִּנְפָקֵי מִינַּאי בְּנִין דְּלָא מַעַלּוּ. א"ל: בַּהֲדֵי כַּבְשֵׁי דְרַחֲמָנָא לָמָּה לָךְ? מַאי דְּמִפַּקְדַתְּ אִיבָּעֵי לָךְ לְמֶעְבַּד,
וּמַה דְּנִיחָא קַמֵּיהּ קוּדְשָׁא בְּרִיךְ הוּא – לֶעְבֵּיד. אֲמַר לֵיהּ: הַשְׁתָּא הַב לִי בְּרַתָּךְ, אֶפְשָׁר דְּגָרְמָא זְכוּתָא דִּידִי וְדִידָךְ וְנָפְקִי
מִנַּאי בְּנִין דְּמַעַלּוּ. א"ל: כְּבָר נִגְזְרָה עָלֶיךָ גְּזֵירָה. אֲמַר לֵיהּ: בֶּן אָמוֹץ, כַּלֵּה נְבוּאָתְךָ וָצֵא! כָּךְ מְקוּבְּלַנִי מִבֵּית אֲבִי אַבָּא – °אֲפִי'
חֶרֶב חַדָּה מוּנַּחַת עַל צַוָּארוֹ שֶׁל אָדָם אַל יִמְנַע עַצְמוֹ מִן הָרַחֲמִים. אִתְּמַר נַמִּי, רִבִּי יוֹחָנָן וְרִבִּי *(אֱלִיעֶזֶר) דְּאָמְרֵי
איוב יג תַּרְוַיְיהוּ: אֲפִילּוּ חֶרֶב חַדָּה מוּנַּחַת עַל צַוָּארוֹ שֶׁל אָדָם אַל יִמְנַע עַצְמוֹ מִן הָרַחֲמִים, שֶׁנֶּא': °"הֵן יִקְטְלֵנִי לוֹ אֲיַחֵל" (ב).§
א"ר

**כל** פרשה שהיתה חביבה על דוד כו'. וא"ת: מאי 'כל הפרשיות'? והא לא אשכחן שום פרשה אחרת שמתחלת באשרי ומסיימת באשרי אלא היא! וי"ל דלאו דוקא "פתח באשרי וסיים באשרי", אלא חתימה מעין פתיחה, כמו תהלה, שפתח ב'תהלה' וסיים ב'תהלה', "תהלת ה' ידבר פי". וכן הרבה פרשיות שמתחילות בהללויה ומסיימות בהללויה:
גדול

**אמר** לה ההוא מינא לברוריא. ברוריא היא בתו של ר' חנינא בן תרדיון והיא היתה אשתו של ר' מאיר ואית' בפירקא קמא דמסכת ע"ז (דף יח) ברוריא דביתהו דר' מאי' ברתי' דר' חנניה בן תרדיון הואי וכבר למדה הרבה חכמות לפני החכמים כדאמרינן בפסחים בפ' תמיד (דף סב:) אמר ליה ומה ברוריא דביתהו דר' מאיר ברתי' דר' חנניה בן תרדיון דהות גמרא תלת מאה (משמעי) [שמעתתא] ביומא מתלת מאה רבותא:
**למה** נסמכה פרשת אבשלום לפרשת גוג ומגוג. פרש' גוג ומגוג הוא המזמור הראשון שכתוב בו יתיצבו מלכי ארץ *)קשה תרבות רעה בתוך ביתו של אדם יותר ממלחמת גוג ומגוג והתם בפרק לפני אידיהן של גוים (ע"ז דף ג) גרסי' לעתיד באים אומות העולם ומתגיירין ומניחין תפילין בראשיהן ותפילין בזרועותיהן ומזוזה בפתחיהן כיון שרואין מלחמת גוג ומגוג אומר להם על מי אתם באים על ה' ועל משיחו שנא' (תהלים ב) למה רגשו גוים [וגו'] יתיצבו מלכי ארץ מיד כל אחד ואחד מנתק מוסרותיו והולך לו שנא' ננתקה את מוסרותימו וגו' וכולא ברייתא:

*) פה ניכר חסרון קצת. ועי' לעיל ז' ב'.

## הגהות הב"ח

(א) גמ' מאי משמע אמר רבה בר ר' שילא כצ"ל ותיבות דעל יום המיתה נאמר נמחק: (ב) שם הן יקטלני לו איחל לסוף יהב ליה ברתיה נפק מיניה מנשה ורבשקה יומא חדא ארכבינהו אכתפיה לאמטויינהו לבי מדרשא אמר חד מינייהו חזי רישא דאבא למטוי ביה גלדאי וחד אמר חזי רישא דאבא לאקרובי עליה לעכו"ם חבטינהו בארעא מנשה חיה ורבשקה מית קרי אנפשיה וכלי כליו רעים [ישעיה לב] אמר רב חנן אפילו בעל: (ג) רש"י ד"ה סמוכים וכו' סמוכים לעד סמיכת כל:

## גליון הש"ס

**גמ'** בעי רחמי. עיין תענית כג ב ובזוה"ק פ' וירא במדרש הנעלם בפ' המכסה אני מאברהם: **שם** דנפקי מינאי. עי' טורי אבן ר"ה יז ב ד"ה ל"ק: **שם** אפילו חרב חדה. עי' תוס' נדה טז ב ד"ה הכל:

[נ"ל אלעזר]

**אבי אבא שחפה את ההיכל.** שלמה: שגנז ספר רפואות. כדי שיבקשו רחמים: גירר עצמות אביו. לפי שהיה רשע – בזהו, ולא נהג בו כבוד בקבורתו להוציאו כהוגן במטות זהב וכסף: סתם מי גיחון. מי שלוח, בדברי הימים (ב לב). ולמה – כדי שלא יבאו מלכי אשור וימצאו מים לשתות. ולא זהו גיחון הנהר הגדול, דההוא לאו בא"י הוא, אלא מעין קטן הוא, סמוך לירושלים, שנאמר "והורדתם אותו אל גיחון" (מ"א א) ומתרגמינן: ותחתון יתיה לשילוחא: עבר ניסן בניסן. קס"ד: משנתקדש החדש לשם ניסן נמלך לעבר את השנה ועשאו אדר. כמו שנאמר בדברי הימים (ב ל) "ויועץ המלך (חזקיהו) לעשות הפסח בחדש השני": ביום שלשים של אדר. ואע"פ שלא נתקדש החדש, שעדיין לא באו עדים: התולה בזכות עצמו. שאומר בתפלתו: עשה לי בזכותי, כגון חזקיהו שאמר "זכר נא את אשר התהלכתי לפניך" (א) וגו': פרועה. מגולה, שניטלה (ב) תקרה שלה: הרוצה להנות. משל אחרים: יהנה. ואין איסור בדבר: כאלישע. כמו שמצינו באלישע שנהנה: והרוצה שלא להנות. משל אחרים: אל יהנה. ואין בדבר לא משום גסות רוח ולא משום שנאה: כשמואל הרמתי. כמו שמצינו בשמואל הרמתי, שלא רצה להנות: כי שם ביתו. לעיל מיניה כתיב "והיה מדי שנה בשנה וסבב בית אל והמצפה ושפט את ישראל" וסמיך ליה "ותשובתו הרמתה כי שם ביתו", וכי איני יודע ששם ביתו? אלא אכולהו מקומות דקרא דלעיל מיניה קאי, שכל מקום שהיה הולך שם היה נושא כל כלי תשמישי בית עמו ואהל חנייתו, שלא להנות מן אחרים: בהוד יפיה. בדדיה: תפלה לעני. דרך עניות: יכוין את רגליו. זו אצל זו: ורגליהם רגל ישרה. נראין כרגל אחד: *הקורא מכאן ואילך לא הפסיד. שהרי הוא כאדם שקורא אחת מכל הפרשיות שבתורה, ואע"פ שלא יצא ידי ק"ש – יש לו קבול שכר כעוסק בתורה: **מתני'** יטה. על צדו: "בשכבך". דרך שכיבה: יעמוד. דכתיב "ובקומך": כדרכו. או בקימה, או בשכיבה, או בישיבה, או מהלך:

גמ'

תורה אור

**גדול** הקורא ק"ש בעונתה יותר מהעוסק בתורה. תימה. אפי' תפלה נמי, דהא אמרינן פ"ק דשבת: (דף יא.) כגון אנו מפסיקין בין לק"ש בין לתפלה! וי"ל: דהכי קאמר: יותר מהעוסק בתורה פעם אחרת, שלא בשעת ק"ש. אבל העוסק בתורה בשעת ק"ש – לא איירי, ואפילו בתפלה פוסק: שנאמר

א"ר חנן: אפי' בעל החלומות אומר לו לאדם למחר הוא מת – אל ימנע עצמו מן הרחמים, שנאמר: °"כי ברב חלמות והבלים ודברים הרבה כי את האלהים ירא". מיד: °"ויסב חזקיהו פניו אל הקיר ויתפלל אל ה'". מאי 'קיר'? אמר רשב"ל: מקירות לבו, שנא': °"מעי מעי אוחילה קירות לבי וגו'". ר' לוי אמר: על עסקי הקיר; אמר לפניו: רבונו של עולם, ומה שונמית שלא עשתה אלא קיר אחת קטנה – החיית את בנה, אבי אבא שחפה את ההיכל כולו בכסף ובזהב – על אחת כמה וכמה. °"זכר־נא את אשר התהלכתי לפניך באמת ובלב שלם והטוב בעיניך עשיתי" – מאי "והטוב בעיניך עשיתי"? א"ר יהודה אמר רב: שסמך גאולה לתפלה. ר' לוי אמר: שגנז ספר רפואות. תנו רבנן: *ששה דברים עשה חזקיהו המלך, על ג' הודו לו ועל ג' לא הודו לו. על ג' הודו לו: גנז ספר רפואות – והודו לו, כתת נחש הנחשת – והודו לו, גירר עצמות אביו על מטה של חבלים – והודו לו. ועל ג' לא הודו לו: סתם מי גיחון – ולא הודו לו, קצץ דלתות היכל ושגרם למלך אשור – ולא הודו לו, עבר ניסן בניסן – ולא הודו לו. ומי לית ליה לחזקיהו: °"החדש הזה לכם ראש חדשים" – *זה ניסן ואין אחר ניסן?! אלא, טעה בדשמואל; *דאמר שמואל: אין מעברין את השנה ביום שלשים של אדר, הואיל וראוי לקובעו ניסן, סבר: 'הואיל וראוי' לא אמרינן.§ א"ר יוחנן משום ר' יוסי בן זמרא: כל התולה בזכות עצמו – תולין לו בזכות אחרים, וכל התולה בזכות אחרים – תולין לו בזכות עצמו. משה תלה בזכות אחרים, שנא': °"זכר לאברהם ליצחק ולישראל עבדיך" – תלו לו בזכות עצמו, שנאמר: °"ויאמר להשמידם לולי משה בחירו עמד בפרץ לפניו להשיב חמתו מהשחית"; חזקיהו תלה בזכות עצמו, דכתיב: "זכר־נא את אשר התהלכתי לפניך" – תלו לו בזכות אחרים, שנא': °"וגנותי *אל העיר הזאת להושיעה למעני ולמען דוד עבדי". והיינו דריב"ל; דאמר ריב"ל, מאי דכתיב: °"הנה לשלום מר לי מר"? – אפי' בשעה ששיגר לו הקב"ה שלום – מר הוא לו.§ °"נעשה נא עליית קיר קטנה". רב ושמואל, חד אמר: עלייה פרועה היתה וקירוה, וחד אמר: אכסדרה גדולה היתה וחלקוה לשנים. בשלמא למ"ד אכסדרה – היינו דכתיב 'קיר', אלא למ"ד עלייה – מאי 'קיר'? שקירוה. בשלמא למ"ד 'עלייה' – היינו דכתיב 'עליית', אלא למ"ד אכסדרה – מאי 'עליית'? *מעולה שבבתים. "ונשים לו שם מטה ושלחן וכסא ומנורה". אמר אביי ואיתימא ר' יצחק: הרוצה להנות – יהנה כאלישע, ושאינו רוצה להנות אל יהנה כשמואל הרמתי שנאמר: "ותשובתו הרמתה כי שם ביתו". וא"ר יוחנן: *שכל מקום שהלך שם – ביתו עמו. °"ותאמר אל אישה הנה נא ידעתי כי איש אלהים קדוש הוא". א"ר יוסי בר' חנינא: מכאן, שהאשה מכרת באורחין יותר מן האיש. 'קדוש הוא', מנא ידעה? רב ושמואל, חד אמר: שלא ראתה זבוב עובר על שלחנו; וחד אמר: סדין של פשתן הציעה על מטתו ולא ראתה קרי עליו. 'קדוש הוא' א"ר יוסי בר' חנינא: הוא קדוש, ומשרתו אינו קדוש, (שנא':) °"ויגש גיחזי להדפה". א"ר יוסי בר' חנינא: שאחזה בהוד יפיה. "עובר עלינו תמיד" א"ר יוסי בר' חנינא משום רבי אליעזר בן יעקב: כל המארח תלמיד חכם בתוך ביתו ומהנהו מנכסיו – מעלה עליו הכתוב כאילו מקריב תמידין. וא"ר יוסי בר' חנינא משום ראב"י: *אל יעמוד אדם במקום גבוה ויתפלל, אלא במקום נמוך ויתפלל, שנא': °"ממעמקים קראתיך ה'". תניא נמי הכי: *לא יעמוד אדם לא על גבי כסא ולא ע"ג שרפרף ולא במקום גבוה ויתפלל, אלא במקום נמוך ויתפלל, לפי שאין גבהות לפני המקום, שנאמר "ממעמקים קראתיך ה'" וכתיב: °"תפלה לעני כי יעטף". וא"ר יוסי בר' חנינא משום ראב"י: המתפלל צריך שיכוין את רגליו, שנא': °"ורגליהם רגל ישרה". (א"ר יצחק א"ר יוחנן) וא"ר יוסי בר' חנינא משום ראב"י: מאי דכתיב: °"לא תאכלו על הדם" – [ג]לא תאכלו קודם שתתפללו על דמכם. (א"ד) א"ר יצחק *א"ר יוחנן א"ר יוסי בר' חנינא משום ראב"י: כל האוכל ושותה ואח"כ מתפלל – עליו הכתוב אומר: °"ואתי השלכת אחרי גוך", אל תקרי 'גוך' אלא 'גאיך'. אמר הקב"ה: לאחר שנתגאה זה – קבל עליו מלכות שמים.§ "ר' יהושע אומר, עד ג' שעות".§ אמר רב יהודה אמר שמואל: [ד]הלכה כרבי יהושע.§ "הקורא מכאן ואילך לא הפסיד".§ אמר רב חסדא אמר מר עוקבא, ובלבד שלא יאמר 'יוצר אור'. מיתיבי: "הקורא מכאן ואילך לא הפסיד כאדם שהוא קורא בתורה, אבל מברך הוא שתים לפניה ואחת לאחריה" – תיובתא דרב חסדא! תיובתא. איכא דאמרי, אמר רב חסדא אמר מר עוקבא: מאי 'לא הפסיד' – שלא הפסיד ברכות. תניא נמי הכי: [ה]"הקורא מכאן ואילך לא הפסיד כאדם שקורא בתורה, אבל מברך הוא שתים לפניה ואחת לאחריה. א"ר מני: גדול הקורא ק"ש בעונתה יותר מהעוסק בתורה, מדקתני: הקורא מכאן ואילך לא הפסיד כאדם הקורא בתורה", מכלל דקורא בעונתה – עדיף.§

**מתני'** *בית שמאי אומרים: בערב – כל אדם יטה ויקרא, ובבקר יעמוד, שנאמר: °"ובשכבך ובקומך"? – ובית הלל אומרים: כל אדם קורא *כדרכו שנאמר: ובלכתך בדרך אם כן למה נאמר ובשכבך ובקומך בשעה שבני אדם שוכבים ובשעה שבני אדם עומדים. א"ר טרפון: אני הייתי בא בדרך והטיתי לקרות כדברי ב"ש, וסכנתי בעצמי מפני הלסטים. אמרו לו: כדי היית לחוב בעצמך, שעברת על דברי ב"ה.§

גמ'

תורה אור (מראי מקומות בגליון): קהלת ה; ישעיה לח; ירמיה ד; ישעיה לח; שמות יב; שם לב; תהלים קו; מלכים ב יט; ישעיה לח; מלכים ב ד; שמואל א ז; מלכים ב ד; שם; תהלים קל; שם קב; יחזקאל א; ויקרא יט; מלכים א יד; דברים ו

מסורת הש"ס: מקום שנהגו קף נ.; סנהדרין פ"ק קף; שייך לעיל ט: במה; עי' רש"א בח"א; [נדרים נו. מנחות; נדרים קף לח.; תוספתא לסנהדרין פ"ב; תוספתא פרק ג'; [לפמ"ש תוס' נזיר כט. ד"ה ה"ג ע"ש ניחא הגה' לל"ל יוחנן אר"י ברבי חנינא]; ספרי פרשת ואתחנן; [עי' תוס' לקמן יג: ד"ה על וכו' וכן בכ"מ יש סס ל: בעמילה]

עין משפט נר מצוה:

מד א מיי' פ"ה מהל' תפלה הלכה ז סמג עשין יט טוש"ע או"ח סימן צ ס"א:

מה ב מיי' שם הלכה ד וסמג שם טור שו"ע או"ח סי' צח ס"א:

מו ג מיי' פ"ג שם [ה"ד] סמג שם טוש"ע או"ח סימן פט [ס"ג]:

מז ד מיי' פ"א מהל' ק"ש הלכה יא סמג עשין יח טוש"ע או"ח סימן נח ס"ו:

מח ה מיי' שם הלכה ג' טור שו"ע שם סעיף ז:

מט ו מיי' פ"ב שם הלכה ב וסמג שם טוש"ע או"ח סימן סג ס"א:

**רב נסים גאון**

תנו רבנן ו' דברים [ששה] עשה חזקיהו מלך יהודה הודו לו וכו' גירר עצמות אביו על מטה של חבלים. ומפרש רבנן טעמא דמילתא מהו שגרם לו לעשות בעצמו' אביו כן במס' סנהדרין (דמ"ז) בפ' נגמר הדין כי נתכוון כי היכי דתיהוי ליה כפרה: וינגש גיחזי להדפה אמר (ריש לקיש) [ר' יוסי בר חנינא] שדחפ' בהוד יופיה. בגמ' דבני מערבא בפ' כל ישראל יש להן חלק (הלכה ז) ובפ' שני דיבמות (הלכה ג) אמר ר' יוסי בר חנינא שנתן ידיו בהוד שביופיה בין דדיה:

**הגהות הב"ח** (א) רש"י ד"ה התולה וכו' לפניך וגו' הס"ד ואח"כ מ"ה מר הוא לו על שאמר לו למען דוד עבדי הס"ד: (ב) ד"ה פרוע וכו' תקרה ומעזיבה שלה:

**גליון הש"ס** גמ' מאי קיר. ירושלמי [ברכות פ"ד] ופ' חלק ושם איתא עוד דרשות בזה: **שם** כל המארח ת"ח. עי' יומא ע"א א ובכתובות קה ב: **במשנה** והטיתי כו'. עי' תוס' יבמות יד א ד"ה לא עשו:

גמ' בשלמא ב"ה קא מפרשי טעמייהו וטעמא דב"ש, אלא ב"ש – מ"ט לא אמרי כב"ה? אמרי לך ב"ש: א"כ, נימא קרא 'בבקר ובערב', מאי 'בשכבך ובקומך', בשעת שכיבה – שכיבה ממש, ובשעת קימה – קימה ממש. וב"ש, האי 'ובלכתך בדרך' מאי עביד להו? –ההוא מבעי להו לכדתניא: 'בשבתך בביתך' – פרט לעוסק במצוה, 'ובלכתך בדרך' – פרט לחתן, מכאן אמרו: הכונס את הבתולה – פטור, ואת האלמנה – חייב. מאי משמע? –אמר רב פפא: כי דרך, מה דרך רשות, אף כל – רשות. –מי לא עסקינן דקא אזיל לדבר מצוה, ואפילו הכי אמר רחמנא לקרי! –אם כן, לכתוב רחמנא 'בשבת ובלכת', מאי 'בשבתך ובלכתך'? – בשבת דידך ובלכת דידך הוא דמחייבת, הא דמצוה – פטירת. –אי הכי, אפילו כונס את האלמנה נמי! –האי טריד והאי לא טריד. –אי משום טרדא, אפילו טבעה ספינתו בים נמי! וכי תימא ה"נ, אלמה א"ר אבא בר זבדא אמר רב: אבל חייב בכל המצות האמורות בתורה, חוץ מן התפילין, שהרי נאמר בהם פאר, שנאמר: 'פארך חבוש עליך'! (יחזקאל כד) –התם – טריד טרדא דמצוה, הכא – טריד טרדא דרשות. (א) וב"ש –ההוא מבעי להו: פרט לשלוחי מצוה. וב"ה אמרי: ממילא ש"מ דאפילו בדרך נמי קרי. ת"ר, בה"א: עומדין וקורין, יושבין וקורין, ומטין וקורין, הולכין בדרך וקורין, (ב) עושין במלאכתן וקורין. ומעשה ברבי ישמעאל ור' אלעזר בן עזריה שהיו מסובין במקום אחד, והיה ר' ישמעאל מוטה ור' אלעזר בן עזריה זקוף. כיון שהגיע זמן קריאת שמע, הטה רבי אלעזר וזקף ר' ישמעאל. אמר לו רבי אלעזר בן עזריה לר' ישמעאל: ישמעאל אחי, אמשול לך משל, למה הדבר דומה? – משל לאחד שאומרים לו: זקנך מגודל, אמר להם: יהיה כנגד המשחיתים. אף כך אתה, כל זמן שאני זקוף – אתה מוטה, עכשיו כשאני הטתי – אתה זקפת! אמר לו: אני עשיתי כדברי ב"ה, ואתה עשית כדברי ב"ש; ולא עוד אלא שמא יראו התלמידים ויקבעו הלכה לדורות. מאי "ולא עוד"? –וכי תימא, בית הלל נמי אית להו מטין – ה"מ דמטה ואתא מעיקרא, אבל הכא – כיון דעד השתא הוית זקוף והשתא מוטה, אמרי ש"מ כב"ש סבירא להו, שמא יראו התלמידים ויקבעו הלכה לדורות. תני רב יחזקאל: עשה כדברי ב"ש – עשה, כדברי ב"ה – עשה. רב יוסף אמר: עשה כדברי ב"ש – לא עשה ולא כלום, דתנן: מי שהיה ראשו ורובו בסוכה ושלחנו בתוך הבית – ב"ש פוסלין, וב"ה מכשירין. אמרו להם ב"ה לב"ש: מעשה שהלכו זקני ב"ש וזקני ב"ה לבקר את ר' יוחנן בן החורנית. מצאוהו שהיה ראשו ורובו בסוכה ושלחנו בתוך הבית, ולא אמרו לו כלום. אמרו להם: משם ראיה?! אף הם אמרו לו: א"כ היית נוהג, לא קיימת מצות סוכה מימיך. רב נחמן בר יצחק אמר: עשה כדברי בית שמאי – חייב מיתה, דתנן אמר ר"ט: אני הייתי בא בדרך והטתי לקרות כדברי ב"ש, וסכנתי בעצמי מפני הלסטים. אמרו לו: כדאי היית לחוב בעצמך, שעברת על דברי ב"ה. מתני' בשחר מברך שתים לפניה ואחת לאחריה, ובערב מברך שתים לפניה ושתים לאחריה, אחת ארוכה ואחת קצרה. מקום שאמרו להאריך – אינו רשאי לקצר, לקצר – אינו רשאי להאריך, לחתום – אינו רשאי שלא לחתום, שלא לחתום – אינו רשאי לחתום. גמ' מאי מברך? –אמר ר' יעקב א"ר אושעיא: יוצר

**רש"י**

גמ' בשבתך בביתך פרט לעוסק במצוה. לקמיה מפרש מאי משמע: ובלכתך בדרך פרט לחתן. ואע"ג דחתן נמי עוסק במצוה הוא, אי לאו קרא יתירה לא נפקא לן מקרא קמא, דכיון דעוסק במצוה לא כתיב בקרא בהדיא, אלא מיעוטא בעלמא הוא דקא דרשינן מ'ביתך' וממעטינן מיניה עוסק במלאכת מצוה דאיכא טרדא. אבל חתן דטרדא דמחשבה בעלמא הוא, שמחשב על עסק בתולים, אי לאו קרא יתירה – לא ממעטינן: הכונס את הבתולה פטור. שטרוד במחשבת בעילת מצוה: מאי משמע. "פרט לעוסק במצוה"? כי דרך. 'בשבתך' ו'בלכתך' הוקשו ל'דרך': מי לא עסקינן כו'. כלומר: מנלן דבדרך רשות לחודא איירי קרא, הא קרא 'דרך' סתמא כתיב, וממילא משתמע נמי מיניה דרך מצוה, ואפילו הכי אמר רחמנא ליקרי: אי משום טרדא. דמחשבה פטרת ליה, אפילו טבעה ספינתו נמי: אלמה אמר רבי אבא. כמו: למה אמר (ג) אע"פ שטרוד בצערו חייב בכל המצות, חוץ מן התפילין, שנאמר בהם "פאר" ליחזקאל: "פארך חבוש עליך" וגו', וכיון דבעו פאר, ואבל מתגולל בצערו בעפר – אין זה פאר: טריד טרדא דמצוה. וכיון דאנן מיעוטא בעלמא דרשינן פרט לחתן, מספיק לן אם ממעטת מיניה טרדא דמצוה: וב"ה אמרי לך. נהי נמי דקרא למדרש מיניה פרט לחתן אתא ממילא ש"מ בלכת דידך הוא דמחייבת, אלמא – בדרך נמי קרי: עוסקין במלאכתן וקורין. לקמן מוקמינן לה, בפרק שני (ד' טז.): הטה ר' אלעזר בן עזריה. כב"ש: לאחד שאמרו לו זקנך מגודל אמר להם יהיה זה כנגד המשחיתים. משל שלך דומה לאחד שאומרים לו: זקנך נאה ומגודל, והוא אומר להם: הואיל וקלסתם אותו – אף הוא יהיה כנגד המשחיתים, הגדול הזה יהיה נתון לתער ולמספריים שאביא עליו ואשחיתנו: עכשיו שאני הטתי. הרי אני כמקלס את מעשיך שהיית מוטה ואתה זקפת: ב"ה נמי אית להו מטין. דבמטין נמי שרו, כדאמרינן לעיל "מטין וקורין": אבל עכשיו, כיון דעד השתא היית זקוף ועכשיו הטית אם לא נזקפתי אני יראו התלמידים ויקבעו הלכה: לא קיימת כו'. וכי היכי דעשה כדברי ב"ה לא עשה ולא כלום לדברי ב"ש, אף העושה כדברי ב"ש לא עשה ולא כלום לדברי ב"ה: מתני' בשחר מברך שתים וכו'. כדאמר בברכות ירושלמי: שבע ברכות הללו על שם (תהלים קיט) "שבע ביום הללתיך": אחת ארוכה ואחת קצרה. אשתים לאחריה דערבית קאי (נ"א: ארוכה – אמת ואמונה, קצרה – השכיבנו): לחתום. בברוך: שלא לחתום. כגון ברכת הפירות ומצות: גמ' מאי מברך. שתים לפניה דשחר, מאי ניהו: יוצר

**תוספות**

שנאמר בהם פאר. פרש"י: ואבל מעולל בעפר קרנו, ואין נאה לתת פאר תחת אפר. וא"ת: ולמה לי האי טעמא, תיפוק ליה מדאמר ליחזקאל 'פארך חבוש עליך' – מכלל דלכולי עלמא אסור! ותירץ השר מקוצי דצריך טעמא של רש"י כי היכי דלא נילף שאר מצות מתפילין מקל וחומר. א"נ: צריך טעמא דרש"י לחייבו בתפילין לאחר יום ראשון, דלא שייך מעולל בעפר קרנו אלא ביום ראשון דוקא: תני רב יחזקאל עשה כבית שמאי עשה ורב יוסף אמר עשה כב"ש לא עשה ולא כלום. וא"ת: פשיטא דאין הלכה כמותן. וי"ל: הואיל וב"ש מחמירים על האדם טפי מב"ה, לא שייך לומר פשיטא, דהא ד"עשה כב"ש לא עשה ולא כלום" – היינו היכא דב"ש מקילין וב"ה מחמירין, אבל הכא בק"ש – לא פסלי ב"ה דברי ב"ש. אבל תימא: א"כ, מה מייתי מסוכה כו' 'לא קיימת מצות סוכה כו''. ופירש"י דכי היכי דמי שעשה כב"ה לא עשה ולא כלום לב"ש, אף העושה כב"ש לא עשה ולא כלום לב"ה, ומאי קא מדמה? התם – פסלי ב"ש לגמרי מה דמכשרי ב"ה, אבל הכא – קרא קרית שמע כב"ש אליבא דב"ה יצא! ע"כ פירש הר"ר שמעיה: דקא מדמה הכי מדקאמר 'לא קיימת', אע"ג דמן הדין יצא, שהרי ראשו ורובו בסוכה אינו אסור אלא גזירה שמא ימשך אחר שלחנו. כה"ג גבי ק"ש, אע"ג דמן הדין יצא בדיעבד, כיון דלב"ה אין נכון כדאיתא במתניתין 'כדאי היית לחוב בעצמך', אם עשה כב"ש לב"ה לא עשה ולא כלום [וע' תוספות סוכה ג. ד"ה דאמר]: אחת ארוכה ואחת קצרה. פירש רש"י: 'ארוכה' – אמת ואמונה, 'קצרה' – השכיבנו. ותימה: דהשכיבנו נמי ארוכה הרבה, ותדע – מדלא קא חשיב לה בתוספתא בהדי הקצרות. ועוד, פעמים שמאריכין הרבה בתוספת כמו "אור יום הנף". ועוד: אמת ואמונה פעמים שמקצרין בה מאד, כדאמרינן לקמן למ"ד אין אומרים פרשת ציצית בלילה, הוא קא מסיים "מודים אנחנו לך שהוצאתנו ממצרים" וכו' בפרק "היה קורא" (לקמן דף יד ע"ב). ונראה לר"ת: דהכל קאי (ד) ב'אמת ואמונה'; אחת ארוכה ואחת קצרה, כלומר: בין יאריך בה בין יקצר בה, כדלקמן. וכן אשכחנא התם (יבמות ד' מג.): "אחת ארוסות ואחת נשואות אחת בתולות ואחת בעולות": מקום שאמרו לקצר. כגון בברכת פירות ובברכת המצות, אין לו להאריך: ורבנן

**עין משפט נר מצוה**

נ א מיי' פ"ד מהלכות ק"ש הלכה א סמג עשין יח טור שו"ע או"ח סימן ע סעיף ג:

נא ב מיי' פ"ד מהלכות תפילין הלכה יג ופ"ד מהלכות אבילות הלכה ט סמג עשין [דרבנן] ב טוש"ע או"ח סימן לח סעיף ה וטור שו"ע יו"ד סימן שפח סעיף א:

נב ג (מיי' פ"ב מהלכות ק"ש הלכה ב) טוש"ע או"ח סי' ס"ג סעיף ב:

נג ד מיי' פ"א מהלכות ק"ש הלכה ה סמ"ג עשין י"ט טוש"ע או"ח סימן נט וסימן רלו סעיף א:

[עי' רש"י ותוס' סוכה כה. ד"ה ובלכתך וכו' דגרסו להיפך וכ"ה בתוספתא פ"א]

יש גורסין ומוסיפין בזה עי' רש"א בשם הילקוט וא"צ להגיה דכיון דצריכא ליה לב"ה למימר ממילא ש"מ בהאי סברא לחודיה שיטתם נכון אבל זהו ודאי שמקשה על ב"ש ל"ל ב' פסוקים:

**מסורת הש"ס**

[בבקר כן יתכן להיות]

[ז. סוכה דף כה.]

[לקמן דף טז:]

[ז: סוכה דף כה. טו. כתובות דף ו: שמחות פ"ו]

[א ספרי פרשת ואתחנן]

[ג. ז: כח. עירובין קד: יג: כט: וש"נ]

## רב נסים גאון

והא אמר רב אבא בר זבדא אמר רב אבל חייב בכל מצו' האמורו' בתורה חוץ מן התפילין מפני שנאמר בהן פאר בפ' ואלו מגלחין במועד (דט"ו) גרסי' אבל אסור להניח תפילין מדקאמר ליה רחמנ' ליחזקאל (יחזקאל כד) פארך חבוש עליך מכלל דכל עלמא אסירי ובסוף פרק חזקת (ב"ב דף ס) כך דרשינן על ראש שמחתי אמר ר' יצחק זה אפר מקלה שבראש חתנים בעא מיניה רב פפא היכא מנח ליה אמר ליה במקום תפילין (ישעיה סא) לשום לאבלי ציון לתת להם פאר תחת אפר מיכן למדנו שהתפילין נאמר בהן פאר:

## הגהות הב"ח

(א) גמ' טריד טרדא דרשות (וב"ה אמרי וכו' נמי קרי) תא"מ ונ"ב ס"א וב"ה הא כתיב בשבתך בביתך ובלכתך בדרך למה לי ש"מ ותיבת וב"ש ההוא מבעי להו פרט לשלוחי מצוה נמחק: (ב) שם בדרך וקורין עוסקין במלאכתן: (ג) רש"י ד"ה אלמה וכו' למה אמר אבל אע"פ שטרוד: (ד) תוד"ה אחת וכו' דהכל קאי אאמת:

נד א מיי' פ"א מהלכות ק"ש הלכה ו טוש"ע או"ח סימן נט סעיף א:
נה ב מיי' שם סמג עשין יט טור שו"ע או"ח סימן ס סעיף א:
נו ג מיי' פ"ז מהלכות תפלה הלכה י טור שו"ע או"ח סימן מז סעיף ז:
נז ד מיי' שם טוש"ע שם סעיף ב:
נח ה מיי' שם טוש"ע שם סעיף ה:
נט ו מיי' פ"ו מהלכות תמידין הלכה ד:

"יוצר אור ובורא חשך". (א) לימא: יוצר אור ובורא נוגה! כדכתיב קאמרינן. - אלא מעתה: "עשה שלום ובורא(ב) רע", מי קא אמרינן כדכתיב?! אלא, כתיב 'רע' וקרינן 'הכל' *לישנא מעליא, הכא נמי - לימא 'נוגה' לישנא מעליא! - אלא אמר רבא: *אכדי להזכיר מדת יום בלילה ומדת לילה ביום. בשלמא מדת לילה ביום - כדאמרינן: "יוצר אור ובורא חשך", אלא מדת יום בלילה היכי משכחת לה? - אמר אביי: "גולל אור מפני חשך וחשך מפני אור". ואידך מאי היא? - אמר רב יהודה אמר שמואל: "אהבה רבה". וכן אורי ליה רבי אלעזר *לר' פדת בריה: 'אהבה רבה'. תניא נמי הכי: באין אומרים 'אהבת עולם' אלא 'אהבה רבה'. ורבנן אמרי: 'אהבת עולם', וכן הוא אומר "ואהבת עולם אהבתיך על כן משכתיך חסד". א"ר יהודה אמר שמואל: גהשכים לשנות, עד שלא קרא ק"ש צריך לברך, משקרא ק"ש א"צ לברך, שכבר נפטר ב'אהבה רבה'. אמר רב הונא: למקרא - צריך לברך, ולמדרש - א"צ לברך; ור' אלעזר אמר: למקרא ולמדרש - צריך לברך, למשנה - א"צ לברך; ור' יוחנן אמר: אף למשנה נמי צריך לברך, [אבל לתלמוד א"צ לברך]. ורבא אמר: דאף לתלמוד צריך (לחזור ו) לברך; *דאמר רב חייא בר אשי: זמנין סגיאין הוה קאימנא קמיה דרב לתנויי פרקין בספרא דבי רב, הוה מקדים וקא משי ידיה ובריך, ומתני לן פרקין. מאי מברך? א"ר יהודה אמר שמואל: אשר קדשנו במצותיו וצונו לעסוק בדברי תורה. ור' יוחנן מסיים בה הכי: *הערב נא ה' אלהינו את דברי תורתך בפינו ובפיפיות עמך בית ישראל ונהיה אנחנו וצאצאינו וצאצאי עמך בית ישראל כלנו יודעי שמך ועוסקי תורתך, ברוך אתה ה' המלמד תורה לעמו ישראל. ורב המנונא אמר: אשר בחר בנו מכל העמים ונתן לנו את תורתו. ברוך אתה ה' נותן התורה. (*) אמר רב המנונא: זו היא מעולה שבברכות. הלכך לימרינהו לכולהו. § תנן התם, *ואמר להם הממונה: ברכו ברכה אחת! והם ברכו, וקראו עשרת הדברות, 'שמע', 'והיה אם שמוע', 'ויאמר', וברכו את העם ג' ברכות: אמת ויציב, ועבודה, וברכת כהנים, ובשבת מוסיפין ברכה אחת למשמר היוצא. מאי 'ברכה אחת'? כי הא דרבי אבא ור' יוסי בר אבא אקלעו להההוא אתרא, בעו מנייהו: מאי 'ברכה אחת'? לא הוה בידייהו. ואתו שיילוהו לרב מתנה, לא הוה בידיה. אתו שיילוהו לרב יהודה, אמר להו: הכי אמר שמואל 'אהבה רבה'. *ואמר רבי זריקא אמר רבי אמי א"ר שמעון בן לקיש: 'יוצר אור'. כי אתא רב יצחק בר יוסף אמר: הא דרבי זריקא לאו בפירוש אתמר אלא מכללא אתמר, דאמר ר' זריקא א"ר אמי אמר ר' שמעון בן לקיש: זאת אומרת - ברכות אין מעכבות זו את זו. אי אמרת בשלמא 'יוצר אור' הוו אמרי - היינו דברכות אין מעכבות זו את זו, דלא קא אמרי 'אהבה רבה'; אלא

תורה אור: ישעיה מה; ירמיה לא

[אולי שגגת הדפוס הוא]

יוצר אור ובורא חשך (ג) (עושה שלום ובורא רע). לקמיה מפרש אידך: מאי היא דהיינו ברכה דישתבח? אינה מן המנין שהיא לאחרי פסוקי דזמרה כמו ברכת הלל ואומרים אותה קודם זמן קריאת שמע אם ירצו: כדכתיב קאמרי'. כתיב בקרא "יוצר אור ובורא חשך עושה שלום ובורא רע": שכבר נפטר באהבה רבה. שיש בה מעין ברכת התורה. "ותן בלבנו ללמוד וללמד לשמור ולעשות ולקיים את כל דברי תלמוד תורתך ותלמדם חקי רצונך": מדרש. הוא קרוב למקרא, כגון מכילתא וספרא וספרי שהם מדרשי מקראות: *לגמרא אין צריך לברך. אפילו קודם אהבה רבה קאמר, והכי מוכח מילתא בפרק שני*: אף לגמרא צריך לברך. שהוא עיקר התורה שממנו הוראה יוצאה. גמרא היינו סברת טעמי משנה, ותירוצי משניות הסותרות זו את זו, וחסורי מחסרא: ומברך. ברכת התורה: ורבי יוחנן מסיים בה הכי. דבעי פתיחה בברוך וחתימה בברוך: הערב נא ה' אלהינו. יערבו עלינו לעסוק בהם מאהבה: ברוך אתה ה' המלמד תורה לעמו ישראל. גרסינן, ולא גרסינן "למדני חקיך" שאין זו ברכה והודאה על שעבר אלא לשון בקשה, ודוד כי אמרה (בתהלים קיט) לא לשם ברכה אמרה אלא בלשון בקשה. והכי קאמר: ה' שאתה ברוך - למדני חקיך: וזו היא מעולה שבברכות. התורה, לפי שיש בה הודאה למקום וקילוס לתורה ולישראל: תנן התם. במסכת תמיד: אמר להם הממונה. והוא סגן הכהנים, כדאיתא ביומא: "היינו סגן היינו ממונה" (בפירש"י שם טו): ברכו ברכה אחת. לקמן מפרש מאי היא. ומן הברכות שלפני ק"ש היא, דהתם מסדר לכוליה סדר עבודת השחר וקאמר דלאחר שסדרו האברים על גבי הכבש ומלחום ירדו ובאו להם ללשכת הגזית לקרות את שמע, והדר תני: אמר להם הממונה ברכו ברכה אחת והם ברכו וקראו עשרת הדברות: וברכו את העם. עם העם: ועבודה. בשביל העבודה שעשו היו מברכין אחריה "רצה ה' אלהינו עבודת עמך ישראל ואשי ישראל ותפלתם תקבל ברצון. ברוך המקבל עבודת עמו ישראל ברצון". אי נמי "שאותך לבדך ביראה נעבוד": וברכת כהנים. לברך את העם ובשאר תפלה לא היה להם פנאי ואף זמן קריאת שמע לא הגיע, כדאמר במסכת יומא (דף לז ע"ב): הקורא את שמע עם אנשי משמר ועם אנשי מעמד - לא יצא, לפי שאנשי משמר מקדימין וכו': מוסיפין ברכה אחת. לקמיה מפרש לה: למשמר היוצא. שהמשמרות מתחלפות ביום השבת, כדאמרינן במסכת סוכה (דף נו:): משמר היוצא עושה תמיד של שחר ומוספין, ומשמר הנכנס עושה תמיד של בין הערבים ובזיכין: מאי ברכה אחת. דקתני רישא, איזו מן הברכות הוא אומר: לאו בפירוש אתמר. לא שמע מפי ר"ל שאמ' בפירוש מאי ברכה אחת יוצר אור: זאת אומרת. דקתני ברכו ברכה אחת: ברכות אין מעכבות זו את זו. בירך את האחת ולא בירך את השניה נפקא מיהא ידי חובתו בההיא שבירך, ואין חברתה מעכבת, לומר שאין זו מועלת בלא זו. ומהכא שמע רבי זריקא דס"ל לר"ל דהך ברכה אחת יוצר אור היא: אי אמרת בשלמא יוצר אור הוו אמרי. ולא אהבה רבה, ואע"ג דמטא ליה זימנא שאף בלילה ראוי לומר, כל שכן דכיון דאמרי "יוצר אור" ודאי מטיא זמנה, ואפ"ה לא אמרי אלא יוצר אור ותו לא אמרי לה, היינו דקאמר שמע מינה ברכות אין מעכבות זו את זו: אלא

[פסחים ג. וש"נ] [לקמן יב. ע"ש] [נ"ל בפרק שני] [עי' תוס' נדה ... ואמר] לקמן דף יד: [עי' תוס' כתובו' ... ד"ה כל הברכ' פסחים קד: ד"ה] תמיד דף לב:

ורבנן אמרי אהבת עולם וכו'. הלכך תקינו לומר בשחרית "אהבה רבה" ובערבית "אהבת עולם": שכבר נפטר באהבה רבה. עד הלכך נימרינהו לכולהו. בירושלמי יש הא דאמרי' שכבר נפטר באהבה רבה - והוא ששנה על אתר, פירוש: לאלתר, שלמד מיד באותו מקום. ונשאל להרב ר' יצחק: כגון אנו, שאין אנו לומדין מיד לאחר תפלת השחר, שאנו טרודין והולכים כך בלא למוד עד אמצע היום או יותר, אמאי אין אנו מברכין ברכת התורה פעם אחרת כשאנו מתחילין ללמוד? והשיב ר"י: דלא קיימא לן כאותו ירושלמי הואיל וגמר' שלנו לא אמרו, ואין צריך לאלתר ללמוד. ועוד: אפי' לפי הירושלמי דוקא אהבה רבה - דלא הוי עיקר ברכה לברכת התורה, דעיקר אהבה רבה לק"ש נתקן, ובשביל היא אינו נפטר מברכת התורה, אלא אם ילמוד מיד וגם לא יעשה היסח הדעת. אבל ברכת "אשר בחר בנו" וברכת "לעסוק בדברי תורה" שהן עיקר לברכת התורה - פוטרת כל היום. וא"ת: מאי שנא מסוכה שצריך לברך על כל סעודה וסעודה "לישב בסוכה"? וי"ל: דשאני תורה שאינו מייאש דעתו, דכל שעה אדם מחוייב ללמוד, דכתיב "והגית בו יומם ולילה" והוי כמו יושב כל היום בלא הפסק; אבל אכילה בסוכה יש שעה קבועה. וא"ת: מפני מה אין אנו מברכין "לישן בסוכה"? וי"ל: דברכה דאכילה שמברכין 'לישב' פוטרתו. א"נ, משום שמא לא יישן והוי ברכה לבטלה, שהרי אין בידו לישן כל שעה שירצה. והיה אומר ר"ת: כשאדם עומד ממטתו בלילה (בשחרית) ללמוד שא"צ לברך ברכת התורה, מפני שברכת התורה של אתמול שחרית פוטרת עד שחרית אחרת, ולא נהירא. והצרפתים נהגו לומר פסוקים(ה) וברכת כהנים וגם "אלו דברים שאין להם שיעור" שהיא משנה, (פ"א דפאה) ו"אלו דברים שאדם אוכל פירותיהן" כו' שהיא *ברייתא (מס' שבת קכז.), מפני הירושלמי דבעי שילמוד על אתר. אבל א"צ, כמו שכתבתי כבר: ה"ג ברוך אתה ה' המלמד תורה לעמו ישראל. אבל לא גרס "למדני חקיך" שאין זו ברכה אלא בקשה שאמר דוד: וברכת כהנים. ואין זה דוכן, שהרי לא היו עומדים לדוכן עד לאחר הקטרת אמורים, דאמרי' בתענית (פ"ד ד' כו:): שלשה פעמים ביום הכהנים נושאין כפיהם וכו'. וא"כ, הוה ליה למתני ד' פעמים; אחד לפני הקטרה ואחד לאחר הקטרה! אלא בלא נשיאות כפים אמרו ברכת כהנים, כמו שאנו אומרים: משום

[מיוחסת כנ"ל]

גליון הש"ס

בגמ' לעסוק כו'. בריי"ף הגירסא על ד"ת שם ועוסקי כו'. בריי"ף הגירסא ולומדי תורתך לשמה שם הלכך כו'. בריי"ף והרא"ש הגירסא אמר ר"פ הלכך

(*) ברב אלפס אי' והא דרב המנונא מעולה כו'

הגהות ה[ב"ח]

(א) גמ' ולי[מא] (ב) שם שלום ... הכל מי קא ... כדכתיב: (ג) ר[ש"י] יוצר וכו' ובורא ... לקמיה מפרש: (ד) ד"ה שכבר וכו' ובשבילו אינו ... היא נתקן: (ה) ... לברכת כה[נים]

אלא אי אמרת "אהבה רבה" הוו אמרי – מאי "ברכות אין מעכבות זו את זו"? דלמא האי דלא אמרי 'יוצר אור' – משום דלא מטא זמן 'יוצר אור', וכי מטא זמן 'יוצר אור' – הוו אמרי! *–ואי מכללא מאי? –דאי מכללא, לעולם 'אהבה רבה' הוו אמרי, וכי מטא זמן 'יוצר אור' – הוו אמרי ליה, ומאי "ברכות אין מעכבות זו את זו"? – [א]סדר ברכות.§ "וקורין עשרת הדברות שמע והיה אם שמוע ויאמר אמת ויציב ועבודה וברכת כהנים". א"ר יהודה אמר שמואל: אף בגבולין בקשו לקרות כן, אלא שכבר בטלום מפני תרעומת המינין. תניא נמי הכי, ר' נתן אומר: בגבולין בקשו לקרות כן, אלא שכבר בטלום מפני תרעומת המינין. רבה בב"ח סבר למקבעינהו בסורא, א"ל רב חסדא: כבר בטלום מפני תרעומת המינין. אמימר סבר למקבעינהו בנהרדעא, א"ל רב אשי: כבר בטלום מפני תרעומת המינין.§ "ובשבת מוסיפין ברכה אחת למשמר היוצא".§ מאי ברכה אחת? א"ר חלבו: [ב]משמר היוצא אומר למשמר הנכנס: מי ששכן את שמו בבית הזה הוא ישכין ביניכם אהבה ואחוה ושלום וריעות.§ "מקום שאמרו להאריך".§ פשיטא, [ג]היכא דקא נקיט כסא דחמרא בידיה וקסבר דשכרא הוא ופתח ומברך אדעתא דשכרא וסיים בדחמרא – יצא, דאי נמי אם אמר "שהכל נהיה בדברו" יצא, דהא תנן: *"על כולם אם אמר 'שהכל נהיה בדברו' – יצא." אלא, היכא דקא נקיט כסא דשכרא בידיה וקסבר דחמרא הוא, (א) פתח ובריך אדעתא דחמרא, וסיים בדשכרא, מאי? בתר עיקר ברכה אזלינן, או בתר חתימה אזלינן? – ת"ש: [ד]שחרית, פתח ב'יוצר אור' וסיים ב'מעריב ערבים' – לא יצא, פתח ב'מעריב ערבים' וסיים ב'יוצר אור' – יצא; ערבית, פתח ב'מעריב ערבים' וסיים ב'יוצר אור' – לא יצא, פתח ב'יוצר אור' וסיים ב'מעריב ערבים' – יצא; כללו של דבר: הכל הולך אחר החתום. – שאני התם דקאמר: "ברוך יוצר המאורות". – הניחא לרב *דאמר "כל ברכה שאין בה הזכרת השם אינה ברכה" – שפיר, אלא לר' יוחנן דאמר: "כל ברכה שאין בה מלכות אינה ברכה", מאי איכא למימר? –אלא, כיון דאמר רבה בר עולא: *כדי להזכיר מדת יום בלילה ומדת לילה ביום, כי קאמר ברכה ומלכות מעיקרא אתרוייהו קאמר. ת"ש מסיפא, "כללו של דבר: הכל הולך אחר החתום". 'כללו של דבר' לאתויי מאי – לאו לאתויי הא דאמרן? –לא, לאתויי נהמא ותמרי. ה"ד? אילימא דאכל נהמא וקסבר דתמרי אכל, ופתח אדעתא דתמרי וסיים בדנהמא – היינו בעיין! –לא צריכא: כגון דאכל תמרי וקסבר נהמא אכל, ופתח בדנהמא וסיים בדתמרי – [יצא], דאפילו סיים בדנהמא נמי יצא; מאי טעמא – דתמרי נמי מיזן זייני.§ אמר רבה בר *חיננא סבא משמיה דרב: [ה]כל שלא אמר 'אמת ויציב' שחרית ו'אמת ואמונה' ערבית – לא יצא ידי חובתו, שנאמר: °"להגיד בבקר חסדך ואמונתך בלילות".§ ואמר רבה בר חיננא [סבא] משמיה דרב: [ו]המתפלל, כשהוא כורע – כורע ב'ברוך' וכשהוא זוקף – זוקף בשם. אמר שמואל: מאי טעמא דרב – דכתיב: °'ה' זוקף כפופים'. מתיבי: °"מפני שמי נחת הוא"! –מי כתיב 'בשמי'? 'מפני שמי' כתיב. אמר ליה *שמואל לחייא בר רב: *בר אוריאן, תא ואימא לך מלתא מעלייתא דאמר אבוך! הכי אמר אבוך: כשהוא כורע – כורע ב'ברוך', כשהוא זוקף – זוקף בשם.
רב

תהלים צב | תהלים קמו | מלאכי ב

**רש"י**

אלא אי אמרת. הך ברכה דקאמרי 'אהבה רבה', היכי ש"מ דאין מעכבות זו את זו? דלמא האי דלא אמרי 'יוצר אור' – משום דלא מטא זמניה הוא, וכי מטא זמניה – אמרי לה! ואע"ג דקרו אינהו ק"ש לא מטא זמניה, כדאמרינן בעלמא (יומא לז:): "הקורא את שמע עם אנשי משמר לא יצא, שאנשי משמר מקדימין": ואי מכללא מאי. וכי אמר ליה מכללא, מאי גריעותא איכא, דקאמר "לאו בפירוש אתמר"? הא שפיר מצי למשמע מכללא ד'יוצר אור' קא אמרי! ומשנינן: ליכא למשמע מהכא, דילמא לעולם אימא לך אהבה רבה וכו': סדר ברכות. אם הקדים המאוחרות: בקשו. לקבוע עשרת הדברות בקריאת שמע: מפני תרעומת המינין. שלא יאמרו לעמי הארץ: אין שאר תורה אמת, ותדעו שאין קורין אלא מה שאמר הקדוש ב"ה ושמעו מפיו בסיני: המינין. גוים תלמידי ישו: פתח בדשכרא וסיים בדחמרא. תחלת הברכה אמר ע"מ 'שהכל', וכיון שהגיע למלך העולם נזכר שהוא יין, ואמר 'פרי הגפן' – פשיטא לן דיצא, דהא אפילו סיים כל הברכה לדעת פתיחתה ואמר 'שהכל' יצא על היין דתנן וכו': אלא. קא מבעיא לן: פתח אדעתא דחמרא, כדי לסיים "בפה"ג", וכשהגיע למלך העולם נזכר שהוא שכר וסיים 'שהכל', מהו? בתר עיקר ברכה אזלינן. ועיקר ברכה אדעתא דיין אמרה, והוי כמו שסיים ביין – ואין ברכת היין מוליאה ידי ברכת שכר, שאין השכר מן הגפן: פתח ביוצר אור. כלומר אדעתא דלימא יוצר אור: וסיים במעריב ערבים. כשאמר 'מלך העולם' נזכר, וסיים "אשר בדברו מעריב ערבים": שאני התם וכו'. כלומר: דלמא פתיחה אינה כלום, והא דקתני "יצא" – לפי שחוזר וחותם בה ברוך יוצר המאורות, וע"י חתימתה אמר דיצא. *אלא 'שהכל' שאין חותם בה בברוך, ופתיחתה אדעתא דבורא פרי הגפן הוא, אימא דלא יצא: מאי איכא למימר. היכי נפיק משום חתימתה, הא אין מלכות בחתימתה: ה"ג אלא כיון דאמר כו'. אלא לא תימא משום חתימתה יצא, אלא פתיחתה נמי מעלייתא היא, ולא תפשוט מיניה לחמרא ושכרא; דלגבי ברכות ערבית ושחרית הוא דמצי למימר דכי פתח בזו וסיים בזו יצא, דהא כי פתח בשחרית אדעתא דמעריב ערבים הוה דעתיה לאדכורי בה מדת יום בלילה כגון "גולל אור", וכי פתח ערבית אדעתא דיוצר אור הוה דעתיה לאדכורי בה מדת לילה כגון "ובורא חשך", הלכך אדעתא דתרוייהו הויא: לאו לאתויי הא דאמרן. כגון שכרא וחמרא: היינו בעיין.(ב) דהא ברכת התמרים על העץ ועל פרי העץ אינה עולה לברכת הלחם, ואי בהא פשטת הכל הולך אחר חתום ברכות – הוא הדין לחמרא ושכרא: כל מי שלא אמר ברכת אמת ויציב. כמו שתקנוה וכן אמת ואמונה בערבית לא יצא: שנא' להגיד בבקר חסדך. וברכת 'אמת ויציב' כולה על חסד שעשה עם אבותינו היא, שהוציאם ממצרים ובקע להם הים והעבירם. וברכת 'אמת ואמונה' מדבר בה אף על העתידות, שאנו מצפים שיקיים לנו הבטחתו ואמונתו לגאלנו מיד מלכים ומיד עריצים ולשום נפשנו בחיים, ולהדריכנו על במות אויבינו, כל אלה הנסים התדירים תמיד: כשהוא כורע. באבות ובהודאה, כורע בברוך וזוקף את עצמו כשהוא מזכיר את השם, על שם "ה' זוקף כפופים" (תהלים קמו): נחת. לשון הכנעה.
כחיזרא

**תוספות**

משום דלא מטא זמן יוצר אור. דנהי דשחיטת התמיד משיעלה עמוד השחר. פי' רש"י: מיהו לא הוה שעה לומר יוצר אור כדאמרי' הקורא כו', ויכול לסבור הברייתא כותיקין*:

ברכה אחת למשמר היוצא וכו'. תימא קצת מאי היא, הואיל ולית בה לא שם ולא מלכות: פתח ואמר בא"י אלהינו מלך העולם, והיה סבור שהיה יין והבין שהיה שכר, ואחר שהבין שהיה שכר סיים שהכל: לא לאתויי נהמא. ופירש רב אלפס: השתא דלא אפשיטא בעיין – אזלינן לקולא, ואפילו פתח בחמרא וסיים בשכרא יצא. ור"י הי' אומר לחומרא דצריך לברך פעם אחרת. ומיהו היה אומר ר"ת: אם היה יודע בבירור שטעה בדבורו שאמר "בורא פרי העץ" תחת (בורא) פרי הגפן– דבתוך כדי דבור יכול לחזור בו. וכן בי"ט בחתימה של יום טוב, אם טעה בין מקדש ישראל והזמנים ואמר מקדש השבת וחזר בתוך כדי דבור יצא, – אחרי שהוא יודע שהוא י"ט. והקשה הר"ר יעקב מקינון: מאי קא מבעיא ליה, והא ודאי מצות אינן צריכות כוונה! והיה אומר הר"י דהיינו בשומע תפלה אחורי בית הכנסת ולא נתכוין לצאת, אבל היכא דנתכוון לברך על היין ונמצא שכר – לא מהני: להגיד בבקר חסדך. חסד שהקדוש ב"ה עשה לנו במצרים. 'ואמונתך', פי': מדבר על העתיד, שאנו מצפים שישמור הבטחתו ואמונתו ויגאלנו מיד המלכים. ובסוף ברכה חוזר לגאולה דפרעה כדי לסמוך ל'גאל ישראל'. א"נ ע"ד המדר' (רבה איכה ג): 'חדשים לבקרים רבה אמונתך', שאדם מאמין ומפקיד רוחו בידו ומחזירה בלא יגיעה: אמת ויציב וכו'. לא קאי על השכינה, אלא קאי א'הדבר הזה' וכו'. וכן איתא בהר"ס. ואיתא בירושלמי: האי מרגניתא דלית ביה טימא, פירוש: שאין לה שומא – כל מה שמשבח מתגני לה, כדאמר לקמן (ד' לג ב) בחד דפתח ואמר "האל הגדול הגבור והנורא" והיה מאריך הרבה, וא"ל ר' חנינא: סיימת לשבחי דמרך?! כי כל פה לא יוכל לספר שבחו:
כרע

**עין משפט נר מצוה**

ס א מיי' פ"א מהלכות ק"ש הלכה ח טוש"ע או"ח סימן ס' סעיף ג:
סא ב מיי' פ"ו מהלכות תמידין הלכה ד:
סב ג מיי' פ"ח מהלכות ברכות הלכה יא (סמג עשין כז) טור ש"ע או"ח סי' רט סעיף א ב:
סג ד מיי' פ"א מהלכות ק"ש הלכה ח (סמג עשין יח) טוש"ע או"ח סימן נט סעיף ב:
סד ה מיי' פ"א מהל' ק"ש הלכה ז טוש"ע או"ח סימן סו סעיף י:
סה ו מיי' פ"ה מהלכות תפלה הלכה י סמג עשין יט טור ש"ע או"ח סימן קיג סעיף ז:

**רב נסים גאון**

כבר בטלום מפני תרעומת המינין. בתלמוד ארץ ישראל של זה הפרק פירשה בדין היה שיהו קורין עשרת הדברות בכל יום מפני מה אין קורין אותן מפני טענת המינין שלא יהו אומרים אלו לבדם ניתנו למשה בסיני: מקום שאמרו להאריך אינו רשאי לקצר לקצר אינו רשאי להאריך לחתום אינו רשאי שלא לחתום פירשוהו בתוספת' (פרק א') אלו ברכות שמקצרין המברך על הפירות ועל המצות כו' ואלו ברכות שמאריכין בהן ברכות של תעניות וברכות של ראש השנה ושל יום הכפורים כו' ובגמ' דבני מערבא (פרק א) גרסי ר' יודן מטבע קצר פותח בברוך ואינו חותם בברוך מטבע ארוך פותח בברוך וחותם בברוך: הניחא למאן דאמר כל ברכה שאין בה הזכרת השם אינה ברכה. עיקר חלוקה של רב ור' יוחנן בפרק כיצד מברכין (דף מ) ובגמ' דבני מערבא בפרק הרואה מקום (הלכה א) גרסי ר' זעירה בר' יהודה בשם רב כל ברכה שאין עמה מלכות אינה ברכה אמר ר' תנחומא ואנא אמינא טעמא (תהלים קמה) ארוממך אלוהי המלך:

[בגיטין סב. וכן במנחות נג. בר אוריין פירש"י בן תורה אכן ביומא עת. ובסוכה מג: וע"ז לא: ובחגיגה יד: איתא בר אריא בר אוריא ולא פירש"י כלום]

**מסורת הש"ס**

תוס' יומא לז: ד"ה אמר אביי
מ: יבמות ס: ב"ב חולין לג. [נ"ה קיא:]
לקמן מ.
לקמן מ.
[לעיל יא: ע"ש]
[תגיגה יד. ע"ש]

**הגהות הב"ח**

גמ' לחמרא הוא (ב) רש"י ד"ה היינו וכו' הדא ברכת.

כ"א חנינא וכן לקמן
כצ"ל
כ"א אבל

**גליון הש"ס**

ג' ד"ה לא כו' א כו' ולא שייך הכא ספק ברכות לקולא א"ח סימן ר"ט ס"ק קשה כן דכבר כתב א בפסחים קב ע"א דשב"ס ד"ה להודיעך לל"ש כן אלא בברכת המצות דהברכות אינן מעכבות. אבל בברכת הנהנין אסור לאכול בלא ברכה ע"ש. ולא הוי כאן חשש ברכה לבטלה. דאם לא יברך יהא אסור לו לשתות. אח"ז ראיתי באבן העוזר (סימן רי"ד) שכ"כ מסברא דנפשיה ולא הביא דברי הרש"א.
מ"ש לקמן (מ"ט ע"ב) בתוס' ד"ה ר"מ: בא"ד שאמר בפה"ע תחת בפה"ג. משמע מזה דאם בירך על היין בפה"ע דלא יצא. [וכ"כ המג"א סימן ר"ח ס"ק כ"ב בשם תשובת ר"י הלוי] ותמוה לי. דהא יין יש פרי עליו. דהא מברכין בפה"ג וא"כ שפיר מברך בפה"ע. אלא דהוי' לו לברר יותר שהוא מגפן. וא"כ לא גרע מבירך שהכל דקיי"ל דיוצא. אח"ז מצאתי בעזה"י בתשובת גינת וורדים חלק או"ח סכ"ט דהעלה לעיקר דיוצא:

רב ששת אכי כרע – כרע כחיזרא, כי קא זקיף – זקיף כחיויא.§ ואמר רבה בר חיננא סבא משמיה דרב: בכל השנה כולה אדם מתפלל "האל הקדוש", "מלך אוהב צדקה ומשפט", חוץ מעשרה ימים שבין ראש השנה ויום הכפורים שמתפלל "המלך הקדוש" ו"המלך המשפט". ורבי אלעזר אמר: אפילו אמר 'האל הקדוש' – יצא, שנאמר: °"ויגבה ה' צבאות במשפט והאל הקדוש נקדש בצדקה". אימתי "ויגבה ה' צבאות במשפט" – אלו עשרה ימים שמר"ה ועד יוה"כ, וקאמר 'האל הקדוש'. מאי הוה עלה? אמר רב יוסף: 'האל הקדוש' ו'מלך אוהב צדקה ומשפט'; רבה אמר: 'המלך הקדוש' ו'המלך המשפט'. והלכתא כרבה.§ ואמר רבה בר חיננא סבא משמיה דרב: כל שאפשר לו לבקש רחמים על חבירו ואינו מבקש – נקרא חוטא. שנאמר: °"גם אנכי חלילה לי מחטא לה' מחדל להתפלל בעדכם". אמר רבא: אם ת"ח הוא(א) צריך שיחלה עצמו עליו. מ"ט? אילימא משום דכתיב °"ואין חלה מכם עלי (ואין) [ו]גולה את אזני" – דילמא מלך שאני? אלא, מהכא: °"ואני בחלותם לבושי וגו'".§ ואמר רבה בר חיננא סבא משמיה דרב: כל העושה דבר עבירה ומתבייש בו – מוחלין לו על כל עונותיו, שנאמר: °"למען תזכרי ובשת ולא יהיה לך עוד פתחון פה מפני כלמתך בכפרי לך לכל אשר עשית נאם ה' אלהים". – דילמא צבור שאני? –אלא, מהכא: °"ויאמר שמואל אל שאול למה הרגזתני להעלות אתי, ויאמר שאול צר לי מאד ופלשתים נלחמים בי *וה' סר מעלי ולא ענני עוד גם ביד הנביאים גם בחלמות ואקראה לך להודיעני מה אעשה", ואילו "אורים ותמים" לא קאמר – משום דקטליה לנוב עיר הכהנים. ומנין דאחילו ליה מן שמיא – שנא' °"(ויאמר שמואל אל שאול) [ו] מחר אתה ובניך עמי", *וא"ר יוחנן: 'עמי' – במחיצתי. ורבנן אמרי, מהכא: °"והוקענום לה' בגבעת שאול בחיר ה'", יצתה בת קול ואמרה: 'בחיר ה''. אמר ר' אבהו בן זוטרתי אמר רב יהודה בר זבידא: בקשו לקבוע פרשת בלק בקריאת שמע, ומפני מה לא קבעוה – משום טורח צבור. מ"ט? אילימא משום דכתיב בה: °"אל מוציאם ממצרים" – לימא פרשת רבית ופרשת משקלות דכתיב בהן יציאת מצרים! –אלא אמר ר' יוסי בר אבין: משום דכתיב בה האי קרא: *°"כרע שכב כארי וכלביא מי יקימנו". ולימא האי פסוקא ותו לא! גמירי: כל פרשה דפסקה משה רבינו – פסקינן, דלא פסקה משה רבינו – לא פסקינן. פרשת ציצית מפני מה קבעוה? א"ר יהודה בר חביבא: מפני שיש בה *חמשה דברים: מצות ציצית, יציאת מצרים, עול מצות, ודעת מינים, הרהור עבירה, והרהור ע"ז. בשלמא הני תלת – מפרשן; עול מצות – דכתיב: °"וראיתם אתו וזכרתם את כל מצות ה'", ציצית – דכתיב: "ועשו להם ציצית וגו'", יציאת מצרים – דכתיב: "אשר הוצאתי וגו'", אלא דעת מינים, הרהור עבירה, והרהור ע"ז מנלן? – דתניא: "אחרי לבבכם" – זו מינות, וכן הוא אומר: °"אמר נבל בלבו אין אלהים", "אחרי עיניכם" – זה הרהור עבירה, שנאמר: °"ויאמר שמשון אל אביו אותה קח לי כי היא ישרה בעיני", "אתם זונים" – זה הרהור ע"ז, וכן הוא אומר: °"ויזנו אחרי הבעלים".§ **מתני'** גמזכירין יציאת מצרים בלילות. *א"ר אלעזר בן עזריה: *הרי אני כבן שבעים שנה, ולא זכיתי שתאמר יציאת מצרים בלילות עד שדרשה *בן זומא. שנא': °"למען תזכר את יום צאתך מארץ מצרים כל ימי חייך". 'ימי חייך'–הימים, 'כל ימי חייך'–הלילות; וחכ"א: 'ימי חייך'–העוה"ז, *'כל'–להביא לימות המשיח.§ **גמ'** *תניא, אמר להם בן זומא לחכמים: וכי מזכירין יציאת מצרים לימות המשיח?! והלא כבר נאמר: °"הנה ימים באים נאם ה' ולא יאמרו עוד חי ה' אשר העלה את בני ישראל מארץ מצרים, כי אם חי ה' אשר העלה ואשר הביא את זרע בית ישראל מארץ צפונה ומכל הארצות אשר הדחתים שם"! אמרו לו: לא שתעקר יציאת מצרים ממקומה, אלא שתהא שעבוד מלכיות עיקר, ויציאת מצרים טפל לו. כיוצא בו אתה אומר: °"לא יקרא שמך עוד יעקב כי אם ישראל יהיה שמך".

לא

תורה אור: ישעיה ה | שמואל א יב | שם כב | תהלים לה | יחזקאל טז | שמואל א כח | שם | שמואל ב כא | במדבר כג | שם כד | שם טו | תהלים יד | שופטים יד | שם ח | דברים טז | ירמיה כג | בראשית לה

**רש"י**

כחיזרא. שבט ביד אדם, וחובטו כלפי מטה בבת אחת: זקיף כחיויא. בנחת ראשו תחלה ואח"כ גופו, שלא תראה כריעתו עליו כמשוי: כחיויא. כנחש הזה, כשהוא זוקף עצמו מגביה הראש תחלה וזוקף מעט מעט: המלך הקדוש. לפי שבימים הללו הוא מראה מלכותו לשפוט את העולם: המלך המשפט. כמו מלך המשפט. כמו "נושאי הארון הברית" (יהושע ג) – כמו "ארון הברית". וכן "המסגרות המכונות" (מלכים ב טז) – שהוא כמו "מסגרות המכונות". וכן "העמק הפגרים" (ירמיה לא) כמו "עמק הפגרים": ה"ג: ואם תלמיד חכם הוא וצריך לרחמים צריך שיחלה עצמו עליו. אם ת"ח הוא זה שצריך לרחמים – צריך שיחלה חבירו עצמו עליו: בחלותם. על דואג ואחיתופל הוא אומר, שהיו ת"ח: למען תזכרי ובושת. סיפיה דקרא "בכפרי לך את כל אשר עשית": גם בחלומות גם בנביאים. ולא אמר לו "גם באורים", לפי שנתבייש ממנו, שלא יאמר לו: אתה גרמת לעצמך שלא נענית באורים ותומים, לפי שהרגת את הכהנים: ורבנן. סברי מהכא שמעינן דאחילו לו: והוקענום. גבעונים אמרו לדוד בסוף ימיו שהיה רעב ג' שנים "ויבקש דוד בה' ויאמר ה' אל שאול ואל בית הדמים על אשר המית את הגבעונים", שהרג את הכהנים שהיו מספיקים לגבעונים לחם ומים, שהגבעונים נתנם יהושע חוטבי עצים ושואבי מים למזבח. (ב)"ויאמר דוד אל הגבעונים ובמה אכפר לכם וברכו את נחלת ה'", והם אמרו לו "יותן לנו שבעה אנשים מבניו והוקענום בגבעת שאול", ובת קול יצאה וסיימה אחריהם "בחיר ה'", דודאי הם לא אמרו "בחיר ה'", שהרי לגנותו היו באין ולא לכבודו: פרשת רבית. "אל תקח מאתו נשך ותרבית וגו'" (ויקרא כה), וסמיך ליה יציאת מצרים: ופרשת משקלות. "אבני צדק וגו'" (ויקרא יט), סיפיה דקרא "אשר הוצאתי אתכם וגו'": כרע שכב. דדמי ל'בשכבך ובקומך', שהקדוש ב"ה שומרנו בשכבנו ובקומנו לשכב שלוים ושקטים כארי וכלביא: ולימא האי פסוקא. וליכא טורח לצבור: עול מצות. "ועשיתם את כל מצותי": מינות. אותם ההופכים טעמי התורה למדרש טעות ואליל: וכן הוא אומר אמר נבל בלבו אין אלהים. ואין לך נבל מן ההופך דברי אלהים חיים: מתני' מזכירין יציאת מצרים בלילות. פרשת ציצית בק"ש, ואע"פ שאין לילה זמן ציצית, דכתיב "וראיתם אותו וזכרתם", אומרים אותה בלילה מפני יציאת מצרים שבה: כבן שבעים שנה. כבר הייתי נראה זקן, ולא זקן ממש, שבאת עליו שיבה יום שהעבירו רבן גמליאל מנשיאותו ומינו רבי אלעזר בן עזריה נשיא, כדאיתא לקמן בפרק "תפלת השחר" (ד' כח.) ואותו היום דרש בן זומא מקרא זה: גמ'

**תוספות**

כרע כחיזרא. ולקמן (ד' כח:) אמרינן עד שיראה איסר וכו'(ג) לא סגי בכריעה לבד וראשו זקוף, אלא בעי נמי שיכוף הראש. וכן איתא בירושלמי דפרקין, ובלבד שלא ישוח יותר מדאי. אמר רבי ירמיה: ובלבד שלא יעשה כהדין חרדונא, והיינו תרגום ירושלמי של צב (ויקרא יא), והצב כשהוא שוחה ראשו זקוף. ובר"ה ויו"כ שאנו שוחין כל שעה בתפלה צריך ליזהר שיגביה קודם שיסיים הברכה, רק שיכרע בברוך ושיגביה מיד, דאמרינן לקמן סוף 'אין עומדין' (ד' לד.): אם בא לשחות תחלת כל ברכה וסוף כל ברכה – מלמדין אותו שלא ישחה:

והלכתא כותיה דרבה. דצריך לחתום "המלך הקדוש" ו"המלך המשפט", ואם לא אמר–מחזירין אותו. וכן 'זכרנו' ו'מי כמוך' ו'כתוב לחיים' ו'בספר חיים' – מחזירים אותו אם לא אמר, דכל המשנה ממטבע שטבעו חכמים אינו יוצא ידי חובתו. וכן פסק רבינו יהודה: אם ספק לו אם אמר אם לא אמר – מחזירים אותו, כדאיתא בירושלמי דתענית פ"ק: היה מתפלל ואינו יודע אם הזכיר טל ומטר ואם לאו – כל שלשים יום בחזקת שלא למוד. פירוש: שלא אמר, אלא כמו שהוא למוד עד עתה שלא אמר כן. אחר כן – בחזקת שהזכיר, והוא הדין לכל הדברים שצריך להזכיר – כך הדין. ואם כן בעשרת ימי תשובה דליכא שלשים יום – צריך לחזור. *ור"ח כתב דאין מחזירין אותו מכל אותן דברים דלא פסק בספר בפירוש, והביא ראיה לדבריו: בקשו לקבוע פרשת בלק בפרשת ק"ש ומפני מה לא קבעוה וכו'. איתא בירושלמי דאותן ג' פרשיות שתקנו בקריית שמע לפי שבהן עשרת הדברות ועיין בו ותמצא הכל:

הדרן עלך מאימתי

**עין משפט נר מצוה**

סו א מיי' פ"ה מהלכות תפלה הלכה יב טור שו"ע או"ח סימן קיג סעיף ו:

סז ב מיי' פ"ב שם הלכה יח סמג עשין י"ט טור שו"ע או"ח סי' קיח וסי' תקפב סעיף א:

סח ג מיי' פ"א מהלכות ק"ש הלכה ג:

**רב נסים גאון**

זה ששנינו אמר רבי אלעזר בן (עזריא) [עזריה] הרי אני כבן שבעים שנה. מיפרשא מילתיה בפרק תפלת השחר (דף כח) במעשה שהיה בין רבן גמליאל ור' יהושע בעת שהסכימו חכמים להעביר את רבן גמליאל מגדולתו ולהמליך תחתיו את ר' אלעזר בן עזריה אמר והא בר תמניסרי אנא ולית לי חיוראתא אירחיש ליה ניסא והדרו ליה תמניסרי דארי חיוראתא והיינו דתנן אמר ר' אלעזר בן עזרי' הריני כבן ע' שנה ולא בן שבעים:

נ"ל ור"ח

**הגהות הב"ח**

(א) גמ' אם ת"ח הוא וצריך לרחמים צריך שיחלה: (ב) רש"י ד"ה והוקענום וכו' מים למזבח ויקרא המלך לגבעונים ויאמר דוד אל הגבעונים מה אעשה לכם ובמה אכפר וברכו: (ג) תוס' ד"ה כרע וכו' איסר וכו' פי' לא סגי:

גי' מהרש"א הן עם כלביא יקום עד יאכל טרף וכ"ה בהדיא בתנחומא

**גליון הש"ס**

תוס' ד"ה כרע כו' שיגביה כו'. עי' תוס' לקמן ל"ד ע"א ד"ה ומתלתו: תוס' ד"ה והלכתא כו' מחזירין אותו. עיין תוס' לקמן לד ע"א ד"ה אמצעיות:

ספרי פ' ראה

מכילתא פרשת בא פ' ט"ז

מכילתא שם תוספתא פ"א

**מסורת**

[ואלהים]

[עירובין נג:]

[תענית כז: מגי']

ס"א ששה

[לקמן כח.]

דברים טז

בדפוסי' אחר חייך

ירמיה כג

בראשית לה

**גמ'** לא שיעקר יעקב ממקומו. שהרי עליו שקראו הקב"ה יעקב אחר זאת ברכתו למצרים, שנאמר "ויאמר אלהים לישראל ויאמר יעקב יעקב ויאמר הנני" (בראשית מו): הנני עושה חדשה. בתר "אל תזכרו ראשונות" כתיב: בתחלה אב לארם. לאנשי מדינתו, שמארץ ארם היה, שנאמר "בעבר הנהר ישבו אבותיכם" (יהושע כד), ואומר "אל ארם נהרים אל עיר נחור" (בראשית כד). אב לכל העולם. "כי אב המון גוים" (שם יז): שרי. לשון יחיד משמע, שרתי: מסדר שבחיה. דמעיקרא אשר בחרת בו בהיות שמו אברם ושמת שמו אברהם:

הדרן עלך מאימתי

לא שיעקר יעקב ממקומו, אלא ישראל עיקר ויעקב טפל לו; וכן הוא אומר: "אל תזכרו ראשנות וקדמניות אל תתבננו", "אל תזכרו ראשנות" – זה שעבוד מלכיות, "וקדמניות אל תתבננו" – זו יציאת מצרים, "הנני עשה חדשה עתה תצמח" – תני רב יוסף: זו מלחמת גוג ומגוג. *משל, למה הדבר דומה – לאדם שהיה מהלך בדרך ופגע בו *זאב וניצל ממנו, והיה מספר והולך מעשה זאב; פגע בו ארי וניצל ממנו, והיה מספר והולך מעשה ארי; פגע בו נחש וניצל ממנו, שכח מעשה שניהם והיה מספר והולך מעשה נחש; אף כך ישראל – צרות אחרונות משכחות את הראשונות.§ "אברם הוא אברהם" – בתחלה נעשה אב לארם, ולבסוף נעשה אב לכל העולם כולו. "שרי היא שרה", בתחלה נעשית שרי לאומתה, ולבסוף נעשית שרה לכל העולם כולו.§ תני בר קפרא: כל הקורא לאברהם 'אברם' – עובר בעשה, שנאמר: "והיה שמך אברהם". רבי אליעזר אומר: עובר בלאו, שנאמר: "ולא יקרא עוד [את] שמך אברם". אלא מעתה הקורא לשרה 'שרי' הכי נמי?! – התם, קודשא בריך הוא אמר לאברהם: "שרי אשתך לא תקרא את שמה שרי כי שרה שמה". – אלא מעתה, הקורא ליעקב 'יעקב' ה"נ?! – שאני התם, דהדר אהדריה קרא, דכתיב "ויאמר אלהים לישראל במראות הלילה ויאמר יעקב יעקב". מתיב רבי יוסי בר אבין ואיתימא רבי יוסי בר זבידא: "אתה הוא ה' האלהים אשר בחרת באברם"! – אמר ליה: התם נביא הוא דקא מסדר לשבחיה דרחמנא מאי דהוה מעיקרא.§

# הדרן עלך מאימתי

**היה** *קורא בתורה והגיע זמן המקרא, אם כוון לבו – יצא. בפרקים שואל מפני הכבוד ומשיב, ובאמצע – שואל מפני היראה ומשיב, דברי ר' מאיר. ר' יהודה אומר: באמצע שואל מפני היראה ומשיב מפני הכבוד, ובפרקים שואל מפני הכבוד, ומשיב שלום לכל אדם. אלו הן בין הפרקים: בין ברכה ראשונה לשניה, בין שניה ל'שמע', בין 'שמע' ל'והיה אם שמוע', בין 'והיה אם שמוע' ל'ויאמר', בין 'ויאמר' ל'אמת ויציב'. ר' יהודה אומר: בין 'ויאמר' ל'אמת ויציב' לא יפסיק. אמר ר' יהושע בן קרחה: *למה קדמה פרשת "שמע" ל"והיה אם שמוע" – *כדי שיקבל עליו עול מלכות שמים תחלה, ואחר כך מקבל עליו עול מצות; 'והיה אם שמוע' ל'ויאמר' – ש'והיה אם שמוע' נוהג בין ביום ובין בלילה, 'ויאמר' אינו נוהג אלא ביום בלבד.§

**גמ'** ש"מ: *מצות צריכות כוונה! מאי אם כוון לבו – לקרות. לקרות?! והא קא קרי! – בקורא להגיה.§ ת"ר: ק"ש ככתבה, דברי רבי, וחכ"א: בכל לשון. מ"ט דרבי? אמר קרא: 'והיו' – בהוייתן יהו. ורבנן מאי טעמייהו? אמר קרא: 'שמע' – בכל לשון שאתה שומע. ולרבי נמי, הא כתיב 'שמע'! ההוא מבעי ליה: השמע לאזניך מה שאתה מוציא מפיך. *ורבנן? סברי להו כמאן דאמר: לא השמיע לאזנו – יצא. ולרבנן נמי הא כתיב 'והיו'! ההוא מבעי להו שלא יקרא למפרע. ורבי, שלא יקרא למפרע מנא ליה? נפקא ליה מ'דברים' 'הדברים'. ורבנן? – 'דברים' 'הדברים' לא דרשי. למימרא דסבר רבי דכל התורה כולה בכל לשון נאמרה, דאי סלקא דעתך בלשון הקודש נאמרה – 'והיו' דכתב רחמנא למה לי? איצטריך, משום דכתיב 'שמע'. למימרא דסברי רבנן דכל התורה כולה בלשון הקודש נאמרה, דאי סלקא דעתך בכל לשון נאמרה – 'שמע' דכתב רחמנא למה לי? איצטריך, משום דכתיב 'והיו'.§ ת"ר: 'והיו' – שלא יקרא למפרע. 'הדברים על לבבך' יכול תהא כל הפרשה צריכה כוונה, תלמוד לומר: 'האלה' – עד כאן צריכה כוונה, מכאן ואילך אין צריכה כוונה, דברי ר' אליעזר, א"ל רבי עקיבא: הרי הוא אומר

אשר

**היה** קורא בתורה. פרשת ק"ש: והגיע זמן המקרא. זמן ק"ש: בפרקים. בין הפסקות, ולקמן מפרש להו במתניתין בין *פרשה ראשונה לשניה, בין שניה לשמע כו': שואל מפני הכבוד. שואל בשלום אדם נכבד שראוי להקדים לו שלום: ומשיב. שלום אם הקדימו לו. ובגמרא פריך: כיון דשואל פשיטא דמשיב: ובאמצע. באמצע הברכה או הפרשה: מפני היראה. אדם שהוא ירא מפניו שלא יהרגהו, אבל מפני הכבוד לא. ר"י. בגמרא מפרש פלוגתייהו: בין ויאמר לאמת ויציב לא יפסיק. בגמרא (ד' יד) מפרש טעמייהו: והיה אם שמוע נוהג בין ביום בין בלילה. דמשתעי בתלמוד תורה, דכתיב "ולמדתם אותם את בניכם" (דברים יא): ויאמר אינו נוהג אלא ביום. דמשתעי בציצית, שאינה נוהגת אלא ביום, דכתיב "וראיתם אותו" – פרט לכסות לילה (שבת דף כז:): **גמ'** ש"מ מצות צריכות כוונה. שיהא מתכוין לשם מצוה, ותקשה לרבה דאמר במסכת ראש השנה (דף כח.) "התוקע לשיר יצא": כוון לקרות. אבל לצאת ידי מצוה לא בעינן שיהא מתכוין, אלא לקרות בתורה בעלמא: הא קא קרי. הא בקורא קא עסיק תנא ואתי, דקתני היה קורא בתורה: בקורא להגיה. את הספר אם יש בו טעות, דאפילו לקריאה נמי לא מתכוין: ככתבה. בלשון הקודש: מדברים הדברים. דהוה ליה למכתב "והיו דברים האלה" (דברים ו) למדרש שיקראו הדברים כסדרן ולא למפרע כגון "ובשעריך ביתך מזוזות": לימא קסבר ר' וכו'. מדאיצטריך ליה קרא לק"ש שתהא ככתבה, סבירא ליה שאר כל התורה בכל לשון נאמרה לקרות: משום דכתיב שמע. דלא תדרוש שמע בכל לשון שאתה שומע כרבנן: עד כאן. עד "על לבבך":

אשר

**היה** קורא אם כוון לבו יצא. בירושלמי אמרינן(א) ברכות אין מעכבות דאע"פ שלא אמר שתים לפניה ושתים לאחריה – יצא. דאם לא כן תקשי מאי מהני אם כוון לבו, הרי לא בירך תחלה. ואף הא(ג) בפ"ק (ד' יא.) מסקינן סדר ברכות אין מעכבות, הא ברכות מעכבות! וי"ל: דהתם איירי בצבור. דיקא נמי, דקתני "אמר להם הממונה". **ובאמצע** שואל מפני וכו'. ופסק רבינו שמעיה: דבמקום שאסור לספר – אסור לדבר אפילו בלשון הקודש. וכן משמע מתוך מתניתין. ובירושלמי קאמר אפילו באמצע הפסוק, רב הונא בשם רב יוסף אמר: 'ודברת בם' – מכאן שיש לך רשות לדבר בם. והיינו נמי דאמרי' בפ"ק דיומא (דף יט:) 'ודברת בם' – ולא בתפלה, פירוש: שאין משיבין בה מפני הכבוד: **בקורא** להגיה. פירש בקונטרס שאין מתכוין לקרות. תימה: אלמא הא קא קרי! ע"כ נראה: בקורא להגיה שאינו קורא התיבות כהלכתן וכנקודתן אלא ככתיבתן קרי כדי להבין בחסרות ויתרות כמו לטטפת ומוזות. "ואם כוון לבו" לאו דוקא, אלא כלומר: לקרות כדין כנקודתן וכהלכתן: **וחכמים** אומרים בכל לשון. אומר הר"י דהלכה כחכמים, דהלכה כרבי מחבירו ולא מחביריו (עירובין ד' מו:). ועוד, דרבנן סבירא להו כמאן דאמר לא השמיע לאזנו יצא, – וכותיה פסקינן לקמן (ד' טו:): *__בלשון__ הקדש נאמרה. פירש רש"י פרק שני דמגילה (ד' יז: ושם): לקרות בתורה. ולא נהירא, דהא עזרא תיקן קריאת התורה, ומקמי דאתא עזרא 'והיו' למה לי? וי"ל: דמיירי בפרשיות המחוייבין לקרות דאורייתא, כמו פרשת זכור. *אי נמי: מקרא בכורים, ווידוי מעשר, ופרשת חליצה, שמצוה בתורה לקרותן – ואפ"ה בכל לשון נאמרה בסיני שכל דבור ודבור שהיה יוצא מפי הקב"ה היה מתחלק לשבעים לשון*: **עד** כאן מצות כוונה. עד "בכל מאדך", שני פסוקים אלו מדברים ביחוד ה', באהבתו וביראתו:

אשר

°) [ועיין בן קרחה פירשו תוס' בשבת קנ. וב"ב קיג. וע' תוס' פסחים קיב. ובכורות נח.]

עין משפט נר מצוה

א א מיי' פ"ב מהלכות ק"ש [הל' א] סמג עשין יח טור שו"ע או"ח סי' ס סעיף ד:
ב ב מיי' שם הלכה טו טז סמג שם טוש"ע או"ח סי' סו סעיף א:
ג ג ד מיי' שם הלכה י סמג שם טוש"ע שם סעיף ה:
ד ה מיי' פ"ג מהלכות ציצית הלכה ה סמג עשין כו טוש"ע או"ח סימן יח סעיף א:
ה ו מיי' פ"ב מהלכות [ק"ש ושופר הלכה ד] סמג שם טוש"ע או"ח סימן סב סעיף ד:
ו ז מיי' פ"ב מהל' ק"ש הלכה י סמג עשין יח טוש"ע או"ח סימן סב סעיף ב:

## רב נסים גאון

**מותיב** ר' יוסי בר אבין ואיתימא ר' יוסי בר זבדא אתה אברהם מי לא הדר קרייה רחמנא אברם ובתוספתא נמי [ספ"א דמכילתין] בענין זה המקום אברם הוא אברהם אע"פ שחזר וקרא את אברהם אברם אינו לגנאי אלא לשבח כו' הוא אברם עד שלא נדבר עמו הוא אברהם משנדבר עמו ויש ששואלין למה נשתנו שמו של אברהם ושמו של יעקב ולא נשתנה שמו של יצחק ופשטה של שאלה זו כי אברהם ויעקב אבותיהם קראום באותן השמות ולפיכך גידלם הקב"ה בשמות שקרא להן הוא אבל יצחק הקב"ה קראו בזה השם קודם שנולד כדכתיב (בראשית יז) אבל שרה אשתך יולדת לך בן וקראת את שמו יצחק ואית במכילתא דר' ישמעאל [בפ' בא] יצחק לא נשתנה שמו למה שנקרא שמו מפי הקב"ה ובגמרא דבני מערבא (בסיפא דהאי פירקא) מפני מה נשתנה שמו של אברהם ושמו של יעקב ושמו של יצחק לא נשתנה אילו אבותיהם קראו אותן בשמן אבל יצחק הקב"ה קראו. ארבעה נקראו עד שלא נולדו יצחק וישמעאל יאשיה ושלמה:

סליק פירקא קמא

פירקא תנינא

**שמעת** מינה מצות צריכות כוונה. איתיה להדיא דהא מילתא בפרק ראוהו בית דין במסכת ראש השנה (דף כח) דקאמר אלמא קא סבר רבא מצות אין צריכות כוונה ואיתיביה אביי כמה תיובתא ולבסוף אוקמי' אלא אמר רבא לצאת לא בעי כוונה לעבור בזמנו לא בעי כוונה שלא בזמנו בעי כוונה:

## גליון הש"ס

**גמ'** כל הקורא כו'. מג"א סימן קנו ועיין פר"ח ס"ס ס"ז:
פרק היה קורא
**גמ'** ההוא מבע"ל כו'. עיין תוס' סוטה י"ז ע"ב ד"ה דכתיב: **תוס'** ד"ה בלשון כו' דהא עזרא כו'. עיין מג"א ריש סימן קל"ה:

מסורת הש"ס: ע"א ומכילתא פ' בא | ע"ז ב: ד"ה ולהו אשה סקיה לפניהם גי' אחרת | [נ"ל ברכה] | תוספתא פ"א | [ר"ה דף כח.] | תוס' לקמן יז. | פסחים קיד: | מגילה דף יז. | סוטה לב: ד"ה ורבנן

אשר אנכי מצוך היום על לבבך" – מכאן אתה למד שכל הפרשה כולה צריכה כוונה. אמר רבה בר בר חנה אמר ר' יוחנן: הלכה כר"ע. איכא דמתני לה אהא, דתניא: *הקורא את שמע צריך שיכוין את לבו; ר' אחא משום ר' יהודה אומר: כיון שכוון לבו בפרק ראשון – שוב אינו צריך. אמר רבה בר בר חנה אמר ר' יוחנן: הלכה כר' אחא שאמר משום ר' יהודה. תניא אידך: 'והיו' – שלא יקרא למפרע, 'על לבבך' – ר' זוטרא אומר: עד כאן – מצות כוונה, מכאן ואילך – מצות קריאה; רבי יאשיה אומר: עד כאן – מצות קריאה, מכאן ואילך – מצות כוונה. מ"ש מכאן ואילך מצות קריאה – דכתיב 'לדבר בם', הכא נמי הא כתיב 'ודברת בם'! ה"ק: עד כאן – מצות כוונה וקריאה, מכאן ואילך – קריאה בלא כוונה. ומאי שנא עד כאן מצות כוונה וקריאה – דכתיב 'על לבבך' 'ודברת בם', התם נמי הא כתיב 'על לבבכם' 'לדבר בם'! ההוא מבעי ליה לכדרבי יצחק, *דאמר: "ושמתם את דברי אלה" – צריכה שתהא שימה כנגד הלב. § אמר מר, "ר' יאשיה אומר: עד כאן – מצות קריאה, מכאן ואילך – מצות כוונה". מ"ש מכאן ואילך מצות כוונה – משום דכתיב 'על לבבכם' – הכא נמי הא כתיב 'על לבבך'! ה"ק: עד כאן – מצות קריאה וכוונה, מכאן ואילך – כוונה בלא קריאה. ומ"ש עד כאן מצות קריאה וכוונה – דכתיב 'על לבבך' 'ודברת בם' – התם נמי הא כתיב 'על לבבכם' 'לדבר בם'! ההוא בדברי תורה כתיב, וה"ק רחמנא: אגמירו בנייכו תורה כי היכי דליגרסו בהו. § ת"ר: "שמע ישראל ה' אלהינו ה' אחד" – עד כאן צריכה כוונת הלב, דברי ר"מ. אמר רבא: הלכה כר"מ. תניא, סומכוס אומר: כל המאריך ב'אחד' – מאריכין לו ימיו ושנותיו. אמר רב אחא בר יעקב: ובדל"ת. אמר רב אשי: ובלבד שלא יחטוף בחי"ת. ר' ירמיה הוה יתיב קמיה דר' [חייא בר אבא] חזייה דהוה מאריך טובא. א"ל: כיון דאמליכתיה למעלה ולמטה ולארבע רוחות השמים, תו לא צריכת. § אמר רב נתן בר מר עוקבא אמר רב יהודה: 'על לבבך' בעמידה. 'על לבבך' סלקא דעתך?! אלא אימא: עד 'על לבבך' – בעמידה, מכאן ואילך לא. ורבי יוחנן אמר: כל הפרשה כולה בעמידה. ואזדא ר' יוחנן לטעמיה, דאמר רבה בר בר חנה א"ר יוחנן: הלכה כר' אחא שאמר משום ר' יהודה. § ת"ר: שמע ישראל ה' אלהינו ה' אחד – זו ק"ש של ר' יהודה הנשיא. א"ל רב לר' חייא: לא חזינא ליה לרבי דמקבל עליה מלכות שמים. אמר ליה: *בר פחתי! *בשעה שמעביר ידיו על פניו מקבל עליו עול מלכות שמים. חוזר וגומרה, או אינו חוזר וגומרה? בר קפרא אומר: אינו חוזר וגומרה; רבי שמעון ברבי אומר: חוזר וגומרה. א"ל: בר קפרא לר"ש ברבי: בשלמא לדידי דאמינא אינו חוזר וגומרה – היינו דמהדר רבי אשמעתא דאית בה יציאת מצרים. אלא לדידך דאמרת חוזר וגומרה, למה ליה לאהדורי? כדי להזכיר יציאת מצרים בזמנה. אמר ר' אילא בריה דרב שמואל בר מרתא משמיה דרב: אמר "שמע ישראל ה' אלהינו ה' אחד" ונאנס בשינה – יצא. אמר ליה רב נחמן לדרו עבדיה: בפסוקא קמא – צערן, טפי – לא תצערן. אמר ליה רב יוסף לרב יוסף בריה דרבה: אבוך היכי הוה עביד? אמר ליה: בפסוקא קמא הוה קא מצער נפשיה, טפי לא הוה מצער נפשיה. אמר *רב יוסף: פרקדן לא יקרא קריאת שמע. מקרא הוא דלא ליקרי, הא מיגנא – שפיר דמי? והא רבי יהושע בן לוי *לייט אמאן דגני אפרקיד! אמרי: מיגנא, כי מצלי – שפיר דמי. מקרא, אע"ג דמצלי – נמי אסור. והא ר' יוחנן מצלי וקרי! שאני ר' יוחנן דבעל בשר הוה. § "ובפרקים שואל וכו'". § משיב מחמת מאי? אילימא מפני הכבוד – השתא משאל שאיל, אהדורי מבעיא?! אלא: שואל מפני הכבוד ומשיב שלום לכל אדם. אימא סיפא: "ובאמצע – שואל מפני היראה ומשיב", משיב מחמת מאי? אילימא מפני היראה – השתא משאל שאיל, אהדורי מבעיא?! אלא מפני הכבוד: היינו-דר"י! דתנן, ר"י אומר: באמצע – שואל מפני היראה ומשיב מפני הכבוד, ובפרקים – שואל מפני הכבוד ומשיב שלום לכל אדם! חסורי מחסרא והכי קתני: בפרקים – שואל מפני הכבוד ואין צריך לומר שהוא משיב, ובאמצע – שואל מפני היראה ואין צריך לומר שהוא משיב, דברי ר"מ; רבי יהודה אומר: באמצע – שואל מפני היראה ומשיב מפני הכבוד. ובפרקים

תורה אור: דברים ו / שם יא / שם ו

**רש"י** איכא דמתני לה. להא דרבה בב"ח: בפרק ראשון. כל פרשת שמע: ע"ב מצות כוונה כו'. כולה מפרש לה והזיל: [א] א"ר יאשיה עד כאן: מצות כוונה כו'. קס"ד לכוונה בלא קריאה: מכאן ואילך. פרשת "והיה אם שמוע": שתהא שימה כנגד הלב. דקא פרק ראשון: מצות כוונה כו'. "ושמתם" דכתיב לאו בקריאה וכוונה קאי, אלא בשימת תפילין של יד שיהא שם אותם על גובה של יד כנגד הלב על קבורת הזרוע – כרדו"ן. ס"ג: ההוא בדברי תורה כתיב. כדמוכח קרא "ולמדתם אותם את בניכם וגו'": עד כאן. פסוק ראשון לבדו: ובדל"ת. ולא בחי"ת, דכל כמה דאמר אחד בלא דל"ת לא משתמע מידי, ומה בצע בהארכתו? אבל בדל"ת יאריך עד כשיעור שיעשנו בלבו יחיד בשמים בארץ ולארבע רוחותיה, כדמפרש לקמן: ובלבד שלא יחטוף בחי"ת. בשביל אריכות הדל"ת לא ימהר בקריאתה, שלא יקראנה בחטף [א] בלא פתח, ואין זה כלום: דאמליכתיה למעלה וכו'. שהארכת שיעור שתחשוב בלבך ה' אחד בשמים ובארץ וארבע רוחותיה: בעמידה. אפי' לב"ה דאמרי [לעיל יא.] עוסקין במלאכתן וקורין, ומהלכין וקורין – מודים הם שצריך לעמוד במקום אחד עד המקרא הזה, לפי שעד כאן מצות כוונה: לא חזינא דמקבל עליה מלכות שמים. שהיה שונה לתלמידיו מקודם זמן ק"ש, וכשהגיע הזמן לא ראיתיו מפסיק: חוזר וגומרה. לאחר שעמדו התלמידים: דקא מהדר. לשנות לתלמידים בכל יום שמעתא דאית בה יציאת מצרים במקום פרשת ציצית ואמת ויציב: בזמנה. בזמן ק"ש: בפסוקא קמא צערן. אם ראיתני מנמנם – צערני עד שאנער יפה בפסוק ראשון: פרקדן. שוכב על גבו ופניו למעלה: לייט אמאן דגני אפרקיד. שמא יתקשה אברו בתוך שנתו ונראה לרבים, והוא דרך גנאי: מיגנא. לישן: כי מצלי שפיר דמי. כשהוא מוטה על צדו מעט – שפיר דמי, אבל מקרי ק"ש, אפילו מצלי נמי אסור – שמקבל עליו מלכות שמים דרך שררה וגאוה: לכל אדם. אפילו אינו נכבד: חסורי מחסרא. דהוה ליה למתני בתרווייהו "אין צריך לומר" – ותו ליכא למקשי מידי: אחי

**תוספות** אשר אנכי מצוך. דאי כדקא אמרת הוה ליה למכתב "אשר צויתיך", ד"מצוך" משמע אפילו מכאן ואילך. ומ"מ, אצטריך "האלה", דאי לאו הכי, הוה אמינא דאף פרשה שנייה בכלל: אמר רבא הלכה כרבי מאיר. והכי הלכתא, דקיי"ל כרבא דהוא בתראה: על לבבך בעמידה. בירושלמי מפרש: לאו דאי היה יושב, עומד, אלא דאם היה מהלך – עומד. אע"ג דב"ה אמרי כל אדם קורא כדרכו – מ"מ, מצוה מן המובחר לעמוד כשהוא מהלך, לפי שאינו מיושב כל כך ואינו יכול לכוין כשהוא מהלך כאשר היה עומד; וכן הלכה דמהלך בדרך מצוה לעמוד בפסוק א', ובענין כונה בפסוק ראשון לבד. וכן איתא בתנחומא:* רב יהודה בשם שמואל אמר אסור לקבל עליו עול מלכות שמים כשהוא מהלך, אלא יעמוד ויקרא, וכשיגיע ל"ואהבת" ילך לדרכו: שואל מפני היראה וכו'. ר"מ ור' יהודה הלכה כרבי יהודה, דאמר "אפילו באמצע משיב מפני הכבוד". א"כ, נראה שמותר לענות קדיש וקדושה באמצע ק"ש, דאין לך מפני הכבוד גדול מזה, אבל באמצע י"ח – אסור, דמשמע (ג) לקמן בפ' אין עומדין (ד' לא.) *דבין גאולה לתפלה אין לענות, וכל שכן בתפלה עצמה. ומי שמתפלל לבדו וש"צ מגיע ל"מודים" – ישחה ל"מודים", אבל לא יאמר 'מודים'. *ודוקא שהיה באמצע הברכה, אבל בסוף הברכה – לא, דנראה ככורע בשביל הברכה, ואמרינן (לקמן ד' לד.) דאין לכרוע בכל ברכות אלא באותן שתקנו חכמים. ור"ת היה רגיל שהיה ממתין ב"עושה פלא" כדי לענות קדיש וקדושה עם הצבור, והי' סובר אפי' שהה כדי לגמור את הכל – אינו חוזר לראש: ימים

**עין משפט נר מצוה**
ז א מיי' פ"ב מהלכות ק"ש ה"א סמג עשין יח טור שו"ע או"ח סימן ס סעיף ה וכסימן סג סעיף ז:
ח ב ג ד מיי' שם הלכה ט סמג שם טוש"ע או"ח סי' סא סעיף ו ח:
ט ה מיי' שם הלכה ג סמג שם טוש"ע או"ח סימן סג סעיף ג:
י ו טור וש"ע או"ח סימן סא סעיף ו:
יא ז מיי' שם סמג שם טוש"ע או"ח סי' סג סעיף ה:
יב ה מיי' שם הלכה ב טוש"ע (או"ח) שם ס"א: ריש פרשת לך

ר"ל ממאי לאמרי' התם א"ח דבר לאחר אמת ויציב וכגירסת הרי"ף והרא"ש ע"ש כ"ה בתלמי גרסתו והוא דחוק ולענ"ד צ"ל למשמע לעיל ע: [ועי' תוס' לקמן כא: ד"ה עד]

**רב נסים גאון**
ההוא מיבעי לי' לכדר' יצחק דאמר ר' יצחק צריכה שתהא שימה כנגד הלב. אתפילין של יד קאי ועיקרה במס' דמנחות (דף לז) בפרק הקומץ את המנחה: שאני ר' יוחנן דבעל בשר הוה. איתיה לפירושיה בבבא מציעא בפ' השוכר את הפועלין (דף פד) אמר (רבא) [רב פפא] אבריה דר' יוחנן בת ה' קבין ואמרי לה בת ג' קבין:

[פי' בן גדולים עיין שבת ג: כט. נזיר נט. וברש"י שם]

**גליון הש"ס**
גמ' זו ק"ש של ר"ה. עי' בר"י בפרקין יא. ד"ה מתני' שאומנין: תוס' ד"ה שואל כו' דמשמע כו'. עי' תשובת בא"ר שבע סימן י:

**מסורת הש"ס**
תוספתא פ"ב
ספרי פרשה [מנחות לז:]
[שלא ירגלו עי' מסביבן ומתגנו בר פחתי וע' אחרים]
נדה קף יד.
[תיבת לייט קלושין לג: ושב]

**הגהות הב"ח**
[א] רש"י ד"ה בחטף (בלא)
(א) רש"י ד"ה עד כאן ותיבת נמחק: (ב) תום' מפני היראה וכו' י"ח אסור דמשמע בפ' מכ"א ע

אַחִי. כָּךְ שְׁמוֹ: תַּנָּא דְּבֵי רַבִּי חִיָּיא. שֶׁהָיָה שׁוֹנֶה בְּבֵית רַבִּי חִיָּיא: מַהוּ שֶׁיַּפְסִיק. לִשְׁאֵלַת שָׁלוֹם: יָמִים שֶׁהַיָּחִיד גּוֹמֵר בָּהֶן אֶת הַהַלֵּל. שֶׁהוּא חוֹבָה לְכָל אָדָם, וְהֵם אֶחָד וְעֶשְׂרִים יוֹם בַּשָּׁנָה, כִּדְאָמְרִינַן בְּמַסֶּכֶת עֲרָכִין (ד' י.): מַהוּ שֶׁיִּטְעוֹם. אֶת הַתַּבְשִׁיל לָדַעַת אִם צָרִיךְ מֶלַח אוֹ תַּבְלִין: מְטַעֶמֶת. טְעִימַת תַּבְשִׁיל: רְבִיעֲתָא. רְבִיעִית הַלּוֹג: חִדְלוּ לָכֶם מִן הָאָדָם. כְּשֶׁיֵּשׁ לָכֶם לַעֲסוֹק בִּכְבוֹד הַמָּקוֹם אַל תִּתְעַסְּקוּ בִּכְבוֹד אָדָם, דְּאִי לָאו הָכִי – לָמָּה לֵיהּ לְחִדּוּל: וּשְׁמוּאֵל. לָא דָּרֵישׁ לְשׁוֹן בָּמָה, אֶלָּא כְּמַשְׁמָעוֹ: בַּמֶּה חֲשַׁבְתּוֹ לָזֶה שֶׁהִקְדַּמְתָּ כְּבוֹדוֹ לִכְבוֹדִי: שׁוֹאֵל מִפְּנֵי הַכָּבוֹד. וְהָא ק"ש קוֹדֶם תְּפִלָּה הוּא, וְקָתָנֵי "שׁוֹאֵל": תַּרְגְּמָהּ ר' אַבָּא. לְהָא דְּרַב וּשְׁמוּאֵל דְּאָסְרֵי: בְּמַשְׁכִּים לְפִתְחוֹ. אֲבָל פְּגָעוֹ בַּדֶּרֶךְ – שׁוֹאֵל: ה"ג. אָמַר רַב אִידִי בַּר אָבִין אָמַר רַב יִצְחָק בַּר אֲשִׁיאָן אָסוּר לָאָדָם לַעֲשׂוֹת חֲפָצָיו קוֹדֶם שֶׁיִּתְפַּלֵּל*: צֶדֶק. תְּפִלָּה, שֶׁמַּצְדִּיקוֹ לְבוֹרְאוֹ, וְהָדַר "וְיָשֵׂם פְּעָמָיו" לְדַרְכֵי חֲפָצָיו: אַל תִּקְרֵי שָׂבֵעַ אֶלָּא שֶׁבַע. יָלִין בַּל יִפָּקֵד מִן הַשָּׁמַיִם בַּחֲלוֹם – הֲרֵי הוּא רַע, לְכָךְ אֵין מַשְׁגִּיחִין לְפָקְדוֹ: וה'

תורה אור

וּבַפְּרָקִים – שׁוֹאֵל מִפְּנֵי הַכָּבוֹד וּמֵשִׁיב שָׁלוֹם לְכָל אָדָם. תַּנְיָא נַמִּי הָכִי: הַקּוֹרֵא אֶת שְׁמַע וּפָגַע בּוֹ רַבּוֹ אוֹ גָּדוֹל הֵימֶנּוּ, בַּפְּרָקִים – שׁוֹאֵל מִפְּנֵי הַכָּבוֹד וא"צ לוֹמַר שֶׁהוּא מֵשִׁיב, וּבָאֶמְצַע – שׁוֹאֵל מִפְּנֵי הַיִּרְאָה ואצ"ל שֶׁהוּא מֵשִׁיב, דִּבְרֵי ר' מֵאִיר; ר' יְהוּדָה אוֹמֵר: בָּאֶמְצַע – שׁוֹאֵל מִפְּנֵי הַיִּרְאָה וּמֵשִׁיב מִפְּנֵי הַכָּבוֹד, וּבַפְּרָקִים – שׁוֹאֵל מִפְּנֵי הַכָּבוֹד וּמֵשִׁיב שָׁלוֹם לְכָל אָדָם. בְּעָא מִינֵּיהּ אֲחִי תַּנָּא דְּבֵי רַבִּי חִיָּיא מֵרַבִּי חִיָּיא: א בַּהַלֵּל וּבַמְּגִלָּה מַהוּ שֶׁיַּפְסִיק? (א) אָמְרִינַן ק"ו: ק"ש דְּאוֹרַיְיתָא פּוֹסֵק – הַלֵּל דְּרַבָּנָן מִבַּעְיָא, אוֹ דִּלְמָא *פִּרְסוּמֵי נִיסָּא עֲדִיף? א"ל: פּוֹסֵק וְאֵין בְּכָךְ כְּלוּם. אָמַר רַבָּה: ב יָמִים שֶׁהַיָּחִיד גּוֹמֵר בָּהֶן אֶת הַהַלֵּל – בֵּין פֶּרֶק לְפֶרֶק פּוֹסֵק, בְּאֶמְצַע הַפֶּרֶק אֵינוֹ פּוֹסֵק; וְיָמִים שֶׁאֵין הַיָּחִיד גּוֹמֵר בָּהֶן אֶת הַהַלֵּל – אֲפִי' בְּאֶמְצַע הַפֶּרֶק פּוֹסֵק. אִינִי?! וְהָא רַב בַּר שַׁבָּא אִיקְלַע לְגַבֵּיהּ דְּרָבִינָא, וְיָמִים שֶׁאֵין הַיָּחִיד גּוֹמֵר אֶת הַהַלֵּל הֲוָה, וְלָא פְּסֵיק לֵיהּ! שָׁאנֵי רַב בַּר שַׁבָּא דְּלָא חָשִׁיב עֲלֵיהּ דְּרָבִינָא.§ בְּעֵי מִינֵּיהּ אַשְׁיָאן תַּנָּא דְּבֵי ר' אַמֵּי מֵר' אַמֵּי: הַשְּׁרוּי בְּתַעֲנִית מַהוּ שֶׁיִּטְעוֹם? אֲכִילָה וּשְׁתִיָּה קַבִּיל עֲלֵיהּ – וְהָא לֵיכָּא, אוֹ דִּילְמָא הֲנָאָה קַבִּיל עֲלֵיהּ – וְהָא אִיכָּא? א"ל: טוֹעֵם וְאֵין בְּכָךְ כְּלוּם. תַּנְיָא נַמִּי הָכִי: ג מְטַעֶמֶת אֵינָהּ טְעוּנָה בְּרָכָה, ד וְהַשָּׁרוּי בְּתַעֲנִית טוֹעֵם וְאֵין בְּכָךְ כְּלוּם. עַד כַּמָּה? ר' אַמֵּי וְר' אַסִּי טָעֲמֵי עַד שִׁיעוּר רְבִיעֲתָא.§ אָמַר רַב: ה כָּל הַנּוֹתֵן שָׁלוֹם לַחֲבֵירוֹ קוֹדֶם שֶׁיִּתְפַּלֵּל – כְּאִילּוּ עֲשָׂאוֹ בָּמָה, שֶׁנֶּאֱמַר: "חִדְלוּ לָכֶם מִן הָאָדָם אֲשֶׁר נְשָׁמָה בְּאַפּוֹ כִּי בַּמֶּה נֶחְשָׁב הוּא", *אַל תִּקְרֵי 'בַּמֶּה' אֶלָּא 'בָּמָה'. וּשְׁמוּאֵל אָמַר: בַּמֶּה חֲשַׁבְתּוֹ לָזֶה וְלֹא לֶאֱלוֹהַּ. מְתִיב רַב שֵׁשֶׁת: "בַּפְּרָקִים – שׁוֹאֵל מִפְּנֵי הַכָּבוֹד וּמֵשִׁיב"! תַּרְגְּמָהּ ר' אַבָּא: בְּמַשְׁכִּים לְפִתְחוֹ. (א"ר יוֹנָה א"ר זֵירָא: כָּל הָעוֹשֶׂה חֲפָצָיו קוֹדֶם שֶׁיִּתְפַּלֵּל – כְּאִילּוּ בָּנָה בָּמָה. א"ל: 'בָּמָה' אָמְרַתְּ? א"ל: לָא, אָסוּר קָא אָמִינָא, וּכְדְרַב אִידִי בַּר אָבִין. ד)אָמַר רַב אִידִי בַּר אָבִין אָמַר רַב יִצְחָק בַּר אֲשִׁיאָן: ו אָסוּר לוֹ לָאָדָם לַעֲשׂוֹת חֲפָצָיו קוֹדֶם שֶׁיִּתְפַּלֵּל, שֶׁנֶּאֱמַר: "צֶדֶק לְפָנָיו יְהַלֵּךְ וְיָשֵׂם לְדֶרֶךְ פְּעָמָיו". וְאָמַר רַב אִידִי בַּר אָבִין אָמַר רַב יִצְחָק בַּר אֲשִׁיאָן: ז כָּל הַמִּתְפַּלֵּל וְאח"כ יוֹצֵא לַדֶּרֶךְ – הקב"ה עוֹשֶׂה לוֹ חֲפָצָיו, שֶׁנֶּאֱמַר: "צֶדֶק לְפָנָיו יְהַלֵּךְ וְיָשֵׂם לְדֶרֶךְ פְּעָמָיו".§ וְא"ר יוֹנָה א"ר זֵירָא: *כָּל הַלָּן שִׁבְעַת יָמִים בְּלֹא חֲלוֹם נִקְרָא רַע, שֶׁנֶּאֱמַר: "וְשָׂבֵעַ יָלִין בַּל יִפָּקֶד רָע", אַל תִּקְרֵי 'שָׂבֵעַ' אֶלָּא 'שֶׁבַע'. א"ל: רַב אַחָא בְּרֵיהּ דְּרַבִּי חִיָּיא בַּר אַבָּא, הָכִי א"ר חִיָּיא א"ר יוֹחָנָן: כָּל הַמַּשְׂבִּיעַ עַצְמוֹ מִדִּבְרֵי תוֹרָה וְלָן – אֵין מְבַשְּׂרִין אוֹתוֹ בְּשׂוֹרוֹת רָעוֹת, שֶׁנֶּאֱמַר: "וְשָׂבֵעַ יָלִין בַּל יִפָּקֶד רָע".§ "אֵלּוּ הֵן בֵּין הַפְּרָקִים וכו'".§ א"ר אַבָּהוּ א"ר יוֹחָנָן: ח הֲלָכָה כר' יְהוּדָה דְּאָמַר, בֵּין 'אֱלֹהֵיכֶם' לֶ'אֱמֶת וְיַצִּיב' לֹא יַפְסִיק. *א"ר אַבָּהוּ א"ר יוֹחָנָן: מַאי טַעְמֵיהּ דְּרַבִּי יְהוּדָה – דִּכְתִיב: וה'

[שבת קף כג:] נ"א עד שיתפלל
ישעיה ב
*סוטה ד:
עי' רש"א
תהלים פה
משלי יט
נה: [וסם איתא וכ"ה בשאלתות בפ' מקץ]
[נ"ל ואמר]

**ימים** שהיחיד גומר בהם את ההלל. לאו דוקא יחיד, אלא אפילו לצבור קורא יחיד, כיון שאין כל ישראל ביחד כמו שהיו בשחיטת פסחים בי"ד בניסן. ולאו דוקא גומר, דודאי קי"ל דימים שאין יחיד גומר את ההלל אין חובה לאמרו כלל אפילו בדילוג, דהכי משמע בערכין (פ"ב ד' י:) דחשיב כ"א יום דיחיד גומר בהן את ההלל ופריך "ר"ה וי"כ נמי לימא", משמע דבשאר ימים טובים כמו בראשי חדשים פשיטא ליה דאין לומר, מדלא חשיב יותר מכ"א יום, וגם מדלא קאמר "לגמור בר"ה וביו"ה" דאז הוה משמע דבשאר ימים טובים כמו בר"ח – ודאי אין גומרין אבל קורין, אבל עתה משמע אפילו קורין לא. וכן משמע בפרק בתרא דתענית (ד' כח:): רב איקלע לבבל, חזנהו דהוו קא קרו בר"ח, סבר לאפסוקינהו – פירוש: שהיה סובר שהיו גומרים אותו – כיון דחזא דקא מדלגי דלוגי אמר: ש"מ מנהג אבותיהם בידיהם, אלמא: דימים דאין גומרין בהן הלל – אין חובה לאמרו, ומה שאנו אומרין אותו – היינו משום מנהג. וכתוב במחזור ויטרי: כיון שאינו אלא מנהג בעלמא – לא מברכינן עליה, כדאמר פרק "לולב וערבה" (סוכה ד' מד:) אין מברכין על דבר שהוא מנהג. ומיהו אומר ר"ת דאינו ראיה, דאטלטול ודאי לא מברכינן, אבל על מצוה – פשיטא דמברכינן דהא חזינן כל יו"ט שני אינו אלא מנהגא – ומברכין. והכא נמי משמע דמברכין, דאי לא מברכין – מאי הפסקה שייך בה? ועוד ראיה דמברכינן על מנהגא – מהא דרב על לבי כנישתא וכו', ואם לא ברכו בתחלה, אמאי לא הרגיש רב דהוה מנהגא עד שדלגו? אלא בוודאי ברכו, מפני שמברכים בטוב על מנהגא, ובשביל כן לא הרגיש עד הדלוג. וא"ת: אמאי לא אסיק אדעתיה אם ברכו 'לקרות' או 'לגמור'? וי"ל: דבכך אין לחוש, שבטוב יכול לברך 'לגמור' אפי' כשהוא מדלג, או איפכא. ומה שמברכין כך על הדלוג 'לקרות' וכשהן גומרין 'לגמור' – כדי שלא יטעו, ומשום הכי לא היה יכול להבין מתוך הברכה עד הדלוג. ויש שרוצין לומר דיחיד האומר הלל בימים שאין גומרין שאין לו לברך. ומיהו, השר מקוצי היה אומר: דכיון שרצה לחייב עצמו – מברך, ואין זה ברכה לבטלה, מידי דהוה אלולב(ב) ואתפילין דהני נשי מברכות אע"ג שאינן חייבות, ובלילי פסחים יש שמברכין פעמים, בתחלה 'לקרות' ואחר הסעודה, אחר 'שפוך', מברכין 'לגמור', ומייתי ראיה מירושלמי (דפרק א') מההיא דמייתי עלה דכל הברכות *פותחין ב"ברוך", חוץ מן הברכות הסמוכות לחברתה וברכת הפירות והמצות, ופריך בירושלמי עלה: והא איכא גאולה! פירוש: 'אשר גאלנו' דסמוכה לחברתה, ואמאי פותחת ב"ברוך"? שנייא דאם שמעה בבה"כ – יצא. ופריך: והרי סופה – פירוש: 'יהללוך' דאינה סמוכה, שהסעודה מפסקת ואפ"ה אינה פותחת ב"ברוך" – ומשני: שתים הנה, אחת להבא ואחת לשעבר. פירוש: אחת להבא – זו היא אותה ברכה שמברכין אחר אכילה 'לגמור' ולאותה ברכה היא סמוכה. אחת לשעבר – היינו אותה שבירך קודם אכילה. אלמא: דמברכין שני פעמים. אבל זה הפירוש אינו מיושב, דהרי(ג) סיפא משמע דקאי אברכה ד'אשר גאלנו', דקאי בה מתחלה! אלא ודאי אברכה ד'אשר גאלנו' קאי. כאשר אפרש, מיהו משמע בירושלמי כאשר פירשתי תחלה שהיו מברכין ב' פעמים תחלה וסוף. אבל אומר ר' יהודה דזו היא תמיהא גדולה, מאחר שבירך קודם אכילה אמאי מפסיק ואוכל בינתים? שהרי בימים שאין יחיד גומר בהן את ההלל, כיון שבירך תחלה כמו הכא – אינו מותר לפסוק אלא מפני הכבוד; דאי בשלא בירך – אמאי לא יפסיק באמצע אפילו שלא מפני הכבוד, הא לא היה מפסיק שום ברכה! אלא נראה: הא דפריך בירושלמי "הרי גאולה", דמשמע דמברכין עליה בתחלה – איירי באדם שעושה הסדר בבת אחת, שאז אינו מפסיק, שאינו צריך, אבל אנו שמפסיקין לאכול אין לנו לברך כלל לא בתחלה ולא בסוף. והא דקאמר בירושלמי והרי(ד) סיפא – זהו 'אשר גאלנו' דחותמת ב"ברוך", ואמאי והא הודאה בעלמא היא כברכת פירות, ואמאי חותמת בברוך! ומשני: שתים הנה, שתי גאולות, אחת להבא ואחת לשעבר, פירוש לעתיד כמו 'יגיענו', וגם היא ארוכה קצת, וגם יש בה לשעבר כמו "אשר גאלנו מגאולת מצרים" – לפיכך חותמת ב"ברוך". ומה שהקשה מ"יהללוך" שאינה סמוכה, לפי מה שפרשתי עתה, ואפ"ה אינה פותחת בברוך – יש ליתן טעם, לפי שהיא הודאה בעלמא, ואפילו שהיא ארוכה קצת – תקנו בה חתימה ולא פתיחה, כמו "אלהי נשמה". וכן משמע בירושלמי שהיה דרכן לומר הלל בבית הכנסת, ואח"כ שותין כוסות שלהם בביתם בלא שום סדר, דבעי בירושלמי (פ' ע"פ): שתאן בבת אחת מהו? פירוש: זה אחר זה, בלא הלל וסדר בינתים, מהו?(ה) שמעינן מן הדא דא"ר יוחנן: הלל, אם שמעה בבית הכנסת – יצא. וכן משמע בתוספתא *דמי שלא היה יודע ונכנס בבית הכנסת וכו'. והשתא נמי מיושב, דבשביל כך פותחת ברכה ד'אשר גאלנו' ב"ברוך" – דטעמא שאינה סמוכה, כי הא דאם קרא הלל בבהכ"נ יצא: **או** דילמא הנאה קביל עליה. האי לישנא משמע דמיירי בתענית יחיד שקבל עליו אבל בתענית הכתוב – לא: **טועם** ואין בכך כלום. פירש ר"ח: שחוזר ופולט, דלא חשיב הנאה מן הטעימה, אבל בולע – לא, אפילו בשאר תעניות, ומשום הכי הפולט אינו צריך ברכה – שאינו נהנה: **במשכים** לפתחו. וכן הלכה, אבל פגעו באקראי – מותר: למה

[פותחות וחותמות בברוך כצ"ל רש"א]
*פרק ע"פ

יג א טור וש"ע או"ח סימן תרכב סעיף ב:
יד ב מיי' פ"ג מהלכות חנוכה הלכה ט טור ש"ע או"ח סימן תכב סעיף ד [ובסי' תפח סעי' א] ובסימן תרמד סעיף א:
טו ג מיי' פ"א מהלכות ברכות הלכה ב סמג (הלכות ברכות) עשין כז טוש"ע או"ח סימן רי סעיף ב:
טז ד מיי' פ"א מהלכות תענית הלכה יד טוש"ע או"ח סימן תקסז סעיף א [רב אלפס תענית פ"א דף קעב]:
יז ה מיי' פ"ו מהלכות תפלה הלכה ד סמג עשין יט טור ש"ע או"ח סימן פט סעיף ב:
יח ו [מיי' שם סמג שם טוש"ע] שם סעיף ג:
[ו מיי' שם טוש"ע שם וע"ש בב"י]
יט ז מיי' פ"ב מהלכות ק"ש הלכה יז סמג עשין יח טוש"ע או"ח סימן סו סעיף ה:

## רב נסים גאון

**אמר** (רבא) [רבה] ימים שהיחיד גומר בהן את ההלל כו'. איתיה לפירושייהו במסכתא תענית בפ' בג' פרקים בשנה (דף כח) דאמר ר' יוחנן משום ר' שמעון בן יהוצדק י"ח ימים יחיד גומר בהן את ההלל כו' והתם נמי אמרינן אמר (רבה) [רבא] זאת אומרת הלל דראש חודש לאו דאורייתא ולפיכך התיר רבא לפסוק בו אפי' באמצע הפרק:

## גליון הש"ס

**גמ'** מטעמת כו'. עי' ילקוט ש"א י"ד בפסוק ויפדו העם את יונתן:

הגהות הב"ח

°"וה' אלהים אמת". חוזר ואומר 'אמת', או אינו^ירמיה^ חוזר ואומר 'אמת'? א"ר אבהו א"ר יוחנן: חוזר ואומר 'אמת'. רבה אמר: אאינו חוזר ואומר 'אמת'. ההוא דנחית קמיה דרבה, שמעיה רבה דאמר 'אמת אמת' תרי זימני; אמר רבה: כל אמת אמת תפסיה להאי! אמר רב יוסף: כמה מעליא הא שמעתתא, דכי אתא רב שמואל בר יהודה, אמר, אמרי במערבא: ערבית - "דבר אל בני ישראל ואמרת אליהם אני ה' אלהיכם אמת". אמר ליה אביי: מאי מעליותא? והא אמר רב כהנא אמר רב: לא יתחיל, ואם התחיל - גומר! וכי תימא 'ואמרת אליהם' לא הוי התחלה - והאמר רב שמואל בר יצחק אמר רב: 'דבר אל בני ישראל' - לא הוי התחלה, 'ואמרת אליהם' - הוי התחלה! אמר רב פפא: קסברי במערבא, 'ואמרת אליהם' - נמי לא הויא התחלה, עד דאמר "ועשו להם ציצית". אמר אביי: הלכך, אנן אתחולי מתחלינן - דקא מתחלי במערבא, וכיון דאתחלינן - מגמר נמי גמרינן, דהא אמר רב כהנא אמר רב: לא יתחיל, ואם התחיל - גומר. חייא בר רב אמר: אמר "אני ה' אלהיכם" - צריך לומר 'אמת', לא אמר "אני ה' אלהיכם" - אינו צ"ל 'אמת'. והא בעי לאדכורי יציאת מצרים! -דאמר הכי: מודים אנחנו לך ה' אלהינו שהוצאתנו מארץ מצרים ופדיתנו מבית עבדים ועשית לנו נסים וגבורות על הים ושרנו לך. § "אמר ר' יהושע בן קרחה, למה קדמה פרשת שמע וכו'". § תניא, ר"ש בן יוחי אומר: בדין הוא שיקדים 'שמע' ל'והיה אם שמוע' - שזה ללמוד וזה ללמד; 'והיה אם שמוע' ל'ויאמר' - שזה *ללמוד וזה לעשות. אטו 'שמע', ללמוד אית ביה, ללמד ולעשות לית ביה?! והא כתיב: 'ושננתם', 'וקשרתם', 'וכתבתם'! ותו, 'והיה אם שמוע' ללמד הוא דאית ביה, ולעשות לית ביה?! והא כתיב: 'וקשרתם', 'וכתבתם'! אלא הכי קאמר: בדין הוא שתקדם 'שמע' ל'והיה אם שמוע' - שזה ללמוד וללמד ולעשות, 'והיה אם שמוע' ל'ויאמר' - שזה יש בה ללמד ולעשות, 'ויאמר' - אין בה אלא לעשות בלבד. ותיפוק ליה מדרבי יהושע בן קרחה! חדא ועוד קאמר; חדא - כדי שיקבל עליו עול מלכות שמים תחלה ואח"כ יקבל עליו עול מצות, ועוד - משום דאית בה הני מילי אחרנייתא. רב במשי ידיה וקרא ק"ש, ואנח תפילין, (א) וצלי. והיכי עביד הכי? והתניא: גהחופר כוך למת בקבר - פטור מק"ש ומן התפלה ומן התפילין ומכל מצות האמורות בתורה, הגיע זמן ק"ש - עולה ונוטל ידיו ומניח תפילין וקורא ק"ש ומתפלל! הא גופא קשיא! רישא אמר 'פטור', וסיפא 'חייב'! -הא לא קשיא: דסיפא - בתרי, ורישא - בחד. מ"מ קשיא לרב! -רב כרבי יהושע בן קרחה סבירא ליה, דאמר: עול מלכות שמים תחלה ואח"כ עול מצות. אימר דאמר רבי יהושע בן קרחה - להקדים קריאה לקריאה, קריאה לעשיה מי שמעת ליה?! ותו, מי סבר ליה כרבי יהושע בן קרחה? והאמר *רב חייא בר אשי: זמנין סגיאין הוה קאימנא קמיה דרב, ומקדים ומשי ידיה ומברך ומתני לן פרקין, ומנח תפילין והדר קרי ק"ש! וכ"ת בדלא מטא זמן ק"ש - א"כ, מאי אסהדתיה דרב חייא בר אשי! -לאפוקי ממ"ד "למשנה אין צריך לברך" קמ"ל דאף למשנה נמי צריך לברך. -מ"מ קשיא לרב! -שלוחא הוא דעוית. § אמר עולא: "כל הקורא ק"ש בלא תפילין - כאילו מעיד עדות שקר בעצמו. א"ר חייא בר אבא א"ר יוחנן: כאילו הקריב עולה בלא מנחה וזבח בלא נסכים. § ואמר רבי יוחנן: הרוצה שיקבל עליו עול מלכות שמים שלמה - יפנה

[נ"ל ללמד]

לעיל דף יא:

---

רש"י

וה' אלהים אמת. לכך אין מפסיקין בין 'אני ה' אלהיכם' ל'אמת': כל אמת אמת תפסיה להאי. ריהטא של אמת תפסתו לזה: הא שמעתתא. דרב שמואל בר יהודה אמר אמרי במערבא וכו'. ק"ש של ערבית אין קורין בה פרשת ציצית כולה לפי שאין מצות ציצית בלילה, אבל מתחילין אותה ומפסיקים בה ומדלגים ואומרים 'אני ה' אלהיכם אמת': לא יתחיל. אין צריך להתחיל 'ויאמר' ערבית: אתחולי מתחלינן. דהא מתחלי במערבא: אמר אני ה' אלהיכם. דהיינו פרשת ציצית: צריך לומר אמת. כדכתיב 'וה' אלהים אמת': והא בעי לאדכורי יציאת מצרים. דתנן (לעיל ד' יב:) "מזכירין יציאת מצרים בלילות", ואי לא אמר 'אמת ואמונה' ולא אמר פרשת ציצית, היכי מדכר יציאת מצרים: ושרנו לך. "מי כמכה באלים וגו'" "מלכותך ראו בניך" עד "גאל ישראל" ו"השכיבנו": שזה ללמוד. "ודברת בם": וזה ללמד. "ולמדתם אותם את בניכם", ואם לא למד תחלה - היאך ילמד את בניו: וזה לעשות. ו'ויאמר' אין בה אלא עשייה: וקשרתם. דתפילין: וכתבתם. דמזוזה, עשייה היא: רב משי ידי. פעם אחת ראוהו שעשה כן: והיכי עביד הכי. שהקדים ק"ש לתפילין: כוך. קבר שחופרין בקירות מערה, ארכו ד' ורחבו ז' טפחים: פטור מק"ש. דהעוסק במצוה פטור מן המצוה, כדאמרינן בפ"ק (ד' יא.) 'בשבתך בביתך' - פרט לעוסק במצוה: וסיפא בתרתי. והכי קאמר: אם שנים הם - מניח את חבירו חופר והוא עולה ומקיים מצות ק"ש ותפילין ותפלה וחוזר למלאכה, וחבירו יעלה ויניח תפילין ויקרא ק"ש ויתפלל: מ"מ. תפילין קודמים לק"ש: עול מצות. דהנחת תפילין עול מצוה הוא: קריאה לקריאה. 'שמע' שהוא קבלת מלכות שמים ל'והיה אם שמוע' שהוא קבלת עול מצות: ומקדים. משכים: ומברך. על התורה: ומתני פרקין. אלמא(ב) מקדים הוא לעסוק בתורה, דהיינו[א] עשייה דמצוה, מקמי מלכות שמים: שלוחא הוא דעוית. השליח קלקל, שאיחר להביא לו תפילין מעיקרא, *והגיע זמן ק"ש והוזקק לקרות כדי שלא יעבור הזמן, וכי מטי שלוחא דתפילין - אנחינהו: כאילו מעיד עדות שקר בעצמו. לישנא מעליא: כאילו הקריב עולה בלא מנחה. שחייבו הכתוב להקריב עמה שנאמר (במדבר כח) "ועשירית האיפה וגו'", אף הקורא ואינו מקיים - אינו גומר את המצוה: נסכים. הוא היין המתנסך על גבי המזבח אחר העולה והזבח, כדכתי' "ונסכיהם חצי ההין וגו'" (שם), וה"ה דמצי למימר כאילו הקריב עולה בלא מנחה ונסכים, דהא עולה נמי טעונה נסכים אלא לישנא דקרא נקט "עולה ומנחה זבח ונסכים": יפנה

ס"א וחביב לק

הגהות ר... [א] רש"י ... פרקין כו' ... נמחק עשייה

---

תוספות

למה קדמה פרשת שמע לוהיה אם שמוע. וא"ת: תיפוק ליה דקדמה בתורה? וי"ל דהכי קאמר: למה קדמה אף לפרשת ציצית דקדמה לכולן? אלא ודאי אין אנו חוששין לזה שהיא קודמת בתורה, משום דאמרינן "אין מוקדם ומאוחר", וא"כ היה לנו להקדים "והיה" - שהיא מדברת בלשון רבים:

ויאמר אינה נוהגת אלא ביום. מכאן משמע כר' שמעון דאמר בפ' "התכלת" (מנחות ד' מג.) דציצית מ"ע שהזמן גרמא, וכן איתא בקדושין (פ"ק ד' לג:) דקאמר "ציצית מצות עשה שהזמן גרמא". וא"ת: א"כ, למ"ד (מנחות מא.) ציצית חובת טלית הוא, ואפילו מונחת בקופסא - אפ"ה חייבת בציצית, היכי אשכחן שיהא הזמן גרמא? וי"ל: דאם היה כסות המיוחד ללילה - פטור. והכי איתא בירושלמי דקדושין, אמר להם ר"ש: אי אתם מודים לי דציצית מ"ע שהזמן גרמא, שהרי כסות לילה פטור מן הציצית; א"ר אילא: טעמא דרבנן שאם היה מיוחד ליום ולילה שחייב בציצית:

ומנח תפילין ומצלי. ומהכא משמע שמותר להניח תפילין בין גאולה לתפלה. וכן בטלית מניח אדם טליתו בין גאולה לתפלה. וכן מצינו שרבי יצחק ברבי יהודה שלא אחר טליתו ושהה השליח והכבר קרא ק"ש בברכותיה, ונתעטף בטליתו וגמר שמונה עשרה, והביא ראיה מהכא מההיא דרב. מ"מ יש לחלק בין תפילין לטלית; דעיקר ק"ש ותפלה שייכי בתפילין, כדאמר בסמוך "כאילו מעיד עדות שקר בעצמו". פירוש: באדון שלוה שהוא קורא "והיו לטוטפת ולאות על ידך" - ואין, ותפלה נמי כדאמרן: "קרי ק"ש ומתפלל* - זו היא מלכות שמים", אבל ציצית שאינו אלא חובת טלית, שאם יש לו טלית חייב, ואם אין לו - פטור מציצית ויכול לקרות ק"ש בלא ציצית - ודאי הוי הפסקה. והר"ר משה מקוצי היה אומר: דאפי' מכאן אין ראיה, דמצי למימר הניח תפילין בלא ברכה, ולאחר י"ח ממשמש בהם ומברך עליהם, ובהכי סגי שגם מותר להתעטף בטלית בעת שידיו מטונפות, ואחר שיטול ידיו - ימשמש בטליתו ומברך:

ומכל מצות האמורות בתורה. וא"ת: וכי ק"ש לא הוה בכלל מצות האמורות בתורה? וי"ל: דאי לא תני בהדיא ק"ש, הוה אמינא דדוקא הני דלית להו קביעות זמן, אבל ק"ש דקביע להו זמן - לא הואיל וזמן עובר, קמ"ל:

עולה בלא מנחה. ה"ה דמצי למימר בלא נסכים, שהרי עולה נמי טעונה נסכים, אלא לישנא דקרא נקט "עולה ומנחה וגו'":

אמאן

---

כ א טוש"ע או"ח סימן סו סעיף ו:
כא ב שם סעיף ח:
כב ג ד מיי' פ"ד מהל' ק"ש הלכה ג סמג עשין יח טור וש"ע או"ח סימן עא סעיף ה ו וביורה דעה סימן שסה סעיף א:
כג ה מיי' פ"ד מהלכות תפילין הלכה כו טוש"ע או"ח סימן כה סעיף ד [רב אלפס כאן ובהלכות תפילין דף טו. וע"ש הגוסחא]:

## רב נסים גאון

לאפוקי ממאן דאמר למשנה אינו צריך לברך. בעל זו המימרא רב הונא ועיקרה בפרק ראשון (דף יא:):

## הגהות הב"ח

(א) גמ' ואנח תפילין ומצלי והיכי: (ב) רש"י ד"ה ומתני פרקין אלמא. נ"ב מפרש הקושיא מכח [שלמד] קודם ק"ש כי [על זה שייך] אחר כך לומר וכי תימא בדלא מטי זמן ק"ש דאי [מהא דמנח תפילין והדר קרי מאי קאמר וכ"ת וכו' הא כיון דלא מטי זמן] ק"ש גם זמן תפילין [לא מטא לכך] פירש רש"י דקושיא הוא [מהא דעסק קודם] בתורה. רק קשה למה [לא מקשה] באמת מכח [מהא דמנח תפילין ולא] יצטרך לומר וכ"ת ואפשר לתרץ [דה"ק וכי תימא בדלא] מטי זמן ק"ש והיה מתחיל בעשיית מצוה דהיינו [לימוד וכיון דהתחיל] להתעסק בעשיית מצוה הניח תפילין שהוא ג"כ עשיית מצוה קודם ק"ש זה אינו דא"כ מאי מקשה אחר כך אם כן [מאי אסהדתיה דרחב"א דילמא זהו אסהיד דהיכא דלא מטי זמן קריאת שמע והתחיל [בעשיית מצוה] שהוא לימוד יניח תפילין כשיגיע [הזמן קודם ק"ש] וע"ש [ואם נפרש ללימוד לא מקרי עשיה פי' קך] [ותו מי סבר לה כר' יהושע] ב"ק והאמר וכו' אלמא] דאף בקריאה לא סבר כר' יהושע ב"ק [דמלמוד קודם ק"ש והלימוד] הוה קודם למצוה אבל לפי פירש"י [משמע ללימוד מיקרי] עשיה:

איפנה ויטול ידיו, ויניח תפילין ויקרא ק"ש ויתפלל, וזו היא מלכות שמים שלמה. א"ר חייא בר אבא א"ר יוחנן: כל הנפנה ונוטל ידיו ומניח תפילין וקורא ק"ש ומתפלל - מעלה עליו הכתוב כאלו בנה מזבח והקריב עליו קרבן, דכתיב: "ארחץ בנקיון כפי ואסובבה את מזבחך ה'". (תהלים כו) א"ל רבא: לא סבר לה מר כאילו טבל? דכתיב: 'ארחץ [בנקיון]' ולא כתב 'ארחיץ [כפי]'. א"ל רבינא לרבא: חזי מר האי צורבא מרבנן דאתא ממערבא ואמר: מי שאין לו מים לרחוץ ידיו - מקנח ידיו בעפר ובצרור ובקסמית! א"ל: שפיר קאמר, מי כתיב ארחץ 'במים'?! 'בנקיון' כתיב - כל מידי דמנקי. דהא רב חסדא לייט אמאן דמהדר אמיא בעידן (א) צלותא, והני מילי - לק"ש, אבל לתפלה - מהדר. ועד כמה? עד פרסה. והני מילי - לקמיה, אבל לאחוריה - אפילו מיל אינו חוזר; [ומינה] - מיל הוא דאינו חוזר, הא פחות ממיל חוזר.

**מתני'** הקורא את שמע ולא השמיע לאזנו - יצא; ר' יוסי אומר: לא יצא. קרא ולא דקדק באותיותיה, ר' יוסי אומר: יצא, רבי יהודה אומר: לא יצא. הקורא למפרע - לא יצא. קרא וטעה - יחזור למקום שטעה.

**גמ'** מאי טעמא דר' יוסי - משום דכתיב: 'שמע' - השמע לאזנך מה שאתה מוציא מפיך. ות"ק סבר: 'שמע' - בכל לשון שאתה שומע. ור' יוסי - תרתי שמע מינה. תנן התם: חרש המדבר ואינו שומע - לא יתרום, ואם תרם - תרומתו תרומה. מאן תנא חרש המדבר ואינו שומע, דיעבד - אין, לכתחלה - לא? אמר רב חסדא: ר' יוסי היא, דתנן: הקורא את שמע ולא השמיע לאזנו - יצא, (ב) דברי רבי יהודה; ר' יוסי אומר: לא יצא. עד כאן לא קאמר ר' יוסי לא יצא - אלא גבי ק"ש דאורייתא, אבל תרומה - משום ברכה הוא, וברכה דרבנן, ולא בברכה תליא מילתא. וממאי דר' יוסי היא? דילמא ר' יהודה היא; ואמר גבי ק"ש נמי: דיעבד - אין, לכתחלה - לא! תדע, דקתני, 'הקורא' - דיעבד אין, לכתחלה - לא! אמרי: האי דקתני 'הקורא' להודיעך כחו דר' יוסי דאמר: דיעבד נמי לא, דאי ר' יהודה - אפי' לכתחלה נמי יצא. - במאי אוקימתא - כר' יוסי, ואלא הא דתניא: לא יברך אדם בהמ"ז בלבו, ואם בירך - יצא, מני? לא ר' יוסי ולא ר' יהודה; דאי ר' יהודה - הא אמר: לכתחלה נמי יצא, אי ר' יוסי - דיעבד נמי לא! - אלא מאי - ר' יהודה, ודיעבד - אין, לכתחלה - לא? אלא הא דתני ר' יהודה בריה דרבי שמעון בן פזי: "חרש המדבר ואינו שומע תורם לכתחלה", מני? לא ר' יהודה ולא ר' יוסי; אי ר' יהודה - הא אמר: דיעבד - אין, לכתחלה - לא, אי ר' יוסי - הא אמר: דיעבד - נמי לא! - אלא לעולם רבי יהודה, ואפי' לכתחלה נמי, ולא קשיא: הא דידיה, הא דרביה, דתנן, רבי יהודה אומר משום ר' אלעזר בן עזריה: הקורא את שמע - צריך שישמיע לאזנו, שנאמר: "שמע ישראל ה' אלהינו ה' אחד". (דברים ו) אמר ליה רבי מאיר: הרי הוא אומר "אשר אנכי מצוך היום על לבבך" - אחר כונת הלב הן הן הדברים. השתא דאתית להכי, אפילו תימא: רבי יהודה כרביה סבירא ליה, ולא קשיא, הא - רבי מאיר, הא - רבי יהודה. תנן התם: הכל כשרים לקרות את המגילה חוץ מחרש שוטה וקטן, ורבי יהודה מכשיר בקטן. מאן תנא חרש דיעבד נמי לא? אמר רב מתנה: רבי יוסי היא, דתנן: הקורא את שמע ולא השמיע לאזנו - יצא, דברי ר' יהודה; רבי יוסי אומר: לא יצא.(ג) ממאי דרבי יוסי היא, ודיעבד נמי לא, דילמא

## רש"י

יפנה. לנקביו: דכתיב ארחץ בנקיון. משמע ארחץ כל הגוף ולא כתיב ארחיץ כפי - לדרשה אתא, לומר שמעלה עליו שכר רחיצת כפיו כאלו טבל כל גופו: קסמית. קיסם: לק"ש. בעידנא דק"ש, שזמנה קבוע, פן יעבור הזמן, אבל לתפלה דכל היום זמנה הוא - צריך למהדר אמיא:

**מתני'** ולא דקדק באותיותיה. לפרשן יפה בשפתיו:

**גמ'** תרתי ש"מ. כי דרשת נמי 'שמע' - בכל לשון שאתה שומע, ש"מ נמי דצריך להשמיע לאזנו: לא יתרום. לפי שאינו שומע הברכה שהוא מברך עליה: מאן תנא כו' לא יצא. אפי' בדיעבד ה"מ כו': ברכה דרבנן היא. דאמור רבנן (פסחים ד' ז:): 'כל המצות כולן מברך עליהן עובר לעשייתן': וממאי דר' יוסי היא. קס"ד האי דמוקמי לה כר' יוסי משום דסבירא לן דר' יהודה לכתחלה נמי מכשיר: דילמא רבי יהודה היא. וק"ש נמי: דיעבד - אין, לכתחלה - לא. ה"ג, ול"ג אפילו: משום רבי יוסי. להודיעך כחו, דאפילו דיעבד נמי לא יצא: בלבו. שלא השמיע לאזנו: ואי רבי יוסי דיעבד נמי לא. דהא בהמ"ז דאורייתא היא, "ואכלת ושבעת וברכת" (דברים ח): אלא מאי ר' יהודה. וק"ש דיעבד אין לכתחלה לא, והא דתרומה וברכת המזון - דרבי יהודה: אלא רבי יהודה לכתחלה קאמר. והא דרבי יהודה בריה דרבי שמעון בן פזי רבי יהודה היא, ודתרומה ר' יוסי היא, ומודה הוא דברכות דרבנן דיעבד שפיר דמי. והא דברכת המזון רבי יהודה היא משמיה דרביה רבי אלעזר בן עזריה דאומר 'צריך שישמיע לאזנו' וכל 'צריך' לכתחלה משמע, הא דיעבד - שפיר דמי: אחר כוונת הלב כו'. ואפילו לכתחלה נמי אינו צריך: השתא דאתית להכי. דאשמעת לן פלוגתא דר"מ: אפילו תימא ר' יהודה. דאמר 'בק"ש נמי יצא', דיעבד - אין, לכתחלה - לא, והא דברכת המזון ודתרומה - רבי יהודה היא, ודקא קשיא לך דרבי יהודה בריה דר"ש בן פזי מני - רבי מאיר היא, דמכשר לכתחלה: מאן תנא חרש דיעבד נמי לא. דקתני גבי שוטה: לא יצא. דיעבד הוא: וממאי. ד"חוץ מחרש" דקאמר דיעבד הוא, ורבי יוסי היא דפסיל דיעבד: *ולכתחלה הוא דלא. הא דיעבד שפיר דמי. ובהא איכא למימר דאפילו רבי יהודה מודה דלא שמעינן דפליג בק"ש אלא דיעבד:

מדסיפא

## תוספות

**אמאן** דמהדר אמיא בעידן ק"ש. ויש ספרים דגרסי: הני מילי לק"ש אבל לתפלה לא, דקאמר רשב"ל (פסחים מו.) "לגבל ולתפלה ד' מילין". ונראה דלא גרסינן ליה, דהוא הדין לענין צלותא נמי מטעם שלא יעבור זמן תפלה, דמאי שנא ק"ש מתפלה? וגם יש לקמן פרק "מי שמתו" (ד' כב.), בטלוה לנטילותא כדרב חסדא דלייט אמאן דמהדר אמיא בעידן צלותא, ומדלא הזכיר שם ק"ש - משמע דבכל ענין מותר. והיא דרשב"ל דאמר "ולתפלה ד' מילין" פירש ר"י: להתפלל שם במנין:

**דילמא** ר' יהודה היא. וא"ת: ר' יהודה היא, והלא אין נזכר ר' יהודה ברישא! וי"ל דפשיטא, מדסיפא ר' יהודה - רישא נמי ר' יהודה,(ד) ופליגי במילתא דר' יהודה:

**להודיעך** כחו דרבי יוסי. וא"ת: לשמעינן כחו דרבי יהודה, דכח דהתירא עדיף! וי"ל: כיון דרבי יהודה לא דריש 'השמע לאזנך' - אין כאן שום חדוש, ופשיטא לכתחלה,(ה) ומהיכא תיתי לאוסרו? אי שרי דיעבד הוא הדין לכתחלה: **אי** ר' יוסי דיעבד נמי לא. וא"ת: לעולם אימא לך רבי יוסי היא, וברכת המזון שאני, דלא כתיב ביה 'שמע'! דבשלמא תרומה דלעיל ומגילה דלקמן שהן מדרבנן - יש לדמותם לק"ש שתקנו שצריך שישמיע לאזנו כמו בק"ש, ותקנו ממש שלא יצא כמו בק"ש, אבל בבהמ"ז שהיא מדאורייתא, כיון דלא כתיב ביה 'שמע' למה יש לנו לתקן שלא יצא אם לא השמיע לאזנו, כיון דמה"ת יצא? וי"ל: כיון שתקנו שצריך להשמיע לאזנו כמו בק"ש, הואיל ומדרבנן מיהא צריך להשמיע - אין לחלק בין ק"ש ובין בהמ"ז, דאפילו בדיעבד אית לן למימר שלא יצא: **ורבי** יהודה מכשיר בקטן. וא"ת: באיזה קטן מיירי? אי בקטן שלא הגיע לחנוך - הא אמרינן בפרק "ראוהו בית דין" (ר"ה ד' כט.) 'כל שאינו מחויב בדבר אינו מוציא את הרבים', ומ"ט דר' יהודה דמכשיר? ואי בהגיע לחנוך - מאי טעמייהו דרבנן דאסרי? הרי קריאת מגילה דרבנן, ואמרי' קטן שהגיע לחנוך מדרבנן - כגדול, ופוטר דרבנן, כדאמר לקמן בפרק 'מי שמתו' (ד' כ:) דקטן מוציא אביו שלא אכל אלא כזית, דהיינו דרבנן. וי"ל: שאני ברכת המזון שהיא חומרא יתירא יותר מדאורייתא, ובקל נפטרים ממנה כדאמרי' לקמן (שם) 'והם החמירו על עצמם או בכזית או בכביצה'.* א"נ: התם ליכא בקטן אלא חד "דרבנן", דמיירי שהקטן אכל כדי שביעה - לכך אתי דרבנן ומוציא דרבנן, אבל הכא דגבי קטן איכא תרתי "דרבנן", דהמגילה דרבנן והקטן דרבנן - אינו יכול להוציא היכא דליכא אלא חד "דרבנן":

דילמא

## עין משפט נר מצוה

כד א טור וש"ע או"ח סימן ב סעיף ו:
כה ב ג מיי' פ"ג מהל' ק"ש הלכה א' ופ"ד מהלכות תפלה הלכה ב ג סמג עשין יח טוש"ע או"ח סימן ד סעיף כב וסימן לב סעיף ד ה ו וסימן רלג סעיף ב:
כו ד מיי' פ"ב מהלכות ק"ש הלכה ח סמג עשין יח טור ש"ע או"ח סימן סב סעיף ג:
כז ה מיי' וסמג שם טוש"ע שם סעיף א:
כח ו מיי' שם הלכה יא (סמג שם) טוש"ע או"ח סימן סד סעיף א:
כט ז מיי' פ"ד מהלכות תרומות הלכה ד:
ל ח מיי' פ"א מהלכות מגילה הלכה ב סמג עשין דרבנן ד טור ש"ע או"ח סי' תרפט סעיף ב:

## רב נסים גאון

**אבל** לתפלה מהדר ועד כמה עד פרסה. ידוע כי הפרסה ארבעת מילין ובמסכת פסחים בפ' אלו עוברין בפסח (דף מו) אמרינן אמר ר' אבהו אמר ריש לקיש לגבל ולתפלה ולנטילת ידים ד' מילין ואיתמר עלה אמר ר' יוסי בר' חנינא לא שנו אלא לפניו אבל לאחריו אפי' מיל אינו חוזר אמר רב אחא בר יעקב ומינה מיל הוא דאינו חוזר הא פחות ממיל חוזר ודכוותה בשחיטת חולין בפרק העור והרוטב (דף קכג) ומזה העיקר אמרי' הכא אבל לתפלה מהדר ועד כמה עד פרסה ובמס' מגילה (דף ג) אמרי' שעורא דמיל כמה הוי כמחמתן לטבריא ובפ' אלו עוברין בפסח (דף מו) נמי שיעורא דמיל כמה הוי כממגדל נוניא לטבריא:

## הגהות הב"ח

(א) גמ' דמהדר אמיא בעידן צלותא [והני מילי וכו' פחות ממיל חוזר] תא"מ. וכ"כ ס"א אינו ולשון האלפסי הוא: (ב) שם דתנן הקורא וכו' לאזנו יצא ר' יוסי אומר כצ"ל ותיבת דברי רבי יהודה נמחק וכן בסמוך: (ג) שם וממאי דר' יוסי: (ד) תוס' ד"ה דילמא וכו' רישא נמי ר' יהודה הס"ד והשאר נמחק: (ה) תד"ה להודיעך וכו' ופשיטא דלכתחלה שרי ומהיכא תיתי:

## גליון הש"ס

**תוס'** ד"ה אמאן כו' ומדלא הזכיר. ע' תוס' שבת יא ע"א ד"ה כגון רשב"י:

**דילמא** ר' יהודה וחסורי מחסרא וכו'. תימה: דאין זה בשום מקום דקאמר חסורי מחסרא ולאוקמי אליבא דחד תנא; ועוד: לוקמיה כר' יוסי ובלא חסורי מחסרא! וי"ל: משום דלקמן פסקינן כר' יהודה, לכך ניחא לאוקמיה אליבא דר' יהודה:

**אבל** בשאר מצות יצא. וא"ת: הא לעיל אמר דשאר מצות ילפינן מק"ש, כגון תרומה ומגילה וברכת המזון? וי"ל: דרב יוסף פליג אסוגיא דלעיל: **בין** הדבקים. *רב אלפס מוסיף: כגון 'וחרה אף', דאם לא יתן ריוח אז נראה כמו וחרף, וכן מוסיף 'וראיתם אותו', 'וזכרתם את', 'ועשיתם את' שצריך ליתן ריוח בין מ"ס שבסוף תיבה לאל"ף שבתחלת תיבה שאחרי. וכן צריך [א] להתיז זיי"ן של 'תזכרו' שלא ישמע סי"ן – למען שיהיה לנו שכר מצות, ולא לנו לעשו' על מנת לקבל פרס: אהלים

דילמא רבי יהודה היא ולכתחלה הוא דלא, הא דיעבד שפיר דמי! –לא ס"ד, דקתני חרש דומיא דשוטה וקטן; מה שוטה וקטן – דיעבד נמי לא, אף חרש – דיעבד נמי לא. ודילמא, הא כדאיתא והא כדאיתא? –ומי מצית לאוקמה כרבי יהודה, והא מדקתני סיפא: רבי יהודה מכשיר בקטן – מכלל דרישא לאו רבי יהודה היא! –ודילמא כולה ר' יהודה היא, ותרי גווני קטן, וחסורי מחסרא והכי קתני: הכל כשרין לקרות את המגילה חוץ מחש"ו, בד"א – בקטן שלא הגיע לחנוך, אבל קטן שהגיע לחנוך – אפילו לכתחלה כשר, דברי רבי יהודה, שרבי יהודה מכשיר בקטן. –במאי אוקימתא – כר"י, ודיעבד – אין, לכתחלה – לא, אלא הא דתני ר"י בריה דר' שמעון בן פזי: חרש המדבר ואינו שומע תורם לכתחלה, מני? לא ר' יהודה ולא ר' יוסי; אי ר' יהודה, דיעבד – אין, לכתחילה – לא, אי ר' יוסי, דיעבד נמי לא! – אלא מאי – ר' יהודה, ואפילו לכתחלה נמי? אלא הא דתניא: *לא יברך אדם ברכת המזון בלבו, ואם בירך – יצא, מני? לא ר' יהודה ולא ר' יוסי; אי רבי יהודה – הא אמר אפי' לכתחלה נמי, ואי ר' יוסי – הא אמר אפי' דיעבד נמי לא! לעולם ר' יהודה היא, ואפילו לכתחלה נמי, ולא קשיא: הא דידיה, הא דרביה, דתניא, א"ר יהודה משום ר' אלעזר בן עזריה: הקורא את שמע צריך שישמיע לאזנו, שנאמר: "שמע ישראל", אמר לו ר' מאיר, הרי הוא אומר: "אשר אנכי מצוך היום על לבבך" – אחר כוונת הלב הן הן הדברים. השתא דאתית להכי, אפי' תימא: ר' יהודה כרביה ס"ל, ולא קשיא, הא – ר' יהודה, הא – רבי מאיר. א"ר חסדא אמר רב שילא: [א]הלכה כרבי יהודה שאמר משום רבי אלעזר בן עזריה, והלכה כרבי יהודה. וצריכא, דאי אשמעינן הלכה כר' יהודה – הוה אמינא: אפילו לכתחלה, קמ"ל: הלכה כר' יהודה שאמר משום ר' אלעזר בן עזריה. ואי אשמעינן הלכה כרבי יהודה שאמר משום ר' אלעזר בן עזריה – הוה אמינא: *צריך, ואין לו תקנה, קמ"ל: הלכה כרבי יהודה. אמר רב יוסף: מחלוקת בק"ש, אבל בשאר מצות – דברי הכל לא יצא, דכתיב: °"הסכת ושמע ישראל". (דברים כז) מיתיבי: לא יברך אדם ברכת המזון בלבו, ואם בירך – יצא! אלא אי אתמר, הכי אתמר: אמר רב יוסף: מחלוקת בק"ש, דכתיב: "שמע ישראל", [ב]אבל בשאר מצות – דברי הכל יצא. והכתיב: "הסכת ושמע ישראל"! ההוא בדברי תורה כתיב.§ "קרא ולא דקדק באותיותיה". א"ר טבי א"ר יאשיה: הלכה כדברי שניהם להקל.§ וא"ר *טבי א"ר יאשיה, מאי דכתיב: °"שלש (משלי ל) הנה לא תשבענה שאול ועצר רחם", וכי מה ענין שאול אצל רחם? אלא לומר לך: מה רחם מכניס ומוציא – אף שאול מכניס ומוציא; והלא דברים ק"ו: ומה רחם שמכניסין בו בחשאי – מוציאין ממנו בקולי קולות, שאול שמכניסין בו בקולי קולות – אינו דין שמוציאין ממנו בקולי קולות! מכאן תשובה לאומרים אין תחיית המתים מן התורה.§ תני ר' אושעיא קמיה דרבא: 'וכתבתם' – הכל בכתב, אפילו צואות. א"ל: דאמר לך מני – *ר' יהודה היא, דאמר גבי סוטה 'אלות' כותב, 'צואות' אינו כותב; והתם הוא דכתיב: °"וכתב את האלות האלה", (במדבר ה) אבל הכא דכתיב 'וכתבתם' – אפי' צואות נמי. –אטו טעמיה דר' יהודה משום דכתיב 'וכתב'?! *טעמיה דר' יהודה משום דכתיב 'אלות', אלות – אין, צואות – לא! – אצטריך, סד"א: נילף 'כתיבה' 'כתיבה' מהתם – מה התם – אלות – אין, צואות – לא, אף הכא נמי – צואות – לא, כתב רחמנא, 'וכתבתם' – אפי' צואות.§ תני רב עובדיה קמיה דרבא: 'ולמדתם' – [ג]שיהא למודך תם, שיתן ריוח בין הדבקים. עני רבא בתריה: כגון *'על לבבך', 'על לבבכם', 'בכל לבבך', 'בכל לבבכם', 'עשב בשדך', 'ואבדתם מהרה', 'הכנף פתיל', 'אתכם מארץ'. א"ר חמא ברבי חנינא: כל הקורא ק"ש ומדקדק באותיותיה מצננין לו גיהנם, שנאמר: °"בפרש שדי מלכים בה תשלג בצלמון", (תהלים סח) אל תקרי 'בפרש' אלא 'בפרש', אל תקרי 'בצלמון' אלא 'בצלמות'.§ ואמר רבי חמא ברבי חנינא: למה נסמכו אהלים

מדסיפא ר' יהודה. דקתני "ר' יהודה מכשיר בקטן": ודילמא כולה ר' יהודה היא וחסורי מחסרא והכי קתני: הכל כשרין לקרות את המגילה חוץ מחש"ו. והא כדאיתא והא כדאיתא: בד"א. דקטן לכתחלה לא – בקטן שלא הגיע לחנוך, אבל הגיע לחנוך – אפי' לכתחלה שרי. הגיע לחנוך מצות, כגון בן תשע ובן עשר, כדאמרינן ביומא פרק בתרא (ד' פב.): במאי אוקימתא. למתניתין דמגילה: כר' יהודה. ואשמעת לן דכי אמר ר' יהודה בק"ש יצא – דיעבד קאמר ולא לכתחלה: אלא הא דתני כו' תורם. וא"ע"פ שהוא צריך לברך ואין אזניו שומעות, מני. אלא מאי. בעית למימר דר' יהודה היא דק"ש אפי' לכתחלה קאמר, כי היכי דתיקו הא דר' יהודה בריה דר' שמעון בן פזי אליביה, והאי דאפליגו בדיעבד להודיעך כחו דר' יוסי: אלא הא דתניא כו'. מני: לעולם ר' יהודה[א] אפי' לכתחלה מכשיר. ודמגילה – רבי יוסי היא, ואפי' דיעבד נמי פסיל. והא דתורם לכתחלה – ר' יהודה, והא דברכת המזון – דרביה הוא דאמר ר' יהודה משום רבי אלעזר בן עזריה: צריך להשמיע לאזנו, והאי לישנא לכתחלה משמע, אבל דיעבד – יצא: השתא דאתית להכי. דאשמעתן הא פלוגתא דר"מ: אפי' תימא ר' יהודה. דאמר בק"ש יצא, דיעבד – אין, לכתחלה – לא, ומתני' דמגילה לכתחלה היא דפסלה לחרש, ור' יהודה היא. והא דברכת המזון נמי ר' יהודה היא ודקא קשיא לך הא דר"י בריה דר' שמעון בן פזי מני – ר"מ היא, דמכשיר לכתחלה: הלכה כר' יהודה. דק"ש שלא השמיע לאזנו יצא: הוה אמינא. דר' יהודה לכתחלה נמי אמר, והאי דאפליג בדיעבד משום דרבי יוסי: ואין לו תקנה. אפילו לדיעבד: בשאר מצות. בכל הברכות: ההוא. "הסכת ושמע" בדברי תורה כתיב, כדאמרי' בפ' "הרואה" (ד' סג:): כתתו עצמכם על דברי תורה: ולא דקדק. שמגמגם: הלכה כדברי שניהם להקל. הלכה כר' יהודה דלא בעי שמיעה, והלכה כר' יוסי דלא בעי דקדוק: שאול ועוצר רחם. פסוק הוא בספר משלי "שלש הנה לא תשבענה": רחם מכניס. הזרע, ומוציא הולד: שאול. קבר: שמכניסין בו בקולי קולות. של בכי ומספד: וכתבתם. ואפילו צואות. שמתחלת כתיבה תמה ושלימה: שבפרשה כגון "וקשרתם וכתבתם" צריך לכתוב בתפילין ומזוזות: דאמר לך מני. הא דאצטריך ליה קרא לרבות צואות לכתיבה: רבי יהודה היא. דשמעינן גבי כתיבת פרשת סוטה משום דלא כתיב ביה 'וכתבתם' אלא 'וכתב' דאמר: אלות – אין, צואות – לא, כגון "והשביע אותה הכהן", "ואמר הכהן", דתנן (סוטה ד' יז): רבי יהודה אומר, כל עצמו אינו כותב אלא "יתן ה' אותך לאלה ולשבועה": משום אלה הוא. דמשמע מיעוטא, הא לא כתיב מיעוטא – הוה משמע כולה מלתא מ"וכתב", והכא דליכא מיעוטא – למה ליה לרבויינהו מ"וכתבתם": בין הדבקים. תיבות המדובקות זו בזו, אם אינך מפרידן כשהתיבה השניה מתחלת באות שהתיבה שמלפניה נגמרת הוא קורא אותן שתי אותיות באות אחת, אם אינו מתעכב ליתן ריוח ביניהם כדמפרש רבא: בפרש שדי. אם תפרש שדי ותבדיל תיבות של מלכות שמים, "מלכים בה תשלג *בצלמון" – התורה אשר בה ימלוכו תשלג ותלבין לך את צל המות: אהלים

לא א מיי' פ"ב מהלכות ק"ש הלכה ח סמג עשין יח טור שו"ע או"ח סימן סב סעיף ג:

לב ב מיי' פ"א מהלכות ברכות הלכה ז סמג עשין כז טוש"ע או"ח סימן קפה סעיף ב ובסימן רו סעיף ג:

[ברב אלפס שלפנינו ליתא אלא הך דזיי"ן של תזכרו בשם הירושלמי אמנם ברא"ש ובטור סימן סא איתא כל זה וכתב הב"י שכ"כ הר"ר יונה בספר היראה ע"ש]

לג ג מיי' פ"ב מהלכות ק"ש הלכה ח ט סמג עשין יח טוש"ע או"ח סימן סא סעיף כ:

לד ד מיי' שם הלכה ח ט טור ר"ס סב:

**רב נסים גאון**

תני ר' (יאשיה) [אושעיא] קמיה דרבא וכתבתם הכל בכתב ואפי' צוואות נמי אמר ליה דאמר לך מני ר' יהודה היא דאמר גבי סוטה אלות כותב צוואות אינו כותב. עיקר דבריו של ר' יהודה במס' סוטה בפ' היה מביא את מנחתה (דף יז) בא לו לכתוב המגילה מאיזה מקום היה כותב ר' יהודה אומר כל עצמו לא היה כותב אלא יתן ה' אותך וגו' ובאו המים המאררים וגו' ואינו כותב ואמרה האשה אמן אמן:

**הגהות הגר"א**

[א] תוס' ד"ה בין כו' וכן צריך כו'. נ"ב ירוש':

**הגהות**

(א) רש"י ד"ה ר' יהודה היא.

[מגילה יט:]

[עירובין מח. יבמות ע. גיטין מו: הוריות ה. ט.]

סנהדרין צב.

[סוטה קד יז.]

[ע"ש בסוגיא]

[הגך הס ב ובהלכות ב נמלאים בכסלר]

[וכערוך ערך העגנן בלמון]

אהלים לנחלים, דכתיב: "כנחלים נטיו כגנות עלי נהר כאהלים נטע וגו'", לומר לך: מה נחלים מעלין את האדם מטומאה לטהרה – אף אהלים מעלין את האדם מכף חובה לכף זכות.§ הקורא למפרע לא יצא וכו'.§ רבי אמי ורבי אסי הוו קא קטרין ליה גננא לר' אלעזר, אמר להו: אדהכי והכי איזיל ואשמע מלתא דבי מדרשא, ואיתי ואימא לכו. אזל אשכחיה לתנא דקתני קמיה דר' יוחנן: *קרא וטעה ואינו יודע להיכן טעה, (א) באמצע הפרק – יחזור *לראש, בין פרק לפרק – יחזור לפרק ראשון, בין כתיבה לכתיבה – יחזור לכתיבה ראשונה. אמר ליה ר' יוחנן: לא שנו אלא שלא פתח ב'למען ירבו ימיכם', אבל פתח ב'למען ירבו ימיכם' – סרכיה נקט ואתי. אתא ואמר להו: אמרו ליה: *אלו לא באנו אלא לשמוע דבר זה – דיינו.§ **מתני'** האומנין קורין בראש האילן ובראש הנדבך, מה שאינן רשאין לעשות כן בתפלה. *חתן פטור מק"ש לילה הראשונה, ועד מוצאי שבת אם לא עשה מעשה. ומעשה בר"ג שנשא אשה וקרא לילה הראשונה; אמרו לו תלמידיו: *למדתנו רבינו שחתן פטור מק"ש! אמר להם: איני שומע לכם לבטל הימני מלכות שמים אפי' שעה אחת.§ **גמ'** *ת"ר: האומנין קורין בראש האילן ובראש הנדבך, ומתפללין בראש הזית ובראש התאנה, ושאר כל האילנות – יורדים למטה ומתפללין. ובעל הבית – בין כך ובין כך יורד למטה ומתפלל, לפי שאין דעתו מיושבת עליו. רמי ליה רב מרי ברה דבת שמואל לרבא, תנן: האומנין קורין בראש האילן ובראש הנדבך, אלמא: לא בעי כונה; ורמינהי: הקורא את שמע צריך שיכוין את לבו, שנאמר: "שמע ישראל", ולהלן הוא אומר: "הסכת ושמע ישראל", מה להלן ב'הסכת' אף כאן ב'הסכת'! אשתיק. א"ל: מידי שמיע לך בהא? – א"ל: הכי אמר רב ששת: והוא שבטלין ממלאכתן וקורין. – והתניא, *בית הלל אומרים: עוסקין במלאכתן וקורין! – לא קשיא: הא בפרק ראשון, הא בפרק שני. *ת"ר: הפועלים שהיו עושין מלאכה אצל בעל הבית – קורין ק"ש ומברכין לפניה ולאחריה, ואוכלין פתן (ב) ומברכין לפניה ולאחריה, [ז] ומתפללין תפלה של שמונה עשרה אבל אין יורדין לפני התיבה ואין נושאין כפיהם. והתניא: מעין י"ח! – אמר רב ששת, לא קשיא: *הא – ר"ג, הא ר' יהושע. – אי ר' יהושע, מאי איריא פועלים, אפילו כל אדם נמי! – אלא אידי ואידי ר"ג, ולא קשיא: [ח] כאן – בעושין בשכרן, כאן – בעושין בסעודתן. והתניא: *הפועלים שהיו עושים מלאכה אצל בעל־הבית קורין ק"ש ומתפללין, ואוכלין פתן ואין מברכים לפניה, [א] אבל מברכין לאחריה שתים, כיצד – *ברכה ראשונה כתקונה, שניה – פותח בברכת הארץ וכוללין "בונה ירושלים" בברכת הארץ; במה דברים אמורים – בעושין בשכרן, אבל עושין בסעודתן או שהיה בעל הבית מיסב עמהן – מברכין כתיקונה.§ "חתן פטור מק"ש".§ *תנו רבנן: *"בשבתך בביתך" – פרט לעוסק במצוה, "ובלכתך בדרך" – פרט לחתן, מכאן אמרו: הכונס את הבתולה – פטור, ואת האלמנה חייב. מאי משמע? – אמר רב פפא: כי דרך, מה דרך – רשות, אף הכא נמי – רשות. מי לא עסקינן דקאזיל לדבר מצוה, ואפילו הכי אמר רחמנא ליקרי! אם כן, לימא קרא 'בלכת', מאי 'בלכתך' – שמע מינה: בלכת דידך הוא דמחייבת, הא דמצוה – פטירת. אי

**רש"י**

אהלים לנחלים. "כנחלים נטיו כאהלים נטע": אף [אהלים]. בתי מדרשות. אהלים לשון נטיעה נופלת בהם, שנאמר "ויטע אהלי אפדנו" (דניאל יא): קטרין ליה גננא. קושרין לו חופה, להשיאו אשה: יחזור לראש. כגון שהיה יודע שבפרק זה טעה ודלג, אבל אינו יודע באיזה מקום בו טעה: בין פרק לפרק. שיודע שגמר הפרשה וצריך להתחיל פרשה אחרת, ואינו יודע באיזה מהן: יחזור לפרק ראשון. להפסק ראשון (ג) "והיה אם שמוע": בין כתיבה לכתיבה. שיודע שצריך לומר 'וכתבתם' ואינו יודע אם ראשון אם שני: (ד) וא"ר יוחנן. לתנא וכו': סרכיה נקט. *אין לטעות מכאן עד 'אמת ויציב' וא"צ לחזור אלא ל'אמת', שהפרשה שגורה בפיו: מתני' האומנין. שהם עסוקים במלאכתן בראש האילן או בראש הנדבך והגיע זמן ק"ש קורין לשם מיד: נדבך. בנין של אבנים, כמו "נדבכין די אבן גלל" (עזרא ו): מה שאינן רשאין לעשות כן בתפלה. דצלותא רחמי היא ובעי כוונה הלכך אין מתפללין בראש האילן ובראש הנדבך, דמסתפי דילמא נפלי, דאין יכולין לעמוד שם אלא על ידי הדחק ומחמת בעתותא לא מצי מכווני: גמ' ומתפללין בראש הזית ובראש התאנה. בזמן שעוסקין בהן, מפני שענפיהם מרובים ויכולין לעמוד שם שלא בדוחק, ואין שם פחד ליפול לפיכך מתפללין בראשם, אבל בשאר אילנות – אין מתפללין: בין כך ובין כך. כלומר: בין מתאנה בין משאר אילנות: יורד ומתפלל. דהא אינו משועבד למלאכה, שהוא ברשות עצמו: לפי שאין דעתו מיושבת עליו. מבעתותו, ואם הקלו אצל פועלים מפני בטול מלאכה, לא הקלו אצל בעל הבית: ברה דבת שמואל. בכמה מקומות קרי ליה בר רחל. ובת שמואל היתה ונשבית לבין העמים, כדאמר בכתובות (דף כג.) ובא עליה אחד ונתעברה הימנו ואח"כ נתגייר. ושמיה איסור, כדאמרי' בב"ב (דף קמט.): רב מרי בריה הורתו שלא בקדושה הוה, לכך לא היה נקרא על שם אביו: תנן האומנין קורין בראש האילן. אפי' בזמן שהן עסוקין, אלמא: לא בעי כוונה: שבטלין ממלאכתן וקורין. כדי שיהיו קורין בכוונה רשאין להיבטל ממלאכתן: פרק ראשון. פרשת שמע בעי כוונה: קורין את שמע ומברכין לפניה ולאחריה. כתקונה, וכן בזמן תפלה: אבל אין יורדין לפני התיבה. אין רשאין ליבטל ממלאכתן ולירד לפני התיבה לעשות שלוחי צבור, שיש שם בטול מלאכה יותר מדאי: מעין שמונה עשרה. "הביננו לדעת דרכיך כו'" שכולל *י"ח ברכות בברכה אחת, וג' ראשונות וג' אחרונות כהלכתן: הא ר"ג הא רבי יהושע. דתנן בפרק תפלת השחר (דף כח:): ר"ג אומר בכל יום ויום מתפלל אדם י"ח ברכות, רבי יהושע אומר מעין י"ח: עושין בשכרן. שנוטלין שכר פעולתן לבד סעודתן – צריכין למהר המלאכה ומתפללין מעין י"ח: אבל עושין בסעודתן. בשביל האכילה לבדה מתפללין י"ח: והתניא. בניחותא, דיש חלוק בין עושין בשכרן לעושין בסעודתן: ואין מברכין לפניה. שאינה מן התורה: אבל מברכין לאחריה. שהיא מן התורה, דכתיב "ואכלת ושבעת וברכת" (לקמן דף מח:): וכוללין. *שני ברכות באחת, שברכת הארץ ובנין ירושלים דומות: בשבתך בביתך פרט לעוסק במצוה. כבר פירשתיה בפרק ראשון (דף יא.):

**תוספות**

אהלים לנחלים. פי' הקונטרס דכתיב "כנחלים נטיו כאהלים נטע". ולי נראה דאהלים דהאי קרא לאו לשון אהל אלא לשון בשמים, אלא נראה מדסמיך 'מה טובו אהליך' ל'כנחלים נטיו': **הקורא** את שמע ואינו יודע להיכן טעה חוזר לראש. פי': מטעם שאינו יודע מהיכן טעה. אבל אם היה יודע מהיכן טעה, שדלג תיבה או פסוק – אינו צריך לחזור אלא מאותו פסוק ואילך, וכן בהלל ומגילה: **מעשה** בר"ג שנשא אשה וקרא ק"ש בלילה ראשונה. לאו מעשה לסתור הוא, דקמ"ל: אם גדול הוא ובוטח בעצמו שיוכל להתכוין, והוא ראוי ליטול את השם – הרשות בידו: **לפי** שאין דעתו מיושבת עליו. ואם תאמר: תיפוק ליה משום דאמרינן לעיל (דף י:) 'לא יעמוד אדם במקום גבוה ויתפלל'! ויש לומר: דהתם איירי על גבי כסא או ספסל, אבל באילן שעלה שם לעשות מלאכתו – הוי כמו עלייה: **הא** בפרק ראשון. לאו דוקא נקט פרק א'. דהיינו אליבא דרבא, ורבא אמר לעיל (יג:) פסוק ראשון לבד, והכי הלכתא: **אפי'** כל אדם נמי. וא"ת: הא שאר כל אדם רשות ופועלים חובה. וי"ל: דפשיטא ליה כיון שיכול לומר מעין י"ח, אין זה שום חדוש אם הפועלים אומרים אפילו לכתחלה: *וחותם בברכת הארץ. אע"ג דמדאורייתא הם, יש כח ביד חכמים לעקור דבר מן התורה הואיל וטרודים במלאכת בעל הבית: אי

**עין משפט נר מצוה**

לד א מיי' פ"ב מהלכות ק"ש הלכה יג יד סמג עשין יח טור שו"ע או"ח סימן סד סעיף ג ג:
לה ב מיי' שם הלכה ד סמג שם טור שו"ע או"ח סימן סג סעיף ח:
לו ג מיי' פ"ד מהלכות ק"ש הלכה א סמג שם טור שו"ע או"ח סימן ע סעיף ג:
לז ד ה מיי' פ"ה מהל' תפלה הלכה ח טור שו"ע או"ח סימן צ סעיף ג:
לח ו מיי' פ"ב מהלכות ק"ש הלכה ד סמג שם טוש"ע או"ח סימן סג סעיף ז:
לט [ז ח מיי' פ"ה מהל' תפלה הלכה ח] ז מיי' פ"ב מהלכות ברכות הלכה ב:
מ ח מיי' וסמג שם טור שו"ע או"ח סימן קצא סעיף א:

**רב נסים גאון**

למה נסמכו אהלים לנחלים. והוא שנאמר בתורה (במדבר כד) משמו של בלעם מה טובו אהליך יעקב כנחלים נטיו:

[לכאורה נ"ל פותח אמנם גם הכ"מ פ"ב מהלכות ברכות דין ב העתיק לדברי תוס' הללו וחותם וכו' ולכן נ"ל דהיה הגי' לפניהם כמ"ש הטור סימן קצא שניה פותח וכו' וכולל וכו' וחותם בברכת הארץ]

**הגהות הב"ח**

(א) גמ' להיכן טעה יחזור לראש באמצע הפ' יחזור לתחלת הפרק בין פרק לפרק כצ"ל: (ב) שם ואוכלין פתן ואין מברכין לפניה) תא"מ. ונ"ב האלפסי והאשר"י גורסי ומברכין לפניה וכו' הוא בטור בסימן קצ"א: (ג) רש"י ד"ה יחזור לפרק וכו' ראשון ויתחיל והיה אם: (ד) שם ד"ה ואמר ליה ר' יוחנן:

**הגהות הגר"א**

[א] גמ' ואין מברכין לפניה. נ"ב וכ"ה גירסת תוס' (ביומא עט ע"א) ובסוכה כו ע"ב ובחולין קז ע"א) אבל גירסת רי"ף והגאונים ומברכין לפניה וכ"ה בתוספתא וכ"כ הרשב"א אבל ליתא בתוספתא שלנו:

**מסורת הש"ס**

במדבר כד; [עי' ברכש"א]; תוספתא פ"ב; תחלת הפרק כנ"ל; [לקמן כו: שבת מה.]; כתובות דף ו:; נ"א לא; תוספתא פ"ב; לעיל יג.; דברים כז; תוספתא פ"ב; [לקמן כח:]; תוספתא פ"ב ע"ש; לקמן דף מו.; יא. סוכה כ"ה; זבות דף ו. (שמחו' פ"ו); (כנ"ל וכ"ה בא"ז); [נ"ל שתים]; [עי' תוס' סוכה כה. ד"ה ובלכתך]

מתני'

השמ"ס רש"י ד"ה ואין מברכין לפניה שאינה מן התורה. עי' לקמן (דף לה ע"א) תוס' ד"ה לפניו וד"ה אלא. ויומא (דף עט ע"א) תוס' ד"ה ולא בירך. ובסוכה (דף כו ע"ב) תוס' ד"ה ולא בירך. וחולין (דף קז ע"א) תוס' ד"ה ולא בירך: תוס' ד"ה וחותם כו' במלאכת בעה"ב. עי' לקמן (דף מו ע"א) תדע דהטוב והמטיב לאו דאורייתא שהרי פועלים עוקרים אותה. ונ"ע:

מא א (מיי' פ"ד מהלכות תפילין הלכה יג) ופ"ד מהלכות אבל הלכה ט [סמג עשין דרבנן ב] טוש"ע או"ח סי' לח סעיף ה וביו"ד סימן שפח סעיף א:
מב ב מיי' פ"א ה"ב ופ"ה מהלכות אבילות ה"ג סמג עשין מד"ס ב טור שו"ע י"ד סימן שפא סעיף א:
מג ג מיי' פ"ד מהלכות ק"ש הלכה ז טור שו"ע או"ח סימן ע סעיף ג:
מד ד מיי' פי"ב מהל' אבל הלכה יב טור שו"ע יו"ד סימן שעז סעיף א:
[מד] [ה] מיי' פ"ד מהלכות נחלות הלכה ה טוש"ע חו"מ סימן רעט סעיף ה:

**אי** הכי מאי איריא בתולה. אי אמרת בשלמא דטעמא משום טרדא – שפיר, אלא מאחר שהוא תולה הטעם במצוה – אלמנה נמי: **אסטנים** אני. ואיכא צער אם לא היה רוחץ, דאינו אסור לרחוץ בימי אבלו אלא משום תענוג. וגם לחוף ראשו אי אית ליה ערבוביא ברישיה – שרי. אפי' תוך שבעה. וכן התיר רבינו שמואל ליולדת אבלה לרחוץ תוך שבעה, ולרחוץ נמי בתשעה באב. וכן משמע נמי במס' יומא (ד' עז:) "מי שיש לו חטטין בראשו סך כדרכו ביום הכפורים ואינו חושש", אע"ג דסיכה כשתיה ביוה"כ. וכן משמע בירושלמי: אבל אסור ברחיצה, הדא דתימא – ברחיצה של תענוג, אבל ברחיצה שאינה של תענוג – מותר, כהדא דאיתמר: מי יש לו חטטין ברישיה וכו': **אנינות** לילה דרבנן. וא"ת: והרי אונן נמי אינו נוהג אלא במעשר, אבל לענין רחיצה דאבילות "דרבנן" הוא, וא"כ לעולם אימא לך דאנינות לילה "דאורייתא" הוי גבי מעשר! ויש לומר: דאי איתא דהוי דאורייתא גבי מעשר, גבי שאר דברים דרבנן – נמי הוה לן למגזר, דכל דתקון רבנן כעין דאורייתא תקון: **אין** עומדין עליהם בשורה. דילמא אתי לאסוקי ליוחסין:

**מתני'** רחץ לילה הראשון שמתה אשתו. ונקברה בו ביום, ואע"פ שאבל אסור ברחיצה – הוא רחץ, כדאמר טעמא: אסטנים אני, והוא אדם מעונג ומפונק: **גמ'** קסבר אנינות לילה דרבנן. ואע"פ שהיה ליל יום המיתה וכתיבא אנינות באורייתא, דכתיב "לא אכלתי באוני ממנו" (דברים כו), ופחות מיום אחד אינו אנינות דילפי רבנן מ"ואחריתה כיום מר", קסבר ר"ג אין לילה של אחריו עם היום אלא מדרבנן הוא כשאר ימי האבל, וגבי אסטנים לא גזור בה רבנן. פלוגתייהו דתנאי היא בזבחים (ד' צט:) באנינות לילה אי מדאורייתא אי מדרבנן: **אין** עומדין עליהם בשורה. כשחוזרים מבית הקברות היו עושים שורות סביב האבל ומנחמין אותו, ואין שורה פחותה מעשרה: ברכת אבלים. ברכת רחבה, שמברכין אותו סעודה ראשונה משל אחרים, ומברכין שם ברכת אבלים, והיא מפורשת בכתובות פרק ראשון (ד' ח.): לאנפילון. בית קטן שלפני טרקלין הגדול: נכוים בפושרים. כלומר: סבור הייתי שתבינו דבר ברמז מועט, שראיתם אותי סר מעליכם ליכנס לאנפילון: הוי. לשון גניחה וצעקה: אין קורין אבות. לישראל: אלא לשלשה. אברהם יצחק ויעקב, לאפוקי שבטים: אלא לארבע. שרה, רבקה, רחל ולאה: אבא פלוני אמא פלונית. לא בבניהם קאמר, אלא בשאר בני אדם, כעין שאנו קורין עכשיו 'מר פלוני', 'מרת פלונית', כך היו רגילין לומר אבא פלוני ואמא פלונית: 'כן אברכך'. ו'כמו חלב ודשן'. תרי קראי דסמיכי להדדי: רננות. שפתים: בפורינו. בגורלנו: אחרית ותקוה. שתהא אחריתנו טובה, ונראה מה שקוינו: ותקננו. לשון תקון: ונשכים ונמצא יחול לבבנו ליראה את שמך. שלא יתגבר עלינו יצר הרע בהרהור הלילה לסור מאחריך ביום, אלא כשנשכים בכל בקר נמצא לבבנו מייחל לך: ותבא לפניך קורת נפשנו. כלומר ספוק צרכנו וקורת רוחנו: ותביט ברעתנו. תדע ותתן לבך ברעה הבאה עלינו: מעזי פנים. שלא יתגרו בי: ומעזות פנים. שלא יוציאו עלי לעז ממזרות: שאינו בן ברית. שאינו מהול: ואע"ג דקיימי קצוצי עליה דרבי. שהיו שוטרים עומדין במלכות אנטונינוס להכות ולהנקם בכל העומדים עליו: בפמליא

– אי הכי מאי איריא הכונס את הבתולה, אפי' כונס את האלמנה נמי! – הכא טריד, והכא לא טריד. – אי משום טרדא – אפילו טבעה ספינתו בים נמי! *אלמה אמר רבי אבא בר זבדא אמר רב: אבל חייב בכל מצות האמורות בתורה, [א]חוץ מן התפילין, שהרי נאמר בהן פאר, שנאמר: °"פארך חבוש עליך וגו'"! – אמרי: התם טרדא דרשות, הכא טרדא דמצוה.§ **מתני'** *רחץ לילה הראשון שמתה אשתו, אמרו לו תלמידיו: *למדתנו רבינו *[ב]שאבל אסור לרחוץ! אמר להם: איני כשאר בני אדם, אסתנים אני. *וכשמת טבי עבדו קבל עליו תנחומין; אמרו לו תלמידיו: *למדתנו רבינו שאין מקבלין תנחומין על העבדים! אמר להם: אין טבי עבדי כשאר כל העבדים, כשר היה. *[ג]חתן אם רוצה לקרות קריאת שמע לילה הראשון – קורא. רבן שמעון בן גמליאל אומר: *לא כל הרוצה ליטול את השם יטול.§ **גמ'** מ"ט דרבן (שמעון בן) גמליאל? קסבר *אנינות לילה דרבנן, דכתיב: °"ואחריתה כיום מר", ובמקום איסטנים לא גזרו ביה רבנן.§ "וכשמת טבי עבדו וכו'".§ ת"ר: עבדים ושפחות אין עומדין עליהם בשורה, ואין אומרים עליהם ברכת אבלים ותנחומי אבלים. *מעשה ומתה שפחתו של רבי אליעזר נכנסו תלמידיו לנחמו. כיון שראה אותם עלה לעלייה – ועלו אחריו; נכנס לאנפילון – נכנסו אחריו, נכנס לטרקלין – נכנסו אחריו; אמר להם: כמדומה אני שאתם נכוים בפושרים, עכשיו אי אתם נכוים אפילו בחמי חמין! לא כך שניתי לכם: [ד]עבדים ושפחות אין עומדין עליהם בשורה ואין אומרים עליהם ברכת אבלים ולא תנחומי אבלים?! אלא מה אומרים עליהם – כשם שאומרים לו לאדם על שורו ועל חמורו שמתו: "המקום ימלא לך חסרונך", כך אומרים לו על עבדו ועל שפחתו: "המקום ימלא לך חסרונך". תניא אידך: עבדים ושפחות אין מספידין אותן; ר' יוסי אומר: אם עבד כשר הוא, אומרים עליו: הוי איש טוב ונאמן ונהנה מיגיעו! אמרו לו: אם כן, מה הנחת לכשרים.§ ת"ר: *אין קורין אבות אלא לשלשה, ואין קורין אמהות אלא לארבע. אבות מאי טעמא? אילימא משום דלא ידעינן אי מראובן קא אתינן אי משמעון קא אתינן – אי הכי, אמהות נמי – לא ידעינן אי מרחל קא אתינן אי מלאה קא אתינן! אלא: עד הכא – חשיבי, טפי – לא חשיבי. תניא אידך: *[ה] עבדים ושפחות אין קורין אותם 'אבא פלוני' ו'אמא פלונית', ושל ר"ג היו קורים אותם 'אבא פלוני' ו'אמא פלונית'. מעשה לסתור?! – משום דחשיבי.§ א"ר אלעזר: מאי דכתיב: °"כן אברכך בחיי בשמך אשא כפי" – "כן אברכך בחיי" – זו ק"ש, "בשמך אשא כפי" – זו תפלה. ואם עושה כן עליו הכתוב אומר: °"כמו חלב ודשן תשבע נפשי", ולא עוד אלא שנוחל שני עולמים, העוה"ז והעולם הבא, שנאמר: °"ושפתי רננות יהלל פי".§ ר' אלעזר בתר דמסיים צלותיה אמר הכי: יהי רצון מלפניך ה' אלהינו שתשכן בפורינו אהבה ואחוה ושלום ורעות, ותרבה גבולנו בתלמידים, ותצליח סופנו אחרית ותקוה, ותשים חלקנו בגן עדן, ותקננו בחבר טוב ויצר טוב בעולמך, ונשכים ונמצא *יחול לבבנו ליראה את שמך, ותבא לפניך קורת נפשנו לטובה. רבי יוחנן בתר דמסיים צלותיה אמר הכי: יהי רצון מלפניך ה' אלהינו שתציץ בבשתנו ותביט ברעתנו ותתלבש ברחמיך ותתכסה בעזך ותתעטף בחסידותך ותתאזר בחנינותך ותבא לפניך מדת טובך וענותנותך. ר' זירא בתר דמסיים צלותיה אמר הכי: יהי רצון מלפניך ה' אלהינו שלא נחטא ולא נבוש ולא נכלם *מאבותינו. ר' חייא בתר דמצלי אמר הכי: יהי רצון מלפניך ה' אלהינו שתהא תורתך אומנותנו, ואל ידוה לבנו ואל יחשכו עינינו. רב בתר צלותיה אמר הכי: יהי רצון מלפניך ה' אלהינו שתתן לנו חיים ארוכים, חיים של שלום, חיים של טובה, חיים של ברכה, חיים של פרנסה, חיים של חילוץ עצמות, חיים שיש בהם יראת חטא, חיים שאין בהם בושה וכלימה, חיים של עושר וכבוד, חיים שתהא בנו אהבת תורה ויראת שמים, חיים שתמלא לנו את כל משאלות לבנו לטובה. רבי בתר צלותיה אמר הכי: *יהי רצון מלפניך ה' אלהינו ואלהי אבותינו שתצילנו מעזי פנים ומעזות פנים, מאדם רע ומפגע רע, מיצר רע, מחבר רע, משכן רע, ומשטן המשחית, *ומדין קשה ומבעל דין קשה, בין שהוא בן ברית בין שאינו בן ברית. ואע"ג דקיימי קצוצי עליה דרבי. רב ספרא בתר צלותיה אמר הכי: יהי רצון מלפניך ה' אלהינו שתשים שלום בפמליא

תורה אור: יחזקאל כד; עמוס ח; תהלים סג; שם; שם

[לעיל יא. וש"נ]; שמחות פ"ו; כ"א לא; מו"ק דף טו:; שמחות פ"א הכ; כ"א לא; פסחים דף נה.; [עי' פירש"י לק]; [פסחים נב. זבר]; שמחות פ"א הכ; שמחות פ"א הכ; שמחות פ"א הכ; [פי' תאות לבב ערך יחול]; [פי' יותר מאבו בערך הנ"ל]; שבת דף ל:; [ושולין אנו בקושי. בערך]

בפמליא של מעלה ובפמליא של מטה, ובין התלמידים העוסקים בתורתך, בין עוסקין לשמה בין עוסקין שלא לשמה. וכל העוסקין שלא לשמה, יהי רצון שיהו עוסקין לשמה. ר' אלכסנדרי בתר צלותיה אמר הכי: יהי רצון מלפניך ה' אלהינו שתעמידנו בקרן אורה ואל תעמידנו בקרן חשכה, ואל ידוה לבנו ואל יחשכו עינינו. איכא דאמרי: הא רב המנונא מצלי לה, ור' אלכסנדרי בתר דמצלי אמר הכי: רבון העולמים, גלוי וידוע לפניך שרצוננו לעשות רצונך, ומי מעכב? שאור שבעיסה ושעבוד מלכיות; יהי רצון מלפניך שתצילנו מידם, ונשוב לעשות חוקי רצונך בלבב שלם. רבא בתר צלותיה אמר הכי: *אלהי, עד שלא נוצרתי איני כדאי ועכשיו שנוצרתי כאילו לא נוצרתי, עפר אני בחיי, ק"ו במיתתי, הרי אני לפניך ככלי מלא בושה וכלימה, יהי רצון מלפניך ה' אלהי שלא אחטא עוד, ומה שחטאתי לפניך מרק ברחמיך הרבים אבל לא ע"י יסורין וחלאים רעים. והיינו וידוי דרב המנונא זוטי ביומא דכפורי. מר בריה דרבינא כי הוה מסיים צלותיה אמר הכי: [א]אלהי, נצור לשוני מרע ושפתותי מדבר מרמה ולמקללי נפשי תדום ונפשי כעפר לכל תהיה, פתח לבי בתורתך ובמצותיך תרדוף נפשי, ותצילני מפגע רע מיצר הרע ומאשה רעה ומכל רעות המתרגשות לבא בעולם, וכל החושבים עלי רעה מהרה הפר עצתם וקלקל מחשבותם, יהיו לרצון אמרי פי והגיון לבי לפניך ה' צורי וגואלי.§ רב ששת כי הוה יתיב בתעניתא, בתר דמצלי אמר הכי: [ב]רבון העולמים, גלוי לפניך, בזמן שבית המקדש קיים אדם חוטא ומקריב קרבן, ואין מקריבין ממנו אלא חלבו ודמו ומתכפר לו; ועכשיו ישבתי בתענית ונתמעט חלבי ודמי, יהי רצון מלפניך שיהא חלבי ודמי שנתמעט כאילו הקרבתיו לפניך על גבי המזבח ותרצני. *ר' יוחנן כי הוה מסיים ספרא דאיוב אמר הכי: סוף אדם למות, וסוף בהמה לשחיטה, והכל למיתה הם עומדים. אשרי מי שגדל בתורה ועמלו בתורה ועושה נחת רוח ליוצרו, וגדל בשם טוב ונפטר בשם טוב מן העולם, ועליו אמר שלמה °"טוב שם משמן טוב ויום המות מיום הולדו".§ מרגלא בפומיה דר"מ: גמור בכל לבבך ובכל נפשך לדעת את דרכי ולשקוד על דלתי תורתי, נצור תורתי בלבך ונגד עיניך תהיה יראתי, שמור פיך מכל חטא וטהר וקדש עצמך מכל אשמה ועון, ואני אהיה עמך בכל מקום. מרגלא בפומייהו דרבנן דיבנה: אני בריה וחברי בריה, אני מלאכתי בעיר והוא מלאכתו בשדה, אני משכים למלאכתי והוא משכים למלאכתו, כשם שהוא אינו מתגדר במלאכתי כך אני איני מתגדר במלאכתו, ושמא תאמר: אני מרבה והוא ממעיט – *שנינו: אחד המרבה ואחד הממעיט ובלבד שיכוין לבו לשמים. מרגלא בפומיה דאביי: לעולם יהא אדם ערום ביראה, °[ג]"מענה רך *משיב חמה", ומרבה שלום עם אחיו ועם קרוביו ועם כל אדם, ואפילו עם גוי בשוק, כדי שיהא אהוב למעלה ונחמד למטה, ויהא מקובל על הבריות. אמרו עליו על רבן יוחנן בן זכאי שלא הקדימו אדם שלום מעולם ואפילו גוי בשוק. מרגלא בפומיה דרבא: תכלית חכמה תשובה ומעשים טובים; שלא יהא אדם קורא ושונה ובועט באביו ובאמו וברבו ובמי שהוא גדול ממנו בחכמה ובמנין, שנאמר: °"ראשית חכמה יראת ה' שכל טוב לכל עושיהם". *'לעושים' לא נאמר אלא 'לעושיהם' – לעושים לשמה, ולא לעושים שלא לשמה. וכל העושה שלא לשמה נוח לו שלא נברא. מרגלא בפומיה דרב: [לא כעולם הזה העולם הבא,] [ד]העולם הבא אין בו לא אכילה ולא שתיה ולא פריה ורביה ולא משא ומתן ולא קנאה ולא שנאה ולא תחרות, אלא צדיקים יושבין ועטרותיהם בראשיהם ונהנים מזיו השכינה, שנאמר: °"ויחזו את האלהים ויאכלו וישתו".§ גדולה הבטחה שהבטיחן הקב"ה לנשים יותר מן האנשים, שנא' °"נשים שאננות קמנה שמענה קולי בנות בוטחות האזנה אמרתי". א"ל רב לר' חייא: נשים במאי זכיין? *באקרויי בנייהו לבי כנישתא, ובאתנויי גברייהו בי רבנן, ונטרין לגברייהו עד דאתו מבי רבנן.§ כי הוו מפטרי רבנן מבי ר' אמי, ואמרי לה מבי ר' חנינא, אמרי ליה הכי: עולמך תראה בחייך, ואחריתך לחיי העולם הבא, ותקותך לדור דורים. לבך יהגה תבונה, פיך ידבר חכמות ולשונך ירחיש רננות, עפעפיך יישירו נגדך, עיניך יאירו במאור תורה ופניך יזהירו כזוהר הרקיע, שפתותיך יביעו דעת וכליותיך תעלוזנה מישרים, ופעמיך ירוצו לשמוע דברי עתיק יומין. כי הוו מפטרי רבנן מבי רב חסדא ואמרי לה מבי ר' שמואל בר נחמני, אמרו ליה הכי: °"אלופינו מסבלים וגו'". "אלופינו מסבלים" – רב ושמואל, ואמרי לה רבי יוחנן ור' אלעזר, חד אמר: 'אלופינו' בתורה, ו'מסבלים' במצות. וחד אמר: 'אלופינו' בתורה ובמצות, ו'מסבלים' ביסורים.

אין

רש"י

בפמליא של מעלה. בחבורת שרי האומות. שבשרים של מעלה יש תגר ביניהם, איכך יש קטטה בין האומות, כדכתיב "ועתה אשוב להלחם עם שר פרס" (דניאל י): ובפמליא של מטה. בחבורת החכמים: בקרן אורה. בזוית אורה: ומי מעכב. שאין אנו עושים רצונך: שאור שבעיסה. יצר הרע שבלבבנו, המחמיצנו: איני כדאי. לא הייתי חשוב והגון להיות נוצר: ועכשיו שנוצרתי. מה חשיבותי, הרי אני כאילו לא נוצרתי: ק"ו. שבמיתתי עפר אני: מרק. כלה וכסס: כי הוה מסיים ספרא דאיוב. על שם שאיוב נפטר בשם טוב: מרגלא בפומיה. דבר זה רגיל בפיו: אני. העוסק בתורה בריה אני וכן חברי עם הארץ בריה הוא: אני מלאכתי בעיר. כלומר: נוחה מלאכתי ממלאכתו: מתגדר. מתגדל לתפוס אומנותי: ושמא תאמר. הדין עמו שאינו מתגדר במלאכתי, שאילו היה תופס אומנותי לא היה לו לב פתוח להרבות בתורה כמותי, והיה ממעיט ואין לו שכר: שנינו. שיש לו שכר לממעיט כמו למרבה: ובלבד שיכוין לבו לשמים. ואגב קרבנות הוא, במנחות בסופה*: ערום ביראה. להערים בכל מיני ערמה ליראת בוראו: תכלית חכמה. עיקרה של תורה שיהא עמה תשובה ומע"ט: העושה שלא לשמה נוח לו שלא נברא. פירוש: שאינו לומד כדי לקיים אלא לקנטר. דבפרק "מקום שנהגו" (ד' נ:) אמרי': רבא רמי, כתיב 'עד שמים חסדך', וכתיב 'מעל השמים', כאן – בעוסק שלא לשמה כו'. והתם איירי במקיים כדי שיכבדוהו. וכן משמע בירושלמי דפירקין: ויאכלו וישתו. שבעו מזיו השכינה כאילו אכלו ושתו: גדולה הבטחה. שהרי קראן "שאננות ובוטחות": לבי כנישתא. תינוקות של בית רבן היו רגילין להיות למדים לפני רבן בבית הכנסת: בי רבנן. בית המדרש, ששם שונים משנה וגמרא: ונטרן לגברייהו. ממתינות לבעליהן, ונותנות להם רשות ללכת וללמוד תורה בעיר אחרת: מפטרי רבנן. זה מזה, שהיה נוטל רשות מחבירו לשוב לביתו ולאחריו: עולמך תראה בחייך. כל צרכיך תמצא: פיך ידבר חכמות. בלשון ברכה היו אומרים: יישירו. לשון יושר, שתהא מבין בתורה כהלכה:

כל

תוספות

ונפשי כעפר לכל תהיה. מה עפר אינו מקבל כליה לעולם – כן יהי רצון שזרעי לא יכלה לעולם, כמו שהוא אומר "והיה זרעך כעפר הארץ": אני בריה וחברי בריה. כלומר: יש לו לב כמוני להבחין בין טוב לרע: העושה שלא לשמה נוח לו שלא נברא. וא"ת: האמר רב יהודה אמר רב, פרק "מקום שנהגו" (ד' נ:): לעולם יעסוק אדם בתורה ובמצות אפילו שלא לשמה, שמתוך שלא לשמה בא לשמה! וי"ל: דהכא איירי שאינו לומד אלא לקנטר חביריו, והתם איירי שלומד ע"מ שיכבדוהו*:

פרק

תורה אור



מה א טור ושו"ע או"ח סי' קכב סעיף א:
מו ב טור ושו"ע סימן תקסה סעיף ד:
מז ג מיי' פ"ה מהלכות דעות הלכה ז:
מח ד מיי' פ"ח מהל' תשובה הלכה ב:

[וע"ע תענית ז. תוספות ד"ה וכל העוסק ותוס' פסחים נ: ד"ה וכאן ותוס' נזיר כג: ד"ה שמתוך ותוס' סוטה כב: ד"ה לעולם]

[ישיב כל"ל]

ס"א ללומדיהם לא נאמר אלא לעושיהם

## רב נסים גאון

ועפעפיך יישירו נגדך. איתי' מפרש במסכתא מגילה בפרק הקורא את המגילה למפרע (דף יח) אמר לי' רמי בר [חמא] לרבי ירמיה מדיפתי מאי (משלי ד) ועפעפיך יישירו נגדך אמר ליה אלו דברי תורה שכתב בהן (שם כג) התעיף עיניך בו (ישרים) [אפילו הכי מיושרין] הן אצל ר' מאיר:

## גליון הש"ס

ברש"י ד"ה אני כו' וכן חברי עם הארץ. עי' סוכה דף נט ע"א תוס' ד"ה הלוקח:



[דף קי:]

[יומא פו.]

[ר' יוחנן כי הוה ספרא דאיוב]

קהלת ז

קי. לעיל ה: [וש"נ]

משלי טו

תהלים קיא

שמות כד

ישעיה לב

סוטה דף כא.

תהלים קמד

"אין פרץ" – שלא תהא סיעתנו כסיעתו של דוד שיצא ממנו אחיתופל, "ואין יוצאת" – שלא תהא סיעתנו *כסיעתו של שאול שיצא ממנו דואג האדומי, "ואין צווחה" – שלא תהא סיעתנו כסיעתו של אלישע שיצא ממנו גחזי, "ברחובותינו" – שלא יהא לנו בן או תלמיד שמקדיח תבשילו ברבים, כגון ישו הנוצרי.§ "שמעו אלי אבירי לב הרחוקים מצדקה". רב ושמואל, ואמרי לה רבי יוחנן ורבי אלעזר, חד אמר: כל העולם כולו נזונין בצדקה – והם נזונין בזרוע; וחד אמר: כל העולם כולו נזונין בזכותם, והם – אפילו בזכות עצמן אין נזונין; כדרב יהודה אמר רב, דאמר רב יהודה אמר רב: בכל יום ויום בת קול יוצאת *מהר חורב ואומרת: כל העולם כולו נזונין בשביל חנינא בני, וחנינא בני – די לו בקב חרובין מערב שבת לערב שבת. ופליגא דרב יהודה, דאמר רב יהודה: מאן 'אבירי לב' – גובאי טפשאי. אמר רב יוסף: תדע, דהא לא איגייר גיורא מינייהו. אמר רב אשי: בני מתא מחסיא אבירי לב נינהו, דקא חזו יקרא דאורייתא תרי זמני בשתא ולא קמגייר גיורא מינייהו.§ *חתן אם רוצה לקרות וכו'". *למימרא, דרבן שמעון בן גמליאל חייש ליוהרא ורבנן לא חיישי ליוהרא – והא איפכא שמעינן להו! דתנן: מקום שנהגו לעשות מלאכה בתשעה באב – עושין, מקום שנהגו שלא לעשות – אין עושין, ובכל מקום תלמידי חכמים בטלים; רבן שמעון בן גמליאל אומר: לעולם יעשה כל אדם את עצמו כתלמיד חכם. קשיא דרבנן אדרבנן, קשיא דרבן שמעון בן גמליאל אדרבן שמעון בן גמליאל! – אמר רבי יוחנן: מוחלפת השיטה. רב שישא בריה דרב אידי אמר: לעולם לא תחליף, דרבנן אדרבנן לא קשיא: ק"ש כיון דכ"ע קא קרו ואיהו נמי קרי – לא מיחזי כיוהרא, *הכא, כיון דכולי עלמא עבדי מלאכה ואיהו לא קא עביד – מיחזי כיוהרא; דרבן שמעון בן גמליאל אדרבן שמעון בן גמליאל לא קשיא: *התם בכוונה תליא מילתא, ואנן סהדי דלא מצי לכווני דעתיה. אבל *הכא, הרואה אומר: מלאכה הוא דאין לו, פוק חזי *כמה בטלני איכא בשוקא.§

## הדרן עלך היה קורא

**מי** *שמתו מוטל לפניו – פטור מק"ש, (ב) ומן התפלה ומן התפילין, ומכל מצות האמורות בתורה. נושאי המטה וחלופיהן וחלופי חלופיהן, את שלפני המטה ואת שלאחר המטה; את שלפני המטה צורך בהם – פטורים, ואת שלאחר המטה צורך בהם – חייבין, ואלו ואלו פטורים מן התפלה. קברו את המת וחזרו, אם יכולין להתחיל ולגמור עד שלא יגיעו לשורה – יתחילו, ואם לאו – לא יתחילו. העומדים בשורה, הפנימיים – פטורים, והחיצונים – חייבים. (*נשים ועבדים וקטנים פטורים מק"ש ומן התפילין וחייבין בתפלה ובמזוזה ובברכת המזון.)§

**גמ'** מוטל לפניו – אין, ושאינו מוטל לפניו – לא; ורמינהי: *מי שמתו מוטל לפניו – אוכל בבית אחר, ואם אין לו בית אחר – אוכל בבית חבירו, ואם אין לו בית חבירו – עושה מחיצה ואוכל, ואם אין לו דבר לעשות מחיצה – מחזיר פניו ואוכל, ואינו מיסב ואוכל, ואינו אוכל בשר ואינו שותה יין, ואינו מברך ואינו מזמן, ואין

---

**פרץ** זה אחיתופל. שפרץ פרצה במלכות בית דוד. "יוצאת" זה דואג שיצא לתרבות רעה, כדמפרש ב"חלק" (דף קו:) גבי ווי שיצא זה: **צווחה** זה גחזי. שהיה מצורע, וכתיב ביה "טמא טמא יקרא" והיינו צווחה: **והם** נזונין בזרוע.

כל העולם כולו נזונין בצדקה. בצדקתו של הקב"ה, ולא בזכות שבידן: והם נזונין בזרוע. בזכות שבידם, ובצדיקים משתעי קרא וקרי להו רחוקים מצדקתו של הקב"ה: אינן נזונין. שאין להן כדי לרכיס ומתפרנסים בקושי: ופליגא דרב יהודה. דאיהו אמר 'אבירי לב' היינו רשעים: גובאי. שם אומה היא בבבל. ובמסכת קדושין (פ"ד דף ע:) אמרינן שהיו מן הנתינים: שבחא דאורייתא תרי זמני בשתא. שהיו נאספים שם ישראל באדר לשמוע בהלכות הפסח מדרש דרב אשי, ובאלול לשמוע הלכות החג: *לא כל הרוצה וכו'. אם לא הוחזק חכם וחסיד לרבים אין זה אלא גאוה, שמראה בעצמו שיכול לכוין לבו: אמרי אינשי עבידתא הוא דלית ליה. הרואה אותו שאינו עושה מלאכה אינו מבין שמחמת תשעה באב הוא בטל, אלא אין לו מלאכה לעשות: פוק חזי כמה בטלני איכא בשוקא. אף בימי מלאכה:

הדרן עלך היה קורא

**מי** שמתו כו' פטור מלקרות ק"ש. לפי שהוא טרוד במחשבת קבורתו, והויא דומיא דחתן דפטור משום טירדא דמצוה: וחלופיהן. שכן דרך שמתחלפין לשאת, לפי שהכל חפצין לזכות בו: את שלפני המטה. שיעסקו בו כשיגיע המטה אצלם: ושלאחר המטה. שנשאוהו כבר: שלפני המטה צורך בהם פטורים. אם צריכים לשאתו – פטורים: ושלאחר המטה. אף אם צורך בהם – חייבים, הואיל שכבר יצאו ידי חובתן מן המת: ואלו ואלו פטורין מן התפלה. דלאו דאורייתא היא. ורבותינו פירשו: לפי שיש להם עוד שהות, ולי נראה שאין זה לשון פטור: לשורה. שהיו מנחמין את האבל בהקף שורה סביבותיו כשחוזרים מן הקבר: **גמ'** שאינו מוטל לפניו. כגון הוא בבית אחד והמת בבית אחר: אוכל בבית אחר. דנראה כלועג לרש וכו': ואינו מיסב. כדרך המסובים בחשיבות על צדו השמאלית ובמטה: ואינו מברך. ואינו צריך לברך ברכת המוציא: ואינו מזמן. אינו צריך לברך ברכת המזון: ואין

---

*בתקעות "יוסם בזרוע עדיך בלו" ולא גרסינן "עדיך לא בלו": **תרי** זימני בשתא. אבל בעצרת שאינו אלא יום אחד לא היו כל כך מתאספין, ושמא ניסא איתרחיש להו. וראיתי בספר העתים שסבר הרב רבי יהודה בר ברזילי שמשמע שהיה עמוד של אש יורד מן השמים עליהם בכלה דאלול ובכלה דאדר: **רב** שישא בריה דרב אידי אמר לעולם לא תחליף. פר"ח דהלכה כרב *ששת דהוא בתראה, והלכה כרשב"ג דלאמר לא כל הרוצה ליטול את השם יטול, (א) ובכל מקום ששנה רבן שמעון בן גמליאל במשנתינו הלכה כמותו, חוץ מערב ולידן וראיה אחרונה (כתובות עז.), וכן פסק ר"ח. ומיהו, אנו שבשום פעם אין אנו מכוונים היטב, גם חתן יש לקרות, דאדרבה נראה כיוהרא אם לא יקרא, כלומר: אני מכוין בכל שעה. אבל לעשות מלאכה בתשעה באב – אין לעשות מלאכה:

הדרן עלך היה קורא

**מי** שמתו מוטל לפניו. רש"י גריס "מי שמתו" אחר "תפלת השחר", אבל נראה לר"י שהוא אחר "היה קורא", דאיירי בספיקי מק"ש, וכאן מתחיל נמי מפטור ק"ש, ובירושלמי גריס כמו כן: **פטור** מק"ש. בירושלמי מפרש טעמא: א"ר בון: כתיב "למען תזכור כו' כל ימי חייך" – ימים שאתה עוסק בחיים, ולא ימים שאתה עוסק במתים. הכי גרסינן: "פטור מקריאת שמע ומן התפלה ומן התפילין": **הכי** גריס רש"י – שלאחר המטה אפילו המטה צריכה להם – חייבין, לפי שלעולם לא היו רגילים לשאת שכבר נשאו חלקם. ותימה קצת הלשון לפרש, מאי קאמר "אפי' צריכה להם", והלא לא היו נושאין כלל את המת! לכך נראה כגרסת הספרים: שלפני המטה ושלאחר המטה, את שהמטה צריכה להם – פטורין ואין צריכה להם – חייבין: **אלו** ואלו פטורין מן התפלה. אבל בק"ש ובתפילין שהן מדאורייתא – חייבים. וקשה דקאמר מי שמתו מוטל לפניו דפטור מן קריאת שמע ומן התפילין וכו', כל שכן דפטור מן התפלה, אלא לא בעי למיתני ברישא אלא החלוק שבין נושאי המטה למתו מוטל לפניו: **ואינו** מברך. פרש"י: ואין זקוק לברך. ומשמע מתוך פירושו שאם רצה לברך – רשאי. מיהו בירושלמי קאמר: אם רצה להחמיר – אין שומעין לו. לכך נראה לומר: אינו מברך – אינו רשאי לברך. ומפרש בירושלמי למה, וקאמר מפני כבודו של מת. אי נמי – מפני שאין לו מי שישא משאו. ופריך והתניא פטור מנטילת לולב, וקא ס"ד דמיירי ביו"ט ובו אינו טרוד לישא משאו, ומשני: תפתר בחול, פי': בחולו של מועד. והתניא

---

מט א ב מיי' פ"ה מהל' תענית הלכה י סמג עשין מד"ס ג טור שו"ע או"ח סי' תקנד סעיף כב:
א ג מיי' פ"ד מהלכות אבילות הלכה ו ופ"ד מהלכות ק"ש הלכה ג סמג עשין יח כ טוש"ע או"ח סימן עא סעיף א:
ב ד מיי' פ"ד מהלכות (אבל) [ק"ש] הלכה ד טור שו"ע אורח חיים סימן עב סעיף א [וביו"ד סימן שנח סעיף א]:
ג ה ו מיי' (פ"ד) [ספ"ו] מהל' תפלה ופ"ד מהלכות ק"ש הלכה א סמג עשין יח טוש"ע או"ח סימן קו סעיף א:
ד ז מיי' פ"ד מהלכות אבל הלכה ו סמג עשין מד"ס ב טוש"ע יו"ד סימן שמא סעיף א וטוש"ע או"ח סימן עא סעיף ה:

### רב נסים גאון

**אמר** רב אשי הני בני מתא מחסיא אבירי לב נינהו דקא חזו יקרא דאורייתא תרי זמני בשתא. היינו תרי ירחי דכלה חודש אדר וחודש אלול והתם בבבא מציעא (אמרינן) בפ' השוכר את הפועלים (דף פו) אמרינן אמר כו' רבה בר נחמני אגב שמדא נח נפשיה אכלו ביה קורצי בי מלכא איכא גברא חד מיהודאי דקא מפגר תריסר אלפי גברי ירחא בקייטא וירחא בסיתוא מכרגא ובפרק השואל (דף לז) אמרי איהו שאיל להו בזמן דכלה:

סליק פרק ב'

### הגהות הב"ח

(א) תוס' ד"ה רב שישא וכו' ובכל מקום: פרק ג (ב) שם במשנה פטור מקריאת שמע ומן התפילין כצ"ל ותיבת ומן התפלה נמחק:

### גליון הש"ס

ברש"י שבחא דאורייתא כו' הלכות החג. כו'. עי' רש"י לקמן ל ע"א ד"ה שבבלה לרגלים כו' ועלרת כו':

---

[הערוך מהפך למעלה כאן פי' של שאול כו' וכו' בטעמא]

תורה אור

ישעיה מו

חולין קד פו. כד: [בתענית כד: דלא גרסינן כ ודע דגם בחולי]

פסחים קה נה.

פס נה:

שמחות פ"י

[משנה לקמן כ.]

מ"ק דף כג: שם

ואין מברכין עליו. אין צריך שיברכו לו אחרים בברכת הלחם: ואין מזמנין עליו. אין מצטרף עם שלשה לזימון: תשמיש המטה איכא בינייהו. לר"ש חייב אבל בעונה בשבת: קתני מיהת פטור מק"ש ומכל ברכות. ואפילו כשהוא אוכל בבית חברו: תרגמא. להא דתני פטור במי שאין לו בית אחר, דקאמר מחזיר פניו ואוכל: רב אשי אמר. לעולם אפילו, ומתניתין נמי אפילו בבית אחר נמי פטר ליה, דכל שמוטל עליו לקוברו קרי מוטל לפניו: ויקם אברהם וגו' וכתיב "ואקברה מתי מלפני". והיא שעתא לאו לפניו הוה: משמרו. אדם אחר שאינו קרובו אלא משמרו: תופס ד' אמות לק"ש. שאסור לקרות בתוך ארבע אמות שלו, משום לועג לרש: פטור מק"ש. משום דעוסק במצוה: חוששין לעכברים. תנא קמא חייש לעכברים אפי' בספינה: דסקיא. מרלוף גדול של עור: ואם היה מתירא. וצריך לרכוב על הסוס ולרוץ: אלא אסיפא. אם היה מתירא רוכב: מלוה ה' חונן דל. קרי ביה מלוה את המקום מי שחונן את הדל, ואין לך דל מן המת והמלוה אותו כאלו מלוה את המקום: דלייה. הגביהו: לא שנית. לא חזרת עליו פעם שנית כדי שתתבונן בו: אלו צדיקים. ומאי "יודעים שימותו" - נותנים אל לבם יום המיתה ומושכים ידיהם מן העבירה, ורשעים "אינם יודעים מאומה" - שעושים עצמם כאינם יודעים ומוטעים: הוא הכה. הפיל את השנים של דורות משני מקדשים שלא היה בהם כמותו: אריאל. זה בית המקדש, שנאמר "הוי אריאל אריאל קרית חנה דוד" (ישעיהו כט): מואב. על שם שבנאו דוד דאתי מרות המואביה:

גזיזי

תורה אור

ואין מברכין עליו ואין מזמנין עליו, ופטור מקריאת שמע ומן התפלה ומן התפילין ומכל מצות האמורות בתורה; ובשבת - מיסב ואוכל בשר ושותה יין, ומברך ומזמן, ומברכין עליו ומזמנין עליו, וחייב בכל המצות האמורות בתורה; *רשב"ג אומר: מתוך שנתחייב באלו נתחייב בכולן. וא"ר יוחנן: מאי בינייהו - תשמיש המטה איכא בינייהו. קתני מיהת "פטור מקריאת שמע ומן התפלה ומן התפילין ומכל מצות האמורות בתורה"! אמר רב פפא: תרגמא אמחזיר פניו ואוכל. רב אשי אמר: כיון שמוטל עליו לקוברו - כמוטל לפניו דמי, שנאמר: °"ויקם אברהם מעל פני מתו", ונאמר: "ואקברה מתי מלפני" - כל זמן שמוטל עליו לקוברו כמוטל לפניו דמי.§ מתו - אין, אבל משמרו - לא, והתניא: המשמר את המת אע"פ שאינו מתו - פטור מק"ש ומן התפלה ומן התפילין ומכל מצות האמורות בתורה. משמרו - אע"פ שאינו מתו, מתו - אע"פ שאינו משמרו. מתו ומשמרו אין, אבל מהלך בבית הקברות - לא, והתניא: אלא יהלך אדם בבית הקברות ותפילין בראשו וספר תורה בזרועו וקורא, ואם עושה כן עובר משום °"לועג לרש חרף עושהו"! התם תוך ארבע [אמות] הוא דאסור, חוץ לארבע אמות חייב, דאמר מר: *מת תופס ד' אמות לק"ש, הכא - חוץ לד' אמות נמי פטור.§ גופא: בהמשמר את המת אע"פ שאינו מתו - פטור מקריאת שמע ומן התפלה ומן התפילין ומכל מצות האמורות בתורה. היו שנים - זה משמר וזה קורא, וזה משמר וזה קורא. בן עזאי אומר: היו באים בספינה - מניחו בזוית זו ומתפללין שניהם בזוית אחרת. מאי בינייהו? אמר רבינא: "חוששין לעכברים" איכא בינייהו. מר סבר: חיישינן, ומר סבר: לא חיישינן.§ ת"ר: גהמוליך עצמות ממקום למקום - הרי זה לא יתנם בדסקיא ויתנם על גבי חמור וירכב עליהם, מפני שנוהג בהם מנהג בזיון. ואם היה מתירא מפני גוים ומפני לסטים - מותר, וכדרך שאמרו בעצמות כך אמרו [ד] בספר תורה. אהייא? אילימא ארישא - פשיטא, מי גרע ספר תורה מעצמות! אלא אסיפא.§ אמר רחבה *אמר רב יהודה: דכל הרואה המת ואינו מלוהו - עובר משום "לועג לרש חרף עושהו". ואם הלוהו מה שכרו? אמר רב אסי, עליו הכתוב אומר: °"מלוה ה' חונן דל", °"ומכבדו חונן אביון".§ רבי חייא ורבי יונתן הוו שקלי ואזלי בבית הקברות, הוה קשדיא תכלתא דרבי יונתן. אמר ליה רבי חייא: [ה] דלייה, כדי שלא יאמרו "למחר באין אצלנו ועכשיו *מחרפין אותנו". אמר ליה: ומי ידעי כולי האי?! והא כתיב: °"והמתים אינם יודעים מאומה"! אמר ליה: *אם קרית - לא שנית, אם שנית - לא שלשת, אם שלשת - לא פירשו לך: °"כי החיים יודעים שימותו" - אלו צדיקים שבמיתתן נקראו חיים, שנאמר: °"ובניהו בן יהודע בן איש חי רב פעלים מקבצאל הוא הכה את שני אריאל מואב והוא ירד והכה את הארי בתוך הבור ביום השלג";

בן

[בראשית כג | משלי יז | משלי יט | שם יד | קהלת ט | מ"ק טז: | שם | שמואל ב כג | סוטה דף מג:]

[כמ"ק איתא רבן גמליאל וכן איתא בשמחות]

[בשאלתות פ' חיי שרה אי' אמר רב יהודה אמר רב]

נ"א מלעיגין.

והתניא פטור מתקיעת שופר אית לך למימר בחול ולא בי"ט? בתמיה, ומשני, א"ר חנינא: שהוא זקוק להכין לו ארון ותכריכין, כדתנן (שבת קנא.): מחשיכין על התחום להביא לו ארון ותכריכין, כמו שהוא נושא משאו דמי. אלמא משמע דבשבתות וי"ט אינו רשאי לברך ולהתפלל, דטרוד להחשיך לו על התחום להביא ארון ותכריכין, וקשיא מסיפא, דקתני: בשבת מברכין עליו ומזמנין עליו, וכן תניא נמי בירושלמי: בד"א? - בחול, אבל בשבת מיסב ואוכל ומברך ועונים אחריו אמן. ואומר הר"י דפליגי אהדדי רישא וסיפא בירושלמי. ורבי נתנאל היה אומר דאפשר לישבו, דודאי אם דעתו להחשיך על התחום - אז יש לנו לומר דטרוד להחשיך ואינו רשאי לברך, אבל בסיפא, מיירי בשאין דעתו להחשיך על התחום, ומיהו האי טעמא לא שייך לטעמא דמשום כבודו. ומן הירושלמי דמשני דפטור מנטילת לולב, דמיירי בחול המועד דטרוד לישא משאו, למדנו שבחול המועד שייך אנינות כשמתו מוטל לפניו. וכיון דכשמוטל לפניו שייך אנינות, כי מוטל עליו לקוברו כמוטל לפניו דמי. וכן איפכא, מי שמתו מוטל לפניו ואין עליו לקוברו - אינו נוהג אנינות, וכן משמע בירושלמי: נמסר לרבים - אוכל בשר ושותה יין, נמסר לכתפים - כנמסר לרבים, ועל כרחך נמסר לרבים ר"ל אפי' לפניו, דאי שלא לפניו - תיפוק ליה שמיד חל עליו אבלות משילא מפתח ביתו, וכיון דלא חל עליה אנינות א"כ אדם שאינו יכול לקבור מתו, כגון אדם שמת בבית האסורים ואין המושל מניחו לקוברו - נראה שאין חייב לנהוג בו אנינות שהרי אין זה מוטל עליו לקברו, מפני שאינו יכול לפדותו ולהוציאו לקברו. כדתניא במסכת שמחות (פ"ב): נתיאשו בעליו מלקוברו - מתאבלין עליו, ופסיק מיניה תורת אנינות. מיהו, באותו שתפסו מושל גם אבילות אינו חייב, דלא דמי לנתיאשו מלקוברו(א) שסם אינו קוברו תו, אבל הכא עדיין הוא מצפה אם יוכל לעשות פשרה עם המושל להניחו לקברו, וכן מעשה דר' אליעזר בר"ש בבבא מציעא (ד' פד:) דפסק מלות אנינות. ומעשה שמתה אחותו של ר"ת בשבת והודיעו לו במוצאי שבת בעיר אחרת, ואכל בשר ושתה יין, ואמר כיון שיש לה בעל שחייב בקבורתה - אינו אסור בבשר וביין. ואפשר שגם ר"ת אם היה בעיר עצמו היה מיקל מאותו הטעם: **וספר** תורה בזרועו וקורא. והוא הדין דעל פה אסור לקרות: **וירכב** עליהם. אבל אי מפסילן לאחוריו על החמור - שפיר דמי, וכן בס"ת. ואפילו אם בדעתך לאסור ס"ת, אבל בנביאים ובכתובים שפיר דמי, *מדנקט ס"ת, ולא מסתבר לומר משום שריותא דגוים ולסטים דהא פשיטא דמותר, דלמה יהיה אסור? ועוד, דבהדיא אמר בירושלמי: דסקיא מלאה ספרים או שהיו בה עצמות של מת - הרי זה מפשילן לאחוריו ורוכב עליו*: **אלא** אסיפא משום לסטים מותר לרכוב עליהם. וה"ה לאחוריו מותר אפילו בלא לסטים: **למחר** באין אצלנו ועכשיו מחרפין אותנו. ותימה: והא אמרי' בפ' "התכלת" (מנחות דף מא.): הסיא שעתא ודאי רמינן ליה. פי': נותנין ציצית בטליתותיהן(ב) משום לועג לרש! וי"ל דה"פ: הכא דמביישין אותם במה שהחיים מצווים והמתים אינם מצווים וגדול המצווה וכו',(ג) והסיא ד"התכלת" היינו דרמו חוטים למתים ועכשיו אנו מסלקין אותן, *ומאי שנא? אומר ר"ת: דוקא הם שהיו רגילים כולם בחייהם ללבוש טלית בד' כנפות וללבוש ציצית, וגם לכל העוסקים בהם יש להם ציצית - והוה "לועג לרש" אם לא היה להם ציצית, או משום דכתיב 'לדורתם', לדור תם, אבל אנו שגם בחיינו אין מנהגינו ללבוש תמיד ציצית, אי הוי רמינן להו הוי כמו לועג לרש. וכ"ת: נשים לאותם שהיה להם בחייהם - א"כ יהיה לועג לרש לאחרים. ועוד אר"ת שמשמע מאנשי לותי"ר(ד) דמסירים הציצית, דציצית עולה למנין תרי"ג עם ח' חוטין וחמשה קשרים, ואם לובש ציצית - נראה כאילו קיים כל התורה, ומיחזי כשיקרא. וזה לא נהירא, דגם חיים עתה למה לובשים? הלא לא קיימו כל התורה כולה! ומיהו, י"ל דאנו סומכים על מסכת שמחות (פי"ב) שלוה אבא שאול לבניו הטילו תכלת מאפיליוני, ואע"פ שהגמרא חולק עליו יש דברים שאנו מניחין הגמרא שלנו ואנו עושין כספרים החיצונים. כמו מחזון ישעיה כפסיקתא, וכמו 'ויחל' שיש בגמרא (מגילה דף לא.) דבתענית קורין ברכות וקללות, ובמסכת סופרים (פי"ז) - מפרש ויחל. והריצב"א היה רגיל שלא להסירם מן הכנף, אלא לקושרם ולהדקם בתוך הכנף לאפוקי נפשיה מפלוגתא אם הם חייבין בציצית - יש להם ציצית, ואם לאו - הרי הם מכוסין*: **שני** אריאל מואב. על שם דוד ושלמה שבנו את הבית, ובאו מרות המואביה:

בן

[ומיהו נראה דאף בס"ת ש"ד מדנקט בסיפא ס"ת כנ"ל רש"א]

[ודקאמר אלא אסיפא כנ"ל והב"א רש"א]

[ומאי טעמא כנ"ל רש"א]

[ועיין תוספות פסחים מ: ד"ה אבל ותוס' ב"ב עד ע"א ד"ה פסקי ותוס' נדה ס"א: ד"ה אבל ותוס' ע"ג סה: ד"ה אבל]

ה א מיי' פ"ד מהלכות תפילין הלכה כג ופי"ד מהלכות אבל הלכה יג [ופ"י מהל' ס"ת הלכה ו] סמ"ג עשין כב טוש"ע או"ח סימן מה סעיף א וסימן עא סעיף ז [וטור שו"ע יו"ד סימן רפב סעיף ד וסי' שסז סעיף ב ג]:

ו ב מיי' פ"ד מהלכות ק"ש הלכה ג טוש"ע או"ח סימן עא סעיף ג ד וביו"ד סימן שמא סעיף ו':

ז ג מיי' פי"ד מהלכות אבל הלכה י"ד סמג עשין ב טור שו"ע יו"ד סימן תג סעיף יו:

[ד מיי' פ"י מהל' ס"ת הלכה יא טוש"ע י"ד סי' רפב סעיף ג']

ח ד (מיי' וסמג שם) טור שו"ע יו"ד סימן שסא סעיף ג

[ה טוש"ע או"ח סי' כג סעיף א' וביו"ד סי' שסז סעיף ד]:

## רב נסים גאון

פרק ג

**דאמר** מר מת תופש ד' אמות לקרית שמע. עיקרה במסכתא סוטה בפרק משוח מלחמה (דף מג) כי אתא רב דימי אמר ר' יוחנן משום ר' אליעזר בן יעקב מת תופש ד' אמות לקרית שמע דכתיב (משלי יז) לועג לרש חרף עושהו:

## הגהות הב"ח

(א) תום' ד"ה ואינו מברך וכו' לנתייאשו מלקוברו שסוב אינו קוברו אבל: (ב) תום' ד"ה למחר וכו' ציצית בטליתותיהן וליכא משום לועג. [ע"ש במנחות ותראה דהגהתו צ"ע]: (ג) בא"ד וגדול המצווה וכו' וקשה מהסיא דהתכלת: (ד) בא"ד מאנשי לותי"ר הא דמסירים הציצית משום דציצית עולה:

גוזי דברדא. חתיכות של ברד וקרח שקורין גלצו"ן בלע"ז, והיינו ביום השלג: ונחת וטבל *לקרייו. כדי לעסוק בתורה: דתנא ספרא דבי רב. תורת כהנים: חלל רשע. על צדקיהו הוא אומר, ועדיין בימי יחזקאל חי היה וקורהו 'חלל': לקריתא. להתעסק בעבודת אחוזתם: איעקר תלמודייהו. אשתכח תלמודם מגרסתם. אייקר – הוכבד עליהם מחמת שכחה: צערא דידהו. צער גופם ממש, כגון עקיצת רמה: שתי רוחות. של שתי ילדות מתות. ונשמע. ונדע (א)מה גזרו היום פורענות בעולם, שהעולם נדון בר"ה: הפרגוד. מחיצה המבדלת בין מקום השכינה:

"בן איש חי", אטו כולי עלמא בני מתי נינהו?! אלא, "בן איש חי" – שאפי' במיתתו קרוי חי; "רב פעלים מקבצאל" – שריבה וקבץ פועלים לתורה; "והוא הכה את שני אראל מואב" – שלא הניח כמותו לא במקדש ראשון ולא במקדש שני; "והוא ירד והכה את הארי בתוך הבור ביום השלג" – איכא דאמרי: דתבר גוזי דברדא ונחת *וטבל, איכא דאמרי דתנא סיפרא דבי רב ביומא דסיתוא. "והמתים אינם יודעים מאומה" – אלו רשעים שבחייהן קרויין מתים, שנאמר: °"ואתה חלל רשע נשיא ישראל". ואי בעית אימא, מהכא: °"על פי שנים עדים או (על פי) שלשה עדים יומת המת". חי הוא! אלא: המת מעיקרא.§ *בני ר' חייא נפוק לקרייתא איעקר להו תלמודייהו, הוו קא מצערי לאדכוריה. א"ל חד לחבריה: ידע אבון בהאי צערא? א"ל אידך: מנא ידע? והא כתיב: °"יכבדו בניו ולא ידע"! א"ל אידך: ולא ידע? והא כתיב: °"אך בשרו עליו יכאב ונפשו עליו תאבל", ואמר רבי יצחק: *קשה רמה למת *כמחט בבשר החי. אמרי: בצערא דידהו – ידעי, בצערא דאחרינא – לא ידעי. ולא? והתניא: *מעשה בחסיד אחד שנתן דינר לעני בערב ר"ה בשני בצורת והקניטתו אשתו והלך ולן בבית הקברות. ושמע שתי רוחות שמספרות זו לזו, אמרה חדא לחברתה: חברתי, בואי ונשוט בעולם ונשמע מאחורי הפרגוד מה פורענות בא לעולם. אמרה לה חברתה: איני יכולה שאני קבורה במחצלת של קנים, אלא לכי את ומה שאת שומעת אמרי לי. הלכה היא ושטה ובאה. ואמרה לה חברתה: חברתי מה שמעת מאחורי הפרגוד? אמרה לה: שמעתי, שכל הזורע ברביעה ראשונה, ברד מלקה אותו. הלך הוא וזרע ברביעה שניה. של כל העולם כולו – לקה, שלו – לא לקה. לשנה האחרת הלך ולן בבית הקברות, ושמע אותן שתי רוחות שמספרות זו עם זו. אמרה חדא לחברתה: בואי ונשוט בעולם ונשמע מאחורי הפרגוד מה פורענות בא לעולם. אמרה לה: חברתי, לא כך אמרתי לך: איני יכולה שאני קבורה במחצלת של קנים? אלא לכי את ומה שאת שומעת בואי ואמרי לי. הלכה ושטה ובאה. ואמרה לה חברתה: חברתי, מה שמעת מאחורי הפרגוד? אמרה לה: שמעתי, שכל הזורע ברביעה שניה שדפון מלקה אותו. הלך וזרע ברביעה ראשונה. של כל העולם כולו – נשדף, ושלו לא נשדף. אמרה לו אשתו: מפני מה *אשתקד של כל העולם כולו לקה ושלך לא לקה, ועכשיו של כל העולם כולו נשדף ושלך לא נשדף? סח לה כל הדברים הללו. אמרו: לא היו ימים מועטים עד שנפלה קטטה בין אשתו של אותו חסיד ובין אמה של אותה ריבה. אמרה לה: לכי ואראך בתך שהיא קבורה במחצלת של קנים. לשנה האחרת הלך ולן בבית הקברות ושמע אותן רוחות שמספרות זו עם זו. אמרה לה: חברתי, בואי ונשוט בעולם ונשמע מאחורי הפרגוד מה פורענות בא לעולם. אמרה לה: חברתי, הניחיני, דברים שביני לבינך כבר נשמעו בין החיים. אלמא ידעי! – דילמא איניש אחרינא שכיב ואזיל ואמר להו.§ ת"ש: דזעירי הוה מפקיד זוזי גבי אושפיזכתיה, עד דאתי ואזיל לבי רב, שכיבה. אזל בתרה לחצר מות. אמר לה: זוזי היכא? אמרה ליה: זיל שקלינהו מתותי *בצנורא דדשא בדוך פלן, ואימא לה לאימא תשדר לי מסרקאי וגובתאי דכוחלא בהדי פלניתא דאתיא למחר. אלמא ידעי! – [דלמא] דומה קדים ומכריז להו. ת"ש: דאבוה דשמואל הוו קא מפקדי גביה זוזי דיתמי, כי נח נפשיה לא הוה שמואל גביה. הוו קא קרו ליה בר אכיל זוזי דיתמי. אזל אבתריה לחצר מות. אמר להו: בעינא אבא. אמרו ליה: אבא טובא איכא הכא. אמר להו: בעינא אבא בר אבא. אמרו ליה: אבא בר אבא נמי טובא איכא הכא. אמר להו: בעינא אבא בר אבא אבוה דשמואל, היכא? – אמרו ליה: סליק למתיבתא דרקיעא. אדהכי חזייה ללוי דיתיב אבראי. אמר ליה: אמאי יתבת אבראי, מאי טעמא לא סלקת? אמר ליה, דאמרי לי: כל כי הנך שני דלא סליקת למתיבתא דרבי אפס ואחלישתיה לדעתיה – לא מעיילינן לך למתיבתא דרקיעא. אדהכי והכי אתא אבוה, חזייה דהוה קא בכי ואחיך. אמר ליה: מאי טעמא קא בכית? אמר ליה: דלעגל קא אתית. מאי טעמא אחיכת? – דחשיבת בהאי עלמא טובא. אמר ליה: אי חשיבנא – נעיילוה ללוי, ועיילוהו ללוי. אמר ליה: זוזי דיתמי היכא? אמר ליה: זיל שקלינהו באמתא דרחיא, עילאי ותתאי – דידן, ומיצעי – דיתמי. אמר ליה: מאי טעמא עבדת הכי? – אמר ליה: אי גנובי גנבי – מגנבו מדידן, אי אכלה ארעא – אכלה מדידן. אלמא דידעי! – דילמא שאני שמואל, כיון דחשיב – קדמי ומכרזי *"פנו מקום". ואף ר' יונתן הדר ביה, דאמר רבי שמואל בר נחמני אמר ר' יונתן: מנין למתים שמספרים זה עם זה? שנאמר: °"ויאמר ה' אליו זאת הארץ אשר נשבעתי לאברהם ליצחק וליעקב לאמר", מאי 'לאמר' – אמר הקדוש ברוך הוא למשה: לך אמור להם לאברהם ליצחק וליעקב שבועה שנשבעתי לכם כבר קיימתיה לבניכם. ואי

---

בן איש חי אטו כולי עלמא. בספרים מדויקים כתיב 'חי' וקרינן 'חיל' ומן הכתיב דייק הכי, שלא כתיב חיל אלא חי: ספרא דבי רב. מ'האריא' דריש, שהוא חמור שבספרים: בתוך הבור. שהוא באמצע הספרים: אלמא ידעי. מדקאמר לעגל קא אתית. ולא מצי לשנויי כדלעיל דומה קדים ואמר להו, דהיינו דוקא לאחר, אבל כל כך לא היה מקדים – דהוא עצמו אינו יודע: אפילו

בריביעה ראשונה. יורה שלש רביעיות הן: בכירה, שניה ושלישית. ראשונה – בי"ז במרחשון, שניה – בכ"ג, שלישית – בר"ח כסליו: ברד מלקה אותו. שעתיד ברד ליפול סמוך לרביעה *ראשונה ומה שנזרע כבר הוקשה, והברד שוברו; והנזרע בשניה עדיין רך הוא ואינו נשבר בשביל הברד, כענין שנאמר "והפשתה והשעורה נכתה והחטה והכוסמת לא נכו" (שמות ט): שדפון. מלקה הרך ואינו משדף הקשה: אלמא ידעי. דברים האמורים בין החיים: לחצר מות. לבית הקברות: בצנורא דדשא. בחור מפתן הבית שהדלת סובב אותו: מסרקאי. מסרק שלי: גובתא. קנה, ובשביל שמתה ילדה אמרה כן לעגמת נפש: בהדי פלניתא דאתיא למחר. לקבורה: אלמא ידעי. מה שעושין, שידעה זו שזו גוססת ונטויה למות: דלמא דומה. מלאך שהוא ממונה על המתים קדים ומכריז להו: עכשיו יבא פלוני. אבל שאר דברי החיים אינם יודעים: בעינא אבא. מבקש אני את אבא, כך היה שמו: א"ל. המתים נגלו לו כאילו הם חוץ מקבריהם ויושבים בעגולה: חזייה. שמואל ללוי *חברו שהיה יושב חוץ לישיבה של שאר מתים: כל כי הנך שני. מספר השנים שלא נכנסת בישיבתו של רבי אפס במסכת כתובות בפרק "הנושא את האשה" (דף קג:): חזייה. שמואל לאבוה דקא בכי וחייך: דלעגל אתית. במהרה תקבר: באמתא דרחיא. כל בנין מושב הרחיים קרוי אמת הרחיים: אלמא ידעי. מי חשוב בין החיים: זאת הארץ. במיתת משה כתיב: ואי

---

רב נסים גאון

דילמא דומה הוא דקדים מכריז להו. במסכת סנהדרין בפרק כל ישראל יש להן חלק (דף לד) אמר ר' יוחנן אותו מלאך שהוא ממונה על הרוחות דומה שמו: ת"ש דאבוה דשמואל הוו מפקדי גביה זוזי דיתמי אמר ליה דאמרו לי כל הנך שני דלא עיילת למתיבתא דר' אפס הכא נמי לא תיעול. איתיה לפירושה במסכת כתובות בפרק (דף קג) דתנו רבנן בשעת פטירתו של רבי כו' אמר להם לחכמי ישראל אני צריך נכנסו חכמי ישראל אצלו אמר להם אל תספדוני בעיירות והושיבו ישיבה לאחר ל' יום שמעון בני חכם גמליאל בני נשיא חנינא בר חמא ישב בראש ודאמרי' עלה לא קביל עליה ר' חנינא שהיה ר' אפס גדול ממנו ב' שנים ומחצה יתיב ר' אפס ברישא ויתיב ר' חנינא אבראי ואתא לוי יתיב גביה ומשום הכא לא עיילוה ללוי למתיבתא דרקיעא עד דבעא שמואל רחמי עליה ועיילוה:

הגהות הב"ח

(א) רש"י ד"ה שתי וכו' מתות הס"ד ואח"כ מ"ה כולי ונשוט ונלע:

גליון הש"ס

גמ' ואף ר' יונתן הדר ביה. עי' סוטה דף לד ע"ב תוס' ד"ה אבותי. רש"י ד"ה ונחת כו' כדי לעסוק בתורה. עי' ב"ק דף פ"ב ע"ב תוס' ד"ה אתא.

---

מסורת הש"ס

וכתרגום רב יוסף א' יא איתא שנוע שנגע בשרך אחד

[ג"ל שניה]

[עיין תוס' ב"ק פ"ב ע"ב ד"ה אתא]

[כמס' עו"ג מו. ד"ה בני רבי חייא וחזקי' שמן]

[סוטה דף י. מח:]

ס"א הבירו

[אבות דר"נ פ"ג]

ג"א צנורא

[כתובות עז:]

[כלומר שקא קדמיתא ערוך וערי' תוי"ט ב"ב פ"ג מ"ג]

תורה אור: יחזקאל כא; דברים יז; איוב יד; שם; דברים לד

ואי ס"ד דלא ידעי. אין מבינין כלום אלא לצערא דגופא: המספר אחר המת. בגנותו של מת אחר מיתתו: קניא מטללא. קנה גדול וכבד נפל מן הגג: טללא. גג: ארנקא דמוחיה. גולגולתו: והמטים עקלקלותם. לעיל מיניה כתיב "היטיבה ה' לטובים" וסמיך ליה "והמטים עקלקלותם", והמכריעים את חובותם יותר על זכיותם להטותם לכף חובה: יוליכם ה' את פועלי האון. לגיהנם: בכ"ד מקומות. השתא משמע מלינו שנדו חכמים בני אדם בכ"ד מקומות לכבוד הרב לפי שלא נהגו כבוד לרבם: הוא היה אומר. עקביא בן מהללאל במסכת עדיות: אין משקין.

תורה אור

ואי ס"ד דלא ידעי – כי אמר להו: מאי הוי? – אלא מאי, דידעי? – למה ליה למימר להו? – לאחזוקי ליה טיבותא למשה. אמר רבי יצחק: כל המספר אחרי המת כאלו מספר אחרי האבן. איכא דאמרי: דלא ידעי; ואיכא דאמרי: דידעי ולא איכפת להו. איני? והא אמר רב פפא: חד אישתעי מילתא בתריה דמר שמואל ונפל קניא מטללא ובזעא לארנקא דמוחיה! שאני צורבא מרבנן, דקודשא בריך הוא תבע ביקריה. אמר רבי יהושע בן לוי: כל המספר אחר *מטתן של תלמידי חכמים נופל בגיהנם, שנא': "והמטים עקלקלותם יוליכם ה' את פועלי האון שלום על ישראל", אפילו בשעה ששלום על ישראל "יוליכם ה' את פועלי האון". תנא דבי ר' ישמעאל: אם ראית תלמיד חכם שעבר עבירה בלילה – אל תהרהר אחריו ביום, שמא עשה תשובה. "שמא" סלקא דעתך? אלא: ודאי עשה תשובה. והני מילי – בדברים שבגופו, אבל בממונא – עד דמהדר למריה.§ ואמר ר' יהושע בן לוי: אבכ"ד מקומות בית דין מנדין על כבוד הרב, וכולן שנינו במשנתנו. אמר ליה ר' אלעזר: היכא? אמר ליה: לכי תשכח. נפק דק ואשכח תלת: המזלזל בנטילת ידים, והמספר אחר מטתן של תלמידי חכמי', והמגיס דעתו כלפי מעלה. בהמספר אחר מטתן של תלמידי חכמים מאי היא? *דתנן, הוא היה אומר: אין משקין לא את הגיורת ולא את המשוחררת; וחכמים אומרים: גמשקין. ואמרו לו: מעשה בכרכמית, שפחה משוחררת בירושלים, והשקוה שמעיה ואבטליון! – ואמר להם: דוגמא השקוה; ונדוהו, ומת בנדויו, וסקלו בית דין את ארונו. דוהמזלזל בנטילת ידים מאי היא? *דתנן, א"ר יהודה: חס ושלום שעקביא בן מהללאל נתנדה, שאין עזרה ננעלת על כל אדם בישראל בחכמה ובטהרה וביראת חטא כעקביא בן מהללאל. אלא את מי נדו – את אלעזר בן חנוך שפקפק בנטילת ידים; וכשמת – שלחו בית דין והניחו אבן גדולה על ארונו. *ללמדך: השכל המתנדה ומת בנדויו – ב"ד סוקלין את ארונו. המגיס דעתו כלפי מעלה מאי היא? *דתנן, שלח לו שמעון בן שטח לחוני המעגל: צריך אתה להתנדות, ואלמלא חוני אתה גוזרני עליך נדוי, אבל מה אעשה שאתה *מתחטא לפני המקום ועושה לך רצונך כבן שמתחטא על אביו ועושה לו רצונו, ועליך הכתוב אומר "ישמח אביך ואמך ותגל יולדתך". ותו ליכא? והא איכא דתני רב יוסף: *תודוס איש רומי הנהיג את בני רומי להאכיל גדיים מקולסין בלילי פסחים; שלח ליה שמעון בן שטח: אלמלא תודוס אתה גוזרני עליך נדוי, שאתה מאכיל את ישראל קדשים בחוץ! – *במשנתנו קאמרינן, והא ברייתא היא. ובמתני' ליכא? והא איכא הא *דתנן: חתכו חוליות ונתן חול בין חוליא לחוליא, ר' אליעזר מטהר, וחכמים מטמאים, וזהו תנורו של עכנאי; מאי עכנאי? אמר רב יהודה אמר שמואל: מלמד, שהקיפוהו הלכות כעכנאי זה וטמאוהו; ותניא: *אותו היום הביאו כל טהרות שטיהר ר"א ושרפום לפניו, ולבסוף ברכוהו! – אפילו הכי, נדוי במתני' לא תנן. אלא בכ"ד מקומות היכא משכחת לה? – ר' יהושע בן לוי מדמה מילתא למילתא, ור' אלעזר לא מדמה מילתא למילתא.§ "נושאי המטה וחלופיהן".§ *ת"ר: זאין מוציאין את המת סמוך לק"ש, ואם התחילו אין מפסיקין. איני? והא רב יוסף אפקוהו סמוך לק"ש! – *אדם חשוב שאני.§ שלפני המטה ושלאחר המטה.§ ת"ר: חהעוסקים בהספד, בזמן שהמת מוטל לפניהם – נשמטין אחד אחד וקורין, אין המת מוטל לפניהם – הן יושבין וקורין והוא יושב ודומם, הם עומדים ומתפללין והוא עומד ומצדיק עליו את הדין, ואומר: רבון העולמים, הרבה חטאתי לפניך ולא נפרעת ממני אחד מני אלף, יהי רצון מלפניך ה' אלהינו שתגדור פרצותינו ופרצות כל עמך בית ישראל ברחמים. אמר אביי: [י] לא מבעי ליה לאיניש למימר הכי, *דארשב"ל, וכן תנא משמיה דרבי יוסי: לעולם אל יפתח אדם פיו לשטן; ואמר רב יוסף: מאי קראה – שנאמר: "כמעט כסדום היינו", מאי אהדר להו נביא – "שמעו דבר ה' קציני סדום".§ "קברו את המת וחזרו וכו'". אם יכולים להתחיל ולגמור את כולה – אין, אבל פרק אחד או פסוק אחד – לא. ורמינהו: קברו את המת וחזרו, אם יכולין להתחיל ולגמור אפילו פרק אחד או פסוק אחד! הכי נמי קאמר: טאם יכולין להתחיל ולגמור אפי' פרק אחד או אפילו פסוק אחד עד שלא יגיעו לשורה – יתחילו ואם לאו – לא יתחילו.§

העומדים

[תהלים קכה] [משלי כג] [ישעיה א]

**רש"י:** אם קינא לה בעלה ונסתרה: לא את הגיורת. ד"בני ישראל" אמור בפרשה (במדבר ה) – פרט לאשת גר ועבד משוחרר: בכרכמית. כך שמה, או על שם מקומה: דוגמא השקוה. על שהיו (א) דומים להם הם השקוה, שהיו שמעיה ואבטליון מבני בניו של סנחריב כדאמרינן בגיטין בפרק "הנזקין" (דף נז:): ר' יהודה. פליג אדלעיל דקתני שנדו את עקביא: שאין עזרה ננעלת. בפרק ה' דפסחים (דף סד:), שהיו שערי העזרה ננעלים כששוחטין פסחים של כל כת וכת, שהפסח נשחט בג' כתות: על כל אדם בישראל. כלומר: כשהיתה ננעלת עליהם, והיינו כשנתמלאה פה לפה לא היה בכולם אדם חשוב בחכמה ויראת חטא כעקביא: אלעזר בן חנוך שפקפק. זילזל, והיינו נמי לכבוד הרב שעבר ע"פ הגוזרים על הידים: אלמלא חוני אתה. שיש שמך בגדולה ובחשיבות: צריך אתה להתנדות. לפי שהטריח לפני המקום על עסק גשמים "לא כך שאלתי" כמה פעמים וכבוד המקום כבוד הרב הוא: מתחטא. לשון חוטא, נקל בלבו לחטוא לאביו ולהטריחו על תאותו: מקולסים. צלויים כשהן שלמין, ותולין כרעיהן וקרסוליהן וקרביהם סביבותן בשפוד, ועל שם כך קורהו מקולס שהוא לשון מזויין, כדמתרגם "וכובע נחושת על ראשו" (שמואל א יז) – וקולסא דנחשא: בלילי פסחים. זכר לפסח שצולהו שלם, שנאמר בו "על כרעיו ועל קרבו" (שמות יב), כלומר עם כרעיו ועם קרבו: גוזרני עליך נדוי. והיינו נמי לכבוד הרב, שאסרו חכמים את הדבר לפי שהוא קרוב להאכיל את ישראל קדשים בחוץ שהרואה סבור שהקדישו לשם פסח: חתכו חוליות. תנור של חרס שהוא עשוי ככלי ומטלטל, ותחלת ברייתו מן הטיט ומצרפו בכבשן כשאר קדרות, ואם נטמא הצריכו הכתוב נתיצה, ואם נתנו בענין זה שחתכו סביב סביב כחוליות עגולות, וחזר וחיברו בטיט של חול בין חוליא לחוליא, רבי אליעזר מטהר עולמית שאינו עוד ככלי חרס, שלא נצרף בכבשן, וחכמים מטמאין: בעכנאי. כנחש זה שכורך עצמו בעגולה: כל טהרות. שנעשו בתנור זה או שנגעו באוירו. והיה רבי אליעזר מטהרן, והם שרפום: וברכוהו. לפי שהרבה מאד לחלוק בדבר זה כדאמרינן בבבא מציעא בפרק "הזהב" (דף נט:): נדוי במתני' לא תנן. הא דברכוהו – בברייתא הוא דתני לה: מדמה מילתא למילתא. כל מקום שרואה במתניתין שנחלק היחיד על הרבים מחלוקת גדולה, או אחד מן החכמים שמדבר קשה כנגד גדול הימנו: אומר לאוי היה כאן נדוי: אין מוציאין את המת. לקברו: סמוך לקריאת שמע. לפי שמתבטלין מן הקריאה: אין המת מוטל לפניהם. שהמת בבית אחר והם מספידין אותו כאן. ויש מפרשין: שנתון לצד אחר: והוא יושב ודומם. הכל: למימר הכי. לא נפרעת ממני, דמשמע הפרע:

הרואה

**תוספות:** אפי' בשעה ששלום על ישראל. והיינו לאחר מיתתו, דלא אתו לאנצויי בהדי המספרים בגנותם. מהכא משמע דאיירי לאחר מיתה: דוגמא השקוה. פרש"י: לפי שהיתה גיורת כמותם, שהיו גרים. וכן משמע בירושלמי דמועד קטן (פ"ג): מהו דוגמא – דכוות'. בערוך פירש: *דוגמא השקוה – מי צבע, אבל לא היו מרים ממש, ולא מחקו התורה עליה אלא ליראה אותה:

מדלגין

**עין משפט נר מצוה:**

ט א מיי' פ"ז מהלכות תלמוד תורה הלכה יד טוש"ע יו"ד סימן שלד סעיף מג:

י ב מיי' שם והלכה יב טוש"ע יו"ד סימן רמג סעיף ז ובסימן שלד סעיף מז:

יא ג מיי' פ"ב מהלכות סוטה הלכה ו:

יב ד מיי' פ"ו מהלכות ברכות הלכה י"ט סמג עשין כז טור שו"ע או"ח סי' קנח סעיף ט:

יג ה מיי' פ"ז מהלכות ת"ת הלכה ד טוש"ע יו"ד סימן שלד סעיף ג:

[ובס רב האי גאון והערוך גרס דוכתא ופי' כפירש"י ע"ש ערך דגם]

יד ו מיי' פ"ח מהלכות חמץ ומצה הלכה יא טוש"ע או"ח סימן תעו סעיף א:

טו ז מיי' פי"ב מהלכות כלים הלכה ה:

טז ח מיי' פ"ד מהלכות ק"ש הלכה ד סמג עשין יח טוש"ע או"ח סימן עב סעיף ב טור שו"ע יו"ד סימן שנח סעיף ב:

יז ט מיי' שם הלכה ה סמג שם טוש"ע או"ח סי' עב סעיף ג [וביו"ד סימן שד"מ סעיף יב]: [י] [רמ"א בהגה' שו"ע יוד סי' שעו סעיף ב]:

יח י מיי' שם הלכה ו סמג שם טוש"ע שם סעיף ד:

[ועי' פירש"י דהכא אמנם במשנה דתענית לא פי' כלום אלא הנקרא פורפייק בלע"ז אכן במנחות סז. כתב רש"י ד"ה ונתחטא נטייל כמו בן מתחטא לפני אביו ע"כ אבל בבכורות נז: כתב רש"י סד"ה והכתיב נתחטא לשון ירידה וחבירו במס' תענית בן המתחטא לפני אביו ע"כ ודע דהרע"ב מ"ח פ"ג דתענית כתב מתחטא מתגעגע וכתב התוי"ט דלשון ארמית היא כמ"ש בערוך כי הילדים רכים ת"י אתוס טלייא מחטיין]

## רב נסים גאון

מעשה בתודוס איש רומי שהנהיג את בני רומי לאכול גדיי' מקולסים בלילי פסחים. גרסינן במסכת פסחים בפ' מקום שנהגו (ד' נג) איבעיא להו תודוס איש רומי גברא רבה הוה או בעלי אגרופים הוה תא שמע את זו דרש תודוס איש רומי כו' שמע מינה גברא רבה הוה שמע מינה ר' יוסי בר אבין אמר מטיל מלאי לכיס של תלמידי חכמים הוה דאמר ר' יוחנן כל המטיל מלאי לכיס של תלמידי חכמים זוכה ויושב בישיבה של מעלה שנא' (קהלת ז) כי בצל החכמה בצל הכסף ובגמרא דבני מערבא (מו"ק פ"ג ה"א) אמרי מהו תודוס אמר

**מסורת הש"ס:** עדיות פ"ה מ"ו | פסחים סד: | מ"ק טו. | תענית דף יט. | פסחים נג. ע"ש ביצה כג. ע"ש תוספתא פ"ב | [עירובין נג. מנחות לח:] עדיות פ"ז כלים פ"ה מ"י ב"מ נט | [ב"מ דף נט:] | שמחות פ"י | לקמן ס. כתובות ח:

## הגהות הב"ח

(א) רש"י ד"ה דוגמא השקוה על שהיו הם דומין לה השקוה:

## גליון הש"ס

גמ' ואר"י מאי קראה שנא' כמעט כסדום. עיין מו"ק דף יח ע"א תוס' ד"ה ואסתייעא:

ר' חנינא דהוה משלח פרנסתן דרבנן: **חתכו** חוליות ונתן חול בין חוליא לחוליא ר' אליעזר מטהר וחכמים מטמאין וזהו תנורו של עכנאי ואמר רב יהודה אמר שמואל למה נקרא שמו עכנאי שהקיפוהו דברים כעכנא וטימאוהו. איתה מיפרשא בבבא מציעא בפרק הזהב (דף נט) ומי שלא עיין בה לשם אינה מתפרשת לו מיכן לפי שלא הוזכר ממנה כאן אלא כפי הצורך בענין נמנו וביוכוהו בלבד וכלל המעשה כולו לשם פירשוהו ולפי שהוא קשה ומשתבשין בפירושה ישר בעיני לפרש תורף דבריה בקיצור כפי שלמדתי מדברי אדוננו האיי גאון ז"ל החלוקה היתה בין ר' אליעזר והחכמים חבריו בתנור שנעשה חוליות של טיט מתחלתו ואחר כן הניחו אותן החוליות אחת על גבי חברתה עד שנגמר התנור ועמד על מתכונתו וכשהיו מרכיבין החוליות אחת על גבי חברתה היו נותנין חול בנתים סבר ר' אליעזר כי זה התנור הואיל והחול נתון בין כל חוליא וחוליא וכשמבקש אדם לפורקו ולהחזירו חוליות כמו שהיה מתחלה יכול הוא לפי כי חוליות שלו לא נדבקו זו בזו ולא נצמדו זו לזו ולפיכך יהא דינו עכשיו בשעה שהוא מוקם כדין שהיה לחוליות שלו קודם הקמתו ואם נפל באוירו של זה התנור שרץ אינו מטמא ולא יהא דינו כדין התנור שחוליותיו מצומדין ומדובקין זו בזו שאמר בו הכתוב (ויקרא יא) תנור וכירים יותץ והחכמים החולקים עליו לא היה אצלם הפרש בין נתן חול בין החוליות שלו בין לא נתן אלא בין כך ובין כך טמא הוא אצלם כדין שאר כלי חרש שמיטמאין מאוירן והיו דנין כנגד ר' אליעזר על זה הדבר ונשאו ונתנו בה הרבה ורצה ר' אליעזר להביא ראיה לדבריו ולסייעם מדרך שהיא נוהגת כמנהג סימנים וראיות והיא מדמות למעשה מופת ולא קיבלום החכמים ולא נתקיימו אצלם לפי שכן דרכו של עולם להתנהג בכיוצא בהן ולפיכך אמרו לו אין מביאין ראיה מן החרוב אין מביאין ראיה מאמת המים כלומר כי אין בזה דבר שהוא סותר למנהגו של עולם ומשנה סדרי בראשית כדי שיהא לך לראיה אלא לעולם אין ההלכה מתקיימת אלא לפי מה שנתברר מן הקבלה של מרובין והיינו דברי חכמים ובגמרא דאלו מגלחים דבני מערבא (הלכה א) הזכירו זה המעשה ואמרו כל הלין שבחא ולית הלכתא כר' אליעזר אמר ר' חנינא משנתנה לא נתנה אלא אחרי רבים להטות ולית לר' אליעזר ידע

שאחרי

יט א מיי' פ"ד מהלכות ק"ש הלכה ו סמג עשין יח טוש"ע או"ח סימן עב סעיף ה: [וכתוספתא פ"ג דשמחות]

כ ב מיי' פ"י מהלכות כלאים הלכה כט סמג לאוין רפג טוש"ע יו"ד סימן שג:

כא ג מיי' פ"ג מהלכות אבל הלכה יד טוש"ע יו"ד סימן שעב סעיף א:

כב ד ה מיי' פ"ו מהל' קרבן פסח הלכה ח:

כג ו מיי' פ"ג מהלכות אבל הלכה יג וטוש"ע יו"ד סימן שעג:

כד ז מיי' פי"א מהלכות גזילה ואבדה הלכה יג [והלכה יג ופ"ב] סמג עשין עד טוש"ע חו"מ סימן רסג סעיף ב ג.

הָעוֹמְדִים בַּשּׁוּרָה וכו'. § *ת"ר: שורה הרואה פנימה – פטורה, ושאינה רואה פנימה – חייבת, רבי יהודה אומר: הבאים מחמת האבל – פטורין, מחמת עצמן – חייבין. § אמר רב יהודה אמר רב: המוצא כלאים בבגדו פושטן אפי' בשוק, מ"ט – "אין חכמה ואין תבונה ואין עצה לנגד ה'" – *כ"מ שיש חלול השם אין חולקין כבוד לרב. מתיבי: קברו את המת וחזרו, ולפניהם ב' דרכים, אחת טהורה ואחת טמאה, בא בטהורה – באין עמו בטהורה, בא בטמאה – באין עמו בטמאה, משום כבודו. אמאי? לימא: "אין חכמה ואין תבונה לנגד ה'"! תרגמה רבי אבא בבית הפרס דרבנן. דאמר רב יהודה אמר שמואל: מנפח אדם בית הפרס והולך; ואמר רב יהודה בר אשי משמיה דרב: בית הפרס שנדש טהור. § ת"ש, דאמר ר' אלעזר בר צדוק: מדלגין היינו על גבי ארונות של מתים לקראת מלכי ישראל, ולא לקראת מלכי ישראל בלבד אמרו אלא אפי' לקראת מלכי אומות העולם, שאם יזכה – יבחין בין מלכי ישראל למלכי אומות העולם. אמאי? לימא: "אין חכמה ואין תבונה ואין עצה לנגד ה'"! כדרבא, דאמר רבא: דבר תורה, אהל, כל שיש בו חלל טפח – חוצץ בפני הטומאה, ושאין בו חלל טפח – אינו חוצץ בפני הטומאה, ורוב ארונות יש בהן חלל טפח, וגזרו על שיש בהן משום שאין בהן, ומשום כבוד מלכים לא גזרו בהו רבנן. § ת"ש: *גדול כבוד הבריות שדוחה [את] לא תעשה שבתורה. ואמאי? לימא: "אין חכמה ואין תבונה ואין עצה לנגד ה'"! – תרגמה רב בר שבא קמיה דרב כהנא בלאו ד"לא תסור". אחיכו עליה: לאו ד"לא תסור" דאורייתא היא! אמר רב כהנא: *גברא רבה אמר מילתא לא תחיכו עליה, כל מילי דרבנן אסמכינהו על לאו ד"לא תסור", ומשום כבודו שרו רבנן. § *ת"ש: "והתעלמת מהם" – פעמים שאתה מתעלם מהם ופעמים שאין אתה מתעלם מהם; הא כיצד – אם היה כהן והיא בבית הקברות, או היה זקן ואינה לפי כבודו, או שהיתה מלאכתו מרובה משל חברו, לכך נאמר: "והתעלמת". אמאי? לימא: "אין חכמה ואין תבונה ואין עצה לנגד ה'"! שאני התם, דכתיב: "והתעלמת מהם". וליגמר מינה! – *איסורא ממונא לא ילפינן. § ת"ש: "ולאחותו" *מה תלמוד לומר? הרי שהיה הולך לשחוט את פסחו ולמול את בנו ושמע שמת לו מת, יכול יחזור ויטמא – אמרת לא יטמא. יכול כשם שאינו מטמא להם כך אינו מטמא למת מצוה, ת"ל: "ולאחותו" – לאחותו הוא דאינו מטמא, אבל

תורה אור: משלי כא | דברים יז | שם כב | במדבר ו

**רש"י**

הרואה פנימה. את חלל הסקף אחורי שורה הפנימית, והאבל יושב שם: מחמת עצמן. ולא מחמת כבוד, שלא באו לנחם אלא לראות את המתאבל: אין חכמה. אין חכמה חשובה נגד ה': אחת טמאה. שיש בה קבר: בא בטהורה. האבל: בבית הפרס. דלא מטמא אלא מדרבנן. והוא שדה שנחרש בו קבר, ועשו חכמים שמא נדלדלו כלי המחרישה את העצמות, והדורס עליהן מסיטן, ועצם כשעורה מטמא במגע ובמשא ולא באהל, וכיון דמדרבנן הוא דאסור, רבנן הוא דאחלוהו ליקרייהו גבי אבל: מנפח אדם. לפניו, שאם יש שם עצם יראנו. דלאו דאורייתא הוא לא חיישינן ומזלזלינן ביה כולי האי למיסמך אנפיחה. והך דדיקה – לעושה פסח אישתרי, ולא לאוכלי תרומה, כדאמרינן ב"חומר בקדש" (חגיגה דף כה:): שנדש. ברגלים: לקראת מלכי ישראל. הרי לכבוד הבריות עוברים על "נפש לא יטמא" (ויקרא כא) דהא ר' אלעזר בר צדוק כהן הוה, כדאמרינן בבכורות (דף לו.): מדלגין. מארון לארון: דבר תורה. הלכה למשה מסיני: אינו חוצץ בפני הטומאה. דנקראת טומאה רצוצה, ובוקעת ועולה: את לא תעשה. קס"ד כל ל"ת קאמר: בלאו דלא תסור וגו'. אחיכו עליה. אינהו סבור דהכי אמרו לו דבר תורה והוא עומד בפני הכבוד – יעבור עליו, והא האי נמי דאורייתא הוא: כל מילי דרבנן וכו'. והכי קאמר להו: דבר שהוא מדברי סופרים נדחה מפני כבוד הבריות, וקרי ליה ל"ת – משום דכתיב לא תסור. ודקא קשיא לכו דאורייתא הוא, רבנן אחלוהו ליקרייהו לעבור על דבריהם היכא דאיכא כבוד הבריות, כגון לטלטל בשבת אבנים של בית הכסא לקנוח (שבת דף פא:), או מי שנפסקה ציצית טליתו בכרמלית לא הצריכוהו להניח טליתו שם ולילך לביתו ערום (מנחות דף לח.): והיא בבית הקברות. האבדה: ואינה לפי כבודו. אין האבדה חשובה לפי כבודו להשיבה: או שהיתה מלאכתו מרובה. שאם בטל ממלאכתו לרדוף אחריה יתרים על דמי האבדה, ולא ירצו הבעלים להשיב לו יותר ממה שמשיב להם, ונמצא הוא מפסיד: ונגמר מינה. לגבי כלאים, דאמרן: פושטן אפילו בשוק: ממונא. קל מאיסורא: ולאחותו מה תלמוד לומר. בנזיר כתיב "כל ימי הזירו לה' על נפש מת לא יבא", וסמיך ליה "לאביו ולאמו לאחיו ולאחותו לא יטמא להם" דהא כולהו בכלל "על נפש מת לא יבא" היו, ולמה יצאו? 'לאביו' – פרט למת מצוה, 'לאמו' מה תלמוד לומר? משום מת מצוה לא איצטריך, דמ'לאביו' נפקא, ודרשי ליה בספרי ללמוד שאם היה נזיר זה כהן, דהוו עליה שתי קדושות אף הוא, לאמו הוא דלא יטמא, אבל מטמא הוא למת מצוה. 'לאחיו' מה תלמוד לומר? הרי שהיה כ"ג והוא נזיר, אף הוא 'לאחיו' לא יטמא, אבל מטמא למת מצוה. ו'לאחותו' מה תלמוד לומר? אם אינו ענין לזה, תנהו ענין למי שהולך לשחוט את פסחו ולמול – את בנו שמטמא למת מצוה: ושמע שמת לו מת. מקרוביו, יכול יטמא להם: אמרת לא יטמא. הואיל ועונת שחיטת הפסח היא, וחלה עליו חובת הפסח שהוא בכרת אם יטמא בטל מלעשות פסח. ולמול את בנו נמי (א) מצות כרת היא. ואית דאמרי בערבי פסחים נמי קאמר, דמילת זכריו מעכב הפסח: אבל

**תוספות**

מדלגין היינו על גבי ארונות. תימה לפ"ה דפי' גולל = כיסוי של ארון, דתניא: *"כל אשר יגע על פני השדה" לרבות גולל ודופק, וא"כ גם הגולל מטמא באהל, והיאך היו מדלגין עליו? וי"ל: דלא קשה, דהא תני' בשמחות (פ"ד הלכה כא): *כל טומאה שאין הנזיר מגלח עליה – אין כהן מוזהר עליה, וגולל ודופק אין נזיר מגלח עליהן, כדתנן במס' נזיר פרק "כהן גדול" (דף נד.). והיה אומר ר"ת דליתי' להאי כללי, דהא אמר התם: רביעית דם אין הנזיר מגלח עליו עד שיהא חצי לוג, ואפילו הכי כהן מוזהר עליו, כדאמרינן בפרק "בהמה המקשה" (חולין דף עב.) דרביעית דם הבא מב' מתים טמא באהל. ומפקינן ליה מ"על כל נפשות מת לא יבא". וי"ל: דהתם מכל מקום הוי שם טומאה שהנזיר מגלח עליה, אבל גולל ודופק אינו כלל בנזיר, ולכך אין כהן מוזהר עליו. אי נמי, הא ברייתא סברה מקצת הראשונים [נזיר נג.] שהיו אומרים רביעית דם גם במגלחת נזיר, ומיהו, תימה אמאי אין המת מטמא באהל, כיון שהכסוי עצמו מקבל טומאה, דכל דבר המקבל טומאה – אינו חוצץ בפני הטומאה, אם כן מטמא באהל! וי"ל: דאין מטמא אלא כל מילון שבו, אבל כל פנימי – טהור, כדתנן במסכת אהלות בפט"ו (משנה ט): חבית שהיא מלאה משקין טהורים ומוקפת צמיד פתיל ונעשאת גולל לקבר, הנוגע בה מטמא טומאת שבעה והחבית והמשקין טהורין – לפי שכל פנימי כולו טהור. ומיהו, תימה לפ"ה דפירש בפ"ק דערובין (דף טו:)(ב) גבי אין עושין מבעלי חיים גולל ודופק לקבר, ופי' גולל היינו כסוי הארון וכי עושין מבעלי חיים כסוי לארון?(ג) ע"כ פר"ת: דגולל היינו מצבה, וכן דרך בני אדם ליתן בהמה על הקבר לסימן עד שיתנו עליו מצבה*).

רוב ארונות יש להם חלל טפח. וי"ל שראש הארון פתוח, שאם היה סתום, אדרבה, כי יש בו פותח טפח – מטמא, ואפילו כל הריקן שבו, כדאמרינן במסכת אהלות בפ"ו (משנה ו): נפש אטומה, הנוגע בה מן הצדדין – טהור, פי' בכל הריקן, מפני שטומאה בוקעת ועולה בוקעת ויורדת, ואם היה מקום הטומאה טפח ע"ט(ד) על רום טפח – הנוגע בה מכל מקום טמא, מפני שהוא כקבר סתום. אלמא: בקבר סתום אינו מטמא כל סביביו אלא כשיש עליו טפח, אבל בטומאה רצוצה אינו מטמא אלא כנגד הטומאה ולא מצד הריקן. ובפרק "המוכר פירות" (ב"ב דף ק:) יש להאריך **): ולאחותו מה ת"ל. גבי נזיר כתיב "על (כל נפשות) [נפש] מת לא יבא" וכתיב בתריה "לאביו ולאמו לאחיו ולאחותו לא יטמא", וכולהו יתירי נינהו דמנפש מת נפקא, ודרשינן: 'לאביו' מה תלמוד לומר? לגופיה לא איצטריך– דהא מ"נפש מת" נפקא כולהו, ולא בא אלא להוציא מת מצוה שמותר לטמא בו. 'לאמו' מה תלמוד לומר? לגופיה לא איצטריך, ולהתיר מת מצוה דמלאביו נפקא, אלא להביא שאם היה נזיר וכהן שיש עליו שתי קדושות – אין הכתוב מזהירו מלטמא אלא לאמו, אבל מטמא הוא למת מצוה. 'לאחיו' מה תלמוד לומר? שאם היה כהן גדול ונזיר דקדושתו חמור, דגם בלא נזירות אסור לטמא לקרוביו, אעפ"כ: לאחיו הוא דאינו מטמא, אבל מטמא הוא למת מצוה, ואם אינו ענין לנזיר גרידא ולא לכהן הדיוט נזיר, תנהו ענין לכ"ג נזיר. 'ולאחותו' מה תלמוד לומר? הרי שאם היה כ"ג ונזיר והלך לשחוט פסחו ולמול את בנו, דאיכא מצות טובא, אפ"ה 'לאחותו' הוא דאינו מטמא, אבל מטמא למת מצוה: אמרת לא יטמא. מפני שקאי על אדם שהוא נזיר וכהן גדול ועושה פסח, משמע דעושה פסח גרידא – רשאי לטמא לקרובים. ותימה, דבזבחים (פ"ב דף ק.) גבי מעשה דיוסף הכהן שמתה אשתו בערב פסח וטמאוהו אחיו בע"כ, ופריך מהא ברייתא דהכא דקאמר לא יטמא, ומאי פריך? דילמא שאני הכא דמיירי דכל קדושות האלו בו, כדפרישי', אבל עושה פסחו גרידא, אימא רשאי לטמא! על כן נראה לפרש: אמרת לא

*) [בכסף קנה: ד"ה על שמכסים [illegible]] **) [וע"ש תוס' [illegible]]

**מסורת הש"ס**

תוספתא פ"ב דשמחות פ"ו

[עירובין סג. סנהדרין פב. שבועות ל:]

עירובין דף לו: פסחים דף לב: מו"ק דף ה: חגיגה דף כה: כתובות דף כח: בכורות דף כז. נדה דף נז. [ועיין בכל המקומות ותמצא שינוי נוסחאות בתמרלים]

מנחות דף לז: [שבת פא: לב: מגילה ג: עירובין מא:]

[גיטין דף נה. נדה דף נ:]

סנהדרין דף יח: כ"מ דף ל:

[כתובות מ: מו: קדושין ג. ב"מ כ: מגילה ג: נזיר מח. סנהדרין לה: זבחים ק.]

**הגהות הב"ח**

(א) רש"י ד"ה אמרת וכו' נמי מצוה שיש בה כרת היא: (ב) תום' ד"ה מדלגין וכו' תימה לפ"ה דאמרינן פ"ק דעירובין אין כצ"ל. ותיבת גבי נמחק: (ג) בא"ד כסוי לארון. נ"ב עי' כתובו' ד: בד"ה עד שיסתום וכס"פ שואל קנב מפור' יותר וע"ש: (ד) ד"ה רוב וכו' טפח על טפח ברום טפח וכו' אלא כשיש:

**רב נסים גאון**

שאחרי רבים להטות לא הקפיד אלא על ידי ששרפו מטהרותיו בפניו פירוש עכנה נקבה של נחשים וזה שנתכוונו לדמותו לדברים בעכנה מפני שהקיפו דבריהן עליו בראיות ברורות שאין עליהן פירכא והתקיפו עליו באתקפות מהוורות שנשברו דבריו ולא מצא מהן מנוס בעכנה זו שאם מקפת על שום דבר ומהרת עליו לא יהיה לו ממנה מפלט ודהוותה התם בבבא קמא בפרק הגוזל בתרא (דף קיז) עכנה עכנה (פתחי) [פתח] פיך ויכנס הרב אצל התלמוד. וזה שאמרו יצאת בת קול ואמרה מה לכם אצל ר' אליעזר שהלכה כמותו בכ"מ ראיתי בו ב' תשובות האחת כי בת קול לא אמרה שהלכה כמותו בדבר זה אלא בכל מקום סתם הוא שאמרה ואיפשר לומר כי בכל מקום ולותי זה המקום היתה כוונתה או מה שרומזה לו שטעמו שאין הלכה כר' אליעזר בזה הדבר ויהיו דברי בת קול נבונים וקיימים והשנית שלא היתה לבת הבונה אלא לנסות את החכמים אם יניחו הקבלה שקבלו והגמרא שבפיהם בשביל בת קול אם לאו ודומה למה שכתב (דברים יג) כי מנסה ה' אלהיכם אתכם ונהנה נודע עם כל זאת בירור קבלתם וזה שאמר ר' יהושע (דברים ל) לא בשמים היא כלומר כי תורת ה' תמימה והבור נתנה לנו בסיני והודיענו כי אינו מחליף ממנה דיבור אחד ואין בתורתנו חסרון ולא ספק כדי שנצטרך אל ראיה מן השמים ולא מקום בתלמוד שיש בו ור' יהושע היא דאמר אין משגיחין בבת קול מיכן היא עיקרו והברכה שבירכוהו לר' אליעזר שהיא כינוי לנידוי פירשו במסכת סנהדרין בסוף פרק ד' מיתות (דף סח) כי בשעת פטירתו התירוהו כמו שאמרו עמד ר' יהושע על רגליו ואמר הותר הנדר הותר הנדר: העומדים בשורה הפנימיים פטורין. במס' סנהדרין בפרק כהן גדול (די"ט) אמרינן אמר ר' מנשיא בר עות שאילית את ר' יאשיה רבה מבית עילמין דהוצל ואמר לי אין שורה פחותה מיו"ד בני אדם ואין אבלים מן המנין: תרגמה ר' אבא בבית הפרס דרבנן. איתה לפירושא דבית

[illegible]

תורה אור

א אֲבָל מְטַמֵּא הוּא לְמֵת מִצְוָה, אַמַּאי? לֵימָא: "אֵין חָכְמָה וְאֵין תְּבוּנָה וְאֵין עֵצָה לְנֶגֶד ה'". – שָׁאנֵי הָתָם, דִּכְתִיב "וּלְאַחוֹתוֹ" – וְלִיגְמַר מִינַּהּ! – *שֵׁב וְאַל תַּעֲשֶׂה שָׁאנֵי. § אֲמַר לֵיהּ רַב פַּפָּא לְאַבָּיֵי: מַאי שְׁנָא רִאשׁוֹנִים דְּאִתְרְחִישׁ לְהוּ נִיסָּא, וּמַאי שְׁנָא אֲנַן דְּלָא מִתְרְחִישׁ לַן נִיסָּא? *אִי מִשּׁוּם תָּנוּיֵי – בִּשְׁנֵי דְרַב יְהוּדָה כּוּלֵּי תָּנוּיֵי בִּנְזִיקִין הֲוָה, וַאֲנַן קָא מַתְנִינַן שִׁיתָּא סִדְרֵי! וְכִי הֲוָה מָטֵי רַב יְהוּדָה בְּעוּקְצִין *"הָאִשָּׁה שֶׁכּוֹבֶשֶׁת יָרָק בִּקְדֵרָה" וְאָמְרִי לַהּ *"זֵיתִים שֶׁכְּבָשָׁן בִּטְרָפֵיהֶן טְהוֹרִים" אָמַר: "הֲוָיוֹת דְּרַב וּשְׁמוּאֵל קָא חָזֵינָא הָכָא", וַאֲנַן קָא מַתְנִינַן בְּעוּקְצִין תְּלֵיסַר מְתִיבָתָא! וְאִילּוּ רַב יְהוּדָה, כִּי הֲוָה שָׁלֵיף חַד מְסָאנֵיהּ – אָתֵי מִטְרָא, וַאֲנַן קָא מְצַעֲרִינַן נַפְשִׁין וּמִצְוַח קָא צָוְחִינַן – וְלֵית דְּמַשְׁגַּח בַּן! – אֲמַר לֵיהּ: קַמָּאֵי הֲווֹ קָא מָסְרֵי נַפְשַׁיְיהוּ אַקְּדוּשַּׁת הַשֵּׁם, אֲנַן לָא מָסְרִינַן נַפְשִׁין אַקְּדוּשַּׁת הַשֵּׁם. כִּי הָא דְּרַב אַדָּא בַּר אַהֲבָה חַזְיֵיהּ לְהַהִיא כּוּתִית דַּהֲוַת לְבִישָׁא *כַּרְבַּלְתָּא בְּשׁוּקָא, סָבַר דְּבַת יִשְׂרָאֵל הִיא, קָם קַרְעֵיהּ מִינַּהּ; אִגַּלַּאי מִילְּתָא דְּכוּתִית הִיא, שַׁיְימוּהָ בְּאַרְבַּע מְאָה זוּזֵי. א"ל: מַה שְּׁמֵךְ? אָמְרָה לֵיהּ: מָתוּן. אֲמַר לַהּ: מָתוּן מָתוּן אַרְבַּע מְאָה זוּזֵי שָׁוְיָא. § רַב גִּידֵּל הֲוָה רְגִיל דַּהֲוָה קָא אָזֵיל וְיָתֵיב אַשַּׁעֲרֵי דִּטְבִילָה, אָמַר לְהוּ: הָכִי טְבִילוּ וְהָכִי טְבִילוּ. אָמְרֵי לֵיהּ רַבָּנַן: לָא קָא מִסְתְּפֵי מָר מִיֵּצֶר הָרַע?(א) אָמַר לְהוּ: דָּמְיָין בְּאַפַּאי כִּי קָאקֵי חִיוּרֵי. *ר' יוֹחָנָן הֲוָה רְגִיל דַּהֲוָה קָא אָזֵיל וְיָתֵיב *אַשַּׁעֲרֵי דִּטְבִילָה, אָמַר: כִּי סָלְקָן בְּנוֹת יִשְׂרָאֵל וְאָתְיָין מִטְּבִילָה מִסְתַּכְּלָן בִּי, וְנֶהֱוֵי לְהוּ זַרְעָא דְּשַׁפִּירֵי כְּוָותִי. אָמְרֵי לֵיהּ רַבָּנַן: לָא קָא מִסְתְּפֵי מָר מֵעֵינָא בִּישָׁא? אָמַר לְהוּ: אֲנָא *מִזַּרְעָא דְּיוֹסֵף קָא אָתֵינָא, דְּלָא שָׁלְטָא בֵּיהּ עֵינָא בִּישָׁא, דִּכְתִיב: °"בֵּן פֹּרָת יוֹסֵף בֵּן פֹּרָת עֲלֵי עָיִן", וְאָמַר רַבִּי אַבָּהוּ: אַל תִּקְרֵי "עֲלֵי עָיִן" אֶלָּא "עוֹלֵי עָיִן". רַבִּי יוֹסֵי בְּרַבִּי חֲנִינָא אָמַר מֵהָכָא: °"וְיִדְגּוּ לָרֹב בְּקֶרֶב הָאָרֶץ" מַה דָּגִים שֶׁבַּיָּם מַיִם מְכַסִּין עֲלֵיהֶם וְאֵין עַיִן הָרָע שׁוֹלֶטֶת בָּהֶם – אַף זַרְעוֹ שֶׁל יוֹסֵף אֵין עַיִן הָרָע שׁוֹלֶטֶת בָּהֶם. וְאִב"א: עַיִן שֶׁלֹּא רָצְתָה לָזוּן מִמַּה שֶּׁאֵינוֹ שֶׁלּוֹ – אֵין עַיִן הָרָע שׁוֹלֶטֶת בּוֹ. §

**מתני'** ב נָשִׁים וַעֲבָדִים וּקְטַנִּים פְּטוּרִין מִקְּרִיאַת שְׁמַע וּמִן

[רש"א מ"ז] תענית כד: סנהדרין קו: ע"ש
בראשית מט
שם מח

## רש"י

אֲבָל מְטַמֵּא הוּא לְמֵת מִצְוָה. וְהוּא כְּבוֹד הַבְּרִיּוֹת, וְדוֹחֶה דְּבַר תּוֹרָה: שֵׁב וְאַל תַּעֲשֶׂה שָׁאנֵי. דְּבָרִים רַבִּים מִפְּנֵי סְיָיג וּמִפְּנֵי כְּבוֹד הַבְּרִיּוֹת, הֵיכָא דְּאֵינוֹ עוֹקֵר דָּבָר בְּמַעֲשֵׂה יָדַיִם, אֶלָּא יוֹשֵׁב בִּמְקוֹמוֹ, וּדְבַר תּוֹרָה נֶעֱקָר מֵאֵלָיו. כְּגוֹן תְּקִיעַת שׁוֹפָר וְלוּלָב בְּשַׁבָּת, וְסָדִין בְּצִיצִית, וְדִכְוָותַיְיהוּ טוּבָא בִּיבָמוֹת (דף צ:). אֲבָל מְעַקֵּר בְּיָדַיִם – לָא. וְהַלּוֹבֵשׁ כִּלְאַיִם עוֹקְרוֹ בְּמַעֲשֶׂה מַמָּשׁ, שֶׁהוּא לוֹבְשׁוֹ. וְטוּמְאַת גּוּפֵי' שֶׁהוּתְּרָה לְכֹהֵן וּלְנָזִיר לִיטַּמֵּא לְמֵת מִצְוָה, דְּקָא מְעַקֵּר בְּיָדַיִם מִפְּנֵי כְּבוֹד הַבְּרִיּוֹת דְּלָאו שֵׁב וְאַל תַּעֲשֶׂה הוּא, הַיְינוּ טַעְמָא דְּלָא גָּמְרִינַן מִינֵּיהּ – דְּהָתָם (ג) לָאו כְּבוֹד הַבְּרִיּוֹת הוּא דְּדָחֵי לָא תַּעֲשֶׂה דִּידֵיהּ. דְּמֵעִיקָּרָא כְּשֶׁנִּכְתַּב ל"ת דְּטוּמְאָה – לֹא עַל מֵת מִצְוָה נִכְתַּב, כְּשֵׁם שֶׁלֹּא נִכְתַּב עַל הַקְּרוֹבִים. אֲבָל הֲשָׁבַת אֲבֵדָה וּפֶסַח – לְכָל יִשְׂרָאֵל נֶאֱמַר, וְאֵצֶל כְּבוֹד הַבְּרִיּוֹת נִתְּנוּ לִדְחוֹת, ע"כ הַיְינוּ דְּדַחְיָין אֵינָהּ בְּיָדַיִם אֶלָּא בִּישִׁיבָתוֹ תִּדָּחֶה הַמִּצְוָה. אֲבָל כִּלְאַיִם דְּבְמַעֲשֶׂה יָדָיו יִדָּחֶה – הִזְהִיר בְּאַזְהָרָתוֹ: בִּנְזִיקִין הֲוָה. לֹא הָיוּ גְּדוֹלִים בְּכָל גְּמָרָא שֶׁל ד' סְדָרִים אֶלָּא *בִּתְלָתָא בָּבֵי שֶׁלָּנוּ. וְהַאי מִילְּתָא נָקַט הָכָא מִשּׁוּם דְּמַיְירֵי שֶׁמּוֹסְרִין נַפְשָׁם עַל קְדוּשַּׁת הַשֵּׁם, וְעַד הַשְׁתָּא אַיְירֵי נָמֵי בְּמִי שֶׁמְּבַזֶּה עַצְמוֹ עַל קְדוּשַּׁת הַשֵּׁם לִפְשׁוֹט כִּלְאַיִם בַּשּׁוּק: הָאִשָּׁה שֶׁכּוֹבֶשֶׁת יָרָק אוֹ זֵיתִים שֶׁכְּבָשָׁן בִּטְרָפֵיהֶן. מִשְׁנָה הִיא בְּמַס' עוּקְצִין*: טְהוֹרִים. שֶׁמּוֹסְקִין זֵיתִים עִם הֶעָלִין כְּדֵי לְאָחֳזָן בָּהֶן, דְּהָווּ לְהוּ עָלִין יָד לַזֵּיתִים לַהֲבִיא לָהֶם טוּמְאָה, כִּדְאָמְרִינַן בְּ"הָעוֹר וְהָרוֹטֶב" (דף קיח.) שֶׁהַיָּד מְבִיאָה טוּמְאָה עַל הָאוֹכֶל. וְאִם כְּבָשָׁן בִּטְרָפֵיהֶן בְּחוֹמֶץ – בָּטְלָה תּוֹרַת יָד מִן הֶעָלִין, לְפִי שֶׁהַכְּבִישָׁה מְרַכַּכְתָּן וּמְרַסַּכְתָּן וְאֵינָן רְאוּיִין שׁוּב לֶאֱחוֹז בָּהֶן: הֲוָיוֹת דְּרַב וּשְׁמוּאֵל קָא חָזֵינָא הָכָא. כְּלוֹמַר: טַעַם הַמִּשְׁנִיּוֹת הַלָּלוּ קָשֶׁה עָלַי כְּכָל הַקּוּשְׁיוֹת שֶׁהָיוּ שְׁנֵי רַבּוֹתַי מִתְקַשִּׁין בָּהֶן בְּכָל הַגְּמ': בִּתְלֵיסַר מְתִיבְתָּא. בִּי"ג פָּנִים, יֵשׁ בֵּינֵינוּ מִשְׁנָה וּבָרַיְיתָא שֶׁל שִׁשָּׁה סְדָרִים, וּמַסֶּכֶת עוּקְצִין גַּם הִיא בִּי"ג פָּנִים כְּגוֹן מִשְׁנַת רַבִּי וְר' חִיָּיא וּמִשְׁנַת בַּר קַפָּרָא וְלֵוִי וְתַנָּא דְּבֵי שְׁמוּאֵל. וְהָכִי אָמְרִינַן בְּמַסֶּכֶת נְדָרִים: (דף מא.) רַבִּי מַתְנֵי הִלְכְתָא בִּי"ג פָּנִים: כַּרְבָּלְתָּא. שֵׁם לְבוּשׁ חָשׁוּב כְּמוֹ "פַּטְּשֵׁיהוֹן וְכַרְבְּלָתְהוֹן" (דניאל ג): מָתוּן מָתוּן. לְשׁוֹן מָאתַן: ד' מֵאוֹת. ב' פְּעָמִים ב' מֵאוֹת. כְּלוֹמַר: הַשֵּׁם גָּרַם לִי. לָשׁוֹן אַחֵר: מָתוּן מָתוּן לְשׁוֹן הַמְתָּנָה; אִם הִמְתַּנְתִּי הָיִיתִי מִשְׁתַּכֵּר ד' מֵאוֹת זוּז: כִּי קָאקֵי חִיוּרֵי. אֲוָוזִים לְבָנִים: ר' יוֹחָנָן. אָדָם יָפֶה תּוֹאַר הָיָה, דְּאָמְרִי' בְּ"הַשּׂוֹכֵר אֶת הַפּוֹעֲלִים" (דף פד.) שׁוּפְרֵיהּ דְּר' אֲבָהוּ מֵעֵין שׁוּפְרֵיהּ וְכוּ': עוֹלֵי עַיִן. מְסוּלָּקִין מִן הָעַיִן שֶׁאֵינָהּ שׁוֹלֶטֶת בָּהֶן: שֶׁלֹּא רָצְתָה לָזוּן. לֵיהָנוֹת מֵאֵשֶׁת אֲדוֹנָיו: **מתני'** נָשִׁים וַעֲבָדִים וּקְטַנִּים פְּטוּרִים מִקַּ"שׁ. שֶׁהִיא מ"ע שֶׁהַזְּמַן גְּרָמָא, וְקַיְי"ל בְּקִדּוּשִׁין (דף כט.) דְּנָשִׁים פְּטוּרוֹת מִדְּאוֹרַיְיתָא. וּתְפִילִּין נָמֵי מ"ע שֶׁהַזְּמַן גְּרָמָא, דְּקָסָבַר לַיְלָה וְשַׁבָּת לָאו זְמַן תְּפִילִּין נִינְהוּ: קְטַנִּים. אֲפִי' קָטָן שֶׁהִגִּיעַ לְחִינּוּךְ לֹא הֵטִילוּ עַל אָבִיו לְחַנְּכוֹ בְּקַ"שׁ, לְפִי שֶׁאֵינוֹ מָצוּי אֶצְלוֹ תָּמִיד כְּשֶׁמַּגִּיעַ זְמַן קַ"שׁ: וּמִן

## תוספות

לא יטמא – אפי' עושה פסחו גרידא. וא"ת: מהיכא פשיטא ליה אמרת לא יטמא? וי"ל כדפירש"י: דלא אתי עשה שאין בו כרת כטומאת קרובים, וידחה עשה שיש בו כרת כגון עושה פסח, וגם מילה שייך בה כרת. וא"ת: התם דפריך על מעשה דיוסף הכהן, מנ"ל [לתלמודא] דהכא מיירי בעושה פסחו לחוד? וי"ל: מדלא כייל גבי עושה פסחו כמו גבי אחרים מי שהיה נזיר וכהן הדיוט. דמעיקרא נקט נזיר לחוד, ואח"כ נזיר וכהן הדיוט וכו'. וא"ת: מנא ליה (לתלמודא) דהאי קרא בעושה פסחו ולמול את בנו? הא קרא כתיב בנזיר! וי"ל: אם אינו ענין בנזיר, דהא כתיבי פסוקים אחרים דמטמא במת מצוה, תנהו ענין להולך לשחוט פסחו וכו'. והשר מקוצי מיישב פירש"י: דמיירי הכא דיש בו כל הקדושות הללו כו'. ומ"מ פריך התם גבי יוסף הכהן, דע"כ אף בעושה פסח גרידא אינו רשאי לטמא. דאי ס"ד עושה פסח מטמא לקרובים, 'ולאחותו' למה לי למימר דמטמא למת מצוה? כיון דמטמא לקרובים אלמא עושה פסחו אינו מעלה עליו שום חומרא טפי – א"כ פשיטא דמטמא למת מצוה. וכי תימא: מכל מקום לריך קרא דמטמא למת מצוה, מפני שיש בו ג' קדושות נזיר וכהן ועושה פסח. ולעולם אימא לך דעושה פסח גרידא מטמא לקרובים – לא היא, דהא כבר שמעינן מלאביו ולאמו ולאחיו דנזיר וכ"ג לא מהני מידי למת מצוה. א"כ, ע"כ קראי לא אצטריכו אלא למעלה דפסח. ולמה לי, פשיטא דאי מטמא לקרובים – כ"ש למת מצוה. ואע"ג דאצטריך קרא ד'לאמו' לכהן הדיוט ונזיר דמטמא למת מצוה, אע"ג דכתב קרא דמטמא לקרובים ואצטריך קרא שהן ב' קדושות אע"ג דשמעינן כבר דמעלה דנזיר לא מהני מידי למת מצוה מ'לאביו', ה"מ – כהן דקדושתו קדושת עולם, ומשום הכי יש לנו לומר כי יש לו שתי קדושות דטפי קדושה ולכך אצטריך קרא. אבל עושה פסח שקדושתו לפי שעה, אם אתה מתיר לו לקרובים – ה"ה למת מצוה מכ"ש, דמאי חזית ליתן לו קדושה טפי גבי מת מצוה יותר מן הקרובים. א"נ יש לפרש בקוצר הברייתא; מדתניא גרידא על ישראל נזיר, ואח"כ נזיר וכהן הדיוט, ואח"כ נזיר וכ"ג, וא"כ מסברא יש לנו לומר (כי יש) דאינו מטמא לקרובים כמו נזיר וכלהו אינך, ודוק מעלמך: **שב ואל תעשה** שאני. וא"ת: נזיר וכ"ג קום עשה הוא דיטמא למת! ותירץ רש"י: דקרא גלי לן דלאו ד"לא יטמא" לא נאמר גבי מת מצוה. ולא נהירא, דא"כ כל מקום דאמרי' שעשה דוחה ל"ת, לקרי שב ואל תעשה וכו' והיאך קרי ליה דחייה? אימא שאינו דחייה, דהתם לא נאמר הלאו! ועוד: דהא מילה ותמיד ופסח דדחו שבת כדאמרינן פרק "אלו דברים" (פסחים דף סט:) אלמא: מקרי שפיר דחייה! אלא נראה: דמנזיר לא גמרינן, דמה לנזיר – שכן ישנו בשאלה; וכן מכהן, מה לכהן – שכן לאו שאינו שוה בכל: **זיתים** שכבשן בטרפיהן טהורים. פירש הקונטרס: כיון דכבשן בקדרה בטלים מתורת יד להביא טומאה. ולא נהירא, דא"כ מאי האי דקאמר עלה שלא נכבשו אלא למראה, מה נתינת טעם יש דבטלינהו מתורת יד? לכך נראה לפרש: דטהורים משום דאותן עלין לא חשיבי אוכל שאין ראויין לאכילה אלא ע"י אותה כבישה בקדרה, שלא נכבשו אלא למראה. כלומר: מה שכבש העלין עמהן – לא כבשן אלא להראות שהזיתים נאים וחדשים, ומשום הכי טהורים. אבל כבשן להיות ראויין לאכילה – משעה שהן מתוקנין לראויה אכילה טמאים: **תליסר** מתיבתא. יש מפרשין: תליסר ישיבות יש בנו שבקיאים. ותליסר לאו דוקא, אלא לשון הרגיל בגמ' כמו תליסר (חולין מד:) זוזי פשיטי. ורש"י פי' בע"א*): **וקטנים** פטורים מק"ש. פירש הקונטרס: קטן שהגיע לחנוך. ולא נהירא, דהא פרק "לולב הגזול" (סוכה דף מב.) אמרי': קטן היודע לשמור תפילין אביו חייב לקנות לו תפילין, אלמא כשהגיע לחנוך דשייך ביה תפילין – חייב בתפילין. ובק"ש נמי יש לחייבו יותר מתפילין, מדלאשמעינן התם קטן היודע לדבר אביו מלמדו תורה ופסוק ראשון של ק"ש. ונראה לר"ת: דמיירי בקטן שלא הגיע לחנוך. ומיהו, סיפא דקתני וחייבין בתפלה היה ר"י רוצה לומר: דמיירי בקטן שהגיע לחנוך. דאי לא הגיע – לא הוו להו לחייבו בתפלה. ולא נהירא, דאם כן לא הוו להו קטנים דומיא דנשים ועבדים, שפטורים בכל ענין וקטנים אינם פטורים אלא בשלא הגיע, ואין יודע לשמור תפיליו. ופי' ר"ת: דלעולם איירי בכל קטן שלא הגיע לחנוך, ומ"מ חייבין בתפלה – וקאי אנשים ועבדים. א"כ אמאי תנא קטנים בהדי נשים ועבדים וכל כיון דלא הגיעו לחנוך. וא"ת: א"כ אמאי תנא קטנים כלל? וי"ל: דכך דרך התנא לשנות יחד נשים ועבדים וקטנים שלא הגיעו לחנוך, כמו: נשים ועבדים וקטנים פטורים מסוכה (סוכה דף כח.): בתפלה

*) וע"ע רש"י שבת קיט. ד"ה תריסר וב"ב קלג: ד"ה עליהם ורש"י ותוס' חולין נה: ד"ה תריסר וע"ל תליסר:

## רב נסים גאון

לאביו ולאמו לאחיו ולאחותו לא יטמא זה שדבר הכתוב בכל אלו הקרובין צריך היה הדבר להזכיר את כולם שאי אפשר שיזכיר דבר שאין בו תלמוד כדכתיב (דברים לב) כי לא דבר רק הוא מכם ואין לנו דרך לידע לאיזה תלמוד נכתבו כולם אלא מקבלת החכמים ז"ל לפי שאם באנו לעיין בהם מדרך דעתנו היה עולה על לבנו כי בהזכירו את האב שמעלתו למעלה מכולם והאם עם הבנים חייבים בכבודו לא היה צריך להזכיר את השאר והיינו אומרים אם הזהיר הכתוב שלא יטמא לאב שהוא עדיף מכולם כל שכן לשאר קרובים שהן פחותין ממנו ולא היינו יודעין מה צורך היה לו להזכיר האם והאח והאחות עד ששמענו קבלה של חכמים שבידיהם ופירושם ואמרו כי לאביו ולאמו צריך הדבר להזכיר את שניהם שאם היה מזכיר את אחד מהן לא היינו למדין ממנו חברו לפי שכל אחד מהם יש לו מעלה מיוחדת לו ואינה כחברו שהאב עדיף מן האם שבנו מיוחס אחריו ולא אחר האם והאם יש לה יתרון על האב מפני שהיא ודאי אמו ואביו אינו ודאי אלא חזקה שאפשר שתזנה אמו ותהר לזנונים ויהיה זה הבן מאיש אחר זולתי בעלה ולפיכך הוצרך לומר לאביו ולאמו ואיתא במסכת נזיר בפרק כהן גדול ונזיר אינן מטמאין לקרוביהן (דף מט) לאביו ולאמו למה לי צריכא דאי כתב רחמנא אביו הוה אמינא היינו טעמא דלא מיטמא ליה משום דחזקה בעלמא הוא אבל אמו (היא) ודאי לילדתיה ליטמא לה ואי כתב רחמנא אמו הוה אמינא אמו היא דלא מיטמי לה דלא אזיל זרעה בתרה אבל אביו כיון דאמר רחמנא (במדבר א) למשפחותם לבית אבותם אימא ליטמי ליה קמ"ל ועוד אמרו (שם דף מח) אם הוצרך לומר אביו ואמו למה הוכיר עוד את אחיו והלא אין צריך להזכירו שכבר היה נלמד מאביו ואמו וזה שהזכיר את אחיו לא לצורך עצמו נאמר אלא ללמד על מת מצוה שאין לו קוברין נאמר שמותר לנזיר להטמא לו ולהתעסק בקבורתו כדתניא לאחיו אינו מיטמא אבל מטמא למת מצוה ונשתיירה עדיין אחותו ושאלנו עליה למה הוצרך הכתוב עוד להזכירה ולאחותו מה תלמוד והשבנו כי הוצרך להזכירה ללמד ממנה תוספת תלמוד שהרי אפי' אם היה הולך לעשות מצוה ונזדמן לו מת מצוה שיניח את המצוה שהיה סובר לעשותה ויטמא למת מצוה ויתעסק בו עד שיקברנו ולפיכך הזכיר הכתוב את אחותו כי שהזכיר אחיו ללמדנו כי הנזיר מטמא למת מצוה בזמן שאינו מתעסק במצוה אחרת והזכירנו עוד לידע אם בזמן בשהוא עוסק במצוה ניחנה ויתעסק במת מצוה אם לאו אתא ולאחותו ללמד כי מת מצוה קודם כמו שאמרו הרי שהיה הולך לשחוט את פסחו ולמול את בנו כו' ת"ל ולאחותו לאחותו הוא דאינו מיטמא אבל מיטמא למת מצוה ודרשינן ליה תו בדרך אחרת לאביו הוא דאינו מיטמא אבל מיטמא למת מצוה ולאמו אינו מיטמא אבל מיטמא שאם היה כהן והוא נזיר לאחיו שאם היה כהן גדול והוא נזיר לאחיו אינו מטמא אבל מטמא למת מצוה ולאחותו מה תלמוד לומר הרי שהיה הולך לשחוט את פסחו ולמול את בנו כו' מכל מקום לא למדנו אלא ממת מצוה ולאחותו מה תלמוד: **ואילו** רב יהודה כי הוה מטי בעוקצין באו לבדנו את שבכבר הוכרנו: האשה שכובשת ירק בקדרה. זו המשנה בתחלת פרק שני דמסכת טהרות ואמרי

## עין משפט נר מצוה

כה א מיי' פ"ג מהלכות אבל הלכה ח טור שו"ע יו"ד סימן שע"ד סעיף ח:

כו ב מיי' פ"ד מהלכות ק"ש סמג עשין יח טור ושו"ע או"ח סימן ע סעיף א ב:

## מסורת הש"ס

[עי' תוס' ב"מ ל: ד"ה אלא ותוס' שבועות ל: ד"ה אבל ועי' יבמות ג: תוד"ה כולהו]

טהרות פ"ב משנה א

עוקצין פ"ב משנה א [ועי' רש"י סנה' קו: ורש"י בתענית כד:]

[ובסנהדרין ובתענית פירש"י בסדר נזיקין ע"ש]

[פי' בגד חשוב כגון כרבלתא דתרנגולא שאין דרך בנות ישראל להתכסות בו שהוא פריצות ומביא לידי עבירה. ערוך]

ב"מ פד. [כל הענין] וע"ש [ועי' תוס' ב"מ פד. ד"ה יתיב]

לקמן נה: סוטה לו: ב"ב קיח:

## הגהות הב"ח

(א) גמ' לא קא מסתפי מר מיצר הרע. נ"ב הא דלא אמרו ליה מעינא בישא כדאמרי' גבי ר' יוחנן היינו משום דלא הוו מסתכלי ביה וקפיד ביה עינא בישא אבל ר"י שהיה גדול ויפה תואר א"כ היה גדל אבל קשיא אמאי לא אמרו לר"י לא קא מסתפי מר מיצר הרע וי"ל משום דר"י מכוין לשם שמים ולא חש ליצר הרע:

## גליון הש"ס

גמ' רב גידל הוה רגיל כו'. ויתיב כו' עי' תוס' פסחים קי ע"ב ד"ה האי מאן:

אומן התפילין, וחייבין בתפלה וּבמזוזה וּבברכת המזון.§ גמ' "ק"ש", פשיטא! מצות עשה שהזמן גרמא הוא, *וכל מצות עשה שהזמן גרמא נשים פטורות! -מהו דתימא: הואיל ואית בה מלכות שמים - קמ"ל. "ומן התפילין".§ פשיטא! - מהו דתימא: הואיל ואתקש למזוזה - קמ"ל.§ "וחייבין בתפלה".§ דרחמי נינהו.(א) -מהו דתימא: הואיל וכתיב בה "ערב ובקר וצהרים", כמצות עשה שהזמן גרמא דמי - קמ"ל.§ "ובמזוזה" פשיטא! -מהו דתימא: הואיל ואתקש לתלמוד תורה - קמשמע לן. "ובברכת המזון" פשיטא! -מהו דתימא: הואיל וכתיב "בתת ה' לכם בערב בשר לאכל ולחם בבקר לשבע" כמצות עשה שהזמן גרמא דמי - קמ"ל.§ *אמר רב אדא בר אהבה: נשים חייבות בקדוש היום דבר תורה. -אמאי? מצות עשה שהזמן גרמא הוא, וכל מצות עשה שהזמן גרמא נשים פטורות! -אמר אביי: מדרבנן. -א"ל רבא: והא "דבר תורה" קאמר! ועוד, כל מצות עשה נחייבינהו מדרבנן! - אלא אמר רבא: אמר קרא "זכור" ו"שמור" - כל שישנו בשמירה ישנו בזכירה, והני נשי, הואיל ואיתנהו בשמירה - איתנהו בזכירה.§ א"ל רבינא לרבא: נשים בברכת המזון, דאורייתא או דרבנן? למאי נפקא מינה? לאפוקי רבים ידי חובתן. אי אמרת (בשלמא) דאורייתא - אתי דאורייתא ומפיק דאורייתא, (אלא *אי) אמרת דרבנן - הוי "שאינו מחויב בדבר", *וכל שאינו מחויב בדבר - אינו מוציא את הרבים ידי חובתן. מאי? ת"ש, *באמת אמרו: בן מברך לאביו, ועבד מברך לרבו, ואשה מברכת לבעלה; אבל אמרו חכמים: תבא מארה לאדם שאשתו ובניו מברכין לו. אי אמרת בשלמא דאורייתא - אתי דאורייתא ומפיק דאורייתא, אלא אי אמרת דרבנן - אתי דרבנן ומפיק דאורייתא?! - ולטעמיך, קטן בר חיובא הוא?! - אלא, הכי במאי עסקינן - כגון שאכל שיעורא דרבנן, דאתי דרבנן ומפיק דרבנן. דרש רב עוירא, זמנין אמר לה משמיה דר' אמי וזמנין אמר לה משמיה דר' אסי: אמרו מלאכי השרת לפני הקב"ה: רבש"ע, כתוב בתורתך "אשר לא ישא פנים ולא יקח שחד", והלא אתה נושא פנים לישראל, דכתיב: "ישא ה' פניו אליך". אמר להם: וכי לא אשא פנים לישראל?! שכתבתי להם בתורה: "ואכלת ושבעת וברכת את ה' אלהיך", והם מדקדקים [על] עצמם *עד כזית ועד כביצה.§ מתני' בעל קרי מהרהר בלבו ואינו מברך לא לפניה ולא לאחריה; ועל המזון מברך לאחריו ואינו מברך לפניו. רבי יהודה אומר: מברך לפניהם ולאחריהם.§ גמ' אמר רבינא, זאת אומרת: הרהור כדבור דמי. דאי סלקא דעתך לאו כדבור דמי, למה מהרהר? -אלא מאי הרהור כדבור דמי, יוציא בשפתיו! -*כדאשכחן בסיני. ורב חסדא אמר: *הרהור לאו כדבור דמי. דאי סלקא דעתך הרהור כדבור דמי - יוציא בשפתיו! -אלא מאי - הרהור לאו כדבור דמי, למה מהרהר? -אמר רבי אלעזר: כדי שלא יהו כל העולם עוסקין בו והוא יושב ובטל. -ונגרוס בפרקא אחרינא!(ב) -אמר רב אדא בר אהבה: בדבר שהצבור עוסקין בו. והרי

**רש"י**

ומן התפילין. משום דסתם קטן אינו יודע לשמור גופו שלא יפיח בהן: וחייבין בתפלה. דתפלה רחמי היא, ומדרבנן היא, ותקנוה אף לנשים ולחנוך קטנים: ובמזוזה ובברכת המזון. מזוזה מצות עשה שלא הזמן גרמא ובגמרא פריך: פשיטא: ברכת המזון. בגמרא בעי לה דאורייתא או דרבנן: גמ' מהו דתימא נקיש תפלין למזוזה. דכתיב "וקשרתם" "וכתבתם", מה מזוזה נשים חייבות - אף תפילין נשים חייבות, קמשמע לן: הכי גרסינן: תפלה דרחמי נינהו. ולא גרס פשיטא, דהא לאו דאורייתא היא: נקיש מזוזה לתלמוד תורה. דכתיב (דברים יא) "ולמדתם אותם את בניכם" וסמיך ליה "וכתבתם". מה תלמוד תורה נשים פטורות - ואע"ג דאין הזמן גרמא - רחמנא פטרינהו, דכתיב "את בניכם" ולא בנותיכם - אף מזוזה נשים פטורות, קמ"ל דנשים חייבות, דכתיב "למען ירבו ימיכם" גברי בעו חיי נשי לא בעו חיי? בתמיה: קדוש היום מ"ע שהזמן גרמא הוא. "זכור את יום השבת לקדשו" (שמות כ) - זכרהו על היין: בשמירה. ד"לא תעשה מלאכה" (שם): והני נשי איתנהו בשמירה. דתנן (קדושין דף כט.): כל מצות לא תעשה, בין שהזמן גרמא בין שאין הזמן גרמא - נשים חייבות, דהשוה הכתוב אשה לאיש לכל עונשים שבתורה: נשים בברכת המזון דאורייתא. דכתיב "ואכלת ושבעת", (דברים ח), והוה ליה מצות עשה שאין הזמן גרמא: או דרבנן. דכתיב "על הארץ הטובה אשר נתן לך" (שם), והארץ לא נתנה לנקבות להתחלק. ואי משום בנות צלפחד - חלק אביהם הם דנטלו, שהיה מיוצאי מצרים: בן. קטן: מברך. ברכת המזון לאביו, אם אין אביו יודע לברך: שיעורא דרבנן. כגון כזית לר"מ וכביצה לרבי יהודה, דמדאורייתא "ואכלת ושבעת וברכת" כתיב, אבל בשיעור כי האי - לא מחייב אלא מדרבנן, והלכך אתי קטן דרבנן ומפיק גדול: עד כזית עד כביצה. עד כזית לר"מ, עד כביצה לר' יהודה. דתנן (לקמן דף מה.): עד כמה מזמנין, ר"מ אומר עד כזית, ר' יהודה אומר: עד כביצה: מתני' בעל קרי. מתקנת עזרא ואילך שתקן טבילה לבעלי קריין לעסוק בתורה, כדאמרינן בב"ק בפרק "מרובה" (דף פב:): מהרהר. ק"ש בלבו, כשמגיע זמן המקרא: ואינו מברך. אפילו בהרהור: לא לפניה ולא לאחריה. כיון דברכות לאו מדאורייתא מחייב, לא אצרכוהו רבנן: ועל המזון מברך לאחריו. דחיובא דאורייתא הוא: ואינו מברך לפניו. דלאו דאורייתא הוא: רבי יהודה אומר וכו'. בגמ' מפרש לה: גמ' כדבור דמי. וכל אדם נמי יוצא ידי חובתו בהרהור: למה מהרהר. מה מועיל: כדאשכחן בסיני. שהפרישן מאשה דכתיב "אל תגשו אל אשה" (שמות יט). ועל פרשה זו סמך עזרא לתקן טבילה לבעלי קריין קודם שיעסקו בתורה, דכתיב (דברים ד) "והודעתם לבניך" וסמיך ליה "יום אשר עמדת לפני ה' אלהיך בחורב", כדאמרינן לקמן בפרקין (דף כא:): אלא

**תוספות**

בתפלה פשיטא כיון דכתיב "ערב ובקר וצהרים אשיחה ואהמה" - כמצות עשה שהזמן גרמא הוי, קמ"ל דרחמי נינהו. ורש"י לא גריס ליה, שהרי תפלה דרבנן היא, ומאי מ"ע שייכי ביה? ומ"מ יש ליישב, דהא הלל דרבנן ונשים פטורות מהאי טעמא, דמצות עשה שהזמן גרמא הוא. כדאמרינן בסוכה (דף לח.): מי שהיה עבד ואשה או קטן מקרין אותו - עונה אחריהן מה שהם אומרים, דאין השומע פטור מקריאתן, כיון שהם פטורים: איכא דגרסי בברכת המזון פשיטא. ומשני: כיון דכתיב "בתת ה' לכם בערב בשר לאכול ולחם בבקר לשבוע" כמ"ע שהזמן גרמא הוא, קמ"ל: נשים בברכת המזון דאורייתא או דרבנן. פי' הקונטרס: דסלקא דעתך דלא מחייבי מדאורייתא משום דכתיב "על הארץ הטובה" ונשים לא נטלו חלק בארץ. ומה שנטלו בנות צלפחד - חלק אביהם נטלו. ותימה: כהנים ולוים נמי תבעי, שהרי לא נטלו חלק בארץ, וא"כ לא יוציאו אחרים ידי חובתן בברכת המזון! אלא י"ל: דטעמא משום דכתיב "על בריתך שחתמת בבשרנו ועל תורתך שלמדתנו", ונשים ליתנהו לא בברית ולא בתורה. ואמרינן לקמן (דף מט.): מי שלא אמר ברית ותורה בברכת המזון - לא יצא ידי חובתו. והשתא קא מבעיא ליה כיון דלא מצו למימר ברית ותורה, לא הוו אלא מדרבנן, או דלמא כיון דלא שייך בהו - הוי שפיר דאורייתא. והא דלקמן - מיירי באנשים, דשייכי בברית ובתורה:

בעל קרי מהרהר בלבו ואינו מברך לא לפניה ולא לאחריה. פי': אפילו בהרהור, כדמשמע בגמ'. והיינו טעמא דשרינא טפי בק"ש מברכות - משום דק"ש דאורייתא וברכות דרבנן. ואפי' למ"ד ק"ש דרבנן - היינו היכא דהזכיר יציאת מצרים, אבל מתניתין שלא הזכיר יציאת מצרים, שלא התירו לו לומר "אמת ויציב". והוי ק"ש דאורייתא, ו"אמת ויציב" דרבנן - שהרי הזכיר יציאת מצרים בק"ש. ואין להקשות: נתקן לימא "אמת ויציב" ולא לימא ק"ש! דהא עדיף לימא ק"ש, דאית ביה נמי מלכות שמים: יוציא בשפתיו. כיון דשרית ליה הרהור אע"פ שהוא כדבור לענין לצאת ידי ק"ש, כמו כן מקרי דבור לענין דמקרי עוסק בתורה, ומדשרית ליה להרהר, אע"פ שהוא בעל קרי - תתיר לו גם דבור: כדאשכחן בסיני. פירוש: אף ע"ג דכדבור דמי לענין שיהא, מ"מ לאו כדבור דמי לענין שיהא בעל קרי אסור להרהר, כדאשכחן בסיני דהיה שם דבור והיו צריכין לטבול. ואע"פ שהיו שותקין - שומע כעונה (סוכה לח:):

ורב חסדא אמר לאו כדבור דמי. ר"ח פירש דהלכה כרב חסדא, מדמדרי רב אדא ורבי אלעזר למלתיה - שמע מיניה כוותיה קיימי, ולא יצא בקריאת שמע בהרהור: והרי

**עין משפט נר מצוה**

כז א מיי' פ"ד מהלכות תפילין הלכה יג סמג עשין כב טוש"ע או"ח סימן לח סעיף ג:
כח ב מיי' פ"א מהל' תפלה הלכה ב סמג עשין יט טוש"ע או"ח סימן קו סעיף ב:
כט ג מיי' פ"ה מהלכ' מזוזה הלכה י סמג עשין כג טוש"ע יו"ד סימן רצא סעיף ג:
ל ד מיי' פ"ה מהלכות ברכות הלכה א סמג עשין כז טוש"ע או"ח סימן קפו סעיף א:
לא ה מיי' פ"ט מהל' ש"ש הלכה א סמג עשין כט טוש"ע או"ח סימן רעא סעיף ב: [ה מיי' פ"ה מה' ברכות הלכה א' טוש"ע שם]
לב ו מיי' פ"ה מהלכות ברכות הלכה טו:
לג ז ח מיי' פ"ה שם הלכה טו ועז סמג עשין כז טוש"ע או"ח סימן קפו סעיף ב:
לד (ט) מיי' פ"ד מהל' ק"ש הלכה ח סמג עשין יח טוש"ע או"ח סימן פח:
לה (י) טוש"ע או"ח סי' סב סעיף ג (ד):

**רב נסים גאון**

לה זותים שכבשן בטרפיהן זו המשנה בתחלת פרק ב' דמסכת עוקצין: ורב יהודה כי הוה שליף חד מסאניה אתי מיטרא. איתיה לפירושה במסכת תענית בפרק סדר תעניות האלו (דף כד) והיינו דאמרי' רב יהודה חזנהו להנהו בי תרי דהוו קא פרצי בריפתא אמר שמע מינה איכא שבעא בעלמא יהב עיניה הוה כפנא אמרו ליה רבנן לרב כהנא בריה דרב נחוניא שמעיה מר דשכיח קמיה נעשייה דליפוק לשוקא עשייה נפק לשוקא חזא כינופיא אמר להו מאי האי [א"ל] אכוספא דתמרי דקא מיזדבן אמר שמע מינה איכא כפנא אמר ליה לשמעיה שלוף לי מסאני שלף ליה חד מסאנא בעא למישלף אידך אתא אליהו כו' ובפרק כל היד המרבה לבדוק דמסכת נדה (דף יג) אמרי' שאני רב יהודה דאימתא דמאריה עליה (קרי) [דקרי] עליה שמואל עליה דרב יהודה אין זה ילוד אשה: ר' יוחנן הוה אזיל ויתיב אשערי טבילה אמר כי סלקן בנות ישראל מטבילה נפגען בי דניהוי להו בני שפירי כוותי. אתה מוצא שהזכירו שבח יופיו בבבא מציעא בפרק השוכר את הפועלים (דף פד) אמר ר' יוחנן אנא אשתיירי משפירי ירושלים האי מאן דבעי מיחזי שופריה דר' יוחנן נייתי כסא דכספא מבי סלקי כו': קריאת שמע ותפילין הויין להו מצות עשה שהזמן גרמא וכל מצות עשה שהזמן גרמא נשים פטורות וכל מצות עשה שלא הזמן גרמא אחד אנשים ואחד נשים חייבין. פירשו בברייתא (קדושין דף לג) איזו היא מצות עשה שהזמן גרמא סוכה ולולב שופר וציצית ואיזו היא מצות עשה שלא הזמן גרמא מזוזה ומעקה ומציאת אבדה ושילוח הקן: אקיש מזוזה לתלמוד תורה מה תלמוד תורה נשים פטורי אף מזוזה נמי פטורי קמ"ל. הא נמי איתה בפירקא קמא דקידושין (דף לד) דאקשינן הרי תלמוד תורה פריה ורביה ופדיון הבן דמצות עשה שלא הזמן גרמא ונשים פטורות ואמרינן (שם דף ל) ותלמוד תורה גופה מנלן דכתיב ולמדתם אותם את בניכם ולא בנותיכם: כדאשכחן בסיני דבר דבור אסור הרהור מותר. במסכת שבת בפרק ר' עקיבא (דף פו) אמרי' אמר ר' בר אבין ור' חנינא בר אבין דאמרי תרוייהו ניתנה תורה לטבולי יום ואמר עלה אמימר ראוה קאמינא ואעפ"כ מי שאירע לו קרי בלילי ו' בסיון דההיא שתא כבר שמע את הדברות ולא סגיא דלא הרהר ר

**מסורת הש"ס**

קדושין דף כט. [וש"נ]
[שבועות דף כ: ע"ש]
[נ"ל ואי]
ר"ה דף כט.
[עי' תוס' לעיל טו וד"ה ר' יהודה]

**הגהות הב"ח**

(א) גמ' דרחמי נינהו מהו דתימא וכו' קמ"ל וכו' נ"ב ברוב הספרים גרסי ליה: (ב) שם בפרק' אחרינ'. נ"ב בהל' דרך ארץ בפרק כ"ב.

**גליון הש"ס**

גמ' ומן התפלין פ' עיין תוס' עירובין דף צו ע"א ד"ה לא ס"ד: ובמזוזה פשיטא. עיין קדף י"ח ע"ב ד"ה ... : שם בבהמ"ז דאורייתא או דרבנן: שם שאכל שיעורא דרבנן: שם לאתויי דרבנן. עיין תוס' ד"ה הא לא ... 

והרי תפלה דדבר שהצבור עסוקין בו, ותנן: היה עומד בתפלה ונזכר שהוא בעל קרי – לא יפסיק אלא יקצר, טעמא דאתחיל, הא לא אתחיל – לא יתחיל! שאני תפלה, דלית בה מלכות שמים. והרי ברכת המזון לאחריו, דלית בה מלכות שמים, ותנן: על המזון מברך לאחריו ואינו מברך לפניו! אלא: ק"ש וברכת המזון – דאורייתא, ותפלה – דרבנן. § אמר רב יהודה: (א) מנין לברכת המזון לאחריה מן התורה – שנאמר: "ואכלת ושבעת וברכת". (דברים ח) מנין לברכת התורה לפניה מן התורה – שנאמר: "כי שם ה' אקרא הבו גדל לאלהינו". (שם לב) אמר ר' יוחנן: למדנו ברכת התורה לאחריה מן ברכת המזון מקל וחומר, וברכת המזון לפניה מן ברכת התורה מקל וחומר; ברכת התורה לאחריה מן ברכת המזון מקל וחומר: ומה מזון שאין טעון לפניו – טעון לאחריו, תורה שטעונה לפניה – אינו דין שטעונה לאחריה; וברכת המזון לפניה מן ברכת התורה מק"ו: ומה תורה שאין טעונה לאחריה – טעונה לפניה, מזון שהוא טעון לאחריו – אינו דין שיהא טעון לפניו. איכא למפרך: (ב) מה למזון – שכן נהנה, ומה לתורה – שכן חיי עולם! ועוד, תנן: על המזון מברך לאחריו ואינו מברך לפניו! תיובתא. § אמר רב יהודה: ספק קרא קריאת שמע ספק לא קרא – אינו חוזר וקורא, ספק אמר "אמת ויציב" ספק לא אמר – חוזר ואומר "אמת ויציב". מאי טעמא – קריאת שמע דרבנן, 'אמת ויציב' דאורייתא. מתיב רב יוסף: "ובשכבך ובקומך"! (שם ו) אמר ליה אביי: ההוא בדברי תורה כתיב. תנן: בעל קרי מהרהר בלבו ואינו מברך לא לפניה ולא לאחריה, ועל המזון – מברך לאחריו ואינו מברך לפניו. ואי ס"ד "אמת ויציב" דאורייתא – לברוך לאחריה! מאי טעמא מברך – אי משום יציאת מצרים – הא אדכר ליה בקריאת שמע. ונימא הא ולא לבעי הא! – קריאת שמע עדיפא, דאית בה תרתי. ור' אלעזר אמר: א ספק קרא קריאת שמע ספק לא קרא – חוזר וקורא ק"ש, ספק התפלל ספק לא התפלל – אינו חוזר ומתפלל. ורבי יוחנן אמר: * ב ולואי שיתפלל אדם כל היום כולו. § ואמר רב יהודה אמר שמואל: ג היה עומד בתפלה ונזכר שהתפלל – פוסק, ואפילו באמצע ברכה. – איני?! והאמר רב נחמן: כי הוינן בי רבה בר אבוה, בען מיניה, הני בני בי רב דטעו ומדכרי דחול בשבת, מהו שיגמרו? ואמר לן: ד גומרין כל אותה ברכה! – הכי השתא! התם – גברא בר חיובא הוא, ורבנן הוא דלא אטרחוהו משום כבוד שבת, אבל הכא – הא צלי ליה. ואמר רב יהודה אמר שמואל: ה התפלל ונכנס לביהכ"נ ומצא צבור שמתפללין, אם יכול לחדש בה דבר – יחזור ויתפלל, ואם לאו – אל יחזור ויתפלל. וצריכא: דאי אשמעינן קמייתא, ה"מ – יחיד ויחיד,

או

רש"י

אלא יקצר. כל ברכה וברכה: דלית בה מלכות שמים. אין "מלך העולם" בברכות של י"ח: ה"ג: והרי ברכת המזון לפניה דאית בה מלכות שמים כו'. לישנא אחרינא: שאני תפלה דלית בה מלכות שמים. קבלת מלכות שמים, כדאיתא בק"ש שמקבל עליו את השם לאדון ולמלך מיוחד. ולהאי לישנא גרסינן: והרי ברכת המזון לאחריו דלית בה מלכות שמים. ולשון זה נראה שהוא עיקר, מדמשני ליה: אלא ק"ש וברכת המזון דאורייתא והאי בלאחריו עסקינן. ולי ללישנא קמא – הא לא איירי בברכת המזון לאחריו בלאתקפתיה, דלהדרי תלמודא עילויה. אלא ק"ש וברכת המזון דאורייתא כו'. ואית דגרסי הכא בלשון קושיא: ק"ש דרבנן היא, אלא ק"ש דאית בה מלכות שמים, וברכת המזון דאורייתא – לאפוקי תפלה דרבנן, ואין בה מלכות שמים. למאן דגרס הכי מפרשינן לקמן "בשכבך ובקומך" – בדברי תורה כתיב: כי שם ה' אקרא. כשבא משה לפתוח בדברי שירה אמר להם לישראל: אני אברך תחלה, ואתם ענו אחרי אמן. "כי שם ה' אקרא" בברכה, אתם – "הבו גודל לאלהינו" באמן. הכי מפרשי לה במסכת יומא (דף לז.). שאינו טעון לפניו. כלומר: שאין עליו לו מקרא מפורש לברך לפניו: טעון לאחריו. כדכתיב "ואכלת ושבעת וברכת": תורה שטעונה לפניה. כדאמרן: איכא למפרך. בתרוייהו. כשאתה בא ללמוד תורה מן המזון איכא למפרך: מה למזון – שכן נהנה. וכשאתה בא ללמוד מזון מן התורה, איכא למפרך: מה לתורה – שכן חיי העולם הבא: ק"ש דרבנן. לקמן פריך לה: אמת ויציב דאורייתא היא. שמזכיר בה יציאת מצרים, דחיובה דאורייתא היא, דכתיב "למען תזכור את יום צאתך מארץ מצרים" (דברים טז): דאית בה תרתי. יציאת מצרים ומלכות שמים: חוזר וקורא ק"ש. קסבר: ק"ש דאורייתא היא: ולואי שיתפלל אדם כל היום. בהלכות גדולות פסק: הלכה כרבי יוחנן בספק, והלכה כשמואל בודאי התפלל: מהו שיגמרו. את הברכה אם נזכר באמצע הברכה באחת מן הברכות שטעה: יחיד ויחיד. כשהתפלל תחלה היה יחיד, וכשנכנס שהתפלל והתחיל להתפלל היה ביחיד:

או

תוספות

והרי תפלה דדבר שהצבור כו'. וא"ת: אמאי שבק בבא דק"ש דקתני בגווה, דדבר שהצבור עסוקין בו וקתני אינו מברך לפניה כו'? וי"ל: משום רבותא דתפלה, פריך מיניה, אע"ג דתפלה מעומד ונראה לכל שאין זה עומד כמותם אפילו הכי אמרינן: אם לא התחיל לא יתחיל. וא"ת: כיון דלא ידע טעמא דבסמוך, יקשה גם לרבינא מה לי ק"ש וברכת המזון יותר מתפלה? וי"ל: לרבינא ניחא, כיון דהרהור כדבור דמי – יש להצריכו בק"ש ובברכת המזון שהם מדאורייתא, יותר מתפלה דרבנן. אבל לרב חסדא, כיון דהרהור אינו כלום, רק שלא יהא יושב ובטל – מה לי ק"ש מה לי תפלה: הא אי לא אתחיל לא יתחיל. וא"ת: אימא דלדבור קאמר, הא בהרהור שפיר דמי? וי"ל: דמשמע דלא יתחיל – אפי' בהרהור, מדלא קאמר: יקצר בדבור או יהרהר בארוכות: הכי גרסי': אלא ק"ש וברכת המזון דאורייתא ותפלה דרבנן, ולא גרסינן מידי בתר הכי עד אמר רב יהודה אמר רב. פי' הקונטרס: ק"ש דאורייתא כיון שאינו אומר 'אמת ויציב' כדפי' במתניתין. ויש ספרים גורסים *ק"ש דרבנן הוא. ומשני: אלא ק"ש אית בה מלכות שמים, וברכת המזון דאורייתא ותפלה דרבנן. וכן הגירסא בפ"ה. וקשה, דבמתניתין פי' דק"ש דאורייתא לכולי עלמא, כיון שלא אמר 'אמת ויציב', דבהכי מיירי מתניתין. וגם יש ספרים גורסים שאני תפלה דלית בה מלכות שמים. והרי ברכת המזון דלית בה מלכות שמים – ותנן: על המזון מברך לאחריו וכו'; אלא היינו טעמא דק"ש אית בה מלכות שמים, וברכת המזון דאורייתא, ותפלה דרבנן. וגם על גירסא זו קשה כדפירש'. ספק לא אמר אמת ויציב – חוזר. ותימה: הא ע"כ צריך לומר שהוא מסופק גם מק"ש. שאם היה ברור לו מק"ש וספק מ'אמת ויציב' – לא יהיה מן התורה, כיון שהזכיר יציאת מצרים בק"ש. ואם כן, הואיל ומסופק משניהם יחזור לק"ש דאית בה תרתי, מלכות שמים ויציאת מצרים, דהכי עדיף מלומר 'אמת ויציב', דליכא אלא חדא כדאמר בסמוך גבי מתני'. ואומר ר"י: דודאי מתני' גבי בעל קרי שידענו בו שלא אמר ק"ש ולא 'אמת ויציב' כלל, ואנו רוצים להתיר לו, הלכך טוב הוא יותר שיאמר ק"ש דאיכא תרתי. אבל הכא, שהוא ספק אם אמר 'אמת ויציב', ומספקא ליה אם אמר שניהם כדפרישית – טוב הוא יותר שיאמר 'אמת ויציב' מלומר ק"ש. דכשיאמר 'אמת ויציב' שמא יש לתלות שתקן הכל. דאם קרא כבר 'אמת ויציב' – גם קרא ק"ש כבר, דמסתמא התפלל כדרך תפלה ק"ש ואח"כ 'אמת ויציב' – ויצא ידי שתיהן. וכי נמי תימא דלא אמר כבר שתיהן – מ"מ שמא אמר ק"ש ולא אמר 'אמת ויציב' שזה יכול להיות, ועתה כשיאמר 'אמת ויציב' – נמצא שהשלים הכל. וכי תימא: שמא לא קרא לא זה ולא זה? כיון דספיקא הוא – כולי האי לא אטרחוהו רבנן לחזור שניהם. אבל אם יאמר ק"ש – אין זו תקנה גמורה כל כך, דשמא קרא ק"ש אחרת ולא יצא כלל במה שעושה עתה. ואם ברור שלא אמר כבר ק"ש, אם כן לא אמר נמי 'אמת ויציב' – שאין רגילות לומר 'אמת ויציב' בלא ק"ש, ואם כן כשיאמר מעתה ק"ש לא תקן כלל ולא יצא מדי ספקו. עוד אמר הר"ר שמעון דמיירי שפיר שאינו מסופק אלא מ'אמת ויציב' אבל ברור הוא שקרא ק"ש. ואפילו הכי הוי 'אמת ויציב' דאורייתא, שר"ל ספק לא אמר 'אמת ויציב' עם פרשת ציצית שמסופק אי לא אמר לא פרשת ציצית ולא 'אמת ויציב' ואם כן לא הזכיר כלל יציאת מצרים וכולה מילתא דיציאת מצרים קרי ליה 'אמת ויציב', לפי דטעם 'אמת ויציב' הוי משום יציאת מצרים והלכך הוי פרשת ציצית בכלל 'אמת ויציב': ההוא בדברי תורה כתיב. והא דאמרינן לעיל בפרק קמא (דף ג.): בערב משום דכתיב "ובשכבך" אסמכתא בעלמא הוא*:

ורבי יוחנן אמר: ולואי שיתפלל אדם כל היום. אומר ר"י דהלכה כרבי יוחנן, ודוקא בספק התפלל; אבל ודאי התפלל – לא. *תדע, דהא מסתמא לא פליג אהא דאמר רב יהודה אמר שמואל בסמוך ונזכר שהתפלל פוסק וכו'. וכן אם יכול לחדש דבר בתפלתו:

עין משפט נר מצוה

לו א מיי' פ"ב מהלכות ק"ש הלכה יג סמג עשין יט טוש"ע או"ח סימן סז:

לז ב ג מיי' פ"י מהל' תפלה הלכה ו סמג עשין יט טוש"ע או"ח סימן קז סעיף א:

לח ד מיי' שם הלכה ז סמג שם טוש"ע או"ח סי' רסח סעיף ב:

לט ה מיי' פ"א מהלכות תפלה הלכה ט סמג שם טוש"ע או"ח סימן קז סעיף א:

[עיין תוס' סוטה לב: ד"ה ורבי]

[ועי' תוס' סוטה לב ע"ב ד"ה ורבי ותוס' מנחות מג ע"ב ד"ה ואיזו]

גליון הש"ס

גמ' אינו חוזר וקורא. עי' ברבינו יונה לעיל פ"ב י"א ד"ה באמצע: שם מ"ט ק"ש דרבנן. עי' בב"ק פז ע"א תוס' ד"ה וכן היה ר"י פוטרו מכל המצות האמורות בתורה ובסוטה לב ע"ב תוס' ד"ה ורבי ובמנחות מג ע"ב תוס' ד"ה ואיזו: רש"י ד"ה שאינו כו' כלומר שלא מצינו. וכיוצא בזה בב"מ פח ע"ב ועיין קדושין טו ע"ב תוס' ד"ה א"ק: תוס' ד"ה ור"י כו' אבל ודאי התפלל. עי' לקמן כט ע"א תוס' ד"ה מפני:

מסורת הש"ס

לקמן דף כב:

[יומא] פ' בא ולקמן דף מח: ע"ש

הגהות הב"ח

(א) גמ' אמר ר' יהודה מנין לברכת [המזון]: (ב) שם מה למזון. לקמן בפ' שלשה סוף דף מח:

[רב] יהודה אמר [ליתא ...]ן איתא ברי"ף וברא"ש]

פסחים דף נד:

לקמן כט. ד"ה מפני]

עד

מ א [טוש"ע או"ח סי' קט סעיף א]:
ב מיי' פ"י מהלכות תפלה הלכה טז סמג עשין יט טור שו"ע או"ח סימן קט סעיף א:
מא ג מיי' פ"ח שם הלכה ו טור שו"ע או"ח סימן נה סעיף א:
מב ד מיי' פ"י שם הלכה טז טור שו"ע או"ח סימן קד סעיף ז:
מג ה מיי' פי"א מהל' עו"ג הלכה טו סמג לאוין נה טור יו"ד סימן קטע:
מד ו מיי' פ"ב מהלכות איסורי ביאה הי"ג טוש"ע אה"ע סי' טו:



תורה אור

אוֹ צִבּוּר וְצִבּוּר, אֲבָל יָחִיד לְגַבֵּי צִבּוּר כְּמַאן דְּלָא צַלֵּי דָּמֵי – קמ"ל; וְאִי אַשְׁמְעִינַן הָכָא – מִשּׁוּם דְּלָא אַתְחֵיל בָּהּ, אֲבָל הָתָם דְּאַתְחֵיל בָּהּ, אֵימָא לָא – צְרִיכָא.§ אָמַר רַב הוּנָא: הַנִּכְנָס לְבֵית הַכְּנֶסֶת וּמָצָא צִבּוּר שֶׁמִּתְפַּלְּלִין, אאִם יָכוֹל לְהַתְחִיל וְלִגְמוֹר עַד שֶׁלֹּא יַגִּיעַ ש"ץ לְ"מוֹדִים" – יִתְפַּלֵּל, וְאִם לָאו – אַל יִתְפַּלֵּל; ריב"ל אָמַר: באִם יָכוֹל לְהַתְחִיל וְלִגְמוֹר עַד שֶׁלֹּא יַגִּיעַ ש"צ לִקְדוּשָּׁה – יִתְפַּלֵּל, וְאִם לָאו – אַל יִתְפַּלֵּל. בְּמַאי קָא מִפַּלְגִי? מָר סָבַר: יָחִיד אוֹמֵר קְדוּשָּׁה; וּמָר סָבַר: אֵין יָחִיד אוֹמֵר קְדוּשָּׁה. *וְכֵן אָמַר רַב אַדָּא בַּר אַהֲבָה: *מִנַּיִן שֶׁאֵין הַיָּחִיד אוֹמֵר קְדוּשָּׁה – שֶׁנֶּאֱמַר: °"וְנִקְדַּשְׁתִּי בְּתוֹךְ בְּנֵי יִשְׂרָאֵל" – גכָּל דָּבָר שֶׁבִּקְדוּשָּׁה לֹא יְהֵא פָּחוֹת מֵעֲשָׂרָה. (ויקרא כב) מַאי מַשְׁמַע? דְּתָנֵי *רַבְּנַאי אָחוּהַ דְּרַבִּי חִיָּיא בַּר אַבָּא: אַתְיָא "תּוֹךְ" "תּוֹךְ". כְּתִיב הָכָא: "וְנִקְדַּשְׁתִּי בְּתוֹךְ בְּנֵי יִשְׂרָאֵל" וּכְתִיב הָתָם: °"הִבָּדְלוּ מִתּוֹךְ הָעֵדָה הַזֹּאת", (במדבר טז) *מַה לְּהַלָּן עֲשָׂרָה, אַף כָּאן עֲשָׂרָה. וּדְכוּלֵּי עָלְמָא מִיהַת מִפְסַק לָא פָּסֵיק. אִיבַּעְיָא לְהוּ: מַהוּ לְהַפְסִיק לְ"יְהֵא שְׁמוֹ הַגָּדוֹל מְבוֹרָךְ"? כִּי אֲתָא רַב דִּימִי אֲמַר, ר' יְהוּדָה *ור"ש תַּלְמִידֵי דְּרַבִּי יוֹחָנָן אָמְרִי: לַכֹּל אֵין מַפְסִיקִין, חוּץ מִן "יְהֵא שְׁמוֹ הַגָּדוֹל מְבוֹרָךְ", שֶׁאֲפִילּוּ עוֹסֵק בְּמַעֲשֵׂה מֶרְכָּבָה – פּוֹסֵק. וְלֵית דהִלְכְתָא כְּוָותֵיהּ.§ "ר' יְהוּדָה אוֹמֵר, מְבָרֵךְ לִפְנֵיהֶם וּלְאַחֲרֵיהֶם". לְמֵימְרָא דְּקָסָבַר רַבִּי יְהוּדָה בַּעַל קֶרִי מוּתָּר בְּדִבְרֵי תוֹרָה? וְהָאָמַר ריב"ל: מִנַּיִן לְבַעַל קֶרִי שֶׁאָסוּר בְּדִבְרֵי תוֹרָה – *שֶׁנֶּאֱמַר: °"וְהוֹדַעְתָּם לְבָנֶיךָ וְלִבְנֵי בָנֶיךָ" (דברים ד) וְסָמִיךְ לֵיהּ "יוֹם אֲשֶׁר עָמַדְתָּ וגו'" – מַה לְּהַלָּן בַּעֲלֵי קְרָיִין אֲסוּרִין, אַף כָּאן – בַּעֲלֵי קְרָיִין אֲסוּרִין! וְכִי תֵּימָא: *רַבִּי יְהוּדָה *לָא דָּרֵישׁ סְמוּכִים, וְהָאָמַר *רַב יוֹסֵף: אֲפִילּוּ מַאן דְּלָא דָּרֵישׁ סְמוּכִים בְּכָל הַתּוֹרָה – בְּמִשְׁנֵה תוֹרָה דָּרֵישׁ. דְּהָא רַבִּי יְהוּדָה לָא דָּרֵישׁ סְמוּכִין בְּכָל הַתּוֹרָה כּוּלָּהּ, וּבְמִשְׁנֵה תוֹרָה דָּרֵישׁ. וּבְכָל הַתּוֹרָה כּוּלָּהּ מְנָא לָן דְּלָא דָּרֵישׁ – דְּתַנְיָא, *בֶּן עַזַּאי אוֹמֵר: נֶאֱמַר °"מְכַשֵּׁפָה לֹא תְחַיֶּה" (שמות כב) וְנֶאֱמַר "כָּל שׁוֹכֵב עִם בְּהֵמָה מוֹת יוּמָת", סְמָכוֹ עִנְיָן לוֹ, לוֹמַר: מַה שּׁוֹכֵב עִם בְּהֵמָה בִּסְקִילָה – האַף מְכַשֵּׁפָה נַמִּי בִּסְקִילָה; אֲמַר לֵיהּ ר' יְהוּדָה: וְכִי מִפְּנֵי שֶׁסְּמָכוֹ עִנְיָן לוֹ נוֹצִיא לָזֶה לִסְקִילָה?! אֶלָּא: אוֹב וְיִדְּעוֹנִי בִּכְלַל כָּל הַמְכַשְּׁפִים הָיוּ, וְלָמָּה יָצְאוּ – לְהַקִּישׁ לָהֶן, וְלוֹמַר לְךָ: מָה אוֹב וְיִדְּעוֹנִי בִּסְקִילָה – אַף מְכַשֵּׁפָה בִּסְקִילָה. וּבְמִשְׁנֵה תוֹרָה מְנָא לָן דְּדָרֵישׁ – דְּתַנְיָא, רַבִּי אֱלִיעֶזֶר אוֹמֵר: *ונוֹשֵׂא אָדָם אֲנוּסַת אָבִיו וּמְפוּתַּת אָבִיו, אֲנוּסַת בְּנוֹ וּמְפוּתַּת בְּנוֹ. ר' יְהוּדָה אוֹסֵר בַּאֲנוּסַת אָבִיו וּבִמְפוּתַּת אָבִיו. וְאָמַר רַב גִּידֵּל אָמַר רַב: מַאי טַעְמָא דר' יְהוּדָה, דִּכְתִיב: °"לֹא יִקַּח אִישׁ אֶת אֵשֶׁת אָבִיו וְלֹא יְגַלֶּה (אֶת) כְּנַף אָבִיו" (דברים כג) – כָּנָף שֶׁרָאָה אָבִיו לֹא יְגַלֶּה. וּמִמַּאי דְּבַאֲנוּסַת אָבִיו כְּתִיב – דִּסְמִיךְ לֵיהּ: "וְנָתַן הָאִישׁ הַשּׁוֹכֵב עִמָּהּ וגו'"! אָמְרִי: אִין, בְּמִשְׁנֵה תוֹרָה דָּרֵישׁ. וְהָנֵי סְמוּכִין מִבָּעֵי לֵיהּ לְאִידָךְ דריב"ל, דְּאָמַר ריב"ל: *כָּל הַמְלַמֵּד לִבְנוֹ תּוֹרָה – מַעֲלֶה עָלָיו הַכָּתוּב כְּאִלּוּ קִבְּלָהּ מֵהַר חוֹרֵב, שֶׁנֶּאֱמַר: °"וְהוֹדַעְתָּם לְבָנֶיךָ וְלִבְנֵי בָנֶיךָ", וּכְתִיב בָּתְרֵיהּ: "יוֹם אֲשֶׁר עָמַדְתָּ לִפְנֵי ה' אֱלֹהֶיךָ בְּחוֹרֵב".§ *תְּנַן: זָב שֶׁרָאָה קֶרִי, וְנִדָּה שֶׁפָּלְטָה שִׁכְבַת זֶרַע, הַמְשַׁמֶּשֶׁת וְרָאֲתָה *דָּם צְרִיכִין טְבִילָה; וְרַבִּי יְהוּדָה פּוֹטֵר. עַד כָּאן לֹא פָּטַר רַבִּי יְהוּדָה אֶלָּא בְּזָב שֶׁרָאָה קֶרִי – דְּמֵעִיקָּרָא לָאו בַּר טְבִילָה הוּא, אֲבָל בַּעַל קֶרִי גְּרֵידָא מְחַיֵּיב! וְכִי תֵּימָא, ה"ה דַּאֲפִילּוּ בַּעַל קֶרִי גְּרֵידָא נַמִּי פָּטַר רַבִּי יְהוּדָה; וְהַאי דְּקָא מִפַּלְגִי בְּזָב שֶׁרָאָה קֶרִי – לְהוֹדִיעֲךָ כֹּחָן דְּרַבָּנַן, אֵימָא סֵיפָא: הַמְשַׁמֶּשֶׁת וְרָאֲתָה *דָּם צְרִיכָה טְבִילָה, לְמַאן קָתָנֵי לַהּ? אִילֵימָא לְרַבָּנַן – פְּשִׁיטָא! הַשְׁתָּא וּמַה זָב שֶׁרָאָה קֶרִי דְּמֵעִיקָּרָא לָאו בַּר טְבִילָה הוּא – מְחַיְּיבִי רַבָּנַן, הַמְשַׁמֶּשֶׁת וְרָאֲתָה *דָּם – דְּמֵעִיקָּרָא בַּת טְבִילָה הִיא – לֹא כָּל שֶׁכֵּן! אֶלָּא לָאו ר' יְהוּדָה הִיא, וְדַוְקָא קָתָנֵי לַהּ

מְשַׁמֶּשֶׁת

או צבור וצבור. בין בראשונה בין בשניה היה עם הצבור, כגון עשרה אחר עשרה, וזה עמהם בשתיהן, ששכח שהתפלל עם הראשונים: רב הונא סבר. יחיד המתפלל עם הצבור אומר "קדוש". הלכך: אם לא גמר עד שלא יגיע ש"ץ ל"קדוש" – לית לן בה. אבל "מודים", אף על פי שיחיד אומר "מודים", אם אינו אומרו עם הצבור – הרואה את כולם כורעים והוא אינו כורע, נראה ככופר במי שחבריו משתחוין לו: מפסק לא פסיק. תפלתו לקדושה לענות עם הצבור, וכן ל"מודים": במשנה תורה דריש. והאי קרא במשנה תורה הוא נאמר: מכשפה לא תחיה. ולא פירש באיזו מיתה תמות, ונאמר אצלו "כל שוכב עם בהמה מות יומת": סמכו ענין לו. סמכתו פרשת "מכשפה לא תחיה" לשוכב עם בהמה: מה שוכב עם בהמה בסקילה. כדאמרינן לה בסנהדרין פרק "ד' מיתות" (דף נד:) בגזרה שוה ד"תהרוגו" דהכא מ"כי הרוג תהרגנו" דמסית, אף מכשף בסקילה: אמר ליה רבי יהודה: וכי מפני שסמכו הענין. לשוכב עם בהמה, נוציא זה המכשף לסקילה שהיא חמורה מכל מיתות שבתורה? אלא מקרא מפורש יש לו במקום אחר שהוא בסקילה: אוב וידעוני בכלל. "לא תחיה" דכל המכשפים היו, ולמה יצאו בפני עצמן כשהפרישן לסקילה, כדכתיב "באבן ירגמו אותם דמיהם בם" – להקיש אליהם את כל הכלל. שזו מדה בתורה, שכל דבר שהיה בכלל ויצא מן הכלל ללמד – לא ללמד על עצמו יצא, אלא ללמד על הכלל כולו יצא: זב שראה קרי וכו'. לענין טבילה שתקן עזרא לבעלי קריין לעסוק בתורה קאי, ולשאר טמאים לא הוצרך. וקאמר הכא: דאם יש לו טומאה אחרת עם הקרי, שאינו יכול לצאת ממנה בטבילה זו כגון זב ונדה שהם טמאים טומאת שבעה – אפילו הכי צריך לטבול לקריו קודם שיעסוק בתורה: פולטת שכבת זרע. הרי היא כבעל קרי: ורבי יהודה פוטר.(א) קס"ד דאין טבילה זו מטהרתו מכל וכל: המשמשת למאן קתני לה. להשמיענו כח מי הוצרכו לחלוק בה: אילימא לרבנן. להודיעך כחן דמחייבי בה: השתא זב שראה קרי. שקדמתו טומאת הזיבה מעיקרא: דמעיקרא. בשעה שראה קרי לאו בר טבילה הוא, ומחייבי ליה רבנן טבילה לקרי לדברי תורה:

משמשת

עד שלא יגיע שליח צבור למודים. וטעמא – לפי שצריך לשוח עם הצבור, שלא יראה ככופר במי שהצבור משתחוין לו. והוא הדין נמי אם יגיע ל'מודים' כששליח צבור יגיע ל'מודים', דשפיר דמי – כיון שהוא משתחוה עם חביריו, אבל אין גמרא פסיקא ליה כי האי גוונא. אבל אין נראה דמשום 'מודים' דרבנן נקט הכי שמלוה לענות – שזה לא מצינו לו עיקר בגמ'. ור"ת היה רגיל כשהיה מתפלל ביחיד, כשהחזן מגיע ל'מודים' – היה כורע עם הקהל בלא אמירה כלל. ודוקא באמצע ברכה, אבל בסוף ברכה – לא, דאמר לקמן (דף לד.) דאסור לשחות בסוף כל ברכה וברכה. מיהו, לכתחלה אין לעשות כן, כדמשמע הכא. וכתב רש"י בסוכה פרק "לולב הגזול" (דף לח:): דאדם המתפלל, ושמע מפי החזן קדיש או קדושה – אינו יכול להפסיק ולענות עם הצבור, אלא ישתוק ויתכוין מעט דשומע כעונה. וי"ל: דלכתחלה אין לעשות כן, דענייה חשיבא טפי הדור מלוה. ור"ת ור"י היו אומרים: דאדרבה, אי שומע כעונה – הוי הפסקה אם שותק. ומ"מ, נהגו העם לשתוק ולשמוע, וגדול המנהג. בירושלמי פרק "תפלת השחר" קאמר: לא התפלל(ב) ובא ומצאן מתפללים מוסף, אם היה יודע שיהיה מתפלל וגומר עד שלא יתחיל ש"ץ כדי לענות אמן – מתפלל, אם לאו – לא יתפלל. באיזה אמן אמרו? פליגי ביה תרי אמוראי, חד אמר: באמן של 'האל הקדוש' וחד אמר: באמן של 'שומע תפלה'. ולא פליגי, כאן – בחול, כאן – בשבת. והא דאמרינן באמן של 'שומע תפלה' – היינו בחול. לכך יש ליזהר לענות אמן ב'האל הקדוש', וגם לענות אמן ב'שומע תפלה'. ומתוך הירושלמי משמע שהיו רגילין לומר י"ח ברכות שלמות במוסף של חול, כגון בר"ח ובחול המועד, ומיהו, אנן סמכינן אהא דאמר פרק "תפלת השחר", (לקמן דף כט.) דקאמר תמני סרי תקון תשסרי לא תקון. ומה שאנו אומרים 'עננו' בין גואל לרופא לא קשה, שאינו אלא לש"ץ, אבל יחיד כוללה ב'ש"ת'. ועוד אומר הר"ר חיים: דאיתא בתוספתא (דפ' ת"ה) בהדיא כמנהגנו, דקאמר התם: ימים שיש בהן קרבן מוסף – כגון ר"ח וח"ה ערבית ושחרית – מתפלל י"ח שלמות ואומר מעין המאורע בעבודה, ואם לא אמר – מחזירים אותו. ובמוספים מתפלל שבע, ואומר קדושת היום באמצע, ובירושלמי נמי, י"ל דטעות סופר הוא, ול"ג של מוסף. אלא: בא ומצאן מתפללין. וכן משמע בירושלמי "פרק מי שמתו" דגם זו המימרא כתובה שם ולא הזכיר של מוסף כלל: אין יחיד מתפלל קדושה. וכן הלכה. אבל המתפלל י"ח עם החזן, לכשיגיע ש"ץ לקדושה יאמר עם השליח צבור "נקדש", וכל הקדושה משלם יכול לענות עם הצבור, דאין זה קרוי יחיד:

ונחזי

## רב נסים גאון

ר' יהודה דלא דריש סמוכין בכל התורה ובמשנה תורה דריש. פירשו לטעמא דמילתא בפרק ט"ו נשים (דף ד) ואמרי ובמשנה תורה מאי טעמא דריש איבעית אימא משום דמוכח ואיבעית אימא משום דמופנה:

[אולי צ"ל ור"ש בן לקיש וע' כתובות קיא:]

[עי' תוס' יבמות דף ד. ד"ה וכי מפני ותוס' קדושין נג. ד"ה וסמיך ליה]

## הגהות הב"ח

(א) רש"י ד"ה ור' יהודה פוטר דקסבר לאין: (ב) תוס' ד"ה עד וכו' בירושלמי וכו' לא התפלל שחרית ובא:

[תיבת וכן ליתא מגילה דף כג:]

[שם ע"ש סנה' כ

[נ"ל ואתיא עד דכתיב עד מה הרעה הזאת כ וכו' כך איתא בו

[ע' תוספות ב"ק אתא]

[פסחים כח:]

יבמות דף ד.

שם סנהדרין דף

יבמות ד. לז. וע"

דברים כג

[קדו' ל. ע"ש]

שם ד

לקמן כו.

[נ"ל נדה]

[נ"ל נדה]

מְשַׁמֶּשֶׁת וְרָאֲתָה נִדָּה אֵינָה צְרִיכָה טְבִילָה, אֲבָל בַּעַל קֶרִי גְּרֵידָא – מְחַיֵּיב! לָא תֵּימָא "מְבָרֵךְ" אֶלָּא "מְהַרְהֵר". וּמִי אִית לֵיהּ לְרַבִּי יְהוּדָה הִרְהוּר?! וְהָתַנְיָא: בַּעַל קֶרִי שֶׁאֵין לוֹ מַיִם לִטְבּוֹל – קוֹרֵא קְרִיאַת שְׁמַע, וְאֵינוֹ מְבָרֵךְ לֹא לְפָנֶיהָ וְלֹא לְאַחֲרֶיהָ, וְאוֹכֵל פִּתּוֹ וּמְבָרֵךְ לְאַחֲרֶיהָ וְאֵינוֹ מְבָרֵךְ לְפָנֶיהָ, אֲבָל מְהַרְהֵר בְּלִבּוֹ וְאֵינוֹ מוֹצִיא בִּשְׂפָתָיו, דִּבְרֵי רַבִּי מֵאִיר. רַבִּי יְהוּדָה אוֹמֵר: בֵּין כָּךְ וּבֵין כָּךְ מוֹצִיא בִּשְׂפָתָיו. אָמַר רַב נַחְמָן בַּר יִצְחָק: עֲשָׂאָן ר' יְהוּדָה כְּהִלְכוֹת דֶּרֶךְ אֶרֶץ.§ דְּתַנְיָא:* °"וְהוֹדַעְתָּם לְבָנֶיךָ וְלִבְנֵי בָנֶיךָ", וּכְתִיב בָּתְרֵיהּ "יוֹם אֲשֶׁר עָמַדְתָּ לִפְנֵי ה' אֱלֹהֶיךָ בְּחֹרֵב", מַה לְּהַלָּן בְּאֵימָה וּבְיִרְאָה וּבִרְתֵת וּבְזִיעַ אַף כָּאן בְּאֵימָה וּבְיִרְאָה וּבִרְתֵת וּבְזִיעַ; מִכָּאן אָמְרוּ: *הַזָּבִים וְהַמְּצוֹרָעִים וּבָאִין עַל נִדּוֹת – מוּתָּרִים לִקְרוֹת בַּתּוֹרָה וּבַנְּבִיאִים וּבַכְּתוּבִים, לִשְׁנוֹת בְּמִשְׁנָה וּגְמָרָא וּבַהֲלָכוֹת וּבָאַגָּדוֹת, אֲבָל בַּעֲלֵי קְרָיִין אֲסוּרִים; רַבִּי יוֹסֵי אוֹמֵר: שׁוֹנֶה הוּא בִּרְגִילִיּוֹת וּבִלְבַד שֶׁלֹּא *יַצִּיעַ אֶת הַמִּשְׁנָה; רַבִּי יוֹנָתָן בֶּן יוֹסֵף אוֹמֵר: מַצִּיעַ הוּא אֶת הַמִּשְׁנָה וְאֵינוֹ מַצִּיעַ אֶת (א) הַגְּמָרָא; רַבִּי נָתָן בֶּן *אֲבִישָׁלוֹם אוֹמֵר: אַף מַצִּיעַ אֶת הַגְּמָרָא וּבִלְבַד שֶׁלֹּא יֹאמַר אַזְכָּרוֹת שֶׁבּוֹ; רַבִּי יוֹחָנָן הַסַּנְדְּלָר תַּלְמִידוֹ שֶׁל רַבִּי עֲקִיבָא מִשּׁוּם ר"ע אוֹמֵר: לֹא יִכָּנֵס לַמִּדְרָשׁ כָּל עִיקָּר וְאָמְרִי לַהּ: לֹא יִכָּנֵס לְבֵית הַמִּדְרָשׁ כָּל עִיקָּר; ר' יְהוּדָה אוֹמֵר: שׁוֹנֶה הוּא בְּהִלְכוֹת דֶּרֶךְ אֶרֶץ. מַעֲשֶׂה בְּרַבִּי יְהוּדָה שֶׁרָאָה קֶרִי וְהָיָה מְהַלֵּךְ עַל גַּב הַנָּהָר. אָמְרוּ לוֹ תַּלְמִידָיו: רַבֵּינוּ, שְׁנֵה לָנוּ פֶּרֶק אֶחָד בְּהִלְכוֹת דֶּרֶךְ אֶרֶץ! יָרַד וְטָבַל וְשָׁנָה לָהֶם. אָמְרוּ לוֹ: לֹא כָּךְ לִמַּדְתָּנוּ רַבֵּינוּ: שׁוֹנֶה הוּא בְּהִלְכוֹת דֶּרֶךְ אֶרֶץ?! אָמַר לָהֶם: אע"פ שֶׁמֵּיקֵל אֲנִי עַל אֲחֵרִים, מַחְמִיר אֲנִי עַל עַצְמִי.§ תַּנְיָא, ר' יְהוּדָה בֶּן בְּתֵירָא הָיָה אוֹמֵר: *אֵין דִּבְרֵי תוֹרָה מְקַבְּלִין טוּמְאָה. מַעֲשֶׂה בְּתַלְמִיד אֶחָד שֶׁהָיָה מְגַמְגֵּם לְמַעְלָה מֵרַבִּי יְהוּדָה בֶּן בְּתֵירָא. אָמַר לֵיהּ: בְּנִי, פְּתַח פִּיךָ וְיָאִירוּ דְּבָרֶיךָ; שֶׁאֵין דִּבְרֵי תוֹרָה מְקַבְּלִין טוּמְאָה, שֶׁנֶּאֱמַר °"הֲלֹא כֹה דְבָרִי כָּאֵשׁ נְאֻם ה'" מָה אֵשׁ אֵינוֹ מְקַבֵּל טוּמְאָה אַף דִּבְרֵי תוֹרָה אֵינָן מְקַבְּלִין טוּמְאָה.§ אָמַר מָר: מַצִּיעַ אֶת הַמִּשְׁנָה וְאֵינוֹ מַצִּיעַ אֶת הַגְּמָרָא. מְסַיַּיע לֵיהּ לְרַבִּי אֶלְעַאי; דְּאָמַר רַבִּי אֶלְעַאי אָמַר ר' אַחָא בַּר יַעֲקֹב מִשּׁוּם רַבֵּינוּ: הֲלָכָה, מַצִּיעַ אֶת הַמִּשְׁנָה וְאֵינוֹ מַצִּיעַ אֶת הַגְּמָרָא. כְּתַנָּאֵי: מַצִּיעַ אֶת הַמִּשְׁנָה וְאֵינוֹ מַצִּיעַ אֶת הַגְּמָרָא, דִּבְרֵי רַבִּי מֵאִיר; רַבִּי יְהוּדָה בֶּן גַּמְלִיאֵל אוֹמֵר מִשּׁוּם רַבִּי חֲנִינָא בֶּן גַּמְלִיאֵל: זֶה וָזֶה אָסוּר; וְאָמְרֵי לַהּ: זֶה וָזֶה מוּתָּר. מ"ד זֶה וָזֶה אָסוּר – כְּרַבִּי יוֹחָנָן הַסַּנְדְּלָר, מ"ד זֶה וָזֶה מוּתָּר – כְּרַבִּי יְהוּדָה בֶּן בְּתֵירָא. *אָמַר רַב נַחְמָן בַּר יִצְחָק נָהוּג עָלְמָא כְּהָנֵי תְּלָת סָבֵי: כְּרַבִּי אֶלְעַאי בְּרֵאשִׁית הַגֵּז, כְּרַבִּי יֹאשִׁיָּה בְּכִלְאַיִם, כְּרַבִּי יְהוּדָה בֶּן בְּתֵירָא בד"ת. כְּרַבִּי אֶלְעַאי בְּרֵאשִׁית הַגֵּז – דְּתַנְיָא, *רַבִּי אֶלְעַאי אוֹמֵר: רֵאשִׁית הַגֵּז אֵינוֹ נוֹהֵג אֶלָּא בָּאָרֶץ. כְּרַבִּי יֹאשִׁיָּה בְּכִלְאַיִם – כִּדְכְתִיב: °"(כַּרְמְךָ) לֹא תִזְרַע [כַּרְמְךָ] כִּלְאָיִם", *רַבִּי יֹאשִׁיָּה אוֹמֵר: לְעוֹלָם *אֵינוֹ חַיָּיב עַד שֶׁיִּזְרַע חִטָּה וּשְׂעוֹרָה וְחַרְצָן בְּמַפּוֹלֶת יָד. כְּרַבִּי יְהוּדָה בֶּן בְּתֵירָא בְּדִבְרֵי תוֹרָה, דְּתַנְיָא, רַבִּי יְהוּדָה בֶּן בְּתֵירָא אוֹמֵר: אֵין דִּבְרֵי תוֹרָה מְקַבְּלִין טוּמְאָה.§ כִּי אֲתָא זְעֵירִי, אָמַר: בַּטְּלוּהָ לִטְבִילוּתָא, וְאָמְרִי לַהּ: בַּטְּלוּהָ לִנְטִילוּתָא. מַאן דְּאָמַר "בַּטְּלוּהָ לִטְבִילוּתָא" – כְּרַבִּי יְהוּדָה בֶּן בְּתֵירָא. מַאן דְּאָמַר "בַּטְּלוּהָ לִנְטִילוּתָא" – כִּי הָא *דְּרַב חִסְדָּא לָיֵיט אַמַּאן דִּמְהַדַּר אַמַּיָּא בְּעִידָּן צְלוֹתָא.§ תָּנוּ רַבָּנַן: בַּעַל קֶרִי שֶׁנִּתְּנוּ עָלָיו תִּשְׁעָה קַבִּין מַיִם – טָהוֹר; נַחוּם אִישׁ גַּם זוֹ לְחָשָׁהּ לְרַבִּי עֲקִיבָא, וְרַבִּי עֲקִיבָא לְחָשָׁהּ לְבֶן עַזַּאי, וּבֶן עַזַּאי יָצָא וּשְׁנָאָהּ לְתַלְמִידָיו בַּשּׁוּק. פְּלִיגִי בַּהּ תְּרֵי אָמוֹרָאֵי בְּמַעְרְבָא, רַבִּי יוֹסֵי בַּר אָבִין וְרַבִּי יוֹסֵי בַּר זְבִידָא: חַד תְּנֵי 'שְׁנָאָהּ' וְחַד תְּנֵי 'לְחָשָׁהּ'. מַאן דִּתְנֵי 'שְׁנָאָהּ' מִשּׁוּם בִּטּוּל תּוֹרָה, וּמִשּׁוּם בִּטּוּל פְּרִיָּה וּרְבִיָּה. וּמַאן דִּתְנֵי 'לְחָשָׁהּ' – (ב)שֶׁלֹּא יְהוּ תַּלְמִידֵי חֲכָמִים מְצוּיִים אֵצֶל נְשׁוֹתֵיהֶם כְּתַרְנְגוֹלִים. אָמַר רַבִּי יַנַּאי: שָׁמַעְתִּי שֶׁמְּקִילִּין בָּהּ וְשָׁמַעְתִּי שֶׁמַּחְמִירִין בָּהּ, וְכָל הַמַּחְמִיר בָּהּ עַל עַצְמוֹ מַאֲרִיכִין לוֹ יָמָיו וּשְׁנוֹתָיו. אָמַר ריב"ל: מַה טִּיבָן שֶׁל טוֹבְלֵי שַׁחֲרִין? – מַה טִּיבָן?! הָא אִיהוּ דְּאָמַר: בַּעַל קֶרִי אָסוּר בְּדִבְרֵי תוֹרָה! –הָכִי קָאָמַר: מַה טִּיבָן בְּאַרְבָּעִים סְאָה? אֶפְשָׁר בְּתִשְׁעָה קַבִּין, מַה טִּיבָן בִּטְבִילָה? אֶפְשָׁר בִּנְתִינָה! אָמַר רַבִּי חֲנִינָא: גָּדֵר גָּדוֹל גָּדְרוּ בָּהּ, דְּתַנְיָא: מַעֲשֶׂה בְּאֶחָד שֶׁתָּבַע אִשָּׁה לִדְבַר עֲבֵירָה. אָמְרָה לוֹ: רֵיקָא! יֵשׁ לְךָ אַרְבָּעִים סְאָה שֶׁאַתָּה טוֹבֵל בָּהֶן? מִיָּד פֵּירַשׁ.§ אָמַר לְהוּ רַב הוּנָא לְרַבָּנַן: רַבּוֹתַי, מִפְּנֵי מָה אַתֶּם מְזַלְזְלִין בִּטְבִילָה זוֹ? אִי מִשּׁוּם צִינָּה, אֶפְשָׁר בְּמֶרְחֲצָאוֹת! אֲמַר לֵיהּ רַב חִסְדָּא: *°וְכִי יֵשׁ טְבִילָה בְּחַמִּין?! אֲמַר לֵיהּ: רַב אַדָּא בַּר אַהֲבָה קָאֵי כְּוָותָךְ. רַבִּי זֵירָא הֲוָה יָתֵיב בְּאַגְּנָא דְּמַיָּא בֵּי מְסוּתָא. אֲמַר לֵיהּ לְשַׁמָּעֵיהּ: זִיל וְאַיְיתִי לִי תִּשְׁעָה קַבִּין וּשְׁדֵי עִלָּוַאי. אֲמַר לֵיהּ רַבִּי חִיָּיא בַּר אַבָּא: לָמָּה לֵיהּ לְמָר כּוּלֵּי הַאי? וְהָא יָתֵיב בְּגַוַּויְיהוּ! אֲמַר לֵיהּ: כְּאַרְבָּעִים סְאָה; מָה אַרְבָּעִים סְאָה בִּטְבִילָה וְלֹא בִּנְתִינָה אַף תִּשְׁעָה קַבִּין בִּנְתִינָה וְלֹא בִּטְבִילָה.§ רַב נַחְמָן תַּקֵּין חַצְבָא בַּת תִּשְׁעָה קַבִּין. כִּי אֲתָא רַב דִּימִי אָמַר, רַבִּי עֲקִיבָא וְרַבִּי יְהוּדָה גְּלוֹסְטְרָא אָמְרוּ: לֹא שָׁנוּ אֶלָּא לְחוֹלֶה לְאוֹנְסוֹ, אֲבָל לְחוֹלֶה הַמַּרְגִּיל אַרְבָּעִים סְאָה. אָמַר רַב יוֹסֵף: אִתְּבַר חַצְבֵיהּ דְּרַב נַחְמָן. כִּי אֲתָא רָבִין אָמַר: *בְּאוּשָׁא הֲוָה עוּבְדָּא בְּקִילְעָא

---

**רש"י**

*מְשַׁמֶּשֶׁת וְרָאֲתָה נִדָּה. דְּטוּמְאַת קֶרִי קָדְמָה, וּכְשֶׁרָאֲתָה הַקֶּרִי רְאוּיָה הָיְתָה לִטְבּוֹל מִיָּד: לֹא כָּל שֶׁכֵּן. דְּלָא אָתְיָא טוּמְאַת נִדָּה שֶׁהִיא אַחֲרוֹנָה, וּמַפְקַעְתָּהּ לִטְבִילָה שֶׁנִּתְחַיְּיבָה בָּהּ כְּבָר: אֶלָּא לָאו רַבִּי יְהוּדָה. קָתָנֵי לְהוֹדִיעֲךָ דַּאֲפִי' הֵיכָא דְּקָדַם הַקֶּרִי – אָתְיָא טוּמְאַת נִדָּה וּמַפְקַעְתָּה טְבִילָה, דְּאֵין טְבִילָה אֶלָּא הַמְטַהֶרֶת; וְאִי לְרַבִּי יְהוּדָה לֵית לֵיהּ תַּקָּנַת עֶזְרָא, לָמָּה לֵיהּ לְאַשְׁמוֹעִינַן בְּהָא? כָּל בַּעֲלֵי קְרָיִין נַמֵי לָא בָּעֵי טְבִילָה לְדִבְרֵי תוֹרָה! הִלְכָּךְ, עַל כָּרְחָךְ דַּוְקָא קָתָנֵי לַהּ: לָא תֵּימָא. בְּמַתְנִי' 'מְבָרֵךְ' אֶלָּא 'מְהַרְהֵר': עֲשָׂאָן ר' יְהוּדָה. לְבִרְכַּת הַמָּזוֹן: כְּהִלְכוֹת ד"א. שֶׁמּוּתָּר לִשְׁנוֹתָהּ בַּעַל קֶרִי, כִּדְבָרָיו: מַה לְּהַלָּן בְּאֵימָה. דִּכְתִיב "וַיַּרְא הָעָם וַיָּנוּעוּ וְגוֹ'" (שמות כ): מִכָּאן אָמְרוּ. כָּל הַטְּמֵאִים מוּתָּרִים בַּתּוֹרָה, שֶׁאַף הֵם יְכוֹלִים לִהְיוֹת בְּאֵימָה וּבִרְתֵת. אֲבָל בַּעַל קֶרִי אֵינוֹ אֶלָּא מִתּוֹךְ קַלּוּת רֹאשׁ וְגַסּוּת הַדַּעַת: וּבוֹעֲלֵי נִדּוֹת. אִם טָבְלוּ לְקִרְיָין לְדִבְרֵי תוֹרָה הַטְּבִילָה אֵינָהּ עוֹלָה לָהֶם לְטַהֲרָם מִטּוּמְאַת בּוֹעֵל נִדָּה שֶׁהִיא שִׁבְעַת יָמִים, אֲבָל לְתַקָּנַת עֶזְרָא עוֹלָה לָהֶם כִּדְתְנַן בְּמַתְנִיתִין "זָב שֶׁרָאָה קֶרִי וְנִדָּה כו' צְרִיכִין טְבִילָה": בִּרְגִילִיּוֹת. מִשְׁנָיוֹת הַשְּׁגוּרוֹת בְּפִיו, שֶׁהוּא מוֹלִיכָן מִפִּיו בִּמְרוּצָה וְאֵין צָרִיךְ לְהַאֲרִיךְ בָּהֶן: שֶׁלֹּא יַצִּיעַ. בְּטַעֲמֵי פֵּירוּשֵׁיהֶן: וְאֵינוֹ מַצִּיעַ אֶת הַמִּדְרָשׁ גָּרְסִי'. מִפְּנֵי שֶׁצָּרִיךְ הוּא תָּמִיד לְהַזְכִּיר בּוֹ אֶת הַפְּסוּקִים שֶׁהוּא דּוֹרֵשׁ: אַזְכָּרוֹת. שֶׁבַּמִּקְרָאוֹת הַנִּדְרָשִׁים: לֹא יִכָּנֵס לַמִּדְרָשׁ כָּל עִיקָּר. לֹא לְהַצִּיעַ וְלֹא לִשְׁנוֹת, אֲבָל לְבֵית הַמִּדְרָשׁ הוּא נִכְנָס וְשׁוֹתֵק: הִלְכוֹת דֶּרֶךְ אֶרֶץ. כְּגוֹן דַּרְכָּן שֶׁל ת"ח שֶׁהִיא בָּרַיְיתָא*, וּפֶרֶק "בֶּן עַזַּאי" הַנּוֹתֵן אַרְבָּעָה דְּבָרִים אֵל לִבּוֹ: מְגַמְגֵּם וְקוֹרֵא. בַּעַל קֶרִי הָיָה: נִרְאֶה בְּעֵינַי דְּה"ג: א"ר אֶלְעַאי הֲלָכָה כו'. וְלָא גָּרְסִינַן מְסַיַּיע לֵיהּ: מִשּׁוּם רַבֵּינוּ. רַב: כִּי הָנָךְ תְּלָת סָבֵי. וְכוּלְּהוּ לְקוּלָּא: אֵינוֹ נוֹהֵג אֶלָּא בָּאָרֶץ. בִּשְׁחִיטַת חוּלִּין יְלֵיף טַעְמָא, בְּפֶרֶק "הַזְּרוֹעַ": חִטָּה וּשְׂעוֹרָה וְחַרְצָן. שְׁלָשְׁתָּן בְּמַפּוֹלֶת יָד, דַּהֲווּ לְהוּ כִּלְאֵי זְרָעִים וְכִלְאֵי הַכֶּרֶם כְּאַחַת: לִטְבִילוּתָא. דְּבַעֲלֵי קְרָיִין: חַד תָּנֵי. בֶּן עַזַּאי, לְחָשָׁהּ לְתַלְמִידִים: מִשּׁוּם בִּטּוּל פְּרִיָּה וּרְבִיָּה. שֶׁהָיוּ נִמְנָעִים מִתַּשְׁמִישׁ מִפְּנֵי טוֹרַח הַטְּבִילָה: שֶׁמְּקִילִּין בָּהּ. בְּמֶרְחֲצָאוֹת, אוֹ בִּנְתִינַת תִּשְׁעָה קַבִּין: שֶׁמַּחְמִירִין בָּהּ. בְּאַרְבָּעִים סְאָה: שֶׁל טוֹבְלֵי שַׁחֲרִין. בַּעֲלֵי קְרָיִין הַטּוֹבְלִין שַׁחֲרִית: וְהָא אִיהוּ אָמַר כו'. לְעֵיל בְּרֵישׁ שְׁמַעְתִּין: אֶפְשָׁר בִּנְתִינָה. תִּשְׁעָה קַבִּין. וְאע"ג דְּלָא תָּנָא לְקַמָּן אֶלָּא בְּחוֹלֶה, (ג)סְתָם תַּלְמִידֵי חֲכָמִים חוֹלִים הֵם, כִּדְאָמַר בְּמַסֶּכֶת נְדָרִים (דף מט:), כְּמַאן מְצַלִּינַן אַקְּלִירֵי וְאַמְּרִיעֵי כְּרַבִּי יוֹסֵי. קְלִירֵי – חוֹלִין, מְרִיעֵי – רַבָּנָן: גָּדֵר גָּדוֹל גָּדְרוּ. בַּמֶּה שֶׁהִצְרִיכוּ בְּאַרְבָּעִים סְאָה: שֶׁתָּבַע אִשָּׁה. אוֹתָהּ אִשָּׁה פְּנוּיָה הָיְתָה, וַחֲכָמִים גָּזְרוּ עַל הַיִּחוּד אַף עַל הַפְּנוּיָה: אַתֶּם מְזַלְזְלִים. לִנְהוֹג כְּרַבִּי יְהוּדָה בֶּן בְּתֵירָא: אֶפְשָׁר בְּמֶרְחֲצָאוֹת. חַמִּין: קָאֵי כְּוָותָךְ. דְּבָעֵי טְבִילָה זוֹ בְּמִקְוֶה כִּשְׁאָר טְבִילוֹת: בְּאַגְּנָא דְּמַיָּא. גִּיגִית: תַּקֵּין חַצְבָא. לִיתֵּן מַיִם לְתַלְמִידִים עֲלֵיהֶם שַׁחֲרִית קוֹדֶם קְרִיאַת הַתּוֹרָה: לֹא שָׁנוּ. דְּסַגִּי בִּנְתִינָה אֶלָּא בְּחוֹלֶה שֶׁרָאָה קֶרִי לְאוֹנְסוֹ: הַמַּרְגִּיל. וּמַמְשִׁיךְ אֶת הַקֶּרִי עָלָיו, שֶׁמְּשַׁמֵּשׁ מִטָּתוֹ: אִתְּבַר חַצְבֵיהּ. אֵינוֹ צָרִיךְ לָנוּ, דְּחוֹלֶה לְאוֹנְסוֹ לָא שְׁכִיחַ: בְּקִילְעָא

---

**עין משפט נר מצוה**

מה א מיי' פ"ד מהלכות ק"ש הלכה ח סמג עשין יח טוש"ע או"ח סימן פח:

מו ב מיי' פ"י מהלכות בכורים הלכה א סמג עשין קמג טוש"ע י"ד סי' שלג סעיף א:

מז ג מיי' פ"ח מהלכות כלאים הלכה יג סמג לאוין רפ טוש"ע י"ד סי' רצו סעיף א:

מח ד מיי' פ"ד מהל' ק"ש הלכה ח ופ"ד מהל' תפלה הל' ד (ופ"א מהל' ברכות הל' ט) ופ"י מהל' ספר תורה הל' ח סמג עשין יח טוש"ע א"ח סי' פח טוש"ע י"ד סי' רפב סעיף ט:

מט ה מיי' פ"ה מהלכות דעות הל' ד ופ"ד מהלכות תפלה הלכה ד סמג לאוין פא טוש"ע או"ח סי' פח וסי' רמ סעיף א וטוש"ע אה"ע סי' כה סעיף ב:

נ ו טור א"ח סי' רמא:

נא ז טוש"ע י"ד סימן רא סעיף עה:

נב ח טור א"ח בב"י סי' פח:

[עיין תוספות יומא לח: ד"ה ולא ותוס' כתובות קד: ד"ה שני]

**רב נסים גאון**

מה ארבעים סאה בטבילה ולא בנתינה. פירשו בברייתא דשיעור מקוה שכשר לטבילה מ' סאה ואיתה להא ברייתא בפרק ערבי פסחים (דף קט) ובעירובין בפרק מבוי (דף יד): **עזרא** תיקן להן טבילה לבעלי קריין. זו אחת מי' תקנות שתיקן עזרא ומפרשא בבבא קמא בפ' מרובה (דף פב) ובגמ' דהקורא את המגילה עומד דבני מערבא (הלכה א):

[עי' ברש"י קדושין לט. ד"ה לא קי"ל וכו' וטעמיה דרבי יאשיה לא ידענא וכו' ועי' תוס' בקדושין שם ובכורות נ"ד. סד"ה דגן ובתוס' חולין פב: ד"ה ולאפוקי מה שכתבו בזה]

**הגהות הב"ח**

(א) גמ' מציע את (הגמ') תז"מ. וכ"ב גי' רש"י המדרש וכן בכל העמוד: (ב) רש"י ד"ה אפשר וכו' דלא תנא לה אלא בחולה. נ"ב בסמוך בסוף עמוד זה:

**גליון הש"ס**

רש"י ד"ה ובועלי נדות אם טבלו לקריין. עי' מ"ל פ"ג ה"ג מהל' ביאת המקדש:

---

**מסורת הש"ס**

[וגם ד"ה לכ"ש וגם לא לאו שייכים לסוף ע"ב לעיל בסמוך]

דברים ד

[מ"ק טו.]

תוספתא פ"ב

[ערך לנו פי' שלא לאחרים ודבר זה אנו מק"ו מסיני אם אסור ללמד לכ"ש]

כמס' ד"א פ"ג

תוס' ב"ק פ"ב: ד"ה אתא

ירמיה כג

חולין קלו:

שם: וקלח:

דברים כב

לט. חולין פב: קלו: בכורות נד.

לעיל טו.

תענית יג.

בקילעא דרב אושעיא, אתו ושאלו לרב אסי, אמר להו: לא שנו אלא לחולה המרגיל, אבל לחולה לאונסו פטור מכלום. א"ר יוסף: אצטמיד חצביה דרב נחמן.§ מכדי כולהו אמוראי ותנאי בדעזרא קמיפלגי, ונחזי עזרא היכי תקן! אמר אביי: עזרא תקן לבריא המרגיל מ' סאה, ובריא לאונסו – ט' קבין. ואתו אמוראי ופליגי בחולה; מר סבר: חולה המרגיל כבריא המרגיל, וחולה לאונסו כבריא לאונסו; ומר סבר: חולה המרגיל כבריא לאונסו, וחולה לאונסו פטור מכלום. אמר רבא: נהי דתקן עזרא טבילה, נתינה מי תקן? והאמר מר: *עזרא תקן טבילה לבעלי קריין! אלא אמר רבא: עזרא תקן טבילה לבריא המרגיל מ' סאה. ואתו רבנן והתקינו לבריא לאונסו ט' קבין. ואתו אמוראי וקא מיפלגי בחולה; מר סבר: חולה המרגיל כבריא המרגיל, וחולה לאונסו כבריא לאונסו; ומר סבר: לבריא המרגיל מ' סאה וחולה המרגיל כבריא לאונסו, ט' קבין, אבל לחולה לאונסו – פטור מכלום. אמר רבא: אהלכתא, בריא המרגיל וחולה המרגיל – ארבעים סאה, ובריא לאונסו – תשעה קבין, אבל לחולה לאונסו – פטור מכלום.§ *ת"ר: בעל קרי שנתנו עליו ט' קבין מים – טהור; בד"א – לעצמו, אבל לאחרים – ארבעים סאה; ר' יהודה אומר: מ' סאה מכל מקום. ר' יוחנן וריב"ל ור"א ור' יוסי בר' חנינא, חד מהאי זוגא וחד מהאי זוגא ארישא. חד אמר: הא דאמרת "במה דברים אמורים לעצמו אבל לאחרים מ' סאה" – לא שנו אלא לחולה המרגיל, אבל לחולה לאונסו – ט' קבין; וחד אמר: כל לאחרים – אפילו חולה לאונסו – עד דאיכא מ' סאה. וחד מהאי זוגא וחד מהאי זוגא אסיפא. חד אמר: הא דאמר רבי יהודה "מ' סאה מכל מקום" – לא שנו אלא בקרקע, אבל בכלים – לא; וחד אמר: אפי' בכלים נמי. בשלמא למ"ד אפי' בכלים – היינו דקתני: "ר' יהודה אומר מ' סאה מכל מקום" אלא למ"ד "בקרקע – אין, בכלים – לא" "מכל מקום" לאתויי מאי? – לאתויי מים שאובין. רב פפא ורב הונא בריה דרב יהושע ורבא (ברבי) בר שמואל כריכו ריפתא בהדי הדדי. א"ל רב פפא: הבו לי לדידי לברוך, דנפול עילואי ט' קבין. אמר להו רבא (ברבי) [בר] שמואל, תנינא: במה דברים אמורים – לעצמו, אבל לאחרים – מ' סאה; אלא, הבו לי לדידי לברוך, דנפול עילואי ארבעים סאה. אמר להו רב הונא: הבו לי לדידי לברוך, דליכא עילואי לא האי ולא האי. רב חמא טביל במעלי יומא דפסחא להוציא רבים ידי חובתן. ולית הלכתא כוותיה.§

**מתני'** *היה עומד בתפלה ונזכר שהוא בעל קרי – לא יפסיק, אלא יקצר. ירד לטבול, אם יכול לעלות ולהתכסות ולקרות עד שלא תהא הנץ החמה – יעלה ויתכסה ויקרא, ואם לאו – יתכסה במים ויקרא; ולא יתכסה לא במים הרעים ולא במי המשרה, עד שיטיל לתוכן מים. *וכמה ירחיק מהן ומן הצואה – ד' אמות.§

**גמ'** ת"ר: היה עומד בתפלה ונזכר שהוא בעל קרי – לא יפסיק אלא יקצר. היה קורא בתורה ונזכר שהוא בעל קרי – אינו מפסיק ועולה, אלא מגמגם וקורא; ר"מ אומר: אין בעל קרי רשאי לקרות בתורה יותר מג' פסוקים. תניא אידך: גהיה עומד בתפלה וראה צואה כנגדו – מהלך לפניו עד שיזרקנה לאחוריו ד' אמות. והתניא: לצדדין! – ל"ק: הא – דאפשר, הא – דלא אפשר. דהיה מתפלל ומצא צואה במקומו, אמר רבה: אע"פ שחטא – תפלתו תפלה. מתקיף ליה רבא: והא "זבח רשעים תועבה"! אלא אמר רבא: הואיל וחטא, *אע"פ שהתפלל – תפלתו תועבה.§ ת"ר: ההיה עומד בתפלה ומים שותתין על ברכיו – פוסק עד שיכלו המים, וחוזר ומתפלל. להיכן חוזר? רב חסדא ורב המנונא, חד אמר: חוזר לראש; וחד אמר: ולמקום שפסק. לימא בהא קמיפלגי, מר

מר

**רש"י**

בקילעא. כניסת הבית, חדר שלפני הטרקלין שקורין פורטיג"ו בלע"ז: אצטמיד. נתחזקו חבריו ותלמידו, כלומר: לוהך לנו עוד בו: וקא מיפלגי אמוראי. רב דימי ורבין: דאמר מר. גבי עשר תקנות, בב"ק בפרק 'מרובה': אמר רבא הלכתא וכו'. אפלוגתא דאמוראי הוא דפסק רבא דפליגי אליבא דרבנן. מיהו, השתא אנן כרבי יהודה בן בתירא נהגינן כדאמר רב נחמן לעיל, ורב נחמן בר יצחק בתרא הוה: לעצמו. לעסוק בתורה לעצמו, אבל ללמד לאחרים – מ' סאה: ור"י אומר מ' סאה מ"מ. מ' סאה שאמרו בכל ענין שהן, ולקמן מפרש לה: חד מהאי זוגא וחד מהאי זוגא. פליגי ארישא בפירושא דמילתא דת"ק: אסיפא. דר' יהודה: ל"ש אלא בקרקע. לא קיימא מ"מ דר' יהודה לאכשורי בכלי אתא, דאין כשר אלא מ' סאה בקרקע, ולקמן בעי: א"כ מאי מ"מ. אבל לאחרים מ' סאה. והכא נמי דלאפוקי אחרים ידי חובתן – כלאחרים דמי: דנפול עילואי. לאו דוקא, אלא טבלתי בט' סאה: לא האי ולא האי. לא הורגלתי לא לזו ולא לזו, שלא ראיתי קרי: טבל. ובירך רגיל היה לעשות כן, דהו"ל ללמד אחרים. ובשאר ימות השנה לא היה טובל, אלא נותן עליו ט' קבין: ולית הלכתא כוותיה. דכי היכי דלעצמו בנתינה – לאחרים נמי בנתינה. אי נמי, דקיי"ל כרבי יהודה בן בתירא:

מתני' לא יפסיק. תפלתו לגמרי אלא יקצר כל ברכה וברכה ואומר כל הברכות בקוצר: במים הרעים. מים סרוחים: עד שיתן לתוכן מים. ובגמרא (ד' כה:) (א) מפרש כמה מיא רמי ואזיל ומפרש לה בחסורי מחסרא והכי קתני: לא יקרא אצל מי רגלים עד שיתן לתוכן מים; וכמה ירחיק מהם. ממי רגלים: גמ' מגמגם. בגמגום: יותר מג' פסוקים. כגון בבית הכנסת דאי אפשר לפחות. כדתנן (מגילה פ"ג ד' כג:) הקורא בתורה לא יפחות משלשה פסוקים: והתניא לצדדין. א"ל להלך עד שתהא לאחוריו: דאפשר. לילך לפניו, עד שתהא לאחוריו: לא אפשר. כגון יש נהר לפניו – מתהלך לצדדים:

מר

**תוספות**

ונחזי עזרא היכן תקן. בהרבה מקומות(ב) גבי שאר תקנות לא פריך גמרא הכי, אלא שאני הכא דדבר הרגיל בכל יום הוא, על כן אנו זכורים: ולית הלכתא כוותיה. דטבילה בכל יום ארבעים סאה, אלא אפילו לאחרים נמי סגי בתשעה קבין, אי נמי, הכי פירושו: ולית הלכתא כוותיה אלא כר' יהודה בן בתירה, דאמר דברי תורה אין מקבלין טומאה. וי"מ: דוקא לתורה, אבל לתפלה צריך *טבילה. ופי' ר"י: דלא שנא. והטובל בערב יוה"כ אין לו לברך, והמברך הוי ברכה לבטלה:

*אלא דכולי עלמא חוזר לראש. וה"ה דהו"מ לאוקמי דכולי עלמא אין חוזר לראש. ומדלא מוקי הכי ש"מ דהלכה דחוזר לראש. וכן לקמן, (ג) בסדיא אמר ר' אבהו חוזר לראש. ותימה, דבמסכת ר"ה (דף לד:) א"ר יוחנן שמע תשע תקיעות בט' שעות ביום יצא, אלמא: תקיעות מצטרפות אע"ג דשהה כדי לעשות כולם. וכן במגילה (פ"ב ד' יח:) נמי, דאמרינן אמר רב אין הלכה כרבי מונה, דאמר אם שהה חוזר לראש, דקאמר נקוט דרב בידך! ואומר השר מקוצי: דיש לחלק, דשאני הכא דאין ראוי לקרות. וכן לקמן (ד' כד:) דרבי אבהו אזל במבואות המטונפות, דהתם כ"ע מודו דחוזר לראש, אבל היכא דגברא חזי, כמו מגילה ושופר, כולי עלמא מודו דאינו חוזר לראש אלא למקום שפסק. ורבינו יהודה פירש:(ד) דהכא לא מצי למימר דכולי עלמא דאין חוזר לראש, ודבהא קמיפלגי, דהא לכ"ע הוי גברא חזי כיון דאינו חוזר לראש, אבל ודאי אי הו"מ למימר הכי – הוה אמר ליה:

והא זבח רשעים תועבה. פר"י: דדוקא במקום שהיה יכול להסתפק ולתלות שיש שם צואה: אע"פ שהתפלל תפלתו תועבה. והוי מעוות לא יוכל לתקן. ור"י פי': דיחזור ויתפלל:

ממתין עד שיכלו המים. במשתין על גבי קרקע, או ע"ג בגדים ואין שם טופח על מנת להטפיח; כדמשמע לקמן (ד' כה.) כגון דעביד טיף טיף, שנבלעין מהרה, כן פי' הרב רבי יוסף. ומיהו נראה, אפילו אם יש בהן טופח על מנת להטפיח – מותרין, כיון דמדאורייתא אינן אסורין אלא כנגד העמוד בלבד, ורבנן הוא דגזור, וכיון שעומד כבר בתפלתו – לא אטרחוהו רבנן לחזור בתפלה:

חיישינן

**עין משפט נר מצוה**

נג א מיי' פ"ד מהל' תפלה הלכה ו:

נד ב מיי' פ"ב מהלכות ק"ש הלכה ז:

נה ג ד מיי' פ"ד מהל' תפלה הל' ט סמג עשין יט טוש"ע א"ח סימן פא סעיף ב:

[ע' תוספו' חולין קכב: ד"ה לגבל]

[שייך לדף כג.]

נו ה מיי' וסמג שם טוש"ע א"ח סימן עו סעיף א:

נז ו ז מיי' שם הל' יג סמג שם טוש"ע א"ח סימן עח:

**רב נסים גאון**

היה עומד בתפלה ונזכר שהוא בעל קרי לא יפסיק. אמרי' עלה בתלמוד ארץ ישראל (פ"ג הלכה ה') מתניתא ברבים אבל בינו לבין עצמו מפסיק וכו' מאיר ברם כר' יהודה אפי' בינו לבין עצמו אינו מפסיק כשאין לו מים לטבול אבל יש לו מים לטבול אפי' ר' יהודה מודה שהוא מפסיק:

**הגהות הב"ח**

(א) במשנה רש"י ד"ה עד שיתן וכו' ובגמ' פריך כמה: (ב) תוס' ד"ה ונחזי וכו' בהרבה מקומות. נ"ב בפרק אין עומדין דף ל"ג גבי הבדלה פריך תלמודא נמי הכי וצריך לומר ג"כ כמ"ש התוספות הכא: (ג) ד"ה אלא וכו' וכן לקמן. נ"ב סוף דף כ"ד: (ד) בא"ד ורבינו יהודה פירש. נ"ב עיין בספר נחלה לגבי סימן ו' ס"ה תמצא כאור לדברים אלו:

**מסורת**

ב"ק פב.

תוספתא פ"ב

[לעיל כא.]

מגילה כז:

[ע' פירש"י לקמן כה: ד"ה מי המשרה]

משלי כא

[עי' תוס' ערוב סכות]

נ"א מאי תקנתא להדר ולצלי

מר סבר: *אם שהה כדי לגמור את כולה – חוזר לראש; ומר סבר: למקום שפסק. אמר רב אשי: האי "אם שהה" "אם לא שהה" מיבעי ליה! – *אלא, אדכולי עלמא אם שהה כדי לגמור את כולה – חוזר לראש, *והתם בדלא שהה קמיפלגי; דמר סבר: גברא דחויא הוא, ואין תפלתו תפלה; ומר סבר: גברא חזיא הוא, ותפלתו תפלה.§ תנו רבנן: בהנצרך לנקביו – אל יתפלל, ואם התפלל – תפלתו תועבה. אמר רב זביד ואיתימא רב יהודה: לא שנו אלא שאינו יכול לשהות בעצמו, אבל אם יכול לשהות בעצמו – תפלתו תפלה. ועד כמה? – אמר רב ששת: געד פרסה. איכא דמתני לה אמתניתא: במה דברים אמורים – כשאין יכול לעמוד על עצמו, אבל אם יכול לעמוד על עצמו – תפלתו תפלה. ועד כמה? אמר רב זביד:(א) *עד פרסה. אמר רבי שמואל בר נחמני אמר רבי יונתן: *דהנצרך לנקביו הרי זה לא יתפלל, משום שנאמר: "הכון לקראת אלהיך ישראל". ואמר רבי שמואל בר נחמני אמר רבי יונתן: מ"ד "שמור רגלך כאשר תלך אל בית האלהים" שמור עצמך שלא תחטא, ואם תחטא – הבא קרבן לפני. "וקרוב לשמע *(דברי חכמים)", אמר רבא: הוי קרוב לשמוע דברי חכמים שאם חוטאים מביאים קרבן ועושים תשובה; "מתת הכסילים [זבח]" – אל תהי ככסילים שחוטאים ומביאים קרבן ואין עושים תשובה; "כי אינם יודעים לעשות רע", אי הכי, צדיקים נינהו! אלא, אל תהי ככסילים שחוטאים ומביאים קרבן, ואינם יודעים אם על הטובה הם מביאים אם על הרעה הם מביאים; אמר הקב"ה: בין טוב לרע אינן מבחינים, והם מביאים קרבן לפני?! רב אשי ואיתימא רב חנינא בר פפא אמר: שמור נקביך בשעה שאתה עומד בתפלה לפני.§ תנו רבנן: *ההנכנס לבית הכסא – חולץ תפילין ברחוק ד' אמות, ונכנס. אמר רב אחא בר רב הונא אמר רב ששת: לא שנו אלא בית הכסא קבוע, אבל בית הכסא עראי – חולץ ונפנה לאלתר. וכשהוא יוצא – מרחיק ד' אמות ומניחן, מפני שעשאו בית הכסא קבוע. איבעיא להו: מהו שיכנס אדם בתפילין לבית הכסא קבוע להשתין מים? רבינא שרי, רב אדא בר מתנא אסר. אתו שיילוה לרבא, אמר להו: אסור, חיישינן שמא יפנה בהן; ואמרי לה: שמא יפיח בהן. תניא אידך: הנכנס לבית הכסא קבוע – חולץ תפיליו ברחוק ד' אמות, ומניחן בחלון הסמוך לרשות הרבים ונכנס, וכשהוא יוצא – מרחיק ד' אמות ומניחן, דברי בית שמאי. ובית הלל אומרים: אוחזן בידו ונכנס; ר"ע אומר: אוחזן בבגדו ונכנס. בבגדו ס"ד?! זימנין מישתלי להו ונפלי! אלא אימא: אוחזן בבגדו ובידו ונכנס, ומניחם בחורין הסמוכים לבית הכסא; [ח] ולא יניחם בחורין הסמוכים לרשות הרבים, שמא יטלו אותם עוברי דרכים ויבא לידי חשד. ומעשה בתלמיד אחד שהניח תפיליו בחורין הסמוכים לרשות הרבים, ובאת זונה אחת ונטלתן, ובאת לבית המדרש ואמרה: ראו מה נתן לי פלוני בשכרי! כיון ששמע אותו תלמיד כך, עלה לראש הגג ונפל ומת. באותה שעה התקינו "שיהא אוחזן בבגדו ובידו ונכנס.§ תנו רבנן: בראשונה היו מניחין תפילין בחורין הסמוכין לבית הכסא, ובאין עכברים ונוטלין אותן. התקינו שיהו מניחין אותן בחלונות הסמוכות לרשות הרבים, ובאין עוברי דרכים ונוטלין אותן; התקינו שיהא אוחזן בידו ונכנס. אמר רבי מיאשא *בריה דריב"ל: הלכה, טגוללן כמין ספר ואוחזן בימינו כנגד לבו. אמר רב יוסף בר מניומי אמר רב נחמן: ובלבד שלא תהא רצועה יוצאת מתחת ידו טפח. אמר רבי יעקב בר אחא אמר רבי זירא: כלא שנו אלא שיש שהות ביום ללבשן, אבל אין שהות ביום ללבשן – עושה להן כמין כיס טפח, ומניחן. *אמר רבה בר בר חנה אמר רבי יוחנן: ביום – גוללן כמין ספר ומניחן בידו כנגד לבו, ובלילה – עושה להן כמין כיס טפח, ומניחן. אמר אביי: לא שנו אלא בכלי שהוא כליין, אבל בכלי שאינו כליין – אפילו פחות מטפח. אמר מר זוטרא ואיתימא רב אשי: תדע, שהרי פכין קטנים מצילין באהל המת. ואמר רבה בר בר חנה: כי הוה אזלינן בתריה דרבי יוחנן, כי הוה בעי למיעל לבית הכסא, כי הוה נקיט ספרא דאגדתא – הוה יהיב לן, כי הוה נקיט תפילין – לא הוה יהיב לן, אמר: הואיל ושרונהו רבנן – נינטרן.

**רש"י**

דמר סבר. כל המפסיק בתפלתו אם שהה כדי לגמור כולה – חוזר לראש. כדאמרינן גבי ק"ש לקמן בפירקין (דף כד:), ובשהה קא מיפלגי הכא: האי אם שהה אם לא שהה מיבעי ליה. דרב חסדא ורב המנונא מיבעי ליה לאפלוגי בין שהה ללא שהה, ומדלא אפליג שמע מינה: אפילו בדלא שהה קאמר: גברא דחויא הוא. כשהתחיל להתפלל והיה צריך לנקביו דחוי הוא מלהתפלל, הלכך מה שהתפלל אינה תפלה – וחוזר לראש: ומר סבר גברא חזיא. אע"פ שאינו יכול להמתין עד שיסיים תפלתו – תפלה ראויה היא מה שהתפלל קודם שתיתה: ועד כמה. יכול להעמיד עצמו מנקביו שיהא מותר להתחיל בתפלה: איכא דמתני. להאי, 'במה דברים אמורים' במתניתא גופא, ולא משמעתא דרב זביד ורב יהודה. וכי איירי אינהו – בשיעורא הוא דאיירי: שמור עצמך שלא תחטא. ותצטרך רגלך ללכת אל בית האלהים להביא חטאת: הוי קרוב לשמוע. תשובה בהבאת קרבנך, מתת אותו ככסילים בלא תשובה: שמור נקביך. מבין רגליך, כמו "להסך את רגליו", (שמואל א כד) שמור נקביך שלא יפיחו: בית הכסא קבוע. שיש בו נוחה, וכל בתי כסאות שבגמרא על פני השדה הם, בלא חפירה: עראי. שזה מתחיל עכשיו לעשותו בית הכסא: חולץ ונפנה לאלתר. ויאחז תפילין בידו, כדאמרינן לקמן. ובקבוע נמי אוחזן בידו, אלא שצריך לחלצן ברחוק ד' אמות, שבזמן שהם בראשו הם בגלוי וגנאי הדבר: מהו שיכנס בתפיליו. כשהן בראשו קאמר: שמא יפנה בהן. גדולים: בחורים הסמוכים לבית הכסא. לפנים מן הגדר בשדה שהוא נפנה בה, נותנן בחורים שבכותל: בחורים הסמוכים לרשות הרבים. חורי כותלי מחיצות השדה, שאין עכברים מצוין במקום הילוך בני אדם, והוא יכנס לאחורי הגדר לפנות: גוללן. ברצועות שלהן: שלא תצא רצועה. שיש בה קדושה שהרי בהן הוא קושרן, ובקשר נראה בעשייתו כמין דל"ת על שם אחת מאותיות של שדי, והשי"ן עשויה בכותלי הקציצה החיצונה, והיו"ד עשויה בראש רצועת תפילין של יד, ורצועה קטנה מאד כפוף ראשה ונראית כמין יו"ד: ואוחזן בימינו. שלא בבגדו, כדי שלא יפלו: ביום. כשהוא חולצן בשביל בית הכסא גוללן כמין ספר כדאמרן: ובלילה. כשהוא חולצן בביתו על מנת להניע עד הבקר: עושה להם כיס טפח. דחללו טפח, דחשיב הכלי אהל להפסיק בינם לקרקע: לא שנו. דבעי טפח אלא בכלי שהוא כליין. כיס העשוי לצרכן; דכליין קרוב להיות בטל אצלם, הילכך בעינן דבר הניכר שיהא חוצץ בפניהם: שהרי פכין קטנים מצילין. בהיקף צמיד פתיל באהל המת, ואף על גב דלא הוי טפח – חיילי: אמר הואיל ושרונהו רבנן. לאוחזן בידו משום שמירתן: נינטרן

**תוספות**

חיישינן שמא יפנה בהן ואסור. ודוקא בבית הכסא קבוע חיישינן שמא יפנה בהן, אבל בבית הכסא עראי שאין רגילים לפנות שם – מותר להשתין בהן, ולא חיישינן שמא יפנה בהן. והא דתניא לקמן "לא ישתין בהן אפילו בבית הכסא עראי" – היינו דוקא כשאוחזן בידו, דחיישינן שמא ישפשף בהן הניצוצות אם יפלו מים על רגליו, או יגע באמה: שהרי פכין קטנים מצילין באהל המת. ועל כרחך מטעם אויר הוא, דאי לית בהו אויר כלל לא היו מצילין, דהוי כמו אוכלין שגבלן בטיט, שמקבלין טומאה באהל המת: דברים

**מסורת הש"ס**

כד: ר"ה לד:

[ס' ד"ה אלא]

תוספתא פ"ב

[ע' ועי' הגוסחא בעין יעקב]

שבת סב.

[ב"ח נ"ל קודם קב בר אחא רש"ל]

**תורה אור**

והכא

עמוס ד

קהלת ד

**עין משפט נר מצוה**

נח א מיי' פ"ד מהל' תפלה הלכה יג סמג עשין יט טוש"ע או"ח סימן קב סעיף ה:

נט ב ג מיי' שם הל' י' סמג שם טוש"ע או"ח סימן נב סעיף א:

ס ד מיי' וסמג שם טוש"ע שם סעיף א ג:

סא ה ו מיי' פ"ד מהל' תפילין הלכה יז סמג עשין כב טוש"ע או"ח סימן מג סעיף ה [רב אלפס כאן ובהל' תפילין דף עה]:

סב ז מיי' וסמג שם טוש"ע שם סעיף א: [ח מיי' שם]:

סג ח ט י מיי' וסמג שם טור שו"ע שם סעיף ה':

סד כ ל מיי' שם הלכה יט סמג שם טוש"ע שם סעיף ו:

ואיתימא רב יהודה עד פרסה כצ"ל רש"ל

**רב נסים גאון**

**פכין** קטנים מצילין באהל המת. עיקרה בסיפרי (פרשת חקת) וכל כלי פתוח בכלי חרש הכתוב מדבר מה ת"ל פתוח ואפילו כל שהוא (והואיל והוא) [הוא] טמא באהל המת לפיכך אם יהיה מוקף בצמיד פתיל מציל על מה שבתוכו כדמפרש התם נמי וכל כלי פתוח מיכן אמרו כלים מצילין בצמיד פתיל באהל המת ואמרו עוד טמא הוא אין ת"ל הוא אלא הוא שיציל על עצמו ובשבת בפ' אמר רבי עקיבא (דף פד) ובבבא קמא בפ' כיצד הרגל מועדת (דף כה) גרסי' תניא מפץ במת מנין ודין הוא ומה פכין קטנים שטהורין בזב טמאין במת:

[בר בריה כצ"ל וכ"ה בשאלתות פ' בא וכן איתא לקמן כד:]

**הגהות הב"ח**

(א) גמ' איכא דמתני לה במתניתא וכו' אמר רב זביד אמר רב יהודה עד פרסה:

**גליון הש"ס**

**תוס'** ד"ה שהרי וכו' שמקבלין טומאה באהל המת. כדאיתא זבחים קף ג ע"א:

נִנְטְרָן. יְשַׁמְּרוּנִי. אַכְנִיסֵם עִמִּי וְיִשְׁמְרוּנִי מִן הַמַּזִּיקִין: לֹא יֶאֱחוֹז בְּיָדוֹ וְכוּ׳ וְיִתְפַּלֵּל. שֶׁאֵין דַּעְתּוֹ מְיוּשֶּׁבֶת עָלָיו בִּתְפִלָּה, שֶׁהֲרֵי לִבּוֹ תָּמִיד עֲלֵיהֶן שֶׁלֹּא יִפְּלוּ מִיָּדוֹ: וְלֹא יִישַׁן בָּהֶן. שֶׁמָּא [א] יָפִיחַ: הֲרֵי אֵלּוּ כַּיּוֹצֵא בָּהֶן. לְעִנְיַן תְּפִלָּה, שֶׁדּוֹאֵג עֲלֵיהֶן שֶׁלֹּא תִּפּוֹל הַסַּכִּין וְתַזִּיקֵנוּ, וְהַקְּעָרָה תִּשָּׁפֵךְ וְהַמָּעוֹת יֹאבְדוּ, וְהַכִּכָּר יִטָּנֵף: לֵית הִלְכְתָא כִּי הָא מַתְנִיתָא. דְּקָתָנֵי "לֹא יַשְׁתִּין בִּתְפִלִּין": דְּבֵית שַׁמַּאי הִיא. דְּאָמְרֵי לְעֵיל "מַנִּיחָן בַּחַלּוֹן הַסָּמוּךְ לְר״ה וְלֹא יַכְנִיסֵם בְּיָדוֹ וְיִכָּנֵס": דְּאִי ב״ה. הָא אָמְרֵי לְעֵיל "אוֹחֲזָן בְּיָדוֹ וְנִכְנָס": בֵּית הַכִּסֵּא עֲרַאי. כְּגוֹן לְהַשְׁתִּין״ שֶׁאֵין אָדָם הוֹלֵךְ בִּשְׁבִילָם לְבֵית הַכִּסֵּא. וְהַפַּעַם הַזֹּאת נַעֲשָׂה הַמָּקוֹם הַזֶּה בֵּית הַכִּסֵּא תְּחִלָּה: שֶׁהִתַּרְתִּי לְךָ כָּאן. בְּבֵית הַכִּסֵּא קָבוּעַ: אָסַרְתִּי לְךָ כָּאן. בְּבֵית הַכִּסֵּא עֲרַאי: מַאי לָאו תְּפִילִּין. שֶׁאָמְרוּ בֵּית הִלֵּל "אוֹחֲזָן בְּיָדוֹ וְנִכְנָס לְבֵית הַכִּסֵּא קָבוּעַ", וּלְהַשְׁתִּין בָּהֶם אֲסָרוּ, כִּדְמְפָרֵשׁ טַעְמָא לְקַמָּן: הָא לָא שָׁרוּ. בְּבֵית הַכִּסֵּא קָבוּעַ: כִּי תַּנְיָא הַהִיא. לָאו לְעִנְיַן תְּפִילִּין תַּנְיָא, אֶלָּא לְעִנְיַן גִּלּוּי טֶפַח וּטְפָחַיִם. דְּלַגְּדוֹלִים אֵינוֹ מְגַלֶּה אֶלָּא טֶפַח, וְלַקְּטַנִּים מְגַלֶּה טְפָחַיִם. וְעַלָּהּ קָאֵי, גִּלּוּי טְפָחַיִם שֶׁהִתַּרְתִּי לְךָ כָּאן – אָסַרְתִּי לְךָ כָּאן: לְאַחֲרָיו טֶפַח. וְלֹא יוֹתֵר, מִשּׁוּם צְנִיעוּת: וּלְפָנָיו טְפָחַיִם. מִשּׁוּם קִילּוּחַ מֵי רַגְלַיִם הַמַּתָּזִין לְמֶרְחוֹק: מַאי לָאו כּו׳. וְהַיְינוּ דְּקָאָמַר לְעֵיל: דְּבָרִים שֶׁהִתַּרְתִּי לְךָ בְּבֵית הַכִּסֵּא עֲרַאי, אָסַרְתִּי לְךָ בְּקָבוּעַ: אֶלָּא אִידִי וְאִידִי בִּגְדוֹלִים. וּמִתּוֹךְ שֶׁהוּא דּוֹחֵק עַצְמוֹ לִגְדוֹלִים הוּא בָּא לִידֵי קְטַנִּים. הִלְכָּךְ: בָּאִישׁ מִלְּאַחֲרָיו טֶפַח, וּמִלְּפָנָיו טְפָחַיִם; וּבָאִשָּׁה מִלְּפָנֶיהָ וְלֹא כְּלוּם. וְהָכִי קָאָמַר: הָא דִּלְעֵיל דְּבָרִים שֶׁאָסַרְתִּי לְךָ בָּאִשָּׁה, הִתַּרְתִּי לְךָ בָּאִישׁ: אִי הָכִי. דִּלְעִנְיַן טֶפַח וּטְפָחַיִם קָתָנֵי, דְּבָרִים שֶׁהִתַּרְתִּי לְךָ כָּאן אָסַרְתִּי לְךָ כָּאן: הָא דְּקָתָנֵי עֲלָהּ. בְּסֵיפָא דִּידָהּ, וְזֶה הוּא ק״ו שֶׁאֵין עָלָיו תְּשׁוּבָה. בְּדָבָר הַזֶּה יֵשׁ לְךָ לַהֲשִׁיבֵנִי ק״ו, וְאֵין לִי עָלָיו תְּשׁוּבָה לְהַחֲזִיר לָךְ. אִי אָמְרַתְּ בִּשְׁלָמָא בִּתְפִילִּין קָאָמַר, וּכְדְאַמְרַן, וּב״ש הִיא – הַיְינוּ דְּקָתָנֵי דְּיֵשׁ כָּאן לְהַקְשׁוֹת קַל וָחוֹמֶר: הַשְׁתָּא בֵּית הַכִּסֵּא קָבוּעַ שָׁרֵי – בֵּית הַכִּסֵּא עֲרַאי מִיבַּעְיָא! וְאֵין לִי תְּשׁוּבָה לַהֲשִׁיבְךָ עָלָיו. אֶלָּא אִי אָמְרַתְּ לְעִנְיַן טֶפַח וּטְפָחַיִם, מַאי ק״ו יֵשׁ לְהַקְשׁוֹת כָּאן: אוֹרְחָא דְּמִילְּתָא הָכִי הוּא. שֶׁהָאִישׁ צָרִיךְ לְגַלּוֹת לְפָנָיו וְלֹא הָאִשָּׁה: תְּיוּבְתָּא דְּרָבָא אָמַר רַב שֵׁשֶׁת. דַּאֲמַר בֵּית שַׁמַּאי הִיא וְלֹא בֵּית הִלֵּל, דְּאִם כֵּן לָא מַשְׁכַּחַת מִידֵי לְאוֹקְמַהּ הַךְ בָּרַיְיתָא דְּקָתָנֵי "מַאי שֶׁהִתַּרְתִּי לְךָ כָּאן אָסַרְתִּי לְךָ כָּאן": דְּלֵיכָּא נִיצוֹצוֹת. שֶׁיְּהֵא צָרִיךְ לְשַׁפְשֵׁף בִּימִינוֹ מֵעַל רַגְלָיו: בֵּית הַכִּסֵּא עֲרַאי. לִקְטַנִּים: דְּאִיכָּא נִיצוֹצוֹת. הַנִּיתָּזִין עַל גַּבֵּי רַגְלָיו. וְאָמְרִינַן בְּמַסֶּכֶת יוֹמָא (דף ל.): מִצְוָה לְשַׁפְשֵׁף, שֶׁאָסוּר לָאָדָם שֶׁיֵּלֵךְ כְּנִילוֹנוֹת שֶׁעַל גַּבֵּי רַגְלָיו, שֶׁמָּא יִרְאֶה כְּכְרוּת שָׁפְכָה וְנִמְצָא מוֹצִיא לַעַז עַל בָּנָיו שֶׁהֵם מַמְזֵרִים. הִילְכָּךְ, אִי אֶפְשָׁר לֶאֱחוֹז תְּפִילִּין בְּיָדוֹ: הָא מִילְּתָא. דִּתְפִילִּין דְּבֵית הַכִּסֵּא עֲרַאי וְקָבוּעַ: תֵּיתֵי לַהּ בְּתוֹרַת טַעְמָא. לְהַתִּיר בְּבֵית הַכִּסֵּא קָבוּעַ אֶת הָאָסוּר בְּבֵית הַכִּסֵּא עֲרַאי מִשּׁוּם טַעְמָא דְּנִילוֹנוֹת: דְּאִי אַתְיָא לַהּ בְּתוֹרַת ק״ו. לוֹמַר: דִּין הוּא לְהָקֵל בְּבֵית הַכִּסֵּא עֲרַאי קַל וּלְהַחְמִיר בְּבֵית הַכִּסֵּא[ה] חָמוּר וְלֹא תָּזוּל בָּתַר טַעְמָא אֶלָּא בָּתַר חוּמְרָא וְקוּלָּא, וַאֲנַן עָבְדִינַן אִיפְּכָא – אֵין לִי עָלָיו מַה לַהֲשִׁיבְךָ, שֶׁאֵין לִי לִמְצוֹא שֶׁיְּהֵא בְּשׁוּם מָקוֹם בֵּית הַכִּסֵּא עֲרַאי חָמוּר מִן הַקָּבוּעַ, שֶׁאוּכַל לַהֲשִׁיבְךָ: אִם הִתַּרְתִּי בְּקָבוּעַ שֶׁהוּא קַל בְּדָבָר פְּלוֹנִי – נַתִּיר בְּשֶׁל עֲרַאי שֶׁהוּא חָמוּר בָּהּ. אֲבָל טַעְמָא אִיכָּא לְמַאי דְּעָבְדִינַן, דְּהָכָא אִיכָּא נִילוֹנוֹת וְהָכָא לֵיכָּא. וְדָבָר זֶה לָאו קַל וָחוֹמֶר, לָא קַל וְלָא חָמוּר: הַנִּכְנָס לִסְעוּדַת קֶבַע. וּגְנַאי הוּא שֶׁיִּצְטָרֵךְ לִנְקָבָיו בְּתוֹךְ הַסְּעוּדָה: מְהַלֵּךְ עֲשָׂרָה פְּעָמִים כּו׳. וּבְכָל פַּעַם וּפַעַם בּוֹדֵק עַצְמוֹ וְיוֹשֵׁב אוּלַי יוּכַל לְהִפָּנוֹת שֶׁהַהִילּוּךְ מוֹרִיד הַגְּדוֹלִים לַנֶּקֶב: חוֹלֵץ תְּפִילָּיו. שֶׁמָּא יִשְׁתַּכֵּר בַּסְּעוּדָה וְיִתְגַּנֶּה בִּתְפִילָּיו: וְכֵן הָדוּר לוֹ. שֶׁיְּהוּ מְזוּמָּנִים לוֹ, וְיַחֲזוֹר וְיָנִיחֵם בִּשְׁעַת בְּרָכָה: בְּאַפַּרְקְסוּתֵיהּ. סוּדָר שֶׁל רֹאשׁוֹ: עִם מְעוֹתָיו. לֹא עִם הַמָּעוֹת מַמָּשׁ, אֶלָּא שְׁנֵי קְשָׁרִים זֶה אֵצֶל זֶה: ה״ג: הָא דְּאַזְמְנֵיהּ הָא דְּלָא אַזְמְנֵיהּ. לִהְיוֹת סוּדָר לִתְפִילִּין, דְּכֵיוָן דְּאַזְמְנֵיהּ – שׁוּב אָסוּר לָצוּר בּוֹ מָעוֹת, מֵאַחַר שֶׁהִקְנוּ לְכָךְ: צַר בֵּיהּ. אִי אַזְמְנֵיהּ – אִין, אִי לָא אַזְמְנֵיהּ – לָא קָדֵישׁ וְשָׁרֵי לְמֵיצַר בֵּיהּ. דְּהָכִי תַּנְיָא בְּהֶדְיָא בְּסַנְהֶדְרִין (מח:): הִנִּיחַ בּוֹ תְּפִילָּיו – יָנִיחַ בּוֹ מָעוֹת: וּלְאַבָּיֵי דְּאָמַר הַזְמָנָה מִילְּתָא הִיא. גַּבֵּי אוֹרֵג בֶּגֶד לְמֵת, בְּסַנְהֶדְרִין בְּפֶרֶק "נִגְמַר הַדִּין" (ד׳ מז:): מַהוּ שֶׁיַּנִּיחַ תְּפִילָּיו תַּחַת מְרַאֲשׁוֹתָיו. בַּלַּיְלָה כְּשֶׁהוּא יָשֵׁן: לְמַעְלָה מְרַאֲשׁוֹתָיו, וְעָלָיו נוֹתֵן הַתְּפִילִּין אוֹ לְמַטָּה מְרַאֲשׁוֹתָיו יוֹצֵא מָקוֹם מִן הַמִּטָּה: אִם הָיָה מָקוֹם גָּבוֹהַּ ג׳ טְפָחִים.

כל

**דברים** שהתרתי לך כאן כו׳. ולא בעי לשנויי דברים שהתרתי לך בבית הכסא עראי אסרתי לך בקבוע – דאסור לפנות בגדולים ותפילין בראשו, אבל להשתין מותר, משום דלא אשכחן בברייתא, אבל הך דטפח וטפחיים – אשכחן ליה בברייתא בהדיא. הר״ר יוסף:

והא

נִנְטְרָן. אָמַר רָבָא: כִּי הֲוָה אָזְלִינַן בָּתְרֵיהּ דר״נ כִּי הֲוָה נָקֵיט סִפְרָא דְאַגַּדְתָּא – יָהֵיב לָן, כִּי הֲוָה נָקֵיט תְּפִילִּין – לָא יָהֵיב לָן, אָמַר: הוֹאִיל וְשַׁרְוִנְהוּ רַבָּנַן – נִינְטְרָן.§ ת״ר: *אלֹא יֶאֱחֹז אָדָם תְּפִילִּין בְּיָדוֹ וס״ת בִּזְרוֹעוֹ וְיִתְפַּלֵּל, בוְלֹא יַשְׁתִּין בָּהֶן מַיִם, *גוְלֹא יִישַׁן בָּהֶן לֹא שֵׁינַת קֶבַע וְלֹא שֵׁינַת עֲרַאי. אָמַר שְׁמוּאֵל: דסַכִּין, וּמָעוֹת, וּקְעָרָה, וְכִכָּר הֲרֵי אֵלּוּ כַּיּוֹצֵא בָּהֶן. אָמַר רָבָא אָמַר רַב שֵׁשֶׁת: לֵית הִלְכְתָא כִּי הָא מַתְנִיתָא – דב״ש הִיא. דְּאִי ב״ה – הַשְׁתָּא בֵּית הַכִּסֵּא קָבוּעַ שָׁרֵי, בֵּית הַכִּסֵּא עֲרַאי מִיבַּעְיָא?! מֵיתִיבִי: "דְּבָרִים שֶׁהִתַּרְתִּי לְךָ כָּאן, אָסַרְתִּי לְךָ כָּאן", מַאי לָאו תְּפִילִּין? אִי אָמְרַתְּ בִּשְׁלָמָא בֵּית הִלֵּל – "הִתַּרְתִּי לְךָ כָּאן" – קָבוּעַ, "אָסַרְתִּי לְךָ כָּאן" – בֵּית הַכִּסֵּא עֲרַאי; אֶלָּא אִי אָמְרַתְּ ב״ש – הָא לֹא שָׁרוּ וְלֹא מִידֵי! –כִּי תַּנְיָא הַהִיא לְעִנְיַן טֶפַח וּטְפָחַיִם. דְּתָנֵי חֲדָא: כְּשֶׁהוּא נִפְנֶה – מְגַלֶּה לְאַחֲרָיו טֶפַח וּלְפָנָיו טְפָחַיִם. וְתַנְיָא אִידָךְ: לְאַחֲרָיו טֶפַח, וּלְפָנָיו וְלֹא כְלוּם. מַאי לָאו אִידִי וְאִידִי בְּאִישׁ, וְלֹא קַשְׁיָא: כָּאן לִגְדוֹלִים, כָּאן לִקְטַנִּים. – וְתִסְבְּרָא?! אִי בִּקְטַנִּים לְאַחֲרָיו טֶפַח לָמָּה לִי! אֶלָּא, אִידִי וְאִידִי בִּגְדוֹלִים, וְלֹא קַשְׁיָא: הָא בְּאִישׁ, הָא בְּאִשָּׁה. –אִי הָכִי, הָא דְּקָתָנֵי עֲלָהּ: *"וְזֶהוּ ק״ו שֶׁאֵין עָלָיו תְּשׁוּבָה", מַאי "אֵין עָלָיו תְּשׁוּבָה"? דַּרְכָּא דְּמִלְּתָא הָכִי אִיתָא! אֶלָּא לָאו – תְּפִילִּין, וּתְיוּבְתָּא דְּרָבָא אָמַר רַב שֵׁשֶׁת, תְּיוּבְתָּא. מִכׇּל מָקוֹם קַשְׁיָא: הַשְׁתָּא בֵּית הַכִּסֵּא קָבוּעַ שָׁרֵי, בֵּית הַכִּסֵּא עֲרַאי לֹא כׇּל שֶׁכֵּן?! –הָכִי קָאָמַר: בֵּית הַכִּסֵּא קָבוּעַ דְּלֵיכָּא נִיצוֹצוֹת – שָׁרֵי, בֵּית הַכִּסֵּא עֲרַאי דְּאִיכָּא נִיצוֹצוֹת – אָסְרֵי. אִי הָכִי, אַמַּאי 'אֵין עָלָיו תְּשׁוּבָה'? תְּשׁוּבָה מְעַלְּיְתָא הִיא! –הָכִי קָאָמַר: הָא מִילְּתָא תֵּיתֵי לַהּ בְּתוֹרַת טַעְמָא וְלָא תֵּיתֵי לַהּ בְּק״ו, דְּאִי אָתְיָא לַהּ בְּתוֹרַת ק״ו – זֶהוּ ק״ו שֶׁאֵין עָלָיו תְּשׁוּבָה.§ *ת״ר: ההָרוֹצֶה לִיכָּנֵס לִסְעוּדַת קֶבַע – מְהַלֵּךְ עֲשָׂרָה פְּעָמִים ד׳ אַמּוֹת, אוֹ ד׳ פְּעָמִים י׳ אַמּוֹת, וְיִפָּנֶה, ואח״כ נִכְנָס. אָמַר ר׳ יִצְחָק: הַנִּכְנָס לִסְעוּדַת קֶבַע – חוֹלֵץ תְּפִילָּיו ואח״כ נִכְנָס. וּפְלִיגָא דר׳ חִיָּיא, דא״ר חִיָּיא: ומַנִּיחָן עַל שֻׁלְחָנוֹ, וְכֵן הָדוּר לוֹ. וְעַד אֵימַת? אָמַר רַב נַחְמָן בַּר יִצְחָק: חעַד זְמַן בְּרָכָה.§ תָּנֵי חֲדָא: צוֹרֵר אָדָם תְּפִילָּיו עִם מְעוֹתָיו בְּאַפַּרְקְסוּתוֹ, וְתַנְיָא אִידָךְ: לֹא יָצוּר! לָא קַשְׁיָא: הָא – דְּאַזְמְנֵיהּ, הָא – דְּלָא אַזְמְנֵיהּ; *דְּאָמַר רַב חִסְדָּא: טהַאי סוּדָרָא דִּתְפִילִּין דְּאַזְמְנֵיהּ לְמֵיצַר בֵּיהּ תְּפִילִּין, צַר בֵּיהּ תְּפִילִּין, אָסוּר לְמֵיצַר בֵּיהּ פְּשִׁיטֵי, אַזְמְנֵיהּ וְלָא צַר בֵּיהּ, צַר בֵּיהּ וְלָא אַזְמְנֵיהּ – שָׁרֵי לְמֵיצַר בֵּיהּ זוּזֵי. וּלְאַבָּיֵי, דְּאָמַר *הַזְמָנָה מִילְּתָא הִיא, אַזְמְנֵיהּ אע״ג דְּלָא צַר בֵּיהּ; צַר בֵּיהּ, אִי אַזְמְנֵיהּ – אָסִיר, אִי לָא אַזְמְנֵיהּ – לָא.§ בְּעָא מִינֵּיהּ רַב יוֹסֵף בְּרֵיהּ דְּרַב נְחוּנְיָא מֵרַב יְהוּדָה: מַהוּ שֶׁיַּנִּיחַ אָדָם תְּפִילָּיו תַּחַת מְרַאֲשׁוֹתָיו? יתַּחַת מַרְגְּלוֹתָיו לָא קָא מִיבַּעְיָא לִי – שֶׁנּוֹהֵג בָּהֶן מִנְהַג בִּזָּיוֹן, כִּי קָא מִיבַּעְיָא לִי – תַּחַת מְרַאֲשׁוֹתָיו, מַאי? –א״ל, הָכִי אָמַר שְׁמוּאֵל: כמוּתָּר, אֲפִילּוּ אִשְׁתּוֹ עִמּוֹ. מֵיתִיבִי: לֹא יַנִּיחַ אָדָם תְּפִילָּיו תַּחַת מַרְגְּלוֹתָיו מִפְּנֵי שֶׁנּוֹהֵג בָּהֶם דֶּרֶךְ בִּזָּיוֹן, אֲבָל מַנִּיחָן תַּחַת מְרַאֲשׁוֹתָיו; וְאִם הָיְתָה אִשְׁתּוֹ עִמּוֹ – אָסוּר; הָיָה מָקוֹם שֶׁגָּבוֹהַּ ג׳ טְפָחִים אוֹ נָמוּךְ ג׳ טְפָחִים – מוּתָּר. תְּיוּבְתָּא דִּשְׁמוּאֵל! תְּיוּבְתָּא. אָמַר רָבָא: אע״ג דְּתַנְיָא תְּיוּבְתָּא דִּשְׁמוּאֵל – הִלְכְתָא כְּוָותֵיהּ. מ״ט?

כָּל

סה א מיי׳ פ״ה מהל׳ תפלה הלכה ה סמג עשין יט טור ש״ע או״ח סימן צו סעיף א:
סו ב מיי׳ פ״ד מהלכות תפילין הלכה יח סמג עשין כב טור וש״ע או״ח סימן מג סעיף א:
סז ג מיי׳ שם הל׳ טו סמג שם טוש״ע א״ח סימן מד:
סח ד מיי׳ פ״ה מהלכו׳ תפלה הלכה ה סמג עשין יט טוש״ע או״ח סימן צו סעיף א:
סט ה מיי׳ פ״ה מהל׳ דעות ה״ו טור ש״ע או״ח סימן ג סעיף ז:
ע ו מיי׳ פ״ד מהלכות דעות הלכה ב:
עא ז ח מיי׳ פ״ד מהל׳ תפילין הלכה טז סמג עשין כב טוש״ע או״ח סימן מ סעיף ח:
עב ט מיי׳ שם הל׳ ט סמג שם טוש״ע או״ח סי׳ מב סעיף ג:
עג י כ מיי׳ שם הל׳ כד סמג שם טוש״ע או״ח סי׳ מ סעיף ג:

**רב נסים גאון**

**ולאביי** דאמר הזמנה מילתא היא. עיקר דבריו של אביי במס׳ סנהדרין בפ׳ נגמר הדין (דף מז) איתמר האורג בגד למת אביי אמר אסור ורבא אמר מותר אביי אמר אסור הזמנה מילתא היא:

**הגהות הב״ח**

(א) רש״י ד״ה לאו אתיא וכו׳ בבית הכסא קבוע חמור:

**גליון הש״ס**

**רש״י** ד״ה ולא ייש בהן שמא יפיח. עיין סוכה ד׳ כו ע״א וצ״ע:

סוכה מח:
[שם כו.]
[ב״מ נה.]
שבת פב.
סנהדרין מח.
[שם מז: מח. מנחות לד:]

**הגהות**
[א] רש״י ד״ה ולא יישן בהן שמא י

כל לנטורינהו טפי עדיף.(א) והיכא מנח להו? — אמר ר' ירמיה: אבין כר לכסת שלא כנגד ראשו. והא תני רבי חייא: מניחן בכובע תחת מראשותיו! דמפיק ליה למורשא דכובע לבר. *בר קפרא צייר להו בכילתא ומפיק למורשהון לבר. רב ששא בריה דרב אידי במנח להו אשרשיפא ופרים סודרא עילוייהו. אמר רב המנונא בריה דרב יוסף: זימנא חדא הוה קאימנא קמיה דרבא ואמר לי: זיל אייתי לי תפילין. ואשכחתינהו בין כר לכסת שלא כנגד ראשו, והוה ידענא [ב]דיום טבילה הוה, ולאגמורן *הלכה למעשה הוא דעבד.§ בעי מיניה רב יוסף בריה דרב נחוניא מרב יהודה: שנים שישנים במטה אחת, מהו שזה יחזיר פניו ויקרא ק"ש, וזה יחזיר פניו ויקרא ק"ש? א"ל הכי אמר שמואל: ואפילו אשתו עמו. מתקיף לה רב יוסף: אשתו ולא מיבעיא אחר?! גאדרבה! *אשתו כגופו, דאחר לאו כגופו! מיתיבי: שנים שישנים במטה אחת — זה מחזיר פניו וקורא, וזה מחזיר פניו וקורא; ותניא אחריתי: הישן במטה ובניו ובני ביתו בצדו — הרי זה לא יקרא ק"ש אא"כ היתה טלית מפסקת ביניהן. ואם היו בניו ובני ביתו קטנים — מותר. בשלמא לרב יוסף לא קשיא: הא — באשתו, הא — באחר. אלא לשמואל קשיא! —אמר לך שמואל: לרב יוסף מי ניחא?! והתניא: היה ישן במטה,(ב) ובניו ובני ביתו במטה — לא יקרא ק"ש אא"כ היתה טליתו מפסקת ביניהן! אלא מאי אית לך למימר — אשתו לרב יוסף תנאי היא, לדידי נמי תנאי היא.§ אמר מר: "זה מחזיר פניו וקורא ק"ש". והא איכא עגבות! מסייע ליה לרב הונא, דא"ר הונא: עגבות אין בהם משום ערוה. לימא מסייע ליה לרב הונא: *האשה יושבת וקוצה לה חלתה ערומה מפני שיכולה לכסות פניה בקרקע, אבל לא האיש. תרגמה רב נחמן בר יצחק: זכגון שהיו פניה טוחות בקרקע.§ אמר מר: "אם היו בניו ובני ביתו קטנים — מותר." ועד כמה? —אמר רב חסדא: תינוקת בת שלש שנים ויום אחד, ותינוק בן ט' שנים ויום אחד. איכא דאמרי: חתינוקת בת י"א שנה ויום אחד, ותינוק בן שתים עשרה שנה ויום אחד, *אידי ואידי עד כדי °"שדים נכנו ושערך צמח". אמר ליה רב כהנא לרב אשי: התם אמר רבא "אע"ג דתיובתא דשמואל הלכתא כוותיה דשמואל", הכא מאי? —אמר ליה: *אטו כולהו בחדא מחתא מחתינהו?! אלא: היכא דאיתמר איתמר, והיכא דלא איתמר לא איתמר. א"ל רב מרי לרב פפא: שער יוצא בבגדו מהו? קרא עליה: שער, שער.§ א"ר יצחק: טפח באשה ערוה. למאי? אילימא לאסתכולי בה — והא *א"ר ששת: למה מנה הכתוב תכשיטין שבחוץ עם תכשיטין שבפנים — לומר לך: טכל המסתכל באצבע קטנה של אשה כאילו מסתכל במקום התורף! 'אלא: באשתו, ולק"ש. אמר רב חסדא: שוק באשה ערוה, שנאמר: °"גלי שוק עברי נהרות", וכתיב °"תגל ערותך וגם תראה חרפתך". *אמר שמואל: כקול באשה ערוה, שנא' °"כי קולך ערב ומראך נאוה". אמר רב ששת: לשער באשה ערוה, שנא' °"שערך כעדר העזים".§ אמר ר' חנינא: אני ראיתי את רבי שתלה תפיליו. מיתיבי: מהתולה תפיליו יתלו לו חייו. *דורשי חמורות אמרו °"והיו חייך תלאים לך מנגד" זה התולה תפיליו! —לא קשיא, הא — ברצועה, הא — בקציצה. ואיבעית אימא: לא שנא רצועה ולא שנא קציצה — אסור, וכי תלה רבי — נבכיסתא תלה. אי הכי, מאי למימרא? — מהו דתימא: תיבעי הנחה כספר תורה, קמ"ל.§ ואמר ר' חנינא: אני ראיתי את רבי סשגיהק ופיהק, ונתעטש, ורק וממשמש

תורה אור: יחזקאל טז; ישעיה מז; שם; שיר ב; שם ד; דברים כח

**והא** תני רבי חייא מניחן בכובע תחת מראשותיו. ואם תאמר: אימא בכובע שלא כנגד ראשו, שהרי בברייתא דלעיל נמי תני "תחת מראשותיו" ולא פריך מיניה, משום דמצינן לפרושי שלא כנגד ראשו! ואומר(ו) הרב: דא"כ מאי איריא בכובע? אפילו שלא בכובע נמי. אלא ש"מ דמיירי אפילו כנגד ראשו! ומ"מ קשיא ליטני דמיירי באשתו עמו, דבעיא כלי בתוך כלי! וצ"ע:

**שנים** שהיו ישנים במטה. וא"ת: והלא רואה ערות עצמו! וי"ל: שיוציא ראשו לחוץ. וא"ת: והרי לבו רואה את הערוה! וי"ל: דקסבר לבו רואה את הערוה מותר, אי נמי: חולץ בבגדו כנגד לבו:

**והתניא** היה ישן במטה ובני ביתו וכו'. פי' רש"י: אשתו בכלל ביתו. ולא נהירא, חדא: דלא אשכחן אשתו דמקריא בני ביתו. ועוד, לפירושו הול"ל והא קתני כאן, כיון דאברייתא דלעיל קאי, אבל מדקאמר "והתניא" משמע דברייתא אחרת היא! ואומר ה"ר יוסף דגרסינן "היה ישן במטה ואשתו ישנה בצדו — לא יחזיר פניו ויקרא אא"כ היתה טלית מפסקת בינו לבינה":

וממשמש

**כל לנטורינהו טפי עדיף.** להו מבזיוני, (ג)כמה שהוא מוזהר על שמירתן מן העכברים ומן הגנבים טפי עדיף להו מבזיוני: **בכובע.** הוא הכיס שלהם: **למורשא דכובע.** שהתפילין נכרין בבליטתן בקצה הכיס, והוא כמורשא: **צייר להו בכילתא.** ביריעה הפרוסה סביבו' מטתו קושרן: **ומפיק למורשהון לבר.** בליטת הקשר שהתפילין בולטין מן היריעה היה הופך לצד החוץ, ולא לצד המטה: **אשרשיפא.** ספסל: **יום טבילה הוה.** יום שטבלה אשתו, דהוה ליה ליל תשמיש. והיינו כשמואל דאמר אפילו אשתו עמו: **ולאגמורן הלכה למעשה.** מה שצוני להביאם לו לא עשה אלא ללמדני הלכה לעשות מעשה כשמואל: **ואפילו אשתו עמו.** (ד)שיחזיר פניו. דכל זמן שהן פונים פנים כנגד פנים, פשיטא ליה דאסור, דאיכא הרהור נגיעת ערוה על ידי חברי תשמיש: **אשתו כגופו.** ורגיל בה, וליכא הרהור כולי האי: **בשלמא לרב יוסף.** דאמר אשתו היא דשריא, אבל אחר — לא, מתרץ להו למתניתא הא באשתו, הא באחר. והא דקתני בני ביתו — אינו אשתו: **היה ישן במטה ובני ביתו.** ואשתו בכלל ביתו: **לדידי נמי.** בין אשתו בין אחר, פלוגתא דהני תנאי היא: **הא איכא עגבות.** דנגעי אהדדי: **וקוצה חלתה ערומה.** ואף על פי שערום אסור לברך, אשה יושבת מותרת, שבישיבתה פניה שלמטה מכוסים בקרקע: **אבל לא האיש.** מפני שהביצים והגיד בולטין ונראין. ואף על פי שמגולות עגבותי' — והיינו סייעתא: **כגון שהיו פניה טוחות.** דבוקות ומכוסות בקרקע. טוחות משמע לשון שעיעות, טיח חלק שאינה בולטת, אפלטיירש"א בלע"ז: **בת שלש ובן תשע.** שהוא זמן שהן באין לכלל ביאה: **בת י"א ובן י"ב.** זמן שהן באות לכלל שערות ושדיהן נכונים, שמשם ואילך באות לכלל [ביאה] שאדם מתאוה להן: **התם אמר רבא.** גבי תפילין תחת מראשותיו דקאמר שמואל אפי' אשתו עמו, הלכה כשמואל: **הכא.** גבי שנים שהם ישנים, דקא שרי שמואל באשתו עמו, מאי: **מחתא מחתינהו.** באריגה אחת *ארגתם: **יצא שערו בבגדו.** שנקב בגדו כנגד זקן התחתון, ויצא מן השער בנקב, מהו? מי הוי ערוה לקרות ק"ש כנגדו או לא: **שער שער.** כלומר: מה בכך: **לאסתכולי בה.** אם אשת איש היא: **תכשיטין שבפנים.** כומז דפוס של בית הרחם שהיו עושין לבנותיהן, ונוקבין כתלי בית הרחם כדרך שנוקבין את האזנים ותוחבין אותו, כדי שלא יזדקקו להן זכרים: **עם תכשיטין שבחוץ.** אצעדה וצמיד, הן הביאו אותן על כפרת הרהור עבירה שנסתכלו בבנות מדין: **לאשתו ולק"ש.** אם טפח מגולה בה — לא יקרא ק"ש כנגדה: **שוק.** *באשת איש: **ערוה.** להסתכל, וכן באשתו לק"ש: **גלי שוק.** וכתיב בתריה תגל ערותך: **קולך ערב.** מדמשבח לה קרא בגוה — שמע מינה תאוה היא: **התולה תפיליו.** ביתד, יתלו חייו: **דורשי רשומות.** קשרים וסתומים הכלולים בתורה. דורשי חמורות גרסינן, והיא היא: **זה התולה תפיליו.** שהתורה חייו של אדם (ה)ורמז לך הכתוב שיתלו חייו: **ברצועה.** והקציצה למטה, גנאי הוא להם. אבל תולה הוא אותם בקציצה, ותהא הקציצה מונחת על היתד והרצועה למטה: **בכיסתא תלה.** בתוך תיקן היו, ותלה התיק: **שגיהק.** ריט"ייר בלע"ז, פעמים שאדם מוציא מגופו לפיו נפיחה מתוך שובעו וריחה כריח המאכל שאכל: **פיהק.** באליי"ר בלע"ז, חיך מלקוחיו פותח להוציא רוח הפה מלא, כאדם שרוצה לישן או שעמד משינה: **ונתעטש.** שטרנוד"ר בלע"ז. ויש שדורשים גיהק נוטריקון גו הקיס סטריליי"ר פיהק — פיו הקיס: **ורק.** ע"ג קרקע: וממשמש

עד א מיי' וסמג טוש"ע שם:
עה ב טוש"ע או"ח סימן רמ סעיף (ו) [ה]:
עו ג מיי' פ"ג מהלכות ק"ש הלכה יח סמג עשין יח טוש"ע או"ח סימן עג סעיף ב:
עז ד מיי' שם טוש"ע שם סעיף א:
עח ה ו מיי' פ"ה מהל' ברכות הלכה כ סמג עשין כז טור ש"ע או"ח סי' עד סעיף ד ובסי' רו סעיף ג' [וביו"ד סי' שכח סעיף א]:
עט ז מיי' פ"ג מהלכות ק"ש הלכה יח סמג עשין יח טוש"ע או"ח סימן עג סעיף ג:
פ ח מיי' שם הל' יט טוש"ע שם סעיף ד:
פא ט מיי' פכ"א מהל' איסו"ב הל' ב סמג לאוין קכו טוש"ע אה"ע סי' כא סעיף א:
פב י מיי' פ"ג מהל' ק"ש הל' טז סמג עשין יח טוש"ע או"ח סי' עה סעיף א:
פג כ [מיי' פ"א מהל' איסו"ב הלכה ב טוש"ע] אה"ע סי' כא סעיף א:
פד ל [מיי' שם] טוש"ע או"ח סי' עה סעיף ב וטוש"ע אה"ע סי' כא סעיף א:
פה מ נ מיי' פ"ד מהל' תפילין הל' ט סמג עשין כב טוש"ע או"ח סי' מ סעיף א:
פו ס מיי' פ"ד מהלכות תפלה הל' יא סמג עשין יט טוש"ע או"ח סי' צז סעיף א:

[שבת קמח. פסחים מב. חולין נח:]

**רב נסים גאון**

**מסייעא** ליה לרב הונא דאמר רב הונא עגבות אין בהן משום ערוה. הא מילתא מיפרשא בפ' ב' דמס' חלה בגמ' דבני מערבא (הלכה א') הדא אמרה עגבות אין בהם משום ערוה הדא דאיתמר לברכה אבל להביט אפי' כל שהוא אסור להביט כההיה דתני המסתכל בעקיבה של אשה כמסתכל בבית הרחם והמסתכל בבית הרחם כאילו בא עליה: **והאמר** רב ששת למה מנה הכתוב תכשיטין שבחוץ עם תכשיטין שבפנים. מפרש' לה במס' שבת בפ' במה אשה (ד' סד) ונקרב את קרבן ה' אמר ר' אלעזר עגיל זה דפוס של דדין כומז זה דפוס של בית הרחם אמר ליה רבא אטו מקרא לא שמעת מיניה כומז כאן מקום זמה והנה כבר הזכיר

[...]ות פ' בא איתה רב פפא
[נד. כולה כנו: כ"ב ע"ג עד. סנהדרין יח.]
[...]ות סו. מנחות נג: בכורות לה:]
חלה פ"ב משנה ג
[קדושין פא:]
[נו: פירש"י ביחר ביאור ע"ש]
שבת סד:
[קדושין ע.]
[פסחים נב. חולין קלד:]
[ב"ח באו"ח סי' ע"ה על דברי רש"י הללו]

[הג]הות הב"ח (א) גמרא טפי עדיף מבזיוני והיכא: (ב) שם היה ישן במטה ובני ביתו כנ"ל ותיבת ובניו נמחק: (ג) רש"י ד"ה כל לנטורינהו וכו' מבזיוני כיון שהוא: (ד) ד"ה ואפילו אשתו עמו והוא שיחזיר: (ה) ד"ה זה התולה תפיליו שהתפילין חייו של אדם. נ"ב בפרק התכלת דף מ"ד ואמר ריש לקיש כל המניח תפילין מאריך ימים שנאמר אדני עליהם יחיו: (ו) תוס' ד"ה והא תני וכו' ואומר הרב רבינו יוסף לא"כ:

[גליו]ן הש"ס תוס' ד"ה והתניא כו' דלא אשכחן אשתו דמקריא בני ביתו. עי' פסחים דף נט ע"ב תוס' ד"ה ולא יפחתו. ועי' פר"ח או"ח בלקוטיו (סימן רל"ח):

פז א טוש"ע או"ח סי' צז סעיף ג:
פח ב טוש"ע שם סעי' ד:
פט ג [טור שו"ע שם ס"א]
[ד [מיי' פ"ד מהל' תפלה הל' יא טוש"ע] שם סעיף א:
צ ה טוש"ע או"ח סי' קג סעיף ג:
צא ו ז מיי' פ"ד מהל' תפלה הלכה יא סמג עשין יט טור שו"ע או"ח סימן צז סעיף ב:
צב ח ט מיי' פ"ה שם הלכה ט סמג שם טוש"ע או"ח סימן קא סעיף ב:
צג י מיי' פ"ד שם הל' יא סמג שם טוש"ע או"ח סי' קג סעי' א:
צד כ מיי' שם הל' יב טוש"ע שם סעי' ב:
צה ל מיי' פ"ג מהלכות ק"ש הלכה יז סמג עשין יח טוש"ע או"ח סימן עד סעיף א:
צו מ ש"ע י"ד סי' רמו סעיף כו בהגה:
צז נ מיי' שם הלכה ד סמג שם טוש"ע א"ח סימן פה סעיף ב:
צח ס ע מיי' שם הלכה יד ופ"ב שם הל' יב טוש"ע או"ח סימן פה סעי' א וסי' סה סעי' א וסי' עח:
צט פ מיי' פ"ג שם הל' יז סמג שם טוש"ע א"ח סי' עד סעיף ו:

ומשמש בבגדו, אבל לא היה מתעטף. וכשהוא מפהק – היה מניח ידו על סנטרו. מיתיבי: המשמיע קולו בתפלתו – הרי זה מקטני אמנה, המגביה קולו בתפלתו – הרי זה מנביאי השקר, מגהק ומפהק – הרי זה מגסי הרוח. המתעטש בתפלתו – סימן רע לו, ויש אומרים:(א) ניכר שהוא מכוער. הרק בתפלתו – כאילו רק בפני המלך! בשלמא מגהק ומפהק לא קשיא: כאן – לאונסו, כאן – לרצונו, אלא מתעטש אמתעטש קשיא! מתעטש אמתעטש נמי לא קשיא: כאן – מלמעלה, כאן – מלמטה; דאמר רב זירא: הא מילתא אבלעא לי בי רב המנונא, ותקילא לי ככולי תלמודאי: המתעטש בתפלתו – סימן יפה לו, כשם שעושים לו נחת רוח מלמטה כך עושין לו נחת רוח מלמעלה. אלא רק ארק קשיא! רק ארק נמי לא קשיא: אפשר כדרב יהודה; דאמר רב יהודה: היה עומד בתפלה ונזדמן לו רוק – מבליעו בטליתו, ואם טלית נאה הוא – מבליעו באפרקסותו. רבינא הוה קאי אחורי דרב אשי, נזדמן לו רוק, פתקיה לאחוריה. א"ל: לא סבר לה מר להא דרב יהודה "מבליעו באפרקסותו"?! א"ל: אנינא דעתאי. המשמיע קולו בתפלתו הרי זה מקטני אמנה. אמר רב הונא: לא שנו אלא שיכול לכוון את לבו בלחש, אבל אין יכול לכוון את לבו בלחש – מותר; וה"מ – ביחיד, אבל בציבור – אתי למיטרד ציבורא. רבי אבא הוה קא משתמיט מיניה דרב יהודה, דהוה קא בעי למיסק לארעא דישראל, דאמר רב יהודה: כל העולה מבבל לא"י עובר בעשה, שנאמר: "בבלה יובאו ושמה יהיו עד יום פקדי אותם נאם ה'". אמר: איזיל ואשמע מיניה מילתא מבית וועדא, והדר אפיק. אזל אשכחיה לתנא דקתני קמיה דרב יהודה: היה עומד בתפלה ונתעטש – ממתין עד שיכלה הרוח וחוזר ומתפלל, איכא דאמרי: היה עומד בתפלה וביקש להתעטש – מרחיק לאחריו ד' אמות ומתעטש, וממתין עד שיכלה הרוח, וחוזר ומתפלל; ואומר: רבש"ע, יצרתנו נקבים נקבים חלולים חלולים, גלוי וידוע לפניך חרפתנו וכלימתנו בחיינו, ובאחריתנו רמה ותולעה; ומתחיל ממקום שפסק.[א] אמר ליה:(ב) אילו לא באתי אלא לשמוע דבר זה – דיי. ת"ר: היה ישן בטליתו ואינו יכול להוציא את ראשו מפני הצנה – חוצץ בטליתו על צוארו וקורא ק"ש. וי"א: על לבו. ותנא קמא – הרי לבו רואה את הערוה! קסבר: לבו רואה את הערוה מותר. אמר רב הונא א"ר יוחנן: היה מהלך במבואות המטונפות – מניח ידו על פיו וקורא ק"ש. א"ל רב חסדא: האלהים! אם אמרה לי ר' יוחנן בפומיה – לא צייתנא ליה. איכא דאמרי, אמר רבה בר בר חנה אמר ריב"ל: היה מהלך במבואות המטונפות – מניח ידו על פיו וקורא ק"ש. א"ל ר' חסדא: האלהים! אם אמרה לי ריב"ל בפומיה – לא צייתנא ליה. ומי אמר ר' הונא הכי? והאמר רב הונא: ת"ח אסור לו לעמוד במקום הטנופת – לפי שאי אפשר לו לעמוד בלי הרהור תורה! – לא קשיא, כאן – בעומד, כאן – במהלך. ומי אמר רבי יוחנן הכי? והאמר רבה בר בר חנה א"ר יוחנן: בכל מקום מותר להרהר בדברי תורה – חוץ מבית המרחץ ומבית הכסא! וכי תימא, הכא נמי, כאן בעומד כאן במהלך; איני?! והא רבי אבהו הוה קא אזיל בתריה דרבי יוחנן, והוה קא קרי ק"ש, כי מטא במבואות המטונפות אשתיק. א"ל לר' יוחנן: להיכן אהדר? א"ל: אם שהית כדי לגמור את כולה – חזור לראש! הכי קאמר ליה: לדידי – לא סבירא לי, לדידך דסבירא לך – אם שהית כדי לגמור את כולה חזור לראש. תניא כותיה דרב הונא, תניא כותיה דרב חסדא. תניא כותיה דרב הונא: המהלך במבואות המטונפות – מניח ידו על פיו וקורא ק"ש. תניא כותיה דרב חסדא: היה מהלך במבואות המטונפות – לא יקרא ק"ש; ולא עוד אלא שאם היה קורא ובא – פוסק. לא פסק מאי? אמר ר' מיאשה בר בריה דריב"ל: עליו הכתוב אומר "וגם אני נתתי להם חקים לא טובים ומשפטים לא יחיו [בהם]". ר' אסי אמר:(ג) "הוי מושכי העון בחבלי השוא". רב אדא בר אהבה אמר מהכא: "כי דבר ה' בזה". ואם פסק מה שכרו? אמר ר' אבהו: עליו הכתוב אומר: "ובדבר הזה תאריכו ימים". אמר רב הונא: היתה טליתו חגורה לו על מתניו – מותר לקרות ק"ש. תניא נמי הכי: היתה טליתו, של בגד ושל שק, חגורה על מתניו – מותר לקרות ק"ש; אבל

ירמיה כז | יחזקאל כ | ישעיה ה | במדבר טו | דברים לב

**וממשמש** בבגדו. פרש"י: להעביר הכינה העוקצתו, אבל לא מתעטף אם נפלה טליתו, ותרי מילי נינהו. ור"ח פי' דחדא מילתא היא; פי' ממשמש בבגדו – תקן(ה) שלא יפול מעל ראשו, אבל אם נפל מעל ראשו – לא היה מתעטף, שהרי היא הפסקה אם מתעטף כיון שנפל לגמרי, אבל לתקן קצת שלא יפול – לא הוי הפסקה:

**ואומר** רבון העולמים. מיד כשגומר תפלתו, ואח"כ מתחיל ממקום שפסק:

**אמר** ליה לדידי לא סבירא לי. פירוש: משום תרתי מילי, חדא: דסבירא לי דאינו חוזר לראש, דאמר רבי יוחנן (ר"ה דף לד:): שמע תשע תקיעות בתשע שעות יצא. ועוד, דסבירא לי מניח ידו על פיו, ואם כן הוי ליה רשאי, אלא לדידך דסבירא לך דחייב להפסיק וכו':

**בחבלי** השוא. כלומר: בחנם מושכים עליהם עון, כי טוב היה שלא היו מקיימין אותו כלל:

*__פסק__ רבינו חננאל כרב חסדא דאסור לקרות ק"ש אפילו צואה תחת בגדו על בשרו, וס"ל "כל עצמותי תאמרנה" (תהלים לה). °דאע"ג דר' חסדא תלמיד דר' הונא הוה, לאומרא אזלינן. ורב אלפס פסק כרב הונא, מדאקשי גמרא מיניה ביומא פרק "הממונה" (ד' ל.):

וממשמש בבגדו. להעביר הכינה העוקצתו: אבל לא היה מתעטף. אם נפלה טליתו – לא היה נוטלה ומתעטף, שלא להפסיק: על סנטרו. מנטו"ן בלע"ז. שלא תראה פתיחת פיו: הרי זה מקטני אמנה. כאילו אין הקב"ה שומע תפלת לחש:(ד) ומגביה קולו. הרי זה מנביאי השקר. דכתיב ויקראו בקול גדול (מלכים א' יח): המגהק והמפהק הרי זה מגסי הרוח. וי"א: ניכר שהוא מכוער. גרסינן: אלא אעטוש קשיא. דאין עטוש אלא לאונסו: למטה. מפיח בקול. ותקילא לי ככולי תלמודאי. שקולה עלי וחביבה, לפי שהיה רגיל להתעטש: כשם שעושים לו נחת רוח. שהעטוש נחת רוח לאדם, כך עושים לו נחת רוח מלמעלה. מן השמים, למלאות שאלתו: אפשר כדרב יהודה. להבליעו באפרקסותו = סודר שבראשו, ושני ראשין תלויין בפניו: פתקיה. זרקו: משתמיט מיניה. לא היה נראה אליו, לפי שהיה רבי אבא חפץ לעלות לא"י ורב יהודה אוסר לו, לפיכך לא היה נכנס לבית המדרש: ואשמע מיניה מילתא. מתוך. מבית וועדא. מבית המדרש: ונתעטש. מלמטה: עד שיכלה הרוח. מגופו, שנודף מאותו רוח: וחוזר לתפלה. למקום שפסק: ואומר. בתוך התפלה, דהא מופסקת ועומדת כבר על ידי הרוח, לפיכך יכול להפסיק נמי ולומר דבר זה באמצע: חוצץ בטליתו על צוארו. מה שיש מן הטלית ולמעלה מן כתפיו מדביק בצוארו, ונמצא ערום קאמר: לדידי לא סבירא לי. לא הייתי מזקיקו להפסיק: בחבלי השוא. בחבלים שאינם חזקים, אלא נוחין להנתק הן מושכין העון על עצמם: אף זה. על ידי דבור בעלמא הוא נענש: ובדבר הזה. בשביל דבור זה שנזהרתם עליו, תאריכון ימים: היתה טליתו חגורה על מתניו. לכסותו ממתניו ולמטה, אע"פ שממתניו ולמעלה הוא ערום – קורא ק"ש: אבל

תורה אור

תיבת וכשהוא ליתא מן מפירש"י נכתב

ס"א איבעי

[מנחות יז.]

הגהות

[א] גמרא ממקום שפסק (וכו"מ כתוב דל"ג)

שבת מא. כתו

מבית וועדא כל"ל רש"א

[כ"ה ברא"ש איתא הריח]

[לעיל טז. שב

שבת מ. קנ. ע"ג מג: זבח

ר"ה לה:

[לעיל כג.]

תוספתא פ"ב

## רב נסים גאון

הזכיר טבעת שהוא תכשיט שבחוץ עם כומז שהוא תכשיט שבפנים ובתר הכי הוזכרה שמעתא דרב ששת והתם היא עיקרה ולא הוזכרה בכאן אלא כדי להקשות ממנה:

## הגהות הב"ח

(א) גמ' המגהק והמפהק וכו' ויש אומרים (ניכר שהוא מכוער) תא"מ ונ"ב ס"א שהוא עכן: (ב) שם אמר אילו כל"ל ותיבת ליה נמחק: (ג) שם ר' אסי אמר מהכא הוי מושכי: (ד) רש"י ד"ה הרי זה וכו' לתא הס"ד ואח"כ מ"ה המגביה הרבה הרי זה מנביאי: (ה) תוס' ד"ה וממשמש וכו' תקן בגדו שלא יפול:

## גליון הש"ס

תום' ד"ה פסק ר"ח וכו' דאע"ג דר"ח וכו'. עי' בב"מ (דף ל"ג ע"א):

אבל לתפלה – עד שיכסה את לבו. וא"ר הונא: שכח ונכנס בתפילין לבית הכסא – מניח ידו עליהן עד שיגמור. עד שיגמור ס"ד?! –אלא כדאמר ר"נ בר יצחק: עד שיגמור עמוד ראשון. ולפסוק לאלתר וליקום! –משום דרשב"ג; דתניא, רשב"ג אומר: עמוד החוזר מביא את האדם לידי הדרוקן. סילון החוזר – מביא את האדם לידי ירקון.§ אתמר: צואה על בשרו, או ידו מונחת בבית הכסא; רב הונא אמר: מותר לקרות ק"ש; רב חסדא אמר: אסור לקרות ק"ש. אמר רבא: מ"ט דרב הונא – דכתיב "כל הנשמה תהלל יה". ורב חסדא אמר: אסור לקרות ק"ש. מ"ט דרב חסדא – דכתיב "כל עצמותי תאמרנה ה' מי כמוך".§ אתמר: ריח רע שיש לו עיקר, רב הונא אמר: מרחיק ד' אמות וקורא ק"ש; ורב חסדא אמר: מרחיק ד' אמות ממקום שפסק הריח, וקורא ק"ש. תניא כוותיה דרב חסדא: לא יקרא אדם ק"ש, לא כנגד צואת אדם ולא כנגד צואת כלבים, ולא כנגד צואת חזירים, ולא כנגד צואת תרנגולים, ולא כנגד צואת אשפה שריחה רע; ואם היה מקום גבוה עשרה טפחים או נמוך עשרה טפחים – יושב בצדו וקורא ק"ש, ואם לאו – מרחיק מלוא עיניו; וכן לתפלה. ריח רע שיש לו עיקר – מרחיק ד' אמות ממקום הריח, וקורא ק"ש. אמר רבא, לית הלכתא כי הא מתניתא (בכל הני שמעתתא) אלא כי הא דתניא: לא יקרא אדם ק"ש לא כנגד צואת אדם ולא כנגד צואת חזירים ולא כנגד צואת כלבים בזמן שנתן עורות לתוכן. בעו מיניה מרב ששת: ריח רע שאין לו עיקר מהו? אמר להו: אתו חזו הני ציפי דבי רב, דהני גנו והני גרסי. וה"מ – בדברי תורה, אבל בק"ש – לא; ודברי תורה נמי לא אמרן אלא דחבריה, אבל דידיה – לא.§ אתמר, צואה עוברת; אביי אמר: מותר לקרות ק"ש; רבא אמר: אסור לקרות ק"ש. אמר אביי מנא אמינא לה – דתנן: הטמא עומד תחת האילן והטהור עובר – טמא, טהור עומד תחת האילן וטמא עובר – טהור, ואם עמד – טמא; וכן באבן המנוגעת. ורבא אמר לך: התם – בקביעותא תליא מילתא, דכתיב: "בדד ישב מחוץ למחנה מושבו", הכא: "והיה מחניך קדוש" אמר רחמנא, והא ליכא.§ א"ר פפא: פי חזיר כצואה עוברת דמי. פשיטא! –לא צריכא, אע"ג דסליק מנהרא. א"ר יהודה: ספק צואה – אסורה; ספק מי רגלים – מותרים. א"ד, אמר רב יהודה: ספק צואה, בבית – מותרת, באשפה – אסורה; ספק מי רגלים – אפילו באשפה נמי מותרין. סבר לה כי הא דרב המנונא, דאמר רב המנונא: לא אסרה תורה אלא כנגד עמוד בלבד, וכדרבי יונתן. דר' יונתן רמי: כתיב "ויד תהיה לך מחוץ למחנה ויצאת שמה חוץ", וכתיב: "ויתד תהיה לך וגו' וכסית את צאתך"! הא כיצד – כאן בגדולים, כאן בקטנים; אלמא: קטנים לא אסרה תורה אלא כנגד עמוד בלבד. הא נפול לארעא – שרי, ורבנן הוא דגזרו בהו, וכי גזרו בהו רבנן – בודאן, אבל בספקן לא גזור. ובודאן עד כמה? אמר רב יהודה אמר שמואל: כל זמן שמטפיחין; וכן אמר רבה בב"ח א"ר יוחנן: כל זמן שמטפיחין; וכן אמר עולא: כל זמן שמטפיחין. גניבא משמיה דרב אמר: כל זמן שרשומן ניכר. א"ר יוסף: שרא ליה מריה לגניבא! השתא צואה, אמר רב יהודה אמר רב: כיון שקרמו פניה מותר, מי רגלים מיבעיא?! – א"ל אביי: מאי חזית דסמכת אהא – סמוך אהא! דאמר רבה בר רב הונא אמר רב: צואה, אפילו כחרס – אסורה. והיכי דמי צואה כחרס? אמר רבה בב"ח א"ר יוחנן: כל זמן שזורקה ואינה נפרכת; וא"ד: כל זמן שגוללה ואינה נפרכת. אמר רבינא: הוה קאימנא קמיה דרב יהודה מדיפתי, חזא צואה, אמר לי: עיין אי קרמו פניה אי לא. א"ד, הכי א"ל: עיין אי מפלאי אפלויי. מאי הוי עלה? אתמר: צואה כחרס; אמימר אמר: אסורה; ומר זוטרא אמר: מותרת. אמר רבא, הלכתא: צואה כחרס אסורה, ומי רגלים כל זמן שמטפיחין. מיתיבי: מי רגלים כל זמן שמטפיחין – אסורין, נבלעו או יבשו – מותרים; מאי לאו נבלעו דומיא דיבשו, מה יבשו – דאין רשומן ניכר, אף נבלעו – דאין רשומן ניכר, הא רשומן ניכר – אסור, אע"ג דאין מטפיחין! – ולטעמיך, אימא רישא: כל זמן שמטפיחין הוא דאסור, הא רשומן ניכר – שרי! – אלא: מהא ליכא למשמע מינה. לימא כתנאי: כלי שנשפכו ממנו מי רגלים – אסור לקרות ק"ש כנגדו, ומי רגלים עצמן שנשפכו – נבלעו – מותר, לא נבלעו – אסור; ר' יוסי אומר: כל זמן שמטפיחין. מאי נבלעו ומאי לא נבלעו דקאמר ת"ק? אילימא נבלעו – דאין מטפיחין, לא נבלעו – דמטפיחין, ואתא ר' יוסי למימר: כ"ז שמטפיחין הוא דאסור, הא רשומן ניכר שרי! – היינו ת"ק! אלא: נבלעו – דאין רשומן ניכר, לא נבלעו – דרשומן ניכר, ואתא ר' יוסי למימר: כ"ז שמטפיחין הוא דאסור, הא רשומן ניכר – שרי! –לא, דכ"ע כ"ז שמטפיחין הוא דאסור, הא רשומן ניכר – שרי; והכא

תהלים קנ | שם לה | ויקרא יג | דברים כג | שם | שם

**רש"י**

אבל לתפלה. צריך הוא להראות את עצמו כעומד לפני המלך ולעמוד באימה, אבל ק"ש אינו מדבר לפני המלך: הדרוקן. חולי המעכב את הרגלים: סילון. של מי רגלים: ירקון. חולי ששמו גלנוי"ה: ידיו בבית הכסא. מחילה יש אינו לבין בית הכסא, ופשט ידיו לפנים מן המחילה: כל הנשמה. הפה והחוטם בכלל ההילול, ולא שאר אברים: שיש לו עיקר. שהצואה מונחת שם ומסרחת; ושאין לו עיקר – הפחת רוח: מרחיק ד' אמות. מן העיקר, ואע"פ שהריח בא אליו, וכגון שהיה לאחוריו, שאינו רואה אותה: ממקום שפסק הריח. שהריח כלה שם: לא כנגד צואת אדם כו'. ואע"פ שאין ריח: לית הלכתא כי הא מתניתא. דלעיל, דאסר צואת כלבים וחזירים בשאין בהם עורות: בזמן שיש בהן עורות. אצואת כלבים וחזירים קאי, שדרכן לתתן בעבוד העורות. אבל צואת אדם – אפי' בלא עורות, שהרי אין דרכן לתתן שם הלכך ע"כ בלא עורות קאמר: שאין לו עיקר. הפחת רוח: ציפי. מחצלות, של בית המדרש: דהני גנו והני גרסי. ואע"פ שדרך הישנים להפיח: וה"מ לגרסא. משום דלא אפשר: אבל לק"ש. יצא לחוץ ויקרא: אבל לדידיה. הפיח הוא עצמו, ממתין עד שיכלה הריח: צואה עוברת. אדם שנושאים לפניו גרף של רעי להעבירו: מותר לקרות. וא"צ להפסיק: הטמא עומד תחת האילן. ולא בנושא את המת קאי, דמת לא שנא עומד ול"ש יושב ול"ש הולך – אהל הוא. וגבי מצורע קתני לה בת"כ, דגלי ביה רחמנא ישיבה דכתיב בדד ישב מחוץ למחנה מושבו. [מושבו] טמא. מכאן אמרו: עומד נמי כיושב דמי, דקביע, אבל מהלך לא קביע: אבן המנוגעת. הרי היא כמצורע, שהקישה הכתוב זאת התורה לכל נגע הצרעת ולנתק ולצרעת הבגד ולבית (ויקרא יד): פשיטא. דפי חזיר אינו בלא צואה: בבית מותר. דאין דרך להניח צואה בבית: לא אסרה תורה. במי רגלים, לקרות, אלא כנגד עמוד הקלוח בלבד: ויצאת שמה חוץ. ולא הצריכו כסוי וכתיב וכסית: עד כמה. ישהו על גבי קרקע ויהא אסור: שרא ליה מריה. ימחול לו רבונו, דודאי שקר העיד משמיה דרב. היבשה נפרכת היא יותר מן הלחה: איכא דאמרי. חומרא היא, אף ע"פ שאם זורקה נפרכת, הואיל ואינה נפרכת מגלגול – לחה היא: קרמו. לשון קרום, טיל"א, כלומר: גלד מעט: אי מפלאי אפלויי. אם יש בה סדקים סדקים – יבשה היא, ושרי: מאי הוי עלה. דמי רגלים: נבלעו. בארץ: יבשו. על גבי אבנים בחמה:

בטופח

**תוספות**

לית הלכתא כי הא מתניתא אלא כי הא דתניא כו'. פרש"י: לית הלכתא כי הא מתניתא דלעיל דאסרה צואת כלבים וחזירים אפי' בשאין בהם עורות, אבל בצואת אדם לא שייך ואסור בכל ענין. משמע אבל בצואת תרנגולים לא איירי רבא, ובהדיא ברייתא לא גרס צואת תרנגולים כלל ולא פליג בהא אמתניתא דלעיל, ולפי זה יש לאסור צואת תרנגולין. ואומר רבינו יהודה: דדוקא כשהן בלול שלהם, שיש שם סרחון גדול, אבל בתרנגולים ההולכים בבית – אין חוששין. ובירושלמי* יש דלהדומים בלבד יש לחוש, *ולא ידעינן לפרש. ועוד קאמר מרחיקין מגללי בהמה ד' אמות, ר' שמואל ברבי יצחק אומר: ובלבד של חמור:

ריח רע שאין לו עיקר. י"מ דבתי כסאות שלנו בעומק, אם יש בהן מחילה מפסקת, הויא כמו ריח רע שאין לו עיקר, כמו בתי כסאות דפרסאי לקמן (ד' כו.) והרי

**עין משפט נר מצוה**

ק א [מיי' פ"ד מהלכות תפלה הלכה ז] וטוש"ע שם ובסי' לא סעיף ח:

קא ב מיי' פ"ד מהל' תפלין הל' כ סמג עשין כב טוש"ע א"ח סי' מג סעיף ח:

קב ג מיי' פ"ג מהל' ק"ש הלכה יא טוש"ע או"ח סימן עו סעיף ז:

קג ד מיי' שם הל' יב סמג עשין יח טור שו"ע א"ח סי' עו סעיף ח:

קד שם סעיף ח: [בגהות מרדכי פירש לפי שבארץ אדום היו השערים מצויים כלאי כתובות סד: והוא מאכילין התרנגולין שעורי' וצואתן מסרחת וע' ב"י סי' עט]

קה ו [מיי' שם הלכה ט טוש"ע]. שם סעי' ב:

קו ז מיי' פ"ד מהלכות תפלה הלכה ח סמג שם טור שו"ע או"ח סי' ל סעיף כו:

קז ח מיי' פ"ג מהלכות ק"ש הל' ו סמג שם טור שו"ע אורח חיים סימן עט סעיף [א] ד:

קח ט י כ [מיי' שם הל' יד טור שו"ע] שם סעיף ט:

קט ל מיי' שם הלכה יג סמג שם טוש"ע א"ח סימן עו סעיף ג:

קי מ מיי' פ"י מהלכות טומאת צרעת הל' יב: תוספתא פ"ב

קיא נ מיי' פ"ג מהל' ק"ש הלכה יג סמג עשין יח טוש"ע או"ח סימן עו סעיף ג:

קיב ס ע מיי' שם הל' טו [ועיין בכ"מ] טור שו"ע שם סעי' ז:

קיג פ מיי' שם הל' ז סמג שם טוש"ע או"ח סי' פב סעי' א [וסעיף ב]:

**רב נסים גאון**

ריח רע שיש לו עיקר. גרסי בני מערבא [בפירקין הלכה ה] אמר רב חסדא* מסוף ריח רע ד' אמות הדא דאיתמר לאחריו אבל לפניו עד מקום שעיניו רואות כהדא ר' בא וחבריה הוו יתבין קמי פונדקייה ברמשא אמרין מהו למימר מילי דאורייה אמרין מכיון דאילו הוה ביממא הוינן חמין ליה ואסור ברם כדון אסור:

**גליון הש"ס**

גמ' כאן בקטנים. ע' בכורות מ"ד ע"ב תוס' ד"ה אימתי: רש"י ד"ה בזמן שיש כו' שדרכן לתתן כו'. עי' ברש"י כתובות ע"ז ע"א ד"ה מקמץ וצ"ע: שם בעבוד העורות. וכן איתא בילקוט פ' בא בפסוק ולא יחרץ כלב לשונו. ולא עוד אלא שזכו לעבד עורות מצואתן ולכתוב בהם סת"ס:

**מסורת הש"ס**

מד: לקמן סב: תמיד כז:

יומא ל.

כנגד אשפה כצ"ל (ח"מ)

[י"ף וברא"ש ליתא]

לג: נגעים פי"ג תוספתא דנגעים ת"כ פרשה מצורע

קכא. וע"ש בכס"מ ... כב. כז. יבמות עו. ... לג. פה: ב"ב קד. ... שם: ע"ג כב. עב. ... לח. זבחים פט: ... קט. נדה לג: ... סוטה קדושין ה:

**הגהות הגר"א**

[א] גמ' ולא כנגד אשפה [ב] שם (ולא כנגד חזירים) תא"מ ונ"ב תוספתא ל"ג לה:

והכא, בטופח על מנת להטפיח איכא בינייהו.§ "ירד לטבול, אם יכול לעלות כו'". לימא תנא סתמא כר' אליעזר, דאמר: *עד הנץ החמה! –אפי' תימא ר' יהושע, ודלמא כותיקין; *דא"ר יוחנן: ותיקין היו גומרין אותה עם הנץ החמה.§ "ואם לאו – יתכסה במים ויקרא". והרי לבו רואה את הערוה! –א"ר אלעזר, ואי תימא ר' אחא בר אבא בר אחא משום רבינו: [א]במים עכורין שנו, דדמו כארעא סמיכתא, שלא יראה לבו ערותו. ת"ר: מים צלולין – ישב בהן עד צוארו וקורא; וי"א: עוכרן ברגלו, ות"ק – והרי לבו רואה את הערוה! –קסבר: לבו רואה את הערוה – מותר. והרי עקבו רואה את הערוה! –קסבר: עקבו רואה את הערוה – מותר. אתמר: עקבו רואה את הערוה – מותר. נוגע, אביי אמר: אסור, ורבא אמר: מותר. רב זביד מתני לה להא שמעתא הכי. רב חיננא בריה דרב איקא מתני לה הכי: נוגע – דברי הכל אסור; רואה, אביי אמר: אסור, רבא אמר: מותר, *לא נתנה תורה למלאכי השרת. [ב]והלכתא: נוגע – אסור, רואה – מותר.§ אמר רבא: [ג]צואה בעששית – מותר לקרות ק"ש כנגדה, [ד]ערוה בעששית – אסור לקרות ק"ש כנגדה. צואה בעששית מותר לקרות ק"ש כנגדה – דצואה בכיסוי תליא מילתא, והא מיכסיא; ערוה בעששית אסור לקרות ק"ש כנגדה °"ולא יראה בך ערות דבר" אמר רחמנא, והא קמיתחזיא.§ אמר אביי: [ה]צואה כל שהוא – מבטלה ברוק; אמר רבא: [ו]וברוק עבה. אמר רבא: [ז]צואה בגומא – מניח סנדלו עליה וקורא ק"ש. בעא מר בריה דרבינא: [ח]צואה דבוקה בסנדלו מאי? תיקו.§ *אמר רב יהודה: [ט]גוי ערום – אסור לקרות ק"ש כנגדו. מאי איריא גוי, אפילו ישראל נמי! – ישראל – פשיטא ליה דאסור, אלא גוי איצטריכא ליה; מהו דתימא: הואיל וכתיב בהו °"אשר בשר חמורים בשרם", אימא כחמור בעלמא הוא – קמ"ל: דאינהו נמי איקרו ערוה, דכתיב °"וערות אביהם לא ראו".§ "ולא יתכסה לא במים הרעים ולא במי המשרה, עד שיטיל לתוכן מים". וכמה מיא רמי ואזיל? אלא ה"ק: [י]לא יתכסה לא במים הרעים ולא במי המשרה כלל; ומי רגלים – עד שיטיל לתוכן מים, ויקרא. ת"ר: *כמה יטיל לתוכן מים – כל שהוא; ר' זכאי אומר: [כ]רביעית. אמר רב נחמן: מחלוקת – לבסוף, אבל בתחילה – כל שהן; ורב יוסף אמר: [ל]מחלוקת – לכתחילה, אבל לבסוף – דברי הכל רביעית. אמר ליה רב יוסף לשמעיה: אייתי לי רביעיתא דמיא, כר' זכאי. *ת"ר: [מ]גרף של רעי ועביט של מי רגלים – אסור לקרות ק"ש כנגדן, ואף ע"פ שאין בהן כלום, ומי רגלים עצמן – עד שיטיל לתוכן מים. וכמה יטיל לתוכן מים? כל שהוא; ר' זכאי אומר: רביעית. בין לפני המטה בין לאחר המטה; רבן שמעון בן גמליאל אומר: לאחר המטה – קורא, לפני המטה – אינו קורא, אבל מרחיק הוא ארבע אמות וקורא; ר"ש בן אלעזר אומר: אפי' בית מאה אמה – לא יקרא עד שיוציאם, או שיניחם תחת המטה. איבעיא להו: היכי קאמר(א) אחר המטה – קורא מיד, לפני המטה – מרחיק ארבע אמות וקורא; או דילמא הכי קאמר: לאחר המטה – מרחיק ד' אמות וקורא, לפני המטה – אינו קורא כלל? ת"ש, דתניא ר"ש בן אלעזר אומר: [נ]אחר המטה – קורא מיד, לפני המטה – מרחיק ארבע אמות; רבן שמעון בן גמליאל אומר: אפי' בית מאה אמה – לא יקרא עד שיוציאם או שיניחם תחת המטה. בעיין איפשיטא לן, מתנייתא קשיין אהדדי! –איפוך בתרייתא. –מה חזית דאפכת בתרייתא? איפוך קמייתא! –מאן שמעת ליה דאמר: *כוליה בית כארבע אמות דמי – ר"ש בן אלעזר היא.§ אמר רב יוסף, בעאי מיניה מרב הונא: מטה פחות משלשה – פשיטא לי דכלבוד – דמי; שלשה, ארבעה, חמשה, ששה, שבעה, שמנה, תשעה, מהו? א"ל: לא ידענא. עשרה, ודאי לא מיבעי לי. אמר אביי: שפיר עבדת דלא איבעיא לך, כל עשרה רשותא אחריתי היא. אמר רבא, הלכתא: פחות משלשה – כלבוד דמי, עשרה – רשותא אחריתי היא, משלשה עד עשרה – היינו דבעא מיניה רב יוסף מרב הונא ולא פשט ליה. אמר רב: הלכה כר"ש בן אלעזר; וכן אמר באלי א"ר יעקב *בריה דבת שמואל: הלכה כרבי שמעון בן אלעזר; ורבא אמר: אין הלכה כר"ש בן אלעזר.§ רב אחאי איעסק ליה לבריה בי רב יצחק בר שמואל בר מרתא, עייליה לחופה ולא הוה מסתייעא מילתא. אזל בתריה לעיוני, חזא ספר תורה דמנחא. אמר להו: איכו השתא לא אתאי סכנתון לברי! דתניא: [ס]בית שיש בו ספר תורה או תפילין – אסור לשמש בו את המטה עד שיוציאם או שיניחם כלי בתוך כלי. אמר אביי: לא שנו [ע]אלא בכלי שאינו כליין, אבל בכלי שהוא כליין – אפילו עשרה מאני כחד מאנא דמי. אמר רבא: גלימא אקמטרא

תורה אור: דברים כג | יחזקאל כג | בראשית ט

**רש"י**

בטופח ע"מ להטפיח איכא בינייהו. ת"ק בעי על מנת להטפיח, ור' יוסי מחמיר: לימא תנא סתמא כר' אליעזר. והלכה כמותו: דילמא לותיקין. קמייתא מתני' עם הנץ החמה, אבל לכ"ע עד שלש שעות: והרי לבו רואה את הערוה. קס"ד כל אבר שאין דרכו לראות את הערוה, [ורואה] אותו בשעה שקורא בתורה, קרינן ביה ולא יראה בך ערות דבר: לא נתנה תורה למלאכי השרת. שאין להם ערוה, על כרחנו יש לנו ערוה, ואין אנו יכולים להשמר מכל זה: (ב)כל שהוא. מעט: ברוק. רוקק עליה ומכסה אותה ברוק: בעששית. לנטירנ"א בלע"ז. כלומר: מחילת זכוכית או קלף דק מפסיק בנתיים והיא נראית: בכסוי תליא מילתא. וכסית את צאתך: מים הרעים. סרוחים: *מי המשרה. ששורים שם הפשתן והקנבוס והם מסריחים: וכמה מיא רמי ואזיל. כמה ישליך לתוכם ויבטלם, הלא מרובין הם: ומי רגלים. מועטין, והם בכלי, והוא בא לקרות ק"ש אצלם: לבסוף. שמי רגלים בכלי וזה נותן לתוכן מים, בההיא קאמר ר' זכאי רביעית: אבל לכתחלה. שקדמו המים למי רגלים, דברי הכל כל שהוא. שכשמטיל מי רגלים בכלי לבסוף ראשון ראשון שנופל לתוך המים מתבטל, ואע"פ שהם רבים והולכין – כבר בטלו: אייתי לי רביעתא. אפי' בתחלה: גרף ועביט. שניהם כלי חרס הם, אלא של רעי קרוי גרף, ושל מי רגלים קרוי עביט: אסור לקרות ק"ש כנגדם. הואיל ומיוחדין לכך, ואע"פ שאין בתוכן כלום: ומי רגלים עצמן. בכלי שאינו מיוחד להם: בין לפני המטה. שאין המטה מפסקת בינו לבינם: בין לאחר המטה. שהמטה מפסקת ביניהם – אסור: או שיניחם תחת המטה. גרסינן – ולא גרסינן כלי בתוך כלי: תחת המטה. כאילו היו טמונים בארץ: היכי קאמר. רשב"ג: בעיין איפשיטא לן. שאלתנו נתפרשה לנו בחלוק שבין לפני המטה ולאחר המטה: מתנייתא מיהו קשיין. שהוחלפה שיטתן: מאן שמעת ליה וכו'. לא ידעתי היכן היא: פשיטא לי. במניחן תחת המטה ורגליה קצרים, שאין הימנה ולקרקע שלשה טפחים, כלבוד דמי, והרי הן כטמונים: עשרה ודאי. לא שאלתי – ממנו – דנראה כאילו אינה תחתיה, מאחר שיש הפסק כל כך אין זה כסוי: עייליה לחופה ולא הוה מסתייעא מילתא. דנשואין, שלא היה יכול לבעול: סכנתון לברי. כמעט סכנתם את בני למות בעונש העון: אפילו עשרה מאני. וכולן כליין כחד מאנא דמי: אקמטרא

**תוספות**

והרי לבו רואה את הערוה. פירש ר"י: מדפריך גמרא הכי בפשיטות משמע דלבו רואה את הערוה אסור. אלא דרבינו שמעיה תלמידו של רש"י פסק כת"ק, דלבו רואה את הערוה מותר. ומיהו בסמוך משמע דאסור, דלא פליגי הני אמוראי אלא בעקבו רואה את הערוה אבל בלבו רואה את הערוה – כ"ע מודו דאסור: והלכתא נוגע עקבו אסור. וטעמא דגזרינן נוגע עקבו – שמא יגע בידיו: גרף של רעי. פי' רש"י: של חרס בלוע. משמע לפירושו: אבל כלי דלא בלע כגון זכוכית – אפשר דשרי[א]: ובלבד שיטיל בהן רביעית מים. אבל בגרף אפשר דלא מהני מים: ספר

**עין משפט נר מצוה**

קיד א מיי' פ"ב (ופ"ג) מהל' ק"ש הלכה ז סמג עשין יח טוש"ע או"ח סי' עד סעיף ב:
קטו ב מיי' שם פ"ג הלכה יז טוש"ע שם סעיף ה:
קטז ג מיי' שם הלכה י סמג שם טוש"ע א"ח סי' עו סעיף א:
קיז ד מיי' שם הלכה טז סמג שם טוש"ע א"ח סי' עה סעיף ה:
קיח ה ו מיי' שם הלכה יא סמג שם טוש"ע או"ח סי' עו סעיף ו:
קיט ז ח מיי' שם טוש"ע שם סעי' ב:
קכ ט מיי' שם הלכה טז סמג שם טוש"ע או"ח סי' עה סעיף ד:
קכא י מיי' שם פ"ב הלכה ז טוש"ע או"ח סי' עד סעיף ב (וסימן פו):
קכב כ ל מיי' שם פ"ג הלכה י טוש"ע או"ח סי' עז סעיף א:
קכג מ (נ) מיי' שם הל' יב סמג שם טוש"ע או"ח סימן פז סעיף א: [נ טור שם]:
קכד ס ע מיי' פ"ד מהל' תפילין הל' כד ופ"י מהל' ס"ת הל' ז סמג עשין כב טוש"ע או"ח סימן מ סעיף ב ובסי' רמ סעיף ו [וב"י סי' רפב ס"ח]:

**רב נסים גאון**

לימא תנן סתמא כר' אליעזר דאמר עד הנץ החמה. (דאמר) [עיקר] מחלוקת ר' אליעזר ור' יהושע בפירקא קמא (דף ט) דהא מסכתא: מאן שמעת ליה דאמר כל הבית כולו כד' אמות דמי ר' שמעון בן אלעזר. עיקר דבריו של ר' שמעון בן אלעזר בתוספתא דעירובין (פ"ג) ובגמרא בפרק עושין פסין (דף כג.) אמר רבי שמעון בן אלעזר כל אויר שתשמישו לדירה כגון דיר וסהר ומוקצה וחצר אפילו בית ה' כורין אפילו בית י' כורין מותר שמעינן מיהא דר' שמעון היה מתיר לטלטל כל כי האי שיעור' מפני שתשמישו לדירה וכולו כד' אמות דמי ליה: אמר רב יוסף בעו מיניה מרב הונא פחות מג' כלבוד דמי. עיקרא דהא מילתא דכל פחות מג' כלבוד דמי שנוי במשנה ובהרבה מקומות וגם בתוספתא ואנו מזכירים מה שנמצא בידינו במסכת כלאים בפרק קרחת הכרם (משנה ד) שנינו מחיצת הקנים אם אין בין קנה לקנה ג' טפחים כדי שיכנס הגדי הרי זה כמחיצה ובתוספתא נמי דכוותה ובפרק קמא דעירובין (דף טז:) מקיפין ג' חבלים כו' מקיפין בקנים ובלבד שלא יהא בין קנה לחברו ג' טפחים ובגמרא דהאי פירקא (שם דף טז.) תא שמע ג' מדות במחיצה כו' והיא שנויה בתוספת' כלאים (פרק ד) ובמתני' (סוכה פרק א דף טז.) המשלשל דפנות מלמעלה למטה אם גבוהות מן הארץ ג' טפחים פסולה משום דנפקא לה מתורת לבוד והא דאמרינן הכא עשרה רשותא אחריתי היא איתיה לעיקרא בפירקא קמא דשבת (דף ו.) בברייתא דתנו רבנן ד' רשויות לשבת כו' [וכן בסוכה דף ה ע"ש]:

**מסורת הש"ס**

[לעיל ט:]
לעיל דף ט: לקמן כו.
[דיבור זה [ודבור הס] שייך לעיל במשנה כב
יומא ל. קדושין נד. [מעילה יז:]
[שבת קנ. ע"ש]
[נזיר לח.]
תוספתא פ"ב
[עירובין מב:]
[ע' פירש"י לעיל טז. ברה]

**הגהות הגר"א**

[א] בתוס' סד"ה נמחק ב' נקודו' הס (דד"ה גרף וד"ה ו הוא לדבור אחד בלפו"י וכ"מ במ ולא כרש"א):

**הגהות הב"ח**

(א) גמ' היכי קאמר רשב"ג אחר המטה: (ב) רש"י ד"ה כל שהוא וד"ה ברוק נ"ל אחר ד"ה בכסוי:

**גליון הש"ס**

רש"י ד"ה אבל כו' כבר בטלו. עי' ע"ג דף עג ע"א תוס' ד"ה כי אתא: רש"י ד"ה מאן שמעת ליה כו' לא ידעתי כו'. וכן ברש"י שבת טז: ד"ה למ"ד. יז. ד"ה הניחא. מט: ד"ה לא זזו. קז: ד"ה הטפויין. קלח: ד"ה באלס וד"ה זה הקץ. עו: מ: ד"ה דרב אחא. פסחים לד: ד"ה תנא [פ"א. ד"ה אבל]. קטז: ברשב"ם ד"ה נלות. יומא יט. ד"ה שער הדלקה. עב: ד"ה הא כמ"ד: פה. ד"ה ולוי הסדר. סוכה כז: ד"ה שלא העמיד. כח. ד"ה שיחות. כט. ד"ה בשביל. מז. ד"ה שיר. נב: שבעה. ביצה טו: ד"ה ופירותיה. כה: ד"ה נלף. תענית סוף פ"ב ד"ה שמעיה. מגילה יד. ד"ה נבואה. סוטה לז: ד"ה אלא זה. מט. ד"ה זיו החכמה. קדושין ל. ד"ה לא זזו. ב"ק ה: ד"ה ולמ"ד. נז: ד"ה לא א"א. סנהדרין יד. ד"ה טורמוסין. מח: ד"ה והלא. ע: בפת. שבועות לז. ד"ה לא א"א. זבחים כב. ד"ה והא תנא. נו: ד"ה לב' ימים. מנחות קה: ד"ה שמעינן. חולין [מו: ד"ה נלרך] נ: ד"ה איסטומכא. נב. ד"ה בר זכאי. נה: ד"ה והרי. קכו: ד"ה גולל. קלא. ד"ה תשעה. ערכין י. ד"ה ולא מוסיפין. יא: ד"ה אלא ד"ה מתשעה. תמורה טו: ד"ה כיולא. כח: ד"ה נעבד נמי:

אַקַמְטְרָא – אִכְּכְלִי בְּתוֹךְ כְּלִי דָּמֵי. אָמַר רַבִּי יְהוֹשֻׁעַ בֶּן לֵוִי: ס"ת – צָרִיךְ לַעֲשׂוֹת לוֹ מְחִיצָה עֲשָׂרָה. מָר זוּטְרָא אִיקְּלַע לְבֵי רַב אַשִׁי, חַזְיֵיהּ לְדוּכְתֵּיהּ דְּמָר בַּר רַב אַשִׁי דְּמַנַּח בֵּיהּ סֵפֶר תּוֹרָה וְעָבֵיד לֵיהּ מְחִיצָה עֲשָׂרָה. אָמַר לֵיהּ: כְּמַאן – כְּרַבִּי יְהוֹשֻׁעַ בֶּן לֵוִי? בְּאֵימַר דְּאָמַר רַבִּי יְהוֹשֻׁעַ בֶּן לֵוִי – דְּלֵית לֵיהּ בֵּיתָא אַחֲרִינָא, מָר הָא אִית לֵיהּ בֵּיתָא אַחֲרִינָא! אָמַר לֵיהּ: *לָאו אַדַּעְתַּאי.§ "כַּמָּה יַרְחִיק מֵהֶן וּמִן הַצּוֹאָה – אַרְבַּע אַמּוֹת". אָמַר רָבָא אָמַר רַב סְחוֹרָה אָמַר רַב הוּנָא: גלֹא שָׁנוּ אֶלָּא לַאֲחוֹרָיו, אֲבָל לְפָנָיו – מַרְחִיק מְלֹא עֵינָיו, וְכֵן לִתְפִלָּה. אִינִי?! וְהָא אָמַר רַפְרָם בַּר פַּפָּא אָמַר רַב חִסְדָּא: עוֹמֵד אָדָם כְּנֶגֶד בֵּית הַכִּסֵּא וּמִתְפַּלֵּל! –הָכָא בְּמַאי עָסְקִינַן – בְּבֵית הַכִּסֵּא שֶׁאֵין בּוֹ צוֹאָה. אִינִי?! וְהָאָמַר *רַב יוֹסֵף בַּר חֲנִינָא: דבֵּית הַכִּסֵּא שֶׁאָמְרוּ – אע"פ שֶׁאֵין בּוֹ צוֹאָה, וּבֵית הַמֶּרְחָץ שֶׁאָמְרוּ – אע"פ שֶׁאֵין בּוֹ אָדָם! –אֶלָּא, הָכָא בְּמַאי עָסְקִינַן: בַּחֲדָתִי. *–וְהָא מִיבָּעֲיָא לֵיהּ לְרָבִינָא: ההִזְמִינוֹ לְבֵית הַכִּסֵּא מַהוּ, יֵשׁ זִימּוּן אוֹ אֵין זִימּוּן? –כִּי קָא מִיבָּעֲיָא לֵיהּ לְרָבִינָא – לְמֵיקַם עֲלֵיהּ לְצַלּוֹיֵי בְּגַוֵּיהּ. אֲבָל כְּנֶגְדּוֹ – לֹא. אָמַר רָבָא: והָנֵי בָּתֵּי כִסְאֵי דְּפַרְסָאֵי, אע"ג דְּאִית בְּהוּ צוֹאָה – כִּסְתוּמִין דָּמוּ.§ **מתני'** *זָב שֶׁרָאָה קֶרִי, וְנִדָּה שֶׁפָּלְטָה שִׁכְבַת זֶרַע, וְהַמְשַׁמֶּשֶׁת שֶׁרָאֲתָה נִדָּה – [ז] צְרִיכִין טְבִילָה, וְרַבִּי יְהוּדָה (ז) פּוֹטֵר. **גמ'** אִיבַּעְיָא לְהוּ: בַּעַל קֶרִי שֶׁרָאָה זִיבָה, לר' יְהוּדָה מַהוּ? כִּי פָּטַר רַבִּי יְהוּדָה הָתָם בְּזָב שֶׁרָאָה קֶרִי – דְּמֵעִיקָּרָא לָאו בַּר טְבִילָה הוּא, אֲבָל בַּעַל קֶרִי שֶׁרָאָה זִיבָה, דְּמֵעִיקָּרָא בַּר טְבִילָה הוּא – מְחַיֵּיב, אוֹ דִּילְמָא לָא שְׁנָא? –תָּא שְׁמַע: הַמְשַׁמֶּשֶׁת וְרָאֲתָה נִדָּה צְרִיכָה טְבִילָה, וְרַבִּי יְהוּדָה פּוֹטֵר. וְהָא מְשַׁמֶּשֶׁת וְרָאֲתָה נִדָּה כְּבַעַל קֶרִי שֶׁרָאָה זִיבָה דָּמְיָא, וְקָא פָּטַר רַבִּי יְהוּדָה – ש"מ. תָּנֵי רַבִּי חִיָּיא בְּהֶדְיָא: בַּעַל קֶרִי שֶׁרָאָה זִיבָה – צָרִיךְ טְבִילָה, וְרַבִּי יְהוּדָה פּוֹטֵר.§

## הדרן עלך מי שמתו

**תְּפִלַּת** הַשַּׁחַר עַד חֲצוֹת, ר' יְהוּדָה אוֹמֵר: חעַד ד' שָׁעוֹת. תְּפִלַּת *הַמִּנְחָה עַד הָעֶרֶב; רַבִּי יְהוּדָה אוֹמֵר עַד פְּלַג הַמִּנְחָה. תְּפִלַּת הָעֶרֶב אֵין לָהּ קֶבַע; *וְשֶׁל מוּסָפִים כָּל הַיּוֹם, °(ר' יְהוּדָה אוֹמֵר: עַד ז' שָׁעוֹת)? **גמ'** וּרְמִינְהוּ: מִצְוָתָהּ טעִם הָנֵץ הַחַמָּה, כְּדֵי שֶׁיִּסְמוֹךְ גְּאוּלָּה לִתְפִלָּה וְנִמְצָא מִתְפַּלֵּל בַּיּוֹם! –כִּי תַּנְיָא הַהִיא – לְוָתִיקִין, *דא"ר יוֹחָנָן: וָתִיקִין הָיוּ גּוֹמְרִים אוֹתָהּ עִם הָנֵץ הַחַמָּה. וכ"ע עַד חֲצוֹת וְתוּ לָא?! וְהָאָמַר רַב מָרִי בְּרֵיהּ דְּרַב הוּנָא בְּרֵיהּ דר' יִרְמְיָה בַּר אַבָּא אָמַר רַבִּי יוֹחָנָן: יטָעָה וְלֹא הִתְפַּלֵּל עַרְבִית – מִתְפַּלֵּל בְּשַׁחֲרִית שְׁתַּיִם, כשַׁחֲרִית – מִתְפַּלֵּל בְּמִנְחָה שְׁתַּיִם! –כּוּלֵּי יוֹמָא מְצַלֵּי וְאָזֵיל, עַד חֲצוֹת – יָהֲבִי לֵיהּ שְׂכַר תְּפִלָּה בִּזְמַנָּהּ, מִכָּאן וְאֵילָךְ – לשְׂכַר תְּפִלָּה יָהֲבִי לֵיהּ, שְׂכַר תְּפִלָּה בִּזְמַנָּהּ – לָא יָהֲבִי לֵיהּ.§ אִיבַּעְיָא לְהוּ: טָעָה וְלֹא הִתְפַּלֵּל מִנְחָה, מַהוּ שֶׁיִּתְפַּלֵּל עַרְבִית ב'? את"ל טָעָה וְלֹא הִתְפַּלֵּל עַרְבִית מִתְפַּלֵּל שַׁחֲרִית ב' – מִשּׁוּם דְּחַד יוֹמָא הוּא, דִּכְתִיב °"וַיְהִי עֶרֶב וַיְהִי בֹקֶר יוֹם אֶחָד", אֲבָל הָכָא – תְּפִלָּה בִּמְקוֹם קָרְבָּן הִיא, וְכֵיוָן דַּעֲבַר יוֹמוֹ בָּטֵל קָרְבָּנוֹ; אוֹ דִילְמָא, כֵּיוָן דִּצְלוֹתָא רַחֲמֵי הִיא – כָּל אֵימַת דְּבָעֵי מְצַלֵּי וְאָזֵיל? –ת"ש: דְּאָמַר רַב הוּנָא בַּר יְהוּדָה א"ר יִצְחָק א"ר יוֹחָנָן: מטָעָה וְלֹא הִתְפַּלֵּל מִנְחָה – מִתְפַּלֵּל עַרְבִית ב', וְאֵין בָּזֶה מִשּׁוּם "דַּעֲבַר יוֹמוֹ בָּטֵל קָרְבָּנוֹ". מֵיתִיבִי: °"מְעֻוָּת נלֹא יוּכַל לִתְקֹן וְחֶסְרוֹן לֹא יוּכַל לְהִמָּנוֹת"; *"מְעֻוָּת לֹא יוּכַל לִתְקֹן" – זֶה שֶׁבִּטֵּל ק"ש שֶׁל עַרְבִית וק"ש שֶׁל שַׁחֲרִית, אוֹ תְּפִלָּה שֶׁל עַרְבִית, אוֹ תְּפִלָּה שֶׁל שַׁחֲרִית: "וְחֶסְרוֹן לֹא יוּכַל לְהִמָּנוֹת" – זֶה שֶׁנִּמְנוּ חֲבֵירָיו לִדְבַר מִצְוָה וְלֹא נִמְנָה עִמָּהֶם! –א"ר יִצְחָק א"ר יוֹחָנָן: הָכָא בְּמַאי עָסְקִינַן – סשֶׁבִּטֵּל בְּמֵזִיד. אָמַר רַב אַשִׁי: דַּיְקָא נַמִי דְּקָתָנֵי "בִּטֵּל" וְלֹא קָתָנֵי "טָעָה" – ש"מ.§

תָּנוּ

---

**רש"י**

אַקַמְטְרָא. אַרְגָּז שֶׁל סְפָרִים. וּבִמְגִילָּה (דף כו:) קַמְטְרֵי דִּסְפָרֵי, וְכֵן תִּרְגֵּם יוֹנָתָן וּבְגִנְזֵי בְּרוֹמִים (יחזקאל כז) – חָלְמִין דִּזְהִירִין מַחֲתִין בְּקַמְטְרִין, וכן לַאֲשֶׁר עַל הַמֶּלְתָּחָה (מלכים ב י) – לְדַעַל קַמְטְרָא: כִּכְלִי בְּתוֹךְ כְּלִי דָּמֵי. דְּהָא גְּלִימָא לָאו כֵּלְיָין הוּא: מְחִיצָה עֲשָׂרָה. וְאִם לָאו – לֹא יְשַׁמֵּשׁ: לְדוּכְתֵּיהּ. בִּמְקוֹם מִטָּתוֹ: לָאו אַדַּעְתַּאי. לֹא נָתַתִּי לִבִּי: כְּנֶגֶד בֵּית הַכִּסֵּא. בְּרָחוֹק אַרְבַּע אַמּוֹת: דְּלֵית בֵּהּ צוֹאָה. שֶׁפִּינּוּ אוֹתָהּ: בֵּית הַמֶּרְחָץ. אָסוּר לְהַרְהֵר בּוֹ: דְּפַרְסָאֵי. בַּחֲפִירָה הָיוּ, וּפִיהֶם בְּרָחוֹק מִן הַגּוּמָא וְהוּא בְּשִׁיפּוּעַ, וְהָרְעִי מִתְגַּלְגֵּל וְנוֹפֵל לְגוּמָא: מתני' זָב שֶׁרָאָה קֶרִי. אע"פ שֶׁטָּמֵא טוּמְאַת שִׁבְעָה מִשּׁוּם זִיבָה, וְאֵין טְבִילָה זוֹ מְטַהַרְתּוֹ – אפ"ה צָרִיךְ טְבִילָה לְדִבְרֵי תוֹרָה, כְּתַקָּנַת עֶזְרָא מִשּׁוּם קֶרִי. וְכֵן נִדָּה, אִם בָּאָה לְהִתְפַּלֵּל י"ח: שֶׁפָּלְטָה שִׁכְבַת זֶרַע. הֲרֵי הִיא כְּבַעַל קֶרִי, כִּדְאַשְׁכְּחַן בְּסִינַי שְׁלֹשֶׁת יָמִים אַל תִּגְּשׁוּ אֶל אִשָּׁה (שמות יט), לְפִי שֶׁשִּׁכְבַת זֶרַע מְטַמְּאָה בִּפְלִיטָתוֹ כָּל שְׁלֹשָׁה, וּלְאַחַר מִכָּאן כְּבָר הִסְרִיחַ בְּגוּפָהּ וְאֵין רָאוּי עוֹד לְהַזְרִיעַ לִהְיוֹת עוֹד וָלָד נוֹצָר הֵימֶנָּה. וה"פ: נִדָּה שֶׁפָּלְטָה עִמָּהּ הַתַּשְׁמִישׁ שֶׁשִּׁמְּשָׁה אֶתְמוֹל קוֹדֶם שֶׁרָאֲתָה: וְרַבִּי יְהוּדָה פּוֹטֵר. קָא סָלְקָא דַּעְתָּךְ הַשְׁתָּא הוֹאִיל וְטוּמְאַת זִיבָה קוֹדֶמֶת, וַהֲרֵי הוּא טָמֵא טוּמְאָה חֲמוּרָה, וְאֵינוֹ אוֹסַרְתּוֹ בְּדִבְרֵי תוֹרָה, כִּדְאַמְרִינַן בְּפִרְקִין הַזָּבִים וְהַמְצוֹרָעִים מוּתָּרִים, תּוּ לֹא אָתְיָא טוּמְאַת קֶרִי דְּקִילָּא וְאָסְרָה לֵיהּ: גמ' לָאו בַּר טְבִילָה הוּא. לְדִבְרֵי תוֹרָה, וְאע"פ שֶׁטּוּמְאָתוֹ חֲמוּרָה, וְתוּ לֹא אָתֵי קֶרִי וּמַצְרִיךְ לֵיהּ:

הַדְרָן עֲלָךְ מִי שֶׁמֵּתוֹ

**תְּפִלַּת** הַשַּׁחַר: עַד הָעֶרֶב. עַד חֲשֵׁכָה: עַד פְּלַג הַמִּנְחָה. בַּגְּמָרָא מְפָרֵשׁ לָהּ: אֵין לָהּ קֶבַע. כָּל הַלַּיְלָה זְמַנָּהּ, וּבַגְּמָרָא מְפָרֵשׁ מַאי לְשׁוֹן אֵין לָהּ קֶבַע: גמ' מִצְוָתָהּ. שֶׁל קְרִיאַת שְׁמַע: לְוָתִיקִין. הַמַּקְדִּימִין לְמִצְוֹת וּמְחַזְּרִים לַעֲשׂוֹת דָּבָר בִּזְמַנּוֹ וּמִצְוָתוֹ, מַקְדִּימִים (א) לְאַחַר הָנֵץ הַחַמָּה לְהִתְפַּלֵּל. וְכִי תְּנַן בְּמַתְנִי' – לַמְאַחֲרִים, שֶׁלֹּא יְאַחֵר יוֹתֵר מֵחֲצוֹת, שֶׁמִּשָּׁם וְאֵילָךְ עָבַר הַזְּמַן: וְכוּלֵּי עָלְמָא. שְׁאָר הַמִּתְפַּלְּלִין הַמְאַחֲרִין עַד חֲצוֹת יְכוֹלִין לְאַחֵר וְתוּ לָא: בְּמִנְחָה. הַיְינוּ אַחַר חֲצוֹת: אִם תִּימְצֵי לוֹמַר. כְּלוֹמַר: אִם תְּשִׁיבֵנִי בִּשְׁאֵלָתִי מִמַּה שֶּׁאָמַרְנוּ טָעָה וְלֹא הִתְפַּלֵּל עַרְבִית וכו': וְכֵיוָן דַּעֲבַר יוֹמוֹ בָּטֵל קָרְבָּנוֹ. וְאֵינוֹ מַקְרִיבוֹ בַּיּוֹם אַחֵר אִם זְמַנּוֹ קָבוּעַ, כְּגוֹן: *מוּסָפִים שֶׁל כָּל יוֹם וָיוֹם:

מַבְדִּיל

---

**תוספות**

**ספר** תורה עושה לו מחיצה. ודוקא ספר תורה, וגם בחומשים יש להחמיר כמו בספר תורה, אבל בשאר ספרים דיין בכסוי בעלמא: הדרן עלך מי שמתו

**תפלת** השחר עד חצות וכו' תפלת המנחה עד הערב. וא"ת: אמאי לא קתני גבי תפלת המנחה כל היום, כמו גבי תפלת המוספין? וי"ל: דזמן מוספין הוא כל היום, אפילו משחרית, שהרי קרבנות יכול להקריב מיד אחר התמיד – א"כ גם תפלת מוספין יכול להתפלל מיד מן הבקר, מה שאין כן במנחה, (ג) אלא משש שעות ומחצה, והכי נמי בפ"ק דע"ג (ד' ד:): לא ליצלי איניש צלותא דמוספין בתלת שעי קמייתא בריש שתא ביחיד כו', אלמא: בשאר ימות השנה יכול להתפלל. ולהכי מקדים תפלת המנחה לתפלת המוספין, משום שהיא תדירה בכל יום, אע"פ שתפלת מוספין קודמת:

**טעה** ולא התפלל ערבית מתפלל בשחרית שתים. וא"ת: והאמר רב לקמן (ד' מ:): תפלת ערבית רשות, וקי"ל כותיה באיסורי! ועוד קשה, דאמר לקמן (ד' ל:): טעה ולא התפלל "יעלה ויבוא" בלילה – אין מחזירים אותו, משום דאין מקדשין את החדש בלילה, ולמה ליה האי טעמא, תיפוק ליה דתפלת ערבית רשות! וי"ל: הא דאמרינן דתפלת ערבית רשות – היינו לגבי מצוה אחרת והיא עוברת, דאז אמרינן תדחה תפלת ערבית מפניה, אבל לחנם אין לו לבטלה. *ומיהו, אם איחר עד המנחה נראה דעבר זמנו בטל קרבנו, כיון ששהה כל כך, ולאחר ב' תפלות לא מצינו שתיקנו חכמים לחזור ולהתפלל אם שכח. ואפילו תפלה אחת אם בטל במזיד – לא יוכל לתקן, ובסמוך קרי ליה מעוות לא יוכל לתקון:

**איבעיא** להו טעה ולא התפלל תפלת מנחה כו'. לא בעי אם טעה ולא התפלל תפלת מוסף – דהא ודאי אינו מתפלל בערבית, דהיאך יקרא את הקרבנות וכבר עבר זמן מוסף! וגם לא תיקנו שבע ברכות של מוסף אלא משום "ונשלמה פרים שפתינו", ובזה ודאי "עבר זמנו בטל קרבנו". אבל שאר תפלות דרחמי נינהו, ולואי שיתפלל אדם כל היום כולו, ואין כאן "עבר זמנו" בתפלה אחרת:

טעה

---

**עין משפט נר מצוה**

קכה א [טוש"ע שם ושם] ב מיי' פ"י מהל' ס"ת הלכה ז טוש"ע או"ח סימן רמ סעיף ו [וביו"ד שם]:

קכו ג מיי' פ"ג מהל' ק"ש הל' ח' טוש"ע או"ח סי' עט סעיף א:

קכז ד מיי' שם הלכ' ב' סמג עשין יח טוש"ע או"ח סימן פג סעיף א:

קכח ה מיי' שם הלכה ג טוש"ע שם סעיף ב:

קכט ו טוש"ע שם סעיף ז:

קל ז מיי' פ"ד מהל' ק"ש הלכה ח ופ"ד מהל' תפלה הל' ה (סמג עשין יח טור או"ח סי' פח):

א ח ט מיי' פ"ג מהל' תפלה הלכה א סמג עשין יט טוש"ע או"ח סי' פט סעיף א:

ב י מיי' שם הלכה ט סמג שם טוש"ע או"ח סי' קח סעיף ב:

ג כ מיי' שם טוש"ע שם סעיף א:

ד ל מיי' שם הל' א טוש"ע או"ח סי' פט סעיף א:

ה מ מיי' שם הל' ט טוש"ע או"ח סי' קח סעיף ב וסימן רלד סעיף ב:

ו נ ס מיי' שם הל' ח טוש"ע שם סי' קח סעיף ז:

[ועי' תוס' יומא פז: ד"ה והאמר ותוס' חגיגה ט: ד"ה או]

**הגהות הב"ח**

(א) רש"י ד"ה לותיקין וכו' מקדימין (א ב) להתפלל לאחר הנץ החמה וכי תנן: (ב) תוס' ד"ה תפלת וכו' משא"כ במנחה דאינה אלא משש:

[ע' תוס' פסחים קז. ד"ה סמוך וכו' שני טעמים שנקרא תפלת המנחה]

כ"א ל"ג

לעיל דף ט: ודף כה:

---

**מסורת הש"ס**

[...] ע"ש בפירש"י [...] נט: ביצה כב. [...] לג. פא: כתובות [...]רין ה: מנחות לה: חולין ו.]

[...]ש איתא ר' יוסי]

[...] נדרים ז. שבת י.]

לעיל דף כח:

[...]' לקמן כז. ד"ה וטלו

תמידין

בראשית א

קהלת א

חגיגה דף ט:

תנו רבנן: [א]טעה ולא התפלל מנחה בערב שבת – מתפלל בליל [א] שבת שתים, [ב]טעה ולא התפלל מנחה בשבת – מתפלל במוצאי שבת שתים של חול, מבדיל בראשונה ואינו מבדיל בשניה, ואם הבדיל בשניה ולא הבדיל בראשונה – שניה עלתה לו, ראשונה לא עלתה לו. למימרא, דכיון דלא אבדיל בקמייתא כמאן דלא צלי דמי ומהדרינן ליה? ורמינהו: *[ג]טעה ולא הזכיר גבורות גשמים בתחיית המתים ושאלה [ד]בברכת השנים – מחזירין אותו, [ה]הבדלה בחונן הדעת – אין מחזירין אותו, מפני שיכול לאומרה על הכוס! – קשיא.§ איתמר, רבי יוסי ברבי חנינא אמר: תפלות אבות תקנום; רבי יהושע בן לוי אמר: [ו]תפלות כנגד תמידין תקנום. תניא כוותיה דר' יוסי ברבי חנינא, ותניא כוותיה דרבי יהושע בן לוי. תניא כוותיה דרבי יוסי בר' חנינא: אברהם תקן תפלת שחרית – שנא' °"וישכם אברהם בבקר אל המקום אשר עמד שם" *ואין עמידה אלא תפלה, שנאמר: °"ויעמד פינחס ויפלל". יצחק תקן תפלת מנחה – שנאמר: °"ויצא יצחק לשוח בשדה לפנות ערב", ואין שיחה אלא תפלה, שנאמר: °"תפלה לעני כי יעטף ולפני ה' ישפך שיחו". יעקב תקן תפלת ערבית – שנאמר: °"ויפגע במקום וילן שם", *ואין פגיעה אלא תפלה, שנאמר: °"ואתה אל תתפלל בעד העם הזה ואל תשא בעדם רנה ותפלה ואל תפגע בי". ותניא כוותיה דר' יהושע בן לוי: *מפני מה אמרו תפלת השחר עד חצות – שהרי תמיד של שחר קרב והולך עד חצות; ורבי יהודה אומר: עד ארבע שעות, שהרי תמיד של שחר קרב והולך עד ארבע שעות. ומפני מה אמרו תפלת המנחה עד הערב – שהרי תמיד של בין הערבים קרב והולך עד הערב; רבי יהודה אומר: עד פלג המנחה, שהרי תמיד של בין הערבים קרב והולך עד פלג המנחה. ומפני מה אמרו תפלת הערב אין לה קבע – שהרי אברים ופדרים שלא נתעכלו מבערב קרבים והולכים כל הלילה; ומפני מה אמרו של מוספין כל היום – שהרי קרבן של מוספין קרב כל היום; רבי יהודה אומר: עד שבע שעות, שהרי קרבן מוסף קרב והולך עד שבע שעות. ואיזו היא [ז]מנחה גדולה – משש שעות ומחצה ולמעלה; ואיזו היא מנחה קטנה – מתשע שעות ומחצה ולמעלה. איבעיא להו: רבי יהודה פלג מנחה קמא קאמר, או פלג מנחה אחרונה קאמר? תא שמע: דתניא, ר' יהודה אומר: [ח]פלג המנחה אחרונה אמרו, והיא י"א שעות חסר רביע. נימא תיהוי תיובתיה דר' יוסי בר' חנינא! אמר לך ר' יוסי בר' חנינא: לעולם אימא לך תפלות אבות תקנום, ואסמכינהו רבנן אקרבנות. דאי לא תימא הכי – תפלת מוסף לר' יוסי בר' חנינא מאן תקנה? אלא: תפלות אבות תקנום, ואסמכינהו רבנן אקרבנות.§ רבי יהודה אומר: עד ארבע שעות. איבעיא להו: *עד ועד בכלל, או דילמא, עד ולא עד בכלל? תא שמע: ר' יהודה אומר עד פלג המנחה. אי אמרת בשלמא עד ולא עד בכלל – היינו דאיכא בין ר' יהודה לרבנן, אלא אי אמרת עד ועד בכלל – ר' יהודה היינו

היינו

---

**רש"י**

מבדיל בראשונה. פעם ראשונה מתפלל בשביל תפלה של עכשיו – לפיכך אומר בה הבדלה בחונן הדעת, והשניה היא בשביל תשלומי תפלת שבת – אינו מבדיל בה: שניה עלתה לו. בשביל תפלת מ"ש, וראשונה לא עלתה לו שאינה כלום, שאין לו להקדים (א) תפלה שעבר זמנה לתפלה שזמנה עכשיו. והשניה נמי לא עלתה לו לשל שבת, הואיל והבדיל בה גילה דעתו שאינה של שבת, והיא תחשב לשל ערבית: אבות תקנום. כדקתני בברייתא לקמיה: כנגד תמידים תקנום. אנשי כנסת הגדולה: רבי יהודה. ס"ל שאין תמיד של שחר קרב אלא עד ארבע שעות: אברים. של עולות. ופדרים. של שאר קרבנות, שנזרק דמן קודם שקיעת החמה, קרבין כל הלילה וכנגדן תקנו תפלת ערבית: מנחה גדולה. אם בא להקדים תמיד של בין הערבים אינו יכול להקדימו קודם שש שעות ומחצה, דבין הערבים כתיב ביה מכי ינטו צללי ערב, משהשמש נוטה למערב, דהיינו משש שעות ומחצה ולמעלה. דאמר מר: חצי שש וחצי שבע – חמה עומדת בראש כל אדם, באמצע הרקיע (פסחים ד' צד.): מנחה קטנה. זמן תמיד של בין הערבים בכל יום מתשע שעות ומחצה ולמעלה, דכתנן בתמיד נשחט (ד' נח.): נשחט בשמונה ומחצה וקרב בתשע ומחצה, והכא מפרש טעמא: פלג מנחה אחרונה. חלק את ב' שעות ומחצה הנותרים ביום, ותמצא פלג אחרון של מנחה מי"א שעות חסר רביע ולמעלה: דאי לא תימא הכי. דמודה רבי יוסי ברבי חנינא דרבנן אסמכינהו אקרבנות: תפלת המוספין מאן תקנה. אלא: ע"כ רבנן אסמכינהו אקרבנות, וכי עיינו במוספין ולא מצאו תפלה כנגדה – עמדו הם ותקנוה: עד ועד בכלל. לרבי יהודה הוא דקא בעי, דאילו לרבנן – עד ולא עד בכלל:

---

**תוספות**

טעה ולא התפלל מנחה בע"ש וכו' טעה ולא התפלל מנחה בשבת מתפלל ערבית שתים. דהיינו של מוצאי שבת ומבדיל בראשונה וכו'. כתב רבינו יהודה: אם טעה ולא הזכיר ר"ח במנחה – לא יתפלל עוד בלילה. דלמה יתפלל עוד, הרי כבר התפלל כל תפלת המנחה מבעוד יום, לבד ר"ח שלא הזכיר, א"כ אין מרויח כלום אם יחזור ויתפלל במוצאי ר"ח. הרי לא יזכיר עוד תפלת ר"ח, וי"ח כבר התפלל. ולא דמי להא דאמר הכא: טעה ולא התפלל מנחה בשבת דמתפלל ערבית בחול שתים, פירוש: של חול, משום שלא התפלל כלל, א"כ ירויח תפלת י"ח כשמתפלל במ"ש, אע"פ שלא יזכיר של שבת. ואת"ה: והלא הוא מתפלל יותר ממה שהוא חייב להתפלל, שלא היה לו להתפלל כי אם ז' ברכות והוא מתפלל י"ח! בכך אין לחוש, שגם בשבת היה דין שיתפלל כל י"ח, רק שלא הצריכוהו מפני הטורח. נמצא שמרויח כל תפלתו. אבל כשטעה ולא הזכיר של ר"ח, כבר התפלל – א"כ לא ירויח כלום אם יתפלל במוצאי ר"ח. (דהא) [וה"ה] נמי אם התפלל במנחה בשבת י"ח שלמות ולא הזכיר של שבת – נראה דלמ"ש לא יתפלל שתים, דכבר התפלל י"ח ברכות. ומיהו ברב אלפס לא משמע כן, דאפי' היכא דאינו מרויח כלום מצריך להתפלל פעם אחרת. וזה לשונו, שכתב אהא דקאמר שמבדיל בראשונה ואינו מבדיל בשניה, ואם לא הבדיל בראשונה והבדיל בשניה – שניה עלתה לו, ראשונה לא עלתה לו, דאיבעי ליה לאקדומי תפלת שניה ברישא (דהכי) [דהיא] חובה; וכיון דלא אבדיל ברישא ואבדיל בבתרייתא גלי דעתיה דהך בתרייתא היא חובה, הלכך בעי למהדר ולצלויי זימנא אחריתי כדי להקדים חובת שעתיה ברישא. ואי אבדיל בתרוייהו, אע"ג דלא מיבעי ליה למעבד הכי – לא מחוייב לאהדורי, ואי לא אבדיל אפילו בחדא מנהון – לא מהדרינן ליה, דתניא: טעה ולא הזכיר הבדלה ב'חונן הדעת' – אין מחזירין אותו, מפני שיכול לאומרה על הכוס. עכ"ל. אלמא: דמצריך להתפלל זימנא אחריתי, אף על גב שלא יחזור ויתפלל פעם שניה יותר מבראשונה. כך היה נראה לה"ר משה מאלאוו"ר מתוך לשון האלפסי:

קשיא. תימה: אמאי לא משני דמיירי קודם שהעשירו? דאמרינן לקמן בפרק "אין עומדין" (דף לג.): העשירו קבעוה על הכוס! וי"ל: דלא אשכחן ברייתא דנשנית בין שתי תקנות:

יצחק תקן תפלת המנחה. ואע"ג דאמרינן (יומא כח:): צלותא דאברהם מכי שחרי כתלי! וי"ל: היינו אחר שתקנה יצחק:

ואין שיחה אלא תפלה שנאמר "תפלה לעני כי יעטוף". תימה: דבפ"ק דע"ז (ד' ז: וע"ש) מוכיח דשיחה [זו] תפלה מויצא יצחק "לשוח בשדה"! י"ל: דכיוצא בו מצינו במגילה (פ"ק ד' יג.) "ויהי אומן את הדסה" ואין הדסה אלא צדיקים דכתיב "והוא עומד בין ההדסים", ובפרק "חלק" (סנהדרין ד' נג.) הוא אומר להיפך:

יעקב תקן תפלת ערבית. תימה. דאמר בפרק גיד הנשה (חולין ד' צא:): "וילך חרנה", כי מטי לחרן בעי למיהדר, אמר: אפשר שעברתי במקום וכו', אלמא דהתם מוכח דהתפלל ערבית ביום, מאחר שהתפלל כבר והוה דעתיה למהדר; וקשה למתניתין דפרק קמא, דקאמר שאינו(ב) זמן תפלה עד צאת הכוכבים! ולפי מה שפירשנו דקי"ל כר' יהודה דאמר עד פלג המנחה – ניחא, ויפה מנהג שלנו, *דאדרבה טוב להתפלל מבעוד יום קצת:

עד פלג המנחה. תימה: מנא ליה הא? בשלמא עד תשע שעות ומחצה דעד אותו זמן הוי תפלת המנחה – ניחא, דהיינו מנחה קטנה, אבל הא מנא ליה? וי"ל: דר' יהודה ס"ל דתפלה כנגד קטרת תקנוה, דכתיב "תכון תפלתי קטרת לפניך" (תהלים קמא):

איבעיא להו עד ועד בכלל וכו'. תימה: דאמר בנדה פרק "הרואה כתם" (ד' נח:): כל שיעורי חכמים להחמיר חוץ מכגרים של כתמים, אלמא – עד ולא עד בכלל! וי"ל: אי אמרי' עד ועד בכלל יש בו גם חומרא שיתפלל ולא אמרי' עבר זמנו בטל קרבנו, ואפי' במזיד:

תא

---

**עין משפט נר מצוה**

ז א מיי' פ"ו [פ"י] מהל' תפלה הלכה טו סמג עשין יט טוש"ע או"ח סימן קח סעי' ט:
ח ב מיי' שם טוש"ע שם סעיף י:
ט ג מיי' שם הלכה ח סמג שם טור וש"ע או"ח סי' קיד סעיף ו:
י ד מיי' שם הלכה ט סמג שם טוש"ע או"ח סי' קיז סעיף ד:
יא ה מיי' שם הלכה יד טוש"ע או"ח סימן רצד סעיף א:
יב ו מיי' פ"א מהלכות תפלה הלכה ה ו טוש"ע או"ח סימן קח סעיף ז [רב אלפס ברכות פ"ג דף יד ב]:
יג ז ח מיי' פ"ג שם הל' ד סמג שם טוש"ע או"ח סי' רל"ג סעיף א:

**הגהות הב"ח**

(א) רש"י ד"ה שניה עלתה וכו' שאין לו להקדים. נ"ב פירוש דודאי הוא לא הקדים ראשונה לתשלומין א"כ מסתמא [דעתו היה] על חובה ולשם [חובה לא] עלתה משום דלא הבדיל בה ע"כ ואם כן דאמרינן דמסתמא דעתו [היה] לחובה משום דלא הבדיל בה א"כ תעלה שניה לו לשם שבת דהרי לא הקדים תפלת תשלומין לחובה ע"כ מפרש רש"י דהואיל והבדיל בשניה גילה דעתו שאינה של שבת והוא תחשב לשל ערבית ר"ל בשעה שהתפלל ראשונה אמרינן דעתו היה לשם חובה אבל כשהתפלל שניה והבדיל בה אז גילה דעתו שאינה של שבת: (ב) תוס' ד"ה יעקב וכו' דפרק קמא דקאמר שאינו. נ"ב [אע"ג דלא] אמרו זמן לצאת הכוכבים אלא לענין ק"ש מ"מ כיון דקי"ל לצריך לסמוך גאולה לתפלה [בערבית] א"כ בע"כ דתפלת ערבית אחר צאת הכוכבים:

**הגהות הגר"א**

[א] גמ' בליל שבת. נ"ב שתים של שבת. כ"ה ברי"ף ושאר פוסקים:

**גליון הש"ס**

גמ' תפלות אבות תקנום. עי' תענית (דף כ"ח ע"א) ברש"י ד"ה הלכו: שם ואין שיחה אלא תפלה. בשאלתות פרשת לך לך איתא שנאמר אשפוך לפניו שיחי. וכן הוא בתוס' (דף ל"ד ע"ב) ד"ה ואין: תוס' ד"ה ואין כו' להיפך. וכן בסנהדרין (ד' נ"ג ע"ב) ואין כסף אלא צדיקים שנאמר ואכרה לי. ובחולין (דף צ"ב ע"א) אומר בהיפוך:

**מסורת הש"ס**

תוספתא פ"ג לקמן כט: (תענית ג:)
[לעיל ו:]
[תענית ז: ה. סוטה יד. סנהדרין לה:]
תוספתא פ"ג ע"ש
[עירובין כב: פסחים ... ר"ה ל: סוכה מח: מנחות סח: חולין מו: ערכין יח: נדה נח:]
[ועיין פסקי תוס' הקומץ רבה סימן קי]

**תורה אור**

בראשית יט | תהלים קו | בראשית כד | תהלים קב | בראשית כח | ירמיה ז

הַיְינוּ רַבָּנָן. דקס"ד, רַבִּי יְהוּדָה פְּלַג אַחֲרוֹן שֶׁל מִנְחָה אַחֲרוֹנָה קָאָמַר: מִתְפַּלֵּל שֶׁל מִנְחָה וכו'. רַבָּנָן לְטַעֲמַיְיהוּ, דְּאָמְרִי: תְּפִלַּת הַמּוּסָפִים כָּל הַיּוֹם, כְּמוֹ שֶׁל מִנְחָה, הִלְכָּךְ תָּדִיר קוֹדֵם. ור' יְהוּדָה לְטַעְמֵיהּ דְּאָמַר מוּסָפִין עַד שֶׁבַע שָׁעוֹת וְתוּ לָא, וְהָוְיָא לָהּ מִצְוָה עוֹבֶרֶת, וְשֶׁל מִנְחָה יֵשׁ לָהּ עוֹד שֶׁהוּת עַד פְּלַג הַמִּנְחָה: שְׁתֵּי תְּפִלּוֹת בַּהֲדֵי הֲדָדֵי. חֲצִי הָאַחֲרוֹן שֶׁל שָׁעָה שְׁבִיעִית הוּא זְמַן לִשְׁתֵּיהֶן, דְּהָא אָמַר מִנְחָה גְּדוֹלָה מִשֵּׁשׁ שָׁעוֹת וּמֶחֱצָה וּלְמַעְלָה: הֵיכִי מַשְׁכַּחַתְּ לַהּ. הֲרֵי עָבַר זְמַן הַמּוּסָפִים מִשֶּׁעָבְרָה שָׁעָה שִׁשִּׁית: פְּלַג רִאשׁוֹנָה. שֶׁל מִנְחָה אַחֲרוֹנָה וְעַד בִּכְלָל; וְאַף עַל גַּב דְּתַנָּא יָהֵב סִימָנָא לִפְלַג אַחֲרוֹנָה דְּקָתָנֵי: אֵיזוֹ פְּלַג מִנְחָה מי"א שָׁעוֹת חָסֵר רְבִיעַ, ה"ק כו': אַף אֲנַן נָמֵי תְּנֵינָא. לְרַבִּי יְהוּדָה עַד וְעַד בִּכְלָל: שֶׁמְּמָאֲנִין אֶת הַקְּטַנָּה'. קְטַנָּה שֶׁהִשִּׂיאַתָּה אִמָּהּ לְאַחַר מִיתַת אָבִיהָ, דְּמִדְּאוֹרָיְיתָא אֵין קִדּוּשֶׁיהָ כְּלוּם; שֶׁהֲרֵי קְטַנָּה אֵינָהּ בַּת דַּעַת, וְאֶת אִמָּהּ לֹא זִכְּתָה תּוֹרָה לִהְיוֹת לָהּ כֹּחַ לְקַדְּשָׁהּ אֶלָּא לָאָב, שֶׁנֶּאֱמַר אֶת בִּתִּי נָתַתִּי לָאִישׁ הַזֶּה (דברי' כב). וּמִיהוּ, רַבָּנָן תִּקִּינוּ לָהּ קִדּוּשִׁין לְהַצְרִיכָהּ מִיאוּן, כְּדֵי שֶׁיִּשָּׂאוּהָ וְלֹא תְּהֵא לִזְנוּת. לְפִיכָךְ, אִם מֵיאֲנָה לְאַחַר זְמַן וְאָמְרָה אִי אֶפְשִׁי בּוֹ – יוֹצֵאת וּמוּתֶּרֶת לְכָל אָדָם, וְאֵינָהּ צְרִיכָה הֵימֶנּוּ גֵּט. וְהֵעִיד ר' יְהוּדָה בֶּן בָּבָא שֶׁפְּעָמִים שֶׁמִּצְוָה עַל בֵּית דִּין לְלַמְּדָהּ שֶׁתְּמָאֵן בּוֹ, כְּגוֹן: שְׁנֵי אַחִים נְשׂוּאִין שְׁתֵּי אֲחָיוֹת יְתוֹמוֹת, אַחַת גְּדוֹלָה וְקִדּוּשֶׁיהָ קִדּוּשֵׁי תּוֹרָה וְאַחַת קְטַנָּה שֶׁאֵין קִדּוּשֶׁיהָ אֶלָּא מִדְּרַבָּנָן, וּמֵת בַּעֲלָהּ שֶׁל גְּדוֹלָה בְּלֹא בָנִים וְנָפְלָה לִפְנֵי אָחִיו לְיִבּוּם, וְנִמְצֵאת זְקוּקָה לוֹ מִן הַתּוֹרָה, וְזִיקָה זוֹ אוֹסֶרֶת אֶת אִשְׁתּוֹ עָלָיו מִשּׁוּם אֲחוֹת זְקוּקָה שֶׁהִיא כַּאֲחוֹת אִשְׁתּוֹ. וא"ר אֱלִיעֶזֶר בְּמַסֶּכֶת יְבָמוֹת (דף קט.): מְלַמְּדִין קְטַנָּה זוֹ שֶׁתְּמָאֵן בְּבַעְלָהּ, וְתַעֲקוֹר קִדּוּשֶׁיהָ לְמַפְרֵעַ, וְתַעֲשֶׂה כָּל בְּעִילוֹתֶיהָ כְּאִלּוּ הֵן שֶׁל זְנוּת כְּדֵי לְהַתִּיר אֶת בַּעְלָהּ לְיַבֵּם אֶת אֲחוֹתָהּ, דִּתְנַן: נוֹשְׂאִין עַל הָאֲנוּסָה וְעַל הַמְפוּתָּה (יבמות דף לז.) – וְהֵעִיד רַבִּי יְהוּדָה בֶּן בָּבָא בַּיּוֹם שֶׁנִּשְׁנֵית עֵדִיּוֹת שֶׁהֲלָכָה כר"א: ע"פ עֵד אֶחָד. שֶׁאָמַר לָהּ: מֵת בַּעְלֵךְ בִּמְדִינַת הַיָּם (יבמות דף קכב.): שֶׁנִּסְקַל תַּרְנְגוֹל. שֶׁנִּיקֵּר קָדְקֳדוֹ שֶׁל תִּינוֹק בִּמְקוֹם שֶׁהַמּוֹחַ רוֹפֵף, וְנִיקֵּב אֶת מוֹחוֹ, וּסְקָלוּהוּ כְּמִשְׁפַּט שׁוֹר שֶׁנָּגַח אֶת הָאָדָם, דִּכְתִיב (שמות כא) הַשּׁוֹר יִסָּקֵל וְגָמְרִינַן בג"ש שׁוֹר שׁוֹר מִשַּׁבָּת, לַעֲשׂוֹת כָּל בְּהֵמָה חַיָּה וָעוֹף כְּשׁוֹר (ב"ק ד' נד:): וְעַל יַיִן בֶּן אַרְבָּעִים יוֹם. שֶׁיָּצָא מִכְּלָל יַיִן מִגִּתּוֹ, וּבָא לִכְלָל יַיִן גָּמוּר וְקָרֵינַן בֵּיהּ נֶסֶךְ שֵׁכָר (במדבר כח): בְּאַרְבַּע שָׁעוֹת. וְתוּ לָא, אַלְמָא כְּרַבִּי יְהוּדָה ס"ל, וְקָאָמַר בְּאַרְבַּע שָׁעוֹת; אַלְמָא לְרַבִּי יְהוּדָה עַד וְעַד בִּכְלָל: הֲלָכָה כְּרַבִּי יְהוּדָה. דמתני', דְּאֵין תָּמִיד שֶׁל שַׁחַר קָרֵב לְאַחַר אַרְבַּע שָׁעוֹת, וה"ה לִתְפִלָּה: בִּבְחִירְתָּא. עֵדִיּוֹת קָרֵי בְּחִירְתָּא, שֶׁהֲלָכָה כְּאוֹתָן עֵדִיּוֹת: כְּשֶׁהוּא אוֹמֵר כְּחוֹם הַיּוֹם הֲרֵי שֵׁשׁ שָׁעוֹת אָמוּר. כְּלוֹמַר: מָצִינוּ בְּמָקוֹם אַחֵר שֶׁשִּׁינָּה הַכָּתוּב בִּלְשׁוֹנוֹ וְאָמַר וְהוּא יוֹשֵׁב פֶּתַח הָאֹהֶל כְּחוֹם הַיּוֹם, וְלֹא אָמַר כְּחוֹם הַשֶּׁמֶשׁ אֶלָּא הַיּוֹם; מַשְׁמַע כָּל הַמְּקוֹמוֹת חַמִּין בֵּין חַמָּה בֵּין צֵל – הוּא מְדַבֵּר בְּשָׁעָה שִׁשִּׁית: הָא מָה אֲנִי מְקַיֵּים וְחַם הַשֶּׁמֶשׁ. דְּמַשְׁמַע: הַשֶּׁמֶשׁ חַם וְהַצֵּל צוֹנֵן: בְּאַרְבַּע שָׁעוֹת. דְּאִילּוּ קוֹדֶם אַרְבַּע שָׁעוֹת, אַף הַשֶּׁמֶשׁ צוֹנֵן: מַנִּי. הָא דְּמַשְׁמַע דְּאַרְבַּע לָאו בֹּקֶר הוּא, דְּהָא כְּתִיב וַיִּלְקְטוּ אוֹתוֹ בַּבֹּקֶר בַּבֹּקֶר וְחַם הַשֶּׁמֶשׁ וְנָמָס הַנּוֹתָר, וּמִדְּמוֹקֵי וְנָמָס בְּאַרְבַּע שָׁעוֹת מִכְּלָל דְּלָאו זְמַן לְקִיטָה הוּא, וְלָאו בֹּקֶר מִיקְּרֵי: אַרְבַּע שָׁעוֹת נָמֵי צַפְרָא הוּא. דְּהָא אָמְרַתְּ עַד וְעַד בִּכְלָל, וְגַבֵּי תָּמִיד כְּתִיב תַּעֲשֶׂה בַבֹּקֶר: לִשְׁנֵי בְקָרִים. שֶׁלֹּא הָיוּ לוֹקְטִים אֶלָּא בְּשָׁלֹשׁ שָׁעוֹת רִאשׁוֹנוֹת, שֶׁהוּא בֹּקֶר רִאשׁוֹן: הָתָם אָמַר רַב כָּהֲנָא. גַּבֵּי תְּפִלַּת הַשַּׁחַר: שֶׁל שַׁבָּת בְּעֶרֶב שַׁבָּת. שֶׁקִּבֵּל עָלָיו שַׁבָּת מִבְּעוֹד יוֹם: שְׁמַע מִינַּהּ. כְּרַבִּי יְהוּדָה ס"ל, דְּאָמַר מִפְּלַג הַמִּנְחָה אָזֵיל לֵיהּ זְמַן תְּפִלַּת הַמִּנְחָה וְעָיֵיל לֵיהּ זְמַן תְּפִלַּת עַרְבִית: וְלָא פַּסְקֵיהּ לִצְלוֹתֵיהּ. כְּלוֹמַר: לֹא הִפְסִיק בֵּין רַבִּי יִרְמְיָה וְלַכּוֹתֶל, לַעֲבוֹר לְפָנָיו וְלֵישֵׁב בִּמְקוֹמוֹ, אֶלָּא עָמַד עַל עָמְדוֹ: כנגד

תא שמע ושל מוספין כל היום ורבי יהודה אומר עד שבע שעות ותניא היו לפניו וכו'. ולא גרסינן אימא סיפא ושל וכו', שאינו במשנה, שדברי רבי יהודה שאמר "עד שבע שעות" אינו במשנה, ויש ספרים שהגיהו אותו במשנה, ומיהו בכל הספרים הישנים אינו. וא"ת: ורבי למה לא הזכיר אותו במשנה? וי"ל: משום דלא ס"ל כוותיה בהא דאמר עד שבע שעות, אבל בהא דקאמר עד ארבע שעות ס"ל כוותיה, משום דתנן בבחירתא כוותיה. ובהיא דפלג המנחה נמי, משום דאמרינן לקמן דעבד כמר עבד ודעבד כמר עבד, דהכי פירושא דעבד כר' יהודה (עבד) דאמר מפלג המנחה ליליא הוא עבד, ומשום הכי מנחה לא. אבל אין לפרש הכל בתפלת המנחה, ועבד כרבי יהודה שהתפלל מנחה קודם פלג, דפשיטא דרבנן מודו בשיעורו דרבי יהודה:

דרב צלי של שבת בע"ש. תימה: דהא אמרינן בפרק "במה מדליקין" (ד' כג:) ובלבד שלא יקדים ושלא יאחר! ויש לומר: דהתם בשאינו מקבל עליו שבת מיד, אבל הכא איירי שמקבל עליו שבת מיד הלכך לא הויא הקדמה. וטעמא משום דס"ל כרבי יהודה, וכן הנך דלקמן שהתפללו של מ"ש בשבת היינו משום דסבירא להו כרבי יהודה לענין תפלת הערב, שהיא שעה ורביע קודם הלילה, אעפ"כ [אין] אסור לעשות מלאכה(א) *במ"ש מיד לאחר פלג [בע"ש] המנחה. וכן לענין תוספת שבת (*וט' [ויו"ט] בלא) וי"ה, דקי"ל שהוא מן התורה, *אם כן לא צריך שיעור גדול כל כך: [אפ"ה] ולא

הַיְינוּ רַבָּנָן! אֶלָּא מַאי? *עַד וְלֹא עַד בִּכְלָל – אֵימָא סֵיפָא וְשֶׁל מוּסָפִין כָּל הַיּוֹם, ר' יְהוּדָה אוֹמֵר: עַד שֶׁבַע שָׁעוֹת; וְתַנְיָא: *הָיוּ לְפָנָיו שְׁתֵּי תְּפִלּוֹת, אַחַת שֶׁל מוּסָף וְאַחַת שֶׁל מִנְחָה – מִתְפַּלֵּל שֶׁל מִנְחָה וְאַחַר כָּךְ שֶׁל מוּסָף, שֶׁזּוֹ תְּדִירָה וְזוֹ אֵינָהּ תְּדִירָה; רַבִּי יְהוּדָה אוֹמֵר: מִתְפַּלֵּל שֶׁל מוּסָף וְאַחַר כָּךְ שֶׁל מִנְחָה, שֶׁזּוֹ עוֹבֶרֶת וְזוֹ אֵינָהּ עוֹבֶרֶת. אִי אָמְרַתְּ בִּשְׁלָמָא עַד וְעַד בִּכְלָל – הַיְינוּ דְּמַשְׁכַּחַתְּ לְהוּ שְׁתֵּי תְּפִלּוֹת בַּהֲדֵי הֲדָדֵי; אֶלָּא אִי אָמְרַתְּ עַד וְלֹא עַד בִּכְלָל – הֵיכִי מַשְׁכַּחַתְּ לְהוּ שְׁתֵּי תְּפִלּוֹת בַּהֲדֵי הֲדָדֵי? כֵּיוָן דְּאָתְיָא לַהּ שֶׁל מִנְחָה אָזְלָא לַהּ שֶׁל מוּסָפִין! -אֶלָּא מַאי, עַד וְעַד בִּכְלָל? קַשְׁיָא רֵישָׁא: מַאי אִיכָּא בֵּין רַבִּי יְהוּדָה לְרַבָּנַן? -מִי סָבְרַתְּ דְּהַאי 'פְּלַג מִנְחָה' פְּלַג אַחֲרוֹנָה קָאָמַר?! פְּלַג רִאשׁוֹנָה קָאָמַר, וְהָכִי קָאָמַר: אֵימַת נָפֵיק פְּלַג רִאשׁוֹנָה וְעָיֵיל פְּלַג אַחֲרוֹנָה? מִכִּי נָפְקֵי י"א שָׁעוֹת חָסֵר רְבִיעַ.§ אָמַר רַב נַחְמָן: אַף אֲנַן נָמֵי תְּנֵינָא, *רַבִּי יְהוּדָה בֶּן בָּבָא הֵעִיד חֲמִשָּׁה דְּבָרִים: אשֶׁמְּמָאֲנִין אֶת הַקְּטַנָּה, וְשֶׁמַּשִּׂיאִין באֶת הָאִשָּׁה עַל פִּי עֵד אֶחָד, וְעַל גתַּרְנְגוֹל שֶׁנִּסְקַל בִּירוּשָׁלַיִם עַל שֶׁהָרַג אֶת הַנֶּפֶשׁ, וְעַל דיַיִן בֶּן אַרְבָּעִים יוֹם שֶׁנִּתְנַסֵּךְ עַל גַּבֵּי הַמִּזְבֵּחַ, *וְעַל התָּמִיד שֶׁל שַׁחַר שֶׁקָּרַב בְּאַרְבַּע שָׁעוֹת; ש"מ: ועַד וְעַד בִּכְלָל, ש"מ. אָמַר רַב כָּהֲנָא: זהֲלָכָה כְּרַבִּי יְהוּדָה, הוֹאִיל *וּתְנַן בִּבְחִירְתָּא כְּוָותֵיהּ.§ *"וְעַל תָּמִיד שֶׁל שַׁחַר שֶׁקָּרַב בְּאַרְבַּע שָׁעוֹת". מַאן תְּנָא לְהָא, *דִּתְנַן: °"וְחַם הַשֶּׁמֶשׁ וְנָמָס" – בְּאַרְבַּע שָׁעוֹת. אַתָּה אוֹמֵר בְּאַרְבַּע שָׁעוֹת, אוֹ אֵינוֹ אֶלָּא בְּשֵׁשׁ שָׁעוֹת? כְּשֶׁהוּא אוֹמֵר: °"כְּחֹם הַיּוֹם" – הֲרֵי שֵׁשׁ שָׁעוֹת אָמוּר, הָא מָה אֲנִי מְקַיֵּים "וְחַם הַשֶּׁמֶשׁ וְנָמָס" – בְּאַרְבַּע שָׁעוֹת. מַנִּי? לָא רַבִּי יְהוּדָה וְלָא רַבָּנַן! אִי רַבִּי יְהוּדָה – עַד אַרְבַּע שָׁעוֹת נָמֵי צַפְרָא הוּא, אִי רַבָּנַן – עַד חֲצוֹת נָמֵי צַפְרָא הוּא! -אִי בָּעֵית אֵימָא: רַבִּי יְהוּדָה, אִי בָּעֵית אֵימָא: רַבָּנַן. אִי בָּעֵית אֵימָא רַבָּנַן – אָמַר קְרָא: "בַּבֹּקֶר בַּבֹּקֶר" – חַלְקֵהוּ לִשְׁנֵי בְקָרִים; וְאִי בָּעֵית אֵימָא רַבִּי יְהוּדָה, הַאי בֹּקֶר יְתֵירָא – לְהַקְדִּים לוֹ שָׁעָה אַחַת. דְּכוּלֵּי עָלְמָא מִיהָא "וְחַם הַשֶּׁמֶשׁ וְנָמָס" בְּאַרְבַּע שָׁעוֹת, מַאי מַשְׁמַע? אָמַר רַבִּי אַחָא בַּר יַעֲקֹב, אָמַר קְרָא: "וְחַם הַשֶּׁמֶשׁ וְנָמָס", אֵיזוֹ הִיא שָׁעָה שֶׁהַשֶּׁמֶשׁ חַם וְהַצֵּל צוֹנֵן? הֱוֵי אוֹמֵר בְּאַרְבַּע שָׁעוֹת.§ "תְּפִלַּת הַמִּנְחָה עַד הָעֶרֶב וכו'". אֲמַר לֵיהּ רַב חִסְדָּא לְרַב יִצְחָק: הָתָם אָמַר רַב כָּהֲנָא "הֲלָכָה כְּרַבִּי יְהוּדָה הוֹאִיל וּתְנַן בִּבְחִירְתָּא כְּוָותֵיהּ", הָכָא מַאי? אִישְׁתִּיק וְלָא אֲמַר לֵיהּ וְלָא מִידֵּי. אָמַר רַב חִסְדָּא: נֶחֱזֵי אֲנַן, מִדְּרַב מְצַלֵּי שֶׁל שַׁבָּת בְּעֶרֶב שַׁבָּת מִבְּעוֹד יוֹם – ש"מ הֲלָכָה כְּרַבִּי יְהוּדָה. אַדְּרַבָּה, מִדְּרַב הוּנָא וְרַבָּנַן לָא הֲווּ מְצַלּוּ עַד אוּרְתָּא, שְׁמַע מִינַּהּ אֵין הֲלָכָה כְּרַבִּי יְהוּדָה! הַשְׁתָּא דְּלָא אִתְּמַר הִלְכְתָא לָא כְּמָר וְלָא כְּמָר, חדַּעֲבַד כְּמָר – עֲבַד, וְדַעֲבַד כְּמָר – עֲבַד.§ רַב אִיקְּלַע לְבֵי גְּנִיבָא וְצַלֵּי שֶׁל שַׁבָּת בְּעֶרֶב שַׁבָּת, וַהֲוָה מְצַלֵּי רַבִּי יִרְמְיָה בַּר אַבָּא לַאֲחוֹרֵיהּ דְּרַב, וְסַיֵּים רַב וְלָא פַּסְקֵיהּ לִצְלוֹתֵיהּ דְּרַבִּי יִרְמְיָה. שְׁמַע מִינַּהּ תְּלָת: שְׁמַע מִינַּהּ טמִתְפַּלֵּל אָדָם שֶׁל שַׁבָּת בְּעֶרֶב שַׁבָּת, וּשְׁמַע מִינַּהּ מִתְפַּלֵּל תַּלְמִיד אֲחוֹרֵי רַבּוֹ, וּשְׁמַע מִינַּהּ יאָסוּר לַעֲבוֹר כְּנֶגֶד הַמִּתְפַּלְּלִין. מְסַיַּיע לֵיהּ לְרַבִּי יְהוֹשֻׁעַ בֶּן לֵוִי, דְּאָמַר רַבִּי יְהוֹשֻׁעַ בֶּן לֵוִי: אָסוּר לַעֲבוֹר כְּנֶגֶד הַמִּתְפַּלְּלִין. -אִינִי?! וְהָא רַבִּי אַמֵּי וְרַבִּי אַסִּי חָלְפִי! – רַבִּי אַמֵּי וְרַבִּי אַסִּי חוּץ לְאַרְבַּע אַמּוֹת הוּא דְּחָלְפִי. – וְרַבִּי יִרְמְיָה הֵיכִי עָבֵיד הָכִי? וְהָא אָמַר רַב יְהוּדָה אָמַר רַב: לְעוֹלָם אַל יִתְפַּלֵּל אָדָם לא

תורה אור: שמות טז; בראשית יח

חולין נח. ד"ה כל שיעורין; לקמן דף כח.; ע"ז משנה א נדה דף ח.; מנחות סד: ד"ה ועל; [נד: בכורות כו.]; דר"ף פרשת בשלח

הגהות הב"ח (א) תוס' ד"ה דרב וכו' במ"ש מיד לאחר פלג המנחה. וכן לענין תוספת ... אין צריך להוסיף ... פלג המנחה:

יד א מיי' פ"ז מהלכות יבום וחליצה הלכה טו טוש"ע אה"ע סימן קנה סעיף יח:
טו ב מיי' פי"ב מהל' גרושין הלכה טו סמג עשין נ טוש"ע אה"ע סי' יז סעיף ג:
טז ג מיי' פ"י מהלכות נזקי ממון הלכה ב סמג עשין סו:
יז ד מיי' פ"ו מהל' איסורי מזבח הל' ט:
יח ה מיי' פ"א מהל' תמידין הל' ב סמג עשין קצ:
יט ו ז מיי' פ"ג מהל' תפלה [הל' א] סמג עשין יט טוש"ע או"ח סי' פ"ט סעיף א:
כ ח מיי' שם הלכה ד סמג שם טוש"ע או"ח סי' רלג סעיף א:
כא ט מיי' שם הלכה ז סמג עשין כט טור שו"ע או"ח סימן רסז סעיף ב:
כב י מיי' פ"ה מהל' תפלה הלכה ו סמג עשין יט טוש"ע או"ח סי' קב סעיף ד:

רב נסים גאון

העיד ר' יהודה בן בבא על חמשה דברים. הא דתני על התרנגול שנסקל בירושלים [על] שהרג את הנפש כבר מפורש בתלמוד ארץ ישראל במסכת עירובין בפרק המוצא תפילין (הלכה א) והכי גרסינן ראו (נ"א ראה) מוחו של תינוק רופף והלך וניקרו וזה הדבר ידוע הוא כי התינוקות מוחיהן פתוחין ונראה להן רפרוף מתחת העור שעל המוח וניקר אותו מקום עד שנקבו והרגו לתינוק וזה התרנגול ראוי להורגו מן הכתוב כי אין הפרש לשור לתרנגול ולכל בעלי חיים שברשותו אבולהי אמר רחמנא סקל יסקל השור: הואיל ותנן (בבתריתא) [בבחירתא] כוותיה ומאי היא מס' עדיות פ"ו מ"א שזו המשנה שנויה בה העיד ר' יודה בן בבא:

גליון הש"ס

גמ' שממאנין את הקטנה. קטנות כצ"ל (וכמבואר בנדה ח:): שם ועל תמיד של שחר. עי' ברש"י מגלי' ... ועי' מנחות ד' סד ע"ב תוס' ד"ה ועל: שם לאחוריה דרב. תפלה של חול. כן הוא בבה"ג:

עין משפט
נר מצוה

כג א מיי׳ פ״ה מהל׳ ת״ת הלכה ו סמג עשין יט טוש״ע או״ח סי׳ צ סעיף כד [וכי״ד סימן רמב סעיף טז]:
כד ב מיי׳ שם הל׳ ה סמג עשין יג טוש״ע יו״ד סי׳ רמב סעיף יו:
לעיל לחומרא כנ״ל רש״א
כה ג מיי׳ שם הל׳ ב טוש״ע שם סעי׳ ב:
כו ד מיי׳ שם הלכה ט טוש״ע שם סעי׳ כד:
כז ה מיי׳ שם טוש״ע או״ח סימן צ סעיף כה:
כח ו ז טוש״ע א״ח סימן רסג סעיף יד:
כט ח מיי׳ פ״ג מהלכות תפלה הל׳ ז (ופכ״ט מהלכות שבת הל׳ י״א) סמג עשין כט טור שו״ע א״ח סי׳ רסז סעיף ב:
ל ט מיי׳ וסמג שם טור שו״ע או״ח סי׳ רצג סעיף ג:
לא י מיי׳ פ״ג מהלכות תפלה הלכה ו:
לב כ מיי׳ פ״א מהל׳ תפלה הלכה ו ופ״ג הל׳ ו ז ופ״ט הלכה ט סמג עשין יט טור או״ח סי׳ רלה רלו רלז:

רב נסים גאון

**אמר** רבא [כו׳] להזיע וקודם גזירה. איתה מיפרשה במס׳ שבת בפ׳ כירה (דף מ.) אמר ר׳ שמעון בן פזי אמר ר׳ יהושע בן לוי משום בר קפרא בתחלה היו רוחצין בחמין שהוחמו מערב שבת כו׳ ראו שאין הדבר עומד התירו להן חמי טבריא ועדיין זיעה במקומה עומדת הודיענו בכאן כי רבי שהתפלל של שבת בערב שבת כבר קיבלה לשבת עילויה ואיחייב לשבות ונאסרו עליו החמין לרחוץ בהן ולא נכנס במרחץ אלא להזיע בלבד וזה המעשה היה קודם שגזרו חכמים על הזיעה לפי מה שיש בהלכה שהזכרנוה אסרו להן להזיע: **אמרי** [עד] כמה נצעריה וניזיל בר״ה צעריה בבכורות צעריה. האי דצעריה בראש השנה שנוי הוא בפרק אם אינן מכירין אותו (דף כה.) דתנן ועוד באו שנים ואמרו ראינוהו בזמנו שלח לו רבן גמליאל גוזר אני עליך שתבא אצלי במקלך ובמעותיך ביום הכפורים שחל להיות בחשבונך ובבכורות (עוד) בפרק כל פסולי המוקדשים (דף לו.) פירשו מעשה (אחר) [אחד] שאירע לר׳ יהושע עם רבן גמליאל דכסיף ליה קמי רבנן והעמידו על רגליו ברבים עד שנכנסה קנאה בלב כל העם שהיו לשם ושיתקו את המתורגמן וזו היא הגירסא של זו המעשה ר׳ צדוק הוה ליה בוכרא רמא ליה שערי בסלי נצרין של ערבה קלופה בהדי דאכיל איבזע שיפותיה אתא לקמיה דר׳ יהושע אמר ליה כלום חלקנו בין בור לחבר אמר ליה הין בא לפני רבן גמליאל אמר ליה לאו אמר ליה והלא ר׳ יהושע אמר לי הין המתן עד שיכנסו בעלי תריסין לבית המדרש כיון שנכנסו עמד השואל ושאל כלום חלקנו בין בור לחבר אמר לו ר׳ יהושע לאו אמר לו רבן גמליאל והלא משמך אמרו לי הין אמר לו עמוד על רגליך ויעידו ר׳ יהושע על רגליו ואמר אלמלי אני (מת) [חי] והוא (חי) [מת] יכול החי להכחיש את (החי) [המת] עכשיו שאני חי והוא חי היאך חי יכול להכחיש את החי היה רבן גמליאל יושב ודורש ור׳ יהושע עומד כל העם ואמרו לחוצפית התורגמן העמד: **נוקי** לר׳ עקיבא לית ליה זכות אבות. איתה בסנהדרין בפרק כל ישראל יש להן חלק (דף לו) מבני בניו של סיסרא למדו תורה בירושלים ומאן אינון ר׳ עקיבא ואיתה הניזקין דמסכת גיטין (דף נז): **נוקי** לר׳ אלעזר בן עזריה שהוא חכם ועשיר והוא עשירי לעזרא הסופר. החכמה שלו גלויה היא וידועה הלא תראה היאך אמר ר׳ יהושע אין דור יתום שר׳ אלעזר בן עז בתוכו באותה המעשה האמור במסכת חגיגה בפרק א׳ (דף ג) והעושר שלו נמי כבר גרסי׳ בפרק (במה אשה) [נ״ל במה בהמה] (שבת דף נד) י״ב אלפי עגלי הוה מעשר ר׳ אלעזר בן עזריה מעדריה כל שנ קדושין בפרק האיש מקדש (דף מט) על מנת שאני עשיר אין אומרים כר׳ אלעזר בן חרסום וכר׳ אלעזר בן עזריה וייחוסו לעזרא הסופר נמי איתה במנחות בפרק כל המנחות באות מצה (דף נג) אמרו לר׳ פרידא (רב עוירא) [ר׳ עזרא] בריה דרב אבטולס דהוא עשירי לר׳ אלעזר בן עזריה דהוא עשירי לעזרא קאי אבבא ובגמרא דפירקין דבני מערבא [הלכה ח] וגם (בפסחים בפרק תמיד) [נ״ל בתענית כ גרסינן הלכו ומינו את ר׳ אלעזר בן עזריה בן י״ז שנה ונתמלא כל ראשו שיבה והיה ר׳ עקיבא יושב ומצטער ואומר לא שהוא בן תורה יותר ממני אלא שהוא בן גדולים יותר ממני אשרי אדם שזכו לו אבו אדם שיש לו יתד להתלות בה ומה היתה יתידתו של ר׳ אלעזר בן עזריה שהיה עשירי לעזרא:

לא* כנגד רבו ולא אחורי רבו; ותניא, רבי אליעזר אומר: המתפלל אחורי רבו, והנותן שלום לרבו, והמחזיר שלום לרבו, *והחולק על ישיבתו של רבו, והאומר *דבר שלא שמע מפי רבו – גורם לשכינה שתסתלק מישראל! – שאני רבי ירמיה בר אבא, דתלמיד חבר הוה. והיינו *דקאמר ליה רבי ירמיה בר אבא לרב: מי בדלת? אמר ליה: אין, בדילנא, ולא אמר, מי בדיל מר? § ומי בדיל? והאמר רבי אבין: פעם אחת התפלל רבי של שבת בערב שבת, ונכנס למרחץ ויצא ושנה לן פרקין ועדיין לא חשכה! *אמר רבא: ההוא דנכנס להזיע, וקודם גזירה הוה. איני? והא אביי שרא ליה לרב דימי בר ליואי לכברויי סלי! – ההוא טעותא הואי. – וטעותא מי הדרא? והא אמר אבידן: פעם אחת נתקשרו שמים בעבים, כסבורים העם לומר חשכה הוא, ונכנסו לבית הכנסת והתפללו של מוצאי שבת בשבת, ונתפזרו העבים וזרחה החמה, ובאו ושאלו את רבי, ואמר: הואיל והתפללו – התפללו! – שאני צבור, דלא מטרחינן להו. § א״ר חייא בר אבין: רב צלי של שבת בערב שבת, רבי יאשיה מצלי של מוצאי שבת בשבת. רב צלי של שבת בערב שבת. אומר קדושה על הכוס, או אינו אומר קדושה על הכוס? ת״ש: דאמר רב נחמן אמר שמואל: מתפלל אדם של שבת בערב שבת ואומר קדושה על הכוס. והלכתא כוותיה. רבי יאשיה מצלי של מוצאי שבת בשבת. אומר הבדלה על הכוס או אינו אומר הבדלה על הכוס? ת״ש דאמר רב יהודה אמר שמואל: מתפלל אדם של מוצאי שבת בשבת, ואומר הבדלה על הכוס. אמר ר׳ זירא אמר רבי אסי אמר ר׳ אלעזר א״ר חנינא אמר רב: בצד עמוד זה התפלל ר׳ ישמעאל בר׳ יוסי של שבת בערב שבת. כי אתא עולא, אמר: בצד תמרה הוה ולא בצד עמוד הוה, ולא ר׳ ישמעאל ברבי יוסי הוה אלא ר׳ אלעזר בר׳ יוסי הוה, ולא של שבת בערב שבת הוה אלא של מוצאי שבת בשבת הוה. § "תפלת הערב אין לה קבע". מאי "אין לה קבע"? אילימא דאי בעי מצלי כוליה ליליא – ליתני תפלת הערב כל הלילה! אלא מאי "אין לה קבע"? כמאן דאמר: *תפלת ערבית רשות. דאמר רב יהודה אמר שמואל: תפלת ערבית, רבן גמליאל אומר: חובה, ר׳ יהושע אומר: *רשות. אמר אביי: הלכה כדברי האומר חובה. ורבא אמר: הלכה כדברי האומר רשות. § ת״ר: מעשה בתלמיד אחד שבא לפני ר׳ יהושע, א״ל: תפלת ערבית רשות או חובה? אמר ליה: רשות. בא לפני רבן גמליאל, א״ל: תפלת ערבית רשות או חובה? א״ל: חובה. א״ל: והלא ר׳ יהושע אמר לי רשות! א״ל: *המתן עד שיכנסו בעלי תריסין לבית המדרש. כשנכנסו בעלי תריסין, עמד השואל ושאל: תפלת ערבית רשות או חובה? א״ל רבן גמליאל: חובה. אמר להם רבן גמליאל לחכמים: כלום יש אדם שחולק בדבר זה? אמר ליה ר׳ יהושע: לאו. א״ל: והלא משמך אמרו לי רשות! אמר ליה: יהושע, עמוד על רגליך ויעידו בך! עמד רבי יהושע על רגליו ואמר: אלמלא אני חי והוא מת – יכול החי להכחיש את המת, ועכשיו שאני חי והוא חי – היאך יכול החי להכחיש את החי? היה רבן גמליאל יושב ודורש, ור׳ יהושע עומד על רגליו, עד שרננו כל העם ואמרו לחוצפית התורגמן: עמוד! ועמד. § אמרי: עד כמה נצעריה וניזיל? בר״ה אשתקד צעריה, בבכורות במעשה דר׳ צדוק צעריה, הכא נמי צעריה, תא ונעבריה! מאן נוקים ליה? נוקמיה לרבי יהושע? בעל מעשה הוא; נוקמיה לר׳ עקיבא? דילמא עניש ליה, דלית ליה זכות אבות; אלא נוקמיה לר׳ אלעזר בן עזריה, דהוא חכם והוא עשיר והוא עשירי לעזרא. הוא חכם – דאי מקשי ליה מפרק ליה, והוא עשיר – דאי אית ליה לפלוחי לבי קיסר אף הוא איזיל ופלח, והוא עשירי לעזרא – דאית ליה זכות אבות ולא מצי עניש ליה. אתו ואמרו ליה: ניחא ליה למר דליהוי ריש מתיבתא? אמר להו: איזיל ואימליך באינשי ביתי. אזל ואמליך בדביתהו. אמרה ליה: דלמא

עיין רש״ל ורש״א

[לעיל ד: שבת טו:]

חלק קי. וע״ש
סוכה דף כח. כלה
[עירובין מ:]
[ביצה לב.]
ס״א רשות כדברי האומר אמר הלכה האומר רשות פז:
[בכורות לו. וע]

רש"י

כנגד רבו. אצל רבו, ומראה כאילו הם שוים: אחורי רבו. נמי יוהרא הוא: שלום לרבו. כשאר כל אדם שלום עליך ולא אמר לו שלום עליך רבי: והיינו דקאמר ליה. אותו היום שהתפלל רב של שבת בערב שבת אמר ליה רבי ירמיה: מי בדלת מן המלאכה הואיל וקבלת עליך שבת בתפלתך: ולא אמר ליה מי בדיל מר. שמע מינה: תלמיד חבר הוי ליה: לבית המרחץ. סלקא דעתך – לאחר שגזרו על הזיעה ועל הרחיצה בשבת, כדאמרי׳ במסכת שבת בפרק כירה שהסיקוה (ד׳ מ.). אלמא: אע״ג דצלי, לא בדיל מאיסורי שבת: אמר רבא להזיע. נכנס להזיע מחמת חום בית המרחץ, ולא נתן עליו מים: וקודם גזרה. עד שלא גזרו על הזיעה. ובכל דוכתא דאמרינן כדאמר רבא להזיע כו׳ – מהכא אמרינן: לכברויי סלי. לעשן אותן בגפרית לאחר שהתפלל של שבת בערב שבת: טעותא הואי. לא קבל עליו תוספת שבת משעת תפלה מדעת, אלא יום המעונן היה וכסבור חשכה ואחר כך זרחה חמה: הואיל והתפללו התפללו. ולא הצריכם להתפלל משתחשך, אלמא: תפלה היא; ואע״פ שלא הותרו במלאכה, התם הוא דלא לעבור על ד״ת, אבל לענין תוספת אע״ג דבטעות הוה, תוספת הוא ע״י תפלה, הואיל ואמר תפלה קבלה היא: בעלי תריסין. חכמים המנצחים זה את זה בהלכה: היאך יכול החי להכחיש את החי. על כרחי אני צריך להודות שאמרתי לו רשות: התורגמן. שהיה עומד לפני רבן גמליאל ומשמיע לרבים את הדרשה מפי רבן גמליאל: עמוד. שתוק: אשתקד. שנה שעברה: בראש השנה. במסכת ראש השנה (דף כה.), שאמר לו: גוזר אני עליך שתבא אצלי במקלך ובמעותיך ביום הכפורים שחל להיות בחשבונך: בבכורות. במסכת בכורות (דף לו.): במעשה דרבי צדוק. בבכורות הוא. ר׳ צדוק הוה ליה בוכרא, ואמר ליה רבן גמליאל לר׳ יהושע: עמוד על רגליך כו׳ כי הכא: תא ונעבריה. נסלק אותו מן הנשיאות: בעל מעשה הוא. והוה ליה לרבן גמליאל צערא טפי: לית ליה זכות אבות. ודילמא עניש ליה רבן גמליאל: מעברין לך. יורידוך מן הנשיאות בשביל אחר:

תוספות

**ולא** אחורי רבו. פירש רש״י: משום יוהרא. ויש מפרש: שנראה כמשתחוה לרבו: **והנותן** שלום לרבו והמחזיר שלום. פירוש: כשאר בני אדם, שאינו אומר ׳שלום עליך רבי׳ והיינו דאמרינן (נ״ק דף עג:) כדי שאילת תלמיד לרב. אי נמי, הסוגה לכתחלה קאמר, ובתלמיד חבר דשרי, ככל הני דלקמן: **הואיל** והתפללו וכו׳. הכא נמי נימא *לענין[א] חומרא ואמאי שרי ליה. ובקונטרס פי׳ בפנים אחר: **שאני** צבור. אע״ג דלא מטא זמן *אין[ב] איסורא איסור בעשיית מלאכה, אף על גב דטעותא הוא: **צלי** של מוצאי שבת וכו׳. יש לומר דהכא מיירי שיש לו צורך מצוה לעשות במוצאי שבת, כגון ללכת למול תינוק ולא יהיה לו יין להבדלה אם לא יקדים, דודאי צריך להוסיף מחול על הקדש דאורייתא, אבל בחנם לא. ופשיטא שלא היו ממהרים להבדיל ולהתפלל של מוצאי שבת בשבת, דגם במלאכה אסור עם חשיכה: **הלכה** כדברי האומר רשות. לאו דוקא רשות, אלא כדפרישית לעיל (ד׳ כו.); ולכך נקרא רשות – לבטלה עבור מצוה אחרת העוברת: **והלכתא** כוותיה דרב. ונראה לכך תקנו פסוקים וקדיש בין גאולה לתפלה, דרשות היא: [ע׳ תוס׳ לעיל ד: ד״ה אמר ר״י]: ושל

הגהות
(א) תוס׳ ד״ה הואיל וכו׳ נמי נימא לעיל לחומרא ואמאי שרי: (ב) וכו׳ אין איסורא כנ״ל ותיבת נמחק:

גליון הש״ס
גמ׳ והמחזיר ברי״ף ובכל״ש והמחזיר שלום לתלמיד חבר קודשין ד׳ מ״ו ד״ה נראין. ע׳ גזרה הוה. ע׳ ע״ב ברש״י מעשה. וברשב״ם:

דלמא מעברין לך? אמר לה: [לשתמש אינש] יומא חדא בכסא דמוקרא ולמחר ליתבר. אמרה ליה: לית לך חיורתא. ההוא יומא בר תמני סרי שני הוה, אתרחיש ליה ניסא ואהדרו ליה תמני סרי דרי חיורתא. היינו דקאמר ר' אלעזר בן עזריה: *הרי אני "כבן" שבעים שנה, ולא "בן" שבעים שנה. תנא: אותו היום סלקוהו לשומר הפתח *ונתנה להם רשות לתלמידים ליכנס. שהיה ר"ג מכריז ואומר: *כל תלמיד שאין תוכו כברו – לא יכנס לבית המדרש. ההוא יומא אתוספו כמה ספסלי. א"ר יוחנן: פליגי בה אבא יוסף בן דוסתאי ורבנן, חד אמר: אתוספו ארבע מאה ספסלי; וחד אמר: שבע מאה ספסלי. הוה קא חלשא דעתיה דר"ג, אמר: דלמא ח"ו מנעתי תורה מישראל. אחזו ליה בחלמיה חצבי חיורי דמליין קטמא. ולא היא, ההיא ליתובי דעתיה הוא דאחזו ליה.§ תנא: עדיות בו ביום נשנית, וכל היכא דאמרינן "בו ביום" – ההוא יומא הוה. ולא היתה הלכה שהיתה תלויה בבית המדרש שלא פירשוה. ואף ר"ג לא מנע עצמו מבית המדרש אפילו שעה אחת, דתנן: *בו ביום בא יהודה גר עמוני לפניהם בבית המדרש, אמר להם:(א) מה אני לבא בקהל? א"ל ר"ג: אסור אתה לבא בקהל; א"ל ר' יהושע: ב מותר אתה לבא בקהל. א"ל ר"ג: והלא כבר נאמר: °"לא יבא עמוני ומואבי בקהל ה'"! א"ל ר' יהושע: וכי עמון ומואב במקומן הן יושבין?!(ב) *כבר עלה סנחריב מלך אשור ובלבל את כל האומות, שנאמר: °"ואסיר גבלות עמים ועתודותיהם שושתי ואוריד כאביר יושבים", *וכל דפריש – מרובא פריש. אמר לו ר"ג: והלא כבר נאמר: °"ואחרי כן אשיב את שבות בני עמון נאם ה'" – וכבר שבו. אמר לו ר' יהושע: והלא כבר נאמר: °"ושבתי את שבות עמי ישראל" – ועדיין לא שבו. מיד התירוהו לבא בקהל.§ אר"ג: הואיל והכי הוה, איזיל ואפייסיה לר' יהושע. כי מטא לביתיה, חזינהו לאשיתא דביתיה דמשחרן. א"ל: מכותלי ביתך אתה ניכר שפחמי אתה. א"ל: אוי לו לדור שאתה פרנסו, *שאי אתה יודע בצערן של ת"ח ג במה הם מתפרנסים ובמה הם נזונים. אמר לו: נעניתי לך, מחול לי! לא אשגח ביה. עשה בשביל כבוד אבא! פייס. אמרו: מאן ניזיל ולימא להו לרבנן? אמר להו ההוא כובס: אנא אזילנא. שלח להו ר' יהושע לבי מדרשא: מאן דלביש מדא ילבש מדא, ומאן דלא לביש מדא יימר ליה למאן דלביש מדא 'שלח מדך ואנא אלבשיה'?! אמר להו ר"ע לרבנן: טרוקו גלי, דלא ליתו עבדי דר"ג ולצערו לרבנן. א"ר יהושע: מוטב דאיקום ואיזיל אנא לגבייהו. אתא, טרף אבבא. א"ל: ד מזה בן מזה יזה, ושאינו לא מזה ולא בן מזה יאמר למזה בן מזה: מימיך מי מערה ואפרך אפר מקלה? א"ל ר"ע: רבי יהושע, נתפייסת? כלום עשינו אלא בשביל כבודך! למחר אני ואתה נשכים לפתחו. אמרי: היכי נעביד? נעבריה – *גמירי: מעלין בקדש ואין מורידין! נדרוש מר חדא שבתא ומר חדא שבתא – אתי לקנאויי! אלא: לדרוש ר"ג *תלתא שבתי, וראב"ע חדא שבתא. והיינו דאמר מר: *שבת של מי היתה – של ראב"ע היתה. ואותו תלמיד – ר' שמעון בן יוחאי הוה.§ ה"ושל מוספין כל היום". א"ר יוחנן: ו ונקרא פושע. ת"ר: *היו לפניו שתי תפלות, אחת של מנחה ואחת של מוסף – מתפלל של מנחה ואח"כ מתפלל של מוסף, שזו תדירה וזו אינה תדירה. ר' יהודה אומר: מתפלל של מוסף ואח"כ מתפלל של מנחה, שזו מצוה עוברת וזו מצוה שאינה עוברת. *א"ר יוחנן, ז הלכה: מתפלל של מנחה ואח"כ מתפלל של מוסף. ר' זירא כי הוה חליש מגירסיה, הוה אזיל ויתיב אפתחא דבי ר' נתן בר טובי, אמר: כי חלפי רבנן אז איקום מקמייהו ואקבל אגרא. נפק אתא ר' נתן בר טובי, א"ל: מאן אמר הלכה בי מדרשא? א"ל, הכי א"ר יוחנן: אין הלכה כר' יהודה דאמר: מתפלל אדם של מוסף ואח"כ מתפלל של מנחה. א"ל: רבי יוחנן אמרה?! אמר ליה: אין. *תנא מיניה ארבעין זמנין. א"ל: חדא היא לך, או חדת היא לך? א"ל: חדת היא לי, משום דמספקא לי בר' יהושע בן לוי.§ אריב"ל: ח כל המתפלל תפלה של מוספין לאחר שבע שעות לר' יהודה, עליו הכתוב אומר: °"נוגי ממועד אספתי ממך היו". מאי משמע דהאי "נוגי" לישנא דתברא הוא? כדמתרגם רב יוסף: "תברא אתי על שנאיהון דבית ישראל על דאחרו זמני מועדיא דבירושלים". א"ר אלעזר: כל המתפלל תפלה של שחרית לאחר ארבע שעות לר' יהודה, עליו הכתוב אומר: "נוגי ממועד אספתי ממך היו". מאי משמע דהאי "נוגי" לישנא דצערא הוא? דכתיב: °"דלפה נפשי מתוגה". רב נחמן בר יצחק אמר, מהכא: °"בתולותיה נוגות והיא מר לה".
רב

**רש"י**

ה"ג. דלמא מעברין לך? אמר לה: יומא חדא בכסא דמוקרא ולמחר ליתבר. ול"ג מעלין בקדש: **כסא דמוקרא.** *כוס זכוכית יקרה שקורין לה בלשון ישמעאל ערקי"א. ואומרים בני אדם במשל הדיוט: יום אחד ישתמש בו בעליו ויתכבד בו, ואם ישבר – ישבר: **לית לך חיורתא.** אין לך שערות לבנות של זקנה, ונאה לדרשן להיות זקן: **י"ח דרי חיורתא.** י"ח שורות של זקנה: **קא חלשא דעתיה דר"ג.** כשראה שנתוספו היום תלמידים רבים, והיה דואג שלא יענש כמה שמנעם בימיו מללמוד: **דמליין קטמא.** כלומר: אף אלו אינם ראויים: **תלויה.** בספק, שלא פירשוה. מתוך שרבו התלמידים רב החדוד והפלפול: **לאשיתא דביתיה דמשחרן.** כותלי ביתו של ר' יהושע שהיו שחורות: **שפחמי אתה.** עושה פחמים. וי"א: נפח: **נעניתי לך.** דברתי למולך יותר מן הראוי: **דלביש מדא.** הרגיל ללבוש המעיל ילבש. כלומר: הרגיל בנשיאות יהיה נשיא: **מזה בן מזה.** כהן בן כהן, יזה את מי חטאת **אפר מקלה.** אפר הקלוי בתנורים ובכירות, כלומר: אפר סתם: **שבת של מי היתה.** במסכת חגיגה: **ואותו תלמיד.** ששאל תפלת ערבית רשות או חובה רשב"י הוא: **ונקרא פושע.** המאחר כ"כ: **מתפלל של מנחה.** מאחר שהגיע זמנה, כדי להקדימה בתחלת זמנה, שלא יקרא פושע גם עליה: **ואח"כ של מוספין.** הואיל ואיחר, *זמנה אינו עובר. דהא אמרי רבנן: ושל מוספים כל היום: **שזו מצוה עוברת.** ר' יהודה לטעמיה, דאמר עד שבע שעות ותו לא: **כי חלפי רבנן.** תלמידים היוצאים מבית ר' נתן: **מאן אמר הלכה בי מדרשא.** מי מבני הישיבה אמר בבית המדרש שהלכה כר' יהודה: **חדא היא לך או חדת היא לך.** אחת היא לך – שלא למדת דבר משמו של ר' יוחנן אלא זו בלבד, לכך חביבה היא לך; או חדשה היא לך, שהיית סבור שאחד מן האחרים אמרה: ה"ג. **א"ל חדת היא לי דמספקא לי בר' יהושע בן לוי.** סבור הייתי שרבי יהושע בן לוי אמרה: **אמר ריב"ל.** גרסי' ול"ג דאמר: **ממועד.** מחמת שהעבירו מועדי התפלות והחגים, יהיו נוגים ואסופים וכלים:
לא

**תוספות**

**ושל** מוספין כל היום. הקשה הרב רבינו שמשון ז"ל, דאמרי' בפרק "תמיד נשחט" (דף נח.): מוספין בשש, בזיכין בשבע! וכ"ת: ה"מ למצוה, אבל דיעבד כל יומא נמי זמניה הוא, הרי *במשנה (פ"ג ד' יד) משמע שהמוספין היו נשחטין עם התמיד ונקטרין עמו! ותירץ: דהתם מיירי בשבת*.

**הלכה** מתפלל של מנחה ואח"כ מתפלל של מוסף. מכאן יש ליזהר ביוה"כ להתפלל תפלת שחרית קודם שש שעות וממלא, דהיינו קודם שיגיע שעת המנחה, דאל"כ היו צריכין להתפלל תפלת המנחה קודם. והר"י אומר דאינו צריך, דהא דקאמר שיתפלל תפלת המנחה קודם – היינו כשיש לו לעשות לצרכיו, שלא יוכל להתפלל תפלת המנחה בזמנה וצריך להתפלל שניהם מיד, כגון שהיה לו לילך לסעודה גדולה, כמו לנשואין, ומתירא שמא ימשוך בסעודתו או שישתכר. אבל אם היה לו שהות להתפלל אחר תפלת מוסף תפלת המנחה בזמנה, אין לו להקדים תפלת המנחה אלא יתפלל כסדר, מוסף ואח"כ מנחה: **כדמתרגם** רב יוסף על דאחרו זמני מועדיא. ואי משתעי ברגלים אין שייך לומר לשון איחור, שהרי אין להם תשלומין, אלא ע"כ בתפלה משתעי קרא:
כיון

**עין משפט נר מצוה**

לג א מיי' פ"ד מהלכות ת"ת הלכה א טוש"ע יו"ד סי' רמו סעיף ז:
[ג"ל ביומא ד' ע. כ"כ המג"א סימן רפ"א ועיין רש"ל וכס"ל]
לד ב מיי' פי"ב מהל' איסורי ביאה הלכה כה סמג לאוין קטו טוש"ע אה"ע סימן ד סעיף י:
לה ג מיי' פ"א מהל' ת"ת הלכה ט ופ"ו מהל' מתנות עניים הלכה יח:
לו ד מיי' פ"א מהל' מלכים הל' ז טוש"ע י"ד סימן רמה סעיף כב בהגה:
לז ה ו מיי' פ"ג מהל' תפלה הלכה ה סמג עשין יט טוש"ע או"ח סימן רפו סעיף א:
לח ז מיי' שם הל' יא טוש"ע שם סעיף ד:
לט ח שם סעיף א:

**מסורת הש"ס**

(ועי' פירש"י לקמן לח. ד"ה כסא)
[לעיל פ"א דף יב:]
[דוגמתו יומא עב:]
ל"ל וזמנה רש"ל
[יומא נג. וע' תוס' מגילה יב: וחוס' יבמות טו: וכסוטה ע. ד"ה מנימין]
מס' ידים פ"ד משנה ד'
דברים כג
ישעיה י
[יומא פד: יבמות טז: כתובות טו. קדושין עג. זבחים עג.]
ירמיה מט
עמוס ט
[יומא יב: עג. מגילה ט: כח: הוריות יב: שבת כח: [תמיד לח:] מנחות לט. לט. וכס מפיק לה מקרא וג"ע לשון גמירי]
[יותר נכון לגרוס תרתי וכ"ה בהקדמת הרמב"ם לפי' המשניות ביבמות] [חגיגה ג.] [לעיל כז:]
[זבחים יב. לא.]
[פסחים עב. מגילה ז: כתובות כב: נ.]
צפניה ג
תהלים קיט איכה א

**הגהות הב"ח**

(א) גמ' אמר להם (מה אני) תא"מ. ונ"ב ס"א מותר: (ב) שם במקומן הן יושבין והלא ככר:

ס"א ואוי לה לספינה שאתה קברניטה

**גליון הש"ס**

**גמ'** מכותלי ביתך. עיין תשב"ץ ח"א ענין קמב: **שם** ונקרא פושע. עיין לקמן (דף מ"ג ע"ב): **שם** כי הוה חליש מגירסא. עיין עירובין (דף כ"ח ע"ב):

**רב נסים גאון**

וזה שאמרו כל בו ביום דאמרינן ההוא יומא איתמר. יש במשנה הרב' מזה הענין כגון האי דתנן במס' ידים (פ"ג מ"ה) אמ' ר' שמעון בן עזאי מקובל אני מפי ע"ב זקנים ביום שהושיבו את ר' אלעזר בן עזריה בראש ששיר השירים וקהלת מטמאין את הידי' אמר ר' עקיבא חס ושלום וכו' (פ"ד מ"א) בו ביום נמנו וגמרו על עריבת [הרגלים] בו ביום אמרו [משנה ג] כל הזבחים וכו' ובתוספתא

[ב'ידים פ"ג] בו ביום עמד יהודה גר עמוני: **אמר** רבן גמליאל השתא איזיל ואפייסיה לר' יהושע אזל חזינהו לאשיתא דביתיה דהוו קא משחרן כו'. ופירשו בגמרא דבני מערבא אזל ואשכח לר' יהושע יתיב עביד מחטין אמר ליה מן אילין את חיי אמר ליה עד כדון את בעי מידע אוי לדור שאתה פרנסו. והאי דאמר ליה עשה בשביל כבוד בית אבא כלומר בשביל הלל הזקן זקני שהיה מזרע דוד כדגרסינן בפ' יציאות השבת (דף טו) הלל ושמעון גמליאל ושמעון נהגו נשיאותן בפני הבית ק' שנה וזה רבן גמליאל הנזכר בכאן הוא בנו של רבן שמעון בן גמליאל שהוא רביעי להלל הזקן דהוי ליה רבן גמליאל חמישי להלל ובנו רבן שמעון ששי להלל ובנו ר' יהודה הנשיא שהוא רבי והוא רבינו הקדוש הוי שביעי להלל הזקן ואיתא במסכת שבת בפרק במה בהמה (דף נו) רבי דאתי מדוד מהפך בזכותיה דדוד ובגמרא דפרק אחרון דתענית דבני מערבא (הלכה ג) אמרי אמר לוי מגילת יוחסין מצאו בירושלים וכתוב בה הלל מן דוד ואיתא בפ' אע"פ שאמרו בכתובות (ד' סב) בדקו במשפחות רבי אתי משפטיה בן אביטל. והאי דאמרינן אעפ"כ לא עברוה לר' אלעזר בן עזריה פירשו בתלמוד ארץ ישראל אלא מינו אותו אב בית דין והיינו דאמר מר שבת של מי היתה של ר' אלעזר בן עזריה היתה ואיתא בפירקא קמא דחגיגה (דף ג) תנו רבנן מעשה בר' יוחנן בן ברוקא ור' אלעזר חסמא שהלכו להקביל את פני ר' יהושע בפקיעין אמר להם מה חידוש היה היום בבית המדרש אמרו לו תלמידיך אנחנו ומימיך אנו שותין אמר להן אעפ"כ אי אפשר לבית המדרש בלא חידוש שבת של מי היתה אמרו לו שבת של ר' אלעזר בן עזריה:

לא על לפרקא דרב יוסף. שהיה ראש הישיבה בפומבדיתא, והיה דורש בשבת קודם תפלת המוספין, ולאחר הדרשה היו הולכים לבית הכנסת ומתפללים תפלת המוספין: בצבור שנו. אם הוא בבהכ"נ עם הצבור, לא יקדים להתפלל: מתני' מה מקום. כלומר: מה טיבה: גמ' ולא אכשל. וישמחו חברי על כשלוני. הרי רעות שתים, שיכשלו על ידי שאגרום להם *שיענשו: מיושבי קרנות. חנוונים, או עמי הארץ, שעוסקים בדבר שיחה: מההגיון. לא תרגילום במקרא יותר מדאי, משום דמשכא. לשון אחר: משיחת ילדים: דעו לפני מי וכו'. כדי שתתפללו ביראה ובכוונה: עמוד הימיני. שני עמודים העמיד שלמה באולם, שם הימני יכין ושם השמאלי בועז (מלכים א ז). הימיני לעולם חשוב: פטיש. המפולץ, פי"ק בלע"ז: אוסרני. חובש אותי: מיתת עולם. לעוה"ב: הייתי בוכה. מאימת משפטו, אם לדין מוליכין אותי לפניו: עד כאן. בתמיה, כלומר: ולא יותר ממורא בשר ודם ולואי. שיהא כמורא בשר ודם, שאם כן תחדלו מעבירות הרבה: עבירה. בסתר, ממורא הבריות, ויודע שהכל הוא גלוי להקב"ה, ואינו מניח בכך: מפני הטומאה. טומאת אהל המת בכל הבית: לחזקיהו שבא. אלי ללוותי: מתני' מעין שמונה עשרה. בגמרא מפרש: הושיע ה' וכו'. זו תפלה קצרה: בכל פרשת העבור כו'. מפרש בגמרא: אם אינו יכול לירד. שאין לו מי שיאחז את חמורו: יחזיר את פניו. לצד ירושלים: באסדא. כמו ותשם בסד רגלי (איוב יג) = בית הסהר שקורין ליפ"ש בלע"ז. לשון אחר: עצים המקושרים זה עם זה הרבה יחד, ובלשון מקרא קורא אותם רפסודות (ד"ה ב) ובלע"ז – רדיי"ל, ובלשון אשכנז – ולו"ס ומשיטין בנהר להוליכן ממקום למקום ויולכין להלך עליהן כמו בספינה: גמ' הבו לה' בני אלים. שהוא רמז לאבות וגבורות וקדושת השם, כדאמרינן בראש השנה (דף לב.): מנין שאומרים אבות? ת"ל הבו לה' בני אלים כו': שיתפקקו. שיראו הפקקים, הם הקשרים. כמו ששנינו* (ב"ב פ:) בקנים ובגפנים מן הפקק (ב) שלמעלה, והוא הקשר שבחלל הקנה פקוק וסתום שם: איסר. שני קמטים, אחד מלמטה ואחד מלמעלה וכאיסר רוחב בשר באמצע: דמצער נפשיה. שהוא ניכר שחפץ לכרוע, אלא שהוא מצטער: ביבנה תקנוה. לאחר זמן מרובה: הפקולי. מוכר פקולי, כמו צמר גפן שקורין קוטו"ן: והשקיף

כיון שהגיע זמן תפלת המנחה אסור לטעום כלום וכו'. ולית ליה לרבי יהושע מפסיקין, ואפילו מן האכילה, ולא היא: לייט

רב אויא חלש ולא אתא לפרקא דרב יוסף. למחר כי אתא, בעא אביי לאנוחי דעתיה דרב יוסף. א"ל: מ"ט לא אתא מר לפרקא? א"ל: דהוה חליש לבאי ולא מצינא. א"ל: אמאי לא טעמת מידי ואתית? א"ל: לא סבר לה מר להא דרב הונא? דאמר רב הונא: אסור לו לאדם שיטעום כלום קודם שיתפלל תפלת המוספין! -א"ל: איבעי ליה למר לצלויי צלותא דמוספין ביחיד, ולטעום מידי ולמיתי! -א"ל: ולא סבר לה מר להא דא"ר יוחנן: אאסור לו לאדם שיקדים תפלתו לתפלת הצבור?! -א"ל: לאו אתמר עלה: א"ר אבא: בבצבור שנו?! ולית הלכתא; גלא כרב הונא ולא כריב"ל; כרב הונא – הא דאמרן, כריב"ל – דאריב"ל: *כיון שהגיע זמן תפלת המנחה, אסור לו לאדם שיטעום כלום קודם שיתפלל תפלת המנחה.§ מתני' ר' נחוניא בן הקנה היה מתפלל בכניסתו לבית המדרש וביציאתו תפלה קצרה. אמרו לו: מה מקום לתפלה זו? אמר להם: בכניסתי אני מתפלל שלא יארע דבר תקלה על ידי, וביציאתי אני נותן הודאה על חלקי. גמ' ת"ר: דבכניסתו מהו אומר? יהי רצון מלפניך ה' אלהי שלא יארע דבר תקלה על ידי, ולא אכשל בדבר הלכה וישמחו בי חברי, ולא אומר [א] על טמא טהור ולא על טהור טמא, ולא יכשלו חברי בדבר הלכה ואשמח בהם. ביציאתו מהו אומר? מודה אני לפניך ה' אלהי ששמת חלקי מיושבי בית המדרש ולא שמת חלקי מיושבי קרנות, שאני משכים והם משכימים – אני משכים לדברי תורה והם משכימים לדברים בטלים, אני עמל והם עמלים – אני עמל ומקבל שכר והם עמלים ואינם מקבלים שכר, אני רץ והם רצים – אני רץ לחיי העולם הבא והם רצים לבאר שחת.§ ת"ר: הכשחלה ר' אליעזר, נכנסו תלמידיו לבקרו. אמרו לו: רבינו, למדנו אורחות חיים ונזכה בהן לחיי העולם הבא. אמר להם: הזהרו בכבוד חבריכם, ומנעו בניכם מן ההגיון, והושיבום בין ברכי תלמידי חכמים, וכשאתם מתפללים – דעו לפני מי אתם עומדים, ובשביל כך תזכו לחיי העולם הבא. וכשחלה רבי יוחנן בן זכאי, נכנסו תלמידיו לבקרו. כיון שראה אותם התחיל לבכות. אמרו לו תלמידיו: נר ישראל, עמוד הימיני, פטיש החזק, מפני מה אתה בוכה? אמר להם: אילו לפני מלך בשר ודם היו מוליכין אותי, שהיום כאן ומחר בקבר, שאם כועס עלי – אין כעסו כעס עולם, ואם אוסרני – אין איסורו איסור עולם, ואם ממיתני – אין מיתתו מיתת עולם, ואני יכול לפייסו בדברים ולשחדו בממון – אעפ"כ הייתי בוכה; ועכשיו שמוליכים אותי לפני ממ"ה הקב"ה, שהוא חי וקיים לעולם ולעולמי עולמים, שאם כועס עלי – כעסו כעס עולם, ואם אוסרני – איסורו איסור עולם, ואם ממיתני – מיתתו מיתת עולם, ואיני יכול לפייסו בדברים ולא לשחדו בממון; ולא עוד, אלא שיש לפני שני דרכים, אחת של גן עדן ואחת של גיהנם, ואיני יודע באיזו מוליכים אותי – ולא אבכה?! אמרו לו: רבינו, ברכנו! אמר להם: יהי רצון שתהא מורא שמים עליכם כמורא בשר ודם. אמרו לו תלמידיו: עד כאן?! -אמר להם: ולואי! תדעו, כשאדם עובר עבירה אומר: "שלא יראני אדם". בשעת פטירתו, אמר להם: פנו כלים מפני הטומאה, והכינו כסא לחזקיהו מלך יהודה שבא.§ מתני' רבן גמליאל אומר: בכל יום ויום מתפלל אדם שמונה עשרה. רבי יהושע אומר: מעין י"ח. ר"ע אומר: יאם שגורה תפלתו בפיו – מתפלל י"ח, ואם לאו – מעין י"ח. ר"א אומר: העושה תפלתו קבע אין תפלתו תחנונים. ר' יהושע אומר: ההולך במקום סכנה מתפלל תפלה קצרה, ואומר: הושע ה' את עמך את שארית ישראל, בכל פרשת העבור *יהיו צרכיהם לפניך, ברוך אתה ה' שומע תפלה. היה רוכב על החמור – ירד ויתפלל, ואם אינו יכול לירד – יחזיר את פניו, ואם אינו יכול להחזיר את פניו – יכוין את לבו כנגד בית קדשי הקדשים. היה מהלך בספינה או באסדא – יכוין את לבו כנגד בית קדשי הקדשים.§ גמ' הני י"ח כנגד מי? א"ר הלל בריה דר' שמואל בר נחמני: *כנגד י"ח אזכרות שאמר דוד ב"הבו לה' בני אלים". רב יוסף אמר: כנגד י"ח אזכרות שבקריאת שמע.(א) א"ר תנחום אמר רבי יהושע בן לוי: כנגד שמונה עשרה חוליות שבשדרה. ואמר ר' תנחום אמר רבי יהושע בן לוי: חהמתפלל צריך שיכרע עד שיתפקקו כל חוליות שבשדרה; עולא אמר: טעד כדי שיראה איסר כנגד לבו; רבי חנינא אמר: כיון שנענע ראשו שוב אינו צריך. אמר רבא: יוהוא – דמצער נפשיה ומחזי כמאן דכרע.§ הני תמני סרי, תשסרי הויין! אמר רבי לוי: ברכת הצדוקים ביבנה תקנוה. כנגד מי תקנוה? א"ר לוי: לרבי הלל בריה דרבי שמואל בר נחמני – כנגד °"אל הכבוד הרעים", לרב יוסף – כנגד "אחד" שבקריאת שמע; לר' תנחום א"ר יהושע בן לוי – כנגד חוליא קטנה שבשדרה. ת"ר: *שמעון הפקולי הסדיר י"ח ברכות לפני רבן גמליאל על הסדר ביבנה. אמר להם ר"ג לחכמים: כלום יש אדם שיודע לתקן ברכת הצדוקים? עמד שמואל הקטן ותקנה, לשנה אחרת שכחה. והשקיף

לט א ב מיי' פ"י מהל' תפלה הלכה יו סמג עשין יט טוש"ע או"ח סימן נ סעיף י:
מ ג מיי' פ"ו שם הלכה ד סמג שם טוש"ע או"ח סימן רפו סעיף ג:
מא ד מיי' וסמג שם טור ש"ע א"ח סי' רלב סעיף ג:
מב ה מיי' פ"י מהל' ברכות הלכה כג כד סמג עשין כז טוש"ע או"ח סי' קי סעיף ח:
מג ו טור וש"ע או"ח סימן א סעיף א:
מד ז מיי' פ"ב מהל' תפלה הלכה ב סמג עשין יט טור ש"ע א"ח סי' קי סעיף א:
מה ח ט מיי' פ"ה שם הלכה יב סמג שם טוש"ע א"ח סימן קיג סעיף ד:
מו י כ מיי' שם טוש"ע שם סעיף ה:

## רב נסים גאון

רבן גמליאל אומר בכל יום אדם מתפלל י"ח. בתלמוד ארץ ישראל הזכירו עוד טעמים אחרים (כעין) [אולי צ"ל על שתקנו] י"ח תוספת על מה שיש בתלמודינו דאמרינן ר' חנניה בשם ר' פינחס כנגד י"ח פעמים שאבות כתובין בתורה אברהם יצחק ויעקב אם יאמר לך אדם י"ט הן אמור לו והנה ה' נצב עליו לית הוא מינהון אם יאמר לך אדם י"ז הן אמור לו ויקרא בהן שמי ושם אבותי מינהון הוא ר' שמואל בר נחמני בשם ר' יונתן כנגד י"ח ציוויים שכתב בפרשת משכן שני אמר ר' חייא בר אדא ובלבד מן ואתו אהליאב בן אחיסמך עד סופיה דסיפרא: היה יושב בספינה או באסדא. בגמ' דבני מערבא גרסי היא אסדא היא רפסודות דכתיב (דברי הימים ב ב) ונביאם לך רפסודות על ים יפו:

## הגהות הב"ח

(א) גמ' אזכרות שבק"ש ר' תנחום א"ר יהושע בן לוי אמר כנגד: (ב) רש"י ד"ה שיתפקקו וכו' מן הפקק ולמעלה:

## גליון הש"ס

גמ' כשחלה ר"א. במס' דרך ארץ רבה פ"ג איתא ר"א בן עזריה. וע"ש עוד איזה שינויים: שם הני י"ח כנגד מי. עי' מדרש תנחומא ר"פ וירא עוד איזה טעמים. ושם איתא דריב"ל אמר נגד י"ח אזכרות שאמר דוד בהבו לה' בני אלים:

(ע' בתי"ט)
שבת קנ ט:
הגהות [א] גמ' ול... טמא טהור ו... טמא. כל זה קודם ול...
(תענית כה:)
נ"י ויהיו
תוספתא פ"ג תהלים כט
שם
מגילה יז:

## גמרא

והשקיף בה שתים ושלש שעות ולא העלוהו. אמאי לא העלוהו? והאמר רב יהודה אמר רב: טעה בכל הברכות כולן – אין מעלין אותו, בברכת הצדוקים – מעלין אותו, חיישינן שמא מין הוא! שאני שמואל הקטן, דאיהו תקנה. וניחוש דלמא הדר ביה! אמר אביי, גמירי: טבא לא הוי בישא. ולא?! והכתיב °"ובשוב צדיק מצדקתו ועשה עול"! ההוא רשע מעיקרו, אבל צדיק מעיקרו – לא. ולא?! והא *תנן: אל תאמין בעצמך עד יום מותך, שהרי *יוחנן כ"ג שמש בכהונה גדולה שמנים שנה ולבסוף נעשה צדוקי! *אמר אביי: הוא ינאי הוא יוחנן. רבא אמר: ינאי לחוד ויוחנן לחוד, ינאי – רשע מעיקרו, ויוחנן – צדיק מעיקרו. הניחא לאביי, אלא לרבא קשיא! אמר לך רבא: צדיק מעיקרו נמי, דלמא הדר ביה. אי הכי, אמאי לא אסקוהו? שאני שמואל הקטן דאתחיל בה. דאמר רב יהודה אמר רב, ואיתימא רבי יהושע בן לוי: לא שנו אלא שלא התחיל בה, אבל התחיל בה – גומרה.§ הני שבע דשבתא כנגד מי? א"ר חלפתא בן שאול: כנגד שבעה קולות שאמר דוד על המים. הני תשע דר"ה כנגד מי? א"ר יצחק דמן קרטיגנין: כנגד תשעה אזכרות שאמרה חנה בתפלתה, דאמר מר: *בראש השנה נפקדה שרה רחל וחנה. הני עשרים וארבע דתעניתא כנגד מי? א"ר חלבו: כנגד כ"ד רננות *שאמר שלמה בשעה שהכניס ארון לבית קדשי הקדשים. אי הכי, כל יומא נמי נמרינהו! אימת אמרינהו שלמה – ביומא דרחמי, אנן נמי ביומא דרחמי אמרי להו.§ "רבי יהושע אומר מעין שמנה עשרה". מאי מעין שמונה עשרה? רב אמר: מעין כל ברכה וברכה, ושמואל אמר: "הביננו ה' אלהינו לדעת דרכיך, ומול את לבבנו ליראתך, ותסלח לנו להיות גאולים, ורחקנו ממכאובינו, ודשננו בנאות ארצך, ונפוצותינו מארבע תקבץ, והתועים על דעתך ישפטו, ועל הרשעים תניף ידיך, וישמחו צדיקים בבנין עירך ובתקון היכלך ובצמיחת קרן לדוד עבדך ובעריכת נר לבן ישי משיחך, טרם נקרא [א] אתה תענה, ברוך אתה ה' שומע תפלה". *לייט עלה אביי אמאן דמצלי "הביננו".§ אמר רב נחמן אמר שמואל: כל השנה כולה מתפלל אדם "הביננו", חוץ ממוצאי שבת וממוצאי ימים טובים, מפני שצריך לומר הבדלה ב"חונן הדעת". מתקיף לה רבה בר שמואל: ונימרה ברכה רביעית בפני עצמה! מי לא תנן, *ר"ע אומר: אומרה ברכה רביעית בפני עצמה; ר' אליעזר אומר: בהודאה! *אטו כל השנה כולה מי עבדינן כר' עקיבא, דהשתא נמי נעביד?! כל השנה כולה מאי טעמא לא עבדינן כר"ע – תמני סרי תקון, תשסרי לא תקון, הכא נמי – שבע תקון, תמני לא תקון. מתקיף לה מר זוטרא: ונכללה מכלל "הביננו ה' אלהינו המבדיל בין קדש לחול"! קשיא.§ אמר רב ביבי בר אביי: כל השנה כולה מתפלל אדם "הביננו" חוץ מימות הגשמים, מפני שצריך לומר שאלה בברכת השנים. מתקיף לה מר זוטרא: ונכללה מכלל "ודשננו בנאות ארצך ותן טל ומטר"! אתי לאטרודי. אי הכי, הבדלה ב"חונן הדעת" נמי אתי לאטרודי! אמרי: התם כיון דאתיא בתחלת צלותא – לא מטריד, הכא כיון דאתיא באמצע צלותא – מטריד. מתקיף לה רב אשי: ונימרה ב"שומע תפלה"! דא"ר תנחום אמר רב אסי: טעה ולא הזכיר גבורות גשמים בתחיית המתים – מחזירין אותו, שאלה בברכת השנים – אין מחזירין אותו, מפני שיכול לאומרה ב"שומע תפלה", והבדלה ב"חונן הדעת" – אין מחזירין אותו, מפני שיכול לאומרה על הכוס! – טעה שאני.§ גופא, א"ר תנחום אמר רב אסי: טעה ולא הזכיר גבורות גשמים בתחיית המתים – מחזירין אותו, שאלה בברכת השנים – אין מחזירין אותו, מפני שיכול לאומרה ב"שומע תפלה", והבדלה ב"חונן הדעת" – אין מחזירין אותו, מפני שיכול לאומרה על הכוס. מיתיבי: *טעה ולא הזכיר גבורות גשמים בתחיית המתים – מחזירין אותו, שאלה בברכת השנים – מחזירין אותו, והבדלה ב"חונן הדעת" – אין מחזירין אותו, מפני שיכול לאומרה על הכוס! ל"ק: הא ביחיד, הא בצבור. בצבור מ"ט לא – משום דשמעה משליח צבור, אי הכי, האי "מפני שיכול לאומרה ב'שומע תפלה'" – "מפני ששומע משליח ציבור" מיבעי ליה! אלא, אידי ואידי ביחיד, ול"ק: הא – דאדכר קודם "שומע תפלה", הא

## רש"י

והשקיף. חשב לזכור אותה. לשון סוכה, כדמתרגמינן וישקף ואסתכי (בראשית יט): רשע מעיקרו. ושב מרשעתו, פעמים שחוזר ונעשה רשע: הוא ינאי. ששנינו בקידושין (פ"ג דף סו.) שהרג חכמי ישראל: ינאי רשע מעיקרו. ונעשה צדיק, וחזר לרשעתו: דאתחיל בה. התחיל לאומרה וטעה באמצעיתה: לא שנו. הא דאמר רב יהודה מעלין אותו: שבעה קולות. במזמור קול ה' על המים (תהלים כט): שאמרה חנה. בפרשת עלץ לבי (ש"א ב): כ"ד רננות. בפרשת ויעמוד שלמה (מלכים א ח). רנה, תפלה, תחנה כלהון כ"ד איכא: ביומא דרחמי. שנצרך לבקש רחמים, שדבקו שערים זה בזה ולא היו מניחין להכניס ארון לבית קדשי הקדשים, כדאמרי' במועד קטן (דף ט.): מעין כל ברכה. אומר בקוצר, ומברך על כל אחת ואחת: הביננו. ואינו מברך אלא שומע תפלה בכל הברכות שבין שלש ראשונות לשלש אחרונות. הביננו כנגד אתה חונן, ומול את לבבנו כנגד השיבנו, לסלוח לנו – כנגד סלח לנו, להיות גאולים – כנגד גאולה, וכן כולם: בנאות ארצך. לשון נוה, כמו בנאות דשא ירביצני (תהלים כג), והוא כנגד ברכת השנים. והתועים על דעתך. העוברים על דבריך: ישפטו. כנגד צדקה ומשפט. לשון אחר: והתועים במשפט על דעתך ישפטו, השיבם ללמדם לשפוט כדבריך, וכן עיקר נראה לי וכן בס"ג: לייט עלה אביי. לפי שמדלג הברכות וכוללן בברכה אחת: כל השנה מי עבדינן כרבי עקיבא. כלומר: כשאנו מתפללין י"ח שלמות מי עבדינן כר' עקיבא לומר ברכה רביעית בפני עצמה, דהשתא כשמתפללין הביננו נעביד כוותיה: שבע תקון. שלש ראשונות ושלש אחרונות והביננו: ונכללה. להבדלה: מכלל. בתוך הביננו, כדרך שהוא כוללה בחונן הדעת. ויאמר: הביננו ה' אלהינו המבדיל בין קדש לחול לדעת דרכיך: לאטרודי. לטעות: בתחלת. התפלה יכול אדם לכוין דעתו יותר מן האמצע: גבורות גשמים. הזכרה בעלמא היא, לפיכך מחזירין אותו, שאינה תפלה שיכול לאומרה בשומע תפלה: ביחיד. מחזירין אותו: בצבור. יחיד המתפלל עם הצבור: דאדכר קודם ש"ת. אין מחזירין אותו, שיכול לאומרה בשומע תפלה:
תחנונים

תורה אור: יחזקאל יח

## תוספות

**לייט** עלה אביי אמאן דמצלי הביננו. והכי קי"ל. ויש ספרים דמסיק: ה"מ במתא, אבל בדרך שרי, כדמשמע במכילתין (א) גבי רבי יוסי וכו':

**ונכללה** בהביננו. והא דאמרינן בפ"ק דנדה (דף ח:): כל השנה כולה מתפלל אדם י"ח, חוץ ממוצאי יה"כ מפני טורח צבור מפני התענית, וי"א שמתפללים י"ח שלימות מפני שצ"ל הבדלה ב'חונן הדעת'. ותימה: אמאי לא פריך ונכללה ב'הביננו'? – וי"ל: דלא דמי, דהתם כל השנה כולה מתפלל י"ח ואין לנו להקשות ונכללה מכלל, כדי לשנות המנהג של כל השנה. אבל הכא, שכל השנה מתפלל 'הביננו', פריך שפיר: למה לי לשנות המנהג בשביל 'אתה חוננתנו' ונכללה ב'הביננו':

**מפני** שיכול לאומרה בשו"ת. כדאמר (לקמן לא.): (עו"ג דף ח) שואל אדם צרכיו ב'שו"ת'. ודוקא צרכיו, כגון שיש לו חולה בתוך ביתו או שצריך שדהו מים דהוא מעין תפלה, וכן שאלה. אבל הזכרה והבדלה ושאר שבחים – אסור שאינה מעין 'שו"ת'. ונראה שכל האומר "ברוך אתה ה' שו"ת" אחר שסיים דברי תחנונים מיושב – מגונה, כדאמרי' (מגילה דף יח.): מכאן ואילך אסור לספר בשבחו של מקום, כלומר: להוסיף ברכות על אלו. ואפילו אם בא להתפלל שמנה עשרה עוד פעם אחרת – אסור שנראה כמוסיף על הברכות. והא דאמר לעיל (דף כא.): ולואי שיתפלל אדם כל היום (ב) – היינו דוקא ספק התפלל, אבל ודאי – אוקמינן לעיל שפוסק אפי' באמצע ברכה, כשמואל בפרק "מי שמתו" (שם). ומה ששליח צבור שונה בהן – היינו להוציא רבים ידי חובתן, ומה שמתפלל בלחש – היינו כדי להסדיר תפלתו, כדמוקמינן בפרק בתרא דר"ה (דף לד:):

## עין משפט נר מצוה

מז א ב מיי' פ"י מהל' תפלה הל' ג סמג עשין יט טוש"ע או"ח סי' קכ"ו סעיף א:
מח ג ד ה מיי' פ"ב שם הל' ג ד סמג שם טוש"ע או"ח סימן קי סעיף א:
מט ו מיי' פ"י שם הל' ח סמג שם טוש"ע א"ח סי' קיד סעיף ה:
נ ז מיי' שם הלכה ט סמג שם טוש"ע א"ח סי' קיז סעיף ד:
נא ח מיי' שם הל' יד סמג שם טוש"ע א"ח סימן לל"ד סעיף א:
נב ט מיי' שם הל' ט סמג שם טוש"ע א"ח סימן קי"ז סעיף ה:

## רב נסים גאון

הני כ"ד דתעניתא כנגד מי אמר ר' חלבו כנגד כ"ד רננות שאמר שלמה. הא מילתא פרשוה בתלמוד ארץ ישראל בפירקין ובפרק ב' דתענית (הלכה ב) ר' חלבו ור' שמואל כנגד כ"ד פעמים רנה תפלה תחנה שכתובין בפרשת שלמה ואית בגמרא בפ' משקין בית השלחין (מועד קטן דף ט) ובפרק כל ישראל יש להם חלק (דף קז) בשעה שבנה שלמה את בית המקדש ובקש להכנים ארון לבית קדש הקדשים דבקו שערים זה בזה אמר כ"ד רננות כו':

## הגהות הב"ח

(א) תוס' ד"ה לייט וכו' במכילתין. נ"ב לעיל בפ"ק דף ג' וע"ש בתוס' בד"ה היה לך: (ב) ד"ה מפני וכו' היינו דווקא בספק התפלל אבל בוודאי התפלל אוקמינן:

## הגהות הגר"א

[א] טרם נקרא אתה תענה. נ"ב כי אתה עונה בכל כו'. גי' רי"ף ורא"ש ועיין רמב"ם:

## מסורת הש"ס

אבות פ"ב מ"ד
[יומא ט.]
נ"ל ואמר
יא. יבמות סד:]
[ב"ק ע. סנהדרין קז:]
קדושין לג: וש"נ]
[לקמן לג. נדה ח.
[לקמן לג:]
פ"ג לעיל כו: [לקמן לג. תענית ג:

**הָא** – דְּאִדְכַּר בָּתַר "שׁוֹמֵעַ תְּפִלָּה".§ אָמַר רַבִּי תַּנְחוּם אָמַר רַב אַסִּי אָמַר ר' יְהוֹשֻׁעַ בֶּן לֵוִי: אטָעָה וְלֹא הִזְכִּיר שֶׁל ר"ח בַּעֲבוֹדָה – חוֹזֵר לָעֲבוֹדָה, נִזְכַּר בְּהוֹדָאָה – חוֹזֵר לָעֲבוֹדָה, בְּ"שִׂים שָׁלוֹם" – חוֹזֵר לָעֲבוֹדָה, וְאִם סִיֵּים – חוֹזֵר לָרֹאשׁ. אָמַר רַב פַּפָּא בְּרֵיהּ דְּרַב אַחָא בַּר אַדָּא: הָא דַּאֲמַרַן "סִיֵּים חוֹזֵר לָרֹאשׁ" – לֹא אֲמַרַן אֶלָּא שֶׁעָקַר רַגְלָיו, אֲבָל לֹא עָקַר רַגְלָיו – חוֹזֵר לָעֲבוֹדָה. א"ל: מְנָא לָךְ הָא? א"ל: מֵאַבָּא מָרִי שְׁמִיעַ לִי, וְאַבָּא מָרִי מֵרַב. אָמַר רַב נַחְמָן בַּר יִצְחָק: הָא דַּאֲמַרַן "עָקַר רַגְלָיו חוֹזֵר לָרֹאשׁ" – לֹא אֲמַרַן אֶלָּא שֶׁאֵינוֹ רָגִיל לוֹמַר תַּחֲנוּנִים אַחַר תְּפִלָּתוֹ, אֲבָל רָגִיל לוֹמַר תַּחֲנוּנִים אַחַר תְּפִלָּתוֹ – חוֹזֵר לָעֲבוֹדָה. אִיכָּא דְּאָמְרִי, אָמַר רַב נַחְמָן בַּר יִצְחָק: בהָא דַּאֲמַרַן כִּי לֹא עָקַר רַגְלָיו חוֹזֵר לָעֲבוֹדָה – לֹא אֲמַרַן אֶלָּא שֶׁרָגִיל לוֹמַר תַּחֲנוּנִים אַחַר תְּפִלָּתוֹ, אֲבָל אִם אֵינוֹ רָגִיל לוֹמַר תַּחֲנוּנִים אַחַר תְּפִלָּתוֹ – חוֹזֵר לָרֹאשׁ.§ "ר' אֱלִיעֶזֶר אוֹמֵר: הָעוֹשֶׂה תְּפִלָּתוֹ קֶבַע וכו'". מַאי "קֶבַע"? א"ר יַעֲקֹב בַּר אִידִי אָמַר רַבִּי אוֹשַׁעְיָא: גכֹּל שֶׁתְּפִלָּתוֹ דּוֹמָה עָלָיו כְּמַשּׂוֹי; וְרַבָּנַן אָמְרִי: דכֹּל מִי שֶׁאֵינוֹ אוֹמְרָהּ בִּלְשׁוֹן תַּחֲנוּנִים; רַבָּה וְרַב יוֹסֵף דְּאָמְרִי תַּרְוַיְיהוּ: כֹּל שֶׁאֵינוֹ יָכוֹל לְחַדֵּשׁ בָּהּ דָּבָר. א"ר זֵירָא: אֲנָא יָכֵילְנָא לְחַדּוּשֵׁי בָּהּ מִילְּתָא, וּמִסְתְּפִינָא דִּלְמָא מִטְרִידְנָא. אַבָּיֵי בַּר אָבִין וְר' חֲנִינָא בַּר אָבִין דְּאָמְרֵי תַּרְוַיְיהוּ: כֹּל שֶׁאֵין מִתְפַּלֵּל עִם דִּמְדּוּמֵי חַמָּה, דא"ר חִיָּיא בַּר אַבָּא א"ר יוֹחָנָן: *מִצְוָה הלְהִתְפַּלֵּל עִם דִּמְדּוּמֵי חַמָּה; וא"ר זֵירָא: מַאי קְרָאָה – °"יִירָאוּךָ עִם שָׁמֶשׁ וְלִפְנֵי יָרֵחַ דּוֹר דּוֹרִים". (תהלים עב) *לַיְיטִי עֲלָהּ בְּמַעַרְבָא אַמָּאן דִּמְצַלֵּי עִם דִּמְדּוּמֵי חַמָּה, מַאי טַעְמָא? דִּלְמָא מִיטְּרְפָא לֵיהּ שַׁעְתָּא.§ "רַבִּי יְהוֹשֻׁעַ אוֹמֵר, הַמְהַלֵּךְ בִּמְקוֹם סַכָּנָה מִתְפַּלֵּל תְּפִלָּה קְצָרָה וכו' בְּכָל פָּרָשַׁת הָעִבּוּר". מַאי 'פָּרָשַׁת הָעִבּוּר'? אָמַר רַב חִסְדָּא אָמַר מָר עוּקְבָא: אֲפִי' בְּשָׁעָה שֶׁאַתָּה מִתְמַלֵּא עֲלֵיהֶם עֶבְרָה כְּאִשָּׁה עוּבָּרָה – יִהְיוּ כָּל צָרְכֵיהֶם לְפָנֶיךָ. אִיכָּא דְּאָמְרִי, אָמַר רַב חִסְדָּא אָמַר מָר עוּקְבָא: אֲפִילּוּ בְּשָׁעָה שֶׁהֵם עוֹבְרִים עַל דִּבְרֵי תוֹרָה – יִהְיוּ כָּל צָרְכֵיהֶם לְפָנֶיךָ. ת"ר: *הַמְהַלֵּךְ בִּמְקוֹם גְּדוּדֵי חַיָּה וְלִסְטִים מִתְפַּלֵּל תְּפִלָּה קְצָרָה. וְאֵיזוֹ הִיא תְּפִלָּה קְצָרָה? ר' אֱלִיעֶזֶר אוֹמֵר: "עֲשֵׂה רְצוֹנְךָ בַּשָּׁמַיִם מִמַּעַל, וְתֵן נַחַת רוּחַ לִירֵאֶיךָ מִתַּחַת, וְהַטּוֹב בְּעֵינֶיךָ עֲשֵׂה, בא"י שׁוֹמֵעַ תְּפִלָּה". ר' יְהוֹשֻׁעַ אוֹמֵר: [א] "שְׁמַע שַׁוְעַת עַמְּךָ יִשְׂרָאֵל וַעֲשֵׂה מְהֵרָה בַּקָּשָׁתָם, בא"י שׁוֹמֵעַ תְּפִלָּה". רַבִּי אֶלְעָזָר בְּרַבִּי צָדוֹק אוֹמֵר: "שְׁמַע צַעֲקַת עַמְּךָ יִשְׂרָאֵל וַעֲשֵׂה מְהֵרָה בַּקָּשָׁתָם, בא"י שׁוֹמֵעַ תְּפִלָּה". אֲחֵרִים אוֹמְרִים: "צָרְכֵי עַמְּךָ יִשְׂרָאֵל מְרוּבִּין וְדַעְתָּם קְצָרָה, יְהִי רָצוֹן מִלְּפָנֶיךָ ה' אֱלֹהֵינוּ שֶׁתִּתֵּן לְכָל אֶחָד וְאֶחָד כְּדֵי פַרְנָסָתוֹ וּלְכָל גְּוִיָּה וּגְוִיָּה דֵּי מַחְסוֹרָהּ, [ב] בָּרוּךְ אַתָּה ה' שׁוֹמֵעַ תְּפִלָּה". אָמַר רַב הוּנָא: והֲלָכָה כַּאֲחֵרִים.§ אָמַר לֵיהּ אֵלִיָּהוּ לְרַב יְהוּדָה אֲחוּהּ דְּרַב סַלָּא חֲסִידָא: זלָא תִּרְתַּח וְלָא תֶּחֱטֵי, לָא תִּרְוֵי וְלָא תֶּחֱטֵי, וּכְשֶׁאַתָּה יוֹצֵא לַדֶּרֶךְ – הִמָּלֵךְ בְּקוֹנְךָ וָצֵא. מַאי 'הִמָּלֵךְ בְּקוֹנְךָ וָצֵא'? אָמַר רַבִּי יַעֲקֹב אָמַר רַב חִסְדָּא: זוֹ תְּפִלַּת הַדֶּרֶךְ. וְאָמַר רַבִּי יַעֲקֹב אָמַר רַב חִסְדָּא: כָּל הַיּוֹצֵא לַדֶּרֶךְ צָרִיךְ לְהִתְפַּלֵּל תְּפִלַּת הַדֶּרֶךְ. מַאי תְּפִלַּת הַדֶּרֶךְ? ח"יְהִי רָצוֹן מִלְּפָנֶיךָ ה' אֱלֹהַי שֶׁתּוֹלִיכֵנִי לְשָׁלוֹם וְתַצְעִידֵנִי לְשָׁלוֹם וְתִסְמְכֵנִי לְשָׁלוֹם, [ג] וְתַצִּילֵנִי מִכַּף כָּל אוֹיֵב וְאוֹרֵב בַּדֶּרֶךְ, וְתִשְׁלַח בְּרָכָה בְּמַעֲשֵׂי יָדַי, [ד] וְתִתְּנֵנִי לְחֵן לְחֶסֶד וּלְרַחֲמִים בְּעֵינֶיךָ וּבְעֵינֵי כָל רוֹאַי, [ה] בא"י שׁוֹמֵעַ תְּפִלָּה. אָמַר אַבָּיֵי: טלְעוֹלָם לִישַׁתֵּף

---

תַּחֲנוּנִים. כְּגוֹן אֱלֹהַי נְצוֹר לְשׁוֹנִי מֵרָע שֶׁאָנוּ אוֹמְרִים בַּעֲמִידָה אַחַר תְּפִלָּה: אֲבָל אִם אֵינוֹ רָגִיל. הָוְיָא סִיּוּם תְּפִלָּתוֹ כַּעֲקִירָה, אֲפִילּוּ לֹא עָקַר: כְּמַשּׂוֹי. וְהַיְינוּ לְשׁוֹן קֶבַע, חוֹק קָבוּעַ הוּא עָלַי לְהִתְפַּלֵּל וְצָרִיךְ אֲנִי לָצֵאת יְדֵי חוֹבָתִי(א): מִי שֶׁאֵינוֹ יָכוֹל. לְכַוֵּין לִבּוֹ לִשְׁאוֹל צְרָכָיו: לְחַדֵּשׁ תורה אור בָּהּ דָּבָר. כְּבַקָּשָׁתוֹ, וְהַיְינוּ לְשׁוֹן קֶבַע – כַּיּוֹם (ב)כֵּן אֶתְמוֹל כֵּן מָחָר: דִּילְמָא מִטְרִידְנָא. שֶׁמָּא אֶטְעֶה, וְלֹא אֵדַע לַחֲזוֹר לַמָּקוֹם שֶׁהִפְסַקְתִּי: שֶׁאֵינוֹ מִתְפַּלֵּל עִם דִּמְדּוּמֵי חַמָּה. וְהַיְינוּ לְשׁוֹן קֶבַע – תְּפִלָּתוֹ עָלָיו חוֹק קָבוּעַ לָצֵאת יְדֵי חוֹבָה, וְאֵינוֹ מַקְפִּיד לַחֲזוֹר אַחַר שְׁעַת מִצְוָה וְעֵת רָצוֹן: עִם דִּמְדּוּמֵי חַמָּה. תְּפִלַּת יוֹצֵר עִם הָנֵץ הַחַמָּה, וּתְפִלַּת הַמִּנְחָה עִם שְׁקִיעַת הַחַמָּה: יִירָאוּךָ עִם שָׁמֶשׁ. זוֹ תְּפִלַּת יוֹצֵר(ג): וְלִפְנֵי יָרֵחַ. זוֹ מִנְחָה: לַיְיטֵי בְּמַעַרְבָא. עַל מִי שֶׁמַּשְׁהֶה תְּפִלַּת הַמִּנְחָה עַד דִּמְדּוּמֵי חַמָּה, שֶׁמָּא תִּטָּרֵף לוֹ הַשָּׁעָה ע"י אוֹנֶס וְעָבַר הַזְּמַן: בְּכָל פָּרָשַׁת הָעִבּוּר וכו'. כְּמוֹ פְּרִישַׁת הָעִבּוּר: אפי' בְּשָׁעָה שֶׁאַתָּה מִתְמַלֵּא עֲלֵיהֶם עֶבְרָה כְּאִשָּׁה עוּבָּרָה. וְהָכִי מַשְׁמַע בְּכָל עִנְיְנֵי פְּרִישַׁת הָעִבּוּר כְּגוֹן עֶבְרָה *בְּעֶבְרָה: יִהְיוּ כָּל צָרְכֵיהֶם. גְּלוּיִם לְפָנֶיךָ לְרַחֵם עֲלֵיהֶם: אֲפִילּוּ בְּשָׁעָה שֶׁהֵם עוֹבְרִים. וּלְשׁוֹן פָּרָשַׁת הָעִבּוּר – שֶׁהֵן פּוֹרְשִׁין לַעֲבֵירָה: עֲשֵׂה רְצוֹנְךָ בַּשָּׁמַיִם. שֶׁאֵין שָׁם חֵטְא, וְאֵין רְצוֹנְךָ עֲלֵיהֶם אֶלָּא לְטוֹב, וַעֲבוֹר לַתַּחְתּוֹנִים עַל רְצוֹנְךָ: וְתֵן. לָהֶם לִירֵאֶיךָ: נַחַת רוּחַ. שֶׁלֹּא יִתְעַרְבֵּב רוּחָם עַל יְדֵי הַבְּרִיּוֹת, כְּגוֹן ע"י חַיּוֹת וְלִסְטִים: וְהַטּוֹב בְּעֵינֶיךָ עֲשֵׂה. אַתָּה לָהֶם. וְדוּגְמָא זוֹ מָצִינוּ בְּסֵפֶר שׁוֹפְטִים: (י) וַיֹּאמְרוּ בְנֵי יִשְׂרָאֵל חָטָאנוּ עֲשֵׂה אַתָּה לָנוּ (כטוב) [כְּכָל הַטּוֹב] בְּעֵינֶיךָ אַךְ הַצִּילֵנוּ וגו': שַׁוְעַת. לְשׁוֹן גְּנִיחָה יוֹתֵר מִתְּפִלָּה: וְדַעְתָּם קְצָרָה. וְאֵינָם יוֹדְעִים לְפָרֵשׁ צָרְכֵיהֶם: לֹא תִּרְתַּח וְלֹא תֶּחֱטֵי. לֹא תִּכְעוֹס, שֶׁמִּתּוֹךְ הַכַּעַס אַתָּה בָּא לִידֵי חֵטְא: לֹא תִּרְוֵי. לֹא תִּשְׁתַּכֵּר בַּיַּיִן: הִמָּלֵךְ. טוֹל רְשׁוּת: לִישַׁתֵּף

---

**הא** דאדכר (אחר) [בתר] שומע תפלה. אז ודאי מחזירין אותו. מיהו, אם לא עקר רגליו – אינו צריך לחזור לראש, ולא לברכת השנים, אלא חוזר ל'שומע תפלה'. וכן משמע בירושלמי פ' "אין עומדין", דקאמר: אם לא שאל בברכת השנים מחזירין אותו, ולהיכן חוזר? ר' שמעון בשם ר' יוחנן אמר: בר"ח אם עקר רגליו חוזר לראש, ואם לאו – חוזר לעבודה, ה"נ, אם עקר רגליו – חוזר לראש, ואם לאו – חוזר ל'שומע תפלה'. אלמא משמע בהדיא דאינו חוזר אלא ל'שומע תפלה' כי לא עקר רגליו. מיהו הירושלמי פליג אגמרא דידן בגבורות גשמים; דהכא קתני: "לא הזכיר גבורות גשמים מחזירין אותו", ולא קאמר לאומרו ב'שומע תפלה', ובירושל' קאמר: אם לא שאל בברכת השנים – אומרה ב'שומע תפלה'. ודכוותה אם לא הזכיר גבורות גשמים בתחיית המתים – מזכיר ב'שומע תפלה'. ומה אם שאלה שהיא מדוחק אומרה ב'שומע תפלה', הזכרה שהיא מריוח לא כ"ש. אלמא דבהדיא איתא התם דחוזר בגבורות גשמים ל'שומע תפלה'! ואפשר להיות שהגמרא שלנו לא חשש לפרשו – משום הקל וחומר, כדאיתא בירושלמי. והא דקתני: לא הזכיר גבורות גשמים מחזירין אותו – איירי שלא הזכיר כלל ב'שומע תפלה', והא ליתא, דהא במסקנא מוקי האי מימרא בנזכר קודם שומע תפלה משום פירכא דשאלה. ובירושלמי קאמר: היה עומד בטל והזכיר של גשם מחזירין אותו, פי' בימות הקיץ, ופריך: והא תניא: בטל וברוחות לא חייבו חכמים להזכיר, והכי פריך: כי היכי דאם לא הזכיר כלל מטל אינו עיכוב, ואם היה רוצה להזכיר – מזכיר, ה"נ, אם עמד בטל והזכיר של גשם – אין לחוש, דלא גרע מלא הזכיר טל כלל. ומשני: דלא דמי ההוא דמקל ומללי, לההוא דמללי ולא מקל. פי': מקלל, כלומר: אינו דומה כשעומד בטל והזכיר של גשם – שהוא סימן קללה, למי שאינו מזכיר כלל לא טל ולא גשם, שאינו מקלל. וכן הלכה למעשה: שאם עומד בשל טל והזכיר של גשם – דמחזירין אותו, ואם לא הזכיר משניהם כלל – אין מחזירין אותו. והדר קאמר בירושלמי: קאי בגשם והזכיר בשל טל – אין מחזירין אותו. ופריך מהכא, והתניא: או שלא הזכיר גבורות גשמים מחזירין אותו, ומשני: הא דאדכר, הא דלא(ד) אדכר, הא דלא אדכר לא טל ולא מטר לכך מחזירין אותו, הא דהזכיר של טל ומטר. ולא נהירא, דפשיטא אם הזכיר שניהם – דאין מחזירין אותו, ואם לא הזכיר כלל – פשיטא דמחזירין אותו! אלא ודאי יש לפרש: הא דאדכר טל, הא דלא אדכר כלל לא טל ולא מטר, לפיכך מחזירין אותו. אבל אם הזכיר טל אף בימות הגשמים – אין מחזירין אותו. לכך יש בני אדם שאומרים כל שעה טל מתוך שהם רגילים, אם כן בימות הגשמים אם שכח 'מוריד הגשם' – אין מחזירין אותו: **טעה** ולא הזכיר של ראש חדש בעבודה חוזר לעבודה. ובהלכות גדולות פי': דוקא ביחיד, אבל בצבור אינו חוזר מפני ששומעה מש"צ. מיהו, צריך לדקדק מפי החזן כל אות ואות של תפלה אע"פ שהוא בקי, דהא אמרינן בראש השנה (פ"ד דף לד:): כשם שמוציא את שאינו בקי – כך מוציא הבקי. ואע"ג דאמרינן התם: לא פטר רבן גמליאל אלא העם שבשדות משום דאניסי וטרידי אבל *טעה – לא, יש לומר: היינו שלא התפלל כלל, אבל היכא שהתפלל כבר – לא חשבינן ליה כאילו לא התפלל כלל. וה"ה לכל דבר שמחזירין אותו אי הדר שמע ליה משלוחא דצבורא מראש ועד סוף – נפיק. והרב ר"מ פסק: דוקא שכח להזכיר של ר"ח, אבל שכח ברכה שלמה – מחזירין אותו, ואינו יוצא בשמיעתו משליח צבור (וע"ע תוס' ר"ה לד: ד"ה כך): **איכא** דאמרי אמר רב נחמן וכו'. רב אלפס פסק כאיכא דאמרי, דברגיל לומר תחנונים ולא עקר רגליו – אינו חוזר לראש, ואם אינו רגיל – גם כי לא עקר רגליו – חוזר לראש, ואם עקר גם כי רגיל לומר תחנונים כמו 'אלהי נצור לשוני' חוזר לראש:

**כל** שאינו יכול לומר תחנונים. פי' ר"ח: דאם יכול לומר לשון תחנונים, אפי' עליו כמשא – הוי תפלה מעליא, דלא בעינן אלא לשון תחנונים בלבד: והיכי

---

עין משפט נר מצוה

**נד** א ב מיי' פ"י מהל' תפלה הלכה י סמג עשין יט טוש"ע או"ח סי' תכב סעיף א:

**נה** ג ד מיי' פ"ד שם הלכה טז סמג שם טוש"ע או"ח סימן לח סעיף ג:

**נו** ה מיי' פ"ג שם הל' ד סמג שם טוש"ע או"ח סי' פט סעיף א ובסי' רלג סעיף א:

**נז** ו מיי' פ"ד שם הל' יט סמג שם טוש"ע או"ח סי' קי סעיף ג:

**נח** ז מיי' פ"א מהלכות דעות הלכה ד ופ"ב הלכה ג:

**נט** ח ט מיי' פ"י מהל' ברכות [ע"ש ולא תמצא והב"י סי' קי תמה על הרמב"ם שהשמיט] סמג עשין (כז) [יט] טוש"ע או"ח סימן קי סעיף ד:

הגהות הב"ח

(א) רש"י ד"ה כמשוי וכו' ידי חובתי הס"ד ואחר כך מתחיל הדבור מי שאינו אומר בלשון תחנונים. מי שאינו: (ב) ד"ה לחדש וכו' קבע כהיום כן: (ג) ד"ה יירא‍וך וכו' תפלת יוצר. נ"ב ע' לעיל ד' ט ע"ב פירש"י דקאי אק"ש: (ד) תום' ד"ה הא לאדכר וכו' דלא אדכר פירוש הא דלא אדכר לא טל ולא מטר לכך מחזירין אותו הא דאדכר דהזכיר:

הגהות הגר"א

[א] גמ' (רי"א שמע שועת עמך ישראל ועשה מהרה בקשתם בא"י ש"ת) תא"מ ונ"ב בתוספתא ל"ג לה: [ב] שם די מחסורה. נ"ב והטוב בעיניך עשה. גירסת רי"ף ורמב"ם ורא"ש: [ג] שם ותסמכני לשלום. נ"ב ותחזירני לביתי לשלום: [ד] שם (ותשלח ברכה במעשה ידי) תא"מ: [ה] שם ובעיני כל רואי. נ"ב כי אתה שומע כו'. טור:

מסורת הש"ס

[וע' רש"א בחדושי א]

שבת דף קיח:

[קדושין לג: ושם נסמן]

תוספתא פ"ג

[בטור לא כנ"ל וכ"ה ברא"ש]

לישתף איניש נפשיה בהדי צבורא. היכי נימא? – יהי רצון מלפניך ה' אלהינו שתוליכנו לשלום וכו'. אימת מצלי? – אמר רבי יעקב אמר רב חסדא: [א]משעה שמהלך בדרך. עד כמה? –אמר רבי יעקב אמר רב חסדא: [ב]עד פרסה. והיכי מצלי לה? –רב חסדא אמר: מעומד; רב ששת אמר: [ג]אפילו מהלך. רב חסדא ורב ששת הוו קאזלי באורחא, קם רב חסדא וקא מצלי. א"ל רב ששת לשמעיה: מאי קא עביד רב חסדא? אמר ליה: קאי ומצלי. א"ל: אוקמן נמי לדידי ואצלי, *מהיות טוב אל תקרא רע.§ מאי איכא בין "הביננו" לתפלה קצרה? – [ד]הביננו – בעי לצלויי ג' קמייתא וג' בתרייתא, וכי מטי לביתיה לא בעי למהדר לצלויי; בתפלה קצרה – לא בעי לצלויי לא ג' קמייתא ולא ג' בתרייתא, וכי מטי לביתיה בעי למהדר לצלויי. והלכתא: [ה]הביננו – מעומד, תפלה קצרה – בין מעומד בין מהלך.§ "היה רוכב על החמור וכו'". ת"ר: *היה רוכב על החמור והגיע זמן תפלה, אם יש לו מי שיאחז את חמורו – ירד למטה ויתפלל, ואם לאו – ישב במקומו ויתפלל; רבי אומר: [ו]בין כך ובין כך – ישב במקומו ויתפלל, לפי שאין דעתו מיושבת עליו. אמר רבא ואיתימא רבי יהושע בן לוי: הלכה כרבי.§ ת"ר: *[ז]סומא ומי שאינו יכול לכוין את הרוחות – יכוין לבו כנגד אביו שבשמים, שנא' °"והתפללו אל ה'"; היה [ח]עומד בח"ל – יכוין את לבו כנגד ארץ ישראל שנא': °"והתפללו אליך דרך ארצם"; היה עומד בארץ ישראל – יכוין את לבו כנגד ירושלים, שנאמר: °"והתפללו אל ה' דרך העיר אשר בחרת"; היה עומד בירושלים – יכוין את לבו כנגד בית המקדש, שנאמר: °"והתפללו אל הבית הזה"; היה עומד בבית המקדש – יכוין את לבו כנגד בית קדשי הקדשים, שנאמר: °"והתפללו אל המקום הזה"; היה עומד בבית קדשי הקדשים – יכוין את לבו כנגד בית הכפורת; היה עומד אחורי בית הכפורת – יראה עצמו כאילו לפני הכפורת; נמצא: עומד במזרח – מחזיר פניו למערב, במערב – מחזיר פניו למזרח, בדרום – מחזיר פניו לצפון, בצפון – מחזיר פניו לדרום; נמצאו כל ישראל מכוונין את לבם למקום אחד. א"ר אבין ואיתימא ר' אבינא: מאי קראה – °"כמגדל דויד צוארך בנוי לתלפיות", תל שכל פיות פונים בו.§ אבוה דשמואל ולוי [ט]כי הוו בעו למיפק לאורחא הוו מקדמי ומצלי, וכי הוה מטי זמן ק"ש קרו. כמאן; כי האי תנא – דתניא: *השכים לצאת לדרך – מביאין לו שופר ותוקע, לולב ומנענע, מגילה וקורא בה, וכשיגיע זמן ק"ש קורא. השכים לישב בקרון או בספינה – מתפלל, וכשיגיע זמן ק"ש קורא; רשב"א אומר: בין כך ובין כך קורא ק"ש ומתפלל, כדי שיסמוך גאולה לתפלה. במאי קמיפלגי? – [י]מר סבר: תפלה מעומד עדיף; ומר סבר: מסמך גאולה לתפלה עדיף. מרימר ומר זוטרא הוו מכנפי בי עשרה בשבתא דרגלא ומצלו, והדר נפקי לפרקא. רב אשי מצלי בהדי צבורא ביחיד מיושב, כי הוה אתי לביתיה הדר ומצלי מעומד. אמרי ליה רבנן: ולעביד מר כמרימר ומר זוטרא! –אמר להו: טריחא לי מלתא. –ולעביד מר כאבוה דשמואל ולוי! –אמר להו: לא חזינא להו לרבנן קשישי מינן דעבדי הכי.§

**מתני'** ר' אלעזר בן עזריה אומר: אין תפלת המוספין אלא בחבר עיר, וחכ"א: [כ]בחבר עיר ושלא בחבר עיר; ר' יהודה אומר משמו: כל מקום שיש שם חבר עיר – יחיד פטור מתפלת המוספין. **גמ'** ר' יהודה היינו ת"ק! איכא בינייהו: יחיד שלא בחבר עיר; ת"ק סבר: פטור, ור' יהודה סבר: חייב. א"ר הונא בר חיננא אמר ר' חייא בר רב: הלכה כר' יהודה שאמר משום ראב"ע. א"ל רב חייא בר אבין: שפיר קאמרת, דאמר שמואל: מימי לא מצלינא צלותא דמוספין ביחיד בנהרדעא

תורה אור: מלכים א ח | שם | שם | דה"ב ו | מלכים א ח | שיר ד

**רש"י**

לישתף נפשיה. אל יתפלל תפלה קצרה בלשון יחיד אלא בלשון רבים, שמתוך כך תפלתו נשמעת: עד כמה. זמנה להתפלל: עד פרסה. אבל לא לאחר שהלך פרסה. ובה"ג מפרש: עד כמה יבקש לילך שיהא צריך להתפלל – עד פרסה, אפי' אין לו לילך אלא עד פרסה, אבל דרך פחות מפרסה – אין צריך להתפלל תפלה זו: רב ששת. מאור עינים הוה: מהיות טוב אל תקרא רע. הואיל ואני יכול להתפלל מעומד, שהרי חבורתי עומדת, לא אקרא רע להתפלל מהלך, ואע"פ שמותר: וכי מטי לביתיה בעי מהדר לצלויי. שהרי לא התפלל כלום מתפלת י"ח: שאין דעתו מיושבת עליו. שקשה עליו עכוב הדרך: לכוין את הרוחות. לצד ארץ ישראל; כדבעינן למימר תל שהכל פונים בו: אחורי בית הכפורת. במערב העזרה היו י"א אמה חצר מכותל בית קדשי הקדשים לכותל מערבי של עזרה, והעומד שם מחזיר פניו לבית הכפורת למזרח: הוו מקדמי. קודם היום: בקרון ובספינה. היכא בעתותא דמיא: קורא ק"ש. ימתין עד שיגיע זמן ק"ש ויקראנה, ואח"כ יתפלל: תפלה מעומד עדיף. שיכול לכוין את לבו. לפיכך היו מקדימין להתפלל מעומד בביתם, שלא יטרכו להתפלל בדרך במהלך: בשבתא דרגלא. שלפני פסח ועצרת וסוכות. ומרימר בעירו ומר זוטרא בעירו, היו הדרשנים. ושחרית היו העם הולכים לבית המדרש, וכשמגיע זמן ק"ש – קורין, והדרשן דורש והעם נשמטים ומתפללים איש איש לבדו. ולכך, הם היו מאספין להם י' שחרית קודם שילכו לבית המדרש וקורין ק"ש ומתפללים בסמיכת גאולה לתפלה, והדר נפקי לפרקא ודרשי: ומצלי בהדי צבורא. ל"ג: רב אשי. היה ראש ישיבה במתא מחסיא ודורש. והוא לא היה מתפלל קודם בית המדרש, אלא כשמגיע זמן ק"ש לוחש הרבה יחד למתורגמן העומד לפניו, ובעוד שהמתורגמן משמיע לרבים הוא קורא את שמע, וסומך גאולה לתפלה ומתפלל מיושב. שלא היה רוצה לצאת, שלא להטריח את הצבור לקום מפניו: בהדי צבורא. בשעה שהצבור נשמטין ומתפללין. אי נמי: בהדי צבורא – כמו שהוא יושב בתוך הצבור, כלומר שאינו יוצא. וכי הוה אתי לביתי' חוזר ומתפלל מעומד לכוין את לבו: טריחא לי מילתא. לאחר בית המדרש עד שאתפלל: ולעביד מר כאבוה דשמואל ולוי. שמתפללין קודם היום בביתם מעומד ולא תטרך לב' תפלות. ומשום מסמך גאולה לתפלה, כיון דמצלו קודם ק"ש – לא קפדי: לא חזינן להו לרבנן קשישי מינן דעבדי הכי. שיקדימו תפלה לקריאת שמע. הלכך: כיון דממתין מתפלה עד זמן ק"ש, מצוה לסמוך תפלה אחר גאולה, לפיכך מתפלל מיושב במקומו. ולפי שאין דעתו מיושבת עליו כ"כ – צריך לחזור ולהתפלל בביתו: מתני' אין תפלת המוספין אלא בחבר עיר. לא תקנוה אלא בצבור. חבר עיר – חבורת העיר, אבל לא ליחיד: משמו. של ראב"ע: כל מקום כו'. ובגמ' פריך: היינו ת"ק אליבא דראב"ע: גמ' יחיד שלא בחבר עיר. יחיד הדר בעיר שאין שם עשרה, לת"ק אליבא דרבי אלעזר דאמר לא תקנוה אלא בעשרה – יחיד זה פטור, ולרבי יהודה אין יחיד פטור אלא במקום עשרה, ששליח צבור פוטרו:
בנהרדעא

[ב"ק פא:] | תוספתא פ"ג | תוספתא פ"ג | תוספתא פ"ג

**תוספות**

והיכי מצלי לה. אתפלת הדרך קאי. ורב ששת אמר אפי' מהלך. וקי"ל כרב ששת. ומיהו, בתוספ' פסק ה"ר יוסף כרב חסדא, וכן רב אלפס פי', דרב חסדא עדיפא ליה טפי:

מאי איכא בין הביננו לתפלה קצרה. תימה: לימא דאיכא בינייהו, דתפלה קצרה אינו מתפלל אלא במקום סכנה. ו"הביננו" מתפלל אפילו שלא במקום סכנה! וי"ל דהכי קא בעי: מאי בינייהו, כל א' במקומו, תפלה קצרה במקום סכנה, ו"הביננו" שלא במקום סכנה:

הלכה כרבי. שלא ירד למטה. ואפי' שלא במקום סכנה, ואפילו במהלך מתפלל, ואינו צריך להחזיר פניו כנגד ירושלים:

היה עומד בח"ל יכוין כנגד ארץ ישראל. ול"ג לבו, דאפניו קאי; כדקתני סיפא: היה עומד במזרח מחזיר פניו למערב:

לתלפיות תל שכל פיות פונים בו. וכהך שמעתתא קי"ל. וכן מסקינן ב"לא יחפור" (ב"ב כה:) דקאמר: אתון דקיימיתון לצפונא דא"י – אדרימו. ולא כהני אמוראי דלעיל (שם) דפליגי אי השכינה במזרח או במערב. עכשיו אנו במערבה של א"י. על כן אנו פונין למזרח:

אבוה דשמואל ולוי הוו מקדמי ומצלו. פירש רש"י: קודם עמוד השחר. ולא נראה, דאם כן לא היו יוצאין בו כלל,(א) דעדיין אינו יום! לכך נראה כפי' ר"ח: דמשעלה עמוד השחר קאמר, והוו מקדמי קודם הנץ החמה קאמר, ועדיין אינו עיקר זמן תפלה:

מסמך גאולה לתפלה עדיף. מלהתפלל מעומד, והכי פסקי בה"ג הלכה כר"ש בן אלעזר. ומשמע די"ח ברכות מותר להתפלל בדרך במהלך, ואין צריך לעמוד. וא"ת: ומ"ש מהביננו, דמסקינן לעיל דמעומד דוקא? וי"ל: דשאני הביננו שהיא קצרה, ואין כאן בטול דרך כ"כ כמו בי"ח ברכות. ועוד פירש הר"ס: דהכא כי הדר לביתיה מצלי מעומד, כדאמרינן בסמוך: רב אשי מצלי בהדי צבורא ביחיד מיושב כדי לקרות ק"ש בשעתא; וכי הדר לביתי' מצלי מעומד. ור"ת פסק כאבוה דשמואל ולוי; ומיהו, מדקאמר רב אשי "לא חזינן לרבנן קשישי דקא עבדי הכי" משמע דאין הלכה כמותם:

אין

**עין משפט נר מצוה**

ם א ב טוש"ע א"ח סי' קי סעיף ז:
סא ג שם סעיף ד:
סב ד ה מיי' פ"ב מהל' תפלה ה"ב [וספ"ד] טוש"ע שם סעיף א ג:
סג ו מיי' פ"ה שם הלכה ב סמג עשין יט טור שו"ע או"ח סי' צד סעיף ד:
סד ז מיי' שם הלכה ג טוש"ע שם סעיף ג:
סה ח מיי' שם הלכה ג טוש"ע שם סעיף א:
סו ט י טוש"ע או"ח סי' פט סעיף ח:
סז כ טוש"ע או"ח סי' רפו סעיף ב:

**רב נסים גאון**

אמר ליה אוקמן לדידי נמי ואצלי מהיות טוב אל תקרא רע. התם בבבא קמא בפרק מרובה (ד' פא) אמרינן מהלכין בשבילי הרשות שלמה אמרה כדתניא הרי שכלו פירותיו מן השדה ואינו מניח בני אדם ליכנס בתוך שדהו מה הבריות אומרות עליו מה הנאה יש לו לפלוני ומה הבריות מזיקות אותו עליו הכתוב אומר מהיות טוב אל תקרא רע ומתמהינן מהיות טוב אל תקרא רע קרא הוא ומתרצי' אין כתיב כי האי גוונא (משלי ג) אל תמנע טוב מבעליו:

**הגהות הב"ח**

(א) תוס' ד"ה אבוה וכו' לא היו יוצאין כלל בתפלה דיום כיון דעדיין אינו יום:

**גליון הש"ס**

גמ' היה עומד אחורי בית הכפורת. עי' ברכינו יונה פ"ק דף ו' ע"א וכדף הספר דף ה' ע"ב: רש"י ד"ה בשבתא דרגלא וכו' ועצרת. עי' לעיל י"ז ע"ב ברש"י ד"ה שבתא ותוס' שם ד"ה תרי זימני:

בנהרדעא, לבר מההוא יומא דאתא פולמוסא דמלכא למתא ואטרידו רבנן ולא צלו, וצלי לי ביחיד, והואי יחיד שלא בחבר עיר. יתיב רבי חנינא קרא קמיה דר' ינאי, ויתיב וקאמר: הלכה כר' יהודה שאמר משום ר' אלעזר בן עזריה. א"ל: *פוק קרא קראיך לברא! דאין הלכה כרבי יהודה שאמר משום ראב"ע. א"ר יוחנן: אני ראיתי את רבי ינאי דצלי והדר צלי. א"ל רבי ירמיה לר' זירא: אודילמא מעיקרא לא כוון דעתיה, ולבסוף כוון דעתיה? א"ל: *חזי מאן גברא רבא דקמסהיד עליה! *ר' אמי ור' אסי באע"ג דהוו להו תליסר בי כנישתא בטבריא, לא הוו מצלו אלא ביני עמודי היכא דהוו גרסי. איתמר, רב יצחק בר אבדימי משום רבינו אמר: הלכה כר' יהודה שאמר משום ראב"ע. רבי חייא בר אבא צלי והדר צלי. א"ל רבי זירא: מאי טעמא עביד מר הכי? אילימא משום דלא כוון מר דעתיה – והאמר ר"א: געולם ימוד אדם את עצמו, אם *יכול לכוין את לבו – יתפלל, ואם לאו – אל יתפלל! –אלא דלא אדכר מר דריש ירחא, והתניא: טעה ולא הזכיר של ר"ח [א](א) בערבית – אין מחזירין אותו מפני שיכול לאומרה בשחרית, דבשחרית – אין מחזירין אותו מפני שיכול לאומרה במוספין, *במוספין – אין מחזירין אותו מפני שיכול לאומרה במנחה! –א"ל: לאו איתמר עלה, א"ר יוחנן, – הבצבור שנו.§ כמה ישהה בין תפלה לתפלה? רב הונא ור"ח, חד אמר: וכדי שתתחונן דעתו עליו; וחד אמר: כדי שתתחולל דעתו עליו. מאן דאמר כדי שתתחונן דעתו עליו – דכתיב: °"ואתחנן אל ה'"; ומ"ד כדי שתתחולל דעתו עליו – דכתיב °"ויחל משה". אמר רב ענן אמר רב: זטעה ולא הזכיר של ר"ח ערבית – אין מחזירין אותו, לפי שאין בית דין מקדשין את החדש אלא ביום. אמר אמימר: מסתברא מילתא דרב בחדש מלא, אבל בחדש חסר – מחזירין אותו. א"ל רב אשי לאמימר: מכדי רב טעמא קאמר, חמה לי חסר ומה לי מלא! אלא, לא שנא.§

## הדרן עלך תפלת השחר

**אין** טעומדין להתפלל אלא מתוך כובד ראש. חסידים הראשונים היו שוהין שעה אחת ומתפללין, כדי שיכוונו לבם לאביהם שבשמים. °אפי' המלך שואל בשלומו לא ישיבנו, ואפי' נחש כרוך על עקבו לא יפסיק.§ **גמ'** מנא ה"מ? א"ר אלעזר, דאמר קרא: °"והיא מרת נפש". –ממאי? דילמא חנה שאני, דהות מרירא לבא טובא! אלא א"ר יוסי בר' חנינא מהכא: °"ואני ברב חסדך אבוא ביתך אשתחוה אל היכל קדשך ביראתך". –ממאי, דילמא דוד שאני, דהוה מצער נפשיה ברחמי טובא! –אלא אמר ר' יהושע בן לוי, מהכא: °"השתחוו לה' בהדרת קדש", אל תקרי בהדרת אלא בחרדת. – ממאי? דילמא לעולם אימא לך, הדרת ממש, כי הא דרב יהודה הוה מציין נפשיה והדר מצלי! – אלא א"ר נחמן בר יצחק מהכא: °"עבדו את ה' ביראה וגילו ברעדה".§ *מאי "וגילו ברעדה"? א"ר אדא בר מתנא אמר *רבה: במקום גילה שם תהא רעדה. אביי הוה יתיב קמיה דרבה, חזייה דהוה קא בדח טובא, אמר: "וגילו ברעדה" כתיב! א"ל: אנא תפילין מנחנא. ר' ירמיה הוה יתיב קמיה דר' זירא, חזייה דהוה קא בדח טובא אמר ליה, °"בכל עצב יהיה מותר" כתיב! – א"ל: אנא תפילין מנחנא. מר בריה דרבינא עבד הילולא לבריה, חזנהו לרבנן דהוו קבדחי טובא, אייתי

---

**רש"י**

בנהרדעא. לפי שיש שם לבור, והשליח פוטרני: פולמוסא. חיל: דצלי והדר צלי. ולמה ליה ב' תפלות? אלא: אחת של שחרית ואחת של מוספין, ש"מ לית ליה דראב"ע: ודילמא מעיקרא לא כוון דעתיה. ותרווייהו דשחרית: מאן גברא רבא דקמסהיד עליה. רבי יוחנן שהעיד על הדבר, יפה דקדק שבשביל תפלת המוספין היתה: משום רבינו. רב: בצבור שנו. דאין מחזירין, משום דשמע ליה מש"ץ, ואיכא מקלת הזכרה, אבל ביחיד צריך לחזור. ובה"ג מפרש לה בש"צ משום טירחא דצבורא, אבל יחיד הדר: טעה ולא הזכיר במוספין. שהתפלל אתה חונן: כמה ישהה בין תפלה לתפלה. מי שיש עליו לחזור ולהתפלל, או משום דטעה או משום מוספין, כמה ישהה בין זו לזו: שתתחונן. שתהא דעתו מיושבת לערוך דבריו בלשון תחנה: שתתחולל. לשון חילוי; והיא היא, אלא בלישנא בעלמא פליגי: בחדש מלא. כשהחדש שעבר מלא עושין ר"ח ב' ימים, הלכך יכול לאומרה למחר דערבית של מחר ר"ח גמור יותר מן הראשון: מכדי טעמא קאמר. שאין מקדשין את החדש בלילה:

הדרן עלך תפלת השחר

**כובד** ראש. הכנעה: שוהין שעה אחת. במקום שבאו להתפלל: גמ' אשתחוה אל היכל קדשך ביראתך. מתוך יראה: מציין נפשיה. מקשט עצמו בבגדיו: עבדו את ה' ביראה. תפלה, שהיא לנו במקום עבודה, עשו אותה ביראה: *בכל עצב יהיה מותר. כשאדם מרעה את עצמו עצב – יהיה לו שכר: דהוה קא בדח טובא. יותר מדאי, ונראה כפורק עול: תפילין מנחנא. והם עדות שממשלת קוני ומשרתו עלי: כסא

---

**תוספות**

*ה"ג: **אין** הלכה כרבי יהודה שאמר משום ראב"ע. אלא הלכה כרבנן, וכן פסק ר"ח. דלהכי מייתי(ב) רבי אמי ור' אסי שהיו מתפללים ביחיד כרבנן ביני עמודי דגרסי, לאשמעינן דהלכה כרבנן: **והתניא** טעה ולא הזכיר של ר"ח בערבית אין מחזירין אותו. ל"ג ליה. דהא אמרינן בסמוך טעה ולא הזכיר של ר"ח – אין מחזירין אותו, לפי שאין מקדשין כו'. אי נמי: אי איתא – אגב אחרינא נקט ליה: **כמה** ישהה בין תפלה לתפלה. כגון: אדם שטעה ורוצה להתפלל שנית, וכן בין תפלת שחרית לתפלת המוספין: **כדי** שתתחולל דעתו עליו. ומפרש בירושלמי דהיינו כשילך ארבע אמות: **לפי** שאין מקדשין את החדש כו'. פי' לעיל בריש פרקין (דף כו.): מה שמקשין ותיפוק ליה משום רשות! משום דהיינו דוקא לעשות מצוה אחרת עוברת. וי"מ: דוקא בלילה ראשונה אין מחזירין אותו – לפי שאין מקדשין החדש בלילה, אבל בלילה שניה מחזירין אותו – שכבר מקודש מיום שלפניו, ולא נראה לחלק: **מסתברא** מילתא דרב בחדש מלא. כלומר: שהיה אותו שלפניו מלא, דאז יכול לאומרה בערבית של מחר שהוא עיקר. והיה אומר ה"ר יצחק: לכל דבר שאמרו חכמים "אין מחזירין אותו" – כגון יעלה ויבא בערבית ועל הנסים – לא מיבעיא אם עקר רגליו(ג) ופתח בברכה שלאחריה – דאין מחזירין אותו, אלא אפילו לא עקר אלא שסיים אותה ברכה שתקנו בה לאומרה – אין מחזירין אותו. ולא נהירא לרבינו אלחנן, דהא חזינן בברכת המזון דאותן שאמרו חכמים מחזירין, וגם אותן שאין מחזירין – שוין, היכא דלא עקר רגליו, כדאמר לקמן (דף מט.) אם שכח של שבת וסיים הברכה כולה ועדיין לא התחיל בברכת 'הטוב והמטיב' – אומר ברוך אשר נתן שבתות למנוחה כו'. וקאמר נמי התם: אם טעה ולא הזכיר של ר"ח קודם שעקר רגליו, דהיינו קודם שיתחיל ברכת 'הטוב והמטיב' דאותה קורא עקר רגליו, אומר: ברוך אשר נתן ראשי חדשים וכו'. אלמא: היכא דלא עקר – אלו ואלו שוין, ואם עקר רגליו שהתחיל בברכת 'הטוב והמטיב' של שבת – חוזר לראש, ושל ר"ח – מעוות לא יוכל לתקון, והכי נמי: יחזור(ד) באותה ברכה, אם לא התחיל בברכה שלאחריה. ומיהו, אין ראיה מהתם, דשאני התם בברכת המזון שכבר בירך ג' ברכות, וברכת 'הטוב והמטיב' לאו דאורייתא היא, על כן אין מחזירין אותו לגמרי כי אין דומה שם הפסק כל כך. ואין להביא ממנו ראיה לי"ח ברכות, דאם יחזירוהו בדבר שאין לו לחזור – הוי כמו הפסקה. ועוד, דאין להביא ראיה לכאן; דאם היית אומר היכא שלא עקר רגליו בי"ח ברכות שהיה לו לחזור – א"כ היה צריך לחזור לרצה, ואין זה הגון. ומיהו, אומר ר"י דראה את ר"ת דהיכא דלא עקר רגליו חזר ל'רצה', אפי' בדברים שאין מחזירין, כגון 'על הנסים', וכן עמא דבר:

הדרן עלך תפלת השחר

**אל** תקרי בהדרת אלא בחרדת. תימה: אמאי לא מוכח בהדיא מדכתיב בתריה "חילו מלפניו כל הארץ"? וי"ל: היינו קרא דכתיב במזמור "הבו לה' בני אלים", ומההוא קרא בעי להוכיח במסכת מגילה (דף יז:) שאומרים אבות וגבורות וקדושת השם, וי"ח ברכות תקנו כנגד האזכרות, ומשום הכי דייק מאותו קרא שכתוב באותה פרשה אבל אותו ד"חילו" וגו' אינו כתוב באותה פרשה: אייתי

---

**עין משפט נר מצוה**

סח א מיי' פ"ד מהל' תפלה הלכה טו ופ"י הלכה א [טוש"ע או"ח סימן קא סעיף א]:
סט ב מיי' פ"ח מהלכות תפלה הלכה ג סמג עשין יט טוש"ע א"ח סי' צ סעיף יח:
ע ג מיי' פ"ד שם הל' טו סמג שם טוש"ע או"ח סי' קא סעיף א):
עא ד ה מיי' פ"י שם הלכה יב סמג שם טוש"ע או"ח סימן קכו סעיף ג:
עב ו מיי' שם הל' טו סמג שם טור שו"ע או"ח סי' קה:
עג ז ח מיי' שם הלכה יא סמג שם טוש"ע או"ח סי' תכב סעיף א:
א ט מיי' פ"ד שם הל' טז סמג שם טוש"ע או"ח סי' צג סעי' ב:
ב י מיי' פ"ה שם הל' ה סמג שם טוש"ע א"ח סימן צח סעיף ו:

[הרי"ף ורא"ש לא גרסי זה ועי' בטור סימן קכ"ו ותכ"ב]

**הגהות הב"ח**

(א) גמ' ולא הזכיר של ר"ח (בערבית וכו'. בשחרית) תא"מ. ונ"ב ס"א אין זה: (ב) תוס' ד"ה אין הלכה כו' דלהכי מייתי הכא רבי אמי וכו' ביחיד ביני עמודי היכא דהוו גרסי כצ"ל ותיבת כרבנן נמחק: (ג) ד"ה מסתברא וכו' עקר רגליו ופתח נ"ב פי' או פתח: (ד) בא"ד וה"נ יחזור לאותה ברכה:

**הגהות הגר"א**

[א] גמ' של ר"ח בערבית. נ"ב רי"ף וש"פ ל"ג אלא בשחרית אין כו' לבד:

**גליון הש"ס**

מתני' אפי' המלך. עי' יומא י"ט ע"ב תוס' ד"ה כס:

---

**מסורת הש"ס**

[יבמות מ. כתובות] [חולין ז.] לעיל דף ח. [עי' תוס' לקמן לד יכוין] [דבורי רש"י נתספס]

תורה אור: דברים ג; שמות לב; שמואל א א; תהלים ה; שם כט; יומא ז:; [רב כ"ל]; שם ב; משלי יד

אַיְיתִי כָּסָא דְמוֹקְרָא, בַּת אַרְבַּע מְאָה זוּזֵי, וּתְבַר קַמַּיְיהוּ, וְאַעֲצִיבוּ. רַב אַשִׁי עֲבַד הִילּוּלָא לִבְרֵיהּ, חֲזָנְהוּ לְרַבָּנַן דַּהֲווּ קָא בָּדְחִי טוּבָא, אַיְיתִי כָּסָא *דְזוּגִיתָא חִיוָּרְתָּא וּתְבַר קַמַּיְיהוּ, וְאַעֲצִיבוּ. אָמְרוּ לֵיהּ רַבָּנַן לְרַב הַמְנוּנָא זוּטִי בְּהִלּוּלָא דְּמָר בְּרֵיהּ דְּרָבִינָא: לִישְׁרֵי לַן מָר! –אָמַר לְהוּ: וַוי לָן דְּמִיתְנַן, וַוי לָן דְּמִיתְנַן! אָמְרֵי לֵיהּ: אֲנַן מָה נַעֲנֵי בַּתְרָךְ? –א"ל: *הֵי תּוֹרָה וְהֵי מִצְוָה דְּמַגְנוּ עֲלַן? א"ר יוֹחָנָן מִשּׁוּם רשב"י: א אָסוּר לְאָדָם שֶׁיְּמַלֵּא שְׂחוֹק פִּיו בָּעוֹלָם הַזֶּה, שֶׁנֶּאֱמַר: °"אָז יִמָּלֵא שְׂחוֹק פִּינוּ וּלְשׁוֹנֵנוּ רִנָּה", אֵימָתַי – בִּזְמַן שֶׁ"יֹּאמְרוּ בַגּוֹיִם הִגְדִּיל ה' לַעֲשׂוֹת עִם אֵלֶּה". אָמְרוּ עָלָיו עַל ר"ל, שֶׁמִּיָּמָיו לֹא מִלֵּא שְׂחוֹק פִּיו בעוה"ז מִכִּי שְׁמָעָהּ מר' יוֹחָנָן רַבֵּיהּ.§ ת"ר: ב אֵין עוֹמְדִין לְהִתְפַּלֵּל לֹא מִתּוֹךְ דִּין, וְלֹא מִתּוֹךְ דְּבַר הֲלָכָה, אֶלָּא מִתּוֹךְ הֲלָכָה פְּסוּקָה. וְהֵיכִי דָּמֵי הֲלָכָה פְּסוּקָה? אָמַר אַבָּיֵי: כִּי הָא דר' זֵירָא, *דְּאָמַר ר' זֵירָא: ג בְּנוֹת יִשְׂרָאֵל הֶחְמִירוּ עַל עַצְמָן, *שֶׁאֲפִילּוּ רוֹאוֹת טִיפַּת דָּם כְּחַרְדָּל – יוֹשֶׁבֶת עָלֶיהָ שִׁבְעָה נְקִיִּים. רָבָא אָמַר: כִּי הָא דְּרַב הוֹשַׁעְיָא, דְּאָמַר רַב הוֹשַׁעְיָא: *מַעֲרִים ד אָדָם עַל תְּבוּאָתוֹ וּמַכְנִיסָהּ בְּמוֹץ שֶׁלָּהּ, כְּדֵי שֶׁתְּהֵא בְּהֶמְתּוֹ אוֹכֶלֶת וּפְטוּרָה מִן הַמַּעֲשֵׂר. ואב"א: כִּי הָא דְּרַב הוּנָא, *דא"ר הוּנָא א"ר זְעִירָא: ה הַמַּקִּיז דָּם בְּבְהֵמַת קָדָשִׁים – אָסוּר בַּהֲנָאָה, וּמוֹעֲלִין בּוֹ. רַבָּנַן עָבְדִי כְּמַתְנִיתִין, רַב אַשִׁי עָבֵיד כִּבְרַיְיתָא.§ ת"ר: *ו אֵין עוֹמְדִין לְהִתְפַּלֵּל לֹא מִתּוֹךְ עַצְבוּת, וְלֹא מִתּוֹךְ עַצְלוּת, וְלֹא מִתּוֹךְ שְׂחוֹק, וְלֹא מִתּוֹךְ שִׂיחָה, וְלֹא מִתּוֹךְ קַלּוּת רֹאשׁ, וְלֹא מִתּוֹךְ דְּבָרִים בְּטֵלִים – אֶלָּא *מִתּוֹךְ שִׂמְחָה שֶׁל מִצְוָה. וְכֵן לֹא יִפָּטֵר אָדָם מֵחֲבֵרוֹ לֹא מִתּוֹךְ שִׂיחָה, וְלֹא מִתּוֹךְ שְׂחוֹק, וְלֹא מִתּוֹךְ קַלּוּת רֹאשׁ, וְלֹא מִתּוֹךְ דְּבָרִים בְּטֵלִים – אֶלָּא מִתּוֹךְ [א] דְּבַר הֲלָכָה, שֶׁכֵּן מָצִינוּ בַּנְּבִיאִים הָרִאשׁוֹנִים שֶׁסִּיְּימוּ דִּבְרֵיהֶם בְּדִבְרֵי שֶׁבַח וְתַנְחוּמִים. [ב] וְכֵן תָּנָא *מָרִי בַּר בְּרֵיהּ דְּרַב הוּנָא בְּרֵיהּ דר' יִרְמְיָה בַּר אַבָּא: אַל יִפָּטֵר אָדָם מֵחֲבֵירוֹ אֶלָּא מִתּוֹךְ דְּבַר הֲלָכָה, שֶׁמִּתּוֹךְ כָּךְ זוֹכְרֵהוּ. כִּי הָא *דְּרַב כָּהֲנָא אַלְוְיֵיהּ לְרַב שִׁימִי בַּר אַשִׁי מִפּוּם נַהֲרָא עַד בֵּי צִנְיָתָא דְּבָבֶל; כִּי מְטָא לְהָתָם, א"ל: מָר, וַדַּאי דְּאָמְרִי אֱינָשֵׁי: הָנֵי צִנְיָתָא דְּבָבֶל אִיתְנְהוּ מֵאָדָם הָרִאשׁוֹן וְעַד הַשְׁתָּא? א"ל: אַדְכַּרְתַּן מִילְּתָא דְּרַבִּי יוֹסֵי בְּרַבִּי חֲנִינָא, דְּאָמַר ר' יוֹסֵי בְּרַבִּי חֲנִינָא: מַאי דִּכְתִיב °"בְּאֶרֶץ אֲשֶׁר לֹא עָבַר בָּהּ אִישׁ וְלֹא יָשַׁב אָדָם שָׁם", וְכִי מֵאַחַר דְּלֹא עָבַר הֵיאַךְ יָשַׁב? אֶלָּא לוֹמַר לְךָ: כָּל אֶרֶץ שֶׁגָּזַר עָלֶיהָ אָדָם הָרִאשׁוֹן לְיִשּׁוּב – נִתְיַשְּׁבָה, וְכָל אֶרֶץ שֶׁלֹּא גָּזַר עָלֶיהָ אָדָם הָרִאשׁוֹן לְיִשּׁוּב – לֹא נִתְיַשְּׁבָה. רַב מָרְדְּכַי אַלְוְיֵיהּ *לְרַבִּי שִׁימִי בַּר אַשִׁי מֵהַגְרוֹנְיָא וְעַד בֵּי כֵּיפֵי, וְאָמְרִי לָהּ: עַד בֵּי דּוּרָא.§ ת"ר: *הַמִּתְפַּלֵּל ז צָרִיךְ שֶׁיְּכַוֵּין אֶת לִבּוֹ לַשָּׁמַיִם. אַבָּא שָׁאוּל אוֹמֵר, סִימָן לַדָּבָר: °"תָּכִין לִבָּם תַּקְשִׁיב אָזְנֶךָ". תַּנְיָא, *א"ר יְהוּדָה: כָּךְ הָיָה מִנְהָגוֹ שֶׁל ר"ע, ח כְּשֶׁהָיָה מִתְפַּלֵּל עִם הַצִּיבּוּר – הָיָה מְקַצֵּר וְעוֹלֶה, מִפְּנֵי טוֹרַח צִבּוּר, ט וּכְשֶׁהָיָה מִתְפַּלֵּל בֵּינוֹ לְבֵין עַצְמוֹ – אָדָם מַנִּיחוֹ בְּזָוִית זוֹ וּמוֹצְאוֹ בְּזָוִית אַחֶרֶת, וְכָל כָּךְ לָמָּה – מִפְּנֵי כְּרִיעוֹת וְהִשְׁתַּחֲוָיוֹת.§ א"ר חִיָּיא בַּר אַבָּא: * י לְעוֹלָם יִתְפַּלֵּל אָדָם בְּבַיִת שֶׁיֵּשׁ בּוֹ חַלּוֹנוֹת, שֶׁנֶּאֱמַר: °"וְכַוִּין פְּתִיחָן לֵיהּ וגו'". *יָכוֹל יִתְפַּלֵּל אָדָם כָּל הַיּוֹם כֻּלּוֹ – כְּבָר מְפוֹרָשׁ עַל יְדֵי דָּנִיֵּאל: °"וְזִמְנִין תְּלָתָא וגו'". יָכוֹל מִשֶּׁבָּא לַגּוֹלָה הוּחֲלָּה? – כְּבָר נֶאֱמַר: °"דִּי הוּא עָבֵד מִן קַדְמַת דְּנָא". יָכוֹל יִתְפַּלֵּל אָדָם לְכָל רוּחַ שֶׁיִּרְצֶה? – ת"ל °"(לְקָבֵל) [נֶגֶד] יְרוּשְׁלֶם". יָכוֹל יְהֵא כּוֹלְלָן בְּבַת אַחַת – כְּבָר מְפוֹרָשׁ ע"י דָּוִד, דִּכְתִיב: °"עֶרֶב וָבֹקֶר וְצָהֳרַיִם וגו'". יָכוֹל יַשְׁמִיעַ קוֹלוֹ בִּתְפִלָּתוֹ? – כְּבָר מְפוֹרָשׁ עַל יְדֵי חַנָּה, שֶׁנֶּאֱמַר: °"וְקוֹלָהּ לֹא יִשָּׁמֵעַ". יָכוֹל *יִשְׁאַל אָדָם צְרָכָיו ואח"כ יִתְפַּלֵּל? – כְּבָר מְפוֹרָשׁ עַל יְדֵי שְׁלֹמֹה, שֶׁנֶּאֱמַר: °"לִשְׁמֹעַ אֶל הָרִנָּה וְאֶל הַתְּפִלָּה", "רִנָּה" – זוֹ תְּפִלָּה, "תְּפִלָּה" – זוֹ בַּקָּשָׁה. אֵין אוֹמֵר דָּבָר *(בַּקָּשָׁה) אַחַר אֱמֶת וְיַצִּיב, אֲבָל כ אַחַר הַתְּפִלָּה – אֲפִי' כְּסֵדֶר וִדּוּי שֶׁל יוה"כ אוֹמֵר. אִיתְּמַר נַמִי, אָמַר רַב חִיָּיא בַּר אַשִׁי אָמַר רַב: *אע"פ שֶׁאָמְרוּ שׁוֹאֵל אָדָם צְרָכָיו בְּ"שׁוֹמֵעַ תְּפִלָּה" אִם בָּא לוֹמַר אַחַר תְּפִלָּתוֹ, אֲפִילּוּ כְּסֵדֶר שֶׁל יוה"כ – אוֹמֵר.§ אָמַר רַב הַמְנוּנָא: כַּמָּה הִלְכְתָא גַּבְרְוָותָא אִיכָּא לְמִשְׁמַע מֵהָנֵי קְרָאֵי דְחַנָּה: °"וְחַנָּה הִיא מְדַבֶּרֶת עַל לִבָּהּ" – ל מִכָּאן לַמִּתְפַּלֵּל צָרִיךְ שֶׁיְּכַוֵּין לִבּוֹ. "רַק שְׂפָתֶיהָ נָעוֹת" – מ מִכָּאן לַמִּתְפַּלֵּל שֶׁיַּחְתּוֹךְ בִּשְׂפָתָיו. "וְקוֹלָהּ לֹא יִשָּׁמֵעַ" – נ מִכָּאן, שֶׁאָסוּר לְהַגְבִּיהַּ קוֹלוֹ בִּתְפִלָּתוֹ. "וַיַּחְשְׁבֶהָ עֵלִי לְשִׁכֹּרָה" – ס מִכָּאן, *שֶׁשִּׁכּוֹר אָסוּר לְהִתְפַּלֵּל, "וַיֹּאמֶר אֵלֶיהָ עֵלִי עַד מָתַי תִּשְׁתַּכָּרִין וגו'" – א"ר אֶלְעָזָר: מִכָּאן, לָרוֹאֶה בַּחֲבֵרוֹ דָּבָר

(תהלים קכו; ירמיה ב; תהלים י; דניאל ו; שם; שם; תהלים נה; שמואל א א; מלכים א ח; שמואל א א)

**רש"י**

כַּסָּא דְמוֹקְרָא. *כּוֹס שֶׁל זְכוּכִית לְבָנָה: לִישְׁרֵי לָן מַר. שִׁירָה: הֵי תּוֹרָה וְהֵי מִצְוָה דְּמַגְנוּ עֲלָן. הֵיכָן הַתּוֹרָה שֶׁעָסַקְנוּ וְהֵיכָן הַמִּצְוֹת שֶׁאָנוּ מְקַיְּימִין, שֶׁיָּגֵינוּ עָלֵינוּ מִדִּינָהּ שֶׁל גֵּיהִנֹּם: הֲלָכָה פְּסוּקָה. שֶׁאֵינָהּ צְרִיכָה עִיּוּן, שֶׁלֹּא יְהֵא מְהַרְהֵר בָּהּ בִּתְפִלָּתוֹ: יוֹשֶׁבֶת עָלֶיהָ ז' נְקִיִּים. לְבַד מֵאוֹתוֹ יוֹם שֶׁפּוֹסֶקֶת. וְהַתּוֹרָה לֹא הִצְרִיכָה ז' נְקִיִּים אֶלָּא לְזָבָה, שֶׁנֶּאֱמַר וְאִם טָהֲרָה מִזּוֹבָהּ, וְאֵין זָבָה אֶלָּא הָרוֹאָה שְׁלֹשָׁה יָמִים רְצוּפִין בְּתוֹךְ י"א יוֹם שֶׁבֵּין נִדָּה לְנִדָּה: וּמַכְנִיסָהּ. הַבַּיִת: בְּמוֹץ שֶׁלָּהּ. קוֹדֶם שֶׁיִּזְרֶה אוֹתָהּ, שֶׁאֵין מִתְחַיֵּיב בְּמַעֲשֵׂר מִן הַתּוֹרָה אֶלָּא בִּרְאִיַּית פְּנֵי הַבַּיִת וּמִשֶּׁנִּמְרַח בַּכְּרִי. אֲבָל לִפְנֵי מֵירוּחַ אֵין רְאִיַּית פְּנֵי הַבַּיִת קוֹבַעְתּוֹ. דִּגְבֵי תְּרוּמָה וּמַעֲשֵׂר כְּתִיב דָּגָן – רֵאשִׁית דְּגָנְךָ (דברים יח) וְהוּא הַמֵּירוּחַ. לְפִיכָךְ כְּשֶׁמַּכְנִיסָהּ לַבַּיִת קוֹדֶם מֵירוּחַ לֹא הוּקְבְּעָה לְמַעֲשֵׂר מִן הַתּוֹרָה, וְרַבָּנָן הוּא דְּאַסְרוּ אֲכִילַת קֶבַע בְּדָבָר שֶׁלֹּא נִגְמַר מְלַאכְתּוֹ, אֲבָל אֲכִילַת עֲרַאי לֹא אַסְרוּ. וּמַאֲכַל בְּהֵמָה עֲרַאי הוּא, דִּתְנַן בְּמַסֶּכֶת פֵּאָה (פ"א מ"ו): מַאֲכִיל לִבְהֵמָה חַיָּה וָעוֹף עַד שֶׁיִּמָּרַח. הִלְכָּךְ: בְּהֶמְתּוֹ אוֹכֶלֶת וּפְטוּרָה, אֲבָל אִיהוּ אָסוּר בַּאֲכִילַת קֶבַע: אָסוּר בַּהֲנָאָה וּמוֹעֲלִין בּוֹ. וְאַע"ג דְּקַיְי"ל אֵין מוֹעֲלִין בְּדָמִים, וְיָלְפִינַן לָהּ מִקְּרָאֵי בְּמַסֶּכֶת יוֹמָא (דף נט:) וּבִשְׁחִיטַת חוּלִּין (דף קיז.), ה"מ – כְּשֶׁנִּשְׁחֲטוּ בָּעֲזָרָה דְּאִיכָּא לְמֵימַר נְתַתִּיו לָכֶם עַל הַמִּזְבֵּחַ לְכַפֵּר (ויקרא יז), לְכַפֵּר נְתַתִּיו לָךְ וְלֹא לִמְעִילָה. אֲבָל בְּדַם הַקָּזָה – מוֹעֲלִין. כְּלוֹמַר: אִם נֶהֱנָה – מֵבִיא קָרְבַּן מְעִילָה. וְהָנָךְ הָוְיָין הֲלָכוֹת פְּסוּקוֹת שֶׁאֵין עֲלֵיהֶן קוּשְׁיוֹת וּפֵירוּקִים שֶׁיְּהֵא צָרִיךְ לְהַרְהֵר בָּהֶן: כְּמַתְנִיתִין. מִתּוֹךְ כּוֹבֶד רֹאשׁ: כִּבְרַיְיתָא. מִתּוֹךְ הֲלָכָה פְּסוּקָה: שִׂיחָה. לֵיצָנוּת: מִתּוֹךְ קַלּוּת רֹאשׁ. חִילּוּף שֶׁל כּוֹבֶד רֹאשׁ. מִתּוֹךְ זְחוּת לֵב וְעָתָק: אֶלָּא מִתּוֹךְ שִׂמְחָה(א). כְּגוֹן דִּבְרֵי תַּנְחוּמִים שֶׁל תּוֹרָה; כְּגוֹן סָמוּךְ לִגְאוּלַּת מִצְרַיִם, אוֹ סָמוּךְ לִתְהִלָּה לְדָוִד שֶׁהוּא שֶׁל שֶׁבַח וְתַנְחוּמִין, כְּגוֹן רְצוֹן יְרֵאָיו יַעֲשֶׂה, שׁוֹמֵר ה' אֶת כָּל אוֹהֲבָיו, וּכְגוֹן מִקְרָאוֹת הַסְּדוּרוֹת בִּתְפִלַּת עַרְבִית: כִּי לֹא יִטּוֹשׁ ה' אֶת עַמּוֹ, וְכַיּוֹצֵא בָּהֶן: אַלְוְיֵיהּ. לִיוָּהוּ בַּדֶּרֶךְ: צִנְיָתָא. דְּקָלִים: אַדְכַּרְתַּן מִילְּתָא כו'. וְזֶה שֶׁאוֹמְרִים מִימוֹת אָדָם הָרִאשׁוֹן הֵם, שֶׁהוּא גָּזַר עַל אוֹתוֹ מָקוֹם לְיִשּׁוּב דְּקָלִים: אִם תָּכִין לִבָּם. אָז תַּקְשִׁיב אָזְנֶךָ: זִמְנִין תְּלָתָא. שַׁחֲרִית, מִנְחָה וְעַרְבִית: יָכוֹל מִשֶּׁבָּא לַגּוֹלָה הוּחֲלָּה. הַתְּפִלָּה הַזֹּאת. הוּחֲלָּה כְּמוֹ נִתְחַלָּה, אֲבָל קוֹדֶם לָכֵן לֹא הָיָה רָגִיל בְּכָךְ: יָכוֹל יְהֵא כּוֹלְלָן. לְשָׁלֹשׁ תְּפִלּוֹת הַלָּלוּ בְּשָׁעָה אַחַת: יָכוֹל יִשְׁאַל צְרָכָיו. כְּגוֹן בְּרָכוֹת דְּאַתָּה חוֹנֵן עַד ש"ת, וְאַח"כ יִתְפַּלֵּל שָׁלֹשׁ בְּרָכוֹת רִאשׁוֹנוֹת, שֶׁהֵן שֶׁל שֶׁבַח: רִנָּה זוֹ תְּפִלָּה. שֶׁל שֶׁבַח: בַּקָּשָׁה. שְׁאֵלַת צְרָכָיו: אַחַר אֱמֶת וְיַצִּיב. קוֹדֶם ג' רִאשׁוֹנוֹת: שֶׁצָּרִיךְ

**תוספות**

אייתי כסא דזוגיתא חיורתא. מכאן נהגו לשבר זכוכית בנשואין: *במקום גילה שם תהא רעדה. פשוטו של מקרא: עבדו את ה' ביראה, וכשיבא יום רעדה תגילו. והכי מפורש בירושלמי: עבדו את ה' ביראה היינו תפלה דאיקרי עבודה, *כדתניא בספרי (פ' עקב) "ולעבדו בכל לבבכם" – זו תפלה:

המקיז דם בבהמת קדשים וכו'. וקשה, דאמר בפ"ג דע"ז (דף מד.) גבי דמים חיצונים ודמים פנימיים של קרבנות: אלו ואלו נמכרים לגננים לזבל, אלמא דאין מועלין בהן! *וי"ל: דהתם היינו לאחר זריקת דמים וכבר נתכפרו בעלים, מה שאין כן הכא: רבנן עבדי כמתניתין. וכותייהו קי"ל. ולכן אין מתפללין מתוך קלות ראש ושחוק, אלא מתוך כובד ראש ושמחה של מצוה, כגון שעסק בדברי תורה. ולכן נהגו לומר פסוקי דזמרה ואשרי קודם תפלה: רב אשי עביד כברייתא. ירושלמי: לא יעמוד ויתפלל אלא מתוך דבר הלכה, א"ר ירמיה: העוסק בצרכי צבור כעוסק בדברי תורה דמי: שכן מצינו בנביאים הראשונים שסיימו דבריהם בדברי שבח ותנחומין. ומקשה בירושלמי חוץ מירמיה וכו', והא כתיב "כי אם מאס מאסתנו" (איכה ה). מיהו *מהדרא קרא דסוף תרי עשר וקהלת לא פריך מידי, שחוזר בטוב בדברי תנחומין, ולא מיירי בפורענות דישראל: ומוצאו בזוית אחרת. תימה: דאמר לקמן (דף לד.): הבא לשחות בסוף כל ברכה וברכה מלמדין אותו שלא ישחה! ותירץ הר"ר יוסף: דהכא מיירי בתחנונים שהיה אומר אחר י"ח ברכות. ולא נהירא, דהא מי"ח קאמר! ונראה להר"י דודאי בסוף כל ברכה אסור לשחות, אבל באמצע הברכה מיהא מותר לשחות, והכי מיירי הכא, וכשהיה מגיע לסוף הברכה היה זוקף. ולכן נהגו העולם בראש השנה וביום הכפורים שמתפללין זכרנו, ובכן תן, ותמלוך – שוחים כשמגיעים לפסוקים. ובסוף ברכה זוקפין, שאין לשחות בסוף ברכות אלא היכא דתקון: דבר

**מסורת הש"ס**

' לעיל כח. פירש"י ד"ה כסא]
' תוס' שבת כ: ד"ה אין ' ב"מ כט: וחולין פד: ד"ה בזוגיתא]
ציין כעין יעקב הגירסא
פירש"י ותו' במגילה שם
חוס דף קז. ע. מנחות סז: נדה טו: [ע"ז מח:]
מעילה יב: [ע"ש]
תוספתא פ"ג
שבת ל: פסחים קיז.
עירובין סד.
סוטה מו:
תוספתא פ"ג
תוספתא שם
לקמן לד:
תוספתא שם
שם
שם
שמואל א א
מלכים א ח
רי"ף ורא"ש ל"ג
ע"ז ח.
שמואל א א
עירובין סד.

**עין משפט נר מצוה**

ג א טוש"ע א"ח סימן תקס סעיף ה:
[וכ"א להדיא תענית ב.]
ד ב מיי' פ"ד מהלכות תפלה הלכה יח סמג עשין יט טוש"ע או"ח סי' צג סעיף ג:
[וע' תוס' יומא נט: ד"ה הוא ותוס' מעילה יב: ד"ה המקיז]
ה ג מיי' פי"א מהלכות איסורי ביאה הל' ד סמג לאוין קיא טוש"ע י"ד סי' קפג:
[רב אלפס כאן ובשבועות פ"ב דף רפ"ט]:
ו ד מיי' פ"ג מהל' מעשר הלכה ו טוש"ע י"ד סימן שלא סעיף פד:
ז ה מיי' פ"ב מהלכות מעילה הלכה יא סמג עשין רי:
ח ו מיי' פ"ד מהלכות תפלה הל' יח סמג עשין יט טוש"ע א"ח סי' צג סעיף ב:
ט ז מיי' שם הלכה טז סמג שם טוש"ע א"ח סימן נח סעי' א:
י ח מיי' פ"ו שם הלכה ב טו"ע א"ח סי' נג סעיף יא:
יא ט טור א"ח סי' קד:
יב י מיי' פ"ה מהלכות תפלה הלכה ו סמג שם טוש"ע א"ח סימן ל סעיף ד:
יג כ מיי' פ"ו שם הל' ב טוש"ע א"ח סימן קיט סעיף א:
יד ל מיי' פ"ד שם הל' טו סמג שם טוש"ע א"ח סי' נח סעי' א:
טו מ נ מיי' פ"ה שם הלכה ט סמג שם טור שו"ע א"ח סי' קא סעיף ב:
טז ס מיי' פ"ד שם הל' יז סמג שם טור וש"ע א"ח סי' נט סעיף א:

**הגהות הב"ח**

(א) רש"י ד"ה אלא מתוך שמחה של מצוה כגון:

**הגהות הגר"א**

[א] גמ' אלא מתוך דבר הלכה. רשום קו על תיבת דבר הלכה וצ"ל שמחה של מצוה: [ב] שם וכן תנא כו' תז"מ:

[לרב אשי כ"ה בסוטה מו: וכ"ה רש"י בגיטין נט. ד"ה זילו ע"ש שכך מוכח וע"ע ברכ"ש ביצה ו. ד"ה א"ל]

**גליון הש"ס**

גמ' כבר מפורש על ידי חנה. עי' יומא עג ע"ב: שם יכול ישאל אדם צרכיו. עי' לקמן לב ע"א:

*דבר אשאינו הגון צריך להוכיחו. "ותען חנה ותאמר לא אדוני" – אמר עולא ואיתימא רבי יוסי ברבי חנינא, אמרה ליה: לא אדון אתה בדבר זה, ולא רוח הקודש שורה עליך, שאתה חושדני בדבר זה. איכא דאמרי, הכי אמרה ליה: לא אדון אתה, לאו איכא שכינה ורוח הקודש גבך, שדנתני לכף חובה ולא דנתני לכף זכות, מי לא ידעת דאשה קשת רוח אנכי?! "ויין ושכר לא שתיתי" – אמר רבי אלעזר: מכאן, לנחשד בדבר שאין בו שצריך להודיעו. "אל תתן את אמתך לפני בת בליעל" – אמר רבי אלעזר: מכאן, לשכור שמתפלל כאילו עובד ע"ז, כתיב הכא "לפני בת בליעל", וכתיב התם °"יצאו אנשים בני בליעל מקרבך", מה להלן ע"ז, אף כאן – ע"ז. "ויען עלי ויאמר לכי לשלום" – אמר רבי אלעזר: מכאן, לחושד את חברו בדבר שאין בו שצריך לפייסו; ולא עוד, אלא שצריך לברכו, שנאמר: "ואלהי ישראל יתן את שלתך".§ "ותדר נדר ותאמר ה' צבאות", אמר רבי אלעזר: מיום שברא הקב"ה את עולמו, לא היה אדם שקראו להקב"ה "צבאות" עד שבאתה חנה וקראתו צבאות; אמרה חנה לפני הקב"ה: רבש"ע, מכל צבאי צבאות שבראת בעולמך קשה בעיניך שתתן לי בן אחד?! משל למה הדבר דומה – למלך בשר ודם שעשה סעודה לעבדיו, בא עני אחד ועמד על הפתח, אמר להם: תנו לי פרוסה אחת! ולא השגיחו עליו, דחק ונכנס אצל המלך. א"ל: אדוני המלך, מכל סעודה שעשית קשה בעיניך ליתן לי פרוסה אחת?! "אם ראה תראה", א"ר אלעזר: אמרה חנה לפני הקב"ה: רבש"ע, אם 'ראה' – מוטב, ואם לאו – 'תראה', אלך ואסתתר בפני אלקנה בעלי, וכיון דמסתתרנא משקו לי מי סוטה, ואי אתה עושה תורתך פלסתר, שנאמר: °"ונקתה ונזרעה זרע". הניחא למאן דאמר אם היתה עקרה נפקדת – שפיר, אלא למאן דאמר אם היתה יולדת בצער יולדת בריוח, נקבות – יולדת זכרים, שחורים – יולדת לבנים, קצרים – יולדת ארוכים, מאי איכא למימר? *דתניא: "ונקתה ונזרעה זרע" – מלמד, בשאם היתה עקרה נפקדת, דברי ר' ישמעאל; א"ל רבי עקיבא: אם כן, ילכו כל העקרות כולן ויסתתרו, וזו שלא קלקלה *נפקדת! אלא: מלמד שאם היתה יולדת בצער – יולדת בריוח, קצרים – יולדת ארוכים, שחורים – יולדת לבנים, אחד – יולדת שנים. מאי "אם ראה תראה" – *דברה תורה כלשון בני אדם.§ "בעני אמתך", "אל תשכח את אמתך", "ונתתה לאמתך". א"ר יוסי בר' חנינא: ג' אמתות הללו למה – אמרה חנה לפני הקב"ה: רבש"ע, *שלשה בדקי מיתה בראת באשה, ואמרי לה: שלשה דבקי מיתה, ואלו הן: נדה וחלה והדלקת הנר, כלום עברתי על אחת מהן?§ "ונתתה לאמתך זרע אנשים" מאי "זרע אנשים"? אמר רב: גברא בגוברין; ושמואל אמר: זרע שמושחה שני אנשים, ומאן אינון – שאול ודוד; ורבי יוחנן אמר: זרע ששקול כשני אנשים, ומאן אינון – משה ואהרן, שנאמר: °"משה ואהרן בכהניו ושמואל בקוראי שמו"; ורבנן אמרי: "זרע אנשים" – זרע שמובלע בין אנשים. כי אתא רב דימי, אמר: לא ארוך ולא גוץ, (א) ולא קטן ולא אלם, ולא צחור ולא גיחור, ולא חכם ולא טפש.§ "אני האשה הנצבת עמכה בזה", – אמר ריב"ל: גמכאן, שאסור לישב בתוך ארבע אמות של תפלה! "אל הנער הזה התפללתי", – א"ר אלעזר: שמואל מורה הלכה לפני רבו היה, שנאמר: "וישחטו את הפר ויביאו את הנער אל עלי", משום ד"וישחטו את הפר" הביאו הנער אל עלי?! אלא, אמר להן עלי: קראו כהן, ליתי ולשחוט. חזנהו שמואל דהוו מהדרי בתר כהן למישחט, אמר להו: למה לכו לאהדורי בתר כהן למישחט? דשחיטה בזר כשרה! אייתוהו לקמיה דעלי, אמר ליה: מנא לך הא? אמר ליה: *מי כתיב "ושחט הכהן"?! "והקריבו הכהנים" כתיב! המקבלה ואילך מצות כהונה; מכאן לשחיטה שכשרה בזר. אמר ליה: מימר שפיר קא אמרת, מיהו, מורה הלכה בפני רבך את – וכל *המורה הלכה בפני רבו חייב מיתה. אתיא חנה וקא צווחה קמיה: "אני האשה הנצבת עמכה בזה וגו'". אמר לה: שבקי לי דאענשיה, ובעינא רחמי ויהיב לך רבא מיניה. אמרה ליה: "אל הנער הזה התפללתי".§ "וחנה היא מדברת על לבה" – אמר רבי אלעזר משום רבי יוסי בן זמרא: על עסקי לבה. אמרה לפניו: רבונו של עולם, כל מה שבראת באשה לא בראת דבר אחד לבטלה, עינים לראות, ואזנים לשמוע, חוטם להריח, פה לדבר, ידים לעשות בהם מלאכה, רגלים להלך בהן, דדים להניק בהן; דדים הללו שנתת על לבי למה, לא להניק בהן?! תן לי בן ואניק בהן. ואמר רבי אלעזר משום רבי יוסי בן זמרא: וכל היושב בתענית בשבת – קורעין לו גזר דינו של שבעים שנה, ואף על פי כן חוזרין ונפרעין ממנו דין עונג שבת. *מאי תקנתיה? אמר רב נחמן בר יצחק: חליתיב תעניתא לתעניתא.§ ואמר רבי אלעזר: חנה הטיחה דברים כלפי מעלה, שנאמר: "ותתפלל על ה'" – מלמד, שהטיחה דברים כלפי מעלה. ואמר רבי אלעזר: אליהו הטיח דברים כלפי מעלה, שנאמר: °"ואתה הסבת את לבם אחרנית". א"ר שמואל בר רבי יצחק: מנין שחזר הקב"ה והודה לו לאליהו – דכתיב

## רש"י

שצריך להודיעו. הנחשד צריך לנקות את עצמו, ולהודיע את חושדו שאין בו אותו דבר מגונה: לפני בת בליעל. אל תתנני כבת בליעל לחשדני בשכרות: ואסתתר. אתייחד עם אחרים, ויחשדני בעלי: פלסתר. שקר: שלש אמתות. דריש להו לשון מיתה: בדקי מיתה. שהאשה נבדקת בהן בשעת הסכנה, שאם ימצא בה אחד מהם תמות: נדה וחלה והדלקת נר. של שבת, על ג' עברות הללו נשים מתות. וטעמא יליף במסכת שבת (ד' לא:): שמובלע בין אנשים. רב דימי מפרש לה: לא ארוך ולא גוץ וכו': אלם. פי': עב: *צחור. רו"ש בלע"ז: גיחור. שהוא לבן יותר מדאי: ולא חכם. יותר מדאי, שלא יהיה תימה בעיני הבריות, ומתוך שנדברין בו שולטת בו עין הרע: הנצבת עמכה. משמע אף הוא עמה בעמידה: אל הנער הזה. על זה ולא לאחר. מכאן שחטאה לעלי ורצה לענשו ולהתפלל שיתן לה בן אחר: והקריבו הכהנים. אמרו בפרק קמא דחגיגה (דף יא.): והקריבו – זה קבלת הדם: של שבעים שנה. כלומר: אפילו נגזר עליו מנעוריו. לפי שתענית קשה בשבת, לפי שהכל מתענגים בו והוא מתענה: תעניתא לתעניתא. יתענה למחר: ותתפלל על ה'. כך כתוב הוא במקרא, ולא גרסינן הכא אל תקרי: שחזר והודה לאליהו. לדבריו הודה לאחר זמן, בנבואת נביאים אחרים: דכתיב

תורה אור

## תוספות

דבר שאינו הגון. פירוש: אע"ג דליכא איסורא דאורייתא, פשיטא, "הוכח תוכיח" כתיב (ויקרא יט):

גברא בגוברין. פי': אדם שיהא חשוב לימנות בין אנשים:

*מכאן ששכור אסור להתפלל. ירושלמי במסכת תרומות, פרק קמא: רבי זירא בעי קמיה דרבי אמי: שכור מהו שיברך? א"ל: "ואכלת ושבעת וברכת", ואפילו מדומדם. פירוש: ואפי' הוא שתוי ושכור כל כך שאינו יכול לדבר כראוי, דהכי משמע "ושבעת וברכת":

מכאן שאסור לישב בד' אמות של תפלה. בין מלפניו (בין מלאחריו) ובין מן הצדדין. ופירשו תשובת הגאונים דוקא ביושב ובטל, אבל אם היה עוסק בק"ש ובברכותיה וכיוצא בהם – אפילו יושב שפיר דמי:

[עמכה] עמך משמע בתוך ארבע אמות – משום דכתיב עמכה מלא בה"א, כלומר: שלא היה יושב בתוך ארבע אמות שלה, כי אם בחמישית:

מורה הלכה בפני רבך את. ואף ע"פ שלא למד עדיין בפניו, מ"מ גדול הדור היה, ובא ללמוד לפניו:

כל היושב בתענית בשבת. פירש ר"ח: בתענית חלום, וכן איתא במדרש תהלים. וכשיושב בתענית חלום בשבת צריך פי' בה"ג שאומר 'עננו' באלהי נצור, ואפילו קובע ברכה לעצמו, כיון שאינו בתוך י"ח: גדולה

## עין משפט נר מצוה

יז א מיי' פ"ו מהלכות דעות הלכה ז סמג עשין יא:

[שייך לעיל עמוד א]

יח ב מיי' פ"ג מהלכות סוטה הלכה כב:

יט ג מיי' פ"ה מהל' תפלה הלכה ו סמג עשין יט טוש"ע או"ח סימן קב סעיף א:

כ ד ה מיי' פ"ט מהל' ביאת המקדש הלכה ו ופ"ה מהל' מעשה הקרבנות הל' א ופ"א מהל' פסולי המוקדשין הלכה א סמג לאוין שט:

כא ו מיי' פ"ו מהלכות ת"ת הלכה ג סמג עשין יג טוש"ע יו"ד סימן רמב סעיף ד:

כב ז ח מיי' (פ"ל מהל' שבת הל' ט) ופ"א מהל' תעניות הל' יב סמג עשין ג טוש"ע או"ח סי' רפח סעיף ד:

## מסורת הש"ס

ערכין טז:

[אחור קסוף רו"ש בלע"ז לקמן [ברש"י לקמן בכורות קף פירש"י לקמן במעלני יו"ש ל]

רש"ל מ"ז

דברים יג

במדבר ה

סוטה כו. [וע' הסיטה וע"ש ובתוס' מנחות]

נ"א נפסדת

[יבמות עא. כתובות סז: קדושין יז: גיטין מא: נדרים ג. ב"מ לא: לב: ע"ז כז. סנהדרין נו. סד: פה: מכות יב. זבחים קח: כריתות יא. ערכין ג. נדה לב: מד.]

שבת לב.

תהלים צט

זבחים לב. [יומא כז. מנחות יט.]

עירובין סג.

[תענית יב:]

מלכים א יח

## הגהות הב"ח

(א) גמ' ולא קטן. נ"ב פי' שהוא דק ביותר ולא אלם פירוש שהוא עב הרבה לשון ואולים:

## גליון הש"ס

תוס' ד"ה מורה וכו' ובא ללמוד לפניו. עי' תס"ד סימן קל"ח:

דכתיב ואשר הרעותי. רישא דקרא אוספה הצולעה והנדחה אקבצה ואשר הרעותי – אני גרמתי להם שבראתי יצר הרע: אלמלא שלש מקראות הללו. שמעידין שיש ביד הקדוש ברוך הוא לתקן יצרנו, ולהסיר יצר הרע ממנו: נתמוטטו רגלינו במשפט. אבל עכשיו יש לנו פתחון פה. שהוא גרם לנו שברא יצר הרע: הטיח. לשון זריקה, כמו כמטחוי קשת (בראשית כא): אין ארי נוהם. שמח ומשתגע ומזיק: מלי כריסיה זני בישי. מילוי הכרס הוא ממיני חטאים הרעים. זני מתרגמינן למיניהו – לזנוהי (בראשית א): הרף ממני. הראהו שיש כח בידו למחול ע"י תפלה: הניחה לי. תורה אור

משמע שהיה אוחז בו: שלש רגלים. אברהם יצחק ויעקב: שהחלהו. הפליג בו, אנוי"ר בלע"ז: נדרו. דבורו שאמר ואכלם: שמסר עצמו למיתה. ויחל לשון חלל: שהחלה עליהם מדת רחמים. כמו יחולו על ראש יואב (ש"ב ג), לשון הניח: שאחזתו אחילו. גרס: אשתא דגרמי. מוליי"ר בלע"ז: אשר נשבעת להם בך. שנאמר בעקדת יצחק בי נשבעתי (בראשית כב): עד כאן. עד ככוכבי השמים: מכאן ואילך דברי הרב. אמר לו אעשה כדבריך: דברים שאמרת לי. בסנה אמרת לי אעלה אתכם מעני מצרים אל ארץ טובה ורחבה (שמות ג): החייתני. בפני האומות: עלה

[סוכה נב: ע"ש] [מגילה כד:] [יומא פו: סנהדרין קב.]

מיכה ז דכתיב: "ואשר הרעתי".§ *אמר רבי חמא ברבי חנינא: אלמלא שלש מקראות הללו – נתמוטטו רגליהם של שונאי ישראל: חד, דכתיב: "ואשר
ירמיה יח הרעתי", וחד, דכתיב: "הנה כחמר ביד היוצר כן אתם בידי בית ישראל"; וחד,
יחזקאל לו דכתיב: "והסרתי את לב האבן מבשרכם ונתתי לכם לב בשר". רב פפא
שם אמר, מהכא: "ואת רוחי אתן בקרבכם ועשיתי את אשר בחקי תלכו". ואמר
במדבר יא רבי אלעזר: משה הטיח דברים כלפי מעלה, שנאמר: "ויתפלל משה אל ה'",
אל תקרי "אל" ה' אלא "על" ה', שכן דבי רבי אליעזר בן יעקב *קורין לאלפי"ן(א)
דברים א עייני"ן ולעייני"ן אלפי"ן. דבי רבי ינאי אמרי, מהכא: "ודי זהב", מאי "ודי זהב"? אמרי
*דבי ר' ינאי, כך אמר משה לפני הקב"ה: רבונו של עולם, בשביל כסף וזהב
שהשפעת להם לישראל עד שאמרו די – הוא גרם שעשו את העגל. אמרי דבי
ר' ינאי: אין ארי נוהם מתוך קופה של תבן אלא מתוך קופה של בשר. אמר
רבי אושעיא: משל, לאדם שהיתה לו פרה כחושה ובעלת אברים, האכילה
כרשינין והיתה מבעטת בו. אמר לה: מי גרם ליך שתהא מבעטת בי – אלא
כרשינין שהאכלתיך. אמר רבי חייא בר אבא אמר ר' יוחנן: משל, לאדם אחד
שהיה לו בן, הרחיצו וסכו, והאכילו והשקהו, ותלה לו כיס על צוארו, והושיבו
על פתח של זונות, מה יעשה אותו הבן שלא יחטא? אמר רב אחא בריה
הושע יג דרב הונא אמר רב ששת: היינו דאמרי אינשי "מלי כרסיה זני בישי" שנאמר: "כמרעיתם וישבעו שבעו
דברים ח וירם לבם על כן שכחוני"; רב נחמן אמר, מהכא: "ורם לבבך ושכחת את ה'"; ורבנן אמרי, מהכא: "ואכל
שם לב ושבע ודשן ופנה"; ואי בעית אימא, מהכא: "וישמן ישורון ויבעט". אמר רבי שמואל בר נחמני אמר רבי
הושע ב יונתן: מנין שחזר הקדוש ברוך הוא והודה לו למשה – שנאמר: "וכסף הרביתי *להם וזהב עשו לבעל".§ נ"ל לה
שמות לב "וידבר ה' אל משה לך רד" מאי "לך רד"? אמר רבי אלעזר, אמר לו הקדוש ב"ה למשה: משה, רד מגדולתך!
כלום נתתי לך גדולה אלא בשביל ישראל, ועכשיו ישראל חטאו(ב) – אתה למה לי? מיד תשש כוחו של משה
דברים ט ולא היה לו כח לדבר. וכיון שאמר: "הרף ממני ואשמידם", אמר משה: דבר זה תלוי בי – מיד עמד ונתחזק
בתפלה ובקש רחמים. משל, למלך(ג) שכעס על בנו והיה מכהו מכה גדולה, והיה אוהבו יושב לפניו ומתירא
לומר לו דבר. אמר המלך: אלמלא אוהבי זה שיושב לפני הרגתיך! אמר: דבר זה תלוי בי – מיד עמד
שמות לב והצילו. "ועתה הניחה לי ויחר אפי בהם ואכלם ואעשה אותך לגוי גדול וגו'" – אמר רבי אבהו: אלמלא מקרא
כתוב אי אפשר לאומרו; מלמד, שתפסו משה להקדוש ברוך הוא כאדם שהוא תופס את חבירו בבגדו,
שם ואמר לפניו: רבונו של עולם, אין אני מניחך עד שתמחול ותסלח להם. "ואעשה אותך לגוי גדול וגו'" –
אמר רבי אלעזר, אמר משה לפני הקדוש ב"ה: רבונו של עולם, ומה כסא של שלש רגלים אינו יכול
לעמוד לפניך בשעת כעסך, כסא של רגל אחד על אחת כמה וכמה! ולא עוד אלא שיש בי בושת פנים
שם מאבותי. עכשיו יאמרו: ראו פרנס שהעמיד עליהם, בקש גדולה לעצמו ולא בקש עליהם רחמים. "ויחל
משה את פני ה'" – אמר רבי אלעזר:(ד) מלמד שעמד משה בתפלה לפני הקדוש ברוך הוא עד שהחלהו; *ורבא [אולי צ"ל ורב]
במדבר ל חגיגה י אמר: עד *שהפר לו נדרו, כתיב הכא "ויחל" וכתיב התם "לא יחל דברו", *ואמר מר: הוא אינו מיחל אבל [נ"ל שהתיר וכ"ה בילקוט ובע"י והוא נכון כלאחא נדרים עז: וב"ב קכ. וע' תוספות בכורות לו. ד"ה מפירין]
שמות לב אחרים מוחלין לו. ושמואל אמר: מלמד שמסר עצמו למיתה עליהם, שנאמר: "ואם אין מחני נא מספרך".
[רב יצחק אמ' מלמד כו' כצ"ל וכ"ה בילקוט ובע"י] *אמר רבא אמר רב יצחק: מלמד שהחלה עליהם מדת רחמים. ורבנן אמרי: מלמד שאמר משה לפני
[ע"ז ז.] הקב"ה: רבש"ע, *חולין הוא לך מעשות כדבר הזה. "ויחל משה את פני ה'". תניא, רבי אליעזר הגדול אומר:
גיטין ע. מלמד שעמד משה בתפלה לפני הקדוש ברוך הוא עד שאחזתו אחילו. *מאי אחילו? אמר רבי אלעזר:
שם אש של עצמות. מאי אש של עצמות? אמר אביי: אשתא דגרמי. "זכור לאברהם ליצחק ולישראל עבדיך אשר
נשבעת להם בך" – מאי 'בך'? אמר רבי אלעזר, אמר משה לפני הקדוש ב"ה: רבונו של עולם, אלמלא נשבעת
להם בשמים ובארץ הייתי אומר כשם ששמים וארץ בטלים – כך שבועתך בטלה. ועכשיו שנשבעת להם
בשמך הגדול, מה שמך הגדול חי וקיים לעולם ולעולמי עולמים – כך שבועתך קיימת לעולם ולעולמי עולמים.
שם "ותדבר אליהם ארבה את זרעכם ככוכבי השמים וכל הארץ הזאת אשר אמרתי". האי "אשר אמרתי"? "אשר אמרת"
מיבעי ליה! – אמר רבי אלעזר: עד כאן דברי תלמיד מכאן ואילך – דברי הרב. ורבי שמואל בר נחמני אמר: אלו
ואלו דברי תלמיד,(ה) אלא כך אמר משה לפני הקדוש ברוך הוא: רבונו של עולם, דברים שאמרת לי "לך אמור
במדבר יד להם לישראל" בשמי הלכתי ואמרתי להם בשמך; עכשיו מה אני אומר להם? "מבלתי יכלת ה'" "יכול ה'" מיבעי
ליה! – אמר רבי אלעזר, אמר משה לפני הקב"ה: רבש"ע, עכשיו יאמרו אומות העולם: תשש כחו כנקבה
ואינו יכול להציל. אמר הקב"ה למשה: והלא כבר ראו נסים וגבורות שעשיתי להם על הים! – אמר לפניו:
רבונו של עולם, עדיין יש להם לומר: למלך אחד – יכול לעמוד, לשלשים ואחד מלכים – אינו יכול לעמוד.
שם אמר ר' יוחנן: מנין שחזר הקדוש ברוך הוא והודה לו למשה – שנאמר: "ויאמר ה' סלחתי כדברך". תני דבי רבי
שם ישמעאל: כדבריך עתידים אוה"ע לומר כן. אשרי תלמיד שרבו מודה לו. "ואולם חי אני". אמר רבא אמר רב יצחק:
ע"ז ז: מלמד, שאמר לו הקדוש ב"ה למשה: משה, החייתני בדבריך.§ *דרש רבי שמלאי: לעולם יסדר אדם שבחו
דברים ג של הקב"ה ואחר כך יתפלל. מנלן – ממשה דכתיב "ואתחנן אל ה' בעת ההיא"; וכתיב "ה' אלהים אתה החלות
להראות את עבדך את גדלך ואת ידך החזקה אשר מי אל בשמים ובארץ אשר יעשה כמעשיך וכגבורותיך", וכתיב
בתריה "אעברה נא ואראה את הארץ הטובה וגו'". (סימן: מעשי"ם, צדק"ה, קרב"ן, כה"ן, תעני"ת, מנע"ל, ברז"ל).§
אמר

כג א מיי' פ"א מהלכות תפלה הלכה ב:

## הגהות הב"ח

(א) גמ' קורין לאלפי"ן. נ"ב פרש"י פ' הקורא עומד דהיינו בדרש' אבל בתפלה איסורא איכא ע"ש ד' כ"ד ע"ב: (ב) שם ועכשיו ישראל חטאו (אתה למה לי) תא"מ ונ"ב ס"א למה לך גדולה: (ג) שם משל למלך ב"ו שכעס: (ד) שם א"ר אלעזר (מלמד שעמד וכו' שהחלהו) תא"מ ונ"ב ס"א מלמד שהתפלל משה עד שהחלה אביי אמר עד שהחלה להקב"ה: (ה) שם דברי תלמיד הן אלא:

## רב נסים גאון

**ואולם** חי אני אמר לו הקב"ה למשה משה החייתני בדבריך. זה הדבר קשה היה בפני התלמידים והיו מלעיזים בו עלינו החולקין על דברי רבותינו ז"ל ואמנם כי פשוטו של זה הדבר נראה שאינו מתקבל על הדעת שמשתבשין בה ואני ברחמי שמיא פירשתיה פירוש צח וביארתי טעמיה ביאור יפה שהוא שוה לענין הכתוב ולסברא והרי אנו מזכירין המימרא כללא כדגרסי' בגמ' ואחר כן נאמר פירושה (במדבר יד) מבלתי יכולת ה' יכול ה' מיבעי ליה אמר ר' אלעזר אמר משה לפני הקב"ה רבש"ע עכשיו יאמרו אומות העולם תשש [כחו] כנקבה ואין בו כח להצילם אמר לו בן עמרם והלא כבר ראו נסים וגבורות שעשיתי על הים אמר לפניו רבונו של עולם יאמרו לפני מלך אחד יכול לעמוד בפני ל"א (מלך) [מלכים] אינו יכול לעמוד אמר ר' יוחנן מנין שחזר הקב"ה והודה למשה שנא' (שם) ויאמר ה' סלחתי כדבריך תנא דבי ר' ישמעאל כדבריך עתידין אומות העולם לומר אשרי תלמיד שרבו מודה לו ואולם חי אני אמר רבא א"ר יצחק אמר לו הקב"ה למשה משה החייתני בדבריך עד כאן היא הדרשה שנאמרה בזה הפסוק ופירושה אנו מזכירין דע לך כי החיים והיכולת שתי מדות הן ממדותיו של הקב"ה שהן מדות עצמו וגדולתו שאינן נחלפין ממנו כלל כי הכח והיכולת אינם נמצאים אלא במי שהוא חי ומי שהוא חי העולמים שלא יתמו שנותיו אי אפשר שלא יהיה יכול וזה הדבר אע"פ שהוא שריר ומקויים בסברא יש לו חיזוק מן הכתוב והיינו דכתב רחמנא (דברים לב) כי אשא אל שמים ידי ואמרתי חי אנכי לעולם פתח בזכרון היד שהוא היכולת וסיים בזכר החיים ואמר חי אנכי לעולם כי היכולת קיימת לו לעולם מפני שהוא חי העולמים ובעת שאירע מעשה המרגלים ואמר הקב"ה להשמידם לאומתו נגש הנביא עליו השלום בתפלה בעדם ואמר בכלל דבריו מבלתי יכולת ה' ולפי שידע הקב"ה כי אמת דבר וכי אם הוא משמיד את העם במדבר ואינו מכבש לפניהן את ארץ כנען האומות אומרים עליו כי קצרה ידו ותשש כחו ואינו יכול לעמוד כנגד ל"א (מלך) [מלכים] ולגרשם מפני בניו ולפיכך קבל תפלתו בעדם ונעתר לו ואמר סלחתי כדברך ואמר לו אחר כן ואולם חי אני הודיע לנביאו שבודאי אילו השמידם לעם היו האומות אומרים שאין לו יכולת ולא היו מכירין גבורתו והואיל ואין מתברר להם שהוא יכול גם כן אין מתברר להם שהוא חי והנה בשביל עתירת הנביא בעד העם הודו האומות כי יש להקב"ה החיים לעלמין ונתברר להם שהוא חי וקיים וזכה הנביא לשבח בשביל זה הדבר כי בשביל עתירתו נודעה גדולתו של מלכנו ועצמו וגבורתו ונתפרסמו בקצות הארץ ונתברר ונתקיים כי הקב"ה יתעלה שמו חי בעצמו ולפיכך א"ל רחמנא ואולם חי אני אחר שאמר כדברך תיכף לה ודרשי ליה רבנן החייתני בדבריך כלומר שבשביל עתירתך גרם הדבר ונתברר לאומות שאני חי וזה הוא צד התירוץ של זה הדבר והיה נעלם מאד וסייעני הקב"ה לגלותו ולפרשו ולא ראיתי אדם שקדמני לזה התירוץ וזה הפירוש יהיה שמור בידך:

**עין משפט נר מצוה**

**כד** א מיי' פט"ו מהל' תפלה הלכה ג סמג עשין כ טוש"ע או"ח סי' קכח סעיף לה:

**כה** ב טוש"ע או"ח סי' לח סעיף ה:

**כו** ג מיי' פ"ד מהל' תפלה הלכה טז סמג עשין יט טור וש"ע או"ח סי' לג סעיף א:

**כז** ד ה מיי' פ"ו שם הל' ט סמג שם טור וש"ע או"ח סימן קד סעיף א:

**כח** ו מיי' שם טוש"ע שם סעיף ב:

**כט** ז מיי' שם טוש"ע שם סעיף א:

**תוספות**

**גדולה** תפלה יותר ממעשים טובים. בלא תפלה, שהרי משה רבינו ע"ה אף על פי שהיו בידו מעשים טובים הוצרך לתפלה:

**כל** המאריך בתפלתו ומעיין בה. פירוש: שמצפה שתבא בקשתו לפי שכוון בתפלתו. תימה: דהכא משמע דעיון תפלה לאו מעליותא הוא. וכן משמע פ' "הרואה" (לקמן נה.): ג' דברים מזכירין עוונותיו של אדם, וקאמר עיון תפלה. ולא כן משמע בפ' "מפנין" (שבת קכז.) דקאמר: אדם אוכל פירותיהן בעוה"ז, וקא חשיב עיון תפלה, אלמא מעליותא הוא! וכן משמע "בגט פשוט" (ב"ב קסד:), דקאמר: משלשה דברים אין אדם ניצול בכל יום וקאמר: עיון תפלה, פירוש: שאין אדם מעיין בה, אם כן משמע שהוא טוב! וי"ל: דתרי עיון תפלה יש: עיון תפלה דהכא – המצפה שתבא בקשתו, ועיון תפלה דהתם – שמכוין את לבו לתפלה*:

**אל** דמעתי אל תחרש. פרש"י: דדייק מדיוקא, מדלא קאמר "ודמעתי תראה" ש"מ שהיא נראית בכל פעם. ואין להתפלל רק שתתקבל:

**קודם** תפלתו מנין שנא' "אשרי יושבי ביתך". ולפיכך תקנו לומר זה הפסוק קודם תהלה לדוד, לאפוקי מהנהו דאמרי 'אשרי' הרבה. אבל

ב"מ נט.

[וע"ע תוס' שבת קיח: ובר"ה טז: וב"ב קסד:]

**רב נסים גאון**

**אפילו** המלך שואל בשלומו לא ישיבנו. ושנינו עוד בתוספתא הכותב את השם אפי' המלך שואל בשלומו לא ישיבנו היה כותב ה' או ו' שמות כיון שגמר אחד מהן משיב שאילת שלום ואיתא להא ברייתא בגמרא דבני מערבא דפירקין: **תנו** רבנן מעשה בחסיד אחד שהיה מתפלל בדרך איתא בבבא קמא בפ' הגוזל (דף קג.) כל מעשה בחסיד אחד אינו אלא ר' יהודה בן בבא או ר' יהודה בר' אלעאי ואיתא דכוותה בתמורה (דף טו) בפרק יש בקרבנות הצבור:

**גמרא**

אמר ר' אלעזר: גדולה תפלה יותר ממעשים טובים. שאין לך גדול במעשים טובים יותר ממשה רבינו, אעפ"כ לא נענה אלא בתפלה, שנאמר: "אל תוסף דבר אלי" (דברים ג) וסמיך ליה "עלה ראש הפסגה". וא"ר אלעזר: גדולה תענית יותר מן הצדקה. מאי טעמא – זה בגופו וזה בממונו. וא"ר אלעזר: גדולה תפלה יותר מן הקרבנות שנא' "למה לי רב זבחיכם" (ישעיה א) וכתיב "ובפרשכם כפיכם" (א). א"ר יוחנן: *כל כהן שהרג את הנפש לא ישא את כפיו, שנא' "ידיכם דמים מלאו" (שם). *וא"ר אלעזר: מיום שחרב בית המקדש ננעלו שערי תפלה, שנאמר: "גם כי אזעק ואשוע שתם תפלתי" (איכה ג), ואע"פ ששערי תפלה ננעלו שערי דמעה לא ננעלו, שנאמר: "שמעה תפלתי ה' ושועתי האזינה אל דמעתי אל תחרש" (תהלים לט). רבא לא גזר תעניתא ביומא דעיבא משום שנא' "סכתה בענן לך מעבור תפלה" (איכה ג). וא"ר אלעזר: מיום שחרב בית המקדש נפסקה חומת ברזל בין ישראל לאביהם שבשמים, שנא' "ואתה *קח לך מחבת ברזל ונתתה אותה קיר ברזל בינך ובין העיר" (יחזקאל ד). § א"ר חנין א"ר חנינא: כל המאריך בתפלתו אין תפלתו חוזרת ריקם. מנא לן – ממשה רבינו שנא': "ואתפלל אל ה'" (דברים ט), וכתיב בתריה "וישמע ה' אלי גם בפעם ההיא". איני?! והא *א"ר חייא בר אבא א"ר יוחנן: כל המאריך בתפלתו ומעיין בה – סוף בא לידי כאב לב, שנא': "תוחלת ממשכה מחלה לב" (משלי יג) מאי תקנתיה – יעסוק בתורה, שנא' "ועץ חיים תאוה באה" (שם) ואין עץ חיים אלא תורה, שנאמר: "עץ חיים היא למחזיקים בה" (שם ג)! – לא קשיא, הא – דמאריך ומעיין בה, הא – דמאריך ולא מעיין בה. א"ר חמא בר' חנינא: אם ראה אדם שהתפלל ולא נענה יחזור ויתפלל שנאמר: "קוה אל ה' חזק ויאמץ לבך וקוה אל ה'" (תהלים כז). ת"ר, ארבעה צריכין חזוק ואלו הן: תורה, ומעשים טובים, תפלה, ודרך ארץ. תורה ומעשים טובים מנין – שנא' "רק חזק ואמץ מאד לשמר *לעשות ככל התורה" (יהושע א). 'חזק' – בתורה, 'ואמץ' – במעשים טובים. תפלה מנין – שנא' "קוה אל ה' חזק ויאמץ לבך וקוה אל ה'"; דרך ארץ מנין – שנא' "חזק ונתחזק בעד עמנו וגו'" (שמואל ב י). § "ותאמר ציון עזבני ה' וה' שכחני" (ישעיה מט). היינו עזובה היינו שכוחה! אמר ר"ל, אמרה כנסת ישראל לפני הקב"ה: רבש"ע, אדם נושא אשה על אשתו ראשונה – זוכר מעשה הראשונה, אתה עזבתני ושכחתני. –אמר לה הקב"ה: בתי, י"ב מזלות בראתי ברקיע ועל כל מזל ומזל בראתי לו שלשים חיל ועל כל חיל וחיל בראתי לו שלשים לגיון ועל כל לגיון ולגיון בראתי לו שלשים רהטון ועל כל רהטון ורהטון בראתי לו שלשים קרטון ועל כל קרטון וקרטון בראתי לו שלשים גסטרא ועל כל גסטרא וגסטרא תליתי בו שלש מאות וששים וחמשה אלפי רבוא כוכבים כנגד ימות החמה – וכולן לא בראתי אלא בשבילך ואת אמרת עזבתני ושכחתני?! "התשכח אשה עולה" (שם)? אמר הקב"ה: כלום אשכח עולות אילים [א] ופטרי רחמים שהקרבת לפני במדבר?! אמרה לפניו: רבש"ע, הואיל ואין שכחה לפני כסא כבודך שמא לא תשכח לי מעשה העגל? –אמר לה: "גם אלה תשכחנה" (שם). אמרה לפניו: רבש"ע, הואיל ויש שכחה לפני כסא כבודך שמא תשכח לי מעשה סיני? – אמר לה: "ואנכי לא אשכחך" (שם). והיינו דא"ר אלעזר א"ר אושעיא: מאי דכתיב "גם אלה תשכחנה" – זה מעשה העגל, "ואנכי לא אשכחך" – זה מעשה סיני. § "חסידים הראשונים היו שוהין שעה אחת". מנא הני מילי? א"ר יהושע ב"ל: אמר קרא "אשרי יושבי ביתך" (תהלים פד). ואמר ר' יהושע ב"ל: המתפלל צריך לשהות שעה אחת אחר תפלתו שנא' "אך צדיקים יודו לשמך ישבו ישרים את פניך" (שם קמ). תניא נמי הכי: המתפלל צריך שישהא שעה אחת קודם תפלתו, ושעה אחת אחר תפלתו. קודם תפלתו מנין – שנא' "אשרי יושבי ביתך". לאחר תפלתו מנין – דכתיב "אך צדיקים יודו לשמך ישבו ישרים את פניך". תנו רבנן: חסידים הראשונים היו שוהין שעה אחת ומתפללין שעה אחת וחוזרין ושוהין שעה אחת. וכי מאחר ששוהין תשע שעות ביום בתפלה, תורתן היאך משתמרת, ומלאכתן היאך נעשית? אלא מתוך שחסידים הם – תורתם משתמרת ומלאכתם מתברכת. § "אפילו המלך שואל בשלומו לא ישיבנו". אמר רב יוסף: לא שנו אלא למלכי ישראל אבל למלכי אומות העולם פוסק. מיתיבי: המתפלל וראה אנס בא כנגדו, ראה קרון בא כנגדו – לא יהא מפסיק אלא מקצר ועולה! – לא קשיא: הא – דאפשר לקצר (*יקצר, ואם לאו – פוסק.) ת"ר: מעשה בחסיד אחד שהיה מתפלל בדרך, בא הגמון אחד ונתן לו שלום ולא החזיר לו שלום, המתין לו עד שסיים תפלתו. לאחר שסיים תפלתו א"ל: ריקא, והלא כתוב בתורתכם "רק השמר לך ושמר נפשך" (דברים ד) וכתיב "ונשמרתם מאד לנפשתיכם" (שם), כשנתתי לך שלום למה לא החזרת לי שלום? אם הייתי חותך ראשך בסייף מי היה תובע את דמך מידי?! א"ל: המתן לי עד שאפייסך בדברים. א"ל: אילו היית עומד לפני מלך בשר ודם ובא חברך ונתן לך שלום – היית מחזיר

**רש"י**

עלה ראש הפסגה. בדבר תפלה זו נתרציתי להראותך אותה: ובפרשכם כפיכם. אי לאו דגדולה תפלה, כיון דאמר למה לי רוב זבחיכם למה לי תו ובפרשכם? הא אפילו זבחיכם לא ניחא ליה: אל תחרש. מדלא (ב) כתיב את דמעתי תראה, ש"מ: נראית היא לפניו, ואין צריך להתפלל אלא שתתקבל לפניו: ונתתה אותה קיר ברזל. סימן למחיצת ברזל המפסקת בינו לבינם: ומעיין בה. מצפה שתעשה בקשתו על ידי תפלתו, סוף שאינה נעשית ונמצאת תוחלת ממושכת חנם. והיה כאב לב כשאדם מצפה ואין תאותו באה: תוחלת. לשון חלוי ותקוה: ועץ חיים תאוה באה. סופו של מקרא הוא: קוה. והתחזק, ולא תמשוך ידך, אלא חזור וקוה: צריכין חיזוק. שיתחזק אדם בהם תמיד בכל כחו: דרך ארץ. אם אומן הוא – לאומנותו, אם סוחר הוא – לסחורתו, אם איש מלחמה הוא – למלחמתו: שלשים חיל. ראשי גייסות וחבורות חלוקות: לגיון וקרטון וגסטרא. שמות של סדרה, כגון שלטון, והגמון, ודוכס, ופחה: עולה. כמו עולות וקרבנות: גם אלה. מעשה העגל שאמרו "אלה אלהיך ישראל" (שמות לב): ואנכי זה מעשה סיני. שנאמר בו "אנכי ה' אלהיך" (שמות כ): יושבי ביתך. והדר יהללוך: יודו לשמך. והדר ישבו ישרים את פניך: תשע שעות. לשלש תפלות: תורתם משתמרת. מתוך לבם, שאין תלמודם משתכח: אבל למלכי אומות העולם פוסק. שלא יהרגנו: הא דאפשר לקצר. כגון שממהר לגמור תפלתו: אבל

[ע' תוס' סנהדרין בתוס' דיבמות שנאמר]

בן אדם קח לך

לקמן נה.

נ"ל לעשות

**הגהות הב"ח**

(א) גמ' שנאמר ובפרשכם כפיכם וגו' ידיכם דמים: (ב) רש"י ד"ה אל תחרש מדלא. נ"ב ובב"מ דף נ"ט פי' בע"א ע"ש:

**הגהות הגר"א**

[א] גמ' עולות (אילים) תז"מ ונ"ב אשים:

**גליון הש"ס**

**גמ'** כל כהן שהרג. בהגהה מוהרי"ב ז"ל וכן בתוס' יבמות (דף ז.) ד"ה שנאמר. וע' בתוי"ט סוף פרק ז' דבכורות: **תוס'** ד"ה גדולה וכו' בלא תפלה. וע' תשובת מהרשד"ם חא"ח סי' ל':

[ברב אלפס אי' והא דלא אפשר לקצר אפשר לקצר מקצר ואי לא מפסיק]

אבל עקרב פוסק. ונוטלו. לפי שהעקרב *מסוכן לעקוץ יותר משהנחש מוכן לישוך: אין מעידין עליו. לומר לאשתו: מת בעליך, להתירה לינשא, פעמים שאין האריות רעבים ואין אוכלין אותו: נחשים ועקרבים. או זה או זה, מעידים עליו שמת, אלמנה: מועד הנחש לישוך: אגב איצצא. כשנופל עליהם ודוחקם הזיקוהו: שור תם. שלא נגח אדם: מועד. שנגח ג' פעמים: בדקולא. סל, שתולין בו תבן בראשו ואוכל: ושדי דרגא. כלומר, הזהר ממנו הרבה: ביומי ניסן. שעברו ימי הסתיו שהלך יבשה, ועכשיו רואה אותה מגלה דשאים וזהו דעתו עליו, ונכנס בו יצר הרע. ערוד. מן הנחש והצב בא, שמזדקקין זה עם זה ויוצא משניהם ערוד*: את חורו. שהוא יוצא משם. ומת הערוד. מצאתי בה"ג, אמרי במערבא: כשהערוד נושך את האדם אם הערוד קודם למים – מת האדם, ואם האדם קודם למים – מת הערוד. ונעשה נס לר' חנינא ונקבע מעין מתחת עקבו: מתני' מזכירין גבורות גשמים. משיב הרוח, שאינו לשון בקשה אלא לשון הזכרה ושבח. ושואלין. ותן טל ומטר, לשון בקשה: והבדלה בחונן הדעת. במוצאי שבת אתה חוננתנו: גמ' מתוך שהיא חכמה. המכיר יודע להבדיל בין קדש לחול ובין טמא לטהור: בין שתי אותיות. בין שתי הזכרות: במילתה מיהא גדולה היא. במקום שצריכה נקמה – דבר גדול הוא: שתי נקמות הללו למה. אחת לרעה – להנקם מן הגוים שלא קבלו את התורה: ואחת לטובה. כדאמרינן בב"ק (דף לח.): מפארן הופיע והפקיר ממונן לישראל, שור של ישראל שנגח שור של גוי – פטור: הופיע. גלה והפקיר, כשלא קבלו את התורה: העשירו. לקנות יין: קבעוה על הכוס. ואף נשכחה תקנת עזרא, וכשחזרו והעניו – קבעוה בתפלה, ונחלקו היאך יאמרוה: בתחלה. כשעלו מן הגולה והיו דחוקים: קדושות. קדוש היום: מפני שיכול. משמע: אם ירצה שלא לחזור ולהתפלל, הא אם אמרה בתפלה – א"נ לאומרה על הכוס: ואנא שמעית. אני שמעתי: חוזר לראש. לתפלה ולכוס.
הלכתא

מחזיר לו?! – א"ל: לאו. ואם היית מחזיר לו, מה היו עושים לך? א"ל: היו חותכים את ראשי בסייף. – א"ל: והלא דברים ק"ו; ומה אתה שהיית עומד לפני מלך בשר ודם *שהיום כאן ומחר בקבר – כך, אני שהייתי עומד לפני מלך מלכי המלכים הקב"ה שהוא חי וקיים לעד ולעולמי עולמים – על אחת כמה וכמה! מיד נתפייס אותו הגמון, ונפטר אותו חסיד לביתו לשלום.§ "אפי' נחש כרוך על עקבו לא יפסיק". אמר רב ששת: לא שנו אלא נחש, אבל עקרב – פוסק. מיתיבי: *נפל לגוב אריות אין מעידין עליו שמת, נפל לחפירה מלאה נחשים ועקרבים – מעידין עליו שמת! – שאני התם, דאגב איצצא מזקי. א"ר יצחק: ראה שוורים פוסק, דתני רב אושעיא: *מרחיקין משור תם חמשים אמה, ומשור מועד – כמלוא עיניו. תנא משמיה דר' מאיר: ריש תורא בדקולא – סליק לאיגרא, ושדי דרגא מתותך. אמר שמואל: הני מילי – בשור שחור וביומי ניסן, מפני שהשטן מרקד לו בין קרניו. ת"ר: *מעשה במקום אחד שהיה ערוד והיה מזיק את הבריות, באו והודיעו לו לר' חנינא בן דוסא. אמר להם: הראו לי את חורו! הראוהו את חורו, נתן עקבו על פי החור, יצא ונשכו ומת אותו ערוד. נטלו על כתפו והביאו לבית המדרש. אמר להם: ראו בני, אין ערוד ממית אלא החטא ממית. באותה שעה אמרו: אוי לו לאדם שפגע בו ערוד ואוי לו לערוד שפגע בו ר' חנינא בן דוסא.§ מתני' *מזכירין גבורות גשמים בתחיית המתים ושאלה בברכת השנים, והבדלה בחונן הדעת; *ר"ע אומר: אומרה ברכה רביעית בפני עצמה; רבי אליעזר אומר: בהודאה.§ גמ' "מזכירין גבורות גשמים". מאי טעמא? *אמר רב יוסף: מתוך ששקולה כתחיית המתים, לפיכך קבעוה בתחיית המתים. "ושאלה בברכת השנים". מאי טעמא? אמר רב יוסף: מתוך שהיא פרנסה לפיכך קבעוה בברכת פרנסה. "הבדלה בחונן הדעת". מ"ט? א"ר יוסף: מתוך שהיא חכמה קבעוה בברכת חכמה; ורבנן אמרי: מתוך שהיא חול לפיכך קבעוה בברכת חול.§ א"ר אמי: גדולה דעה שנתנה בתחלת ברכה של חול. וא"ר אמי: *גדולה דעה שנתנה בין שתי אותיות, שנאמר: "כי אל דעות ה'". וכל מי שאין בו דעה אסור לרחם עליו, שנאמר: "כי לא עם בינות הוא על כן לא ירחמנו עושהו". אמר רבי אלעזר: גדול מקדש שנתן בין ב' אותיות, שנאמר: "פעלת ה' מקדש ה'". וא"ר אלעזר: כל אדם שיש בו דעה – כאילו נבנה בית המקדש בימיו; דעה נתנה בין שתי אותיות, מקדש נתן בין שתי אותיות. מתקיף לה *רב אחא קרחינאה: אלא מעתה, גדולה נקמה שנתנה בין שתי אותיות שנאמר: "אל נקמות ה'"! – אמר ליה: אין, במילתה מיהא גדולה היא. והיינו דאמר עולא: שתי נקמות הללו למה? אחת לטובה ואחת לרעה, לטובה – דכתיב: "הופיע מהר פארן", לרעה – דכתיב: "אל נקמות ה' אל נקמות הופיע".§ "רבי עקיבא אומר אומרה ברכה רביעית כו'". א"ל רב שמן בר אבא לר' יוחנן: מכדי אנשי כנסת הגדולה תקנו להם לישראל ברכות ותפלות קדושות והבדלות, נחזי(א) היכן תקון. – א"ל: בתחילה קבעוה בתפלה, העשירו – קבעוה על הכוס, חזרו והענו – קבעוה בתפלה, והם אמרו: המבדיל בתפלה צריך שיבדיל על הכוס. איתמר נמי, אמר ר' חייא בר אבא אמר רבי יוחנן: אנשי כנסת הגדולה תקנו להם לישראל ברכות ותפלות קדושות והבדלות. בתחלה קבעוה בתפלה, העשירו – קבעוה על הכוס, חזרו והענו – קבעוה בתפלה, והם אמרו: המבדיל בתפלה צריך שיבדיל על הכוס. איתמר נמי, רבה ורב יוסף דאמרי תרוייהו: המבדיל בתפלה צריך שיבדיל על הכוס. אמר *רבא, *ומותבינן אשמעתין: *טעה ולא הזכיר גבורות גשמים בתחיית המתים ושאלה בברכת השנים – מחזירין אותו, והבדלה בחונן הדעת – אין מחזירין אותו, מפני שיכול לאומרה על הכוס! – לא תימא "מפני שיכול לאומרה על הכוס" אלא אימא "מפני שאומרה על הכוס". איתמר נמי, אמר רבי בנימין בר יפת: שאל ר' יוסי את ר' יוחנן בצידן ואמרי לה, ר' שמעון בן יעקב דמן צור את ר' יוחנן, ואנא שמעית: המבדיל בתפלה, צריך שיבדיל על הכוס או לא? ואמר ליה: צריך שיבדיל על הכוס.§ איבעיא להו: המבדיל על הכוס, מהו שיבדיל בתפלה? – אמר רב נחמן בר יצחק: קל וחומר מתפלה: ומה תפלה דעיקר תקנתא היא – אמרי: המבדיל בתפלה צריך שיבדיל על הכוס; המבדיל על הכוס, דלאו עיקר תקנתא היא – לא כ"ש! תני ר' *אחא אריכא קמיה דרב חיננא: המבדיל בתפלה משובח יותר ממי שיבדיל על הכוס, ואם הבדיל בזו ובזו – *ינוחו לו ברכות על ראשו. הא גופא קשיא! אמרת, המבדיל בתפלה משובח יותר ממי שיבדיל על הכוס, אלמא: תפלה לחודה סגי, והדר תני: אם הבדיל בזו ובזו – ינוחו לו ברכות על ראשו, וכיון דנפיק ליה בחדא – איפטר, והויא *ברכה שאינה צריכה; ואמר רב ואיתימא ר"ל, ואמרי לה ר' יוחנן ור"ל דאמרי תרוייהו: כל המברך ברכה שאינה צריכה – עובר משום: "לא תשא"! אלא, אימא הכי: אם הבדיל בזו ולא הבדיל בזו – ינוחו לו ברכות על ראשו. בעא מיניה רב חסדא מרב ששת: טעה בזו ובזו* מהו? – אמר ליה: טעה בזו ובזו – חוזר לראש.
אמר

אבל עקרב פוסק. בירושלמי קאמר דאם היה נחש מרתיע לבא כנגדו – פוסק, לפי שבא כנגדו בכעס מתכוון להזיקו. ומיהו לא מצינו אם פסק שיחזור לראש, מדלא קאמר: ואם פסק חוזר לראש, אבל לתחלת ברכה מיהא יחזור. ואם טעה בג' ראשונות או בג' אחרונות – חוזר לתחלת הג': בגבות – בראשונות, ובעבודה – באחרונות, כדאמרינן לקמן בפרקין (דף לד.).
אמר

ל א ב מיי' פ"ו מהל' תפלה הלכה ט (סמג עשין יט) טוש"ע או"ח סי' קד סעיף ג:
לא ג מיי' פי"ג מהל' גירושין הלכה יז (סמג לאוין נ) טוש"ע אה"ע סי' יז סעי' כט:
לב ד ה ו מיי' פ"י מהל' תפלה סמג עשין יט טוש"ע או"ח סימן קד סעיף ז:
לג ו מיי' פ"ב מה' תפלה הלכה טו סמג שם טוש"ע או"ח סי' קיד סעי' א:
לד ז מיי' שם הל' טו סמג שם טוש"ע או"ח סי' קיז סעי' א:
לה ח מיי' שם הלכה ז יב סמג שם טוש"ע או"ח סימן רצד סעי' א:
לו י מיי' פ"י שם הלכה ח סמג שם טוש"ע או"ח סי' קיד סעי' ה:
לז כ מיי' שם הל' ט סמג שם טוש"ע או"ח סי' קיז סעי' ד:
לח ל מיי' שם הל' יד סמג שם טוש"ע או"ח סי' רצד סעיף א:
לט מ טור או"ח סי' רצד:
מ נ מיי' פכ"ט מהל' שבת הלכה טו סמג עשין כט טוש"ע או"ח סי' רצו סעי' ו ובסמ"ג רצו סעי' ח ד [רב אלפס לקמן פ"ח]:
מא ס טוש"ע או"ח סי' רצד סעיף א:

לעיל כט. נדה ח.

## רב נסים גאון

אפי' נחש כרוך על עקבו לא יפסיק אמר רב ששת לא שנו אלא נחש אבל עקרב פוסק. בתלמוד ארץ ישראל פירשו טעמא דמלתא ואמרי הא עקרב מפסיק למה משום דמחיא וחזרה ומחיא: באותה שעה אמרו אוי לו לאדם שפגע בו ערוד ואוי לו לערוד שפגע בו ר' חנינא בן דוסא. פירשו עוד בתלמוד ארץ ישראל ואמרו מאי עיסקא דהדין חברברה אלא כד הוא נכית לבר נשא אין בר נשא קדים למיא חברברה מיית ואין חברברה קדים למיא בר נשא מיית אמרון ליה תלמידוי רבי ולא הרגשתה יבא עלי ממה שהיה לבי מכוון בתפלתי לא הרגשתי אמר ר' יצחק בן אלעזר ברא לו הקב"ה מעיין מתחת כפות רגליו לקיים מה שנאמר (תהלים קמה) רצון יראיו יעשה: מזכירין גבורות גשמים בתחיית המתים. פירשו בתלמוד ארץ ישראל כשם שתחיית המתים חיים לעולם כך ירידת גשמים חיים לעולם ר' חייא בר אבא שמע ליה מן הדא קרייה (הושע ו) יחיינו מיומים ונדעה נרדפה לדעת את ה' ויבא כגשם לנו ובבראשית רבה דר' הושעיא (פרשה יג) דר' חייא בר אבא אמר שקולה כנגד תחיית המתים ר' אבא בריה דר' חייא בר אבא אף חכמים קבעו אותה בתחיית המתים בזו יד ובזו יד פתיחה ובזו פתיחה בזו יד (יחזקאל לז) היתה עלי יד ה' ובזו יד (תהלים קמה) פותח את ידך בזו פתיחה (יחזקאל לז) הנני פותח את קברותיכם ר' יודן בשם ר' אלעזר בר אבינה בזו שירה ובזו שירה (ישעיה מב) ירונו יושבי סלע ובזו שירה (תהלים סה) יתרועעו אף ישירו:

נ"א מוכן
[חולין קכז.]
[לעיל כח:]
יבמות קכא.
פסחים קיד.
[תוס' פ"ג]
תענית דף כ.
[דבורי רש"י נדפסו בטעות וצריך להפכם]
סנהד' צב. ע"ש
שמואל א ב
ישעיה כז
שמות טו
שם ע"ש
תהלים צד
דברים לג
[שבת קנ: ע"ש פסחי' קה: קז.]
נ"ל רבה [קדו' נ: וש"נ] תוספתא פ"ג
לעיל כו: כט.
[ע' שבת קיח. קיט:]
[שבת לה. מגיל' כה. ע"ש]
[יומא ע. סוטה מח.]
שמות כ
[עי' פירושו בכל"ש]

הגהות הב"ח (א) גמ' ניחזי היכן תיקון. נ"ב בפרק מי שמתו. דף כב ע"ב גבי טבילת בעלי קרי פריך תלמודא נמי הכי וע"ש בתוס':

גליון הש"ס גמ' נתן עקבו על פי החור. עיין יפה מראה בתענית (פרק ג סימן יז) ד"ה מפלתו:

אמר ליה רבינא לרבא: הלכתא מאי? – אמר ליה: כי קידוש, מה קידוש אף על גב דמקדש בצלותא מקדש אכסא, אף הבדלה נמי – אע"ג דמבדיל בצלותא מבדיל אכסא.§ "ר' אליעזר אומר: בהודאה". ר' זירא הוה רכיב חמרא, הוה קא שקיל ואזיל ר' חייא בר אבין בתריה. אמר ליה, ודאי דאמריתו משמיה דר' יוחנן: הלכה כר' אליעזר ביום טוב שחל להיות אחר השבת? – אמר ליה: [א] אין. *הלכה – מכלל דפליגי! –ולא פליגי?! והא פליגי רבנן! –אימר דפליגי רבנן – בשאר ימות השנה, ביום טוב שחל להיות אחר השבת מי פליגי? –והא פליג ר' עקיבא! *–אטו כל השנה כולה מי עבדינן כר' עקיבא, דהשתא ניקו ונעביד כוותיה?! כל השנה כולה מאי טעמא לא עבדינן כרבי עקיבא? – דתמני סרי תקון, תשסרי לא תקון, הכא נמי – שב תקון, תמני לא תקון! –אמר ליה: לאו "הלכה" אתמר, אלא "מטין" אתמר. [ב] *דאתמר, ר' יצחק בר אבדימי אמר משום רבנו: הלכה, ואמרי לה: מטין. ר' יוחנן אמר: מודים; ור' חייא בר אבא אמר: נראין. אמר ר' זירא: נקוט דרבי חייא בר אבא בידך. *דדייק וגמר שמעתא מפומא דמרה שפיר כרחבא דפומבדיתא. דאמר רחבא *אמר ר' יהודה: אהר הבית סטיו כפול היה, והיה סטיו לפנים מסטיו. אמר רב יוסף: אנא לא האי ידענא ולא האי ידענא, אלא מדרב ושמואל ידענא דתקינו לן מרגניתא בבבל: בותודיענו ה' אלהינו את משפטי צדקך ותלמדנו לעשות חקי רצונך, ותנחילנו זמני ששון וחגי נדבה [ד] ותורישנו קדושת שבת וכבוד מועד וחגיגת הרגל. בין קדושת שבת לקדושת יום טוב הבדלת ואת יום השביעי מששת ימי המעשה קדשת, הבדלת וקדשת את עמך ישראל בקדושתך, ותתן לנו וכו'.§ **מתני'** *האומר *ג"על קן ציפור יגיעו רחמיך" ו"על טוב יזכר שמך", ד"מודים" "מודים" –משתקין אותו.§ **גמ'** בשלמא "מודים" "מודים" משתקין אותו – משום דמיחזי כשתי רשויות, ו"על טוב יזכר שמך" – נמי משמע על הטובה ולא על הרעה, *ותנן: החייב אדם לברך על הרעה כשם שמברך על הטובה. אלא, "על קן צפור יגיעו רחמיך" מ"ט? – פליגי בה תרי אמוראי במערבא, רבי יוסי בר אבין ורבי יוסי בר זבידא; חד אמר: מפני שמטיל קנאה במעשה בראשית, וחד אמר: מפני שעושה מדותיו של הקדוש ברוך הוא רחמים, ואינן אלא גזרות. ההוא דנחית קמיה דרבה ואמר: אתה חסת על קן צפור אתה חוס ורחם עלינו. אמר רבה: כמה ידע האי צורבא מרבנן לרצויי למריה! –א"ל אביי: והא "משתקין אותו" תנן! *ורבה נמי – לחדודי לאביי הוא דבעי.§ ההוא דנחית קמיה דר' חנינא, ואמר: האל הגדול הגבור והנורא והאדיר והעזוז והיראוי החזק והאמיץ והודאי והנכבד. המתין לו עד דסיים, כי סיים א"ל: סיימתינהו לכולהו שבחי דמרך?! למה לי כולי האי? אנן הני תלת דאמרינן – אי לאו דאמרינהו משה רבנו באורייתא, ואתו אנשי כנסת הגדולה ותקנינהו בתפלה – לא הוינן יכולין למימר להו, ואת אמרת כולי האי ואזלת! משל, למלך בשר ודם שהיו לו אלף אלפים דינרי זהב, והיו מקלסין אותו בשל כסף, והלא גנאי הוא לו.§ ואמר *רבי חנינא: *זהכל בידי שמים – חוץ מיראת שמים, שנאמר: °"ועתה ישראל מה ה' אלהיך שואל מעמך כי אם ליראה". אטו יראת שמים מילתא זוטרתא היא?! והא"ר חנינא משום ר' שמעון בן יוחי: אין לו להקב"ה בבית גנזיו אלא אוצר של יראת שמים, שנאמר: °"יראת ה' היא אוצרו"! – אין, לגבי משה מילתא זוטרתא היא. דאמר ר' חנינא: משל, לאדם שמבקשים ממנו כלי גדול ויש לו – דומה עליו ככלי קטן, קטן ואין לו – דומה עליו ככלי גדול.§ "מודים מודים – משתקין אותו". אמר ר' *זירא, חכל האומר "שמע" "שמע" – כאומר "מודים" "מודים" דמי. מיתיבי: הקורא את שמע וכופלה – הרי זה מגונה. מגונה הוא דהוי, שתוקי לא משתקינן ליה! – לא קשיא: הא – דאמר מילתא מילתא ותני לה, והא – דאמר פסוקא פסוקא ותני ליה. אמר ליה רב פפא לאביי: ודילמא מעיקרא לא כוון דעתיה, ולבסוף כוון דעתיה? –אמר ליה: חברותא

**רש"י**

הלכתא מאי. המבדיל בתפלה צריך שיבדיל על הכוס, או לא: ביום טוב שחל להיות אחר השבת. שאין מתפללין אתה חונן: ה"ג הלכה מכלל דפליגי, ולא פליגי, והא פליגי רבנן אימר דפליגי רבנן בשאר ימות השנה בי"ט שחל להיות אחר השבת, מי פליגי והא פליג ר"ע אטו כל השנה מי עבדינן כר"ע דהשתא נעביד וכו' – והכי *פריך: א"ל רבי זירא: [ג] הלכה מכלל דפליגי?! בתמיה, ופריך הגמרא: ולא פליגי? והא פליגי רבנן וכו': והא פליג ר' עקיבא. לומרה ברכה רביעית לעצמה, ואצטרי' למימר הלכה כר"א לאפוקי מדר"ע: אטו כל השנה כולה מי עבדינן כר"ע דהשתא נעביד כוותיה. דאצטריך למימר הלכה כר"א: הלכה. מ"ד הלכה – דרשינן לה בפרקין, ומ"ד מטין – מדרש לא דרשינן ברבים, אבל אורויי מורינן ליחיד לעשות כר"א בי"ט שחל להיות בא' בשבת, ומ"ד נראין – אורויי נמי לא מורינן, ואי עביד לא מהדרינן עובדא: מודים. חכמים לר"א בי"ט שחל להיות אחר השבת: נקוט דר' חייא בר אבא בידך. שהוא מדקדק בלשון רבו, וקובע בו סימנים שלא יתחלף לו נראין במטין או במודים: כרחבא. שהיה מדקדק בלשון רבו ואומר סטיו כפול היה ואע"פ שבלשון משנה קורהו אצטבא, בפסחים ובסוכה על גב האצטבא, הוא דקדק בלשון רבו ולא אמר אצטבא כפולה היתה. יש פותרין הא דרחבא מדאמר ר' יהודה דדייק ספיקי דרבוותיה אי מדרבי יהודה אי מדרב יהודה. וקשיא לי בגוה טובא, חדא – דרחבא לא ראה רבי יהודה מימיו, לא רבי יהודה ברבי אלעאי ולא ר' יהודה *נשיאה. ועוד: כולהו אמוראי נמי דייקו לומר דבר בשם אומרו. ועוד: ליכא למימר מהא דדייק לישנא דשמעתא, אלא ספיקי דרבוותא: סטיו כפול. אצטבאות זו לפנים מזו, בהיקף עגול, לישב שם: לא האי ידענא כו'. לא נראין ולא מודים ולא מטים: ותודיענו. לומר במקום ותתן לנו ולכשיגיע בין קדושת שבת לקדושת י"ט וכו' הבדלת וקדשת את עמך ישראל בקדושתך יאמר ותתן לנו ה' אלהינו מועדים לשמחה וכו', ומסיים מקדש ישראל והזמנים: בתפלתו: מתני' האומר. על קן צפור יגיעו רחמיך. אנשים שהיו מראים עצמם כמתכוונים להעמיק בלשון תחנונים, ואומרים: רחום וחנון אתה, ועל קן צפור יגיעו רחמיך, שאמרת לשלח את האם. או שאומר: על טוב שאתה עושה לנו יזכר שמך, או שאומר: מודים מודים – משתקין אותו: גמ' שמטיל קנאה. לומר: על אלה חס, ולא על שאר בריותיו: מדותיו. מצותיו, והוא לא לרחמים עשה, אלא להטיל על ישראל חקי גזרותיו; להודיע שהם עבדיו ושומרי מצותיו וגזרות חוקותיו, אף בדברי' שיש לשטן ולגוים להשיב עליהם, ולומר מה צורך במצוה זו: ורבה נמי לחדודי לאביי הוא דבעי. שישיב לו מה שהשיב: אי לאו דאמרינהו משה. האל הגדול הגבור והנורא אשר לא ישא פנים ולא יקח שוחד (דברים י): ותקנינהו בתפלה. כשהתפלל עזרא על מעל הגולה, בספר עזרא (נחמיה ט): הכל בידי שמים. כל הבא על האדם ביד הקב"ה; כגון ארוך, קצר, עני, עשיר, חכם, שוטה, לבן, שחור, הכל בידי שמים. הוא אבל צדיק ורשע אינו בא על ידי שמים, את זו מסר בידו של אדם, ונתן לפניו שני דרכים, והוא יבחר לו יראת שמים: מילתא מילתא ותני לה. כל תיבה ותיבה חוזר ושונה – מגונה הוי, שתוקי לא משתקינן ליה, שאין זה דומה למקבל עליו שתי מלכיות, אלא למתלוצץ. אמר פסוק שלם ותני ליה – משתקינן ליה, דמחזי כשתי רשויות:
חברותא

**עין משפט נר מצוה**

מב א מיי' פ"ה מהל' בית הבחירה הל' א:
מג ב מיי' פ"ב מהל' תפלה הלכה יב סמג עשין יט טוש"ע או"ח סי' תצא סעיף ב:
[נ"ל פירושא]
מד ג מיי' פ"ט מהל' תפלה הל' ז סמג שם:
מה ד מיי' שם הלכה ד סמג שם טוש"ע או"ח סימן קכא סעיף ב:
מו ה מיי' פ"י מהלכות ברכות הלכה ג סמג עשין כז טוש"ע או"ח סימן רכב סעיף ג:
מז ו מיי' פ"ט מהל' תפלה הל' ז טוש"ע או"ח סימן קיג סעיף ט:
מח ז מיי' פ"ה מהל' תשובה הל' א:
מט ח מיי' פ"ב מהל' ק"ש הלכה יא סמג עשין יח טוש"ע או"ח סי' סא סעיף ט:

## רב נסים גאון

**אמר** ר' זירא נקוט דר' חייא בר אבא בידך דגמר שמעתתא מפומיה דרביה. איתא בפרק כיצד מברכין על הפירות (דף לח) מה ענין בנימין בר יפת אצל ר' חייא בר אבא ר' חייא בר אבא דייק שמעתא מפומיה דרביה ר' חייא בר אבא כל ל' יומין הוה מהדר לתלמודיה קמיה דר' יוחנן רביה ואית דכוותה בפ' כיסוי הדם (דף פו) דשחיטת חולין ובפ' המביא אשם תלוי דכריתות (דף כז):
**מודים** מודים משתקין אותו. בתלמוד ארץ ישראל נתנו הפרש בזה הדבר ואמרו הדה דאיתמר בצבור אבל ביחיד תחנונים הם ובגמ' דמגילה (ירושלמי פרק ד הלכה י) אמרו ודכוותה אמן אמן שמע שמע:

[ברב אלפס וברא"ש סדר המשנה דהכא בזה"ל האומר יברכוך טובים הרי זה דרך המינות האומר על קן צפור וכו' וע"ש פירש"י ורבינו יונה וכן במה שפי' הרא"ש ודע שכסדר הזה נשנית ג"כ במשנה דמגילה כה. מכון ממש]

## הגהות הגר"א

[א] גמ' (א"ל אין) תא"מ: [ב] צ"ל איתמר: [ג] רש"י ד"ה ה"ג כו' (א"ל ר' זירא) תא"מ: [ד] גמ' (ותנחילנו זמני ששון וחגי נדבה) תא"מ ונ"ב ברמב"ם ל"ג לה:

**תורה אור**
נדה טז: מגלה כה.
דברים י

## גליון הש"ס

**גמ'** אלא מטין אתמר. עיין תשובת דבר שמואל (סימן קיד):
**במתני'** האומר על קן צפור. ע' זוה"ק פ' אמור על פסוק אדם ובהמה תושיע ה'. ובמדרש רבה פרשת כי תצא (פ"ו):

**מסורת הש"ס**
[שבת קו: ושם
[לעיל כט.]
עירובין מו:
[לקמן לח: פסר
פסחים יג: נב:
מגילה כה.
לקמן דף נד. [ו
[עירובין יג. נזיר נט: זבחים מג: נדה ל: מח
[ע' תוס' מגילה
ישעיה לג
מגילה שם [סוט

חברותא כלפי שמיא. מנהג שנוהג אדם בחברו ינהג אצל המקום, ולא יזהר בתפלתו: מחינן ליה. כלומר: מלמדין אותו שיכוין ומכין אותו אם ירגיל בכך: מרזפתא. קורנס, "ותשם את המקבת בידה" מתרגמינן "מרזפתא" (שופטים ד): מתני' ולא יהא סרבן באותה שעה. לפי שאר יורדין לפני התיבה כשאומרים לו "לך רד" צריך לסרב פעם אחת, כלומר איני כדאי לכך, כדאמרי' לקמן בשמעתין. אבל זה – לא יסרב, מפני שגנאי הוא שתהא התפלה מופסקת כל כך: מתחלת הברכה שטעה זה. אם דלג א' מן הברכות ואמר אחרת, ואינו יודע לשוב ולאחוז סדרו – יתחיל העובר תחתיו אותה ברכה שדלג זה, ואומר משם ולהלן: לא יענה אמן אחר הכהנים. הש"ץ בסוף כל ברכה וברכה: מפני הטירוף. שלא תטרף דעתו ויטעה. לפי שש"צ הוא צריך להתחיל ברכה שניה, ולומר לפני הכהנים כל תיבה ותיבה, כדאמרינן במס' סוטה (דף לט:). ובענותו אמן לא יוכל לכוין מהר ולהתחיל בברכה שלאחריו: אם אין שם כהן אלא הוא. החזן: לא ישא את כפיו. שמא לא יוכל לחזור לתפלתו לדעת לכוין להתחיל ב"שים שלום", שדעתו מטורפת מאימת הצבור: ואם הבטחתו. כלומר: אם בטוח הוא שאין דעתו מטורפת מאימת הצבור: גמ' יסרב. כשאומרים לו לך, יעשה עצמו כלא רוצה, כלומר: איני כדאי: שהקדיחתו. לשון שריפה, כמו כי אש קדחה באפי (דברים לב): מהבהב. כלומר: מזמין עצמו כמו נגער לעמוד: אין להן סדר. ואם דלג ברכה אחת ואח"כ נזכר בה – אומרה, אף שלא במקומה: מתחלת הברכה שטעה זה. וממילא משתמע דגומר ממנה והלאה, אלמא על סדרה צריך לחזור ולאומרה: חדא ברכתא נינהו. ודקתני מתני' מתחלת הברכה שטעה זה – היינו אתה חונן: ונפטר. נוטל רשות: א"צ להזכיר שמו. של חולה: תחלה וסוף. במודים, ולך נאה להודות:

תורה אור

*חברותא כלפי שמיא מי איכא?! אי לא כוון דעתיה מעיקרא – מחינן ליה במרזפתא דנפחא עד דמכוין דעתיה.§ מתני' (*האומר יברכוך טובים – הרי זה דרכי מינות.) [א]העובר לפני התיבה וטעה – יעבור אחר תחתיו, ולא [ב]יהא סרבן באותה שעה. מהיכן [ג]הוא מתחיל? מתחלת הברכה שטעה *זה. [ד]העובר לפני התיבה לא יענה אמן אחר הכהנים מפני הטרוף, [ה]ואם אין שם כהן אלא הוא – לא ישא את כפיו. *ואם הבטחתו שהוא נושא את כפיו וחוזר לתפלתו – רשאי. גמ' ת"ר: [ו]העובר לפני התיבה – צריך לסרב, ואם אינו מסרב – דומה לתבשיל שאין בו מלח, ואם מסרב יותר מדאי – דומה לתבשיל שהקדיחתו מלח. כיצד הוא עושה – פעם ראשונה יסרב, שניה *מהבהב, שלישית – פושט את רגליו ויורד. *ת"ר: שלשה רובן קשה ומיעוטן יפה, ואלו הן: שאור, ומלח, וסרבנות.§ אמר רב הונא: [ז]טעה בשלש ראשונות – חוזר לראש, באמצעיות – חוזר ל"אתה חונן", באחרונות – חוזר ל"עבודה"; ורב אסי אמר: אמצעיות אין להן סדר. מתיב רב ששת: "מהיכן הוא חוזר – מתחלת הברכה שטעה זה", *תיובתא דרב הונא! –אמר לך רב הונא: אמצעיות – כולהו חדא ברכתא נינהו. אמר רב יהודה: [ח]לעולם אל ישאל אדם צרכיו לא בשלש ראשונות, ולא בשלש אחרונות, אלא באמצעיות. דא"ר חנינא: ראשונות – דומה לעבד שמסדר שבח לפני רבו, אמצעיות – דומה לעבד שמבקש פרס מרבו, אחרונות – דומה לעבד שקבל פרס מרבו [ט]ונפטר והולך לו.§ *ת"ר: מעשה בתלמיד אחד *שירד לפני התיבה בפני רבי אליעזר והיה מאריך יותר מדאי. א"ל תלמידיו: רבינו, כמה ארכן הוא זה! – אמר להם: כלום מאריך יותר ממשה רבינו?! דכתיב ביה: (דברים ט) "את ארבעים היום ואת ארבעים הלילה וגו'". שוב מעשה בתלמיד א' שירד לפני התיבה בפני ר"א והיה מקצר יותר מדאי. א"ל תלמידיו: כמה קצרן הוא זה! א"ל: כלום מקצר יותר ממשה רבינו?! דכתיב: (במדבר יב) "אל נא רפא נא לה". א"ר יעקב אמר רב חסדא: כל המבקש רחמים על חבירו אין צריך להזכיר שמו, שנאמר: "אל נא רפא נא לה", ולא קמדכר שמה דמרים.§ ת"ר: * [י]אלו ברכות שאדם שוחה בהן: באבות תחלה וסוף, בהודאה תחלה וסוף, ואם בא לשוח בסוף כל ברכה וברכה ובתחלת כל ברכה וברכה – מלמדין אותו שלא ישחה. אר"ש בן פזי אריב"ל משום בר קפרא: הדיוט – כמו שאמרנו. כהן

*אמר 'מודים מודים' – משתקין אותו. ירושלמי: הדא דתימא – בצבור, אבל ביחיד – תחנונים הם: *אמר פסוקא וכפליה. פי' בקונטרס: משתקין אותו דמחזי כעושה ב' רשויות. ובה"ג ובפר"ח מפרש איפכא: פסוקא – אין משתקין אותו, מיהו מגונה הוי. אך לשון הגמרא לא משמע כפי'. ואותן בני אדם שאומרים ב' או ג' פעמים שמע ישראל ביוה"כ – משתקין אותם לפירש"י, ולפר"ח – מגונה מיהא הוי. או שמא אין לחוש רק כשקורא ק"ש בעונתה, ומקבל עליו עול מלכות שמים, ומ"מ טוב שלא לומר, אך מה שאומרים "ה' הוא האלהים" ז' פעמים ביוה"כ ויום ערבה, כנגד ז' רקיעים משבחים לבורא שהוא דר למעלה מז' – מנהג כשר הוא. וגם מצינו בקרא שתי פעמים "ה' הוא האלהים" גבי אליהו (מלכים א יח): מהיכן הוא מתחיל? מתחלת הברכה שטעה בה. ירושלמי: בטיטי אשתתק באופנים, אתון שיילון לר' בון, אמר להו בשם ריב"ל: זה שעבר תחתיו יתחיל ממקום שפסק. ופריך: והתנן מתחיל מתחלת הברכה שטעה בה! אמר להו: מכיון דעניתון קדושת השם, כמי שהוא תחלת הברכה דמי: לא יענה אמן אחר הכהנים מפני הטרוף. תימה: תיפוק ליה דמפסיק תפלה אם עונה אמן! וי"ל: מאחר שלא אמר האי טעמא, ש"מ דעניית אמן לא חשיב ליה הפסקה – מאחר שצורך תפלה הוא. אבל לקרות כהנים לדוכן אומר ר"ת שאין ש"צ יכול לקוראם, דחשיב הפסקה לתפלה אם קוראם, אלא אחד מבני הקהל קוראם. והא דאמרינן בסוטה פ' "אלו נאמרים" (ד' לח.): לשנים קורא כהנים וכו' – לאו אשליח צבור קאי, אלא אחזן. כדתניא בספרי (פרשת נשא) "אמור להם" – מלמד שהחזן אומר להם: אמרו. וחזן לאו היינו שליח צבור; דחזן היינו המתעסק בצרכי צבור. וכן משמע נמי בסוטה (ד' לט:), דלאו אשליח צבור קאי; דמעיקרא קאמר "אין הכהנים רשאין להתחיל בברכה עד שיכלה הדבור מפי הקורא", פי': הקורא 'כהנים' ואח"כ אומר: אין שליח צבור רשאי וכו', משמע דשנים הם. ויש שהיו רוצים לומר דכמו כן אין ש"צ רשאי להקרות 'יברכך' לכהנים, דכמו כן הוי הפסקה. אמנם רבינו יהודה פי' דבהדיא יש במדרש "טעמי יתרות וחסרות": "אמור להם" – מלמד ששליח צבור אומר להם על כל דבור ודבור. וכן יש שרוצים להתיר לשליח צבור עצמו לקרות 'כהנים', אפילו לפי' ר"ת. דמה דפי' דהויא הפסקה – היינו דוקא בימיהם, מיד כשסיימו ברכת הודאה לא היו אומרים: "או"א אבותינו ברכנו בברכה", כדמשמע בסוטה (שם) דקאמר: אין הקורא רשאי לקרות כהנים עד שיכלה אמן מפי הצבור, פי': אמן שעונין בסיום ברכת הודאה, אלמא משמע שלא היו אומרים אלא כהנים מיד. אבל עכשיו, שהורגלו לומר 'אלהינו' בלשון ברכה ותפלה – אין זה הפסק, דלא גרע מעניית אמן דהכא דלא חשיבא הפסק, כדפרישית*: אמצעיות אין להן סדר. פי' בקונטרס: ואם דלג ברכה אחת ואחר כך נזכר בה שלא במקומה – אומרה במקום שנזכר. ולא נהירא; דהא תנן במגילה (פ"ב ד' יז.): "הקורא את המגילה למפרע לא יצא", ותניא (שם): וכן בהלל, וכן בק"ש, וכן בתפלה! לכך נראה כפירוש רשב"ם ורב אלפס, ד"אין להן סדר" דקאמר – היינו שיתחיל במקום שדלג הברכה, ומשם ואילך יאמר הכל על הסדר, אבל ודאי לא יתחיל ב'אתה חונן' כמו בג' ראשונות וג' אחרונות שחוזר לראש. וראיה, מדתניא בתוספתא דמכילתין: *הקורא את שמע והשמיט בה פסוק אחד – לא יקרא אותו פסוק בפני עצמו, אלא מתחיל מאותו פסוק ואילך וגומר עד סופה. ותניא נמי בפ"ב דמגילה (ד' יח:) שאם השמיט פסוק א' במגילה – שקורא על הסדר מאותו פסוק ואילך, והתם משוי תפלה למגילה לענין הך מילתא כדפרישית. ובה"ג פסק כרב אסי, דאמר אמצעיות אין להם סדר; חדא – דרב הונא כתלמיד לגבי רב אסי כדאמרינן בכמה מקומות אמר רב הונא אמר רב אסי: ועוד – דלרב הונא צריך לדחוק ולשנויי מתניתין דכולהו חדא ברכתא נינהו, ואשנויי דחיקי לא ניקום ונסמוך. ועוד – דרב אסי ורב ששת קיימי בחד שיטתא, ועוד – דבשל סופרים הלך אחר המיקל. וא"כ אדם שטעה ודלג ברכה אחת באמצעיות, או שלא אמר 'המלך המשפט' בין ר"ה ליוה"כ, דקי"ל בפ"ק (דף יב:) דמחזירין אותו – לא יחזור ל'אתה חונן', אלא לאותה ברכה שדלג, ומשם ואילך יאמר על הסדר, כדפי' רשב"ס. והיכא שטעה בג' ראשונות: כגון שטעה בחתימתן, או לא הזכיר בין ר"ה ליוה"כ בברכת אבות, 'זכרנו' או בחתיית המתים 'מי כמוך', או שלא אמר 'המלך הקדוש' חוזר לראשונה. והיכא שטעה בשלש אחרונות: כגון שטעה כמו כן בחתימתן, או שלא הזכיר בין ראש השנה ליוה"כ בשים שלום 'בספר חיים טובים', או 'וכתוב לחיים טובים' בהודאה – חוזר ל'עבודה'. וטעמא: דכיון שכולה שבח – הוי כברכה א'. ותענית צבור שש"צ קובע ברכה לעצמו, שאומר 'עננו' בין 'גואל' ל'רופא', אם שכחה ונזכר בה קודם סיום תפלה – אין מחזירין אותו, כיון שהיה צריך לחזור ולומר על הסדר כפי' רשב"ס א"כ הויא ברכה לבטלה אם מחזירין אותו. אבל לפי' הקונטרס היה אומרה במקום שנזכר, ואין כאן ברכה לבטלה: אל ישאל אדם צרכיו לא בג' ראשונות ולא בג' אחרונות. פי' ר"ח ורבינו האי: דוקא ליחיד, אבל צרכי צבור – שואלין. ולכך אנו אומרים 'זכרנו' וקרובץ ו'יעלה ויבא' בהם. ותדע דלדוקא יחיד קאמר, שהרי עיקר ברכות אחרונות צרכי צבור הם*: מלמדין אותו שלא ישחה. וא"ת: וישחה, ומה בכך! וי"ל: שלא יבא לעקור דברי חכמים, שלא יאמרו כל אחד מחמיר כמו שהוא רוצה, ואין כאן תקנת חכמים. וחיישינן[א] ליוהרא:

קידה

עין משפט נר מצוה

[שייך לדף לג:]

[ג"ז שייך לשם]

נ א מיי' פ"י מהלכות תפלה הלכה ג סמג עשין יט טוש"ע או"ח סי' קכו סעיף ב:

נא ב מיי' שם טוש"ע שם ובסי' נג סי"ז:

נב ג מיי' שם הלכה ד סמג שם טוש"ע שם סימן קיט סעיף ג ובסי' קכו סעיף ב:

נג ד מיי' פי"ד מהל' נשיאת כפים הל' ה סמג עשין כ טוש"ע או"ח סימן קכח סעיף יט:

נד ה מיי' שם פט"ו הלכה י טוש"ע שם סעיף כ:

נה ו טוש"ע או"ח סי' נג סעיף טז:

נו ז מיי' פ"י מהל' תפלה הלכה א ד סמג עשין יט טוש"ע או"ח סי' קכו סעיף ב:

נז ח מיי' פ"א שם הלכה ד ופ"ו שם הל' ג סמג שם טוש"ע או"ח סי' קיב סעיף א:

נח ט מיי' פ"ה שם הל' יא סמג עשין יט טוש"ע או"ח סי' קכג סעיף א:

נט י מיי' פ"ה שם הל' יוד סמג שם טוש"ע או"ח סי' קיג סעיף א:

## רב נסים גאון

תנו רבנן אלו ברכות שאדם שוחה בהן כו'. פי' בתלמוד ארץ ישראל בפ' מאימתי קורין הכל שוחין בהודאה עם שליח צבור ר' זעירא אמר ובלבד במודים כו' תני ובלבד שלא ישוח יותר מדאי ובגמ' דד' אבות נזיקין (בבא קמא דף טז) איתא שדרו של אדם לסוף (ע') [שבע] שנה נעשה נחש והני מילי הוא דלא כרע במודים ובגמ' דסוטה בפ' אלו נאמרים בכל לשון (דף מ) אמרי בזמן ששליח צבור אומר מודים העם מה הם אומרים:

## הגהות הב"ח

(א) תוס' ד"ה מלמדין וכו' וחיישינן ליוהרא. נ"ב כלומר ועוד חיישינן ליוהרא:

[וע"ע תוס' מנחות מד. ד"ה כל כהן כו']

## גליון הש"ס

רש"י ד"ה מתחלת הברכה וכו' וממילא כו'. עיין בקרבן נתנאל שמגלה גירסא בקלף. תיובתא דרב אסי לימא תהוי תיובתא דר"ה אמר לך ר"ה: גמ' אר"ש בן פזי אריב"ל. במדרש רבה בראשית פרשה לט איתא ריב"ש בשם ריב"ל אמר כ"ג תחלת כל ברכה שוחה והמלך בתחלת כל ברכה ובסוף כל ברכה שוחה. רבי סימון בשם ריב"ל אמר המלך משהיה כורע לא היה נזקף:

מסורת הש"ס

מגילה דף כה.

שם [ועמ"ש לעיל לג: גירסת הרי"ף ורא"ש]

נ"א בה

[סוטה לח:]

[פירוש יענוש בראשון]

גיטין ע. ע"ש

[נ"ל תיובתא דרב אסי לימא תהוי תיובתא דרב הונא וכו' כך היה הגירסא לפני רש"י וע' בסוף ס' קרבן נתנאל]

מכילתא דר"י פרשת בשלח

[לפי שמצוה להתפלל במקום נמוך כדאיתא לעיל י: הלכך קתני ירד לפני רש"י ר"ה לב. ד"ה ירד]

במדבר יב

[תוספתא פ"א]

[פ"ב]

[וע"ע תוס' ע"ג ת. ד"ה אם בא]

עין משפט
נר מצוה

ס א מיי' פ"ה מהלכות תפלה הלכה י:
סא ב מיי' שם הל' יג סמג עשין יט:
סב ג מיי' שם הל' יד ופ"ט שם הלכה ה טוש"ע או"ח סי' קלא סעיף א:
סג ד מיי' פ"י מהלכות תפלה סמג שם טור שו"ע או"ח סימן קא סעיף א:

[כוונת התו' מהא דאמרי' לעיל כו: ואין שיחה אלא תפלה]

סד ה מיי' פ"ו מהלכות דעות הלכה ב:
סה ו מיי' פ"ח מהל' תשובה הל' ז:
סו ז מיי' פ"ט מהלכות תשובה הל' ב ופי"ב מהל' מלכים הל' ב:
סז ח מיי' פ"ז מהל' תשובה הלכה ד:
סח ט מיי' פ"ה מהל' תפלה הלכה ו סמג עשין יט טוש"ע או"ח סי' צ סעיף ד:
סט י טוש"ע שם סעי' ה:
ע כ מיי' פ"ב מהל' תשובה הל' ה טוש"ע או"ח סי' תרז סעיף ב:

תורה אור

כֹּהֵן גָּדוֹל – בְּסוֹף כָּל בְּרָכָה וּבְרָכָה, וְהַמֶּלֶךְ – תְּחִלַּת כָּל בְּרָכָה וּבְרָכָה וְסוֹף כָּל בְּרָכָה וּבְרָכָה. אָמַר רַבִּי יִצְחָק בַּר נַחְמָנִי, לְדִידִי מְפָרְשָׁא לִי מִינֵּיהּ דריב"ל: אהֶדְיוֹט – כְּמוֹ שֶׁאָמַרְנוּ, כֹּהֵן גָּדוֹל – תְּחִלַּת [א] כָּל בְּרָכָה וּבְרָכָה, הַמֶּלֶךְ – כֵּיוָן שֶׁכָּרַע, שׁוּב אֵינוֹ זוֹקֵף, שֶׁנֶּאֱמַר: °"וַיְהִי כְּכַלּוֹת שְׁלֹמֹה לְהִתְפַּלֵּל וגו' קָם מִלִּפְנֵי מִזְבַּח ה' מִכְּרֹעַ עַל בִּרְכָּיו" (מלכים א ח). ת"ר: *בקִידָּה – עַל אַפַּיִם, שֶׁנֶּאֱמַר: °"וַתִּקֹּד בַּת שֶׁבַע אַפַּיִם אֶרֶץ" (שם א), כְּרִיעָה – עַל בִּרְכַּיִם, שֶׁנֶּאֱמַר: "מִכְּרֹעַ עַל בִּרְכָּיו", הִשְׁתַּחֲוָאָה – זוֹ פְּשׁוּט יָדַיִם וְרַגְלַיִם, שֶׁנֶּאֱמַר: °"הֲבוֹא נָבוֹא אֲנִי וְאִמְּךָ וְאַחֶיךָ לְהִשְׁתַּחֲוֹת לְךָ אָרְצָה" (בראשית לז). *אָמַר רַב חִיָּיא בְּרֵיהּ דְּרַב הוּנָא: חֲזֵינָא לְהוּ לְאַבַּיֵּי וְרָבָא גדְּמַצְלוּ אַצְלוּיֵי.§ תָּנֵי חֲדָא: הַכּוֹרֵעַ בְּהוֹדָאָה הֲרֵי זֶה מְשׁוּבָּח; וְתַנְיָא אִידָךְ: הֲרֵי זֶה מְגוּנֶּה! לָא קַשְׁיָא: הָא – בַּתְּחִלָּה, הָא – לְבַסּוֹף. רָבָא כָּרַע בְּהוֹדָאָה תְּחִלָּה וָסוֹף. אָמְרִי לֵיהּ רַבָּנַן: אַמַּאי קָא עָבֵיד מָר הָכִי? – אֲמַר לְהוּ: חֲזֵינָא לְרַב נַחְמָן דְּכָרַע, וַחֲזֵינָא לֵיהּ לְרַב שֵׁשֶׁת דְּקָא עָבַד הָכִי. – וְהַתַּנְיָא: הַכּוֹרֵעַ בְּהוֹדָאָה הֲרֵי זֶה מְגוּנֶּה! – הַהִיא – בְּהוֹדָאָה שֶׁבְּהַלֵּל. – וְהַתַּנְיָא: הַכּוֹרֵעַ בְּהוֹדָאָה וּבְהוֹדָאָה שֶׁל הַלֵּל הֲרֵי זֶה מְגוּנֶּה! – כִּי תַּנְיָא הַהִיא – בְּהוֹדָאָה דְּבִרְכַּת הַמָּזוֹן.§ **מתני'** הַמִּתְפַּלֵּל וְטָעָה – סִימָן רַע לוֹ, וְאִם שְׁלִיחַ צִבּוּר הוּא – סִימָן רַע לְשׁוֹלְחָיו, מִפְּנֵי *שֶׁשְּׁלוּחוֹ שֶׁל אָדָם כְּמוֹתוֹ. אָמְרוּ עָלָיו עַל ר' חֲנִינָא בֶּן דּוֹסָא, שֶׁהָיָה מִתְפַּלֵּל עַל הַחוֹלִים וְאוֹמֵר, "זֶה חַי וְזֶה מֵת". אָמְרוּ לוֹ: מִנַּיִן אַתָּה יוֹדֵעַ? אָמַר לָהֶם: אִם שְׁגוּרָה תְּפִלָּתִי בְּפִי – יוֹדֵעַ אֲנִי שֶׁהוּא מְקוּבָּל, וְאִם לָאו – יוֹדֵעַ אֲנִי שֶׁהוּא מְטוֹרָף.§ **גמ'** אֵהַיָּיא? א"ר חִיָּיא אָמַר רַב סָפְרָא מִשּׁוּם חַד דְּבֵי רַבִּי: בָּאָבוֹת. אִיכָּא דְּמַתְנֵי לַהּ אַבָּרַיְיתָא: הַמִּתְפַּלֵּל דצָרִיךְ שֶׁיְּכַוֵּין אֶת לִבּוֹ בְּכוּלָּן, וְאִם אֵינוֹ יָכוֹל לְכַוֵּין בְּכוּלָּן – יְכַוֵּין אֶת לִבּוֹ בְּאַחַת; א"ר חִיָּיא אָמַר רַב סָפְרָא מִשּׁוּם חַד דְּבֵי רַבִּי: בָּאָבוֹת. "אָמְרוּ עָלָיו עַל רַבִּי חֲנִינָא וכו'". מְנָא הָנֵי מִילֵּי? א"ר יְהוֹשֻׁעַ בֶּן לֵוִי, דְּאָמַר קְרָא: °"בּוֹרֵא נִיב שְׂפָתַיִם שָׁלוֹם שָׁלוֹם לָרָחוֹק וְלַקָּרוֹב אָמַר ה' וּרְפָאתִיו". א"ר חִיָּיא בַּר אַבָּא *א"ר יוֹחָנָן: הכָּל הַנְּבִיאִים כּוּלָּן לֹא נִתְנַבְּאוּ אֶלָּא לְמַשִּׂיא בִּתּוֹ לְתַלְמִיד חָכָם וּלְעוֹשֶׂה פְּרַקְמַטְיָא לת"ח וּלְמְהַנֶּה ת"ח מִנְּכָסָיו, אֲבָל תַּלְמִידֵי חֲכָמִים עַצְמָן – °"עַיִן לֹא רָאָתָה אֱלֹהִים זוּלָתְךָ יַעֲשֶׂה לִמְחַכֵּה לוֹ". וְאָמַר רַבִּי חִיָּיא בַּר אַבָּא אָמַר רַבִּי יוֹחָנָן: וכָּל הַנְּבִיאִים כּוּלָּן לֹא נִתְנַבְּאוּ אֶלָּא לִימוֹת הַמָּשִׁיחַ, אֲבָל לָעוֹלָם הַבָּא – "עַיִן לֹא רָאָתָה אֱלֹהִים זוּלָתְךָ". וּפְלִיגָא דִּשְׁמוּאֵל, *דְּאָמַר שְׁמוּאֵל: זאֵין בֵּין העוה"ז לִימוֹת הַמָּשִׁיחַ אֶלָּא שִׁעְבּוּד מַלְכֻיּוֹת בִּלְבַד, שֶׁנֶּאֱמַר: °"כִּי לֹא יֶחְדַּל אֶבְיוֹן מִקֶּרֶב הָאָרֶץ". וא"ר חִיָּיא בַּר אַבָּא א"ר יוֹחָנָן: כָּל הַנְּבִיאִים כּוּלָּן לֹא נִתְנַבְּאוּ אֶלָּא לְבַעֲלֵי תְשׁוּבָה, אֲבָל צַדִּיקִים גְּמוּרִים – "עַיִן לֹא רָאָתָה אֱלֹהִים זוּלָתְךָ". וּפְלִיגָא דר' אֲבָהוּ, דא"ר רַבִּי אֲבָהוּ: מָקוֹם חשֶׁבַּעֲלֵי תְשׁוּבָה עוֹמְדִין – צַדִּיקִים גְּמוּרִים אֵינָם עוֹמְדִין, שֶׁנֶּאֱמַר: °"שָׁלוֹם שָׁלוֹם לָרָחוֹק וְלַקָּרוֹב". לָרָחוֹק בְּרֵישָׁא וַהֲדַר לַקָּרוֹב. וְרַבִּי יוֹחָנָן אָמַר לָךְ: מַאי "רָחוֹק" – שֶׁהָיָה רָחוֹק מִדְּבַר עֲבֵירָה מֵעִיקָּרָא, וּמַאי "קָרוֹב" – שֶׁהָיָה קָרוֹב לִדְבַר עֲבֵירָה(א) וְנִתְרַחֵק מִמֶּנּוּ הַשְׁתָּא. *מַאי "עַיִן לֹא רָאָתָה?" אָמַר רַבִּי יְהוֹשֻׁעַ בֶּן לֵוִי: זֶה יַיִן הַמְשׁוּמָּר בַּעֲנָבָיו מִשֵּׁשֶׁת יְמֵי בְרֵאשִׁית; רַבִּי *שְׁמוּאֵל בַּר נַחְמָנִי אָמַר: זֶה עֵדֶן שֶׁלֹּא שָׁלְטָה בּוֹ עֵין כָּל בְּרִיָּה. שֶׁמָּא תֹּאמַר, אָדָם הָרִאשׁוֹן הֵיכָן הָיָה? – בַּגַּן. וְשֶׁמָּא תֹּאמַר: הוּא גַּן, הוּא עֵדֶן – תַּלְמוּד לוֹמַר: °"וְנָהָר יֹצֵא מֵעֵדֶן לְהַשְׁקוֹת אֶת הַגָּן", גַּן לְחוּד וְעֵדֶן לְחוּד.§ ת"ר: מַעֲשֶׂה שֶׁחָלָה בְּנוֹ שֶׁל ר"ג, שִׁגֵּר שְׁנֵי ת"ח אֵצֶל רַבִּי חֲנִינָא בֶּן דּוֹסָא לְבַקֵּשׁ עָלָיו רַחֲמִים. כֵּיוָן שֶׁרָאָה אוֹתָם עָלָה לַעֲלִיָּיה וּבִקֵּשׁ עָלָיו רַחֲמִים. בִּירִידָתוֹ, אָמַר לָהֶם: לְכוּ – שֶׁחֲלָצַתּוּ חַמָּה. אָמְרוּ לוֹ: וְכִי נָבִיא אַתָּה?! אָמַר לָהֶן: לֹא נָבִיא אָנֹכִי וְלֹא בֶן נָבִיא אָנֹכִי, אֶלָּא כָּךְ מְקוּבְּלַנִי: אִם שְׁגוּרָה תְּפִלָּתִי בְּפִי – יוֹדֵעַ אֲנִי שֶׁהוּא מְקוּבָּל, וְאִם לָאו – יוֹדֵעַ אֲנִי שֶׁהוּא מְטוֹרָף. יָשְׁבוּ וְכָתְבוּ וְכִוְּונוּ אוֹתָהּ שָׁעָה. וּכְשֶׁבָּאוּ אֵצֶל ר"ג, אָמַר לָהֶן: הָעֲבוֹדָה! לֹא חִסַּרְתֶּם וְלֹא הוֹתַרְתֶּם, אֶלָּא כָּךְ הָיָה מַעֲשֶׂה, בְּאוֹתָהּ שָׁעָה חֲלָצַתּוּ חַמָּה וְשָׁאַל לָנוּ מַיִם לִשְׁתּוֹת. וְשׁוּב מַעֲשֶׂה בְּרַבִּי חֲנִינָא בֶּן דּוֹסָא שֶׁהָלַךְ לִלְמוֹד תּוֹרָה אֵצֶל ר' יוֹחָנָן בֶּן זַכַּאי, וְחָלָה בְּנוֹ שֶׁל ריב"ז. אָמַר לוֹ: חֲנִינָא בְּנִי, בַּקֵּשׁ עָלָיו רַחֲמִים וְיִחְיֶה. הִנִּיחַ רֹאשׁוֹ בֵּין בִּרְכָּיו וּבִקֵּשׁ עָלָיו רַחֲמִים – וְחָיָה. אָמַר רַבִּי יוֹחָנָן בֶּן זַכַּאי: אִלְמָלֵי הֵטִיחַ בֶּן זַכַּאי אֶת רֹאשׁוֹ בֵּין בִּרְכָּיו כָּל הַיּוֹם כּוּלּוֹ – לֹא הָיוּ מַשְׁגִּיחִים עָלָיו. אָמְרָה לוֹ אִשְׁתּוֹ: וְכִי חֲנִינָא גָּדוֹל מִמְּךָ?! אָמַר לָהּ: לָאו, אֶלָּא הוּא דּוֹמֶה כְּעֶבֶד לִפְנֵי הַמֶּלֶךְ, וַאֲנִי דּוֹמֶה כְּשַׂר לִפְנֵי הַמֶּלֶךְ.§ *וְאָמַר רַבִּי חִיָּיא בַּר אַבָּא אָמַר רַבִּי יוֹחָנָן: טאַל יִתְפַּלֵּל אָדָם אֶלָּא בְּבַיִת שֶׁיֵּשׁ שָׁם חַלּוֹנוֹת, שֶׁנֶּאֱמַר: °"וְכַוִּין פְּתִיחָן לֵיהּ בְּעִלִּיתֵהּ (לְקֳבֵל) [נֶגֶד] יְרוּשְׁלֶם". אָמַר רַב כָּהֲנָא: יחָצִיף עָלַי מַאן דְּמַצְלֵּי בְּבִקְתָּא. וְאָמַר רַב כָּהֲנָא: *כחָצִיף עָלַי מַאן דִּמְפָרֵשׁ חֶטְאֵיהּ, שֶׁנֶּאֱמַר: °"אַשְׁרֵי נְשׂוּי פֶּשַׁע כְּסוּי חֲטָאָה".§

## הדרן עלך אין עומדין

**קידה** על אפים. ומייתי קרא. אע"ג דאשכחן נמי בענין אחר, יש לומר דקים ליה מקבלה דקידה על אפים, ומייתי קרא דמסייעו: **חזינא** לאביי ורבא דמצלו אצלויי. פירוש: שהיו מטין על צדיהן: **יכוין** לבו באחת מהן. והא דאמרי' בסוף פרק "ת"ה" (דף ל:) לעולם ימוד אדם דעתו אם יכול לכוין – יתפלל, ואם לאו – אל יתפלל, יש לפרש התם נמי באחת מהן: **חציף** עלי מאן דמצלי בבקתא. וא"ת: הכתיב "ויצא יצחק *לשוח בשדה" (בראשית כד), וי"ל: דהתם מיירי בהר המוריה, כדאמרי' בפסחים פרק "האשה" (ד' פח.): לא כיצחק שקראו שדה וכו'. א"נ: בקתא דהכא מיירי בבקעה, במקום שרגילין שם בני אדם לעבור והולכי דרכים: **כסוי** חטאה. וטעמא: לפי שאז מתבייש על חטאו. אבל אם מפרש חטאיו דומה שאינו מתבייש עליו, ואמרינן לעיל פרק קמא (ד' יב:): כל העושה דבר ומתבייש – מוחלים לו מיד:

הדרן עלך אין עומדין

כֹּהֵן גָּדוֹל בְּסוֹף כָּל בְּרָכָה. כָּל מַה שֶּׁהוּא גָּדוֹל בְּיוֹתֵר צָרִיךְ לְהַכְנִיעַ וּלְהַשְׁפִּיל עַצְמוֹ: אֵינוֹ זוֹקֵף. עַד שֶׁיִּגְמוֹר: קָם מִלִּפְנֵי מִזְבַּח ה' מִכְּרוֹעַ. רֵישֵׁיהּ דִּקְרָא "וַיְהִי כְּכַלּוֹת שְׁלֹמֹה" לְהִתְפַּלֵּל וַהֲדַר "קָם מִכְּרוֹעַ": אַרְצָה. לְשׁוֹן מִשְׁתַּטֵּחַ מַשְׁמַע: דִּמְצַלּוּ אַצְלוּיֵי. כְּשֶׁנּוֹפְלִין עַל פְּנֵיהֶם אֵין פּוֹשְׁטִין יְדֵיהֶם וְרַגְלֵיהֶם, אֶלָּא מַטִּין עַל צִדֵּיהֶן: בַּתְּחִלָּה. כּוֹרֵעַ: חֲזֵינָא לְרַב נַחְמָן דְּכָרַע. תְּחִלָּה וָסוֹף: בְּהוֹדָאָה דְּהַלֵּל. "הוֹדוּ לַה' כִּי טוֹב": **מתני'** אִם שְׁגוּרָה. אִם סְדוּרָה תְּפִלָּתִי בְּפִי בִּמְרוּצָה וְאֵינִי נִכְשָׁל, וּתְחִנָּתִי נוֹבַעַת מִלִּבִּי אֶל פִּי, כָּל מַה שֶּׁאֲנִי חָפֵץ לְהַאֲרִיךְ בְּתַחֲנוּנִים: שֶׁהוּא מְטוֹרָף. הַחוֹלֶה לָשׁוֹן אַחֵר: [*לָשׁוֹן] טוֹרְפִין לוֹ תְּפִלָּתוֹ בְּפָנָיו*, כְּלוֹמַר: הַתְּפִלָּה שֶׁהִתְפַּלְּלוּ עָלָיו מְטוֹרֶפֶת וּטְרוּדָה מִמֶּנּוּ וְאֵינָהּ מְקוּבֶּלֶת: **גמ'** אֵהַיָּיא. בְּהֵיכָא, וּבְאֵיזוֹ מִן הַבְּרָכוֹת הָוֵי טָעוּת בְּסִימָן רַע: בָּאָבוֹת. שֶׁהוּא תְּחִלַּת הַתְּפִלָּה, רֶמֶז הוּא שֶׁאֵין חָפֵץ בָּהּ: בּוֹרֵא נִיב שְׂפָתַיִם. כְּשֶׁהַנִּיב בָּרִיא בָּאָדָם – אָז מוּבְטָח עַל הַשָּׁלוֹם: לֹא נִתְנַבְּאוּ. הַטּוֹבוֹת וְהַנֶּחָמוֹת: עַיִן לֹא רָאָתָה. לֹא נִרְאֵית וְלֹא נִגְלֵית לְשׁוּם נָבִיא: רָחוֹק. שֶׁהָיָה רָחוֹק כָּל יָמָיו מִן הָעֲבֵירָה, דְּהַיְינוּ צַדִּיק מֵעִיקָּרוֹ: חֲלָצַתּוּ חַמָּה. שְׁלָפַתּוּ, נִיטְּלָה מִגּוּפוֹ הַחַמָּה, הוּא הַחוֹלִי הַקּוֹדְחוֹ. חֲלָצַתּוּ – לְשׁוֹן *חָלַץ מֵהֶם: לֹא חִסַּרְתֶּם. שָׁעָה: כְּעֶבֶד. בֶּן בַּיִת, נִכְנָס וְיוֹצֵא שֶׁלֹּא בִּרְשׁוּת: כְּשַׂר לִפְנֵי הַמֶּלֶךְ. שֶׁאֵינוֹ רָגִיל לָבֹא לְפָנָיו: חַלּוֹנוֹת. שֶׁגּוֹרְמִין לוֹ שֶׁיְּכַוֵּין לִבּוֹ, שֶׁהוּא מִסְתַּכֵּל כְּלַפֵּי שָׁמַיִם וְלִבּוֹ נִכְנָע: דִּמְצַלֵּי בְּבִקְתָּא. בְּבִקְעָה, שֶׁכְּשֶׁהוּא בְּמָקוֹם צְנִיעוּת חָלָה עָלָיו אֵימַת מֶלֶךְ, וְלִבּוֹ נִשְׁבָּר:

הדרן עלך אין עומדין

## רב נסים גאון

**אמר** ר' חייא בריה דרב הונא חזינא לאביי ורבא דכי נפלי על אנפיהו מצלו אצלויי. איתא במס' מגילה בפ' הקורא את המגילה עומד יושב (דף כב) רב איקלע (לבית) [לבבל] בתענית צבור נפל כולי עלמא על אפייהו רב לא נפל מאי טעמא רצפה של אבנים היתה ומשום אבן משכית אית דאמר דמשום האי טעמא הוו אביי ורבא מצלו אצלויי. במס' ע"ז בגמ' דבני מערבא בפ' ר' ישמעאל (הלכה א) אמרו עליה אי אתה משתחוה אבל אתה משתחוה על אבני בית המקדש רב מפקד לדבי רב אחא ר' אמי מפקד לאנשי ביתיה כד תהוון נפקין לתעניתא לא תהוון רבעין כאורחכון ר' יונה רבע על סיטריה ר' אחא רבע על סיטריה: **אמר** רב (ששת) [כהנא] חציף עלאי מאן דמפרש חטאיה שנא' (תהלים לב) אשרי נשוי פשע כסוי חטאה. אית בפרק יום הכפורים (דף פו) רב רמי כתיב אשרי נשוי פשע כסוי חטאה וכתיב (משלי כח) מכסה פשעיו לא יצליח לא קשיא כאן בחטא מפורסם כאן בחטא שאינו מפורסם רב זוטרא בר טוביה אמר לא קשיא כאן בעבירות שבין אדם לחבירו כאן בעבירות שבין אדם למקום:

## הגהות הב"ח

(א) גמ' לדבר עבירה מעיקרא ונתרחק:

## הגהות הגר"א

[א] גמ' כהן גדול תחלת. נ"ב וסוף:

מסורת ה[ש"ס]

כל"ל תוי"ט
(לעיל ה:) מגילה כב: שבו
[מגילה כב: ע"ש]
[הושע ה]
[חגיגה י: קדושי' נדרים עב: נזיר' נו. מנחות לג:]
ישעיה נז
סנהדרין לט.
שם סד
שבת סג. קנא: פ' סנהדרין שם [ו
דברים טו
ישעיה נז
סנהדרין שם
[שם איתא ר"ל]
בראשית ב
[לעיל לא. ע"ש]
דניאל ו
סוטה ז: ע"ש
תהלים לב

**כיצד** מברכין וכו' חוץ מן היין. שמתוך חשיבותו קבעו לו ברכה לעצמו, וכן הפת: בורא מיני דשאים. לפי שיש בכלל פרי האדמה דשאים וזרעים כגון קטניות, ורבי יהודה בעי היכר ברכה לכל מין ומין: **גמ'** קדש הלולים. בנטע רבעי כתיב, ומשמע שני הלולים טעון באכילתו כשאוכלנו בשנה הרביעית שהוא מותר באכילה: האי מיבעי ליה. הלולים לשון חלולים; חד מינייהו אתא לאורויי: אחליה והדר אכליה, הוציאהו לחולין ע"י פדיון אם באת לאוכלו חוץ לירושלים, וחד: ללמדך שלא נאמרה תורת רבעי אלא בכרם, שנאמר קדש הלולים – דבר שמהללין בו טעון חלול, וזהו יין: שאין אומרים. הלוים שיר של קרבן במקדש אלא על היין, כשמנסכין נסכי מזבח: הניחא למ"ד כו'. כולה סיומא דפרכא הוא, וה"ק: הניחא הא דילפת ברכה מהכא למאן דתני נטע רבעי – דאית ליה כל פירות האילן בתורת רבעי, ולא דריש מהכא דבר דטעון הלול טעון חלול – אייתר ליה חד הלול לברכה: מאי איכא למימר. הא מיבעי ליה למדרש שאין חלול אלא במקום הלול: חד תני כרם רבעי. בכל מקום שיש במשנה נטע רבעי תני איהו "כרם": הניחא אי יליף בג"ש. דריש למלתיה בג"ש, ואייתר ליה חד הלול לברכה: אשכחן לאחריו. כדאשכחן בברכת המזון דכתיב "ואכלת ושבעת וברכת" (דברים ח): חייב בעוללות. "וכרמך לא תעולל" (ויקרא יט). איזהו עוללות – כל שאין להן פסיגין לא כתף ולא נטף, אלא שורה יחידית של ענבים: קמה תוכיח. דאשכחן דאברכה רחמנא ברכה דכתיב "תאכל בה לחם" וגו' (דברים ח) וסמיך ליה ואכלת ושבעת וברכת: צד מזבח. יין לנסכים, וסלת למנחות: ז' מינין. האמורים ב"ארץ חטה ושעורה" וגו' (שם ח) ובתרייהו כתיב "ואכלת ושבעת וברכת": שכן טעונים בכורים. דהכי אמרינן במנחות (פ"ט ד' פד:): נאמר כאן "ארץ" – *"כי תבא אל הארץ" (דברים כו), ונאמר להלן "ארץ חטה ושעורה". מה להלן שבח הארץ – אף כאן שבח הארץ: אלא סברא הוא. דלתרווייהו אית להו פירכא; למאן דתני כרם ויליף ברכה מז' המינים איכא פירכא – שכן טעונים בכורים. ולמאן דתני נטע רבעי איכא למפרך – התינח מידי דבר נטיעה, דלאו בר נטיעה מנלן? אלא סברא הוא, דכיון דנהנה צריך להודות למי שבראם: מעל. כנהנה מן ההקדש, דכתיב "לה' הארץ ומלואה" כדאמרינן לקמן: לאחר ברכה. הרי היא לבני אדם: גוזל

תורה אור

**כיצד** מברכין על הפירות? [א]על פירות האילן הוא אומר: "בורא פרי העץ" חוץ מן היין, שעל היין הוא אומר: "בורא פרי הגפן"; ועל [ב]פירות הארץ הוא אומר: "בורא פרי האדמה", חוץ מן הפת, שעל [ג]הפת הוא אומר: "המוציא לחם מן הארץ"; *[ד]ועל הירקות הוא אומר: "בורא פרי האדמה", רבי יהודה אומר: "בורא מיני דשאים".§ **גמ'** מנא ה"מ? *דתנו רבנן: °"קדש הלולים לה'" – מלמד שטעונים ברכה לפניהם ולאחריהם, מכאן אמר ר"ע: אסור לאדם שיטעום כלום קודם שיברך –והאי "קדש הלולים" להכי הוא דאתא?! האי מיבעי ליה, חד: דאמר רחמנא – °אחליה והדר אכליה; ואידך: דבר הטעון שירה – טעון חלול, ושאינו טעון שירה – אין טעון חלול, וכדר' שמואל בר נחמני א"ר יונתן; *דאמר ר' שמואל בר נחמני א"ר יונתן: מנין [ד] שאין אומרים שירה אלא על היין – שנאמר: °"ותאמר להם הגפן החדלתי את תירושי המשמח אלהים ואנשים", אם אנשים משמח – אלהים במה משמח? מכאן, שאין אומרים שירה אלא על היין! הניחא למאן דתני [ה] "נטע רבעי", אלא למאן דתני "כרם רבעי" מאי איכא למימר? דאתמר: ר' חייא ור' שמעון ברבי, °חד תני: "כרם רבעי", וחד תני: "נטע רבעי"! ולמאן דתני "כרם רבעי" – הניחא אי יליף ג"ש, דתניא: ר' אומר, נאמר כאן: °"להוסיף לכם תבואתו", ונאמר להלן °"ותבואת הכרם" – מה להלן כרם אף כאן כרם. אייתר ליה חד "הלול" לברכה; ואי לא יליף גזרה שוה – ברכה מנא ליה? ואי נמי יליף גזרה שוה – אשכחן לאחריו, לפניו מנין! הא לא קשיא, [ה]דאתיא בקל וחומר: *כשהוא שבע מברך – כשהוא רעב לא כל שכן? אשכחן כרם, שאר מינין מנין? דיליף מכרם, מה כרם דבר שנהנה וטעון ברכה – אף כל דבר שנהנה טעון ברכה. –איכא למפרך: מה לכרם שכן חייב בעוללות! קמה תוכיח. מה לקמה – שכן חייבת בחלה! כרם יוכיח. *וחזר הדין: לא ראי זה כראי זה ולא ראי זה כראי זה, הצד השוה שבהן – דבר שנהנה וטעון ברכה, אף כל דבר שנהנה טעון ברכה. –מה להצד השוה שבהן – שכן יש בו צד מזבח! ואתי נמי זית דאית ביה צד מזבח. –וזית מצד מזבח אתי?! והא בהדיא כתיב ביה כרם, דכתיב: °"ויבער מגדיש ועד קמה ועד כרם זית!" אמר *רב פפא: °"כרם זית" – אקרי, כרם סתמא – לא אקרי. מ"מ קשיא: מה להצד השוה שבהן שכן יש בהן צד מזבח! אלא: דיליף לה משבעת המינין – מה שבעת המינין דבר שנהנה וטעון ברכה, אף כל דבר שנהנה טעון ברכה. מה לשבעת המינין שכן חייבין בבכורים! ועוד: התינח לאחריו, לפניו מנין? –הא לא קשיא; דאתי בקל וחומר: כשהוא שבע מברך – כשהוא רעב לכ"ש. ולמאן דתני "נטע רבעי" – הא תינח כל דבר נטיעה. דלאו בר נטיעה, כגון בשר ביצים ודגים, מנא ליה? –אלא, סברא הוא: אסור לו לאדם שיהנה מן העולם הזה בלא ברכה.§ ת"ר: [ו]אסור לו לאדם שיהנה מן העוה"ז בלא ברכה, *וכל הנהנה מן העוה"ז בלא ברכה – מעל. מאי תקנתיה – ילך אצל חכם. –ילך אצל חכם – מאי עביד ליה?! הא עביד ליה איסורא! – אלא אמר רבא: ילך אצל חכם מעיקרא וילמדנו ברכות, כדי שלא יבא לידי מעילה. אמר רב יהודה אמר שמואל: כל הנהנה מן העוה"ז בלא ברכה – כאילו נהנה מקדשי שמים, שנא': °"לה' הארץ ומלואה". ר' לוי רמי: כתיב "לה' הארץ ומלואה", וכתיב: °"השמים שמים לה' והארץ נתן לבני אדם"! לא קשיא, כאן – קודם ברכה, כאן

**כיצד** מברכין. לא שייך להקשות: תנא היכא קאי דקתני 'כיצד', כדפריך בריש מכילתין (ד' ב.) – משום דהכא סברא הוא לברך, כדמסיק בגמרא דאסור ליהנות מן העולם הזה בלא ברכה. אי נמי, י"ל: דקאי אמתני' ד"מי שמתו" (ד' כ:), דקתני: בעל קרי מברך לאחריו ואינו מברך לפניו, והכי נמי שייך הכא לברך על כל דבר ודבר, ע"כ קאמר הכא 'כיצד מברכין':

**אחליה** והדר אכליה. תימה: למה לי קרא? הא בפ"ב דקדושין (ד' נד:) גמרינן קדש קדש ממעשר שני, א"כ נילף ממעשר שני! וי"ל: אי לאו קרא דהלולים, הוה אמינא דאדרבה, נילף לחומרא קדש קדש משביעית ואין לו פדיון. עוד פי' רבינו חיים כהן: אי מהתם, הוה אמינא כי מעשר שני ממש, ודוקא בזמן שמעשר שני נוהג, כמו בשנה ראשונה ושניה ורביעית וחמישית לשמטה נוהג חלול, אבל שלישית וששית שמעשר עני דוקא – אימא לא, קמ"ל חלולים*:

**שאין** אומרים שירה אלא על היין. פירוש: אין אומרים שירה על שום אכילת מזבח, כגון זריקת דמים ונסוך המים, כי אם על היין. אבל ודאי מצינו שירה בלא יין, כגון הלל שבשחיטת פסחים (תמיד נשחט ד' סד.) [ע"ש בתוספות]:

**ולמאן** דתני כרם רבעי וכו'. ועתה קיימא לן דרבעי נוהג אף בח"ל. מיהו, בכרם נוהג ולא בשאר אילנות, דכל המיקל בארץ הלכה כמותו בח"ל. *וכרם רבעי בזמן הזה מחללין על שוה פרוט', ושוחקו ומטילו לנהר. וכן מפורש בשאלתות דרב אחאי [פרשת קדושים סימן ק]:

**ואתי** נמי זית במה הצד. וא"ת: איכא למפרך: מה להצד השוה שכן חייבים בלקט, דפרט בכרם היינו לקט, משא"כ בזית דאין בו לקט! וי"ל: דניחא ליה למפרך פירכא אפילו יהא הצד השוה חשוב למיתי זית מיניה, מ"מ קאמר דשאר מינים לא ידע מיניה:

**תינח** לאחריו. דעיקר ברכה לאחריו, כדכתיב "ואכלת ושבעת וברכת": **לפניו** לכ"ש. לאו ק"ו הוא, דאם כן תהא ברכה דלפניו מדאורייתא, ולעיל פרק 'מי שמתו' (דף כא.) משמע גבי בעל קרי דלאו דאורייתא הוא. ואפי' רבי יהודה לא פליג אלא משום דעשאן כהלכות דרך ארץ (שם ד' כב.*):

**דבר** שאין גדולו מן הקרקע. כגון בשר וחלב. וא"ת: מאי איריא בשר, אפילו ירקות נמי לא אתיא ליה! וי"ל דאיכא למימר: קמה תוכיח. ולפי' רש"י ניחא, דגרים "דלאו בר נטיעה מנין", וליכא למימר דאתא משאר אילנות, דאיכא למפרך – מה להנך שכן חייבים בפאה: **אלא** סברא הוא אסור לאדם שיהנה כו'. וקרא דנסיב לעיל – אסמכתא בעלמא, והגמרא היה סבור מתחלה דלמוד גמור הוא:

כאן

[לקמן לז.] [קדושים פ"ג פ"ו] [ויקרא יט] [ערכין יא. יב.] [שופטים ט] [ויקרא יט] [דברים כב] [תביא מארנך] [עין ה: כא. וש"נ] [שופטים טו] [ב"מ פ"ז:] [תוספתא פ"ד] [תהלים כד] [שם קטו]

[ועי' תוס' ב"ק סט: ד"ה קדש וכו' ביתר ביאור ותו' קדושין נג: ד"ה גמר]

[ועי' היטב תוס' קדושין ב: ד"ה אתרוג]

[לקמן מח: ע"ש פירש"י ד"ה כשהוא שבע וכו' וד"ה כשהוא רעב וכו']

[וע"ע תוס' יומא עט. ותוס' סוכה כו: ותוס' חולין קז. ד"ה ולא]

## עין משפט נר מצוה

א א מיי' פ"ח מהל' ברכות סמג עשין כז טוש"ע או"ח סימן רב סעיף א:

ב ב מיי' וסמג שם טור שו"ע א"ח סימן רג סעיף א:

ג ג מיי' פ"ג שם הל' ב סמג שם טוש"ע א"ח סי' קסז סעיף ב:

ד ד מיי' פ"ח שם סמג שם טוש"ע א"ח סימן רה סעיף א:

[ד] מיי' פ"ג מהל' כלי המקדש הלכה ב:

[ה] מיי' פ"ט מהלכות מעשר שני טוש"ע י"ד סימן רלד סעיף ז ובהג"ה שם:

ה ה ו מיי' פ"א שם הל' ב סמג שם טור א"ח סימן רי סעיף א:

## גליון הש"ם

**גמ'** אחליה והדר אכליה. בירושלמי פ"ז דפאה אמר אהך דרשה דהכא לא מתמנעי רבנן בין ה' לח'. וכן הוא בירושלמי פ"ז דשבת על דרשה דאלה הדברים אלו ל"ט מלאכות: **שם** חד תני כרם רבעי. עי' סוטה מג ע"ב רש"י ד"ה קלא ולע"ג: **שם** כרם זית איקרי. וכעין זה חולין קלט ע"ב וש"נ:

**תום'** ד"ה ולמאן כו' שוה פרוטה. וכן הוא ברבינו יונה ובש"ע ותמוה לי כיון דילפינן חלול חלול ממעשר ליבעי חלול על דבר שעליו צורה ול"ע:

**כאן** לאחר ברכה. וכן בפ' "כל כתבי" (שבת ד' קיט.) אמרי' כשהיו מניחים השולחן היו אומרים "לה' הארץ ומלואה", וכשהיו מסלקין השולחן היו אומרים "השמים שמים לה' והארץ נתן לבני אדם":

**כאן** בזמן שישראל עושין רצונו של מקום שנאמר "ואספת דגנך". וא"ת: והא לקמן בזמן שאין ישראל עושין רצונו של מקום מוקמי' ליה! וי"ל: דמיירי ודאי שעושין רצונו, אבל אין עושין רצונו כ"כ, דאינם צדיקים גמורים. ועוד י"ל: דפליג ליה אהא דלקמן, שבא לפרש מה בין עושים ואין עושין, *והכא בעושים ואין עושים כי הדדי (א) ניינהו.

**דרך** טרקסמון. פירש"י: היינו לדאורייתא, אבל מדרבנן גם חצר קובעת, כדמשמע בפ' "יוצא דופן" (נדה ד' מז.), איזהו חצר שחייב במעשר וכו', וכן מוכח בפ' "המביא" (ביצה ד' לה.):

**טובא** גריר. מכאן משמע שאסור לשתות יין בערב פסח מן המנח' ולמעלה. ואם רוצה לשתות צריך לשתות הרבה, דטובא מגריר גריר: לה

כאן – לאחר ברכה.§ א"ר חנינא בר פפא: כל הנהנה מן העוה"ז בלא ברכה כאילו גוזל להקב"ה וכנסת ישראל, שנא': "גוזל אביו ואמו ואומר אין פשע חבר הוא לאיש משחית"; ואין אביו אלא הקב"ה, שנא' "הלא הוא אביך קנך"; ואין אמו אלא כנסת ישראל, שנא': "שמע בני מוסר אביך ואל תטוש תורת אמך". מאי "חבר הוא לאיש משחית"? א"ר חנינא בר פפא: חבר הוא לירבעם בן נבט שהשחית את ישראל לאביהם שבשמים.§ ר' חנינא בר פפא רמי: כתיב "ולקחתי דגני בעתו וגו'" וכתיב: "ואספת דגנך וגו'"! – ל"ק: כאן בזמן שישראל עושין רצונו של מקום, כאן בזמן שאין ישראל עושין רצונו של מקום. ת"ר: א"ואספת דגנך", – מה ת"ל – לפי שנא': "לא ימוש ספר התורה הזה מפיך", יכול דברים ככתבן? ת"ל: "ואספת דגנך" – הנהג בהן מנהג דרך ארץ, דברי ר' ישמעאל; ר"ש בן יוחי אומר: אפשר אדם חורש בשעת חרישה, וזורע בשעת זריעה, וקוצר בשעת קצירה, ודש בשעת דישה, וזורה בשעת הרוח, תורה מה תהא עליה? אלא: בזמן שישראל עושין רצונו של מקום – מלאכתן נעשית ע"י אחרים, שנא': "ועמדו זרים ורעו צאנכם וגו'". ובזמן שאין ישראל עושין רצונו של מקום – מלאכתן נעשית ע"י עצמן, שנא': "ואספת דגנך"; ולא עוד, אלא שמלאכת אחרים נעשית על ידן, שנא': "ועבדת את אויבך וגו'". אמר אביי: הרבה עשו כרבי ישמעאל – ועלתה בידן, כר' שמעון בן יוחי – ולא עלתה בידן. א"ל רבא לרבנן: במטותא מינייכו, ביומי ניסן וביומי תשרי לא תתחזו קמאי, כי היכי דלא תטרדו במזונייכו כולא שתא. אמר רבה בר בר חנה א"ר יוחנן משום רבי יהודה בר' אלעאי: בא וראה שלא כדורות הראשונים דורות האחרונים, דורות הראשונים עשו תורתן קבע ומלאכתן עראי – זו וזו נתקיימה בידן, דורות האחרונים שעשו מלאכתן קבע ותורתן עראי – זו וזו לא נתקיימה בידן.§ ואמר רבה בר בר חנה אר"י משום ר"י בר' אלעאי: *בא וראה שלא כדורות הראשונים דורות האחרונים; דורות הראשונים היו מכניסין פירותיהן דרך *טרקסמון – כדי לחייבן במעשר, דורות האחרונים מכניסין פירותיהן דרך גגות דרך חצרות דרך קרפיפות – כדי לפטרן במן המעשר; *דא"ר ינאי: אין הטבל מתחייב במעשר עד שיראה פני הבית, שנא' "בערתי הקדש מן הבית"; ור' יוחנן אמר: אפי' חצר קובעת, שנא': "ואכלו בשעריך ושבעו".§ "חוץ מן היין וכו'". מאי שנא יין? אילימא משום דאשתני לעלויא, אשתני לברכה? והרי שמן, דאשתני לעלויא ולא אשתני לברכה! *דאמר רב יהודה אמר שמואל, וכן א"ר יצחק א"ר יוחנן: שמן זית מברכין עליו "בפה"ע"! אמרי: התם משום דלא אפשר, היכי נבריך? נבריך "בורא פרי הזית" – פירא גופיה זית אקרי. – ונבריך עליה "בורא פרי עץ זית"! – אלא אמר מר זוטרא: חמרא – זיין, משחא – לא זיין. ומשחא לא זיין?! והתנן: "הנודר גמן המזון מותר במים ובמלח", והוינן בה: מים ומלח הוא דלא אקרי מזון, הא כל מילי אקרי מזון, נימא תיהוי תיובתא דרב ושמואל, דאמרי: אין מברכין "בורא מיני מזונות" אלא בה' המינין בלבד! וא"ר הונא: באומר "כל הזן עלי"; אלמא משחא זיין! – אלא: חמרא סעיד, ומשחא לא סעיד. – וחמרא מי סעיד?! *והא רבא דהוה שתי חמרא כל מעלי יומא דפסחא כי היכי דנגרריה ללביה וניכול מצה טפי! – טובא גריר, פורתא סעיד. – ומי סעיד כלל?! והכתיב: "ויין ישמח לבב אנוש ולחם לבב אנוש יסעד וגו'" נהמא הוא דסעיד, חמרא לא סעיד! – אלא: חמרא אית ביה תרתי – סעיד ומשמח, נהמא – מסעד סעיד, שמוחי לא משמח. אי הכי נבריך עליה שלש ברכות! לא קבעי אינשי סעודתייהו עלויה. א"ל: רב נחמן בר יצחק לרבא: אי קבע עלויה סעודתיה מאי? א"ל: לכשיבא אליהו ויאמר אי הויא קביעותא, השתא מיהא *בטלה דעתו אצל כל אדם.§ גופא: אמר רב יהודה אמר שמואל, וכן א"ר יצחק א"ר יוחנן: השמן זית מברכין עליו "בורא פרי העץ". היכי דמי? אילימא ודקא שתי ליה (משתה) – אוזוקי מזיק ליה! *דתניא: זהשותה שמן של תרומה – משלם את הקרן ואינו משלם את החומש, חהסך שמן של תרומה – משלם את הקרן ומשלם את החומש! אלא: דקא אכיל ליה על ידי פת. אי הכי, הויא ליה פת עיקר והוא טפל; ותנן, *זה הכלל: טכל שהוא עיקר ועמו טפלה – מברך על העיקר ופוטר את הטפלה! אלא: דקא שתי ליה ע"י אניגרון; דאמר רבה בר בר שמואל: *אניגרון – מיא דסלקא, *אנסיגרון – מיא דכולהו

גוזל להקב"ה. את ברכתו: וכנסת ישראל. שכשחטאו הפירות לוקין: אין פשע. ולפי שהוא מיקל, רואים האחרים ולמדין ממנו לעשות כן, ליהנות מן העולם בלא ברכה. ולכך נקרא זה המיקל "חבר לאיש משחית": לירבעם בן נבט. שחטא והחטיא את ישראל, כך הוא חוטא ומחטיא: בזמן שעושין רצונו. הדגן שלהם, וכשאין עושים רצונו – נוטלו ומראה להם שהוא שלו: דברים ככתבן. שלא יעסוק בדרך ארץ: הנהג בהם. עם דברי תורה: מנהג דרך ארץ. שאם תבא לידי צורך הבריות סופך ליבטל מדברי תורה: אפשר. בתמיה: אפשר כדבריך: ביומי ניסן. ימי הקציר: ביומי תשרי. דריכת הגתות והבדים: דרך טרקסמון. דרך שערי החצר והבית: פני הבית. פתח כניסה ויציאה: אין הטבל מתחייב במעשר. מן התורה. אבל אכילת קבע אסור לאכול מדרבנן: זית אקרי. והוה ליה בורא פרי הפרי, שהפרי קרוי זית; ואין זו בריאת שמים כי בידי אדם היא בריאה זו. אבל גבי גפן, הגפן היא העץ, והענבים הם פרי הגפן: חמרא זיין. להכי חשיב לקבוע לו ברכה לעצמו: ואמר רב הונא. הא דקתני מותר במים ובמלח ואסור בשאר אוכלין ומשקין – לאו באומר קונם מזון עלי, דאין מזון אלא מה' מיני דגן – חטין ושעורין וכוסמין ושבולת שועל ושיפון. אלא באומר: כל הזן עלי קונם; וכל מילי נהי דלא אקרו מזון, מיהו מיזן זייני, בר ממים ומלח. אלמא: משחא זיין: סעיד. חשיב טפי ממזון: והכתיב ויין ישמח לבב אנוש. וסיפא דקרא "ולחם לבב אנוש יסעד", משמע: אבל יין אינו אלא משמח. ומשני: לאו כדקאמרת, אלא: לחם יסעד ולא ישמח, אבל יין סועד ומשמח: אי הכי. דזיין וסעיד, מזון הוא, ולברך עליה שלש ברכות לאחריו! ואנן אמרינן לקמן בפרקין (דף לז.): כל שהוא משבעת המינין ולא מין דגן – חכמים אומרים: ברכה אחת: אוזוקי מזיק. לגופיה, ואין זו אכילה שטעונה ברכה. דגבי ברכה "ואכלת" כתיב: דתני'. דלאו בר אכילה היא: השותה שמן של תרומה. בשוגג: משלם את הקרן. כשאחד מזיק את חבירו בממונו: ואין משלם חומש. דגבי חומש אכילה כתיב ואיש "כי יאכל קדש בשגגה" (ויקרא כב), פרט למזיק: ע"י הפת. משום לפתן: ע"י אניגרון. מין מאכל הוא, ונותנים לתוכו שמן, ושנוי במשנה בכמה מקומות: דאמר רבה בר שמואל. לא אתא הכא אלא לפרושי לן מאי ניהו: מיא דסלקא. מים שנשלקו בהן תרדין: דכולהו

ו א מיי' פ"ג מהל' תלמוד תורה הלכה ז טוש"ע י"ד סי' רמו סעיף כא [בהגה] וטוש"ע או"ח סי' קנו:
ז ב מיי' פ"ג מהל' מעשר הלכה ו ופרק ד שם סמג עשין קלה טוש"ע י"ד סי' שלא סעיף פג:
ח ג טוש"ע י"ד סי' ריז סעיף יט:
ט ד טוש"ע או"ח סימן תע"א סעיף א:

והכא בעושין ועושין ואין עושין כי הדדי כנ"ל ופי' דלקמן מפרש מה בין עושין ואין עושין כל כך כסברת התוס' בתירוץ א' ואין עושין כלל ואיכא ג' בבות דע"כ צ"ל דס"ל הכי כיון דמיישב הני ב' פסוקים דהאי קרא דועמדו זרים איירי בעושין ומפיק מיניה דאפי' אסיפת דגן אינם צריכים לעשות כמ"ש מלאכת דגן באותו קרא ועמדו זרים ורעו צאנכם ובני נכר אכריכם וקרא דואספת דגנך איירי באין עושין ע"כ פי' דאין עושין כ"כ דאל"כ קשה במאי מוקמת לקרא דולקחתי דגני אבל הכא לר"ח כ"פ אי ס"ד דאית ליה האי סברא למיפק מהאי קרא דועמדו זרים אפי' מלאכת אסיפת דגן למה ליה להקשות הני תרי קראי אהדדי ולקחתי דגני מואספת דגנך עדיפא מיניה ה"ל להקשות קרא דולקחתי דגני אקרא דועמדו זרים דמשמע אפי' זרים יעשו בשבילן אלא ודאי דלא מפיק מידי מהאי קרא כמו ר' ישמעאל וא"כ צ"ל ראיה אלא לב' מעלות אלו לאין עושין כלל ולעושין אבל לעושין ואין עושין כ"כ אין לו שום ראיה לחלק ביניהם וכי הדדי נינהו ואם כן ע"כ פליגי אהדדי:

י ה ו מיי' פ"ח מהלכות ברכות הלכה ב סמג עשין כז טוש"ע א"ח סי' רב סעיף ד:
יא ז מיי' פ"י מהלכות תרומה הלכה יא:
יב ח שם הלכה א:
יג ט מיי' פ"ג מהלכות ברכות הל' ה סמג עשין כז טוש"ע א"ח סי' רב סעיף ד ובסימן רד סעי' יב ובסי' ריב ס"א:

### הגהות הב"ח

(א) תוס' ד"ה כאן בזמן וכו' כי הדדי. נ"ב בענינים בעלמא הם תוספים את הדגן אלא שאם אין עושין לוקח הדגן מרשותם:

### גליון הש"ס

תוס' ד"ה כאן בזמן. ועוד י"ל כו'. עי' תשובת רשב"ש (חא"ח סי' ל"ט).

תוספתא פ"ו דתרומות | שבועות כג. [יומא עו.]

גיטין דף פח. | [עפירש"י והו' | שם וב"מ פז: | [לקמן לו.] | ערובין כו: וכן | פסחים קז: | [פסחים מז. ם | לקמן מא. מד. | [נ"ל אכסגרון ביומא עו. וכב' אי' בערוך

דכולהו שלקי. א"כ, הוה ליה אניגרון עיקר ושמן טפל. ותנן, זה הכלל: כל שהוא עיקר ועמו טפלה – מברך על העיקר ופוטר את הטפלה! הכא במאי עסקינן – בחושש בגרונו. דתניא: *החושש בגרונו – לא יערענו בשמן תחלה בשבת, אבל נותן שמן הרבה לתוך אניגרון ובולע. – פשיטא! – *מהו דתימא: כיון דלרפואה קא מכוין – לא לבריך עליה כלל, קמ"ל: כיון דאית ליה הנאה מיניה בעי ברוכי. § קמחא דחיטי – רב יהודה אמר: "בורא פרי האדמה", ורב נחמן אמר: "שהכל נהיה בדברו". א"ל רבא לרב נחמן: לא תפלוג עליה דרב יהודה, דר' יוחנן ושמואל קיימי כוותיה; דאמר *רב יהודה אמר שמואל, וכן א"ר יצחק א"ר יוחנן: שמן זית – מברכין עליו "בורא פרי העץ"; אלמא: אע"ג דאשתני – במלתיה קאי; ה"נ, אע"ג דאשתני – במלתיה קאי! מי דמי? התם – לית ליה עלויא אחרינא, הכא – אית ליה עלויא אחרינא בפת. וכי אית ליה עלויא אחרינא לא מברכינן עליה "בורא פרי האדמה" אלא "שהכל"?! והא"ר זירא אמר רב מתנא אמר שמואל: אקרא חייא וקמחא דשערי מברכינן עלייהו "שהכל נהיה בדברו", מאי לאו, דחיטי – "בורא פרי האדמה"! לא, דחיטי נמי, "שהכל נהיה בדברו". ולשמעינן דחיטי וכ"ש דשערי! אי אשמעינן דחיטי – הוה אמינא: ה"מ דחיטי, אבל דשערי לא לבריך עליה כלל – קמ"ל. ומי גרע ממלח וזמית?! *דתנן: *על המלח ועל הזמית אומר "שהכל נהיה בדברו"! אצטריך, סד"א: מלח וזמית – עביד איניש דשדי לפומיה, אבל קמחא דשערי, הואיל וקשה לקוקיאני – לא לבריך עליה כלל; קמ"ל: כיון דאית ליה הנאה מיניה – בעי ברוכי. § *קורא – רב יהודה אמר: "בורא פרי האדמה"; ושמואל אמר: "שהכל נהיה בדברו". רב יהודה אמר "בורא פרי האדמה" – פירא הוא, ושמואל אמר "שהכל נהיה בדברו" – הואיל וסופו להקשות. אמר ליה שמואל לרב יהודה: *שיננא! כוותך מסתברא, דהא צנון סופו להקשות ומברכינן עליה "בורא פרי האדמה". ולא היא, צנון נטעי אינשי אדעתא דפוגלא, דקלא – לא נטעי אינשי אדעתא דקורא. וכל היכא דלא נטעי אינשי אדעתא דהכי – לא מברכינן עליה?! והרי צלף, דנטעי אינשי אדעתא דפרחא, ותנן: על מיני נצפה על העלין ועל התמרות אומר: "בורא פרי האדמה" ועל האביונות ועל הקפריסין אומר: "בורא פרי העץ"! – אמר רב נחמן בר יצחק: צלף – נטעי אינשי אדעתא דשותא, דקלא – לא נטעי אינשי אדעתא דקורא. ואע"ג דקלסיה שמואל לרב יהודה, הלכתא כוותיה דשמואל. § אמר רב יהודה אמר רב: צלף של ערלה בחוצה לארץ – זורק את האביונות ואוכל את הקפריסין. למימרא, דאביונות פירי וקפריסין לאו פירי?! ורמינהו: על מיני נצפה על העלים ועל התמרות אומר "בורא פרי האדמה", ועל האביונות ועל הקפריסין אומר "בורא פרי העץ"! – הוא דאמר כר"ע. דתנן, *רבי אליעזר אומר: צלף – מתעשר תמרות ואביונות וקפריסין, ר"ע אומר: אין מתעשר אלא אביונות בלבד, מפני שהוא פרי. – ונימא: הלכה כרבי עקיבא! – אי אמר הלכה כרבי עקיבא, הוה אמינא – אפי' בארץ, קמ"ל: *כל המיקל בארץ – הלכה כמותו בחוצה לארץ, אבל בארץ לא. – ונימא: הלכה כרבי עקיבא בחוצה לארץ, דכל המיקל בארץ – הלכה כמותו בח"ל! – אי אמר הכי, הוה אמינא: הנ"מ – גבי מעשר אילן, דבארץ גופא מדרבנן, אבל גבי ערלה דבארץ מדאורייתא – אימא בח"ל נמי נגזור, קמ"ל. § רבינא אשכחיה למר בר רב אשי דקא זריק אביונות וקאכיל קפריסין. א"ל: מאי דעתך – כר' עקיבא דמיקל, ולעביד מר כב"ש דמקילי טפי! דתנן: *צלף, ב"ש אומרים: כלאים בכרם, וב"ה אומרים: אין כלאים בכרם, אלו ואלו מודים שחייב בערלה. הא גופא קשיא! אמרת צלף, ב"ש אומרים: כלאים בכרם, אלמא מין ירק הוא, והדר תני: אלו ואלו מודים שחייב בערלה, אלמא מין אילן הוא! – הא לא קשיא; ב"ש ספוקי מספקא להו, ועבדי הכא לחומרא והכא לחומרא. מ"מ, לב"ש הוה ליה ספק ערלה, ותנן: *ספק ערלה בא"י – אסור, ובסוריא – מותר, ובח"ל – יורד ולוקח

**רש"י**

דכולהו שלקי. כל מיני ירק שלוק: החושש בגרונו. וצריך לתת בו שמן הרבה, דהוה ליה שמן עיקר ואניגרון טפל: לא יערענו בשמן. בשבת, דמשהי ליה בתוך גרונו ואינו בולעו, וכיון דלא בלע ליה – מוכחא מילתא דלרפואה הוא. וחכמים גזרו על כל רפואות הנכרות משום שחיקת סממנים שהיא מלאכה: תחלה. כלומר: לכתחלה לא יתן השמן בפיו לשם ערעור, כי אם לשם בליעה, ואם בא להשהותו – ישהנו: דאית ליה הנאה מיניה. לבד הרפואה יש לו הנאת אכילה: והלכתא וכו'. עד פטר להו לא גרסינן ומה"ג הוא: קמחא דחיטי. אוכל קמח חטים כמות שהיא: בורא פרי האדמה. כשאר כוסס חטין, דתניא לקמן בפרקין (ד' לז.) שמברך "בורא פרי האדמה": דאשתני. נגרע, הואיל ולא אשתני לעלויא מעלייתא: במלתיה קאי. והוה ליה ככוסס חטין: הכא אית ליה עילויא אחרינא. הלכך: יצא מכלל פרי, ולכלל דרך אכילתו לא בא. אבל השמן מיד בא בשנויו לכלל דרך אכילתו, ועיקר הפרי לכך נטעוהו – הלכך פרי הוא: מאי לאו. מדאמר שערי, מכלל דס"ל בחטי – "בפה"א", דחשיב: ומי גרע ממלח וזמית. והיכי תיסק אדעתין דלא תבעי ברכה: זמית. שלמיר"א(א): קוקיאני. תולעים שבמעיים: דאית ליה הנאה. באכילה: קורא. רך של דקל – כשענפיו גדלים בכל שנה ושנה כדרך כל האילנות, הנוסף בשנה זו רך ובשנה שניה מתקשה ונעשה עץ: צנון סופו להקשות. שאם אינו תולשו בעתו הוא מתקשה כעץ: אדעתא דפוגלא. לאכלו כשהוא רך, ושמו פוגלא: צלף. מין עץ: אדעתא דפרחא. שם פריו: מיני נצפה. הוא צלף, לפי שגדלים בו כמה מיני אכילה קרי ליה מיני: תמרות. בתוך העלים גדלים כמין תמרות, ובולטין בעלה, כמו בעלין של ערבה: אביונות. הוא הפרי: קפריסין. הוא קליפה גדולה שסביבות הפרי, כעין קליפה הגדילה סביב אגוזים דקים: צלף נטעי אינשי אדעתא דשותא. לאכול את העלים ואת התמרות, שאינן ממעטין את האילן בכך: דקלא לא נטעי אינשי אדעתא. לאכול את הקורא, שהאוכלו ממעט ענפי האילן: ערלה בחוצה לארץ. מדברי סופרים היא: דכל המיקל בארץ. בערלה, הלכה כמותו בחוצה לארץ. דכיון דאינה מן התורה, הלך אחר המיקל: גבי מעשר. דהא דר"ע לגבי מעשר איתמר. דמעשר פירות האילן דבארץ גופה דרבנן, שהתורה לא חייבה לעשר אלא דגן תירוש ויצהר: כלאים בכרם. קסבר מין ירק הוא: מ"מ לב"ש הוה ליה ספק ערלה וכו'(ב). האי מ"מ מסקנא דפירכא דרבינא הוא, ולמימר שאף הפרי עצמו מותר בחוצה לארץ, דהא בארץ ספק הוא ותנן ספק ערלה כו': ובסוריא. ארם צובה שכבש דוד והוסיפה על גבול ארץ ישראל: ובחוצה לארץ. הלוקח מן החשוד על הערלה ויודע הוא שיש בפרדסו זקנות ונטיעות: יורד ולוקח. הימנו, אף על פי שספק הוא אם יביא מן הנטיעות: ובלבד

**תוספות**

לא יערענו. פירש"י: להשהותו. וא"ת: א"כ, לפלוג וליתני בדידה: מאי איריא ע"י אניגרון – אפילו בעיניה שרי לבלעו לאלתר, דהא אינו אסור אלא לערער, דהיינו להשהותו. ע"כ פי' הר"י: לא יערענו – אפי' בבליעה בלא שהייה, שכל שתייה שאינה אלא לרפואה קרי ליה ערעור, ואפי' כשבולעו. והיינו טעמא דמתסר – משום דקא מוכחא מילתא דלרפואה קא מכוין. א"נ יש ליישב פירוש רש"י: לא יערענו – להשהותו, אבל נותן הוא לתוך אניגרון – ואפילו להשהותו, או בולעו(ג) בעיניה בלא שהייה: כיון דאית ליה הנאה מיניה בעי ברוכי. ונראין הדברים(ד) דאם אדם שותה *משקין; אם המשקין רעים לשתות דלית ליה הנאה מיניה – לא בעי ברוכי, ואי אית ליה הנאה מיניה בלא הרפואה – בעי ברוכי: והלכתא שכתוב בספרים לא גרסי'. דלשון ה"ג הוא עד קמחא וכו': קמחא דחיטי. נראה דלא מיירי בקמחא ממש, דאם כן לא שייכא ביה ברכה ד"בורא פרי האדמה", אלא מיירי בקמחא שקורין איסקלא"טיר, או בקמח שעושין משבולת שועל שמייבשין בתנור: לא נטעי אינשי אדעתא דקורא. וסבר גמ' כוותיה דשמואל. וא"כ, אותן לולבי גפנים דלא נטעי אינשי אדעתא דהכי, מברכינן עלייהו "שהכל נהיה בדברו". ואותן שקדי', כשהם רכים אוכלים קליפתם החיצונה ולא נטעי להו אדעתא דהכי למיכל להו כשהן רכים כי אם לאכול הגרעינין שלהן כשיתבשלו, מברך עלייהו נמי "שהכל": קליפי

**עין משפט נר מצוה**

יד א ב מיי' פ"ח מהל' ברכות הל' ב סמג עשין כז טוש"ע או"ח סי' רב סעיף ד:
טו ג מיי' פכ"א מהלכות שבת הל' כד טוש"ע או"ח סי' שכח סעיף לב [רב אלפס שבת ס"פ י"ד דף מז]:
טז ד טוש"ע או"ח סי' רד סעיף ח:
יז ה מיי' פ"ג מהלכות ברכות הלכה ב סמג עשין כו טוש"ע או"ח סי' רח סעיף ה:
יח ו ז ח מיי' פ"ח שם הלכה ג ד ה סמג שם טוש"ע או"ח סי' רד סעיף א:
יט ט טוש"ע או"ח סי' רג סעיף ח:
כ י מיי' פ"ח מהלכות ברכות הלכה ו סמג שם טוש"ע או"ח סי' רב סעיף ו:
כא כ מיי' פ"י מהל' מ"ש ונטע רבעי הלכה ג סמג עשין קלו טוש"ע יו"ד סימן רצד סעיף ג:
כב ל מיי' פ"ב מהל' תרומה הלכה ד:
כג מ מיי' פ"ה מהל' כלאים הל' כ טוש"ע יו"ד סי' רצו סעיף טו:
כד נ מיי' פ"י מהלכות מאכלות אסורות הל' יא סמג לאוין קמד טוש"ע יו"ד סימן רצד סעיף ט י:

**מסורת הש"ס**

תא פ"ע דתרומות דשביעית [תוספתא שבת פי"ג]

[לעיל לה:]

[ג"ל דתניא]

עירובין ד' כח.

[ז] נה. קנב. עירובין יג. חגיגה טו: ר"ה כ"ד: ... קדושין ... שבת: ב"ב קלג: עו"ג סנהדרין פ: כריתות ... נדה יג. כה:]

מעשרות פ"ד משנה ו

שבת דף קלט.

[ספק' פ"ה דכלאים]

ו פ"ג משנה ט קדושין לח:

לקמן מ: נדרים נה:

[פי' בערוך מרק והטור בא"ח סי' ר"ד פי' מי מלח ורבינו האי פירש זומית שהוא הקלף]

**גליון הש"ס**

קוקיאני. וקשה ... כלאחת שבת דף קט:

**רב נסים גאון**

אי אמר הכי הוה אמינא הני מילי מעשר (ירק) [אילן] דבארץ גופיה מדרבנן. שנינו במסכת ראש השנה בפ' א' באחד בתשרי ראש השנה לשנים ולשמטים וליובלו' לנטיעה ולירקות ובברייתא (שם דף יב) לירקות ולמעשרות ואמרינן לירקות מאי ניהו מעשר ירק היינו מעשרות תנא דרבנן וקתני דאורייתא וליתני דאורייתא ברישא איידי דחביבה ליה אקדמה ותנא דידן תנא דרבנן וכל שכן דאורייתא ובמסכת יומא בפרק יום הכפורים (דף פג) איתא נמי גוזזין כרישין ואוכל ואינו צריך לעשר והני מילי ירק דרבנן ובתחיל' מסכת מעשרות דבני מערבא אמרי ירקות מנין איסי בן עקביא אומר המעשרות לירק מדבריהן לפי שהכתוב לא זכר אלא זרע הארץ ופרי העץ כדכתיב וכל מעשר הארץ מזרע הארץ מפרי העץ אבל ירק מדרבנן הוא כדפרשי':

**הגהות הב"ח**

(א) רש"י ד"ה זמית שלמייר"א. נ"ב פי' מי מלח: (ב) ד"ה מ"מ לב"ש וכו' ערלה וכו' וכולי האי

מ"מ: (ג) תוס' ד"ה לא יערענו וכו' או בולעו. נ"ב והאי ובולע כלומר או בולעו: (ד) ד"ה כיון וכו' ונראין הדברים. נ"ב עיין לקמן דף ל"ח ע"א גבי שתיתא רכה:

**קליפי** אגוזים והגרעינים חייבין בערלה. דפירי נינהו. מכאן יש לברך על הגרעינין של גודגדניות, וגרעיני אפרסקין, ושל תפוחים וכל מיני גרעינים של פירות בורא פרי העץ: **אין** קוצצין אילנות בשביעית. וא"ת: בלא שביעית נמי, תיפוק ליה דאסור משום "לא תשחית את עצה" (דברים כ)! וי"ל: דלא טעין קבא, דלא שייך ביה לא תשחית, כדאיתא פרק "לא יחפור" (ב"ב כו.). אי נמי: איירי דמעולה בדמים לעשות ממנה קורות, דאז *לא שייך לא תשחית. ומיהו, משום איסורא דשביעית איכא "לאכלה" – ולא לסחורה, ולא להפסד: **שיעורו** כפול הלבן. ופחות מכאן לא הוי פירא. מכאן יש ללמוד דעל בוסר פחות מפול לא מברכינן עליה "בורא פרי העץ" אלא "בורא פרי האדמה": לשון ה"ג **והלכתא** כמר בר רב אשי מדלגבי ערלה לאו פירא הוא וכו'. והיה אומר הר"מ: דלגבי ערלה לאו פירא הוא – היינו משום דכל המיקל בארץ הלכה כמותו בח"ל. אבל בארץ – ודאי הוי פירא, ומברכין עליו "בורא פרי העץ" ובברכות ליכא חלוק בין בארץ לח"ל: **ברטיבא.** כגון ליטואר"ו בלעז, מברכינן עליה "בורא פרי האדמה", אבל יבישתא לא מברכינן עליה. וכן הלכה בזנגבילא שקורין זינזי"ברו בלעז, וכן[(א)] קל"ו של גרופל"י שאין רגילים לאכול [אלא] ברטיבא כגון בליטואר"ו – אין מברכין עליהם כלל ביבשתא. אבל עץ של קנמון שקורין קניל"א – מברכין עליו "בורא פרי האדמה", מפני שרגילין לאכלו ביובש, וגם הוא גדל על הארץ כמו קנים. ועל צוקר"ו מברכין "בורא פרי העץ" כי "יערי עם דבשי" (שיר ה) – זה צוקר"ו. ואגוז שקורין מוסקד"א מברכין "בורא פרי העץ", שגם נוהגין לאכול אותו ביובש: **כל** שיש בו מחמשת המינין מברכין עליו "בורא מיני מזונות". וכן קלייריט"ש בלע"ז שעושים מקמח ומים או מחלב – מברכין עליהם "בורא מיני מזונות". וכן כשנותנים קמח לתוך פולין או לתוך עדשים או כרישים, וכן לתוך שקדים שעושין לחולה, אם עושין אותו כדי שיסעוד הלב – אז צריך לברך "בורא מ"מ"; ואם לדבק[(ב)] בעלמא – אינו צריך לברך "בורא מ"מ". וטוב להחמיר ולגמעו בתוך הסעודה לאחר ברכת "המוציא", ופטור ממנה נפשך:

ולוקח, ובלבד שלא יראנו לוקט! – רבי עקיבא במקום ר"א עבדינן כוותיה, *וב"ש במקום ב"ה אינה משנה. ותיפוק ליה דנעשה שומר לפרי, ורחמנא אמר: "וערלתם ערלתו את פריו" – [א]את הטפל לפריו, ומאי ניהו – שומר לפרי! אמר רבא: היכא אמרינן דנעשה שומר לפרי – היכא דאיתיה בין בתלוש בין במחובר, הכא – במחובר איתיה, בתלוש ליתיה. איתיביה אביי: *[ב]פיטמא של רמון מצטרפת, והנץ שלו אין מצטרף; מדקאמר "הנץ שלו אין מצטרף", אלמא דלאו אוכל הוא, ותני' גבי ערלה: *[ג]קליפי רמון והנץ שלו, קליפי אגוזים [ד]והגרעינין – חייבין בערלה! –אלא אמר רבא: היכא אמרינן דנעשה להו שומר לפירי – היכא דאיתיה בשעת גמר פירא, האי קפרס ליתיה בשעת גמר פירא. איני?! והאמר רב נחמן אמר רבה בר אבוה: *הני מתחלי דערלה – אסירי, הואיל ונעשו שומר לפירי; ושומר לפירי אימת הוי – בכופרא, וקא קרי ליה שומר לפירי! רב נחמן סבר לה כרבי יוסי; דתנן, *רבי יוסי אומר: סמדר – אסור מפני שהוא פרי, ופליגי [ה]רבנן עליה. מתקיף לה רב שימי מנהרדעא: ובשאר אילני מי פליגי רבנן עליה?! והתנן: *מאימתי אין קוצצין את האילנות בשביעית? ב"ש אומרים: כל האילנות משיוציאו; וב"ה אומרים: [ו]החרובין משישרשרו, והגפנים משיגרעו והזיתים משיניצו, ושאר כל האילנות – משיוציאו; ואמר רב אסי: הוא בוסר, הוא גרוע, הוא פול הלבן. פול הלבן ס"ד?! אלא אימא: [ז]שיעורו כפול הלבן. מאן שמעת ליה דאמר: בוסר – אין, סמדר – לא – רבנן, וקתני: שאר כל האילנות משיוציאו! אלא אמר רבא: היכא אמרינן דהוי שומר לפרי – היכא דכי שקלת ליה לשומר מיית פירא, הכא – כי שקלת ליה לא מיית פירא. הוה עובדא ושקלוה לנץ דרמונא – ויבש רמונא, ושקלוה לפרחא דביטיתא – ואיקיים ביטיתא *(והלכתא כמר בר רב אשי, דזריק את האביונות ואכיל את הקפריסין. ומדלגבי ערלה לאו פירא נינהו – [ח]לגבי ברכות נמי לאו פירא נינהו, ולא מברכינן עליה "בורא פרי העץ", אלא "בורא פרי האדמה".)§ פלפלי – רב ששת אמר: "שהכל"; רבא אמר: [ט]לא כלום. ואזדא רבא לטעמיה. דאמר *רבא: [י]כס פלפלי ביומי דכפורי – פטור, כס זנגבילא ביומא דכפורי – פטור. מיתיבי: *היה ר"מ אומר, ממשמע שנאמר: "וערלתם ערלתו את פריו", איני יודע שעץ מאכל הוא?! אלא מה ת"ל "עץ מאכל" – להביא עץ שטעם עצו ופריו שוה, ואיזהו – זה הפלפלין, ללמדך שהפלפלין חייבין בערלה, וללמדך שאין ארץ ישראל חסרה כלום, שנאמר: "ארץ אשר לא במסכנת תאכל בה לחם לא תחסר כל בה"! לא קשיא: [כ]הא ברטיבתא, הא ביבשתא. *אמרי ליה רבנן למרימר: [ל]כס זנגבילא ביומא דכפורי – פטור. והא אמר *רבא: [מ]האי המלתא דאתיא מבי הנדואי – שריא, ומברכין עליה "בפה"א"! לא קשיא: הא ברטיבתא, הא ביבשתא.§ חביץ קדרה, וכן דייסא; רב יהודה אמר: "שהכל נהיה בדברו"; רב כהנא אמר: "[נ]בומ"מ". בדייסא גרידא כ"ע לא פליגי ד"בומ"מ", כי פליגי – בדייסא כעין חביץ קדרה, רב יהודה אמר: "שהכל" – סבר דובשא עיקר; רב כהנא אמר: "בורא מיני מזונות" – סבר סמידא עיקר. א"ר יוסף: כוותיה דרב כהנא מסתברא, דרב ושמואל דאמרי תרוייהו: כל שיש בו מחמשת המינין מברכין עליו "בורא מיני מזונות".§ גופא, רב ושמואל דאמרי תרוייהו: [ס]כל שיש בו מחמשת המינין מברכין עליו "בורא מיני מזונות"; ואיתמר נמי, רב ושמואל דאמרי תרוייהו: כל שהוא מחמשת המינין מברכין עליו "בורא מיני מזונות". וצריכא: דאי אשמעינן "כל שהוא" – הוה אמינא משום דאיתיה בעיניה, אבל על ידי תערובות – לא, קמ"ל

**ובלבד שלא יראנו.** החבר כשהוא לוקט מן הנטיעות: **אינה משנה.** ואין זה ספק אלא ודאי: **ותיפוק ליה.** דאי נמי ר' עקיבא דאמר לענין מעשר דלאו פירא נינהו, לענין ערלה אסירי קפריסין דהוה ליה שומר: **בתלוש ליתיה.** סופו שנופל הימנו כשמגיע להתבשל: **פיטמא** של רמון. הפרח שבראשו, כעין שיש לתפוחים ולספרגלין: **מצטרפת.** לכביצה, לטומאת אוכלין: **והנץ שלו.** נץ ברמון כקפרס באביונות: **אין מצטרף.** אע"ג דקי"ל "בהעור והרוטב" (ד' קיז:) שומרים מצטרפין לטומאה קלה דהיינו טומאת אוכלין. הני מילי – קליפת האגוז והרמון, אבל הנץ שומר על גבי שומר הוא ואין מצטרף; והכי אמרינן "בהעור והרוטב" (ד' קיט:): **חייבים בערלה.** דרחמנא רבינהו מ"את פריו" – הטפל לפריו, והאי נץ ליתיה שומר בתלוש, שכשמתייבש נופל מעל הקליפה: **קפרס ליתיה בגמר פירא.** כשמגיע סמוך לבשולו הוא נופל ממנו: **מתחלי.** בתמרי כקפרס בצלף: **בכופרא.** כשהתמרים קטנים קודם בשולם: **סבר לה כר' יוסי.** דכופרא הוי פרי ואע"פ שלא נגמר לפיכך שומר שלו חשוב שומר: **סמדר אסור.** ענבים כיון שנפל הפרח וכל גרגיר נראה לעצמו קרוי סמדר. וקאמר ר' יוסי, כיון שבא לכלל סמדר קרוי פרי. ואסור משום ערלה: **ופליגי רבנן עליה.** והלכה כרבים. **הלכך:** אביונות בעוד שהקפריסין בהן – לאו פירי נינהו, ולא מיקרו קפריסין שומר לפרי: **בשאר אילנות.** חוץ מן הענבים: **אין קוצצין בשביעית.** דרחמנא אמר "לאכלה" ולא להפסד: **משיוציאו.** את הפרי: **משישרשרו.** משיראו בהן כמין שרשרות של חרובין: **משיגרעו.** שהענבים גסים כגרוע, ולקמן מפרש לה: **משיניצו.** משיגדל הנץ סביב: **הוא בוסר הוא גרוע.** כל מקום שהזכירו בוסר – הוא גרוע: **פול הלבן ס"ד.** הא בענבים קיימינן: **מאן שמעת ליה דאמר.** גבי ענבים בוסר הוא דהוי פרי, אבל סמדר לא: **רבנן.** הוא דפליגי עליה דר' יוסי במסכת ערלה, וקאמרי בשאר אילנות דמשיוציאו הוי פרי הראוי: **ביטיתא.** אביונות: **כס פלפלי.** כל דבר שאדם אוכל שלא כדרכו מיקרי כסיסה. **פטור.** **מכתא:** המלתא. ליטואר"ו בלע"ז: **שריא.** אין בה לא משום בשול גוים ולא משום געול גוים: **הנדואי.** כושיים: **חביץ קדרה.** מין מאכל קפוי, כמו חלב שמקפיאוהו בקיבה, כך עושין מאכל קפוי בקדרה. ולקמן מפרש לה: קמחא ודובשא ומשחא, וקרו ליה אברוש"ט: **דייסא.** של חטים כתושות במכתשת. **דייסא כעין חביץ קדרה.** לקמן מפרש לה: חטי דמתברי בכשיתא ויהבו בהו דובשא, ועביד להו כקדירה: **סמידא.** סלת.

תורה אור: ויקרא יט

[ביצה יג: יבמות ע.]
עוקצין פ"ב מ"ג [חולין קיח:]
ערלה פ"א משנה ח
פסחים דף נב:
ערלה פ"א משנה ז
שביעית פ"ד משנה יוד פסחים דף נב:
מהרש"ל מ"ז כי הוא מבעל ה"ג ולאו מן הגמ' וכן הוא להדיא ברא"ש
יומא פא:
שם סוכה לה. [ע"ש בפירש"י ומהר"ם ליפשב]
[ביומא איתא א"ל רבינא]
יומא שם

כה א טוש"ע י"ד סי' רצד סעיף ב:
כו ב מיי' פ"ה מהל' טומאת אוכלין הלכה ה:
כז ג מיי' פ"י מהל' מ"ש ונטע רבעי הל' יג טוש"ע י"ד סי' רצד סעיף ה:
כח ד מיי' שם וטור ש"ע י"ד סימן רצד סעיף ח:
[כדאיתא בב"ק נח:]
כט ה מיי' שם:
ל ו ז מיי' פ"ה מהל' שמיטה ויובל הלכה יח טוש"ע או"ח סימן רב סעיף ב:
לא ח מיי' פ"ח מהל' ברכות הלכה ו סמג עשין כז טוש"ע או"ח סי' רב סעיף ב:
לב ט י כ ל מיי' שם הל' ז וסמג שם ומיי' פ"ב מהל' שביתת עשור הלכה ו סמג לאוין סט טוש"ע או"ח סי' תריב סעיף ט ועי' טוש"ע י"ד סי' קיג סעיף ח:
לג מ טוש"ע או"ח סי' רב סעיף ו:
לד נ מיי' פ"ג מהל' ברכות הל' ד סמג עשין כז טוש"ע או"ח סי' רח סעיף ב וסעיף ט:

**רב נסים גאון**
**מאימתי** אין קוצצין את האילנות בשביעית. ומפני מה אין קוצצין מפני שאמר הכתוב והיתה שבת הארץ לכם לאכלה ודרשי' לה לאכלה ולא להפסד ובמסכת דפסחים בפרק מקום שנהגו (דף נב) כדאמרינן ר' אילא קץ בפנייתא דשביעי' אקשי' עליה והיכי עבד הכי לאכלה אמר רחמנא ולא להפסד וכו' ומפרקינן בסופה אלא ר' אילא ברנסחני קץ כלומר שאין באין לידי גמר פרי ולכך התיר ר' אילא לקוצן והכין אמר בהלכות בפירוש' דנסחני כפניות דנסחני דקרו להו גופרי מברכין עליהן בורא פרי העץ דכיון דלא עבדי פירא אחריני היינו פירייהו ואית בבבא קמא בפ' החובל בחברו (דף נח) אמר רב דיקלא דטעין קבא אסור למקצייה והא אמן תנן ובכמה יהא בזיתים ולא יקוצנו רובע שאני זיתים דחשיבי וזו המשנה היא אע"פ שהיא בשביעית לא הקשו ממנה עליה דרב אלא משיעורא דאית ביה הוא רובע ורב אמר קב אלא מהו דברי רב אמר קב השנים קאמר ואנן מוזהרין בשביעית בלבד מפני שכל דבר שיש בו הפסד הוא אסור מן הכתוב דכתיב (דברים כ) לא תשחית את עצה הלא תראה כי כל שרשי עציו עקרים ויש הנאה מעציו יותר מפריו מותר לקוצו הואיל והוא משתבר בקציעתו אינו עובר עליו משום לא תשחית כדאמרי' אמר רבינא ואם היה מעולה בדמים מותר ואיתא בברייתא נמי סיועא זה רק עץ אשר תדע זה אילן מאכל כי לא עץ מאכל הוא זה אילן סרק וכי מאחר שסופנו לרבות כל דבר מה ת"ל כי לא עץ מאכל הוא להקדים סרק למאכל יכול אפי' מעולה בדמים ת"ל רק ואיתא בבבא בתרא בפרק לא יחפור (דף כו) מאי דמסייע לה ובסוף פ' הישן תחת המטה (סוכה דף כט) הזכירו ענשו של דבר ואמרו בשביל ד' דברים מאורות לוקין ואחד מהן קוצצי אילנות טובים וזה הדבר בשאר השנים אבל בשביעית אין מותר לקוץ מהפירות אלא לאחר שנגמרין כגון כפניאתא דנסחני דהוא גמר פירי דידהו דרחמנא אמר תהיה כל תבואתה לאכול ואמרי' בגמ' מלמד שאינה נאכלת אלא כל מה שנקצץ ממנה קודם גמר פירי הרי הפסידו ורחמנא אמר לאכלה ולא להפסד דתנן (שביעית פרק ד משנה י) כל האילן כיון שבא לעונת המעשרות מותר לקוצו:

**הגהות הב"ח** (א) תום' ד"ה ברטיבא וכו' וכן מסמר של גרופל"י שאין: (ב) ד"ה כל שיש וכו' ואם לדבק. נ"ב ע"ל דף ל"ט ע"א:

**גליון הש"ס** גמ' כל שיש בו כו'. ע' לקמן מ"א ע"ב תוס' ד"ה אלא כו'. עי' פסחים נ"ב ע"ב [illegible] **רש"י** ד"ה משיוציאו [illegible] **תוס'** ד"ה כל כו'. ואם לדבק. לקמן ל"ט ע"א: **בא"ד** א"צ לברך כו'. [illegible] **בא"ד** בתוך הסעודה. [illegible]

קמ"ל, 'כל שיש בו'. ואי אשמעינן 'כל שיש בו', הוה אמינא כל שיש בו חמשת המינים – אין, אבל אורז ודוחן – לא, משום דע"י תערובת; אבל איתיה בעיניה – נימא אפילו אורז ודוחן נמי מברכין עליו "בורא מיני מזונות" קמ"ל: כל שהוא מחמשת המינים הוא דמברכין עליו 'בורא מיני מזונות'; לאפוקי אורז ודוחן, דאפילו איתיה בעיניה – לא מברכינן "בורא מיני מזונות".§ ואורז [ודוחן] לא מברכינן "בורא מיני מזונות"?! והתניא: הביאו לפניו פת אורז ופת דוחן – מברך עליו תחלה וסוף כמעשה קדרה; וגבי מעשה קדרה תניא: בתחלה מברך עליו "בורא מ"מ" ולבסוף מברך עליו ברכה אחת מעין שלש! –כמעשה קדרה, ולא כמעשה קדרה; כמעשה קדרה – דמברכין עליו תחלה וסוף; ולא כמעשה קדרה, דאילו במעשה קדרה – בתחלה "בורא מיני מזונות" ולבסוף ברכה אחת מעין ג', ואילו הכא, בתחלה מברך עליו "שהכל נהיה בדברו", ולבסוף "בורא נפשות רבות וחסרונן על כל מה שברא". –ואורז לאו מעשה קדרה הוא? והתניא, אלו הן מעשה קדרה: חילקא, טרגיס, (א) סולת, *זריז, וערסן, ואורז! –הא מני – רבי יוחנן בן נורי היא; דתניא, *רבי יוחנן בן נורי אומר: אורז מין דגן הוא, וחייבין על חמוצו כרת, ואדם יוצא בו ידי חובתו בפסח; אבל רבנן לא. –ורבנן לא?! והתניא: *הכוסס את החטה מברך עליה "בורא פרי האדמה"; טחנה אפאה ובשלה, בזמן שהפרוסות קיימות – בתחלה מברך עליה "המוציא לחם מן הארץ" ולבסוף מברך עליה ג' ברכות, אם אין הפרוסות קיימות – בתחלה מברך עליה "בורא מיני מזונות" ולבסוף מברך עליה ברכה אחת מעין ג'; הכוסס את האורז מברך עליו "ב"פ האדמה"; טחנו, אפאו ובשלו, אף על פי שהפרוסות קיימות – בתחלה מברך עליו "בורא מיני מזונות", ולבסוף מברך עליו ברכה אחת מעין שלש. מני? אילימא ר' יוחנן בן נורי היא, דאמר "אורז מין דגן הוא" – "המוציא לחם מן הארץ" ושלש ברכות בעי ברוכי! אלא לאו – רבנן היא, ותיובתא דרב ושמואל! תיובתא.§ אמר מר: הכוסס את החטה מברך עליה "בורא פרי האדמה". והתניא: "בורא מיני זרעים"! –לא קשיא: הא ר' יהודה, והא רבנן; דתנן, *ועל ירקות(ב) אומר: "בורא פרי האדמה"; ר' יהודה אומר: "בורא מיני דשאים".§ אמר מר: הכוסס את האורז – מברך עליו "בורא פרי האדמה", טחנו אפאו ובשלו, אע"פ שהפרוסות קיימות – בתחלה מברך עליו "בורא מיני מזונות", ולבסוף ברכה אחת מעין שלש. –והתניא: לבסוף ולא כלום! –אמר רב ששת: לא קשיא: הא ר"ג והא רבנן. דתניא, *זה הכלל: כל שהוא משבעת המינים, רבן גמליאל אומר: שלש ברכות, וחכמים אומרים: ברכה אחת מעין שלש. ומעשה ברבן גמליאל והזקנים שהיו מסובין בעלייה ביריחו, והביאו לפניהם כותבות ואכלו, ונתן רבן גמליאל רשות לר' עקיבא לברך. קפץ ובירך רבי עקיבא ברכה אחת מעין שלש. אמר ליה רבן גמליאל: עקיבא, עד מתי אתה מכניס ראשך בין המחלוקת! א"ל: רבינו, אע"פ שאתה אומר כן וחבריך אומרים כן, למדתנו רבינו: *יחיד ורבים הלכה כרבים. רבי יהודה אומר משמו: כל שהוא משבעת המינים ולא

*לעיל לה. | תוספתא פ"ד | [ר"ה י. וש"נ]

**רש"י**

קמ"ל כל שהוא. דאע"ג דכולהו מחד מינא, בעינן דליהוי מחמשת המינין, ואי לא, לא מברכינן עליה בורא מיני מזונות: אורז. מי"ל: דוחן. פנ"ך: כמעשה קדרה. ברכה שמברכין על מעשה קדרה של חמשת מינין: ברכה אחת מעין ג'. בשלהי פרקין (דף מד.) מפ' לה על המחיה כו': ואורז לאו מעשה קדרה. דקא מספקא ליה מכלל מעשה קדרה לברכה אחרת: אלו הן מעשה קדרה. לענין ברכה: חילקא טרגיס זריז וערסן. מפרש להו במועד קטן (ג) (פ"ב יג:): חילקא. חטי דמתברי בתחילתא חדא לתרתי: טרגים. חדא לתלת: זריז. חדא לארבע: ערסן. חדא לחמש: הא מני. הך מתניתא דקתני אורז כמעשה קדרה, רבי יוחנן בן נורי: ה"ג אבל רבנן לא ורבנן לא והתניא כו'. ול"ג והלכתא. ומהלכות גדולות הוא: הכוסס. כמות שהיא: אפאה ובשלה. לאחר שאפאה בתנור ועשאה לחם, חזר ובשלה במים: שהפרוסות קיימות. שלא נמוחו בבשולן: ברכה אחת מעין ג'. "על המחיה ועל הכלכלה", ובשלהי פרקין (דף מד.) מפרש לה: אלא לאו רבנן היא. וקתני "במ"מ", ותיובתא דרב ושמואל: הא רבי יהודה כו'. הא דקתני "בורא מיני זרעים" – ר' יהודה היא, דקתני לכל מין ומין מעין ברכתו, כדמפרש לקמן בפירקין (דף מ.) אליביה. הלכך, לירקות "בורא מיני דשאים". לחטין דזרעים נינהו "בורא מיני זרעים". ולרבנן, בין זרעים בין ירקות – "בפה"א" ולא בעינן לכל מין ומין מעין ברכתו: ולא כלום. כלומר אין טעון מברכות פירות ארץ ישראל ולא כלום, אלא "בורא נפשות רבות", ככל מידי דליתיה משבעת המינין: כותבות. הם תמרים, (ד) והם "דבש" האמור בשבעת המינין, שהדבש זב מן התמרים: קפץ ובירך. לאחריהן: משמו. של ר"ג:

**תוספות**

בורא נפשות רבות וחסרונם. כמו לחם ומים, שאי אפשר בלא הם. *ועל כל מה שברא להחיות בהם נפש כל חי" כלומר: על כל מה שבעולם, שגם אם לא בראם יכולין העולם לחיות בלא הם, שלא בראם כי אם לתענוג בעלמא, כמו תפוחים וכיוצא בהן. ומסיים "ברוך חי העולמים" – ובירושלמי "ברוך אתה ה' חי העולמים":

אם הפרוסות קיימות. יש מפרשים דהיינו כשהלחם אינו שרוי במים כ"כ שאם יקח הפרוסה שלא ישבר: רש"י פי': אורז = מי"ל. ויש מפרשים ר"יזו, ולהאי פירוש יש לפרש דדוחן היינו מי"ל:

תיובתא דרב ושמואל. באורז; אבל אדוחן לא הוי תיובתא, ואפשר דהוי הלכתא כוותייהו ולא מברכין עליה "בורא מיני מזונות":

הכוסס חטה צריך לברך עליה "בורא פרי האדמה". שהרי אפילו בקמחא דחיטי אמרינן לעיל(ה) מברכין עליה "בפה"א". ולרב נחמן לא ס"ל הכי – משום דאשתנו. ומיהו בלאחריו יש לספק מאי מברכין: אם מברכין "על המחיה ועל הכלכלה" ומסיים "על האדמה ועל פרי האדמה", דלא אשכחן ברכת על המחיה ועל הכלכלה אלא היכא דבריך עלייהו ברישא קודם אכילה "בורא מיני מזונות". ור"ת הגיה במחזור שלו "על האדמה ועל פרי האדמה כו'", וחזר בו, דלא אשכחן בשום מקום הך ברכה. דלקמן (דף מד.) מפרש ברכה אחת מעין ג' וקאמר בחמשת המינים 'על הארץ ועל המחיה', ועל ז' המינים 'על הארץ ועל הפירות', ועל האדמה ועל פרי האדמה – לא הזכיר. ועוד, מדקאמר הכא על הכוסס את החטה מברך "בורא פרי האדמה", וקאמר בהדיא טחנו ואפאו פת עד "אם אין הפרוסות קיימות בתחלה מברך בורא מ"מ ולבסוף ברכה אחת מעין שלש", ומדלא קתני הכא גבי כוסס החטה מברך לאחריו ברכה אחת מעין שלש, ש"מ: דבכוסס ליכא ברכה לאחריו מעין ג'. והא דקאמר כל שהוא מין דגן ולא עשאו פת וכו' וחכמים אומרים ברכה אחת מעין ג' – מיירי דעבדינהו כעין דייסא, דחשיבא אז אכילתו. אבל הכוסס את החטה חי דלא חשיבא אכילתו כ"כ, אע"ג דהיא מן חמשת המינים – אינו מברך לאחריו ברכה מעין שלש, אלא "בורא נפשות רבות וכו'". ומיהו אומר הר"י: שיש לספק, שמא חכמים כיילי ליה בההוא מין דגן ולא עשאו פת וכו', וחכמים אומרים: ברכה אחת מעין שלש. ונכון להחמיר, שאין לאכול קליות או חטים שלוקות אלא בתוך הסעודה, שאז ברכת המזון פוטרתן, אם לא נתמעכו יפה דהוו כמו דייסא, ובירושלמי יש שגם האמוראים היו מסופקים, דקאמר: הדין דאכיל סלת, פירוש: קליות, מאי מברך בסופה? רבי ירמיה אמר: לא אכלית סלת מן יומא וכו':

נתן ר"ג רשות לר' עקיבא לברך. סבור(ו) היה שיברך ג' ברכות כמו שהיה סובר. וא"ת: לר"ג הא קי"ל *דאין מזמנין על הפירות! וי"ל: דר"ג היה סבור שהיה מברך על כל ז' מינין ג' ברכות שלמות, וכי בירך ר"ע מעין ג' – לעצמו דוקא, דקי"ל אין מזמנין על הפירות, ואחרים המסובין ברכו כל אחד לעצמו. וא"ת: לר"ג דאמר ג' ברכות שלמות וס"ל דמזמנים על ז' המינים, אי ס"ל דברכה טעונה כוס – א"כ(ז) יזמנו, וא"כ יזמנו לעולם! וי"ל: דיכול להיות שלא ישתה כלל מן כוס של ברכה. וא"ת: מ"מ, לאותו המברך שהוא טועם – צריך לברך פעם אחרת, וא"כ אין לדבר סוף! וי"ל: היכא דאינו שותה בקביעות רק מלא לוגמיו – מודה ר"ג, דאל"כ וכי לית ליה לר"ג ברכה אחת מעין שלש בשום מקום: [וע"ע תוס' פסחים קה: ד"ה ש"מ]:

**עין משפט נר מצוה**

[עי' ב"ח סימן רז ובעט"ז סק]

לה א מיי' פ"ג מהל' ברכות הל' יוד סמג עשין כז טוש"ע או"ח סי' רח סעיף ח:

לו ב מיי' שם הלכה ד סמג שם טוש"ע שם סעיף ב:

לז ג מיי' פ"ה ופ"ו מהל' חמץ ומצה סמג לאוין עט טוש"ע או"ח סימן תנג סעיף א:

לח ד מיי' פ"ג מהל' ברכות הל' ב טוש"ע או"ח סי' רח סעיף ד:

לט ה מיי' שם הל' ח סמג עשין כז טוש"ע או"ח סי' קסח סעיף י:

מ ו ז [מיי' שם הלכה י] סמג שם טוש"ע או"ח סי' רח סעיף ז:

**הגהות הב"ח**

(א) גמ' טרגיס זריז כצ"ל ותיבת סולת נמחק: (ב) שם ועל הירקות הוא אומר: (ג) רש"י ד"ה חילקא וכו' במועד קטן. נ"ב ס"פ מי שמתו דף י"ג: חילקא טרגיס וטיסני חילקא חדא לתרתי טרגיס חדא לתלת טיסני חדא לארבע: (ד) שם ד"ה כותבות וכו' תמרים והוא דבש: (ה) תוס' ד"ה הכוסס וכו' אמרינן לעיל. נ"ב ריש ל"ו: (ו) ד"ה נתן וכו' סבור שיהא מברך: (ז) בא"ד טעונה כוס א"כ יזמנו לעולם כצ"ל ותיבות יזמנו וא"כ נמחק:

**גליון הש"ס**

גמ' הכוסס כו'. עי' רש"י [לעיל לו ע"א ד"ה קמח] ועי' מגילה ז ע"ב ד"ה לאיכסויה [וביומא פ"א ד"ה שכוסס]: תוס' ד"ה הכוסס כו' שמא חכמים כיילי ליה בההוא וכו' ועי' לקמן מ"ד ע"א: תוס' ד"ה נתן כו' דאינו שותה בקביעות רק מלא לוגמיו. עי' לקמן ע"א תוס' ד"ה בלל:

[חולין קו. וע"ש בתוס' ד"ה וש"נ]

(א) ולא מין דגן הוא, או מין דגן ולא עשאו פת, ר״ג אומר: שלש ברכות, וחכ״א: ברכה אחת; כל שאינו לא משבעת המינין ולא מין דגן, כגון פת אורז ודוחן – ר״ג אומר: ברכה אחת מעין שלש, וחכ״א: ולא כלום. במאי אוקימתא – כר״ג, אימא סיפא דרישא: אם אין הפרוסות קיימות – בתחלה מברך עליה "בורא מיני מזונות", ולבסוף מברך עליה ברכה אחת מעין שלש, מני? אי ר״ג – השתא אכותבות ואדייסא אמר ר״ג ג׳ ברכות, אם אין הפרוסות קיימות מיבעיא?! אלא פשיטא – רבנן, אי הכי קשיא דרבנן אדרבנן! אלא, לעולם רבנן, ותני גבי אורז: ולבסוף אינו מברך עליו ולא כלום.§ אמר רבא: האי ריהטא דחקלאי דמפשי ביה קמחא – מברך "במ״מ". מ״ט – דסמידא עיקר. דמחוזא דלא מפשי ביה קמחא – מברך עליו "שהכל נהיה בדברו". מ״ט – דובשא עיקר. *והדר אמר רבא: [א]אידי ואידי "במ״מ"; דרב ושמואל דאמרי תרווייהו: כל שיש בו מחמשת המינים מברכין עליו "בורא מיני מזונות".§ א״ר יוסף: *האי חביצא דאית ביה פרורין כזית – בתחלה מברך עליו "המוציא לחם מן הארץ" ולבסוף מברך עליו שלש ברכות; דלית ביה פרורין כזית – בתחלה מברך עליו "בורא מיני מזונות", ולבסוף ברכה אחת מעין שלש. אמר רב יוסף: מנא אמינא לה – *דתניא: [ב]היה עומד ומקריב מנחות בירושלים, אומר: ברוך שהחיינו וקימנו והגיענו לזמן הזה; נטלן לאכלן – מברך "המוציא לחם מן הארץ", ותני עלה: [ג]וכולן פותתן כזית. א״ל אביי: אלא מעתה, לתנא דבי ר׳ ישמעאל דאמר, ׳פורכן עד שמחזירן לסלתן׳, ה״נ דלא בעי ברוכי "המוציא לחם מן הארץ"?! וכי תימא ה״נ, והתניא: לקט מכולן כזית ואכלן, אם חמץ הוא – ענוש כרת, ואם מצה הוא – אדם יוצא בו ידי חובתו בפסח! הכא במאי עסקינן – בשערסן. אי הכי, אימא סיפא: והוא שאכלן בכדי אכילת פרס, ואי בשערסן – האי ׳שאכלן׳?! ׳שאכלו׳ מיבעי ליה! –הכא במאי עסקינן – בבא מלחם גדול. מאי הוה עלה? אמר רב ששת: [ד]האי חביצא, אף על גב דלית ביה פרורין כזית – מברך עליו "המוציא לחם מן הארץ". אמר רבא: [ה]והוא דאיכא עליה תוריתא דנהמא. [ו]טרוקנין חייבין בחלה. [א] וכי אתא רבין א״ר יוחנן: טרוקנין [ב] פטורין מן החלה. מאי טרוקנין? אמר אביי: כובא דארעא. ואמר אביי: [ז]טריתא פטורה מן החלה. מאי טריתא? איכא דאמרי: גביל מרתח, ואיכא דאמרי: [ח]נהמא דהנדקא; ואיכא דאמרי: [ט]לחם העשוי לכותח. תני רבי חייא: לחם העשוי לכותח פטור מן החלה. והא תניא: חייב בחלה! התם כדקתני טעמא, ר׳ יהודה אומר: [י]מעשיה מוכיחין עליה, עשאן כעבין

**חביצא** דאית ביה פרורין. פרש״י: כמו שלניקו״ק, (ג) וא״ת: והתניא לעיל דזמן שהפרוסות וכו׳, אין הפרוסות קיימות – לא יברך עליהן המוציא, אע״ג דאית ביה כזית! וי״ל: דרב יוסף מפרש ליה הפרוסות קיימות – היינו בכזית, ואין הפרוסות קיימות – בשאין בהן כזית, וכן מפרש נמי בירושלמי. וא״ת: ואיך מדמה רב יוסף פרורי מנחות לפרורי חביצא? וי״ל: כיון שנטגנין בשמן – כנתבשלו דמי. ומיהו קשה ד׳לקט מכולן כזית׳ דקאי אחמשת המינין ולא אמנחות, כמו שאפרש, והתם (ד) נמי לא מיירי בשנתבשלו, ומאי מדמה לחביצא שהוא מבושל? לכך נ״ל: חביצא – היינו פרורין הנדבקים יחד על ידי מרק, או על ידי חלב, כמו חביצא דתמרי – *שהן נדבקין:

**היה** עומד ומקריב מנחות. פרש״י: בעל הבית המתנדב מנחה, ודוחק גדול הוא, דהיה עומד ומקריב – משמע בכהן המקריב, וכן לישנא "נטלן לאכלן" משמע דאכהן קאי. ונראה בכהן העומד להקריב ראשון במשמרתו, וכ״ד משמרות היו וכל שבת מתחדשת משמרה אחרת, אם כן כל משמרה אינה משמרת אלא ב׳ פעמים בשנה, וכיון שיש להם זמן קבוע – מברכין שהחיינו, ולא כפירש״י דמנחות דמיירי בכהן שלא הקריב מעולם:

**לקט** מכולן. פירש״י דקאי אמנחות ולא נהירא; דא״כ, היכי קאמר "דאם חמץ הוא וכו׳" והא אמרינן (מנחות ד׳ נב:): כל המנחות באות מצה!– ונראה דקאי אחמשת מינין, וה״ק: לקט מכל מיני לחמים כזית כו׳:

**אמר** רבא והוא דאיכא עליה תוריתא דנהמא. וכן קיימא לן, דרבא בתרא הוא, ולא בעינן שיהו בפרורין כזית, כיון דאיכא תוריתא דנהמא לענין המוציא, ואפילו נתבשלו לפירוש רש״י. והא דמשמע בירושלמי דפרוסות קיימות הן בכזית – היינו לפי שכן דרך להיות תוריתא דנהמא בכזית, אבל פעמים דאפילו בפחות מכזית איכא תוריתא דנהמא, ואפילו ביותר מכזית ליכא תוריתא דנהמא. ונראה דהיינו כשנותני׳ הפרורין (ה) במים, ואם המים מתלבנים מחמת הפרורין – אזלא ליה תוריתא דנהמא. וכן היה רגיל רבינו דוד ממי״ץ ללבן פרורין במים בלילה כדי לאכלן בשחר בלא ברכת המוציא ובלא ברכת המזון, שלא לאחר, כדי שיתחזק ראשו ויוכל להגיד ההלכה:

**לחם** העשוי לכותח פטור מן החלה. והיינו כשעשאו כלמודים, ופירש״י: עיסה שמיבשים בחמה. וקשה, דהא אמרינן במסכת חלה (פ״א משנה ה), כל שתחלתו עיסה וסופו סופגנין – חייבין בחלה, וכל שתחלתו סופגנין וסופו עיסה – חייבין נמי בחלה, ושתחלתו סופגנין וסופו נמי סופגנין – פטור מן החלה! ופסק ר״ת: אם כן, בניבל״ש וריסולא״ש דתחלתן עיסה – מברכין עליהן ׳המוציא׳ וחייבין בחלה, אף על פי דסופן סופגנין. ומתחלה היה ר״ל ר״ת דלדוקא חייבין בחלה, דמצות חלה בעודן עיסה, דכתיב "עריסותיכם", והואיל שהיו מתחלה עיסה – חייבין בחלה, אבל מן ׳המוציא׳ פטורים, דעכשיו הם סופגנין. ול״נ דהא לעיל קתני "נטלן לאכלן מברך עליהן המוציא" גבי מנחה, אף על פי דעכשיו הם סופגנין שהמנחות מטוגנות בשמן. ורימשי״ש אף על גב דחייבין בחלה שהיו עיסה מתחלה – פטורין מ׳המוציא׳, ואין מברכין עליהם אלא "בורא מיני מזונות", דלית להו תוריתא דנהמא, ואחר כך ברכת מעין שלש "על המחיה ועל הכלכלה". ור׳ יחיאל ז״ל היה מסופק

ולא (ג) מין דגן. שבמין דגן יש חילוק, שאם עשאו פת – הכל מודים שמברך לאחריו ג׳ ברכות: או. אף אם מין דגן הוא אלא שלא עשאו פת, בשתים אלו נחלקו ר״ג וחכמים: במאי אוקימתא. להאי דלעיל דקתני "ולבסוף ברכה אחת מעין שלש": כר״ג – אימא סיפא דרישא. דהיא מתני׳, דמתני׳ גבי הכוסס את החטה דהיא רישא דידה, וקתני סיפא "אין הפרוסות קיימות" כו׳: השתא. אפילו אדייסא אמר ר״ג במתניתין בתרייתא, או מין דגן ולא עשאו פת – מברך אחריו ג׳ ברכות: אין הפרוסות קיימות. שבתחלתו פת ממש היה: מיבעיא. וכשמוחה מי גרע מדייסא? אלא לאו רבנן היא. דאמרי גבי דייסא ברכה אחת והאי נמי משמוח – לאו פת הוא, והוי כדייסא: והלכתא. לא גרסינן: ריהטא. הוא חביץ קדרה: דחקלאי. בני כפר: דמפשי ביה קמחא. שמרבים בו קמח: דמחוזא. בני כרך: חביצא. כעין שלניי״קוק, שמפררין בתוך האלפס לחם: מנא אמינא לה. דאפרורין כזית מברכין המוציא: היה. ישראל עומד: ומקריב מנחות. ונקנה לכהן להקריבה: אומר ברוך שהחיינו. אם לא הביא מנחות זה ימים רבים: נטלן לאכלן. הכהן: ותני עלה. כלומר ותנן על המנחות; מנחת מחבת ומנחת מרחשת הקריבות כשהן אפויות: וכולן פותתן. כלומר: כולן קודם קמיצה; ועושה אותן פתיתין כזיתים דכתיב "פתות אותה פתים" (ויקרא ב). אלמא: פתיתין כזיתים מברך עליהן "המוציא": פורכן. למנחות האפויות על המחבת ועל המרחשת קודם קמיצה, עד שמחזירן לסלתן: הכי נמי. דפליג אהא דקתני מברך "המוציא": והתניא לקט מכולן. פתיתי המנחות: כזית כו׳. ומדקאמר "יוצא בו ידי חובתו בפסח" משום אכילת מצה, דמצות עשה היא דכתיב "בערב תאכלו מצות", והכא לחם בעינן, דכתיב בה "לחם עוני", אלמא: לחם הוי, ומברך "המוציא". וקא מתניתין על כרחך רבי ישמעאל היא, דהא קתני לקט מכולן כזית – אלמא בפתיתין פחותין מכזית קאי: בשערסן. כשחזר וגבלן יחד וחזר ואפאן. ערסן לשון עריסותיכם: והוא שאכלן בכדי אכילת פרס. שלא ישהה משהתחיל לאכול שיעור כזית עד שגמר אכילת השיעור יותר מכדי אכילת חצי ככר של שמנה ביצים דהוי חציו ארבעה ביצים שזהו לירוק שיעור אכילה. ואם שהה יותר – אין האכילה מצטרפת, והוה ליה כאוכל חצי זית היום וחצי זית למחר, ואין בו חיוב כרת אם חמץ הוא: ואי בשערסן והוא שאכלו. לשון יחיד מיבעי ליה: הב״ע. ובשלא ערסן היא, ודקאמרת; והא דקתני חשיב למיהוי לחם – בבא מלחם גדול ונשאר מן הלחם שלא נפרס כולו. אבל אם נפרס כולו – לא חשיבי פתיתין הפחותין מכזית, ולא מברכינן "המוציא", ואין יוצא בהן ידי חובת מצה בפסח:

תוריתא דנהמא. תואר הלחם: כובא דארעא. עושה מקום חלל בכירה, ונותן בתוכו מים וקמח, כמו שעושין באלפס: גביל מרתח. נותנים קמח ומים בכלי, ומחממין בכף, ושופכי׳ על הכירה כשהיא נסקת: נהמא דהנדקא. בצק שאופין בשפוד ומושחים אותו תמיד בשמן או במי ביצים ושמן: לחם העשוי לכותח. אין אופין אותו בתנור אלא בחמה: כעבין

(מעין זה שבת נסמן)

מנחות עה:

סס

מא א מיי׳ פ״ג מהל׳ ברכות הלכה ד סמג עשין כז טוש״ע או״ח סי׳ רח סעיף ב:

מב ב מיי׳ פ״ו מהל׳ תמידין ומוספין הלכה יח:

מג ג מיי׳ פי״ג מהל׳ מעשה הקרבנות הלכה יא:

מד ד ה מיי׳ פ״ג מהל׳ ברכות הל׳ ח סמג עשין כז טוש״ע או״ח סי׳ קסח סעיף י:

מה ו ז מיי׳ פ״ו מהל׳ בכורים הל׳ יב סמג עשין קמא טוש״ע י״ד סי׳ שכט סעיף ה וטוש״ע או״ח סי׳ קסח סעיף טו:

מו ח ט טוש״ע או״ח שם סעיף טז:

מז י מיי׳ פ״ו מהל׳ בכורים הל׳ יד סמג עשין קמא טוש״ע י״ד סי׳ שכט סעיף ז:

הגהות הב״ח

(א) גמ׳ ולאו מין דגן וכו׳ וחכמים אומרים ברכה אחת מעין שלש שאינו: (ב) רש״י ד״ה ולאו מין: (ג) תוס׳ ד״ה חביצ׳ וכו׳ כמו של נייקו״ק. נ״ב כלומר שנתבשלו וא״כ קשה מדתניא לעיל וכו׳: (ד) בא״ד והתם לא מיירי בשנתבשלו מ״מ מאי מדמה: (ה) ד״ה תוריתא דנהמא וכו׳ במים דאם המים וכו׳ רב דוד ממיץ לשרות פרורים במים כל הלילה:

הגהות הגר״א

[א] גמ׳ (טרוקנין חייבין בחלה). תא״מ: [ב] שם כי אתא רבין א״ר טרוקנין חייבין בחלה. כצ״ל:

כְּעָבִין. עֲרוּכָה וּמְקוּשֶּׁטֶת כִּגְלוּסְקָאוֹת נָאוֹת, גַּבֵּי דַּעֲשׂוּיָה דְּלָלֶחֶם עֲשָׂאָהּ: כִּלְמוּדִין. כִּנְסָרִים בְּעָלְמָא, שֶׁלֹּא הִקְפִּיד עַל עֲרִיסָתָהּ. וְדוּגְמָתוֹ שָׁנִינוּ "בְּמוֹעֵד קָטָן" (פ"ג דף יג.): עוֹשֶׂה לוֹ לִמּוּדִין – לוּחִין, לְבוֹר שֶׁל יַיִן לְכַסּוֹתוֹ: זֵיעָה בְּעָלְמָא הוּא. וְאֵינוֹ פְּרִי לְבָרֵךְ עָלָיו "בּוֹרֵא פְּרִי הָעֵץ": וְחוֹמֶץ סְפוּנְיוֹת. סוֹפֵי עֲנָבִים שֶׁאֵין מִתְבַּשְּׁלִים עוֹלָמִית, וְעוֹשִׂים מֵהֶן חוֹמֶץ: מְחַיֵּיב קֶרֶן וְחוֹמֶשׁ. לְשׁוֹתֶה מִמֶּנּוּ בְּשׁוֹגֵג: וְר' יְהוֹשֻׁעַ פּוֹטֵר. דְּזֵיעָה בְּעָלְמָא הוּא, וְאֵין שֵׁם תְּרוּמָה חָל עָלָיו, וְאֵין לְךָ פְּרִי הַנִּיתָּן לְמַשְׁקֶה אֶלָּא זֵיתִים וַעֲנָבִים בִּלְבַד, וְהַיְינוּ כְּמַר בַּר רַב אַשִׁי: טְרִימָא מַהוּ. מַה מְּבָרְכִין עָלָיו? וְשֵׁם טְרִימָא – כָּל דָּבָר הַכָּתוּשׁ קְלָת וְאֵינוֹ מְרוּסָּק: לָא הֲוָה אַדַּעְתָּא דְּרָבָא. לֹא הָיָה מֵבִין מַהוּ שׁוֹאֵל: א"ל. רָבִינָא לְהַהוּא מֵרַבָּנָן: אֵיזוֹ טְרִימָא אַתָּה שׁוֹאֵל: דְּקוּרְטְמֵי. כַּרְכּוֹם, שֶׁכּוֹתְשִׁים אוֹתוֹ וְנוֹתְנִין בּוֹ יַיִן וְשׁוֹתִין: אוֹ דְּשׁוּמְשְׁמֵי. לְהוֹצִיא שַׁמְנָן: אוֹ דְּפוּרְצָנֵי. כְּתִישַׁת עֲנָבִים לָתֵת לְתוֹךְ הַחַרְצַנִּים מַיִם לַעֲשׂוֹת תֶּמֶד: א"ל רָבָא: חֲשִׁילְתָּא קָא אָמְרַתְּ. מִתּוֹךְ דִּבְרֵי רָבִינָא הֵבִין רָבָא אֶת הַשְּׁאֵלָה. א"ל: דָּבָר מָעוּךְ שָׁאַלְתַּנִי. כְּמוֹ "בֵּיעֵי חֲשִׁילָתָא" "דִּשְׁחִיטַת חוּלִּין" (דף מג.): מוּתָּר לַעֲשׂוֹת מֵהֶן טְרִימָא. שֶׁאֵינוֹ מַפְסִידָהּ, אַלְמָא דְּבְמִילְּתָא' קָאֵי. וְכֵיוָן דְּהָכִי הוּא – מְבָרְכִין עֲלֵיהּ "ב"פ הָעֵץ": שְׁתִיתָא. מַאֲכָל הֶעָשׂוּי מִקֶּמַח קְלָיוֹת שֶׁנִּתְיַבְּשׁוּ בַּתַּנּוּר בְּעוֹד שֶׁהַשִּׁבֳּלִים לַחִים*: עָבָה לַאֲכִילָה עֲבִידָא. וּבְמִילְּתָא' קָיְימָא: שֶׁבּוֹחֲשִׁין. מְגִיסִין בְּכַף לְעָרְבוֹ יָפֶה בְּמֵימָיו: זֵיתוֹם הַמִּצְרִי. מְפוֹרָשׁ בְּמַסֶּכֶת פְּסָחִים (דף מב:*): וְכָל הַמַּשְׁקִים שׁוֹתֶה. אַלְמָא לַאֲכִילָה מְכַוֵּין וּרְפוּאָה מִמֵּילָא הָוְיָא. הָכָא נָמֵי – לַאֲכִילָה מְכַוֵּין כו'(א): ה"ג וּצְרִיכָא דְּרַב וּשְׁמוּאֵל. וְאַע"ג דְּתַנְיָא לְעִנְיַן שַׁבָּת דְּאוֹכֶל הוּא וּמוּתָּר לְאָכְלוֹ בְּשַׁבָּת, אִיצְטְרִיךְ לְמֵימַר דְּטָעוּן בְּרָכָה: ה"ג דסד"א כֵּיוָן דִּלְרְפוּאָה קָא מְכַוֵּין לָא לִבְעֵי בְּרָכָה קמ"ל כֵּיוָן דְּמִתְהֲנֵי מִינֵּיהּ. שֶׁהֲרֵי מַאֲכָל הוּא – בָּעֵי בָּרוֹכֵי: וְהִלְכְתָא. ל"ג, וּמֵהֲלָכוֹת גְּדוֹלוֹת הוּא: דְּאַפֵּיק מַשְׁמַע. שֶׁהוֹצִיא כְּבָר, וְהָא וַדַּאי בְּרָכָה הֲגוּנָה, דִּלְשֶׁעָבַר בָּעֵינַן, שֶׁהֲרֵי כְּבָר הוֹצִיא הַלֶּחֶם הַזֶּה מִן הָאָרֶץ שֶׁהוּא בָּא לֵיהָנוֹת הֵימֶנּוּ: דִּכְתִיב אֵל מוֹצִיאָם מִמִּצְרַיִם. וּכְשֶׁנֶּאֶמְרָה פָּרָשַׁת בִּלְעָם כְּבָר יָצְאוּ: הַמּוֹצִיא לְךָ מַיִם. וּכְבָר הוֹצִיא: וְרַבִּי נְחֶמְיָה סָבַר דְּמַפִּיק מַשְׁמַע. שֶׁעָתִיד לְהוֹצִיא, דִּכְתִיב "הַמּוֹצִיא אֶתְכֶם" וּכְשֶׁנֶּאֱמַר פָּסוּק זֶה לְמֹשֶׁה עֲדַיִין לֹא יָצְאוּ, וְ"הַמּוֹצִיא לְךָ מַיִם" – עֲדַיִין הָיָה מוֹצִיא, כָּל יְמֵי הֱיוֹתָם בַּמִּדְבָּר: דְּאַפֵּיקִית יָתְכוֹן. שֶׁאֲנִי הוּא שֶׁהוֹצֵאתִי אֶתְכֶם: אַשְׁמְעִינַן

מסופק אם וירמשי"ש חייבין בחלה משום(ג) עושה עיסתו בלק כדי לחלקה – פטורין מן החלה, דלית בהו שיעורא. הכא גבי וירמשיי"ש נמי פעמים מחלקן, שאין משימין שיעור חלה בקדרה אחת אך היה מצריך ליקח חלה בלא ברכה בשביל הספק. וכל דבר שתחלתו סופגנין וסופו עיסה—חייבין בחלה וב'המוציא', דקיי"ל כרבי יוחנן פרק "כל שעה" (פסחים לז.). דפליגי ר' יוחנן ור"ל במעשה אילפס, ופליגי בבלילתו רכה, דהיינו תחלתו סופגנין וסופו עיסה, אם נאפה בתנור או בכירה או באילפס בלא מים ושמן. דר"ל ס"ל דלא הוה חייב אלא כשנאפה בתנור, והאי קאי מתניתין תחלתו סופגנין וסופו עיסה דחייב בחלה, אבל באילפס פטור. ורבי יוחנן מחייב, דמעשה אילפס סופו עיסה קרינן ביה. רק שלא יהיה משקין באילפס – דהכי איתא בירושלמי: כל שהאור תחתיו – חייב בחלה ומברכין עליו 'המוציא'. אבל אנילי"ש אין מברכין עליו 'המוציא', דלא הוי אלא גובלא בעלמא. ומיהו, אם קבע סעודתיה עלייהו, כמו בפורים – מברך 'המוציא'. וכל דבר שתחלתו סופגנין וגם סופו – כגון הני סופגנין שמטגנין אותן בשמן שקורין בוניי"ש – *פטורין מן החלה: **מר** זוטרא קבע סעודתיה עלויה. וכן נ"ל, אי קבע סעודתיה עליה – מברכין עליה 'המוציא'. וכן צוה הר"מ בפורים, שקובעין סעודתן עליהן, לברך 'המוציא' בפת תחלה כדי לפוטרן מברכה, שהיה מסופק אי הוה קביעותייהו קביעות או לא: **האי** דובשא דתמרי מברכין עלויה שהכל. וכן משקין מכל מיני פירות בר מתירוש ויצהר, כדאמרינן גבי ערלה. *ולאפוקי מה"ג שפירש דמיירי שנתן לתוכן מים. ושכר דידן, אע"ג דשמא יש בהן כזית בכדי אכילת פרס – לא מברכין עליו "בורא מיני מזונות" אלא 'שהכל'. ואפי' לרב ושמואל דאמרי כל שיש בו מחמשת המינין מברכין עליו "בורא מיני מזונות" – הכא לא הוי בהו ממש שעורים(ג) ואין שכר אלא טעמא בעלמא. ועוד: משום שיש בו עלויה אחרינא בפת, ועוד – בשתיה אומר 'שהכל': **ושוין** שבוחשין. רבי(ד) ור' יוסי פליגי גבי נותן מים לתוך המורסן ובקלישה איירי, מדקתני 'ובוחשין' ולא קתני לשון גבול, והכי דייקינן התם: **ואי** ס"ד לרפואה עבדי ליה, רפואה בשבת מי שרי. דסובר דכיון(ה) דכל שעקרו לרפואה, ואין רגילות לעשותו לצורך אכילה – אסור בשבת וכו': **והא** תנן כל האוכלין וכו'. דמשמע מדנקט כל האוכלין דאפי'(ו) כל שעקרו לרפואה כיון שראוי לאכילה שפיר דמי, מדנקט 'כל'. ומסיק הגמרא וצריכא דרב ושמואל דפשיטא(ז) דמתניתין שריא, אף על פי שעומד לרפואה, אבל דרב ושמואל אשמעינן דלא נימא כיון דעקרו לרפואה – לא לבריך עליה כלל, קא משמע לן: כיון דמתהני מיניה בעי ברוכי. ומכל מקום, לא יברך אלא 'שהכל', כיון שאינו עשוי לסעוד כי אם לשתות. ואם כן, כל דבר שיש בו מחמשת המינין ואינו עשוי לסעוד כי אם לשתות, כגון שכר וכיוצא בו – מברך 'שהכל', וכהאי גוונא פסק בה"ג: והלכתא שתיתא עבה – מברך "בורא מיני מזונות", קלישתא – מברך 'שהכל', ואף על פי שלרפואה נעשית, היכא דאית ליה הנאה מיניה – מברך: והלכתא

תורה אור

כְּעָבִין – חַיָּיבִין, כִּלְמוּדִין – פְּטוּרִים. א"ל אַבַּיֵי לְרַב יוֹסֵף: הַאי כּוּבָא דְּאַרְעָא מַאי מְבָרְכִין עֲלָוֵיהּ? א"ל: מִי סָבְרַתְּ נַהֲמָא הוּא?! אגּוּבְלָא בְּעָלְמָא הוּא וּמְבָרְכִין עֲלָוֵיהּ "בּוֹרֵא מִינֵי מְזוֹנוֹת". מָר זוּטְרָא בקָבַע סְעוּדָתֵיהּ עֲלָוֵיהּ, וּבֵרֵךְ עֲלָוֵיהּ, "הַמּוֹצִיא לֶחֶם מִן הָאָרֶץ" וְשָׁלֹשׁ בְּרָכוֹת. אָמַר מָר בַּר רַב אַשִׁי: גוְאָדָם יוֹצֵא בָּהֶן יְדֵי חוֹבָתוֹ בְּפֶסַח, מ"ט – °"לֶחֶם עוֹנִי" קָרֵינַן בֵּיהּ. דברים טז וְאָמַר מָר בַּר רַב אַשִׁי: דהַאי דּוּבְשָׁא דְּתַמְרֵי מְבָרְכִין עֲלָוֵיהּ "שֶׁהַכֹּל נִהְיָה בִּדְבָרוֹ". מ"ט? – זֵיעָה בְּעָלְמָא הוּא. כְּמַאן? כִּי הַאי תַּנָּא, דִּתְנַן: *דְּבַשׁ תְּמָרִים, וְיֵין תַּפּוּחִים, וְחוֹמֶץ סְפוּנְיוֹת, וּשְׁאָר מֵי פֵּירוֹת שֶׁל תְּרוּמָה – רַבִּי אֱלִיעֶזֶר מְחַיֵּיב קֶרֶן וְחוֹמֶשׁ, וְרַבִּי יְהוֹשֻׁעַ הפּוֹטֵר. א"ל: הַהוּא מֵרַבָּנַן לְרָבָא: טְרִימָא מַהוּ? לָא הֲוָה אַדַּעְתֵּיהּ דְּרָבָא מַאי קָאָמַר לֵיהּ. יָתֵיב רָבִינָא קַמֵּיהּ דְּרָבָא, א"ל: דְּשׁוּמְשְׁמֵי קָא אָמְרַתְּ, אוֹ דְּקוּרְטְמֵי קָא אָמְרַתְּ, אוֹ דְּפוּרְצָנֵי קָא אָמְרַתְּ? אַדְּהָכִי וְהָכִי אַסְקֵיהּ רָבָא לְדַעְתֵּיהּ, אָמַר לֵיהּ: חֲשִׁילְתָּא וַדַּאי קָא אָמְרַתְּ, וְאַדְכַּרְתַּן מִלְּתָא הָא דְּאָמַר רַב אַסִי: והַאי תַּמְרֵי שֶׁל תְּרוּמָה – מוּתָּר לַעֲשׂוֹת מֵהֶן טְרִימָא, וְאָסוּר לַעֲשׂוֹת מֵהֶן שֵׁכָר. וְהִלְכְתָא: זתַּמְרֵי וְעָבְדִינְהוּ טְרִימָא – מְבָרְכִין עֲלָוַיְיהוּ "בּוֹרֵא פְּרִי הָעֵץ". מַאי טַעְמָא – בְּמִלְּתַיְיהוּ קַיְימֵי כִּדְמֵעִיקָּרָא.§ שְׁתִיתָא, רַב אָמַר: "שֶׁהַכֹּל נִהְיָה בִּדְבָרוֹ", וּשְׁמוּאֵל אָמַר: "בּוֹרֵא מִינֵי מְזוֹנוֹת". אָמַר רַב חִסְדָּא: וְלָא פְּלִיגִי, חהָא בְּעָבָה הָא בְּרַכָּה; עָבָה – לַאֲכִילָה עָבְדִי לָהּ, רַכָּה – לִרְפוּאָה קָא עָבְדִי לָהּ. מְתִיב רַב יוֹסֵף: *וְשָׁוִין, [ח] שֶׁבּוֹחֲשִׁין אֶת הַשְּׁתוּת בְּשַׁבָּת [ט] וְשׁוֹתִין זֵיתוֹם הַמִּצְרִי; וְאִי ס"ד לִרְפוּאָה קָא מְכַוֵּין, רְפוּאָה בְּשַׁבָּת מִי שָׁרֵי?! א"ל אַבַּיֵי: וְאַתְּ לָא תִּסְבְּרָא?! וְהָא *תְּנַן: טכָּל הָאוֹכָלִין אוֹכֵל אָדָם לִרְפוּאָה בְּשַׁבָּת וְכָל הַמַּשְׁקִין שׁוֹתֶה! אֶלָּא מָה אִית לָךְ לְמֵימַר? – גַּבְרָא לַאֲכִילָה קָא מְכַוֵּין, ה"נ – גַּבְרָא לַאֲכִילָה קָא מְכַוֵּין. לִישָּׁנָא אַחֲרִינָא: אֶלָּא מָה אִית לָךְ לְמֵימַר – גַּבְרָא לַאֲכִילָה קָא מְכַוֵּין וּרְפוּאָה מִמֵּילָא קָא הָוְיָא, ה"נ – לַאֲכִילָה קָא מְכַוֵּין וּרְפוּאָה מִמֵּילָא קָא הָוְיָא. וּצְרִיכָא דְּרַב (וּשְׁמוּאֵל): דְּאִי מֵהַאי, – ה"א לַאֲכִילָה קָא מְכַוֵּין וּרְפוּאָה מִמֵּילָא קָא הָוְיָא; אֲבָל הָכָא, *כֵּיוָן דִּלְכַתְּחִילָּה לִרְפוּאָה קָא מְכַוֵּין, לָא לִבָרֵיךְ עֲלָוֵיהּ כְּלָל – קמ"ל: כֵּיוָן דְּאִית לֵיהּ הֲנָאָה מִינֵּיהּ, בָּעֵי בָּרוֹכֵי.§ "שֶׁעַל הַפַּת הוּא אוֹמֵר הַמּוֹצִיא וכו'".§ ת"ר: מָה הוּא אוֹמֵר? "הַמּוֹצִיא לֶחֶם מִן הָאָרֶץ", רַבִּי נְחֶמְיָה אוֹמֵר: "מוֹצִיא לֶחֶם מִן הָאָרֶץ". אָמַר רָבָא: בְּ"מוֹצִיא" כּוּלֵּי עָלְמָא לָא פְּלִיגִי דְּאַפֵּיק מַשְׁמַע, דִּכְתִיב: °"אֵל מוֹצִיאָם מִמִּצְרַיִם", כִּי פְּלִיגִי – בְּ"הַמּוֹצִיא"; רַבָּנַן סָבְרִי: "הַמּוֹצִיא" – דְּאַפֵּיק מַשְׁמַע, דִּכְתִיב: °"הַמּוֹצִיא לְךָ מַיִם מִצּוּר הַחַלָּמִישׁ"; וְרַבִּי נְחֶמְיָה סָבַר: "הַמּוֹצִיא" – דְּמַפִּיק מַשְׁמַע, שֶׁנֶּאֱמַר: °"הַמּוֹצִיא אֶתְכֶם מִתַּחַת סִבְלוֹת מִצְרַיִם". וְרַבָּנַן? – הַהוּא, הָכִי קָאָמַר לְהוּ קוּדְשָׁא בְּרִיךְ הוּא לְיִשְׂרָאֵל: כַּד מַפֵּיקְנָא לְכוּ עָבֵידְנָא לְכוּ מִלְּתָא כִּי הֵיכִי דְּיָדְעִיתוּ דַּאֲנָא הוּא דְּאַפֵּיקִית יָתְכוֹן מִמִּצְרַיִם, דִּכְתִיב: °"וִידַעְתֶּם כִּי אֲנִי ה' אֱלֹהֵיכֶם הַמּוֹצִיא". מְשַׁתַּבְּחִין לֵיהּ רַבָּנַן לְרַבִּי זֵירָא [אֶת] בַּר רַב זְבִיד אֲחוּהּ דר"ש בַּר רַב זְבִיד דְּאָדָם גָּדוֹל הוּא, וּבָקִי בִּבְרָכוֹת הוּא. אָמַר לְהֶם: לִכְשֶׁיָּבֹא לְיֶדְכֶם הֲבִיאוּהוּ לְיָדִי. זִמְנָא חֲדָא אִיקְּלַע לְגַבֵּיהּ, אַפֵּיקוּ לֵיהּ רִיפְתָּא, פָּתַח וְאָמַר "מוֹצִיא". אָמַר: זֶה הוּא שֶׁאוֹמְרִים עָלָיו דְּאָדָם גָּדוֹל הוּא וּבָקִי בִּבְרָכוֹת הוּא?! בִּשְׁלָמָא אִי אָמַר "הַמּוֹצִיא" – אַשְׁמְעִינַן

במדבר כג · דברים ח · שמות ו · שם

פי"א מ"ב חולין קכ: · לקמן דכא כך ע"ש עירובין כט: · ושבת קו. · שבת קנו. · קט: יומא מט. · רש"ל מ"ז לעיל לו. · [וע' תוס' פסחים לו: ד"ה דכ"ע] · [תרומות פי"א מ"ג]

מח א ב מיי' פ"ג מהל' ברכות הלכה ט טוש"ע או"ח סימן קסח סעיף טו:
מט ג מיי' פ"ו מהל' חמץ ומצה הל' ו טוש"ע או"ח סי' תסא סעיף ב:
נ ד מיי' פ"ח מהלכות ברכות הלכה ב סמג עשין כז טוש"ע או"ח סי' רב סעיף ח:
נא ה ו מיי' פי"א מהל' תרומות הלכה ב:
נב ז מיי' פ"ח מהל' ברכות הל' ד סמג עשין כז טוש"ע או"ח סי' רב סעיף ו:
נג ח [מיי' פ"ג שם הל' ג] טוש"ע או"ח סי' רח סעי' ו
[ח מיי' פכ"א מהל' שבת הל' לג טוש"ע או"ח סי' שכ"א סעיף י"ד]
[ט מיי' שם הלכה כב]
נד ט מיי' פכ"א מהל' שבת הל' כב סמג לאוין סה טוש"ע או"ח סי' שכח סעיף לז:

**הגהות הב"ח**

(א) רש"י ד"ה וכל המשקים וכו' מכוין כו' ס"ד ואחר כך מ"ה ה"ג. ולריכא וכו' ברכה הס"ד ואחר כך מ"ה דסד"א: (ב) תוס' ד"ה לחם וכו' וירמשיי"ש חייבים בחלה משום דתנן העושה עיסתו בלק כדי לחלקה פטורה מן החלה דלית בהו שיעורא א"כ הכא: (ג) ד"ה האי דובשא וכו' דאין שכר אלא וכו' ועוד בשתיה נ"ב עיין בסוף עמוד זה: (ד) ד"ה ושוין שבוחשין רבי יוסי בר יהודה פליג גבי נותן מים. נ"ב פ' מי שהחשיך סוף דף קנה: (ה) ד"ה ואי וכו' דכיון שעקרו כל"ל ותיבת דכל נמחק: (ו) ד"ה והתניא וכו' דאפילו שעקרו כל"ל ותיבת כל נמחק: (ז) בא"ד דפשיטא למתני' דשרי בשבת כיון שעומד לאכילה אע"ג דעיקרו לרפואה אבל לרב:

**גליון הש"ס**

גמ' ור"נ סבר המוציא דמפיק משמע. ע' עירובין י"ט ע"ב וצ"ע: רש"י ד"ה כלמודין כנסרים. ע' תוי"ט פ"ה מ"ט דכלים: רש"י ד"ה שתיתא מאכל העשוי כו'. וכ"ל רש"י מלכים א יב:

**נה** א מיי' פ"ג מהל' ברכות הל' ב סמג עשין כז טוש"ע או"ח סי' קסז סעיף ב:

**נו** ב ג ד מיי' פ"ח מהל' ברכות סמג שם טוש"ע או"ח סי' רה סעיף א [וכסימן רב סעיף יב]:

**נז** ה מיי' פ"ו מהל' חמץ ומצה הלכה ו סמג עשין מא טוש"ע או"ח סי' תסא סעיף ד:

**נח** ו מיי' פ"ז מהלכות חמץ ומצה הלכה יג סמג עשין מא טוש"ע או"ח סי' תעג סעיף ה:

**נט** ז מיי' פ"א מהל' ברכות הל' ב ופ"ג הל' יב סמג עשין כז טוש"ע או"ח סימן רי סעיף א:

אשמעינן טעמא, ואשמעינן דהלכתא כרבנן; אלא דאמר "מוציא" מאי קמ"ל? –ואיהו דעבד – לאפוקי נפשיה מפלוגתא. והלכתא א"המוציא לחם מן הארץ", דקי"ל כרבנן, דאמרי: דאפיק משמע.§ "ועל הירקות אומר וכו'". קתני ירקות דומיא דפת – מה פת שנשתנה ע"י האור, אף ירקות נמי שנשתנו ע"י האור. אמר רבנאי משמיה דאביי, בזאת אומרת: שלקות מברכין עליהן "בורא פרי האדמה" (*ממאי – מדקתני ירקות דומיא דפת.) דרש רב חסדא משום רבינו, ומנו – רב: שלקות מברכין עליהם "בורא פרי האדמה"; ורבותינו היורדין מארץ ישראל, ומנו – עולא משמיה דר' יוחנן אמר: שלקות מברכין עליהן "שהכל נהיה בדברו"; ואני אומר: גכל שתחלתו "בורא פרי האדמה", שלקו – "שהכל נהיה בדברו"; וכל שתחלתו "שהכל נהיה בדברו", שלקו – "בורא פרי האדמה". בשלמא כל שתחלתו "שהכל נהיה בדברו" שלקו "בפה"א" – משכחת לה בכרבא וסלקא וקרא; אלא כל שתחלתו "בפה"א" שלקו – "שהכל", היכי משכחת לה? א"ר נחמן בר יצחק: משכחת לה דבתומי וכרתי. דרש רב נחמן משום רבינו, ומנו – שמואל: שלקות מברכין עליהם "בפה"א"; וחברינו היורדים מארץ ישראל, ומנו – עולא, משמיה דר' יוחנן אמר: שלקות מברכין עליהן "שהכל נהיה בדברו"; ואני אומר: במחלוקת שנויה. דתניא: *יוצאין ברקיק השרוי ובמבושל שלא נמוח, דברי ר"מ, ור' יוסי אומר: היוצאים ברקיק השרוי, אבל לא במבושל, אע"פ שלא נמוח. ולא היא, דכ"ע – שלקות מברכין עליהן "בפה"א", ועד כאן לא קאמר ר' יוסי התם – אלא משום דבעינן טעם מצה וליכא, אבל הכא – אפי' רבי יוסי מודה.§ אמר ר' חייא בר אבא א"ר יוחנן: שלקות מברכין עליהם "בפה"א", ור' בנימין בר יפת א"ר יוחנן: שלקות מברכין עליהם "שהכל נהיה בדברו". א"ר נחמן בר יצחק: קבע עולא *לשבשתיה כר' בנימין בר יפת. *תהי בה ר' זירא: וכי מה ענין ר' בנימין בר יפת אצל ר' חייא בר אבא? ר' חייא בר אבא – *דייק וגמיר שמעתא מרבי יוחנן רביה, ורבי בנימין בר יפת – לא דייק; ועוד, רבי חייא בר אבא *כל תלתין יומין מהדר תלמודיה קמיה דר' יוחנן רביה, ור' בנימין בר יפת לא מהדר; ועוד, בר מן דין ובר מן דין, דההוא תורמסא *דשלקי ליה שבע זמנין בקדרה ואכלי ליה בקנוח סעודה, אתו ושאלו לר' יוחנן, ואמר להו: מברכין עלויה "בורא פרי האדמה"; ועוד, אמר ר' חייא בר אבא: אני ראיתי את ר' יוחנן שאכל זית מליח ובירך עליו תחלה וסוף. אי אמרת בשלמא שלקות במילתייהו קיימי – בתחלה מברך עליו "בורא פרי העץ" ולבסוף מברך עליו ברכה אחת מעין שלש, אלא אי אמרת שלקות לאו במילתייהו קיימי, בשלמא בתחלה מברך עליו "שהכל נהיה בדברו", אלא לבסוף מאי מברך? –דילמא: "בורא נפשות רבות וחסרונן על כל מה שברא". מתיב רב יצחק בר שמואל: *ירקות שאדם יוצא בהן ידי חובתו בפסח – יוצא בהן ובקלח שלהן, אבל לא כבושין ולא שלוקין ולא מבושלין; ואי ס"ד במילתייהו קאי – שלוקין אמאי לא? –שאני התם, דבעינן טעם מרור – וליכא.§ אמר ליה רבי ירמיה לרבי זירא: רבי יוחנן היכי מברך על זית מליח? כיון דשקילא לגרעיניה

בצר

**תוספות**

**והלכתא** המוציא וכו'. ואע"פ דבמוציא כ"ע לא פליגי דאפיק משמע. *ובירושלמי מפרש טעמא: כדי שלא לערב האותיות, כגון 'העולם' – 'מוציא'. ואע"ג דל'לחם מן' נמי איכא עירוב, שאני התם דקרא כתיב (תהלים קד) "מצמיח חציר לבהמה ועשב לעבודת האדם להוציא לחם מן הארץ". ועל כן יש לבצוע בשתי ידיו בעשר אצבעות נגד י' תיבות שבמקרא זה: **מדקתני** ירקות דומיא דפת. לא הוי ירקות דומיא דפת, שהרי פת אישתני לעלויא, ויש ירקות שאין משתנות לעלויא. אלא כלומר: מה הפת אין בשול מגרע את הברכה, אף הירקות נמי – במלתייהו קיימי, ולא מגרע להו הבשול: **משכחת** לה בתומי וכרתי. וא"ת: והרי נראה לעינים דהבשול משביחן! וי"ל: דהיינו בשביל הבשר והמלח שבתוכן. ונראין הדברים שכל דבר שהוא כל כך טוב מבושל כמו חי, וחי כמו מבושל, כמו מיני קטניות, וכן תפוחים – יש להן ברכה הראשונה, שכל כך שוין מבושלין כמו חיין. ומטעם זה מברכינן נמי על היין מבושל "בורא פרי הגפן", °שכל כך הוא טוב אחר הבשול כמו קודם לכן. וקרא וסלקא וכרוב וכיוצא בהן, שטובין יותר מבושלין מחיין, כשהן חיין – מברכין עליהם 'שהכל', ומבושלין – 'ב"פ האדמה'. וכן אותן ערמוניות וחבושים שאינן ראוין לאכלן חיין כמו מבושלין, בתחלה מברכין עליהן 'שהכל' ומבושלין 'בורא פרי העץ'. אך אותן ערמוניות שקורין לומיברד"ש – מברך עליהן 'בורא פרי העץ' אפילו בתחלה. וכל דבר המתקלקל בבשולו, כגון תומי וכרתי וכיוצא בהן, כשהן חיין – מברך עליהן 'בורא פרי האדמה', ומבושלים – 'שהכל', כך נראה לרבינו יהודה. ומיהו הרב אלפס פסק בשלקות,(ד) דאשתני לגריעותא ע"י בשולן, אומר 'בורא פרי האדמה' כרב נחמן, דאמר שלקות מברכין עליהן 'בורא פרי האדמה' דר' חייא בר אבא קאי נמי כוותיה. ובכל שלקות איירי ר' חייא בר אבא, אף באותן דמשתנים לגריעותא – מדפליג להו גמרא אהדדי ר' חייא בר אבא ור' בנימין בר יפת. ואגוז מטוגן בדבש – מברך עליו 'בורא פרי העץ', דאגוז עיקר: **כל** תלתין יומין מהדר תלמודיה. לאו דוקא כל תלמודו, אלא כל מה שהיה לומד בשלשים יום – היה חוזר הכל לפניו ביום שלשים ואחד: **זית** מליח. ומליח כרותח:

בכלר

**רש"י**

**אשמעינן טעמא.** פירושא דקרא, כמו שפירשנוהו ולמדנו פירושו: **ואשמעינן הלכה כרבנן.** ד"המוציא" – דאפיק הוא: **מאי קמשמע לן.** הכל מודים בזו: **אף ירקות שנשתנו כו'.** ואפילו הכי במילתייהו קיימי, ומברכין עלייהו "בורא פרי האדמה": **שלקות.** כל ירק שלוק: **דרש רב חסדא.** כך: **משום רבינו.** רב: **שלקות אומר בורא פרי האדמה ורבותינו כו' ומאן נינהו עולא אמר רבי יוחנן שהכל.** הרי הדבר במחלוקת: **ואני אומר.** ליישב דבריהם שאינן חלוקין; יש מהן "פרי האדמה" ויש מהן "שהכל": **כל.** ירק הנאכל חי שתחלתו ב"פ האדמה", שלקו – אפקיה ממלתיה לגריעותא ומברך "שהכל". ולקמן מוקי לה בתומי וכרתי: **וכל.** ירק שאין דרכו לאכול חי, שמתחלתו אם אכלו חי – "שהכל" הוא מברך: **שלקו.** והביאו לדרך אכילתו, הוא עיקר פריו – ומברך "בורא פרי האדמה": **דרש רב נחמן.** כך: **משום רבינו.** שמואל: **שלקות מברך בורא פרי האדמה וחברינו כו'.** רב נחמן חשוב, ולא קרי לעולא רבותינו: **אמר שלקות שהכל ואני אומר.** שהם חלוקין בפלוגתא דרבי מאיר ורבי יוסי. ודברי שמואל ודברי ר' יוחנן בכל מיני ירקות הן, וחלוקין זה על זה; שמואל כר"מ דאמר מבושל קאי במלתיה, ור' יוחנן קאי כר' יוסי: **יוצאין ברקיק השרוי.** במים, ידי אכילת מצה של מצוה, וקרינן ביה "לחם עוני": **אבל לא במבושל.** דתו לאו לחם איקרי: **אפילו ר' יוסי מודה.** דלענין ברכה במילתיה קאי: **אמר רב נחמן קבע עולא לשבשתיה כר' בנימין.** (א)עולא שאמר משום ר' יוחנן לעיל "שהכל", למד וקבע שבושו כרבי בנימין, עד שנתקעה בלבו, ועכשיו אומר בבית המדרש בשם רבי יוחנן: **תהי בה ר' זירא.** במחלוקת זו שהוזכרה בבית המדרש וכי מה ענין להזכיר דברי ר' בנימין (ב)אצל דברי רבי חייא בר אבא במחלוקת בית המדרש, הרי אינו כדאי לחלוק עליו: **בר מן דין ובר מן דין.** לבר משתי ראיות הללו שאמרתי שאין רבי בנימין(ג) כלום אצל רבי חייא, יש לנו עוד ראיה שלא אמר רבי יוחנן מימיו שלקות שהכל: **וא"ל בורא פרי האדמה.** אלמא: אע"ג דשלקיה קאי במלתיה: **שאכל זית מליח.** שהיה מלוח זה כמה ימים, וקי"ל (פסחים עו.): מליח כרותח: **אבל לא כבושין.** בירקות של מרור היא שנויה בפרק "כל שעה" (דף לט.), לומר שאין יוצאין בהן שלוקין משום מרור, אלמא – לאו במלתייהו קיימי. שלוק הוי נימוח טפי ממבושל: **דבעינן טעם מרור וליכא.** אבל לענין ברכה – שם פרי עליו:

בצר

**מסורת הש"ס**

ירושלמי פ"ו ה"א

[ברי"ף ורא"ש זה]

פסחים מא.

פי' שבשוך למודו

[עי' פירש"י בכ ד"ה תהי]

[לעיל לג: וש"נ]

[חולין פו: ע"ש]

[ביצה כה:]

פסחים לט.

**הגהות הב"ח**

(א) רש"י ד"ה אמר רב נחמן וכו' כרבי בנימין בר יפת עולא וכו' כר' בנימין בר יפת עד שנתקעה: (ב) ד"ה תהי וכו' כרבי בנימין בר יפת אצל: (ג) ד"ה בר מן וכו' רבי בנימין בר יפת כלום: (ד) תוס' ד"ה משכחת וכו' ה"ר אלפס פסק בשלקות אע"ג דאשתנו לגריעותא על ידי בשולן ג"כ אומר בורא:

**גליון הש"ס**

גמ' והלכתא המוציא. עי' תורת חיים סנהדרין ע"ב ע"א ד"ה רי"א:

תוס' ד"ה משכחת לה וכו' שכל כך הוא טוב אחר הבישול כמו קודם לכן. עי' מתני' ספ"ב דתרומות ובר"ש שם:

ס א מיי' פ"ד מהלכות מאכלות אסורות הל' א [טוש"ע או"ח סי' תפו].
סא ב טוש"ע או"ח סי' ריא סעיף ג.
סב ג טוש"ע או"ח סי' רה סעיף ד.
סג ד מיי' פ"ג מהל' ברכות הל' ו טוש"ע או"ח סי' רה סעיף ב.
סד ה מיי' פ"ח מהל' ברכות הלכה ד סמג שם טוש"ע או"ח סימן רה סעיף ב.
סה ו מיי' פט"ו מהל' תרומות הלכה י"ב ופ"א מהל' טומאת אוכלין הלכה ז:

בצר ליה שיעורא! – אמר ליה: מי סברת כזית גדול בעינן?! כזית בינוני בעינן (והא איכא), וההוא דאייתו לקמיה דרבי יוחנן – זית גדול הוה, דאע"ג דשקלוה לגרעינותיה פש ליה שיעורא. *דתנן: [א]זית שאמרו – לא קטן ולא גדול אלא בינוני, וזהו אגורי. ואמר רבי אבהו: לא אגורי שמו אלא אברוטי שמו, ואמרי לה: סמרוסי שמו, ולמה נקרא שמו אגורי – ששמנו אגור בתוכו.§ נימא כתנאי, דהנהו תרי תלמידי דהוו יתבי קמיה דבר קפרא, הביאו לפניו כרוב ודורמסקין ופרגיות, נתן בר קפרא רשות לאחד מהן לברך, קפץ ובירך על הפרגיות, לגלג עליו חבירו. כעס בר קפרא, אמר: לא על המברך אני כועס אלא על המלגלג אני כועס; אם חבירך דומה כמי שלא טעם טעם בשר מעולם – אתה על מה לגלגת עליו?! חזר ואמר: לא על המלגלג אני כועס אלא על המברך אני כועס. ואמר: אם חכמה אין כאן, זקנה אין כאן?! תנא: ושניהם לא הוציאו שנתן. מאי לאו בהא קא מיפלגי; דמברך סבר: שלקות ופרגיות "שהכל נהיה בדברו", הלכך חביב עדיף; ומלגלג סבר: שלקות "ב"פ האדמה", פרגיות – "שהכל נהיה בדברו", [ב]הלכך פירא עדיף! – לא, דכ"ע שלקות ופרגיות "שהכל נהיה בדברו", והכא בהאי סברא קא מיפלגי; מר סבר: חביב עדיף, ומר סבר: כרוב עדיף, דזיין.§ אמר ר' זירא, כי הוינן בי רב הונא אמר לן: הני גרגלידי דלפתא, פרמינהו פרימא רבא – "בפה"א", פרימא זוטא – "שהכל נהיה בדברו". וכי אתאן לבי רב יהודה אמר לן: [ג]אידי ואידי "בפה"א", והאי דפרמינהו טפי – כי היכי דנמתיק טעמיה. אמר רב אשי, כי הוינן בי רב כהנא אמר לן: תבשילא דסלקא דלא מפשו בה קמחא – "בורא פרי האדמה", דלפתא, דמפשו בה קמחא טפי – "בורא מיני מזונות"; והדר אמר: [ד]אידי ואידי "בורא פרי האדמה", והאי דשדי בה קמחא טפי – לדבוקי בעלמא עבדי לה. אמר רב חסדא: *תבשיל של תרדין – יפה ללב וטוב לעינים, וכ"ש לבני מעים. אמר אביי: והוא דיתיב אבי תפי ועביד *תוך תוך.§ אמר רב פפא: פשיטא לי, [ה]מיא דסלקא – כסלקא, ומיא דלפתא – כלפתא, ומיא דכולהו שלקי – ככולהו שלקי. בעי רב פפא: מיא דשיבתא מאי, למתוקי טעמא עבדי, או לעבורי זוהמא עבדי לה? ת"ש: *[ו]השבת, משנתנה טעם בקדירה – אין בה משום תרומה ואינה מטמאה טומאת אוכלים. שמע מינה: למתוקי טעמא עבדי לה, שמע מינה.§ אמר רב חייא בר אשי: פת צנומה בקערה מברכין עליה "המוציא". ופליגא דר' חייא, דאמר ר' חייא: צריך שתכלה ברכה עם הפת. מתקיף לה רבא: מאי שנא צנומה דלא – משום דכי כליא ברכה אפרוסה קא כליא; על הפת נמי, כי קא גמרה – אפרוסה גמרה! אלא

**רש"י**

בצר ליה שיעורא. וגבי ברכת פירות הארץ אכילה כתיבה, ואכילה בכזית: כזית שאמרו. לענין שיעור כל אכילות: אגור בתוכו. מזומן לצאת ממנו, שאינו נבלע בפרי כמשקה תפוחים ותותים אלא אגור כמשקה ענבים: דורמסקין. אף הן שלקות מעשב שקורין אקדלשי"ט בלע"ז. כך ראיתי בפירוש בבא קמא של רבינו יצחק ברבי יהודה. אבל כאן פירש פרונ"ש וכן שמעתי אני כאן ובבבא קמא (פ"י דף קטז:) פרונ"ש. ואי אפשר להעמידה, דא"כ הרי ברכתו "ב"פ העץ" והאיך קדם וברך על הפרגיות שברכתן "שהכל" ואינם כדברים חשובים כדמפרש ואזיל: שלא טעם טעם בשר. ונעשה הבשר חביב עליו: פרגיות. בשר עוף שקורין פרדרי"ש: זקנה אין כאן. הלא זקן אני, והיה לו לשאלני על איזה מהן יברך לפטור את שאר המינין. ודברים הללו אינן באין ללפת את הפת אלא שלא מחמת הסעודה הן באין, ואמרינן לקמן (דף מא:) דטעונין ברכה לפניהם ואין הפת פוטרתן: דמברך סבר שלקות. דכרוב ודורמסקין "שהכל" ברכתן כפרגיות, דעל דבר שאין גדולו מן הארץ כגון בשר, ביצים ודגים תנא במתניתין *"שהכל". וכיון דברכותיהם שוות – חביב עדיף: ומלגלג סבר שלקות בורא פרי האדמה. שהיא ברכה חשובה לעצמה לדברים חשובים, והיה לו להקדימו: כרוב עדיף דזיין. דתניא לקמן (דף מד:) כרוב למזון ותרדין לרפואה: גרגלידי דלפתא. ראשי לפתות: פרמינהו. מנוסיי"ר בלע"ז, לשון קניבת ירק: פרימא זוטא. גריעותא היא, ובשלקא חי קאי: אבי תפי. על מקום שפיתת הקדירה: ועביד תוך תוך. כלומר: שמבשלק ונמחה מאד, וקול רתיחתו נשמעת כקול תוך תוך: מיא דסלקא. תבשיל של תרדין: כסלקא. לענין ברכה: דשיבתא. ירק שנותנין מעט בקדירה למתק בעלמא ולא לאכלו, אני"ט בלע"ז: למתוקי טעמא עביד. ומברכין על מימי תבשילו "ב"פ האדמה": השבת אין בה. כבד שלה משנתנה בקדרה והוציאוה אין בה שוב משום איסור תרומה, דהוה ליה כעץ בעלמא. מדקתני "משנתנה טעם" ש"מ לטעמא עבידא: פת צנומה. יבשה, שנתנה בקערה לשרות. וכן כנומות – דקות*: צריך שתכלה. ברכת "המוציא" עם פריסת הפרוסה מן הפת, והאי פרוס ועומד הוא: אפרוסה (בליא). כיון דאמרת עם פריסת הפרוסה תכלה מאי חשיבותא ומאי אהניא:

**תוספות**

בצר ליה שיעורא. היינו דוקא בברכה שלאחריו – דבעינן שיעור, אבל בברכה שלפניו – אפילו פחות מכשיעור, דאסור ליהנות בעולם הזה בלא ברכה בין לענין אכילה בין לענין שתיה. אבל בברכה שלאחריו – בעינן שיעור מלא לוגמיו. על כן יש ליזהר לשתות מכוס של ברכה מלא לוגמיו, כדי שיברך לאחריו מעין ג' ברכות. והר"י היה אומר בורא נפשות, כיון דלאו ברכה חשובה היא – אפי' בבציר משיעורא מברכינן 'בורא נפשות רבות'. ולא נראה, דכיון ד'בורא נפשות' תקנוה כנגד 'על הגפן' כי היכי ד'על הגפן' בעי שיעורא, ב'בורא נפשות רבות' נמי בעי שיעורא. ובירושלמי: ר' יוחנן היכי בריך אזית? הא לא הוי שיעורא! וקאמר משום בריה. דאפילו לא אכל אלא פרידה אחת של ענב או פרידה אחת של רמון – בעי ברוכי, משום דבבריה מברכין אפילו פחות מכזית. וחולק על גמרא דידן, כדמשמע הכא. א"כ, אין הלכה כמותו של ירושלמי. (א) וה"ר יוסי היה מפרש שהירושלמי אינו חולק על הגמרא שלנו, דהכא מיירי שהוסרו הגרעינים ונמלח – אם כן לא היה כברייתו, אבל אם אכלו שלם, אפי' אם היה פרידה אחת של רמון – מברך עליו תחלה וסוף. וגמרא ירושל' היה סבור שהזית היה שלם, ולכך הוצרך לתרץ באותו ענין דאכל פרידה *דבריה, ואינן חולקים יחד. ועוד יש בירושלמי: היכא דבריך אתורמוסא למיכליה ונפל מידיה ושקל אחרינא – בעי ברוכי זמנא אחריתי. ופריך: מאי שנא מאמת המים? פירוש: דמברך לשתות, והני אזלי והני אחריני נינהו, וא"צ לברך פעם אחרת! ומשני: הכא הוה דעתו מתחלה לזה, שהיה יודע שילכו להן, אבל בתורמוסא לא ידע שיפלו מידו. ויאמר 'ברוך שם כבוד מלכותו לעולם ועד' משום דהוה ברכה לבטלה. וכן נכון לומר על כל ברכה לבטלה 'בשכמל"ו'. **דורמסקין.** פירש"י פרונ"ש. ולא נראה, דבסמוך משמע דמברכין עליהן 'בורא פרי האדמה' וא"כ 'בורא פרי העץ' בעי ברוכי! ונראה שהוא מין כרוב. **נתן בר קפרא רשות לאחד מהן לברך.** ונראה דמיירי בברכה שלפניו; דאי בשל אחריו – הא אמרינן (חולין קו.) דאין מזמנין על הפירות, (ב) ומיירי בהסבו. ואנו אין לנו שום הסבה אלא על הפת. ולכך צריך לברך כל אחד על כל דבר חוץ בפירות הן ביין: **חביב עדיף.** וכן הלכה: אם יש לו שני מיני פירות לפניו – חביב עדיף. ו'בורא פרי האדמה' עדיפא מ'שהכל נהיה בדברו', דמבוררת טפי וחשובה לעצמה מקרים. ויברך על אותו המין שייך בו פרי האדמה, אף על פי שאותו המין שיש לברך עליו 'שהכל' חביב עליו. ואם לפניו פירות שהברכות שוות, ואחד מהן הוא מז' המינין – יברך תחלה על אותו של ז' המינין, דעדיפי: **מיא דסלקא בסלקא.** מברכין עליה 'בורא פרי האדמה' אף על פי שאין בה אלא מים וטעם הירקות – מברך עליהן כאשר יברך על הירקות. אע"ג דאמרינן לעיל דמי פירות זיעה בעלמא הוא – יש לחלק: **פת** צנומה בקערה מברכין עליה "המוציא לחם מן הארץ", ופליגא דר' חייא. וא"ת: היכי מיירי? אם יש שלמה לפניו – הא אמרינן בסמוך דכ"ע שלמה עדיף! ואי ליכא אלא צנומה – היכי פליג עלה ר' חייא, הא מסקינן לעיל (דף לז:) פרורין אף על פי שאין בהן כזית מברכין עליהן 'המוציא', הואיל ואית בהו תוריתא דנהמא! וי"ל: כגון דליכא שלמה לפניו, ובלע מן הצנומה. רב חייא בר אשי סבר דהוי כמו שלמה, מאחר שהיא חביבה – [מברך עליה]. ור' חייא ס"ל: צריך שתכלה ברכה עם הפת, ואם כן בעינן שתכלה הברכה עם בליעת הפת, וכיון שבלועה קודם לכן – שלמה עדיף, אבל אי ליכא שלמה – מודה שיברך על הפרורים *'המוציא לחם מן הארץ': והלכתא

כלים פי"ז משנה ח
[לקמן מ:]
[דבריה היה ואינן כו' כל"ל]
עירובין כט.
[פסחים עד.]
[בראשית מא]
גמרה [עי' פ"ג נדה נח:]
[שם מנחות עה: ד"ה אפילו]

**הגהות הב"ח**

(א) תוס' ד"ה בצר וכו' וה"ר יוסף היה מפרש:

**גליון הש"ס**

רש"י ד"ה דורמסקין כו' הרי ברכתו בפה"ע. ק"ל הא גם בפה"ע עדיף משהכל אלא דהמברך סבר דשלקות מברך שהכל. וא"כ ג"כ בפה"ע אין ברכתו שהכל מבואר בסוגיא גבי זית מליח ול"ע: רש"י ד"ה ועביד תוך וכו' כקול תוך תוך. עי' פסחים עד ע"א ברש"י ד"ה ר' ישמעאל: תוס' ד"ה בצר וכו' מלא לוגמיו כדי שיברך. עי' לעיל ל"ז ע"א תוס' ד"ה נתן ל"ג: בא"ד היה אומר. עי' לקמן מ"ט ע"ב תוס' ד"ה ור"ש: תוס' ד"ה נתן וכו' ומיירי בהסבו. עי' חולין ק"ו ע"א תוס' ד"ה מ':

אלא אמר רבא מברך ואח"כ בוצע. (א) וגומר כל הברכה, ואח"כ מפריש הפרוסה, דכלייה ברכה קמה שלם: פתיתין ושלמין אמר רב הונא. אם רצה מברך על הפתיתין, ואם הפתיתין גדולים מן השלמין – צריך לברך עליהן: כתנאי. הא דאמרת פרוסה של חטין ושלמה של שעורין כו' תנאי היא: אבל לא חצי בצל גדול. ואע"פ שיש בו יותר מקטן שלם: במקום שיש כהן. ונותנו לו מיד: במקום שאין כהן. צריך לישראל שיצניענו עד שימצא כהן ליתנו לו, וחצי בצל אין מתקיים: יוצא ידי שניהם. ידי מחלוקת של רב הונא ורבי יוחנן: מניח פרוסה תחת השלמה. ונמלאו שתיהן בידו, ובוצע או משתיהן או מן השלמה: לחם עוני כתיב. ודרכו של עני בפרוסה, לפיכך צריך שיראה כבוצע מן הפרוסה: אכולא שירותא. פרוסה גדולה שהיה די לו לכל הסעודה בשבת: ריפתא דערובא. שערבו בו לאמול ערובי חצירות: טול

והלכתא כרבא דמברך ואח"כ בוצע. פי': שלא יפריש הפרוסה מן הפת עד אחר הברכה. ויש שנוהגין לברך ברכת 'המוציא' קודם שיחתוך, כדי שתהא הפת שלמה בשעת ברכה. ואין המנהג נכון לעשות,(ב) דהוי היסח הדעת בין הברכה לאכילה. ומיהו, בשבת נכון להחמיר ולברך קודם שיחתוך, שלא תשמט ידו לבצוע קודם שתכלה הברכה שאז לא יהיה לו לחם משנה, ובפרק "שלשה שאכלו" (לקמן מז.) מסקינן דלעינן עד שתכלה אמן מפי העונין, שלא יבצע קודם. ויש שמצריכים רשיה שצריך לסיים הברכה קודם שיבצע מדתני רבי חייא בירושלמי: אין מברכין על הפת אלא בשעה שהוא פורס, והיינו משום שאם יפרוס קודם הברכה שמא תפול הפרוסה מידו, ולא יוכל לאכול פרוסה אחרת שיבצע בלא ברכה אלא יצטרך לחזור(ג) ולברך, ויש כאן ברכה לבטלה. אבל אם (*לא) היה צריך לברך על כל הפת ולא יוכל לפרוס קודם הברכה, אז אם תפול הפרוסה אינו מברך על פרוסה אחרת, ויפטר בברכה ראשונה: מברך על הפתיתין ופוטר את השלמין. פירש"י: אם הפתיתין והשלמין שוין – יברך על איזה שירצה, ואם הפתיתין גדולים – צריך לברך על הפתיתין לפטור את השלמין. ור' יוחנן אומר: על השלמין מצוה מן המובחר, אפי' אם הפתיתין גדולי' טפי. ותימה: א"כ, סברא הפוכה, דלרב הונא פתיתין שהם גדולים עדיפי, ולר' יוחנן שלמין עדיפי, ואין סברא לומר דפליגי בהפוך סברות. ועוד תימה: אמאי שינה בסמוך לשונו דנקט לשון פרוסה של חטין? ע"כ פירש רבינו תם: דמיירי בפתיתין גדולים ושלמים קטנים. וה"פ: אמר רב הונא מברך על הפתיתין, כלומר: אם ירצה והוא הדין על השלמין, אם ירצה. ורבי יוחנן אמר: שלמין עיקר. וכן הלכה כרבי יוחנן, דהא רב ורבי יוחנן – הלכה כר' יוחנן, וכל שכן לגבי רב הונא שהלכה כמותו, שהיה תלמידו של רב, דדוקא באמוראי בתראי אמרינן הלכה כבתראי:

(פי' מהרש"א ומהרש"ל)

תורה אור

אלא אמר רבא: מברך ואח"כ בוצע. נהרדעי עבדי כר' חייא, ורבנן עבדי כרבא. אמר רבינא, אמרה לי אם: אבוך עביד כר' חייא, דאמר ר' חייא: צריך שתכלה ברכה עם הפת, ורבנן עבדי כרבא. והלכתא [א]כרבא, דאמר: מברך ואח"כ בוצע. § איתמר, הביאו לפניהם פתיתין ושלמין; אמר רב הונא: מברך על הפתיתין ופוטר את השלמין, ור' יוחנן אמר: [ב]שלמה מצוה מן המובחר, אבל פרוסה של חטין ושלמה מן השעורין – דברי הכל מברך על הפרוסה של חטין ופוטר את השלמה של שעורין. א"ר ירמיה בר אבא: כתנאי; *[ג]תורמין בצל קטן שלם אבל לא חצי בצל גדול. ר' יהודה אומר: לא כי, אלא חצי בצל גדול. מאי לאו בהא קמיפלגי, דמר סבר: חשוב עדיף, ומר סבר שלם עדיף! – היכא דאיכא כהן – כולי עלמא לא פליגי דחשוב עדיף, כי פליגי – דליכא כהן. *דתנן: [ד]כל מקום שיש כהן – תורם מן היפה, וכל מקום שאין כהן – תורם מן המתקיים, ר' יהודה אומר: אין תורם אלא מן היפה. אמר רב נחמן בר יצחק: *וירא שמים יוצא ידי שניהם, ומנו? מר בריה דרבינא. דמר בריה דרבינא [ה]מניח פרוסה בתוך השלמה ובוצע. תני תנא קמיה דרב נחמן בר יצחק: מניח הפרוסה בתוך השלמה ובוצע ומברך. אמר ליה: מה שמך? א"ל: שלמן. א"ל: שלום אתה ושלמה משנתך, ששמת שלום בין התלמידים. אמר רב פפא: הכל מודים [ו]בפסח שמניח פרוסה בתוך שלמה ובוצע. מאי טעמא – "לחם עני" כתיב. א"ר *אבא: [ז]ובשבת חייב אדם לבצוע על שתי ככרות. מ"ט – "לחם משנה" כתיב. א"ר אשי: חזינא ליה לרב כהנא [ח]דנקיט תרתי ובצע חדא. ר' זירא [ט]הוה בצע אכולא שירותא. א"ל רבינא לרב אשי: *והא קא מתחזי כרעבתנותא! אמר [ליה]: כיון דכל יומא לא קא עביד הכי, והאידנא קא עביד – לא מתחזי כרעבתנותא. *רב אמי ורב אסי [י] כי הוה מתרמי להו ריפתא דערובא מברכין עליה "המוציא לחם מן הארץ", אמרי: הואיל ואתעביד ביה מצוה חדא – נעביד ביה מצוה אחריתי.
אמר

אבל פרוסה של חטין ושלמה מן השעורים ד"ה מברך על הפרוסה של חטין. דחיטי עדיפי, משום דאקדמיה קרא. אבל פתיתין ושלמין ממין אחד, אפילו יהיו הפתיתין מפת נקיה והשלמין מפת קיבר – מברך על השלמין כדאיתא בתוספתא (פרק ד): שלמין דגלוסקאות ושלמין דבעל הבית – מברך על השלמין דגלוסקאות; פרוסה דגלוסקאות ושלמין דבעל הבית – מברך על השלמין דבעל הבית; פת כשר ופת של גוי – מברך על הכשר (תחלה). וכן אמרינן בירושלמי: פת טהור ופת טמא – מברך על הטהור. אבל אם פת של גוי חביב ונקי ופת של ישראל אינו חביב – מברך לאיזה שירצה. כדאיתא בירושלמי: פת נקי טמא ופת קיבר טהור – מברך לאיזה שירצה. אבל רבינו שמשון נוהג לסלק הפת לבן של גוי מעל השלחן עד לאחר ברכת 'המוציא'. שני שלמין ממין אחד, אם אחד יותר נקי – מברך על הנקי, דחביב ליה טפי: כתנאי כו'. פירש רש"י: חצי בצל גדול קרי חשוב, לפי שיש בו יותר מבצל קטן שלם. ולא נראה, דהא לכאורה משמע דלהכי נקט חצי בצל גדול(ד) משום דיש בחצי בצל גדול כמו בקטן שלם, ולא יותר. ועוד, דאם כן לא הוי דומיא דחשוב דגבי פרוסה של חטין דקאי עלה, דהתם שוין. ויש לפרש: דכהדדי שוין הם, אבל דגדול טוב יותר לאכילה מן הקטן. ועוד פירש רש"י: דמייתי תנאי אסיפא, דמברך על הפרוסה של חטין ופוטר את השלמה של שעורים, ומר סבר: חשוב עדיף, ומר סבר: חטין דמקדמי בקרא עדיפי. אבל א"א לפרש דחטין עדיפי משום שפת של חטין חשוב מפת של שעורים, דהא פי' דמין אחד פת נקיה ופת קיבר השלם עדיף: ומר סבר שלם עדיף. וא"ת: מנא ליה הא?(ה) אימא דחטין חשיבי טפי משום דאקדמיה קרא! ויש לומר דהכי מדמה: דהתם אע"ג דמסברא חשוב לכהן עדיף, דכתיב (במדבר יח) "בהרימכם את חלבו ממנו", ואפי' הכי קאמר דשלם עדיף, ה"נ: נימא שלם עדיף מפתיתין של חטין, אע"ג דאקדמיה קרא. והדין עם רש"י שלא רצה לפרש כתנאי אפלוגתייהו דרבי יוחנן ורב הונא, שהרי למאי דמפרש(ו) לרב הונא כשהן שוין מברך על איזו שירצה, א"כ לא קפיד אחשיבות ולא אשלמות, וא"כ מאי כתנאי איכא? ולפר"ת נמי, דפי' דמברך על הפתיתין גדולים אם ירצה, ואי בעי בריך על השלמים קטנים, אלמא: לא חשיב ליה עדיף, אלא כי הדדי נינהו לרב הונא, וא"כ לא מצי קאי כתנאי אפלוגתא דפתיתין: כל היכא דאיכא כהן כ"ע לא פליגי דחשיב עדיף. ונהי דלעיל קאמר פתיתין גדולים ושלמים קטנים דמברך על השלמים – היינו דוקא לברכה, דלא איכפת ליה שיברך בגדול דלמה יברך בגדול, הואיל ואינו נקי מזה. אבל גבי נתינה לכהן איכא נפקותא דיתן לו הגדול החשוב טפי, דניחא ליה: מניח פרוסה בתוך השלמה ובוצע. פירש רש"י: ובוצע לשתיהן, או בוצע לשלמה בלבד, והיינו ע"י שניהן דכיון שהניח הפרוסה תחת השלמה נראה כמו שבוצע נמי אפרוסה ודוקא בוצע לשלמה. אבל לא רצה לפרש ובוצע לאיזה מהן שירצה, או לפרוסה או לשלמה, דמדקאמר לתוך השלמה – משמע דהשלמה עיקר. ולפי' רש"י ה"פ: ירא שמים יוצא ידי שניהם כדרב הונא וכדר' יוחנן בפתיתין ושלמה. ולפי' ר"ת לא מצינו לפרש הכי, דקאי אפתיתין שהרי אינו צריך לעשות כן, אלא יברך על השלמה ודי בכך לכ"ע, דאפילו רב הונא לא קאמר אלא על הפרוסה אם ירצה, אבל פשיטא אם בירך על השלמה – יצא. ונראה *לפירוש ר"ת: שניהם קאי אשני לחמים, אפרוסה של חטים ושלמה של שעורים: הכל מודים בפסח שמניח הפרוסה בתוך השלמה ובוצע. מאי טעמא? – "לחם עוני" כתיב. משום דכתיב "לחם עוני" מניח הפרוסה תחת השלמה ונראה כבוצע על הפרוסה. ומ"מ, אין לבצוע כי אם על השלמה, ועל הפרוסה יברך 'על אכילת מצה'. וכורכים ואוכלים משתיהן יחד כדי שיהא נראה כבוצע על הפרוסה, וכן המנהג. אבל אין לעשות 'המוציא' וגם 'על אכילת מצה' מן הפרוסה, דהוי כעושה מצות חבילות חבילות. ונראה לי דהא הוי ברכה של נהנין, ואינם נקראים חבילות חבילות, דהא אקידוש מברכים וברכת היין. ורבינו מנחם מווינ"א היה רגיל לעשות הכל על הפרוסה, ואין השלמה באה כי אם בשביל לחם משנה. והר"י היה רגיל לברך תחלה ברכת 'המוציא' על שתיהן, קודם שיבצע, ואחר כך מברך 'על אכילת מצה' ובוצע משתיהן אחר כך, ואין זה חבילות מאחר שהיה עושה על שתיהן. ופעמים מפיק הר"י נפשיה מפלוגתא ולא היה רוצה לשנות המנהג, והיה מברך על השלמה תחלה 'המוציא' והיה בוצע קצת, ולא היה מפרידה עד שיברך על הפרוסה 'על אכילת מצה', ובוצע משתיהן יחד:
הביאו

סו א מיי' פ"ז מהלכות ברכות הל' ב סמג עשין כז טוש"ע או"ח סי' קסז סעיף א:
סז ב מיי' שם הל' ד סמג שם טוש"ע או"ח סי' קסח סעיף א:
סח ג מיי' פ"ה מהל' תרומות הלכה ב:
סט ד שם הלכה א:
ע ה מיי' פ"ז מהלכות ברכות הלכה ד סמג עשין כז טוש"ע או"ח סי' קסח סעיף א:
עא ו מיי' פ"ח מהל' חמץ ומצה הלכה ו טוש"ע או"ח סי' תעה סעיף א [רב אלפס כאן וכפ' ע"פ דף קנט]:
עב ז ח מיי' פ"ז מהל' ברכות הל' ד ופ"ל מהל' שבת הל' ט סמג עשין כט טוש"ע או"ח סי' רעד סעיף א: [רב אלפס כאן ובשבת פט"ו דף מז. ובע"פ דף קנט]:
עג ט מיי' פ"ז מהלכות ברכות הל' ז טוש"ע שם סעיף ב:
[י שו"ע או"ח סי' שלו סעי' ב בהגהה]:

הגהות הב"ח
(א) רש"י ד"ה אלא וכו' בוצע וגומר כל: (ב) תוס' ד"ה והלכתא וכו' לעשות כן דהוי היסח: (ג) בא"ד אלא יצטרך לחזור. נ"ב דתני בירושלמי היכא דבריך אתורמוסא ולמיכליה ונפל מידיה וכו' וע' לעיל בדף יב ד"ה בר לעיל ליה: (ד) ד"ה כתנאי וכו' דהו"ל לומר אבל לא גדול שאינו שלם אלא נקט חצי: (ה) ד"ה ומר וכו' הא איכא למימר דחטין: (ו) בא"ד למאי דמפרש רש"י לרב הונא דכשהן שוין:

גליון הש"ס
גמ' א"ל שלמן. מלינו שם זה בסוף מגילת רות ושם הוא מלא וי"ו.

תרומות פ"ב מ"ה
שם מ"ד [מנחות נה.]
[שבת סא.]
דברים טז
שבת קיז:
שמות טז
כתובות נו:
שבת שם
[ונראה דצ"ל כר"ת וקאי לשני כו"ל]

אמר רב: טול ברוך, טול ברוך" אינו צריך לברך, "הבא מלח, הבא לפתן" – צריך לברך; ור' יוחנן אמר: אפי' "הביאו מלח, הביאו לפתן" – נמי א"צ לברך; "גביל לתורי גביל לתורי" – צריך לברך; ורב ששת אמר: אפילו "גביל לתורי" נמי אינו צריך לברך, דאמר רב יהודה אמר רב: [ג] אסור לאדם שיאכל קודם שיתן מאכל לבהמתו, שנא': "ונתתי עשב בשדך לבהמתך" והדר "ואכלת ושבעת". § אמר רבא בר שמואל משום רבי חייא: אין הבוצע רשאי לבצוע עד שיביאו מלח או לפתן לפני כל אחד ואחד. רבא בר שמואל אקלע לבי ריש גלותא, אפיקו ליה ריפתא ובצע להדיא. אמרו ליה: הדר מר משמעתיה? אמר להו: לית דין צריך בשש. § ואמר רבא בר שמואל משום רבי חייא: אין מי רגלים כלים אלא בישיבה. אמר רב כהנא: ובעפר תיחוח אפילו בעמידה; ואי ליכא עפר תיחוח – יעמוד במקום גבוה וישתין למקום מדרון. § ואמר רבא בר שמואל משמיה דר' חייא: אחר כל אכילתך אכול מלח, ואחר כל שתייתך שתה מים, ואי אתה נזוק. תניא נמי הכי: אחר כל אכילתך אכול מלח, ואחר כל שתייתך שתה מים, ואי אתה נזוק. תניא אידך: אכל כל מאכל ולא אכל מלח, שתה כל משקין ולא שתה מים, ביום – ידאג מן ריח הפה, ובלילה – ידאג מפני אסכרה. § ת"ר: המקפה אכילתו במים – אינו בא לידי חולי מעים, וכמה? אמר רב חסדא: קיתון לפת. אמר רב מרי א"ר יוחנן: הרגיל בעדשים אחת לשלשים יום – מונע אסכרה מתוך ביתו. אבל כל יומא, לא. מ"ט – משום דקשה לריח הפה. ואמר רב מרי א"ר יוחנן: הרגיל בחרדל אחת לשלשים יום – מונע חלאים מתוך ביתו, אבל כל יומא לא. מ"ט – משום דקשה לחולשא דלבא. אמר רב חייא בר אשי אמר רב: הרגיל בדגים קטנים אינו בא לידי חולי מעים; ולא עוד אלא שדגים קטנים מפרין ומרבין ומבריאין כל גופו של אדם. א"ר חמא ברבי חנינא: הרגיל בקצח אינו בא לידי כאב לב. מיתיבי, רשב"ג אומר: קצח – אחד מששים סממני המות הוא, והישן למזרח גרנו – דמו בראשו! לא קשיא: הא בריחו, הא בטעמו. אימיה דרבי ירמיה אפיא ליה ריפתא, ומדבקא ליה ומקלפא ליה. § "ר' יהודה אומר: בורא מיני דשאים". א"ר זירא ואיתימא ר' חיננא בר פפא: אין הלכה כרבי יהודה. וא"ר זירא ואיתימא ר' חיננא בר פפא: מ"ט דרבי יהודה – אמר קרא: "ברוך ה' יום יום", וכי ביום מברכין אותו ובלילה אין מברכין אותו?! אלא לומר לך: כל יום ויום תן לו מעין ברכותיו; הכא נמי, כל מין ומין תן לו מעין ברכותיו. וא"ר זירא ואיתימא ר' חיננא בר פפא: בוא וראה שלא כמדת הקב"ה מדת בשר ודם: מדת בשר ודם – כלי ריקן מחזיק, מלא אינו מחזיק; אבל הקב"ה אינו כן – מלא מחזיק, ריקן אינו מחזיק, שנאמר: "ויאמר אם שמוע תשמע", אם שמוע – תשמע, ואם לאו – לא תשמע. ד"א: אם שמוע בישן – תשמע בחדש, ואם יפנה לבבך – שוב לא תשמע. §

**מתני'** בירך על פירות האילן "בורא פרי האדמה" – יצא, ועל פירות הארץ "בורא פרי העץ" – לא יצא. ועל כולם, אם אמר "שהכל נהיה בדברו" – יצא. §

**גמ'** מאן תנא דעיקר אילן ארעא היא? אמר רב נחמן בר יצחק: ר' יהודה היא, דתנן: יבש המעין ונקצץ האילן – מביא ואינו קורא; ר' יהודה אומר: מביא וקורא. § "על פירות הארץ וכו'". פשיטא! – א"ר נחמן בר יצחק: לא נצרכה אלא לר' יהודה דאמר "חטה מין אילן היא"; דתניא: אילן שאכל ממנו אדם הראשון, רבי מאיר אומר: גפן היה, שאין לך דבר שמביא יללה על האדם אלא יין, שנאמר: "וישת מן היין וישכר"; רבי נחמיה אומר: תאנה היתה, שבדבר שנתקלקלו בו נתקנו, שנאמר: "ויתפרו עלה תאנה"; ר' יהודה אומר: חטה היתה, שאין התינוק יודע לקרות אבא ואמא עד שיטעום טעם דגן. ס"ד אמינא, הואיל ואמר רבי יהודה חטה מין אילן היא, ליברך עליה "בורא פרי העץ" – קמשמע לן: היכא מברכינן "בורא פרי העץ" – היכא דכי שקלת ליה לפירי איתיה לגווזא והדר מפיק, אבל

---

**רש"י**

טול ברוך. הבוצע קודם שטועם מן הפרוסה בצע ממנה והושיט למי שאצלו, וא"ל: טול מפרוסת הברכה. אף על פי ששח בינתיים – אין צריך לחזור לברך. ואף על גב דשיחה הויא הפסקה כדאמרינן במנחות (פרק ג' דף לו.): סח בין תפילין לתפילין צריך לברך, וכן בכסוי הדם, הך שיחה צורך ברכה, ולא מפסקת: הביאו מלח. נמי אין צריך לברך, שאף זו צורך ברכה שתהא פרוסה של ברכה נאכלת בטעם: גביל לתורי. גבול את המורסן במים לצורך השוורים: ובצע ליה להדיא. כלומר: מיד, ולא המתין למלח ולפתן: בשש. עכוב, כמו: "בושש רכבו" (שופטים ה). כלומר: פת נקיה היא זו, ואין צריכה לפתן: אין מי רגלים כלים. מן הגוף אלא בישיבה, לפי שכשהקלוח קרוב לפיסוק הוא דואג שלא יפלו נצוצות על רגליו ומפסיק: בעפר תיחוח. ליכא נצוצות: אסכרה. בו"ן מלנ"ט: המקפה אכילתו במים. שותה מים הרבה אחר אכילתו עד שאכילתו צפה במים. "ויצף הברזל" – מתרגמינן "וקפא פרזלא" (מלכים ב ו): מונע אסכרה. שהחולי בא מחמת עכור בני מעים, והעדשים משלשלים: קצח. רבותינו מפרשים ניי"לא בלע"ז, אבל אני שמעתי מין זרעים שזורעין אותו בארץ ישמעאל: למזרח גורנו. של קצח, שרוח מערבית רוח לחה ומתונתה היא, ומכנסת הריח בתוך הגוף: הא בריחו הא בטעמו. הריח קשה, והטעם טוב: מדבקא ליה. בריפתא עד שקלטו הטעם: ומקלפא ליה. בשביל הריח: כל יום ויום. בשבת מעין שבת, ביום טוב מעין יו"ט: כלי מלא. אדם חכם: אם שמוע. פעם אחת, סופך שתטה אזן פעם אחרת: אם תשמע בישן. ששנית ושלשת מה ששמעת אשתקד: דעיקר אילן ארעא היא. דעיקר כל הפירות היא הארץ, והכל גדל הימנה: יבש המעין ונקצץ האילן. היה לו בית השלחין וכו' מעין שהוא משקהו ממנו, וקצר בכורים ממנו ואחר כך יבש המעין. וכן שדה האילן וקצץ בכורים ממנו, ואח"כ נקצץ האילן: מביא ואינו קורא. שאינו יכול לומר "מן האדמה אשר נתתה לי", דכיון דיבש המעין ונקצץ האילן ממנה בטלה לה ארעא: מביא וקורא. שהארץ היא עיקר: שהוא הביא יללה. זה הביא מיתה: שאין התינוק יודע לקרא אבא ואמא. וזה נקרא עץ הדעת: גווזא. הענף של עץ: מפיק. פירי אחריני: חוץ

---

**תוספות**

הבא מלח כו' צריך לברך. דהוי היסח הדעת. והכי אמרי' בפ"ג דמנחות (דף לו.): סח בין תפילין לתפילין – צריך לברך, וכן הלכה. אם סח בין ברכת 'המוציא' לאכילה, או בין ברכת קידוש לשתיה – צריך לחזור ולברך, אי לאו מילתא דשייכא לסעודה כמו 'טול ברוך'. וכן בשחיטה – צריך לחזור ולברך, אי לאו ממילתא דשחיטה, כמו "הטעו יותר בהמות ותרנגולים לשחוט" או שיאמר "אחוז היטב שלא ישמט לך שלא תפסל השחיטה" – אין זו הפסקה. ואנו אין אנו רגילים להביא על השלחן לא מלח ולא לפתן, משום דפת שלנו חשוב והרי הוא כי ההוא דאמר בסמוך לית דין צריך בשש. מיהו, רבי מנחם היה מדקדק מאד להביא מלח על השלחן, כדאיתא במדרש: כשישראל יושבין על השלחן וממתינין זה את זה עד שיטלו ידיהם והן בלא מצות, השטן מקטרג עליהם וברית מלח מגין עליהם:

רבי יהודה היא דתנן יבש המעין וכו'. ונראה דהלכה כרבי יהודה דסתם לן תנא כוותיה, ואם בירך על פירות האילן 'בורא פרי האדמה' – יצא: יבש המעין כו'. יש מפרשים: לכך מביא ואינו קורא מפני שאינו נראה כמשבח להקב"ה, אלא כקובל על מה שנתן לו אדמה שאינה ראויה לפירות:

איתיה לגווזא והדר אתי. מהכא נראה דתותים ופריזי"ש ובונטונ"ש וכיוצא בהן – מברכין עליהם 'בורא פרי העץ', שהרי דרך העץ להתקיים ימים, רבים וכי שקיל הפרי בשנה זו – הדר אתי פרי באותו העץ עצמו. *מיהו הרב רבי מנחם היה מביא ראיה מירושלמי ממסכת כלאים *דמברכין על כל מיני דאטד 'בורא פרי האדמה', דקאמר התם: הסנין ואטדין מין אילן הם ואינן כלאים בכרם. ופריך: והתניא אלו הן מיני דשאים הקונדס והאטד! ומשני: תמן – לברכה, והכא – לכלאים. אלמא: לענין ברכה מיני דשאין.(א) ומיהו, לדברי הכל פריזי"ש צריך לברך עליהם 'בפה"ע' דאינו גדל על אטדין ועצו מתקיים משנה לשנה:

(וע' תוס' בכורות ח. ד"ה באילן וכו') (סוף פ"ה)

**הגהות הב"ח**

(א) תוס' ד"ה איתיה וכו' מיני דשאין הן ומיהו:

**גליון הש"ס**

גמ' סד"א הואיל ואר"י חטה מין אילן. ע' שבת קנ ע"ב תוס' ד"ה כוותיה.

---

**עין משפט נר מצוה**

עד א ב מיי' פ"א מהל' ברכות הל' ח סמג עשין כז טוש"ע או"ח סי' קסז סעיף ו וסימן רו סעיף ג:
[ב] מיי' פ"ט מהלכות עבדים הל' ח סמג עשין פז וז"ל ומקדימין מזון הבהמות והעבדים לסעודת עצמן הרי הוא אומר כעיני עבדים אל יד אדוניהם כעיני שפחה אל יד גברתה וגו' ע"ק:
עה ג ד מיי' פ"ד מהל' ברכות הלכה ג סמג עשין כז טוש"ע או"ח סי' קסז סעיף ה:
[בגיטין איתא שיטעום בלום עד שיתן וכו' וכן איתא בר"ף ובר"ש]
עו ה מיי' פ"ד מהל' תפילין הל' יח טוש"ע או"ח סי' ג סעיף יג:
עז ו ז טוש"ע או"ח סי' קע סעיף כב בהגה וטוש"ע יו"ד סי' קטו סעי' ו:
עח ח מיי' פ"ד מהל' דעות הלכה ט:
עט ט מיי' שם הלכה ט:
פ י מיי' פ"ח מהלכות ברכות הלכה א סמג עשין כז טוש"ע או"ח סימן רח סעיף ד:
פא כ מיי' שם הלכה י וסמג שם טוש"ע או"ח סי' רו סעיף א:
פב ל מיי' פ"ד מהל' בכורים הלכה יב:
פג מ טוש"ע או"ח סי' רג סעיף ב:

**מסורת הש"ס / תורה אור**

[חולין פז.] גיטין סב. [ג איתא שמואל ואיתא אמר רב הונא אמר רב] דברים יא יומא ל. ד"ה מגוה [לקמן נז:] [מסכת כלה] מלת ר' וכס"א איתא ר' חנינא תהלים סח סוכה מו. סוכה מו. שמות טו [לעיל יב.] ביכורים פ"א משנה ו [סנהדרין ע. ע"ש] בראשית ט [סנהדרין ע: וכו' ומ"ש תוס' ד פירשו בענין אחר] שם ג

אבל היכא דכי שקלת ליה לפירי ליתיה לגוואזא דהדר מפיק – לא מברכינן עליה "בורא פרי העץ" אלא "בפה"א".§ "ועל כולן אם אמר שהכל וכו'".§ איתמר, רב הונא אמר: חוץ מן הפת ומן היין; ורבי יוחנן אמר: *אפי' פת ויין. נימא כתנאי: *ראה פת ואמר "כמה נאה פת זו ברוך המקום שבראה" – יצא. ראה תאנה ואמר: "כמה נאה תאנה זו ברוך המקום שבראה" – יצא, דברי ר' מאיר; ר' יוסי אומר: "כל המשנה ממטבע שטבעו חכמים בברכות – לא יצא ידי חובתו. נימא, רב הונא דאמר כר' יוסי, ור' יוחנן דאמר כר' מאיר! – אמר לך רב הונא: אנא דאמרי אפי' לר' מאיר; עד כאן לא קאמר ר' מאיר התם – אלא היכא דקא מדכר שמיה דפת, אבל היכא דלא קא מדכר שמיה דפת – אפילו ר' מאיר מודה. ור' יוחנן אמר לך: אנא דאמרי אפילו לרבי יוסי, עד כאן לא קאמר ר' יוסי התם – אלא משום דקאמר ברכה דלא תקינו רבנן, אבל אמר "שהכל נהיה בדברו" דתקינו רבנן – אפילו ר' יוסי מודה. בנימין רעיא כרך ריפתא [ג]ואמר: "בריך מריה דהאי פיתא". אמר רב: יצא. והאמר רב: כל ברכה שאין בה הזכרת השם אינה ברכה! –דאמר: "בריך רחמנא מריה דהאי פיתא". והא בעינן שלש ברכות! מאי [ד]'יצא' דקאמר רב – נמי, יצא ידי ברכה ראשונה. מאי קמשמע לן – אע"ג דאמרה בלשון חול, תניא, *"ואלו נאמרים בכל לשון: פרשת סוטה, וידוי מעשר, וקריאת שמע, ותפלה, וברכת המזון"! אצטריך, סד"א; הני מילי – דאמרה בלשון חול כי היכי דתקינו רבנן בלשון קדש, אבל לא אמרה בלשון חול כי היכי דתקינו רבנן בלשון קדש אימא לא – [ה]קמ"ל.§ גופא, *אמר רב: °כל ברכה שאין בה הזכרת השם – אינה ברכה. *ורבי יוחנן אמר: כל ברכה שאין בה מלכות – אינה ברכה. אמר אביי: כוותיה דרב מסתברא, *דתניא: °"לא עברתי ממצותיך ולא שכחתי". 'לא עברתי' – מלברכך, 'ולא שכחתי' – מלהזכיר שמך עליו, ואילו מלכות לא קתני. *ור' יוחנן – תני 'ולא שכחתי' מלהזכיר שמך ומלכותך עליו.§

**מתני'** *ועל דבר שאין גדולו מן הארץ אומר: "שהכל נהיה בדברו". על החומץ ועל הנובלות ועל הגובאי אומר: "שהכל נהיה בדברו"; *ר' יהודה אומר: כל שהוא מין קללה אין מברכין עליו. היו לפניו מינין הרבה, ר' יהודה אומר: אם יש ביניהן מין שבעה – עליו הוא מברך; וחכ"א: מברך על איזה מהן שירצה.§ **גמ'** תנו רבנן: [ט]על דבר שאין גדולו מן הארץ, כגון: בשר בהמות חיות ועופות ודגים, אומר "שהכל נהיה בדברו"; על החלב ועל הביצים ועל הגבינה אומר 'שהכל'; *על הפת שעפשה, ועל היין שהקרים, ועל התבשיל שעבר צורתו אומר 'שהכל'; *על המלח ועל הזמית ועל כמהין ופטריות אומר 'שהכל'. למימרא, דכמהין ופטריות לאו גדולי קרקע נינהו?! והתניא: *הנודר מפירות הארץ – אסור בפירות הארץ ומותר בכמהין ופטריות, ואם אמר "כל גדולי קרקע עלי" – אסור אף בכמהין ופטריות! אמר אביי: מירבא רבו מארעא, מינקי לא ינקי מארעא. והא "על דבר שאין גדולו מן הארץ" קתני! – תני: על דבר שאין יונק מן הארץ.§ "ועל הנובלות".§ מאי נובלות? ר' זירא ור' אילעא, חד אמר: [כ]בושלי כמרא. וחד אמר: תמרי דזיקא. תנן, ר' יהודה אומר: כל שהוא מין קללה אין מברכין עליו; בשלמא למ"ד בושלי כמרא – היינו דקרי ליה מין קללה, אלא למאן דאמר תמרי דזיקא – מאי מין קללה? אשארא. איכא דאמרי: בשלמא למאן דאמר בושלי כמרא – היינו דמברכינן עלייהו 'שהכל'; אלא למ"ד תמרי דזיקא 'שהכל'?! "בורא פרי העץ" מבעי ליה לברוכי! –אלא: בנובלות סתמא – כ"ע לא פליגי דבושלי כמרא נינהו, כי פליגי – בנובלות תמרה. *דתנן: [ל]הקלין שבדמאי: השיתין, והרימין, והעוזרדין,(א) בנות שוח, ובנות שקמה, וגופנין, ונצפה, ונובלות תמרה. שיתין – אמר רבה בר בר חנה א"ר יוחנן: מין תאנים,[א](ב) רימין – כנדי; העוזרדין – טולשי; בנות שוח – *אמר רבה בר בר חנה א"ר יוחנן: תאיני [ב] חיוורתא;(ג) בנות שקמה – אמר רבה בר בר חנה א"ר יוחנן: דובלי. [ג](ד) גופנין – שילהי גופני; נצפה – פרחה; נובלות תמרה – ר' אילעא ור' זירא, חד אמר: בושלי כמרא, וחד אמר: תמרי דזיקא. בשלמא למ"ד בושלי כמרא – היינו דקתני: הקלין שבדמאי – ספיקן הוא דפטור, הא ודאן חייב; אלא למאן דאמר תמרי דזיקא, ודאן חייב?! הפקרא נינהו! הכא במאי עסקינן – שעשאן גורן. *דא"ר יצחק א"ר יוחנן משום ר' אליעזר בן יעקב: [מ]הלקט והשכחה והפאה שעשאן גורן – הוקבעו למעשר. איכא דאמרי: בשלמא

סוטה לב. | לעיל יב. | [לקמן מט.] | דברים כו | נדרים נה: | ב"ב דף לה: | [לעיל לו. נד] | נדרים שם | דמאי פ"א מ"א | ע"ז יז. [וע' | סוטה מג:

**רש"י**

חוץ מן הפת ומן היין. כדאמרינן לקמן (דף מג.) שגורם ברכות הרבה לעצמו בקדוש ובהבדלה ובברכת חתנים: ידי ברכה ראשונה. ברכת הזן: פרשת סוטה. כשהכהן משביעה: וידוי מעשר. "בערתי הקדש מן הבית" (דברים כו): מלברכך. "ברוך אשר קדשנו במצותיו וצונו להפריש תרומה ומעשר": מתני' הנובלות. מפרש בגמ': גובאי. חגבים טהורים: מין קללה. חומץ ונובלות וגובאי על ידי קללה הן באין: גמ' שהקרים. בוטי"ר בלע"ז: מירבא רבו מארעא. מלחלוחית הארץ הם גדלים על העצים ועל הכלים: בושלי כמרא. כמו שרופי חמה, שבשלם השרב החום ויבשו ונתמרים הם. כמרא = חום, כמו: "מכמר בשרא" (פסחים דף נח.): תמרי דזיקא. שהרוח משירן: אשארא. אחומץ וגובאי פליג ר' יהודה: פרי העץ בעי ברוכי. שהרי לא נשתנו לקלקול: הקלין שבדמאי. פירות שהקלו חכמים בדמאי שלהן, שהלוקחן מעם הארץ אין צריך לעשרן. אלו הן: השיתין כו'. שאינן חשובים, ואין ע"ה חש עליהם מלעשרן: טולשי. קולמשי: שילהי גופני. ענבים סמוניות: הא ודאי. אם ידוע שלא הופרש מהן מעשר: שעשאן גורן. העני, או מי שלקטן, העמיד מהן ערימת כרי: הלקט והשכחה והפאה. אע"פ שפטורים מן המעשר לקטן עני ועשאן גורן – הוקבעו למעשר מדרבנן, דמאן דחזי סבר שתבואת קרקעו היא: בשלמא

תורה אור | תוספתא פ"ו

**תוספות**

ורבי יוחנן אמר אפי' פת ויין. וכן הלכה. דרב ור' יוחנן הלכה כר' יוחנן, וכ"ש לגבי רב הונא שהיה תלמידו של רב: נימא רב הונא כר' יוסי. וא"ת: היכי מצי סובר רב הונא כר' יוסי? הא רב הונא מודה בשאר דברים חוץ מפת ויין שאם אמר 'שהכל' – יצא, ואילו ר' יוסי סבר דלא יצא דכל המשנה ממטבע כו'! וי"ל: דמצי למימר דאפילו ר' יוסי לא קאמר לא יצא – אלא ב'ברוך המקום' שאינה ברכה כלל, אבל ב'שהכל' – מודה:

אמר אביי כוותיה דרב מסתברא כו'. י"מ: דמסתברא ברייתא כוותיה. ומיהו: רב אלפס פסק כר' יוחנן, וכן פסק ר"י דכל ברכה שאין בה מלכות שמים – אינה ברכה. ולכך היה אומר ר"י שאם היה מדלג מלכות של ברכת המוציא – שצריך לחזור ולברך, ואפי' דלג תיבת 'העולם' בלבד, ד'מלך' לבד אינו מלכות. וברכות *של שמונה-עשרה אין בהן מלכות דאינן באין בפתיחה, ובחתימה אין שייך מלכות. אבל 'אלהי אברהם' הוי כמו מלכות. דאברהם אבינו המליך הקב"ה על כל העולם, שהודיע מלכותו. ומעין שבע דמאלי בשבת הואיל ויש בה 'האל הקדוש שאין כמוהו' הוי כמו מלכות, כמו 'שמע ישראל ה' אלהינו ה' אחד' דהוי במקום מלכות. *ולפי מה דפרישית דכל היכא דכתיב 'אלהי אברהם' הוי כמו מלכות ניחא, ולר' יוחנן לא קשיא דלא(ה) תני מלכותך דאטו כרוכלא כל האי ליתני וליזיל: אבל

**עין משפט נר מצוה**

פד א מיי' פ"ח מהל' ברכות הלכה י סמג עשין כז טוש"ע או"ח סי' קסז ס"י ובסי' רו ס"א:
פה ב מיי' פ"א מהל' ברכות הלכה ה סמג שם:
פו ג ד טוש"ע או"ח סי' קסז סעיף י וסימן קפז סעיף א:
פז ה מיי' פ"א מהלכות ברכות הלכה ו:
פח ו מיי' שם הלכה ה סמג שם טוש"ע א"ח סימן ריד:
פט ז מיי' שם פ"ח הל' ח טוש"ע או"ח סי' רד סעיף א (ב):
צ ח ט מיי' שם [והל' א] סמג שם טוש"ע או"ח שם סעיף א:
צא י מיי' פ"ט מהל' נדרים הל' א סמג לאוין רמב טוש"ע י"ד סי' רפו סעיף כג:

[עמ"ש תוס' לקמן מט. ד"ה ברוך]

צב כ מיי' פ"ח מהל' ברכות הלכה ח סמג שם טוש"ע או"ח סי' רב ס"ט וסי' רד ס"א:
צג ל מיי' פי"ג מהל' מעשר הלכה א:
צד מ מיי' פ"ב מהל' תרומות הלכה ט:

[ר"ה לב:]

**גליון הש"ס**

גמ' כל ברכה שאין בה הזכרת השם. עי' לקמן דף נ"ד ע"ב תוס' ד"ה פטריתון: רש"י ד"ה הלקט וכו' ועשאן גורן. ע' בב"ק דף נ"ד ע"א בפירש"י ד"ה מרחו:

ספרי פ' כי תבא

[כ"ה הגי' גם ברא"ש ובהגהת הרש"ל אמנם מתו' ד"ה אמר אביי משמע דלא גרסינן]

נ"א על החלב ועל הגבינה ועל הביצים אומר שהכל

**רב נסים גאון**

על החומץ ועל הגובאי ועל הנובלות הוא אומ' שהכל נהיה בדברו. גרסי בני מערבא החמיץ יינו אומר ברוך דיין האמת בא לאכלו אומר שהכל נהיה בדברו ראה גובאי אומר ברוך דיין האמת בא לאכלו אומר שהכל נהיה בדברו נובלות שנשרו אומר ברוך דיין האמת בא לאכלן אומר שהכל: השיתין אמר רבה בר בר חנה אמר ר' יוחנן מיני תאיני פירשו בתלמוד ארץ ישראל דדמאי (פרק א הלכה א) אלו הן השיתין ר' שמעון בריה דר' אבא אמר שהן יוצאות מתחת העלין ואמרי תו במסכת שביעית בפרק בנות שוח (הלכה א) תני רבן שמעון בן גמליאל אומר מהוצאת העלין עד הפגים נ' יום מן הפגים ועד השיתין הנובלות נ' יום ומן השיתין ועד התאנים נ' יום:

**הגהות הב"ח**

(א) גמ' והעוזרדין. נ"ב באלפס פ' חבית פרש"י שפירלינ"ג בלשון אשכנז: (ב) שם שיתין אמר רבה ב"ב חנה א"ר יוחנן מין תאנים נ"ב פי' תאנים מדבריות: (ג) שם תאיני חוורתא. נ"ב פירוש הגדלים מג' שנים לג' שנים ומתג' (ד) שם דובלי. נ"ב פירוש תאנה המורכבת בערמון ופירוש פרחה עיין לעיל דף ל"ו ע"א: (ה) תוס' ד"ה אמר וכו' דלא כתיב ומלכותך עליו דאטו:

בשלמא למ"ד תמרי דזיקא – היינו דהכא קרי לה 'נובלות' סתמא, והתם קרי לה תמרה, אלא למ"ד בושלי כמרא – ניתני אידי ואידי 'נובלות' סתמא, או אידי ואידי 'נובלות תמרה'! – קשיא.

"היו לפניו מינין הרבה כו'". § אמר עולא: מחלוקת בשברכותיהן שוות, דרבי יהודה סבר: מין שבעה עדיף, ורבנן סברי: מין חביב עדיף. אבל בשאין ברכותיהן שוות – ד"ה מברך על זה וחוזר ומברך על זה. מיתיבי: היו לפניו צנון וזית – מברך על הצנון ופוטר את הזית! – הב"ע – כשהצנון עקר. אי הכי, אימא סיפא; ר' יהודה אומר: מברך על הזית, שהזית ממין שבעה; (א) לית ליה לר' יהודה הא דתנן: *כל שהוא עיקר ועמו טפלה – מברך על העיקר ופוטר את הטפלה?! וכי תימא ה"נ דלית ליה, והתניא: רבי יהודה אומר, אם מחמת צנון בא הזית – מברך על הצנון ופוטר את הזית! – לעולם בצנון עיקר עסקינן, וכי פליגי רבי יהודה ורבנן – במילתא אחריתי פליגי, וחסורי מחסרא והכי קתני: היו לפניו צנון וזית – מברך על הצנון ופוטר את הזית. בד"א – כשהצנון עיקר, אבל אין הצנון עיקר – ד"ה מברך על זה וחוזר ומברך על זה; ושני מינין בעלמא שברכותיהן שוות – מברך על איזה מהן שירצה. רבי יהודה אומר: מברך על הזית, שהזית ממין שבעה. פליגי בה רבי אמי ורבי יצחק נפחא; חד אמר מחלוקת בשברכותיהן שוות, דרבי יהודה סבר: מין שבעה עדיף, ורבנן סברי: מין חביב עדיף, אבל בשאין ברכותיהן שוות – דברי הכל מברך על זה וחוזר ומברך על זה; וחד אמר: אף בשאין ברכותיהן שוות נמי מחלוקת. בשלמא למאן דאמר בשברכותיהן שוות מחלוקת – שפיר, אלא למאן דאמר בשאין ברכותיהן שוות פליגי – במאי פליגי? – א"ר ירמיה: להקדים. דאמר רב יוסף ואיתימא רבי יצחק: *כל המוקדם בפסוק זה מוקדם לברכה, שנאמר: °"ארץ חטה ושערה וגפן ותאנה ורמון ארץ זית שמן ודבש". (דברים ח) ופליגא דרבי חנן, דא"ר חנן: *כל הפסוק כולו לשיעורין נאמר. 'חטה' – דתנן: *הנכנס לבית המנוגע וכליו על כתפיו וסנדליו וטבעותיו בידיו – הוא והן טמאין מיד; היה לבוש כליו, וסנדליו ברגליו, וטבעותיו באצבעותיו – הוא טמא מיד, והן טהורין *עד שישהא בכדי אכילת פרס, (ב) פת חטין ולא פת שעורין, מיסב ואוכלן בלפתן. 'שערה' – דתנן: *עצם כשעורה מטמא במגע ובמשא, ואינו מטמא באהל. 'גפן' – כדי רביעית יין לנזיר. 'תאנה' – כגרוגרת להוצאת שבת. 'רמון' – כדתנן: *כל כלי בעלי בתים שיעורן

---

**רש"י**

בשלמא למ"ד. נובלות דדמאי תמרי דזיקא, ונובלות דמתני' אוקימנא בבושלי כמרא, היינו דהכא קרי להו נובלות תמרה ובמתני' קרי להו נובלות סתמא: בשברכותיהן שוות. כגון זיתים ותפוחים, דתרוייהו "ב"פ העץ", ובא לפטור את שתיהן בברכה אחת: חביב עדיף. איזה שירצה דמתניתין – את החביב עליו משמע: אבל בשאין ברכותיהן שוות ד"ה. אין ברכה אחת פוטרתן, ושוב אין כאן מחלוקת. ואע"ג דתנן (לעיל דף מ.): בירך על פירות האילן "ב"פ האדמה" יצא – ה"מ בחד מינא וטעה ובירך עליה "ב"פ האדמה", אבל צנון וזית ובירך על הצנון – לא נפטר זית: פשיטא לא גרסינן עד מיתיבי – חדא: שאין זו שיטת הגמ'. מעיקרא קשיא ליה פשיטא דלא איצטריך למימרא, והדר קשיא היכי מצי למימרא. ועוד: דלאו פשיטא היא, אי לאו דאשמעינן עולא ה"א צנון פוטר את הזית, דהתנן בירך על פירות האילן "ב"פ האדמה" – יצא: שהיה צנון עיקר. שבשבילו התחיל האכילה, ולא אכל זית אלא להפיג חורפו של צנון, דהוה ליה זית טפל. ותנן (דף מד.): כל שהוא עיקר ועמו טפלה – מברך על העיקר ופוטר את הטפלה: מברך על זה כו'. וכאן לא נחלקו: ושני מינים בעלמא. כגון זית ותפוח שברכותיהן שוות, והאחד ממין שבעה, בזה נחלקו: חד אמר מחלוקת בשברכותיהן שוות. וכדאמרן: ה"ג. וחד אמר אף בשאין ברכותיהן שוות נמי מחלוקת. ומפרש לה ואזיל: במאי פליגי. הא ודאי לא מפטרי בחדא ברכה: אמר ר' ירמיה בלהקדים פליגי. ולא גרסי' אבל בשברכותיהן שוות מברך על אחד מהן שירצה. דהשתא בשאינן שוות מקפיד ר' יהודה על הקדמתן. ואמר: מין שבעה עדיף, כשבא לפטור זו בזו – לא כ"ש: דאמר ר' יצחק כו'. אלמא: קפדינן אהקדמה, ור' יהודה אית ליה דר' יצחק, הלכך כל שכן היכא דחד לאו ממין שבעה, דמין שבעה עדיף. ורבנן לית להו דר' יצחק במקום חביב, דחביב עדיף: ופליגא דרבי חנן. הא דר' יצחק דאמר המוקדם קודם לברכה. אלמא קרא לשבח א"י בא, שיש בה פירות החשובים הללו, ומנאן כסדר חשיבותם. ופליג אדר' חנן דאמר לא בא הכתוב להודיע שבח חשיבות הפירות בטעם שלהם, אלא שבחה של א"י שיש בה פירות ששיעורי תורה נתלין בהן. וכיון דהכי הוא – לא הקפיד הכתוב על סדרן, שהרי בזו כולן שוין: בבית המנוגע. כתיב "והבא אל הבית יטמא עד הערב" (ויקרא יד). ולא כתיב כבוס בגדים "והאוכל בבית יכבס את בגדיו" (שם) – כשוהא שיעור אכילה ואפילו לא יאכל, מדכתיב בסיפיה "והשוכב בבית יכבס את בגדיו". הלכך: הנכנס בו ונושא את בגדיו עמו שלא כדרך מלבושו – אין אלו בגדיו, וטמאים מיד, שאף בהן אני קורא "והבא אל הבית". וכשהוא לבוש בהן – בעי שהייה: אכילת פרס. חצי ככר שמשיערו בו חכמים את העירוב; *שהוא כולו מזון שתי סעודות, וחציו – מזון סעודה אחת: פת חטין. נאכלת מהר: מיסב. דרך הסבה, שהיא נאכלת מהר, שאינו פונה אנה ואנה: ואינו מטמא באהל. הלכה למשה מסיני הוא: כדי רביעית יין לנזיר. אכל חרצנים וזגים ולולבין כשיעור רביעית יין – חייב. ואין שיעור רביעית יין ורביעית מים שוין, לפי שהיין עב והמים קלושין ויש ברביעית יין יותר ממה שיש ברביעית מים, כדאמרינן (במנחות קז.) [בשבת (דף עז.)] גבי רביעית דם שיכול לקרוש ולעמוד על כזית משום דסמיך, אבל מידי דקליש לא הוה רביעית דידיה כזית: להוצאת שבת. דתנן: המוציא אוכלין כגרוגרת (שבת עו:), והיא תאנה יבשה: שיעורן

**תוספות**

אבל בשאין ברכותיהן שוות. פירש"י: כגון צנון וזית, ושוב אין כאן מחלוקת, כיון שאין האחד פוטר את חבירו, אפי'(ג) ר' יהודה מודה דאין עדיפות בשבעת המינים, אלא מברך על איזה שירצה תחלה החביב לו, ואחר כך יברך על השני. וכן יש לפרש דרבי יהודה מודה לחכמים, הואיל ולא פי' הגמרא, מוטב שנאמר שיחיד מודה לרבים ולא רבים מודים ליחיד. והקשה רש"י: ולברך על הצנון ולפטר את הזית, דהא תנן לעיל בירך על פירות האילן 'ב"פ האדמה' יצא! ותירץ: דשאני התם שאין שם אלא חד מינא, וטעה ובירך 'ב"פ האדמה', אבל הכא כשבירך 'ב"פ האדמה' על הצנון לא פטר את חברו שהוא 'ב"פ העץ' אפי' בדיעבד. וא"ת: הא אמרינן לעיל (דף לט.) גבי עובדא דבר קפרא דברכת 'בורא פרי האדמה' חשיבא טפי מ'שהכל', לפי שמבוררת טפי, א"כ גם 'ב"פ העץ' חשיבא טפי מברכת 'ב"פ האדמה'! וי"ל: דלא חשיב 'ב"פ העץ' כל כך מ'ב"פ' האדמה כמו שחשוב 'בורא פרי האדמה' מ'שהכל'. ומ"ש בהלכות גדולות ד'ב"פ' העץ תקדים ל'ב"פ האדמה' דמבוררת טפי – היינו לפי המסקנא דלקמן, דפליגי בשאין ברכותיהן שוות, וקי"ל כר' יהודה. אבל להאי לישנא דאמרי' דלא פליגי בשאין ברכותיהן שוות – לא מתוקם פסק דהלכות גדולות, כדפירשנו לעיל: מיתיבי היו לפניו צנון וזית מברך על הצנון וכו'. ופריך: אלמא דמברך 'ב"פ האדמה' אפילו לפטור 'ב"פ העץ', אפילו לגבי זית שהוא משבעת המינים, וכ"ש קליות שהן כמו כן משבעת המינין, דמברך עליהן 'ב"פ האדמה' לפטור את *התפוחים! לכן צריך להנהיג הכי, כדפירשית *לעיל באין ברכותיהן שוות, כמו תפוחים וקליות: א"ר ירמיה להקדים דא"ר יוסף וכו'. פירש"י והר"י לפי גרסא זו, אתיא הא דאמר רב יוסף כל המוקדם כר' יהודה דוקא. אבל ר' שמעיה גרים: אמר רב יוסף וכו' ואתיא אליבא דרבנן, ומיירי שאין חביבין זה מזה, דהא אזלינן בתר מוקדם. דאי בחביבין – פשיטא דחביב קודם, דהא אפילו בשאר מינין לגבי שבעת המינין אמרי רבנן דמברך על איזה שירצה, ומילתא דרב יוסף מילתא באפי נפשה. ולא נהירא, דבסמוך משמע דגרס: דאמר רב יוסף, ואתיא כר' יהודה דוקא, דקאמר רב חסדא ורב המנונא הוו יתבי בסעודתא וכו', א"ל: לא סבר לה מר להא דרב יוסף דאמר כל המוקדם וכו': במאי פליגי. כלומר: מאי טעמא דר' יהודה דאמר שבעת המינין עדיף, מאי עדיפות שייכא בהו, אחר שאין יכולין לפטור שאר מינין? ומשני: דהעדיפות הוי מן ההקדמה: גפן כדי רביעית יין וכו'. פי': אם אכל עלין או לולבין כדי רביעית יין – חייב, אבל אם אכל מהן כדי רביעית מים – לא מחייב, דקליסי והולכין בקל חוץ מן הכלי. אבל כי משערין ביין צריך שיעורא טפי, שהיין הוא עב ומחזיק גודש קצת קודם שיפול מן הכוס רביעית יין, ואם היה מים היה (ד)יוצא יותר מרביעית*: כלי בעלי בתים. גבי כלי עץ מתניא: אייתו

---

**עין משפט נר מצוה**

צה א ב מיי' פ"ח מהל' ברכות הל' יג סמג עשין כז טוש"ע או"ח סי' רי"א סעיף א:
צו ג מיי' וסמג שם טוש"ע או"ח שם סעיף ד:
צז ד מיי' פי"ז מהלכות טומאת צרעת הל' ז:
צח ה שם הלכה ו:
צט ו מיי' פ"ג מהל' טומאת מת הל' ב:
ק ז מיי' פ"ה מהלכות נזירות הלכה ב סמג לאוין רכ:
קא ח מיי' פי"ח מהל' שבת הל' א:
קב ט מיי' פ"ו מהל' כלים הלכה ב:

**הגהות הב"ח**

(א) גמ' ממין שבעה וכו' לית ליה: (ב) שם אכילת פרס תנא פת חטין וכו' ואוכלה בלפתן: (ג) תוס' ד"ה אבל וכו' דאפילו רבי יהודה: (ד) ד"ה גפן וכו' היה הוצאה יותר:

עיין מהרש"א ומהרש"ל [נראה דהך דפירשית הוא סיום דבור התוס' ומתחיל דבור חדש מן באין ברכותיהן שלעיל על הגמ' לעיל ופי' כמו תפוחים וכו' ותיבת לעיל הוא כמו שציינו הרבה פעמים כשנתספחו דבורי תוס' להורות מקום שזה שייך לעיל והמעתיקים שגו והדפיסו הכל לדבור אחד (וכן הגיה הגאון מהר"מ מווילנא)]

**גליון הש"ס**

גמ' כל המוקדם בפסוק. עי' טורי אבן חגיגה דף י"ב ע"ב ד"ה ואת הארץ.

**מסורת הש"ס**

לעיל לט: ולקמן מד.
יומא פ. סוכה ה: עמ' נגעים פי"ג
מגורע פ"ד פ"ה
אהלות פ"ב
שבת קיב: עירובין ד [כל]
[עירובין פב:]
[וע"ע תוס' עירובין ד. ותוס' סוכה ו.]

שיעורן ברמונים. "ארץ זית שמן" – אמר ר' יוסי ברבי חנינא: ארץ שכל שיעוריה כזיתים. כל שיעוריה סלקא דעתך?! והא איכא הנך דאמרן! אלא: ארץ שרוב שיעוריה כזיתים. "דבש" – [א]*ככותבת הגסה ביום הכפורים. *ואידך? הני שיעורין בהדיא מי כתיבי?! *אלא מדרבנן, וקרא אסמכתא בעלמא.§ רב חסדא ורב המנונא הוו יתבי בסעודתא, אייתו לקמייהו תמרי ורמוני, שקל רב המנונא בריך אתמרי ברישא. אמר ליה רב חסדא: לא סבירא ליה מר להא דאמר רב יוסף ואיתימא ר' יצחק: כל המוקדם בפסוק זה קודם לברכה?! – אמר ליה: [ב]זה שני ל"ארץ", וזה חמישי ל"ארץ". – אמר ליה: מאן יהיב לן נגרי דפרזלא ונשמעינך.§ איתמר: הביאו לפניהם תאנים וענבים בתוך הסעודה; אמר רב הונא: טעונים ברכה לפניהם ואין טעונים ברכה לאחריהם.§ וכן אמר רב נחמן: טעונים ברכה לפניהם ואין טעונים ברכה לאחריהם; ורב ששת אמר: טעונין ברכה בין לפניהם בין לאחריהם, שאין לך דבר שטעון ברכה לפניו ואין טעון ברכה לאחריו אלא פת הבאה בכסנין בלבד. ופליגא דר' חייא, *דא"ר חייא: פת פוטרת כל מיני מאכל, [ג]יין פוטר כל מיני משקים. אמר רב פפא, [ד]הלכתא: דברים הבאים מחמת הסעודה בתוך הסעודה – אין טעונים ברכה לא לפניהם ולא לאחריהם, ושלא מחמת הסעודה בתוך הסעודה – טעונים ברכה לפניהם ואין טעונים ברכה לאחריהם; לאחר הסעודה – טעונים ברכה בין לפניהם בין לאחריהם. שאלו את בן זומא, מפני מה אמרו: דברים הבאים מחמת הסעודה בתוך הסעודה אינם טעונים ברכה לא לפניהם ולא לאחריהם? אמר להם: הואיל ופת פוטרתן, אי הכי, יין נמי נפטריה פת! – [ה]שאני יין, דגורם

שיעורן ברמונים. ניקב כמוציא רמון – טהור. בעלי בתים חסים על כליהם הלכך ניקב כמוציא קטניות – מצניעו לזיתים, ניקב כמוציא זית – משתמש לאגוזים, ניקב כמוציא אגוז – משתמש בו רמונים. אבל של אומן העומד למכור לא הוי שיעוריה בהכי: שרוב שיעוריה. אכילת חלב דם נותר ופיגול: דבש. האמור בתורה הוא דבש תמרים, וכותבת היא תמרה: זה שני לארץ. "ארץ זית שמן ודבש" דכתיב בסיפיה דקרא הפסיק "ארץ" את הסדר, וחזר לעשות זיתים ותמרים חשובים (א)מתאנים ורמונים. שהרמון חמישי ל"ארץ" הכתובה בראש המקרא, ודבש שני ל"ארץ" הכתובה בסופו: מאן יהיב לן נגרי דפרזלא. רגלים של ברזל: ונשמעינך. נשמשך, ונלך אחריך תמיד: הביאו לפניהם תאנים וענבים בתוך הסעודה. ולא ללפת את הפת. דא"כ – הוו להו טפלה, ואין חולק בדבר שאין טעון ברכה לא לפניו ולא לאחריו. אלא: לפעמים שבא למתק את פיו בתוך הסעודה בפירות: מברך לפניהם. דלאו טפלה נינהו: ולא לאחריהם. דבהמ"ז פוטרתן: בין לפניהם בין לאחריהם. דלא פטר אלא מידי דזיין, והני לא זייני: פת הבאה בכסנין. לאחר אכילה ובהמ"ז היו רגילים להביא כיסנין, והן קליות, לפי שיפין ללב כדאמרי' בעלמא (עירובין כט:) הני כיסני דמעלו ללבא. ומביאין עמהן פת שנלושה עם תבלין כעין אובליא"ש שלנו, ויש שעושין אותן כמין צפורים ואילנות ואוכלין מהן דבר מועט. ומתוך שנותנים בה תבלין הרבה ואגוזים ושקדים ואכילה מועט – לא הטעינוה ברכה מעין ג', מידי דהוה אפת אורז ודוחן, דאמרינן בפרקין (דף לז:) בתחלה "בורא מיני מזונות" ולבסוף ולא כלום: פת פוטרת. בין לפניהם בין לאחריהם: דברים הבאים מחמת הסעודה. ללפת בהן את הפת: אין טעונין ברכה. דהוו להו טפלה. הלכך: כל מידי, בין מזון בין פירות, שהביאו ללפתן – אין בו ברכה לא לפניו ולא לאחריו: שלא מחמת הסעודה בתוך הסעודה. כגון דייסא, וכן כרוב ותרדין, שאינן לפתן ובאין למזון ולשובע: טעונין ברכה לפניהן. דלאו טפלה נינהו, ואינן בכלל לחם דנפטר בברכת המוציא: ולא לאחריהן. דמיני מזון נינהו, וברכת המזון פוטרתן: דברים הרגילין לבא לאחר סעודה. כגון פירות, אפי' הביאן בתוך הסעודה שלא מחמת לפתן: טעונין ברכה בין לפניהן בין לאחריהם. דאין ברכת המזון פוטרתן, דלאו מזוני נינהו: דגורם

אייתו לקמייהו תמרי ורמוני. ולא ללפת בהן את הפת. דאם כן הוו להו פת עיקר והן טפלה, ותנן (דף מד.): מברך על העיקר ופוטר את הטפלה: זה שני לארץ. מ"מ, היכא דאיכא חטה וזית או שעורים ותמרים, אע"ג דשוין לארץ, מכל מקום המוקדם בפסוק דהיינו ל"ארץ" ראשון, יקדים לברכה: הביאו לפניהם תאנים וענבים בתוך הסעודה. וכגון שאין באין ללפת את הפת אלא לקנוח סעודה: אלא פת הבאה בכסנין. דטעון ברכה לפניו ואין טעון ברכה לאחריו רק "בורא נפשות רבות". מידי דהוה אאורז ודוחן, דאמרי' לעיל (דף לז:) בתחלה מברך "במ"מ" ולבסוף ולא כלום, הואיל ונתנו בהן שקדים הרבה. ופי' רש"י: אפי' אם אכל מהן אחר בהמ"ז קאמר. ולא נהירא, חדא: דאמרי' לעיל כל שיש בו מחמשת המינין צריך ברכה מעין שלש. ועוד: אמאי קאמר כיסנין, לימא נמי אורז ודוחן! ע"כ צריך לפרש דמיירי בתוך הסעודה, קודם בהמ"ז, דמיירי בה, וה"ק: חוץ מן הפת הבאה בכיסנין, בתוך הסעודה קודם ברכהמ"ז, דאין טעון ברכה לאחריו, דפטר ליה בהמ"ז אפי' לרב ששת משום דהוי דבר מועט; אבל בלא סעודה, אף לאחריו צריך לברך מעין ג' ברכות. ולהכי לא נקט פת אורז ודוחן, שהרי אפילו בלא סעודה נמי אין צריכין ברכה מעין ג' לאחריו: לא קי"ל כרב ששת אלא כרב הונא ורב נחמן, דאין הלכה כיחיד במקום רבים. ה"ג: ויין פוטר כל מיני משקין. ולכאורה מיירי ביין בלא סעודה. דאי בהדי פת – תיפוק ליה דפטר ליה פת, דאפי' יין נמי הוה לומר הספר בסמוך דפטור, אי לאו טעמא דקובע ברכה לעצמו. אלא מיירי בלא סעודה, ואפ"ה יין פוטר. ולית הלכתא כוותיה, שהרי מפת פוטרת אין הלכה כמותו, אלא כפסק רב פפא, א"כ גם מהא דקאמר יין פוטר וכו' לית הלכתא כוותיה: הלכתא דברים הבאים בתוך הסעודה מחמת הסעודה. פי' הקונטרס: ללפת בהן את הפת – אין טעונין ברכה, דהוו להו טפלה. ולא נהירא, דא"כ מתני' היא (דף מד.), דמברך על העיקר ופוטר את הטפלה, ומאי קמ"ל? ועוד קשה: דפריך בסמוך יין נמי נפטריה פת, ומאי קשה, והלא כששותים היין אינו טפלה לפת, ואנן במידי דטפל לפת מיירינן? ואין לפרש לפירוש הקונטרס יין נפטריה פת – כששורה פתו ביינו קאמר דהוה ליה יין טפל, דהא לא אשכחן שיברך עליו בענין זה! אלא ודאי מיירי בשתיה. ועוד קשה מה שפי' רש"י: דברים הבאים שלא מחמת הסעודה בתוך הסעודה – כגון דייסא ותרדין וכרוב שאינן של לפתן, ובאין לזון ולשבוע טעונים ברכה לפניהם – דלאו טפלה נינהו, ומיהו פטורין מברכת המזון – דמיני מזון נינהו. ולא נהירא, דאמרי' במתני' ברך על הפת פטר את הפרפרת, ובגמ' מפרש דהוא הדין כל מעשה קדרה. ודברים הרגילים לבא לאחר הסעודה, פירש"י: כמו פירות, ואפי' הביא אותן בתוך הסעודה שלא מחמת לפתן – טעונים ברכה. בין לפניהם – דלאו טפלה נינהו, ובין לאחריהם – דאין ברכת המזון פוטרתן דלאו מזון נינהו; דהיינו כרב ששת דאמר לעיל הביאו לפניו תאנים ורמונים בתוך הסעודה דטעונים ברכה בין לפניהם בין לאחריהם, והוי דלא כהלכתא, דקיי"ל כרב נחמן וכרב הונא כדפרישית לעיל. על כן פי' ר"י: דברים הבאים מחמת הסעודה בתוך הסעודה כלומר: הרגילים לבא מחמת הסעודה בפת, שרגילים לאכלן עם הפת כגון בשר ודגים וכל מיני קדרה, והביאן בתוך הסעודה – אין טעונין ברכה לפניהם ולאחריהם, אפי' אכלן בתוך הסעודה בפני עצמן בלא פת, דכיון דמשום פת הם באין – הפת פוטרתן. אבל דברים שאין דרכן לבא בתוך הסעודה, כגון תמרים ורמונים ושאר כל פירות שאין רגילים ללפת בהן את הפת – טעונין ברכה לפניהן, דכיון דלאו משום לפתן אתו – אין הפת פוטרתן, והיינו כר"נ וכרב הונא דלעיל, דאמרי דטעונין ברכה לפניהן ולא לאחריהן: לאחר הסעודה גרסי' ותו לא ולא גרסי' דברים הבאים בהך סיפא – והכי פירושו: אם הביאו דברים שהזכרנו אחר הסעודה. פי': לאחר שמשכו את ידיהם מן הפת, שוב אין הפת פוטרתן כלל, והוי כמו שאכלן בלא שום סעודה. ובין דברים הרגילים לבא מחמת הסעודה, ובין דברים שאין רגילים לבא מחמת הסעודה – טעונים ברכה לפניהם ולאחריהם, דאכל דברים דלעיל קאי, ועכשיו אין לנו דין זה, דאין מנהג שלנו למשוך ידינו מן הפת כלל עד לאחר בהמ"ז, אלא כל שעה שאנו אוכלין פירות או שום דבר קודם בהמ"ז דעתנו לאכול פת כל שעה, וקיי"ל כפסק דרב פפא: אי הכי יין נמי נפטריה פת. דודאי יין מחמת סעודה אתי, שהוא שותה כמה פעמים, דאי לאו הסעודה לא ישתה, ולפטריה פת! ומשני: שאני יין דגורם ברכה לעצמו. פירש"י: דבהרבה מקומות הוא בא, ומברכין עליו אע"פ שאין צריכין לשתות כגון בקידוש וברכת אירוסין. ורשב"א פי': משום דצריך לברך על היין "בורא פרי הגפן", ובתחלה כשהוא בענבים "בורא פרי העץ", ועל שאר משקין "שהכל נהיה בדברו". ומיהו, אומר ר"ת: דבשאר משקין כמו מים ושכר הבאים מחמת הסעודה – פת פוטרתן, דאפי' יין הוה פוטר אי לאו דקובע ברכה לעצמו, ולא כמחזור ויטרי שכתב שמברכין למים ברכה בכל פעם ופעם, ואפי' בתוך הסעודה דהוי כנמלך. והא דלא פריך הכא (ב)מהן משום דיין זיין אבל מים לא זייני, כדאמר (לעיל לה.): "הנודר מן המזון" וכו', ופשיטא דלא פטר להו פת – דאינה בכלל ברכת הפת: מיהו

קג א מיי' פ"ב מהלכות שביתת עשור הל' א סמג לאוין סט טוש"ע או"ח סי' תריב סעיף א:

קד ב מיי' פ"ח מהל' ברכות הל' יג סמג עשין כז טוש"ע או"ח סי' ריא סעיף ד:

קה ג טוש"ע או"ח סי' קעד סעיף ב:

קו ד מיי' פ"ד מהלכות ברכות הל' יא סמג שם טוש"ע או"ח סימן קעז סעיף א ב:

[ע' תוס' סוכה ו. ד"ה אלא]

קז ה טוש"ע או"ח סי' קעד סעיף א ז:

הגהות הב"ח

(א) רש"י ד"ה זה שני וכו' חשובים מרמונים שהרמון כצ"ל ותיבת מתאנים נמחק: (ב) תום' ד"ה אי הכי וכו' כנמלך וכו' דלא פריך הכא מיין אלא משום דיין.

בעירובין ובסוכה הש"ס אלא הלכתא

חולין קיא:

דגורם ברכה לעצמו.§ רב הונא אכל *תליסר ריפתי בני תלתא תלתא בקבא ולא בריך. א"ל רב נחמן: עדי כפנא! אלא: אכל שאחרים קובעים עליו סעודה צריך לברך. רב יהודה הוה עסיק ליה לבריה בי רב יהודה בר חביבא, אייתו לקמייהו פת הבאה בכסנין. כי אתא, שמעינהו דקא מברכי "המוציא". אמר להו: מאי 'ציצי' דקא שמענא? דילמא "המוציא לחם מן הארץ" קא מברכיתו?! –אמרי ליה: אין; דתניא רבי מונא אמר משום רבי יהודה: פת הבאה בכסנין מברכין עליה "המוציא", ואמר שמואל: הלכה כרבי מונא. אמר להו: אין הלכה כרבי מונא אתמר. אמרי ליה: והא מר הוא דאמר משמיה דשמואל, לחמניות – מערבין בהן ומברכין עליהן "המוציא"! – שאני התם דקבע סעודתיה עלייהו, אבל היכא דלא קבע סעודתיה עלייהו – לא. רב פפא איקלע לבי רב הונא בריה דרב נתן, בתר דגמר סעודתייהו אייתו לקמייהו מידי למיכל, שקל רב פפא וקא אכיל. אמרי ליה: לא סבר לה מר "גמר אסור מלאכול"?! –אמר להו: סלק אתמר. *רבא ורבי זירא איקלעו לבי ריש גלותא, לבתר דסליקו תכא מקמייהו שדרו להו *ריסתנא מבי ריש גלותא, רבא אכיל ורבי זירא לא אכיל. א"ל: לא סבר לה מר "סלק אסור מלאכול"?! –א"ל: אנן אתכא דריש גלותא סמכינן.§ אמר רב: הרגיל בשמן – שמן מעכבו. אמר רב אשי, כי הוינן בי רב כהנא אמר לן: כגון אנן דרגילינן במשחא – משחא מעכבא לן. ולית הלכתא ככל הני שמעתתא, אלא כי הא דאמר רבי חייא בר אשי אמר רב, שלש תכיפות הן: *תכף לסמיכה שחיטה, תכף לגאולה תפלה, תכף לנטילת ידים ברכה. אמר אביי, אף אנו נאמר: תכף לתלמידי חכמים ברכה, שנאמר: °"ויברכני ה' בגללך". איבעית אימא מהכא, שנאמר: °"ויברך ה' את בית המצרי בגלל יוסף".§ **מתני'** ברך על היין שלפני המזון – פטר את היין שלאחר המזון, ברך על הפרפרת שלפני המזון – פטר את הפרפרת שלאחר המזון, ברך על הפת – פטר את הפרפרת, על הפרפרת – לא פטר את הפת; בש"א: אף לא מעשה קדרה. היו *יושבין – כל אחד מברך לעצמו, הסבו – אחד מברך לכולן. בא

בראשית ל
שם לט

**רש"י**

דגורם ברכה לעצמו. בכמה מקומות הוא כאן, ומברכין עליו ואע"פ שלא היו צריכים לשתייתו: רב הונא אכל תליסר ריפתי. מפת הבאה בכסנין ולא בירך אחריו: אמר רב נחמן עדי כפנא. גרסי': עדי. אלו, כלומר: אלו לרעבון נאכלו, ואכילה מרובה כזו לא נקבעת מברכה. אלא, כל שאחרים קובעין אכילתן בכך – טעונין בהמ"ז, כך פירש רב האי. ורבותינו פירשו: תליסר ריפתי מפת שלנו, ולא בירך אחריו משום דלא שבע, וקרא כתיב (דברים ח) "ואכלת ושבעת וברכת", וכך פי' רב יהודאי בה"ג. ואינו נ"ל, דלית ליה לרב הונא "והם החמירו על עצמן עד כזית ועד כביצה" (לעיל דף כ:) ודלא כר"מ ודלא כר' יהודה (לקמן דף מט:): לחמניות. אובליא"ש בלע"ז: אסור מלאכול. עד שיברך בהמ"ז, ויחזור ויברך על הבא לפניו. דכיון דגמר – הסח דעתי' מברכה ראשונה ומסעודתיה: סלק אתמר. אם סלק השלחן וכל האוכל מעל השלחן, ועדיין לא ברכו – אסור לאכול: ריסתנא. אמינישטרשיו"ן: אתכא דריש גלותא סמכינן. ואין סילוקתנו סלוק, שדעתנו אם יצא משאות מאת פניו אלינו נאכל: הרגיל בשמן. למשוח ידיו אחר אכילה: שמן מעכבו. לענין ברכה, שאפילו גמר וסלק ולא משח ידיו – עדיין סעודה קיימת ואוכל בלא ברכה: ולית הלכתא ככל הני שמעתתא. אין סיום סעודה תלוי לא בגמר ולא בסלוק ולא בשמן, אלא במים אחרונים, כ"ז שלא נטל מים אחרונים – הוא מותר לאכול, ומשנטל – אסור לאכול: לנטילת ידים. דמים אחרונים – בהמ"ז, ולא יאכל כלום עד שיברך על מזונו: תכף לת"ח. המקריבו אליו ומארחו בביתו: ברכה. בביתו: מתני' ברך על היין כו'. נוהגין היו להביא קודם אכילה כוס יין לשתות, כדתניא לקמן (דף מג.) כיצד סדר הסבה כו'. ומביאין לפניהם פרפראות להמשיך אכילה, כגון פרגיות ודגים, ואח"כ מביאין השלחן, ולאחר גמר סעודה יושבים ושותים ואוכלים. ומה הן אוכלים – פרפראות, כגון כיסני דמעלו ללבא, ולחמניות, והוא יין ופרפרת שלאחר המזון, ושניהם קודם בהמ"ז: מעשה קדרה. חלקא טרגים(א) וטיסני: היו יושבים. בלא הסבת מטות. שמוטים על לדיהן שמאלית על המטה, ואוכלין ושותין בהסבה: כל אחד ואחד מברך לעצמו. דאין קבע סעודה בלא הסבה: בא

**תוספות**

מיהו ר"י ור"ת היו אומרים שלא לברך כלל אשאר משקין הבאין בתוך הסעודה וטעמא – דפת פוטרת כל הדברים הבאים בשבילה. והשתא יין פוטר כל מיני משקין – לפי שעיקר משקה הוא, והוא ראש לכל מיני משקין, ולכך הוא העיקר והן טפלין לו לענין ברכה. והלכך: משקין הבאין מחמת הסעודה שבאין בשביל הפת לשרות המאכל, וגם א"א לאכילה בלא שתיה, והלכך פת פוטרתן, חוץ מן היין, כדקאמר גמרא טעמא, ולהאי טעמא ניחא מה שאנו מברכים בפסח על החזרת על אכילת מרור, לבד: שהעולם מקשים: אמאי אין מברכין נמי ב"פ האדמה? וב"פ האדמה דשאר ירקות אינו פוטר. כדקאמרינן התם: כיון דאיכא הגדה – והלל אסח דעתיה אלא ודאי טעמא הוי: כיון דרחמנא קבעיה חובה, דכתיב על מצות ומרורים יאכלוהו הוי כמו דברים הרגילין לבא מחמת הסעודה, דפת פוטרתן: **לחמניות.** פרש"י: אובליא"ש. ולא נהירא, דא"כ אפילו לא קבע נמי(ב) לבריך המוציא שהרי הוא לחם גמור, שהרי סופו עיסה! ונראה לפרש דהיינו ניל"ש. מיהו כי קבע סעודתיה עליה מברך עליו המוציא, כמו בפורים. מיהו רבינו שמשון פירש דאין לברך עליו המוציא, דהוי כמו דייסא: **סלק** אתמר. משמע שדרכן היה(ג) לסלק השלחן קודם בהמ"ז. ולכאורה, קשה למנהג שלנו שאנו מקפידים שלא לסלק הלחם קודם(ד). ושמא בימיהם נמי לא היו מסלקין השלחן מקמי המברך כי אם מלפני שאר המסובין. לפי שהיו להן שלחנות קטנים, וכל אחד לפני עצמו אוכל על שלחנו. אבל אנו שרגילים לאכול כולנו על שלחן אחד – אין נאה לסלק השלחן עד לאחר ברכת המזון: **רבי** זירא לא אכל. תימה(ה), לפי מה שמפרשים העולם הב לן ונבריך – אסור למשתי בלא ברכה שלפניו, אמאי לא אכל? לבריך עליה וליכול! ושמא היה תבשיל שהיה בו פת, והיה צריך ברכת המוציא ונט"י, וטורח היה לעשות כל כך: **אתכא** דריש גלותא סמכינן. מי ששכח לאכול אפיקומן, ואמר הב לן ונבריך – אינו היסח הדעת, דאנן אתכא דרחמנא סמכינן. ואם שכח וברך ולא אכל אפיקומן – א"צ לחזור(ו), דכל מצות לשם מצוה עשויות. והא דאמרינן* כי אמר הב לן ונבריך אסור למשתי, וכן אסורים כולן – היינו דוקא כי אמר בעל הבית, אבל לא אורח (וכי אסורים כולן היינו כי אמר בעה"ב אבל בשביל אורח אינן נאסרין), ואף איהו גופא יכול לחזור ולאכול עם בעה"ב: **אתכא** דריש גלותא סמכינן. וכשרגיל לאכול מיני פירות, ומביאין להם בזה אחר זה, יש אומר שצריך לברך אכל חד וחד, לפי שאינן יודעים אם יתן להם בעה"ב יותר. ונראה שאין צריך לברך, לפי שסומכין על שלחן בעה"ב, והיינו דבי ריש גלותא: **תכף** לנטילת ידים ברכה. והלכך: כיון שנטל ידיו באחרונה לאחר סעודה – אסור לאכול עד שיברך, והוא הדין אם אמר הב לן ונבריך אפי' בלא נטילה*: **ברך** על הפת פטר את הפרפרת. נראה דמיירי בפרפרת שבתוך הסעודה, דאי בפרפרת שלאחר הסעודה – הא פסק רב פפא *דברים הבאים לאחר סעודה טעונין ברכה לפניהם ולאחריהם. ורש"י פירש: פרפרת – מיני דגים ופרגיות. וקצת קשה, א"כ מאי קמ"ל דברך על הפרפרת דלא פטר את הפת? ונראה כפירוש ר"ח, דפירש דפרפרת – פת לנומה בקערה, דלית בה תוריתא דנהמא, דמברכין עליה בורא מיני מזונות והשתא ניחא דאצטריך לאשמעינן ברך על הפרפרת לא פטר את הפת אע"ג דהוא מין פת וכן משמע בגמרא דחשיב פרפרת *מעשה קדרה ומעשה קדרה היינו חלקא טרגים וטיסני כדאמרינן לעיל (לז.): **הסבו** אחד מברך לכלן. ואנו אין לנו הסבה אלא בפת בלבד, ופת מהני אפי' בלא הסבה, דדוקא לדידהו שהיו אוכלים בהסבה – היו צריכים הסבה. אלא: ישיבה שלנו הוי קביעות לנו כהסבה דידהו, שהם היו רגילים כל אחד להסב על מטתו ועל שלחנו, אבל עכשיו כולנו אוכלים על שלחן אחד, וכשאנו אוכלין יחד – היינו קביעותינו. והכא דקאמר היו יושבין וכו' – בגמרא משמע דמיירי בין בברכת המוציא בין בברכת המזון; בהמ"ז – כעובדא דתלמידי דרב. בברכת המוציא – מההיא דפליגי ביין אי בעי הסבה, ומיהו, בני אדם האוכלים בדרך והולכים ולא ישבו – כל אחד מברך לעצמו. וא"ת: מאי שנא דבמוגמר אפילו לא הסבו אחד מברך לכולם? בירושלמי פריך, ומשני: משום דבמוגמר כולם נהנים ביחד, אבל אכילה ושתיה אינה באה אלא לזה אחר זה: אע"פ

**עין משפט נר מצוה**

קח א ב מיי' פ"ג מהל' ברכות הל' ט סמג עשין כז טוש"ע או"ח סי' קסח סעיף ו ז:
קט ג ד שם סעיף ו וסעיף ח:
קי ה מיי' פ"ד מהלכות ברכות הלכה ז סמג שם טוש"ע או"ח סימן קעט סעיף ב:
קיא ו מיי' פ"ג מהל' מעשה קרבנות הלכה יב:
קיב ז מיי' פ"ז מהל' תפלה הל' יז טוש"ע או"ח סי' קיא סעיף א:
קיג ח מיי' פ"ד מהל' ברכות הלכה יב סמג עשין כז טוש"ע או"ח סי' קעט סעיף א ובסי' קסו:
קיד ט מיי' פ"ד מהל' ברכות הלכה יב סמג שם טור או"ח סימן קעו:
קטו י טור או"ח סימן קעו:
קטז כ מיי' פ"א מהל' ברכות הלכה יב סמג שם טוש"ע או"ח סי' קסז סעיף יח וסימן ריג סעיף א:

**רב נסים גאון**

שלש תכיפות הן תכף לסמיכה שחיטה. בתלמוד ארץ ישראל בפ' מאימתי קורין אמר תכף לסמיכה שחיטה דכתיב (ויקרא א) וסמך ושחט. תכף לנטילת ידים ברכה [שנאמר] (תהלים קלד) שאו ידכם קדש וברכו את ה'. תכף לגאולה תפלה שנאמר (שם יט) יהיו לרצון אמרי פי מה כתיב בתריה יענך ה' ביום צרה ובגמ' דפ"ב דשחיטת קדשים (דף לג) אמרי תכף לסמיכה שחיטה דאורייתא:

**הגהות הב"ח**

(א) רש"י ד"ה מעשה קדרה חלקא טרגים. נ"ב ע"ל דף לז ע"ב: (ב) תוס' ד"ה לחמניות וכו' לא קבע נמי לריך לברך וכו' שהרי תחלתו וסופו עיסה: (ג) ד"ה סלק וכו' משמע שדרכן. נ"ב פירוש מדקאמר לבתר דסליקו תכא וכו': (ד) ד"ה הלחם קודם. נ"ב כלומר ולמה לא מסלקין גם השלחן: (ה) ד"ה רבי זירא וכו' תימה. נ"ב וכ"כ התוספות פרק כסוי הדם סוף דף פו וכ"כ הרא"ש לשם: (ו) ד"ה אתכא דריש גלותא וכו' א"צ לחזור ולאכול לכל:

[ווע"ע תוס' סוטה לט. ד"ה כל כהן]

**גליון הש"ס**

גמ' אלא כי הא דאמר רבי חייא. עי' ברמב"ן במלחמות פ"ב דשבת בד"ה ועוד כתב הרי"ף הא דרב גידל: שם גמ' שלש תכיפות הן. עי' לקמן דף נ"ב ע"ב תוס' ד"ה תכף: רש"י ד"ה לנטילת ידים דמים אחרונים. כך מבואר בסוגיין. אבל בדברים ובירושלמי פ' א"ע מבואר דקאי על נטילה ראשונה. ועיין תוס' סוטה דף ל"ט ע"א ד"ה כל וכו':

**מסורת הש"ס**

[פו' ב"ב קנג: ד"ה תא ועי' רש"י ותוס' ב"ת קיט. ד"ה תליסר]

[רבה]

חלק ולקמן דף נ: [ע"ש דיסתנא]

מנחות צג. [ביצה כ.]

[גי' לאכול כ"ה הגי' בה שבמשניות אכן שלמי וכרי"ף ורא"ש וכ"ה שבאלתות ליתא וכ"מ ע"ב ד"ה הסבו אין]

לעיל מא:

[*מעין מעשה קדירה וכ"ה ברא"ש]

קיז א מיי' פ"ז מהל' ברכות הל' יג סמג עשין כז טור או"ח סי' קעד:

[ע' תוס' עירובין לב. ד"ה ר"ש]

קיח ב מיי' פ"ד מהל' ברכות הל' יב סמג וטור שם:

קיט ג טוש"ע שם ס"ד:

קכ ד מיי' פ"ד מהל' ברכות הל' יב סמג וטור שם:

קכא ה ו מיי' פ"ד מהל' ברכות הל' ו סמג שם טוש"ע או"ח סימן קטו:

קכב ז ח מיי' פ"א מהל' ברכות הל' יב סמג שם טוש"ע או"ח סי' קסז סעיף יא:

**רב נסים גאון**

**והוא** אומר על המוגמ'. גרסי' בגמ' דבני מערבא (הלכה ו) מה בין מוגמר ובין יין מוגמר כולן מריחין יין אחד הוא שהוא טועם פשיטא של זו הבעיא דמוגמר אע"ג דמילתא ידועה היא שאין מביאין אותו אלא לאחר הסעוד' אחד מברך לכולן ולפיכך שאל השואל מפני מה היין הבא בתוך המזון כל אחד ואחד מברך לעצמו והמוגמר אחד מברך לכולן יין אחד טועם ומברך כל אחד לעצמו:

**הגהות הב"ח**

(א) רש"י ד"ה נהר וכו' שמו הס"ד ואח"כ מ"ה א"ד כיון דאמרו ניזיל וניכול בדוכתא פלן רישא דוקא:

**גליון הש"ס**

**תוס'** ד"ה הסבו אין וכו'. תימה אמאי מקשה. עי' רשב"א בחידושיו שבת דף נ"ט ע"ב ד"ה הא יש עליה תותס:

בא להם יין בתוך המזון – כל אחד ואחד מברך לעצמו. אחר המזון – אחד מברך לכולם, והוא אומר על המוגמר, ואע"פ שאין מביאין את המוגמר אלא לאחר סעודה.§ **גמ'** אמר רבה בר בר חנה א"ר יוחנן: לא שנו אלא בשבתות וימים טובים, הואיל ואדם קובע סעודתו על היין, אבל בשאר ימות השנה – מברך על כל כוס וכוס. אתמר נמי, אמר רבה בר מרי א"ר יהושע בן לוי: לא שנו אלא בשבתות וימים טובים, ובשעה שאדם יוצא מבית המרחץ, ובשעת הקזת דם, הואיל ואדם קובע סעודתו על היין, אבל בשאר ימות השנה – מברך על כל כוס וכוס. רבה בר מרי איקלע לבי רבא בחול, חזייה דבריך לפני המזון והדר בריך לאחר המזון, א"ל: *יישר, וכן אמר ריב"ל. רב יצחק בר יוסף איקלע לבי אביי בי"ט, חזייה דבריך אכל כסא וכסא. א"ל: לא סבר לה מר להא דריב"ל?! –א"ל: נמלך אנא.§ איבעיא להו: בא להם יין בתוך המזון, מהו שיפטור את היין שלאחר המזון? אם תימצי לומר "ברך על היין שלפני המזון פוטר את היין שלאחר המזון" – משום דזה לשתות וזה לשתות, אבל הכא דזה לשתות וזה לשרות – לא; או דילמא לא שנא? –רב אמר: פוטר, ורב כהנא אמר: אינו פוטר. רב נחמן אמר: פוטר, ורב ששת אמר: אינו פוטר. רב הונא ורב יהודה וכל תלמידי דרב אמרי: אינו פוטר. איתיביה רבא לרב נחמן: בא להם יין בתוך המזון – כל אחד ואחד מברך לעצמו, לאחר המזון – אחד מברך לכולם! א"ל, הכי קאמר: אם לא בא להם יין בתוך המזון אלא לאחר המזון – אחד מברך לכולם.§ "ברך על הפת – פטר את הפרפרת, על הפרפרת – לא פטר את הפת; ב"ש אומרים: אף לא מעשה קדרה". איבעיא להו: ב"ש ארישא פליגי, או דילמא אסיפא פליגי? דקאמר תנא קמא: ברך על הפת פטר את הפרפרת וכ"ש מעשה קדרה, ואתי ב"ש למימר: לא מיבעיא פרפרת – דלא פטרה להו פת, אלא אפילו מעשה קדרה – נמי לא פטרה; או דילמא אסיפא פליגי, דקתני: ברך על הפרפרת לא פטר את הפת, פת הוא דלא פטר, אבל מעשה קדרה – פטר. ואתו ב"ש למימר: ואפי' מעשה קדרה נמי לא פטר – תיקו.§ "היו יושבין כל אחד ואחד כו'". הסבו – אין, לא הסבו – לא. ורמינהו: *עשרה שהיו הולכים בדרך, אע"פ שכולם אוכלים מככר אחד – כל אחד ואחד מברך לעצמו; ישבו לאכול, אע"פ שכל אחד ואחד אוכל מככרו – אחד מברך לכולם. קתני "ישבו", אע"פ שלא הסבו! – אמר רב נחמן בר יצחק, כגון דאמרי: ניזיל וניכול לחמא בדוך פלן. כי נח נפשיה דרב, אזלו תלמידיו בתריה. כי הדרי, אמרי: ניזיל וניכול לחמא אנהר דנק. בתר דכרכי יתבי וקא מיבעיא להו: הסבו דוקא תנן, אבל ישבו – לא, או דילמא כיון דאמרי ניזיל וניכול ריפתא בדוכתא פלניתא – כי הסבו דמי? לא הוה בידייהו. קם רב אדא בר אהבה

אהדר

[שבת נג. סג: פסחים נג: ב"ק ק. שבועות מ: יז: עה: עו:]

[גי' אחרת בנוסחת הגמ']

[תוספתא פ"ה]

**רש"י**

**בא** להם יין בתוך המזון כו'. בגמ' מפרש טעמא (ד' מג.): **והוא** אומר על המוגמר. אותו שבירך על היין הוא מברך על המוגמר. שהיו רגילים להביא לפניהם אחר אכילה אבקת רוכלין על האש במחתות לריח טוב ומברכים עליו "בורא עצי בשמים": **לאחר סעודה.** לאחר בהמ"ז, שאינו מגמרי סעודה אפי' הכי מי שבירך על היין שהתחיל בברכות אחרונות – גומרן: **גמ' לא שנו.** דיין שלפני המזון פוטר את שלאחר המזון: **אלא בשבתות כו'.** דדעתו לישב אחר המזון ולשתות, וכי בריך ברישא – אדעתא דהכי בריך: **על כל כוס וכוס.** דהוה כנמלך ומתחיל בשתיה בכל חד וחד: **יישר.** יפה עשית: **וכן אמר ריב"ל.** לעשות: **לא סבר לה מר כו'.** דבי"ט לאו נמלך הוא: **נמלך אנא.** איני רגיל לקבוע סעודה על היין: **בא להם יין בתוך המזון.** וקודם המזון לא בא להם: **אם תמצי לומר.** להביא ראיה ממשנתנו דקתני דיין שלפני המזון פוטר את שלאחר המזון – אינה ראיה, דהתם זה לשתות וזה לשתות, אבל שבתוך המזון – לשרות אכילה שבמעיו הוא בא, ולא היו רגילין לשתות בתוך הסעודה אלא מעט, **לשרות:** **לאחר המזון אחד מברך לכולן.** קס"ד דה"ק: דכשהביאו יין שני אחר המזון – אחד מברך לכולן, והא תנא ליה דכל אחד ואחד יברך על שבתוך המזון לעצמו, וקא מצריך תו ברכה על שלאחר המזון: **פטר את הפרפרת.** אע"פ שאין צורך סעודה למלוי הכרס, אלא לגמר אכילה: **וכל שכן מעשה קדרה.** שהוא לאכול, לזון ממש: **בדוך פלן.** במקום פלוני. דקבעו להם מתחלה מקום בדבור ועצה והזמנה – הוי קביעות. אבל ישבו מאליהן במקום אחד יחד – אינה קביעות: **אזלו תלמידיו בתריה.** דקברוהו בעיר אחרת: **נהר דנק.** כך שמו(א): *רישא דוקא. דקתני היו יושבים – בלא הזמנת מקום הוא, דלא הוי קביעות. אבל אנו שהזמנינהו לכך – הוי קביעות, ואחד מברך לכולן:

אהדר

**תוספות**

**ואע"פ** שאין מביאין את המוגמר אלא לאחר סעודה. וככר ברכו ברכת המזון ויש הפסק בין יין למוגמר:

**ורב** ששת אמר אינו פוטר ורב נחמן אמר פוטר וכל תלמידי דרב וכו'. ונראה דהלכה כתלמידי דרב, דרב ששת קאי כוותייהו והלכתא כותיה דר"נ בדיני *וכרב ששת באיסורי. ואע"ג דקי"ל *דרב ושמואל הלכה כרב באיסורי, שאני הכא דכל תלמידי דרב פליגי עליה, מסתמא כך שמעו מרב. [בכורות מט:] מיהו, אין אנו צריכין לאותו פסק, דאין אנו מושכין ידינו מן הפת כלל. ונראה דיין שלפני סעודה פוטר את היין שבתוך הסעודה, אע"ג דפסקינן הכא דיין שבתוך הסעודה אינו פוטר יין דלאחר הסעודה – שאני הכא דזה לשרות וזה לשתות, אבל זה לשתות וזה לשרות – פוטר שפיר, כגון יין שלפני הסעודה פוטר שבתוך הסעודה. ומה דנקט שבתות וי"ט – לאו דוקא, דה"ה אם קבעו סעודה על היין בשאר ימות החול. ואם הביא אדם יין לפני הסעודה לשתות בתוך הסעודה, פשיטא דיין דלפני סעודה פוטרתו, כיון דדעתיה למשתי. וכן יין של קידוש פוטר יין שבתוך הסעודה, וכן הבדלה, אם הביא על שלחנו להבדיל דפוטר יין שלאחרי כן, שבתוך הסעודה. ושבתות וי"ט לאו דוקא, ולא אתא למעוטי אלא נמלך. ואפילו את"ל דדוקא נקט שבתות וי"ט, מ"מ יש לומר, ה"מ – לענין שבא לפטור יין שלאחר המזון שהוא אחר שמשכו ידיהם מן הפת, שאין רגילות לקבוע לשתות יין לאחר המזון בקביעות, אלא בשבתות וימים טובים ולא בשאר ימים. אבל לענין לפטור יין שבתוך המזון, שרגילות לשתות – ודאי אפילו בשאר ימים פטר ליה יין שלפני המזון, אע"פ דזה לשתות וזה לשרות. דעד כאן לא איבעיא לן אלא אי לשרות, דלא חשיב, מפיק לשתות. אבל לשתות, דחשיב טפי, דהיינו יין שלפני המזון, פשיטא דפוטר יין דלשרות. וכן משמע נמי בערבי פסחים (דף קא.) גבי שקדשו בב"ה, דר' יוחנן אמר: אף ידי יין נמי יצאו, ואין צריך לחזור ולברך על היין שבתוך הסעודה. אע"ג דקדשו שלא במקום סעודה ס"ל לרבי יוחנן מדיצאו ידי קידוש – מידי יין נמי יצאו. ואף על גב דאיתותב רבי יוחנן – היינו דוקא בשינוי מקום, א"כ נראה משם דה"ה להבדלה, דאין לחלק בין הבדלה לקידוש. ולאפוקי מהני דחולקין ואמרי דוקא קידוש פוטר, משום דאין קידוש אלא במקום סעודה, אבל יין של הבדלה – לא פטר, אפילו הבדיל לאחר נטילה. דהכי מיירי הא דפסקינן דיין שלפני המזון פוטר היין שבתוך המזון דכבר נטל ידיו. והכי משמע בסמוך מתוך הברייתא, כילד סדר הסבה וכו'. מיהו, נראה כיון דנטל ידיו ודעתו לאכול ולשתות שם – פוטר אפילו דהבדלה, כדפריש מההיא דערבי פסחים. ועוד: דלא גרע יין דהבדלה מיין שלפני הסעודה דפטר. ומיהו, יש שמחמירין להבדיל קודם נטילת ידים לאפוקי נפשייהו מפלוגתא, דאז ודאי צריך לברך אחריו ברכה מעין שלש ולא פטר יין שבתוך המזון: **יין** שבתוך המזון מהו שיפטור יין שלאחר המזון. ומיירי דלא הוה להו יין לפני המזון: **הסבו אין לא הסבו לא.** תימה: אמאי מקשה מדיוקא? *ותקשי ליה מרישא בהדיא, דקתני היו יושבים מברך כל אחד לעצמו! וי"ל: דאי מרישא הוה אמינא שישבו בשביל עסק אחר, שלא היה דעתם מתחלה לאכול, אבל אם ישבו אדעתא לאכול – אפילו בלא הסבה נמי מהניא:

[ועי' תוס' ש... אלא]

**עשרה** בני אדם שהיו מהלכין כו' ניזיל וניכול לחמא כו' כישבו והסבו דמיא. והשתא ניחא הא דפריש במתניתין דמיירי בין בברכת המוציא בין בברכת המזון, כדמשמע הכא מתוך הברייתא דעשרה בני אדם וכו'. וא"ת: אמאי המתינו למיבעי עד ברכת המזון, והיאך ברכו על הפת מתחלה? וי"ל: שמא מיירי דישבו לאכול זה אחר זה, וברך כל אחד לעצמו המוציא:

כל

אהדר קרעיה לאחוריה, וקרע קריעה אחרינא. אמר: נח נפשיה דרב וברכת מזונא לא גמרינן! עד דאתא ההוא סבא, רמא להו מתניתין אברייתא ושני להו: כיון דאמרי ניזיל וניכול לחמא בדוך פלן – כהסבו דמי.§ "הסבו – אחד מברך". אמר רב: לא שנו אלא פת דבעי הסבה, אבל יין לא בעי הסבה. ור' יוחנן אמר: אאפילו יין נמי בעי הסבה. איכא דאמרי, אמר רב: לא שנו אלא פת – דמהניא ליה הסבה, אבל יין – לא מהניא ליה הסבה. ורבי יוחנן אמר: אפילו יין נמי מהניא ליה הסבה. מיתיבי: *כיצד סדר הסבה? אורחין נכנסין ויושבין על גבי ספסלין ועל גבי קתדראות עד שיתכנסו כולם. הביאו להם מים כל אחד ואחד נוטל ידו אחת, בא להם יין – כל אחד ואחד מברך לעצמו; עלו והסבו ובא להם מים, אף על פי שכל אחד ואחד נטל ידו אחת – חוזר ונוטל שתי ידיו. בא להם יין, אף על פי שכל אחד ואחד ברך לעצמו – אחד מברך לכולם. להאיך לישנא דאמר רב: לא שנו אלא פת דבעי הסבה, אבל יין לא בעי הסבה – קשיא רישא! – שאני אורחין דדעתייהו למיעקר. ולהאיך לישנא דאמר רב: לא שנו אלא פת דמהניא ליה הסבה, אבל יין לא מהניא ליה הסבה – קשיא סיפא! – שאני התם, דמגו דקא מהניא ליה הסבה לפת, מהניא ליה הסבה ליין.§ "בא להם יין בתוך המזון". *שאלו את בן זומא: מפני מה אמרו ב"בא להם יין בתוך המזון – כל אחד ואחד מברך לעצמו, לאחר המזון – אחד מברך לכולם"? אמר להם: הואיל ואין בית הבליעה פנוי.§ "והוא אומר על המוגמר כו'". מדקתני "והוא אומר על המוגמר" – מכלל דאיכא עדיף מיניה, *ואמאי? הואיל והוא נטל ידיו [א] תחלה באחרונה. מסייע ליה לרב, דאמר רב חייא בר אשי *אמר רב: גהנוטל ידיו תחלה באחרונה – הוא מזומן לברכה. *רב ורבי חייא הוו יתבי קמיה דרבי בסעודתא. א"ל רבי לרב: קום משי ידך! חזייה דהוה מרתת, אמר ליה רבי חייא: *בר פחתי! עיין בברכת מזונא קאמר לך.§ אמר רבי זירא אמר רבא בר ירמיה: דמאימתי מברכין על הריח – משתעלה תמרתו. א"ל רבי זירא לרבא בר ירמיה: והא לא קא ארח! – אמר ליה: ולטעמיך "המוציא לחם מן הארץ" דמברך – והא לא אכל! אלא – דעתיה למיכל, הכא נמי דעתיה לארוחי. אמר רבי חייא בריה דאבא בר נחמני אמר רב חסדא אמר רב, ואמרי לה אמר רב חסדא אמר זעירי: הכל המוגמרות מברכין עליהן "בורא עצי בשמים", חוץ וממושק שמן חיה הוא, שמברכין עליו "בורא מיני בשמים". מיתיבי: אין מברכין "בורא עצי בשמים" אלא על אפרסמון של בית רבי. ועל אפרסמון של בית קיסר, ועל ההדס שבכל מקום! תיובתא. אמר ליה רב חסדא לרב יצחק: האי משחא דאפרסמון מאי מברכין עלויה? – א"ל הכי אמר רב יהודה: "בורא שמן ארצנו". א"ל: בר מיניה דר' יהודה דחביבא ליה ארץ ישראל, לכולי עלמא מאי? – א"ל: הכי אמר רבי יוחנן: ז"בורא שמן ערב". אמר ר' אדא בר אהבה: האי כשרתא מברכין עלויה "בורא עצי בשמים", אבל משחא כבישא – לא; ורב כהנא אמר: אפילו משחא כבישא, אבל משחא טחינא – לא; נהרדעי אמרי: חאפי' משחא טחינא. אמר

**רש"י**

אהדר קרעיה לאחוריה. קרע שקרע בהספד רבו החזיר החלוק לאחוריו, ומה שלאחור לפנים, כדי לקרוע קרע אחר, להראות אבל עכשיו כיום המיתה, על שהיו צריכים להוראה ואין יודעים להורות: רמי להו כו'. כדרמינן לעיל, ועל כרחך מבעי ליה לאוקומי ברייתא בהכי וקתני אחד מברך לכולם דקביעות הוא: הביאו להם מים. כך היו רגילים: נוטל ידו אחת. לקבל בה כוס ששותה לפני המזון: עלו. על המטות והסבו: חוזר ונוטל ב' ידיו. שצריך לאכול בשתיהן. אע"פ שכל אחד ואחד ברך לעצמו. צריכין עוד ברכה, שאין ברכה ראשונה פוטרתו; שאין הראשון קרוי שלפני המזון, שאינו במקום סעודה, והאי בתרא הוא יין שלפני המזון: אחד מברך לכולן. דכיון דהסבו הוקבעו: קשיא רישא. דקתני: כל אחד ואחד מברך לעצמו: שאני אורחין דדעתייהו למיעקר. סופן למיעקר ולעלות ולהסב במקום אחר, שאין זה מקום המסיבה, אלא כאן ישבו עד שיתכנסו כל הקרואים. ודרך בעלי בתים עשירים היה לזמן לסעודתם אורחים עניים, להכי קרי להו אורחים. והא דאמר רב: יין לא בעי הסבה אלא ישיבה בעלמא – שלא בשעת סעודה קאמר, או בשעת סעודה ובמקום סעודה: הואיל ואין בית הבליעה פנוי. ואין לב המסובין אל המברך, אלא לבלוע: מכלל דאיכא עדיף מיניה. ואפ"ה: כיון דאתחיל בהדא – עביד לאידך: הנוטל ידיו תחלה. במים אחרונים, הוא מזומן לבהמ"ז: חזייה. רבי חייא לרב: דהוה מרתת. שמא רואה ידי מלוכלכות, או שמא האכלתי באכילה יותר מדאי: עיין בברכת מזונא קאמר לך. כאן נתן לך רשות לברך בהמ"ז, שהנוטל ידיו תחלה הוא מברך: על הריח. של מוגמר: תמרתו. קיטור העשן שמתמר ועולה: הא לא ארח. לא הריח בו עדיין, ולא נהנה: מברכין עליהן בורא עצי בשמים. ואע"פ שנשרף ואינו בעין אלא שהתימור עולה: חוץ ממושק. מוסג"א בלע"ז: שהוא מן חיה. מן הרעי של חיה: מיתיבי אין מברכין בורא עצי בשמים אלא על אפרסמון. שהעץ עצמו בא לפנינו: של בית רבי ושל בית קיסר. נקט הני משום שאינו מצוי אלא בבית מלכים ובעלי גדולה: ועל ההדס שבכל מקום. וה"ה לכל הדומה להם, שהעץ עצמו מריח בלא שרפה אלא דהדס שכיח, ודברו חכמים בהווה בכל מקום. ומוגמר לא מברכינן אלא "בורא מיני בשמים": משחא דאפרסמא מאי מברכין. על ריחו: שמן ארצנו. שהיה גדל ביריחו ועל שם הריח היתה נקראת יריחו. והוא פנג האמור בספר יחזקאל (כ"ז) "יהודה וא"י המה רוכליך בחיטי מנית ופנג" – כך ראיתי בספר יוסף בן גוריון: בר מיניה דרב יהודה. אל תביא לי ראיה מדבריו בזו: כשרתא. קושט: משחא כבישא. שמן שבו טמון הקושט והשמן מריח מן הבושם שבתוכו: לא. הואיל ואין נראה לעינינו אלא השמן: משחא טחינא. שטחנו בו כשרתא:

סמלק

**תוספות**

כל אחד נוטל ידו אחת. מפני *כבוד הברכה ולא דמי לנוטל ידיו לפירות דהוי מגסי הרוח, כיון שאינו נוטל שתי ידיו: בא להם יין וכו'. אע"ג דיין שלפני המזון פוטר יין שלאחר המזון, כל שכן זה שלפניו הוא. שאני הכא כיון שעלו להסב – הוי שנוי מקום וצריך לברך: הואיל ואין בית הבליעה פנוי. וי"מ: כשאומר סברי מורי והם מניחין לאכול כדי לשמוע הברכה ולענות אמן, שיהיו פטורים. וכן משמע בירושלמי גבי הך ברייתא: הני מילי – באורחין, אבל בבעל הבית – פטור, מפני שהכל פונים אל בעל הבית. תני רבי חייא: אף בעל הבית בתוך ביתו. ואין נראה לרבינו אלחנן, דכיון שתקנו חכמים שיברך כל אחד לעצמו – אינו יוצא כלל בברכת חבירו; וגם שלא תחלוק בין פנוי לשאינו פנוי, דאתי למטעי. והטוב והמטיב יש מפרש שפוטר לאחרים לכולי עלמא, דהכי משמע הטוב – לעצמו והמטיב – לאחריני שהם שותים ממנו. ורבינו יחיאל היה אומר דלא היא, דשייך נמי אין בית הבליעה פנוי, ולא פליג בין הטוב ובין ברכת היין; דמשום האי טעמא הטוב לדידיה ומטיב לאחריני – אינו פוטר אחרים. דהא המטיב שייך אפי' שלא בפני המטיבין לו, כדאמרי' לקמן בפרק הרואה (דף נט:): אמרו לו, ילדה אשתך זכר, אומר ברוך הטוב והמטיב. הטוב – לדידיה והמטיב – לאשתו, אע"ג דאין אשתו אצלו. אבל צריך עיון קצת מהבדלה שאנו מבדילין ועומדים, היאך אנו פוטרין זה את זה מיין ומהבדלה. אחרי שאין אנו לא יושבים ולא מסובין? ושמא י"ל: מתוך שקובעין עצמן כדי לצאת ידי הבדלה – קבעי נמי אכולה מילתא. ולכך נאה וטוב למבדיל, וגם לשומעים, שישבו בשעת הבדלה שאז יהיה נראה כקבע – ופוטר אותם: כל המוגמרות מברכין עליהן בורא עצי בשמים. אע"פ שנשרפו ואין עצי בשמים בעין: ועל ההדס שבכל מקום. בעל הלכות גדולות לא גריס תיובתא, ומשני: תנא הדס וכל דדמי ליה. כלומר: שעיקרו לריח, לאפוקי תפוחים וחבושים שאין עיקרן לריח אלא לאכול. ומי שהולך בבית שיש שם בשמים, ויש שם מיני בשמים שמריח בהן, ומספקא ליה אי ממין עץ אי ממין אדמה הוא, יש מפרשים שמברך שהכל נהיה בדברו, דעל כולן אם ברך שהכל – יצא. והרב רבינו משה מקוצי היה אומר שיברך בורא מיני בשמים: משחא כבישא. פי' ר"ח: שמענו שכובשין מרבותינו שומשמין וורד ועצי בשמים זמן מרובה, וקולטין השומשמין ריח של בשמים, וסוחטים וטוחנים אותם, ויש בו ריח של בשמים. ומשחא טחינא קרוב לטחינתו נותנים עליהם עצי בשמים, ואינו קולט כל כך הריח:

שמן

**עין משפט נר מצוה**

[ועי' מ"ש תוס' פסחים קטו. ד"ה כל שטיבולו כו' ותו' חגיגה יח: ד"ה הנוטל]

קכג א מיי' פ"א מהל' ברכות שם סמג עשין כז טור או"ח סי' קעד טוש"ע או"ח סימן ריג סעיף א:

קכד ב מיי' פ"ד מהל' ברכות הלכה יב סמג שם טוש"ע או"ח סי' קעד סעיף ח:

קכה ג מיי' פ"ז מהל' ברכות הלכה יב סמג שם טוש"ע א"ח סי' קפא סעיף ו:

קכו ד מיי' פ"ט מהל' ברכות הל' ב סמג שם טוש"ע או"ח סימן רטז סעיף יב:

קכז ה מיי' שם טוש"ע שם סעיף יג:

קכח ו מיי' שם והל' א טוש"ע שם סעיף ב:

קכט ז מיי' שם הלכה ג טוש"ע שם סעיף ד:

קל ח מיי' שם טוש"ע שם סעיף ה:

**הגהות הגר"א**

[א] גמ' (ואמאי הואיל והוא נטל ידיו באחרונה) נמחק:

**גליון הש"ס**

גמ' שאני התם דמגו דקא מהניא ליה הסבה. עי' לעיל דף ל"ט ע"א ברש"י ד"ה זקנה ובתוס' ד"ה נתן:

**מסורת הש"ס**

תוספתא פ"ד

תוספתא פ"ד

ז עד באחרונה

לקמן מו:

[שם]

ולים [שבת ג. בן גדולים וע' מ"ש לעיל יג:]

אמר רב גידל אמר רב: האי סמלק מברכין עלויה "בורא עצי בשמים". אמר רב חננאל אמר רב: הני חלפי דימא מברכין עלייהו "בורא עצי בשמים". אמר מר זוטרא: מאי קראה – "והיא העלתם הגגה ותטמנם בפשתי העץ". (רב משרשיא אמר): האי נרקום דגינוניתא מברכין עלויה "בורא עצי בשמים", דדברא – "בורא עשבי בשמים". אמר רב ששת: הני סיגלי מברכין עלייהו "בורא עשבי בשמים". אמר מר זוטרא: האי מאן דמורח באתרוגא או בחבושא אומר "ברוך שנתן ריח טוב בפירות".§ אמר רב יהודה: האי מאן דנפיק ביומי ניסן וחזי אילני דקא מלבלבי, אומר: ברוך שלא חיסר בעולמו כלום וברא בו בריות טובות ואילנות טובות להתנאות בהן בני אדם. אמר רב זוטרא בר טוביה אמר רב: מנין שמברכין על הריח – שנאמר: "כל הנשמה תהלל יה", איזהו דבר שהנשמה נהנית ממנו ואין הגוף נהנה ממנו – הוי אומר זה הריח. ואמר רב זוטרא בר טוביה אמר רב: עתידים בחורי ישראל שיתנו ריח טוב כלבנון, שנאמר: "ילכו יונקותיו ויהי כזית הודו וריח לו כלבנון". ואמר רב זוטרא בר טוביה אמר רב, מאי דכתיב: "את הכל עשה יפה בעתו" מלמד, שכל אחד ואחד יפה לו הקב"ה אומנתו בפניו. אמר רב פפא, היינו דאמרי אינשי: תלה ליה קורא לדבר אחר – ואיהו דידיה עביד.§ ואמר רב זוטרא בר טוביה אמר רב: אבוקה כשנים, וירח כשלשה. איבעיא להו: אבוקה כשנים בהדי דידיה, או דילמא אבוקה כשנים לבר מדידיה? –ת"ש: וירח כשלשה. אי אמרת בשלמא בהדי דידיה – שפיר, אלא אי אמרת לבר מדידיה – ארבעה למה לי? והאמר מר: לאחד – נראה ומזיק, לשנים – נראה ואינו מזיק, לשלשה – אינו נראה כל עיקר! אלא לאו שמע מינה אבוקה כשנים בהדי דידיה, שמע מינה.§ ואמר רב זוטרא בר טוביה אמר רב, ואמרי לה אמר רב חנא בר ביזנא אמר רבי שמעון חסידא, ואמרי לה אמר רבי יוחנן משום רבי שמעון בן יוחי: נוח לו לאדם שיפיל עצמו לתוך כבשן האש ואל ילבין פני חברו ברבים. מנלן – מתמר, שנאמר: "היא מוצאת וגו'".§ ת"ר: הביאו לפניו שמן והדס, ב"ש אומרים: מברך על השמן ואח"כ מברך על ההדס; וב"ה אומרים: מברך על ההדס ואח"כ מברך על השמן. אמר ר"ג: אני אכריע. שמן – זכינו לריחו וזכינו לסיכתו, הדס – לריחו זכינו, לסיכתו לא זכינו. א"ר יוחנן: הלכה כדברי המכריע. רב פפא איקלע לבי רב הונא בריה דרב איקא, אייתו לקמייהו שמן והדס, שקל רב פפא בריך אהדס ברישא והדר בריך אשמן. אמר ליה: לא סבר לה מר הלכה כדברי המכריע?! – אמר ליה, הכי אמר רבא: (א) הלכה כב"ה. ולא היא, [א] לאשתמוטי נפשיה הוא דעבד.§ ת"ר: הביאו לפניהם שמן ויין, ב"ש אומרים: אוחז השמן בימינו ואת היין בשמאלו, מברך על השמן וחוזר ומברך על היין; ב"ה אומרים: אוחז את היין בימינו ואת השמן בשמאלו, מברך על היין וחוזר ומברך על השמן. וטחו בראש השמש, ואם שמש ת"ח הוא – טחו בכותל, מפני שגנאי לתלמיד חכם לצאת לשוק כשהוא מבושם.§ ת"ר: ששה דברים גנאי לו לתלמיד חכם: אל יצא כשהוא מבושם לשוק, ואל יצא יחידי בלילה, ואל יצא במנעלים המטולאים, ואל יספר עם אשה בשוק, ואל יסב בחבורה של עמי הארץ, ואל יכנס באחרונה לבית המדרש; ויש אומרים: אף לא יפסיע פסיעה גסה, ואל יהלך בקומה זקופה. "אל יצא כשהוא מבושם לשוק" – א"ר אבא בריה דר' חייא בר אבא אמר רבי יוחנן: במקום שחשודים על משכב זכור. אמר רב ששת: לא אמרן אלא בבגדו, אבל בגופו – זיעה מעברא ליה. אמר רב פפא: ושערו כבגדו דמי; ואמרי לה, כגופו דמי. "ואל יצא יחידי בלילה" – משום חשדא, ולא אמרן אלא דלא קביע ליה עידנא, אבל קביע ליה עידנא – מידע ידיע דלעידניה קא אזיל. "ואל יצא במנעלים המטולאים" – מסייע ליה לרבי חייא בר אבא, דאמר ר' חייא בר אבא: גנאי הוא לתלמיד חכם שיצא במנעלים המטולאים. איני?! והא ר' חייא בר אבא נפיק! – אמר מר זוטרא בריה דרב נחמן: בטלאי על גבי טלאי. ולא אמרן אלא בפנתא, אבל בגילדא – לית לן בה; ובפנתא [ב] לא אמרן אלא באורחא אבל בביתא – לית לן בה; ולא אמרן אלא בימות החמה, אבל בימות הגשמים – לית לן בה. "ואל יספר עם אשה בשוק" – אמר רב חסדא: ואפילו היא אשתו. תניא נמי הכי: אפילו היא אשתו, ואפילו היא בתו, ואפילו היא אחותו – לפי שאין הכל בקיאין בקרובותיו. "ואל יסב בחבורה של עמי הארץ" – מאי טעמא? – דילמא אתי לאמשוכי בתרייהו. "ואל יכנס אחרונה לבית המדרש" – משום דקרו ליה פושע. וי"א: "אף לא יפסיע פסיעה גסה" – דאמר מר: פסיעה גסה נוטלת אחד מת"ק ממאור עיניו של אדם. מאי תקנתיה? להדריה בקידושא דבי שמשי. "ואל יהלך בקומה זקופה" – דאמר מר: [ג] המהלך בקומה זקופה אפילו ארבע אמות, כאילו דוחק רגלי שכינה, דכתיב: "מלא כל הארץ כבודו".§

מתניתין

**רש"י**

סמלק. יסמי"ן קורין לו בלשון ישמעאל, והוא מין עשב שיש בו שלש שורות של עלין זו למעלה מזו ושלשה עלין לכל שורה: חלפי דימא. בושם שקורין אשפי"ג. והוא שבולת נרד, ועשוי כעין גבעולי פשתן, (ב) דאשכחן גבעולין דאיקרי עץ: נרקום. חבצלת השרון, בה"ג: דגנוניתא. הגדל בגינה: סיגלי. ויול"ש בלע"ז: חבושין. קודוניי"ש בלע"ז: להתנאות. ליהנות: כלבנון. שמריחין עליו ופרחיו: יפה לו אומנתו. ואפי' בורסי נאה לו אומנתו בעיניו. ועשה הקדוש ב"ה כן שלא יחסר העולם אומנות: קורא. רך הגדל בדקל, תלה אותו לחזיר והוא יגלגלנו באשפה שזו היא אומנתו: אבוקה כשני בני אדם. לענין היוצא בלילה, דאמר מר: אל יצא אדם יחידי בלילה: וירח כשלשה. ויש חלוק בין שנים לשלשה, כדלקמן: לאחד נראה. השד ומזיקו: היא מוצאת והיא שלחה וגו'. ואילו בהדיא לא אמרה: אלו הסימנים של יהודה הם, ולו אני הרה. אלא: לאיש אשר אלה לו אנכי הרה, אם יודה – יודה, ואם לאו – אשרף, ולא אלבין פניו: שמן והדס. בסוף הסעודה. שמן – לסוך ידיו להעביר זוהמת האוכלים, והדס – להריח, כמו שאמרנו: אני אכריע. לצד בית שמאי: זכינו לריחו ולסיכתו. כגון משחא כבישא, הלכך שמן עדיף: ולא היא. לא אמר רבא הלכתא כב"ה, אלא רב פפא אכסיף לפי שטעה, והשמיט עצמו בכך: שמן ויין. זהו יין שלאחר המזון, ואין זה כוס של ברכה: חוזר ומברך על היין. כגון בחול, שאין היין קבע, ואין היין שלפני המזון פוטרו: שמן בימינו. לפי שעליו מברך תחלה: מברך על השמן. "בורא שמן ערב": וטחו בראש השמש. כדי שלא יצא בידיו מבושמות בשוק, שגנאי הוא לתלמיד חכם: שחשודים על משכב זכור. מבשמין עצמם כדי שיתאוו להם: ושערו כבגדו דמי. דלא שכיח ביה זיעה: ואמרי לה כגופו. דשכיח ביה זיעה: משום חשדא. של זנות: דלא קביע ליה עידנא. שלא קבעו לו רבו קביעות ללמדו בלילה: בפנתא. אנפוני"א בלע"ז, שעל גבי הרגל: גילדא. עקב, שקורין סול"א: בימות הגשמים. הטיט מכסהו: אפי' היא אשתו. שאין הכל מכירין בה וחושדין אותו: דקרו ליה פושע. מתעצל: בקידושא דבי שמשי. ששותה כוס של קידוש בשבת בלילה:

מתני'

**תוספות**

שמן והדס. האי שמן – להריח הוא. דאי להעביר הזוהמא – הא אמרינן בפרק אלו דברים (לקמן נג.) דאין מברכין עליו:

הכי אמר רבא הלכתא כבית הלל ולא היא לאשתמוטי נפשיה הוא דקא עביד. כך כתוב בספרים שלנו ובפירוש רש"י. אבל רב אלפס פסק כרבא, משמע שלא היה גורס בספרו ולא היא וכו':

*האי מאן דמורח באתרוגא וחבוש' מברך וכו'. ודוקא כשמריח בהם אבל אם בא לאכול מהם אין לברך ברכת ריח כי אם ברכת אכילה:

בא/וכלי

**עין משפט נר מצוה**

קלא א ב מיי' פ"ט מהל' ברכות הל' ו סמג עשין כז טוש"ע או"ח סי' רטז סעיף ז:

קלב ג מיי' שם טוש"ע שם סעיף ט:

קלג ד טוש"ע שם סעיף ח:

[שייך לעיל קודם ד"ה שמן]

קלד ה מיי' שם הל' א טוש"ע שם סע"ב:

קלה ו מיי' פ"י מהל' ברכות הל' יג סמג שם טוש"ע או"ח סי' רכו:

קלו ז מיי' פ"ט מהל' ברכות סמג שם טוש"ע או"ח סי' רטז סעיף א:

קלז ח מיי' פ"ו מהל' דעות הלכה ח:

קלח ט מיי' פ"ט מהל' ברכות הל' ג סמג עשין כז טוש"ע א"ח סי' רטז סעיף יא:

קלט י מיי' פ"ז מהל' ברכות הלכה יד ופ"ט הלכה ד סמג שם טור או"ח סי' רי"ב וטור וש"ע או"ח סימן רו סעיף ד:

קמ כ ל מ נ מיי' פ"ה מהל' דעות הל' ט:

קמא ס שם הלכה ז:

קמב ע שם הלכה ב:

קמג פ צ שם הלכה ח:

**רב נסים גאון**

ששה דברים גנאי לתלמיד חכם אל יצא יחידי בלילה. ובמסכת שחיטת חולין בפ' גיד הנשה (דף צא) אמרינן ויאבק איש עמו אמר ר' יצחק מכאן לתלמיד חכם שלא יצא יחידי בלילה. ויש אומרים אף אל יהלך בקומה זקופה ובפרק האשה נקנית (קדושין דף לא) אמרינן אמר ר' יהושע בן לוי אסור לאדם שיהלך ד' אמות בקומה זקופה שנאמר (ישעיה ו) מלא כל הארץ כבודו:

[ז"ל רמ"ע מפאנו ס"ס ה' רב פפא מסברא דנפשיה פליג על ר' יוחנן ולא מחמת כסופא הוא דבעי לאשתמוטי אלא במדת חסידות ותלה הגדולה ברבו ואי לאו דקים ליה דהכי הלכתא לא עביד עובדא בנפשיה והכי קי"ל בכל דוכתא מעשה רב]

מס' ד"א זוטא פ"ו

**הגהות הב"ח**

(א) גמ' הלכה כב"ה (ולא היא וכו' דעבד) תא"מ. ונ"ב האלפסי לא גרס ליה: (ב) רש"י ד"ה חלפי וכו' גבעולי פשתן מאי קרא דאשכחן:

[הרמב"ם לא הזכיר אלא החלוק בין ימות החמה לאסור וימות הגשמים מותר אבל ההפרש בין פנתא לגילדא וכן בין לאורחא או בביתו השמיט אמנם הרי"ף בברכות ויותר ביאור בשבת פ' אלו קשרים הביא כל דרכים אלו ועי' בלחם משנה הל' דעות פ"ה דין ט]

**מסורת הש"ס / מראי מקומות**

תורה אור

יהושע ב | תהלים קנ | הושע יד | קהלת ג | בראשית לח | ישעיה ו

[נ"ל אמר רב משרשיא] | [ר"ה יא.] | [נ"ל בחורי ישראל שטעמו טעם חטא וכו' ע"י] | [גי' הערוך והוא אזיל ע"ש ערך קר] | ב"מ נט. כתובות סוטה י: | [ע' תוספות פסחים ד"ה אין ותו' ב"ב ד"ה הכרעה] | [תוס' פ"ה] | [ע' חולין לא. פסחים] | זבחים יט. | [שבת קיד. ע"ש] | גי' רש"ל עצל שם [תענית י:] [ע' תוס' י: ד"ה פסיעה]

גליון הש"ס גמ' ולא היא לאשתמוטי נפשיה. עי' בקרבן עדה בירושלמי נזיר פ"ז דף כ"ה ד"ה איתניה ואנא מלקי. ועי' בתשובת הרלב"ח דף רע"ט ד"ה וכר מן דין: רש"י ד"ה סמלק וכו' והוא מין עשב. כדאמרינן אח"כ הני סגלי. מבואר דסיגלי יסמין. וכמו שפי' רש"י סיגלי (ויול"ש בלע"ז). ועי' רש"י על התורה (בראשית ל יד) ובראב"ע שם: רש"י ד"ה מברך על השמן בורא שמן ערב. עי' לקמן נ"ג ע"א ברש"י ד"ה אין מברכין עליו:

הגהות הגר"א [א] גמ' (ולא היא לאשתמוטי נפשיה הוא לעבד) נמחק ונ"ב הרי"ף ל"ג: [ב] שם (ובפנתא ל"א אלא באורחא אבל בביתא ל"ל בה) תא"מ: [ג] שם (דאמר מר המהלך בקומה זקופה אפי' ד"א כאלו דוחק רגלי שכינה) תא"מ ונ"ב הרי"ף ל"ג לה:

עין משפט נר מצוה

קד א מיי' פ"ג מהל' ברכות הלכה ה והלכה ז סמג עשין כח טוש"ע או"ח סימן ריב סעיף א:
קמה ב מיי' פ"ג שם הל' ג והלכה יא סמג שם טוש"ע או"ח סי' רח סעיף א:
קמו ג מיי' פ"ג מהל' ברכות הלכה יג ופ"ח הל' יד סמג שם טוש"ע או"ח סי' רח:
קמז ד מיי' וסמג שם טוש"ע א"ח סימן רח סעיף י:

**מתני'** *הביאו לפניו מליח(א) תחלה ופת עמו – מברך על המליח ופוטר את הפת, שהפת טפלה לו. *זה הכלל: כל שהוא עיקר ועמו טפלה – מברך על העיקר ופוטר את הטפלה.§ **גמ'** ומי איכא מידי דהוי מליח עיקר ופת טפלה?! אמר רב אחא בריה דרב עוירא אמר רב אשי: באוכלי פירות גנוסר שנו. *אמר רבה בר בר חנה: כי הוה אזלינן בתריה דרבי יוחנן למיכל פירות גנוסר, כי הוינן בי מאה – מנקטינן ליה לכל חד וחד עשרה עשרה, וכי הוינן בי עשרה – מנקטינן ליה כל חד וחד מאה מאה, וכל מאה מינייהו *הוה מחזיק להו צנא בר תלתא סאוי *ואכיל להו. ומשתבע דלא טעים זיונא. זיונא ס"ד?! אלא אימא: מזונא. רבי אבהו אכיל עד דהוה שריק ליה דודבא מאפותיה; ורב אמי ורב אסי הוו אכלי עד דנתור מזייהו. רשב"ל הוה אכיל עד דמריד, ואמר להו רבי יוחנן לדבי נשיאה, והוה משדר ליה רבי יהודה נשיאה באלושי אבתריה ומייתי ליה לביתיה.§ כי אתא רב דימי, אמר: עיר אחת היתה לו לינאי המלך בהר המלך, שהיו מוציאים ממנה ששים רבוא ספלי טרית לקוצצי תאנים מע"ש לע"ש. כי אתא רבין, אמר: אילן אחד היה לו לינאי המלך בהר המלך, שהיו מורידים ממנו ארבעים סאה גוזלות משלוש בריכות בחדש. כי אתא ר' יצחק, אמר: עיר אחת היתה בארץ ישראל וגופנית שמה, שהיו בה שמנים זוגות אחים כהנים נשואים לשמנים זוגות אחיות כהנות. ובדקו רבנן מסורא ועד נהרדעא, ולא אשכחו בר מבנתיה דרב חסדא דהוו נסיבן לרמי בר חמא ולמר עוקבא בר חמא, ואע"ג דאינהי הוו כהנתא – אינהו לא הוו כהני. אמר רב: כל סעודה שאין בה מלח אינה סעודה. אמר רבי חייא בר אבא א"ר יוחנן: כל סעודה שאין בה *שריף אינה סעודה.§

**מתני'** אכל ענבים ותאנים ורמונים – מברך אחריהם שלש ברכות, דברי רבן גמליאל; וחכ"א: ברכה אחת (מעין שלש). ר"ע אומר: אפי' אכל שלק והוא מזונו – מברך עליו ג' ברכות. *השותה מים לצמאו – מברך "שהכל נהיה בדברו"; ר' טרפון אומר: *"בורא נפשות רבות וחסרונן".§ **גמ'** מ"ט דר"ג? – דכתיב: °"ארץ חטה ושערה וגו'", וכתיב: "ארץ אשר לא במסכנת תאכל בה לחם וגו'", וכתיב: °"ואכלת ושבעת וברכת את ה' אלהיך". ורבנן? – "ארץ" הפסיק הענין. ור"ג נמי, "ארץ" הפסיק הענין! – ההוא מבעי ליה למעוטי הכוסס את החטה. א"ר יעקב בר אידי א"ר חנינא: בכל שהוא מחמשת המינין – בתחלה מברך עליו "בורא מיני מזונות", ולבסוף ברכה אחת מעין שלש. אמר רבה בר מרי אריב"ל: כל שהוא משבעת המינין – בתחלה מברך "בורא פרי העץ" ולבסוף ברכה אחת מעין שלש.§ א"ל אביי לרב דימי: מאי ניהו [א] ברכה אחת מעין שלש? – א"ל: גאפירי דעץ – "על העץ ועל פרי העץ ועל תנובת השדה ועל ארץ חמדה טובה ורחבה שהנחלת לאבותינו לאכול מפריה ולשבוע מטובה, רחם ה' אלהינו על ישראל עמך ועל ירושלים עירך ועל מקדשך ועל מזבחך ותבנה ירושלים עיר קדשך במהרה בימינו והעלנו לתוכה *ושמחנו בה כי אתה טוב ומטיב לכל". דחמשת המינין – "על המחיה ועל הכלכלה ועל תנובת השדה כו'" וחותם "על הארץ ועל המחיה". מיחתם במאי חתים? כי אתא [ב] רב דימי אמר: רב חתים בר"ח "ברוך מקדש ישראל וראשי חדשים". הכא מאי? – רב חסדא אמר: "על הארץ ועל פירותיה"; ור' יוחנן אמר: "על הארץ ועל הפירות". א"ר עמרם: *ולא פליגי, הא – לן, והא – להו. מתקיף לה ר"נ בר יצחק: אינהו אכלי ואנן מברכין?! דאלא איפוך: רב חסדא אמר: "על הארץ ועל הפירות"; ר' יוחנן אמר: "על הארץ ועל פירותיה".
אמר

רש"י

**מתני'** מליח. כל דבר מלוח: **גמ'** פירות גנוסר. פירות ארץ ים כנרת חשובים מן הפת: זיונא. משמע מידי דבר אכילה: מזונא. דבר הסועד: דשריק דודבא מאפותיה. שהזבוב מחליק ממצחו. מתוך צהלת פניו בשרו מחליק: עד דמריד. דעתו מטרפת: באלושי. אוכלוסי בני אדם: ספלי טרית. ספלים מלאים חתיכות דג חתוך, שקורים טוני"א: לקוצצי תאנים. למאכל פועלים שקוצצים תאנים, והיו מרובים עד שכל אלו צריכין להם למאכל: בריכות. קוביי"ש בלע"ז: משלש בריכות בחדש. ג' פעמים בחדש מורידים ממנו כך: שמנים זוגות אחים. שנים שנים אחים היו כולם, וכן נשותיהם: שריף. תבשיל לא שיש בו מרק, כמו: שורפה חיה: **מתני'** מברך אחריהם ג' ברכות. ר"ג לטעמיה, דאמר לעיל בפירקין (דף לז.): כל שהוא מז' המינים מברך אחריו ג' ברכות: אפילו אכל שלק. של ירק: והוא מזונו. שסמך עליו למזון: וחסרונן. צרכי ספוקן: **גמ'** וברכת. אכולהו קאי. ובההוא קרא ג' ברכות רמיזי, כדאמרינן בפרק "שלשה שאכלו" (דף מח:): ארץ הפסיק הענין. ולא קאי "וברכת" אלא אלחם, דסמיך ליה: ור"ג ההוא. הפסקה לפרושי חטה דכתיב בקרא קמא אחטה; ולמעוטי שאם כססה כמות שהיא – אין זו בכלל ברכה, אא"כ עשאה לחם: חמשת המינים. כולם מין דגן: חטין ושעורין וכוסמין ושבולת שועל ושיפון. כוסמין – מין חטה, שבולת שועל ושיפון – מין שעורה: מברך עליו ב"מ מזונות. אם עשאו תבשיל: כל שהוא מז' המינים. משאר ז' המינים האמורים בפסוק, ואינו מין דגן: אפירי דעץ על העץ ועל פרי העץ ועל ארץ חמדה טובה ורחבה. אתרוייהו קאי, כולה עד סופה: רב חתים בר"ח כו'. אע"ג דדמיא לתרתי: הכא מאי. מי מחתמינן בתרתי כהאי גוונא, כגון "על הארץ ועל הפירות" ולא הויא חתימה בשתים ממש, כדמפרש לה בפרק שלשה שאכלו (דף מט.): הא לן והא להו. רב חסדא מבבל, ובבבל חתמי "על הארץ ועל פירותיה"; ור' יוחנן מארץ ישראל, והתם חתמי "על הפירות": ואנן מברכינן. "על פירותיה". ארץ ישראל להודה קאי, ואנן לא אכלינן מינייהו ומברכים עלייהו:
קופרא

תוספות

**באוכלי** פירות גנוסר שנו. שהמליח עיקר, שהוא בא להשיב הלב שנחלש מפני מתיקות הפירות, והפת שלאחריו טפל ואינו בא אלא בשביל המליח. וא"ת: פירות הוי עיקר, ומליח טפל, ולבריך על הפירות ולפטר כולהו! וי"ל: דמיירי שלא אכל הפירות באותו מעמד. א"נ: בשעה שאכל פירות גנוסר לא היה שם עדיין מליח ופת, דלא היה יודע שיחלש לבו מחמת המתיקות: **מברך** על המליח. ואף על גב דאשמעינן דפת פוטר את הפרפרת, איצטריך לאשמעינן דפעמים דפת טפל: **רבי** עקיבא אומר אפי' אכל שלק והוא מזונו כו'. ולא דמי להיא דלעיל (דף לז.) דר"ג נתן רשות לר"ע לברך וכו', דשאני הכא דאיקבע מזוניה עליה: **על** העץ ועל פרי העץ. אבל על היין מברכים על הגפן ועל פרי הגפן, דכיון דיין קובע ברכה לעצמו משום חביבותיה – הוא הדין לאחריו. ובחתימה יש שחותמין על הארץ ועל הפירות ויש שחותמין על הגפן ועל פרי הגפן. מיהו, לכאורה משמע דא"צ לשנות החתימה – שהרי אין אנו משנין רק לומר פרי הגפן במקום פרי העץ, אבל בעלמא היכא דלא מברכינן על העץ, – אלא בסתמא על הארץ ועל הפירות – ביין נמי אין לשנות. ובס' המיימוני מצריך להזכיר בה מעין המאורע בשבת ובי"ט. וכן משמע בירו'. ומיהו, לא נהגו העולם כן, ויכול להיות מה שמזכירים מעין המאורע – היינו דוקא בימיהם, שהיו רגילין לקבוע איין ואמיני פירות, אבל האידנא – לא קבעי. ופר"ת: היכא דאכיל מיני מזונות כגון דייסא ותאנים ושתי חמרא מברך ברוך אתה ה' אמ"ה על המחיה ועל הכלכלה על הגפן ועל פרי הגפן ועל העץ ועל פרי העץ ועל תנובת השדה וכו' וחותם בא"י אמ"ה על הארץ ועל המחיה ועל הפירות. ולא הוי חתימה בשתים, דהארץ היא המוציאה המחיה והפירות: **אינהו** מיכל אכלי ואנן מברכין. משמע שאין נראה למקשן שידברו האמוראים דבבל בשביל בני ארץ ישראל. כי כך פר"ת גבי (קדושין כט:) לעולם ישא אשה ואחר כך ילמוד תורה, ותנא אחריתי: ילמוד תורה ואחר כך ישא אשה; ומסיק: הא לן והא להו. ופירש ר"ת: דר' יוחנן היה מדבר בשביל תלמידיו שהיו מבבל. דשמא הכא קשיא ליה למקשן דבאותה שעה שאמר רב חסדא הא מילתא לא היה לפניו שום תלמיד מא"י, וכן לא שום תלמיד מבבל לפני רבי יוחנן. וא"כ לא היה מזכיר רב חסדא שהיה מבבל, כי אם לבני בבל ולהכי פריך היאך יברכו בני בבל על הארץ ועל פירותיה, משמע דקאי דוקא על פירות של ארץ ישראל, והם אינם אוכלים אותן:
עבידנא

ואכיל להו לכולהו כצ"ל רש"ל

הגהות הב"ח
(א) במשנה מליח בתחלה:

הגהות הגר"א
[א] מאי ניהו ברכה א' מעין ג'. נ"ב א"ל דחמשת מינים על המחיה ועל הכלכלה כו' עד טוב ומטיב לכל וחותם על הארץ ועל המחיה אפירי דעץ על העץ ועל פרי העץ. דחמרא על הגפן ועל פרי הגפן. מיחתם במאי חתים רב חסדא אמר כו'. כן הוא גי' רי"ף ורא"ש ולגי' שלנו צ"ע למה לא פשט מה' מינים: [ב] שם (כי אתא רב דימי א"ר חתים בר"ח ברוך מקדש ישראל ור"ח הכא מאי) תא"מ:

גליון הש"ס
גמ' למעוטי הכוסס את החטה. ע' לעיל ל"ז ע"א תוס' ד"ה הכוסס:

[ע' תוס' לעיל לז. ד"ה בורא ותוס' לקמן מה. ד"ה ר"ט]

לעיל לה: מח.
עירובין ל.
לא הוה רש"ל
עירובין יד.
דברים ח
שם
[בבנינה כי אתה ה' טוב וכו']
[יומא כח: ביצה ה. קדושין כט: סוכה ... ביצה יד: ב"ב קמז.]

עין משפט
נר מצוה

קמח א ב ג מיי' פ"ח מהל' ברכות הל' א סמג עשין כז טוש"ע או"ח סי' רד סעיף א ז ובסימן רז:

קמט ד מיי' פ"ח מהל' ברכות הלכה ח:

קנ ה טוש"ע או"ח סי' רטז סעיף א:

קנא ו ז מיי' פ"ח מהל' ברכות הל' א סמג שם טוש"ע או"ח סימן רד סעיף ז:

**עבידנא** ככולהו. וכן אנו נוהגין כרב אשי, דמברכינן בתר מיא ובתר ירקא בורא נפשות רבות: **ולבני** מערבא דמברכין הכי בתר וכו'. ואנן לא עבדינן כבני מערבא. דדוקא לדידהו שהיה דרכם לסלקם בלילה שייכא ברכה דלשמור חקיו, כדכתיב ושמרת את החקה הזאת למועדה מימים וגו'. אבל אנו שמסלקין אותן בחלי היום, או אפי' נסלקן בלילה – לא שייך חקה. ודוקא לדידהו דקסברי לילה לאו זמן תפילין הוא ומימים ימימה אתא למעוטי לילות – שייכא ברכה דחקה. אבל אנן דקי"ל* דלילה זמן תפילין הוא, ואנן *משימין הפסוק ושמרת החקה וגו' בפסח, ומה שאין אנו מניחים אותן בלילה – מפני שמא יפיח בהן; אפי' נמתין לסלקן עד הלילה – לא מברכינן. אע"ג דאנן קיימא לן דשבת וי"ט לאו זמן תפילין, אפ"ה – לא מברכינן, דדוקא לדידהו דסבירא להו חקה קאי אתפילין מברכי'. ותדע, שהרי אינהו נמי לא היו מברכין אלא אתפילין לחודייהו, משום דכתיב בהו חקה, אבל אשאר מצות כגון ציצית ולולב וסוכה – לא היו מברכין (וה"ה הכא) וקשה, דהוי מצי לשנויי הכי: לאפוקי שאר מצות, אפי' לבני מערבא*:

מנחות לו:

נ"ל מוקמינן

רש"ל מ"ז

[בתוס' סוכה לט. ד"ה אבל לפניו וכו' ובתוס' נדה נא: ד"ה ולבני מערבא ישוב על זה ודע דבתוס' נדה שם מבוארים הדברים יפה וע"ע תוס' מנחות לו: ד"ה ושמרת]

אָמַר רַב יִצְחָק בַּר אַבְדִּימִי מִשּׁוּם רַבֵּינוּ: אעַל הַבֵּיעָא וְעַל מִינֵי קוּפְרָא בַּתְּחִלָּה מְבָרֵךְ "שֶׁהַכֹּל" וּלְבַסּוֹף "בּוֹרֵא נְפָשׁוֹת רַבּוֹת וכו'". אֲבָל יַרְקָא – לָא; ור' יִצְחָק אָמַר: באֲפִילּוּ יַרְקָא, אֲבָל מַיָּא – לָא; וְרַב פַּפָּא אָמַר: גאֲפִילּוּ מַיָּא. מָר זוּטְרָא עָבֵיד כְּרַב יִצְחָק בַּר אַבְדִּימִי, וְרַב שִׁימִי בַּר אַשִׁי עָבֵיד כר' יִצְחָק, וְסִימָנָךְ: חַד כִּתְרֵי וּתְרֵי כְּחַד. א"ר אַשִׁי: אֲנָא זִמְנָא דְּכִי מַדְכַרְנָא עָבֵידְנָא כְּכוּלְּהוּ. *תְּנַן: דכָּל שֶׁטָּעוּן בְּרָכָה לְאַחֲרָיו טָעוּן בְּרָכָה לְפָנָיו, וְיֵשׁ שֶׁטָּעוּן בְּרָכָה לְפָנָיו וְאֵין טָעוּן בְּרָכָה לְאַחֲרָיו. בִּשְׁלָמָא לְרַב יִצְחָק בַּר אַבְדִּימִי – לְאַפּוֹקֵי יַרְקָא, לר' יִצְחָק – לְאַפּוֹקֵי מַיָּא, אֶלָּא לְרַב פַּפָּא לְאַפּוֹקֵי מַאי? –לְאַפּוֹקֵי מִצְוֹת. וְלִבְנֵי מַעַרְבָא דְּבָתַר דְּמִסַּלְּקִי תְּפִלַּיְיהוּ מְבָרְכִי "אקב"ו לִשְׁמוֹר חֻקָּיו" – לְאַפּוֹקֵי מַאי? –לְאַפּוֹקֵי הרֵיחָנֵי: א"ר יַנַּאי א"ר: כָּל שֶׁהוּא כְּבֵיצָה – בֵּיצָה טוֹבָה מִמֶּנּוּ. כִּי אֲתָא רָבִין אָמַר: טָבָא בֵּיעֲתָא מְגוּלְגַּלְתָּא מִשִּׁיתָּא קַיְיסֵי סוּלְתָּא. כִּי אֲתָא רַב דִּימִי אָמַר: טָבָא בֵּיעֲתָא מְגוּלְגַּלְתָּא מִשִּׁיתָּא, מְטוּוִיתָא מֵאַרְבַּע, מְבוּשַּׁלְתָּא – כָּל שֶׁהוּא כְּבֵיצָה בֵּיצָה טוֹבָה הֵימֶנּוּ, לְבַר מִבִּשְׂרָא.§ "רע"א: אֲפִילּוּ אָכַל שֶׁלֶק כו'". וּמִי אִיכָּא מִידֵי דְּהָוֵה שֶׁלֶק מְזוֹנֵי?! א"ר אַשִׁי: בְּקֶלַח שֶׁל כְּרוּב שָׁנוּ. ת"ר: *טְחוֹל – יָפֶה לַשִּׁינַּיִם וְקָשֶׁה לִבְנֵי מֵעַיִם, כְּרֵישִׁין – קָשִׁין לַשִּׁינַּיִם וְיָפִין לִבְנֵי מֵעַיִם. כָּל יָרָק חַי מוֹרִיק, וְכָל קָטָן מַקְטִין, וְכָל נֶפֶשׁ מֵשִׁיב אֶת הַנֶּפֶשׁ, וְכָל קָרוֹב לַנֶּפֶשׁ מֵשִׁיב אֶת הַנֶּפֶשׁ. כְּרוּב לְמָזוֹן וּתְרָדִין לִרְפוּאָה, אוֹי לוֹ לַבַּיִת שֶׁהַלֶּפֶת עוֹבֶרֶת בְּתוֹכוֹ. אָמַר מָר: טְחוֹל – יָפֶה לַשִּׁינַּיִם וְקָשֶׁה לִבְנֵי מֵעַיִם. מַאי תַּקַּנְתֵּיהּ? –נִלְעֲסֵיהּ וְנִשְׁדְּיֵיהּ. כְּרֵישִׁין – קָשִׁין לַשִּׁינַּיִם וְיָפִין לִבְנֵי מֵעַיִם. מַאי תַּקַּנְתֵּיהּ? –לִישַׁלְקִינְהוּ וְנִבְלְעִינְהוּ. כָּל יָרָק חַי מוֹרִיק. א"ר יִצְחָק: בִּסְעוּדָה רִאשׁוֹנָה שֶׁל אַחַר הַקָּזָה. וא"ר יִצְחָק: כָּל הָאוֹכֵל יָרָק קוֹדֶם אַרְבַּע שָׁעוֹת – אָסוּר לְסַפֵּר הֵימֶנּוּ. מַאי טַעְמָא? מִשּׁוּם רֵיחָא. וא"ר יִצְחָק: אָסוּר לְאָדָם שֶׁיֹּאכַל יָרָק חַי קוֹדֶם אַרְבַּע שָׁעוֹת. אַמֵּימָר וּמָר זוּטְרָא וְרַב אַשִׁי הֲווּ יָתְבֵי, אַיְיתוּ קַמַּיְיהוּ יָרָק חַי קוֹדֶם אַרְבַּע שָׁעוֹת, אַמֵּימָר וְרַב אַשִׁי אֲכוּל וּמָר זוּטְרָא לָא אֲכַל. אָמְרוּ לֵיהּ: מַאי דַּעְתָּיךְ – דא"ר יִצְחָק: כָּל הָאוֹכֵל יָרָק קוֹדֶם אַרְבַּע שָׁעוֹת אָסוּר לְסַפֵּר הֵימֶנּוּ, מִשּׁוּם רֵיחָא – וְהָא אֲנַן דְּקָא אָכְלִינַן וְקָא מִשְׁתַּעֲיַת בַּהֲדַן! אָמַר לְהוּ: אֲנָא כְּאִידָךְ דר' יִצְחָק ס"ל, דא"ר יִצְחָק: אָסוּר לְאָדָם שֶׁיֹּאכַל יָרָק חַי קוֹדֶם אַרְבַּע שָׁעוֹת. כָּל קָטָן מַקְטִין. אָמַר רַב חִסְדָּא: אֲפִילּוּ גַּדְיָא בַּר זוּזָא. וְלָא אֲמַרַן אֶלָּא דְּלֵית בֵּיהּ רִבְעָא, אֲבָל אִית בֵּיהּ רִבְעָא – לֵית לָן בָּהּ. כָּל נֶפֶשׁ מֵשִׁיב נֶפֶשׁ. אָמַר רַב פַּפָּא: אֲפִילּוּ גִּילְדָנֵי דְּבֵי גִילֵי. כָּל הַקָּרוֹב לַנֶּפֶשׁ מֵשִׁיב אֶת הַנֶּפֶשׁ; אָמַר רַב אַחָא בַּר יַעֲקֹב: עוּנְקָא. א"ל רָבָא לְשַׁמָּעֵיהּ: כִּי מַיְיתִית לִי אוּמְצָא דְּבִשְׂרָא, טְרַח וְאַיְיתִי לִי מֵהֵיכָא דִּמְקָרַב לְבֵי בָּרוּךְ. כְּרוּב לְמָזוֹן וּתְרָדִין לִרְפוּאָה. כְּרוּב, לְמָזוֹן אִין וְלִרְפוּאָה לָא?! וְהָתַנְיָא: *שִׁשָּׁה דְּבָרִים מְרַפְּאִין אֶת הַחוֹלֶה מֵחָלְיוֹ וּרְפוּאָתָן רְפוּאָה, וְאֵלּוּ הֵן: כְּרוּב, וּתְרָדִין, וּמֵי סִיסִין *דְּבַשׁ, [א] וְקֵיבָה, וְהֶרֶת, וְיוֹתֶרֶת הַכָּבֵד! אֶלָּא אֵימָא: כְּרוּב אַף לְמָזוֹן. אוֹי לוֹ לַבַּיִת שֶׁהַלֶּפֶת עוֹבֶרֶת בְּתוֹכוֹ. אִינִי?! וְהָא אָמַר לֵיהּ רָבָא לְשַׁמָּעֵיהּ: כִּי חָזֵית לִיפְתָּא בְּשׁוּקָא – לָא תֵּימָא לִי: בְּמַאי כָּרְכַתְּ רִיפְתָּא! אָמַר אַבָּיֵי: מִבְּלִי בָּשָׂר; וְרָבָא אָמַר: מִבְּלִי יַיִן. אִיתְּמַר, רַב אָמַר: מִבְּלִי בָּשָׂר; וּשְׁמוּאֵל אָמַר: מִבְּלִי עֵצִים; וְרַבִּי יוֹחָנָן אָמַר: מִבְּלִי יַיִן. א"ל רָבָא לְרַב פַּפָּא: *סוּדָנִי, אֲנַן תַּבְרִינַן לָהּ בְּבִשְׂרָא וְחַמְרָא, אַתּוּן דְּלָא נְפִישׁ לְכוּ חַמְרָא – בְּמַאי תַּבְרִיתוּ לָהּ? –א"ל: בְּצִיבֵי. כִּי הָא דְּבִיתְהוּ דְּרַב פַּפָּא בָּתַר דִּמְבַשְּׁלָא לָהּ – תַּבְרָא לָהּ בִּתְמָנַן אוּפֵי פַּרְסַיְיתָא.§ תָּנוּ רַבָּנַן: דָּג קָטָן מָלִיחַ פְּעָמִים שֶׁהוּא מֵמִית – בְּשִׁבְעָה, בְּשִׁבְעָה עָשָׂר, וּבְעֶשְׂרִים וְשִׁבְעָה; וְאָמְרִי לָהּ: בְּעֶשְׂרִים וּשְׁלֹשָׁה. וְלָא אֲמַרַן אֶלָּא בְּמַטְוֵי וְלָא מַטְוֵי, אֲבָל מַטְוֵי שַׁפִּיר – לֵית לָן בָּהּ; וּדְלָא מַטְוֵי שַׁפִּיר לָא אֲמַרַן אֶלָּא דְּלָא שָׁתָה בָּתְרֵיהּ שִׁכְרָא, אֲבָל שָׁתָה בָּתְרֵיהּ שִׁכְרָא לֵית לָן בָּהּ.§ ו"וְהַשּׁוֹתֶה מַיִם לִצְמָאוֹ וכו'". לְאַפּוֹקֵי מַאי? – א"ר אִידִי בַּר אָבִין: זלְאַפּוֹקֵי לְמַאן

דחנקתיה

[נ"ל יבש וכן הוא לקמן נז: וכן איתא בעו"ג כט. ע"ש פרש"י]

[בערוך פי' סודני ירא שמים כדכתיב סוד ה' ליראיו וע' ברש"י מנחות עח. ונדה יב:]

הגהות הגר"א

[א] גמ' (דבש) תז"מ:

קוּפְרָא. כָּל מִינֵי בָּשָׂר: אֲבָל יַרְקָא לָא. צָרִיךְ לְבָרוֹכֵי אַחֲרֶיהָ: חַד כִּתְרֵי. מָר זוּטְרָא שֶׁהוּזְכַּר כָּאן יָחִיד, בְּלֹא שֵׁם אָבִיו – עָבֵיד כְּרַב יִצְחָק בַּר אַבְדִּימִי, שֶׁהוּזְכַּר בִּשְׁמוֹ וּבְשֵׁם אָבִיו: וּתְרֵי כְּחַד. מָר בַּר רַב אַשִׁי שֶׁהוּזְכַּר בִּשְׁמוֹ וּבְשֵׁם אָבִיו, עָבֵיד כר' יִצְחָק שֶׁהוּזְכַּר יָחִיד: כְּכוּלְּהוּ. אַף כְּרַב פַּפָּא: כָּל שֶׁטָּעוּן בְּרָכָה. מִשְׁנָה הִיא בְּמַסֶּכֶת נִדָּה: לְמַעוּטֵי יַרְקָא. וכ"ש מַיָּא: לְמַעוּטֵי מִצְוֹת. אֵין מְבָרְכִין כְּשֶׁמְּסַלְּקִין תְּפִילִּין וְצִיצִית וְאַחַר תְּקִיעַת שׁוֹפָר וְלוּלָב: כָּל שֶׁהוּא כְּבֵיצָה. אֵין לְךָ מִין מַאֲכָל שִׁיעוּר כְּבֵיצָה שֶׁלֹּא תְּהֵא בֵּיצָה טוֹבָה לַגּוּף מִמֶּנּוּ: מְגוּלְגַּלְתָּא. צְלוּיָה לַחָה וְרַכָּה, שֶׁשּׂוֹרְפִין אוֹתָהּ: קַיְיסֵי. מִדּוֹת מַחֲזִיקוֹת לוֹג: מְגוּלְגַּלְתָּא מִשִּׁיתָּא. טוֹבָה מִשִּׁשָּׁה קַיְיסֵי: מְטוּוִיתָא. צְלוּיָה קָשָׁה, טוֹבָה מֵאַרְבַּע קַיְיסֵי: מְבוּשַּׁלְתָּא. בְּמַיִם. עֲלָהּ א"ר יַנַּאי: כָּל שֶׁהוּא כְּבֵיצָה בֵּיצָה טוֹבָה מִמֶּנּוּ: בְּקֶלַח שֶׁל כְּרוּב שָׁנוּ. שֶׁהוּא מָזוֹן, דְּתַנְיָא לְקַמָּן כְּרוּב לְמָזוֹן: כְּרֵישִׁין. כַּרְתִּי: כָּל יָרָק חַי מוֹרִיק. נוֹטֵל תּוֹאַר הַפָּנִים: כָּל קָטָן. שֶׁלֹּא גָּדַל כָּל צָרְכּוֹ. וּלְקַמָּן מְפָרֵשׁ כַּמָּה כָּל צָרְכּוֹ: כָּל נֶפֶשׁ. דָּבָר חַי הַמְהַלֵּךְ שָׁלֵם, כְּגוֹן דָּגִים קְטַנִּים שֶׁגְּדָלוּ כָּל צָרְכָּן: הַקָּרוֹב לַנֶּפֶשׁ. הָאוֹכֵל מִן הַבְּהֵמָה בְּמָקוֹם חִיּוּת שֶׁלָּהּ. וּלְקַמָּן מְפָרֵשׁ לָהּ: אוֹי לַבַּיִת. לַכְּרֵס, הָאוֹכֵל לֶפֶת: נִלְעֲסֵיהּ. כּוֹסְסוֹ וּמַשְׁלִיכוֹ: לִישַׁלְקִינְהוּ. בִּקְדֵרָה הַרְבֵּה, שֶׁלֹּא יִצְטָרֵךְ לְכוֹסְסוֹ בְּשִׁינָּיו: קוֹדֶם אַרְבַּע שָׁעוֹת. שֶׁאֵינוֹ זְמַן סְעוּדָה; וְהָרֵיחַ קָשֶׁה לִבְנֵי אָדָם הַמְסַפְּרִים עִמּוֹ קוֹדֶם אֲכִילָה, שֶׁהַגּוּף רֵיקָן: כְּאִידָךְ דר' יִצְחָק סְבִירָא לִי. אֲבָל אָסוּר לְסַפֵּר – לָא סְבִירָא לִי: בַּר זוּזָא. כְּלוֹמַר: שָׁמֵן וְטוֹב שֶׁשָּׁוֶה זוּז: דְּלֵית בֵּיהּ רִבְעָא. שֶׁלֹּא גָּדַל עַד רְבִיעִית שֶׁלּוֹ. כְּגוֹן: טָלֶה רְבִיעִית שֶׁל אַיִל, גְּדִי כְּדֵי רְבִיעִית שֶׁל שָׂעִיר גָּדוֹל, וְכֵן כָּל דָּבָר: גִּילְדָנֵי דְּבֵי גִילֵי. דָּגִים קְטַנִּים מְאֹד וּמְלוּיִין בֵּין הַקָּנִים בָּאֲגַם, וְאֵין דַּרְכָּן לִגְדּוֹל יוֹתֵר. אֲבָל דָּג קָטָן מִמִּין דָּג גָּדוֹל, וְלֹא גָּדַל רוֹבַע – זֶה הוּא קָטָן מַקְטִין: עוּנְקָא. צַוָּאר. מְקוֹם בֵּית הַשְּׁחִיטָה, וְסָמוּךְ לַלֵּב וְלַמֵּעַיִם: לְבֵי בָּרוּךְ. לְמָקוֹם שֶׁבֵּרְכוּ שָׁם עַל הַשְּׁחִיטָה: וּמֵי סִיסִין. תַּבְשִׁיל שֶׁל פּוֹלִיאוֹ"ל: וְהֶרֶת. וולדיר"א, שֶׁהַוָּלָד נוֹצָר בּוֹ: יוֹתֶרֶת הַכָּבֵד. טַרְפְּשָׁא דְּכַבְדָּא, שֶׁקּוֹרִין איבר"ש: מִבְּלִי בָּשָׂר. הִיא קָשָׁה אֲבָל כְּשֶׁמְּבַשְּׁלָהּ עִם בָּשָׂר שָׁמֵן מַתִּישׁ כֹּחָהּ: מִבְּלִי יַיִן. כְּשֶׁאֵין שׁוֹתֶה אַחֲרֶיהָ יַיִן: מִבְּלִי עֵצִים. שֶׁאֵינוֹ שׁוֹלְקָהּ הַרְבֵּה: סוּדָנִי. בַּעַל שֵׁכַר תְּמָרִים. ור' פַּפָּא מוֹכֵר שֵׁכָר הָיָה, כִּדְאָמַר בְּ"אֵיזֶהוּ נֶשֶׁךְ" (ד' סה.) טַרְשָׁא דְּרַב פַּפָּא שִׁכְרָא לָא פָּסֵיד, וְאָמַר רַב פַּפָּא: אִי לָאו דִּרְמַאי שִׁכְרָא לָא אִיעַתַּרִי (פסחים קיג.) וְהוּא נִקְרָא סוּדָנִי, כִּדְאָמְרִינַן: תַּמְרֵי בְּחַלּוּזָךְ לְבֵי סוּדָנָא רְהוֹט (שם): דְּלָא נְפִישׁ לְכוּ חַמְרָא. שֶׁשּׁוֹתֵי שֵׁכָר אַתֶּם: בְּמַאי תַּבְרִיתוּ לָהּ. לְכֹחוֹ שֶׁל לֶפֶת: אוּפֵי פַּרְסַיְיתָא. בִּקְעִיּוֹת שֶׁל עֵצִים גְּדוֹלוֹת הָיְתָה שׂוֹרֶפֶת תַּחַת קְדֵרַת הַלֶּפֶת: פְּעָמִים שֶׁהוּא מֵמִית. וְאֵלּוּ הֵן: בְּיוֹם שִׁבְעָה יָמִים לִמְלִיחָתוֹ, אוֹ בְּיוֹם שִׁבְעָה עָשָׂר, אוֹ בְּיוֹם שִׁבְעָה וְעֶשְׂרִים:

מאי

מסו[רת]

נדה נח:

[שבת קי.

[לקמן נז:

דחנקתיה אומצא.§ רבי טרפון אומר: "בורא נפשות רבות וחסרונן".§ *אמר ליה רבא בר רב חנן לאביי, ואמרי לה לרב יוסף: הלכתא מאי? -אמר ליה: *אפוק חזי מאי עמא דבר.§

# הדרן עלך כיצד מברכין

*שלשה שאכלו כאחת חייבין לזמן. אכל דמאי, ומעשר ראשון שנטלה תרומתו, מעשר שני והקדש שנפדו, והשמש שאכל כזית, והכותי – מזמנין עליו. אכל טבל, ומעשר ראשון שלא נטלה תרומתו, ומעשר שני והקדש שלא נפדו, והשמש שאכל פחות מכזית, והגוי – אין מזמנין עליו. נשים ועבדים וקטנים אין מזמנין עליהן. *עד כמה מזמנין? עד כזית; ר' יהודה אומר: עד כביצה.§

גמ' מה"מ? אמר רב אסי: דאמר קרא °"גדלו לה' אתי ונרוממה שמו יחדו". רבי אבהו אמר מהכא: °"כי שם ה' אקרא הבו גדל לאלהינו". אמר רב חנן בר *אבא: מנין לעונה אמן שלא יגביה קולו יותר מן המברך – שנאמר: "גדלו לה' אתי ונרוממה שמו יחדו". אמר ר' שמעון בן פזי: מנין שאין המתרגם רשאי להגביה קולו יותר מן הקורא – שנאמר: °"משה ידבר והאלהים יעננו בקול"; שאין תלמוד לומר "בקול", ומה תלמוד לומר "בקול" – בקולו של משה. תניא נמי הכי: אין המתרגם רשאי להגביה קולו יותר מן הקורא, ואם אי אפשר למתרגם להגביה קולו כנגד הקורא – ימעך הקורא קולו ויקרא.§ אתמר: שנים שאכלו כאחת; פליגי רב ורבי יוחנן, חד אמר: אם רצו לזמן מזמנין; וחד אמר: אם רצו לזמן – אין מזמנין. תנן: שלשה שאכלו כאחת חייבין לזמן; שלשה – אין, שנים – לא! –התם חובה, הכא רשות. תא שמע: *שלשה שאכלו כאחת – חייבין לזמן ואין רשאין ליחלק; שלשה אין, שנים – לא! –שאני התם, דקבעו להו בחובה מעיקרא. תא שמע: השמש שהיה משמש על השנים – הרי זה אוכל עמהם אע"פ שלא נתנו לו רשות, היה משמש על השלשה – הרי זה אינו אוכל עמהם אלא אם כן נתנו לו רשות! –שאני התם, דניחא

תהלים לד | דברים לב | שמות יט

**רש"י**

מאי עמא דבר. היאך נוהגים. וכבר נהגו לברך בתחלה "שהכל" ולבסוף "בורא נפשות רבות וחסרונן על כל מה שברא".

הדרן עלך כיצד מברכין

שלשה שאכלו וכו' לזמן. להזדמן יחד לצרוף ברכה בלשון רבים כגון "נברך": שנטלה תרומתו. קס"ד (א) תרומת מעשר שלו, שעל הלוי להפריש: מעשר שני שנפדה. להתירו באכילה חוץ לירושלים ואת פדיונו יעלה לירושלים, ויאכל: והשמש. ששמש בסעודה ואכל עמהם כזית כדי להצטרף עמהם לזמון. ובכל הני אצטריך לאשמעינן אע"ג דדמו לאיסור – אין כאן ברכה בעבירה, כדמפרש וחזיל בגמרא: עד כמה מזמנין. כמה יאכל עמהם ויתחייב עמהם בזימון. ונפקא מינה – להוציאם ידי חובתן, אם יתנו לו הכוס לברך: גמ' מה"מ. דשלשה צריכים לברכת צירוף: גדלו לה' אתי. הרי שלשה. וכן "אקרא, הבו גודל" – היחיד אומר לשנים: אינן רשאין ליחלק. ולברך כל אחד לעצמו, דמפקעי לה לתורת זמון: שלשה אין שנים לא. ה"פ: דמדקתני אין רשאין ליחלק שמע מינה דשלשה מזמנין, שנים אין מזמנין ואפילו רצו. דאי קאמרת שנים נמי אם רצו מזמנין, אמאי אין האחד רשאי ליחלק? ליזיל הוא, ולא מפקעת ברכת זמון בהכי, ויזמנו השנים שאני התם דהוקבעו בחובה מעיקרא. ואי אזיל הוא מפקעת להו חובה, וקמו להו ברשות; וגדול המצווה ועושה ממי שאינו מצווה ועושה: אוכל עמהם. אין כאן גאוה, דניחא להו דמייתי להו לידי זמון. ואי שנים מזמנין, אמאי ניחא להו? בלאו דידיה נמי, אי בעו מזמני: דניחא

עירובין יד: | שם פסחים נב. מנחות לה: | [לקמן נ.] | [נט: יומא עט: לקמן מט: ד"ה עד כמה] | כ"א בשאלתות פרשת יתרו | [לקמן נ.] | [ל' עד אלא מנאך ונ"ב אין כאן מקומו]

**תוספות**

דחנקתיה אומצא. ודוקא מים, שאין לו הנאה כי אם לשתות מים לצמאו, והנאה דחנקתיה אומצא אין זה נחשב הנאה. אבל שאר משקים, שלעולם הגוף נהנה מהן – בכל ענין מברך ואפילו חנקתיה אומצא, כדאמרינן לעיל (דף לו.). ואע"ג דלרפואה אתי בעי ברוכי. ורב עמרם פירש: דדוקא לפניו לא בעי ברוכי, אבל לאחריו חייב ורבינו משה פירש: דלא היא, דהואיל ואינו נהנה – אפילו לאחריו לא בעי ברכה: רבי טרפון אומר בורא נפשות רבות וכו'. פירוש: לפניו. ופוק חזי מאי עמא דבר, והנה נהגו העולם לברך לאחריו. אבל לא מצינו לפרש דפליגי בלאחריו, דתנא קמא סבר דמברך לפניו ולא לאחריו ורבי טרפון סבר אף לאחריו יברך בורא נפשות רבות, דאם כן – כי פריך לעיל מרב פפא דמברך (ליקשי), [לסייעיה] ממלתיה דרבי טרפון שהוא תנא*:

הדרן עלך כיצד מברכין

שלשה שאכלו כאחת. בירושלמי פריך: הכא את אמרת חייבים לזמן, והכא את אמרת אין רשאין ליחלק. ועתה לכאורה אין זה קשה. וכן לקמן (דף נ.) פריך: תנינא חדא זימנא שאין רשאין ליחלק, היינו משום דחייבים לזמון! ול"נ דהכי פריך: הכא את אמרת דאין רשאין ליחלק, דמשמע: אם גמרו אכילתן יחד – אינן רשאין ליחלק, אבל האחד רשאי לגמור סעודתו ולברך קודם חברו. וחייבין לזמן משמע: דחובת זימון עליהם, ואינן רשאין לגמור סעודתן זה בלא זה. ומשני שמואל: כאן בתחלה כאן בסוף. איזהו בתחלה ואיזהו בסוף? פליגי בה תרי אמוראי, חד אמר: נתנו דעתם לאכול – זהו בתחלה, אכלו כזית – זהו בסוף. וחד אמר: אכלו כזית – זהו בתחלה, נתנו דעתם לאכול – זהו בסוף. ורב אלפס תופס דרך *ראשון עיקר, וה"פ: נתנו דעתם לאכול, כלומר שהתחילו מתחלה לאכול ביחד – זהו בתחלה; או ודאי חובת זימון עליהם. אכלו כזית – זהו בסוף, כלומר: אם האחד התחיל קודם חברו בכזית – או ודאי אם גמרו סעודתם יחד חייבים לזמן, אבל רשאין לגמור זה בלא זה ולברך: אבל טבל אין מזמנין עליו. תימה: דאמר בערכין (דף ד.) הכל מצטרפין לזמון, כהנים לוים וישראלים. ופריך: פשיטא! ומשני: לא צריכא – אף על גב דכהן אוכל תרומה וישראל חולין. אלמא: אף על גב דתרומה אסורה לישראל, אחרי שהכהן יכול לצרף עם ישראל, לאכול בחולין – מצטרפין לזמון. והכא נמי: נהי דחד מנייהו אכל טבל, דאין ראוי לאחרים. אמאי אינן מזמנין? ויש לומר: דאכילת טבל לאו שמה אכילה, דלא חזיא אף לכהן, אבל תרומה – לכל הפחות ראויה לכהן האוכלה, *והוא הדין אם אכלו שלשתן טבל – דאין חייבים לזמן, כדאמרינן (ב"ק פ"ט דל"ד): הרי שגזל סאה חטין וטחנה ואפאה ואכלה ומברך עליהן – אינו מברך אלא מנאץ. מכאן היה אומר רבינו יהודה דשלשה שאכלו, והאחד היה מודר הנאה מן השנים והוא אוכל משלו – יכול להצטרף עמהם לזימון, דנהי דאינו ראוי לאכול עמו, הם ראוים לאכול עמהם – וכן לענין הנזהר מפת של גוי. אבל אם שלשתן מודרין הנאה זה מזה – אין מצטרפין, אע"פ שיכולים לשאול על נדרם – דהשתא מיהא לא אתשילו: בקולו של משה. וא"ת: היכי מייתי ראיה ממשה, והא צריך לאתויי דמשה היה מתרגם ולא היה מרים קולו יותר מהקב"ה שהיה קורא והוא מביא שהקב"ה היה קורא ומשה היה מתרגם? ופירש רב אלפס: בקולו של משה, מסתמא משה בכל כחו היה עונה כדי להשמיע קולו לכל העם, אבל הקב"ה לא היה צריך להרים קולו – שהרי לא היה מדבר אלא למשה לבד, ואפילו הכי היה מגביה קולו, כדי שלא יהא קולו של משה המתרגם רם יותר מקולו של הקב"ה שהיה קורא: אם רצו לזמן אין מזמנין. פירש"י: וכן לענין המוציא ושאר ברכות – אין האחד מברך להוציא חברו, לגבי הא דאמר אביי נקטינן שנים שאכלו כאחת מצוה ליחלק ולברך כל אחד לעצמו בין ברכת המוציא בין ברכת המזון, לשון רש"י לקמן. ולא נהירא, דלעיל פרק כיצד מברכין (דף לט.) בעובדא דבר קפרא, נתן בר קפרא רשות לאחד לברך ושנים הוו התם. ועוד, אי הוו שלשה התם לא היו שם אלא פירות! וכן נמי אמרינן לקמן (דף נג.) דעל המאור אחד מברך לכולן! ע"כ נ"ל: דברכה ראשונה – מוציאין זה את זה שנים לכ"ע, והטעם: הואיל ויושבין לאכול יחד – דעתן לצרף, ואחד מברך להוציא חברו. אבל בברכה של סוף סעודה, שמסתלקין זה מזה – צריך לברך כל אחד לעצמו. ויש מתרצים דיש חלוק בין ברכת המוציא – דלא הויא כי אם דרבנן – ע"כ מוציאין זה את זה, אבל בבהמ"ז שהיא מדאורייתא – לשם החמירו*: שלשה שאכלו כאחד אין רשאין ליחלק. מפרש"י: אמאי אין רשאין ליחלק האחד מפני השנים, כיון דב' נמי מזמנין, ליזיל הוא, והא לא מיפק' ברכת זמון. תימה: דילמא טעמא דאין רשאין ליחלק – משום דיפטרו לשלישי מברכת הזמון. וגם הוא אין לו להפקיע ממנו ברכת הזמון! וי"ל: דעיקר פרכתו סמיך אסיפא, דקתני: ד' אין רשאין ליחלק, אע"ג דאיכא שנים מכאן וב' מכאן והוי כמו וכו', וכה"ג תמצא בהרבה מקומות. ותימה: א"כ אמאי לא מקשי מן הסיפא בהדיא? ע"כ פירש רבינו יהודה: דודאי פריך מרישא, וה"ק: דליכא למימר דמשום היחיד קאמר – דא"כ ה"ל למימר אין היחיד רשאי ליחלק, אי נמי אין אחד מהם רשאי ליחלק. אבל מדקתני: אין רשאין ליחלק, משמע מכלהו פקע זמון אם נסתלק אחד מהם: והא

**עין משפט נר מצוה**

קנבא [מיי' שם] טוש"ע או"ח סימן רד סעיף ז:
א ב מיי' פ"ה מהלכות ברכות הלכה ב סמג עשין כז טוש"ע או"ח סימן קצב סעיף א:
ב ג מיי' פ"א מהלכות ברכות הל' כ סמג שם:
ג ד טוש"ע או"ח סימן קצט סעיף א:
ד ה שם סעיף ב:
ה ו מיי' שם הלכה יט סמג שם טוש"ע או"ח סי' קצו סעיף א:
ו ז מיי' פ"ה מהל' ברכות הלכה ז סמג שם טוש"ע או"ח סימן קצט סעיף ד:
ז ח מיי' שם טוש"ע שם סעיף ו:

[ועיין רש"י עירובין יד: ד"ה ר"ט]

ח ט מיי' שם הלכה ח סמג שם טוש"ע או"ח סי' קפד סעיף ו וסימן קצו סעיף ד:
ט י מיי' פ"א מהלכות ברכות הל' יד סמג שם טוש"ע או"ח סימן קכד סעיף יב:
י כ מיי' פ"ד מהלכות ת"ת הלכה ג ופי"ב מהל' תפלה הל' יא טוש"ע או"ח סי' קמה ס"א וטור י"ד סי' רמה:
יא ל מיי' פ"ה מהלכות ברכות הלכה י סמג עשין כז טוש"ע או"ח סי' קצג סעיף א:
יב מ טוש"ע שם וכסי' קע סעיף כא:

**הגהות הב"ח**

(א) רש"י ד"ה שנטלה תרומתו קס"ד. נ"ב נ"ל דמשום סיפא קאמר רש"י קס"ד וע"ל דף מ"ז ע"ב ול"נ שהוא ט"ס וזה קאי אסיפא אלא שלא נטלה תרומתו וק"ל שוב ראיתי בשבת דף קכז פרש"י לשם וכ"ש תרומה גדולה שעל ישראל להפריש והפרישו קודם וכו' ע"ש וזה חסר כאן:

**גליון הש"ס**

תוס' ד"ה אבל טבל כו' ואפאן ואכלן ומברך. שם ליתא כן. אלא ואפאה והפריש חלה ובירך ונ"ע: תוס' ד"ה שלשה שאכלו כאחד אין רשאין ליחלק כו' סמיך אסיפא. כעין זה בתוס' גיטין דף פ' ע"ב תוס' ד"ה זו דברי ר"מ וש"נ:

[ועמ"ש תוס' בהריכות בביאור הדברים בחולין קו. ד"ה וש"מ]

דניחא להו דמקבע להו בחובה (מעיקרא). ת"ש: *א נשים מזמנות לעצמן, ועבדים מזמנים לעצמן, נשים ועבדים וקטנים אם רצו לזמן – אין מזמנין; (*והא נשים אפילו מאה) והא מאה [א] נשי כתרי גברי דמיין, וקתני: נשים מזמנות לעצמן ועבדים מזמנין לעצמן! –שאני התם, דאיכא דעות. –אי הכי אימא סיפא: נשים ועבדים אם רצו לזמן אין מזמנין, אמאי לא? והא איכא דעות! –שאני התם – משום פריצותא.§ תסתיים דרב דאמר "אם רצו – לזמן אין מזמנין" דאמר רב דימי בר יוסף אמר רב: שלשה שאכלו כאחת ויצא אחד מהם לשוק – קוראין לו ומזמנין עליו; טעמא – דקוראין לו, הא לא קוראין לו – לא! –שאני התם, דאקבעו להו בחובה מעיקרא. אלא, תסתיים דר' יוחנן הוא דאמר "אם רצו לזמן – אין מזמנין". דאמר רבה בר בר חנה א"ר יוחנן: שנים שאכלו כאחת –אחד מהן יוצא בברכת חבירו. והוינן בה; מאי קא משמע לן? תנינא: *בשמע ולא ענה – יצא! ואמר רבי זירא: לומר שאין ברכת הזימון ביניהם, תסתיים. א"ל רבא בר רב הונא לרב הונא: והא רבנן דאתו ממערבא אמרי: אם רצו לזמן – מזמנין, מאי לאו דשמיע להו מרבי יוחנן? –לא, דשמיע להו מרב מקמי דנחית לבבל.§ גופא, אמר רב דימי בר יוסף אמר רב: גשלשה שאכלו כאחת ויצא אחד מהם לשוק – קוראין לו ומזמנין עליו. אמר אביי: והוא דקרו ליה ועני. אמר מר זוטרא: ולא אמרן אלא בשלשה, אבל בעשרה – עד דנייתי. מתקיף לה רב אשי: אדרבה, איפכא מסתברא! תשעה – (א) נראין כעשרה, שנים אין נראין כשלשה! דוהלכתא כמר זוטרא. מ"ט – *כיון דבעי לאדכורי שם שמים. בציר מעשרה לאו אורח ארעא.§ אמר אביי, נקיטינן: שנים שאכלו כאחת – מצוה ליחלק. *תניא נמי הכי: השנים שאכלו כאחת – מצוה ליחלק; במה דברים אמורים – כששניהם סופרים, אבל אחד סופר ואחד בור – סופר מברך, ובור יוצא. אמר רבא, *הא מילתא אמריתא אנא, ואיתמרה משמיה דרבי זירא כוותי: ושלשה שאכלו כאחת – אחד מפסיק לשנים ואין שנים מפסיקין לאחד. ולא?! והא רב פפא אפסיק ליה לאבא מר בריה, איהו וחד! –שאני רב פפא *דלפנים משורת הדין הוא דעבד.§ יהודה בר מרימר ומר בר רב אשי ורב אחא מדיפתי כרכי ריפתא בהדי הדדי, לא הוה בהו חד דהוה מופלג מחבריה לברוכי להו; (*יתבי וקא מיבעיא להו), הא דתנן: שלשה שאכלו כאחת חייבין לזמן – הני מילי היכא דאיכא אדם גדול, אבל היכא דכי הדדי נינהו – חלוק ברכות עדיף. בריך איניש (ג) לנפשיה, אתו לקמיה דמרימר, אמר להו: ידי ברכה – יצאתם, זידי זימון – לא יצאתם. וכי תימרו ניהדר ונזמן – *אין זימון למפרע.§ בא ומצאן כשהן מברכים, מהו אומר אחריהם? רב זביד אמר: "ברוך ומבורך"; רב פפא אמר: עונה אמן. ולא פליגי: חהא דאשכחינהו דקא אמרי "נברך", והא דאשכחינהו דקא אמרי "ברוך"; אשכחינהו דקא אמרי "נברך" – אומר "ברוך ומבורך", אשכחינהו דקא אמרי "ברוך" – עונה אמן. תני חדא: העונה אמן אחר(ג) ברכותיו הרי זה משובח, ותניא אידך: הרי זה מגונה! –לא קשיא: טהא – ב"בונה ירושלים", הא – בשאר ברכות. אביי עני ליה בקלא כי היכי דלשמעו פועלים וליקומו, ד"הטוב והמטיב" לאו דאורייתא. רב אשי עני ליה בלחישא, כי היכי דלא נזלזלו ב"הטוב(7) והמטיב".
רבי

**רש"י**

דניחא להו דמקבע להו בחובה. דגדול המצווה ועושה: אם רצו אין מזמנים. כדמפרש טעמא לקמן: שאין קביעותן נאה משום פריצותא, בין דנשים בין דמשכב זכור דעבדים בקטנים: דאפילו מאה כתרי דמיין. לענין חובה, דאין חייבות לזמן, ואם רצו – מזמנין, והוא הדין לשנים: דאיכא דעות. דאע"ג דלענין חובה אינן חייבות; לענין רשות – דעות שלשה חשיבי להודות טפי משני אנשים, דאיכא משום "גדלו לה' אתי": קוראין לו. להודיעו שהם רוצים לזמן, ויפנה אליהם במקום מעמדו, ודי להם בכך: ומזמנין עליו. ואע"פ שאינו בא אצלם: ואמר רבי זירא: לומר שאין ברכת הזימון ביניהן. לא בא ללמדנו אלא שאין צריכין זימון. דכיון דאחד יוצא בברכת חברו אשמעינן דאין זימון, דאי יש זימון – ברכת שניהם היא, שהרי אומר "נברך" והוא עונה "ברוך הוא": לאו דשמיע להו מרבי יוחנן. דבר מערבא הוא. דאילו רב – בבבל הוה, ובני מערבא היכא שמיע להו: והוא דקרו ליה ועני. שסמוך הוא אצלם, ועונה "ברוך הוא": לא אמרן. דלא צריך למיתי גבייהו – אלא שלשה, אבל עשרה שיצטרפו משום הזכרת השם – עד דאתי גבייהו: נראין כעשרה. דאין אדם ממהר להבחין בין עשרה לתשעה: מצוה ליחלק. ולברך כל אחד בפני עצמו, בין ברכת "המוציא" בין ברכת המזון: אחד מפסיק לשנים. אם גמרו השנים סעודתן ורוצין לזמן, דרך ארץ הוא שיהא האחד מפסיק את סעודתו עד שיזמנו עליו עד ברכת הזן, דהיינו ברכת זימון, וחוזר וגומר סעודתו. אבל שנים אין עליהם להפסיק בשביל היחיד, וימתין עד שיגמרו: לפנים משורת הדין. לאחשוביה: לא הוה בהו(ה). מופלג בחכמה ובזקנה מן השנים: דאיכא אדם גדול. שהגדול מברך, כדפסקינן לקמן הלכתא (דף מז.): בא ומצאן. אחד מן השוק בא ומצא שלשה שהיו מזמנין: ברוך ומבורך. דלא מצי למימר "שאכלנו משלו": הא דקאמר ברוך ומבורך. כדאשכחינהו דקאמר המזמן "נברך", אבל אשכחינהו דענו "ברוך הוא" – עונה בתרייהו אמן: הא בבונה ירושלים. שהיא סוף הברכות, הרי זה משובח. וכן בסוף ברכות דקריאת שמע, שחרית וערבית, ו"אחר כל ברכותיו" דקתני בברייתא "הרי זה משובח" – אחר גמר כל ברכותיו קאמר. ו"אחר כל ברכותיו" דקתני "הרי זה מגונה" – בסוף כל ברכה וברכה קאמר: כי היכי דלשמעו פועלים. וידעו שנגמרה כל הברכה, שהרי אין המברך עונה אמן אלא לבסוף: וליקומו. לעבידתייהו. ואי משום דקמספקע להו מ"הטוב והמטיב" – לא איכפת ליה, דקסבר דלאו דאורייתא היא, אלא ביבנה תקנוה על הרוגי ביתר שנתנו לקבורה: רב אשי עני. להאוא אמן בלחישה כי היכי דלא לשמעו וידעו שגמר הברכות ויזלזלו ב"הטוב והמטיב". ומיהו, משום דסוף כל ברכותיו היא, ותניא בברייתא "ה"ז משובח" – לא סגי דלא עני ליה:
קטינא

**תוספות**

והא מאה נשי כתרי גברי דמיין. לענין קבוץ תפלה, ולענין כל דבר שבעשרה – ואפילו הכי חשבינן להו כשלשה, וה"ה לשנים, אבל לא מצי למימר כחד דמיין, דאינן יכולות לזמן, דהא קתני נשים מזמנות לעצמן, ורש"י פירש: כתרי – לענין חובה, דאין חייבות לזמן, ואם רצו מזמנות, והוא הדין לשנים:

שאני התם דאיכא דעות. מכאן משמע דנשים יכולות לזמן לעצמן. וכן עשו בנות רבינו אברהם, חמיו של רבינו יהודה, ע"פ אביהן. ומיהו, לא נהגו העולם כן; וקשה: אמאי לא נהגו? מדקתני מזמנות משמע דקאמר חייבות לזמן! וי"ל: דנשים מזמנות לעצמן, היינו: אם רצו לזמן – מזמנות. וכן משמע קצת הלשון מדקתני בסמוך נשים ועבדים אם רצו לזמן אין מזמנין. ועוד, דמדמה ליה הגמרא לשנים משמע דחובה ליכא. והא דקאמר בריש ערכין (דף ג. ושם) הכל מחויבין בזימון לאתויי נשים, לענין רשות קאמר, ולא לענין חובה. ונשים צריך עיון אם יוצאות בברכת הזימון של אנשים מאחר שאין מבינות. ויש מביאין ראיה שיוצאות מדאמר לקמן: סופר מברך ובור יוצא, מכאן משמע שאף הנשים יוצאות בבהמ"ז שלנו. מיהו, יש לדחות אותה ראיה, דשאני בור – שמבין בלשון הקדש ויודע קצת מאי קאמר אבל אינו יודע לברך. אבל נשים, שאינן מבינות כלל – מצי למימר דלא נפקי. והא דאמרי' במגילה (פ"ב ד' יז.) לועז ששמע אשורית יצא – פרסומי ניסא בעלמא שאני כדאמרינן התם (דף יח.) האחשתרנים בני הרמכים מי ידעינן מאי ניהו:

אי הכי אימא סיפא. לא גרס אי הכי דהא אפי' מעיקר' נמי הוה מצי למפרך מסיפא דאין מזמנין:

רב זביד אמר ברוך הוא ומבורך. ובה"ג פסק: ברוך הוא ומבורך שמו תמיד לעולם ועד. ואי הוה עשרה עני בתרייהו: ברוך הוא אלהינו ומבורך שמו תמיד לעולם ועד:

הא בבונה ירושלים הא בשאר ברכות. פר"ח וה"ג די"מ בכל ברכה וברכה כגון אחר ישתבח וכיוצא בו. ומיהו, פוק חזי מאי עמא דבר – שלא נהגו לענות אמן אלא אחר בונה ירושלים דבהמ"ז:

רב אשי עני ליה בלחישה. וכן פסק בה"ג. ועוד, לדידן ליכא פועלים – אפילו אביי מודה: לא

**עין משפט נר מצוה**

יג א מיי' פ"ה מהלכות ברכות הלכה ז סמג עשין כז טוש"ע או"ח סי' קצט סעיף ו:
יד ב מיי' פ"א שם הל' יא סמג שם טוש"ע או"ח סי' ריג סעיף ב:
טו ג ד מיי' פ"ה שם הלכה יג וסמג שם טוש"ע או"ח סימן קצד סעיף ב:
טז ה מיי' שם הל' טו סמג שם טוש"ע או"ח סי' קצג סעיף א:
יז ו מיי' פ"ז שם הל' ו סמג שם טוש"ע או"ח סי' ר סעיף א:
יח ז טוש"ע או"ח סימן קצד סעיף א:
יט ח מיי' פ"ה שם הל' יז סמג שם טוש"ע או"ח סי' קצח סעיף א:
כ ט מיי' פ"א שם הל' טז סמג שם טוש"ע או"ח סי' קפח סעיף א ובסי' רטו סעיף א:
כא י טוש"ע או"ח סי' קפח סעיף ב:

**הגהות הב"ח**

(א) גמ' נראין כעשרה. נ"ב ע"ל סוף דף מ"ז: (ב) שם בריך איניש אינש לנפשיה: (ג) שם אחר כל ברכותיו: (ד) שם דלא לזלזלו רבנן בהטוב: (ה) רש"י ד"ה לא הוה בהו חד מופלג:

**הגהות הגר"א**

[א] גמ' והא נשים אפי' מאה (והא מאה) תא"מ:

[ערכין ג.]
[ל' תיבות הללו מוכן ומלכרי רב דגרים והא אפי' כתרי גברי דמיין]
סוכה לח: [ע"ש]
מגילה כג:
חולין קו.
[מנחות מ:]
[לעיל ז. וש"נ]
[לקמן נ.]
[נ"ל אמרי וכ"א בכי"ף ורא"ש]

קְטִינָא חֲרִיךְ שָׁקֵי. כָּךְ הָיוּ קוֹרִין לְר' זֵירָא. וְטַעֲמָא מְפָרֵשׁ בְּבָבָא מְצִיעָא "בְּהַשּׂוֹכֵר אֶת הַפּוֹעֲלִים" (דף פה.): כִּי מְטָא לְמִשְׁרֵי. לִשְׁנָא דְּשֵׁירוּתָא, כְּלוֹמַר: לִפְרוֹס בִּרְכַּת "הַמּוֹצִיא" וְלֶאֱכוֹל: רַב הוּנָא דְּמִבָּבֶל. הַיְינוּ רַב הוּנָא סְתָמָא; וּלְפִי שֶׁעַכְשָׁיו הָיָה ר' זֵירָא בְּאֶרֶץ יִשְׂרָאֵל בִּמְקוֹם ר' אַבָּהוּ, וְהָיָה עוֹלֶה מִבָּבֶל, קָאָמַר הָכִי: קְרוֹבִים לָעִיר. שֶׁיָּכוֹל לְהַלְוֹתָן בַּעַל הַבַּיִת תָּמִיד וּלְדַעַת מַה הֵן צְרִיכִין: נְכָסָיו. קַרְקָעוֹת: עַד הֵיכָן בִּרְכַּת הַזִּמּוּן. שֶׁצְּרִיכִין לִהְיוֹת שְׁלֹשָׁה, וּכְשֶׁהֵן שְׁנַיִם לֹא יֹאמְרוּהָ: בִּרְכַּת הַמָּזוֹן שְׁתַּיִם וְשָׁלֹשׁ*. פְּעָמִים שֶׁהֵם שְׁתֵּי בְּרָכוֹת, פְּעָמִים שֶׁהֵם שָׁלֹשׁ. כֵּיצַד: כְּשֶׁהֵם שְׁלֹשָׁה — הֵן שָׁלֹשׁ בְּרָכוֹת, וּכְשֶׁהֵם שְׁנַיִם — הֵן שְׁתֵּי בְּרָכוֹת, כִּדְמְפָרֵשׁ וְאָזֵיל: דְּקָסָבַר. בִּרְכַּת זִמּוּן. עַד הַזָּן וּכְשֶׁהֵם שְׁנַיִם אֵין אוֹמְרִים אֶלָּא בִּרְכַּת הָאָרֶץ וּ"בוֹנֵה יְרוּשָׁלַיִם": וּמַאן דְּאָמַר שָׁלֹשׁ וְאַרְבַּע. כְּשֶׁהֵן שְׁנַיִם הֲרֵי שָׁלֹשׁ: "הַזָּן", וּבִרְכַּת הָאָרֶץ, וּ"בוֹנֵה יְרוּשָׁלַיִם". וּכְשֶׁהֵם שְׁלֹשָׁה הֵם מוֹסִיפִים "נְבָרֵךְ" עַד "וּבְטוּבוֹ חָיִינוּ": מוֹקִים לַהּ. לֹא גָּרְסִינַן. וְהָכִי גָּרְסִי': וְהָא דְּתַנְיָא שְׁתַּיִם וְשָׁלֹשׁ בְּבִרְכַּת פּוֹעֲלִים דְּאָמְרִי בִּרְכַּת הָאָרֶץ וּ"בוֹנֵה יְרוּשָׁלַיִם" בַּחֲדָא בְּרָכָה אֵין כָּאן אֶלָּא בִּרְכַּת "הַזָּן" וּבִרְכַּת הָאָרֶץ, וּכְשֶׁהֵם שְׁלֹשָׁה מוֹסִיפִין "נְבָרֵךְ" — הֲרֵי שָׁלֹשׁ: דְּאָמַר מָר. לְעֵיל בְּפֶרֶק שֵׁנִי (דף טז.): שֶׁהֲרֵי פּוֹתֵחַ בָּהּ בְּבָרוּךְ. וְאִי דְּאוֹרַיְיתָא הִיא, הָוְיָא סְמוּכָה לַחֲבֶרְתָּהּ — וְאֵין פּוֹתְחִין בָּהּ בְּבָרוּךְ: כִּדְתַנְיָא כו' יֵשׁ מֵהֶן כו'. כְּגוֹן בִּרְכַּת פֵּירוֹת וּמִצְוֹת פּוֹתֵחַ וְאֵינוֹ חוֹתֵם. וְטַעְמָא מְפָרֵשׁ בְּ"עַרְבֵי פְסָחִים" (דף קה.) מִשּׁוּם דְּכוּלָּהּ חֲדָא הוֹדָאָה, וְאֵין הֶפְסֵק דָּבָר תְּחִנָּה אוֹ דָּבָר אַחֵר בְּתוֹכָהּ, כְּמוֹ שֶׁיֵּשׁ בְּקִידּוּשׁ, "כִּי הוּא יוֹם תְּחִלָּה לְמִקְרָאֵי קוֹדֶשׁ" וְ"הִנְחַלְתָּנוּ": וְיֵשׁ

(נ"ל קיבל) (מתפח) הגוסחא שנים ושלשה (א"ש וכן בטוש"ע או' יודקק)

ר' זֵירָא חֲלַשׁ, עַל לְגַבֵּיהּ ר' אַבָּהוּ, *קַבִּיל עֲלֵיהּ: אִי *מִתְפַּח קְטִינָא חֲרִיךְ שָׁקֵי — עָבֵידְנָא יוֹמָא טָבָא לְרַבָּנַן. אִתְפַּח, עֲבַד סְעוּדְתָא לְכוּלְּהוּ רַבָּנַן. כִּי מְטָא לְמִשְׁרֵי, אֲמַר לֵיהּ לְר' זֵירָא: לִישְׁרֵי לַן מָר! — א"ל: לָא סְבַר לַהּ מָר לְהָא דְר' יוֹחָנָן דְּאָמַר: א בַּעַל הַבַּיִת בּוֹצֵעַ? שְׁרָא לְהוּ. כִּי מְטָא לְבָרוֹכֵי, אֲמַר לֵיהּ: נִבְרֵיךְ לַן מָר! — אֲמַר לֵיהּ: לָא סָבַר לַהּ מָר לְהָא דְּרַב הוּנָא דְּמִן בָּבֶל דְּאָמַר: בּוֹצֵעַ מְבָרֵךְ? וְאִיהוּ כְּמַאן סְבִירָא לֵיהּ? — כִּי הָא דְּאָמַר ר' יוֹחָנָן מִשּׁוּם ר' שִׁמְעוֹן בֶּן יוֹחַי: בַּעַל הַבַּיִת בּוֹצֵעַ ב וְאוֹרֵחַ מְבָרֵךְ. בַּעַל הַבַּיִת בּוֹצֵעַ — כְּדֵי שֶׁיִּבְצַע בְּעַיִן יָפָה, וְאוֹרֵחַ מְבָרֵךְ — כְּדֵי שֶׁיְּבָרֵךְ(א) בַּעַל הַבַּיִת. מַאי מְבָרֵךְ — [ב] "יְהִי רָצוֹן שֶׁלֹּא יֵבוֹשׁ בַּעַל הַבַּיִת בָּעוֹלָם הַזֶּה וְלֹא יִכָּלֵם לָעוֹלָם הַבָּא"; וְרַבִּי מוֹסִיף בָּהּ דְּבָרִים: "וְיַצְלִיחַ מְאֹד בְּכָל נְכָסָיו, וְיִהְיוּ נְכָסָיו וּנְכָסֵינוּ מוּצְלָחִים וּקְרוֹבִים לָעִיר, וְאַל יִשְׁלוֹט שָׂטָן לֹא בְּמַעֲשֵׂי יָדָיו וְלֹא בְּמַעֲשֵׂי יָדֵינוּ, וְאַל *יִזְדַּקֵּר לֹא לְפָנָיו וְלֹא לְפָנֵינוּ שׁוּם דְּבַר הִרְהוּר חֵטְא וַעֲבֵירָה וְעָוֹן מֵעַתָּה וְעַד עוֹלָם". § ג עַד הֵיכָן בִּרְכַּת הַזִּמּוּן? רַב נַחְמָן אָמַר: עַד "נְבָרֵךְ"; וְרַב שֵׁשֶׁת אָמַר: עַד "הַזָּן". נֵימָא כְּתַנָּאֵי; דְּתָנֵי חֲדָא: ד בִּרְכַּת הַמָּזוֹן שְׁנַיִם(ב) וּשְׁלֹשָׁה; וְתַנְיָא אִידָךְ: שְׁלֹשָׁה וְאַרְבָּעָה. סְבָרוּהָ, דְּכוּלֵּי עָלְמָא "הַטּוֹב וְהַמֵּטִיב" לָאו דְּאוֹרַיְיתָא הִיא; מַאי לָאו בְּהָא קָמִיפַּלְגִי, מַאן דְּאָמַר 'שְׁתַּיִם וְשָׁלֹשׁ' — קָסָבַר עַד 'הַזָּן', וּמַאן דְּאָמַר שָׁלֹשׁ וְאַרְבַּע — קָסָבַר עַד "נְבָרֵךְ"! — לָא, רַב נַחְמָן מְתָרֵץ לְטַעֲמֵיהּ וְרַב שֵׁשֶׁת מְתָרֵץ לְטַעֲמֵיהּ. רַב נַחְמָן מְתָרֵץ לְטַעֲמֵיהּ; דְּכ"ע עַד "נְבָרֵךְ", מַאן דַּאֲמַר: 'שָׁלֹשׁ וְאַרְבַּע' — שַׁפִּיר, וּמ"ד 'שְׁתַּיִם וְשָׁלֹשׁ' — אָמַר לָךְ: הָכָא בְּבִרְכַּת פּוֹעֲלִים עָסְקִינַן, דְּאָמַר מָר:(ג) *פּוֹתֵחַ בְּ"הַזָּן" וְכוֹלֵל 'בּוֹנֵה יְרוּשָׁלַיִם' בְּבִרְכַּת הָאָרֶץ. רַב שֵׁשֶׁת מְתָרֵץ לְטַעֲמֵיהּ; דְּכ"ע עַד "הַזָּן", מ"ד שְׁתַּיִם וְשָׁלֹשׁ — שַׁפִּיר, וּמ"ד שָׁלֹשׁ וְאַרְבַּע — קָסָבַר: *"הַטּוֹב וְהַמֵּטִיב" דְּאוֹרַיְיתָא הִיא.§ אָמַר רַב יוֹסֵף: תֵּדַע ד"הַטּוֹב וְהַמֵּטִיב" לָאו דְּאוֹרַיְיתָא — ה שֶׁהֲרֵי פּוֹעֲלִים עוֹקְרִים אוֹתָהּ. אָמַר רַב יִצְחָק בַּר שְׁמוּאֵל בַּר מָרְתָא מִשְּׁמֵיהּ דְּרַב: תֵּדַע דְ'הַטּוֹב וְהַמֵּטִיב' לָאו דְּאוֹרַיְיתָא — שֶׁהֲרֵי פּוֹתֵחַ בָּהּ בְּ"בָרוּךְ" וְאֵין חוֹתֵם בָּהּ בְּ"בָרוּךְ". כִּדְתַנְיָא: * ה כָּל הַבְּרָכוֹת כּוּלָּן פּוֹתֵחַ בָּהֶן בְּ"בָרוּךְ" וְחוֹתֵם בָּהֶן בְּ"בָרוּךְ" חוּץ מִבִּרְכַּת הַפֵּירוֹת, וּבִרְכַּת הַמִּצְוֹת, וּבְרָכָה הַסְּמוּכָה לַחֲבֶרְתָּהּ, וּבְרָכָה אַחֲרוֹנָה שֶׁבִּקְרִיַּת שְׁמַע; יֵשׁ מֵהֶן שֶׁפּוֹתֵחַ בָּהֶן בְּ"בָרוּךְ" וְאֵין חוֹתֵם בְּ"בָרוּךְ", וְיֵשׁ

(לעיל טז.) (לקמן מט.) (פסחים קד:)

**לא** סבר לה מר להא דאמר ר"ה דמן בבל כו'. מיהו, יש לישב הני תרי לישני דר' יוחנן: כשבעל הבית מסב עמהם — ודאי הוא בוצע ואורח מברך וכו', אבל כשאין בעל הבית מסב עמהן — הגדול שבהן יעשה המוציא, וגם הוא יברך ברכת המזון:

**עד** היכן ברכת הזמון וכו'. פירש רש"י: ממתין עד הזן והזן בכלל. שנים אינם מברכין הזן ולא נהירא דברכת הזן דאורייתא, ואיך יחיד פטור מינה? ועוד: הא קיימא לן כרב ששת באיסורי, ולדידיה יחיד אומר שנים, ובכל דוכתא נקט שלש ברכות, ודוחק לומר דלא מיירי אלא ביש זמון לרב ששת! ועוד: דמעשים בכל יום דיחיד מברך שלש ברכות. ועוד: דמדתניא לקמן בפרקין (דף מח:) *וברכת — זו ברכת הזמון, את ה' אלהיך — זו ברכת הזן, וקשה לרב ששת, יאמר הזן — זו ברכת הזמון! לכן יש לפרש דקאי אדלעיל, דקאמר אחד מפסיק לשנים, ובעי נמי: [עד] היכ' צריך להמתין — עד שיברכו השנים — עד נברך, ורב ששת אמר: עד שיגמרו הזן, ומשם ואילך יכול היחיד לאכול. ולא משום דחשיב ברכת הזן מזמון [א], דודאי יחיד נמי מתחייב מהזן, אלא משום דכיון דנברך אינה ברכה — אינו אומרה לבדה, אלא יגמור עמה גם ברכת הזן שהיא ברכה. והשתא ניחא דקיימא לן שפיר כרב ששת, וכפירוש זה איתמר בירושלמי: **ולמאן** דאמר שנים ושלשה קסבר עד הזן. ופירש"י: שנים — ליחיד, ושלשה — לזמון. ולפי שיטתו פירש כן, ודוחק גדול הוא כדפרישית; וכי יחיד פטור מברכת הזן שהיא דאורייתא? ועוד: הואיל וקאי אברכתא, אמאי נקט לשון זכר שנים ושלשה — הוה ליה למנקט לשון נקבה שתים ושלש! לכך נראה פירוש של רב אלפס דקאי אבני אדם, והכי קאמר: ברכת זמון בשנים ושלשה בני אדם היכא שכל אחד אינו יודע כי אם ברכה אחת, למאן דאמר שנים ושלשה קא סבר עד הזן, כלומר ברכת הזמון עד הזן, שמברך עד סוף הזן דכולה כברכה אחת של זמון היא. ולהכי קאמר שנים או שלשה, כלומר: לפעמים נשלמה בשנים, והוא הדין באחד, אבל נקט שנים לרבותא. ופעמים בשלשה בני אדם, שאחד יברך מנברך עד הזן, והשני נודה לך והשלישי עד בונה ירושלים, אבל לתנאין אין לברך, אם האחד אינו יודע כי אם חצי ברכה, אבל רביעי לא, דנברך לבד לא חשיב ברכה, ולכך אי אפשר לחלק לשנים נברך והזן. ומאן דאמר בד', קסבר עד נברך, דנברך חשיב ברכה אחת בפני עצמה, והזן ברכה אחרת. והיינו בד', שארבעה בני אדם מברכין אותן: שאחד יאמר נברך, והשני הזן, והשלישי נודה לך והרביעי — עד בונה ירושלים:

**כל** הברכות כולן פותחות בברוך וחותמות בברוך חוץ מברכת הפירות וברכת המצות וברכה הסמוכה לחברתה וברכה אחרונה שבקריית שמע. והא לך הסדר: ברכת אשר יצר אינה סמוכה לנטילת ידים, דנטילה שייכא בלא אשר יצר, והרבה פעמים אומרה לבדה. אלהי נשמה אמאי אינה פותחת בברוך? דאינה סמוכה לאשר יצר וכו', כגון אם לא בא מן הנקבים דידיו טהורות — אין צריך לברכת אשר יצר! וצריך לומר: הואיל ואין בה אלא הודאה בעלמא אינה פותחת בברוך, ומכל מקום חותמת בברוך — הואיל וארוכה קצת. וכן נמי צריך לומר גבי אתה הוא עד שלא נברא העולם וכו'. וכל הני ברכות קטנות כל אחת ברכה לעצמה, כדאמרן בעלמא: *כד הוה מהלך — הוה מברך מצעדי גבר, וכן כולן. ועוד: דהוו קצרות והויין כברכת הפירות. יהי רצון למי היא סמוכה? ואומר רבינו תם: שהיא מן הברכה ברוך אתה ה' המעביר שינה מעיני וכו' וצריך לומר ויהי רצון. ואם תאמר: והלא כל הברכות כולן צריך לומר בחתימתן מעין פתיחתן. והא ליכא? וי"ל: דשפיר הוי מעין פתיחה סמוך לחתימה איכא ותגמלני חסדים טובים והיינו גמילות חסדים — שהקב"ה מעביר שינה מן האדם ומחדש כחו; כדאמרינן במדרש: חדשים לבקרים וגו' — שהוא מחזיר הנשמה שלמה ושקטה בגוף כאשר היתה בתחלתה, אע"פ שהיתה עייפה, והיינו כעין פתיחתה. ולעסוק בדברי תורה והערב נא — הכל ברכה אחת היא, וצריך לומר והערב נא. וישתבח סמוכה לברוך שאמר, ולכך יש ליזהר שלא לספר ביניהם, אע"פ שיש הפסק טובא פסוקי דזמרה — מכל מקום לא מפסקי. וזה ניחא ברכה אחרונה שבק"ש אמת כו', אמת היא סמוכה אל אהבה וכו', ופסוקי ק"ש לא מפסקי. ואם תאמר: ברכה אחרונה למי שהוא קורא בתורה, אמאי צריכה לפתוח בברוך? הא סמוכה לחברתה לברכה ראשונה! ויש לומר: לפי שהיו רגילים *שלא היו מברכים רק הראשון ברכה ראשונה. והאחרון ברכה אחרונה, ואיכא הפסק גדול בין ראשון לאחרון. *שוב שתקנו שתיהן לכל א' וא' משום הנכנסין ומשום היוצאים, לא זזה ממקומה:

והטוב

(לקמן ס:) (מגילה כא.) (אחריס כך תר כן שתקנו)

*א משום הנכנסין ומשום היוצאין שוב לא זזה ממקומה]

---

עין משפט נר מצוה

כב א מיי' פ"ז מהלכות ברכות הל' ב סמג עשין כז טוש"ע או"ח סי' קסז סעיף יז:
כג ב מיי' וסמג שם טוש"ע או"ח סימן רא סעיף א:
[ב מיי' פ"ב שם הל' ז טוש"ע שם]:
כד ג מיי' פ"ה שם הל' ב סמג שם טוש"ע או"ח סי' ר סעיף ב:
כה ד טוש"ע א"ח סי' קלד סעיף ג:
כו ה מיי' פ"א מהלכות ברכות הל' ה ופי"א הלכה א סמג שם:

[שם איתא וברכת זו ברכת הזן את ה' אלהיך זו ברכת הזימון אמנם לכאורה נראה עיקר כגירסת תוס' מפני שיהיה כסדר]

## רב נסים גאון

ר' זירא חלש קביל עליה ר' אבהו אי מיתפח קטין חריך שאקי. הדבר שבשבילו נקרא ר' זירא בזה השם מפורש בבבא מציעא בפרק השוכר את הפועלים (דף פה) ר' זירא כי סליק לארץ ישראל יתיב ש' תעניתא ק' קמייתא כי היכא דלישתכח תלמודא דבבל מיניה כי היכי דלא ניטרח בגירסיה ק' מצעייתא דלא נישכוב ר' אילעא (בגמ' איתא ר' אלעזר) בשניה ונפלן עליה מילי דצבורא ק' בתרייתא כי היכי דלא נישלוט בו נורא דגיהנם כל ל' יומין הוה בדיק נפשיה שגר תנורא סליק יתיב בגויה לא הוה קא שלטא ביה נורא יומא חד יהבו ביה רבנן עינייהו וחרך שאקי וקרו ליה קטין חריך שאקיה ובמס' סנהדרין בפרק אחד דיני ממונות (דף לז) הנהו בריוני דהוו בשיבבותיה דר' זירא כי נח נפשיה דר' זירא אמרי עד האידנא הוה קטין חריך שאקי דהוה בעא עלן רחמי כו'.

## הגהות הב"ח

(א) גמ' שיברך לבעל הבית: (ב) שם ברכת המזון שתים ושלש ותניא אידך שלש וארבע סברוה: (ג) שם דאמר מר ברכה ראשונה פותח בברכת הארץ וכוללים בונה ירושלים:

## הגהות הגר"א

[א] תוס' ד"ה עד היכן. ולא משום דחשיב ברכת הזן מזמון כו'. וכזה נכתב לאחייה סי"ב (ועי' בדברי רבינו בא"ח סי' קצ"ב):

## גליון הש"ס

גמ' שהרי פועלי' עוקרין. עי' לעיל דף ט"ז ע"א תוס' ד"ה והוא ול"ע:

ויש מהן שחותם בהן ב"ברוך" ואין פותח ב"ברוך". ו"הטוב והמטיב" פותח ב"ברוך" ואין חותם ב"ברוך", מכלל דברכה בפני עצמה היא. ואמר רב נחמן בר יצחק: תדע ד"הטוב והמטיב" לאו דאורייתא – שהרי עוקרין אותה בבית האבל. כדתניא: *מה הם אומרים בבית האבל? "ברוך הטוב והמטיב"; ר"ע אומר: "ברוך דיין האמת". "הטוב והמטיב" אין, "דיין אמת" לא?! – אלא אימא: אף "הטוב והמטיב". מר זוטרא איקלע לבי רב אשי איתרע ביה מילתא, פתח ובריך: א"הטוב והמטיב, אל אמת דיין אמת, *שופט בצדק לוקח במשפט, ושליט בעולמו לעשות בו כרצונו כי כל דרכיו משפט, שהכל שלו ואנחנו עמו ועבדיו, ובכל אנחנו חייבים להודות לו ולברכו, גודר פרצות בישראל הוא יגדור את הפרצה הזאת בישראל לחיים". בלהיכן הוא חוזר? רב זביד משמיה דאביי אמר: חוזר לראש, ורבנן אמרי: למקום שפסק. והלכתא: למקום שפסק.§ א"ל ריש גלותא לרב ששת: אע"ג דרבנן קשישי אתון, פרסאי בצרכי סעודה בקיאי מינייכו, בזמן שהן שתי מטות – גדול מסב בראש ושני לו למעלה הימנו, ובזמן שהם שלש – גדול מסב באמצע, שני לו למעלה הימנו, שלישי לו למטה הימנו. אמר ליה: וכי בעי אישתעויי בהדיה, *מתריץ תרוצי ויתיב ומשתעי בהדיה! – א"ל: שאני פרסאי דמחוי ליה במחוג. מים ראשונים מהיכן מתחילין? אמר ליה: מן הגדול. – ישב גדול וישמור ידיו עד שנוטלין כולן?! – א"ל: לאלתר מייתו תכא קמיה. מים אחרונים מהיכן מתחילין? – אמר ליה: מן הקטן. וגדול יתיב וידיו מזוהמות עד שנוטלין כולן?! א"ל: לא מסלקי תכא מקמיה עד דמטו מיא לגביה. אמר רב ששת: אנא מתניתא ידענא דתניא, *כיצד סדר הסבה: גבזמן שהן שתי מטות – גדול מסב בראש ושני לו למטה הימנו, בזמן שהן שלש מטות – גדול מסב בראש, שני לו למעלה הימנו, שלישי לו למטה הימנו. דמים הראשונים מתחילין מן הגדול, המים אחרונים, בזמן שהם ה' – מתחילין מן הגדול, ובזמן שהם מאה – מתחילין מן הקטן עד שמגיעים אצל ה', וחוזרין ומתחילין מן הגדול; ולמקום שמים אחרונים חוזרין – לשם ברכה חוזרת. מסייע ליה לרב, דא"ר חייא בר אשי אמר רב: *כל הנוטל ידיו באחרונה תחלה – הוא מזומן לברכה.§ רב ורבי חייא הוו יתבי בסעודתא קמיה דרבי. אמר ליה רבי לרב: קום משי ידך! חזייה דקא מרתת, אמר ליה: בר פחתי! עיין בברכת מזונא קאמר לך. ת"ר: זאין מכבדין – לא בדרכים, ולא בגשרים ולא

ויש מהם חותם ולא פותח. כגון ברכה הסמוכה לחברתה, שהרי כבר פתח בברכה ראשונה. וברכה אחרונה שבקריאת שמע "אמת ויציב", "אמת ואמונה", שאע"פ שק"ש מפסיק בינתים – אברכות דלפניה סמוכה, והויא לה סמוכה לחברתה: הטוב והמטיב וכו'. דלאו סמוכה לחברתה היא שאינה מברכת המזון, אלא על קבורת הרוגי ביתר תקנוה: שהרי עוקרים אותה בבית האבל. אליבא דר"ע: להיכן הוא חוזר. מי שנצטרף לזימון, ואמרן לעיל אליבא דרב ששת: ברכת זימון עד "הזן", והולך זה להיות מפסיק אכילתו עד שיגמור המברך ברכת "הזן", וחזר זה שהפסיק לשנים וגמר סעודתו, להיכן הוא חוזר לברך לאחר שיגמור סעודתו? חוזר לראש. לתחלת "הזן", שהרי נתחייב בזימון שבתחלה הוקבע בג': למקום שפסק. לברכת הארץ, כשאר יחיד: ה"ג אף על גב דרבנן אתון, פרסאי בצרכי סעודה בקיאי מינייכו: בזמן שהן שתי מטות. רגילין היו לאכול בהסבה על צדו השמאלית, מוטה ורגליו לארץ, איש איש על מטה אחת: בזמן שהן שנים גדול מסב בראש. כלומר: מסב תחלה על מטתו: ושני לו למעלה הימנו. מטת השני אצל מראשותיו של גדול: ובזמן שהן שלשה גדול מסב באמצע, שני לו למעלה הימנו, שלישי לו למטה הימנו. אצל מרגלותיו: אמר ליה. רב ששת לריש גלותא: וכי בעי אשתעויי מתריץ תרוצי ויתיב. ואם רצה הגדול לדבר עם שני לו – צריך הוא לזקוף עצמו ממסיבתו, לישב זקוף, דכל זמן שהוא מוטה אינו יכול לדבר עמו, לפי שהשני לו אחורי ראשו של גדול הוא, ופני הגדול מסובין אצל אחר, וטוב לו שישב שני לו למטה הימנו, וישמע דבריו כשהוא מוטה: במחוג. מראים בידיהם ובאצבעותיהם ברמיזה: מים ראשונים מהיכן מתחילין. רב ששת קא"ל לריש גלותא: מהיכן מתחילין פרסיים מים ראשונים: לאלתר מייתו תכא קמיה. שלחן שלו מביאין מיד לפניו ואוכל. ולפני כל אחד ואחד היו מביאין שלחן קטן: לא מסלקי תכא. מקמי גדול, עד דמשו כולהו. ובעוד שהוא אוכל האחרים נוטלין מים אחרונים: שני לו למטה הימנו. שאם הולך גדול לספר עמו לא יהא צריך לזקוף: ובזמן שהם ג' שני לו למעלה הימנו. ואם בא לספר – מספר עם השלישי לו. ואם בא לספר עם השני לו – טוב הוא שיזקוף, ואל ישפיל את השני לו לפני קטן ממנו, שיהא הוא למטה וקטן ממנו למעלה הימנו: מתחילין מן הגדול. ולאלתר מעיילי תכא קמיה: ובזמן שהם מאה. לאו דוקא, דה"ה עשרה ולכל יותר מחמשה. שגנאי הוא שיסלקו השלחן מלפני הגדול כשיטול ידיו, וימתין שם יושב ובטל עד שיטלו כלם. לפיכך, כשהם יותר מחמשה – מתחילין מן הקטן היושב בסוף, ואין מסלקין שלחן מלפני הגדול עד שיגיעו המים לחמשה שאצלו: וחוזרים ומתחילין מן הגדול. ונוטלין שלחן מלפניו: למקום שמים אחרונים חוזרים. כשמגיעים לחמשה, אם נטל הגדול – מברך, ואם נוח לאחר ליטול קודם לו – הוא מברך: הנוטל ידיו באחרונה תחלה. אותו שנוטל בתחלת החמשה האחרונים, קורא "תחלה" באחרונה: אין מכבדין. לומר "היה אתה קודם": לא בדרכים. הולכי דרכים, לומר לגדול הימנו "לך לפני": ולא

והטוב והמטיב. וא"ת: ואמאי פותחת בברוך? והלא סמוכה לחברתה היא! ויש לומר: דנתקנה בפני עצמה, (היא) בשביל הרוגי ביתר*. וא"ת: אמאי אינה חותמת בברוך? וי"ל: משום דקצרה היא, רק שתקנו לאחר כך שלש מלכיות ושלש גמולות ושלש הטבות. ונאמן אתה של ברכת ההפטרה הוא מן הברכה העליונה*, ולכך הוא נכתב גדול – שבימים הראשונים היו רגילין לעמוד כל הקהל ולומר בקול רם נאמן אתה וכו' כשהיה התינוק מגיע שם: להיכן הוא חוזר. פירש רש"י: דקאי לאחד דפסיק לשנים וממתין לאחרים עד הזן, והיכן חוזר לאחר סעודתו? רבנן אמרי: למקום שפסק, והלכתא: למקום שפסק. ותימה: דא"כ, היכי הלכתא למקום שפסק אחרי שאכל אחר כך, פשיטא דיחזור אפילו להזן דהא הזן דאורייתא! ע"כ צריך לומר דקאי אהא דאמרינן לעיל, דהמברך אומר נברך שאכלנו משלו והמסובין עונים ברוך שאכלנו משלו ובטובו חיינו. להיכן הוא חוזר המברך לאחר שיענו המסובין – חוזר לראש, שהמברך חוזר ואומר נברך שאכלנו משלו ובטובו חיינו. ורבנן אמרי – למקום שפסק, שאומר ברוך שאכלנו משלו, וכן הלכתא: והר"מ מאייבר"א פירש: דקאי אשלשה שאכלו, ויצא אחד מהם לשוק, קוראים לו ומזמנים עליו. ולעיל נמי, הכי פירושו: עד היכן מקום זימון, שצריך להו לאותו אחד דקרו ליה ועני – עד נברך, ומכאן ואילך – ילך לדרכו, ואינם צריכים האחרים עוד לצירופו. והכא בעי, לאותו מן השוק להיכן הוא חוזר – למקום שפסק, דהיינו: למר – מהזן ואילך, ולמר מנברך. והשתא ניחא דלא קשה מהזן – שהרי לא *ספר בינתיים: מר זוטרא איקלע לבי רב אשי איתרע ביה מילתא. וכוותיה קיימא לן. והכי מברכין: בא"י, אמ"ה האל הטוב והמטיב, אל אמת דיין אמת שופט בצדק ולוקח במשפט ושליט במעשיו, ואנחנו עבדיו ועמו, ובכל אנחנו חייבין להודות לו ולברכו, גודר פרצות בישראל הוא יגדור פרצה זאת מעלינו ומעל האבל שבתוכנו לחיים ולשלום. הרחמן הוא ימלוך עלינו לעולם ועד וגו'. ופירש בה"ג: דאין לומר במשפט דקיימא לן בפ' במה בהמה יוצאה (דף נה:) דיש מיתה בלא חטא ויש יסורין בלא עון. ומיהו, בכך אין למחקו: בזמן שהן שתי מטות גדול מסב בראש שני לו למעלה הימנו. דהיינו: כלפי ראשו, שמסב על המטה דרך שמאל, ולמטה מקרי דרך מרגלותיו, דהיינו מימינו. ובזה מדקדק רב ששת דאם כן בעי גדול לתרוצי כפשוטיה כשמדבר עם השני, כיון שהשני למעלה הימנו. ולקמן במתניתא גרס: גדול מסב בראש, השני למטה הימנו וזהו כלפי מרגלותיו, והוא מימינו, ואז לא מתריץ ויתיב כי בעי לאשתעויי בהדי שני: אין מכבדין וכו'. וא"ת: הא אמרינן בשבת בפ' במה בהמה (ד' נא.): לוי ורב הונא בר חייא הוו קא אזלי באורחא קדמה חמריה דרב הונא לחמרא דלוי, בעי רב הונא לאפוקי מדעתיה דלוי כו', אלמא מכבדים בדרכים! וי"ל: כשיצאו לדרך כאחד – מכבדין בדרכים, אבל אם כל אחד ילך לדרכו ופגעו זה בזה ואירע להם דרך למקום אחד – אין מכבדים: אין

[כדאיתא לקמן מח:]

[ויתר ביאור תמצא בתו' פסחים קז: ד"ה חוץ]

כז א מיי' פ"ב מהלכות ברכות הלכה ח סמג עשין כז טוש"ע או"ח סי' קפט סעיף ב טוש"ע י"ד סימן שעט סעיף א:

כח ב מיי' שם פ"ה הל' ב טוש"ע או"ח סי' [קלב סעיף א ובסי'] ר סעיף ב:

כט ג מיי' פ"ז מהל' ברכות הל' א סמג שם:

ל ד מיי' וסמג שם טוש"ע או"ח סימן קסה סעיף ב:

לא ה ו מיי' שם הל' יב סמג שם טוש"ע או"ח סי' קפא סעיף ו:

לב ז מיי' שם [שו"ע י"ד סי' רמב סעיף יז בהגה]:

[עי' רש"א ועי' מג"א סי' קפג ס"ק יא דל"ל סעד]

[מס' שמחות ע"ש]

שם

[תרגום של בשל בשלמא ובת בערוך ערך טי']

תוספתא פ"ה

לעיל מג. ע"ש

## רב נסים גאון

שאני פרסאי דבמחוג מחוו והיו מבירין זה את זה ברמיזותיו של זה ומבין כל אחד מהן מה שחבירו אומר ובפ"ק דמסכת חגיגה (דף ה) ר' יהושע בן חנניה הוה קאי בי קיסר אחוי ליה ההוא מינא עמא דאהדרינהו מאריה לאפיה מינייהו אחוי ליה איהו ידו נטויה עלינו אמרו ליה לר' יהושע בן חנניה מאי אחוי לך עמא דאהדרינהו מאריה לאפיה מיניה ומאי אחוית ליה ידו נטויה עלינו אמרו ליה להוא מינא מאי אחוית ליה עמא דאהדרינהו מאריה לאפיה מיניה ומאי אחוי לך לא ידענא אמרי גברא דלא ידע מאי מחוו ליה במחוג יתיב [בגמ' איתא יחוי] קמיה מלכא וקטלוה:

## גליון הש"ס

תוס' ד"ה להיכן וכו'. ולמר מנברך נ"ל מן נודה לך [רש"א]:

וְלֹא בְּיָדַיִם מְזוֹהָמוֹת. רָבִין וְאַבַּיֵי הֲווּ קָא אָזְלִי בְּאוֹרְחָא, קַדְמֵיהּ חֲמָרֵיהּ דְּרָבִין לְדְאַבַּיֵי, וְלָא אֲמַר לֵיהּ 'נֵיזִיל מָר'. אֲמַר: מִדְּסָלֵיק הַאי מֵרַבָּנַן מִמַּעַרְבָא גַּס לֵיהּ דַּעְתֵּיהּ. כִּי מְטָא לְפִתְחָא דְּבֵי כְנִישְׁתָּא, אֲמַר לֵיהּ: נֵיעוֹל מָר. אֲמַר לֵיהּ: וְעַד הַשְׁתָּא לָאו מָר אֲנָא?! –אֲמַר לֵיהּ, הָכִי אָמַר רַבִּי יוֹחָנָן: אֵין מְכַבְּדִין אֶלָּא בְּפֶתַח שֶׁיֵּשׁ בָּהּ מְזוּזָה. *דְּאִית בַּהּ מְזוּזָה אִין, דְּלֵית בַּהּ מְזוּזָה – לָא? אֶלָּא מֵעַתָּה, בֵּית הַכְּנֶסֶת וּבֵית הַמִּדְרָשׁ דְּלֵית בְּהוּ מְזוּזָה, הָכִי נָמֵי דְּאֵין מְכַבְּדִין?! אֶלָּא אֵימָא: בְּפֶתַח הָרָאוּי לִמְזוּזָה.§ אָמַר רַב יְהוּדָה בְּרֵיהּ דְּרַב שְׁמוּאֵל בַּר שֵׁילַת מִשְּׁמֵיהּ דְּרַב: אֵין הַמְסוּבִּין רַשָּׁאִין לֶאֱכוֹל כְּלוּם עַד שֶׁיִּטְעוֹם הַבּוֹצֵעַ. יָתֵיב רַב סַפְרָא וְקָאָמַר: לִטְעוֹם אִיתְּמַר. לְמַאי נָפְקָא מִינַּהּ – *שֶׁחַיָּיב אָדָם לוֹמַר בִּלְשׁוֹן רַבּוֹ. ת"ר: *שְׁנַיִם מַמְתִּינִין זֶה לָזֶה בִּקְעָרָה, שְׁלֹשָׁה אֵין מַמְתִּינִין, הַבּוֹצֵעַ הוּא פּוֹשֵׁט יָדוֹ תְּחִלָּה, וְאִם בָּא לַחֲלוֹק כָּבוֹד לְרַבּוֹ אוֹ לְמִי שֶׁגָּדוֹל הֵימֶנּוּ – הָרְשׁוּת בְּיָדוֹ. רַבָּה בַּר בַּר חָנָה הֲוָה עָסֵיק לֵיהּ לִבְרֵיהּ בֵּי רַב שְׁמוּאֵל בַּר רַב קְטִינָא, קְדֵים וְיָתֵיב וְקָמַתְנֵי לֵיהּ לִבְרֵיהּ: אֵין הַבּוֹצֵעַ רַשַּׁאי לִבְצוֹעַ עַד שֶׁיִּכְלֶה אָמֵן מִפִּי הָעוֹנִים. רַב חִסְדָּא אָמַר: מִפִּי רוֹב הָעוֹנִים. א"ל רָמִי בַּר חָמָא: מ"ש רוּבָּא – דְּאַכַּתִּי לָא כְּלְיָא בְּרָכָה, מִיעוּטָא נָמֵי לָא כְּלְיָא בְּרָכָה! –א"ל: שֶׁאֲנִי אוֹמֵר, כָּל הָעוֹנֶה אָמֵן יוֹתֵר מִדַּאי אֵינוֹ אֶלָּא טוֹעֶה.§ ת"ר: *אֵין עוֹנִין לֹא אָמֵן חֲטוּפָה, וְלֹא אָמֵן קְטוּפָה, וְלֹא אָמֵן יְתוֹמָה, וְלֹא יִזְרוֹק בְּרָכָה מִפִּיו. בֶּן עַזַּאי אוֹמֵר: כָּל הָעוֹנֶה אָמֵן יְתוֹמָה – יִהְיוּ בָּנָיו יְתוֹמִים, חֲטוּפָה – יִתְחַטְּפוּ יָמָיו, קְטוּפָה – יִתְקַטְּפוּ יָמָיו, וְכָל הַמַּאֲרִיךְ בְּאָמֵן מַאֲרִיכִין לוֹ יָמָיו וּשְׁנוֹתָיו. רַב וּשְׁמוּאֵל הֲווּ יָתְבִי בִּסְעוּדְתָּא, אֲתָא רַב שִׁימִי בַּר חִיָּיא הֲוָה קָמְסַרְהֵב וְאָבֵיל. א"ל רַב: מַה דַּעְתָּךְ – לְאִיצְטָרוֹפֵי בַּהֲדַן? אֲנַן אֲכַלְנָא לַן! –א"ל שְׁמוּאֵל: אִלּוּ מַיְיתוּ לִי *אַרְדִּילַיָּא, וְגוֹזָלַיָּא לְאַבָּא – מִי לָא אָכְלִינַן?! תַּלְמִידֵי דְּרַב הֲווּ יָתְבִי בִּסְעוּדְתָּא, עָל רַב אַחָא. אָמְרִי: אֲתָא גַּבְרָא רַבָּא דִּמְבָרֵךְ לָן. אָמַר לְהוּ: מִי סְבָרִיתוּ דְּגָדוֹל מְבָרֵךְ?! עִיקָּר שֶׁבִּסְעוּדָּה מְבָרֵךְ. וְהִלְכְתָא: גָּדוֹל מְבָרֵךְ, אע"ג דְּאָתָא לְבַסּוֹף.§ "אָכַל דְּמַאי וכו'". הָא לָא חֲזֵי לֵיהּ! –*כֵּיוָן דְּאִי בָּעֵי – מַפְקַר לְהוּ לְנִכְסֵיהּ וְהָוֵי עָנִי, וַחֲזֵי לֵיהּ, דִּתְנַן: *מַאֲכִילִין אֶת הָעֲנִיִּים דְּמַאי וְאֶת הָאַכְסַנְיָא דְּמַאי. וְאָמַר רַב הוּנָא: תָּנָא, ב"ש אוֹמְרִים: אֵין מַאֲכִילִין אֶת הָעֲנִיִּים וְאֶת הָאַכְסַנְיָא דְּמַאי.§ "מַעֲשֵׂר רִאשׁוֹן שֶׁנִּטְּלָה תְּרוּמָתוֹ". *פְּשִׁיטָא! –לָא צְרִיכָא אֶלָּא שֶׁהִקְדִּימוֹ בְּשִׁבֳּלִים, וְהִפְרִישׁ מִמֶּנּוּ תְּרוּמַת מַעֲשֵׂר וְלֹא הִפְרִישׁ מִמֶּנּוּ תְּרוּמָה גְּדוֹלָה; וּכְדר' אַבָּהוּ, דְּאָמַר ר' אַבָּהוּ אָמַר רֵישׁ לָקִישׁ: *מַעֲשֵׂר רִאשׁוֹן שֶׁהִקְדִּימוֹ בְּשִׁבֳּלִים – פָּטוּר מִתְּרוּמָה גְּדוֹלָה, שֶׁנֶּאֱמַר: "וַהֲרֵמֹתֶם מִמֶּנּוּ תְּרוּמַת ה' מַעֲשֵׂר מִן הַמַּעֲשֵׂר" – מַעֲשֵׂר מִן הַמַּעֲשֵׂר אָמַרְתִּי לְךָ, וְלֹא תְּרוּמָה גְּדוֹלָה וּתְרוּמַת מַעֲשֵׂר מִן הַמַּעֲשֵׂר. אָמַר לֵיהּ *רַב פַּפָּא לְאַבַּיֵי: אִי הָכִי, אֲפִילּוּ הִקְדִּימוֹ בִּכְרִי נָמֵי! –אֲמַר לֵיהּ: עָלֶיךָ אָמַר קְרָא מִכֹּל

**רש"י**

וְלֹא בְּיָדַיִם מְזוֹהָמוֹת. בִּנְטִילַת מַיִם אַחֲרוֹנִים: מִמַּעַרְבָא. לְפִי שֶׁהָיָה רָבִין רָגִיל לַעֲלוֹת מִבָּבֶל לְא"י, וְלוֹמַר הוּא דְּבָרָיו מִשְּׁמוֹ שֶׁל ר' יוֹחָנָן: בְּפֶתַח הָרָאוּי לִמְזוּזָה. כְּלוֹמַר: בִּכְנִיסַת כָּל פְּתָחִים, לְמַעוּטֵי דְּרָכִים וּפִרְצוֹת: לִטְעוֹם אִיתְּמַר. אֵין חִלּוּק בַּדָּבָר, אֶלָּא שֶׁחַיָּיב לוֹמַר בִּלְשׁוֹן רַבּוֹ: קָדֵים. רַבָּה בַּר בַּר חָנָה לֵישֵׁב עַל הַשּׁוּלְחָן וְלִשְׁנוֹת לִבְנוֹ הִלְכוֹת סְעוּדָּה. לְפִי שֶׁהֶחָתָן רָגִיל לִבְלוֹעַ, וְהָיָה מְלַמְּדוֹ הֵיאַךְ יַעֲשֶׂה: לִבְצוֹעַ. לִפְרוֹס הַפְּרוּסָה מִן הַפַּת: עַד שֶׁיִּכְלֶה אָמֵן מִפִּי הָעוֹנִים. אָמֵן אַחַר בִּרְכַּת "הַמּוֹצִיא", דְּאַף עֲנִיַּית אָמֵן מִן הַבְּרָכָה הִיא, וְאָמְרִי' בְּפֶרֶק "כֵּיצַד מְבָרְכִין" (דף לט:): צָרִיךְ שֶׁתִּכְלֶה בְּרָכָה קוֹדֶם בְּצִיעָה. חֲטוּפָה. שֶׁקּוֹרִין אֶת הָאָלֶף בַּחֲטָף וְלֹא בְּפַתָּח*, וְאוֹמֵר אֲמֵן וְהוּא צָרִיךְ לוֹמַר אָמֵן: קְטוּפָה. שֶׁמְּחַסֵּר קְרִיאַת הַנּוּ"ן, שֶׁאֵינוֹ מוֹצִיאָהּ בַּפֶּה שֶׁתְּהֵא נִכֶּרֶת: יְתוֹמָה. שֶׁלֹּא שָׁמַע הַבְּרָכָה, אֶלָּא שֶׁשָּׁמַע שֶׁעוֹנִין אָמֵן. וְהָא דְּאָמְרִי' בְּ"הֶחָלִיל" (סוכה נא:) שֶׁבְּאַלֶכְּסַנְדְּרִיָּא שֶׁל מִצְרַיִם הָיוּ מְנִיפִים בְּסוּדָרִים כְּשֶׁהִגִּיעַ עֵת לַעֲנוֹת אָמֵן – אַלְמָא לָא שָׁמְעֵי וְקָא עָנוּ! הָנְהוּ מֵידַע יָדְעֵי שֶׁהֵם עוֹנִים אַחַר בְּרָכָה, וְעַל אֵיזוֹ בְּרָכָה הֵם עוֹנִים, אֶלָּא שֶׁלֹּא הָיוּ שׁוֹמְעִים אֶת הַקּוֹל: וְלֹא יִזְרוֹק בְּרָכָה מִפִּיו. בִּמְהִירוּת, שֶׁדּוֹמֶה עָלָיו כְּמַשָּׂא, אֶלָּא שֶׁחוֹק קָבוּעַ הוּא לוֹ: וְקָא מְסַרְהֵב וְאָבֵיל. מְמַהֵר לֶאֱכוֹל, כְּדֵי לְהִצְטָרֵף לְזִימּוּן וִיזַמְּנוּ עָלָיו: אֲכִילְנָא לָן. גָּמַרְנָה לָן סְעוּדָתֵנוּ קוֹדֶם שֶׁבָּאתָ, וְאִי אַתָּה מְחַיְּיבֵנוּ עוֹד בְּזִימּוּן: אִילּוּ מַיְיתוּ לִי אַרְדִּילַיָּא וְגוֹזָלַיָּא לְאַבָּא. שְׁמוּאֵל חֲבִיבִין עָלָיו אַרְדִּילַיָּא בִּקְנוּחַ סְעוּדָה – וְהֵן כְּמֵהִין וּפִטְרִיּוֹת, וּלְרַב הָיוּ חֲבִיבִין גּוֹזָלוֹת. וּשְׁמוּאֵל הָיָה קוֹרֵא לְרַב "אַבָּא" לִכְבוֹדוֹ: מִי לָא אָכְלִינַן. הִלְכָּךְ לָא גָּמְרָה סְעוּדָתָא וּמִצְטָרֵף: עִיקָּר שֶׁבִּסְעוּדָּה. אֶחָד מֵאוֹתָן שֶׁהָיוּ בִּתְחִלַּת הַהֲסִבָּה: הָא לָא חֲזֵי לֵיהּ. וְהָוְיָא לָהּ בִּרְכַּת זִמּוּן הַבָּאָה בַּעֲבֵירָה, וּכְתִיב (תהלים י) "בּוֹצֵעַ בֵּרֵךְ נִאֵץ ה'", וְאָמַר מָר(א) (בב"ק דף צד.) הֲרֵי שֶׁגָּזַל סְאָה שֶׁל חִטִּים וּטְחָנָהּ וַאֲפָאָהּ וּבֵרֵךְ עָלֶיהָ – אֵין זֶה מְבָרֵךְ אֶלָּא מְנָאֵץ: דְּמַאי. חָשׁוּד הַלְּקוּחִים מֵע"ה, סָפֵק עִשְּׂרָן סָפֵק לֹא עִשְּׂרָן: אַכְסַנְיָא. חַיִל שֶׁל מֶלֶךְ שֶׁמַּטִּיל עַל בְּנֵי הָעִיר לְזוּנָם בְּשׁוּבָם מִמִּלְחַמְתּוֹ. וַהֲרֵי הֵם כַּעֲנִיִּים, לְפִי שֶׁהֵם שֶׁלֹּא בִּמְקוֹמָם: מַאֲכִילִים אֶת הָעֲנִיִּים דְּמַאי. דְּרוֹב עַמֵּי הָאָרֶץ מְעַשְּׂרִים הֵם, וְחוּמְרָא דְּרַבָּנָן בְּעָלְמָא הוּא: שֶׁהִקְדִּימוֹ בְּשִׁבֳּלִים. לֵוִי קָדַם אֶת הַכֹּהֵן וְנָטַל מַעֲשֵׂר בְּשִׁבֳּלִים קוֹדֶם שֶׁנָּטַל כֹּהֵן תְּרוּמָה גְּדוֹלָה. וְהַכֹּהֵן הָיָה לוֹ לִיטּוֹל תְּרוּמָה גְּדוֹלָה תְּחִלָּה א' מִנ' דְּרַחֲמָנָא קַרְיֵיהּ "רֵאשִׁית" וּכְתִיב (שמות כב): "מְלֵאָתְךָ וְדִמְעֲךָ לֹא תְאַחֵר". נִמְצֵאת תְּרוּמָה גְּדוֹלָה שֶׁל כֹּהֵן בְּתוֹךְ הַמַּעֲשֵׂר הַזֶּה אֶחָד מֵחֲמִשִּׁים שֶׁבּוֹ, לְבַד מִתְּרוּמַת מַעֲשֵׂר שֶׁעַל הַלֵּוִי לְהַפְרִישׁ תְּרוּמָה מִמַּעַשְׂרוֹ: וּכְדְרַבִּי אַבָּהוּ. אַשְׁמְעִינַן מַתְנִי' דְּהָכִי הוּא כִּדְרַבִּי אַבָּהוּ, דְּפָטַר לֵיהּ לַלֵּוִי מִתְּרוּמָה גְּדוֹלָה שֶׁבּוֹ:

**תוספות**

אין המסובין רשאין לטעום עד שיטעום המברך. ותימה מההוא סבא דערבי פסחים (דף קו.) דגמין ושתי, אלמא: דשתי קודם המברך! שמא יש חלוק בין אכילה לשתיה. אי נמי, יש לומר: דלא שתה, אלא להראות לו מעשה, שלא היה צריך לומר יותר. ובירושלמי יש: כשיש לכל אחד ככרו או כוסו בידו – יכולים לשתות אפילו קודם המברך, וגבי ההוא סבא היה לו כוסו בידו. והכי איתא בירושלמי: אמר רבי בון בשם רב אין המסובין רשאין לטעום עד שיטעום המברך. ריב"ל אמר: שותין אע"פ שלא שתה המברך. ולא פליגי: רבי בון בשם רב – שזקוק לכוס אחד, דריב"ל – דהיה להל אחד רוקו בידו. ורן וזהו רדיוו שמשון בחופה אחת, שבלע החתן המוציא, והיה בולע רבינו שמשון הפת שהיה לפניו ואוכל. והשר מקוצי היה אומר: אם בלע המברך ונתן לכל אחד חלקו – אין צריך להמתין כל אחד עד שיטעום המברך. והא דאמרי' הכא אין המסובין רשאין לטעום כו' – היינו להקדים ולבלוע מן הפת שבלע המברך, אבל אחר שנתן לכל אחד חלקו – אין קפידא. וכן צריך לומר בסמוך הבולע הוא פושט ידיו תחלה לטבול פתו, ואם בא לחלוק כבוד לרבו – רשאי. ולמאי? והא אין המסובין רשאין לטעום וכו', ואין לומר דמן הטבול לחודיה קאמר, אך המברך אוכל קודם – דא"כ מה כבוד היה זהו? אבל לפי מה שפירשתי – ניחא. ויש מפרש: פושט ידיו תחלה בקערה להתחיל באכילה, ומכאן משמע שאין צריך למזוג מכוס ברכה לשאר כוסות היכא שיש בפני האורחים כוסות שאינן פגומות, אבל אם אותן כוסות פגומות – יש קפידא*:

אמן יתומה. שאין שומע הברכה מפי המברך, ועונה אחר האחרים ששמעו אמן. תימה: דהא אמרינן בסוכה (פ"ה דף נא:): באלכסנדריא של מצרים שהיה שם קהל גדול ולא היו יכולים כולם לשמוע מפי המברך והיו מניפים בסודרים כדי שידעו חתימת הברכות, ויענו אמן! וי"ל: שהיו יודעים באיזו ברכה החזן עומד, אמנם לא היו שומעים אותו. אבל הכא מיירי שאינם יודעים כלל היכן החזן עומד ומתפלל, ובאיזו ברכה הוא עומד, אלא עונה אחר האחרים בלא שמיעה ולא ידיעה*:

כל המאריך באמן מאריכין לו ימיו ושנותיו. ובלבד שלא יאריך יותר מדאי. וטעמא: לפי שאין קריאת התיבה כמשמעה כשהוא מאריך יותר מדאי. ומסקנא דמלתא דאין הבולע רשאי לבלוע עד שיכלה אמן מפי רוב העונים:

אילו מייתו לי ארדיליא וכו'. משמע דכן הלכה, דרב נמי לא פליג. אבל אי אמר הב לן ונבריך שהסיחו דעתם מלאכול – אין שלישי מצטרף עמהם:

והלכתא גדול מברך. ומיהו, אם הגדול נותן רשות לקטן לברך – שפיר, כדאשכחן (לעיל מג. מו:) דאמר ליה לרב משי ידך וכו':

ומאכילין את האכסניא דמאי. מיירי באכסניא ישראל, ומוטלין עליהם לזונם, והם כעניים, ודוקא דמאי, אבל טבל – לא, דקספו להו איסור. מיהו ואי נמי – באכסניא של גוים, שהטיל עליהם המלך. מכל מקום – דוקא דמאי, אבל טבל – לא, דאם כן פורע חובו מממונו של כהן*: ואמר רב הונא תנא בש"א אין מאכילין. וא"ת: רב הונא טעמא דב"ש אתא לאשמעי'? דהכי פריך בכמה דוכתין! ויש לומר: דקא משמע לן: דאי משכחת תנא דאמר, אין מאכילין – בית שמאי היא, ולא תיחוש לאותה משנה או ברייתא: אמר



**עין משפט נר מצוה**

לג א מיי' פ"ז מהלכות ברכות הל' יב סמג עשין כז טוש"ע או"ח סי' קפא סעיף ו:
לד ב מיי' שם הל' ה סמג שם טוש"ע או"ח סי' קסז סעיף טו:
לה ג מיי' שם הלכה ו סמג שם טוש"ע או"ח סי' קע סעיף ב:
לו ד מיי' שם הלכה ה סמג שם טוש"ע או"ח סי' קסז סעיף יז:
לז ה מיי' שם טוש"ע שם סעיף טז:
לח ו מיי' פ"א שם הל' יד סמג שם טוש"ע או"ח סי' קכד סעיף ח: [illegible] ט טוש"ע או"ח סי' קנז סעיף א:
מ ח מיי' שם ופ"ז הל' ב סמג שם טוש"ע או"ח סי' רא סעיף א:
מא ט מיי' פ"א מהל' מעשר הלכה יא:
מב י מיי' פ"א מהל' ברכות הלכה כ:
מג כ מיי' פ"ג מהלכות תרומות הלכה יג טור יו"ד סי' שלא:

**רב נסים גאון**

אין מכבדין לא בדרכים אלא בפתח הראוי למזוזה. אית לפירוש פתחים הראויים למזוזה ושאינן ראויין במסכת יומא בפ"ק (דף יא) ובמנחות בפרק הקומץ את המנחה (דף לג):
אין עונין לא אמן חטופה ולא אמן קטופה ולא אמן יתומה כו'. איתא בגמרא דבני מערבא בס"פ אלו דברים שבין בית שמאי וב"ה אי זו היא אמן יתומה ההן דחייב בברכה והוא עאני ולא ידע מה עאני:
אבל דמאי. פירשוהו בתלמוד ארץ ישראל בפרק הדין אבל פירות ספק נתקנו ספק לא נתקנו מזמנין ובפ"ק דעירובין (דירושלמי הלכה י) נמי אמרינן דמאי דמיי תיקן לא תיקן כלומר שיש בו ספק אם הוציא ממנו מעשר אי לא ולפיכך חייב להוציא ממנו תרומת מעשר ונקראת תרומת מעשר של דמאי ובמשנה סוף מסכת מעשר שני יוחנן כהן גדול העביר הודאת המעשר ובימיו אין אדם צריך לשאול על הדמאי ובמסכת סוטה בפרק עגלה ערופה (דף מח) תניא אף הוא ביטל את הוידוי וגזר על הדמאי עמד ותיקן להם הלוקח פירות מעם הארץ מפריש תרומת מעשר ונותנה לכהן וזו הברייתא בתוס' סוטה [ס"פ יג]:

**הגהות הב"ח**

(א) רש"י ד"ה הא לא חזי וכו' ואמר מר. נ"ב פ"ק דסנהדרין:

**מסורת הש"ס**

[ע' תוס' יומא יא: ד"ה ין ותוס' מנחות לג. ד"ה והא] — יומא פ"א מ"ג שבת טו. [ברכות ה.] ובספתא פ"ה גיטין נט: — [תוספתא מגילה פ"ג] — [פסחים קיט:] — [ע' נדרים פב: גיטין לא: שבת קכז: עירובין לא: פסחים לה: סוכה לה:] — [ע' עירובין פסחים סס] — ביצה יג: — תמורה ה: — [ע' תוס' שבת יג. ד"ה ע' דנותן, סוף תוס' ב"מ קא: ד"ה ותורה] — דמאי פ"ג מ"א עירובין יז: — [ועי' תוס' תו' עירובין יז: ד"ה ואת אכסניא]
תורה אור: במדבר יח

"מכל *מעשרותיכם תרימו". ומה ראית? האי אידגן והאי לא אידגן. § "מעשר שני והקדש שנפדו". פשיטא! הב"ע – [א]כגון שנתן את הקרן ולא נתן את החומש, *והא קמ"ל: דאין חומש מעכב. "השמש שאכל כזית". פשיטא! מהו דתימא שמש לא קבע – קמ"ל. § "והכותי מזמנין עליו". אמאי? לא יהא אלא עם הארץ, ותניא: [ב]אין מזמנין על ע"ה! אביי אמר: בכותי חבר. רבא אמר: אפילו תימא בכותי ע"ה, והכא בע"ה דרבנן דפליגי עליה דר' מאיר עסקינן; דתניא: *איזהו ע"ה? כל שאינו אוכל חוליו בטהרה, דברי ר"מ; וחכמים אומרים: כל שאינו מעשר פירותיו כראוי, והני כותאי – עשורי מעשרי כדחזי, דבמאי דכתיב באורייתא מזהר זהירי *דאמר מר: כל מצוה שהחזיקו בה כותים – הרבה מדקדקין בה יותר מישראל. ת"ר: *איזהו ע"ה? כל שאינו קורא ק"ש ערבית ושחרית, דברי ר' אליעזר, רבי יהושע אומר: כל שאינו מניח תפילין, בן עזאי אומר: כל שאין לו ציצית בבגדו, ר' נתן אומר: כל שאין מזוזה על פתחו, ר' נתן בר יוסף אומר: כל שיש לו בנים ואינו מגדלם לת"ת, *אחרים אומרים: אפי' קרא ושנה ולא שמש ת"ח הרי זה ע"ה. א"ר הונא: הלכה כאחרים. רמי בר חמא לא אזמין עליה דרב מנשיא בר תחליפא דתני סיפרא וספרי והלכתא. כי נח נפשיה דרמי בר חמא, אמר רבא: לא נח נפשיה דרמי בר חמא אלא דלא אזמין ארב מנשיא בר תחליפא. והתניא, אחרים אומרים: אפילו קרא ושנה ולא שמש ת"ח הרי זה ע"ה! – שאני רב מנשיא בר תחליפא דמשמע להו לרבנן, ורמי בר חמא הוא דלא דק אבתריה. ל"א: דשמע שמעתתא מפומייהו דרבנן וגרים להו – כצורבא מרבנן דמי. § "אכל טבל ומעשר וכו'". טבל – פשיטא! – לא צריכא – בטבל טבול מדרבנן. ה"ד – בעציץ שאינו נקוב. "מעשר ראשון כו'". פשיטא! – לא צריכא – כגון שהקדימו בכרי. מהו דתימא: כדאמר ליה רב פפא לאביי – קמ"ל, כדשני ליה. "מעשר שני וכו'". פשיטא! לא צריכא שנפדו ולא נפדו כהלכתן; מעשר שני – כגון שפדאו על גבי אסימון, ורחמנא אמר: °"וצרת הכסף בידך" – *כסף שיש (לו) עליו צורה, הקדש – שחללו על גבי קרקע ולא פדאו בכסף, ורחמנא אמר: °"ונתן הכסף וקם לו". "והשמש שאכל פחות מכזית". פשיטא! – אידי דתנא רישא 'כזית', תנא סיפא 'פחות מכזית'. "והנכרי אין מזמנין עליו". פשיטא! הכא במאי עסקינן – [ג]בגר שמל ולא טבל, *דאמר רבי זירא א"ר יוחנן: לעולם אינו גר עד שימול ויטבול, וכמה דלא טבל גוי הוא. § "נשים ועבדים וקטנים אין מזמנין עליהן". אמר רבי *יוסי: קטן המוטל בעריסה מזמנין עליו. והא תנן: נשים ועבדים וקטנים אין מזמנין עליהם! – הוא דאמר כרבי יהושע בן לוי, דאמר ריב"ל: אף על פי שאמרו קטן המוטל בעריסה אין מזמנין עליו – אבל עושין אותו סניף לעשרה. ואמר ריב"ל: תשעה ועבד מצטרפין. מיתיבי: *מעשה ברבי אליעזר שנכנס לבית הכנסת ולא מצא עשרה, ושחרר עבדו והשלימו לעשרה; שחרר אין, לא שחרר לא! – תרי איצטריכו, שחרר חד ונפיק בחד. והיכי עביד הכי? והאמר רב יהודה: *כל המשחרר עבדו עובר בעשה, שנאמר: °"לעולם בהם תעבודו"! – לדבר מצוה שאני. – מצוה הבאה בעבירה היא! – מצוה דרבים שאני.(א) ואמר ריב"ל: לעולם ישכים אדם לבית הכנסת כדי שיזכה וימנה עם עשרה הראשונים. שאפילו מאה באים אחריו – קבל עליו שכר כולם. *שכר כולם – סלקא דעתך?! אלא אימא: נותנין לו שכר כנגד כולם. § אמר רב הונא: תשעה וארון מצטרפין. א"ל רב נחמן: וארון גברא הוא?! – אלא אמר רב הונא: תשעה נראין כעשרה מצטרפין. אמרי לה: כי מכנפי; ואמרי לה: כי מבדרי. אמר רבי אמי: שנים ושבת מצטרפין. אמר ליה רב נחמן: ושבת גברא הוא?! – אלא אמר רבי אמי: שני תלמידי חכמים המחדדין זה את זה בהלכה מצטרפין. מחוי רב חסדא: כגון אנא ורב ששת. מחוי רב ששת: כגון אנא ורב חסדא. § א"ר יוחנן: קטן פורח מזמנין עליו. תנ"ה: קטן שהביא שתי שערות מזמנין עליו, ושלא הביא שתי שערות – אין מזמנין עליו, ואין מדקדקין בקטן. הא גופא קשיא! אמרת: הביא שתי שערות – אין, לא הביא – לא, והדר תני: אין מדקדקין בקטן, לאתויי מאי? לאו לאתויי

תורה אור: במדבר יח | דברים יד | ויקרא כז

**רש"י**

מכל מעשרותיכם. בפרשת לוים כתיב "ואל הלוים תדבר", וכתיב בהאי קרא "את כל תרומת ה'" – כל צד תרומה שבו חייבים להפריש ממנו: האי אידגן. משעה שנתמרח בכרי נעשה דגן, וכיון דאיקרי דגן – חלה עליו רשות כהן תחלה, דכתיב "ראשית דגנך תתן לו". אבל בשבלים לא אידגן, ולא חלה עליו רשות כהן: מעשר שני והקדש. אם הבעלים פודין אותו מוסיפין חומש: לא קבע. אין לו קביעות, לפי שהולך ובא: והכא בע"ה דרבנן. ברייתא דקתני, "אין מזמנין על ע"ה" – בע"ה דרבנן: דפליגי עליה דר"מ. וקאמרי כשאינו מעשר פירותיו, הלכך כותי מזמנין עליו – דעשורי מעשר: איזהו עם הארץ. שדברו חכמים בכל מקום: שלא שמש ת"ח. הוא הגמרא התלויה בסברא, שהיו נותנים לדברי משנה טעם והיו מתקפים יחד ועוסקים בכך, והיא דוגמת הגמרא שסדרו האמוראים: לא אזמין עליה. רמי בר חמא לא רצה לצרפו לשלשה לזימון: דמשמע. משמש: ורמי בר חמא הוא דלא דק. לא בדק לשאול מדת רב מנשיא: שלא נטלה תרומתו. קס"ד: תרומת מעשר קאמר: פשיטא. דאין מזמנין דהיינו טבל: שהקדימו בכרי. לאחר שנתמרח והוקבע לתרומה מן התורה, קדם לוי את הכהן ונטל מעשר ראשון תחלה, ואחד מחמשים שבו היה ראוי לתרומה גדולה לכהן. ו"שלא ניטלה תרומתו דקתני" – לאו תרומת מעשר קאמר, אלא תרומה גדולה: מהו דתימא כדאמר ליה רב פפא לאביי. לעיל; אי הכי, אפילו הקדימו בכרי נמי – קמ"ל: אסימון. כסף שלא נקבע בו צורה, וקורין לו פלוו"ן בלע"ז: עד שימול ויטבול. ביבמות (ד' מו:) נפקא לן מ"ויקח משה את הדם ויזרוק על העם" ואין הזאה בלא טבילה: סניף. חבור לזימון עשרה. וכי אמר רב אסי – נמי לעשרה קאמר: מצוה דרבים. להוציא רבים ידי חובתם בקדושה: תשעה נראין כעשרה. מפרש ואזיל לה: אמרי לה כי מכנפי. הוו נראים כעשרה, שאין אדם מבחין בהן כל כך, מתוך שהן יחד: ואמרי לה כי מבדרי. נראין טפי מרובין: שני תלמידי חכמים המחדדין זה את זה בהלכה מצטרפין. להיות שלשה: קטן פורח. שהביא סימנים, ולא בא לכלל שניו: לאתויי

**תוספות**

אמר רב הונא הלכה כאחרים. והאידנא אין אנו מדקדקים ורגילים אנו לזמן בעמי הארץ. כדאמרינן בחגיגה (פ"ג דף כב.): כמאן מקבלינן האידנא סהדותא מע"ה – כמאן, כרבי יוסי, כדי שלא יהא כל אחד הולך ובונה במה לעצמו*: מצוה דרבים שאני. מכאן קשה לה"ג, דפירש דמי שמת לו מת בי"ט האחרון דאבילות נוהג, ולא אתי י"ט האחרון דרבנן ודחי אבילות דאורייתא, דכתיב (עמוס ח) ואחריתה כיום מר. דהכא חזינן דאתיא תפלה דרבנן ודחיא קרא דלעולם בהם תעבודו! וכן משמע נמי בריש כתובות (דף ד.): גבי חתן נוהג ז' ימי המשתה, ואח"כ נוהג ז' ימי אבילות, ומדשבעת ימי המשתה מבטלין אבלות דאורייתא – כל שכן יום טוב שני: קטן פורח מזמנין עליו. פרש"י: שהביא שתי שערות, ועדיין לא הגיע לי"ג שנה ויום אחד. ולא נהירא. דא"כ אמאי אמר בסמוך לאתויי קטן פורח? היינו שהביא שתי שערות דקתני בברייתא בהדיא! ע"כ פר"ת: קטן פורח – בתוך י"ג שנה ועדיין לא הביא שתי שערות ידועות, שאינן גדולות כדי לכוף ראשן לעיקרן שכן הוא שיעורם, ולהכי קרי ליה פורח – שפרחו ולמחו בו שערות אבל אינן גדולות כל השיעור. והשתא ה"פ: אמרת הביא, דמשמע הביא דוקא, והדר קתני אין מדקדקין בקטן דמשמע אפילו לא הביא, אלא ש"מ לאתויי קטן פורח, ואתי סיפא לגלויי רישא דמה שהוא אומר ברישא הביא שתי שערות – היינו פורחות, שאינן שערות ממש, ובדפירש, שנכנס בתוך י"ג שנה. ואר"ת: והא אמרינן לעיל קטן המוטל בעריסה עושין אותו סניף! וי"ל: דהתם איירי בעשרה והכא מיירי בשלשה, או שמא פליגי אהדדי: ולית

**עין משפט נר מצוה**

מד א מיי' פ"ה מהל' ברכות הלכה כ:
[וע"ע תוס' חגיגה כב. ד"ה כמאן]
מה ב טוש"ע או"ח סי' קנט ס"ג [דהאידנא מזמנין]:
מו ג טוש"ע שם סעיף ז:
[עי' תוס' שבת קכז: ד"ה הא קמ"ל]
מז ד מיי' פי"ג מהל' אסורי ביאה הלכה ו סמג לאוין קטז טוש"ע יו"ד סי' רסח סעיף ב:
מח ה ו מיי' פ"ט מהל' עבדים הל' ו סמג עשין פו טוש"ע יו"ד סי' רסז סעיף עט:
מט ז מיי' פ"ח מהל' תפלה הלכה א סמג עשין יט טוש"ע או"ח סי' נ סעיף יד [רב אלפס לעיל דף ו. וברא"ש שם סימן ז]:

**הגהות הב"ח**

(א) גמ' מצוה דרבים שאני. נ"ב עמ"ש במס' גיטין דף מ"ג ע"ב ול"ע גם נ"ע משמעה ערוכה לגיטין דף מ"א היכא דעבד הוא חציו עבד וחציו בן חורין דכופין את רבו לשחררו כדי לקיים מצות פריה ורביה אף שאינו מצוה דרבים ובני ה"ר הכרך השיב דשאני בעבד שהוא חציו עבד וחציו בן חורין וכן בשפחה שחציה בת חורין לפי הכבות המתקנן בגיטין דף מ"ג כי שם שהוא בעצמו דהיינו כגון עשה עבירה שחרר חציו והנית חציו א"כ הוא נקרא פושע שגרם שעבד או שפחה לא יוכלו לישא עבד ושפחה וקיים לא תהו בראה אלא לשבת ע"כ קונסין אותו אף לעבור עבירה לשחררם לגמרי כדי לזכות לעבד ושפחה כיון דהוא הגורם להם העבירה והוא כעין שכתבו תוס' לשם דהיכא דהוא פושע שוב אין מזכין אותו בה"ג כאן דאיפכא היכא שהתחיל העבירה כופין לו לעשות עבירה כדי לזכות לעבד אבל זה אינו דהא היכא שהתחיל העבירה בזה היכא דמשחרר חצי עבדו הוא קונה ומקנסין למ"ד [בכסף פליגי ומוקי למתניתין] דכסף בעבד של שני שותפים דלאו קונה לו"ה וכופין רבו שני לשחררו והוא לא פשע ולא גרם לו העבירה שוב מצאתי בתוספות למסכת שבת דף ד' שכתבו דגם מצות פ"ו הוא כמו מצוה גדולה ומ"מ הוא דוחק וכן כתבו תוס' במסכת עירובין דף לב ע"ב ד"ה ולא לעבר עם הארץ כו':

**גליון הש"ס**

גמ' תשעה וארון. עי' שבת לב ע"א תוס' ד"ה על שקורין ובמהרש"א שם:

**מסורת הש"ס**

[מתנותיכם כל"ל ס... עירובין לא: ד"ה [רשב"א] וכן איתא בשבת קכז: וכן במדבר יח פכ"ט]
[גיטין סא. תוספו' פ"ג]
[קדושין עו. גיטין ז.]
סוטה כב. ע"ש
[עי' תוס' לעיל כ... אחרים]
[ב"מ מז:]
[ועי' תוס' שבת קכ ונתן]
יבמות מו:
[נ"ל רב אסי מפרש"י ד"ה סניף]
גיטין לח:
גיטין שם ויקרא כה [סוכה ל: ב"ק צד.]
[מגילה כב:]

לאתויי קטן פורח. ולית הלכתא ככל הני שמעתתא אלא כי הא *דאמר רב נחמן: אקטן היודע למי מברכין – מזמנין עליו. אביי ורבא הוו יתבי קמיה דרבה, אמר להו רבה: למי מברכין? אמרי ליה: לרחמנא. –ורחמנא היכא יתיב? רבא אחוי לשמי טללא, אביי נפק לברא אחוי כלפי שמיא. אמר להו רבה: תרוייכו רבנן הויתו. היינו דאמרי אינשי: *בוצין בוצין מקטפיה ידיע.§ וא"ר יהודה בריה דרב שמואל בר שילת משמיה דרב: בתשעה אכלו דגן ואחד אכל ירק – מצטרפין. א"ר זירא, בעאי מיניה מרב יהודה: שמנה מהו? שבעה מהו? ג–א"ל: לא שנא. ששה(א) *ודאי לא מבעיא לי. א"ל רבי ירמיה: שפיר עבדת דלא איבעיא לך, התם טעמא מאי – משום דאיכא רובא, הכא נמי – איכא רובא. ואיהו סבר: *דרובא דמינכר בעינן.§ ינאי מלכא ומלכתא כריכו ריפתא בהדי הדדי, ומדקטל להו לרבנן – לא הוה ליה איניש לברוכי להו. אמר לה לדביתהו: מאן יהיב לן גברא *דמברך לן? אמרה ליה: אשתבע לי דאי מייתינא לך גברא – דלא מצערת ליה. אשתבע לה. אייתיתיה לשמעון בן שטח אחוה, אותביה בין דידיה לדידה. אמר ליה: חזית כמה יקרא עבדינא לך! –אמר ליה: לאו את קא מוקרת לי, אלא אורייתא היא דמוקרא לי, דכתיב °"סלסלה ותרוממך *תכבדך כי תחבקנה". אמר לה: קא חזית דלא מקבל מרות! יהבו ליה כסא לברוכי. אמר: היכי אבריך – "ברוך שאכל ינאי וחביריו משלו"? שתייה לההוא כסא. יהבו ליה כסא אחרינא ובריך. א"ר אבא בריה דרב חייא בר אבא (*א"ר יוחנן): שמעון בן שטח *דעבד – לגרמיה הוא דעבד, דהכי אמר ר' חייא בר אבא אר"י: לעולם אינו מוציא את הרבים ידי חובתן עד שיאכל כזית דגן.(ב) מיתיבי, רשב"ג אומר: עלה והסב עמהם, האפילו לא טבל עמהם אלא בציר, ולא אכל עמהם אלא גרוגרת אחת – מצטרף! –איצטרופי מצטרף, אבל להוציא את הרבים ידי חובתן – עד שיאכל כזית דגן. איתמר נמי, אמר רב חנא בר יהודה משמיה דרבא: אפי' לא טבל

**רש"י**

לאתויי קטן פורח. שאין מדקדקין בו אם בא לכלל שנים או לאו. ומה הן שנים – י"ג שנים ויום אחד: טללא. גג(ג): מקניה. מקן שלו, מקטנותו: בוצין. דלעת ואית דגרסי מ"קטפיה" וקטף הוא שרף האילן, כלומר: משעה שהוא חונט ויוצא מתוך השרף, ניכר אם יהיה טוב: ואיהו סבר. רבי זירא שהיה קובל (ד) ומתחרט על שלא שאל על הששה, סבר: דילמא רובא דמנכר שפיר בעינן דליכול דגן, ואי בעי מיניה ששה לא היה מתיר: ינאי מלכא. ממלכי בית חשמונאי היה, והרג חכמי ישראל שבאו לפסלו מן הכהונה, במסכת קידושין (דף סו.): סלסלה ותרוממך. סיפיה דקרא: "תכבדך כי תחבקנה": היכי אבריך. ולא נהניתי, אומר: נברך שאכל ינאי וחביריו משלו? כלומר: שמעון בן שטח דעבד. שבירך להוציאם ידי חובתם בשביל כוס אחד ששתה: לגרמיה הוא דעבד. אין אדם מודה לו: עד שיאכל כזית דגן. ומכי אכל כזית דגן מיהא מפיק, אף על גב דכזית דגן שיעורא דרבנן הוא, כדאמר בפרק "מי שמתו" (דף כ:). מיהו, כיון דמיחייב מדרבנן – מחוייב בדבר קרינן ביה. ומוציא רבים ידי חובתן. וא"ת: בקטן שהגיע לחינוך הא לא אמר הכי? ההוא אפי' מדרבנן לא מיחייב, דעליה דאבוה(ה) הוא דרמי לחנוכיה. ובעל ה"ג פסק דוקא דאכלו איניהו כזית או כביצה דכוותיה, אבל אכלו ושבעו – לא מפיק, ואי אפשר להעמידה. דהא ינאי וחבריו אכלו ושבעו, ואפקינהו שמעון בן שטח. ואע"ג דלגרמיה הוא דעבד – טעמא משום דלא אכל כזית דגן, הא אכל כזית דגן – הכי נמי: ובשבת

**תוספות**

ולית הלכתא ככל הני שמעתתא אלא כי הא קטן היודע. משמע דקאי נמי ארבי יוחנן; ולא נהירא, שהרי אין דרך הגמרא שסותר דברי אמוראים והברייתא שהביא ראיה לדברי ר' יוחנן בלא שום טעם. וי"ל: דקאי אקטן פורח, כלומר: קטן פורח(ו) מזמנין עליו – היינו דוקא היודע למי מברכין, ותרוייהו בעינן. ולפירושינו נ"ל: דלא מייתי עובדא דאביי ורבא לענין אזמוני עלייהו, אלא לפרש מהו קטן היודע למי מברכין. דמסתמא לא פורחים הוו, דאם כן, מהו רבותייהו אם יודעים למי מברכין? ורבה נמי דעבד – היינו להראות שיש בהם בינה והם קטנים, ולא מזמנין עלייהו. ואומר ר"ת: אף על פי דלית הלכתא ככל הני שמעתתא, מזהו הורה ריב"ל דאמר קטן ממש עושין אותו סניף לעשרה. והכא דבעינן פורח ויודע – היינו דוקא בשלשה. ולית הלכתא ככל הני שמעתתא – לא קאי אריב"ל. ודיקא נמי, שהרי מפסיק הגמרא בינתיים באותו מעשה [דר' אליעזר] דלעולם ישכים אדם, ותניא כוותיה. אלא קאי אהני שמעתתא דבתר תניא כוותיה דישכים, כגון: תשעה וארון, ושבת ושנים, ותשעה נראין כעשרה, ושנים מחדדים, וקטן פורח. אע"ג דתנא ברייתא הכי לאתויי פורח, יעמידנה רב נחמן באינו יודע למי מברכין, והיינו נמי כריב"ל דאמר לעיל קטן אין מזמנין עליו. פי': מוטל בעריסה, עד שידע למי מברכין, אבל עושין אותו סניף לעשרה. פי': לברכת המזון, וה"ה לתפלה דהכא לא פליג רב נחמן, דכי בעי יודע ופורח כדפי' – ה"מ לזמון שלשה, אבל לסניף – מודה לריב"ל דסניף לעשרה, וה"ה לתפלה קטן מצטרף. ודיקא נמי, דפריך עלה ממעשה דר' אליעזר שהיה לתפלה, לריב"ל דמיירי בזהמ"ז. ומיהו, תימה: דבנ"ר (פ' נא) קאמר עלה דריב"ל: הלא הוא דמיתא – לברכת המזון, אבל לתפלה – לא, והיה אומר ר"ת: דאין הלכה כן, לפי שחולק על הגמרא שלנו. דודאי ריב"ל לענין תפלה נמי קאמר, מדפריך מעובדא דר' אליעזר דמיירי בתפלה. ויש מצרפין קטן לתפלה רק שיהא חומש בידו, ואומר ר"ת: דמנהג שטות הוא, דכי היכי דאמר אטו חומש גברא הוא? ה"נ: אטו ארון גברא הוא? ועוד: הא דקאמר קטן מצטרף – היינו אפי' בלא חומש. ועוד: דלא חזינן בשום דוכתא דמהני, אלא בעובדא דעבור השנה שסעולין בעליה, בפרקי דרבי אליעזר (פ"ח), דקאמר בשלשה מעברין את השנה. ר' אליעזר אומר: בעשרה, ואם נתמעטו – מביאין ספר תורה ועושין עגולה וכו', ואין מזכיר שם שיהא הקטן אותו ספר תורה. והתם נמי לא קאמר אלא ספר תורה שעשוי בגליון, אבל חומשין שלנו – לא. ומיהו קאמר בירושלמי, א"ר יוסי:(ז) זמנין אכלית עם ר' חלפתא אבא ועם ר' חנינה בר סרסי חבירי ולא מזמנין עלוי עד שהבאתי שתי שערות. ומשם משמע להצטרף לזמון לא עבדין עד שיביא שתי שערות, הא לתפלה עבדי. ומתוך ירושלמי זה פי' ר"י דאין עושין קטן סניף לעשרה לא לתפלה ולא לברכת המזון. וגם היה אומר ר"י שגם רבינו תם עצמו לא היה נוהג לעשות כן קטן סניף לעשרה ולא עשה מעשה. והלכך אפי' חומש בידו לא מהני דלפירשנו, כיון דלא אתהני קטן לבדו גם חומש בידו לא אתהני. ומיהו, *קטן פורח ויודע למי מברכין, משמע שמברכין עליו גם בשלשה, כברייתא וליכא מאן דפליג. וזה לשון רבינו שפוסק, מסקנא דמלתא: אין עושין קטן סניף לעשרה לזמון ולתפלה ולשלשה עד שיביא שתי שערות, כעובדא דר' יוסי ברבי חלפתא בירושלמי, והא דאמרינן בירושלמי: קטן וס"ת עושין אותו סניף. אומר ר"י: דגרס התם קטן לס"ת, כלומר: סניף לקריאת התורה קאמר ודוקא התם כדאיתא במגילה (פ"ג דף כג.) דקטן עולה למנין שבעה, דקאמר: הכל עולין למנין שבעה, אפי' קטן אפי' אשה, אי לאו משום כבוד צבור, אבל לשאר דברים – לא. ואפי' אם אשכחן בשום דוכתא דקטן [וחומש מצטרף] אפי' לתפלה – היינו דוקא העשוי בגליון, אבל חומשין שלנו לא. ולפי' ר"ת חומש אינו מועיל כלל כדי קטן, אבל קטן לחוד הוי סניף, כדקאמר גבי עובדא דר' אליעזר. ור"ת פי' דהסיה ירושלמי דרבי יוסי בר' חלפתא – דוקא בשלשה מיירי: **אביי** ורבא הוו יתבי וכו'. ואם תאמר: היכי דמי, אי הוו קטנים פורחים, מאי רבותא הוה בהו שהביטו כלפי מעלה? אלא לריך לומר: דהאי לאו לאזמוני עלייהו קא מנסי להו, כי היו קטנים טובא; אלא לנסותינהו קא עביד שהיה בהם בינה: **תשעה** שאכלו דגן ואחד ירק מצטרפין. והכי הלכתא, שאחד שאכל ירק או שתה כוס יין – מצטרף, ואפילו נברך שאכלנו יכולין לומר, שהרי שתיה בכלל אכילה. ויש שרוצים לומר דהיינו דוקא לזמון עשרה, אבל לשלשה – לא מצטרפי, דהרי לעיל נמי מחמרינן טפי בצירוף שלשה מעשרה. ומיהו, בירושלמי תני: שנים שאכלו פת ואחד ירק – מזמנין, וכן פסק ר"י בתוספתו. והשר מקוצי מפרש דאין הלכה כאותה ברייתא דירושלמי; חדא: שהרי מסיק עלה התם: מתני' כרבן שמעון בן גמליאל, כלומר: ורבנן פליגי, דלא מצטרפי, ואין הלכה כיחיד. ועוד: דא"כ קשה דרבי יוחנן אדר' יוחנן; דהכא א"ר יוחנן דלעולם אינו מוציא עד שיאכל כזית דגן, הא מצטרף – שפיר. אפי' לא טעם אלא שתיה, כעובדא דר"ש בן שטח, ובירושלמי קא"ר יוחנן: לעולם אין מזמנין עד שיאכל כזית, ומשמע אפי' *מצטרף. אלא ש"מ: כאן לעשרה, ובירושלמי איירי בזמון שלשה. ולהשלים לעשרה אפי' איכא שנים ושלשה ששתו – מצטרפין, ושתיה בכלל אכילה, ולא קפדינן אלא ארובא דמינכר: **עד** שיאכל כזית דגן. משמע, שאם אכל כזית דגן – שיכול להוציא אף אחרים שאכלו על השובע. ותימה: והרי כזית אינו חייב אלא מדרבנן. והיכי אתי דרבנן ופטר דאורייתא? דהא אמרינן בפרק מי שמתו (ד' כ:): תבא מארה למי שאשתו ובניו מברכים לו, ולא מצי לאוקומי [הא] דשרו לקטן שיכול להוציא אביו – אלא בדאכל אביו כזית, דאתי קטן דרבנן שהגיע לחינוך, ופטר אביו שאינו חייב אלא מדרבנן. הא אם אכל אביו כדי שביעה – אינו יכול לפטרו! ופרש"י: דמחויב דרבנן מחויב קרינן ביה, אבל קטן

**עין משפט נר מצוה**

נ א מיי' פ"ה מהלכות ברכות הלכה ז סמג עשין כז טוש"ע או"ח סי' קצט סעיף י:

נא ב ג ד ה מיי' שם הל' ח וסמג שם טוש"ע או"ח סי' קצז סעיף ב:

נב ו טוש"ע שם סעיף ד:

תיבת ודאי הוא ר"ת וד' אכלו ירק (כ"מ). ויש גורסים וי דא וכ"ה בילקוט ובזה א"ש דברי רש"י ד"ה ואיהו: [ועי' לעיל כ"ה ע"ב פחות מג' כו' שלשה ארבעה כו' תשעה מהו כו' עשרה ודאי לא מיבעיא לי. הריעב"ץ]

[לפמ"ש מהרש"א בח"א אין זה כנוסח הגמ' אלא רש"י מפרש ע"פ סוטה דקראה ע"ש ועי' תוס' עירובין סג. ד"ה בלר וכו' מ"ש בשם הירושלמי וע"ע תו' כ"ק לב: ד"ה משולש]

**מסורת הש"ס**

[ערכין ג.]

[גי' הערוך בנין [illegible] ידיעי ע"ש ומצאתי בתוס' סוכה נו: ד"ה בוצינא דגרסי בוצינא מקטפי' ידיע]

[עו"ג לז:]

[עיין תוס' פסחים קג: ד"ה כיון]

משלי ד

[ג' תיבות הללו נראה לטעות הדפוס הוא]

[קטן פורח כפי' ר"ח ויודע כצ"ל]

נ"ל להצטרף

**רב נסים גאון**

ינאי מלכא כריך ריפתא ולא הוה ליה איניש דמברך ליה אמרה ליה דביתהו השתא דקטלת לכולהו רבנן מאן מברך לך. איתא מפורש ומבוארא במס' קדושין בפ' האומר לחברו (דף סו) שנתגלגלה [ותקה] [הרעה] ע"י אלעזר בן פועירה וע"י יהודה בן גדידיה ויהרגו כל חכמי ישראל והיה העולם משתומם עד שבא שמעון בן שטח והחזיר את התורה ליושנה ובמס' סוטה בפ' עגלה ערופה (ד' מז) אמרי' כד קטל ינאי מלכא לרבנן אמטינהו [illegible] לשמעון בן שטח ואיתא נמי בפ' כל ישראל יש להם חלק (דף קז) ובתלמוד א"י דהאי פירקא אמרי' ש' נזירים עלו בימי שמעון בן שטח ק"נ מהן מצאו להן פתח וק"נ לא מצאו להן פתח שלח שמעון בן שטח לגבי ינאי מלכא אמר ליה איכא הכא שלש מאות נזירין ואינון בעיין תשע מאה קורבנין הב לי פלגא מן דידך ואנא יהיב פלגא מן דידי שלח ליה ת"נ אזל לישנא בישא ואמר ליה דלא יהב ליה מן דיליה כלום שמע ינאי מלכא וכעס דחיל שמעון בן שטח וערק בתר יומין סלקין בני נשי דרבבן מן מלכותיה דפרס לגבי ינאי מלכא מדאכלין אמרין נהירין אנן דהוה הכא [חד גבר סב וכו'] ועיקרה דמילתא בבראשית דר' הושעיא בפרשת וירא יעקב כי יש שבר במצרים דקשיא הא אדאית בגמ' דידן כי אפשר שתכף זה המעשה וזה הכעס שנפל בלבו של ינאי המלך על ר' שמעון בן שטח אירע זה המעשה הנזכר והוא שנאמר בו נזרקה בו מינות ויהרגו כל חכמי ישראל וכשראה שמעון בן שטח חשש שמא יתאנה עליו ויענישנו על אותו המעשה שהיה והלך ונתחבא עד שקבלה אחותו עליו אמונת שלום מן המלך ואחר כן יצא מהמחבא ונכנס אצלו וזה ששלח לו מן הנזירין הב פלגא מדידך ואנא יהיב פלגא מדידי אמת הוו דבריו כי כמו שעיין בנדריהם וחקרם יפה עד שנתברר לו שאינן קיימין והורה להן שפטורין הם מלהביא קרבן עליהם כדמפרש באותו המעשה ק"נ מצאו להם פתח היה לו לומר פלגא מדידי כלומר מתורתו והוראתו וזהו צד התירוץ שלו וכבר שאלו המלך בשביל הדבר הזה והחזיר לו תשובה בזה הענין כדאמרינן (שם) אתא עאל יתיב בין מלכא למלכתא אמר ליה אפלית בי אמר ליה לא אפלית בך את מן ממונך ואנא מן אורייתי דכתיב (קהלת ז) כי בצל החכמה בצל הכסף:

**גליון הש"ס**

גמ' אביי ורבא כו'. [illegible] ורבה בר רב חנן: רש"י ד"ה עד שיאכל כו' ההוא אפי' מדרבנן כו'. וק"ל [illegible] וצ"ע:

**הגהות הב"ח** (א) גמ' לא שנא ששה (ולאי) תז"מ ונ"ב רש"י גורס ווי: (ב) שם כזית דגן וכדתניא רשב"ג אומר עלה והסב: (ג) רש"י ד"ה טללא גג הס"ד ואח"כ מ"ה בוצין דלעת מקניה וכו' מקטנותו ואית דגרסי: (ד) ד"ה ואיהו וכו' שהיה קובל. נ"ב נראה שהיה גורס בגמרא ששה ווי לא קמיבעיא לי שהיה מילר על שלא שאל אותו וכ"א להדיא בב"ר פ' נ"א: (ה) ד"ה עד שיאכל וכו' דעליה דאבוה: (ו) תוס' ד"ה ולית וכו' כלומר קטן פורח דמזמנין: (ז) בא"ד אמר ר' יוסי כמה זמנין אכלית:

**עין משפט נר מצוה**

נג א ב מיי' פ"ב מהל' ברכות הלכה ה סמג עשין כז טור או"ח סי' קפז וקפח:

נד ג מיי' שם הלכה ה וסמג שם טוש"ע או"ח סי' קפח סעיף ד ה:

נה ד ה מיי' שם הל' ג סמג שם טור או"ח סי' קפז:

טבל עמהם אלא בציר, ולא אכל עמהם אלא גרוגרת אחת – מצטרף, ולהוציא את הרבים ידי חובתם – אינו מוציא עד שיאכל כזית דגן.§ אמר רב חנא בר יהודה משמיה דרבא הלכתא: אכל עלה ירק ושתה כוס של יין – מצטרף, להוציא – אינו מוציא עד שיאכל כזית דגן. אמר רב נחמן: משה תקן לישראל ברכת "הזן" בשעה שירד להם מן, יהושע תקן להם ברכת הארץ(א) כיון שנכנסו לארץ, דוד ושלמה תקנו "בונה ירושלים". דוד תקן "על ישראל עמך ועל ירושלים עירך", ושלמה תקן "על הבית הגדול והקדוש", "הטוב והמטיב" ביבנה תקנוה כנגד הרוגי ביתר. דאמר רב מתנא: *אותו היום שניתנו הרוגי ביתר לקבורה תקנו ביבנה "הטוב והמטיב", "הטוב" – שלא הסריחו, "והמטיב" – שניתנו לקבורה.§ תנו רבנן, סדר ברכת המזון כך היא: ברכה ראשונה – ברכת "הזן", שניה – ברכת הארץ, שלישית – "בונה ירושלים", רביעית – "הטוב והמטיב", ובשבת – מתחיל בנחמה ומסיים בנחמה ואומר קדושת היום באמצע; רבי אליעזר אומר: רצה לאומרה בנחמה – אומרה, בברכת הארץ – אומרה, בברכה שתקנו חכמים ביבנה – אומרה. וחכמים אומרים: אינו אומרה אלא בנחמה בלבד. חכמים היינו תנא קמא! –איכא בינייהו דיעבד.§ *תנו רבנן: מנין לברכת המזון מן התורה? שנאמר: "ואכלת ושבעת[א] וברכת" – *זו ברכת הזן, "את ה' אלהיך" – זו ברכת הזימון, "על הארץ" – זו ברכת הארץ, "הטובה" – זו בונה ירושלים, וכן הוא אומר: "ההר הטוב הזה והלבנון", "אשר נתן לך" – זו הטוב והמטיב. אין לי אלא לאחריו, לפניו מנין? אמרת קל וחומר, *כשהוא שבע מברך כשהוא רעב לא כל שכן? [ג] רבי אומר: [אינו צריך,] "ואכלת ושבעת וברכת" – [ג] זו ברכת הזן, אבל ברכת הזימון – מ"גדלו לה' אתי" נפקא, "על הארץ" – זו ברכת הארץ, "הטובה" – זו בונה ירושלים, וכן הוא אומר "ההר הטוב הזה והלבנון", "הטוב והמטיב" – ביבנה תקנוה. אין לי אלא לאחריו, לפניו מנין? תלמוד לומר: "אשר נתן לך" – משנתן לך. רבי יצחק אומר: אינו צריך, הרי הוא אומר "וברך את לחמך ואת מימיך", אל תקרי "וברך" אלא "וברך", ואימתי קרוי לחם – קודם שיאכלנו. ר' נתן אומר: אינו צריך, הרי הוא אומר: "כבאכם העיר כן תמצאון אותו בטרם יעלה הבמתה לאכול כי לא יאכל העם עד באו כי הוא יברך הזבח אחרי כן יאכלו הקראים". וכל כך למה? לפי שהנשים דברניות הן. ושמואל אמר: כדי להסתכל ביפיו של שאול, דכתיב: "משכמו ומעלה גבה מכל העם". ורבי יוחנן אמר: לפי שאין מלכות נוגעת בחברתה אפי' כמלא נימא.§ ואין לי אלא ברכת המזון, ברכת התורה מנין? אמר ר' ישמעאל: ק"ו, על חיי שעה מברך – על חיי עוה"ב לא כ"ש? רבי חייא בר נחמני תלמידו של רבי ישמעאל אומר משום רבי ישמעאל: אינו צריך, הרי הוא אומר: "על הארץ הטובה אשר נתן לך", ולהלן הוא אומר: "ואתנה לך את לחת האבן והתורה והמצוה וגו'". ר"מ אומר: מנין שכשם שמברך על הטובה כך מברך על הרעה? ת"ל: "אשר נתן לך ה' אלהיך"(ב) – דיינך, בכל דין שדנך, בין מדה טובה ובין מדה פורענות. רבי יהודה בן בתירה אומר: אינו צריך, הרי הוא אומר: "טובה", "הטובה"; *"טובה" – זו תורה, וכן הוא אומר: "כי לקח טוב נתתי לכם", "הטובה" – זו בנין ירושלים, וכן הוא אומר "ההר הטוב הזה והלבנון".§ תניא, רבי אליעזר אומר: כל שלא אמר "ארץ חמדה טובה ורחבה", בברכת הארץ ו"מלכות בית דוד" ב"בונה ירושלים" – לא יצא ידי חובתו; נחום הזקן אומר: צריך שיזכור בה ברית. רבי יוסי אומר: צריך שיזכור בה תורה. פלימו אומר: צריך שיקדים ברית לתורה, שזו נתנה בשלש בריתות וזו

**רש"י**

ובשבת מתחיל בנחמה. כלומר: אינו צריך לא לסיים ולא להתחיל בשל שבת, אלא מתחיל ומסיים בנחמה. בנין ירושלים קרי נחמה, כל היכי דמתחיל בין "רחם" בין "נחמנו": בברכה שתקנו חכמים. ב"הטוב והמטיב": איכא בינייהו דיעבד. לרבנן בתראי מהדרינן ליה: בדתנא קמא גרסינן אשר נתן לך זו הטוב והמטיב ולא גרסינן ביבנה תקנוה אלא בדרבי(ג): כשהוא שבע. מצוה לברך ולהודות על שבעו: כשהוא רעב. והוא בא להפיק את רעבו ע"י בריאתו של הקב"ה לא כל שכן, שזה צריך לברך להקב"ה יותר: אינו צריך. לק"ו זה (ד) ולא גרסי' בדרבי "אשר נתן לך" – זה "הטוב והמטיב": אלא וברך את לחמך. ברך על לחמך: כי הוא יברך הזבח ואחרי כן יאכלו הקרואים. למדך שטעון לברך לפני אכילה. על הזבח הוא אומר: "ברוך אשר קדשנו במצותיו וצונו לאכול את הזבח". והיכן צונו? – "והבשר תאכל" (דברים יב): וכל כך למה. היו מאריכות בדבריהן: שאין מלכות נוגעת בחברתה. לפי ששמואל היה מנהיג את ישראל, ושאול היה נוטל את השררה משדבר שמואל אליו, ואורך דברים עכב לפי שעה: בין מדה טובה. התורה מדה טובה היא: ומלכות בית דוד בבונה ירושלים. שעל ידו נתקדשה ירושלים: צריך שיזכור בה ברית. בברכת הארץ, שעל ידי ברית נתנה לאברהם בפרשת מילה (בראשית יז) "ונתתי לך ולזרעך אחריך את ארץ מגוריך": צריך שיזכור בה תורה. שאף בזכות התורה והמצות ירשו את הארץ, שנאמר "למען תחיון ורביתם ובאתם וירשתם את הארץ" (דברים ח): צריך שיקדים ברית לתורה. כגון "על בריתך שחתמת בבשרנו ועל תורתך שלמדתנו ועל חיים שהנחלתנו": תורה נתנה(ה) בשלש בריתות. בשלשה מקומות נתנה התורה לישראל: בסיני, ובאהל מועד, ובהר גריזים ובערבות מואב. ובכל אחד נכרתה ברית, כדתניא במסכת סוטה (דף לז.): ארור בכלל וארור בפרט וכו'. וכן באהל מועד שנאמר (דברים כח) "אלה דברי הברית אשר צוה ה' את משה לכרות את בני ישראל בארץ מואב מלבד הברית אשר כרת אתם בחורב". וכתיב (שם כט) "ושמרתם את דברי הברית" וגו':

מילה

**תוספות**

קטן שהגיע לחינוך – לא מיקרי מחויב דרבנן, דאביו חייב לחנכו אבל עליו אין שום חיוב. וקשה לפירושו: מכל מקום, כיון שאינו מן התורה, אינו מוציא אחרים שמחויבים! ועוד: דוחק לומר בקטן שהגיע לחינוך קרי אינו מחויב מדרבנן, דאם אינו מחויב אפילו מדרבנן – אם כן אינו פוטר את אביו! ובה"ג פירש: דאחד שאכל כזית – אינו יכול להוציא אחרים שאכלו כדי שביעה, דלא אתי דרבנן ופוטר דאורייתא. אבל כשלא אכלו גם האחרים רק כזית – פוטר אותם. ולא היא, דהא סמכינן אעובדא דינאי וחבריו, והם אכלו כדי שביעה, ואפילו הכי קא חזינן דקא פטר להו שמעון בן שטח. אלא נראה לחלק: דקטן שאינו בר חיוב כלל דאורייתא, אפילו אכל כדי שביעה – הלכך אינו מחויב בדבר קרינן ביה. ולכך לא מפיק ליה אי אכל שיעורא דאורייתא. אבל גדול. שהוא בר חיובא מן התורה, כי אכיל כדי שביעה מחויב בדבר קרינן ביה, אפילו לא אכל כלל. כדאמרי' בראש השנה (פ"ג ד' כט.): כל הברכות אף על פי שיצא – מוציא חוץ מברכת הלחם וברכת היין, והיינו טעמא – דכל ישראל ערבין זה בזה. והוא הדין בברכת המזון, אף ע"פ שיצא – מוציא כדפרישית. וכזית דגן אינו צריך אלא שיוכל לומר שאכלנו משלו:

**מתחיל** בנחמה. פי' הקונטרס: לאו דוק' מתחיל בנחמה ומסיים אלא כלומר – דאין צריך להזכיר של שבת לא בפתיחה ולא בנחמה, אלא באמצע. אבל מתחיל ומסיים בנחמת ירושלים, כמו בחול, שאומר רחם וחותם בבונה ירושלים. ויש שמתחילין בנחמנו וחותמים בנחמת ציון עירך ובבנין ירושלים. ונותנים טעם לדבריהם דרחם הוי לשון תחנה, ואין אומרים תחנונים בשבת. אבל נחם אינו לשון תחנונים, אלא כמו והנחם על הרעה לעמך (שמות לב), ולא נהירא, דהכל משמע לשון תחנונים. ואין להקפיד, אפילו אי הוי לשון בקשה, כדאמר בירושלמי דשבת בפרק אלו קשרים: מהו לומר רוענו זוננו פרנסנו בשבת? א"ל: טופס ברכות כך הוא. ומנהג שטות הוא המשנה ברכה של חול: **ברית** ותורה. אין צריך להזכיר ברית ותורה וחיים ומזון, דדי להזכיר על בריתך שחתמת בבשרנו ועל תורתך שלמדתנו וכו', דהיינו ברית ותורה. והגמרא – לסימנא בעלמא נקטיה:

מאן

**רב נסים גאון**

**דאמר** רב מתנה אותו היום שניתנו הרוגי ביתר לקבורה תיקנו הטוב והמטיב. בסוף מסכת תענית (דף כו) שנינו אמר רבן שמעון בן גמליאל לא היו ימים טובים לישראל כחמשה עשר באב ואמרי' בגמ' רב מתנה אמר יום שניתנו הרוגי ביתר בו לקבורה הודיענו רב מתנה כי הדבר שגרם לעשות את יום ט"ו באב בשמחה היא קבורת אלו ההרוגים ואיתא למעשה דביתר וכמה נהרגו בה והיאך נתגלגל הדבר מפרש במסכת גיטין בפרק הניזקין (דף נז) ובגמ' דסוף תענית דבני מערבא:

**שזו** ניתנה בג' בריתות. הכין מפרש בספרי (פרשת ראה) כנגד ג' בריתות שכרת הקב"ה עם ישראל אחד בחורב ואחד בערבות מואב ואחד בהר גריזים ובהר עיבל ובמס' סוטה בפ' ואלו

[ויתכן לפרש זו ברכת הזימון את ה' אלהיך זו ברכת הזן וכן העתיקו תוס' לעיל מו. ד"ה על היכן]

**הגהות הב"ח**

(א) גמ' ברכת הארץ בשעה שנכנסו: (ב) שם ה' אלהיך אשר דיינך: (ג) רש"י ד"ה בדתנא קמא כו' אלא בדרבי ולא גרסינן בדרבי אשר נתן לך זה הטוב והמטיב הס"ד: (ד) ד"ה אינו צריך לק"ו זה הס"ד ואח"כ מ"ה אלא: (ה) ד"ה תורה נתנה וכו' בסיני וכו' תנאי פלוני כל ברכה לחד תנא מוזכרת גריזים והר עיבל ומכניס אהל מועד ולאידך תנא הר סיני ואהל מועד תנא הוא דכללות נאמרו בסיני ופרטות באהל מועד וע"ש בפ' אלו נאמרים דף לז.:

**הגהות הגר"א**

[א] גמ' וברכת זו ברכת הזימון את ה' אלהיך זו ברכ' הזן. כצ"ל: [ב] שם כשהוא רעב לא כ"ש. כצ"ל: [ג] שם ר' ישמעאל אומר. כצ"ל (וע' בירוש): [ד] שם וברכת. נ"ב את ה' אלהיך:

**מסורת הש"ס**

תענית לא. ב"ב קכא.

מכילתא פ' בא [תוס' פ"ו ע"ש לעיל כח.]

[לעיל לה.]

שבת ל. מ"ק כח. יומא לח: תענית ה:

[לעיל ה. וש"נ]

**תורה אור**

דברים ח | שם ג | תהלים לד | שמות כג | שמואל א ט | שם | שמות כד | דברים ח | לקמן נד. | משלי ד

**גליון הש"ס**

גמ' יהושע תקן. תשב"ץ ח"ב (ענין קס)

וזו נתנה בי"ג בריתות. ר' *אבא אומר: אצריך שיאמר בה הודאה תחלה וסוף, והפוחת – לא יפחות מא', וכל הפוחת מא' הרי זה מגונה. וכל החותם 'מנחיל ארצות' בברכת הארץ ו'מושיע את ישראל' ב"בונה ירושלים" – הרי זה בור, בוכל שאינו אומר 'ברית ותורה' בברכת הארץ ו'מלכות בית דוד' ב"בונה ירושלים" – לא יצא ידי חובתו. מסייע ליה לר' אילעא, דא"ר אילעא א"ר יעקב בר אחא משום רבינו: כל שלא אמר 'ברית ותורה' בברכת הארץ ו'מלכות בית דוד' ב"בונה ירושלים" – לא יצא ידי חובתו. פליגי בה אבא יוסי בן דוסתאי ורבנן, חד אמר: "הטוב והמטיב" צריכה מלכות, וחד אמר: אינה צריכה מלכות; מאן דאמר "צריכה מלכות" – קסבר: דרבנן, ומאן דאמר אינה צריכה מלכות – *קסבר: דאורייתא.§ ת"ר: מהו חותם? ב"בנין ירושלים"; רבי יוסי בר' יהודה אומר: "מושיע ישראל". "מושיע ישראל" אין, "בנין ירושלים" לא?! – אלא אימא: אף 'מושיע ישראל'. רבה בר רב הונא איקלע לבי ריש גלותא, פתח בחדא וסיים בתרתי. אמר רב חסדא: גבורתא למחתם בתרתי! והתניא, רבי אומר: אין חותמין בשתים! גופא, רבי אומר: אין חותמין בשתים. איתיביה לוי לרבי: ג"על הארץ ועל המזון"! –ארץ דמפקא מזון. "על הארץ ועל הפירות"! –ארץ דמפקא פירות; "מקדש ישראל והזמנים"! –ישראל דקדשינהו לזמנים; "מקדש ישראל וראשי חדשים"! –ישראל דקדשינהו לראשי חדשים; "מקדש *השבת וישראל והזמנים"! –חוץ מזו. ומאי שנא? –הכא–חדא היא, התם – תרתי, כל חדא וחדא באפי נפשה. וטעמא מאי אין חותמין בשתים – לפי *שאין עושין מצות חבילות חבילות. מאי הוי עלה? א"ר ששת: פתח ב"רחם על עמך ישראל" חותם ב"מושיע ישראל", פתח ב"רחם על ירושלים" – חותם ב"בונה ירושלים". ורב נחמן אמר: דאפי' פתח ב"רחם על ישראל" חותם ב"בונה ירושלים", משום שנאמר: ה"בונה ירושלים ה' נדחי ישראל יכנס", אימתי "בונה ירושלים ה'" – בזמן ש"נדחי ישראל יכנס".§ אמר ליה רבי זירא לרב חסדא: ניתי מר ונתני! –אמר ליה: ברכת מזונא לא גמירנא ותנויי מתנינא?! –אמר ליה: מאי האי? –אמר ליה: דאקלעי לבי ריש גלותא וברכי ברכת מזונא, וזקפי רב ששת לקועיה עלי כחויא. –ואמאי? –דלא אמרי לא ברית ולא תורה ולא מלכות. –ואמאי לא אמרת? –כדרב חננאל אמר רב, דאמר רב חננאל אמר רב: לא אמר ברית ותורה ומלכות – יצא. ברית – לפי שאינה בנשים, תורה ומלכות – לפי שאינן לא בנשים ולא בעבדים. –ואת שבקת כל הני תנאי ואמוראי ועבדת כרב.§ אמר רבה בב"ח א"ר יוחנן: "הטוב והמטיב" צריכה מלכות. מאי קמ"ל? – *כל ברכה שאין בה מלכות לא שמה ברכה, והא א"ר יוחנן חדא זימנא! –א"ר זירא: לומר שצריכה שתי מלכיות, חדא דידה, וחדא ד"בונה ירושלים". –אי הכי, ניבעי תלת – חדא דידה, וחדא ד"בונה ירושלים" וחדא דברכת הארץ! –אלא, ברכת הארץ מאי טעמא לא? משום דהוייא לה ברכה הסמוכה לחברתה, "בונה ירושלים" נמי לא תבעי דהוייא לה ברכה הסמוכה לחברתה! –ה"ה דאפילו "בונה ירושלים" נמי לא בעיא, אלא אידי דאמר מלכות בית דוד – לאו אורח ארעא דלא אמר מלכות שמים. רב פפא אמר, הכי קאמר: "צריכה שתי מלכיות לבר מדידה.§ יתיב רבי זירא אחורי דרב גידל, ויתיב רב גידל קמיה דרב הונא ויתיב וקאמר: טעה ולא הזכיר של שבת, אומר: "ברוך שנתן שבתות למנוחה לעמו ישראל באהבה לאות ולברית. ברוך מקדש השבת". אמר ליה: מאן אמרה? –רב הדר יתיב וקאמר: טעה ולא הזכיר של יום טוב אומר "ברוך שנתן ימים טובים לעמו ישראל לשמחה ולזכרון, ברוך מקדש ישראל והזמנים". א"ל: מאן אמרה? – רב. הדר יתיב וקאמר: טעה ולא הזכיר של ראש חודש אומר "ברוך שנתן ראשי חדשים לעמו ישראל לזכרון", ולא ידענא – אי אמר בה 'שמחה' אי לא אמר בה 'שמחה', אי חתים בה אי לא חתים בה, אי דידיה אי דרביה. גידל בר מניומי הוה קאי קמיה דרב נחמן, טעה רב נחמן והדר

תורה אור: תהלים קמז

[ס"א אינו] [לעיל יב. מ:]

## רש"י

מילה נתנה בי"ג בריתות. *בפרשת מילה שנתנה לאברהם אבינו הם כתובים: תחלה וסוף. *"נודה ה' אלהינו" ו"על כולם ה' אלהינו אנו מודים לך": מ"ד צריכה מלכות קסבר דרבנן. הלכך לאו ברכה הסמוכה לחברתה היא, שאינה מברכת הארץ: ומ"ד אינה צריכה מלכות קסבר דאורייתא היא. ומברכת הארץ היא, כדאמר לעיל: (דף מח:) "אשר נתן לך" – זה הטוב והמטיב, והויא לה ברכה הסמוכה לחברתה. ומיהו, פותח בה בברוך – לפי שפתיחתה היא חתימתה, שכולה הודאה אחת היא ואינה (א) הפסקה, ודומה לברכת הפירות והמצות: בונה ירושלים לא. בתמיה. אם חתם בונה ירושלים לאו חתימה היא? הלא עיקר ברכה דירושלים היא: אלא אימא אף מושיע. אם בא לחתום "מושיע ישראל" ולאחתם "בונה ירושלים" –יצא, שתשועת ישראל היא בנין ירושלים: פתח בחדא. כשהתחיל בברכה לא אמר "רחם ה' על ישראל עמך ועל ירושלים עירך" אלא אחת מהן, וכשחתם חתם בשתים "מושיע ישראל ובונה ירושלים": אין חותמין בשתים. שדומין לעושין מצות חבילות; כי היכי דאמר (פסחים קב:): אין אומר ב' קדושות על כוס אחד: מקדש השבת וישראל והזמנים. והכא ליכא למימר ישראל מקדשי לשבת וזמנים, דאילו זמנים תלויין בב"ד לקדש חדשים ע"פ הראייה, אבל שבת קדישא וקיימא: חוץ מזו ומ"ש הכא חדא היא. אין כאן אלא ברכת מקדש, שמברך להקב"ה שמקדש השבת והזמנים. אבל "מושיע ישראל" ו"בונה ירושלים" – תרתי מילי נינהו, ואין כוללים ב' דברים בברכה אחת. ולא גרס הא בהא תליא; ובה"ג גרס הכי: חוץ מזו, ומ"ש – הני תרתי קדושי נינהו, ומודה רבי דחתמינן בהו בשתים, אבל נחמה חדא מילתא היא ובחדא בעי למחתם. ואינו נ"ל, דא"כ אית ליה לרבי חותמין בשתים, והכא ה"ט דהא בהא תליא; ולא היה לו לכלול ולומר אין חותמין בשתים. ועוד: רבי כי אמרה – לאו אנחמה אמרה: פתח בעל עמך ישראל כו'. דבעינן חתימה מעין פתיחה: ור"נ כו'. "בונה ירושלים" תשועת ישראל היא, דכתיב (תהלים קמז) "בונה ירושלים ה'" ואז "נדחי ישראל יכנס": לאו אורח ארעא דלא אמר מלכות שמים. ב"בונה ירושלים", הלכך מהדר לה ב"הטוב והמטיב" (*ואומר: מלך העולם הטוב והמטיב): שתי מלכיות. כגון: אבינו מלכנו אדירנו בוראנו גואלנו קדושנו קדוש יעקב רועינו רועה ישראל המלך הטוב והמטיב לכל וכו': לבר מדידה. שפותחת "ברוך אתה ה' אלהינו מלך העולם" וכו': ויתיב רב גידל וקאמר טעה כו' א"ל. רב הונא לרב גידל מאן אמרה: ולא ידענא. רבי זירא קאמר לה: לא ידענא אי אמר רב גידל לזכרון ולשמחה אי לא אמר לשמחה; ואי אמרה משמיה דרב אי לא אמרה: אי חתים בה. "מקדש ישראל וראשי חדשים", אי לא חתים: והדר

[תוי"ט נדרים פ"ג מי"א ד"ה שנכרתו] [תנא (זה) הוא רב' אבא בשמו רבי אבא עי' ערוך ערך רב] [לעיל מו.] [ביצה יז.] [ס"א אינו]

## תוספות

מאן דאמר אינה צריכה מלכות קסבר דאורייתא. הקשה רש"י: הואיל והיא דאורייתא, אמאי פותחת בברוך? הא סמוכה היא! ותירץ: דקצרה היא, והויא הודאה בעלמא, כברכת פירות וכברכת מצות. ותימה: אמאי שינו אותה יותר משאר ברכות הסמוכות, שחותמות ולא פותחות? הואיל ודאורייתא היא – היה לנו להאריך בה, ולחתום בברוך ולא לשנות משאר סמוכות! וי"ל: דאין ה"נ, ולמאן דאית ליה שהיא דאורייתא – היה חותם ולא פותח, וכן איתא בתוספתא [פ"א] בהדיא: ר' יוסי הגלילי היה מאריך בה וחותם. ומיהו אנן קי"ל שהיא מדרבנן, ולכך צריכה מלכות, כדאמר: צריכה שתי מלכיות, בר מדידה: לומר שצריכה ב' מלכיות בר מדידה. חדא דבונה ירושלים דלאו אורח וכו', וגם בה אין יכולין לומר מלכות דהא סמוכה היא, ע"כ אומרה בהטוב והמטיב והואיל ואמר בה מלכות דבונה ירושלים דלאו אורח ארעא וכו', אמר נמי דברכת הארץ, אע"פ שהיא סמוכה לחברתה, הואיל ולא נתקנו בזה אחר זה; דיהושע תקן ברכת הארץ, ומשה תקן ברכת הזן, מש"ה נקט מלכות דלא הוי סמוכות. ומיהו, אנן הואיל ונתקנו על הסדר – אין אנו פותחין בברוך. ויש שנוהגין לומר בבונה ירושלים מלכות: ברוך שנתן שבתות למנוחה וכו'. וא"ת: והא סמוכה היא! וי"ל: הואיל ולא נתקנה שם אלא לאומרה לפרקים, כששכח רצה והחליצנו – אין זה קרוי סמוכה, וצריך פתיחה בברוך. ובברכות של י"ח – ברכות כולם סמוכות לברכות אל חי וקים. אי נמי: אלהי אברהם – היינו מלכות, *כדאמרינן (לעיל ד' ז:): משנברא העולם לא היה אדם שקראו להקב"ה אדון, עד שבא אברהם וקראו אדון שנא' אדני אלהים מה תתן לי (בראשית טו). ואם הוא י"ט כולל ואומר ברוך שנתן שבתות למנוחה וי"ט לעמו ישראל לשמחה, וכן כי מקלע שבת ור"ח: אי

## עין משפט נר מצוה

נו א מיי' פ"ב מהלכות ברכות הלכה ג סמג עשין כז טור או"ח סי' קפז:

נז ב מיי' שם והלכה ד סמג שם טוש"ע שם סעיף ג ד ובסי' קפח סעיף ג:

נח ג מיי' שם הלכה ג סמג שם טור או"ח סימן קפז:

נט ד מיי' שם הל' ד סמג שם טוש"ע או"ח סי' קפח סעיף ז:

ס ה מיי' שם הלכה ז סמג שם טוש"ע או"ח סי' קפט סעיף א:

סא ו ז מיי' שם הל' יב סמג שם טוש"ע או"ח סי' קפח סעיף ו:

סב ח מיי' שם הל' יג טוש"ע שם סעיף ז [ובסי' תכל]:

## רב נסים גאון

ואלו נאמרין בכל לשון שנינו הפכו פניהם כלפי הר גרזים כו' (דף לז) תנו רבנן ברוך בכלל ברוך בפרט וכן בסיני וכן בערבות מואב שנא' (דברים כח) אלה דברי הברית אשר צוה ה' את משה וגו' מלבד הברית אשר כרת אתם בחורב וכתיב (שם כט) ושמרתם את דברי הברית הזאת ואדונינו האי גאון ז"ל כתב בפירושו דברכות הכי ג' דתורה מפרשי רבנן האמורין בלוחות שניות (שמות לד) הנה אנכי כורת ברית (שם פסוק כז) כרתי אתך ברית (בחורב) (שם פסוק כח) ויכתוב על הלוחות כמכתב הראשון את דברי הברית:

[ועי' תוס' לעיל מ: ד"ה אמר אביי]

[פסחים קב: סוטה ח. טעמא דבעינן שיהא לבו פנוי למצוה אחת ולא יפנה עצמו הימנה כ"כ תוס' מ"ק ח: ד"ה לפי וכו']

## הגהות הב"ח

(א) רש"י ד"ה ומ"ד אינה וכו' אחת היא ואין בה הפסקה. נ"ב ע"ל בפרש"י דף מו סוף ע"א:

## גליון הש"ס

גמ' והתניא ר' אומר אין חותמין בשתים. עי' פסחים דף קב ע"ב תוס' ד"ה וליתו הלכתא. שם לאכרבב"ח אר"י הטוב והמטיב צריכה מלכות מאי קמ"ל. ק"ל הא לעיל פליגי בזה בן דוסתאי ורבנן וצ"ע [עי' רשב"א]: רש"י ד"ה ומ"ד א"צ מלכות וכו' ומיהו פותח בה בברוך לפי שפתיחתה היא חתימתה עיין לעיל דף מו ע"א ד"ה הטוב והמטיב לאו דאורייתא וגם לא נזכר מלכות בברייתא וצ"ע:

וְהָדַר לְרֵישָׁא. אֲמַר לֵיהּ: מַאי טַעְמָא עָבֵיד מָר הָכִי? אֲמַר לֵיהּ, דַּאֲמַר רַבִּי שֵׁילָא אָמַר רַב: טָעָה – חוֹזֵר לָרֹאשׁ. וְהָא אָמַר רַב הוּנָא אֲמַר רַב: טָעָה – אוֹמֵר: "בָּרוּךְ שֶׁנָּתַן"! אֲמַר לֵיהּ: לָאו אִיתְּמַר עֲלָהּ, אָמַר רַב מְנַשְּׁיָא בַּר תַּחְלִיפָא אֲמַר רַב: לֹא שָׁנוּ אֶלָּא שֶׁלֹּא פָּתַח בְּ"הַטּוֹב וְהַמֵּטִיב", אֲבָל פָּתַח בְּ"הַטּוֹב וְהַמֵּטִיב" – חוֹזֵר לָרֹאשׁ.§ אָמַר רַב אִידִי בַּר אָבִין אָמַר רַב עַמְרָם אָמַר רַב נַחְמָן אָמַר שְׁמוּאֵל: טָעָה וְלֹא הִזְכִּיר שֶׁל רֹאשׁ חֹדֶשׁ בִּתְפִלָּה – מַחֲזִירִין אוֹתוֹ, [א] בְּבִרְכַּת הַמָּזוֹן – אֵין מַחֲזִירִין אוֹתוֹ. אֲמַר לֵיהּ רַב (א) אָבִין לְרַב עַמְרָם: מַאי שְׁנָא תְּפִלָּה וּמַאי שְׁנָא בִּרְכַּת הַמָּזוֹן? –אֲמַר לֵיהּ: אַף לְדִידִי קַשְׁיָא לִי, וּשְׁאֵילְתֵּיהּ לְרַב נַחְמָן, וַאֲמַר לִי: מִינֵּיהּ דְּמָר שְׁמוּאֵל לָא שְׁמִיעַ לִי, אֶלָּא נֶחֱזֵי אֲנַן, תְּפִלָּה דְּחוֹבָה הִיא – מַחֲזִירִין אוֹתוֹ; בִּרְכַּת מְזוֹנָא, דְּאִי בָּעֵי אָכֵיל אִי בָּעֵי לָא אָכֵיל – אֵין מַחֲזִירִין אוֹתוֹ. –אֶלָּא מֵעַתָּה, [ב] שַׁבָּתוֹת וְיָמִים טוֹבִים דְּלָא סַגִּי דְּלָא אָכֵיל, הָכִי נַמִי דְּאִי טָעֵי הָדַר! –אֲמַר לֵיהּ: אִין, דַּאֲמַר רַבִּי שֵׁילָא אֲמַר רַב: טָעָה – חוֹזֵר לָרֹאשׁ. וְהָא אָמַר רַב הוּנָא אֲמַר רַב: טָעָה – אוֹמֵר "בָּרוּךְ שֶׁנָּתַן"! – לָאו אִיתְּמַר עֲלָהּ: [ג] לֹא שָׁנוּ אֶלָּא שֶׁלֹּא פָּתַח בְּ"הַטּוֹב וְהַמֵּטִיב", אֲבָל פָּתַח בְּ"הַטּוֹב וְהַמֵּטִיב" – חוֹזֵר לָרֹאשׁ.§ "עַד כַּמָּה מְזַמְּנִין וכו'". לְמֵימְרָא, דְּרַבִּי מֵאִיר חָשֵׁיב לֵיהּ כַּזַּיִת וְרַבִּי יְהוּדָה כַּבֵּיצָה – וְהָא אִיפְּכָא שְׁמַעִינַן לְהוּ! *דִּתְנַן: [ד] וְכֵן מִי שֶׁיָּצָא מִירוּשָׁלַיִם וְנִזְכַּר שֶׁהָיָה בְּיָדוֹ בְּשַׂר קֹדֶשׁ, אִם עָבַר צוֹפִים – שׂוֹרְפוֹ בִּמְקוֹמוֹ, וְאִם לָאו – חוֹזֵר וְשׂוֹרְפוֹ לִפְנֵי הַבִּירָה מֵעֲצֵי הַמַּעֲרָכָה. עַד כַּמָּה הֵם חוֹזְרִים? רַבִּי מֵאִיר אוֹמֵר: זֶה וָזֶה בִּכְבֵיצָה; וְרַבִּי יְהוּדָה אוֹמֵר: [ה] זֶה וָזֶה בִּכְזַיִת! –אָמַר רַבִּי יוֹחָנָן: מוּחְלֶפֶת הַשִּׁיטָה. אַבָּיֵי אָמַר: לְעוֹלָם לָא תֵּיפוֹךְ, הָכָא בִּקְרָאֵי פְּלִיגֵי, ר' מֵאִיר סָבַר: *"וְאָכַלְתָּ" – זוֹ אֲכִילָה, "וְשָׂבָעְתָּ" – זוֹ שְׁתִיָּה, וַאֲכִילָה [ו] בִּכְזַיִת. וְרַבִּי יְהוּדָה סָבַר: *"וְאָכַלְתָּ וְשָׂבָעְתָּ" – אֲכִילָה שֶׁיֵּשׁ בָּהּ שְׂבִיעָה, וְאֵיזוֹ זוֹ – כַּבֵּיצָה. הָתָם – בִּסְבָרָא פְּלִיגֵי, ר' מֵאִיר סָבַר: חֲזָרָתוֹ *כְּטוּמְאָתוֹ – מַה טּוּמְאָתוֹ בִּכְבֵיצָה, אַף חֲזָרָתוֹ בִּכְבֵיצָה; וְר' יְהוּדָה סָבַר: חֲזָרָתוֹ כְּאִיסּוּרוֹ – מָה אִיסּוּרוֹ בִּכְזַיִת, אַף חֲזָרָתוֹ בִּכְזַיִת.§ **מתני'** כֵּיצַד מְזַמְּנִין? [ז] בִּשְׁלֹשָׁה – אוֹמֵר: "נְבָרֵךְ", בִּשְׁלֹשָׁה וָהוּא – אוֹמֵר: "בָּרְכוּ". בַּעֲשָׂרָה – אוֹמֵר: "נְבָרֵךְ אֱלֹהֵינוּ", בַּעֲשָׂרָה וָהוּא – אוֹמֵר: "בָּרְכוּ"; אֶחָד עֲשָׂרָה, וְאֶחָד עֲשָׂרָה רִבּוֹא. בְּמֵאָה – הוּא אוֹמֵר: "נְבָרֵךְ לַה' אֱלֹהֵינוּ", בְּמֵאָה וָהוּא – אוֹמֵר: "בָּרְכוּ". וּבָאֶלֶף הוּא אוֹמֵר: "נְבָרֵךְ לַה' אֱלֹהֵינוּ אֱלֹהֵי יִשְׂרָאֵל", בָּאֶלֶף וָהוּא אוֹמֵר: "בָּרְכוּ", בְּרִבּוֹא – אוֹמֵר: "נְבָרֵךְ לַה' אֱלֹהֵינוּ אֱלֹהֵי יִשְׂרָאֵל אֱלֹהֵי צְבָאוֹת יוֹשֵׁב הַכְּרוּבִים עַל הַמָּזוֹן שֶׁאָכַלְנוּ", בְּרִבּוֹא וָהוּא – אוֹמֵר: "בָּרְכוּ". כָּעִנְיָן שֶׁהוּא מְבָרֵךְ כָּךְ עוֹנִים אַחֲרָיו: "בָּרוּךְ ה' אֱלֹהֵינוּ אֱלֹהֵי יִשְׂרָאֵל אֱלֹהֵי צְבָאוֹת יוֹשֵׁב הַכְּרוּבִים עַל הַמָּזוֹן שֶׁאָכַלְנוּ". ר' יוֹסֵי הַגְּלִילִי אוֹמֵר: לְפִי רוֹב הַקָּהָל הֵם מְבָרְכִים, שֶׁנֶּאֱמַר: °"בְּמַקְהֵלוֹת בָּרְכוּ אֱלֹהִים ה' מִמְּקוֹר יִשְׂרָאֵל". אָמַר ר' עֲקִיבָא: מַה מָּצִינוּ בְּבֵית הַכְּנֶסֶת – אֶחָד מְרוּבִּים וְאֶחָד מוּעָטִים אוֹמֵר "בָּרְכוּ אֶת ה'". רַבִּי יִשְׁמָעֵאל אוֹמֵר: "בָּרְכוּ אֶת ה' הַמְבוֹרָךְ".§ **גמ'** אָמַר שְׁמוּאֵל: [י] לְעוֹלָם אַל יוֹצִיא אָדָם אֶת עַצְמוֹ מִן הַכְּלָל. תְּנַן: בִּשְׁלֹשָׁה וָהוּא – אוֹמֵר: "בָּרְכוּ"! – אֵימָא: אַף

---

**רש"י**

וְהָדַר לְרֵישָׁא. לִתְחִלַּת בִּרְכַּת הַמָּזוֹן. כִּדְאָמְרִינַן (לעיל דף כט:) גַּבֵּי תְּפִלָּה: עָקַר אֶת רַגְלָיו – חוֹזֵר לָרֹאשׁ, הָתָם הוּא דְּחִיקָה עֲקִירַת רַגְלַיִם, אֲבָל הָכָא סִיּוּם הַבְּרָכָה הוּא עֲקִירַת רַגְלַיִם: מִי שֶׁיָּצָא מִירוּשָׁלַיִם. לְעֵיל מִינֵּיהּ מַיְירֵי: הַהוֹלֵךְ לִשְׁחוֹט אֶת פִּסְחוֹ וְנִזְכַּר שֶׁיֵּשׁ לוֹ חָמֵץ בְּתוֹךְ בֵּיתוֹ, אִם יָכוֹל לַחֲזוֹר וּלְבַעֵר וְלַחֲזוֹר לְמִצְוָתוֹ – יַחֲזוֹר וִיבַעֵר, וְאִם לָאו – יְבַטֵּל בְּלִבּוֹ, וְכֵן מִי שֶׁיָּצָא מִירוּשָׁלַיִם וְנִזְכַּר שֶׁיֵּשׁ בְּיָדוֹ בְּשַׂר קוֹדֶשׁ וְנִפְסַל בִּיצִיאָתוֹ חוּץ לַחוֹמָה: אִם עָבַר צוֹפִים. מָקוֹם שֶׁיָּכוֹל לִרְאוֹת מִשָּׁם בֵּית הַמִּקְדָּשׁ: לִפְנֵי הַבִּירָה. מָקוֹם בְּהַר הַבַּיִת שֶׁיֵּשׁ שָׁם בֵּית הַדֶּשֶׁן גָּדוֹל שֶׁשּׂוֹרְפִין פְּסוּלֵי קָדָשִׁים קַלִּים, כִּדְאָמְרִינַן בִּזְבָחִים, בְּפֶרֶק "טְבוּל יוֹם" (דף קד:): זֶה וָזֶה. חָמֵץ וּבְשַׂר קוֹדֶשׁ: חֲזָרָתוֹ כְּטוּמְאָתוֹ. גָּרְסִינַן. שִׁיעוּר חֲזָרָתוֹ כְּשִׁיעוּר טוּמְאָתוֹ; מִידֵי דְּחָשִׁיב לְעִנְיַן טוּמְאָה – חָשִׁיב זֶה לְעִנְיַן חֲזָרָה: **מתני'** בִּשְׁלֹשָׁה וְהוּא אוֹמֵר בָּרְכוּ. דְּהָא בְּלָאו דִּידֵיהּ אִיכָּא זִימּוּן. וְכֵן כּוּלָּם: אֶחָד עֲשָׂרָה וְאֶחָד עֲשָׂרָה רִבּוֹא. כְּלוֹמַר: הַכֹּל שָׁוֶה, מִשֶּׁרְאוּיִים לְהַזְכִּיר אֶת הַשֵּׁם – אֵין צְרִיכִין לְשַׁנּוֹת, וּבַגְּמָ' פָּרֵיךְ הָא קָתָנֵי סֵיפָא בְּמֵאָה וְהוּא אוֹמֵר כו': לְפִי רוֹב הַקָּהָל הֵם מְבָרְכִים. כְּמוֹ שֶׁאָמַר, שֶׁיֵּשׁ חִילּוּק בֵּין מֵאָה לַעֲשָׂרָה וּבֵין מֵאָה לָאֶלֶף וּבֵין אֶלֶף לְרִבּוֹא, וְהָא דְּקָתָנֵי אֶחָד עֲשָׂרָה וְאֶחָד עֲשָׂרָה רִבּוֹא – ר"ע הִיא, דְּאָמַר: מַה מָּצִינוּ בְּבֵית הַכְּנֶסֶת מִשֶּׁהִגִּיעוּ לַעֲשָׂרָה אֵין חִילּוּק בֵּין רַבִּים בֵּין מוּעָטִים – אַף כָּאן אֵין חִילּוּק. הָכִי מוֹקֵי לָהּ בַּגְּמָרָא. **גמ'** אַל יוֹצִיא אֶת עַצְמוֹ. אע"פ שֶׁבִּשְׁלֹשָׁה הוּא רָאוּי לוֹמַר לִשְׁלֹשָׁה "בָּרְכוּ", טוֹב לוֹ שֶׁיֹּאמַר "נְבָרֵךְ", וְאַל יוֹצִיא עַצְמוֹ מִכְּלַל הַמְבָרְכִים: תְּנַן בִּשְׁלֹשָׁה וְהוּא אוֹמֵר בָּרְכוּ. אַלְמָא הָכִי עָדִיף, כְּלוֹמַר: רַבִּים אַתֶּם וַאֲפִילּוּ אֵינִי עִמָּכֶם: אַף

תורה אור

---

**תוספות**

**אי בעי** אכיל ואי בעי לא אכיל. וא"ת: והא הוי ר"ח מיומי דלא להתענות בהון במגילת תענית? וי"ל: דהכי פירושו: אי בעי אכיל ואי בעי לא אכיל פת, שחייבנו בברכת המזון. אבל ביום טוב צריך לאכול פת. ותימה, דאמרינן בסוכה (פ"ב דף כז.): אי בעי אכיל ואי בעי לא אכיל, חוץ מלילה הראשונה, דיליף ט"ו ט"ו מחג המצות! וי"ל, דה"פ: שאינו צריך לאכול בסוכה אם לא ירצה, אבל בשביל יו"ט – צריך לאכול. וא"ת: מנ"מ אם צריך לאכול בשביל יו"ט או בשביל סוכות? *ומיהו, אומר רבינו יהודה דנפקא מינה: כגון שירדו גשמים ואכלו חוץ לסוכה, דהשתא אם לכבוד יו"ט – שפיר, אבל אם בשביל סוכה – ביו"ט ראשון צריך לחזור ולאכול בסוכה לאחר שיפסקו הגשמים, דילפינן ט"ו ט"ו מחג המצות, אבל בשאר ימים – אינו צריך. והא דאמרינן בפרק אלו דברים (פסחים ד' סח:): מר בריה דרבינא הוה יתיב בתעניתא כולה שתא משמע שהיה מתענה ביום טוב! מפרש ר"י: דבתענית חלום, קאמר אבל בשאר תעניות – אסור. וסעודה שלישית של שבת, היה מסופק ר"י דשמא אי בעי לא אכיל אלא מיני תרגימא, כדפי' ר"ח, כדאמרי' בסעודת סוכה. ומיהו, בכתובות פרק אע"פ (דף סד:) חשיב גבי משרה אשתו על ידי שליש שלש סעודות משל שבת, א"כ משמע דכולן שוות! ועוד: כיון דילפינן *ממן – אלמא דשוות הן. ומיהו, אם אכל סעודה רביעית ושכח של שבת – לא הדר לרישא, דודאי אי בעי לא אכיל הך סעודה רביעית כלל: **עד** כמה מזמנין וכו'. ה"ה ברכת המזון בלא זימון, אלא רבותא אשמעינן דאפילו על כזית – מזמנין: **אם** עבר צופים. פירש"י בפסחים (פ"ג ד' מט.): מקום שאמו צופים, ול"נ. דא"כ ה"ל למימר: וכמדתו לכל רוח, כדקאמר התם [נג:] גבי מודיעים ולפנים! אלא י"ל: שאינו מקום, וצופים הוי לשון ראיה. וה"פ: אם הרחיק מירושלים כ"כ שאינו יכול לראות ירושלים – שורפו במקומו: **רבי מאיר** סבר ואכלת זו אכילה, ואכילה בכזית. ואומר הר"י: דהני קראי אסמכתא בעלמא נינהו, דמדאורייתא בעינן שביעה גמורה, כדאמר פרק מי שמתו (ד' כ:): וכי לא אשא פנים לישראל וכו'. וכן אמרינן התם: בן מברך לאביו, ומוקים לה במאן דאכיל שיעורא דרבנן, ופירש"י: היינו כזית או כביצה. ועוד: אי כזית או כביצה הוי דאורייתא – איזה שיעור דרבנן? וקי"ל בכזית, דלפי מה שמחליף רבי יוחנן קאמר רבי יהודה בכזית, ור' מאיר ורבי יהודה הלכה כרבי יהודה. וגם לאביי דלא מחליף, ור"מ אית ליה עד כזית נראה דהלכה כר"מ בכזית. אף על גב דבעלמא *ר"מ ורבי יהודה הלכה כרבי יהודה, בהא הלכה כר"מ דהא קים ליה ר' יוחנן בשיטתו לעיל, *דאינו מוציא רבים ידי חובתן עד שיאכל כזית, וכן לעיל *גבי שאכל כזית מליח. וכן פסק בה"ג ור"ח ושאלתות. *ולענין שתיה אומר ר"י דיש להחמיר ולברך עליו אפילו בפחות ממלא לוגמיו. אף על גב דלענין יום הכפורים ליתא – לא ילפינן מינה לענין ברכה. תדע: דלענין ברכת המזון – בכזית, ולענין יום הכפורים – עד דהוי דוקא *ככותבת: **נברך** אלהינו גרסינן ולא גרסינן נברך לאלהינו בלמ"ד – דדוקא גבי שיר והודאה כתיב למ"ד, כמו שירו לה' הודו לה' גדלו לה', אבל גבי ברכה לא מצינו זה הלשון. וכן מפורש בסדר רב עמרם: **אמר** ר"ע: מה מצינו בבית הכנסת אחד עשרה כו'. משמע דרבי יוסי הגלילי מודה בבית הכנסת, מדקאמר מה מצינו וכו', כלומר: שאתה מודה לי. ומאי שנא דפליגי בברכת המזון, ומודו בבית הכנסת? ויש לומר: דודאי לא חלקו בין עשרה למאה בתפלה, דאלו נכנסים ואלו יוצאים, ולאו אדעתיה דש"צ. אבל בברכת המזון, שהן קבועין ומעורבין שם יחד אין לטעות בזה, שאין יוצאין עד לאחר ברכת המזון: **לעולם** אל יוציא אדם את עצמו מן הכלל. ופריך בירושלמי מן הקורא בתורה ומן החזן שאומר ברכו. ומפרש: כיון שאומר המבורך – אין זה מוציא עצמו מן הכלל: **תנן** בשלשה והוא אומר ברכו. ס"ד השתא דברכו עדיף, משום דברכו היינו לווי לברך את השם, אבל נברך אינו אלא נטילת רשות: אלא

[שבת קיז:]

שייך למשנה לעיל מה.

[עירובין פב:]

---

**עין משפט נר מצוה**

סג א מיי' פ"ב מהלכות ברכות הל' יג סמג עשין כז טוש"ע או"ח סי' קפח סעיף ז ובסי' תכב:

סד ב ג מיי' שם הל' יב טוש"ע שם ס"ו:

סה ד ה מיי' פ"ד מהל' פסולי המוקדשין הלכה ח:

סו ו ז מיי' פ"ה מהל' ברכות הל' ב ד סמג עשין כז טוש"ע או"ח סי' קצב סעיף א:

[ועי' היטב תוס' סוכה כז. ד"ה אי בעי]

---

**רב נסים גאון**

**מר** סבר חזרתו כטומאתו מה טומאתו בכביצה. עיקרה בתורת כהנים יכול יטמא כל שהוא ת"ל אשר יאכל הא אינו מטמא אלא בכביצה ובגמרא דיום הכפורים (דף פ) אמרינן תניא ר' אומר כל איסורין שבתורה בכזית חוץ מטומאת אוכלין בכביצה כו' מנלן א"ר אבהו אמר ר' אלעזר דאמר קרא מכל האוכל אשר יאכל אוכל שאתה יכול לאוכלו בבת אחת שיערו חכמים שאין בית הבליעה יתר מביצת תרנגולת ולענין איסורין אמרי' (סוכה ו) ארץ זית שמן ארץ שרוב שיעוריה כזיתים ועיקרו בתורת כהנים אשר תאכל אין אכילה בפחות מכזית ובגמ' דפרק גיד הנשה (חולין דף צו) אמרי' ור' יהודה אכילה כתיבה בה ואכילה בכזית והתם נמי אמרי' (שם דף קב) אבר מן החי צריך כזית מ"ט אכילה כתיב ביה ובכמה רבות בתלמוד ומינה ילפינן לנוגע ולנושא ששיערו חכמים בכזית ברבנא בתורת כהנים [בפרשת אמור] והכי איתא בת"כ [פ' שמיני] נבלה וטרפה לא יאכל לטמאה בה אבל שאין לה טומאה בה את אכילה וכו' יכול נבלת בהמה מטמא בגדים בבית הבליעה מק"ו ת"ל בה בה אתה מטמא בבית הבליעה ואין אתה מטמא בנבלת בהמה בבית הבליעה א"כ למה נאמר האוכל ליתן שיעור מה האוכל בכזית אף הנוגע והנושא בכזית: **בשלשה** והוא אומר ברכו. אמר שמואל לעולם אל יוציא אדם את עצמו מן הכלל ואסיקנא דנברך עדיף למה נהגו העם בספר תורה לומר הקורא ברכו ואינו אומר נברך ופירוקה כי הקורא בס"ת כיון שהצריכוהו לומר המבורך לא יצא מן הכלל והרי בירך הוא תחלה קודם הצבור ובברכת המזון אם הוא אומר ברכו את שאכלנו משלו הרי הוציא את עצמו מן הכלל והכי אמרינן בתלמוד ארץ ישראל שמואל אמר אני איני מוציא את עצמי מן הכלל התיבון הרי הקורא בתורה אומר ברכו אמר ר' אבין מכיון דהוא אומר המבורך אף הוא אינו מוציא עצמו מן הכלל והוא פירוק יפה וחביב:

---

**מסורת הש"ס**

פסחים מט. ודף פח.

[יומא עט:]

[שם פא.]

[פסחים מט: פח. קכח.]

תהלים סח

[מח.] [לח.]

פ' יחזרו קודש סימן נב

[ועי' תוס' יומא עט. ד"ה ולא בירך באריכות]

**הגהות הב"ח**

(א) גמ' אמר ליה רב אבין לרב עמרם [illegible]:

**גליון הש"ס**

תוס' ד"ה אם עבר כו' כו' הוי לשון ראיה. לקמן סא ע"ב ברש"י ד"ה מן הצופים: תוס' ד"ה ר"מ סבר ולענין שתיה אומר ר"י דיש להחמיר ולברך. ק"ל הא שייך להחמיר לברך בברכה ספיקא להקל וכו':

אף "בָּרְכוּ", ומ"מ "נְבָרֵךְ" עָדִיף. דַּאֲמַר רַב אַדָּא בַּר אַהֲבָה: אָמְרֵי בֵּי רַב, תְּנֵינָא: ו' נֶחֱלָקִין עַד י'; אִי אָמְרַתְּ בִּשְׁלָמָא "נְבָרֵךְ" עָדִיף – מש"ה נֶחֱלָקִין, אֶלָּא א"א "בָּרְכוּ" עָדִיף – אַמַּאי נֶחֱלָקִין? אֶלָּא לָאו ש"מ "נְבָרֵךְ" עָדִיף – ש"מ. תַּנְיָא נַמִּי הָכִי: *בֵּין שֶׁאָמַר "בָּרְכוּ" בֵּין שֶׁאָמַר "נְבָרֵךְ" אֵין תּוֹפְסִין אוֹתוֹ עַל כָּךְ, *וְהַנַּקְדָּנִין תּוֹפְסִין אוֹתוֹ עַל כָּךְ. *וּמִבִּרְכוֹתָיו שֶׁל אָדָם נִיכָּר אִם ת"ח הוּא אִם לָאו. כֵּיצַד? רַבִּי אוֹמֵר: "וּבְטוּבוֹ" – הֲרֵי זֶה ת"ח, "וּמִטּוּבוֹ" – ה"ז בּוּר. א"ל אַבָּיֵי לְרַב דִּימִי: וְהָכְתִיב °"וּמִבִּרְכָתְךָ יְבֹרַךְ (אֶת) בֵּית עַבְדְּךָ לְעוֹלָם"! בִּשְׁאֵלָה שָׁאנֵי. בִּשְׁאֵלָה נַמִּי, הָכְתִיב °"הַרְחֶב פִּיךָ וַאֲמַלְאֵהוּ"! – הַהוּא בד"ת כְּתִיב. תַּנְיָא, רַבִּי אוֹמֵר: "בְּטוּבוֹ חָיִינוּ" – הֲרֵיזֶה ת"ח, "חַיִּים" – הֲרֵיזֶה בּוּר. *נְהַרְבְּלָאֵי מַתְנֵי אִיפְּכָא, וְלֵית הִילְכְתָא כִּנְהַרְבְּלָאֵי. אָמַר רַבִּי יוֹחָנָן: "נְבָרֵךְ שֶׁאָכַלְנוּ מִשֶּׁלּוֹ" – הֲרֵי זֶה ת"ח, "לְמִי שֶׁאָכַלְנוּ מִשֶּׁלּוֹ" – הֲרֵי זֶה בּוּר. אֲמַר לֵיהּ רַב אַחָא בְּרֵיהּ דְּרָבָא לְרַב אָשֵׁי: וְהָא אָמְרִינַן *"לְמִי שֶׁעָשָׂה לַאֲבוֹתֵינוּ וְלָנוּ אֶת כָּל הַנִּסִּים הָאֵלּוּ"! – א"ל: הָתָם מוֹכְחָא מִילְּתָא, מַאן עָבֵיד נִיסֵּי – קוּדְשָׁא ב"ה. א"ר יוֹחָנָן: (א) "בָּרוּךְ שֶׁאָכַלְנוּ מִשֶּׁלּוֹ" – הֲרֵיזֶה ת"ח, "עַל הַמָּזוֹן שֶׁאָכַלְנוּ" – הֲרֵי זֶה בּוּר.* א"ר הוּנָא בְּרֵיהּ דְּרַב יְהוֹשֻׁעַ: לָא אָמְרַן אֶלָּא בג', דְּלֵיכָּא שֵׁם שָׁמַיִם, אֲבָל בַּעֲשָׂרָה דְּאִיכָּא שֵׁם שָׁמַיִם – מוֹכְחָא מִילְּתָא, כִּדְתְנַן: כְּעִנְיָן שֶׁהוּא מְבָרֵךְ כָּךְ עוֹנִין אַחֲרָיו: "בָּרוּךְ ה' אֱלֹהֵי יִשְׂרָאֵל אֱלֹהֵי הַצְּבָאוֹת יוֹשֵׁב הַכְּרוּבִים עַל הַמָּזוֹן שֶׁאָכַלְנוּ".§ "אֶחָד עֲשָׂרָה וְאֶחָד עֲשָׂרָה רִבּוֹא". הָא גּוּפָא קַשְׁיָא! אָמְרַתְּ: אֶחָד עֲשָׂרָה וְאֶחָד עֲשָׂרָה רִבּוֹא – אַלְמָא כִּי הֲדָדֵי נִינְהוּ, וַהֲדַר קָתָנֵי: בְּמֵאָה אוֹמֵר, בְּאֶלֶף אוֹמֵר, בְּרִבּוֹא אוֹמֵר! – אָמַר רַב יוֹסֵף, לָא קַשְׁיָא: הָא ר' יוֹסֵי הַגְּלִילִי, הָא ר"ע; דִּתְנַן, ר' יוֹסֵי הַגְּלִילִי אוֹמֵר: לְפִי רוֹב הַקָּהָל הֵם מְבָרְכִין, שֶׁנֶּאֱמַר: °"בְּמַקְהֵלוֹת בָּרְכוּ אֱלֹהִים". אר"ע, מָה מָצִינוּ בְּבֵית הַכְּנֶסֶת וכו'." ור"ע, הַאי קְרָא דְּרַבִּי יוֹסֵי הַגְּלִילִי מַאי עָבֵיד לֵיהּ? מִיבְּעֵי לֵיהּ לִכְדְתַנְיָא; *הָיָה ר' מֵאִיר אוֹמֵר: מִנַּיִן שֶׁאֲפִי' עוּבָּרִין שֶׁבִּמְעֵי אִמָּן אָמְרוּ שִׁירָה עַל הַיָּם – שֶׁנֶּאֱמַר: "בְּמַקְהֵלוֹת בָּרְכוּ אֱלֹהִים ה' מִמְּקוֹר יִשְׂרָאֵל". -וְאִידָךְ? מִ"מָּקוֹר" נָפְקָא. אָמַר רָבָא: הֲלָכָה כר"ע. רָבִינָא וְרַב חָמָא בַּר בּוּזִי אִקְלְעוּ לְבֵי רֵישׁ גָּלוּתָא, קָם רַב חָמָא וְקָא מְהַדַּר אַבֵּי מֵאָה. א"ל רָבִינָא: לָא צְרִיכַתְּ, הָכִי אָמַר רָבָא: הֲלָכָה כר"ע.§ אָמַר רָבָא: כִּי אָכְלִינַן רִפְתָּא בֵּי רֵישׁ גָּלוּתָא מְבָרְכִינַן ג' ג'. וְלִיבָרְכוּ י'! – שָׁמַע רֵישׁ גָּלוּתָא וְאִיקְפַּד. -וְנִיפְּקוּ בְּבִרְכְתָא דְּרֵישׁ גָּלוּתָא! – אַיְּדֵי דְּאָוְשׁוּ כ"ע לָא שָׁמְעֵי. אָמַר רַבָּה תּוֹסְפָאָה: הָנֵי ג' דְּכָרְכֵי רִפְתָּא בַּהֲדֵי הֲדָדֵי, וְקָדֵים חַד מִינַּיְיהוּ וּבָרֵיךְ לְדַעְתֵּיהּ, אִינּוּן נָפְקִין בְּזִמּוּן דִּידֵיהּ, אִיהוּ לָא נָפֵיק בְּזִמּוּן דִּידְהוּ, *לְפִי שֶׁאֵין זִמּוּן לְמַפְרֵעַ.§ "ר' יִשְׁמָעֵאל אוֹמֵר". רַפְרַם בַּר פָּפָּא אִקְלַע לְבֵי כְּנִישְׁתָּא דַּאֲבֵי גִּיבַר, קָם קְרָא בְּסִפְרָא וְאָמַר: "בָּרְכוּ אֶת ה'", וְאִשְׁתִּיק וְלָא אָמַר "הַמְבוֹרָךְ". אָוְשׁוּ כ"ע: "בָּרְכוּ אֶת ה' הַמְבוֹרָךְ"! אָמַר רָבָא: פַּתְיָא *אוּכָּמָא, בַּהֲדֵי פְּלוּגְתָּא לְמָה לָךְ? וְעוֹד: הָא נְהוּג עָלְמָא כְּרַבִּי יִשְׁמָעֵאל.§

**מתני'** *ג' שֶׁאָכְלוּ כְּאַחַת – אֵינָן רַשָּׁאִין לֵיחָלֵק, וְכֵן ד' וְכֵן חֲמִשָּׁה; ו' – נֶחֱלָקִין, עַד עֲשָׂרָה; וַעֲשָׂרָה – אֵין נֶחֱלָקִין, עַד כ'. שְׁתֵּי חֲבוּרוֹת שֶׁהָיוּ אוֹכְלוֹת בְּבַיִת אֶחָד, בִּזְמַן שֶׁמִּקְצָתָן רוֹאִין אֵלּוּ אֶת אֵלּוּ – הֲרֵי אֵלּוּ מִצְטָרְפִין לְזִמּוּן, וְאִם לָאו – אֵלּוּ מְזַמְּנִין לְעַצְמָן וְאֵלּוּ מְזַמְּנִין לְעַצְמָן. אֵין מְבָרְכִין עַל הַיַּיִן עַד שֶׁיִּתֵּן לְתוֹכוֹ מַיִם, דִּבְרֵי ר' אֱלִיעֶזֶר; וחכ"א: מְבָרְכִין.§

**גמ'** מַאי קמ"ל? תְּנֵינָא חֲדָא זִימְנָא: *ג' שֶׁאָכְלוּ כְּאַחַת חַיָּיבִין לְזַמֵּן! –הָא קמ"ל, כִּי הָא דְּאָמַר רַבִּי אַבָּא אָמַר שְׁמוּאֵל: ג' שֶׁיָּשְׁבוּ לֶאֱכוֹל כְּאַחַת וַעֲדַיִין לֹא אָכְלוּ – אֵינָן רַשָּׁאִין לֵיחָלֵק.(ג) ל"א: אָמַר רַבִּי אַבָּא [א] אָמַר שְׁמוּאֵל, הָכִי קָתָנֵי: ג' שֶׁיָּשְׁבוּ לֶאֱכוֹל כְּאַחַת, אע"פ שֶׁכָּל אֶחָד וְאֶחָד אוֹכֵל מִכִּכָּרוֹ – אֵינָן רַשָּׁאִין לֵיחָלֵק. אִי נַמִּי: כִּי הָא דְּרַב הוּנָא, דְּאָמַר רַב הוּנָא: ג' שֶׁבָּאוּ מג' חֲבוּרוֹת – אֵינָן רַשָּׁאִין לֵיחָלֵק. אָמַר רַב חִסְדָּא: וְהוּא – שֶׁבָּאוּ מג' חֲבוּרוֹת שֶׁל ג' בְּנֵי אָדָם. אָמַר רָבָא: וְלָא

תורה אור: שמואל ב ז | תהלים סח

---

**רש"י**

אף ברכו. שפיר דמי. ומיהו, טוב לו להיות מן המברכים: תנינא. סייעתא לשמואל: ששה נחלקין. אם רצו ליחלק ולזמן אלו לעצמן ואלו לעצמן – רשאין. הן, שהרי יש זימון כאן וכאן. כלומר: וכן ז' וכן ח' לשתי חבורות, וכן ט' לשתי חבורות, עד עשרה. אבל אם היו עשרה – חלה עליהן הזכרת השם, ואם יחלקו לא יהיה שם הזכרה – אין נחלקין עד שיהיו שם עשרים: ה"ג ואי אמרת ברכו עדיף אמאי ששה נחלקין. אם ירצו, הא מעיקרא יכולין לומר "ברכו", והשתא תו לא אמרי: אלא לאו ש"מ. אף "ברכו" קאמר מתני', וכיון דמתני' אף "ברכו" קאמר, מסתברא היא שטוב לו לאדם להיות מן המברכים, וסייעתא דשמואל. וגירסא הכי איתא ששה (ג)עד עשרה ואי אמרת "ברכו" דוקא, אמאי ששה נחלקין? אלא לאו ש"מ אף "ברכו", ש"מ: תנ"ה. דמתניתין אף "ברכו" קאמר: והנקדנין. דווקנין, תופסין אותו על שהוציא עצמו מן הכלל: ומטובו הרי זה בור. שממעט בתגמוליו של מקום, דמשמע דבר מועט כדי חיים: בשאלה שאני. שהשואל שואל כעני על פתח, שאינו מריס ראש לשאול שאלה גדולה: הרחב פיך. לשאול כל תאותך: חיים ה"ז בור. דהוציא עצמו מן הכלל: מתני איפכא. "חיים" עדיף, שכולל את כל חיי עולם: נברך שאכלנו משלו. משמע שהוא יחידי שהכל אוכלים משלו: למי שאכלנו משלו. משמע מרובים הן, זה זן את זה וזה זן את זה, ולפי דבריו מברך את בעל הבית: התם מוכחא מילתא. דבמעשה נסים ליכא למימר מרובין: כדתנן על המזון שאכלנו. ולא קתני (ד)משלו: ואידך. עוברים ממקור נפקא ואנן ממקהלות דרשינן: הלכה כר"ע. בכהמ"ז, דאחד עשרה ואחד עשרה רבוא: מברכינן תלתא תלתא. ריש גלותא מאריך בסעודתו, ואנן כל ג' וג' שגמרו סעודתן מזמנין בקול נמוך, ויושבין אחר הברכה עד שגמר ריש גלותא ויזמנו הוא והיושבין אצלו בקול רם. ולקמן פריך: וניפקו בברכה דריש גלותא: שמע ריש גלותא. אם היו מזמנין י' י' היה צריך המברך להגביה קולו, וישמע ריש גלותא ויחרה לו שאנו עושין חבורה לעצמנו בפרהסיא, אע"ג דמפקי נפשייהו מידי זמון של הזכרת השם, וכי הדר מזמן ריש גלותא בהזכרת השם לאו אינהו נפקי ביה, כדאמר רבה תוספאה דאין זמון למפרע – אפ"ה ניחא להו בהכי, משום דאוושי כולי עלמא, שהיו שם מסובין רבים ואין קול המברך נשמע: ובריך לדעתיה. לעצמו בלא זימון: למפרע. משבירך, וידי זמון לא יצא: פתיא. כלי חרס, כדאמר (ע"ז ד' לג:): הני פתיותא דבי מכסי: בהדי פלוגתא למה לך. טוב לך לאחוז דברי רבי ישמעאל, שאף ר"ע מודה דכי אמר "המבורך" טפי עדיף, אלא שאין צריך:

**מתני'** אינן רשאין ליחלק. דאיתחייבו להו בזמון: וכן ד'. אין הג' מזמנין והיחיד יחלק מהם, דאיהו נמי איקבע בחובת זמון: ששה נחלקים. כדי זמון לכאן וכדי זמון לכאן: עד עשרה. אבל עשרה אין נחלקים, דאיתחייבו להו בזמון הזכרת השם עד שיהא עשרים, ואז יחלקו אם ירצו לשתי חבורות: **גמ'** ג' שבאו משלש חבורות. וכדמסיים רב חסדא שבאו מג' חבורות של ג' בני אדם בכל חבורה, ונתחייבו אלו בזמון, ועמד אחד מכל חבורה ונצטרפו שלשה לחבורה אחת – חייבין לזמן ואינן רשאין ליחלק שכבר הוקבעו. ואפילו לא אכלו אלו השלשה משנצטרפו יחד, שכבר גמרו סעודתן עם הראשונים:

---

**תוספות**

**אלא** ש"מ נברך עדיף. לאו דוקא עדיף, אלא: כי הדדי נינהו. ועדיף היינו חשוב; *כמו הקישא עדיף וג"ש עדיף פ' איזהו מקומן (ד' מח.), ר"ל – דההיקש חשוב ואין לבטלו מפני הג"ש. וה"נ קאמר: נברך חשוב כמו ברכו, ולפיכך לא יוציא עצמו מן הכלל. והקונטרס מוחק עדיף, ומיהו אתי שפיר עדיף כדפי': **על** המזון הרי זה בור. דמשמע דמברך לבעל הבית המאכילו. דאי לרחמנא למה הוא מזכיר מזון? בלא מזון יש הרבה לברכו: **אמר** רבא הלכה כר"ע. פירש ר"ת: דהכי קיי"ל, והלכך בין בעשרה בין במאה בין ברבוא – אומר נברך אלהינו על המזון שאכלנו. אבל בג' לא יזכיר על המזון כדאמר לעיל. וגם בעשרה – אם אינו רוצה להזכיר על המזון – הרשות בידו, ואומר ובטובו חיינו: **שלשה** שישבו לאכול כאחד. אף על פי שהיו אוכלין בככר, שכל אחד ואחד אוכל מככרו – אינן רשאין ליחלק. כלומר: אף על פי שהן אוכלין בככרות, וס"ד אין זה צרוף ולא חל עליהם חובת זימון – אפ"ה אינן רשאין ליחלק: *__אבל__ אי אקדימו ואזמינו עלייהו בדוכתייהו. פי': שאכל כל אחד מהשלשה והפסיק לשתים שהיו מסובין עמו עד הזן כדאיתא לעיל (דף מה:): פרח חובת זמון מעליהם. כלומר: פטורין מן הזמון ורשאין עתה ליחלק, ורש"י לא פירש כן:

שחלקוה

---

**עין משפט נר מצוה**

[ועי' חולין כו ריש ע"א]

סז א ב ג ד (ה) טוש"ע או"ח סי' קצב ס"א: [ה מיי' פ"ה מהל' ברכות הלכה ד:]

סח ו טוש"ע או"ח סי' קנג סעיף ח:

סט ז מיי' פ"ה מהלכות ברכות הל' יד סמג עשין כז טוש"ע או"ח סי' קצ סעיף א:

[גי' הערוך והנקדנין פי' המדקדק שלא בדבר לצורך ובלשון ערבי קורין אותו אלמנקר כגון תרגולת המנקר באשפה ערוך ערך נקר]

ע ח מיי' פ"ע מהלכות תפלה הלכה ח ופ"ב הלכה ה סמג עשין יט טוש"ע או"ח סי' נה סעיף א [וכסי' קצג סעיף ז]:

עא ט מיי' פ"ה מהל' ברכות הל' י סמג עשין כז טוש"ע או"ח סי' קצג סעיף א:

עב י מיי' שם הלכה יב סמג שם טוש"ע או"ח סי' קצה סעיף א:

עג כ ל מיי' שם הל' יא סמג שם טוש"ע או"ח סי' קצג סעיף ד:

עד מ נ מיי' שם סמג שם טוש"ע או"ח שם סעיף ה:

**הגהות הב"ח**

(א) גמ' א"ר יוחנן ברוך שאכלנו. נ"ב ובאשר"י (מגיה) [ובגירסתו] נברך וקאי אדר' יוחנן נברך: (ב) שם אינן רשאין ליחלק ל"א א"ר אבא וכו' אע"פ שכל אחד ואחד אוכל מככרו לעצמו אינן רשאין ליחלק: (ג) רש"י ד"ה אלא לאו וכו' ששה נחלקין עד עשרה: (ד) ד"ה כדתנן וכו' ולא קתני משלו נ"ב באשר"י (מגיה) [ובגירסתו] ג"כ שלו וכן במשנה.

**הגהות הגר"א**

[א] גמ' ל"א אמר ר' אבא. נ"ב כאן ג' ל"א מתחלפות הלה"ש ל"ג לה וריי"ף ל"ג לראשונה.

[פסחים פח. מגילה יד: ע"ז טו: ע"ש פירש"י לשבת]

**מסורת הש"ס**

[תוספתא פ"ה] | [מסכת ברכו' פ"א] | [סנהדרין יז.] | [פסחים קטז:] | [ל"י כמאן דמברך מזון רי"ף ורא"ש] | [סוטה ל:] | [לעיל מה:] | [שם] | [שם]

עה א מיי' פכ"ו מהל' כלים הל' יב:

עו ב מיי' פ"ה מהלכות ברכות הל' יב סמג עשין כז טוש"ע או"ח סי' קצה סעיף א:

עז ג ד ה ו מיי' פ"ז שם הלכה ט סמג שם טוש"ע או"ח סי' קס סעיף יב וסימן רעב סעיף א:

עח ז מיי' שם וסמג שם טוש"ע א"ח סימן קעא סעיף ד:

עט ח מיי' פ"ח שם הל' יב סמג שם טוש"ע א"ח סי' קעב סעיף א:

פ ט מיי' שם טוש"ע שם סעיף ב:

ולא אמרן – אלא דלא אקדימו הנך ואזמון עלייהו בדוכתייהו, אבל אזמון עלייהו בדוכתייהו – פרח זימון מינייהו. אמר רבא: מנא אמינא לה? *דתנן: אמטה שנגנבה חציה, או שאבדה חציה, או שחלקוה אחין או שותפין – טהורה. החזירוה – מקבלת טומאה מכאן ולהבא. מכאן ולהבא – אין, למפרע – לא, אלמא: כיון דפלגוה פרח לה טומאה מינה, ה"נ: כיון דאזמון עלייהו – פרח זימון מינייהו.§ "ב' חבורות וכו'". תנא: באם יש שמש ביניהם – שמש מצרפן. "אין מברכין על היין". ת"ר: יין, *געד שלא נתן לתוכו מים – אין מברכין עליו "ב"פ הגפן" אלא "בורא פרי העץ" ונוטלין ממנו לידים, משנתן לתוכו מים – מברכין עליו "בורא פרי הגפן" ואין נוטלין [א] ממנו לידים, דברי ר"א; וחכ"א: בין כך ובין כך מברכין עליו "ב"פ הגפן" דואין נוטלין הימנו לידים. כמאן אזלא הא *דאמר שמואל: העושה אדם כל צרכיו בפת, כמאן? כר' אליעזר. א"ר יוסי ברבי חנינא: *מודים חכמים לר"א בכוס של ברכה, שאין מברכין עליו עד שיתן לתוכו מים. מ"ט? –אמר רב אושעיא: בעינן מצוה מן המובחר. ורבנן – למאי חזי? -א"ר זירא: וחזי לקורייטי.§ ת"ר, *זד' דברים נאמרו בפת: אין מניחין בשר חי על הפת, ואין מעבירין כוס מלא על הפת, ואין זורקין את הפת, ואין סומכין את הקערה בפת. אמימר ומר זוטרא ורב אשי כרכו ריפתא בהדי הדדי איתי לקמייהו תמרי ורמוני, שקל מר זוטרא פתק לקמיה דרב אשי דסתנא, א"ל: לא סבר לה מר להא דתניא: אין זורקין את האוכלין?! –ההיא – בפת תניא. –והתניא: כשם שאין זורקין את הפת כך *אין זורקין את האוכלין! –א"ל, והתניא: אף על פי שאין זורקין את הפת אבל זורקין את האוכלין! –אלא לא קשיא: יהא – במידי דממאיס, הא – במידי דלא ממאיס. ת"ר: *כממשיכין יין בצנורות לפני חתן ולפני כלה, וזורקין לפניהם קליות ואגוזים בימות החמה אבל לא בימות הגשמים, אבל לא גלוסקאות – לא בימות החמה ולא בימות הגשמים.§ א"ר יהודה: שכח והכניס אוכלין לתוך פיו בלא ברכה – מסלקן לצד א' ומברך. תניא חדא: בולען; ותניא אידך: פולטן; ותניא אידך: מסלקן! –ל"ק: חהא דתניא בולען – במשקין, טוהא דתניא פולטן – במידי דלא ממאיס, והא דתניא מסלקן – במידי דממאיס.

במידי

**רש"י**

ולא אמרן אלא דלא אקדימו הנך. חבורות שפרשו אלו מהן ואזמון עלייהו דהני. כגון: אם היו ארבעה בכל חבורה ונשאר בכל אחת כדי זימון, והפורשים הללו היו צריכים לצאת לשוק קודם שגמרו החבורות את סעודתם: אבל אזמון עלייהו. דהני. כגון: שנצטרפו אלו עמהם לזימון, כדאמר' לעיל קורין לו ומזמנים עליו, ובירכו החבורות, ואלו לא היו שם אלא (א) כדי "נברך" ו"ברוך הוא", ועכשיו הם באים לברך – לא מזמני, דפרח מינייהו חובת זימון, ותו לא הדר עלייהו: מטה טמאה שנגנבה חציה אלמא כיון דפלגוה. פקע שם מטה מינה, ושם טומאה. אע"ג דהדר הדרוה והרי היא מטה – לא הדרה טומאתה. הכא נמי, כיון דפקע שם שלשה מינייהו בהפרדם, ושם זימון ע"י שזימנו הראשונים עליהם – אע"ג דהדרי לכלל שם שלשה, לא הדרי לכלל זימון. אבל כי לא אזמון לא פקע חובת זימון מהן, אף (ב) לפי פרידתם: אם יש שמש ביניהם. שמשמש לשתיהם: שמש מצרפן. אע"פ שאין אלו רואין את אלו, כגון יריעה פרוסה ביניהם: אין מברכין עליו ב"פ הגפן. לפי שהיה יינם חזק מאד ואין ראוי לשתיה בלא מים, הלכך אכתי לא אשתני למעליותא ולא זו מברכתו הראשונה, והרי הוא כענבים, וברכתו "ב"פ העץ": ונוטלין ממנו לידים. דשם מים עליו, דמי פירות בעלמא מקרי: משנתן לתוכו מים. שם יין עליו, ואין נוטלין אלא במים[ב]. לשון אחר הכי גרסי': יין עד שלא נתן לתוכו מים – מברכין עליו "ב"פ העץ" ואין נוטלין הימנו לידים, משנתן לתוכו מים – מברכין עליו "בורא פרי הגפן" ונוטלין הימנו לידים דברי ר' אליעזר. וחכ"א: בין כך ובין כך מברכין עליו "ב"פ הגפן" ואין נוטלין ממנו לידים. וטעמייהו דרבנן משום הפסד אוכלין. כך מצאתי בהלכות גדולות אצל קידוש והבדלה, [ג] ובדקתי בתוספתא ולא גרסינן בה הכי אלא כמו שהוא בספרים: כר"א. דאמר נוטלין הימנו לידים ולא חייש להפסד אוכלין: למאי חזי. לשתיה דמברכין עליו ברכת היין: לקורייטי. פייסו"ן בלע"ז, ובלשון חכמים: אנומלית ואלונתית: אין מעבירים כוס מלא על הפת. שלא ישפך על הפת ותהא הפת בזויה: פתק. זרק: דסתנא. אמיניסטרישו"ן בלע"ז, מנה של בשר מבושל: מידי דממאיס. שמתמעך בזריקתו, כגון תאנים שבשלו כל צרכם ותותים: דלא ממאיס. רמון ואגוז וכל דבר קשה: ממשיכין יין בצנורות. משום סימן טוב. ואין כאן משום בזיון והפסד לפי שמקבלים אותו בראש פי הצנור בכלי: בימות החמה. שאין טיט בדרכים: אבל לא גלוסקאות. שהרי אף בימות החמה הן נמאסין בזריקתן: בולען. בלא ברכה: פולטן. ומברך, וחוזר ואוכלן: משקין. בולען, שאי אפשר לסלקן לאחד מלוגמיו ולברך, ולא לפולטם שמפסידן: פולטן במידי דלא ממאיס. במה שנתנו בפיו ויכול לחזור ולאוכלו:

במידי

**תוספות**

שחלקוה אחין או שותפין טהורה. תימה: דאמר בסוכה (פ"ק דף טז.) מטה מטמאה אברים כגון ארוכה ושתי כרעים! ולי נראה: דהתם איירי שיכול להחזירה כאשר בתחלה ולתקנה, שהכרעים בעין והדיוט יכול להחזירה. וא"ת: אמאי לא פריך הכא מכל כלי שנשבר וטהור, אלמא כיון דפלגוה פרח לה טומאה! ול"נ: דשאני התם – שאינו ראוי עוד להצטרף הכלי יחד ולקבל טומאה אפילו מכאן ולהבא, ולא הוי דומיא דשלשה בני אדם דהוו ראוים עוד להצטרף לזמון: שמש מצרפן לזמון. וה"ה בשני בתים ובני אדם עומדים ומשמשין מזו לזו – מצטרפין, וכן איתא בירושלמי, ובלבד שישמעו ברכת המזון מפי המברך, והא דנקט במתני' בית [אחד] – משום חדוש דסיפא, דאפילו בבית אחד אם לאו – אין מזמנין. וכן בבית חתנים כשאוכלים בחופה בב' בתים ובני אדם משמשין מזו לזו – מצטרפין, ובלבד שישמעו ברכת המזון מפי המברך: בורא פרי העץ ונוטלין ממנו לידים. פירש"י: כי לא נתן לתוכו מים לא הוי אלא כמי פירות. ומכאן משמע דמי פירות כשרין לנטילת ידים. ויש לחלק בין הני דאמרינן בפרק כל הבשר (דף קז.) דאחזותא קפדיתו. ומיהו, יש מפרשים: לנטילת ידים בעינן מים דכתיב וידיו לא שטף במים: כמאן אזלא הא דאמר שמואל וכו' כר' אליעזר. לכאורה משמע ממאי דאמר ר"א נוטלין וכו'. ותימה דאמרינן בפרק במה טומנין (ד' נ:): אימר דאמר שמואל במידי דלא ממאיס במידי דממאיס מי אמר? וא"כ, היכי מוקים לה הא דשמואל כר"א, דהא יין מידי דממאיס בנטילת ידים, ובמידי דממאיס מודה שמואל! ועוד קשה: דהכא משמע דאין הלכה כשמואל, מדמוקי לה כר"א, ובפרק שני דבילה (ד' כא:) קאמר סתמא דגמ' דסופלי לחיותא בי"ט דמטלטלין להו אגב רפתא כשמואל משמע דקי"ל כוותיה! וי"ל: דהכא לא קאמר אלא לדברי ר"א(ג) דסבר לה כשמואל, ועדיפא מיניה קאמר – שמתיר אפילו היכא דממאיס, ולא נחת כאן אלא לפרש טעמא דר"א, כדפירשנו. ובה"ג אמר דהלכה כרבנן דהכא, והלכה נמי כשמואל. דכי קאמר שמואל – הני מילי מידי דלא ממאיס, אבל מידי דממאיס לא, ודלא כפי'(ד) ר"ת שפסק דלא כשמואל מדמוקי ליה כר"א, אלא ודאי קיימא לן כשמואל כדפירשנו. ואם כן, מותר לסמוך הקערה בפת היכא דלא ממאיס. וי"א דצריך לאכלו אח"כ. ויש נוהגים לאכול דייסא בפת, הואיל ואוכלין הפת אח"כ, אבל במס' סופרים אוסרו, דאמרינן במס' סופרים (פ"ג): אין אוכלין אוכלין באוכלין אא"כ היה אוכלן בבת אחת, ושמא ההיא דלא כשמואל: מודים חכמים לר"א בכוס של ברכה שאין מברכין עליו עד שיתן לתוכו מים. תימה: דאמרינן לקמן ד' דברים נאמרו בכוס של ברכה חי ומלא! וי"ל: דבעינן שיתנו חי לתוך הכוס ואח"כ ימזגנו. אי נמי: בעינן חי מן החבית. אי נמי: קאי אכוס עצמו, ומאי חי – שלם, כדאיתא במכות (ד' טז:): ריסק ט' נמלים ואחד חי וכו', אלמא דאותו חי היינו שלם, ה"נ – בעינן שיהא הכוס שלם בלא *שבירה: למאי חזי. פי': ולמאי אשתני לעילויא? ומשני: לקורייטי. וכן הלכה כרבנן, דיין חי מברכין עליו בורא פרי הגפן, דאמרינן (פסחים קח:): שתאן חי – יצא: אין זורקין את האוכלים. בהני שלשה מודה שמואל: אין מעבירין כוס מלא על הפת, וגם אין חותכין עליו בשר חי, ואין זורקין את הפת אפילו לא ממאיס, וכן שאר אוכלין אסור לזרוק במידי דממאיס: ולא בימות הגשמים. אע"פ שבאגוזים אין האוכל נמאס בתוכו, מ"מ כשאין נופלים בטיט נמאסים. ומיהו, עכשיו שדרכן לזרוק חטים בבית חתנים צריך ליזהר שלא יזרקום אלא במקום נקי:

מעיקרא

**מסורת הש"ס**

כלים פי"ח מ"ט

[תוספתא פ"ד]

שבת נ: קמג.

ב"ב נז:

[ע"ז ל: ע"ש]

מס' ד"א פ"ט [חמשה דברים על האוכלין]

[מס' סופרים פ"ג]

[תוספתא פ"ח]

[וע"ע תוס' שבת עו: ד"ה כדי ובעירובין כט: ופסחים קח: ד"ה שתאן וב"ב נז: ד"ה עד]

**הגהות הב"ח**

(א) רש"י ד"ה אבל אזמון וכו' אלא עד כדי: (ב) ד"ה מטה וכו' אף לפני פרידתם: (ג) תוס' ד"ה כמאן וכו' וי"ל וכו' ר' אליעזר דסבר: (ד) בא"ד ודלא כפירוש רבינו חננאל שפסק דלא:

**הגהות הגר"א**

[א] גמ' ונוטלין ממנו כו' ואין נוטלין. נ"ל להיפך כל"א שברש"י (וכירושלמי ריש פ"ו יין בזמן שהוא כמות שהוא מברכין עליו בפה"ע ואין נוטלין ממנו לידים בזמן שהוא מזוג אומר עליו בפה"ג ונוטלין ממנו לידים דברי ר"א וחכ"א בין חי בין מזוג אומרים עליו בפה"ג ואין נוטלין ממנו לידים אמר ר' אבא משום איבוד אוכלין כו' גירסת רבינו שם. וז"ש בגמ' כאן כמאן כו' כר"א דוקא לטעמייהו דרבנן משום איבוד אוכלין כמ"ש בירושלמי וכמ"ש בשנות אליהו ראיה מזבחים כ"ב אבל רבינו בא"ח סי' ק"ס לקח ראיה כה"ה ועי"ש): [ב] רש"י ד"ה (ונוטלין ממנו עד אלא במים. תא"מ: [ג] שם (ובדקתי בתוספתא ול"ג בה הכי אלא כמו שהוא בספרים תא"מ (הגירסא רבינו בתוספתא ג"כ להיפך):

במידי דלא ממאיס נמי, לסלקינהו לצד אחד וליברך! - תרגמא רב יצחק קסקסאה קמיה דרבי יוסי בר אבין משמיה דרבי יוחנן; משום שנאמר: "ימלא פי תהלתך". בעו מיניה מרב חסדא: מי שאכל ושתה ולא ברך - מהו שיחזור ויברך? - אמר להו: מי שאכל שום וריחו נודף, יחזור ויאכל שום אחר כדי שיהא ריחו נודף?! אמר רבינא: הלכך, אפילו גמר סעודתו יחזור ויברך, דתניא: טבל ועלה, אומר בעלייתו: ברוך אשר קדשנו במצותיו וצונו על הטבילה. ולא היא, התם - מעיקרא גברא לא חזי, הכא - מעיקרא גברא חזי, והואיל ואידחי אידחי. תנו רבנן: אספרגוס - יפה ללב וטוב לעינים וכ"ש לבני מעים, והרגיל בו - יפה לכל גופו, והמשתכר הימנו - קשה לכל גופו. מדקתני יפה ללב, מכלל דבחמרא עסקינן, וקתני: וכל שכן לבני מעים, והתניא: ללע"ט יפה לרמ"ת קשה! - כי תניא ההיא - במיושן, כדתנן: קונם יין שאני טועם, שהיין קשה לבני מעים, אמרו לו: והלא מיושן יפה הוא לבני מעים, ושתק - [ג] אסור בחדש ומותר במיושן, שמע מינה. תנו רבנן ששה דברים נאמרו באספרגוס: אין שותין אותו אלא כשהוא חי ומלא, מקבלו בימין ושותהו בשמאל, ואין משיחין אחריו, ואין מפסיקין בו, ואין מחזירין אותו אלא למי שנתנו לו, ורק אחריו, ואין סומכין אותו אלא במינו. והתניא: אין סומכין אותו אלא בפת! - לא קשיא הא בדחמרא, הא בדשכרא. תני חדא: ללע"ט יפה לרמ"ת קשה, ותניא אידך: לרמ"ת יפה ללע"ט קשה! - לא קשיא; הא בדחמרא, הא בדשכרא. תני חדא: רק אחריו לוקה, ותניא אידך: לא רק אחריו לוקה! - לא קשיא: הא בדחמרא, הא בדשכרא. א"ר אשי: השתא דאמרת לא רק אחריו לוקה - מימיו נזרקין אפילו בפני המלך. א"ר ישמעאל בן אלישע, שלשה דברים סח לי סוריאל שר הפנים: אל תטול חלוקך בשחרית מיד השמש ותלבש; ואל תטול ידיך ממי שלא נטל ידיו; ואל תחזיר כוס אספרגוס אלא למי שנתנו לך, מפני שתכספית, ואמרי לה: אסתלגנית של מלאכי חבלה מצפין לו לאדם ואומרים: אימתי יבא אדם לידי אחד מדברים הללו וילכד. אמר ריב"ל, שלשה דברים סח לי מלאך המות: אל תטול חלוקך שחרית מיד השמש ותלבש; ואל תטול ידיך ממי שלא נטל ידיו; ואל תעמוד לפני הנשים בשעה שחוזרות מן המת, מפני שאני מרקד ובא לפניהן וחרבי בידי ויש לי רשות לחבל. ואי פגע מאי תקנתיה? - לינשוף מדוכתיה ארבע אמות, אי איכא נהרא - ליעבריה, ואי איכא דרכא אחרינא - ליזיל בה, ואי איכא גודא ליקו אחוריה, ואי לא - ליהדר אפיה ולימא: "ויאמר ה' אל השטן יגער ה' בך וגו'" עד דחלפי מיניה. א"ר זירא א"ר אבהו, ואמרי לה במתניתא תנא, עשרה דברים נאמרו בכוס של ברכה: טעון הדחה, ושטיפה, חי, ומלא, עיטור, ועיטוף, נוטלו בשתי ידיו, ונותנו בימין, ומגביהו מן הקרקע טפח, ונותן עיניו בו; ויש אומרים: אף משגרו במתנה לאנשי ביתו. אמר ר' יוחנן, אנו אין לנו אלא ארבעה בלבד: הדחה, שטיפה, חי, ומלא. תנא: הדחה מבפנים ושטיפה מבחוץ. א"ר יוחנן: כל המברך על כוס מלא - נותנין לו נחלה בלי מצרים, שנאמר: "ומלא ברכת ה' ים ודרום ירשה". ר' יוסי בר חנינא אומר: זוכה ונוחל שני עולמים, העולם הזה והעולם הבא. "עיטור" - רב יהודה מעטרהו בתלמידים, רב חסדא מעטר ליה בנטלי. [ד] אמר ר' חנן: ובחי. אמר רב ששת: ובברכת הארץ. "עיטוף" - רב פפא מעטף ויתיב, רב אסי פריס סודרא על רישיה. "נוטלו בשתי ידיו" - א"ר חיננא בר פפא: מאי קראה - "שאו ידיכם קדש וברכו את ה'". "ונותנו לימין". א"ר חייא בר אבא אמר ר' יוחנן, ראשונים שאלו: שמאל מהו שתסייע לימין? אמר רב אשי: הואיל וראשונים איבעיא להו ולא איפשט להו, אנן

תורה אור: תהלים עא | זכריה ג | דברים לג | תהלים קלד

---

**רש"י**

במידי דלא ממאיס נמי. למה לי פולטן? לסלקינהו לצד אחד: יחזור ויאכל שום אחר. כדי שיסריח יותר. כלומר: יוסיף על סרחונו [א] *ויעשה ברכה לבטלה: *מי שאכל ושתה ולא ברך. (א) לפניהם קודם אכילה ברכת המוציא וברכת היין: מהו שיחזור וכו'. [ב] לאחר אכילה ושתיה: הלכך. כיון דאם נזכר באמצע יכול לברך, אפי' גמר סעודתו נמי יכול לברך: על הטבילה. אלמא אע"ג דטבל הויא ברכה: התם מעיקרא לא חזי. דרוב טבילות משום קרי הם, ובעלי קריין אסורים בברכות, שהם דברי תורה כדאמרינן בפרק "מי שמתו" (דף כ:). ודחוי מעיקרא לאו דחוי הוא, ולכי מתקן הדר מברך, אבל האי מעיקרא איחזי, וכיון דגמר אידחי, והואיל ואידחי - אידחי: אספרגוס. כוס שהיו שותים בכל בקר אליבא ריקנא לרפואה: דבחמרא עסקינן. דאמרינן לקמן בשמעתין אספרגוס ללע"ט יפה ואוקמינן בשל יין. וסימן לע"ט: לב, עין, טחול. וכ"ש לבני מעים. קושיא היא. כלו': בחמרא קתני, וכ"ש לבני מעים, והתניא לקמן, לרמ"ת קשה, אספרגוס של יין, וסימן רמ"ת: ראש, מעים, תחתוניות: כי תניא ההיא. דקתני וכ"ש לבני מעים: ביין מיושן. של ג' שנים. כדתנן בבבא בתרא (דף צח.): ישן - משל אשתקד, מיושן - משל שלש שנים: קונם יין שאני טועם. הקונם יהא עלי יין שאני טועם: אלא חי. יין חי שאינו מזוג: אין מפסיקין בו. אלא שותהו בבת אחת: ואין סומכין אותו. לאכול אחריו מיד: בדחמרא. סמיכתו בפת: בדשכרא. סמיכתו במינו, אם שכר תמרים הוא - סומכו בתמרים, ואם של תמרים הוא - סומכו בתמרים: לוקה. חולי: בדחמרא. לא ירוק: בדשכרא. אם לא רק מים הבאים בפיו אחריו לוקה: אפילו בפני המלך. ירוק ואל יתעכב: סוריאל. מלאך חשוב לבא לפני הקב"ה: אל תטול חלוקך. שחרית מיד השמש אלא אתה בעצמך טלהו ממקום שהוא שם ותלבשנו: תכספית. שם חבורת שדים: איסתלגנית. שם חבורת מלאכי חבלה: אימתי יבא אדם לידי אחד מן הדברים הללו וילכד. רבי ישמעאל עלה לרקיע על ידי שם, בברייתא דמעשה מרכבה: גודא. כותל: כוס של ברכה. ברכת המזון: הדחה ושטיפה וכו'. כולהו מפרש להו ואזיל: מן הקרקע. אם ע"ג קרקע הסב ואם על גבי שלחן - מגביהו מן השלחן: במתנה. דרך דורון וחשיבות: לאנשי ביתו. לאשתו: חי. שמוזגו במים לאחר שנתנו בכוס חי. אבל לברך עליו חי הא אמרן במתני'* אין מברכין, אי נמי, חי כלע"ז פרי"ק להביאו מן החבית לשמו: מעטרהו בתלמידים. תלמידיו סובבין אותו כשהוא מברך: בנטלי. כוסות: ובברכת הארץ. כשמגיע לברכת הארץ מוסיף עליה: מעטף. מתעטף: אנן

[עי' רש"א] | ה"ד"ה מהו שיחזור וכו' קודם ד"ה יחזור ויאכל | פסחים ז: | נדרים סו. ע"ש | [לעיל נ:] | וסוי' חמא"ה

---

**תוספות**

מעיקרא גברא לא חזי. תימה: והלא טמא אינו אסור לברך! ובקונטרס פירש דבעלי קריין אסורים בדברי תורה. וי"ל: דמיירי בטבילת גרים, ומפני אותה טבילה הצריכו לכל שאר טבילות לברך לאחר טבילה. וכן בנט"י, שפעמים אדם בא מבית הכסא ואין אדם ראוי לברך עד לאחר הנטילה, נהגו העם לברך כל שאר ברכת ידים לאחר נטילה*:

אין לנו אלא ארבעה דברים. ומיהו לא משמע (כן) דפליג ר' יוחנן אההיא דנותנו לימינו, כדאמרי' לקמן: א"ר יוחנן ראשונים שאלו מהו שתסייע שמאל לימין, משמע שכן היו נוהגים. ומיהו, מדהאמוראים היו עושים עיטור ועיטוף, משמע שהיו מחמירים על עצמן והיו זהירים בכולן; ולפיכך יש להחמיר בכוס של ברכה:

שטיפה חי ומלא. ירושלמי דסוף פירקין, א"ר אחא: שלשה דברים נאמרו בכוס של ברכה: מלא, עיטור ומודח. ושלשתן מקרא נפתלי שבע רצון ומלא ברכת ה', שבע - עיטור, רצון - מודח, ומלא - כמשמעו: שטיפה מבחוץ והדחה מבפנים. ופי' ר"י: דוקא שאין הכוס יפה, שיש בו שיורי כוסות. אבל אם הוא יפה - בלאו הכי שפיר דמי, דלא בעינן אלא שיהא כוס של ברכה יפה: זוכה לשני עולמות. פי' הרב רבי יוסף ממרשייליא: מדהוה ליה למכתב ים ודרום רש, וכתב ירשה, הרי יו"ד ה"א יתירה. וביו"ד ה"א נבראו שני עולמות, כדאמרינן בהתכלת (מנחות ד' כט:): כי ביה ה' צור עולמים (אל תקרי צור, אלא צר וכו'): שמאל מהו שתסייע לימין. בכוסות גדולות מיירי, או בראש חדש טבת שחל להיות בשבת שהוא בחנוכה, או בנישואין, וצריך להאריך בברכת המזון.

אין

---

**עין משפט נר מצוה**

פא א מיי' פי"א מהל' ברכות הל' ז סמג עשין כז טוש"ע י"ד סי' רסח סעיף ב:

פב ב מיי' פ"ד שם הל' ב טוש"ע או"ח סי' קסז סעיף ח:

[ועי' תוס' פסחים ז: ד"ה על]

פג ג ש"ע או"ח סי' ד סעיף יח:

פד ד ש"ע י"ד סימן שנט סעיף ב:

פה ה ו מיי' פ"ז שם הל' טו סמג שם טוש"ע או"ח סי' קפג סעי' א ב ג:

פו ו שם סעיף ד:

**רב נסים גאון**

ללע"ט יפה לרמ"ת רע. סימן הוא. ובהלכות גדולות מפרש ללב לעין לטחול יפה לראש למעים לתחתוניות רע: עשרה דברים נאמרו בכוס של ברכה כו'. בפרקין בגמ' דבני מערבא אמרי אמר ר' אחא ג' דברים נאמרו בכוס של ברכה עטור ומודח ומלא ושלשתן בפסוק אחד (דברים לג) נפתלי שבע רצון ומלא שבע עטור רצון מודח ומלא כמשמעו אמר ר' חייא אם עשיתם כן מה כתוב תמן ים ודרום ירשה אתה זוכה לירש העולם הזה והעוה"ב:

[כל זה ליתא לפנינו שם]

**הגהות הב"ח**

(א) רש"י ד"ה מי שאכל ושתה ולא ברך אברכה לפניהם קאי:

**הגהות הגר"א**

[א] רש"י ד"ה יחזור כו' (ויעשה ברכה לבטלה) תא"מ: [ב] שם ד"ה מהו שיחזור כו' באמצע אכילה ושתיה. כצ"ל (ערש"א): [ג] גמ' ושתק מותר במיושן. כצ"ל: [ד] שם מעטר ליה בנטלי חי אמר רב ששת על הכל גו'. כצ"ל (וכ"כ רבינו בא"ח סי' קפ"ג):

**גליון הש"ס**

גמ' אל תטול חלוקך. מג"א סי' ד סק"א.

[עי' לעיל נ: תוס' ד"ה מודים. ועי' תוס' סנהדרין ע. ד"ה חי]

[בהכה"ש ליתא לכל זה גם בהרי"ף נדפס בפנים בין שני חצאי עיגולים וכן מוחק ד"ה של הגליון ועיקר הגה' שהיה לפני רב אלפס כך ליתא חי אמר רב ששת על ברכת הארץ וכ"כ ר' יונה וכ"כ ב"י]

סימן קפג ע"ש וע"ע תוס' שבת עו: ד"ה כדי ותוס' עירובין כט: ותוס' פסחים קח: ותוס' בבא בתרא נז: ד"ה עד וכו' מה שפירש ר"ח על מה דאמרינן בברכת הארץ נגד פירש"י דהכא]

[א ב מיי' פכ"ט מהל' שבת הל' ז]
פז א ב ג ד סמג עשין כז טוש"ע או"ח סי' קפג סעיף ד:
פח ה מיי' פ"ז מהלכות ברכות הלכה טו טוש"ע שם סעיף ו:
פט ו מיי' פ"ד שם הל' א סמג שם טוש"ע או"ח סי' קפג סעיף ט:
א ז מיי' פכ"ט מהל' שבת הלכה ו ז סמג עשין כט טוש"ע או"ח סי' רעא סעיף י:
[ז מיי' פכ"ט מהלכות שבת הל' כד טוש"ע או"ח סי' רלח סעיף א]:
ב ח מיי' פ"ט מהל' ברכות הל' ח ט ופכ"ט מהל' שבת הל' כה סמג עשין כז כט טוש"ע או"ח סי' ריז סעיף ב ה ו וסי' רצז סעיף ב וסי' רצח סעיף יב:
[ח מיי' פ"ב מהלכות ברכות הל' יד ופ"ד הל' א טוש"ע או"ח סי' קפד ס"ה]:
ג ט [מיי' פ"ז מהלכות ברכות הלכה יד] טוש"ע או"ח סי' קעד סעיף ג:
ד י מיי' פ"א מהלכות ברכות הלכה יג סמג עשין כז טוש"ע או"ח סי' רטו סעיף ב:

**אין** מסיחין על כוס של ברכה. פירש"י: שלא יסיח (דעת) המברך משנתנו לו כוס של ברכה, וה"ה המסובין שאין רשאין להסיח דבעינן שיתכוין שומע ומשמיע, וגם אין להפסיק השומעים בשיחת חולין כמו שאין המברך רשאי להסיח. ואע"פ שאמר התם (פרק בתרא דר"ה ד' לד:): שמע תשע תקיעות בתשע שעות ביום – יצא, משמע שהשומע סח בינתים ואפילו הכי יצא, אך לכתחלה אין לעשות כן. ומיהו, נראה דהיינו דוקא בשעה שהמברך שותק מעט בין ברכה לברכה, אבל בשעה שהוא מברך, אם היה מדבר – אפילו בדיעבד לא יצא:

**והלכתא** בכולהו יושב ומברך. לפי שברכת המזון דאורייתא החמירו בה להיות יושב ומברך. שהרי עשרה דברים נאמרו בו, מה שאין כן בשאר ברכות. והוא נוטריקון, ואכלת ושבעת שב עת וברכת לברכת המזון, מפי רבי משה אלברט:

הדרן עלך שלשה שאכלו

א אנן נעבד לחומרא. ב "ומגביהו מן הקרקע טפח" – א"ר אחא בר חנינא: מאי קראה – °"כוס ישועות אשא ובשם ה' אקרא". ג "ונותן עיניו בו" – כי היכי דלא ניסח דעתיה מיניה. ד "ומשגרו לאנשי ביתו במתנה" – כי היכי דתתברך דביתהו.§ עולא אקלע לבי רב נחמן, כריך ריפתא בריך ברכת מזונא, יהב ליה כסא דברכתא לרב נחמן. א"ל רב נחמן: לישדר מר כסא דברכתא לילתא. א"ל: הכי א"ר יוחנן: אין פרי בטנה של אשה מתברך אלא מפרי בטנו של איש, שנאמר: °"וברך פרי בטנך" – "פרי בטנה" לא נאמר אלא "פרי בטנך". תניא נמי הכי, ר' נתן אומר: מנין שאין פרי בטנה של אשה מתברך אלא מפרי בטנו של איש – שנאמר: "וברך פרי בטנך" – "פרי בטנה" לא נאמר אלא 'פרי בטנך'. אדהכי שמעה ילתא, קמה בזיהרא ועלתה לבי חמרא ותברא ד' מאה דני דחמרא. א"ל רב נחמן: נשדר לה מר כסא אחרינא, שלח לה: כל האי נבגא דברכתא היא. שלחה ליה: ממהדורי מילי ומסמרטוטי כלמי.§ א"ר אסי: ה"אין מסיחין על כוס של ברכה. ואמר רב אסי: אין מברכין על כוס של פורענות. מאי כוס של פורענות? א"ר נחמן בר יצחק: כוס שני. תנ"ה: השותה כפלים לא יברך, משום שנאמר: °"הכון לקראת אלהיך ישראל" – והאי לא מתקן. א"ר אבהו, ואמרי לה במתניתא תנא: האוכל ומהלך – מברך מעומד, וכשהוא אוכל מעומד – מברך מיושב, וכשהוא מיסב ואוכל – יושב ומברך. ו והלכתא: בכולהו יושב ומברך.§

## הדרן עלך שלשה שאכלו

**אלו** *דברים שבין בית שמאי ובין בית הלל בסעודה: ב"ש אומרים, מברך על היום ואח"כ מברך על היין, וב"ה אומרים: ז מברך על היין ואחר כך מברך על היום. ב"ש אומרים: נוטלין לידים ואח"כ מוזגין את הכוס, וב"ה אומרים: מוזגין את הכוס ואח"כ נוטלין לידים. ב"ש אומרים: מקנח ידיו במפה ומניחה על השולחן, וב"ה אומרים: על הכסת. ב"ש אומרים: מכבדין את הבית ואח"כ נוטלין לידים, וב"ה אומרים: נוטלין לידים ואח"כ מכבדין את הבית. *ב"ש אומרים: נר ומזון בשמים והבדלה, וב"ה אומרים: נר ובשמים מזון והבדלה. ב"ש אומרים: "שברא מאור האש", וב"ה אומרים: [ז] "בורא מאורי האש". ח אין מברכין לא על הנר ולא על הבשמים של גוים ולא על הנר ולא על הבשמים של מתים, ולא על הנר ולא על הבשמים של ע"ז, ואין מברכין על הנר עד שיאותו לאורו. מי שאכל ושכח ולא בירך, ב"ש אומרים: יחזור למקומו ויברך, וב"ה אומרים: יברך במקום שנזכר. ועד מתי מברך? [ח] עד כדי שיתעכל המזון שבמעיו. *בא להן יין אחר המזון, אם אין שם אלא אותו כוס – בית שמאי אומרים: מברך על היין ואח"כ מברך על המזון, ובית הלל אומרים: ט מברך על המזון ואח"כ מברך על היין. י ועונין אמן אחר ישראל המברך, ואין עונין אמן אחר כותי המברך, עד שישמע כל הברכה כולה.§ **גמ'** *תנו רבנן, דברים שבין ב"ש וב"ה בסעודה: ב"ש אומרים, מברך על היום ואח"כ מברך על היין, שהיום גורם ליין שיבא וכבר קדש היום ועדיין יין לא בא; וב"ה אומרים: מברך על היין ואח"כ מברך על היום, שהיין גורם לקדושה שתאמר. *דבר אחר: ברכת היין תדירה וברכת היום אינה תדירה. תדיר ושאינו תדיר – תדיר קודם. והלכה כדברי ב"ה. מאי "ד"א"? – וכי תימא התם תרתי והכא חדא – ה"נ תרתי נינהו: ברכת היין תדירה וברכת היום אינה תדירה, תדיר ושאינו תדיר – תדיר קודם. "והלכה כדברי ב"ה" – פשיטא! דהא נפקא בת קול! – איבעית אימא: קודם בת קול, ואיבעית אימא: לאחר בת קול, ורבי

תהלים קטז | דברים ז | עמוס ד

אנן נעבד לחומרא. שלא תסייע שמאל לימין בשעת ברכה: שמעה ילתא. שלא ישגר לה כוס של ברכה: קמה בזיהרא. עמדה בכעס: כל האי נבגא דברכתא היא. כל יין שבקנקנים ככוס של ברכה הוא, שתי ממנו: נבגא. כוס, כמו: לשתי מר *אנבגא: ממהדורי מילי. ממחזירי בעיירות ירבו תמיד דברים ומסמרטוטי כלמי. ומתמלקי בגדים בלויים ומורטטים ירבו כנים. כנים מתרגמי' כלמתא: אין מסיחין. משאחזו עד שיברך: כוס שני. שהוא של זוגות, והעומד (א) על שלחנו ושתי זוגות ניזוק על ידי שדים: כפלים. זוגות: הכון לקראת(ב). בדברים נאים ולא בדברי פורענות: מסב. במטה דרך הסבה: והלכתא. בכולהו יושב ומברך:

הדרן עלך שלשה שאכלו

**אלו** דברים וכו' בסעודה. שנחלקו בהלכות סעודה: מברך על היום. בקידוש שבתות וימים טובים: ואחר כך מוזגין את הכוס. יין הבא לפני המזון, כדאמרינן בפרק "כיצד מברכין" (דף מג.): הסבו אע"פ שנטל כו', הביאו להם יין וכו', וקאמרי ב"ש נוטלין לידים ואחר כך שותים את הכוס ואוכלים סעודתם בההיא נטילה. וב"ה אומרים: מוזגין את הכוס ושותין אותו, ואחר כך נוטלין לידים. וטעמא דתרווייהו מפרש בגמרא: ומקנח ידיו במפה. מנטילת מים ראשונים: ומניחה על השולחן. ומקנח בה ידיו תמיד מזוהמת התבשיל: וב"ה אומרים. על הכר או על הכסת יניחנה אחרי כן, ושם יקנח בה ידיו תמיד. וטעמא מפרש בגמ': מכבדין את הבית. מקום שאכלו שם אם הסבו על גבי קרקע – מכבדים את הקרקע, או אם הסבו על השלחן – מכבדין את השלחן משיורי אוכלין שנתפזרו עליו: ואחר כך נוטלין לידים. מים אחרונים: נר ומזון. מי שאין לו אלא כוס אחד במוצאי שבת מניחו עד לאחר המזון, וסודר עליו נר ומזון ובשמים והבדלה כו': אין מברכים על הנר ועל הבשמים של גוים ושל מתים. טעם דכולהו מפרש בגמרא: שיאותו. שיהו נהנים ממנו: עד כדי שיתעכל המזון. מפרש שיעורא בגמ': מברך על היין. בגמרא מפרש פלוגתייהו: עונין אמן אחר ישראל המברך. אפילו לא שמע אלא סוף ברכה, אבל לא לאחר כותי, שמא ברך להר גרזים: **גמ'** שהיום גורם ליין שיבא. כוס זה לא בא אלא בשביל שבת לקידוש: וכבר קדש היום. משקבלו עליו, או מצאת הכוכבים: ועדיין יין לא בא. לשלחן, וכשם שקודם לכניסה כך קודם לברכה: שהיין גורם לקדושה שתאמר. שאם אין יין לא מקדשין, והמקדש על הפת – גם הוא במקום יין וברכת הפת קודמת: תדיר קודם. נפקא לן במסכת זבחים מהאי קרא דכתיב במוספין "מלבד עולת הבקר אשר לעולת התמיד תעשו את אלה". "מלבד" משמע לאחר שהקרבתם התמיד תקריבו המוספין, וקא דרשינן "אשר לעולת התמיד" קרא יתירה, למילף דבשביל שהיא תמיד הקדימה הכתוב, ומכאן אתה למד לכל התמידין:

[קדושין ע.] | תורה אור | פסחים קיד. סוכה | פסחים קג. | [לקמן נג.] | תוספתא פ"ה [פסחים] [סוכה נו.] | פסחים שם [קיד.] נא.

## רב נסים גאון

**תדיר** ושאינו תדיר תדיר קודם. עיקרו במשנת זבחים בפ"י (דף פט) ובמשנת הוריות בפרק אחרון (דף יג) כל התדיר מחבירו הוא קודם את חבירו ואמרינן בגמרא מנא הני מילי אמר אביי דאמר קרא (במדבר כח) מלבד עולת הבוקר אשר לעולת התמיד מכדי כתיב עולת הבוקר עולת התמיד למה לי מאי קאמר רחמנא האי דתדיר קדים ברישא:

## הגהות הב"ח

(א) רש"י ד"ה כוס שני וכו' והעומד מעל: (ב) ד"ה הכון לקראת אלהיך בדברים:

## גליון הש"ס

**גמ'** ומשגרו לאנשי ביתו. עי' תוי"ט ריש סוטה ד"ה רי"א:

*ורבי יהושע היא, דאמר: אין משגיחין בבת קול. וסברי בית שמאי דברכת היום עדיפא?! והתניא: *הנכנס לביתו במוצאי שבת – מברך על היין ועל המאור ועל הבשמים ואחר כך אומר הבדלה, ואם אין לו אלא כוס אחד – מניחו לאחר המזון ומשלשלן כולן לאחריו! – והא, ממאי דב"ש היא, דלמא ב"ה היא? – לא ס"ד, דקתני מאור ואח"כ בשמים, ומאן שמעת ליה דאית ליה האי סברא – ב"ש; *דתניא, א"ר יהודה: לא נחלקו בית שמאי וב"ה על המזון שבתחלה ועל הבדלה שהיא בסוף, על מה נחלקו? על המאור ועל הבשמים(א) – ב"ש אומרים: מאור ואחר כך בשמים, וב"ה אומרים: בשמים ואחר כך מאור. – וממאי דבית שמאי היא ואליבא דרבי יהודה, דילמא בית הלל היא, ואליבא דרבי מאיר? – לא ס"ד, דקתני הכא במתניתין: בית שמאי אומרים, נר ומזון בשמים והבדלה, ובית הלל אומרים: נר ובשמים מזון והבדלה; והתם בברייתא קתני: אם אין לו אלא כוס אחד – מניחו לאחר המזון ומשלשלן כולן לאחריו, שמע מינה דבית שמאי היא ואליבא דרבי יהודה. ומכל מקום קשיא! – קא סברי בית שמאי: *שאני עיולי יומא מאפוקי יומא, עיולי יומא – כמה דמקדמינן ליה עדיף, אפוקי יומא – כמה דמאחרינן ליה עדיף, כי היכי דלא להוי עלן כמשוי. וסברי ב"ש(ב) ברכת המזון טעונה כוס?! והא תנן: בא להם יין לאחר המזון, אם אין שם אלא אותו כוס – בית שמאי אומרים: מברך על היין ואחר כך מברך על המזון. מאי לאו דמברך עילויה ושתי ליה! – לא, דמברך עילויה ומנח ליה. והאמר מר: *המברך צריך שיטעום! – דטעים ליה. והאמר מר: *טעמו – פגמו! – דטעים ליה בידיה. – והאמר מר: *כוס של ברכה צריך שיעור, והא קא פחית ליה משיעוריה! – דנפיש ליה טפי משיעוריה. – והא, "אם אין שם אלא אותו כוס" קתני! – תרי לא הוי, ומחד נפיש. – והא תני רבי חייא, ב"ש אומרים: מברך על היין ושותהו, ואחר כך מברך ברכת המזון! – אלא: תרי תנאי ואליבא דב"ש. "ב"ש אומרים וכו'". *ת"ר, ב"ש אומרים: נוטלין לידים ואח"כ מוזגין את הכוס, שאם אתה אומר מוזגין את הכוס תחלה – גזרה *שמא יטמאו משקין שאחורי הכוס מחמת ידיו, ויחזרו ויטמאו את הכוס. וליטמו ידים לכוס! – ידים שניות הן, *ואין שני עושה שלישי בחולין אלא על ידי משקין. וב"ה אומרים: מוזגין את הכוס ואחר כך נוטלין לידים, שאם אתה אומר נוטלין לידים תחלה, גזרה שמא יטמאו משקין שבידים מחמת הכוס, ויחזרו ויטמאו את הידים. וניטמי כוס לידים! – אין כלי מטמא אדם. – וניטמי למשקין שבתוכו! – הכא בכלי שנטמאו אחוריו במשקין עסקינן, דתוכו טהור וגבו טמא. *דתנן: כלי שנטמאו אחוריו במשקין – אחוריו טמאים, תוכו

**ור' יהושע היא.** דבבא מציעא בתנורו של עכנאי בפ' "הזהב" (ד' נט:). **ומשלשלן.** לשון שלשלת, כלומר: סודרן לאחר המזון: **וממאי דב"ש היא כו'.** אלמא לב"ש מאור ואח"כ בשמים, וכן ברייתא נמי מאור ואחר כך בשמים קאמר, אלמא ב"ש היא. וקתני יין ברישא וקתני הבדלה: **ודילמא ב"ה היא ואליבא דר"מ.** דתנן במתניתין ב"ה אומרים נר ובשמים, ואמר בגמרא ר"מ היא: **לא סלקא דעתך.** לאוקמי ברייתא כמתניתין; דמתני' קתני – מזון באמצע, וברייתא קתני משלשלן כולן לאחריו, כר' יהודה דאמר על המזון שבתחלה, ומדקתני לרבי יהודה מאור ואח"כ בשמים, בית שמאי היא: **ומ"מ קשיא.** דברכת היין קדמה להבדלה: **קידוש** עיולי הוא והבדלה אפוקי היא: **ברכה טעונה כוס.** ברכת המזון, דקתני מניחו לאחר המזון: **והתנן.** מתני' בפרקין: **בא להן.** כל ימות השנה קאמר: **אחר המזון.** ובתוך המזון לא בא להם, וכשגמרו סעודתם בא להם לפני ברכת המזון: **מאי לאו דשתי ליה.** וה"ק ב"ש: אם רצה מברך על היין ושותהו, ואין צריך להניחו לברכת המזון: **טעמו פגמו.** לברכת המזון ולקידוש ולהבדלה, בפרק "ערבי פסחים" (ד' קה:): ה"ג **אלא תרי תנאי אליבא דב"ש.** תנא דמתני' ותנא דר' חייא (*). תנא דרבי חייא אליבא דב"ש אמר: אין ברכה טעונה כוס. ותנא דמתניתין דלעיל דרבי יהודה אליבא דב"ש סבר: ברכה טעונה כוס: **גזרה שמא יטמאו משקין.** שנפלו באחורי הכוס מחמת ידים. דתנן (פרה פ"ח מ"ז): כל הפוסל את התרומה מטמא משקים להיות תחלה, ויחזרו ויטמאו את הכוס. וב"ש סברי: אסור להשתמש בכוס שאחוריו טמאות, כדלקמן: **וליטמו ידים לכוס.** למה ליה דקאמר משקין שאחורי הכוס, בלא משקין נמי מטמו ידים לכוס: **אלא ע"י משקין.** שהמשקין נעשין ראשונים מדרבנן. וא"ת: כלי אינו מקבל טומאה אלא מאב הטומאה! – הני מילי מדאורייתא, וחכמים גזרו שיהו משקים ראשונים מטמאים כלי, גזרה משום משקים זב וזבה שהן אבות הטומאה, כגון רוקו ומימי רגליו: **וב"ה אומרים כו'.** בתוספתא ה"ג לה: וב"ה אומרים: אחורי הכוס לעולם טמאים. דבר אחר: תכף לנט"י סעודה. למאי דקיישיתו שלא יטמאו הידים את אחורי הכוס לאו חששא היא, שאפילו לכתחלה מותר להשתמש בכלי שאחוריו טמאים ותוכו טהור, כגון זה שמטמא אחוריו מחמת משקין, דאמרינן ביה בשמעתין תוכו טהור. הלכך: מוזגין ושותין את הכוס תחלה קודם נטילה. שאם אתה אומר נוטלין לידים תחלה – שמא יהו אחורי הכוס טמאין, גזרה שמא לא יהו הידים נגובות יפה ממי הנטילה, ויטמאו המשקין שבידים מחמת כוס, והן נעשים תחלה ויחזרו ויטמאו את הידים, ונמצא אוכל בידים מסואבות: **ונטמי כוס לידים.** למה לי משקין בידים, אפי' ידים נגובות נמי יטמא כוס לידים! וכיון דהכי הוא, נהי נמי דבכוס שלפני המזון עביד ב"ה תקנתא, דשותהו קודם נטילה, כוסות הבאין בתוך המזון מה תהא עליהן? הלא מטמאין את הידים: **אין כלי מטמא אדם.** כלומר: כלי כזה שנטמא בולד הטומאה אינו מטמא את הידים. דקיי"ל כרבנן דפליגי עליה דרבי יהושע במסכת ידים (פ"ג מ"א) בכלים שנטמאו במשקין ואומר: את שנטמא באב הטומאה – מטמא את הידים, ושנטמא בולד הטומאה – אינו מטמא את הידים, שאין שני עושה שני. ואע"פ שהספר מטמא את הידים - אין למדים הימנו. הלכך, כוסות שבתוך המזון שהידים נגובין - אינן מטמאין את הידים. ואם תאמר: פעמים שיש משקין תבשיל טופח על הידים – אין תורת משקין עליו אלא תורת אוכל: **בכלי שנטמאו אחוריו במשקין.** בכלי שטף קאמר, דאילו כלי חרס אין מטמאין מגבן אפילו בטומאה דאורייתא: **שנטמאו אחוריו במשקין.** אין לך משקה שאינו ראשון לטומאה, שאף אם נגע בשני עשאוהו חכמים תחלה: **אחוריו טמאין.** אף על פי שאין אדם וכלים מקבלין טומאה מן התורה אלא מאב הטומאה גזרו חכמים*) שיהו משקין מטמאין כלים מפני שמצינו משקה שהוא אב הטומאה לטמא אדם וכלים מה"ת, כגון זובו של זב ורוקו ומימי רגליו, גזרו על כל המשקין טמאין שיטמאו כלים:

*) [שבת יד:]

תוכו

**ורבי יהושע היא דאמר אין משגיחין בבת קול.** ואם תאמר: א"כ קשה הלכתא אהלכתא; דהיא דרבי יהושע דתנור של עכנאי קי"ל כרבי יהושע, וקי"ל כב"ה! וי"ל: דדוקא התם קאמר דאין משגיחין בבת קול, דהבת קול היה כנגד הרוב, וכבר אמרה תורה אחרי רבים להטות (שמות כג), אבל ב"ה היו רבים. אע"פ שמייתי רבי יהושע הכא, אע"ג דלא דמי דשאני התם דהבת קול היה כנגד הרוב, האי תנא סבר טפי מרבי יהושע דאמר אין משגיחין בבת קול, אע"פ שהרוב מסייע לבת קול הואיל וב"ש מחדדי טפי. וא"ת: מ"ש דבקדוש והבדלה מברכין קודם על היין, ובברכת המזון אין מברכין עד לאחר שלש ברכות? וי"ל: דהיכי נעביד, אם נברך קודם ברכת המזון – א"כ יהא ברכת המזון היסח הדעת; דבשלמא בשאר ברכות לא עקר נפשיה משתיה, דבקדוש היה רוצה לאכול, ובהבדלה היה רוצה לשתות, אבל בברכת המזון עקר נפשיה משתיה: **מניחו עד לאחר המזון.** הכא משמע שמותר לטעום קודם הבדלה. תימה, הא אמימר בת טוות (ע"פ דף קו.), פי' לן מעונה, לפי שלא היה לו יין להבדיל עליו! וי"ל: דשאני אמימר שהיה סבור שיהיה לו כוס למחר, או מחמיר על עצמו היה, והכא שאני, דקסבר ברכת המזון טעונה כוס ולכך מניחו לברכת המזון: **טעמו פגמו.** פרשב"ם: דוקא לקדוש ולהבדלה צריך שלא יהא פגום, אבל לשתות – צריך לברך עליו אע"פ שהוא פגום, דאסור ליהנות מן העוה"ז בלא ברכה. וקדוש והבדלה נמי לא אמרן אלא במקום דאפשר, אבל אי אפשר – מברך אפי' אפגום, ונותן לתוכו מים. כדאיתא בירושלמי: רבי יונה טעים אכסא ומתקן ליה, פי': לאחר ששתה ממנו הוסיף עליו כל שהוא מים או יין, והיה מברך עליו: **גזרה שמא יטמאו משקין שבידים.** אבל בתוך הסעודה ליכא למיחש שהרי אדם מנגב ידיו יפה קודם אכילה, כדאמרי': *האוכל בלא ניגוב ידים וכו', אבל בשתיה אין אדם מדקדק לנגב ידיו כל כך:

תכף

מסורת הש"ס: [עירובין ז. ב"מ נט: חולין מד. יבמות יד. פסחים קיד.] · תוספתא פ"ה (פסחים קג.) · תוספתא פ"ה פסחים קג: קה: · עי' במהרש"א מה שהגיה בדברי רש"י אלו · [פסחים קה:] · [עירובין מ: פסחים קה:] · [פסחים שם] · [שם] · תוספתא פ"ה · [ע' תו' עירובין ד. ד"ה היא ובחולין פז: ד"ה כל ובכריתות יג: ד"ה וחלב] · חגיגה כב: בכורות לח. כלים פכ"ה מ"ו נדה ז:

עין משפט נר מצוה:

ה א מיי' פכ"ט מהלכות שבת הל' טז טוש"ע או"ח סי' קפב סעיף ג:

ו ב מיי' פי"א מהל' אבות הטומאות הלכה ב:

ז ג מיי' פ"ז שם הל' ה:

ח ד מיי' פ"ח שם הלכה א:

ט ה מיי' פ"ז שם הל' ג ופי"ג מהל' כלים הלכה ז:

הגהות הב"ח

(א) גמ' ועל הבשמים ב"ש אומרים: (ב) שם וסברי ב"ש (ברכת המזון) תא"מ ונ"ב ס"א וכן הוא בפירש"י ברכה:

## רב נסים גאון

**ור' יהושע היא דאמר** אין משגיחין בבת קול. עיקר שלו הוא שאמר ר' יהושע בפרק הזהב (ב"מ דף נט) במעשה תנורו של עכנאי לא בשמים היא (דברים ל) כבר נתנה לנו על הר סיני וכו' כבר הזכרנוה לשעבר. ואלו האותאבות (נ"ל הקושיות) שנזכרו בכאן המברך צריך שיטעום וטעמו פגמו וכוס של ברכה צריך שיעור כולן ענפים יוצאין מן ההיא ברייתא דאקשו מינה כבר והתניא הנכנס לביתו במוצאי שבתות כו' ואיתא מיפרשא בפ' ערבי פסחים (דף קה) כי כשהזכירו זו הברייתא לשם אמרינן עלה שמע מינה מהא מתניתא ה' שמע מינה המבדיל בתפלה צריך שיבדיל על הכוס וש"מ ברכה טעונה כוס וש"מ כוס של ברכה צריך שיעור וש"מ המברך צריך שיטעום וש"מ טעמו פגמו: **וניטמו** ידים לכוס ידים שניות הן. עיקרה דטומאת ידים גזירה דרבנן היא וכי גזרו בהו רבנן טומאה לתרומה אבל לחולין לא והיא אחת מי"ח דבר שגזרו בו ביום ואיתא מיפרשא בפ' יציאות השבת (דף יג) מאי נינהו י"ח דבר דתנן ואלו פוסלין את התרומה והספר והידים ואמרינן ידים מ"ט גזרו בהו רבנן טומאה מפני שהידים עסקניות הן וזו המשנה בסוף מס' זבים ומדקתני ואלו פוסלין את התרומה מכלל שהידים שניות הן כי השני הוא שפוסל את התרומה על העיקר שכבר הקדמנוהו בתחלת המסכת כי השני עושה שלישי בתרומה ולא בחולין ואיתא בפ"א דמסכת טהרות (נ"ל דתוספת' טהרות) הידים מטמאות אחד בקודש ופוסלות את התרומה ואין ידים לחולין ובגמ' דאין דורשין דבני מערבא (הלכה ה) גרסי' מתוך שאתה אומר לו ידיו שניות אף הוא בודל מן התרומה ולא מחמת משקה גזרו עליהם ויהיו תחלה ק"ו ומה אם טבול יום שהוא דבר תורה אינו אלא פוסל ידים שהן מדבריהם לא כ"ש ד"א כלום גזרו על הידים לא מפני כדי שיהא בודל מן התרומה מתוך שאתה אומר לו ידיו שניות אף הוא בודל מן התרומה ותנן בפרה פ' י"א (משנה ה) כל הטעון ביאת מים מדברי סופרי' מטמא את הקודש ופוסל את התרומה ומותר בחולין ובמשנת ידים בפ"ג התמיהו ואמרו לו לר"ע היכן מצינו שהידים תחלה

ואמרינן תו והיד מטמאת את חברתה דברי ר' יהושע וחכ"א ידים שניות הן ואין שני עושה שני ולפי זה הטעם אין הידים מטמאין את הכוס אבל המשקין שאחוריו מטמאין מחמת ידים כדתנן במס' פרה (פ"ח משנה ז) כל הפוסל את התרומה מטמא את המשקין להיות תחלה חוץ מטבול יום ובפרק אור לי"ד (פסחים ד' יז) הן אומרין משקין הבאין מחמת ידים ובפרק יציאות השבת (דף יד) אמרי' האוכלין שנטמאו במשקין משקין דמאי אי נימא במשקין שנטמאו מחמת שרץ דאורייתא היא דכתיב (ויקרא יא) וכל משקה אשר ישתה אלא דנגעו במשקין הבאין מחמת (שרץ) [ידים] וגזרו רבנן על משקין הבאין מחמת ידים משום משקין הבאין מחמת שרץ ובתוספתא טבול יום (פרק ד) תנא חומר בידים מטבול יום וכו' ומטמאין את המשקין לעשותן תחלה ולפי שעיקר טומאת ידים מדרבנן היא הוי ספיקה טהור כדתנן במס' טבול יום (פ"ב משנה ג) חומר בטבול יום מבידים שספק טבול יום פוסל את התרומה והידים ספיקן טהור. גזירה שמא יטמאו משקין שבידים מחמת הכוס זה הכוס קאי בטומאת אחוריים כדתנן בפרק חומר בקודש (חגיגה כ) אחוריים ותוך ובית הצביעה לתרומה כלומר שאחוריו נטמאו במשקין ואעפ"כ תוכו טהור וכל שהוא בענין הזה הרי הוא מטמא את המשקים והמשקין עוד מטמאים דברים אחרים כדתנן בטהרות בפרק ח' (משנה ז) משקין שנטמאו באחורי כלי מטמאין אחד ופוסלין אחד ובתוספתא כלים (פ"ג) משקין טהורין הנתונין על הארץ ונגע בהן כוס שאחוריו טמאין או בית צביעתו נטמאו משקין וטומאת אחוריים מדרבנן היא כדתניא בתורת כהנים [בפ' שמיני] רבי אומר תדע שאין טומאת משקין לכלים מן התורה [אלא מד"ס שאין טומאה מן התורה] מטמאה את כלי שטף מאחריו שאין תוכו טמא ואין לך טומאת אחוריים אלא במשקין בלבד ובתרומה אבל בקודש הכל טמא דתנן

אחורים

י א טוש"ע או"ח סי' קסו:
יא ב ג מיי' פ"ו מהל' ברכות הלכה יט סמג עשין כז טוש"ע או"ח סי' קפ סעיף ב:
יב ד מיי' פכ"ט מהל' שבת הלכה כד סמג עשין כט טוש"ע או"ח סי' רצז סעיף א:
יג ה ו מיי' וסמג שם טוש"ע או"ח סי' רצח סעיף א:
יד ז מיי' שם הלכה כה ופ"ט מהל' ברכות הל' יג סמג שם טוש"ע או"ח סי' רצח סעיף ו וסי' רצז סעיף ב:

תוכו ואוגנו ואזנו וידיו טהורין, נטמא תוכו – נטמא כולו. במאי קא מיפלגי? – ב"ש סברי: אסור להשתמש בכלי שנטמאו אחוריו במשקין, גזרה משום ניצוצות, וליכא למגזר שמא יטמאו המשקין שבידים בכוס; וב"ה סברי: מותר להשתמש בכלי שנטמאו אחוריו במשקין, אמרי: ניצוצות לא שכיחי, ואיכא למיחש שמא יטמאו משקין שבידים מחמת הכוס. *ד"א: תכף לנט"י סעודה. מאי ד"א? –ה"ק להו ב"ה לב"ש: לדידכו דאמריתו "אסור להשתמש בכלי שאחוריו טמאין" דגזרינן משום ניצוצות, אפ"ה – הא עדיפא, דתכף לנט"י סעודה.§ "ב"ש אומרים, מקנח וכו'". ת"ר, *בית שמאי אומרים: מקנח ידיו במפה ומניחה על השלחן, שאם אתה אומר על הכסת – גזרה שמא יטמאו משקין שבמפה מחמת הכסת, ויחזרו ויטמאו את הידים. –ונטמייה כסת למפה! –אין *כלי מטמא כלי. –ונטמייה כסת לגברא גופיה! –אין כלי מטמא אדם. ובה"א: על הכסת, שאם אתה אומר על השלחן, גזרה שמא יטמאו משקים שבמפה מחמת השולחן, ויחזרו ויטמאו את האוכלין. –ולטמא שלחן לאוכלין שבתוכו! –הכא בשלחן שני עסקינן, ואין *שני עושה שלישי בחולין אלא ע"י משקין. במאי קמיפלגי? – ב"ש סברי: אסור להשתמש בשלחן שני, גזרה משום אוכלי תרומה; וב"ה סברי: מותר להשתמש בשלחן שני, אוכלי תרומה זריזין הם. ד"א: אין נט"י לחולין מן התורה. מאי ד"א? –הכי קאמרי להו ב"ה לב"ש: וכי תימרו מ"ש גבי אוכלין דחיישינן, ומ"ש גבי ידים דלא חיישינן – אפילו הכי הא עדיפא, דאין נט"י לחולין מן התורה. מוטב שיטמאו ידים דלית להו עיקר מדאורייתא – ואל יטמאו אוכלים דאית להו עיקר מדאורייתא.§ "בש"א, מכבדין וכו'". *ת"ר, בש"א: מכבדין את הבית ואחר כך נוטלין לידים, שאם אתה אומר נוטלין לידים תחלה, נמצא אתה מפסיד את האוכלין. (א) אבל נט"י לב"ש תחלה – לא סבירא להו, מ"ט – משום פירורין. ובה"א: אם שמש תלמיד חכם הוא, נוטל פירורין שיש בהן כזית, ומניח פירורין שאין בהן כזית. מסייע ליה לר' יוחנן, *דא"ר יוחנן: פירורין שאין בהם כזית מותר לאבדן ביד. במאי קמיפלגי? ב"ה סברי: אסור להשתמש בשמש ע"ה; וב"ש סברי: מותר להשתמש בשמש ע"ה. א"ר יוסי בר חנינא א"ר הונא: בכוליה פרקין הלכה כב"ה, בר מהא דהלכה כב"ש. ור' אושעיא מתני איפכא, ובהא נמי הלכה כב"ה.§ "בש"א, נר ומזון וכו'". *רב הונא בר יהודה איקלע לבי רבא, חזייה לרבא דבריך אבשמים ברישא. א"ל: מכדי ב"ש וב"ה אמאור לא פליגי; *דתניא, בש"א: נר ומזון בשמים והבדלה. ובה"א: נר ובשמים מזון והבדלה! – עני רבא בתריה: זו דברי ר"מ, אבל ר' יהודה אומר: לא נחלקו ב"ש וב"ה על המזון שהוא בתחלה ועל הבדלה שהיא בסוף. על מה נחלקו – על המאור ועל הבשמים, שבש"א: על המאור ואח"כ בשמים, ובה"א: בשמים ואח"כ מאור. וא"ר יוחנן: נהגו העם כב"ה אליבא דרבי יהודה.§ "בש"א, שברא כו'". אמר *רבא: ב"ברא" כ"ע לא פליגי דברא משמע, כי פליגי ב"בורא", ב"ש סברי: "בורא" – דעתיד למברא; וב"ה סברי: "בורא" נמי דברא משמע. מתיב רב יוסף: "יוצר אור ובורא חשך", "יוצר הרים ובורא רוח", "בורא השמים ונוטיהם"! אלא א"ר יוסף: ב"ברא" ו"בורא" כ"ע לא פליגי דברא משמע, כי פליגי – ב"מאור" ו"מאורי"; דב"ש סברי: חדא נהורא איכא בנורא, וב"ה סברי: טובא נהורי איכא בנורא. תניא נמי הכי, אמרו להם ב"ה לב"ש: הרבה מאורות יש באור.§ "אין מברכין כו'". בשלמא נר – משום דלא שבת, אלא בשמים מ"ט לא? –אמר רב יהודה אמר רב: הכא במסבת גוים עסקינן, מפני שסתם מסבת גוים לע"ז היא. הא מדקתני סיפא: "אין מברכין לא על הנר ולא על הבשמים של ע"ז", מכלל דרישא לאו בע"ז עסקינן! – א"ר חנינא מסורא: "מה טעם" קאמר, מה טעם אין מברכין לא על הנר ולא על הבשמים של גוים – מפני שסתם מסבת גוים לע"ז. ת"ר: אור ששבת מברכין עליו, ושלא שבת – אין מברכין עליו. (*מאי שבת) ומאי לא שבת? אי

**רש"י**

תוכו ואוגנו ואזנו וידיו טהורין. דכיון דטומאה זו דרבנן היא, עבדו בה היכרא דלידעו דמדרבנן היא, כי היכי דלא לשרוף עלה תרומה וקדשים, והקילו בה, וכן מפורש (בבכורות דף לח.) אוגנו שפתו הכפולה לצד חוץ, אזנו כמו אזן הקדירה, ידיו כלי שיש לו יד, כגון מחבת: גזרה משום ניצוצות. שמא יתזו ניצוצות מתוכה על אחוריו, ויטמאו משקין שבאחוריו, ויטמאו את הידים. הלכך, נוטלים לידים תחלה שלא יטמאו את אחורי הכוס, ולמאי דמפרשי ב"ה מחמת אחוריו – לאו חששה הוא, דהא אסור להשתמש ביה: וב"ה סברי מותר להשתמש בו. הלכך לחששה דידן איכא למיחש, אבל לחששה דידכו – ליכא למיחש, דלא איכפת לן אם יטמאו אחוריו: הא עדיפא. למזוג הכוס תחלה ואח"כ נט"י תכף לסעודה, ולא אתיא חששה דניצוצות ומפקעה הלכתא. וזו מהלכות סעודה היא: משקין שבמפה. שמא יהיה משקה טופח עליה מחמת נגוב הידים, ויחזרו ויטמאו את הידים כשיקנח בה תמיד בתוך הסעודה: ונטמייה כסת למפה. בלא משקים: אין כלי. שאינו אב הטומאה, מטמא כלים ולא אדם, והוא יזהר שלא יגעו ידיו בכסת, אם ראשונה היא לטומאה: מחמת שלחן. כדמפרש לקמיה, דסברי ב"ה מותר להשתמש בשלחן שני: משום אוכלי תרומה. שהשני פוסל את התרומה: אפילו הכי הא עדיפא. לחוש שמא אירע מקרה שישתמשו בשלחן שני, ולא יפייחנה על גבי השלחן שלא תטמא את האוכלין מחמת משקין שבה, מלחוש שלא תטמא מחמת כסת ותחזור ותטמא את הידים: מפסיד את האוכלין. שמים אחרונים נתזין עליהם ונמאסים: ה"ג בתוספתא בה"א אם שמש ת"ח הוא – נוטל פירורין שיש בהן כזית ומניח פירורין שאין בהם כזית: מתני איפכא. מפיך בהך סיפא דב"ש לב"ה ודב"ה לב"ש, וקבע בהא נמי הלכה כב"ה: וא"ר יוחנן. גרסי': דברא משמע. לשעבר. ויפה לאומרו, שעל בריית האור שברא בששת ימי בראשית משבחין אותו, לפי שבמו"ש נברא כדאמרינן בפסחים (פ"ד דף נד.): בורא. דבר שהוא בורא תמיד, והא לא שייכא הכא, שהרי כבר נברא: הרבה מאורות. שלהבת אדומה לבנה וירקרקת: משום דלא שבת. ממלאכת עבירה, שהגוי עושה מלאכה לאורו, ותניא לקמן אור שלא שבת – אין מברכין עליו, הואיל ונעבדה בו עבירה: במסבת גוים. לאכילה, לסעודה:
אי

**תוספות**

תכף לנטילת ידים סעודה. והאי דלא חשיב ליה לעיל בפ' כ"מ (דף מב.) בהדי אידך תכיפות – משום דשנויה *במשנה לא חש למתנייה: דבר אחר אין נטילת ידים לחולין מן התורה וכו'. יש ספרים שכתוב בהן: הכי קאמרי להו *ב"ש לבית הלל, אפילו לדידכו דאמריתו אסור להשתמש בשלחן שני משום אוכלי תרומה, הא עדיפא דאין נטילת ידים לחולין מן התורה, מוטב וכו' ואל יטמאו וכו'. ול"נ, דהא קאמרי בית שמאי דאסור להשתמש בשלחן שני, ודוחק לומר כמו שפירש רש"י שמא במקרה בעלמא ישתמש. אלא נראה כספרים שכתוב בהן: מאי דבר אחר, הכי קאמרי להו ב"ה לב"ש, וכ"ת מ"ש גבי אוכלין דחיישינן ומ"ש גבי ידים דלא חיישינן וכו', והשתא לא הוי האי דבר אחר כי ההיא דלעיל שאינו צריך לטעם ראשון, אבל הכא האי ד"א לא בא אלא לפרש טעמא דב"ה קאמר, וליישב דבריהם:
פירורין דלית בהו כזית מותר לאבדן ביד. מיהו, קשה לעניותא כדאמרינן בפרק כל הבשר (דף קה:): בכוליה פירקין הלכה כב"ה לבר מהא. וא"ת: והא בההוא דיחזור למקומו ויברך משמע דהלכה כב"ש לקמן (דף נג:) בשמעתין מדעבדי אמוראי בתרייהו! י"ל: דלא חשיב לה, משום דהתם אפילו ב"ה מודו לב"ש, אלא שלא הטריחוהו *לכך: נהגו העם כב"ה אליבא דרבי יהודה. תימא: דאנן אפילו לכתחלה נוהגין כן, ובפרק *הדר (דף סב:) אומר: נהגו – אורויי לא מורינן, ואי עבד הכי – לא מהדרינן ליה! וי"ל: דהתם איכא אמוראי דפליגי, חד אמר הלכה, והוה פירוש הלכה לכתחלה, ומורינן הכי, א"כ נהגו דקאמר אידך – הוי דיעבד. אבל הכא יכול להיות דאין כאן אלא נהגו *גרידא: בברא כ"ע ל"פ. וא"ת: הואיל ול"פ בלשון ברא, אמאי אמר בורא? וי"ל: דלשון קרא עדיף: וכי

**הגהות הב"ח**

(א) גמ' מפסיד את האוכלין (אבל נ"י וכו' משום פירורין) תא"מ ונ"ב ס"א לא גרסי זה:

**רב נסים גאון**

**אִי נֵימָא לָא שָׁבַת** מֵחֲמַת מְלָאכָה וַאֲפִי' הִיא מְלָאכָה שֶׁל הֶיתֵּר. כְּגוֹן שֶׁל חוֹלֶה וְשֶׁל חַיָּה, קָאָמַר דְּאֵין מְבָרְכִין: **עַשְׁשִׁית.** לנטירנ"א: **שֶׁהָיְתָה דּוֹלֶקֶת וְהוֹלֶכֶת.** מֵעֶ"שׁ, וּבְבֵית יִשְׂרָאֵל: **לְמ"שׁ מְבָרְכִין.** לְפִי שֶׁלֹּא נֶעֶבְדָה בָּהּ עֲבֵירָה, שֶׁלֹּא הוּדְלְקָה בְּשַׁבָּת: **גּוֹי שֶׁהִדְלִיק מִיִּשְׂרָאֵל.** מִשֶּׁחָשְׁכָה מ"שׁ: **הַךְ אִיסּוּרָא אָזְלָא.** מִתּוֹךְ שֶׁשַּׁלְהֶבֶת דּוֹלֶקֶת וְהוֹלֶכֶת, קַמָּא קַמָּא פָּרַח לֵיהּ: **הַמּוֹצִיא שַׁלְהֶבֶת לר"ה.** בְּשַׁבָּת – חַיָּיב. וּמוֹקְמִינַן לָהּ בְּמַסֶּכֶת בֵּיצָה כְּגוֹן דְּשַׁיְיפֵיהּ לַחֶרֶס מִשְׁחָא וְאַתְלֵי בָּהּ נוּרָא, דְּגַחֶלֶת לֵיכָּא אֶלָּא שַׁלְהֶבֶת, וּמִשּׁוּם חֶרֶס לָא מִחַיַּיב, דְּלֵית בָּהּ שִׁיעוּרָא: **מַה שֶּׁעָקַר לֹא הִנִּיחַ.** וְהוֹצָאַת שַׁבָּת לָא מִחַיְּיבָא עַד דְּאִיכָּא עֲקִירָה מֵרְשׁוּת זוֹ וַהֲנָחָה בִּרְשׁוּת זוֹ: **גְּזֵירָה מִשּׁוּם גּוֹי רִאשׁוֹן וְעַמּוּד רִאשׁוֹן.** אִי שָׁרֵית בְּגוֹי שֶׁהִדְלִיק מִגּוֹי מִשֶּׁחָשְׁכָה, אָתֵי לְבָרוֹכֵי בְּגוֹי שֶׁהִדְלִיק מִבְּעוֹד יוֹם, וּבְאוֹתוֹ אוּר עַצְמוֹ שֶׁלֹּא נִתּוֹסֵף מִשֶּׁחָשְׁכָה, כְּגוֹן שֶׁמְּבָרֵךְ עָלָיו סָמוּךְ לַחֲשֵׁכָה מִיָּד: **גָּדוֹל מוּכְחָא מִלְּתָא דְּגוֹי הוּא.** וְאֵין צָרִיךְ לִבְדּוֹק אַחֲרָיו, דְּאִי אִיתָא דְּיִשְׂרָאֵל הוּא לֹא הָיָה מְמַהֵר סָמוּךְ לַחֲשֵׁכָה מִיָּד לֶאֱחוֹז הָאוּר בְּיָדוֹ: **כְּפִי הַכִּבְשָׁן.** שֶׁשּׂוֹרְפִים בּוֹ אֲבָנִים לְסִיד. אִם עָבֶה כְּאוּר הַיּוֹצֵא מִפִּי הַכִּבְשָׁן – נְהוֹרָא בָּרְיָא הִיא, וּלְהִשְׁתַּמֵּשׁ לְאוֹרָהּ הִיא נַעֲשֵׂית: **וְאִם לָאו.** לָאו לְאוֹרָהּ נַעֲשֵׂית, אֶלָּא לְבַשֵּׁל, וְאֵין מְבָרְכִין אֶלָּא עַל שֶׁנַּעֲשָׂה לְהָאִיר: **בִּתְחִלָּה.** בִּתְחִלַּת שְׂרֵפַת אֲבָנִים אֵין הָאוּר לְהָאִיר: **בַּסּוֹף.** לְאַחַר שֶׁנִּשְׂרְפוּ הָאֲבָנִים רוּבָּן מַדְלִיקִין אוּר גָּדוֹל מִלְּמַעְלָה לְמָרֵק שְׂרֵפַת הָאֲבָנִים, וּמִשְׁתַּמְּשִׁין נָמֵי לְאוֹרָהּ: **שֶׁל תַּנּוּר. בַּסּוֹף מְבָרְכִין עָלָיו,** לְאַחַר שֶׁהוּסַּק הַתַּנּוּר וְהַפַּת בְּתוֹכָהּ מַדְלִיקִין קִסְמִין דַּקִּין בְּפִיו לְהָאִיר וְלִקְלוֹט חוּמּוֹ לְתוֹכוֹ, וְכֵיוָן דְּמִשְׁתַּמֵּשׁ לְאוֹרוֹ – מְבָרְכִין עָלָיו: **אוּר שֶׁל בֵּית הַכְּנֶסֶת.** בִּדְאִיכָּא אָדָם חָשׁוּב – לִכְבוֹדוֹ הִדְלִיקוּהָ; וְלֹא שֶׁצָּרִיךְ לָאוּר, אֶלָּא לְכָבוֹד בְּעָלְמָא, וְאֵין מְבָרְכִין עָלָיו: **לֵיכָּא אָדָם חָשׁוּב.** לְהָאִיר לָהֶם הִדְלִיקוּהָ, וּמְבָרְכִין: **הָא וְהָא דְּאִיכָּא אָדָם חָשׁוּב.** וְאִי אִיכָּא חַזָּנָא – שַׁמָּשׁ שֶׁאוֹכֵל בְּבֵית הַכְּנֶסֶת, אַף לְאוֹרָהּ עֲשׂוּיָה שֶׁיֹּאכַל הַחַזָּן לְאוֹרָהּ, וּמְבָרְכִין: **הָא וְהָא דְּאִיכָּא חַזָּנָא.** וְאִיכָּא סַהֲרָא שֶׁהַחַזָּן יָכוֹל לֶאֱכוֹל לְאוֹרָהּ – אֵין מְבָרְכִין עַל הַנֵּר, שֶׁלֹּא לְהָאִיר הִדְלִיקוּהָ אֶלָּא לִכְבוֹד אָדָם חָשׁוּב: **מִפְּנֵי בִּטּוּל בֵּית הַמִּדְרָשׁ.** שֶׁבִּזְמַן שֶׁאֶחָד מְבָרֵךְ לְכוּלָּם הֵם צְרִיכִים לִשְׁתּוֹק מִגִּרְסָתָם כְּדֵי שֶׁיִּתְכַּוְּנוּ כּוּלָּם וְיִשְׁמְעוּ אֵלָיו וְיַעֲנוּ אָמֵן: **מַרְפֵּא.** לְאָדָם הַמִּתְעַטֵּשׁ, שֶׁרְגִילִים לוֹמַר "אֲסוּתָא": **נֵר. לִכְבוֹד הַמֵּת עֲבִידָא:** **בְּשָׂמִים עֲבִידֵי לְעַבּוֹרֵי רֵיחָא.** דִּסְרָחוֹנוֹ שֶׁל מֵת עֲבִידֵי, וְלֹא לְהָרִיחַ: **כֹּל.** מֵת שֶׁהוּא חָשׁוּב לְהוֹצִיא לְפָנָיו נֵר בַּיּוֹם, אִם הוֹצִיאוּהוּ בַּלַּיְלָה בְּמוֹצָאֵי שַׁבָּת לִקְבוּרָה – אֵין מְבָרְכִין עַל אוֹתוֹ נֵר, דְּלִכְבוֹד עֲבִידָא וְלֹא לְהָאִיר: **וְכֹל.** מֵת שֶׁאֵינוֹ חָשׁוּב לְהוֹצִיא נֵר לְפָנָיו בַּיּוֹם אֶלָּא בַּלַּיְלָה, מְבָרְכִין עָלָיו אִם הוֹצִיאוּהוּ בְּמוֹצָאֵי שַׁבָּת לִקְבוּרָה: **מְבָרְכִין עָלָיו.** דִּלְהָאִיר עֲבִידָא: **בְּשָׂמִים.** שֶׁמּוֹלִיךְ אָדָם אִסְטְנִיס לְבֵית הַכִּסֵּא לְהַעֲבִיר מִמֶּנּוּ רֵיחַ רַע שֶׁל בהכ"ס – אֵין מְבָרְכִין עָלָיו: **וְשֶׁמֶן הֶעָשׂוּי לְהַעֲבִיר אֶת הַזּוּהֲמָא.** שֶׁמְּבִיאִים בְּסוֹף הַסְּעוּדָה לָסוּךְ יָדַיִם מְזוֹהָמוֹת, וְהוּא מְבוּשָּׂם בִּבְשָׂמִים: **אֵין מְבָרְכִין עָלָיו.** "בּוֹרֵא עֲצֵי בְשָׂמִים" אֶלָּא "בּוֹרֵא שֶׁמֶן עָרֵב" מְבָרְכִין אִם שֶׁמֶן שֶׁל אֲפַרְסְמוֹן הוּא – וְהָא דְּאָמַר בְּ"כֵּיצַד מְבָרְכִין" (דף מג.) הַאי מִשְׁחָא כְּבִישָׁא וּטְחִינָה מְבָרְכִין עָלָיו "בעצ"ב" – לָא בְּבָא בְּתוֹךְ הַסְּעוּדָה קָאָמַר, אֶלָּא בְּבָא לְהָרִיחַ: **לְגַמֵּר אֶת הַכֵּלִים.** לְבַשֵּׂם בַּעֲשָׁנוֹ אֶת הַבְּגָדִים: **בִּטְבֶרְיָא.** הָיוּ רְגִילִים לְגַמֵּר עַרְבֵי שַׁבָּתוֹת וּבְצִפּוֹרִי בְּמוֹ"שׁ:
לא

תורה אור

**אִי נֵימָא,** לָא שָׁבַת מֵחֲמַת מְלָאכָה אֲפִילּוּ מִמְּלָאכָה דְּהֶתֵּירָא – וְהָתַנְיָא: אוֹר שֶׁל חַיָּה וְשֶׁל חוֹלֶה מְבָרְכִין עָלָיו! – אָמַר רַב נַחְמָן בַּר יִצְחָק: מַאי שָׁבַת – שֶׁשָּׁבַת מֵחֲמַת מְלֶאכֶת עֲבֵירָה. תַּנְיָא נַמִי הָכִי: עַשָּׁשִׁית שֶׁהָיְתָה דּוֹלֶקֶת וְהוֹלֶכֶת כָּל הַיּוֹם כּוּלּוֹ – לְמוֹצָאֵי שַׁבָּת מְבָרְכִין עָלֶיהָ.§ תָּנוּ רַבָּנַן: גּוֹי שֶׁהִדְלִיק מִיִּשְׂרָאֵל וְיִשְׂרָאֵל שֶׁהִדְלִיק מִגּוֹי – מְבָרְכִין עָלָיו, גּוֹי מִגּוֹי – אֵין מְבָרְכִין עָלָיו. מַאי שְׁנָא גּוֹי מִגּוֹי דְּלָא – מִשּׁוּם דְּלָא שָׁבַת, אִי הָכִי יִשְׂרָאֵל מִגּוֹי נַמִי, הָא לָא שָׁבַת! – וְכִי תֵּימָא, הָךְ אִיסּוּרָא אֲזַל לֵיהּ וְהָא אַחֲרִינָא הוּא וּבִידָא דְּיִשְׂרָאֵל קָא מִתְיַלְּדָא – אֶלָּא הָא דְּתַנְיָא: הַמּוֹצִיא שַׁלְהֶבֶת לִרְשׁוּת הָרַבִּים חַיָּיב, אַמַּאי חַיָּיב? מַה שֶּׁעָקַר לֹא הִנִּיחַ וּמַה שֶּׁהִנִּיחַ לֹא עָקַר! אֶלָּא: לְעוֹלָם דְּאִיסּוּרָא נַמִי אִיתֵיהּ, וְכִי קָא מְבָרֵךְ – אַתּוֹסֶפְתָּא דְּהֶתֵּירָא קָא מְבָרֵךְ. אִי הָכִי, גּוֹי מִגּוֹי נַמִי! – אִין הָכִי נַמִי, גְּזֵירָה מִשּׁוּם גּוֹי רִאשׁוֹן וְעַמּוּד רִאשׁוֹן.§ תָּנוּ רַבָּנַן: הָיָה מְהַלֵּךְ חוּץ לַכְּרַךְ וְרָאָה אוֹר, אִם רוֹב גּוֹיִם – אֵינוֹ מְבָרֵךְ, אִם רוֹב יִשְׂרָאֵל – מְבָרֵךְ. הָא גּוּפָא קַשְׁיָא! אָמְרַתְּ: אִם רוֹב גּוֹיִם – אֵינוֹ מְבָרֵךְ, הָא מֶחֱצָה עַל מֶחֱצָה – מְבָרֵךְ; וַהֲדַר תָּנֵי: אִם רוֹב יִשְׂרָאֵל – מְבָרֵךְ, הָא מֶחֱצָה עַל מֶחֱצָה – אֵינוֹ מְבָרֵךְ! – בְּדִין הוּא דַּאֲפִי' מֶחֱצָה עַל מֶחֱצָה נַמִי מְבָרֵךְ, וְאַיְּידֵי (דתני) רֵישָׁא רוֹב גּוֹיִם – תְּנָא סֵיפָא רוֹב יִשְׂרָאֵל.§ ת"ר: הָיָה מְהַלֵּךְ חוּץ לַכְּרַךְ וְרָאָה תִּינוֹק וַאֲבוּקָה בְּיָדוֹ, בּוֹדֵק אַחֲרָיו, אִם יִשְׂרָאֵל הוּא – מְבָרֵךְ, אִם גּוֹי הוּא – אֵינוֹ מְבָרֵךְ. מַאי אִירְיָא תִּינוֹק, אֲפִי' גָּדוֹל נַמִי! – אָמַר רַב יְהוּדָה אָמַר רַב: הָכָא בְּסָמוּךְ לִשְׁקִיעַת הַחַמָּה עָסְקִי', גָּדוֹל – מוּכְחָא מִלְּתָא דְּוַדַּאי גּוֹי הוּא, תִּינוֹק – אֵימַר יִשְׂרָאֵל הוּא אַקְרֵי וְנָקֵיט.§ ת"ר: הָיָה מְהַלֵּךְ חוּץ לַכְּרַךְ וְרָאָה אוֹר, אִם עָבֶה כְּפִי הַכִּבְשָׁן – מְבָרֵךְ עָלָיו, וְאִם לָאו – אֵינוֹ מְבָרֵךְ עָלָיו. תָּנֵי חֲדָא: אוֹר שֶׁל כִּבְשָׁן מְבָרְכִין עָלָיו, וְתַנְיָא אִידָךְ: אֵין מְבָרְכִין עָלָיו! לָא קַשְׁיָא: הָא – בִּתְחִלָּה, הָא – לְבַסּוֹף. תָּנֵי חֲדָא: אוֹר שֶׁל תַּנּוּר וְשֶׁל כִּירַיִם מְבָרְכִין עָלָיו, וְתַנְיָא אִידָךְ: אֵין מְבָרְכִין עָלָיו! – לָא קַשְׁיָא: הָא בִּתְחִלָּה, הָא לְבַסּוֹף. תָּנֵי חֲדָא: אוֹר שֶׁל בֵּית הַכְּנֶסֶת וְשֶׁל בֵּית הַמִּדְרָשׁ מְבָרְכִין עָלָיו, וְתַנְיָא אִידָךְ: אֵין מְבָרְכִין עָלָיו! ל"ק: הָא – דְּאִיכָּא אָדָם חָשׁוּב, הָא – דְּלֵיכָּא אָדָם חָשׁוּב. וְאִי בָּעֵית אֵימָא: הָא וְהָא דְּאִיכָּא [א] אָדָם חָשׁוּב, וְלָא קַשְׁיָא: הָא דְּאִיכָּא חַזָּנָא, הָא דְּלֵיכָּא חַזָּנָא, ואב"א: הָא וְהָא דְּאִיכָּא חַזָּנָא, וְלָא קַשְׁיָא: הָא דְּאִיכָּא סַהֲרָא, וְהָא דְּלֵיכָּא סַהֲרָא.§ ת"ר: הָיוּ יוֹשְׁבִין בְּבֵית הַמִּדְרָשׁ וְהֵבִיאוּ אוֹר לִפְנֵיהֶם. בש"א: כָּל אֶחָד וְאֶחָד מְבָרֵךְ לְעַצְמוֹ, וּבה"א: אֶחָד מְבָרֵךְ לְכוּלָּן, מִשּׁוּם שֶׁנֶּאֱמַר: "בְּרׇב עָם הַדְרַת מֶלֶךְ". בִּשְׁלָמָא ב"ה מְפָרְשִׁי טַעְמָא, אֶלָּא בֵּית שַׁמַּאי מַאי טַעְמָא? –קָסָבְרִי: מִפְּנֵי בִּיטּוּל בֵּית הַמִּדְרָשׁ. תַּנְיָא נַמִי הָכִי: שֶׁל בֵּית רַבָּן גַּמְלִיאֵל לֹא הָיוּ אוֹמְרִים "מַרְפֵּא" בְּבֵית הַמִּדְרָשׁ מִפְּנֵי בִּיטּוּל בֵּית הַמִּדְרָשׁ.§ אֵין מְבָרְכִין לֹא עַל הַנֵּר וְלֹא עַל הַבְּשָׂמִים שֶׁל מֵתִים". מ"ט? נֵר – לִכְבוֹד הוּא דַּעֲבִידָא, בְּשָׂמִים – לְעַבּוֹרֵי רֵיחָא הוּא דַּעֲבִידִי. אָמַר רַב יְהוּדָה אָמַר רַב: כֹּל שֶׁמּוֹצִיאִין לְפָנָיו בַּיּוֹם וּבַלַּיְלָה אֵין מְבָרְכִין עָלָיו, וְכֹל שֶׁאֵין מוֹצִיאִין לְפָנָיו אֶלָּא בַּלַּיְלָה – מְבָרְכִין עָלָיו. אָמַר רַב הוּנָא: בְּשָׂמִים שֶׁל בֵּית הַכִּסֵּא, וְשֶׁמֶן הֶעָשׂוּי לְהַעֲבִיר אֶת הַזּוּהֲמָא – אֵין מְבָרְכִין עָלָיו. לְמֵימְרָא, דְּכׇל הֵיכָא דְּלָאו לְרֵיחָא עֲבִידָא לָא מְבָרְכִין עֲלֵיהּ, מֵתִיבִי: הַנִּכְנָס לַחֲנוּתוֹ שֶׁל בַּשָּׂם וְהֵרִיחַ רֵיחַ, אֲפִילּוּ יָשַׁב שָׁם כָּל הַיּוֹם כּוּלּוֹ – אֵינוֹ מְבָרֵךְ אֶלָּא פַּעַם אֶחָד, נִכְנָס וְיָצָא, נִכְנָס וְיָצָא – מְבָרֵךְ עַל כָּל פַּעַם וּפַעַם; וְהָא הָכָא דְּלָאו לְרֵיחָא הוּא דַּעֲבִידָא וְקָמְבָרֵךְ! –אִין, לְרֵיחָא נַמִי הוּא דַּעֲבִידָא, כִּי הֵיכִי דְּנֵירְחוּ אֱינָשֵׁי וְנֵיתוּ וְנִזְבּוּן מִינֵּיהּ. תָּנוּ רַבָּנַן: הָיָה מְהַלֵּךְ חוּץ לַכְּרַךְ וְהֵרִיחַ רֵיחַ, אִם רוֹב גּוֹיִם – אֵינוֹ מְבָרֵךְ, אִם רוֹב יִשְׂרָאֵל – מְבָרֵךְ. רַבִּי יוֹסֵי אוֹמֵר: אֲפִי' רוֹב יִשְׂרָאֵל נַמִי אֵינוֹ מְבָרֵךְ, מִפְּנֵי שֶׁבְּנוֹת יִשְׂרָאֵל מְקַטְּרוֹת לִכְשָׁפִים. –אַטּוּ כּוּלְּהוּ לִכְשָׁפִים מְקַטְּרָן?! – ה"ל מִיעוּטָא לִכְשָׁפִים, וּמִיעוּטָא נַמִי לְגַמֵּר אֶת הַכֵּלִים, אִשְׁתַּכַּח רוּבָּא דְּלָאו לְרֵיחָא עָבִיד, וְכָל רוּבָּא דְּלָאו לְרֵיחָא עָבִיד – לָא מְבָרֵךְ. אָמַר ר' חִיָּיא בַּר אַבָּא אָמַר רַבִּי יוֹחָנָן: הַמְהַלֵּךְ בְּעַרְבֵי שַׁבָּתוֹת בִּטְבֶרְיָא וּבְמוֹצָאֵי שַׁבָּתוֹת בְּצִיפּוֹרִי וְהֵרִיחַ רֵיחַ – אֵינוֹ מְבָרֵךְ, מִפְּנֵי שֶׁחֶזְקָתוֹ אֵינוֹ עָשׂוּי אֶלָּא לְגַמֵּר בּוֹ אֶת הַכֵּלִים. תָּנוּ רַבָּנַן: הָיָה מְהַלֵּךְ בְּשׁוּק שֶׁל עֲבוֹדָה זָרָה, נִתְרַצָּה לְהָרִיחַ – הֲרֵי זֶה חוֹטֵא.§
וְאֵין

**וכי** תימא הך איסורא אזיל ליה. ה"מ לאקשויי: אי הכי גוי מגוי נמי! אלא עדיפא מיניה פריך, דה"מ לשנויי כדמשני בסמוך: **גזירה** משום גוי ראשון וגוי ראשון משום עמוד ראשון וכו'. חדא גזרה היא דגזרו חכמים כל אש גוי שביד הגוי, דאי לא הא לא קיימא הא. אבל גוי שהדליק מישראל וישראל מגוי – מברכין עליו, והכי קיימא לן: **הא** דאיכא אדם חשוב. אם כן משום כבודו של חשוב, ולא לאורה, כך פרש"י. ור"ח פירש איפכא: באדם חשוב – לאורה, ודליכא אדם חשוב – עשוי לכבוד בית הכנסת: **אין** מברכין עליו. פירש"י: מיהו מברכין עליו ברוך שברא שמן ערב. והא דאמר לעיל בכיצד מברכין (ד' מג.): האי משחא כבישא מברכין עליו בורא עצי בשמים – היינו בבא להריח ולא מיירי בתוך הסעודה: באכילה

טו א ב מיי' פכ"ט מהל' שבת הל' כז טוש"ע או"ח סי' רצח סעיף ה:
טז ג מיי' שם הל' כו טוש"ע או"ח שם סעי' כט:
יז ד (מיי' פ"ו מהל' שבת הלכה יג סמג עשין כט):
יח ה (ו) מיי' פכ"ט מהל' שבת הלכה כו סמג עשין (כו) כט טוש"ע או"ח סי' רצח סעיף ז וסי' רנ"ד סעיף ז:
[ו טוש"ע שם]:
גי' הערוך למ"ש מכבה ומדליקה עי' בערך עששית וברכ לאלפס כך לי' תנ"ה עששית שהיתה דולקת והולכת כל היום כולו מביאין ממנה אור להבדלה ועי' ברא"ש
יט ז מיי' שם סמג עשין (כח) כט טוש"ע או"ח סי' רצח סעיף ח:
כ ח ט (י) מיי' שם טוש"ע שם סעיף יא: [י טוש"ע שם]:
כא כ שם סעיף יב:
כב ל מיי' פ"ד מהל' ת"ת הל' ט טוש"ע יו"ד סי' רמו סעיף יז:
כג מ טור (טוש"ע) או"ח סי' רצח [סעיף יב]:
כד נ מיי' פ"ט מהל' ברכות הלכה כ סמג עשין כז (וכט) טוש"ע או"ח סי' ריז סעיף ב וסי' רצז סעיף ב:
כה ס מיי' פ"ט מהלכות ברכות הלכה ה סמג עשין כז טוש"ע או"ח סי' ריז סעיף ה:
כו ע מיי' שם הל' ח טוש"ע שם סעיף ג:

הגהות הגר"א

[א] גמ' הא לליכא אדם חשוב ואבו"ה הא והא לאורה. נ"ב גירסת ר"ח לליכא:

גליון הש"ס

גמ' מתוס על מתלה נמי מבכך. עי' פר"ח יו"ד סי' קי"ח סק"ז: רש"י ד"ה מרפא כו' שרגילים לומר כו'. והוא בפרקי דר"א פרק נ"ב מיום שנבראו שמים וארץ לא היה אדם חולה אלא אם היה בדרך או בשוק והיה עוטש ונשמתו יוצאת מנחיריו עד שבא יעקב אבינו וביקש רחמים ואמר רבון כל העולמים אל תקח נפשי ממני עד שאצוה את בני ובנותי ונעתר לו לפיכך חייב אדם לומר בעטישתו חיים שנהפך המות הזה לאור שנאמר עטישותיו תהל אור:

תוספתא דשבת פ"י
[דתנא]
תוספתא פ"ה ע"ש
משלי יד
(ספ"ה) [רפ"ח] עי' ש"ש היטב ופי' ק"ח
תוספתא פ"ה

**באכילה** מרובה. ד' מילין, כך פירש"י. ולי נראה דזה מועט יותר מאכילה מועטת, אלא נראה לפרש איפכא: אכילה מרובה כל זמן שהוא למא, דאין שם קצבה, אבל מועט – ד' מילין: **והייתם** קדושים אלו מים אחרונים. דוקא להם שהיו רגילין ליטול ידיהם אחר הסעודה, מפני מלח סדומית. אבל אנו שאין מלח סדומית מצוי בידינו, ואין אנו רגילין ליטול אחר הסעודה – אין הנטילה מעכבת עלינו לברך. ומיהו, אנשים מעונגים הרגילין ליטול ידיהן אחר הסעודה – ודאי להם מעכבת הנטילה לברך ברכת המזון, וצריכים ליטול את ידיהם קודם בהמ"ז*:

הדרן עלך אלו דברים

"ואין מברכין על הנר עד שיאותו". אמר רב יהודה אמר רב: לא 'יאותו' יאותו ממש, אלא: כל שאילו עומד בקרוב ומשתמש לאורה, ואפילו בריחוק מקום. וכן אמר רב אשי: בריחוק מקום שנינו. מיתיבי: היתה לו נר טמונה בחיקו או בפנס, או שראה שלהבת ולא נשתמש לאורה, או נשתמש לאורה ולא ראה שלהבת – אינו מברך עד שיראה שלהבת וישתמש לאורה; בשלמא משתמש לאורה ולא ראה שלהבת – משכחת לה דקיימא בקרן זוית, אלא ראה שלהבת ולא נשתמש לאורה היכי משכחת לה, לאו דמרחקא? – לא, כגון דעמיא ואזלא.§ ת"ר: גחלים לוחשות – מברכין עליהן, אוממות – אין מברכין עליהן. היכי דמי לוחשות? – אמר רב חסדא: כל שאילו מכניס לתוכן קיסם ודולקת מאיליה. איבעיא להו: אוממות או עוממות? – ת"ש, דאמר רב חסדא בר אבדימי: "ארזים לא עממהו בגן אלהים". ורבא אמר: יאותו ממש. וכמה? אמר עולא: כדי שיכיר בין איסר לפונדיון; חזקיה אמר: כדי שיכיר בין מלוזמא של טבריא למלוזמא של ציפורי. רב יהודה מברך אדבי אדא דיילא. רבא מברך אדבי גוריא בר חמא. אביי מברך אדבי בר אבוה. אמר רב יהודה אמר רב: אין מחזרין על האור כדרך שמחזרים על המצות. א"ר זירא: מריש הוה מהדרנא, כיון דשמענא להא דרב יהודה אמר רב – אנא נמי לא מהדרנא, אלא אי מקלע לי ממילא – מבריכנא.§ "מי שאכל וכו'". אמר רב זביד ואיתימא רב דימי בר אבא: מחלוקת בשכח, אבל במזיד – ד"ה יחזור למקומו ויברך. פשיטא, "ושכח" תנן! – מהו דתימא: ה"ה אפילו במזיד, והאי דקתני "ושכח" – להודיעך כחן דב"ש, קמ"ל. תניא, אמרו להם ב"ה לב"ש: לדבריכם, מי שאכל בראש הבירה ושכח וירד ולא ברך, יחזור לראש הבירה ויברך?! – אמרו להן ב"ש לב"ה: לדבריכם, מי ששכח ארנקי בראש הבירה, לא יעלה ויטלנה?! לכבוד עצמו הוא עולה – לכבוד שמים לא כל שכן? הנהו תרי תלמידי, חד עביד בשוגג כב"ש – ואשכח ארנקא דדהבא, וחד עביד במזיד כב"ה – ואכליה אריא. רבה בב"ח הוה קאזל בשיירתא, אכל ואשתלי ולא בריך; אמר: היכי אעביד? אי אמינא להו "אנשאי לברך" – אמרו לי: בריך, (א) כל היכא דמברכת לרחמנא מברכת. מוטב דאמינא להו אנשאי יונה דדהבא. אמר להו: אנטרו לי, דאנשאי יונה דדהבא. אזיל ובריך, ואשכח יונה דדהבא, ומאי שנא יונה – דמתילי כנסת ישראל ליונה, דכתיב: "כנפי יונה נחפה בכסף ואברותיה בירקרק חרוץ", מה יונה אינה ניצולת אלא בכנפיה, אף ישראל אינן ניצולין אלא במצות.§ "עד אימתי הוא וכו'". כמה שיעור עכול? – א"ר יוחנן: כל זמן שאינו רעב; וריש לקיש אמר: כל זמן שיצמא מחמת אכילתו. א"ל: רב ימר בר שלמיא למר זוטרא, ואמרי לה רב ימר בר שיזבי למר זוטרא: מי אמר ריש לקיש הכי? והאמר רב אמי אמר ריש לקיש: כמה שיעור עכול – כדי להלך ארבע מילין! – ל"ק: כאן באכילה מרובה, כאן באכילה מועטת.§ "בא להם יין וכו'". למימרא, דישראל אע"ג דלא שמע כולה ברכה עונה, וכי לא שמע היכי נפיק? – אמר חייא בר רב: בשלא אכל עמהן. וכן אמר רב נחמן אמר רבה בר אבוה: בשלא אכל עמהן. א"ל רב לחייא בריה: ברי, חטוף ובריך. וכן אמר רב הונא לרבה בריה: חטוף ובריך. למימרא, דמברך עדיף ממאן דעני אמן, והתניא, ר' יוסי אומר: גדול העונה אמן יותר מן המברך! א"ל ר' נהוראי: השמים! כן הוא; תדע, שהרי גוליירין יורדין ומתגרין [במלחמה] וגבורים יורדין ומנצחין. – תנאי היא, דתניא: אחד המברך ואחד העונה אמן במשמע, אלא שממהרין למברך יותר מן העונה אמן. בעי מיניה שמואל מרב: מהו לענות אמן אחר תינוקות של בית רבן? – אמר ליה: אחר הכל עונין אמן חוץ מתינוקות של בית רבן הואיל ולהתלמד עשויין. וה"מ בדלא עידן מפטריהו, אבל בעידן מפטריהו – עונין.§ ת"ר: שמן מעכב את הברכה, דברי רבי זילאי; רבי זיואי אומר: אינו מעכב; רבי אחא אומר: שמן טוב מעכב; ר' זוהמאי אומר: כשם שמזוהם פסול לעבודה – כך ידים מזוהמות פסולות לברכה. אמר רב נחמן בר יצחק: אנא לא זילאי ולא זיואי ולא זוהמאי ידענא, אלא מתניתא ידענא; דאמר רב יהודה אמר רב, ואמרי לה במתניתא תנא: "והתקדשתם" – אלו מים ראשונים, "והייתם קדשים" – אלו מים אחרונים, "כי קדוש" (ב) – זה שמן, "אני ה' אלהיכם" – [א] זו ברכה.§

# הדרן עלך אלו דברים

---

**רש"י**

לא יאותו ממש. שאפילו לא נהנה ממנו מברכין עליו. ומאי עד שיאותו – עד שיהא אורו ראוי ליהנות ממנו לעומדים סמוך לו, ואז מברכים עליו אפי' הרחוקים ממנו, ובלבד שיראוהו: בפנס. בעששית: יאותו ממש. עומד בסמוך: וכמה. הוא צריך להיות בסמוך: מלוזמא. משקל: רב יהודה. היה מברך על אור שבבית אדא דיילא. ורחוק מביתו היה, רב יהודה לטעמיה דלא בעי סמוך: רבא מברך אדבי גוריא בר חמא. סמוך לביתו היה, רבא לטעמיה דאמר סמוך בעינן: אין מחזרי' על האור. אם אין לו אור א"צ לחזר אחריו: חד עבד בשוגג כב"ש. אע"פ ששגג ונעקר מן המקום ע"י שכחה החמיר על עצמו כב"ש, וחזר למקום שאכל ובירך: חד עבד במזיד. נעקר ממקום שאכל במזיד כדי לברך במקום אחר, שהולך לילך: אנשאי יונה דדהבא. שכחתי יונה של זהב: יונה אינה נצולת אלא בכנפיה. או בורחת, או נלחמת בראשי אגפיה: באכילה מרובה. ד' מילין: בא להם יין אחר המזון. הא פריש לה בגמרא בריש פרקין; לב"ש אין ברכת המזון טעונה כוס, ולב"ה טעונה כוס: היכי נפיק. קס"ד באחד מן המסובין עסקינן במתני': חטוף וברך. כשמושיטין כוס של ברכה הוי מחזר שיתנוהו לך ותברך: במשמע. העונה והמברך במשמע "קומו ברכו את ה' אלהיכם" בס' עזרא (נחמיה ט) ואומר ויברכו שם כבודך, והיא עניית אמן שבמקדש. במסכת תענית (פ"ב דף טז: ולקמן דף סג.) מפרש: "קומו ברכו" – בתחלת ברכה, "ויברכו שם כבודך" – (שם) במקום עניית אמן, שבמקדש אומר בשכמל"ו: שממהרין למברך. ליתן שכר: אחר תינוקות. כשלומדים ברכות מפי רבן: הואיל ולהתלמד עשויין. שאין מתכוונים לברך אלא ללמוד: אבל בעידן מפטרייהו. כשאומרים ההפטרה ומברכין בתורה ובנביא – עונין אחריהן אמן: שמן מעכב את הברכה. שמן שהיו רגילין להביא בסוף הסעודה לסוך אחר הסעודה את הידים, אחר מים אחרונים, להעביר את הזוהמא: מעכב את הברכה. שאסור לזמן עד שיובא, וכן לענין שמעכב ברכות כל דבר הבא בקנוח סעודה (ג) שמותר לאכלו בלא ברכה עד שיסכוהו: שמן טוב. שיש בו בשמים, מעכב את הברכה למי שרגיל (ד) בו:

הדרן עלך אלו דברים

---

**תורה אור**: יחזקאל לא; תהלים סח; ויקרא כ

**מסורת הש"ס**: (תוספתא פ"ה); פסחים עה: ע"ש; [בערוך פי' מטע]; [שבת מטו. קל. וש"נ מה. סנהדר' לג.]; נזיר סו:

---

**עין משפט נר מצוה**

כז א שו"ע או"ח סימן רלח סעיף טו:
כח ב מיי' פכ"ט מהל' שבת הלכה כו סמג עשין כט טוש"ע או"ח שם סעיף ט:
כט ג מיי' שם הל' כה טוש"ע שם סעיף ד:
ל ד מיי' שם הלכה כו טוש"ע שם סעיף א:
לא ה ו מיי' פ"ד מהל' ברכות הל' א סמג עשין כז טוש"ע או"ח סי' קפ"ד סעיף א:
[וע"ע תוס' חולין קה. ד"ה מים]
לב ז (מיי' פ"ב מהל' ברכות הלכה יד) [הרמב"ם לא הביא לכל זה ועי' בל"מ טעם רחוק] סמג שם טוש"ע או"ח שם סעיף ה:
לג ח מיי' פ"א מהל' ברכות הל' יא שו"ע או"ח סי' ריג סעיף ג:
לד ט מיי' שם הל' יג סמג עשין כז טוש"ע או"ח סי' רטו סעיף ב:
לה י טוש"ע או"ח סי' רא סעיף ד:
לו כ מיי' שם הלכה יג טו סמג שם טוש"ע או"ח סי' רטו סעיף ב ג:
לז ל מיי' פ"ז מהלכות ברכות הל' יא יב סמג שם טוש"ע או"ח סימן קפא סעיף א י:

**רב נסים גאון**

כדי שיכיר בין מלוזמא של טבריא למלוזמא של ציפורי. הא פירושה בתלמוד ארץ ישראל כדי שיהא יודע להבחין בין מטבע למטבע ובגמ' דאין עומדין [בירושלמי הלכה ב] אמרו העונין אמן צריכין ליתן עיניהם בנר ועיניהם בכוס:

**הגהות הב"ח**

(א) גמ' אמרי לי בריך הכא כל היכא וכו' יונה דדהבא הדר ואזיל ובריך וכו' מאי שנא יונה דנקט דמתלין וכו' אלא במצות ל"א מה יונה זו כנפיה מגינות עליה אף ישראל מצות מגינות עליהן עד אימתי (ב) שם כי קדוש אני זה שמן הטוב אני ה': (ג) רש"י ד"ה מעכב את הברכה וכו' בקנוח סעודה שאסור לאוכלו: (ד) ד"ה שמן וכו' שרגיל. נ"ב עיין בפ' כילד מברכין דף מב:

[בערך גליור כתב הרב המוסף הערוך פי' בלשון יוני משרתים של אנשי המלחמה ע"ש]:

**הגהות הגר"א**

[א] גמ' בסוף הפרק (ה' אלהיכם) תא"מ (ודריש לה מקרא דס"פ שמיני וכ"ה בא"דרת אליהו שם):

**הרואה** מקום שנעשו בו נסים לישראל, אומר: "ברוך שעשה נסים לאבותינו במקום הזה". מקום שנעקרה ממנו עבודה זרה, אומר: "ברוך שעקר עבודה זרה מארצנו". על הזיקין, ועל הזועות, ועל הרעמים, ועל הרוחות, ועל הברקים אומר: "ברוך שכחו וגבורתו מלא עולם". על ההרים ועל הגבעות, ועל הימים, ועל הנהרות, ועל המדברות אומר: "ברוך עושה בראשית". רבי יהודה אומר: הרואה את הים הגדול אומר: "ברוך שעשה את הים הגדול", בזמן שרואהו לפרקים. על הגשמים, ועל בשורות טובות, אומר: "ברוך הטוב והמטיב". על בשורות רעות, אומר: "ברוך דיין האמת". בנה בית חדש, וקנה כלים חדשים, אומר: "ברוך שהחיינו וקיימנו והגיענו לזמן הזה". מברך על הרעה מעין על הטובה, ועל הטובה מעין על הרעה. והצועק לשעבר – הרי זו תפלת שוא; היתה אשתו מעוברת, ואומר: "יהי רצון שתלד אשתי זכר" – הרי זו תפלת שוא; היה בא בדרך ושמע קול צוחה בעיר, ואומר: "יהי רצון שלא תהא בתוך ביתי" – הרי זו תפלת שוא. § הנכנס לכרך מתפלל שתים, אחת בכניסתו ואחת ביציאתו; בן עזאי אומר: ארבע, שתים בכניסתו ושתים ביציאתו, נותן הודאה על שעבר וצועק על העתיד. § חייב אדם לברך על הרעה כשם שמברך על הטובה, שנאמר: "ואהבת את ה' אלהיך בכל לבבך וגו'" 'בכל לבבך' – בשני יצריך, ביצר טוב וביצר הרע; "ובכל נפשך" – אפילו הוא נוטל את נפשך, "ובכל מאדך" – בכל ממונך. ד"א: "בכל מאדך" – בכל מדה ומדה שהוא מודד לך הוי מודה לו. לא יקל אדם את ראשו כנגד שער המזרח, שהוא מכוון כנגד בית קדשי הקדשים. ולא יכנס להר הבית במקלו, ובמנעלו, ובפונדתו, ובאבק שעל רגליו, ולא יעשנו קפנדריא; ורקיקה – מקל וחומר. כל חותמי ברכות שבמקדש היו אומרים: "עד העולם". משקלקלו הצדוקים ואמרו אין עולם אלא אחד – התקינו שיהו אומרים: "מן העולם ועד העולם". § והתקינו שיהא אדם שואל את שלום חברו בשם, שנאמר: "והנה בעז בא מבית לחם ויאמר לקוצרים: ה' עמכם, ויאמרו לו: יברכך ה'"; ואומר: "ה' עמך גבור החיל"; ואומר: "אל תבוז כי זקנה אמך"; ואומר: "עת לעשות לה' הפרו תורתך". רבי נתן אומר: הפרו תורתך משום עת לעשות לה'. § **גמ'** מנא הני מילי? אמר רבי יוחנן, דאמר קרא: "ויאמר יתרו ברוך ה' אשר הציל וגו'". אניסא דרבים מברכינן, אניסא דיחיד לא מברכינן?! והא ההוא גברא דהוה קא אזיל בעבר ימינא, נפל עליה אריא, אתעביד ליה ניסא ואיתצל מיניה; אתא לקמיה דרבא, וא"ל: כל אימת דמטית להתם – בריך "ברוך שעשה לי נס במקום הזה"! ומר בריה דרבינא הוה קאזיל בפקתא דערבות וצחא למיא, אתעביד ליה ניסא איברי ליה עינא דמיא ואישתי. ותו, זימנא חדא הוה קאזיל ברסתקא דמחוזא ונפל עליה גמלא פריצא, איתפרקא ליה אשיתא, על לגוה; כי מטא לערבות, בריך: ברוך שעשה לי נס בערבות ובגמל, כי מטא לרסתקא דמחוזא, בריך: ברוך שעשה לי נס בגמל ובערבות! – אמרי: אניסא דרבים כולי עלמא מיחייבי לברוכי, אניסא דיחיד – איהו [א] חייב לברוכי. § תנו רבנן: הרואה מעברות הים, ומעברות הירדן, מעברות נחלי ארנון, אבני אלגביש במורד בית חורון, ואבן שבקש לזרוק עוג מלך הבשן על ישראל, ואבן שישב עליה משה בשעה שעשה יהושע מלחמה בעמלק, ואשתו של לוט, וחומת יריחו שנבלעה במקומה – על כולן צריך שיתן הודאה ושבח לפני המקום. בשלמא מעברות הים, דכתיב: "ויבאו בני ישראל בתוך הים ביבשה", מעברות הירדן, דכתיב: "ויעמדו הכהנים נשאי הארון ברית ה' בחרבה בתוך הירדן הכן וכל ישראל עוברים בחרבה עד אשר תמו כל הגוי לעבור את הירדן". אלא מעברות נחלי ארנון מנלן? – דכתיב: "על כן יאמר בספר מלחמת ה' את והב בסופה וגו'", תנא: "את והב בסופה" – שני מצורעים היו דהוו מהלכין בסוף מחנה ישראל, כי הוו קא חלפי ישראל אתו אמוראי (א) עבדי

**הרואה** מקום שנעשו בו נסים לישראל. כגון הנך דקתני לקמן: מעברות הים והירדן ונחלי ארנון כו': זיקין וזועות ורעמים. מפרש בגמרא: מלא עולם. לפי שאלו נראין או נשמעין למרחוק: ברוך עושה בראשית. ובגמרא (דף נט.) פריך: אטו הנך דלעיל לאו מעשה בראשית נינהו: לפרקים. מפרש בגמרא (שם ע"ב). ולפי שהוא חשוב וגדול מכלן קבע ליה רבי יהודה ברכה לעצמו: מברך על הרעה מעין על הטובה. דיין האמת: ועל הטובה מעין על הרעה. הטוב והמטיב. ובגמרא מפרש היכי דמי: הנכנס לכרך. המהלך בדרך וצריך לעבור כרך, ושם מצויים מושלים רעים ומחפשים עלילות: אחת בכניסתו. מתפלל שיכניסנו לשלום. ביציאתו. מתפלל שיוציאנו לשלום. ארבע. כדמפרש: נותן הודאה על שעבר וצועק על העתיד, נמצאו ד', כדמפרש בגמרא: חייב אדם לברך על הרעה כו'. מפרש בגמרא: ד"א בכל מאדך. מדות מדודות לך, בין מדה טובה בין מדת פורענות: לא יקל ראש. לא ינהג קלות ראש: כנגד שער מזרחי. חוץ להר הבית אשר בחומה הנמוכה אשר לרגלי הבית במזרח, לפי שכל השערים מכוונים זה כנגד זה, שער מזרח, שער עזרת נשים, ושער עזרת ישראל, ופתח האולם וההיכל, ובית קדשי הקדשים בימי מקדש ראשון, כשהיה ארון: טרקסין: בפונדתו. חגור חלול ונותנין בו מעות: מק"ו. בגמרא מפרש ליה: כל חותמי ברכות שבמקדש היו אומרים עד העולם. במסכת תענית (פ"ב דף טז:) אמרינן: אין עונין אמן במקדש, המברך אומר בסוף כל ברכה "ברוך אתה ה' אלהי ישראל מן העולם ועד העולם", וכן כולם. והעונין אומרים: "ברוך שם כבוד מלכותו לעולם ועד". ויליפינן לה מקרא דתפלת עזרא וסיעתו. ושמעינן הכא דבמקדש ראשון לא היו אומרים אלא "ברוך ה' אלהי ישראל עד העולם": משקלקלו הצדוקים. ואמרו אין עולם אלא זה: התקינו. עזרא וסיעתו שיהו אומרים "מן העולם ועד העולם", לומר שני עולמות יש, להוציא מלב הצדוקים הכופרים בתחיית המתים: שיהא אדם שואל לשלום חבירו בשם. בשמו של הקב"ה, ולא אמרינן מזלזל הוא בכבודו של מקום בשביל כבוד הבריות להוציא שם שמים עליו. ולמדו מבועז שאמר "ה' עמכם", ומן המלאך שאמר לגדעון "ה' עמך גבור החיל": ואומר אל תבוז כי זקנה אמך. למוד מדברי זקני אומתך לעשות מה שראית שעשו הם. ובגמ' מפרש מאי ואומר: ואומר עת לעשות לה' הפרו תורתך. פעמים שמבטלים דברי תורה כדי לעשות לה'. אף זה, המתכוין לשאול לשלום חברו זה רצונו של מקום, שנאמר "בקש שלום ורדפהו", מותר להפר תורה ולעשות דבר הנראה אסור: **גמ'** ה"ג:

**הרואה** וכו' אומר ברוך שעשה נסים לאבותינו וכו'. פירש רבי' שמעיה: דכל הני ברכות צריכות להזכרת שם ומלכות ברוך אתה ה' אלהינו מלך העולם. וכן כתב רבינו שמשון מקוצי, כי הר"י היה רגיל לברך על הברקים ברוך אתה ה' אלהינו מלך העולם שכחו וגבורתו מלא עולם. וכן פר"י ומייתי ירושלמי דפירקין: רבי זעירא כו' כל ברכה שאין בה וכו'. ונראה לרבינו: דדוקא לרואה משלשים יום לשלשים יום דומיא דרואה ים הגדול לפרקים. דאמר בירושלמי דפרקים היינו שלשים יום: **שעקר** עבודה זרה מארצנו. בירושלמי מתני: כשנעקרה עבודה זרה מכל ארץ ישראל: **על** הנהרות. לאו על כל נהרות איירי, אלא ארבע נהרות דכתיבי בקרא, כמו חדקל ופרת.
אבני

א א מיי' פ"י מהלכות ברכות הל' ט סמג עשין כז טוש"ע או"ח סי' ריח סעיף א:
ב ב ג מיי' שם הל' טו סמג שם טוש"ע או"ח סי' רכז סעיף א:
ג ד מיי' שם טוש"ע או"ח סי' ריח ג וסי' רכב סעיף ב:
ד ה מיי' שם הלכה ג סמג שם טוש"ע או"ח סי' רכב סעיף ג:
[עי' תוספות לקמן נט. ד"ה על]
ה ו ז מיי' שם הלכה כב כה כו סמג שם טוש"ע או"ח סי' רל סעיף א:
ו ח מיי' פ"ז מהל' בית הבחירה הלכה ב סמג עשין קסד:
ז ט טוש"ע או"ח סי' ריח סעיף ה:
[עי' תוס' סוכה מו. ד"ה העושה וכו' מ"ש בשם רב שרירא גאון]
ח י מיי' פ"י מהלכות ברכות הלכה ט סמג עשין כז טוש"ע שם סעיף ב:
ט כ מיי' שם טוש"ע שם סעיף ד:
י ל שם סעיף א:

בכ"י ובכי"י ובמשנה שבמשניות הגי' המינין [מכות כג:]

משלי כג

**הגהות הב"ח**
(א) גמ' אתו אמוראי עשו להו בנחלי ארנון עבדי להו:

**הגהות הגר"א**
[א] גמ' אניסא דיחיד איהו. נ"ב ובריה ובר בריה. גירסת הגאונים והרי"ף:

מנלן דמברכינן אניסא א"ר יוחנן דאמר קרא: "ויאמר יתרו ברוך ה' אשר הציל אתכם" וגו': בעבר ימינא. שם מדינה בדרומו של פרת: בפקתא. בקעה: ערבות. שם מקום: וצחא למיא. צמא למים: ברסתקא. בשוק: גמלא פריצא. גמל משוגע, שעסקיו רעים: אתפרקא ליה אשיתא. נפלה חומת בית שהיה סמוך לו, ונכנס לתוך הבית מפני הגמל: מעברות הים. מקום שעברו ישראל בים סוף: ומעברות הירדן. בימי יהושע: מעברות נחלי ארנון. לקמן מפרש מאי ניסא: במורד בית חורון. בימי יהושע היה, בספר יהושע (י): ואבן שבקש עוג. לקמן מפרש:
עבדי

עין משפט נר מצוה

שייך לע"א

[הנזכר בירושלמי הביאו הרא"ש סי' א]

יא א טוש"ע או"ח סי' ריח סעיף ח:

יב ב מיי' פ"י מהלכות ברכות הל' ח סמג עשין כז טוש"ע או"ח סי' ריט ס"א:

יג ג מיי' שם טוש"ע שם סעיף ב:

יד ד מיי' שם טוש"ע שם סעיף ג:

טו ה שם סעיף ז:

[הטור באו"ח סי' ריט העתיק דברי תוס' הללו בזה"ל וכיון דלא אפסיקא עבדינן לחומרא ובעינן תרוייהו]

[לעיל מ:]

[כל זה מוחק המעי"ט]

עבדי להון נקירותא וטשו בהון, אמרי: כי חלפי ישראל הכא נקטלינון, ולא הוו ידעי דארון הוה מסגי קמייהו דישראל והוה ממיך להו טורי מקמייהו; כיון דאתא ארון, אדבקו טורי בהדי הדדי וקטלינון, ונחת דמייהו לנחלי ארנון. כי אתו את והב, חזו דמא דקא נפיק מביני טורי, אתו ואמרי להו לישראל ואמרו שירה, היינו דכתיב: (במדבר כא) °"ואשד הנחלים אשר נטה לשבת ער ונשען לגבול מואב". אבני אלגביש – מאי אבני אלגביש? תנא: אבנים שעמדו על גב איש וירדו על גב איש; עמדו על גב איש – זה משה, דכתיב: (שם יב) °"והאיש משה ענו מאד", וכתיב: (שמות ט) °"ויחדלו הקלות והברד ומטר לא נתך ארצה". ירדו על גב איש – זה יהושע, דכתיב: (במדבר כז) °"קח לך את יהושע בן נון איש אשר רוח בו", וכתיב: (יהושע י) °"ויהי בנוסם מפני בני ישראל הם במורד בית חורון וה' השליך עליהם אבנים גדלות".§ אבן שבקש עוג מלך הבשן לזרוק על ישראל – גמרא גמירי לה. אמר: מחנה ישראל כמה הוי – תלתא פרסי, איזיל ואיעקר טורא בר תלתא פרסי ואישדי עלייהו ואיקטלינהו. אזל עקר טורא בר תלתא פרסי ואייתי על רישיה, ואייתי קודשא בריך הוא עליה קמצי ונקבוה ונחית בצואריה; הוה בעי למשלפה, משכי שיניה להאי גיסא ולהאי גיסא ולא מצי למשלפה, והיינו דכתיב: (תהלים ג) °"שני רשעים שברת"; וכדר' שמעון בן לקיש, *דא"ר שמעון בן לקיש: מאי דכתיב "שני רשעים שברת" – אל תקרי "שברת" אלא "שרבבת". *משה כמה הוה – עשר אמות, שקיל נרגא בר עשר אמין שוור עשר אמין, ומחייה בקרסוליה וקטליה.§ ואבן שישב עליה משה – דכתיב: (שמות יז) °"וידי משה כבדים ויקחו אבן וישימו תחתיו וישב עליה". ואשתו של לוט – שנאמר: (בראשית יט) °"ותבט אשתו מאחריו ותהי נציב מלח". וחומת יריחו שנבלעה – דכתיב: (יהושע ו) °"ותפל החומה תחתיה". בשלמא כולהו – ניסא, אלא אשתו של לוט, פורענותא הוא! – דאמר "ברוך דיין האמת". – והא "הודאה ושבח" קתני! – [א]תני: על לוט ועל אשתו מברכים שתים, על אשתו אומר: "ברוך דיין האמת", ועל לוט אומר: "ברוך זוכר את הצדיקים". *א"ר יוחנן: אפילו בשעת כעסו של הקב"ה זוכר את הצדיקים, שנאמר: (בראשית יט) °"ויהי בשחת אלהים את ערי הככר ויזכר אלהים את אברהם וישלח את לוט מתוך ההפכה וגו'". וחומת יריחו שנבלעה. והא נפלה! שנאמר: (יהושע ו) °"ויהי כשמע העם את קול השופר ויריעו העם תרועה גדולה, ותפל החומה תחתיה! –כיון דפותיה ורומה כי הדדי נינהו, משום הכי אבלעה בלועי.§ אמר רב יהודה אמר רב: *[ב]ארבעה צריכין להודות – יורדי הים, הולכי מדברות, ומי שהיה חולה ונתרפא, ומי שהיה חבוש בבית האסורים, ויצא. יורדי הים מנלן – דכתיב: (תהלים קז) °"יורדי הים באניות וגו' המה ראו מעשי ה'", ואומר: "ויעמד רוח סערה יעלו שמים ירדו תהומות", ואומר: "יחוגו וינועו כשכור", ואומר: "ויצעקו אל ה' בצר להם וממצוקתיהם יוציאם", ואומר: "יקם סערה לדממה", ואומר: "וישמחו כי ישתקו", ואומר: "יודו לה' חסדו ונפלאותיו לבני אדם". הולכי מדברות מנלן – דכתיב: "תעו במדבר בישימון דרך עיר מושב לא מצאו ויצעקו אל ה' וידריכם בדרך ישרה", "יודו לה' חסדו". מי שחלה ונתרפא – דכתיב: "אוילים מדרך פשעם ומעונותיהם יתענו כל אכל תתעב נפשם וגו'", "ויזעקו אל ה' בצר להם וגו'", "ישלח דברו וירפאם וגו'", "יודו לה' חסדו". מי שהיה חבוש בבית האסורין, מנלן? דכתיב: "ישבי חשך וצלמות וגו'", "כי המרו אמרי אל וגו'", ואומר: "ויכנע בעמל לבם וגו'", ואומר: "ויזעקו אל ה' בצר להם", ואומר: "יוציאם מחשך וצלמות וגו'", ואומר: "יודו לה' חסדו". מאי מברך? – אמר רב יהודה: [ג]"ברוך גומל חסדים טובים". [א] אביי אמר: וצריך לאודויי קמי עשרה, דכתיב: (שם שם) °"וירוממוהו בקהל עם וגו'". מר זוטרא אמר: ותרין מינייהו רבנן, שנאמר: °"ובמושב זקנים יהללוהו". מתקיף לה רב אשי: ואימא כולהו רבנן! –מי כתיב "בקהל זקנים"?! "בקהל עם" כתיב. –ואימא: [ד]בי עשרה שאר עמא, ותרי רבנן! – קשיא. רב יהודה חלש ואתפח, על לגביה רב חנא בגדתאה ורבנן, אמרי ליה: בריך רחמנא דיהבך ניהלן ולא יהבך לעפרא. אמר להו: [ה]פטרתון יתי מלאודויי. והא אמר אביי: בעי אודויי באפי עשרה! –דהוו בי עשרה. והא איהו לא קא מודה! – לא צריך, דעני בתרייהו אמן.§ אמר רב יהודה: שלשה צריכין שימור, ואלו הן: חולה, חתן, וכלה, במתניתא תנא: חולה, חיה, חתן, וכלה. ויש אומרים: אף אבל. ויש אומרים: אף תלמידי חכמים בלילה. ואמר רב יהודה, שלשה דברים [המאריך בהן] מאריכין ימיו ושנותיו של אדם: המאריך בתפלתו, והמאריך על שלחנו, והמאריך בבית הכסא. והמאריך בתפלתו, מעליותא היא?! והאמר רבי חייא בר אבא א"ר יוחנן: כל

**תוספות**

*אבני אלגביש במורד בית חורון. וה"ה מקום שנפל שם מחנה סנחריב, דלא גרע מזקיה מאלפס *המסוים, אלא לא חש לפרש לפי שידוע המקום סביב ירושלים. ועוד היה נראה לרבינו יהודה כיון שאין הנס ידוע ע"פ המקום כי הנך – אין מברכין עליו אלא אותם שנעשה להם הנס. וכן כל אדם מברך על ניסו, אף על פי שאינו ניכר מתוך המקום:

ארבעה צריכין להודות יורדי הים וכו'. ובתהלים לא חשיב כזה הסדר, אלא חשיב הולכי המדבר ראשון דקרא נקט סדר המסוכנין יותר תחלה וגמרא נקט המצויין תחלה: ואימא בי עשרה ותרי רבנן. *ועבדי לחומרא, ואפילו ליכא תרי רבנן. ונהגו העולם לברך אחר שקורא בתורה. ודוקא בחולה שנפל למטה, אבל חש בראשו או במעיו ואינו מוטל למטה – לא. ה"ר יוסף:

פטרתון יתי מלאודויי. וא"ת: והא אמרינן*, ברכה שאין בה מלכות אינה ברכה! וי"ל: דרב יהודה היה מתלמידי דרב, ורב סבר לעיל בפרק כיצד מברכין (דף מ:) דלא בעינן אלא הזכרת השם (או מלכות ורחמנא היינו מלכות):

**רש"י**

עבדי להון נקירותא. מערות מעברות נחלי ארנון עמק עמוק היו ישראל צריכים לעבור בתוכו עמק, עשו אמוריים מערות בגדי ההרים ונחבאו שם: וטשו. נחבאו: מסגי. עוגר: ממיך טורי. משפיל הרים, ומתפשטין זה לצד זה עד שהעמק שוה: חזו דמא. כשחזרו ההרים למקומן: ואשד. ושפך: אשר נטה לשבת ער. ההר שבעבר העמק נטה ונתפשט לצד חברו ההר אשר לצד עבר מואב. ושם ארץ מואב ער: שעמדו. באויר: לא נתך ארצה. לא הגיע לארץ, אלא עמדו באויר(א): מחנה ישראל כמה הוי תלתא פרסי. עוג חשב כן בלבו. מחנה ישראל תלתא פרסי, דכתיב (במדבר לג) "ויחנו מבית הישימות עד אבל השטים". ואמר רבה בר בר חנה: לדידי חזי לי ההוא דוכתא והוה תלתא פרסי אורכא ותלתא פרסי פותיא (עירובין פ"ה ד' נה:): קמצי. נמלים: שרבבת. לשון *אשתרבובי אשתרבוב, ירדו וגדלו למטה: משה כמה הוי עשר אמין. שהרי הוא הקים את המשכן (ב)ודרשי' הקים את עצמו לקומת המשכן, וכתיב ביה "עשר אמות אורך הקרש" (שמות לו): שוור. קפץ למעלה: בקרסוליה. קבילי"א בלע"ז: וידי משה כבדים. ואינו יכול לפושטן כל היום אלא אם כן תומכים בזרועותיו, ויקחו אבן וישימו תחתיו: תחתיה. משמע: במקומה, ואי אפשר זו אלא על ידי בליעה: דאמר ברוך דיין האמת. פורענותא הוא: זוכר את הצדיקים. שזכר את אברהם: כיון דפותיה ורומה כי הדדי הוו. ואין נפילה ניכרת בה אם לא נבלעה, משום הכי אבלעה, והוא דרך נפילה לחומה כזו: צריכין להודות. כשיוצאין מן הסכנה: וירוממוהו בקהל עם. בסוף פרשת המזמור(ג): ואתפח. נתרפא: בגדתאה. שם עירו בגדד, היא עיר החשובה שבבבל משתרבבה: שימור. מן המזיקין: חולה. שהורע מזלו, לפיכך השד מתגרה בו. וכן חיה – אשה שילדה, וכן אבל: חתן וכלה ותלמידי חכמים. מקנאתו מתגרה בהם: והמאריך על שלחנו. שמתוך כך עניים באין ומתפרנסים: והמאריך בבית הכסא. רפואה היא לו: מעיין

**מסורת הש"ס**

[סוכה ה. קדושין מ]

[מגילה טו: סוטה]

[בכורות מד.]

[וע"ע פירוש רש"י סז. וכתובות ז: י:]

**הגהות הב"ח**

(א) רש"י ד"ה לא נתך וכו' באויר הס"ד ואח"כ מ"ה אמר עוג חשב כן בלבו הס"ד ואח"כ מ"ה מחנה וכו' תלתא פרסי מחנ' ישראל: (ב) ד"ה משה וכו' הקים את המשכן שנאמר ויקם משה את המשכן ודרשינן הקים: (ג) ד"ה וירוממוהו וכו' המזמור כתיב הס"ד:

[בשאלתות פ' וישלח סי' כ"ו איתא דאמר ר"י]

[תשובת רב האי גאון על דלא קחשיב הנך ד' לצריכין להודות כסדר הנאמר בפסוק עי' בערוך ערך ארבע ותמצא נחת וכלל דבריו דבקרא סדורין מה שבכיח טפי ובגמרא מסדר לפום הקרובין לסכנה וע"ע בתוס' ד"ה ארבעה וכו' שכתבו להיפך וע"ע בתוס' לשבת ב. ד"ה יציאות וכן מפרש רב האי בד' צריכין להודות ע"ש היטב]

**הגהות הגר"א**

[א] גמ' חסדים טובים (רשום קו על מלות הללו) וכ"ב לחייבים טובות שגמלני כל טוב. רי"ף ורא"ש:

**גליון הש"ס**

גמ' דכתיב וירוממוהו בקהל עם. וקהל מקרי עשרה כמו שפירש"י כתובות ז ע"ב ד"ה במקהלות: שם אמר רב יהודה שלשה צריכין שמור. מג"א סי' רל"ט ס"ק ז: שם וי"א אף אבל. עיין רבינו יונה פ"ק דמסכתין דף ד ע"ב ד"ה שנאמר: שם ג' דברים המאריך בהן מאריכין. עי' לעיל מז ע"א ונע"ק [ערש"א בח"א]: תד"ה ארבעה כו' המצויין תחלה. עי' ריש שבת בתוס' ד"ה יציאות:

מעיין בה. אומר בלבו שתיעשה בקשתו לפי שהתפלל בכוונה: כאב לב. שאין בקשתו נעשית: תוחלת. לשון תפלה, כמו "ויחל משה" (שמות לב): מזכירין עונותיו. שעל ידיהן מסתכלים למעלה במעשיו, לומר: בוטח זה בזכויותיו, נראה מה הם! קיר נטוי. מקום סכנה: מוסר דין. בוטח הוא בזכויותיו שחברו יהיה נענש על ידו: ה"ג: הא דמעיין (א) הא דלא מעיין: לולבי גפנים. וילי"ש בלע"ז: מוריני בהמה. כל בשר שבבהמה שאינו חלק אלא דומה למורג חרוץ שאינו חלק, כמו החיך והלשון והכרס הפנימי ובית הכוסות: התולה. שאינו יושב, אלא על ברכיו, שמתוך כך נקביו נפתחין יותר מדאי: הכי גרסינן. הא דמאריך ותלי, הא דמאריך ולא תלי: למגדלי חזירים ומלוי ברבית. שממון מרובה בלא טורח, ושמחים בחלקם, לכך פניהם צהובים: הימנותא. לשון שבועה. כלומר: באמונה, שתיהן אסורות לי: ואברכה מברכיך. ומברכך. ברכת המזון מברך לבעל הבית: מת קודם לאחיו. דכתיב "וימת יוסף וכל אחיו" (שמות א): צריכים רחמים. צריכים לבקש רחמים שיבואו, לפי שהם בידו של הקב"ה, ואין להם לשום לבא אלא ברשותו: ראה קראתי בשם. "ראה" משמע: (ב) הישב בלבבך מה עיניך בדבר! לך אמור לו לבצלאל: עשה משכן ארון וכלים. שכן הם סדורים בפרשת "כי תשא": "ראה קראתי בשם וגו' את אהל מועד ואת הארון לעדות" וכל הפרשה. ומשה אמר לו: עשה ארון וכלים, כגון שלחן ומנורה ואחר כך משכן, דס"ל לר' שבספר שהם סדורים ב"ויקחו לי תרומה": אמר לו: אותיות שנבראו בהן שמים וארץ. על ידי צירופן. ובספר יצירה תני להו: כל חלום ולא טוות. כל חלומות יראה אדם ולא יראה אחד מאותן שהוא שרוי בתענית, שאינו טוב. טוות – לשון תענית, כמו "ובת טוות" האמור בדריוש (דניאל ו): דלא מפשר. שלא פתרוהו: כאגרתא דלא מקריא. לא טוב ולא רע הוא, שכל החלומות הולכין אחר הפתרון: עדיף מחלמא טבא. שמביא את האדם לידי תשובה: עציבותיה מסתייה. דיו (ג) עצבונו, מה שהאדם מתעצב עליו מבטל את החלום: אפילו לדידי. שאני מאור עינים: בדיחותיה מפכחא ליה. (ד) מבטליה: מנגדא. מלקות. קשה לגוף האדם יותר ממלקות, לפי שדואג ממנו: זה חלום רע. מיראתו ישוב ויכנע: והשיח

*כל המאריך בתפלתו ומעיין בה סוף בא לידי כאב לב שנאמר: °"תוחלת ממשכה מחלה לב". *וא"ר יצחק: שלשה דברים מזכירים עונותיו של אדם, ואלו הן: קיר נטוי, ועיון תפלה, ומוסר דין על חבירו לשמים! – הא לא קשיא, (א)הא – דמעיין בה, הא – דלא מעיין בה. והיכי עביד – דמפיש ברחמי. והמאריך על שלחנו – דלמא אתי עניא ויהיב ליה, דכתיב °"המזבח עץ שלוש אמות גבה", וכתיב °"וידבר אלי זה השלחן אשר לפני ה'". *פתח במזבח וסיים בשלחן! ר' יוחנן ור' אלעזר דאמרי תרוייהו: כל זמן שבהמ"ק קיים – מזבח מכפר על ישראל, ועכשיו – שלחנו של אדם מכפר עליו. והמאריך בבית הכסא מעליותא הוא? *והתניא, עשרה דברים מביאין את האדם לידי תחתוניות: האוכל עלי קנים, ועלי גפנים, ולולבי גפנים, ומוריני בהמה, ושדרו של דג, ודג מליח שאינו מבושל כל צרכו, והשותה שמרי יין, והמקנח בסיד ובחרסית, והמקנח בצרור שקינח בו חבירו, וי"א: אף התולה עצמו בבית הכסא יותר מדאי! – לא קשיא, הא – דמאריך ותלי, הא – דמאריך ולא תלי. כי הא דאמרה ליה ההיא מטרוניתא לר' יהודה בר' אלעאי: *פניך דומים למגדלי חזירים ולמלוי ברבית. – אמר לה: הימנותא! לדידי תרוייהו אסירן; אלא, עשרים וארבעה בית הכסא איכא מאושפיזאי לבי מדרשא, דכי אזילנא בדיקנא נפשאי בכולהו.§ ואמר רב יהודה, שלשה דברים מקצרים ימיו ושנותיו של אדם: מי שנותנין לו ס"ת לקרות ואינו קורא, כוס של ברכה לברך ואינו מברך, והמנהיג עצמו ברבנות. ס"ת לקרות ואינו קורא – דכתיב °"כי הוא חייך וארך ימיך". כוס של ברכה לברך ואינו מברך – דכתיב °"ואברכה מברכיך". והמנהיג עצמו ברבנות – *דא"ר חמא בר חנינא: מפני מה מת יוסף קודם לאחיו – מפני שהנהיג עצמו ברבנות.§ ואמר רב יהודה אמר רב, שלשה צריכים רחמים: מלך טוב, שנה טובה, וחלום טוב. מלך טוב – דכתיב °"פלגי מים לב מלך ביד ה'". שנה טובה – דכתיב °"תמיד עיני ה' אלהיך בה *מראשית השנה ועד אחרית שנה". חלום טוב – דכתיב °"ותחלימני *(ותחייני)". אמר רבי יוחנן: שלשה דברים מכריז עליהם הקב"ה בעצמו, ואלו הן: רעב, ושובע, ופרנס טוב. רעב – דכתיב °"כי קרא ה' לרעב וגו'", שובע – דכתיב °"וקראתי אל הדגן והרביתי אתו", פרנס טוב – דכתיב °"(*ויאמר) ה' אל משה לאמר ראה קראתי בשם בצלאל וגו'". אמר רבי יצחק: אין מעמידין פרנס על הצבור אלא אם כן נמלכים בצבור, שנא' °"ראו קרא ה' בשם בצלאל". אמר לו הקדוש ברוך הוא למשה: משה, הגון עליך בצלאל? אמר לו: רבונו של עולם, אם לפניך הגון – לפני לא כל שכן? אמר לו: אף על פי כן, לך אמור להם. הלך ואמר להם לישראל: הגון עליכם בצלאל? אמרו לו: אם לפני הקדוש ברוך הוא ולפניך הוא הגון – לפנינו לא כל שכן? א"ר שמואל בר נחמני א"ר יונתן: בצלאל על שם חכמתו נקרא. בשעה שאמר לו הקדוש ברוך הוא למשה: לך אמור לו לבצלאל עשה לי משכן ארון וכלים, הלך משה והפך, ואמר לו: עשה ארון וכלים ומשכן. אמר לו: משה רבינו, מנהגו של עולם – אדם בונה בית ואחר כך מכניס לתוכו כלים, ואתה אומר: עשה לי ארון וכלים ומשכן! כלים שאני עושה – להיכן אכניסם? שמא כך אמר לך הקב"ה: עשה משכן ארון וכלים. אמר לו: שמא בצל אל היית וידעת! אמר רב יהודה אמר רב: יודע היה בצלאל לצרף אותיות שנבראו בהן שמים וארץ. כתיב הכא °"וימלא אתו רוח אלהים בחכמה *ובתבונה ובדעת", וכתיב התם °"ה' בחכמה יסד ארץ כונן שמים בתבונה" וכתיב °"בדעתו תהומות נבקעו". אמר רבי יוחנן: אין הקדוש ברוך הוא נותן חכמה אלא למי שיש בו חכמה, שנא' °"יהב חכמתא לחכימין ומנדעא לידעי בינה". שמע רב תחליפא בר מערבא ואמרה קמיה דרבי אבהו, אמר ליה: אתון מהתם מתניתו לה, אנן מהכא מתנינן לה – דכתיב °"ובלב כל חכם לב נתתי חכמה".§ אמר רב חסדא: *כל חלום ולא טוות. ואמר רב חסדא: חלמא דלא מפשר – כאגרתא דלא מקריא. ואמר רב חסדא: לא חלמא טבא מקיים כוליה, ולא חלמא בישא מקיים כוליה. ואמר רב חסדא: חלמא בישא עדיף מחלמא טבא. וא"ר חסדא: חלמא בישא – עציבותיה מסתייה, חלמא טבא – חדוייה מסתייה. אמר רב יוסף: חלמא טבא – אפילו לדידי בדיחותיה מפכחא ליה. ואמר רב חסדא: חלמא בישא קשה מנגדא, שנאמר: °"והאלהים עשה שיראו מלפניו" ואמר רבה בר בר חנה א"ר יוחנן: זה חלום רע. °"הנביא אשר אתו חלום יספר חלום ואשר דברי אתו ידבר דברי אמת מה לתבן את הבר נאם ה'", וכי מה ענין בר ותבן אצל חלום? אלא אמר ר' יוחנן משום ר' שמעון בן יוחי: *כשם שאי אפשר לבר בלא תבן – כך אי אפשר לחלום בלא דברים בטלים. אמר ר' ברכיה: חלום, אף על פי שמקצתו מתקיים – כולו אינו מתקיים, מנא לן – מיוסף דכתיב °"והנה השמש והירח וגו'" והיא

לך אמור לבצלאל: עשה משכן ארון וכלים. ואם תאמר: היכא אשכחן שאמר הקדוש ברוך הוא לעשות משכן תחלה? הרי בפרשת תרומה כתיב ארון תחלה! ויש לומר דבפרשת כי תשא כתיב את אהל מועד ואת הארון לעדות:

שבע

יז א טוש"ע או"ח סימן לח סעיף ה:
יח ב טוש"ע או"ח סי' רא סעיף ג:

הגהות הב"ח

(א) רש"י ד"ה ה"ג הא דמעיין בה הא דלא מעיין בה הס"ד: (ב) ד"ה ראה וכו' ראה משמע (הסיג בלבבך) תא"מ ונ"ב ס"א הכן את לבבך: (ג) ד"ה עציבותיה מסתייה (דיו) תא"מ ונ"ב ס"א די לו: (ד) ד"ה בדיחותיה וכו' ליה טיבותיה מבטלתו. נ"ב ס"א דלא מתקיים עליו כלל.

מרשית חסר א' כתיב
והחייני
יחזקאל לו
וידבר

[בפ' ויקהל פסוק ל"א כתיב בתבונה בלא וי"ו אבל בפ' כי תשא ל"א פסוק ג' כתיב ואמלא אותו רוח אלהים בחכמה ובתבונה ובדעת ולכן יתכן להיות כתוב הכא ואמלא אותו וגו' והוא קרא מוקדם]

לעיל לב: | [ר"ה טז:] | משלי יג | יחזקאל מא | שם | תענית כז: ע"ש | שבת פא. ע"ש | ריש מט: ע"ש | סוטה יג: ע"ש | דברים ל | בראשית יב | משלי כא | דברים יא | ישעיה לח | מ"ב ח | שמות לא | שם לה | שם | משלי ג | שם | דניאל ב | שמות לא | קהלת ג | ירמיה כג | נדרים ח. | בראשית לז

יט א טוש"ע או"ח סי' רכ סעיף א:
כ ב טוש"ע או"ח סימן קל:

והחיא שעתא. דהלם אמיה לא הות: יצפה. שיתקיים: מיוסף. שלא נתקיימו השתחוואות הללו עד עשרים ושתים שנה, כשירד יעקב למצרים, שכבר היה הרעב שתי שנים דכתיב "כי זה שנתים הרעב" (בראשית מה): לאדם טוב מראין לו חלום רע. כדי שידאג ולא יחטא, ושיכפר לו עונותיו: לאדם רע מראין לו חלום טוב. כדי לשמחו, שיאכל עולמו: ודוד לא ראה חלום טוב והא כתיב וכו'. לא גרסינן הכי, אלא גרסינן: והא כתיב "לא תאונה אליך רעה" וגו'. קשיא לרב הונא, דאמר: לאדם טוב מראין לו חלום רע. ומשני: איהו לא חזי אחריני

**שבע** זמנין לגזרו עלך. כך הוא הלשון: שבע זמנין לגזרו עלך. ויש מפרש: דשבע זמנין לריך לומר הלשון טבא חזאי, וכן לענות אחריו. אבל ר"י לא היה רגיל לאומרו אלא שלש פעמים: **פותרי** חלומות. פירש ר"י: דמזל שעת הלידה גריס, ואין הדבר תלוי בחכמה:

הרואה

[עי' פירש"י דהכא וגירסתו וכן הגירסא בעי"י לאדם טוב מראין לו חלום רע ולאדם רע מראין לו חלום טוב תניא נמי הכי וכו']

והחיא שעתא אמיה לא הות. א"ר לוי: לעולם יצפה אדם לחלום טוב עד כ"ב שנה. מנלן – מיוסף, דכתיב °"אלה תלדות יעקב יוסף בן שבע עשרה שנה וגו'", וכתיב °"ויוסף בן שלשים שנה בעמדו לפני פרעה וגו'". מן שבסרי עד תלתין כמה הוי – תלת סרי, ושב דשבעא ותרתי דכפנא – הא כ"ב. § אמר רב הונא: לאדם *טוב אין מראין לו חלום טוב, ולאדם רע אין מראין לו חלום רע. תניא נמי הכי: כל שנותיו של דוד לא ראה חלום טוב, וכל שנותיו של אחיתופל לא ראה חלום רע.(א) והכתיב °"לא תאנה אליך רעה", *ואמר רב חסדא אמר רב ירמיה בר אבא: שלא יבהילוך לא חלומות רעים ולא הרהורים רעים, "ונגע לא יקרב באהלך" – שלא תמצא אשתך ספק נדה בשעה שאתה בא מן הדרך! – אלא: איהו לא חזי ליה, אחריני חזו ליה. -וכי לא חזא איהו מעליותא הוא?! והאמר ר' זעירא: *כל הלן שבעה ימים בלא חלום נקרא רע, שנאמר: °"ושבע ילין בל יפקד רע", אל תקרי "שבע" אלא "שבע"! -אלא הכי קאמר: דחזא ולא ידע מאי חזא. אמר רב הונא בר אמי אמר ר' פדת א"ר יוחנן: הרואה חלום ונפשו עגומה ילך ויפתרנו בפני שלשה. יפתרנו?! והאמר רב חסדא: חלמא דלא מפשר כאגרתא דלא מקריא! – אלא אימא: איטיבנו בפני שלשה. ליתי תלתא ולימא להו: חלמא טבא חזאי. ולימרו ליה הנך: טבא הוא, וטבא ליהוי, רחמנא לשוייה לטב. שבע זמנין לגזרו עלך מן שמיא דלהוי טבא, ויהוי טבא. ולימרו ג' הפוכות, וג' פדויות, ושלש שלומות. שלש הפוכות – °"הפכת מספדי למחול לי פתחת שקי ותאזרני שמחה", °"אז תשמח בתולה במחול ובחרים וזקנים יחדו והפכתי אבלם לששון וגו'", °"ולא אבה ה' אלהיך לשמע אל בלעם ויהפך וגו'". § שלש פדויות – דכתיב °"פדה בשלום נפשי מקרב לי וגו'", °"ופדויי ה' ישבון וגו'", °"ויאמר העם אל שאול היונתן ימות אשר עשה הישועה וגו'". שלש שלומות – דכתיב °"בורא ניב שפתים שלום שלום לרחוק ולקרוב אמר ה' ורפאתיו", °"ורוח לבשה את עמשי וגו'", °"ואמרתם כה לחי ואתה שלום וביתך שלום וגו'". אמימר ומר זוטרא ורב אשי הוו יתבי בהדי הדדי, אמרי: כל חד וחד מינן לימא מלתא דלא שמיע ליה לחבריה. פתח חד מינייהו ואמר: [ג]האי מאן דחזא חלמא ולא ידע מאי חזא, ליקום קמי כהני בעידנא דפרסי ידייהו, ולימא הכי: רבש"ע, אני שלך וחלומותי שלך, חלום חלמתי ואיני יודע מה הוא, בין שחלמתי אני לעצמי ובין שחלמו לי חבירי ובין שחלמתי על אחרים, אם טובים הם – חזקם ואמצם כחלומותיו של יוסף, ואם צריכים רפואה – רפאם כמי מרה על ידי משה רבינו, וכמרים מצרעתה, וכחזקיהו מחליו, וכמי יריחו על ידי אלישע, וכשם שהפכת קללת בלעם הרשע לברכה – כן הפוך כל חלומותי עלי לטובה ומסיים בהדי כהני, דעני צבורא אמן. ואי [א] לא – לימא הכי: "אדיר במרום שוכן בגבורה, אתה שלום ושמך שלום, יהי רצון מלפניך שתשים עלינו שלום". פתח אידך ואמר: האי מאן דעייל למתא ודחיל מעינא בישא, לנקוט זקפא דידא דימיניה בידא דשמאליה, וזקפא דידא דשמאליה בידא דימיניה, ולימא הכי: אנא פלוני בר פלוני *מזרעא דיוסף קאתינא דלא שלטא ביה עינא בישא, שנאמר: °"בן פרת יוסף בן פרת עלי עין וגו'", אל תקרי "עלי עין" אלא "עולי עין". ר' יוסי בר' חנינא אמר מהכא: °"וידגו לרב בקרב הארץ" מה דגים שבים מים מכסים עליהם ואין עין רעה שולטת בהם, אף זרעו של יוסף אין עין רעה שולטת בהם. ואי דחיל מעינא בישא דיליה – ליחזי אטרפא דנחיריה דשמאליה. פתח אידך ואמר: האי מאן דחליש, יומא קמא – לא לגלי כי היכי דלא לתרע מזליה, מכאן ואילך – לגלי. *כי הא דרבא, כי הוה חליש – יומא קמא לא מגלי, מכאן ואילך א"ל: לשמעיה, פוק אכריז: רבא חלש. מאן דרחים לי – לבעי עלי רחמי, ומאן דסני לי – לחדי לי, וכתיב °"בנפל אויבך אל תשמח ובכשלו אל יגל לבך פן יראה ה' ורע בעיניו והשיב מעליו אפו". § שמואל כי הוה חזי חלמא בישא אמר: °"וחלמות השוא ידברו". כי הוה חזי חלמא טבא אמר: וכי החלומות השוא ידברו? והכתיב °"בחלום אדבר בו". רבא רמי: כתיב "בחלום אדבר בו" וכתיב "וחלמות השוא ידברו"! – לא קשיא, כאן – ע"י מלאך, כאן – ע"י שד. א"ר ביזנא בר זבדא א"ר עקיבא א"ר פנדא א"ר נחום א"ר בירים משום זקן אחד, ומנו – ר' בנאה: עשרים וארבעה פותרי חלומות היו בירושלים, פעם אחת חלמתי חלום והלכתי אצל כולם, ומה שפתר לי זה לא פתר לי זה – וכולם נתקיימו בי, לקיים מה שנאמר: *"כל החלומות הולכים אחר הפה. אטו "כל החלומות הולכים אחר הפה" קרא הוא?! – אין, וכדרבי אלעזר, דא"ר אלעזר: מנין *שכל החלומות הולכין אחר הפה – שנאמר: °"ויהי כאשר פתר לנו כן היה". אמר רבא: והוא דמפשר ליה מעין חלמיה, שנאמר: °"איש כחלמו פתר". °"וירא שר האפים" – מנא ידע? א"ר אלעזר: מלמד שכל אחד ואחד הראוהו חלומו ופתרון חלומו של חבירו. *א"ר יוחנן: השכים ונפל לו פסוק לתוך פיו – הרי זו נבואה קטנה. ואמר ר' יוחנן, ג' חלומות מתקיימין: חלום של שחרית וחלום שחלם לו חבירו, וחלום שנפתר בתוך חלום. ויש אומר: אף חלום שנשנה, שנאמר: °"ועל השנות החלום וגו'". § אמר ר' שמואל בר נחמני א"ר יונתן: אין מראין לו לאדם אלא מהרהורי לבו, שנאמר: °"אנת מלכא רעיונך על משכבך סלקו", ואיבעית אימא מהכא °"ורעיוני לבבך תנדע". אמר רבא: תדע, דלא מחוו ליה לאיניש לא דקלא דדהבא, ולא *פילא דעייל בקופא דמחטא. §

אמר

תורה אור

חזו ליה חלום רע: וכי לא חזי איהו מעליותא הוא. כיון דלא חזי חלום רע כדקאמר "שלא יבהילוהו", וחלום טוב לא כל שכן דלא חזי – דהא קתני כל ימיו של דוד לא ראה חלום טוב, אם כן לא חזי חלום כלל: אלא שבע. שבעה לילות ילין ולא יפקד בשום חלום – הרי הוא רע, ושונאים אותו ואין מראין לו כלום: ומשני: דחזי ולא ידע מאי חזי. אדם טוב מראין לו חלום טוב, ועד שלא יקיץ – משכחת ממנו, כדי שלא ישמח: זקפא. גודל: עלי עין. עולי עין. שלטין על העין, ולא העין עולה בהן: אטרפא דנחיריה דשמאליה. דופן השמאלי של חוטמו: האי מאן דחליש. מי שחלה(ב): דסני לי לחדי לי. ומתוך כך ישוב חרון אף מעלי: הרהורי לבו. מה שהוא מהרהר ביום: רעיונך. מחשבותיך. וכן כל לשון רעיון שבמקרא אינו לשון רצון, אלא לשון מחשבה וזה יוכיח: "ורעיוניה יבהלוניה" (דניאל ד'). וכי רצונו של אדם מבהלו? אלא מחשבותיו מבהלין אותו: דקלא דדהבא. דבר שלא הורגל לראות ולא הרהר בו מעולם: קופא דמחטא. נקב המחט:

קיסר

בראשית לז | שם מא | תהלים צא | משלי יט | תהלים ל | ירמיה לא

סנהדרין קג. | לעיל יז. ע"ש | דברים כג | תהלים נה | ישעיה נז | ישעיה לח | שמואל א יד | דה"א יב | שמואל א כה | בראשית מט | שם מח | [נדרים מ.] | משלי כד | זכריה י | במדבר יב | [עי' תו' סנה' ונתן] | בראשית מא | שם מ | שם מא | דניאל ב | שם

## רב נסים גאון

**אמימר** ומר זוטרא ורב אשי הוו יתבי בהדי הדדי אמרי כל חד וחד מינן נימא מילתא דלא שמיע ליה לחברי' פתח חד מינייהו ואמר האי מאן דחזאי חלמא ולא ידע מאי חזאי ניקו קמי כהני בעידנא דפרסין כהני ידיהו. מפרש טעמא דמילתא במדרש ילמדנו רבינו בפרשת נשא הנה מטתו שלשלמה ששים גבורים אלו ס' אותיות שבברכת כהנים כולם אחוזי חרב שכל אחד ואחד שמו של הקב"ה נזכר בו יברכך ה' יאר ה' ישא ה' איש חרבו על ירכו מה ראתה ירך נזכרת כן אפילו רואה אדם בחלומו החרב שלופה ונתונה בצוארו וקוטע את ירכו משכים לבוקר והולך לבית הכנסת מפחד שראה בלילות בחלומו ורואה את הכהנים נושאין את כפיהם והחלום הרע מתבטל ממנו לכך נאמר מפחד בלילות:

לעיל כ. ב"מ פד. ב"ב קיח: סוטה לו:

## הגהות הב"ח

(א) גמ' חלום רע אימי והכתיב לא: (ב) רש"י ד"ה האי מאן דחליש מי שחלה יומא קמא לא לגלי לא יגלה יום ראשון שמא יתרע מזליה הס"ד:

## הגהות הגר"א

[א] גמ' דעני לבורא אמן ואי כו'. נ"ב וכ"ה בטוש"ע אבל גירסת רי"ף ורא"ש וכי מהדרי כהני אפייהו לימא הכי כו':

[לקמן נו.] | בראשית מא | [לקמן נז: וקנ"ע] | [ב"מ לח:]

אמר ליה קיסר לר' יהושע בר' *(חנניא): אמריתו דחכמיתו טובא, אימא לי מאי חזינא בחלמאי! אמר ליה: חזית דמשחרי לך פרסאי וגרבי בך, ורעיי בך שקצי בחוטרא דדהבא. הרהר כוליה יומא, ולאורתא חזא. אמר ליה שבור מלכא לשמואל: אמריתו דחכמיתו טובא, אימא לי מאי חזינא בחלמאי! אמר ליה: חזית דאתו רומאי ושבו לך, וטחני בך קשייתא ברחייא דדהבא. הרהר כוליה יומא ולאורתא חזא. § בר הדיא מפשר חלמי הוה, מאן דיהיב ליה אגרא – מפשר ליה למעליותא, ומאן דלא יהיב ליה אגרא – מפשר ליה לגריעותא. אביי ורבא חזו חלמא, אביי יהיב ליה זוזא ורבא לא יהיב ליה. אמרי ליה: אקרינן בחלמין °"שורך טבוח לעיניך וגו'". לרבא אמר ליה: פסיד עסקך ולא אהני לך למיכל מעוצבא דלבך, לאביי א"ל: מרווח עסקך, ולא אהני לך למיכל מחדוא דלבך. אמרי ליה: אקרינן °"בנים ובנות תוליד וגו'", לרבא – אמר ליה כבישותיה, לאביי א"ל: בנך ובנתך נפישי, ומינסבן בנתך לעלמא, ומדמיין באפך כדקא אזלן בשביה. אקריין °"בניך ובנותיך נתנים לעם אחר", לאביי א"ל: בנך ובנתך נפישין, *את אמרת לקריבך, והיא אמרה לקריבה, ואכפה לך ויהבת להון לקריבה, דהוי כעם אחר. לרבא א"ל: דביתהו שכיבא, ואתו בניה ובנתיה לידי איתתא אחריתי, *דאמר רבא אמר ר' ירמיה בר אבא אמר רב: מאי דכתיב "בניך ובנתיך נתנים לעם אחר" – זו אשת האב. אקרינן בחלמין °"לך אכל בשמחה לחמך", לאביי אמר ליה: מרווח עסקך, ואכלת ושתית וקרית פסוקא מחדוא דלבך. לרבא אמר ליה: פסיד עסקך, טבחת ולא אכלת, ושתית וקרית(א) לפכוחי פחדך. אקרינן °"זרע רב תוציא השדה", לאביי א"ל מרישיה, לרבא א"ל מסיפיה. אקרינן °"זיתים יהיו לך בכל גבולך וגו'", לאביי א"ל מרישיה, לרבא א"ל מסיפיה. אקרינן °"וראו כל עמי הארץ וגו'", לאביי א"ל: נפק לך שמא דריש מתיבתא הוית, אימתך נפלת בעלמא. לרבא אמר ליה: בדיינא דמלכא אתבר, ומתפסת בגנבי, ודייני כולי עלמא קל וחומר מינך. למחר אתבר בדיינא דמלכא, ואתו(ב) ותפשי ליה לרבא. אמרי ליה: חזן חסא על פום דני. לאביי א"ל: עיף עסקך כחסא, לרבא א"ל: מריר עסקך כי חסא. אמרי ליה: חזן בשרא על פום דני. לאביי אמר ליה: בסים חמרך ואתו כולי עלמא למזבן בשרא וחמרא מינך. לרבא אמר ליה: תקיף חמרך, ואתו כולי עלמא למזבן בשרא למיכל ביה. אמרי ליה: חזן חביתא דתלי בדיקלא, לאביי אמר ליה: מדלי עסקך כדיקלא. לרבא אמר ליה: חלי עסקך כתמרי. אמרי ליה: חזן רומנא דקדחי אפום דני, לאביי אמר ליה: עשיק עסקך כרומנא. לרבא אמר ליה: קאוי עסקך כרומנא. אמרי ליה: חזן חביתא דנפל לבירא, לאביי א"ל: מתבעי עסקך, *כדאמר "נפל פתא בבירא ולא אשתכח". לרבא א"ל: פסיד עסקך ושדי ליה לבירא. אמרי ליה: חזינן בר חמרא דקאי אאיסדן ונוער, לאביי אמר ליה: מלכא הוית, וקאי אמורא עלך. לרבא א"ל: פטר חמור (ג) גהיט מתפילך. א"ל: לדידי חזי לי ואיתיה! –אמר ליה: וא"ו ד"פטר חמור" ודאי גהיט מתפילך. § לסוף אזל רבא לחודיה לגביה, אמר ליה: חזאי דשא בריתא דנפל, אמר ליה: אשתך שכבא. אמר ליה: חזאי *ככי ושני דנתור, א"ל: בנך ובנתך שכבן. אמר ליה: חזאי תרתי יוני דפרחן, א"ל: תרי נשי מגרשת. אמר ליה: חזאי תרי גרגלידי דלפתא, אמר ליה: תרין קולפי בלעת. אזל רבא ההוא יומא ויתיב בי מדרשא כוליה יומא, אשכח הנהו תרי סגי נהורי דהוו קמנצו בהדי הדדי, אזל רבא לפרוקינהו – ומחוהו לרבא תרי, דלו למחוייה אחריתי, אמר: מסתיי, תרין חזאי! לסוף אתא רבא ויהיב ליה אגרא, א"ל: חזאי *אשיתא דנפל. א"ל: נכסים בלא מצרים קנית. א"ל: חזאי אפדנא דאביי דנפל וכסיין אבקיה, א"ל: אביי שכיב ומתיבתיה אתיא לגבך. א"ל: חזאי אפדנא דידי דנפיל, ואתו כולי עלמא שקיל לבינתא לבינתא, א"ל: שמעתתך מבדרן בעלמא. א"ל: חזאי דאבקע רישי ונתר מוקרי, א"ל: *אודרא מבי סדיא נפיק. א"ל: אקריון הללא מצראה בחלמא. א"ל: ניסא מתרחשי לך. הוה קא אזיל בהדיה בארבא, אמר: בהדי גברא דמתרחיש ליה ניסא למה לי? בהדי דקא סליק נפל סיפרא מיניה, אשכחיה רבא וחזא דהוה כתיב ביה: *כל החלומות הולכין אחר הפה. אמר: רשע! בדידך קיימא וצערתן כולי האי! כולהו מחילנא לך, בר מברתיה דרב חסדא. יהא רעוא דלמסר ההוא גברא לידי דמלכותא דלא מרחמו עליה. אמר: מאי אעביד? גמירי: *דקללת חכם אפילו בחנם היא באה, וכ"ש רבא – דבדינא קא לייט, אמר: איקום ואגלי, *דאמר מר: גלות מכפרת עון. קם גלי לבי רומאי, אזל יתיב אפתחא דריש *טורזינא דמלכא. ריש טורזינא חזא חלמא, א"ל: חזאי חלמא דעייל מחטא באצבעתי, א"ל: הב לי זוזא! ולא יהב ליה, לא א"ל ולא מידי. א"ל: חזאי דנפל תכלא בתרתין אצבעתי, א"ל: הב לי זוזא! ולא יהב ליה, ולא א"ל. א"ל: חזאי דנפל תכלא בכולה ידא, א"ל: נפל תכלא בכולהו שיראי. שמעי בי מלכא ואתיוה לריש טורזינא, קא קטלי ליה. א"ל: אנא אמאי? אייתו להאי דהוה ידע ולא אמר! אייתוהו לבר הדיא, אמרי ליה: אמטו זוזא דידך חרבו שיראי

רש"י

קיסר. מלך רומי, והיה לו תגר עם פרסיים: מאי חזינא. מאי אראה בלילה בחלום? משחרי לך פרסאי. עושים בך עבודת המלך. כמו: לא תמרא דחד מנהון שחרית (תרגום במדבר יז). ולשון חכמים: (ספרי פ' דברים) הדבק לשחור וישתחוו לך: ושבו לך. ישללוך בשבי: וטחנו בך קשייתא. יכופו אותך לטחון גרעיני תמרים: שבור(ד). מלך פרס. פסיד עסקך. תתקלקל פרקמטיא שלך: ולא אהני לך למיכל. מתוך צערך לא יטעם לך שום מאכל: מרווח עסקך. ומתוך שמתמהך לא תתאוה לאכול, שתהיה שבע בשמחתך: והיא. אפשך: לפכוחי פחדך. להפיג דאגתך: מרישיה. "זרע רב תוציא השדה": בדיינא דמלכא. אוצר שתכשיטי המלך שם ישבר על ידי גנבים, ויעלילו עליך לומר שאתה גנבתם: קל וחומר מינך. אם רבא נחשד – כל שכן שיחשדונו, וזהו "ויראו ממך": חסא. חזרת: עיף עסקך. כפול בריות, כחזרת שהיא רחבה וכפולה: מריר עסקך. שנאוי לכל ומר יהיה הסחורה שלך: חביתא. הם היו משתכרים ביין: חלי עסקך. מתוק, כלומר: שתתן סחורתך בזול: דקדחי. גדלה: עשיק עסקך. ביוקר תמכרנו: כמו "עשיק לגנבך" (ב"מ ד' נב.): לרבא א"ל: קאוי עסקך. לשון קהוי, הכל ישנאוהו: מתבעי עסקך. יתבקש עסקך ויחזרו אחריו לקנות: דקאי אאיסדן. מראשותיו, כדמתרגמינן "מראשותיו" – אסדוהי (בראשית כח): מלכא הוית. ראש ישיבה, הדורש והמתורגמן עומד עליו באמורא להשמיע בקול רם לרבים, כקול חמור הנוער: וי"ו דפטר חמור גהיט מתפילך. בפרשת "והיה כי יביאך": "וכל פטר חמור תפדה בשה" והוא חסר וי"ו, ובתפילין של רבא כתבו הכותב מלא ואח"כ מחקו, והיינו גהיט = מחוק: דשא בבריתא. דלת חילון שבבית: אתתך מתה. השומרת את הבית: ככי. שיניים הפנימיות, שקורין מסילא"ר: תרתי נשי מגרשת. שאשתו של אדם קרויה יונה דכתיב: "יונתי תמתי": תרין קולפי בלעת. מכת מקל עב בראשו כראשי לפתות: בלא מצרים. נחלה בלא מצרים, כלומר קרקעות רחבים ורבים: וכסיין אבקיה. כסוי עפר הפורח מתפולת החומה: ונתר מוקרי. נשר מוחו: אודרא מבי סדיא. המוכין יוצאין מן הכר שבמראשותיו: הללא מצראה. הלל שאנו קורין בפסח. לפי שיש הלל אחר הקרוי הלל הגדול, קורין לזה הלל המצרי: ניסי מתרחשי לך. שע"י נסים נקרא ניסן. שעל כל צרה הבאה לישראל אומרים אותו על גאולתן: הוה קא אזיל. בר הדיא בהדיה דרבא: בארבא. בספינה: אמר בהדי גברא דמתרחיש ליה ניסא למה לי. שמא כאן יארע לו הנס שתטבע הספינה והוא יגל: בדידך קיימא. בך הוא תלוי הפתרון אם לטובה אם לרעה, והפכת לי לרעה: אשתו של רבא. בת רב חסדא היתה: טורזינא דמלכא. שומר אוצר המלך: נפל תכלא. תולע: שיראי

תורה אור / מסורת הש"ס (margins): חנניא | דברים כח | שם | שם | כג. קדושין מה: | [ושם איתא רב רבא אמר רב] | קהלת ט | דברים כח | שם | [שבת סו:] | ב בשו"ג כח. ע' שם ד"ה ככי | [לעיל נה:] | מכות יא. | סנהדרין לז: | ך טרזא פי' שומר המטעלים | (ויסוד לחומת ביתו כך פירש"י ב"ק נ. ד"ה לאושין וכו' ע"ש ובערוך פי' כותל) | [גי' הערוך אודרא פי' נוצה]

הגהות הב"ח

(א) גמ' וקרית פסוקא לפכוחי: (ב) שם ותפשי ליה לרבא דחיל כולי עלמא ואמרי רבא איתפיס אנן לא כל שכן אמרי ליה: (ג) שם גהיט מתפילך עיין רבא ואשכח וא"ו דפטר חמור גהיט בתפלה לסוף אזל: (ד) רש"י ד"ה שבור מלכא מלך פרס:

גליון הש"ס

גמ' א"ל אשתך שכבא. עי' לקמן דף ס"ב ע"א תוס' ד"ה רבא:

שיראי דמלכא. מעילים של מלך: דאצטליק. נחלק לב', ודוגמתו ב"העור והרוטב" (דף קכה.) דלגי מלגך: יעצו עליך רעה. והם הלחיים – פה שיעץ עליך רעה. ניכר בחוטם שמתחמם ומוליא הבל, על כן הוא קרוי חרון אף: חרון אף. לא תצטרך למעשה ידיך. שתתעשר: באדרותא מיתת. בכבוד והדר תמות: אמו בעל. דומיא דשמן שהוא בתוך הזית, השקה את אמו: קטיף לי כוכבא. עקרתי כוכב בחלום: גנבת. שנמשלו לכוכבים. הוו רגילין לעשות לה חופה של הדס בכניסתה לחופה, וקורין לה

תורה אור

הינומא, כדאמרינן בכתובות (דף טו:): "שיצאתה בהינומא וראשה פרוע": טונא דאסא. טולא דאסא(ב): שכבי משלחת. ממית הפשטת: אם כן. דלית לך נכסי, ואבוך לא שכיב הכא: קפא. דאמרי לך – היא כשורה, שבלשון פרס ויון קורין לכשורה קפא: דיקא. הוא עשרה. שבלשון יוני קורין לעשרה דיקא. והכי אמרי לך: יש לך ממון בקורה עשירית: דריש עשרה. קורה שבראש עשרה: שלש שלומות הם. שלש חלומות המבשרים שלום: ופרשו כאשר בסיר. חלמא. פורענותא היא: ובכל קנינך. לשון מרובה הוא, אף קנים הרבה – קנה של בינה הוא: קרא קורא קירא קניא. קרא = דלעת, כדאמרינן לקמן: הרואה דלועין בחלום ירא שמים הוא, לשון "דלו עיני למרום" (ישעיה לח): קורא. רך הגדל בענפי הדקל בכל שנה, כדרך שאר אילנות ולשנה שניה הוא מתקשה ונעשה עץ: קירא. שעוה: קניא. קנה: האוכל מבשרו. בחלום: בין ברדוף. כשהוא רץ: גם עלה. קרוב לנוטריקון של גמל: פלא נעשה לו. כמו שנעשה לפינחס, כדאמרינן בסנהדרין (דף פב:).

דמסרגא

שיראי דמלכא! כפיתו תרין ארזי בחבלא, אסור חד כרעיה לחד ארזא וחד כרעיה לחד ארזא, ושרו לחבלא עד דאצטליק(א) רישיה, *אזל כל חד וחד וקם אדוכתיה ואצטליק ונפל בתרין.§ שאל בן דמא בן אחותו של ר' ישמעאל את ר' ישמעאל: ראיתי שני לחיי שנשרו. אמר: שני גדודי רומי יעצו עליך רעה, ומתו. אמר ליה בר קפרא לרבי: ראיתי חוטמי שנשר, אמר ליה: חרון אף נסתלק ממך. אמר ליה: ראיתי שני ידי שנחתכו, אמר ליה: לא תצטרך למעשה ידיך. אמר ליה: ראיתי ב' רגלי שנקטעו, אמר ליה: על סוס אתה רוכב. חזאי דאמרי לי: באדר מיתת וניסן לא חזית, אמר ליה: באדרותא מיתת, ולא אתית לידי נסיון. אמר ליה ההוא מינא לר' ישמעאל: ראיתי שאני משקה שמן לזיתים, אמר ליה: בא על אמו. אמר ליה: חזאי דקטיף לי כוכבא, אמר ליה: בר ישראל גנבת. אמר ליה: חזאי דבלעתי לכוכבא. אמר ליה: בר ישראל זבנתיה, ואכלת לדמיה. אמר ליה: חזאי עיני דנשקן אהדדי, אמר ליה: בא על אחותו. אמר ליה: חזאי דנשקי סיהרא, אמר ליה: בא על אשת ישראל. אמר ליה: חזאי דדריכנא בטונא דאסא. אמר ליה: בא על נערה המאורסה. אמר ליה: חזאי טונא מעילאי והוא מתתאי, אמר ליה: משכבך הפוך. אמר ליה: חזאי עורבי דהדרי לפורייה, אמר ליה: אשתך זנתה מאנשים הרבה. אמר ליה: חזאי יוני דהדרי לפורייה, אמר ליה: נשים הרבה טמאת. אמר ליה: חזאי דנקיט תרי יוני ופרחן, אמר ליה: תרתי נשי נסבת ופטרתינון בלא גט. אמר ליה: חזאי דקליפנא ביעי, אמר ליה: שכבי קא משלחת. אמר ליה: כולהו איתנהו בי, בר מהא דליתיה! אדהכי והכי אתיא האי איתתא, ואמרה ליה: האי גלימא דמכסא – דגברא פלוני הוא, דמית ואשלחתיה. אמר ליה: חזאי דאמרי לי: שבק לך אבוך נכסי בקפודקיא? אמר ליה: אית לך נכסי בקפודקיא? אמר ליה: לאו. אזל אבוך לקפודקיא? אמר ליה: לאו. -אם כן: קפא – כשורא, דיקא – עשרה, זיל חזי קפא דריש עשרה, שהיא מלאה זוזי, אזל

בראשית כו אשכח שהיא מלאה זוזי.§ אמר רבי חנינא: הרואה באר בחלום – רואה שלום, שנאמר: °"ויחפרו עבדי יצחק
משלי ח בנחל וימצאו שם באר מים חיים". ר' נתן אומר: מצא תורה, שנאמר: °"כי מצאי מצא חיים" וכתיב הכא
"באר מים חיים". רבא אמר: חיים ממש. אמר רבי חנן, שלש שלומות הן: נהר, צפור, וקדרה. נהר – דכתיב
שם סו °"הנני נטה אליה כנהר שלום", צפור – דכתיב °"כצפרים עפות כן יגן ה' צבאות וגו'", קדרה – דכתיב °"ה' ישעיה סו שם לא
תשפת שלום לנו". אמר ר' חנינא: ובקדרה שאין בה בשר *שנינו: °"ופרשו כאשר בסיר וכבשר בתוך [שנאמר כנ"ל וכ"ה בילקוט ישעיה סוף רמז רלט]
מיכה ג קלחת".§ אמר ר' יהושע בן לוי: הרואה נהר בחלום ישכים ויאמר "הנני נטה אליה כנהר שלום", קודם
ישעיה נט שיקדמנו פסוק אחר – °"כי יבא כנהר צר". הרואה צפור בחלום ישכים ויאמר "כצפרים עפות כן יגן וגו'",
משלי כז קודם שיקדמנו פסוק אחר – °"כצפור נודדת מן קנה וגו'". הרואה קדרה בחלום ישכים ויאמר "ה' תשפת
שלום לנו", קודם שיקדמנו פסוק אחר – °"שפת הסיר שפת". הרואה ענבים בחלום ישכים ויאמר °"כענבים יחזקאל כד
הושע ט במדבר", קודם שיקדמנו פסוק אחר – °"ענבמו ענבי רוש". הרואה הר בחלום ישכים ויאמר °"מה נאוו על דברים לב
ישעיה נב ההרים רגלי מבשר", קודם שיקדמנו פסוק אחר – °"על ההרים אשא בכי ונהי". הרואה שופר בחלום ישכים
ירמיה ט ויאמר °"והיה ביום ההוא יתקע בשופר גדול", קודם שיקדמנו פסוק אחר – °"תקעו שופר בגבעה". הרואה ישעיה כז
הושע ה כלב בחלום ישכים ויאמר °"ולכל בני ישראל לא יחרץ כלב לשנו", קודם שיקדמנו פסוק אחר °"והכלבים שמות יא
ישעיה נו עזי נפש". הרואה ארי בחלום ישכים ויאמר °"אריה שאג מי לא ירא", קודם שיקדמנו פסוק אחר – °"עלה עמוס ג
ירמיה ד אריה מסבכו", הרואה תגלחת בחלום ישכים ויאמר °"ויגלח ויחלף שמלתיו", קודם שיקדמנו פסוק אחר
בראשית מא (°"כי) אם גלחתי וסר ממני כחי". הרואה באר בחלום ישכים ויאמר °"באר מים חיים", קודם שיקדמנו שופטים טז
שיר ד פסוק אחר – °"כהקיר ביר מימיה". הרואה קנה בחלום ישכים ויאמר °"קנה רצוץ לא ישבור", קודם שיקדמנו ירמיה ו
ישעיה מב פסוק אחר – °"הנה בטחת *לך על משענת הקנה הרצוץ". תנו רבנן: הרואה קנה בחלום – יצפה לחכמה, בד"י חסר מלת לך והוא קרא בישעיה ל"ו
מלכים ב יח שנאמר: °"קנה חכמה", קנים – יצפה לבינה, שנאמר: °"ובכל קנינך קנה בינה". אמר רבי זירא: קרא, קורא,
משלי ד שם קירא, קניא – כולהו מעלו לחלמא. תניא: אין מראין דלועין אלא למי שהוא ירא שמים בכל כחו. הרואה
דברים לג שור בחלום ישכים ויאמר °"בכור שורו הדר לו", קודם שיקדמנו פסוק אחר – °"כי יגח שור את איש".
שמות כא תנו רבנן, חמשה דברים נאמרו בשור: האוכל מבשרו – מתעשר, נגחו – הויין ליה בנים שמנגחים בתורה,
נשכו – יסורין באים עליו, בעטו – דרך רחוקה נזדמנה לו, רכבו – עולה לגדולה. והתניא: רכבו – מת! –לא קשיא:
זכריה ט הא – דרכיב הוא לתורא, הא – דרכיב תורא לדידיה.§ הרואה חמור בחלום – יצפה לישועה, שנאמר: °"הנה מלכך
יבוא לך צדיק ונושע הוא עני ורכב על חמור". הרואה חתול בחלום, באתרא דקרו ליה שונרא – נעשית
לו שירה נאה, שינרא – נעשה לו שינוי רע. הרואה ענבים בחלום, לבנות בין בזמנן בין שלא בזמנן – יפות,
[ע' סנהדרין נג.] שחורות, בזמנן – יפות, שלא בזמנן – רעות. הרואה סוס *לבן בחלום, בין בנחת בין ברדוף – יפה לו, אדום –
בנחת יפה, ברדוף קשה. הרואה ישמעאל בחלום – תפלתו נשמעת, ודוקא ישמעאל בן אברהם, אבל טייעא
בעלמא – לא. הרואה גמל בחלום – מיתה נקנסה לו מן השמים והצילוהו ממנה. אמר רבי חמא ברבי
בראשית מו שמואל ב יב חנינא: מאי קראה – °"אנכי ארד עמך מצרימה ואנכי אעלך גם עלה". רב נחמן בר יצחק אמר מהכא – °"גם
[לקמן נז:] ה' העביר חטאתך לא תמות". הרואה פינחס בחלום – פלא נעשה לו, *הרואה פיל בחלום – פלאות נעשו
לו, פילים – פלאי פלאות נעשו לו. והתניא: כל מיני חיות יפין לחלום, חוץ מן הפיל ומן הקוף! לא קשיא,
הא

[עי' בע"י]

הגהות הב"ח

(א) גמ' עד דאוצטליק אמר רבא לא מחוורתא ליה עד דאוצטליק רישיה אלא וכו' ואוצטליק רישיה ונפל בתרין: (ב) רש"י ד"ה טונא וכו' דאסא הס"ד ואח"כ מ"ה משכבו הפך בלומה נערה היא מלמעלה והוא מלמטה הס"ד ואח"כ מ"ה שכבי קא משלחת:

## רב נסים גאון

**דתני** רב יוסף אין מראין דלועין אלא ליראי שמים. כבר שאלני עליה תלמיד מבני ספרד היש לה טעם ואני לא קבלתי בה כלום וגם לא נשאלתי עליה קודם לכן מעולם ונמתי לו כי זאת קבלה היא ביד החכמי' ולא נודע לי שהזכירו בה טעם אבל נראין הדברים בעיני שאפשר שיהו דומים יראי שמים לדלועין שכשם שהדלועין אין בכל פירות הארץ גדולים מהם ואעפ"כ אינן מתגשאין על הארץ אלא כל זמן שהן גדלין ופרין הן מוסיפין נמיכות בארץ כך הן יראי שמים אין כל הבריות שמעלתו גבוהה ממעלתם ולא עדיף מהם כדדרשינן בהאי פסוקא (איוב כח) הן יראת ה' היא חכמה וסור מרע בינה שכן בלשון יוני קורין לאחת הינא לפי שמפורש בפ' ב"מ (שבת דף לא:) ואעפ"כ כל זמן שמוסיף להן הקב"ה גדולה וכבוד ונשיאות הן מוסיפין ענוה ונמיכו' בענין שמפורש במדרש ילמדנו רבינו שהתורה *)סולמה ענוה דכתיב (משלי כב) עקב ענוה יראת ה' ובתרה יראה דכתיב (תהלים קיא) ראשית חכמה יראת ה' ובפרק יציאות השבת בגמ' דבני מערבא (הלכה ג) אמר ר' יצחק בן אלעזר כל שעשת חכמה עטרה לראשה עשת ענוה עקב לסולייסה דכתיב ראשית חכמה יראת ה' וכתיב עקב ענוה יראת ה' ובגמ' דידן בסוף פירקא דכיסוי הדם (חולין דף פט) אמר הקב"ה לישראל חושק אני בכם שאפי' בשעה שאני משפיע לכם גדולה אתם ממעטין עצמכם לפני נתתי גדולה לאברהם אמר (בראשית יח) ואנכי עפר ואפר נתתי גדולה למשה ואהרן אמרו (שמות טז) ונחנו מה נתתי גדולה לדוד אמר (תהלים כב) ואנכי תולעת ולא איש ולפיכך אפשר שתהא כוונתן של חכמים בדימוי יראי שמים לדלועים בשביל הדבר הזה ועוד נשמענה מגופה של מלה דלועין דלו עיני למרום וזו היא מדת יראי שמים כמו שאמר חזקיה (ישעיה לח) דלו עיני למרום כלומר שהן בוטחין בו ומצפין אליו ומחכים לטובו והיה ישר בעיני השואל זה הפירוש גם בעיני כל התלמידים שהיו לשם ולפיכך כתבתיו בזה המקום:

*) סולמה כ"ה לפנינו בתנחומא בראשית

הא – דמסרג, הא – דלא מסרג. הרואה הונא בחלום – נס נעשה לו. חנינא חנניא יוחנן – נסי נסים נעשו לו. *הרואה הספד בחלום – מן השמים חסו עליו ופדאוהו. והני מילי – בכתבא.§ העונה "יהא שמיה רבא מברך" – מובטח לו שהוא בן העולם הבא. הקורא ק"ש – *ראוי שתשרה עליו שכינה, אלא שאין דורו זכאי לכך. המניח תפילין בחלום – יצפה לגדולה, (דברים כח) שנאמר: °"וראו כל עמי הארץ כי שם ה' נקרא עליך וגו'". *ותניא, רבי אליעזר הגדול אומר: אלו תפילין שבראש. המתפלל בחלום – סימן יפה לו, והני מילי – דלא סיים. הבא על אמו (משלי ז) בחלום – יצפה לבינה, שנאמר: °"כי אם לבינה תקרא". הבא על נערה מאורסה – יצפה לתורה, (דברים לג) שנאמר: °"תורה צוה לנו משה מורשה קהלת יעקב", *אל תקרי "מורשה" אלא *"מאורסה". הבא על אחותו בחלום – יצפה (משלי ז) לחכמה, שנאמר: °"אמר לחכמה אחתי את". הבא על אשת איש בחלום – מובטח לו שהוא בן העולם הבא, וה"מ – דלא ידע לה ולא הרהר בה מאורתא.§ א"ר חייא בר אבא: הרואה חטים בחלום – ראה שלום, שנאמר: (תהלים קמז) °"השם גבולך שלום חלב חטים ישביעך". הרואה שעורים בחלום – סרו עונותיו, שנאמר:

(ישעיה ו) °"וסר עונך וחטאתך תכפר". אמר רבי זירא: אנא לא סלקי מבבל לא"י עד דחזאי שערי בחלמא. הרואה גפן טעונה בחלום – אין אשתו מפלת נפלים, שנאמר: (תהלים קכח) °"אשתך כגפן פריה". שורקה – יצפה למשיח, שנאמר: (בראשית מט) °"אסרי לגפן עירה ולשרקה בני אתנו". הרואה תאנה בחלום – תורתו משתמרת בקרבו, שנאמר: (משלי כז) °"נוצר תאנה יאכל פריה". הרואה רמונים בחלום, זוטרי – פרי עסקיה כרמונא, רברבי – רבי עסקיה כרמונא, פלגי – אם ת"ח הוא – יצפה לתורה, שנאמר: (שיר ח) °"אשקך מיין הרקח מעסיס רמני", ואם ע"ה הוא – יצפה למצות, שנאמר: (שם ד) °"כפלח הרמון רקתך". מאי "רקתך" – *אפילו ריקנין שבך מלאים מצות כרמון. הרואה זיתים בחלום, זוטרי – פרי ורבי וקאי עסקיה כזיתים, וה"מ – פירי, אבל אילני – הויין ליה בנים מרובין, שנאמר: (תהלים קכח) °"בניך כשתלי זיתים וגו'". איכא דאמרי: הרואה זית בחלום – שם טוב יוצא לו, שנאמר: (ירמיה יא) °"זית רענן יפה פרי תאר קרא ה' שמך". הרואה שמן זית בחלום – יצפה למאור תורה, שנאמר: (שמות כז) °"ויקחו אליך שמן זית זך". הרואה תמרים בחלום – תמו עונותיו, שנאמר: (איכה ד) °"תם עונך בת ציון". אמר רב יוסף: הרואה עז בחלום – שנה מתברכת לו, עזים – שנים מתברכות לו, שנאמר: (משלי כז) °"ודי חלב עזים ללחמך". הרואה הדס בחלום – נכסיו מצליחין לו, ואם אין לו נכסים – ירושה נופלת לו ממקום אחר. אמר עולא, ואמרי לה במתניתא תנא: והוא דחזא בכנייהו. הרואה אתרוג בחלום – הדור הוא לפני קונו, שנאמר: (ויקרא כג) °"פרי עץ הדר כפת תמרים". הרואה לולב בחלום – אין לו אלא לב אחד לאביו שבשמים. הרואה אווז בחלום – יצפה לחכמה, שנאמר: (משלי א) °"חכמות בחוץ תרנה". והבא עליה – הוי ראש ישיבה. אמר רב אשי: אני ראיתיה ובאתי עליה, וסלקית לגדולה. הרואה תרנגול בחלום – יצפה לבן זכר, תרנגולים – יצפה לבנים זכרים, תרנגולת – יצפה לתרביצה נאה וגילה. הרואה ביצים בחלום – תלויה בקשתו, נשתברו – נעשית בקשתו, וכן אגוזים, וכן קשואים, וכן כל כלי זכוכית, וכן כל הנשברים כאלו.§ הנכנס לכרך – נעשו לו חפציו, שנאמר (תהלים קז) °"וינחם אל מחוז חפצם". המגלח ראשו בחלום – סימן יפה לו, ראשו וזקנו – לו ולכל משפחתו. היושב בעריבה קטנה – שם טוב יוצא לו, בעריבה גדולה – לו ולכל משפחתו, וה"מ – דמדליה דליי. הנפנה בחלום – סימן יפה לו, שנאמר (ישעיה נא) °"מהר צעה להפתח", וה"מ – דלא קנח. העולה לגג בחלום – עולה לגדולה, ירד – יורד מגדולתו. אביי ורבא דאמרי תרווייהו: כיון שעלה – עלה. הקורע בגדיו בחלום – קורעים לו גזר דינו. העומד ערום בחלום, בבבל – עומד בלא חטא, בארץ ישראל – ערום בלא מצות. הנתפש לסרדיוט – שמירה נעשית לו, נתנוהו בקולר – הוסיפו לו שמירה על שמירתו, וה"מ – בקולר, אבל חבלא בעלמא – לא. הנכנס לאגם בחלום – נעשה ראש ישיבה, ליער – נעשה ראש לבני כלה. רב פפא ורב הונא בריה דרב יהושע חזו חלמא, רב פפא דעייל לאגמא – נעשה ראש ישיבה, רב הונא בריה דרב יהושע דעייל ליער – נעשה ראש לבני כלה. איכא דאמרי: תרווייהו לאגמא עיילי, אלא רב פפא דתלי טבלא – נעשה ראש ישיבה, רב הונא בריה דרב יהושע דלא תלי טבלא – נעשה ראש לבני כלה. אמר רב אשי: אנא עיילית לאגמא, ותלאי טבלא ונבחי בה נבוחי. תני תנא קמיה דר"נ בר יצחק: המקיז דם בחלום – עונותיו מחולין לו. והתניא: עונותיו סדורין לו! (יומא פח.) *מאי סדורין – סדורין לימחל. תני תנא קמיה דרב ששת: הרואה נחש בחלום – פרנסתו מזומנת לו, נשכו – נכפלה לו, הרגו – אבדה פרנסתו. אמר ליה רב ששת: כל שכן שנכפלה פרנסתו! ולא היא, רב ששת הוא דחזא חויא בחלמיה וקטליה.§ תני תנא קמיה דרבי יוחנן: כל מיני משקין יפין לחלום חוץ מן היין, יש שותהו וטוב לו, ויש שותהו ורע לו; יש שותהו וטוב לו – שנאמר: (תהלים קד) °"ויין ישמח לבב אנוש", ויש שותהו ורע לו – שנאמר: (משלי לא) °"תנו שכר לאובד ויין למרי נפש". אמר ליה רבי יוחנן לתנא, תני: תלמיד חכם לעולם טוב לו, שנאמר: (שם ט) °"לכו לחמו בלחמי ושתו ביין מסכתי".

אמר

[בפירש"י בעמוד ב' ד"ה דמסרג] [ב"ק נה. ע"ש] [סנהדרין יח.] [מנחות לה: [מגילה טז: וטוס יז. חולין פט.]] [פסחים מט.] [סנהדרין נט.] [עירובין יט. חגיגה כז. מגילה ו. סנהדרין לז.]

דמסרג. שיש לו אוכף על גביו – *יפה: נס נעשה לו. נו"ן כנגד נו"ן, וכגון שראה השם כתוב: חנינא. נוני"ן הרבה, נסים רבים: והני מילי בכתבא. אכולהו קאי, שראה הונא או חנינא או תיבה זו של הספד כתובה, דמשמע חסו עליו ופדאוהו: דלא סיים. שנעור משנתו קודם שנסתלק, סימן הוא שסמוך אצל הקב"ה: מובטח לו שהוא בן העולם הבא. ונוטל חלקו וחלק חברו בגן עדן, דדמי לאשת איש: פלגי. רמונים שנחלקו: יצפה לתורה. שנאמר "אשקך מיין הרקח" היינו תורה: מעסיס רמוני. הנמלך מן הרמונים: נכסיו מצליחין. כהדס זה, שעליו משולשים זה על זה, כמין קליעה: בכנייהו. על כנם, במקומם, כמחובר: הוי ראש ישיבה. שמכריז ומלוה לרבים: אני ראיתיה וכו'. ועל כן נעשיתי ראש ישיבה במתא מחסיא: תרביצא. גינה, אי נמי: בהמ"ד תרביצא נאה וגילה נוטריקון של תרנגול: תלויה בקשתו. בספק, כביצים הללו שהאוכל סתום בם: נשתברו. נתגלה האוכל: וינחם אל מחוז. היינו כרך: חפצם. סימן הוא להיות חפציו נעשים: המגלח. סימן גדולה ותפארת היא לו, כמו "ויגלח ויחלף" וגו' (בראשית מא): בעריבה. בספינה: דמדלי. שהולכת בגובה של ים: הנפנה. סימן הוא שסרחונו וגנותו נפרש ויוצא מעליו: והוא דלא קנח. שלא המאיס ידיו: בבבל עומד בלא חטא. לפי שחו"ל אין לה זכיות אלא עון יש בישיבתה, וזה עומד ערום בלא אותם עונות: בא"י. שהרבה מצות תלויות בה וזה העומד ערום – סימן שהוא ערום ממצותיה: הנתפש לסרדיוט. שומרין אותו שלא יברח, אלמא: סימן שמירה הוא ששומרים אותו מידי היזק: אגם. שיש בו קנים גדולים וקטנים וסמוכים זה לזה – סימן לראש ישיבה, שהגדולים והקטנים מתקבלים יחד קבוץ גדול ובאים לשמוע דרשה מפיו: יער. אילנות גדולים ואינן סמוכים זה לזה, אף זה סימן לראש לתלמידי הרב והוא ראש לבני כלה, שמפרש לתלמידים שמועתם אחר שעמד הרב והם מחזרין על שמועתם ויש תלמידים שלא ידינו בדברי הרב כל הצורך, וזה מבינה להם: תלי טבלא. נראה לו שהיה זוג ועינבל תלוי בצוארו ומשמיע קול, והוא סימן לראש ישיבה שמשמיע קול לרבים: ונבחי בה נבוחי. קשקשתי בה בקול: עונותיו מחולין לו. לפי שהעונות קרויין אדומים, שנאמר "אם יאדימו כתולע", (ישעיה א) ואומר "נכתם עונך", (ירמיה ב) וסימן הוא שפורשין ממנו: פרנסתו מזומנת. כנחש שעפר לחמו, ומצוי לו בכל מקום: הרגו. לנחש: כל שכן שנכפלה לו. שהרי נתגבר עליו: ולא היא. אלא רב ששת דורש להנאתו, לפתור חלומו לטובה: יש שותהו כו'. לפיכך אין לעמוד על פתרונו:

השכים

## רב נסים גאון

הרואה את הנחש בחלומו פרנסה מזומנת לו. זה הדבר בנוי על העיקר שהזכירוהו בפ' יוה"כ (דף עה) תניא ר' יוסי אומר בוא וראה שלא כמדת הקב"ה מדת בשר ודם כו' קלל את הנחש עלה לגג מזונותיו עמו ירד למטה מזונותיו עמו ולפי שפרנסתו מצויה לו בכל מקום לפיכך הרואהו בחלומו פרנסה מזומנת לו:

**עין משפט נר מצוה**

כ א מיי' פ"י מהלכות ברכות הלכה ט סמג עשין כז טוש"ע או"ח סי' רכד סעיף א:
כא ב ג מיי' שם טוש"ע שם סעיף ב:
כב ד שם סעיף ג:
כג ה מיי' שם טוש"ע שם ובסי' ריח סעיף ז:
כד ו טוש"ע סימן רכד סעיף ד:

[באדר"נ פ"מ ליתא וכזה אתי שפיר שלשה נביאים]

**תוספות**

**הרואה** מרקולים. בתוספתא תנן במקום מרקולים דהכא עבודה זרה. וא"כ, לאו דוקא מרקולים אלא לפי שבמקומו של תנא היו עובדים לה. ועתה אין אנו רגילים לברך לפי שאנו רואים אותה בכל יום, וכל הנך הרואים אמרו לעיל דהוי משלשים יום לשלשים יום: **הרואה** מרקולים. פירש ר"י: לא ידענא אמאי נקט מרקולים יותר משאר עבודה זרה. ונראה לי דא"צ לברך רק במקום שבונים עבודה זרה, או שהועמדה שם מחדש – ולכך נקט מרקולים, שרוגמין בה אבנים בכל יום והוי כמגדל עבודה זרה אבל לא על עבודה זרה קבועה שם מקודם. ובירושלמי יש נעקרה עבודה זרה ממקום אחד ונתנה למקום אחר, במקום שנתנה אומר ברוך שנתן ארך אפים לעוברי רצונו, ובמקום שנעקרה אומר ברוך שעקר עבודה זרה מן המקום הזה:

**רש"י**

השכבים. העומד ממטתו ונפל לו פסוק בפיו: שיר השירים. כולו יראת שמים וחבת המקום בלב כל ישראל: רבי ישמעאל בן אלישע. מהרוגי המלכות היה והפשיטו עור קרקפתו בחייו: חוץ מן הפיל והקוף והקפוד. שמשונין במראיהן: קפוד. חיה שדומה לקוף ויש לה זנב ארוך ושמה מרטינ"א: דמסרג. אוכף על גביו, וי"א: נתון בא֗פסר: חוץ ממר. פסו"ר בלע"ז: פסל. דולויי"ר: דחזנהו בקתייהו. שראויין למלאכתן לחבל ולהשחית: פגי תמרה. שלא בשלו כל צרכן: בכנייהו. במחובר, אבל בתלוש סימן הוא למכות כדמפשר ליה *בר הדיא לרבא קולפי בלעת: תכלת. ירוק הוא, ומי שפניו ירוקים חולה הוא: קריא. יבנ"ך: קפופא. לואיט"א בלע"ז, ויש לה לסתו' כלחיי אדם לפיכך הן מגונים: קורפראי. טלפ"א: גודגדניות. ליראי"ש: כפניות. מין תמרים רעים: שמש. חמה זורחת: קול. של מיני זמר, או קול ערב של אשה: עטוש. אשטרנוד"ר: מהר צועה. מי שצריך להריק מעיו. הרקת כלי נקראת צעיה, שנאמר (ירמיה מח): ושלחתי לו צועים וצעוהו וכליו יריקו, במוצב כתיב: ותחלימני והחייני. בחזקי' כתיב: תרדין. בלי"ן: מי סיסין. בשול פוליאו"ל: והרת. וידלייר"א, שהשליל בתוכה: יותרת הכבד. איידר"ש של בהמה: ומברין. לשון בריאות: ותגלחת. אם מגלח: זוטרי. יפין: מסאנא וסנדלא. סימן יוצאי חוץ הוא, שמוציא אחרים מן הבית: עפרא. סימן הוא שרמז להם קבורה: לב עובדיהם. על פושעי ישראל מתפלל: כבשן של אש. חפירה שהושק בה כבשנם של חנניה מישאל ועזריה: מקום שנוטלין ממנו עפר. מקום יש בבבל שאין בהמה יוצאה משם אם אין נותנים עליה עפר מעפר המקום. והוא סימן השמד ומקללותיה של בבל היא. וביסוד מהר"ר יצחק ראיתי שנוטלים משם עפר לטיט לבנייני המקום, וסוף סוף אותו מקום אין בו ישוב ולא זרע ולא נטיעה: גוזר ומקיים. שגזר להשמידה וקיים: נתקללה

**גמרא**

*אמר רבי יוחנן: השכים ונפל פסוק לתוך פיו – הרי זה נבואה קטנה. תנו רבנן, *שלשה מלכים הם: הרואה דוד בחלום – יצפה לחסידות, שלמה – יצפה לחכמה, אחאב – ידאג מן הפורענות. ג' נביאים הם: הרואה ספר מלכים – יצפה לגדולה, *יחזקאל – יצפה לחכמה, ישעיה – [א] יצפה לנחמה, ירמיה – ידאג מן הפורענות.§ שלשה כתובים גדולים הם: הרואה ספר תהלים – יצפה לחסידות, משלי – יצפה לחכמה, איוב – ידאג מן הפורענות. שלשה כתובים קטנים הם: הרואה שיר השירים בחלום – יצפה לחסידות, קהלת – יצפה לחכמה, קינות – ידאג מן הפורענות. הרואה מגלת אסתר – נס נעשה לו. שלשה חכמים הם: הרואה רבי בחלום – יצפה לחכמה, ראב"ע – יצפה לעשירות, רבי ישמעאל בן אלישע – ידאג מן הפורענות. שלשה תלמידי חכמים הם: הרואה בן עזאי בחלום – יצפה לחסידות, בן זומא – יצפה לחכמה, אחר – ידאג מן הפורענות. כל מיני חיות יפות לחלום, חוץ מן הפיל והקוף והקפוד. והאמר מר: הרואה *פיל בחלום – פלא נעשה לו! לא קשיא, הא – דמסרג, הא – דלא מסרג. כל מיני מתכת יפין לחלום, חוץ ממר פסל וקרדום, והני מילי – דחזנהו בקתייהו. כל מיני פירות יפין לחלום, חוץ מפגי תמרה. כל מיני ירקות יפין לחלום, חוץ מראשי לפתות. והאמר רב: לא איעתרי עד דחזאי ראשי לפתות! – כי חזא – בכנייהו חזא. כל מיני צבעונין יפין לחלום, חוץ מן התכלת. כל מיני עופות יפין לחלום, חוץ מן *קריא וקפופא וקורפראי. [הגו"ף הגו"ף מעי"ן משיב"ן ומרחיבי"ן, סימן]. ג' נכנסין לגוף ואין הגוף נהנה מהן: גודגדניות, וכפניות, ופגי תמרה. שלשה אין נכנסין לגוף והגוף נהנה מהן, אלו הן: רחיצה, וסיכה, ותשמיש. שלשה מעין העולם הבא, אלו הן: שבת, שמש, ותשמיש. תשמיש דמאי? אילימא תשמיש המטה – הא מכחש כחיש! – אלא: תשמיש נקבים. שלשה משיבין דעתו של אדם, אלו הן: קול ומראה וריח. שלשה מרחיבין דעתו של אדם, אלו הן: דירה נאה, ואשה נאה, וכלים נאים.§ [חמש"ה וששה"ה ועשר"ה סימן]§ חמשה אחד מששים, אלו הן: אש, דבש, ושבת, ושינה, וחלום. אש – אחד מששים לגיהנם, דבש – אחד מששים למן, שבת – אחד מששים לעולם הבא, שינה – אחד מששים למיתה, חלום – אחד מששים לנבואה. ששה דברים סימן יפה לחולה, אלו הן: עטוש, זיעה, שלשול, קרי, ושינה, וחלום. עטוש – דכתיב °"עטישותיו תהל אור", זיעה – דכתיב °"בזעת אפיך תאכל לחם", שלשול – דכתיב °"מהר צעה להפתח ולא ימות לשחת", קרי – דכתיב °"יראה זרע יאריך ימים", שינה – דכתיב °"ישנתי אז ינוח לי", חלום – דכתיב °"ותחלימני והחייני". *ששה דברים מרפאין את החולה מחליו ורפואתו רפואה, אלו הן: כרוב, ותרדין, וסיסין יבשין, וקיבה, והרת, ויותרת הכבד, וי"א: אף דגים קטנים. ולא *עוד אלא, שדגים קטנים מפרין ומברין כל גופו של אדם. עשרה דברים מחזירין את החולה לחליו, וחליו קשה, אלו הן: האוכל בשר שור, בשר שמן, בשר צלי, בשר צפרים, וביצה צלויה, ותגלחת, ושחלים, והחלב, והגבינה, והמרחץ. וי"א: אף אגוזים, וי"א: אף קשואים. תנא דבי ר' ישמעאל: *למה נקרא שמן 'קשואים'? – מפני שהן קשים לגוף כחרבות. איני? והכתיב °"ויאמר ה' לה שני גוים בבטנך", *אל תקרי "גוים" אלא "גיים", וא"ר יהודה אמר רב: אלו אנטונינוס ורבי, שלא פסק משלחנם לא צנון ולא חזרת ולא קשואין, לא בימות החמה ולא בימות הגשמים! – לא קשיא, הא – ברברבי, הא – בזוטרי.§ ת"ר: מת בבית – שלום בבית, אכל ושתה בבית – סימן יפה לבית, נטל כלים מן הבית – סימן רע לבית. תרגמא רב פפא במסאנא וסנדלא, כל דשקיל שכבא מעלי, בר ממסאנא וסנדלא, כל דיהיב שכבא מעלי, בר מעפרא וחרדלא.§ "מקום שנעקרה ממנו עבודת גלולים". תנו רבנן, *הרואה מרקולים אומר: "ברוך שנתן ארך אפים לעוברי רצונו". מקום שנעקרה ממנו עבודה זרה אומר: "ברוך שעקר עבודה זרה מארצנו, וכשם שנעקרה ממקום זה כן תעקר מכל מקומות ישראל, והשב לב עובדיהם לעבדך". ובח"ל אין צריך לומר "והשב לב עובדיהם לעבדך" – מפני שרובה גויים. רשב"א אומר: אף בחוץ לארץ צריך לומר כן, מפני שעתידים להתגייר, שנאמר: °"אז אהפך אל עמים שפה ברורה".§ דרש רב המנונא: הרואה בבל הרשעה צריך לברך חמש ברכות; ראה בבל אומר "ברוך שהחריב בבל הרשעה"; ראה ביתו של נבוכדנצר אומר: ברוך שהחריב ביתו של נבוכדנצר הרשע; ראה גוב של אריות או כבשן האש אומר: ברוך שעשה נסים [ג] לאבותינו במקום הזה; ראה מרקולים אומר: ברוך שנתן ארך אפים לעוברי רצונו. ראה מקום שנוטלין ממנו עפר אומר: ברוך אומר ועושה גוזר ומקיים. רבא כי הוה חזי חמרי דשקלי עפרא, טריף להו ידא על גבייהו ואמר: רהוטו צדיקי למעבד רעותא דמרייכו. מר בריה דרבינא כי הוה מטי לבבל, הוה שקיל עפרא בסודריה ושדי לברא, לקיים מה שנא' °"וטאטאתיה במטאטא השמד". אמר רב אשי: אנא הא דרב המנונא לא שמיע לי, אלא מדעתאי בריכתינהו לכולהו.

אמר

**תורה אור / מסורת הש"ס (גליון)**

איוב מא | בראשית ג | ישעיה נא | ישעיה נג | איוב ג | שם לח | בראשית כה | צפניה ג | ישעיה יד

[לעיל נה: וקל"ע] [אדר"נ פ"מ וע"ש] [לעיל נו.] [לעיל נו:] [גי' הערוך קריא סם וינשוף תרגום קליא וקפופא] [לעיל מ.] לעיל מד: ע"ג כט. [ע"ג יא. וכט.] [עי' תוס' ע"ג יא. ד"ה לא צנון] [בכל הספרים ותקונים כתיב גיים והקרי גוים ומלוה להסביר] [תוספתא פ"ו]

**הגהות הגר"א**

[א] גמ' וישעי' יצפה לנחמה) תא"מ: [ב] שם שעשה נסים לאבותינו. נ"ל לצדיקים.

**גליון הש"ס**

גמ' כל מיני עופות. עי' נדה דף כ"ג ע"א בתוס' ד"ה קריא שהוא לשם גירסא אחרת כאן:

**רב נסים גאון**

**הרואה** ר' עקיבא בחלומו יצפה לחסידות. אית בפרק כל ישראל יש להן חלק (דף קי) שנא' אספו לי חסידי אלו ר' עקיבא וחבריו שמסרו נפשם לזביחה על דברי תורה ואמרי' (שם) אמר רבה בר בר חנה שבקה ר' עקיבא לחסידותיה: **הרואה** ר' אלעזר בן עזריה יצפה לחכמה לפי שנתמנה בישיבה והוא בן י"ח שנה והיה הוא כבר חכם מאד כמו שאתה מוצא (חגיגה דף ג) אמר ר' יהושע עליו אין דור יתום שר' אלעזר בן עזריה שרוי בתוכו ואמרו בשבחו (גיטין דף סז) ר' אלעזר בן עזריה קופה של בשמים כלומר שהיה מאסף החכמות ומסדר אותם ושנינו (סוטה דף מט) משמת ראב"ע בטלה עטרת החכמים ואע"פ שר"ע הגיע למעלה יתירה וגדולה בחכמה שאפי' משה רבינו כשהראהו הקב"ה דורות העתידין כשראה את ר' עקיבא אמר לפני הקב"ה רבש"ע יש לך אדם כזה ואתה נותן תורה ע"י כמפורש בפ' הקומץ את המנחה (מנחות ד' כט) מיהו לא התחיל ללמוד ולגרום עד שהיה בן מ' שנה כמו שאמרו (בסלהי ספרי) ר' עקיבא למד תורה בן מ' שנה ושימש את החכמים מ' שנה ופרנס את ישראל מ' שנה ואפשר שחסידותו היתה יתירה על חכמתו ולפיכך הוא משובח בחסידות: **ר' ישמעאל בן אלישע** ידאג מן הפורענות מפני שבימיו היו ישראל עומדין בצרות וגזירות ומלחמות בסוף זמן בית שני וכבר נשבה בנערותו ופדאהו ר' יהושע בן חנניה כמפורש בפ' הניזקין (גיטין דף נח) מעשה בר' יהושע בן חנניה שהלך לכרך גדול של רומי אמרו לו תינוק אחד יש בבית הסוהר כו' אמרו לא זז משם עד שפדאו בממון הרבה לא היו ימים מועטים עד שהורה הוראה בישראל ומנו ר' ישמעאל בן אלישע ואיתא בסוף גמ' דהוריות דבני מערבא ושימש בכהונה גדולה כדאמרי' בפ' מאימתי קורין (דף ז) תניא אמר ר' ישמעאל בן אלישע פעם אחת נכנסתי לבית קה"ק להקטיר קטורת לפני לפנים וקודם חרבן הבית נהרג עם רבן שמעון בן גמליאל דתניא במכילתא דר' ישמעאל כשנהרג ר' שמעון ור' ישמעאל אמר להן ר' עקיבא לתלמידיו התקינו עצמיכם לפורענות שאילו טובה עתידה לבא בדורנו בתחלה לא היו מקבלין אותה אלא רבן שמעון ור' ישמעאל ועכשיו גלוי לפני מי שאמר והיה העולם שפורענות גדולה עתידה לבוא בדורנו ונסתלקו אלו מבינותינו שנא' (ישעיה נז) הצדיק אבד וגו' ובפ' עגלה ערופה דמס' סוטה (דף מח) ובפ' דיני ממונות דתחלת סנהדרי' (דף יא) אמרי' ת"ר משמתו נביאים

*אמר רבי ירמיה בן אלעזר: נתקללה בבל – נתקללו שכניה, נתקללה שומרון – נתברכו שכניה. נתקללה בבל נתקללו שכניה, דכתיב °"ושמתיה למורש קפד ואגמי מים". נתקללה שומרון נתברכו שכניה, דכתיב °"ושמתי שומרון לעי השדה למטעי כרם וגו'".§ ואמר רב המנונא: [א]הרואה אוכלוסי ישראל, אומר: "ברוך חכם הרזים". אוכלוסי גוים אומר: °"בושה אמכם וגו'". ת"ר: *הרואה אוכלוסי ישראל אומר: "ברוך חכם הרזים". שאין דעתם דומה זה לזה, ואין פרצופיהן דומים זה לזה. בן זומא ראה אוכלוסא על גב מעלה בהר הבית, אמר: "ברוך חכם הרזים", וברוך שברא כל אלו לשמשני. הוא היה אומר: כמה יגיעות יגע אדם הראשון עד שמצא פת לאכול: חרש, וזרע, וקצר, ועמר, ודש, וזרה, וברר, וטחן, והרקיד, ולש, ואפה, ואח"כ אכל, ואני משכים ומוצא כל אלו מתוקנין לפני. וכמה יגיעות יגע אדם הראשון עד שמצא בגד ללבוש: גזז ולבן ונפץ וטוה וארג, ואחר כך מצא בגד ללבוש, ואני משכים ומוצא כל אלו מתוקנים לפני. כל *אומות שוקדות ובאות לפתח ביתי, ואני משכים ומוצא כל אלו לפני. הוא היה אומר: אורח טוב *מהו אומר – כמה טרחות טרח בעל הבית בשבילי, כמה בשר הביא לפני, כמה יין הביא לפני, כמה גלוסקאות הביא לפני, וכל מה שטרח – לא טרח אלא בשבילי. אבל אורח רע מהו אומר – מה טורח טרח בעל הבית זה? פת אחת אכלתי, חתיכה אחת אכלתי, כוס אחד שתיתי, כל טורח שטרח בעל הבית זה – לא טרח אלא בשביל אשתו ובניו. על אורח טוב מהו אומר – °"זכור כי תשגיא פעלו אשר שררו אנשים". על אורח רע כתיב – °"לכן יראוהו אנשים וגו'". °"והאיש בימי שאול זקן בא באנשים" אמר *רבא ואיתימא רב זביד ואיתימא רב אושעיא: זה ישי אבי דוד שיצא באוכלוסא, ונכנס באוכלוסא, ודרש באוכלוסא. אמר עולא: נקיטינן – אין אוכלוסא בבבל. תנא: אין אוכלוסא פחותה מששים רבוא.§ ת"ר: [ב]הרואה חכמי ישראל אומר "ברוך שחלק מחכמתו ליראיו", [ג]חכמי אומות העולם – אומר "ברוך שנתן מחכמתו [א] לבריותיו". [ד]הרואה מלכי ישראל אומר "ברוך שחלק מכבודו ליראיו", מלכי אומות העולם – אומר "ברוך שנתן מכבודו [ב] לבריותיו". א"ר יוחנן: *[ה]לעולם ישתדל אדם לרוץ לקראת מלכי ישראל, ולא לקראת מלכי ישראל בלבד אלא אפי' לקראת מלכי אומות העולם, שאם יזכה – יבחין בין מלכי ישראל למלכי אומות העולם. רב ששת סגי נהור הוה, הוו קאזלי כולי עלמא לקבולי אפי מלכא, וקם אזל בהדייהו רב ששת. אשכחיה ההוא מינא אמר ליה: חצבי לנהרא, כגני לייא?! אמר ליה: תא חזי דידענא טפי מינך. חלף גונדא קמייתא, כי קא אוושא אמר ליה ההוא מינא: אתא מלכא. אמר ליה רב ששת: לא קאתי. חלף גונדא תניינא, כי קא אוושא אמר ליה ההוא מינא: השתא קא אתי מלכא. אמר ליה רב ששת: לא קא אתי מלכא. חליף תליתאי, כי קא שתקא, אמר ליה רב ששת: ודאי השתא אתי מלכא. אמר ליה ההוא מינא: מנא לך הא? אמר ליה: דמלכותא דארעא כעין מלכותא דרקיעא; דכתיב °"צא ועמדת בהר לפני ה' והנה ה' עבר ורוח גדולה וחזק מפרק הרים ומשבר סלעים לפני ה' לא ברוח ה' ואחר הרוח רעש לא ברעש ה' ואחר הרעש אש לא באש ה' ואחר האש קול דממה דקה". כי אתא מלכא, פתח רב ששת וקא מברך ליה. אמר ליה ההוא מינא: למאן דלא חזית ליה קא מברכת?! ומאי הוי עליה דההוא מינא? איכא דאמרי: חברוהי כחלינהו לעיניה, ואיכא דאמרי: רב ששת*) *נתן עיניו בו, ונעשה גל של עצמות.§ ר' שילא *[ו]נגדיה להההוא גברא דבעל גויה. אזל אכל ביה קורצי בי מלכא, אמר: איכא חד גברא ביהודאי דקא דיין דינא בלא הרמנא דמלכא. שדר עליה פריסתקא, כי אתא אמרי ליה: מה טעמא נגדתיה להאי? אמר להו: דבא על חמרתא. אמרי ליה: אית לך סהדי? אמר להו: אין. אתא אליהו, אדמי ליה כאיניש, ואסהיד. אמרי ליה: אי הכי בר קטלא הוא! – אמר להו: אנן מיומא דגלינן מארעין לית לן רשותא למקטל, אתון – מאי דבעיתון עבידו ביה. עד דמעייני ביה בדינא, פתח ר' שילא ואמר: °"לך ה' הגדלה והגבורה וגו'". אמרי ליה: מאי קאמרת? אמר להו: הכי קאמינא – בריך רחמנא דיהיב מלכותא בארעא כעין מלכותא דרקיעא, ויהב לכו שולטנא ורחמי דינא. אמרו: חביבא עליה יקרא דמלכותא כולי האי! יהבי ליה קולפא, אמרו ליה: דון דינא. כי הוה נפיק, אמר ליה ההוא גברא: עביד רחמנא ניסא לשקרי הכי?! –אמר ליה: רשע! לאו חמרי איקרו? דכתיב °"אשר בשר חמורים בשרם". חזייה דקאזיל למימרא להו דקרינהו חמרי, אמר: האי רודף הוא, *והתורה אמרה: אם בא להרגך – השכם להרגו, מחייה בקולפא וקטליה. אמר: הואיל ואתעביד לי ניסא בהאי קרא – דרשינא ליה: "לך ה' הגדלה" – זו מעשה בראשית, וכן הוא אומר °"עשה גדלות עד אין חקר". "והגבורה" – זו יציאת מצרים, שנאמר: °"וירא ישראל את היד הגדלה וגו'". "והתפארת" – זו חמה ולבנה שעמדו לו ליהושע, שנאמר: °"וידם השמש וירח עמד וגו'". "והנצח" – זו מפלתה של רומי, וכן הוא אומר °"ויז נצחם על בגדי וגו'". "וההוד" – זו מלחמת נחלי ארנון – שנאמר: °"על כן יאמר בספר מלחמות ה' את והב בסופה וגו'". "כי כל בשמים ובארץ" – זו מלחמת סיסרא, שנאמר: °"מן שמים נלחמו הכוכבים ממסלותם וגו'". "לך ה' הממלכה" – זו מלחמת עמלק, וכן הוא אומר °"כי יד על כס יה". "והמתנשא" – זו מלחמת גוג ומגוג, וכן הוא אומר °"הנני אליך גוג נשיא ראש משך ותבל". "לכל לראש" – אמר *רב חנן בר רבא אמר ר' יוחנן: אפילו ריש גרגיתא מן שמיא מנו ליה. במתניתא תנא משמיה דרבי עקיבא: "לך ה' הגדלה" – זו קריעת ים סוף, "והגבורה" – זו מכת בכורות, "והתפארת" – זו מתן תורה, "והנצח" – זו ירושלים, "וההוד" – זו בית המקדש.§

תנו

*) [גי' הערוך מלתא אמר רב ששת ונפקו בוטיטא דנורא וכבינהו לעיניה ערוך ערך בטט א']

---

נתקללה בבל נתקללו שכניה. כלומר: אוי לרשע אוי לשכנו: קאת וקפוד. חיות ועופות רעים ומזיקין את השכנים. אבל עי השדה ומטעי כרם שנתקללו בה ערי ישראל – הנאה היא לשכנים: אוכלוסי. חיל גדול של ששים רבוא: חכם הרזים. היודע מה שבלב כל אלו: לשמשני. שהם חורשים וזורעים, ואני מוצא מוכן: כל אומות שוקדות ובאות לפתחי. עשיר היה, והכל באין אצלו לסחורה: שאם יזכה. לעולם הבא ויראה בכבוד מלך המשיח: יבחין. כמה יתר כבוד נוטלי שכר מצות יותר ממה שהיה כבוד האומות בעוה"ז: חצבי לנהרא. הכדין השלמים הולכים לנהר לשאוב מים: כגני לייא. השבורים להיכן? כלומר: למה הולכים? ואף אתה שאתה סומא ולא תראהו, להיכן תלך: גונדא. כת: ורחמי דינא. אוהבים משפט: *כחלינהו לעיניה. נקרו לעיניו: קולפא. מקל לרדות: התורה אמרה אם בא להרגך השכם להרגו. אם במחתרת וגו' (שמות כב). לפי שבא על עסקי נפשות, שיודע הוא שאם ימצא ותמצאנו חותר לא תעמיד עצמך מלהציל ממונך, והוא בא לדעת כן שיקום עליך ויהרגך, אמרה תורה: השכם אתה והרגהו: הממלכה זו מלחמת עמלק. דכתיב בה כסא מלכות – כי יד על כס יה (שמות יז), כלומר: על ידי מלחמה לה' בעמלק יתעלה כסאו: המתנשא. מדכתיב לשון נשיאות משמע על נשיא ראש משך ותובל: לכל לראש. לכל הקם להיות לראש הוא מתנשא, כלומר: שהוא גוזר ומעמידו: ריש גרגיתא. בור הממונה על החופרין חפירות למלאותן מים כדי להשקות בהן שדותיהן:

ברוך

תורה אור

---

[שייך לעיל קודם ד"ה ורחמי דינא]

כה א מיי' פ"י מהלכות ברכות הל' יא סמג עשין כז טוש"ע או"ח סי' רכד סעיף ה:

כו ב מיי' שם טוש"ע שם סעיף ו:

כז ג מיי' שם טוש"ע שם סעיף ז:

כח ד מיי' שם טוש"ע שם סעיף ח:

כט ה שם סעיף ט:

ל ו מיי' פי"ב מהלכות איסורי ביאה הלכה ב סמג לאוין קיב טוש"ע אה"ע סי' טז סעיף א:

---

## רב נסים גאון

נביאים האחרונים חגי זכריה ומלאכי נסתלקה רוה"ק מישראל אף הוא אומר בשעת מיתתו שמעון וישמעאל לחרבא ושאר עמא לביזא ועקן סגיאן עתידין למיתי על עמא עיקרה דהא בריי' בתוס' סוטה ובפ' העור והרוטב במסכת שחיטת חולין (דף קכג) אמרו אל תתמה שהרי קרקפלו של ר' (יהושע) [ישמעאל] מונח בראשי מלכים: *) שלשה תלמידין הן בן עזאי ובן זומא ואחר. הני בן עזאי ובן זומא הן חשובין יושבין בראש התלמידין כדתנן במס' קדושין בפ' האיש מקדש (דף מט) על מנת שאני תלמיד אין אומרים כשמעון בן עזאי ושמעון בן זומא ובפירקא קמא דמס' הוריות (דף ג) אמרי' או תלמיד וראוי להוראה אלא (מי שחסידותו) [אולי צ"ל שבן עזאי היה חסידותו] יתירה על חכמתו והאי אחר הוא אלישע בן אבויה וגם הוא היה גדול בחכמה ומזורז ובקי בתלמידים מיהו כיון שאירע לו אותו המאורע המפור' בחגיגה בפ' אין דורשין בעריות (דף יד) וקצץ בנטיעות נקרא אלישע אחר מפני שחזר לאחוריו ובפרק האשה נקנית (קדושין ד' לט) ובפרק שילוח הקן (חולין דף קמב) אמרי אלמלא לא דרשיה אחר להאי קרא כרבי יעקב בר ברתיה לא חטא ואחר מאי חזא איכא דאמרי כי האי גוונא חזא ואיכא דאמרי לישניה דגברא רבה חזא דהוה [גריר] ליה דבר אחר אמר פה שהפיק מרגליות ילחך עפר נפק חטא ולפיכך מי שרואהו בחלומו ידאג מן הפורענ': *) גדגדניו' *(הזיכום) בפרק בכל מערבין (עירובין ד' כח) (ואינון) [משמע דאינון] הינדקוקי ובטיית אלא הנדקוקה כי השמועה שנאמרה משמו של רב מערבין בגודגדניות כדאקשינן עליה מברי' מסקינן בה איבעי תימא כי קאמר רב בהינדוקי ובפרקין בגמרא דבני מערבא גרסי בר שילת בשם רב פעפועין וגודגדניות וחלגלוגות מערבי בהון בעון קומוי אילין אינון אמר לון קקולי והנדקוקי ופרפחני: *) הרוא' את המרקולי'. היא ע"ז וכבר מפורש כי בתחלה מציבין ג' אבנים ב' מהן סדורין על גבי קרקע אחת בצד חברתה והשלישית על גביהן כדתניא (ע"ז דף נ) אלו הן אבני מרקולים אחת מיכן ואחת מיכן ואחת על גביהן ואמר רבא כי תניא ההיא בעיקר מרקולים כל שהוא מוצב בזה המעשה נקרא מרקולים והיו עובדין אותו והיה עבודתו שמשליך אבן כלפי אותן האבנים המוצבין (כדתניא) [כדתנן] בסנהדרין פ' ד' מיתות (דף ס) הזורק אבן למרקולים זו היא עבודתו כלומר ישראל שעשה כן בשוגג חייב חטאת במזיד בלא התראה ענוש כרת ואם התרו בו נסקל ואמרי' בגמ' (שם דף סד) ואע"ג דקא מיכוון למירגמה ובמס' ע"ז בפ' ר' ישמעאל (דף נ) איתא להא ברייתא שהזכרנוה ובב"מ בפ' אלו מציאות שלו (דף כה) כאבני בית קולים חייב להכריז ואלו הן אבני בית קולים אחת מיכן ואחת מיכן ואחת באמצע:

**התורה** אמרה הבא להורגך השכם להורגו היינו דאמר רחמנא (שמות כב) אם במחתרת ימצא הגנב והכה וגו' והתם בסנהדרין בפרק בן סורר ומורה (דף עב) תנינן הבא במחתרת נידון משום סופו ואמרינן בגמ' אמר רבא מ"ט דמחתרת חזקה אין אדם מעמיד עצמו על ממונו והאי מימר אמר אי אזילנא וקאי לאפאי מריה בביתיה ולא שביק לי קטילנא ליה ואמרה תורה בא להרגך השכם להרגו:

---

עירובין יח:

ישעיה יד

מיכה א

ירמיה נ

[תוספתא פ"ו]

[נ"ל אומניות]

[ג' תו' ב"מ כג: ד"ה באוכלוסא]

איוב לו

שם לז ש"א יז [יבמות עו: ע"ש]

[לעיל ט: יט:]

מלכים א יט

בת לז. [כ"ב עה. סנהד' ק.]

ד"ה א כט

יחזקאל כג

[לקמן סב: סנהדרין עב.]

איוב ט

שמות יד

יהושע י

ישעיה סג

במדבר כא

שופטים ה

שמות יז

יחזקאל לח לט

[ב"ב לא: ושם איתא א"ר חנן ב"ר אמר רב וכו' ותוס' מייתי ליה בהדי אלו מימרות שאמר בשם רב ע"ש]

### הגהות הגר"א

[א] גמרא לבריותיו. נ"ב כ"ו: [ב] שם לבריותיו. נ"ב לכ"ו:

בָּרוּךְ מַצִּיב גְּבוּל אַלְמָנָה. כְּגוֹן בְּיִשּׁוּב בַּיִת שֵׁנִי: אַמַּאי. קָא מִתְנַחַתְּ: נָפַל לֵיהּ בְּתִלָּא. שֶׁנָּפַל לוֹ וְנַעֲשָׂה תֵּל: דַּיּוֹ לָעֶבֶד שֶׁיְּהֵא כְּרַבּוֹ. שֶׁהֲרֵי בֵּית הַמִּקְדָּשׁ חָרֵב, שֶׁהוּא בֵּיתוֹ שֶׁל הקב"ה: כִּכְלִי אוֹבֵד. וּכְשֵׁם כְּלִי לְאַחַר י"ב חֹדֶשׁ מִשְׁתַּכַּחַת מִן הַלֵּב, דְּיֵאוּשׁ בְּעָלִים לְאַחַר י"ב חֹדֶשׁ בְּפֶרֶק אֵלּוּ מְצִיאוֹת (ד' כח.): מִי שֶׁמָּצָא כְּלִי אוֹ שׁוּם מְצִיאָה חַיָּיב לְהַכְרִיז שָׁלֹשׁ רְגָלִים, וְאִם נִמְצָא אַחַר הַסֻּכּוֹת צָרִיךְ לְהַמְתִּין וּלְהַכְרִיז בְּפֶסַח וּבַעֲצֶרֶת וּבֶחָג, דְּהַיְינוּ י"ב חֹדֶשׁ, וְשׁוּב אֵין צָרִיךְ לְהַכְרִיז: אֲשֶׁר חָלַק וְשֶׁהֶחֱיָינוּ. דִּלְאַחַר שְׁלֹשִׁים יוֹם הָוֵה: מֵחָכְמָתוֹ לִירֵאָיו. כְּרַב חֲנִינָא דְּחַכִּים טְפֵי: בַּהֲקָנִים. לינטיליו"ש, כַּעֲדָשִׁים: כּוּשִׁי. שָׁחוֹר הַרְבֵּה: *גִּיחוֹר. אָדוֹם הַרְבֵּה, רו"ש בְּלַעַ"ז: לַוְוקָן. לָבָן יוֹתֵר מִדַּאי: קִפֵּחַ. בֶּטֶן גָּדוֹל, מִתּוֹךְ עָבְיוֹ נִרְאֵית קוֹמָתוֹ מְקוּפַּחַת. לָשׁוֹן אַחֵר: קִפֵּחַ – אָרוֹךְ הַרְבֵּה, וּפַרְצוּפוֹ שָׁמוּט וּבוֹלֵט דְּמִכּוֹעָר *קָוֵי: הַדַּרְנִיקוֹס. רודא"ש. לָשׁוֹן אַחֵר: פִּיו עָקוֹם: פְּתוּיֵי רֹאשׁ. שֶׁשְּׂעָרוֹ כִּנְמָטָא כָּל שְׂעָרוֹ דָּבוּק זֶה בָּזֶה. פלטודי"ר בְּלַעַ"ז: אוֹמֵר בָּרוּךְ מְשַׁנֶּה אֶת הַבְּרִיּוֹת. דְּמִמְּעֵי אִמָּן הָווּ: קִטֵּעַ. שֶׁנִּקְטְעוּ יָדָיו. הָכָא הוּא דְּקִטֵּעַ מַשְׁמַע דְּיָדַיִם הוּא מִשּׁוּם דְּקָתָנֵי תַּרְתֵּי קִטֵּעַ וְחִגֵּר. אֲבָל הֵיכָא דְּקָתָנֵי קִטֵּעַ לְחוּד – מַשְׁמַע דְּרַגְלַיִם, כִּדְתְנַן (שבת פ"ו ד' סה:): הַקִּטֵּעַ יוֹצֵא בְּקַב שֶׁלּוֹ: הֵיכָא דְּאִיתְרַע לֵיהּ בָּתַר דְּאִתְיְלִיד. לְאַחַר שֶׁנּוֹלַד נוֹלְדוּ בּוֹ: אוֹמֵר בָּרוּךְ דַּיַּין הָאֱמֶת. דּוּמְיָא דְּקִטֵּעַ, וְקִטֵּעַ בָּתַר דְּאִתְיְלִיד הוּא: קִפּוֹף. עוֹף שֶׁקּוֹרִין ווֹלטי"ר, וְיֵשׁ לוֹ לְסָתוֹת וּלְחָיַיִם כְּאָדָם: כּוֹכְבָא דְּשָׁבִיט. כּוֹכָב הַיּוֹרֵד כְּמִין בָּרָק מִמָּקוֹם לְמָקוֹם, וְאָרוֹךְ כְּשֵׁבֶט שֶׁהוּא יוֹרֶה, וְנִרְאֶה כְּמוֹ שֶׁפּוֹתֵחַ רָקִיעַ: וּגְמִירֵי דְּלָא עָבַר כִּסְלָא. שֶׁלֹּא נִמְצָא מַעֲבִיר מַזַּל כְּסִיל כְּשֶׁהוּא שָׁבִיט: כִּסְלָא. כְּסִיל: רַב הוּנָא אָמַר. מַאי זִיקִין וִילוֹן הוּא דְּמִקְרַע וּמִתְחֲזֵי רָקִיעַ דֶּרֶךְ הַקְּרִיעָה כְּרוֹמַח: כְּתִיב עוֹשֶׂה עָשׁ כְּסִיל וְכִימָה. דְּקַדְמֵיהּ לֵיהּ כְּסִיל לְכִימָה: הָא כֵּיצַד. מְלַמֵּד שֶׁשְּׁנֵיהֶן שָׁוִין: שֶׁאִלְמָלֵא חַמָּה שֶׁל כְּסִיל וְכוּ'. כְּסִיל שׁוֹלֵט בִּימוֹת הַחַמָּה – לְהָכִי אַקְדְּמֵיהּ קְרָא. כִּימָה שׁוֹלֵט בִּימוֹת הַגְּשָׁמִים וּלְהָכִי אַקְדְּמֵיהּ קְרָא: עַקְרָב. הַיְינוּ כִּימָה, וּמִמַּזַּל טָלֶה הוּא: נְהַר דִּינוּר. מַתֶּשֶׁת כֹּחוֹ שֶׁל עַקְרָב: עוּקְצָא דְּעַקְרַבָּא. זְנַב הָעַקְרָב: מַעֲדַנּוֹת כִּימָה. קִשּׁוּרִים שֶׁל כִּימָה: כְּמֵאָה כּוֹכְבֵי. יֵשׁ בֵּין הַכּוֹכָבִים שֶׁל כִּימָה, שֶׁהֵן כֹּחָהּ שֶׁל כִּימָה: אָמְרִי לָהּ דְּמִכַּנְפֵי. אוֹתָן שֶׁהֵן כֹּחָהּ שֶׁל כִּימָה, וְאָמְרִי לָהּ דְּמִבַּדְּרָן: יוּתָא אָמְרִי לָהּ. דְּקַיְימָא בִּזְנַב טָלֶה, וְאָמְרִי לָהּ דְּקַיְימָא בְּרֵישׁ עֶגְלָא: רֵישָׁא דְּעֶגְלָא. רֹאשׁוֹ שֶׁל עֵגֶל, וְהַיְינוּ מַזַּל שׁוֹר. וְהוּא נִמְשָׁךְ אַחַר מַזַּל טָלֶה, רֹאשׁ הַשּׁוֹר סָמוּךְ לִזְנַב טָלֶה, שֶׁכֵּן הַסֵּדֶר: טָלֶה שׁוֹר תְּאוֹמִים: וּמִסְתַּבְּרָא כְּמַאן דְּאָמַר זָנָב. הַיְינוּ כּוֹכָבִים הָעֲשׂוּיִין כְּזָנָב, מִדִּכְתִיב וְעַיִשׁ עַל בָּנֶיהָ תְנֻחֵם: אַלְמָא חֲסֵרָה. וְהַאי זָנָב מֶחֱזֵי כְּטַרְפָּא דְּטָרֵיף:

כַּטַּרְפָּא

[ועי' רש"י לעיל גיחור] [ועי' בכורות מה והיינו להדיא ול"ע על הפי' תמה המ"א והניח בל"ע הערוך בבכור בכ"ף ניחא] [מ"ק ח: ע"ש] [תוספתא פ"ו] [פי' מי שאין רי אלא רחבה ערוך] [עו"ג כ. ע"ש]

תורה אור

ת"ר: הָרוֹאֶה בָּתֵּי יִשְׂרָאֵל, בְּיִשּׁוּבָן אוֹמֵר – "בָּרוּךְ מַצִּיב גְּבוּל אַלְמָנָה", בְּחוּרְבָּנָן אוֹמֵר – "בָּרוּךְ דַּיַּין הָאֱמֶת". בָּתֵּי אוּמּוֹת הָעוֹלָם, בְּיִשּׁוּבָן אוֹמֵר – "בֵּית גֵּאִים יִסַּח ה'" (משלי טו), בְּחוּרְבָּנָן אוֹמֵר – "אֵל נְקָמוֹת ה' אֵל נְקָמוֹת הוֹפִיעַ" (תהלים צד). עוּלָּא וְרַב חִסְדָּא הֲווּ קָא אָזְלִי בְּאוֹרְחָא, כִּי מְטוֹ אַפִּתְחָא דְּבֵי רַב חָנָא בַּר חֲנִילַאי, נְגַד רַב חִסְדָּא וְאִתְנַח. אֲמַר לֵיהּ עוּלָּא: אַמַּאי קָא מִתְנַחַתְּ? *וְהָאָמַר רַב: אֲנָחָה שׁוֹבֶרֶת חֲצִי גּוּפוֹ שֶׁל אָדָם, שֶׁנֶּאֱמַר: "וְאַתָּה בֶן אָדָם הֵאָנַח בְּשִׁבְרוֹן מָתְנַיִם וגו'" (יחזקאל כא), ור' יוֹחָנָן אָמַר: אַף כָּל גּוּפוֹ שֶׁל אָדָם, שֶׁנֶּאֱמַר: "וְהָיָה כִּי יֹאמְרוּ אֵלֶיךָ עַל מָה אַתָּה נֶאֱנָח וְאָמַרְתָּ אֶל שְׁמוּעָה [כִּי בָאָה] וְנָמֵס כָּל לֵב וגו'" (שם)! – א"ל: הֵיכִי לָא אֶתְנַח? בֵּיתָא דַּהֲווּ בַּהּ שִׁיתִּין אַפָּיָיתָא בִּימָמָא וְשִׁיתִּין אַפָּיָיתָא בְּלֵילְיָא, וְאָפְיָין לְכָל מַאן דִּצְרִיךְ. וְלָא שָׁקַל יְדָא מִן כִּיסָא, דְּסָבַר: דִּילְמָא אָתֵי עָנִי בַּר טוֹבִים, וְאַדְּמָטוּ לֵיהּ לְכִיסָא קָא מִכְסִיף. וְתוּ, הֲווּ פְּתִיחִין לֵיהּ אַרְבְּעָה בָּבֵי לְאַרְבַּע רוּחָתָא דְּעָלְמָא, וְכָל דַּהֲוָה עָיֵיל כַּפְיָין נָפֵיק כִּי שְׂבַע. וְהָווּ שָׁדוּ לֵיהּ חִטֵּי וְשַׂעֲרֵי בִּשְׁנֵי בַּצּוֹרֶת אַבָּרַאי, דְּכָל מַאן דִּכְסִיפָא מִילְּתָא לְמִשְׁקַל בִּימָמָא אָתֵי וְשָׁקֵיל בְּלֵילְיָא. הַשְׁתָּא נְפַל בְּתִלָּא, וְלָא אֶתְנַח?! – אֲמַר לֵיהּ, הָכִי אָמַר ר' יוֹחָנָן: מִיּוֹם שֶׁחָרַב בֵּית הַמִּקְדָּשׁ נִגְזְרָה גְּזֵירָה עַל בָּתֵּיהֶן שֶׁל צַדִּיקִים שֶׁיֶּחֱרָבוּ, שֶׁנֶּאֱמַר: "בְּאָזְנָי ה' צְבָאוֹת אִם לֹא בָּתִּים רַבִּים לְשַׁמָּה יִהְיוּ גְּדֹלִים וְטוֹבִים מֵאֵין יוֹשֵׁב" (ישעיה ה). וְאָמַר ר' יוֹחָנָן: עָתִיד הַקָּדוֹשׁ בָּרוּךְ הוּא לְהַחֲזִירָן לְיִשּׁוּבָן, שֶׁנֶּאֱמַר: "שִׁיר הַמַּעֲלוֹת לְדָוִד הַבֹּטְחִים בַּה' כְּהַר צִיּוֹן" (תהלים קכה), מָה הַר צִיּוֹן עָתִיד הַקָּדוֹשׁ בָּרוּךְ הוּא לְהַחֲזִירוֹ לְיִשּׁוּבוֹ, אַף בָּתֵּיהֶן שֶׁל צַדִּיקִים עָתִיד הקב"ה לְהַחֲזִירָן לְיִשּׁוּבָן. חַזְיֵיהּ דְּלָא מְיַישַּׁב דַּעְתֵּיהּ, א"ל: דַּיּוֹ לָעֶבֶד שֶׁיְּהֵא כְּרַבּוֹ. ת"ר: הָרוֹאֶה קִבְרֵי יִשְׂרָאֵל אוֹמֵר: "בָּרוּךְ אֲשֶׁר יָצַר אֶתְכֶם בַּדִּין וְזָן אֶתְכֶם בַּדִּין, וְכִלְכֵּל אֶתְכֶם בַּדִּין, וְאָסַף אֶתְכֶם בַּדִּין, וְעָתִיד לַהֲקִימְכֶם בַּדִּין". מָר בְּרֵיהּ דְּרָבִינָא מְסַיֵּים בַּהּ מִשְּׁמֵיהּ דְּרַב נַחְמָן: "וְיוֹדֵעַ מִסְפַּר כּוּלְּכֶם, וְהוּא עָתִיד לְהַחֲיוֹתְכֶם וּלְקַיֵּים אֶתְכֶם, בָּרוּךְ מְחַיֵּה הַמֵּתִים". קִבְרֵי גוֹיִם אוֹמֵר "בּוֹשָׁה אִמְּכֶם וגו'" (ירמיה נ). אָמַר ריב"ל: הָרוֹאֶה אֶת חֲבֵירוֹ לְאַחַר שְׁלֹשִׁים יוֹם אוֹמֵר: "בָּרוּךְ שֶׁהֶחֱיָינוּ וְקִיְּמָנוּ וְהִגִּיעָנוּ לַזְּמַן הַזֶּה", לְאַחַר י"ב חֹדֶשׁ – אוֹמֵר "בָּרוּךְ מְחַיֵּה הַמֵּתִים". אָמַר רַב: *אֵין הַמֵּת מִשְׁתַּכֵּחַ מִן הַלֵּב אֶלָּא לְאַחַר שְׁנֵים עָשָׂר חֹדֶשׁ, שֶׁנֶּאֱמַר: "נִשְׁכַּחְתִּי כְּמֵת מִלֵּב הָיִיתִי כִּכְלִי אֹבֵד" (תהלים לא). רַב פַּפָּא וְרַב הוּנָא בְּרֵיהּ דְּרַב יְהוֹשֻׁעַ הֲווּ קָאָזְלִי בְּאוֹרְחָא, פַּגְעוּ בֵּיהּ בְּרַב חֲנִינָא בְּרֵיהּ דְּרַב אִיקָא, אֲמַרוּ לֵיהּ: בַּהֲדֵי דַּחֲזֵינָךְ בְּרֵיכִינַן עֲלָךְ תַּרְתֵּי: "בָּרוּךְ אֲשֶׁר חָלַק מֵחָכְמָתוֹ לִירֵאָיו" וְ"שֶׁהֶחֱיָינוּ". אֲמַר לְהוּ: אֲנָא נָמֵי, כֵּיוָן דַּחֲזֵיתִינְכוּ חֲשַׁבְתִּינְכוּ עֲלַאי כְּשִׁיתִּין רִבְּוָון בֵּית יִשְׂרָאֵל, וּבְרֵיכְנָא עֲלַיְיכוּ תְּלָתָא, הָנָךְ תַּרְתֵּי וּ"בָרוּךְ חֲכַם הָרָזִים". אֲמַרוּ לֵיהּ: חַכִּימַת כּוּלֵּי הַאי?! *יְהָבוּ בֵּיהּ עֵינַיְיהוּ וְשָׁכֵיב. אָמַר ריב"ל: הָרוֹאֶה אֶת הַבַּהֲקָנִים אוֹמֵר "בָּרוּךְ מְשַׁנֶּה הַבְּרִיּוֹת". מֵיתִיבֵי: רָאָה *אֶת הַכּוּשִׁי וְאֶת הַגִּיחוֹר וְאֶת הַלַּוְוקָן וְאֶת הַקִּפֵּחַ וְאֶת הַנַּנָּס *וְאֶת הַדַּרְנִיקוֹס אוֹמֵר "בָּרוּךְ מְשַׁנֶּה אֶת הַבְּרִיּוֹת". אֶת הַקִּטֵּעַ וְאֶת הַסּוּמָא וְאֶת *פְּתוּיֵי הָרֹאשׁ וְאֶת הַחִגֵּר וְאֶת הַמּוּכֶּה שְׁחִין וְאֶת הַבַּהֲקָנִים אוֹמֵר "בָּרוּךְ דַּיַּין אֱמֶת"! – ל"ק, הָא – מִמְּעֵי אִמּוֹ, הָא – בָּתַר דְּאִתְיְלִיד. דַּיְקָא נָמֵי, דְּקָתָנֵי דּוּמְיָא דְּקִטֵּעַ, שְׁמַע מִינַּהּ. ת"ר: הָרוֹאֶה פִּיל קוֹף וְקִפּוֹף אוֹמֵר "בָּרוּךְ מְשַׁנֶּה אֶת הַבְּרִיּוֹת". רָאָה *בְּרִיּוֹת טוֹבוֹת וְאִילָנוֹת טוֹבוֹת אוֹמֵר "בָּרוּךְ שֶׁכָּכָה לוֹ בְּעוֹלָמוֹ". "עַל הַזִּיקִין". מַאי זִיקִין? אָמַר שְׁמוּאֵל: *כּוֹכְבָא דְּשָׁבִיט. וְאָמַר שְׁמוּאֵל: נְהִירִין לִי שְׁבִילֵי דִּשְׁמַיָּא כִּשְׁבִילֵי דִּנְהַרְדְּעָא, לְבַר מִכּוֹכְבָא דְּשָׁבִיט דְּלָא יָדַעְנָא מַאי נִיהוּ. וּגְמִירִי דְּלָא עָבַר כִּסְלָא, וְאִי עָבַר כִּסְלָא – חָרֵב עָלְמָא. וְהָא קָא חָזֵינַן דְּעָבַר! – זִיוֵיהּ הוּא דְּעָבַר, וּמִתְחֲזֵי כִּדְעָבַר אִיהוּ. רַב הוּנָא בְּרֵיהּ דְּרַב יְהוֹשֻׁעַ אָמַר: וִילוֹן הוּא דְּמִקְרַע, *דְּמִגַּלְגַּל וּמַחֲזֵי נְהוֹרָא דִּרְקִיעָא. רַב אָשֵׁי אָמַר: כּוֹכְבָא הוּא דְּעָקַר מֵהַאי גִּיסָא דְּכִסְלָא, וְחָזֵי לֵיהּ חַבְרֵיהּ מֵהָךְ גִּיסָא וּמִבְעִית, וּמֶחֱזֵי כְּמַאן דַּעֲבַר. שְׁמוּאֵל רָמֵי: כְּתִיב "עֹשֶׂה עָשׁ כְּסִיל וְכִימָה" (איוב ט) וּכְתִיב "עֹשֶׂה כִימָה וּכְסִיל" (עמוס ה). הָא כֵּיצַד: אִלְמָלֵא חַמָּה שֶׁל כְּסִיל – לֹא נִתְקַיֵּים עוֹלָם מִפְּנֵי צִינָּה שֶׁל כִּימָה, וְאִלְמָלֵא צִינָּה שֶׁל כִּימָה – לֹא נִתְקַיֵּים עוֹלָם מִפְּנֵי חַמָּה שֶׁל כְּסִיל. וּגְמִירֵי, אִי לָאו עוּקְצָא דְּעַקְרַבָּא דִּמְנַח בִּנְהַר דִּינוּר – כָּל מַאן דַּהֲוָה טְרִיקָא לֵיהּ עַקְרַבָּא לָא הֲוָה חָיֵי. וְהַיְינוּ דְּקָאָמַר לֵיהּ רַחֲמָנָא לְאִיּוֹב "הַתְקַשֵּׁר מַעֲדַנּוֹת כִּימָה אוֹ מֹשְׁכוֹת כְּסִיל תְּפַתֵּחַ" (איוב לח). מַאי כִּימָה? אָמַר שְׁמוּאֵל: כְּמֵאָה כּוֹכְבֵי. אָמְרִי לָהּ דְּמִכַּנְפֵי, וְאָמְרִי לָהּ דְּמִבַּדְּרָן. מַאי עָשׁ? אָמַר רַב יְהוּדָה: יוּתָא. מַאי יוּתָא? אָמְרִי לָהּ: זְנַב טָלֶה, וְאָמְרִי לָהּ: רֵישָׁא דְּעֶגְלָא. וּמִסְתַּבְּרָא כְּמַאן דְּאָמַר זְנַב טָלֶה, דִּכְתִיב "וְעַיִשׁ עַל בָּנֶיהָ תַנְחֵם" (שם) אַלְמָא חַסְרָה, וּמִתְחַזְיָא כְּטַרְפָּא

כְּטַרְפָּא

[כתובות סב.] [כ"ב יז.] [גי' הערוך ברדניקוס פי' גאון שהוא איש שקומתו ארוכה יותר מאשר בני אדם] [עי' ערוך מה שפי' בשם רב האי גאון] [מלת דמגלגל ליתא בכ"י ולא בתוס' וכן בע"י ליתא אכן בערוך ערך ויל גרס וילון הוא דמגלגל ומתחזי נהורא דרקיע]

**הרואה** חבירו אחר שלשים יום אומר שהחיינו. אומר ר"י: דוקא חבירו החביב עליו, אבל בענין אחר – לא: **וילון** הוא דמקרע ומחזי נהורא ברקיע. לפי הענין משמע דלא רב הונא לתרץ דלא עבר כסלא, ולא קאי אמתניתין לפרושי מאי זיקין. דהא רב אשי דבתריה קאי אשנויא דלא עבר כסלא, ודלא כפירוש רש"י:

על

לא א מיי' פ"י מהל' ברכות הל' יוד סמג עשין כז טוש"ע או"ח סי' רכד סעיף ז:
לב ב מיי' שם הל' יא טוש"ע שם סעי' יא:
לג ג מיי' שם הל' יוד טוש"ע שם סעיף יב:
לד ד מיי' פ"י מהל' ברכות הל' ב סמג עשין כז טוש"ע או"ח סי' רכה סעיף א:
לה ה מיי' שם הל' יב טוש"ע שם סעיף ח:
לו ו מיי' שם טוש"ע שם סעיף ט:
לז ז מיי' שם טוש"ע שם סעיף ח:
לח ח מיי' שם הל' יג טוש"ע שם סעיף ט:
לט ט מיי' שם הל' יד וסמג שם טוש"ע או"ח סי' רכז סעיף א:

## רב נסים גאון

**הרואה** את הכושי ואת הגיחור ואת הלווקן וכו'. שנינו במס' בכורות בפ' מומין אלו (דף מה) הכושי והגיחור והלווקן והכיפח והננס כו' פסולין באדם כשרין בבהמה ופירשנא בגמ' כושי אוכמא גיחור סומקא לווקן חוורא כיפח גיבח [בס הגי' גבוה] וכדאמר רב פפא אריכא שמוטא סניא ננס יודע הוא בלשון חכמים שהוא הקצור בקומה:

בְּטַרְפָּא דְטָרֵיף. וְהַאי דְּאָזְלָא בָּתְרָהּ – דַּאֲמַרָה לָהּ: הַב לִי בְּנַי! שֶׁבְּשָׁעָה שֶׁהקב"ה בִּקֵּשׁ לְהָבִיא מַבּוּל לָעוֹלָם, נָטַל שְׁנֵי כוֹכָבִים מִכִּימָה וְהֵבִיא מַבּוּל לָעוֹלָם, וּכְשֶׁבִּקֵּשׁ לְסָתְמָהּ – נָטַל שְׁנֵי כוֹכָבִים מֵעָיִשׁ וּסְתָמָהּ. וְלִיהְדַּר לָהּ?* – אֵין הַבּוֹר מִתְמַלֵּא מֵחוּלְיָתוֹ, אִי נַמִי: *אֵין קַטֵּיגוֹר נַעֲשֶׂה סַנֵּיגוֹר. וְלִיבְרֵי לָהּ תְּרֵי כּוֹכְבֵי אַחֲרִינֵי! – °"אֵין כָּל חָדָשׁ תַּחַת הַשָּׁמֶשׁ". א"ר נַחְמָן: עָתִיד הקב"ה לְהַחֲזִירָן לָהּ, שֶׁנֶּאֱמַר: °"וְעַיִשׁ עַל בָּנֶיהָ תַנְחֵם".§ "וְעַל הַזְּוָעוֹת". [א]מַאי זְוָעוֹת? א"ר קְטִינָא: גּוֹהָא. רַב קְטִינָא הֲוָה קָאָזֵיל בְּאוֹרְחָא, כִּי מְטָא אַפִּתְחָא דְּבֵי אוֹבָא טַמְיָא גְּנַח גּוֹהָא. אֲמַר: מִי יָדַע אוֹבָא טַמְיָא הַאי גּוֹהָא מַהוּ? רְמָא לֵיהּ קָלָא: קְטִינָא קְטִינָא, אַמַּאי לָא יָדַעְנָא? בְּשָׁעָה שֶׁהקב"ה זוֹכֵר אֶת בָּנָיו שֶׁשְּׁרוּיִים בְּצַעַר בֵּין אוּמּוֹת הָעוֹלָם מוֹרִיד שְׁתֵּי דְמָעוֹת לַיָּם הַגָּדוֹל, וְקוֹלוֹ נִשְׁמָע מִסּוֹף הָעוֹלָם וְעַד סוֹפוֹ, וְהַיְינוּ גּוֹהָא. א"ר קְטִינָא: אוֹבָא טַמְיָא כַּדִּיב הוּא, וּמִילֵּיהּ כַּדִּיבִין. אִי הָכִי – גּוֹהָא גּוֹהָא מִיבְּעֵי לֵיהּ! –וְלָא הִיא, גּוֹהָא גּוֹהָא עֲבִיד, וְהַאי דְּלָא אוֹדֵי לֵיהּ – כִּי הֵיכִי דְּלָא לִיטְעֵי כּוּלֵּי עָלְמָא אַבַּתְרֵיהּ. וְרַב קְטִינָא דִּידֵיהּ אָמַר: סוֹפֵק כַּפָּיו, שֶׁנֶּאֱמַר: °"וְגַם אֲנִי אַכֶּה כַפִּי אֶל כַּפִּי וַהֲנִחֹתִי חֲמָתִי". רַבִּי נָתָן אוֹמֵר: אֲנָחָה מִתְאַנֵּחַ, שֶׁנֶּאֱמַר: °"וַהֲנִחוֹתִי חֲמָתִי בָּם וְהִנֶּחָמְתִּי". וְרַבָּנַן אָמְרִי: בּוֹעֵט בָּרָקִיעַ, שֶׁנֶּאֱמַר: °"הֵידָד כְּדֹרְכִים יַעֲנֶה אֶל כָּל יֹשְׁבֵי הָאָרֶץ". רַב אַחָא בַּר יַעֲקֹב אָמַר: דּוֹחֵק אֶת רַגְלָיו תַּחַת כִּסֵּא הַכָּבוֹד, שֶׁנֶּאֱמַר: °"כֹּה אָמַר ה' הַשָּׁמַיִם כִּסְאִי וְהָאָרֶץ הֲדֹם רַגְלָי".§ "וְעַל הָרְעָמִים". [ב]מַאי רְעָמִים? אָמַר שְׁמוּאֵל: עֲנָנֵי בְּגַלְגְּלָא, שֶׁנֶּאֱמַר: °"קוֹל רַעַמְךָ בַּגַּלְגַּל הֵאִירוּ בְרָקִים תֵּבֵל רָגְזָה וַתִּרְעַשׁ הָאָרֶץ". וְרַבָּנַן אָמְרִי: עֲנָנֵי דְּשָׁפְכִי מַיָּא לַהֲדָדֵי, שֶׁנֶּאֱמַר: °"לְקוֹל תִּתּוֹ הֲמוֹן מַיִם בַּשָּׁמַיִם". רַב אַחָא בַּר יַעֲקֹב אָמַר: בַּרְקָא תַּקִּיפָא דְּבָרֵיק בַּעֲנָנָא, וּמִתַּבַּר גִּזְיֵזֵי דְּבַרְזָא. רַב אַשִׁי אָמַר: עֲנָנֵי *חַלְחוּלֵי מְחַלְחְלִי, וְאָתֵי זִיקָא וּמְנַשֵּׁב אַפּוּמַיְיהוּ, וְדָמֵי כְּזִיקָא עַל פּוּם דָּנֵי. וּמִסְתַּבְּרָא כְּרַב אַחָא בַּר יַעֲקֹב – דְּבָרֵיק בַּרְקָא וּמִנְהֲמִי עֲנָנֵי, וְאָתֵי מִטְרָא.§ "וְעַל הָרוּחוֹת". [ג]מַאי רוּחוֹת? אָמַר אַבַּיֵּי: זַעְפָּא. וְאָמַר אַבַּיֵּי: גְּמִירִי, דְּזַעְפָּא בְּלֵילְיָא לָא הָוֵי. וְהָא קָא חֲזֵינַן דְּהָוֵי! – הַהוּא דְּאַתְחוּלֵי בִּימָמָא. וְאָמַר אַבַּיֵּי: גְּמִירִי, דְּזַעְפָּא תַּרְתֵּי שַׁעֵי לָא קָאֵי, לְקַיֵּים מַה שֶּׁנֶּאֱמַר: °"לֹא תָקוּם פַּעֲמַיִם צָרָה". –וְהָא קָא חֲזֵינַן דְּקָאֵי! –דְּמַפְסִיק בֵּינֵי בֵּינֵי.§ וְעַל הַבְּרָקִים אוֹמֵר "בָּרוּךְ שֶׁכֹּחוֹ וּגְבוּרָתוֹ מָלֵא עוֹלָם". [ד]מַאי בְּרָקִים? אָמַר רָבָא: בַּרְקָא. וְאָמַר רָבָא: בַּרְקָא יְחִידָאָה, וּבַרְקָא חִיוָּרָא, וּבַרְקָא יְרוֹקְתָא, וַעֲנָנֵי דְּסָלְקָן בְּקֶרֶן מַעֲרָבִית וְאָתְיָין מִקֶּרֶן דְּרוֹמִית, וְתַרְתֵּי עֲנָנֵי דְּסָלְקָן חֲדָא לְאַפֵּי חַבְרְתָהּ – כּוּלְּהוּ קַשְׁיָין. לְמַאי נַפְקָא מִינָּהּ – לְמִבְעֵי רַחֲמֵי. וְהָנֵי מִילֵּי – בְּלֵילְיָא, אֲבָל בְּצַפְרָא לֵית בְּהוּ מַמָּשָׁא. *אָמַר רַבִּי שְׁמוּאֵל בַּר יִצְחָק: הָנֵי עֲנָנֵי דְּצַפְרָא לֵית בְּהוּ מַמָּשָׁא, דִּכְתִיב: °"וְחַסְדְּכֶם כַּעֲנַן בֹּקֶר וגו'". א"ל רַב פָּפָּא לְאַבַּיֵּי, הָא אָמְרִי אִינָשֵׁי: כַּד מִפְתַּח בָּבֵי מִטְרָא, בַּר חַמָּרָא, מוֹךְ שַׂקָּיךְ וּגְנֵי! –לָא קַשְׁיָא, הָא – דִּקְטַר בְּעֵיבָא, הָא – דִּקְטַר בַּעֲנָנֵי. אָמַר ר' אֲלֶכְּסַנְדְּרִי אָמַר ר' יְהוֹשֻׁעַ בֶּן לֵוִי: לֹא נִבְרְאוּ רְעָמִים אֶלָּא לִפְשׁוֹט עַקְמוּמִית שֶׁבַּלֵּב, שֶׁנֶּאֱמַר: °"וְהָאֱלֹהִים עָשָׂה שֶׁיִּרְאוּ מִלְּפָנָיו". וא"ר אֲלֶכְּסַנְדְּרִי אמר ריב"ל: הָרוֹאֶה אֶת הַקֶּשֶׁת בֶּעָנָן צָרִיךְ שֶׁיִּפּוֹל עַל פָּנָיו, שֶׁנֶּאֱמַר: °"כְּמַרְאֵה הַקֶּשֶׁת אֲשֶׁר יִהְיֶה בֶעָנָן וגו' וָאֶרְאֶה וָאֶפֹּל עַל פָּנָי". *לַיְיטֵי עֲלָהּ בְּמַעֲרָבָא, מִשּׁוּם דִּמְחֲזֵי כְּמַאן דְּסָגֵיד לְקַשְׁתָּא. אֲבָל בְּרוּכֵי וַדַּאי מְבָרֵךְ. מַאי מְבָרֵךְ – "בָּרוּךְ זוֹכֵר הַבְּרִית". בְּמַתְנִיתָא תָּנָא, ר' יִשְׁמָעֵאל בְּנוֹ שֶׁל ר' יוֹחָנָן בֶּן בְּרוֹקָא אוֹמֵר: "נֶאֱמָן בִּבְרִיתוֹ וְקַיָּים בְּמַאֲמָרוֹ". *א"ר פָּפָּא: הִלְכָּךְ נֵימְרִינְהוּ לְתַרְוַיְיהוּ, [ה]"בָּרוּךְ זוֹכֵר הַבְּרִית *וְנֶאֱמָן בִּבְרִיתוֹ וְקַיָּים בְּמַאֲמָרוֹ".§ "עַל הֶהָרִים וְעַל הַגְּבָעוֹת". אַטּוּ כָּל הָנֵי דַּאֲמַרַן עַד הַשְׁתָּא, לָאו מַעֲשֵׂה בְרֵאשִׁית נִינְהוּ? וְהָכְתִיב °"בְּרָקִים לַמָּטָר עָשָׂה"! – אָמַר אַבַּיֵּי: כְּרוֹךְ וּתְנִי. רָבָא אָמַר: [ו]הָתָם מְבָרֵךְ תַּרְתֵּי, "בָּרוּךְ שֶׁכֹּחוֹ מָלֵא עוֹלָם" וְ"עוֹשֶׂה מַעֲשֵׂה בְרֵאשִׁית", הָכָא – "עוֹשֶׂה מַעֲשֵׂה בְרֵאשִׁית" אִיכָּא, "שֶׁכֹּחוֹ מָלֵא עוֹלָם" – לֵיכָּא.§ אריב"ל: הָרוֹאֶה רָקִיעַ בְּטָהֳרָתָהּ אוֹמֵר "בָּרוּךְ עוֹשֶׂה *בְרֵאשִׁית". אֵימָתַי? אָמַר אַבַּיֵּי: כִּי אָתָא מִטְרָא כּוּלֵּי לֵילְיָא, וּבְצַפְרָא אָתָא אִסְתָּנָא, וּמְגַלְיָא לְהוּ לִשְׁמַיָּא. וּפְלִיגֵי דְּרַפְרָם בַּר פָּפָּא א"ר חִסְדָּא, דְּאָמַר רַפְרָם בַּר פָּפָּא א"ר חִסְדָּא: מִיּוֹם שֶׁחָרַב בהמ"ק לֹא נִרְאֵית רָקִיעַ בְּטָהֳרָתָהּ, שֶׁנֶּאֱמַר: °"אַלְבִּישׁ שָׁמַיִם קַדְרוּת וְשַׂק אָשִׂים כְּסוּתָם".§ ת"ר

**רש"י**

כְּטַרְפָּא דְּטָרֵיף. דָּבָר שֶׁהוּא חָסֵר וּסְתָמוּהוּ מִגּוּפוֹ שֶׁעֲשָׂאוּהוּ כְּנוּס וּמִתְחֲזֵי כִּמְכָה בְּקוֹרְנָס. טַרְפָּא דְּטָרֵיף = מוּכֶּה בְּהַכָּאוֹת, כְּמוֹ "אֵילָה טְרוּפָה". ל"א דְּמִתְחֲזְיָא כִּדְטַרְפָּא מְטָרֵף נִדְבָּק יַחַד, וְעָשׂוּי סְנִיפִין כְּמִין חִיבּוּר: וְהַאי דְּאָזְלָא. עַיִשׁ אַחַר כִּימָה: דַּאֲמַרָה לָהּ הַב לִי בְּנַי. שְׁנֵי כּוֹכָבִים שֶׁלִּי: וְלִיהְדַר. לְכִימָה אוֹתָן כּוֹכָבִים עַצְמָן שֶׁנָּטַל הֵימֶנָּה: גּוֹהָא. בְּלָשׁוֹן קוֹרִין רְעִידַת הָאָרֶץ גּוֹהָא: אוֹבָא טַמְיָא. בַּעַל אוֹב שֶׁל עֲצָמוֹת שֶׁעוֹשֶׂה כִּשּׁוּף בְּעַצְמוֹת הַמֵּת. טַמְיָא – עֲצָמוֹת. וְדוֹמֶה לוֹ בְּמַסֶּכֶת כֵּלִים: בֵּית מָלֵא טַמְיָא. וּפֵי' רַבֵּינוּ הַאי: מְלָא טַמְיָא – בַּיִת שֶׁהוּא מָלֵא עֲצָמוֹת. וְהָכִי רָאִיתִי עַל זֶה מִבְּרֵאשִׁית רַבָּה, דְּקָתָנֵי הֲדְרִיָּינוּס שְׁחִיק טַמְיָא – הַיְינוּ שְׁחִיק עֲצָמוֹת. וְאֵין לְפָרֵשׁ אוֹב טָמֵא – שֶׁאֵין הַלָּשׁוֹן: גְּנַח גּוֹהָא. וּמִתְגַּעֵשׁ וּתִרְעַשׁ, כְּלוֹמַר: נִזְדַּעְזְעָה הָאָרֶץ מְאֹד מְאֹד. גְּנַח גּוֹהָא חֲדָא מִילְּתָא הִיא, וְכֵן הַלָּשׁוֹן: גּוֹהָא גּוֹהָא מִיבְּעֵי לֵיהּ. שְׁנֵי פְּעָמִים הָיָה לוֹ לְהִזְדַּעְזֵעַ, כְּנֶגֶד שְׁתֵּי דְּמָעוֹת: סוֹפֵק כַּפָּיו. וּמֵאוֹתוֹ קוֹל מִזְדַּעְזַעַת הָאָרֶץ. שֶׁמָּצִינוּ שֶׁכַּפָּיו סוֹפֵק שֶׁנֶּאֱמַר "גַּם אֲנִי אַכֶּה כַפִּי אֶל כַּפִּי" (יחזקאל כא): אֲנָחָה מִתְאַנֵּחַ. וּמֵאוֹתָהּ אֲנָחָה מַרְעִיד הַקַּרְקַע, וּמָצִינוּ שֶׁמִּתְאַנֵּחַ שֶׁנֶּאֱמַר "וַהֲנִיחוֹתִי חֲמָתִי בָּם", (יחזקאל ה) כְּבַיָּכוֹל הָאָדָם שֶׁיֵּשׁ לוֹ קִימָה וּמִתְאַנֵּחַ וּמִתְנַחֵם דַּעְתּוֹ וְעוֹשֶׂה לוֹ נַחַת רוּחַ: וְהִנֶּחָמְתִּי. אֶנָּחֵם עַל הָרָעָה שֶׁעָשִׂיתִי לָהֶן: הֵידָד כְּדוֹרְכִים יַעֲנֶה. שֶׁדּוֹרֵךְ וּבוֹעֵט בָּרָקִיעַ: וְהָאָרֶץ הֲדוֹם רַגְלָי. כְּגוֹן שֶׁדְּחָקָהּ תַּחַת כִּסֵּא הַכָּבוֹד וּמַגִּיעַ בְּעִיטוּתוֹ עַד לָאָרֶץ, שֶׁהִיא הֲדוֹם רַגְלָיו: עֲנָנֵי בְּגַלְגְּלָא. עֲנָנִים מִתְחַכְּכִין וּמִתְחַכְּכִין, וְנִשְׁמָע הַקּוֹל. לָשׁוֹן אַחֵר: הָעֲנָנִים פּוֹגְעִין בַּגַּלְגַּל וּמִתְגַּלְגְּלוֹת עִם הַגַּלְגַּל כְּבַעַל כְּרָחָם, וְאוֹתוֹ הַקּוֹל הַיְינוּ רְעָמִים: בַּרְקָא. בְּרָקִים שֶׁל אֵשׁ: וּמִתַּבַּר גִּזְיֵזֵי דְּבַרְזָא. וְאוֹתוֹ הַקּוֹל הַיְינוּ רְעָמִים. גִּזְיֵזֵי = גלצ"ש, חֲתִיכוֹת שֶׁל בָּרָד: חַלְחוּלֵי מְחַלְחְלִי. עֲנָנֵי, וּמְנַשֵּׁב זִיקָא עֲלַיְיהוּ, וְהַיְינוּ רְעָמִים: מְנַהֲמִי עֲנָנֵי. הוֹמוֹת הָעֲנָנִים: זַעְפָּא. סופטורבי"ל: בַּרְקָא. אישלוזי"ר, לְשׁוֹן מַבְרִיק – נָהָר: בַּרְקָא יְחִידָאָה. שֶׁלֹּא הִבְרִיק אֶלָּא פַּעַם אֶחָד: וּבַרְקָא חִיוָּרָא וּבַרְקָא יְרוֹקְתָא כּוּלְּהוּ קַשְׁיָין. שֶׁאֵינָם שֶׁל בְּרָכָה: דְּסָלְקָן חֲדָא לְאַפֵּי חַבְרְתָהּ. שֶׁשְּׁנֵי עֲנָנִים פּוֹגְעִים זֶה אֶת זֶה: עֲנַן בֹּקֶר. לֹא קָבוּעַ: כַּד מִפְתַּח בָּבֵי מִטְרָא בַּר חַמָּרָא מוֹךְ שַׂקָּיךְ וּגְנֵי. אִם כְּשֶׁתִּפְתַּח דְּלָתֶיךָ בַּבֹּקֶר יֵרֵד לְךָ מָטָר, לְךָ אֲנִי אוֹמֵר – חַמָּר הַהוֹלֵךְ מִמָּקוֹם לְמָקוֹם לְהָבִיא תְּבוּאָה – מוֹךְ שַׂקָּיךְ וּגְנֵי = כְּפוֹל שַׂקְּךָ תַּחְתֶּיךָ וְתִישַׁן עָלָיו, וְלֹא תֵּלֵךְ אָנֶה וָאָנָה לְהָבִיא תְּבוּאָה, לְפִי שֶׁיִּהְיוּ הַחִטִּים בְּזוֹל בִּשְׁבִיל הַגֶּשֶׁם: ה"ג הָא דִּקְטַר בְּעֵיבָא. נִתְקַשְּׁרוּ הַשָּׁמַיִם בְּעַב עָבֶה אָז טוֹב, כִּי יֵרֵד גֶּשֶׁם רַב: הָא דִּקְטַר בַּעֲנָנָא. עָנָן קָלוּשׁ, הוּא עֲנַן בֹּקֶר שֶׁאֵין בּוֹ מַמָּשׁ: צָרִיךְ שֶׁיִּפּוֹל עַל פָּנָיו. לְפִי שֶׁהוּא מַרְאֶה כְּבוֹד ה': כְּרוֹךְ וּתְנֵי. בְּכוּלְּהוּ "בָּרוּךְ עוֹשֶׂה בְרֵאשִׁית" וּ"בָרוּךְ שֶׁכֹּחוֹ מָלֵא עוֹלָם". כְּרוֹךְ וּתְנֵי לְכוּלְּהוּ בַּחֲדָא בָּבָא, וְעַל כּוּלָּם שְׁתֵּי בְּרָכוֹת הַלָּלוּ: עַל הֶהָרִים. לֹא מָצֵי לְבָרוֹכֵי "מָלֵא עוֹלָם" שֶׁאֵינָן בְּמָקוֹם אֶחָד, אֶלָּא כָּל אֶחָד וְאֶחָד בִּמְקוֹמוֹ: אוֹמֵר בָּרוּךְ עוֹשֶׂה בְרֵאשִׁית. שֶׁכָּךְ הָיְתָה בְּרִיָּיתוֹ, וְאַחַר כָּךְ כִּסּוּהוּ עֲנָנִים: אִסְתָּנָא. רוּחַ צְפוֹנִית: בִּתְקוּפָתָהּ

**תוספות**

*עַל הרוחות אומר שכחו וגבורתו מלא עולם. ירושלמי: מתני' כשבאים בזעם, אבל כשבאין בנחת אומר: ברוך עושה בראשית:

הִלְכָּךְ נימרינהו לתרווייהו. אומר ר"י: דאין חותמין בברוך בברכה זו. והיכי מברך – ברוך אתה ה' אלהינו מלך העולם נאמן בבריתו וקיים בשבועתו וזוכר הברית:

רָבָא אמר התם מברך שכחו וגבורתו מלא עולם ועושה מעשה בראשית. פי': אומר או האי או האי, איזה שירצה. וכן פירש רב אלפס:

*הִלְכָּךְ נימרינהו לתרווייהו. רוב ההודאות ואל ההודאות. לפיכך תקנו בישתבח אחר סיום הברכה ברוך אתה ה' אל מלך גדול בתשבחות אל ההודאות: הטוב

**עין משפט נר מצוה**

[שייך לעיל במשנה נד]

מ א ב ג ד מיי' פ"י מהלכות ברכות הל' יד סמג עשין כז טוש"ע או"ח סי' רכז סעיף א:

מא ה מיי' שם הלכה טז סמג שם טוש"ע או"ח סי' רכט סעיף א:

מב ו מיי' שם הלכה יד טו וסמג שם טוש"ע או"ח סימן רכז סעיף א:

שייך מע"ל [חגיגה יג: ר"ה כו. קדושין ה.]

**מסורת הש"ס ותורה אור השלם**

[שבת פ:]

תורה אור

סנהדרין עז.

קהלת א

איוב לח

יחזקאל כא

יחזקאל ה

ירמיה כה

ישעיה סו

תהלים עז

ירמיה י

פי' חולין קלג.

נחום א

תענית ו: ע"ש

הושע ו

קהלת ג

יחזקאל א

[יומא יג: וש"נ]

ב ס:] תענית ז. מגילה כח:

[נ"ל נאמן בלא וא"ו. הגר"א באו"ח סי' רכט ס"ק א]

תהלים קלה

מעשה

ישעיה נ

מג א מיי' פ"י מהלכות ברכות הל' יח סמג עשין כז טוש"ע או"ח סי' רכט סעיף ב:
[וכן משמע כנ"ל]
מד ב מיי' שם הל' טו סמג שם טוש"ע או"ח סי' ריח סעיף ג וסי' רכל סעיף יג:
מה ג טוש"ע או"ח סי' רכח סעיף ב:
מו ד מיי' שם הלכה ו סמג שם טוש"ע או"ח סי' רכא סעיף א:
מז ה ו ז ח מיי' שם הלכה ה טוש"ע שם סעיף ב:
מח ט מיי' שם הל' ז סמג שם טוש"ע או"ח סי' רכב סעיף א:
מט י טוש"ע או"ח סי' רכג סעיף א:
נ כ מיי' וסמג שם טוש"ע שם סעיף ב:
נא ל מיי' פ"ד מהלכות ברכות הל' ג סמג שם טוש"ע או"ח סימן קעה סעיף א:
נב מ מיי' שם הלכה ט סמג שם טוש"ע או"ח סי' קעה סעיף א:
[ועי' היטב תוס' פסחים קא. ד"ה שינוי יין]
נג נ מיי' שם טוש"ע שם סעיף ז:
נד ס מיי' פ"י מהלכות ברכות הל' א סמג שם טוש"ע או"ח סי' רכג סעיף ג:
[ע מיי' שם]:

**הטוב** והמטיב. אבל אשינוי לחם ואשינוי בשר – אין מברכין הטוב והמטיב. דדווקא איין דאית ביה תרתי, דסעיד ומשמח – מברכין הטוב והמטיב. אבל בשר ולחם לא. ופרשב"ם בערבי פסחים: (דף קא. ושם) דדוקא כשהאחרון משובח מברכים הטוב והמטיב, אבל בכיוצא בו – לא. *אך בירושלמי דכילד מברכין, א"ר אבא בר רב הונא: צריך לברך על יין חדש וישן. שינוי יין א"צ לברך, שינוי מקום צריך לברך, היסח הדעת כשינוי מקום. משמע דוקא כשהאחרון ישן – דעדיף טפי. ור"ת פי': דאפי' אין האחרון חשיב, רק שלא ישתנה לגריעותא יותר מדאי(א) ומסייס בה רבי על כל חבית וחבית שהיה פותח היה מברך הטוב והמטיב, ומשמע דלא קפיד אם האחרון משובח אם לאו. אע"ג דישן אידכר בסוף, מ"מ נימא דרבי פליג עליה. ולפרשב"ם יעמידנה להך דרבי במסופק אם האחרון טוב, ומספק היה מברך על כל אחד שמא משובח הוא. אך ר"ת מפרש דעובדא דרבי בא לחלק כדפי'. וי"מ דההוא דחדש וישן מיירי בברכת בורא פרי הגפן דומיא דשינוי מקום דבתר הכי, אבל לא מצינו כן בגמרא שלנו*:

**התם** דאיכא בני חבורה דשתו בהדיה. וה"ה אם אשתו ובניו עמו, אבל יחיד לא, ואפילו שהחיינו אין מברך יחיד על שינוי יין, דלא אשכחן יחיד שמברך שהחיינו רק אחדתא. וכן כל פרי חדש כשאכלו מברך שהחיינו כדאמרינן בסוף בכל מערבין (עירובין מ:): **ורבי** יוחנן אמר אפי' קנה כיוצא בהם. והלכתא כר' יוחנן אליבא דלישנא בתרא אפילו קנה והדר קנה שהיו לו כלים חדשים כיוצא באלו – צריך לברך. דקי"ל כרבי יוחנן לגבי דרב מכ"ש דלגבי רב* הלכתא כוותיה. ואומר ר"י: דוקא בבגדים חשובים דומיא דבית חדש נקט כלים חדשים, אבל שאינם חשובין כ"כ כמו מנעלים ואנפליאות וחלוק וכיוצא בהן – אין צריך לברך. בירושלמי, א"ר חייא בר אבא: לא סוף דברים חדשים, אלא אפי' שחקים כאילו חדשים הן. ר' יעקב בשם רבי חייא בר אבא אמר: קנה – אומר שהחיינו; ניתן לו – אומר הטוב והמטיב; לבש בגדים – אומר מלביש ערומים. ול"ע בגמרא שלנו דלא אשכחן הטוב והמטיב אלא בדאיכא אחרינא בהדיה: [רב הונא]

תורה אור

תנו רבנן: [א]הרואה חמה בתקופתה לבנה בגבורתה וכוכבים במסילותם ומזלות כסדרן, אומר "ברוך עושה בראשית". ואימת הוי? –אמר אביי: כל כ"ח שנין, והדר מחזור ונפלה תקופת ניסן בשבתאי באורתא דתלת נגהי ארבע.§ "ר' יהודה אומר: הרואה הים וכו'". "לפרקים" עד כמה? אמר רמי בר אבא א"ר יצחק: בעד שלשים יום. ואמר רמי בר אבא א"ר יצחק: הרואה פרת אגשרא דבבל אומר "ברוך עושה בראשית". גוהאידנא דשניוה פרסאי – מבי שבור ולעיל, רב יוסף אמר: מאיהי דקירא ולעיל. ואמר רמי בר אבא: הרואה דגלת אגשרא דשביסתנא אומר "ברוך עושה בראשית". מאי °'חדקל'? – א"ר אשי: שמימיו חדין [בראשית ב] וקלין. מאי *'פרת' – שמימיו פרין ורבין. ואמר רבא: האי דחריפי בני מחוזא – משום דשתו מיא דדגלת, האי דגיחורי – משום דמשמשי בימָמא, והאי דניידי עינייהו – משום דדיירו בבית אפל.§ "על הגשמים כו'". ועל הגשמים "הטוב והמטיב" מברך?! *והא"ר אבהו, ואמרי לה במתניתא תנא: דמאימתי מברכין על הגשמים – משיצא חתן לקראת כלה. מאי מברכין? אמר רב יהודה: ה"מודים אנחנו לך על כל טפה וטפה שהורדת לנו", ורבי יוחנן מסיים בה הכי: "אילו פינו מלא שירה כים וכו' אין אנו מספיקין להודות לך ה' אלהינו... עד "תשתחוה", [ב] בא"י רוב ההודאות". ו'רוב ההודאות' ולא כל ההודאות?! –אמר רבא: אימא "האל ההודאות". א"ר פפא: הלכך זנימרינהו לתרוייהו "רוב ההודאות והאל ההודאות", ואלא קשיא! – ל"ק, הא – דשמע משמע, הא – דחזא מחזי. דשמע משמע – היינו בשורות טובות, ותנן: על בשורות טובות אומר "ברוך הטוב והמטיב"! –אלא אידי ואידי דחזי מחזי, ולא קשיא, הא – דאתא פורתא, הא – דאתא טובא. ואב"א: הא והא דאתא טובא, ולא קשיא, זהא – דאית ליה ארעא, הא – דלית ליה ארעא. –אית ליה ארעא "הטוב והמטיב" מברך?! והא (*תנן): בנה בית חדש וקנה כלים חדשים אומר "ברוך שהחיינו והגיענו לזמן הזה", [ג] שלו ושל אחרים – אומר "הטוב והמטיב"! –לא קשיא, חהא – דאית ליה שותפות, הא – דלית ליה שותפות, והתניא: טקצרו של דבר על שלו הוא אומר "ברוך שהחיינו וקיימנו", על שלו ועל של חבירו – אומר "ברוך הטוב והמטיב".§ וכל היכא דלית לאחרינא בהדיה לא מברך "הטוב והמטיב"?! – והתניא, אמרו ליה: ילדה אשתו זכר, אומר "ברוך הטוב והמטיב"! –התם נמי, דאיכא אשתו בהדיה, דניחא לה בזכר. ת"ש: כמת אביו והוא יורשו, בתחלה אומר "ברוך דיין האמת" ולבסוף הוא אומר "ברוך הטוב והמטיב"! –התם נמי, דאיכא אחי דקא ירתי בהדיה. ת"ש: *שינוי יין א"צ לברך, לשינוי מקום צריך לברך. וא"ר יוסף בר אבא א"ר יוחנן: מאע"פ שאמרו "שינוי יין א"צ לברך", אבל אומר "ברוך הטוב והמטיב"! –התם נמי, נדאיכא בני חבורה דשתו בהדיה.§ ס"בנה בית חדש וקנה כלים חדשים וכו'". א"ר הונא: לא שנו אלא שאין לו כיוצא בהן, אבל יש לו כיוצא בהן – א"צ לברך. ור' יוחנן אמר: [ע] אפילו יש לו כיוצא בהן צריך לברך. מכלל

בתקופתה. מקום שהיא חוזרת שם לתחלת היקפה, היא שעת תליית המאורות, ומאז התחילה להקיף ולשמש: אימת הוי. חמה בתקופתה קאי: כל כ"ח שנים. של תקופת ניסן, *שבסוף כ"ח, כשחוזר מחזור גדול של חמה להיות תקופה נופלת בשעת תליית המאורות, בשבתאי היא שעה תחלת ליל ד': באורתא דתלת נגהי ד'. שהעריב שמשו של ג' בשבת ויתחיל ליל ד': נגהי. ליל, כדאמר בפסחים בשמעתא קמייתא (דף ג.) דאיכא דוכתא דקרו ללילא נגהי: שבתאי. שם שעה ראשונה של ליל ד', שבאותה שעה נתלו מאורות. ושבע שעות הן וחוזרות חלילה שצ"ם חנכ"ל. תמלא בהקף סדרן של עולם סימני שעות תחלת הלילות: ככנ"ש חל"ם; מולאי שבת כוכב. תחלת ליל ב' – צדק, תחלת ליל ג' – נוגה, תחלת ליל רביעי – שבתאי, תחלת ליל ה' – חמה, תחלת ליל ששי – לבנה, תחלת ליל שבת – מאדים. וסדר תחלת הימים כעלות השחר: חל"ס ככנ"ש. ותקופה מושכת מחברתה ז' שעות ומחצה, כלומר מתאחרת אחר היום והשעה שנפלה בה חברתה ז' שעות ומחצה. הרי שלשים שעות לארבע תקופות. הרי יום ורביע לשנה. לד' שנים – חמשה ימים. למדת שאין תקופה נופלת בתחלת הלילה אלא לסוף ד' שנים, שהוא מחזור קטן. וז' מחזורים קטנים – למחזור גדול. וסימניך: דכ"ז הגא"ו, הרי שאינה באה לתחלת ליל ד', אלא מכ"ח שנים לכ"ח שנים. בראש כל מחזור קטן באה לתחלת הלילה, ובראש מחזור הגדול באה לתקופה הראשונה שהוא תחלת ליל ד': אגשרא דבבל אומר ברוך עושה בראשית. קים להו שלא נשתנה פרת מהלוכו ע"י אדם משם ולמעלה, אבל משם ולמטה הסיבוהו בני אדם דרך אחרת: והאידנא דשניוה פרסאי. מלמעלה לגשר, אין מברך עליו עושה בראשית אלא מאיהי דקירא ולעיל. איהי דקירי שם מחוז שהוא על הפרת: חדין. חריפין מיא וקלין לשקול במאזנים, וטובים לשתות שאין מכבידין את הגוף: ה"ג: והאי דגיחורי משום דמשמשי בימָמא. לפיכך בניהן אדומין כאדמומית היום, רו"ש בלע"ז: דניידי עינייהו. עיניהם נדים ונעים: משיצא חתן לקראת כלה. שהמים קבולין על הארץ, וכשהטפה נופלת עליהן טפה התחתונה בולטת לקראתה: שמע משמע. שבשרוהו לאמר ירדו גשמים בלילה, אומר "הטוב והמטיב": אתה פורתא. מודים אנחנו לך: אתא טובא. "הטוב והמטיב": אית ליה ארעא. "הטוב והמטיב", שהטיב לו: בנה בית חדש. [ד]שכולו שלו, אומר שהחיינו: שלו ושל אחרים. הטוב והמטיב: ה"ג: (והתנן) בנה בית חדש וכו' לא קשיא הא דאית ליה שותפות הא דלית ליה שותפות. ול"ג אלא הא והא דאית ליה ארעא. וה"פ: תירוצא דשנינן קמי בדוכתיה, "מודים אנחנו לך" – בדלית ליה ארעא, "הטוב והמטיב" – בדאית ליה. ודקא קשיא לך בנה בית חדש אומר "שהחיינו" – לא קשיא, ההוא דבנה בית חדש שאין לו שותפות בה ועליה מברך שהחיינו, אבל גשמים בדאית ליה ארעא – טובה שיש לו שותפות בה היא, שהרי כל מי שיש לו קרקע שותף עמו בטובה זו: והתניא. בניחותא: קצרו של דבר. [ה]כלומר: כללו של דבר: ולבסוף הוא אומר הטוב והמטיב. על בשורות הירושה שנשארה לו ירושה מאביו, שכן בשרוהו מת אביו ויורשו, כלומר: הניח נכסים: שינוי יין. שתה יין בסעודה והביאו לו יין אחר טוב מן הראשון – אין צריך לברך "בורא פרי הגפן": שינוי מקום. יצא מכאן והלך לבית אחר והביאו לו יין: ר"י אמר אפילו יש לו כיוצא בהן. מירושה, הואיל ולענין קנייה חדש היא אצלו – צריך לברך: קנה

## רב נסים גאון

על הגשמי' ועל בשורו' טובות הוא אומר ברוך הטוב והמטיב. גרסי' בגמ' דבני מערבא מה ראו לסמוך בשורות טובות לירידת גשמים ר' ברכיה בשם ר' לוי על שם מים קרים על נפש עיפה ושמועה טובה וגו' ועיקרה בבראשית דר' אושעיא והכין אמר התם מה שמועה ב' הטוב והמטיב:

## הגהות הב"ח

(א) תום' ד"ה הטוב וכו' יותר מדאי דהכי מסיים בה ר':

## הגהות הגר"א

[א] גמ' לבנה בגבורתה וכוכבים במסילותם ומזלות כסדרן. נ"ב גי' הרי"ף ורא"ש בטהרתה במשמרותם בעתם: [ב] שם עד תשתחוה. נ"ב וירוממו את שמך מלכנו. גירסת רי"ף ורא"ש: [ג] שם (שלו ושל אחרים אומר הטוב והמטיב) תא"מ: [ד] רש"י ד"ה בנה בית חדש עד ד"ה ס"ג. נמחק: [ה] שם ד"ה קצרו של דבר. כלומר כללו של דבר שכולו שלו אומר שהחיינו שלו ושל אחרים הטוב והמטיב. כצ"ל:

שבתחלת
[בכורות נה:]
תענית ו: ע"ש
[תניא]
[תענית]
פסחים קא.

גליון הש"ס

גמ' ולימת הוי אביי. בערוך ערך ... היה לו הגירסא ולו אמר אביי. וע"ש ... פירושים על בתקופה:

דקנה וחזר וקנה דברי הכל אין צריך לברך. דהא רבי יוחנן לא אמר צריך לברך אלא משום דלענין קנייה חדש הוא: ואיכא דאמרי כו' מכלל דכי יש לו וקנה דברי הכל צריך לברך. דהא רב הונא לא אמר אין צריך לברך אלא דקנה, וחזר וקנה דליכא חדוש כלל. אבל יש לו וקנה דאיכא חדוש – מודה הוא דצריך: בין כך ובין כך. בין שיש לו בין שאין לו. הואיל ולא קנה הראשונים ועכשיו קנה – צריך לברך: לא כר' מאיר ולא כרבי יהודה. דאפילו רבי יהודה לא פליג אלא ביש לו וקנה, אבל בקנה וחזר וקנה – לא: דמסקא ארעא שרטון. לימ"ך, מחמת המים, והוה ליה לזבל: השתא מיהא רעה היא. שמתקלקלת תבואה של שנה זו, ומברך "ברוך דיין האמת": ועל הטוב שהיא מעין הרעה. יברך "הטוב והמטיב": מאי היא. כגון דאשכח מציאה: שלא יסריח. הזרע, אלא יקלוט ויהיה ולד, ולאחר שלשה ימים אם לא קלט כבר הסריח, ואין תפלה מועלת: שלא יהא סנדל. שלא תתעבר אשתו ולד אחר, ויהיה פוחת צורתו של ראשון, ודומה לדג של ים ששמו סנדל. הכי אמרינן במס' נדה (דף כה:): סנדל דומה לסנדל של ים, ומתחלתו ולד היה אלא שנרצף. משל לאדם שסטר את חבירו והחזיר צורתו לאחוריו: ומי מהני. תפלה לזכר אפילו בתוך ארבעים יום, והלא הדבר תלוי בהזרעה תחלה: הכי גרסינן: משכחת לה דמהניא, כגון שהזריעו שניהם בבת אחת: כל היכי דדרשת ליה להאי קרא. מדריש לחדא משמעות: מסיפיה לרישיה מדריש. מי שנכון לבו בטוח בה' – משמועה רעה לא ירא: בדברי תורה כתיב. אשרי אדם מפחד תמיד – שמא תשתכח ממנו, שמתוך כך הוא מחזיר לשנותם תמיד: תנו רבנן. בן עזאי אומרה דאמר: שתים בכניסתו ושתים ביציאתו: לית לן בה. יזהר בעצמו שלא יפשע, או אם פשע כבר אל יכנס במקום סכנה: בי בני. בית המרחץ: מתותיה. חפירה שהמים נופלים לתוכה, ובני אדם רוחצים על גבי תקרה שעל גבה: בחד אבריה. בזרועו החזיק אחד או שנים, וזה בזה החזיקו עד מאה ואחד: היינו דרבי אחא. דבעי אודויי שהוצלתי לשלום: שאין דרכן של בני אדם וכו'. כלומר: לא היה להם לעסוק ברפואות אלא לבקש רחמים: התכבדו

תורה אור

מכלל דכי קנה וחזר וקנה – דברי הכל אין צריך לברך. וא"ד, אמר רב הונא: לא שנו אלא שלא קנה וחזר וקנה, אבל קנה וחזר וקנה – אין צריך לברך. ור' יוחנן אמר: אפילו קנה וחזר וקנה – צריך לברך. מכלל דכי יש לו וקנה – דברי הכל צריך לברך. מיתיבי: בנה בית חדש ואין לו כיוצא בו, קנה כלים חדשים ואין לו כיוצא בהם – צריך לברך, יש לו כיוצא בהם – אין צריך לברך, דברי ר"מ. ר' יהודה אומר: בין כך ובין כך – צריך לברך. בשלמא ללישנא קמא, רב הונא – כר"מ, ורבי יוחנן – כרבי יהודה, אלא ללישנא בתרא, בשלמא רב הונא – כרבי יהודה, אלא רבי יוחנן, דאמר כמאן? לא כר"מ ולא כרבי יהודה! –אמר לך רבי יוחנן: הוא הדין דלרבי יהודה, קנה וחזר וקנה – נמי צריך לברך, והא דקא מיפלגי ביש לו וקנה – להודיעך כחו דר"מ, דאפי' קנה ויש לו – אין צריך לברך, וכל שכן קנה וחזר וקנה, דאין צריך לברך. –וליפלגו בקנה וחזר וקנה דאין צריך לברך, להודיעך כחו דר' יהודה! –*כח דהתירא עדיף ליה.§

ב"מברך על הרעה כו'". היכי דמי? –כגון דשקל בדקא בארעיה, אף על גב דטבא היא לדידיה, דמסקא ארעא שירטון ושבחא – השתא מיהא רעה היא. ג"ועל הטובה כו'". היכי דמי? –כגון דאשכח מציאה, אף על גב דרעה היא לדידיה, דאי שמע בה מלכא שקיל לה מיניה – השתא מיהא טובה היא.§ ד"היתה אשתו מעוברת ואמר יהי רצון שתלד כו' הרי זו תפלת שוא". ולא מהני רחמי?! מתיב רב יוסף: "ואחר ילדה בת ותקרא את שמה דינה", מאי "ואחר"? אמר רב: לאחר שדנה לאה דין בעצמה ואמרה: י"ב שבטים עתידין לצאת מיעקב, ששה יצאו ממני, וארבעה מן השפחות – הרי עשרה, אם זה זכר – לא תהא אחותי רחל כאחת השפחות! מיד נהפכה לבת, שנא' "ותקרא את שמה דינה"! –*אין מזכירין מעשה נסים. ואיבעית אימא: מעשה דלאה – בתוך ארבעים יום הוה. כדתניא: שלשה ימים הראשונים – יבקש אדם רחמים שלא יסריח, משלשה *ועד ארבעים – יבקש רחמים שיהא זכר, מארבעים יום ועד שלשה חדשים – יבקש רחמים שלא יהא סנדל, משלשה חדשים ועד ששה – יבקש רחמים שלא יהא נפל, מששה ועד תשעה – יבקש רחמים שיצא בשלום. –ומי מהני רחמי? והא"ר יצחק בריה דרב אמי: *איש מזריע תחלה – יולדת נקבה, אשה מזרעת תחלה – יולדת זכר, שנאמר: "אשה כי תזריע וילדה זכר"! –הכא במאי עסקינן – כגון שהזריעו שניהם בבת אחת.§ "היה בא בדרך". ת"ר, מעשה בהלל הזקן שהיה בא בדרך ושמע קול צווחה בעיר, אמר: מובטח אני שאין זה בתוך ביתי. ועליו הכתוב אומר "משמועה רעה לא יירא נכון לבו בטח בה'". אמר רבא: כל היכי דדרשת להאי קרא, *מרישיה לסיפיה – מדריש, מסיפיה לרישיה – מדריש. מרישיה לסיפיה מדריש – "משמועה רעה לא יירא" מה טעם – "נכון לבו בטח בה'". מסיפיה לרישיה מדריש: "נכון לבו בטח בה'" – "משמועה רעה לא יירא". ההוא תלמידא דהוה קא אזיל בתריה דרבי ישמעאל ברבי יוסי בשוקא דציון. חזייה דקא מפחיד, אמר ליה: חטאה את, דכתיב "פחדו בציון חטאים". אמר ליה: *והכתיב "אשרי אדם מפחד תמיד"! – אמר ליה: ההוא בדברי תורה כתיב. יהודה בר נתן הוה שקיל ואזיל בתריה דרב המנונא, אתנח. אמר ליה: יסורים בעי ההוא גברא לאתויי אנפשיה?! דכתיב "כי פחד פחדתי ויאתיני ואשר יגרתי יבא לי" –והא כתיב: "אשרי אדם מפחד תמיד" –ההוא בדברי תורה כתיב.§ "הנכנס לכרך". ת"ר, ה בכניסתו מהו אומר: "יהי רצון מלפניך ה' אלהי שתכניסני לכרך זה לשלום". נכנס, אומר: "מודה אני לפניך ה' אלהי שהכנסתני לכרך זה לשלום". בקש לצאת, אומר: "יהי רצון מלפניך ה' אלהי ואלהי אבותי שתוציאני מכרך זה לשלום". יצא, אומר: "מודה אני לפניך ה' אלהי שהוצאתני מכרך זה לשלום, וכשם שהוצאתני לשלום כך תוליכני לשלום, ותסמכני לשלום, ותצעידני לשלום, ותצילני מכף כל אויב ואורב בדרך". אמר רב מתנא: ל"ש אלא בכרך שאין דנין והורגין בו, אבל בכרך שדנין והורגין בו – לית לן בה. א"ד, אמר רב מתנא: אפילו בכרך שדנין והורגין בו, זימנין דלא מתרמי ליה אינש דיליף ליה זכותא.§ ת"ר, ו הנכנס לבית המרחץ אומר: "יהי רצון מלפניך יי' אלהי שתצילני מזה וכיוצא בו, ואל יארע בי דבר קלקלה ועון, ואם יארע בי דבר קלקלה ועון – תהא מיתתי כפרה לכל עונותי". אמר אביי: לא לימא איניש הכי, דלא לפתח פומיה לשטן; *דאמר ר"ל וכן תנא משמיה דר' יוסי: לעולם אל יפתח אדם פיו לשטן. אמר רב יוסף: מאי קראה – דכתיב "כמעט כסדם היינו לעמורה דמינו", מאי אהדר להו נביא – "שמעו דבר יי' קציני סדם וגו'". כי נפיק מאי אומר? א"ר אחא: "מודה אני לפניך יי' אלהי שהצלתני מן האור". ר' אבהו על לבי בני, אפחית בי בני מתותיה, אתרחיש ליה ניסא קם על עמודא שזיב מאה וחד גברי בחד אבריה, אמר: היינו דר' אחא. דאמר רב אחא: [א] ז הנכנס להקיז דם אומר "יהי רצון מלפניך יי' אלהי שיהא עסק זה לי לרפואה ותרפאני, [ב] כי אל רופא נאמן אתה ורפואתך אמת, לפי שאין דרכן של בני אדם לרפאות אלא שנהגו". אמר אביי: לא לימא איניש הכי, *דתני דבי רבי ישמעאל: "ורפא ירפא" ח מכאן שניתנה רשות לרופא לרפאות. כי קאי מאי אומר? – אמר רב אחא: "ברוך רופא חנם".[ג] §

הנכנס

[ביצה ב: גיטין מח: עד: נח. נדה נט:]

בראשית ל

כח: חולין מג.]

[ועי' תוס' סנהדרין כב. ד"ה ארבעים]

כח. לא. ע"ש

ויקרא יב

תהלים קיב

[לקמן סג. סנהדרין ע.]

ישעיה לג

גיטין נה:

משלי כח

איוב ג

יט. כתובות ח:

ישעיה א

ב"ק פה.

שמות כא

[פי' על זה כתב רש"י ביצה ב: ד"ה התירא ועי' בכ"מ פ"י מה"ב ה"א]

נה א (מיי' פ"י מהל' ברכות סמג עשין כז) טוש"ע או"ח סימן רכג סעיף ג:
נו ב ג מיי' שם הלכה ד (סמג שם) טוש"ע או"ח סי' רכב סעיף ד:
נז ד ה מיי' שם הלכה [כב] כה סמג שם טוש"ע או"ח סימן רל סעיף א:
נח ו מיי' שם הלכה כ טוש"ע שם סעיף ג:
נט ז מיי' שם הל' כא טוש"ע שם סעיף ד:
ס ח טוש"ע י"ד סימן שלו סעיף א:

הגהות הגר"א

[א] גמ' (לא"ד אחא תא"מ: [ב] שם (ותרפאני כי א"ר נ"א ורפואתך אמת לפי) תא"מ ונ"ב כי רופא חנם אתה: [ג] שם חנם. נ"ב וכ"ה ברא"ש אבל גירסת בה"ג והרמב"ם חולים:

גליון הש"ס

גמ' כח דהתירא כו'. עי' רש"ל פסחים ק"ב ע"א ד"ה להודיעך כחו ועי' א"ר סי' כב: שם כל היכי דדרשת להאי קרא. כעין זה לקמן סג ע"א: רש"י ד"ה שלא יהא סנדל. שלא תתעבר. עי' נדה דף כה ע"ב תוס' ד"ה קמ"ל:

סא א ב מיי' פ"ז מהל' תפלה הלכה ה סמג עשין יט טוש"ע או"ח סי' ג סעיף א:
סב ג ד מיי' שם וסמג שם טוש"ע או"ח סי' ו סעיף א:
סג ה מיי' שם הלכה א ב סמג שם טוש"ע או"ח סי' רלט סעיף א:
סד ו ז מיי' שם הל' ג ד ו סמג שם טוש"ע או"ח סי' מו סעיף א:
סה ח מיי' פ"ג מהל' ציצית הל' ח סמג שם טוש"ע או"ח סי' ח סעיף ה:
סו ט מיי' פ"ד מהלכות תפילין הל' ד סמג עשין כב טוש"ע או"ח סי' כה סעיף ה:
סז י מיי' שם טוש"ע שם סעיף ט [וכסעיף ה בהגה]:
סח כ מיי' פ"ז מהל' תפלה הלכה ד סמג עשין יט טוש"ע או"ח סי' ד סעיף א וסי' מו סעיף א:
סט ל מיי' פ"י מהל' ברכות הל' ג סמג עשין כז טוש"ע או"ח סי' רכב סעיף ג:
ע מ טוש"ע או"ח סימן רל סעיף ה:

**אשר** יצר את האדם בחכמה. בתנחומא: ויברא אלהים את האדם, א"ר בון: בחכמה – שהתקין מזונותיו ואח"כ בראו. היינו דאמר בסנהדרין בס"פ אחד דיני ממונות (דף לח.): לכך נברא בערב שבת – כדי שיכנס לסעודה מיד, וע"כ יסדו אשר יצר את האדם בחכמה: **מפליא** לעשות. משום דאמרינן בב"ר: כי גדול אתה ועושה נפלאות אתה אלהים לבדך, אדם עושה נאד אפילו יש בו נקב אחד מלא מחט סדקית – הרוח יוצא ואינו יכול לשמור בו יין, והקב"ה ברא נקבים נקבים באדם ושומר הרוח שאינו יוצא ממנו: **כי** שמע קול תרנגולא אומר: ברוך שנתן לשכוי בינה להבחין. והוא הדין אפילו כי לא שמע, דאין ברכה זו אלא להבחנה על הנאת האורה, שתרנגול מבחין והוא נהנה מן האור: **כי** פרים סודרא על רישיה. וה"ה לכל כובע ולכל כסוי. ודוקא כשנהנה, אבל אם אינו נהנה כגון שהוא שוכב על מטתו – לא יברך לא זו, ולא מלביש ערומים, ולא ברכות כיוצא בהן, כיון שלא נהנה. כדמשמע בפרק שלישי דמגילה (דף כד:) גבי מי שלא ראה מאורות מימיו, דכולי עלמא בעי שיהנה מן האורה: **אשר** קדשנו במצותיו וצונו להניח תפילין. כיון דתחלת הנחתו בזרועו יש לברך להניח. אבל בשל ראש מברך על מצות ולא להניח, שכבר התחיל והניח אחד מהם. ובפ' הקומץ (מנחות לו. ושם) אמר: לא סח – מברך אחת, סח – מברך שתים. פי"ה: דעל שתי התפילין קאמר, דמברך ברכה אחת על שתיהן בלא סח בינתים. ודוחק לומר דלא הוצרכו שתי ברכות דלהניח ועל מצות אלא כשסח ועבר עבירה. לכן פר"ת: דעל של ראש שהיא גמר מצוה ועיקר, דיש בה ד' בתים ושי"ן – מברך על מצות. אבל סח – חוזר ומברך שתים על של ראש. וכן בשימושא רבא דגאונים. ולפר"ת גבי סח מברך שתים, אם יניח של ראש לבד – דאין מעכבין זה את זה – מברך שתים על של ראש בלבד. ומה שלא הזכיר הגמ' על של ראש בלבד מברך שתים – לפי שאין רגילות כלל להניח זה בלא זה דתפילין בי בר חבו שכיחי (ב"מ ד' כט:). וכן פי' רבינו תם בתשובותיו, וכן רבינו אלחנן בסדר תקון תפלה שלו כתב כן:

התכבדו וכו'. אל המלאכים המלוים אותו הוא אומר, שנאמר "כי מלאכיו יצוה לך" (תהילים צא): שאם יפתח. אחד מהם – מן החללים, כגון הלב או הכרס או המעים: או אם יסתם אחד מהם. מן הנקבים הפתוחים, כגון הפה או החוטם או פי הטבעת. "יפתח" קאי אחללים, "יסתם" קאי אנקבים: קצירי. חולים: רופא כל בשר. כנגד היציאה, שהיא רפואת כל הגוף: ומפליא לעשות. כנגד שהגוף חלול כמו נאד, והנאד הזה אם יש בו נקב אין הרוח עומד בתוכו, והקב"ה ברא את האדם בחכמה וברא בו נקבים נקבים הרבה, ואעפ"כ הרוח בתוכו כל ימי חייו, וזו היא פליאה וחכמה: ותהא מטתי שלמה. שלא יהא פסול ורשע בזרעי: לשכוי. תרנגול, דאיכא דוכתא דקרו לתרנגול שכוי כדאמרינן בר"ה (דף כו.): הכי גרסי': אילימא כשם שמברך על הטובה "הטוב והמטיב", כך מברך על הרעה "הטוב והמטיב", והתנן על בשורות טובות "הטוב והמטיב" ועל שמועות רעות אומר "ברוך דיין האמת": לקבולינהו בשמחה. לברך על מדת פורענות בלבב שלם: באלהים. לשון דיין, כמו "עד האלהים יבא דבר שניהם" (שמות כב): ובת בדברא. ולן בשדה: הוה בהדיה תרנגולא. להקיצו משנתו:

תורה אור

[א]הנכנס לבית הכסא, אומר: "התכבדו מכובדים קדושים משרתי עליון, תנו כבוד לאלהי ישראל, הרפו ממני עד שאכנס ואעשה רצוני ואבא אליכם". אמר אביי: לא לימא איניש הכי, דלמא שבקי ליה ואזלי. אלא לימא: [ב]"שמרוני שמרוני, עזרוני עזרוני, סמכוני סמכוני, המתינו לי המתינו לי, עד שאכנס ואצא שכן דרכן של בני אדם". [ג]כי נפיק אומר: "ברוך אשר יצר את האדם בחכמה וברא בו נקבים נקבים *חללים חללים גלוי וידוע לפני כסא כבודך שאם יפתח אחד מהם או אם יסתם אחד מהם אי אפשר לעמוד לפניך". [א] מאי חתים? – אמר רב: "רופא חולים". אמר שמואל: קא שוינהו *אבא לכולי עלמא קצירי! אלא: "רופא כל בשר". רב ששת אמר: "מפליא לעשות". *א"ר פפא: הלכך [ד]נמרינהו לתרוייהו, "רופא כל בשר ומפליא לעשות". § [ה]הנכנס לישן על מטתו אומר מ"שמע ישראל" עד "והיה אם שמוע". ואומר "ברוך המפיל חבלי שינה על עיני ותנומה על עפעפי ומאיר לאישון בת עין. יהי רצון מלפניך ה' אלהי שתשכיבני לשלום, ותן חלקי [ב] בתורתך, ותרגילני לידי מצוה, ואל תרגילני לידי עבירה, ואל תביאני לידי חטא, ולא לידי עון, ולא לידי נסיון, ולא לידי בזיון, וישלוט בי יצר טוב ואל ישלוט בי יצר הרע ותצילני מפגע רע ומחלאים רעים ואל יבהלוני חלומות רעים והרהורים רעים, ותהא מטתי שלמה לפניך, והאר עיני פן אישן המות, ברוך אתה ה' המאיר לעולם כולו בכבודו". [ו]כי מתער, אומר: "אלהי, נשמה שנתת בי טהורה, אתה יצרתה בי, אתה נפחתה בי, ואתה משמרה בקרבי, ואתה עתיד ליטלה ממני ולהחזירה בי לעתיד לבא, כל זמן שהנשמה בקרבי מודה אני לפניך ה' אלהי ואלהי אבותי רבון כל העולמים אדון כל הנשמות, ברוך אתה ה' המחזיר נשמות לפגרים מתים". [ז]כי שמע קול תרנגולא, לימא: "ברוך אשר *נתן לשכוי בינה להבחין בין יום ובין לילה". כי פתח עיניה, לימא: "ברוך פוקח עורים". כי *תריץ ויתיב, לימא: "ברוך מתיר אסורים". כי לביש, לימא: "ברוך מלביש ערומים". כי זקיף, לימא: "ברוך זוקף כפופים". כי נחית לארעא, לימא: "ברוך רוקע הארץ על המים". כי מסגי, לימא: "ברוך המכין מצעדי גבר". כי סיים מסאניה, לימא: "ברוך שעשה לי כל צרכי". כי אסר המייניה, לימא: "ברוך אוזר ישראל בגבורה". כי פרים סודרא על רישיה, לימא: "ברוך עוטר ישראל בתפארה". [ח]כי מעטף בציצית, לימא: "ברוך אשר קדשנו במצותיו וצונו להתעטף בציצית". [ט]כי מנח *תפילין אדרעיה, לימא: "ברוך אשר קדשנו במצותיו וצונו להניח תפילין". [י]ארישיה, לימא: "ברוך אשר קדשנו במצותיו וצונו על מצות תפילין". [כ]כי משי ידיה, לימא: "ברוך אשר קדשנו במצותיו וצונו על נטילת ידים". כי משי אפיה, לימא: "ברוך המעביר חבלי שינה מעיני ותנומה מעפעפי, ויהי רצון מלפניך ה' אלהי שתרגילני בתורתך ודבקני במצותיך, ואל תביאני לא לידי חטא ולא לידי עון ולא לידי נסיון ולא לידי בזיון, וכוף את יצרי להשתעבד לך, ורחקני מאדם רע ומחבר רע, ודבקני ביצר טוב ובחבר טוב בעולמך, ותנני היום ובכל יום לחן ולחסד ולרחמים בעיניך ובעיני כל רואי, ותגמלני חסדים טובים, ברוך אתה ה' גומל חסדים טובים לעמו ישראל". § "חייב אדם לברך כו'". מאי "חייב לברך על הרעה כשם שמברך על הטובה"?! – אילימא: כשם שמברך על הטובה "הטוב והמטיב", כך מברך על הרעה "הטוב והמטיב" – והתנן: על בשורות טובות אומר "הטוב והמטיב", על בשורות רעות אומר "ברוך דיין האמת"! – אמר רבא: לא נצרכה [ל]אלא לקבולינהו בשמחה. אמר ר' אחא משום ר' לוי: מאי קרא – "חסד ומשפט אשירה לך ה' אזמרה", אם חסד – אשירה, ואם משפט – אשירה. רבי שמואל בר נחמני אמר: מהכא – *"בה' אהלל דבר באלהים אהלל דבר", "בה' אהלל דבר" – זו מדה טובה, "באלהים אהלל דבר" – זו מדת פורענות. רבי תנחום אמר: מהכא "כוס ישועות אשא ובשם ה' אקרא", "צרה ויגון אמצא ובשם ה' אקרא". ורבנן אמרי מהכא "ה' נתן וה' לקח יהי שם ה' מבורך". אמר רב הונא אמר רב משום רבי מאיר, וכן תנא משמיה דר' עקיבא: [מ]לעולם יהא אדם רגיל לומר "כל דעביד רחמנא לטב עביד". כי הא, דרבי עקיבא דהוה קאזיל באורחא, מטא לההיא מתא, בעא אושפיזא לא יהבי ליה. אמר: כל דעביד רחמנא *לטב. אזל ובת בדברא, והוה בהדיה תרנגולא וחמרא ושרגא. אתא זיקא כבייה לשרגא, אתא שונרא אכליה לתרנגולא, אתא אריה אכליה לחמרא. אמר: כל דעביד רחמנא לטב. ביה בליליא אתא גייסא, שבייה למתא. אמר להו: לאו אמרי לכו "כל מה שעושה הקדוש ברוך הוא הכל

[גירסת הרי"ף חלולים ועי' ב"י]

[פירושו תמצא בר מז. ד"ה אלו]

[לעיל נט. וש"נ]

[עי' ברא"ש פירוש]

[עמ"ש על הגליון סב:]

[מנחות לו. מב:]

תהלים קא

שם נו

שם קטז

איוב א

[תענית כא.]

הגהות הגר"א

[א] גמ' לעמוד לפניך. נ"ב אפי' שעה אחת: [ב] שם ותן חלקי. נ"ב זו היא תוספת של ר"ע גאון:

[באלהים אהלל דבר בה' אהלל דבר כך איתא בקרא וכן ברב אלפס העתיק על נכון]

הכל לטובה. אילו היה נר דלוק – היה הגייס רואה אותי, ואילו היה החמור נוער או התרנגול קורא – היה הגייס בא ושובה אותי: והא קחזינן דמזיקא. שמזקת: אוי לי מיוצרי. אם אלך אחרי יצרי, ואם לא אלך אחריו – אוי לי מיצרי המיגעני בהרהורים: דו פרצופין. שני פרצופין בראו תחלה, אחד מלפניו ואחד מאחריו, ולאחר לשנים ועשה מן האחד חוה: אחור וקדם צרתני. לשון צורה, דהיינו שני פרצופין: זכר ונקבה בראם. משמע: מתחלת בריאתם תרי הוו: היינו דכתיב ויבן. שהיה צריך בנין: מאי ויבן. והלא כבר נבנית כדי לקבל את הפירות. שאם יהיה קצר מלמטה ורחב מלמעלה תהא התבואה דוחפת את הכתלים מלמעלה לכאן ולכאן, שהמשא מכביד עליהם: שושבין. משתדל בחופתו ובזיווגו: ולמ"ד פרצוף. ומתחלתו היה מצד אחד זכר ונקבה מצד אחר: הי מינייהו סגי ברישא. איזהו פרצוף היה מהלך לפנים: אפי' היא אשתו. גנאי הדבר: נזדמנה לו על הגשר. אשת איש, והיא לפניו. יסלקנה לצדדין. על שיעבור לפניה: אחורי אשה בנהר. אחורי אשת איש, מגבהת בגדיה מפני המים, והוא מסתכל בה: יד ליד לא ינקה רע. אפילו כמשה רבינו שקבל תורה מימינו של הקב"ה לא ינקה רע, וקרא באשה משתעי: עם הארץ. לא שמש תלמידי חכמים, שלא למד משנה זו ששנינו: לא יהלך אדם אחורי אשה ואפילו היא אשתו: ולמאי דקאמר רב נחמן. שהלך אחריה ממש, אם כן אפילו בי רב, עם תינוקות של בית רבן, נמי לא קרא: בשעה שהצבור מתפללים. דכיון שאינו נכנס נראה כפורק עול ומבזה בית הכנסת: ואי דרי מידי. אין כאן גנאי, דמוכחא מילתא דהאי דלא נכנס מפני המשאוי: ואי איכא פתחא אחרינא. אין כאן בזוי, דמאן דחזי סבר בפתחא אחרינא ליעול: יביע. לשון אבעבועות. כל משקה מסריח מעלה רתיחה ואבעבועות: חטאת. לשון חטה דריש ליה: כליות יועצות. את הלב: עושה כן: והלב מבין. מה יש לו לעשות, אם ישמע לעצת הכליות אם לאו. ומנין שהכליות יועצות – שנאמר (תהלים טז) "אברך את ה' אשר יעצני" אף לילות יסרוני כליותי. ומנין שהלב מבין – שנאמר (ישעיה ו) "ולבבו יבין": לשון מחתך. הדבור, להוציא מפיו: וחפה. הם השפתים, גומר ומוציאו: ושוחקת

הכל לטובה"! ואמר רב הונא אמר רב משום ר' מאיר: לעולם יהיו דבריו של אדם מועטין לפני הקב"ה, שנאמר: "אל תבהל על פיך ולבך אל ימהר להוציא דבר לפני האלהים כי האלהים בשמים ואתה על הארץ על כן יהיו דבריך מעטים".§ דרש רב נחמן בר רב חסדא: מאי דכתיב "וייצר ה' אלהים את האדם" בשני יודי"ן – שני יצרים ברא הקב"ה, אחד יצר טוב ואחד יצר רע. מתקיף לה רב נחמן בר יצחק: אלא מעתה, בהמה דלא כתיב בה "וייצר" – לית לה יצרא?! והא קא חזינן דמזקא ונשכא ובעטא! אלא כדר"ש בן פזי, דאמר *ר' שמעון בן פזי: אוי לי מיוצרי ואוי לי מיצרי. אי נמי: כדר' ירמיה בן אלעזר, דאמר ר' ירמיה בן אלעזר: דו פרצופין ברא הקב"ה באדם הראשון, שנאמר: "אחור וקדם צרתני".§ "ויבן ה' אלהים את הצלע", *רב ושמואל; חד אמר: *פרצוף, וחד אמר: זנב. בשלמא למאן דאמר "פרצוף" – היינו דכתיב "אחור וקדם צרתני", אלא למאן דאמר "זנב", מאי "אחור וקדם צרתני"? – כדרבי אמי, דאמר ר' אמי: "אחור" למעשה בראשית "וקדם" לפורענות. בשלמא "אחור למעשה בראשית" – דלא אברי עד מעלי שבתא, אלא "וקדם לפורענות" פורענות דמאי? אילימא *פורענות דנחש – והתניא, *רבי אומר: בגדולה מתחילין מן הגדול, ובקללה מתחילין מן הקטן. בגדולה מתחילין מן הגדול – דכתיב *"וידבר משה אל אהרן ואל אלעזר ואל איתמר בניו הנותרים קחו וגו'". בקללה מתחילין מן הקטן – בתחלה נתקלל נחש, ולבסוף נתקללה חוה, ולבסוף נתקלל אדם! –אלא פורענות דמבול, דכתיב "וימח את כל היקום אשר על פני האדמה מאדם ועד בהמה", ברישא אדם והדר בהמה. בשלמא למאן דאמר פרצוף – היינו דכתיב "וייצר" בשני יודין, אלא למאן דאמר זנב, מאי "וייצר"? – כדר"ש בן פזי, דאמר ר' שמעון בן פזי: אוי לי מיוצרי אוי לי מיצרי. בשלמא למאן דאמר פרצוף היינו דכתיב "זכר ונקבה בראם", אלא למאן דאמר זנב – מאי "זכר ונקבה בראם"? – כדר' אבהו, דרבי אבהו *רמי: כתיב "זכר ונקבה בראם" וכתיב "כי בצלם אלהים עשה את האדם"! הא כיצד – בתחלה עלה במחשבה לבראת ב', ולבסוף לא נברא אלא אחד. בשלמא למאן דאמר פרצוף – היינו דכתיב "ויסגר בשר תחתנה", אלא למאן דאמר זנב מאי "ויסגר בשר תחתנה"? – א"ר ירמיה ואיתימא רב זביד ואיתימא רב נחמן בר יצחק: לא נצרכה אלא למקום חתך. בשלמא למ"ד זנב – היינו דכתיב "ויבן", אלא למ"ד "פרצוף" – מאי "ויבן"? – לכדר"ש בן מנסיא, *דדרש ר"ש בן מנסיא: מאי דכתיב "ויבן ה' את הצלע" – מלמד שקלעה הקב"ה לחוה והביאה לאדם הראשון, שכן בכרכי הים קורין לקליעתא בנייתא. דבר אחר: 'ויבן', אמר רב חסדא, ואמרי לה במתניתא תנא: מלמד שבנאה הקב"ה לחוה כבנין אוצר, מה אוצר זה קצר מלמעלה ורחב מלמטה, כדי לקבל את הפירות – אף אשה קצרה מלמעלה ורחבה מלמטה, כדי לקבל את הולד. "ויביאה אל האדם" א"ר ירמיה בן אלעזר: מלמד שנעשה הקב"ה שושבין לאדם הראשון; מכאן למדה תורה דרך ארץ שיחזור גדול עם קטן בשושבינות ואל ירע לו.§ ולמאן דאמר פרצוף הי מינייהו סגי ברישא? אמר רב נחמן בר יצחק: מסתברא דגברא סגי ברישא, דתניא: *לא יהלך אדם אחורי אשה בדרך ואפי' אשתו, נזדמנה לו על הגשר – יסלקנה לצדדין, וכל העובר אחורי אשה בנהר – אין לו חלק לעולם הבא. *תנו רבנן: המרצה מעות לאשה מידו לידה כדי להסתכל בה – אפילו יש בידו תורה ומעשים טובים כמשה רבינו – לא ינקה מדינה של גיהנם, שנאמר: "יד *ליד לא ינקה רע" – לא ינקה מדינה של גיהנם. א"ר נחמן: מנוח עם הארץ היה, דכתיב "וילך מנוח אחרי אשתו". מתקיף לה רב נחמן בר יצחק: אלא מעתה גבי אלקנה, דכתיב "וילך אלקנה אחרי אשתו", וגבי אלישע דכתיב "ויקם וילך אחריה" הכי נמי אחריה ממש?! אלא – אחרי דבריה ואחרי עצתה, הכא נמי – אחרי דבריה ואחרי עצתה. א"ר אשי: ולמאי דקאמר רב נחמן מנוח עם הארץ היה – אפי' בי רב נמי לא קרא, שנאמר: "ותקם רבקה ונערותיה ותרכבנה על הגמלים ותלכנה אחרי האיש" ולא לפני האיש. א"ר יוחנן: אחורי ארי ולא אחורי אשה, אחורי אשה ולא אחורי עכו"ם, אחורי עכו"ם ולא אחורי בהכנ"ס בשעה שהצבור מתפללין. ולא אמרן אלא דלא דרי מידי, ואי דרי מידי – לית לן בה, ולא אמרן אלא דליכא פתחא אחרינא, ואי איכא פתחא אחרינא – לית לן בה, ולא אמרן אלא דלא רכיב חמרא, אבל רכיב חמרא – לית לן בה, ולא אמרן אלא דלא מנח תפילין, אבל מנח תפילין – לית לן בה.§ אמר רב: יצר הרע דומה לזבוב, ויושב בין שני מפתחי הלב, שנא' "זבובי מות יבאיש יביע שמן רוקח". ושמואל אמר: כמין חטה הוא דומה, שנאמר: "לפתח חטאת רובץ". ת"ר: שתי כליות יש בו באדם, אחת יועצתו לטובה ואחת יועצתו לרעה. ומסתברא דטובה לימינו ורעה לשמאלו, דכתיב "לב חכם לימינו ולב כסיל לשמאלו".§ תנו רבנן: *כליות יועצות, לב מבין, לשון מחתך, פה גומר, ושט מכניס ומוציא כל מיני מאכל, קנה מוציא קול ריאה

וכל העובר אחרי אשה בנהר אין לו חלק לעוה"ב. פי': אם רגיל בכך, לפי שיבא לידי ניאוף וסופו יורד לגיהנם: אלא מעתה גבי אלקנה דכתיב וילך אלקנה אחרי אשתו וגו'. שבוש הוא, שאין פסוק זה בכל המקרא, ול"ג ליה*: ר"ע

עא א מיי' פכ"א מהל' איסורי ביאה הל' כב סמג לאוין קכו טוש"ע אה"ע סי' כא סעיף א:
עב ב מיי' פ"ו מהלכות תפלה הל' א סמג עשין יט טוש"ע או"ח סי' צ סעיף ח:

עי' במהרש"ל הגירסא שהביא בשם ילקוט פ' שופטים [עמ"ש בס"ד או"ח על הגליון בעירובין יח:]

קהלת ה | בראשית ב | תהלים קלט | [עירובין יח.] | בראשית ב | [פי' הערוך גוף] | [תענית טו: ע"ש] | ויקרא י | [בתענית איתא פסוק אחר] | בראשית ז | שם ה | שם ט | שם ב | משלי יא | שופטים יג | מלכים ב ד | בראשית כד | לעיל ח: | קהלת י | בראשית ד | קהלת י

עין משפט נר מצוה

עג א מיי' פ"ה מהל' יסודי התורה הל' ז סמג עשין ג:

עד ב מיי' פ"ז מהלכות בית הבחירה הל' ה:

עה ג שם הלכה ח:

עו ד מיי' שם הלכה ט טוש"ע או"ח סימן ג סעיף ה:

מסורת הש"ס

שואבת כל מיני משקין. אע"פ שהן נכנסין בכרס דרך הושט, הריאה מוללתן ושואבתן מבעד לדופני הכרס: זורקת בו טפה. מרה, ומניחתו מן הכעס: שוחק. שחוק: קרקבן. בעוף, הוא המסס בבהמה: טוחן. המאכל: אף. החוטם: נעור. מקיצו משנתו: נעור הישן וישן הנעור. שנתחלפה ובאה השינה מן האף והקיבה נעורת: נמוק והולך לו. מתנונה והולך לו ונמשך למיתה. לשון אחר: נעור הישן – הקיבה, ונמצאו קיבה ואף נעורים שאינו ישן כלל. או ישן הנעור – ונמצאו שניהם ישנים, ואינו נעור כי אם בקושי: ולבי חלל בקרבי. יצר הרע הרי הוא כמת בקרבי, שיש בידי לכופו: נאם פשע לרשע וגו'. אמר דוד: בקרב לבי יש. ואומר אני שהפשע נאם לרשע. כלומר: שהיצר הרע אומר לרשע: אל יהא פחד אלהים לנגד עיניך. אלמא – יצר הרע שופטו, עד שמרחיקו שאינו מתפחד מיוצרו: כי יעמוד. הקב"ה: לימין אביון להושיע משופטי נפשו. ש"מ: יש לך אדם שיש לנפשו שני שופטים: לא שבק מר חיי לכל בריה. אם אתה מן הבינונים – אין לך צדיק גמור בעולם: לרשיעי גמורי. העולם הזה, שאין להם בעולם הבא כלום, וצריכין ליטול שכרן כאן. כגון אחאב שהיה עשיר מאד, דקאמר ליה בן הדד "כספך וזהבך לי הוא" (מלכים א כ): לצדיקי גמורי העוה"ב. שאין להם בעוה"ז כלום, כגון רבי חנינא בן דוסא שדי לו בקב חרובין מערב שבת לערב שבת (*תענית כד:): לכך נאמר בכל מאדך. מן החביב עליך: והיה מקבל עליו עול מלכות שמים. קורא קריאת שמע: ממתים ידך יי' ממתים. מידך היה לו למות, ולא מידי בשר ודם: מן הצופים. מקום שיכולין לראות משם הר הבית, ומשם והלאה אין יכולין לראותו: וברואה. שיכול לראות משם, פרט אם מקום נמוך הוא: ובשאין גדר. מפסיק בינו להר הבית: ובזמן שהשכינה שורה. שבית המקדש קיים: הנפנה ביהודה לא יפנה מזרח ומערב. אחוריו למזרח ופניו למערב, ולא אחוריו למערב ופניו למזרח, מפני שירושלים בארץ יהודה היא בצפונה של ארץ יהודה, בגבול שבין יהודה לבנימין, ויש מארץ יהודה הימנה [למזרח] עד סוף ארץ ישראל והימנה למערב עד סוף ארץ ישראל, שארץ יהודה על פני כל אורך ארץ ישראל היא מן המזרח למערב כרלועה ארוכה וקצרה. ואם יפנה מזרח ומערב יהיה פרועו לצד ירושלים, או פרועו שלפניו או פרועו שלאחריו. אבל צפון ודרום – יפנה, ובלבד שלא יפנה כנגד ירושלים ממש, בדרומה של ארץ יהודה: ובגליל. שהיא בצפונה של א"י, לא יחזיר פניו לצפון ולדרום אלא מזרח ומערב: ה"ג: וחכמים אוסרין. ולא גרסינן: בכל מקום: חכמים היינו ת"ק. דאמר: לא יפנה, ולא מפליג בין רואה ללא רואה בין בזמן הבית בין בזמן הזה: איכא בינייהו צדדים. דיהודה וגליל, שאינן כנגד ירושלים ממש. לתנא קמא – לדדין נמי אסירי, דהא הנפנה ביהודה קאמר, כל יהודה משמע. ורבנן בתראי סברי: כנגד ירושלים ממש אסור, אבל לצדדין מותר. דהא אדר' יוסי קיימי, דאמר לא אסרו אלא ברואה, אבל ברחוק לא, ואפילו כנגד ירושלים ממש. ואתו רבנן למימר: וחכמים אוסרים, אפילו שלא ברואה ואפילו בזמן הזה ומיהו נגד ירושלים לא: בדר' עקיבא גרסינן בכל מקום, הלכך בחוצה לארץ נמי קאמר: הוו שדיין ליה לבני. לבנים שישב עליהן לפנות היו מתוקנים וזקופות על לדיהן ראשון א' למזרח והשני למערב, לבנה אחת לצפון ולבנה אחת לדרום, והוא יושב על האחת ונפנה בינתים, נמצא הוא נפנה צפון ודרום. ולא היה רוצה לפנות בבבל מזרח ומערב לפי שבבל במזרחה של ארץ ישראל עומדת, שלא יהא פרועו לא מלפניו ולא מלאחריו לצד ארץ ישראל: אזל אביי שדנהו צפון ודרום. לראות אם יקפיד רבו על כך, אי סבירא ליה כר"ע דאמר בחו"ל נמי קפדינן עלה דמילתא:

אחר

תורה אור

ריאה שואבת כל מיני משקין, כבד כועס, מרה זורקת בו טפה ומניחתו, טחול שוחק, קרקבן טוחן, קיבה ישנה, אף נעור. נעור הישן, ישן הנעור – נמוק והולך לו. תנא: אם שניהם ישנים או שניהם נעורים – מיד מת.§ תניא, רבי יוסי הגלילי אומר: צדיקים יצר טוב שופטן, שנאמר: °"ולבי חלל בקרבי". (תהלים קט) רשעים – יצר רע שופטן, שנאמר: °"נאם פשע לרשע בקרב לבי אין פחד אלהים לנגד עיניו", (שם לו) בינונים – זה וזה שופטן, שנאמר: °"יעמד לימין אביון להושיע משפטי נפשו". (שם קט) אמר *רבא: כגון אנו בינונים. אמר ליה אביי: לא שביק מר חיי לכל בריה! ואמר רבא: לא איברי עלמא אלא לרשיעי גמורי או לצדיקי גמורי. אמר רבא: לידע אינש בנפשיה אם צדיק גמור הוא אם לאו. אמר רב: לא איברי עלמא אלא לאחאב בן עמרי ולר' חנינא בן דוסא. לאחאב בן עמרי – העולם הזה, ולרבי חנינא בן דוסא – העולם הבא.§ "ואהבת את י"י אלהיך". *תניא, ר' אליעזר אומר: אם נאמר "בכל נפשך" למה נאמר "בכל מאדך"? ואם נאמר "בכל מאדך" למה נאמר "בכל נפשך"? אלא: אם יש לך אדם שגופו חביב עליו מממונו – לכך נאמר "בכל נפשך", ואם יש לך אדם שממונו חביב עליו מגופו – לכך נאמר "בכל מאדך". *רבי עקיבא אומר: "בכל נפשך" – *אפילו נוטל את נפשך. תנו רבנן: פעם אחת גזרה מלכות הרשעה שלא יעסקו ישראל בתורה, בא פפוס בן יהודה ומצאו לרבי עקיבא שהיה מקהיל קהלות ברבים ועוסק בתורה. אמר ליה: עקיבא, אי אתה מתירא מפני מלכות? אמר לו: אמשול לך משל, למה הדבר דומה – לשועל שהיה מהלך על גב הנהר, וראה דגים שהיו מתקבצים ממקום למקום, אמר להם: מפני מה אתם בורחים? אמרו לו: מפני רשתות שמביאין עלינו בני אדם. אמר להם: רצונכם שתעלו ליבשה, ונדור אני ואתם כשם שדרו אבותי עם אבותיכם? אמרו לו: אתה הוא שאומרים עליך פקח שבחיות?! לא פקח אתה, אלא טפש אתה! ומה במקום חיותנו אנו מתיראין, במקום מיתתנו על אחת כמה וכמה! אף אנחנו, עכשיו שאנו יושבים ועוסקים בתורה, שכתוב בה °"כי הוא חייך וארך ימיך" (דברים ל) – כך, אם אנו הולכים ומבטלים ממנה – עאכ"ו. אמרו: לא היו ימים מועטים עד שתפסוהו לר"ע וחבשוהו בבית האסורים, ותפסו לפפוס בן יהודה וחבשוהו אצלו. אמר לו: פפוס! מי הביאך לכאן? אמר ליה: אשריך רבי עקיבא שנתפסת על דברי תורה, אוי לו לפפוס שנתפס על דברים בטלים. בשעה שהוציאו את ר' עקיבא להריגה זמן ק"ש היה, והיו סורקים את בשרו במסרקות של ברזל, והיה מקבל עליו עול מלכות שמים. אמרו לו תלמידיו: רבינו, עד כאן?! אמר להם: כל ימי הייתי מצטער על פסוק זה "בכל נפשך" – אפילו נוטל את נשמתך, אמרתי: מתי יבא לידי ואקיימנו, ועכשיו שבא לידי לא אקיימנו?! היה מאריך ב"אחד" עד שיצתה נשמתו ב"אחד". יצתה ב"ק ואמרה: אשריך ר"ע שיצאה נשמתך ב"אחד". אמרו מלאכי השרת לפני הקב"ה: זו *תורה וזו שכרה? °"ממתים ידך י"י ממתים וגו'"! (תהלים יז) – אמר להם: "חלקם בחיים". יצתה בת קול ואמרה: אשריך ר"ע *שאתה מזומן לחיי העוה"ב.§ "לא יקל אדם את ראשו כנגד שער המזרח שהוא מכוון כנגד בית קדשי הקדשים וכו'". אמר רב יהודה אמר רב: לא אמרו אלא מן הצופים ולפנים, וברואה. איתמר נמי, א"ר אבא בריה דרבי חייא בר אבא, הכי אמר רבי יוחנן: לא אמרו אלא מן הצופים ולפנים, וברואה, ובשאין גדר, ובזמן שהשכינה שורה. ת"ר: הנפנה ביהודה לא יפנה מזרח ומערב אלא צפון ודרום, ובגליל לא יפנה אלא מזרח ומערב. ורבי יוסי מתיר, שהיה ר' יוסי אומר: לא אסרו אלא ברואה, ובמקום שאין שם גדר, ובזמן שהשכינה שורה. וחכמים אוסרים. חכמים היינו ת"ק! –איכא בינייהו צדדין. תניא אידך: הנפנה ביהודה לא יפנה מזרח ומערב אלא צפון ודרום, ובגליל – צפון ודרום אסור, מזרח ומערב מותר. ורבי יוסי מתיר, שהיה רבי יוסי אומר: לא אסרו אלא ברואה. רבי יהודה אומר: בזמן שבית המקדש קיים – אסור, בזמן שאין בית המקדש קיים – מותר. רבי עקיבא אוסר בכל מקום. רבי עקיבא היינו ת"ק! –איכא בינייהו חוץ לארץ. רבה הוו שדיין ליה לבני מזרח ומערב, אזל אביי שדנהו צפון ודרום, על רבה תרצנהו. אמר: מאן האי דקמצער לי? אנא כר' עקיבא סבירא לי, דאמר: בכל מקום אסור.§

תניא

[לעיל יז:]

[בע"י ובילקוט איתא והוא נכון לפמ"ש עירובין ה. ד"ה והא אמר אביי מר חבירו]

פסחים כה. סנהדרין עד. יומא פב.

[ובילקוט רמז תתל"ד ר' עקיבא אומר נאמר בכל נפשך בכל מאדך אלא מדה ומדה שהוא לך בין במדת הטוב במדת הפורענות]

[מנחות כט:]

[עי' תוס' כתובות קג: מזומן וכו']

רבי עקיבא אוסר בכל מקום. מזרח אחוריו ופניו למערב, ומסקינן אפילו בחוץ לארץ ומפרש בירושלמי ובלבד שאין שם כותל: רבה

*תניא, אמר רבי עקיבא: פעם אחת נכנסתי אחר ר' יהושע לבית הכסא, ולמדתי ממנו ג' דברים: למדתי שאין נפנין מזרח ומערב אלא צפון ודרום, אולמדתי שאין נפרעין מעומד אלא מיושב, בולמדתי שאין מקנחין בימין אלא בשמאל. אמר ליה בן עזאי: עד כאן העזת פניך ברבך! -א"ל: *תורה היא וללמוד אני צריך. תניא, בן עזאי אומר: פעם אחת נכנסתי אחר רבי עקיבא לבית הכסא, ולמדתי ממנו ג' דברים: למדתי שאין נפנין מזרח ומערב אלא צפון ודרום, ולמדתי שאין נפרעין מעומד אלא מיושב, ולמדתי שאין מקנחין בימין אלא בשמאל. אמר לו ר' יהודה: עד כאן העזת פניך ברבך! -אמר לו: תורה היא וללמוד אני צריך. רב כהנא על, גנא תותיה פורייה דרב. שמעיה דשח ושחק ועשה צרכיו, אמר ליה: *דמי פומיה דאבא כדלא שריף תבשילא! א"ל: כהנא, הכא את? פוק, דלאו ארח ארעא. אמר לו: תורה היא וללמוד אני צריך.§ *מפני מה אין מקנחין בימין אלא בשמאל? אמר רבא: מפני שהתורה ניתנה בימין, שנאמר: °מימינו אש דת למו. רבה בר בר חנה אמר: מפני שהיא קרובה לפה. ור' שמעון בן לקיש אמר: מפני שקושר בה תפילין. רב נחמן בר יצחק אמר: מפני שמראה בה טעמי תורה. כתנאי, רבי אליעזר אומר: מפני שאוכל בה. ר' יהושע אומר: מפני שכותב בה. ר' עקיבא אומר: מפני שמראה בה טעמי תורה. א"ר תנחום בר חנילאי: כל הצנוע בבית הכסא נצול משלשה דברים: מן הנחשים, ומן העקרבים, ומן המזיקין. ויש אומרים: אף חלומותיו מיושבים עליו. ההוא בית הכסא דהוה בטבריא, כי הוו עיילי ביה בי תרי אפי' ביממא מתזקי, רבי אמי ורבי אסי הוו עיילי ביה חד וחד לחודיה ולא מתזקי. אמרי להו רבנן: לא מסתפיתו? -אמרי להו: אנן קבלה גמירינן, קבלה דבית הכסא - צניעותא ושתיקותא, קבלה דיסורי - שתיקותא ומבעי רחמי. אביי מרביא ליה [אמיה] אמרא למיעל בהדיה לבית הכסא. ולרביא ליה גדיא! - שעיר בשעיר מיחלף. רבא, מקמי דהוי רישא - מקרקשא ליה בת רב חסדא אמגוזא בלקנא, בתר דמלך - עבדא ליה כוותא, ומנחא ליה ידא ארישיה. אמר עולא: גאחורי הגדר - נפנה מיד, ובבקעה - כל זמן שמתעטש ואין חברו שומע. איסי בר נתן מתני הכי, [ג'] אחורי הגדר - כל זמן שמתעטש ואין חברו שומע, דובבקעה - כל זמן שאין חברו רואהו. מיתיבי: *היוצאין מפתח בית הבד ונפנין לאחורי הגדר והן טהורין! -בטהרות הקלו. ת"ש: *כמה ירחקו ויהיו טהורין - כדי שיהא רואהו! -שאני אוכלי טהרות, דאקילו בהו רבנן. רב אשי אמר: ומאי "כל זמן שאין חברו רואה" דקאמר איסי בר נתן - כל זמן שאין חברו רואה את פרועו, אבל לדידיה חזי ליה. ההוא ספדנא דנחית קמיה דרב נחמן, אמר: האי צנוע באורחותיו הוה. א"ל רב נחמן: את עיילת בהדיה לבית הכסא, וידעת אי צנוע אי לא? דתניא: אין קורין צנוע - אלא למי שצנוע בבית הכסא. ורב נחמן, מאי נפקא ליה מיניה? -משום דתניא: *כשם שנפרעין מן המתים - כך נפרעין מן הספדנין ומן העונין אחריהן.§ *תנו רבנן: איזהו צנוע - זה הנפנה בלילה במקום שנפנה ביום. איני?! *והאמר רב יהודה אמר רב: טלעולם ינהיג אדם את עצמו שחרית וערבית, כדי שלא יהא צריך להתרחק! ותו, רבא ביממא הוה אזיל עד מיל, ובליליא א"ל לשמעיה: פנו לי דוכתא ברחובה דמתא. וכן אמר ליה רבי זירא לשמעיה: חזי מאן דאיכא אחורי בית חבריא, דבעינא למפני! -לא תימא 'במקום' אלא אימא "כדרך שנפנה ביום". רב אשי אמר: אפילו תימא 'במקום' - לא נצרכה אלא לקרן זוית. גופא, אמר רב יהודה אמר רב: לעולם ינהיג אדם את עצמו שחרית וערבית, כדי שלא יהא צריך להתרחק. תניא נמי הכי, בן עזאי אומר: השכם וצא, הערב וצא, כדי שלא תתרחק. משמש ושב, ואל תשב ותמשמש, שכל היושב וממשמש - אפי' עושין כשפים באספמיא - באין עליו. ואי אנשי ויתיב ואח"כ משמש, מאי תקנתיה? -כי קאי לימא הכי: לא לי לא לי, לא תחים ולא תחתים, לא הני ולא מהני, לא חרשי דחרשא ולא חרשי דחרשתא.§

תניא

---

אחר רבי יהושע וכו'. וביהודה הוה: עד כאן. כלומר: כל זה העזת פניך בפני רבך, שנסתכלת בכל אלו: דשח ושחק. עם אשתו, שיחה בטלה של ריצוי תשמיש: ועשה צרכיו. ושימש מטתו: כדלא שריף תבשילא. כאדם רעב, כמו שלא שמשת מטתך מעולם שאתה נוהג קלות ראש זה לתאותך: שריף. הומי"ר בלע"ז: שקרובה לפה. רגילין להושיטה לפה: שקושר בה תפילין. בזרוע שמאלו: טעמי תורה. נגינות טעמי מקרא של תורה נביאים וכתובים, בין בניקוד שבספר בין בהגבהת קול ובגלגול נעימות הנגינה של פשטא ודרגא ושופר מהפך, מוליך ידו לפי טעם הנגינה, ראיתי בקוראים הבאים מארץ ישראל: מן הנחשים ומן העקרבים ומן המזיקין. דמתוך צניעותו מתנהג בנחת ובשתיקה, ואין הנחשים מרגישים להתקנאות בו. ואף המזיקין חסין עליו: חלומותיו מיושבין עליו. שאין המזיקין מבהילין אותו: קבלה. מסורת ומנהג שקבלנו מרבותינו בבית הכסא: קבלה דיסורי שתיקותא. שלא יבעט ביסורין הבאים עליו: מרביה ליה אימרא. מגדלת לו שה, ומלמדתו שהולך עמו תמיד: שעיר. שד של בית הכסא דומה לשעיר, ועליהם נאמר (ישעיה יג) "ושעירים ירקדו שם": אמגוזא בלקנא. נותנת אגוז בספל של נחשת ומקרקשת בו מבית, והוא נפנה כנגדה מבחוץ: בתר דמלך. ונעשה ראש ישיבה צריך שימור טפי מפני המזיקים. *שמתקנאים השדים בתלמידי חכמים יותר משאר בני אדם: כוותא. חלון, כנגד מקום שהוא נפנה שם אחורי הבית: אחורי הגדר נפנה מיד. ואין צריך להתרחק כלום: ובבקעה. צריך להתרחק כדי שלא ישמע חברו עטושים של מטה. אבל אין צריך להתרחק עד כדי שלא יראהו: רב אשי אמר וכו'. לא גרסינן עד לקמן דמוקי לאיסי בר נתן בהכי: יוצאין מפתח בית הבד. משמרי טהרות של שמן בית הבד, אם הוצרכו לפנות יוצאים מפתח בית הבד ונפנין לאחורי הגדר שלפני הפתח, ואין חוששין שמא בתוך כך יכנס עם הארץ ויגע, אלמא: נפנין לאחורי הגדר מיד: בטהרות הקלו. בשביל שמירת טהרות הקלו בבית הכסא: כמה ירחקו. שומרי טהרות: כדי שיהא רואהו. וכיון דאינו יכול להתרחק יותר, על כרחך אם הוצרך לפנות - יפנה, תיובתא דאיסי דבעי שלא יראנו: דאקילו בהו רבנן. בשביל שמירתן הקלו בבית הכסא: אבל לדידיה חזי ליה. אבל הוא עצמו את חברו יכול לראות, ולא ירחיק: במקום שנפנה ביום. מתרחק מבני אדם בלילה כביום: ינהיג אדם עצמו. לפנות: שחרית. קודם היום: וערבית. משחשכה: כדי שלא יהא צריך להתרחק. אלמא: אין מתרחקין בלילה: פנו לי דוכתא. מבני אדם: כדרך שנפנה ביום. לענין פרוע טפח וטפחיים, כדאמרינן בפרקי קמאי (פ"ג ד' כג:) ומיושב כדאמרינן לעיל: לקרן זוית. אם יש קרן זוית סמוך צריך להסתפק שם בלילה כביום, ולא יפנה בגלוי: משמש. בצרור או בקיסם לפתוח נקבים, כדאמרינן במסכת שבת (ד' פב.). לשון אחר: משמש מושב שלא יהא מלוכלך. ולשון ראשון הגון, דאח"כ למה לי משום כשפים? תיפוק לי כיון שישב כבר מלוכלכים בגדיו, ומה יועיל משמושו? לא לי לא לי. לא תוכלו לי: לא תחים ולא תחתים. הם שמות הכשפים העשויים ע"י תחבולות: לא הני ולא מהני. לא כולן ולא מקצתן: לא חרשי דחרשא ולא חרשי דחרשתא. ולא מכשפות מכשף זכר, ולא מכשפות מכשפה נקבה. לשון אחר: לא הני ולא מהני = לא יצלח ולא יועיל עוד מכשפות:

על

---

**רבא** מקמי דהוה רישא כו' בתר דמלך עבדה ליה כוותא ומנחא ליה ידא כו'. תימה: דע"כ לא מלך רבא עד אחר פטירתו של אביי, כדמשמע לעיל *בעובדא דבר הדיא, וכן בכתובות דקאמר: חומה דביתהו דאביי אתיא לקמיה דרבא, בסוף פרק אע"פ (ד' סה.). וזהו תימה, דלעיל (ד' נו.) משמע דראה בחלום פטירתה קודם פטירתו דאביי! וי"ל: מכל מקום לא נפטרה עד אחר אביי:

סליקו תוספות דמסכת ברכות

---

עז א מיי' פ"ה מהלכות דעות הלכה ו טוש"ע או"ח סי' ג סעיף ב:
עח ב מיי' שם טוש"ע שם סעיף י:
ג ד טוש"ע שם סעיף ח:
עט [ג ד מיי' שם]:
פ ה ו מיי' פי"ג מהל' טומאת משכב ומושב הלכה ב:
פא ז מיי' פ"ה מהלכות דעות הל' ו טוש"ע או"ח סי' ג סעיף ח:
פב ח טוש"ע י"ד סימן שדמ סעיף א [וברא"ש פ"ג דמ"ק סי' קי]:
פג ט מיי' פ"ה מהלכות דעות הל' ו טוש"ע או"ח סי' ב סעי' ו בהגה:
פד י מיי' שם טוש"ע או"ח סי' ג סעיף יב:

---

ד"א פ"ז
[מגילה כח.]
חגיגה ה:
[לעיל כד:]
דברים לג
פ"י מ"ב
שם
[ע"ז מז:]
[הוריות יג:]
[אדר"נ פ"מ וכד"א פ"ז]
[נו.]
[פי' כשם שנפרעין מן המת אם הוא חוטא כך נפרעין מן הספדנין שאומרים עליו שהוא צדיק. ערוך]

תניא, בן עזאי אומר: על כל משכב שכב – חוץ מן הקרקע, על כל מושב שב – חוץ מן הקורה. אמר שמואל: *שינה בעמוד השחר – כאסטמא לפרזלא, יציאה בעמוד השחר – כאסטמא לפרזלא. בר קפרא הוה מזבן מילי בדינרי: עד *דכפנת – אכול, עד דצחית – שתי, עד דרתחא קדרך – שפוך. קרנא קריא ברומי – בר מזבין תאני, תאני דאבוך זבין! אמר להו אביי לרבנן: כי עייליתו בשבילי דמחוזא למיפק ביה בחקלא, לא תחזו לא להך גיסא ולא להך גיסא, דלמא יתבי נשי ולאו אורח ארעא לאסתכולי בהו. *רב ספרא על לבית הכסא, אתא רבי אבא נחר ליה אבבא, אמר ליה: ליעול מר! בתר דנפק, אמר ליה: עד השתא לא עיילת לשעיר, וגמרת לך מילי דשעיר?! לאו הכי תנן: *מדורה היתה שם, ובית הכסא של כבוד, וזה היה כבודו: מצאו נעול – בידוע שיש שם אדם, מצאו פתוח – בידוע שאין שם אדם, אלמא: לאו אורח ארעא הוא! –והוא סבר: מסוכן הוא, *דתניא, רבן שמעון בן גמליאל אומר: עמוד החוזר – מביא את האדם לידי הדרוקן. סילון החוזר – מביא את האדם לידי ירקון. רבי אלעזר על לבית הכסא, אתא

ההוא *רומאה דחקיה, קם ר' אלעזר ונפק. אתא דרקונא שמטיה לכרכשיה, קרי עליה רבי אלעזר: °"ואתן אדם תחתיך" °אל תקרי "אדם" אלא אדום.§ °"ואמר להרגך ותחס עליך", "ואמר"?! "ואמרתי" מיבעי ליה! "ותחס"?! "וחסתי" מיבעי ליה! – אמר רבי אלעזר, אמר לו דוד לשאול: מן התורה – בן הריגה אתה, שהרי רודף אתה, *והתורה אמרה: בא להרגך השכם להרגו. אלא, צניעות שהיתה בך – היא חסה עליך, ומאי היא – דכתיב °"ויבא אל גדרות הצאן על הדרך ושם מערה ויבא שאול להסך את רגליו". תנא: גדר לפנים מן גדר, ומערה לפנים ממערה. °"להסך" – אמר ר' אלעזר: מלמד שסיכך עצמו כסוכה. °"ויקם דוד ויכרת את כנף המעיל אשר לשאול בלט" אמר ר' יוסי בר' חנינא: כל המבזה את הבגדים סוף אינו נהנה מהם, שנאמר: °"והמלך דוד זקן בא בימים ויכסהו בבגדים ולא יחם לו".§ °"אם ה' הסיתך בי ירח מנחה" אמר רבי אלעזר: אמר ליה הקב"ה לדוד: 'מסית' קרית לי? הרי אני מכשילך בדבר שאפי' תינוקות של בית רבן יודעים אותו, דכתיב °"כי תשא את ראש בני ישראל לפקדיהם ונתנו איש כפר נפשו וגו'". מיד °"ויעמד שטן על ישראל", וכתיב °"ויסת את דוד בהם לאמר לך מנה את ישראל". וכיון דמנינהו לא שקל מינייהו כופר, דכתיב °"ויתן ה' דבר בישראל מהבקר ועד עת מועד" מאי "עת מועד"? –אמר שמואל סבא חתניה דרבי חנינא משמיה דרבי חנינא: משעת שחיטת התמיד עד שעת זריקתו. רבי יוחנן אמר: עד חצות ממש. °"ויאמר למלאך המשחית בעם רב" אמר רבי אלעזר, אמר ליה הקב"ה למלאך: טול לי רב שבהם, שיש בו ליפרע מהם כמה חובות. באותה שעה מת אבישי בן צרויה ששקול כרובה של סנהדרין.§ °"ובהשחית ראה ה' וינחם", מאי ראה? אמר רב: ראה יעקב אבינו, דכתיב °"ויאמר יעקב כאשר ראם". ושמואל אמר: אפרו של יצחק ראה, שנאמר: °"אלהים יראה לו השה". רבי יצחק נפחא אמר: כסף כפורים ראה, שנאמר: °"ולקחת את כסף הכפורים מאת בני ישראל וגו'". רבי יוחנן אמר: בית המקדש ראה, דכתיב °"בהר ה' יראה". פליגי בה ר' יעקב בר אידי ורבי שמואל בר נחמני, חד אמר: כסף הכפורים ראה, וחד אמר: בית המקדש ראה. ומסתברא כמאן דאמר בית המקדש ראה, שנאמר: °"אשר יאמר היום בהר ה' יראה".§ "לא יכנס אדם להר הבית במקלו וכו'". *מאי קפנדריא? אמר רבא: קפנדריא כשמה. ורב חנא בר אדא משמיה דרב סמא בריה דרב מרי אמר: כמאן דאמר אינש "אדמקיפנא אדרי – איעול בהא". אמר רב נחמן אמר רבה בר אבוה: [א]הנכנס לבית הכנסת על מנת שלא לעשותו קפנדריא – מותר לעשותו קפנדריא. רבי אבהו אמר: [ב]אם היה שביל מעיקרו – מותר. אמר ר' חלבו אמר רב הונא: [ג]הנכנס לבית הכנסת להתפלל – מותר [א] לעשותו קפנדריא שנאמר: °"ובבא עם הארץ לפני ה' במועדים וגו'".§ "ורקיקה מקל וחומר". אמר רב ביבי אמר ר' יהושע בן לוי: [ד]כל הרוקק בהר הבית בזמן הזה – כאילו רוקק בבת עינו, שנאמר: °"והיו עיני ולבי שם כל הימים". אמר רבא: רקיקה בבית הכנסת – שריא, מידי דהוה אמנעל. מה מנעל, בהר הבית – אסור, בבית הכנסת – מותר, אף רקיקה – בהר הבית הוא דאסור, בבית הכנסת שרי. אמר ליה רב פפא לרבא, ואמרי לה רבינא לרבא, ואמרי לה רב אדא בר מתנא לרבא: אדיליף ממנעל, נילף מקפנדריא! –אמר ליה: תנא יליף ממנעל, ואת אמרת מקפנדריא! מאי היא? דתניא: [ה]*לא יכנס אדם להר הבית לא במקלו שבידו, ולא במנעלו שברגלו, *ולא במעות הצרורים לו בסדינו, ובפונדתו מופשלת לאחוריו, ולא יעשנה קפנדריא, ורקיקה מקל וחומר ממנעל, ומה מנעל שאין בו דרך בזיון *אמרה תורה °"של נעליך מעל רגליך" רקיקה שהיא דרך בזיון – לא כל שכן. רבי יוסי בר יהודה אומר: אינו צריך, הרי הוא אומר °"כי אין לבוא אל שער המלך בלבוש שק", והלא דברים קל וחומר: ומה שק שאינו מאוס לפני בשר ודם – כך, רקיקה שהיא מאוסה, לפני מלך מלכי המלכים – לא כל שכן? –אמר ליה: אנא הכי קאמינא: נימא הכא לחומרא והכא לחומרא, ואימא

**רש"י**

על כל מושב שב חוץ מן הקורה. שמא תפול: **כאסטמא לפרזלא.** אליי"ר בלע"ז, שמועיל לברזל, כך מועיל לגוף יציאה להפנות: **אדכפנת אכול.** שאם תשהה תעבור ממך תאות המאכל, ואין המאכל מועיל: **עד דרתחא קדרך שפוך.** קודם שתצטנן, משל הוא זה: כשאתה צריך לנקביך – שפוך, ואל תשהה אותם: **קרנא קריא ברומי.** אם תשמע קול קרן ברומי, הוא סימן למבקשי תאנים לקנות ולהוליך למקום אחר: **בר מזבין תאני, תאני דאבוך זבין.** אם אין אביך בבית – הזהר אתה בנו למכור תאניו בעוד שיש תובעים: **בשבילי.** שביל קטן שפונים בו לשדות: **נחר ליה אבבא.** לידע אם יש שם אדם. נחר = טוסי"ר בלע"ז: **אמר ליה.** ר' אבא לרב ספרא: **עד כאן לא עיילת לשעיר.** שאינן צנועין בבית הכסא: **וגמרת לך מילי דשעיר.** שאינך צנוע: **לאו הכי תנן.** במסכת תמיד: **מדורה היתה שם.** בעזרה, היסק גדול של אור להתחמם שם הכהנים המסיכים רגליהם בבית הכסא, שצריכין טבילה, כדתנן במסכת יומא (ד' כח.): כל המסיך [ב] רגליו טעון טבילה: **ובית הכסא של כבוד.** אלמא: אין מספרים בבית הכסא, ואת אמרת: ליעול מר! **והוא סבר.** רב ספרא שמהר לומר: ליעול מר, סבר מסוכן הוא בעמוד החוזר, אם ישוב לאחוריו ויחזור העמוד: **הדרוקן.** כרסו נפה:

**דרקונא.** נחש: **שמטיה לכרכשיה.** חלחולת שהרעי יוצא בו, שקורין טבחיא: **ואמר להרגך ותחס עליך.** דוד אמר לשאול כן בצאתו מן המערה שנכנס בה לפנות, וכרת דוד את כנף מעילו. ואמר להרגך – הקב"ה התיר לי להרגך: **התורה אמרה וכו'.** "אם במחתרת ימצא הגנב" וגו' (שמות כב), וכבר פירשנוהו למעלה במעשה דר' שילא (ד' נח.): **צניעות שראיתי בך.** שנכנס למערה בשביל הצנע, ואף שם נהג צניעות, כדמפרש ואזיל: **שסכך רגליו.** בבגדיו כסוכה: **שיש בו ליפרע כמה.** שיש במיתתו כדי לכפר על כמה עונות: **ובהשחית ראה ה' וינחם.** מקרא הוא באותה פרשה בדברי הימים: **כסף כפורים ראה.** שנתן במנין ראשון של ישראל למשכן, והוא כפר על מנין זה. שהרי לזכרון נתן, כדכתיב: "והיה לבני ישראל לזכרון לכפר", ועכשיו הוצרכו כפרתו: **כשמה.** כמשמעה, פירוש שמה: **אדמקיפנא אדרי איעול בהא.** בעוד שאני מקיף כל שורות הבתים הללו אכנס כאן, לקצר דרכי: **אדרי.** שורות: **קפנדריא.** טרי"א בלע"ז: **מעיקרא.** קודם שנבנה עליו בית הכנסת: **נילף מקפנדריא.** לאיסורא, דתנן במסכת מגילה (ד' כח.): אין עושין בית הכנסת קפנדריא: **תנא יליף.** רקיקה ממנעל: **פונדתו.** אזור חלול שנותנין בו מעות: **ואימא**

**עין משפט נר מצוה**

פה א ב (ליתא ברמב"ם) ג מיי' פי"א מהל' תפלה הלכה י סמג עשין יט טוש"ע או"ח סי' קנא סעיף ה:

פו ד מיי' פ"ז מהלכות בית הבחירה הלכה ז סמג עשין קסד:

פז ה מיי' שם הלכה ב:

**הגהות הגר"א**

[א] שם הנכנס לבהכ"נ להתפלל מותר. נ"ב גירסת הרי"ף מצוה וכן הרא"ש במגילה.

[ב] רש"י ד"ה כל המיסך כו' אלמא אין כו'. נ"ב וצ"ע למה לא פירש כמ"ש בתמיד למיחמה לגא כו'.

**גליון הש"ס**

גמ' אל תקרי אדם. עי' יבמות ס"א ע"א תוס' ד"ה ואין.

**מסורת הש"ס**

[עי' בערוך ערך אסטמא ועי' עוד במוסף הערוך ערך פן ו' שפירש השתנה מלשון אם שוניהם מלכים ב יח]

[בערוך ערך כפן הדברים אלו על דכן יפה ע"ש]

תורה אור

תמיד כז.

שם כו.

שם ולעיל כה. מד:]

[עי' תוספות ב"ק לח. ד"ה אלא] ישעיה מג

שמואל א כד

[לעיל נח. סנהדרין עב:] שמואל א כד

שם

שמואל א כו

מלכים א א

שמות ל

שמואל ב כד

דה"א כא

שם

שם

דה"א כא

בראשית לב

שם כב

בראשית כב

שמות ל

בראשית כב

שם

מגילה כט. ע"ש

יחזקאל מו

מלכים א ט

[תוספתא פ"ז]

[עי' תוס' ב"מ כו. ד"ה בכור ותוס' פסחים ז. ד"ה בכור]

שמות ג

[עי' תוספות חגיגה ד: ד"ה כי תבואו]

אסתר ד

ואימא: הר הבית דאסור במנעל - ליליפא ממנעל, אבל (ב"ה) דשרי במנעל, אדיליף ממנעל ולהיתר - נילף מקפנדריא ולאיסור! - אלא אמר *רבא: כי ביתו. מה ביתו, אקפנדריא - קפיד איניש, ארקיקה ומנעל - לא קפיד איניש, אף ב"ה: אקפנדריא הוא דאסור, רקיקה ומנעל שרי. § "כל חותמי ברכות שבמקדש וכו'". כל כך למה - לפי שאין עונין אמן במקדש. *ומנין שאין עונין אמן במקדש - שנאמר: "קומו ברכו את ה' אלהיכם מן העולם עד העולם". ואומר "ויברכו (את) שם כבודך ומרומם על כל ברכה ותהלה". יכול כל הברכות כולן תהא להן תהלה אחת - ת"ל "ומרומם על כל ברכה ותהלה", על כל ברכה וברכה - תן לו תהלה. § "התקינו שיהא אדם שואל בשלום חברו וכו'". *מאי "ואומר"? - וכי תימא: בעז מדעתיה דנפשיה קאמר - ת"ש "ה' עמך גבור החיל". וכי תימא: מלאך הוא דקאמר ליה לגדעון - ת"ש "אל תבוז כי זקנה אמך". ואומר "עת לעשות לה' הפרו תורתך". אמר רבא: האי קרא *מרישיה לסיפיה מדריש, מסיפיה לרישיה מדריש. מרישיה לסיפיה מדריש: "עת לעשות לה'" מאי טעם - משום "הפרו תורתך". מסיפיה לרישיה מדריש: "הפרו תורתך" מ"ט - משום "עת לעשות לה'". *תניא, הלל הזקן אומר: בשעת המכניסין - פזר, בשעת המפזרים - כנס. ואם ראית דור שהתורה חביבה עליו - פזר, שנאמר: "יש מפזר ונוסף עוד", ואם ראית דור שאין התורה חביבה עליו - כנס, שנאמר "עת לעשות לה' הפרו תורתך". דרש בר קפרא: זלת - *קבוץ קנה מינה, באתר דלית גבר - תמן הוי גבר. אמר אביי: ש"מ: *באתר דאית גבר - תמן לא תהוי גבר. פשיטא! - לא נצרכה אלא בששניהם שוין. דרש בר קפרא: איזוהי פרשה קטנה שכל גופי תורה תלוין בה - "בכל דרכיך דעהו והוא יישר ארחתיך". אמר רבא: אפילו לדבר עבירה. *דרש בר קפרא: לעולם ילמד אדם את בנו אומנות נקיה וקלה. מה היא? אמר רב חסדא: מחטא דתלמיותא. תניא, ר' אומר: לעולם אל ירבה אדם רעים בתוך ביתו, שנא' "איש רעים להתרועע". תניא, ר' אומר: אל ימנה אדם אפטרופוס בתוך ביתו, שאלמלי לא מינה פוטיפר את יוסף אפטרופוס בתוך ביתו - לא בא לאותו דבר. § תניא, *ר' אומר: למה נסמכה פרשת נזיר לפרשת סוטה - לומר לך *שכל הרואה סוטה בקלקולה יזיר עצמו מן היין. אמר חזקיה בריה דר' פרנך אמר רבי יוחנן: למה נסמכה פרשת סוטה לפרשת תרומות ומעשרות - לומר לך: כל שיש לו תרומות ומעשרות ואינו נותנן לכהן - סוף נצרך לכהן על ידי אשתו, שנאמר: "ואיש את קדשיו לו יהיו" וסמיך ליה "איש איש כי תשטה אשתו" וכתיב "והביא האיש את אשתו וגו'". ולא עוד אלא - סוף שנצרך להן, שנאמר: "ואיש את קדשיו לו יהיו". אמר רב נחמן בר יצחק: ואם נתנן - סוף מתעשר, שנאמר: "איש אשר יתן לכהן לו יהיה" - לו יהיה ממון הרבה. א"ר הונא בר ברכיה משום רבי אלעזר הקפר: כל המשתף שם שמים בצערו - כופלין לו פרנסתו, שנאמר: "והיה שדי בצריך וכסף תועפות לך". ר' שמואל בר נחמני אמר: פרנסתו מעופפת לו כצפור, שנאמר: "וכסף תועפות לך". א"ר טבי א"ר יאשיה: כל המרפה עצמו מדברי תורה - אין בו כח לעמוד ביום צרה, שנאמר: "התרפית ביום צרה צר כחכה". א"ר אמי בר מתנה אמר שמואל: ואפילו מצוה אחת, שנאמר: "התרפית" - מכל מקום. § אמר רב ספרא, ר' אבהו הוה משתעי: כשירד חנינא בן אחי רבי יהושע לגולה היה מעבר שנים וקובע חדשים בחוצה לארץ. שגרו אחריו שני ת"ח רבי יוסי בן כיפר ובן בנו של זכריה בן קבוטל. כיון שראה אותם, אמר להם: למה באתם? אמרו ליה: ללמוד תורה באנו. הכריז [עליהם]: אנשים הללו גדולי הדור הם, ואבותיהם שמשו בבית המקדש, כאותה ששנינו: *זכריה בן קבוטל אומר: הרבה פעמים קריתי לפניו בספר דניאל. התחיל הוא מטמא והם מטהרים, הוא אוסר והם מתירים. הכריז עליהם: אנשים הללו של שוא הם, של תהו הם. אמרו לו: כבר בנית - ואי אתה יכול לסתור, כבר גדרת - ואי אתה יכול לפרוץ. אמר להם: מפני מה אני מטמא ואתם מטהרים, אני אוסר ואתם מתירים? - אמרו לו: מפני שאתה מעבר שנים וקובע חדשים בחו"ל. - אמר להם: והלא עקיבא בן יוסף היה מעבר שנים וקובע חדשים בחו"ל? - אמרו לו: הנח רבי עקיבא, שלא הניח כמותו בארץ ישראל. א"ל: אף אני לא הנחתי כמותי בא"י. - אמרו לו: גדיים שהנחת נעשו תישים בעלי קרנים, והם שגרונו אצלך, וכן אמרו לנו: לכו ואמרו לו בשמנו: אם שומע - מוטב, ואם לאו - יהא בנדוי. ואמרו

תורה אור: נחמיה ט | שם | רות ב | שופטים ו | משלי כג | תהלים קיט | משלי יא | משלי ג | משלי יח | במדבר ה | שם | איוב כב | משלי כד

---

ואימא הר הבית דאסור במנעל. ילפינן רקיקה מיניה לאיסורא בקל וחומר, אבל בית הכנסת דשרי במנעל לא נילף רקיקה להתירא, דרקיקה מחמירא, אלא ילפינן מקפנדריא לאיסורא: ויברכו שם כבודך. "בשכמל"ו" עונים. והמברך אומר: "ברוך ה' אלהי ישראל מן העולם ועד העולם". מפרש בתוספתא שתקנו מן העולם ועד העולם להודיע שאין העוה"ז לפני העוה"ב כלום, אלא כפרוזדור לפני הטרקלין. כלומר: הנהיגו בברכותיו בעוה"ז כדי להיות רגילים לעוה"ב שכולו ארוך: תהלה אחת. שיענו פעם אחת: בשכמל"ו: על כל הברכות. בסוף ברכה אחרונה: וכי תימא בועז מדעתיה עבד. ולא גמרינן מיניה: תא שמע. דגמרינן ממלאך שאמר לגדעון: וכי תימא מלאך הוא דקאמר ליה לגדעון. כלומר: לא שאל בשלומו ולא ברכו, אלא בשליחות קאמר, מאת המקום לבשרו שהשכינה עמו, ולא גמרינן מיניה: תא שמע אל תבוז כי זקנה אמך. אל תבוז את בועז לאמר מדעתו עשה, אלא ללמוד מזקני ישראל כי יש לו על מי שיסמוך, שנאמר "עת לעשות לה'": מסיפיה לרישיה כו'. אם באת לדרשו למקרא זה יש לך לדרשו יפה בין בהתחלתו בין בהפוך: מרישיה לסיפיה: עת לעשות לה' משום הפרו. עתים הם לה' לעשות משפט פורעניות בעוברי רצונו - משום דהפרו תורתך: מסיפיה לרישיה. הפרו תורתו עושי רצונו, כגון אליהו בהר הכרמל (מלכים א יח) שהקריב בבמה בשעת איסור הבמות משום עת לעשות סייג וגדר בישראל לשמו של הקדוש ברוך הוא: בשעת המכניסים. שאין חכמי הדור מרבים תורה לתלמידים: פזר. אתה, לשנות לתלמידים: בשעת המפזרים. שהגדולים שבדור מרבילים תורה: כנס. אתה, ולא תטול שררה עליהם. דאף זו לכבוד שמים היא למחות במדת הענוה, וכתיב "עת לעשות לה' הפרו תורתך": ואם ראית דור שאין התורה חביבה עליו כנס. ואל תטיל דברי תורה לבזיון: הפרו תורתך. מלפזרה בשעה שהכנוס לשם שמים: הכי גרסינן: זלת קבוץ קנה מינה. אם ראית פרקמטיא בזול - קבוץ וקנה מינה ואסוף, שסופה להתייקר: פשיטא. הא דאמרי לה ליה פשיטא שלא יורה אדם הלכה בפני רבו! למה ליה לאביי למשמע מכללא: בששניהן שוין. אם באת במקום תלמיד חכם ואין גדול ממנו - אל תטול עטרה לדרוש במקומו: בכל דרכיך. אפילו לעבור עבירה: דעהו. תן לב אם לורך מלוה הוא, כגון אליהו בהר הכרמל - עבור עליה: מחטא דתלמיותא. ברוסי"ד שלגנבוי"ש, שהספירות עשויות שורות שורות כתלמי מענה: להתרועע. להתרוצץ: אפוטרופוס. מכניס ומוציא נכסיו: כל שיש לו תרומות ומעשרות ואינו נותנן לכהן סוף שנצרך לו על ידי אשתו. שעושית סוטה. ה"ג: ואיש את קדשיו לו יהיו וסמיך ליה איש איש כי תשטה אשתו וכתיב והביא האיש את אשתו: איש את קדשיו לו יהיו. שמעכב קדשיו אצלו ואינו נותנן לכהנים וללוים: סוף שנצרך להן. שנעשה עני, וצריך לבא ליטול מעשר עני: לו יהיו. לעצמו יצטרכו: המשתף שם שמים בצערו. שמברך על רעה "דיין האמת", או שמבקש רחמים מלפניו בצרכיו: בצריך. בצרכיך: תועפות. לשון כפילה, כדמתרגמינן "וכפלת" - ותעיף (שמות כו): התרפית. מדברי תורה, ביום צרה צר כחכה: ואפילו מצוה אחת. אם נתרפה ממנה, כשבאה לידו ולא חש להתעסק בה - צר כחו: התרפית מכל מקום. אף במצוה אחת משמע: מעבר שנים וכו'. ותנן: אין מעברין את השנים אלא ביהודה, דכתיב "לשכנו תדרשו" - כל דרישות שאתה דורש לא יהו אלא בשכנו של מקום, בפ"ק דסנהדרין (דף יא:): שגרו אחריו. למחות בידו: כבר בנית. שהגדלת שמנו לומר: גדולי הדור הם: והלא עקיבא בן יוסף עשה כן. דתנן ביבמות, א"ר עקיבא: כשירדתי לנהרדעא לעבר שנים, בפרק בתרא "האשה שהלך בעלה וצרתה" (דף קכב.): ואמרו

---

## רב נסים גאון

עת לעשות לה' הפרו תורתך. פירוש טעמו בגמרא דבני מערבא ר' יוסי אומר אם נתישנו דברי תורה בפיך אל תבוז להם מאי טעמא (משלי כג) ואל תבוז כי זקנה אמך אמר ר' זעירא אם נזדקנה אומתך עמוד וגדרה כשם שעשה אלקנה שהיה מדריך את ישראל לפעמי רגלים מה טעם (ש"א א) ועלה האיש ההוא מעירו:

---

עין משפט נר מצוה:

פח א מיי' פי"א מהל' תפלה הלכה ח סמג עשין יט טוש"ע או"ח סי' קנא סעיף ה:

פט ב מיי' שם הלכה י טוש"ע או"ח שם סעיף ז וסי' ג סעיף יג:

צ ג מיי' פ"ד מהלכות תשובה הלכה טו:

צא ד מיי' פכ"ב מהל' איסורי ביאה הלכה טו סמג לאוין קכו טוש"ע אה"ע סי' כב סעיף טז:

מסורת הש"ס: [נ"ל בית הכנסת] | [בדפו"י הגי' רב] | תענית טז: סוטה מ: | [מכות כג:] | [לעיל ס. סנהדרין ע.] | [תוספתא פ"ז] | תוספות סוטה כב: בשנוי וכו' ותריכת פירוש' בסוגיא דהכא | קדושין פב: ע"ש | [סוטה ב.] | [נזיר ב.] | יומא יח:

[עי' גירסת הערוך בערך קפן]

[אמר רב פפא היינו דאמרי אינשי גנבא אפום מחתרתא רחמנא קרי קוף הוא הנוסח בע"י]

צב א טוש"ע י"ד סי' רמב סעי' לח בהג"ה:
צג ב מיי' פ"ג מהלכות ת"ת הלכה יב סמג עשין יב טוש"ע י"ד סימן רמו סעיף כח:

ואמרו לאחינו שבגולה. שלא ישמעו לו: יעלו להר. לאחד ההרים, להתנהג בחוקות העמים לבנות במות: אחיה יבנה מזבח. אדם גדול היה, וראש לבני הגולה: חנניה. הוא חנניה *אחי רבי יהושע: ינגן בכנור. לפני הבמה, לפי שחנניה לוי היה, כדתנן במסכת ערכין (ד' יא:): מעשה בר' יהושע בן חנניה שהלך לסייע את רבי יוחנן בן גודגדא בהגפת דלתות. אמר לו: חזור בך שאתה מן המשוררים ואני מן השוערים: לכרם. על שם שהיו יושבים שורות שורות, ככרם זה הנטוע שורות שורות: בכבוד אכסניא. מכניסי אורחים בבתים: ראש המדברים. במסכת שבת מפרש לה, ב"במה מדליקין" (דף לג:): שנים עשר מיל. שלש פרסאות. מחנה ישראל מבית הישימות עד אבל השטים, *תלתא פרסי: אמרה תורה כו'. כלומר קראו הכתוב "מבקש ה'": כשם שאני הסברתי לך פנים כך אתה הסבר פנים. והיינו דכתיב פנים בפנים: הרב בכעס. עליהם, משום מעשה העגל: ותלמיד בכעס. וגם אתה מראה להם כעס, שהרחקת אהלך ממחנה: אם אתה מחזיר האהל למקומו גרסינן: והיינו דכתיב ושב אל המחנה. השב האהל למחנה, ואם לאו – משרתך יהושע בן נון נער לא ימיש מתוכה, שישמש תחתיך. ואף על פי שהשיבו לאחר שנתרצה הקב"ה לישראל, והוקם המשכן, לא יצא דבר לבטלה. לא גרסינן "ומשרתו יהושע" וגו': הסכת. עשו כתות – כתות. דריש הס כמו עשו: כתתו עצמכם. ודרשי נמי הס כמו עשה, עשו עצמכם כתותים להצטער על דברי תורה: זאת התורה. היכן מצויה – באדם שממית עצמו באהלי תורה: הס ואחר כך כתת. שתוק, כמו ויהס כלב (במדבר יג), שתוק והאזן לשמועתך עד שתהא שגורה בפיך ואף על פי שאינה מיושבת לך, ואחר כך כתתנה והקשה עליה מה שיש לך להקשות, ותרץ תרוצין עד שתתישב לך: יהגה. יעיין: מיץ חלב יוציא חמאה. המוציא את החלב שמצץ משדי אמו על דברי התורה – חמאה היא לו: ומיץ אף. המוציא כעס רבו וסובלו – יוציא הלכות דם לעומתם: דתנן. שדיני ממונות עמוקים הם, והרוצה שיתחכם יעסוק בדיני ממונות שאין מקצוע בתורה גדול מהם: המנבל עצמו. ששואל לרבו כל ספקותיו, ואף על פי שיש בהם שחבריו מלעיגים עליו: ואם זמות. שסתמת פיך מלשאול. לשון זמם – טבעת של רצועה שחוסמים בחוטם בהמה שעסקיה רעים, ונותנים אותו בשפתיה לחוסמם יחד ולסותמן, סופך שתתן יד לפה כששואלוך ולא תדע להשיב: עשית חסד. שהאכילם. שנאמר "ויבא אהרן וכל זקני ישראל לאכל לחם" וגו' (שמות יח): חמות. אשתו של עובד אדום: וח' כלותיה. שהיו לה מח' בניה: שנאמר

[עירובין נה:]
ע"ז ז. חולין מד: כ
[שבת לג: מנחות כו

תורה אור

ואמרו לאחינו שבגולה: אם שומעין – מוטב, ואם לאו – יעלו להר, אחיה יבנה מזבח, חנניה ינגן בכנור, ויכפרו כולם ויאמרו: אין להם חלק באלהי ישראל. מיד געו כל העם בבכיה ואמרו: חס ושלום! יש לנו חלק באלהי ישראל. וכל כך למה? – משום שנאמר: °"כי מציון תצא תורה ודבר ה' מירושלים". בשלמא הוא מטהר והם מטמאין – לחומרא, אלא הוא מטמא והם מטהרין, היכי הוי? והא *תניא: אחכם שטמא – אין חברו רשאי לטהר, אסר – אין חברו רשאי להתיר! קסברי: כי היכי דלא נגררו בתריה.§ תנו רבנן: כשנכנסו רבותינו לכרם ביבנה היו שם רבי יהודה ורבי יוסי ור' נחמיה ור' אליעזר בנו של רבי יוסי הגלילי, פתחו כולם בכבוד אכסניא ודרשו. פתח רבי יהודה ראש *המדברים בכל מקום בכבוד תורה ודרש: °"ומשה יקח את האהל ונטה לו מחוץ למחנה", והלא דברים קל וחומר, ומה ארון ה' שלא היה מרוחק אלא שנים עשר מיל אמרה תורה: °"והיה כל מבקש ה' יצא אל אהל מועד", תלמידי חכמים שהולכים מעיר לעיר וממדינה למדינה ללמוד תורה – על אחת כמה וכמה.§ °"ודבר ה' אל משה פנים אל פנים". אמר ר' יצחק: אמר לו הקדוש ברוך הוא למשה: משה, אני ואתה נסביר פנים בהלכה. איכא דאמרי, כך אמר לו הקדוש ברוך הוא למשה: כשם שאני הסברתי לך פנים – כך אתה הסבר פנים לישראל, והחזר האהל למקומו. °"ושב אל המחנה וגו'". אמר רבי אבהו, אמר לו הקדוש ברוך הוא למשה: *עכשיו יאמרו הרב בכעס ותלמיד בכעס, ישראל מה תהא עליהם? אם אתה מחזיר האהל למקומו – מוטב, ואם לאו – יהושע בן נון תלמידך משרת תחתיך. והיינו דכתיב "ושב אל המחנה". אמר רבא: אף על פי כן לא יצא הדבר לבטלה, שנאמר: °"ומשרתו יהושע בן נון נער לא ימיש מתוך האהל".§ ועוד פתח ר' יהודה בכבוד תורה ודרש: °"הסכת ושמע ישראל היום הזה נהיית לעם". וכי אותו היום נתנה תורה לישראל? והלא אותו יום סוף ארבעים שנה היה! אלא ללמדך: שחביבה תורה על לומדיה בכל יום ויום כיום שנתנה מהר סיני. אמר ר' תנחום בריה דר' חייא איש כפר עכו: תדע, שהרי אדם קורא קריאת שמע שחרית וערבית, וערב אחד אינו קורא – דומה כמי שלא קרא קריאת שמע מעולם. 'הסכת' – עשו כתות כתות ועסקו בתורה, לפי שאין התורה נקנית אלא בחבורה. כדר' יוסי ברבי חנינא, *דאמר ר' יוסי ברבי חנינא: מאי דכתיב °"חרב (על) הבדים ונואלו" – חרב על שונאיהם של תלמידי חכמים שיושבים בד בבד ועוסקים בתורה. ולא עוד אלא שמטפשים, כתיב הכא "ונואלו", וכתיב התם °"אשר נואלנו". ולא עוד אלא שחוטאים – שנאמר: "ואשר חטאנו". איבעית אימא מהכא °"נואלו שרי צען". דבר אחר: "הסכת ושמע ישראל" – כתתו עצמכם על דברי תורה, כדאמר ריש לקיש. *דאמר ריש לקיש: במנין שאין דברי תורה מתקיימין אלא במי שממית עצמו עליה – שנאמר: °"זאת התורה אדם כי ימות באהל". דבר אחר: "הסכת ושמע ישראל" – הס ואחר כך כתת. כדרבא, *דאמר רבא: לעולם ילמוד אדם תורה ואחר כך יהגה.§ אמרי דבי ר' ינאי: מאי דכתיב °"כי מיץ חלב יוציא חמאה ומיץ אף יוציא דם ומיץ אפים יוציא ריב", במי אתה מוצא חמאה של תורה – במי שמקיא חלב שינק משדי אמו עליה. "ומיץ אף יוציא דם" – כל תלמיד שכועס עליו רבו פעם ראשונה ושותק – זוכה להבחין בין דם טמא לדם טהור. "ומיץ אפים יוציא ריב", כל תלמיד שכועס עליו רבו פעם ראשונה ושניה ושותק – זוכה להבחין בין דיני ממונות לדיני נפשות. *דתנן, ר' ישמעאל אומר: הרוצה שיתחכם יעסוק בדיני ממונות, שאין לך מקצוע בתורה יותר מהן, שהן כמעין נובע. אמר ר' שמואל בר נחמני: מאי דכתיב °"אם *נבלת בהתנשא ואם זמות יד לפה" – כל המנבל עצמו על דברי תורה – סופו להתנשא, ואם זמם – יד לפה.§ פתח ר' נחמיה בכבוד אכסניא ודרש: מאי דכתיב °"ויאמר שאול אל הקיני לכו סרו רדו מתוך עמלקי פן אוסיפך עמו ואתה עשיתה חסד עם כל בני ישראל", והלא דברים קל וחומר: ומה יתרו שלא קרב את משה אלא לכבוד עצמו – כך, המארח תלמיד חכם בתוך ביתו, ומאכילו ומשקהו ומהנהו מנכסיו – על אחת כמה וכמה.§ פתח ר' יוסי בכבוד אכסניא ודרש: °"לא תתעב אדמי כי אחיך הוא לא תתעב מצרי כי גר היית בארצו", והלא דברים קל וחומר: ומה מצריים שלא קרבו את ישראל אלא לצורך עצמן, שנאמר: °"ואם ידעת ויש בם אנשי חיל ושמתם שרי מקנה על אשר לי" – כך, המארח תלמיד חכם בתוך ביתו, ומאכילו ומשקהו ומהנהו מנכסיו – על אחת כמה וכמה. פתח ר' אליעזר בנו של ר' יוסי הגלילי בכבוד אכסניא ודרש: °"ויברך ה' את עובד אדם (הגתי) בעבור ארון האלהים", והלא דברים ק"ו: ומה ארון שלא אכל ושתה, אלא כבד ורבץ לפניו – כך, המארח תלמיד חכם בתוך ביתו, ומאכילו ומשקהו, ומהנהו מנכסיו – עאכ"ו. מאי היא ברכה שברכו? – אמר רב יהודה בר זבידא: זו חמות וח' כלותיה שילדו ששה ששה בכרס אחד, שנאמר

ישעיה ב
שמות לג
שם לג
שם
שם
שם
דברים כז
ירמיה נ
במדבר יב
ישעיה יט
ע"ז יט.
במדבר יט
משלי ל
ב"ב קעה.
משלי ל
[נדה כז.]
שמואל א טו
דברים כג
בראשית מז
שמואל ב ו

[ז"ל התקבי בשורש עכשו ויש שכותבין עכשיו ביו"ד ואינו צריך]
תענית ז. מכות י.
שבת פג: גיטין נז:
במדבר יט

## רב נסים גאון

תנו רבנן כשנכנסו רבותינו לכרם ביבנה. בגמרא דבני מערבא ובפסחים בפ' תמיד נשחט גרסינן תמן תנינן זה מדרש דרש ר' אלעזר בכרם ביבנה וכי כרם היה שם אלא אלו תלמידי חכמים שהן עשוין שורות שורות ככרם: פתח ר' יהודה ראש המדברים בכל מקום. מפורש במסכת שבת בפרק במה מדליקין (דף לג) אמרו יהודה שעילה יתעלה

## גליון הש"ס

גמ' ששה בכרס אחד. בנוה לדרך פרשה שמות כתב בשם המפרשים דז' חדרים יש באשה שלשה מימין ושלשה משמאל ואחד באמצע אם תתעבר מימין יהיו זכרים ובשמאל נקבות ובאמצע טומטום או אנדרוגינוס ונתעברו מכל החדרים רק לא מאמצע דטומטום הוי סימן קללה:

שנאמר: °"פעלתי השמיני"(א) וכתיב °"כי ברכו אלהים" °"כל אלה [מבני] (ל) עבד אדם המה ובניהם ואחיהם (אנשי) [איש] חיל בכח לעבדה ששים ושנים לעבד אדם".§ אמר ר' אבין הלוי: *כל הדוחק את השעה – שעה דוחקתו, וכל הנדחה מפני השעה – שעה נדחית מפניו, מדרבה ורב יוסף. *דרב יוסף סיני, ורבה עוקר הרים. אצטריכא להו שעתא, *שלחו להתם: סיני ועוקר הרים איזה מהם קודם? שלחו להו: סיני קודם, *שהכל צריכין למרי חטיא. אף על פי כן לא קבל עליו ר' יוסף, דאמרי ליה כלדאי: מלכת תרתין שנין. מלך רבה עשרין ותרתין שנין, מלך רב יוסף תרתין שנין ופלגא. כל הנך שני דמלך רבה, אפילו אומנא לביתיה לא קרא.§ ואמר רבי אבין הלוי: מאי דכתיב °"יענך ה' ביום צרה ישגבך שם אלהי יעקב", "אלהי יעקב" ולא אלהי אברהם ויצחק – מכאן לבעל הקורה שיכנס בעביה של קורה. ואמר רבי אבין הלוי: כל הנהנה מסעודה שתלמיד חכם שרוי בתוכה כאילו נהנה מזיו שכינה, שנאמר: °"ויבא אהרן וכל זקני ישראל לאכל לחם עם חתן משה לפני האלהים". וכי לפני אלהים אכלו? והלא לפני משה אכלו! אלא לומר לך: כל הנהנה מסעודה שתלמיד חכם שרוי בתוכה – כאילו נהנה מזיו שכינה. *ואמר רבי אבין הלוי: הנפטר מחברו [א] אל יאמר לו "לך בשלום" אלא "לך לשלום". שהרי יתרו שאמר לו למשה °"לך לשלום" – עלה והצליח, דוד שאמר לו לאבשלום °"לך בשלום" – הלך ונתלה. ואמר רבי אבין הלוי: [ב] הנפטר מן המת אל יאמר לו "לך לשלום" אלא "לך בשלום", שנאמר: °"ואתה תבוא אל אבתיך בשלום".§ אמר רבי לוי בר חייא: אהיוצא מבית הכנסת ונכנס לבית המדרש ועוסק בתורה – *זוכה ומקבל פני שכינה, שנאמר: °"ילכו מחיל אל חיל יראה אל אלהים בציון". אמר רבי חייא בר אשי אמר רב: *תלמידי חכמים אין להם מנוחה לא בעולם הזה ולא בעולם הבא, שנאמר: "ילכו מחיל אל חיל יראה אל אלהים בציון".§ *אמר רבי אלעזר אמר רבי חנינא: תלמידי חכמים מרבים שלום בעולם, שנאמר: °"וכל בניך למודי ה' ורב שלום בניך", אל תקרי "בניך" אלא "בוניך". °"שלום רב לאהבי תורתך ואין למו מכשול" °"יהי שלום בחילך שלוה בארמנותיך" °"למען אחי ורעי אדברה נא שלום בך" °"למען בית ה' אלהינו אבקשה טוב לך" °"ה' עז לעמו יתן ה' יברך את עמו בשלום".§

## הדרן עלך הרואה וסליקא לה מסכת ברכות

**רש"י**

שנאמר פעלתי השמיני. בני עובד אדום קא חשיב בדברי הימים. וקא חשיב תמניא, והיא תשיעית. כל אחת ילדה ששה, הם חמשים וארבע, הוסיף עליהם שמונה בנים הראשונים, הרי ששים ושנים לעובד אדום: הדוחק את השעה. כגון אבשלום שבקש למלוך בחזקה: **אצטריכא להו שעתא**. להיות אחד מהם ראש ישיבה. אצטריכא להו גרסי', הוצרכו להם חכמים: סיני. היו קורין לרב יוסף, שהיה בקי בברייתות הרבה: עוקר הרים. לרבה בר נחמני, שהיה מחודד יותר בפלפול: למרי חטיא. למי שמקנן תבואה למכור, כלומר: למי שמקנן שמועות: דאמרי ליה כלדאי. לרב יוסף: מלכת תרתין שנין. אמר: אם אמלוך תחלה אמות לסוף שנתים ונדחה מפני השעה ולא אבה למלוך, והשעה עמדה לו שלא הפסיד שנותיו בכך: **אומנא לביתיה לא קרא**. לא נהג כל אותן השנים שום צד שררה, וכשהיה צריך להקיז דם היה הולך לבית הרופא ולא היה שולח לבא אליו: שיאחז בעובי הקורה. אם בא לטלטלה ממקום למקום לתתה בבנין. כלומר: יעקב שכל הבנים שלו וטרח בגידולם, יבקש עליהם רחמים: הנפטר מן המת. כשהיו מוליכים ארונות ממקום למקום לקבורה היו מלוים אותו מעיר לעיר, וחוזרים אלו ואחרים מלוים אותו משם והלאה, והחוזרים קרי נפטרים נוטלין רשות להפטר ממנו: אין להם מנוחה. מישיבה לישיבה וממדרש למדרש:

הדרן עלך הרואה וסליקא לה מסכת ברכות

**מסורת הש"ם**

[ערוכין יג:] עירוכין ל. [מ"ק יב.] הוריות יד. [ב"ב קמה:]

דה"א כו · שם · תהלים כ · שמות יח · שם ד · שמואל ב טו · בראשית טו

[מ"ק כט. ע"ש] · שם · ...מות קכב: נזיר סו: תמיד לב: כריתו' כח: · שם כט

**הגהות הב"ח**

(א) גמ' שנאמר פעולתי ...שמיני כי ברכו אלהים ...תיב כל אלה מבני עובד אדום המה ובניהם:

**גליון הש"ם**

...מ' כל הדוחק את השעה. ...א רסי' קנו ע"א: **שם** ...' הנהגה מסעודה מג"א ...ף סי' קנו ורס"י תקס"ח סק"ה:

**עין משפט נר מצוה**

צג א טוש"ע או"ח סי' קנה סעיף א:

שם שם

[מ"ק כט. ע"ש]

[א] מג"א סי' ק"י סק"ט

[ב] [רמב"ם פ"ד מהל' אבל ה"ד]

תהלים פד · ישעיה נד · תהלים קיט · שם קכב · שם שם · שם

**רב נסים גאון**

תלמידי חכמים אין להם מנוחה. בגמרא דבני מערבא במסכת שביעית בפרק רביעי פירשו כי זו היגיעה שהן יגעין היא (משבחין) [שמשבחין] ומקלסין וגורסין בתורה כדאמרי' ר' יונה בשם ר' חייא בר אשי עתידין חברין להתיגע מבתי כנסיות לבתי מדרשות מאי טעמא דכתיב (תהלים פד) ילכו מחיל אל חיל:

סליקא לה להא מסכתא